AMERICA'S PREMIER GUNMAKERS

10
4
BROWNING ARMS COMPANY MORGAN, UTAH & MONTREAL P.Q.
ONE OF FIVE THOUSAND

AMERICA'S PREMIER
GUNMAKERS
Collector's Edition

K.D. KIRKLAND

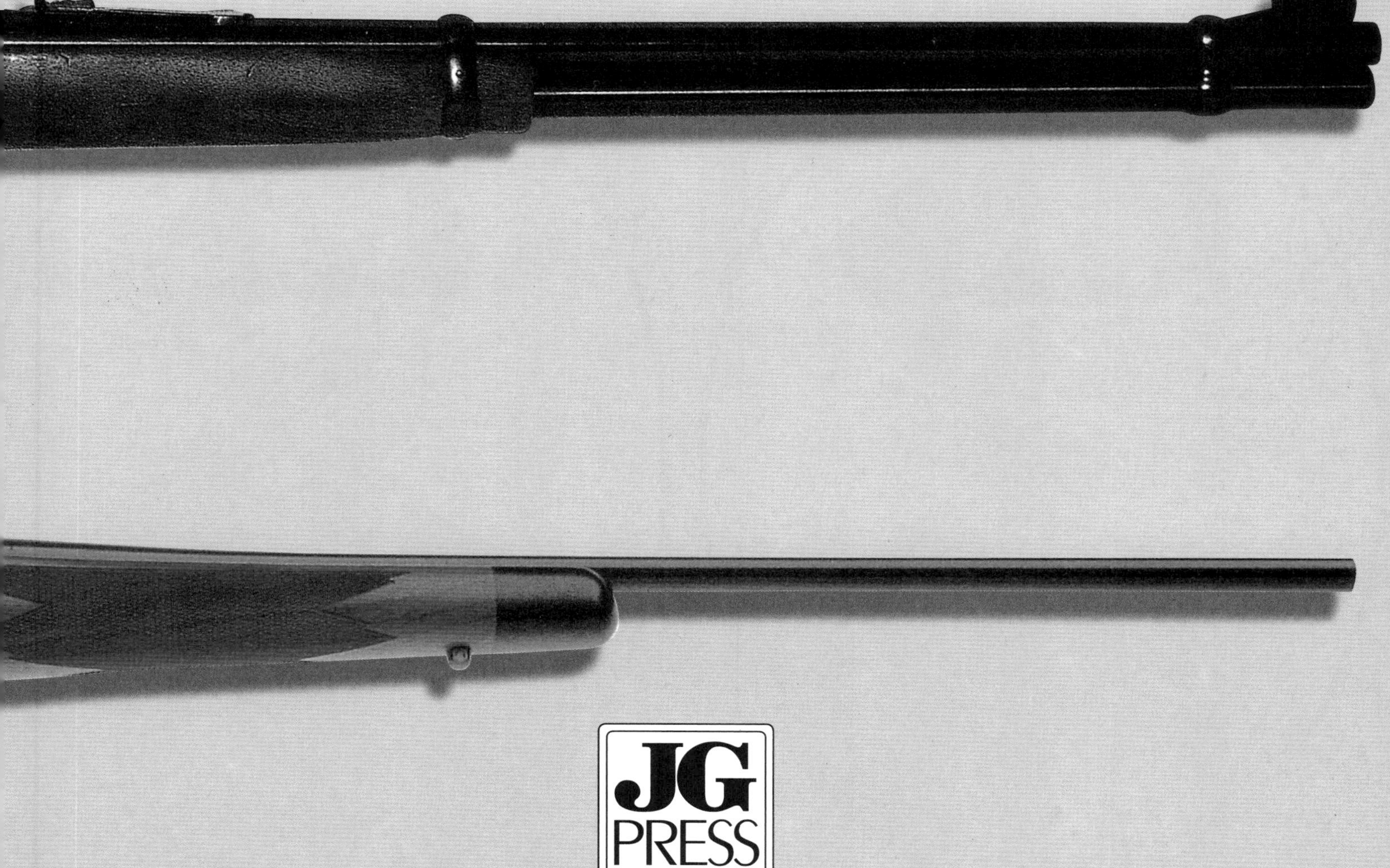

JG PRESS

Published by World Publications Group, Inc.
140 Laurel Street
East Bridgewater, MA 02333
www.wrldpub.com

10-ISBN 1-4643-0175-1
13-ISBN 978-1-4643-0175-9

Jacket design by Kevin Ullrich

Printed in China by Toppan Leefung Printing Limited

Designed by Ruth DeJauregui
Edited and captioned by Timothy Jacobs and Marie Cahill

Page 1: **This Model 1100 Field Grade shotgun is a fine example of Remington gunmaking skill.** ***Pages 2—3, from top to bottom:*** **A .36 caliber Colt Navy revolver of the Civil War era; a super-high quality 'One of Five Thousand' Browning automatic pistol; a classic Model 94 Winchester lever action, in .357 caliber; and a Remington Model 700 Mountain Rifle, in .280 caliber.** ***These pages, left to right:*** **The prolific John Moses Browning, founder of Browning Arms; Samuel Colt, inventor and founder of Colt Firearms; Eliphalet Remington II, inventor and founder of Remington Arms; and Oliver F Winchester, founder of Winchester Repeating Arms Company.**

Acknowledgements
The author wishes to thank Paul Thompson of Browning NA, Nola Clavio and George K Bukovsky of Remington Arms/El du Pont de Nemours & Co, Inc, Mark A Sweetland of Rumrill-Hoyt, Inc and Janice Murphy at US Repeating Arms for their gracious and invaluable assistance. The author and publisher wish to thank Bruce Kaye at Theodore Roosevelt National Park, Elizabeth Holmes at Buffalo Bill Historical Center, Oster Loh at Olin Corporation, Wayne Boyer and Dennis Clark of Trader's Den in Logan, Utah. The author and publisher would also like to acknowledge the books *John M Browning, American Gunmaker,* by John Browning and Curt Gentry, and *Remington Arms, An American History,* by Alden Hatch, published in 1956 by Rinehart & Company, Inc, from which much of our historical information has been adapted. Finally, special thanks go to Sylvia Kirkland for her assistance in preparing the manuscript.

Photo Credits
All Browning photos courtesy of Browning NA; Colt photos courtesy of Colt Industries; Remington photos courtesy of El du Pont de Nemours & Co, Inc; and all Winchester photos courtesy of Buffalo Bill Historical Center, Cody, Wyoming except the following:

American Graphic Systems Archives 11, 45, 47, 101 (all), 140 (bottom), 114, 331 (bottom), 368 (all), 399
Mike Badrocke 74-75, 78-79
Barker Texas History Center, Prints and Photographs Collection, University of Texas, Austin 134 (middle)
John Batchelor 120-121 (all), 122-123, 134-135 (top), 142-143, 154-155, 162-163, 166-167, 170-171, 174-175, 178-179, 182-183, 190-191, 198-199, 206-207, 214-215
Brompton Books Archives 262, 424-425
The Church of Jesus Christ of Latter Day Saints, Visual Resources Library 36 (bottom)
Cinema Shop 160 (right), 163 (top), 200-201, 204-205, 212 (bottom), 233, 254 (bottom), 301, 308-309, 383, 392, 394-395, 416 (bottom right)
© RE DeJauregui 240, 286-287, 320-321
Denver Public Library, Western History Division 398-399
Dover 133, 137 (middle)
El du Pont de Nemours & Co, Inc via Rumrill-Hoyt 220-221 (all), 222-223, 226-227, 246-247, 302-303, 306-307
Robert Hunt Picture Library 261 (bottom)
Ian V Hogg 50, 51, 76 (top), 178 (bottom)
Lloyd G Ingles, California Academy of Sciences 409 (center)
J&J Kidd 46-47, 54-55, 86-87, 330-331, 335, 338-339, 350-351 (all), 354-355 (all), 358-359, 362-363, 404-405 (all)
© KD Kirkland 86 (bottom), 100, 112 (all), 113, 226 (bottom), 298-299, 303 (bottom), 304-305, 432
Library of Congress 131 (bottom)
Lowie Museum of Anthropology, University of California, Berkeley 393
The National Archives 128 (top), 160 (left), 249 (all), 257
Olin Industries, Incorporated 327, 331 (center), 333, 336, 337, 339, 357, 365 (center), 366, 367, 369 (all), 372 (top), 373, 376, 379, 380, 381, 382, 384, 385, 386, 387, 389, 390, 391(bottom), 392 (right), 397 (bottom), 402, 403, 406 (bottom), 407, 410, 416 (top, bottom left), 418, 419
Peter Newark's Western Americana 178 (middle), 251 (bottom), 259, 276, 423 (top)
Royal Artillary Institution, Museum of Artillary at the Rotunda, London
Joseph Coughlan 198 (bottom), 251 (center), 426 (bottom)
Seaver Center for Western History Research, Los Angeles County Museum 138-139 (both), 142 (bottom), 146-147, 163 (bottom), 250-251, 256-257, 254-255 (top)
Smithsonian Institution 284 (top)
National Anthropological Archives 128 (bottom)
South Dakota State Historical Society 254-255 (bottom)
Theodore Roosevelt National Park Visitor Center, Medora, North Dakota 364 (all), 365 (top, bottom)
Mike Trim 78 (bottom right)
US Air Force 74 (top), 75 (right) 76-77, 78 (bottom left), 79 (top), 186, 241, 361
US Army 53, 180 (top), 189 (both), 263, 422
John Pinderhughes 427 (bottom left)
US Department of Defense 181, 190-191 (bottom)
US Navy 258, 397 (top)
US Repeating Arms Company 348, 359 (bottom), 360-361 (second from bottom), 401 (all), 406 (top), 408-409 (all), 410-411(bottom) 412-413 (top, bottom), 413 (all), 414-415 (all), 417
© Bill Yenne 311, 420

Table of Contents

Browning **6**
Jonathan Browning and His Guns 10
John Moses Browning 14
John M Browning's Pistols and Rifles 24
John M Browning's Shotguns 54
Browning's Machine Guns and Aircraft Cannon 66
Fabrique Nationale 82
Newer Browning Pistols and Rifles 86
Newer Browning Shotguns and Bows 94
Browning Craftsmanship and Special Editions 102

Colt **118**
The Arms of Samuel Colt 122
Metallic Cartidges 154
Great Colts of the Nineteenth Century 158
The Evolution of the Modern Colt Revolver 166
Automatic Pistols and Rifles 174
Craftsmanship in the Twentieth Century 182
Excellence and Art 206
The Tradition Continues 214

Remington **218**
A Remington History 222
Civilian Arms 226
Military Arms 246
Remington Ammunition 270
Eliphalet Remington's First Gun 286
How E Remington Entered the Arms Trade 302
The Death of E Remington Senior 306
A Glossary of Remington Arms 310

Winchester **322**
Oliver F Winchester's Company 326
Winchester and the Age of Smokeless Powder 334
The Company Enters the Twentieth Century 350
The Western Cartridge Company 358
Winchester Today 362
Major Browning Winchester Models 370
Major Winchesters Through the Years 388

Glossary of Terms **420**

Index **428**

America's Premier Gunmakers

BROWNING

Stephen

Previous pages: A beautifully crafted Browning Gold Classic automatic pistol. *These pages:* Two excellent Browning hammerless doubles, manufactured by Miroku Firearms Mfg of Japan. Note the master engraving and the fine wood stocks. These are shotguns that would be at home both on the field and on display.

Jonathan and His

Above: The Cylinder Repeating Rifle—one of Jonathan Browning's first designs. *Below:* Jonathan Browing's lathe, on which his son John M Browning would learn the art of gunsmithing. *At right:* Abraham Lincoln traded yarns with Jonathan Browning.

Browning Guns

The Father of the Son

Jonathan Browning, destined to be the father of one of the world's great gunmakers, was born on 22 October 1805 at Brushy Fork of Bledsoe Creek in Summer County, Tennessee. He was an industrious, talented fellow, and fixed up his first gun at the tender age of 13, while he was apprenticed to a local blacksmith.

By the time he was 19, Jonathan was considered to be a competent gunsmith, and he forged his own tools for his gunsmithing work. Some of these tools were still in use in the twentieth century, as Jonathan's son John Moses Browning found the old tools also served him well in his shop in Ogden, Utah.

On 9 November 1826, one month after he became 21, Jonathan married Elizabeth Stalcup. Their first child was born in August of the following year, and Jonathan's first gun shop was established at Brushy Fork. He worked there from 1824 to 1834.

While none of them survive, at least some of the guns he made at Brushy Fork saw action in the Seminole Wars of 1836, and in the Civil War (to which many combatants brought their own personal weapons).

Jonathan eventually moved to Quincy, Illinois, then a settlement of 753 people. He invented both his Slide Bar Repeating Rifle and his Cylinder Repeating Rifle in Quincy—descriptions of both of which follow this biography. His gunsmithing business in Quincy flourished, and he entered a period of comfortable prosperity about the time he was elected Justice of the Peace. By the time he was 35, Jonathan had eight children.

Through his lawyerly cousin, Orville H Browning, Jonathan made the acquaintance of a young Illinois lawyer by the name of Abraham Lincoln. Lincoln spent the night in the Jonathan Browning home on at least two different occasions, and the wise, folksy cameraderie between the two men was a Browning family staple for generations.

Also during his middle 30's, Jonathan became interested in religion. The Church of Jesus Christ of Latter-Day Saints,

commonly referred to as the Mormon Church, had its beginnings in New York state. Due to continuous persecution, church leader Joseph Smith led the Mormons to the banks of the Mississippi River and founded a settlement which he named Nauvoo (from the Hebrew word denoting a beautiful place). Within a year they had filled the swamp and turned Nauvoo into a city laid out in large square blocks with over 250 houses. Converts were arriving in large numbers, and in a few short years, Nauvoo became the largest city in Illinois. Sometime in 1840, Jonathan was converted to Mormonism, and shortly thereafter, moved to Nauvoo where he set up a two story brick residence, with the first floor serving as his gun shop.

On 27 June 1844, Joseph Smith and his brother Hyrum were murdered by a mob in Carthage, Illinois. Brigham Young became leader of the Mormons. Figuring that the persecution wouldn't stop, he immediately began to follow through on an old contingency plan to leave what was then the United States and settle the Latter-Day Saints in the Rocky Mountains.

In the midst of this exodus, a message arrived from the President of the United States requesting that the Mormons supply 500 or so volunteers for the war against Mexico which was then raging. Jonathan Browning added himself to the lists of the Mormon Battalion but Brigham Young forbad him to go.

Jonathan's gunmaking skills were far more important to the success of the Mormon migration to the west, than any fighting skills he could offer to the US in the war with Mexico. So it was that Jonathan provided the Utah pioneers with both his Slide Repeating Rifle and his Cylinder Repeating Rifle, both of which operated according to the tenets of simple construction, easy operation and accurate efficiency.

Above: **Jonathan Browning, father of John M Browning.** ***Below:*** **Jonathan Browning's home and gunsmith shop at Brushy Fork of Bledsoe Creek, Tennessee.** ***Right:*** **Jonathan Browning's home in Nauvoo, Illlinois.** ***Far right:*** **Map tracing the Mormon Exodus from Nauvoo, Illinois to Salt Lake City, Utah. Jonathan Browning's guns aided the Mormons in their journey westward.**

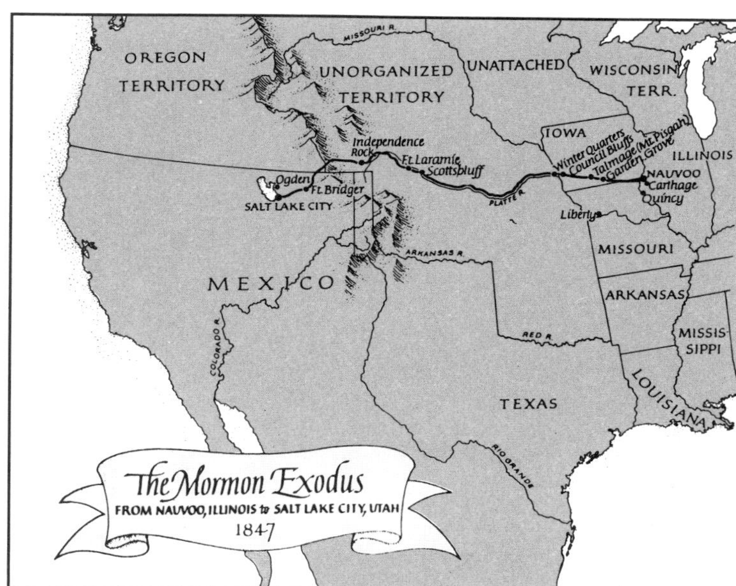

The Brownings and some of their Mormon companions were told to set up a settlement for a while at Kanesville, Iowa, and here they paused in their exodus.

On 24 July 1947, Brigham Young led the advance company of pioneers down into the Salt Lake Valley, and in 1852, Jonathan was permitted to load his wagons and follow the westward trail. Jonathan settled his family in Ogden, Utah. He never again applied himself to the inventing of new guns, as his talents at being a mechanic and engineer were in great demand, due to the constant battle for survival against the elements in that frontier community.

Jonathan and Elizabeth had 11 children by then, and two years after their arrival, he married Elizabeth Clark, who became the mother of John Moses Browning, his brother Matt, and a daughter who died in infancy. A few years later, he married Sarah Emmett, who bore him seven more children, for a grand total of 22! Jonathan Browning died on 21 June 1879 in his 74th year. He had had time enough to become glad in the knowledge that he had sired, in the person of his son John Moses, a greater gunmaker than himself, and had helped to give direction to his talent.

Jonathan Browning's Guns

Slide Bar Repeating Rifle. This is a percussion repeating rifle of approximately .45 caliber, with an ingenious magazine that holds five (or 25) shots. It has a 40.3-inch octagon barrel, and weighs 9.9 pounds.

One of the earliest known American repeating rifles, this firearm was invented by Jonathan Browning sometime between 1834 and 1842 while he was residing in Quincy, Illinois. It was never patented, but was manufactured by its inventor during his residences in Quincy and Nauvoo, Illinois; and Kanesville, Iowa—altogether, from 1842—1852. The total number manufactured is not known.

The Slide Bar Repeater has a number of particularly ingenious features, including its five-shot magazine (a 25-shot variant was available) that takes hand loads. The mechanism centers around a rectangular iron bar with five percussion chambers—for the hand loads—bored in it. This slides through an aperture at the breech and is manually operated.

Since it is an underhammer firearm, the shooter can ease his index finger forward from the trigger to cock the rifle, thus never having to drop the gun from his shoulder during a firing session. Also, having the percussion chambers located in the bar permits comparatively fast 'mass production' loading, and provides the single-barrel firearm with the capability of firing five (or 25) shots in comparatively rapid succession. A thumb-operated lever, on the right-hand side of the breech, forces the slide against the barrel as each load moves into line with the bore. This creates a gas-tight seal.

The Jonathan Browning Slide Repeating Rifle is not only one of the earliest repeating rifles ever made, it is also one of the simplest—both in its small number of parts and its ease of operation.

Slide Bar Repeating Rifle

Cylinder Repeating Rifle. This is a six shot repeating percussion rifle of approximately .45 caliber, with a six-shot cylindrical magazine. It has a 29.9-inch half octagon, half 16-sided barrel and weighed 12.1 pounds.

The Cylinder Repeating Rifle was invented by Jonathan Browning during his residence in Quincy, sometime between 1834 and 1842. Like the Slide Repeating Rifle, it was never patented. Also, this rifle was not manufactured after Browning arrived in Utah in 1852. The total number manufactured is not known.

The powder and ball are loaded into the cylinder chambers and a percussion cap is placed on each nipple. The rifle is cocked by drawing back the hammer, but there is no mechanism for revolving the cylinder when the hammer is cocked; the cylinder has to be rotated manually after each shot.

The front edge of the cylinder has a tapered cone around each chamber which fits into the breech of the barrel. There is a conical cam in the rear of the receiver, which, when engaged, jams the cylinder tight against the breech of the barrel. This cam traverses horizontally through the receiver immediately to the rear of the cylinder.

John Moses

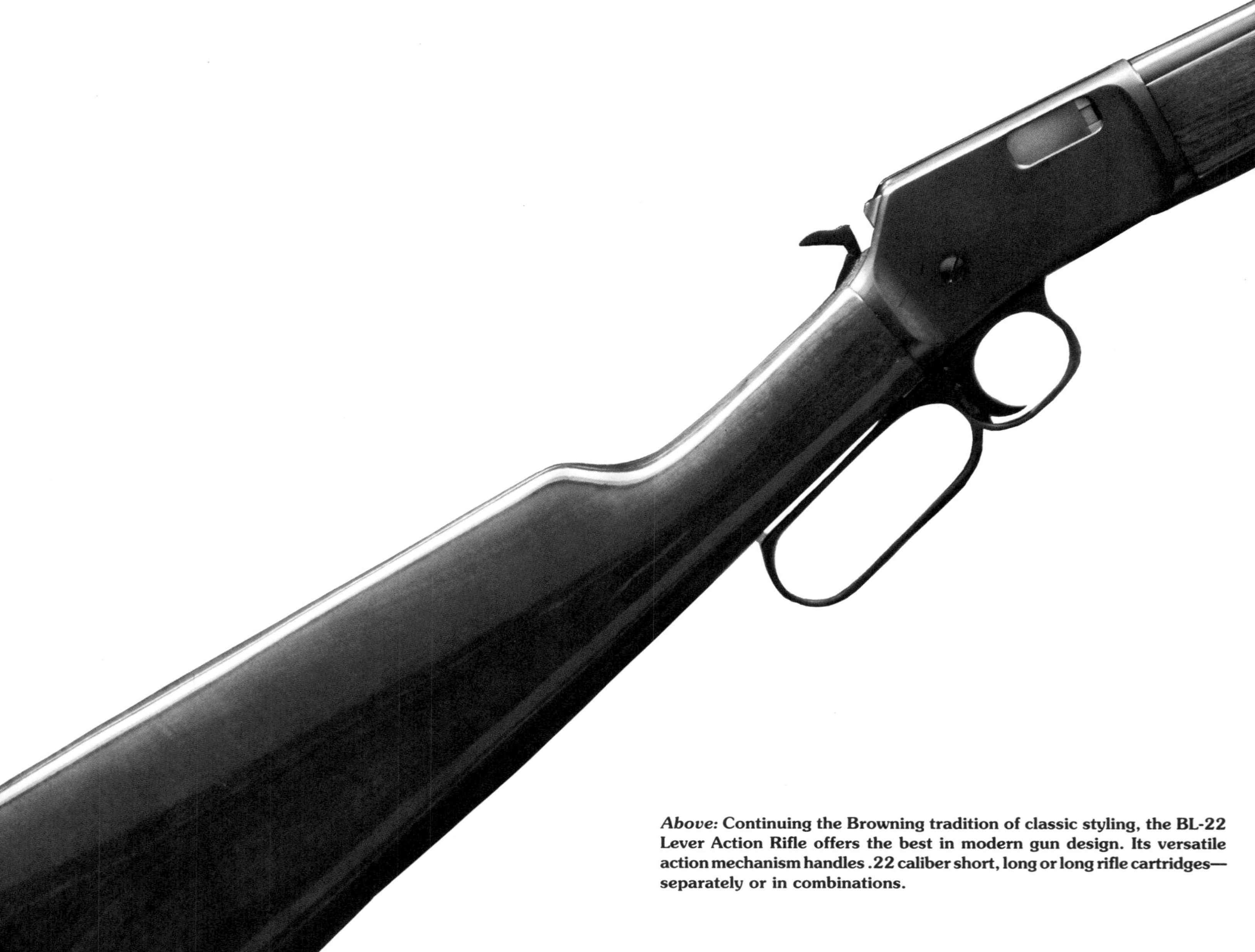

Above: **Continuing the Browning tradition of classic styling, the BL-22 Lever Action Rifle offers the best in modern gun design. Its versatile action mechanism handles .22 caliber short, long or long rifle cartridges—separately or in combinations.**

Browning

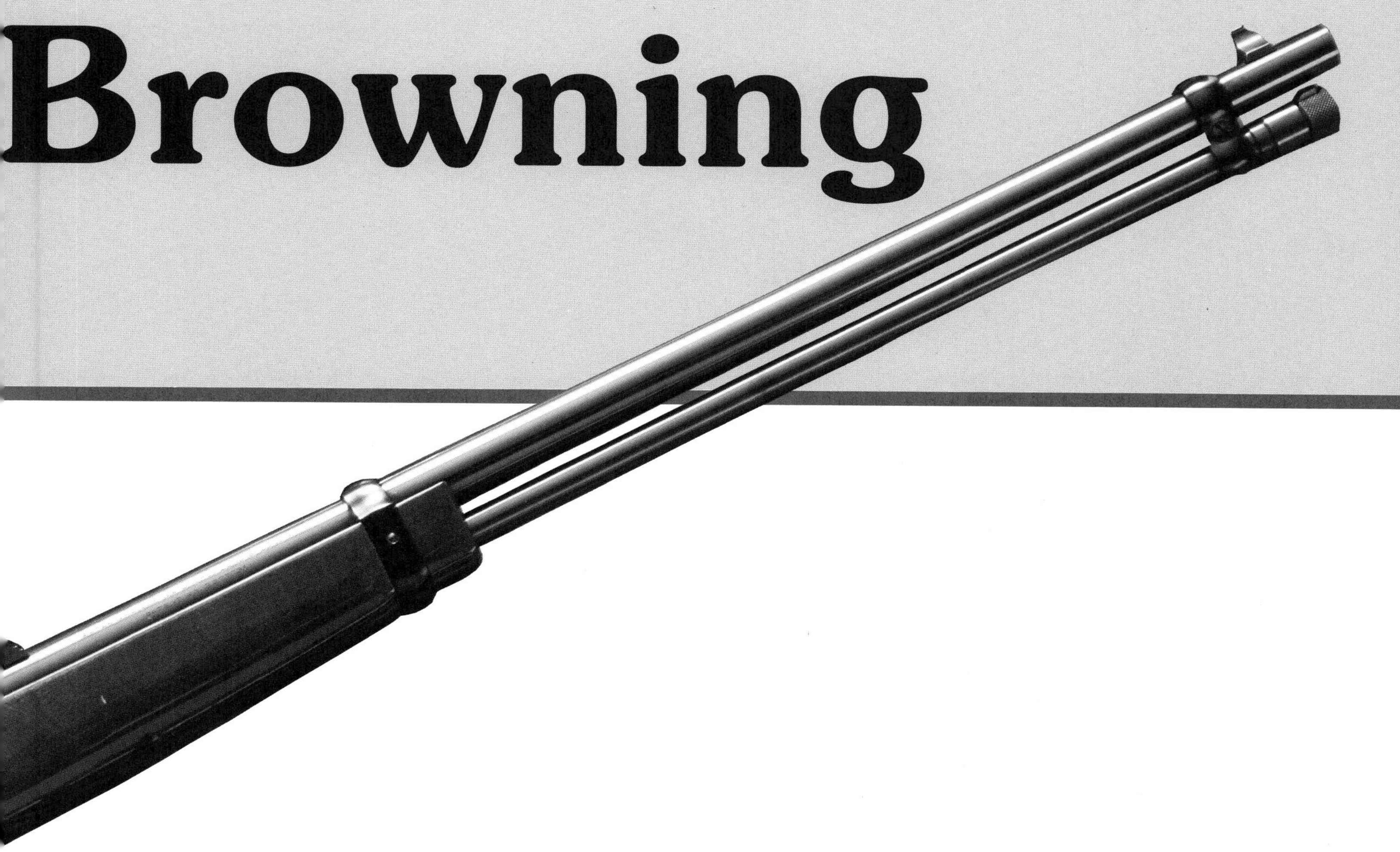

The Man of Inventions

John Moses Browning was born 29 January 1855 in Ogden, Utah. His first toddling steps were toward his dad's gun shop. Family remembrances indicate that he actually started his career at about age six when he dragged a box into the shop to serve as his own work bench and, about a year later, the seven year old was beginning to take himself seriously as a gunsmith. The first gun that John made was composed of the smashed barrel of an old flint lock, a stick of wood, a piece of wire and a scrap of tin.

In 1869, the transcontinental railroad was completed and the Mormons were no longer isolated, but were tangibly connected to both coasts of the country. Just as Utah then stood astride a growing America, so in a few years would John Browning find himself squarely astride new firearms developments. His father had watched the percussion lock gradually replace the flintlock, and now John witnessed the passing of the percussion lock and the introduction of the cartridge firearm.

His father's gun shop was reconditioned in 1873, and it was here in 1878 that John invented the first of his many famous guns—the 1878 Single Shot Rifle, for which John received $8000 from the Winchester Repeating Arms Company.

Thus began a long and profitable relationship between Winchester and Browning. When he was just 27 years old, John invented what would later become the Model 86 Winchester. This was a milestone in firearms design, and it was so efficient that it remained in the Winchester line for over 70 years. In 1887, he invented a lever action repeating shotgun.

John Browning did most of his designing in his own head, and before undertaking the making of a particular model, he had it completely visualized through completion. He never thought that faculty to be unique; he supposed that it was a common attribute. He would, however, use sketches and templates to prove to himself that the designs were indeed sound mechanical concepts.

Although he drew no blueprints, he would make numerous measurements, and would carefully denote them. When the work was going well, John often whistled or sang, and once commented that the sounds of the machines and tools were an orchestra to his ear. Whenever he became stumped over some particular difficulty he fell silent, and when frustration built to a certain point, he simply worked harder as though the tension generated a heat that consumed all obstacles.

Once, he was asked how he managed to create a gun of precise parts and functions with no other instruments of measurement than an inside and outside caliper, a compass (which also served as a scriber), a foot rule graduated down to 64ths and a little spirit level he'd inherited from his father. He smiled and replied, 'Why, I went at the job about the same way I've gone at every other job. I find a good starting place, a fixed point—like the North Star—from which I make exact calculations and then I calculate.'

Once a model was completed, he spent considerable time testing it in the hills behind Ogden and even asked his wife, Rachel, to operate the various prototypes to see if she could

easily work the mechanism. This same inventive process went on all his life, model after model.

As was noted earlier, John's association with the Winchester Repeating Arms Company began with their purchase of his Single Shot in 1883 and lasted 19 years until 1902. During that period John—being freed from the burdens of running an arms-manufacturing shop—was able to devote nearly all of his time to inventing. And invent he did! For nearly 20 years Winchester's new firearms were all Brownings (although never known as such), and 34 of the guns purchased by Winchester were never manufactured; the Winchester line could not have absorbed them, but by purchasing them, Winchester kept them out of the hands of its own competitors.

In effect, Winchester was employing John to work exclusively for them and instead of paying him a fixed salary, he was given his asking price for every gun design he submitted. John's prices were high but at the same time Winchester became the world's leading manufacturer of sporting arms. Browning had more patents for firearms designs than any other American inventor during that period.

Browning invented the Winchester Model 1894 Lever Action Repeating Rifle which has been acclaimed 'the most popular hunting rifle ever built, bar none!' The model 1894 was America's first smokeless-powder sporting rifle. It is interesting to note that all of John's rifle designs for Winchester were designed for black powder cartridges, and yet were later adapted to the much more powerful smokeless cartridges, with only a change of barrel steel. John's philosophy was stated thusly: 'If anything can happen to a gun it probably will sooner or later.' He therefore set his margins of safety far in excess of merely adequate requirements, as if to say, 'make it strong enough, then double it.'

Because of John M Browning's genius, Winchester was the only company in the world with a complete line of sporting arms with not a single model facing a competitor that was even remotely dangerous. By 1900, fully 75 percent of the repeating sporting arms on the American market, both lever and pump action, were of John Browning's invention.

However, Winchester's monopoly was to end in 1902 when its president, TG Bennett, refused to pay Browning royalties for a new invention known as the automatic shotgun. In all of its dealings with Browning the Winchester Company had never paid him a royalty but simply bought his inventions outright. However, an automatic shotgun had no precedent, and Browning figured that it would sell like hotcakes, and righfully wanted in on its sales as a pioneering innovator, while Winchester concluded that it would take too long to perfect, and so refused his offer.

Winchester regretted this mistake, for more than 54 years were to pass before another successful autoloading shotgun was developed. Also, thus was cemented the already extant, and eventually long, Browning association with Fabrique Nationale of Herstal, Belgium—who did accept John Browning's offer.

The automatic shotgun, machine guns, and pistols of John M Browning owed their birth to an event in the fall of 1889. At a shooting match, John's attention was riveted by the clump of sweet clover that stood over to one side of his brother Will's shooting stand: it was forcefully moved by the muzzle blast of Will's gun. John thought, 'Now, why can't we use all that wasted energy to help operate the gun?' When he had rounded up his brothers and they ran back towards the gunshop, everyone knew that John was in an inventing frame of mind.

'Yes, sir!' John exclaimed, from the sheer excitement of the idea that was still expanding in his mind, 'An idea, as

Above and below: **Two views of a Browning Single Shot Rifle—John M Browning's first firearm. A 'falling block' style rifle, this was a successful beginning of a great career for John M Browning.** ***Left:*** **Rachel Teresa Child, shortly before she married John M Browning.** ***Above:*** **Matt Browning, a favorite among John's many brothers.**

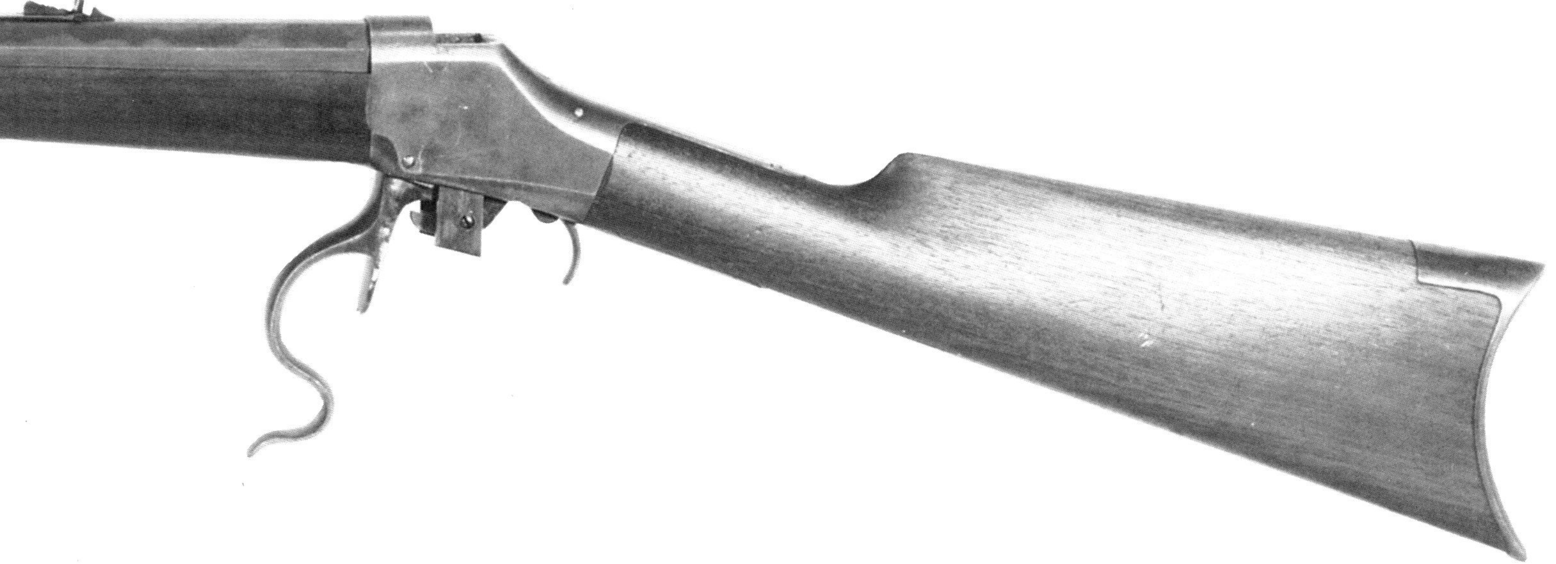

Pappy used to say—biggest one I ever had. Get that damn horse going, Matt.'

'Why, it might even be possible to make a fully automatic gun,' he surmised aloud, 'one that would keep firing as long as you had ammunition.'

As soon as they reached the shop, John took an old .44 caliber Model 73 and wired it to a board, with the rifle lying flat on its side. They nailed the board to the floor. Then they drilled a hole slightly bigger than the old rifle's bore size in a length of two-by-four, and then put it on the floor about a quarter inch from the barrel, with the board's hole lined up with the rifle's bore.

'What happens to that block of wood is what we want to see,' John explained. After a few safety precautions had been arranged they were ready to begin. When they touched the rifle off, the board came to rest only when its momentum had been spent in a ricocheting course of leaps from one obstacle to another. The gas pressure from the rifle proved to be every bit as powerful as John had surmised upon his observation of the sweet clover at the shooting match.

Turning to his brothers he said, 'You know, we may not be more than 10 years away from a pretty good automatic machine gun.' Speaking of that moment later, John's brother Matt said, 'John had Ed and me as excited as a couple of kids at a circus. And then he tells us that we may have a pretty good machine gun, in 10 years.' John was really arguing with himself aloud. He admitted that it did look as though they had stumbled onto something new, the possibility of an automatic gun, operated by the gas that had been wasted since the first shot was fired through a barrel. But, he cautioned, they shouldn't get too excited. 'But,' he concluded, 'it ought to be interesting. Anyhow, Ed, in the morning we'll make a gas-operated gun.' 'Figure doing it by noon?' Ed asked with an in-on-the joke wryness. 'Hardly,' John replied. 'About four o'clock I'd guess.' The laughter broke the tension of that momentous day.

On 22 November 1890 John's brother, Matt Browning, sat down and wrote a letter which in time would have tremendous military significance. It was written in long hand on Browning Brothers' stationary and was addressed to Colt's Patent Firearms Manufacturing Company of Hartford, Connecticut. Complete with the author's homespun usages, it read:

Dear Sirs:

We have just completed our new Automatic Machine Gun & thought we would write to you to see if you are interested in that kind of a gun. We have been at work on this gun for some time & have got it in good shape. We made a small one first which shot a 44 W.C.F. charge at the rate of about 16 times per second & weighed about 8#. The one we have just completed shoots the 45 Gov't chge about 6 times per second & with the mount weighs about 40#. It is entirely automatic and can be made as cheaply as a common sporting rifle. If you are interested in this kind of gun we would be pleased to show you what it is & how it works as we are intending to take it down your way before long. Kindly let us hear from you in relation to it at once.

Yours very truly,
Browning Bros

Above and below right, respective views: **The prototype, and a refined version, of Browning's gas-operated machine gun.** ***Below:*** **Browning with his 37mm aircraft cannon.** ***Overleaf:*** **Browning automatic shotguns.**

Browning's first gas-operated machine gun could fire 600 rounds per minute, while Gatlings of that period had a rate of fire of 1000 rounds a minute but required manual rotation of the mechanism to be fired. By 1895, John's gas-operated machine gun had been developed to such a high degree of efficiency that it was officially adopted by the United States Navy. His first automatic shotgun patent was filed in 1900, and by that year, both Fabrique Nationale and Colt's Patent Firearms Manufacturing Company had Browning Automatic Pistols in production.

All this was accomplished with no curtailment in John's inventing of more conventional rifles and shotguns, as well as miscellaneous inventions such as a machine for loading of machine gun belts invented in 1899 at the request of the Ordinance Board. The Browning Automatic Rifle was officially adopted by the United States in 1917 while the Government .45 Caliber Automatic Pistol had become the official United States military sidearm six years earlier in 1911.

In 1917 the US Government offered John Browning $750,000 for rights to his automatic firearms, and Browning patriotically accepted this sum, knowing that, had the Government paid him standard royalties for the use of these designs, he would have received almost 13 million dollars.

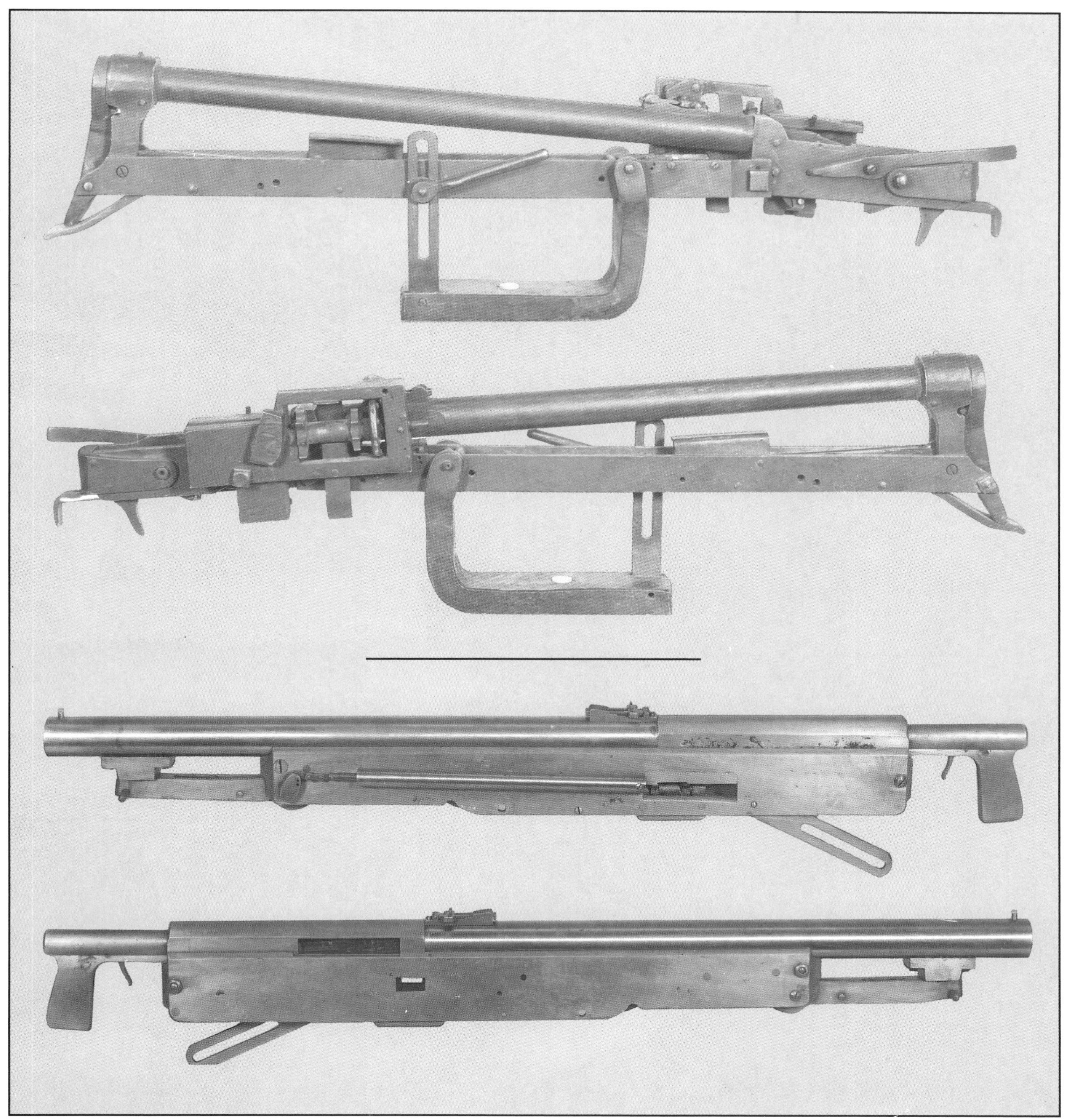

SPECIAL STEEL-12 GAUGE-SHELLS 2¾
SAVE this Booklet...
on the Operation and Care of
GENUINE BROWNING
under and Automatic Shotguns
BROWNING
ARMS COMPANY
Reg. U. S. Pat. Off.
ST. LOUIS, MISSOURI

In September 1918, Browning tested his .50 caliber machine gun, which was the 'big brother' to the .30 caliber machine gun that had seen lots of action in World War I. Both of these machine guns saw heavy use—both on the ground, and as aircraft armament—in World War II, and are still in limited use at the present time. In a report from the commanding officer of the US Army Air Force dated November 1943, the .50 caliber Browning machine gun was cited as 'the most outstanding aircraft gun of the Second World War.'

Even Reichsmarshall Herman Goering admitted that 'If the German Air Force had had the Browning .50 caliber, the Battle of Britain would have turned out differently.' To date, no fewer that 66 different known models of the Browning Recoil Machine Gun have been made. The latest aircraft models were stepped up to a cyclic rate of fire of 1300 rounds per minute in the .30 caliber and 1200 per minute in the .50 caliber. Indeed, 'Browning' has come to be a household word. The term 'browning' appears in many French dictionaries as a common noun, uncapitalized, defined as 'one of the pistols designed by the American inventor, John M Browning.'

John M Browning died the day after Thanksgiving 1926 at the Fabrique Nationale plant in Liège, Belgium. The cause of his death was attributed to heart failure. A bronze plaque hangs in the Fabrique Nationale factory in Liège. On it is the likeness of a man, neither young nor old but balding, with a medium-full mustache, an intent serious look in his the eyes, and just a hint of amusement in the lines of his mouth. The French on the plaque reads, in English,

'To the Memory of John M Browning 1855—1926. Thirty years previous, he came to this place from Ogden to have his first automatic pistol manufactured, and on the 26th of November, 1926, while he was busily engaged at work, death overtook the greatest firearms inventor the world has ever known.'

In his lifetime John M Browning took out a total of 128 patents covering more than 80 separate and distinct firearms. Upon John Browning's death the presidency of Browning Arms went to John's son, Val, a respected firearms inventor in his own right with 38 patents to his name, and a generous benefactor of colleges and hospitals. Val was even decorated by Belgian royalty. In turn, Val Browning's son, John Val, was president of Browning Arms for 14 years until just before it was acquired by Fabrique Nationale in 1977.

Today, John M Browning's designs remain the staples of the firearms industry, however, the involvement of the Browning family in the company ended with the FN stock buyout. Today, Browning North America, headquartered in Mountain Green, Utah, has divested itself of all product lines not directly related to hunting and fishing.

Firearms manufacturing is split between Asia and Europe with two-thirds of the guns being built by Miroku, a Japanese company that has made only Browning guns for the past 20 years. Fabrique Nationale itself makes the other one third. With total sales approaching $150 million a year, Browning is clearly the market leader in sales of high quality rifles and shotguns as well as home safes.

In January 1988, Browning acquired 37 percent interest in Winchester. Browning Arms has a heritage and a pride in true craftsmanship that continues to satisfy its firearms buffs from generation to generation.

Below: **The Browning shop in Ogden, Utah, at about the turn of the century.** ***Right:*** **The patent drawings for Browning's John M Browning's Single Shot Rifle.**

J. M. BROWNING.
Breech-Loading Fire-Arm.

No. 220,271. Patented Oct. 7, 1879.

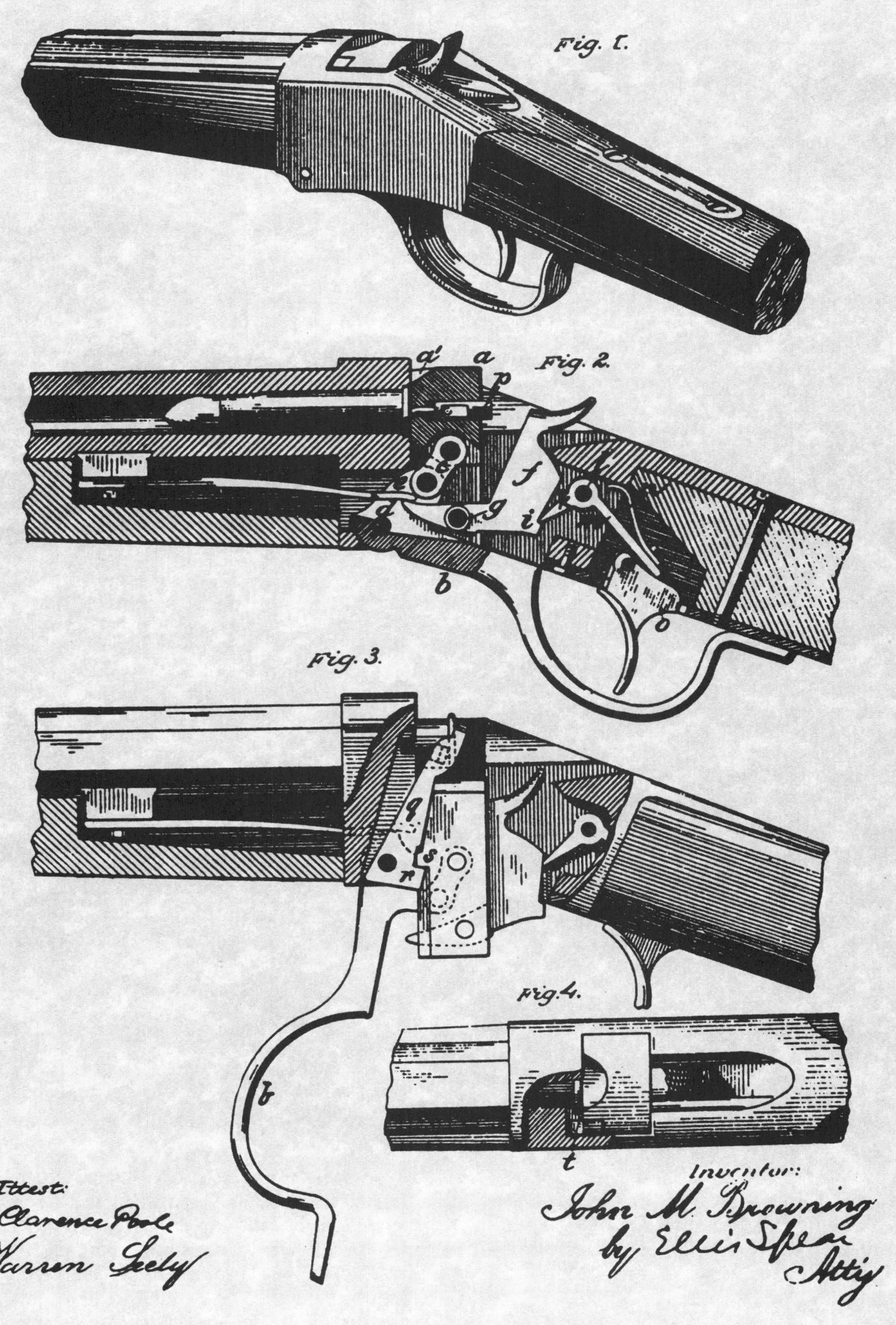

John M
Pistols

A Selection of John M Browning's Pistols

Semiautomatic .38 Caliber Pistol. This is a gas-operated semiautomatic pistol of .38 caliber, with a pistol-grip magazine, a hammer safety and fixed sights. It has a 5.75-inch barrel and weighs 2.1 pounds. It was the first of John M Browning's many semiautomatic pistol designs and was invented in 1894–95. This pistol is a logical outgrowth of Browning's development of the gas-operation principle, which during the preceding five years he had applied primarily to machine gun models.

A gas vent is located on the top of the barrel a short distance from the muzzle, over which is positioned a piston lever, linked to the breech bolt. As the expanding gases from the detonating cartridge pass through the vent, sufficient pressure is exerted on the lever to force it upward and rearward in an arc. The rearward movement opens the breech bolt, causing it to extract and eject the fired cartridge and cock the hammer.Then, as the lever and breech bolt return to their forward position, a fresh cartridge is fed into the chamber, readying the pistol for the next round.

The patent application for this firearm was filed 14 September 1895, and US Patent Number 580,923 was granted 20 April 1897. On 3 July 1895, the pistol was test-fired by officials of Colt's Patent Firearms Manufacturing Company in Hartford, Connecticut. On 24 July 1896, American manufacturing and sales rights on this pistol (and three others) were assigned to the Colt Firearms Company.

This agreement became the basis for all subsequent agreements between Browning and Colt, even though this particular pistol was never commercially produced. From the day of the agreement, Colt has produced semiautomatic pistols exclusively of the basic Browning design.

.38 Caliber Pistol

Semiautomatic .32 Caliber Pistol. This is a blowback-operated semiautomatic pistol of .32 caliber, with a pistol-grip magazine, a hammer safety and fixed sights. It has a six inch barrel and weighs two pounds. John M Browning invented this pistol in the fall of 1895, and it differs from his first semi-auto design in that the blowback principle, not gas pressure per se, is the basis of its operation. It was test-fired by Colt officials on 14 January 1896, and American

Browning's and Rifles

A weapon renowned for its performance and reliability, the 9mm Hi-Power automatic pistol *above* is one of the many Browning designs manufactured by Fabrique Nationale in Liège, Belgium. The last of John M Browning's pistol designs, it incorporates the improvements and innovations of a quarter century of pistol design.

manufacturing and sales rights were assigned to Colt on 24 July 1896. The patent application was filed 31 October 1896, and US Patent Number 580,926 was granted 20 April 1897. This pistol was never commercially produced.

The expanding pressures within the cartridge case act directly on the breech bolt through the cartridge base, forcing it backward and effecting cartridge ejection and cocking during the rearward movement. A spring located above the barrel provides the energy to slam the bolt shut again, and as the bolt is closing, it catches a fresh cartridge from the pistol-grip magazine, shoving it into the chamber, ready for firing. The slide and breech bolt are integral, and as with any blowback action, must provide sufficient inertia to delay rearward movement until the bullet leaves the barrel and gas pressures have partially diminished.

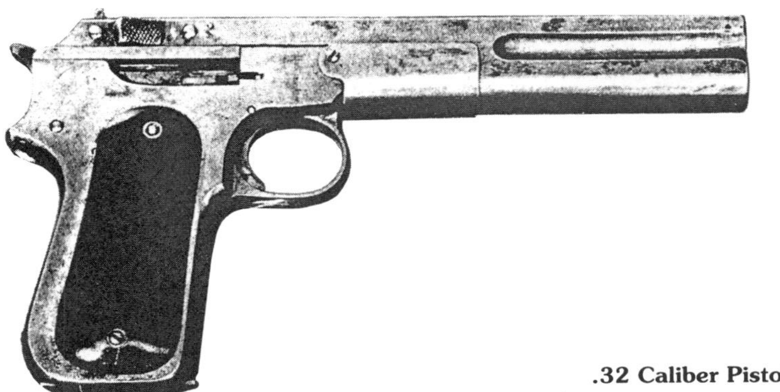

.32 Caliber Pistol

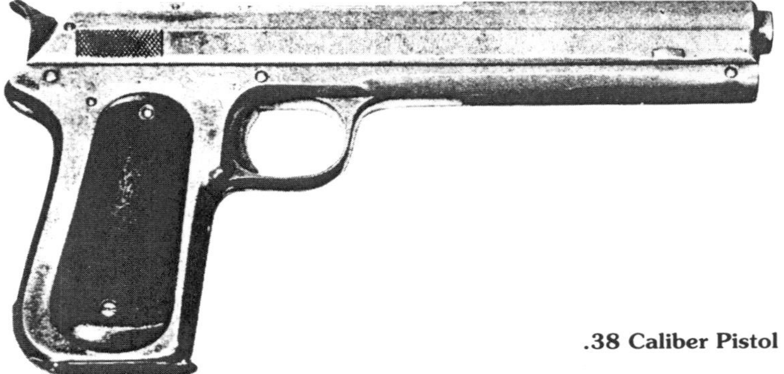

.38 Caliber Pistol

Semiautomatic .38 Caliber Pistols. These are both semiautomatic pistols of .38 caliber, with positive-lock, recoiling barrels. They each have a pistol-grip magazine and a hammer safety. One of these pistols was designed with fixed sights, and the other with no sights. Both have an 8.9-inch barrel and weigh two pounds. These two pistols were forerunners of the Colt Model 1900. They were invented in 1896 and manufacturing and sales rights were assigned to Colt on 24 July of that same year.

Patent Application Number 67 was filed on 31 October 1896 and US Patent Number 580,924 was granted on 20 April 1897. Patent Application Number 68 was filed on 7 November 1901, and US Patent Number 708,794 was granted on 9 September 1902. Neither of these pistols was commercially produced.

These are the first Browning pistols to employ a positively locked, recoiling barrel. The top of the barrel has tranverse ribs and recesses which fit into corresponding ribs in the slide. Each end of the barrel is attached to a link which, when the barrel is in battery position, presses the barrel tightly upward against the slide and thereby interlocks these ribs and recesses. Thus, in firing, the barrel and slide are locked together with a secure seal at the breach.

In discharging a cartridge, the barrel and slide recoil—locked together until the bullet has left the barrel and gas pressures diminish—at which point the barrel links draw the barrel downward out of the locking recesses, freeing it. The slide alone continues to move rearward, accomplishing the extraction, ejection and cocking functions in the process. The slide is slammed shut by springs, and as it shuts, it chambers a new cartridge from the pistol-grip magazine, readying the firearm for another shot.

Both of these pistols were originally designed to eject from the top, and were later modified to eject from the side.

Semiautomatic .38 Caliber Pistol. This is a short recoil operated semiautomatic pistol of .38 caliber, with a pistol-grip magazine, both hammer and grip safety and fixed sights. It has a 5.9-inch barrel, and weighs two pounds. This pistol was the first pistol to employ Browning's famous grip safety. It was invented by John M Browning in 1896. The patent application was filed on 31 October 1896, and US Patent Number 580,925 was granted on 20 April 1897. The firearm was submitted to Colt in the spring of 1896, and American manufacturing and sales rights were granted the company on 24 July 1896. This pistol was never commercially produced.

This semiautomatic pistol employs a rotating barrel which locks to the slide. It consists of a cylinder-shaped frame which contains a cylinder-shaped slide. The barrel, enclosed by the recoil spring, is wholly contained in the slide. Located near the breech end of the barrel are three pairs of locking lugs which fit into corresponding grooves in the slide and lock the barrel and slide together.

When the gun is fired, the barrel and slide recoil together for a short distance. Upon recoil, two camming studs near

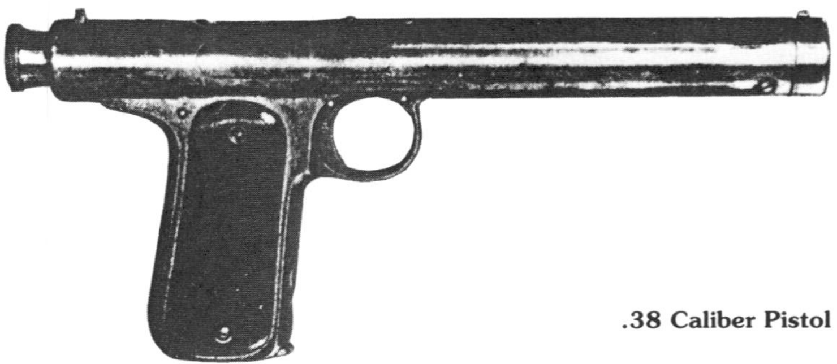

.38 Caliber Pistol

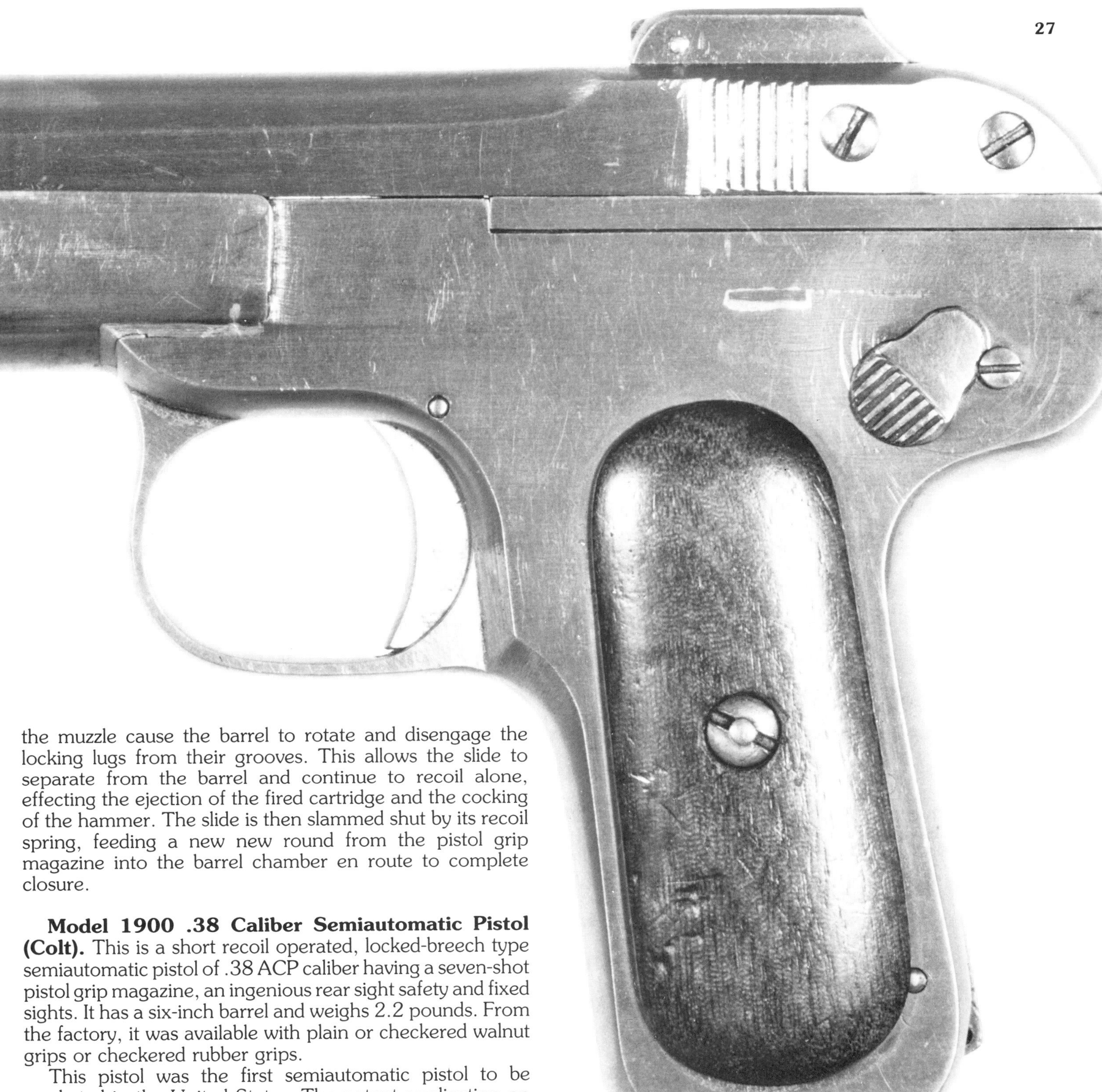

***Above:* The Model 1900 .32 caliber semiautomatic pistol was the first Browning designed automatic pistol ever maufactured. Produced by Fabrique Nationale, it was immediately popular.**

the muzzle cause the barrel to rotate and disengage the locking lugs from their grooves. This allows the slide to separate from the barrel and continue to recoil alone, effecting the ejection of the fired cartridge and the cocking of the hammer. The slide is then slammed shut by its recoil spring, feeding a new new round from the pistol grip magazine into the barrel chamber en route to complete closure.

Model 1900 .38 Caliber Semiautomatic Pistol (Colt). This is a short recoil operated, locked-breech type semiautomatic pistol of .38 ACP caliber having a seven-shot pistol grip magazine, an ingenious rear sight safety and fixed sights. It has a six-inch barrel and weighs 2.2 pounds. From the factory, it was available with plain or checkered walnut grips or checkered rubber grips.

This pistol was the first semiautomatic pistol to be marketed in the United States. The patent application on this firearm was filed 31 October 1896, and US Patent Number 580,924 was granted on 20 April 1897. It was tested by Colt on 29 June 1896, selected for production in 1898 and was placed on the market in February 1900. Its rear sight operated as a safety when pushed down—in which case it blocked the firing pin from the hammer.

Two modified versions appeared in 1902. In the 1902 Sporting Model the safety-sight was replaced with an adjustable rear sight, the hammer was changed from spur to stub round, and as a safety feature a shorter firing pin was used; this last feature soon became a Colt standard. In the 1902 Military Model, capacity was increased to eight rounds, a slide stop was added and the pistol grip was made larger.

Model 1900 .38 Caliber Pistol

Above:* The Colt Pocket Model 1903. Advertisements for the Automatic Colt Pistol *(left opposite)* and the New Service Model Ace...a natural for military shooters *(right opposite).

Model 1900 .32 Caliber Pistol

In 1903 a short-barrel Pocket Model was introduced. The Sporting Models of 1900 and 1902 were discontinued in 1908, the Pocket Model in 1927, and the Military Model in 1928. Total production figures on this pistol are at best approximate. Not only were several numbering systems used for the serial numbers, but large blocks of numbers were set aside for pistols which were—as far as can be determined—never manufactured. Numbering on the military model started at a high figure, then receded, then started back up again. It is estimated that an approximate total of 111,890 of the Sporting, Military and Pocket Models were produced.

Model 1900 .32 Caliber Semiautomatic Pistol (Fabrique Nationale). This is a hammerless, blowback-operated semiautomatic pistol of .32 ACP (7.65mm Browning) caliber, with a seven-shot pistol grip magazine, a thumb safety and fixed sights. It has a four-inch barrel, weighs 1.4 pounds and has factory walnut grips. This was the first Browning-designed semiautomatic pistol to go into production with any firm.

This gun was invented early in 1897. The patent application was filed 28 December 1897, and US Patent Number 621,747 was granted on 21 March 1899. It was shown to Colt officials and a representative of Belgium's Fabrique Nationale shortly after, and on 17 July 1897, a contract between Browning and Fabrique Nationale was signed, authorizing the firm to manufacture the pistol for all markets outside the United States. Actual production commenced in 1899, thus entitling this design to the above stated claim. The FN .32 Caliber Model 1900, as it was listed by Fabrique Nationale, became immediately popular, and demand was exceptional—100,000 had been produced by August 1904, and 500,000 had been produced by 1909. This model was discontinued in 1910 and was replaced by FN Model 1910, after a total production of 724,450 units.

Model 1911 Government .45 Caliber Automatic Pistol (Colt, Remington and Others). This is a short recoil-operated, locked-breech, semiautomatic pistol which has been manufactured in a wide variety of calibers, including .22, .38, .38 Super, .45 ACP and 9mm. In .45 ACP caliber, this firearm has a seven-shot pistol-grip magazine, comes equipped with manual, grip and magazine safeties and has fixed sights. With a standard barrel of five inches (the original was 3.8 inches), weighs 2.4 pounds, and has a wide variety of grip styles, including diamond-checkered walnut, plain checked walnut and Colt plastic.

Invented in 1905, this is one of John M Browning's most famous designs. The original was the pilot model for what has, for over a half century, been the official United States military sidearm. The patent application for the pistol was

Military Model
Semiautomatic
.45 Caliber Pistol

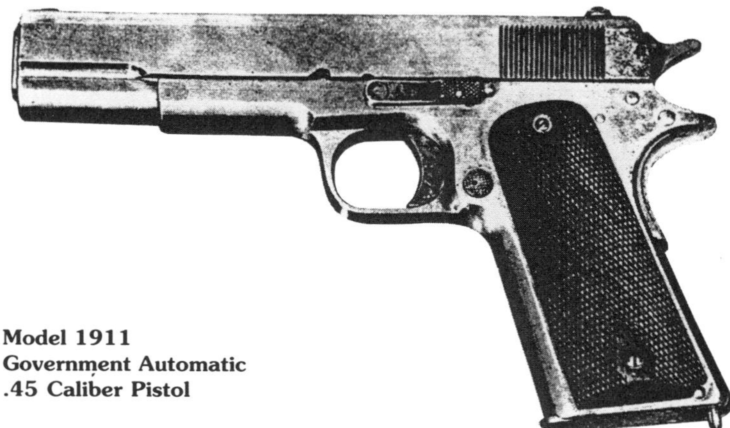

Model 1911
Government Automatic
.45 Caliber Pistol

filed on 17 February 1910, and US Patent Number 984,519 was granted on 14 February 1911. A second patent application—covering the details of the mechanical safety—was filed 23 April 1913 and US Patent Number 1,070,582 was granted 19 August 1913.

Colt commenced production in late 1905 with the first models reaching the market in the spring of 1906. The model was considered a commercial success and remained on the market in essentially its original design form until 1911, although some slight modifications had been made in 1909 and 1910.

The US government automatic pistol trials in March 1911 brought in a recommendation for adoption. Upon ratification, adoption became official on 29 March 1911, and the first Military Model was manufactured by Colt on 31 December of that year. A commercial model, identical with the Military Model except for markings, appeared on the market on 9 March 1912.

Slight changes in both of these models have been made over the years. The most important was the traditional Browning improvement of redesigning the pistol's parts so that they served several functions, thereby improving an already efficient design by reducing the total number of parts and simplifying the firearm. These changes were covered by a 1913 Browning patent.

In 1929 Colt brought out the Super .38 Model, which was patterned after the .45 Model 1911, but was chambered for the .38 caliber cartridge. In 1931, .22 caliber was added

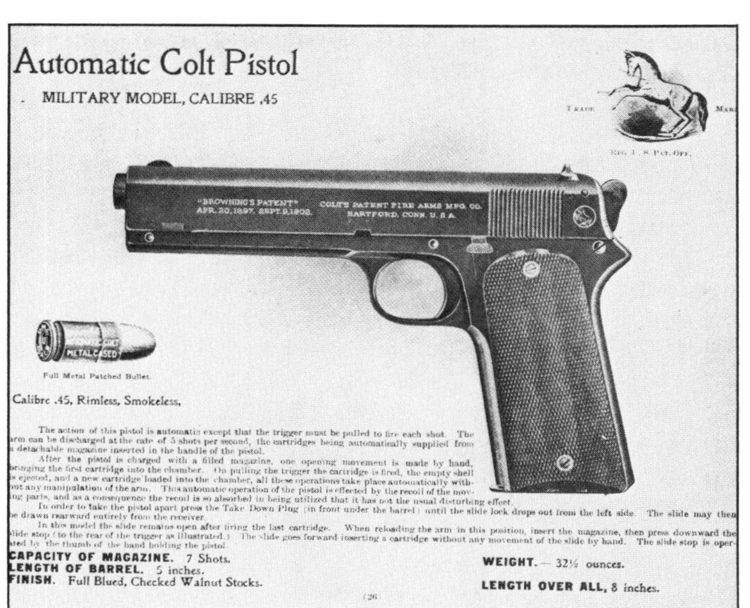

Automatic Colt Pistol

MILITARY MODEL, CALIBRE .45

Full Metal Patched Bullet.

Calibre .45, Rimless, Smokeless,

The action of this pistol is automatic except that the trigger must be pulled to fire each shot. The arm can be discharged at the rate of 5 shots per second, the cartridges being automatically supplied from a detachable magazine inserted in the handle of the pistol.

After the pistol is charged with a filled magazine, one opening movement is made by hand, bringing the first cartridge into the chamber. On pulling the trigger the cartridge is fired, the empty shell is ejected, and a new cartridge loaded into the chamber, all these operations take place automatically without any manipulation of the arm. This automatic operation of the pistol is effected by the recoil of the moving parts, and as a consequence the recoil is so absorbed in being utilized that it has not the usual disturbing effect.

In order to take the pistol apart press the Take Down Plug (in front under the barrel) until the slide lock drops out from the left side. The slide may then be drawn rearward entirely from the receiver.

In this model the slide remains open after firing the last cartridge. When reloading the arm in this position, insert the magazine, then press downward the slide stop (to the rear of the trigger as illustrated.) The slide goes forward inserting a cartridge without any movement of the slide by hand. The slide stop is operated by the thumb of the hand holding the pistol.

CAPACITY OF MAGAZINE. 7 Shots.
LENGTH OF BARREL. 5 inches.
FINISH. Full Blued, Checked Walnut Stocks.

WEIGHT.—32½ ounces.
LENGTH OVER ALL, 8 inches.

(26)

to the design roster, with the .22 Ace Pistol. This was followed by two deluxe-grade models in 1933—the .45 National Match Pistol and the .38 Super Match. The Commander, a lightweight model weighing 1.7 pounds, was made available in 1949. This model was available in .45 ACP, .38 Super and 9mm calibers. In 1957, Colt brought out another deluxe .45 caliber target pistol, the Gold Cup National Match. A counterpart in .38 caliber, the .38 National Match, appeared in 1960.

Although these models cover a wide range of grades, all stick closely to the Model 1911 in basic design specifications. One exception is the .22 Service Ace, introduced in 1937. Based on the Model 1911, it contained modifications by another designer which enabled the shooter to get the same recoil or 'kick' with .22-caliber cartridges as with .45 ACPs,

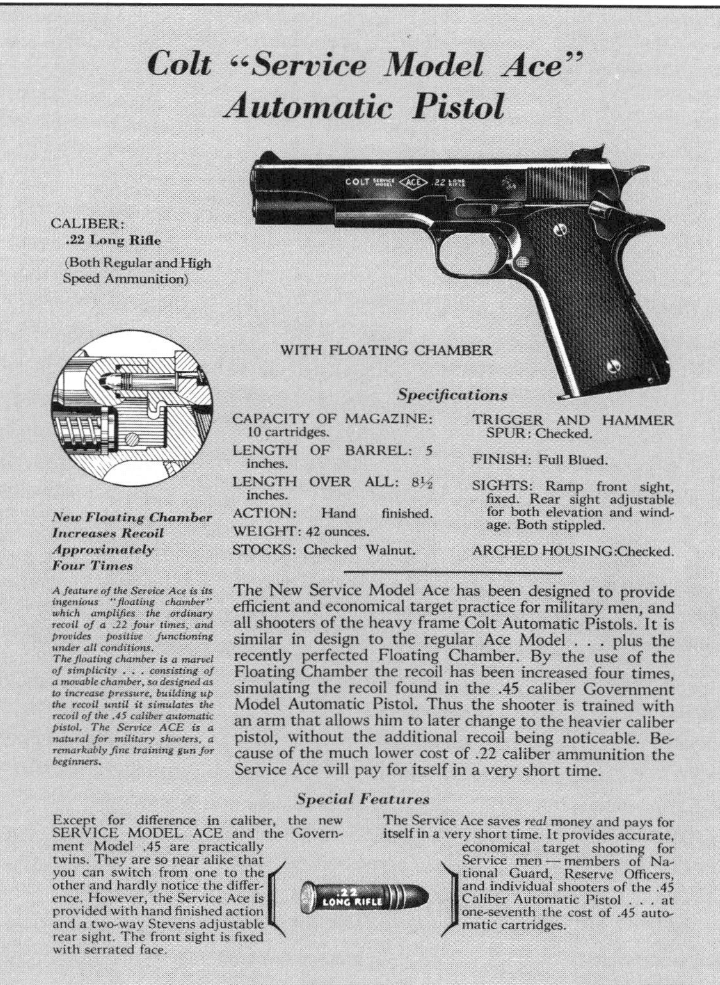

Colt "Service Model Ace" Automatic Pistol

CALIBER:
.22 Long Rifle
(Both Regular and High Speed Ammunition)

WITH FLOATING CHAMBER

New Floating Chamber Increases Recoil Approximately Four Times

A feature of the Service Ace is its ingenious "floating chamber" which amplifies the ordinary recoil of a .22 four times, and provides positive functioning under all conditions.
The floating chamber is a marvel of simplicity . . . consisting of a movable chamber, so designed as to increase pressure, building up the recoil until it simulates the recoil of the .45 caliber automatic pistol. The Service ACE is a natural for military shooters, a remarkably fine training gun for beginners.

Specifications

CAPACITY OF MAGAZINE: 10 cartridges.
LENGTH OF BARREL: 5 inches.
LENGTH OVER ALL: 8½ inches.
ACTION: Hand finished.
WEIGHT: 42 ounces.
STOCKS: Checked Walnut.

TRIGGER AND HAMMER SPUR: Checked.
FINISH: Full Blued.
SIGHTS: Ramp front sight, fixed. Rear sight adjustable for both elevation and windage. Both stippled.
ARCHED HOUSING:Checked.

The New Service Model Ace has been designed to provide efficient and economical target practice for military men, and all shooters of the heavy frame Colt Automatic Pistols. It is similar in design to the regular Ace Model . . . plus the recently perfected Floating Chamber. By the use of the Floating Chamber the recoil has been increased four times, simulating the recoil found in the .45 caliber Government Model Automatic Pistol. Thus the shooter is trained with an arm that allows him to later change to the heavier caliber pistol, without the additional recoil being noticeable. Because of the much lower cost of .22 caliber ammunition the Service Ace will pay for itself in a very short time.

Special Features

Except for difference in caliber, the new SERVICE MODEL ACE and the Government Model .45 are practically twins. They are so near alike that you can switch from one to the other and hardly notice the difference. However, the Service Ace is provided with hand finished action and a two-way Stevens adjustable rear sight. The front sight is fixed with serrated face.

The Service Ace saves *real* money and pays for itself in a very short time. It provides accurate, economical target shooting for Service men — members of National Guard, Reserve Officers, and individual shooters of the .45 Caliber Automatic Pistol . . . at one-seventh the cost of .45 automatic cartridges.

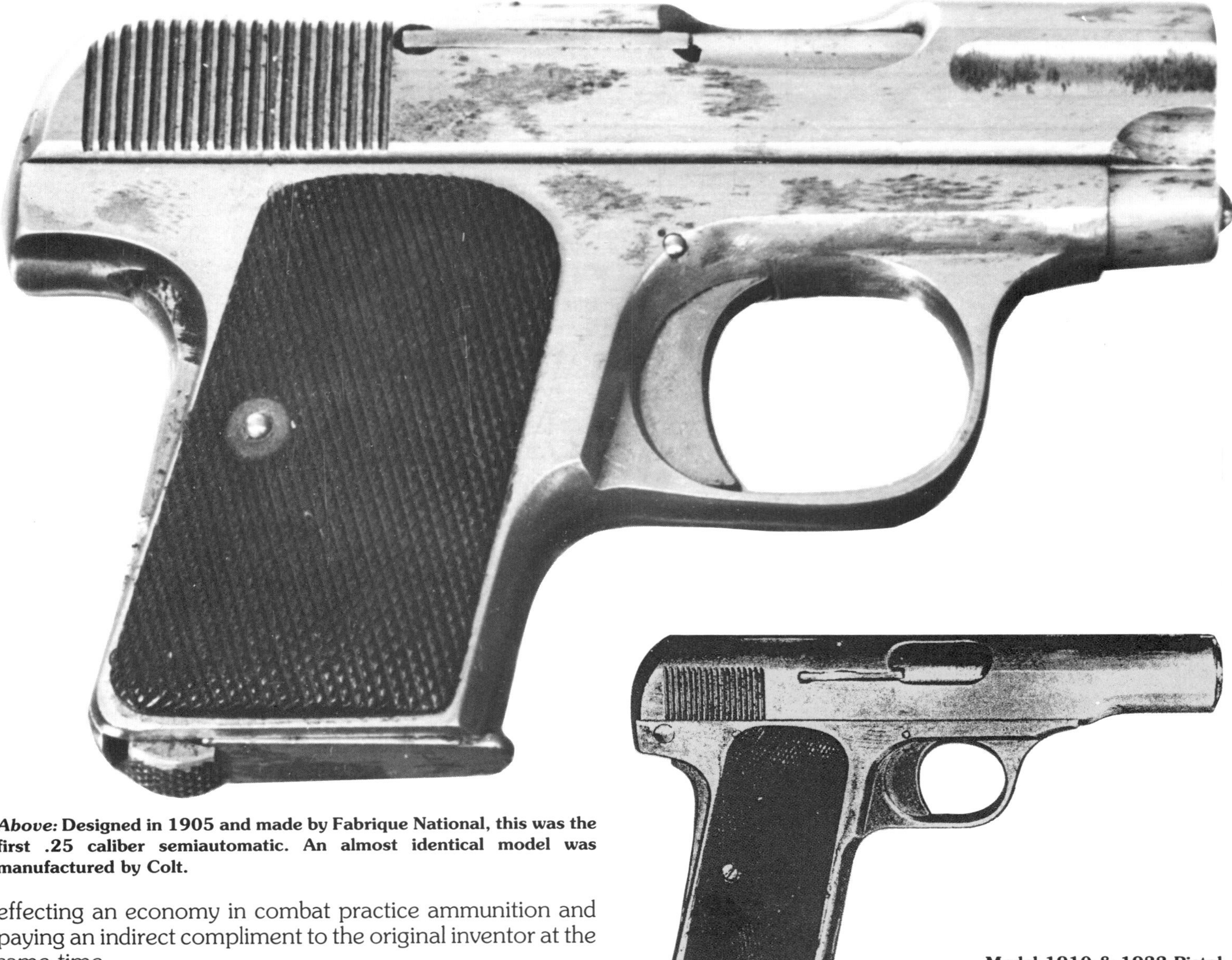

***Above:* Designed in 1905 and made by Fabrique National, this was the first .25 caliber semiautomatic. An almost identical model was manufactured by Colt.**

effecting an economy in combat practice ammunition and paying an indirect compliment to the original inventor at the same time.

Manufacture of the two Ace models was discontinued in 1940, but because the stock of parts for these was so large, Ace pistols were sold until 1947. Altogether, 10,935 units of the Ace and 13,800 units of the Service Ace were manufactured. Likewise, the .45 National Match and the .38 Super Match were discontinued in 1940; but they were still numbered with the regular commercial models for years afterward.

Between 1911 and the beginning of World War I, approximately 100,000 of the official Government Model 1911s were produced for the US Armed Forces. In 1917, the Ordinance Department, in an attempt to step up production, contracted with nine companies to produce the pistol. Of these nine, however, only the Remington Arms Company actually entered production before the war ended. For the duration, Colt produced 488,450 and Remington 21,676 units, for a wartime total of 510,126 pistols overall.

During World War II, an estimated 1,800,000 Government Model 1911s were made. Under a licensing agreement similar to that of World War I, Colt and Ithaca each produced about 400,000 units; Remington-Rand, Inc produced about 900,000 units; and the Union Switch and Signal Company produced about about 50,000 units.

After visiting all the factories which, in peace and war, have produced this weapon and examining their records, martial arms authority Lieutenant Colonel RC Kuhn has determined that, just by the end of 1945, total production of the military model was 2,695,212 units—and production has continued 'for lo, these many years since.'

Model 1910 & 1922 Pistol

Semiautomatic .25 Caliber Pistol Model Vest Pocket (Fabrique Nationale, Colt, Browning and Others). This is a blowback-operated, hammerless, semiautomatic pistol in .25 ACP caliber, with a six shot pistol-grip magazine, with thumb, grip and (later models) magazine safeties. This pistol has fixed sights, an overall length of 4.5 inches and weighs 13 ounces. Grips on various examples are black rubber with checked field and checked walnut.

This pistol was the first .25 caliber semiautomatic. It was invented by John M Browning in 1905, and was patented in Belgium that same year. This was the only Colt automatic pistol that was truly hammerless—it was discharged by a striker mechanism.

In the United States, patent application on the gun was filed 21 June 1909, and US Patent Number 947,478 was granted on 25 January 1910. The pistol's size partially accounts for (but is by no means proportionate to) its sales. It was first manufactured by FN in 6.35mm in 1905, and approximately 100,000 were sold within the first five years. Colt obtained license to manufacture the pistol in the United

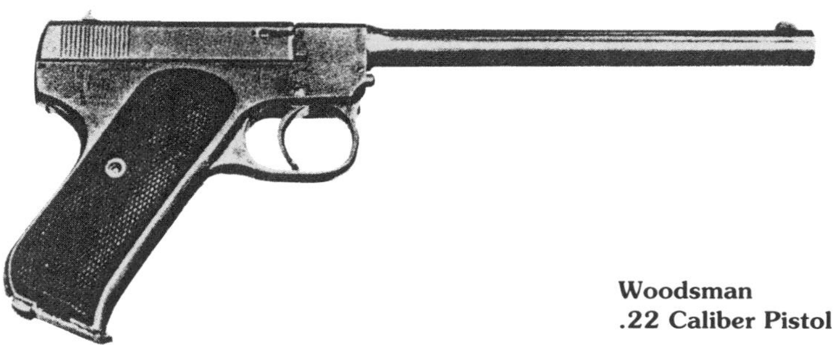

Woodsman
.22 Caliber Pistol

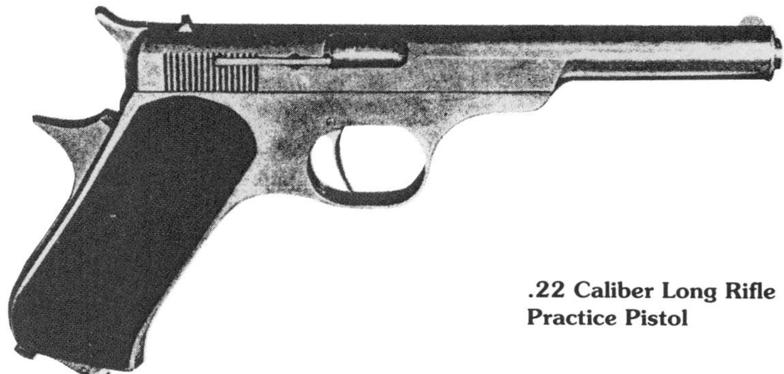

.22 Caliber Long Rifle
Practice Pistol

States and their version, chambered for the .25 caliber ACP cartridge, was introduced in October 1908, with sales numbering 141,000 by 1917. A later Browning Arms Company model, introduced in 1953, also proved highly successful.

The FN and Colt Models are almost identical, except for the thumb safety. The FN safety has a hook which latches into a notch forward of the regular safety notch in the slide and holds the slide to the rear in such a way that the barrel can be easily turned for takedown. The Colt safety has no hook, and has only one notch in the slide which locks the slide when the safety is on. The only other modifications in the Colt model were the addition of a magazine safety in 1917 and a change in sights. The Colt model was discontinued in February 1947, with total production of 420,753 units.

The first FN model was discontinued in 1940, after production of 1,080,408 units. The current Browning and FN Model .25 Caliber followed. In this, the grip safety has been eliminated, and the weight of the pistol has been reduced to 10 ounces in the standard model and 7.8 ounces in the lightweight model; the overall length was reduced to four inches in both. Even before the expiration of Browning's patents, numerous imitations of this gun had appeared on the market, particularly from Spain. Production figures on all models probably number well into the millions.

Woodsman .22 Caliber Semiautomatic Pistol (Colt). This is a blowback-operated, hammerless (concealed hammer), semiautomatic pistol in .22 long rifle caliber (early models, however, handled only low-velocity .22s), with a 10-shot magazine. This pistol has thumb and automatic (breechblock must be fully closed for firing) safeties, fixed rear/bead or partridge-style front sights, and a (after 1933) 4.5 or (pre-1933) 6.5-inch barrel. With the shorter barrel, the Woodsman weighs in at 10 ounces; with the longer barrel, this figure is 1.75 pounds. Grips for all variants tend to be checkered walnut.

The Woodsman pistol was invented in 1914. The patent application was filed on 30 March 1917 and US Patent Number 1,276,716 was granted on 27 August 1918. Colt began production on 29 March 1915, first calling it the 'Colt .22 Automatic Target Pistol.' Not until 1927 was it given the name by which it is best known, 'the Woodsman.' Somewhat of a rarity for the era in which it first appeared, it utilizes a half-length slide which completely separates from the breech end of the barrel.

'Lesmok or semi-smokeless, lubricated cartridge only' was Colt's caution on ammunition for early models. In approximately 1920, a change in magazine design made possible the use of high-speed ammunition. Many owners converted their models before this. It was relatively easy to make the pistol capable of handling high-velocity cartridges—by replacing the original mainspring, housing and recoil spring, and by employing an upgraded magazine.

The 4.5-inch barrel Sport Model was introduced in 1933, followed by the Match Target Woodsman in 1938. This was a deluxe model of the Target Woodsman, with an extra-heavy 6.5-inch barrel, larger grips, new trigger, new sights, an added seven ounces of weight. It represented a radical change in design, with a flat-sided barrel and elongated, curved grips.

Manufacture of all three models was discontinued in 1940, but as a result of a plentiful supply of already-manufactured parts, these pistols remained on the market until June 1947, with a total production of 187,423 units.

Two postwar Woodsman models with familiar names were introduced in May 1947—the Target, with a six-inch barrel, and the Sport, with a 4.5 inch barrel. In December of the same year, Match Target Pistols, with 4.5 or six-inch barrels, were introduced. In 1950, Colt brought out an economy model based on the Woodsman; this had a 4.5 inch barrel, and modifications—on the sights, magazine and other aspects of the Woodsman design—distinguished this as an economy firearm. First designated the 'Challenger,' it was renamed the 'Huntsman' in 1955. In 1959, Colt made a few minor changes in the Target Model and redesignated it the 'Targetsman.'

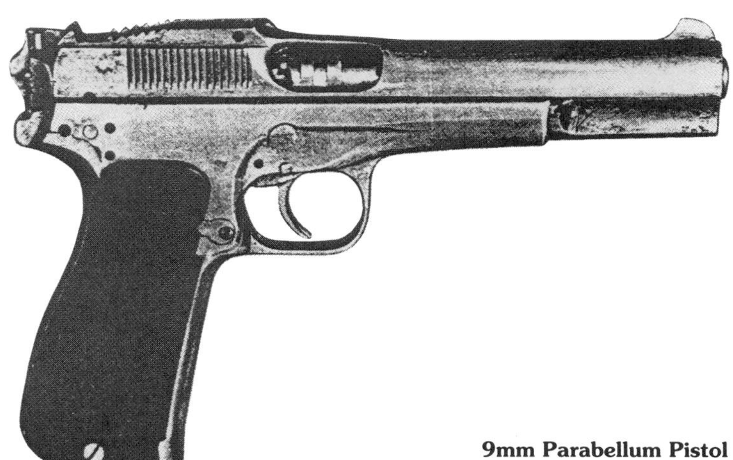

9mm Parabellum Pistol

Semiautomatic Pistol in 9mm Parabellum Caliber. This is a blowback-operated, hammerless (concealed hammer), semiautomatic pistol in 9mm Parabellum caliber, with a pistol-grip magazine, thumb and hammer safeties, and fixed front/elevation rear, sights. It has a 5.7-inch barrel and weighs 2.3 pounds.

The barrel is adapted to move rearward a short distance in a line parallel with the movement of the breechblock and slide without being locked to the breechblock.

Above: Browning's pilot model 9mm pistol. *Right:* John M Browning and his Automatic 22. *Opposite:* A Browning Brothers advertisement in the *Ogden Morning Herald*, touting their wares.

In early 1923, John M Browning was informed that the French Ministry of War was interested in obtaining a semiautomatic pistol of large magazine capacity chambered for the 9mm Parabellum cartridge. Browning completed this model in a few months. This pistol was never patented or commercially produced. It has been seen as a precursor design to Browning's last pistol design, which closely resembled it.

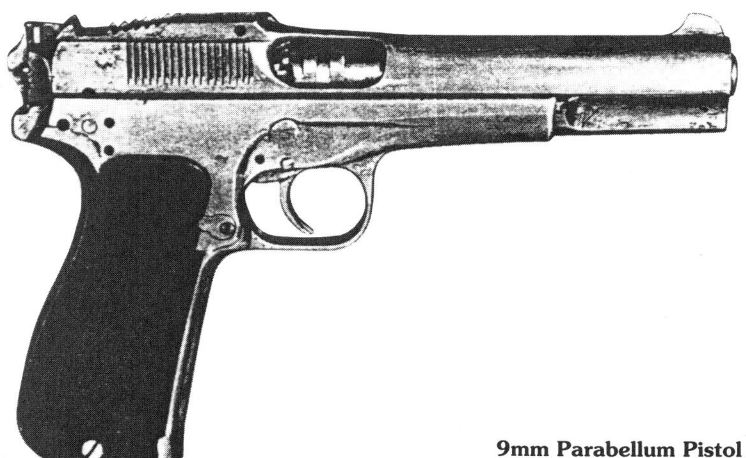

9mm Parabellum Pistol

Semiautomatic Pistol in 9mm Parabellum Caliber (Fabrique Nationale, Browning and Others). This is a short recoil-operated, locked breech, semiautomatic pistol in 9mm Parabellum (9mm Luger) Caliber, with a 13-shot pistol-grip magazine and blade front/fixed rear sights (some military models having graduated-leaf rear sights). This pistol has thumb, hammer and magazine safeties, a 4.6-inch barrel and weighs 2.2 pounds. The grips are checkered wood; military models are also equipped with a quick-takedown shoulder stock which is fastened to the grips so that the pistol can be fired with rifle-like steadiness.

This was John M Browning's last pistol development. The patent application was filed on 28 June 1923, and US Patent Number 1,618,510 was granted on 22 February 1927—three months after John M Browning's death.

This was first produced by Fabrique Nationale in 1935 as the 'Model 1935.' The visible ribs on the breech end of the barrel are engaged by corresponding grooves in the slide which securely lock the two together upon firing. The breechblock is demountably fixed to the slide, so that the breechblock effectively seals the breech against the force of the fired charge. Recoil continues in this locked position until the bullet leaves the bore. Then a camming action tilts the rear of the barrel downward, freeing the slide and the breechblock to continue rearward, effecting the necessary ejection and cocking operations. A spring slams the action shut anew, and as this operation proceeds, a fresh cartridge is shoved from the magazine into the firing chamber by lugs on the moving mechanism.

The Model 1935 was adopted as the official sidearm of the Belgian Army and other European and colonial troops. Over 200,000 were manufactured in Canada for the Chinese Army during World War II. This pistol was, for years, the standard military sidearm of many of the NATO countries, and the Browning Company sold it as a personal and sporting arm as well.

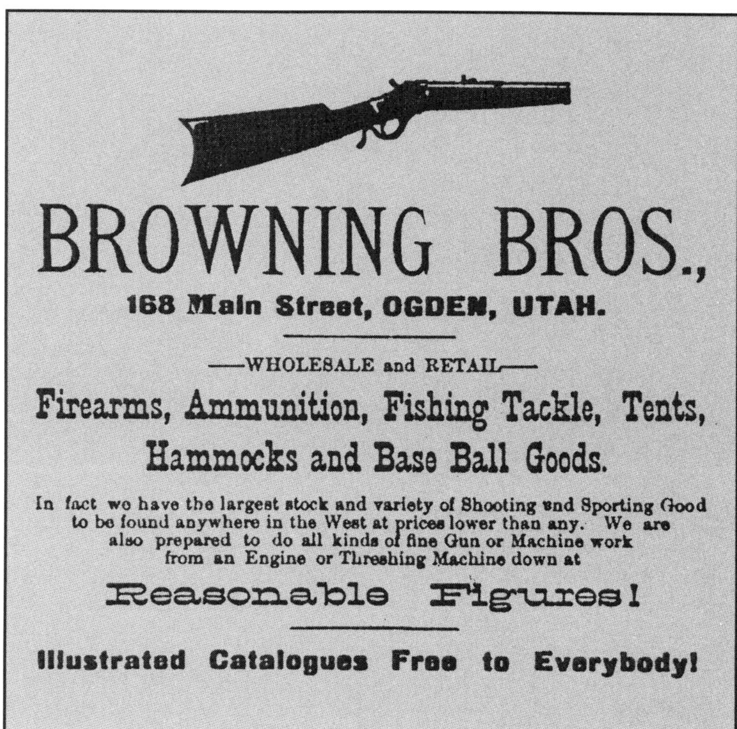

These ornate 9mm Hi-Power pistols were introduced in 1985 to commemorate John Browning's innovative and highly successful automatic pistol design. Engraved on the top of the Classic edition *(right)* is a bald eagle protecting her young from a lynx. On the sides are engraved profiles of an eagle's head and the words 'One of Five Thousand.' The Classic Gold edition *(left)* features similar engraving with inlaid, 18 karat gold highlights and the words 'One of Five Hundred.'

BROWNING ARMS COMPANY MORGAN, UTAH & MONTREAL P.Q.
ONE OF FIVE THOUSAND

A Selection of John M Browning's Rifles

Single Shot Rifle (Browning Brothers and Winchester). This is a single shot falling block rifle which has been adapted to a very wide variety of calibers, ranging from .22 short to .50-90 Sharps. It has both hammer and action safeties (half-cock notch and full-close firing only), windage and elevation-adjustable rear/blade front sights, a variety of barrel lengths from 15 to 30 inches (depending upon model) and, likewise, weight varying from 4.5 to 13 pounds. Since this rifle was made in a wide number of variants, stock styles varied widely also, from a standard rifle type stock to the ornate and heavily styled Schuetzen target model, to the shotgun style featured on that particular variant! Barrels likewise varied—in length, as is noted above, and in configurations from round to octagonal to half-octagonal.

This was John M Browning's first firearm, invented in 1878 when he was 23 years old.The patent was filed 12 May 1879, and US Patent Number 220,271 was granted on 7 October 1879. Production by the Browning Brothers, in Ogden, Utah Territory, began about 1880 and continued until 1883, with a total of approximately 600 rifles manufactured. Manufacturing and sales rights were sold to the Winchester Repeating Arms Company in 1883 and the rifle appeared in 1885 as the Winchester Single Shot Model 1885.

The hammer dropped down with the breechblock when the trigger guard was levered open, and cocking was accomplished by the closing movement. Of course, it could also be cocked by hand.

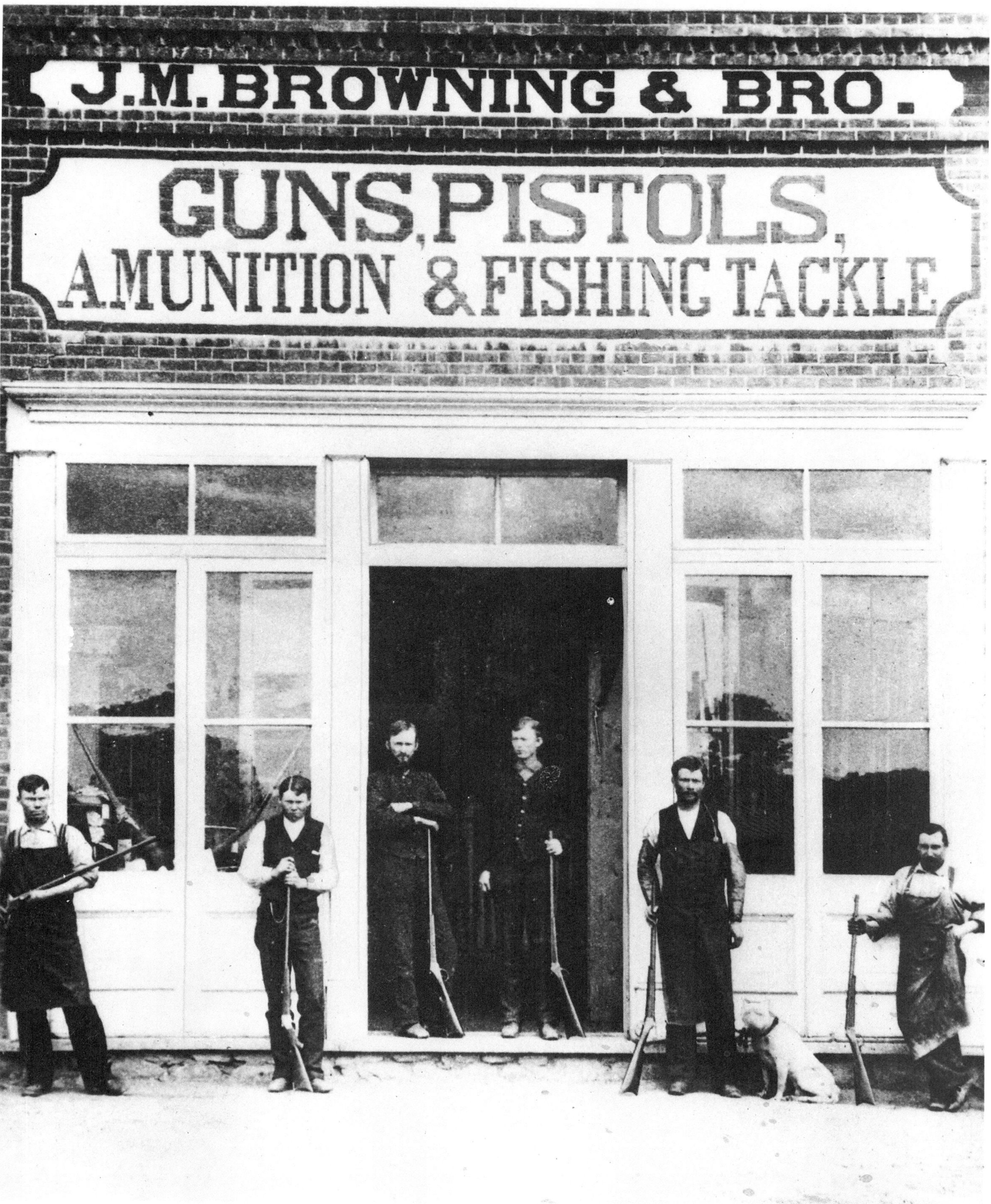

Above left: The inventor at age 18. *Opposite:* The Browning shop and factory as it appears today, and *(above)* as it appeared in 1882. Shown here from left to right are Sam Browning, George Browning, John M Browning, Matthew S Browning, Ed Browning and Frank Rushton.

Overleaf: The Browning tradition of innovation and craftsmanship continues today—*(from the top down)* an A-Bolt 22 Bolt Action, a BL-22 Lever Action Grade II, a BL-22 Lever Action Grade I and a 22 Semi-Auto.

SILENT PLACES
STEWART EDWARD WHITE
GROSSET & DUNLAP
Stewart Edward White
GROSSET & DUNLAP
THEIR YESTERDAYS
WRIGHT
A.L. BURT COMPANY
KEEP THE WAGONS MOVING!
THE RE-CREATION OF BRIAN KENT
WRIGHT
THE BOOK SUPPLY COMPANY
SPOILERS OF THE VALLEY
ROBERT WATSON
THE FORBIDDEN TRAIL
WILLSIE
RIDERS of the TRAIL
JOHNSON
THEIR YESTERDAYS
WRIGHT
THE SPOILERS
REX BEACH
EMERSON HOUGH
THE STRANGE TEEPEE
HART
THE BOOK SUPPLY COMPANY
H.W. RODEN
GRACE HARLOWE OVERLAND SERIES
BLAKISTON
TRIANGLE BOOKS
WAR ON THE RANGE
RUBEL
PHOENIX
THE SILENT CALL
EDWIN MILTON ROYLE
THE SUNSET TRAIL
ALFRED HENRY LEWIS
HEART OF THE SUNSET
REX BEACH
REX BEACH
HEART OF THE SUNSET
YUKON EDITION
THE NIGHT-RIDERS
CULLUM

THE RE-CREATION OF BRIAN KENT
WRIGHT
BACK OF BEYOND
STEWART EDWARD WHITE
ON TIPTOE
WHITE
JIM the CONQUEROR
PETER B. KYNE
Never the Twain Shall Meet
Peter B. Kyne
WEBSTER MAN'S MAN
PETER B. KYNE
A.L. BURT COMPANY
The Young Forester
ZANE GREY
813 K99w Copy 2
GROSSET & DUNLAP
The Dark Road
LEROUX
THE COVERED WAGON
HOUGH
ACROSS THE MESA
WASON
THE RE-CREATION OF
THE BOOK SUPPLY COMPANY
APPLETON
GOLDSMITH
BAD MEN AND GOOD
MacHARG BALMER
EVERY MAN
NICHOLS
Winning the Wilderness
McCarter
MARGARET HILL McCARTER
CYCLONE JIM
REPP
FACE WEST
LULL
HARPERS
THROUGH THE WALL
MOFFETT
COWBOY HUGH
NICHOLS
THE IRON HORSE
EDWIN C. HILL
THE LONE STAR RANGER
ZANE GREY
LEWIS
THE BARRIER
REX BEACH

Above: **An original 1886 Winchester.** ***At bottom:*** **A replica of same that was introduced in 1986 to commemorate the 100th anniversary of its invention.** ***Opposite:*** **The Model 1886 with half magazine.** ***Right:*** **The Four Bs, Utah's premier live-bird team in the 1890s.**

The Single Shot has been adapted to over 33 different calibers, including both rim- and centerfire cartridges—more than any other single shot or repeating rifle known. It was the first Winchester rifle capable of handling the more powerful metallic cartridges of the period.

Through the years the Single Shot was produced in a variety of models. The light carbine (called the 'Baby Carbine') appeared in 1898. The takedown model was introduced in 1910. A special military target version was introduced in 1905; in 1914 it was revamped as the Winder Musket, named in honor of Colonel CB Winder, and was used for training expeditions in World War I. In 1914, the Single Shot was also made into a shotgun, chambered for the three-inch 20-gauge shell.

This firearm was discontinued in all models in 1920. Total production of all models was approximately 140,325, which includes the 600-unit production by the Browning Brothers.

Tubular Magazine Repeating Rifle. This was a bolt action, tubular magazine firearm of indeterminate caliber. The second arm invented by John M Browning was a tubular magazine repeating rifle. Patent was filed 29 March 1882, and US Patent No. 261,667 was granted 25 July 1882. This gun was never manufactured, and no known models survive.

This was probably John M Browning's first tubular magazine design. From the patent application, its bolt action was to have a rotating sleeve with locking shoulders in the receiver. The then-features of this gun were the arrangement of the tubular magazine under the barrel; the receiver, open at the top; and the carrier for elevating cartridges from the magazine to the chamber.

Cartridges are loaded into the magazine through the top of the receiver when the bolt is open. A system of grooves on each side of the inner walls of the receiver guide the cartridges as they are manually forced one by one into the rear opening of the magazine. A spring system in the magazine forces a fresh cartridge onto the spring-loaded carrier at the bottom of the chamber, where, when the bolt is opened, the cartridge is snagged by a lug on the bolt and is thereby slid into the breech when the bolt was closed.

The striker-type firing pin has a finger hook for manual cocking. A spent cartridge is ejected by opening the bolt, which action also allows a fresh cartridge from the magazine to come into position for bolt-loading into the breech.

Lever Action Repeating Rifle. This is a lever action rifle in .45 caliber, with a tubular magazine, an automatic safety and a 26.8-inch octagonal barrel. This rifle weighs 8.8 pounds. It was invented in 1882. Patent was filed 13 September 1882, and US Patent Number 282,839 was granted 7 August 1883. It was never manufactured.

It is a unique firearm in that it operates quite differently from most lever actions. Of very simple construction, the breechblock and finger lever are essentially of one piece. The breech piece is hung to the receiver by the extractor in such a manner that the operating movement causes the rear end of the breech to drop, thereby unlocking the piece, while the forward end, in the receiver, is guided longitudinally by the extractor.

The swinging movement of the combination breechblock and finger piece extracts and ejects the fired shell, and pivots a one-piece carrier upward from the magazine, with a fresh round ready to load when the action is closed. Cocking the hammer is not done automatically, but instead must be done

manually for each round, thus constituting an automatic safety.

When in closed position, the rear end of the breech rests squarely against the recoil-bearing surface in the receiver, holding the front end of the breechblock against the barrel. The purpose of this construction is to provide a lever action rifle of extreme simplicity, with a minimum of parts.

Model 1886 Lever Action Repeating Rifle. This is a lever action repeating rifle in a large variety of calibers—including .45-70 US Government, .40-82 WCF, .45-90 WCF, .40-65 WCF, .38-56 WCF, .50-110, .40-70 WCF, .38-70 WCF, .50-100-450 and .33 WCF—with a choice of either full-length or half-length tubular magazine of varying capacities, depending on the ammunition used. Safeties on this firearm are manual and mechanical, and barrels include 26-inch round, octagon or half octagon, 22-inch round and special barrels and magazines that were finished to owner specifications until 1908. The weight of this arm varies widely depending on specifications and caliber, and stock types range from the sporter with straight or pistol grip, to extra-lightweight, to shotgun, carbine and musket-type stocks.

Invented in 1882–83, this was the first Browning-designed repeating rifle ever manufactured. It was also the first repeating rifle from any source to successfully employ sliding vertical locking lugs—which effectively seal the breech and barrel of the gun. By this same distinction, it was the forerunner of all later Browning lever action rifles. It has been said that practically every improvement since made in lever action rifle design was derived from this design.

Patent was filed 26 May 1884, and US Patent Number 306,577 was on granted 14 October 1884. Purchased by Winchester in October 1884, it appeared on the market in 1886 as the legendary Winchester Model 1886. In 1894, the Model 1886 was converted to a takedown model, and in 1936, it was slightly modified to handle the .348 Winchester cartridge, and became the Model 71.

The Model 1886 was discontinued in 1935 with 159,994 produced, and the Model 71 was discontinued in 1957 with 43,267 produced. The total production for this rifle was 203,261 units, and its production life had spanned 71 years.

Model 1890 .22 Caliber Pump Action Repeating Rifle (Winchester). This is pump action repeating rifle of .22 caliber (short, long, long rifle and WRF) with a tubular magazine of varying capacity (from 15 shorts to 11 long rifles), manual and mechanical safeties and a wide variety of sights. It has a 24-inch octagonal barrel and weighs, depending on stock styling, 5.8 to 6.0 pounds. Available stocks include a standard rifle type, with curved steel butt plate and straight grip, and optional pistol-grip stocks.

The patent application on this gun was filed 13 December 1887, and US Patent Number 385,238 was granted on 26 June 1888. The firearm was produced, and appeared in 1890 as the Winchester .22 Caliber Repeating Rifle Model 1890, and was the first repeating pump action gun manufactured by Winchester. It has been called 'the most popular .22 caliber pump action rifle ever made.'

What distinguished this rifle over previous .22 caliber repeaters was the cartridge carrier-feed mechanism. Pre-

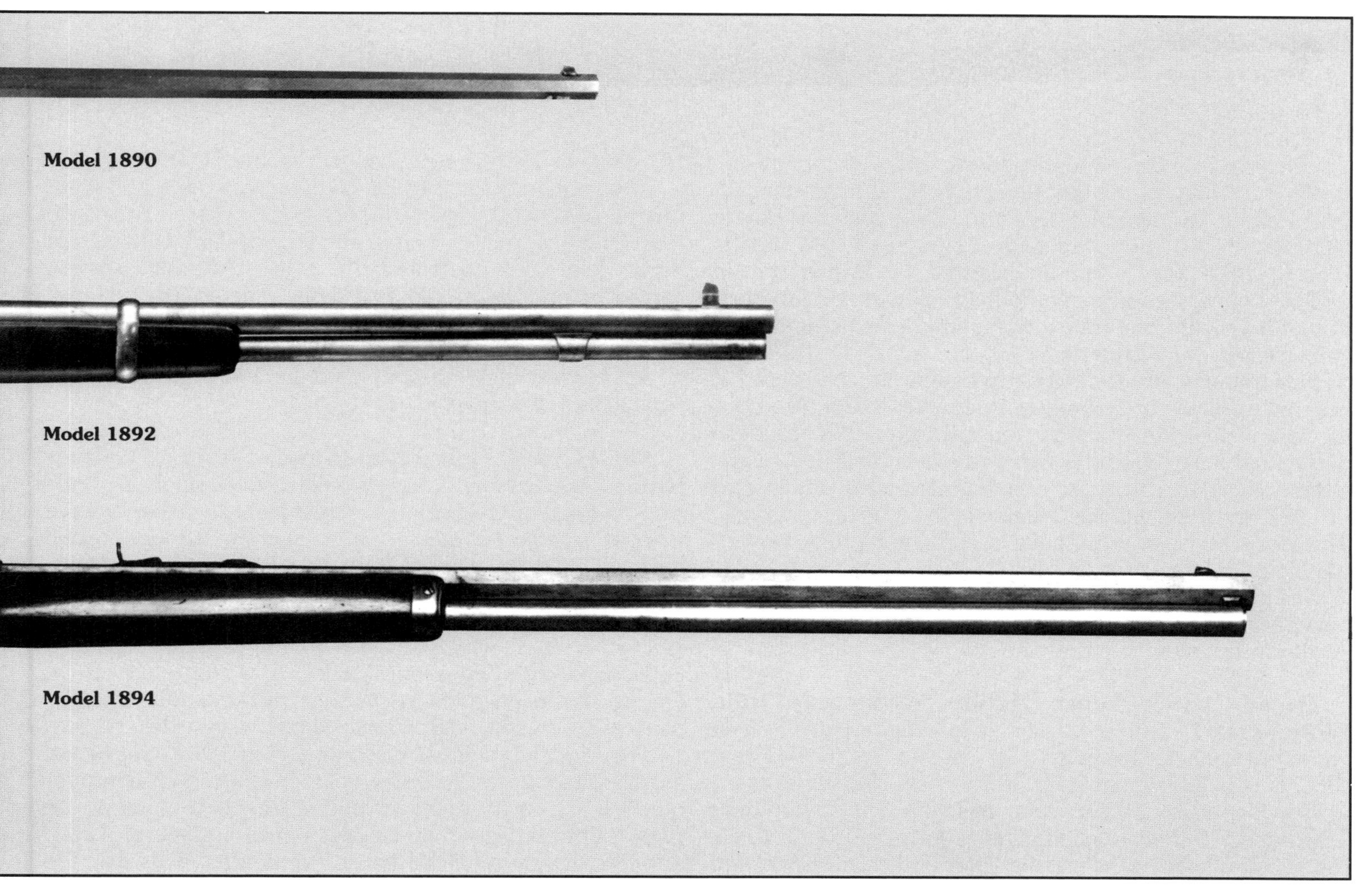

viously, no positive method of handling the .22 caliber short cartridge had been developed. This small cartridge was prone to jam most repeater rifle mechanisms—it was so short that, often, two cartridges would find their way to where only one of them should have been.

Browning's design features a fingerlike cartridge stop on the front of the carrier, which assures that only one .22 short cartridge at a time can fit onto the carrier. When a spent cartridge is ejected from the chamber, the carrier presents the fresh cartridge, ready to be loaded by the mechanism into the chamber.

First manufactured with its barrel permanently mounted to its frame, the Model 1890 was converted to takedown in 1893. The Model '06, introduced in 1906, represents a modification which enabled one rifle to accept all .22-caliber cartridges except the slightly irregular .22 WRF (the Model 1890 versions were not interchangeable). Also, with these changes, a 20-inch round barrel replaced the 24-inch octagonal barrel. In 1932, the Models 90 and '06 were renamed the 'Model 62,' with the introduction on both of a barrel with slightly different specifications, and new sights.

The Models 90 and '06 were discontinued in 1932 with 849,000 and 848,000 produced respectively. The Model 62 was discontinued in 1958 with 409,475 produced. The production total for all variants of this rifle are 2,106,475 units, with a production life of 69 years.

Model 1892 Lever Action Repeating Rifle (Winchester). The Model 1892 is a lever action repeating rifle of either .44-40, .38-40, .32-20 or .25-20 caliber, with a tubular magazine having capacities ranging from five to 17 rounds, both mechanical and manual safeties, and adjustable sights. With barrel lengths ranging from an absolute minimum of 14 inches (special model) to an absolute maximum of 36 inches (special model), the weight of this firearm varied from 5.5 to eight pounds. The Model 1892 was available with a wide variety of stocks.

The 1892 was originally designed with its barrel permanently mounted to its frame, but in 1893 it became available in a takedown model. A modified version with a decreased magazine capacity was introduced in 1924 as the Model 53. Its successor, the Model 65, was introduced in 1933.

The Model 53 was discontinued in 1932 with a production total of 24,916 units; the Model 65 was discontinued in 1947, with a total of 5704; and the Model 92, though not produced except in the carbine model for several years after the introduction of the Model 53, was not officially discontinued until 1941—at which time 1,004,067 had been manufactured. The manufacturing total for all variants combined stands at 1,034,687 units.

Model 1894 Lever Action Repeating Rifle (Winchester). This is a lever action rifle in .32-40 and .38-55 (both black powder), and .25-35, .30-30 and .32 Special (all three, smokeless powder) calibers, with a tubular magazine of various capacities ranging from three to eight cartridges. This design has both manual and mechanical safeties, and adjustable sights. Barrel lengths and styles include 20-inch round, 22-inch round and 26-inch round, octagonal or half octagonal, and weights range from 5.8 to 6.3 pounds for carbine models, from seven to 7.8 pounds for other variants. Stock styles are many and various.

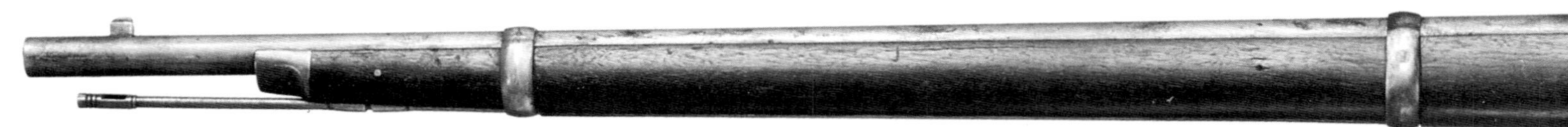

Often called 'the most famous sporting rifle ever produced,' the Model 94 is perhaps best-known as the 'Winchester .30-30.' Patent was filed 19 January 1894, and US Patent Number 524,702 was granted on 21 August 1894, and the Model 1894 was first manufactured by Winchester in 1894—hence, its company monicker. It was revolutionary in that it was the first repeating hunting rifle to handle the smokeless-powder cartridges.

First manufactured with a permanently attached barrel, it became available in a takedown model in 1895. Modified versions include the Model 55, introduced in 1924 (principal differences being a shorter barrel, a redesigned stock and a switch to half-length magazine), and the Model 64, introduced in 1933 (the main difference being in the type of steel used). The Model 55 was discontinued in 1932, and production for the Model 64 halted in 1957.

Still in production as the Model 94 carbine, this rifle has outsold any other manufactured by the Winchester Repeating Arms Company.

Model 1895 Lever Action Repeating Rifle (Winchester). This is a lever action repeating rifle in a variety of calibers, including .30 US Army, .30-40 Krag, .38-72, .40-72 Winchester, .303 British, .35 Winchester, .405 Winchester, .30 Government 1903, .30 Government 1906 and 7.62mm Russian. This firearm has a four to six round box magazine, adjustable sights and both manual and mechanical safeties. Barrel lengths and styles vary from 22 to 36 inches, and round, octagonal or half-octagonal. Weight and stock style varies according to variant specifications.

This was the first non-detachable box-type magazine rifle designed to handle jacketed sharp-nosed bullets. The patent application for this rifle was filed on 19 November 1894, and US Patent Number 549,345 was granted on 5 November 1895. The firearm was first manufactured by Winchester in 1896, and is known as the Winchester Model 95.

Four slightly different versions of the musket appeared between 1895 and 1908—they are as follows. The .30 Army Model/1895 US Army Pattern was adopted by the US Army in 1895. The same year, some 10,000 of these were chambered for the .30-40 Krag cartridge and were purchased by the US Army for use in the Spanish-American War. Prior to America's entry into World War I, 293,816 of these guns were chambered for the 7.62mm Russian cartridge, and were sold to Russia. The fourth of these particular variants was a takedown version that appeared in 1910.

All models were discontinued in 1931, with a total production of 425,881.

Model 1900 Bolt Action Single Shot .22 Caliber Rifle (Winchester). This was a bolt action, single shot rifle of .22 (long and short, interchangeable) caliber with a manual safety, adjustable sights and an 18-inch round barrel. This rifle weighs 2.8 pounds.

The patent application on this gun was filed 17 February 1899, and US Patent Number 632,094 was granted 29 August 1899. It was first listed in the Winchester 1899 catalogue as the Winchester Model 1900 Single Shot Rifle. Designed as a low price, single shot 'plinking' rifle, it was of especially simple construction and has been widely copied.

The Model 1900 was discontinued in 1902; the Model 1902, announced the same year, had a modified trigger guard shape, a short trigger pull, a steel butt plate, a rear peep sight and a slightly heavier barrel. In July of 1904, another slightly modified version appeared. This was the Model 1904, which had a longer, heavier barrel and a modified stock. Another interesting variant is the Model 99 Thumb Trigger Rifle, which also appeared in 1904. This rifle has no conventional trigger; just behind the cocking piece on the bolt is a button called the 'thumb trigger.' When ready to discharge a round, the marksman merely presses down on this button with the thumb to release the firing pin.

In 1928 and the years following, Winchester brought out other variations—the Models 58, 59, 60 and 68. In 1920, a shotgun version, similar to the Model 1902, was announced—this being the Winchester Model 36 Single Shot Shotgun. It was the only American-made shotgun chambered for 9mm paper shells, and was discontinued in

Above: An original Model 95 Lever Action Takedown Rifle. _Below:_ An original Browning Single Shot, introduced as the Winchester Model 1900. _Right:_ An advertisement for the .50-100-450 cartridge, designed especially for the Winchester Model 1886.

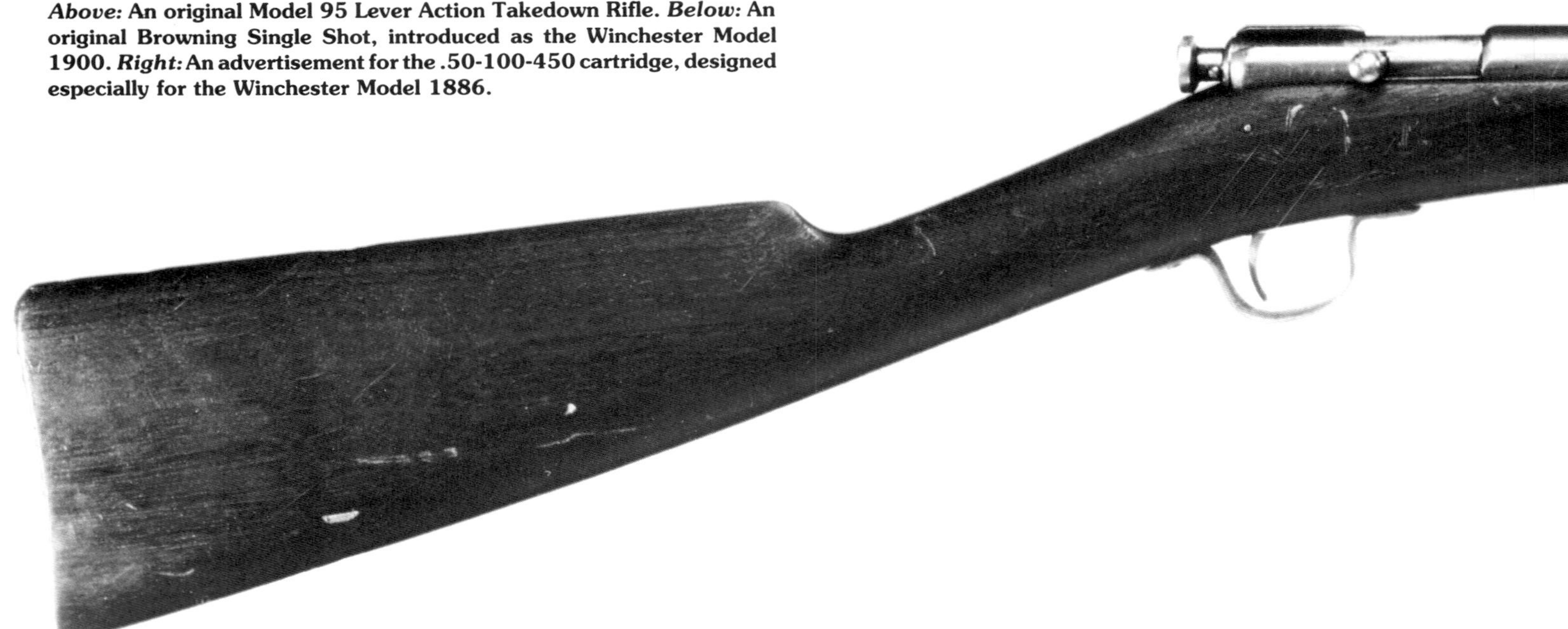

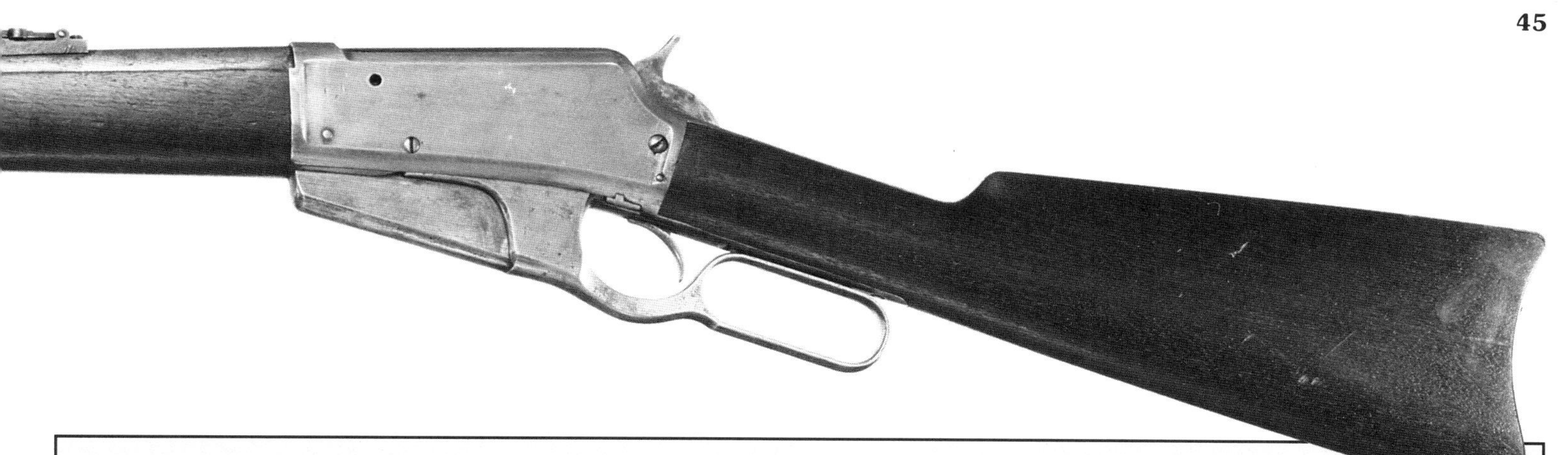

WINCHESTER = Model 1886

.50-100-450.

A New Cartridge.

.50 Caliber,
100 Grains Powder.

450 Grain
Solid Bullet.

LIST PRICE, $48 PER 1000.

To meet the demands of our friends for a .50 caliber carrying a heavy bullet, we are now prepared to furnish the above. The bullet has a penetration of about 16 pine boards 7/8 inch thick, and a trajectory of about 12 inches at 200 yards. This cartridge cannot be fired with good results out of the .50-110-300 rifle, but requires a barrel especially rifled for it.

Winchester Repeating Arms Company,

NEW HAVEN, CONN.

Send for our 112 page catalogue—free.

These two Browning guns were purchased by Mr OE Brownsey, a good friend of Val Browning. *Above:* An over and under with solid field rib, ivory sight and single selective trigger. *At top:* This automatic has a semi-beaver tail fore end of burled walnut with fine checkering, a solid field rib with ivory sight and a walnut butt stock with matching checker pattern. *At left* holding the automatic is Everett L Brownsey, OE Brownsey's son. Everett Brownsey served as mayor of Tombstone, Arizona. *Right:* From an earlier era, a group of Dodge City gunfighters who relied on their Browning designed Winchesters to enforce the law in Tombstone in the days of the Wild West.

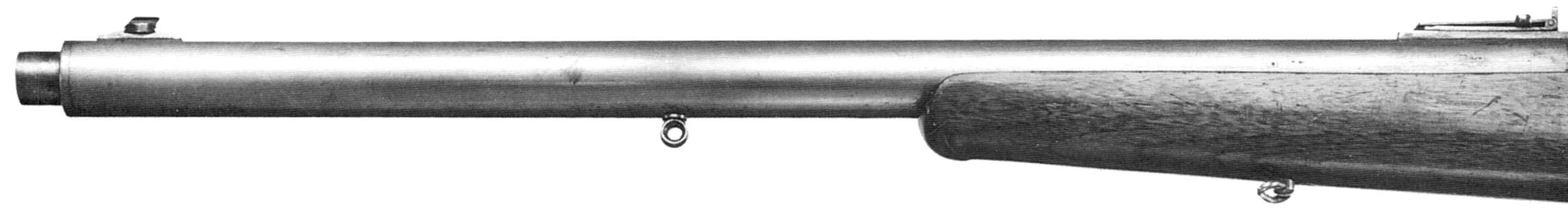

1927. The last variant, the 68, was introduced in 1934 and was discontinued in 1946. The overall production total, including every variant, stands at 1,458,666.

Semiautomatic High Power Rifle (Remington and Fabrique Nationale). This is a recoil-actuated, autoloading rifle in .25, .30, .32 or .35 Remington caliber, with a five-round nondetachable clip magazine, manual safety and adjustable sights. It has a 22-inch barrel and weighs 7.8 pounds. The stock for most examples tends to be of the rifle type with a straight or semi-pistol grip, having a shotgun-style rubber butt plate.

This was the first successful autoloading, high-power rifle in the United States. The basis of its autoloading, semiautomatic mechanism is a rotating bolt head having double lug locks in the barrel extension. The barrel itself recoils inside of a barrel jacket while it is still locked to the bolt. A stop-open latch holds the breechblock open after the last shell is fired.

The patent application for this gun was filed on 6 June 1900, and US Patent Number 659,786 was granted on 16 October 1900. US manufacturing and sales rights were granted to the Remington Arms Company, and the rifle first appeared in 1906 as the Remington Model 8 Autoloading Center Fire Rifle. Fabrique Nationale introduced the gun in Belgium in 1910 as the FN Caliber .35 Automatic Rifle.

The Remington Model 8 was discontinued in 1936, and was replaced by the Model 81 Woodmaster the same year. Modifications introduced by the Woodmaster included an improved stock and a slight weight increase to eight pounds. The Model 81 was discontinued in 1950. The FN model differed from the Remington models in that it had a solid-matted rib barrel, a bead front sight and two-position-folding rear sight (the Models 8 and 81 had adjustable open rear sights), a checked forearm and buttstock and a weight of 8.3 pounds. The FN model was discontinued in 1931, with a total production of 4913 units. As a matter of company policy, production figures are not available on Remington arms.

The Browning Automatic Rifle (Colt, Winchester, Marlin-Rockwell, Fabrique Nationale and others). This is an air-cooled, gas-actuated, automatic rifle in a variety of calibers, including .30-06, 6.5mm, 7mm, 7.62mm and 7.9mm, and having a 20 to 40-round box magazine and complex safety arrangements which are described below. It can be fired at a maximum full-automatic rate of 480 rounds per minute, emptying a 20-round magazine in 2.5 seconds. The World War II-era variant, the M1918A2, has a high rate of 550 rpm.

At top: **Browning's original for the Semiautomatic High Power Rifle.** ***Below, from the top down:*** **Two of the best known American military arms, the BAR and the Government .45 Caliber Automatic Pistol.** ***Opposite:*** **John and Matt Browning on an elk hunt.**

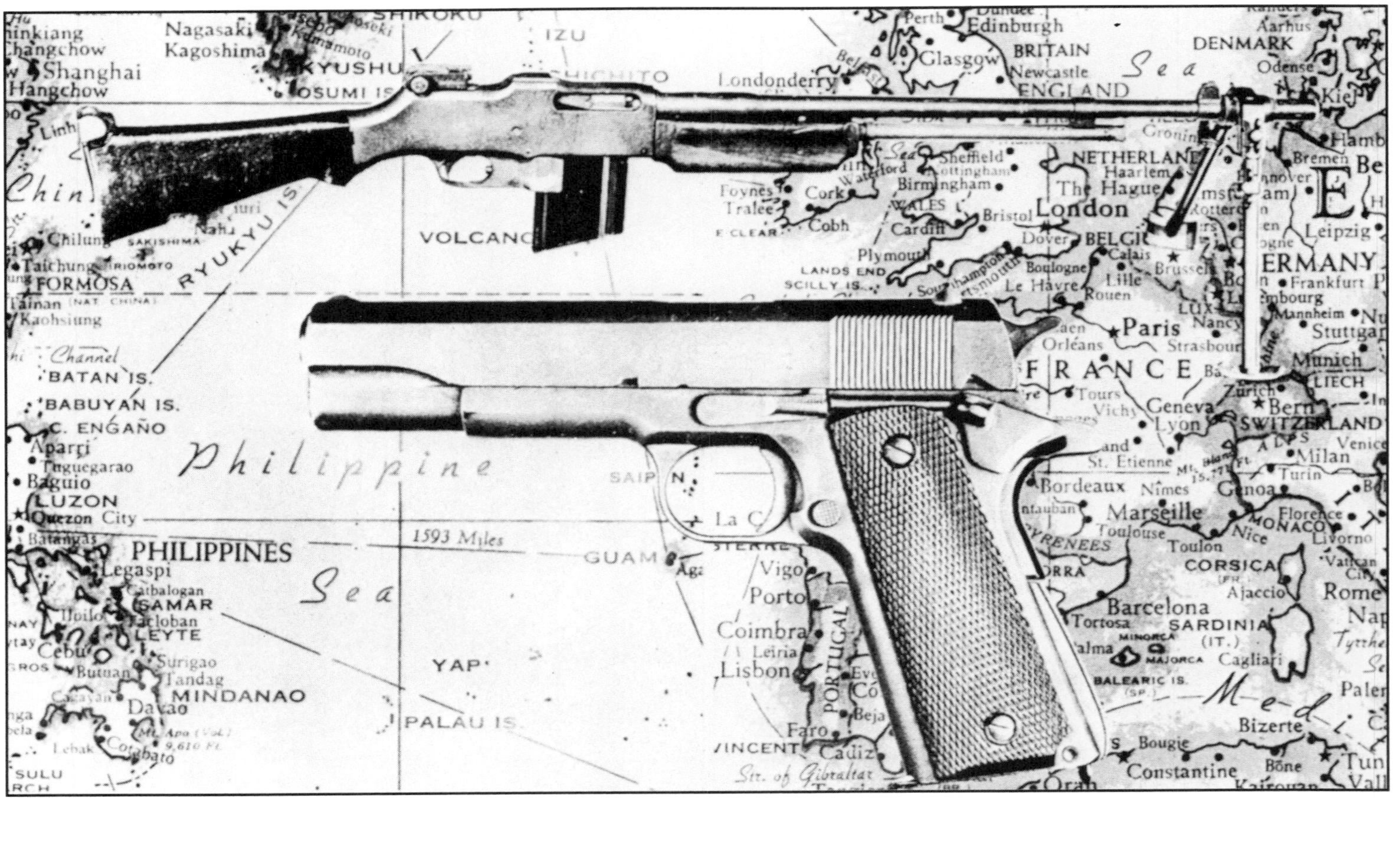

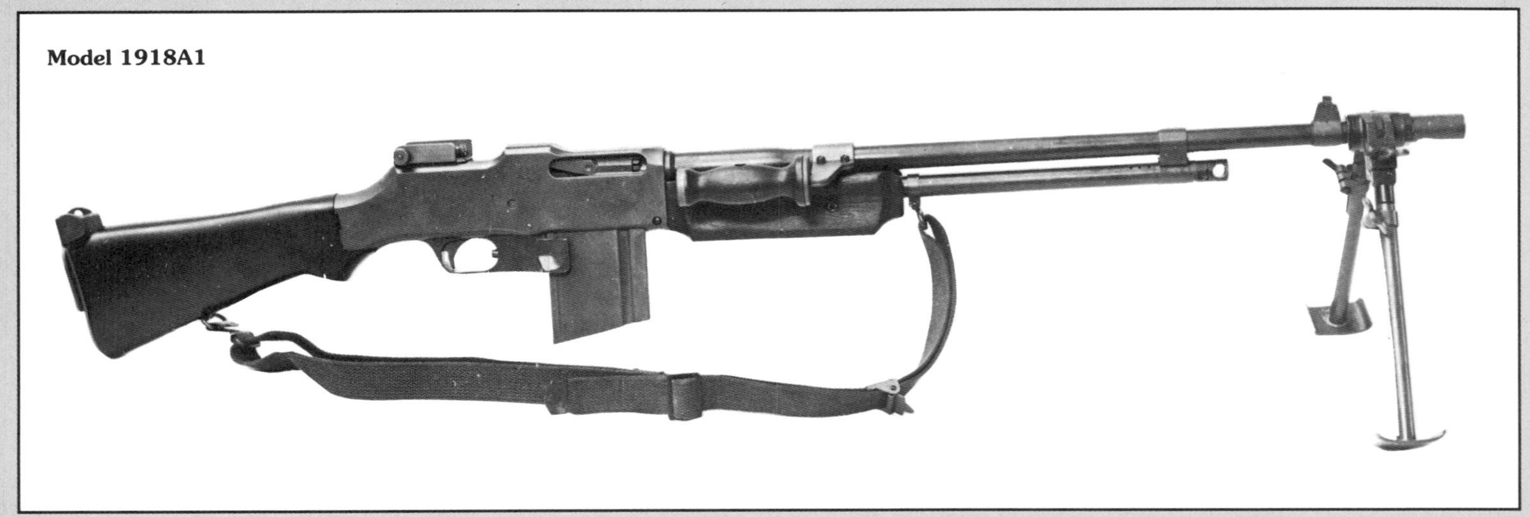
Model 1918A1

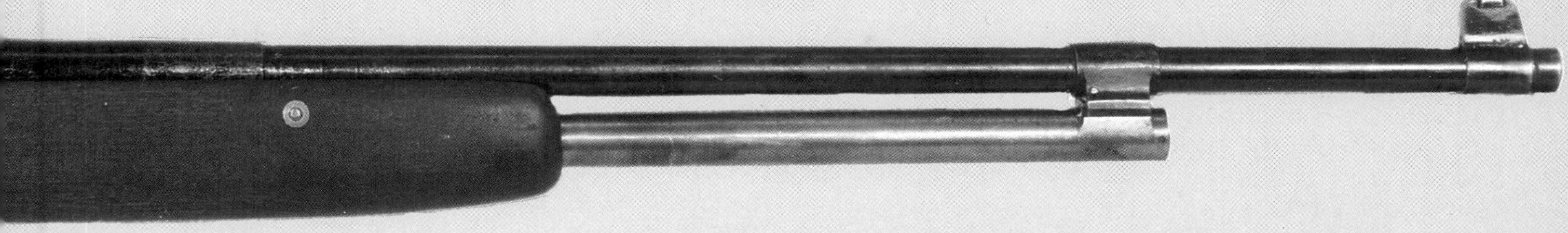

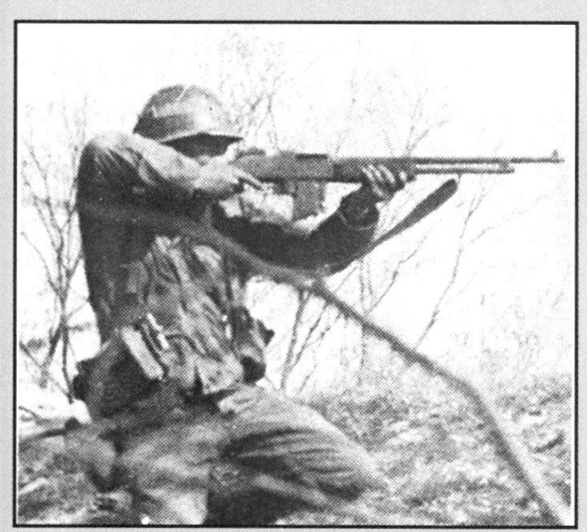

At top: Two views of John M Browning's automatic rifle, made in his shop in Ogden, Utah. A forerunner to the US Automatic Rifle Model 1918, this rifle has uncontrolled top ejection. Another variant of the BAR, the Model 1918A1 *(far left)* has a hinged butt plate and bipod attached just ahead of the fore end stock. *Left:* The Browning Automatic Rifle in action.

Best known as the 'BAR,' it is also known as the Browning Light Machine Rifle Model 1917, the Light Browning, the Colt Automatic Machine Rifle and the Fusil Mitrailleur Browning. This rifle has a 24-inch barrel and weighs approximately 20 pounds with a full magazine. Sights are adjustable, and the stock is a heavy rifle type arrangement.

The safety for this automatic weapon is a fire-control change lever. When the change lever is in its forward position, marked with the letter 'F,' the rifle will shoot one shot with each pull of the trigger. In vertical position, marked with the letter 'A,' the rifle will fire at full automatic. In the rearward position, marked by the letter 'S,' for 'safe,' the weapon will not fire.

On some models, when the 'F' lever is all the way forward, the rate of fire is reduced in such a way that single shots may be effected by jerking and releasing the trigger. On the M1918A2, there is no provision for semiautomatic fire, but this last-mentioned method for firing single shots can be used. The M1918A2 also differs from earlier models in that it is slightly heavier and is equipped with a flash hider and bipod.

The patent application for the first of these designs was filed on 1 August 1917, and US Patent Number 1,293,022 was granted on 4 February 1919. The BAR was officially adopted by the United States Government in 1917 and first saw combat use in July 1918. It is designed for takedown in combat conditions, and its 70 pieces can be completely disassembled and reassembled in 55 seconds.

The BAR has a bolt lock which is pivoted to the rear of the bolt and which rises in and out of locking engagement with a shoulder on the receiver. The rear of the bolt lock is attached to the slide by a link, which is free to reciprocate backward and forward. Attached to the forward part of the barrel is a gas piston which derives its energy from a gas port drilled through the barrel wall. In operation, the piston sends a slide to the rear, and in turn, the slide, through its link connection with the bolt lock, pivots the bolt lock downward—out of locking contact with the receiver.

During World War I, approximately 52,000 BARs were manufactured by Colt, Winchester and Marlin-Rockwell. After World War I, production rights reverted to Colt, and also, by arrangement with John M Browning, Fabrique Nationale began European production in 1920. The FN model is called the Fusil Mitrailleur Leger. Large quantities of this weapon were manufactured for various European countries over the years. It has been widely copied; many nations adopted the BAR or a have had a similar gun in reserve.

In 1922, the US Army brought out its Cavalry Model. In 1933, Colt produced the 'Colt Monitor' for police and bank guard use. In November 1939, there were approximately 87,000 in our war reserve, and approximately 177,000 were produced in this country during World War II. The FN version differed from the Colt model chiefly in having a quicker takedown mechanism—which allowed the barrel to be removed easily for replacement.

Below: John and Rachel Browning at home, a few months before his final trip to Belgium. _Opposite:_ American troops in Europe during WWII. US forces used the BAR during both World War I and II.

John M

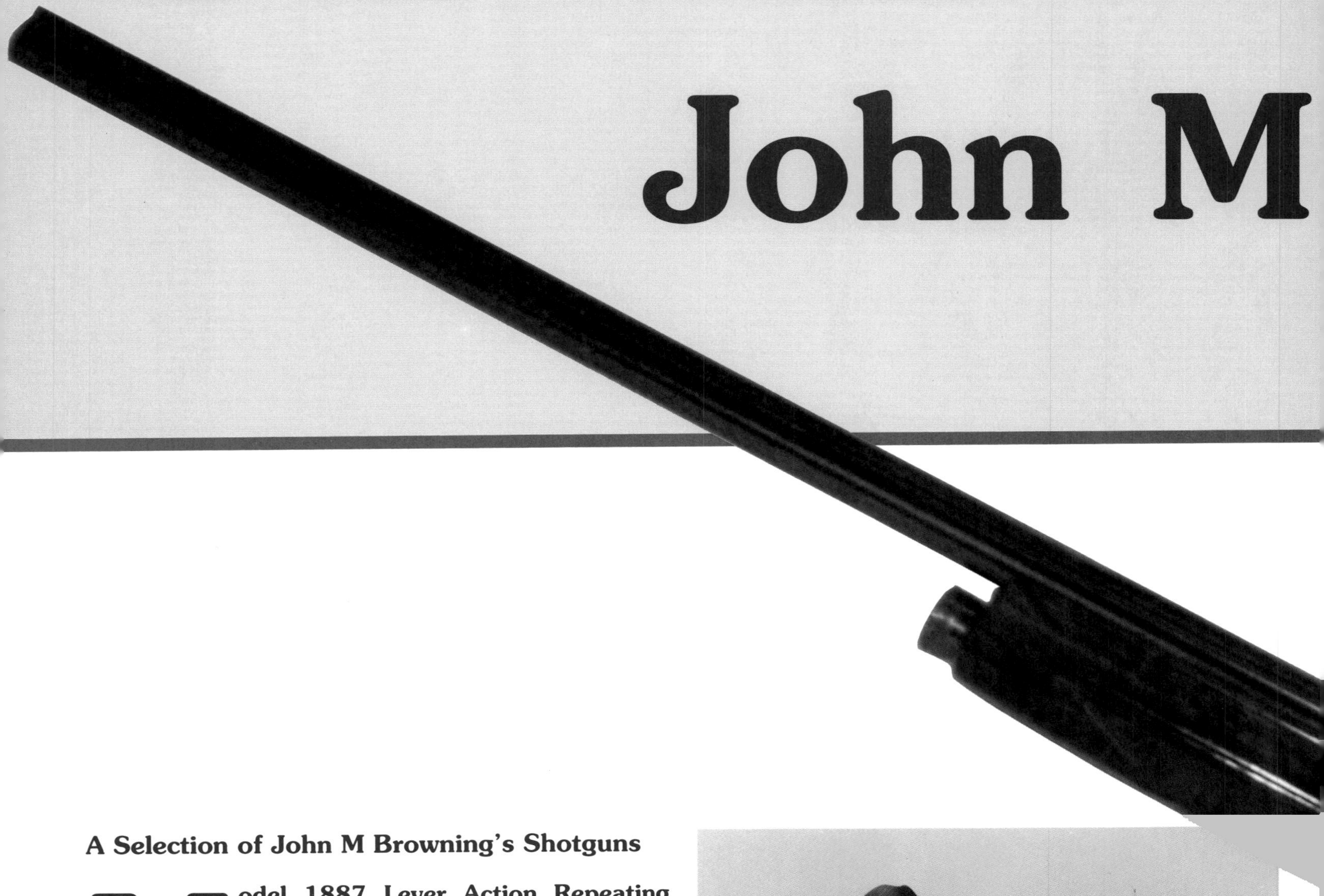

A Selection of John M Browning's Shotguns

Model 1887 Lever Action Repeating Shotgun (Winchester). It is a lever action repeating shotgun in 10 or 12 gauge, with a four-shot tubular magazine (plus one in the chamber), and groove and bead sights. Examples of this shotgun type have 20, 30 or 32-inch barrels, with cylinder bore, riot, standard or full choke. The 10 gauge variants weigh approximately nine pounds, and the 12 gauge variants weigh approximately eight pounds. Stocks for these guns are standard plain with pistol grip and hard rubber butt plate.

This was the first lever action repeating shotgun made in the United States. It has been called 'the first really successful repeating shotgun.' The patent application on this gun was filed on 15 June 1885 and US Patent Number 336,287 was granted on 16 February 1886. Manufacturing and sales rights were sold to the Winchester Repeating Arms Company in 1886, and the manufactured gun appeared in June 1887 as the Winchester Model 1887 Shotgun. Riot gun variants in 10 and 12 gauge were brought out in 1898.

The model 1887 was discontinued in 1899. Redesigned to handle the new smokeless powder loads, it reappeared in 1901—in 10 gauge only—as the Model 1901. This model was discontinued in 1920. Some 64,855 units of the Model 1887 were produced, as were 13,500 units of the Model 1901, for a grand total of 78,355 units overall.

Model 1893 Pump Action Repeating Shotgun (Winchester). This is a pump action shotgun of 12 gauge, with a five-shot tubular magazine and bead and groove sights. Barrel lengths for this gun are 30 and 32 inches, with standard full choke and optional cylinder-bore and modified

Browning's Shotguns

John M Browning's revolutionary automatic shotgun made firearms history even before it was manufactured by precipitating a break between Browning and Winchester. Invented in 1900, the design has remained popular to this day. The sleek Automatic-5 *above* is a current production model. Browning *(at left)* holds an early model of this legendary shotgun.

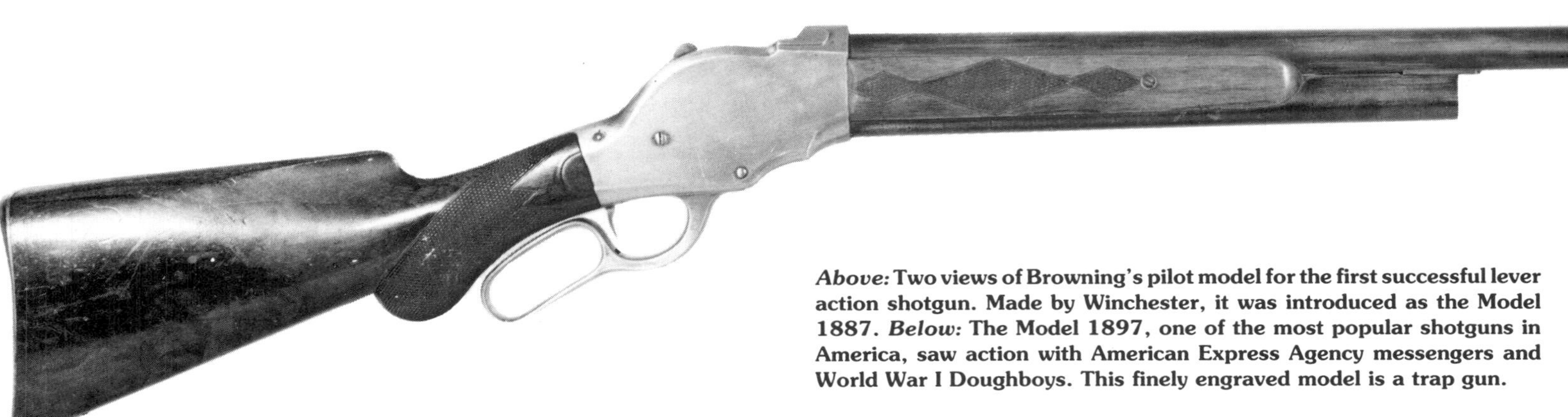

Above: **Two views of Browning's pilot model for the first successful lever action shotgun. Made by Winchester, it was introduced as the Model 1887.** ***Below:*** **The Model 1897, one of the most popular shotguns in America, saw action with American Express Agency messengers and World War I Doughboys. This finely engraved model is a trap gun.**

variants available. The weight for all models is approximately 7.8 pounds, and stocks tend to be plain, with pistol grip and hard rubber butt plate, with options having been available.

This was the first shotgun with a sliding-forearm pump action manufactured by Winchester. The patent application for this gun was filed on 30 June 1890, and US Patent Number 441,390 was granted on 25 November 1890. Manufacturing and sales rights were sold to the Winchester Repeating Arms Company in 1890; the gun was announced in April 1894 as the Winchester Model 1893.

The Model 1893 was discontinued in 1897 when the Model 1897—a much-modified takedown version of the Model 1893—was introduced. Total production for the Model 1893 was 34,050 units.

Model 1897 Pump Action Repeating Shotgun. This is a pump action shotgun in 12 and 16 gauge with a five-shot, tubular magazine, and bead and groove sights. Variant examples had barrel lengths of 20, 22, 26, 28, 30 and 32 inches (plus other variants), with cylinder bore, modified, intermediate, full or Winchester skeet chokes. The weights of the various examples of the Model 1897 are from 7.1 to 7.9 pounds, and standard stocks are plain, with pistol grip and hard rubber butt plate, with optional checkering and other specialties having been available.

This was one of the most popular shotguns in America. Introduced in November 1897, the Model 1897 is a modified version of the Model 1893, with a stronger frame, side ejection, and takedown capability. In addition to its legendary record as a sporting arm, the Model 1897 also saw other usage. It was widely used as a law-enforcement riot gun, and the American Express Agency armed its messengers with Model 1897s for a time. During World War I, this weapon was used by American forces as a trench gun with much effectiveness.

Back in 1897, the Standard, Trap, Pigeon and Brush Gun variants were introduced, and in 1898, the Riot Gun variant was brought out. This was followed by the Tournament Model in 1910, and the Trench Gun—for Armed Forces use during World War I, and for the public in 1920. The Trap Gun was succeeded by the Special Trap Model in 1931, and the Brush, Riot, Trench and Pigeon models were discontinued in 1931, 1935, 1935 and 1939, respectively. The Tournament Model was succeeded in 1931 by the Standard Trap Model, which itself was discontinued in 1939.

The Standard Model 1897 was discontinued in 1957. After all was said and done, the overall production total for all Model 1897 variants was 1,240,700.

Automatic Shotgun (Fabrique Nationale, Browning, Remington and others). This is a long recoil-operated automatic shotgun. The following specifications refer to the most representative group of variants, the Browning Automatic-5 family of shotguns. These come in gauges 12, 16, 20 and three-inch Magnum 12, with a five-shot magazine, except in three-inch Magnum, which has a five-shot capacity with Folding Crimp three-inch shells and a four-shot capacity with Rolled Crimp three-inch shells. Barrel lengths for the Auto-5 run from 26 to 32 inches, depending on type specifications and option package, and include all possible choke borings, including interchangeable, screw-in, choke systems. Weights tend to run from 6.3 to nine pounds, again depending on variant type. Stocks are a standard, hand checkered, French walnut type with semi-

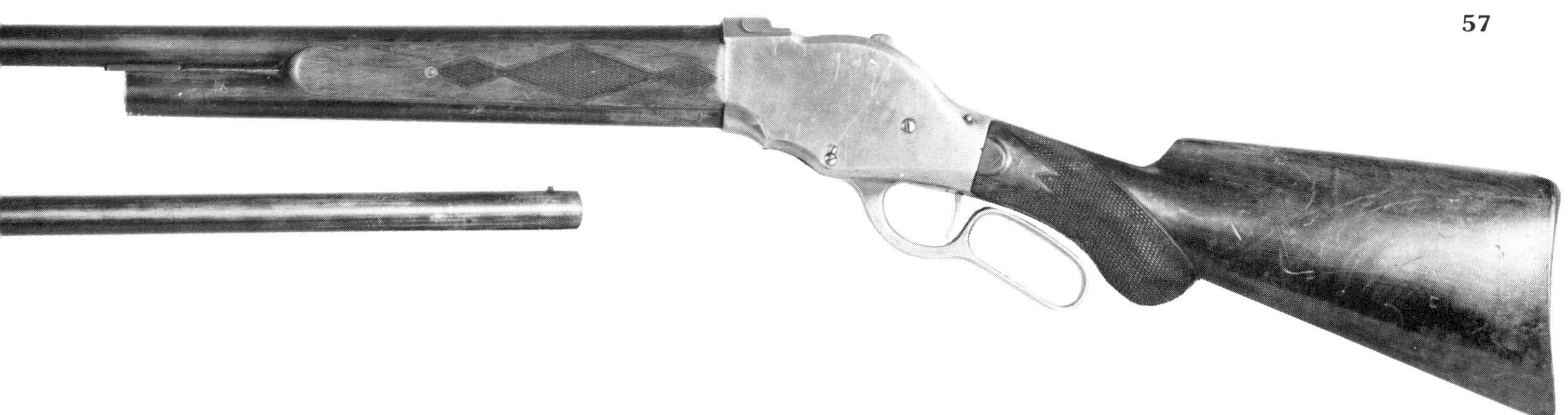

pistol grip, and deluxe engraved specials have been available.

This was the world's first successful automatic shotgun, an unheard-of thing in its day, and immediately successful, selling 10,000 guns in its first year of production. John M Browning took out four patents on this revolutionary firearm. US Patent Number 659,507, filed on 8 February 1900, was granted on 9 October 1900; US Patent Number 689,283, filed on 18 March 1901, was granted on 17 December 1901; US Patent Number 710,094, filed on 11 January 1902, was granted on 30 September 1902; and US Patent Number 812,236, filed on 30 June 1904, was granted on 13 February 1906.

The automatic shotgun was first manufactured by Fabrique Nationale, for the Browning Arms Company, in 1903. In 1905 the Remington Arms Company was licensed to manufacture and sell the gun, bringing it out as the Remington Model 11 Automatic Shotgun. The Browning Automatic-5 is the Browning Arms Company model.

The Automatic utilizes the forces which are generated by firing the cartridge to eject the empty case, to load a fresh round from the magazine into the chamber, and to cock the gun automatically.Through a simple, but highly effective, adjustable friction break and shock absorber, Browning was able to make the gun adaptable to whatever cartridge loads were desired.

The original Browning Automatic Shotgun is in 12 gauge only, with a 28-inch barrel; full, modified or cylinder bore choke; and is chambered for any cartridge up to 2.8 inches. Its weight is about 7.8 pounds and stocks tend to be English walnut with a straight grip. The gun exists in three models, all of them takedown-capable. These represent the Regular, Trap and Messenger (20-inch barrel) guns. While these models are generally of five-shot capacity, there are also two-shot variants.

The Remington model that was manufactured in 1905 is practically identical to the Browning Automatic-5, many of the parts being interchangeable. It differs in the following details. The butt plate is of hard rubber. The stock had a full pistol grip. The safety is of the cross-bolt style but with no finger piece. There is no magazine cut-off. The forearm has a reinforcing dowel which the Automatic-5 does not have. The carrier is of the old style, without the quick-loading feature. The front trigger-plate screw is a pin, and the rear trigger-plate screw has no locking screw. On some of the early Remington models, the carrier latch screw and cartridge stop screw are pins with a transverse locking screw. There is a fiber cushion in the rear of the receiver to stop the breechblock and firing pin. On some early models, the firing pin is identical to the Automatic-5; on later models, the firing pin was changed to a straight cylinder which won't lock when the action is open. There were other very minor differences in detail, depending on the year of manufacture.

Two variations in the Browning gun were offered in 1921—a Police Special, in 12 gauge, and a short-barrel Riot Gun, in 12, 16 and 20 gauge. The Model Sportsman, a three-shot version of the Model 11, with semi-beavertail fore end, was introduced in 1931. All models of the Model 11 and the Model Sportsman were discontinued in 1948. The Remington Model 11-48 Autoloader was introduced in 1949, and except for changes made to streamline the gun and make it easier to manufacture, it still has the same basic action as its predecessor.

The Browning Automatic-5 is still in production and is offered in many different specifications. Combined production figures on this gun cannot even be estimated.

Model 17 Pump Action Shotgun (Remington). This is a pump action, underloading shotgun in 20 gauge, with a five-shot tubular magazine, and groove and bead sights. Barrel lengths for all variants tend to be 18.5, 20, 26, 28, 30 and 32 inches, with standard full choke and optional chokes. The weights for various examples tend to be around 5.3 pounds, and stocks are as follows. Standard and riot models are checkered with a straight grip and hard rubber butt plate, while police models feature a pistol grip only, with no shoulder stock.

001 OF
FIVE HUNDRED
BROWNING GOLD CLASSIC
J.BAERTEN

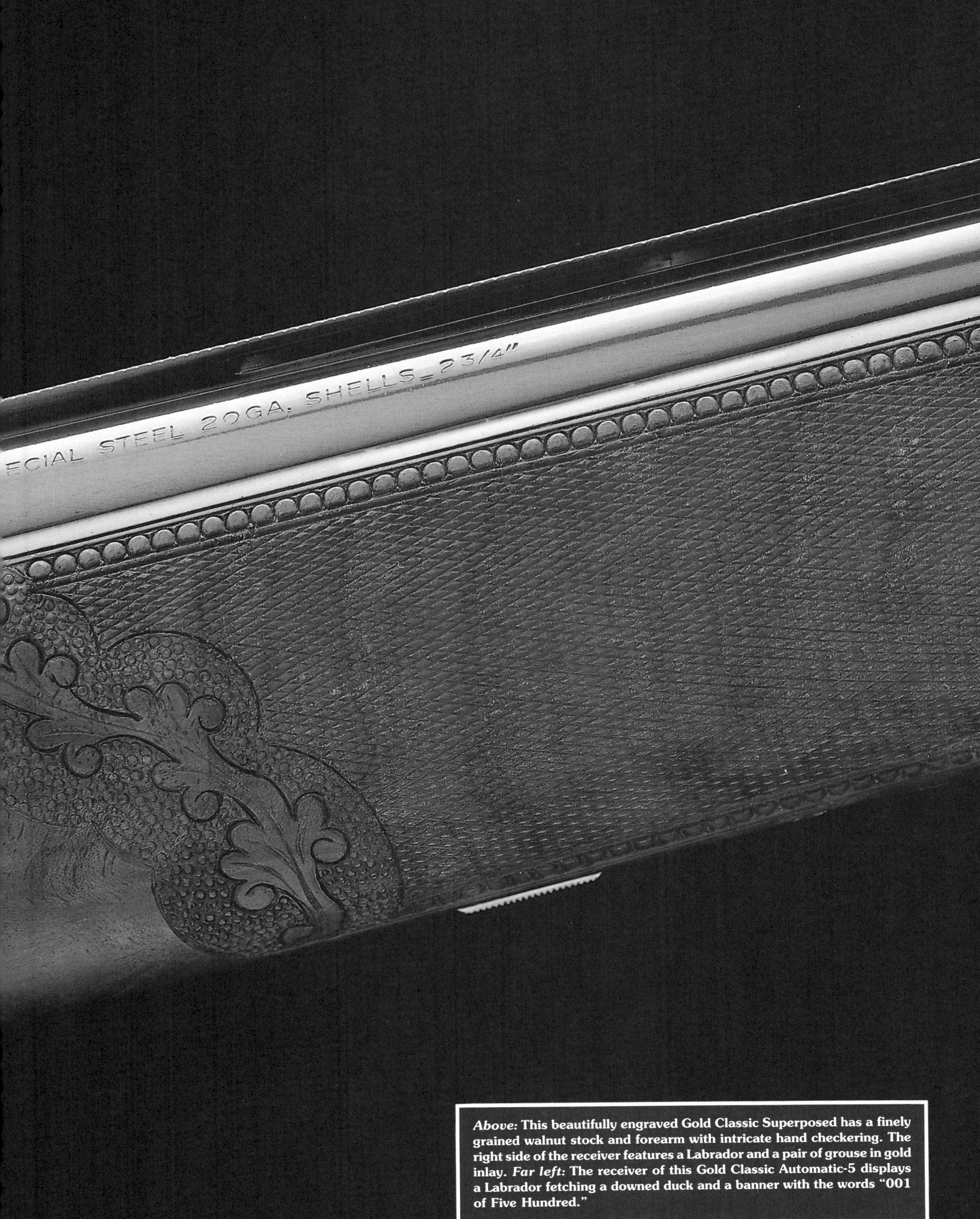

Above: This beautifully engraved Gold Classic Superposed has a finely grained walnut stock and forearm with intricate hand checkering. The right side of the receiver features a Labrador and a pair of grouse in gold inlay. *Far left:* The receiver of this Gold Classic Automatic-5 displays a Labrador fetching a downed duck and a banner with the words "001 of Five Hundred."

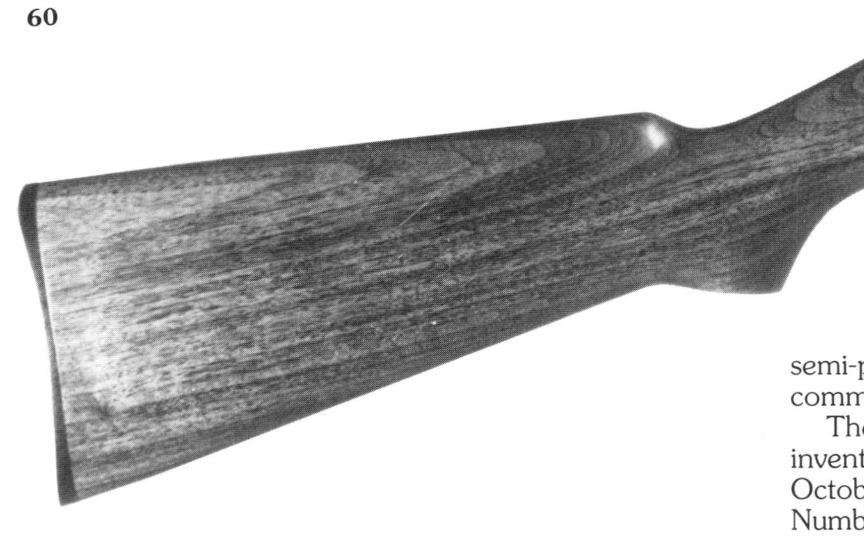

This was John M Browning's last repeating shotgun. The patent for this gun was filed on 26 November 1913, and US Patent Number 1,143,170 was granted on 15 June 1915. The Remington Arms Company was granted manufacturing and sales rights to this model, introducing it in 1921 as the Remington Model 17.

All production was discontinued in 1933. Since its patent expiration, the design has been used with marked success by various manufacturers, with examples being made in all gauges. For instance, the Ithaca Model 37 Pump is of the same basic design except that it is in 12 gauge. No production figures are available on the Model 17.

Superposed Shotgun (Fabrique Nationale and Browning). This is an over and under double-barrel shotgun in 12, 20, 28 and .410 gauge, including Magnum loads,

Model style: Standard, Magnum, Lightning, Lightning Trap, and Broadway Trap 12 gauge; Standard and Lightning 20 gauge; Standard 28 gauge; Standard .410 gauge. Barrel lengths for the Browning Superposed Shotgun run the gamut from 26.5 to 32 inches, with extra barrel sets available for each gun, and can be found in all possible choke borings. Weight also varies widely—from six to 8.1 pounds, depending upon varaint and barrel choice, etcetera. Stocks are a standard hand-checkered, hand-rubbed walnut, with a semi-pistol grip. However, deluxe engraved specials are also common.

The Superposed Shotgun was John M Browning's last invention. Patent applications on this gun were filed on 15 October 1923 and 29 September 1924, and US Patent Numbers 1,578, 638—39 were granted on 30 March 1926. First Produced by Fabrique Nationale in 1930, the Superposed Shotgun appeared in the Browning Arms Company line in 1931.

The barrels are mounted one above the other, rather than side by side, to permit the improved accuracy of a single sighting plane. Shells are placed directly in the two chambers. Automatic ejectors flip out the spent shells when the gun is opened. Unfired shells are merely elevated by the ejectors for easy removal by hand, if desired. This is made possible by the various physical differences between spent and unspent shells.

The first Superposed models had double triggers. Later, John M Browning's son, Val A Browning, designed twin single triggers for the gun, and ultimately the single selective trigger. The twin single triggers differed from the double triggers in that after selecting and shooting one round in one barrel, a second pull on the same trigger would fire the remaining barrel, thus eliminating the necessity of moving the finger from one trigger to the other. In the final version, the single selective trigger fires both barrels, either barrel first, by moving a thumb selector. The Superposed was initially provided only in 12 gauge in the United States. Val A Browning later designed the 20 gauge variant for American sale.

The Browning Superposed is still in production and is currently available in a wide variety of custom specifications.

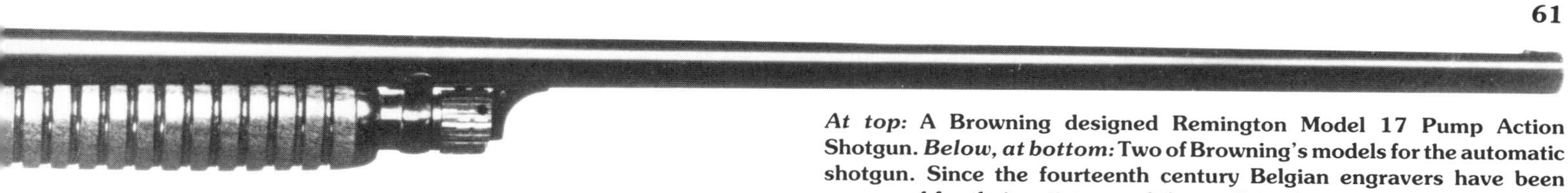

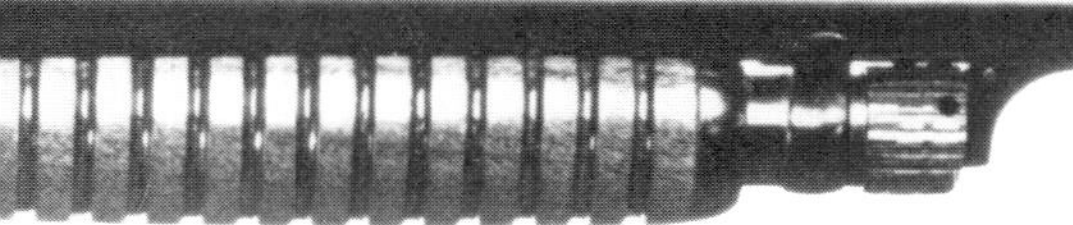

At top: A Browning designed Remington Model 17 Pump Action Shotgun. *Below, at bottom:* Two of Browning's models for the automatic shotgun. Since the fourteenth century Belgian engravers have been renowned for their artistry, and the tradition lives on today at Fabrique Nationale in Liège. *Below:* The Presentation One Superposed, with a pair of gold inlaid mallard ducks on an engraved receiver, is an example of their fine craftsmanship. *Overleaf:* A Black Duck Limited Edition Superposed Shotgun and a BAR Big Game Series Limited Edition.

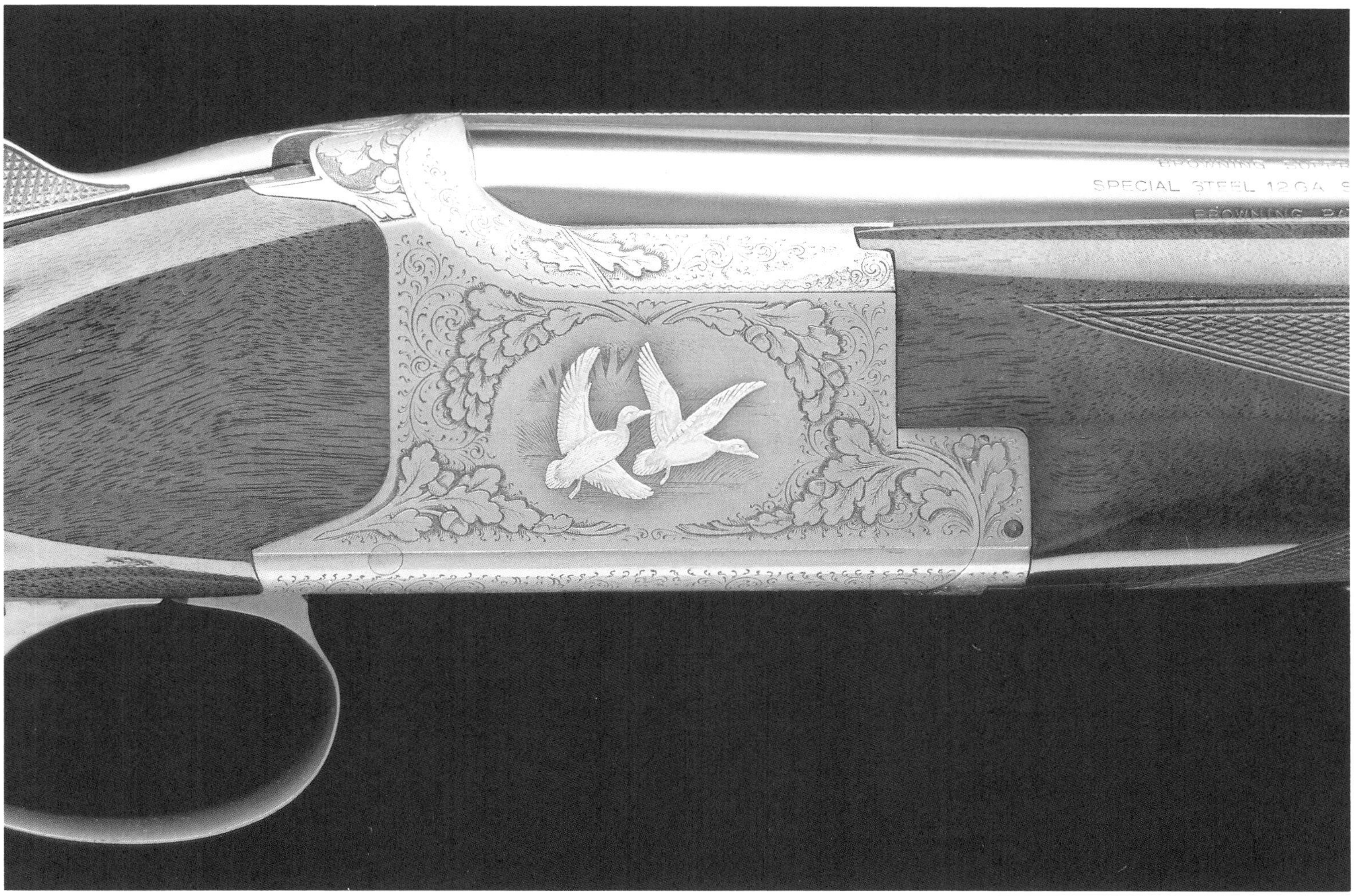

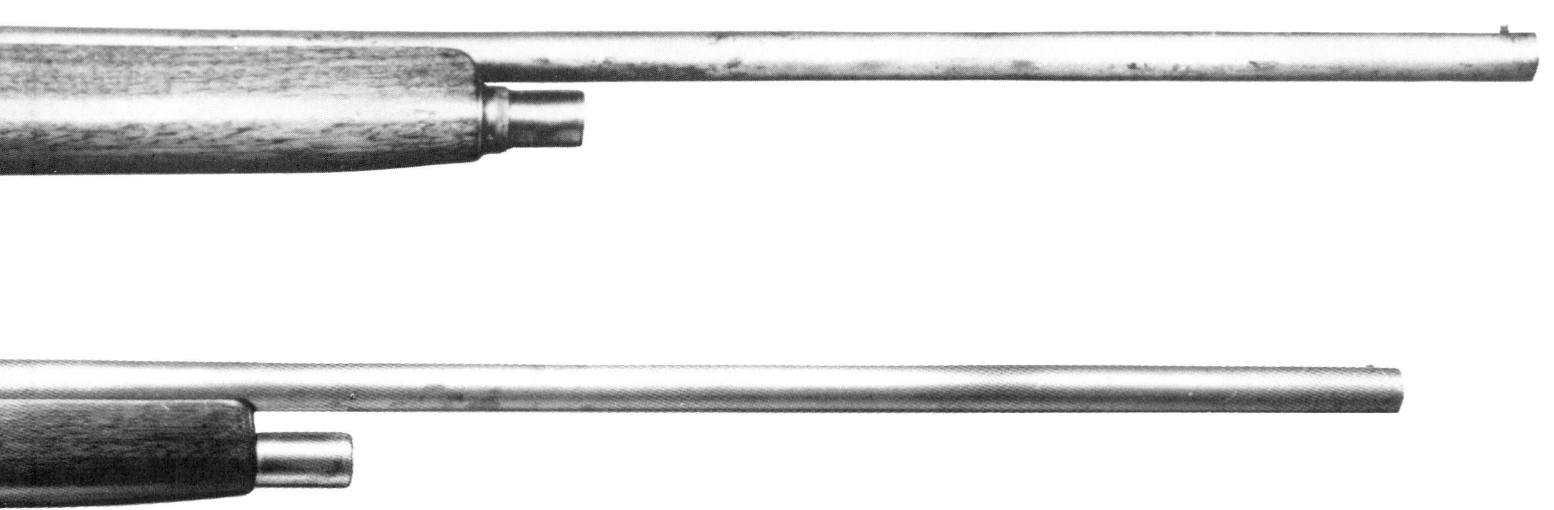

437PY00444
444 OF SIX HUNDRED
BROWNING SUPERPOSED
SPECIAL STEEL 12GA. SHELLS

Little-Known Browning Arms

Among the patents that were assigned to John M Browning, but not specifically mentioned in the previous listings, are 32 patents covering entire firearms for which there are no known surviving models. In addition, several models were often covered by the same patent. It is known, for example, that Browning designed several additional experimental models of both the .45 caliber Government and the .22 caliber long rifle practice pistols. The total of John M Browning's original firearms models is therefore well over 100.

Also, no mention has been made here of the Browning Double Automatic. This shotgun was invented not by John M Browning himself, but by his son Val A Browning—while he was president of the Browning Arms Company. The invention of this firearm is of note here, as it is one of a number of fine examples of the continuing Browning family gunmaking tradition.

To clear up an ongoing confusion, mention should also be made of the FN-Browning Light Automatic Rifle, Caliber .308, the standard infantry rifle for the NATO nations. Despite its name, this weapon was not a Browning invention. The following excerpt from the Fabrique Nationale descriptive brochure on this gun explains why it is so designated:

'The designer of this weapon was Mr DD Saive, Chief of Weapon Design and Development at FN, who, in the course of his career was able to gain an extensive experience in automatic weapons. For many years he collaborated with the great inventor, JM Browning. It is not surprising, therefore, that one finds in this rifle, in several places, features which first appeared in Browning mechanisms (gas intake and piston, wire-spring-actuated extractor, recoil spring housed in the buttstock); and thus it can be said that the weapon is of Browning inspiration—a natural consequence of more than 50 years of continuous collaboration between the FN and Browning companies.'

Of the 44 firearms John M Browning sold to the Winchester Repeating Arms Company, thirty-one were rifles. Of this number only seven were manufactured. Among the 24 not manufactured are a .38 caliber, tubular magazine, lever action rifle; a .30 caliber, box magazine, pump action rifle; and a .30 caliber repeater in which the operant mechanism is very much like a backwards-mounted lever action.

In addition, John M Browning submitted three other rifles to Winchester which were neither patented nor manufactured. These include a .44 caliber pump action repeating rifle, a .22 caliber single shot rifle, and a .45 caliber lever action single shot rifle. It is assumed that these guns were not patented because of previously existing patents, and consequently were not purchased by Winchester, although the models remain in the Winchester Gun Museum.

Also, John M Browning sold 13 shotguns to the Winchester Repeating Arms Company. Of these, only three were manufactured. One of the shotguns John M Browning submitted to Winchester, a 12-gauge, pump action shotgun, was neither patented nor manufactured. It is assumed that this gun was not patented because of previously existing patents and consequently was not purchased by Winchester, although the model remains in the Winchester Gun Museum.

Below: **John M Browning's workbench, with some tools made by his father way back in the 1830s.** ***Opposite:*** **An intricately engraved Superposed steel receiver inscribed with the engraver's name.**

SPECIAL
BROWNING
CLASSIC
J. BAERTEN

Browning's and Aircraft

A Selection of Browning Machine Guns

In the fall of 1889, John M Browning made several experimental models which served as preliminary steps in his development of a gas-operated, fully automatic gun that would fire continuously as long as the trigger is pulled and a supply of cartidges is being fed into it.

The first of these was derived from a Winchester Model 73 lever action. Browning put a hinge on the muzzle end of the barrel which operated a gas flapper that was attached to the modified lever of the rifle. Though this crude machine gun was built in a single day, it worked. Several others were made—all working out the machinations necessary to perfect his gas-operation experiment.

A patent application was filed on 6 January 1890, and US Patent Number 417,782 was granted on 29 March 1892. This was John M Browning's first patent embodying his gas-operation principle for the machine gun. Browning noted in the application that 'This invention is applicable to machine guns and also to firearms.'

The final experiment had a concave cap with a hole in the center which was fitted directly over the muzzle. When the bullet passed down the barrel and through the hole in the cap, the expanding gases that followed the bullet forced this cap forward. Attached to the cap was a spring-loaded operating lever that was connected also to the gun's firing mechanism. When a shot was fired, the cap would move, trigger the operating lever which in turn 'pulled' the trigger, creating an identical repeat process. This could, hypothetically, go on indefinitely, providing the trigger was held in the 'pulled' position, there were enough cartridges to fire and the barrel of the weapon didn't melt from the heat of continuous firing.

This weapon is referred to in Browning's patent as an 'Automatic Magazine Gun.' It fired .44-40 black powder ammo at the rate of 960 rounds per minute, and weighed approximately eight pounds. It was not, however, considered ready for production.

The first Browning Gas-Operated Machine Gun. This is a gas-operated full automatic weapon in .45-70 caliber, with a belt magazine, a cyclic rate of fire of 600

Below: **John M Browning's first gas-operated machine gun, circa 1890–91, made solely for testing. *Opposite:* Browning and an infantry variant of the Model 1917 .30 Caliber Machine Gun.**

Machine Guns Cannon

rounds per minute and a barrel length of 22.5 inches. This gun weighs 40 pounds with its mount.

This was John M Browning's first fully developed machine gun. This gun was invented in 1890–91. The patent application was filed on 3 August 1891 and US Patent Number 471,783 was granted on 29 March 1892.

Browning placed a bracket on the muzzle end of the barrel of this model. On it, a lever was hung on a pivot, so that one end of the lever formed a cap over the front of the muzzle. This cap contained an aperture corresponding to the bore of the barrel, to allow passage of the bullet. The muzzle bracket acted as a spacer to keep the lever cap a short distance forward of the muzzle, thereby forming a small, enclosed gas chamber between the end of the barrel and the cap.

When a shot was fired, the expanding gases following the bullet pushed the cap forward. The cap lever was in turn connected to the action by a series of rods and levers—thus, the forward action of the muzzle cap was the initial impetus which carried through the mechanism, effecting extraction, ejection, feeding, loading and firing of the cartridges automatically.

Gas-Operated Breechloading Gun. The patent application on this gun was filed on 11 July 1892, and US Patent Number 502,549 was granted on 1 August 1893.

A new idea appeared in this model: the energy was not taken from the muzzle—instead, a hole was drilled through the barrel, tapping the high-pressure gases directly behind the bullet before the bullet had left the barrel. Actually, holes were drilled on both sides of the barrel, and a pair of flappers was positioned near these holes.

The flappers were, in turn, attached to the operating rod on the bottom of the barrel. The expanding gas that was tapped from behind the bullet (via the holes) caused both flappers to pivot rearward, imparting motion to the operating rod, and subsequently to the operating mechanism.

One possible reason for this arrangement is that it may have helped to ameliorate the instability at the muzzle which resulted from the unbalanced action of a single flapper. However, as soon as this two-flapper mechanism was created, Browning became aware of many possibilities for simpler mechanisms.

Model 1895 Automatic Machine Gun (Colt). This is a gas-operated machine gun in .30-40 Krag and 6mm Lee Enfield calibers, with a belt magazine and a cyclic rate of fire of 400 rounds per minute. It is an air-cooled weapon, with a 21.5-inch barrel, and weighs 40 pounds.

This was the first fully automatic weapon to be purchased by the United States Government. The first patent application of this gun was filed 7 November 1892, and US Patent Number 544,657 was granted on 20 August 1895. Various modifications of the gun were covered by various US Patents—Number 544,658, filed on 15 March 1893 and granted 20 August 1895; Number 544,659, filed on 11 September 1893 and granted on 20 August 1895; and Number 543,567, filed on 16 April 1895 and granted 30 July 1895.

Arrangements were made with Colt's Patent Firearms Manufacturing Company in 1895 for the gun's manufacture the same year. In January 1896, the Model 95 was tested by the Navy in competitive trials. Its successful performance resulted in the Navy's placing an order with Colt for fifty of these guns. In the hands of US Marines, these Model 1895 Machine Guns saved the foreign legations in Peking during the Boxer Rebellion.

After their use in the Spanish-American War, the Model 95 acquired a nickname—the 'Browning Peacemaker.' At the outbreak of World War I, the Model 1895 comprised a large portion of the United States machine gun arsenal, and though by the second decade of the twentieth century, the gun was outdated, a number were manufactured for military use in the interim before the Model 1917 Browning Heavy Water-Cooled Machine Gun went into production. The Model 1895 was then relegated to training use.

The Model 1895 Machine Gun employed a hole drilled through the barrel near the muzzle, which powered a piston that worked the mechanism of the gun via a swinging lever. When the mechanism was activated, it fed, fired, extracted and ejected the cartridges automatically. The firing cycle was continuous as long as the trigger was depressed and ammunition was supplied, and a very heavy barrel was used on the theory that the extra metal would help prevent heat buildup. The unusual movement of the piston, which swung in a half arc beneath the barrel, gave the gun an additional nickname—'The Potato Digger.'

This gun was discontinued in 1917. Total production figures are not available. Some 1500 were produced during World War I.

Experimental Gas-Operated Firearm. This is an experimental gas-operated machine gun in .44 caliber, with a 20-shot box magazine and a cyclic rate of fire of 720 rounds per minute. It has a 14.5-inch barrel and weighs 7.3 pounds.

This was an important test model, designed to improve upon the ideas that were already in operation on the Model 1895 Machine Gun. After their testing in the Experimental Gas-Operated Firearm, many of these improvements would go into the later models that would see action in some of the most intensive conflicts in our present war-heavy century.

Gas-Operated Breechloading Gun
.44 Caliber Experimental Model

Model 1917 .30 Caliber

Left: A US military model of the Browning Model 1917 .30 Caliber Water-Cooled Machine Gun. During World War I, Browning's son Val taught troops in France how to use this weapon. An air-cooled variant was developed later.

The patent application on this gun was filed 8 December 1894, and US Patent Number 544,661 was granted on 20 August 1895. Because of its hand-forged parts and unfinished appearance, this experimental model is often erroneously assumed to be a very early Browning gas-operated gun.

However, Browning's main purpose in designing it was to effect an improvement in the gas port, which, in all his prior machine guns (including the Colt Model 1895) had undergone little change. As stated in the patent, 'The objects of the invention being to avoid the fouling and clogging of the mechanism by the gases and to prevent the escape of the gases until after the lever shall have commenced its opening movement and received its initial force, and to prevent the lateral spread of the gases and to generally improve and simplify the construction of the gas operated mechanism.'

One very important idea that is present in this experimental gun centers on an alternate method of constructing the gas port. This method entails putting an elbow on the gas vent, so that the force of the gases are applied along the axis of the barrel—enabling the use of a piston to operate the mechanism rather than a swinging arm. This is an idea that has seen much usage since.

Model 1917 .30 Caliber Machine Gun (Colt, Remington, Westinghouse and Others). This is a short recoil-operated, water-cooled and later air-cooled, fully automatic machine gun in .30-06 caliber with a link belt magazine and a 20-inch barrel. Its cyclic rate of fire is 600 rounds per minute (with adjustments in later variants), and it weighs 37 pounds with its water jacket filled, and 22 pounds in air-cooled versions.

Versions of this gun have made history in World Wars I and II, and the Korean War. Until recently, it continued to

Left: **John M Browning testing one of his machine guns.** ***Below:*** **A machine gunbelt loading device, one of Browning's miscellaneous inventions, designed in 1899 at the request of US Army Ordance.**

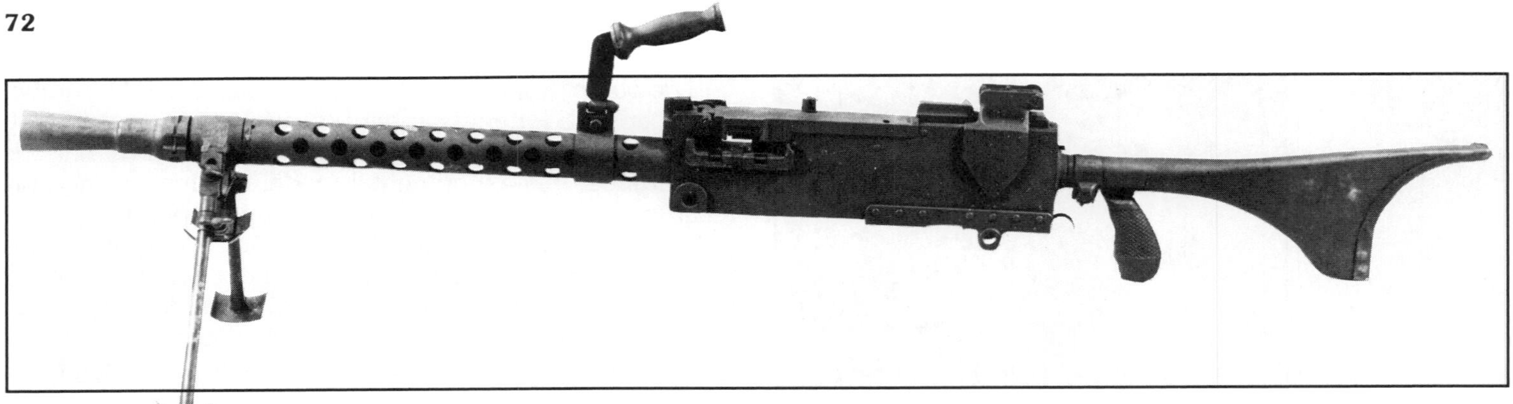

occupy a prominent place in the military arsenal of the United States. All this began back in 1900, when John M Browning invented a machine gun to replace the outdated Model 1895. The patent application for this new gun was filed on 19 June 1900, and US Patent Number 768,934 was granted on 23 July 1901.

Although sometimes referred to as the Browning Model 1901, the design of 1900 was never manufactured, since the government lacked interest in military weapons at the time. Nevertheless, its basic operating features are the same as those of all Browning machine guns since produced.

Browning continued working on the gun intermittently over the years, modifying its mechanism to eject from the bottom rather than the right side, and increasing its rate of fire. The patent application covering these improvements was filed on 3 October 1916, and US Patent Number 1,293,021 was granted on 4 February 1919.

The model embodying these changes—known as the Browning .30 Caliber Heavy Machine Gun—was first publicly demonstrated at Congress Heights, Washington, DC, on 27 February 1917. In May 1917, official tests were held at Springfield Armory. Following the tests, a board appointed by the US Secretary of War recommended its immediate adoption. The first combat use of the Model 1917 was by the 79th Division in France on 26 September 1918.

In the short-recoil system, the barrel and breechblock are locked together when the gun is fired and recoil together for a short distance, until the bullet clears the barrel and the gas pressure diminishes, at which point they unlock, and the breechblock alone continues to recoil. During this time, all this energy compresses the mechanism's springs, so that, as they become unsprung, the springs return all parts to their 'battery,' or firing positions. During the recoil of the breechblock, the fired cartridge is extracted from the barrel and ejected, and a fresh cartridge is fed into the chamber and fired. The firing cycle is continuous as long as the trigger is depressed and a supply of ammunition available.

This model was water-cooled, but Browning also made a later air-cooled variant. This air-cooled weapon was the first

***At top:* The .30 Caliber Air-Cooled Machine Gun was used by American forces during World War I, World War II and the Korean War. *Left:* US soldiers fire the same gun in combat during World War II.**

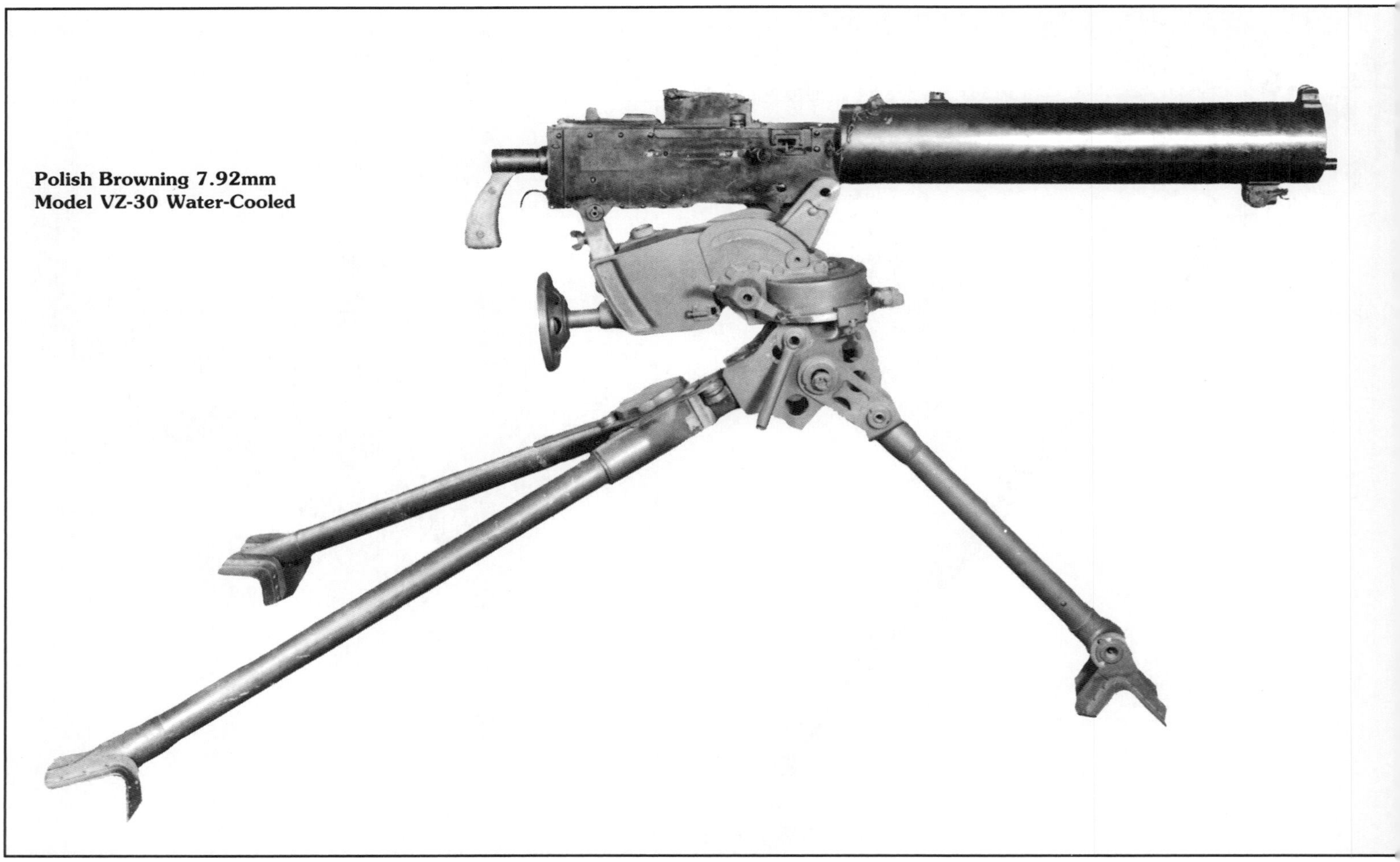

Polish Browning 7.92mm Model VZ-30 Water-Cooled

.30 Caliber Air-Cooled

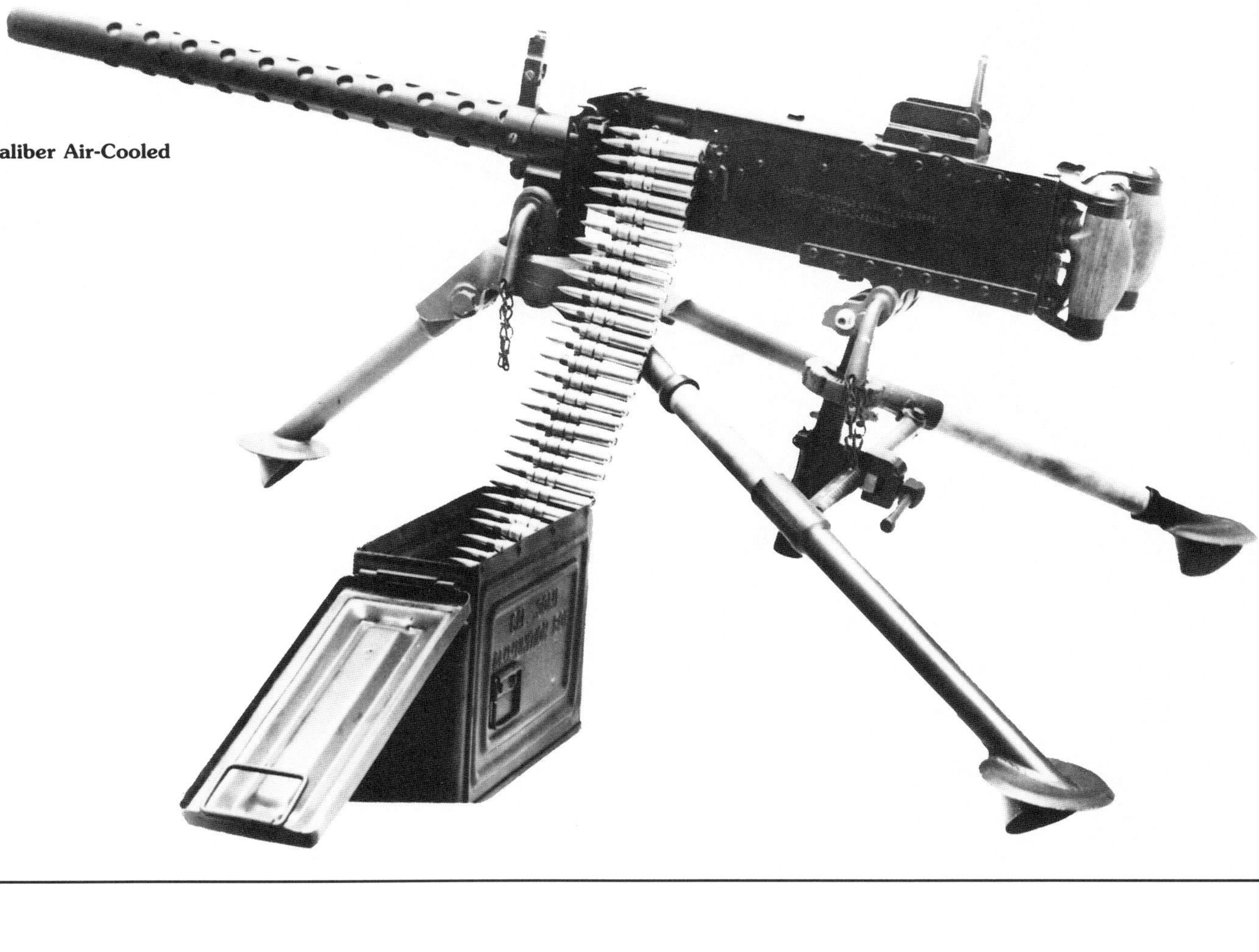

Browning .50 caliber machine guns were standard armament for World War II Allied fighters like this P-51 Mustang *(below). At right* is a section view of same, showing its control cockpit detail. *Far right:* Armorers of the 45th Fighter Squadron, 15th Fighter Group replenish a P-51's guns.

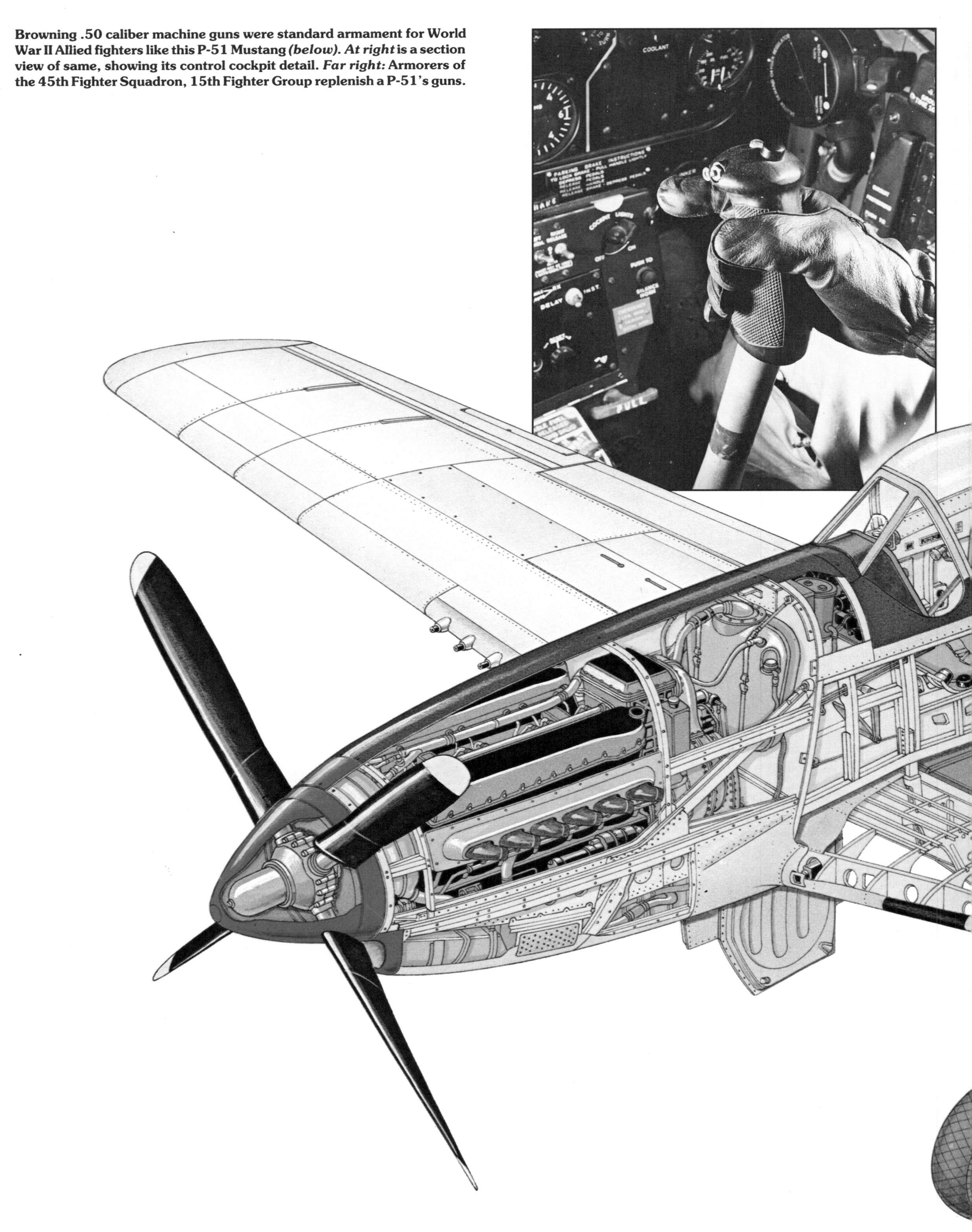

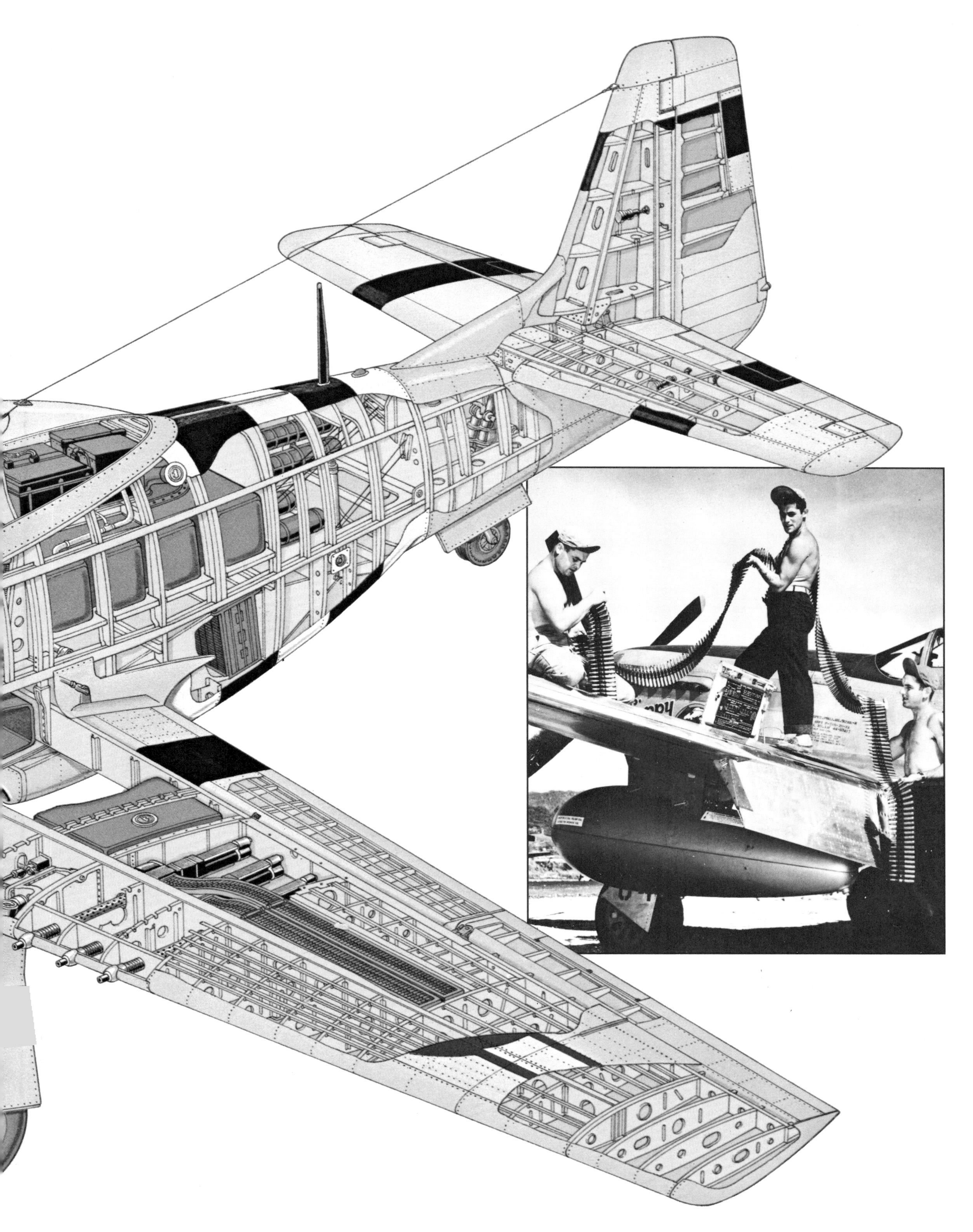

Above: **A Browning .50 caliber M2 on a halftrack in Rome 1944. Here it is being used for air defense.** ***Right:*** **A waist gunner aboard a B-17F at Bovington, England readies his weapon, a Browning .50 Caliber Machine Gun.**

in the US to be successfully used aboard pursuit planes—the pilot looked along his sights and aimed at the target by maneuvering his ship. To enable the use of a forward-mounted machine gun on a fighter plane without literally shooting one's own propeller off, the firing mechanism of the gun was synchronized with the motor of the plane so that the bullets passed through the spaces between the revolving propeller's blades.

The .30 caliber air-cooled Browning, in its diverse configurations, was one of America's most important military weapons in World War II. Many modified versions of this gun have appeared since its invention. It generally weighs approximately 22 pounds, and has an increased rate of fire of approximately 700 rounds per minute, although some aircraft models were stepped up to as high as 1300 rounds per minute for duty in the superheated skies of the 1940s and early 1950s.

The US Government contracted with three companies for World War I production of the Model 1917. Between its official adoption in 1917 and the Armistice of the following year, nearly 43,000 were produced: Westinghouse accounted for 30,150, Remington, 12,000 and Colt 600. Over a million units of the World War II Browning .30M2 were manufactured. Most countries have since acquired similar weapons. Total production can only be estimated as well into the millions.

Browning Water-Cooled Machine Gun in .50 Caliber (Colt and others). This is a short recoil-operated, water-cooled and later air-cooled, machine gun in .50 caliber with a link belt magazine and a 39-inch barrel. This weapon weighs 82 pounds with a full water jacket—air-cooled variants weigh less.

To meet the increased threat of armored combat vehicles in World War I, General John 'Blackjack' Pershing, Commander of the American Expeditionary Forces, requested a machine gun cartridge that was heavier and more powerful than the .30 caliber cartridge then in use by the AEF.

A .50-caliber cartridge was developed—it hurled a 1.8 ounce bullet to a muzzle velocity of 2750 feet per second. To shoot this powerful load, John M Browning developed

Below: A Boeing B-17G of the 401st Bombardment Squadron, 91st Bombardment Group, 1st Combat Bombardment Wing, of the US 8th AF. *Clockwise, from far right:* A sharp-eyed waist gunner and his Browning over North Africa in 1943; gunner positions in a B-17F; another gunner at his Browning.

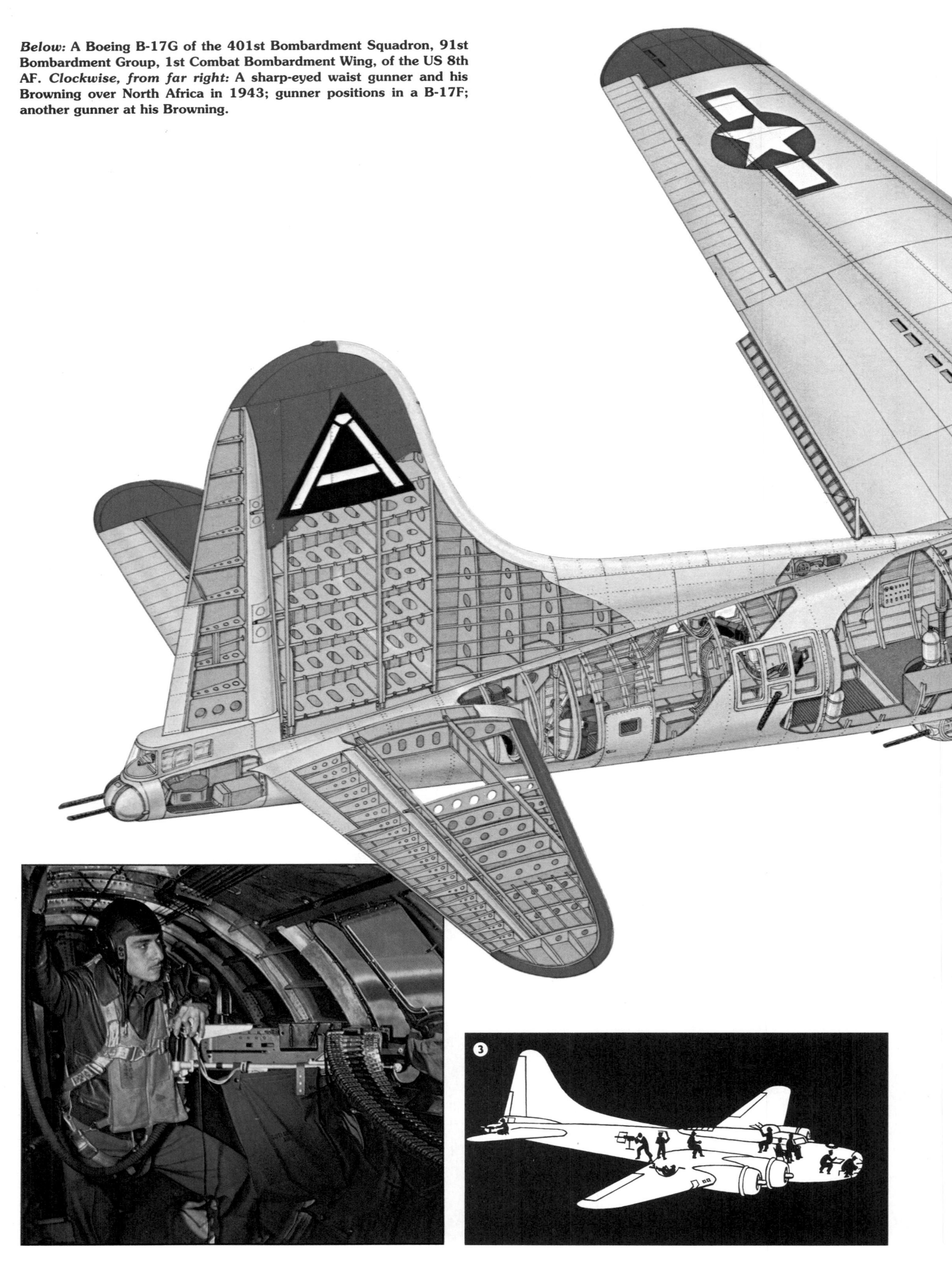

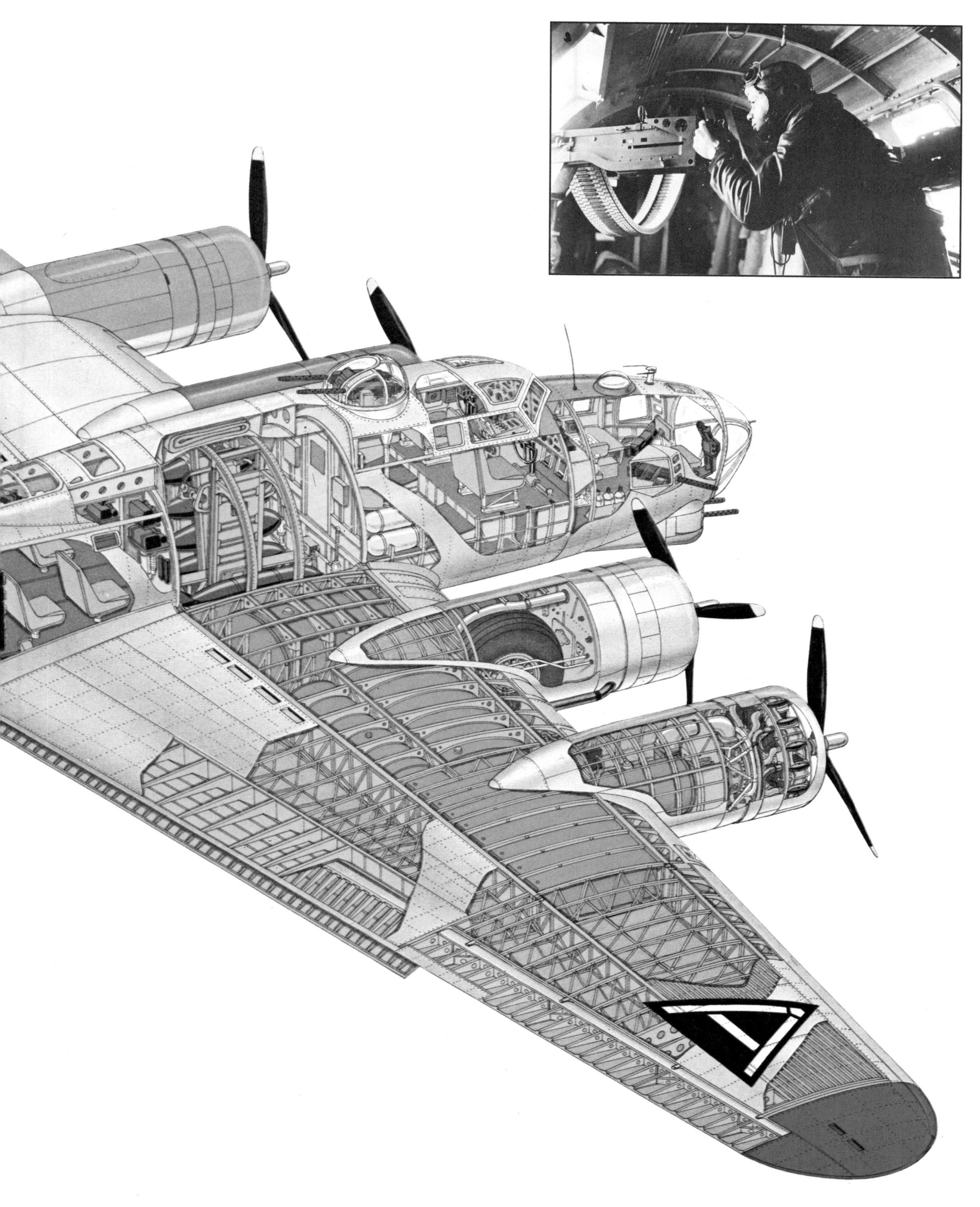

the Browning .50 Caliber Water-Cooled Machine Gun. He began work in July of 1917, and the gun was first test-fired, in Colt's meadow in Hartford, Connecticut, a little over a year later. The patent application for the gun was filed on 31 July 1923, and US Patent Number 1,628,226 was granted on 10 May 1927.

Developed too late to see use in World War I, the Browning .50-Caliber Machine Gun played a prominent role in World War II and the Korean War. This gun has the same basic operating features as the .30 caliber, but through the use of a unique oil buffer the necessary strengthening of the gun is accomplished without a proportional increase in weight. The oil buffer absorbs excess recoil energy, thereby effectively reducing undue strain on the parts. In addition, this oil buffer provides a means of controlling the rate of fire.

Browning also incorporated double spade grips on the .50 caliber, as these gave a two-handed—and thus more stable—control of the gun than did the pistol grip used on the smaller .30 caliber. To date, no less than 66 known models of the Browning recoil-operated machine gun have been manufactured by the US and various Allied countries. The majority of these have been .50 caliber.Other highly effective models which followed the original prototype were the Water-Cooled Infantry, the Water-Cooled Anti-Aircraft Single and Twin Mount, and the Air-Cooled Tank Gun. One of the later aircraft models, the .50M3, was stepped up to a cyclic rate of fire of 1200 rounds per minute.

During World War II, the .50M2 was produced by the following companies: Colt's Patent Firearms Manufacturing Company, High Standard Company, Savage Arms Corporation, Buffalo Arms Corporation, Frigidaire, AC Spark Plug, Brown-Lipe-Chappin, Saginaw Division of General Motors Corporation and Kelsey-Hayes Wheel Company. Of the 3,283,837 Browning machine guns produced in this country during World War II, approximately two million were .50 calibers. Like the Browning .30 caliber, this gun has been widely copied by other countries, and total production can only be estimated as well into the millions.

Necessarily, not all of John M Browning's machine gun and fully automatic weapon mechanisms can be covered here—nor can the work of such important modifiers of original Browning designs as Fred Moore and Colonel S Gordon Green. For those seeking further information, please consult *Volume One of The Machine Gun: History, Evolution and Development of Manual, Automatic and Airborne Repeating Weapons,* by George M Chinn, Lt Col, USMC Retired, published by the Superintendent of Documents, Washington, DC.

John M Browning's Aircraft Cannon

Browning 37mm Aircraft Cannon (Colt, Vickers and others). This is a long recoil-operated aircraft cannon of 37mm caliber with a barrel length of 44 inches and a cyclic rate of fire of 135 rounds per minute. This cannon weighs approximately 313 pounds without magazine attached, and approximately 406 pounds with a 15-shot magazine attached. These specifications are based on the M4 model.

John M Browning began work on his first aircraft cannon in early 1921; three months later, it was successfully test-fired in the hills outside of Ogden. The patent applications for this gun were filed on 15 December 1923, 11 April 1924 and 28 April 1924, and US Patent Numbers 1,525,065—67 were granted on 3 February 1925.

The cannon was successfully demonstrated to US Army officials at the Aberdeen Proving Ground in mid-1921, when it fired a series of one-pound projectiles at a muzzle velocity of 1400 feet per second, and a cyclical rate of 150 rounds per minute. Shortly after, Browning designed two additional models, each firing heavier projectiles—the first at 2000 feet per second, and the second at approximately 3000 feet per second.

In 1929, a small number of these weapons were manufactured by the Vickers Arms Company in England for sale to Spain. The US Government, for a time apathetic to the production of new military weapons, did not renew interest in the gun until 1935, when the Army Air Corps model of Browning's cannon was produced by request. This cannon was entered on the ordnance lists as the M4.

The World War II model, the M9, was used in rather limited quantities by the US Army Air Corps, which eventually decided that such heavy armament was neither practical nor essential. This cannon did, however, see much use in the hands of the Russians. During their most critical defensive combat with Germany, the M9 was their primary aerial cannon. Several thousand of these guns—and the P-39 Bell Aircobra planes on which they were mounted—had been sent to Russia by the US Government. The M9s' high-velocity, armor-piercing projectiles proved to be quite effective against German tanks.

The basis of the long-recoil principle is that both recoil and counter-recoil are controlled by a hydro-spring buffing mechanism. The breechblock is of the vertical, sliding-wedge type. When the projectile is fired and driven down the bore of the barrel, the barrel, breechblock, and locking frame, all locked together, recoil rearward 10 inches before the breechblock cams downward, cocking the hammer, ejecting the empty case, and loading a new shell—at which point, the mechanism locks up and is again ready for firing.

The M9 was principally intended for use by aircraft. It is either mounted to fire through the hub of the propeller or from the wings. With little change, it can be fed from either right or left. The muzzle velocity of its standard round is 3050 feet per second. The total production of all Browning Aircraft Cannons, including World War II, is under 100,000 units.

The United States Government sent several thousand P-39 Bell Aircobra planes mounted with Browning M9s to Russia. With their armor-piercing projectiles, the M9s were a crucial element in the Russians' aerial battles against the Germans. *Above:* A Bell P39D-1 in flight.

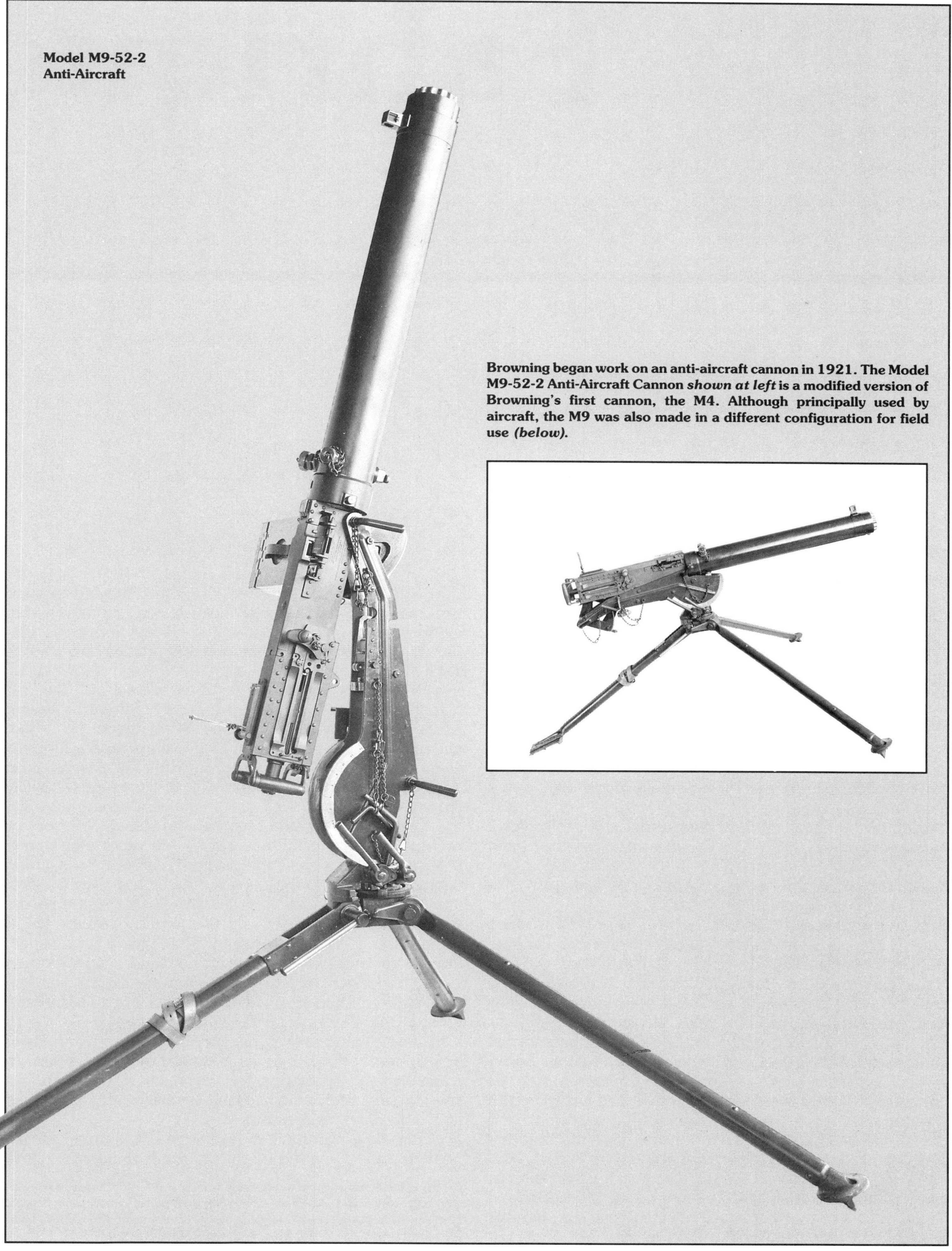

Model M9-52-2
Anti-Aircraft

Browning began work on an anti-aircraft cannon in 1921. The Model M9-52-2 Anti-Aircraft Cannon *shown at left* is a modified version of Browning's first cannon, the M4. Although principally used by aircraft, the M9 was also made in a different configuration for field use *(below)*.

Fabrique

The History

It is quite natural that firearms enthusiasts throughout the world should regard Liège, Belgium as their capital; it has been steeped in gunmaking tradition for nearly six centuries. Indeed, Fabrique Nationale, the historical heir of a firearm manufacturing tradition dating from the fourteenth century has its home in the suburbs of this gracious city of the Meuse Valley.

Way back in the 1500s, metal workers grouped under the name of 'Bon Metier Des Febvres' (the 'Good Guild of Metal Workers') had a central role in the industrial and economic life of Liège. These men were totally dedicated to the manufacturing of guns and military weapons, and to the making of the highest quality gunpowder and projectiles.

In this same era, the Princes-Evaques managed to maintain the Principality of Liège in a state of political neutrality, and made the city's fortune by promoting its weapons to a number of warring neighbor-states.

In the seventeenth century the talent of metal workers from Liège came to be recognized throughout Europe. During this period a Swedish a banker named Louis de Geer financed a dozen iron mills, nail works, gun foundries and arms factories. Many of the workers at these various facilities were workers from the Principality of Liège.

At the Court of the French King Louis XIV, richly adorned firearms were in vogue, and the ability to create a finely-crafted, expensively ornate firearm had become prized as one of the highest arts—and was rewarded richly by the extravagant French royalty. Therefore attracted to the French Court, the great master armorers of the time left their own countries and settled in northwestern France. And from Liège came Adrien Reynier, who became the personal gunsmith to Louis XIV. The guns and pistols of Reynier and his fellow countrymen became renowned as masterpieces of classical arm manufacturing.

In 1672, a proclamation was issued in Liège that required arms makers to have their products tested and hallmarked. Fabrique Nationale's concern for quality and perfection therefore has its roots in that long-ago proclamation, and it is still a source of pride that every FN firearm is thoroughly proven to a very high standard of excellence.

In the eighteenth century, the export of firearms was an ever-increasing source of prosperity for Liège. By 1750, annual firearms production in Liège had reached 100,000 weapons. By 1788, the 70 to 80 arms manufacturers in Liège were exporting more than 200,000 weapons annually at a value of three or four million guilders. And the quality of even the lowest-grade firearms was steadily improving, for, due to the quality demands made by the European aristocracy, increasingly sophisticated firearms manufacturing techniques were steadily being invented. The French Revolution and its aftermath were disastrous for the gunmakers of Liège, and the number of active workshops soon fell to 14, and the government Proof House, where final inspection of firearms took place, fell into disuse. Since French royalty no longer existed, the demand for extremely high-quality firearms had dropped to almost nil. Most orders were now for only the most utilitarian of weapons.

In 1810, an imperial decree reestablished the Proof House, and at about that same time, innovation began to trickle back into the shops, for a production line was set up whereby separately machined parts could be fully assembled after only very small adjustments.

Under the government of Napoleon Bonaparte, tastes in firearms once again turned toward the higher grades, and

In 1984, Browning introduced the Classic and Gold Classic series to commemorate three of John Browning's greatest inventions. *Right, from top to bottom:* The Classic Automatic-5 Shotgun, the Classic Over & Under Shotgun and the Classic 9mm Hi-Power Pistol.

Nationale

technical improvements became the watch word of the day. More than ever before, the gunmakers of Liège were asked to make vast quantities of arms for their Parisian customers.

The 19th century may be called the Golden Age of gunsmithing in Liège, and was marked by significant advances in the craft. A whole range of inventions had contributed to revolutionizing the design and the manufacture of military firearms. In particular, many of these inventions were derived from the percussion-cap principle that was patented by Alexander Forsyth in 1807.

Heretofore, ignition of the powder charge in a firearm was effected by one of several methods—all of which had their own mechanism of application—the wick, or 'match'; the spark-generating friction wheel; and the spark-striking chip of flint. A percussion cap is a small brass or copper cup that contains a small amount of fulminate of mercury, which explodes when struck by a blow. The percussion cap rests on a nipple which is tapped into the the breech of the gun. When it is struck by the firearm's hammer, the charge in the cap expends its energy through the hole in the nipple, igniting the powder charge in the gun's chamber. This was so much more efficient than the wheellock, flintlock or matchlock that its acceptance was rapid and widespread.

Soon enough, experiments with self-contained cartridges of various types resulted in cardboard cartridges made for guns with long, needle-like firing pins. These were inefficient, as the cartridges tended to swell and stick in the chamber. At about the same time, the idea of using paper cartridges in conjunction with percussion caps was leading to the design of many of the weapons that were used in the American Civil War. Shortly after this, however, the percussion cap was made an integral part of a limited-expansion brass cartridge, and the basic mechanism of the modern firearm was formed around this combination.

The progress that was made in the development of the modern cartridge also led to the development of firearms able to fire a varying number of shots. So it was that Collier's revolver appeared in about 1820; and 1835 saw the invention of Colt's revolver; Spencer's repeating rifle appeared in 1860 and Mauser's rifle appeared in 1864. These were followed by the automatic weapons inventions of the late 1880s and early 1890s. Liège's manufacturers adopted these various improvements as soon as they were introduced. In 1870, an idea which later would lead to the creation of Fabrique Nationale began to take shape. Fearing foreign competition, some manufacturers decided to unite. First they established a communal workshop—which was known as the 'Petit Syndicat,' or 'Little Syndicate'—where they made guns for the Belgian Guard.

In 1886, a partnership grouped seven manufacturers under the name of 'Les Fabricants d'Armes Reunis,' or 'The United Arms Makers.' In 1888, following an order for 150,000 repeating rifles from the Belgian Government, the Fabricants d'Armes Reunis, needing help to fulfill the order, induced their direct competitors to become their partners for the sake of fulfilling the government order. Strictly for that purpose, a limited company—actually, more of a coalition—was formed.

The name of the new Company was chosen on 8 December 1888, and it was 'Fabrique Nationale d'Armes de Guerre.' On 1 February 1890, a plot of land was purchased in the territory of Herstal, a commune lying near Liège. Today, the main workshops of Fabrique Nationale Herstal (as the firm is now formally known) firearms division are located on that very plot of ground.

The 'coalition' worked so well that the arms makers decided to keep it going. At the end of the nineteenth century, FN was exploring two new fields: the manufacturing of dual-purpose guns that could be used for both game and target shooting, and the making of bicycles. In 1896 the company board of directors approved the manufacturing of 50,000 .22 caliber sporting rifles, and in 1898, the company invented a bicycle without a chain, the so-called chainless bicycle, a version of which was immediately put into production.

Fabrique Nationale Air-Cooled Machine Gun

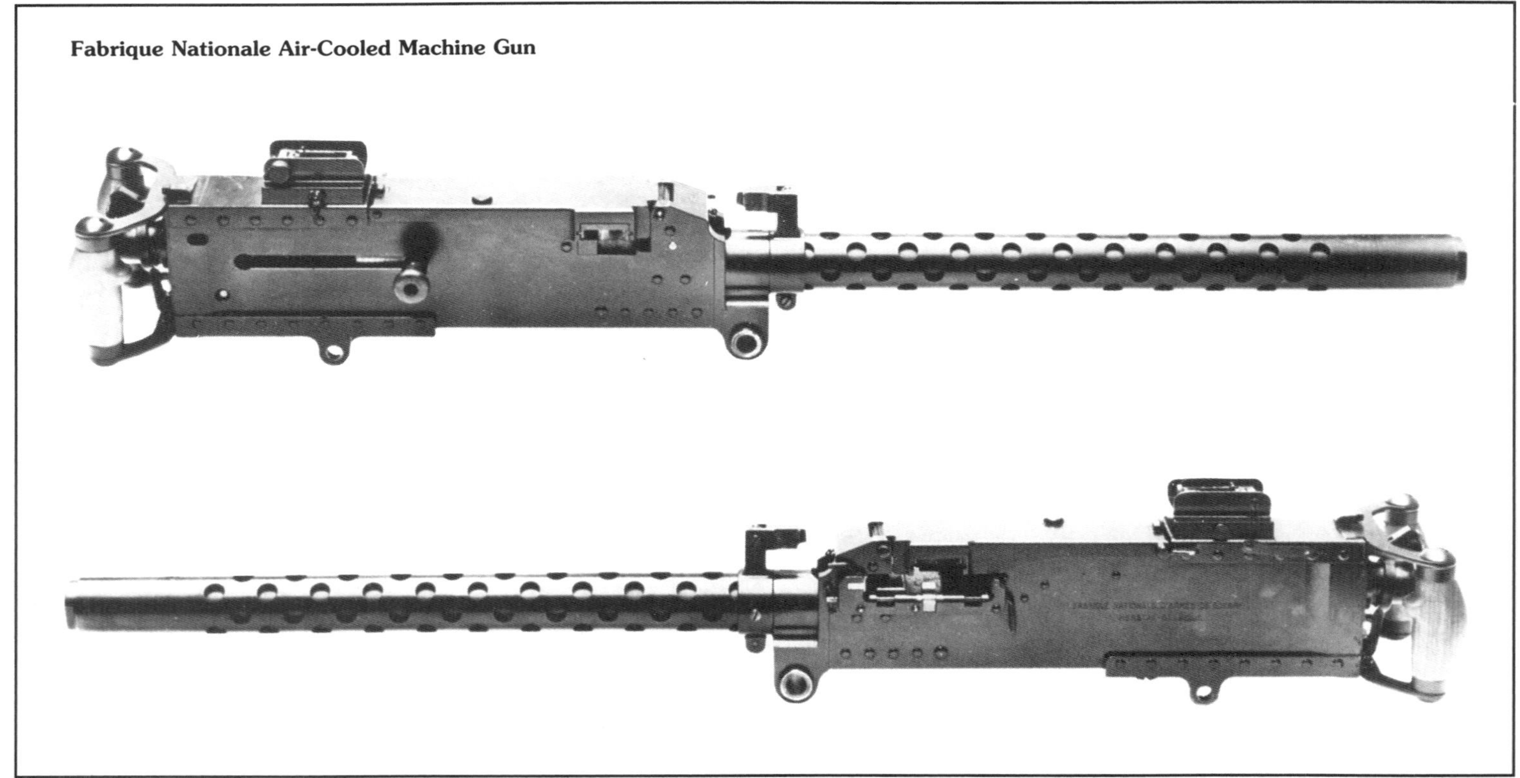

The Browning Era

In 1897, FN's Board of Directors sent its commercial director to the United States to obtain information about the latest improvements in bicycles. During his time in the US, he became acquainted with John Moses Browning and Matthew Browning. John had just applied for a patent covering his Automatic Pistol in .32 Caliber.

Browning offered the license for this pistol to FN who, upon accepting the offer, produced the first pistols of this type in 1899. The superiority of this weapon was soon widely recognized, and in 1900 it was adopted as an official sidearm for the Belgian Army Corps. This was an historic moment—it was the first time that an automatic pistol was accepted into the equipment roster of any nation's regular army.

This was just the beginning of a long and fruitful relationship. In 1902 John M Browning arrived in Herstal with the prototype of an automatic shotgun that he had previously offered, in vain, to American manufacturers. Since FN had had little success in the hunting firearms market, and especially since the .32 semiautomatic had gone over so well, the firm took an immediate interest in this weapon, and a license contract was signed. On the same day, Browning ordered 10,000 shotguns from this license, for sale under his own newly-created 'Browning Firearms Company.'

Since then, FN has manufactured about three million automatic shotguns. The substance of the relationship still maintained by FN with the Browning Company is exemplified in that long-ago agreement. Shortly after selling them the automatic shotgun license, John M Browning acceded to FN's wishes to use his name as a trademark. By granting FN the right to do so, he sealed the consolidation of interests which has, ever since, united the Browning Arms Company and Fabrique National.

As time goes on, one can judge the considerable and far-reaching consequences of that agreement. Now the FN-Browning brand name which is engraved on each firearm that is produced in by the united companies is an assurance, to shooters throughout the world, of perfection in gunmaking.

That maker's mark represents the linking of the centuries-old tradition of Liège's armorers with the inventive genius of the Browning family. Today, FN actually owns the Browning Arms Company, of which Browning Arms North America is an independent subsidiary. The tradition, firmly unified, continues.

Above, clockwise from upper left: **Browning's awards—The Cross of Knighthood of the Order of Leopold, The John Scott Legacy Medal and the gold-inlaid 100,000th FN Model 1900.** ***Left:*** **The Liège shop, where engravers like the one** ***below*** **ply their trade.**

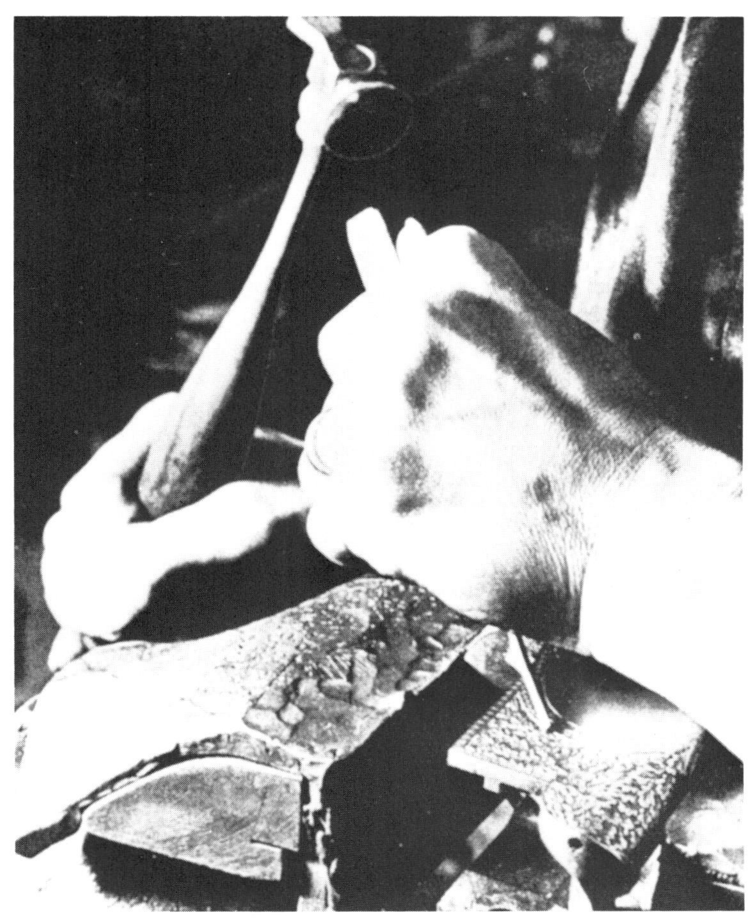

Newer Pistols

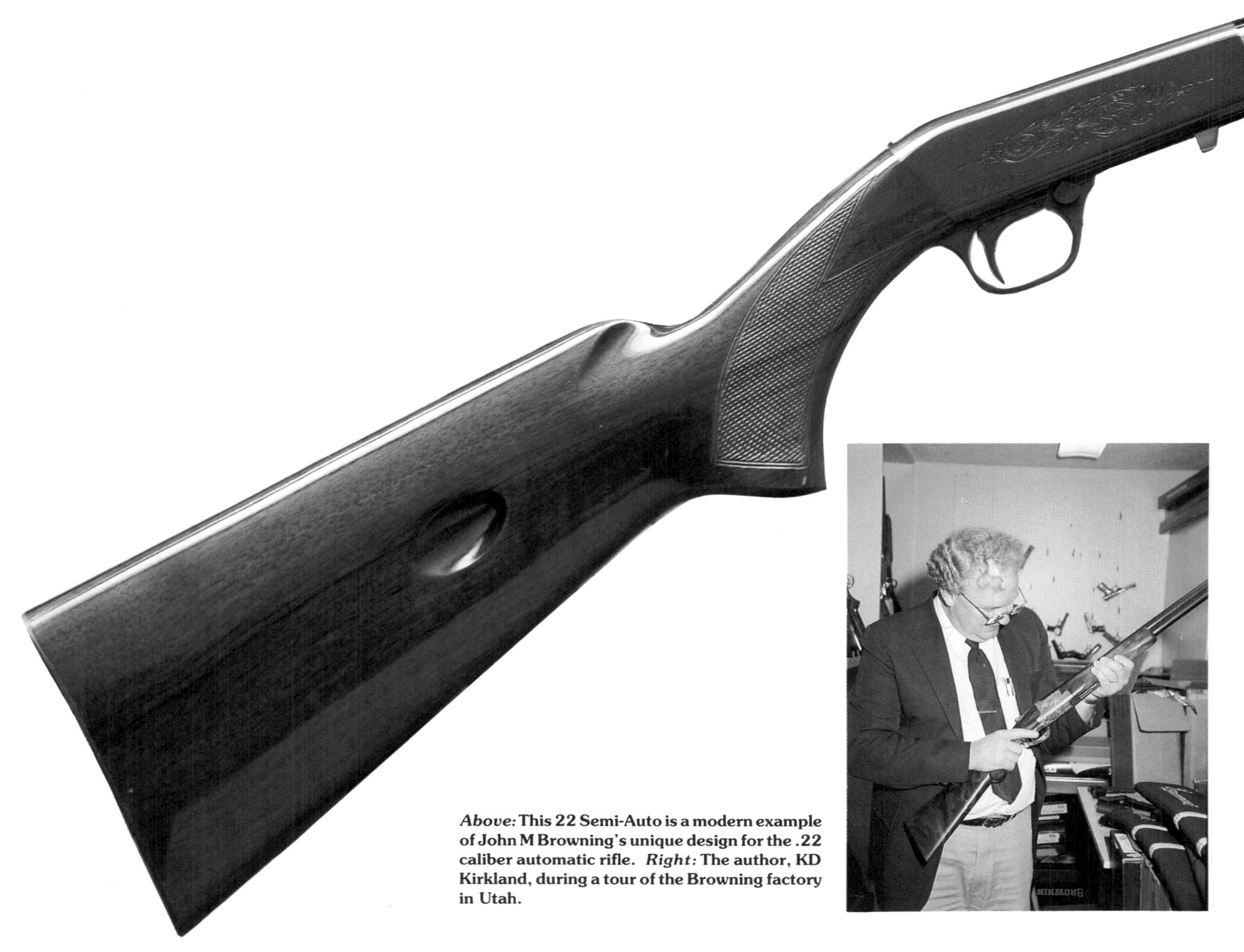

Above: This 22 Semi-Auto is a modern example of John M Browning's unique design for the .22 caliber automatic rifle. *Right:* The author, KD Kirkland, during a tour of the Browning factory in Utah.

Browning and Rifles

Browning Pistols

The following major modern Browning pistols have been manufactured for the Browning Company of Morgan, Utah by Fabrique Nationale d'Armes de Guerre (now Fabrique Nationale Herstal) of Herstal, Belgium; Arms Technology Inc of Salt Lake City, Utah; and by JP Sauer & Sohn of Eckenforde, West Germany. Many of these are either updates of or follow-ons to, original John M Browning designs.

Browning .25 Caliber Automatic Pistol. This is a blowback-operated semiautomatic pistol in .25 ACP and 6.35mm Browning caliber, with a six-shot pistol-grip magazine and a 2.1-inch barrel. This pistol weighs approximately seven ounces, and has standard hard rubber grips, with optional Nacrolac pearl grips having been available. It was manufactured from 1955 to 1969, and is based on the John M Browning design.

Browning .380 Caliber Automatic Pistol. This is a blowback operated, hammerless, semiautomatic pistol in .380 ACP caliber, with a six-shot pistol grip magazine. This pistol has two main variants, the 1955 model and the 1971 model—the former is equipped with fixed sights and a four-inch barrel, and the latter is equipped with adjustable rear/fixed front sights and a 4.4-inch barrel. The 1971 models have plastic thumbrest stocks. The earlier variants weigh 1.3 pounds, and the later variants weigh 1.4 pounds. Production on the 1955 model ended in 1969, and production on the 1971 model ended in 1975. This is essentially an update of the original John M Browning design.

Browning Hi-Power 9mm Automatic Pistol. This is a short recoil-operated, locked breech, semiautomatic pistol in 9mm Parabellum caliber, with a 13-shot pistol grip magazine and blade front/fixed rear sights (optional adjustable rear/ramp front sights are available). This pistol has a 4.6-inch barrel and weighs 2.2 pounds. The grips are checkered walnut or Nacrolac pearl. This pistol has been manufactured from 1955 to date, and is essentially an update of the original production model of the John M Browning design.

Browning Nomad Automatic Pistol. This is a semiautomatic pistol in .22 long rifle caliber, with a pistol grip 10-shot magazine, and barrel lengths of 4.5 and 6.8 inches, with removable blade front/adjustable rear sights. This pistol weighs 2.1 pounds with the 4.5-inch barrel. Plastic stocks are standard on this pistol, which was made from from 1962 to 1974.

Browning Challenger Automatic Pistol. This is a semiautomatic pistol in .22 long rifle, with a ten-shot pistol grip magazine, and removable blade front/adjustable rear sights. Barrel lengths for this pistol range from 4.5 to 6.8 inches, and weighs 2.4 pounds with the latter barrel. This pistol has standard checkered walnut stocks, with finely figured and carved stocks on extra-fine Gold and Renaissance Models. The Challenger was manufactured from 1962 to 1975.

Browning Medalist Automatic Target Pistol. This is a semiautomatic pistol in .22 long rifle caliber, having a 10-shot magazine. Its 6.8-inch barrel has a ventilated rib, and removable blade front/click-adjustable mocrometer rear sights. The pistol weighs 2.9 pounds, and was made from 1962 to 1975.

Browning BDA Double Action Automatic Pistol. This is a locked breech, double action, semiautomatic pistol in 9mm Luger, .38 Super Auto and .45 ACP with a seven to nine-shot magazine (depending on caliber used) and a 4.4-inch barrel. This pistol weighs 1.8 pounds, has fixed sights and plastic grips, and was introduced in 1977.

Browning Rifles

The following are major modern Browning rifles that have been manufactured for Browning of Morgan, Utah, by Fabrique Nationale d'Armes de Guerre (now Fabrique Nationale Herstal) of Herstal, Belgium; Miroku Firearms Mfg Co of Tokyo, Japan; and Oy Sako Ab of Riihimaki, Finland. Many of these are either updates of, or follow-ons to, original John M Browning designs.

Browning .22 Automatic Rifle. This is an autoloading rifle in .22 short and long rifle caliber, with a 15 (short) or 10 (long rifle)-shot tubular magzine in the buttstock and a 19.3 to 24-inch barrel. It weighs approximately five pounds, has open rear/bead front sights and pistol-grip style checkered stock. This rifle has been made from 1965 to date.

Browning High-Power Bolt Action Rifle. This is a bolt action rifle in .270 Winchester, .30-06, 7mm Remington Magnum, .300 H&H Magnum, .300 Winchester Magnum, .308 Norma Magnum, .338 Winchester Magnum, .375 H&H Magnum and .458 Winchester Magnum calibers, with a four to six shot (depending on caliber) magazine and adjustable sights and barrel lengths from 22 to 24 inches. The stock is standard with checkering and pistol grip, Monte Carlo cheekpiece, sling swivels and recoil pad on magnum models.This rifle was made from 1959 to 1974.

Browning High-Power Bolt Action Rifle, Short Action. This is a bolt action rifle (featuring a shortened, light-caliber only version of the standard bolt action) in .222 Remington and .222 Remington Magnum calibers, with a six shot magazine and a 22 to 24-inch barrel, and no factory sights included. This rifle was made from 1963 to 1974.

Browning High-Power Bolt Action Rifle, Medium Action. This is a bolt action rifle (featuring an intermediate-caliber action) in .22-250, .243 Winchester, .264 Winchester Magnum, .284 Winchester Magnum and .308 Winchester calibers, with barrel lengths that range from 22 to 24 inches. This rifle was made from 1963 to 1974.

Browning T-Bolt .22 Repeating Rifle, T-1. This is a straight-pull bolt action rifle in .22 long rifle caliber, with a five-shot clip magazine and peep rear/ramp front sights. It has a 24-inch barrel, weighs six pounds and has a plain

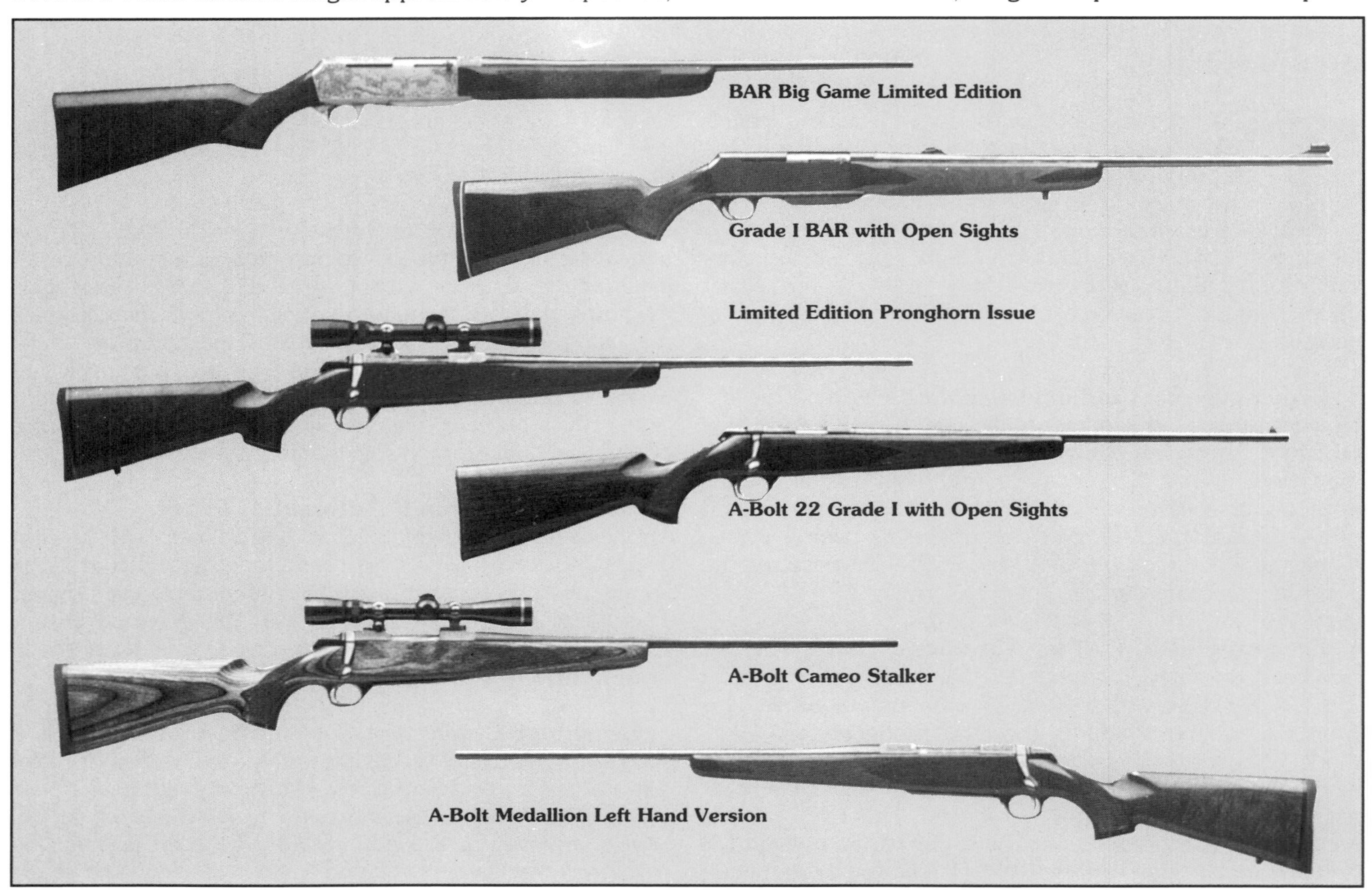
BAR Big Game Limited Edition

Grade I BAR with Open Sights

Limited Edition Pronghorn Issue

A-Bolt 22 Grade I with Open Sights

A-Bolt Cameo Stalker

A-Bolt Medallion Left Hand Version

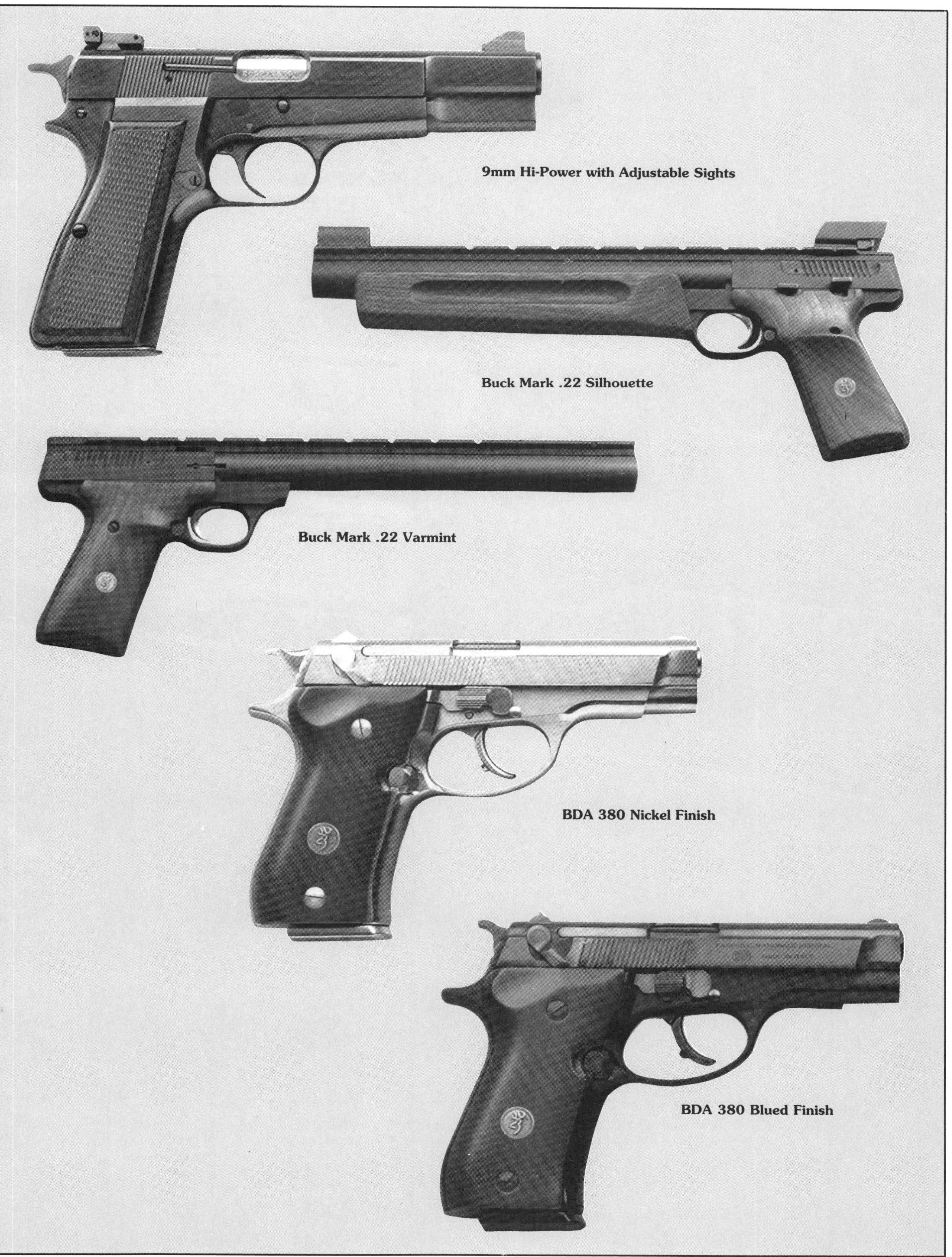

9mm Hi-Power with Adjustable Sights

Buck Mark .22 Silhouette

Buck Mark .22 Varmint

BDA 380 Nickel Finish

BDA 380 Blued Finish

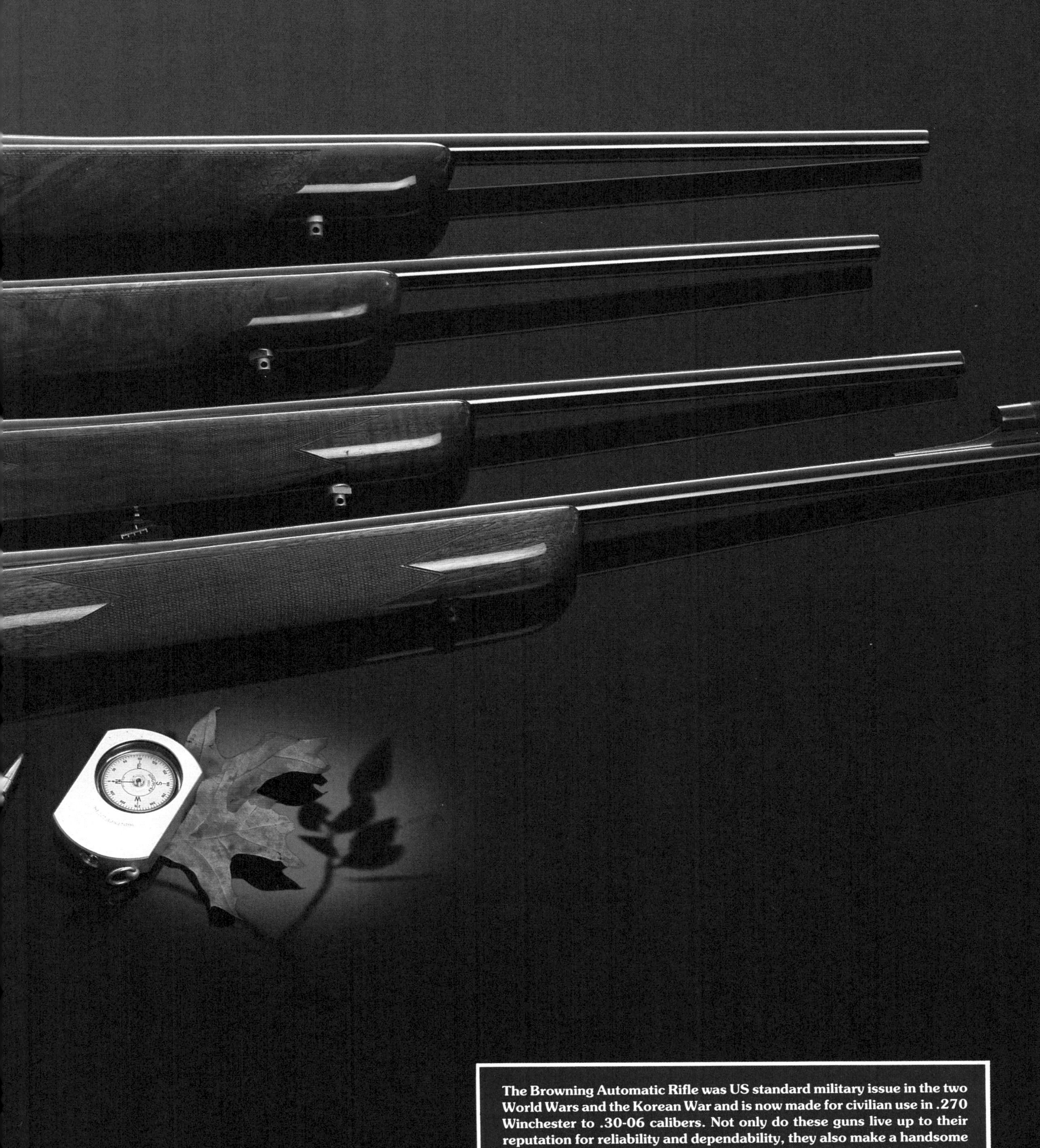

The Browning Automatic Rifle was US standard military issue in the two World Wars and the Korean War and is now made for civilian use in .270 Winchester to .30-06 calibers. Not only do these guns live up to their reputation for reliability and dependability, they also make a handsome addition to any collection. *From top to bottom:* BAR Big Game Series Limited Edition, Grade IV, Grade III and Grade I.

walnut stock with pistol grip. Also available in a left hand model, it was made from 1965 to 1974.

Browning BAR Automatic Rifle. This is a gas-operated semiautomatic rifle in .243 Winchester, .270 Winchester, .308 Winchester and .30-06 calibers, with a four-shot box magazine and folding-leaf rear/hooded ramp front sights and a 22-inch barrel. It weighs about 7.5 pounds and has a checkered French walnut stock that is equipped with sling swivels, and has been manufactured from 1967 to date.

Browning BAR Magnum. This is a gas-operated semiautomatic rifle in .243 Winchester, .270 Winchester, .308 Winchester, .30-06, 7mm Remington Magnum and .300 Winchester Magnum calibers, with a four-shot (three-shot for Magnums) box magazine and folding-leaf rear/hooded ramp front sights and a 24-inch barrel. It weighs about 7.5 pounds and has a checkered French walnut stock that is equipped with sling swivels and a recoil pad. This rifle has been manufactured from 1969 to date.

Browning BL-22 Lever Action Repeating Rifle. This is a 'short-throw' lever action rifle in .22 short, long and long rifle calibers, having a 15 to 22-shot (depending on ammo used) tubular magazine and folding-leaf rear/bead fronts sights with scope mounting grooves on the receiver. It has a 20-inch barrel and weighs five pounds. Its walnut straight-grip stock is furnished with a barrel band. This rifle has been manufactured from 1970 to date.

Browning BLR Lever Action Repeating Rifle. This is a lever action repeating rifle in .243 Winchester, .308 Winchester and .358 Winchester calibers, having a four-round detachable box magazine, adjustable rear/hooded ramp front sights and a 20-inch barrel. It weighs approximately seven pounds and has a checkered walnut straight-grip stock complete with barrel band and recoil pad. This rifle has been made from 1971 to date.

Browning 78 Single Shot Rifle. This is a single shot, falling block rifle in .22-250, 6mm Remington, .243 Winchester, .25-06, 7mm Remington Magnum, .30-06 and .45-70 Government, having open rear/blade front sights on the .45-70 model only—all others have no factory sights. Its barrel length is 24 to 26 inches, with octagon or heavy round styles available, and weighs from 7.8 to 8.8 pounds, depending on caliber and barrel choice. This rifle has a fancy checkered walnut stock; more precisely, the .45-70 model has a straight-grip stock with curved butt plate, while the others have stocks equipped with a Monte Carlo comb, a cheekpiece, a pistol grip with cap and a recoil pad. The Browning 78 Single Shot Rifle has been manufactured from 1973 to date.

Browning offered a limited-edition Bicentennial 78 Set, which included a Model 78 in .45-70 caliber, with receiver engravings that featured a bison and an eagle, plus scroll engraving on top of the receiver, lever, both ends of barrel and butt plate; and a high grade walnut stock and forearm. Also as part of the set, an engraved hunting knife and stainless steel commemorative medallion, were included. Rifle, hunting knife and medallion fit in a custom alderwood presentation case, and the items in each set have matching serial numbers beginning with '1776' and ending in numbers from 1 to 1000. The Bicentennial 78 edition was limited to 1000 sets, and all were made in 1976.

Browning BAR .22 Automatic Rifle. This is a semiautomatic rifle in .22 long rifle caliber, with a 15-shot tubular magazine and a 20.3-inch barrel. It weighs approximately 6.3 pounds and has folding leaf rear/gold bead ramp front sights, with scope mount grooves in the receiver, and a checkered French walnut pistol-grip stock. This rifle was introduced in 1977.

Browning BPR .22 Pump Rifle. This is a hammerless slide-action repeating rifle in .22 long rifle and .22 Magnum rimfire, having a tubular magazine that holds 15 of the former or 11 of the latter ammunition, and has a 20.3-inch barrel. It weighs approximately 6.3 pounds and has folding leaf rear/gold bead ramp front sights, with scope mount grooves in the receiver, and a checkered French walnut pistol-grip stock. The Browning BPR .22 Pump was introduced in 1977.

Below: **These finely finished A-Bolt Centerfire Rifles were designed with the hunter in mind. Because the A-Bolt's 60 degree bolt requires less movement than a 90 degree bolt, the hunter can get back on target quicker for fast follow-up shots. The A-Bolt is the lightest (about seven pounds) Browning bolt action rifle.**

The Pittman-Robertson Act

In 1987, Browning joined in the commemoration of the 50th Anniversary of the Pittman-Robertson Act, which is known officially as the Federal Aid in Wildlife Restoration Act. Pittman-Robertson may well be the single most important piece of legislation ever enacted to benefit wildlife.

Over half a century ago—in 1937—the Pittman-Robertson Act was sponsored by Senator Key Pittman of Nevada and Representative A Willis Robertson of Virginia. This act directs the proceeds of an 11 percent excise tax—on the manufacturing cost of guns and ammunition—specifically to programs involving wildlife management. The fundamental concept was that sportsmen would directly help pay for the needs of wildlife through monies collected by the tax.

This excise tax was heartily supported by sportsmen and the wildlife management community. Recent amendments have broadened it to include archery equipment and pistols as well, and each year, more than $100 million is collected from sportsmen through this tax. Over the past five decades of Pittman-Robertson, more than $1.5 billion has been collected for wildlife.

State wildlife agencies receive portions of these monies according to a formula, the criteria of which are the state's population, its general need and the number of hunting licenses sold in that state. The state proposes conservation or research programs and, if approved, Pittman-Robertson funds will cover up to 75 percent of the cost—or, in dollar terms, three dollars for every one dollar put up by the state.

More than 62 percent of the money collected goes directly into land acquisition. Since the program began, over 3.7 million acres have been purchased to develop and operate wildlife management areas. Purchasing land and improving habitat has always been of utmost importance, as habitat loss is the most significant cause of reduced wildlife populations. Twenty-six percent goes directly into research or surveys. A recent amendment allows about seven percent of the tax to be spent on hunter education programs. The remaining five percent goes to the states for planning and supervision, and for providing and distributing technical information to the pertinent agencies. Funds are used where they are needed most—for both game and protected animals.

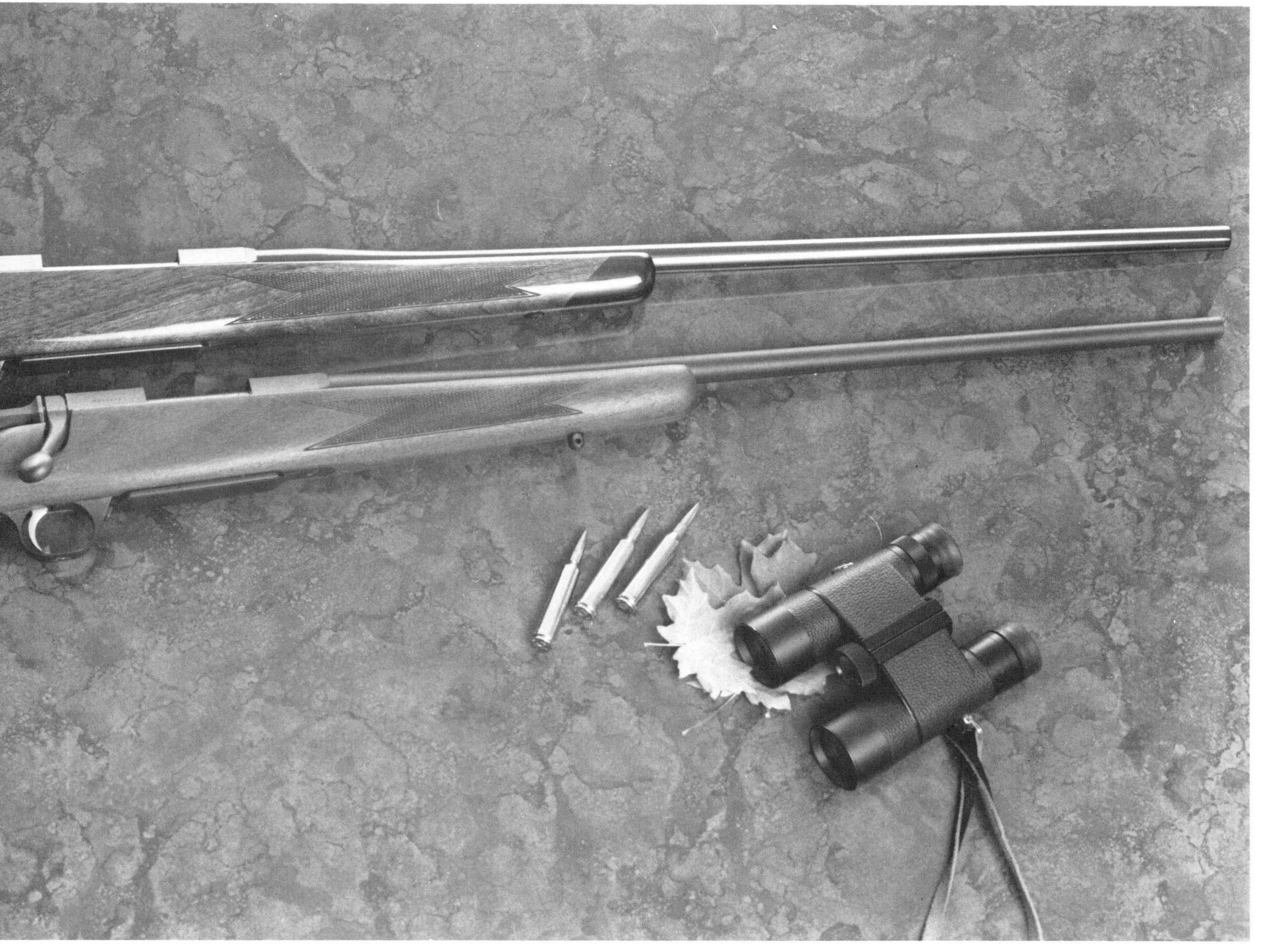

Newer Shotguns

Browning Shotguns

The following Browning shotgun was distributed by Browning of St Louis, Missouri, but was manufactured by Remington Arms Company of Ilion, New York. It is based on the original John M Browning autoloading shotgun design.

Browning Grade I Three or Five Shot Autoloading Shotgun. This is a recoil-operated autoloading shotgun in 20, 16 or 12 gauge, having a two- or four-shot tubular magazine, and a 26- to 32-inch standard barrel with any standard boring. This shotgun weighs from about 6.9 to eight pounds depending on gauge and barrel length, and has a checkered pistol-grip stock. It was available in Special, Special Skeet and Utility Field models. The Grade I Three or Five Shot Autoloading Shotgun was made from 1940 to 1949.

The following are major modern Browning shotguns which have been manufactured for Browning of Morgan, Utah, by Fabrique Nationale d'Armes de Guerre (now Fabrique Nationale Herstal) of Herstal, Belgium, and by Miroku Firearms Mfg Co of Tokyo, Japan. Many of these are either updates of or follow-ons to, original John M Browning designs.

Browning Automatic-5, Standard. This is a recoil-operated shotgun in Magnum 20, 16, Magnum 12 and 12 gauge, with pre-World War II 16-gauge guns having been chambered for 2.6-inch shells, and with standard 16 gauge guns having been discontinued in 1964. With a four-shot magazine and one in the chamber, prewar guns were also available in three-shot models. Barrels for these guns are from 26 to 32 inches in length, and barrel styles include plain, raised matted rib and ventilated rib with a choice of standard chokes. Weight, depending on stylistic treatment, runs from 7.3 to eight pounds. The Browning Automatic-5 can be found in Trap, Magnum 12, Light 12, Buck Special, Magnum 20 and Skeet models, and generally has a checkered pistol-grip stock. It was made from 1900 to 1973.

Browning Sweet 16 Automatic-5. This is a recoil-operated shotgun in 16 gauge, with a four-shot magazine and one in the chamber. Barrel lengths for this gun were from 26 to 32 inches, and included plain with striped matting on top of barrel, raised matted rib and ventilated rib styling. This gun weighed from 7.3 to eight pounds, with a lightweight version that has a gold-plated trigger. The Browning Sweet 16 Automatic-5 was made from 1937 to 1976.

Browning Superposed Hunting Shotguns. These are double-barrel, over and under, box lock shotguns, equipped with selective automatic ejectors and a selective single trigger (earlier models had double triggers, twin selective triggers or a non-selective single trigger). Bores run from .410 to 12 gauge, with any standard choke, and barrel lengths run from 26.5 to 32 inches. Styles include raised matted rib or ventilated rib, with the prewar Lightning model without barrel rib, and the postwar version of same supplied only with a ventilated rib, and weights run from 6.3 to 7.7 pounds. Stocks tend to be checkered, with pistol grip.

The higher-grade Superposed Hunting Shotguns—the Pigeon, Pointer, Diana, Midas and Grade VI models—differ from standard Grade I models in overall quality, engraving, wood and checkering; also, Midas and Grade VI guns are

***Right, above and below:* Delicate scrollwork covers the polished grey receiver of this Grade VI Citori. The left side of the receiver features three mallard drakes. The Grade VI Citori can also be customized with a blued receiver and gold inlay.**

Browning and Bows

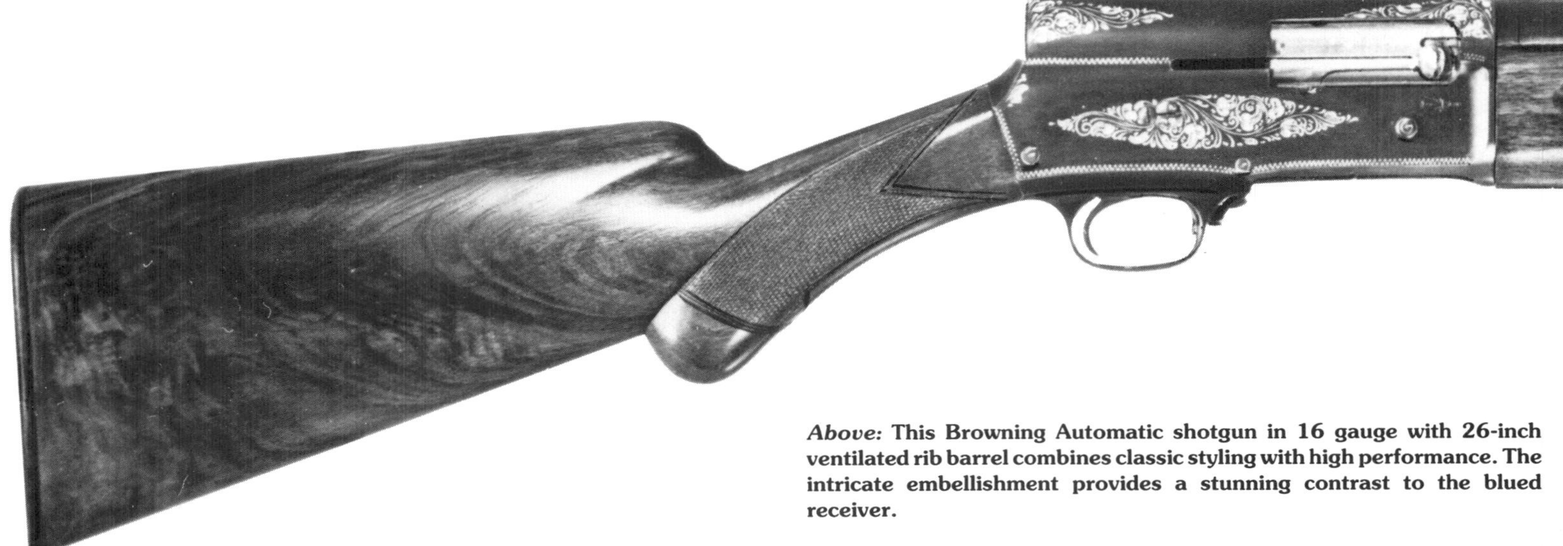

Above: **This Browning Automatic shotgun in 16 gauge with 26-inch ventilated rib barrel combines classic styling with high performance. The intricate embellishment provides a stunning contrast to the blued receiver.**

richly gold-inlaid. Browning Superposed Hunting Shotguns have been made from 1928 to the present.

Browning Double Automatic, Standard Grade (Steel Receiver). This is a short recoil system autoloading shotgun in 12 gauge only, having a two shot capacity, and barrel lengths from 26 to 30 inches. These guns are equipped with any standard choke and weigh about 7.8 pounds, having checkered pistol-grip stocks. They were made from 1955 to 1961.

Browning Twelvette Double Automatic. This is a short recoil system autoloading shotgun in 12 gauge, having a two-shot capacity, and having barrel lengths from 26 to 30 inches, with a wide selection of any standard choke.

This is essentially a lightweight version of the Double Automatic, with an aluminum receiver, and a weight of 6.8 to seven pounds, depending upon barrel length. Receivers for the Twelvette series were anodized in grey, brown and green with silver engraving. The Twelvette was made from 1955 to 1971.

Browning BT-99 Grade I Single Barrel Trap Gun. This is a single-shot, box lock shotgun with an automatic ejector mechanism, in 12 gauge, with a 23- or 24-inch ventilated rib barrel and modified, improved modified or full choke. It weighs about eight pounds and has a checkered pistol-grip stock with beavertail forearm and recoil pad. The BT-99 has been made from 1971 to date.

Browning BSS Hammerless Double Barrel Shotgun. This is a double barrel, side by side, box lock shotgun in 20 and 12 gauge, with automatic ejectors and a non-selective single trigger. Barrels range from 26 to 30 inches, with chokes ranging from improved cylinder and modified, to modified and full, to both barrels in full choke. Barrel styling is a matted solid rib, and weights are approximately seven to 7.3 pounds.

Stocks tend to be checkered pistol-grip, with beavertail forearm variety. This gun has been made from 1972 to date.

Browning Liège Over and Under Shotgun. This is a box lock superposed double barrel shotgun, with automatic

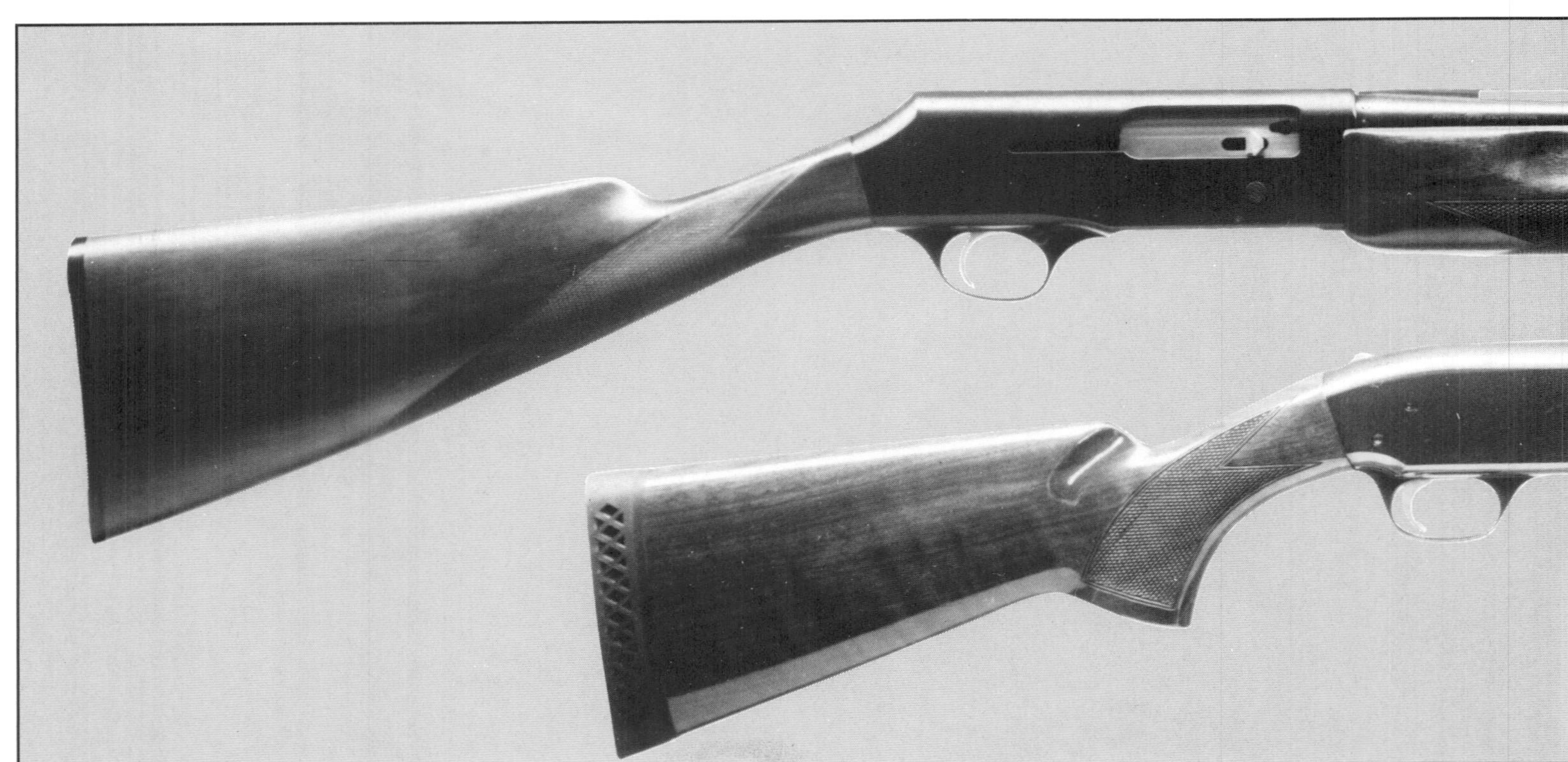

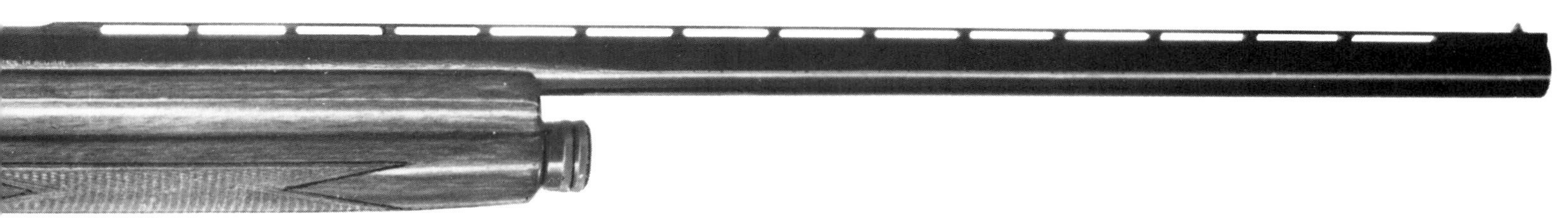

ejectors and a non-selective single trigger in 12 gauge. Barrel lengths range from 26.5 to 30 inches, with choke combinations of improved cylinder and modified, modified and full or both barrels full choke. The barrel style is ventilated rib-type, with gun weights, depending upon length of barrels, ranging from 7.3 to 7.9 pounds. A checkered pistol-grip stock completes the picture for this shotgun that was manufactured from 1973 to 1975.

Browning Citori Over and Under Hunting Shotgun. This is a double barrel, over and under, box lock shotgun in 20 and 12 gauge, having automatic ejectors and a selective single trigger. Barrels range from 26 to 30 inches, with choke combinations including improved cylinder and modified, modified and full and both barrels at full choke. Trap and Skeet models are major variants. With standard ventilated rib styling, weights, depending upon barrel length, run from 6.8 to 7.8 pounds. A checkered pistol-grip stock with recoil pad and semi-beavertail forearm are standard for this shotgun line that was made from 1973 to date.

Browning 2000 Gas Automatic Shotgun. This is a gas-operated autoloading shotgun in 20 and 12 gauge, having a four-shot magazine and barrel lengths from 26 to 30 inches with any standard choke. Plain matted barrel or ventilated rib are available, with gun weights ranging from 6.7 to 7.8 pounds, depending upon gauge and barrel. A checkered pistol-grip stock is standard, and this gun is also available in Field, Magnum, Buck Special, Trap and Skeet Models. The Browning 2000 has been made from 1974 to date.

Browning BPS Pump Shotgun. This is a pump action repeating shotgun in 12 gauge, with a magazine that holds five 2.8- or four 3-inch shells, and has available barrel lengths of from 26 to 30 inches. Chokes offered are improved cylinder, modified or full, with a ventilated rib barrel. This shotgun weighs 7.8 pounds more or less (depending on barrel length). It was introduced in 1977.

Browning Bows

Browning bows are designed by experts. Harry Drake, Browning's master bow designer, is well known to the world of archery. His Special Flight bow designs have dominated the National Archery Association Flight Championships since 1947.

On that date, the National and World Flight Record for the greatest distance an arrow was shot from a hand held bow was established with a Flight Bow designed by Harry Drake. The current World Flight Record for maximum distance from a hand held bow, in both men's and women's professional competition, was set with Drake flight bows.

In addition, every World Flight Record for foot bows since 1959 has been attained with a Drake design. Harry Drake also designed the compound hunting bow that shot a conventional 450 grain broadhead hunting arrow a spectacular 582.8 yards—the greatest flight distance ever recorded for a hunting arrow. This amazing feat was achieved in 1976, at the Utah State Bow Hunters' Annual Shoot.

An outstanding competitor in his own right, Harry Drake currently holds several National Archery Association flight

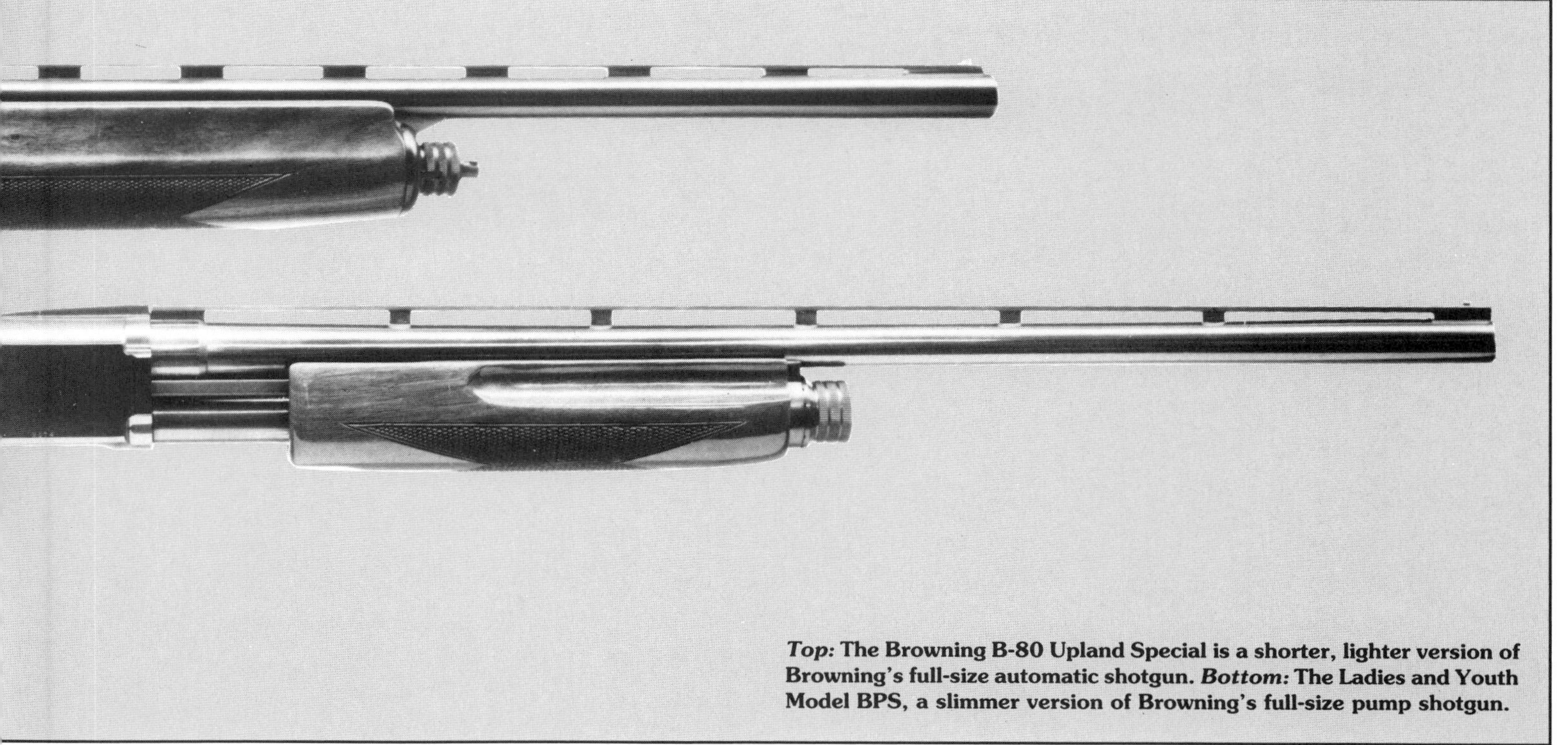

***Top:* The Browning B-80 Upland Special is a shorter, lighter version of Browning's full-size automatic shotgun. *Bottom:* The Ladies and Youth Model BPS, a slimmer version of Browning's full-size pump shotgun.**

From top to bottom: The Limited Edition Superposed Pintail Duck Issue is hand engraved with delicate rosette patterns. Each firearm is inlaid and engraved with 18 karat gold. A handsome complement to this fine shotgun is the Limited Edition Black Duck Issue. Also shown are the Superposed Express Rifle, the Superposed Continental and rifle barrels for the Continental.

records, including the regular foot bow record of over 1542 yards. Harry also holds the honor of having shot an arrow further than any other man in the world. In 1971, using a Harry Drake bow in the Unlimited Foot Bow division, Harry shot an arrow 2028 yards, or 6084 feet! This earned him a place in the Guiness Book of World Records. More to the point, to design a bow and use it to shoot an arrow that far takes a thorough knowledge of how and why a bow limb works.

Browning bows are built for arrow speed, which depends entirely on how well the bow limbs can store and transmit energy. In theory, a bow's stored energy should be equal to, or greater than, the peak draw weight. In practice, this is rarely true. Friction in the cables and cams, combined with limb drag, can reduce a bow's energy by more than 10 percent.

Below: **In addition to its firearms, Browning also produces a line of bows, many of which are the inspirations of master bow designer Harry Drake. Known for their speed and accuracy, Browning bows are made for both hunting and range archery.**

To avoid this loss, Browning mounts its cams in limb notches rather than on bulky metal hangers. This helps the cams to operate smoothly, and doesn't add any unnecessary weight or drag to the limbs—thus, Browning bows utilize more of the bow limb's stored energy.

All Browning compound bows store more foot-pounds of energy than their respective peak draw weights. By comparison, when other bows of competing designs were tested, it was found that many of them stored less than their peak draw weights. On Browning 'four-wheelers,' the cables are attached to extending tuning bars, which allow the bow to be more accurately 'set,' or tuned, which in turn means more of the bow's energy is harnessed and not wasted.

Browning wood handle compound bows incorporate a warm, solid hand-filling riser that has been sculptured into a pistol grip. The African hardwoods that are used combine superior strength with the type of wood grain one is accustomed to seeing on high quality rifles and shotguns. These bows are easy to carry, weigh less than most other comparable bows and are easy to hold on target.

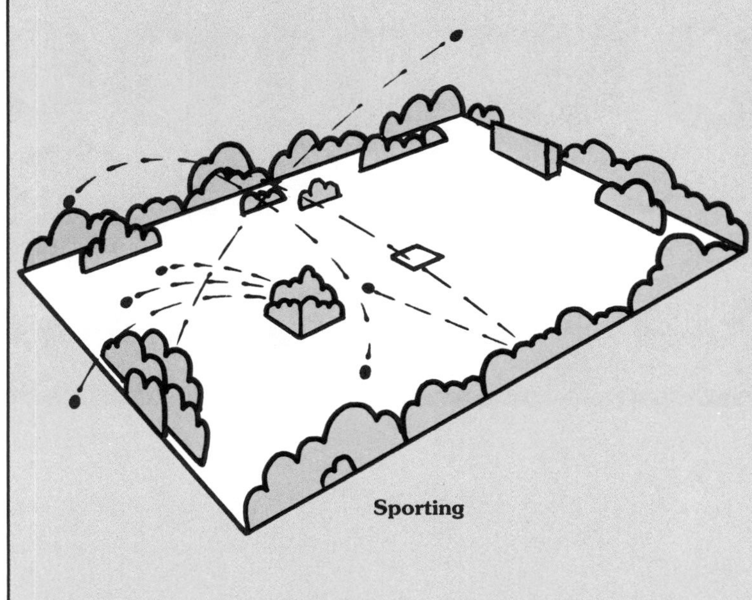
Sporting

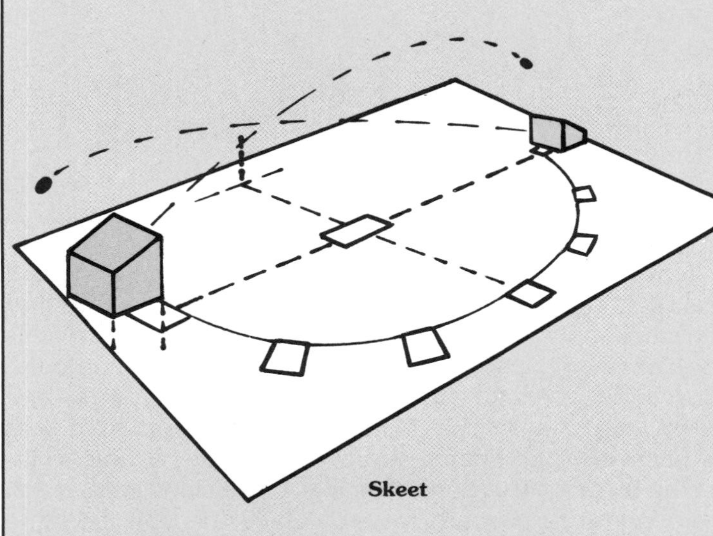
Skeet

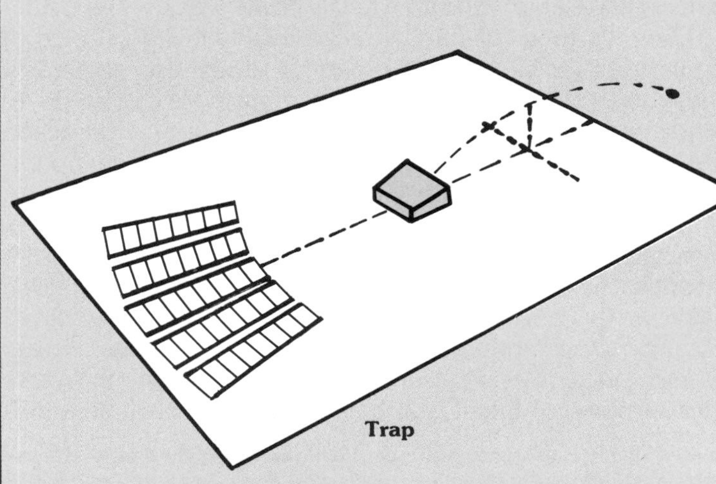
Trap

Shooting Sports

Non-game shooting sports involving shotguns fall into three main categories: Sporting, Skeet and Trap. The technical definition of each is as follows.

Sporting is of British origin, and has not yet been included in the roster of Olympic specialties, as trap and skeet shooting have. Nevertheless, this is a form of clay pigeon shooting that is rapidly gaining in popularity, as it closely replicates the true hunting environment. Clay traps are concealed diversely over a free course where they execute a plethora of throws, imitating high-flying pheasants; bolting rabbits; birds flying in front, and to the side, of the shooter; and game of various types skimming over the ground or rising up from brush. The action takes place both in the woods and out in the open.

Skeet shooting is practiced on a semicircular layout. A release hut is located at each end of the circle's diameter—a distance of 36.8 meters, or 40 yards. The left hut is termed the 'high tower,' and the right one the 'low tower.' The clay pigeons are shot at from eight stations in succession.

First the clay pigeon is thrown from the high tower, and then from the low tower, and so on. The shooter is entitled to one cartridge per clay, and each time, shoots from a different station on the circle. Shots from stations 1, 2, 6 and 7 involve 'doubles' in which clay pigeons are thrown simultaneously from the two towers. The shooter must try to break them with one cartridge per target, taking his first shot at the clay thrown from the nearest hut and his second at the one thrown from the farthest hut.

A complete series of eight stations therefore involves 25 clay pigeons. Skeet shooting is not only an official Olympic sport, but is also an excellent discipline for shooters who want to engage in their favorite sport outside of the regular game season.

Trap shooting is another Olympic specialty, but it is neither necessary to be a champion, nor is it necessary to have a costly trap range at one's disposal to enjoy trap shooting as a rewarding leisure activity.

Shooters are placed at a distance of 15 meters—or approximately 16.4 yards—behind a trench in which one or more throwing machines are installed. These machines are variously adjusted to provide a wide variety of clay pigeon trajectories. These trajectories are circumscribed by the limits established by International Regulations.

The starting order of the machines is purposely random, and the velocity, orientation and height of the clay's flight can vary with every shot. For Olympic events, 15 throwing machines are used; for Universal trench shooting, five machines are used; and for International ball-trap shooting, one machine is used. The shooter is entitled to 2 cartridges per clay. He changes his position for each clay pigeon. A complete trap shooting series is composed of 25 clay pigeons.

Browning and Special

Craftsmanship

Craftsmanship and fine gunmaking are traditions at Browning. Take the exquisite work done on Browning Superposed shotguns for example. Each Browning Superposed is a unique masterpiece, in the best gunmaker's tradition, and a living proof of his love for his craft. Steels are selected for their high strength, taking into account the more than 24 different variants that are determined by the end-use of the part. French walnut is used for the stocks, having been selected for its density and the beauty of its veining and color.

The 84 parts that make up each Superposed are the result of 794 operations conducted on precision machinery; 64 of these parts undergo heat-treating according to their respective functions. In the course of the manufacturing processes, 1490 carefully-designed gauges and measuring tools are used to control 2310 dimensions. Machines then give way to the gunsmiths, who carry out by hand the striking off, fitting in, timing and finishing. The gunsmithing tradition is so strong in these craftsmen that, for example, each barrel filer makes his own tools—which he will then use for the external trueing of the barrels and for smoothing off the upper and side ribs.

This hand work confers individuality and excellence upon each gun. The gunsmiths who assemble the three principal elements of the gun—the action frame, the barrels and the foreend—use the technique of lampblacking, an ingenious method which is both simple and efficient. This ancient process is in fact the only way to 'see' the proper fitting and timing of the parts inside the closed gun. The gunsmith covers the parts in a fine layer of lampblack, or soot, produced by the flame of an oil lamp. He then fits them firmly together before taking them cleanly apart again. If there has been any friction between the parts, the lampblack will have disappeared. The gunsmith can then make any necessary modifications. This operation is repeated several times, until the fitting meets the very severe standards imposed by Browning.

In order to ensure the specified fit between the wood and steel section, the craftsman uses a technique similar to that involving lampblack, but this time, a special red dye is smeared on the action frame, which is then locked onto the stock. The gunsmith then disassembles the parts, and checks the places marked with red dye for proper fit, makes the necessary alterations, and thereby effects a precise fit.

One by one, with a watchmaker's meticulousness, each operating part of the firearm is carefully fitted. At the same time, stocks and foreends are rough cut, shaped, adjusted, carved and smoothed off. Each operation is carried out by hand, with a skill comparable to the fine materials being used. Only patience can succeed in the slow process of crafting steel and wood to a peak of artistry.

Then it's time for hand checkering; this is a process of regularity, precision and sureness of touch, and requires a true woodcrafter's knowingness. The surfaces that are to be engraved are then polished to an impeccable sheen, and the craftsman passes yet another work of art to those who will now adorn it with exquisite engravings.

Fabrique Nationale Herstal perpetuates Liège's traditional engraving of firearms. When asked by a visiting journalist to describe the most important personal quality of a good engraver, a Browning master engraver quickly answered, 'An iron constitution.' Engraving on steel does indeed demand, in addition to a very thorough artistic training, quite unusual powers almost 'spiritual' in their nature. It demands

Select walnut stocks and exquisite engraving exemplify the fine, traditional craftmanship found in today's Browning firearms. *At right, from top to bottom:* A Black Duck Issue Superposed, a Gold Classic Automatic-5 and a Pintail Duck Issue Superposed.

Craftsmanship Editions

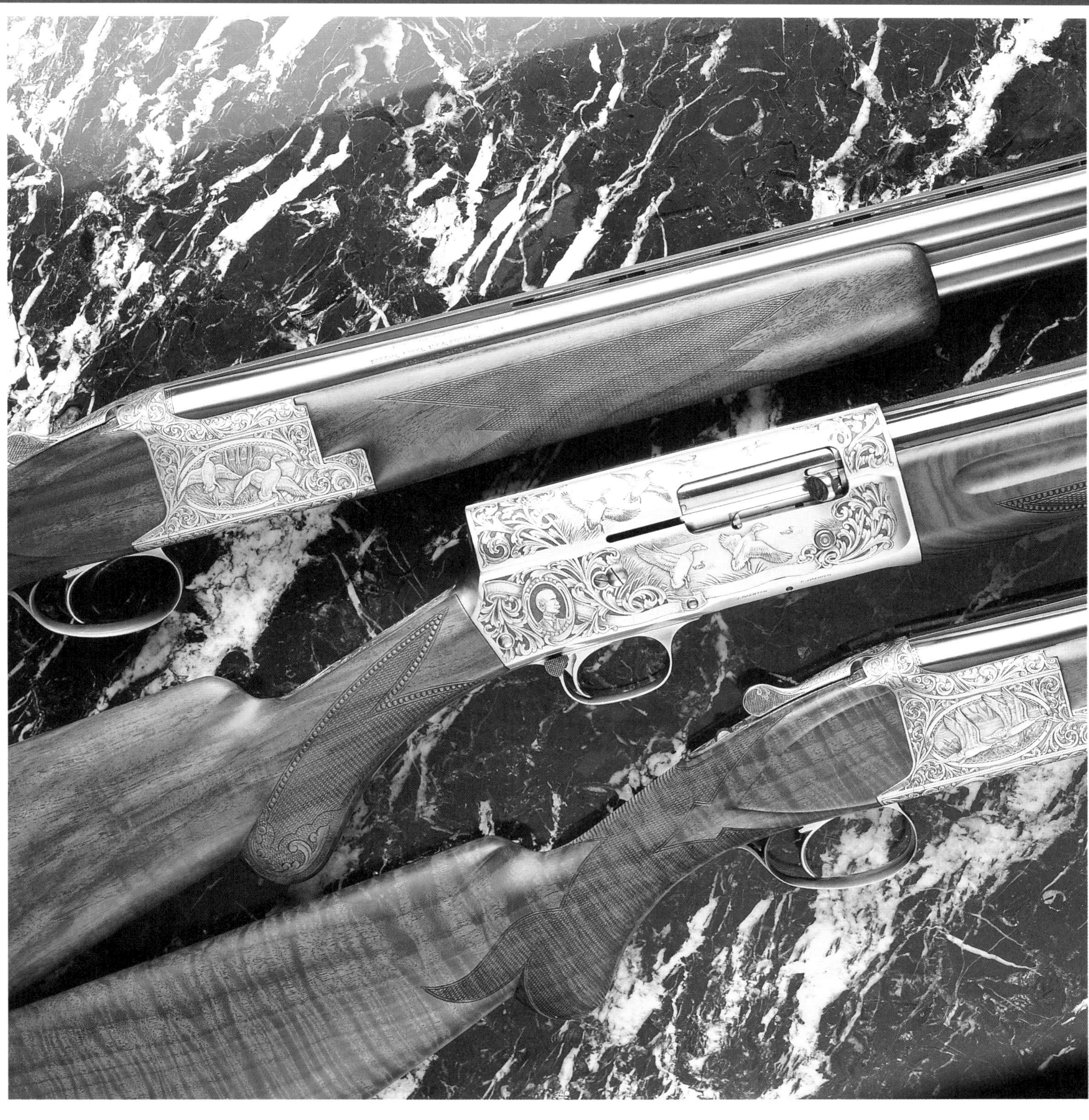

concentration, calmness, sureness of hand and physical endurance to such degrees that only a few men are able to properly do the work.

It is an art that is executed with pointed chisels and a small, flat-headed hammer with which to strike them. With these, the craftsman carves out the drawing with a rare continuity and smoothness of line. It is a technique calling for absolute perfection, because one can not use an eraser on steel.

Browning offers an extremely wide array of classic, fine engraving styles, with accompanying backgrounds, figurative motifs, gold inlay and, in short, absolutely everything there is to offer in the way of firearms embellishment.

The fact that the over and under barrels give the Browning Superposed its characteristic elegance is the happy outcome of a number of functional advantages that result from its design, which has been widely copied. The arrangement of the barrels one above the other give the shooter a better view of the target, and allow faster and more precise aiming. No other double-barrelled shotgun will allow a well-aimed second cartridge to be fired so quickly after the first.

Special Editions

All major gun manufacturers produce special edition firearms and Browning is no exception. The firearms given in the following are among Browning's more famous special editions.

The Two Millionth Browning Automatic-5 Shotgun is a museum-quality firearm that was fit for a king and was actually produced for a President. In early 1970, the Two Millionth Auto-5 was taken from the production line and placed in the hands of Browning's very best Belgian craftsmen to be prepared for presentation to the then United States President, Richard M Nixon, who, under carefully-made arrangements, would then donate the gun to the Smithsonian Institution. Due to political considerations, the presentation to President Nixon and ultimately to the Smithsonian was never made.

The inlaid designs and patterns on the Two Millionth Auto-5 were created by Browning's master engraver, Andre Watrin, whose signature is engraved on the forward portion of the trigger guard. All gold inlay was executed by Master Engraver Jose Baerten and G Vandermissen. The designs on this unique firearm were inspired by an early exposition model Auto-5 that had been embellished by Browning's famous Master Engraver Felix Funken in 1930.

Technically, there is little engraving per se on this superb firearm, because all the decorative work was of 18 and 20 karat gold inlay. The left side of the receiver features a wreath framing the profile of John M Browning; above this is the description 'Browning Automatic Shotgun Number 2,000,000,' surrounded by elaborate border work and three mythological Chimera. The right side of the receiver features a wreath framing the symbol of the city of Liège, Belgium, in addition to elaborate scrollwork and eight

intricately inlaid mythological subjects of varying sizes. The top tang bears the gold inlaid signature of John M Browning, bordered by scrollwork and delicate gold borders.

The scrollwork featured on the receiver, tang, trigger guard and barrel is of 'fleur-de-lis' design. The gunstocks are of the highest grade walnut, featuring superb checkering performed by P Hanauer, Browning's best checkerer and woodcarver. The stock features a pistol-grip cap with a gold-plated oval inlay, bearing the inscription, 'Manufactured by Browning Arms Co, June 6, 1970. Invented by John M Browning, October 9, 1900.' Shipped to the United States on 26 June 1970, the gun was displayed in a special one-of-a-kind Browning Pro-Steel safe, featuring a handsome, full-color wildlife painting on the front door, a specially polished and finished interior, special lighting and a motorized rotating stand that provided a truly dramatic display.

It remained with Browning for some 15 years while the company sought an appropriate and meaningful use for this historic one-of-a-kind firearm. Then, in 1985, Browning offered the shotgun to the National Shooting Sports Foundation for display and auction at the Eighth Annual Shot Show in Houston, Texas. The proceeds from the sale went to the National Shooting Sports Foundation educational programs on safety, ethics and wildlife conservation in the shooting sports.

The Bicentennial Commemorative Superposed is a special limited edition issued to commemorate the United States Bicentennial. Fifty-one Guns were produced in 1976, each one of which celebrates one state of the Union and Washington, DC. The receivers feature side plates engraved with a gold-inlaid hunter and wild turkey on the right side, and the United States flag and bald eagle on the left side, with specific state markings inlaid in gold, and all on a deep blued background. The stocks and forearms are of American walnut, highly figured with decorative checkering. These are among the rarest of Browning firearms and some collectors value them today in excess of $10,000 each in new, unfired condition.

The Jonathan Browning Mountain Rifle commemorates Browning's roots in the Browning family. When Jonathan Browning invented his Cylinder Repeating Rifle, he designed a unique trigger system to operate it. During their development of the Jonathan Browning Mountain Rifle, Browning designers of the late 1970s found that, by making some modifications to this trigger system, they could give black powder enthusiasts a single trigger that functioned both as a standard trigger and as a highly sensitive 'set' trigger.

In addition to being remarkably fast and smooth, this newly patented trigger was amazingly uncomplicated. For the standard trigger, one had simply to cock the hammer

***Opposite:* In contrast to the ornate engraving on the shotguns pictured on page 99, this superposed has a simple yet elegantly engraved receiver. *Below:* The Browning Auto-5 Ducks Unlimited 50th Anniversary Gun of the Year.**

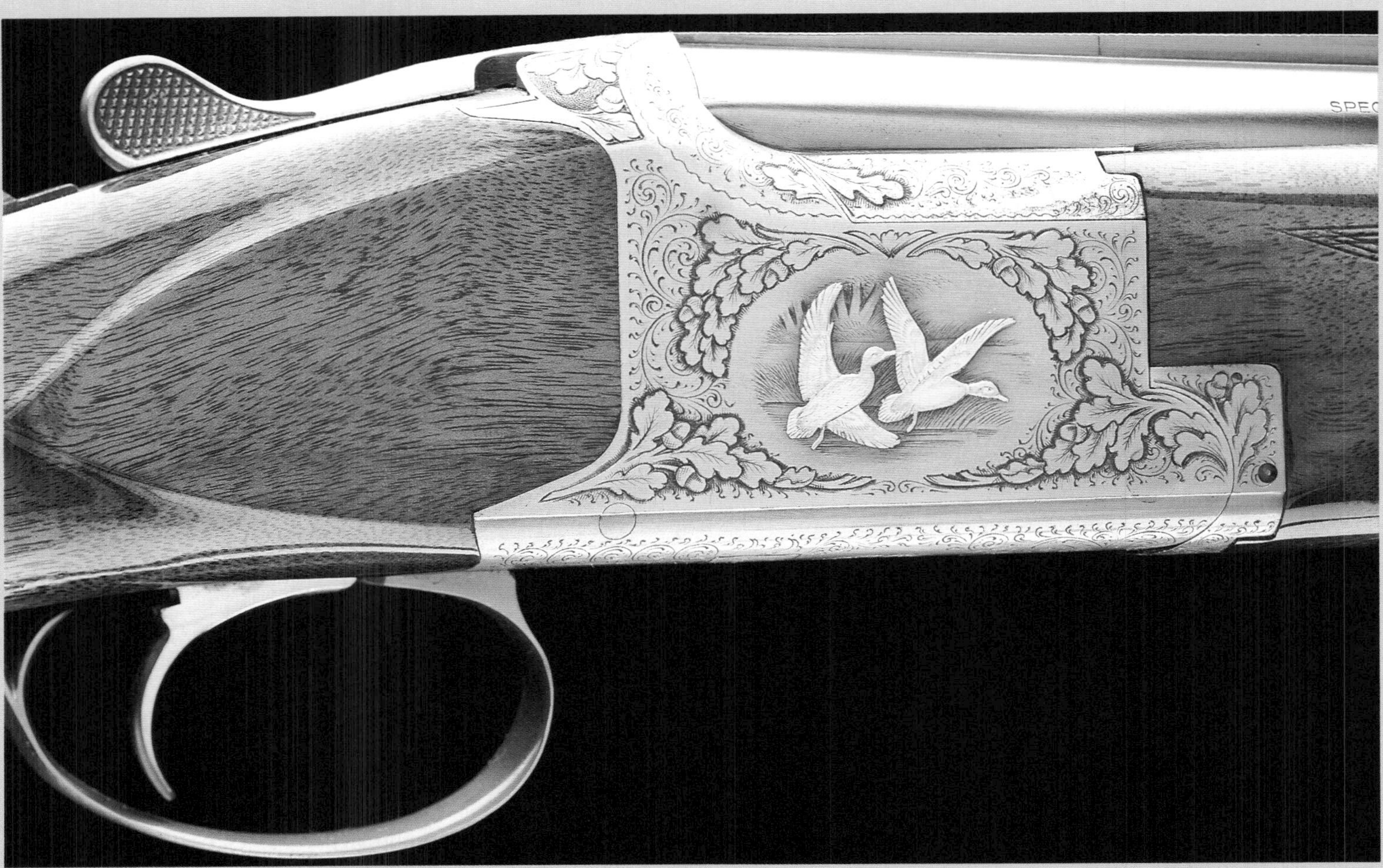

Above: This Presentation One Superposed Shotgun has oak leaf engraving on a silver grey receiver. Embellishing the sides of the receiver are two mallard ducks inlaid in gold. *Below:* This Presentation Two Superposed displays mourning doves in gold inlay on the receiver. The fleur-de-lis design on the receiver is more intricate than the engraving on the Presentation One.

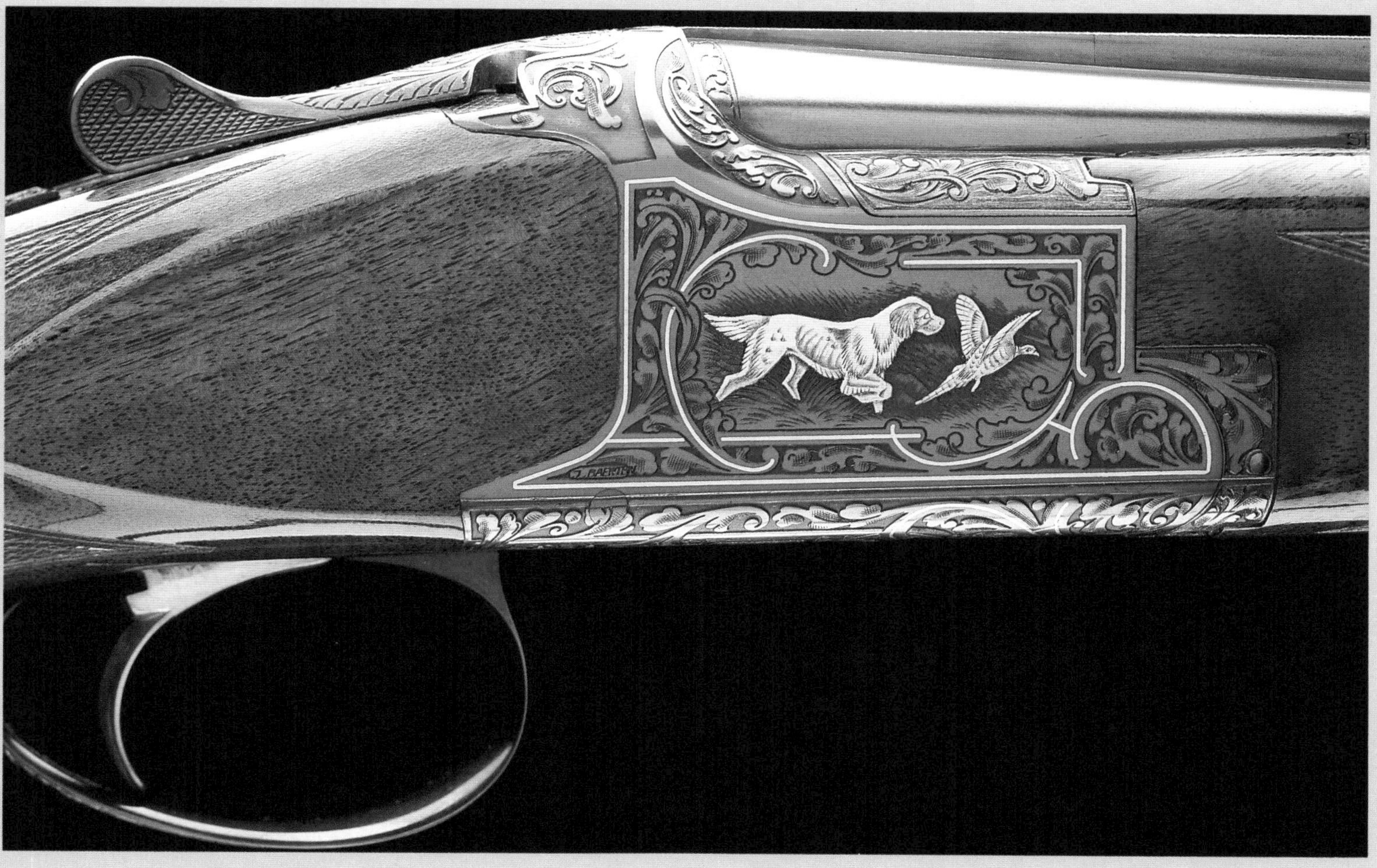

Above: The highly engraved receiver on this Presentation Three Superposed has a gold inlaid border and an English setter flushing a pheasant. *Below:* With its exquisite engraving and high quality finish, the Presentation Four Superposed is gunmaking at its finest. Deep floral carving adorns the receiver, which features a group of waterfowl in gold inlay.

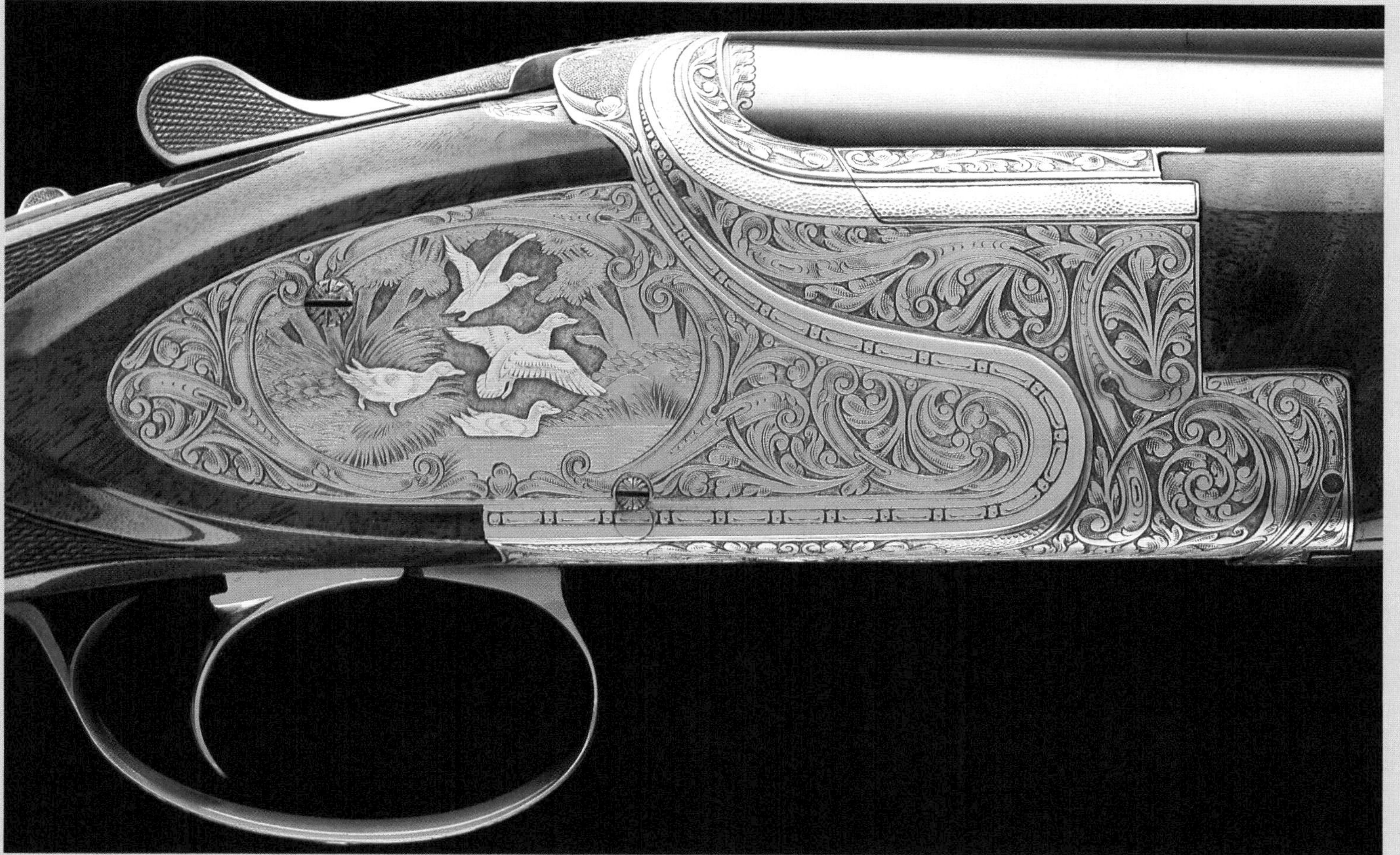

***At top, above and below:* These two guns illustrate the range of custom work. This BAR Big Game has a finely engraved silver grey receiver while the Grade I BAR has a simple, blued receiver.**

and squeeze the trigger. To use the 'set' trigger, the hammer was cocked and the trigger was pushed forward, thus sensitizing it to provide a light let-off that could be preset at between 2 ounces and 2 pounds.

The Mountain Rifle features traditionally-styled adjustable sights, which include a screw adjustment for elevation and drift adjustment for windage, with a sight radius of 21.9 inches, for accurate sighting. The Mountain Rifle is in .45, .50 and .54 caliber, weighs approximately 9.6 pounds and its hooked breech allows the barrel to be easily removed for cleaning. It is complete with a spare nipple and a ramrod of brass-tipped hickory.

Browning's unique, two-piece breech plug system reduces barrel stress and eliminates the danger of pre-ignition due to the presence of residue from previous firings.

The stock of a Jonathan Browning Mountain Rifle is specially selected and seasoned hardwood, finished with a deluxe oil finish and accented with a choice of browned steeled or brass finish on the butt plate, trigger guard and complimentary furniture. The barrel and lock are executed in traditional browned steel finish. A ram's horn on the breech plug adds further distinction to this special edition black powder rifle.

The Limited Edition Waterfowl Superposed Shotguns were featured in Browning's 1980 catalogue. This special edition is devoted to celebrating the mallard duck, and features generous gold inlay life-studies of this regal American bird. Each shotgun in the series has a handsomely gold inlaid and engraved gray steel receiver.

Limited to 500 Belgium-made guns, the edition number of each firearm is written in gold on the bottom of the receiver along with the words 'American Mallard' and that bird's scientific name. Gracing each gun, in 24-karat gold relief against a grayed steel background scene, are the following depictions, which are based on drawings by western wildlife artists Leon Burrows. On the receiver's left side is a quiet pond on a fall morning with a pair of Mallards rising over it. On the receiver's right side, the birds come in over the calm waters of a marsh with wings set for landing. Another pair of Mallards rise to flight on the bottom of the receiver, and the golden head of a drake graces the bottom of the trigger guard.

The stocks of these distinctive firearms are beautifully carved, high grade dark French walnut with a hand-oiled

finish. The forearms feature extremely fine hand checkering, and a distinctive scroll pattern has been cut into the buttstock's rounded pistol grip. A uniquely checkered butt replaces the common or traditional plate. To compliment, display and protect these magnificent firearms, each commemorative Lightning Superposed was provided with a form-fitting, velvet-lined black walnut case.

The Classic and Gold Classic Editions, inaugurated in 1984, have as their focal points three of John M Browning's most appreciated inventions—the Automatic-5, the 9mm Hi-Power Pistol and the Superposed Shotgun.

The Classics are limited editions of 5000 units and feature engraved hunting and wildlife scenes on satin gray steel. Each model is individually inscribed with the engraver's name. In a banner across the right side of the receiver on the shotguns, and across the frame on the Hi-Power, are engraved the words, 'Browning Classic.' The left side similarly displays the words 'One of Five Thousand.'

Limited to runs of 500 pieces, the Gold Classics feature engraving similar to the Classics—with the addition of 18 karat gold inlays which include a portrait of John M Browning, the words 'Browning Gold Classic,' the issue number and each of the various wildlife that appear in the engraved tableaux. These engravings and inlays are set against an exquisite background of grayed steel.

The Auto-5 was technically the first of the Classic and Gold Classic Editions. Its hand-selected, beautifully grained walnut stock and forearm feature a rounded semi-pistol grip that is similar to the traditional style found on early Auto-5s. The right side of the receiver on both Classic and Gold Classic Auto-5 models feature a pair of mallard drakes in flight, with the left displaying a labrador dog retrieving a downed duck.

The Classic 9mm Hi-Power Pistol was introduced in 1985. This ornate commemorative pistol features—on the top of its grayed, solid steel slide—an engraving of a bald eagle protecting her young from a lynx. On the pistol's right and left side are engraved profiles of an eagle's head, and the walnut grips have hand cut checkering and detailed, carved scrollwork. The pistol is complete with an attractive, velvet-lined display case.

The Classic and Gold Classic Over and Under Shotguns have hand-selected, highly figured, dense-grained walnut stocks featuring a traditional straight grip, English styling and Schnabel forearm with intricate hand-checkering. The grayed steel receivers on both editions have delicate scroll engravings and game scenes.

Above: The entire receiver, trigger guard and top tang of this Grade VI Citori feature deep relief engraving. Note that Citori's unique gold plating and engraving process captures an uncannily lifelike image of mallard ducks in flight. *Below:* The Gold Classic Over & Under with its highly figured receiver was made to commemorate the Superposed—John M Browning's last gun design.

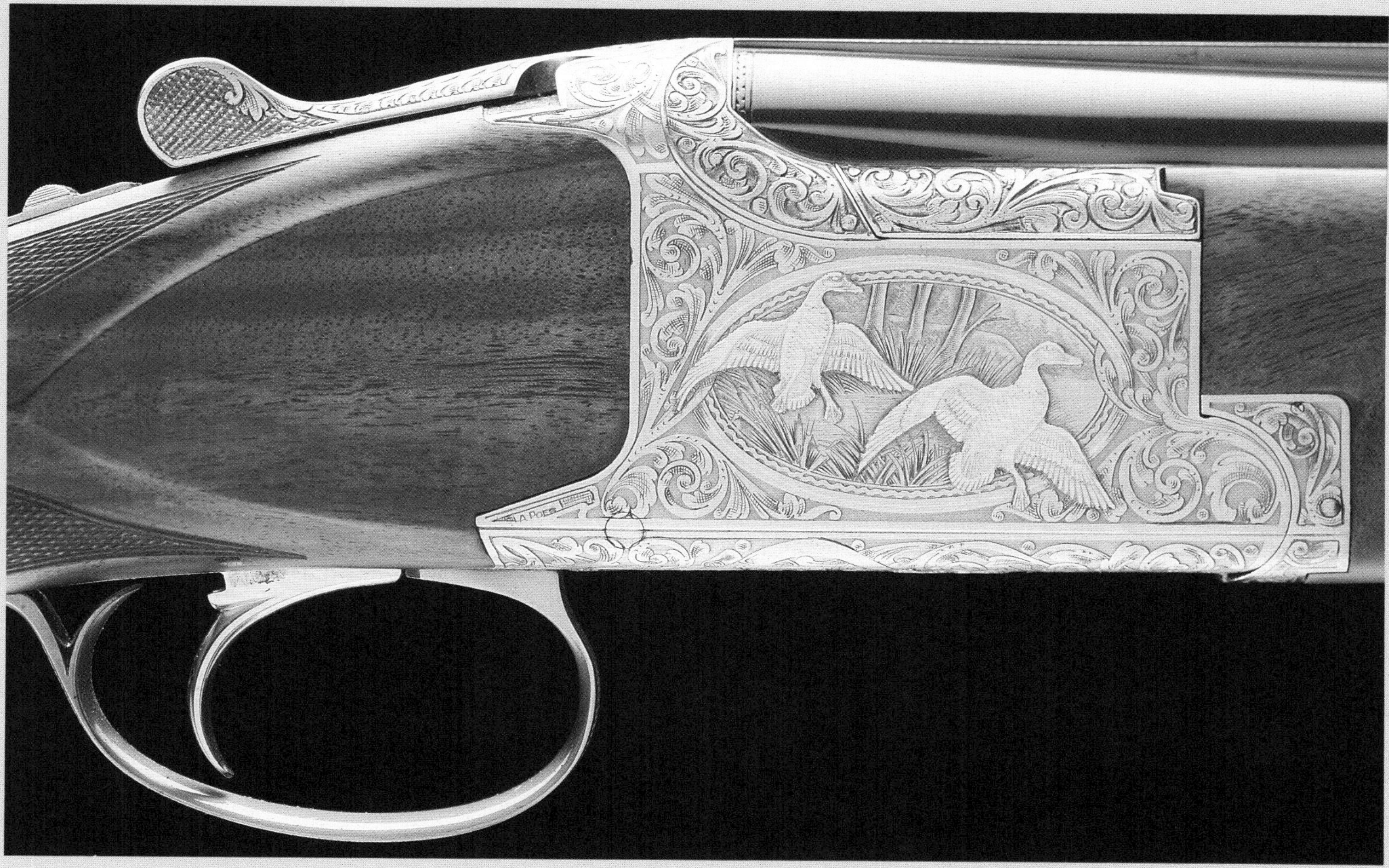

The detailed engraving and gold inlay on the Black Duck Limited Edition Superposed *(above)* and the BAR Big Game Series Limited Edition *(below)* are fine examples of the high quality of firearms embellishment available from Browning's Custom Gun Shop in Belgium.

Above: The headquarters of Browning Arms Company in Morgan, Utah. The machine shop *(below left, below right, opposite)* produces some of the world's finest firearms. Here, the highly skilled workers carry on the tradition of gunmaking that began in the brilliant mind of the most prolific firearms inventor ever known, John Moses Browning. *Overleaf:* These Superposed Shotguns are a testimonial to the Browning tradition.

SERIES I
2HP

White tail Deer

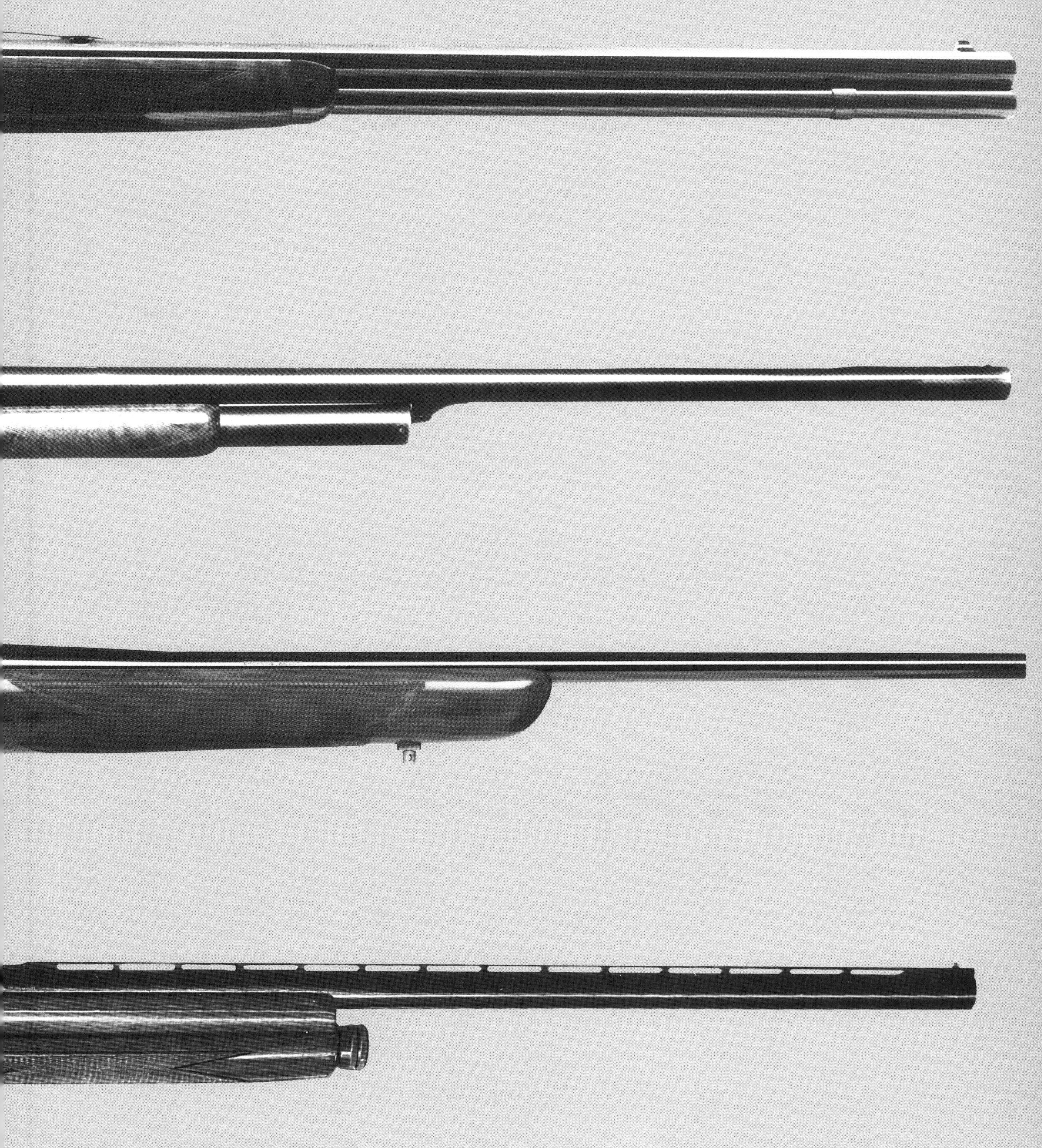

These pages, from top to bottom: A Winchester Model 1886 lever action, the first Browning design manufactured by Winchester; John Browning's personal trap gun, a Model 1897 pump with leather butt stock cover; a Browning Big Game Series Limited Edition automatic hunting rifle, with custom engraving; and a Browning automatic shotgun in 16 gauge with a 26-inch ventilated rib barrel, made in Belgium by Fabrique Nationale.

America's Premier Gunmakers

COLT

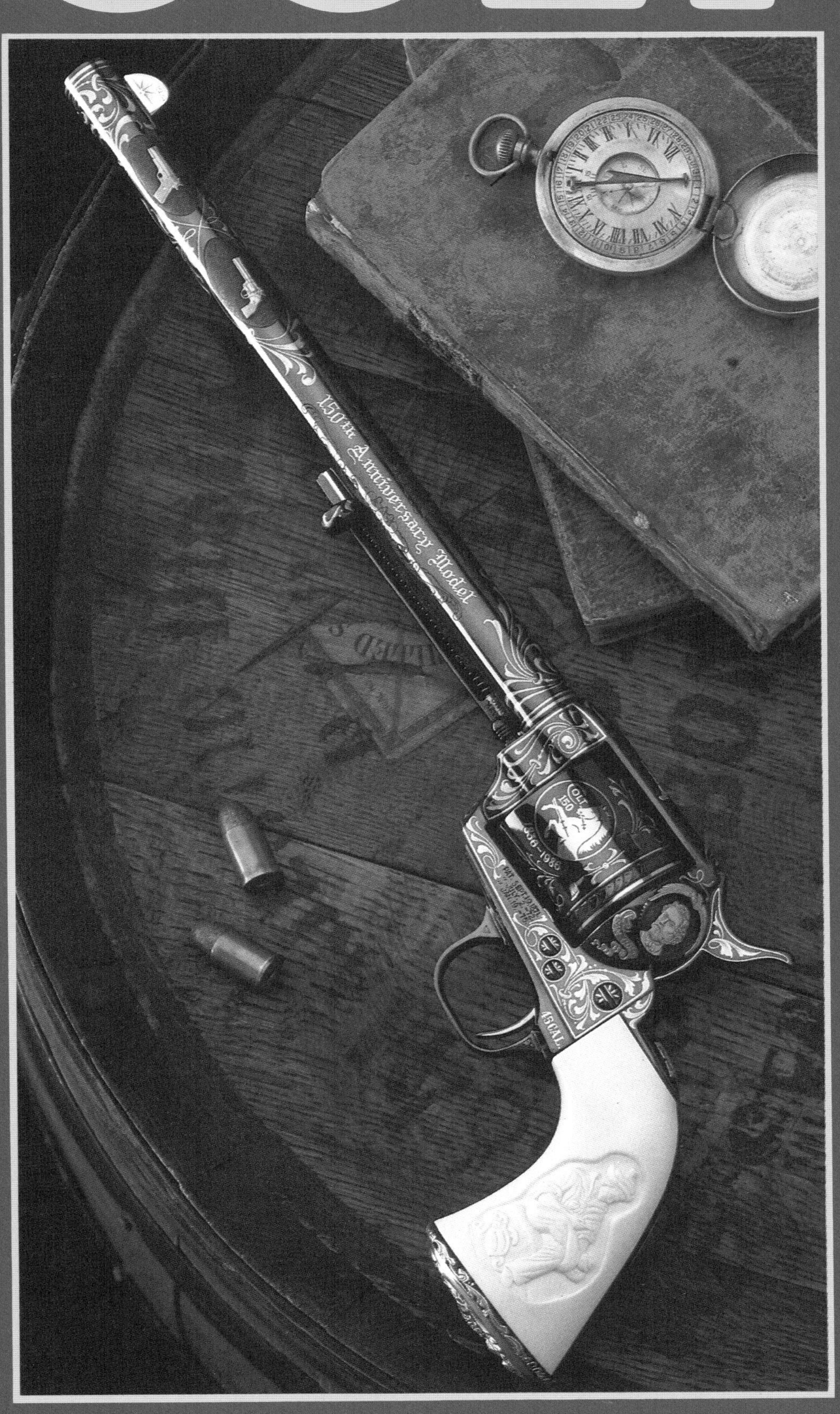

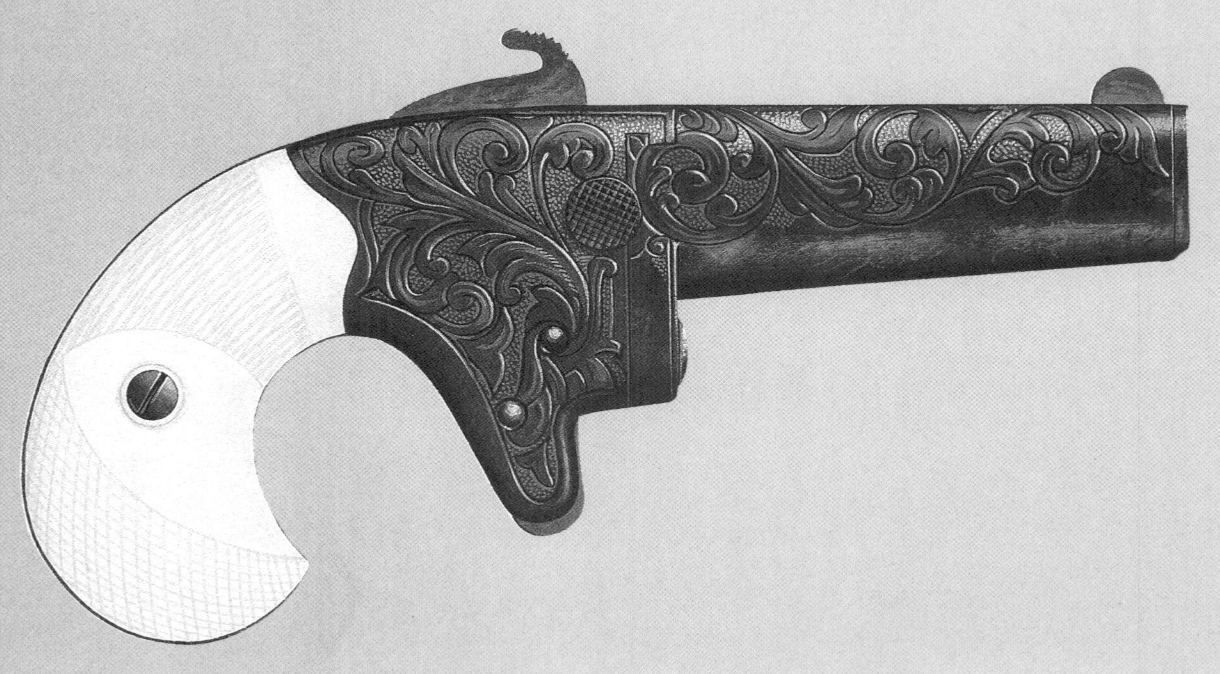

Previous pages: The Colt 150th Anniversary Gun, a Single Action Army Revolver with a Buntline-length barrel in .45 caliber, featuring luxuriant engraving and inlay work. Completed in time for the Anniversary in 1986, the firearm went on exhibition for the year, and was then auctioned for a whopping $150,000! *These pages, from top to bottom:* Presentation-grade Colts: A hammerless automatic pistol, circa 1940; an Old Model Navy percussion cap revolver of the pre-Civil War era; and a Number One Deringer, circa 1870.

The Arms of

Samuel Colt was born in Hartford, Connecticut on 19 July 1814, the son of Christopher and Sarah Caldwell Colt. Samuel was naturally inquisitive. Apparently, between the ages of seven and 16, he owned several pistols and took them apart to discover the details of their mechanism. Later in life, he attended the Academy of Amherst, but his education there was cut suddenly off—due to his experimentations with torpedo designs, which quickly got him into trouble with the authorities. Samuel's father, Christopher, ran a dye shop. Samuel helped out in the shop and this experience, no doubt, gave him a grounding in chemistry and metallurgy.

On 2 August 1830, Samuel, then a boy of 16, sailed on the ship *Corlo*, bound from Boston to Calcutta, India. It was while on this voyage that Colt, watching the ship's wheel and noting both its rotation and its alignments, conceived the use of the revolving cylinder in a firearm. His concepts were then carved into a wooden model of a pistol resembling the 'pepperbox' type of revolver. On his return, Samuel Colt introduced his idea to Mr Anson Chese, who by trade was a gunsmith. From drawings and the wooden model whittled out on the *Corlo*, an all metal model pistol was produced in 1832.

This first pistol model actually blew up in Colt's hand when he tried to fire it. A new model followed, much improved over the first. That second model contained basically three elements that were to make Colt famous. The three elements were: the rotation of a mini-chambered breech in a single-barreled firearm by the action of cocking the hammer; the locking of the cylinder into place in front of the barrel; and the placing of partitions between the bores of the breech, this to insure that when the pistol fired that only one chamber at a time went off.

Colt had a great idea, but he had no money. At one time his father had been well off, but the family dye business had lost money when Colt was very young—his father could be of no help to him. So in 1832, Colt embarked on a lecture tour of the United States and Canada in which he gave lectures on and demonstrations of nitrous oxide or 'laughing gas.' He knew how to draw an audience, and how to keep their attention, if not their complete sanity. He changed the spelling of his name to Coult and inserted the title Doctor in front of it. This, in combination with the novel nature of nitrous oxide, brought him immediate and considerable success.

These antics with laughing gas were, however, only a part of a larger scheme. Colt never forgot that his prime motivation was money to produce his pistols. Various models were produced in 1832, 1833 and 1834, and finally in 1835, Colt quit the lecture circuit and went to Europe where he took out patents in both England and France for his pistols. He returned to America, and US patents were finally granted him on 25 February 1936.

Based on these patents and the unique designs of these firearms, a new company was formed. The 'Patent Arms Manufacturing Company of Paterson, New Jersey, Colt's Patent' was formed in 1836; $150,000 in stock was sold in order to finance the company, and Colt himself received in payment for his services between one and two dollars for each pistol that was manufactured. This company is referred to in firearms history as the Paterson factory. It commenced its operations with high hopes in 1836, went into bankruptcy in 1841 and closed permanently in 1842. But it was a beginning.

From the Paterson factory came the first promotion model revolver. It was a .40 caliber five shot pistol, with a barrel length of 3.25 inches. This was the first Colt revolver and it was produced in 1835. It is interesting to note that this small gun had a forestock made of wood—to make the gun resemble as closely as possible the standard flintlock guns of its time.

Some interesting methods of determining the number of firearms produced in a factory where no exact records exist are employed by firearms collectors and enthusiasts. A particular model of firearm with a known production number is compared to the firearm without known production num-

Samuel Colt

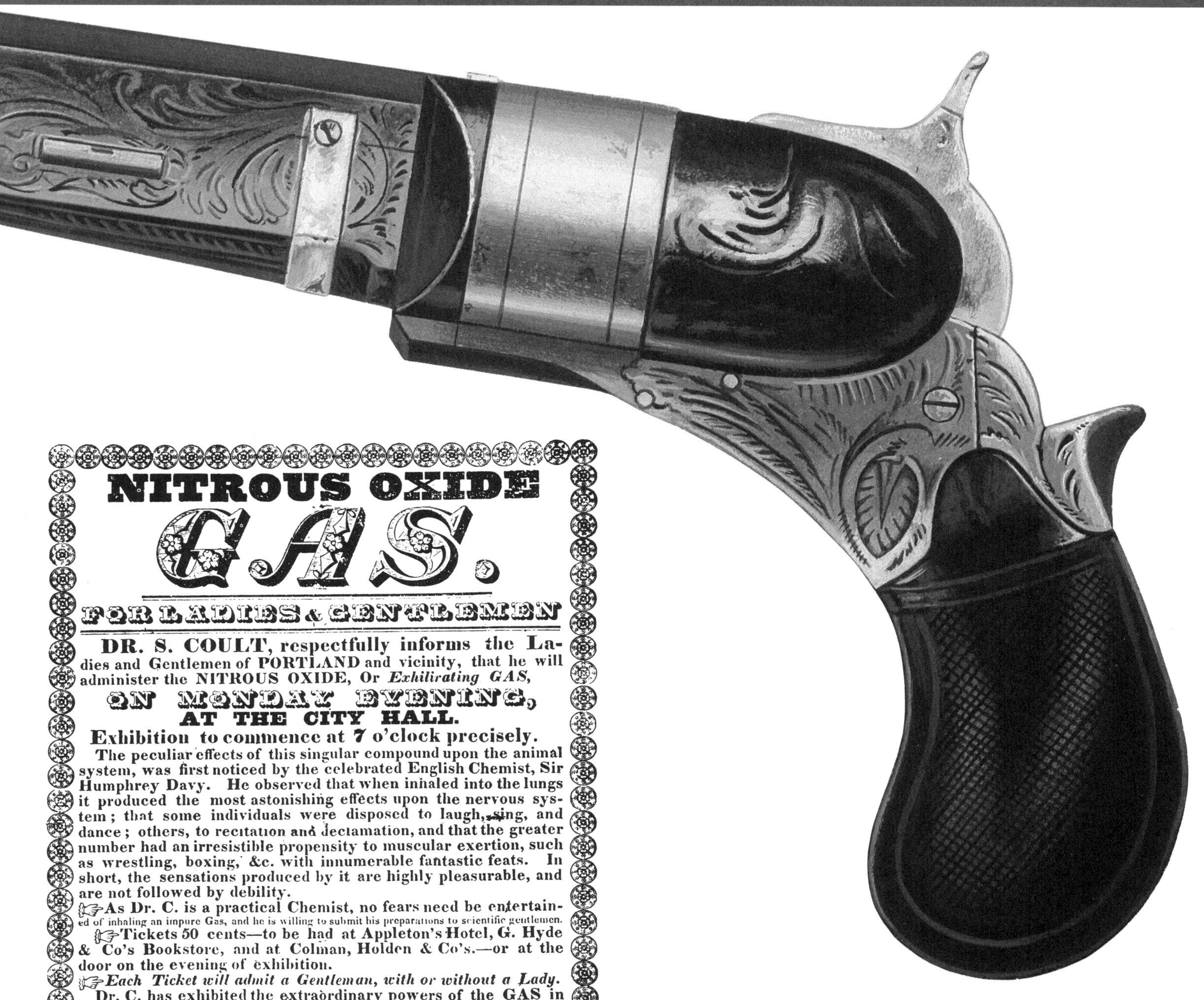

NITROUS OXIDE

GAS.

FOR LADIES & GENTLEMEN

DR. S. COULT, respectfully informs the Ladies and Gentlemen of PORTLAND and vicinity, that he will administer the NITROUS OXIDE, Or *Exhilirating GAS*,

ON MONDAY EVENING,

AT THE CITY HALL.

Exhibition to commence at 7 o'clock precisely.

The peculiar effects of this singular compound upon the animal system, was first noticed by the celebrated English Chemist, Sir Humphrey Davy. He observed that when inhaled into the lungs it produced the most astonishing effects upon the nervous system; that some individuals were disposed to laugh, sing, and dance; others, to recitation and declamation, and that the greater number had an irresistible propensity to muscular exertion, such as wrestling, boxing, &c. with innumerable fantastic feats. In short, the sensations produced by it are highly pleasurable, and are not followed by debility.

☞As Dr. C. is a practical Chemist, no fears need be entertained of inhaling an impure Gas, and he is willing to submit his preparations to scientific gentlemen.

☞Tickets 50 cents—to be had at Appleton's Hotel, G. Hyde & Co's Bookstore, and at Colman, Holden & Co's.—or at the door on the evening of exhibition.

☞*Each Ticket will admit a Gentleman, with or without a Lady.*

Dr. C. has exhibited the extraordinary powers of the GAS in many of the Cities of the United States, to audiences composed of Ladies and Gentlemen of the first respectability—and many Ladies have inhaled the GAS at select Exhibitions. Those Ladies who may be anxious of witnessing the Exhibition, in this city, may be assured, that the City Hall embraces every accommodation for their comfort, and that not a shadow of impropriety attends the Exhibition, to shock the most modest.

He will attend, on reasonable terms, to any applications for private Exhibitions to select parties of Ladies and Gentlemen, if application be made to him at Appleton's, prior to the 16th inst.

☞He will likewise administer the GAS to any gentleman, wishing to inhale it in private, between the hours of 8 and 11, at 50 cents per dose. All persons inhaling the Gas between these hours, have the privilege of admitting two to witness the effects

DOORS OPEN AT HALF PAST SIX O'CLOCK.

PORTLAND, Oct. 13, 1832

Printed at the Argus Office...2 UNION ST.

At left: **Lacking money to manufacture his guns, Samuel Colt, posing as the mysterious 'Dr S Coult,' embarked on a series of nitrous oxide demonstrations to raise the necessary cash. This flyer advertises 'Dr Coult's' presentation. *Above:* This is one of the experimental models Colt had made between 1832–1835, before he took out patents and before the Paterson factory was built.**

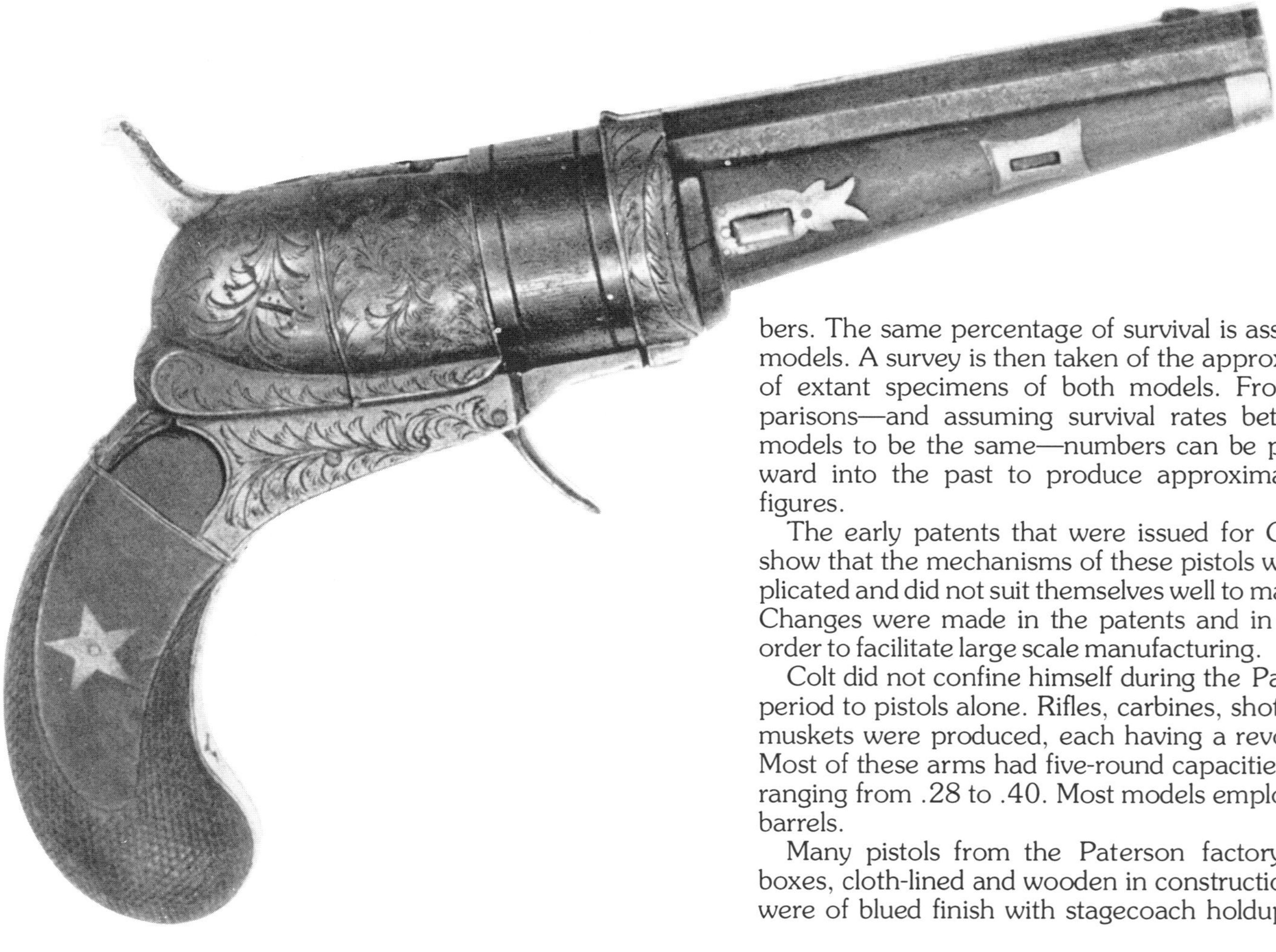

bers. The same percentage of survival is assumed for both models. A survey is then taken of the approximate number of extant specimens of both models. From these comparisons—and assuming survival rates between the two models to be the same—numbers can be projected backward into the past to produce approximate production figures.

The early patents that were issued for Colt's revolvers show that the mechanisms of these pistols were quite complicated and did not suit themselves well to mass production. Changes were made in the patents and in the designs in order to facilitate large scale manufacturing.

Colt did not confine himself during the Paterson factory period to pistols alone. Rifles, carbines, shotguns and even muskets were produced, each having a revolving cylinder. Most of these arms had five-round capacities, with calibers ranging from .28 to .40. Most models employed octagonal barrels.

Many pistols from the Paterson factory were sold in boxes, cloth-lined and wooden in construction. The barrels were of blued finish with stagecoach holdup scenes being

THE UNITED STATES OF AMERICA.

TO ALL TO WHOM THESE LETTERS PATENT SHALL COME:

Whereas SAMUEL COLT, a citizen of the UNITED STATES, hath alleged that he has invented a new and useful improvement in *Fire Arms*, which improvement he states has not been known or used before his application; hath made oath that he does verily believe that he is the true inventor or discoverer of the said improvement; hath paid into the treasury of the United States the sum of thirty dollars, delivered a receipt for the same, and presented a petition to the Secretary of State, signifying a desire of obtaining an exclusive property in the said improvement, and praying that a patent may be granted for that purpose. **These are therefore** to grant, according to law, to the said SAMUEL COLT, his heirs, administrators or assigns, for the term of fourteen years, from the twenty-fifth day of February, one thousand eight hundred and thirty-six, the full and exclusive right and liberty of making, constructing, using and vending to others to be used, the said improvement; a description whereof is given in the words of the said SAMUEL COLT himself, in the schedule hereto annexed, and is made a part of these presents.

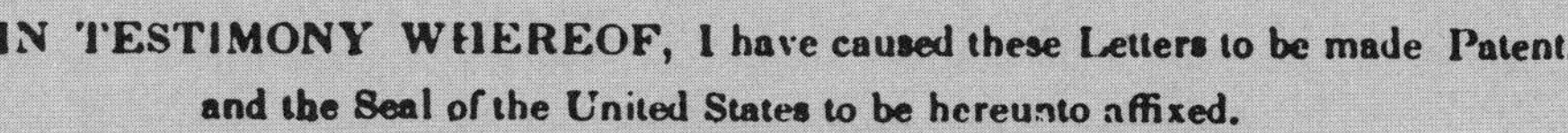

IN TESTIMONY WHEREOF, I have caused these Letters to be made Patent, and the Seal of the United States to be hereunto affixed.

GIVEN under my hand at the City of Washington, this twenty-fifth day of February, in the year of our Lord one thousand eight hundred and thirty-six, and of the independence of the United States of America the sixtieth.

ANDREW JACKSON.

BY THE PRESIDENT,

JOHN FORSYTH,

Secretary of State.

CITY OF WASHINGTON, To WIT:

I Do Hereby Certify, That the foregoing Letters Patent were delivered to me on the twenty-fifth day of February, in the year of our Lord one thousand eight hundred and thirty-six, to be examined; that I have examined the same, and find them conformable to law, and I do hereby return the same to the Secretary of State, within fifteen days from the date aforesaid, to wit on this twenty-sixth day of February, in the year aforesaid.

B. F. BUTLER,

Attorney General of the United States.

Above opposite: The Paterson factory, which opened in 1836 and closed in 1842. *Opposite:* This Promotion Model Revolver, made in 1835, was supposed to have been used in selling stock for Colt's new company. *Above:* Preamble to Patent 138, issued on 25 February 1836.

Overleaf: Clockwise from upper left: A patent drawing for Colt's Revolving Gun, patented 25 February 1836; an exploded view of the same; Colt's Revolving Gun designs for (above) pistol and (below) rifle versions; and a view of Colt's cylinder mechanism.

S Colt—Revolving Gun Patent

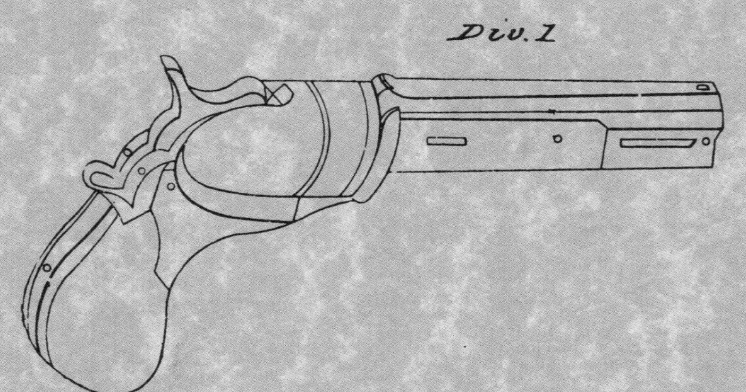

4 Sheets—Sheet 1

S. COLT.

Revolving Gun.

Patented Feb. 25, 1836.

4 Sheets—Sheet 2.

S. COLT.

Revolving Gun.

Patented Feb. 25, 1836.

No138, 25Feb1836

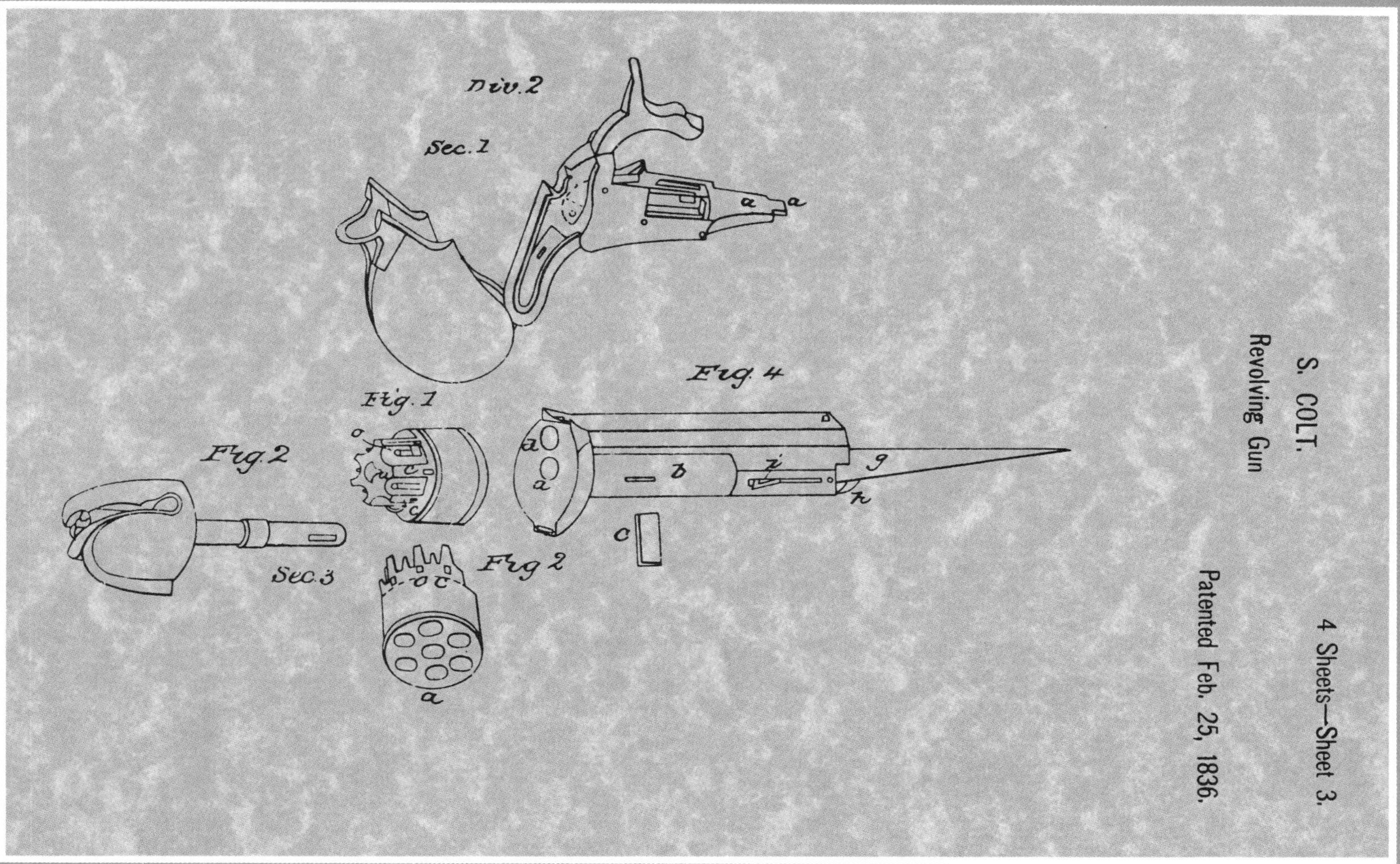

S. COLT.

Revolving Gun

4 Sheets—Sheet 3.

Patented Feb. 25, 1836.

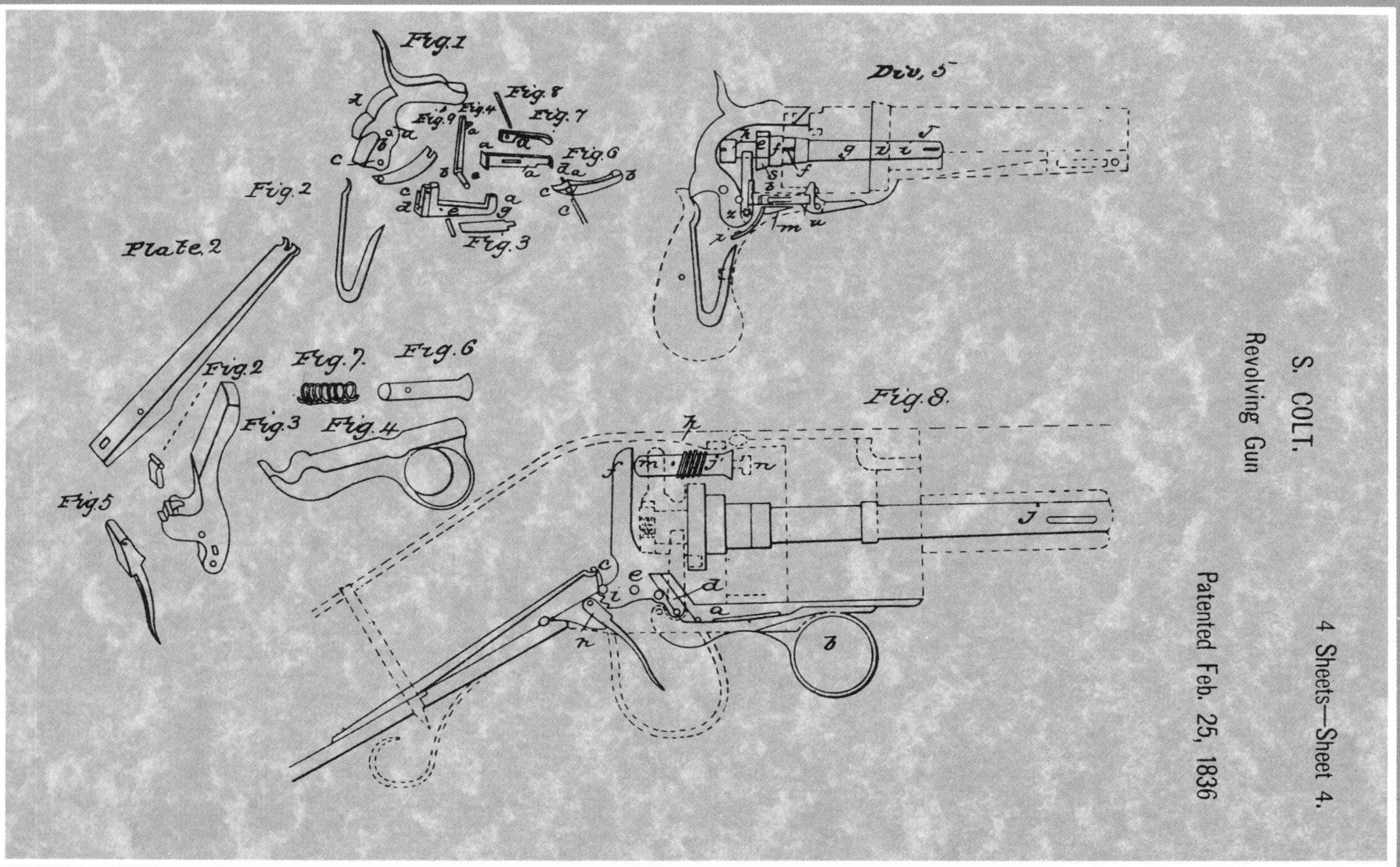

S. COLT.

Revolving Gun

4 Sheets—Sheet 4.

Patented Feb. 25, 1836

Above: **An engraving of the Second Seminole War of 1835,in which Chief Micanopy *(at left)* helped lead the Indians. *At right:* A Paterson Colt cased with accessories. *Below right:* A Paterson Colt and the 1837 Military Pistol. *Bottom right:* The 1837 Paterson Revolving Carbine.**

imprinted in the cylinders. The gun sights were incorporated into the hammer such that when the pistol was cocked and ready for firing, the notch appeared in conjunction with the barrel sight in order to provide aiming capability. A powder flask and magazine-capping device for holding percussion caps were usually included with the boxed pistol, along with a bullet mold, a cleaning rod, and various ingeniously designed tools for disassembling the pistol. Sometimes an extra cylinder was included, thus providing the owner with a total of 10 shots without reloading.

The greatest markets that Colt had for the output of his Paterson Factory were both the South and the Republic of Texas, which at this time was engaged in its war of independence with Mexico. So many of Colt's pistols from the Paterson factory were sold to the Texans that Colt later referred to the regular Paterson model as the 'Texas Arm.'

Even at this early stage, Samuel Colt knew the value of beauty in workmanship and the need for showmanship in the sale of firearms. The Paterson factory was capable of producing special arms, made to order—with differing numbers of shots in the cylinders being available, as well as different kinds of ornamentation. The extravagance of this ornamentation was limited only by the customer's ability to pay for it. It included ornate engravings, inlays and ivory or pearl stocks and handles.

Of course the biggest potential market for firearms was the United States government, and Colt tried in 1837 to get his arms adopted by the government. But government bureaucracy was no less then than what it is today, and Colt was turned down. The Ordnance Board felt that Colt's firearms were too complicated and that therefore they could break down too easily. This, combined with the idea that the flintlock single shot muskets and pistols which were then employed by the army were good enough, led the board to conclude that the status quo was what the government wanted.

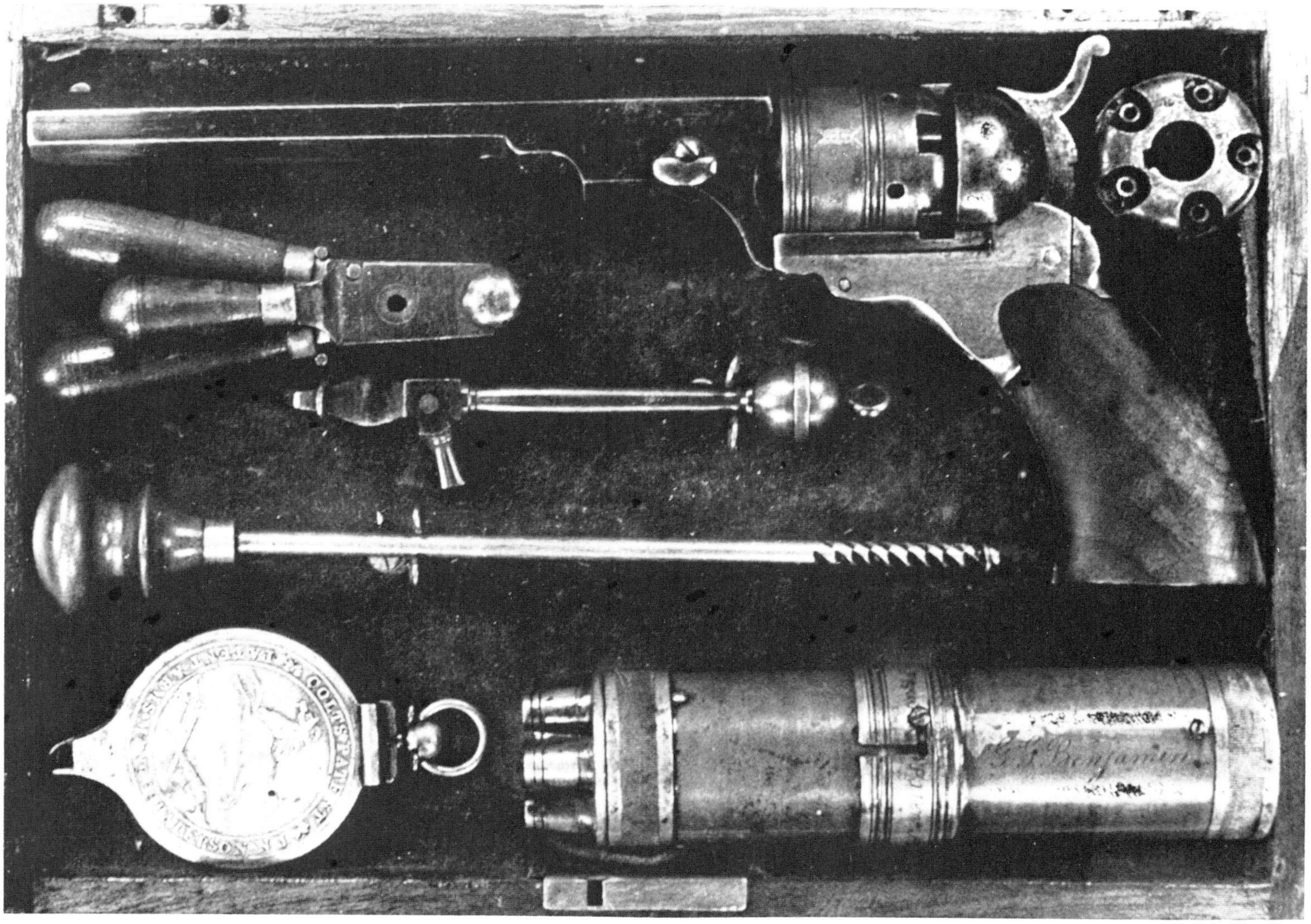

But the bureaucrats in Washington were not the men who would actually be using his weapons. So Colt undertook to place his pistols in the hands of soldiers—who he felt would see at once the advantages of being able to deliver several shots without reloading.

Taking a number of his pistols with him, he journeyed to the seat of the Seminole War in Florida, which was the only war going at the time. Here he sold his arms directly to the officers and the troops who were engaged on a day-to-day basis in warfare with the Indians. Naturally, the soldiers in the field found these weapons to be of tremendous advantage over the arms they were accustomed to using. The clamor went up for the government to procure more of Colt's arms. One army captain flatly testified that Colt's firearms were eight times more efficient as arms then in use. Another officer testified that 'if our enemies knew that we were in possession of such arms, they would be less apt to commence hostilities with us.' It was generally felt by those who had used Colt's pistols that one man armed with one Colt pistol was fully equal to five or six men armed with common muskets.

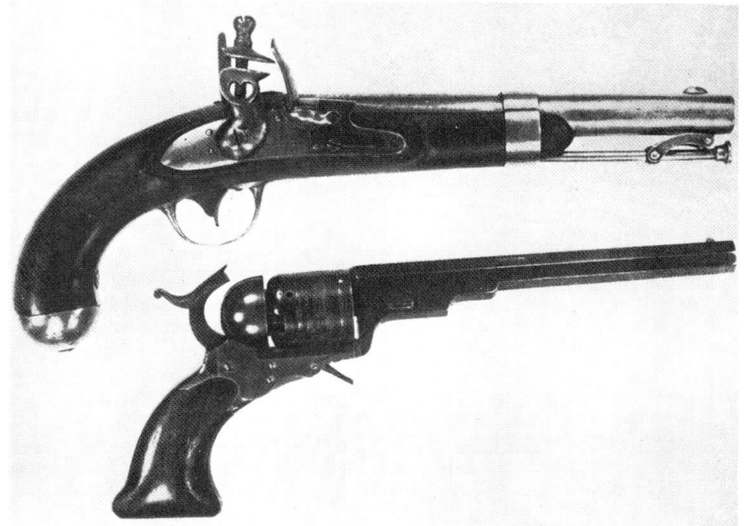

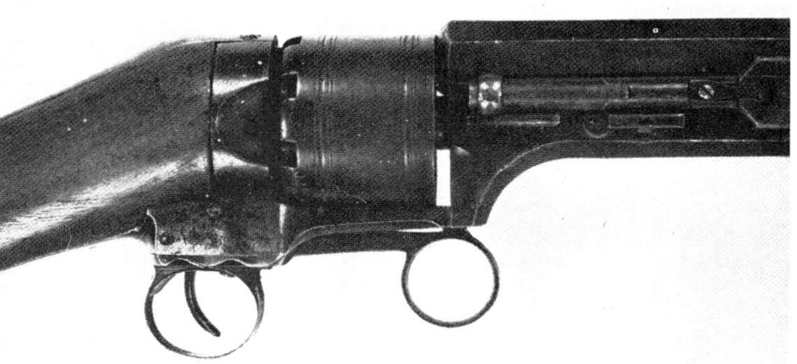

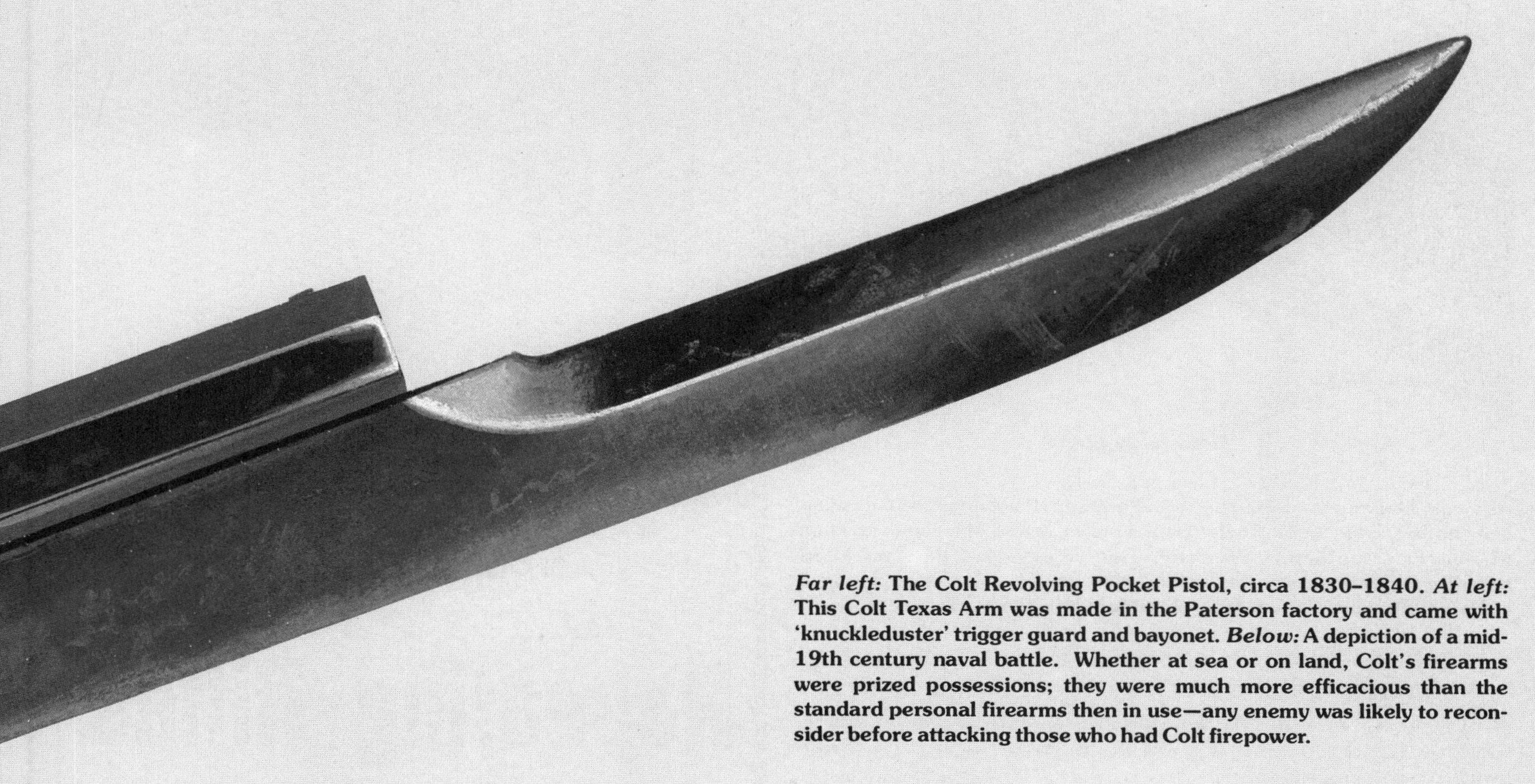

Far left: The Colt Revolving Pocket Pistol, circa 1830–1840. *At left:* This Colt Texas Arm was made in the Paterson factory and came with 'knuckleduster' trigger guard and bayonet. *Below:* A depiction of a mid-19th century naval battle. Whether at sea or on land, Colt's firearms were prized possessions; they were much more efficacious than the standard personal firearms then in use—any enemy was likely to reconsider before attacking those who had Colt firepower.

***Above:* A hammer model of the 1839 Paterson Revolving Rifle (see overleaf caption, page nine). *At right:* An announcement of a demonstration of Colt Paterson arms. *Opposite:* This engraving depicts an 1858 parade, celebrating the laying of the Atlantic Cable, which was presaged by Sam Colt's submarine telegraph cable in New York harbor.**

Unfortunately, while Colt was in Florida selling pistols to men whose lives depended on them, back home his subordinates at the Patent Arms Company were quarreling about management. There are even accounts of some of these employees dueling to the death over their disagreements. Technically, Colt was an employee of the factory, yet it was his ideas and his genius that kept things moving: when he was not personally present, things simply fell apart.

The Paterson Factory came to an end mostly because the guns were sufficiently complicated by design that they had to be made by hand, and that multi-firing arms were not needed by the average man. Time and distance had defeated this first of Colt's factories. It was simply not possible to get enough Colt weapons into the hands of those who needed them and would appreciate them to make the factory profitable. As as result, the 'Patent Arms Manufacturing Company of Paterson, New Jersey, Colt's Patent' closed permanently in 1842.

With the Paterson Factory in bankruptcy, Colt reverted back to (what were for him) his childhood toys—namely, 'torpedoes.' These torpedoes were actually what we would refer to today as mines. Submerged cable, another of his inventions, was used to electrically explode the mine from miles away. In 1842, Congress granted $15,000 for the project, ostensibly to protect US harbors in times of war. Two years later, Congress made a special adjournment to see Colt destroy a ship of over 500 tons, which at that time was under sail and travelling at five knots.

Things submerged intrigued Colt. In the mid-1840s he laid the first underwater telegraph cable in New York harbor.

The year 1845 was pivotal for Colt. Texas had won its independence from Mexico by this time, and had been accepted as a state into the Union. But trouble with Mexico persisted over certain territorial claims in and around the Rio Grande River. General (later President) Zachary Taylor, who had taken part in the Seminole War in Florida, and who may well have been acquainted with Colt's pistols, was sent to southeastern Texas.

BY CONSENT OF THE MAYOR,

AN EXHIBITION OF

COLT'S PATENT

Repeating Rifles

Will be made at the Battery.

On Monday afternoon, 19th inst.

At half past 4 o'clock.

The public are respectfully invited to attend. The instrument may also be examined at the store of Dick & Holmes, Vendue Range, who have a few of them for sale, price $150 each.

SAMUEL COLT, Patentee.

These Rifles are eight times more effective, and very little more expensive than the ordinary Rifle of equal finish.

DICK & HOLMES, Agents.

February 17th, 1838.

E. C. Councell's print, No. 1 Queen-street.

As the prospect for hostilities increased, so did the clamor for Colt's repeaters. All the available Colts were purchased by the government and sent to Texas. Now the guns were available to those men who needed them the most. One of those men was Samuel H Walker. Like Taylor, Walker had fought in the Florida wars and had come into contact with Colt's pistols. Walker was a Texas Ranger who, with 14 other men, had at one time engaged 80 Comanche warriors and lived to tell the tale. Their Colt 'five shooters' had allowed them to kill 33 of the marauding Indians.

The supply of available Colts was meager to begin with, and battlefield losses lessened the stockpiles even further. So Walker took leave of the Army in 1846, at Zachary Taylor's order, and came North to both drum up volunteers for the Mexican campaign—and more importantly, to procure more Colt weapons.

Walker got in touch with Colt. The main question was what could be done about getting back into production. Colt possessed his patents only. He had neither money nor a factory. But the world had finally realized the value of his repeaters, and that realization generated a demand that, to this day, survives.

Even though Colt's patents had reverted to him upon the demise of the Paterson Factory, the models he used to produce the guns were lost. But determination was a trait not lacking in Samuel Colt.

He redesigned one of his earlier pistols from memory, even making certain improvements as he went along. These

improvements mainly incorporated fewer moving parts, thus simplifying the process of manufacture and meeting head-on the government's original objections to the pistols as being too unreliable in a battlefield setting.

Walker wanted 1000 pistols as soon as possible. Colt contacted Eli Whitney, son of the inventor of the cotton gin. Whitney was at that time manufacturing arms for the US government in Whitneyville, Connecticut, and agreed to produce the guns, which were to be six, rather than five shot, repeaters and have nine inch barrels. The precision with which Colt's guns had to be made necessitated that Whitney purchase or fabricate special machinery to produce the parts. The total price per pistol was to be $28.00 (this included the accessories).

After the customary barrage of governmental red tape and delays, Colt's pistols began arriving in Mexico. Colt later claimed that because of the contract arrangements with Whitney, he actually made no money on these pistols. When the contract with Whitney expired, however, Colt did wind up owning all of that specialized machinery that the Whitneyville plant used to produce the weapons. And this collection of specialized lathes, dyes, moldings and the like would later provide Colt with the foundation for his Hartford, Connecticut plant.

Colt sent a matched pair of pistols to Walker as a personal present. But shortly afterwards, Walker was killed in action in October 1847. After Walker's death, one of these pistols was sent back to Colt, who regarded it as one of his most

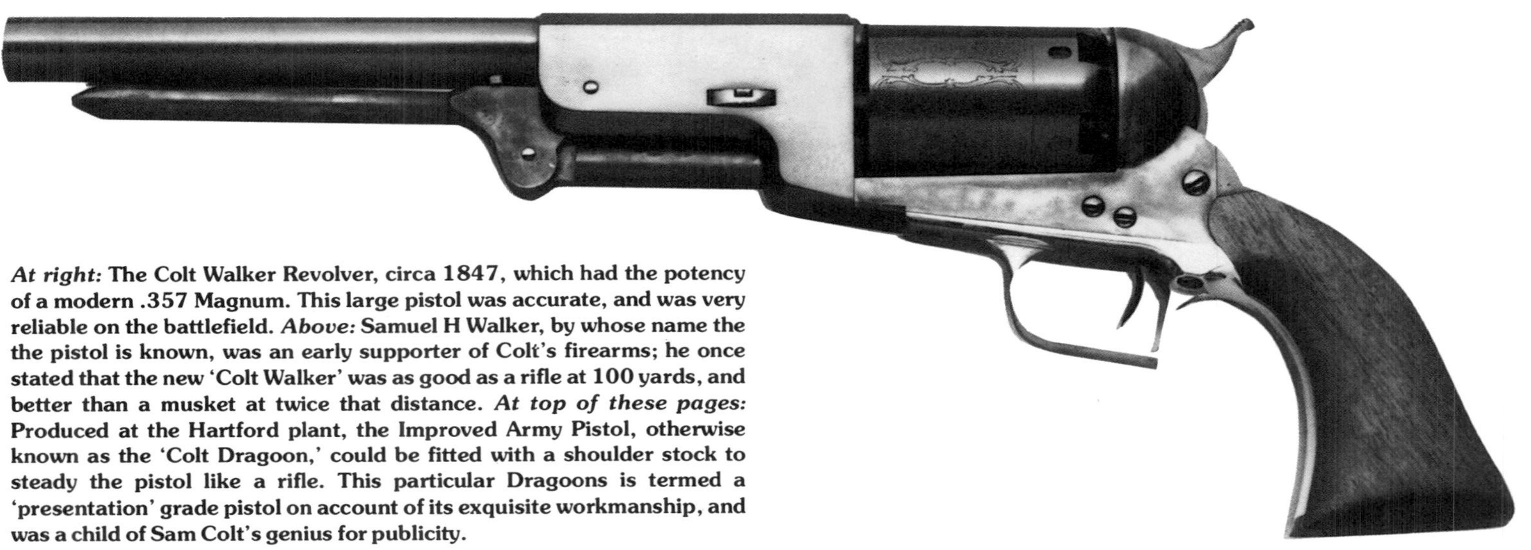

At right: **The Colt Walker Revolver, circa 1847, which had the potency of a modern .357 Magnum. This large pistol was accurate, and was very reliable on the battlefield.** ***Above:*** **Samuel H Walker, by whose name the the pistol is known, was an early supporter of Colt's firearms; he once stated that the new 'Colt Walker' was as good as a rifle at 100 yards, and better than a musket at twice that distance.** ***At top of these pages:*** **Produced at the Hartford plant, the Improved Army Pistol, otherwise known as the 'Colt Dragoon,' could be fitted with a shoulder stock to steady the pistol like a rifle. This particular Dragoons is termed a 'presentation' grade pistol on account of its exquisite workmanship, and was a child of Sam Colt's genius for publicity.**

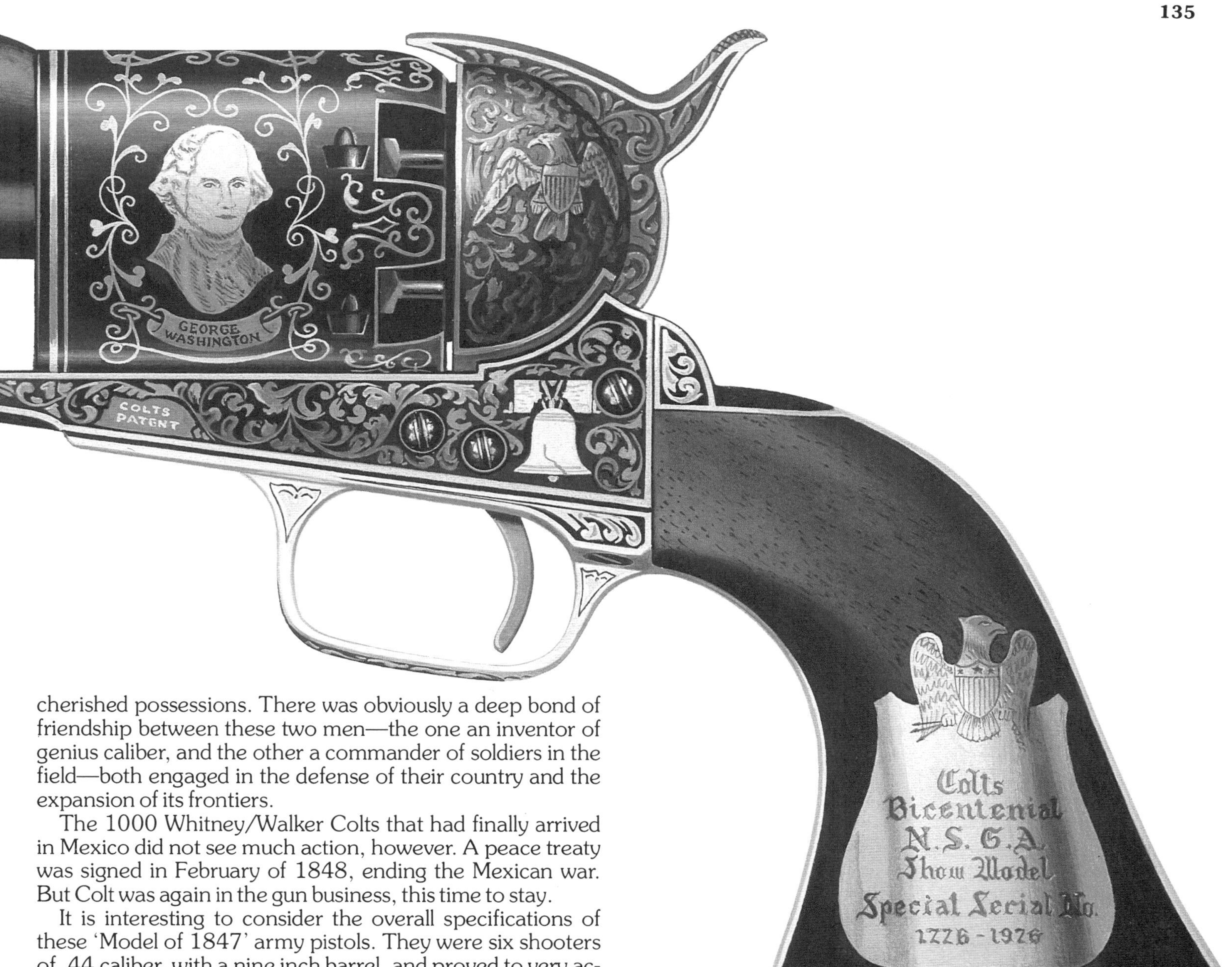

cherished possessions. There was obviously a deep bond of friendship between these two men—the one an inventor of genius caliber, and the other a commander of soldiers in the field—both engaged in the defense of their country and the expansion of its frontiers.

The 1000 Whitney/Walker Colts that had finally arrived in Mexico did not see much action, however. A peace treaty was signed in February of 1848, ending the Mexican war. But Colt was again in the gun business, this time to stay.

It is interesting to consider the overall specifications of these 'Model of 1847' army pistols. They were six shooters of .44 caliber, with a nine inch barrel, and proved to very accurate indeed. Walker stated them to be as good as a rifle at 100 yards, and better than a musket at twice that distance. They weighed four pounds, nine ounces, and displayed the now famous squareback triggerguards made of brass. In firepower, they were about equal to today's .357 Magnums. Quite an achievement for the 1840s! In addition, honoring the man who inspired, in a sense, the design of these pistols, this model is commonly known as the 'Colt Walker.'

Samuel Colt was by nature a showman. He turned this flair for catching the public mind to his advantage by starting the practice of making 'presentation' grade, usually boxed, sets of pistols to give as gifts to powerful and influential people. These specimens were often masterpieces of the gunmaker's art. They were virtually flawless in appearance. Deep bluing was set off by heavy inlays of polished gold flowing over the barrel and other parts in delicate traceries. The grips were often richly carved with ivory insets. Who would not have been (or would not be today) stunned by such a noble gift?

It was at his factory on Pearl Street in Hartford that the large scale production of Colt pistols began. Between the years 1845 and 1852, an average of 1000 firearms per year were produced by the Hartford Factory, including carbines as well as repeating pistols. Times were changing, and the need for firearms was growing. The Gold Rush to California was under way. Pioneers were pushing westward. A general feeling of lawlessness had engulfed the nation, and the need for personal protection had grown. Colt was very aware of these circumstances, and quickly added pocket pistols and belt models to his line of firearms.

One of the most interesting pistols to be produced at the Hartford Factory was the Improved Army Pistol, which is called by collectors the 'Colt Dragoon.' These Dragoons were six shooters of .44 caliber, and were made in both 7.5 and eight inch barrel lengths. The Colt Dragoon was the mainstay of the pistol line until it was superseded by the New Model Army Pistol in 1860.

It is interesting to note that the Dragoons, when sold to both the army and civilians, could be equipped with shoulder stocks that could, in effect, turn the pistol into a rifle. This was feasible because of the overwhelming advantage of accuracy that the Colt weapons possessed in relationship to other weapons of the day. From 1847 until 1860, the total production of Colt Dragoons was about 22,000, and apparently half of these went to civilians.

As the popularity of his guns increased, so did the probability of patent infringements upon Colt's designs. Colt took to imprinting upon each of his firearms 'Colt's Patent,'

Above: The Whitneyville Armory, where the Whitneyville Colts were made in 1847. _At right:_ Part of the original Hartford, Connecticut plant. From this small beginning, the plant expanded on a grand scale _(below right)_: at this stage, the factory was shaped like the letter 'H,' and its entrance was capped by a blue dome covered with gold stars.

and in his advertising the words 'Beware of counterfeits and patent infringements' appeared regularly.

Even though the original Dragoons were of the cap and ball variety, they proved to be extremely popular even after the invention of the center fire cartridge. And in the middle 1970s, 100 years later, Colt Arms bowed to this continuing demand by producing the 'Third Model Dragoon.'

In 1848, Colt so perfected the designs of his weapons, and particularly the Dragoons, that the parts of all of the arms of the same model could be interchanged with parts from other Colts. Again, this was due to the standardization of measurements and the perfecting of the precision of the machinery on which the arms were produced. The simplification of manufacture produced only five moving parts in the Dragoons, as opposed to 17 such parts in earlier models.

There are three basic classifications of Dragoon pistols which are used by collectors today. The Number One Dragoon is the first model that was made at Hartford, and incorporated a round cylinder, square back trigger guard and no roller on the hammer.

The Number Two Dragoon was an improved model that was made after 1849. It featured a round back trigger guard, rectangular cylinder notches, a roller on the hammer and pins between the nipples. The Number Three Dragoon is virtually the same as the Number Two, except that it is fitted with a shoulder stock.

Colt's master patent was granted him by the United States government in 1836 and was due to expire by 1849. But the legal reasoning behind the granting of patents was that a patent was to be issued so that the inventor could have a sufficient amount of time in which to tool up and produce his invention free of competition and, thereby, realize a profit on his idea. Colt, however, was able to prove that he had *not* received a reasonable profit in the 14 years since the patent was issued, and an extension was granted him until 1857.

By the early 1850s, Samuel Colt was a prosperous and influential figure. He was given a commission as a lieutenant colonel in the Connecticut State Militia. Thereafter he referred to himself, rightfully, as Colonel Colt. It is interesting to note, however, that in 1861 the Colonel's official military commission was withdrawn. This was due to the fact that he was far more valuable to his country as an arms inventor and producer than he was as a field commander.

In June of 1856, Samuel Colt married Elizabeth Hart Jarvis. Her brother was vice-president of the Colt Armory at that time. The couple honeymooned in Europe for six months and even attended the coronation of Tsar Alexander II in St Petersburg, Russia. In 1858, Colt sent three sets of firearms engraved and inscribed to the new Tsar. These guns are, by far, the most intricate of the presentation models and presently reside at the Hermitage Museum in Leningrad in the Soviet Union.

The Hartford Plant grew on a grand scale. The main factory building itself was of brick construction and shaped like the letter 'H.' It was three and one half stories high and each parallel section of the 'H' was 500 feet long. The building itself was capped by a large blue dome containing gold stars similar to a Russian Orthodox cathedral.

The Hartford Factory developed into a school of great influence for inventors, technicians and mechanics of the day. Colt's magnetic personality drew many of the best minds in the United States to him. Rollin White at one time worked for Colt and himself patented certain devices which later became the basis for the Smith and Wesson Firearms Company. Francis A Pratt and Amos Whitney were associated with Colt during this period and their partnership later formed the Pratt and Whitney Company, which today manufactures engines of almost every kind.

In 1850, two models of pistols were introduced by Colt. The Model 1849 Pocket Pistol and the Model 1851 Navy Pistol came to the marketplace. Since there is a series of belt and pocket pistols associated with this period of time, it is well to quote from Colt's *Armsmear* publication to differentiate the models involved. 'Pocket Revolvers' with six inch, five inch, four inch and three inch barrels and .31 bore, were introduced about 1848. They were first made without lever rammers and were loaded by removing the cylinder from its pin and using the pin for a rammer.

At right: A prime example of a First Model Hartford Dragoon, circa 1846, with the squarebacked triggerguard typical of the early Colt dragoons. _Below right:_ An Old Model Pocket Pistol of 1850. _Opposite:_ An early 1850s Colt advertisement, showing a Colt Dragoon—as assembled and as disassembled.

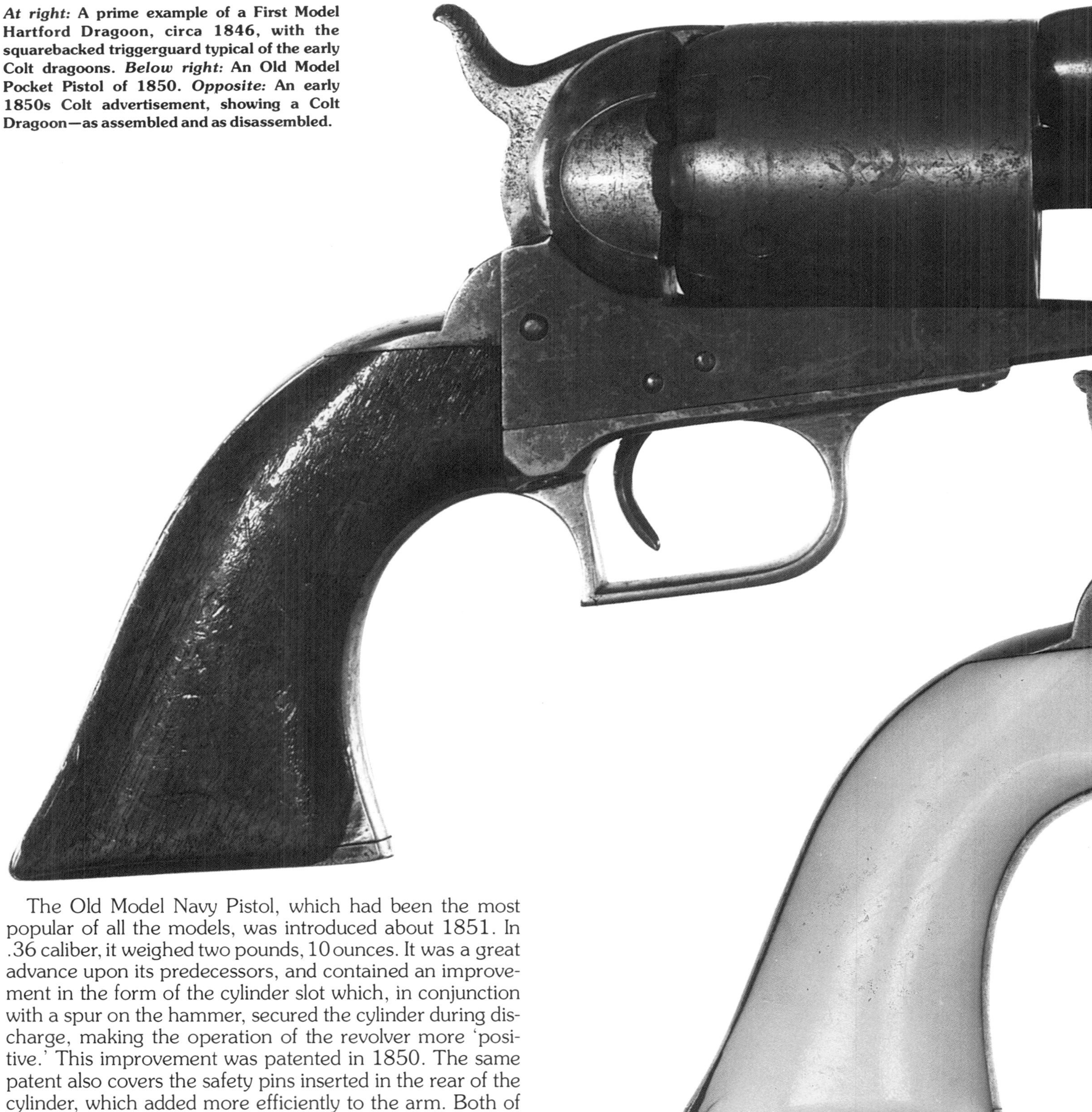

The Old Model Navy Pistol, which had been the most popular of all the models, was introduced about 1851. In .36 caliber, it weighed two pounds, 10 ounces. It was a great advance upon its predecessors, and contained an improvement in the form of the cylinder slot which, in conjunction with a spur on the hammer, secured the cylinder during discharge, making the operation of the revolver more 'positive.' This improvement was patented in 1850. The same patent also covers the safety pins inserted in the rear of the cylinder, which added more efficiently to the arm. Both of these improvements have been retained in nearly all the Colt revolvers made since.

The Old Model Pocket Pistol was improved in 1849 by the introduction of the improved features of the Navy Pistols and has not been materially altered since. It was .31 caliber, and its weight was from 24 to 27 ounces, dependent upon the length of its barrel.

The New Pocket and New Model Police, New Model Army and New Model Navy, were all introduced after 1860. They presented nothing new in principle, but by a better arrangement of parts—and in the Army Model, by less weight—suited the markets better, and were mostly made in .36 caliber, except for the New Model Army in .44 caliber.

The New Pocket Pistol weighed from 25 to 28 ounces, the New Model Police Pistol weighed from 24 1/2 to 26 ounces, the New Model Navy Pistol weighed two pounds 10 ounces, and the New Model Army Pistol weighed two pounds 11 ounces.

Also, during this period, the Sidehammer series of guns was introduced. The thing that made the Sidehammer series unique was that for the first time, a solid frame was employed. This means that the barrel was screwed into the frame, thus making the barrel and frame integral.

It is interesting to note that even on common production

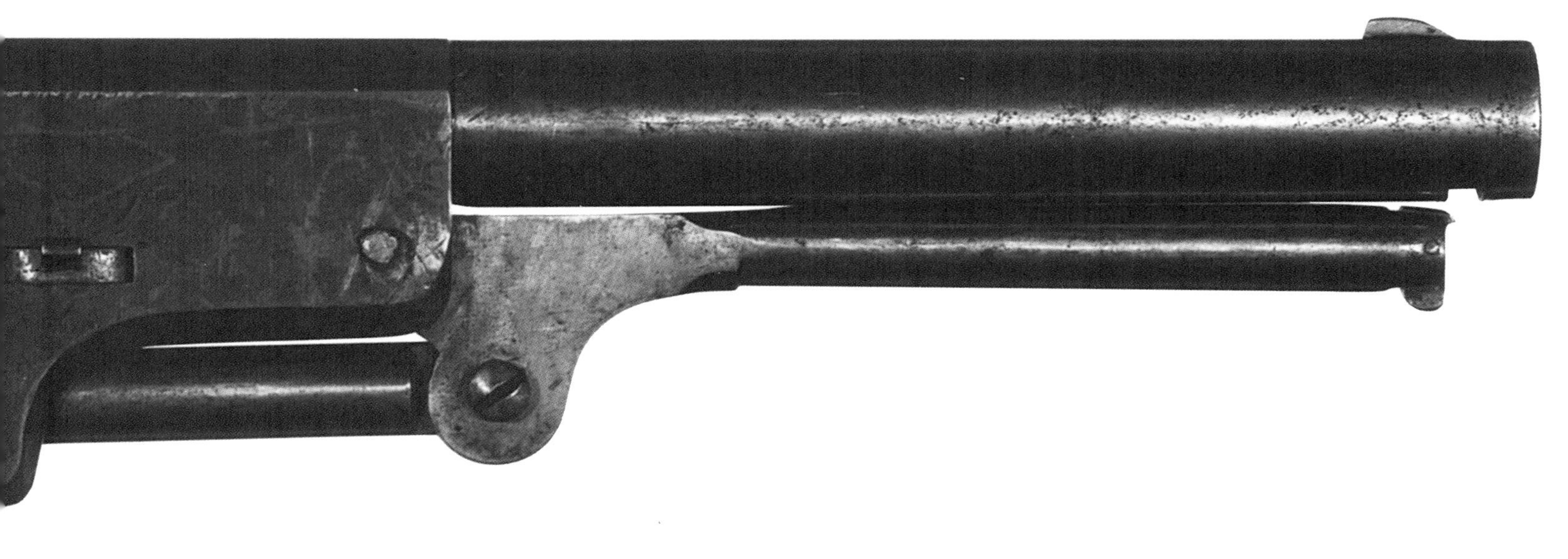

models, the scene that appeared on the cylinders was usually of a fight between pistol-armed men and Indians. Later, these cylinder scenes would change. On the cylinders of the Navy Colts, the scene was generally one of both steam and sailing ships battling one another. The overall motif for these naval battle scenes was taken from an episode in the Texas War of Independence in which Commodore Moore of the Texas Navy defeated a fleet of Mexican vessels which was greatly superior to his own fleet: this actual historical event was used to demonstrate the fact that a man armed with a Colt could defeat a force vastly outnumbering him.

The 1851 Navy Colt was very popular as a belt revolver, because it was lighter than the Dragoon. The Navy Pistol, which was actually used by the Army (and comparatively little by the US Navy), wound up being a favorite dueling weapon among various adversaries in the California Gold Rush period.

In 1849, Colt hired a Mr EK Root as his factory foreman and general superintendent. Root was a mechanical engineer and inventor in his own right. But his talents did not come cheaply. Colt exhibited a fair amount of farsighted wisdom by hiring Mr Root at the price demanded. Colt felt—and was later justified in believing—that it was cheaper, in

Clockwise from immediate above: **The sidearms worn by these cowpokes in this 1927 photo are Colts, underscoring Colt's continued popularity; an Old Model Navy Pistol with shoulder stock; an Old Model Army Pistol, also equipped with a shoulder stock; the Colt London factory, at which the 1849 Model Pocket Pistol and the 1851 Navy Pistol were made; and a pamphlet advertising Colt's London models.**

the long run, to hire expensive men than to hire cheap ones of lesser talents. Indeed, this kind of thinking led Colt to pay his better class workmen $5.00 a day, which at that time was roughly five times the going rate for such labor. But when high wages are paid, high demands can be made and the workers and management at the Hartford Plant lived up to all expectations. Arms were produced rapidly and efficiently. Marketing and advertising schemes, principally under Colt's direction, increased the reputation of Colt's firearms and his markets and orders grew at an astonishing rate.

The United States was not the only nation involved in conflict. This Colt knew and on foreign trips he managed to come in contact with heads of state then involved in regional wars. One such foreign leader was the Sultan of Turkey. Colt presented him with a pair of presentational revolvers, which led the Sultan to immediately order 5000 such arms and make to Colt a personal present of a jewel encrusted gold snuffbox. Later, Colt was to be the recipient of an Order of Turkish Nobility decoration from this same sultan.

Even though the designation 'Colt's Patent' appeared on Colt's firearms, there were always those ready to imitate the genuine article for their own profit. Fortunately, Colt was now wealthy enough to employ a battery of lawyers, who pursued these patent infringements vigorously. Colt's patents basically incorporated three principles in revolver construction: 1) turning the cylinder by the action of cocking the hammer, 2) locking and unlocking the cylinder by the same action of cocking and 3) providing a block between the chambers to prevent simultaneous discharge of several chambers. The infringers always lost and as long as Colt's patent remained intact, they had to search elsewhere for designs.

In 1851, Colt had gone to Europe and had given a series of lectures before the Institute of Civil Engineers at London. These lectures and the ensuing discussions turned into a litany of praise for Colt and his new pistols. The British, at this time, being 'the rulers of the world' had ample need for the latest in weaponry in order to quash the local uprisings, disturbances and disputes that almost continually plagued the Empire.

Colt set up a pistol factory in London in 1853 in order to exploit this market. It was situated at Pimlico on the Thames Bank near Zaruxall Bridge. The arms models made here were the 1849 Model Pocket Pistol and the 1851 Navy Pistol.

Since gunmaking in the British Isles at this time was mainly a piecemeal project, whereby a gun was produced in many different locations—usually backstreet workshops—the London Colt Factory was the source of great amazement to English observers. Not only were all of Colt's guns made under one roof, but the machinery used was of such perfection and precision that it could be run by women whose only former training had been in needlework. The London Factory was all the rage for British society and even Charles Dickens wrote of his tour through it in *Household Words* in 1855.

COLT'S PATENT REPEATING PISTOLS,

ARMY, NAVY, AND POCKET SIZES,

APPROVED OF BY HER MAJESTY'S HON. BOARD OF ORDNANCE, AND THE MOST DISTINGUISHED NAVAL AND MILITARY AUTHORITIES,

AND NOW IN GENERAL USE THROUGHOUT THE WORLD.

MANUFACTURED AT

THAMES BANK, NEAR VAUXHALL BRIDGE;

OFFICES FOR SALE OF ARMS, 1, SPRING GARDENS, COCKSPUR STREET, LONDON.

BEWARE OF COUNTERFEITS AND PATENT INFRINGEMENTS.

Every genuine London-made Weapon is stamped on the barrel—"Address, COL. COLT, *London."*

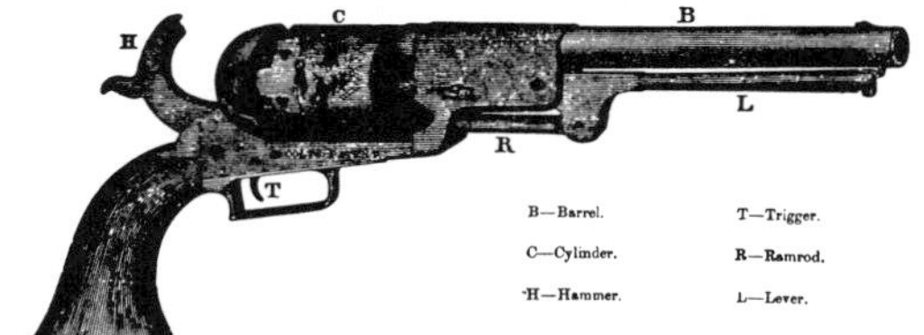

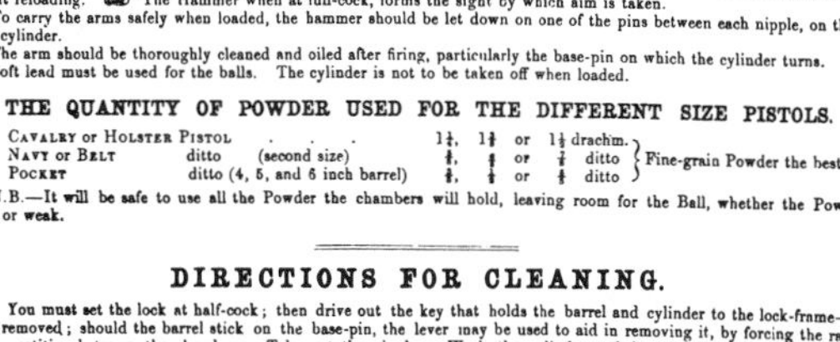

B—Barrel. T—Trigger.
C—Cylinder. R—Ramrod.
H—Hammer. L—Lever.

DIRECTIONS FOR LOADING COLT'S PISTOLS.

First explode a cap on each nipple to clear them from oil or dust, then draw back the hammer to the half-cock, which allows the cylinder to be rotated; a charge of powder is then placed in each chamber, and a ball with the pointed end upwards, without wadding or patch, is put one at a time into the mouths of the chambers, turned under the rammer, and forced down with the lever below the surface of the cylinder, so that they cannot hinder its rotation. This is repeated until all the chambers are loaded. Percussion-caps are then placed on the nipples, when, by drawing back the hammer to the full-cock, the arm is in condition for a discharge by pulling the trigger; a repetition of the same motion produces the like results, viz. six shots without reloading. ☞ The Hammer when at full-cock, forms the sight by which aim is taken.

To carry the arms safely when loaded, the hammer should be let down on one of the pins between each nipple, on the end of the cylinder.

The arm should be thoroughly cleaned and oiled after firing, particularly the base-pin on which the cylinder turns.

Soft lead must be used for the balls. The cylinder is not to be taken off when loaded.

THE QUANTITY OF POWDER USED FOR THE DIFFERENT SIZE PISTOLS.

CAVALRY or HOLSTER PISTOL	. . .	1¼, 1⅜ or 1½ drachm.	Fine-grain Powder the best.
NAVY or BELT	ditto (second size)	[illegible], [illegible] or [illegible] ditto	
POCKET	ditto (4, 5, and 6 inch barrel)	[illegible], [illegible] or [illegible] ditto	

N.B.—It will be safe to use all the Powder the chambers will hold, leaving room for the Ball, whether the Powder is strong or weak.

DIRECTIONS FOR CLEANING.

You must set the lock at half-cock; then drive out the key that holds the barrel and cylinder to the lock-frame—they can be removed; should the barrel stick on the base-pin, the lever may be used to aid in removing it, by forcing the rammer on the partition between the chambers. Take out the nipples. Wash the cylinder and barrel in warm water, dry and oil them thoroughly; oil freely the base-pin on which the cylinder revolves.

TO TAKE THE LOCK TO PIECES, CLEAN, AND OIL.

First—Remove the stock, by turning out the bottom and two rear screws that fasten it to the guard and lock-frame.
Second—Loosen the screw that fastens the mainspring to the trigger-guard, and turn the spring from under the tumbler of the hammer.
Third—Remove the trigger-guard, by turning out the three screws that fasten it to the lock-frame.
Fourth—Turn out the screw, and remove the double spring that bears upon the trigger and bolt.
Fifth—Turn out the screw-pins that hold the trigger and bolt in their places.
Sixth—Turn out the remaining side screw-pin, and remove the hammer with hand attached, by drawing it downwards out of the lock-frame. Clean all the parts and oil them thoroughly.

TO PUT THEM TOGETHER.

Replace the hammer with hand attached, then the bolt, the trigger, the trigger-guard, the mainspring, and finally the handle; returning each of the screws in their proper places, the arm is again fit for use.

☞ The Arms can be obtained, Wholesale and Retail, of the Manufacturer and Patentee,

SAMUEL COLT, 1, SPRING GARDENS, COCKSPUR STREET, LONDON

Or through any respectable Gun Dealer, Mercantile House, Army and Navy or E. I. Agent.

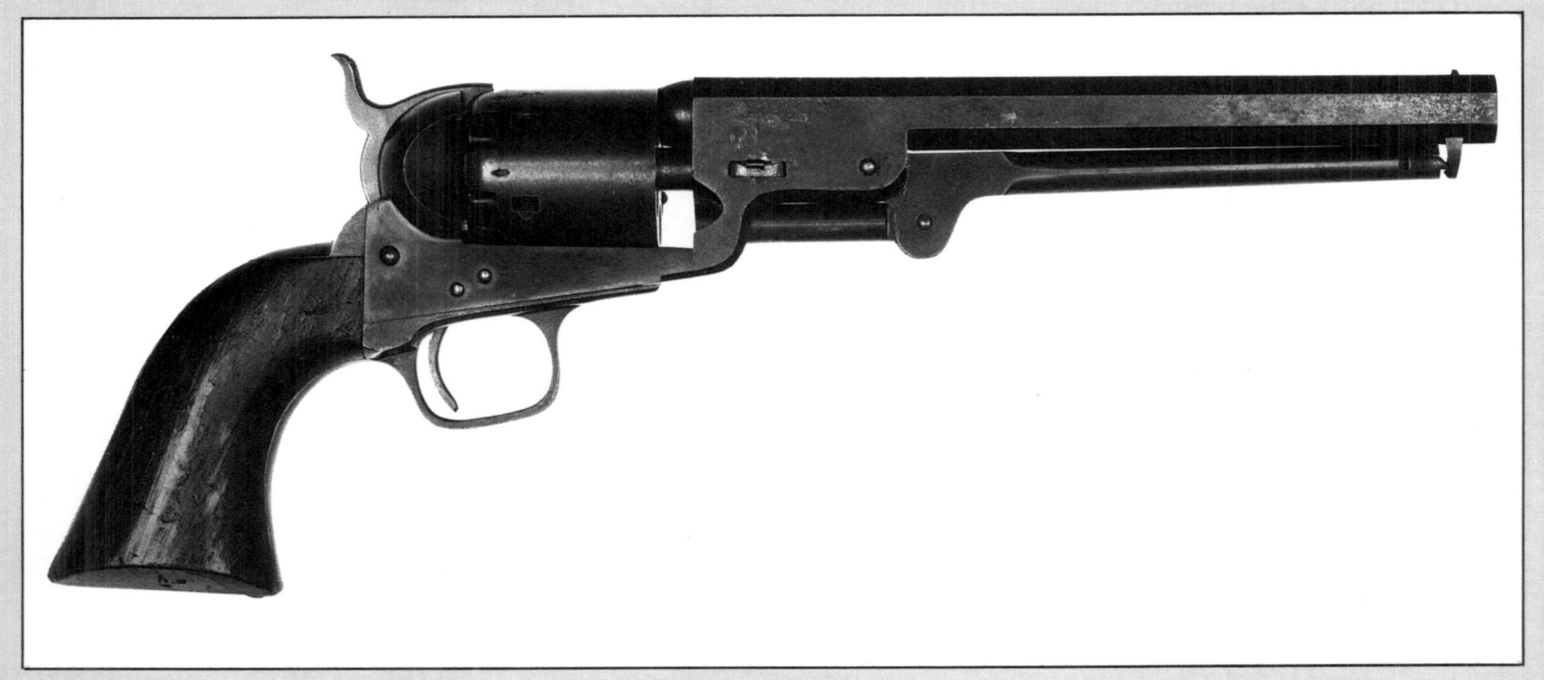

These pages, top to bottom: **An ornate Old Model Navy Pistol, (such pistols were given as gifts to influential people); an engraved New Model Pocket Pistol 'sidehammer Colt,' circa 1855; and a London Colt.**

Charles Dickens Tours Colt's Ill-Fated London Factory (1855)

We are on the threshold of Colonel Colt's factory in the somber and smoky region of Millbank. Under the roof of this low, brickbuilt, barrack-looking building, we are told that we may see what cannot be seen under one roof elsewhere in all England, the complete manufacture of a pistol, from dirty pieces of timber and rough bars of cast steel, till it is fit for the gunsmith's case. To see the same thing in Birmingham and in other places where firearms are made almost entirely by hand labour, we should have to walk about a whole day, visiting many shops carrying on distinct branches of the manufacture; not to speak of the toolmakers, the little screw and pin makers; all of whose work is done here. 'We are independent people,' says my informant, 'and are indebted to no one, save the engine and fixed machine makers.' This little pistol which is just put into my hand will pick into more than 200 parts, every one of which parts is made by a machine. A little skill is required in polishing the wood, in making cases, and in guiding the machines; but mere strength of muscle, which is so valuable in new societies, would find no market here, for the steam engine—indefatigably toiling in the hot, suffocating smell of rank oil, down in the little stone chamber below—performs nine-tenths of all the work that is done here. Neat, delicate-handed little girls do the work that brawny smiths still do in other gunshops. Most of them have been seamstresses and dressmakers, unused to factory work, but have been induced to conquer some little prejudice against it, by the attraction of better pay than they could hope to get by needlework. Even the men have, with scarcely an exception, been hitherto ignorant of gunmaking. No recruiting sergeant ever brought a more miscellaneous group into the barrack-yard, to be drilled more rapidly to the same duty, than these 200 hands have been. Carpenters, cabinet-makers, ex-policemen, butchers, cabmen, hatters, gas-fitters, porters—or at least one representative from each of those trades—are steadily drilling and poring at lathes all day in upper rooms.

The girls here earn from two to three shillings per day; the boys the same. The men get from three to eight shillings per day of 10 hours; while one or two, being quick, clever and reliable, are paid regularly 12 shillings per day. What is commonly called piecework is not the system usually adopted here. It has been found to tempt the men to hurry their work at the expense of a neat finish, and the manager prefers to give a workman six months trial, during which he learns the business of gunmaking by machinery, and he is also sure by that time to have shown what wages he is worth. Only 12 of these people are Americans; one or two Germans, the rest English.

Above: **Charles Dickens—perhaps pondering Colt's unique London factory, whose mass-production techniques were much different than any manufacturing process with which English gunsmiths were acquainted.**

Listening to these facts as my conductor communicates them, we pass into a long room hung with portraits of targets as they appeared after firing at them with Colt's revolvers. All the bullet marks are, of course, very near the bull's eye—which, I hope I am not presumptuous or depreciatory of the great Colt invention in attributing in some measure to the marksman. Beyond this is the storeroom, lined with wooden racks up to the ceiling, which are almost naked now, only five pistols of all the number that are made here—600 a week—being at the moment in store.

Out of the hot atmosphere, and the all-pervading odor of hot oil, we pass a yard ankle deep in iron chips (which make a dry hard road in all weathers, very destructive to leather) into a long outbuilding in which the only genuine smiths are at work. Here the very beginning of the pistols is made—if we except the cutting and polishing of the stock, which have been already described in these pages. There is little of the noise of a smithy here, except the roaring of the furnaces. A workman rams the end of a long bar of steel into the fire, and taking it out glowing with heat, strikes a bit off the end as if it were a stick of peppermint, while his companion—giving it a couple of rough taps upon the anvil—drops the red hot morsel into a die. This die is a plug hole, shaped something like a horseshoe, at the foot of a machine bearing a painful resemblance to a guillotine. While they have been breaking off the bit of steel, a huge screw has been slowly lifting up the iron hammerhead, which plays the part of the axe in the guillotine; and now the great hammer drops, and with one stroke beats the piece of iron to the form of the die. It has cooled to a black heat now, and is shaped something like the sole of a narrow shoe; but it must be heated again and the heel end beat up at right angles to the long part—taking care that it is bent according to the grain of the metal, without which it will be liable to flaw. Thus the shield, and what may be called the body of the pistol, are made in an instant.

In Birmingham, the barrels of firearms are made of old nails that have been knocked about, and which are melted, rolled into sheets, twisted again, and beaten about till they are considered to be tougher and less likely to burst—but the American gunsmiths know nothing about this. They merely beat it with steam hammers; for it would not do to draw it through holes, as thick wire is drawn, or to roll it as with ordinary round bars. These hammers are fixed, five in a frame, where they quiver with a chopping noise too rapidly to count the strokes, over a little iron plate, never touching it, though coming very close. Into the first of these the smith thrusts the red end of the bar, and guides it till it is beaten square. The next hammer beats it smaller, but still square. The next beats it smaller and longer still, but rounder. The fourth hammer beats it round, and the fifth strikes off the exact length for the barrel. This gradual process is absolutely necessary, for the steel will not bear being beaten round the first time; and, although five barrels may be thus forged in one minute, the rapid strokes of these hammers are said to make it quite as tough as the Birmingham plan; which seems to be borne out by the results at the proof-house. On the same floor, the barrels and cylinders, after polishing, are casehardened and tinted blue by burning in hot embers—processes which are well known.

Across the yard strewn with chips of iron again, and through the tool room, where men are turning great screws and other bolts and portions of machinery, we mount to the first floor and enter a long room filled with machines, and rather more redolent of hot rank oil. Considering that the floor supports a long vista of machinery in full action, the place looks clean and neat, and is not very noisy. Girls quietly attending to the boring and rifling of the barrels—having nothing to do but to watch the lathe narrowly, and drop a little oil upon the borer with a feather now and then—men drilling cylinders, holding locks to steam files, cutting triggers, slotting screws, treating cold iron everywhere as if it were soft wood, to be cut to any shape, without straining a muscle. It would be difficult and tedious to describe these machines minutely, although they are very interesting to a spectator, and cannot, I believe, be seen elsewhere. Every one of them is a simple lathe; but it is in the various cutters, borers and riflers that the novelty and ingenuity exist. Where the thing is to be made of eccentric shape, the cutter is of eccentric shape also; and although the superintendent of each machine acquires more or less skill by practice, it is in the perfection of these cutters and borers that the guarantee for uniformity consists. The bores of barrels and cylinders must be mathematically straight, and every one of the many parts must be exactly a duplicate of another. No one part belongs, as a matter of course, to any other part of one pistol; but each piece may be taken at random from a heap, and fixed to and with the other pieces until a complete weapon is formed, that weapon being individualized by a number stamped upon many of its component parts. The advantage of these contrivances is obvious. In every case of revolvers are placed, when sold, a number of such parts of a pistol as are most liable to accident; and with these, any soldier or sailor may, in a few minutes, repair his own weapon.

All this time we have been seeing only the making of little bits of a pistol. Pausing for a moment to see the engraving of a ship in full sail, and other ornamental work—including the maker's name stamped by great pressure on the cylinder—we come into a great room, where all the minute portions are brought to be examined. Here, by means of gauges, but chiefly by the practised eye of the superintendent, each separate article is examined, and rejected if in the slightest degree faulty. From this room the various parts are served out to the workmen who put them together and turn out the complete revolver.

Here is the proving room, where the pistols undergo a preparatory trial, before being sent up for the regular government proof. It is by no means the dark, mysterious iron-plated room in which I have been taught to believe that guns are proved, but an ordinary workshop, with two square wooden pipes, fixed horizontally, and open at the end, breast high. I am invited to prove a pistol, by firing it into one of these pipes which, I am told, afford sufficient protection to the firer in case of a barrel bursting—an event, pains were taken to assure me, of very rare occurrence. After a little practice, I find that a mere novice may, with one hand, discharge the six rounds as rapidly as the eye can wink.

—Charles Dickens
Household Words (Chapter 15, Volume 9)

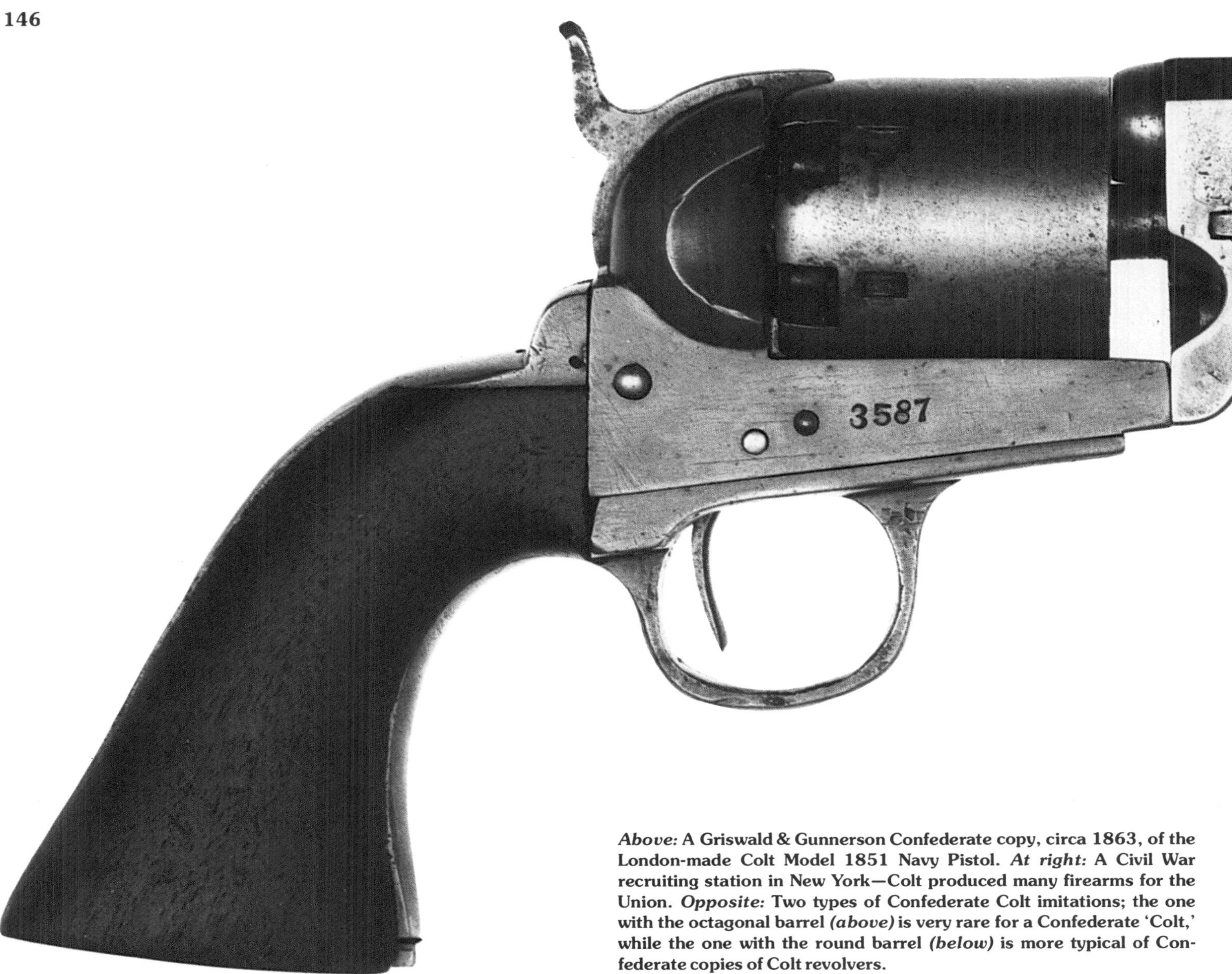

Above: **A Griswald & Gunnerson Confederate copy, circa 1863, of the London-made Colt Model 1851 Navy Pistol. *At right:* A Civil War recruiting station in New York—Colt produced many firearms for the Union. *Opposite:* Two types of Confederate Colt imitations; the one with the octagonal barrel *(above)* is very rare for a Confederate 'Colt,' while the one with the round barrel *(below)* is more typical of Confederate copies of Colt revolvers.**

In 1854, the British government contracted with Colt to produce both large orders of revolvers and of the machinery for the manufacture of muskets.

Colt's genius was not confined merely to inventiveness and public relations. He was an organizer and a manager of the highest grade. He recognized almost from the beginning that in the production of a firearm, some pieces of the gun require more skill to produce than others. Obviously, if the fabrication of one firearm is assigned to one individual, that individual will have to be paid according to the most skilled labor required for those particular parts composing the gun. This was unfair, both to Colt and the employee, as well as the customer. The work, therefore, was divided into various divisions depending on the precision or skill required to produce the individual parts. Pay was graduated according to each worker at the skill level at which he functioned. A system of subcontracting was employed whereby the less skilled workman ran the basic machines and did the routine work while the more skilled men did the actual assembling of the arms and their final finishing.

Because all of the parts of a particular model of gun had to be interchangeable with other specimens of that same model, precision was of the utmost importance. This need led Colt to institute the standardization of gauges used in calibrating the machinery upon which the parts were produced. This meant that, standardization being assured, workmen were able to be paid according to their ability to produce. Henry Ford is traditionally credited with this kind of assembly line process, but it was Colt who had the basic concepts in mind—and in operation—long before Ford came onto the American scene. Only 10 percent of the cost of a given weapon was generally taken up with the wages of the men who ran the machines. Thus, Colt's profitably increased, yet he was able to sell his 'perfect' weapons at a very reasonable price.

All of these mass production techniques and the ideas and attitudes behind them were purely of American vintage. The British employees of Colt's factory in London could never seem to adjust themselves to such processes. Consequently, the London branch of Colt's factory closed in 1857. It was bought by others who attempted to produce Colt's pistols, but if Colt could not make the factory run, no one could. In a short time, the London Pistol Company ceased to exist.

But if Colt's English venture had not proven to be so profitable, his foresight and insight into the political instability of the US did. Colt sensed that because of the slavery issue and other economic factors, the North and the South would almost inevitably go to war. That conflict, he knew, would test the very existence of the Union itself. Being a Connecticut Yankee by birth and owing his success

to the American enterprise in general, Colt undertook to have his Hartford Factory work literally night and day to produce for the US Government in advance of the anticipated hostilities. He wrote to Mr Root, his general manager, to get '5000 or 10,000 ahead of each kind of firearm in production.' He wanted his people to 'make hay while the sun shines.' This they were able to accomplish by working double shifts. And since supply lines were—at this point in time—still undisturbed, the flow of raw materials for the arms were still easily accessible. Thus, when hostilities broke out, Colt was able to supply the government with its immediate and long range needs. By 1862, the Colt plant was, indeed, 'making hay while the sun shines.'

However, the frenzied pace of production had taken its toll on Samuel Colt. He had suffered a personal blow when one of his daughters died and this, combined with his desire to furnish the Union troops with all of the weapons that they needed, led him into a condition of nervous exhaustion. On

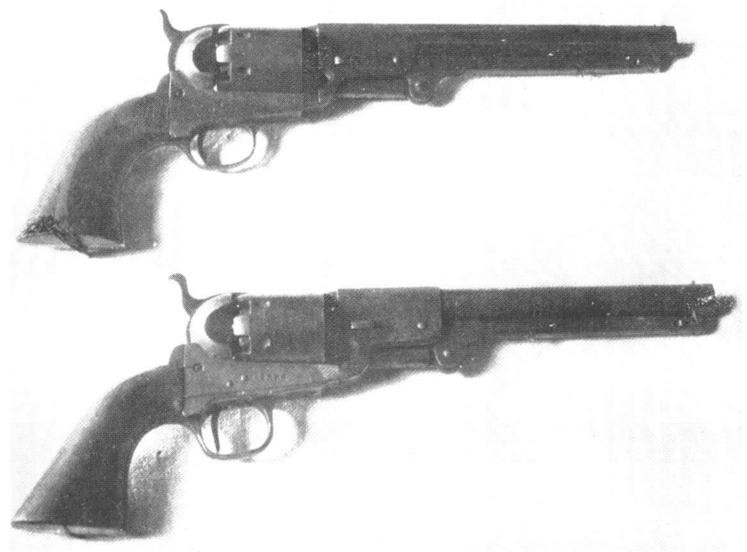

***At top:* Colt's Hartford plant after the fire of 1864. Confederate spies in the plant were suspected of arson. *Above:* Back in the swing of things—the Colt factory as it looked after the rebuilding of the burned factory—1874.** **See also the pre-fire factory photo on page 21.**

his death bed, he was making plans to increase the size and output of the Hartford Factory by two-fold. He even contracted with the government to furnish 75,000 single shot muskets in addition to the revolver orders already filed with him. Colonel Samuel Colt died on 10 January 1862, being only 48 years of age.

His estate consisted of over 100 acres of prime land in Hartford, the largest private armory in the world and a corporation with paid up capital of over $1,000,000. The total value of his estate was estimated at $5,000,000. All of this is the more amazing when one considers that these accomplishments were done in a 14 year period. Not only had Samuel Colt, during this time, supplied his nation with the kinds of weapons that it needed and in sufficient quantities and made for himself a fortune; he had also established a standard of employee welfare that, even by today's standards, would be considered phenomenal. Colt's employees

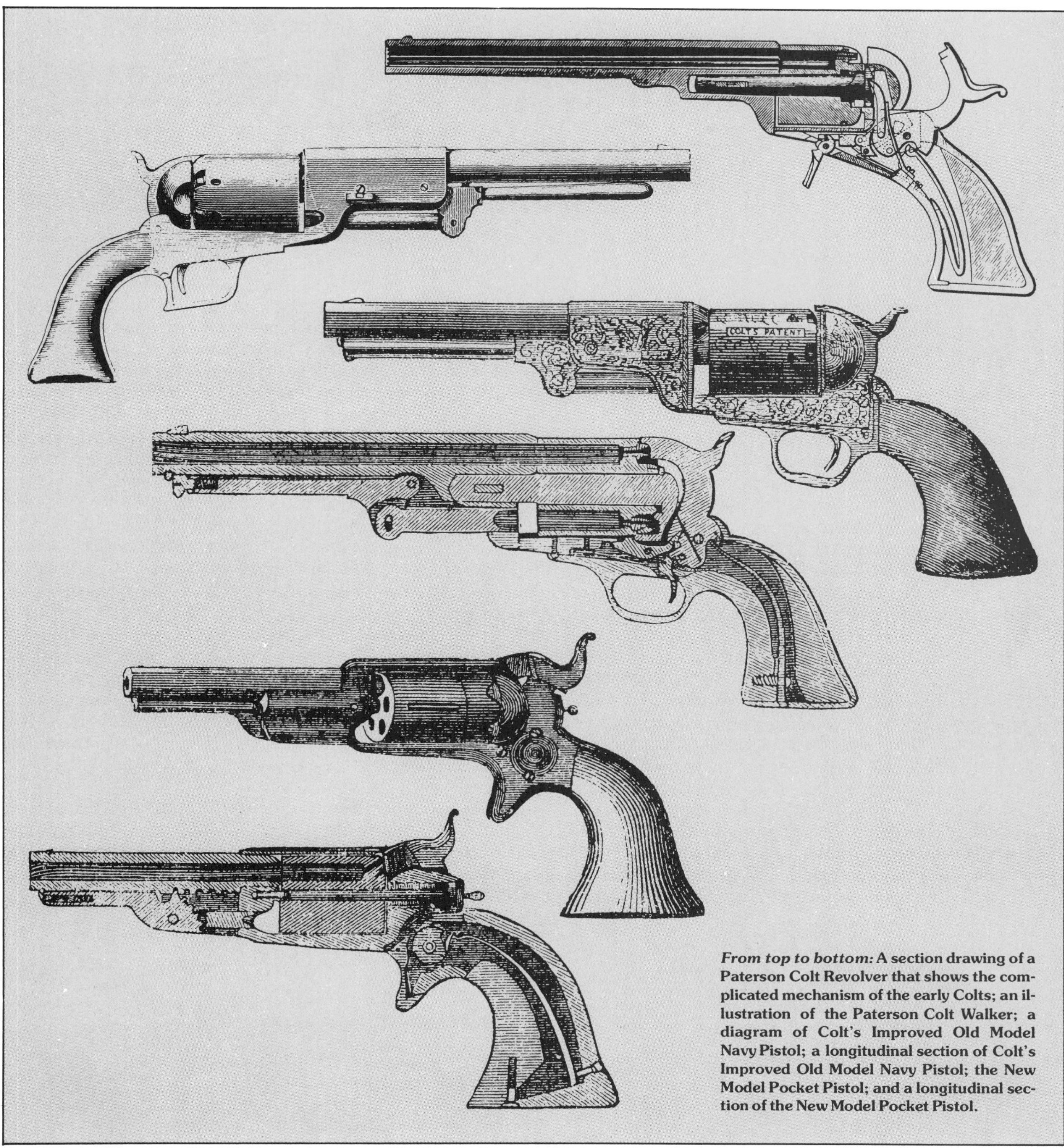

From top to bottom: **A section drawing of a Paterson Colt Revolver that shows the complicated mechanism of the early Colts; an illustration of the Paterson Colt Walker; a diagram of Colt's Improved Old Model Navy Pistol; a longitudinal section of Colt's Improved Old Model Navy Pistol; the New Model Pocket Pistol; and a longitudinal section of the New Model Pocket Pistol.**

worked in heated, well-lit, ventilated rooms with running water and at the highest pay in the country for the class of work that they did. They were even provided with up-to-date homes and a recreation center for their off hours. As a result, their loyalty to him personally and to the company, was unbounded. EK Root was elected the president upon Mr Colt's death.

The last models of Colt revolvers which were introduced before Mr Colt's death were the 1860 Army, the 1861 Navy and the 1862 Police and Pocket Navy. In February 1864, fire swept the old armory of the Hartford plant. The precision machines and floors of the plant had been saturated with nearly 10 years of accumulated oil. Eyewitness accounts attest to the ferocity of the blaze. Historians have speculated about the cause of the fire and most attribute it to Confederate spies in the plant itself. The total loss was nearly three quarters of a million dollars which was partly covered by insurance. It is interesting to note that during Colt's lifetime he carried no insurance, but had never had to worry very much about arson. Luckily, the fire did not occur until near the very end of the Civil War and the plant's destruction did not affect the outcome of the conflict.

A Tour of Colt's Hartford Factory (1857)

Leaving the office we cross the bridge, pass down through the machine shop, engine room, etc, to the rear parallel, an apartment 40 by 50 feet square, the center of which is appropriated as the storeroom for iron and steel. Large quantities of these materials, in bars and rods, are stored here in charge of a responsible party, whose duty it is to fill the orders from the contractors, and render an accurate statement of such deliveries to the main storekeeper's department. This latter system is universal throughout the establishment—thus, materials of all kinds can be readily accounted for, no matter what their state of transposition.

At this point it is well to inform the reader that almost the entire manual labor of the establishment is performed by contract. The contractors are furnished room, power, tools, material, heat, light—in fact all but muscle and brains; themselves, however, and their subordinates are all subject to the immediate government, as prescribed by the code of rules, laid down by the Company. The contractors number some scores—some particular manipulators requiring only their individual exertions, while others employ one to 40 assistants. Many of them are men of more than ordinary ability, and some have rendered themselves pecuniarily comfortable by their exertions.

We now pass into the forge shop, an apartment 40 by 200 feet square, comprising the whole of one arm of the parallel. Along each side range stacks of double-covered forges—the blasts for which, entering and discharging through flues in the walls, carry off the smoke and gases. Here, for the first time in our life, we were in a blacksmith shop in full operation, yet free from smoke and cinders, and with a pure atmosphere. Several kinds of hammers are used—those most in use, however, being 'drops' of the novel construction peculiar to the establishment; they are raised on the endless screw principle, and tripped by a trigger at the will of the operator. All the parts of the firearm composed of iron or steel are forged in swages, in which, although they may have ever so many preliminary operations, the shape is finally completed at a single blow. That some idea may be formed of the amount of work on a single rifle or pistol, we have determined to state the number of separate operations of each portion, and in each department. We adopt the 'Navy' or belt pistol, the weight of which is 38 ounces, as the example. In forging, the number of separate heats are enumerated: lockframe, two; barrel, three; lever, two; rammer, one; hammer two; hand, two; trigger, two; bolt, two; main spring, two; key, two; nipples, two each, 12; thus we find that no less than 32 separate and distinct operations, some of which contain in themselves several subdivisions, are required in the forging for a single pistol.

It is unnecessary to describe all the operations performed by the machines; a few will render the whole understandable. In all there are 36 separate operations before the cylinder is ready to follow the lockframe to the inspector. The barrel goes through 45 separate opera-

Touring Colt's Hartford factory—*opposite, left and right:* The Forging Shop and the Wareroom. *Above:* The dome-topped armory. This was no sweatshop—in fact, employees enjoyed unrivalled good working conditions for that era.

tions on the machines. The other parts are subject to about the following number: Lever, 27; rammer, 19; hammer, 28; hand, 20; trigger, 21; bolt, 21; key, 18; sear spring, 12; 14 screws, seven each, 98; six cones, eight each, 48; guard, 18; handlestrap, five; and stock, five. Thus it will be observed that the greater part of the labor is completed in this department. Even all the various parts of the lock are made by machinery, each having its relative initial point to work from, and on the correctness of which the perfection depends.

As soon as completed the different parts are carried to the story above, which, with the exception of machinery and columns through the center, is an exact counterpart of the room below. It is designated the Inspecting and Assembling Department. Here the different parts are most minutely inspected; this embraces a series of operations which in the aggregate amount to considerable work; the tools to inspect a cylinder, for example, are fifteen in number, each of which must gauge to a hair. The greatest nicety is observed, and it is absolutely impossible to get a slighted piece of work beyond this point. On finishing his examination, the inspector punches his initial letter on the piece inspected, thus pledging his reputation on its quality.

The mountings, consisting of the handlestrap and guard, which are composed of gunmetal, are cast and afterward worked up in the machines in the same manner as the other metal work. The woodwork of the stock is also shaped by machinery.

Each part having been thus far completed in itself, now comes the first uniting or 'assembling,' as the workmen term it. Let us get our Navy pistol in shape; to do so we will want a cylinder, barrel, lockframe, hammer, trigger, bolt, key, mainspring, hand, sear spring, lever, rammer, guard, back strap, stock and a number of peculiar screws. These are readily united by the assembler, and our pistol assumes its material shape, It is now numbered; to make it special, we will designate our number as 138,565; the imprint of the establishment, 'Address Colonel Sam Colt, Hartford, Conn' is also stamped on at this time. It is now carefully taken apart, all the pieces being stamped the particular number of the arm; and thus our barrel, cylinder and etc, each with a quantity of his fellows, are taken away for their final finishing.

Most of the metal work is carried to the dry polishing shop—a room 60 feet square, located in the third story of the center building. Here it is polished on emery and other wheels, about half a yard in diameter, the operatives sitting at their work. After inspection, the barrels and cylinders are handed over for the blueing process—an operation that requires nicety and practical experience. The ovens for this, as well as for the casehardening—to which process all the iron work is submitted—as well as the forges for tempering the springs, etc, are located in the forge shop. From the polishers, the mountings go to the electroplaters—who occupy a room 25 by 40, in the basement of the office building, where they are plated with silver, and afterward burnished. The woodwork returns to the stock maker's shop—a room 60 by 80, in the third story of the center building. This is supplied with power saws, planes, morticing and shaping machines and as throughout the whole establishment, every means is

adopted for labor saving. The stock then comes back for varnishing and the final finishing.

On their final completion, all the parts are delivered to the general storekeeper's department, a room 60 feet wide by 190 feet long, situated in the second story of the central building, and extending over the rear parallel, All the hand tools and materials (except the more bulky kinds) are distributed to the workmen from this place; several clerks are required to parcel the goods out and keep the accounts; in fact, it is a store, in the largest sense of the term, and rather on the wholesale principle at that. On the reception of finished, full sets of the parts of the pistols, they are once more carried up to the assembling room; but this time to another corps of artisans. Guided by the numbers, they are once more assembled; and now, although each portion has associated with scores of its fellows and gone through many distinct operations in distant parts of the establishment, our particular pistol, number 138,565, is reassembled as first united, and the finished firearm is laid on a rack, ready for the prover; of course many others accompany it to the department of this official, which is located in the third story of the rear building. Here each chamber is loaded with the largest charge possible, and practically tested by firing—after which they are cleaned out by the prover and returned to the inspection department. The inspectors again take them apart, thoroughly clean and oil them; then they are for the last time put together and placed in a rack for the final inspection. The parts having been so thoroughly examined and tested, it would seem that this last inspection was scarcely necessary; but, after a short observation, we saw several laid aside. Taking up one with a small mark on the barrel, 'Why do you reject this?' we inquired. 'Pass that today, and probably much larger blemishes would appear tomorrow,' replied Mr T. The order from the Principal is perfection; and a small scratch in the blueing or varnish is sufficient to prevent the arm passing. The finished arm finally passing the inspection, is now returned to the storeroom—from whence, after being papered, they are sent to the wareroom, situated in the basement of the office building; from this they are sent to nearly every portion of the habitable globe.

Besides the great degree of uniformity and precision arrived at by the adaption of machinery in this manufacture, which exactness could be compassed in no other manner, it is stated that a number sufficient to supply the present demand could not be produced by manual labor alone. During the time of our visit we were informed that scarcely less than 100,000 weapons were at that moment in the various stages of progress, yet the whole number of employees was a little less than 600 who, by the aid of mechanical contrivances, turn out an average of 250 finished arms per diem.

In round numbers it might be stated that supposing the cost of an arm to be $100; of this the wages of those who attended to and passed the pieces through the machines was 10 percent, and those of the best class workmen engaged in assembling or putting together, finishing and ornamenting the weapons was also 10 percent, thus leaving 80 percent for the duty done by the machinery.

With the exception of the steam engine and boilers, a majority of the machinery was not only invented, but constructed on the premises. When this department was commenced, it was the intention of the company to manufacture solely for their own use. Some months since, applications were made by several foreign governments to be supplied with machines and the right to operate them. After mature deliberation, it was concluded to supply orders, and on the day of our visit we saw a complete set of machinery, for manufacturing firearms, that will shortly be shipped to a distant land. The company has now determined to incorporate this manufacture as a branch of their regular business.

Employees' Welfare

Although so much care and attention have been exercised in perfecting the armory and its accessories and products, the general welfare of the employees has not been neglected; extensive arrangements for their comfort and convenience are in the course of rapid completion.

And we may here remark that they are deserving of such especial favor; as a body they are mostly young men, many of them having commenced their business life in the establishment. It was, in a measure, necessary to educate men expressly for the purpose, as the manipulation required is not exclusively that of the gunsmith, or of the machinist, but a combination of both of these callings. Taken as a whole, we found them decidedly a reading and thinking community, and we venture the assertion that it would be difficult to produce a counterpart of their mental capacity in the same number of mechanics employed in a manufactory. That they are well compensated for their services is evident from the fact of the payroll amounting to from $1000 to $1200 per day.

The grounds around the armory have been laid out in squares of 500 feet each by streets 60 feet wide; upon these squares are being erected commodious three-story dwellings. Sufficient for about 80 families have already been finished, and are occupied by the employees; the operations will be continued until all who desire are accommodated. These houses have all the conveniences of city life. Gasworks, of sufficient capacity to supply as large a population as can occupy the area, have already been erected and put into operation.

One of the buildings is a beautiful structure known as Charter Oak Hall—so named from its being located on the same avenue as the venerable and time-honored tree, which for centuries braved the storm, and from a singular incident became celebrated in our colonial history. This hall is employed by the operatives for lectures, debates, concerts, balls and etc. The festive occasions are enlivened with music from a band organized from their midst—the instruments, which are most excellent, having been furnished through the liberality of Colonel Colt. A public park, fountains and etc, are in the plans, all of which are being successfully executed.

On the hill overlooking the whole is the palatial residence of the proprietor. It is really a superb edifice, the main building being 50 by 100 feet; it is in the Italian villa style—the ground and outbuildings being on the scale which would naturally be expected of a man of his extended views and liberal taste.

—*United States Magazine* (March 1857)

The tour continues—*clockwise from immediate left:* The Proving Room, the Dry Polishing Room, machinery for stocks and grips, and the main part of the armory—a room that was ranked as the best, most well-arranged and efficient workshop of its time.

Metallic

The history of self-exploding metallic cartridges actually began in France about 1812, with a Monsieur Pauly. The first types of this ammunition were actually made of paper which held the powder and the bullet, and only the rear of the cartridge was brass, with its depression to hold a detonator. When the cartridge was fired, the paper holding the powder and bullet were consumed in the explosion. In later improvements in cartridges of this kind, the paper shells were discarded in favor of a rolled cardboard—somewhat similar to our modern shotgun shells.

In 1847 Monsieur Haulier patented the idea of a self-contained cartridge that employed copper and brass in its construction. These types of shells were of very small caliber, and the first metallic cartridge to come to the United States (in the mid-1850s) was an early .22 short. Once arriving in America, the metallic cartridge soon took on more standard forms of construction, and was also being made in larger calibers.

Of course, these cartridges are the mainstay of the firearms industry today, and the four key elements of their original construction are the four elements common to all cartridges presently. The first of these elements is the case, which is made out of expandable metal, which, even though it expands upon detonation, immediately contracts in size slightly, to allow removal from the chamber. The second element is, of course, the explosive material, a gunpowder of some sort, which is loaded into the case. The third element is the bullet or projectile, which is crimped or fitted into the case in some manner. And the fourth element is the primer, or explosive device, which, when the hammer strikes it, detonates the powder.

When metallic cartridges were first introduced in the mid-1800s, the primer was generally of a fulminate of mercury compound. The explosive was generally black powder, which produced great amounts of smoke and flame, and bullets were generally of pure lead.

By the time of the Civil War, at least two repeating rifles, each employing metallic cartridges, were in use. They were the Henry rifle and the Spencer rifle. These two rifles were in .24 caliber and .56 caliber respectively.

It is interesting to note that the first metallic cartridges were of the 'folded head' type. Their distinguishing feature was that even though they were self contained, they could not be reloaded after they were fired. This proved to be quite a disadvantage, and naturally, other designs were brought forth, particularly by a Mr Bearden, who invented the 'boxer' type of center fire cartridge with a drawn brass case, which could be reloaded.

The ability of Bearden's case to withstand the blow of the hammer and retain its shape was of such tremendous advantage that Army regulations for many years called for soldiers to both save and reload their fired ammo cases.

The metallic cartridge revolution was actually first seen in rifles, not pistols. But it was not long before the idea took shape to use these new cartridges in revolving cylinder handguns. But a particular legal entanglement over a certain patent by Rollin White prevented the use of center fire cartridges in revolving pistols for some years. White had taken out a patent which involved the loading of shot and the recapping of primers from the rear of the cylinder. This concept was later adapted into a rimfire .22 caliber pistol. This particular pistol was never a commercial success, but

Cartridges

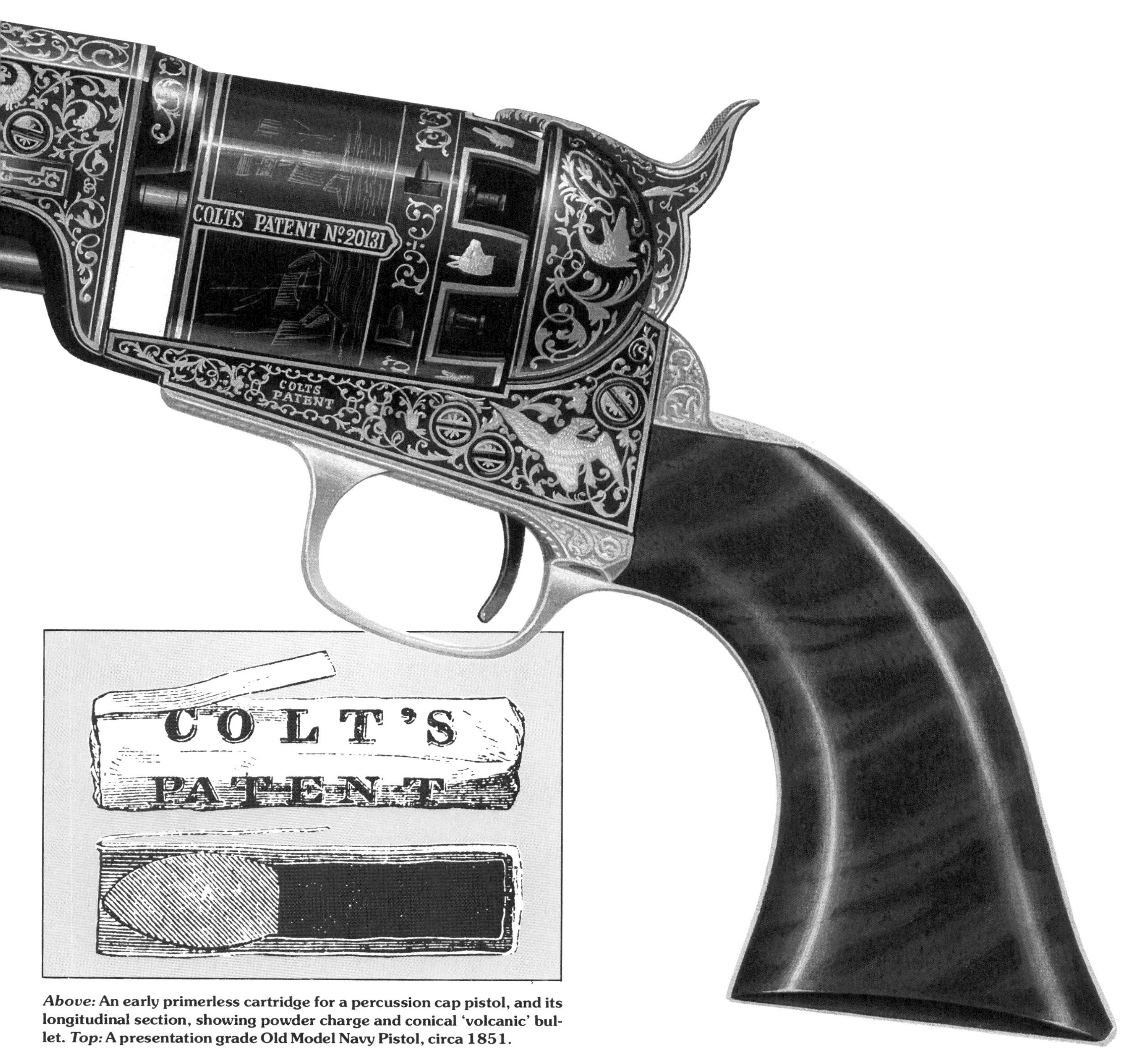

Above: **An early primerless cartridge for a percussion cap pistol, and its longitudinal section, showing powder charge and conical 'volcanic' bullet.** *Top:* **A presentation grade Old Model Navy Pistol, circa 1851.**

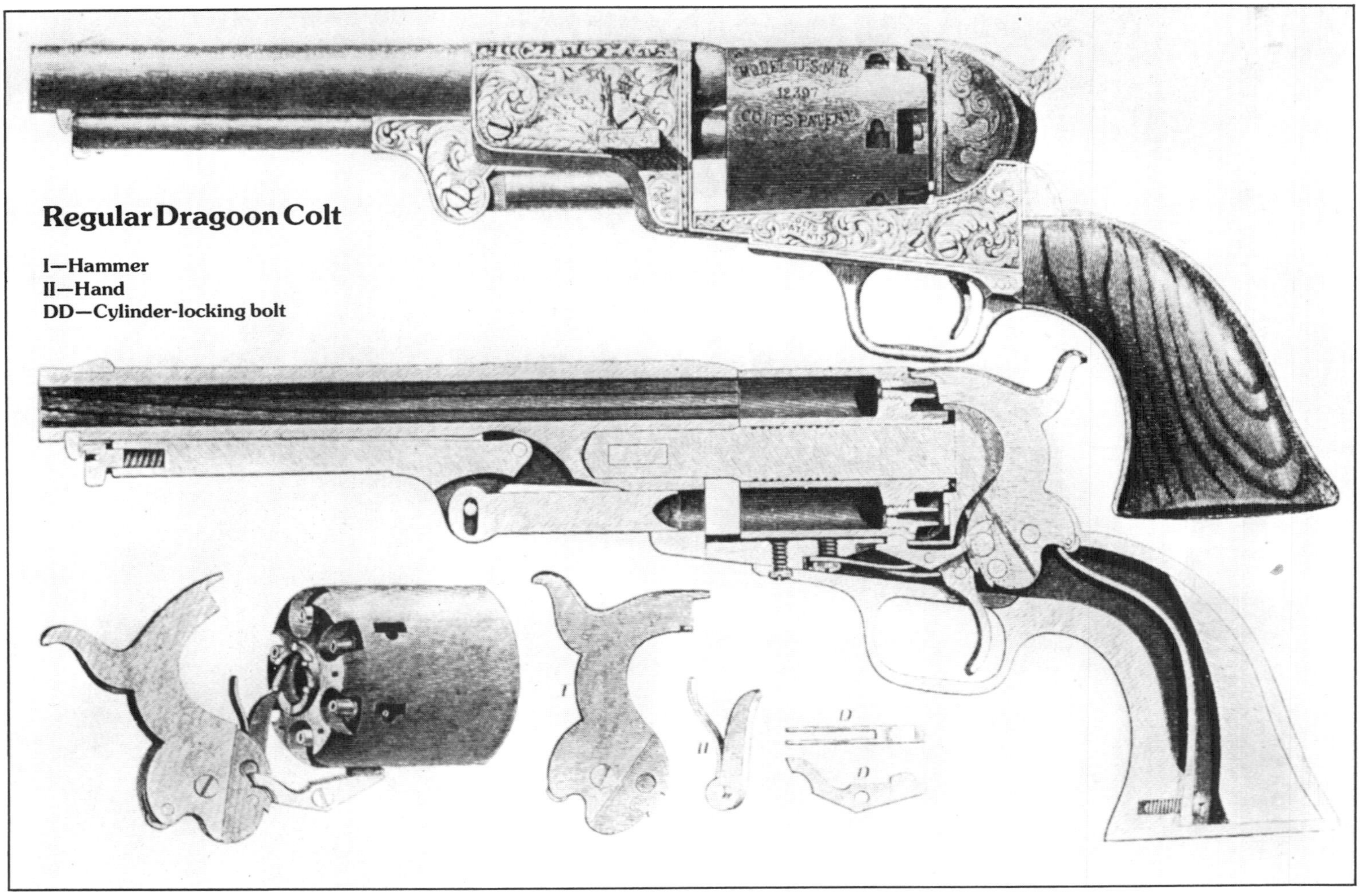

Regular Dragoon Colt

I—Hammer
II—Hand
DD—Cylinder-locking bolt

Above: A section drawing of a Regular Dragoon Colt, a typical Colt design from 1847 to 1855. *Top:* Colt primerless cartridges were made here; these cartridges predated the revolutionary metallic cartridge.

Above opposite: A folded-head cartridge, the first satisfactory metallic center-fire cartridge in use; a modern, solid-head cartridge. *Opposite:* Colt's first metallic cartridge revolver, the Single Action Army.

the ideas behind it were patented, and were therefore unavailable to other arms manufacturers—at least while the patent stood.

Another factor that prevented the quick conversion from cap and ball to cartridges was the fact that cartridges were not widely produced, and were therefore not readily available to the public. But the advantages of cartridges were overwhelming, and where there was a will, a way would be found. The great conversion from cap and ball to cartridges was underway. It would take many turns, but in the end cartridges would win out.

Because the cartridge revolution had first taken place in rifles and long arms, naturally, gun owners wanted to convert their cap and ball pistols to be able to use the same cartridges as their long arms. Since most of the long arms which used cartridges were of .44 caliber, it was natural that the first pistols were of .44 and .45 caliber, also.

Actually, the conversion of a cap and ball pistol into a cartridge pistol was relatively simple. The nipples, which held the caps in place, were simply cut away, leaving an open hole in the rear of the cylinder, large enough to accommodate the cartridge. The hammer was then modified such that when it was released, the primer at the rear of the cartridge was struck forcibly enough to set off the powder. Of course the rammer—which was indispensable for the loading of a cap and ball pistol—was no longer needed, and was usually removed as a part of the conversion process.

But centerfire cartridges were still hard to obtain, and so many folks of the time took to carrying two separate cylinders with them. One of the percussion cap type, and the other of the new cartridge type.

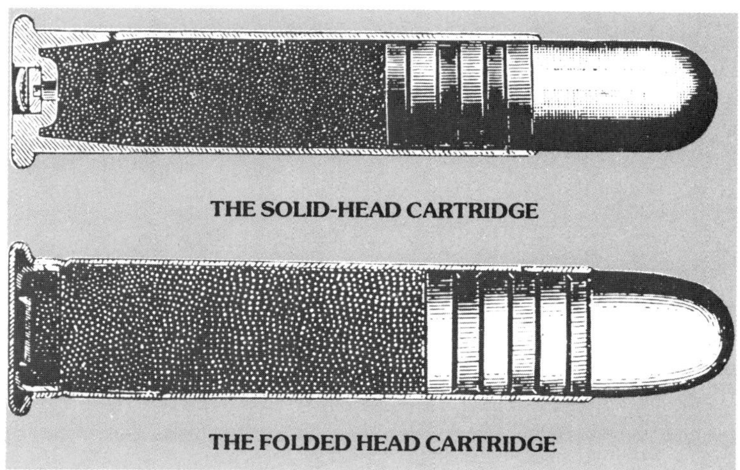

THE SOLID-HEAD CARTRIDGE

THE FOLDED HEAD CARTRIDGE

Later, another alteration of importance took place. This was Mr Thuer's patent which was taken out in 1868. It incorporated small firing pins in the cylinder itself—thus negating the need to alter the cap and ball hammer.

As can be seen from the above, this alteration process from cap and ball to cartridges was momentous enough to generate its own set of patents. The alteration process itself made money for the gunmakers as well. Colt accepted contracts with the government for alterations of all revolvers in the hands of all of the Armed Services of the United States Government in 1872.

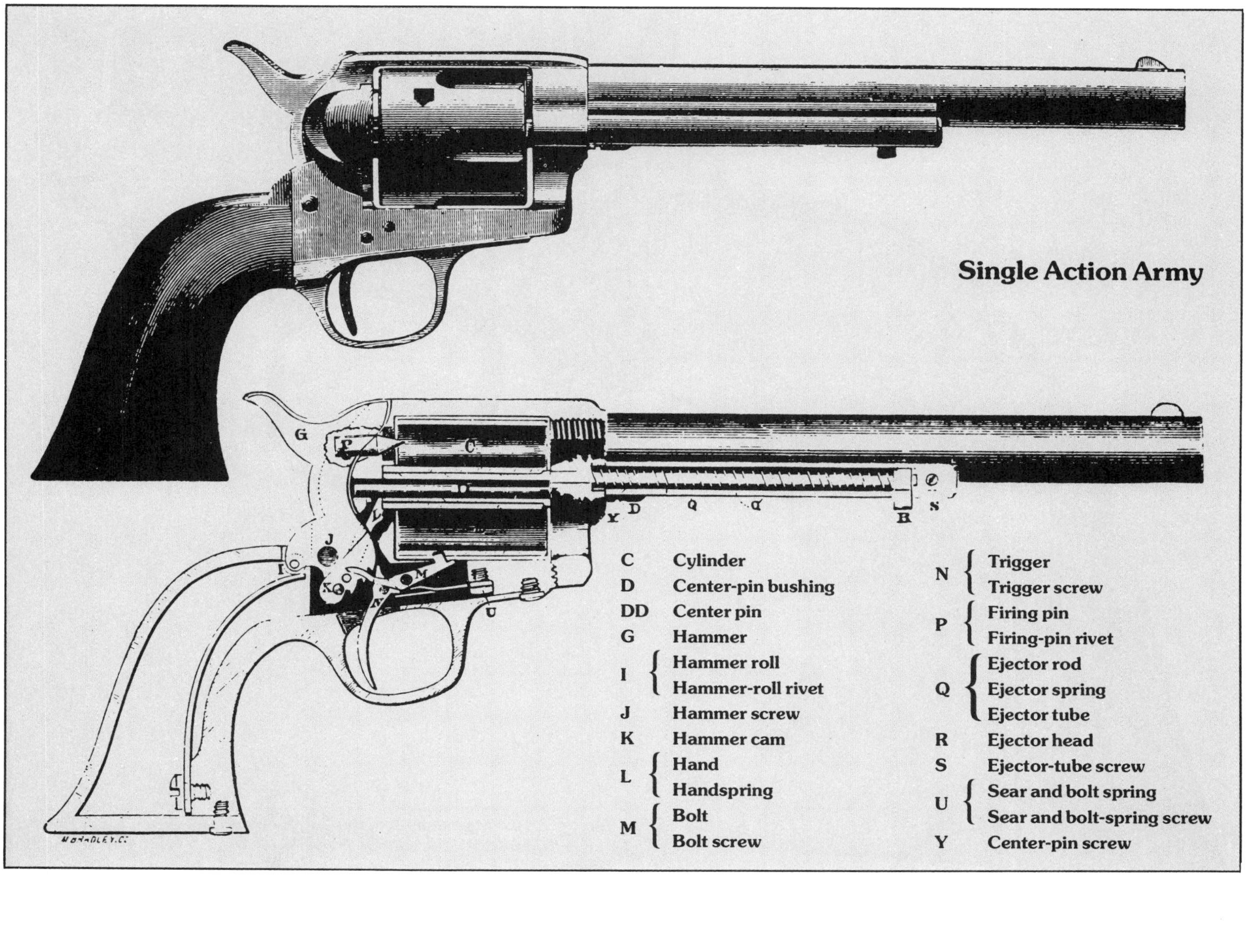

Single Action Army

C	Cylinder	N	Trigger Trigger screw
D	Center-pin bushing	P	Firing pin Firing-pin rivet
DD	Center pin	Q	Ejector rod Ejector spring Ejector tube
G	Hammer	R	Ejector head
I	Hammer roll Hammer-roll rivet	S	Ejector-tube screw
J	Hammer screw	U	Sear and bolt spring Sear and bolt-spring screw
K	Hammer cam	Y	Center-pin screw
L	Hand Handspring		
M	Bolt Bolt screw		

Great Colts Nineteenth

Above: **An ornate example of the Colt Single Action Army Target Model, which is basically the same—aside from its 7.5 inch barrel—as the famous Colt 'Peacemaker' Frontier Model Single Action Army Revolver.**

of the Century

The 'Peacemaker,' The Gun that Won the West

The Peacemaker was the first cartridge pistol produced by the Colt Company. It was first officially known as the New Model Army Metallic Cartridge Revolving Pistol, and later renamed Single Action Army Revolver.

This weapon was a .45 caliber pistol using the new self-contained center-fire cartridges. Up to 40 grains of black powder could be packed behind its 235 grain lead bullet. But the government initially chose to pack only 28 grains of black powder instead of the maximum 40.

The Single Action Army Revolver was initially produced in 1871, and by 1873, the first order of 8000 was placed by the Army's Ordnance Department. There were basically three barrel lengths available for the Single Action Army Revolver, and these were representative of the three basic markets employing such a weapon. The Cavalry Model had a barrel length of 7.5 inches. This was to facilitate long-range accuracy. The standard or Artillery Model had a barrel length of 5.5 inches. And for civilians, a 4.75 inch barrel model was made available.

Since the availability of cartridges was somewhat limited on the frontiers, and since most customers carried both a sidearm as well as a rifle, the Single Action Army was quickly tooled to use .44-40 caliber ammunition, so as to match the caliber of the very popular 1873 Winchester Repeating Rifle. This was not simply a matter of convenience to frontiersmen. The ability to have both of one's firearms chambered for the same cartridge could mean the difference between life and death in certain situations.

There is a particular type of Single Action Army Pistol called the Buntline Special, which has caused some confusion among historians. The Buntline Special got its name, not from anyone at the Colt factory, but rather from a Ned Buntline, who was a prolific writer of the period. Buntline specialized in writing about the Wild West. On trips into the West, he presented various distinguished frontiersmen with Army Colts with 12-inch barrels and shoulder stocks. Wyatt Earp and Bat Masterson were among those to receive such weapons. It is doubtful, however, that there was much practically to pistols with foot-long barrels. They were mainly for gift and show purposes. Obviously, Buntline found it more sensational to write about characters shooting it out in the streets of the Wild West with pistols of extraordinary barrel length rather than more conventional arms.

The Single Action Army Pistol provided the overall pattern for 'six-shooter' type Colt pistols up to the present time. It is the gun that is the most easily recognized as being a Colt by the general public, and indeed its appearance is deeply etched into the American psyche. The Single Action Army became the Frontier Colt. It was the 'Peacemaker' that stood between the law abiding and the outlaws. Wild Bill Hickok and Wyatt Earp (the first marshall of Dodge City, then Wichita, Kansas—and finally Tombstone, Arizona), used their Colts to blaze their way into the history of the Wild West. And of course, desperados and anti-heros had them also. William Bonney, alias Billy the Kid, did his murderous work with Colts. Even the brash and wily General George Armstrong Custer vainly relied on his Single Action Armys when justice was done at the battle of the Little Big Horn.

Legend has it that the renown of the Old Frontier Six-Shooter was such that it was 'not God or the Declaration of Independence that made men free and equal, but, rather,

Left: **General George Custer was known for his pair of fancy Colts.** ***Above:*** **Early cowboy movie star William S Hart brandishes his Peacemakers.** ***Right:*** **Patent drawings for the Peacemaker show metallic cartridges in its chambers, and how its chambers align with its barrel.**

Mr Samuel Colt.' Another legend runs that on a tombstone is inscribed the words 'Here lies poor Bill Adams, he was shot with a Colt Revolver, and of such is the Kingdom of Heaven,' leaving one to wonder whether the realms above are inhabited by men, or pistols—or hopefully a happy combination of both.

When their lives depended on it, men and women depended on their Colt revolver. In the movie *The Shootist*, John Wayne explains to a young boy that to survive a gunfight is not so much a matter of speed and accuracy as it is a matter of being 'willing.' And when men had to rely upon their 'willingness,' they found their Colts to be equally as willing and reliable.

Other Great Revolvers

In the years after the Civil War, the nation was expanding westward, the South was rebuilding, and the overall tenor of the times was one of flux and change, expansion and competition. In this atmosphere, a greater and greater need arose for personal protection. The National Arms Company had begun to produce small, single shot Deringer Pistols in the early 1870s. The Colt Company bought out the National Arms Company, and in so doing, inherited the Deringer line of small handguns. While the general public's concept of a Deringer-type pistol is that the weapon is of small caliber, the original Deringers were actually of .41 caliber, and thus packed quite a punch.

The first center fire pistols to appear on the market were all of single action variety. This meant that the hammer had to be cocked, thus revolving the cylinder before the trigger could be pulled. In the later 1870s, Colt introduced its new Double Action Self-Cocking Center Fire Six-Shot Revolver. The revolving of the cylinder into place was no longer dependent on the cocking of the hammer, but was rather now a function of the pulling of the trigger. When the trigger was pulled, the cylinder would almost instantaneously roll into place, and the hammer would miraculously pull itself into a cocked position and immediately would snap forward, firing the cartridge. This meant that all six shots in the cylinder could be fired as rapidly as the trigger could be pulled. Here was advancement indeed! Colt referred to this first double action pistol as the Lightning Model.

However, this first double action revolver did not meet with as much success as might have been anticipated. The number of internal parts required to produce such lightning speed was greatly increased, thus contributing to the overall weight and complexity of the weapon. Many continued to use their far more simple single action 'Peacemakers.'

By the early 1900s, however, the transition from single action to double action weapons was almost complete. An interesting variation on the double action revolver took

W. MASON.

Revolving Fire-Arms.

No. 158,957. Patented Jan. 19, 1875.

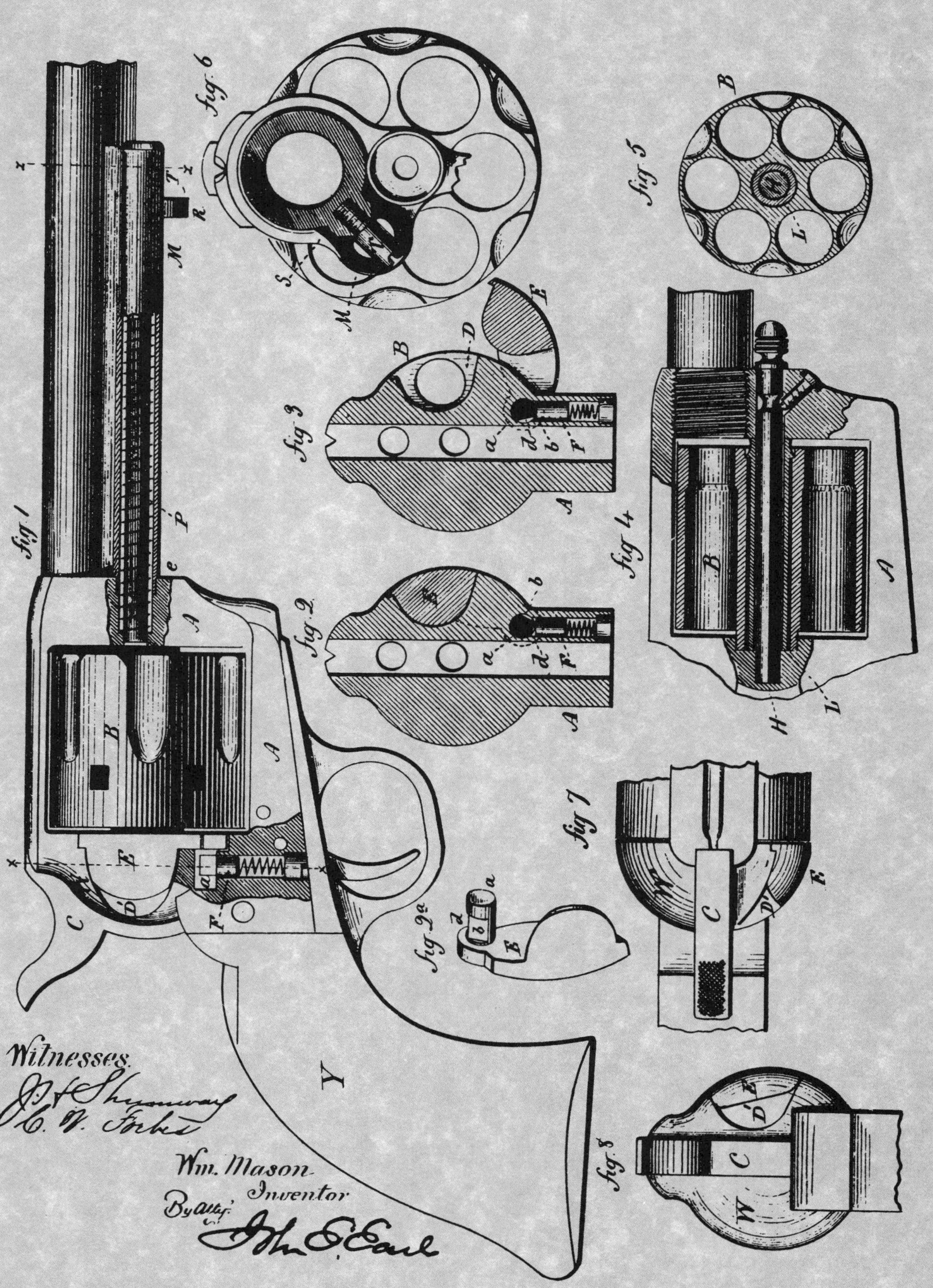

THE GRAPHIC CO. PHOTO-LITH. 39 & 41 PARK PLACE, N.Y.

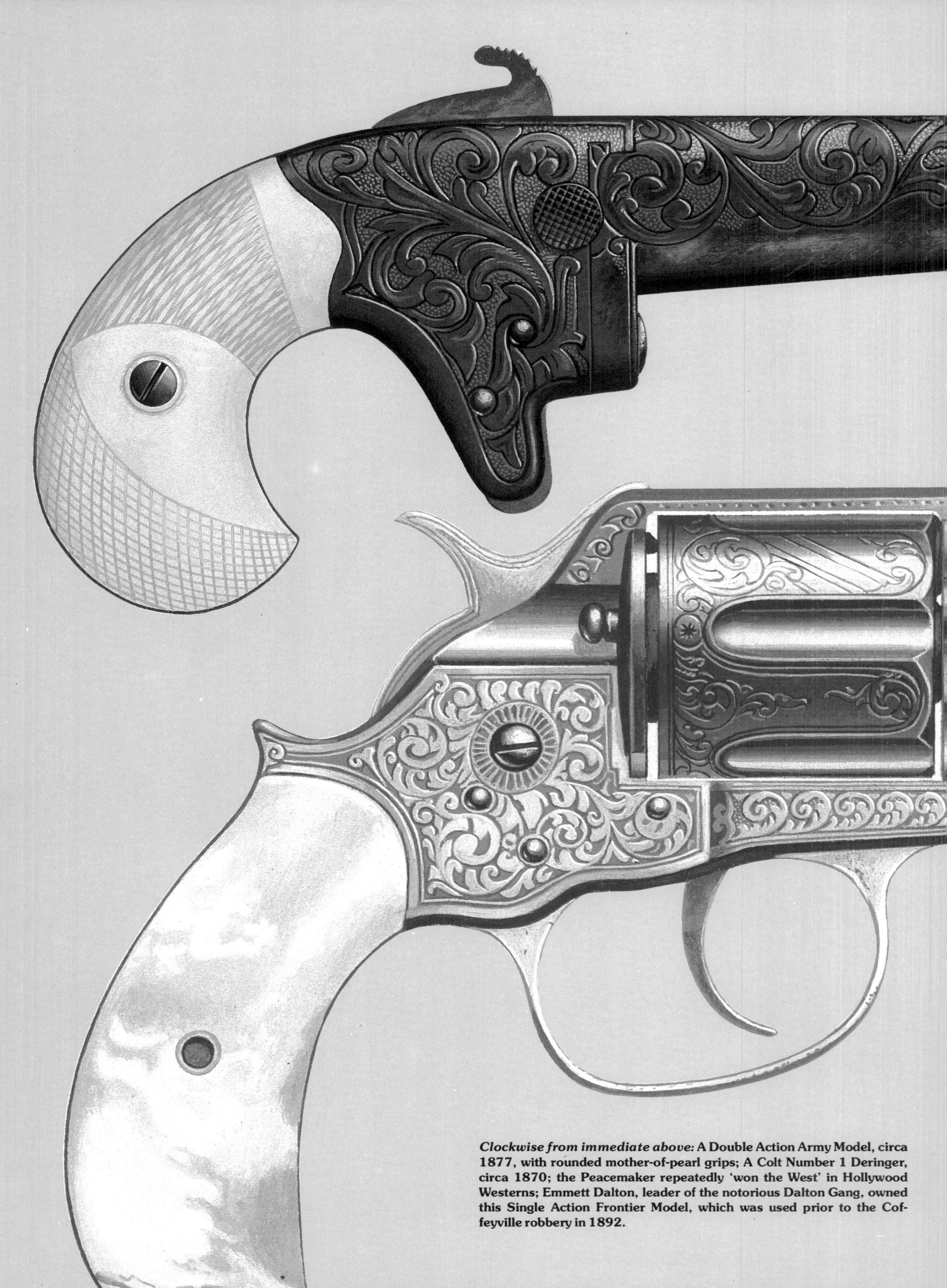

Clockwise from immediate above: A Double Action Army Model, circa 1877, with rounded mother-of-pearl grips; A Colt Number 1 Deringer, circa 1870; the Peacemaker repeatedly 'won the West' in Hollywood Westerns; Emmett Dalton, leader of the notorious Dalton Gang, owned this Single Action Frontier Model, which was used prior to the Coffeyville robbery in 1892.

place in 1902. The government had contracted with Colt to produce some double action army models with wider triggers and enlarged trigger guards. Ostensibly, these weapons were to be used in Alaska, and the customized alterations were such that troops could more easily use the pistols in very severe weather where heavy gloves were required. These pistols originally bound for Alaska were of the .45 caliber variety. At the same time, American troops were engaging foes in the Philippine Islands, half a world away. The standard issue weapon in the Philippines at that time was .38 caliber Double Action Army Pistols. These were found, by experience, not to pack the firepower needed to successfully engage the enemies in deep jungle surroundings. So, in typical Army fashion, the Alaska-customized Colts were sent to the Philippines because of their larger caliber, and proved to be successful weapons. They were known ever after to collectors as Philippine Model Double Action Army Colts.

Colt's Rifles and Shotguns

Colt Firearms is, of course, best known for its production of revolvers and automatic pistols. But it should be noted that the company produced many single shot muskets for the Civil War, and between that time and the early 1900s, produced many different kinds of rifles and shotguns in both single and double-barreled varieties. A General Berdan of the US Army had patented a particular kind of bottlenecked center fire cartridge in the 1860s. The Colt Company built a rifle around this cartridge design known as the Berdan Russian Rifle. In 1870, the Russian Government contracted for the construction of 40,000 of these single shot, breech loading rifles.

In the later 1870s, Colt even produced both hammered and hammerless double-barreled shotguns, but both models were discontinued by 1900.

This business of placing two barrels side by side was, at first, thought to be a profitable idea. In about 1880, Colt produced a .45-70 double-barreled rifle. But the model soon fell into disfavor with the public and was discontinued, probably due to its excessive weight. Winchester had cap-

tured the market in rifles and carbines with their .44-40 caliber weapons. Colt attempted to capitalize on this popularity by bringing out, in 1883, the first Colt repeating rifle using the new cartridge ammunition. It was produced in both the shorter carbine size, as well as the longer rifle size, but only a little over 6000 specimens were produced.

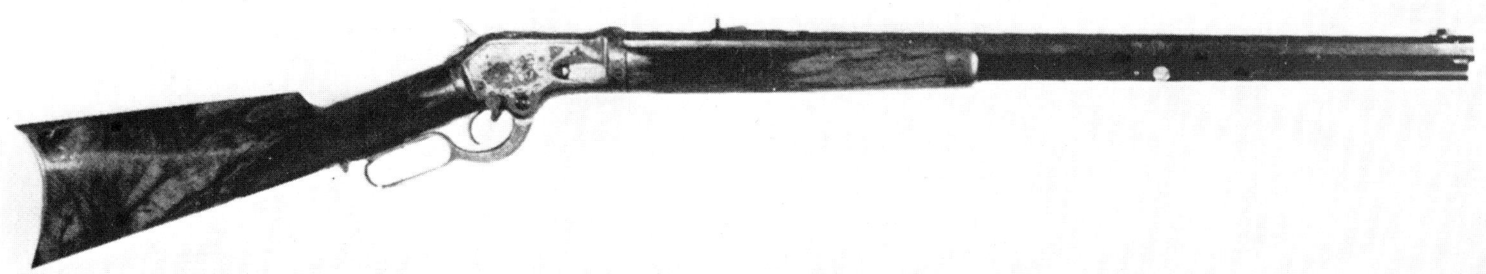

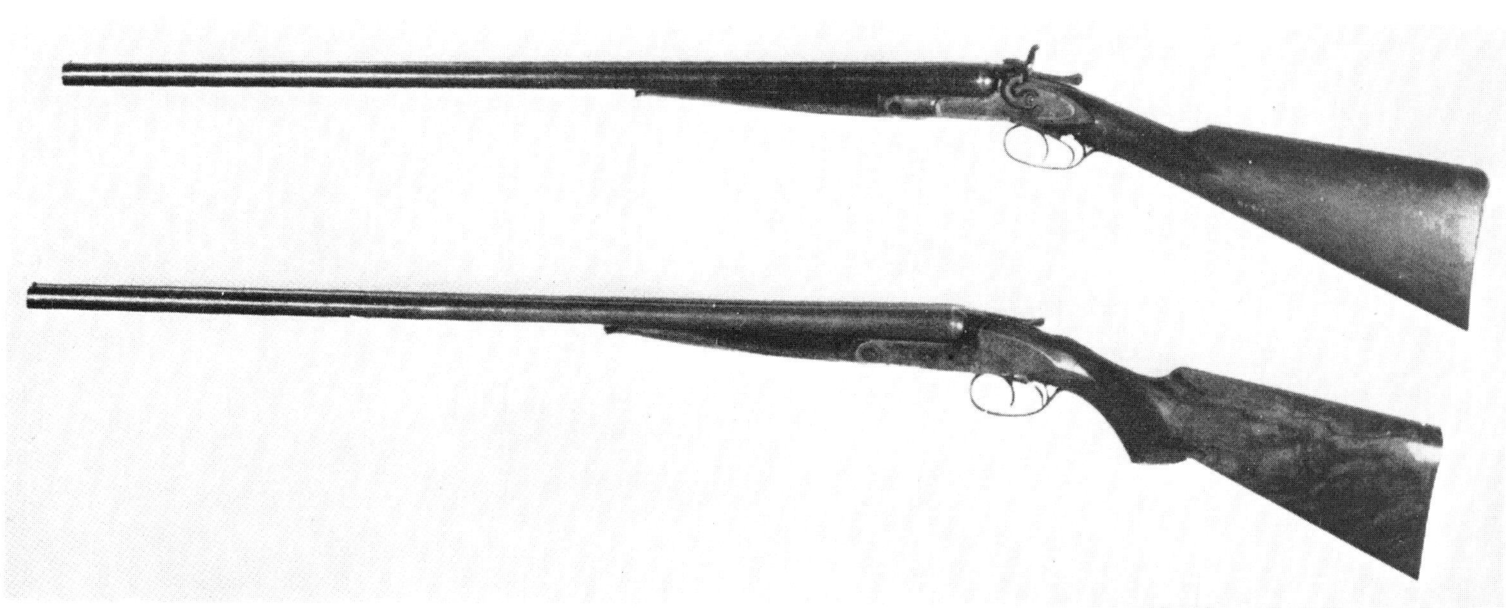

In the mid-1880's, an altogether new type of repeating rifle appeared. It was known as the 'Lightning Magazine Rifle.' It was produced under a Dr Elliot's patents. It incorporated a 'trombone' action, which we know today to be the familiar 'pump' or 'slide action.' The old spent cartridge was ejected from the chamber, and a new one was mechanically inserted into place by the quick sliding action of the hand on a rail mounted parallel to the barrel. This allowed the user of the 'Colt Lightning Pump' to hold the rifle's trigger and work the slide, thus achieving a near-machine gun rate of fire. In some quarters, the Colt Lightning Pump is said to be 'the gun that *should have* won the West.'

But by the early 1900s, profitability was not to be found in the production of sporting arms, but, rather, in the manufacture of the new automatic pistols, rifles and mounted military weapons.

Clockwise from immediately above: **An early ad for Colt's Lightning Pumps; a Lightning Express .44–40 model; a Colt Berdan rifle for the Russian Army; Colt 1855 model revolving sidehammer shotgun (five shots) and rifle (six shots); Colt Phillipine model pistol; Colt's lever action 'Burgess' rifle; and Colt hammer and hammerless shotguns.**

The Evolution Modern Colt

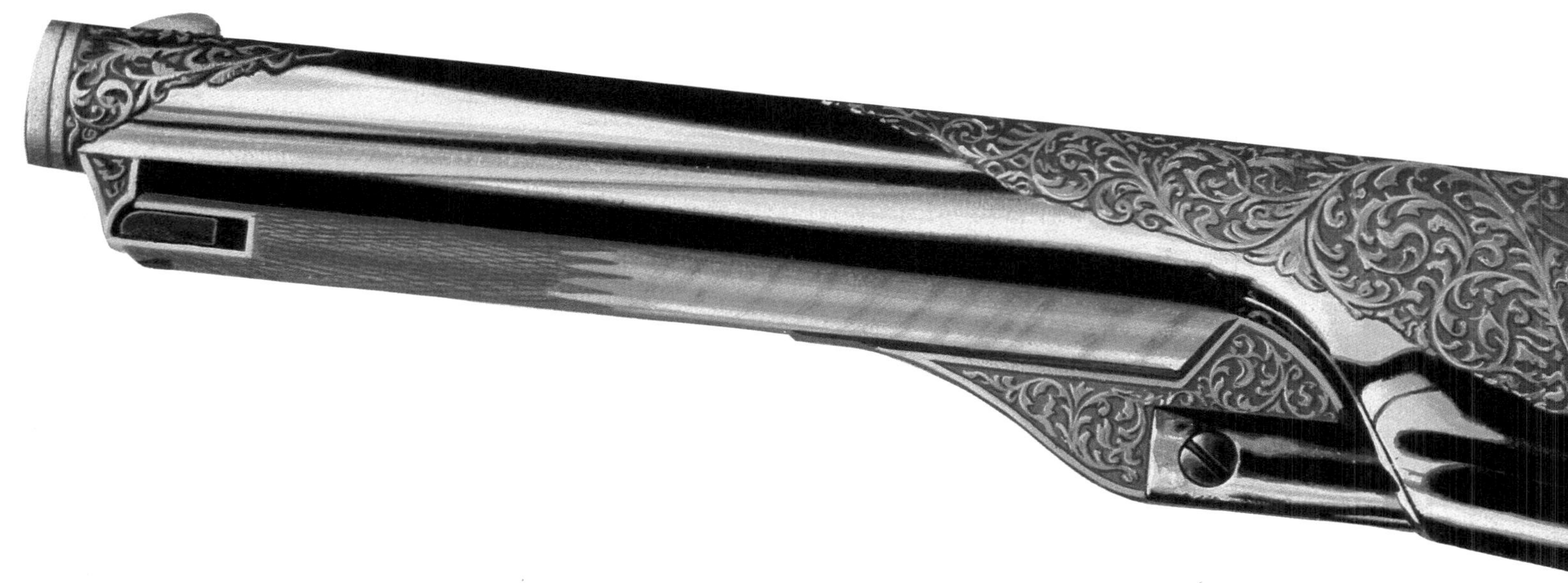

The modern era of Colt revolvers can actually be traced to the early 1890s, when Colt scored a resounding market victory over its competitors by introducing 'swingout' cylinders on its double-action revolvers. Prior to this time, many single and double-action revolvers had to be broken between the breech and the cylinder in order for the cartridges to be loaded. This placed the pistol in an inverted 'V' position in the user's hand. Alternately, many Colt revolvers had a 'reloading notch' offset at the rear of the cylinder. Shells were placed in their chambers by rotating the cylinder until an empty chamber aligned with the reloading notch, at which point the shell was manually loaded into the chamber. The rotating procedure was followed for unloading spent shells, with the exception that, at this point, the 'empties' were pushed out of their chambers with the famous offset ejector rod, which gave the Peacemaker its distinctive head-on appearance. But now the cylinder had only to be released from the overall frame and swung out on hinges in a sideways motion in order to facilitate unloading and loading. Colt was about 10 years ahead of its competitors at Smith and Wesson in this new innovation, and profited immensely by it.

The modern era of Colt Revolvers, at least, began with the Official Police Model, which went by the name of New Navy when it was first introduced in 1889. Variations on this basic model continued in subsequent years. The Pocket Positive, the Police Positive, and the New Service Revolvers are among the most famous of these early truly modern revolvers.

In the 1930s, target shooting became popular to the extent that target type pistols were designed from regular production models. This began a trend that continues to the present day. The features incorporated into a target weapon are usually more advanced than those generally found in common production weapons. In time, these advanced features 'trickle down' into the regular production firearms.

This phenomenon of a shifting awareness that pistols could be used for long range target shooting with great accuracy, and not merely for short range work, and the gradual inclusion of target model features into standard off-the-shelf pistols has laid the foundation for constant improvements in Colt firearms—particularly the revolver series—since the turn of the century.

The history of Colt revolvers from the early 1900s until the mid 1950s is basically a picture of several different models, basically similar to one another, being produced in very large quantities and providing the collectors with an almost insurmountable task of tracing, cataloguing, and documenting this body of firearms. The four standard means of differentiating these different models from one another are noting the size and type of hammer employed, the type of sights, the kind and size of grips, and the barrel and chamber dimensions.

Even employing these methods, the task of documenting different models is sometimes overwhelming. As an ex-

of the Revolver

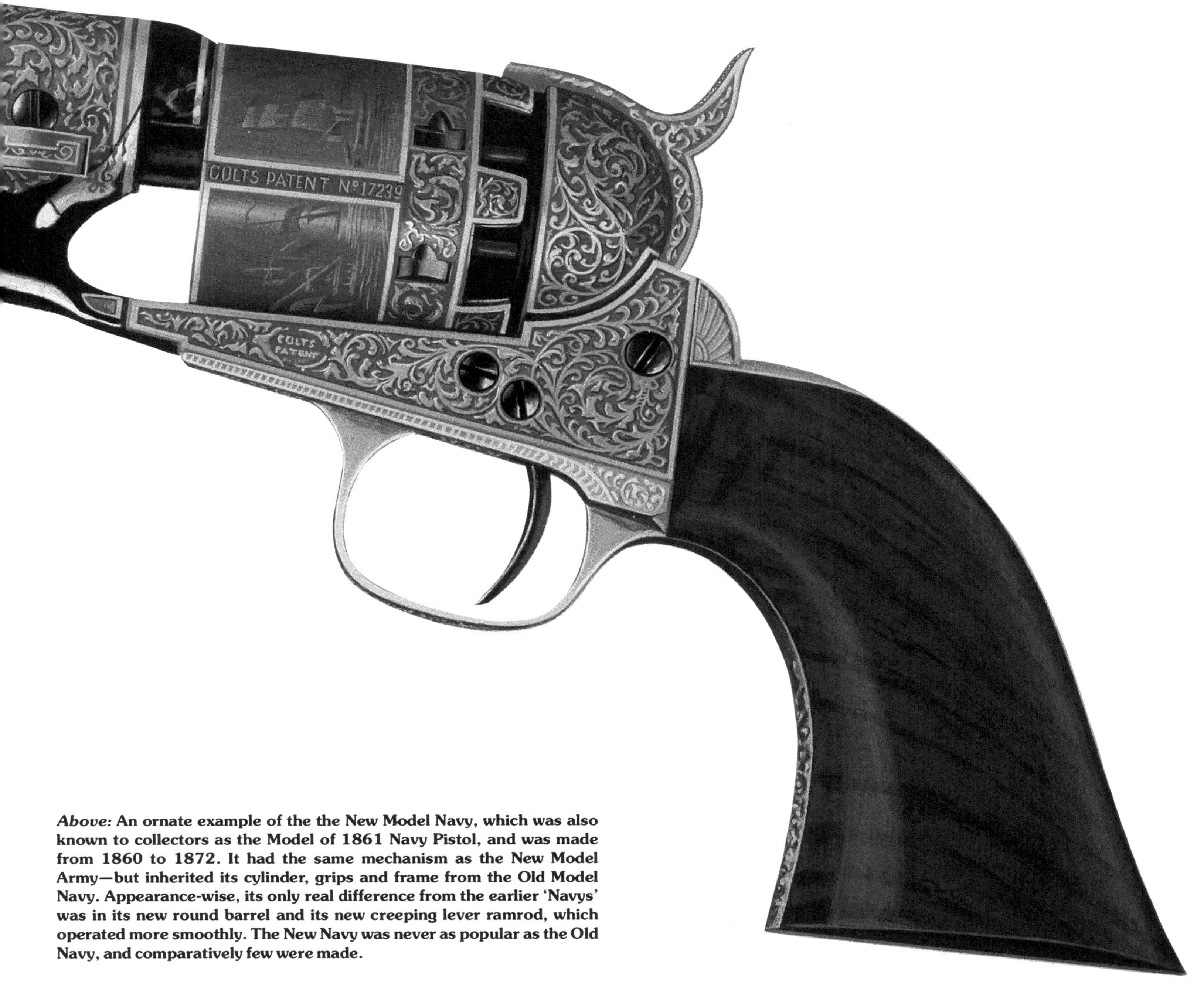

Above: An ornate example of the the New Model Navy, which was also known to collectors as the Model of 1861 Navy Pistol, and was made from 1860 to 1872. It had the same mechanism as the New Model Army—but inherited its cylinder, grips and frame from the Old Model Navy. Appearance-wise, its only real difference from the earlier 'Navys' was in its new round barrel and its new creeping lever ramrod, which operated more smoothly. The New Navy was never as popular as the Old Navy, and comparatively few were made.

ample, the New Service Double Action Revolvers were introduced in 1898. Between then and the middle 1940s, when the model was discontinued, over 350,000 were produced. There were so many serial number runs employed during this time that a collector could specialize in only these New Service Pistols, and probably never be able to acquire a representative specimen of each of the conformations.

It was also during this era that the modern 'snubnosed' pistols gained prominence. In 1837 Samuel Colt had introduced what collectors have since referred to as a 'Baby Paterson Pistol.' It had not proven to be very popular since concealable weapons at that period of American history were not of great importance. But in the 1920s, two snubnosed pistols were introduced into the market place—both of .38 caliber and varying only in barrel lengths. These were the 'Detective Special' and the 'Banker's Special.' Over 400,000 of these particular models have been produced to the present time.

In 1955, the Colt Python came into the hands of eager enthusiasts. This pistol was, and continues to be, the top of Colt's line of revolvers. It is, in the minds of many, without doubt the finest production revolver money can buy. It is available with various grips, triggers, hammers and sights. It is the 'issue weapon' of many police departments around the country. The Python has been the recipient of a veritable galaxy of awards and world records. Every Python, even though produced on an assembly-line basis, both is hand

fitted and features the hand honing of all interior and exterior contact points. Pythons feature ventilated ribs, for greater heat dispersion in the barrel, a fast cocking wide spur hammer and a fully shrouded ejecter rod. The .357 Magnum Python uses both .357 Magnum and .38 Special amunition. The Python features a 'locking hand' which secures the cylinder firmly into place when firing—no other double action revolver of any make incorporates this particular feature.

Up until the Python's introduction, the Officers Model .38 Special had been the premier Colt revolver. It had won numerous NRA center-fire pistol championships. These Officers Models were generally customized privately by

***Counterclockwise from immediate below:* A 1933 advertisement for the Colt Bankers' Special; two pages from the 1940 Colt catalogue—the New Service Revolver was claimed to be able to stop 'any animal on the American Continent'; the Colt Python, Colt's top of the line revolver, was made available to the general public in 1955.**

Colt Officers' Model Target Revolver

WITH NEW HEAVY BARREL

Six Shots
Double Action
Swing-out Cylinder

CALIBERS:
.32 Police Positive. (Using in the same Arm .32 Police Positive (New Police), .32 S. & W. short, .32 S. & W. long, Regular and Sharp Shoulder).
.38 Special. (Using in the same Arm .38 Short Colt; .38 Long Colt; .38 Colt Special; .38 Colt Special Hi-Speed; .38 S. & W. Special (full and mid-range loads); .38 S. & W. Special High Velocity; .38-44 S. & W. Special).
.22 Long Rifle (See page 23).

General Specifications

LENGTHS OF BARREL: 4, 4½, 5, 6 or 7½ inches. Heavy Type Barrel, 6 inch only, on .38 Caliber Model. .32 Caliber 6 inch heavy barrel only.
LENGTH OVER ALL: With 6-inch barrel, 11¼ inches.
STOCKS: Checked Walnut.
TRIGGER: Checked.
ACTION: Super-smooth, hand finished.
SIGHTS: "Patridge" (regularly furnished) or "Bead". Both non-reflecting; Front Sight adjustable for elevation; Rear Sight adjustable for windage.
FINISH: Full Blued; top of frame stippled to eliminate reflection and glare.
BACK STRAP: Checked.
WEIGHT: With 6-inch barrel, (.38 Caliber) 34 ounces; with 6 inch Heavy barrel, 36 ounces.

Heavy Barrel
The Officers' Model is available with Heavy Barrel, (6 inch length only) the same as furnished in the Shooting Master. Adds 2 ounces to weight of gun. Specify Standard or Heavy Barrel in ordering. Both same price.

This Revolver is made from forgings of finest selected steels, every part carefully tested, finished and assembled by hand by skilled workmen. Each Arm is target tested by firing 12 to 18 rounds of various standard loaded ammunition, and a signed 5 shot test target is included with every Arm.
The Colt Officers' Model well merits its reputation as the most popular .38 Caliber Target Revolver produced, maintaining Colt's Standard of Quality, Durability, Accuracy and Safety — the latter being assured by the COLT POSITIVE LOCK — an especially desirable feature for range shooting. Where there are target shooters, there you will find the Colt Officers' Model Target Revolver.

Special Features

Target shooters who like a little extra weight in the muzzle end of their target revolvers will find the Officers' Model with heavy (Shooting Master) barrel, exactly to their liking. Two ounces have been added to the weight of the gun, all in the barrel. It steadies the arm for rapid fire shooting, and balances the gun beautifully. Either standard or heavy type barrels can be furnished. The .22 Caliber model, which weighs 38 ounces with its present barrel, will not be furnished with a heavier barrel. Both .22 and .38 Caliber models handle the High Speed cartridges, the .22 Caliber model being furnished with the Colt Embedded Head Cylinder to eliminate possibility of split cartridge-heads.

SPECIAL

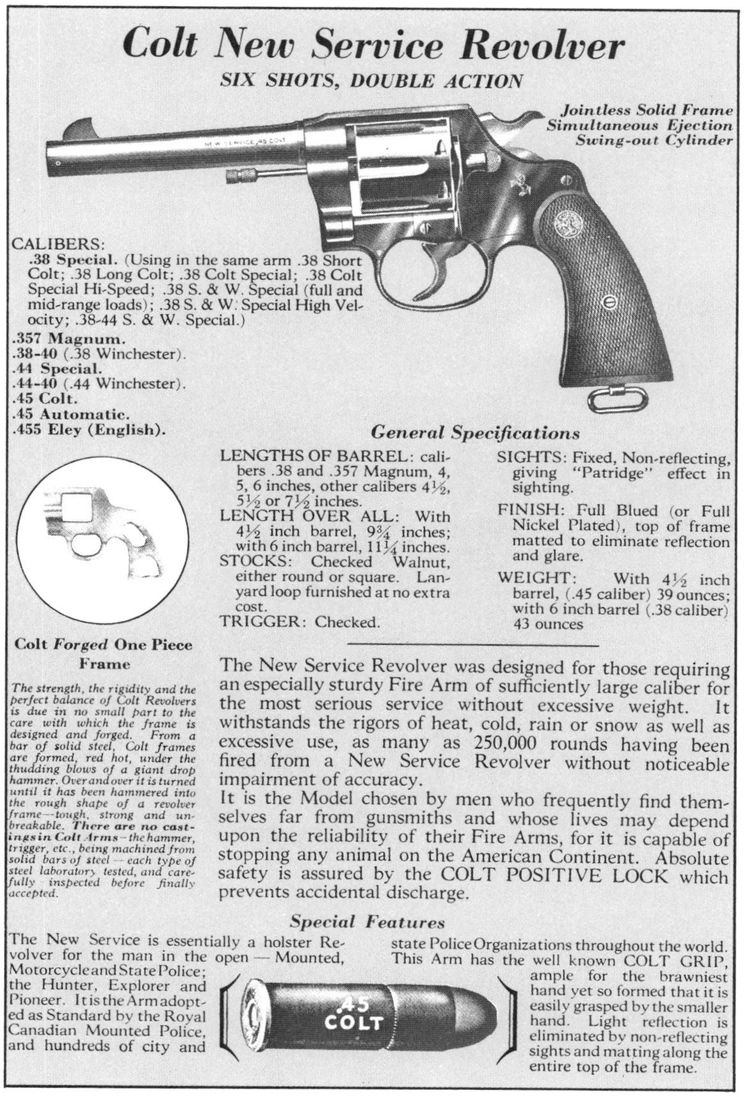

Colt New Service Revolver

SIX SHOTS, DOUBLE ACTION

Jointless Solid Frame
Simultaneous Ejection
Swing-out Cylinder

CALIBERS:
.38 Special. (Using in the same arm .38 Short Colt; .38 Long Colt; .38 Colt Special; .38 Colt Special Hi-Speed; .38 S. & W. Special (full and mid-range loads); .38 S. & W. Special High Velocity; .38-44 S. & W. Special.)
.357 Magnum.
.38-40 (.38 Winchester).
.44 Special.
.44-40 (.44 Winchester).
.45 Colt.
.45 Automatic.
.455 Eley (English).

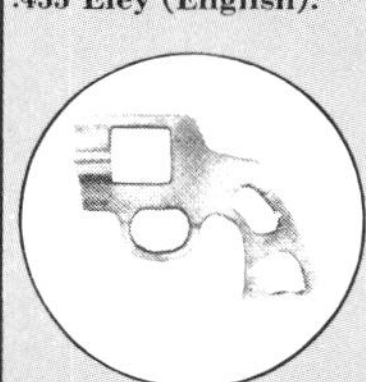

Colt *Forged* One Piece Frame

The strength, the rigidity and the perfect balance of Colt Revolvers is due in no small part to the care with which the frame is designed and forged. From a bar of solid steel, Colt frames are formed, red hot, under the thudding blows of a giant drop hammer. Over and over it is turned until it has been hammered into the rough shape of a revolver frame—tough, strong and unbreakable. ***There are no castings in Colt Arms*** *– the hammer, trigger, etc., being machined from solid bars of steel — each type of steel laboratory tested, and carefully inspected before finally accepted.*

General Specifications

LENGTHS OF BARREL: calibers .38 and .357 Magnum, 4, 5, 6 inches, other calibers 4½, 5½ or 7½ inches.
LENGTH OVER ALL: With 4½ inch barrel, 9¾ inches; with 6 inch barrel, 11¼ inches.
STOCKS: Checked Walnut, either round or square. Lanyard loop furnished at no extra cost.
TRIGGER: Checked.

SIGHTS: Fixed, Non-reflecting, giving "Patridge" effect in sighting.
FINISH: Full Blued (or Full Nickel Plated), top of frame matted to eliminate reflection and glare.
WEIGHT: With 4½ inch barrel, (.45 caliber) 39 ounces; with 6 inch barrel (.38 caliber) 43 ounces

The New Service Revolver was designed for those requiring an especially sturdy Fire Arm of sufficiently large caliber for the most serious service without excessive weight. It withstands the rigors of heat, cold, rain or snow as well as excessive use, as many as 250,000 rounds having been fired from a New Service Revolver without noticeable impairment of accuracy.

It is the Model chosen by men who frequently find themselves far from gunsmiths and whose lives may depend upon the reliability of their Fire Arms, for it is capable of stopping any animal on the American Continent. Absolute safety is assured by the COLT POSITIVE LOCK which prevents accidental discharge.

Special Features

The New Service is essentially a holster Revolver for the man in the open — Mounted, Motorcycle and State Police; the Hunter, Explorer and Pioneer. It is the Arm adopted as Standard by the Royal Canadian Mounted Police, and hundreds of city and state Police Organizations throughout the world. This Arm has the well known COLT GRIP, ample for the brawniest hand yet so formed that it is easily grasped by the smaller hand. Light reflection is eliminated by non-reflecting sights and matting along the entire top of the frame.

knowledgeable gunsmiths. Ventilated ribs and underslung barrel weights had been added to increase their accuracy.

Even though Smith and Wesson had produced .357 Magnums before the Python appeared, it was Colt's idea to produce a *deluxe* Magnum pistol. The name 'Python' actually came from a contest among Colt factory employees, and not from anyone in the advertising division of the company. Stainless steel Pythons would appear later, but the original Python featured a special finish referred to as Colt Royal Blue. This Royal Blue finish is still the most popular today. It is a concession to the fact that the appearance of beautiful, deep blueing is not a function of the blueing procedure itself as much as it is a process of the polishing—which takes place after the blueing. Royal Blue is achieved by the use of extremely fine grit sand papers and crocus cloths that are used on the exterior parts. The Python took the market by storm, even though it was somewhat more expensive than its competitors, the Smith and Wesson Highway Patrolman, the Combat Magnum, and the Smith and Wesson .357 Magnum. Not only was the finish unexpectedly beautiful, but the internal action of the Python was equally as

COLT
PYTHON .357

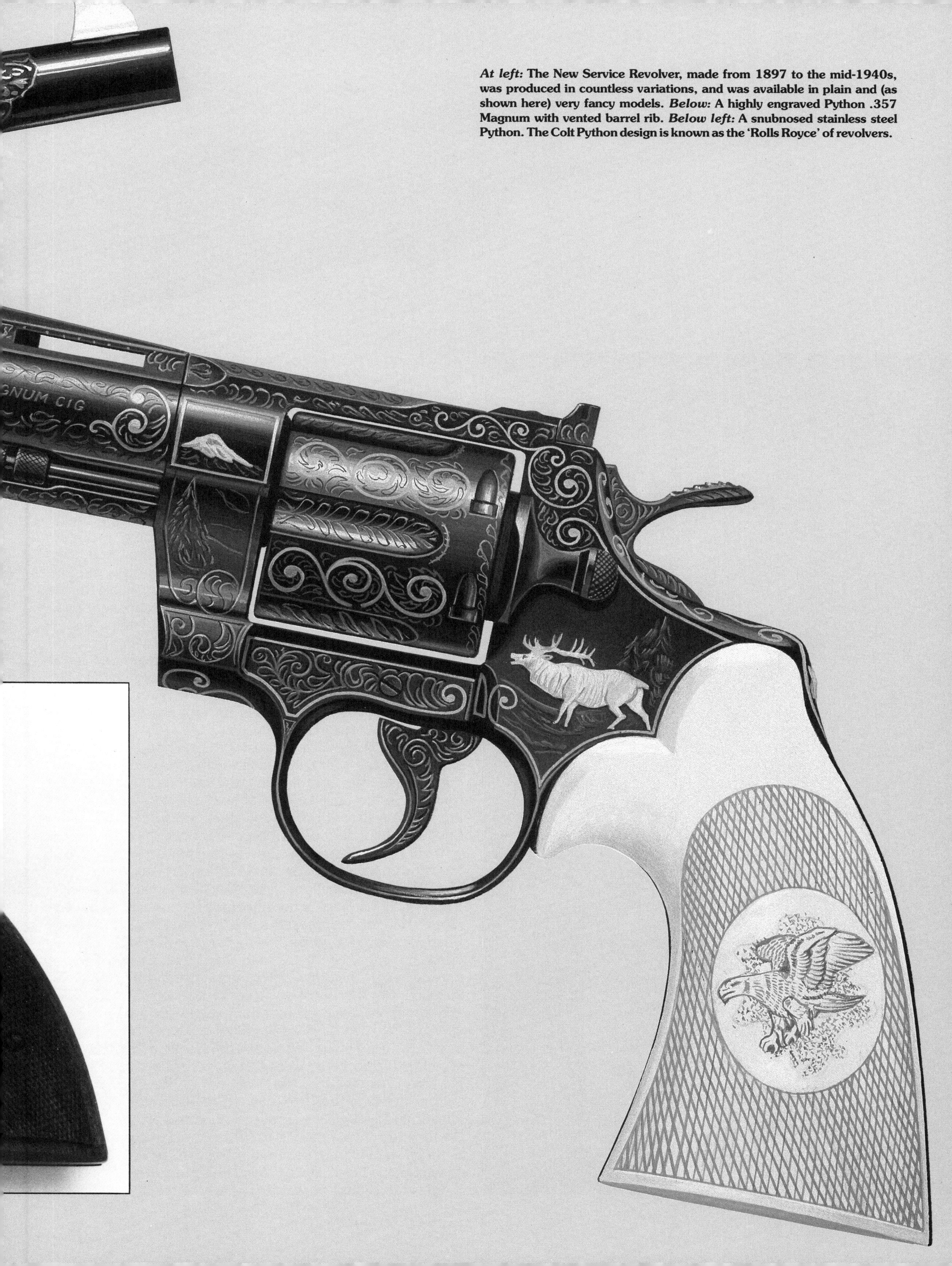

At left: The New Service Revolver, made from 1897 to the mid-1940s, was produced in countless variations, and was available in plain and (as shown here) very fancy models. *Below:* A highly engraved Python .357 Magnum with vented barrel rib. *Below left:* A snubnosed stainless steel Python. The Colt Python design is known as the 'Rolls Royce' of revolvers.

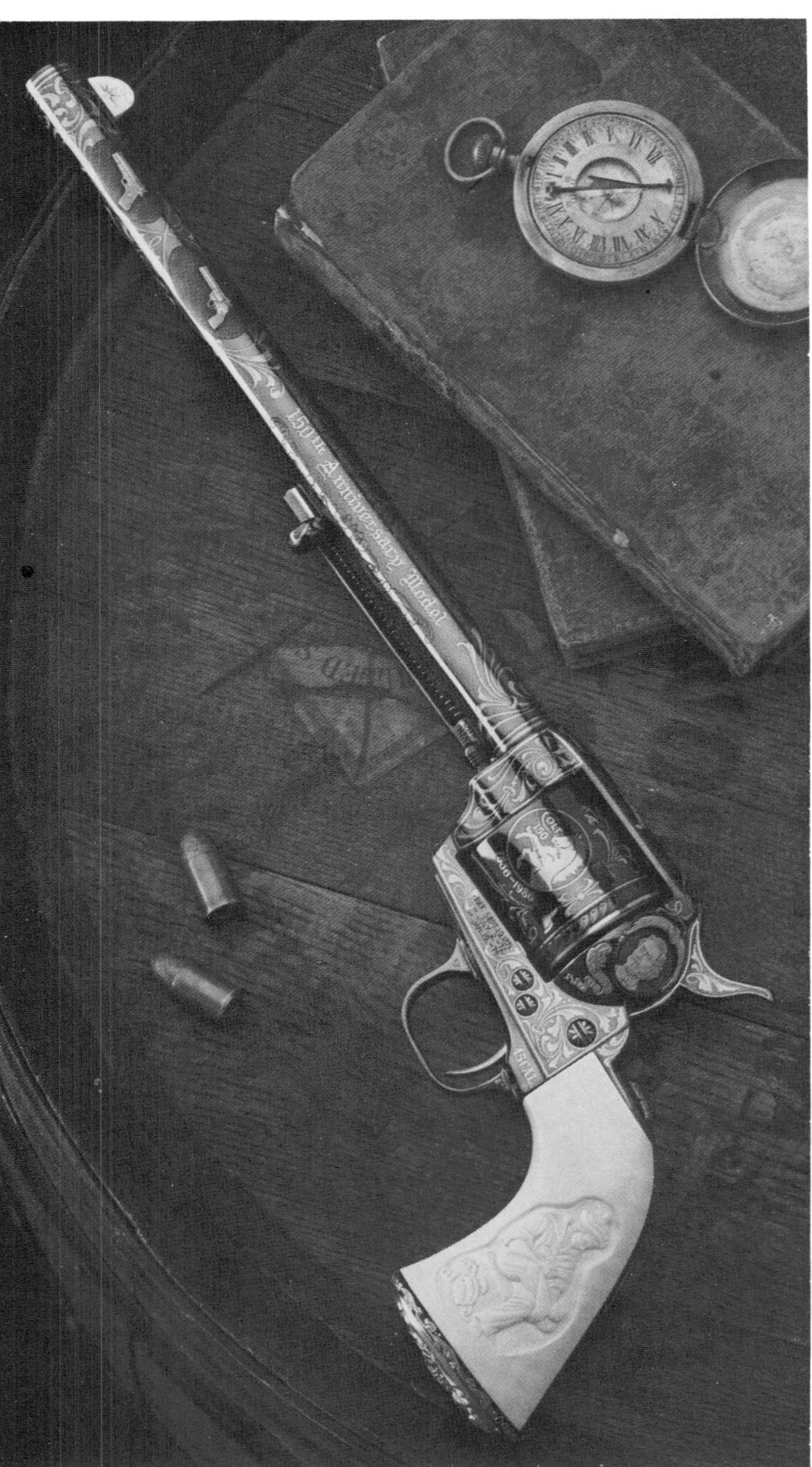

astounding. The internal parts of these first Pythons were hand polished, producing an action that was silky smooth and seemingly friction-free.

The Python is a rather heavy pistol, weighing 34 ounces. The weight is distributed more toward the muzzle, thus offering target shooters a balance which results in more accurate sighting of the target in rapid-fire situations. This increased weight also contributes to the Python's ability to absorb recoil even when using large caliber cartridges.

The Python reigns as the 'Rolls Royce' of revolvers and as the hand gun most enthusiasts dream of owning. From the initial machining of its forged frame to its final polishing, through many hours of hand work, the Python is the pinnacle of American gunsmithing today. It is available in four barrel lengths—2.5 inch, four inch, six inch and eight inch. The finishes are Royal Blue with walnut grips, stainless steel and heavily polished Ultimate stainless steel with black Colt neoprene grips. All Pythons are equipped with red insert front sights and adjustable white outline rear sights. The Python can be considered an investment in a precision double action revolver, and it is currently backed by an unprecedented 10 year limited warranty.

Today, Colt firearms carries on a tradition of innovation stretching back 150 years. Even with sophisticated techniques such as laser bore sighting, the bedrock of Colt's quality still rests in the skilled hands of its craftsmen, working with the timeless strength of forged steel. In 1986, the Custom Shop at Colt undertook its most expansive project in the 150 years of Colt's existence. The 150th Anniversary Exhibition Model, a .45 caliber Colt single action one-of-a-kind Army Model Pistol was auctioned at a black tie affair in Las Vegas in 1986. This revolver is heavily embellished with gold inlaid motifs, border bands, and scroll work. It is appropriately serial numbered 'Colt-150.' The genuine hand carved ivory grips are enhanced by a solid gold butt cap depicting a patriotic eagle, with a small diamond being the eagle's eye. Included with this pistol was a custom designed, solid ebony and cocobolo-wood presentation case with an ivory hand carved Colt medallion insert. Even a leather bound scrapbook, detailing its 1986 Exhibition Tour and a museum quality exhibition case were included. Starting price for the bidding was set at $150,000.00!

Fortunately, one did not have to be invited to the black tie auction in Las Vegas in order to purchase an 'Anniversary Commemorative Colt Pistol.' An 'Anniversary Engraving Sampler' was offered to all Colt customers who purchased a currently-produced blue or nickel finished gun in 1986. This 'Engraving Sampler' was a unique concept, in that the

Collectors' items—Although Colt's 150th Anniversary Exhibition Gun *(opposite)* had a $150,000 auction price tag, a humble old Single Action Army Frontier Model similar to the one *below* (but with serial number 1) fetched $242,000 at an auction at Christie's East in 1981.

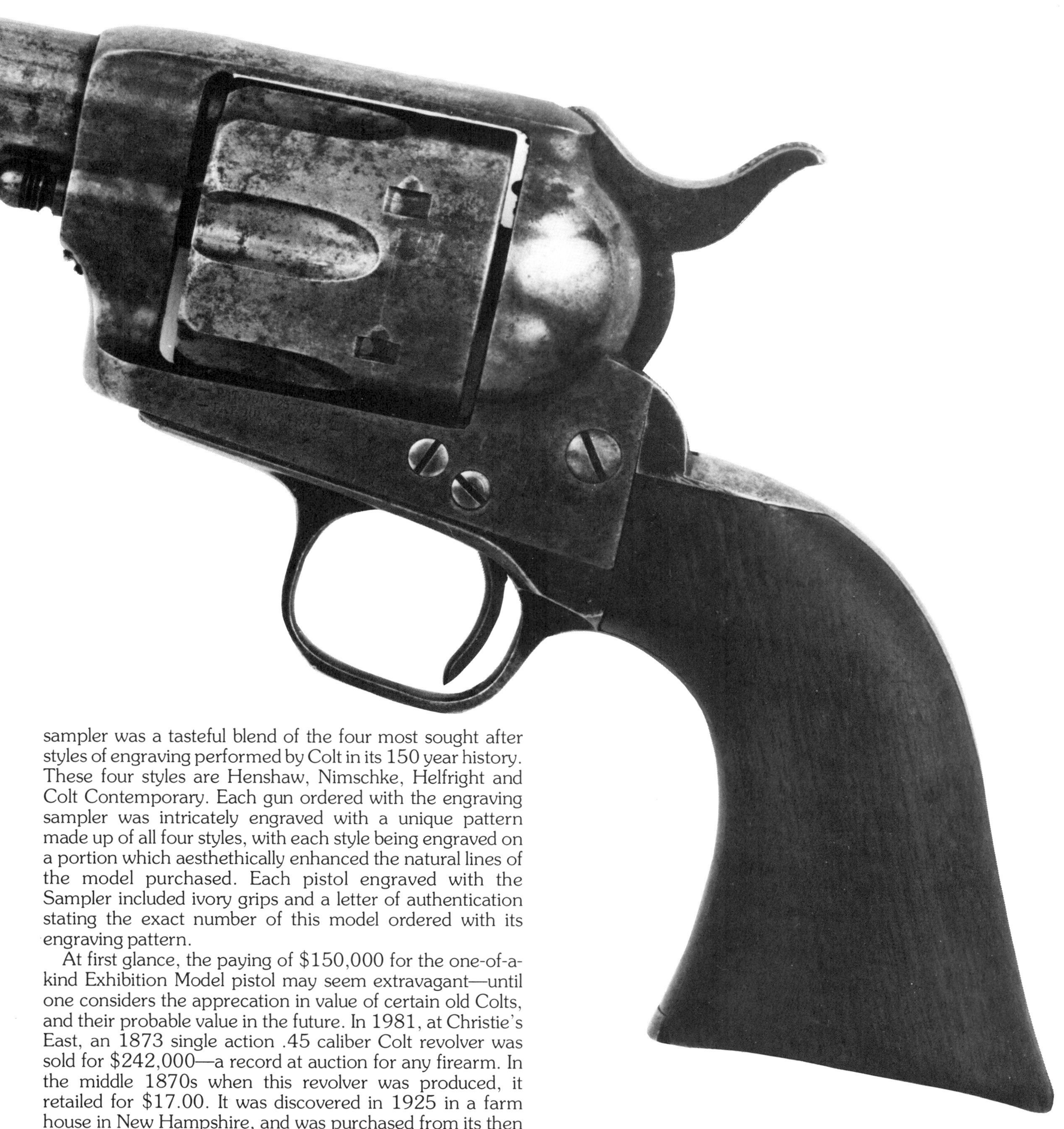

sampler was a tasteful blend of the four most sought after styles of engraving performed by Colt in its 150 year history. These four styles are Henshaw, Nimschke, Helfright and Colt Contemporary. Each gun ordered with the engraving sampler was intricately engraved with a unique pattern made up of all four styles, with each style being engraved on a portion which aesthethically enhanced the natural lines of the model purchased. Each pistol engraved with the Sampler included ivory grips and a letter of authentication stating the exact number of this model ordered with its engraving pattern.

At first glance, the paying of $150,000 for the one-of-a-kind Exhibition Model pistol may seem extravagant—until one considers the apprecation in value of certain old Colts, and their probable value in the future. In 1981, at Christie's East, an 1873 single action .45 caliber Colt revolver was sold for $242,000—a record at auction for any firearm. In the middle 1870s when this revolver was produced, it retailed for $17.00. It was discovered in 1925 in a farm house in New Hampshire, and was purchased from its then owner for $4.00. It is staggering to imagine what a Colt Anniversary Pistol may be worth 20 or 30 years from now.

Automatic and

Colt Automatic Pistol
POCKET MODEL, HAMMERLESS
CALIBERS .32 AND .380
For the Following Cartridges:
Caliber .32 Rimless, Smokeless.
Caliber .380 Rimless, Smokeless.
CAPACITY OF MAGAZINE.
Cal. .32, 8 shots.
Cal. .380, 7 shots.
LENGTH OF BARREL. 3¾ inches.
FINISH. Full Blued or Full Nickel Plated. Checked Walnut Stocks.
WEIGHT. 23 ounces.
LENGTH OVER ALL. 6¾ inches.
This popular Colt Automatic Pistol is a light, well balanced arm; powerful, yet convenient as a personal weapon. Hammerless with a solid breech construction there are no projecting parts, making the arm convenient and dependable for protection. Accidental discharge is made impossible by the Slide Lock as well as the COLT AUTOMATIC GRIP SAFETY. The Slide Lock is thrown on or off by the thumb and not only disconnects the trigger from the operating mechanism but serves as an indicator, showing whether the arm is cocked or not. THE GRIP SAFETY is entirely automatic in operation, locking the mechanism until the pistol is firmly grasped at time of discharge. These two positive safeties absolutely prevent any accidental discharge. In addition, the Caliber .32 (from No. 468097) and Caliber .380 (from No. 92894) are now equipped with a Safety Disconnector similar to that incorporated in the Caliber .25 as described under that model.

At top: **A neat and handy Pocket Model Colt Hammerless Automatic Pistol, circa 1940, and *(above)* a 1926 ad for same from Colt's catalogue.**

Pistols Rifles

The invention in the latter 19th century of a new type of gunpowder caused a revolution in ballistics circles. This new powder burned much more efficiently than did black powder. You could pack more punch into a smaller cartridge, and all sorts of interesting things could be done with larger cartridges. Firearms had to be manufactured with more stress capacity to handle this hot new stuff, and therefore arms technology *really* started to take off. This new powder, incidentally, didn't stink the place up so much as did black powder, and it was called 'smokeless powder.'

The principle of any automatic weapon is very simple. When the initial cartridge is fired, the natural recoil from the explosion is used to do two things—namely, eject the spent shell and reload a new cartridge into the chamber. A 'fully' automatic weapon is one in which only one trigger depression is needed to set off a simultaneous series of shots. The designation 'semi-automatic' is used to differentiate the action from a 'fully-automatic' one in that a 'semi-automatic' will fire, eject and reload only one cartridge per trigger pull. A further differentiation between automatic-type weapons can be made on the basis of whether the energy used to eject the spent cartridge and reload the new one is derived from recoil, or whether it is derived from utilizing expanded gases which are released during the detonation. Most automatic weapons are of the recoil type operation, whereas some larger machine guns are operated on the gas expansion basis.

John M Browning, of Browning Arms fame, is credited with originating the idea of firearms that could load and unload themselves. In experiments in the early 1890s, Browning noticed that when a gun was fired, not only did the projectile fly out of the end of the barrel, but gases were released out that same opening. Browning noticed this phenomenon when he observed that as a gun is fired in close proximity to tall grasses or weeds, the explosion violently disturbs the adjacent foilage. He concluded that there must be some way of utilizing that otherwise wasted energy.

The principle of rapid fire guns, at least, was nothing new to Colt Firearms. From the middle 1860's, Colt had produced the famous Gatling gun. These 10-barreled guns could fire 600 rounds per minute of .45-70 cartridges. But of course, their power to fire at such rates was entirely dependent on the human muscle of the operater. Still, the Gatling guns were the best of the rapid-fire weapons for many years.

John Browning concluded that since Colt was at the forefront of rapid-fire weapons, they would be most interested in his ideas and patents. He was right. In 1895 the Colt/Browning Automatic Gun was brought to the marketplace. This tripod-mounted, air-cooled and belt fed machine gun could fire 400 shots per minute. It was used to great advantage in both the Spanish-American War and in World War I. But, obviously, these kinds of weapons were not intended for the general public. This, however, did not preclude the general populace from wanting handguns that operated on this same automatic principle.

Colt became the first American manufacturer of an automatic pistol in 1900. The Model 1900 was a .38 caliber weapon weighing 37 ounces, having a barrel six inches in length and a magazine capacity of seven shots. These seven shots were of a new straight-cased .38 caliber rimless cartridge that was capable of a velocity of 1260 feet per second—a truly astounding speed for the times. The Model 1900, even though it was manufactured by Colt, was in fact based on the 1897 patents of the Browning Arms Company. On 20 April, 1897, Browning filed a series of four patents which were to remain the benchmarks of automatic

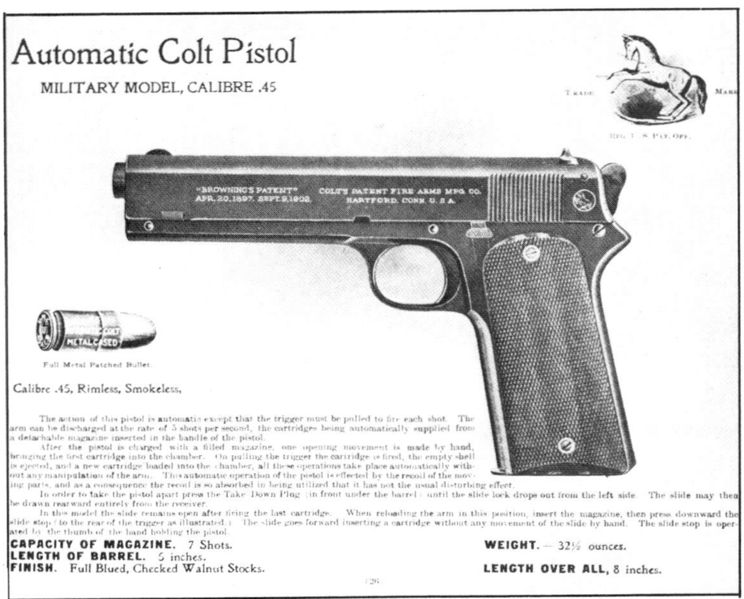

Automatic Colt Pistol

MILITARY MODEL, CALIBRE .45

Full Metal Patched Bullet.

Calibre .45, Rimless, Smokeless,

The action of this pistol is automatic except that the trigger must be pulled to fire each shot. The arm can be discharged at the rate of 5 shots per second, the cartridges being automatically supplied from a detachable magazine inserted in the handle of the pistol.

After the pistol is charged with a filled magazine, one opening movement is made by hand, bringing the first cartridge into the chamber. On pulling the trigger the cartridge is fired, the empty shell is ejected, and a new cartridge loaded into the chamber, all these operations take place automatically without any manipulation of the arm. This automatic operation of the pistol is effected by the recoil of the moving parts, and as a consequence the recoil is so absorbed in being utilized that it has not the usual disturbing effect.

In order to take the pistol apart press the Take Down Plug (in front under the barrel) until the slide lock drops out from the left side. The slide may then be drawn rearward entirely from the receiver.

In this model the slide remains open after firing the last cartridge. When reloading the arm in this position, insert the magazine, then press downward the slide stop (to the rear of the trigger as illustrated.) The slide goes forward inserting a cartridge without any movement of the slide by hand. The slide stop is operated by the thumb of the hand holding the pistol.

CAPACITY OF MAGAZINE. 7 Shots.
LENGTH OF BARREL. 5 inches.
FINISH. Full Blued, Checked Walnut Stocks.

WEIGHT. — 32½ ounces.
LENGTH OVER ALL, 8 inches.

(26)

pistols into the 1940s. Indeed, the date of 'April 20' was so important that it was imprinted onto each weapon for many years. Many innovations followed with succeeding models coming out in 1902, 1903, 1905, 1907, 1908 and 1911. This time frame, from 1897 until 1911, is accounted by many to be one of the most innovative and creative periods in Colt's history. This combination of Browning's originality and Colt's precision manufacturing set down the basics for automatic weapons to this day.

Calibrations for Colt automatic pistols are much simpler than for Colt revolvers. Only .22 rimfire, .25, .32, .380, .38, .38 Special, Super .38, 9mm, .45 and .455 have been produced.

An interesting abbreviation appears beside certain calibers of automatic weapons. This abbreviation, 'ACP,' stands for Automatic Colt Pistol. The 'ACP' shell casings differ from other cartridges in that there is a reduced indenture of rim at the rear of the cartridge. This is to enable the cartridge to be quickly loaded and ejected by the automatic weapon's mechanism.

It is interesting, and somewhat humorous, to note that when the Model 1900 came out, the first people to shoot it had a difficult time getting used to the automatic character of the weapon. Generally, when a person began shooting an automatic pistol, because he did not know what to expect out of this device, his shots were generally far from accurate (to say the least). The Great Unknown was very disquieting to those first automatic shooters. But one quickly caught on to the tremendous advantages of an automatically loading and ejecting weapon. The 'trigger finger' had been rediscovered as a vital part of the human anatomy!

When the first prototype of the Model 1900 was submitted to the US Ordnance Board, their tests proved somewhat inconclusive. The Board stated that, 'This type of pistol has not yet reached such a stage as to justify its adoption in the place of the revolver for Service use.' Reliability was the key question involved in whether the government should abandon the revolver as the military's sidearm weapon of issue and go with the new automatic.

In time, however, the Colt automatic was adopted by the military. Of the 4.7 million Colt automatic pistols that have been produced, the US Government has been the purchaser of at least three million of them. While many different models of automatic pistols have been, and still are, produced by Colt with numberless variations among these different basic styles, the model 1911 and the 1911 A-l still rank as the company's best selling automatics.

Currently, the Gold Cup National Match Mark IV Series 80 is the top of the line Colt automatic pistol. It has a barrel length of five inches and weighs 39 ounces. The Gold Cup is

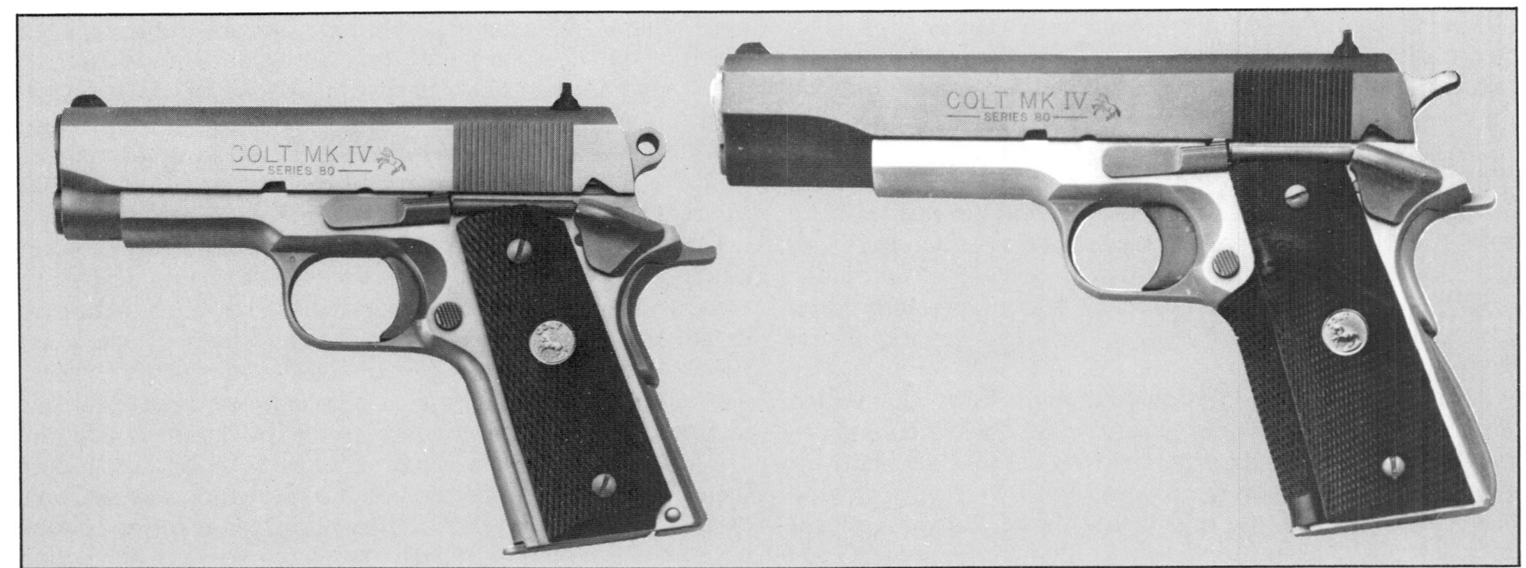

the premier American center-fire automatic target pistol, with its accurizor barrel that tightens shot groupings by as much as 90 percent. This Colt automatic is acclaimed as one of the world's finest match scorers. It features a wide grooved trigger with an adjustable top, serrated target hammer, and flat back-strap mainspring housing. It also features the revolutionary Firing Pin Safety, which allows the bearer to carry a round in the chamber in the 'cocked and locked' position—which enables the shooter to deliver consistent trigger pull on all shots, rather than the heavy first pull of a double action.

From its historic beginnings, Colt has continued to improve its line of automatic pistols to include, *clockwise from left:* the Stainless Steel Gold Cup National Match; the MK IV Combat Elite Series 80; the MK IV Stainless Steel Officer's model; MK IV Series 80 Gold Cup National Match; and a 1905 advertisement which states that the Automatic Colt Pistol is 'automatic except that the trigger must be pulled to fire each shot.'

PATENTED APR 20 1897. SEPT. 9 1902.
DEC 19 1905. FEB 14. 1911. AUG. 19. 1913

Above: A fancy civilian version of the Colt 1911 Model Automatic Pistol, which has for years been the standard sidearm for the US military. *At left:* The terror of latter-19th century military encounters was the manually-cranked Gatling Gun, which Colt produced to the design specs of the Gun's inventor, Dr Gatling (far left).

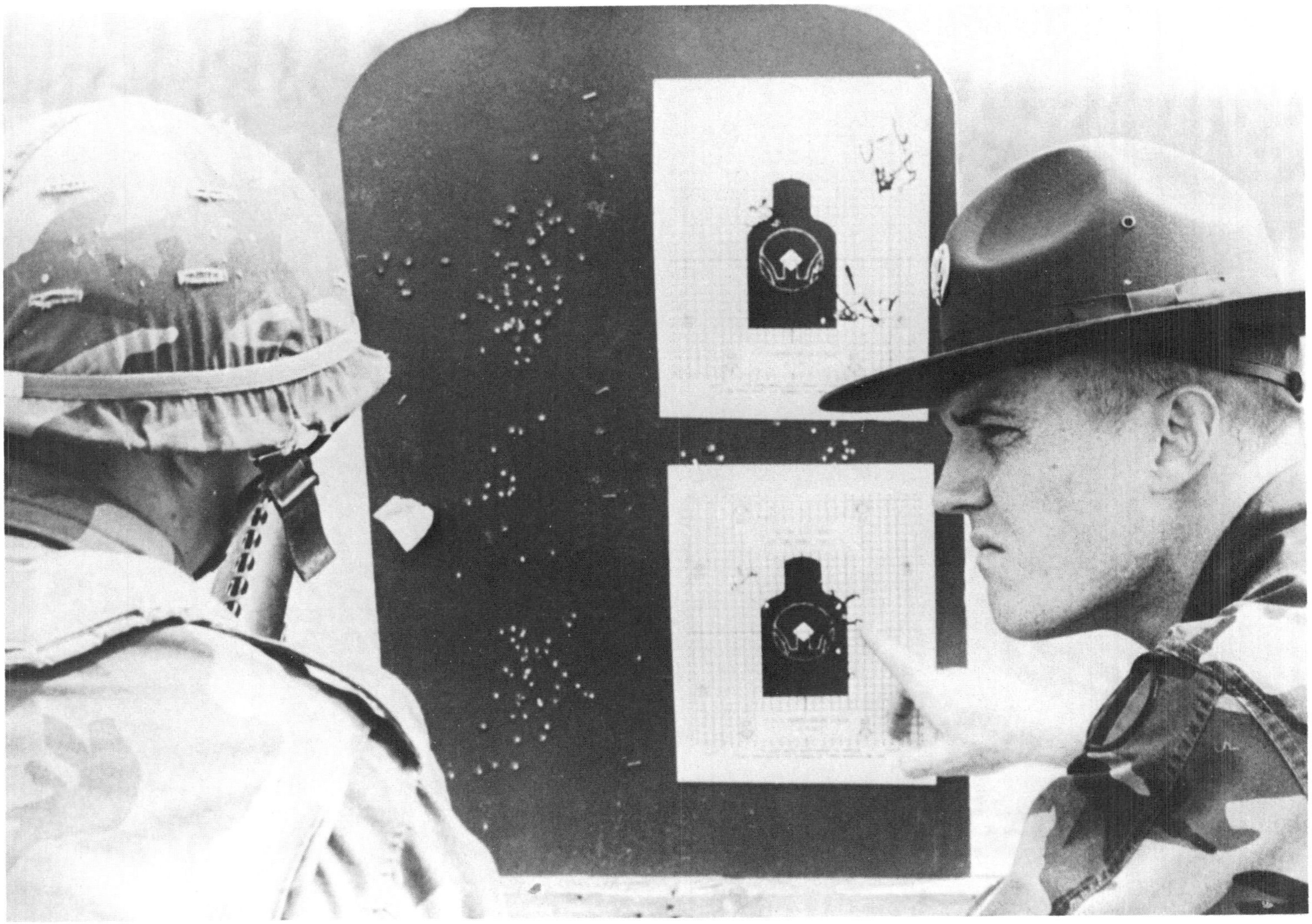

***Above:* This drill sergeant shows a soldier how to 'zero in' his M16 for better accuracy. *Below:* An AR-15 A2 Sporter II—one variant of its military cousin, the M16. *Opposite:* US Marines and their M16s, on guard at the terrorist-bombed US embassy in Beirut, in the early 1980s.**

Undoubtedly, the most famous of Colt's automatic weapons are the AR-15 and M16 Automatic and semi-automatic rifles. The caliber of these rifles is .223.

In the early 1960s, Colt acquired the rights to produce and market the AR-15 rifle from the Armalite Division of the Fairchild Engine and Airplane Corporation. Colt Arms had the connections necessary to place this rifle, in large quantities, into the hands of both law enforcement and government officials. The US Army began contracting for these rifles in 1963, partly at the request of General Curtis LeMay. As US involvement in Southeast Asia increased and the war in Vietnam began to unfold in ever greater ferocity, more and more AR-15 rifles were ordered by the government. So many AR-15s were put on the front lines that the weapon was adopted as the replacement for the then-standard M14 rifle. Because the AR-15 replaced the M14, its name was changed to the M16. Today, however, the designation AR-15 is still to be found on the civilian version of this military weapon known as the Sporter.

As the M16 found its way into different environments of hostilities, variations were produced in accordance with need. Today the M16 is available in carbine, heavy assault rifle, submachine gun, light machine gun and survival pack models, and even is equipable as a grenade launcher.

Colt Industries spent literally millions of dollars in plant production equipment for the M16 as well as a new test range complex built in West Hartford, Connecticut. Even foreign plants are licensed by Colt for the protection of the M16 in Korea, the Philippines and Indonesia. Few products of any type or variety produced by any manufacturer have enjoyed the ready recognizability of the Colt-made M16 Automatic Rifle.

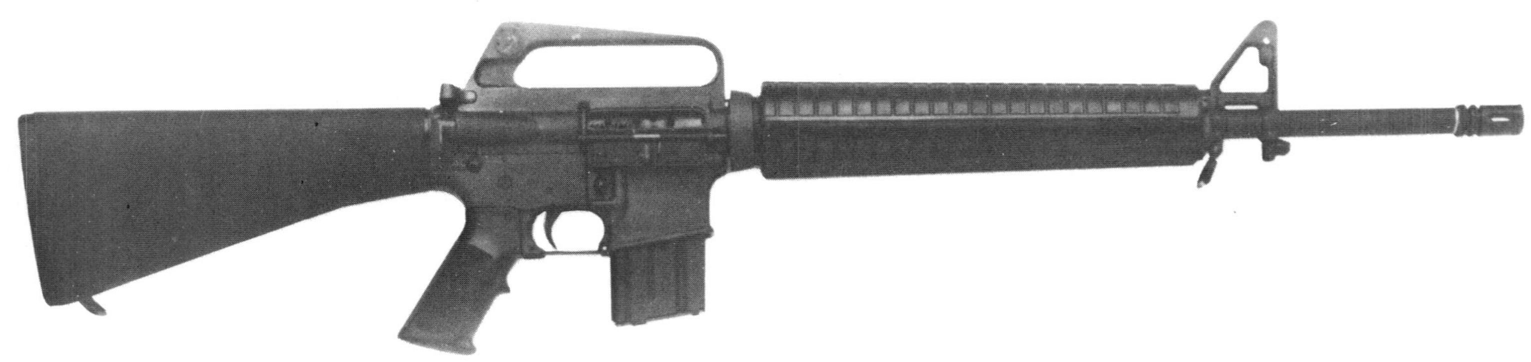

Craftsmanship Twentieth

The following account, in the form of a tour of Colt's Hartford, Connecticut, factory, was originally published in 1940 in *A Century of Achievement*. The insights contained here are as good a view into the heart and soul of Colt's commitment to craftsmanship as they are into the factory itself. Though this selection may be from another time, the spirit and commitment are still alive and well, such that it could have been written yesterday.

Because raw steel is such a vital factor in the production of a firearm, the greatest care is given to its selection. Before a machine even touches it, the steel itself must conform to the most rigid of specifications.

Steel mills have on their order files the specifications which Colt metallurgists have laid down as the kind of steel they want. In a New Jersey mill, a quantity of steel is being made. It is given a heat number. Billet samples of this raw steel before it is rolled into shape are sent to the Colt factory for approval. To the laboratory it goes. It is given a Brinell test to determine its hardness, which is another way to say whether it is machineable or not. Too soft, it will tear; too hard, it will ruin the cutters.

The billet samples are submitted to chemical and physical inspections. They are acid etched to reveal defects. They are fractured three separate times: first for grain size; then hardened, tested for hardness and fractured a second time as hard; and as a final test to determine their toughness, they are drawn and then fractured as drawn.

If the billet samples are OK'd, the steel mill is notified that the particular heat number has been approved and to proceed to roll the steel into the specific pieces and sizes on order by Colt. Steel men often say that the Colt people are 'almost unreasonable' in their demands.

From the steel sheds and laboratory, the forging shop is our first stop. A blank is heated red hot. With long tongs it is placed on the forge. A giant weight, released by the mechanism of a foot pedal, forges the steel between the two dies into shape. Literally it pounds the molecules of steel into the desired shape. I watch the frame of my revolver drop forged into a jointless solid piece. It's a terrifying sight, this drop forging. The drop die weighs between 500 and 600 pounds. It drops six feet exerting a force of over 2000 pounds. Sparks fly 10 or 12 feet when the die hits the steel. The terrific heat and the earsplitting noise conjures an image in the mind of some gigantic monster giving full vent to its fury. Across the alley from the forge shop a battery of punch presses trim off the excess metal resulting from the forging. The trimmed pieces are next placed into a steel drum and shot blasted to smooth their surfaces. We open one of the drums where a number of pistol receivers are tumbling. The term 'shot blasting' is well named. Under heavy air pressure a veritable shower of fine steel shot is blasted over all the surfaces, removing all scale.

Down go the forgings to the grinding room. Each individual receiver or frame is set on a heavily magnetized chuck to hold it tightly in place, and is forced between seg-

in the Century

At top: This heavily-engraved New Model Navy Pistol is evidence of the long Colt tradition of craftsmanly care. *Above:* The Colt armory on the banks of the Connecticut River, in the 1940s.

Colt firearms, such as the Peacekeeper at *above right*, must meet exacting standards. *Immediate right:* Arms expert JH Fitzgerald. *Above:* Colt's Forge Shop—where frames were swaged from solid bars of steel—in the 1940s. *Below:* Heat treating ovens. *Opposite:* Profiling machines.

mented wheels of carborundum whirling in opposite directions. Each piece is ground to the proper thickness, and the top and bottom surfaces are made smooth.

Masters Of Steel

There is probably no more important department in the whole Colt plant than the heat treating room. In this room filled with roaring furnaces, the varying conditions of steel are mastered. Steel is made softer, harder, drawn to fine temper and in a number of ways processed to fit the exact needs that will be demanded of it. For instance, the drop forgings must be normalized before they can be machined. Normalizing the forging prepares the steel so that it can be machined with maximum efficiency—not too soft, not too hard. When all the machining processes are completed, the same pieces are hardened again. Take the slide of an automatic, as an example: it takes a terrible beating. It has to travel back and forth on the receiver every time a shot is fired. Innumerable machine operations are necessary—60 to be exact. After each slide has gone through its machining routine, it is sent back again to the heat treating room to be heat treated. The same thing holds true of barrels and cylinders. Triggers, cranes, latches, sears, firing pins, hammers and etc are also hardened in the heat treating room.

Built Like a Watch But Strong Enough To Stand Dynamite

The number of different and separate machine operations that go into the production of a Colt revolver or automatic pistol is simply staggering.

In the factory office of Mr Harry Stevens, the assistant works manager, is a library of several volumes, each containing a thorough description of all the various and sundry factory operations. There is a whole volume, for instance, describing in detail in sucessive numerical order each and every operation on a Colt Officers' Model Target Revolver. Another covers the 'S' Model which you and I know as the Woodsman .22 Long Rifle Automatic Pistol—incidentally, as sweet a little .22 as ever felt the squeeze of a hand. But let me stick to my story.

In every foreman's office are duplicates of these master factory control books, each foreman having that part which comes under his jurisdiction. Operation Number 86, for example, in the manufacture of a Government Model .45 receiver is to 'hand finish recoil spring hold, slideways, magazine opening and mainspring housing cuts.'

Believe it or not, there are some 1400 separate operations in making a Colt revolver. There are about 1200 separate operations in manufacturing a Colt automatic pistol.

Obviously it would be impossible to attempt to describe any real portion of them. Even if I tried, you would soon get

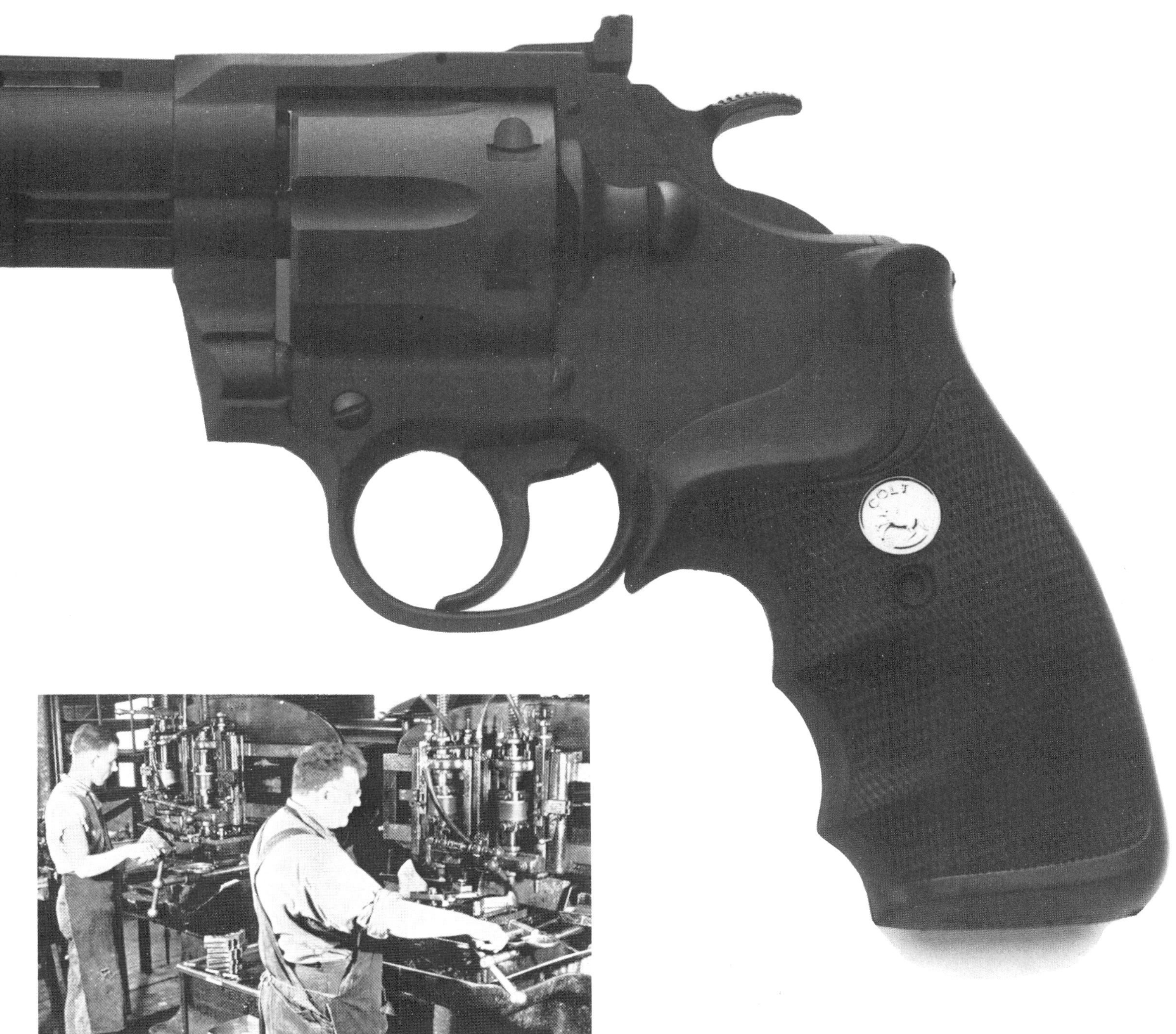

lost in a maze of technical detail. And so would I. The most I can do is to describe a few important operations such as rifling the barrel, drilling the cylinders, filing, fitting, assembling, testing, finishing, blueing... major operations that call for departments of their own.

'Fitz' guides me to one of the big machine rooms. Revolvers and automatics are not made on the same machines. The machine operations on a revolver are in charge of Timothy Trant; the machine operations of an automatic are under the supervision of Britthold Magnusson. We toss a coin to see which we'll go through. Heads it is—Trant wins.

In geometrical arrangement, hundreds of machines are spaced in this great room. Huge batteries of them stretch in rows from one side of the room to the other. Machines are grouped so that, as one operation is complete, the machine to do the following operation is right at hand. Rough and finish milling machines, for example, are side by side. It's really a beautiful sight to watch these hundreds of machines going full blast.

One is immediately aware that careful planning preceded this wonderfully efficient system. Yet such is the history of all progressive manufacturing. You or I go into a plant for the first time. What we see—the efficient layout of machinery, the efficient transportation of power to run those machines, provision made for retooling the machines—are the results of years of planning, of painstaking research, of training and experience. It is so easy and so human to accept all of it with one casual glance without stopping to realize the brains and the energy that were its conception and development.

A frame—drop forged, shot blasted, normalized and ground—comes up to the South Armory, third floor. Immediately, before a single operation is begun, each frame is carefully inspected. Thirty of them are placed on a rack. From then on, each rack goes through as a unit of production.

The first machine operation on a revolver frame is to sidemill it. Next, an especially designed machine shaves out the opening in the frame where the cylinder will eventually

Above: **One of Colt's fine new Diamondback revolvers.** ***At left:*** **A Strategic Air Command airman, his M16 ready, guards a B-1B bomber at Offutt AFB.** ***Below:*** **A master craftsman hand filing a revolver frame.** ***Below right:*** **The first step in producing a perfect barrel.**

go. This is a rough operation, and the opening is next broached to finish size. A broach is a long bar of steel with a series of teeth to form cutting edges. Broaches used in the Colt factory for cutting cylinder or magazine openings will run anywhere from 30 inches to 72 inches long, each cutting tooth being larger than the one preceding and taking off so much metal per tooth, approximately .005 to .0075 of an inch. Sometimes they do 50 pairs of receivers of frames and break. Normally a broach will do a 1000 pairs before wearing out. Edges, of course, must constantly be honed and kept in the sharpest condition.

After broaching, the second side is first rough milled, then finish milled as was the first side. The frame next goes to a profiling machine. A profiling machine is to steel what a shaper is to wood-working. The cutting tool follows a pattern, milling away the metal to form the shapes desired. It is an interesting operation to watch, for one quickly sees the dropforged blank take shape. Drilling the crane hole is next. After drilling, the hole is reamed and counterbored. The operation is a fussy one, the gauge allowing a tolerance of only .001 of an inch. The barrel hole is next drilled, rough and finish reamed, counterbored, threaded and counterbored again. The frame is placed in a drill chuck again and screw and pin holes are bored. The hammer slot is cut.

The trigger hole is cut. A large hole is then cut on the side of the frame... a chunk is literally taken out. There's a lot of work to do on a revolver frame that's beneath the surface (really, inside the frame)... milling that must be done to make room for the working parts that, when the revolver is complete, are hidden underneath the side plate.

More profiling, more contour cutting... profiling for hammer and trigger, profiling inside stocks, profiling for bolt clearance, profiling the trigger guard. More drilling... firing pin hole, recess for recoil plate. And so it goes—through the 145 separate machine operations that go to make a revolver frame.

'Go' and 'No go'—that's what the gauges read. And believe me, mister, that's just what they mean. The operations must stay within these limitations or else. 'No go' means just that... a fast trip to the scrap pile. Split a hair six times, and you have some idea of the tolerances allowed in certain operations... limitations that permit a difference of only .0005 of an inch. Of course not all tolerances are as exacting as this. Some allow .001 of an inch, some .002, a few as high as .003 of an inch. That's pretty accurate, too. Remember that many parts go into a firearm, which is a

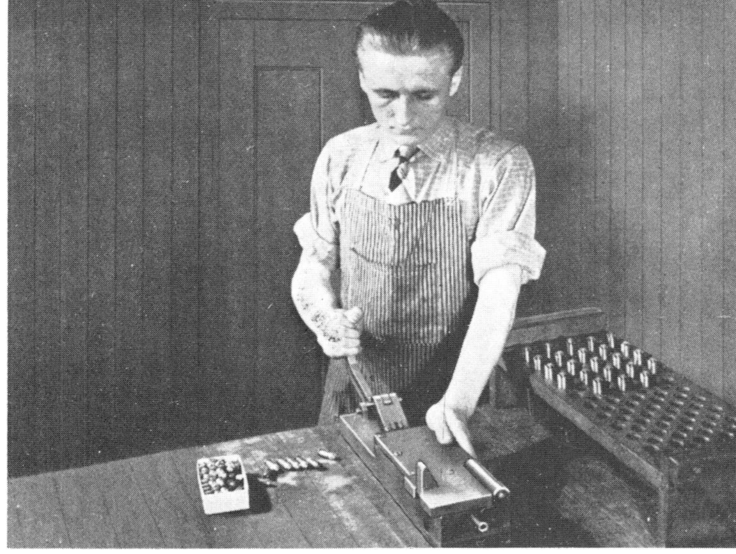

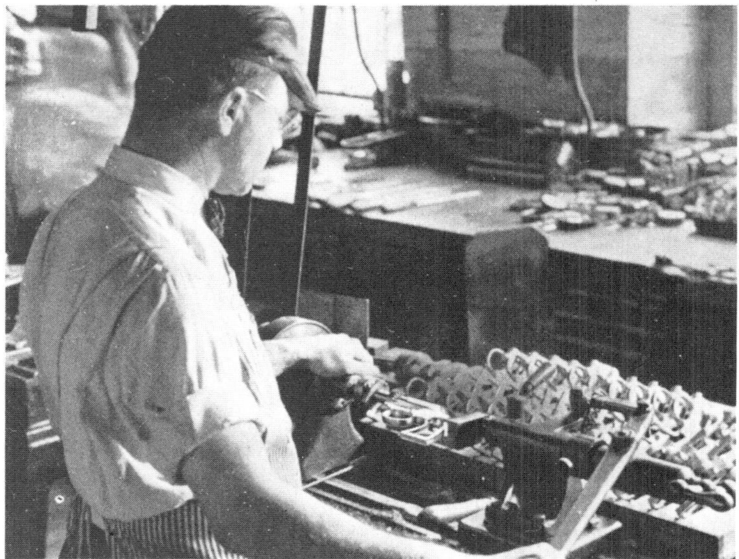

mechanism that you hold in your hand in which the problem of accuracy and precision is quite different that in building a large, heavy machine. Gauges are kept exact by frequent inspections and renewals. On the inspection bench alone, I counted 26 separate and different gauges. Yes, gauges play a leading role in the manufacture of Colt revolvers and automatics. They are the control instruments of production.

Some of the machinery at Colt is very ingenious. There is the regular run of lathes, shapers, drilling machines and etc, but scattered among the conventional machinery are a great many original machines, invented, designed and built in the Colt factory... machines that have no duplicates anywhere in the world. I saw a number of veteran machines that were built many, many years ago still in operation doing their work with efficiency and dispatch.

If you would see an interesting sight, stand on the threshold of one of the huge machine floors in a wing of the Colt factory. There you will see hundreds of machines nestled closely side by side as far as your eye can see. Noisy, yes—but a thrilling sight.

The Magic Touch Of Hands

Hand filing is a very important step in the manufacture of a Colt firearm. On a slide and receiver of an automatic pistol some 40 separate hand filing operations are necessary. On

one operation alone I saw 12 different files used, varying in coarseness from one to four. Files of all kinds littered the benches. Many of them looked alike to me, but each had its purpose and each was used for that purpose. The bench jigs that have been designed to hold the various pieces to be filed are very ingenious.

Fitting a slide to a receiver so that it travels easily, yet has no side play, requires filing skill. If a slide rubs a mite, the high spot is filed down. The slide must work freely without shaking. Filing, as with every operation, is inspected and checked. Handfitted slides and receivers are matched and given serial numbers. In the inspection, the serial numbers are checked to be sure that the receiver and slide have the same numbers.

The smooth yet tight fit of the crane to the revolver frame is another filing operation that demands a masterly touch. It must swing easily, yet be snug. So is the fitting of the hammer—that it may work easily between the frame sides. Filing requires the utmost skill. Most Colt filers have been at their benches for a dozen years or more. They are aristocrats of hand work.

Gauging the height of the firing pin is an operation that demands years of experience. Another is filing the sides of the tang for grips. These must be filed so accurately that light cannot show under the center, otherwise there would be a slight rock when the grips were attached. Fittings are so tailored to each gun that once fitted, they are mated so that there can be no chance of their becoming separated. Important fittings such as cranes, side plates and hammers are individually marked by the fitter, who stamps on them his number—forever identifying his handiwork and imposing on him the responsibility of super accurate work.

Making Colt Barrels

Drilling the barrel hole is a continuous process. A flow of oil of 500 pounds pressure forces the fine chips out as fast as the cutting edge takes them off. The drilling process is delicate. It takes about 10 minutes to drill a five inch barrel. One can honestly say that a Colt barrel 'gets a lot of reaming.' A barrel is machine reamed many times, each reaming making the barrel hole a thousandth or so larger.

Since every barrel tapers inside slightly toward the muzzle end, a generous amount of finish reaming is necessary. The target .38, for instance, must come within half a thousandth

Above: **A soldier in basic training with his M16.** ***At right:*** **General George Patton with his ivory-handled Colt. In the pistol factory—counterclockwise from *above left*: Ensuring that the barrel lines up correctly; 'proof-testing' the barrel; and chambering the cylinder.**

of the exact diameter. Sometimes it is necessary to finish ream a barrel four or five times to acquire this exactness. All along the line, I hold up to the light the barrel that is going into the gun they're building for me. Now they are putting it through the leading and polishing operation. They squirt on a drop or two of hot lead and wipe it through. The hot lead takes out any microscopic ridges and gives the inside of the barrel a high polish. We go to a rifling machine. In rifling, Colt acknowledges no superior. Inserted into the machine, the barrel is rifled. It takes about 20 minutes. Two barrels are on the same machine, each taking its turn as the cam throws the barrel over for its next cut. I hold it to the light again and see a spiral ribbon exactly .0035 deep, a lefthand twist that will spin a bullet accurately to its mark. It is a beautiful sight. No other word describes it.

A lathe turns the outside to exact dimension. The micrometer allows a tolerance of but .002 of an inch. Beyond this tolerance the barrel goes to the scrap heap. And let me say right here lest there be any doubt in your mind, there is a scrap heap at Colt's—never a big one, thanks to efficient workmen carefully supervised. But if there's the slightest doubt as to a tiny flaw or to the accuracy of a given measurement, out the piece goes right then and there. The Colt people bend over backward on this. They demand and they get perfection. A slot is cut and the front sight fitted, wound into place by a brass wire. In a subsequent brazing

Above: A highly-embellished version of the New Model Army Pistol, which was made from about 1860 to 1872. Collectors have since called it the Model of 1860 Army Revolver or the Round-Barreled Army—of the new series of percussion cap revolvers, the Army was the largest. *At left:* Soldiers of the 82nd Airborne gather around a flag during a pause in the action in Grenada; they carried the day with their M16s.

and heat treating process this wire melts in such a manner as to fix the sight as firmly as if it were part of the barrel itself.

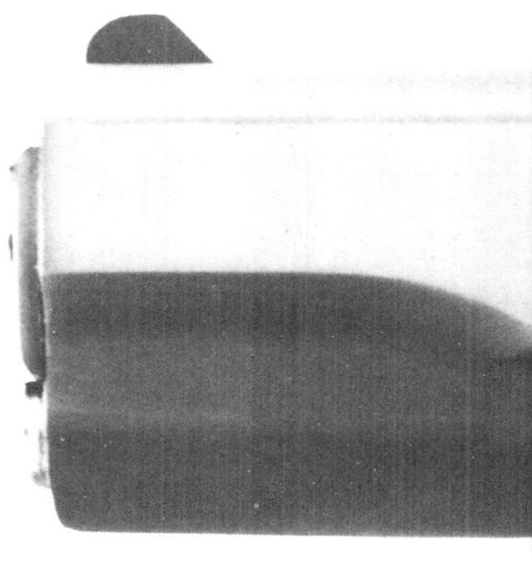

Making The Cylinders

There are 60 separate operations on the cylinder alone. Colt cylinders originate from a solid round bar of specification steel. To the layman, this bar of steel looks like a pipe. It is fed into a wonderfully ingenious machine—an automatic machine which cuts the bar to working length. It is an old machine, built by Colt inventors and mechanics some 40 years ago, but it can be dependably counted on to do its work with accuracy that must have been marvelled at at the time the machine was made. The center hole is bored, first rough bored, finish bored, then reamed three times. It must be accurate to .0005 of an inch. Inspectors look each cylinder over to detect any possible flaw in the steel. It is then ground to finish diameter, the diameter gauge allowing a tolerance of less than .002 of an inch. It is then gauged for trueness of diameter, the gauging showing up any slight eccentricity that might have occurred should any particles of dirt have crept into the arbor upon which the cylinder is held while being ground.

Drilling The Chambers

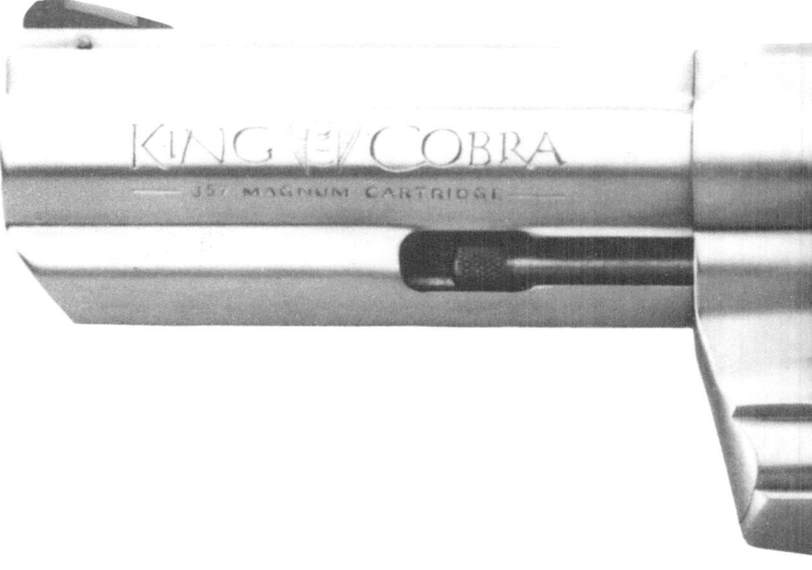

A lathe operation next cuts the cylinder to exact length. Into a drill jig it goes and the six holes are spotted. The bores of the cylinder are drilled half way through from the rear. Then the bores are drilled from the front to complete the process. There is a difference of .0012 between the front and rear ends of the chamber bores. The bores are reamed, first by a boring reamer, then by hand. A milling machine then makes the lightening cuts—the sleeve-like semi-round cuts that you see on the outside of your cylinder at the front end—so-called because their sole purpose is to take out unnecessary weight. Lead cuts are then made to facilitate travel. A coupling is doweled into position. A ratchet rod and ratchet are assembled to the cylinder, and two dowel pins inserted to hold the ratchet in correct and permanent position.

Practically all that remains to complete the cylinder is the fine reaming of the chamber bores. And when I say 'fine reaming,' that is just what I mean. There is no finer industrial reaming done anywhere in the country. The gauges allow no tolerances whatever. Measurements must be held exact to size. Cylinders, all machine operations complete, are sent to the heat treating room for heat treating.

All Colt cylinders turn right: this motion holds the crane tightly against the frame, keeping the chamber and barrel in perfect alignment for every shot.

Fitting And Assembling

From machines to hand filing, to finishing, blueing, assembly, targeting, inspection and finally to stock, is the itinerary of a Colt revolver. Minor machine operations are done en route such as chamfering edges of hammer and trigger slots, gauging fitting stops so that the cylinder will not swing out too far, cutting the safety latch slot and cutting threads inside the frame barrel hole to exact gauge depth and tapering them.

Fitting the cylinder to the frame is an operation assigned only to an expert. Fine files and emery grit are his tools. One man has been fitting cylinders for over 25 years. That has

Opposite: Ranging the barrel and chamber of a Colt revolver, circa 1940. This experienced craftsman had been, as of this photo, on the job for 31 years. *At left:* A Colt Stainless Steel King Cobra .357 Magnum revolver. *Above:* A Delta Elite 10mm Auto pistol. By combining the proven design and reliability of the famous Government Model with a versatile 10mm auto cartridge, the Delta Elite is a highly effective and handy weapon for a variety of applications.

***Above, from bottom:* Stainless steel Officer's ACP; blue Combat Commander; and stainless steel Government Model. *At right, from bottom:* A King Cobra, with short hammer throw for quicker lock time; a Colt Peacekeeper for police work; and the much-renowned Python.**

been his one job—nothing else. He has never worked in any other department.

Facing the barrel hole is exacting to the nth degree. No tolerances are allowed. When the barrel is fitted to the revolver frame, it must screw up tight and when it is tight, the front sight must be perfectly true on top of the barrel.

Probably no single operation in the assembly of a Colt revolver is gauged and inspected more rigidly and more often than ranging or aligning the chamber bores with the barrel. Before it goes to the shooting gallery, the firearm is ranged. It is ranged again after it is returned, and again in the final inspection. Not only that, but the gauging and the inspection work are rechecked by a second inspection. The perfect alignment of cylinder and barrel of every Colt revolver is a demand, a 'must' and a creed. As some indication of the precision employed in ranging, the maximum wear allowable of the range gauges is .0005 of an inch—or the thickness of a human hair split six times.

Polishing Steel To a Mirror-Like Finish

Some idea of the ultra skill employed in the polishing process may be gleaned from the fact that polishers coming to Colt who have worked elsewhere have to go through a training school. Though experts before, they actually are not good enough to do the fine work that Colt demands. Some of the polishing operations, particularly those involving flat surfaces, are so exacting that 98 out of 100 polishers cannot do the work.

The polishing room is literally a room of wheels—wheels and sparks. These wheels are of all types—flat wheels, form wheels, contour wheels—each designed and suited to a certain polishing operation. The actual polishing of a revolver or an automatic is but a fraction of the total time and cost in-

volved. The preparatory work is enormous—keeping the different polishing wheels in order, resetting them with fresh abrasive, breaking new wheels in—all this is preparatory to the actual polishing of the steel. When you stop to consider that practically every Colt model requires a different set of wheels, you begin to understand what I mean when I say the polishing room is a room of wheels. It is mighty interesting to watch how a polishing wheel is reset. A polishing wheel is made of wood and formed to carefully fit the surface it is going to polish. The rim of the wheel is covered with leather. New leather is given a coating of beef tallow and Japanese wax melted together in secret combinations to gain required texture. Most of the leather is imported: American hides, particularly of late, have not been thick enough to stand the gaff. The leather covered wheels are given a thorough bath and are dipped in hot glue. The rim is then rolled in loose abrasive, the coarseness of which is determined by the job assigned each wheel. The new wheels must then be broken in.

From polishing, we go downstairs to the blueing room.

Moisture is the great enemy of the blueing room. With the care that a hospital operation room fights bacteria, so does the Colt blueing room fight moisture. Nothing is overlooked to constantly guard the surfaces of steel against damaging moisture.

Frames, cylinders, barrels, slides, receivers and parts come to the blueing room direct from the polishing department. Side plates and craned are removed. Everything is first given a bath in hot gasoline... gasoline heated to 150 degrees Fahrenheit. This removes all dirt particles, dust or grease that may have gathered on the way down from the polishing room. Hot air is then forced over them to eliminate all presence of moisture, the arch enemy.

After washing and drying, the side plates (in the case of revolvers) are put back on. But they are put on with 'work screws' that hide beneath the surface so that the entire surface can be completely exposed for cleaning and blueing. When finished, blued screws will replace the work screws.

Scenes from the 1940s—*counterclockwise from top:* Large and small parts are polished to a mirror-like finish here in the Polishing Room; two polishers at work; and loading a rack of revolver frames into a blueing furnace. *Above right:* The Colt Detective Special.

All surfaces to be blued are then wiped with a solution of alcohol and whiting—a polishing compound of very fine texture. Wiped with a soft dry cloth, the parts are now chemically clean. From this point on until the blueing process is complete, not a human hand touches a surface to be blued. All this is preparatory to the actual blueing process itself.

A blueing run starts the first thing in the morning. A secret mixture of charred bone and primer is put into the blueing furnaces. The furnaces slowly revolve. Pyrometers control furnace heat. Readings are taken every 15 minutes during the five hours it takes to complete the blueing process, which reaches a high temperature of 650 degrees.

The furnaces are gas fired. Four burners supply the heat in each one, and it is interesting to note that the forward burner is larger to compensate for any heat loss through the doors.

The 'charge' used in the blueing process is ground animal bone charred to chemical purity in a bone pot placed into a white hot furnace at 1400 degrees. Two hundred pounds of bone are charred at a time, burning away all foreign matter.

The 'primer' is bone, soaked in pure petroleum oil. Even the oil is boiled to remove moisture and foreign matter: it must be chemically pure. The primer is what gives off the smoke that keeps free oxygen away from the pieces being blued in the revolving drums. The 'primer' and 'charge' are mixed and put into the furnace before the work goes in.

What is the chemistry of blueing anyway? How does this blueing process impart the handsome and lasting blued steel finish so famous in modern firearms? Blueing is a combination of carbonizing and oxidizing, which, with heat brings the inherent carbon of the steel through the open pores to the surface: all the coloring is done by heat. No particle of bone ever touches the parts being blued—the smoke given off by the 'primer' expels free oxygen from the drum, leaving only sufficient oxygen to allow combustion. The primer and the charge control the composition of gas in the furnace; the heavy carbon dioxide shielding the parts from contact with oxygen. All this calls for expert knowledge and experience in mixing the proper proportions of the primer and charge—not only to obtain the proper color, but to create a smoke that is free from moisture. Otherwise—though blued, the pieces would be pitted.

When you buy a Colt revolver or automatic with full blued finish, a full blued finish is what you get. Even the inside of your barrel is blued. And there is something beautiful about blued steel that even an artist of words could hardly describe.

Over a hundred fabricating hammers a week are used in manufacturing Colt revolvers and automatic pistols. You must wonder how hammers could wear out so quickly. But these are not ordinary hammers. They are lead hammers and are used because lead is softer than steel and therefore can do it no harm. In filing, fitting and assembling it is often necessary to slightly tap the frame with a hammer in order to loosen a side plate or a crane fitting that fits too tightly—for which lead hammers are used. Incidentally, they are made right in the Colt factory—thousands of them. Using lead hammers is just another way with which Colt 'Care-On-Little-Things' is expressed.

All the parts that go into the manufacture of a Colt revolver or automatic—even the incidental ones like the stocks,

the springs, screws and etc—are made right in the Colt plant.

There is a well equipped woodworking shop in which the grips are turned out. Colt grips are made from selected walnut. The actual shaping of a pair of Colt grips is pretty much a matter of conventional wood turning. Finishing them, however, is a horse of another color (no Colt pun intended). The filing, sandpapering and hand finishing require patience that only those who are satisfied with nothing less than best possess. Perhaps the most outstanding machine in this department is the checkering machine. I was thrilled watching this ingenious automatic machine that, with mathematical precision, cuts the tiny but deep grooves that result in checkered grips. Shooters all agree that beautifully deep checkered stocks add security to the grip... essential to firing line confidence.

The proper and dependable action of the firing mechanism's springs constitutes an important function in the operation of a firearm. In the automatic, of course, there are the main spring, the recoil spring and the firing pin spring. Springs in a revolver include the bolt spring, latch spring and ejector rod spring. You might naturally think that

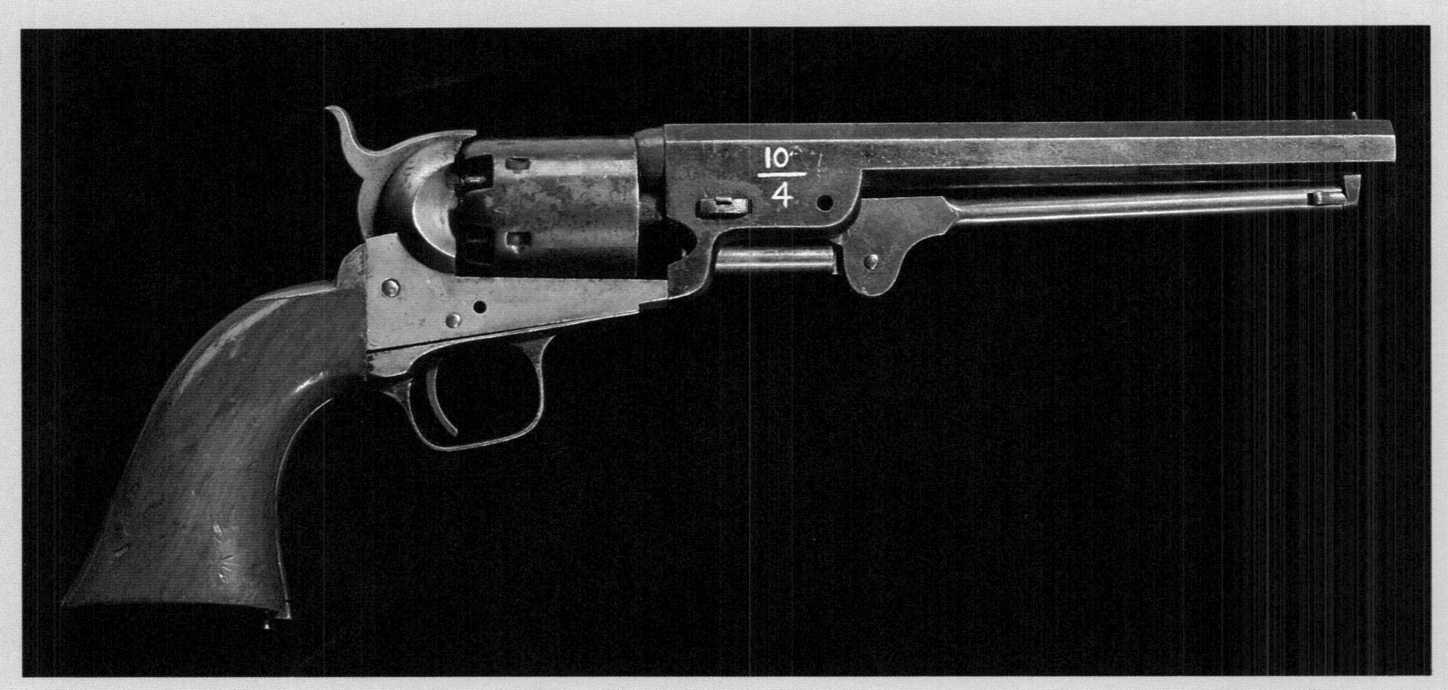
10
4

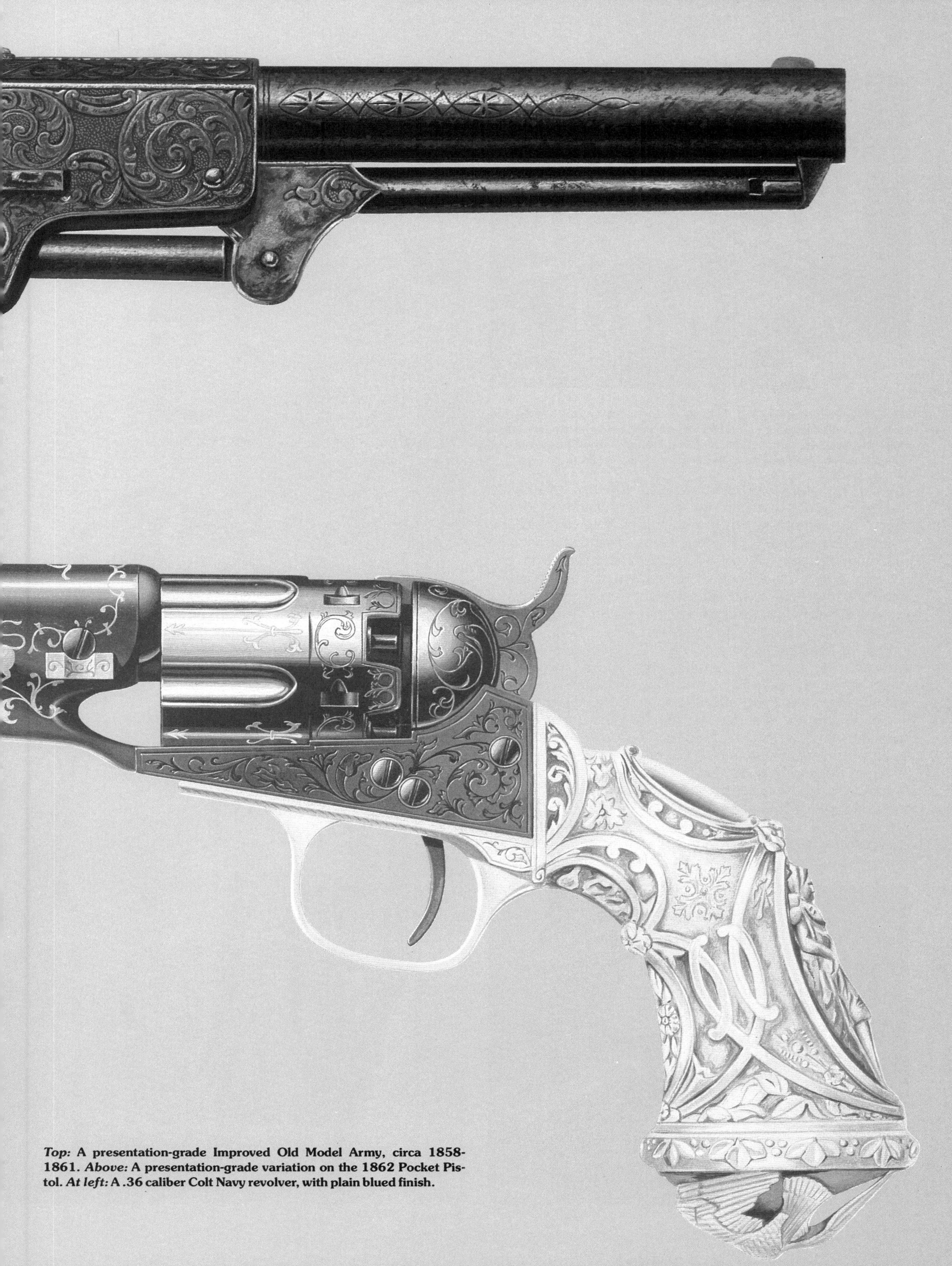

Top: **A presentation-grade Improved Old Model Army, circa 1858-1861.** ***Above:*** **A presentation-grade variation on the 1862 Pocket Pistol.** ***At left:*** **A .36 caliber Colt Navy revolver, with plain blued finish.**

Above: **Hand checkering pistol stocks in the mid-20th century.** ***Below:*** **Note the tools that this assembler used to fit and adjust parts into a finished pistol.** ***At right:*** **John Wayne and Joanna Barnes look on as Kirk Douglas extols his Peacemaker in the movie** ***The War Wagon.***

the Colt company would purchase its springs, but they do not—they make them themselves. The quality of springs that Colt demands is not obtainable anywhere in the country. Years ago Colt's engineers designed and built machines to make springs to the specifications desired. Occasional efforts have been made since that time to determine whether the same specifications could not be met outside the plant, but to date no manufacturer of springs can be found who will meet Colt demands.

First of all, triple A wire is used. The dimensions of the wire must be exact, the number of coils to a given length must be exact, the wright must be exact, and all these specifications must tally after the springs are heat treated to specified temper. A spring is ordinarily just a few coils of wire, but with Colt it is a major part to be fussed over until it's exactly right and unvaryingly efficient.

When the gun has been built, assembled and tested, only one more thing is necessary and then the gun is ready to go to the shipping room as a full fledged Colt. That one thing is inspection—inspection with a capital 'I.' From the shooting gallery, their testor-signed targets accompanying them, Colt firearms go to the inspection room where a veteran of long

Colt "Service Model Ace" Automatic Pistol

CALIBER:
.22 Long Rifle
(Both Regular and High Speed Ammunition)

WITH FLOATING CHAMBER

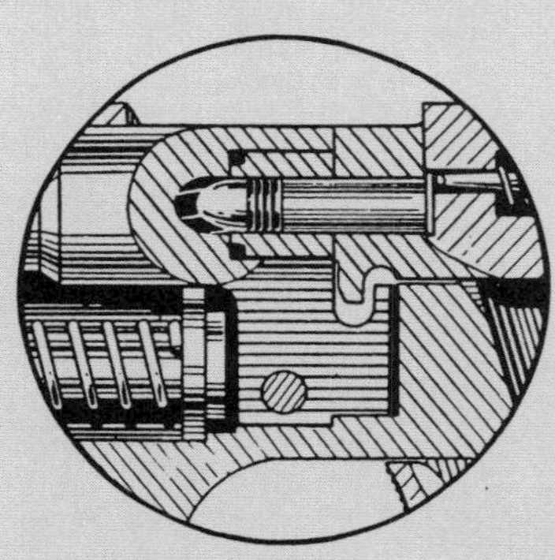

New Floating Chamber Increases Recoil Approximately Four Times

A feature of the Service Ace is its ingenious "floating chamber" which amplifies the ordinary recoil of a .22 four times, and provides positive functioning under all conditions.
The floating chamber is a marvel of simplicity . . . consisting of a movable chamber, so designed as to increase pressure, building up the recoil until it simulates the recoil of the .45 caliber automatic pistol. The Service ACE is a natural for military shooters, a remarkably fine training gun for beginners.

Specifications

CAPACITY OF MAGAZINE: 10 cartridges.

LENGTH OF BARREL: 5 inches.

LENGTH OVER ALL: 8½ inches.

ACTION: Hand finished.

WEIGHT: 42 ounces.

STOCKS: Checked Walnut.

TRIGGER AND HAMMER SPUR: Checked.

FINISH: Full Blued.

SIGHTS: Ramp front sight, fixed. Rear sight adjustable for both elevation and windage. Both stippled.

ARCHED HOUSING: Checked.

The New Service Model Ace has been designed to provide efficient and economical target practice for military men, and all shooters of the heavy frame Colt Automatic Pistols. It is similar in design to the regular Ace Model . . . plus the recently perfected Floating Chamber. By the use of the Floating Chamber the recoil has been increased four times, simulating the recoil found in the .45 caliber Government Model Automatic Pistol. Thus the shooter is trained with an arm that allows him to later change to the heavier caliber pistol, without the additional recoil being noticeable. Because of the much lower cost of .22 caliber ammunition the Service Ace will pay for itself in a very short time.

Special Features

Except for difference in caliber, the new SERVICE MODEL ACE and the Government Model .45 are practically twins. They are so near alike that you can switch from one to the other and hardly notice the difference. However, the Service Ace is provided with hand finished action and a two-way Stevens adjustable rear sight. The front sight is fixed with serrated face.

.22 LONG RIFLE

The Service Ace saves *real* money and pays for itself in a very short time. It provides accurate, economical target shooting for Service men — members of National Guard, Reserve Officers, and individual shooters of the .45 Caliber Automatic Pistol . . . at one-seventh the cost of .45 automatic cartridges.

Colt .45-.22 "Conversion Unit"

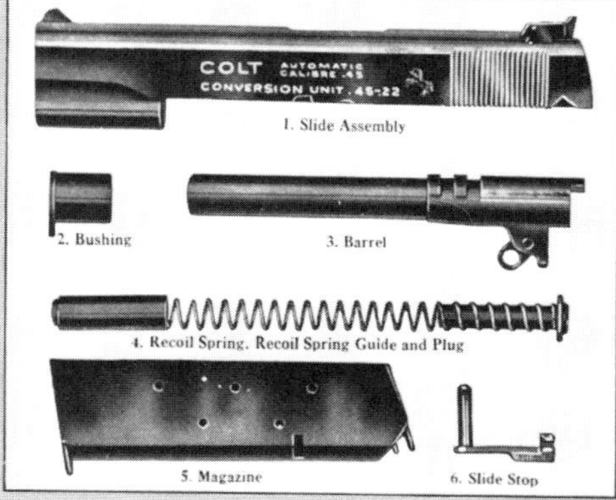

For Converting the Colt Service Model Ace .22 to a .45 Caliber Pistol

The New .45-.22 Conversion Unit converts the recently developed .22 caliber Service Ace (with Floating Chamber) to caliber .45. By simply interchanging the component parts of the Unit with the corresponding parts of the Service Ace, the shooter may shift from .22 caliber ammunition to .45 Automatic cartridges in a very few minutes. The .45-.22 is composed of Match Grade slide, equipped with fixed front sight and either fixed or Stevens adjustable rear sight; selected Match barrel with bushing; recoil spring, recoil spring guide and plug; magazine and slide stop. This new Unit makes it possible for you to secure maximum pleasure from your Colt Service Ace.

years goes over them 'with a fine-toothed comb.' He looks them over thoroughly, gauges certain fittings, ranges them again, checks action and trigger pull, and literally mothers them like they were lost orphans. If they pass final inspection and 9/10ths of them will, they are put into stock in the shipping room, wrapped in soft tissue and boxed. A Colt has to earn its VP—the 'Verified Proof' mark. This is truly a badge of perfection which the final inspectors strike on to the metal after they have given a firearm a 'clean bill of health' to go out into the world and uphold the Colt reputation for building the world's finest hand guns. But a Colt has to earn it—it must pass every test, every inspection by a good margin or else the VP does not go on. The VP mark is held in high honor by Colt workmen. They know, better than anyone else, that when a firearm finally gets its VP it is a true Colt—a thoroughbred.

The thing that impressed me perhaps more than any other single thing in my whole trip through the mammoth Colt plant is the absolute and utter care given to the manufacture of a Colt revolver or automatic pistol. I have seen precision manufacturing before. But never, never have I seen so many—and so minute—gaugings, inspections, regaugings and tests put into the manufacture of a single product.

Not only is meticulous care given to each machine operation, but the deliberate and unhurried hand fittings, the skilled benchwork, is of a character that one might easily and truthfully associate with only the great guilds of medieval craftsmen. Craftsmanship, skill and practical knowledge born only of experience is the important human tool that builds a Colt revolver. Gauges catch any faulty mechanical operation, but the human eye, the human hand and long years of experience are the factors that account for the unchallenged accuracy, the smoothness of operation and the absolute dependability of a Colt.

In my desire to emphasize the skill of the old school I must not give you the impression that the Colt factory is run by old men—by no means: rubbing elbows with these older gentlemen are youthful, keen-eyed, stalwart young men ambitious to carry on the spirit and traditions of each of their crafts. On my travels through the Colt factory, occasionally losing my own bearings in their 50-odd acres of floor space, I made it a particular observation to note in my mind how the problem of developing apprentices was being met. I was deeply impressed with the type of young men serving the plant and the seriousness with which they accept the responsibility of their separate functions. Craftsmanship is in their blood.

Opposite and above: **Ads from Colt's 1940 catalogue.** ***Left:*** **Checking a revolver in Colt's Final Inspection Room.** ***Above left:*** **Testing Officers' Models in the Shooting Gallery.** ***Overleaf:*** **In the Old West, you always had to be prepared—John Wayne and Kirk Douglas test their Colts in one of the many films in which Mr Wayne and Mr Douglas starred.**

Excellence

Above: A rather fancy Single Action Army revolver. The first large revolver for metallic cartridges that was sold by Colt, it was first named the New Model Army Metallic Cartridge Revolving Pistol and is also called the 'Peacemaker' and the 'Frontier Six-Shooter'and has very often been referred to as 'legendary.'

and Art

In the realm of firearms hand engraving, the words 'custom' and 'factory' have similar but distinctive meanings. Custom engraving is the product of a special and specific request by the client to decorate a gun with certain selected patterns and, in some cases, the use of precious metals. Factory engraving is done in more traditional and standardized styles of engraving. Journeymen engravers work on this type of project, whereas the master engravers are assigned the custom work.

Pricing for engraving is generally made on the basis of how much of the firearm is covered with the artwork. Letters of the alphabet denominate this coverage factor. 'A' is one-quarter coverage, 'B' is one-half coverage, 'C' is three-quarters coverage, and 'D' is full coverage.

The Colt Custom Gun Shop performs special services to enhance most Colt products cosmetically and functionally. The time-honored Colt Single Action Army revolver is produced and sold in limited quantities exclusively by the Colt Custom Shop, for sale to collectors of fine firearms. The Custom Shop produced several unique Single Action variations for 1986. These models used the old style black-powder frame design that featured a base pin screw, a round ejector rod head, a three-line patent date rollmark on the frame, an Italic rollmark on the barrel and caliber stamp under the barrel on the .44-40 caliber model.

Colt offers its custom services on all current firearms featured in the standard commercial products catalog, and will consider work on older Colt models—on a case-by-case basis (depending upon availability of replacement parts).

The Custom Gun Shop has historically supplied collectors of fine art with hand engraved firearms of premium quality. Production firearms are enhanced through the time-honored craft of embellishing metal, utilizing the hands of Colt's world-renowned master engravers. Colt engravers handcarve traditional engraving patterns, and inlay both flush and raised reliefs with precious metals to enhance the appearance and worth of firearms submitted to their care. The engravers provide five different scroll patterns: Classic American, (and, upon special request) Oakleaf, Vine, English or Nimschke styles of engraving. Colt master engraving provides the finest balance and detail available today. In addition, each piece is individually signed by the master engraver—and this has historically contributed to greater desirability and value. Additionally, master-engraved firearms can be documented in detail on Colt letterhead by the Colt Historian.

Custom engraving pricing is based on the amount of coverage desired, complexity of style and time required for special requests. The engraving pattern will be designed and quoted by experienced Custom Shop personnel, who can offer the collector valuable insight into the design of a personalized firearm. These truly unique Colts can currently be created in less than a year.

The Custom Shop offers hand engraving performed by journeyman engravers that complements any Colt firearm. Engraving may be special ordered to highlight individual parts of the firearm. The four basic decoration areas of the Single Action Army are the barrel, the cylinder, the frame and the trigger guard/backstrap. Colt hand engraving designs, based on a variation of the American style, are chosen by the engraver. Coverage on other Colt models is consistent with their four traditional coverages, unless a specific quotation is requested. The Colt Custom Gun Shop can deliver these types of orders currently in less than six months.

The Custom Gun Shop accepts requests for limited production (minimum of 50 firearms) Colt firearms. This is ideal for organizations who wish to incorporate mottos, dates and pictures into artwork of their customized firearm. Anniversary, celebration and fund raiser commemorative edition firearms for fraternal, civic, military and law enforcement groups have been successfully created by Colt. The Custom Shop selectively plates guns in gold or silver with the finest detail offered in the industry today, and can hand

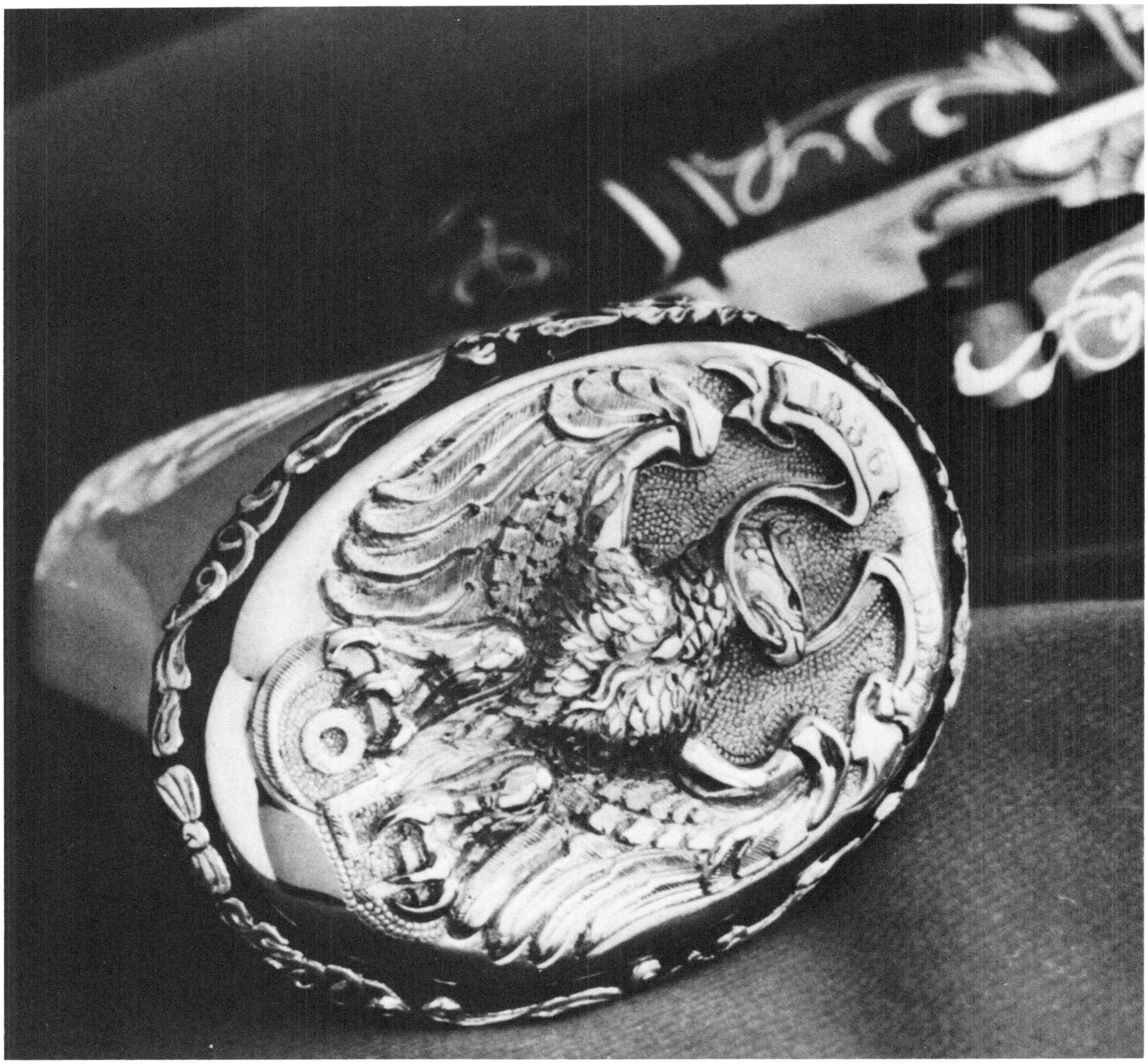

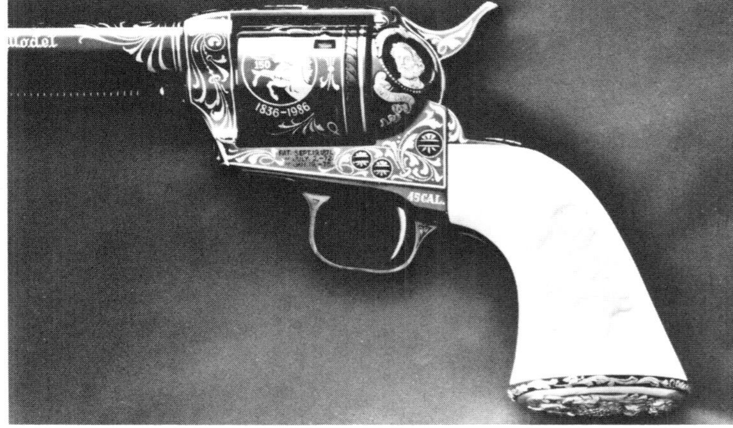

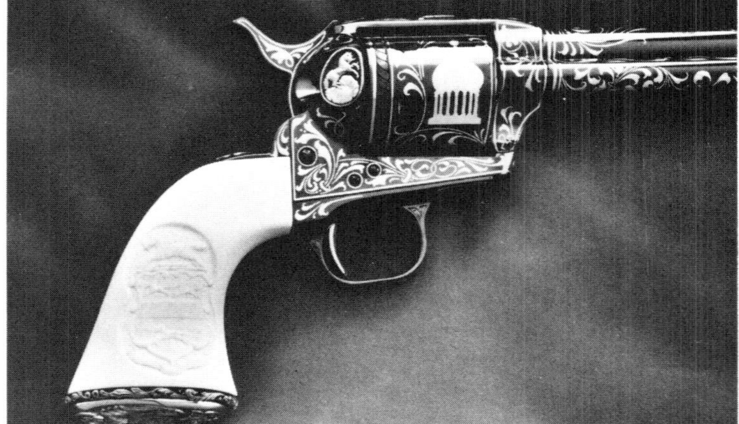

Opposite: Colt's 150th Anniversary Exhibition Gun, based on the 'Peacemaker' of Wild West fame. Grip engravings feature the young Sam Colt whittling the prototype from which the modern revolver would evolve, a head portrait of Colt on the receiver flange, Colt's 'rampant colt' logo on the cylinder, and portraits of the Python Ultimate revolver and Officer's ACP on the barrel. *Top:* The grips butt of the 150th Anniversary Gun. *Above left and right:* A 'flip side' view of its receiver with engravings.

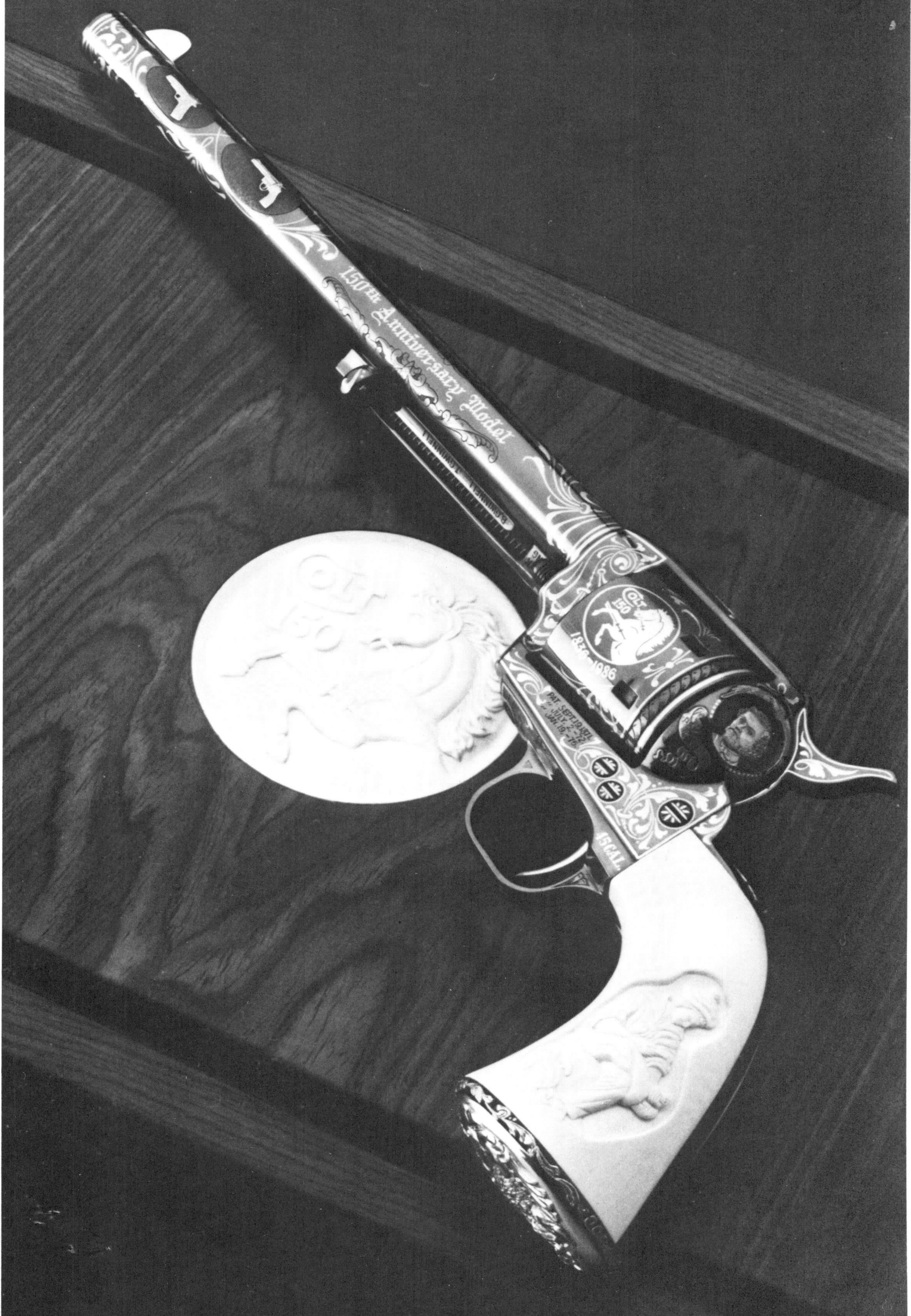
150th Anniversary Model
1836–1986

Above left and right: **Samples from the Colt Custom Shop—inlays, motifs and scroll styles.** ***Below:*** **An ad for Colt ornamentation in 1940.** ***Opposite:*** **A historical letter from the Colt Historian, tracing the history of a collector's Colt by means of factory records.**

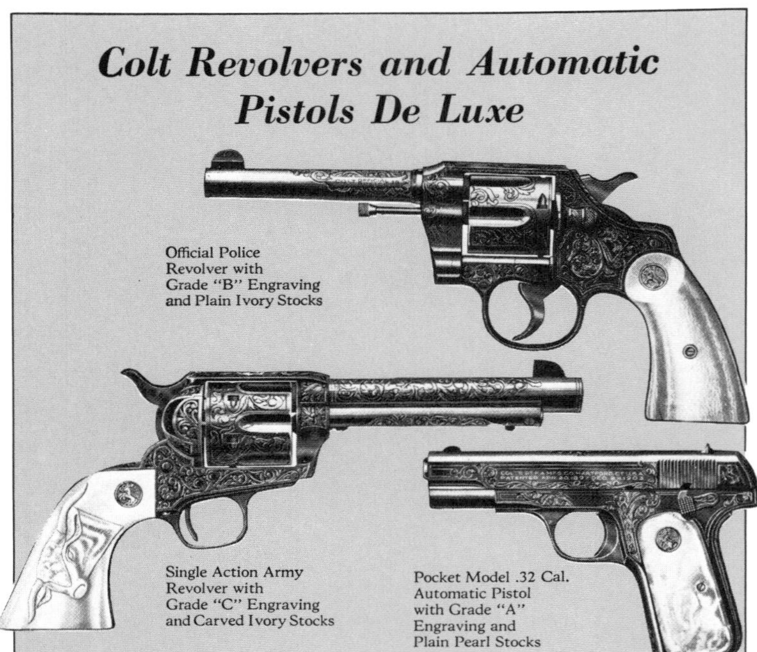

engrave to the specifications of individuals or organizations, polish to presentation grade cosmetic standards and fit guns with unique stocks and stock decorations. Customers may design cosmetic or functional features to create a unique variation on current Colt model offerings and the Custom Shop will fabricate their designs. Unique presentation packaging can be ordered to complement and protect the 'customized' firearms.

Colt Revolvers and Automatic Pistols De Luxe
Official Police Revolver with Grade "B" Engraving and Plain Ivory Stocks
Single Action Army Revolver with Grade "C" Engraving and Carved Ivory Stocks
Pocket Model .32 Cal. Automatic Pistol with Grade "A" Engraving and Plain Pearl Stocks
Whether for presentation purposes, as special match prizes or the favorite Arm of a shooter, Colts may be had in almost any special finish or decoration desired. We have always taken special pride and given the greatest attention to such ornamented Arms. A Colt of any model (except .22 Automatic Pistol) may be fitted with select stocks in choice Pearl or Ivory (either carved or plain). All genuine Colt Pearl or Ivory stocks are identified by the rampant Colt medallion. Special price list of Fancy Stocks, sent upon request.
Engraving may be had in any one of the three grades illustrated in the models shown above. The grade refers only to the amount of engraving desired, "A" representing the minimum, "B" medium grade and "C" the most ornamental. The quality of work is the same in all cases and performed by the same experts.
Also we can furnish Colt Arms with any special design desired, with full gold or silver plating or inlaid State or National seals, etc., also Pearl or Ivory Stocks with inlaid enamel initials or emblems in colors. The work in this department is performed by highly skilled craftsmen only, who have had years of experience in this painstaking and beautiful designing. Estimates for all work of this character are furnished in advance.

The Custom Shop polishers have prided themselves on attention to detail and the quality of finish that is evident in Colt Royal Blue and special plated firearms. The 'Mirror Brite' finish imparts an ultra buffed sheen to all exterior parts of the firearm. Great attention is paid to highlighting surfaces, which results in firearms of high polishing standards.

Colt firearms may be refinished in blue, blue and color case, Colt Guard, Royal Blue and nickel. Prices will vary depending on the model and condition of firearms. All modern firearms returned for refinishing are cleaned, given minor adjustments and test fired.

The Custom Gun Shop can enhance the presentation of any Colt firearm with a select wood presentation case. These fine cases, crafted from oak, cherry or walnut are available with 'French fit'—partitioned interiors of rich velvet. Custom etched or engraved plates may be ordered to further enrich the presentation of guns produced for special awards, retirements, anniversaries or birthdays. All custom

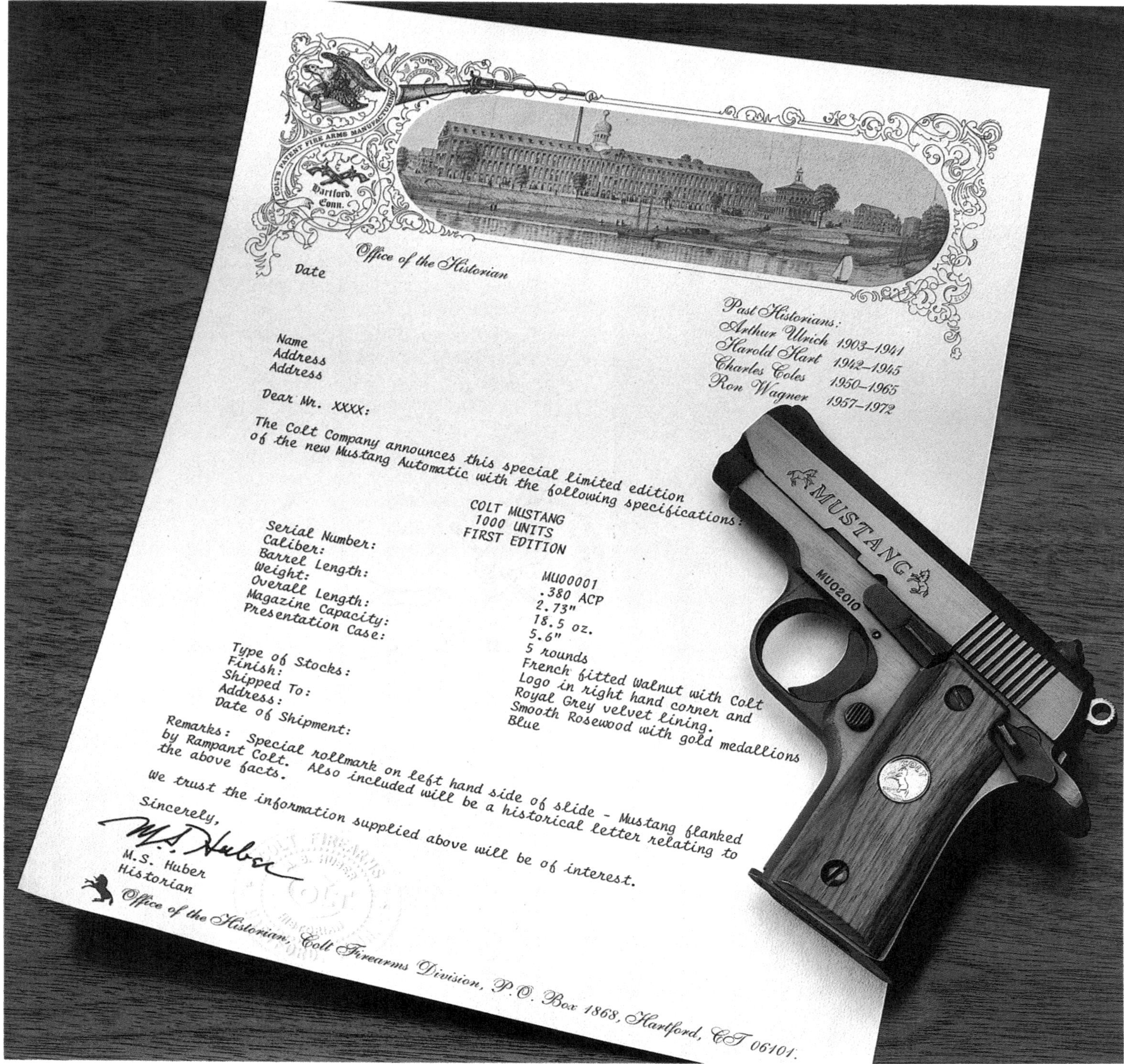

Colt's Patent Fire Arms Manufacturing
Hartford, Conn.

Office of the Historian

Date

Past Historians:
Arthur Ulrich 1903–1941
Harold Hart 1942–1945
Charles Coles 1950–1965
Ron Wagner 1957–1972

Name
Address
Address

Dear Mr. XXXX:

The Colt Company announces this special limited edition of the new Mustang Automatic with the following specifications:

COLT MUSTANG
1000 UNITS
FIRST EDITION

Serial Number:	MU00001
Caliber:	.380 ACP
Barrel Length:	2.73"
Weight:	18.5 oz.
Overall Length:	5.6"
Magazine Capacity:	5 rounds
Presentation Case:	French fitted Walnut with Colt Logo in right hand corner and Royal Grey velvet lining.
Type of Stocks:	Smooth Rosewood with gold medallions
Finish:	Blue
Shipped To:	
Address:	
Date of Shipment:	

Remarks: Special rollmark on left hand side of slide - Mustang flanked by Rampant Colt. Also included will be a historical letter relating to the above facts.

We trust the information supplied above will be of interest.

Sincerely,

M.S. Huber
M.S. Huber
Historian

Office of the Historian, Colt Firearms Division, P.O. Box 1868, Hartford, CT 06101.

cases are manufactured to the highest quality standards to ensure compatibility with the firearms and the setting in which they will be displayed. A choice of blue, red or forest green lining colors are available.

A new line of glass wall/walnut frame presentation cases is available that allows an upright firearm to be viewed from four sides and top while protecting the firearm from the adverse effects of unsupervised handling. These cases are ideal for collector shows and are available on special order for most current models.

The Custom Gun Shop also presents fine, crafted custom grips: grips of ivory, and of rosewood, walnut and bacote woods can be fitted to all Colt models. Grips can be ordered with gold or nickel Rampant Colt medallions to complement the color of the finish selected on the firearm. Colt Single Action Army grips are now crafted with a blind screw hole on the left grip to enhance their appearance. Single Action Army wood grips can now be custom fitted to the traditional one piece configuration upon request. Checkered grips in the fleur-de-lis pattern can be ordered for the Single Action Army in any of the above choices of grip material. Special grip medallions may also be ordered on commissioned products.

The Colt Historian authenticates production and shipping information essential to establishing the value of firearms. A Colt historical letter adds value to any collection piece by adding knowledge about past or current production. Letters serve to assure buyers and sellers that the basic physical characteristics of a gun are consistent with original factory records. Letters also provide valuable documentation for insurance policies that must rely on appraisals and certifications of authenticity. Thus the investor, the history buff and the collector all derive valuable benefits from this unique service.

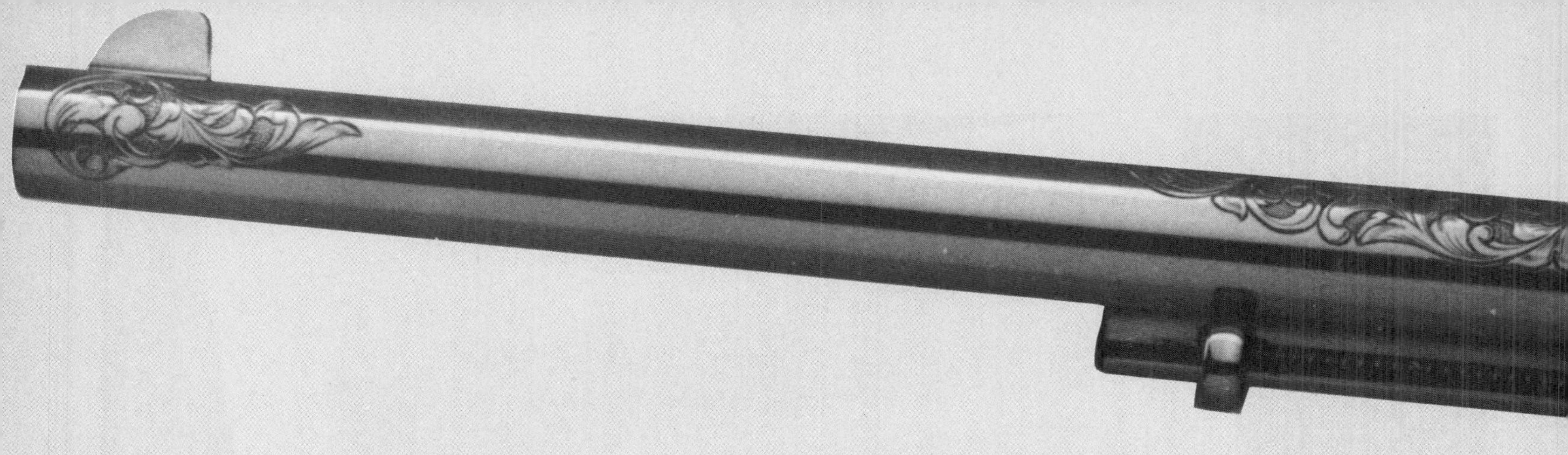

At left: What more could a Wild West enthusiast want? This hobbyist seems pleased with his collection of Log Cabin Library magazines and his beautifully engraved Colt. *Above top and bottom:* A fine-grade Colt 150th Anniversary Commemorative pistol and a Colt 150th Anniversary Engraving Sampler in four styles of engraving.

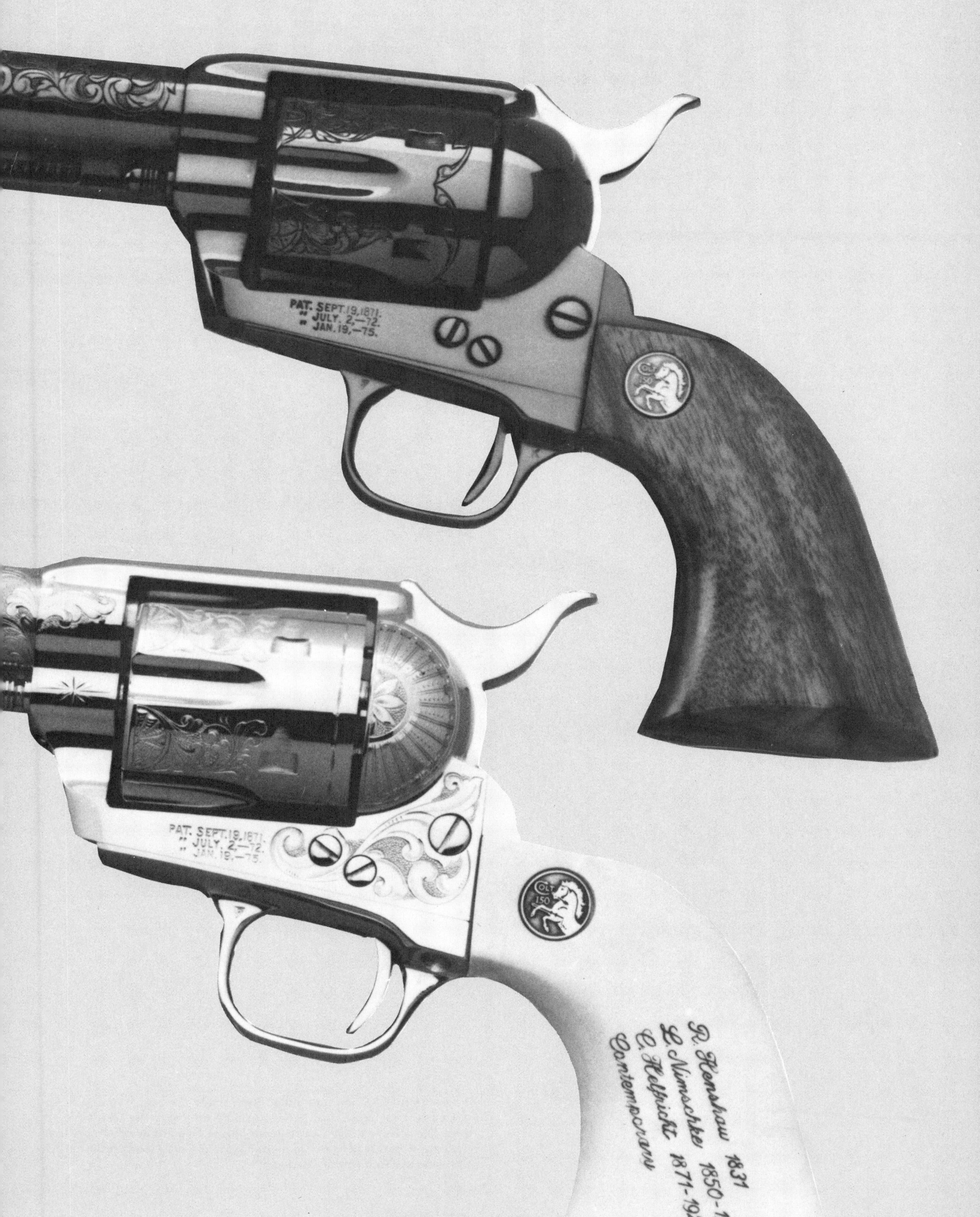
PAT. SEPT.19,1871.
" JULY. 2,—72.
" JAN.19,—75.
PAT. SEPT.19,1871.
" JULY. 2,—72.
" JAN.19,—75.
R. Henshaw 1831
L. Nimschke 1850-190
C. Helfricht 1871-1921
Contemporary

The Tradition

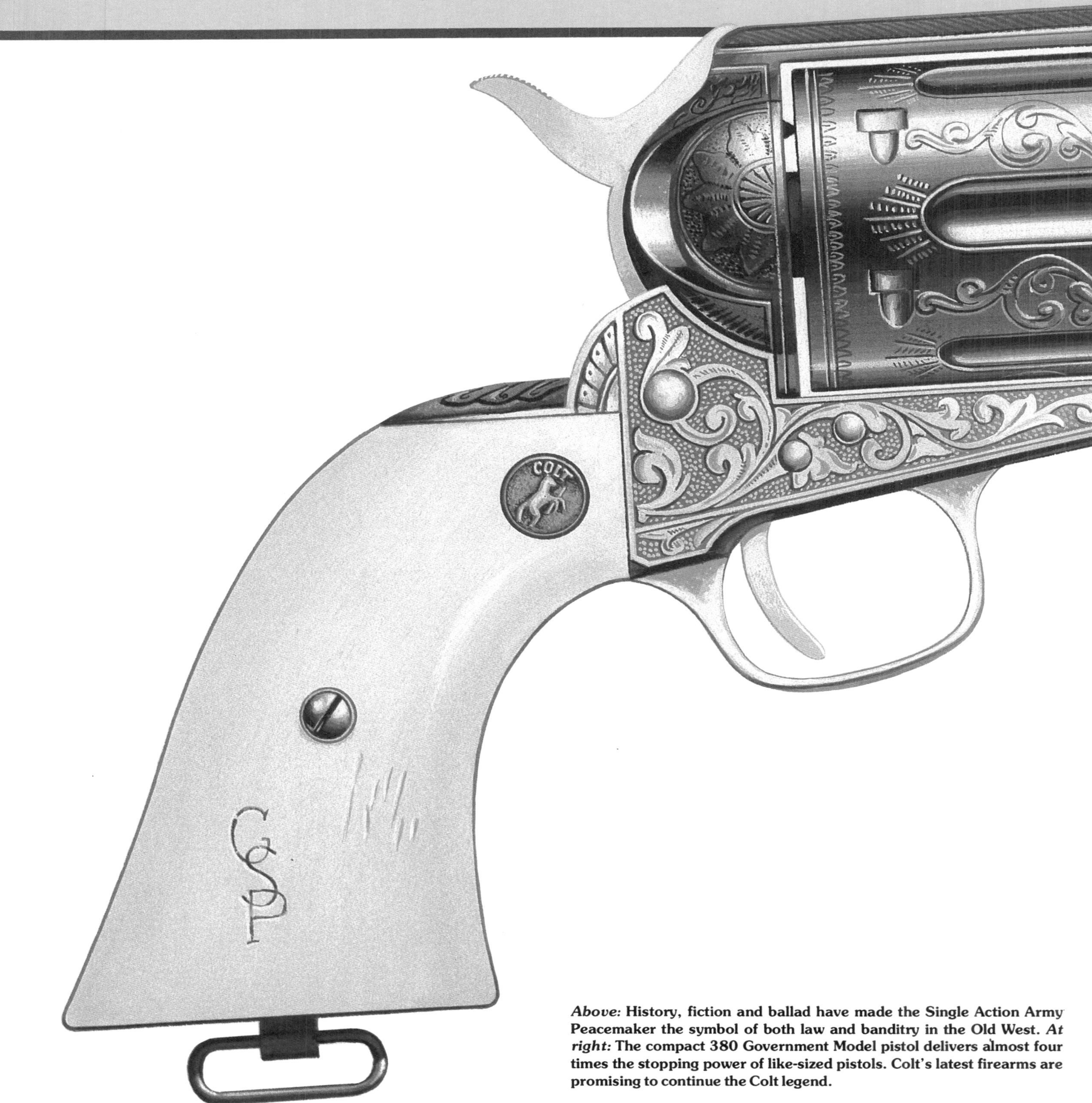

Above: History, fiction and ballad have made the Single Action Army Peacemaker the symbol of both law and banditry in the Old West. *At right:* The compact 380 Government Model pistol delivers almost four times the stopping power of like-sized pistols. Colt's latest firearms are promising to continue the Colt legend.

Continues

Today the tradition of excellence continues on at Colt. Bill Stokes, Vice President of Manufacturing says, 'The bottom line is to build the quality into Colt products at the very beginning rather than repairing them over a period of time.'

Colt employs extensive quality improvement programs in all phases of production and finishing. These programs require supervisors to inspect the production outputs of their respective departments at least twice per day. These inspections are made using gauges, micrometers and other testing apparatus. When a new run of parts is begun, this inspection process is actually a careful observation of *all* parts on that run as opposed to a random sampling.

Those particular parts of a firearm that could affect function and safety are denominated 'critical operations' and extra attention is paid to their fabrication and milling.

Every setup person and supervisor is required by Colt to attend a 22 week training program at Hartford State Technical Institute. The 88 hours of classroom work is taken up with such subjects as reading a blue print, setting up a particular machine properly, and the basic shop math needed to carry out assigned responsibilities.

Colt personnel are also trained in the use of computer aided design and manufacturing processes. Colt is in the midst of a modernization program which will bring these technologies to bear upon its products.

Since the raw materials used in the fabrication of the firearm are just as important as the finished product, Colt's quality control extends 'backwards' to their supplier's operations, as well. Each year, Colt Firearms gives its 'Vendor of the Year Award' to its best supplier on the basis of quality and dependability of delivery.

But quality control does not begin with the raw material and end with the finished product for Colt. Colt Firearms maintains a customer service center as well as 120 local service centers worldwide. Even this service center network is currently being computerized in order to ensure ongoing customer satisfaction.

The history of Colt firearms began with cap and ball pistols and moved through the conversion processes involved in adapting to the new center-fire cartridges. Single action, and then double action revolvers were, and still are, produced. The turn of the century brought the advent of automatic weapons to the Colt line of products. Today, Colt firearms defend the nation as a whole, and its citizenry in particular. The spirit of Samuel Colt lives on.

At top: **Colt's Double Diamond .357 Magnum revolver with vent-rib barrel, adjustable sights, polished finish and fine wooden grips.** ***Above:*** **Colt's compact, sophisticated Double Diamond 45 Automatic.**

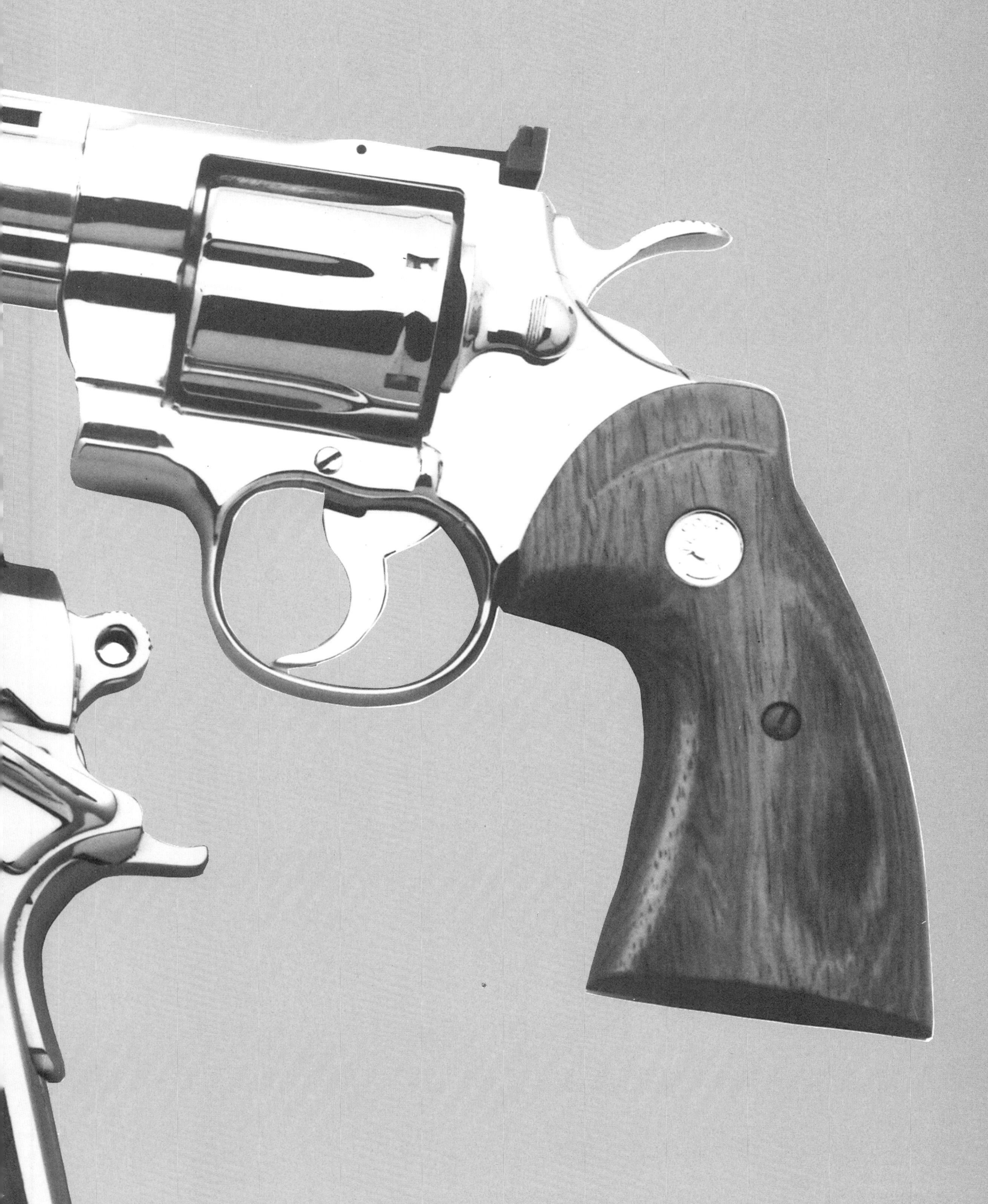

America's Premier Gunmakers
REMINGTON

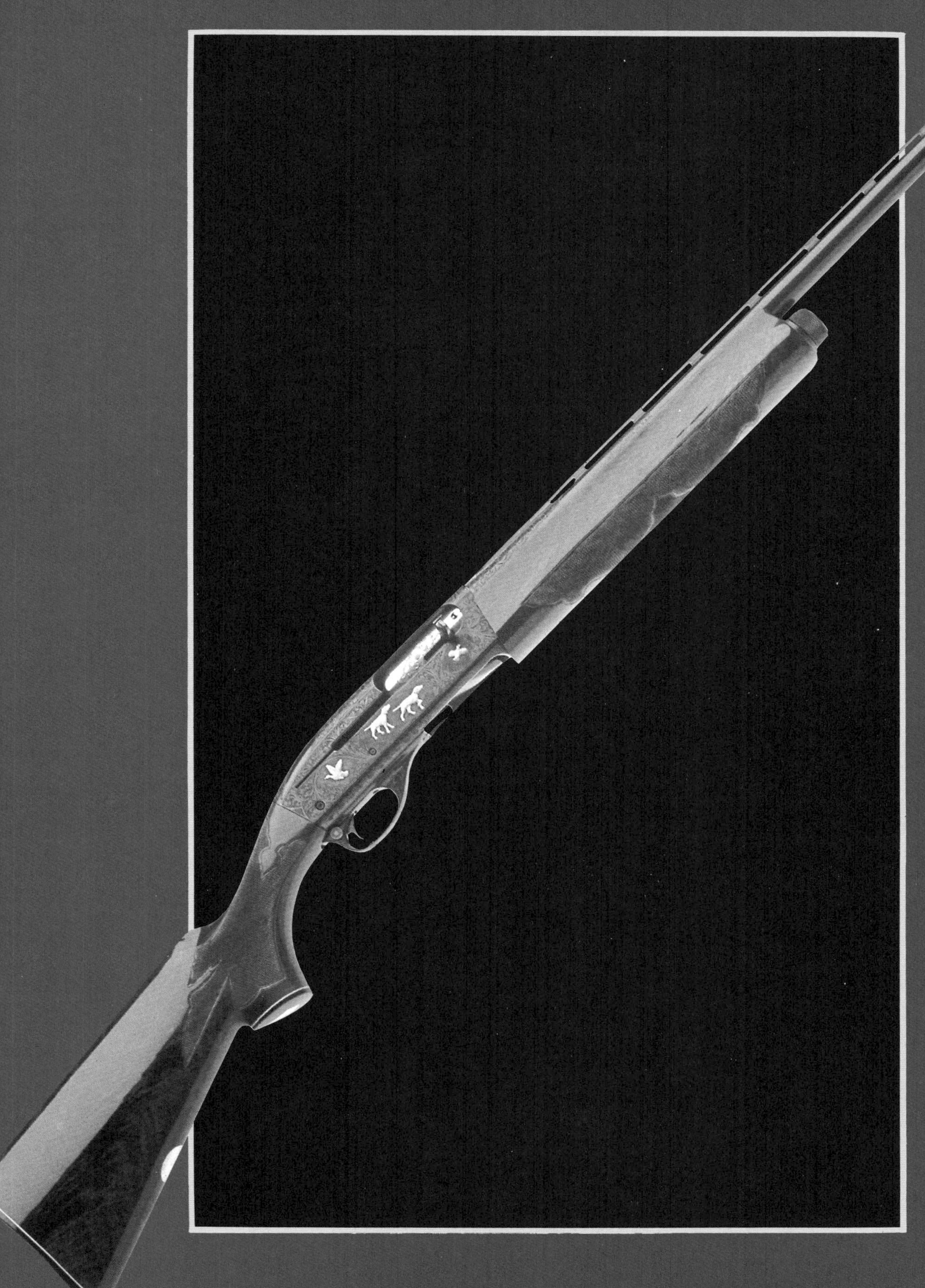

Previous pages: A Model 1100 automatic shotgun with commemorative engraving from Remington's Custom Shop in celebration of the two millionth Model 1100 manufactured. *These pages, top to bottom:* The Model 1100 Special Field automatic shotgun, with four-shot capacity; the legendary Model 700 Mountain Rifle, a favorite in calibers up to .300 Winchester Magnum; and a Model 870 Wingmaster pump shotgun.

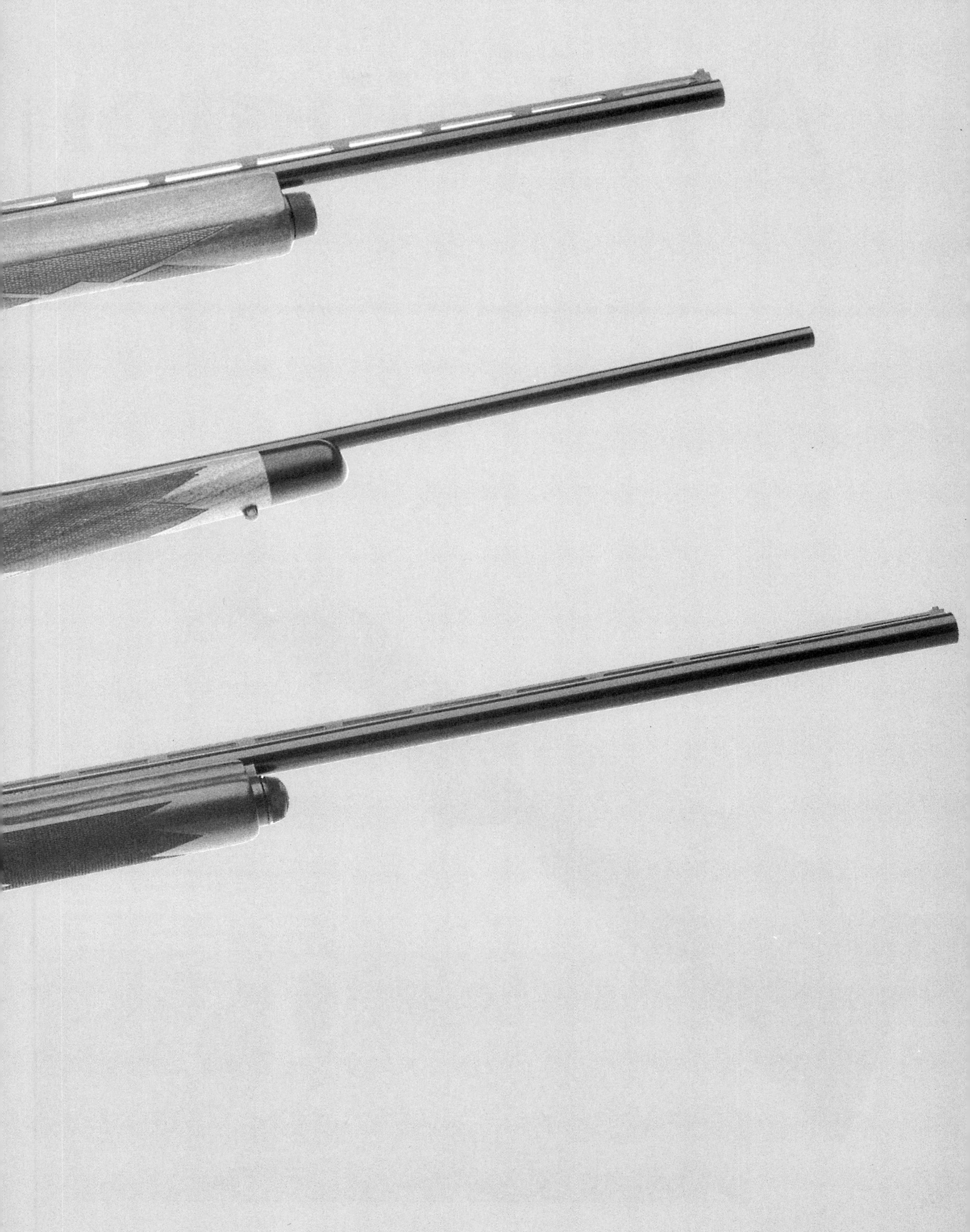

A Remington

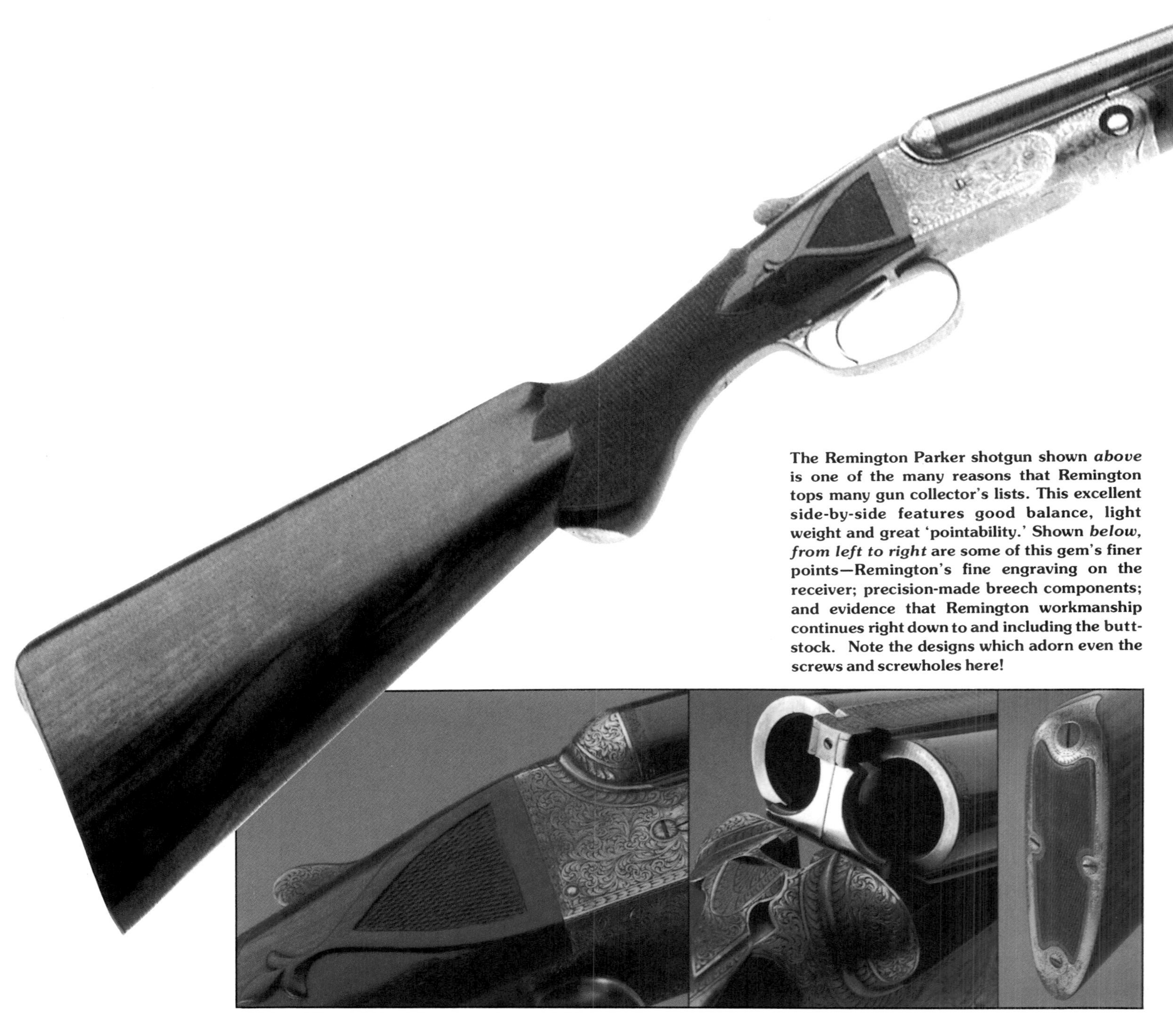

The Remington Parker shotgun shown *above* is one of the many reasons that Remington tops many gun collector's lists. This excellent side-by-side features good balance, light weight and great 'pointability.' Shown *below, from left to right* are some of this gem's finer points—Remington's fine engraving on the receiver; precision-made breech components; and evidence that Remington workmanship continues right down to and including the butt-stock. Note the designs which adorn even the screws and screwholes here!

History

A history of the Remington Arms Company is a miniature panorama of American history itself. In 1816, on the heels of the War of 1812, Eliphalet Remington and his son, Eliphalet Jr, founded the Remington Company just outside of Ilion Gorge, New York.

Demand grew for the workmanship of the Remington father/son duo. Complete rifles were produced on a customized, individual basis, but profits were also to be had in producing barrels for other gunsmiths to be used in their own firearms. Increased demand always follows excellent workmanship, and the Remington business soon outgrew the production capacity of their original forge. In 1828, they moved their operation into Ilion proper, along the banks of the Erie Canal. The Canal at this time was the most important thoroughfare of commercial traffic in this region, and the new location proved to be successful indeed. The same year as the move to Ilion also brought tragedy. Eliphalet, Sr met an accidental death at this time.

The business expanded rapidly, and a year after the move, a second forge was installed to produce barrels, balls, and accessories. Because the Remingtons were selling principally to other gunsmiths, it is not uncommon to find REMINGTON markings on various *parts* of guns produced in this area during this period.

Eliphalet, Jr was now president of the company. He was a gunmaker and manufacturer first and foremost. While he was able to introduce many improvements in the fabrication of firearms and their accompanying parts, he is not remembered as a major innovator of the same genre as Samuel Colt, for example. Remington was a genius at combining the innovations and patents of others. Remington Arms was also a *production* facility, not particularly given to experimentation with untried ideas. So while blazing inventiveness was not a hallmark of Remington Arms, neither was the company dependent on just one invention or set of innovations for its continuing existence. In fact, Remington has one of the longest continuous histories of any US arms manufacturer.

Eventually, Eliphalet Jr's son Philo came into the family business, and the company changed its name to E Remington and Son. John Griffiths of Cincinnati had originally contracted with the US Government to produce 5000 Model 1841 Percussion 'Mississippi' Rifles. He was unable to fulfill his contract and the Remingtons took it over. This afforded them their first opportunity to produce, on a large scale, weapons for the government. Following this first contract, the government awarded the Remingtons a second contract for 7500 more of the same model. Remington had broken into the arms trade in a big way! In 1846–7, Remington also received a US Navy contract for the production of the Jenks Breech-loading Percussion Carbine. In 1851, another contract followed for the production of 7500 Model 1841 Percussion Rifles. By this time, demand was so great for their products that the Remingtons had expanded their manufacturing facilities to nearby Herkimer, New York. In the early 1850s, two more of Eliphalet, Jr's sons—namely, Samuel and Eliphalet III—entered the family business and E Remington and son was changed to E Remington and *Sons* to account for what was now a larger family partnership.

The Remingtons were not willing to confine themselves to the production of rifles and other long arms alone. Samuel Colt had patented his revolving percussion revolver in 1836, and a little over 20 years later—in 1857—the Remingtons introduced their Beals Pocket Revolvers. During the Civil War, Remington—along with all other arms manufacturers in the United States—devoted its complete time and resources to the fabrication of all sorts of firearms for the war effort.

Eliphalet Jr died in 1861, and his son Philo succeeded him as president of the firm. At the end of the Civil War, the company was reorganized as a corporation that retained the name of E Remington and Sons.

The Remington company played a significant role in the great American westward expansion. The company introduced a great variety of pistols and rifles. The most famous of their many lines of products was the 'Rolling Block' series of rifles. These were eagerly purchased by gun merchants both in the United States and abroad. Remington soon found itself squarely in the midst of a very lucrative stream of European contracts to upgrade the various armories of these nations. Samuel Remington died in 1882, and his brother Philo assumed full management of the company. In 1886, the company was in dire financial straits and went into receivership.

The company was acquired by Hartley and Graham in 1888. H and G was a famed New York military and sporting goods firm which had, twenty years earlier, founded the Union Metallic Cartridge Company of Bridgeport, Connecticut.

E Remington and Sons was renamed the Remington Arms Company and functioned as such from 1888 until 1912, when it was merged with the Union Metallic Cartridge Company. From then until 1934, the company was named Remington-UMC. The Great Depression brought yet another reorganization of the company and its name reverted to 'Remington Arms Company, Inc,' by which it is still known today. The DuPont Corporation acquired controlling interest in the firm in 1933.

Unlike other major American gun manufacturers, the definitive history-to-date of Remington Arms has yet to be fully written. There is really no fully documented chronological history of the company. Firearms collectors continue to have a very difficult time in cataloguing and tracing the numerous models and variations of Remington firearms. Often, manufacturing specifications would shift within the same model of gun without being documented by the factory, thus leaving collectors and dealers to surmise for themselves the details and peculiarities of whole lines of Remington products. The Remington Factory at times apparently overproduced, in anticipation of entering into contracts which never materialized. These inventories of parts were then salvaged by being used in other models for which

***Below:* This Remington Sportsman 581 is just one of the fine rifles made by Remington, America's oldest sporting rifle manufacturer. The 581's five-shot capacity and rugged construction make it the ideal 'plinker.' *At right:* The Remington Arms plant at Ilion, in the 1940s.**

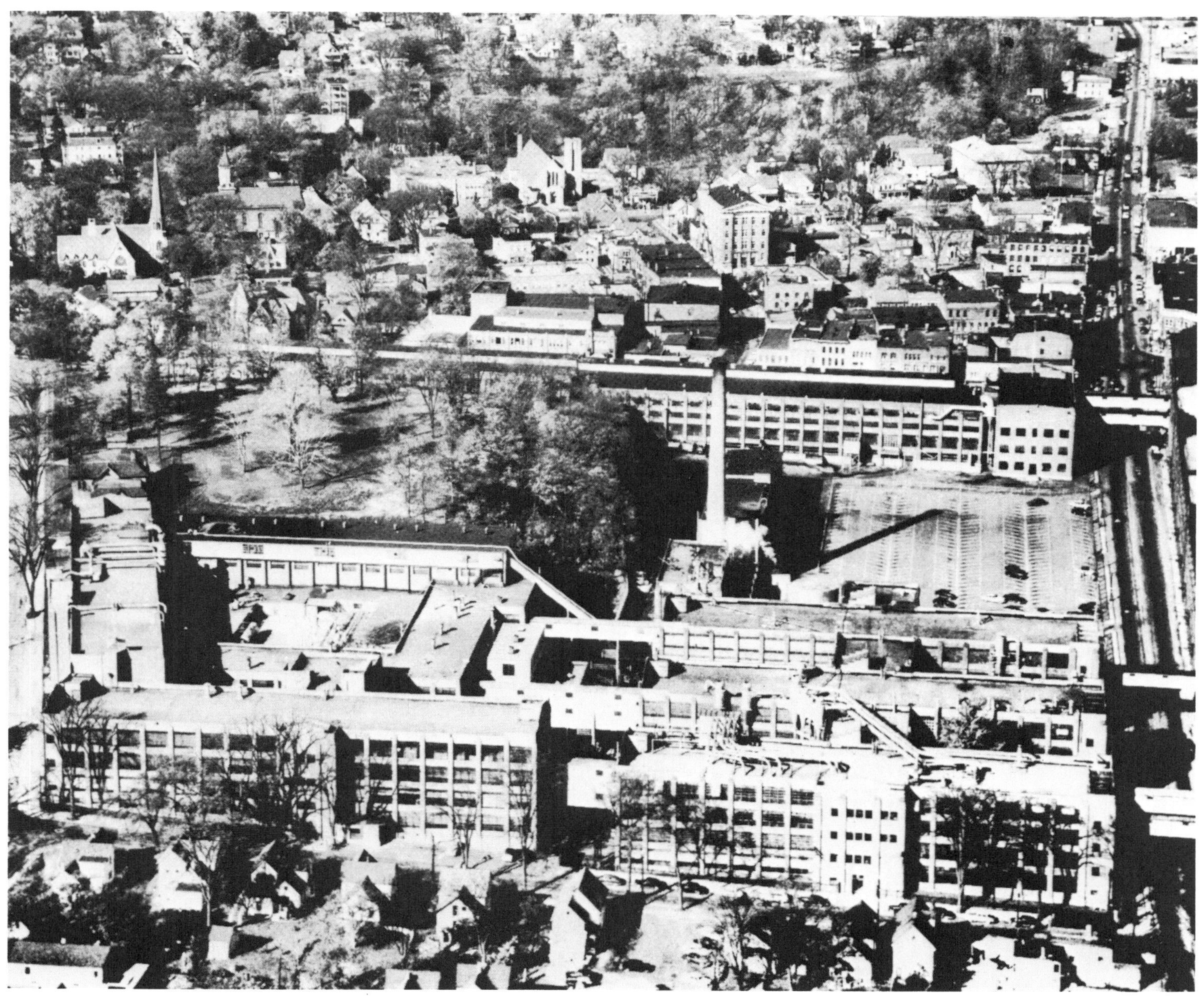

contracts did exist. Thus 'variations' within model runs are numerous and plaguing. Definitive technical data simply does not exist for many Remington models.

Tracing Remington's history as well as documenting model productions is for the most part a trip through uncharted waters. Gun collectors and historians are often at variance one with another as to production details concerning a particular model or variation on a model. These 'grey areas' of Remington history and production are both numerous and intriguing. They provide the historian and researcher with fertile, and sometimes frustrating, fields of endeavor. However, collectors have a difficult time establishing the rarity of certain models; this lends itself to confusions about value and the pricing of certain specimens.

It is interesting to note, also, that engraved Remingtons are somewhat rare. The only real engraving that was done at the factory was apparently on the Magazine Derringer Model. When engraving was done, it was usually very simple in form and basic in design. Most engraving is found on the early percussion handguns, but does not in any way compare to the engraving on contemporaneous Colts. When, however, engraving was performed by Remington, it was accomplished by an acid etching process, in contrast to the rolled design made famous by Colt. Some engraved Remington longarms were produced but they are generally considered to be quite rare.

Boxed sets of Remington pistols are also considered rarities, because Remington Arms did not go in for exquisite presentation-grade specimens, as did some other American manufacturers. Remington did, however, employ 'specialty' grip materials in its production. Ivory and pearl were the most often used materials in Remington decorative grips. The value of a gun thus equipped is considered to generally be a function of its type—in conjunction with the *kind* of *grip material* employed and the overall *condition* of the firearm.

Today, Remington produces numerous lines of both sporting and military weapons. Remington Arms are found at all 'wavelengths' of the firearms spectrum. Remington does offer superb finish and fine wood (and other) stocks. The longest-lasting American gun manufacturer continues to uphold its tradition of offering the public well-made, accurate and superbly finished weapons for a fair price.

Civilian

Above: The Remington Model 700 hunting rifle. *At right:* Montanans Thayne Bowman (white shirt) and Tom Yule (plaid jacket) and their Remington Mohawk .222s, equipped with Leopold scopes, and Tom's son Tim with his Bushnell Sportview 4x-equipped Mohawk.

Arms

Non-military use of firearms generally falls into the categories of hunting and target shooting. Conservation has come to characterize the first group and national and international competitions have come to characterize the second category.

The Remington Arms Company has played a significant role in both of these areas of civilian firearms use. One of the hallmarks of Remington guns is that they are priced for availability. Probably a greater percentage of firearms in private hands in the Unites States are of Remington make than of any other manufacturer. Remingtons are functional, reliable and tend to maintain their value.

Rifles

Firearms literature abounds with never-ending debates about what constitutes the 'perfect' rifle. This debate tends to center around a balance between two points. The first is the caliber desired (which itself tends toward a 'perfection' of its own) and the second is the rifle itself. Choosing a firearm for personal use requires that the purchaser has in mind beforehand the use to which the gun will be put. This involves such considerations as whether one wants exclusively to shoot targets, or shoot *and* go hunting for game, or wants to hunt exclusively; also, if shooting targets, at what ranges and distances will one be shooting, and will it be serious competition shooting; and if hunting, what sort of game and what sort of habitat does this game prefer—and so on. Does one require long range accuracy or does what one would be doing call for sheer muzzle power? The type of action of the gun must also be taken into account; also, the 'convenience' of a rifle—that is, its weight and handling capabilities—are of prime importance in the selection process. The more forethought that is put into choosing a rifle, the greater will be the satisfactions of using that gun in the future.

Probably, the most popular rifle caliber is the .30-06, a caliber that has bagged more brown bears and grizzlies than any other caliber of this century. It is available in a wide variety of bullet styles and weights. Almost all rifle mechanism types are available in .30-06 caliber with the exception of a few lever-actions. While it is true that, technically speaking, no caliber of rifle is 'perfect,' the .30-06 comes about as close as one can come to perfection in an imperfect world.

After World War II, one of the more interesting innovations that occurred in the American gunmaking industry was the introduction of Monte Carlo stocks. The Monte Carlo comb, when incorporated into a stock design, raises the mid part of the stock sufficiently to cause one's cheek to rest at a higher position when looking down the sights. Remington began producing Monte Carlo stocks for many of its models. Firearms writers and critics both raved about and reviled the Monte Carlo design. Some claimed that it reduced perceived recoil when the rifle was fired. Others claimed (and rightfully so) that the Monte Carlo comb actually *increases* perceived recoil. Actually, the Monte Carlo design was simply a way of skirting the inherent design problems of pre-World War II stocks without actually doing anything about them. When soldiers began returning from World War II, their demands on their hunting rifles were greater than before the war. Battlefield experience yielded more sophisticated thinking about what they actually wanted out of their rifles.

Most everyone in this period wanted telescopic sights; but telescopic sights and the old stock designs were not an easy match. The Monte Carlo design at first seemed to come to the rescue, offering a higher cheek position—and thus better eye access to 'scopes'—than the old stocks did. So the band wagon was set into motion, and Remington, along with most other manufacturers, began making Monte Carlo stocks available on their most prominent models.

By the middle-to-late 1970s the Monte Carlo fad had pretty much run its course. In the early 1970s, even before this turn of events, Remington contacted Jim Carmichael—who is generally acknowledged as the dean of modern gun writers—with a request that he design a classic-styled stock for the Model 700 bolt action rifle. Carmichel says that designing the stock was something of an exercise in frustration, but the Model 700 Classic was a result of his labors. The Model 700 Classic certainly looks better than Remington's old Monte Carlo stocks and actually feels better to shoot. This Remington innovation—that of designing a 'classic' stock—forced other gunmakers to follow suit. The 'classic design' has by now superseded the Monte Carlo in most respects. It actually solves the pre-World War II stock design problems by supplying the higher comb needed for telescopic sight shooting *and* eliminates many of the undesirable features of the Monte Carlo design. 'Classic' stocks feature a straight, high comb and reduce perceived recoil. In addition, they generally look a great deal better than Monte Carlos.

Remington had been active in production of weapons for World War I, but with peace in 1918 and the Great Depression of the 1930s, demand virtually dried up for Remington products. The factory at Ilion continued to exist, but shipments of products were few and this period produced considerable losses for the company. During this time, Remington's profitably was mainly due to its cartridge division in Bridgeport. Despite the overall depressed economic circumstances, the DuPont Corporation saw an opportunity in Remington, and purchased controlling interest of the firm in 1933. At this time, Remington was running third in the American arms market behind Winchester and Savage. DuPont's original intention was to close the firearms division of the business and concentrate wholly on the cartridge division. But before doing so, company policy dictated that a survey be taken of the firearms division before closure. George Read was sent from DuPont of Wilmington to Ilion for this purpose. Read would later recommend that the firearms division not be dissolved but rather upgraded and modernized. DuPont followed through by pumping investment dollars into Ilion. New equipment was acquired, fabrication processes were set up, and attempts were made to modernize the whole manufacturing process.

During this time, the most popular bolt action rifle on the market was the Winchester Model 70. Remington undertook to compete with the Model 70 by introducing the Remington Model 720 in 1941. The Model 720 was indeed competitive with Winchester but in 1941 the United States was forced into a war not of its own making. The production of sporting arms was simply set aside for the now immediate problem of emergency war production. It is interesting to note, however, that while Remington was blessed with huge arms contracts from the government for World War II, these contracts resulted in very meager profits for the company. This is an example of a little known historic fact: Arms manufacturers do not generally profit from war.

During World War I, Congress had determined that no manufacturer or transportation agency would engage in war profiteering. When World War II fell upon the nation, Congress was once again determined that windfall profits were to be kept at a minimum. But Remington's factories and facilities had to be expanded and tooled up for the increased war production. This overbuilding and excessive expansion could prove disastrous for Remington after the war was over. DuPont management realized this and undertook an extensive 'Reconversion and Modernization' program to utilize the expanded facilities of the company after the

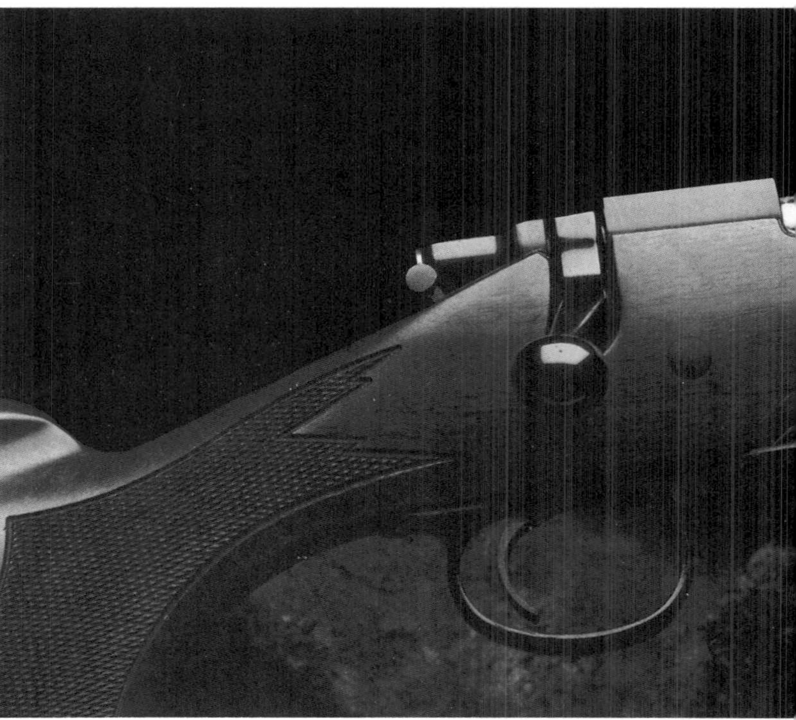

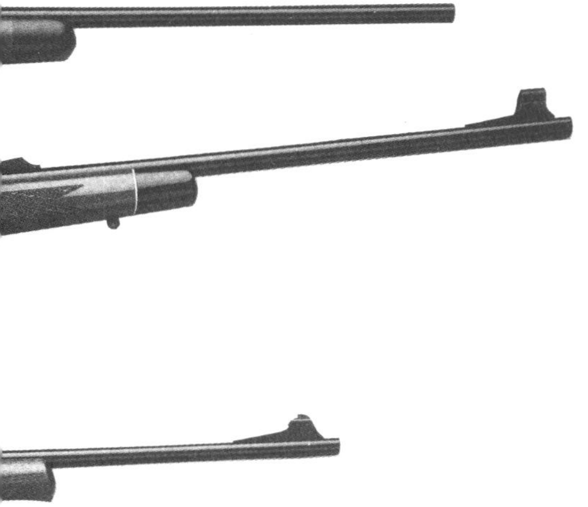

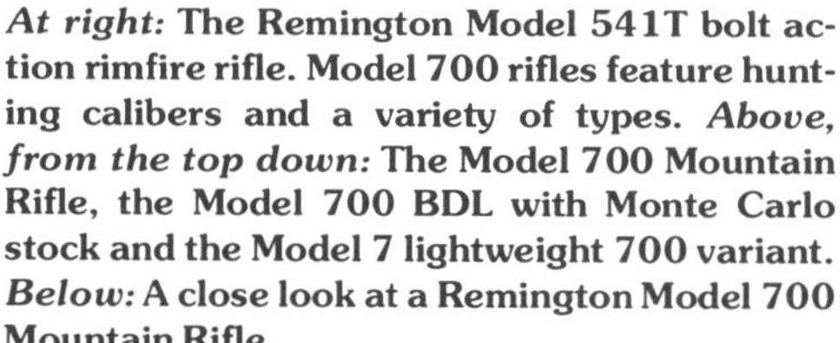

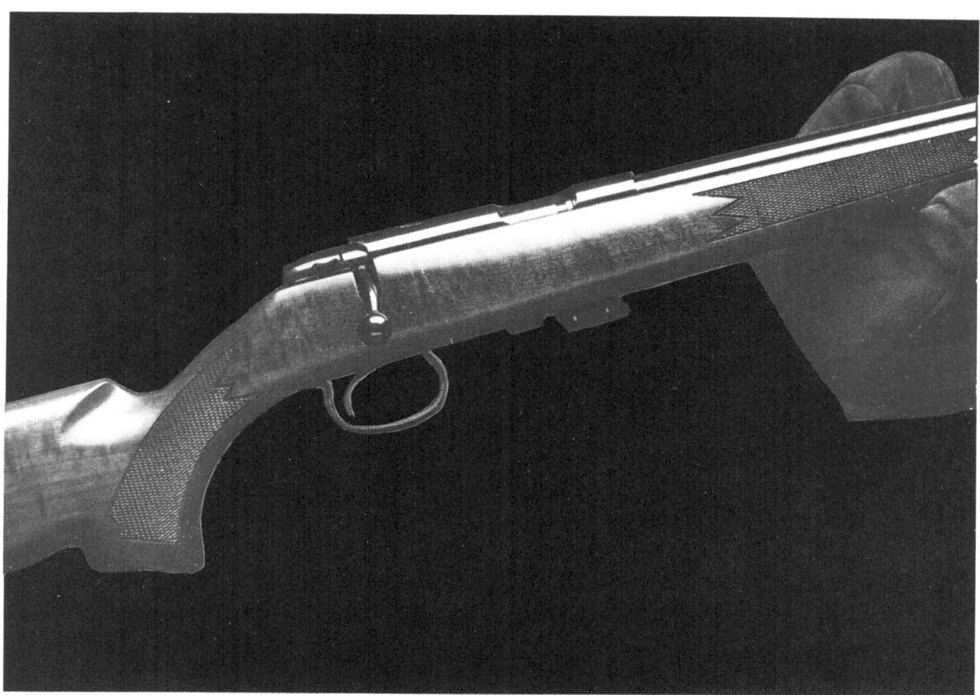

At right: **The Remington Model 541T bolt action rimfire rifle. Model 700 rifles feature hunting calibers and a variety of types. *Above, from the top down:* The Model 700 Mountain Rifle, the Model 700 BDL with Monte Carlo stock and the Model 7 lightweight 700 variant. *Below:* A close look at a Remington Model 700 Mountain Rifle.**

war, and thus insure its continued existence. At the heart of this project was the design and fabrication of the Model 721 and 722 rifles. These rifles had to succeed or Remington Firearms itself would cease to exist.

When crucial times arrived, crucial personalities arose. Mike Walker became the driving force behind the production of the new rifles. Walker hailed from Iowa and had answered an ad in the American Rifle magazine in 1942 when Remington was searching for research engineers. Remington was gathering its engineering talent at this time in order to meet the intensive wartime production schedule. This pool of talent would later prove indispensable to the success of the company. Technically, the Model 721/722 rifle project began on 12 August 1942, when $200 was authorized to prepare a project outline. In 1943, the research and development department spent $11,500 for background research—but it was not until almost at war's end that the project was again a priority.

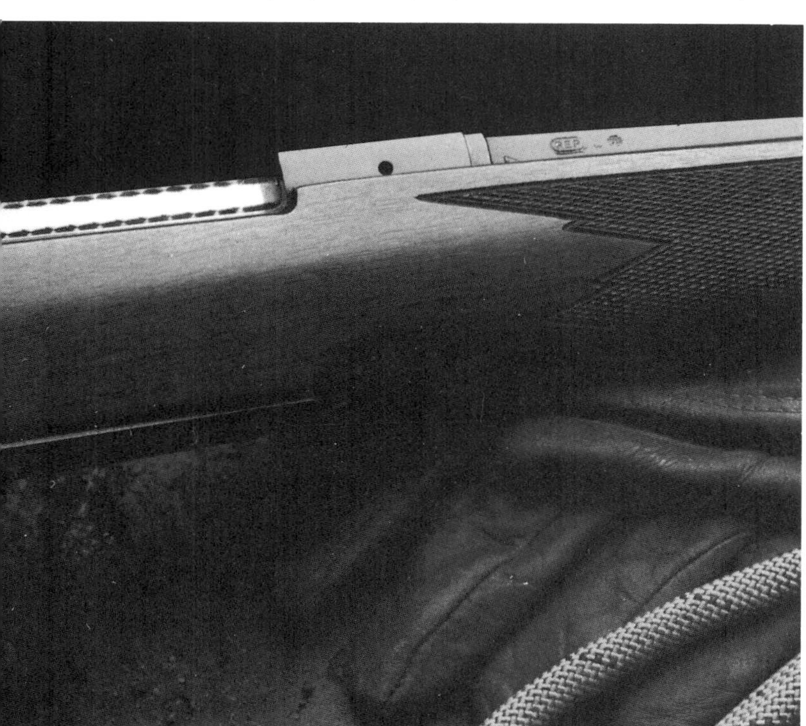

In August of 1944, Walker was placed at the head of the 721/722 project and given $35,000 to begin building prototypes for the new rifles. Walker headed a team of designers which was remarkably small for what was to become such a major weapon project: only three men—Dana McNally, Leon Rix and Knute Reed—were assigned to produce the drawings and fabricate the prototype form.

The feasibility studies that had been done in 1942 established the rough parameters of what the 721/722 rifles should be. These parameters stated that the rifles should be light in weight and fast handling; their production costs must be low enough to provide sufficient profitably for the company; they would have to be capable of being manufactured with mass-production techniques; and the new rifles were not to compete head to head with the Winchester Model 70, but rather were to eat into the Winchester Model 94, Marlin Model 86 and Savage Model 40 markets. The fascinating thing about the model 721/722 project is that it brought to bear a sectional talent in such a way that the rifles that were produced are, even today, bench marks in the production history of center fire weapons. In terms of productivity, the Model 721 rifle only required 60 machine operations, whereas its predecessor, the Model 720, required 250 such operations. Here was efficiency indeed! Because of the unique production processes involved, precision parts could be produced without the high degree of individual workmanship previously needed.

The original 721/722 design drawings called for the rifles to be produced in four barrel lengths ranging from 20 to 26 inches. However, production models were actually produced in 24 and 26 inch lengths. Later 22-inch barrels were offered for some calibers. The 721/722 weighed only 7.25 pounds at the most. By comparison, Winchester's Model 70 weighed 7.75 pounds and most of Remington's other competitors

weighed in at a hefty eight pounds or more. Standard stocks for the 721/722 were cut from American walnut and featured a standard pistol grip with a semi-beavertail forearm; and the two basic stock designs were the iron sight version—which dropped 1.87 inches at the comb and 2.87 inches at the heel—and a high comb stock which dropped 1.38 inches at the comb and 2.19 inches at the heel.

The 721/722s were marketed in five chamberings: .30-06, .270 Winchester, .300 H and H Magnum, .257 Roberts and .300 Savage. The 220 Swift was originally planned for the 721 rifle but was dropped in favor of the Remington .222 cartridge. The .222 Remington is still of universal popularity today as a fine varmint caliber. The introduction of the .222 Remington greatly enhanced the sales of the short-action 722 rifles. In time, other calibers became available for the Model 721, namely the .280 Remington, the .264 Winchester Magnum, the .308 Winchester, the .244 Remington, the .222 Remington Magnum and the .243 Winchester.

The series of tests to which the 721/722 rifles were subjected were extensive almost beyond belief. Various cold, rain, dust and endurance tests were devised. Ice tests and blow-up tests were later added. Machinery was set up to subject the rifles to 50,000-round firings in order to check the wear on the bolt and firing systems. Even gas leak tests were conducted in an 'iron lung' type of device. These last tests were meant to determine safety parameters beyond those generally encountered by hunters. The blow-up tests were by far the most publicized. These tests were conducted in the .30-06 caliber, which was considered to be potentially the most dangerous load fired through the 721/722 rifles. No fewer than five 220-grain cartridges were lodged into the rifles one after the other, and then the weapon was fired. Remington estimated that the internal pressures thus created exceeded 300,000 pounds per square inch. This was testing taken to extraordinary lengths, but it did provide the company with excellent advertising and valuable data concerning the strength of the new actions.

Remington had a fine product, but still had to convince the United States patent office that no one else's patents were being stepped on by this new product. The company's lawyers had to produce written depositions that established when, where and who

At left: The Model 700 is world renowned for its accuracy and strength. Available in 16 calibers, this big game rifle features handcrafted fit and finish—as is implied by this photograph. _Below:_ The potent Remington 660 Carbine with sling and shock pad, and _below left_, without same.

actually worked on the new rifles. The patent people in Washington wanted to examine all of the blow-up test specimens as well as Remington's competitor's specimens.

The 721/722 project was kept a virtual secret at the factory. In the spring of 1947, rumors were surfacing of a new Remington product. At this time, some writers were actually shown the first prototype specimens. They immediately recognized that here were entirely new rifle designs, not just remakes composed of spare military parts. The official announcements were made and actual marketing began in January 1948.

The 721s and 722s were first marketed at more expensive prices than had been originally planned. The 721 retailed for around $80.00 and the 722 for around $75.00. By this time, the Winchester 94 sold for about $60.00 and the Marlin Model 86 went for about $59.00. The purchaser of the Remingtons paid a little more, but got impressively much more. This fact actually made the $110.00 price tag on the Winchester Model 70 seem expensive in comparison to what the buyer was actually getting for his money. The 721/722s were in fact just as good as the Winchester Model 70s at considerably less cost. Many shooters during this period had actually become accustomed to paying upwards of $200.00 for custom rifles built from surplus military parts. Thus a truly fine $80.00 rifle with state-of-the-art performance was a welcome and eagerly sought-after piece of merchandise. Deliveries of various calibers began in 1948 with the .30-06 Springfield coming out in March of that year, followed by the .300 Savage in May, the .270 Winchester and .250 Roberts in July, and, finally, the .300 H and H Magnum in September. Two grades of the rifle were made—the standard and the fancy. The fancy grade was subdivided into various classes: the B Special with a checkered stock of selected walnut, and the D Peerless and F Premier grades which featured progressively finer wood and more detailed engravings.

Obviously, DuPont management was in the firearms game to make money. It was estimated that the 721/722 rifles had to be sold at a 1500 per month clip in order to break even. When one considers the low production sales figures for pre-World War II rifles, a break-even point of 1500 specimens per month was indeed audacious—and the response of the market was overwhelming. People liked the rifles' light weight and good balance. Their speed and smoothness of operation was acclaimed. The clean stock lines and proportions, and the smooth-working, strong receiver were 'winners.' The safety was both noiseless and convenient, and the bolt handle and safety location were designed with low mounted scopes in mind. Even the trigger was adjustable—and best of all, the price was right.

***Below:* The Remington Model 788 is chambered for five calibers from .223 Remington to .308 Winchester, and has nine locking lugs. *At right:* The famous turn-of-the century sharpshooter Annie Oakley, the only woman to ever hold the 'World Champion Shotgun Shot' title, was married to trick shot Frank Butler, who became a Remington salesman. Annie's prowess was amazing, and she most often used Remington rifles and pistols. Here, however, she holds a shotgun which was custom-tailored for her in Great Britain.**

— COPYRIGHT 1899 —
— RICHARD K. FOX —

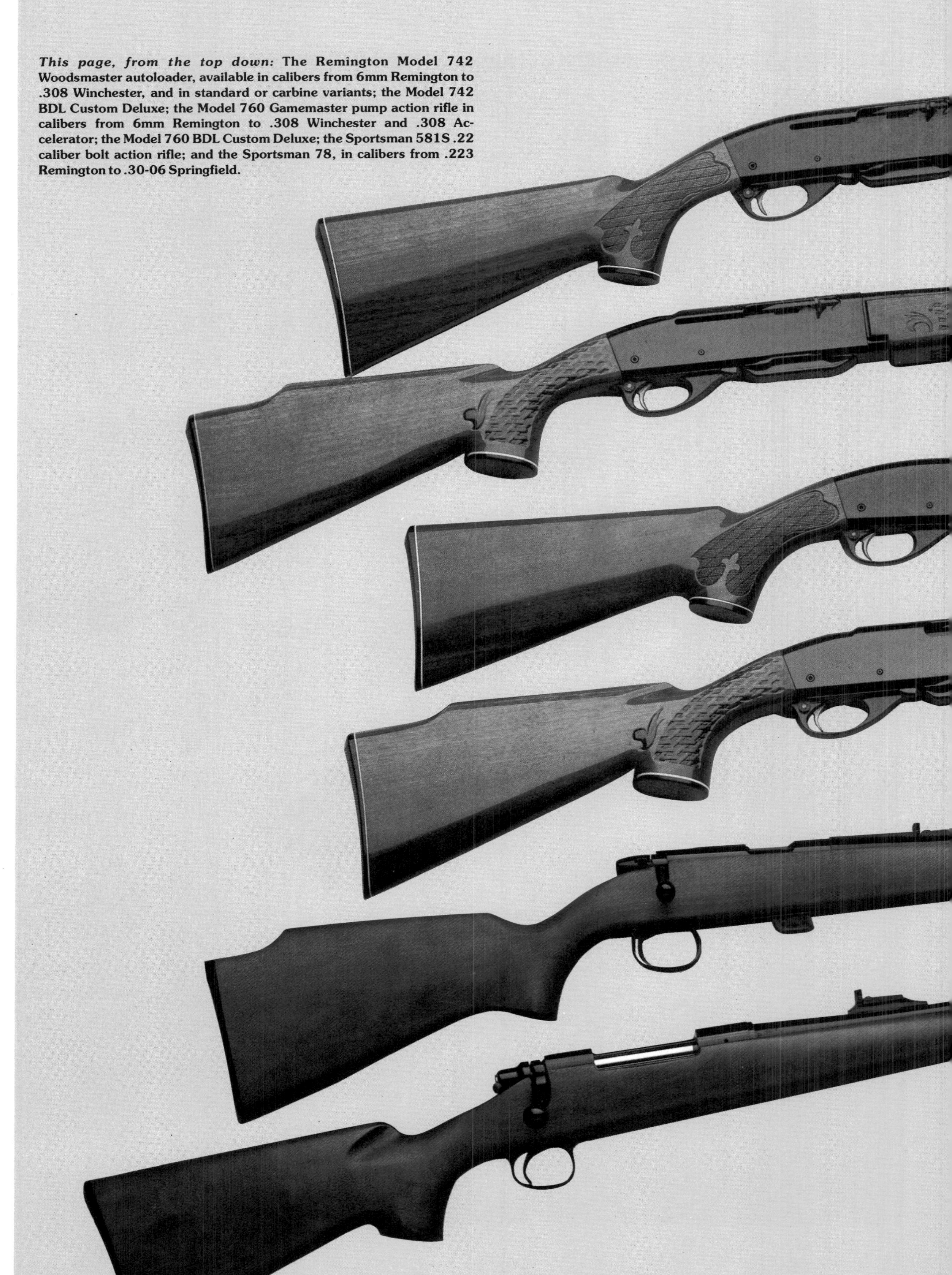

This page, from the top down: The Remington Model 742 Woodsmaster autoloader, available in calibers from 6mm Remington to .308 Winchester, and in standard or carbine variants; the Model 742 BDL Custom Deluxe; the Model 760 Gamemaster pump action rifle in calibers from 6mm Remington to .308 Winchester and .308 Accelerator; the Model 760 BDL Custom Deluxe; the Sportsman 581S .22 caliber bolt action rifle; and the Sportsman 78, in calibers from .223 Remington to .30-06 Springfield.

The first year's production (1949) was approximately 46,000 rifles; sales in 1950 exceeded 50,000. Remington was selling everything it could ship. There was an early demand for checkering on the standard model stocks, but this would have boosted the rifle's base retail price by $10.00 to $15.00 and Remington opted not to checker the stocks. By 1951, sales had slipped slightly back into the 30,000 per year range, although coming years would see times when over 50,000 rifles annually were produced.

In 1962, the Remington model 700 was introduced, and it superseded the 721 and 722. Sales soared again, this time into the 60,000 per year category in the first year of production. Since that time, some years have seen over 100,000 of these rifles produced and sold. The Model 721/722 and their upgraded offspring, the Model 700, have set records as the best selling bolt action rifles in the world to this day.

One of the most interesting innovations generated by Remington Arms was that of the adjustable trigger. Up until the introduction of the Models 721 and 722, most rifle triggers were simply factory-set. But with the introduction of the new Remington rifles after World War II a new phase was coined in the every day usage of the firearms trade: 'The fully adjustable trigger.' This meant that the amount of effort required to pull the trigger in order to release the hammer could be adjusted according to taste. This is made possible via a secondary sear, located at the long end of the trigger lever, which allows the mainspring pressure to be drastically reduced. With only a small amount of pressure on this secondary sear, it is possible to maintain a small amount of contact with the mainspring. Small screws were mounted in the trigger housing which made it possible to adjust the limits of motion within the trigger mechanism—the weight of pull, creep, backlash and depth of sear engagement could be adjusted to suit sportsmen's finger reflexes. Naturally, Remington's competitors followed suit and virtually every deluxe new rifle which has been introduced since Remington's innovation has featured a fully adjustable trigger mechanism.

One objection that has been raised about the Remington Model 700 is that its extraction and ejection mechanism *looks* as if it's too small to be reliable—but looks can deceive. The extraction and ejection mechanism of a rifle is intended to clamp onto the spent shell and eject it from the breech when the bolt is pulled back. When one considers how a Remington Model 700 extractor works, apparent heftiness matters little. Remington extractors are somewhat unique: the more pressure is exerted on them, the tighter they hold onto the shell casing—this is the famous Remington 'ring of steel' bolt face extractor. The extractor derives its strength from the bolt itself and also cannot override the cartridge rim; when overriding takes place, the ejector gets 'stuck,' and fails to eject the spent cartridge. Remington put up with numerous complaints about their miniature extractors. Finally, their engineers concocted a tug of war test between a standard Model 98 Mauser extractor and the Model 700. The two rifle bolts were fitted into a laboratory setup which measured tensile strength. The machine ran the pressure on each extractor up to hundreds and then thousands of pounds. The Mauser extractor let go first. The Remington extractor was triumphant.

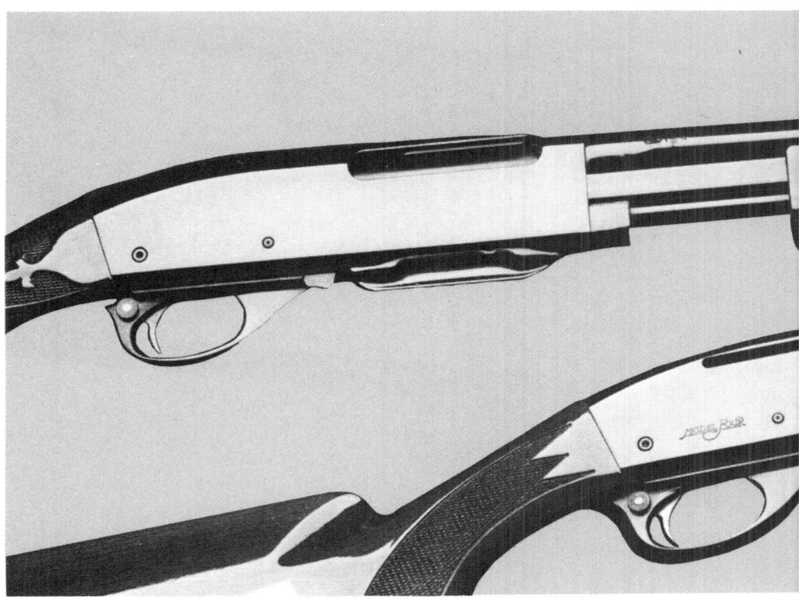

As early as 1874, Remington was involved in the fabrication of beautifully made, single shot target rifles. The American team won an international competition over a crack Irish team that year at Creedmoor, Long Island: the Irish team was fresh off a victory at Wimbledon, England which declared them to be the finest marksmen in the Western World! Important in this victory were specially built 'Creedmoor' long range rifles made for the American team by E Remington and Sons under the supervision of L L Hepburn. Today, Remington's 40-X target rifle stands at the top of the accuracy heap. Many consider the 40-X to be the most accurate center fire rifle ever offered by a major arms manufacturer. Its accuracy is legendary and even rivals the efforts of the best custom gun shops. Today every 40-X that leaves the Remington factory is virtually a dream come true.

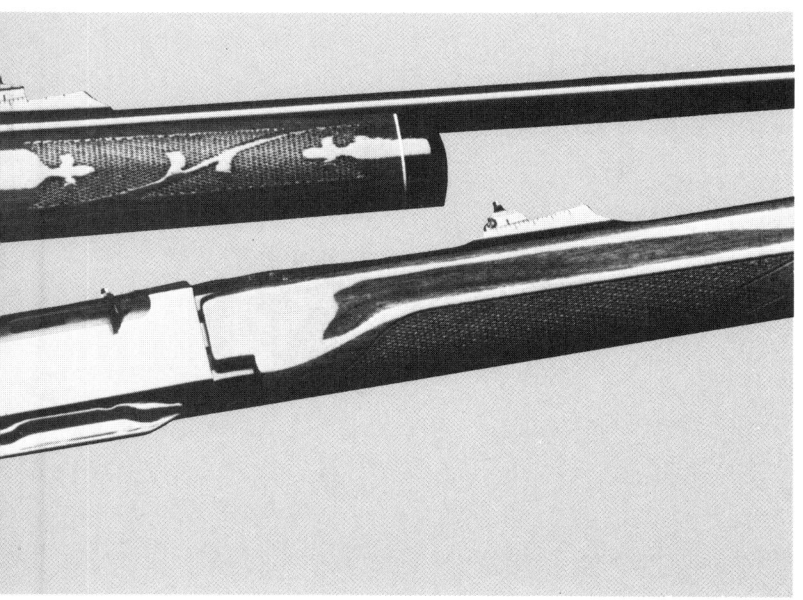

But the accuracy game is not only played by bench rest shooters. Varmint rifles offer superb accuracy as well as conventional hunting features. One of the most accurate varmint rifles that can be had over the counter is the Remington 40-XB. This rifle comes in a variety of calibers from .22 up to .300 Magnum. The barrel is a heavy stainless steel tube. The 40-XB is available in both single shot and repeater models. Ultra-fine trigger pull is optional. Unlike other Remington firearms, 40-XB rifles are produced in Remington's custom shop and are hand built and tested. Each rifle is test fired for accuracy and the test targets are supplied with each rifle. The 40-XB stock profile and dimensions are beautiful to target and varmint shooters; the rifle is a stellar performer.

Remington also manufactures a very accurate varmint rifle known as the Model 700 Varmint Special, which is a variant of the Model 700 Sporter. Both the Model 700 Varmint Special and the 40-XB are direct descendents of the Model 722. The 700s are not custom built or fitted as are the 40-XBs, but they are remarkable for mass-produced weapons.

Shotguns

Remington began producing double-barrel shot guns with the Remington-Whitmore Model of 1874, which was actually a shotgun and rifle combination. This particular 'do-anything' gun was produced from 1874 to 1882, when an actual double-barreled shotgun was produced in both 10 and 12 gauge. In the middle 1890s, Remington upgraded its shotgun technology by marketing a hammerless gun from 1894 until 1900. In 1907 Remington introduced its Model 10A Standard Grade repeating shotgun with slide action. This particular model proved to be quite popular, and continued to be sold into the late 1920s. About the time that the slide action shotgun was introduced, Remington came up with the Model 11A Five Shot Autoloader. This was a hammerless shotgun of the Browning type, with a tubular magazine holding four shells and available in 12, 16 and 20 gauge. Remington did not, however, confine itself to slide action and autoloader shotguns only.

In 1932, the Model 32A Over-and-Under Gun was introduced. This hammerless double-barrel featured automatic ejectors—and later models even incorporated a selective single trigger mechanism. It was available in 12 gauge only, but in various barrel lengths (from 26 to 32 inches) and chokes. Production ceased about 1942. In 1973, Remington introduced the Model 3200 Field Grade Over-and-Under Shotgun, which continues in production today.

The Remington Model 870 is probably the most popular pump action shotgun of all time. In 1950, the first Model 870s appeared. These were five shot slide-action hammerless repeaters in various gauges, all of whose tubular magazines held four shells. Total sales are well over four million pieces. Pump action shotguns are generally used by those hunters who favor the reliability of manual operation especially in inclement weather and rough conditions. The 12 and 20 gauge 870s feature the interchangeable 'Rem Choke,' which is crafted from heat-treated seamless stainless steel and provides a wide variety of choke settings for the individual shotgun.

Today, the Model 870 Pump Action Shotgun comes in six varieties: the Wingmaster, the Special Field, the .410 Field, the Wingmaster Deer Gun, the 20 gauge Youth gun and the Express. There are also two special purpose 870s—namely, the SP Deer Gun and the SP Magnum.

Probably the largest selling *automatic* shotgun of all time is the Remington Model 1100 Automatic Field Gun, which was first introduced in 1963. This gas-operated autoloader is noted for its balance and soft recoil. It is marketed today in three basic varieties: the Magnum, the Field Grade and the Special Field. An array of separately sold barrels of various lengths, chokes and chambers make it possible for the Model 1100 owner to put his gun to its best

These pages, from the top down: **The Remington Model 7600 pump action; the Remington Model 4; the Model 40-XB-BR Benchrest rifle; the New Model 40-XB Kevlar Stock Varmint Special; the Model 40-XR Rimfire rifle; and the Remington Long-Range XR-100 Pistol.**

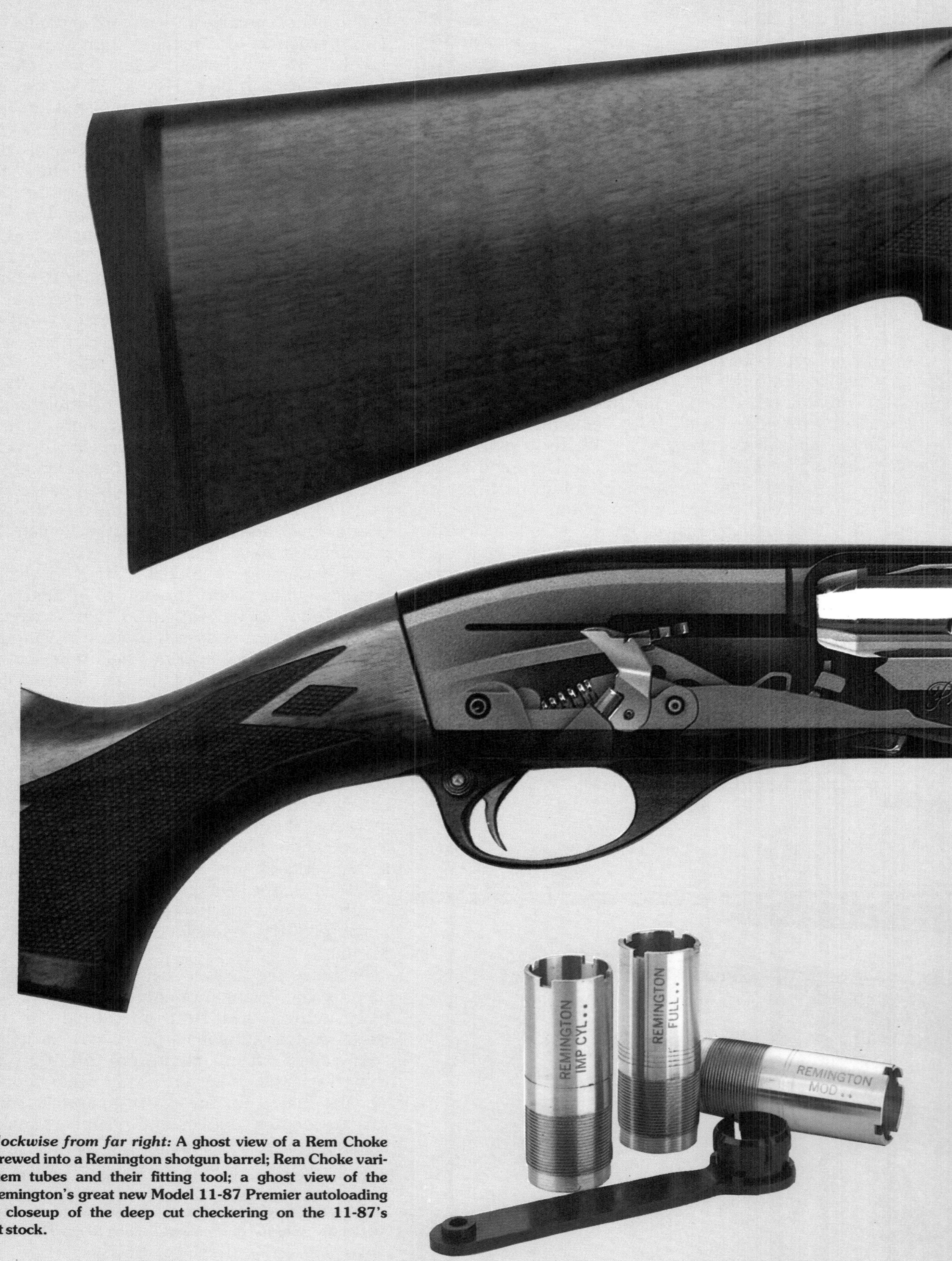

These pages, clockwise from far right: **A ghost view of a Rem Choke choke tube as screwed into a Remington shotgun barrel; Rem Choke variable choke system tubes and their fitting tool; a ghost view of the mechanism of Remington's great new Model 11-87 Premier autoloading shotgun; and a closeup of the deep cut checkering on the 11-87's American Walnut stock.**

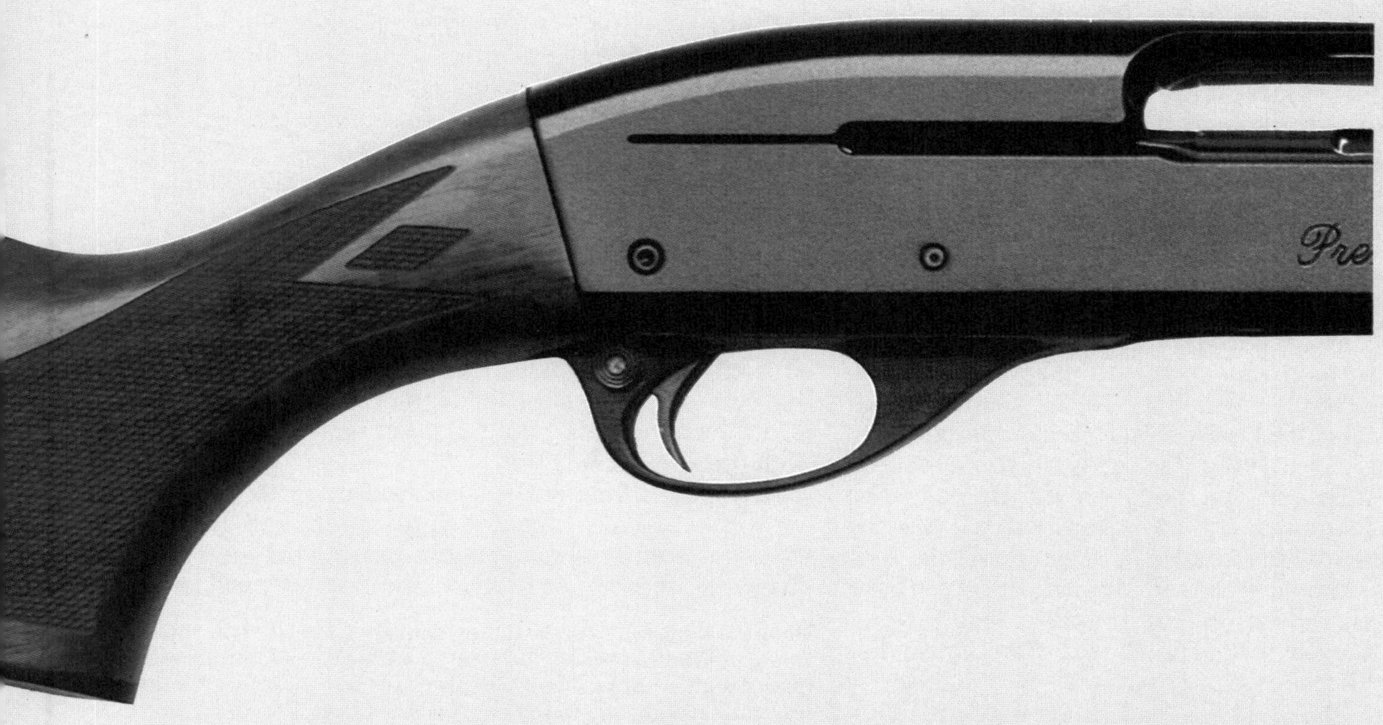

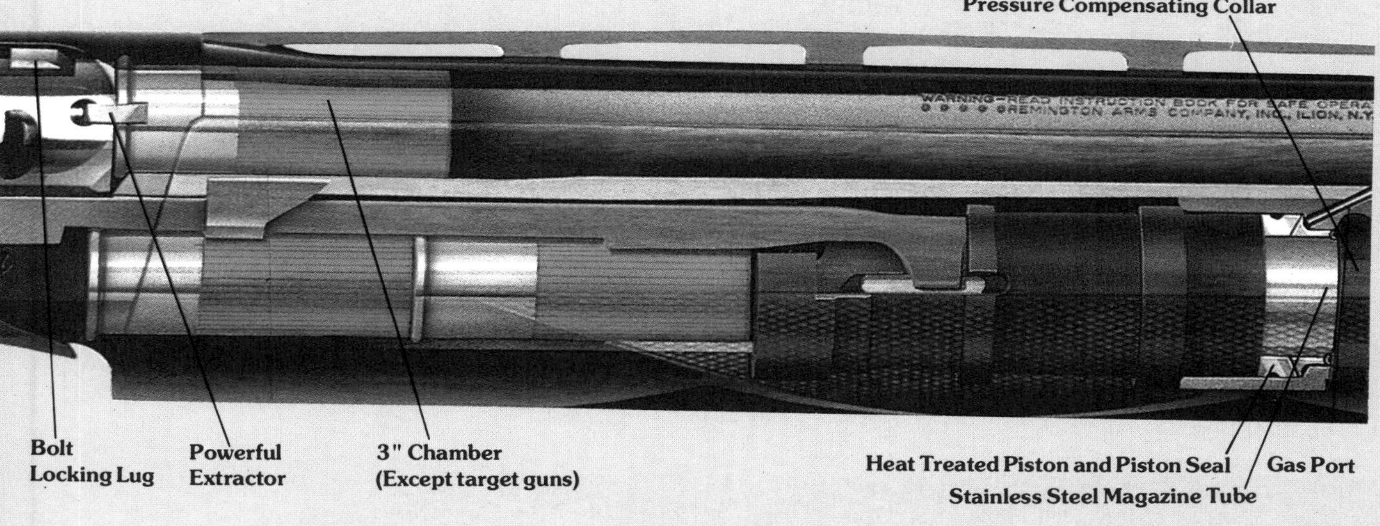
Pressure Compensating Collar
WARNING—READ INSTRUCTION BOOK FOR SAFE OPERA
REMINGTON ARMS COMPANY, INC., ILION, N.Y.
Bolt
Locking Lug
Powerful
Extractor
3" Chamber
(Except target guns)
Heat Treated Piston and Piston Seal
Gas Port
Stainless Steel Magazine Tube

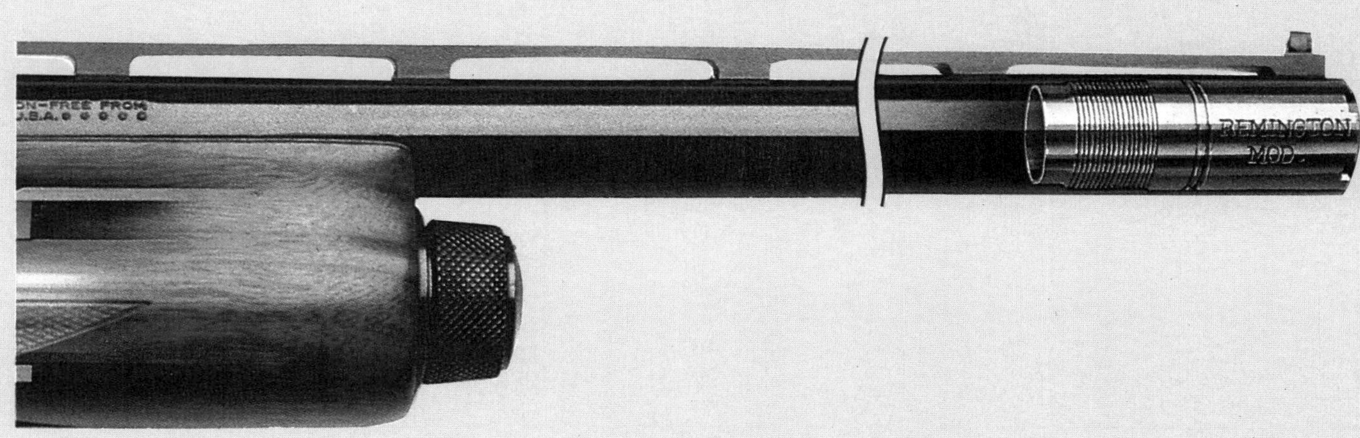
REMINGTON
MOD.

use from upland game to flyaway shooting. The various Model 1100 versions are distinctively decorated with receiver scroll work, usually a high gloss finished stock, white spacers and the now-familiar diamond grip cap inlay.

The top-of-the-line Remington Autoloading Shotgun is presently the Model 11-87 Premier Autoloader, which utilizes a pressure compensating system which enables the shooter to use all loads—from heavy three inch Magnums to light 2.75 inch loads—interchangably. This particular gas system is completely self-cleaning. No matter how many rounds are shot, the compensating spring never has to be removed for maintenance. In lab tests, Remington has proven that its Model 11-87 is literally *twice as durable* as the most popular autoloader currently on the market. The 11-87 Premier features cut (not stamped) checkering and satin finish on an American Walnut stock. The Model 11-87 is also available in Special Purpose Deer Gun and Special Purpose Magnum models.

One of the newest innovations that Remington has introduced into the shotgun world is its SP MultiRange Duplex Shells. These shells are the first and only shotgun loads with a stratified payload; that is, heavier shot is loaded in front of lighter shot so that, when the shell is fired, the heavy shot breaks through any shot-deflecting brush and cover while the lighter shot retains its lethal energy for extended ranges. These multi-range shot shells are marketed in camouflage olive drab hulls with dull black bases. That this concept of two shot sizes in one shell is indisputibly effective is seen from a recent Remington test, in which new SP Duplex BBX4 shells were shot from 40 yards at a target moving 40 miles per hour. The resulting patterns showed 100 percent of the BB shot and 83 percent of the Number Four shot hit within a 30-inch circle. Most all of Remington's shotgun ammunition is available in both lead and steel shot.

Remington remains the only American ammunition company that also manufactures guns, and thus is able to tailor entire shooting systems to unique advantage, given the company's myriad ammunition product lines.

Below and bottom: **This beautiful Remington Model 1100 autoloading trap gun—shown here in 'flip side' views—belongs to proud owner Mr Don Griffith, who has shot it with pleasure for many years. Another avid trap and skeet shooter is Air Force General Curtis LeMay *(at right)*.**

Remington Rifles 1816–1944

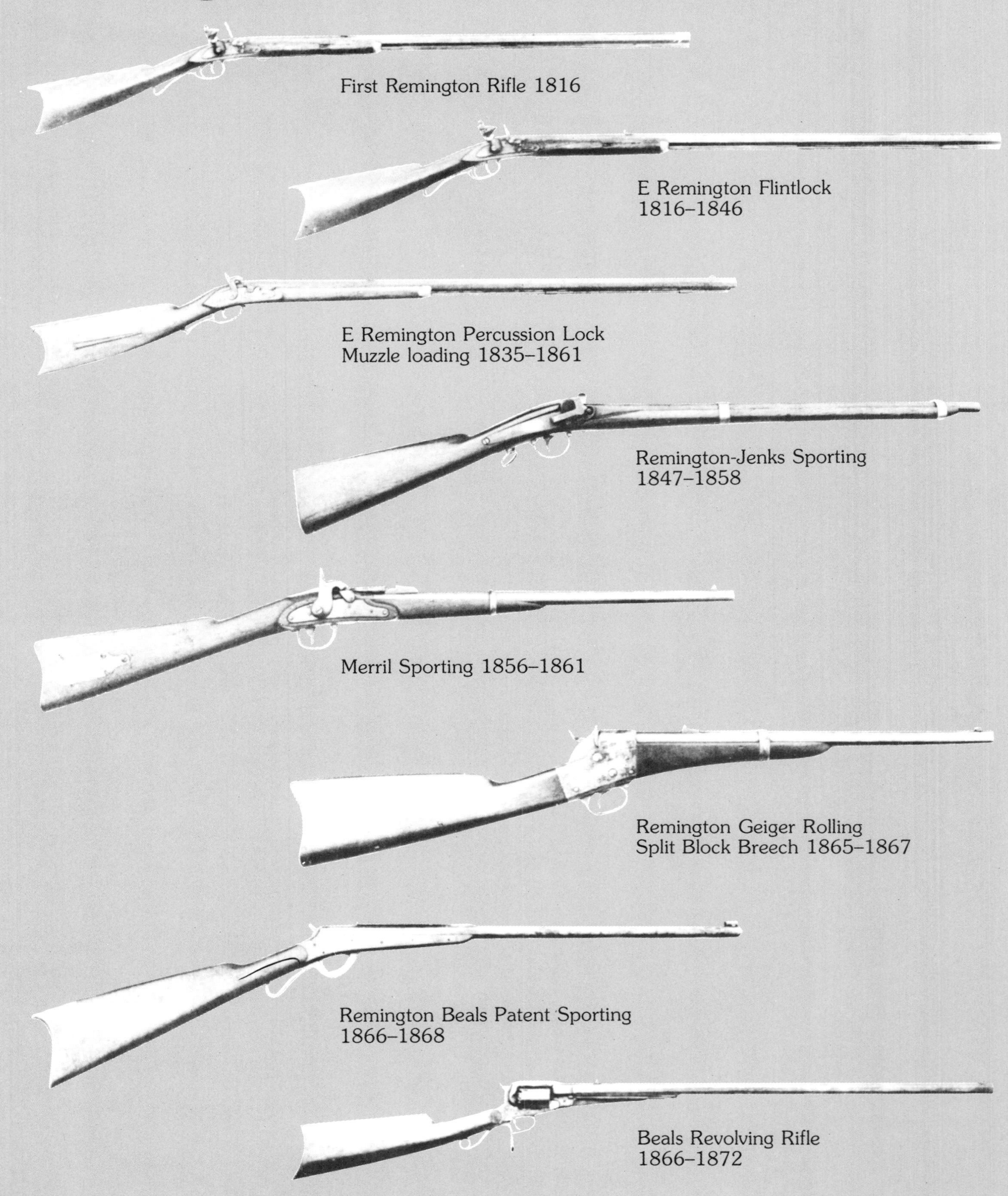

First Remington Rifle 1816

E Remington Flintlock
1816–1846

E Remington Percussion Lock
Muzzle loading 1835–1861

Remington-Jenks Sporting
1847–1858

Merril Sporting 1856–1861

Remington Geiger Rolling
Split Block Breech 1865–1867

Remington Beals Patent Sporting
1866–1868

Beals Revolving Rifle
1866–1872

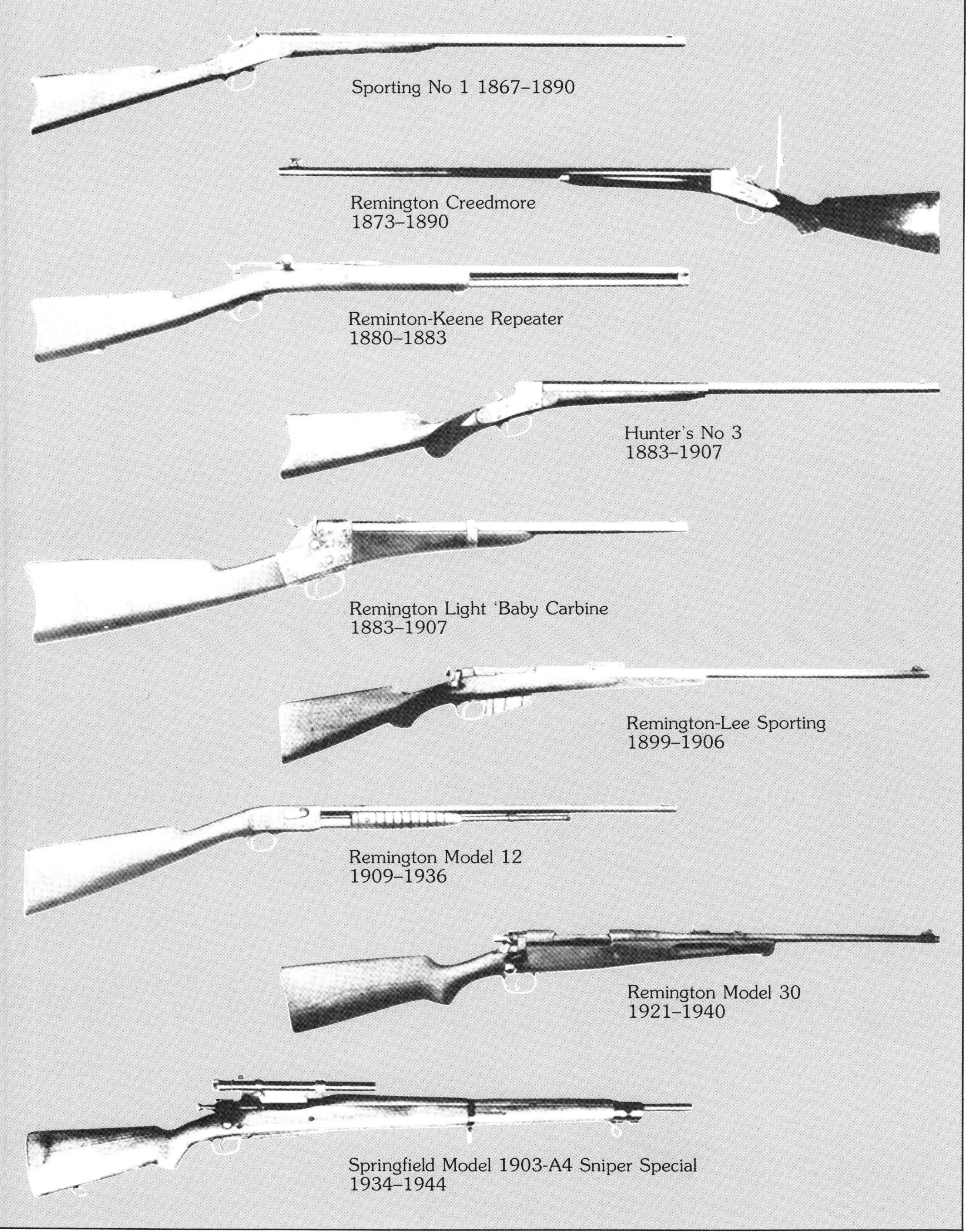
Sporting No 1 1867–1890
Remington Creedmore
1873–1890
Remington-Keene Repeater
1880–1883
Hunter's No 3
1883–1907
Remington Light 'Baby Carbine
1883–1907
Remington-Lee Sporting
1899–1906
Remington Model 12
1909–1936
Remington Model 30
1921–1940
Springfield Model 1903-A4 Sniper Special
1934–1944

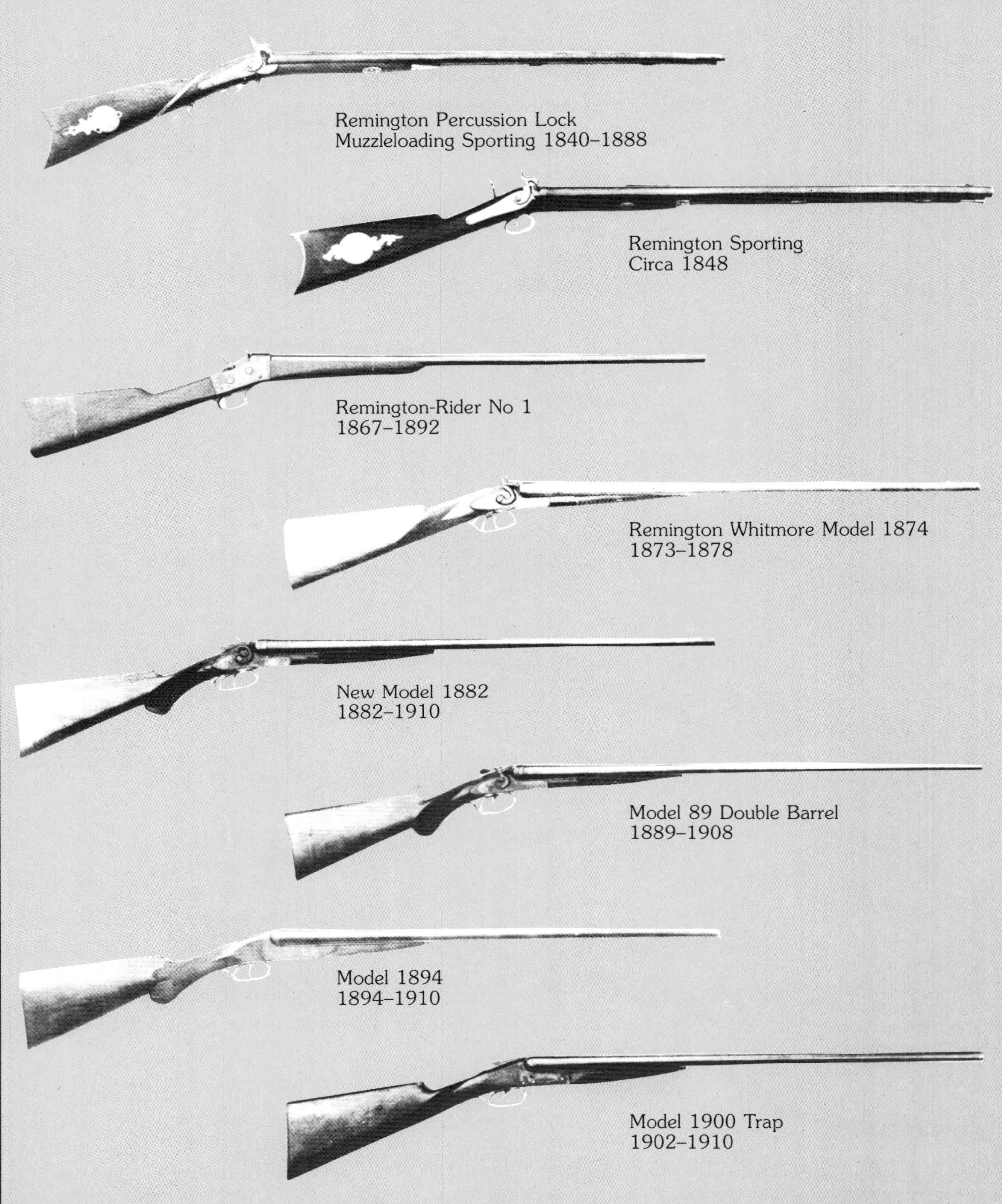

Remington Shotguns 1840–Present
Remington Percussion Lock
Muzzleloading Sporting 1840–1888
Remington Sporting
Circa 1848
Remington-Rider No 1
1867–1892
Remington Whitmore Model 1874
1873–1878
New Model 1882
1882–1910
Model 89 Double Barrel
1889–1908
Model 1894
1894–1910
Model 1900 Trap
1902–1910

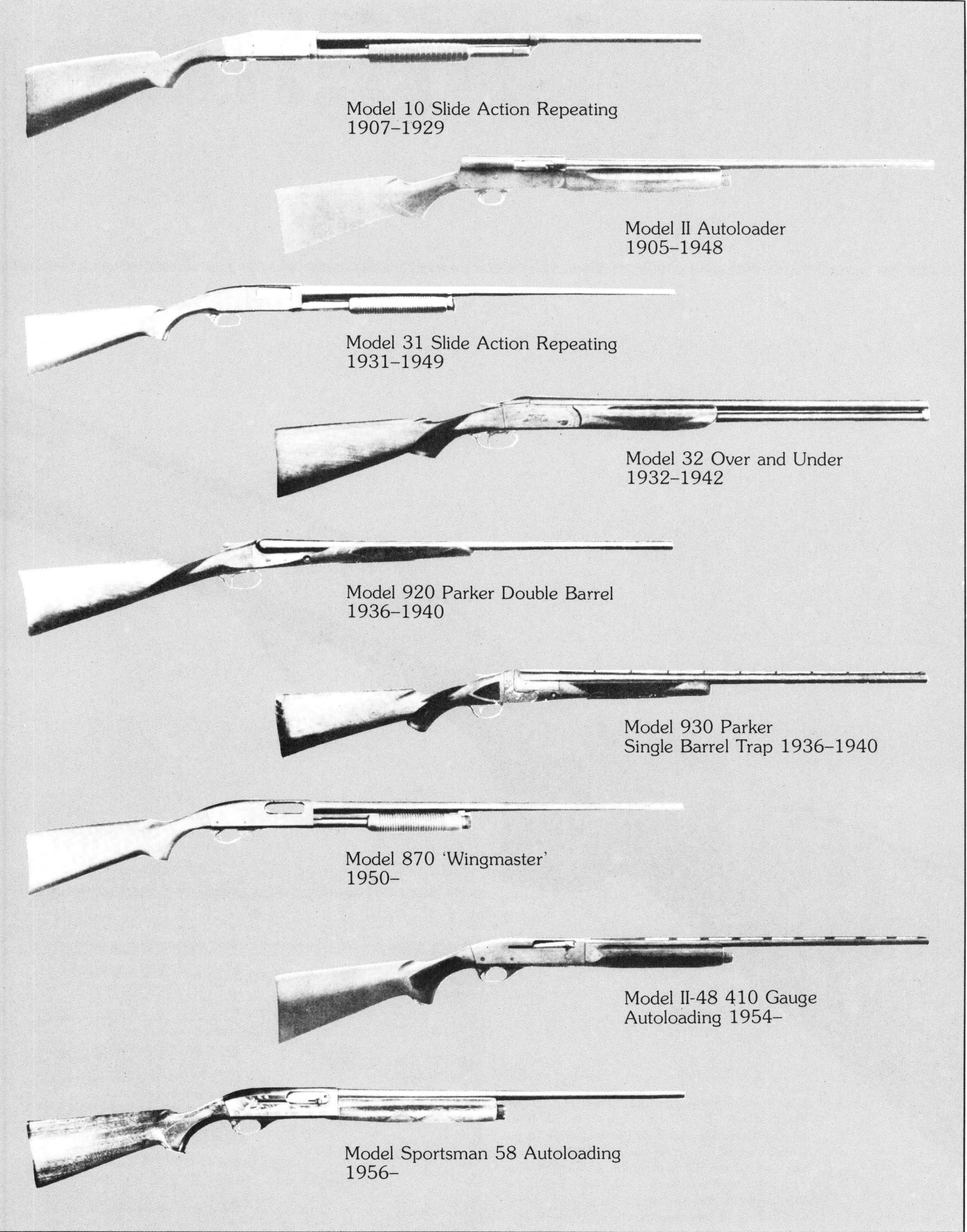

Model 10 Slide Action Repeating
1907–1929

Model II Autoloader
1905–1948

Model 31 Slide Action Repeating
1931–1949

Model 32 Over and Under
1932–1942

Model 920 Parker Double Barrel
1936–1940

Model 930 Parker
Single Barrel Trap 1936–1940

Model 870 'Wingmaster'
1950–

Model II-48 410 Gauge
Autoloading 1954–

Model Sportsman 58 Autoloading
1956–

Military

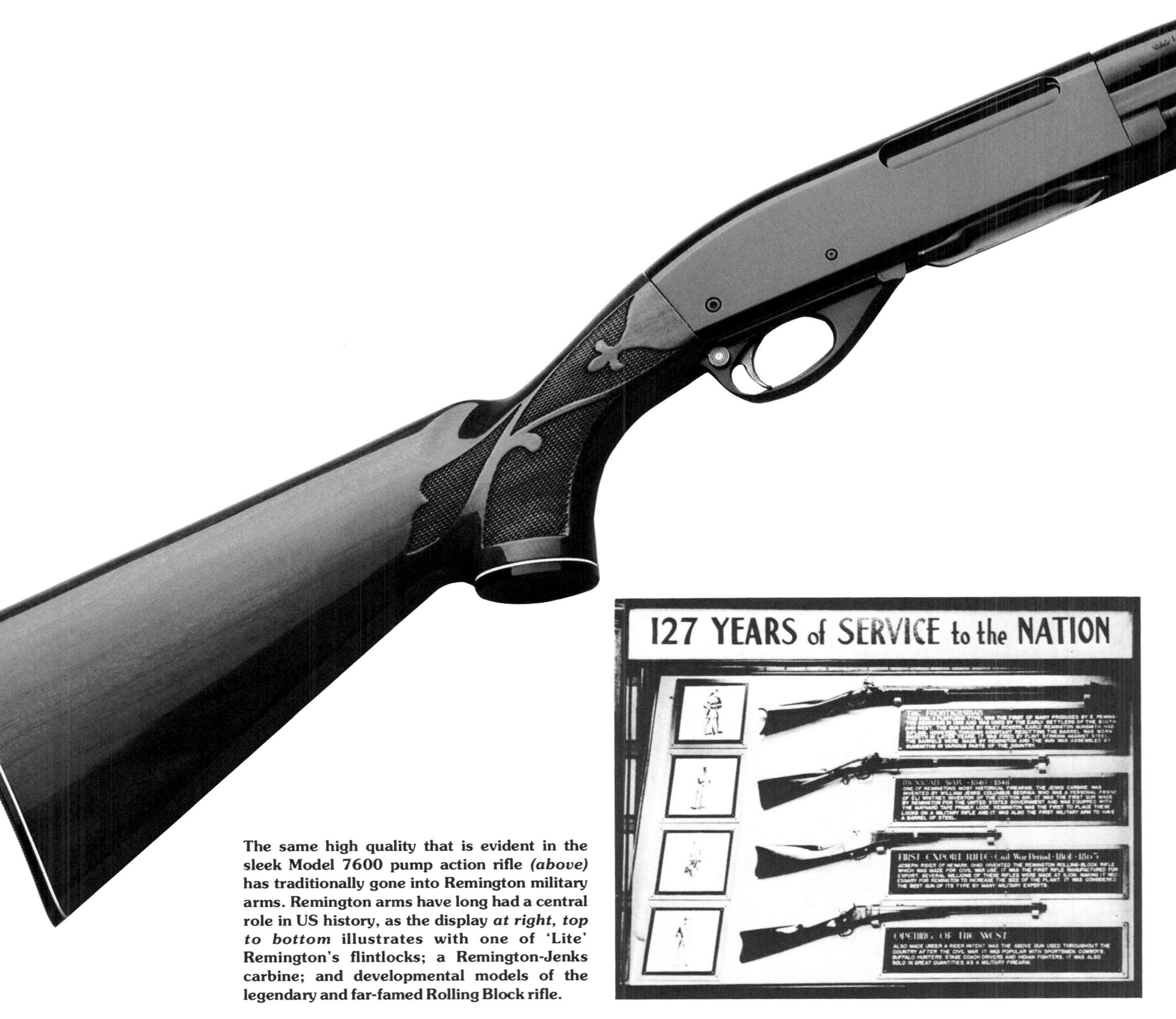

The same high quality that is evident in the sleek Model 7600 pump action rifle *(above)* has traditionally gone into Remington military arms. Remington arms have long had a central role in US history, as the display *at right, top to bottom* illustrates with one of 'Lite' Remington's flintlocks; a Remington-Jenks carbine; and developmental models of the legendary and far-famed Rolling Block rifle.

Arms

In 1845 the United States was preparing for war with Mexico. These preparations were hindered by circumstances in connection with the fact that the army was at that time equipped with muzzle-loading rifled muskets known as the 'Harpers Ferry Rifles.' These were to be produced by the John Griffiths Company of Cincinnati, Ohio, which held a contract from the government to produce 5000 units. The Griffiths Company was unable to fulfill its obligations on time; the government became understandably concerned, and let out the unofficial word to Eliphalet Remington that if he could see his way clear, the government would purchase rifles from him instead. Remington purchased the initial contracts from Griffiths and the government sweetened the deal by ordering an additional 5000 Harpers Ferry Rifles. Remington had to expand his facilities in order to meet this increased demand. He visited Chicopee Falls, Massachusetts and came in contact with the NP Ames Company. At this time, the Ames Company was turning out swords, bayonets and other military paraphernalia. Ames had also just contracted with the Navy for a new carbine invented by William Jenks. Remington bought the Ames Company, including all of its machinery, contracts and guns in various stages of production—as well as the services of his new-found friend, Mr Jenks. Jenks' original design was improved upon at many points. When finally delivered to the US Navy, the Remington-Jenks carbines were rifles with cast steel barrels, which were brightly tinned for protection against salt water, with hardened locks and breechs. The butt plate, trigger guard, sling rings, screws and other fittings were made of brass, polished to a high sheen. They were delivered to Commodore MC Perry's fleet in Vera Cruz in 1847, and were in the hands of his Marine troops when *they* stormed into the fabled Halls of Montezuma.

With the introduction of the Remington-Jenks carbine, the US Armed Forces were finally out of the musket age. A joint Army and Navy board said of the Jenks carbine, 'The board is of the opinion that this carbine combines, in an eminent degree, the two great advantages attending arms loading at the breech—that of propelling the ball with great force and that of being loaded rapidly and easily in situations where the use of the rammer is inconvenient; the later consideration would recommend it for use in boat service and in the fighting tops of vessels as well as in the Cavalry service.' But startling new inventions, even when they carry with them overwhelming advantages, are not always recognized by the 'authorities' in power at the time. Lieutenant Colonel George Talcott of the Ordnance Department was resolutely opposed to the Remington-Jenks rifles. In a letter to the Secretary of War he said: 'A prejudice against all arms loading at the breech is prevalent among officers, and especially the dragoons. That the arms of Mr Jenks, even if found better than others, can be introduced is not to be supposed. As regards the arming of the Second Dragoons with them, Colonel Twiggs has protested in advance against the use by his regiment of any breech loading or patent arms of any kind whatever.

'There are now Colts, Jenks, Hubbels, Nuttings—and I know not how many other kinds of patent arms—that they will ultimately all pass into oblivion cannot be doubted. I am, sir, etc, G Talcott, Lieutenant Colonel of Ordnance.' As it happened, Talcott and Twiggs were the only ones to pass into 'oblivion.'

Before the US military accepted the Jenks carbine,

extraordinarily difficult requirements were imposed upon the Remington-Jenks carbines by the Ordnance Department. One of them was that the Jenks must fire 1500 times without any noticeable deterioration in its performance; the first such test went well until about the 1400th shot, when the nipple on the firing mechanism broke and the gun was subsequently turned down.

But Jenks knew that he had a good idea. He went to Europe and in England and France found governments that were more than willing to give him contracts. That the Europeans found the Jenks carbines very attractive caused the US government to awaken out of its close-minded slumber. In 1858, the Jenks carbine was redesigned to accept cardboard cartridges and was tested by the government once again. This time, the Ordnance Department tests consisted of firing the gun a mere 126 times. Then they loaded it, held it under water for a full minute, and set it aside. The next day the carbine was fired and, though rusted, no difficulty was encountered in putting 50 rounds through it.

By the latter 1850s, Remington was beginning to do an expanded business for other gunsmiths. In their catalogue for 1858, they stated that:

'We have acquired a practical knowledge of the gunmaking business, especially in the manufacture of barrels, which we believe few, if any others, possess, having during that time (40 years) tested a great variety of Iron for the purpose, but having mostly manufactured it ourselves expressly for our own use.

'We have also, for nearly 30 years, been testing the Steel of almost every manufacturer in the world, for our Cast Steel Barrels, and have for a long time had it made to our order expressly for that purpose.

'These repeated and long continued experiments, in procuring the proper material for every variety of Barrel, and an equally long experience in the various methods of working and annealing it, enable us to say, without boasting, that we are now prepared to make Barrels both of Iron and Steel in greater variety and perfection than any other Establishment in this country, if not in the world; having been first in successfully introducing Steel for Sporting Guns, and also for US Rifles and Carbines, and having recently manufactured about 15,000 such for the US Service.'

Prices at this time ran as follows: cast steel barrels, $3.00 each; iron barrels, $2.00 each, Stubbs Twist (Damascus) $4.00 each; and matched barrels for double guns, (cast steel) $6.50 per pair.

The advent of the Civil War found the Union in dire straights. At that time, the government ran only two arsenals—one at Springfield, Massachusetts, and the other at Harpers Ferry, Virginia. But Virginia had seceded from the Union with the advent of war, and the Harpers Ferry arsenal was destroyed in the first days of the conflict. This left the Union with only one arsenal—which could only turn out a few thousand rifles a year. The government turned to Eliphalet Remington with the question, 'How many guns, revolvers and bayonets can you make for us?' The answer to that initial question was astounding. Orders from the Army and the Navy eventually amounted to over $29 million—a staggering sum in those days. At its peak, Remington produced over 200 pistols and nearly 1000 rifles per day for the Union troops. Dropforged bayonets were also produced by Remington during the war; 18,000 Maynard percussion locks were also built and used for the conversion of 1842-vintage flintlock military muskets. A cartridge division of the company was set up which supplied almost 10 million cartridges (which were primerless packets, each containing gunpowder, wadding and a rifle or pistol ball) to the government. Other deliveries included over 125,000 Remington-Beals .44 caliber Army revolvers, 5000 Remington-Beals .36 caliber Navy revolvers and 20,000 carbines. Of course, the bullet molds, reloading tools and other accessories for these firearms were also fabricated by Remington.

Such prodigious output of his factories naturally placed a severe strain on Eliphalet Remington himself. In August of 1861, his doctors diagnosed an inflammation of the bowels which today would be called an appendicitis attack. Overwork had simply caught up with him, and shortly before his death he dictated to his daughter, Maria, the following rather melancholy poem:

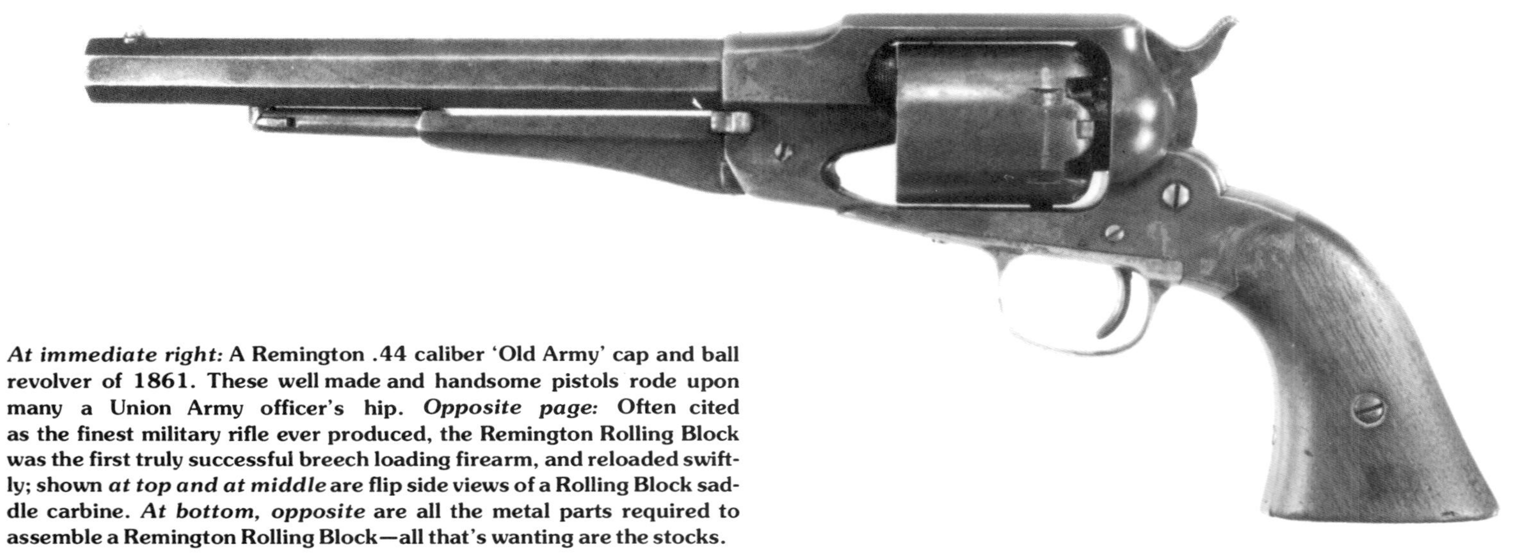

***At immediate right:* A Remington .44 caliber 'Old Army' cap and ball revolver of 1861. These well made and handsome pistols rode upon many a Union Army officer's hip. *Opposite page:* Often cited as the finest military rifle ever produced, the Remington Rolling Block was the first truly successful breech loading firearm, and reloaded swiftly; shown *at top and at middle* are flip side views of a Rolling Block saddle carbine. *At bottom, opposite* are all the metal parts required to assemble a Remington Rolling Block—all that's wanting are the stocks.**

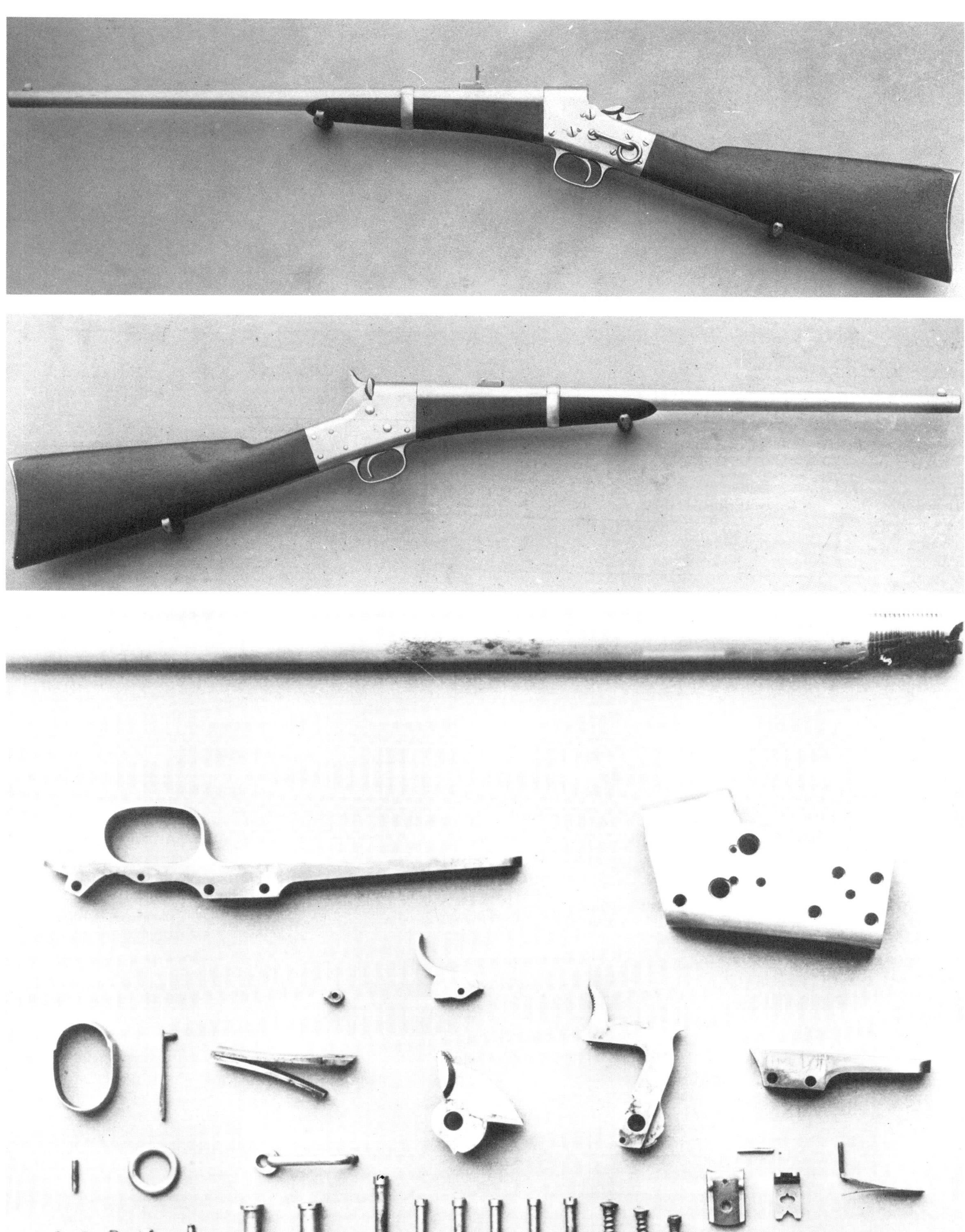

In manhood's strong and vigorous prime
I planted a young Linden tree
Near to my dwelling, which in time
Has spread its branches wide and free.

Oft I have viewed its healthful growth
With something like a parent's pride
Who sees the offspring of his youth
Grow to strong manhood by his side.

But now, old age has damped the flame
That glowed within me at that day
Energy and strength desert my frame
And I am sinking in decay.

But thanks! I've lived and long have shared
Health and vigor like this tree
And when I'm gone let it be spared—
A mute remembrance of me.

On 12 August 1861, Eliphalet Remington died. The business passed to Eliphalet's three sons, Philo, Samuel and Eliphalet, III. The sons continued in the footsteps of their father by importing promising inventors into the company. One such inventor was Leonard M Geiger, whose breech loading mechanism eventually became the basis for the famous Remington Rolling Block Rifle; however, the Geiger gun had a curious breech mechanism through which the hammer struck a rimfire cartridge. The Ordnance Department ordered 20,000 Geiger carbines, but since the Remington Armory was already awash with orders, these guns were manufactured by the Savage Company of Middleton, Connecticut under license from Remington. These guns were delivered in early 1865 and saw action in the last days of the Civil War. It is interesting to note that some of these Geiger carbines were equipped with small coffee grinding mills attached to the stocks; the Union army was not to be without its appropriate condiments around the campfire at night!

The Geiger carbines proved to be very successful against Confederate troops armed with ancient muzzle loaders. But because of the peculiar split-breech arrangement, certain weaknesses were noted in these carbines. An improved Geiger breech loader was presented to the board of the Springfield Arsenal in January of 1865. Competition tests were conducted including 65 other gunmakers—including Sharps, Roberts, Burnsides, Peabody and Henry—but it was shown that the Geiger gun needed further work.

Joseph Rider, in attempting to improve on Geiger's ideas, finally produced a gun that became known as the Remington Rolling Block Rifle. The Rolling Block breech was incredibly strong, easy to operate, and virtually foolproof. These single shot rifles have been praised as the best military arm ever produced. The breech was opened by simultaneously cocking the hammer and rolling the solid breech block straight back with the thumb. The backward motion of the block ejected the empty cartridge. A fresh round was shoved into the chamber, and the breech rolled forward and closed in one continuous motion. A locking lever secured the hammer while the gun was open and locked the breech after it was closed. The firing pin ran through a hole in the solid breech block, with the hammer striking against the back of the pin, as it projected slightly from the block, at the moment of firing. Because of the unique nature of this rolling block system, the greater the recoil, the more securely the mechanism was interlocked; it was literally impossible to blow out a Rolling Block breech—which was capable of handling any ammunition then available.

Both military and sporting Rolling Blocks were produced. There were over a million of the military models and carbines made. The total production of the Rolling Blocks spanned a remarkably long period of gunmaking history, from 1867 until 1934. The Rolling Block was produced in four basic action sizes: the Number 1 Action was the largest of the Rolling Blocks and was chambered for the largest and heaviest calibers; the Number 2 Action was chambered generally for cartridges of medium-size and pistol cartridges; the Number 3 Action was made in rimfire calibers of .22, .25-10 Stevens and .32; and the Number 4 Action was similar to the Number 1 in size and was designed for the 'smokeless high powered cartridges.' This last action was first introduced in 1898 especially for use with the then-new 'smokeless powder' cartridges, and was the last of the large frame Rolling Blocks.

The claim that the Rolling Block action was by far the strongest in the world was not lightly made. According to the report of Alphonse Polain, director

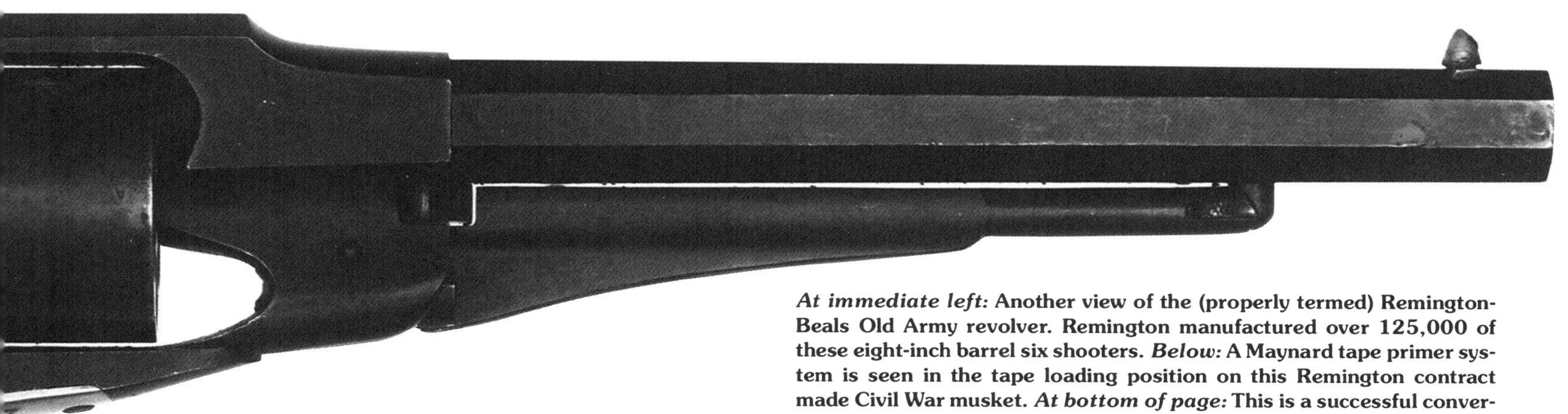

At immediate left: **Another view of the (properly termed) Remington-Beals Old Army revolver. Remington manufactured over 125,000 of these eight-inch barrel six shooters.** ***Below:*** **A Maynard tape primer system is seen in the tape loading position on this Remington contract made Civil War musket.** ***At bottom of page:*** **This is a successful conversion—of a Remington percussion Zouave Rifle of 1863—to the famous Rolling Block action.**

of the proving house at Liege, Belgium, a .50 caliber Remington Rolling Block was loaded with 750 grains of powder (10 times the normal load), 40 balls and two wads. It was fired and the report states that 'nothing extraordinary occurred.' The Spanish government tested Remington Rolling Blocks by soaking them in sea water and then setting them aside to rust. When they were eventually fired, every metal part was coated with a thick film of corrosion but the mechanisms worked flawlessly. Various examining boards in different countries came up with incredible tests to which to subject the Rolling Blocks—the guns were fired over 2500 times continuously; stocks were removed and the guns were fired without them; metallic cartridges were filed down so that they would burst in the chamber; and ram rods were left in the barrels and shot out of them. Never a breech failed. Never a gun burst. All functioned perfectly. *Iron Age Magazine* of 7 March 1872 stated:

'The excellent shooting qualities of the barrels made at E Remington and Sons have been, from the era of the founder, a proverb in mouths of wisest censure. The superiority has been, moreover, quite as generally observed in the barrels of the military as of the sporting rifles. It is possible that a degree of this excellence may be due to the choiceness of material, but the extraordinary care given to the interior finish, the delicate gauging of the chambers, and the exact turning of the muzzles, and more than all, the patient and faithful straightening process, which is never neglected, are probably the general claimants in this instance... The Remingtons, with an honorable pride in the excellence of their production, and correctly estimating the superlative importance of this quality in a barrel, have omitted no care, whether it concerns the experience and skill of artisans, or the severity of intermediate and final inspection, that will secure the merit of precision for their work.' By 1872, the Remington Armory was capable of turning out 1500 guns in a single day, all to exacting standards of quality. After the Civil War, the American arms market had slowed significantly. This was not the case, however, in most European capitals. European generals had studied the Civil War with meticulous care, and learned that muzzle loading arms were a thing of the past. But neither the Prussian Needle gun nor the French Chassepot—which were both breechloaders—could begin to compare with the new American single shot rifles. Opportunity knocked at Remington's door. The two other Remington brothers readily agreed that Sam was their best salesman. His personality was warm and charming. He was socially polished and witty. His *savoir vivre* would make him an instant hit in the extremely exclusive social circles of Europe, and could

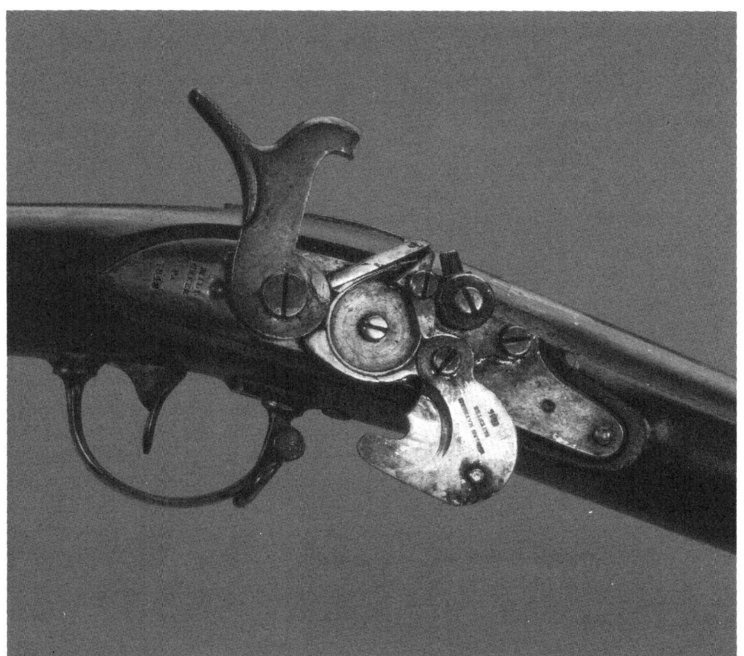

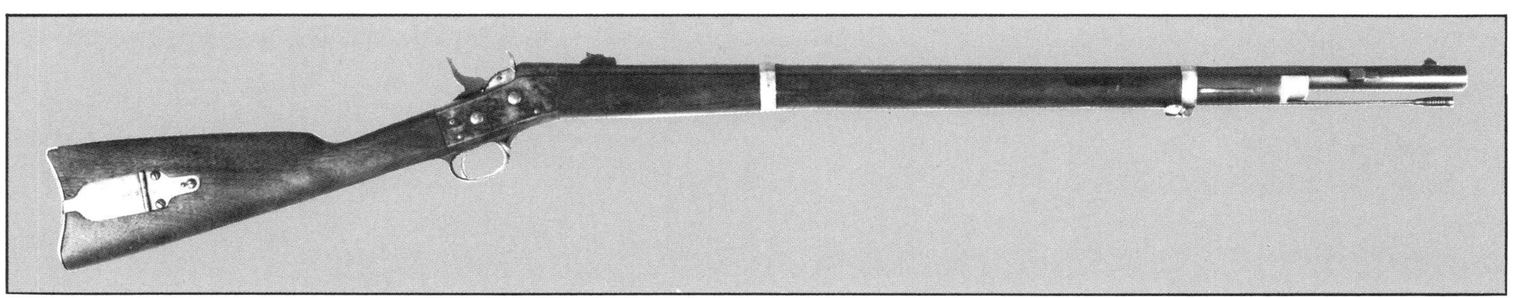

win for the company many valuable contracts totalling millions of dollars. So that Sam could better deal with European royalty, he was elected president of E Remington and Sons in 1866. He sailed to Europe with his wife, Flora, and established headquarters in Paris, where he lived in opulent style. While upper class European society—and particularly, the royal houses—normally excluded tradesmen and industrialists from social events, the makers of firearms were welcomed with open arms. Sam was entertained in most of the royal palaces of Europe and his company's product, the Rolling Block rifle, was eagerly received by kings and military leaders alike.

However, not all of Sam Remington's endeavors met with success. Sometimes an excellent product backed by good salesmanship simply falls victim to sheer misfortune. The Prussian army had decided that the Remington Rolling Block rifles were the guns for them. Accordingly, Sam was invited to their maneuvers near Potsdam. Sam arrived on the scene resplendent in silk hat, Prince Albert coat, and riding a beautiful charger. The King of Prussia, soon to become Kaiser Wilhelm I, welcomed Sam graciously with the request that he would like to personally shoot Sam's rifle. Sam handed the piece to the king, confident of his majesty's approval. The king adjusted the sights, took careful aim at an oak tree about 100 meters away, and pulled the trigger. Nothing happened! A dud cartridge! Lady Luck had betrayed him! The king hurled the gun to the ground in a rage and galloped away leaving Sam Remington to muse upon the furies of Fate.

Remington's losing streak did not last long. At the Imperial Exposition of 1867 in Paris, the High Commission of Firearms unanimously selected the Remington Rolling Block Rifle as the best rifle in the world. The exposition's judges consisted of leading ordnance experts from France, England, Austria, Russia, Prussia, Spain, Italy, Sweden, Holland and Belgium. They awarded Sam Remington the Silver Medal, which was the highest award for both military and sporting firearms. Shortly after this, Ismael Pasha, the great Khedive of Egypt, sent a commission to France to inquire about the latest firearms with which to equip his new Egyptian Army. The Egyptian Commission called on Samuel Remington, who immediately set sail for Cairo to see Khedive Ismael Pasha. A close, personal friendship evolved between them. Khedive Ismael Pasha gave Sam an ancient scimitar of Damascene workmanship. What really impressed the Khedive was the fact that the guns specified in the contract actually arrived on the specified date—such efficiency was a rarity indeed, and must not go unrewarded! Sam Remington found himself owning a parcel of land in the most desirable residential district of Cairo. The only problem with such a gift was that when a parcel of land was given as a gift, the receiver was obligated to build on it or else be guilty of unforgivable discourtesy. Sam built an exquisite marble palace on this piece of property, but never

Below: **Patent drawings for a US Army rifled musket. Remington made many similar arms for the Union during the Civil War.** ***Below right:*** **Patent drawings for the Remington Rolling Block rifle.** ***At right:*** **Late 19th century Remington arms displays, ready for shipping to firearms expositions around the world.**

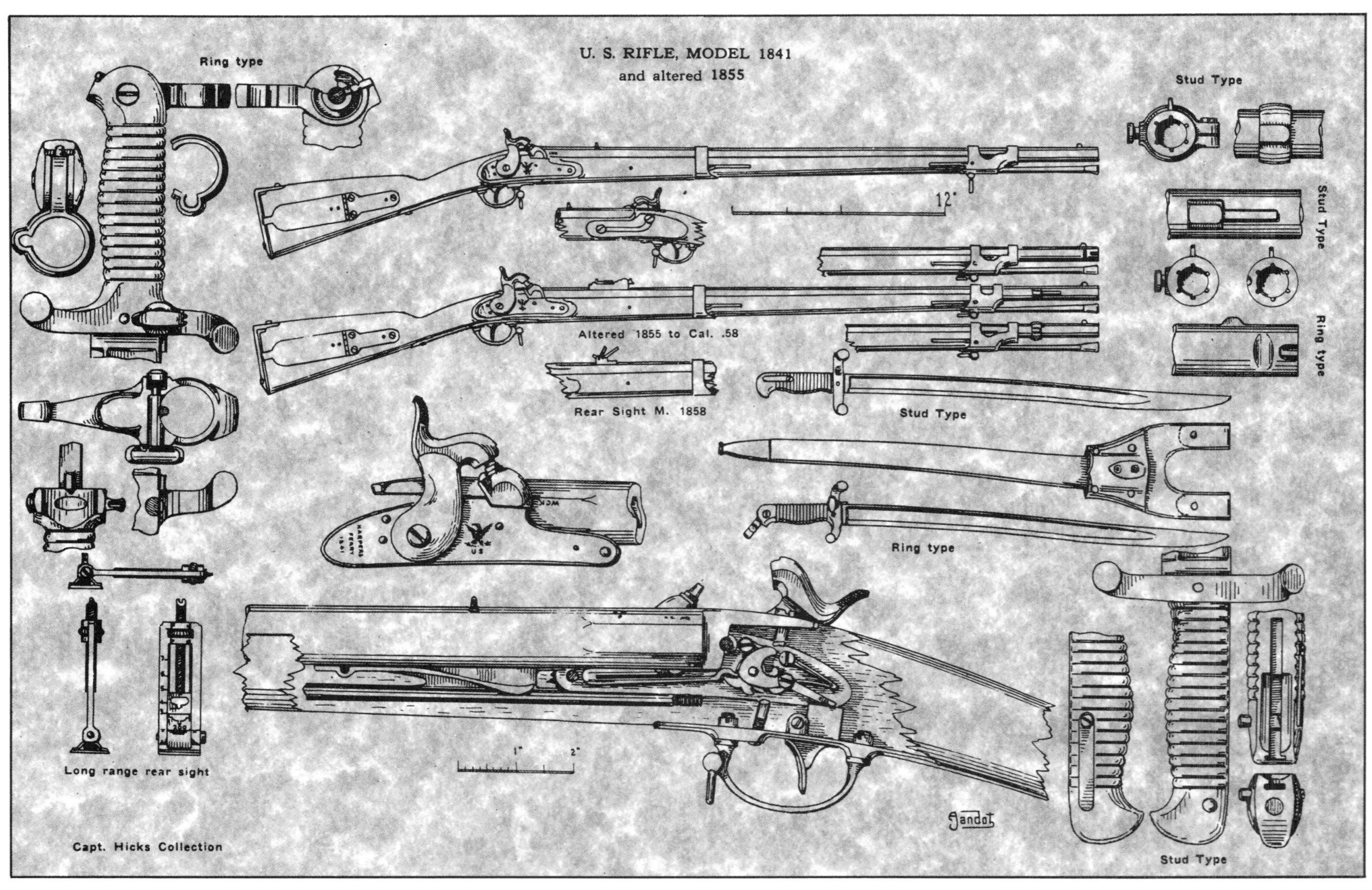

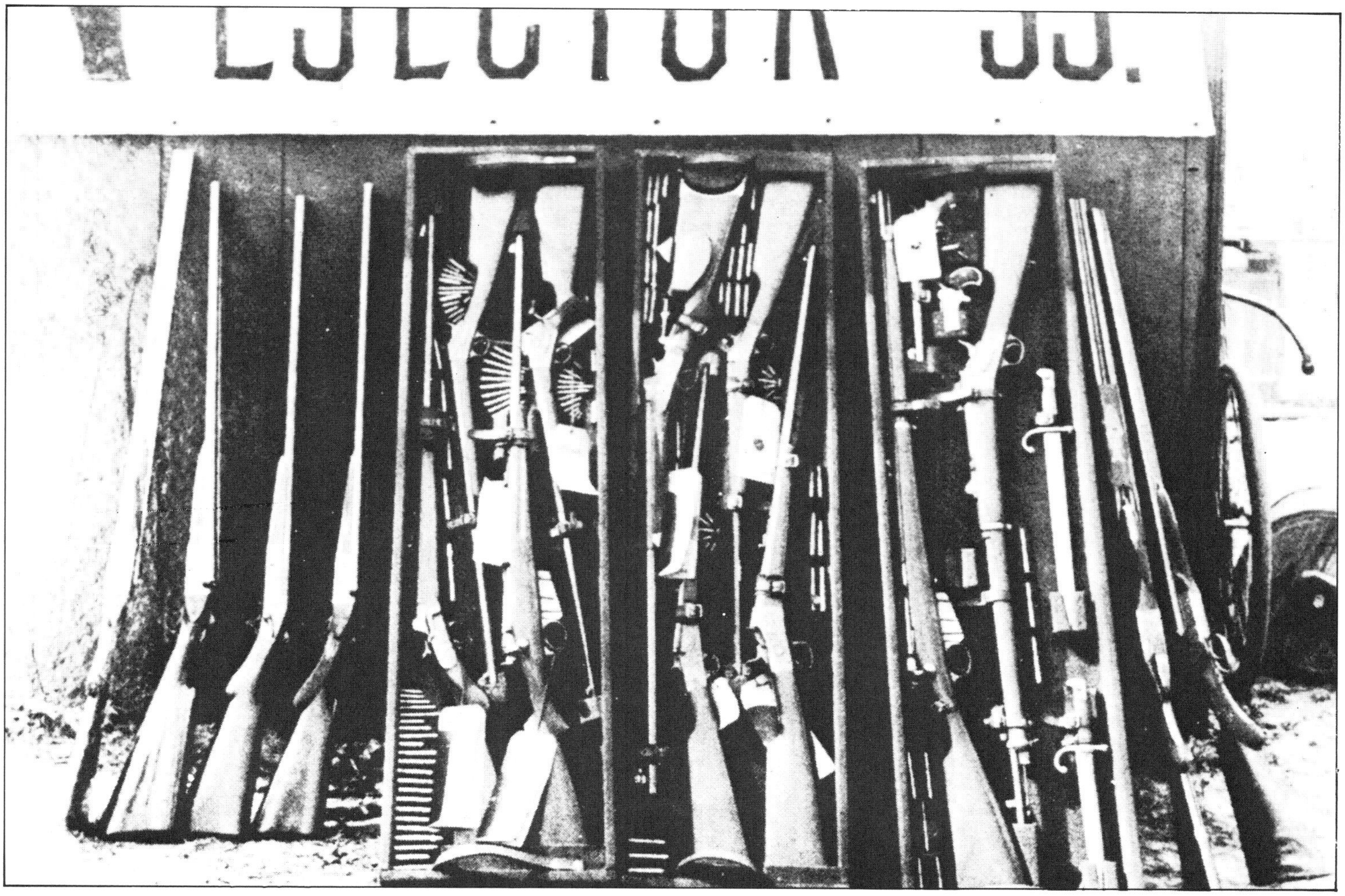

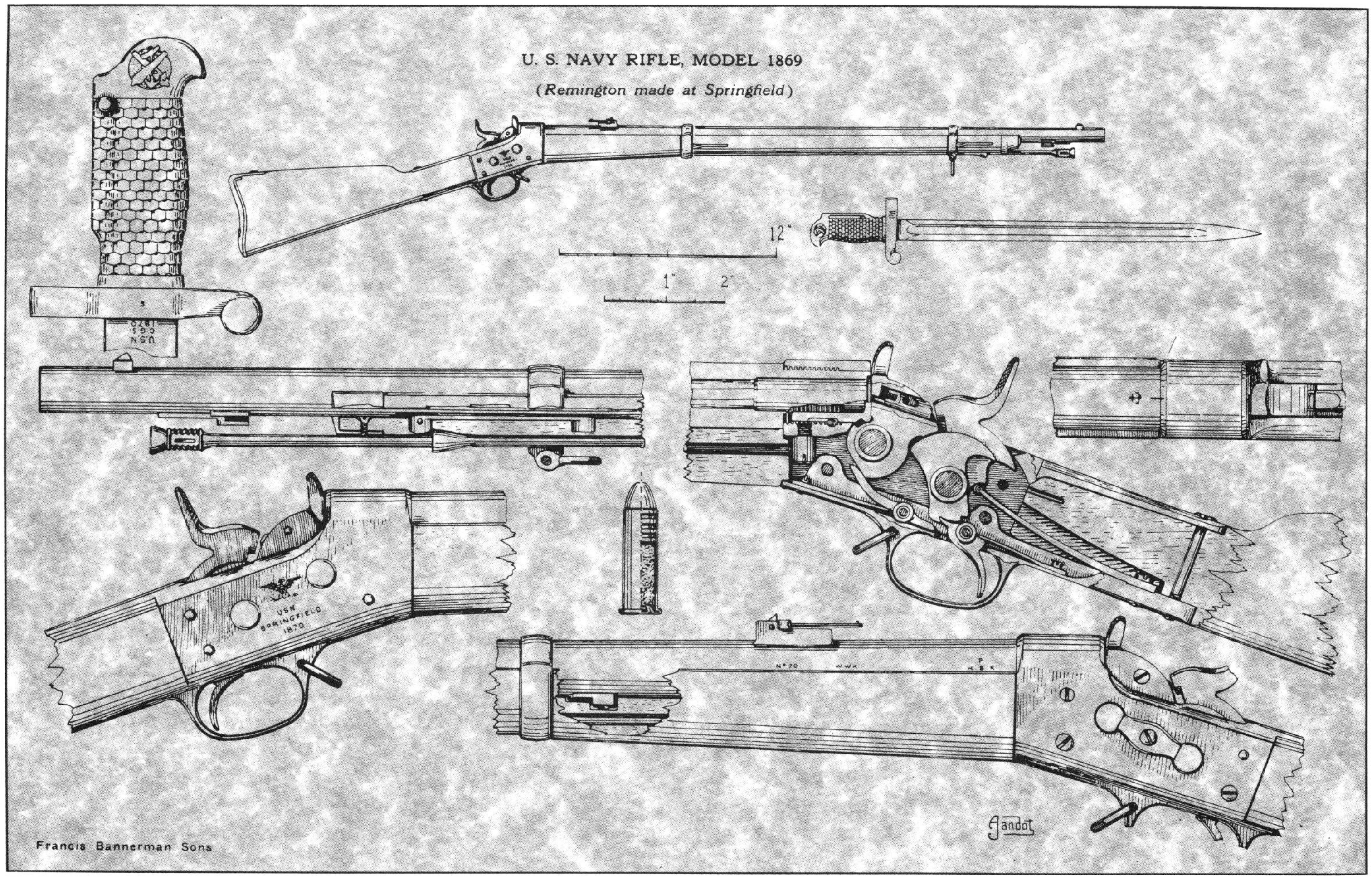
U. S. NAVY RIFLE, MODEL 1869
(*Remington made at Springfield*)
12"
1"
2"
USN
SPRINGFIELD
1870
Francis Bannerman Sons

Remington and the armament of the Indian Wars of the Old West. The lot of the US Cavalry soldier just got better and better weapons-wise; many were issued Remington Rolling Blocks, and eventually light armament evolved to include the bolt action, tubular magazine Remington/Keene rifle, such as is shown *immediately below*—which reloaded fast and held enough ammo in its magazine to preclude reloading with any frequency. The capacious tubular magazine which was located under the barrel of the Remington/Keene contained a long spring which pushed the ammo backward toward the breech, where, as a round was fired and its spent case ejected, another round was fed into the chamber for firing. However, most Indian scouts were supplied with single shot Springfield trap door models, such as those held by the Indians on the left, *at the bottom of the page, below*—in a scene from *Walk the Proud Land*, a Hollywood version of the American Indian Wars. Even famed fighting scouts such as Captain Taylor's squad, shown *at below right*, were issued the old Springfield carbines. Though Springfield was indeed the US Army's standard armorer, Remington was often called upon in times of war to produce such 'contract models' as these standard designs in enormous quantity.

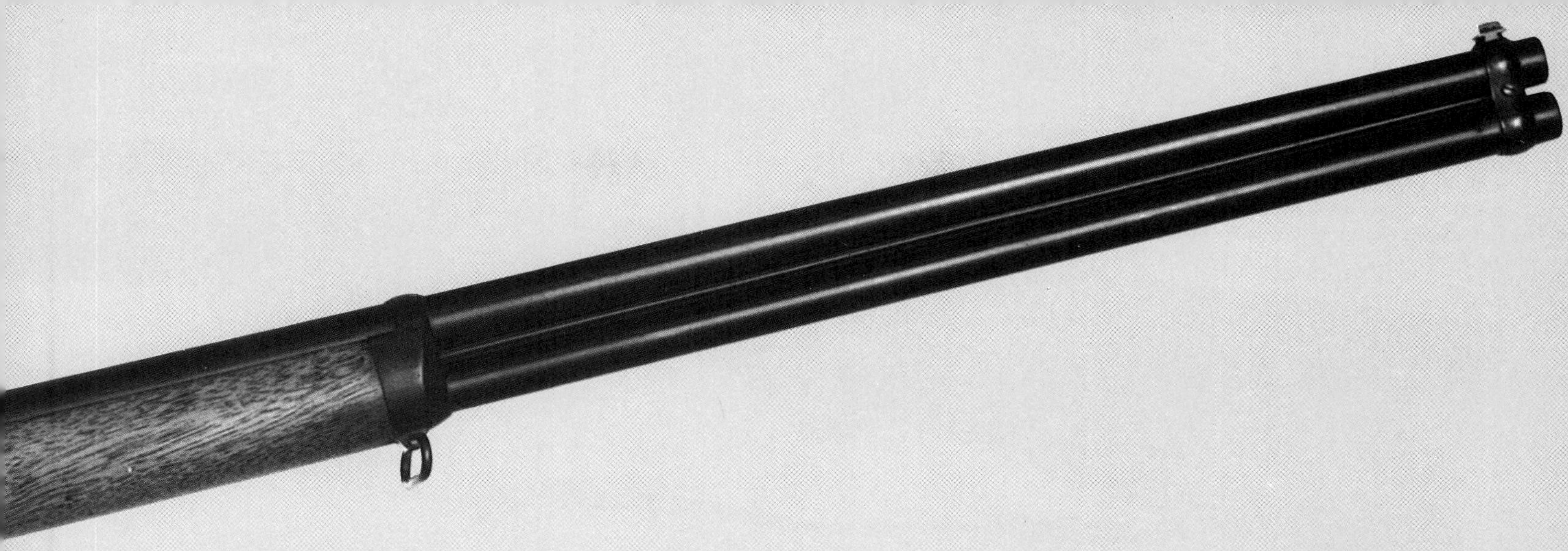

Capt Taylor and his
Noted Indian Scouts
on Drill at Pine Ridge S.D.

Below: **The Remington/Lee bolt action magazine rifle, invented by James Paris Lee, a Remington employee. It revolutionized arms design with its strong bolt action and quickly replaceable magazine clip.** ***Opposite page:*** **Early Remington fan and almost too-avid shooter (see text, this page), General George A Custer.**

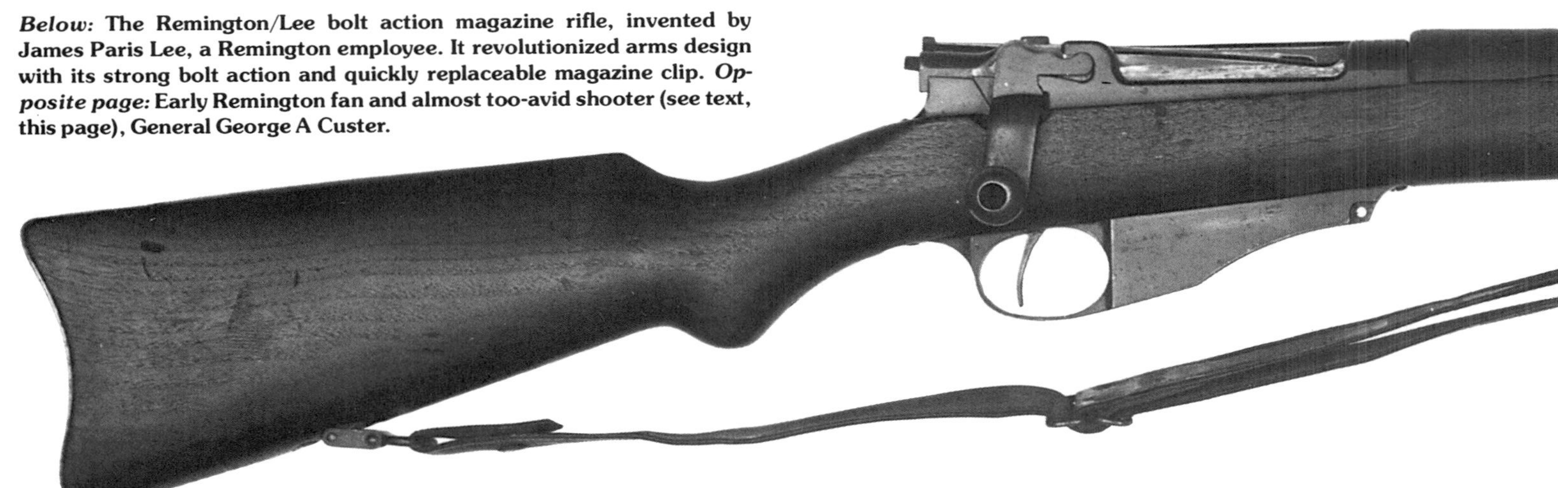

found opportunity to live in it. After his death it was sold to the British Government, who used it until 1952 to entertain VIPs in Cairo.

Historically speaking, one of the most interesting tributes to the virtues of the Remington Rolling Block rifles comes from none other than General George Armstrong Custer. In 1872, the General had purchased a beautiful Remington Sporting Rifle of the finest (F) grade for which he paid $91.50. Apparently he felt that he got his money's worth because he wrote to the Remingtons:

'Headquarters Fort Abraham Lincoln, DT
October 5, 1873

'Messrs Remington & Sons:

Dear Sirs—Last year I ordered from your firm a Sporting Rifle, caliber .50. I received the rifle a short time prior to the departure of the Yellowstone Expedition. The Expedition left Fort Rice the 20th of June, 1873, and returned to Fort Abraham Lincoln, September 21, 1873. During the period of three months I carried the rifle referred to on every occasion and the following list exhibits but a portion of the game killed by me: Antelope 41; buffalo four; elk four; blacktail deer four; American deer three; white wolf two; geese, prairie chickens and other feathered game in large numbers.

'The number of animals killed is not so remarkable as the distance at which the shots were executed. The average distance at which the 41 antelopes were killed was 250 yards by actual measurement. I rarely obtained a shot at an antelope under 150 yards, while the range extended from that distance up to 630 yards.

'With the expedition were professional hunters employed by the Government to obtain game for the troops. Many of the officers and men also were excellent shots, and participated extensively in hunting along the line of march. I was the only person who used one of your Rifles, which, as may properly be stated, there were pitted against it breech-loading rifles of almost every description, including many of the Springfield breechloaders altered to Sporting Rifles. With your Rifle I killed far more game than any other single party, professional or amateur, while the shots made with your rifle were at longer range and more difficult shots than were those made by any other rifles in the command. I am more than ever impressed with the many superior qualities possessed by the system of arms manufactured by your firm, and I believe I am safe in asserting that to a great extent this opinion is largely shared by the members of the Yellowstone Expedition who had the opportunity to make practical tests of the question.'

I am truly yours,
GA Custer
Brevet Major General US Army

During the 1870s and 1880s, the best military weapons in the hands of world armies were still single shot affairs. It was seen that a great improvement could be made by devising a means of better facilitating the loading and ejection of cartridges from rifle breeches. Many mechanisms were invented to meet this end, but few were successful. At first, a magazine-type box was mounted on the side of the rifle, thus allowing the soldier to quickly find his ammunition supply. Later small springs were incorporated into these magazine boxes to allow the shells to be sprung upward as needed. It was not long before the idea caught on of mounting this spring-loaded box beneath the rifle and incorporating it somehow into the breech loading mechanism of the arm, thus creating a new type of repeating rifle. At first this sounded simple, but proved to be somewhat complex to achieve. Various masterpieces of mechanical complication were devised, none of which attracted the favor of military men. It remained for James Paris Lee, a Scottish-born American who worked for Remington, to do the job.

Lee's design was the ultimate in simplicity. The receiver was cut away underneath and a detachable sheet metal box was inserted through the bottom of it. The cartridges rested on an 'elevator' of sorts within this box, or 'magazine,' which was a loaded zig-zag spring. A spring catch held the magazine in place once it was pushed into the rifle. When the bolt was opened, the magazine spring moved a cartridge upward into the receiver. As the rifle bolt was closed, the cartridge was pushed forward into the chamber ready for firing. Soldiers could carry fully loaded magazines on their belts, and were availed of much faster reloading, and thus a greater rate of fire than ever before.

James P Lee was in fact one of the most brilliant of

all the inventors who had worked for the Remingtons. While still employed by the Winchester Arms Company, he had developed a refinement to the lever action repeater which replaced the Winchester Model 73. But he wanted to work at his own ideas for a bolt action magazine rifle, so he came to Philo Remington—who recognized talent, and gave him an entire workshop in the Armory and all of the technical assistance that he needed. Lee patented, on his own, the box magazine in 1879 and Remington began to manufacture the Remington/Lee rifle in 1880. Structural weaknesses in the breech resulted in several fatal shooting accidents, and these weaknesses were remedied. It is a testimony to the soundness of Lee's idea that the design was carried on, even with such early tragedy. Lee eventually perfected the design and made it one of the safest guns in the world. Remington made the Remington/Lee rifle for the Lee Arms Company, which the inventor had organized as a selling agency. In 1884 Lee entered into an agreement with the Remingtons to both manufacture and sell his gun on a royalty basis. But by this time E Remington and Sons was in dire financial straits and eventually went into receivership, upon which Lee recovered the rights to his gun. Later, the British adopted the Lee system, in the form of the famous Lee/Enfield Rifle. This weapon was the standard arm of the British infantry for more than 50 years, even into World War II.

A curious legend surrounds James P Lee. In 1878–79, Lee lived in a room at the Osgood Hotel. He had a habit of bringing his drawings and models home at night, for further work. Remington also then employed a certain German mechanic by the name of Mauser. The story goes that Mauser bored a hole in the floor of his room—which was just above Lee's—and spend many hours flat on his stomach watching what went on below through the hole. The Mauser employed by the Remingtons was in fact the brother of Peter Paul and Wilhelm Mauser, the inventors of the Mauser Repeating Rifle: thus serious questions about the originality of the Mauser design persist. In any event, James P Lee is unquestionably credited with the invention of the box magazine and the Mauser Rifles were not so equipped until a number of years later.

The Spanish American War was a conflict that was short-lived, and thus had little effect on Remington and its partner, the Union Metallic Cartridge Company (UMC). The government did issue contracts, however, and Remington supplied rifles, while UMC made cartridges for the Army as well as brass cases for the six-inch shells with which Admiral Dewey's fleet won the battle of Manila Bay.

The summer of 1914 was one of unusual international tension. War clouds gathered upon the horizon of the world, but no one wanted to believe that war was possible. Archduke Francis Ferdinand, heir to the double Imperial Crown of Austria-Hungary, was shot by a Serbian at Sarejevo. Almost immediately Austria mobilized against Serbia. Russia mobilized against Austria in order to protect Serbia, in what Russia perceived as a religious war. Germany mobilized against France and France countered with its own defensive mobilization. The German armies surged forward and flowed over neutral Belgium. By the time the Germans were halted on the Marne, a short distance from Paris, the Allied governments had taken stock of their arsenals and found themselves in desperate need of guns and ammunition. Purchasing orders began inundating American firearms manufacturers in general, and Remington in particular. America was technically neutral, but its heart and hands were with the Allied cause. At first Remington produced a few thousand old fashioned Lebel rifles for France. Then the British ordered 1,000,000 Enfield

At left: **Admiral Dewey on board the USS *Olympia*, at the Battle of Manila Bay—Remington made rifles, and the Union Metallic Cartridge Company made ammo for the US in the Spanish American War. *At right:* French troops of the 1880s, with Lebel rifles such as those Remington made for France some time later, in World War I.**

rifles with the outlook that 1,000,000 more would be needed. Enfields had never been produced on a truly mass-production basis. It was up to the Remington engineers to retool their facilities to produce a maximum of 2000 guns per day. This meant that 3895 machines, 5905 fixtures, 7000 tools and 3415 gauges had to be revamped and/or fabricated, and mounted. Deliveries were to begin by 1 January 1916. This industrial miracle was actually accomplished a year ahead of schedule! Employment at the Ilion factory went from 1200 in 1914 to over 15,000 by 1917. Just before the United States entered the First World War, the factory turned out 61,000 Enfields for the British in one month!

The Imperial Russian Government was the last of the great Allies to come to Remington for help. But when they did, it was in true Tzarist style. The contract which was signed in 1915 called for one million Russian rifles and 100 million rounds of ammunition. The British contracts were already overwhelming the Ilion and Bridgeport factories. Whole new factories would need to be built in order to accommodate the Russians. In order to insure that his investment was protected the Tzar sent no fewer than 1500 inspectors to the Remington factories to verify that the 5000 Russian rifles that were coming off the assembly line every day met critical standards. The most irritating of these inspectors was a Cossack captain who became known as 'Alexander the Great.' His particular worry was that the rifles might fire accidentally. He would take a gun off of the assembly line, load and cock it and then bang the butt on the concrete floor with all his might. Of course the rifles were too well made to accidentally discharge even when subjected to this kind of punishment, but as many as a dozen rifle stocks per day were cracked in this manner. Officials of the company could do nothing to stop this waste but the gunsmiths could. They filed down the locking mechanism on a particular rifle until the trigger literally hung by a hair of steel. They maneuvered this specimen into Alexander's hands. When the Cossack slammed the butt into the floor, the rifle naturally went off, and the projectile pierced a four inch pipe above Alexander's head sending a stream of water under high pressure into his upturned face, knocking him flat on his back!

By February 1917 the numerous Remington plants were producing at peak levels. Ilion was producing 2400 Enfields a day; the Bridgeport Rifle Factory, 5000 rifles and 5000 bayonets a day; and the Hoboken and Barnum Avenue plants, four million cartridges daily.

Then the unthinkable happened—all that had been Russia for almost 1000 years was overthrown! Tzar Nicholas II and his family were murdered. The Russian nation simply disintegrated into fragments, each fighting for its own survival. A provisional government under Alexander Kerensky was formed but lasted only a short time. Naturally, one of the first acts of the new Russian Republic was to repudiate all contracts that had been entered into by the Tzar's government. Remington had accepted the largest contract—and so was hardest hit. The Russian Revolution cost Remington millions of dollars in lost capital investment,

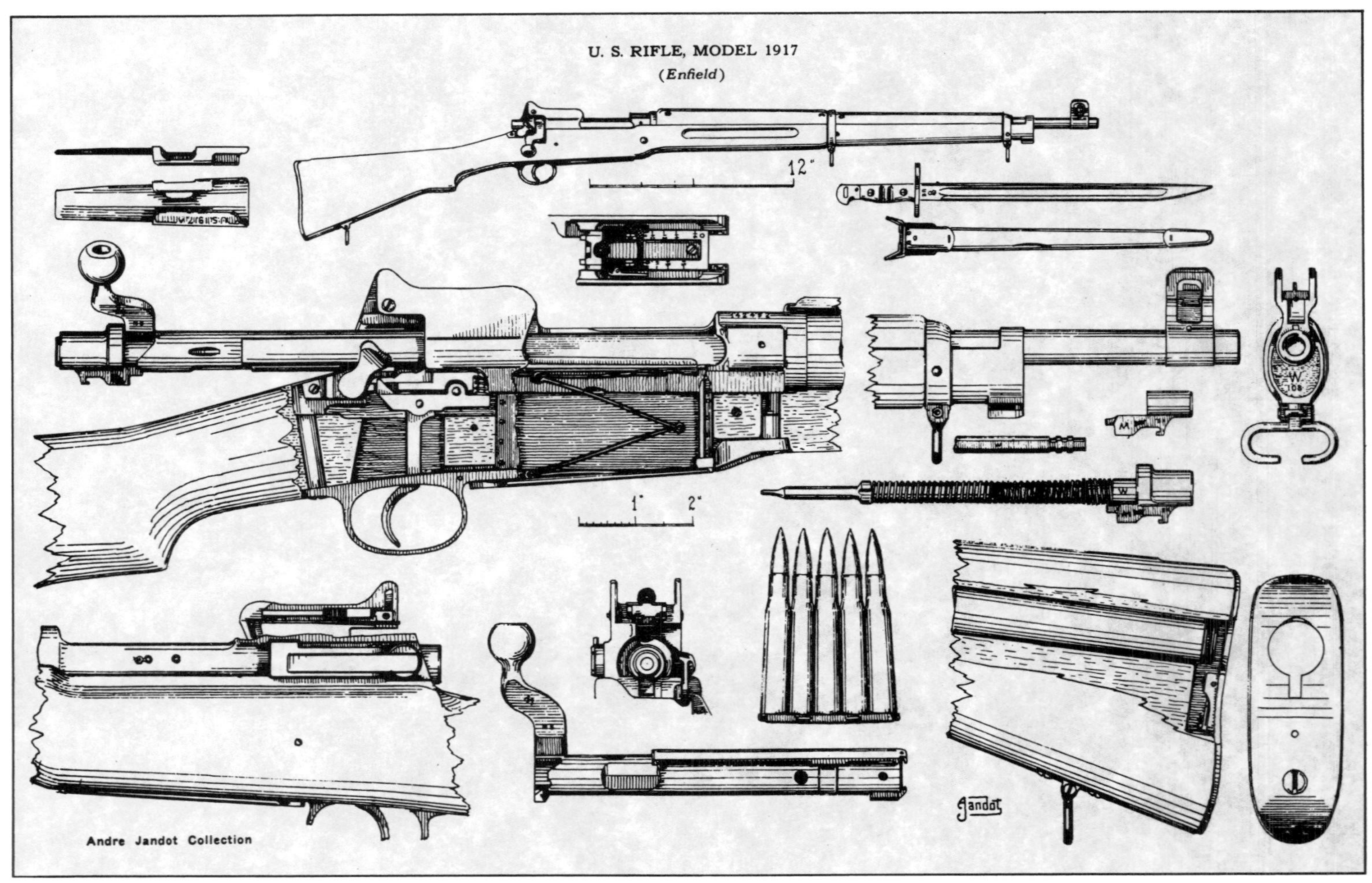

stockpiled hundreds of thousands of unwanted rifles in warehouses, and threw thousands of American workers out of work suddenly. But on 2 April 1917, America entered the War pledging its 'lives, fortunes and sacred honor' to victory. If the war was to be won, America had to arm four million troops in a matter of months. This was partially accomplished by government contracts to purchase 600,000 of the 750,000 Russian rifles already manufactured by Remington; this reduced the company's loss from an estimated $10 million to about $300,000. (It is interesting to note that some of these rifles were later shipped by the US Government to Vladivostok—on the eastern coast of what is now the Soviet Union—to arm the White Russian Army which attempted to rescue that country from the Bolshevicks.)

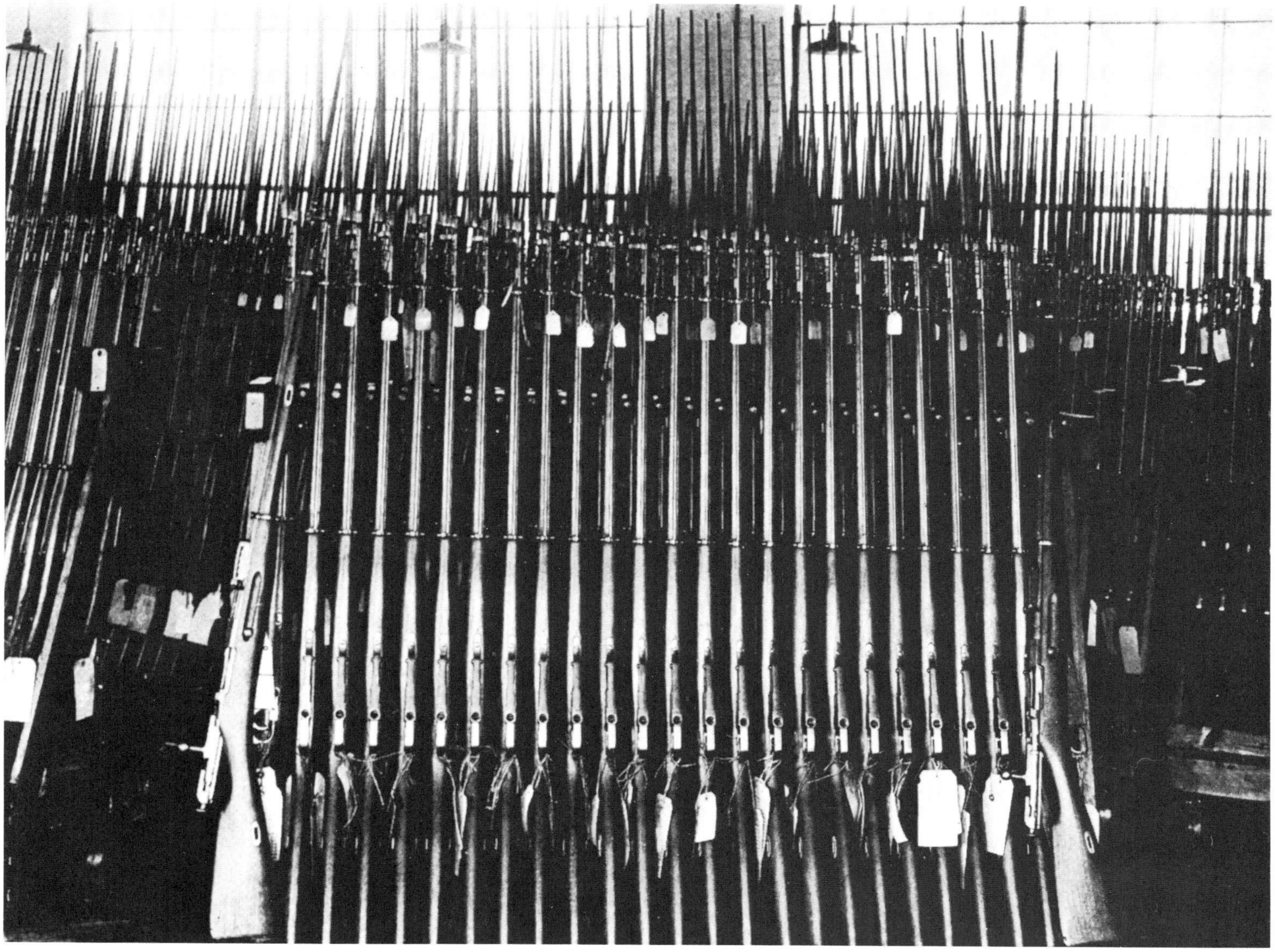

The Army Ordnance Department estimated that at least four million rifles would be needed within two years—at a time when there were approximately 700,000 Springfields in government arsenals, and the total manufacturing capability was 350,000 rifles a year; this left a net deficit of three million guns. Remington engineers suggested a radical solution to this problem. They proposed redesigning the British Enfield to take the Springfield .30-06 cartridge. This new US Enfield would be a far simpler gun to make and could be turned out in huge quantities by both Ilion

During World War I, Remington combined the British Lee/Enfield bolt action design (which was relatively simple for Remington to manufacture) with the new, powerful, Springfield .30-06 cartridge. The result was the potent Model 1917 *(opposite). Above:* Some of the rifles Remington built for the Tzar of Russia. *Below:* US troops in France, in 1917: many carried Remington-made arms.

and other factories.

The new rifle was officially adopted by the Ordnance Department as US Rifle Model 1917. Remington retooled to make it, and other manufacturers also received large orders. By December 1917, production at Ilion was 3000 'M-17s' a day, and by June of that year production peaked at 4000 per day. Total production at Ilion was 545,541, while Remington's Eddystone plant produced 1,181,908 M-17s! By the war's end, over one million M-17s were stored in government arsenals. These were the same guns which would, 23 years later, be shipped to England after the British defeat at Dunkirk. These M-17s would play a pivotal role in saving Great Britain from a Nazi invasion.

Remington's production record for the World War I effort proved that a company whose foundation consisted of making sporting guns and ammunition could become one of the greatest industrial factors in the defense of the United States. Remington had produced 69 percent of all rifles manufactured for American troops during World War I and over 50 percent of all the small arms ammunition for the United States and her Allies. In addition, *all the ammunition* used by the Belgian Army in its four years of war was made by Remington.

In 1929, Remington sales amounted to over $21 million; by 1932, they had fallen below $8 million. At that figure, the company was losing money at the rate of nearly $1 million a year. Under these circumstances, merger or bankruptcy were the only alternatives left. Fortunately for Remington, EI DuPont de Nemours & Company of Delaware would come to the rescue. Some personnel at DuPont were skeptical about entering a new field—that of firearms production—because DuPont had up until this time had as its primary direction chemical operations and production. In the spring of 1933, the DuPont directors voted, but not unanimously, to acquire a controlling interest in Remington common stock.

The outbreak of war in 1939 had virtually no effect upon Remington's profitability. The strict neutrality laws of the United States made it impossible for US arms manufacturers to produce weapons for any country's war effort. But neutrality laws finally gave way to lend-lease agreements, which enabled US manufacturers to meet the growing British demands. British Prime Minister Winston Churchill sent his personal representative, Sir Walter Leighton, to Washington to get rifles from the US at any cost. England was in desperate need of several million improved Enfields, but the new British Enfield rifles were difficult to produce and no one was equipped with the machinery to do the job. If Britain wanted rifles in less than the two-year time span needed to tool up for production, some kind of compromise would have to be found.

The US government at this time had the machinery for making Springfield rifles at the Rock Island arsenal. If the government would lease this machinery to Remington, production of *Springfields* for the British could begin within a year—But the British wanted *Enfields*, not Springfields, and objected; they proposed that Remington retool the Rock Island arsenal machinery to produce the Enfields they wanted.

Remington's president took a strong stand against this proposal. US Army troops were equipped with Springfields, and if the machines were altered they could not produce spare parts if required. As events proved, this was indeed a wise decision. Final agreement with the British was reached in January 1941, and nine months later Springfield rifles began coming off the assembly line three months ahead of schedule. This was indeed a remarkable feat of engineering: the model 1903 Springfield contained 91 parts, whereas the new model A-3 contained only 79; 23 parts, previously requiring forging, were redesigned so that they could be stamped by presses—and only 24 parts remained unchanged. The bulk of these remodeled Springfields were not delivered to the British as America was thrust into the conflict herself on 7 December 1941; it was impossible to supply all of our men with Garands—then the standard US service rifle—so our 'Yanks' also got A-3s; the US Government took over the British supply contract, and Remington was now arming American troops. Had it not been for Remington President CK Davis' stand against retooling for Enfields, the GIs would not have had those guns when they needed them the most.

Remington's rifle production program was prodigious indeed, but did not compare with its production of ammunition. As early as June 1940, British contracts required the Remington Bridgeport facility to increase its production of .30 caliber ammunition by 600 percent and .50 caliber ammunition by 2000 percent! The capacity of the plant was increased with the understanding that at any time the capacity for further expansion would be used solely for the United States government, if needed. The British agreed to this provision and the job was begun. In the late summer of 1940, during the Battle of Britain, Remington was entrusted by the British government with a secret: bullets with an incendiary core. These were needed in .30 and .50 caliber. The incendiary bullet had to have exactly the same ballistic characteristics as both the ordinary lead core bullet, and the tracer bullet—otherwise they would be erratic in their flight. In less than a month, Remington had developed a working model of the bullet and had put it into large scale production. Later, the Army Ordnance Department would describe this accomplishment as, 'one of the vital factors in winning the Battle of Britain.'

In 1940, Remington had been approached by the Army Ordnance Department in Washington to prepare for war. At that time, in all of the Remington organization, there were only 360 men who had any experience with military ammunition. What the Ordnance people were asking for would require 40 times that workforce to be employed at Bridgeport alone. Remington management divided this almost impossible task into two divisions; the company-owned factories, and government plants which had just been constructed for the exigencies of wartime production. Even though DuPont was overloaded with work, they let Remington take some of their best men—which eventually amounted to over 500 supervisory personnel.

***Opposite:* A painting of the World War I Battle of Soissons. In evidence here are Remington-made Model 1917s, fixed with bayonets, in the hands of American 'doughboys.' *Above:* US paratroopers in North Africa prepare for action during World War II: note the Model 1917 leaning against the truck.**

Remington's Lake City Factory was the first modern facility to be designed for the express purpose of making military ammunition. Eventually it would consist of seven distinct manufacturing units—three for .30 caliber, two for .50 caliber, and one for .30 caliber carbine cartridges. Each unit was in fact a complete factory in itself. Raw material went in one end, and finished cartridges came out the other. This was the first time in history that ammunition was made in what was referred to as a closed cycle, meaning a continuous process. This was both a dangerous and difficult way of manufacturing; if through carelessness or mechanical difficulties a number of defective cases were to get into the works, the whole process of production would have to be stopped until they were cleared out. In actuality, this only happened once: the workers' deep sense of their great responsibility made for this extraordinary record of quality control.

It is interesting to note that during the whole of World War II, there was only one serious explosion at a Remington Plant; this occurred at a small storage warehouse at Bridgeport. The Navy had placed a hurried call for ammunition and the regular packing department, already swamped with orders, was strained to fill it. Men were set to work hurriedly nailing up cases and someone, it is thought, drove a nail into a primer. The explosion cost seven people their lives, and

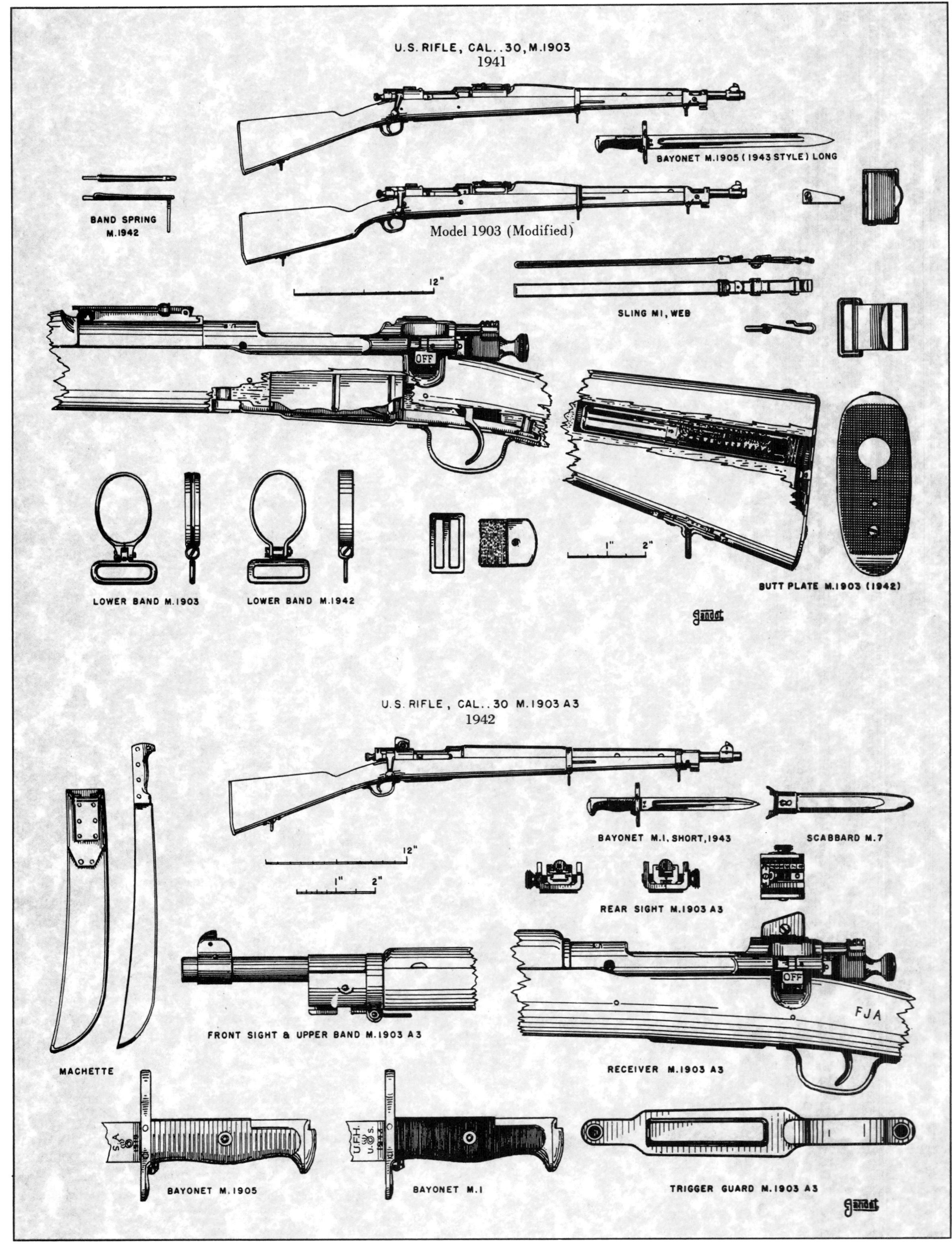
U.S. RIFLE, CAL. .30, M.1903
1941
BAYONET M.1905 (1943 STYLE) LONG
BAND SPRING M.1942
Model 1903 (Modified)
12"
SLING M1, WEB
OFF
1"
2"
LOWER BAND M.1903
LOWER BAND M.1942
BUTT PLATE M.1903 (1942)
Gandot
U.S. RIFLE, CAL. .30 M.1903 A3
1942
BAYONET M.1, SHORT, 1943
SCABBARD M.7
12"
1"
2"
REAR SIGHT M.1903 A3
OFF
FJA
FRONT SIGHT & UPPER BAND M.1903 A3
MACHETTE
RECEIVER M.1903 A3
BAYONET M.1905
BAYONET M.1
TRIGGER GUARD M.1903 A3
Gandot

from that time forward, Remington absolutely refused to compromise safety on government orders no matter how urgent the request.

At its peak, the huge Lake City plant comprised 3800 acres, 25 miles of road, 236 major buildings, 11 miles of railroad track and parking space for 5000 automobiles. The plant had its own hospital, police and fire departments. Originally, the plant was designed to have a daily capacity of two million rounds of .30 caliber cartridges and 640,000 rounds of .50 caliber cartidges. This was stepped up to meet Ordnance Department requirements until, at the end, capacity was over 8.9 million cartridges per day.

But sheer production figures are not the only story. In 1943, over 14,000 people worked at the Remington plant on Barnum Avenue. This plant was unique among ammunition plants for the sheer variety of calibers and types of ammunition that were manufactured at one location. The list included ball, armor piercing, tracer and incendiary bullets; standard military cartridges; a wide variety of primers; shot shells and .22 caliber cartridges for training; and several types of cartridge for special purposes. These included such oddities as .45 caliber revolver cartridges full of birdshot (good for killing snakes) for downed airmen who had parachuted into South Pacific jungles, and 'frangible bullets' for soldiers in training to practice firing live ammunition at an airplane without endangering the pilot.

Remington at war. *Above left:* Design drawings for the Model 1903 Springfield rifle, redesigned by Remington in World War II as the 1903 A3 *(below left). Below:* Design drawings of the M1903 Springfield and M1917 Enfield—and the M1 Garand, which Remington did not manufacture.

Remington licensed the US government and all designated manufacturers *without charge* for all Remington patents and technology—Remington even made its Research and Development Department available to the government. This R and D Department worked on a wide range of projects for both the government as well as private manufacturers. Among Remington R and D accomplishments are the development of a grenade launcher for the Garand rifle, super high-speed artillery projectiles, electrically fired primers for machine guns, a 12 gauge shell to start torpedo gyroscopes, new ballistic instruments and dozens of other devices.

It is clear from a historical perspective, why the government selected Remington to be its chosen instrument in building new cartridge plants. The Ordnance Department had established rigidly high standards of acceptance for military cartridges. These standards had been set up in peace time under the assumption that ammunition thus produced was to be done on a small production basis. When these standards were brought into gigantic mass-production operations, questions naturally arose as to their feasibility—but Remington had faith in its people, and set up standards even tougher than those of Ordnance. As a result, Remington not only met the 'impossible' government specifications—but in some instances actually raised them even *higher*.

Another historically significant fact about the huge expansions; vast training programs; the setting of new standards; the development of new types of ammunitions; the complex organizing of machine tool procurement; *and* the arrangements for obtaining the

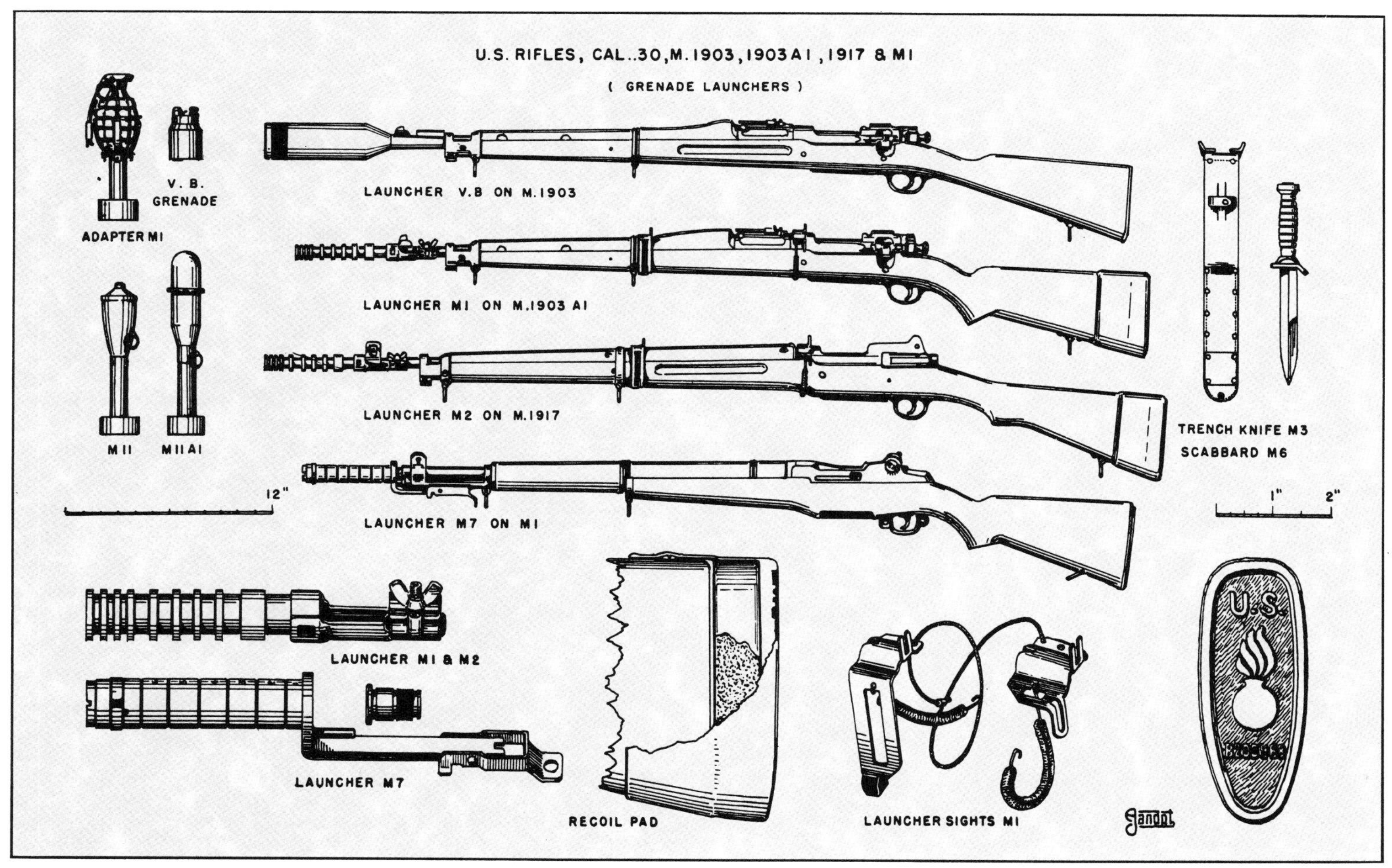

huge stockpiles of raw materials was *planned* and actually *set into motion before* Pearl Harbor. The men who were in the know realized that war was coming, and their far sighted wisdom made for a United States military that was far more prepared for war than is generally supposed. Therefore, when war did arrive, it was only a matter of stepping up an already prodigious capacity for the production of small arms and ammunition. The output of the government's cannily-built new plants was doubled almost overnight. This was due to the streamlining of assembly line designs. For example, production in the units designated to make one million .30 caliber cartridges was raised to two million and units designated for maximum daily production of 640,000 .50 caliber were stepped up to one million. This was possible not simply out of luck, but was the result of far-sighted preparations. Hardly had the great new ammunition plants gone into full production before the US Army found itself practically snowed under by cartridges: as early as July 1942, Ordnance began shifting emphasis away from .30 caliber ammunition, and by the summer of 1943, at the very height of the war, cutbacks in production were ordered.

On 31 December 1943, five full months *before* D Day, the huge Salt Lake City, Utah, plant was ordered to cease operations and was placed in standby condition. Operations at the Denver plant ended on 31 July 1944, and the plant was converted to make fuses for artillery projectiles. All the requirements of the Ordnance Department had been met in 'overflowing' fashion. The government was justifiably lavish in its recognition of Remington's outstanding services during this critical period of American history. On 24 August 1942, the Army/Navy E—for 'Excellent'—pennant was awarded to the Lake City plant. Both the Denver and Bridgeport Works were similarly awarded one month later. The Ilion plant received its award on 9 November 1942 and the Utah plant was honored in September of the following year. Remington's smallest plant at Findlay was given the right to hoist the Pennant of Excellence on 31 August 1944.

Many American corporations expanded fully 100 percent, and some grew up to 500 percent, to meet defense requirements during the war years. Few, if any, expanded over 2000 percent as did Remington: in 1939, there were fewer than 4000 people employed in all Remington plants; at the peak of production in 1943 Remington personnel numbered 82,500! (During this time over 15,000 Remington employees joined various branches of the Armed Services, and replacements were trained for them.)

Remington's safety record is nearly as astounding as its production records. In 1939 the major injury rate was 1.07 per million man hours worked. By 1942, the rate was only 0.88 and in 1943 it dropped to 0.67. Even though Remington plants were producing dangerous commodities, their safety record ranked far better than the average for general industry. Both the Lake City, Kansas and Denver, Colorado Ordnance plants achieved safety records which are among the best all-time performances in the history of industrial safety.

During the World War II years, Remington manufactured no fewer than 1,840,000 rifles and more than 16 *billion* cartridges for the US government. The ammunition statistic represents *41 percent* of all the small-arms ammunition used by the United States during that war for its own forces and for Lend-Lease.

Below: **A sniper version of the Model 1903.** ***At right:*** **Remington handguns.**

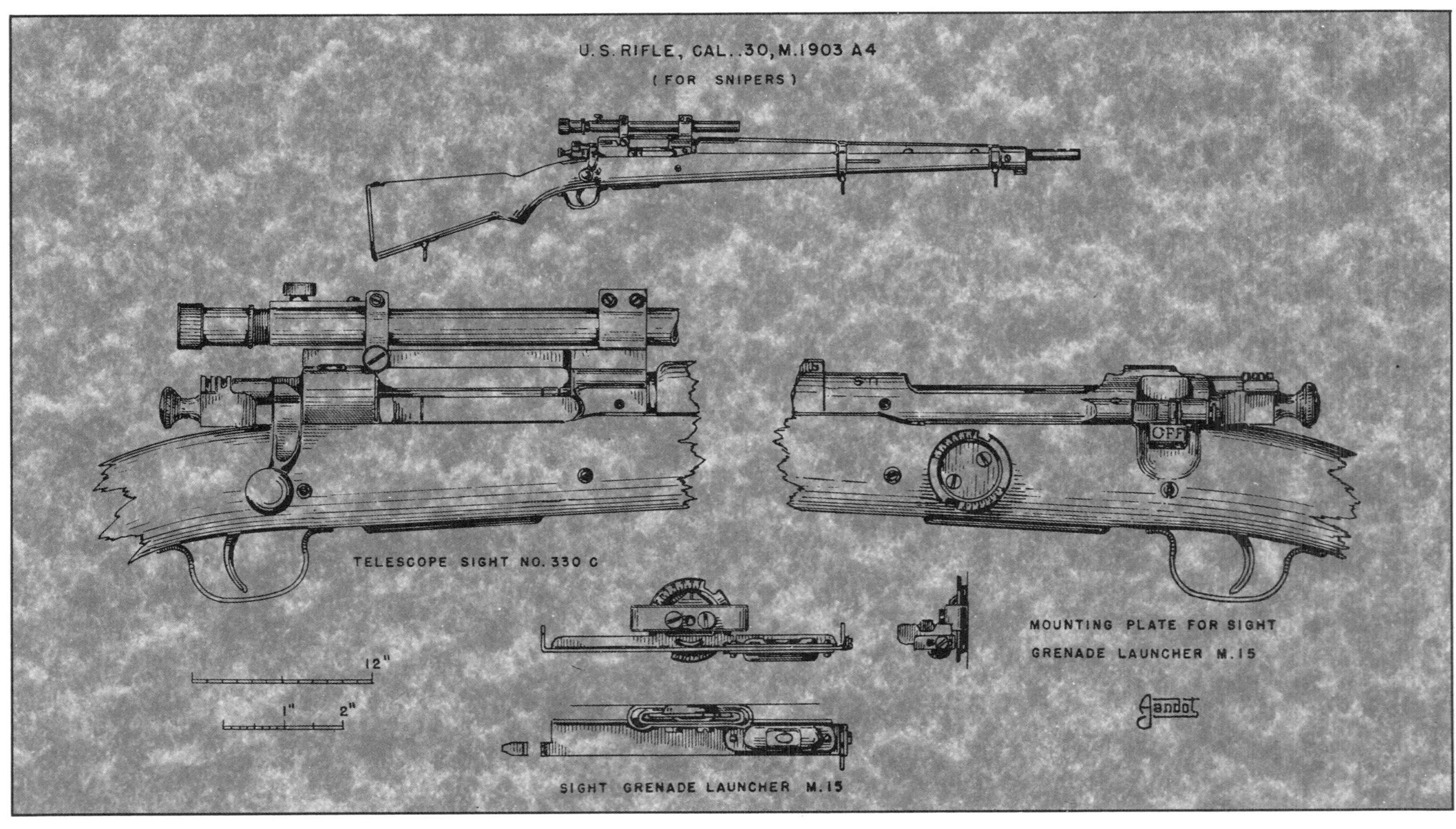

Remington Pistols to 1938
Early Experimental
Rider Pocket
Revolver
1860–1888
'Pocket' Revolver
Conversion 1868–1888
Rider Magazine
Pistol 1871–1888
Model 1871 Army Single
Action 1872–1888
New Line Revolver
No 1 1873–1888
Iroquis Revolver
1878–1888
Mark III Signal
1915–1918
Model 51 Automatic
1918–1934
.45 Automatic
1919 Government
Experimental
Parker 35mm Signal
Pistol Mark I
1938

OCT.
HUNTING TAG
CITIZEN RESIDENT
28802

Many an American GI has dreamed, while on duty across the seas, of returning home to such a familiar setting as this. *These pages:* 'Remington—as American as apple pie.' So implies this homey photograph, taken very early on a chilly autumn morning, of a prime example of the improved Model 870 Wingmaster—one of the world's great pump action shotguns, and a carrier of the Remington tradition of unmatched craftsmanship.

Remington

The history of ammunition actually began in the 13th century, when Roger Bacon experimented with new ways of making what was then called 'Greek fire' by combining saltpeter, sulfur, and charcoal—and eventually blew himself out of this world in the process. Gun powder was thus invented—and not for another 600 years would the formula change appreciably. The first real advance in ammunition technology ocurred when a French gunsmith named Houiller came up with the idea of *encapsulating* projectile and powder, and thus made the first cartridges.

These early cartridges were made of various kinds of paper, cardboard or linen, and were easily broken or ruined by water. In the US Civil War, for example, wastage from such causes consumed 40 percent of the ammunition in the field. Some of these early cartridges had to be bitten open before loading so that the loose powder could spill out to be ignited by the percussion cap. Good teeth were thus a military necessity: for many years, the United States Army ran fresh recruits through severe dental tests to determine whether their teeth met evenly! (These standards were still in place until the middle of World War II when the Pentagon finally decided that no one needed to bite modern cartridges.)

In 1807, a Scottish clergyman named John Forsythe invented the percussion cap, which was simply a pinch of highly volatile fulminate of mercury sandwiched between two small copper disks which were shaped to fit securely over a 'nipple' in the breach of a firearm. When this 'cap' was struck by the hammer, the miniature explosion sent flame through the nipple into the powder charge in the gun's breech. The first half of the 19th century saw these ideas—the cartridge and the percussion cap—evolve into an idea about combining the percussion cap with the cartridge in one unit! German gunsmiths produced the 'needle gun' which was also the first bolt-action rifle: this weapon had, in place of the now-familiar firing pin, a long needle which penetrated the fulminate of mercury-charged base of a thin-walled cartridge, detonating its powder charge. The cartridges, however, were often unreliable and tended to stick in the chamber.

The first cartridge that was truly successful was made by the Maynard Rifle Company in 1851. It consisted of an elongated bullet set into a brass case containing the powder. The percussion cap was a separate affair mounted in the base of the shell. At this same time, Smith and Wesson produced an equally 'developmental' metallic revolver cartridge. The Volcanic Arms Company improvised on these ideas by making a hollow rim around the base of the cartridge and filling it with fulminate of mercury: this was the first practical rim fire cartridge.

With the invention of the metallic cartridge, the supremacy of breech loading guns was fully established. The fact that the brass cartridge would expand from the pressure of the explosion and thus automatically seal in all escaping gases and flames made these kinds of guns truly practical. The US Civil War was fought mainly with percussion cap firearms, but the conflict proved that these were obsolete. Any soldier, whether Blue or Grey, who had seen a Sharps or a Henry or a Remington Geiger wanted such a metallic

At right: **A sampler of Remington ammo types, for all levels of sport. Remington has long been a major contributor to the advance of cartridge ammunition, and offers a full line of rifle, pistol and shotgun ammunition.**

Ammunition

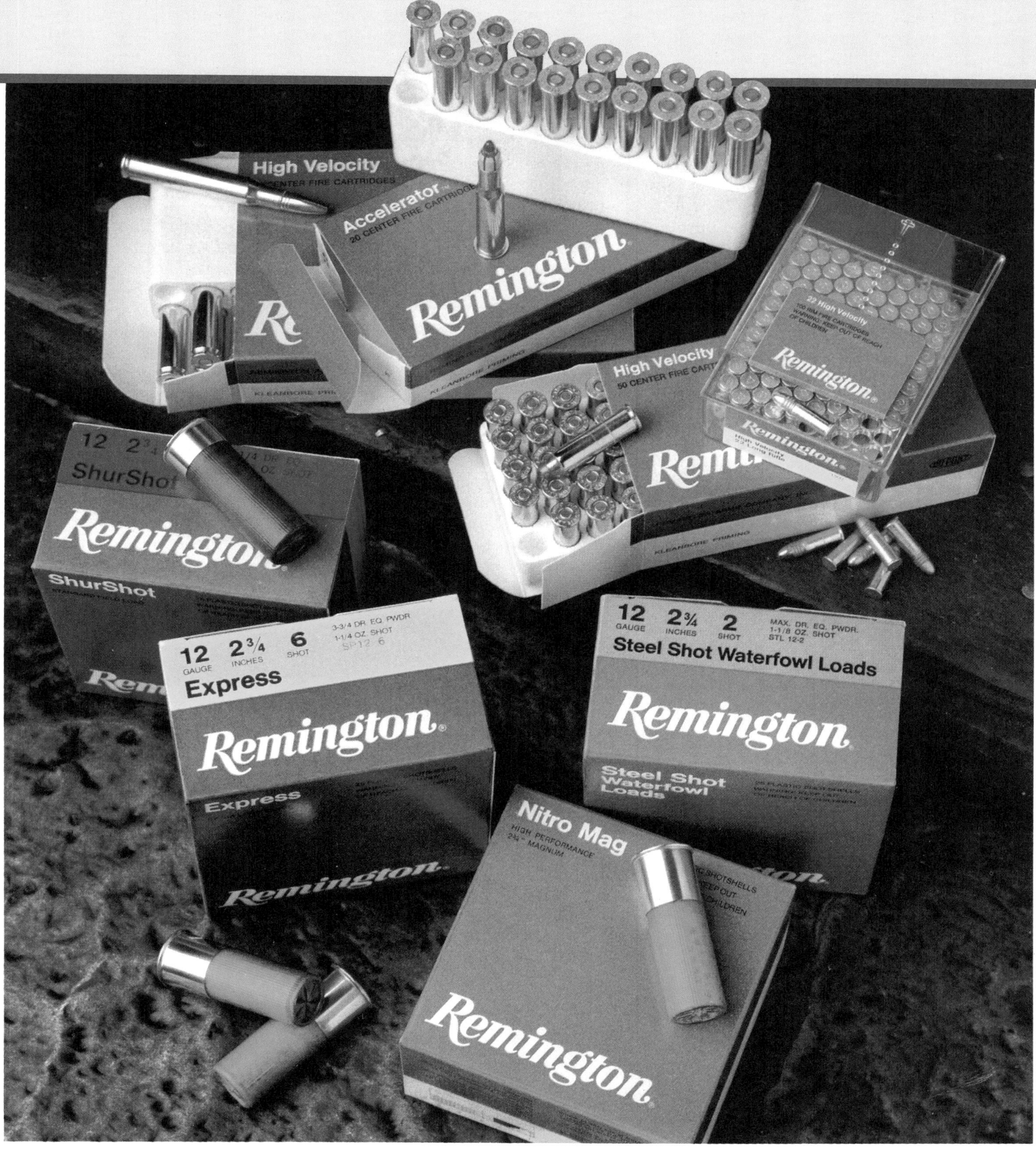

High Velocity
Accelerator
20 CENTER FIRE CARTRIDGES
Remington
KLEANBORE PRIMING
High Velocity
50 CENTER FIRE
22 High Velocity
Remington
12 2¾
ShurShot
Remington
ShurShot
12 GAUGE 2¾ INCHES 6 SHOT
3-3/4 DR. EQ. PWDR
1-1/4 OZ. SHOT
SP12 6
Express
Remington
Express
Remington
12 GAUGE 2¾ INCHES 2 SHOT
MAX. DR. EQ. PWDR.
1-1/8 OZ. SHOT
STL 12-2
Steel Shot Waterfowl Loads
Remington
Steel Shot Waterfowl Loads
Nitro Mag
HIGH PERFORMANCE
2¾ - MAGNUM
Remington

cartridge-firing breech loader.

Marcellus Hartley—perhaps the most brilliant of the arms entrepreneurs of the time—recognized that the trend toward metallic cartridges was fat with the possibility of enormous profits. Gunmakers usually had plenty to do in times of war, but in peace time, sport shooter and hunter would only buy two or perhaps three guns in his lifetime. However, Hartley reasoned that sportsmen would need to buy ammunition every year; thus the ammunition trade with its almost continual cash flow would prove to be a stabilizing influence in the otherwise 'boom and bust' firearms trade. Hartley and his partners bought two small New England cartridge companies—the Crittenden and Tribbals Manufacturing Company of South Coventry, Connecticut, and the CD Leet Company of Springfield, Massachusetts. Crittenden and Tribbals made the ammunition for the Spencer Rifle which Schulyer, Hartley and Graham sold. Hartley later moved the entire business to the Tribbals factory at South Coventry. Then he moved the whole operation to Bridgeport, Connecticut, and on 9 August 1867, incorporated and consolidated it all into the Union Metallic Cartridge Company.

The mechanical wizard AC Hobbs came to work for UMC and was soon put in sole charge of the manufacturing end of the business—a position which he held for over 20 years. During that time, Hobbs personally invented complete machinery complexes to move cartridges production beyond handwork and into all-machine operation. This automation not only vastly increased the speed at which ammunition could be produced and insured quality control but, more importantly, increased the safety factor of the operation as a whole.

One day a rather strange Armenian gentleman known only as Mr Azerian came calling at the UMC headquarters. After being taken on a courtesy tour of the Bridgeport operation, Mr Azerian identified himself as a representative of the Turkish Government and on the spot ordered 10 million rounds of ammunition. This was a staggering order for such a young company—and in time, some of the contract was signed out to the newly organized Winchester Arms Company. This one Turkish contract not only put UMC on its financial feet, but the surplus also assured the success of Winchester Arms.

About this time Colonel Hiram Berdan invented a new bullet configuration: it was accurate up to 300 yards. The Colonel also invented a breech loading mechanism known as the 'Berdan Slam Bang Breech.' This mechanism was used by the United States Army after the Civil War to convert muzzle-loading Springfields into breech loaders, and was also incorporated into the standard rifle of the Imperial Russian Army. Colonel Berdan's clever bullet was an ingenious modification of the then still-new rim fire cartridge. However, Berdan's cartridge had a percussion cap, or 'primer,' embedded in the center of the case surrounded by a flange of reinforcing brass: this 'primer' is known world-wide as the 'Berdan primer.' This was the first practical center fire cartridge and it was first manufactured by UMC at Bridgeport. The advantage of a center fire cartridge over rim fire ammunition was its enormously greater strength—due to the fact that you could make the casing thicker, since the firing pin had no need to dent the center fire case as it did the rimfire case. Much more powder and therefore more power and bullet velocity could now be packed into a metallic cartridge; the center fire was also more sure of firing and less apt to accidental discharge. The increased safety of the center fire cartridge is illustrated in the official report of the tests at the Frankfort Arsenal on 21 April 1868: 'A wooden box

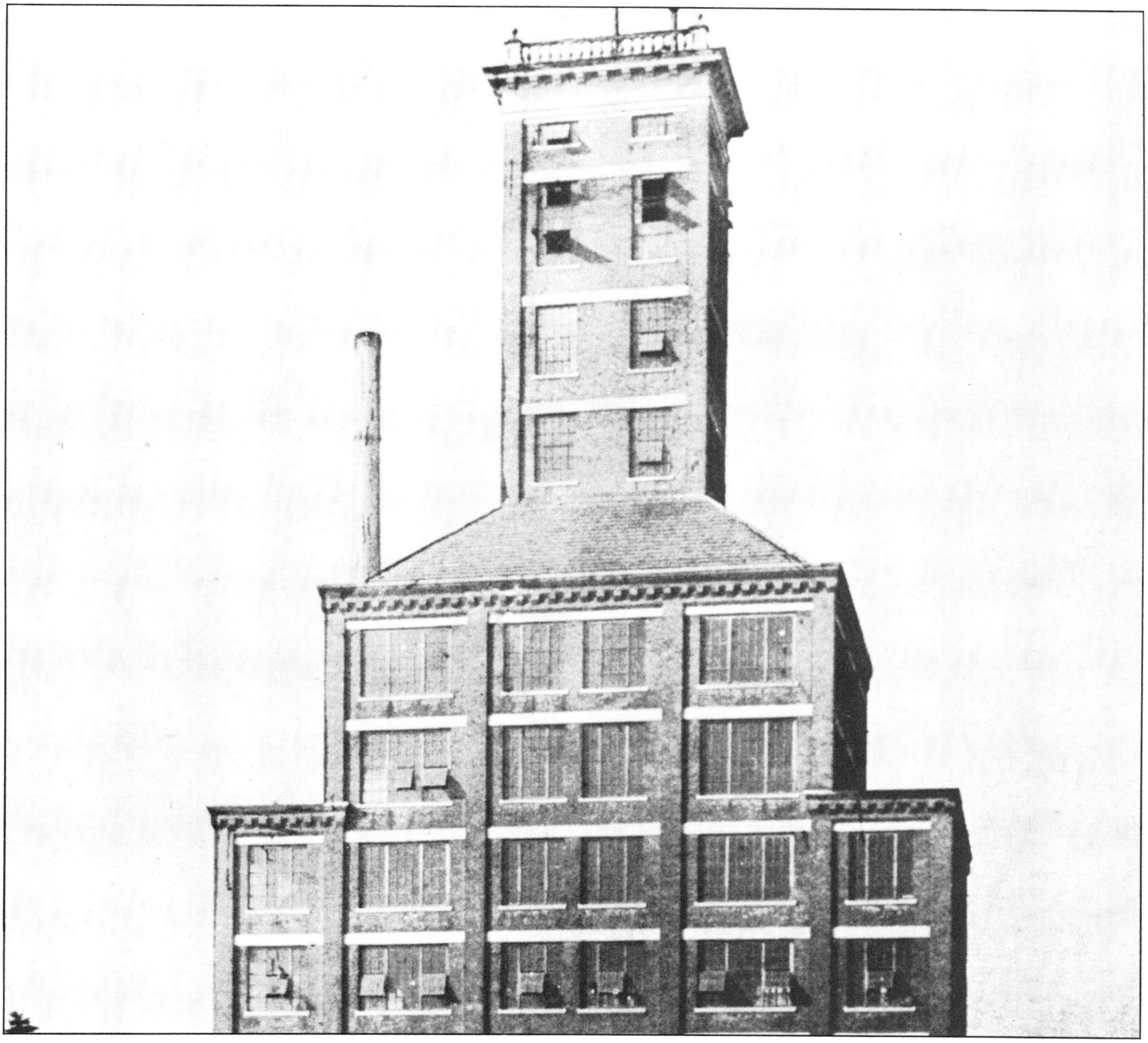

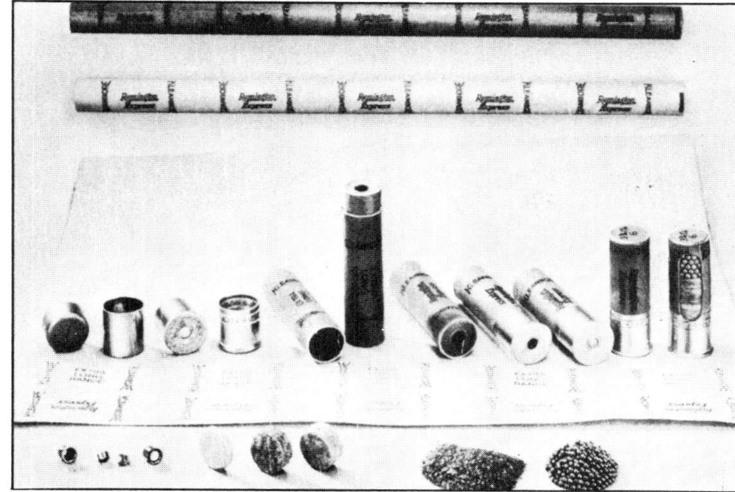

At left: The Union Metallic Cartridge Company, early on. *At top:* A 'shot tower,' in which molten metal falls from its pan *(at right)* into the shot-hardening tank. *Above:* Remington shotgun shell components.

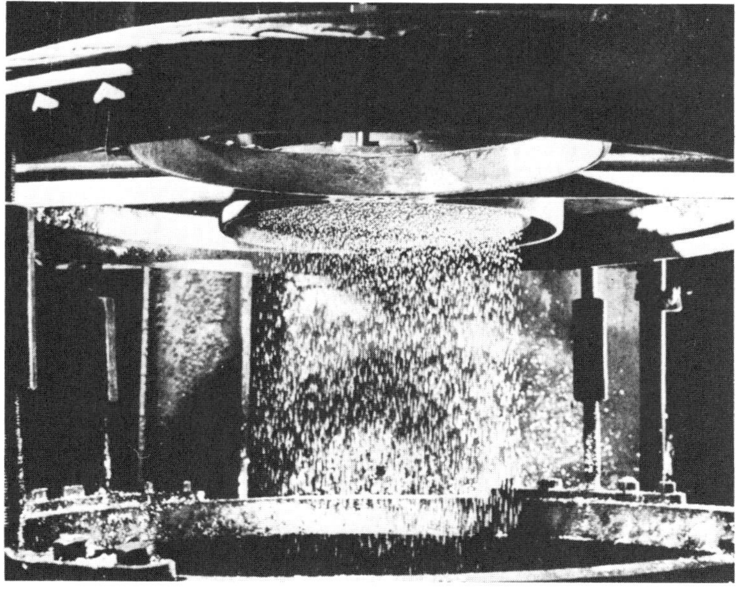

Shotgun Shells

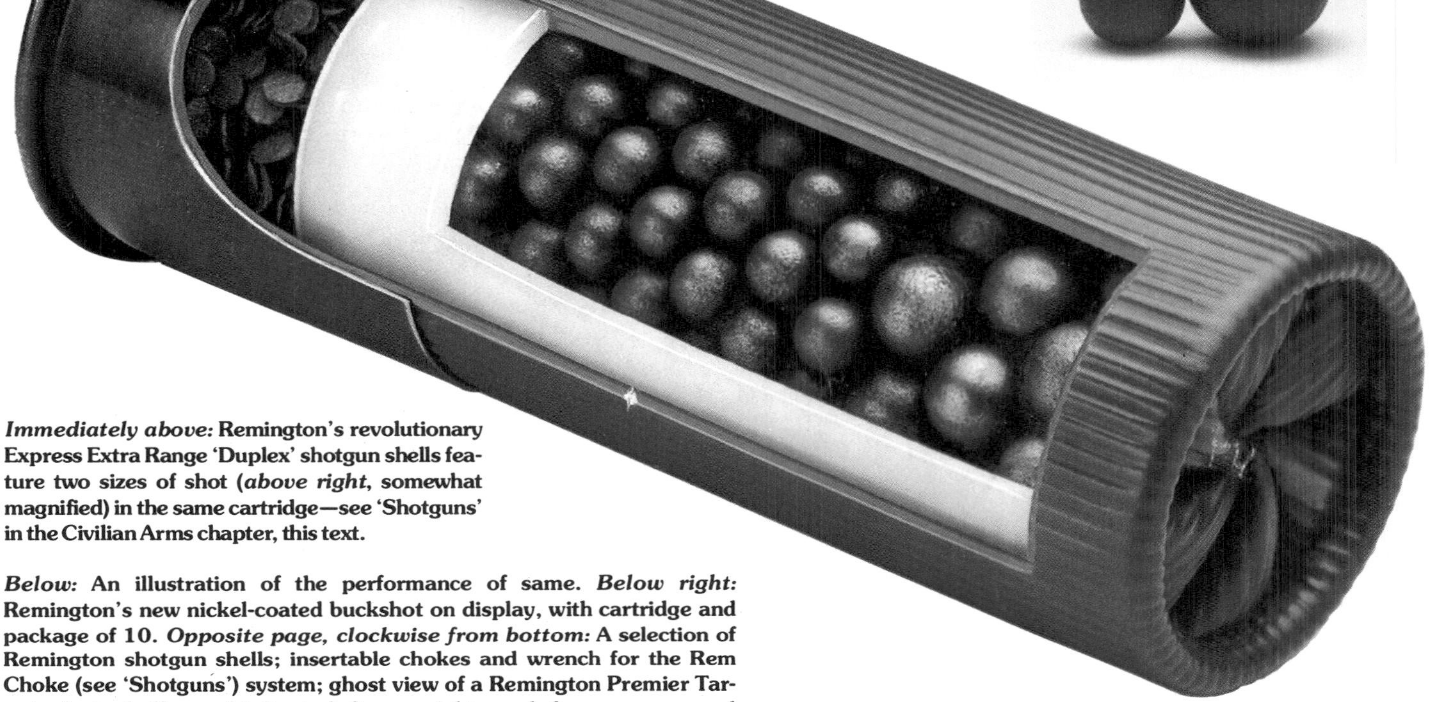

Immediately above: Remington's revolutionary Express Extra Range 'Duplex' shotgun shells feature two sizes of shot (*above right*, somewhat magnified) in the same cartridge—see 'Shotguns' in the Civilian Arms chapter, this text.

Below: An illustration of the performance of same. *Below right:* Remington's new nickel-coated buckshot on display, with cartridge and package of 10. *Opposite page, clockwise from bottom:* A selection of Remington shotgun shells; insertable chokes and wrench for the Rem Choke (see 'Shotguns') system; ghost view of a Remington Premier Target shot shell; sophisticated figure-eight wad from same; and Remington's advanced Premier 209 primers. Remington can coordinate the designs of its ammo and its arms, and thus fulfill any shooter's needs.

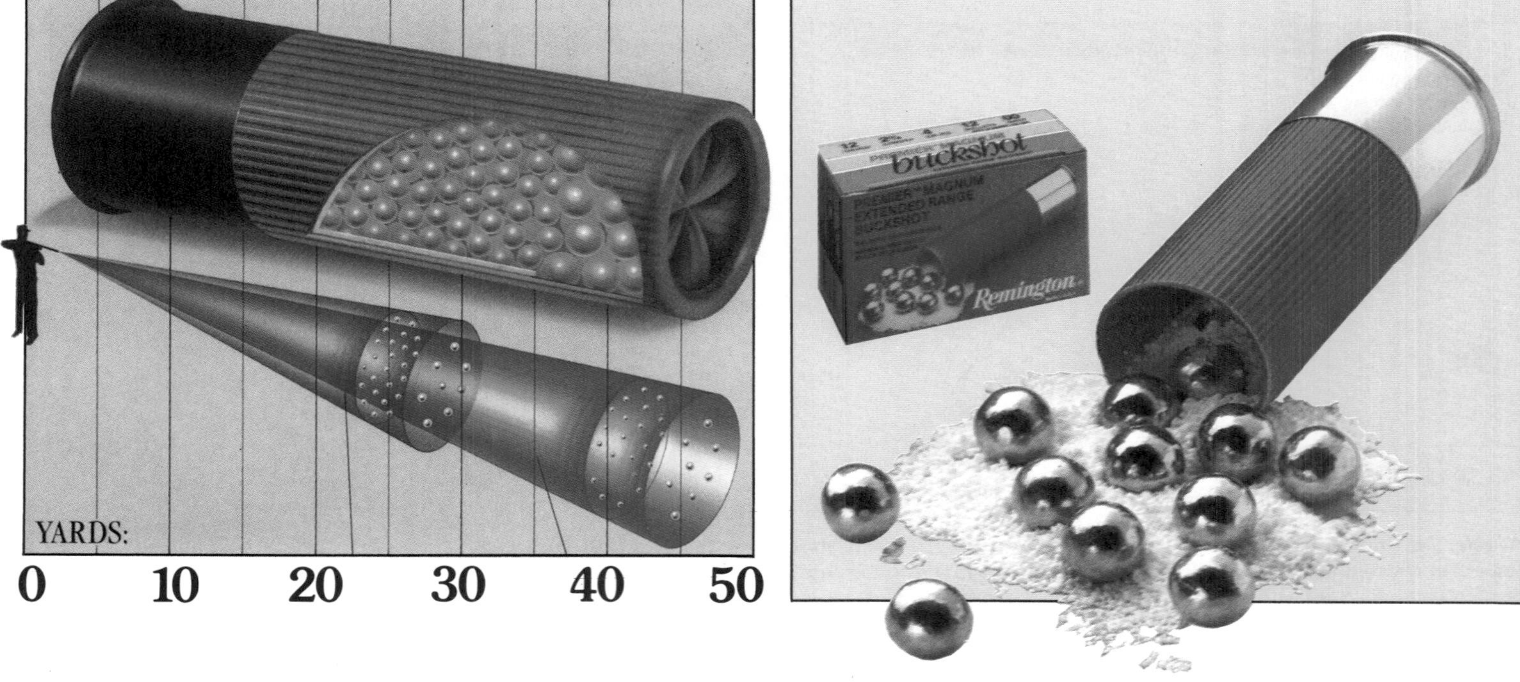

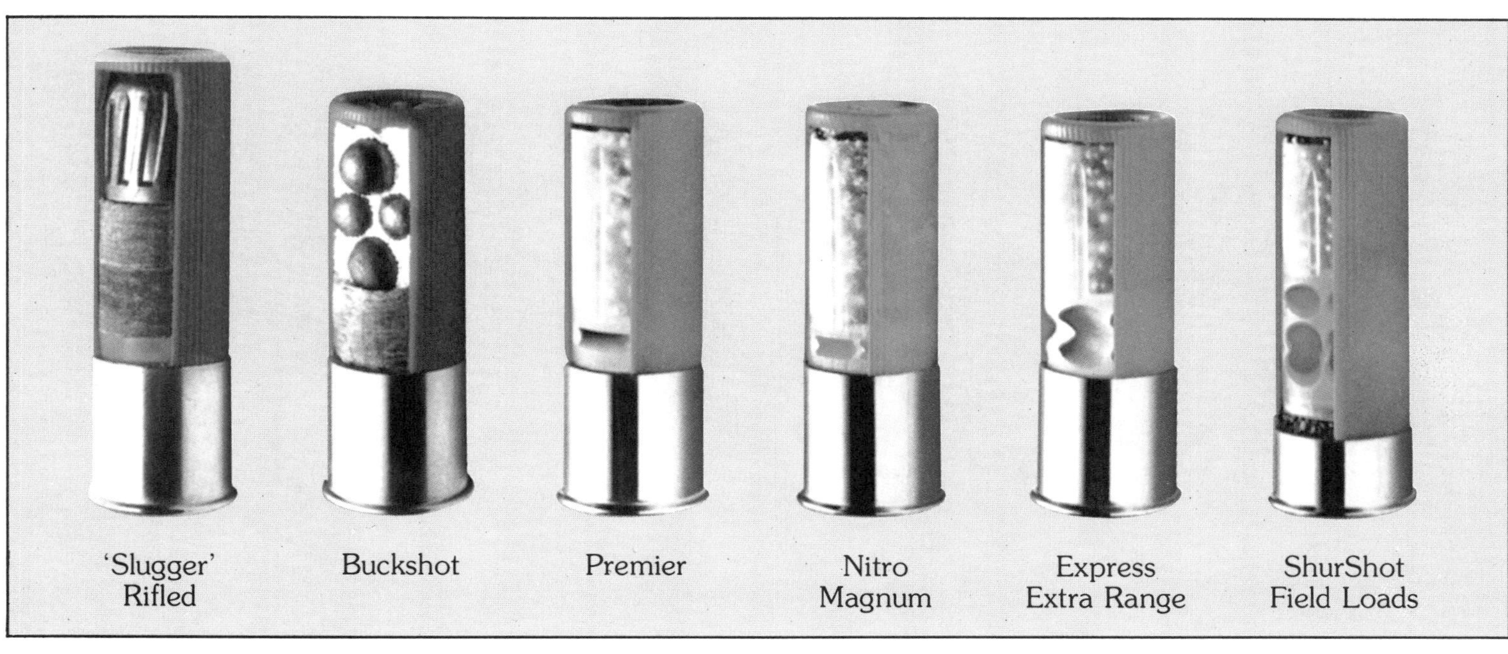
'Slugger' Rifled
Buckshot
Premier
Nitro Magnum
Express Extra Range
ShurShot Field Loads

ready for issue containing 680 metallic cartridges, caliber .50, in paper packages was fired into from the one-inch Gatling Gun. Three shots perforated the box and the upper layer of paper packages, destroying the upper half of the wooden box. The damage done was as follows; 29 cartridges exploded, 97 badly crushed out of shape, but not exploded, 38 loose uninjured, 480 in paper packages uninjured. The trial seemed to prove that the explosion of a caisson or an ammunition dump is robbed of its greatest terrors by being confined to only a small number of the few cartridges that may be struck by an enemy's shot.'

Due to Hobbs' inventive genius and to the terrific pace at which he worked, UMC got into large scale production only a few months after the contract with Berdan was consummated. These events would place UMC almost overnight in a commanding position in small-arms ammunition manufacturing. Unlike many inventions, the Berdan cartridge was an instantaneous success. The gunmakers of America as well as the rest of the world immediately began to adapt their locks to use the center fire principal. This was especially true of the Remingtons, who had just produced the famous Remington Rolling Block Rifle. The combination of the new Remington breech loader and the UMC ammunition was simply unbeatable.

Hartley and his partners became the general sales agents for Remington, thus establishing the close cooperation between the companies which eventually resulted in their merger. The market for center fire ammunition was explosive. The Union Metallic Cartridge Company had one of the fastest growth rates ever recorded in American history. In 1867 it had only about 30 employees and one small factory; only four years later buildings had sprouted up all over the Bridgeport site and production was over 400,000 cartridges per day.

However, fast production and overwhelming quantities did not mean a sacrifice in quality. UMC ammunition was tested to very high standards, and these standards the company took pains to maintain on a rigidly consistent basis. For example, the bark *Forya*, bound from New York to the Russian fortress of Kronstadt with a cargo of 3,645,120 cartridges, was destroyed in a gale. Her deck was stove in, and the crew abandoned the water-logged hulk. Some days

later, the SS *Iowa* found the derelict barely afloat in a North Atlantic steamer lane. With salvage as their incentive, the officers and crew of the *Iowa* pumped out the *Forya* and towed her back to New York. The ammunition which had been under water for five weeks was taken out and shipped to Bridgeport. Tests were conducted and the report states, 'The wet paper boxes were removed and 10,450 of the cartridges were fired, proving them uninjured.' Twenty years later, more of this same lot were tested without a misfire. Another rigorous accidental test of UMC ammunition occurred in 1898; when the US battleship *Maine* was blown up in Havana Harbor, the UMC small arms ammunition aboard her went to the bottom. In 1911, her twisted hull was brought to the surface by Naval engineers and hundreds of these cartridges—which had lain at the bottom of a tropical sea for 13 years—were shot off without a single misfire.

Since UMC was not bound to any special type of arm, like the gunmaking companies were, it was free to make cartridges for everyone. The catalogue for 1872 listed over 30 separate patterns, including center fire, rimfire, cap and ball, and, generally, cartridges applicable to breech loaders of all descriptions—even the Gatling gun! By the early 1900s, the company was able to produce more than 15,000 different loads, varying from BB caps to 10 gauge shot shells. This tremendous variety was due to Hartley's determination that there should be a UMC cartridge for *every* type of gun that was made. This was not simple vanity for the benefit of advertising, but was the cornerstone of his business philosophy. That philosophy proved valid indeed.

With center fire cartridges squarely in the mainstream of the ammunition market, inventiveness lagged until the early 1920s. The fact that gun bores were subject to corrosive build-ups of residue after firing proved the need for general improvements in ammunition. Unless rifles were cleaned almost instantly after a day's shooting, or even after firing only a single shot, the shining bore would be coated with corrosion, and its polished perfection could possibly be ruined forever.

Below: The interior of Marcellus Hartley and partners' firearms and munitions store. Hartley and cohorts formed the Union Metallic Cartridge Company. _Opposite:_ Inside the UMC Bridgeport ammunition factory in the 1870s.

Cartridges

Inside a modern Remington center fire cartridge *(above)*. *At left:* The tip of a Remington Soft Point bullet, a semi-jacketed projectile which features improved mushrooming upon impact for better knockdown power. *At right, from the top down:* A well-mushroomed Soft Point; cutaway views of various Remington bullet types. *Below:* The shiny brass and copper look of modern Remington center fire rifle cartridges. *Opposite, from left to right:* A selection of Remington rimfire ammo—.22 caliber blunt point antisnake bullets; standard .22 long rifle bullets; and .22 caliber hollow point bullets. Note that the first and the last of these are 'hyper velocity' rounds.

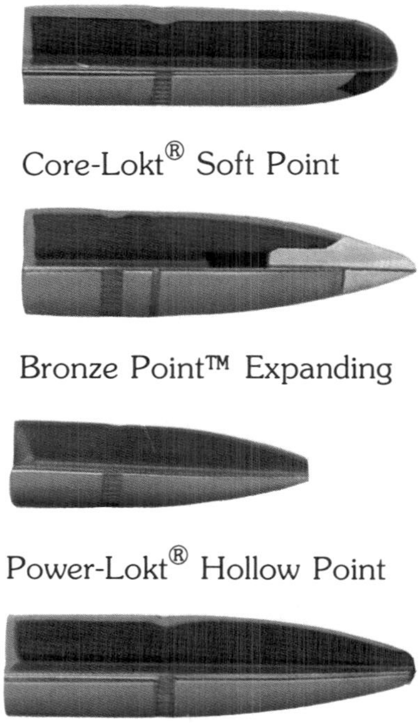

Core-Lokt® Soft Point

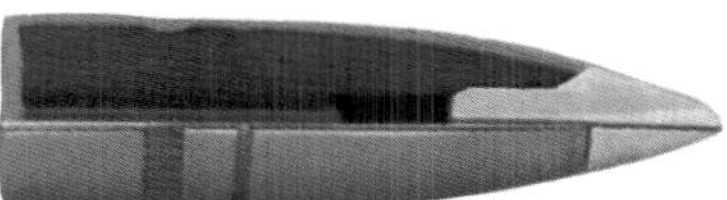

Bronze Point™ Expanding

Power-Lokt® Hollow Point

Core-Lokt Pointed Soft Point

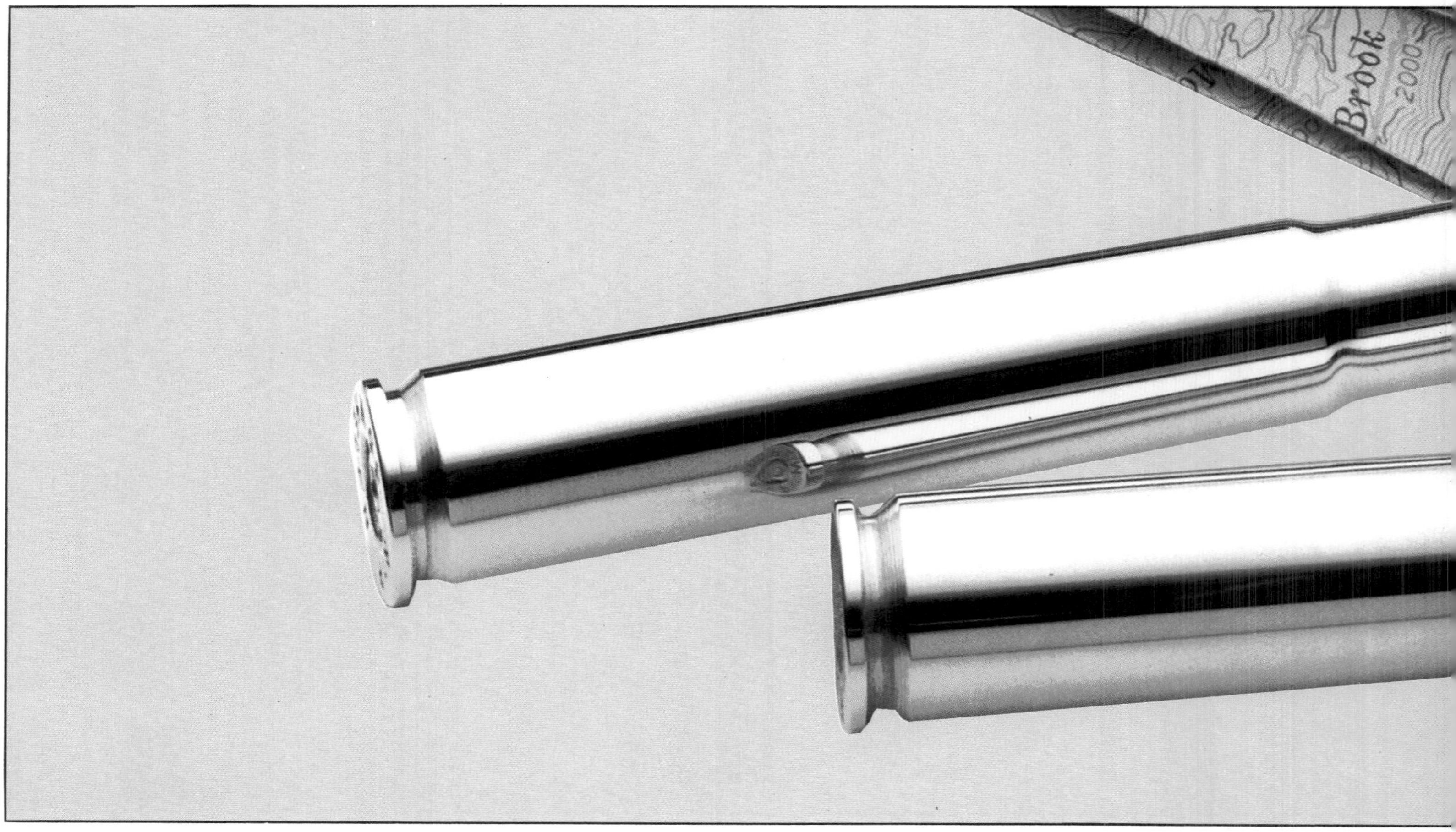

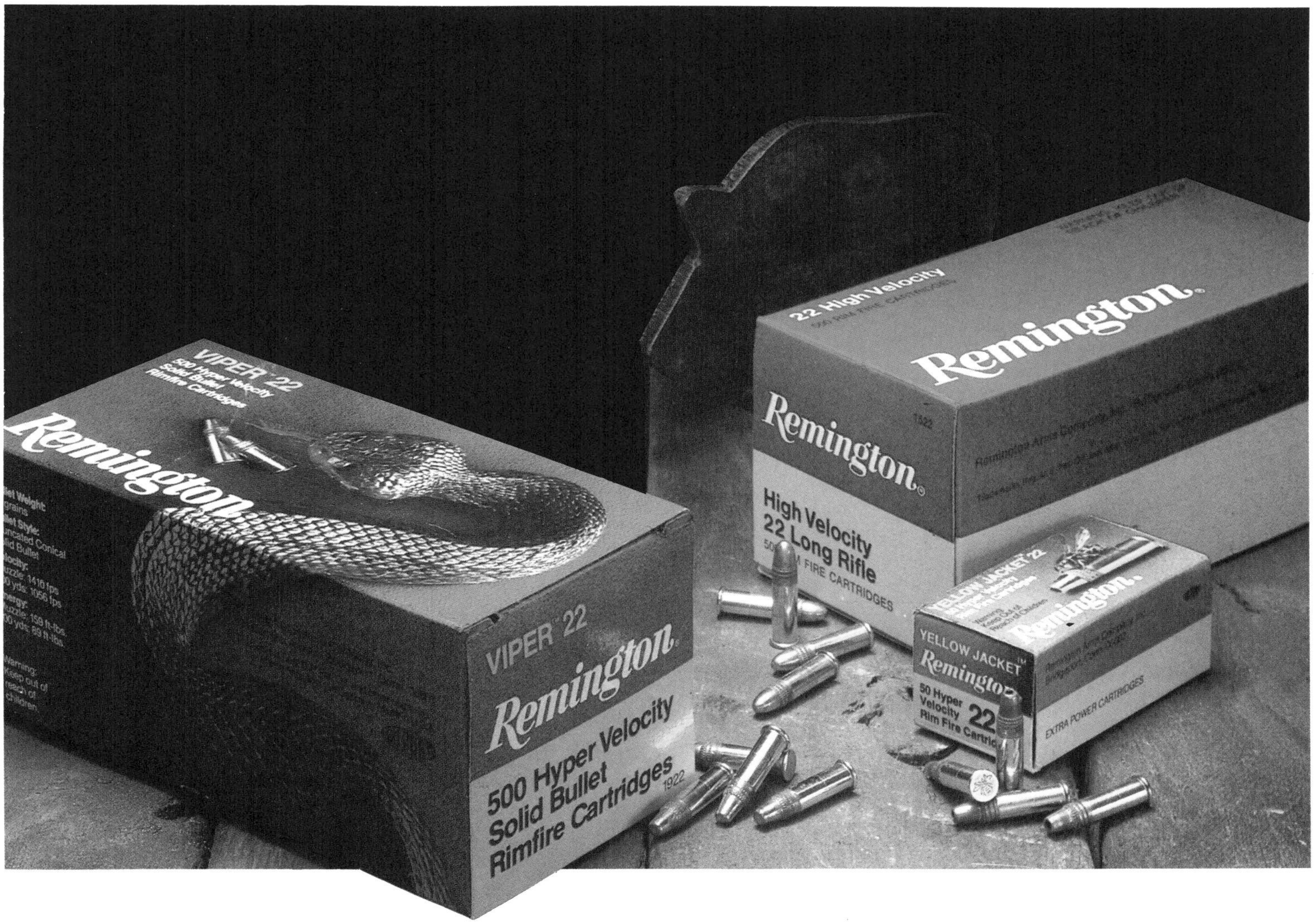

VIPER 22
500 Hyper Velocity
Solid Bullet
Rimfire Cartridges
Remington
VIPER 22
Remington
500 Hyper Velocity
Solid Bullet
Rimfire Cartridges
1922
22 High Velocity
Remington
Remington
High Velocity
22 Long Rifle
YELLOW JACKET 22
Remington
YELLOW JACKET
Remington
50 Hyper
Velocity
Rim Fire Cartridges
22
EXTRA POWER CARTRIDGES

0
30
330
300
270
E
S
FINLAND

This damage was not caused by the erosion of the bullets or the smokeless powder, but by the chemical action of the fulminate of mercury and potassium chlorate used in the primers. Potassium chlorate was the real villain: it is akin to plain table salt, and absorbs water so quickly that even a minute grain would instantly begin a rusting process and eat a tiny hole in the steel.

In 1926 Remington introduced 'Kleanbore' ammunition which freed gunners from the incessant use of cleaning rags and powder solvents.

James E Burns, an imaginative chemist, paid a visit to Remington in the winter of 1924. He spoke of his plans for a trip to Florida, and then pulled out a revolver and began shooting—luckily with only primed empty cartridge cases. He requested that Remington technicians lay the pistol away in a damp place until he returned from his trip in about a month. When he returned, the revolver was examined: the bluing on the outside of the barrel showed streaks of rust—but when a dry rag was run through the barrel, the bore shown with pristine brilliance. Here was a chemical miracle! Burns had discovered a substituted for potassium chlorate in primers.

It took over two years of intensive experimentation before Remington was ready to go on the market with this new noncorrosive primer. The formula finally used contained lead styphnate, which was manufactured by DuPont. Extensive testing was carried out both in

At left: Testing in the 1950s: A Remington technician places cartridges in a machine which simulates adverse conditions that exceed the most rugged of field conditions. *At right:* Another Remington technician tests new means of fabricating aluminum components for firearms during the postwar sporting arms boom of the 1940s and 50s; the war was over, and the hunt was on. *Above left:* A 1912 ad featuring the 'Remington Cubs.'

Remington's laboratories and also by special arrangement with various shooting galleries in New York state. Literally millions of rounds were fired in these tests. The guns in which the ammunition was fired were put through rigorous testing programs in which they were left uncleaned for 18 months after firing anywhere from 25 to 25,000 shots. Throughout the intervening years guns fired from 30,000 to over one million times without cleaning have still shown no signs of corrosion or erosion.

Other specimens were put into laboratory humidifiers which were run at 90 percent humidity at a temperature of 120 degrees. The outside of the barrels of these guns became encrusted with rust but in every case the bores came through in perfect condition. The new priming material formula not only failed to corrode, but actually *protected* the bores of guns through which it was fired. When the time came to actually market the noncorrosive ammunition, Remington held a contest to choose a name for it. Two men, separated by thousands of miles, had the same bright idea. WA Robbins of Jonesboro, Louisiana, and Nelson K Starr of Goshen, Indiana both suggested 'Kleanbore.' They each received a prize from Remington.

Remington introduced 'Kleanbore' ammunition to the general public in 1926, and though it is prudent to clean and oil one's firearm regularly, Kleanbore ammunition has helped to preserve many a gun bore. At present all cartridge companies make noncorrosive ammunition but, as in so many other firearm improvements, it was Remington that pioneered this revolutionary breakthrough.

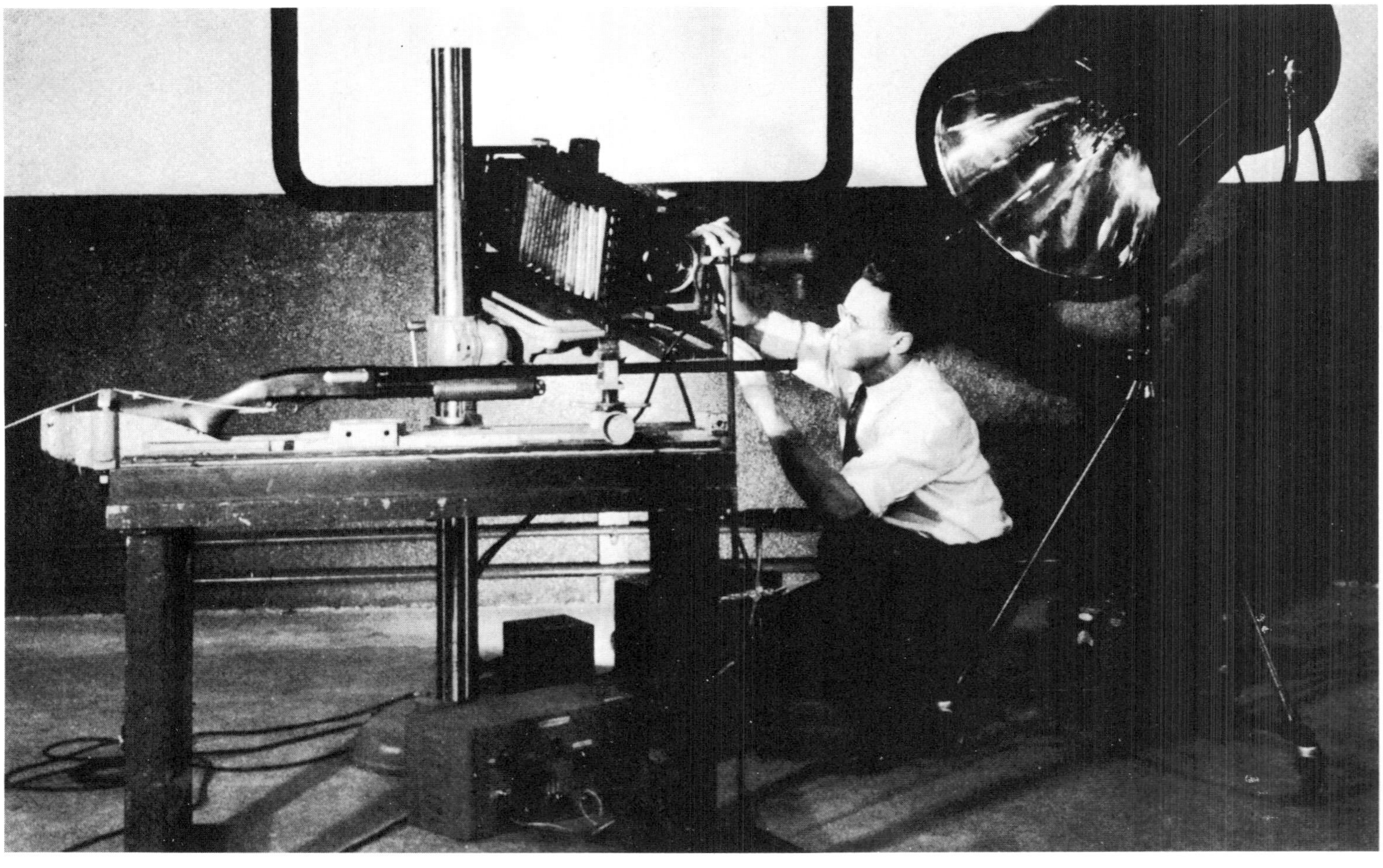

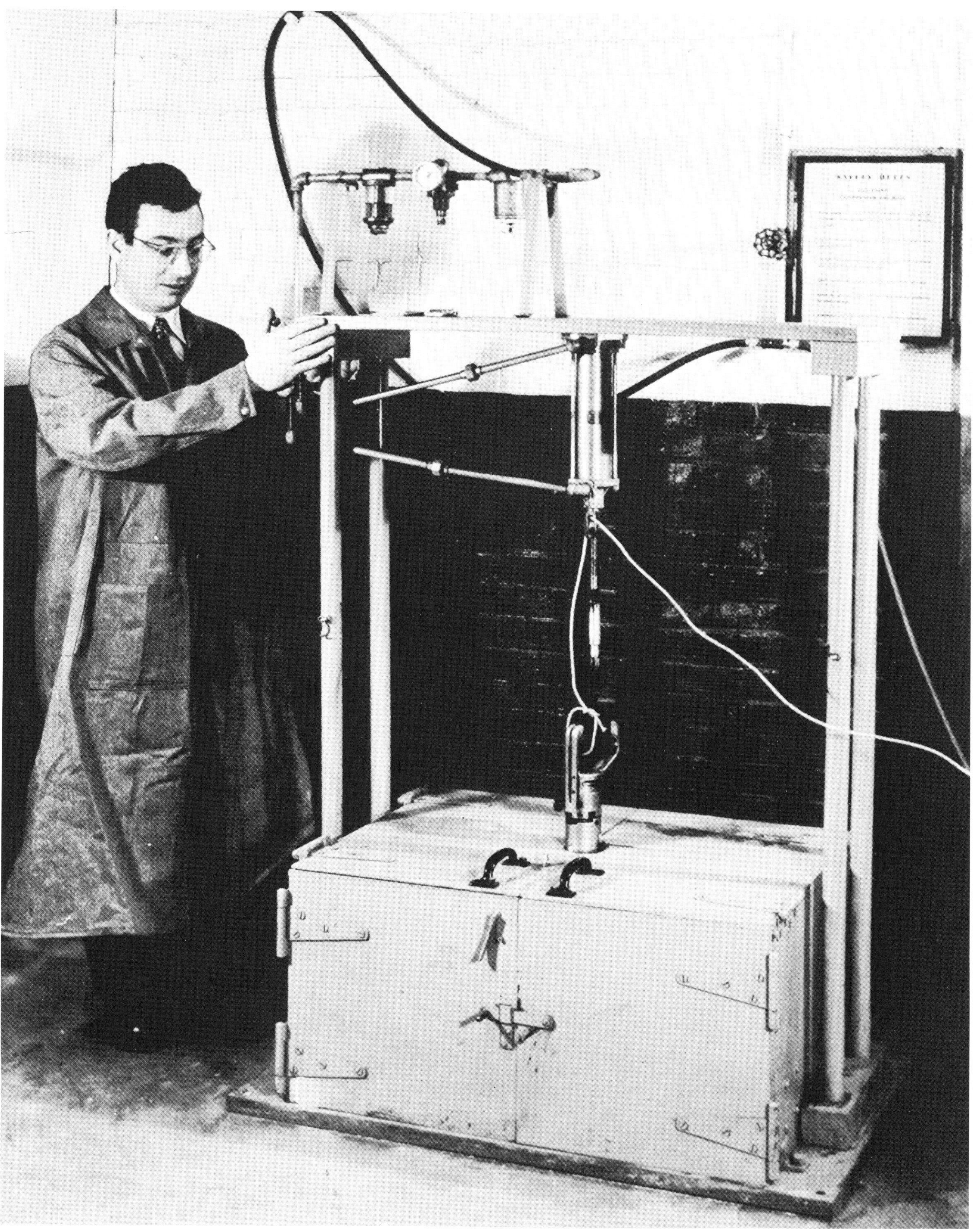

Above: Remington's experimental industrial tools, fasteners and cartridges have long been tested by remote control devices such as this. *Above left:* Features from Remington's famous Peters line of ammunition—the new 'Accelerator' bullets which increase muzzle velocity by almost 30 percent, and Peters .44 Remington Magnum semi-jacketed hollow point bullets. *At left:* Setting up a high-speed photo ballistics study.

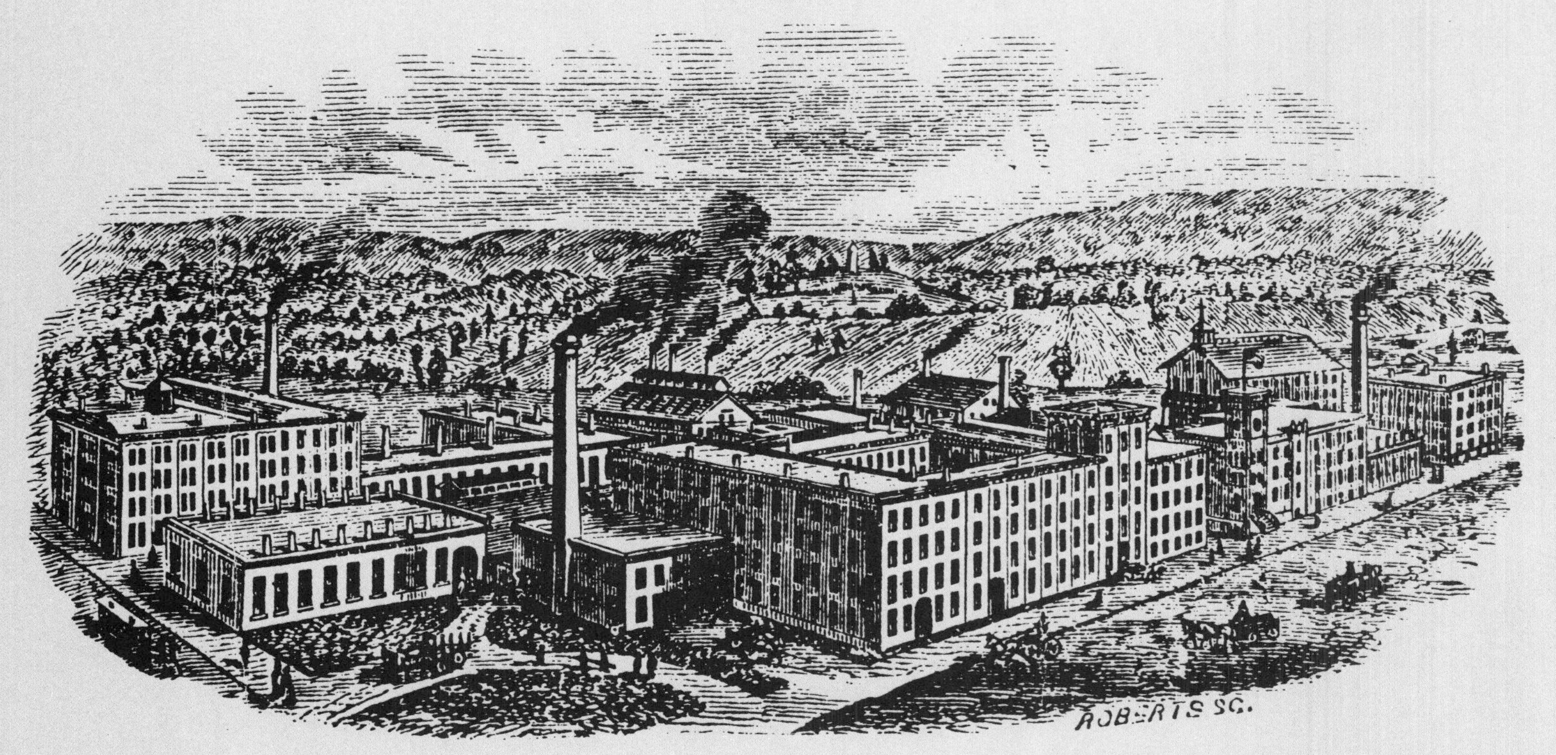
ROBERTS SC.

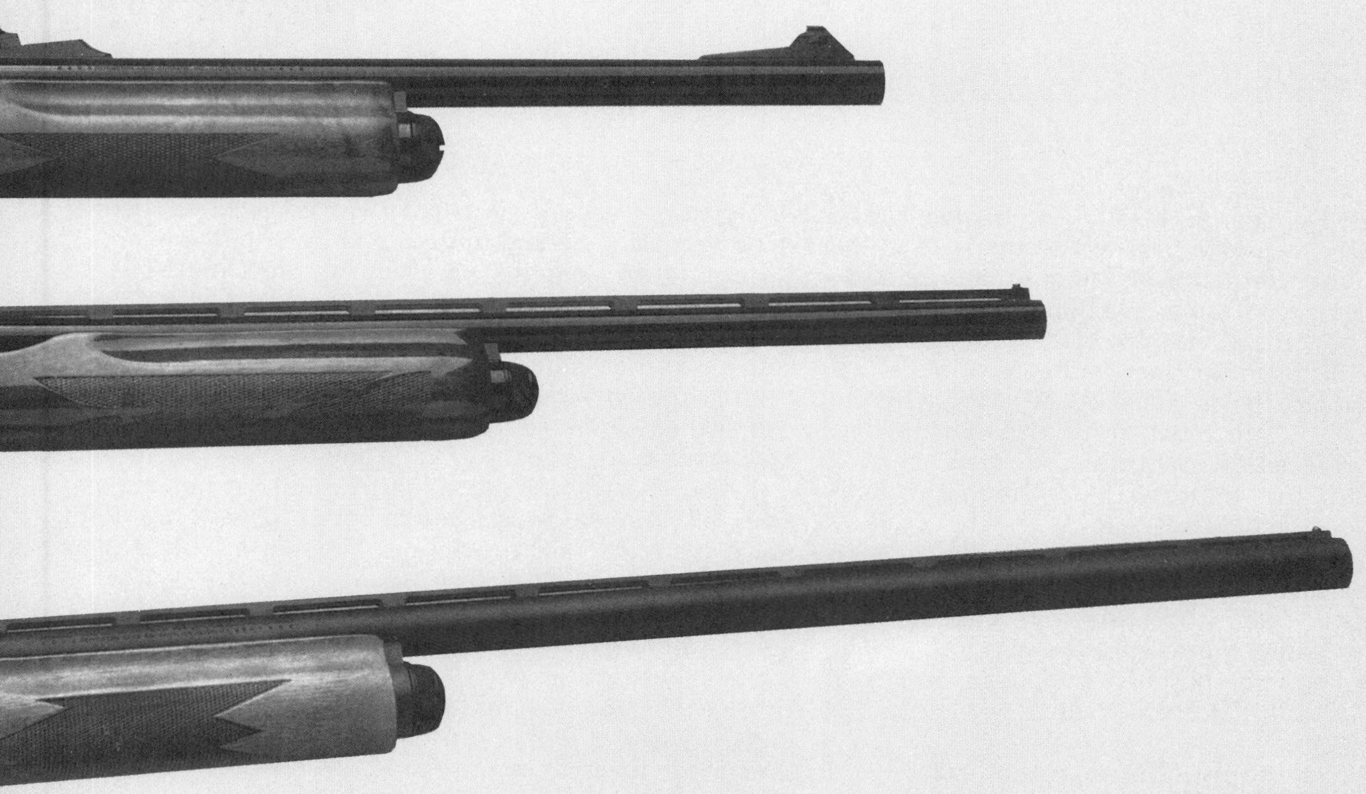

Above, far left: The Remington Armory in Ilion, New York, as it was portrayed by an engraver in 1874. *Above, at top:* Remington accessories for the complete hobbyist—an all-purpose pocket knife and Rem Oil protective firearms lubricant—and an old-fashioned cleaning rod. The firearms shown *on these pages* are, from top to bottom: The Model 870 Wingmaster Deer Gun; the Model 870 20 gauge Youth Gun; and the New Model 870 Express.

Eliphalet First

Eliphalet Remington, II—'Lite' to his family and friends—lay asleep in a soft feather bed in the northeast bedroom of his father's house. Abigail, his young wife, lay beside him. The sun rose at 4:54 AM on that morning early in August 1816, and a first shaft of light, piercing the fringe of trees that rimmed the Remington fields, touched Lite's long, chiseled nose. He awoke, and remembering his plans for the day, heaved himself out of his feathered nest.

Abigail stirred and muttered, 'Is the night over already?'

'Yes,' said Lite. 'But don't you move. The women say you must be extra careful of the first child.'

'You're so good, Lite,' she answered. 'I'll keep him safe for you. Are you going to start the gun today?'

'Sure as shootin',' her husband said. 'The hay is in and things are slow at the forge. Father says I can use it.'

He put on a rough homespun shirt and pantaloons—broadcloth was for Sundays—pulled on his leather half boots, and went down to the hearty New England breakfast his mother had ready for him. He ate quickly, scarcely speaking to his parents, for in his mind he was already working the iron to form the barrel of his gun.

Legend says that young Remington asked his father for a gun; that he was refused on the grounds it was too costly, and that he went straight off and made one for himself. Legend often lies. In an era when game supplied most of the meat for every larder and the forest was still full of bears, wolves, and sleek, dangerous panthers, a gun was not a luxury but a necessity, and Lite Remington was not a man to go off without careful study and planning and make a gun by inspiration.

Remington, having carefully studied methods of gun-making, and having minutely examined all the rifles he could lay hands on, decided that he could make a better gun than he could buy, and he was quite right.

Lite finished his breakfast quickly, kissed his mother, and said to his father, 'Stop by the forge when you can and give me the benefit of your advice.'

'If you don't know more than I do about gun-making after all that studying, you'd better give it up right now,' his father answered. 'But I'll have a look at it all the same.'

Young Remington went out of the kitchen door, being careful not to bang it for Abigail's sake. He cut straight across the hay field in which the cows were now in pasture, toward the tall trees that rimmed the edge of 'the Gulph.' Ignoring the wagon track that quartered down its steep slopes to the ford near the sulphur springs, he slipped and slid down an almost vertical foot path between the great tree trunks that rose branchless for fully 60 feet before spreading out their thick canopy of leaves. The August heat was already on the fields, but in the wooded gorge the air was mostly chilly, and the steady rushing sound of the creek, rippling over its bed of boulders, made it seem cooler still.

The new stone building that housed the forge and smithy, which Lite's father, Eliphalet I, had built the year before, stood right on the water's edge. When it was operating, a wooden flume several hundred feet long carried water from a dam at the bend of the creek

Remington's Gun

Evidence of the oldest commercial firearms business in the United States. *Above:* This sleek Remington Model 600 in .243 Winchester caliber may serve to illustrate what a long way Remington firearms design has come since 'Lite' Remington first hammered out a barrel at he and his father's forge. But the flintlock that he made was no mean gun—its first public shooting trial caused many of the best shots in the land to buy barrels, parts and entire rifles that he, Eliphalet Remington II, had made. This was just the beginning of a way of thinking and a care of making that would enable the Remington Arms company to become, over the years, one of the greatest arms and ammunition makers in the entire world.

above the ford to the big waterwheel with its 12-foot wooden paddles. The water gate would remain shut today; the flume, empty; and the wheel still. Lite would not need them for the job at hand. Remington threw open the big door of the forge and left it so—it would be hot in there later. The interior of the shop was a scene of cluttered order. Nearest the doors was the wooden ox sling—stout, four-poster gallows on which oxen were hoisted to be shod since they could not give their feet to the smith as horses did. On racks along the walls hung dozens of horseshoes and even more of the little half shoes for the oxen's cloven hooves. Wagon wheels with shiny new iron tires leaned against the stone walls. In one corner were piled a heterogeneous assortment of parts for agricultural implements: harrow teeth and cultivator prongs, ox yokes, hoes, crowbars and the metal parts of other farmers' tools—including iron facings for wooden plows (it would be three years yet before Jethro Wood of Cayuga County invented the first all-metal plow).

In another heap were iron parts that the Remingtons made for the grist mills which were springing up on virtually every creek that could get up a sufficient head of water to turn a wheel. Mixed in with them were heavy sleigh shoes, curved to fit over the wooden runners of the only vehicle that could be used in that country from December to March.

In one corner of the shop stood the brick forge, its interior chimney already blackened with soot. Close beside it were the big circular tub bellows, a good six feet in diameter, mounted horizontally on a wooden frame. Within easy reach was the heavy triangular anvil, its iron column secured to a stout wooden block. The tools of the blacksmith's trade were racked handily by—sledge hammers, grooving hammers, wedge-shaped pritchel hammers for punching nail holes in the horseshoes, mandrels, rasps, paring knives, long-handled iron ladles for dishing out molten metal, chisels, gouges, files and powerful scissor tongs for handling the white-hot iron. At the south end of the building nearest to the waterwheel were big grindstones, laboriously cut from a red sandstone cliff in the Gulph.

Lite Remington hung a leather apron from his neck and went straight to the forge, where he started a fire of charcoal, which had been bought from the charcoal burners who worked their pits back in the hills—where the great trees provided an apparently inexhaustible supply of raw material. While the fire was getting started, Remington selected a rod of iron that he himself had smelted down from ore that had been mined in Frank's Fort Gulph, and from scrap iron which had been traded in by the farmers who were the Remington forge's best customers.

It took better than half an hour to get the fire exactly right. Then Lite shoved his bar of iron into the furnace and, swinging on the pole of the bellows, pumped it up and down, forcing jets of air into the coals which sparked and sizzled. The iron rod gradually heated to a cherry red that seemed brighter than the coals. Judging the right instant exactly from long experience, Lite seized the bar with the tongs and expertly swung it across the anvil. Holding it thus with his left hand, he raised a heavy hammer with his right.

Above: **Eliphalet Remington II, aka 'Lite' Remington. *Above right:* The Remington homestead in Ilion, New York, where Lite was born, and in which he lived with his wife Abigail and his parents until the young couple moved into the house *(at right)* which Lite's dad built for them.**

Stop here and take a look at him, for as the first blow rings upon the glowing metal, history will be made, and that small bar of iron will become the first of 10 million guns bearing the name of Remington. Lite had a long, loose-jointed body which in Sunday broadcloth seemed deceptively slender. Now, poised in tension for the blow, thighs and buttocks strained the rough cloth of his trousers, his bare arms were bunched with muscle and the rigid cords of his neck made a perfect pattern of human power.

So far he might have stood as the prototype of the young workman—the essence of physical strength and skill, single of purpose and beautifully adapted to that end. But the head poised on his straining neck seemed strangely out of context with his body: it was delicate, long and well-shaped with curly, dark hair growing to a widow's peak on the high forehead. Lips and nose were finely chiseled, eyebrows delicately sketched above large, dreamy eyes. Even in the flush of furnace heat and hard labor, sweat beading and dripping from the point of his classic nose, Lite Remington looked like a *poet*, which he was!

The hammer described a perfect arc and smashed down on the hot iron, sending up a spray of sparks. With the deceptive ease of practiced skill, Remington struck again and again in ringing rhythm. The end of the rod was beaten flat to a thickness of about one half

of an inch. When it cooled from red to pale pink, Remington swung it back to the bed of the furnace and pumped the bellows once more. Thus he worked it until the rod was changed to a long metal bar, one-half inch wide and one-half inch thick. Then he worked it over again until thickness and width were as nearly uniform as human skill could make them: this was only the first step.

The legend built around that gun has it completed in a single day, but it took a practiced gunsmith a week to make a gun, and must have taken Remington at least that long. After he had forged his length of iron, he took an arbor—the core around which he must build his barrel, for there were as yet no tools in the world that would drill a straight hole through three feet or more of metal—and fixed it in his vise.

Remington brought the strip of iron to red heat again, placed an end of it over the arbor and slowly bent the softened metal around the core so that it fitted in a closed spiral. Every few inches he would have to reheat it. It was close, arduous work, done with painstaking exactitude, for the tightness and evenness of the spiral, and the quality of the weld along its seams, determined the success of the whole undertaking.

While Lite worked, his father came by to offer approval and advice, and farmer customers dropped in to purchase goods and offer their opinions—since in the farm country of those times almost every man had at least a smattering of the blacksmith's craft, every man had his opinions!

The job was done at last. Lite Remington had produced a closed spiral of metal some forty-two inches long with a .4-inch arbor running through it. He laid this spiral in the bed of coals, and this time brought it to white heat. Then he sprinkled borax and sand on it to facilitate the welding process, and seizing it in his tongs pounded it vigorously on the stone floor. This was called 'jumping,' which was meant to jar the malleable edges of the spiral strip against each other so that heat-activated molecules would run together and weld the metal spiral into a solid tube of iron. Because only eight inches could be heated at once, Remington repeated this process six times—and there was the rough barrel of the gun!

Remington then plunged it, with a hiss and flash of steam, into a tub of water to cool. When he could touch it without burning his fingers, he drew out the arbor and eagerly raised the barrel, warm and dripping; he sighted along it to answer the vital question: Was it straight? As far as his eye could tell, it was. Then he looked through it, aiming at the open doors, and it seemed to him there was a slight divergence. To check this, he made a plumb line with a piece of string and a small weight, and dropped it down the tube. About a foot below the muzzle, the string almost touched the side of the barrel.

Marking the spot carefully, Remington rested the tube on two pieces of metal and taking a soft lead hammer tapped it smartly, several times. When he tried his plumb line again it was almost right. Two more slight taps, and now the line ran dead center down the length of the barrel, which was now actually 'as straight as a plumb line.'

E. REMINGTON & SONS

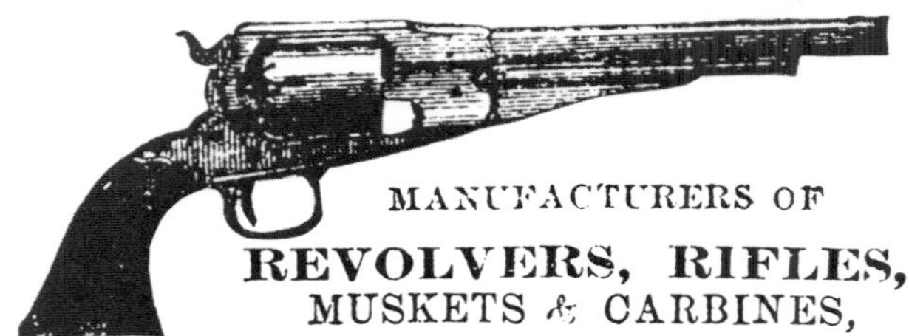

MANUFACTURERS OF
REVOLVERS, RIFLES,
MUSKETS & CARBINES,
For the United States service. Also,
POCKET AND BELT REVOLVERS,
Repeating Pistols, Rifle Canes, Revolving Rifles, Rifle and Shot Gun Barrels and Gun Materials, sold by gun dealers and the trade generally. In these days of house-breaking and robbery, every house, store, bank and office should have one of
REMINGTON'S REVOLVERS.
Parties desiring to avail themselves of the late improvements in Pistols, and superior workmanship and form, will find all combined in the New Remington Revolvers.
Circulars containing cuts and description of our Arms will be furnished upon application.
E. REMINGTON & SONS, Ilion, N Y.
MOORE & NICHOLS, Agents, No. 40
July 6—4m Courtland-st., New York.

For the last day's work on the barrel, Lite needed power. That morning he went first to the dam and hoisted the sluice gate. A fine head of water roared down the flume. Cascading over the end, it smashed down in flying spray on the 12-foot wheel, which shuddered and groaned and began to turn. Inside the forge the grindstones were revolving. Remington drove tapering wooden spindles into both ends of his barrel to act as handles, then pressed it vertically against the grindstone. The abrasive surface bit into the iron, sending forth a bright river of sparks. Lite gradually moved it against the wheel, cutting a flat, smooth surface the length of the barrel. Eight such surfaces were cut to give the barrel the octagon-shape that was then in fashion.

It took the better part of a day to grind the barrel. When it was done, Lite lifted it and caressed the polished metal, but the inside of the barrel was still rough, and he had no tools for reaming and rifling it.

The following day, Remington put on his best black broadcloth suit so that he would be properly attired for a visit to the metropolis of Utica. He slung a knapsack—packed with plenty of meat and bread—over his shoulder, clapped a tall beaver hat on his head, and carrying his barrel in one hand and his father's rifle in the other for protection against various carnivorous animals, set out for town.

Because it was much shorter and easier going than the River Road, he followed the old Oneida Trail along the crests of the hills. As soon as he left his father's fields, he plunged into the great woods; it was a little like diving into clear, cool water. The hot August sun was strained by the almost impenetrable ceiling of leaves to a dim green gloom, through which Lite saw an endless vista of dark, columned tree trunks rising to

Above: The old Remington family forge down in Ilion 'Gulph,' in which Lite Remington learned the blacksmithing business from his dad, Eliphalet Remington, Senior; they made farm implements and general smithing goods, including the occasional rifle barrel. When Lite made his first firearm, a flintlock rifle, response to the accuracy of the arm was overwhelming. Demand for Lite's barrels and complete rifles grew until Lite's dad had to build his son a company headquarters—and house (see caption, page 76). *Above left:* A Remington ad of 9 November 1866.

the high Gothic groining of branches and leaves. The white pole of an occasional birch was like a marker placed to show the way. Except for a thin spread of low ferns, there was no underbrush in that forest—the dense shade killed all vegetation that could not reach up to the light. The great trees stood a good 20 feet apart, so the only obstacles that Remington encountered were an occasional huge log fallen across the trail. Under his feet the forest floor, laid down through centuries by fallen trees and leaves and rotting vegetation, was delightfully springy to walk on.

Though the forest was so vast and dim, Lite did not feel lonely, for it was anything but silent. Indeed, it was as noisily conversational as a county-wide quilting bee. Away above him in the upper stories of the trees there was a tremendous traffic of birds. Crows, blackbirds and jays wrangled and disputed with hoarse croaks and shrill jabbering. Woodcock, plover and partridge talked to each other, and wild pigeons flocked in thousands, cooing low. Squirrels raced up and down the broad, bare tree trunks like flashes of gray light, and, on the ground, sudden scurryings indicated that minks, raccoons and other such valuable varmints were getting out of the way, while occasionally a deer flashed across the field of vision.

Remington noted the lively life around him, but he never broke his easy ground-covering stride, even while his imagination delighted in picturing the creatures who made all that commotion. But fanciful though he was, he probably never produced a mental image of his own angular person, top-hatted and in formal black, pacing through the aboriginal forest.

Except for a charcoal burner's aromatic pit and a thin trickle of humanity that he saw in the deep crack of Frank's Fort Gulph, he encountered no other signs of civilization until, after better than three hours walking, he struck the down slope to Utica. There the forest ended abruptly and he came out in the dazzling sunlight of open fields. Below him were the houses of

Above left: The Remington armory at Ilion, which was built in 1835. *At left:* Ilion, New York, as it was in 1883. The Remington Armory is at photo left. *Below left:* One of the canal barges which transported Remington products on the Erie Canal in the 1850s. *Above:* The Remington Arms plant at the corner of First and Morgan Streets in Ilion, New York, in the 1880s. *Below:* The Ilion plant at full capacity in spring of 1916.

REMINGTON ARMS CO.
ILION. N.Y. 1916.
© W.B.

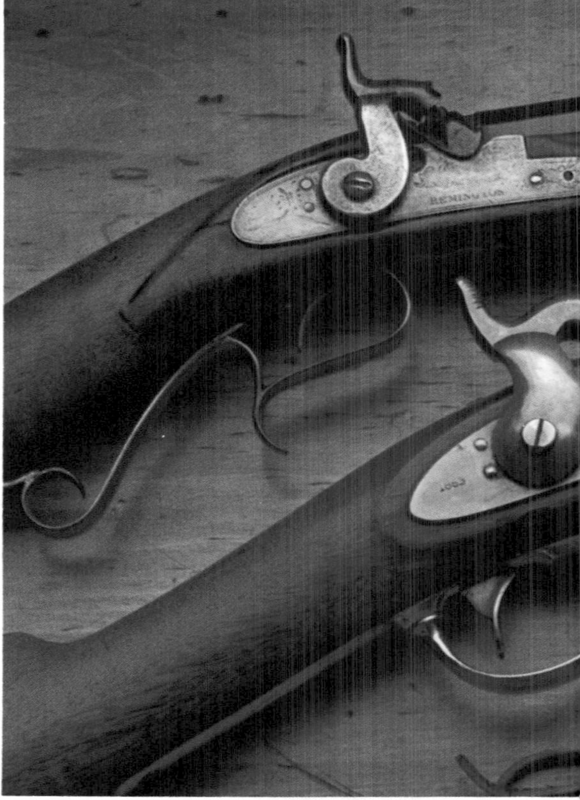

Above: An exemplification of the hand fitting and finishing which goes into every fine Remington firearm. The quality that is so evident in Remington arms throughout the company's history is the result of careful attention to detail—as is witnessed to by the astonishingly rich engraving on the Remington Parker double-barrel shotgun at *above right* (which view also evidences a closeup of the engraved 'Parker' appellation of same). *At above far right* is a portrait of Eliphalet 'Lite' Remington II, with family memorabilia; *at far right* is a very fine grade Remington double derringer from the 1860s amid familiar surroundings; and *at right, left to right*, handsome specimens of a Remington pre-Civil War cap and ball rifle with octagonal barrel, and a Remington cap and ball rifled musket of Civil War vintage with adjustable rear sight.

the fast-growing town, straggling from the hills to cluster thickly at the water's edge. He saw the brand-new mills and factories, fine church spires and the turmoil of commerce along the wharves. The Mohawk River's thin blue band, curving away between the hills, was speckled with activity. It was the one break in the great Appalachian mountain barrier from the Saint Lawrence to the Cumberland Gap, and through it funneled the mass migration of settlers, pouring out of the East to fill the vast vacuum of the fertile Western plains.

The river was crowded with long, high-sided bateaux and the big eight-oared Durham boats, with square sails set before the favoring wind. Oxen drew the new Pennsylvania wagons up the roads that ran along both banks, while other families moved westward on foot or on horseback, and occasionally in fine four-horse coaches.

Nor was all the traffic upriver. The fertile farms of the Mohawk Valley, the Genessee Valley and the Finger Lakes were the breadbasket of the Eastern seaboard. Their produce, and cargoes of salt from the famous salt springs of Syracuse, were floated down the Mohawk in strange lozenge-shaped vessels—half raft, half scow—that were called 'arks.'

Utica, with its population of 1200, was the biggest city Remington knew. As he walked down the steep hill of Genesee Street, it seemed very metropolitan to him and, in fact, it made up in bustle what it lacked in size. He inquired for the shop of Morgan James, a young man about his own age, who was making himself a reputation as a gunsmith.

Remington approached young Mr James with his barrel, and stated his need. James took it in his hands and hefted expertly. He peered along it and through it, and turned it over and over, inspecting the forging with particular care. Lite looked on with the agonized concentration of an artist exhibiting his latest work. This was the first authoritative critique of his labors.

James soon put him out of his misery. 'That's a fine barrel,' he said. 'Straight as a string. It'll only take me a couple of hours to ream it for you, but the rifling is a long job.'

He secured it firmly in the narrow, wooden bed of his rifling machine, and introduced a nut auger mounted on the end of a slender five-foot rod. He turned the rod by a hand crank with infinite care, moving inch by inch into the barrel, cutting a smooth shining surface.

While the gunsmith worked, Remington never moved from the shop. He had no desire to explore the familiar sights of Utica. The grog shops and taverns by the wharves, crowded even at noon with teamsters and river men, were genuinely sickening to his fastidious mind. However, the new mills and the glass and cotton factories interested him intensely, for woven in with the poetic streak in his nature was a hard strand of practical ambition. The two elements of his character were twisted together like the steel and iron of an imported Damascus gun barrel to form the pattern of the man.

On previous visits to town, he had invariably visited its factories to examine new additions to their machinery and discuss economic problems with their owners. The rattle and bang of machinery, the crash of wooden spindles or the grating roar of slow-turning grindstones were a discordant symphony that drew him as strongly in one direction as the music of the forest did in another. It seemed to him a striking evidence of the fantastic prosperity of the times that experienced mill hands now made as much as 200 dollars a year. Where young workmen could do that, the sky was clearly the limit for an ambitious man with a little capital. Remington had every intention of jumping on the band wagon of industrial expansion, and he regarded the forge in the Gulph as a good base from which to leap.

At left: An early 20th century work photo of 'the Howards'—grandfather, father and son—representing 69 years of family craftsmanship at Remington. *Above:* The old Remington office building on East Main Street in Ilion, New York, which originally was Lite Remington's town house. *Below:* An 18th century photo of the Erie Canal at Ilion. See the canal barge photo on page 80. *Overleaf:* A Mohawk 600 with a Leopold 2x7 Vari-XII scope. The name Mohawk refers to the river which flows near Ilion, and the powerful Indian tribe for which it was named.

However, he had no time for factories this day; he wanted to study every move the master gunsmith made. So he ate his lunch in the shop, sharing a slab of ham and cheese and bread with James, while he cross-questioned the gunsmith about his craft.

When the reaming was done, they peered through the barrel in turn to admire its smooth sheen. Then James fastened it in the rifling machine again and, substituting a special cutting tool for the auger, began the infinitely delicate task of cutting spiral grooves inside the barrel. The bit cut a tiny fraction of an inch at a time, and James worked with an intensity that was matched only by his patience.

As soon as the light began to fade, the gunsmith knocked off. Remington spent the night with him and induced James—who loved his trade, and was to become famous at it—to talk about the history and technique of his craft. James began his tale at the beginning of America, and described the clumsy guns with which the Pilgrims had miraculously managed to supply themselves with game. Their matchlocks were so heavy that they usually required a forked stand to steady the barrel, and the charge was ignited by a slow-burning match like a piece of punk for lighting firecrackers. Then had come the wheel lock, in which a clockwork mechanism turned a steel wheel against a piece of flint throwing a stream of sparks into the priming pan. Finally, the familiar flintlock was invented by Dutch chicken thieves, who called it the *snaphance*, or hen snatcher!

All of these guns had been smooth bore and you were lucky to hit the broad end of a potato patch with one. However, German and Swiss immigrants, whose descendants are the Pennsylvania Dutch, brought the *rifle* to America. Their first rifles were German Jaegers weighing 20 pounds or more. They were unwieldy compared to the smooth-bore flintlocks then in general use, but with one you could actually hit a squirrel in the top of a tree. The trouble was that nobody could carry a Jaeger through the woods and besides that, it took special tools and about 10 minutes to reload, by which time the pioneer would likely be out of luck.

The immigrant German gunsmiths went to work on this problem. Through trading ideas among their many small, individual shops they gradually developed a long, graceful rifle that weighed less than 10 pounds and could be fired two or three times a minute. This was the 'Kentucky rifle'—it should have been called the 'Pennsylvania rifle.' It was perfected about 1730, and quickly became the most famous gun in the world.

'It was the rifle made the conquest of the Western wilderness possible,' James told Lite, 'but we Easterners (meaning New Yorkers in the parlance of those pre-Wild West days) were awfully slow about taking it up. We stuck to smooth bores until after the Revolution, and only now are rifles really becoming common hereabouts. It's still hard to get a good barrel. You've made a dandy.'

James finished the rifling job the next morning. When Remington paid him his fee—which was four double reales (two-bit pieces worth twenty-five cents each), still considered viable currency in the country districts—he felt that he had received more than his money's worth.

To complete his barrel, Remington had to bore a small touch hole near its base for the powder train, and had to forge a plug which he would screw into the rear end for the breech block. The firing mechanism was to be the then-universal flintlock. Remington forged the parts and finished them with a hammer, a cold chisel and a file. The lock consisted of a lock-plate to which he brazed a priming pan; a vertical strip of steel, which was held against the priming pan by a powerful spring; and a hammer, actuated by another spring, holding a piece of flint. When the trigger was pulled, the hammer slammed the flint down the face of the steel, uncovering the priming pan and throwing a stream of sparks into the priming powder from whence a flash of fire passed through the touch hole to the main charge.

In the evenings, Lite worked on the stock of the gun, shaping it from a straight-grained block of walnut with a draw knife, and whittling it out so that it fitted flush against the breech block, and exactly accepted the curves of the lock. He smoothed it down with a small block of sandstone—sandpaper had not been invented—and polished it with wild beeswax. The barrel was coated with hazel-brown, an excellent preservative made of uric acid and iron oxide.

On a Saturday evening, he assembled the gun, securing the stock and metal parts with hand-wrought screws and pins.

Not all the game in the world would have induced so strict a Methodist as Lite Remington to fire his gun off on Sunday. Besides, the sound of a shot breaking the Sabbath calm would have brought down on his head the ire of the Godly neighbors. But he would have been less than human had he not swung the new rifle to his shoulder 50 times that day.

He did not need the sun to wake him Monday morning. He took his gun, powder horn, newly molded bullets and greased patches to the field in back of the house. There he loaded with a heaping measure of black powder—might as well know if she'd take it—rammed the powder home and drove in the patch and bullet. He shook a pinch of powder into the priming pan and cocked the gun. Then he laid it on the ground with its butt against a tree, and tied a piece of string to the trigger. If she was going to blow up, he was too prudent to put his face in the way. He backed off, and knew a moment of irresolution while he thought of all the work that gun had cost him. Then he pulled the string.

There was a terrific explosion and the gun gave a convulsive leap spewing clouds of pungent black powder smoke. Lite ran through the choking fumes and picked up his gun: she wasn't hurt a bit.

Then came the real test. Lite reloaded with a normal charge and, aiming carefully at the bole of an ancient oak, pulled the trigger. The crash made his ears ring, and smoke blanked out everything in front of him. When it cleared, he saw the oak absolutely unscathed.

He fired again with the same lack of result, but on the third try, he got the hang of the thing. The bullet hole, centered beautifully in an irregular circle of bark, was the first of many Remington bull's eyes.

***At right:* Early cowboy movie star Tom Mix admires a fine custom shotgun. Remington has long made excellent shotguns, with high-quality finish and meticulous care given to all aspects of each firearm.**

How E
Entered the

It all began in the autumn of 1816, when Eliphalet entered a shooting match. Shooting matches were, at that time, the major sport of America. Tennis, golf and football were yet to be imported; it would be 20 years before the first baseball game was played at Cooperstown a couple of valleys to the south. True, the young men of the frontier had other amusements such as running races, wrestling matches and games of agility and luck, like trying to catch a greased pig. However, all these were minor accomplishments, good enough for a rough-and-tumble afternoon of fun, but were no great shakes compared to the more important art of sending a bullet as straight to the mark as the vagaries of handmade guns and highly variable black powder permitted.

Shooting for food and for survival was an essential element of life; but when shooting for sport, a man might display the skill of which he was most proud. These matches were held wherever a few men could get together in wilderness clearings on the outskirts of growing villages or towns. And the best shots competed on a county-wide basis—this counted as an organized sport in that part of the New World.

It was a county match that Remington entered. He had practiced all through August and September and was rather pleased with his marksmanship and his gun. On that fine October day, he found the crack shots and their fans gathered in a clearing near Crane's Corners. Some wore the buckskin jackets of the frontier, others wore workaday homespun shirts and pantaloons and a few stood about somewhat self-consciously in black broadcloth and beaver hats. Lite was among the last.

There were in the crowd quite a few young women, who had come to watch the menfolk display their prowess. They wore long stout woolen dresses with sunbonnets or shawls on their heads, and they chattered together like squirrels, for it was not too often that they got together for a purely social occasion. The men, too, were in high spirits—boasting of terrific shots and improbable ranges, like bringing down a running buck at 150 yards.

When the shooting began, the horseplay ended—the women stopped talking as everyone tensely waited for the ear-splitting *whomp* of those long, big-caliber rifles and strained to see the result of each shot through heavy clouds of black powder smoke.

Remington seemed as calm as one of those expressionless wooden statues that amateur sculptors of the time liked to carve from tree trunks, but as he laid his gun in a forked rest and sighted along its brown barrel, his nerves were twitching. He was afraid he might make a fool of himself.

Remington Arms Trade

Above: Carrying the Remington tradition, this fine Remington 1100 SA Skeet autoloader comes in 12 or 20 gauge, and right or left-handed versions. *Below:* Tom Yule and Dale, the older of his two sons, adjust sights on their Mohawk 600 .222s.

That he did not do; nor did he win the match—but he placed second, which was not a small thing against the best shots in the Valley.

When it was over, the chronicles say that the county champion came over to congratulate Remington, and examine his gun. Then he asked leave to try it and shot better than he had in the match.

'Where did you get it?' was his question; and one can hear Lite answering with proper pride, 'Made it myself!' It seems that Remington had some difficulty convincing the men who crowded around that he was not boasting. When they saw he was serious, they were really interested. The champ was the first to ask what Lite would charge for a barrel.

Remington did a rapid mental calculation—so much iron, use of the forge, three days' work, a trip to Utica for reaming, a fair profit.

'I figure I could do it for 10 dollars,' he said.

'A fair price. When can I have it?'

Again Remington calculated. 'In about 10 days,' he said.

Other shooters wanted barrels or complete guns. Before Lite left the field, he was in the gun business.

***At right:* Montanan Tom Yule aims through his scope at a far target; Tom's Remington Mohawk 600 is a fine small game rifle, and in .222 caliber it has all the ballistic qualities needed. *Below:* The then-newly invented telephone inspired this 1899 ad for Peters smokeless powder cartridges. Though the dialogue is a bit unlikely, it gets the point across!**

The Death
E Remington

# of Senior

Since building his first gun, young Remington had almost imperceptibly assumed the management of his family's foundry business. His father continued to run the agricultural manufacture and to do most of the building, but the rapidly expanding gun business was in Lite's hands, and the decisions concerning it were his. Soon, Lite's father took charge of building the little frame house on what is now Otsego Street, which was to be his son's temporary headquarters.

All the lumber for it was carted down from the Gulph in big drays pulled by four powerful horses each. Early on the morning of 22 June 1828, Eliphalet Remington I superintended the loading of a dray from the piles of 20-foot planks that were stacked in the drying yard near the sawmill. Then he mounted to the top of the high sweet-smelling load, while a young driver gathered up the reins. It was a hard pull up the hill, but the going was easier on the Cedarville Road. They passed the Remingtons' stone house, went down the hill into the Gulph again and crossed the wooden bridge with the dray's big, iron-tired wheels rumbling on the boards and the measured stamp of the horses' hooves like the rolling thunder of distant cannon.

Where the gorge cut between the crests of the hills its walls were several hundred feet high and a scant 200 feet apart. Here the untouched forest still stood in its somber splendor, and the bright morning was dimmed to a dusk so deep that the teamster halted to light his lanterns. Their yellow light gleamed dimly on the huge boles of the trees, and threw fantastic shadows as the dray moved on.

Beyond the heights, the road pitched sharply downward, and the horses braced themselves against the breeching straps to hold back the load while the driver leaned on the long lever of his brakes. Jolting and swaying, they moved slowly down the steep hill until, where the road made an abrupt curve to follow the course of the creek, they came to a sink hole. As one wheel dropped into it, the strain was all one way on the piled-up timbers. They slid a little between the holding stakes, and the whole load canted suddenly, pitching Remington off and ahead. There was no stopping the momentum of four horses and a heavily-loaded dray. The horrified driver tugged frantically at the reins and braked with all his might, but the equipage rolled inexorably forward, and a six-foot, iron-shod wheel passed over the dark body in the road.

Five days later Eliphalet Remington, father of Eliphalet Remington II—who was even then embarking on one of the greatest American enterprises in history—died in the fine stone house he had built in the wilderness. He died and his son went on, carrying the family name far beyond their little foundry.

Above right: Tradition shines in an F-Grade Remington Custom Shop Model 1100 SA Skeet gun. _At right:_ Part of the Remington Museum in Ilion, New York. _Overleaf:_ Movie star Audie Murphy, and his sawed-off Remington Model 1882 shotgun in the 1960 movie _Hell Bent for Leather._

A Glossary of Remington Arms

Company Update

The close of World War II gave Remington the opportunity to retool its facilities to produce sporting arms. Large numbers of returning GIs were eager to pit themselves against less deadly foes than the war had provided. Hunting in America became a national passion with widespread popularity. North America was literally rediscovered as the habitat of many types of game suitable for sport hunting. Accordingly, Remington marketed numerous models of rifles and shotguns to suit the tastes and needs of everyone from the big game hunter to the field bird shooter. Bolt action rifles, target and sporting rifles, slide-action repeaters and autoloading guns were produced. Many advances were made in both the design of stocks and the ballistic characteristics of ammunition. It was a natural consequence, therefore, that Remington should involve itself heavily in various conservation movements. That same commitment is maintained today.

A glance at modern Remington product catalogues reveals that the company is presently marketing no fewer than three shotgun product lines, a half dozen or so rifle lines and a series of target rifles. All of this is in addition to both center fire and shot shell ammunition of almost countless types, sizes and specifications. However, a large product line has not meant that Remington has slackened its attention to detail. Their Custom Gun Shop caters to those who dream of owning a truly fine firearm. These custom guns are crafted one at a time to the dimensions, taste and style of the buyer. The F Grade Shotgun with Gold is one of two custom-grade shotguns available with personalized inlay and engravings. Various hunting rifles are also available from the custom shop, including the Grade Four Model 700 Rifle, the Model 40-XR Custom Sporter, the Model 700 Safari Grade Rifle, the Model 7 Custom with Kevlar Stock and the Model 700 Custom KS Mountain Rifle. The Custom Shop even produces a handgun known as the New Custom XT-100 Heavy Barrel in .223 Remington.

Recently, Remington undertook to revamp its advertising, marketing and distributing techniques to better serve its many loyal customers. Remington prides itself in being committed to the quality of the hunting life. Their logo reads, very truthfully, 'Remington Country—It's a way of life since 1816.' That committment also produces a rare fact for a modern manufacturer in the world arena today: *Every* part of *every* Remington gun is not only designed, but built *and* tested in the USA.

Remington Handguns

Remington-Beals First Model Beals Pocket Revolver. Made circa1857–1858. Total quantity estimated between 4500 and 5000.

Percussion; .31 caliber. Five-shot round cylinder; three–inch octagon barrel.

Remington-Second Model Beals Pocket Revolver. Made circa 1858–1860. Total of about 1000.

Percussion; .31 caliber. Five-shot round cylinder; three–inch octagon barrel.

Remington-Third Model Beals Pocket Revolver. Made circa 1859–1860. Total quantity about 1000 to 1500.

Percussion; .31 caliber. Five-shot round cylinder; four–inch octagon barrel, spur type trigger.

At top of page: The Remington hunting arms logo—'Remington Country: It's a Way of Life.' *At right:* Tom Yule's sons Tim (left) and Dale (right) with a canine friend. Tim holds his .22 caliber single shot Model 514, and older brother Dale has his dependable Mohawk 600 .222 in hand.

H & I
TRUCK & AUTO SALVAGE

These pages, from immediate right, counterclockwise: **A Remington-Beals Army Model Revolver; a Remington Model 1865 Navy Rolling Block Pistol; a Remington Model 95 Double Derringer; a Remington Number 3 Revolver (which is often erroneously referred to as a 'New Line Number 3 Pistol'); and its design heir, a Remington Number 4 Revolver; a Model 1901 Target Rolling Block Pistol; and a Model 1890 Single Action Army Revolver.**

Remington-Rider Pocket Model Revolver. Made circa 1860–1873; with altered specimens made for .32 rimfire metallic cartridge after 1873. Estimated quantity approximately 20,000.

Percussion; .31 caliber. Five-shot tapering cylinder; three-inch octagon barrel. Large, oval-shaped brass trigger guard.

Remington-Beals Army Model Revolver. Made circa 1860–1862. Quantity made estimated between 2000 and 3000.

Percussion; .44 caliber. Six-shot round cylinder; eight-inch octagon barrel.

Remington-Beals Navy Model Revolver. Made circa 1860–1862. Total quantity estimated at 15,000. Substantially identical in appearance to the Beals Army, but slightly smaller.

Percussion; .36 caliber. Six-shot round cylinder; 7.5-inch octagon barrel.

Remington-Rider Single Shot Derringer, aka 'Parlor Pistol.' Made circa 1860–1863. Total quantity less than 1000.

Remington Zig-Zag Derringer, aka 'Zig-Zag Pepperbox.' Made circa 1861–1862. Total less than 1000.

Caliber .22 short rimfire.

Remington Model 1861 Army Revolver, aka 'Old Model Army.' Made circa 1862. Total quantity estimated between 9000 and 12,000.

Percussion; .44 caliber. Six-shot round cylinder; eight-inch octagon barrel.

Remington New Model Army Revolver. Made circa 1863–1875. Total quantity estimated approximately 132,000.

Percussion; .44 caliber. Six-shot round cylinder; eight-inch octagon barrel.

Remington New Model (Single Action) Belt Revolver. Made circa 1863–1873 in percussion; made in cartridge model subsequent to 1873. Total quantity estimated from 2500 to 3000.

Percussion; .36 caliber. Six-shot round cylinder; 6.5-inch octagon barrel.

Remington-Rider Double Action New Model Belt Revolver. Made circa 1863–1873 in percussion with subsequent production as metallic cartridge model. Total quantity estimated at 5000.

Percussion; .36 caliber. Six-shot round cylinder; 6.5-inch octagon barrel.

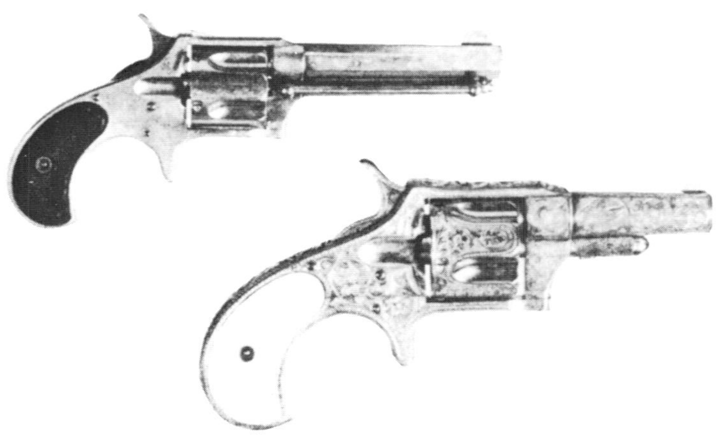

Remington New Model Police Revolver. Made circa 1863–1873 in percussion with subsequent production as factory alterations to cartridge. Total quantity estimated at 18,000.

Percussion; .36 caliber. Five-shot round cylinder with safety notches on cylinder shoulder. Octagon barrel in 3.5–inch, 4.5–inch, 5.5–inch and 6.5–inch lengths.

Remington New Model Pocket Revolver. Made circa 1863–1873 in percussion; subsequent production as metallic cartridge conversions. Total quantity estimated at 25,000.

Percussion; .31 caliber. Five-shot round cylinder; safety notches on cylinder shoulders. Octagon barrel, available in three–inch, 3.5–inch, four–inch and 4.5–inch lengths.

Remington-Elliot Derringer 22 RF, aka 'Pepperbox.' Made circa 1863–1888. Total quantity combined for this .22 caliber with the larger .32 caliber model estimated at 25,000.

Caliber .22 rimfire.

Remington-Elliot Derringer 32 RF, aka 'Pepperbox.' Made circa 1863–1888. Total quantity of this and the .22 caliber type estimated at 25,000.

Caliber .32 rimfire.

Remington Vest Pocket Pistol, aka 'Saw Handle Derringer.' Made circa 1865–1888. Total quantity estimated at approximately 25,000.

Calibers .30, .32 and .41 rimfire.

Remington Model 1865 Navy Rolling Block Pistol. Made circa 1866–1870. Total produced originally estimated at approximately 1000; since revised to approximately 6500.

Caliber .50 rimfire; single shot; 8.5–inch round barrel.

Remington Double Derringer, aka 'model 95 Double Derringer,' aka 'Over-Under Derringer.' Made circa 1866–1935. Total quantity estimated at over 150,000.

Caliber .41 rimfire short; three–inch round, superposed barrels.

Remington-Elliot Single Shot Derringer. Made circa 1867–1888. Total quantity estimated at approximately 10,000.

Caliber .41 rimfire; 2.5–inch round barrel.

Remington Model 1867 Navy Rolling Block Pistol. Made circa early 1870s. Total quantity unknown.

Caliber .50 center fire.

Remington-Rider Magazine Pistol. Made circa 1871–1888. Total quantity estimated at approximately 10,000.

Caliber .32 extra short.

Remington Model 1871 Army Rolling Block Pistol. Made circa 1872–1888. Total quantity approximately 6000 plus.

Caliber .50 center fire. Single shot; eight–inch round barrel.

Remington Number 1 Revolver—New Model (Smoot's Patent). Probably most easily termed 'Remington-Smoot New Model Number 1, aka erroneously 'New Line Revolver Number 1.'

Remington Model 1875 Single Action Army Revolver. Made circa 1875–1889. Total quantity estimated approximately 25,000.

Caliber .44 Remington center fire.

Remington Iroquois Pocket Revolver. Made circa 1878–1888. Total quantity estimated approximately 10,000.

Caliber .22 rimfire. Seven-shot plain or fluted cylinder; 2.25–inch round barrel.

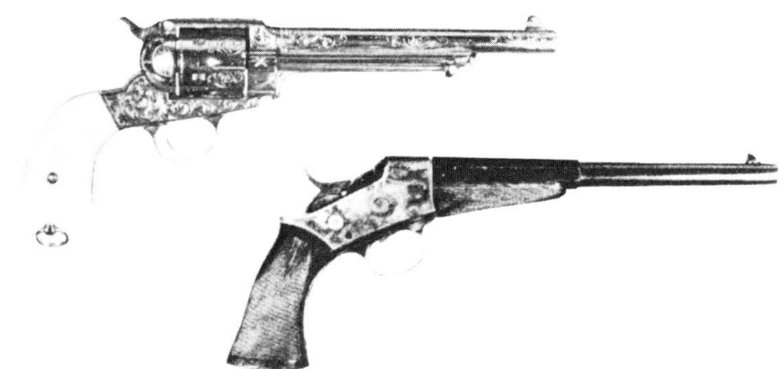

Remington Model 1890 Single Action Army Revolver. Made circa 1891–1894. Total quantity approximately 2000.

Caliber .44–40 center fire. Six-shot cylinder; 5.5–inch or 7.5–inch round barrel.

Remington Model 1891 Target Rolling Block pistol. Made circa 1892–1898. Total quantity shown on factory records at 116; however, larger quantities are possible.

Calibers .22 long and short rimfire; .25 Stevens; .32 S&W rimfire and center fire. Single shot; 10–inch half octagon/half round barrel.

Remington Model 1901 Target Rolling Block Pistol. Made circa 1901–1909. Total of 735 made, as indicated by factory records.

Calibers .22 short and long rifle rimfire; .25-10 rimfire; .44 S&W center fire. Single shot; 10–inch half octagon/half round barrel.

Remington Mark III Signal Pistol. Made circa 1915–1918. Total quantity approximately 24,500.

Ten gauge chambered for a special shot type shell charged with special powder only intended to fire flares. Single shot, nine–inch round iron barrel.

Remington Model 51 Automatic Pistol. Made circa 1918–1934. Total quantity approximately 65,000.

Caliber .32 (seven-shot) and .380 rimless (eight-shot). 3.5–inch round barrel.

Remington Model XP-100 Single Shot Pistol. Made circa 1963 to date. Bolt action.

Caliber .221 Remington Fire Ball; 10.5–inch barrel with ventilated rib; 16.75 inches overall. Weight 3.75 pounds.

Remington Rifles

Remington Model 1863 Percussion Contract Rifle, aka 'Zouave Rifle.' Made circa 1862–1865. Total quantity 12,501. Caliber .58; single shot muzzle loader; 33–inch round barrel.

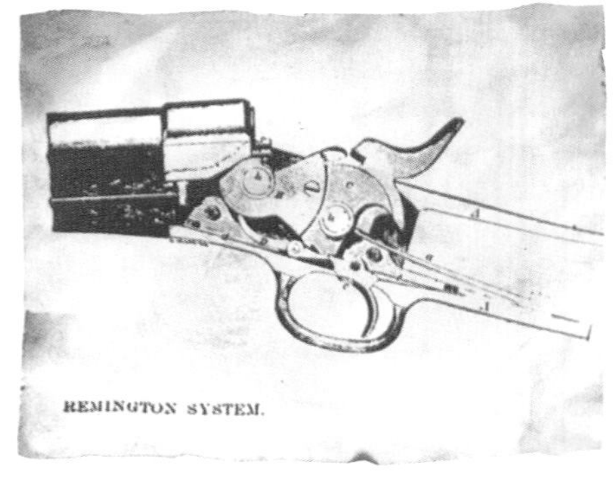

Remington Single Shot Breech-Loading Carbine, aka 'Split Breech Remington.' Made circa 1864–1866.

Calibers .46 and .50 rimfire. The predecessor of the famed 'Rolling Block' design; 20–inch round barrel.

Remington-Beals Single Shot Rifle. Made circa 1866–1868. Quantity unknown; estimated at less than 800.

Remington Revolving Percussion Rifle. Made circa 1866–1879. Total quantity estimated at less than 1000.

Calibers .36 and .44; six-shot round cylinder.

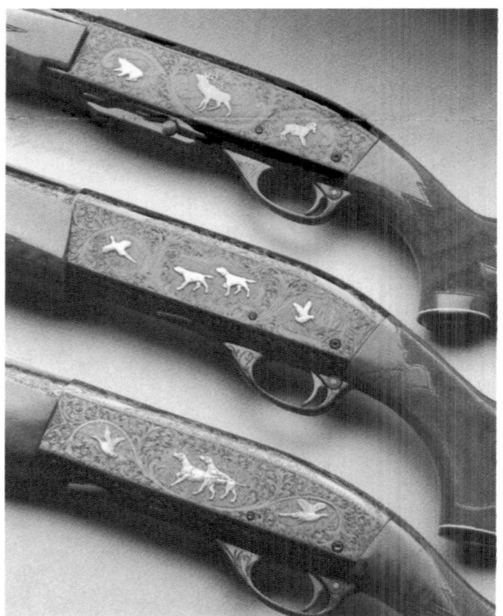

Rifle Cane, aka 'Cane Gun.' Made circa 1858–1866 in percussion; made 1866 to circa 1888 in breech-loading metallic cartridge model. Total quantity estimated at 4500.

Cartridge models made in .22 rimfire and .32 rimfire. Barrel length approximately 26 inches.

Remington Rolling Block Military Rifles and Carbines. Large Number 1 size action. Made circa 1867–1902. Quantity totaling over one million.

Remington US Navy Rolling Block Carbine. Circa 1868–1869. Quantity made estimated 5000.

Caliber .50-70 center fire; 23.75–inch barrel.

Remington Number One Rolling Block Sporting Rifles, Various Types. Overall period all types circa 1868–1902.

Remington Model 1867 Navy Cadet Rolling Block Rifle. Made by Springfield Armory circa 1868 utilizing Remington actions only; the same action as the 1868–1869 Navy Carbine. Quantity made, 498.

Caliber .50-45 center fire cadet cartridge; 23.5–inch round barrel.

Remington New York State Contract Rolling Block Rifles and Carbines. Made for New York State National Guard circa 1872. Total quantity estimated at 15,000.

Rifle has 36–inch barrel.

Sporting Rifle Number 1.

Calibers .40-50, .40-70, .44-77, .45-70, .50-45, .50-70; 23–inch and 30–inch octagon barrels.

These pages, column by column, from top to bottom, starting at left: **Four Rifle Canes; a cutaway of the Rolling Block action; Remington Custom shop designs commemorating the millionth Model 742 auto rifle, the two millionth Model 1100 auto shotgun and Remington's overall 10 millionth gun; a Model 742 Woodsmaster autoloading rifle; the Model 742 Woodsmaster BDL Custom Deluxe; the Model 760 Gamemaster; the Model 760 BDL Custom Deluxe; an era-spanning array of six Remington rifle and shotgun models; Model 2 Sporting Rifle; Remington-Hepburn Number 3 Creedmore; Remington-Hepburn Number 3 Sporting Model.**

Long Range 'Creedmoor' Rifle. Made circa 1873–1890. Quantity estimated as a few thousand.

Calibers .44-90, .44-100, .44-105. 34–inch part octagon/part round barrel.

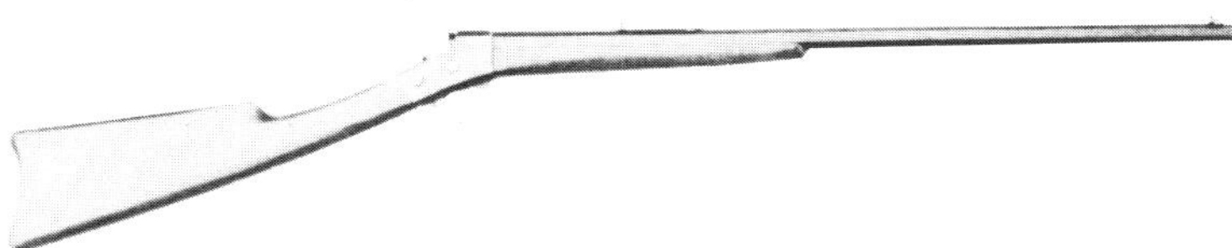

Remington Model 2 Sporting Rifle. Made circa 1873–1910. Exact quantities unknown.

Large variety of rimfire calibers from .22 to .38 as well as center fire from .22 to .38-40; 24–inch and 26–inch octagon barrel standard.

Mid-Range Target Rifle. Made circa 1875–1890.

Calibers .40-70, .44-77, .45-70, .50-70; 28–inch and 30–inch part octagon/part round barrels.

Short Range Rifle. Made circa 1875–1890. Quantity estimated several thousand.

Center fire calibers .38 extra long; .40-50; .44 S&W; .44 extra long. Rimfire calibers .38 extra long; .44 extra long and .46; 26–inch and 30–inch optional octagonal or round barrels.

Black Hills Rifle. Made circa 1877–1882.

Caliber .45-60 center fire; 28–inch round barrel.

Remington-Keene Magazine Bolt Action Rifle. Made circa 1880–1888. Total quantity estimated at 5000.

Caliber .45-70 most widely made and most popular and in demand; also in .40 caliber and .43 caliber. 24.5–inch round barrel standard.

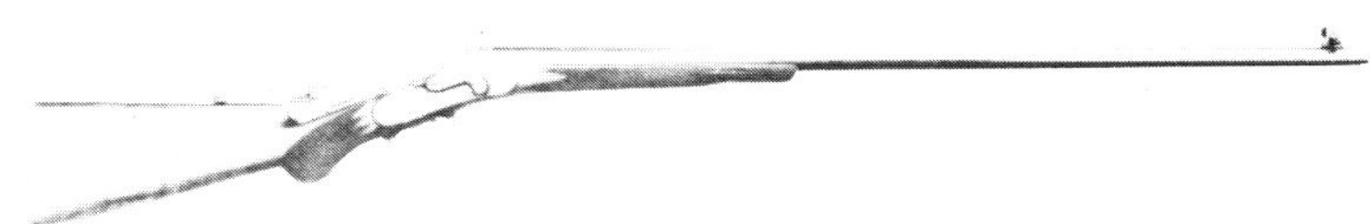

Remington-Hepburn Number 3 Improved Creedmoor. Made circa 1880–1907. Quantity unknown

Remington-Lee Magazine, Bolt Action Rifles. Made circa 1880–1907. Total quantity in excess of 100,000.

Remington-Hepburn Number 3 Long Range Military Rifle. Made circa 1880s; quantity unknown.

Chambered for .44-75-520 Remington straight cartridge; 34–inch round barrel.

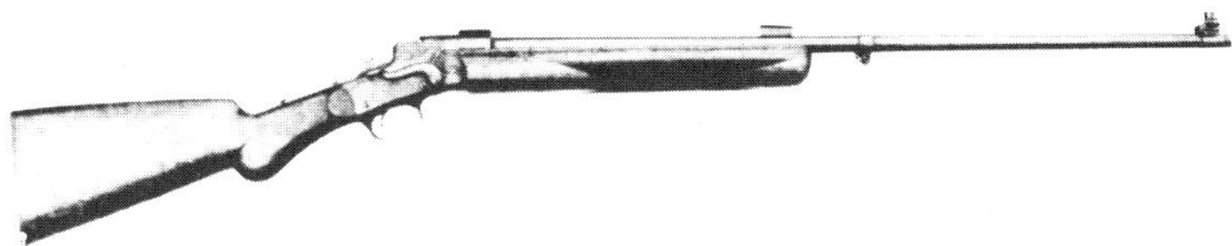

Remington-Hepburn Number 3 Sporting and Target Model. Made circa 1883–1907. Quantities unknown, estimated at 8000 to 10,000.

Listed in a tremendous variety of calibers from .22 Winchester center fire to .50-90 Sharps straight. Barrel lengths 26 inches, 28 inches and 30 inches.

Remington-Hepburn Number 3 Match Rifle. Made circa 1883–1907. Quantity unknown.

Remington Model 1 1/2 Sporting Rifle. Manufactured circa 1888–1897. Estimated several thousand manufactured.

Rimfire calibers .22, .25 Stevens, .25 long, .32, .38 long and extra long. Center fire calibers .32-20, .38-40, .44-40; 24–inch to 28–inch medium weight octagon barrel.

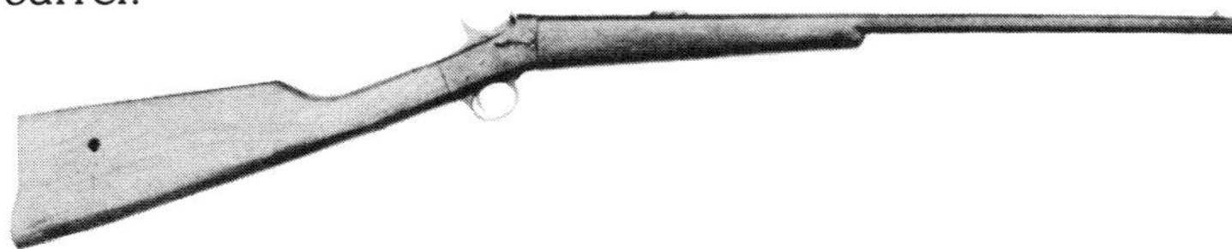

Remington New Model Number 4 Rolling Block Rifle. Made circa 1890–1933. Quantity made estimated at over 50,000.

Chambered for rimfire calibers .22 short, long and long rifle; .25 Stevens; .32 short and long; 22.5–inch octagonal barrels for most production (24–inch also in .32 caliber) with round barrels available in latter years of production.

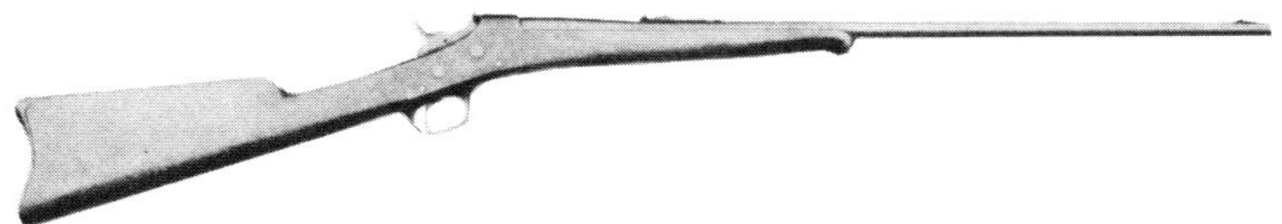

Remington Number 5 Rolling Block Rifles and Carbine. Made circa 1897–1905. Three basic styles. Total quantity estimated at 100,000.

Remington-Hepburn Number 3 High-Power Rifle. Believed introduced around 1900 and made to circa 1907. Quantity unknown.

Calibers .30-30, .30 Government, .32 Special, .32-40 HP, .38-72; 26–inch, 28–inch and 30–inch round barrels standard.

Remington Number 6 Rolling Block Type Rifle. Made circa 1902–1933. Exact quantities unknown, but over 250,000 or more.

Rimfire calibers .22 short, long, long rifle and .32 short and long; also available in smoothbore for shot cartridges; 20–inch round barrel.

Remington Number 7 Rifle, Rolling Block Action. Made circa 1903–1911.

Rimfire calibers .22 short and long rifle, .25-10 Stevens; 24–inch, 26–inch and 28–inch part octagon/part round barrels.

Remington-Hepburn Number Schuetzen Match Rifle, aka 'Underlever Hepburn,' aka 'The Walker-Hepburn.' Made circa 1904–1907.

Calibers .32-40, .38-40, .38-50, .40-65; 30–inch or 32–inch part octagon/part round barrel.

Remington Model 8A Autoloading Rifle. Made circa 1906–1936.

Calibers .25, .30, .32 and .35 Remington. Standard grade. Takedown. Detachable box magazine holds five cartridges; 22-inch barrel. Weight, 7.75 pounds.

Remington Model 12A Slide Action Repeating Rifle. Made circa 1909–1936.

Caliber .22 short, long or long rifle. Standard grade. Hammerless. Takedown. Tubular magazine holds 15 short, 12 long or 10 long rifle cartridges; 22-inch round barrel. Weight, 4.5 pounds.

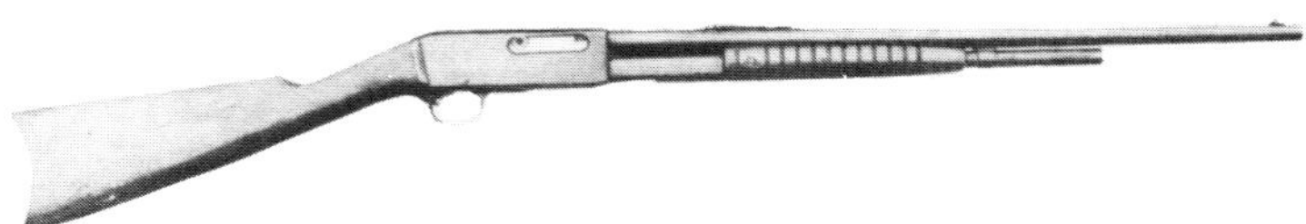

Remington Model 14A High Power Slide Action Repeating Rifle. Made circa 1912–1935.

Calibers .25, .30, .32 and .35 Remington. Standard grade. Hammerless. Takedown, five-shot tubular magazine. 22–inch barrel. Weight about 6.75 pounds.

Remington Model Number 4S 'Military Model' Rolling Block Sporting Rifle, aka 'Boy Scout Rifle.' Made circa 1913–1923. Approximate quantity made estimated from 10,000 to 25,000.

Caliber .22 rimfire short and long; 28–inch round barrel.

Remington Model 16 Autoloading Rifle. Made circa 1914–1928. Closely resembles the Winchester Model 03.

Calibers .22 short, .22 long rifle, .22 Winchester rimfire, .22 Remington Automatic. Takedown, 15-shot tubular magazine in buttstock; 22–inch barrel. Weight, 5.75 pounds.

Remington Model 30A Bolt Action Express Rifle. Made from 1921–1940.

Calibers .25, .30, .32 and .35 Remington, 7mm Mauser, 30-06. Standard grade. Modified M/1917 Enfield Action. Five-shot box magazine; 22–inch barrel. Weight about 7.25 pounds.

Remington Model 24A Autoloading Rifle. Made circa 1922-1935.

Calibers: .22 short, .22 long rifle. Standard grade. Takedown. Tubular magazine in buttstock, holds 15 short or 10 long rifle; 21–inch barrel. Weight about five pounds.

Remington Model 241A 'Speedmaster' Autoloading Rifle.
Calibers .22 short, .22 long rifle. Standard grade. Takedown. Tubular magazine in buttstock, holds 15 short or 10 long rifle; 24–inch barrel. Weight about six pounds.

Remington Model 552A 'Speedmaster' Autoloading Rifle.
Caliber .22 short, long, long rifle. Tubular magazine holds 20 short, 17 long, 15 long rifle; 25–inch barrel. Weight about 5.5 pounds.

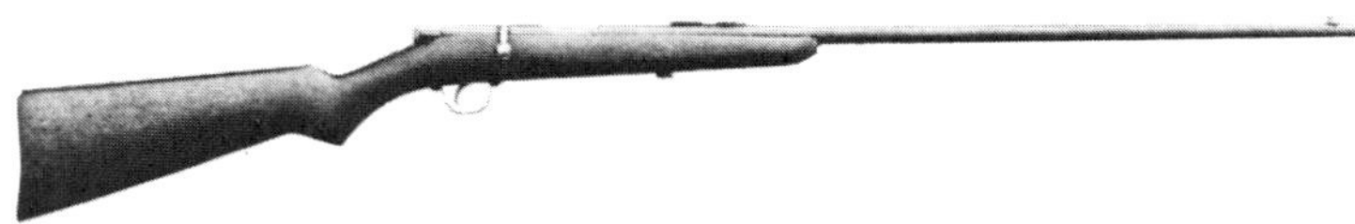

Remington Model 33 Bolt Action Single Shot Rifle. Made circa 1931–1936.
Caliber .22 short, long, long rifle. Takedown; 24-inch barrel. Weight about 4.5 pounds.

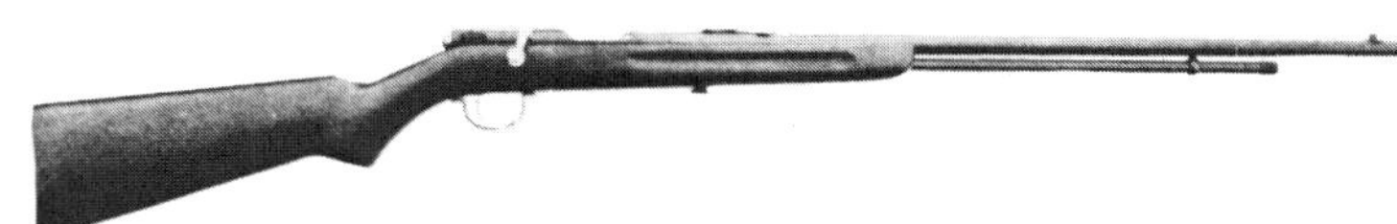

Remington Model 34 Bolt Action Repeating Rifle. Made circa 1932–1936.
Caliber .22 short, long, long rifle. Takedown. Tubular magazine holds 22 short, 17 long or 15 long rifle; 24–inch barrel. Weight about 5.25 pounds.

Remington Model 81A 'Woodmaster' Autoloading Rifle. Made circa 1936–1950.
Calibers .30, .32 and .35 Remington, .300 Savage. Standard grade. Takedown. Five-shot box magazine (not detachable); 22–inch barrel. Weight, 8.25 pounds.

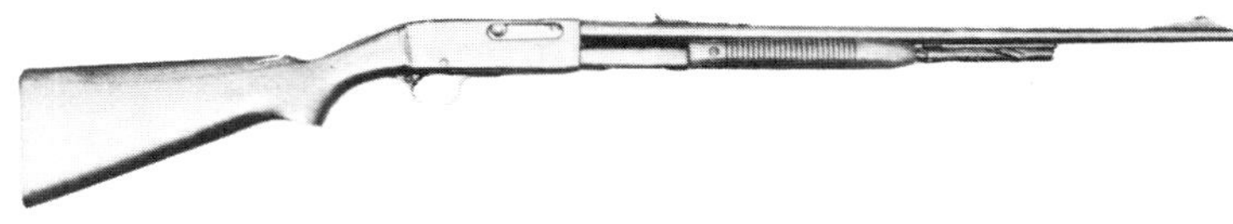

Remington Model 121A 'Fieldmaster' Slide Action Repeating Rifle. Made circa 1936–1954.
Caliber .22 short, long, long rifle. Standard grade. Hammerless. Takedown. Tubular magazine holds 20 short, 15 long or 14 long rifle cartridges. 24-inch round barrel. Weight, six pounds.

Remington Model 141A 'Gamemaster' Slide Action Repeating Rifle. Made circa 1936–1950.
Calibers .30, .32 and .35 Remington. Standard grade. Hammerless. Takedown. Five-shot tubular magazine; 24-inch barrel. Weight about 7.75 pounds.

Remington Model 511A 'Scoremaster' Bolt Action Box Magazine Repeating Rifle. Made circa 1939–1962.
Caliber .22 short, long, long rifle. Six-shot detachable box magazine. Takedown; 25–inch barrel. Weight about 5.5 pounds.

Remington Model 550A Autoloading Rifle. Made circa 1941–1971.
Has 'Power Piston' or floating chamber which permits interchangeable use of .22 short, long or long rifle cartridges. Tubular magazine holds 22 short, 17 long, 15 long rifle; 24–inch barrel. Weight about 6.25 pounds.

Remington Model 521 TL Junior Target Bolt Action Repeating Rifle. Made circa 1947–1969.
Caliber, .22 long rifle. Takedown. Six-shot detachable box magazine; 25–inch barrel. Weight about seven pounds.

Remington Model 721A Standard Grade Bolt Action High Power Rifle. Made circa 1948–1962.
Calibers: .264 Winchester, .270 Winchester, .30-06. Four-shot box magazine; 24–inch barrel. Weight about 7.25 pounds.

Remington Model 722A Standard Grade Bolt Action Sporting Rifle. Made circa 1948–1962. Same as Model 721A, except shorter action.
Calibers .257 Roberts, .308 Winchester, .300 Savage. Weight, seven pounds.

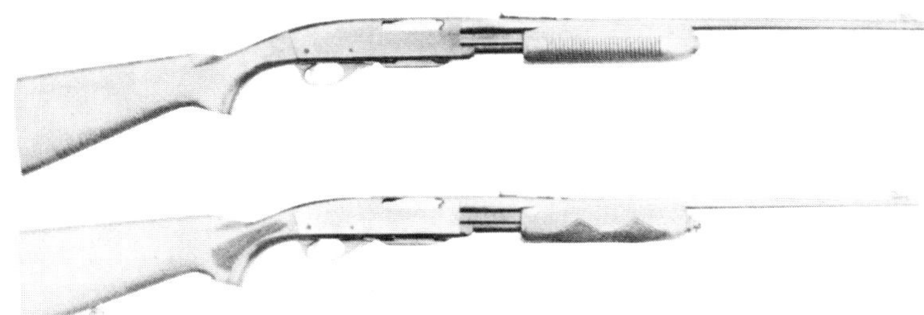

Remington Model 760 'Gamemaster' Standard Grade Slide Action Repeating Rifle. Made circa 1952–date.
Calibers .223 Remington, 6mm Remington, .243 Winchester, .257 Roberts, .270 Winchester, .280 Remington, .30-06, .300 Savage, .308 Winchester, .35 Remington. Hammerless; 22–inch barrel. Weight about 7.5 pounds.

Remington Model 572A 'Fieldmaster' Slide Action Repeater. Made circa 1955–date.
Caliber, .22 short, long, long rifle. Hammerless. Tubular magazine holds 20 short, 17 long, 15 long rifle; 23-inch barrel. Weight about 5.5 pounds.

Remington Model 40X Heavyweight Bolt Action Target Rifle. Made circa 1955–1964. Action similar to Model 722.
Caliber .22 long rifle. Single Shot. Click adjustable trigger; 28–inch heavy barrel. Weight, 12.75 pounds.

***Top to bottom, starting with the extreme left column:* A New Model Number 4; a Number 5; a Number 7; a Model 8A auto; a Model 14A pump; a Model 4S Boy Scout Rifle; a Model 24A auto; a Model 33 bolt action; a Model 34 bolt action; a Model 141 pump; a Model 760; a Model 760 Deluxe; and a Model 40X.**

These pages: A Model 600 Mohawk bolt action carbine in .243 Winchester caliber, with telescopic sight and sling. The stock of this excellent firearm has been customized by its owner, Mr Don Griffith. With a five-shot magazine and weighing 6.5 pounds, this firearm was manufactured from 1963—1971, and many of these fine firearms are still in circulation.

Remington Nylon 66 'Mohawk Brown' Autoloading Rifle. Made circa 1959–date.

Caliber .22 long rifle. Tubular magazine in buttstock holds 14 rounds. 19.5–inch barrel. Weight about four pounds.

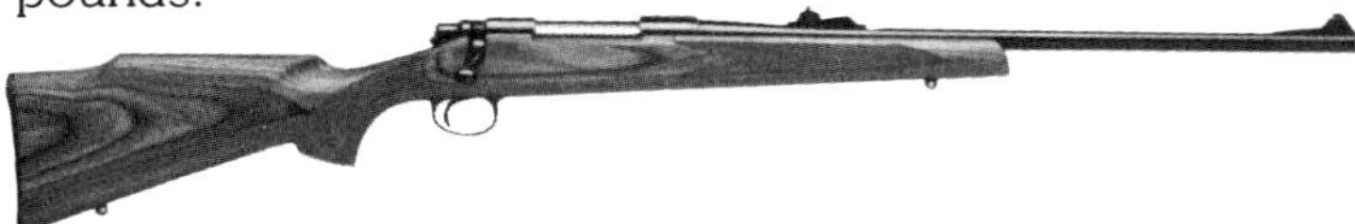

Remington Model 742 'Woodmaster' Automatic Big Game Rifle. Made circa 1960–date.

Calibers 6mm Remington, .243 Winchester, .280 Remington, .30-06, .308 Winchester. Gas-operated semiautomatic. Four-shot clip magazine; 22–inch barrel. Weight, 7.5 pounds.

Remington Nylon 76 Lever Action Repeating Rifle Made circa 1962–1964. Other specifications same as for Nylon 66.

Short-throw lever action.

Remington Model 700ADL Center Fire Bolt Action Rifle. Made circa 1962–date.

Calibers .22-250, .222 Remington, .25-06, 6mm Remington, .243 Winchester, .270 Winchester, .30-06, .308 Winchester, 7mm Remington Magnum. Magazine capacity: six-shot in .222 Remington, four-shot in 7mm Remington Magnum, five-shot in other calibers. Barrel lengths 24–inch in .22-250, .222 Remington, .25-06, 7mm Remington; 22–inch in other calibers. Weight, seven pounds.

Remington Model 660 Bolt Action Carbine. Made circa 1963–1971.

Calibers .222 Remington, 6mm Remington, .243 Winchester, .308 Winchester. Five-shot box magazine (six-shot in .222); 20–inch barrel. Weight, 6.5 pounds.

Above: **A Model 742.** ***Below, from top to bottom:*** **The Model 74 Sportsman autoloader; the Model 76 Sportsman pump action rifle; and the Sportsman 581 bolt action rifle. With a variety of target and hunting sights available, these are versatile firearms.**

Remington Model 600 Bolt Action Carbine. Made circa 1964–1967.

Calibers .222 Remington, 6mm Remington, .243 Winchester, .308 Winchester, .35 Remington five-shot box magazine (six shot in .222 Remington); 18.5–inch barrel with ventilated rib. Weight, six pounds.

Remington Model 40-XB Center Fire Match Rifle. Made circa 1964–date.

Calibers: .222 Remington, .222 Remington Magnum, .223 Remington, .22-250, 6x47mm, 6mm Remington, .243 Winchester, .25-06, 7mm Remington Magnum, .30-06, .308 Winchester (7.62mm NATO), .30-388, .300 Winchester Magnum. Bolt Action single shot; 27.25–inch standard or heavy barrel. Weight, 9.25 pounds heavy barrel.

Remington Model 788 Center Fire Bolt Action Rifle. Made circa 1967–date.

Calibers .222 Remington, .22-250, .223 Remington, 6mm Remington, .243 Winchester, .308 Winchester, .30-30, .44 Remington Magnum. Three-shot clip magazine (four-shot in .222 and .223 Remington); 24–inch barrel in .22s, 22–inch in other calibers. Weights 7.5 pounds with 24–inch barrel, 7.25 pounds with 22–inch barrel.

Remington Model 580 Bolt Action Single Shot Made circa 1967–date.

Caliber .22 short, long, long rifle; 24–inch barrel. Weight, 4.75 pounds.

Remington Model 541-S Custom Sporter Made circa 1972–date.

Caliber .22 short, long, long rifle. Bolt action repeater. Scroll engraving on receiver and trigger guard. Five-shot clip magazine; 24–inch barrel. Weight, 1.5 pounds.

Remington Nylon 66 Bicentennial Commemorative. Made in 1976. Same as Nylon 66, except has commemorative inscription on receiver, celebrating the 200th anniversary of American independence.

Remington Shotguns

Remington-Whitmore Model 1874 Double Barrel Hammer Shotgun and Rifle. Made circa 1874–1882. Total quantity estimated at a few thousand.

Barrels 28–inch and 30–inch, steel standard.

Model 1882 Double Barrel Hammer Shotgun. Made circa 1882–1889. Total quantity estimated at approximately 7500.

Gauges 10 and 12; 28–inch and 30–inch steel or damascus barrels.

Model 1885, Model 1887, Model 1889 Double Barrel Hammer Shotguns. Made circa 1885–1909. Total quantity unknown, estimated over 30,000.

Gauges 10, 12, 16; barrel lengths 28 inches to 32 inches; available in steel or damascus barrels.

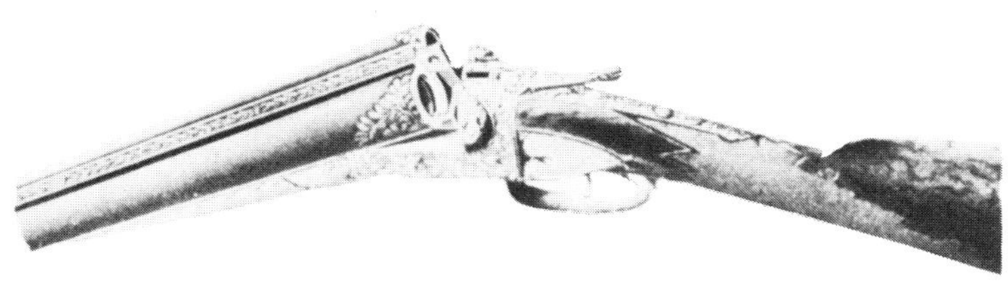

Hammerless Shotguns Model 1894 and Model 1900. Made circa 1894–1910. Total produced unknown.

Gauges 10, 12, 16; barrel lengths from 26 inches to 32 inches, steel or damascus twist.

Remington Model 11A Standard Grade 5-Shot Autoloader. Made circa 1905–1949.

Gauges 12,16 and 20. Hammerless Browning type. Takedown. Tubular magazine holds four shells. Plain, solid rib or ventilated rib barrels; lengths from 26 inches to 32 inches.

Remington Model 10A Standard Grade Slide Action Repeating Shotgun. Made circa 1907–1929.

Gauge, 12. Hammerless. Takedown; six-shot. Five-shell tubular magazine. Plain barrels, 26 inches to 32 inches.

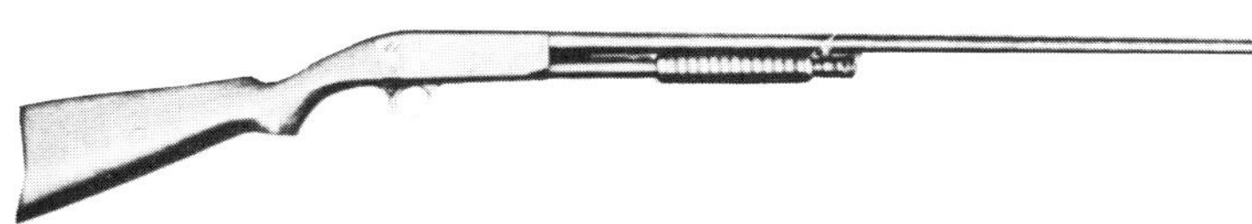

Remington Model 17A Standard Grade Slide Action Repeating Shotgun. Made circa 1921–1933.

Gauge, 12. Hammerless. Takedown. Five-shot. Four-shell tubular magazine. Plain barrels, 26 inches to 32 inches; full, modified or cylinder bore chokes. Weight about 5.75 pounds.

Remington Model 29A Standard Grade Slide Action Repeating Shotgun. Made circa 1929–1933.

Gauge, 12. Hammerless. Takedown. Six–shot. Five-shell tubular magazine. Plain barrels, 26 inches to 32 inches; full, modified or cylinder bore chokes. Weight about 7.5 pounds.

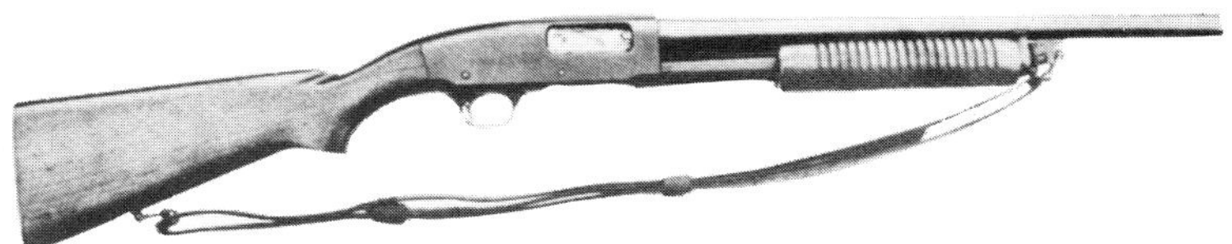

Remington Model 31A Standard Grade Slide Action Repeater.

Gauges 12, 16 and 20. Hammerless. Takedown. Three-shot or five-shot. Tubular magazine holds two or four shells. Plain or ventilated rib barrels; lengths from 26 inches to 32 inches.

Remington Model 32A Standard Grade Over-and-Under Gun. Made circa 1932–1942.

Guage, 12. Hammerless. Takedown. Automatic ejectors. Plain, raised matted solid rib, ventilated rib barrels; 26 inches, 28 inches, 30 inches, 32 inches. Weight about 7.75 pounds.

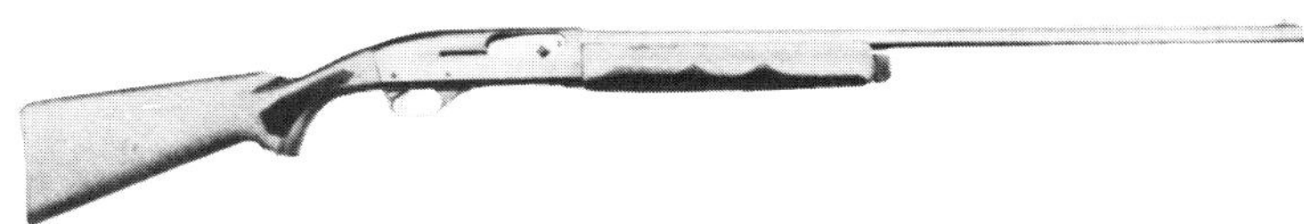

Remington Sportsman-48A Standard Grade 3-Shot Autoloader. Made circa 1949–1959.

Gauges 12, 16 and 20. Streamlined receiver. Hammerless. Takedown.

Remington Wingmaster Model 870AP Standard Grade 5-Shot Slide Action Repeater. Made circa 1950–1963.

Gauges 12, 16 and 20. Hammerless. Takedown. Tubular magazine holds four shells. Plain, matted top surface or ventilated rib barrels; 26-inch improved cylinder, 28-inch modified or full choke, 30-inch full choke (12 gauge only). Weight about seven pounds.

Remington Sportsman-58ADL Autoloader. Made circa 1956–1964.

Gauge, 12. Deluxe grade. Gas-operated; three-shot magazine. Plain or ventilated rib barrels; 26 inches, 28 inches, 30 inches. Weight about seven pounds.

Remington Model 1100 Automatic Field Gun. Made circa 1963–date.

Gauges 12, 16 and 20. Gas-operated. Hammerless. Takedown. Plain or ventilated rib barrels; 30-inch/full, 28-inch/modified or full, 26-inch/improved cylinder. Weights average 7.25 to 7.5 pounds.

Remington Model 3200 Field Grade Over-and-Under Shotgun. Made circa 1973–date.

Gauge, 12. Box lock. Automatic ejectors. Selective single trigger. 2.75–inch chambers. Ventilated rib barrels: 26-inch improved cylinder and modified; 28-inch, modified and full, 30-inch modified and full choke. Weight about 7.75 pounds.

Top to bottom, left to right: **The super fine Remington Special Model 1900, one of the finest doubles ever produced; the Model 17A Standard pump; the Model 31A Standard; and the Sportsman-48A Standard-Grade Autoloader.**

America's Premier Gunmakers
WINCHESTER

Previous pages: Inheritor of the proud Model 94 lever action tradition, this Model 9422M is a handy varmint rifle in .22 Magnum caliber. *These pages, from top to bottom:* A Model 66 Winchester, the model to bear the Winchester Repeating Arms Company name; a Model 73, of the type that Buffalo Bill Cody called 'the Boss'; a Model 86, with greatly improved lever action mechanism; and a Model 94—one of the most popular hunting rifles ever manufactured.

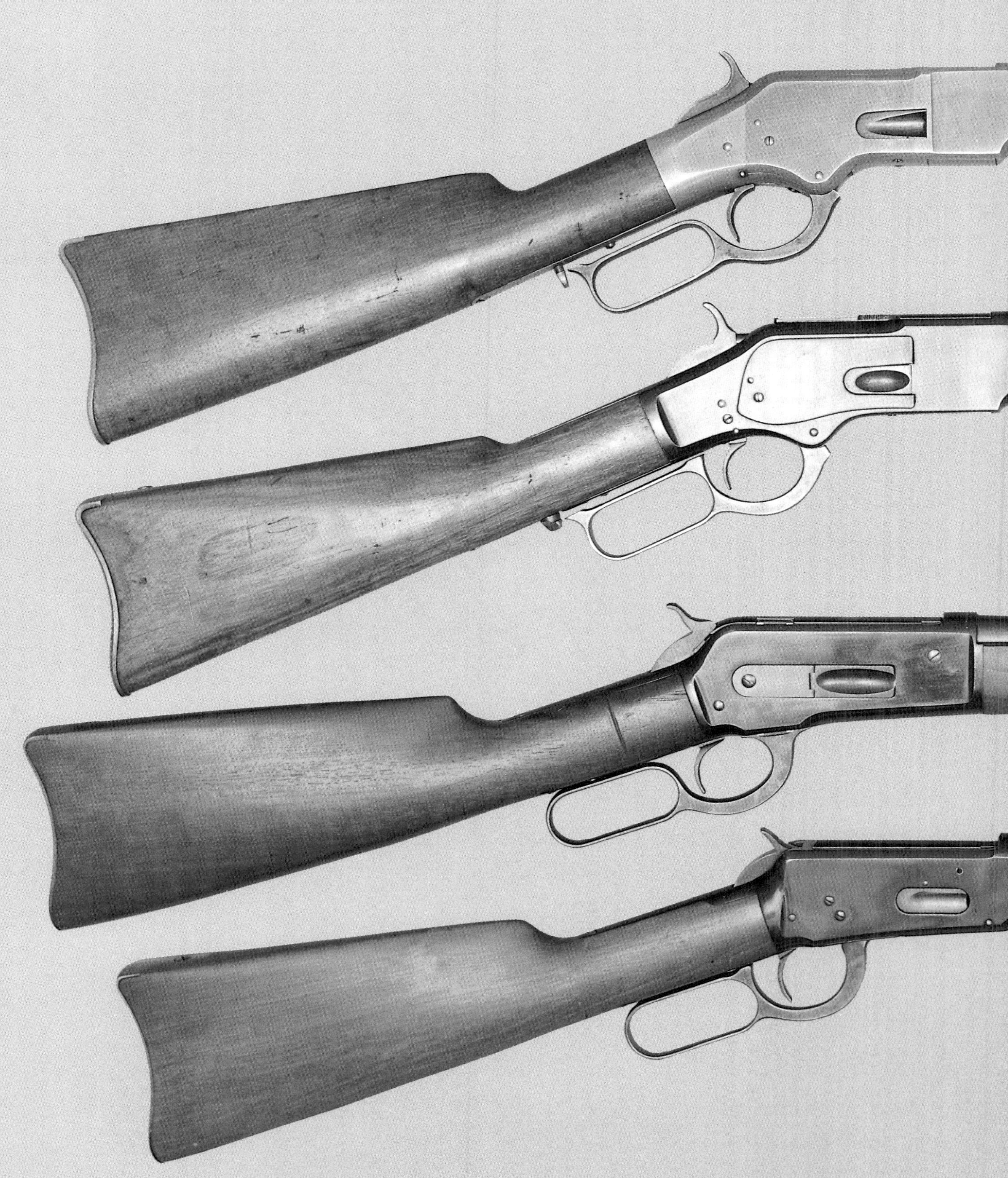

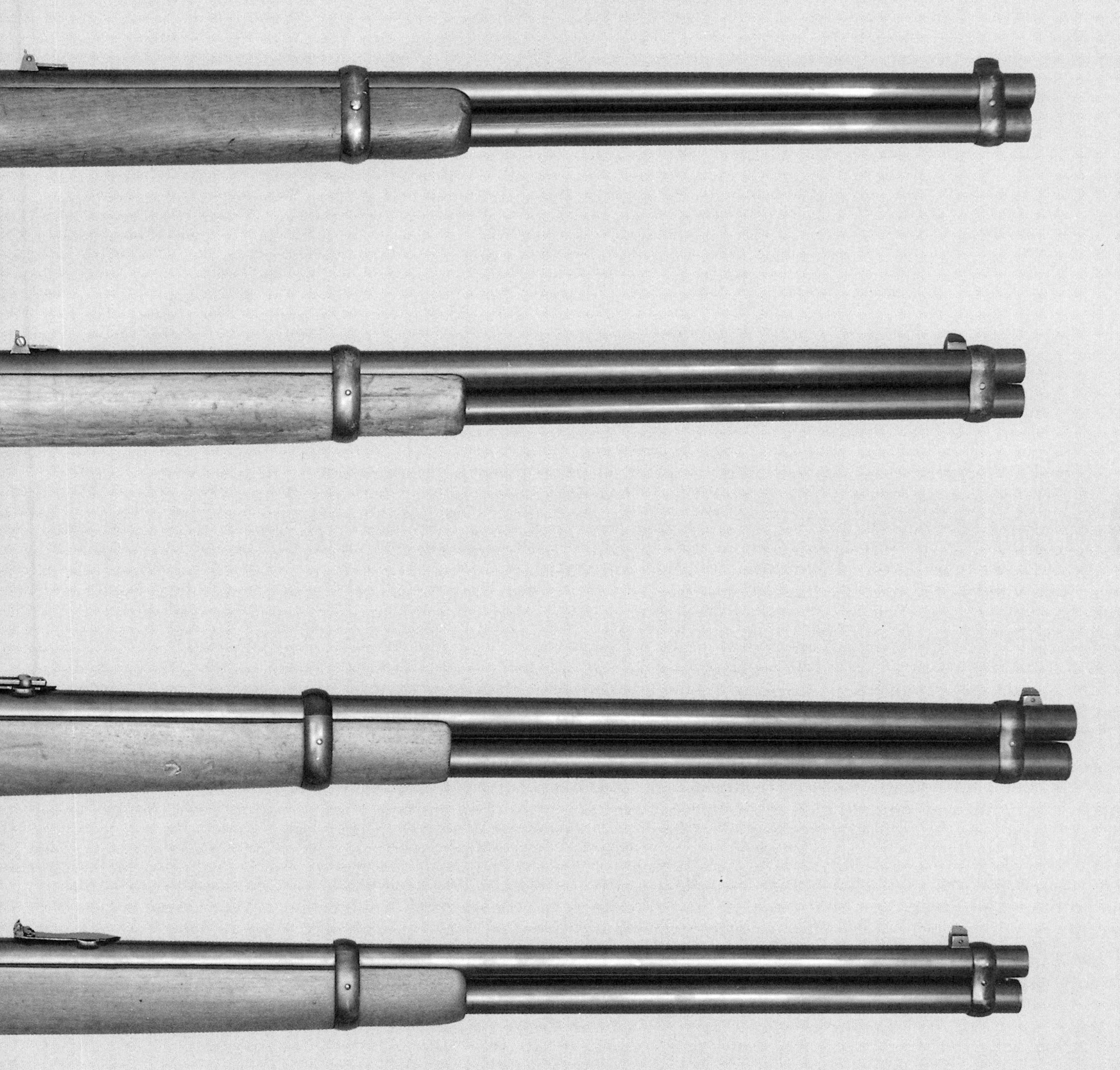

Oliver F

Oliver F Winchester was born in Boston in 1810. His impoverished youth was followed by an apprenticeship with a carpenter. By age 21, he became a master builder, but the world of business lured him to Baltimore where he operated a men's clothing store. In 1848, the now successful Winchester settled in New Haven, Connecticut and established the nation's first shirt factory. This venture made him wealthy and a leading citizen of 'The Elm City,' but he still searched for further opportunities.

Winchester first invested his talent and money in the gun business in 1855, when he became one of the original stockholders of the Volcanic Repeating Arms Company. This company had been formed in Norwich, Connecticut with the goal of developing and marketing a repeating rifle, an item that had long been a gleam in the eye of many inventors. The business failed in February of 1857, despite several cash advances by Winchester totaling over $25,000; however, he did manage to take over all the major claims against the company and bought out the other investors. In April of that year, the company was reorganized as the New Haven Arms Company with Winchester as President and Treasurer.

The company continued production of the Volcanic Arms models and ammunitions but soon hired Benjamin Henry, a wizard gunmaker, to turn the old, rather weak Volcanic lever action and its ammunition into a new, more viable, weapons system. In only three years, Henry's Rifle was ready to be sold. He had not only come close to perfecting the metallic rimfire cartridge, but had given the New Haven Arms Company ammunition that was considerably more potent than their old Volcanic Arms self-contained cartridge-bullets. The new Henry cartridge of .44 caliber propelled a 216 grain bullet at 1200 feet per second. Henry's work ranks as one of the most important developments in firearms history—his repeating rifle was the first truly practical magazine fed, breechloading, repeating firearm.

The Henry Rifle, however, was rejected by the US Army, who preferred the old-fashioned single shot rifle to anything that even hinted of innovation. It took the Civil War to prove once and for all the superiority of the New Haven Arms Company's Henry repeater. Though rejected as armament for federal troops, militias from Connecticut and other states armed themselves with the new lever actions. The demand for ammunition was so great that the US Army, which did eventually purchase 1200 of the rifles, had to buy five million rounds from the company for its volunteer regiments.

By the end of the Civil War, the company's net worth amounted to $354,000, and in February of 1867, its name was changed to the Winchester Repeating Arms Company. The deep recession following the Civil War nearly doomed the enterprise, but a timely order from the Mexican rebel Juarez, as well as various Turkish sultans, supplied sufficient business to ensure the company's continued existence.

Winchester Repeating Arms was housed in a brick building of four floors located at 9 Artizan Street in New Haven and employed 100 workers. The standard workweek at Winchester during this period was from seven o'clock in the morning to six o'clock in the evening (with an hour for lunch Monday through Friday), and Saturday from seven o'clock in the morning to five o'clock in the evening. Only those

Manufactured by the New Haven Arms Company under the direction of Oliver F Winchester, the Henry Repeating Rifle *(above)* was the first practical magazine fed, breechloading, repeating firearm. *At right:* The Volcanic Repeating Arms Company offices in New Haven, Connecticut.

Winchester's Company

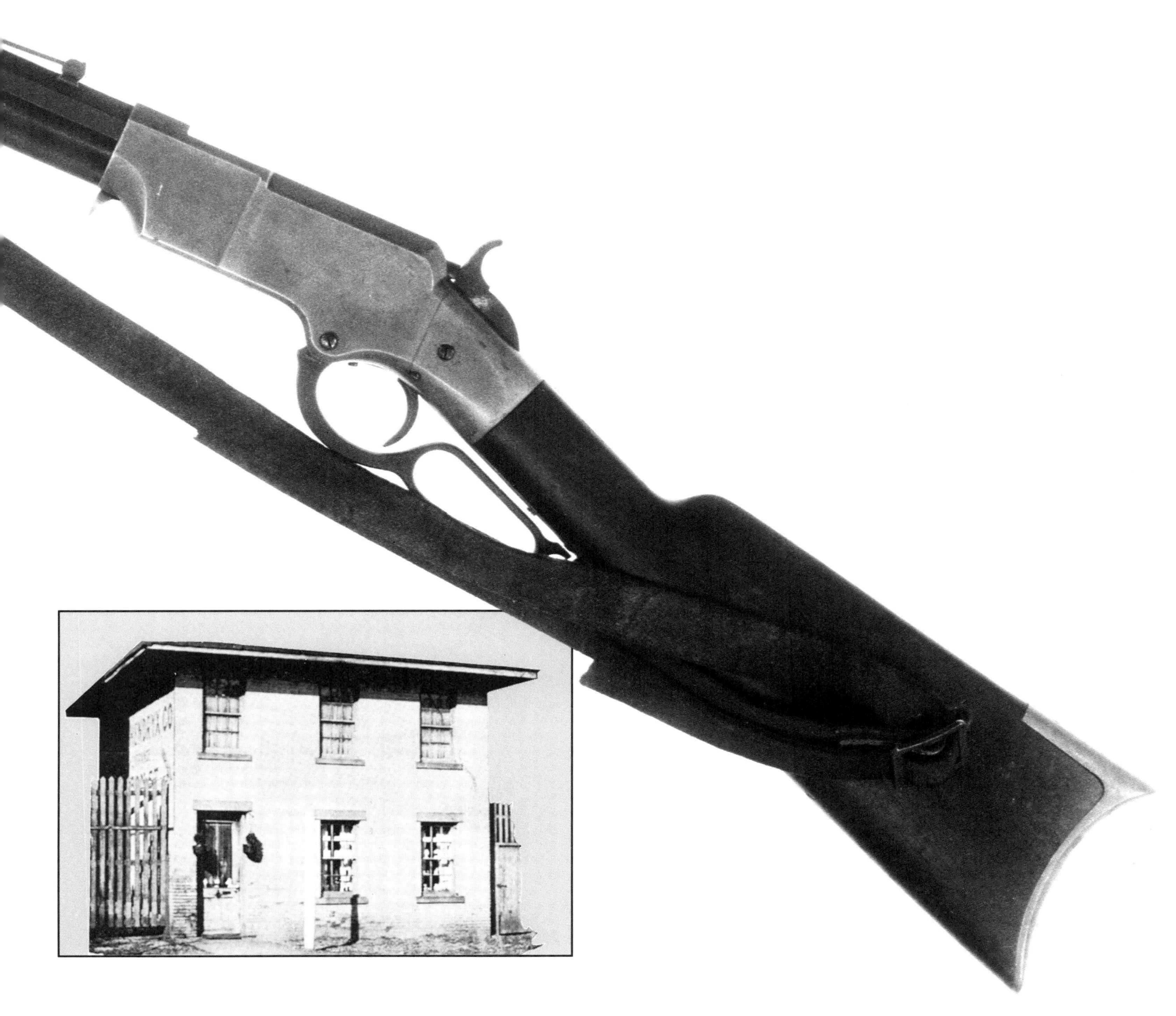

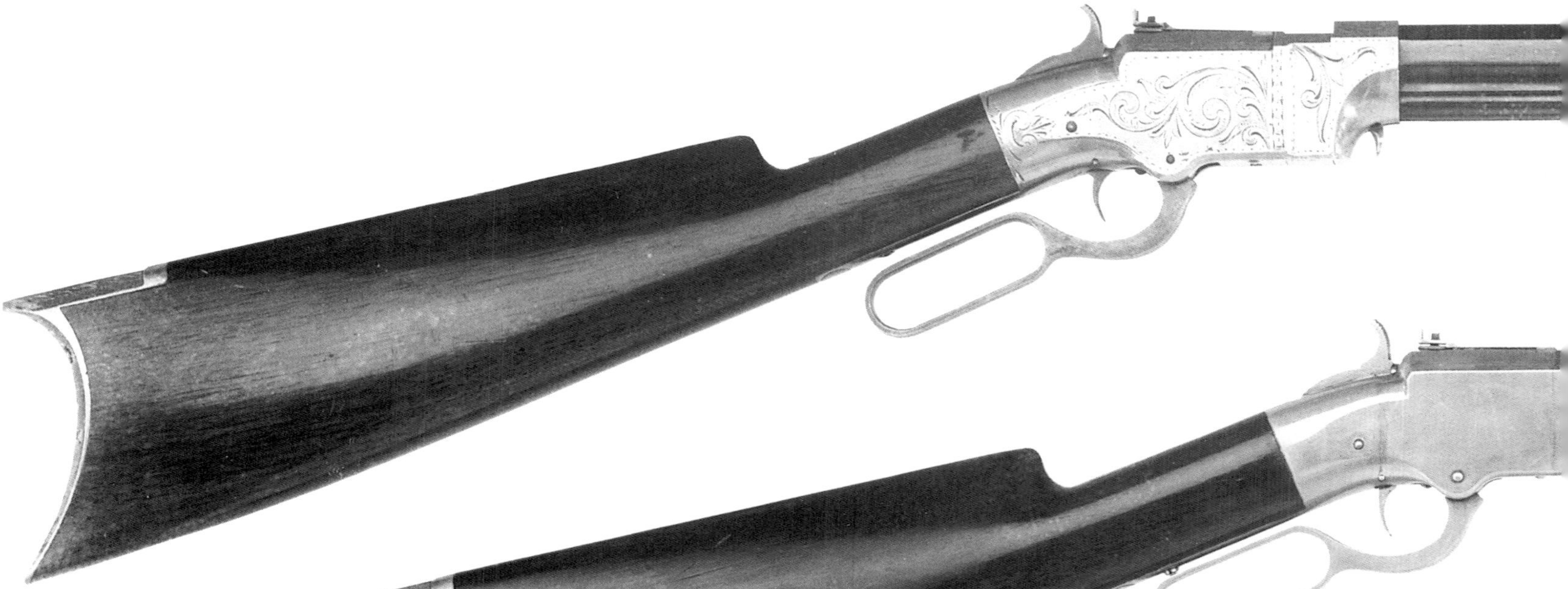

SIXTY SHOTS PER MINUTE

HENRY'S PATENT

REPEATING

RIFLE

The Most Effective Weapon in the World.

This Rifle can be discharged 16 times without loading or taking down from the shoulder, or even loosing aim. It is also slung in such a manner, that either on horse or on foot, it can be **Instantly Used,** without taking the strap from the shoulder.

For a House or Sporting Arm, it has no Equal;

IT IS ALWAYS LOADED AND ALWAYS READY.

The size now made is 44-100 inch bore, 24 inch barrel, and carries a conical ball 32 to the pound. The penetration at 100 yards is 8 inches; at 400 yards 5 inches; and it carries with force sufficient to kill at 1,000 yards.

A resolute man, armed with one of these Rifles, particularly if on horseback, CANNOT BE CAPTURED.

"We particularly commend it for ARMY USES, as the most effective arm for picket and vidette duty, and to all our citizens in secluded places, as a protection against guerilla attacks and robberies. A man armed with one of these Rifles, can load and discharge one shot every second, so that he is equal to a company every minute, a regiment every ten minutes, a brigade every half hour, and a division every hour."—*Louisville Journal.*

Address **JNO. W. BROWN,**
Gen'l Ag't., Columbus, Ohio,
At Rail Road Building, near the Depot.

B. NEVINS' Steam Printing Establishment, No.'s 36, 38 and 40 North High Street, Columbus, Ohio.

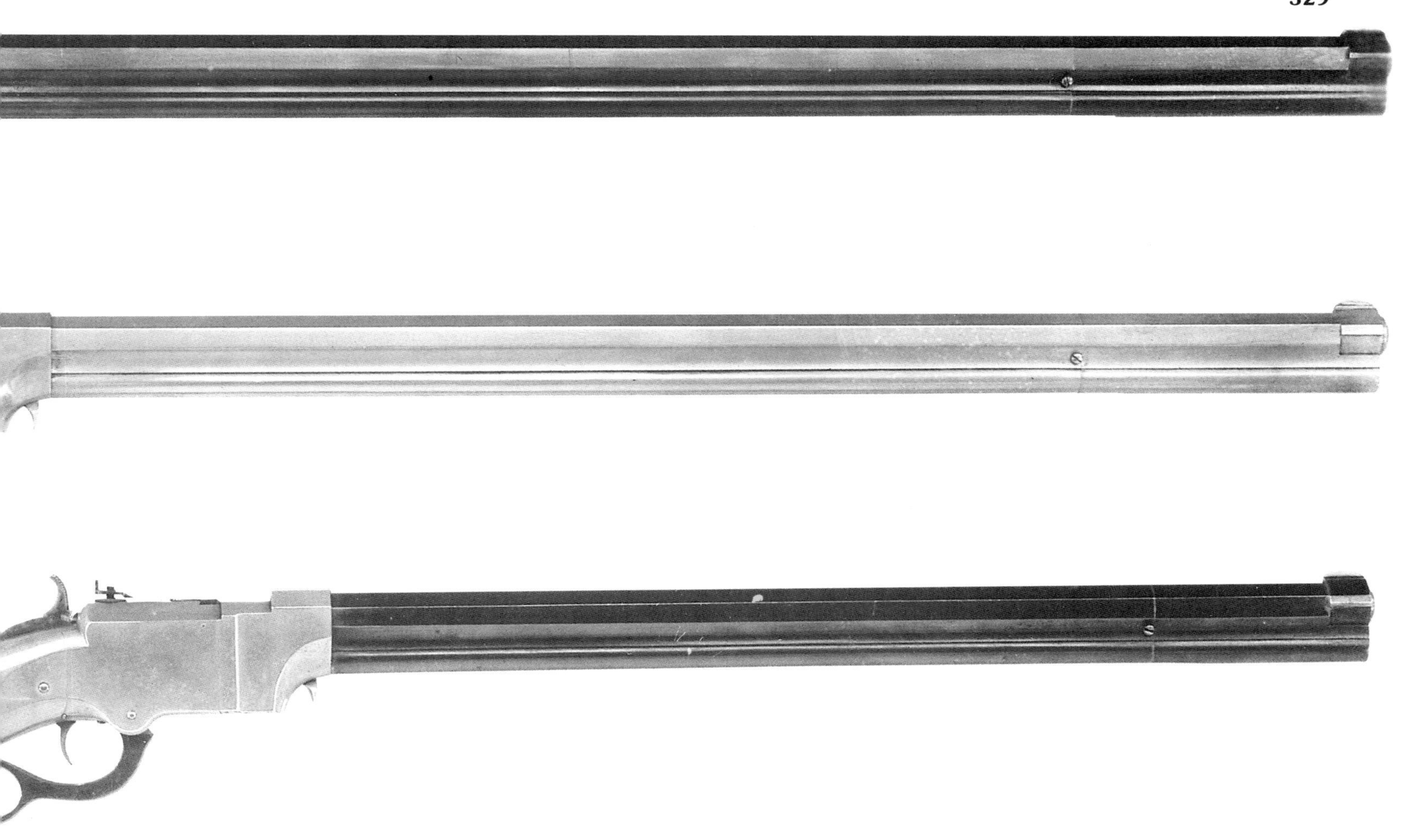

At left: **Benjamin Henry, creator of the famed Henry Repeating Rifle, at about the time of the Civil War.** ***Far left:*** **An advertisement for the Henry Repeating Rifle. These classic firearms *(above, top to bottom)*—two rifles and a carbine—were manufactured by the Volcanic Repeating Arms Company, the forerunner of the New Haven Arms Company.**

employees who had perfect attendance with no tardiness received the full 60 hours pay, and not surprisingly most of the work force lived within easy walking distance of the 'Winchester Works.'

In 1872, a new plant was completed at the corner of Munson and Canal streets (Canal Street would later be renamed Winchester Avenue). These buildings were along the west side of the street, where the Olin 'B' Track parking lot is today located. Most of the original buildings have been torn down in recent years. Of the still-existing buildings, 5-F—built in 1883—and the Custom Shop buildings (6-B)—built in 1887—are the oldest. In 1866, the first gun to bear the name of Winchester—the Model 1866 or, as it was known then, the 'New Model Winchester'—appeared. The '66' was an improved Henry rifle with the addition of a loading port on the side of the receiver and a wood forearm. These two improvements made the difference between a good gun and a true classic.

In 1873 (the first time that the actual year of introduction was used as a Winchester model designation), the Model 1873 Rifle and the world's first center fire metallic cartridge, the .44-40 Winchester, were introduced. The Model 1873 was manufactured from 1873 until 1924, with total production of 720,000 pieces. The largest production year was 1891, when over 41,000 Model 73s were manufactured. Designated 'The Boss' by Buffalo Bill Cody, this was the gun, more than any other, that became legendary. Even more important to the company than the Model 73 itself was that Winchester had entered the general metallic-cased ammunition business. Prior to 1873, Winchester had produced ammunition to fit its own rifles and pistols only.Oliver Winchester's genius lay in being able to organize, manufacture and set up distributing systems that successfully produced and marketed his rifles. He had continually enlarged the company's armory facilities and brought in new and improved machinery. His introduction of new, mass production methods and his relentless emphasis on research had made his firm one of the earliest to profit from the benefits of modern industrial technology. While wages of workers had risen from $1.50 a day to $3.50, Winchester's production costs actually fell. Rifle barrels, for example, went from $800 per hundred to a cost of just under $80 for the same number.The industrial revolution was an era when industrialists, merchants and inventors of every description were hard at work pushing the United States into the forefront of world commerce. Oliver Winchester was a member of this elite group and like his contemporaries he was also not one to shrink from his civic duties, serving as a councilman for the city of New Haven during the Civil War, becoming Lieutenant Governor of the state of Connecticut and in 1878 being instrumental in the formation of the Board of Associated Charities, a forerunner of today's United Fund. On 10 December 1880, Oliver F Winchester died and his son's brother-in-law, William W Converse, was elected to succeed him as President of the firm.

ED SCHIEFFELIN
In 1877 prospector Ed Schieffelin dared to search for silver in the San Pedro Valley - a land frequented by hostile Apaches. He had been warned by troopers at the newly established Camp Huachuca, some 20 miles distant, that all he would find would be his own tombstone. That warning inspired the name of his first claim. Two years later, after the influx of miners to the silver rich hills, the miner's camp became a city known as Tombstone. Schieffelin, having been a prospector since age 17, soon grew restless to explore new country and when offered $ 300,000 for his claims in 1880, he quickly accepted. He left the now prosperous city he had founded, a rich man.
Although wealthy enough to live comfortably for the rest of his life, Schieffelin continued to prospect the West, including Alaska, until his death in Oregon in 1897.

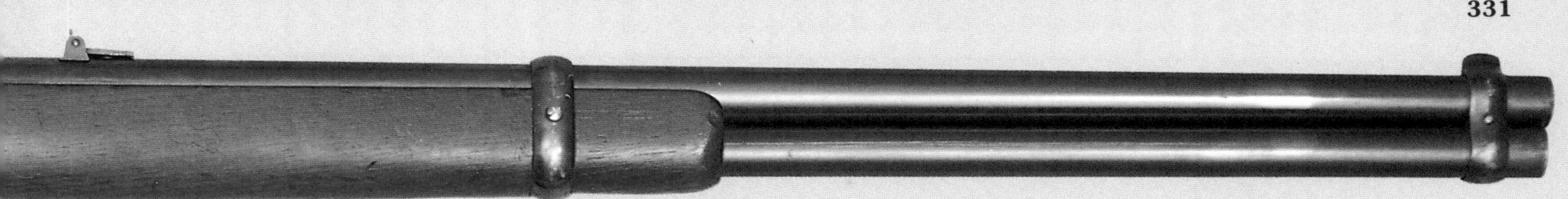

NEW HAVEN ARMS COMPANY,

NEW HAVEN, CONN.,

U. S. A.,

Manufacturers of

Henry's Repeating Rifles,

CARBINES, MUSKETS AND SHOT GUNS,

AND

FIXED AMMUNITION

FOR THE SAME.

HENRY A. CHAPIN, Sec'y. **O. F. WINCHESTER, Pres't.**

At right: **The trade card for the New Haven Arms Company, the manufacturer of the Henry Repeating Rifle.** ***Below left:*** **An exhibit at the Tombstone Courthouse State Historic Park honoring Ed Schiefflin (below), the prospector who discovered the Lucky Cuss Mine that started the rush to Tombstone, Arizona. Schiefflin always carried a Henry Repeating Rifle in his travels.** ***At top:*** **The Winchester Model 66 was an improved version of the Henry Repeating Rifle. The addition of a loading port on the side of the receiver and a wood forearm made a good gun a true classic.**

Winchester and Browning

In 1885, through the hard work and bargaining skills of Thomas G Bennett, who had recently become President of Winchester, a long and profitable agreement between the company and John Moses Browning began. One of Bennett's trips to Browning's headquarters in Ogden, Utah netted the designs for the 1885 Single Shot Rifle and the 1886 Lever Action Rifle for only $8000. These rifles were the first Winchesters adapted to the very long range shooting prevalent in the western United States.

In the ensuing years, Browning sold Winchester over 40 gun designs outright, of which seven rifles and three shotguns were actually manufactured and became the mainstays of the Winchester product line. By the turn of the century, Browning had perfected automatic firearm designs, including his truly groundbreaking automatic (actually, semiautomatic) shotgun.

It was over the issue of Thomas G Bennett's extraordinarily cautious approach to the automatic shotgun design that Winchester lost its special relationship with John Moses Browning. Further difficulty arose from the fact that Browning's designs had previously been sold to Winchester on a fee simple basis that did not include the payment of royalties. With the advent of this new design, Browning expressed a desire to receive royalties for it and other designs to follow. While this was no doubt an exacerbating factor in the deterioration of the Winchester-Browning relationship, it can be seen by the following narrative that it was not the primary difficulty by any stretch of the imagination. Browning's break with Winchester was well publicized, and in later years Browning recalled the circumstances as follows:

'It was not a very dignified parting, I admit, but I was younger then. Bennett was the most conservative of men, and admittedly the automatic was something of an inno-

vation. To put it simply, he was afraid of it, and so were the few men in his confidence. They were afraid that it would take ten years to develop such a gun to the point where it would be a profitable manufacturing article. It doesn't take many weak spots to eat up all the profit.

'Don't think of him as a coward. He enlisted at 16 and fought through the Civil War, coming out a captain. Cowards don't do things like that. But he didn't replace the old 73 and 76 models until competition forced him to it. The 86 pulled him out of that hole. Winchester had a fine record. It was their boast at one time that the company had not borrowed a cent for 40 years. The factory was a temple, and Bennett was the high priest.

'He never had an official of the company present at any of our confabs. His conservativeness worked pretty well. He is a big man, and he looked so solid in his chair that I had the feeling I could come back year after year, find him there, make a deal without any wasted words, and get back to work. It was a comfortable feeling...

'The automatic shotgun put Bennett in a tough position. I'll bet he'd have shelled out a hundred thousand dollars just to have had it banished forever from the earth, leaving him with his levers and pumps. If he made the gun and it proved a failure, as he and his advisors seemed to have half suspected, it would leave a blot on the Winchester name. Even if he made it and it proved a big success, it would seriously hurt one of the best-paying arms in his line—the 97 shotgun. If a competitor got it, and it caught the popular fancy, he'd be left a long jump behind in an important branch of the business. That's why he marked time for two years, and why, once I'd forced a showdown, I got so mad.'

Far left: John M Browning designed numerous firearms for Winchester. Browning and Thomas G Bennett, president of Winchester, _(right)_ ended the relationship following a dispute over the design of Browning's revolutionary automatic shotgun _(below)_.

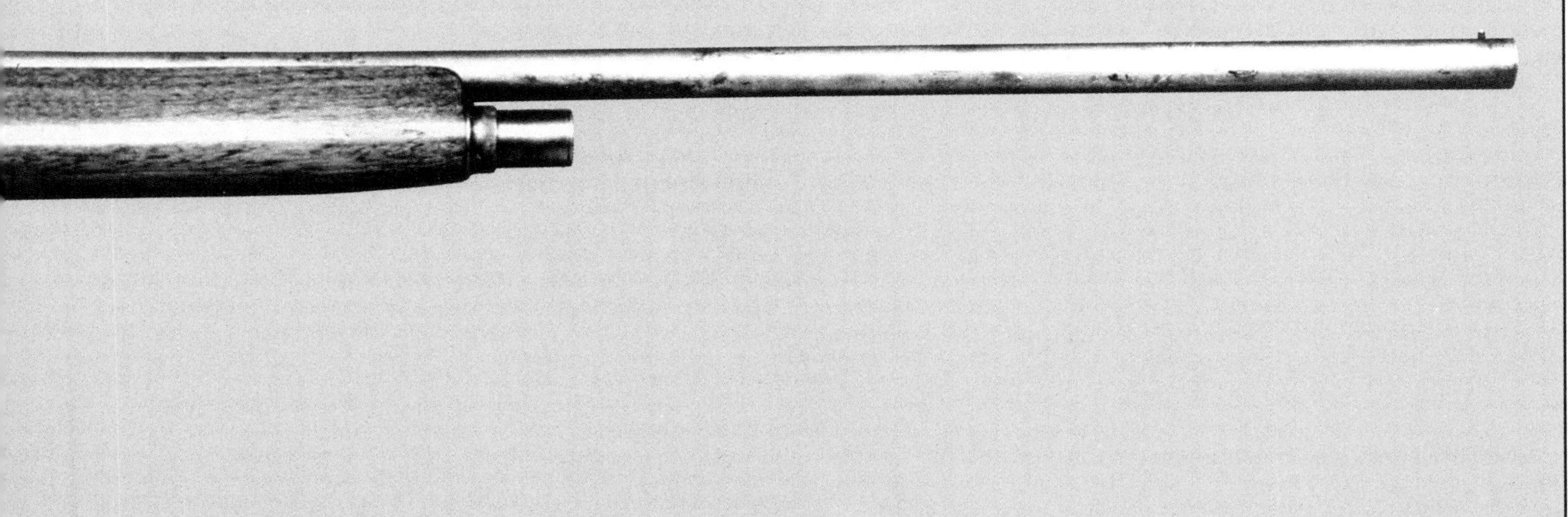

Winchester Smokeless

The decade of the 1880s was a period of great growth in the ammunition business, increasing fivefold while the business climate in general remained stable. Winchester became one of the largest ammunition manufacturers in the world during this period. In 1888 Winchester, in partnership with the Union Metallic Cartridge Company and Marcellus Hartley, bought out the Remington Arms Company of Ilion, New York, but this arrangement was short lived and was officially dissolved in 1896, when all of Winchester's interest was sold to Mr Hartley; the Sherman Anti-Trust Law was chiefly to blame. Still, by 1890 Winchester was the pre-eminent arms and ammunition manufacturer in the United States.

That was an era in which new developments in firearms designs were beginning to grow out of new developments in the type of gunpowder used in cartridges. The old 'black' powder had served for hundreds of years, but was prone to cause any rifle, pistol or shotgun to belch huge clouds of sulfurous smoke with each shot. It could be said that a new era in firearms design arrived when the old black powder formula was incrementally improved upon—by way of a phenomenal chain of developments that resulted in the invention of modern, relatively clean-burning and more efficient 'smokeless' powder.

Black powder had been known for centuries in China before it was introduced into the Western world and put to use in warfare. It is a matter of conjecture who was the first European to discover that a combination of charcoal, sulphur and saltpeter would burn violently enough to propel a projectile. In any event, since its first use in firearms around the middle of the fourteenth century, black powder continued to be made of these ingredients. The charcoal produces gas volume, sulphur the temperature, and saltpeter the oxygen to facilitate fast burning. At first, little care was taken for the quality of the gunpowder—if it worked, it worked, that was all.

Over the years, the importance of using pure ingredients was recognized, and a moderate control over the relative power of each charge was achieved by varying the grain size. Still, the tried and true combination of 75 parts saltpeter, 10 parts sulphur and 15 parts charcoal remained the basic formula for gunpowder.

The lethality of the first weapons using black powder were less important against an enemy than the unnerving effect of the flame and smoke they produced. Gradually, firearms were improved and their superiority was eventually established over the battle-axe, the sword, the spear, the longbow and the crossbow—and the art of war was revolutionized.

Then came the nineteenth century, during which the increase in the efficiency of firearms—especially the rifle—had been rapid.

By 1890, however, technical developments both in guns and ammunition had just about reached the limits imposed by the use of black powder. Little more could be done to improve the equilibrium of weight, barrel length and rifling twist of firearms using this type of propellant. To obtain greater velocities and flatter trajectories with the same calibers and weights of bullets, the powder loads and cartridge cases had been lengthened to the extent that such powerful black powder cartridges as the Sharps .40-90 and the Winchester .40-110-260 Express measured nearly four inches long.

These dimensions made their use in repeating arms very problematic, and even the single shot weapons capable of handling them were about as large and heavy as could be made and still be used as a shoulder arm.

The principal limitations of black powder as a propellant are its incomplete combustion which lessens its efficiency (and hence, its potential power-to-volume ratio) and fouls the barrel of a firearm, the heavy smoke it gives off when fired which not only stinks but also reveals the position of the shooter to an enemy or game, and the fast rate at which it burns after ignition—which would prove to provide a far less powerful 'push' than the comparatively extended burn of smokeless powder.

At right: **This Winchester Model 1893 Pump Action Repeating Shotgun was used to quell an attempted train robbery near Tombstone. Lawman Jeff Milton survived the gunfight, but the outlaw was mortally wounded.**

and the Age of Powder

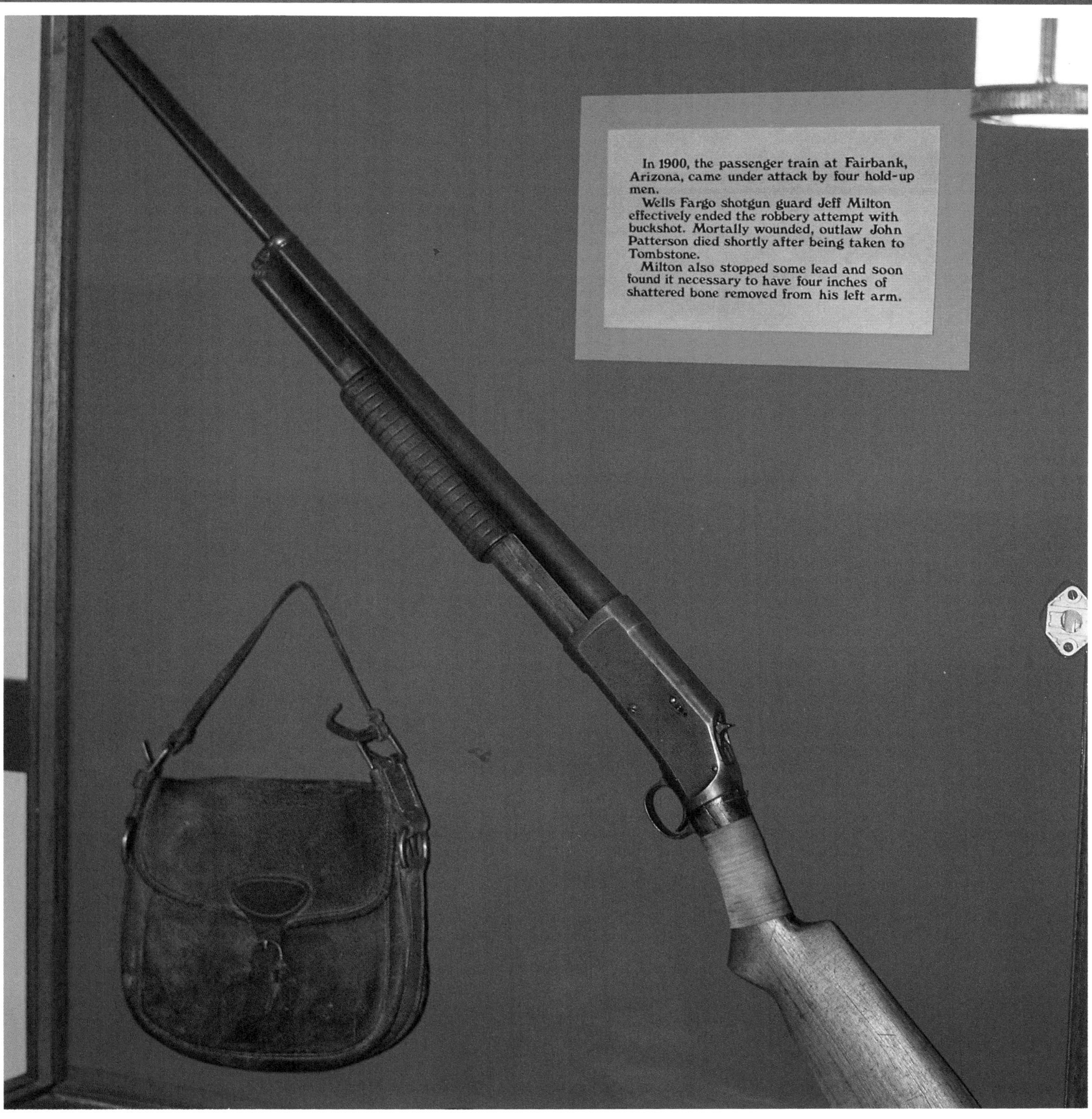

In 1900, the passenger train at Fairbank, Arizona, came under attack by four hold-up men.
Wells Fargo shotgun guard Jeff Milton effectively ended the robbery attempt with buckshot. Mortally wounded, outlaw John Patterson died shortly after being taken to Tombstone.
Milton also stopped some lead and soon found it necessary to have four inches of shattered bone removed from his left arm.

The road to the arms maker's goal of higher velocity, flatter trajectory, and better accuracy and range of shooting could only be unblocked by the development of a propellant superior to black powder. Two discoveries that were made during the 1840s were important to the development of such a superior gunpowder. In 1845, the inventor Schoenbein of Basel, Switzerland first produced nitrocellulose, or 'guncotton,' by nitrating cellulose. A year later an Italian chemist, Asconio Sobero, discovered nitroglycerin, formed by the action of nitric and sulphuric acids on glycerin. Nitrocellulose and nitroglycerin are powerful explosives. They contain carbon and hydrogen in combination with available oxygen to support combustion; both are unstable and capable of rearranging themselves with extreme rapidity into more stable compounds in the form of gases and with a concomitant great increase in volume.

In their original form, neither nitrocellulose nor nitroglycerin are usable for small arms, due to their instability. However, in 1885 a French Government chemist named Vieille discovered that nitrocellulose, when dissolved in ether or alcohol, produces a stable colloid which can be dried and used as a substitute for black powder. It proved impossible, however, to adapt nitroglycerin by a similar process, but within a few years Alfred Nobel and Sir Frederick Able combined nitrocellulose with nitroglycerin to produce a similar product. In both processes, the resulting pasty colloid was easy to handle and could be dried into grains, flakes or cylinders of various sizes. When detonated in the granular form, these mixtures produced very little smoke—hence, the granulated colloids came to be known as 'smokeless powder.'

Powder made by the Vieille process became known as single-base or bulk smokeless. The methods of its manufacture were sufficiently advanced by the late 1880s for powder companies to begin supplying the market in bulk. The powder made by the use of nitroglycerin was called double-base or dense smokeless. More powerful, and originally somewhat more difficult to control, this latter powder was made available during the early 1890s.

In addition to the characteristic the name suggests, smokeless powder burns cleaner than black powder and is by weight and volume many more times as powerful. Even more important is the control which can be exercised over the rate at which it burns. This is done by manufacturing the powder in different shapes and sizes, and by coating the grains with graphite. Slowing down the rate of combustion makes it possible to overcome the inertia of the projectile and start it on its way before the full pressure of the gas is developed. This 'slow' buildup of pressure gives greater velocity to the projectile through an extended push.

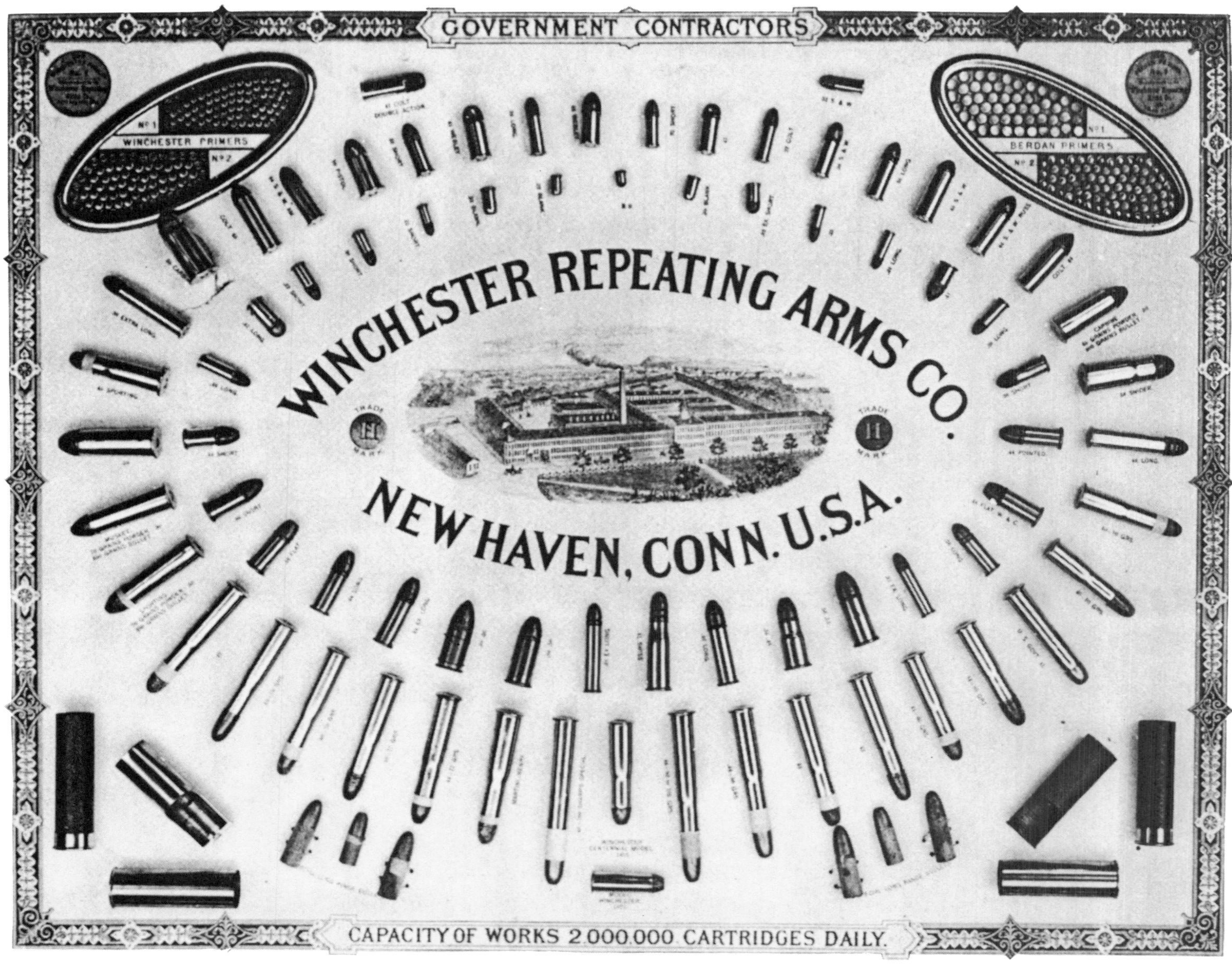

Increased velocity gives flatter trajectories to bullets and improves the accuracy of shooting. The greater power of smokeless powder makes possible both the use of relatively compact cartridges, and increase in potential velocities. In turn, higher velocities make possible the use of lighter bullets which, due to their speed at the moment of impact with a target, have an effect as satisfactory as the large, heavy pieces of lead that were hurled by the heavier-caliber black powder firearms.

While the superior qualities of smokeless powder insured its adoption, the introduction of smokeless powder added to the complexity of design and manufacture of both guns and ammunition. A whole host of chemical, metallurgical, and ballistical problems had to be solved before satisfactory results could be obtained. Among the more immediate consequences was the birth of the modern rifle and the subsequent evolution of guns with greater accuracy. Also, the use of smokeless powder hastened the substitution of scientific methods and laboratory techniques for rule-of-thumb and empirical procedures in the manufacture of guns and ammunition.

One of the major problems affecting all ammunition companies using the early smokeless powder came from the much-increased variety of powder mixtures. Black powder had long been standardized and limited to a few brands. But, in the case of smokeless powder, the different methods used in its manufacture and the wide variety of forms manufactured—each with a different burning speed—combined with the constant experimentation in improving all of the above, smokeless powder became available in dozens of varieties, each with its own particular characteristics.

It was several years before the performance of these various powders could be properly analyzed, and then standardized in ammunition use. To add to the problem, the powder companies at first had great difficulty controlling the quality of smokeless powder. Variations in different batches of the same brands made it even more difficult for ammunition producers to maintain a uniform performance in their own product.

At left: A display of Winchester cartridges, circa 1879. _Below:_ Various early Winchester cartridges, including the cartridge _(center)_ produced by the Volcanic Arms Company.

The greater potency of the new propellant made for a more delicate balance between the kind of powder used, the weight of the bullet and the design of the case; it was somewhat tricky to arrive at optimal performance. Of course, the dangers from overloading were increased, especially after 'double-base' or dense smokeless powder became available.

As one authority pointed out: 'If we load an abnormal amount of smokeless powder into a cartridge, or use a heavier or tighter, or harder bullet, or crowd a lot of powder into a small powder chamber, the pressure curve rises very rapidly. For example, if a maximum safe charge in a certain cartridge gives 50,000 pounds pressure, one grain of additional weight may give 60,000 pounds and cause the brass cartridge case to expand so much that it sticks tightly in the chamber and is difficult to extract, and 3 grains of powder above the maximum charge may give about 75,000 pounds and blow out the primer, and allow gas to get back into the gun's mechanism, and 5 grains above the normal maximum charge may disrupt the case entirely, and the powerful gas escaping to the rear may completely demolish the breech action of the weapon.'

Often the solution of one problem led to another. This is illustrated in connection with bullet design and construction. As we have said, the greater pressure and higher velocity generated by smokeless powder permitted the use of smaller-caliber bullets with the same, or a better, impact on the target than larger calibers using black powder. Decreasing the caliber, however, reduced the diameter of bullets relative to their length. In order to keep them from 'keyholing' or tumbling end-over-end in flight, it became necessary to increase their rate of spin, which was done by increasing the twist of the rifling in the gun barrels. This brought a further complication: when the lead or lead alloy bullets were forced at the greater speed through the rifling, they tended to disintegrate or become deformed.

By 'jacketing,' bullets within a thin layer of gilding metal or cupro-nickel, ammunition companies were able to overcome this tendency of the soft-lead bullets to disintegrate. Furthermore, the hard surface gave the projectile a better hold on the rifling of the gun barrel, increasing its spin and accuracy in flight and resulting in greater penetration of the target.

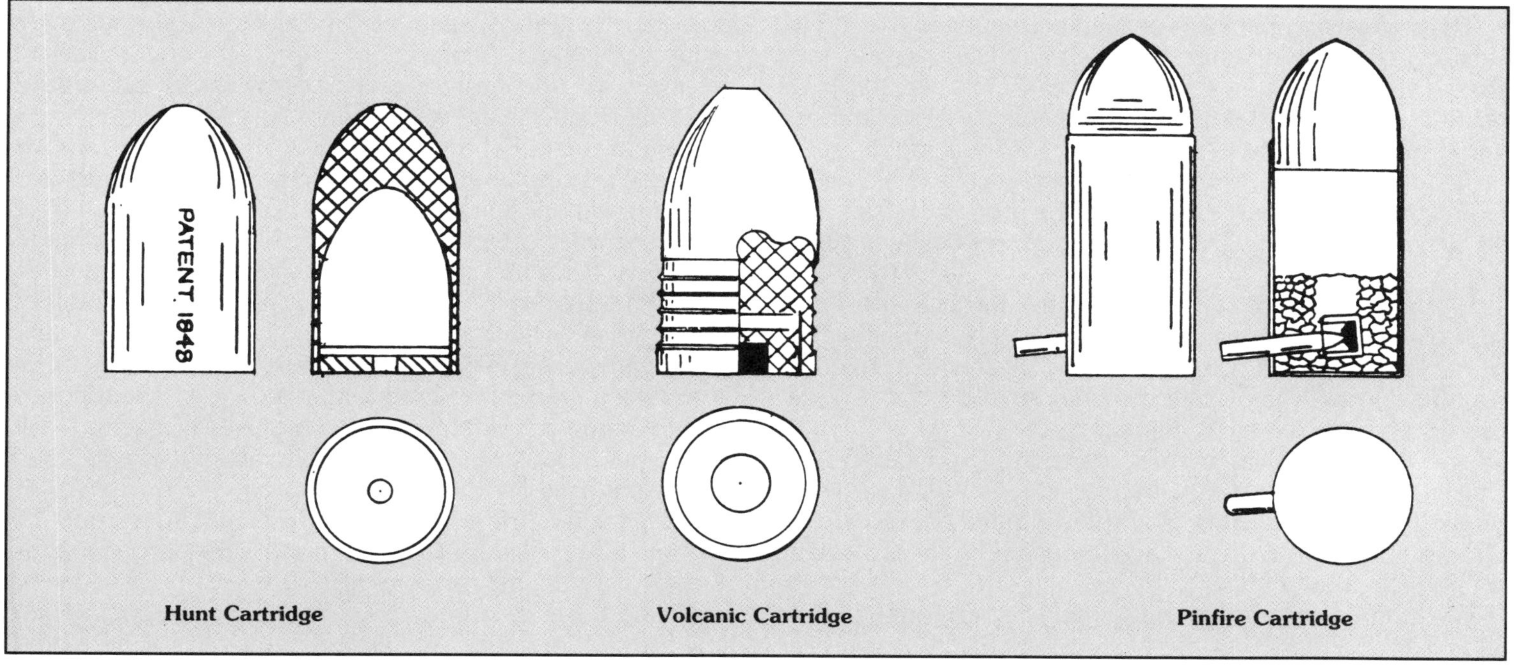

It was then discovered that completely jacketed bullets could penetrate a target without necessarily inflicting any serious damage, which was not a desirable trait for game-hunting cartridges. Finally, a solution was arrived at wherein the noses of jacketed bullets were left uncovered, and this allowed for mushrooming upon impact.

The difference in the penetration of a softnose and a fully jacketed bullet is illustrated by tests made of the WCF (Winchester Center Fire) .30 caliber smokeless powder cartridge. From a distance of 15 feet, the soft-nose bullet went through 12 dry pine boards, each seven-eighths of an inch thick. The fully jacketed bullet penetrated through 35 boards from the same distance.

The adoption of smokeless ammunition was a slow process. Not for some 10 years after the new propellant was first introduced were smokeless loads sufficiently perfected to meet the approval of any large number of shooters.

Winchester began experimenting with smokeless powder as early as 1888. Indicative of the difficulties encountered is the fact that the first announcement of smokeless loads did not come until five years later, the catalog for 1893 carrying the statement that the Company would load, on order, its paper Rival shot shells with smokeless (also known as 'nitro') powder.

The following year the Company announced that it was carrying one product line of loaded smokeless paper shot shells in stock. This was the Winchester Leader, the Rival being changed to black powder. This policy was continued until 1905, when a second smokeless load was added. At the same time the number of hand-loaders' shells (which were empty, but came already primed) to be used with smokeless powder was increased from two to four product lines during the same period.

While the use of smokeless powder in shot shells presented some problems, it proved much more difficult to use the new propellant in metallic cartridges. Winchester management devoted most of its attention to the solution of this latter problem during the succeeding years.

The first smokeless metallic cartridge produced by the Company, the .30 US Army, for use in the Winchester Single Shot and the newly-adopted United States service rifle, the Krag-Jorgensen, was announced in the Company catalog for April 1894.

With the statement that 'new smokeless cartridges will be added as fast as experimental work permits,' the list of smokeless loads was increased to 17 the following year. Actually, in all but four of these cartridges, smokeless powder was substituted for black powder without any attempt to attain higher velocities.

This was explained in the following head note to the list: 'The smokeless cartridges enumerated below may be divided into two classes. In the one class are those cartridges in which black powder has been replaced with smokeless powder. In these, to meet the requirements of the guns for which black powder cartridges were intended, no attempt has been made to get additional velocity. The name of the black powder cartridge has been retained, and the word 'Smokeless' added. The smokeless cartridge in point of excellence differs from the black powder cartridge only in smokelessness and cleanliness. Velocity and penetration remain the same. In the other class, cartridges may be numbered the .236 Navy, .25-35 Winchester, .30 US Army, and .30 Winchester Smokeless. These are purely smokeless cartridges.

'The velocities obtained cannot be gotten with black powder, nor have we been successfully able to use lead or alloys without metal patches (jackets). These are cartridges belonging entirely to the smokeless powder class, and cannot be used with black powder. Their excellence is in high velocity and consequent flat trajectory. The full metal patch gives great penetration. The soft nose bullet will expand to give effects upon animal tissues very much greater than the small caliber would otherwise enable.'

The production of even this rather modest list of smokeless loads had, by 1895, taxed the ingenuity and facilities of the management, and TG Bennett had already taken steps to put the work on a more scientific basis by establishing a laboratory. This laboratory had its beginning in about 1886 when Thomas Addis, the Company's foreign sales agent, purchased a Schultz chronoscope in Europe. This was a device which measured bullet velocities, and evidence of the Company's deepening commitment to the 'scientific approach' came a short time later, when Addis acquired, also in Europe, a Boulenge chronoscope, which was a superior instrument used for the same purpose.

Addis (at such times as he was in New Haven) and TG Bennett did considerable testing with the chronoscopes. These experiments appear to have continued on an intermittent basis, largely when the two men could spare time from other duties, and did bear some fruit after a bit of

1886

.50-100-450.

—A New Cartridge.—

.50 Caliber,
100 Grains Powder.

450 Grain
Solid Bullet.

LIST PRICE, $48 PER 1000.

To meet the demands of our friends for a .50 caliber carrying a heavy bullet, we are now prepared to furnish the above. The bullet has a penetration of about 16 pine boards 7/8 inch thick, and a trajectory of about 12 inches at 200 yards. This cartridge cannot be fired with good results out of the .50-110-300 rifle, but requires a barrel especially rifled for it.

Winchester Repeating Arms Company,

NEW HAVEN, CONN.

Send for our 112 page catalogue–free.

At top: A Winchester Model 1886 .45-90 Caliber WCF Rifle, and an advertisement *(above)* for new high power cartridges for the Model 1886. Cartridges of this sort created a revolution in firearms design.

trial and error: in February 1889, the Company catalog included its first ballistics table, which was expanded in later editions.

With the advent of smokeless powder, laboratory testing had taken on a new significance. After it was clear that the new powder had come to stay, TG Bennett moved to put the laboratory on a more formal basis and, in 1894, he employed Edward Uhl, a recent graduate of the Yale Sheffield Scientific School, to take charge.

This laboratory represented a major step in the direction of scientific control over developmental work and manufacturing processes. This is well illustrated in the case of priming mixtures. Prior to the introduction of the laboratory, the development and production of priming mixtures were entrusted to the primer shop foreman, who had long experience in the work. New mixtures were tried out empirically, and the foreman had a 'little black book' into which he entered the various formulas. This information was available only to the foreman who kept it a closely guarded secret. It is said that the Company did not dare fire the primer shop foreman, for without his little black book, the primer shop would shut down. Adding to the complexity this system imposed, there was always also the possibility that he would go over to a competitor for more money.

The demands for smokeless powder primers made this system inadequate. The new propellant required a different kind of primer 'burn' than did black powder. Hundreds of mixtures were tried, and the configuration of the primer was changed many times before satisfactory results could be obtained. However, with the application of chemical analysis it was not only possible to compound more accurate and satisfactory mixtures, but in the laboratory, the existing formulas lost their mystery and the little black book lost its significance.

Essentially the same condition applied in the case of metal working. The tempering methods used to anneal brass, harden steel and so forth had been evolved over many years of empirical observation. The men in charge of these operations were master craftsmen who had a 'feel' for their work. With the advent of smokeless powder, greater pressures were put upon gun chambers and cartridge cases, and greater heat was generated. The Company, already deep into their fascination with science, gave up on traditional metallurgy and plunged into the laboratory with that aspect of their operations as well.

The importance of metallurgy is illustrated by the following example from 1898, after the laboratory was in operation. Working on a Government order for .30 caliber smokeless ammunition to be used in the Spanish-American War, the Company had lot after lot of ammunition rejected by the Government inspector because of defects. These took the form of 'cut-offs,' or separation of cartridge cases about a half-inch from cartridge bases; splits in the necks of cartridge cases; and weaknesses in casings that allowed expansion in the firing chamber to the point that some cartridges could not be ejected after being fired.

Henry Brewer, a metallurgist par excellence, was brought in to help solve the difficulty. According to him, the cartridges lacked the proper crystal structures in various parts of their designs, and only after careful analysis had the proper crystal structure for each part of the cartridge been arrived at.

As the manufacture of smokeless powder ammunition was pushed ahead, the operations of the laboratory expanded. By 1901, the work had become extensive enough to warrant the establishment of a chemical division and Joseph Wild, a graduate of the Yale Sheffield Scientific School, was put in charge. In 1904 he was succeeded by William Buell, a graduate of the same school, with several years experience in the laboratories of the Pennsylvania Railroad. Buell was an exceptionally able chemical engineer and under his direction the work of the laboratory assumed increasing significance over succeeding years.

Winchester kept the promise it made in 1895 to add new smokeless cartridges as fast as they could be developed. By 1905, the list had grown to 100 and in 1914 the total came to 175. Many of these were available in both full jacketed and softnose bullets, so the actual number of individual loads was probably at least 20 percent greater than indicated.

A considerable number of these new cartridges were still black powder types with smokeless powder substituted, but—as with some of those mentioned earlier in this chapter—with no attempt to achieve higher velocities. These were designed to be used in firearms manufactured before smokeless powder was introduced. Due to the greater pressures developed with smokeless powder, it was dangerous to use high pressure smokeless loads in these black powder firearms.

A second group, including a line of Winchester high velocity cartridges, was described as giving higher velocity and increased muzzle energy, with only a moderate increase in initial pressure. Many of these cartridges could be used safely in the Company's Model 86 and Model 92 rifles, originally designed for black powder ammunition, but users were cautioned against using high velocity cartridges in the Model 73.

The third class of smokeless cartridges were high power loads such as the 6mm Navy, the .30 US Army, the British

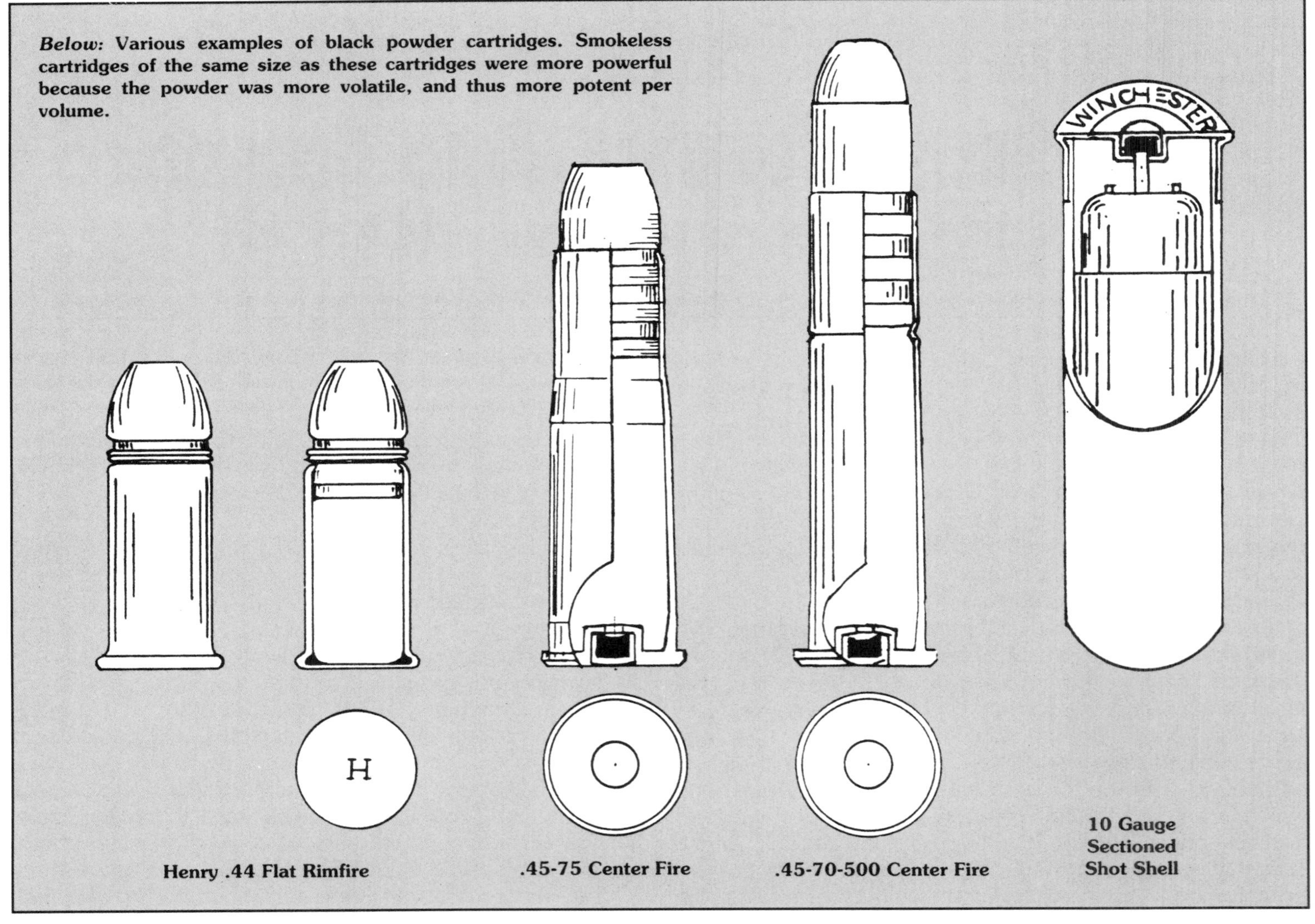

Below: **Various examples of black powder cartridges. Smokeless cartridges of the same size as these cartridges were more powerful because the powder was more volatile, and thus more potent per volume.**

.303, and such Winchester calibers as .30-30, .33, .35 and .405, and could be used safely only in guns designed especially to handle high pressures. Not all of the smokeless loads offered in 1914 had been originally developed by Winchester. In line with its policy of producing a full line of ammunition for all types of firearms, the Company expanded its manufacture to include practically all the new cartridges brought out by the US Government and the other arms and ammunition companies.

While adding smokeless loads to its ammunition line, Winchester did not reduce the manufacture of black powder metallic cartridges and components. Including loaded and empty primed cartridge cases, bullets, blanks and other components, the catalog for 1914 listed approximately the same 375 black powder items that had appeared in 1890.

Beginning in 1911, the Company offered to load rimfire and center fire black powder pistol cartridges with 'Lesmok' at no extra cost. Lesmok was a semi-smokeless powder developed by Du Pont. This powder added a slight degree of muzzle velocity, and hence, accuracy to small caliber ammunition. While it gave off more smoke and caused more bore fouling than smokeless, the fouling was of such a nature that it did not cake and harden in the barrel, and firing did not have to be interrupted for cleaning.

While sales of factory-loaded ammunition had grown enormously over the preceding quarter century, a large number of shooters during the early 1890s still preferred to load or reload their own metallic cartridges. The reasons for this preference are well stated in the following quote from AC Gould's book, *Modern American Rifles,* published in 1892.

'Every person who shoots a rifle will be likely to sometime prepare ammunition. One rarely finds an expert rifleman who uses factory cartridges, especially if he shoots at targets, or where extreme accuracy is desired. Factory made cartridges are expensive and, however excellent when leaving the factories, may rapidly deteriorate by being stored in an unfavorable place. Tyros usually shoot factory cartridges; the old and skillful marksman rarely does. But, besides the questions of economy and more reliability in properly reloaded cartridges, is the necessity of reloading when one is located away from the large cities, where it is impossible to procure the products of the factories.

'If residing in a section where gun dealers are numerous, the great variety of cartridges make a very large stock necessary (if the dealer would keep a full line) and as many of the cartridges would be seldom called for, the stock would become old and deteriorate. Therefore, only the most called-for rimfire and center fire cartridges are found in the average gun store. Thus it seems necessary for a rifleman—if he desires to economize, to have reliable ammunition and to be able to supply himself with such at will—to possess a knowledge of how to reload rifle cartridges.'

Winchester had long supplied the demands of the hand loaders, and continued to advertise the fact that 'shells of all our center fire rifle cartridges are made of extra thickness for this purpose.' A considerable part of the Company's sales was made up of ammunition components, including primed and unprimed empty cartridge cases, wads, bullets and extra primers.

In 1890, the Company listed in its catalog two types of reloading tools, in addition to bullet molds and charge cups for measuring powder. Also included were directions for reloading and recommendations of the best types of powders. Between 1890 and 1915, there was no change in policy and the Company continued to cater to the hand loaders using black powder.

The hand loading of smokeless powder was a different proposition, and beginning in 1898 the Company made every effort to discourage the practice. While this attitude may have been colored by a desire to increase the sale of factory-made ammunition, the main reason was based upon the increasing number of accidents suffered by shooters using hand loaded smokeless cartridges.

As a large number of these accidents involved Winchester firearms, the management was especially interested in taking steps to eliminate them. In the catalog for 1898 the Company, under the heading, 'Reloading Smokeless Powder Cartridges Impractical,' explained its attitude as follows.

'We are constantly in receipt of letters of inquiry regarding the reloading of smokeless powder rifle ammunition, and we therefore make the following general statement.

'It has been the common experience of persons using reloaded smokeless powder cartridges to have a large number of shells so reloaded rupture in the gun. Extensive experiments carried on by the Winchester Repeating Arms Company—and by the Ordnance Department of the United States Army—with shells, guns and smokeless powders of nearly every known manufacture, have alike failed to find a remedy for this difficulty.

'Experiments show that after the first firing with smokeless powder, the metal of the shell undergoes a slow but decided change, the exact nature of which the best experts have as yet failed to determine. No immediate deterioration attends the shooting of smokeless powder: for, by reloading and shooting immediately, the shells may be shot many times with no sign of rupture.

'If, however, the fired shells are not allowed to stand for two or three days, no matter whether they are cleaned or uncleaned; wet or dry; or loaded or unloaded, the result is always the same—namely, the metal becomes brittle, and rupture of the shells at the next discharge is probable.

'For this reason, the Winchester Repeating Arms Company cautions its patrons against the reloading of smokeless powder rifle ammunition, and wishes to do its utmost to discourage this practice.'

It turned out that the cartridge casings had an adverse reaction to the residue left by the primers then being used; with some thought and effort, this danger was overcome. However, the use of the very potent double-base smokeless powder had become more prevalent. This gave birth to a new danger—namely, overloading. This gave rise to the following warning concerning hand loading in the Winchester catalog of 1900.

'The many smokeless powders on the market differ so greatly in their various qualities and characteristics, that their use may be attended with very great danger through improper loading. Many smokeless powders—excellent powders in themselves and perfectly safe and satisfactory if used in the proper amounts and in the cartridges for which they are designed—may become very dangerous when used in other cartridges, or in the wrong amounts.

'Smokeless powder varies greatly in bulk, density, rapidity of combustion chamber pressure and charge required, and for this reason it is very unsafe to load smokeless powder, unless the means of determining the chamber pressures are at hand. Thirty grains of one powder might be a perfectly safe and satisfactory load, while 30 grains of another pow-

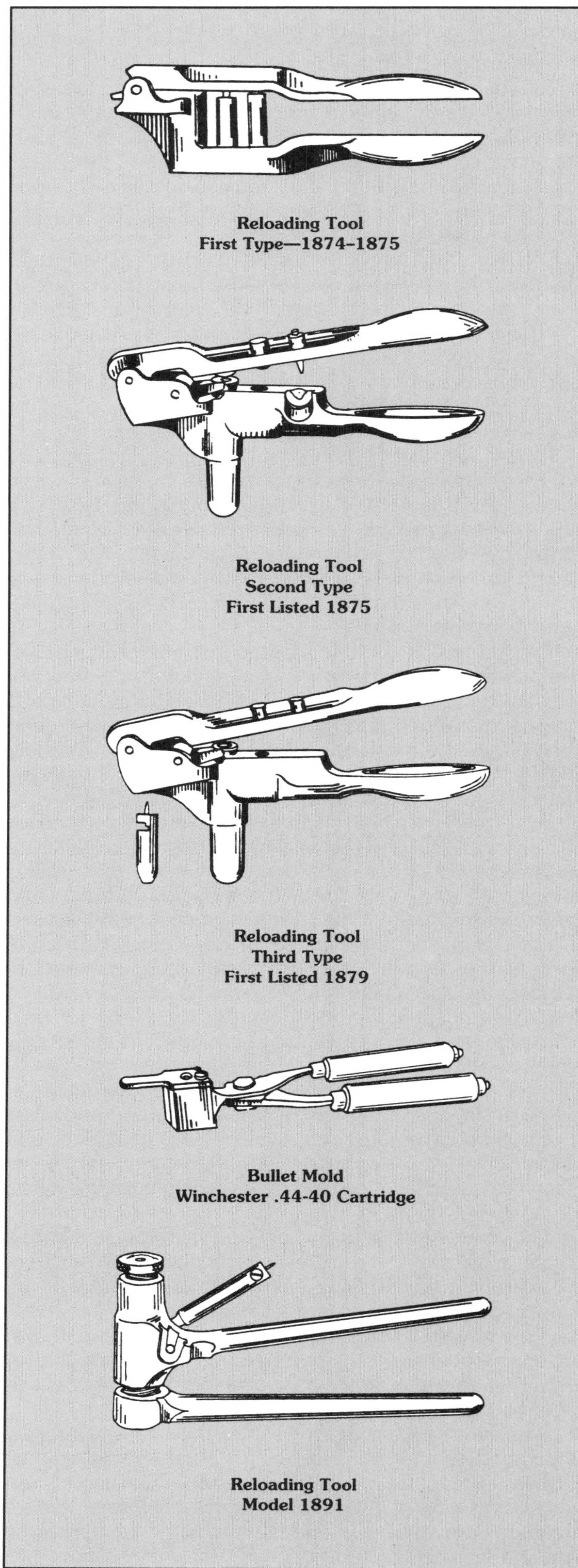

Reloading Tool
First Type—1874–1875

Reloading Tool
Second Type
First Listed 1875

Reloading Tool
Third Type
First Listed 1879

Bullet Mold
Winchester .44-40 Cartridge

Reloading Tool
Model 1891

der in the same cartridge might burst the strongest nickel steel barrel.

'Many things tend to increase the chamber pressure to an extent little to be expected by the novice. An increase of but a few grains in powder charge will sometimes produce the most astonishing results, and what was previously a perfectly safe load may thus be rendered a very dangerous one indeed.'

Winchester was joined in this campaign by the other ammunition manufacturers and by the powder companies. How effective these warnings were in minimizing the hand loading of metallic cartridges is impossible to determine, but the following is an interesting observation by Townsend Whelen, writing in 1918. 'An acquaintance with thousands of riflemen throughout our country enables me to assert that very few of them load their own ammunition.'

There is no question that these warnings helped to alert shooters to the necessity of being aware, more than ever before, of the potency of some of the new grades of gunpowder.

While the advantages of smokeless over black powder were not as striking in shot shells as in rifle ammunition, the relative cleanness and ballistic economy of smokeless were sufficient to bring about its popularity in shotgun ammunition. The smooth bores and larger diameters of shotgun barrels, as compared to the rifling twists and relatively small diameters of rifle barrels, made for a relatively simpler adaption of designs from black powder to smokeless powder ammunition; even so, the difficulties encountered were formidable enough.

As was the case with metallic cartridges, the varieties of smokeless powder types (including the stronger, double-base types) necessitated continual changes in the composition of priming mixtures, and the balance between powder charges and the weight of the shot. Among other things, the greater heat generated by smokeless powder tended to melt shot made of pure lead. Therefore, chilled shot—made by adding antimony as a hardening agent—had to be used. Also, the higher explosive pressures necessitated the use of wads that were more elastic. Beyond that, a number of changes were made in the design of the head and brass portions of the heavy paper shot shells in order to increase their strength.

Because of the higher pressures developed by smokeless loads, all the ammunition companies had trouble with their paper shot shells 'cutting off,' or separating at the junction of the paper body with the brass head of the shell.

On 9 June 1896, John Gardner, superintendent of Winchester's cartridge shop, was granted US Patent 25611 on a method of construction designed to overcome this difficulty. The essential feature of his patent was the use of circumferential grooves around the 'collar' of the brass head of the shell. These grooves not only held the paper part of the cartridge more firmly in place, but also acted as a shock absorber by flattening against the walls of the chamber when the shell was discharged.

The advantages of this type of construction were so obvious that it was quickly adopted by other ammunition companies. Winchester brought suit against these concerns and forced them to abandon its use. However, Gardner's patent covered only the use of grooves around the entire circumference of the brass heads. Winchester's competitors found that they could get the same effects by indenting their name in the same position, and in this way were able to get the same effect without infringing on his patent.

Gardner's patent solved but one of the many problems connected with adapting shotgun ammunition to smokeless powder. Many of the same laboratory techniques applied in the case of smokeless metallic ammunition had to be applied to cure the ailments of smokeless shot shells. Winchester did not reduce its offerings of black powder shot shells because, as was the case with metallic ammunition, smokeless powder did not eliminate the demand for black powder loads.

Many shotguns were still in use which were not strong enough to handle the more powerful smokeless ammunition. Also, the smokeless loads cost more. In 1914, for example, the list price of loaded 'Nublack' 12-gauge black powder shells was $25 per thousand, while the corresponding smokeless loads in the Repeater and Leader brands were quoted at, respectively, $37.50 and $48 per thousand.

In respect to the hand loading of smokeless powder shot shells, Winchester—beyond cautioning against overloading—issued no warnings. On the contrary, beginning in 1895 and continuing thereafter, the Company included tables in its catalog giving the comparative strength of the various kinds of smokeless powder and their equivalents in black powders for the benefit of handloaders.

Also touted in the catalog were the advantages of the Company's empty shot shells that were designed for smokeless hand loads, and also, special wads and primers were added to the line of hand load ammunition components.

Nevertheless, the advent of smokeless powder did have an effect on shot shell hand loading, and contributed to a subsequent decline in the practice. Henry Brewer explained this phenomenon in the following quote.

'Black powder loading was a pretty simple affair, but when smokeless powder came on the market, shot shell loading became very different and much greater knowledge, skill, and experience was required. There were a good many accidents resulting from overloading by inexperienced handloaders. As a result, quite a business was built up in various localities where game shooting was prevalent, by local handloaders who bought the empty shells, powder, wads and shot, and loaded the shells to meet the requirements and whims of their particular customers.

'These handloaders were usually themselves sportsmen and knew the requirements of the local sportsmen, and they also knew from personal experience good loads from poor loads. The local sportsmen came to rely on their advice as to loads and many of them built up a big reputation for their product and had correspondingly large sales.

'This was especially true in the Chesapeake Bay region, noted for its duck and goose hunting. As a matter of fact, these handloaders were doing a better job than the factory loaders, for they were in closer touch with the shooters and were themselves shooters and sportsmen, and were constantly testing the results of their loads in the field.

'From the foregoing, it is apparent that the initial effect of smokeless powder was not to reduce handloading, but to put it more into the hands of specialists. It was only after the ammunition companies noted the popularity of these special loads and decided to expand their own offerings that handloading of smokeless shot shells as well as black powder loads began to decline.'

Until around 1895, neither Winchester nor the Union Metallic Cartridge Company seems to have made any particular effort to push their sales of factory loaded shells. Winchester did not even list loaded shells in its catalog until 1894, and during the early 1890s, there is evidence that both

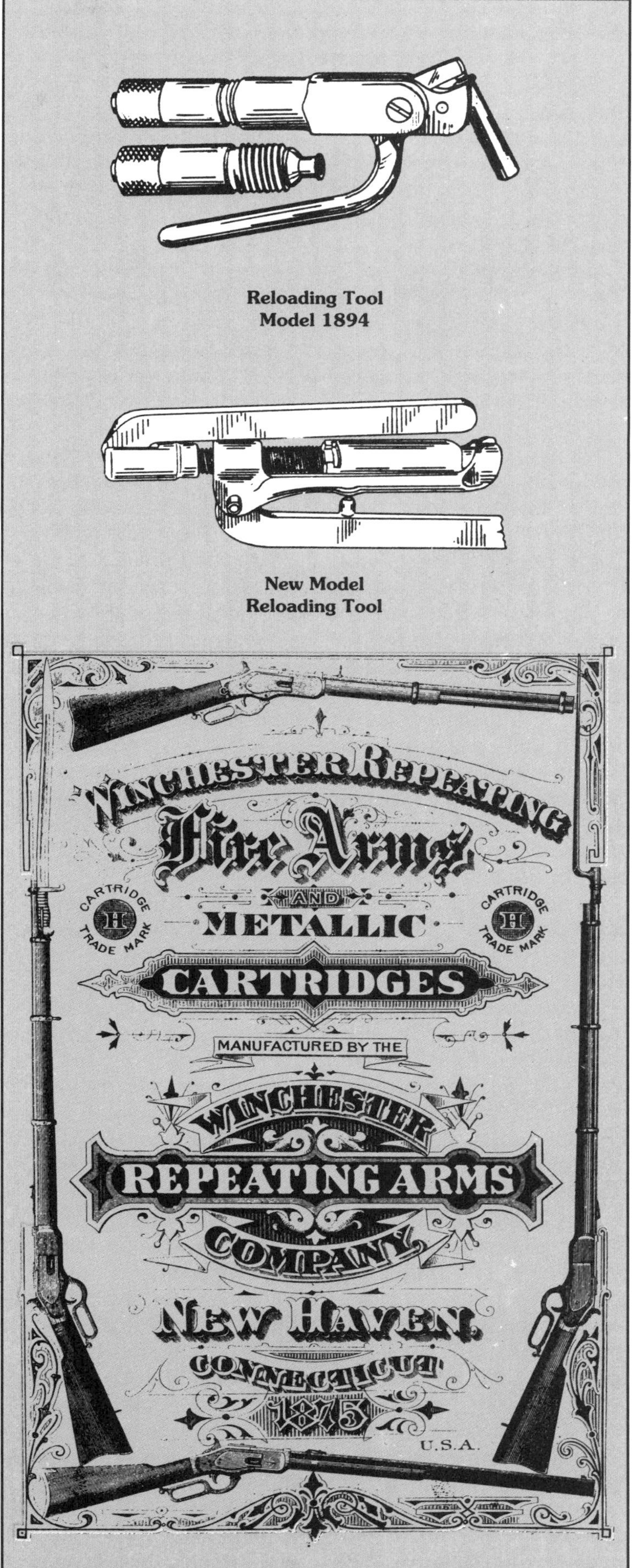

Far left and at top: **Winchester sold a number of reloading tools and bullet molds. The advent of smokeless powder contributed to the decline of hand loading.** ***Above:*** **An advertisement for the Winchester Repeating Arms Company.**

companies were willing to sign an agreement not to load shot shells as long as they and the US Cartridge Company could continue to control the supply of components.

Several considerations apparently led to this lack of enthusiasm. The sale of components was highly profitable, and the early loading machines were relatively inefficient. The cost of factory loaded shells was too high to compete vigorously with hand loading economy, and there was no reason to think that the demand for loaded shells would be very great.

Between 1890 and 1895, the general situation changed. The rise of competing firms not only threatened the Winchester, UMC and USCC control over the manufacture of components, but specialized loading companies were beginning to build up large markets. Machinery had been improved sufficiently to make the margin between costs and selling prices more competitive.

Finally, the sales of factory loaded shells had shown a remarkable increase. Winchester's annual production of loaded shells, for example, grew from 23.2 million in 1890 to 67.5 million in 1895. It may be assumed that the production of loaded shells by UMC and the US Cartridge Company increased in approximately the same proportion.

Noting the success of the special hand loaders, Winchester management decided, in 1896, to expand its offerings of individual shot shell loads, and Bert Claridge was hired to take charge of shot shell loading. This was an excellent choice. Claridge had been in charge of the shot shell loading department of a large sporting goods house in Baltimore. He was an expert shooter, famous among the hunters and sportsmen of the Chesapeake Bay region for the quality of his hand loaded shot shells, and he knew from personal experience what powder-and-shot combination gave the best results under given conditions.

Under Claridge's direction, Winchester's list of shot shell loads began to multiply. He not only increased the number of standard loads, but paid particular attention to 'special orders,' which in many cases developed considerable sales volume. It was Henry Brewer's judgment that 'No other one feature of our loaded shell job played such an important part in building our sales as did Bert Claridge. Under his guidance, we led all the loading companies in smokeless shells, in spite of the fact UMC had always led in black powder Loads. Smokeless loads sold on quality to the more particular shooters, and it was Claridge who put our smokeless loads ahead of all others as to quality.'

This move by Winchester to cater more to the individual demands of shooters was followed by the other ammunition companies, and marked a decline in popularity of hand loading. From the early days of black powder, someone had always been interested in getting special performance from their firearm—a function that hand loading had always pointedly had, and which was now supplied, except for the very particular shooters, by many factory loads.

The demand for factory loaded shot shells continued to expand. Winchester's annual output of loaded shells grew from 67.5 million in 1895 to 243.4 million in 1907.

The use of smokeless powder, plus catering to the demands of individual shooters, multiplied the variety of loads in shot shells. In 1885, just prior to its first sale of loaded shells, Winchester carried only four brands of paper shot shells and two brass shells. In 1914, the catalog listed two types of brass shells, four empty paper shot shells, and six brands of loaded paper shot shells.

This small number of brands completely obscures an almost fantastic increase in individual loads that were being manufactured by the latter date. It was an expansion that was closely related to the relationships among the powder companies, the loading companies, and the users of shot shells. Prior to the advent of factory loaded shells, powder companies had concentrated their sales efforts on the hand loaders. Dealer and jobber connections were carefully built up, and powder companies employed expert shooters as 'missionary salesmen,' whose function was to build up a preference for particular brands of powder.

When the manufacturers started loading shells at the factory, they not unnaturally stressed the qualities of their ammunition and did not feature the powder brands. This move threatened to upset or destroy the whole pattern of consumer-dealer-jobber relationships built up by the powder companies. Not wishing to fight the powder companies in their efforts to expand the sales of factory loads, the ammunition companies began quite early to furnish shot shells loaded with the brand of powder specified by the buyers. This, in itself, added to the multiplicity of different loads; but, because shooters also had preference for different combinations of powder and shot sizes, the companies also extended this option to purchasers.

Even before smokeless powder became widely adopted, the variety of individual shot shell loads had mushroomed. In 1895, just a year after it had first listed loaded shells in its catalog, Winchester was prepared to furnish to its customers, at no extra cost, a choice among 23 combinations of shot-and-powder loads, 16 sizes of shot, and at least 12 brands of powder.

The result was between four and five thousand individual loads. After the introduction of smokeless powder, the list grew steadily—largely because of the increase in powder brands. It has been estimated that, by 1907, Winchester's total allowable loads came to 14,383.

The increased variety of shot shell loads added greatly to the manufacturing problem in this part of the business. The shooting season began in the fall and continued through the winter. Orders began to come in during the late spring and early summer—but until these orders were received and the particular loads were known, production could not begin. The result was intense activity during the summer months, followed by a comparative lull in activity in the off-season.

Assembling the finished product for shipment was a complex task. Each case had to be carefully labeled. Not infrequently, an individual order would call for several varieties of powder. The Company also had to be careful not to have excessive stock on hand at the end of the season—partly because particular loads might not be popular the following season, and partly because shot shells loaded with smokeless powder were subject to extreme deterioration unless very carefully stored.

Beginning around 1901, ammunition companies moved to spread their production over a longer period by making special agreements with jobbers. Under this arrangement, if a jobber would order shells by the carload on or before March 15, he would be allowed to pay for the shipment the following September and still receive a discount. These arrangements were carefully worked out under the supervision of the Ammunition Manufacturers' Association.

Sometime around 1907, the Company began to restrict the extreme variety of their factory loads by listing definite shot sizes for each of the smokeless loads which would be

Above: **A typical ammunition factory during the Civil War era. Notice the number of female workers and the box of .43 caliber cartridges, a popular cartridge of the time.**

furnished at standard prices. Orders for shot sizes not on the standard list were accepted only at an increased price. About the same time, the Company began to restrict its powder loads to specific brands.

While these moves helped somewhat to reduce the variety of loads, no determined attempt was made to actually cut the list of loads until after World War I. In 1921, the various ammunition companies moved to eliminate some 5200 loads from their shot shell lists. These 5200 loads that were eliminated comprised but 10 percent of all their business.

TEXAS
RANGER

With the cooperation of the Department of Commerce, the manufacturers moved to simplify shot shell loads still further. In 1924 a committee, consisting of George R Watrous of the Winchester Repeating Arms Company and HJ Strugnell of the Remington Arms Company, was appointed by the ammunition manufacturers to study the possibility of a further reduction in number of loads. On 1 January 1925, the manufacturers further reduced load combinations to 1747 in all. Further elimination brought the list down to 137, total, by 1947. As you may well suspect, this marked a resurgence in hand loading, as there are always those who are willing to economise—and to take their chances on their own expertise.

Mention has already been made of the importance of improved machinery in loading shot shells. There is some evidence of a considerable improvement in these machines and in the general methods of manufacture during the 1890–1914 period. Available information is lacking for any discussion of these beyond noting a general trend toward increasing labor productivity. It is of interest that, of some 77 patents taken out by Winchester during this period, 51 covered metallic ammunition and shot shell design, 11 applied to primers and 15 to machinery used in the manufacture of both metallic ammunition and shot shells.

Not all the ideas contained in these patents were utilized, of course, but at the same time a number of improvements were introduced which were either not patentable or which the Company felt could be kept secret without being patented. The importance attached to certain of these "secret" manufacturing processes is illustrated by the following experience of Henry Brewer.

While no date is specified, it must have been around 1900 when he was called into the office by TG Bennett, and was told that the Union Metallic Cartridge Company was being sued by a workman who had been injured in their loading room. They had asked Bennett to send someone familiar with loading machines to examine their machines, so he could testify as a loading expert that they were designed and operated with a reasonable degree of safety.

Brewer states, 'Mr Bennett directed that I go to UMC and do whatever I could to help them in the matter. I was greatly elated, because this gave me an opportunity of seeing the UMC loading room—so far as I know, no Winchester representative had ever been in their loading room. It seemed to me a great opportunity to see how they did things—and possibly pick up some good ideas.

At left: **The Winchester Colt Commemorative set, honoring two guns that tamed the Wild West. The receiver of this Winchester Model 94 features a portrait of Oliver F Winchester etched in gold.**

'I therefore said to Mr Bennett, "There is no objection, I suppose, to my keeping my eyes open and seeing what I can see?" Mr Bennett replied, "Now Brewer, you are going there at their request, do what they ask you to do, but don't go prying into things that are none of our business." Mr Arthur Hooper, Vice President, who was sitting at the adjoining desk spoke up, "Why, Tom, there is no objection, is there, to the young man keeping his eyes open?" So I went determined to learn all that I could that might be of help to Winchester.'

Brewer made the most of his opportunity, and when he returned to New Haven, he informed TG Bennett that Union Metallic Cartridge Company had Winchester 'licked a mile in the matter of the cost of loading.' This, he explained, was because the UMC loading machines were operated by one operator each, whereas the Winchester loading machines required four operators. The UMC machines had automatic devices for feeding wads and shells, whereas the Winchester machine required one girl to feed shells and two girls to feed wads, and a boy to tend the machine.

The speed of the Winchester machine was limited to the speed of the girl feeder, and our daily output was generally a little less than 25,000 shells per day, whereas the UMC loading machines were turning out over 30,000 comparable loads per day with only one operator.

Brewer went on to say, 'I suggested to Mr Bennett that we immediately design automatic wad feeds and automatic shell feeds for our loading room, so that we could reduce the number of operators and increase the output to equal that of UMC loaders, and I told him that I thought if we could accomplish this, we could save $50,000 per year.

'Mr Bennett turned to Mr Hooper and said to him, "Hooper, what would you give to be a young man again? Listen to this young man, saving $50,000 a year," and they both had a good-hearted laugh over it. However, Mr Bennett, with his usual confidence in the men under him, approved the plan, authorized our designing automatic feeds—and, after several years of experimental work and very costly building of the automatic feeds, all of our shot shell machines were so equipped.

'This development of automatic feeds again brought attention to automatic shell feeds, and we continued to develop automatic feeds for our various machines, notably in the Paper Shot Shell Department, and in time we developed automatic paper shot shell feeds, which were used in our shot shell headers, our shot shell primers and our other machines.

'When we were saving an amount which I estimated at $200,000 a year, I had great pleasure in going to Mr

Bennett and calling his attention to the fact that he had laughed at me when I said we could save $50,000 a year, and that I now estimated we were saving in excess of $200,000 a year as a result of my two-hour visit to the UMC loading room.'

One problem connected with shot shell manufacture involved the purchase and storage of shot. Prior to 1912, Winchester purchased its shot from outside concerns. Shot was shipped in cloth bags weighing 25 pounds each. These had to be carefully stored and handled to prevent the bags from bursting. Adding to the complexity of shot-handling operations in those days was that, during the course of production, the Company had to handle a large variety of shot sizes.

Because the demand for particular sizes varied from season to season, it was not possible to purchase the required amounts until orders began to come in, without running the danger of building shot inventories beyond current needs. Also—if, for any reason, the required shot failed to arrive by the time it was needed, production schedules were seriously disrupted.

In spite of these difficulties, the Company took no steps to produce its own shot until 1911. In that year, the National Lead Company—which had been Winchester's own source of shot—purchased the US Cartridge Company, and thereby became a direct competitor with Winchester in the ammunition field.

Winchester management was unwilling to have its principal source of shot in the hands of a competitor, and immediately started to build its own shot tower in New Haven. The structure was completed in 1912, at a total cost of $190,000. The tower was nine stories high, and the equipment used was of the latest design and was almost completely automatic.

Conveyors carried the lead to the top floor, where it was melted, poured into sieves to give the required sizes and dropped into a water tank 154 feet below. Sorting, polishing, sizing and inspection were all done mechanically, without the shot being handled by workman. A duplicate set of machinery guarded against a breakdown, and an average of about 50 tons of shot could be produced in a day's operations.

Located close to the shot shell loading rooms, the use of the shot tower greatly simplified Winchester's manufacturing problems. Shot was ordered to be made at the tower in the sizes and amounts needed by the loading room, and was, upon production, transferred directly without the necessity of storage and extra handling. Inventories now kept track of easily-handled lead 'pigs.'

By 1914, Winchester management could look upon its ammunition development with considerable satisfaction. The problems brought about by the introduction of smokeless powder and the expansion of factory loading had been met and brought under control, an impressive list of new cartridges and shot-shell loads had been added to the line, and the addition of the shot tower had further integrated Winchester's ammunition manufacturing processes.

***Below:* The Model 9422 Commemorative Rifle—complete with its own .22 caliber ammunition—honors the Boy Scouts of America. *At right:* The Winchester Shot Tower, which was completed in 1912.**

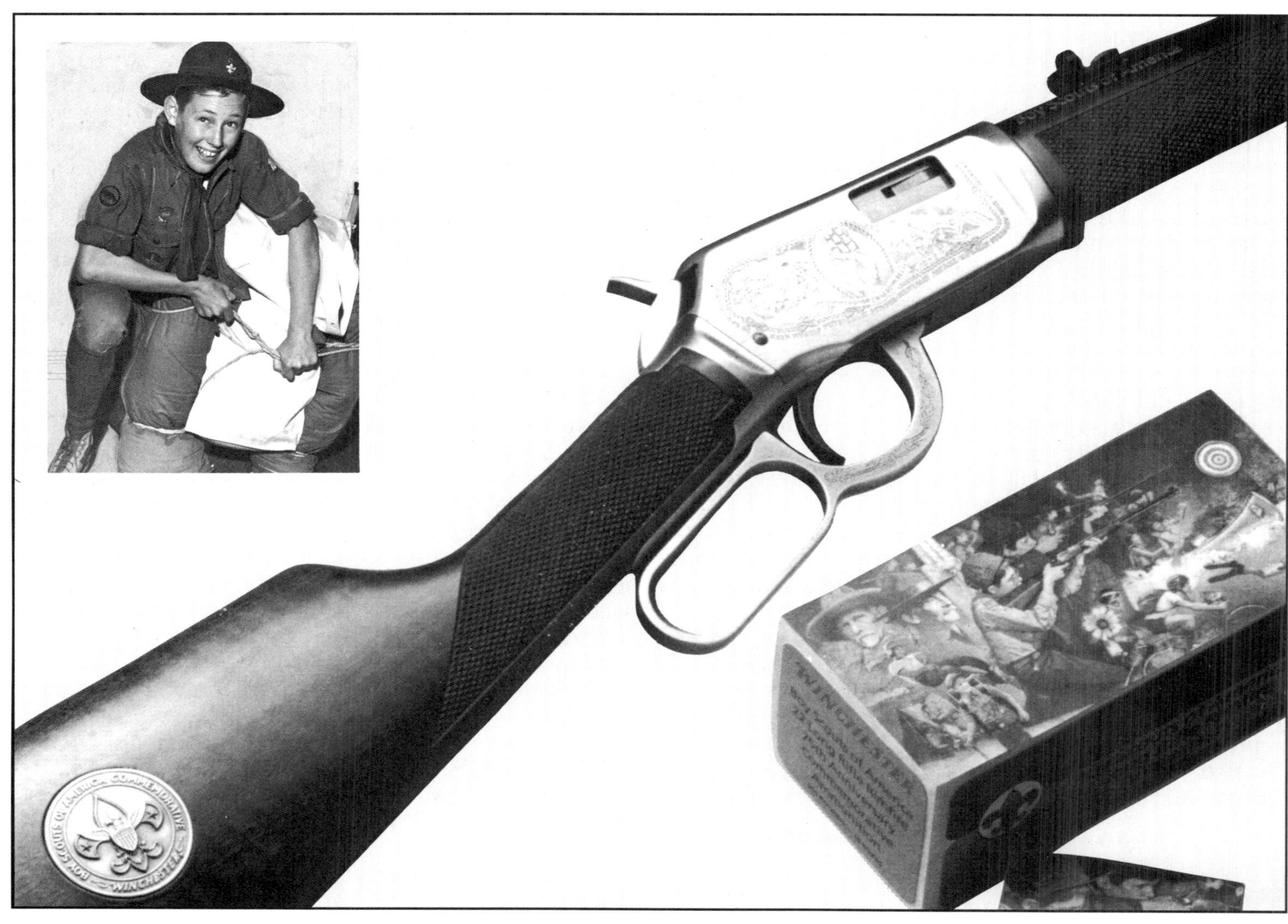

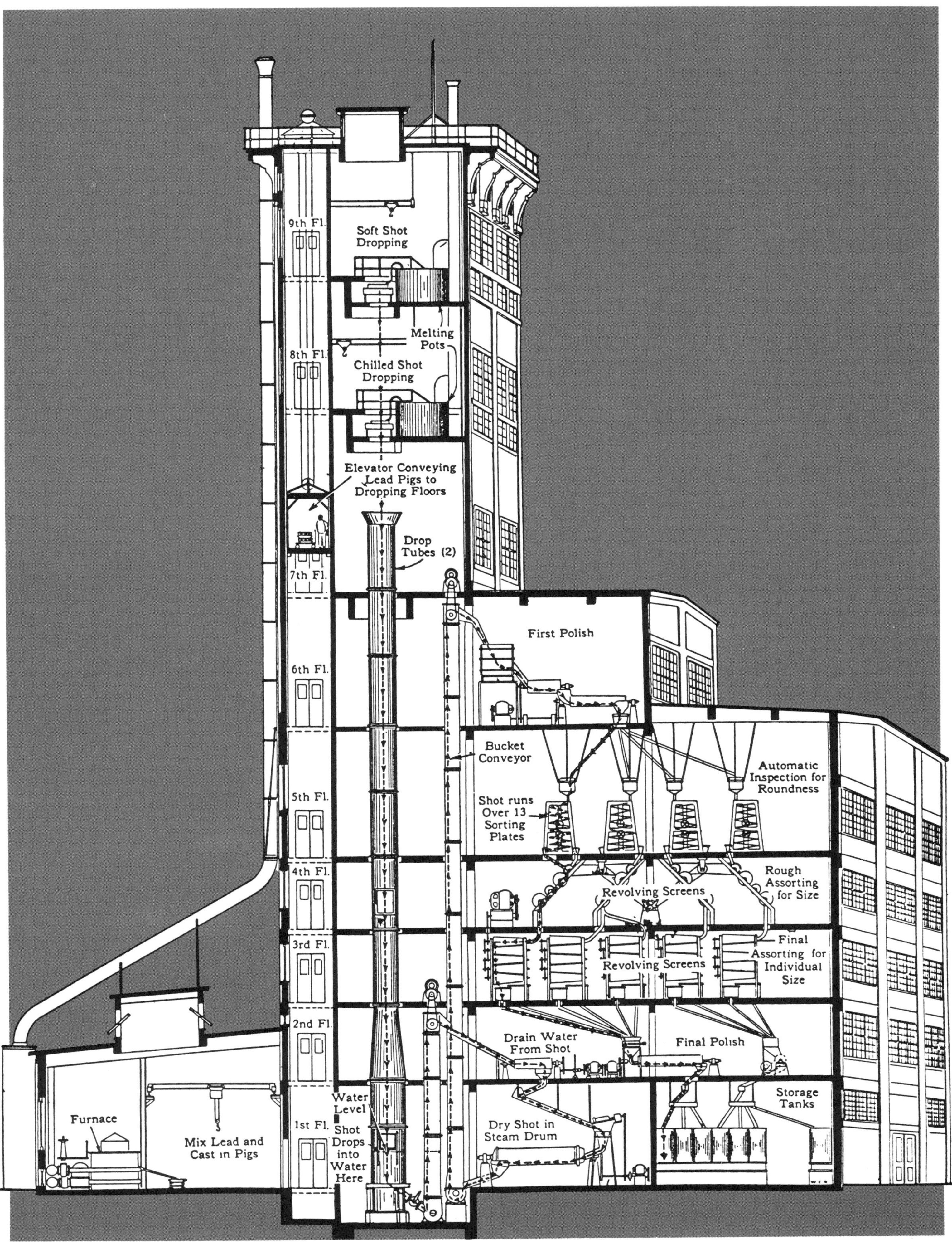

9th Fl.
Soft Shot Dropping
Melting Pots
8th Fl.
Chilled Shot Dropping
Elevator Conveying Lead Pigs to Dropping Floors
Drop Tubes (2)
7th Fl.
First Polish
6th Fl.
Bucket Conveyor
Automatic Inspection for Roundness
5th Fl.
Shot runs Over 13 Sorting Plates
4th Fl.
Rough Assorting for Size
Revolving Screens
3rd Fl.
Final Assorting for Individual Size
Revolving Screens
2nd Fl.
Drain Water From Shot
Final Polish
Water Level
1st Fl.
Shot Drops into Water Here
Storage Tanks
Furnace
Mix Lead and Cast in Pigs
Dry Shot in Steam Drum

The Company Twentieth

By the start of the twentieth century, Winchester's reputation as a manufacturer of quality firearms was well established. *Below:* The Winchester Model 1887, the first successful repeating shotgun. This particular shotgun was used by railway express car guards. *Above:* The Winchester Model 1897, one of the most popular shotguns ever made.

Enters the Century

The 20-year period surrounding the turn of the century was marked by level prices, reflecting a generally stable business atmosphere. This stability was exemplified by Winchester's price list, which had only the most minor changes—most of these additions or deletions to the catalogue—over a period of 24 years. The company prospered, and many new products entered the line, including the Winchester Pump Action; the Model 1890 Rimfire; the Model 92 Center Fire Lever Action; the Model 94, the first Winchester designed for smokeless powder; the Model 97 Pump Shotgun; the Model 1898 Breech Loading Saluting Cannon; the Model 03, the first really successful American semiautomatic and the Model 12.

In 1916, John Edward Otterson was elected as the first Vice President and General Superintendent of Winchester, becoming the first company head who was not a member of the Winchester family. With war impending in Europe, a vast expansion of the old Winchester plant was undertaken to fulfill the war contracts. Winchester became the supplier of Enfields to the British army, eventually delivering over a half million rifles and bayonets to the Western front. When America entered the war in 1917, the company switched to manufacturing arms for the US Army. More than 50,000 Browning Automatic Rifles and several hundred million rounds of ammunition were sold.

During World War I, the short barreled version of the Winchester Model 97 shotgun (widely known as a 'riot gun') was used by the American troops as a trench gun. Groups of American soldiers that were especially skilled at trap shooting were armed with these guns and stationed where they could fire at any hand grenades thrown and thus deflect them from falling into the American trenches.

The Americans generally fired .34 caliber buck shot in their shotguns, each load consisting of six shot pellets. They also employed these guns against German soldiers, and the ensuing German casualties prompted the German government to contact Secretary of State Lansing on 14 September 1918 and protest the use of the shotguns by the American Army, calling attention to the fact that according to the laws of war every prisoner found to have in his possession such guns or ammunition would immediately forfeit his life.

The passage in the Hague Decrees alluded to in the German protest refers to the use of arms calculated to cause 'unnecessary' suffering. The American reply noted that the shotguns did not fall under the Hague ban and that if the Germans carried out their death threat 'in a single instance' the United States Government knew what to do in the way of reprisals and gave notice of its intention to carry them out.

The Americans continued their grisly work, and by November 1918 two more models (the Winchester Hammerless and the Remington) were scheduled to be brought into production when Germany suddenly surrendered. The author's own grandfather was one of these shotgun-toting Dough Boys and remembers him recounting stories of this period.

Employment at Winchester rose to more than 15,000 during the war, the highest it would ever be, but several things went wrong during this period. Prices had been stable for almost 25 years and had lulled the company into signing long term fixed price contracts just as wages and costs of goods were making dramatic upward trends. The expansion of the plant had been carried on haphazardly and new buildings had been erected among the old ones. Instead of increasing efficiency, the expansion had decreased efficiency

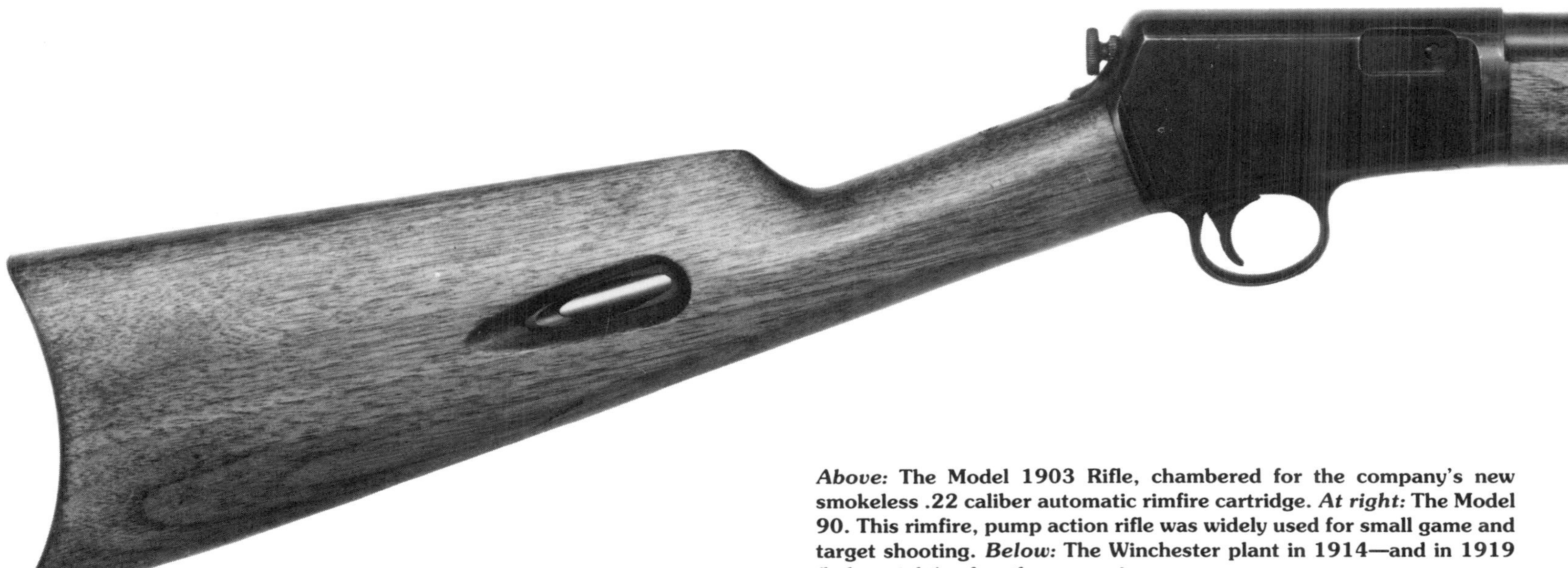

Above: **The Model 1903 Rifle, chambered for the company's new smokeless .22 caliber automatic rimfire cartridge.** ***At right:*** **The Model 90. This rimfire, pump action rifle was widely used for small game and target shooting.** ***Below:*** **The Winchester plant in 1914—and in 1919 (below right), after the expansion.**

by making it impossible to consolidate operations into the new buildings because they were so spread out.

At the end of the war, contracts were cancelled—this idled large portions of the plant principally because sales of sporting arms lagged. But the biggest worry in 1919 was the amount of income tax the company would have to pay for its war years profits. Estimations of the amount of tax actually owed ranged from 18 to 80 percent, and this caused so much concern in management that, in order to be prepared to pay the tax and still leave enough money for 'new projects,' Winchester borrowed $3 million from Kidder Peabody.

This last sum was in addition to a loan of $16 million the company had borrowed to finance the recent expansion, of which only $8 million had been paid off. Even when the income tax problem was resolved with the payment of $3.14 million to the government, the arms and ammunition business was deemed too small to pay off the remaining indebtedness—which now stood at about $17 million dollars total. Therefore, an agreement between the stockholders, Kidder Peabody, Otterson and Louis K Liggett to reorganize the company and expand into new areas was signed.

Mr Liggett was the founder and President of the United Drug Company and had made millions of dollars organizing the first nationwide chain of drug stores and supplying them with his own brands of merchandise under the trade name of Rexall. Kidder Peabody thought very highly of him and considered the Winchester resurrection possible only if he were directly involved in the planning and operation of the new experiment.

In early 1920, the Winchester Company was organized with JE Otterson as President and was divided into two divisions—The Winchester Repeating Arms Company, manufacturer of the firearms and ammunition, and the Winchester Company, which was to establish a chain of Winchester dealer agents and open Winchester retail stores that would sell all of the new Winchester line of home hardware.

This new hardware product line, usually manufactured at the arms plant, included knives, cutlery, fishing equipment, hand tools, skis, wrenches, batteries, flashlights, carpenter tools, ice skates, roller skates, paint, varnish, brushes, baseball bats, athletic equipment, kitchen appliances, washing machines, and the Ice-O-Later gas refrigerator. This major

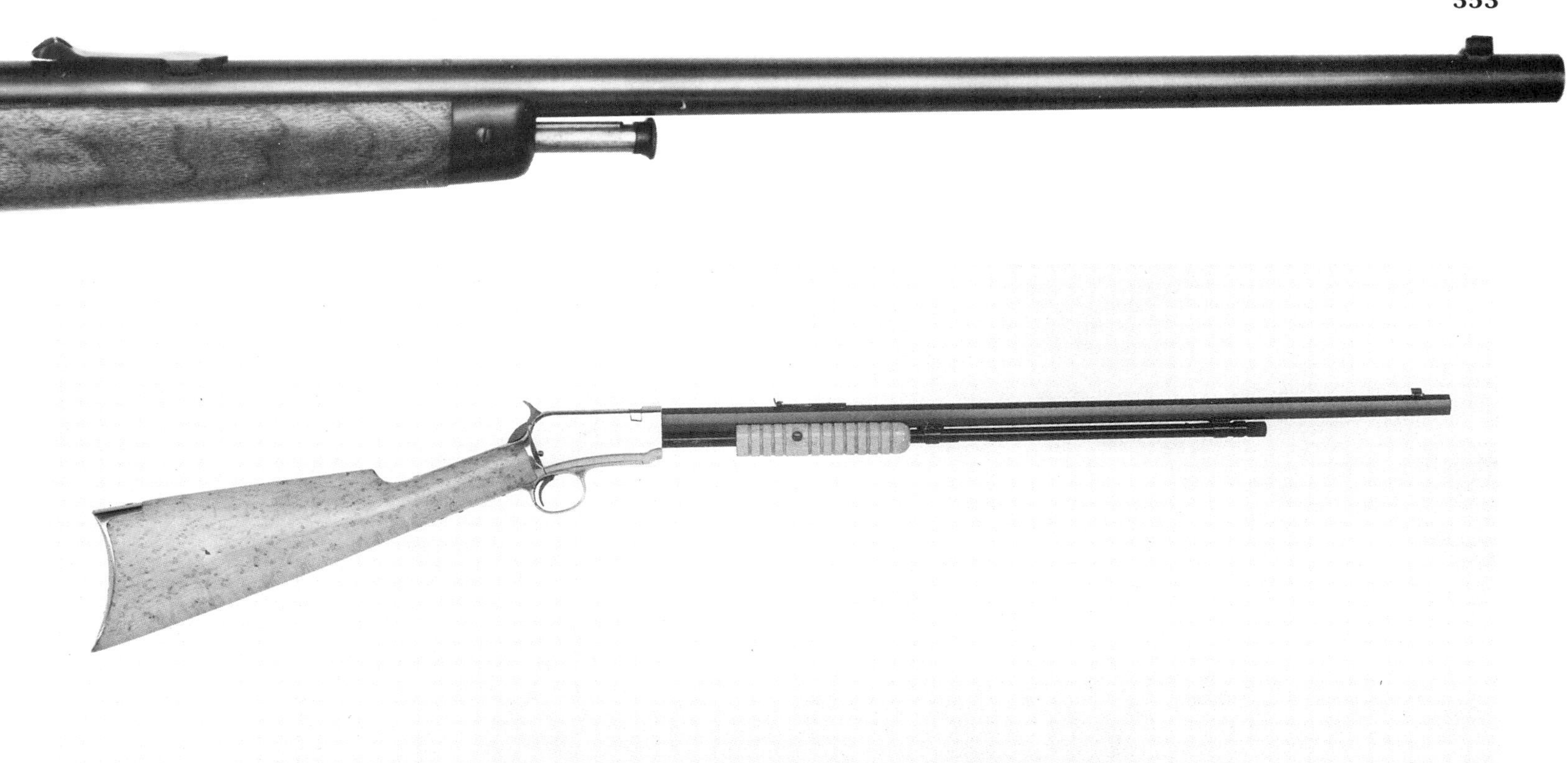

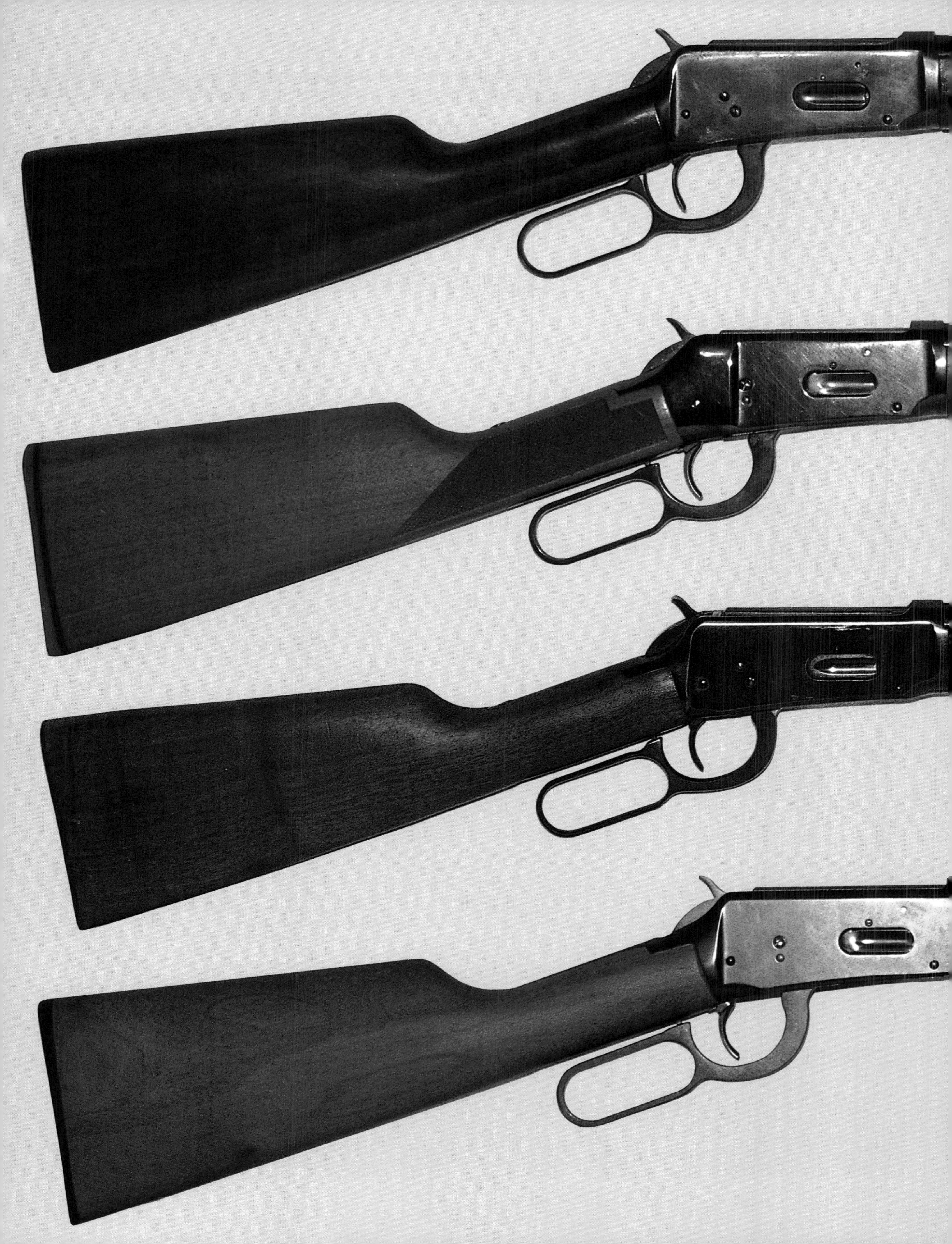

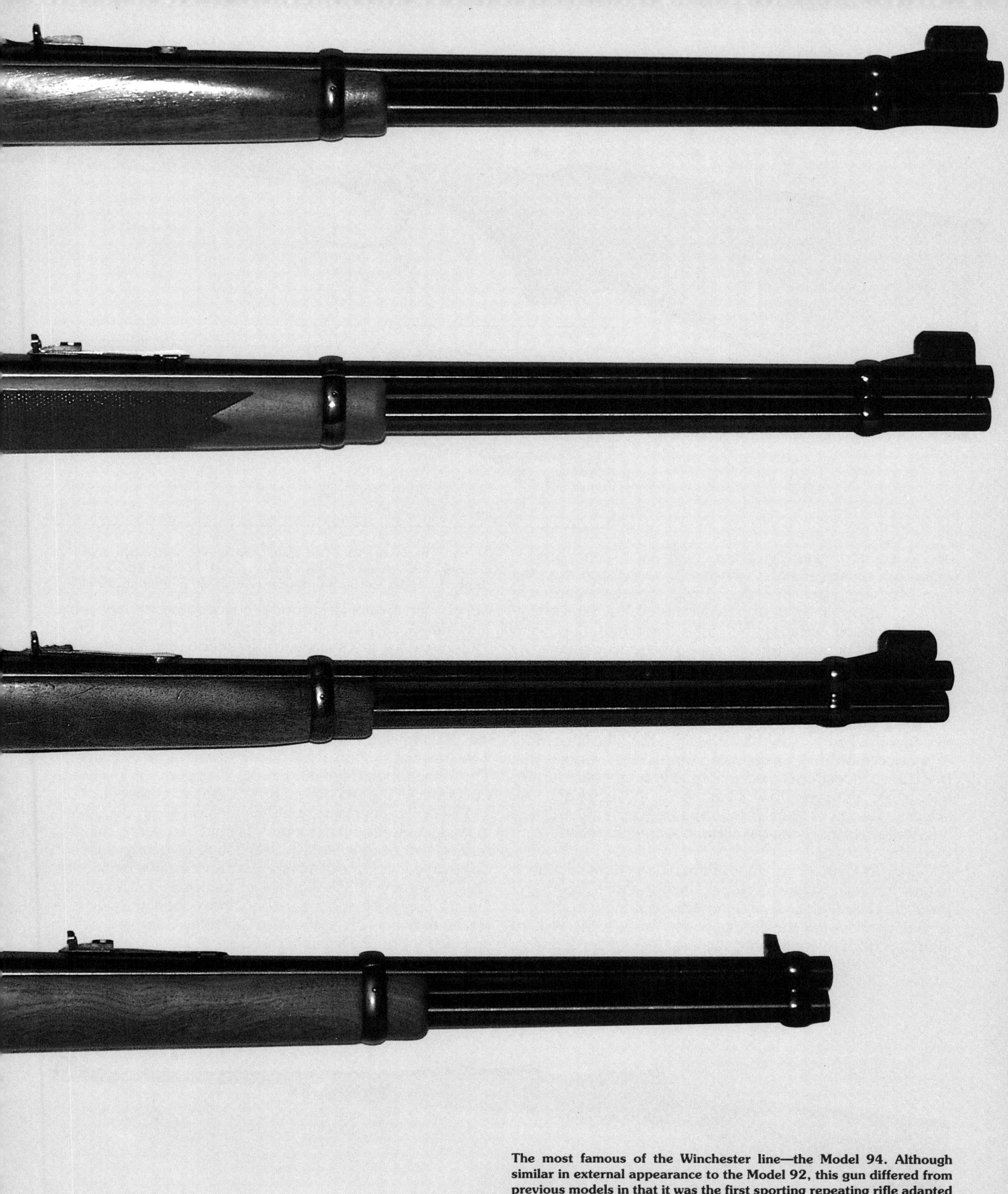

The most famous of the Winchester line—the Model 94. Although similar in external appearance to the Model 92, this gun differed from previous models in that it was the first sporting repeating rifle adapted for the smokeless cartridge. The Model 94 was especially popular in the West, where it quickly became standard equipment for settlers, hunters and ranchers. *Above, from top to bottom:* The Model 94 .32 Special Rifle, the Model 94 .357 Caliber Big Bore, the Model 94 .30-30 Caliber and the Model 94 Trapper Special .30-30 Caliber.

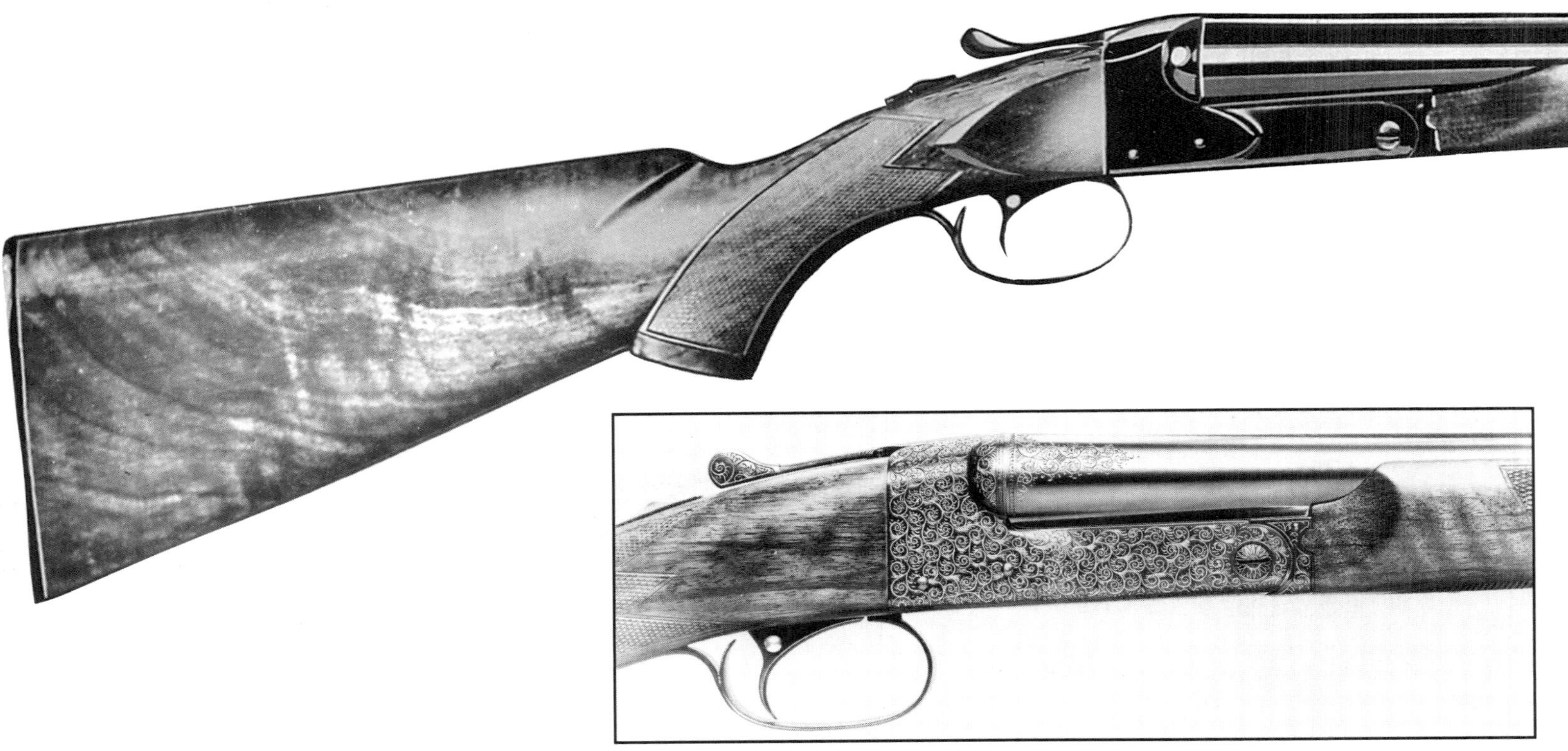

At top: The Model 21 Field Gun. Above: The intricately engraved receiver of the Model 21 Grand American. At bottom: The Model 54. Opposite: In the 1920s, Winchester ventured into other product lines.

expansion into areas that were unfamiliar to the management and technical staffs appears to have been doomed from the very start. In order to buy expertise, hardware manufacturing companies were purchased, but this strategy generally failed because the only companies that were willing to sell out were usually weak and noncompetitive or possessing only obsolete product lines.

As Winchester's acquisitions and expansions roared into the 1920s, their debt service became staggering. Sales of all hardware product lines began to lag and costs continued to run uncontrolled, making all, or nearly all, of the lines more expensive than their respective competitions. Substantial pressure to give special concessions to in-house sales further aggravated the cash flow situation of the company. All available resources were being used to keep the hardware business afloat and keep the numerous creditor wolves from the door.

During this period, arms and ammunition profits continued to perform well; however, a lack of investment in design and production facilities or equipment was beginning to show in declining sales and increasing costs. Despite the lack of attention from management, the engineering departments were continuing to design and produce some fine new arms. The Model 52 rimfire rifle in 1920 and the Model 54 in 1924 were the first successful bolt action rifles produced by Winchester.

With only a minor redesign and facelift, the Model 54 became the Model 70 in 1937. The Model 21 made its debut in 1931. However, firearms sales were not enough to keep the sinking ship afloat and by February of 1929 the Winchester Company was dissolved and a new company, The Winchester Repeating Arms Company of Delaware, took over all the old obligations of the old company.

The dealer agents were disbanded and all products were to be sold on the open market. Within two years, the debt service had become totally debilitating at nearly a million dollars a year, and the company was propelled into bankruptcy on 21 January 1931. Winchester had gone down with the Great Depression. It was to rise again less than one year later on the shoulders of the Western Cartridge Company, which acquired it on 22 December 1931.

THE
WINCHESTER
HERALD
New WINCHESTER PADLOCKS
Modern Protection
WINCHESTER
"AS GOOD AS THE GUN"

WINCHESTER
TRADE MARK
TOOLS
Largest and most complete line of tools offered by any manufacturer under one brand—
WINCHESTER
Fine tools made for exclusive distribution to the retail trade through the stores of Winchester Dealers
WINCHESTER
BIT BRACES

The "Young Idea"
Turns to the Sport of Roller Skating
At the time when the fisherman feels the Izaak Walton rising in him and the shooter grows impatient under the lure of target and trap, the active "young idea" turns to strenuous days in the open. With increasing thousands all over America each year this means that a large outlet for their energy is in the sport of roller skating.
With vigorous municipal and recreation center promotion this healthful, joy-filled sport is growing in popularity every year. Besides the thousands of initiates who will be in the market for the best in roller skates as their first equipment there is that army of old timers to whom new skates will be necessary or who will be ready for better ones this year.
The demand for
WINCHESTER
TRADE MARK
ROLLER SKATES
In 1922 was more than 50% greater than in 1921

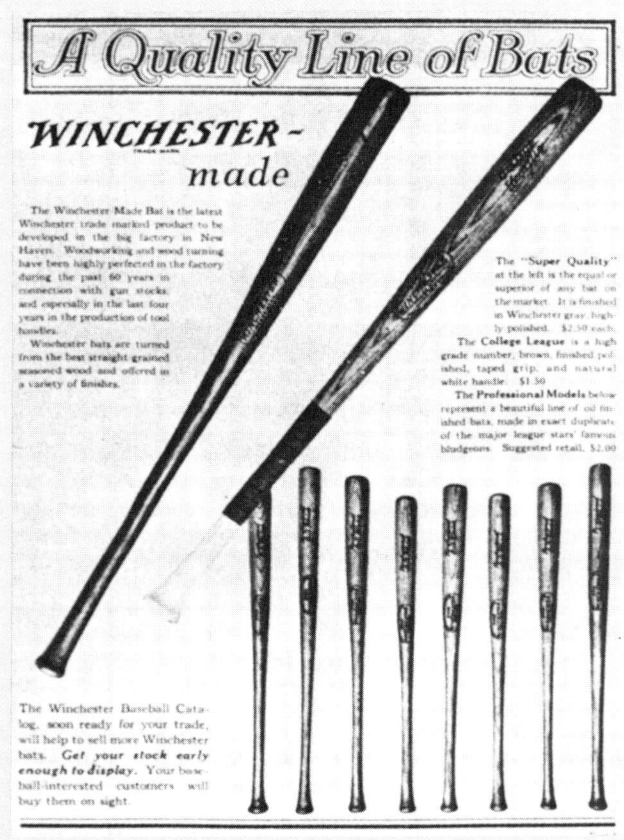
A Quality Line of Bats
WINCHESTER-
TRADE MARK
made
The Winchester Made Bat is the latest Winchester trade marked product to be developed in the big factory in New Haven. Woodworking and wood turning have been highly perfected in the factory during the past 60 years in connection with gun stocks, and especially in the last four years in the production of tool handles.
Winchester bats are turned from the best straight grained seasoned wood and offered in a variety of finishes.
The "Super Quality" at the left is the equal or superior of any bat on the market. It is finished in Winchester gray, highly polished. $2.50 each.
The College League is a high grade number, brown, finished polished, taped grip, and natural white handle. $1.50
The Professional Models below represent a beautiful line of oil finished bats, made in exact duplicate of the major league stars' famous bludgeons. Suggested retail, $2.00
The Winchester Baseball Catalog, soon ready for your trade, will help to sell more Winchester bats. Get your stock early enough to display. Your baseball-interested customers will buy them on sight.

The Cartridge

The Western Cartridge Company had its roots in Franklin W Olin, who founded, in 1892, the Equitable Powder Manufacturing Company of East Alton, Illinois. Initially that company had produced black powder for use in southern Illinois coal mines, but by 1894 had switched its emphasis to production of 'sporting powder' for ammunition. Aware of the growing popularity of factory loaded ammunition, Olin began work on a machine that would load shotgun shells and this invention established the Western Cartridge Company.

Olin believed in 'hands on' involvement in the important elements of developing the company's various product lines and Western's reputation for manufacturing quality products grew until, by the turn of the century, it was a major force in the ammunition business. The reliability of its ammunition earned the Western Cartridge Company commendations from the US and Allied governments during World War I.

Franklin Olin was succeeded by his son, John, who himself was gifted with an inventive mind. Young John shared his father's interest in the technical side of the business, and his interests in the development of smokeless powder for commercial use resulted in the introduction of Western's Super-X ammunition, which is still available today. The demand for these Super-X shells was so great among hunters and sportsmen that the Western Cartridge Company soon rose to a position of absolute dominance in the ammunition industry.

With the purchase of Winchester, the Winchester-Western Company became the largest owner of patents on ammunition and firearms in the world. Relying on the same innovative spirit that started the company, John Olin took an active interest in the development of the ammunition and firearms now produced by Winchester. By 1940, Winchester-Western had introduced 23 new guns to its line and was in a solid position to serve the country once more as World War II approached. By that war's end the company had produced more than 15 billion rounds of ammunition and 1.5 million military arms.

Following the war, Winchester-Western continued to remain on the leading edge of ammunition technology, with a list of innovative firsts that included Ball Powder propellant in 1946, the Baby Magnum shotshell in 1954, the .22 Winchester Magnum Rimfire cartridge in 1959, the Mark 5 shotshell in 1962, the Compression-Formed plastic shotshell in 1964, the Double A target load in 1965, the Super Double X 10 gauge shotshell in 1968, the Silvertip hollow-point load in 1979 and the Super-X 10 gauge Magnum steel shot load in 1982.

Western Company

Introduced in 1924, the Model 54 Rifle *(above)* marked Winchester's entry into the heavy caliber, bolt action field. In 1980, Winchester introduced the Model 23 Shotgun *(below)*, which is manufactured by a subsidiary in Japan. It was the first side-by-side shotgun produced by Winchester in 20 years.

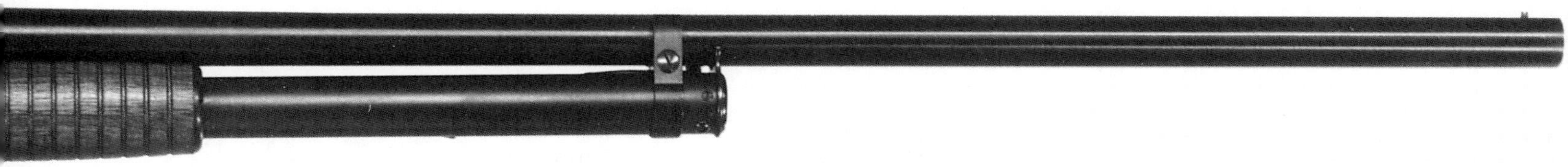

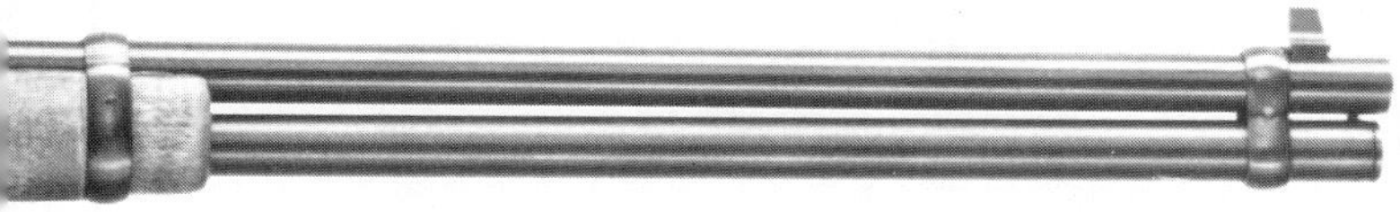

At top and bottom: Two views of the Model 1912 Shotgun. Priced at $20, this gun was an immediate best seller. General Curtis E LeMay *(above)* fires his Model 1912 Trap Gun. *Center, above and below:* The Model 70 Magnum Bolt Action Center Fire Rifle—and the Model 94 Ranger Carbine with Bushnell Sportview 4X scope and see-through mounts.

Winchester

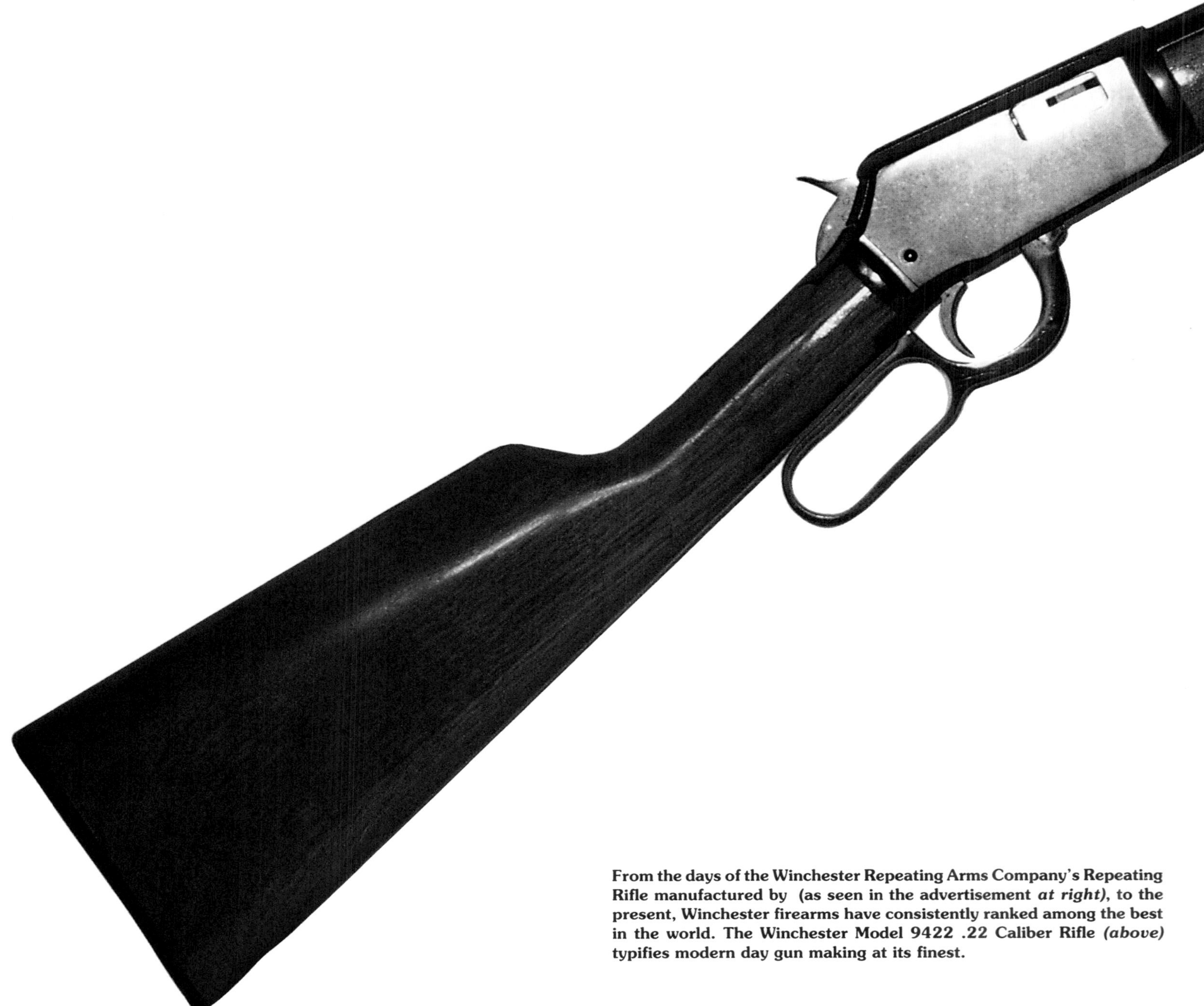

From the days of the Winchester Repeating Arms Company's Repeating Rifle manufactured by (as seen in the advertisement *at right*), to the present, Winchester firearms have consistently ranked among the best in the world. The Winchester Model 9422 .22 Caliber Rifle *(above)* typifies modern day gun making at its finest.

Today

In August 1954, Olin merged with Mattheson Chemcal Corporation to form Olin Mattheson, one of America's largest industrial complexes. In December 1980, Olin's board of directors authorized the disposal of the company's Winchester Sporting Arms business in the United States, and on 20 July 1981 Winchester was sold to the US Repeating Arms Company, which was actually a group of former employees, investors and bankers. Today the firm, though currently under bankruptcy court protection, is still making the famed Winchester rifles under a license from Olin. (It is interesting to note that in January of 1988 Browning acquired 37 percent interest in Winchester arms.)

Olin's Winchester Operations branch continues to manufacture sporting and defense ammunition and market its Japanese-produced line of high-quality over-and-under and side-by-side shotguns. The worldwide operations of today's Winchester include headquarters and an ammunition manufacturing plant (complimented by Olin's brass mill) in East Alton, Illinois; a ball powder propellant manufacturing plant in St Mark's, Florida; and a defense products manufacturing facility at Marion, Illinois.

Winchester operations also include the Lake City Army Ammunition Plant at Independence, Missouri; a Winchester shotshell plant at Anagni, Italy; and another ammunition plant in Australia. Olin-Kodensha (OK Firearms Company) at Tochigi, Japan produces the popular Classic Doubles line of Winchester shotguns. Whatever the future may bring, it is clear that when you load up with Winchester, you load up with a legend.

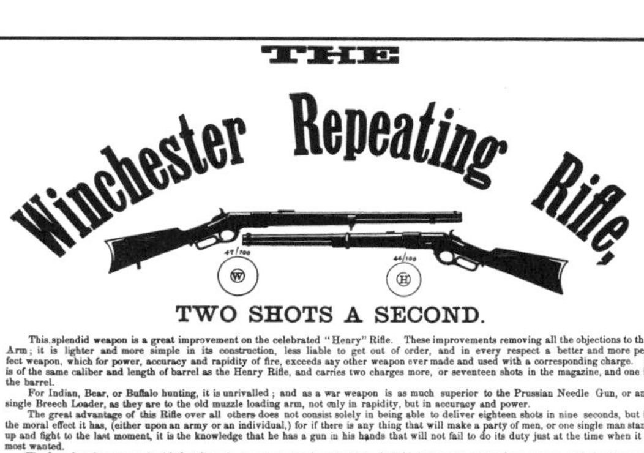

THE

Winchester Repeating Rifle,

47/100 W 44/100 H

TWO SHOTS A SECOND.

This splendid weapon is a great improvement on the celebrated "Henry" Rifle. These improvements removing all the objections to that Arm; it is lighter and more simple in its construction, less liable to get out of order, and in every respect a better and more perfect weapon, which for power, accuracy and rapidity of fire, exceeds any other weapon ever made and used with a corresponding charge. It is of the same caliber and length of barrel as the Henry Rifle, and carries two charges more, or seventeen shots in the magazine, and one in the barrel.

For Indian, Bear, or Buffalo hunting, it is unrivalled; and as a war weapon is as much superior to the Prussian Needle Gun, or any single Breech Loader, as they are to the old muzzle loading arm, not only in rapidity, but in accuracy and power.

The great advantage of this Rifle over all others does not consist solely in being able to deliver eighteen shots in nine seconds, but in the moral effect it has, (either upon an army or an individual,) for if there is any thing that will make a party of men, or one single man stand up and fight to the last moment, it is the knowledge that he has a gun in his hands that will not fail to do its duty just at the time when it is most wanted.

The first thought connected with fast firing is, a great waste of ammunition—but this is in reality quite the contrary; as it is not necessary to commence firing at the enemy when five or six hundred yards off, (for fear of being unable to load up again before he gets right on you), but the fire can be reserved until he is within one hundred, or even fifty yards (with the assurance that before he can get up to you, you can deliver either eighteen or fourteen shots as the case may be, whether you have a Rifle or Carbine), and consequently there is so much greater chance of being able to make every shot count.

The advantage that this Gun possesses over all others for *single individuals* traveling through a wild country, where there is reason to expect a sudden attack either from *robbers or Indians*, cannot be *over-estimated*, as it is well known to all who have used a gun to any extent (especially in close quarters), that there is a *little* uncertainty of its going off; but with this Gun there can be no such feeling, because even though a Cartridge should miss fire, it is drawn from the barrel with *unfailing certainty*, and another placed in its stead, and fired in just *half a second*, thereby giving two chances, even though the enemy should be within twenty feet at the firing of the first shot, which is something that no other Rifle yet built is capable of doing.

For those living in a country where there is reason to expect an attack from *Indians*, (and as it is at times necessary for all the men to be away from home, consequently leaving their wives and children to fight for themselves), this Gun is what has long been wanted; it is so simple in its construction, that a child ten years old can with half an hours instruction, load and fire it with perfect safety, it being impossible to get a cartridge into it otherwise than right.

Another great advantage that it has over all other Rifles is, that it can be loaded and fired as a Single Breech Loader as fast as any other Breech Loading Gun that is built, either in this country or Europe, at the same time having in the magazine in reserve *sixteen shots* that can be used in an emergency as before stated; this last advantage places it far ahead of any other Rifle yet made, whether it is Repeating or Single Loading. With regard to penetration, it is fully equal to any other Rifle that is made, having the same length of barrel, charge of powder and caliber, or bore.

The greatest care is taken in making the barrels, (which are all of steel); the straightening of them is done by the best workmen that can be found; the rifling is also done by experienced men, and with the most improved machinery, consequently with regard to *accuracy* they are equal to the best Target Rifles.

At present but two sizes are made, namely, a rifle with an octagon barrel, twenty-four inches long, and weighing nine and a half pounds, and carrying seventeen shots in the magazine, and one in the barrel, or eighteen shots in all, all of which can be fired by an expert in nine seconds, or at the rate of two shots per second. Also a carbine with a round barrel, twenty inches long, carrying thirteen shots in the magazine, and one in the barrel, or fourteen shots in all, weighing seven and a half pounds; this is especially adapted to the use of cavalry, as for hunting on the western plains. Both these guns use the same charge, or cartridge as is used in the old model Henry Rifle. None are genuine without the letter H or W raised in the end of the copper cartridge.

To the following price list the cost of packing will be added in all cases. Box for single guns seventy-five cents. Cases for ten guns $2.50. Lining boxes with tin for shipment holding ten guns, $3.50 each extra.

Rifles with varnished Stocks and Slings,	$50.00
Carbines with oiled Stocks without Slings,	40.00
Cartridges, per 1000,	20 00
Slings for Carbines,	2.50
Leather Cases,	6.00 to 7.50
Extra finish with plating and engraving will cost from	60 00 to 100.00

CAUTION.

As much of the accuracy and power of any good Rifle depends upon the *care* and accuracy with which the amunition is made, and the quality of the material. We have paid, and still pay great attention to keeping up the quality of our Cartridges, and none are genuine, or of our make, except those that have the letter H or the letter W raised in the metal on the head of the copper shell. All manufacturers are cautioned against using or copying this trade mark. All our arms that have gun metal frames and mountings, use the catridges with the letter H. All cartridges with the letter W, are adapted to the new models, with Iron Frames and mounting, designed expressly for army use.

All buyers who want a reliable article are cautioned against buying any of the poor trash in the market, some of which is offered at one to three, or even five dollars per 1000 less than a good article can be sold for. Sold by all the principal gun dealers in the country.

MANUFACTURED BY THE

WINCHESTER REPEATING ARMS CO.,

New Haven, Conn.

O. P. DAVIS, Sec'y. O. F. WINCHESTER, Pres't.

Theodore Roosevelt

Theodore Roosevelt was born in New York on 27 October 1858. By the time he graduated from Harvard in 1880, he had become both an excellent boxer and an avid sportsman. In 1884, he became a rancher in North Dakota, where he served as a local deputy sheriff. Roosevelt captured these western experiences in his book *Hunting Trips of a Ranchman*, which was published in 1885. It was in this volume that he first expressed his enthusiasm for Winchester rifles.

The Sharps and English Express rifles of his time were noted for their vicious recoil, but when Teddy came into contact with a .45-75 Winchester Model 76 Half Magazine, his lifelong love affair with Winchesters was born. The Model 76 was a pleasure to shoot, it was accurate and handy, and was quite equal to any kind of hunting to be found in North America. In short order, Teddy also acquired a .44 caliber WCF Winchester Model 73, a .45-75 caliber WCF Winchester Model 76, and a Hammerless Top Lever Breechloading Double Shotgun.

When Roosevelt's Rough Riders went to Cuba during the Spanish-American War, Teddy brought along his .30 caliber Winchester Model 95. His exploits as Colonel Roosevelt of the Rough Riders brought him such notoriety that in 1898 he was elected Governor of New York. Roosevelt was elected Vice President of the United States under President McKinley in 1901 and became the 26th President of the United States when the latter was assassinated. He served the remainder of McKinley's term and was returned to the presidency in 1904 by a large majority.

It was during his last year in office that Roosevelt began extensive preparations for his now famous African trip with his son, Kermit, to gather specimens for the Smithsonian Institution. Naturally Teddy wanted to use Winchester rifles and ammunition on the hunt, and so entered into extensive correspondence with the Winchester Company to procure weapons to his exacting specifications.

In his many letters to Winchester, Teddy showed himself to be both impersonal and difficult to please. He became very upset over the way the guns were first made even though he was himself chiefly responsible for the confusion. The management of Winchester, however, saw the inestimable worth of having the President of the United States use their weapons in such a public setting, and so handled the matter with both tact and diplomacy by sparing no effort to give Roosevelt exactly what he wanted.

Teddy's initial choice of weapons was as follows: a .30-40 caliber Model 95, two .405 caliber Model 95s and a .45-70 caliber Model 86. After considerable discussion, it was decided that the company would supply two .405 caliber Model 95 rifles and one .30 caliber Model 95, chambered for the US Government ammunition, as well as all of the ammunition needed for the trip.

The President's great African hunting trip began on 23 March 1909 when he, his son Kermit and a group of naturalists sailed from New York for Mombasa, British East Africa. The party landed in April of that year and spent the next 11 months hunting wild animals. They sent back to the United States a total of 4897 mammals, more than 4000 birds, 2000 reptiles and approximately 500 fishes, besides numerous other specimens. Accounts of the trip written by Roosevelt ran in *Scribner's Magazine* during the years 1909 and 1910 and were later incorporated into his book entitled *African Game Trails.*

Teddy lavishly praised his Winchester weapons in all of these accounts, and Winchester lavishly quoted him in their advertising campaigns. One example read 'Tarlton took his big double-barrel and advised me to take mine as the sun had just set and it was likely to be close work; but I shook my head, for the Winchester .405 is, at least for me personally, the "medicine gun" for lions.'

Far left: **Theodore Roosevelt the hunter, in 1883 with his Model 1876.** ***At bottom:*** **Two views of Roosevelt's finely engraved Model 1876 in .40-60 caliber.** ***At above left:*** **'Teddy' and his hunting companions Wilmont Dow (photo left) and Bill Sewell (photo right).** ***Left, center:*** **The Winchester ammunition wagon for Roosevelt's famed African Safari.**

'Buffalo Bill' Cody

William Frederick Cody promoted himself into the ranks of such legendary Americans as Kit Carson, Daniel Boone, Jim Bridger and 'Wild Bill' Hickok. He was both a superb rider and marksman and, between 1872 and 1916, he recreated the atmosphere of the American West before European and American audiences principally through his now famous Wild West Show.

Cody was never employed by the Winchester company to publicize its products, but Winchesters were associated with him and many of his fellow marksmen in the Wild West Show from the very beginning. Cody was featured in over 200 'nickel novels' (the forerunners to modern comic books) and, either directly or indirectly, was always associated with Winchester firearms, as is evidenced by the following quote from one of those cheap thrillers. 'Buffalo Bill turned in his saddle and sent a dozen shots from his Winchester rattling back up the hill at the savages...Crack! Crack! went Buffalo Bill's Winchester, and howls and yells followed the reports.'

One of Cody's personal Winchester favorites was his smoothbore .44 Caliber Model 73 with which he used shot shells. These shells were necessary for safety reasons, because the shot would disperse and drop harmlessly within the grounds of the exhibition centers. However, this in no way detracted from Cody's marksmanship. He was known to have terrified his wife by shooting coins from between the fingers of his own children (who of course had complete confidence in their father's acumen). Winchester never failed to publicize the fact that its guns were the first choice of such star performers. This semi-elitism became the hallmark of Winchester advertising. A typical example would read:

'Look all the makes over, but if you are not swayed from your purpose of getting the gun with the maximum of strength, safety, ease and certainty, good shooting and good wearing qualities, you will surely select a Winchester. There are other makes, but the Winchester is the only one that has successfully stood every conceivable test that sportsmen could put to it, and also the rigid technical trials of the US Ordnance Board, embracing strength, accuracy, penetration, endurance, excessive loads, defective shells, rust and dust.

'Its popularity with sportsmen and its official endorsement by Government Experts are convincing proof of its reliability and wearing and shooting qualities. Stick to a Winchester and you won't get stuck!'

Far right: **Buffalo Bill Cody, the showman of the American frontier, did much both directly and indirectly to spread the fame of Winchester firearms. In his famous Wild West Show, he and his fellow sharpshooters—including Annie Oakley—used Winchester rifles and ammunition. As the hero of Western nickel novels *(at right, above and below)*, Buffalo Bill was armed with Winchester rifles in his battles against Indians and outlaws.**

Robert Peary

Admiral Robert Peary, had long claimed to be the first man to reach the North Pole on 6 April 1909. While controversy has raged around Peary's achievement one thing is certain: he carried with him a Winchester Model 92. Advertisements such as the following were circulated by Winchester in 1909, under the heading 'The Rifle That Helped Peary Reach the North Pole.' Peary is quoted as saying—

'Personally I always carry a Winchester rifle. On my last expedition I had a Model 1892 .44 caliber Carbine, and Winchester cartridges, which I carried with me right to the North Pole. After I left the ship, I depended upon it to bring down the fresh meat that we needed. Since 1888, both in Nicaragua and in the Arctic regions, I have always used the Winchester Repeaters.

'Each of my Arctic expeditions since '91 has been fitted with these arms. The last expedition carried the .44-40 Carbine, for use on deer, seals, hare and the like, and the .40-82 for use on musk-oxen, walrus and polar bears. In facing the polar bears, in gathering a herd of musk-oxen with the least expenditure of time and priceless ammunition, and in securing the greatest number of walrus out of an infuriated herd in the least time, I desire nothing better than a Winchester Repeater.'

Adolph and 'Plinky' Topperwein

In the early 1900s, Winchester employed the son of a German gunsmith named Adolph Topperwein to represent the company as an exhibition shooter. In 1903, Topperwein married Elizabeth Servaty, who worked in the ammunition loading room at the Winchester plant at New Haven. Until she was married, Mrs Topperwein's acquaintance with shooting had not extended beyond the loading of ammunition, but she quickly proved to have an exceptional talent as a markswoman.

She set her first world's record in trap shooting in 1904 at the World's Fair in St Louis by breaking 967 clay targets out of a possible 1000 and was ever after known as 'Plinky' Topperwein. Winchester immediately arranged to have the Topperweins travel as a team, and they took their place among the world's finest shooters. The couple's feats are indeed impressive.

Plinky once 'shot trap' for a total time of five hours using a pump gun, and hit 1952 clays out of 2000 thrown. Adolph, firing a .22 caliber Winchester rifle at 2.5 inch wooden blocks tossed into the air, shot steadily, eight hours a day for 10 consecutive days, hitting a total of 72,491 blocks, missing only nine. Of the first 50,000 blocks, he missed only four, and had a number of runs of more than 10,000 without a miss, and one perfect run of 14,540.

Even more amazing, Adolph specialized in targeting playing cards held edge-on at a distance, and one of his most astonishing feats involved extinguishing lighted matches that were held by assistants—by shooting backward from a prone position using a mirror to sight the target! He could also hit potatoes thrown directly toward him, break balls thrown over his head from directly behind, and break targets thrown directly in front of him.

His most famous shot was billed as never having been accomplished by any other shooter in the world. In this, he threw balls into the air and broke them, using a rifle with solid bullets while riding a bicycle at full speed. The Topperweins retired from travelling for Winchester in 1940, still retaining their status as excellent mark shooters—despite the fact that Adolph was 70 years old and his wife but a few years younger. They had done much to keep the name of Winchester before the public.

Opposite, above: **Admiral Robert Peary carried a Winchester Model 92 with him on his historic expedition to the North Pole.** ***Opposite, below:*** **The midnight sun on the horizon above the Arctic.** ***Below, left and right:*** **'Plinky' and Adolph Topperwein. For 36 years, the Topperweins represented Winchester as exhibition shooters. Their fancy shots did much to promote the Winchester name.**

Major Winchester

The Winchester Repeating Arms Company put John M Browning *(far right)* to work redesigning the repeating action of the Models 73 and 76. The end result was the Model 1886 *(above)*, a rifle with an exceptionally smooth operating action—capable of handling the heavier, more powerful ammunition loads.

Browning Models

Rifles

Single Shot Rifle. This was John M Browning's first firearm model, invented in 1878 when he was 23 years old. The patent was filed on 12 May 1879, and US Patent Number 220,271 was granted on 7 October 1879. Production by the Browning Brothers in Ogden, Utah Territory, began about 1880 and continued until 1883, with a total of approximately six hundred rifles manufactured. Manufacturing and sales rights were sold to the Winchester Repeating Arms Company in 1883 and the arm appeared in 1885 as the Winchester Single Shot Model 1885.

The Single Shot is a lever action, exposed hammer, fixed barrel single shot rifle. The hammer drops down with the breechblock when the rifle is opened and is cocked by the closing movement. It can also be cocked by hand. The Single Shot has been adapted to over 33 different calibers, more than any other single shot or repeating rifle known. Including both rimfire and center fire types, its loads range from the .22 Short to the .50-90 Sharps. It was the first Winchester rifle capable of handling the most powerful metallic cartridges of the period.

Barrel lengths vary depending on the model, from the light carbine, with a 15-inch barrel, to the 30-inch Schuetzen. Barrel styles are round, octagon, or half octagon. The weight of this arm ranges from 4.5 to 13 pounds, depending on specifications. Model styles include sporting and special sporting rifles, special target rifles, Schuetzen rifle, carbine, musket and shotgun. Stock types are many and various.

Through the years, the Single Shot was produced in a variety of models. The light carbine (called the 'Baby Carbine') appeared in 1898. The takedown model was

introduced in 1910. A special military target version was introduced in 1905; in 1914 it was revamped as the Winder Musket, named in honor of Colonel CB Winder, and was used for training troops in World War I. In 1914 the Single Shot was also made into a shotgun, chambered for the three inch, 20 gauge shell. The Single Shot was discontinued in all models in 1920. Total production of all models was approximately 140,325, which includes the 600 unit production by the Browning Brothers.

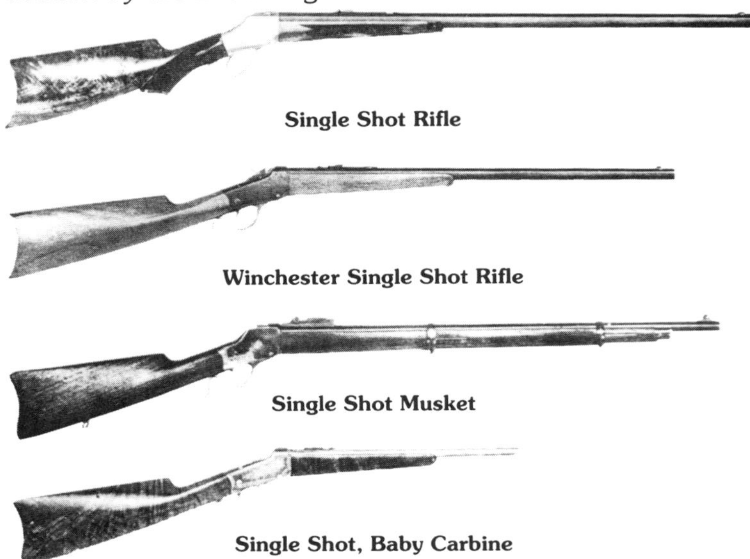

Single Shot Rifle

Winchester Single Shot Rifle

Single Shot Musket

Single Shot, Baby Carbine

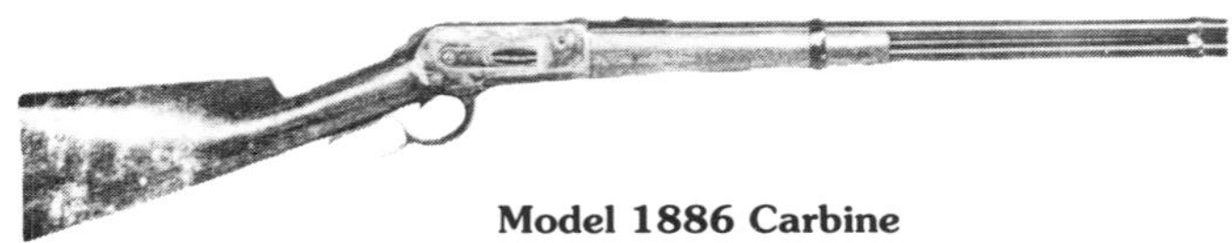

Model 1886 Carbine

Model 1886 Lever Action Repeating Rifle. Invented in 1882–83, this was the first Browning-designed repeating rifle to be manufactured. It was also the first repeating rifle to successfully employ sliding vertical locks, which effectively sealed the breech and barrel of the gun; as such it was the forerunner of all later Browning lever action repeating rifles. The patent was filed on 26 May 1884, and the US Patent No 306,577 was granted on 14 October 1884. Purchased by Winchester in October 1884, it appeared in 1886 as Model 1886.

The 1886 Lever Action is a tubular magazine, fixed barrel repeating rifle in a wide variety of calibers, including .45-70 US Government, .40-82 WCF, .45-90 WCF, 40-65 WCF, 38-56 WCF, .50-110, .40-70 WCF, .38-70 WCF, .50-100-450, .33 WCF. Options included a choice of full or half length tubular magazine of varying capacities, depending on the ammunition used.

Safeties on this firearm are manual and mechanical, and barrels include 26-inch round, octagon or half octagon, and 22-inch round. Special barrels and magazines finished to specifications were available until 1908. Stock types range from the sporter with straight or pistol grip, to extra lightweight, to shotgun, carbine and musket type stocks. The weight varies widely, depending on specifications and caliber.

In 1894, it was converted to a takedown model. In 1936 the Model 1886, slightly modified to handle the .348 Winchester cartridge, became the Model 71. The Model 1886 was discontinued in 1935 with 159,994 produced; the Model 71 was discontinued in 1957 with 43,267 produced—making the total for this gun 203,261 units during a production life of 71 years.

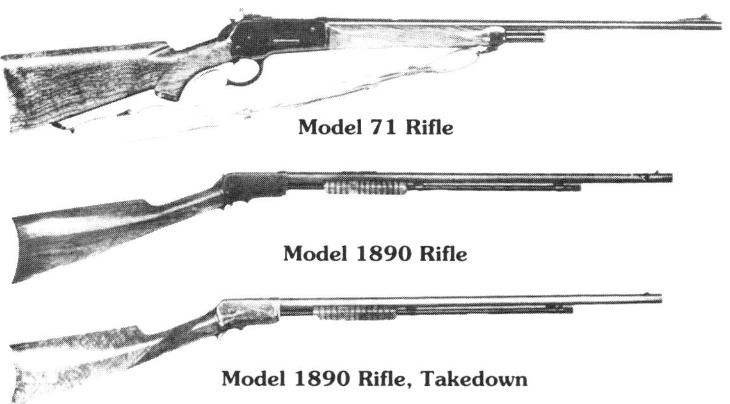

Model 71 Rifle

Model 1890 Rifle

Model 1890 Rifle, Takedown

Model 1890 .22 Caliber Pump Action Repeating Rifle. The patent application for this gun was filed on 13 December 1887, and US Patent Number 385,238 was granted on 26 June 1888. It appeared in 1890 as the Winchester .22 Caliber Repeating Rifle Model 1890, and was the first repeating pump action gun manufactured by Winchester.

The Model 1890 is a tubular magazine repeating rifle of .22 caliber (.22 short, long rifle and WRF; not originally interchangeable) with a tubular magazine of varying capacity (from 15 shorts to 11 long rifles). It has a sliding breechblock, operated by forearm slide, and both manual and mechanical safeties. It has a 24-inch octagon barrel and weighs from 5.75 to six pounds. Available stocks include a standard rifle type, with curved steel butt plate, and straight grip and optional pistol grip stocks.

The Model 1890 has been called 'the most popular .22 caliber pump action rifle ever made.' The radical improvement in this rifle over previous .22 caliber repeaters was the carrier mechanism. Previously no positive method of handling the .22 caliber short cartridges had been developed. Browning suceeded by installing a fingerlike cartridge stop in front of the carrier—this metered one cartridge at a time onto the carrier from the magazine. At the correct instant, when the spent cartridge from the chamber had been ejected, the carrier raised and held the new cartridge in positive alignment with the chamber for loading.

First manufactured with its barrel fixed to the frame, it was converted to takedown in 1893. The Model 06, introduced in 1906, incorporated a modification which enabled one rifle to accept all .22 caliber cartridges, except the .22 WRF. A 20-inch round barrel replaced the 24-inch octagon. In 1932 the Models 90 and 06 were renamed as combined 'Model 62,' with the introduction on both of a barrel with slightly different specifications and new sights. The Models 90 and 06 were discontinued in 1932 with 849,000 and 848,000 produced respectively; the Model 62 was discontinued in 1958 with 409,475 produced—making the total for this gun 2,106,475 units, with a production life of 69 years.

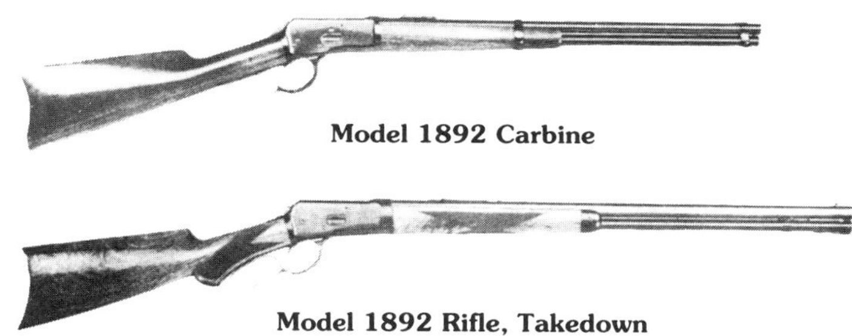

Model 1892 Carbine

Model 1892 Rifle, Takedown

Model 1892 Lever Action Repeating Rifle. This model, first manufactured by Winchester in 1892 and known as the Winchester Model 92, has the same basic design as the Model 1886, and incorporates many of its special features, including the double locking system, covered under US Patent Number 306,577. Two additional patents covered it—Number 465,339, filed on 3 August 1891 and granted on 15 December 1891, and Number 499,005, filed on 19 September 1892 and granted on 6 June 1893.

The Model 1892 is a simplified, lighter version of the Model 86, specifically designed for smaller calibers including .44-40, .38-40, .32-20 and .25-20, with a tubular magazine capacity of from five to 17 rounds. This firearm has both manual and mechanical safeties, and weighs from 5.5 to eight pounds, depending on model and caliber. Barrel lengths and styles include 24-inch round, octagon or half octagon for rifles; 20-inch round for carbines; and 30-inch round for muskets. Shorter barrels from 14 to 20 inches and special lengths up to 36 inches are also available. Stock types include sporting, carbine and musket with straight grips and fancy models with a pistol grip.

Originally, the 1892 was made with its barrel fixed to its frame, but became available in a takedown model in 1893. A modified version with a decreased magazine capacity was introduced in 1924 as the Model 53. Its successor, the Model 65, was introduced in 1933. The Model 53 was discontinued in 1932 with a total production of 24,916 units; the Model 65 was discontinued in 1947, with a total of 5704 units; the Model 92, though not produced except in the carbine model for several years after the introduction of the Model 53, was not officially discontinued until 1941, at which time 1,004,067 units had been manufactured. The manufacturing total for all variants combined stands at 1,034,687 units.

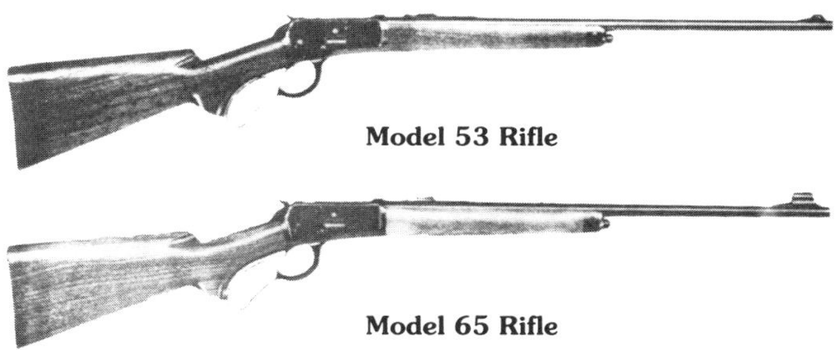

Model 53 Rifle

Model 65 Rifle

Model 1894 Lever Action Repeating Rifle. The patent for this gun was filed on 19 January 1894, and US Patent Number 524,702 was granted on 21 August 1894. It was first manufactured by Winchester in 1894 and was known as the Winchester Model 1894. Often called 'the most famous sporting rifle ever produced,' the Model 94 is

Far left: **The Model 1885 Single Shot Schuetzen Rifle. Although repeating rifles were gaining in popularity during the 1880s, such high-quality single shots as this have never lost their loyal following.**

Above, from top to bottom: **A handsomely engraved Model 1886, an unadorned variant (like the Model 1876 pictured on page 45, the Model 1886 was a favorite of Theodore Roosevelt) and the Model 1906 Slide Action Repeater, which Winchester introduced when it learned that Stevens Arms Company was planning to bring out a new line of repeating rifles chambered for .22 caliber cartridges.** ***At right:*** **An advertisement for the Winchester Repeating Arms Company.**

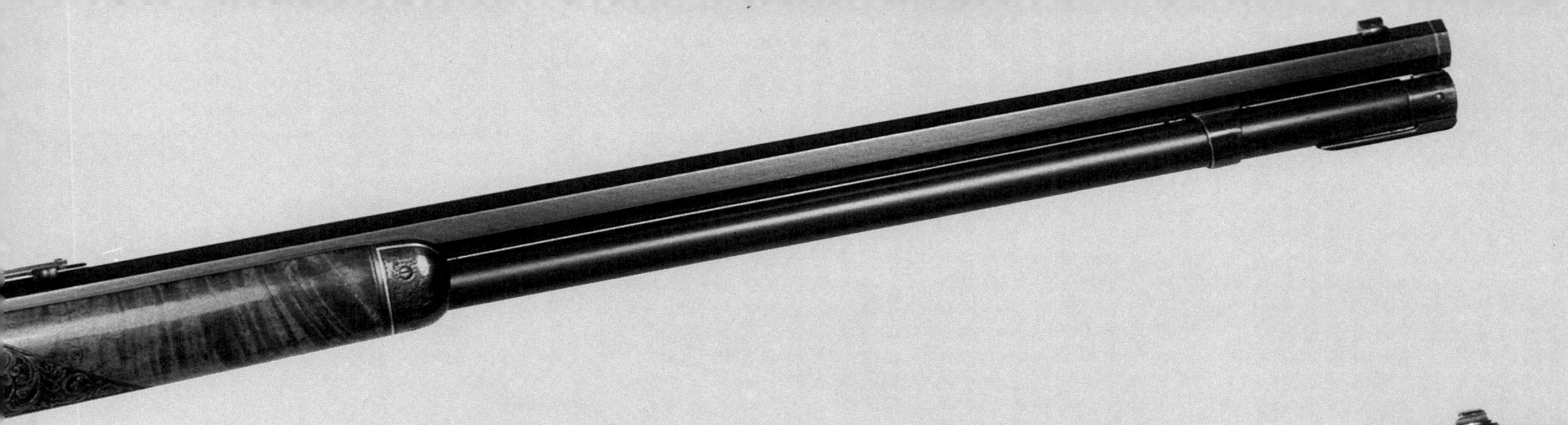

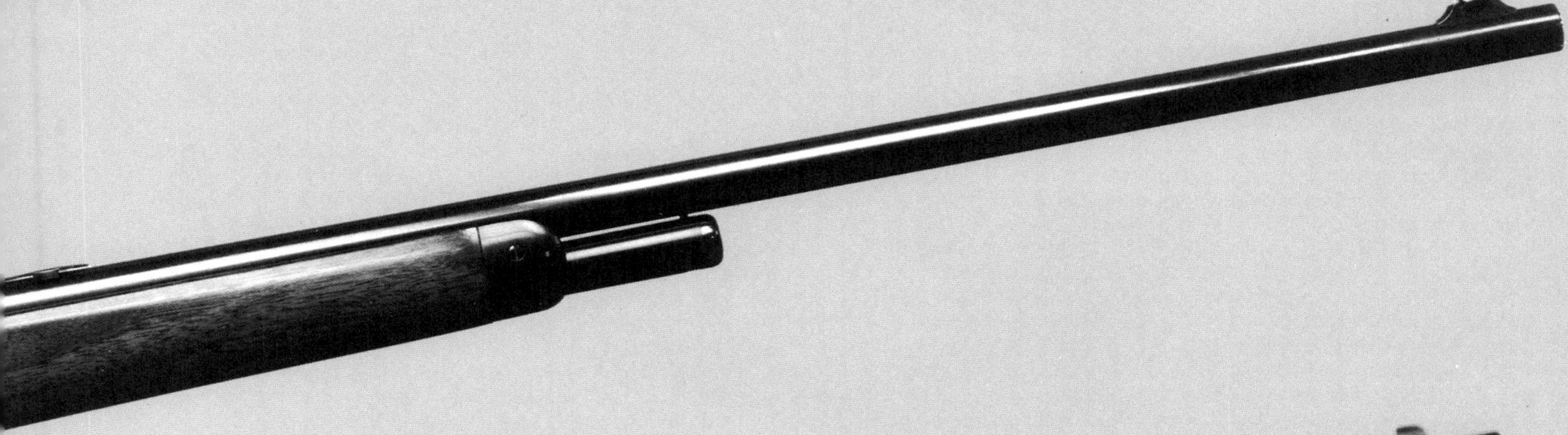

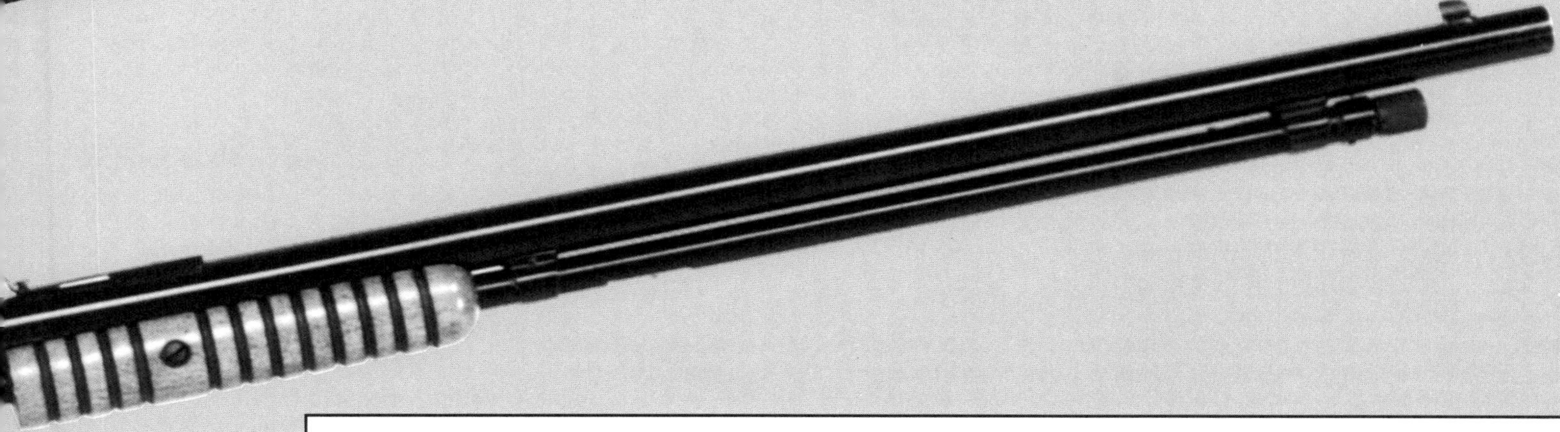

Winchester Repeating
Fire Arms.
Manufactured by the
Winchester
Repeating Arms Company.
New Haven, Connecticut.
Cartridge
H
Trade Mark
44/100.
47/100
Cartridge
W
Trade Mark
Punderson & Crisand, New Haven, Ct

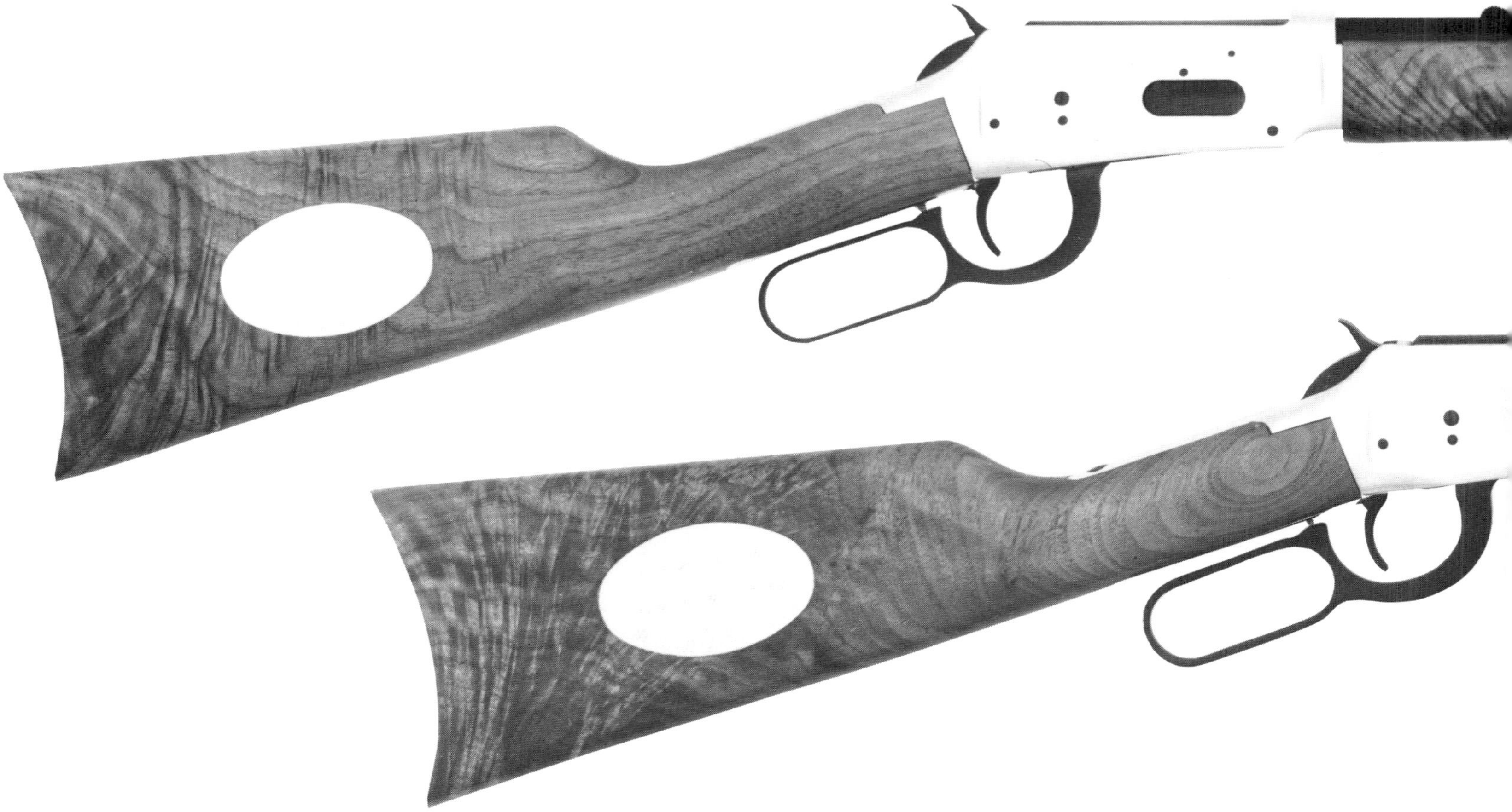

perhaps best known as the 'Winchester .30-30.' It was revolutionary in that it was the first sporting repeating action rifle to handle smokeless powder cartridges.

It is a lever action, tubular magazine, repeating rifle in .32-40 and .38-55 (both black powder) calibers. In 1895, .25-35 and .30-30 were added, and .32 Special in 1902, all three using smokeless powder. This firearm has a tubular magazine of various capacities, ranging from three to eight cartridges, manual and mechanical safeties, and adjustable sights. Barrel lengths and styles are 20-inch round, 22-inch round, octagonal or half octagonal, and weights range from 5.75 to 6.25 pounds for carbine models, to seven to 7.75 pounds for other variants. Model styles include sporting rifle, fancy sporting rifle, extra lightweight rifle and carbine.

First manufactured as a repeater, the Model 94 became available in a takedown model in 1895. Modified versions include the Model 55, introduced in 1924 (the principal differences being a shorter barrel, a redesigned stock and a

Model 1894 Rifle

Model 1894 Rifle, Takedown

Model 64 Rifle

At top, above and below: **The Centennial Model 1894 Rifle and Carbine honoring Oliver F Winchester and Franklin W Olin, respectively, two men who shaped the history of Winchester firearms.** ***At bottom:*** **The Model 55.**

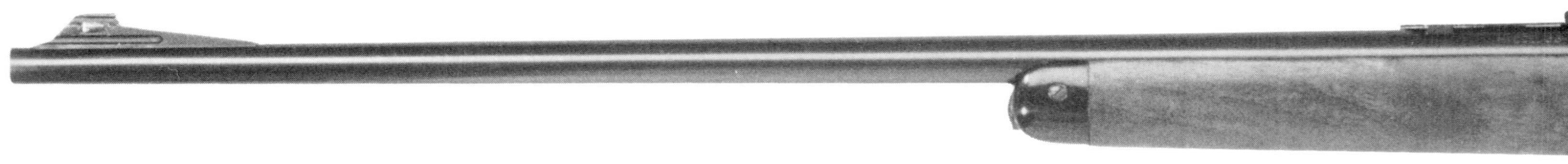

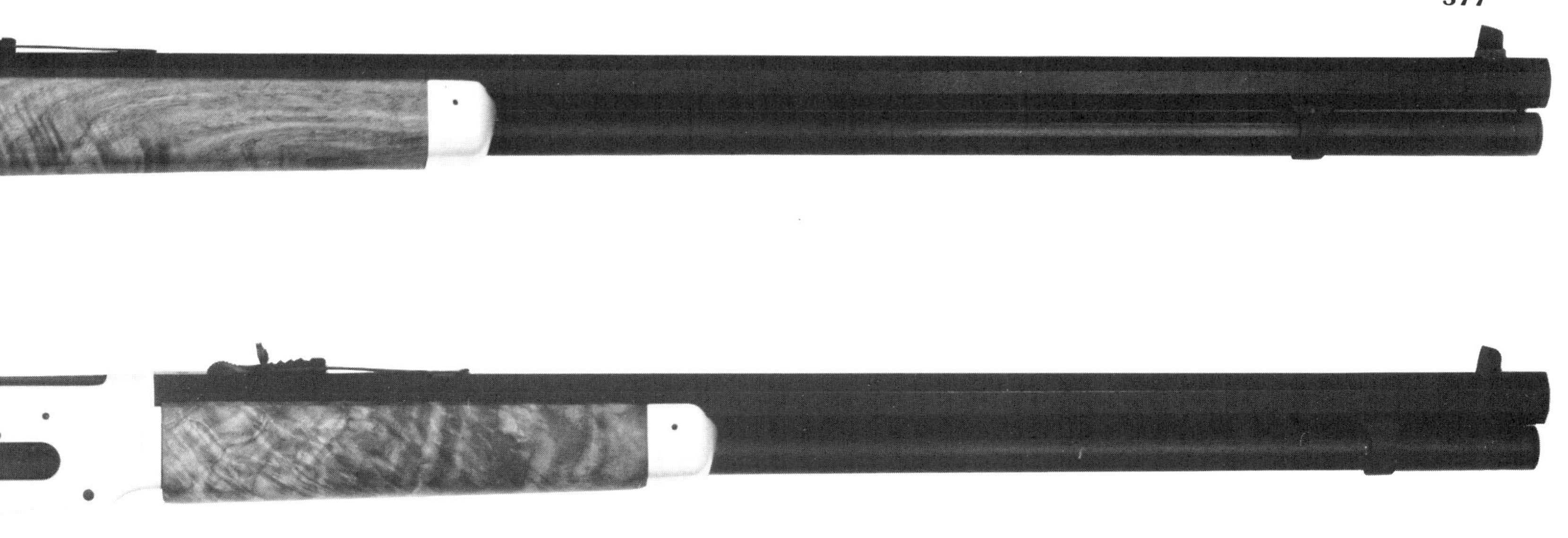

switch to half magazine) and the Model 64, introduced in 1933 (the main difference being the steel used). The Model 55 was discontinued in 1932 and the Model 64 in 1957. Still in production as the Model 94 carbine, this rifle has outsold any other manufactured by the Winchester Repeating Arms Company. Over two and a half million had been produced by 1962.

Model 1895 Lever Action Repeating Rifle. The patent application on this gun was filed on 19 November 1894, and US Patent Number 549,345 was granted on 5 November 1895. It was first manufactured by Winchester in 1896 and was known as the Winchester Model 95. This was the first nondetachable box type magazine rifle designed to handle the jacketed sharp nosed bullets.

It is a lever action rifle, with a wide range of calibers—.30 US Army (Krag), .38-72, .40-72 Winchester, .303 British, .35 Winchester, .405 Winchester, .30 Government 1903, .30 Government 1906, 7.62mm Russian. This firearm has a box magazine of from four to six rounds capacity, and manual and mechanical safeties. Barrel lengths are varied, from 22 to 36 inches in round, octagon or half octagon styles. Weight also varies, depending on barrel and caliber. Available stock types include sporting and fancy sporting, carbine and musket.

Four slightly differing versions of the musket appeared between 1895 and 1908. One, the Musket .30 Army Model 1895 US Army Pattern, was adopted by the US Army in 1895. The same year some 10,000 muskets chambered for the .30-40 Krag cartridge were purchased by the US Army for use in the Spanish-American War. Prior to America's entry into World War I, 293,816 of these guns, chambered for the 7.62mm Russian cartridge, were sold to Russia. A takedown version of the rifle appeared in 1910. Model 95 was discontinued in all models in 1931 with a total production of 425,881 units.

Model 1900 Bolt Action Single Shot .22 Caliber Rifle. The patent application on this gun was filed 17 February 1899, and US Patent Number 632,094 was granted 29 August 1899. It was first listed in the Winchester 1899 catalogue as the Winchester Model 1900 Single Shot Rifle. Designed as a low priced, single shot 'plinking' rifle, it has an especially simple construction and has been widely copied.

It is a bolt action, single shot, takedown rifle of .22 caliber (short and long, interchangeable), with a manual safety. This Single Shot Rifle weighs 2.75 pounds, has an 18-inch round barrel, and is available with a straight grip.

The Model 1900 was discontinued in 1902; the Model 1902, announced the same year, has a modified trigger guard shape, a short trigger pull, a steel butt plate, a rear peep sight and a slightly heavier barrel. In July of 1904, another slightly modified version appeared, the Model 1904, which has a longer, heavier barrel and a differently shaped stock.

An interesting modification is the Model 99 Thumb Trigger Rifle, which also appeared in 1904. This rifle is void either of trigger or trigger guard. Just behind the cocking piece on the bolt is a button called the thumb trigger. When in shooting position, the shooter merely presses downward on this button with the thumb to release the firing pin.

In 1928 and the years following, Winchester brought out other variations, the Models 58, 59, 60 and 68. In 1920, a shotgun version similar to the Model 1902 was announced;

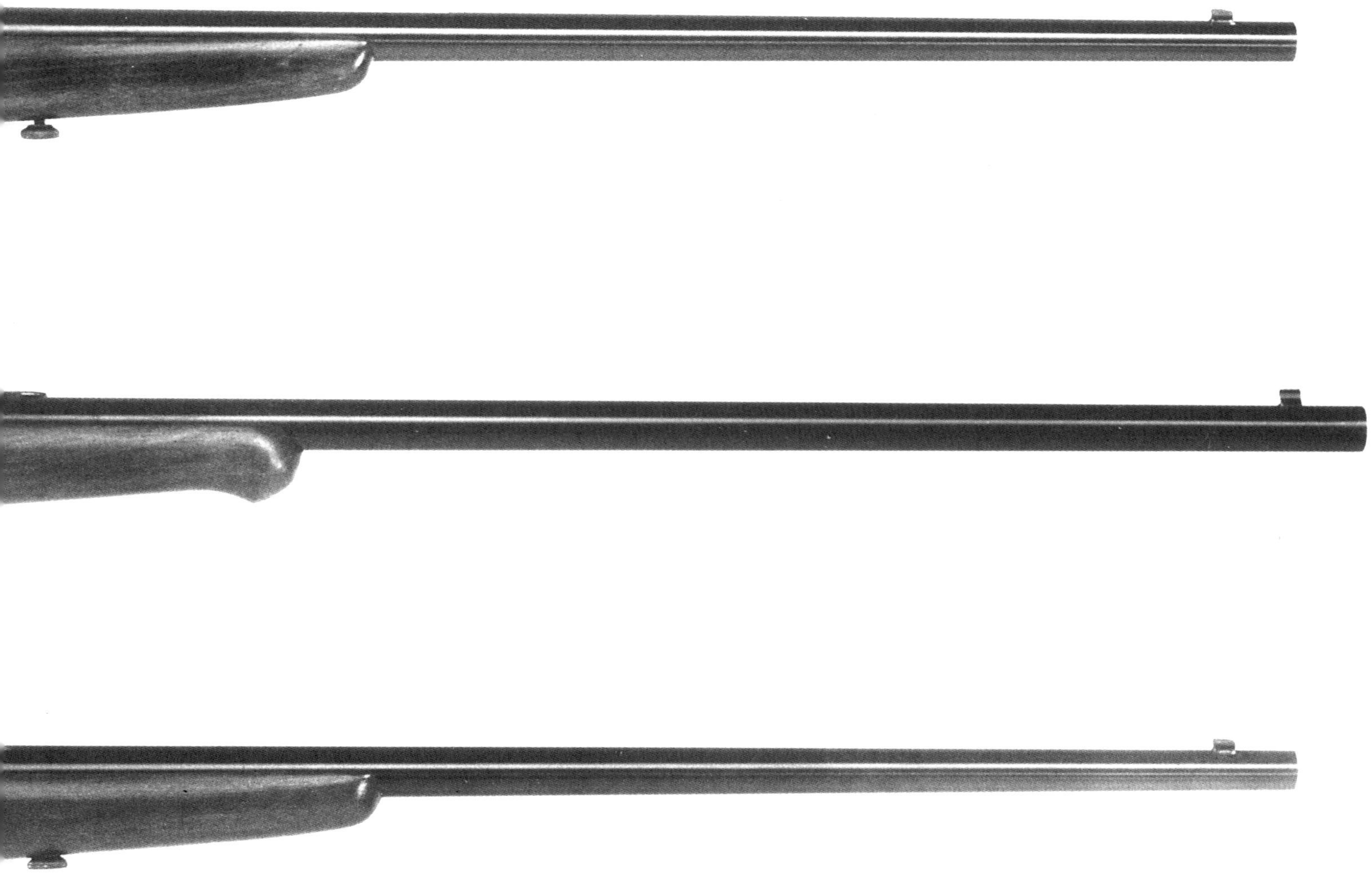

Modifications of the Model 1900 Single Shot Rifle. *Above, from top to bottom:* The Model 99 Thumb Trigger Rifle, which had a button, not a standard trigger, to release the firing pin; the Model 1904 Rifle with a heavy target barrel; and the Model 1902 Rifle, with improved trigger guard and improved trigger pull.

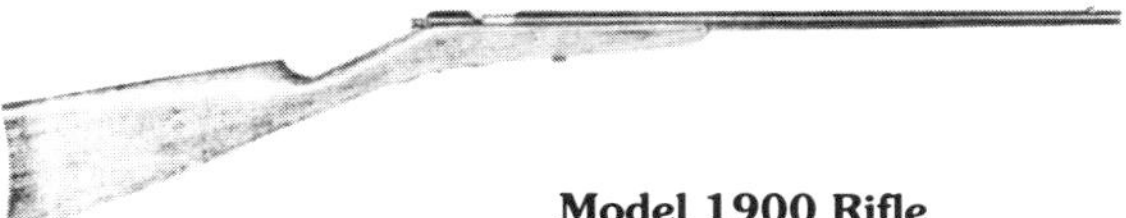

Model 1900 Rifle

this was the Winchester Model 36 Single Shot Shotgun. This is the only American made shotgun chambered for 9mm paper shells; it was discontinued in 1927. The last model, the 68 (introduced in 1934) was discontinued in 1946. Production totals are as follows: Model 1900, 105,000; Model 02, 640,299; Model 04, 302,859; Model 99 Thumb Trigger, 75,433; Model 36 Shotgun, 20,306; Model 58, 38,992; Model 59, 9293; Model 60, 165,754; and Model 68, 100,730 for a total of 1,458,666 units.

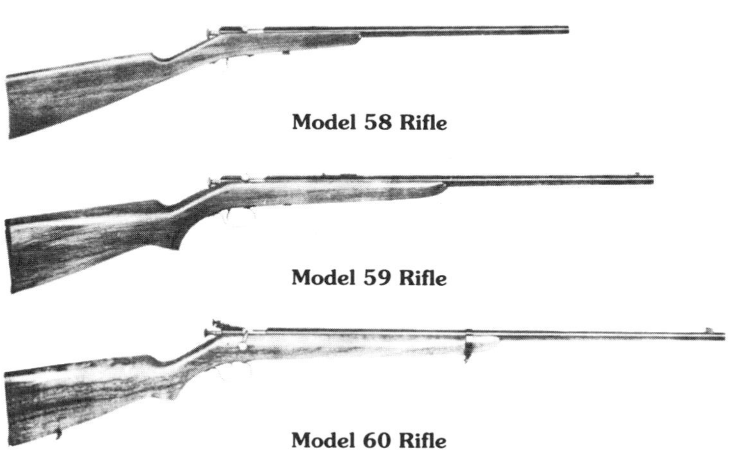

Model 58 Rifle

Model 59 Rifle

Model 60 Rifle

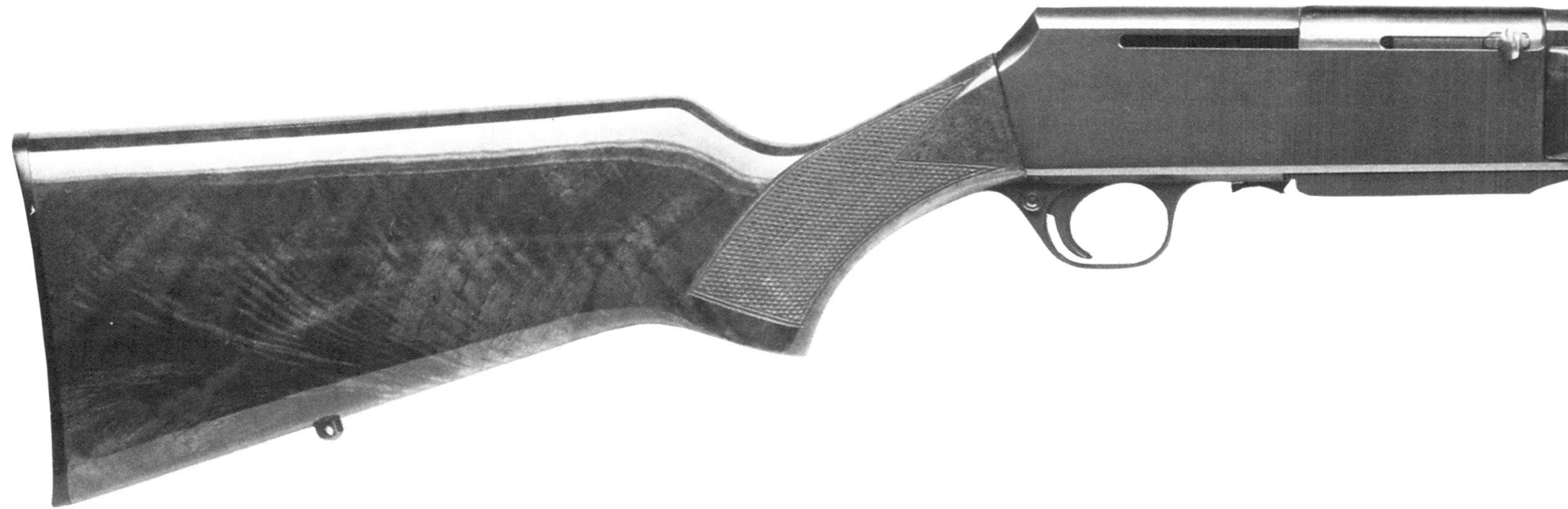

The Browning Automatic Rifle. The Browning Automatic Rifle was invented prior to 1917. The patent application on this gun was filed on 1 August 1917, and US Patent Number 1,293,022 was granted on 4 February 1919. Best known as the BAR, it is also known as the Browning Light Machine Rifle Model 1917, the Light Browning, the Colt Automatic Machine Rifle, and the Fusil Mitrailleur Browning. The BAR was officially adopted by the United States government in 1917 and first saw combat use in July of 1918.

The specifications that follow refer to the Colt Model 1917. It is an air cooled, gas actuated, automatic machine rifle. The BAR has a caliber of .30-06, with a detachable box magazine of either 20 or 40 rounds, staggered arrangement. The safety is a fire control change lever. When the change lever is in its forward position, marked with the letter 'F,' the rifle will shoot one shot with each pull of the trigger. In vertical position, marked with the letter 'A,' the rifle will fire full automatic. In the rearward position, marked by the letter 'S,' the rifle is safe. On some models, the 'F' position, when the lever is all the way forward, merely reduces the rate of fire in such a way that single shots may be fired by quickly pulling and releasing the trigger. It weighs 17.37 pounds with full magazine, and has a 24-inch round barrel. Stock type is standard rifle only, with pistol grip. A takedown, its 70 pieces can be completely disassembled and reassembled in 55 seconds.

A lever on the receiver permits fully automatic or semiautomatic firing. At full automatic, it can be fired at a maximum rate of 480 rounds per minute, emptying a 20 round magazine in two and one-half seconds. This rifle has a bolt lock which pivots to the rear of the bolt, and rises in and out of locking engagement with a shoulder on the receiver. The rear of the bolt lock is attached to the slide by a link, which is free to reciprocate backward and forward. Attached to the forward part of the barrel is a gas piston which derives its energy from a gas port drilled through the barrel wall. In operation, the piston sends a slide to the rear, and, in turn, the slide, through its link connection with the bolt lock, pivots the bolt lock downward out of locking contact with the receiver.

During World War I approximately 52,000 were manufactured by Colt, Winchester, and Marlin-Rockwell. After World War I, production rights reverted to Colt and, by arrangement with John M Browning, Fabrique Nationale began European production in 1920, calling their model the Fusil Mitrailleur Leger. Large quantities of the rifle have since been manufactured for various European countries. It was made in 6.5mm, 7mm, 7.62mm, 7.9mm and .30-06 caliber. It has been widely copied; many nations historically have had the BAR or a similar gun in reserve.

In 1922 the US Army brought out its Cavalry Model. In 1933, Colt produced the 'Colt Monitor' for police and bank guard use. In November 1939, there were approximately 87,000 in our war reserve. Approximately 177,000 were produced in this country during World War II. In comparison with earlier models, the World War II BAR, the M1918-A2, is slightly heavier and equipped with flash hider and bipod. It carries the conventional stock without pistol grip. A decelerating device permits a cyclic rate of fire of 350 to 550 rounds per minute. No mechanical provision is made for semiautomatic fire, but, at a low rate of fire, single shots can be discharged by pulling and quickly releasing the trigger.

The Fabrique Nationale version differed from the Colt model chiefly in having a quicker takedown mechanism which allowed the barrel to be removed easily for replacement. Total production by FN to the end of 1961 was 67,310 units.

***At top:* The Browning Automatic Rifle—aka BAR. *At right:* The original Browning Brothers Store in Ogden, Utah, circa 1882—and the staff of 'The Largest Arms Factory Between Omaha and the Pacific.'**

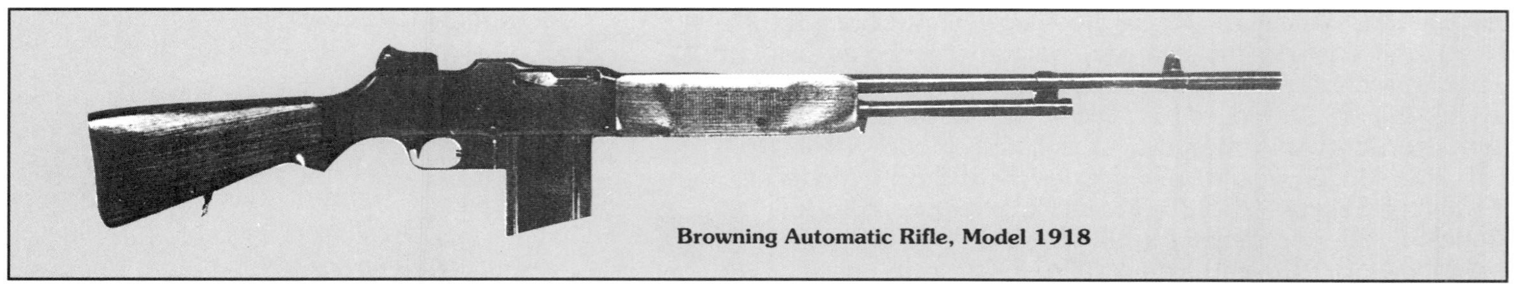

Browning Automatic Rifle, Model 1918

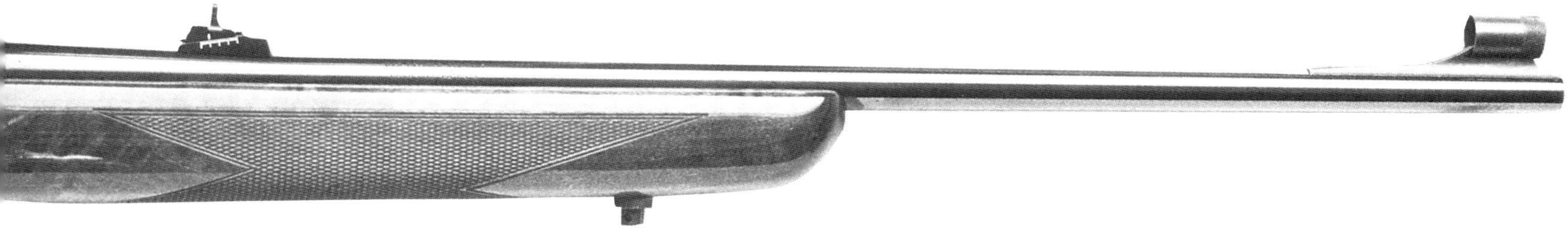

J.M. BROWNING & BRO.
GUNS, PISTOLS,
AMUNITION & FISHING TACKLE

Shotguns

Model 1887 Lever Action Repeating Shotgun. This was the first lever action repeating shotgun made in the United States and has been called 'the first really successful repeating shotgun.' The patent application on this gun was filed on 15 June 1885 and US Patent Number 336,287 was granted on 16 February 1886. Manufacturing and sales rights were sold to the Winchester Repeating Arms Company in 1886, and it appeared in June 1887 as the Winchester Model 1887 Shotgun.

It is a lever action repeating shotgun in 10 and 12 gauge, with a tubular magazine that holds four shells in the magazine and one in the chamber. In 1898, 10 and 12 gauge riot guns were added. Barrel lengths are 30 and 32 inches for both the 10 and 12 gauge, with full chokes and 20 inches for the 10 and 12 gauge riot gun, with cylinder bore. The 10 gauge weighs about nine pounds; the 12 gauge, about eight pounds. The standard stock is plain with a pistol grip and a hard rubber butt plate.

The model 1887 was discontinued in 1899. Redesigned to handle the smokeless powder loads, it reappeared in 1901, in 10 gauge only, as the Model 1901. This model was discontinued in 1920. 64,855 of the Model 1887 were produced and 13,500 of the Model 1901—for a total of 78,355.

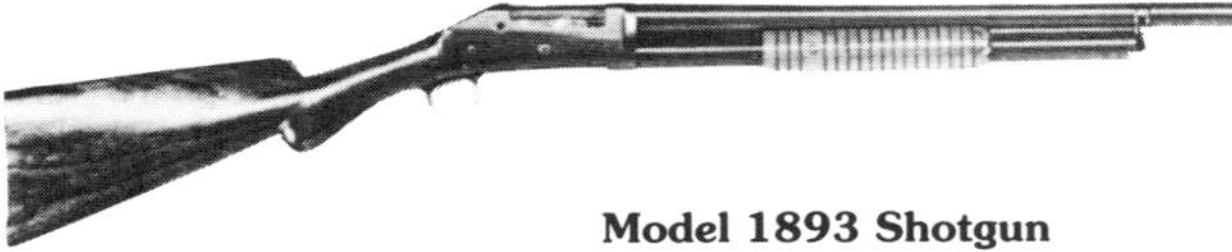

Model 1893 Shotgun

Model 1893 Pump Action Repeating Shotgun. The patent application on this gun was filed on 30 June 1890, and US Patent Number 441,390 was granted on 25 November 1890. Manufacturing and sales rights were sold to the Winchester Repeating Arms Company in 1890; the gun was announced in April 1894 as the Winchester Model 1893. This was the first shotgun with a sliding forearm of pump action manufactured by Winchester.

It is a pump action repeating shotgun in 12 gauge with a five shot, tubular magazine. Barrel lengths are 30 and 32 inches with a full choke—modified choke or cylinder bore specials being available. The Model 1893 weighs about 7.75 pounds and is available in plain stocks with pistol grip and a hard rubber butt plate.

The Model 1893 was discontinued in 1897 when the Model 1897, a modified takedown version of the Model 1893, was introduced. Total production was 34,050 units.

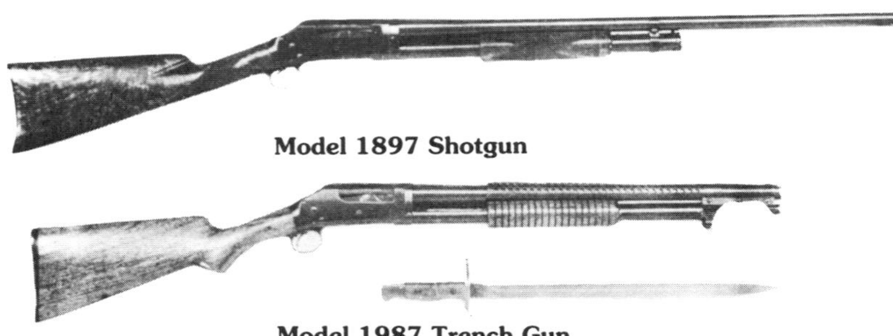

Model 1897 Shotgun

Model 1987 Trench Gun

Model 1897 Pump Action Repeating Shotgun. The Model 1897 is a modified takedown version of the Model 1893, with a stronger frame and side ejection. Introduced in November of 1897, it soon became one of the most popular shotguns in America. It is a pump action repeating shotgun in 12 and 16 gauge (takedown exclusive on the 16, and optional on the 12) with a five shot, tubular magazine. Variant examples have barrel lengths of 20, 22, 26, 28, 30 and 32 inches, with cylinder bore, modified, intermediate, full or Winchester skeet chokes. The weights of the various examples of the Model 1897 are from 7.1 to 7.9 pounds, and standard stocks are plain, with pistol grip and hard rubber butt plate, plus optional checkering and other specialties having been available.

In addition to its great popularity as a sporting arm, the 97 saw other uses. A short barrel version was widely used as a riot gun by law enforcement agencies; also for a time the American Express Company armed its messengers with this

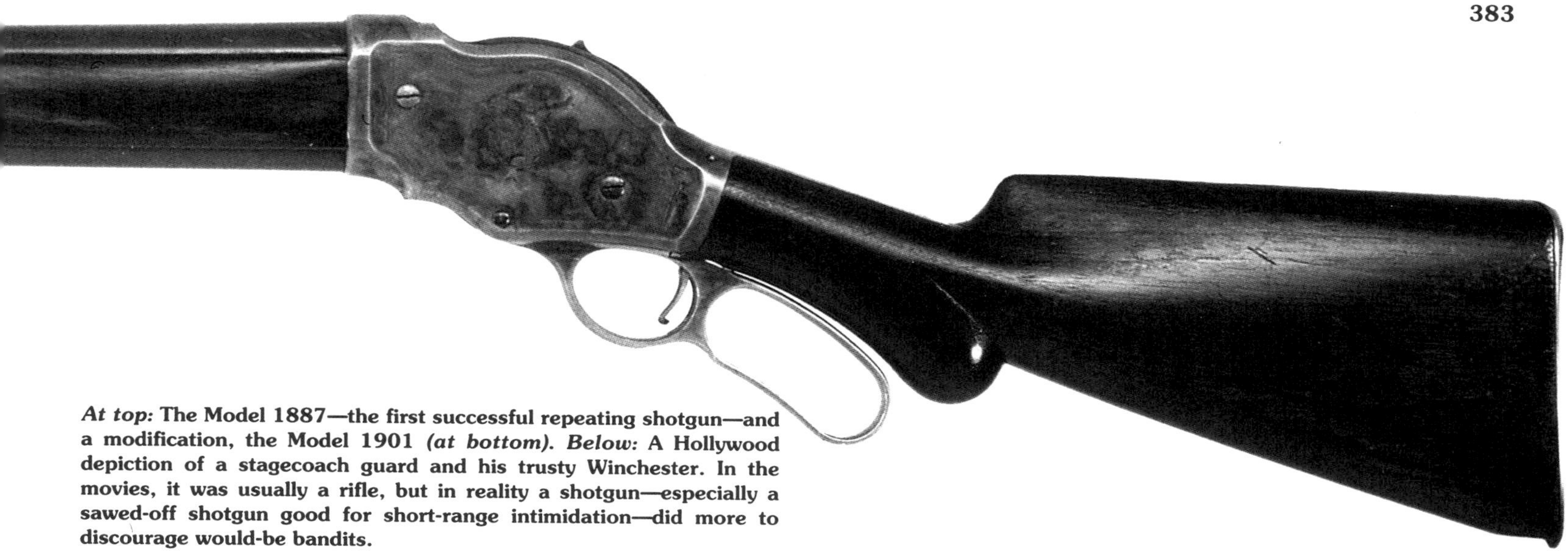

At top: **The Model 1887—the first successful repeating shotgun—and a modification, the Model 1901** ***(at bottom). Below:*** **A Hollywood depiction of a stagecoach guard and his trusty Winchester. In the movies, it was usually a rifle, but in reality a shotgun—especially a sawed-off shotgun good for short-range intimidation—did more to discourage would-be bandits.**

firearm. During World War I the 97 was used by American troops as a trench gun, with considerable success.

The standard, trap, pigeon and brush guns were introduced in 1897, followed by the riot gun, in 1898; the tournament, in 1910, and the trench gun, in 1920, (but previously manufactured for the US Army use in World War I). The trap gun was discontinued in 1931 and was succeeded by the special trap gun, which was discontinued in 1939. Other models were discontinued as follows—the pigeon gun was discontinued in 1939, the brush gun in 1931, the riot gun in 1935 and the trench gun in 1935.

The tournament gun was discontinued in 1931 and was succeeded by the standard trap, which was discontinued in 1939. The standard Model 1897 was discontinued in 1957. Total production for all models stands at 1,240,700.

Winchester's Rare Brownings

John M Browning sold Winchester a total of 44 firearms—31 rifles and 13 shotguns. Of this number, only seven rifles and three shotguns were actually manufactured. Most of the remaining 34 arms, comprising 24 rifles and 10 shotguns, exist only as one-of-a-kind prototype specimens in either the Winchester or Browning Museums.

Among the rarest guns in the world, they are unique in design, functionality and construction. The Winchester Museum also contains three other Browning rifles and one other shotgun that were neither bought by Winchester nor patented for manufacture principally because they infringed previously existing patents.

The following is a listing of these rarest-of-the-rare American firearms.

Rifles

Repeating Rifle in .38 Caliber. The patent application on this gun was filed on 6 March 1884, and US Patent number 312,183 was granted on 10 February 1885. This .38 caliber rifle has a 28-inch octagon barrel and weighs 9.25 pounds. In this lever action, tubular magazine rifle, the locking arrangement of the breechblock is greatly simplified, inasmuch as the lever itself, having a seat in the receiver, acts as the locking lug.

The lever is spring loaded in such a way as to allow the lever to snap in and out of engagement with its socket, or locking shoulder, in the receiver.

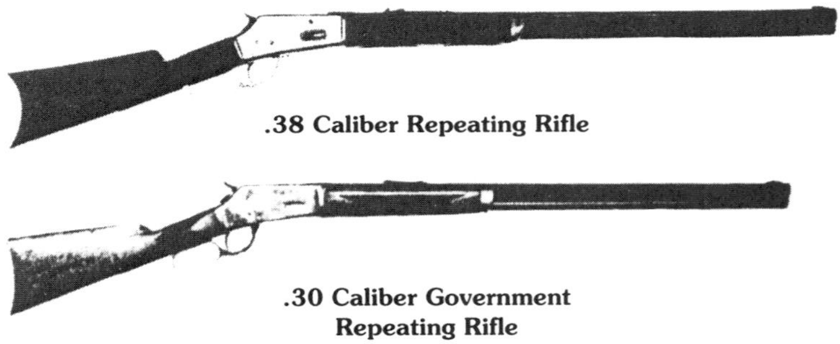

.38 Caliber Repeating Rifle

.30 Caliber Government Repeating Rifle

Lever Action .30 Government Caliber Repeating Rifle. The patent application for this gun was filed on 5 March 1885, and US Patent number 324,296 was granted on 11 August 1885. This lever action, .30 Government caliber, tubular magazine rifle has a 28-inch octagon barrel and weighs 9.25 pounds.

The main novelty of this gun is its locking lug, which is pivoted on the rear of the sliding breechblock in such a manner that the front end rises in and out of locking engagement with the receiver and breechblock. The locking lug also serves as the link between the rotary motion of the lever, and the longitudinal motion of the breechblock.

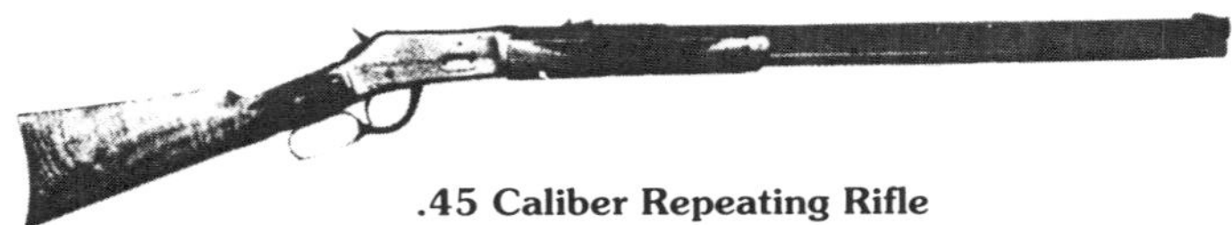

.45 Caliber Repeating Rifle

Lever Action Repeating Rifle in .45 Caliber. The patent application for this gun was filed on 26 May 1885, and US Patent number 324,297 was granted on 11 August 1885. It has a 28-inch octagon barrel and weighs 9.25 pounds. This .45 caliber, lever action, tubular magazine rifle features a toggle locking system, wherein the lever is the front part of the toggle, which 'bears' in a socket in the breechblock.

The rear half of the toggle pivots at the rear, against the receiver, and houses the trigger. Opening the lever flexes the toggle joint and allows the bolt to slide to the rear.

As in many of John M Browning's designs, one part has several functions: the links of the toggle joint serve to form a stout breech locking system, and act as the linkage necessary to reciprocate the breechblock. The action also features a firing pin block which renders the gun safe until the lever piece is fully closed.

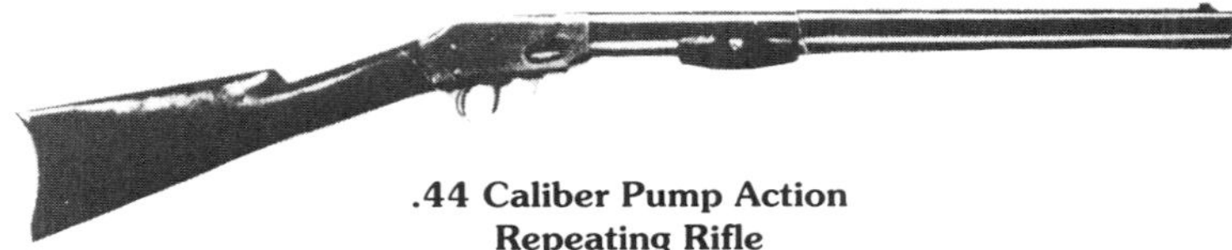

.44 Caliber Pump Action Repeating Rifle

Pump Action Repeating Rifle in .44 Caliber. The patent application on this gun was filed 12 July 1886, and US Patent number 367,336 was granted 26 July 1887. This .44 caliber firearm has a 20-inch round barrel and weighs close to six pounds. It is a pump action rifle having a tubular magazine and a pivoting breechblock, the rear end of which rises into locking engagement with the receiver.

Instead of being placed to the rear of the breechblock, as is most common, the hammer works through a recess nearly in the middle of the breechblock, allowing for a very short receiver. The tail end of the hammer projects into the trigger guard forward of the trigger, allowing the hammer to be cocked or uncocked manually.

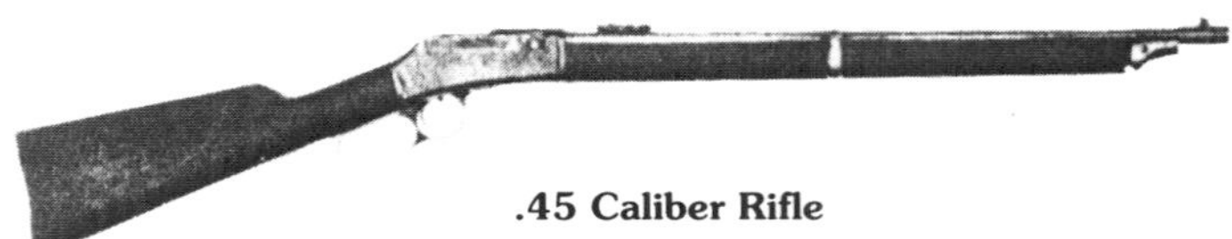

.45 Caliber Rifle

Lever Action Repeating Rifle in .45 Caliber. The patent application on this gun was filed 21 November 1887, and US Patent number 376,576 was granted 17 January 1888. This lever action, tubular magazine .45 caliber rifle has a 22-inch round barrel and weighs 7.2 pounds. It loads through the bottom and ejects from the top of the receiver.

The forward end of the operating lever contains the lock mechanism. The operating lever is hung to the receiver by a link, which extends to the rear. The forward end of the lever is guided by channel cuts in the receiver. The sliding firing pin acts as a hammer and is cocked by the closing movement of the lever.

Lever Action Repeating Rifle in .45-70 Caliber. The patent application on this gun was filed on 18 November 1889, and US Patent number 428,887 was granted on 27 May 1890. This .45-70 caliber, box magazine rifle has a 28-inch round barrel and weighs 8.1 pounds.

In this unique firearm the breechblock, magazine and lever are one unit. With the lever closed the assembly is in locking engagement with the receiver and comprises an effective breech closure. The cartridges ride in the magazine recess in a 'bullet end down position,' with magazine spring pressure urging them forward. Opening the lever turns this whole assembly and brings the cartridges in line with the bore. This rifle can be operated either as a repeater or as a single shot firearm.

A selector lever on the side of the magazine portion urges the top cartridges out of the magazine into loading position. Closing the lever completes the loading cycle. Extraction is to the side and is effected by a combination extractor and pivot slide attached to the breech assembly.

Another interesting feature of this rifle is the firing pin, which acts as its own pivot sear. The front of the firing pin is latched in cocked position by a hardened screw in the receiver. A lever attached to the trigger pushes the rear of the firing pin upward, pivoting the striker out of engagement with the hardened screw.

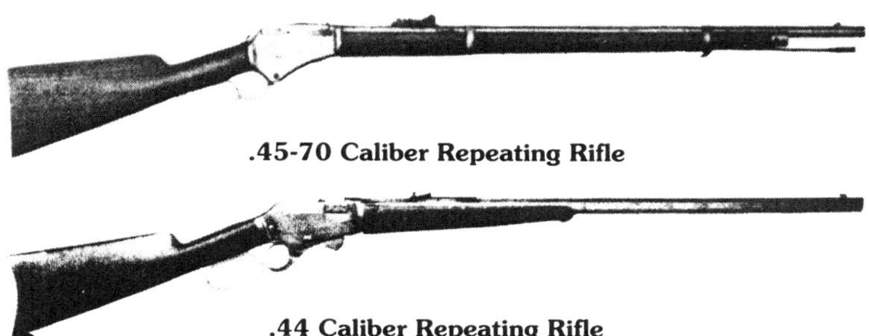

.45-70 Caliber Repeating Rifle

.44 Caliber Repeating Rifle

Lever Action Repeating Rifle in .44 Caliber. This is a lever action, integral revolving magazine rifle, and is very similar to the .45-70 Caliber Lever Action Repeating Rifle. The lever, magazine and breechblock are essentially one piece; the cartridges ride 'bullet down' in the magazine; the magazine is loaded from the bottom and the cartridges are inserted upward, rim first.

The unique feature of this rifle is the arrangement of the firing pin and the method for inserting the cartridges.

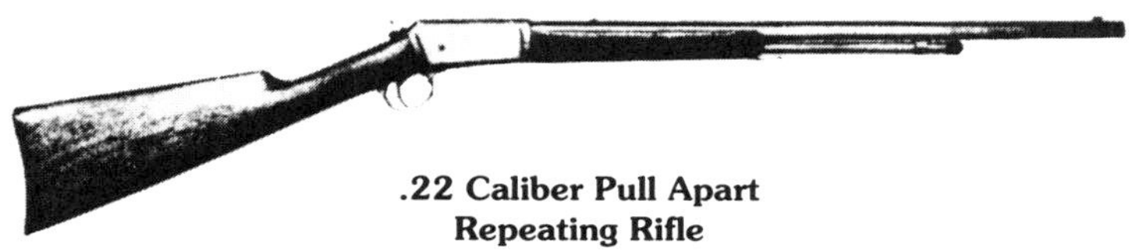

.22 Caliber Pull Apart Repeating Rifle

Pull Apart Repeating Rifle in .22 Caliber. This firearm is of the pull apart variety. Operation of the action is effected by literally pulling it open to its full extension of seven-eighths of an inch, just far enough for its .22 caliber cartridges, which are fed by a carrier from a tubular magazine.

Ignition is by a striker, the rear end of which projects from the rear of the receiver. The two main parts are unlocked from each other by pulling the trigger.

.45 Caliber Repeating Rifle

Lever Action Repeating Rifle in .45 Caliber. This military type rifle, with detachable box magazine, features a locking system with vertically rising locking lugs that are similar to the Winchester 86 and 94 models, but utilizes a striker rather than a hammer.

The novelty in this firearm is the magazine, which is positioned for the most part under the barrel forward of the breech face. The cartridges are pulled rearward out of the magazine onto a carrier by the breech bolt during its rearward movement. The carrier then lifts the cartridges into position for loading by the breech bolt during its forward movement.

.30 Caliber Repeating Rifle

Lever Action Repeating Rifle in .30 Caliber (Number One). In this lever action box magazine rifle, the locking block is pivoted to the receiver immediately to the rear of the hammer, and encloses the hammer on both sides. Initial motion of the lever pivots the locking block downward, allowing the breechblock to slide to the rear. Ejection and loading of the magazine are through the top.

.30 Caliber Repeating Rifle

Lever Action Repeating Rifle in .30 Caliber (Number Two). This military type, box magazine lever action rifle features a novel hammer arrangement. The hammer does not pivot, as is usual in lever action rifles; it is essentially a striker which works in a recess in the upper tang of the receiver, and has an exposed ear for manual cocking. As is the case in most of Browning's lever actions, cocking is automatic with the operation of the lever. Loading is from the top by means of a cartridge clip.

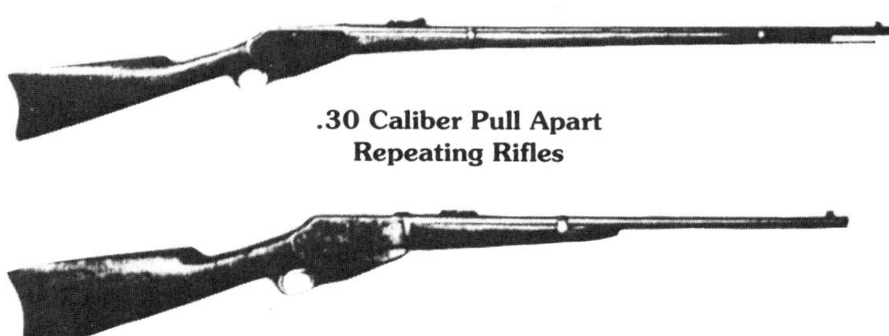

.30 Caliber Pull Apart Repeating Rifles

Pull Apart Repeating Rifle in .30 Caliber. This pull apart musket type rifle, with box magazine, operates in the manner common to pull-apart designs. The receiver and barrel assembly, and the breechblock, trigger guard and stock assembly, separate at a predetermined distance, allowing the end of the breechblock to pick up rounds from the magazine.

Connecting the two main components is a tube, inside of which the hammer works like a piston. The small finger piece at the front of the trigger guard is a sear block safety. The breechblock locks at the rear on a shoulder in the receiver.

A second variant of this design was also sold to Winchester. This model has a safety which locks the sear with the hammer cocked, and also locks the gun against accidental operation.

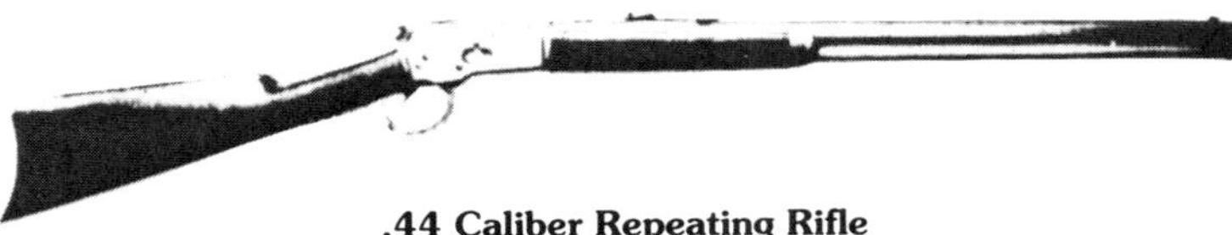

.44 Caliber Repeating Rifle

Lever Action Repeating Rifle in .44 Caliber (Number Three). This lever action, tubular magazine repeating rifle has the same action as the Winchester Model 92. It is identical in principle and differs only in minor detail.

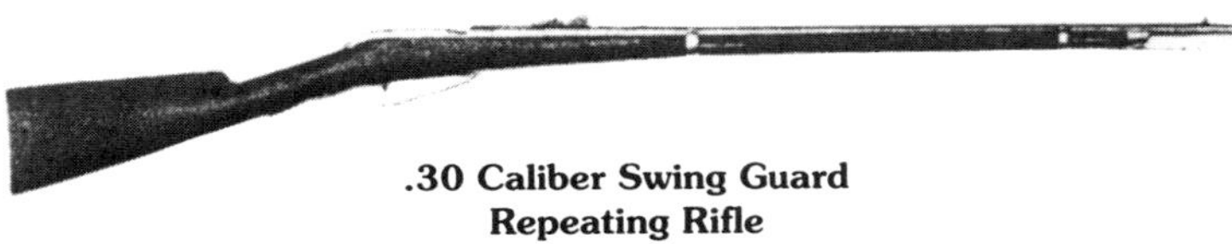

.30 Caliber Swing Guard Repeating Rifle

Swing Guard Repeating Rifle in .30 Caliber. This novel firearm works like a lever action with the lever mounted backward. The trigger is pivoted to the frame at its rear. The front of the guard is latched to the rear of the box magazine by a spring latch.

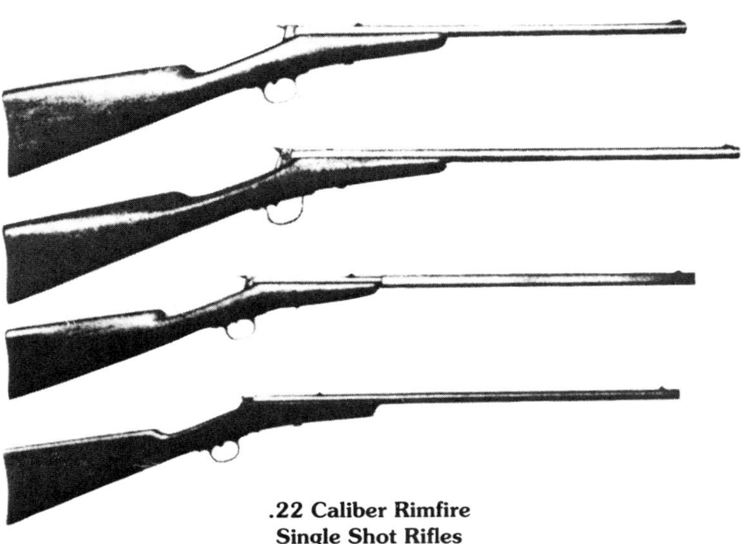

.22 Caliber Rimfire Single Shot Rifles

Rimfire Single Shot Rifle in .22 Caliber. This rifle, like the three models which follow, is of extremely simple design. The breechblock, hammer and trigger are one piece, and operate up and down at about 20 degrees from the vertical. In loading, the breech bolt is pushed down until the tail of the breechblock extends into the trigger guard, and is latched there against the force of the mainspring, which forces the breechblock upward into a locked position with the barrel.

The firing pin is a hardened pin installed rigidly on the face of the breechblock. A thumbpiece projects from the rear of the breechblock for the purpose of pushing it downward into locked position. The tail of the breechblock acts as a trigger. The gun is ready to fire the moment a fresh cartridge is placed in the chamber.

Pulling the trigger allows the breechblock assembly to spring forcibly upward into locked position. The built in firing pin ignites the cartridge simultaneously. Extraction is manual with two clearance cuts on the rear of the barrel to allow the fingers to pick out the cartridge.

A second version of this design differs in the use of a simple pushrod type extractor and a different spring arrangement on the breechblock. The third variant uses a different type of mainspring, and incorporates various minor detail changes. The fourth, and final, variant is unique only in that its replaceable firing pin is screwed into the back of the breechblock.

.30 Caliber Pump Action Repeating Rifle

Pump Action Repeating Rifle in .30 Caliber. This rifle has a box magazine which loads from the bottom. The breechblock is locked into a recess in the left side of the receiver, and is positively held in locking engagement with the receiver by a locking cam on the slide.

The breechblock, instead of rising into a vertical position, moves laterally into a locking position with the receiver. This gun cannot be fired until it is completely locked. The action is very smooth and is suitable for relatively low pressure cartridges.

.40 Caliber Repeating Rifle

Lever Action Repeating Rifle in .40 Caliber. This tubular magazine rifle features a one piece locking block, which lifts vertically as it closes the lever into a recess at the rear of the bolt. The locking block is raised in and out of locking position by a link which also serves as a trigger housing. This arrangement disconnects the trigger from the sear until the action is fully closed.

.236 Caliber Repeating Rifle

Lever Action Repeating Rifle in .236 Caliber. This rifle has a box magazine, and loads and ejects obliquely out the top of the receiver. Its tilting breechblock is guided at the front only, with the rear being left free to follow the lever through its downward arc.

This downward motion of the lever allows for a short receiver. The actuating lever carries the trigger and hammer as a unit. The hammer is cocked by closing the lever. A projection on the rear of the mainspring guide latches the lever in closed position.

.30 Caliber Repeating Rifle

Bolt-sear Lever Action Repeating Rifle in .30 Caliber. In this lever action rifle, the sear is part of the bolt assembly, and acts on a striker, which allows the trigger to pivot as a unit with the lever. The box magazine is attached with a screw and is not freely detachable. The receiver is cut away to conform to a one piece stock. The safety on this is on the top tang to the rear of the receiver.

A second variant of this design has a two piece stock and the magazine is inside the receiver. Its magazine loading arrangement features staggered double rows of cartridges.

Shotguns

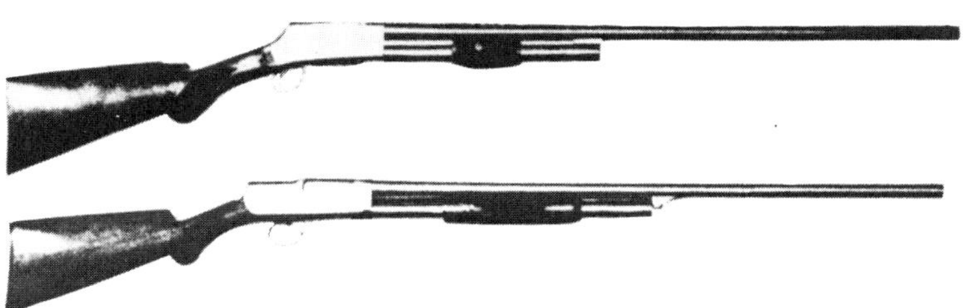

12 Gauge Pump Action Shotguns

Pump Action Shotgun in 12 Gauge. This 12 gauge, pump action shotgun is locked by a turning breechblock which is actuated by a cam slot in the slide. The slot in the receiver to the rear of the ejection opening is the passage or clearance for the large locking lug on the bolt.

The long, rail type locking lug acts as a guide for the cylindrical breechblock as it reciprocates. A standard type carrier elevates the cartridges from the tubular magazine into loading position. On the front of the carrier, however, is a simple dog which serves as a cartridge stop. A second, similar design was also sold to, but not manufactured by, Winchester. A third variant has a pivoting breechblock which locks at the rear of the side of the receiver. The slide which manipulates the breechblock is mounted on the opposite side of the receiver in such a way as to completely close the ejection opening when the gun is closed. The rear end of the magazine can pivot downward free from the receiver, allowing the tube and handle to be used as a wrench for unscrewing the barrel from the receiver.

A fourth variant has a locking system that is unusual but exceptionally strong. Instead of rotating, or pivoting, or being locked by a separate member, the whole breechblock raises vertically in and out of locking engagement with a series of locking lugs spaced along the top of the receiver. Both ends of the breechblock are raised by two links pivoted fore and aft on the slide. The extractor is pivoted to the breechblock to allow for its vertical movement.

The fifth variant incorporates many of the features which later appeared in John M Browning's automatic shotguns and in many of the modern day shotgun designs. The locking block, assembled to and pivoting from the breechblock, is locked to the upper wall of the receiver. As with most modern shotguns, the hammer and trigger mechanism are part of an assembly which is fastened inside an opening at the bottom of the receiver.

The gun has a barrel takedown using interrupted threads with a takeup ring very similar to that used in the Browning .22 Semiautomatic Rifle. The magazine tube pivots to the barrel. When the rear of the magazine is disengaged from the receiver, the tube swings down and is used as a handle to thread the barrel in and out of the receiver.

Pump Action Shotgun in 10 Gauge. This model has a tilting breechblock, which is pivotally mounted at the rear to the receiver. The front of the breechblock tilts down so far that the breechblock itself is used as a carrier, picking the cartridges up from tubular magazine with a 'tray' on top of the breechblock.

The breechblock pauses in its upward movement long enough for the extracting slide, which reciprocates longitudinally, to pick the cartridge off the top of the breechblock and force it into the chamber. The breechblock then completes its upward motion, ready for firing.

A second design, similar to this but differing in minor details, was also sold to, but not manufactured by, Winchester.

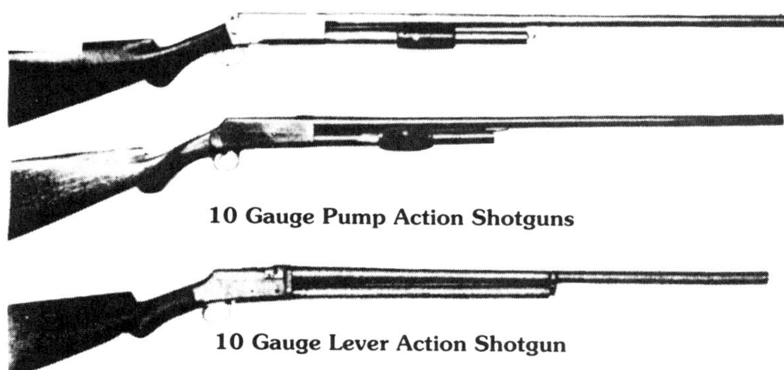

10 Gauge Pump Action Shotguns

10 Gauge Lever Action Shotgun

Lever Action Shotgun in 10 Gauge. This lever action shotgun has a tubular magazine and pistol grip. The finger lever, carrying the entire locking mechanism, is hung to the receiver by a link on the left hand side. The forward end of the link is hung on a pivot in the finger lever; the rear of the link on a pivot in the frame. The upper portion of the finger lever is guided by the receiver.

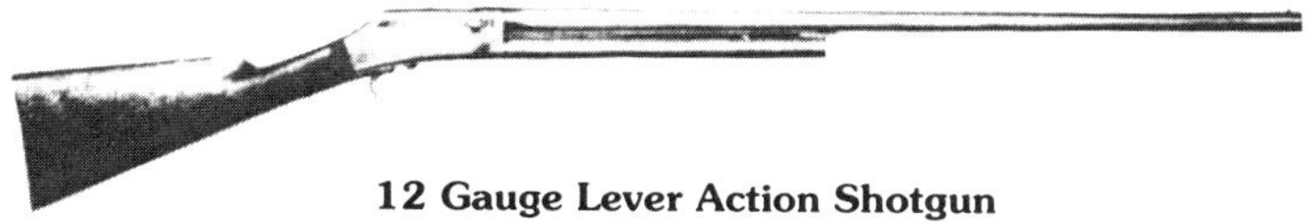

12 Gauge Lever Action Shotgun

Lever Action Shotgun in 12 Gauge. This shotgun has a tubular magazine and a one piece breechblock, trigger guard and lever combined. The breechblock works along a track on the side of the receiver, by means of a round pin visible at the front of the breechblock.

In working the lever, the greater part of the insides of the gun come out of the receiver with the lever. This, and the long lever throw, are two disadvantages of this extremely simple, rugged gun.

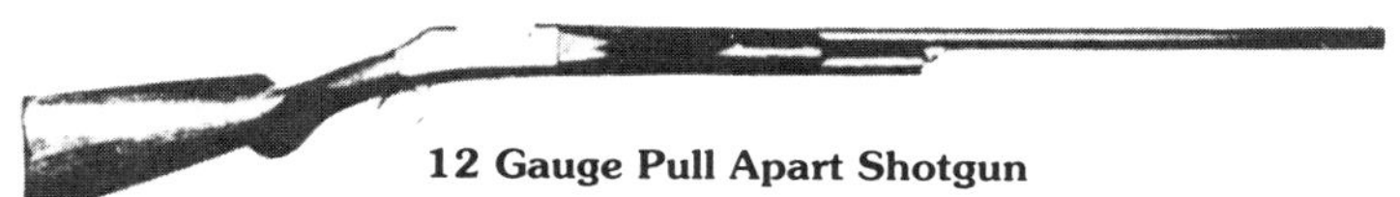

12 Gauge Pull Apart Shotgun

Pull Apart Shotgun in 12 Gauge. Another of John M Browning's pull apart firearms, it only handles the 12 gauge cartridge. A latch is positioned at the front of the trigger guard, to prevent accidental operation. The rear unit, which includes the trigger guard, has a lug projecting forward into the top of the receiver. The lug works on the rear of the breech bolt in such a way as to unlock it from the back of the frame.

In this model, the hammer and mainspring work inside a long tube attached to the receiver. The tube acts as a guide to keep the two essential parts—the stock and trigger assembly and the barrel and receiver assembly—in alignment when the gun is pulled apart.

Major Through the

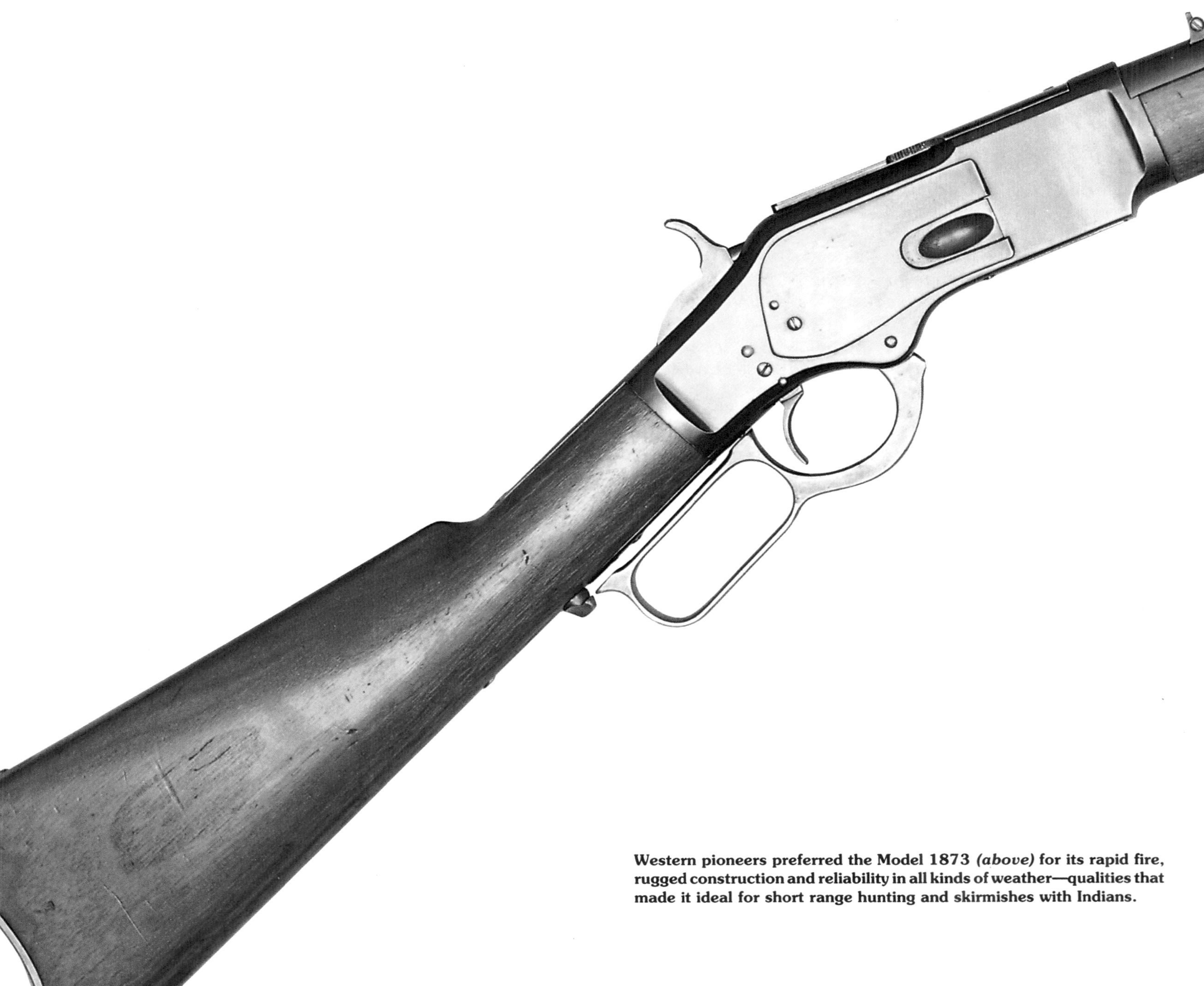

Western pioneers preferred the Model 1873 *(above)* for its rapid fire, rugged construction and reliability in all kinds of weather—qualities that made it ideal for short range hunting and skirmishes with Indians.

Winchesters Years

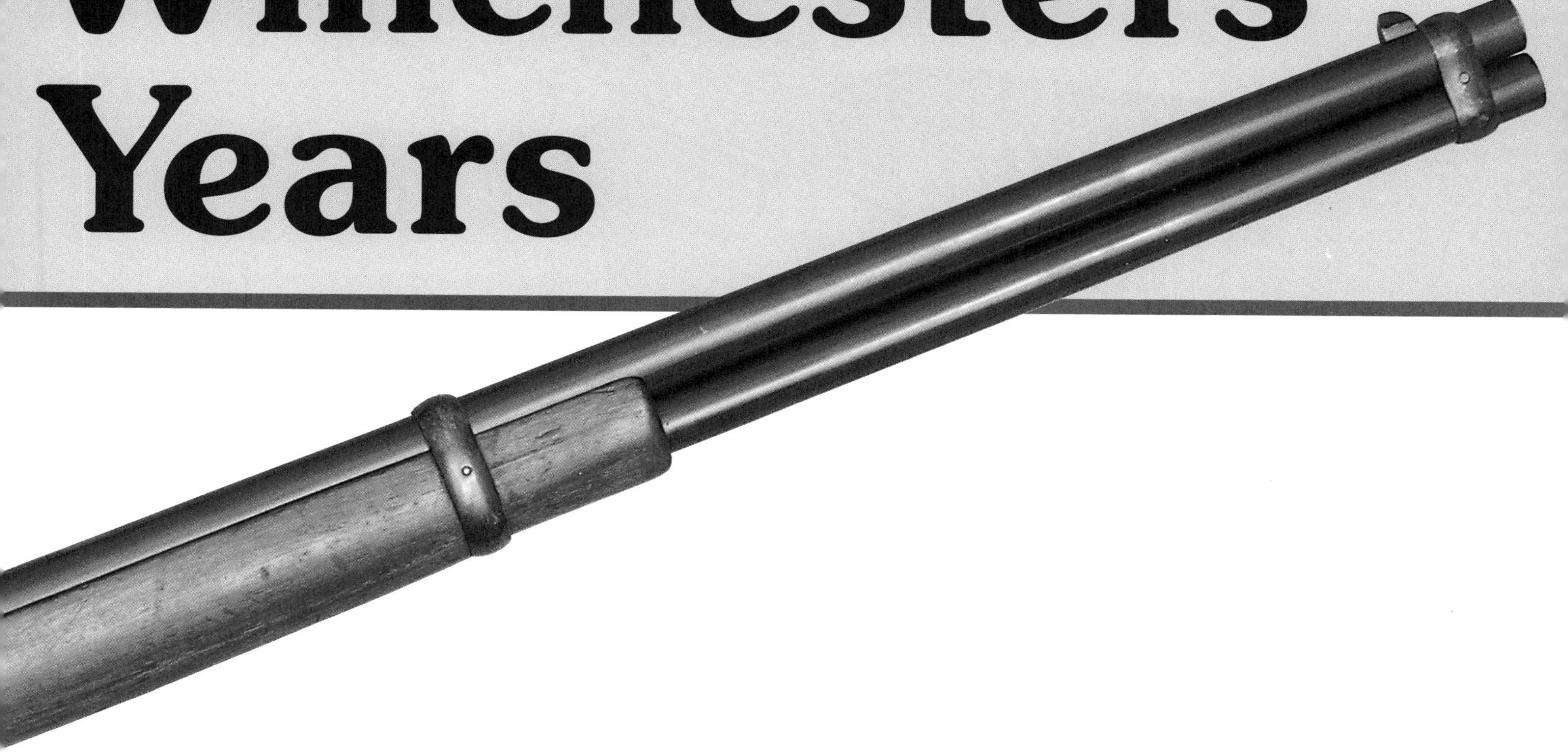

Oliver F Winchester knew that he had the first and best lever-action repeater in the world and did not mind extolling its virtues. In one of his letters, he asks the following historically pertinent questions.

'What would be the value of an army of one hundred thousand infantry and cavalry, thus mounted and armed with a due proportion of artillery, each artilleryman with a repeating carbine slung to his back?

'Certainly the introduction of repeating guns into the army will involve a change of the Manual of Arms. Probably it will modify the art of war; possibly it may revolutionize the whole science of war. Where is the military genius that is to grasp this whole subject, and so modify the science of war as to best develop the capacities of this terrible engine—the exclusive control of which would enable any government (with resources sufficient to keep half a million of men in the field) to rule the world?'

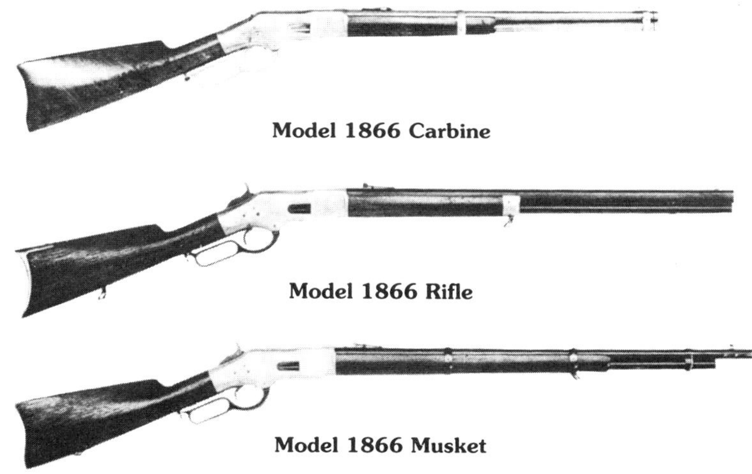

Model 1866 Carbine

Model 1866 Rifle

Model 1866 Musket

The Model 1866. This gun, the first truly operant lever action repeater, was invented by B Tyler Henry and is also known as the Henry Rifle. Various loading methods were developed and patented for the Model 1866 in both 1865 and 1866. Collectors have determined that at least four types of the 1866 were manufactured.

The first model has the Henry drop in the receiver ahead of the hammer, no flare to accommodate the fore end, an additional screw in the upper tang and an inside serial number. The second model has less drop ahead of the hammer and has the fore end flare. The third model has the drop ahead of the hammer but is less pronounced than the preceding two models and has an outside serial number usually in block numerals. The fourth model has slightly less drop in the receiver ahead of the hammer, and the serial number is usually in script numbers between the lever latch and the lower tang screw.

Winchester submitted a specially made Model 1866 to the Army trials in February of 1873. Although this Winchester did not pass all of the tests satisfactorily, it should be noted that none of the repeaters present passed the test. When one considers the details of the testing procedure, one can see why. The first test examined rapidity with aim—the number of shots fired in one minute that strike a target six feet by two feet, at a distance of 100 feet.

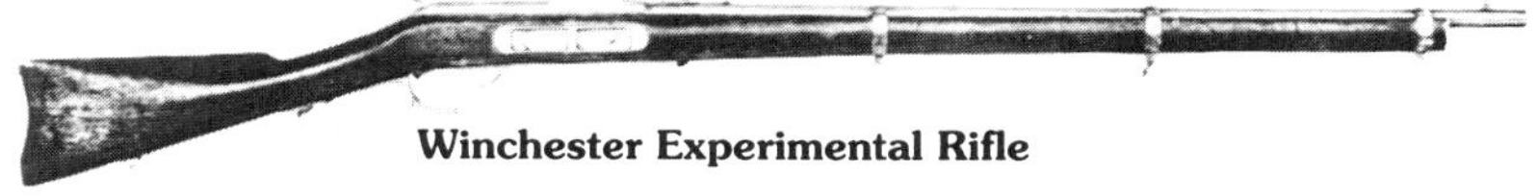

Winchester Experimental Rifle

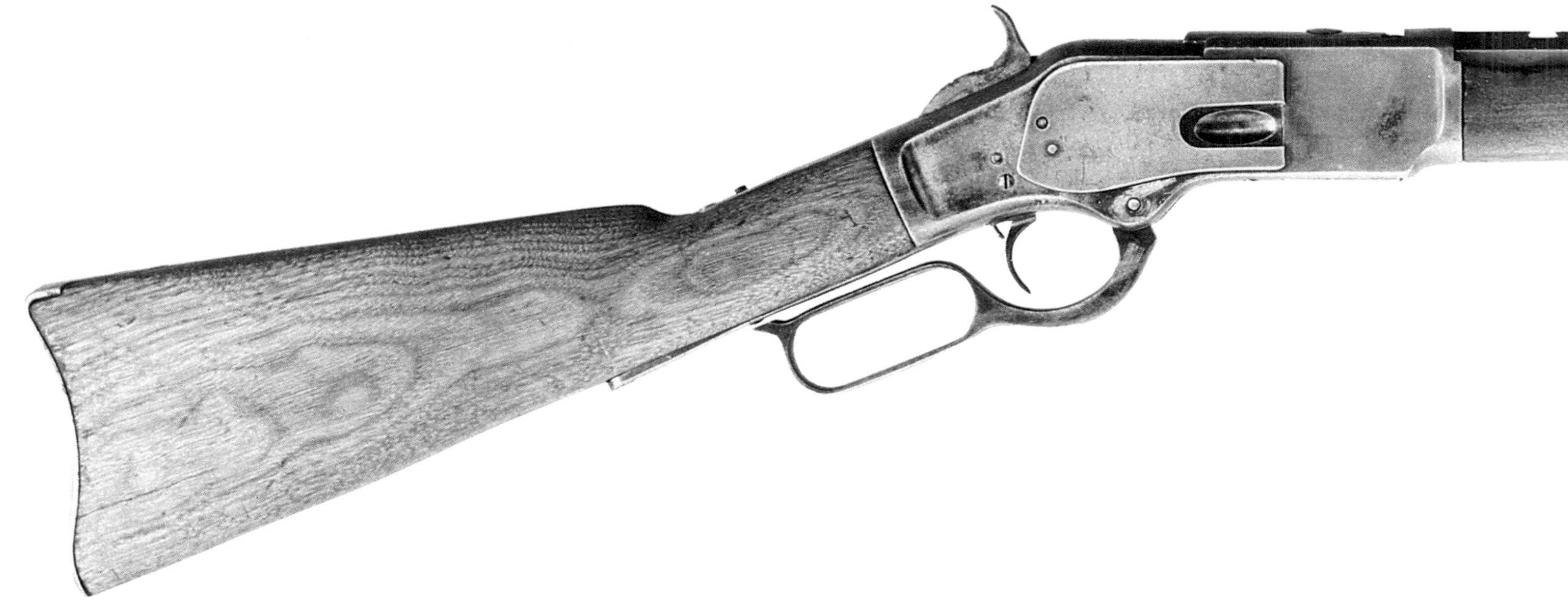

The second tested rapidity at will—the number of shots that can be fired in one minute, irrespective of aim. The third tested endurance. Each gun had to fire 500 continuous rounds, without cleaning, and then the state of the breech mechanism was examined at the end of every 500 rounds. The fourth tested performance with defective cartridges. Each gun was fired once with cartridges that had been cross-filed on the head to nearly the thickness of the metal, cut at intervals around the rim and had a longitudinal cut the whole length of the cartridge from the rim up.

The fifth tested performance under dusty conditions. The gun was placed in a box and exposed to a blast of fine sand dust for several minutes; it was removed from the box, fired 50 rounds, replaced for 5 minutes, removed and fired 50 rounds more. The sixth test examined performance under rusty conditions. The breech mechanism and receiver were cleaned of grease; the chamber of the barrel was then greased and plugged, and the butt of the gun inserted to the height of the chamber in brine for 10 minutes, exposed for 2 days to the open air standing in a rack, and then fired 50 rounds.

The seventh, and final test, examined performance firing overloads. The gun was fired once with 86 grains of powder and one lead ball weighing 450 grains; and again, with 90 grains and one ball; and once again with 90 grains and two balls. The firearm was closely examined after each discharge.

Benito Juarez bought at least 1000 Model 1866s for use in his war with Emperor Maximilian of Mexico. Turkish contracts in 1870 and 1871 accounted for 46,000 muskets and 5000 carbines. The French government also bought 3000 muskets and 3000 carbines from Winchester, and Chili and Peru cooperatively bought a large consignment of 1866 Winchesters at a cost of about $90,000. The Model 1866 was officially discontinued in 1898. Peak production of over 35,000 units had been achieved in 1871.

Model 1873 Carbine

The Model 1873. The Model 1873 is the Winchester best known to collectors and the public alike. Although a tremendous number of variations were produced, collectors have designated at least four separate model types of the '73,' each distinguished by minor structural alterations. The first Model 1873s were manufactured with an iron frame

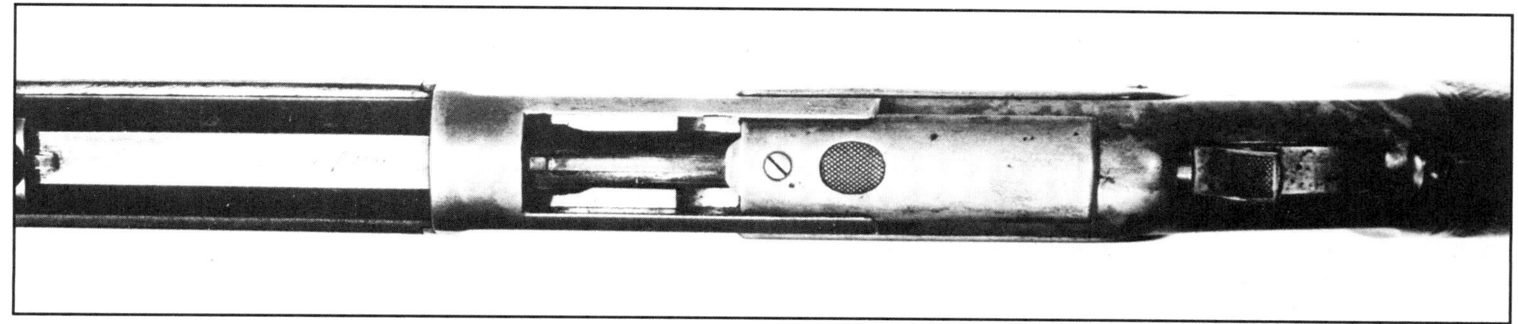

which was later replaced with one of steel, resulting in a lighter gun and lower production costs. A bright blue finish was the standard for the Model 73, with trigger, hammer, lever and internal parts casehardened for greater durability and to minimize wear.

Of particular interest to collectors is a 'cutaway' display Model 73 which was produced in the Winchester Model Shop. This 'cutaway' version featured sectional cuts that enabled Winchester salesmen to show the inner workings of the gun at fairs, exhibits and other public gatherings. Of the few that were produced, no two were sectioned in the same manner.

An interesting, if often misunderstood, variation of the Model 1873 is the 'One of One Thousand.' This version was announced as follows in the 1875 catalog:

'It is the purpose of the manufacturers of these arms to introduce a greater variety than has heretofore been made, to meet the different purposes and uses to which they are applicable, whether for sporting or war. Among these, the demands of amateur sportsmen are the most exacting for an arm that will shoot with unerring accuracy.

'With the perfect machinery and great skill of the men we employ in boring, rifling, straightening, polishing and finishing our barrels, we can always count with confidence upon any

***At bottom:* The Model 66 Carbine. *At top:* The Model 1873 Special Sporting Rifle. For shooters who wanted a premium gun—the Model 1873 One of One Thousand. To collectors of antique firearms, this model is probably the most valuable of all American shoulder arms. *Above:* Detail of barrel marking on a Model 1873 One of One Thousand.**

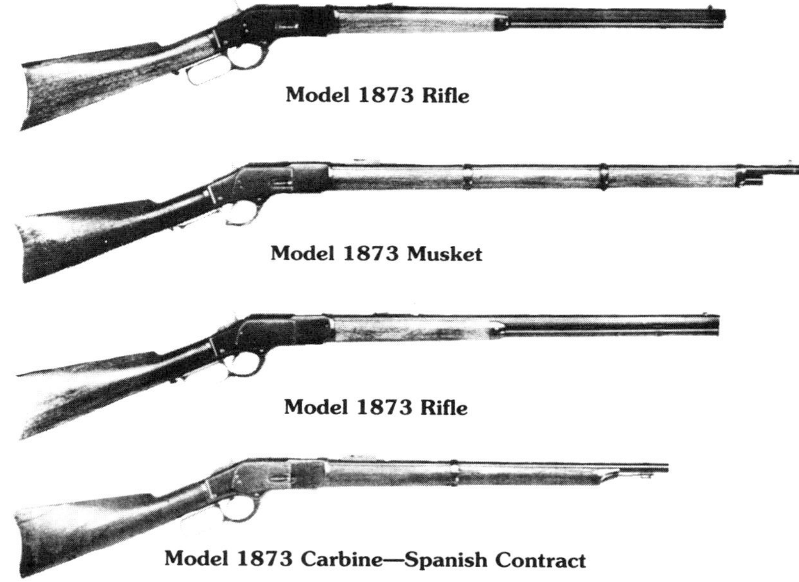

Model 1873 Rifle

Model 1873 Musket

Model 1873 Rifle

Model 1873 Carbine—Spanish Contract

Above: **The Model 1873 One of One Thousand, one of the rarest and finest of the Wild West Winchesters.** ***Left:*** **The infamous Billy the Kid poses with his lever action repeater.** ***Right:*** **Two Indian scouts—one holding a Model 1876—and an Indian school boy, circa 1880.**

barrel shooting with accuracy; but in this as in all other cases, the degree of accuracy will vary. The barrel of every sporting rifle we make will be proved and shot at a target, and the target will be numbered to correspond with the barrel and be attached to it.

'All of the barrels that are found to make targets of extra merit will be made up into guns with set triggers and extra finish and marked, as a designating name, One of One Thousand.'

By 1877, the One of One Thousand was dropped from the catalog but not before a total of 136 of these firearms were produced. Although only 36 of these guns have been found to date, it is believed by most collectors that others are still somewhere in circulation.

The year 1891 saw the greatest Model 73s produced, when over 41,000 were manufactured. Production ceased in 1923 after over 700,000 had been produced.

Model 1876 Carbine

Model 1876 Rifle

The Model 1876. After the introduction of the Model 1873, Winchester conceded that 'the constant calls from many sources, and particularly from the regions in which the grizzly bear and other large game are found, as well as the plains where absence of cover and shyness of game require the hunter to make his shots at long range, made it desirable to build a still more powerful gun than the Model 1873.'

In 1876, at the Philadelphia Centennial Exposition, the Model 1876 first appeared. It was immediately christened the 'Centennial Model,' commemorating the anniversary of the Revolutionary War. The Model 1876 is essentially the same as the Model 73, but is built heavier, to handle the .45-75 WCF cartridge.

In 1886, production of the Model 76 was discontinued, but the last rifle did not leave the factory until over 10 years later. Production figures indicate that a little over 63,000 of

these rifles were manufactured, with most of them having been sold to the Royal Canadian Mounted Police, who used them in the Indian conflicts of Western Canada around the turn of the century. By 1905, the Model 76 had been retired from duty with the Mounties, but not before it had carved a record for dependability and ruggedness. The peak production year was 1884, when over 12,000 were manufactured.

The Model 71. The Winchester 1871, a continuation of the Model 1886, commenced production in 1935. This rifle was chambered only for the .348 Winchester, for which varying bullet weights of 150, 200 and 250 grains were offered. A 24-inch barrel, an open sporting or peep rear sights and hooded front ramp sights were standard. The Model 71 was available in 'Standard Rifle' and 'Deluxe Rifle' grades with the 'Deluxe' having sling loops and slings, a pistol grip cap and checkering. By the time the Model 71 was discontinued in 1958, over 47,000 had been produced.

The Model 53. The Model 53 was introduced in 1924 as a continuation of the Model 1892. Chambered for .25-20, .32-20 and .44-40 cartridges, this rifle has a 22 inch round barrel, a six shot magazine, straight grip and shotgun style butt plate. The Model 53 is considered by collectors to be a rare gun since it was discontinued in 1932 and only about 25,000 were actually produced over a period of 10 years.

The Model 65. Another continuation of the Model 1892, the Model 65 features a shotgun butt stock, uncapped pistol grips and a semi beavertail fore end. The barrel is tapered, generally 22 inches long and the magazine holds seven shots. The Model 65 is chambered for the .218 Bee, the .25-20, and .32-20 cartridges. A total of less than 6000 were manufactured from 1933 to 1947.

The Model 1901. The Model 1901 is a lever action shotgun made for smokeless powder loads and available only in 10 gauge. Its barrel length is 32 inches, with a standard blued overall finish. The Model 1901 did not sell well, principally because the relatively new slide action shotguns of the period were proving themselves far more popular.

The Model 1901 has some safety features, among them a trigger block and a mechanically operated firing pin retractor, both of which prevent accidental discharge. Manufacture of the Model 1901 ceased in 1920, and the remaining guns on hand were shipped to Mexico in the early 1930s.

The Model 64. The Model 64 is a long-lived and very popular continuation model which utilized John M Browning's Model 1894 action. It was introduced in 1933, and was chambered for various cartridges including the .25-35, the .30-30, the .32 Winchester Special and the .219 Zipper. A rapid taper 24-inch barrel is standard, with ramp type front sights. Manufacture of the Model 64 ceased in 1956 but was resumed in 1970.

The Lee Model Winchester. The Lee Winchester is a bolt action rifle which uses a slight upward and then rearward

Left: **A serious Gary Cooper (photo far left), appearing in the 1950 movie *Dallas*, keeps his Winchester Model 1876 close by his side. The Model 76 was introduced to fill the need for a powerful, long range rifle.**

Above: **The wreck of the *Maine*, with Winchesters aboard. *At left:* For over 50 years, the Model 73 Lever Action Repeating Rifle was one of the most popular rifles produced by Winchester.**

pull of the bolt. This type of action is both fast and dependable. Only about 20,000 Lee 'straight pull' models were produced and of these only a small number were fitted as sporting rifles.

Although it had been in use by US Armed forces for many years, sportsmen found it less desirable than most lever actions. The majority of Lee Winchesters—in musket configuration—were sold to the Navy and saw duty in the Spanish-American War. Apparently, a large number of these Lee muskets were on board the *Maine* when it was sunk in Havana Harbor. About 50 of these rifles were recovered from the ship, and were later sold by a New York arms dealer. Manufacture of the Lee Model was discontinued in 1902.

The Model 1898 Winchester Cannon. While the Winchester Cannon is not a true gun because it does not fire projectiles, it has nonetheless proved to be a crowd pleaser for the general public, as well as being a sought-after collectors' item. The cannon is made for 10 gauge black powder blanks only, and the barrel is marked 'Not for Ball.' The earliest of these cannons were made with enamelled metal surfaces and had steel wheels. On later models, rubber tires and chrome plated metal parts were also available at extra cost. The cannons were designed primarily as a starter or salute guns and so were in limited demand. However, nearly 19,000 had been manufactured before they were discontinued in 1958.

Winchester-Western Rifles

Winchester Model 73 Lever Action Repeating Rifle. The Model 73 is chambered for .32-20, .38-40 and .44-40 cartridges. Over 720,000 rifles of this model were manufactured from 1873 to 1924.

Winchester Single Shot Rifle. Designed by John M Browning, this firearm was manufactured from 1885 to 1920 in a variety of models and chambered for most of the popular cartridges of the period, rimfire and center fire, from .22 to .50 caliber. See also the description in the 'Major Browning Winchester Models' section of this text.

Model 1886 Rifle, Takedown

Model 1886 Rifle, Takedown

Winchester Model 86 Lever Action Repeater. Available in solid frame or takedown style, this rifle was made from 1886 to 1935. It is a lever action repeating rifle chambered for .45-70, .38-56, .45-90-300, .40-82-260, .40-65-260, .38-56-255, .38-70-255, .40-70-330, .50-110-300, .50-100-450 and .33 caliber. See also the description in the 'Major Browning Winchester Models' section of this text.

43. MINERS AT HOME.
PHOTO. BY McCLURE

Winchester Model 90 Slide Action Repeater. The Model 90 is a pump action rifle that was chambered for the .22 short, long and .22 long rifle, and the .22 Winchester rimfire cartridge. It was manufactured from 1890 to 1932. See also the description in the 'Major Browning Winchester Models' section of this text.

Winchester Model 92 Lever Action Repeating Rifle. A solid frame or takedown, the Model 92 is chambered for .25-20, .32-20, .38-40 and .44-40 cartridges. It was made from 1892 to 1941. See also the description in the 'Major Browning Winchester Models' section of this text.

Winchester Model 53 Lever Action Repeating Rifle. A modification of the Model 92, this rifle of .25-20, .32-20 or .44-40 caliber was made from 1924 to 1932.

Winchester Model 65 Lever Action Rifle. Manufactured from 1933 to 1947, this design represented an improved version of the Model 53 in .25-20 and .32-20 calibers.

At left:* A vintage photo of miners in their Colorado Gold Rush cabin, with at least one Winchester against the wall. *Above:* Cowhands and a Winchester in Weepah, Nevada in 1927. *Below:* A Winchester-wielding desperado in the motion picture *A Fistful of Dollars.

Special Features

Winchester went to great lengths to please its customers by offering a variety of special order features for their guns in almost every conceivable price range and taste spectrum. Some of these special features were available for only a short time, while others were listed in Winchester catalogs for many years. Some features were standard on one type of gun but were listed as options on other types.

Variations in barrel style and length are just one example of the special features available. Round barrels were standard for all lever action Winchester rifles, but any customer could order an octagonal barrel at additional charge.

'Extra heavy' target barrels were provided for some models and these, whether round or octagonal in shape, were available in any length up to 36 inches. These rifles with heavy barrels were sometimes known as 'Buffalo Rifles.' For a time Winchester offered 'extra light weight' rifles in certain models but these did not prove to be as popular as the standard rifles. If the customer so desired, he could order his rifle with the front half of the barrel rounded and the rear portion octagonal in shape—which provided a finer overall balance in the gun.

The types, sizes, variations and designs of sights available for Winchester guns are no less than legion. They include 'The Winchester Express,' 'The Rocky Mountain Front Sight,' 'The Knife Blade,' 'The Marbles Improved Sight,' 'The Beach Combination Sight,' 'The Vickers-Maxim Sight,' 'The Globe Sight,' 'The Lymans Patent Windgauge Front Sight,' 'The Marbles Duplex,' 'The Caterpillar,' 'The Military Wind Gauge Sight,' 'The Flexible Rear Sight,' 'The Combination Tang Peep Sight,' 'The Mid Range Vernier Peep Sight' and 'The Spirit Lever Sight.'

Winchester even manufactured, for a while, telescopic scopes of high quality with five different reticles in three, four and five power. If a customer wanted a nonglaring sighting plane, he could order a matted barrel in either cross checkered or weaving lines design.

Smoothbore barrels could be ordered if the customer wanted to use shot cartridges. These smoothbore guns were mainly made for exhibition shooters, and were available in a wide variety of calibers. Various rifling twist combinations were also available upon request. Winchester, for many years, ran the following discussion of rifling in its catalogs.

'One of the most difficult things to determine in making rifle barrels is the twist, or rifling, required to shoot a given cartridge to best advantage. Cartridges of different or like caliber containing different weights of powder or lead require a different twist. A proper twist is one which will spin a bullet fast enough to keep it point on to the limit of its range, thus insuring the best possible accuracy.

'If the twist is too slow the flight of the bullet will be untrue, and it will "tumble" or "keyhole," as it is called when a bullet passes through the air in a lengthwise position instead of point on. On the contrary, if the twist is too quick or sharp the bullet will spin so rapidly that it is unsteady in its flight and wobbles like a top when it first begins to spin.

'The only sure way of ascertaining a perfect twist is by calculation and exhaustive practical tests. The Winchester Repeating Arms Company have complete facilities for verifying all calculations for twist, which enables them to determine with positive certainty the twist that will give best results with a given cartridge.'

These special order riflings could be ordered in basically three types—the Medford, the Whitworth or the Alexander Henry, as well as other more exotic styles. Winchester also offered a number of different devices intended to reduce the rifle's blast noise. Other devices were offered to reduce its recoil; these and other options were fitted upon request.

Most Winchesters had stocks made of selected straight grain American walnut. While American walnut was the standard, other woods such as English, Italian, or other imported walnuts, maple (either curly or bird's eye), orangewood or other fruitwoods such as cherry and peach, could be special ordered.

Winchester employed a rigid system of stock grading which included four basic categories—the grain flow of the wood (which was designated as either straight or fancy); the density of the wood (which had a great bearing on the kind of carving or checkering ultimately performed on it); the contrast or grain of the wood (which mainly had to do with its color and shading); and the fitting and finishing of the wood.

Winchester's checkering and carving were generally divided into eight different styles denominated A through H. Styles A and B consisted of carving, while a moderate amount of border carving was used with style C. Style D incorporated carving—usually of oak leaves and acorns—and style E was generally a tasteful combination of checkering and carving. Styles F, G and H carried progressively less carving, and style H (the lowest priced) carried only checkering.

In addition, Winchester offered color casehardening of receivers and butt plates as well as hammers and levers. During this process, the parts were packed in airtight cylinders with a combination of bone meal and leather dust heated to a red hot temperature. The parts were then quenched quickly in water. The quenching step actually controlled the colors that would appear, in an iridescent shimmer on the metal so tempered.

Plating in gold, silver, nickel and chrome was offered on many models. Winchester engraving was generally priced according to coverage and quality, and ranged through 10 grades, although the quality of the workmanship varied slightly from grade to grade. Various scenes were offered in standard patterns, but the customer could have an illustration from a photograph duplicated to his taste. Both American and English scrolls were employed in Winchester engraving, and inscriptions on the engraved gun were done in a variety of patterns consisting of names, dates or other pertinent information.

Also, gold, silver or platinum bands could be inlaid on engraved barrels or receivers if ordered. 'Engraving' means that the lines are cut into the metal, penetrating the surface. 'Inlay work' means that a precious metal is used to fill in the engraved grooves, and 'sculptured designs' refer to precious metal designs that are raised above the surface of the firearm. More often than not, the term 'inlay work' is used to include 'sculptured designs.' The engravers who worked for Winchester have in the past been allowed to choose their own patterns, provided the engravers had sufficient expertise to carry it off, or they could follow the basic styles that were offered in the current catalogs.

Figures of deer have been, by far, the most popular designs—with standing, drinking, listening and pausing stances generally the most used. The elk has also been a popular animal as well as moose, mountain goat, bear and antelope. Some kinds of buffalo and hunting dogs have also been pictured, but these are considered rare animals on older Winchesters, as are scenes which contained more than one animal.

Finally, Winchester has offered extra parts that could be special ordered for various firearms. For example, saber bayonets of 25 inches in length were offered for a number of Winchester muskets, as well as matching leather scabbards with brass fittings. Winchester has also offered saddle rings for firearms.

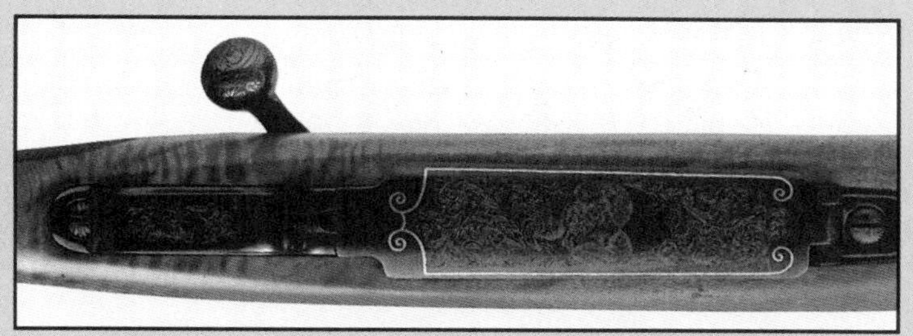

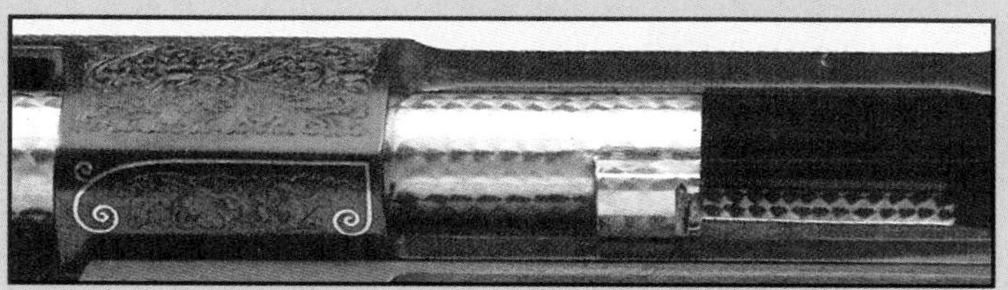

Custom work from Winchester—*right, from top down:* An engraved trigger guard and floor plate; a hand-jewelled bolt and magazine follower; and a hand-engraved receiver with gold inlay. *Below, left and right:* gold inlaid muzzle band and an engraved pistol grip cap. *At bottom, left to right:* Model 70 Exhibition Grade; Model 70 Custom Built; and a Super-X Model 1 Shotgun.

Winchester-Western Shotguns

Winchester Model 1887 Lever Action Repeater. Made from 1887 to 1901, the Model 1887 is a solid frame 10 or 12 gauge shotgun with a four shot tubular magazine. It has a plain 30- or 32-inch barrel, with full choke, and a plain pistol grip stock. It weighs nine pounds in 10 gauge and eight pounds in 12 gauge. See also the description in the 'Major Browning Winchester Models' section of this text.

Model 1887 Shotgun

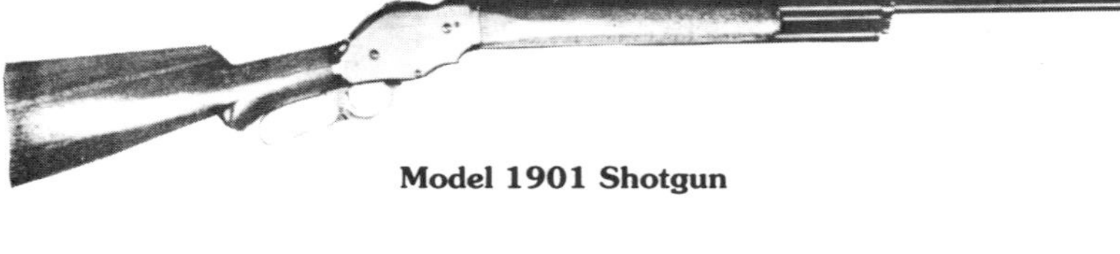

Model 1901 Shotgun

Winchester Model 1901 Lever Action Repeater. The Model 1901 is a redesigned version of the Model 1887, and has the same general specifications. It is available in 10 gauge only and was made from 1901 to 1920.

Winchester Model 97 Slide Action Repeating Shotgun. The Model 97 is a standard grade, takedown or solid frame pump action shotgun in 12 or 16 gauge, with a five shell tubular magazine. Available with barrel lengths of 26 to 32 inches, it weighs about 7.75 pounds and has a plain pistol grip stock and grooved slide handle. This firearm was manufactured from 1897 to 1957. See also the description in the 'Major Browning Winchester Models' section of this text.

Winchester Model 1911 Autoloading Shotgun. The Model 1911 is a hammerless, takedown semiautomatic shotgun in 12 gauge only, with a four shell tubular magazine. It weighs about 8.5 pounds and was made from 1911 to 1925. It should be noted that John M Browning invented the autoloading—or, 'automatic'—shotgun.

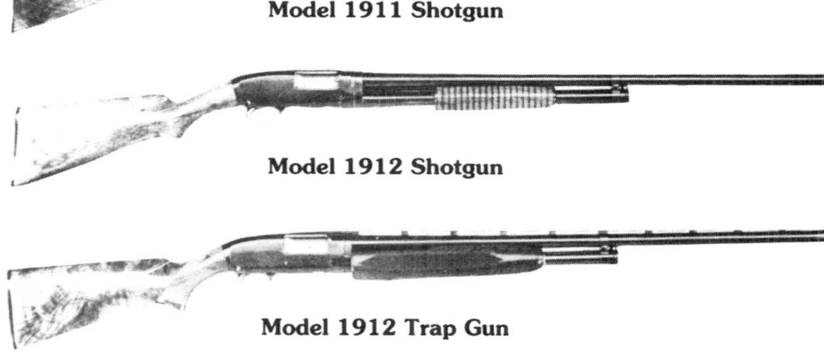

Model 1911 Shotgun

Model 1912 Shotgun

Model 1912 Trap Gun

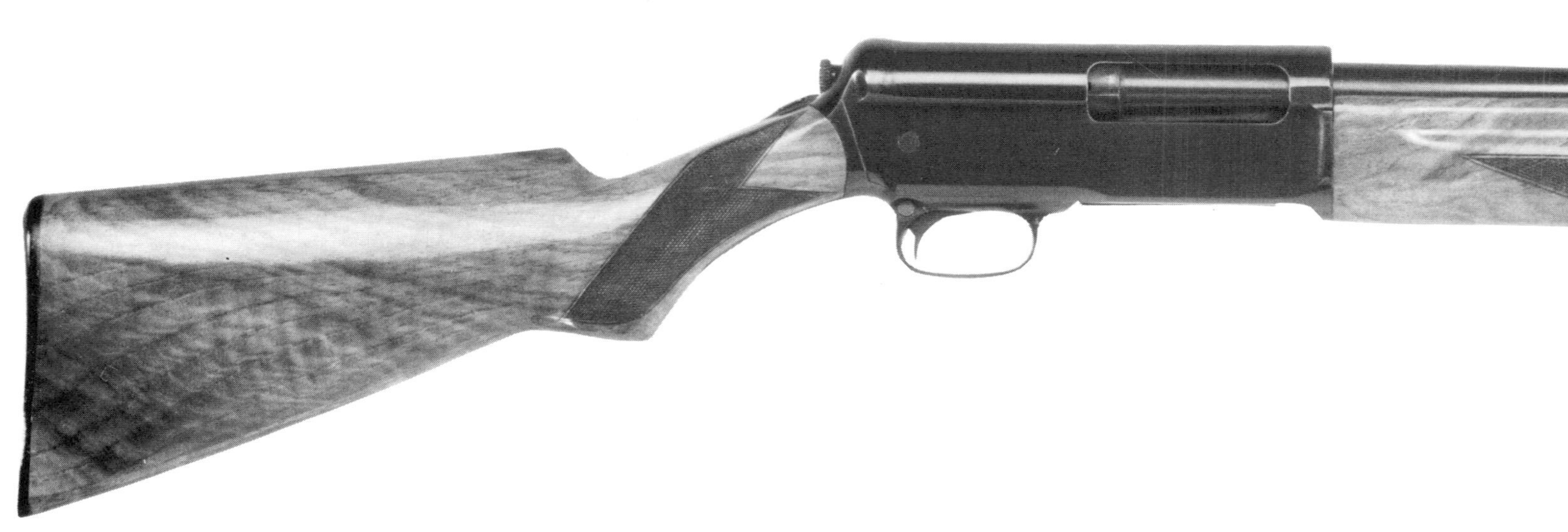

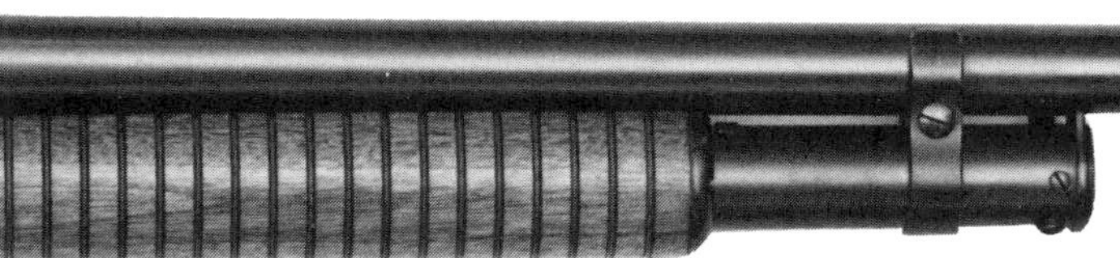

Winchester Model 12 Standard Slide Action Repeating Shotgun. The Model 12 is a hammerless, takedown pump action shotgun in 12, 16, 20 or 28 gauge, with a six shell tubular magazine and barrel lengths of from 26 to 32 inches with full to cylinder chokes. It weighs about 7.5 pounds and was made from 1912 to 1964.

Model 1912 Trench Gun

Winchester Single Shot Lever Action Shotgun. Like the Single Shot Rifle, this 20 gauge shotgun has a falling block action, with a high wall receiver. Available in solid frame or takedown, it has a 3-inch chamber, a 26-inch barrel and weighs about 5.5 pounds. This firearm was manufactured from 1914 to 1916.

Model 20 Shotgun

Winchester Model 20 Single Shot Hammer Gun. The Model 20 is a takedown single shot shotgun chambered for a .410 gauge, 2.5 inch shell. It has a 2-inch barrel with a full choke and was made from 1919 to 1924.

Winchester Model 36 Single Shot Bolt Action Shotgun. The Model 36—a single shot, takedown firearm—uses 9mm short or long, shot shells or 'pumpkin ball' cartridges interchangeably. It weighs about three pounds and was made from 1920 to 1927.

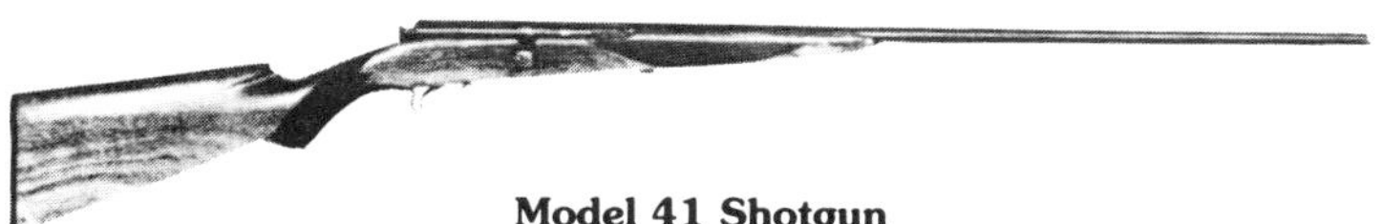

Model 41 Shotgun

Winchester Model 41 Single Shot Bolt Action Shotgun. The Model 41 is a single shot, takedown shotgun chambered for a .410 gauge, 2.5-inch paper shot shell. It has a 24-inch barrel with full choke and was made from 1920 to 1934.

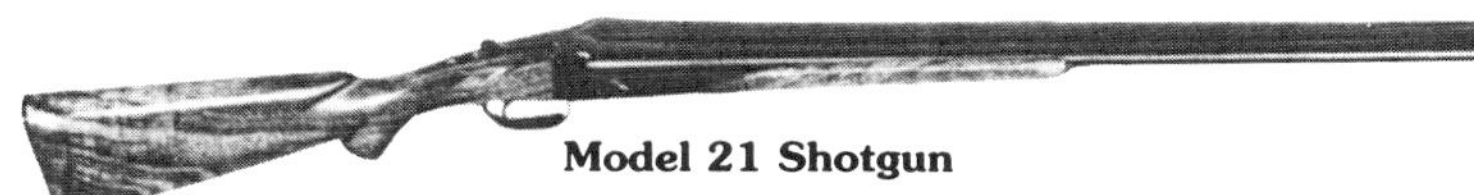

Model 21 Shotgun

Winchester Model 21 Double Barrel Field Gun. The Model 21 is a hammerless, box lock double barreled shotgun with an automatic safety. Made in 12, 16 and 20 gauge, it is available with double triggers or a selective single trigger, and selective or nonselective ejection. This gun was made from 1930 to 1958.

At top: The Model 97 became the standard against which other shotguns were judged. *At bottom:* The Model 1911 Autoloading Shotgun. John M Browning was the genius behind this revolutionary design.

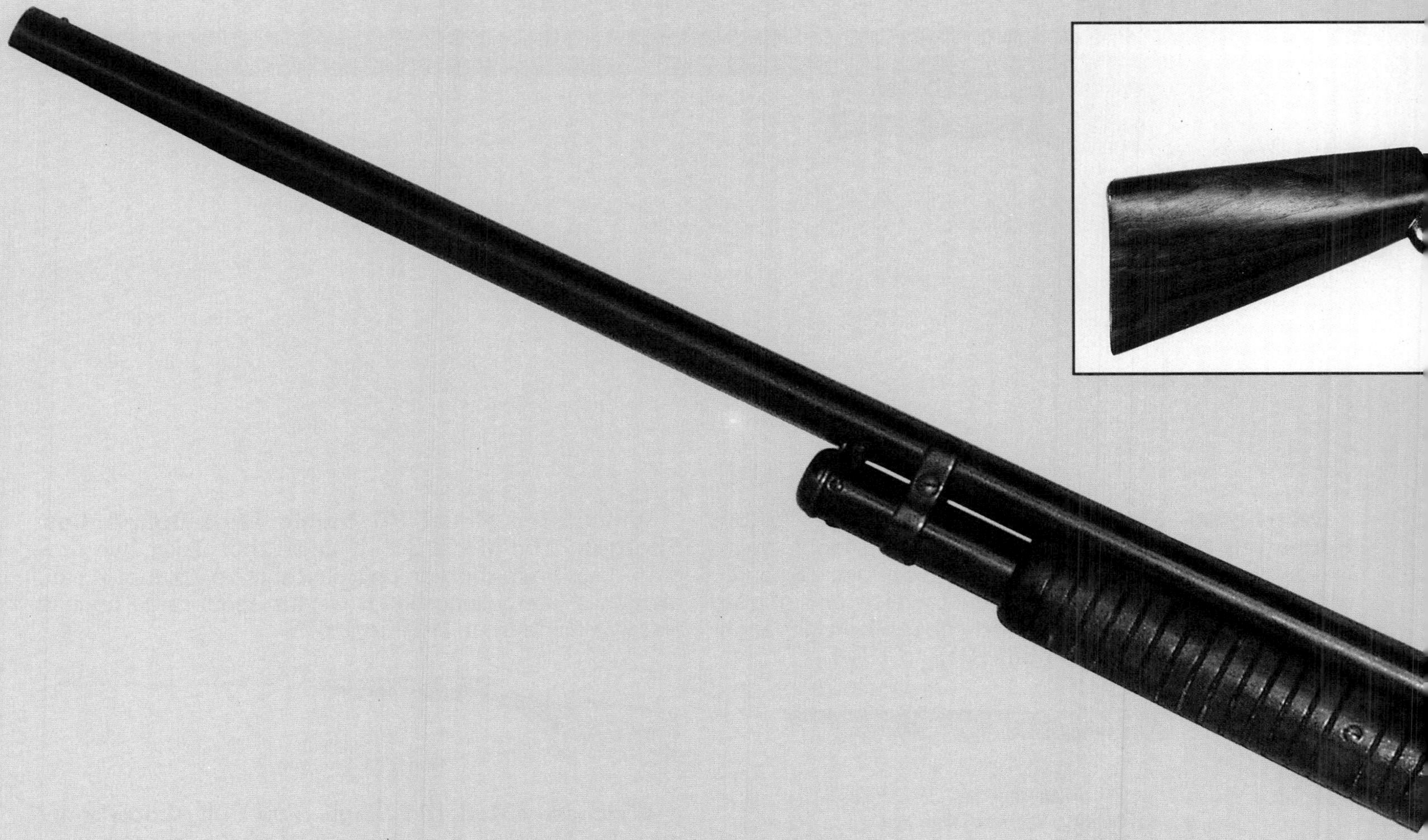

The Model 93 Shotgun *(far right)* was the forerunner of the Model 1897 Shotgun *(above and below)*. The Model 97's refinements corrected a number of weaknesses in the Model 93. The most notable modification was an improved slide lock which kept the gun locked until it was fired, thereby preventing the gun from jamming in case of a misfire.

The Winchester Model 21 –
An American Classic, Built to Your Order.

Coveted by many, possessed by a fortunate few, the Winchester® Model 21 side-by-side shotgun stands alone in its field. Heir to a half-century tradition of excellence, it is a jewel of American custom craftsmanship.

Like a fine painting or rare gem, each Model 21 is unique. In every detail of its year-long construction, it is painstakingly handbuilt to the owner's specifications. Exquisitely grained walnut, superb hand-checkering, intricate hand-engraving and inlays of precious metals are all brought together to create a masterpiece as distinctively yours as your own fingerprint. To fit your shooting requirements, the Model 21 is offered in a selection of gauges, chokes, and barrel lengths.

While not inexpensive, your Model 21 in Grand American or Custom grade will repay you amply in terms of shooting pleasure and in the certain knowledge that you own the finest example of the American gunmaker's art.

For a copy of the Model 21 prospectus, send $10.00 to: The Model 21 Custom Shop, U.S. Repeating Arms Company, 275 Winchester Avenue, New Haven, Connecticut 06511, or call (203) 789-5000.

WINCHESTER.
more than a gun,
an American legend.

Winchester trademarks licensed from Olin Corporation.

Winchester Model 21, Grand American. Since 1959, the Model 21 has been offered only in deluxe models on special order. Each of these custom guns has a full fancy American walnut stock and forearm with fancy checkering, finely polished and hand smoothed working parts with engraved inlays, carved stocks and other extras available at additional cost. Made from 1960, these have been among Winchester's presentation best at a cost of about $10,000.

Model 42 Shotgun

Winchester Model 42 Standard Slide Action Repeating Shotgun. The Model 42 is a hammerless, takedown shotgun in .410 guage. The tubular magazine holds five 3-inch or six 2.5-inch shells. Made from 1933 to 1963, it weighs about six pounds.

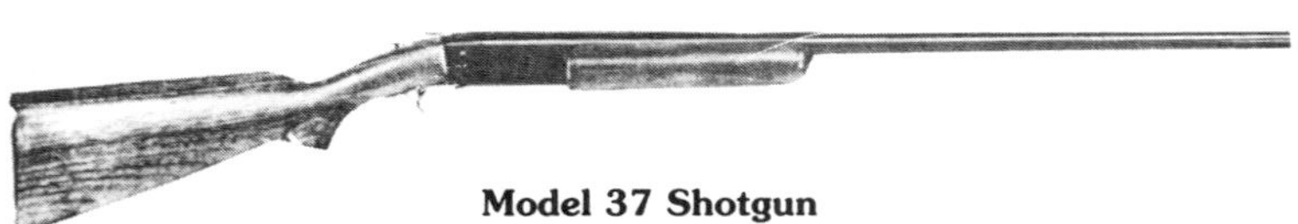

Model 37 Shotgun

Winchester Model 37 Single Barrel Shotgun. The Model 37 is semi-hammerless, takedown shotgun in 12, 16, 20, 28 and .410 gauge with automatic ejection. It was made from 1937 to 1963.

From the first firearms manufactured by the New Haven Arms Company *(right)*, Winchester has maintained a standard of excellence, as is illustrated by the custom built Model 21 seen in the advertisement *above*.

Winchester Model 370 Single Barrel Shotgun. The Model 370 is a takedown shotgun in 12, 16, 20, 28 and .410 gauge with automatic ejection. This firearm was produced from 1968 to 1973.

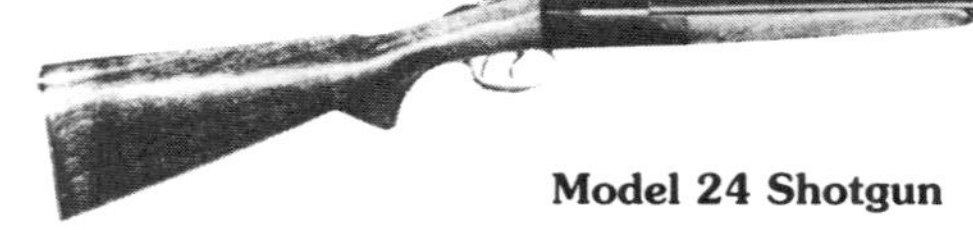

Model 24 Shotgun

Winchester Model 24 Hammerless Double Barrel Shotgun. The Model 24 is a double barreled box lock shotgun with double triggers, plain extractors and automatic safety. Made in 12, 16 and 20 gauge, it was manufactured from 1939 to 1957.

Model 40 Shotgun

Winchester Model 40 Standard Autoloading Shotgun. Made from 1940 to 1941, the Model 40 is an automatic repeating shotgun with a streamlined receiver. Hammerless and takedown-capable, it is available in 12 gauge only, with a four shell tubular magazine.

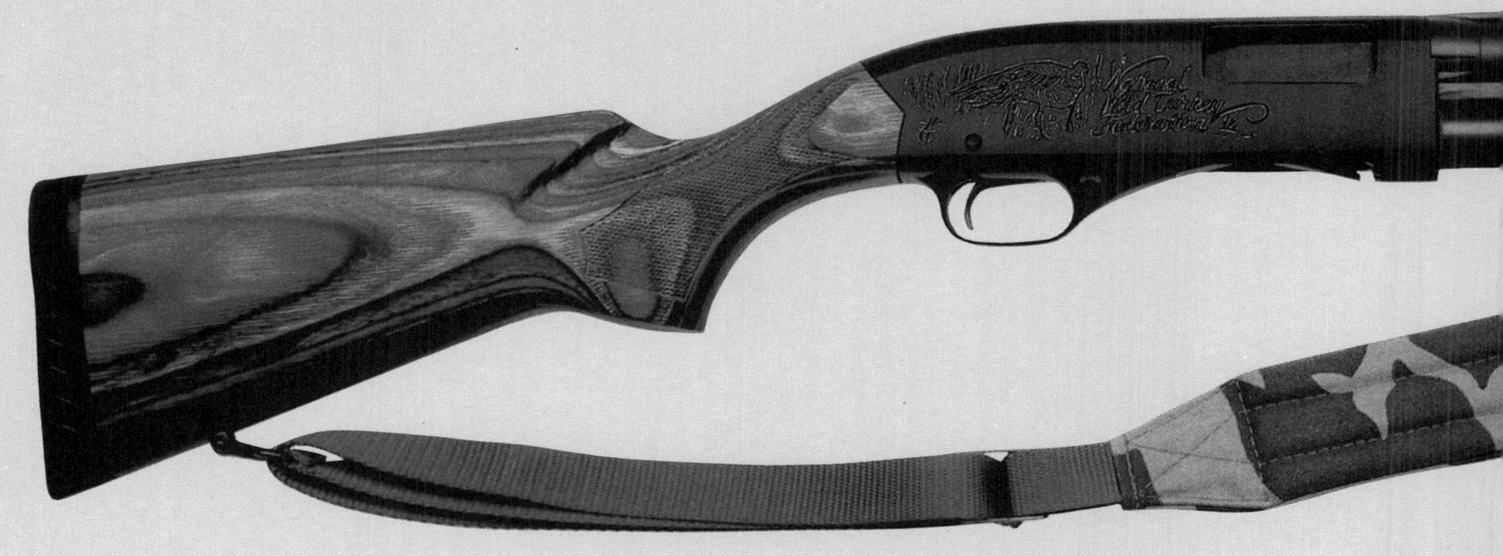

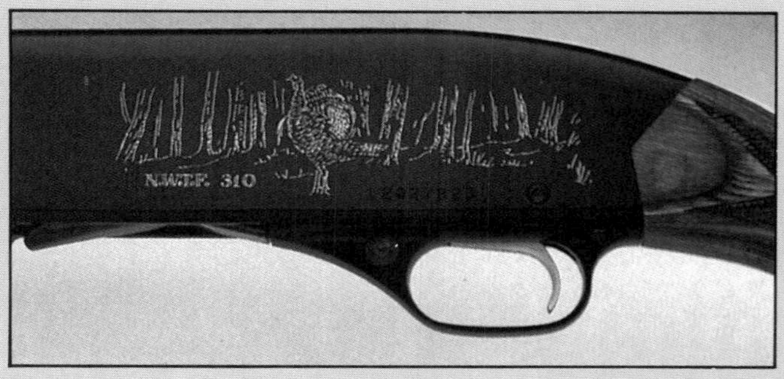

Named the 1987 Gun of the Year by the National Wild Turkey Federation, the Model 1300 Special Turkey Gun *(above)* was introduced as a tribute to the successful restoration of the wild turkey. This 12 gauge, pump action shotgun has a ventilated 22-inch rib barrel, Winchoke system, and a roll-engraved receiver with turkey scenes. It also features military-style lock-up of bolt and barrel *(far right)*. The Collector's Edition Model features an engraved and gold-filled receiver *(left)* and gold-plated trigger, middle and front sights. *Below:* The regular edition Model 1300 Turkey Gun has a satin-finished walnut or laminated WIN-CAM stock and forearm, with roll engraving on the receiver. *Below right:* The Model 1300 CamoPack combines all the features of the regular Turkey Gun with an extra 30-inch Waterfowl barrel.

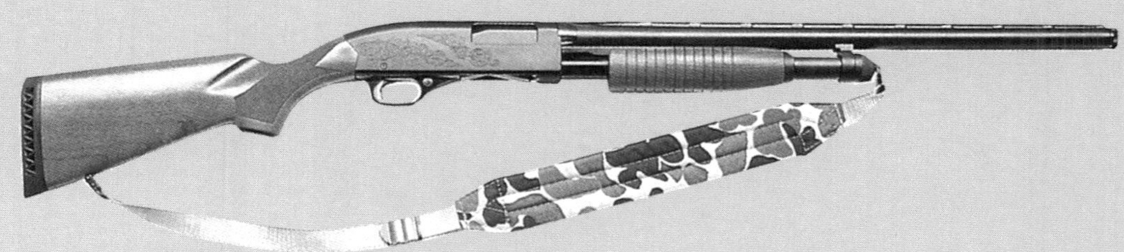

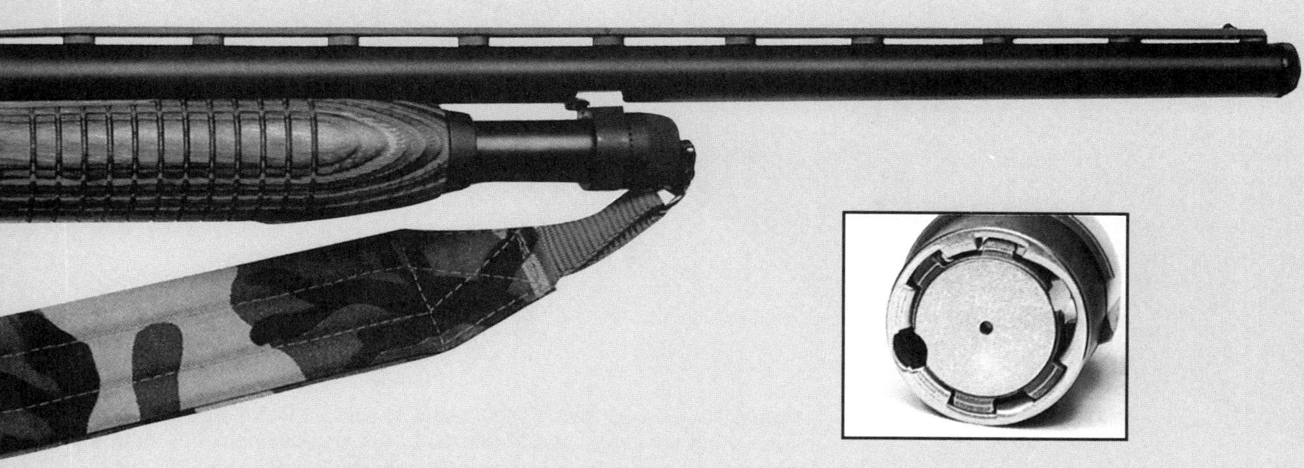

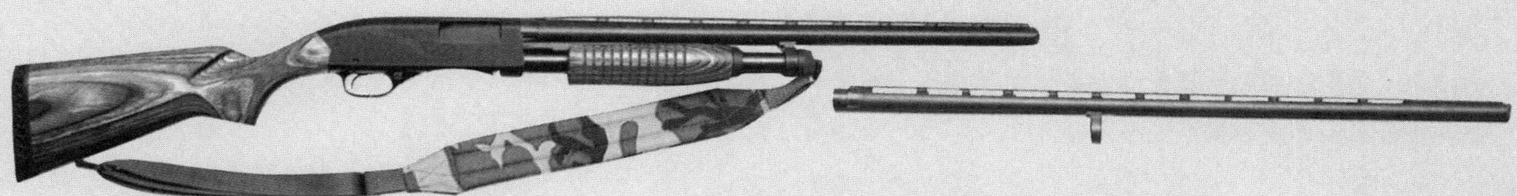

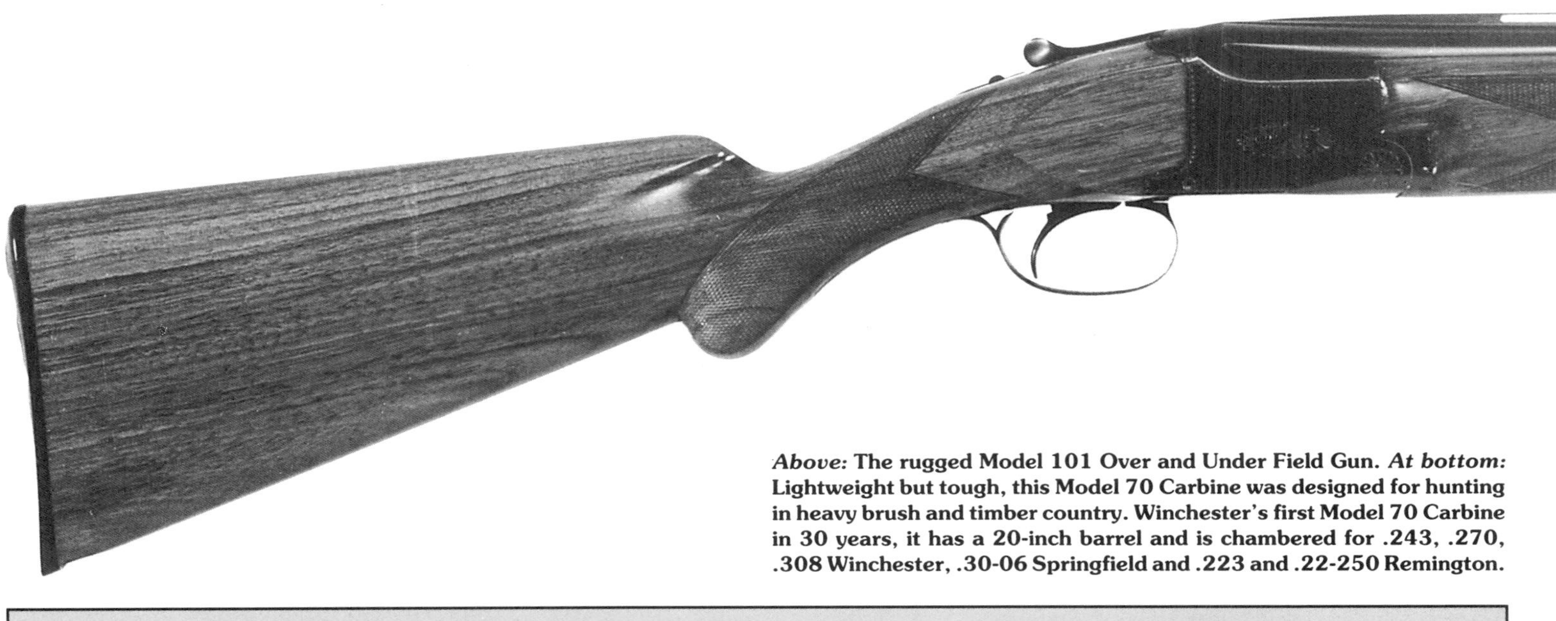

Above: The rugged Model 101 Over and Under Field Gun. *At bottom:* Lightweight but tough, this Model 70 Carbine was designed for hunting in heavy brush and timber country. Winchester's first Model 70 Carbine in 30 years, it has a 20-inch barrel and is chambered for .243, .270, .308 Winchester, .30-06 Springfield and .223 and .22-250 Remington.

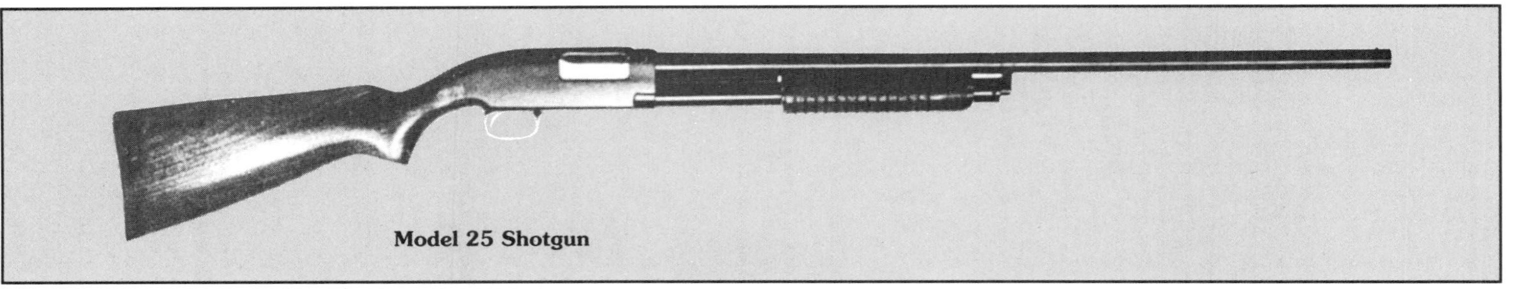

Model 25 Shotgun

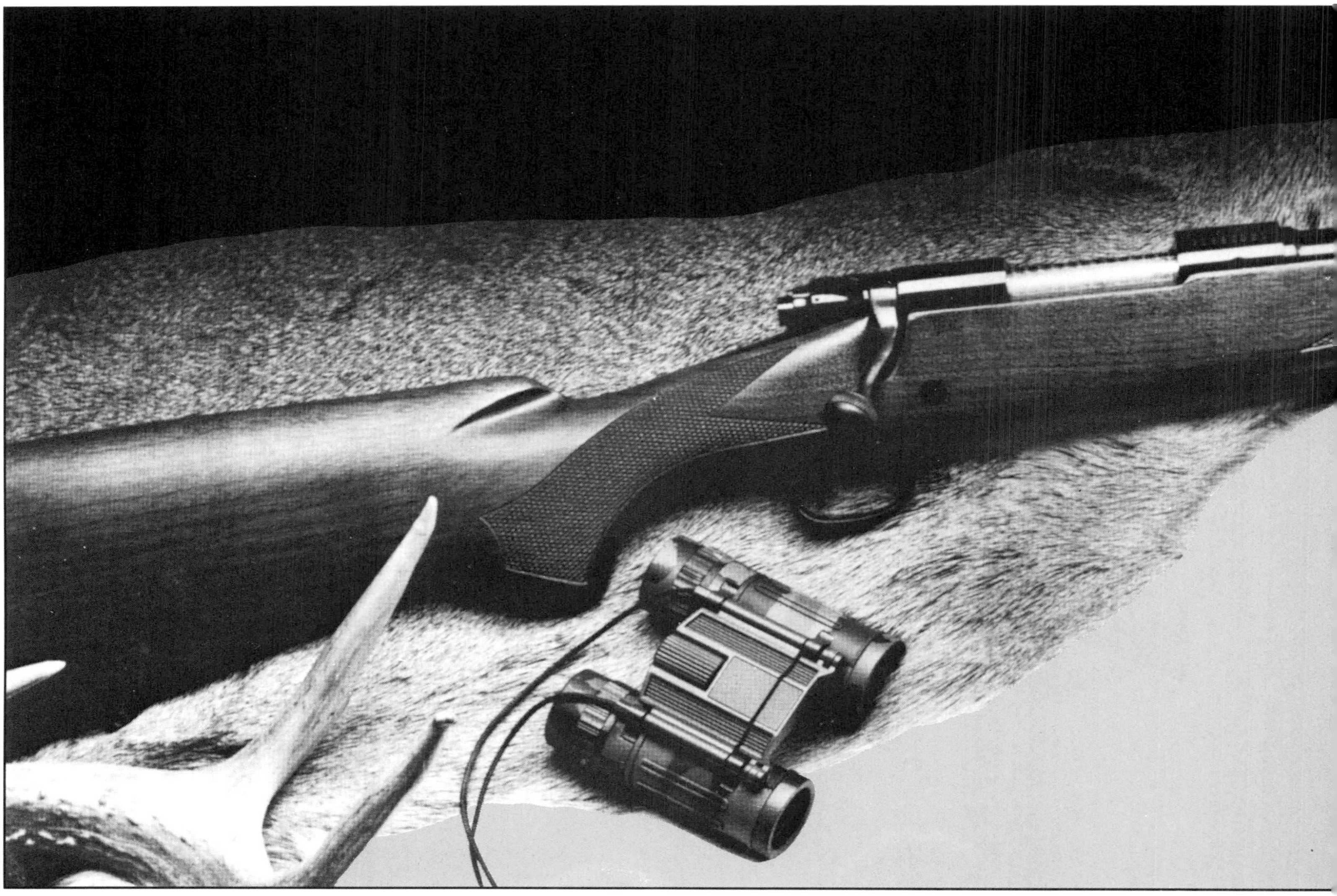

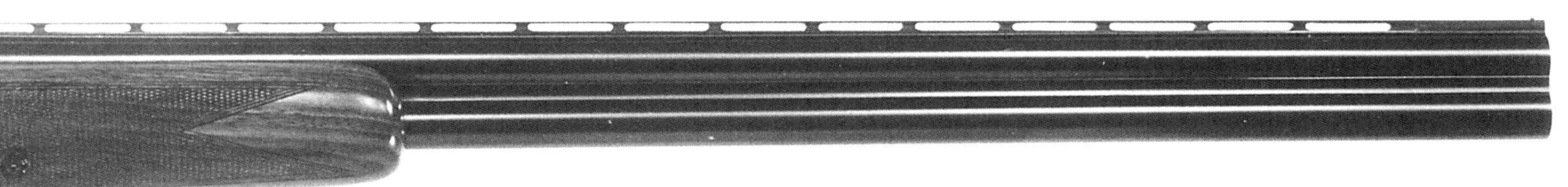

Winchester Model 25 Slide Action Repeating Shotgun. Manufactured from 1949 to 1955, the Model 25 is a hammerless, solid frame 12 gauge shotgun.

Winchester Model 50 Standard Grade Autoloader. Designed with a nonrecoiling barrel and independent chamber, the Model 50 is chambered for 12 or 20 gauge. Production for this model ran from 1954 to 1961.

Winchester Model 59 Autoloading Shotgun. The Model 59 has an alloy receiver and a 'Win Lite' steel and fiberglass barrel. Made from 1959 to 1965, this 12 gauge shotgun has a magazine that holds two shells.

Winchester Model 101 Over and Under Field Gun. The Model 101 is a box lock shotgun with an engraved receiver, automatic ejectors, single selective trigger and combination barrel selector and safety. This gun is chambered for 12 or 28 gauge and has been in production since 1963.

Winchester 'Xpert' Model 96 Over and Under Field Gun. The Model 96 has a box lock action similar to the Model 101. It has a plain receiver, automatic ejectors and a selective single trigger. Made in 12 and 20 gauge, it has been manufactured since 1976.

Winchester Model 1200 Slide Action Field Gun. The Model 1200 is a rotary bolt, takedown style shotgun in 12, 16 and 20 gauge with a four shot magazine. It has been manufactured from 1964 to date.

Winchester Model 1400 Automatic Field Gun. The Model 1400 is a gas operated, front-locking rotary bolt takedown style shotgun in 12, 16 or 20 gauge, with a two shot magazine. It was manufactured from 1964 to 1968.

Winchester Super X Model 1 Automatic Field Gun. Produced since 1974, this 12 gauge takedown shotgun is gas operated.

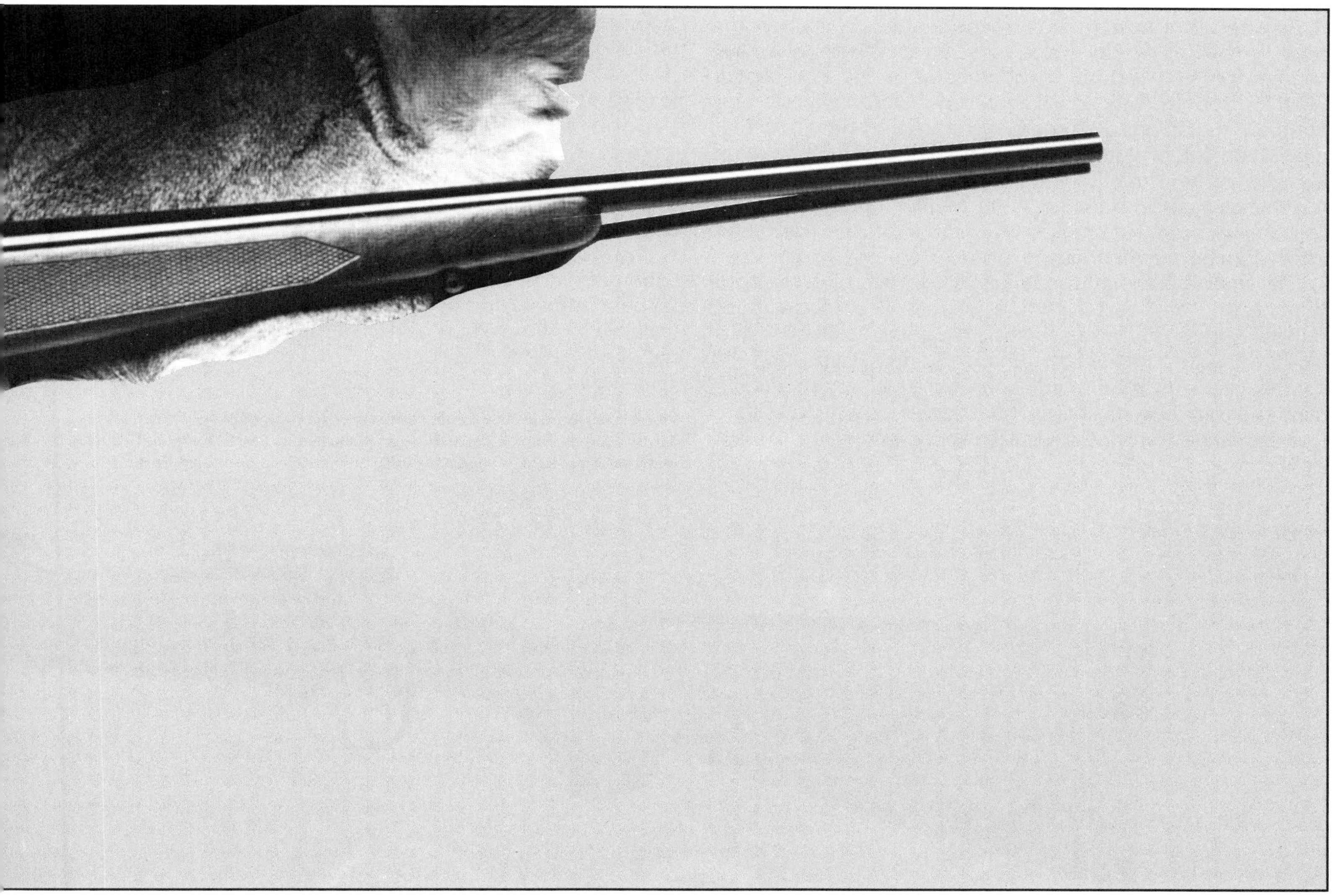

US Repeating Arms Rifles

The following rifles are produced under license from Olin Corporation.

Winchester Model 70 Bolt Action Center Fire Rifle. This bolt action, center fire rifle is avaialable with barrel lengths of 20 to 24 inches, weighs 5.75 to 8.5 pounds and has a magazine capacity of three to five rounds, depending on ammunition. It is available in a wide range of calibers, from .223 Remington to .458 Winchester Magnum.

As a result of having been in continuous production for close to 50 years, the Model 70 has partaken of many refinements and technological advancements. The Model 70 XTR Sporter Rifle series comes in various calibers. The Standard model has a Monte Carlo stock and cheekpiece, a hinged steel floorplate, jeweled bolt, detachable sling swivels, rifle sights, and a 24-inch barrel. The Magnum version has the same sporter features and 24-inch barrel. Available calibers are 7mm Remington Magnum and .264, .300 and .338 Winchester Magnum.

The Special Varmint model has a 24-inch, high strength Winchester steel barrel without sights. The Model XTR Super Express Rifle comes in two big game calibers—.375 H&H Magnum or .458 Winchester Magnum—and its sporter stock is reinforced with two steel crossbolts. In addition, this fine big game rifle comes equipped with a forward sling swivel and adjustable open rear and ramp front sights.

The Model 70 XTR is also available in a Featherweight version, which has a 22-inch barrel, weighs 6.75 pounds and has a receiver drilled and tapped for scope mounting. A special European version of the Featherweight combines the same features with 6.5 X 55 Swedish Mauser caliber chambering. A limited edition .270 Winchester Ultra Grade Featherweight with 24 karat gold hand engraving and custom hand fitting is also available, serial numbered 1 to 1000.

The Model 70 Lightweight Carbine is a light and fast handling utility and brush gun, weighing six pounds with a 20-inch barrel. The Ranger Bolt Action Rifle has a ramp bead front, adjustable rear sights and a one piece American hardwood stock. The Ranger Youth Bolt Action Carbine is size-scaled to fit younger or smaller shooters, weighs 5.75 pounds, has ramp bead front and semibuckhorn folding leaf rear sights and is complete with an American hardwood stock.

The Model 70 Winlite offers the Model 70 bolt action with a fiberglass stock for light weight, strength, accuracy and the ultimate stability for bedding of the barreled action. It is available in four calibers and in barrel lengths of 22 and 24 inches, and its stock has a contoured rubber recoil pad and sling swivel studs.

Above: **Designed for the smaller shooter—the Ranger Bolt Action Carbine.**
Below: **Like the Model 70 Carbine on the previous page, the Model 70 XTR Featherweight Rifle is made for easy carrying in mountain terrain.**

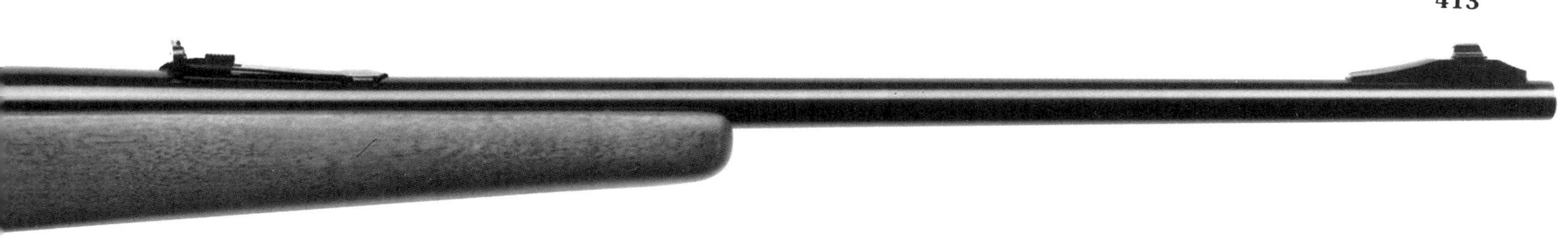

Model 70 XTR Sporter Rifle

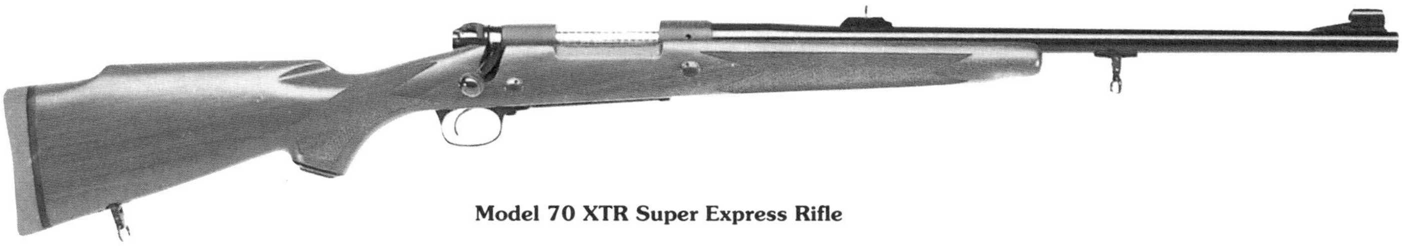

Model 70 XTR Super Express Rifle

Winchester Ranger Youth
Bolt Action Carbine

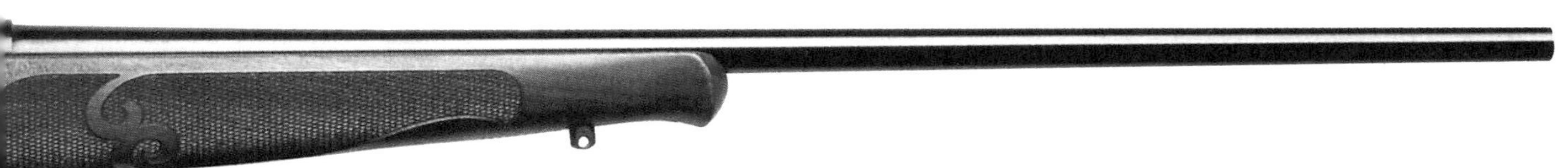

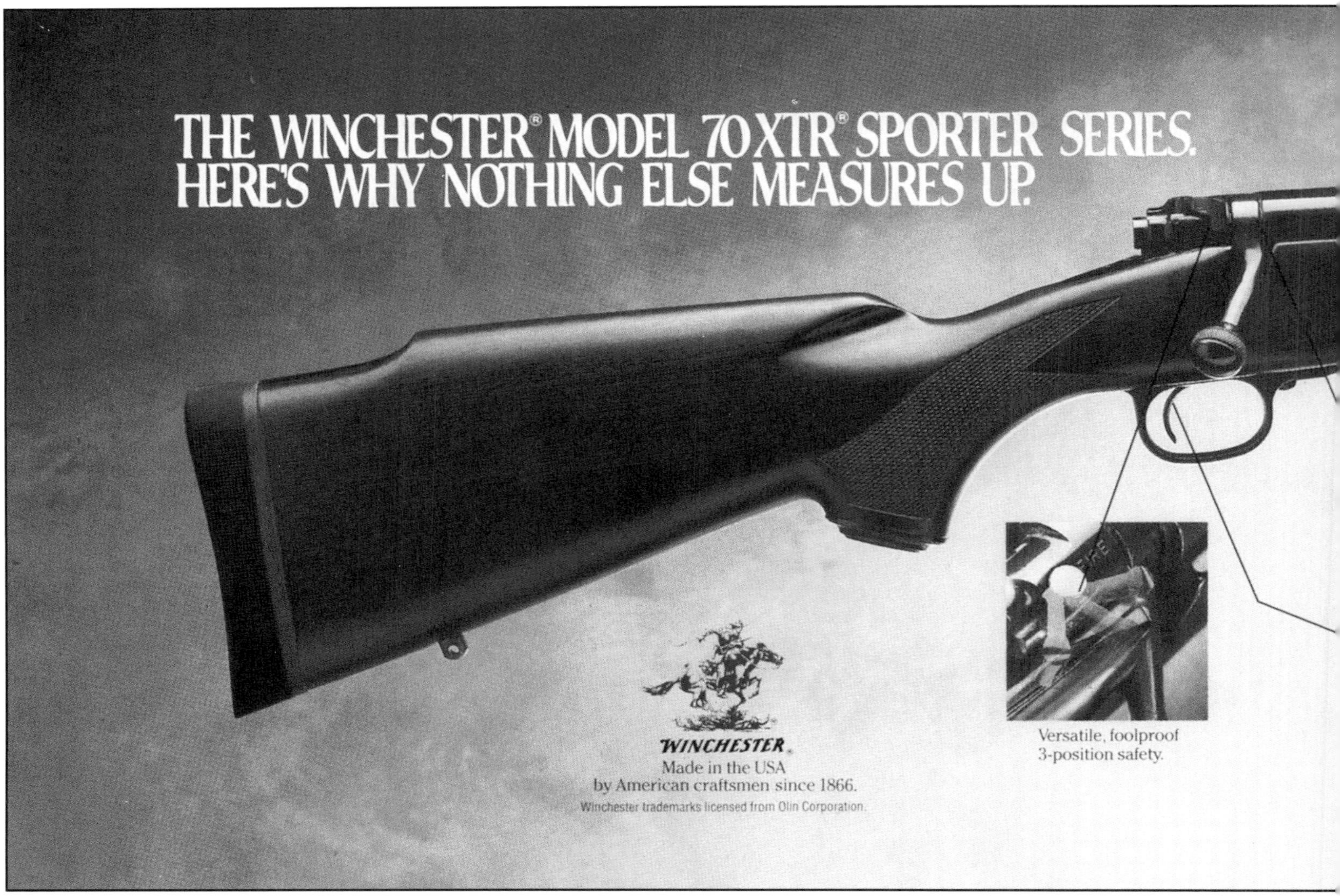

THE WINCHESTER® MODEL 70 XTR® SPORTER SERIES.
HERE'S WHY NOTHING ELSE MEASURES UP.

WINCHESTER.
Made in the USA
by American craftsmen since 1866.
Winchester trademarks licensed from Olin Corporation.

Versatile, foolproof 3-position safety.

Winchester Model 94 Carbines. As a hunting rifle, the Model 94 has achieved legendary status—it is regarded by many as the symbol of the Wild West. The Model 94 is a lever action, center fire rifle with a magazine capacity of five to nine rounds, barrel lengths of 16 to 24 inches and weights of six to seven pounds, depending on the variant.

It is made with a forged steel receiver, designed for side ejection of spent cartridges and top mounting of scopes. Each carbine comes packaged with a thumb hammer extension that is reversible for right- or left-handed use with a scope.

The .30-30 caliber Model 94 XTR Carbine has a 20-inch barrel, dovetailed blade front, and semibuckhorn rear sights. It also has a six round capacity magazine, precise cut checkering and a butt plate. The XTR in 7-30 Waters, developed for higher muzzle velocity and flatter shooting accuracy, features a 24 inch barrel with a dovetailed blade front sight and seven cartridge capacity.

The Model 94 Standard Carbine is available in .30-30 Winchester with a six-shot magazine, 20-inch steel barrel, composition butt plate and dovetailed blade front, and adjustable rear, sights. The compact Trapper Carbine combines a 16-inch barrel with post front sight, and either a five shot magazine in .30-30 Winchester, or .45 Colt and .44 Remington Magnum calibers with nine-shot magazine capacity.

Winchester Range Lever Action Carbine

Model 94 XTR Rifle

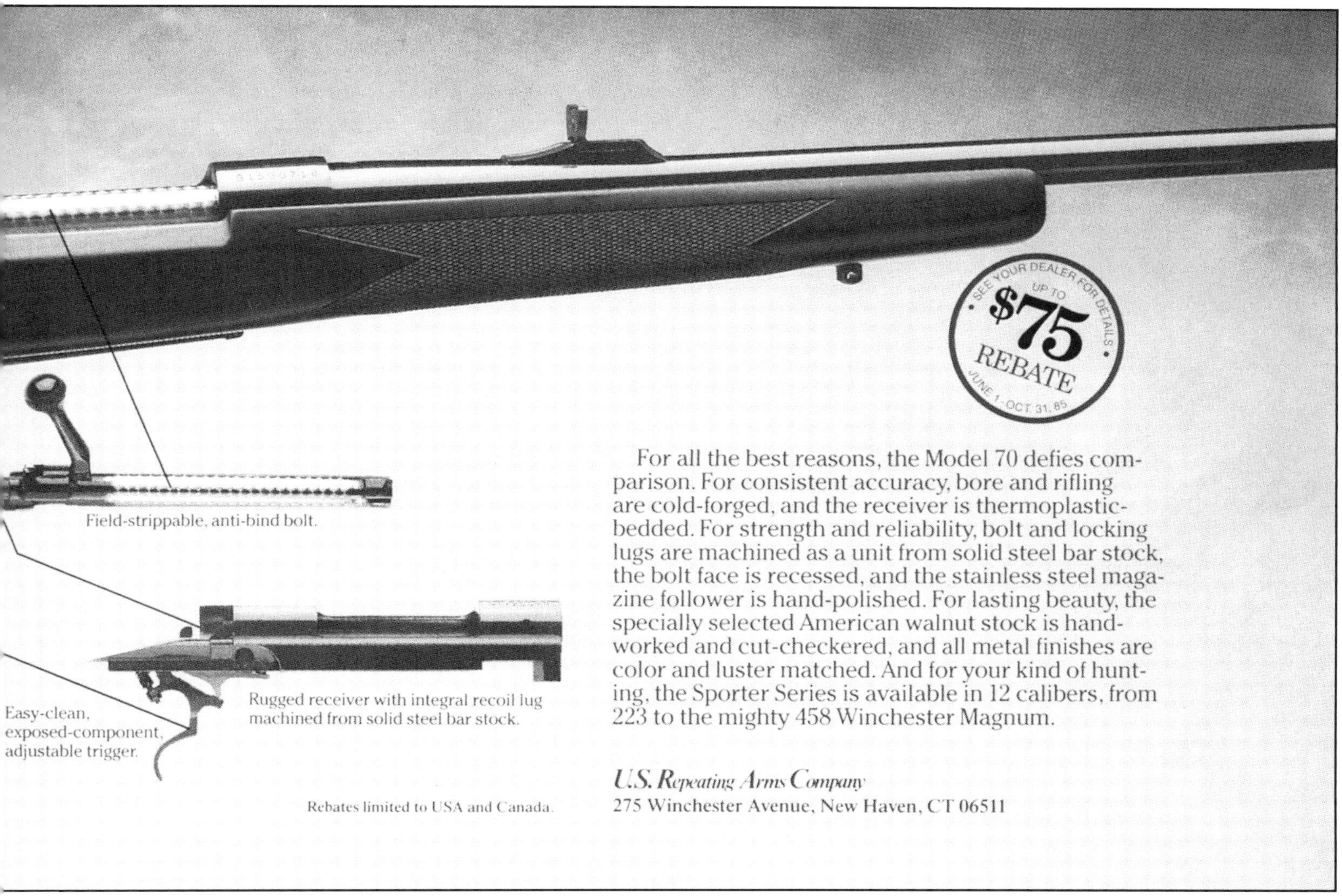

SEE YOUR DEALER FOR DETAILS • UP TO $75 REBATE JUNE 1 - OCT. 31, 85

Field-strippable, anti-bind bolt.

Easy-clean, exposed-component, adjustable trigger.

Rugged receiver with integral recoil lug machined from solid steel bar stock.

For all the best reasons, the Model 70 defies comparison. For consistent accuracy, bore and rifling are cold-forged, and the receiver is thermoplastic-bedded. For strength and reliability, bolt and locking lugs are machined as a unit from solid steel bar stock, the bolt face is recessed, and the stainless steel magazine follower is hand-polished. For lasting beauty, the specially selected American walnut stock is hand-worked and cut-checkered, and all metal finishes are color and luster matched. And for your kind of hunting, the Sporter Series is available in 12 calibers, from 223 to the mighty 458 Winchester Magnum.

U.S. Repeating Arms Company
275 Winchester Avenue, New Haven, CT 06511

Rebates limited to USA and Canada.

***Above:* The Model 70 XTR Sporter combines accuracy with the beauty of an American walnut stock. *Below:* The Model 94 Chief Crazy Horse Commemorative, complete with tribal decorations, honors the Sioux people.**

The Range Lever Action Carbine is a five shot .30-30 caliber with an American hardwood stock, a 20-inch barrel and blade front and semibuckhorn rear sights. For big game hunting the Model 94 Big Bore utilizes .375, .356 or .307 Winchester cartridges. This gun also features side ejection, Monte Carlo stocks of American walnut, sling swivels and a reversible thumb hammer extension. The receiver is forged steel with reinforced side panels, and has been drilled and tapped for top mounting of scopes.

To celebrate Winchester's 120th Anniversary, the company issued limited edition Model 94 carbines commemorating founder Oliver F Winchester, the horse-and-rider trademark, and Chief Crazy Horse. The Chief Crazy Horse Model 94 Winchester celebrates the great Sioux chief and his people, and is beautifully and symbolically engraved. This fine firearm is chambered for the classic .38-55 Winchester cartridge.

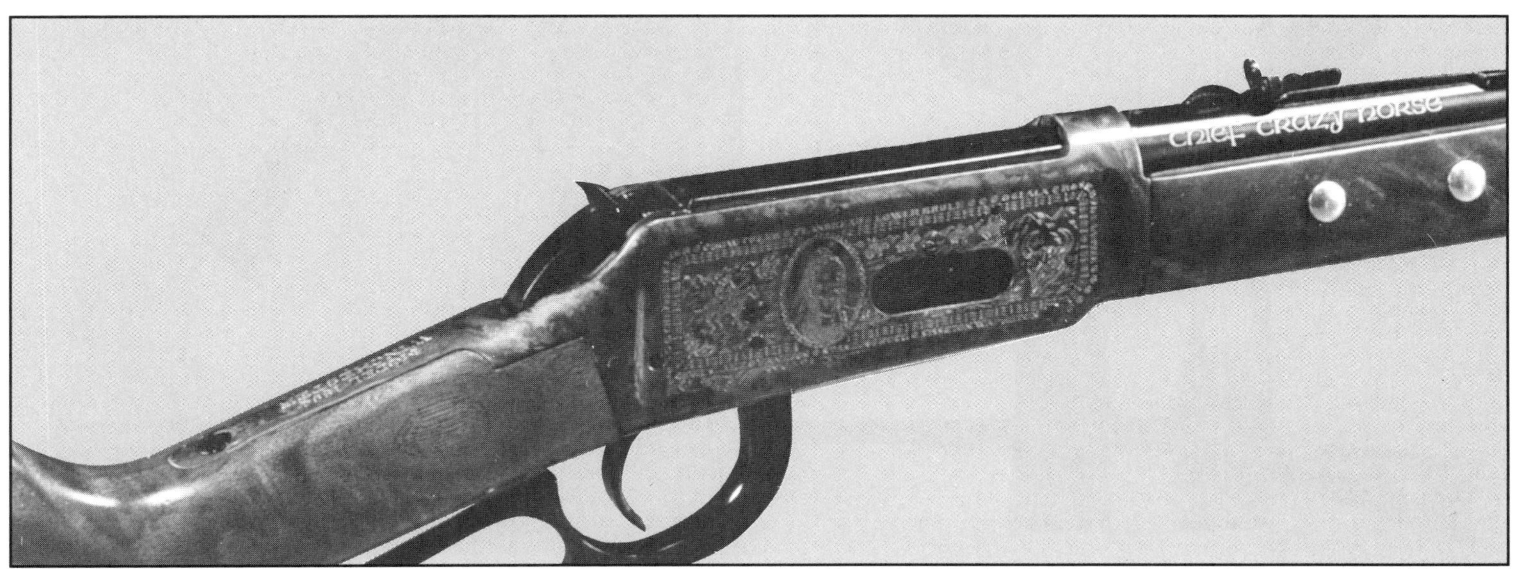

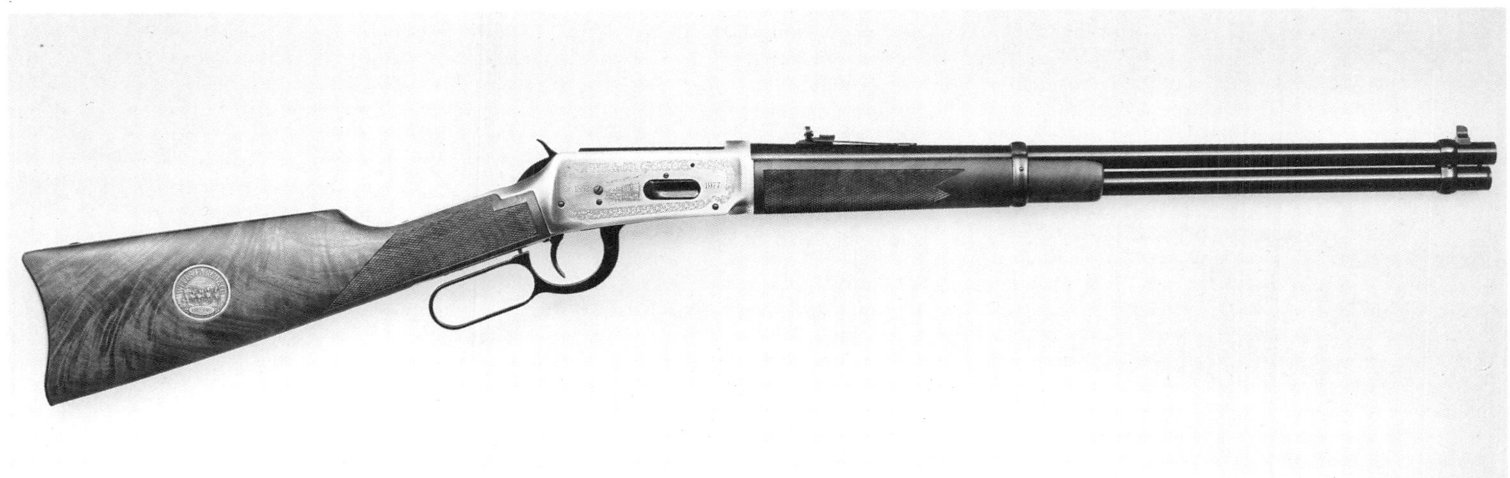

Winchester Model 9422 Rifles. This lever action, rimfire .22 caliber rifle has available barrel lengths of 20.5 inches and 22.2 inches, and weighs from 6.25 pounds to 6.5 pounds. The Model 9422 XTR, considered one of the world's finest production sporting arms, features positive lever action and bolt design for feeding and chambering from any shooting position.

The receiver, frame and finger lever are forged steel; receivers are designed for side ejection of spent cartridges and are grooved for top mounting of scopes. Each rifle has an adjustable thumb hammer extension with half-cock safety, ramped bead front and semibuckhorn rear sights.

The Standard Model 9422 XTR Rifle has a western saddle carbine profile with a straight stock and forearm with barrel band, traditional finger lever and composition butt plate. Model 9422 XTR Classic Rifle features include a satin finish walnut stock with fluted comb and crescent steel butt plate, curved finger lever and undercut pistol grip, and an extended forearm with barrel band and 22.5 inch barrel for long range accuracy.

The Commemorative Models are all limited edition firearms that feature the handsome Winchester engraving, which is designed around historical images and tastefully calligraphed lettering. The Model 9422 Boy Scouts of America Commemorative, complete with commemorative .22 Long ammunition, may well claim to be the the first such honor for that organization. A maximum 15,000 units were manufactured in the mid-1980s.

The .22 caliber, lever action, Annie Oakley Commemorative Model 9422 is the first US firearm to honor a historic American woman. Only 6000 units of the Annie Oakley Rifle were issued.

Above: **The Wells Fargo Commemorative Carbine honors the 125th anniversary of Wells Fargo.** ***Below left:*** **The Bull Buffalo Skull with Blue Tails Gun Mount.** ***Right:*** **The Model 9422 Annie Oakley Commemorative—a tribute to sharpshooter Annie Oakley** ***(below)*****, heroine of the Old West.**

WINCHESTER MODEL 9422 ANNIE OAKLEY™ COMMEMORATIVE

The First Commemorative Winchester® Rimfire Rifle to Honor an American Heroine.

The Annie Oakley Commemorative Model 9422 is a highly decorative 22-caliber rifle . . . a tribute to the sharp-shooting woman who has become a central figure in American folklore.

Annie Oakley gained immense fame in Buffalo Bill's Wild West Show from 1885 to 1902. She created a sensation in America and Europe because of her uncanny accuracy with a rifle. Her highly-publicized use of Winchester firearms was an important factor in establishing the reputation of Winchester guns throughout the world.

It is fitting that this ultimate shooter be honored with the Model 9422, considered one of the world's finest production sporting arms. Its classic styling, accuracy, and feel are the results of superb craftsmanship.

Finger lever, receiver, and barrel bands are antique gold-plated. The receiver is roll-engraved with her portrait and a scene from her show. The barrel is inscribed in gold "Annie Oakley Commemorative." The stock and forearm are select American walnut with a protective high-luster finish.

Functional features include a brass internal magazine tube, half-cock safety, hooded bead front sight and semi-buckhorn rear sight. Internal components are carefully finished for smoothness of action. Positive lever action and bolt design ensure feeding and chambering from any shooting position. Take-down for inspection or cleaning is greatly simplified with a single-screw construction.

In keeping with established traditions for Winchester commemorative rifles, the Annie Oakley 9422 is offered in a limited issue. Six thousand of these special rifles will be produced, bearing serial numbers AOK1 through AOK6000.

The Annie Oakley Commemorative Model 9422 is a decorative, distinctive tribute to a remarkable woman. It will be a treasured possession for collectors, sportsmen, and sportswomen.

ANNIE OAKLEY COMMEMORATIVE

WINCHESTER®

Winchester trademarks licensed from Olin Corporation.

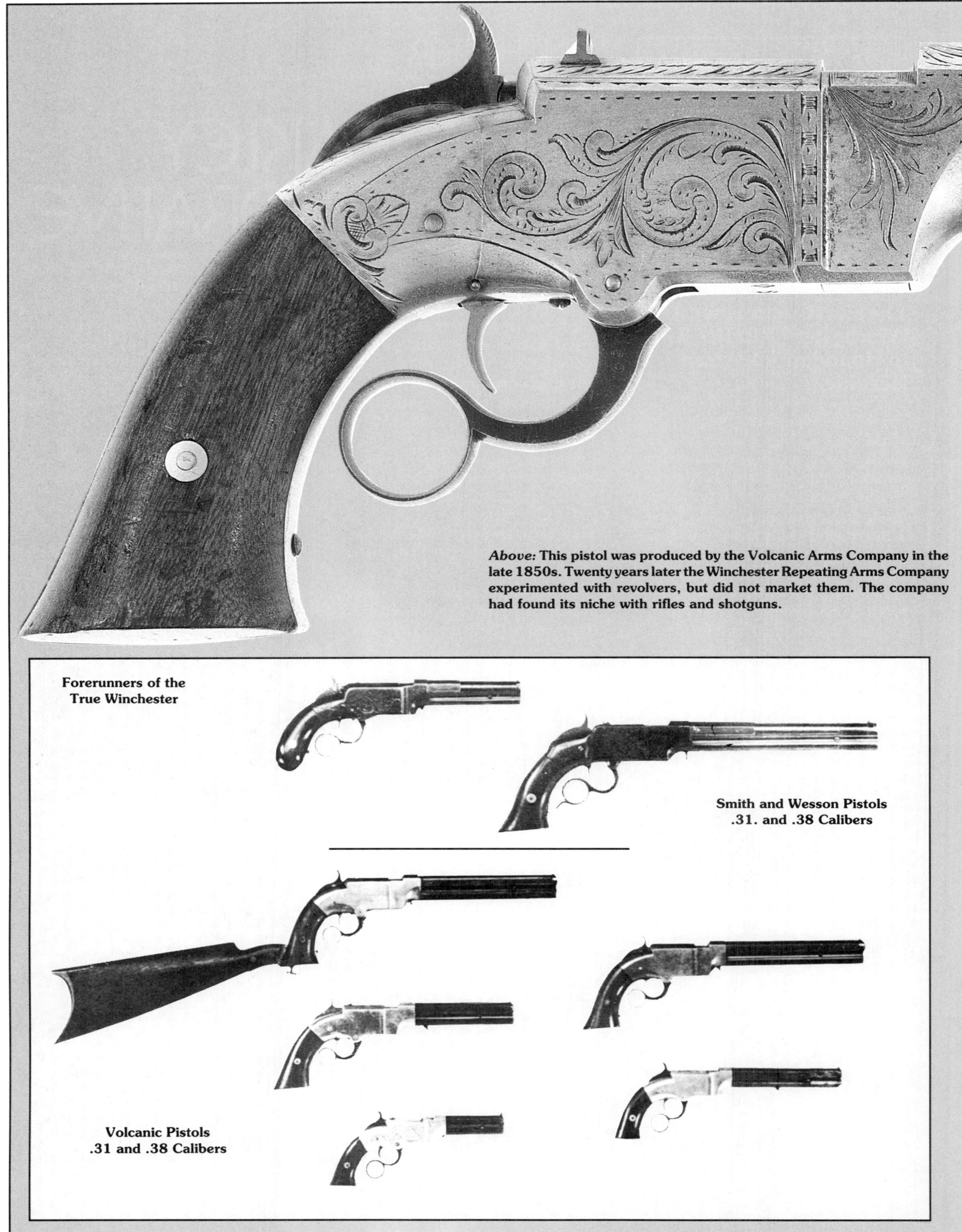

Above: This pistol was produced by the Volcanic Arms Company in the late 1850s. Twenty years later the Winchester Repeating Arms Company experimented with revolvers, but did not market them. The company had found its niche with rifles and shotguns.

Winchester Pistols

In a letter to Ed Martin dated 17 October 1862, Oliver F Winchester mentioned that 3000 revolvers were being produced by the New Haven Arms Company. Technically, these are the first Winchester pistols. They held six shots and retailed for about $15. Historians believe that John Walch, John Parker Lindsay and Cyrus Manville were all involved in the contracting and patenting of these first Winchester pistols.

These 'Walch Revolvers,' as they came to be known, were of two major types: the brass frame model and the iron frame model. The early Winchester Company produced these revolvers from 1860 until 1862. At the Centennial Celebration in Philadelphia in 1876, Winchester displayed models and drawings of a number of proposed pistols that were all built to the same design in three basic model classifications, all featuring solid frame construction.

Apparently Winchester's work on pistols was in the direction of developing a design that would have the solid frame of the unsuccessful Colt revolver and the rapid ejection capability of the Smith and Wesson pistols. All of the Winchester revolvers, of which there were very few, closely followed either their Colt or Smith and Wesson counterparts in exterior appearances. None of these revolvers played an important part in Winchester history, as they were all unsuccessful and were not produced commercially—except for extremely small quantities, usually for government contracts.

For example, Winchester had contracts with the US government for the US Ordnance Trials, and with Imperial Russia. Around the turn of the century, Winchester did produce a .22 Single Shot Bolt Action pistol in limited numbers, but it was never successfully marketed.

The War Department contracted with Winchester to manufacture the Colt Model 1911 .45 Automatic Pistol, but due to war contracts and other business at the time, Winchester subcontracted manufacture of these pistols to other firms. When the Armistice was signed in November of 1918, production ceased after only a few hundred of these automatics were made.

It is interesting to note that, as late as the 1960s, Winchester produced some experimental revolvers that were never marketed. Winchester had made its mark in history with repeating rifles, and wisely never ventured very far into the realm of pistols, which was already dominated by other patents and design innovations.

Winchester Experimental Pistols

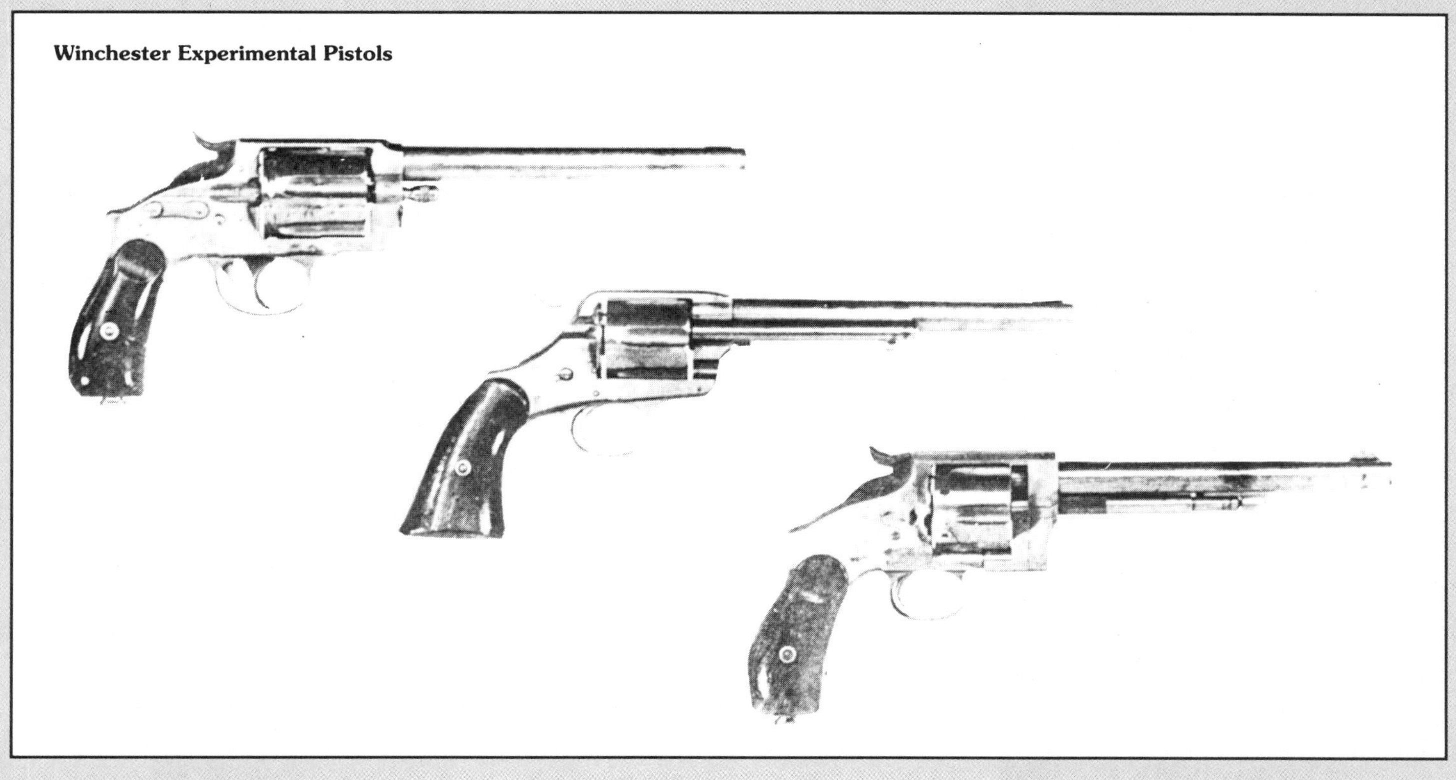

GLOSSARY OF TERMS

Action. Generally defined as the moving parts of a firearm. Three basic 'actions' are prevalent in the world of small firearms. These are: single action, double action and automatic (semi and full).

Anvil. The actual piece of metal in the primer of a centerfire metallic cartridge which comes into direct contact with the priming compound at the blow of the hammer.

Ball. *(see Bullet)*

Barrel. The tube through which the bullet is propelled by the powder explosion. The 'bore' of a barrel is its inside diameter. The 'muzzle' of a barrel is the end furthest from the user. The 'breech' of a barrel is the end nearest the user.

Barrel Key. Sometimes called the 'barrel bolt.' A key which holds the barrel to the center pin of the frame.

Barrel Lug. A block of metal forming the frame of percussion-cap Colt revolvers which was threaded to hold the jointed-lever ramrod in place.

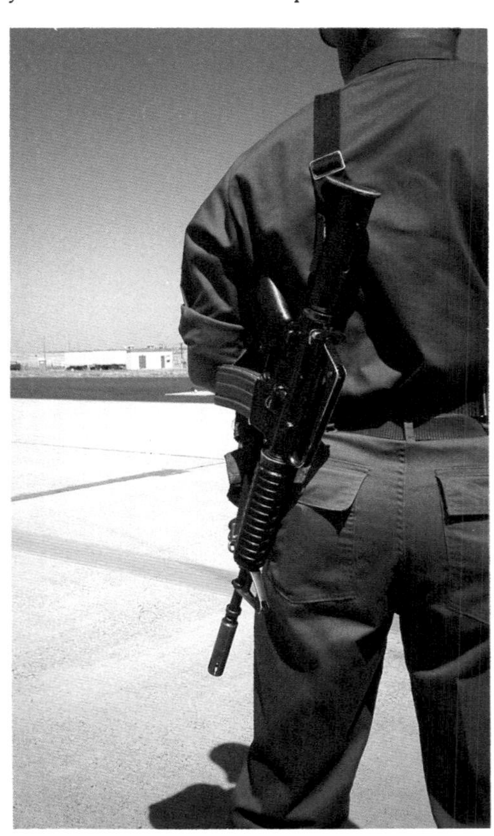

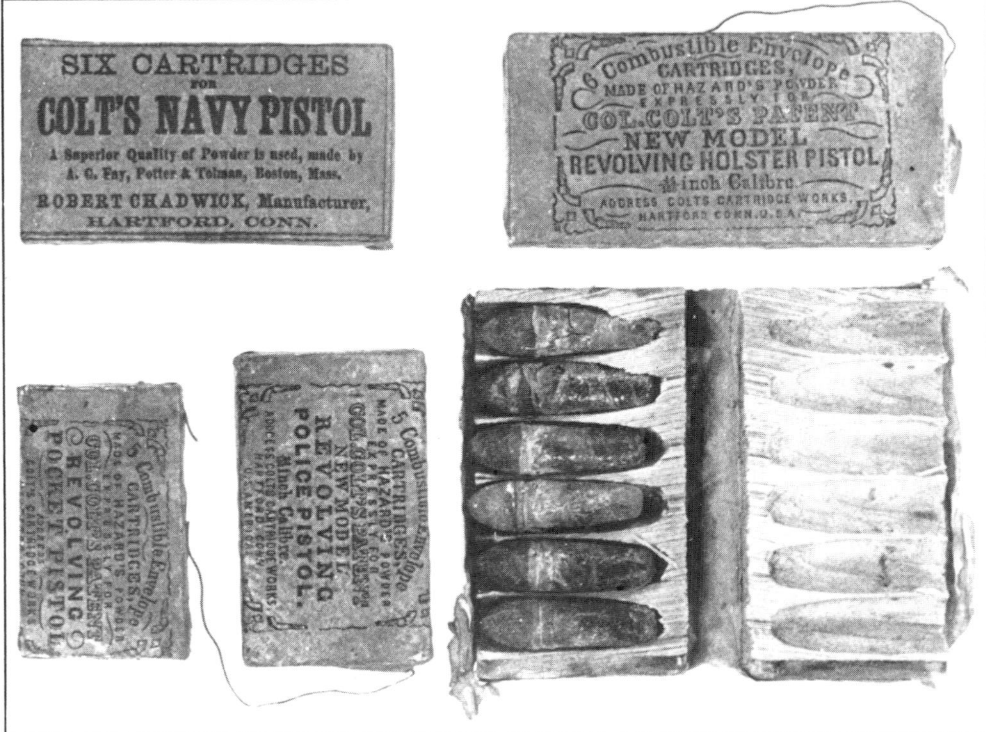

Bore. *(see Barrel)*

Breech. *(see Barrel)*

Bullet. The projectile fired from cartridge firearms. 'Balls' are bullets which are fired from early firearms. 'Shot' is generally thought of as being a collection of bullets or balls fired from the same enclosure.

Butt. Usually the shoulder rest of the wooden stock of a firearm.

Carbine. A shortened rifle.

Cartridge. Technically the housing for the powder or explosive charge, but generally defined as the housing, the charge and projectile together.

Center Fire. A metallic cartridge fired by a primer located in the center of the rear of the shell.

Center Pin. The pin on which the cylinder revolves. At one time referred to as the 'arbor.'

Chamfer. A bevel in the barrel of a percussion cap revolver used to make it easier to load the bullet into the chamber.

Chamber. The bored recessions in the cylinder of a revolver meant to hold the charges.

Cock. An early name for the hammer of a revolver.

Cylinder. The round revolving breech piece bored with chambers which holds the cap, powder and ball or, depending on the modernity of the firearm, the cartridge, of a revolver.

Clockwise from immediate left: **A Colt Mustang 380 (a popular law enforcement backup gun); a security guard at Beale Air Force Base, with his Colt M16 dangling from its shoulder sling; combustible envelope cartridges, made for use in Colt's early percussion cap revolving pistols—these particular cartridges were made under a patent taken out in 1862; the open breech of a Browning Special Steel Superposed shotgun.**

Cylinder-locking Bolt. The bolt which locks the cylinder in such a manner that one of the chambers is always in line with the barrel.

Deringer. A small single-shot pistol made by Henry Deringer of Philadelphia, Pennsylvania. It has come to define all very small pistols usually used for personal protection.

Double Action. A revolver action in which the pulling of the trigger both cocks the hammer and turns the cylinder as well as fires the cartridge.

Ejector. The device for removing the cartridge case from the firearm after it has been fired.

Firing Pin. A small pin in the frame of a firearm that, when struck by the hammer, comes into direct contact with the cartridge and fires it.

Forestock. That part of the wood stock of certain firearms which lies in front of the trigger.

Fulminate Of Mercury. A chemical compound of mercury which explodes when struck by a sharp blow.

Grip or Grips. The usually wood or rubber hold for the hand, by which pistols are held.

Hammer. The hammerlike piece of metal which is released by the action of the trigger and strikes either a firing pin, or directly strikes the primer of the cartridge, thus discharging the load in the firearm's chamber.

Hammer Spring. The spring which provides the energy for the driving force of the hammer. Sometimes called a 'mainspring.'

Loading Gate or **Loading Notch.** In certain cartridge revolvers, this was the opening through which cartridges were put in, and removed from, the cylinder.

Lock. In early literature, the 'lock' can be substituted for our modern word, 'action.'

Matchlock. This was the first type of mechanical ignition system used in a firearm.

Maynard's Tape Primers. An invention in the 1850s which was much like children's caps today. A roll of these primers was inserted into the magazine of a percussion cap pistol and were fed into proximity with powder in the cylinder by the act of cocking the hammer prior to discharge.

Musket. The first kind of shoulder arm widely used by infantry soldiers. Muskets first came into prominence in the 16th and 17th centuries. The standard musket of the 18th and early 19th centuries was .69 caliber smoothbore.

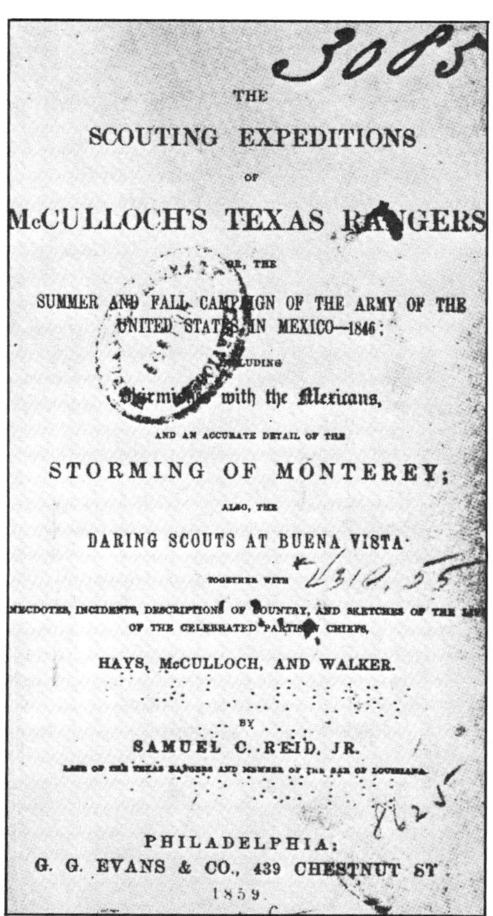
THE
SCOUTING EXPEDITIONS
OF
McCULLOCH'S TEXAS RANGERS;
OR, THE
SUMMER AND FALL CAMPAIGN OF THE ARMY OF THE UNITED STATES IN MEXICO—1846;
INCLUDING
Skirmishes with the Mexicans,
AND AN ACCURATE DETAIL OF THE
STORMING OF MONTEREY;
ALSO, THE
DARING SCOUTS AT BUENA VISTA;
TOGETHER WITH
ANECDOTES, INCIDENTS, DESCRIPTIONS OF COUNTRY, AND SKETCHES OF THE LIVES OF THE CELEBRATED PARTISAN CHIEFS,
HAYS, McCULLOCH, AND WALKER.
BY
SAMUEL C. REID, JR.
LATE OF THE TEXAS RANGERS AND MEMBER OF THE BAR OF LOUISIANA.
PHILADELPHIA:
G. G. EVANS & CO., 439 CHESTNUT ST.
1859.

Nipple. A small protrusion on each chamber of a percussion cap arm upon which the percussion cap is placed.

Pepperbox. A particular kind of cap and ball revolver that involved the turning of a single, large cylinder in which each chamber also formed its own individual barrel.

Percussion Cap. A small copper container open at one end containing a small amount of fulminate of mercury. The cap is placed over the nipple of the cylinder of a cap and ball firearm and provides the ignition charge for the powder when struck by the hammer.

Pistol. A firearm intended for use in one hand only.

Primer. A form of percussion cap mounted into the body of a center fire cartridge.

Ramrod. In old muzzle-loading arms, this was the wood or metal piece used for running the charge down the barrel.

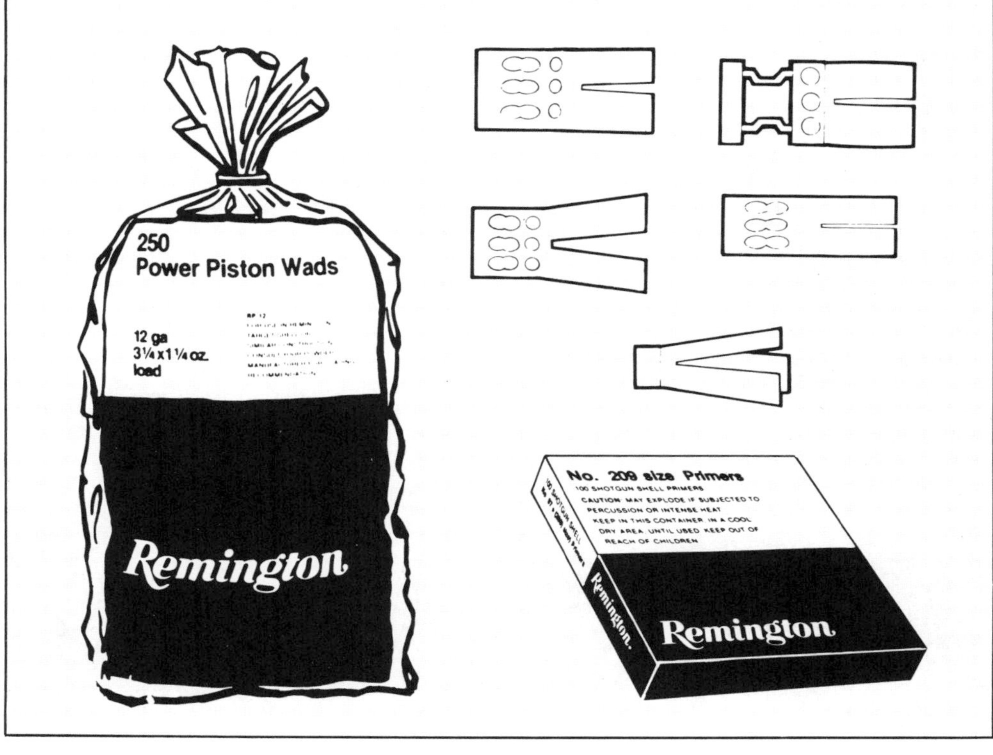

At left: World War II generals whose troops used American firearms: Eisenhower, Patton, Bradley and Hodges. _Above:_ An account of 'the Texas campaign.' _Above right:_ European troops with eighteenth-century weaponry. _At right:_ Remington reloading materials.

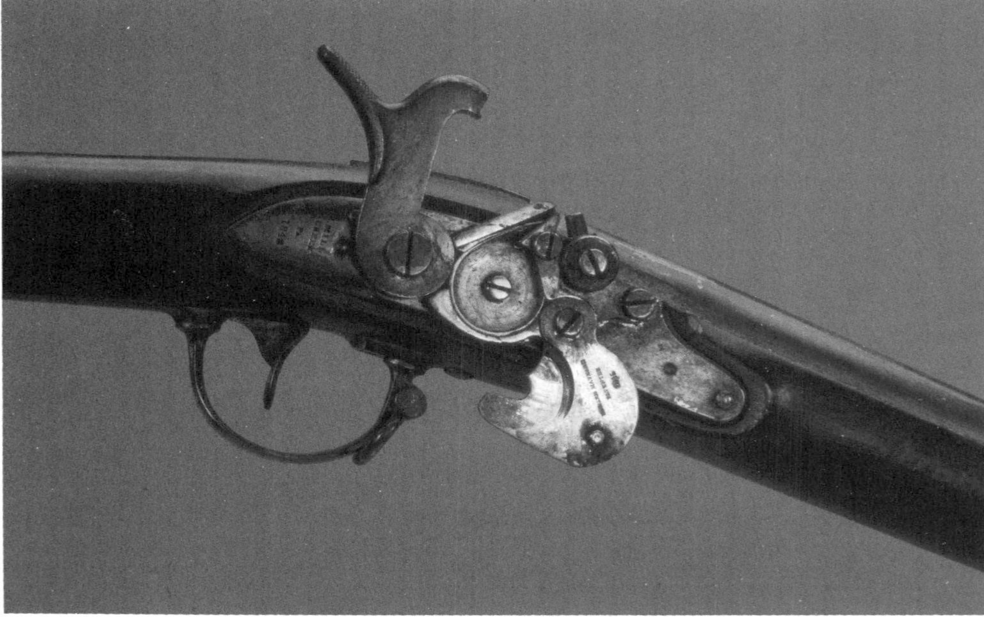

These pages, clockwise from above: **A closeup of the Maynard Tape Priming system; a Colt Heirloom 1 'mirror brite' .45 caliber Officer's ACP; hand-tuning Colt revolver and ACP actions; a publicity photo of Remington 'Hyper Velocity' Yellow Jacket .22 rimfire cartridges; Colt's new Delta automatic pistol and Delta Heavy Barrel (H-Bar) AR-15; and a US soldier samples his tasty rations with his Colt M16 nearby.**

Ratchet. A gear milled with teeth and mounted at the back of the cylinder of a revolver which engages the pawl that turns the cylinder.

Revolver. Short for 'revolving pistol.' Used today to describe any cylinder-revolving handgun.

Rifle. Technically, any firearm whose barrel is grooved, or 'rifled,' on the inside, thus causing the bullet to spin as it is fired. Rifles were invented in Europe in the 16th century and adapted to American use in the early-to-middle 1700s. The Kentucky Rifle is the most famous adaption of the earlier European versions.

Rifling. The particular pattern of grooving on the inside of a barrel which imparts lateral spin to the bullet, thus increasing accuracy by means of gyroscopic force.

Rimfire. A metallic cartridge whose percussion priming mechanism is in the rim, rather than the center, of the cartridge base.

Shot. *(see Bullet)*

Shotgun. A smoothbore gun, made to discharge either shot or a large, soft, hollow 'slug.'

Sight. A device, composed of two parts, used for aiming a weapon. These two parts are: a notch or more sophisticated device at the breech of the barrel and a blade, pin or ball at the muzzle of the barrel.

Single Action. A type of revolver action in which the hammer must be cocked by hand before the trigger can cause it to fall on the charge. The manual cocking of the hammer rotates

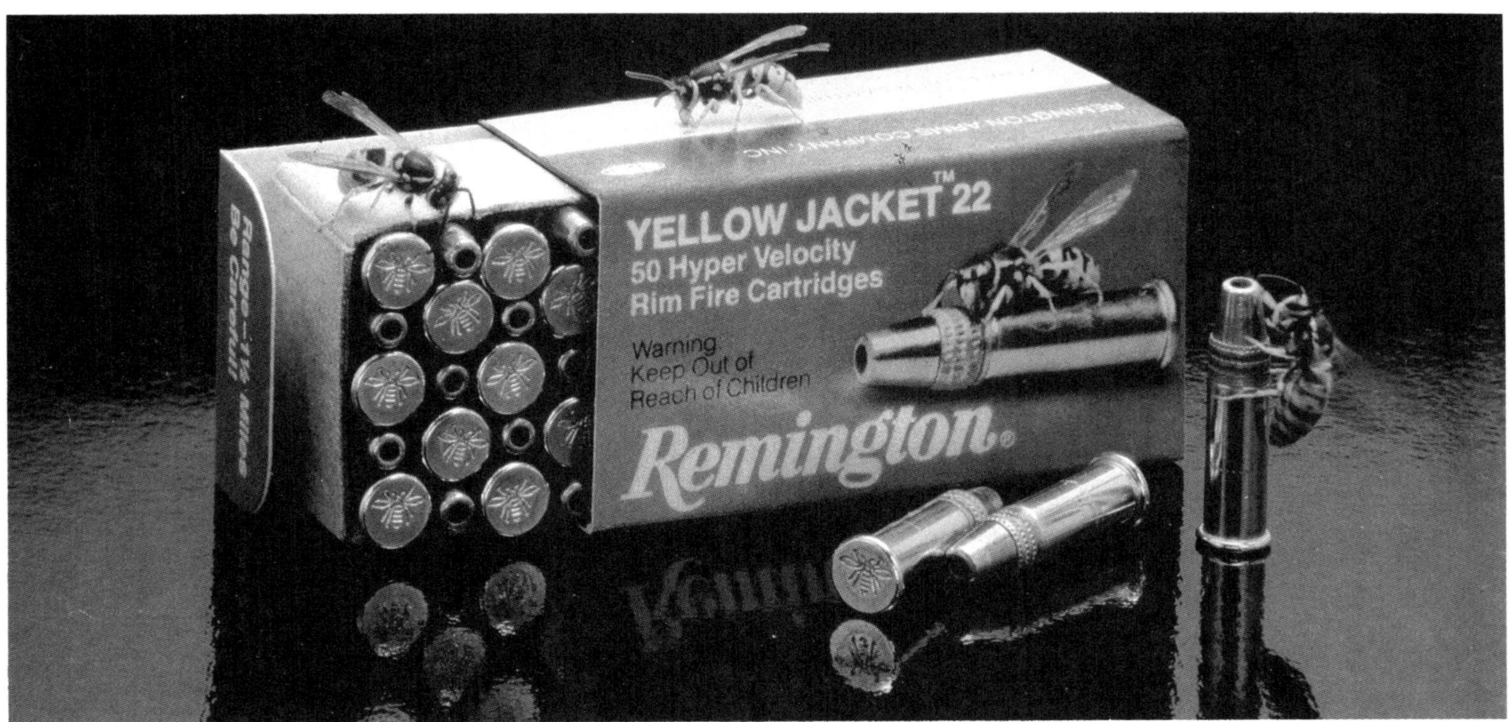

the cylinder and, therefore, the cartridge into its proper position.

Trigger. A lever which, when pulled upon by the finger, engages the firing mechanism of the firearm.

Triggerguard. Generally, a loop of metal surrounding the trigger which prevents its being accidentally struck.

Wheellock. This was the first type of ignition for a firearm that did not require a lighted match to set off the powder. The mechanism was actually a windable, spring-loaded wheel which struck sparks against a piece of flint, thus igniting the weapon's powder charge.

INDEX

Addis, Thomas: 338
Alexander II, Tsar: 136
Ammunition: Browning 16, *20-21*, *37*, *45*, 84; Colt 154-157; Remington 270-285, *427*; Winchester 334-349, *337*, *339*, *340*
Ammunition Manufacturer's Association: 344

Baerten, Jose: 104
Barnes, Joanna: *200*
Bennett, Thomas G: 332, *333*, 338, 347-348
Bennett, TG: 17
Berdan Slam Bang Breech: 272
Berdan Russian Rifle. 164
Berdan, General: 164
Berdan, Colonel Hiram: 272, 276
Black powder: 358, *See also Ammunition: Winchester*
Board of Associated Charities: 329
Bonaparte, Napoleon: 82
Bonney, William: 159
Boone, Daniel: 366
'Boxer' Center Fire cartridge: 154
'Boy Scout Rifle': *See Remington Model 4S*
Bradley, General Omar: *421*
Brewer, Henry: 340, 342, 347
Browning Arms Company: 64, 85, 175
Browning Bows: 97-100, *100*
Browning, Edward: 18
Browning, John Moses: *4*, 11, 13, 15, 16, 17, 21, 22, 24, 26, 28,33, *49*, 52, *52*, 57, 60, 64, 66, 68, 72, 76, 80, 85, 104,105, 175, 332, *333*, *370*, 371, 372, 380, 384
Browning, John Val: 22
Browning, Jonathan: 11, 12, *12*, 13
Browning, Matthew: 13, *17*, 18, *49*, 85

Browning Models

Automatic Gun: 17, 18, 19
Automatic-5, Standard: *58-59*, *83*, 94
Automatic Magazine Gun: 66
Automatic Rifle: 21, 48, 92
Automatic Shotgun: 56-57, 85, 116-117
Automatic .32 Caliber Pistol: *26-27*, 85
BAR Automatic Rifle: *32*, *48-49*, *50*, *51*, 92, *108-109*, *111*
BDA Double Action Automatic Pistol: 88
Bicentennial 78 Set: 92
Bicentennial Commemorative Superposed: 105
BL-22 Lever Action Repeating Rifle: *14-15*, *38-39*, 92
BLR Lever Action Repeating Rifle: 92
BPR .22 Pump Rifle: 92
BPS Pump Shotgun: *96-97*, 97
Breechloading Firearm: *23*, *68*
Browning Peacemaker: *See Colt Model 1895 Automatic Machine Gun*
Browning 78 Single Shot Rifle: 92
BSS Hammerless Double Barrel Shotgun: 96
BT-99 Grade I Single Barrel Trap Gun: 96
Challenger Automatic Pistol: 87-88
Citori Over and Under Hunting Shotgun: *95*, 97, *110*
Classic Edition: 109
Double Automatic: 64, 65, 96
Experimental Gas-Operated Firearm: 68
Gas-Operated Machine Gun: *19*, 66
Gas-Operated Breechloading Gun: 68
Gas-Operated Machine Gun: 19, *19*
Gold Classic Edition: *58-59*, *103*, 109
Grade I Three or Five Shot Autoloading Shotgun: *90-91*, 94
Hi-Power 9mm Automatic Pistol: *2*, *7*, *34-35*, 32-33, 87
High-Power Bolt Action Rifle: 88
Jonathan Browning Mountain Rifle: 105, 108
Jonathan Browning Cylinder Repeating Rifle: *10-11*, 11, 12, 13,
Lever Action Repeating Rifle: 40
Liège Over and Under Shotgun: *83*, 96-97
Light Browning: *See Browning Light Machine Rifle Model 1917*
Light Machine Rifle Model 1917 (BAR): 52
Lightning Superposed: 109
Limited Edition Black Duck Issue: *98-99*, *103*, *111*
Limited Edition Superposed Pintail Duck Issue: *98-99*, *103*
Limited Edition Waterfowl Superposed Shotgun: *62-63*, 108
Medalist Automatic Target Pistol: 88
M9: *See Browning 37mm Aircraft Cannon*
Model '06: *See Winchester Model 1890*
Model 17 Pump Action Shotgun: 57
Model 53: *See Winchester Model 1892*
Model 55 (Rifle): *See Winchester Model 1894*
Model 62: *See Winchester Model 1890*
Model 62 (Rifle): *See Winchester Model 1894*
Model 65 (Rifle) *See Winchester Model 1892*
Model 71: *See Browning Model 1886*
Model 90: *See Winchester Model 1890*
Model 95: *44*, *also see Winchester Model 1895 (Rifle)*
Model 99 Thumb Trigger Rifle: 44
Model 1886 Lever Action Repeating Rifle: *41*, 42, 116-117
Model 1897 Pump Action Repeating Shotgun: 56, 56-57, *116-117*
Model 1901: 72
Model 1902: 27-28, *28*, 29, *29*
Model 1911 Government Automatic Pistol: 28-29, *29*, *48*
Model 1917 Heavy Water-Cooled Machine Gun: 68, *69*
Model 1917 .30 Caliber Air-Cooled Machine Gun: 71
Model 1935: 35
Nomad Automatic Pistol: 87
Rare Brownings: 384-387
Recoil Machine Gun: 22
Revolving Cylinder Rifle: *10-11*
Semiautomatic High Power Rifle: 48, *48-49*
Semiautomatic .38 Caliber Pistol: 24, *24*, 26, *26*
Semiautomatic .32 Caliber Pistol: 24, *26*, *28*
Semiautomatic .25 Caliber Pistol Model Vest Pocket: 30-31, *30*
Semiautomatic Pistol in 9mm Parabellum Caliber: 31, *31*, 33, *33*
Slide Bar Repeating Rifle: 11, 12, 13, *13*
Superposed Shotgun: 60, *61*, *62-63*, *106-107*
Superposed Hunting Shotguns: 94, 96, 102, 104, *421*
Sweet 16 Automatic-5: 94
T-Bolt .22 Repeating Rifle, T-1: 88
Tubular Magazine Repeating Rifle: 40
Twelvette Double Automatic: 96
Two Millionth Browning Automatic-5 Shotgun: 104
Woodsman: *See Colt Woodsman .22 Caliber Semiautomatic Pistol*
.380 Caliber Automatic Pistol: 87
.22 Automatic Rifle: 86-87, 88
.22 Caliber Single Shot Rifle: 64
.25 Caliber Automatic Pistol: *30*, 87
.30 Caliber Air-Cooled: *72*, *73*, 76
.30 Caliber Box Magazine Pump Action Rifle: 64
.30 Caliber Heavy Machine Gun: 72, *74-75*, 105
.30 Caliber Machine Gun: 22
.30 Caliber Repeater: 64
.32 Caliber Semiautomatic: *26-27*, 85
.38 Caliber Tubular Magazine Lever Action Rifle: 64
.44 Caliber Pump Action Repeating Rifle: 64
.45 Caliber Lever Action Single Shot Rifle: 64
.45 Caliber Pistol: 19, *29*
.50 Caliber Machine Gun: 22, 76, 80
12 Gauge Pump Action Shotgun: 64
37mm Aircraft Cannon: *18*, 80, *81*
2000 Gas Automatic Shotgun: 97

Browning, Orville H: 11
Browning, Val A: 22, 60
Buell, William: 340
Buntline Special: 159
Buntline, Ned: 159
Burns, James E: 280
Butler, Frank: 232

Carson, Kit: 366
CD Leet Company: 272
Center Fire cartridge: 159
Chese, Anson: 122
Chief Micanopy: *128*
Child, Rachel Teresa: 15, *16*, *52*
Civil War: 224, 272
Claridge, Bert: 344
Clark, Elizabeth: 15
Clemens, Samuel: 286
Cody, 'Buffalo Bill': 329, 366, *366*, *391*
Coffeyville robbery: 162
Collier's Revolver: 84
Colt, Christopher: 122
Colt Custom Gun Shop: 207, 210-211

Colt Models

Automatic Machine Rifle: *See Browning Model 1917*
Automatic Pistol, Model 380 Government: *214*
Automatic Pistol, Model 1900: 175, 176
Automatic Pistol, Model 1911 Government: 176, *177*, *179*, 193, *195*, 419
Automatic Pistol, Model 1940 Hammerless: *118-119*, *174*
Baby Patterson Pistol: *163*
Bankers' Special: 168, *168*
AR-15 A2 Sporter II: 180, *180*
Berdan Russian Rifle: 164
Buntline Special: 159
Colt Carbines: 124
Colt 150th Anniversary Commemorative pistol: *119*, 172, *212*
Colt 150th Anniversary Engraving Sampler: 172, *212*
Colt 150th Anniversary Exhibition Gun: 172, 173, *173*, *208*
Colt Berdan: *165*
Colt/Browning Automatic Gun: 175
Colt 'Burgess' rifle: *165*
Colt, experimental model: *123*
Colt Heirloom 1 'mirror brite' .45 caliber Officer's ACP: *426*
Colt Lightning Pump: *See Lightning Magazine Rifle*
Colt Number 1 Deringer: *118-119*, *162*
Colt Revolver: 84
Colt Revolving Gun: *125*
Colt Walker Revolver: *134*, 135, *139*

Combat Commander: *194*
Delta Auto pistol: *426*
Delta Elite 10mm Auto pistol: *193*
Delta Heavy Barrel AR-15: *426*
Detective Special: 168, *196*
Diamondback revolver: *187*
Double Action Army Model: 160, *162*, 164, *165*
Double Action Self-Cocking Center Six-Shot Revolver: *See Double Action Army Model*
Double Diamond 45 Automatic: *216*
Double Diamond .357 Magnum revolver: *216*
First Model Hartford Dragoon: *138*
Frontier Model: *See Single Action Army Revolver*
Frontier Six-Shooter: See Single Action Army Revolver
Gatling Gun: 175, *179*
Gold Cup National Match: 29
Improved Army Pistol, 'Colt Dragoon': *134*, 135, 136, *138*
Lightning Model: *See Double Action Army Model*
London Colt: *143*
M14 Automatic Rifle: 180
M16 Automatic Rifle: 180, *180, 189*, 191, *421*
M60 Light Machine Gun: *421*
Mark IV Series weapons: 176, *177*
Military Pistol: *128*
Model 95: 68
Model 1895 Automatic Machine Gun: 68, 72
Model 1900: 24, 27, *27*, 28, *28*
Model 1903 Pocket Pistol: *24*
Model of 1860 Army Revolver: *See New Model Army Pistol*
Model Pocket Pistol: 140
Monitor: 52
Muskets: 124, 164
Mustang 380: *421*
Navy Pistol, 1851: 140, 141, 150-151
New Model Army: 135, 138, 149, 167, *191*
New Model Army Metallic Cartridge Revolving Pistol: *See Single Action Army Revolver*
New Model Navy: 138, 139, 166, *167*, 168, *168, 171, 183*
New Model Pocket Pistol: 138, *143, 149, 199*
New Model Police: 138, 148
New Service Model Ace: *29*
New Service Revolver: *See New Model Navy*
Officers Model Target Revolver: *168*
Officers Model .38 Special: 168
Official Police Model: *See New Model Navy*
Old Model Army Pistol: 135, *140, 199*
Old Model Navy Percussion Cap revolver: *118-119*
Old Model Navy Pistol: *2*, 136, 138, 139, *140, 143, 146, 149, 155*, 167, *199*
Old Model Pocket Pistol: 136, 138, *138, 141*
Patterson Colt: 128, *128*
Patterson Colt Revolver: *139*
Patterson Revolving Carbine: *128*
Patterson Revolving Rifle: *132*
Peacekeeper: *184, 195*
Peacemaker: *See Single Action Army Revolver*
Philippine Model Double Action Army Colt: *See Double Action Army Model*
Pocket Navy: 139
Pocket Positive: *See New Model Navy*
Police Positive: *See New Model Navy*
Promotion Model Revolver: 122, *125*
Python: *168*, 168-169, *171*, 172, *195*
Regular Dragoon Colt: *156*
Revolving Pocket Pistol, Model 1830: *135*
Rifles: 124, 164, *165*
Round-Barreled Army: *See New Model Army Pistol*
Service Model Ace Automatic Pistol: *203*
Shotguns: 124, 164, *165*
Sidehammer series: 138
Single Action Army Revolver: *156*, 158, 159, *160, 160, 162, 166, 173, 197, 206*, 207, 208, 211, *214*
Single Action Army Target Model: *158*
Single Action Metallic Revolver: *See Single Action Army Revolver*
Stainless Steel Gold Cup National Match: *177*
Stainless Steel King Cobra .357 Magnum revolver: *193, 195*
Stainless Steel Officer's ACP: *194*
'Texas Arm': *See Patterson Colt*
Third Model Dragoon: 136
Whitney/Walker Colt: *See Colt Walker Revolver*
Woodsman .22 Long Rifle Automatic Pistol: 31, *31*, 184
Colt, Samuel: *4*, 122, 128-129, 132-133, 134-135, 136, 139, 140-141, 144, 146-147, 148-149, 153, 168, 223
Colt, Sarah Caldwell: 122
Colt's Patent Firearms Manufacturing Company: 18, 19, 24, 68, 80
Converse, William W: 329
Custer, General George A: 159, *160*, 250, *257*

Dalton, Emmett: 162
Dewey, Admiral: 258, *258*
Dickens, Charles: 141, *144*
Douglas, Kirk: *200, 203*
Drake, Harry: 97
DuPont Corporation: 224, 228, 262-263, 280

E Remington and Son: *See Remington Arms Company*
Earp, Wyatt: 159
EI Du Pont de Nemours and Company: *See DuPont Corporation*
Eisenhower, Dwight General: *421*
Emmett, Sarah: 13
Enfield rifle: 351
Equitable Powder Manufacturing Company: 358

Fabrique Nationale: 17, 19, 22, 82, 84, 85
Fairchild Engine and Airplane Corporation: 180
Federal Aid in Wildlife Restoration Act: *See Pittman-Robertson Act*
Fitzgerald, JH: *184*, 185
FN-Browning Light Automatic Rifle: 64
Ford, Henry: 146
Forsyth, Alexander: 84
Funken, Felix: 104
Fusil Mitrailleur Browning: *See Browning Model 1917*
Fusil Mitrailleur Leger: 52

Gardner, John: 342-343
Gatling, Richard J: *179*
Geiger, Leonard: 250
Geiger gun (rifle and carbine): 250
Goering, Reichmarshall Herman: 22
Gould, AC: 341
Green, Colonel S Gordon: 80
Griffiths, John: 223

Hague Decrees: 351
Hanauer, P: 105
Hart, William S: *160*
Hartford State Technical Institute: 215
Hartford Factory: 134, 135, *136*, 136, 140, 147, 148, *148*, 149, 150-151, *151*, 152-153, *153*, 182-183, *183*, 184-185, 187, 188-189, 192, 194-195, 196-197, 200, 203
Hartley, Marcellus: 272, 276-277, 334
Haulier, Monsieur: 154
Henry, Benjamin: 326, *326*, 389
Henry rifle: 154, 326, *326, 329, 331*
Hepburn, LL: 236
Hickok, 'Wild Bill': 159, 366
Hobbs, AC: 272, 276
Hodges, Courtney General: *421*
Hooper, Arthur: 347

Jarvis, Elizabeth Hart: 136
Jenks, William: 247-248
John Griffiths Company: 247
Jonathan Browning Cylinder Repeating Rifle: *10-11*, 11, 12, 13,105
Juarez, Benito: 390

Kidder Peabody: 352
King Louis XIV: 82
Krag-Jorgensen rifle: 338

Lake City Army Ammunition Plant: 363
Lee, James Paris: 256, 258
LeMay, Curtis General: 180, *421*, 240, 241
Lesmok: 341
Liggett, Louis K: 352
Lincoln, Abraham: 11, *11*
London Colt: *143*
London Factory: *140*, 141, 144, 146

Masterson, Bat: 159
Mattheson Chemical Corporation: 363
Mauser's Rifle: 84
Maynard tape primer system: *251*
McKinley, President William: 364
Metallic cartridge: 154, 160
Metallurgy: 339-340
Milton, Jeff: *335*
Mix, Tom: *301*
Monte Carlo stocks: 227-228
Moore, Commodore: 139
Moore, Fred: 82
Morgan, James: 300, 304
Murphy, Audie: *312-313*

National Arms Company: 160
National Lead Company: 348
New Haven Arms Company: 326, *331*, 429
Nicholas II, Tsar: 260
Nixon, Richard M: 104

Oakley, Annie: *233, 366*
Olin, Franklin W: 358, *376*,
Olin, John: 358
Olin Corporation: 422
Olin-Mattheson: 363
Otterson, John Edward: 351, 352

P-39 Bell Airacobra: 80, *80*
Patent Arms Manufacturing Company of Patterson, New Jersey, Colt's Patent: 212, 232
Patterson Factory: 122, 123, *125*, 128, 131, 132-133
Patton, George General: *189, 421*
Pauly, Monsieur: 154
Peary, Admiral Robert: 368, 369
Perry, Commodore MC: 247
Pershing, General John: 76
Peters 'Accelerator' bullets: 282
Pittman-Robertson Act: 93
Potato Digger: *19, also see Winchester Model 1985*
Pratt, Francis A: 136
Pratt & Whitney Company: 136
Pump Action: 351

Reloading tools: *342-343*
Rem Choke choke tube: *238-239*
Rem Oil: *285*
Remington, Abigail: 286, 288
Remington Arms Company, Inc: 48, 60, 223-224, 227-229, 236, 251-252, 258, 284, 343, 347
Remington-Beals Revolvers: 224, *350-351*, 310, 312, *312*
Remington Custom Shop work: *306-307*
Remington, Eliphalet: 223, 241-242, 250, 286, *295*, 307

Remington, Eliphalet 'Lite' Jr: *4*, 223-224, 286-288, *288*, 290-292, 296, 300, 302, 304, 307
Remington, Eliphalet III: 223, 350
Remington-Elliot Deringer 22 RF: 313
Remington, Flora: 252
Remington, Maria: 248
Remington Models
A-3: *See Model 1903 Springfield Rifle*
Black Hills Rifle: 315
'Boy Scout Rifle': *See Remington Model 4S*
Contract models: 256-257
Creedmoor Rifle: 236, *243*, 315
Double Deringer: *294-295, 312*, 313
Enfield Rifle: *See Remington/Lee Rifle*
Geiger gun (rifle and carbine): 250
Hammerless Shotgun Model 1894: 321
'Harpers Ferry Rifles': 247
Iroquois Revolver: *267*, 313
Jenks Breech-loading Percussion Carbine: 223
LT-20 Limited Shotgun: *320*
Lebel Rifles: 258, *259*
Lee/Enfield Rifle: *See Remington/Lee Rifle*
Long Range XR-100 Pistol: *236-237*
M-1 Garand: *236-237*
M-1917 Enfield Rifle: *See US Rifle Model 1917*
Magazine Deringer Model: 225
Marlin Model 86 Rifle: 229, 232
Mark III Signal: *267*, 213
Mauser Repeating Rifle: 258
Mid-Range Target Rifle: 319
Model 11/2 Sporting Rifle: 316
Model 2 Sporting Rifle: 314, *315*
Model 4S 'Military Model' Rolling Block Sporting Rifle: 226, *317*
Model 7 Rifle: *238-239*, 310
Model 8 Autoloading Center Fire Rifle: 48
Model 8A Autoloading Rifle: 316, *317*
Model 10A Standard Grade Slide Action Repeating Shotgun: 321
Model 11A Standard Grade 5-Shot Autoloader: 321
Model 11-87 Premier Shotgun: *238-239*
Model 12A Slide Action Repeating Rifle: 316
Model 14A High Power Slide Action Repeating Rifle: 316, *317*
Model 16 Autoloading Rifle: 316
Model 17: 60
Model 17A Standard Grade Slide Action Repeating Shotgun: 321
Model 24A Autoloading Rifle: 316, *317*
Model 29A Standard Grade Slide Action Repeating Shotgun: 321
Model 31A Standard Grade Slide Action Repeater: 321, *321*
Model 32A Standard Grade Over-and-Under Gun: 321
Model 33 Bolt Action Single Shot Rifle: 317, *317*
Model 34 Bolt Action Repeating Rifle: 317, *317*
Model 40X Heavyweight Bolt Action Target Rifle:236, 320, *320*
Model 40-XB (Center Fire Match Rifle, Varmint and Varmint Special): *236-237*, 237, 320
Model 40-XBBR Benchrest Rifle: *236-237*
Model 40-XR (Custom Sporter Rifle and Rimfire Rifle): *236-237*, 310
Model 51 Automatic: *267*, 313
Model 74 Sportsman Autoloading Rifle: *320*
Model 81 Woodmaster: 48
Model 81A 'Woodmaster' Autoloading Rifle: 317
Model '95 Double Deringer: *See Double Deringer*
Model 121A 'Fieldmaster' Slide Action Repeating Rifle: 317
Model 141A 'Gamemaster' Slide Action Repeating Rifle: 317, *317*
Model 241A 'Speedmaster' Autoloading Rifle: 317
Model 511A 'Scoremaster' Bolt Action Box Magazine Repeating Rifle: 310, 317
Model 521 TL Junior Target Bolt Action Repeating Rifle: 317
Model 541-S Custom Sporter: 320
Model 541-T Bolt Action Rimfire Rifle: *229*
Model 550A Autoloading Rifle: 317
Model 552A 'Speedmaster' Autoloading Rifle: 317
Model 572A 'Fieldmaster' Slide Action Repeater: 317
Model 580 Bolt Action Single Shot: 317
Model 600: *See Mohawk 600*
Model 660 Bolt Action Carbine: *221*, 320
Model 700 Rifles (ADL, BDL, Classic, Hunting, Mountain, Safari, Sporter, Varmint Special): *2-3*, *218*, 228, *228-230*, 236, 310, 320
Model 720 Rifle: 228
Model 721 Rifles (721 and 721A): 229, 231-232, 236, 317
Model 722 (722 and 722A): 229, 231-232, 236, 317
Model 742 (Woodmaster and BDL Custom Deluxe): *234-235*, 315, 317, *317*
Model 760 (Deluxe and 'Gamemaster' Rifles): *234-235*, *315*, 317, *317*
Model 788 Center Fire Bolt Action Rifle: *232*, 320
Model 870 (.410 Field, New Model Express, SP Deer Gun, SP Magnum, Special Field, Wingmaster, Wingmaster AP, Wingmaster Deer Gun and Youth Gun): *218*, 237, *237*, *269*, *284-285*, 321
Model 1100 (Autoloading Trap Gun, SA Skeet Gun and Special Field): *218*, *219*, *240*, *302-303*, *306-307*, *315*
Model 1841 Percussion 'Mississippi' Rifle: 232
Model 1861 Army Revolver: 312
Model 1863 Percussion Contract: 314
Model 1865 Navy Rolling Block Pistol: 313, *313*
Model 1867 (Navy Cadet Rolling Block Rifle and Navy RollingBlock Pistol): 313-314
Model 1871 (Army Single Action and Army Rolling Block Pistol): *267*, 313
Model 1875 Single Action Army Revolver: 313
Model 1882 Shotgun: *308-309*, 321
Model 1885 Double Barrel Hammer Shotgun: 321
Model 1887 Double Barrel Hammer Shotgun: 321
Model 1889 Double Barrel Hammer Shotgun: 321
Model 1890 Single Action Army Revolver: *312*, 313
Model 1891 Target Rolling Block Pistol: 313
Model 1900 Hammerless Shotgun: 321, *321*
Model 1901 Target Rolling Block Pistol: *312*, 313
Model 1903 Springfield Rifle: *264*, *266*
Model 1919 Government Experimental Pistol: *267*
Model 3200 Field Grade Over-and-Under Shotgun: 321
Model 7600 Rifle: *236-237*, *246-247*
Mohawk 600: *226*, *286-287*, *298-299*, *310*, 320
Monte Carlo stocks: 227-228
New Custom XT-100 Heavy Barrel: 314
New Model Army Revolver: 312
New Model Belt Revolver: 312
New Model Number 4 Rolling Block Rifle: 316, *317*
New Model Pocket Revolver: 313
New Model Police Revolver: 313
Number 1 Revolver: *267*, *312*, 313
Number 4 Revolver: *312*
Nylon 66 Rifles: 320
Nylon 76 Lever Action Repeating Rifle: 320, *320*
'Old Model Army': *See Remington Model 1861*
'Old Army' cap and ball Revolver: *248*
'Over-Under Deringer': *See Double Deringer*
'Parlor Pistol': *See Remington-Rider Single Shot Deringer*
Remington-Beals Revolvers: 224, 310, 312, *312*, *350-351*
Remington-Elliot Deringer 22 RF: 313
Remington-Hepburn Number 3: *215*, 215, 216
Remington-Hepburn Number Schuetzen Match Rifle: 216
Remington-Jenks Carbines: *246*, 247-248
Remington-Keene Magazine Bolt Action Rifle: *254-255*, 315
Remington-Lee Magazine, Bolt Action Rifles: 250, *257-263*, 315
Remington-Parker Shotgun: *222-223*, *294-295*
Remington-Rider Pistols: *267*, 312, 313
Remington Third Model Beals Pocket Revolver: 310
Remington-Whitmore Model 1874: 321
Remington-UMC: *See Remington Arms Company*
Revolving Percussion Rifle: 314
Rifle Cane: 314, *315*
Rolling Block Rifle: *246*, *249*, 250-252, *251*, 253,
'Saw Handle Deringer': *See Vest Pocket Pistol*
Single Shot Breech-Loading Carbine: 314
'Split Breech Remington': *See Single Shot Breech-Loading Carbine*
Sportsmans 48A Standard Grade Autoloader: 321, *321*
Sportsman 58 ADL Autoloader: 321
Sportsman 78 Rifle: 234-235
Sportsman 581 Bolt Action Rifle: 224, 320
Sportsman 581-S Rifle: *234-235*
US Enfield Rifle: *See US Rifle Model 1917*
US Rifle Model 1917: *260*, 261-262, *262-263*, *265*
XP-100 Single Shot Pistol: 313
Remington, Philo: 223-224, 350, 258
Remington, Samuel: 223-224
Remington-UMC: *See Remington Arms Company*
Rexall: 352
Reynier, Adrien: 82
Rider, Joseph: 250
Roosevelt, Theodore: 364, *364*
Roosevelt, Kermit: 364, 365
Root, EK: 139, 147, 150
Rough Riders: 346

Saive, DD: 64
Savage Arms Company: 228, 250
Schiefflin, Ed: *331*
Scholes, Christopher Latham: 282
Second Seminole War of 1835: *128*
Seminole War: 129, 132
Servaty, Elizabeth: *See Topperwein, 'Plinky'*

Sherman Anti-Trust Law: 334
Shotgun shells: *274-275*
Skeet Shooting: 101, *101*
Smith, Joseph: 12
Smith & Wesson Combat Magnum: 169
Smith & Wesson Firearms Company: 136, 166, 169
Smith & Wesson Highway Patrolman: 169
Smith & Wesson .357 Magnum: 169
Smokeless powder: 358, *See also Ammunition: Winchester*
Smokeless Powder Sporting Rifle: *See Winchester Model 1894*
Soft Point bullet: *278-279*
Solid-Head cartridge: *156*
Spanish-American War: 364, 377, 397
Special Flight Bow: 97
Spencer rifle: 154
Sporting Shooting: 101, *101*
Springfield Model A-3 Rifle: 263
Springfield Model 1903 Rifle: 263
Springfield trap door models: *254-255*
Stalcup, Elizabeth: 11, 13
Starr, Nelson K: 64
Stevens, Harry: 184
Stokes, Bill: 215
Strugnell, HJ: 347

Talcott, Lt Col George: 31
Topperwein, Adolph: 369, *369*
Topperwein, 'Plinky': 369, *369*
Trant, Timothy: 185
Trap Shooting: 101, *101*
Twain, Mark: *See Samuel Clemens*

Uhl, Edward: 399
Union Metallic Cartridge Company (UMC): 224, 228, 258, 260, 263, 270, *270*, 276-277, *277*, 334, 343, 344, 347
United Drug Company: 352
US Cartridge Company (USCC): 344, 348
US Repeating Arms Company: 363

Vandermissen, G: 104
Volcanic Repeating Arms Company: 326, *326, 329, 428*

'Walker-Hepburn': *See Remington-Hepburn Number Schuetzen Match Rifle*
Walker, Samuel H: 132-133, 134, *134*, 135
Watrous, George R: 347
Wayne, John: 160, *200, 203*
Western Cartridge Company: 356, 358
White, Ed: 148, *148*, 158, *158*
White, Rollin: 136, 154
Whitney, Amos: 136
Whitney, Eli: 134
Whitneyville Armory: 134, *136*
Wild, Joseph: 340
Winchester Center Fire (WCF): 338
Winchester Custom Shop: 329
Winchester laboratory: 338-340
Winchester Models
Browning Automatic Rifle: 351, *379, 380*
Experimental Rifle: *389*
Leader: 338
Lee Model Winchester: 395, 397
'New Model Winchester': *See Model 1866*
Ranger Lever Action Carbine: *414*
Ranger Bolt Action Carbine: *412, 413*
Sharps .40-90: 334, 364
Single Shot, 'Baby Carbine': 371, 372
Single Shot Rifle: *370-371*, 371, 372, *372*, 413
Model 1 Super X Automatic Field Gun: 411
Model 03: 351, *352*
Model 06: 373, *374, See also Model 62*
Model 20: 403, *403*
Model 21: 456, *456*, 403, *403*, 406, *406*
Model 23: *358*
Model 24: 406, *406*
Model 25: *410*, 411
Model 36: 44, 379, 403, *403*
Model 37: 406, *406*
Model 40: 406, *406*
Model 41: 403, *403*
Model 42: 406, *406*
Model 50: 411
Model 52: 356
Model 53: 373, *373*, 395, 399
Model 54: 356, *356, See also Model 70*
Model 55: *376*
Model 58: 378, 379, *379*
Model 59: 378, 379, *379*, 411
Model 60: 378, 379, *379*
Model 62: 373
Model 64: 376, *376*, 377, 395
Model 65: 373, *373*, 395, 399
Model 68: 378, 379
Model 70: 228-229, 231-232, 356, *361, 401, 410*, 412, *412, 413, 415*
Model 71: 373, *373*
Model 73 Lever Action: 66, 258
Model 86: 15
Model 90: *See Model 62*
Model 92: 351
Model 94: 229, 232, *322-323, 347*, 351, *354-355, 361, 378*, 414-415, *414, 415*
Model 94 Chief Crazy Horse Commemorative: 415, *415*
Model 96: 411
Model 97: 333, *350*, 351, *403*
Model 99: 378, *378*, 379
Model 101: *410*, 411
Model 370: 406
Model 1200: 411
Model 1300: *408*
Model 1400: 411
Model 1866: *322-323*, 326, 329, *331*, 333, 389, *389*, 390, *391*
Model 1871: 373, *373*, 395
Model 1873: *322-323*, 329, 333, 340, 346, *388*, 390, *390*, 391, *391*, 392, *392*, 395, *395*
Model 1876: 333, 364, *365*, 392, *392*, 395, *395*
Model 1878 Single Shot Rifle: 15, 16
Model 1885 Single Shot Rifle: *16-17*, 36, 40, 332, 338, 371, *372*, 372
Model 1886 Lever Action Rifle: *322-323*, 332, *339*, 340, 365, *370*, 372, *372*, 373, *374*, 385, 397, *397*
Model 1887: 54, *350*, 382, *383*, 402
Model 1890: 42-43. *42-43*, 351, *352*, 373, *373*, 399
Model 1892: 43, 340, 351, 368, 373, *373*, 395, 399
Model 1893: 54, 56, *60-61*, *335*, 382, *382*
Model 1894: *2-3*, 15, 16, 43, 44, 351, *354-355*, 373, 376, *376*, 385, 395
Model 1895: 44, 364, 365, 377
Model 1897: 56, *56-57*, 333, *350*, 351, 382, *382*, 384, 402
Model 1898: 351, 397
Model 1900: *38-39*, 44, *44*, 378, 379, *379*
Model 1901: 54, 382, *383*, 395, 402, *402*
Model 1902: *378*, 379
Model 1904: *378*, 379
Model 1911: 402, *402, 403*
Model 1912: 351, *361, 402*, 403, *403*
Model 9422: *323, 362*, 416-417
Model 9422 Annie Oakley Commemorative: 416, *416*
Model 9422 Boy Scout Commemorative: *348*
.22 Caliber Pull Apart Repeating Rifle: 385, *385*
.22 Caliber Rimfire Single Shot Rifle: 386, *386*
.236 Caliber Repeating Rifle: 386, *386*
.30 Caliber Bolt-sear Lever Action Repeating Rifle: 386, 386, 387
.30 Caliber Government Repeating Rifle: 384, *384*
.30 Caliber Lever Action Repeating Rifle (Number One): 385, *385*
.30 Caliber Lever Action Repeating Rifle (Number Two): 385, *385*
.30 Caliber Pul Apart Repeating Rifle: 385, *385*
.30 Caliber Pump Action repeating Rifle: 386, *386*
.30 Caliber Repeating Rifle: *385, 386*
.30 Caliber Swing Guard Repeating Rifle: 386, *386*
.38 Caliber Repeating Rifle: 384, *384*
.40 Caliber Repeating Rifle: 386, *386*
.44 Caliber Lever Action Repeating Rifle: 385, *385*
.44 Caliber Lever Action Repeating Rifle (Number Three): 386, *386*
.44 Caliber Pump Action Repeating Rifle: 384, *384*
.44 Caliber Repeating Rifle: *385, 386*
.45 Caliber Lever Action Repeating Rifle: 384, *384*, 385, *385*
.45 Caliber Repeating Rifle: *384, 385*
.45 Caliber Rifle: *384*
.45-70 Caliber Repeating Rifle: 385, *385*
10 Gauge Lever Action Shotgun: 387, *387*
10 Gauge Pump Action Shotgun: 387, *387*
12 Gauge Lever Action Shotgun: 387, *387*
12 Gauge Pull Apart Shotgun: 387, *387*
12 Gauge Pump Action Shotgun: 387, *387*
20 Gauge Single Shot Lever Action Shotgun: 403, *403*
Winchester .30-30: *See Model 1894*
Winchester Repeating Rifle: 159
Winchester Pistols: 418-419
Winchester Sporting Arms: 363
Winder Musket: 372
Winchester Museum: 384
Winchester, Oliver: *5*, 326, 329, *376*, 389, 415, 419
Winchester Operations: 363
Winchester Repeating Arms Company: 15, 16, 17, 22, 36, 54, 228, 258, 272, 352, 326, 329, 341, 343, *343*, 344, 345, 347, 352, *352, 362*, 364, 371, 374, 382, 400
Winchester Special Features: 400-401
Winchester Sporting Arms: 363
Winchester-Western Company: 358
Winder, Colonel CB: 372
World's Fair: 369
World War I: 228, 258, 261-262
World War II: 227-228, 236, 258, 263, 266, 310

Young, Brigham: 12, 13
Yule, Steve: *303, 310*
Yule, Tom: *303-305*

'Zouave Rifle': *See Remington Model 1863 Percussion Contract Rifle*

Overleaf: **A boy and his dog head off into the wilds, with a rifle along for protection against snakes—and to do a little 'plinking' along the way. It's an American image that dates back to the beginnings of the nation itself.**

W9-CJM-272

CALCULUS

SECOND EDITION

CALCULUS

SECOND EDITION

Ross L. Finney

George B. Thomas, Jr.
Massachusetts Institute of Technology

With the collaboration of
Maurice D. Weir
Naval Postgraduate School

 ADDISON-WESLEY PUBLISHING COMPANY

Reading, Massachusetts ▪ Menlo Park, California
New York ▪ Don Mills, Ontario ▪ Wokingham, England ▪ Amsterdam
Bonn ▪ Sydney ▪ Singapore ▪ Tokyo ▪ Madrid ▪ San Juan

Sponsoring Editor: Jerome Grant
Developmental Editor: Elka Block
Managing Editor: Karen Guardino
Production Supervisor: Jack Casteel
Copy Editor: Barbara Flanagan
Proofreader: Joyce Grandy
Text Design: Geri Davis, Quadrata, Inc.
Art Consultant: Joseph Vetere
Art Coordinator: Connie Hulse
Electronic Illustration: Tech-Graphics
Production Editorial Services: Barbara Pendergast
Manufacturing Supervisor: Roy Logan
Marketing Manager: Andy Fisher
Cover Design: Peter Blaiwas

PHOTO CREDITS

xviii, NASA **xx,** Dick Morton; ©1993 Norbert Wu **10,** Dick Smith Photo **61,** AP/Wide World Photos **62,** Paul DeMark, Office of Public Affairs, Humbolt State University **112,** Dick Morton; Breed Technologies, Inc. **145,** AP/Wide World Photos **151,** AP/Wide World Photos **182,** NASA **196,** From *PSSC Physics* 2/E, 1965; D.C. Heath & Co. with Education Development Center, Inc., Newton, MA. Reprinted with permission. **200,** Dick Morton **252,** Paul Lipke/Trireme Trust **261,** Dr. Joshua E. Barnes, University of Hawaii **272,** Mark Rick (both) **339,** Marshall Henrichs **346,** Brian Tucholke/WHOI and Tom Reed, University of Hawaii; Jian Lin **366,** AP/Wide World Photos **423,** AP/Wide World Photos **438,** Dick Morton (both) **465,** © Richard F. Voss/IBM Research **487,** From *PSSC Physics* 2/E, 1965; D.C. Heath & Co. with Education Development Center, Inc., Newton, MA. Reprinted with permission; © Timothy Egan/Woodfin Camp & Associates; Mark Gerson/FPG International Corp. **505,** Susan Van Etten **506,** Reprinted by permission of the Putnam Publishing Group from *Skene's Elements of Yacht Design* by Francis S. Kinney. Copyright© 1927, 1935, 1938, 1962, 1973 by Dodd, Mead and Co.; Susan Van Etten/Karle Proppe **510,** Steven J. Boljonis; Science Source/Photo Researchers **556,** Tom Jorgensen, The University of Iowa **570,** From *PSSC Physics* 2/E, 1965; D.C. Heath & Co. with Education Development Center, Inc., Newton, MA. Reprinted with permission. **628,** Dick Morton; Joseph Nettis/Stock Boston **630,** H. Armstrong Roberts, Inc. **643,** From *PSSC Physics* 2/E, 1965; D.C. Heath & Co. with Education Development Center, Inc., Newton, MA. Reprinted with permission. **690,** Lori Stiles, University of Arizona (both) **750,** Dick Morton **763,** AP/Wide World Photos (both) **770,** From *PSSC Physics* 2/E, 1965; D.C. Heath & Co. with Education Development Center, Inc., Newton, MA. Reprinted with permission. **785,** ©1994 Nelson L. Max, University of California/Biological Photo Service; Graphic by Alfred Gray **792,** From *PSSC Physics* 2/E, 1965; D.C. Heath & Co. with Education Development Center, Inc., Newton, MA. Reprinted with permission **793,** NASA **796,** From *Gardner's Photographic Sketch Book of the Civil War,* Plate 75. Reprinted with permission of Dover Publications, Inc. **798,** Dick Morton **829,** ND Roger-Viollet **876,** Dick Morton **930,** Julia Kimbell (both) **938,** NASA/Jet Propulsion Laboratory

Library of Congress Cataloging-in-Publication Data
Finney, Ross L.
Calculus / Ross L. Finney, George B. Thomas, Jr. — 2nd ed.
p. cm.
Includes index.
ISBN 0-201-54977-8 (set)– ISBN 0-201-54306-0 (Calculus of A Single Variable)
1. Calculus. I. Thomas, George Brinton, 1914– . II. Title.
QA303.F44 1994
515 — dc20
93-31728
CIP

1 2 3 4 5 6 7 8 9 10 VH 9796959493

Preface

This book is written for the standard calculus sequence. Its purpose, in addition to making it possible to learn calculus, is to teach students to use calculus effectively and to show how knowing calculus can pay off in their professional lives. The prerequisites are the usual exposure to algebra, trigonometry, and analytic geometry. Chapter 1 reviews the essentials.

Although this book is livelier and less formal than many traditional calculus texts, the appropriate level of rigor has been maintained. We try to explain things carefully but without belaboring the obvious and without answering questions students aren't yet ready to ask. For example, we state the max-min theorem for continuous functions and use it to prove the Mean Value Theorem, but we do not prove the max-min theorem itself or explore the properties of the real number system on which it depends. We use absolute values to control function outputs in Chapter 1 and show how limit theorems are proved with epsilons and deltas at the end of Chapter 2, but put the more complicated arguments in the appendices.

Highlights of Content Changes in the Second Edition

Chapter 1 now reviews coordinates, increments, and lines in a single introductory section. The presentation of circles includes a review of completing the square. Parabolas are still discussed, but the formal focus-directrix definition has been moved to a later chapter on plane curves. **Chapter 2** (limits) begins with an informal definition motivated by graphs and numerical patterns. The max-min theorem for continuous functions has been moved to Chapter 4 but the Intermediate Value Theorem is still there. **Chapter 3** (derivatives) covers the same material as before, but contains additional numerical and graphical work. **Chapter 4** (applications of derivatives) combines the max-min theorem for continuous functions with the first derivative theorem and the first derivative test into a new introductory section on detecting extreme values of functions. In the chapter's presentation of curve sketching, the emphasis is on how derivatives determine the shape of a function's graph. This enables students not only to analyze the graphs of polynomials and rational functions, but also to identify cusps and to sketch solutions of first order differential equations and initial value problems. **Chapter 5** (integration) begins with a new section on answering practical questions by approximating with finite sums (distance traveled, volume, average value, etc.). It then proceeds into the integral calculus by investigating the limits of such sums. The new **Chapter 6** (transcendental functions) now precedes **Chapter 7** (applications of integration). Chapter 6 also takes a new approach (exponential functions before logarithmic functions) and concludes with a new section treating separable and first order linear differential equations. **Chapter 8** (techniques of integration) is shorter than before. It still covers integration by parts, partial fractions, trigonometric substitutions, tables, and improper integrals, but the remaining trigonometric integrals are treated (as appropriate) in the introductory section and earlier chapters. **Chapter 9** (sequences and series) concludes with a brief subsection on the use of power series in solving first order initial value problems. **Chapter 10** (conic sections, parametrized curves, and polar coordinates) includes the formal definition of parabola that used to be in Chapter 1 and covers equations of conic sections that have been shifted away from the origin. Polar coordinates now use only radian measure. **Chapter 11** (vectors and space) has additional vector-geometry exercises, and **Chapter 12** (vector functions) now takes a vector approach to curvature in the plane. In **Chapter 13** (partial derivatives) the section on differentiability and linearization for functions of two independent variables now comes before the section on the Chain Rule. Directional derivatives are defined in the plane before being introduced in space, and the section on Lagrange multipliers has been expanded to include functions with two constraints (formerly in an appendix). **Chapter 14** (multiple integrals) contains illustrated strategies for finding limits of integration for double integrals in polar coordinates, and for triple integrals in rectangular, cylindrical, and spherical coordinates. **Chapter 15** (vector analysis) has been reordered to place the section on path independence, potential functions, and conservative fields ahead of the presentation of Green's theorem. This completes the work on line integrals before surface integrals are introduced. The chapter also contains a new section on integrals over parametrized surfaces.

Applications and Examples

The applications come from all over. From the life and social sciences, there are applications to determining lung volume (p. 506), restoring normal blood flow in arteries (p. 205), spreading innovation (p. 528), and predicting the consequences of human evolution (p. 385). From business and economics there are applications to inventory control (p. 311), marginal cost and revenue (pp. 143 and 238), and the determination of production levels that are likely to maximize profit or loss (p. 239). From science and engineering, we discuss solar-powered cars (p. 339), colliding galaxies (p. 261), sequential vs. binary search (p. 398), coasting ships (p. 430), and warping railroad tracks (p. 61). From everyday life, we apply calculus to everything from art forgery (p. 338), to baseball (p. 769), the 1989 Loma Prieta earthquake (p. 366), human-powered flight (p. 145), the Concorde's sonic booms (p. 806), and the cost of home electricity (p. 340).

Exercises

Each exercise set is graded to run from routine at the beginning to more challenging toward the end. Within this framework, the exercises generally follow the order of presentation in the text. Most sets contain applications and many contain calculator, graphing utility, and critical thinking exercises. Each section concludes with questions that guide students in writing short descriptions of key ideas. Each chapter concludes with a review list and a set of practice exercises covering the chapter's main points.

Enhancements to Learning

In addition to the attention paid to writing style and content, we have included the following features to make calculus more accessible and easier to use. The book is printed in full color throughout and contains more than 1800 figures. There are **drawing lessons,** step-by-step descriptions of **solution procedures,** and **boxed strategies** for problem solving. The steps in many of the examples are accompanied by **explanatory notes,** and the burden of exposition is carried by art in the body of the text when we feel that pictures and text together will convey ideas better than words alone (see p. 450 for an example). There are entertaining **historical notes** and helpful marginal lists and comments. All of these features were well received in the first edition.

There are also some learning enhancements new to this second edition: New **chapter openers** focus on the day-to-day use of calculus in contemporary careers. There are more **graphing utility** exercises (see, for example, Sections 2.1, 3.5, 4.3, 4.5, 5.4, 6.1, 7.8, and 12.4). In addition to exercises that provide opportunities to use calculators and graphers (denoted by ▦ and ◪), there are **critical thinking** exercises (denoted by ◈) and exercises that ask students to explain the reasoning behind their answers. (Answers to most critical thinking exercises are not supplied in the Answer section in order to encourage students to try solving an exercise before being given the answer.) At the end of every section additional **writing** exercises provide questions that ask students to write short paragraphs about key concepts for themselves. (No answers are supplied for these questions.)

We have increased the **visual emphasis** by including more figures in the text and more graphs in the exercises for students to interpret and explain.

There are more **problem solving** aids than before, and more **marginal sidelights** and enrichment material.

The **exercise sets** have been revised and improved to have a more consistent even-odd pairing and a broader range of mid-level material.

Supplements for Instructors

OmniTest II is a computerized testing system that allows instructors to generate tests, quizzes, and additional practice problems, based on the learning objectives of the text. As an algorithm-driven system, OmniTest II creates multiple versions of the same test by automatically inserting a random selection of numbers into model problems. The numbers, while varied, all produce reasonable answers. Questions may be selected in any combination of open-ended, multiple-choice, and true-false formats. Instructors may assign an instructor code and level of difficulty to each model problem. OmniTest II is available for IBM PC/compatibles.

Printed Test Bank includes 30 test items per text section, covering the section's learning objectives. It contains printed answer keys and student worksheets for each test.
Instructors Solutions Manuals contain solutions for all text exercises.
Answer Book contains short answers to all exercises.
Transparency Masters include a selection of definitions, theorems, proofs, formulas, tables, and figures. These may be copied onto transparency acetates for overhead projection.

Supplements for Students

Student Study Guide By Maurice D. Weir, Naval Postgraduate School. Organized to match the text, this workbook, in a semiprogrammed format, increases student proficiency.
Student Solutions Manuals By Thomas L. Cochran and Michael Schneider of Belleville Area College. These manuals contain worked solutions to odd-numbered exercises.

Software-Related Supplements for Instructors and Students

Analyzer⋆ This program is a tool for exploring functions from calculus and other disciplines. It can graph functions singly or together. It can differentiate, integrate, or iterate a function. It can find roots, extreme values and inflection points, and vertical asymptotes. It can compose functions, graph polar and parametric equations, display families of curves, and make animated sequences with changing parameters. It takes full advantage of flexibility of the Macintosh, allowing input to be either numeric (from the keyboard) or graphic (with a mouse). **Analyzer⋆** runs on Macintosh II, Plus, or better.

The Calculus Explorer Consisting of 27 programs ranging in coverage from functions to vector fields, this software enables instructors and students to use the computer as an "electronic chalkboard." The accompanying manual devotes a section to each program, and includes both examples and exercises. It is available for IBM PC/compatibles.

InSight This calculus demonstration software enhances the understanding of calculus concepts graphically. The program presents ten simulation scenarios. Each scenario describes an application and a related problem and takes the user through the solution visually. The format is interactive. The software is available for IBM PC/compatibles.

The Student Edition of MathCAD A powerful free-form scratchpad, this edition has all the problem-solving capabilities of the professional version. Available for the IBM PC/compatibles.

Mathematical Modeling with MathCAD A workbook of 45 laboratory activities using MathCAD to complement a standard course in calculus.

Laboratories for Calculus I Using Mathematica by Margaret Höft, The University of Michigan at Dearborn. This is a collection of *Mathematica* experiments for the first term of the calculus sequence.

Math Explorations Series Each of the six manuals in this series provides problems and explorations in calculus. Intended for self-paced and laboratory settings, these manuals are an excellent complement to the text.

- **Exploring Calculus with a Graphing Calculator, Second Edition** By Charlene E. Beckman and Ted Sundstrom of Grand Valley State University.
- **Exploring Calculus with Mathematica** By James K. Finch and Millianne Lehmann of the University of San Francisco.
- **Exploring Calculus with Derive** By David C. Arney of the U.S. Military Academy at West Point.
- **Exploring Calculus with Maple** By Mark H. Holmes, Joseph G. Ecker, William E. Boyce, and William L. Seigmann of Rensselaer Polytechnic Institute.
- **Exploring Calculus with Analyzer*** By Richard E. Sours of Wilkes University.
- **Exploring Calculus with the IBM PC Version 2 0** By John B. Fraleigh and Lewis I. Pakula of the University of Rhode Island.

Acknowledgments

We would like to express our thanks and appreciation for the many valuable contributions of the people who reviewed this book as it developed through its various stages:

Mohammed Aziz, *Cedar Valley College*
William Bare, *Berry College*
Martin Bartelt, *Christopher Newport University*
Chris Caldwell, *University of Tennessee at Martin*
Douglas Cameron, *The University of Akron*
Eleanor Canter, *Wentworth Institute of Technology*
Gerry Cox, *Lake Michigan College*
Pamela Crawford, *Randolph Macon College*
Donald Cresswell, *Idaho State University*
Michael Failla, *Harford Community College*
Maureen Fenrick, *Mankato State University*
Marsha Finkel-Babadi, *University of North Florida*
Stuart Goldenberg, *California Polytechnic State University–San Luis Obispo*
Warren Gordon, *City University of New York, Bernard M. Baruch College*
Stanley Gurak, *University of San Diego*
Elizabeth Hawkins, *Shoreline Community College*
Thomas Hern, *Bowling Green State University*
Jeanne Hutchison, *University of Alabama at Birmingham*
Richard Järvinen, *Winona State University*
Kenneth Kalmanson, *Montclair State College*
Marcia Kemen, *Wentworth Institute of Technology*
Leonard Krop, *De Paul University*
Lee LaRue, *Paris Junior College*
Deanna Li, *North Seattle Community College*
Benny Lo, *Ohlone College*
David Manderscheid, *University of Iowa*
Eldon Miller, *University of Mississippi*
Ann Marie Murray, *Hudson Valley Community College*
Greg Naber, *California State University–Chico*
James Nicholson, *Clemson University*
Judith Palagallo, *The University of Akron*
Paul Patten, *North Georgia College*
Julia Polk, *Okallosa-Walton Community College*
Clyde Scandrett, *Naval Postgraduate School*
Kenneth Schoen, *Worcester State College*
Carolyn Showalter, *Ocean County College*
Dennis Snow, *University of Notre Dame*
Charlene Solomon, *Wentworth Institute of Technology*
David Stacey, *Bellevue Community College*
Jack Wilson, *University of North Carolina at Asheville*

We are particularly grateful to Maurice D. Weir at the Naval Postgraduate School, who shared his teaching ideas throughout the preparation of this book and drafted the revisions of some of the later chapters. We appreciate his constant encouragement and thoughtful advice. We would also like to thank Fred Brauer, University of Wisconsin, Madison, for sharing classroom notes on differential equations.

We want to thank Cynthia Hutcherson, who, along with Kelly Locke of Hartnell College and Teresa Henson of the Naval Postgraduate School, provided answers to all the exercises in the text. We also appreciate the work of an excellent team of graduate students from Stanford University—Tanya Kalich, David Cardon, Afshin Bayrooti, and Miguel Abreu—who checked every answer for accuracy.

We owe a special thanks to John R. Martin of Tarrant County Jr. College, Carl Mueller of Georgia Southwestern College, and Jennifer Earles Szydlik of the University of Wisconsin at Madison for reading the text and exercises in galley pages and checking the calculations.

We appreciate all the assistance of the staff at Addison-Wesley. We particularly want to acknowledge the expert advice and assistance provided by Elka Block, Development Editor for this edition. Her attention, talent, and constant support have made a significant contribution to the quality of this revision. We would also like to thank the rest of the Addison-Wesley Finney/Thomas book team: Jack Casteel, Helen Curtis, Geri Davis, Andrew Fisher, Barbara Flanagan, Jerome Grant, Connie Hulse, Kathy Manley, Dick Morton, Barbara Pendergast, and Joe Vetere for their hard work in bringing this text to fruition.

Accuracy

Addison-Wesley is committed to publishing educational materials of high quality. Rigorous editing and proofing procedures ensure the highest level of accuracy possible. This commitment to quality motivates every step of the publishing process. We hope you are satisfied with this text, and welcome any response you may have.

Any errors that remain in the text are the responsibility of the authors. We will appreciate having these brought to our attention. With the enhanced accuracy/quality control process we and Addison-Wesley have put into place with this text, we feel confident that we have made this text as error free as is humanly possible. Your Addison-Wesley representative will be happy to describe the process to you.

Some of our colleagues suggested that since we are so confident about the book's accuracy, we should go one step further, and offer payment for any remaining errors that are found. With this in mind, but primarily because we want to detect any remaining errors quickly and correct them in subsequent printings, we are offering to pay $5 per *mathematical* error to the first person who reports the error. Any mathematical error that has follow-through effects will be counted as at most two errors. Please report any errors to us in care of: Ross L. Finney, Addison-Wesley Publishing Co., One Jacob Way, Reading, MA 01867.

R.L.F., *Monterey, California*
G.B.T., Jr., *State College, Pennsylvania*

Contents

1 Prerequisites for Calculus

OVERVIEW 1

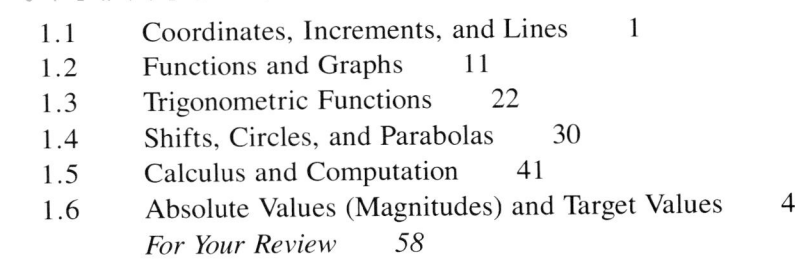

1.1 Coordinates, Increments, and Lines 1
1.2 Functions and Graphs 11
1.3 Trigonometric Functions 22
1.4 Shifts, Circles, and Parabolas 30
1.5 Calculus and Computation 41
1.6 Absolute Values (Magnitudes) and Target Values 48
For Your Review *58*
Practice Exercises *58*

2 Limits and Continuity

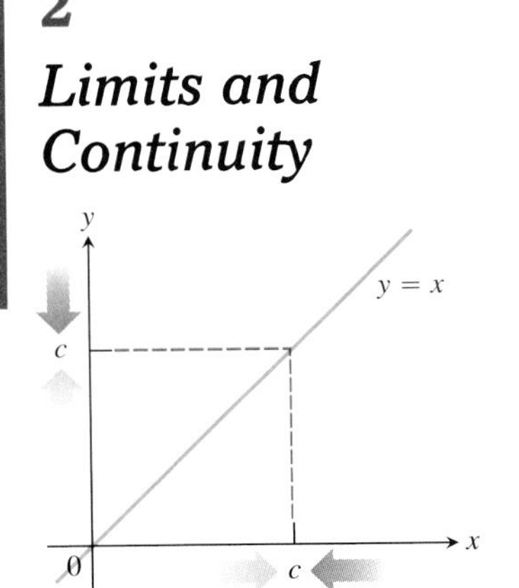

OVERVIEW 63

2.1 Limits of Function Values 63
2.2 Limits Involving Infinity 76
2.3 The Sandwich Theorem and $(\sin\theta)/\theta$ 84
2.4 Continuous Functions 90
2.5 Defining Limits Formally with Epsilons and Deltas 101
For Your Review *109*
Practice Exercises *109*

3 Derivatives

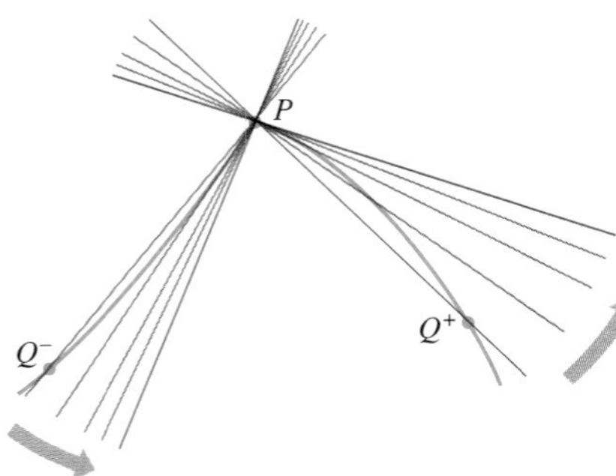

OVERVIEW 113

3.1 Slopes, Tangent Lines, and Derivatives 113
3.2 Differentiation Rules 126
3.3 Velocity, Speed, and Other Rates of Change 138
3.4 Derivatives of Trigonometric Functions 152
3.5 The Chain Rule 159
3.6 Implicit Differentiation and Fractional Powers 168
3.7 Linearizations and Differentials 176
3.8 Newton's Method 187
For Your Review *195*
Practice Exercises *195*

4 Applications of Derivatives

OVERVIEW 201

4.1 Related Rates of Change 201
4.2 Extreme Values of Functions 209
4.3 How y' and y'' Determine the Shape of a Graph 218
4.4 Graphs of Rational Functions — Asymptotes and Dominant Terms 227
4.5 Optimization 234
4.6 The Mean Value Theorem 246
4.7 Antiderivatives, Differential Equations, and Modeling 253
For Your Review *265*
Practice Exercises *266*

5 Integration

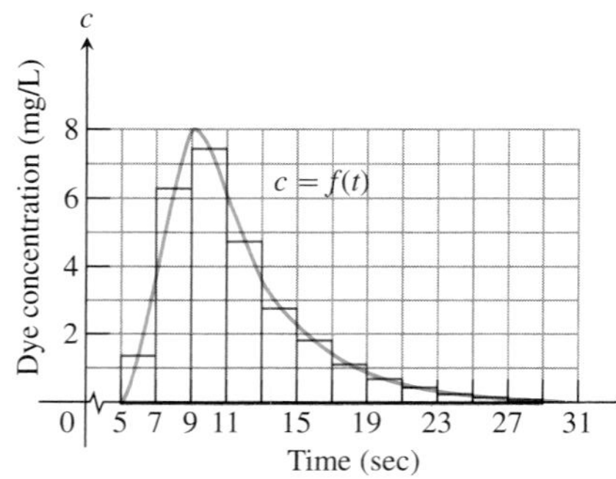

OVERVIEW 271

5.1 Estimating with Finite Sums 271
5.2 Riemann Sums and Definite Integrals 282
5.3 Basic Properties, Area, and the Mean Value Theorem for Integrals 294
5.4 The Fundamental Theorem of Calculus 302
5.5 Indefinite Integrals 313
5.6 Integration by Substitution — Running the Chain Rule Backward 322
5.7 Numerical Integration 331
For Your Review *342*
Practice Exercises *342*

6 *Transcendental Functions*

OVERVIEW 347

6.1 Exponential Functions and the Derivative of e^x 347
6.2 Inverse Functions and Their Derivatives 355
6.3 Logarithmic Functions and the Derivative of $\ln x$ 361
6.4 Exponential and Logarithmic Integrals; $\ln x = \int_1^x \frac{1}{t}\, dt$ 373
6.5 Growth and Decay 379
6.6 L'Hôpital's Rule 388
6.7 Relative Rates of Growth 395
6.8 Inverse Trigonometric Functions 401
6.9 Derivatives of Inverse Trigonometric Functions; Integrals 409
6.10 Hyperbolic Functions 416
6.11 First Order Differential Equations 424
For Your Review *434*
Practice Exercises *435*

7 *Applications of Integration*

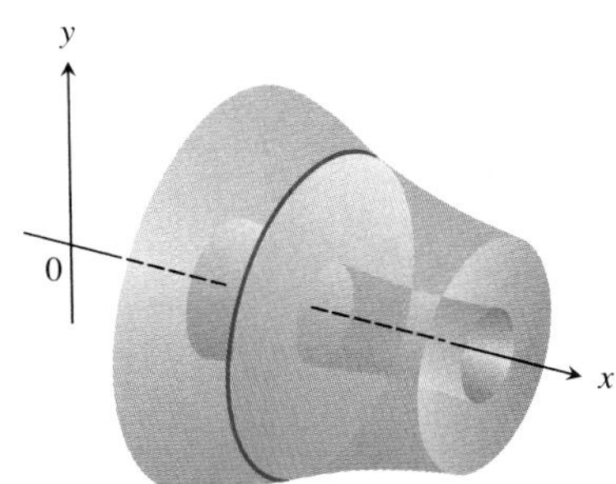

OVERVIEW 439

7.1 Areas Between Curves 439
7.2 Volumes of Solids of Revolution—Disks and Washers 446
7.3 Cylindrical Shells—An Alternative to Washers 456
7.4 Curve Length and Surface Area 462
7.5 Work 472
7.6 Fluid Pressures and Fluid Forces 479
7.7 Centers of Mass 486
7.8 The Basic Pattern and Other Modeling Applications 497
For Your Review *507*
Practice Exercises *507*

8 *Techniques of Integration*

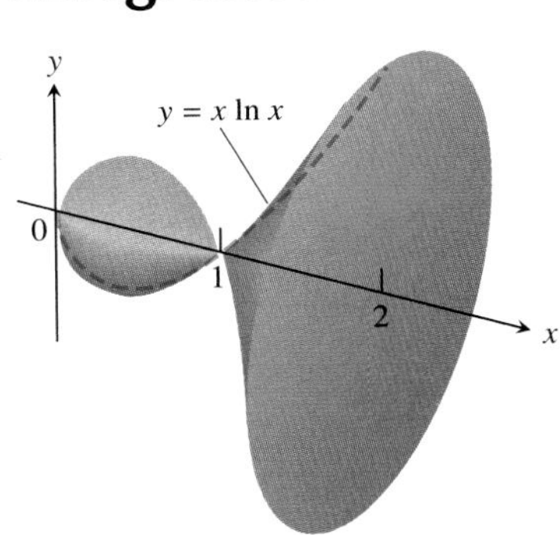

OVERVIEW 511

8.1 Basic Integration Formulas 511
8.2 Integration by Parts 517
8.3 Partial Fractions 524
8.4 Trigonometric Substitutions 529
8.5 Integral Tables 534
8.6 Improper Integrals 542
For Your Review *552*
Practice Exercises *552*

9
Infinite Series

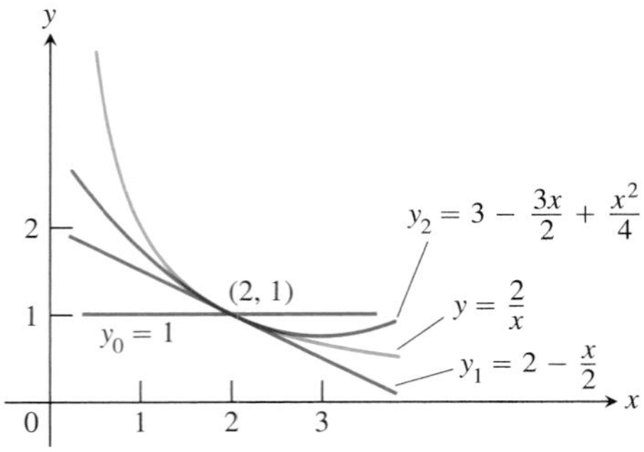

OVERVIEW 557

9.1 Sequences 557
9.2 Infinite Series 567
9.3 Series with Nonnegative Terms — Comparison and Integral Tests 576
9.4 Series with Nonnegative Terms — Ratio and Root Tests 585
9.5 Alternating Series and Absolute Convergence 591
9.6 Power Series 597
9.7 Taylor and Maclaurin Series 605
9.8 Calculations with Taylor Series 619
For Your Review 626
Practice Exercises 626

10
Conic Sections, Parametrized Curves, and Polar Coordinates

OVERVIEW 629

10.1 Conic Sections and Quadratic Equations 629
10.2 The Graphs of Quadratic Equations in x and y; Rotations About the Origin 645
10.3 Parametrizations of Curves 650
10.4 Calculus with Parametrized Curves 656
10.5 Polar Coordinates 662
10.6 Polar Graphs 667
10.7 Polar Equations for Conic Sections 674
10.8 Integration in Polar Coordinates 680
For Your Review 686
Practice Exercises 687

11
Vectors and Analytic Geometry in Space

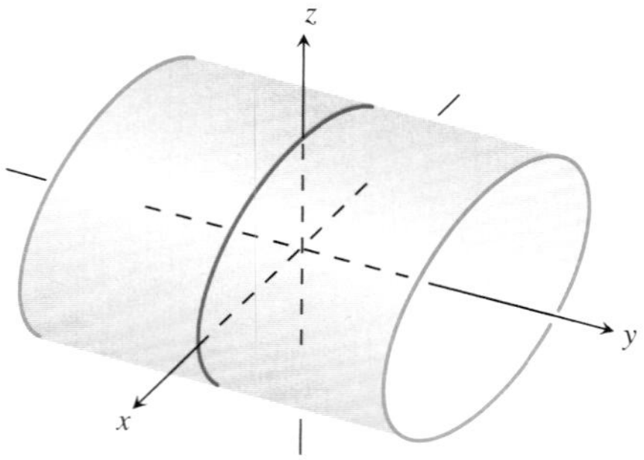

OVERVIEW 691

11.1 Vectors in the Plane 691
11.2 Cartesian (Rectangular) Coordinates and Vectors in Space 700
11.3 Dot Products 710
11.4 Cross Products 718
11.5 Lines and Planes in Space 724
11.6 Surfaces in Space 731
11.7 Cylindrical and Spherical Coordinates 741
For Your Review 746
Practice Exercises 747

12 Vector-Valued Functions

OVERVIEW 751

12.1 Vector-Valued Functions and Space Curves 751
12.2 Modeling Projectile Motion 762
12.3 Arc Length and the Unit Tangent Vector **T** 771
12.4 Curvature, Torsion, and the **TNB** Frame 776
12.5 Planetary Motion and Satellites 788
For Your Review *795*
Practice Exercises *795*

13 Partial Derivatives

(Generated by Mathematica)

OVERVIEW 799

13.1 Functions of Several Independent Variables 799
13.2 Limits and Continuity 808
13.3 Partial Derivatives 814
13.4 Differentiability, Linearization, and Differentials 823
13.5 The Chain Rule 833
13.6 Directional Derivatives, Gradient Vectors, and Tangent Planes 841
13.7 Maxima, Minima, and Saddle Points 853
13.8 Lagrange Multipliers 864
For Your Review *873*
Practice Exercises *873*

14 Multiple Integrals

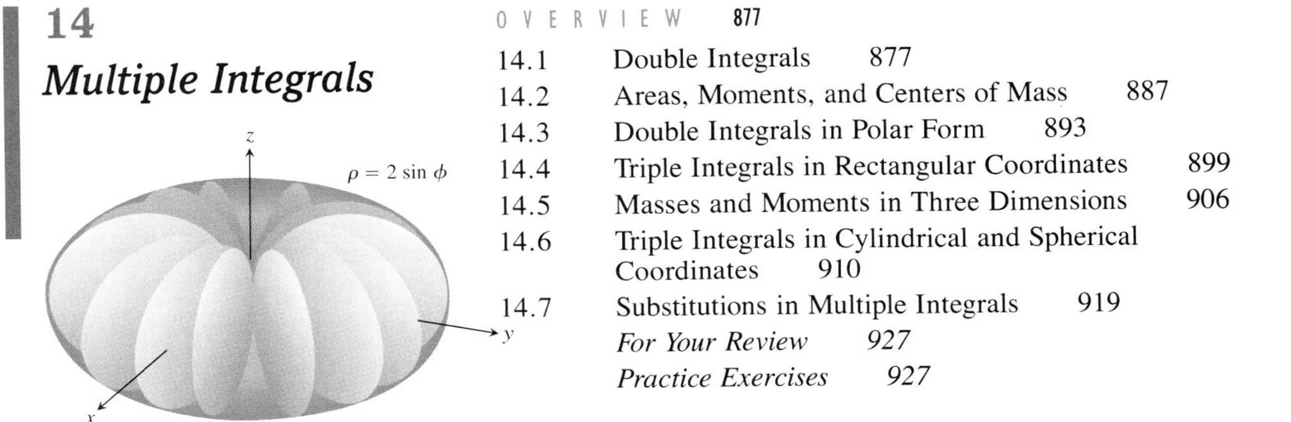

OVERVIEW 877

14.1 Double Integrals 877
14.2 Areas, Moments, and Centers of Mass 887
14.3 Double Integrals in Polar Form 893
14.4 Triple Integrals in Rectangular Coordinates 899
14.5 Masses and Moments in Three Dimensions 906
14.6 Triple Integrals in Cylindrical and Spherical Coordinates 910
14.7 Substitutions in Multiple Integrals 919
For Your Review *927*
Practice Exercises *927*

15 *Integration in Vector Fields*

OVERVIEW 931
15.1 Line Integrals 931
15.2 Vector Fields, Work, Circulation, and Flux 937
15.3 Path Independence, Potential Functions, and Conservative Fields 946
15.4 Green's Theorem in the Plane 954
15.5 Surface Area and Surface Integrals 965
15.6 Parametrized Surfaces 975
15.7 Stokes's Theorem 983
15.8 The Divergence Theorem 993
For Your Review *1001*
Practice Exercises *1001*

Appendices

A.1 Formulas from Precalculus Mathematics A-1
A.2 Proofs of the Limit Theorems in Chapter 2 A-6
A.3 A Proof of the Chain Rule for Functions of a Single Variable A-9
A.4 Mathematical Induction A-10
A.5 Simpson's One-Third Rule A-13
A.6 Limits That Arise Frequently A-14
A.7 Determinants and Cramer's Rule A-16
A.8 Path Independence of $\int \mathbf{F} \cdot d\mathbf{r}$ Implies $\mathbf{F} = \nabla f$ A-24
A.9 Complex Numbers A-25
A.10 Tables for $\sin x$, $\cos x$, $\tan x$, e^x, e^{-x}, and $\ln x$ A-26

Answers A-29

Index I-1

A Brief Table of Integrals T-1

Prologue

What Is Calculus?

Calculus is the mathematics of motion and change. Where there is motion or growth, where variable forces are at work producing acceleration, calculus is the right mathematics to apply. This was true in the beginnings of the subject, and it is true today.

Calculus was first created to meet the mathematical needs of the scientists of the sixteenth and seventeenth centuries, which were mainly mechanical in nature. Differential calculus dealt with the problem of calculating rates of change. It enabled people to define slopes of curves, to calculate the velocities and accelerations of moving bodies, to find the firing angle that gave a cannon its greatest range, and to predict the times when planets would be closest together or farthest apart. Integral calculus dealt with the problem of determining a function from information about its rate of change. It enabled people to calculate the future location of a body from its present position and a knowledge of the forces acting on it, to find the areas of irregular regions in the plane, to measure the lengths of curves, and to locate the centers of mass of arbitrary solids.

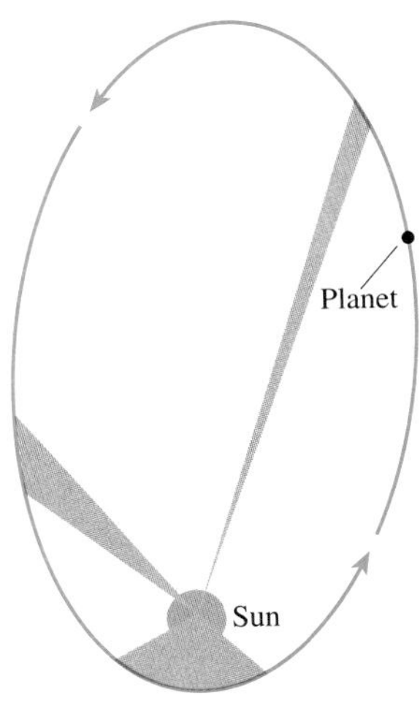

P.1 A planet moving about its sun. The shaded regions have equal areas. According to Kepler's second law, the planet takes the same amount of time to traverse the curved outer boundary of each region. The planet therefore moves faster near the sun than it does farther away.

Before the mathematical developments that culminated in the great unifying discoveries of Sir Isaac Newton (1642–1727) and Baron Gottfried Wilhelm Leibniz (1646–1716), it took the astronomer Johannes Kepler (1571–1630) twenty years of concentration, record-keeping, and arithmetic to discover the three laws of planetary motion that now bear his name:

1. Each planet travels in an ellipse that has one focus at the sun (Fig. P.1).
2. The radius vector from the sun to a planet sweeps out equal areas in equal intervals of time.
3. The squares of the periods of revolution of the planets about the sun are proportional to the cubes of their orbits' semimajor axes. If T is the length of a planet's year and a is the semimajor axis of its orbit, then the ratio T^2/a^3 has the same constant value for all planets in the solar system.

With calculus, deriving Kepler's laws from Newton's laws of motion is but an afternoon's work. Kepler described how the solar system worked—calculus and Newton's laws explained why it worked that way.

Today, calculus and its extensions in mathematical analysis are far reaching indeed, and the physicists, mathematicians, and astronomers who first invented

P.2 Calculus helped us predict that moons would travel in elliptical orbits about their planets; it also helped us to launch cameras and telescopes to observe the planets of our solar system. This photograph shows the Astro-1 group of telescopes on board the space shuttle *Columbia* in December 1990. One of the goals of this mission was to investigate the magnetic fields of Jupiter. We describe the effects of magnetic fields on moving electrical charges with calculus.

the subject would surely be amazed and delighted, as we hope you will be, to see what a profusion of problems it solves and what a wide range of fields now use it in the mathematical models that bring understanding about the universe and the world around us.

Economists use calculus to forecast global trends. Oceanographers use calculus to formulate theories about ocean currents and meteorologists use it to describe the flow of air in the upper atmosphere. Biologists use calculus to forecast population size and to describe the way predators like foxes interact with their prey. Medical researchers use calculus to design ultrasound and x-ray equipment for scanning the internal organs of the body. Space scientists use calculus to design rockets and explore distant planets. Psychologists use calculus to understand optical illusions in visual perception. Physicists use calculus to design inertial navigation systems and to study the nature of time and the universe. Hydraulic engineers use calculus to find safe closure patterns for valves in pipelines. Electrical engineers use it to design stroboscopic flash equipment and to solve the differential equations that describe current flow in computers. Sports equipment manufacturers use calculus to design tennis rackets and baseball bats. Stock market analysts use calculus to predict prices and assess interest rate risk. Physiologists use calculus to describe electrical impulses in neurons in the human nervous system. Drug companies use calculus to determine profitable inventory levels and timber companies use it to decide the most profitable time to harvest trees. The list is practically endless, for almost every professional field today uses calculus in some way.

"The calculus was the first achievement of modern mathematics," wrote John von Neumann (1903–1957), one of the great mathematicians of the present century, "and it is difficult to overestimate its importance. I think it defines more unequivocally than anything else the inception of modern mathematics; and the system of mathematical analysis, which is its logical development, still constitutes the greatest technical advance in exact thinking."*

How to Learn Calculus

Learning calculus is not quite the same as learning arithmetic, algebra, and geometry. In those subjects, you learn primarily how to calculate with numbers, how to simplify algebraic expressions and calculate with variables, and how to reason about points, lines, and figures in the plane. Calculus involves those techniques and skills but develops others as well, with greater precision and at a deeper level. Calculus introduces so many new concepts and computational operations, in fact, that you will no longer be able to learn everything you need in class. You will have to learn a fair amount on your own. What should you do to learn?

1. Read the text carefully. You won't be able to learn all the meanings and connections you need just by attempting the exercises. You will need to read the relevant passages in the book and work through the examples step by step.

**World of Mathematics,* Vol. 4 (New York: Simon and Schuster, 1960), "The Mathematician," by John von Neumann, pp. 2053–2063.

Speed reading won't work here. You are reading and searching for detail in a step-by-step logical fashion. This kind of reading, required of any deep and technical content, takes attention, patience, and practice.

2. Complete the homework exercises, keeping the following principles in mind.

   a) Sketch a diagram whenever possible.
   b) Write your solution in a connected step-by-step logical fashion, as if you were explaining to someone else.
   c) Take a moment to think about why each exercise is there. Why was it assigned? How is it connected to the other assigned exercises?

3. Each time you complete a section of the text, try on your own to write short descriptions of the key points. If you succeed, you probably understand the material. If you do not, you will know where there is a gap in your understanding. There is a list of questions to guide your writing under the heading "Writing for Your own Knowledge" at the end of each section.

Learning calculus is a process—it doesn't come all at once. Be patient, persevere, ask questions, discuss ideas with classmates, and seek help when you need it, right away. The rewards of learning calculus will be very satisfying, both intellectually and professionally.

SAFE DIVE TIMES

KIMBERLY VENTIMIGLIA, a diving instructor in Beverly, MA, teaches prospective divers how to calculate dive times that will keep the amount of nitrogen absorbed from the compressed air they breathe within safe bounds.

The longer and deeper the dive, the greater will be the amount of nitrogen absorbed. The body can tolerate a limited amount of excess nitrogen, but when this limit is exceeded, a diver must pause at a so-called decompression stop one or more times on the way back to the surface to breathe off excess gas.

If the return is too fast, the trapped gas will form harmful (and painful) bubbles in the body's blood and tissues.

The limits to how long one can safely stay at a given depth without needing a decompression stop can be found in U.S. Navy decompression tables or read from a graph based on the tables, like the one shown here.

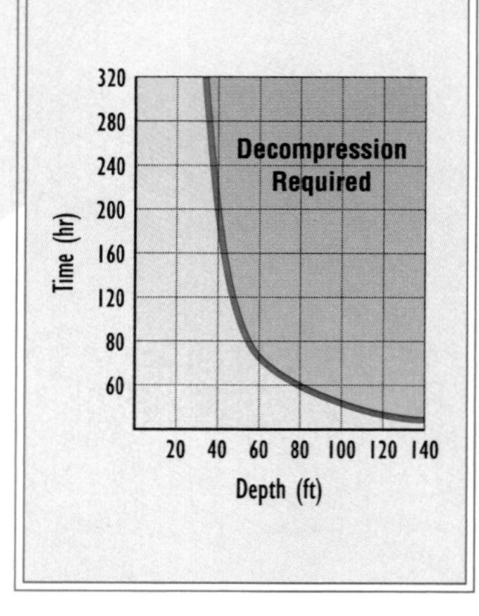

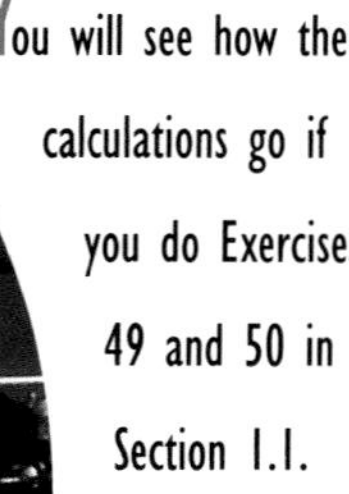

You will see how the calculations go if you do Exercises 49 and 50 in Section 1.1.

OVERVIEW

This chapter reviews what you need to know to start learning calculus. Since calculus, at least at the beginning, is concerned chiefly with motion and change, our emphasis will be on functions and graphs. Functions are the major tools for describing the real world in mathematical terms, all the way from warping railroad track and draining tanks to heartbeats, seasonal temperatures, and efficiency on a factory floor. Graphs enable us to see important changes in behavior and help us to predict the effects of those changes.

1 Prerequisites for Calculus

1.1 Coordinates, Increments, and Lines

The natural setting for learning calculus is the coordinate plane. This section discusses increments and reviews what you need to know about coordinates and lines. The coordinates defined here are often called **Cartesian coordinates,** after their chief inventor, René Descartes (1596–1650). They are also called **rectangular coordinates** because of their right-angled construction.

The Cartesian (Rectangular) Coordinate Plane

Cartesian coordinates locate points in the plane with numbers read from mutually perpendicular number lines called **coordinate axes.** On the horizontal x-axis, the numbers increase from left to right. On the vertical y-axis, the numbers increase in the upward direction. The point where the axes cross is zero on each axis; it is the **origin** of the coordinate system (Fig. 1.1).

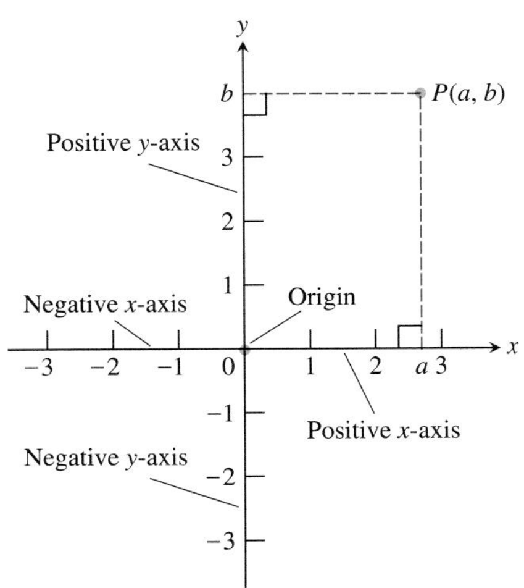

1.1 Cartesian coordinates.

We assign coordinates to a point in the plane by dropping a perpendicular from the point to each axis. If the perpendiculars from a point P meet the x-axis at a and the y-axis at b, then the pair (a, b) (read "a b") is the **coordinate pair** of P. The number a is the **x-coordinate** of P, and b is the **y-coordinate.** The pair (a, b) is an **ordered pair;** it gives the x-coordinate first and the y-coordinate second. To show that P has the coordinate pair (a, b), we sometimes write $P(a, b)$ (read "P a b"). The y-coordinate of every point on the x-axis is zero. The x-coordinate of every point on the y-axis is zero. The origin is the point $(0, 0)$.

The origin divides the x-axis into the **positive x-axis** to the right and the **negative x-axis** to the left. It divides the y-axis into the **positive y-axis** above and the **negative y-axis** below. The axes themselves divide the plane into four regions called **quadrants,** numbered counterclockwise (Fig. 1.2 on the following page).

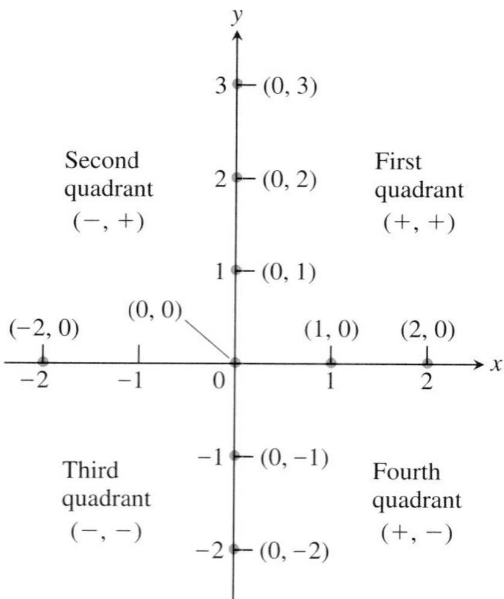

1.2 The points on the axes all have coordinate pairs, but we usually label them with single numbers. Notice the coordinate sign patterns in the quadrants.

A Word About Scales

When we plot data in the coordinate plane or graph formulas whose variables have different units of measure, we do not need to use the same scale on the two axes. If we plot thrust vs. time for a rocket motor, for example, there is no reason to place the mark that shows 1 sec on the time axis the same distance from the origin as the mark that shows 1 lb on the thrust axis. In the plot in Fig. 1.3, which shows how the heart rate typically returns to normal after exercise, the length that shows 1 minute on the time axis shows 10 beats per minute on the vertical axis.

When we graph functions whose variables do not represent physical measurements and when we draw figures in the coordinate plane to study their geometry and trigonometry, we make the scales on the axes identical. A vertical unit of distance then looks the same as a horizontal unit. As on a surveyor's map or a scale drawing, line segments that are supposed to have the same length will look as if they do and angles that are supposed to be congruent will look congruent.

Computer displays and calculator displays are another matter. The vertical and horizontal scales on machine-generated graphs usually differ, and there are corresponding distortions in distances, slopes, and angles. Circles may look like ellipses, rectangles may look like squares, right angles may appear to be acute or obtuse, and so on. Circumstances like these require us to take extra care in interpreting what we see.

Distance

Our first application of coordinates is the calculation of distance.

The distance between points $P_1(x_1, y_1)$ and $P_2(x_2, y_2)$ is

$$d = \sqrt{(x_2 - x_1)^2 + (y_2 - y_1)^2}. \tag{1}$$

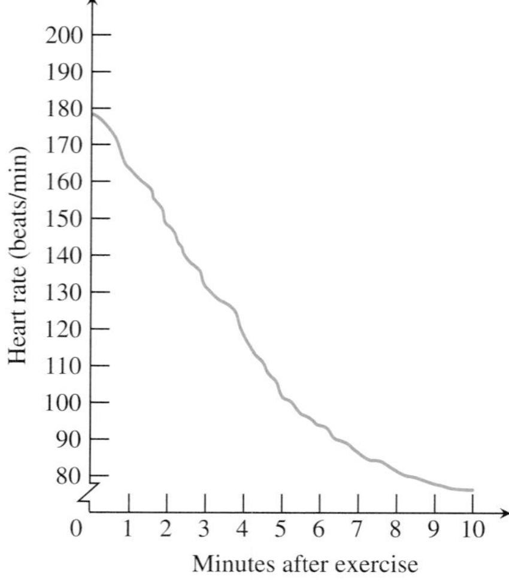

1.3 How the heartbeat returns to a normal rate after running. (Adapted from James F. Fixx's *The Complete Book of Running,* 1977, Random House.)

The formula comes from the Pythagorean theorem (Fig. 1.4).

EXAMPLE 1 The distance between $P_1(-1, 2)$ and $P_2(3, 4)$ is

$$\sqrt{(3 - (-1))^2 + (4 - 2)^2} = \sqrt{(4)^2 + (2)^2} = \sqrt{20} = \sqrt{4 \cdot 5} = 2\sqrt{5}.$$

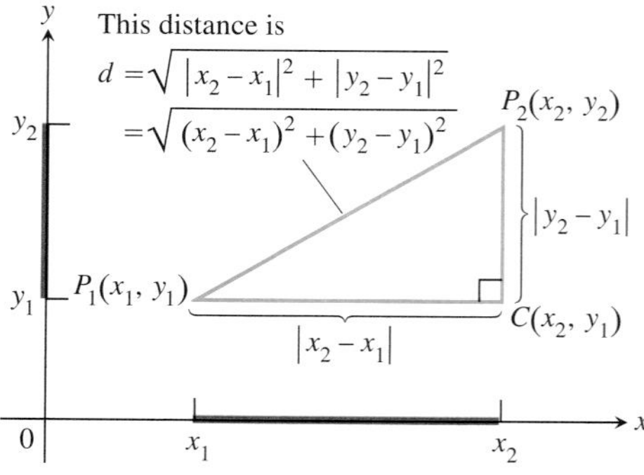

1.4 To find the distance between $P_1(x_1, y_1)$ and $P_2(x_2, y_2)$, apply the Pythagorean theorem to triangle P_1CP_2. Notice the use of absolute values $|x_2 - x_1|$ and $|y_2 - y_1|$ to denote the lengths of the sides.

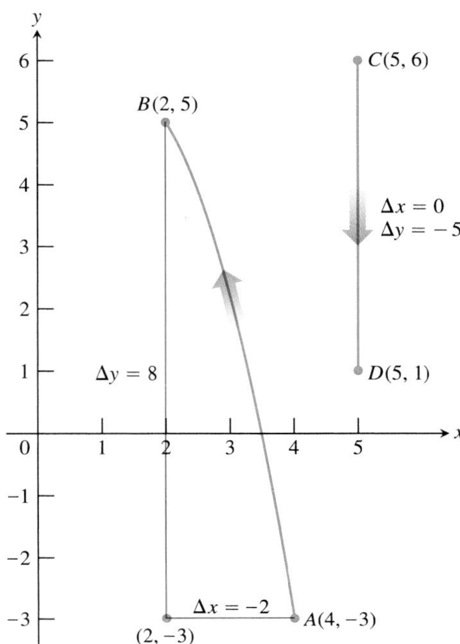

1.5 Coordinate increments may be positive, negative, or zero.

Increments

One of the many reasons calculus has proved to be so useful is that it is the right mathematics for relating a quantity's rate of change to its graph. Explaining that relationship is one of the goals of this book. The basic plan is to define what we mean by the slope of a line and then to build on that idea to define the slopes of curves. Just how this is done will become clear as the book goes on.

To define the slope of a line we start with the notion of increment. When a particle in the plane moves from one point to another, the net changes or increments in its coordinates are found by subtracting the coordinates of its starting point from the coordinates of its stopping point.

Increments are net changes. If a particle moves from (x_1, y_1) to (x_2, y_2), the increments in its coordinates are

$$\Delta x = x_2 - x_1 \quad \text{and} \quad \Delta y = y_2 - y_1. \tag{2}$$

The symbols Δx and Δy are read "delta x" and "delta y." The letter Δ is a Greek capital d for "difference." Neither Δx nor Δy denotes multiplication; Δx is not "delta times x" nor is Δy "delta times y."

EXAMPLE 2 The coordinate increments from $A(4, -3)$ to $B(2, 5)$ are

$$\Delta x = 2 - 4 = -2, \qquad \Delta y = 5 - (-3) = 8$$

(Fig. 1.5). From $C(5, 6)$ to $D(5, 1)$, the increments are

$$\Delta x = 5 - 5 = 0, \qquad \Delta y = 1 - 6 = -5.$$

Slopes of Nonvertical Lines

All lines except vertical lines have slopes. We calculate slopes from changes in coordinates. Once we see how this is done, we will also see why vertical lines do not have slopes.

To begin, let L be a nonvertical line in the plane. Let $P_1(x_1, y_1)$ and $P_2(x_2, y_2)$ be points on L (Fig. 1.6). We call $\Delta y = y_2 - y_1$ the **rise** from P_1 to P_2 and $\Delta x = x_2 - x_1$ the **run** from P_1 to P_2. Since L is not vertical, $\Delta x \neq 0$ and we may define the **slope** of L to be $\Delta y/\Delta x$, the amount of rise per unit of run. It is conventional to denote the slope by the letter m.

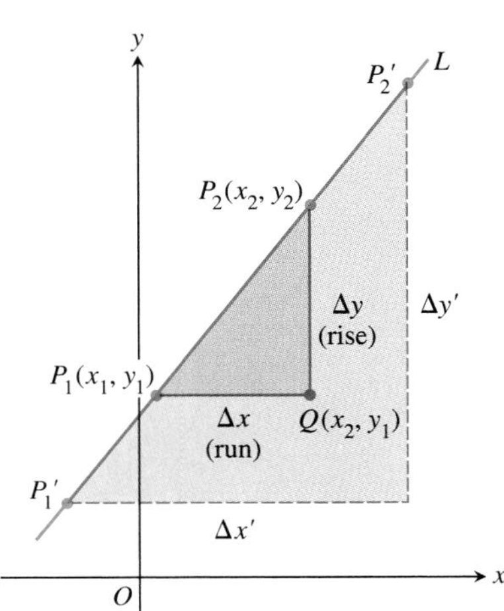

1.6 The slope of line L is

$$m = \frac{\Delta y}{\Delta x} = \frac{\Delta y'}{\Delta x'}.$$

DEFINITION

The **slope** of a nonvertical line is

$$m = \frac{\text{rise}}{\text{run}} = \frac{\Delta y}{\Delta x} = \frac{y_2 - y_1}{x_2 - x_1}. \tag{3}$$

Suppose that instead of choosing the points P_1 and P_2 to calculate the slope in Eq. (3), we choose a different pair of points $P_1{}'$ and $P_2{}'$ on L and calculate

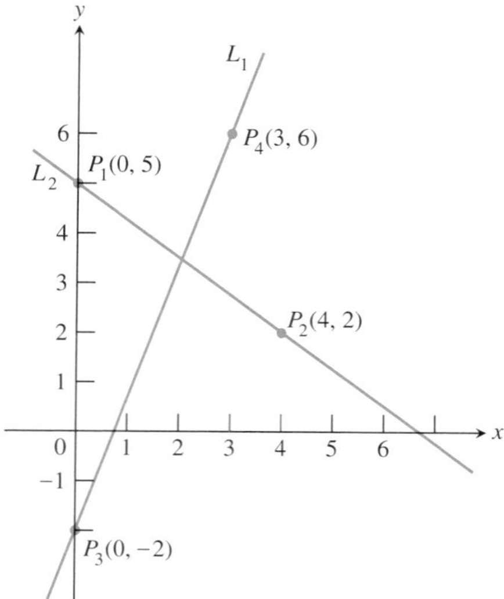

1.7 The slope of L_1 is

$$m = \frac{\Delta y}{\Delta x} = \frac{6 - (-2)}{3 - 0} = \frac{8}{3}.$$

This means that $3\Delta y = 8\Delta x$ for every change of position on the line. The slope of L_2 is

$$m = \frac{\Delta y}{\Delta x} = \frac{2 - 5}{4 - 0} = \frac{-3}{4}.$$

This means that y decreases 3 units every time x increases 4 units.

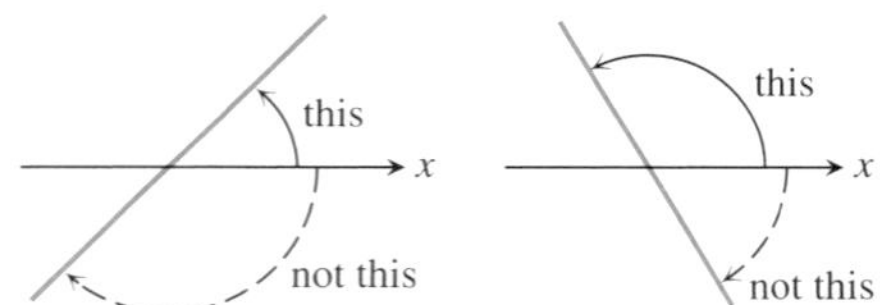

1.8 Angles of inclination are measured counterclockwise from the x-axis.

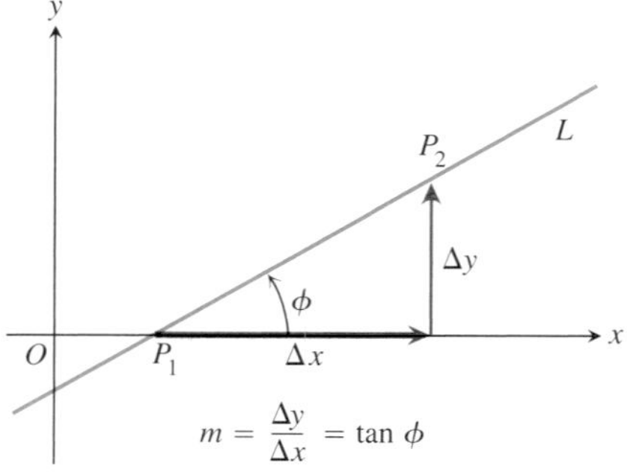

1.9 The slope of a nonvertical line is the tangent of its angle of inclination.

$\Delta y'/\Delta x'$. Will we get the same value for the slope? The answer is yes because $\Delta y/\Delta x$ and $\Delta y'/\Delta x'$ are the ratios of corresponding sides of similar triangles (Fig. 1.6). The slope of a line depends only on how steeply the line rises or falls and not on the points we use to calculate it.

A line that goes uphill as x increases has a positive slope. A line that goes downhill as x increases has a negative slope. (See Fig. 1.7.) A horizontal line has slope zero since its points all have the same y-coordinate, giving $\Delta y = 0$.

Vertical Lines Have No Slope

The formula $m = \Delta y/\Delta x$ is undefined for vertical lines because Δx is always zero along a vertical line. We express this by saying that vertical lines *have no slope.*

Angles of Inclination

The **angle of inclination** of a line that crosses the x-axis is the smallest angle we get when we measure counterclockwise from the x-axis around the point of intersection to the line (Fig. 1.8). The angle of inclination of a horizontal line is taken to be 0°. Thus, an angle of inclination may have any measure from 0° up to but not including 180°.

The slope of a nonvertical line is the tangent of the line's angle of inclination. Figure 1.9 shows why this is true. If m denotes the slope and ϕ the angle, then

$$m = \frac{\Delta y}{\Delta x} = \tan \phi . \tag{4}$$

EXAMPLE 3 The slopes of lines become increasingly large as their angles of inclination approach 90° from either side. A few keystrokes on a calculator will show you that

φ approaching 90° from below	**φ approaching 90° from above**
tan 89.9° ≈ 573	tan 90.1° ≈ − 573
tan 89.99 ≈ 5730	tan 90.01 ≈ − 5730
tan 89.999 ≈ 57300	tan 90.001 ≈ − 57300
tan 89.9999 ≈ 573000	tan 90.0001 ≈ − 573000

We say that the slope of a line "becomes infinite" as its angle of inclination approaches 90°.

Parallel and Perpendicular Lines

Parallel lines have equal angles of inclination. Hence, if they are not vertical, parallel lines have the same slope. Conversely, lines with equal slopes have equal angles of inclination and are therefore parallel.

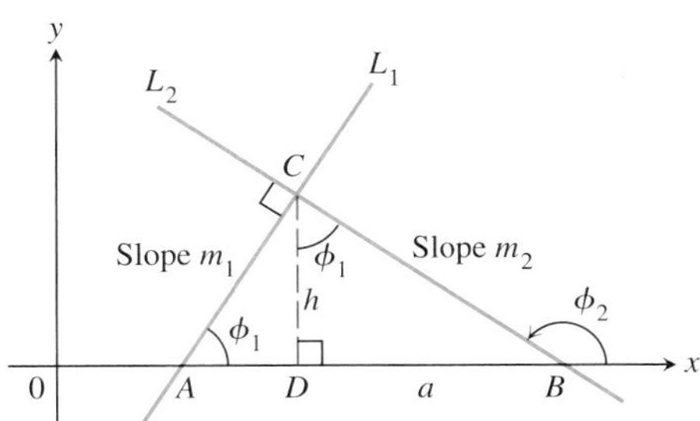

1.10 ΔADC is similar to ΔCDB. Hence ϕ_1 is also the upper angle in ΔCDB. From the sides of ΔCDB, we read $\tan \phi_1 = a/h$.

If neither of two perpendicular lines L_1 and L_2 is vertical, their slopes m_1 and m_2 are related by the equation $m_1 m_2 = -1$. Figure 1.10 shows that

$$m_1 = \tan \phi_1 = \frac{a}{h}, \qquad \text{while} \qquad m_2 = \tan \phi_2 = -\frac{h}{a}. \tag{5}$$

Hence,

$$m_1 m_2 = \left(\frac{a}{h}\right)\left(-\frac{h}{a}\right) = -1 \qquad \text{and} \qquad m_2 = -\frac{1}{m_1}. \tag{6}$$

EXAMPLE 4 The slope of a line perpendicular to a line of slope 3/4 is $-4/3$.

Equations for Lines

DEFINITION

An **equation for a line** is an equation that is satisfied by the coordinates of every point on the line but is not satisfied by the coordinates of points that lie elsewhere.

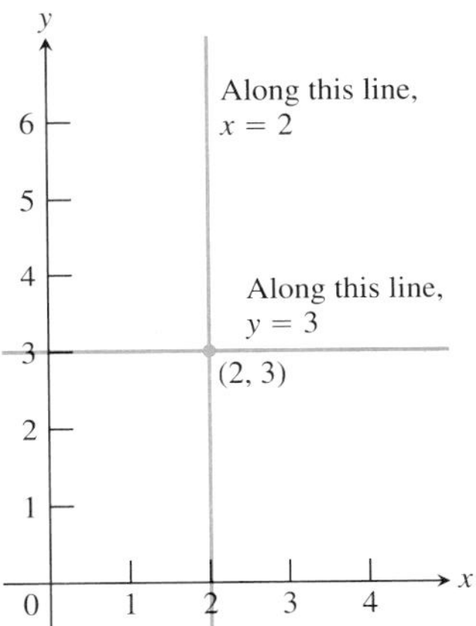

1.11 The standard equations for the horizontal and vertical lines through the point (2, 3) are $y = 3$ and $x = 2$.

Horizontal and Vertical Lines

The standard equations for the horizontal and vertical lines through a point (a, b) are simply $y = b$ and $x = a$ (Fig. 1.11). A point (x, y) lies on the horizontal line through (a, b) if and only if $y = b$. It lies on the vertical line through (a, b) if and only if $x = a$.

Point–Slope Equations To write an equation for a line L that is not vertical, it is enough to know its slope m and the coordinates of a point $P_1(x_1, y_1)$ on it. If $P(x, y)$ is any other point on L (Fig. 1.12), then $x \neq x_1$ and the slope of L is

$$m = \frac{y - y_1}{x - x_1}. \tag{7}$$

Multiplying both sides of Eq. (7) by $x - x_1$ gives

$$y - y_1 = m(x - x_1). \tag{8}$$

We can check right away that Eq. (8) is an equation for L. Every point (x, y) on L satisfies the equation—even the point (x_1, y_1). If $P'(x', y')$ is not on L (Fig. 1.12), the coordinates x' and y' of P' do not satisfy Eqs. (7) and (8) because the slope m' of $P'P_1$ is different from m.

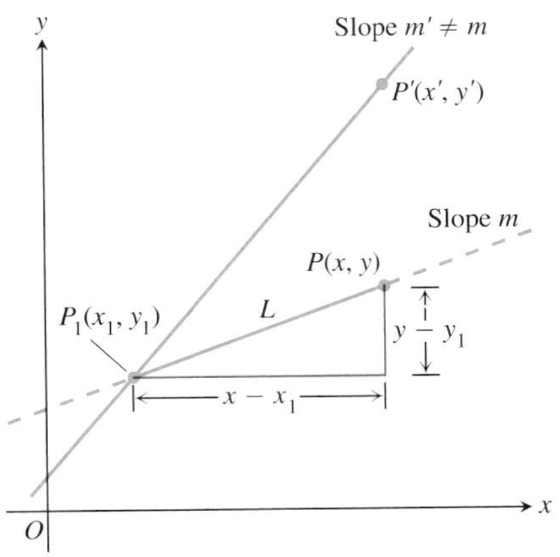

1.12 Point $P(x, y)$ lies on L if and only if $(y - y_1)/(x - x_1) = m$.

DEFINITION

The equation

$$y - y_1 = m(x - x_1) \tag{9}$$

is the **point–slope equation** of the line that passes through the point (x_1, y_1) with slope m.

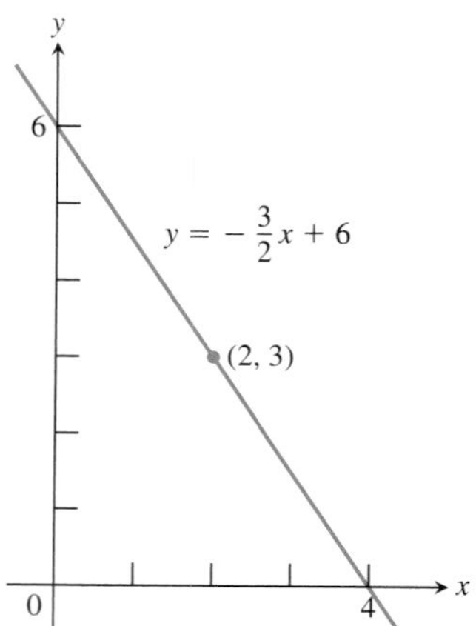

1.13 The line in Example 5.

EXAMPLE 5 Write an equation for the line that passes through the point (2, 3) with slope $-3/2$ (Fig. 1.13).

Solution

$y - y_1 = m(x - x_1)$	Start with the general point–slope equation, Eq. (9).
$y - 3 = -\frac{3}{2}(x - 2)$	Take $m = -3/2$ and $(x_1, y_1) = (2, 3)$.
$y = -\frac{3}{2}x + 3 + 3$	Solve for y . . .
$y = -\frac{3}{2}x + 6.$	. . . and simplify.

EXAMPLE 6 Write an equation for the line through $(-2, -1)$ and $(3, 4)$.

Solution We first calculate the slope and then use Eq. (9).

$$m = \frac{-1 - 4}{-2 - 3} = \frac{-5}{-5} = 1.$$

The (x_1, y_1) in Eq. (9) can be either $(-2, -1)$ or $(3, 4)$:

With $(x_1, y_1) = (-2, -1)$	**With $(x_1, y_1) = (3, 4)$**
$y - (-1) = 1 \cdot (x - (-2))$	$y - 4 = 1 \cdot (x - 3)$
$y + 1 = x + 2$	$y - 4 = x - 3$
$y = x + 1.$	$y = x + 1.$

Same result

Either way, $y = x + 1$ is an equation for the line (Fig. 1.14).

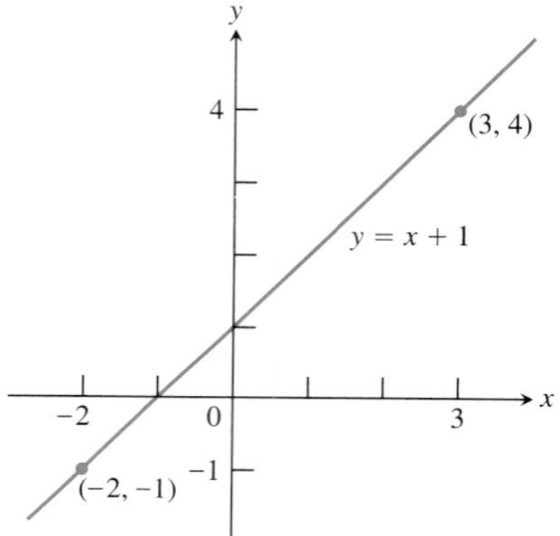

1.14 The line in Example 6.

Slope–Intercept Equations

Figure 1.15 shows a line with slope m and y-intercept b. If we take $(x_1, y_1) = (0, b)$ in the point–slope equation for the line, we find that

$$y - b = m(x - 0). \qquad (10)$$

When rearranged, this becomes

$$y = mx + b. \qquad (11)$$

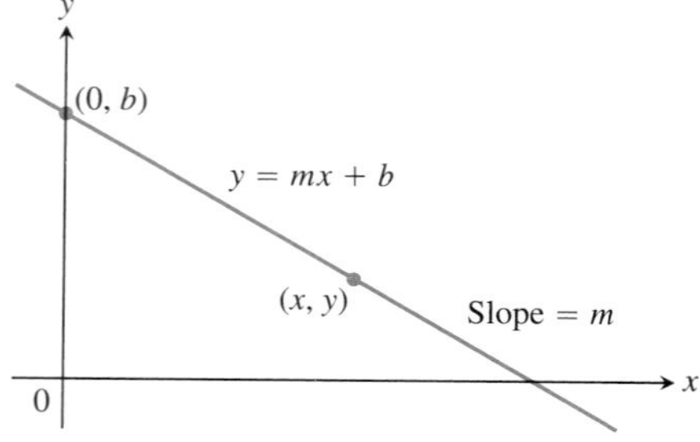

1.15 The line with slope m and y-intercept b. Its standard equation is $y = mx + b$.

DEFINITION

The equation

$$y = mx + b \qquad (12)$$

is the **slope–intercept equation** of the line with slope m and y-intercept b.

Equation (12) is the form we use to find the slope of a line from its equation.

EXAMPLE 7 The slope–intercept equation of the line with slope 2 and y-intercept 5 is

$$y = 2x + 5.$$

EXAMPLE 8 Find the slope and y-intercept of the line $8x + 5y = 20$.

Solution Solve the equation for y to put the equation in slope–intercept form. Then read the slope and y-intercept from the equation:

$$\begin{aligned} 8x + 5y &= 20 \\ 5y &= -8x + 20 \\ y &= -\frac{8}{5}x + 4. \end{aligned}$$

The slope is $m = -8/5$. The y-intercept is $b = 4$.

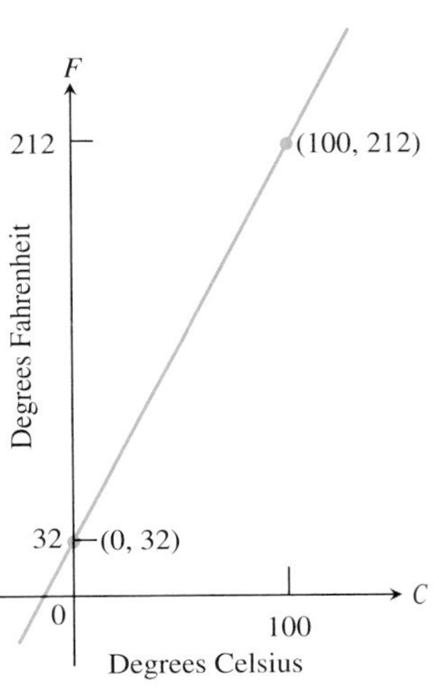

1.16 Fahrenheit versus Celsius temperature.

EXAMPLE 9 *Celsius vs. Fahrenheit.* The standard equation for converting Celsius temperature to Fahrenheit temperature is a slope–intercept equation. If we plot Fahrenheit temperature (F) against Celsius temperature (C) in the CF-plane, the points we plot lie on a straight line (Fig. 1.16). The line passes through the point (0, 32) because 0°C corresponds to 32°F, the freezing point of water. It also passes through (100, 212) because 100°C corresponds to 212°F, the boiling point of water at sea level.

This is enough information to write a formula for F in terms of C. The line's slope is

$$m = \frac{212 - 32}{100 - 0} = \frac{180}{100} = \frac{9}{5}.$$

The F-intercept is

$$b = 32.$$

The resulting slope–intercept equation,

$$F = \frac{9}{5}C + 32, \tag{13}$$

is the formula we seek.

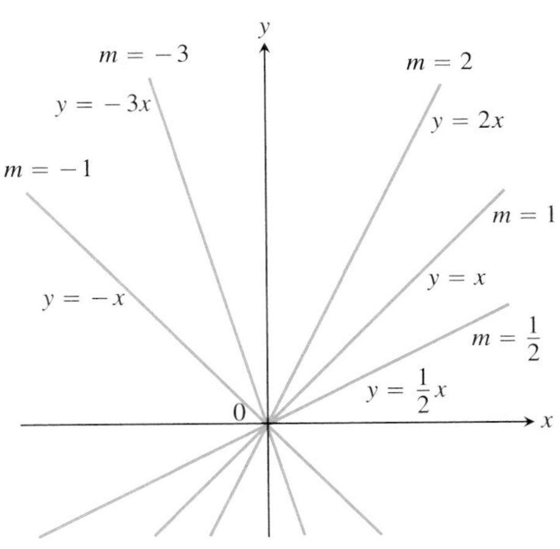

1.17 The line $y = mx$ passes through the origin with slope m.

EXAMPLE 10 *Lines Through the Origin.* When a nonvertical line passes through the origin, its y-intercept is $b = 0$ and the equation $y = mx + b$ simplifies to $y = mx$. The line $y = (1/2)x$ passes through the origin with slope 1/2, the line $y = x$ with slope 1, and the line $y = -x$ with slope -1 (Fig. 1.17).

The General Linear Equation

The equation

$$Ax + By = C \qquad (A \text{ and } B \text{ not both zero}) \tag{14}$$

is called the **general linear equation** because its graph is always a line and because every line has an equation in this form. Notice that all the equations in this section can be arranged in this form. A few of them are in this form already.

Railroad and Highway Grades

Civil engineers calculate the slope of a roadbed by calculating the ratio of the distance it rises or falls to the distance it runs horizontally. They call this ratio the **grade** of the roadbed, usually written as a percentage. Along the coast, railroad grades are usually less than 2%. In the mountains, they may go as high as 4%. Highway grades are usually less than 5%.

In analytic geometry we calculate slopes the same way, but we usually do not express them as percentages.

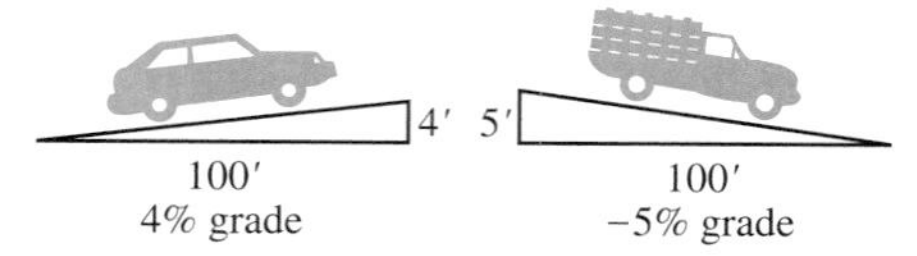

The following summary lists the main facts about lines.

Summary

Slope

1. The slope of the line through $P_1(x_1, y_1)$ and $P_2(x_2, y_2)$, $x_1 \neq x_2$, is

$$m = \frac{\text{rise}}{\text{run}} = \frac{y_2 - y_1}{x_2 - x_1} = \frac{\Delta y}{\Delta x}.$$

2. $m = \tan \phi$ (ϕ is the angle of inclination)
3. Vertical lines have no slope.
4. Horizontal lines have slope zero.
5. For lines that are neither horizontal nor vertical, it is handy to remember:
   a) they are parallel $\Leftrightarrow$ $m_2 = m_1$;
   b) they are perpendicular $\Leftrightarrow$ $m_2 = -1/m_1$.
   (The symbol $\Leftrightarrow$ is read "if and only if.")

Equations for Lines

$x = a$	Vertical line through (a, b)
$y = b$	Horizontal line through (a, b)
$y = mx + b$	Slope–intercept equation
$y - y_1 = m(x - x_1)$	Point–slope equation
$Ax + By = C$	General linear equation (A and B not both zero)

Applications—The Importance of Lines and Slope

Light travels along lines, as do bodies falling from rest in a planet's gravitational field or coasting under their own momentum (like a hockey puck gliding across the ice). We often study such motions by writing equations for the lines. Many important variables are related by linear equations. The relation between Fahrenheit temperature and Celsius temperature is linear (Example 9). So is the relation between water pressure and depth in an ocean or a lake. Once we know that a relation between two variables is linear, we can find the exact relation from any two pairs of corresponding values the same way we find an equation for a line when we know two of its points.

Slope itself is important because it gives a way to say how steep something is (roadbeds, roofs, stairs). The notion of slope also gives a way to measure how rapidly things change in the world around us, as we will see in the chapters ahead.

Exercises 1.1

In Exercises 1–6, find the distances between the given points.

1. $(1, 0)$ and $(0, 1)$ **2.** $(2, 4)$ and $(-1, 0)$

3. $(2\sqrt{3}, 4)$ and $(-\sqrt{3}, 1)$ **4.** $(2, 1)$ and $(1, -1/3)$

5. (a, b) and $(0, 0)$ **6.** $(0, y)$ and $(x, 0)$

In Exercises 7–10, a particle moves from A to B. Find the net changes Δx and Δy in the particle's coordinates.

7. $A(-3, 2)$, $B(-1, -2)$ **8.** $A(-1, -2)$, $B(-3, 2)$

9. $A(-3.2, -2)$, $B(-8.1, -2)$ **10.** $A(\sqrt{2}, 4)$, $B(0, 1.5)$

In Exercises 11–14, plot the points A and B and sketch the line AB. Then find the slope of the line.

11. $A(-1, 2)$, $B(-2, -1)$ **12.** $A(-2, 1)$, $B(2, -2)$

13. $A(2, 3)$, $B(-1, 3)$ **14.** $A(-2, 0)$, $B(-2, -2)$

In Exercises 15–18, find an equation for (a) the vertical line and (b) the horizontal line through the given point.

15. $(-1, 4/3)$ **16.** $(\sqrt{2}, -1.3)$

17. $(0, -\sqrt{2})$ **18.** $(-\pi, 0)$

In Exercises 19–32, write an equation for each line described.

19. Passes through $(-1, 1)$ with slope -1

20. Passes through $(2, -3)$ with slope $1/2$

21. Passes through $(3, 4)$ and $(-2, 5)$

22. Passes through $(-8, 0)$ and $(-1, 3)$

23. Has slope $-5/4$ and y-intercept 6

24. Has slope $1/2$ and y-intercept -3

25. Passes through $(-12, -9)$ and has slope 0

26. Passes through $(1/3, 4)$ and has no slope

27. Has y-intercept 4 and x-intercept -1

28. Has y-intercept -6 and x-intercept 2

29. Passes through $(5, -1)$ and is parallel to the line $2x + 5y = 15$

30. Passes through $(-\sqrt{2}, 2)$ parallel to the line $\sqrt{2}x + 5y = \sqrt{3}$

31. Passes through $(4, 10)$ and is perpendicular to the line $6x - 3y = 5$

32. Passes through $(0, 1)$ and is perpendicular to the line $8x - 13y = 13$

QUICK GRAPHING

Graph the lines in Exercises 33–36 by taking the following steps:

1. Find the x-intercept by setting $y = 0$ in the equation and solving for x.
2. Find the y-intercept by setting $x = 0$ and solving for y.
3. Plot the intercepts and draw the line.

33. $3x + 4y = 12$ **34.** $x + 2y = -4$

35. $\sqrt{2}x - \sqrt{3}y = \sqrt{6}$ **36.** $1.5x - y = -3$

37. Is there anything special about the relationship between the lines $Ax + By = C_1$ and $Bx - Ay = C_2$ $(A \neq 0, B \neq 0)$? Give reasons for your answer.

38. Is there anything special about the relationship between the lines $Ax + By = C_1$ and $Ax + By = C_2$ $(A \neq 0, B \neq 0)$? Give reasons for your answer.

INCREMENTS AND MOTION

39. A particle starts at $A(-2, 3)$ and its coordinates change by increments $\Delta x = 5$, $\Delta y = -6$. Find its new position.

40. A particle starts at $A(6, 0)$ and its coordinates change by increments $\Delta x = -6$, $\Delta y = 0$. Find its new position.

41. The coordinates of a particle change by $\Delta x = 5$ and $\Delta y = 6$ as it moves from $A(x, y)$ to $B(3, -3)$. Find x and y.

42. A particle started at $A(1, 0)$, circled the origin once counterclockwise, and returned to $A(1, 0)$. What were the net changes in its coordinates?

APPLICATIONS

43. *Insulation.* By measuring slopes in Fig. 1.18, estimate the temperature change in degrees per inch for (a) the gypsum wallboard; (b) the fiberglass insulation; (c) the wood sheathing. (Graphs can shift in printing, so your answers may differ slightly from those in the back of the book.)

44. *Insulation.* According to Fig. 1.18, which of the materials in Exercise 43 is the best insulator? the poorest? Explain.

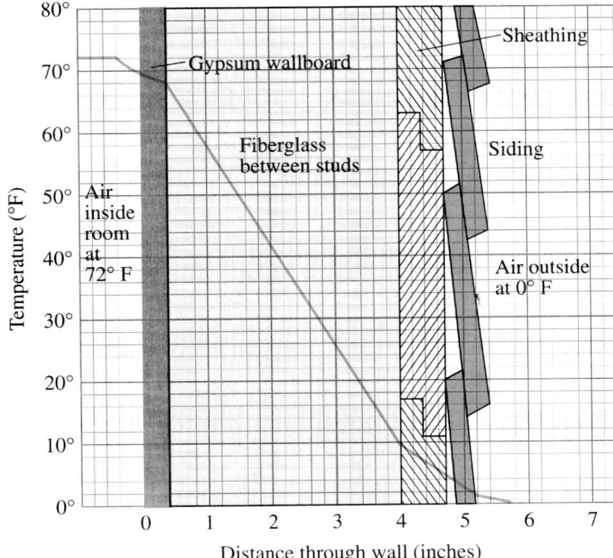

1.18 The temperature changes in the wall in Exercises 43 and 44. (*Source: Differentiation*, by W. U. Walton et al., Project CALC, EDC, Inc. Newton, MA, 1975, p. 25.)

45. *Fahrenheit vs. Celsius.* Is there a temperature at which a Fahrenheit thermometer gives the same reading as a Celsius thermometer? If so, what is it? (See Example 9).

46. *Degrees Kelvin* (K). The Kelvin temperature scale begins by assigning 0 to the lowest temperature that is theoretically possible ("absolute zero") and measuring upward in Celsius-size units from there. Absolute zero measures -273.15 on the Celsius scale, so 273.15 K is equivalent to 0°C. Find equations that express Celsius and Fahrenheit temperature in terms of Kelvin temperature (K).

47. When a ray of light reflects off a flat surface, the angle of reflection is equal to the angle of incidence (Fig. 1.19). Parts (a) and (b) of Fig. 1.19 show different light rays arriving from the second quadrant to reflect off the positive x-axis. In each case, find an equation for the line along which the departing light travels.

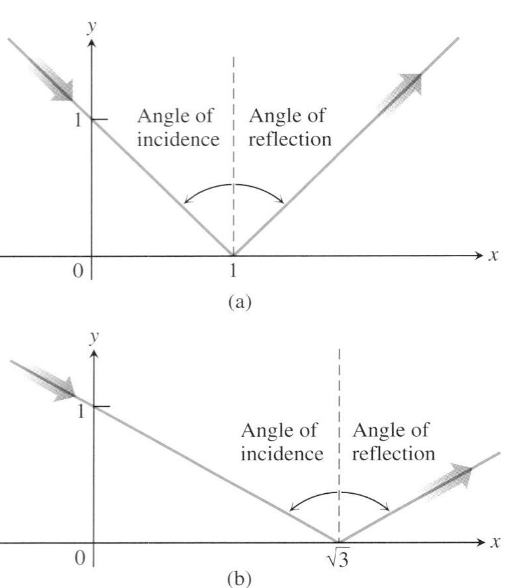

1.19 The paths of the light rays in Exercise 47.

48. *The Mt. Washington Cog Railway.* The steepest part of the Mt. Washington Cog Railway in New Hampshire has a phenomenal 37.1% grade. Along this part of the track, the passengers in the front of the car are 14 ft above those in the rear. About how far apart are the front and rear rows of seats, as measured along the floor of the car?

DECOMPRESSION STOPS

Scuba divers often have to make decompression stops on their way to the surface after deep or long dives. A stop, which may vary from a few minutes to more than an hour, provides time for the safe release of nitrogen and other gases absorbed by the tissues and blood while the body was under pressure. Dives to 33 ft or less do not require decompression stops. Dives to greater depths can be made without return stops if the diver does not stay down too long. The graph in Fig. 1.20 shows the longest times that a diver breathing compressed air may spend at various depths and still surface directly (at 60 ft/min). The times shown are total dive times, not just the times at maximum depth.

The coordinates of the point P in Fig. 1.20 are $x = 70$ and $y = 50$, so a diver going to 70 ft (but no deeper) can return safely without stopping if the total dive time is 50 min or less. Decompression stops are needed for dives plotted above or to the right of the curve, because their times exceed the limits set for their depths. Decompression stops are not needed for dives plotted on the curve or for dives plotted below or to the left of it, because the lengths of these dives do not exceed the limits for their depths. Exercises 49 and 50 are about these time limits.

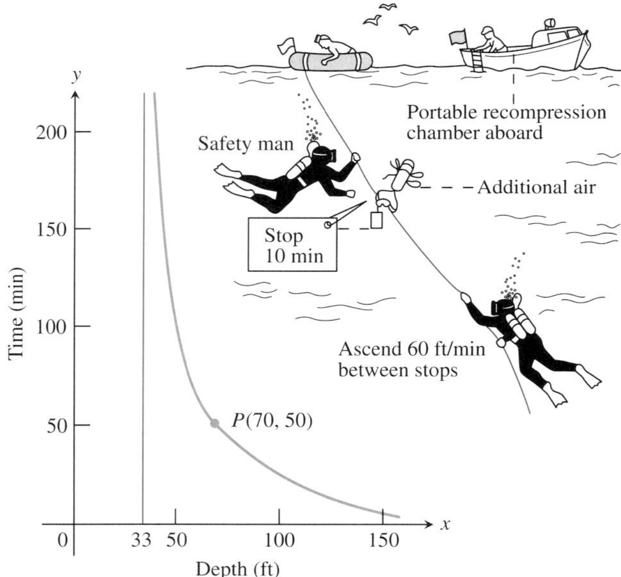

1.20 The coordinates of the points on the curve show how long scuba divers breathing compressed air can safely stay below the surface without a decompression stop. (Data from *U.S. Navy Diving Manual,* NAVSHIPS 250–538.)

49. You have been working at 100 ft below the surface for 1 hr. Do you need a decompression stop on the way up?

50. Which of the following dives need decompression stops and which do not?

a) (40, 100) **b)** (100, 40) **c)** (70, 100) **d)** (50, 50)

GEOMETRY

51. A rectangle with sides parallel to the axes has vertices at $(3, -2)$ and $(-4, -7)$.
    a) Find the coordinates of the other two vertices.
    b) Find the area of the rectangle.

52. The rectangle in Fig. 1.21 has sides parallel to the axes. It is three times as long as it is wide. Its perimeter is 56 units. Find the coordinates of the vertices A, B, and C.

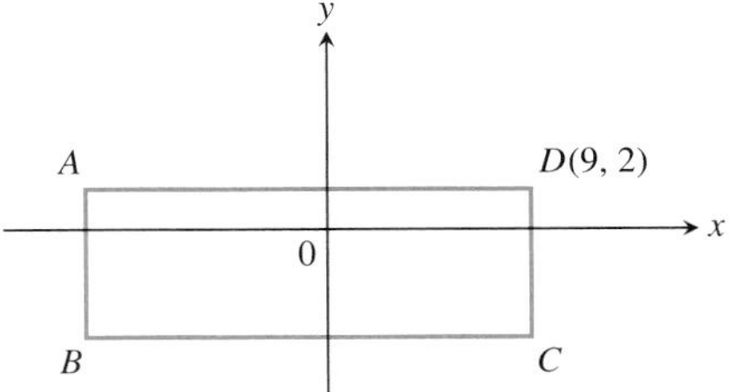

1.21 The rectangle in Exercise 52.

53. The line through the points $(1, 1)$ and $(2, 0)$ cuts the y-axis at the point $(0, b)$. Find b by using similar triangles.

54. A 90° rotation counterclockwise about the origin takes $(2, 0)$ to $(0, 2)$ and $(0, 3)$ to $(-3, 0)$, as shown in Fig. 1.22. Where does the rotation take each of the following points?
    a) $(4, 1)$ b) $(-2, -3)$ c) $(2, -5)$
    d) $(x, 0)$ e) $(0, y)$ f) (x, y)
    g) What point is taken to $(10, 3)$?

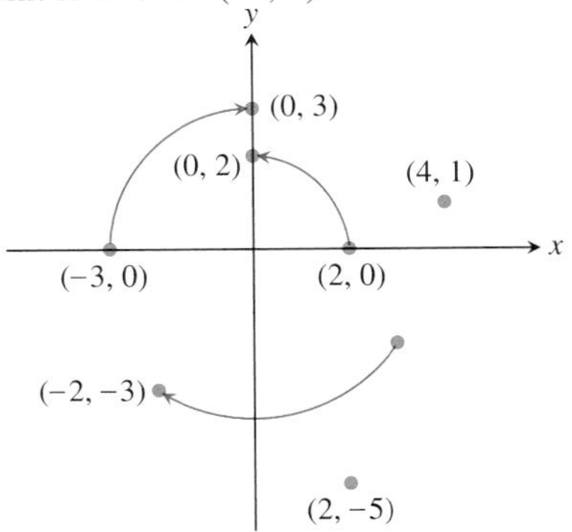

1.22 The points moved by the 90° rotation in Exercise 54.

55. Three different parallelograms have vertices at $(-1, 1)$, $(2, 0)$, and $(2, 3)$. Sketch them and give the coordinates of the missing vertices.

56. How large a slope can you calculate with your calculator? To find out, continue the list of tangent values in Example 3. The best we could do was

$$\tan(89.999\ 99999\ 99) = 57295\ 77951\ 31$$

and

$$\tan(90.000\ 00000\ 01) = -57295\ 77951\ 31.$$

57. For what value of k is the line $2x + ky = 3$ perpendicular to the line $x + y = 1$? For what value of k are the lines parallel?

58. Find the line that passes through the point $(1, 2)$ and the point of intersection of the lines $x + 2y = 3$ and $2x - 3y = -1$.

Writing for Your Own Knowledge

Answer the following questions in writing. Some answers will take only a sentence or two; others may require several paragraphs. Some explanations may also call for graphs or sketches.

1. How do you write an equation for a line when you know the coordinates of two points on the line? when you know the line's slope and the coordinates of a point on the line? when you know the line's slope and y-intercept? Give an example in each case.
2. What are the standard equations for lines perpendicular to the coordinate axes? Give examples.
3. How are the slopes of mutually perpendicular lines related? Give examples.
4. When a line is not vertical, what is the relationship between its slope and its angle of inclination?

EXPLORER PROGRAM

Name a Function	Offers practice in matching formulas to standard graphs.

1.2 *Functions and Graphs*

Functions are the main building blocks of calculus and the major tool for describing relations in the real world in mathematical terms. This section reviews the notions of function and graph and discusses some of the functions that will arise later in our study of calculus.

Functions

The values of one variable quantity often depend on another:

The temperature at which water boils depends on elevation (the boiling point drops as you go up).

The amount by which your savings will grow in a year depends on the interest rate offered by the bank.

The area of a circle depends on the circle's radius.

In each of these examples, the value of one variable quantity, which we might call y, depends on the value of another variable quantity, which we might call x. Since the value of y in each case is completely determined by the value of x, we say that y is a function of x. We say that y is the **dependent variable** of the function, and x is the **independent variable.**

In mathematics, any rule that assigns to each element in one set some element from another set is called a function. The sets may be sets of numbers, sets of number pairs, sets of points, or sets of objects of any kind. The sets do not have to be the same. All the function has to do is assign some element from the second set to each element in the first set (Fig. 1.23). Thus a function is like a machine that assigns an output to every allowable input. The inputs make up the **domain** of the function; the outputs make up the **range** (Fig. 1.24).

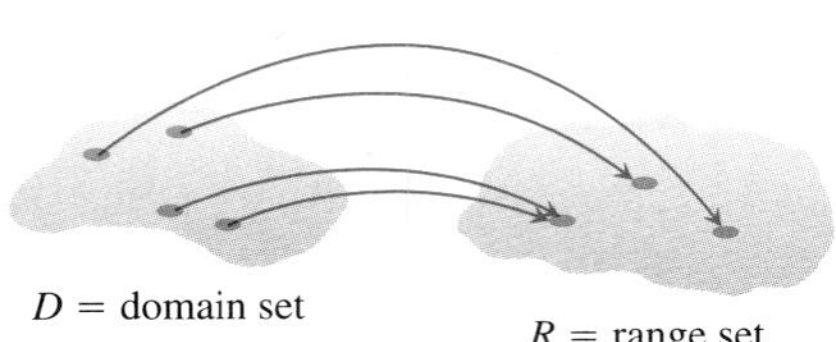

1.23 A function from set D to set R assigns a single element of R to each element in D.

1.24 A flow diagram for a function f.

DEFINITION

A **function** from a set D to a set R is a rule that assigns to each element in D a single element of R.

The word *single* in the definition does not mean that there must be only one element in the function's range, although this can happen for some functions. It means that each input from the domain is assigned exactly one output from the range, no more and no less.

Euler invented a symbolic way to say "y is a function of x":

$$y = f(x), \tag{1}$$

which we read as "y equals f of x." This notation is shorter than the verbal statements that say the same thing.

Euler's notation enables us to give different functions different names just by changing the letters we use. To say that the boiling point of water is a function of elevation, we can write $b = f(e)$. To say that the area of a circle is a function of the circle's radius, we can write $A = g(r)$. (Here we use a g because we just used f for something else.) We have to know what the variables b, e, A, and r mean, of course, for these equations to make sense.

In addition to giving a function a useful name, the notation $y = f(x)$ gives a way to denote specific values of a function. The value of f at $x = a$ can be written as $f(a)$, read "f of a."

EXAMPLE 1 The function A defined by the rule $A(r) = \pi r^2$ gives the area of a circle as a function of its radius r. The area of a circle of radius 2 is

$$A(2) = \pi(2)^2 = 4\pi .$$

Leonhard Euler (1707–1783)

Leonhard Euler, the dominant mathematical figure of his century and the most prolific mathematician who ever lived, was also an astronomer, physicist, botanist, and chemist and an expert in Oriental languages. He was the first scientist to give the function concept the prominence in his work that it has in mathematics today. Euler's collected books and papers fill 72 volumes. (This does not count Euler's enormous correspondence to approximately 300 addressees.) His introductory algebra text, written originally in German (Euler was Swiss), is still read in English translation.

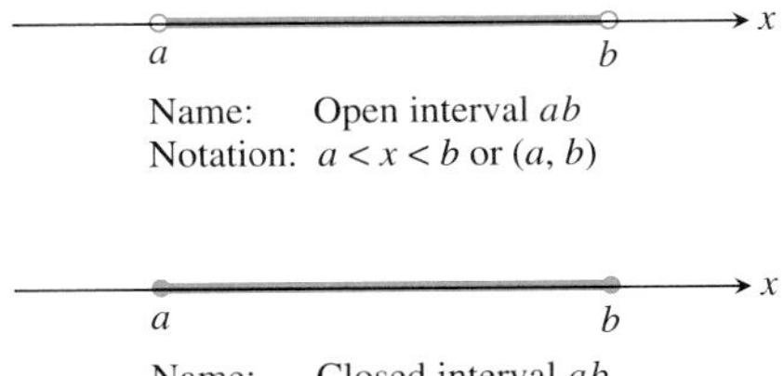

1.25 Open and closed finite intervals.

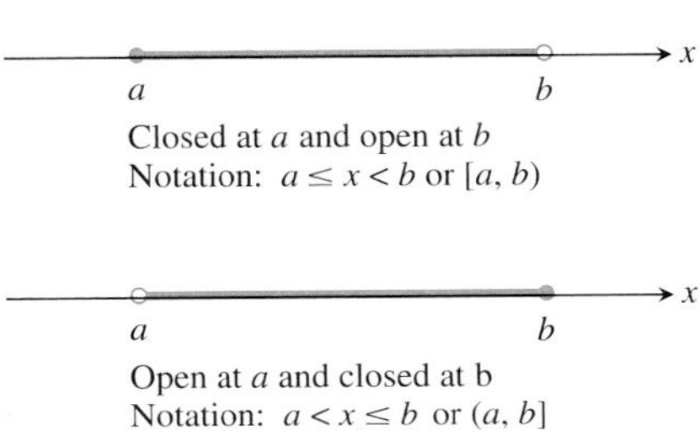

1.26 Half-open finite intervals.

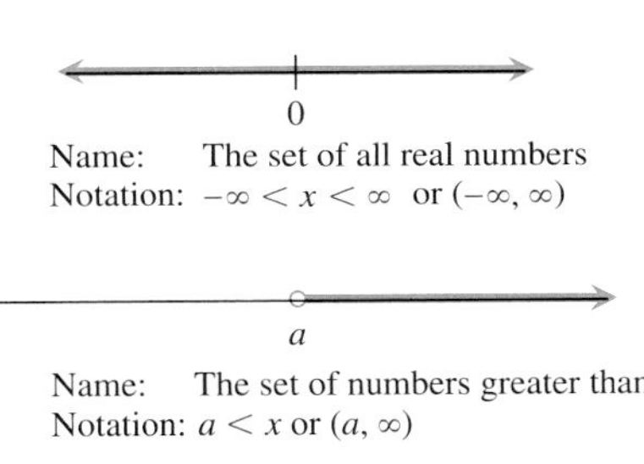

a

Name: The set of numbers greater than or equal to a
Notation: $a \leq x$ or $[a, \infty)$

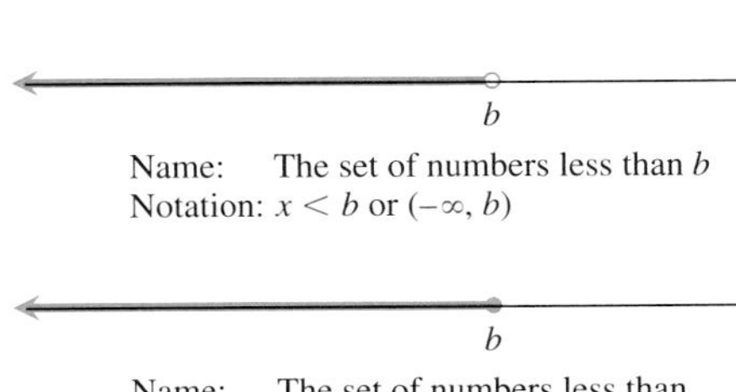

1.27 Rays on the number line and the line itself are called *infinite intervals*. The symbol ∞ (infinity) is used merely for convenience; it does not mean there is a number ∞.

In the context of geometry, the domain of the function $A = \pi r^2$ is the set of all possible radii—in this case the set of all positive real numbers. The range is also the set of positive real numbers.

Real-Valued Functions of a Real Variable

In most of our work, functions have domains and ranges that are sets of real numbers. Such functions are called **real-valued functions of a real variable** and are usually defined by formulas or equations.

EXAMPLE 2 *The Function $y = x^2$.* The formula $y = x^2$ defines the number y to be the square of the number x. If $x = 5$, then $y = 5^2 = 25$.

The domain is the set of allowable x-values—in this case the set of all real numbers. The range, which consists of the resulting y-values, is the set of non-negative real numbers.

Example 2 illustrates another point about defining functions. When we define a function $y = f(x)$ with a formula, and the domain is not stated explicitly, the domain is assumed to be the largest set of x-values for which the formula gives real y-values. This is the function's so-called **natural domain.** If we want to restrict the domain in some way, we must say so. The domain of $y = x^2$ is understood to be the entire set of real numbers. We must write "$y = x^2$, $x > 0$" if we want to restrict the function to positive values of x.

The domains and ranges of many real-valued functions of a real variable are intervals or combinations of intervals. The intervals may be finite (Figs. 1.25 and 1.26) or infinite (Fig. 1.27).

The set of real numbers that lie *strictly between* two fixed numbers a and b is an **open interval.** The interval is "open" at each end because it contains neither of its endpoints. Intervals that contain both endpoints are **closed.** Intervals that contain one endpoint but not both are **half-open.**

The endpoints of an interval make up the interval's **boundary** and are called **boundary points.** The remaining points make up the interval's **interior** and are called **interior points.** Closed intervals contain their boundary points. Open intervals contain no boundary points. Every point of an open interval is an interior point of the interval.

EXAMPLE 3

Function	Domain (x)	Range (y)
$y = x^2$	$(-\infty, \infty)$	$[0, \infty)$
$y = \sqrt{1 - x^2}$	$[-1, 1]$	$[0, 1]$
$y = \dfrac{1}{x}$	$(-\infty, 0) \cup (0, \infty)$	$(-\infty, 0) \cup (0, \infty)$
$y = \sqrt{x}$	$[0, \infty)$	$[0, \infty)$
$y = \sqrt{4 - x}$	$(-\infty, 4]$	$[0, \infty)$

The formula $y = x^2$ gives a real y-value for any real number x.

The formula $y = \sqrt{1 - x^2}$ gives a real y-value for every value of x in the closed interval from -1 to 1. Beyond this domain, the quantity $1 - x^2$ is negative and its square root is not a real number. (Complex numbers are excluded from consideration until Chapter 9.)

The formula $y = 1/x$ gives a real y-value for every x except $x = 0$. *We cannot divide any number by 0.*

The formula $y = \sqrt{x}$ gives a real y-value only when x is positive or zero. The number $y = \sqrt{x}$ is not a real number when x is negative.

In $y = \sqrt{4 - x}$, the quantity $4 - x$ cannot be negative. That is, $4 - x$ must be greater than or equal to 0. In symbols, $0 \le 4 - x$ or $x \le 4$. The formula $y = \sqrt{4 - x}$ gives a real y-value for any x less than or equal to 4.

Graphs and Graphing

The points (x, y) in the plane whose coordinates are the input–output pairs of a function $y = f(x)$ make up the function's **graph.** The graph of the function $y = x + 2$, for example, is the line $y = x + 2$. It is the set of points with coordinates (x, y) in which y equals $x + 2$.

These are the basic steps for graphing a function by hand.

EXAMPLE 4 Graph the function $y = x^2$ over the interval $-2 \le x \le 2$.

Solution **STEP 1:** Make a table of xy-pairs that satisfy the function rule, in this case the equation $y = x^2$.

x	$y = x^2$
−2	4
−1	1
0	0
1	1
2	4

STEP 2: Plot the points (x, y) whose coordinates appear in the table.

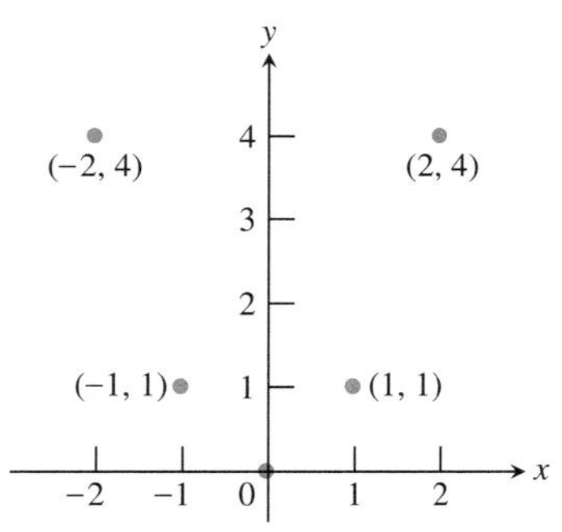

STEP 3: Draw a smooth curve through the plotted points. Label the curve with its equation.

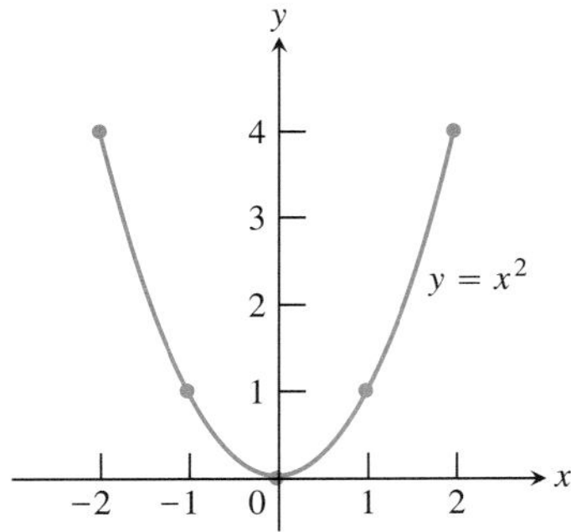

How do we know that the graph of $y = x^2$ doesn't look like one of *these* curves?

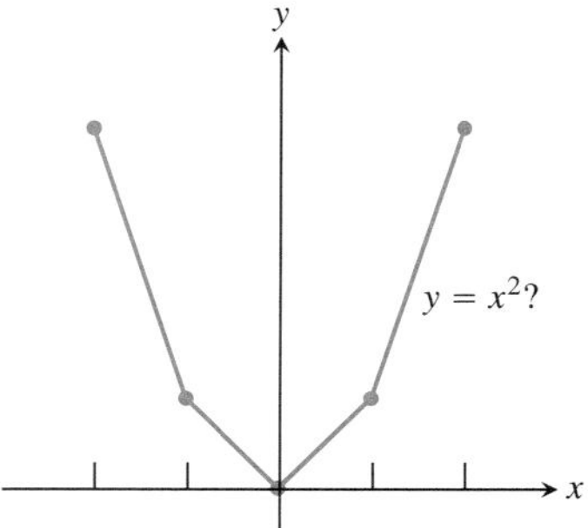

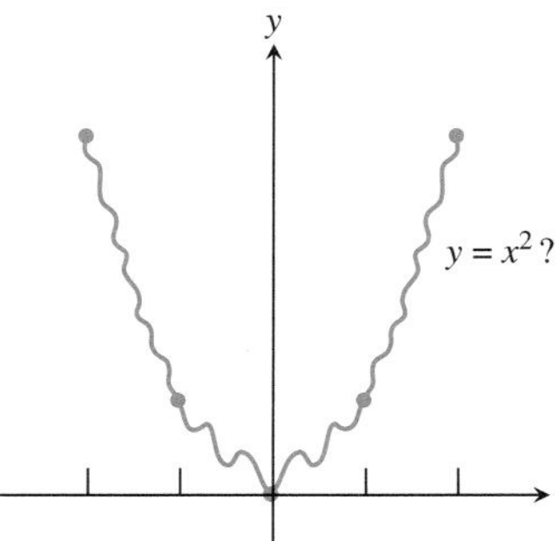

A Useful One-Line Function Table Generator

The following BASIC program will generate a table of values for any function you can key into your calculator or computer. We illustrate the program with the commands for evaluating $y = f(x) = x^3 - 4x$ at six points evenly spaced across the interval $[0, 2]$.

First, call up BASIC and enter the function with the line

```
10 DEF FNF(X) = X ^ 3 – 4*X
```

Then enter the command RUN. Finally, enter the lines

```
FOR X = 0 TO 2 STEP 0.4
PRINT X, FNF(X): NEXT
```

The screen will list the xy pairs for $x = 0$, 0.4, 0.8, 1.2, 1.6, and 2. Decrease the step size to refine the list.

To find out, we might plot more points. But how would we connect *them?* The basic question would still remain: How do we know for sure what the graph does between the points we plot?

The answer lies in calculus, as we will see in Chapter 4. There we will learn to use a marvelous mathematical tool called a *derivative* to find a curve's exact shape between plotted points. Meanwhile, we will have to settle for plotting individual points and connecting them as best we can.

Figure 1.28 shows graphs of functions that arise frequently in calculus. (We will review trigonometric functions in the next section.)

1.28 Useful graphs.

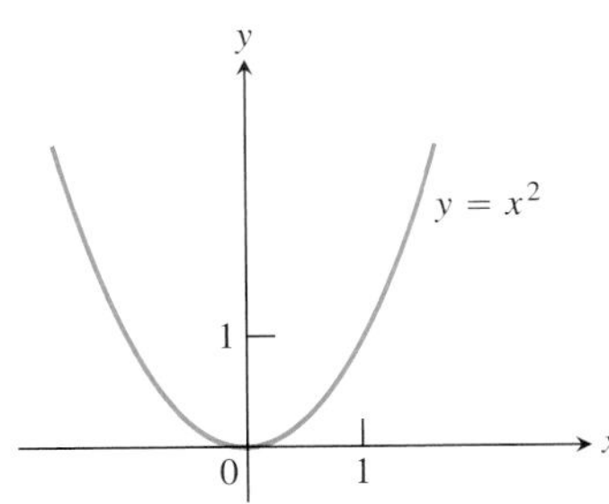

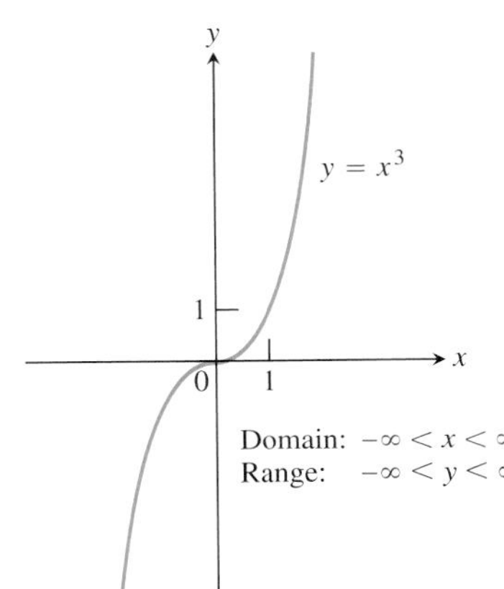

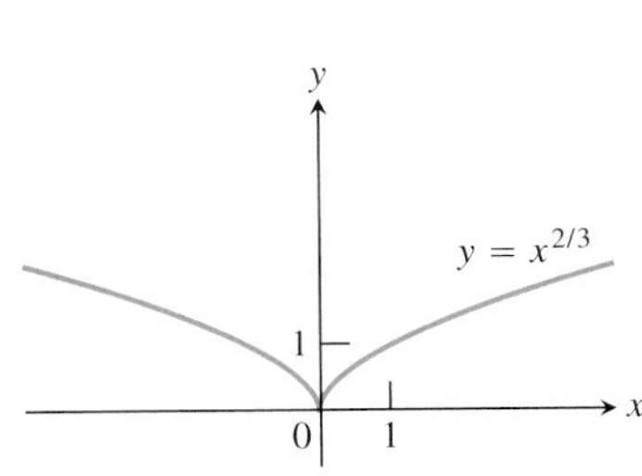

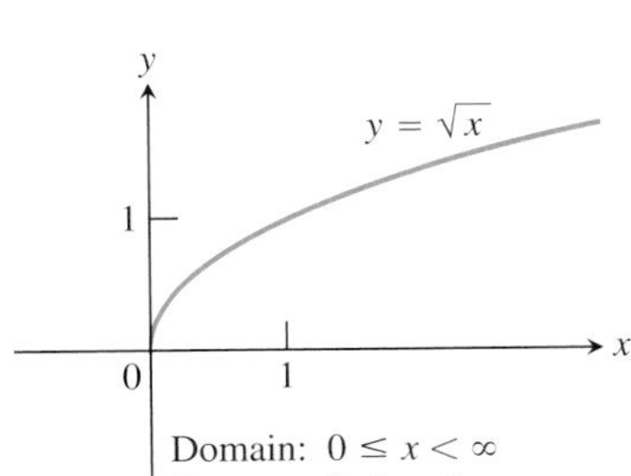

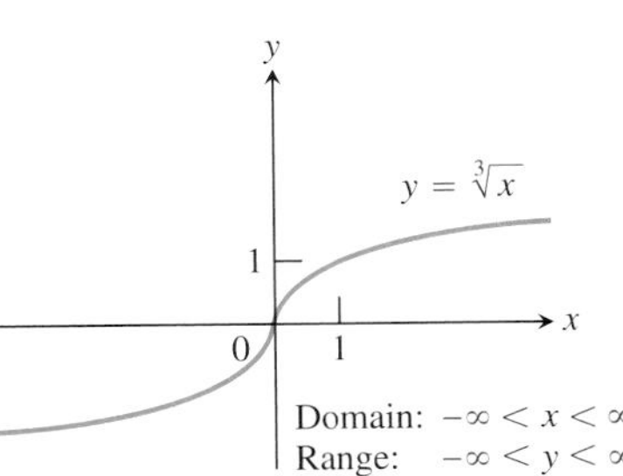

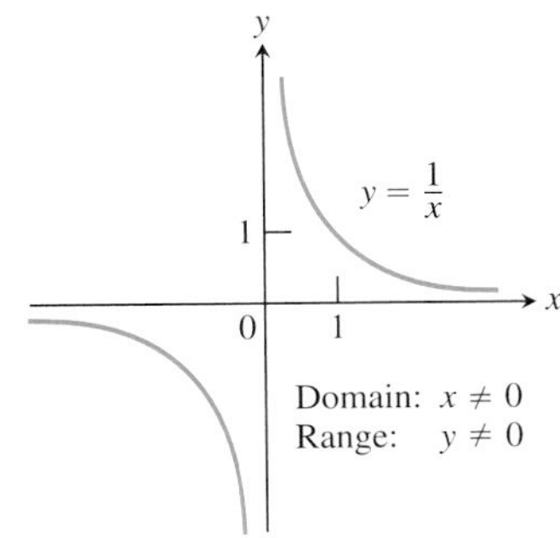

$y = \frac{1}{x^2}$

Domain: $x \neq 0$

Range: $y > 0$

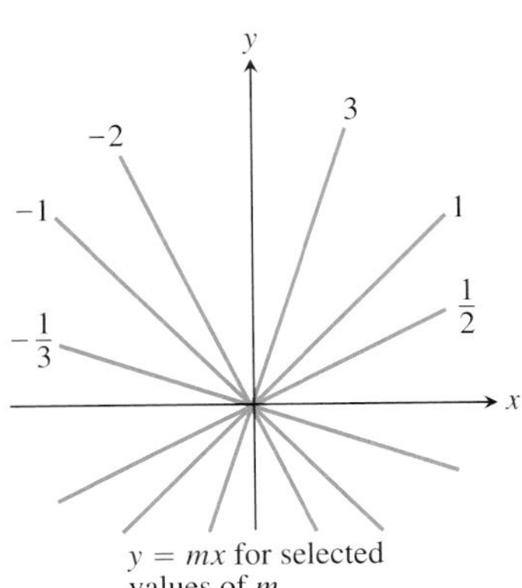

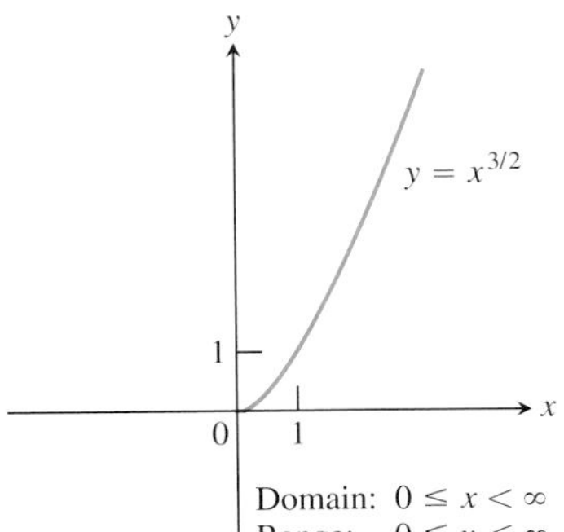

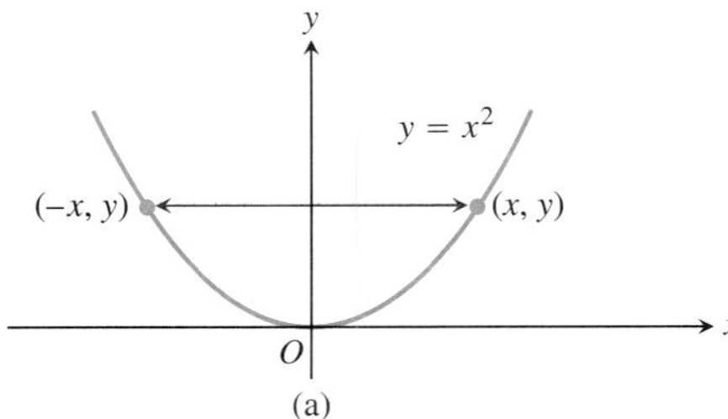

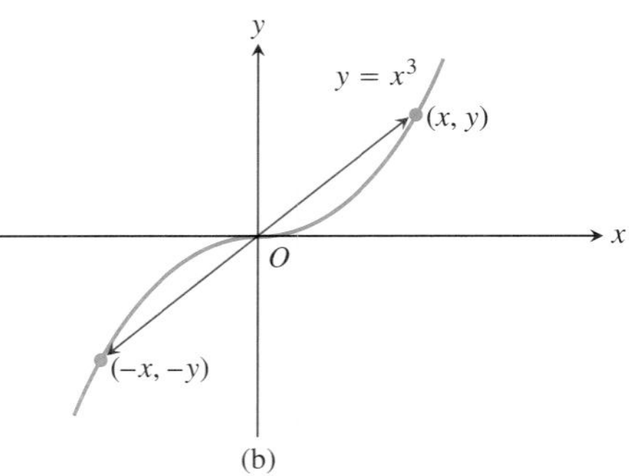

1.29 (a) The graph of $y = x^2$ (an even function) is symmetric about the y-axis. (b) The graph of $y = x^3$ (an odd function) is symmetric about the origin.

Even Functions and Odd Functions—Symmetry

DEFINITIONS

A function $y = f(x)$ is an **even** function of x if $f(-x) = f(x)$ for every x in the function's domain. It is an **odd** function of x if $f(-x) = -f(x)$ for every x in the function's domain.

The names even and odd come from powers of x. If y equals an even power of x, as in $y = x^2$ or $y = x^4$, it is an even function of x (because $(-x)^2 = x^2$ and $(-x)^4 = x^4$). If y equals an odd power of x, as in $y = x$ or $y = x^3$, it is an odd function of x (because $(-x)^1 = -x$ and $(-x)^3 = -x^3$).

Saying that a function $y = f(x)$ is even is equivalent to saying that its graph is symmetric about the y-axis. Since $f(-x) = f(x)$, the point (x, y) lies on the curve if and only if the point $(-x, y)$ lies on the curve (Fig. 1.29a).

Saying that a function $y = f(x)$ is odd is equivalent to saying that its graph is symmetric with respect to the origin. Since $f(-x) = -f(x)$, the point (x, y) lies on the curve if and only if the point $(-x, -y)$ lies on the curve (Fig. 1.29b).

The graphs of polynomials in even powers of x are symmetric about the y-axis. The graphs of polynomials in odd powers of x (no constant terms) are symmetric about the origin.

EXAMPLE 5 *Even, Odd, and Neither*

$f(x) = x^2$	Even function: $(-x)^2 = x^2$ for all x Symmetry about y-axis
$f(x) = x^2 + 1$	Even function: $(-x)^2 + 1 = x^2 + 1$ for all x Symmetry about the y-axis (Fig. 1.30a)
$f(x) = x$	Odd function: $(-x) = -(x)$ for all x Symmetry about the origin
$f(x) = x + 1$	Not odd: $f(-x) = -x + 1$, but $-f(x) = -x - 1$ The two are not equal. Not even: $(-x) + 1 \neq x + 1$ (Fig. 1.30b)

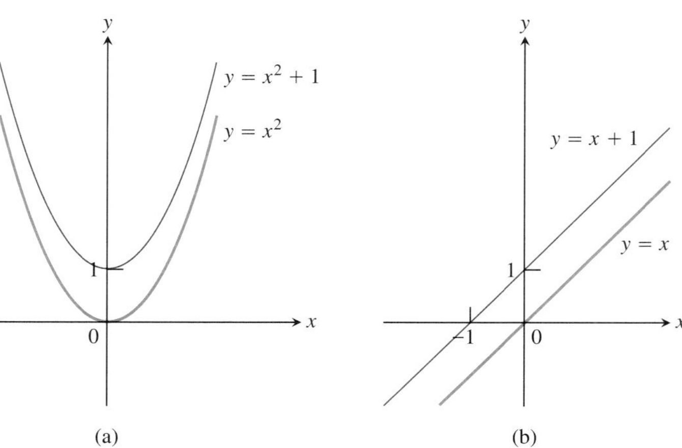

1.30 (a) If we add 1 to $y = x^2$, the resulting function is still even and its graph is still symmetric about the y-axis. (b) If we add 1 to $y = x$, the resulting function is no longer odd. The symmetry about the origin is lost.

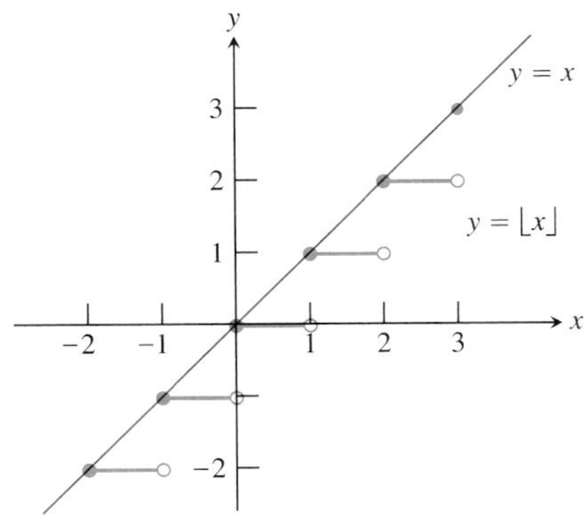

1.31 The graph of $y = \lfloor x \rfloor$ and its relation to the line $y = x$. As the figure shows, $\lfloor x \rfloor$ is less than or equal to x, so it provides an integer floor for x at each point.

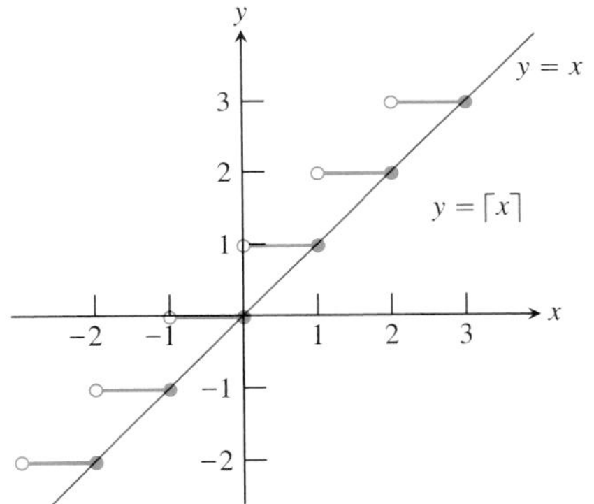

1.32 The graph of $y = \lceil x \rceil$ and its relation to the line $y = x$. As the figure shows, $\lceil x \rceil$ is greater than or equal to x, so it provides an integer ceiling for x at each point.

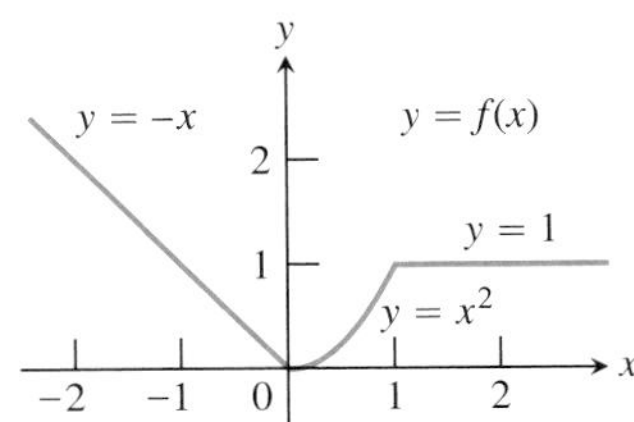

1.33 To graph the function $y = f(x)$ shown here, we apply different formulas to different parts of its domain (Example 7).

Step Functions

The **greatest integer function** $y = \lfloor x \rfloor$ assigns to each real number the greatest integer less than or equal to x. The notation $\lfloor x \rfloor$ is read "the greatest integer in x." Other common notations are $[x]$ and $[\![x]\!]$, read the same way. Figure 1.31 shows the graph.

EXAMPLE 6 *Values of* $y = \lfloor x \rfloor$

Positive	$\lfloor 1.9 \rfloor = 1,\quad \lfloor 2.0 \rfloor = 2,\quad \lfloor 2.4 \rfloor = 2$
Zero	$\lfloor 0.5 \rfloor = 0,\quad \lfloor 0 \rfloor = 0$
Negative	$\lfloor -1.2 \rfloor = -2,\quad \lfloor -0.5 \rfloor = -1$

The notation $y = \lfloor x \rfloor$ comes from computer science, where it is used to denote the result of rounding x down to the nearest integer. You can think of $\lfloor x \rfloor$ as the integer floor for x, and the notation is chosen to suggest just that. The companion function

$$\lceil x \rceil \qquad \text{(integer ceiling for } x\text{)}$$

gives the result of rounding x up to the nearest integer. It gives the least integer greater than or equal to x and is called the **least integer function** (Fig. 1.32).

The greatest and least integer functions are called **step functions** because their graphs look like steps. Their values hold constant for a while and then jump. Other examples of step functions are provided by postal rates, rates for overtime pay, and rates at parking lots. The digital readouts on scales and watches are step functions of weight and time, respectively.

Functions Defined in Pieces

While some functions are defined by single formulas, others are defined by applying different formulas to different parts of their domains.

EXAMPLE 7 The values of the function

$$y = f(x) = \begin{cases} -x & \text{for } x < 0 \\ x^2 & \text{for } 0 \le x \le 1 \\ 1 & \text{for } x > 1 \end{cases}$$

are given by three separate formulas: $y = -x$ when $x < 0$, $y = x^2$ when $0 \le x \le 1$, and $y = 1$ when $x > 1$. However, the function is *just one function*, whose domain is the entire set of real numbers (Fig. 1.33).

EXAMPLE 8 Suppose that the graph of $y = f(x)$ consists of the line segments shown in Fig. 1.34 on the following page. Write a formula for f.

Solution We find formulas for the segments from (0, 0) to (1, 1) and from (1, 0) to (2, 1) and piece them together in the manner of Example 7.

Segment from (0, 0) to (1, 1) The line through (0, 0) and (1, 1) has slope $m = (1 - 0)/(1 - 0) = 1$ and y-intercept $b = 0$. Its slope–intercept equation is $y = x$. The segment from (0, 0) to (1, 1) that includes the point (0, 0) but not the point (1, 1) is the graph of the function $y = x$ restricted to the half-open interval $0 \le x < 1$, namely,

$$y = x, \qquad 0 \le x < 1.$$

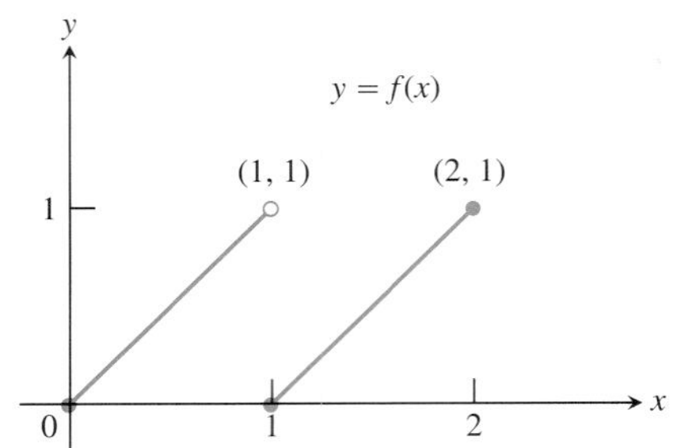

1.34 The graph of the function in Example 8. The segment on the left contains (0, 0) but not (1, 1). The segment on the right contains both of its endpoints.

Segment from (1, 0) to (2, 1) The line through (1, 0) and (2, 1) has slope $m = (1 - 0)/(2 - 1) = 1$ and passes through the point (1, 0). The corresponding point–slope equation for the line is therefore

$$y - 0 = 1(x - 1), \qquad \text{or} \qquad y = x - 1.$$

The segment from (1, 0) to (2, 1) that includes both endpoints is the graph of $y = x - 1$ restricted to the closed interval $1 \le x \le 2$, namely,

$$y = x - 1, \qquad 1 \le x \le 2.$$

Formula for the function $y = f(x)$ shown in Fig. 1.34 We obtain a formula for f on the interval $0 \le x \le 2$ by combining the formulas we obtained for the two pieces of its graph:

$$f(x) = \begin{cases} x & \text{for } 0 \le x < 1 \\ x - 1 & \text{for } 1 \le x \le 2. \end{cases}$$

Sums, Differences, Products, and Quotients

The sum $f + g$ of two functions of x is itself a function of x, defined at any point x that lies in both domains. The same holds for the differences $f - g$ and $g - f$, the product $f \cdot g$, and the quotients f/g and g/f, as long as we exclude any points that require division by zero.

EXAMPLE 9 The functions f and g defined by the formulas

$$f(x) = \sqrt{x} \qquad \text{and} \qquad g(x) = \sqrt{1 - x}$$

can combine in the following ways.

Function	Formula	Domain
f	$f(x) = \sqrt{x}$	$0 \le x$
g	$g(x) = \sqrt{1 - x}$	$x \le 1$
$f + g$	$(f + g)(x) = f(x) + g(x) = \sqrt{x} + \sqrt{1 - x}$	$0 \le x \le 1$ (Intersection of domains of f and g)
$f - g$	$(f - g)(x) = f(x) - g(x) = \sqrt{x} - \sqrt{1 - x}$	$0 \le x \le 1$
$g - f$	$(g - f)(x) = g(x) - f(x) = \sqrt{1 - x} - \sqrt{x}$	$0 \le x \le 1$
$f \cdot g$	$(f \cdot g)(x) = f(x)g(x) = \sqrt{x(1 - x)}$	$0 \le x \le 1$
f/g	$\frac{f}{g}(x) = \frac{f(x)}{g(x)} = \sqrt{\frac{x}{1 - x}}$	$0 \le x < 1$ ($x = 1$ excluded)
g/f	$\frac{g}{f}(x) = \frac{g(x)}{f(x)} = \sqrt{\frac{1 - x}{x}}$	$0 < x \le 1$ ($x = 0$ excluded)

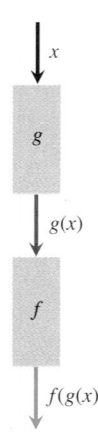

1.35 Two functions can be composed when the range of the first lies in the domain of the second.

Composite Functions

Suppose that the outputs of a function g can be used as inputs of a function f. We can then hook g and f together to form a new function whose inputs are the inputs of g and whose outputs are the numbers $f(g(x))$, as in Fig. 1.35. We say that the function $f(g(x))$ (read "f of g of x") is the **composite** of g and f. It is made by **composing** g and f in the order first g, then f. The usual "stand-alone" notation for this composite is $\boldsymbol{f \circ g}$, which is read "f of g." Thus, the value of $f \circ g$ at x is $(f \circ g)(x) = f(g(x))$.

EXAMPLE 10 Find a formula for $(f \circ g)(x) = f(g(x))$ if $g(x) = x^2$ and $f(x) = x - 7$. Then find $f(g(2))$.

Solution To find $f(g(x))$, we replace x in the formula for $f(x)$ by the expression given for $g(x)$:

$$\begin{aligned} f(x) &= x - 7 \\ f(g(x)) &= g(x) - 7 \\ &= x^2 - 7. \end{aligned}$$

We then find the value of $f(g(2))$ by substituting 2 for x:

$$f(g(2)) = (2)^2 - 7 = -3.$$

Changing the order of composition usually changes the result. In Example 10, we composed $g(x) = x^2$ and $f(x) = x - 7$ in the order first g, then f, to obtain the function $f \circ g$ whose value at x was $f(g(x)) = x^2 - 7$. In the next example, we see what happens when we reverse the order to obtain the composite $g \circ f$.

$f(g(x))$ vs. $g(f(x))$

The parentheses in the notation for composite functions tell which function comes first:

The notation $f(g(x))$ says "first g, then f."
To find $f(g(2))$, find $g(2)$ and then apply f.

The notation $g(f(x))$ says "first f, then g."
To find $g(f(2))$, find $f(2)$ and then apply g.

EXAMPLE 11 Find a formula for $(g \circ f)(x) = g(f(x))$ if $g(x) = x^2$ and $f(x) = x - 7$. Then find $g(f(2))$.

Solution To find $g(f(x))$, we replace x in the formula for $g(x)$ by the expression for $f(x)$:

$$\begin{aligned} g(x) &= x^2 \\ g(f(x)) &= (f(x))^2 \\ &= (x - 7)^2 \end{aligned}$$

To find $g(f(2))$, we substitute 2 for x in the formula for $g(f(x))$:

$$g(f(2)) = (2 - 7)^2 = (-5)^2 = 25.$$

This is different from the number $f(g(2)) = -3$ found in the preceding example.

Exercises 1.2

In Exercises 1–4, write a formula that expresses the first quantity as a function of the second.

1. The perimeter of a square as a function of the length of the square's sides
2. The surface area of a cube as a function of the length of the cube's edges
3. The volume of a sphere as a function of the sphere's radius
4. The surface area of a sphere as a function of the sphere's radius

In Exercises 5–18, find the domain and range of each function. Then graph the function. What symmetries, if any, do the graphs have? Use the graphs in Fig. 1.28 for guidance, as needed. Take advantage of symmetry when you draw.

5. $y = -x^2$
6. $y = (-x)^2$
7. $y = -\dfrac{1}{x}$
8. $y = -\dfrac{1}{x^2}$
9. $y = 2\sqrt{x}$
10. $y = \sqrt{2x}$

11. $y = -\sqrt{x}$

12. $y = \sqrt{-x}$

13. $y = -x^{3/2}$

14. $y = (-x)^{3/2}$

15. $y = (-x)^{2/3}$

16. $y = -x^{2/3}$

17. $y = \dfrac{x^3}{8}$

18. $y = -2\sqrt[3]{x}$

19. Consider the function $y = 1/\sqrt{x}$.

a) Can x be negative?
b) Can x equal zero?
c) What are the domain and range of the function?

20. Consider the function $y = \sqrt{(1/x) - 1}$.

a) Can x equal zero?
b) Can x be greater than 1? Can x be less than 1?
c) What are the domain and range of the function?

In Exercises 21–32, say whether the functions are odd, even, or neither. Try to answer without writing anything down (except the answer).

21. $y = x^4$

22. $y = x^5$

23. $y = x^{-1}$

24. $y = x^{-2}$

25. $y = 2x + 1$

26. $y = 2x + x^2$

27. $y = x^2 - 1$

28. $y = 2x - x^3$

29. $y = \dfrac{3}{x^2 - 1}$

30. $y = \dfrac{2}{x - 1}$

31. $y = \dfrac{4x}{x^2 - 1}$

32. $y = \dfrac{5x^2}{x^2 - 1}$

In Exercises 33–38, find the domain and range of each function. Then graph the function.

33. $y = \lceil 2x \rceil$

34. $y = 2\lceil x \rceil$

35. $y = -\lceil x \rceil$

36. $y = -\lfloor x \rfloor$

37. $y = \dfrac{\lfloor x \rfloor}{2}$

38. $y = \left\lfloor \dfrac{x}{2} \right\rfloor$

39. Graph each function over the given interval.

a) $y = x - \lfloor x \rfloor, \quad -3 \le x \le 3$
b) $y = \lfloor x \rfloor - \lceil x \rceil, \quad -3 \le x \le 3$

40. *Integer Parts of Decimals.* When x is positive or zero, $\lfloor x \rfloor$ is the integer part of the decimal representation of x. What is the corresponding description of $\lceil x \rceil$ when x is negative or zero?

41. Make a table of values with $x = 0$, 1, and 2, and graph the function

$$y = \begin{cases} x, & 0 \le x \le 1 \\ 2 - x, & 1 < x \le 2. \end{cases}$$

42. Make a table of values with $x = 0$, 1, and 2, and graph the function

$$y = \begin{cases} 1 - x, & 0 \le x \le 1 \\ 2 - x, & 1 < x \le 2. \end{cases}$$

Graph the functions in Exercises 43–46.

43. $y = \begin{cases} 3 - x, & x \le 1 \\ 2x, & 1 < x \end{cases}$

44. $y = \begin{cases} 1/x, & x < 0 \\ x, & 0 \le x \end{cases}$

45. $y = \begin{cases} 1, & x < 5 \\ 0, & 5 \le x \end{cases}$

46. $y = \begin{cases} 1, & x < 0 \\ \sqrt{x}, & x \ge 0 \end{cases}$

47. Find a formula for each function graphed.

a)

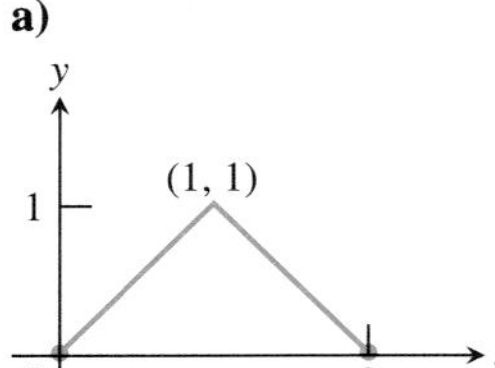

b)

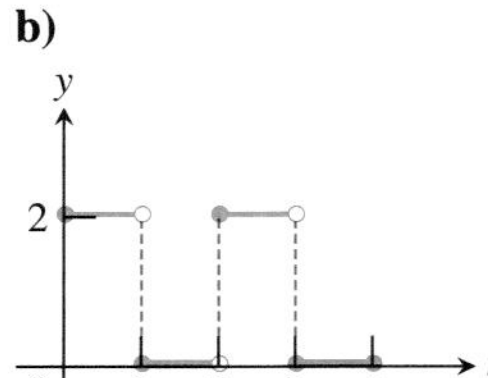

48. Find a formula for each function graphed.

a)

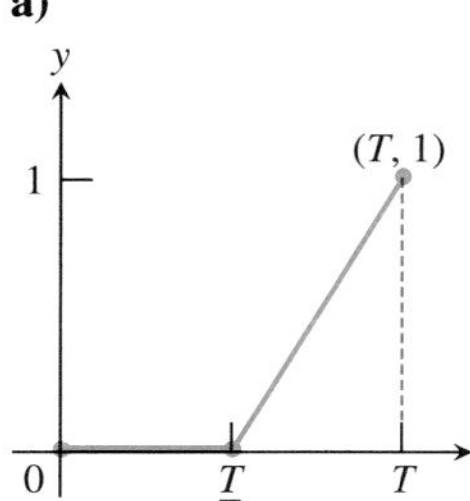

b)

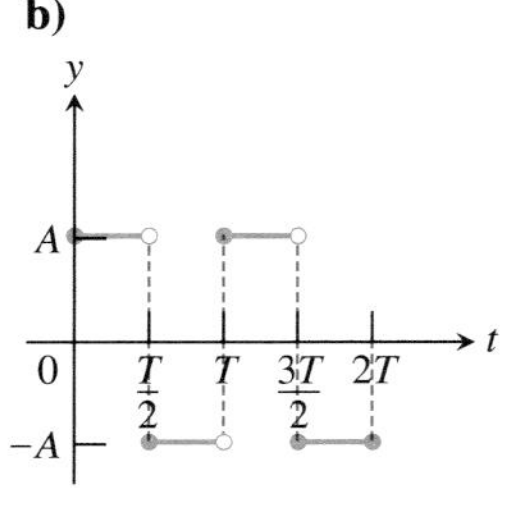

In Exercises 49 and 50, find the domains and ranges of f, g, $f + g$, and $f \cdot g$.

49. $f(x) = x, \quad g(x) = \sqrt{x - 1}$

50. $f(x) = \sqrt{x + 1}, \quad g(x) = \sqrt{x - 1}$

In Exercises 51 and 52, find the domains and ranges of f, g, f/g, and g/f.

51. $f(x) = 2, \quad g(x) = x^2 + 1$

52. $f(x) = 1, \quad g(x) = 1 + \sqrt{x}$

53. If $f(x) = x + 5$ and $g(x) = x^2 - 3$, find the following.

a) $f(g(0))$ **b)** $g(f(0))$
c) $f(g(x))$ **d)** $g(f(x))$
e) $f(f(-5))$ **f)** $g(g(2))$
g) $f(f(x))$ **h)** $g(g(x))$

54. If $f(x) = x - 1$ and $g(x) = 1/(x + 1)$, find the following.

a) $f(g(1/2))$ **b)** $g(f(1/2))$
c) $f(g(x))$ **d)** $g(f(x))$
e) $f(f(2))$ **f)** $g(g(2))$
g) $f(f(x))$ **h)** $g(g(x))$

55. If $u(x) = 4x - 5$, $v(x) = x^2$, and $f(x) = 1/x$, find formulas for the following.

a) $u(v(f(x)))$ **b)** $u(f(v(x)))$
c) $v(u(f(x)))$ **d)** $v(f(u(x)))$
e) $f(u(v(x)))$ **f)** $f(v(u(x)))$

56. If $f(x)=\sqrt{x}$, $g(x)=x/4$, and $h(x)=4x-8$, find formulas for the following.

a) $h(g(f(x)))$ **b)** $h(f(g(x)))$
c) $g(h(f(x)))$ **d)** $g(f(h(x)))$
e) $f(g(h(x)))$ **f)** $f(h(g(x)))$

Let $f(x)=x-3$, $g(x)=\sqrt{x}$, $h(x)=x^3$, and $j(x)=2x$. Express each of the functions in Exercises 57 and 58 as a composite involving one or more of f, g, h, and j.

57. **a)** $y=\sqrt{x}-3$
b) $y=2\sqrt{x}$
c) $y=x^{1/4}$
d) $y=4x$
e) $y=\sqrt{(x-3)^3}$
f) $y=(2x-6)^3$

58. **a)** $y=2x-3$
b) $y=x^{3/2}$
c) $y=x^9$
d) $y=x-6$
e) $y=2\sqrt{x-3}$
f) $y=\sqrt{x^3-3}$

59. Copy and complete the following table.

$g(x)$	$f(x)$	$(f \circ g)(x)$
a) $x-7$	$\sqrt{x}$	
b) $x+2$	$3x$	
c)	$\sqrt{x-5}$	$\sqrt{x^2-5}$
d) $\dfrac{x}{x-1}$	$\dfrac{x}{x-1}$	
e)	$1+\dfrac{1}{x}$	x
f) $\dfrac{1}{x}$		x

60. *A Magic Trick.* You may have heard of a magic trick that goes like this: Take any number. Add 5. Double the result. Subtract 6. Divide by 2. Subtract 2. Now tell me your answer, and I'll tell you what you started with.

Pick a number and try it.

You can see what is going on if you let x be your original number and follow the steps to make a formula $f(x)$ for the number you end up with.

EVEN AND ODD

One of the benefits of knowing that a function is even or odd is that once you know its values on one side of the origin you automatically know its values on the other side. The figures in Exercises 61–64 show portions of the graphs of functions defined on $[-2, 2]$. Copy each figure and complete the graph given so that f is (a) even, (b) odd.

61.

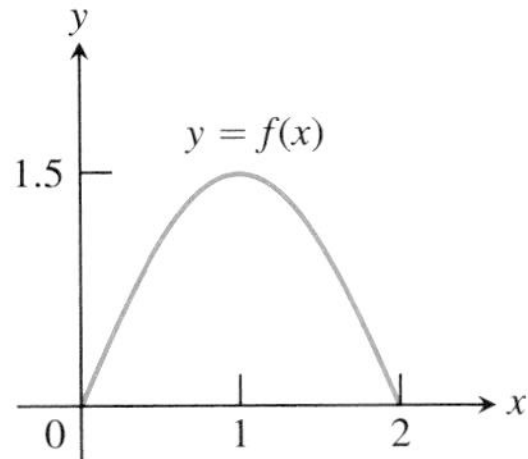

62.

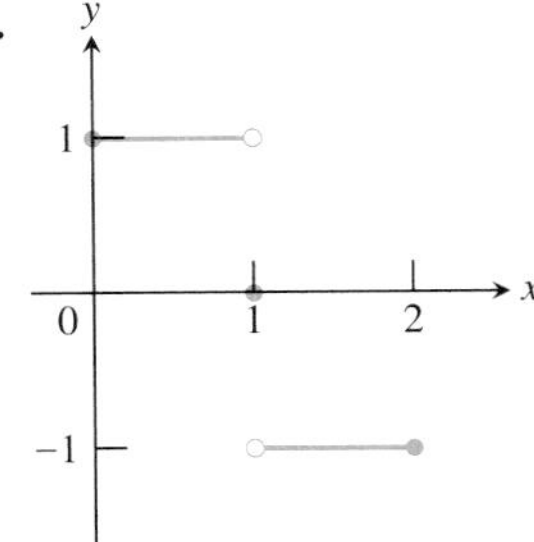

63.

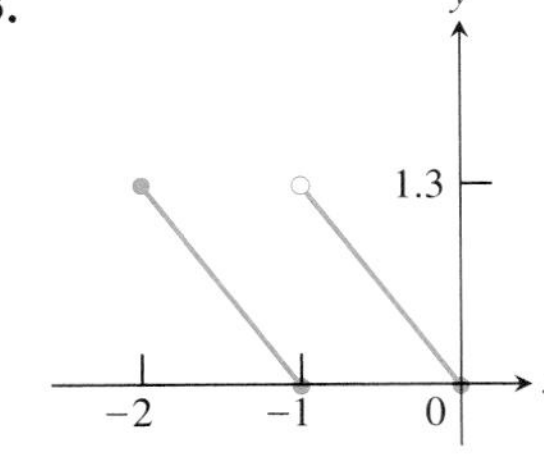

64.

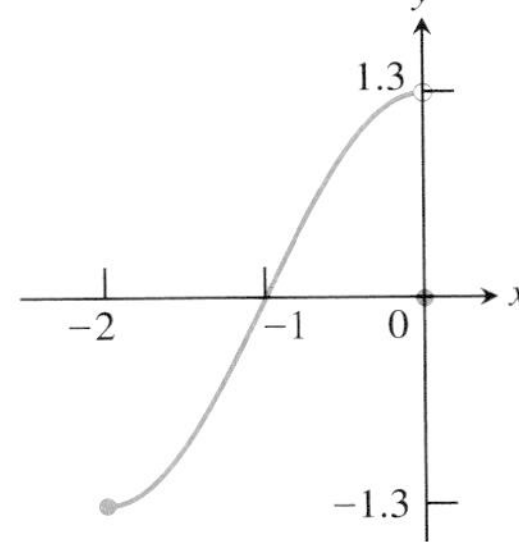

In Exercises 65–68, graph f and give a formula for $g(x)$ so that f is (a) even, (b) odd. Refer to the graphs in Fig. 1.28 as needed.

65. $y=f(x)=\begin{cases} g(x), & x<0 \\ 0, & x=0 \\ 1/x, & x>0 \end{cases}$

66. $y=f(x)=\begin{cases} 1/x^2, & x<0 \\ 0, & x=0 \\ g(x), & x>0 \end{cases}$

67. $y=f(x)=\begin{cases} g(x), & x<0 \\ x^{2/3}, & x\ge 0 \end{cases}$

68. $y=f(x)=\begin{cases} \sqrt[3]{x}, & x\le 0 \\ g(x), & x>0 \end{cases}$

69. Can anything be said about the product of an even function and an odd function? Give reasons for your answer.

70. Can anything be said about the product of two odd functions? What about the square of an odd function? Give reasons for your answers.

Writing for Your Own Knowledge

Answer the following questions in writing. Some answers will take only a sentence or two; others may require several paragraphs. Some explanations may also call for graphs or sketches.

1. What is a function? How do you graph a real-valued function of a real variable? Give examples of functions and their graphs, and describe the domains and ranges.

2. What is an even function? an odd function? What symmetries do the graphs of such functions have? Give examples. Give an example of a function that is neither odd nor even.
3. When is it possible to compose one function with another? Does the order in which functions are composed ever matter?

EXPLORER PROGRAMS

Power Grapher	Graphs functions singly or together. Makes tables of values of functions.
Name a Function	Offers practice in matching formulas to standard graphs.

1.3 Trigonometric Functions

In surveying, navigation, and astronomy, angles are measured in degrees, but in calculus it is best to use radians. We will see why in Section 3.4. In the present section, we use radians and degrees together so that you can practice relating the two.

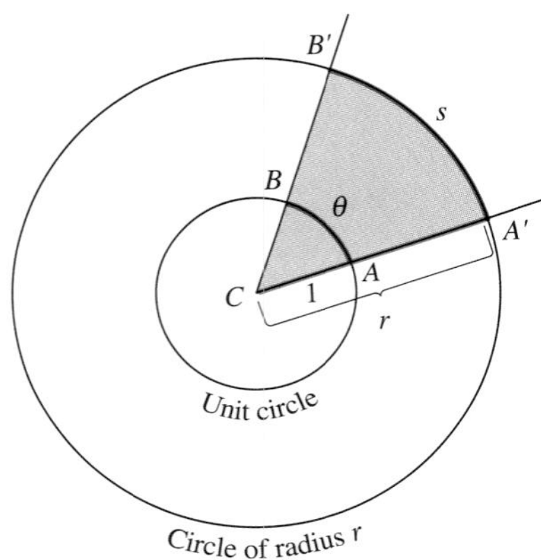

1.36 The radian measure of angle ACB is the length θ of arc AB on the unit circle centered at C. The value of θ can be found from any other circle, however, as the ratio of s to r.

Radian Measure

The **radian measure** of the angle ACB at the center of the unit circle (Fig. 1.36) equals the length of the arc that the angle cuts from the unit circle.

If angle ACB cuts an arc $A'B'$ from a second circle centered at C, then circular sector $A'CB'$ will be similar to circular sector ACB. In particular,

$$\frac{\text{Length of arc } A'B'}{\text{Radius of second circle}} = \frac{\text{Length of arc } AB}{\text{Radius of first circle}}. \tag{1}$$

In the notation of Fig. 1.36, Eq. (1) says that

$$\frac{s}{r} = \frac{\theta}{1} = \theta \quad \text{or} \quad \theta = \frac{s}{r}. \tag{2}$$

When you know r and s, you can calculate the angle's radian measure θ from this equation.

We find the relation between degree measure and radian measure by observing that a semicircle of radius r, which we know has length $s = \pi r$, subtends a central angle of 180°. Therefore,

$$180° = \pi \text{ radians}. \tag{3}$$

Conversion Formulas

$1 \text{ degree} = \frac{\pi}{180} (\approx 0.02) \text{ radians}$

Degrees to radians: multiply by $\frac{\pi}{180}$.

$1 \text{ radian} = \frac{180}{\pi} (\approx 57) \text{ degrees}$

Radians to degrees: multiply by $\frac{180}{\pi}$.

EXAMPLE 1 *Conversions* (Fig. 1.37)

Change 45° to radians: $45 \cdot \frac{\pi}{180} = \frac{\pi}{4}$ rad

Change 90° to radians: $90 \cdot \frac{\pi}{180} = \frac{\pi}{2}$ rad

Change $\frac{\pi}{6}$ radians to degrees: $\frac{\pi}{6} \cdot \frac{180}{\pi} = 30°$

Change $\frac{\pi}{3}$ radians to degrees: $\frac{\pi}{3} \cdot \frac{180}{\pi} = 60°$

Degrees	Radians

1.37 The angles of two common triangles, in degrees and radians.

EXAMPLE 2 An acute angle whose vertex lies at the center of a circle of radius 6 subtends an arc of length 2π (Fig. 1.38). The angle's radian measure is

$$\theta = \frac{s}{r} = \frac{2\pi}{6} = \frac{\pi}{3}. \qquad \text{Eq. (2) with } s = 2\pi,\ r = 6$$

The equation $\theta = s/r$ is sometimes written

$$s = r\theta. \tag{4}$$

This equation gives a handy way to find s when you know r and θ.

EXAMPLE 3 An angle of $3\pi/4$ radians at the center of a circle of radius 8 subtends an arc

$$s = r\theta = 8 \cdot \frac{3\pi}{4} = 6\pi. \qquad \text{Eq. (4) with } r = 8 \text{ and } \theta = 3\pi/4$$

The arc is 6π units long.

EXAMPLE 4 How long is the arc subtended by a central angle of 120° in a circle of radius 4?

Solution The equation $s = r\theta$ holds only when the angle is measured in radians, so we must find the angle's radian measure before finding s:

$$\theta = 120 \cdot \frac{\pi}{180} = \frac{2\pi}{3} \text{ rad} \qquad \text{Convert to radians.}$$

$$s = r\theta = 4 \cdot \frac{2\pi}{3} = \frac{8\pi}{3}. \qquad \text{Then find } s = r\theta.$$

The arc is $8\pi/3$ units long.

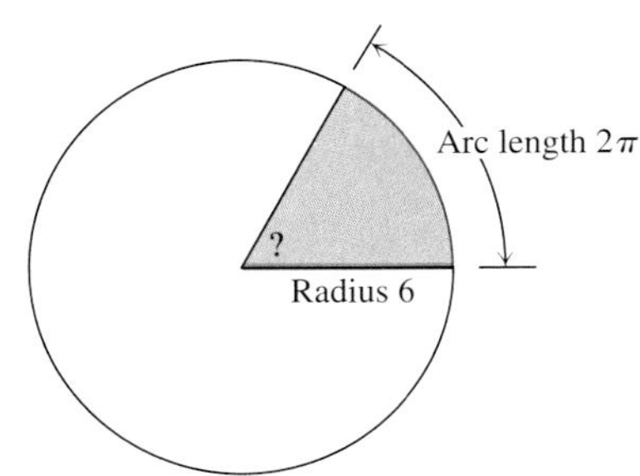

1.38 What is the radian measure of this angle? See Example 2.

When angles are used to describe counterclockwise rotation, the measurements can go arbitrarily far beyond 2π radians, or 360°. Similarly, angles that describe clockwise rotations can have negative measures of all sizes (Fig. 1.39).

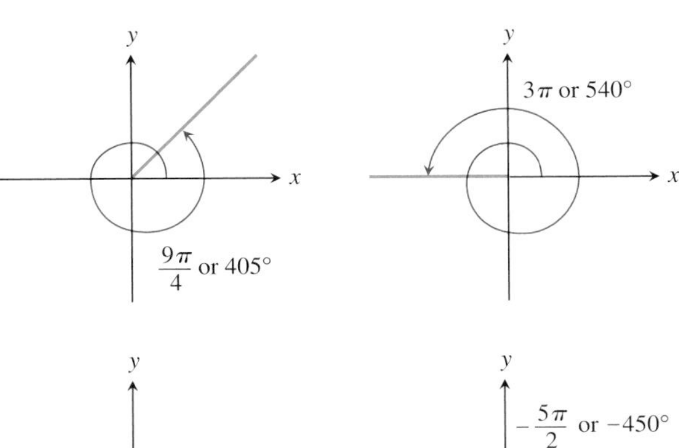

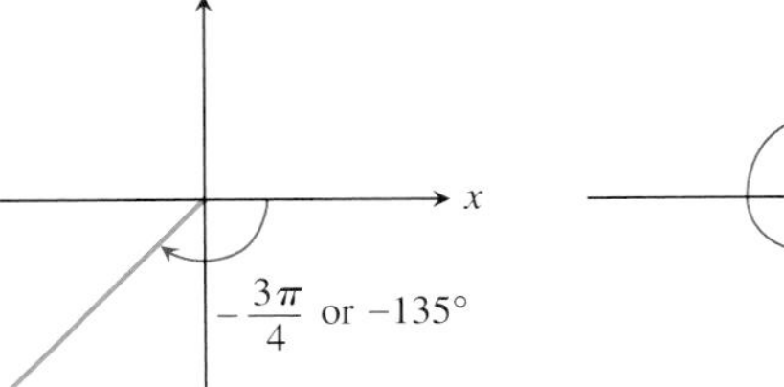

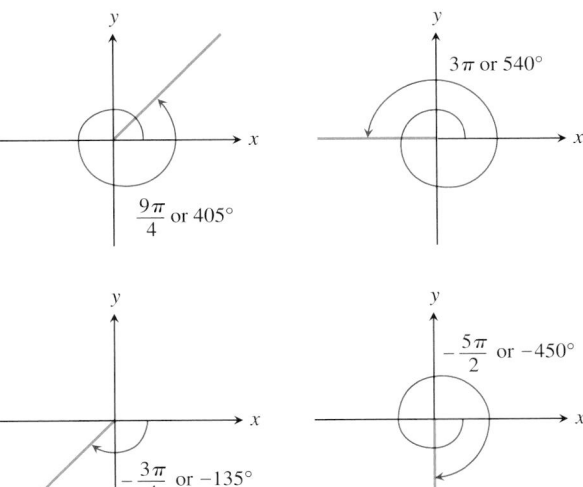

1.39 Angles can have any measure.

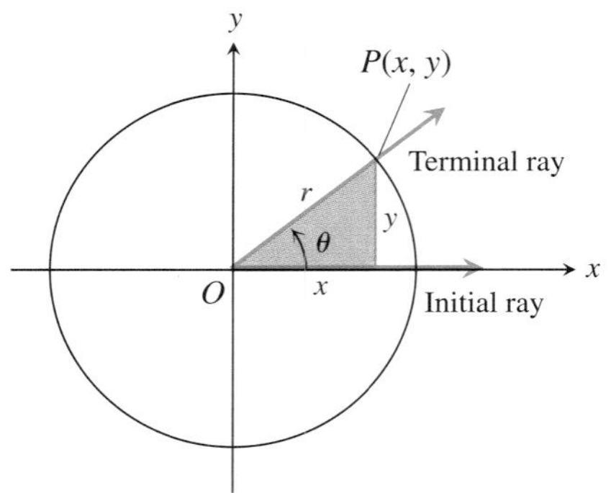

1.40 An angle θ in standard position.

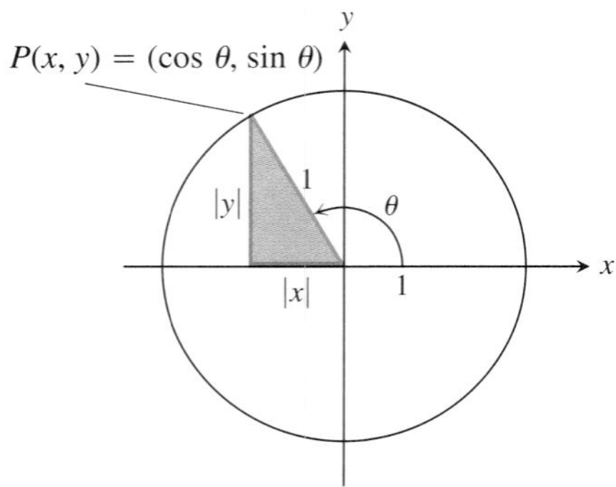

1.41 The acute reference triangle for an angle θ.

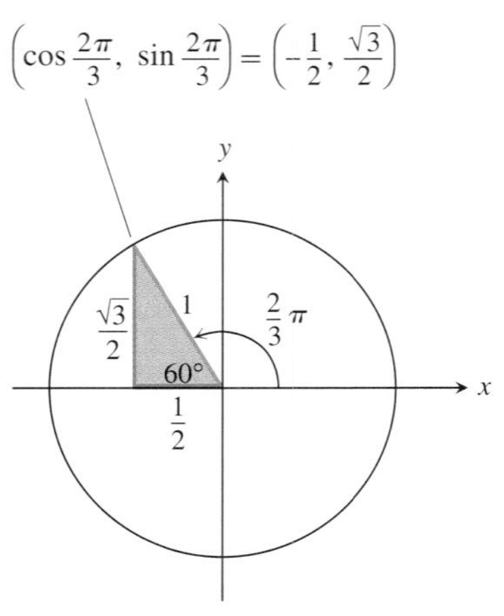

1.42 The triangle for calculating the sine and cosine of $2\pi/3$ radians (Example 5).

The Six Basic Trigonometric Functions

When an angle of measure θ is placed in standard position at the center of a circle of radius r (Fig. 1.40), the six basic trigonometric functions of θ are defined in the following way:

$$\begin{array}{llll} \text{Sine:} & \sin\theta = \dfrac{y}{r} & \text{Cosecant:} & \csc\theta = \dfrac{r}{y} \\ \text{Cosine:} & \cos\theta = \dfrac{x}{r} & \text{Secant:} & \sec\theta = \dfrac{r}{x} \\ \text{Tangent:} & \tan\theta = \dfrac{y}{x} & \text{Cotangent:} & \cot\theta = \dfrac{x}{y} \end{array} \qquad (5)$$

As you can see, $\tan\theta$ and $\sec\theta$ are not defined if $x = 0$. In terms of radian measure, this means they are not defined when θ is $\pm\pi/2$, $\pm 3\pi/2, \ldots$. Similarly, $\cot\theta$ and $\csc\theta$ are not defined for values of θ for which $y = 0$, namely $\theta = 0, \pm\pi, \pm 2\pi, \ldots$. Notice also that

$$\begin{array}{ll} \tan\theta = \dfrac{\sin\theta}{\cos\theta} & \csc\theta = \dfrac{1}{\sin\theta} \\ \sec\theta = \dfrac{1}{\cos\theta} & \cot\theta = \dfrac{1}{\tan\theta} \end{array} \qquad (6)$$

whenever the quotients are defined.

Because $x^2 + y^2 = r^2$ (Pythagorean theorem),

$$\cos^2\theta + \sin^2\theta = \frac{x^2}{r^2} + \frac{y^2}{r^2} = \frac{x^2 + y^2}{r^2} = 1. \qquad (7)$$

The equation $\cos^2\theta + \sin^2\theta = 1$, true for all values of θ, is probably the most frequently used identity in trigonometry.

The coordinates of the point $P(x, y)$ in Fig. 1.40 can be expressed in terms of r and θ as

$$\begin{array}{ll} x = r\cos\theta & \text{Because } x/r = \cos\theta \\ y = r\sin\theta & \text{Because } y/r = \sin\theta \end{array} \qquad (8)$$

Using Triangles to Calculate Sines and Cosines

If the circle in Fig. 1.40 has radius $r = 1$, Eqs. (8) simplify to

$$x = \cos\theta, \qquad y = \sin\theta.$$

We can therefore calculate the values of the cosine and sine from the acute reference triangle made by dropping a perpendicular from the point $P(x, y)$ to the x-axis (Fig. 1.41). The numerical values of x and y are read from the triangle's sides. The signs of x and y are determined by the quadrant in which the triangle lies.

EXAMPLE 5 Find the sine and cosine of $2\pi/3$ radians.

Solution

STEP 1: Draw the angle in standard position and write in the lengths of the sides of the reference triangle (Fig. 1.42).

STEP 2: Find the coordinates of the point P where the angle's terminal ray cuts the circle:

$$\cos \frac{2\pi}{3} = x\text{-coordinate of } P = -\frac{1}{2}$$

$$\sin \frac{2\pi}{3} = y\text{-coordinate of } P = \frac{\sqrt{3}}{2}.$$

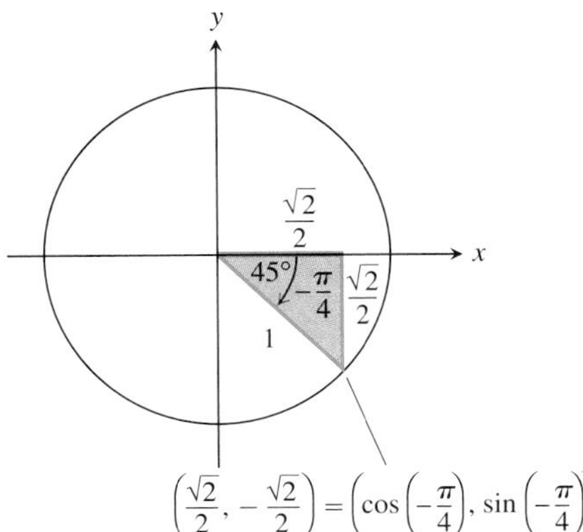

1.43 The triangle for calculating the sine and cosine of $-\pi/4$ radians (Example 6).

EXAMPLE 6 Find the sine and cosine of $-\pi/4$ radians.

Solution

STEP 1: Draw the angle in standard position and write in the lengths of the sides of the reference triangle (Fig. 1.43).

STEP 2: Find the coordinates of the point P where the angle's terminal ray cuts the circle:

$$\cos\left(-\frac{\pi}{4}\right) = x\text{-coordinate of } P = \frac{\sqrt{2}}{2},$$

$$\sin\left(-\frac{\pi}{4}\right) = y\text{-coordinate of } P = -\frac{\sqrt{2}}{2}.$$

Table 1.1 gives the values of the sine, cosine, and tangent for selected values of θ.

TABLE 1.1
Values of $\sin\theta$, $\cos\theta$, and $\tan\theta$ for selected values of θ

Degrees	-180	-135	-90	-45	0	45	90	135	180
θ (radians)	$-\pi$	$-3\pi/4$	$-\pi/2$	$-\pi/4$	0	$\pi/4$	$\pi/2$	$3\pi/4$	π
$\sin\theta$	0	$-\sqrt{2}/2$	-1	$-\sqrt{2}/2$	0	$\sqrt{2}/2$	1	$\sqrt{2}/2$	0
$\cos\theta$	-1	$-\sqrt{2}/2$	0	$\sqrt{2}/2$	1	$\sqrt{2}/2$	0	$-\sqrt{2}/2$	-1
$\tan\theta$	0	1	UND	-1	0	1	UND	-1	0

Graphs

When we graph the six basic trigonometric functions, we usually denote the independent variable by x instead of θ (Fig. 1.44 on the following page). Notice that the graph of $\tan x = (\sin x)/(\cos x)$ "blows up" as x approaches odd-integer multiples of $\pi/2$. Notice the similar behavior of $\cot x = (\cos x)/(\sin x)$ as x approaches integer multiples of π.

Figure 1.45 on the following page shows the graphs of $y = \cos 2x$ and $y = \cos(x/2)$ plotted against the graph of $y = \cos x$. Multiplying x by a number greater than 1 speeds a trigonometric function up and shortens its period (the time for one complete cycle). Multiplying x by a positive number less than 1 slows a trigonometric function down and lengthens its period.

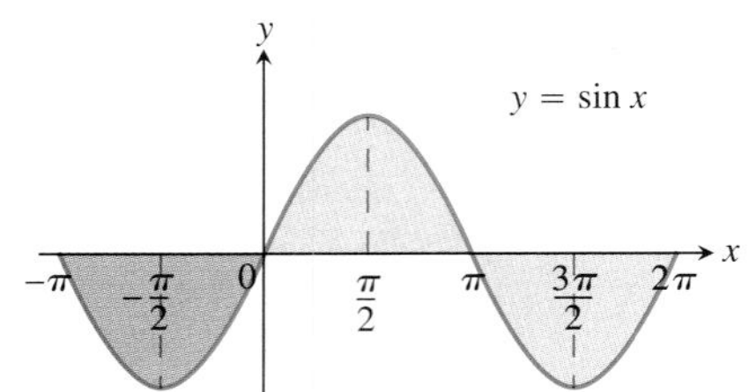

Domain: $-\infty < x < \infty$
Range: $-1 \le y \le 1$

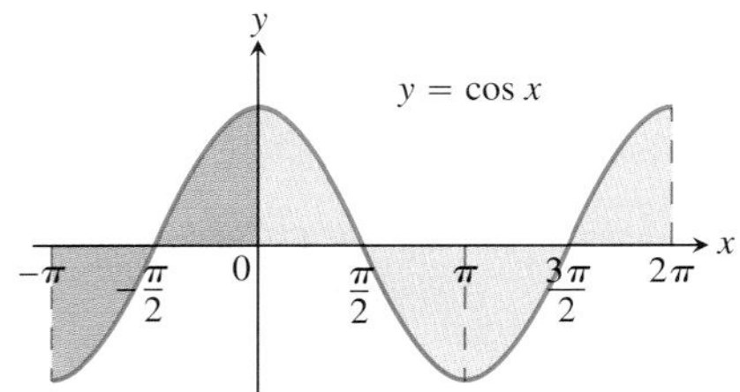

Domain: $-\infty < x < \infty$
Range: $-1 \le y \le 1$

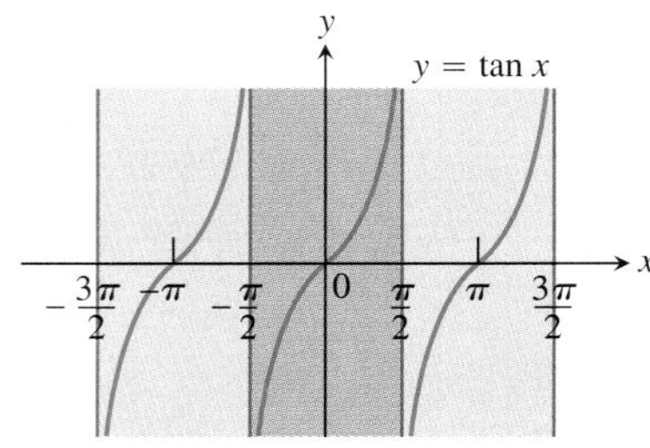

Domain: All real numbers except odd integer multiples of $\pi/2$
Range: $-\infty < y < \infty$

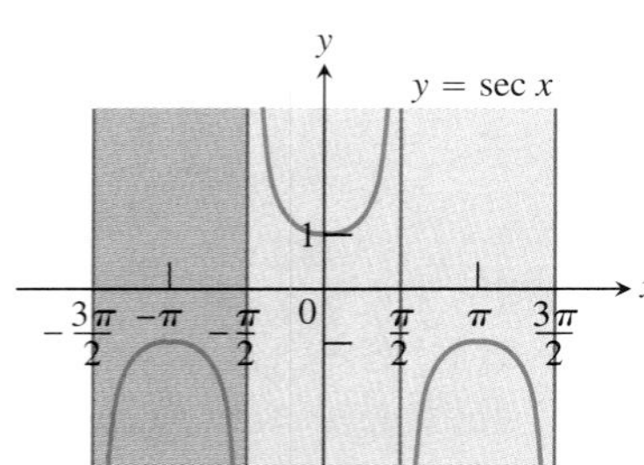

Domain: $x \neq \pm\frac{\pi}{2}, \pm\frac{3\pi}{2}, \ldots$
Range: $y \le -1$ and $y \ge 1$

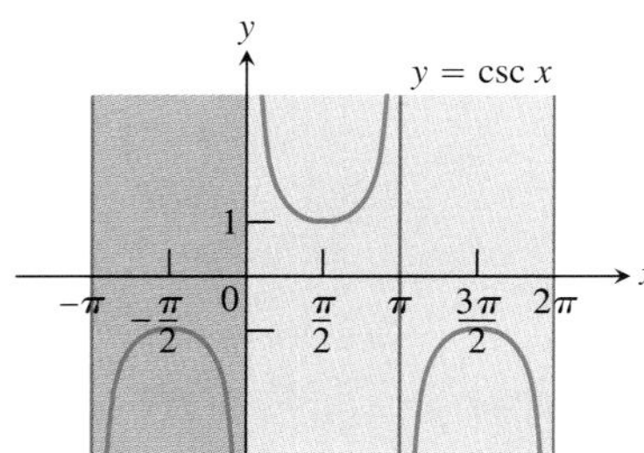

Domain: $x \neq 0, \pm\pi, \pm 2\pi, \ldots$
Range: $y \le -1$ and $y \ge 1$

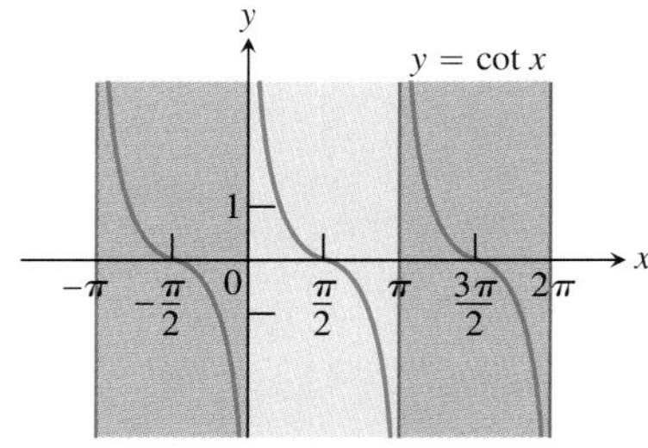

Domain: $x \neq 0, \pm\pi, \pm 2\pi, \ldots$
Range: $-\infty < y < \infty$

1.44 The graphs of the six basic trigonometric functions as functions of radian measure. Each function's periodicity shows clearly in its graph.

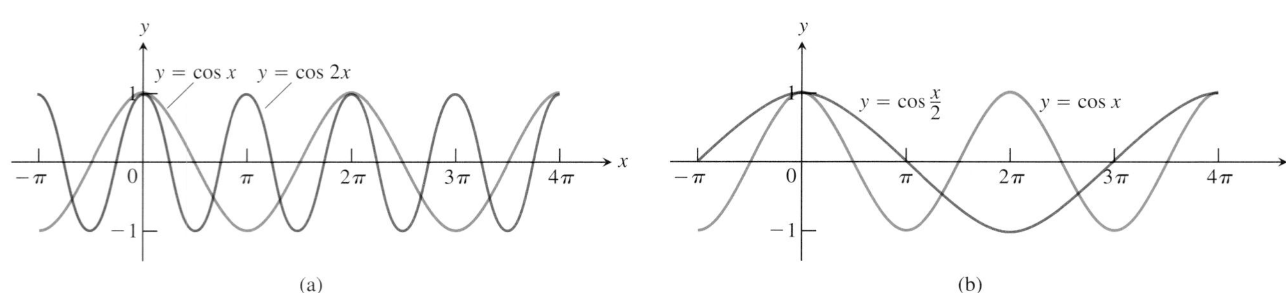

1.45 (a) Multiplying x by 2 speeds the cosine up and shortens the period from 2π to π. (b) Multiplying x by $1/2$ slows the cosine down and lengthens its period from 2π to 4π.

Periodic Functions

Functions like the trigonometric functions whose values repeat at regular intervals are called periodic.

DEFINITION

A function $f(x)$ is **periodic** if there is a positive number p such that, for all x, $f(x+p)=f(x)$. The smallest such value of p is the **period** of f.

As we can see from Fig. 1.44, the sine, cosine, secant, and cosecant functions have period $p = 2\pi$. The tangent and cotangent functions have period $p = \pi$:

Period 2π	Period π	
$\sin(x+2\pi) = \sin x$	$\tan(x+\pi) = \tan x$	
$\cos(x+2\pi) = \cos x$	$\cot(x+\pi) = \cot x$	(9)
$\sec(x+2\pi) = \sec x$		
$\csc(x+2\pi) = \csc x$		

The importance of periodic functions stems from the fact that much of the behavior we study in science is periodic. Brain waves and heartbeats are periodic, as are household voltage and electric current. The electromagnetic field that heats food in a microwave oven is periodic, as are cash flows in seasonal businesses and the behavior of rotational machinery. The seasons are periodic— so is the weather. The phases of the moon are periodic, as are the motions of the planets. There is strong evidence that the ice ages are periodic, with a period of 90,000–100,000 years.

If so many things are periodic, why limit our discussion to trigonometric functions? The answer lies in a surprising and beautiful theorem from advanced calculus that says that every periodic function we want to use in mathematical modeling can be written as an algebraic combination of sines and cosines. Thus, once we learn the calculus of sines and cosines, we will know everything we need to know to model the mathematical behavior of periodic phenomena.

Even vs. Odd

The symmetries in the graphs in Fig. 1.44 reveal that the cosine and secant functions are even and the other four functions are odd:

Even	Odd	
$\cos(-x) = \cos x$	$\sin(-x) = -\sin x$	
$\sec(-x) = \sec x$	$\tan(-x) = -\tan x$	(10)
	$\csc(-x) = -\csc x$	
	$\cot(-x) = -\cot x$	

Angle Sum and Difference Formulas

As you may recall from an earlier course,

$$\cos(A+B) = \cos A\cos B - \sin A\sin B \tag{11}$$

$$\sin(A+B) = \sin A\cos B + \cos A\sin B \tag{12}$$

These formulas hold for all A and B. There are similar formulas for $\cos(A-B)$ and $\sin(A-B)$ (Exercises 39 and 40).

Double-angle (Half-angle) Formulas

It is sometimes possible to simplify a calculation by changing trigonometric functions of θ into trigonometric functions of 2θ. There are four basic formulas for doing this, called **double-angle formulas.** The first two come from setting A and B equal to θ in Eqs. (11) and (12):

$$\cos 2\theta = \cos^2\theta - \sin^2\theta \qquad \text{Eq. (11) with } A = B = \theta \tag{13}$$

$$\sin 2\theta = 2\sin\theta\cos\theta \qquad \text{Eq. (12) with } A = B = \theta \tag{14}$$

The other two double-angle formulas come from the equations

$$\cos^2\theta + \sin^2\theta = 1, \qquad \cos^2\theta - \sin^2\theta = \cos 2\theta.$$

We add to get

$$2\cos^2\theta = 1 + \cos 2\theta,$$

Drawing Lesson

Tip for Graphing sines and cosines: Curve first, scaled axes later

1. The one basic sine and cosine curve:

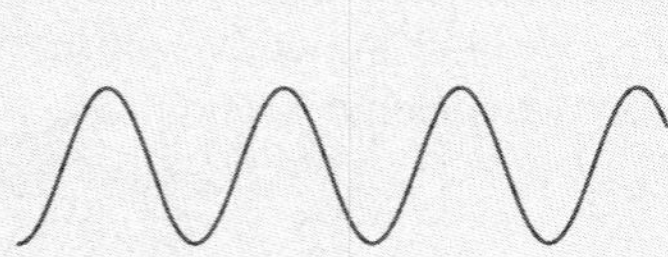

2. The basic curve with appropriately scaled axes in different positions:

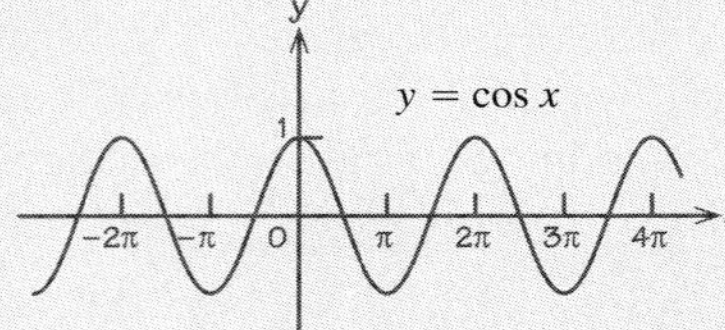

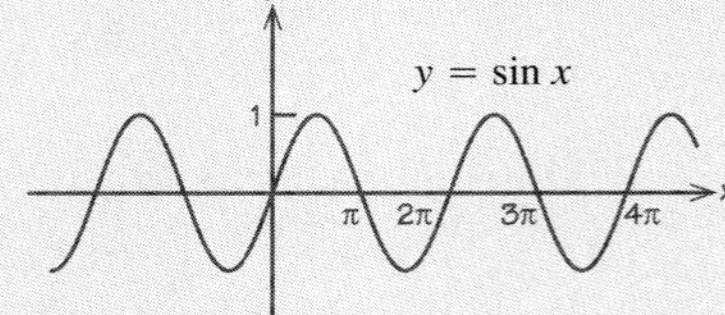

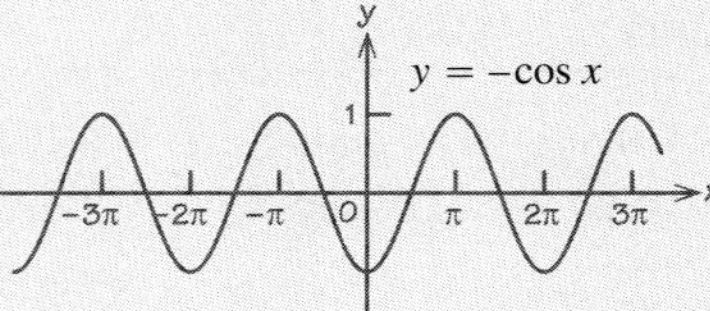

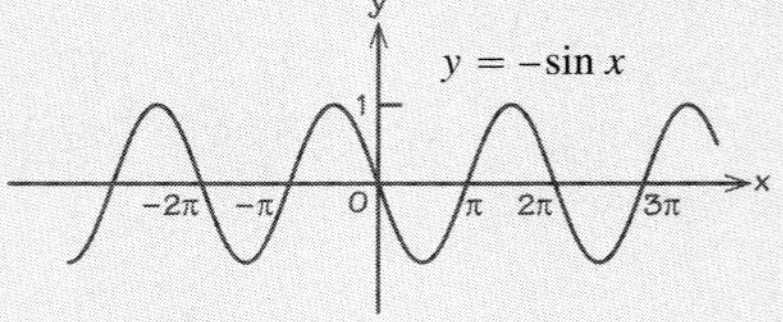

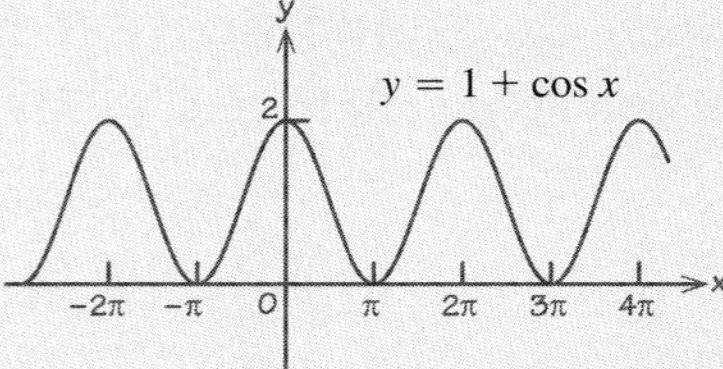

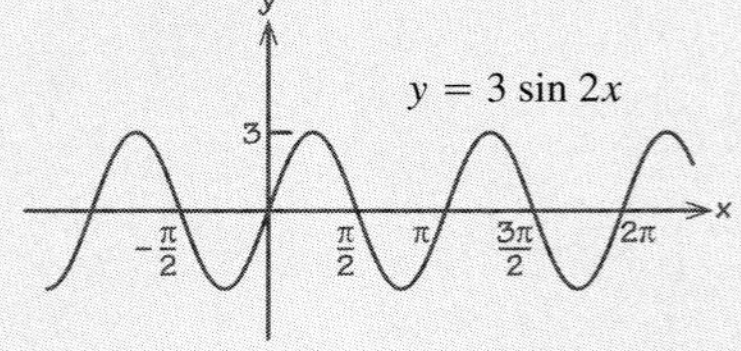

Where to Look for Other Formulas

Additional information is available in Appendix 1 of this book.

subtract to get

$$2\sin^2\theta = 1 - \cos 2\theta,$$

and divide by 2 to get

$$\cos^2\theta = \frac{1+\cos 2\theta}{2} \tag{15}$$

$$\sin^2\theta = \frac{1-\cos 2\theta}{2}. \tag{16}$$

When θ is replaced by $\theta/2$ in Eqs. (15) and (16), the resulting formulas are called **half-angle formulas.** Some books refer to Eqs. (15) and (16) by this name.

Exercises 1.3

Exercises 1 and 2 give angles in degrees. Change them to radians.

1. **a)** 120° **b)** 270° **c)** −60° **d)** −540°

2. **a)** 150° **b)** 405° **c)** −135° **d)** −240°

Exercises 3 and 4 give angles in radians. Change them to degrees.

3. **a)** $\frac{2\pi}{3}$ **b)** $\frac{3\pi}{4}$ **c)** $-\frac{7\pi}{4}$ **d)** $-\frac{7\pi}{2}$

4. **a)** $\frac{5\pi}{4}$ **b)** $\frac{9\pi}{4}$ **c)** $-\frac{3\pi}{2}$ **d)** -4π

5. In a circle of radius 10 m, how long is the arc subtended by a central angle of a) $4\pi/5$ radians? b) 110°?

6. An angle whose vertex lies at the center of a circle of radius 8 subtends an arc of length 10π. Find the angle's radian and degree measures.

7. You want to make an 80° angle by marking an arc on the perimeter of a 12-in.-diameter disk and drawing lines from the ends of the arc to the disk's center. To the nearest tenth of an inch, how long should the arc be?

8. If you roll a 1-m-diameter wheel forward 30 cm over level ground, through what angle will the wheel turn? Answer both in radians (to the nearest tenth) and degrees (to the nearest degree).

9. Copy and complete the following table of function values (θ in radians). If the function is undefined, enter "UND."

θ	$-\pi$	$-2\pi/3$	0	$\pi/2$	$3\pi/4$
$\sin\theta$					
$\cos\theta$					
$\tan\theta$					
$\cot\theta$					
$\sec\theta$					
$\csc\theta$					

10. Copy and complete the following table of function values (θ in radians). If the function is undefined, enter "UND."

θ	$-3\pi/2$	$-\pi/3$	$-\pi/6$	$\pi/4$	$5\pi/6$
$\sin\theta$					
$\cos\theta$					
$\tan\theta$					
$\cot\theta$					
$\sec\theta$					
$\csc\theta$					

Graph the functions in Exercises 11–14 together with the function $y = \sin x$.

11. $y = 2\sin x$ **12.** $y = -\sin x$

13. $y = \sin 2x$ **14.** $y = \sin(x/2)$

Graph the functions in Exercises 15–18 together with the function $y = \cos x$.

15. $y = 2\cos x$ **16.** $y = -2\cos x$

17. $y = \cos 3x$ **18.** $y = \cos(x/3)$

19. Graph $y = \cos x$ and $y = \sec x$ together for $-3\pi/2 \le x \le 3\pi/2$. Comment on the behavior of $\sec x$ in relation to the signs and values of $\cos x$.

20. Graph $y = \sin x$ and $y = \csc x$ together for $-\pi \le x \le 2\pi$. Comment on the behavior of $\csc x$ in relation to the signs and values of $\sin x$.

The formulas in Exercises 21–28 define s as a function of t. Graph the functions in the ts-plane (t-axis horizontal, s-axis vertical). What symmetries do the graphs have?

21. $s = \cot 2t$ **22.** $s = -\tan t$

23. $s = \sec(t/2)$

24. $s = \csc(t/2)$

25. $s = \sin(\pi t)$

26. $s = \cos(\pi t)$

27. $s = \cos\left(\frac{\pi t}{2}\right)$

28. $s = \sin\left(\frac{\pi t}{2}\right)$

29. Graph $y = \sin x$ and $y = \lfloor \sin x \rfloor$ together. What are the domain and range of $\lfloor \sin x \rfloor$?

30. Graph $y = \sin x$ and $y = \lceil \sin x \rceil$ together. What are the domain and range of $\lceil \sin x \rceil$?

31. Consider the function $f(x) = \sqrt{(1 + \cos 2x)/2}$.
   a) How large does $\cos 2x$ become? how small?
   b) How large does $(1 + \cos 2x)/2$ become? how small?
   c) What are the domain and range of f?

32. Consider the function $g(x) = \sqrt{(1 - \cos 2x)/2}$.
   a) How large does $(1 - \cos 2x)/2$ become? how small?
   b) What are the domain and range of g?

Use Eqs. (5) to verify the identities in Exercises 33 and 34.

33. $\sec^2 \theta = 1 + \tan^2 \theta$

34. $\csc^2 \theta = 1 + \cot^2 \theta$

Use the angle sum formulas,

$$\cos(A + B) = \cos A \cos B - \sin A \sin B$$
$$\sin(A + B) = \sin A \cos B + \cos A \sin B$$

to derive the identities in Exercises 35–40.

35. $\cos\left(x - \frac{\pi}{2}\right) = \sin x$

36. $\cos\left(x + \frac{\pi}{2}\right) = -\sin x$

37. $\sin\left(x + \frac{\pi}{2}\right) = \cos x$

38. $\sin\left(x - \frac{\pi}{2}\right) = -\cos x$

39. $\cos(A - B) = \cos A \cos B + \sin A \sin B$

40. $\sin(A - B) = \sin A \cos B - \cos A \sin B$

41. What happens if you take $B = A$ in the identity $\cos(A - B) = \cos A \cos B + \sin A \sin B$? Does the result agree with something you already know?

42. What happens if you take $B = 2\pi$ in the identities

$$\cos(A + B) = \cos A \cos B - \sin A \sin B,$$
$$\sin(A + B) = \sin A \cos B + \cos A \sin B?$$

Do the results agree with something you already know?

43. Evaluate $\cos 15°$ as $\cos(45° - 30°)$.

44. Evaluate $\sin 75°$ as $\sin(45° + 30°)$.

45. Evaluate $\sin \frac{7\pi}{12}$ (radians) as $\sin\left(\frac{\pi}{4} + \frac{\pi}{3}\right)$.

46. Evaluate $\cos \frac{10\pi}{24}$ (radians) as $\cos\left(\frac{\pi}{4} + \frac{\pi}{6}\right)$.

Use double-angle formulas to find the function values in Exercises 47–50 (angles in radians).

47. $\cos^2 \frac{\pi}{8}$

48. $\cos^2 \frac{\pi}{12}$

49. $\sin^2 \frac{\pi}{12}$

50. $\sin^2 \frac{\pi}{8}$

51. *The Tangent Sum Formula.* The standard formula for the tangent of the sum of two angles is

$$\tan(A + B) = \frac{\tan A + \tan B}{1 - \tan A \tan B}.$$

Derive the formula.

52. Derive a formula for $\tan(A - B)$.

Writing for Your Own Knowledge

Answer the following questions in writing. Some answers will take only a sentence or two; others may require several paragraphs. Some explanations may also call for graphs or sketches.

1. What is radian measure?
2. How can you find the values of trigonometric functions from triangles?
3. What is a periodic function?

EXPLORER PROGRAMS

PowerGrapher	Graphs functions singly or together.
Name a Function	Provides practice in matching formulas to graphs.

1.4 *Shifts, Circles, and Parabolas*

This section shows how to change an equation to shift its graph up or down or to the right or left. Knowing about this can help us spot familiar graphs in new locations. It can also help us sketch the graphs of unfamiliar equations more quickly. We practice mostly with circles and parabolas (because they make useful examples in calculus), but the methods apply to other curves as well. We will say more about parabolas and circles in Chapter 10.

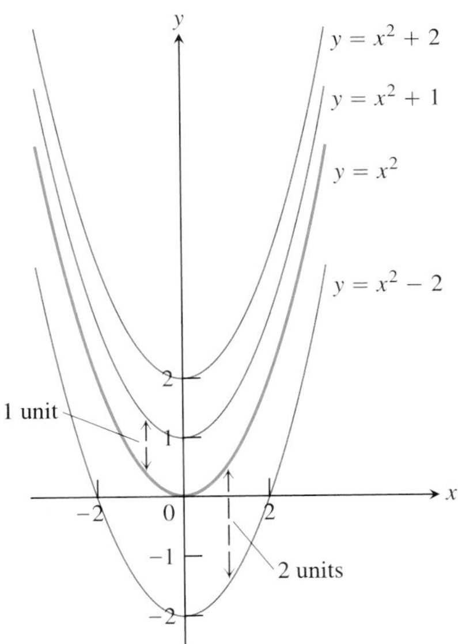

1.46 To shift the graph of $f(x) = x^2$ up (or down), we add positive constants to (or subtract them from) the formula for f.

How to Shift a Graph

To shift the graph of a function $y = f(x)$ straight up, we add a positive constant to the right-hand side of the formula $y = f(x)$.

EXAMPLE 1 Adding 1 to the right-hand side of the formula $y = x^2$ to get $y = x^2 + 1$ shifts the graph up 1 unit (Fig. 1.46).

To shift the graph of a function $y = f(x)$ straight down, we subtract a positive constant from the right-hand side of the formula $y = f(x)$.

EXAMPLE 2 Subtracting 2 from the right-hand side of the formula $y = x^2$ to get $y = x^2 - 2$ shifts the graph down 2 units (Fig. 1.46).

To shift the graph of $y = f(x)$ to the left, we add a positive constant to x.

EXAMPLE 3 Adding 3 to x in $y = x^2$ to get $y = (x + 3)^2$ shifts the graph 3 units to the left (Fig. 1.47).

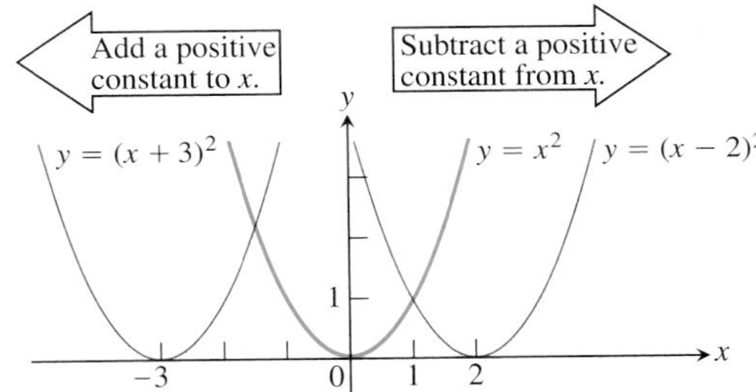

1.47 To shift the graph of $y = x^2$ to the right, we subtract a positive constant from x. To shift the graph to the left, we add a positive constant to x.

To shift the graph of $y = f(x)$ to the right, we subtract a positive constant from x.

EXAMPLE 4 Subtracting 2 from x in $y = x^2$ to get $y = (x - 2)^2$ shifts the graph 2 units to the right (Fig. 1.47).

Shift Formulas

Vertical shifts ($k > 0$)

$y = f(x) + k$	Shifts the graph of f **up** k units
$y = f(x) - k$	Shifts the graph of f **down** k units

Horizontal shifts ($h > 0$)

$y = f(x - h)$	Shifts the graph of f **right** h units
$y = f(x + h)$	Shifts the graph of f **left** h units

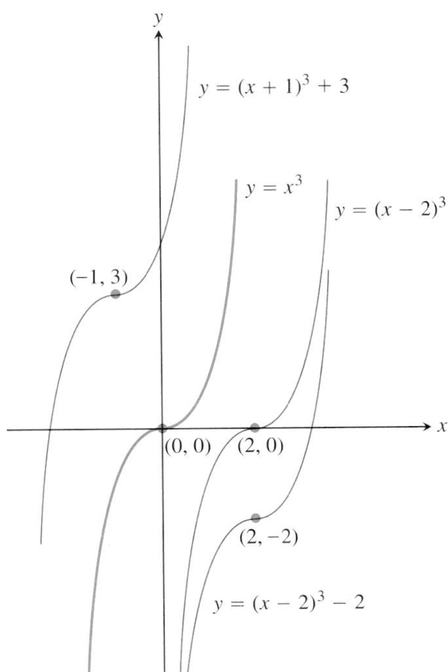

1.48 The graph of $y = x^3$ shifted to three new positions in the xy-plane.

EXAMPLE 5 The graph of $y = (x - 2)^3 - 2$ is the graph of $y = x^3$ shifted 2 units to the right and 2 units down. The graph of $y = (x + 1)^3 + 3$ is the graph of $y = x^3$ shifted 1 unit to the left and 3 units up (Fig. 1.48).

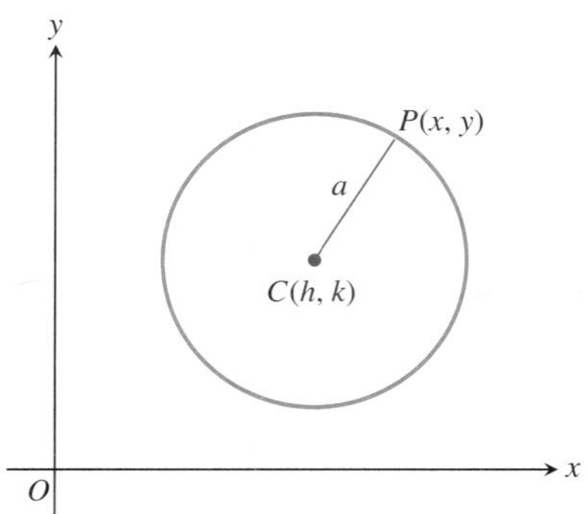

1.49 The standard equation for this circle is $(x - h)^2 + (y - k)^2 = a^2$.

Equations for Circles

As you know, a **circle** is the set of points in a plane whose distance from a given fixed point in the plane is constant. The fixed point is the **center** of the circle; the constant distance is the **radius.** To write an equation for the circle of radius a centered at the point $C(h, k)$, we let $P(x, y)$ denote a typical point on the circle (Fig. 1.49). The length CP equals the radius a, so

$$\sqrt{(x - h)^2 + (y - k)^2} = a \qquad CP = a$$

or

$$(x - h)^2 + (y - k)^2 = a^2. \qquad \text{Both sides squared} \tag{1}$$

The Standard Equation for the Circle of Radius *a* Centered at the Point (*h, k*)

$$(x - h)^2 + (y - k)^2 = a^2 \tag{2}$$

EXAMPLE 6 The standard equation for the circle of radius 2 centered at (3, 4) is

$$(x - 3)^2 + (y - 4)^2 = (2)^2$$

or

$$(x - 3)^2 + (y - 4)^2 = 4.$$

There is no need to square out the x- and y-terms in this equation. In fact, it is better not to do so. The present form reveals the circle's center and radius.

EXAMPLE 7 Find the center and radius of the circle

$$(x - 1)^2 + (y + 5)^2 = 3.$$

Solution Comparing

$$(x - h)^2 + (y - k)^2 = a^2 \qquad \text{with} \qquad (x - 1)^2 + (y + 5)^2 = 3$$

shows that

$$\begin{aligned} -h &= -1 &\quad \text{or} \quad h &= 1 \\ -k &= 5 &\quad \text{or} \quad k &= -5 \\ a^2 &= 3 &\quad \text{or} \quad a &= \sqrt{3}. \end{aligned}$$

The center is the point $(h, k) = (1, -5)$. The radius is $a = \sqrt{3}$.

If an equation for a circle is not in standard form, we can find the circle's center and radius by first converting the equation to standard form. The algebraic technique for doing so is called completing the square (Appendix 1).

EXAMPLE 8 Find the center and radius of the circle

$$x^2 + y^2 + 4x - 6y - 3 = 0.$$

Solution We convert the equation to standard form by completing the squares in x and y:

$x^2 + y^2 + 4x - 6y - 3 = 0$	Start with the given equation.
$(x^2 + 4x \quad) + (y^2 - 6y \quad) = 3$	Gather terms. Move the constant to the right-hand side.
$\left(x^2 + 4x + \left(\frac{4}{2}\right)^2\right) + \left(y^2 - 6y + \left(\frac{-6}{2}\right)^2\right) = 3 + \left(\frac{4}{2}\right)^2 + \left(\frac{-6}{2}\right)^2$	Add the square of half the coefficient of x to each side of the equation. Do the same for y. The parenthetical expressions on the left-hand side are now perfect squares.
$(x^2 + 4x + 4) + (y^2 - 6y + 9) = 3 + 4 + 9$	
$(x + 2)^2 + (y - 3)^2 = 16$	Write each quadratic as a squared linear expression.

With the equation now in standard form, we read off the center's coordinates and the radius: $(h, k) = (-2, 3)$ and $a = 4$.

For circles centered at the origin, h and k are 0 and Eq. (2) simplifies to $x^2 + y^2 = a^2$.

The Standard Equation for the Circle of Radius *a* Centered at the Origin

$$x^2 + y^2 = a^2 \tag{3}$$

The circle of radius 1 unit centered at the origin is called **the unit circle.**

Notice that the circle $(x - h)^2 + (y - k)^2 = a^2$ is the same as the circle $x^2 + y^2 = a^2$ with its center shifted from the origin to the point (h, k). The shift formulas we have been using for graphs of functions apply to equations of any kind. Shifts to the right and up are accomplished by subtracting positive values of h and k from x and y. Shifts to the left and down are accomplished by adding positive values of h and k to x and y.

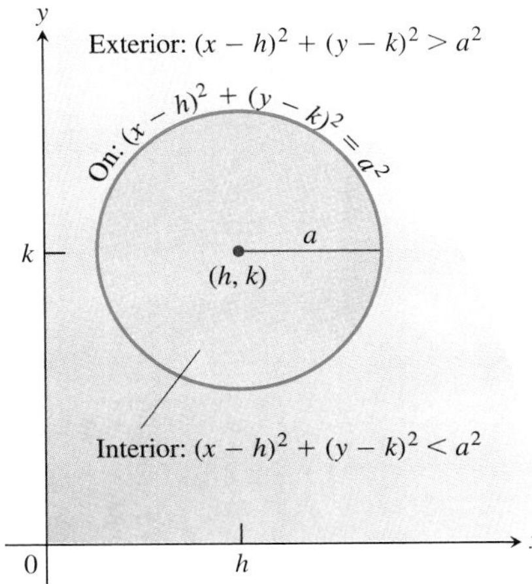

1.50 The interior and exterior of the circle $(x - h)^2 + (y - k)^2 = a^2$.

EXAMPLE 9 If the circle $x^2 + y^2 = 25$ is shifted 2 units to the left and 3 units up, its new equation is $(x + 2)^2 + (y - 3)^2 = 25$. As Eq. (2) says it should be, this is the equation of the circle of radius 5 centered at $(h, k) = (-2, 3)$.

Interior and Exterior

The points that lie inside the circle $(x - h)^2 + (y - k)^2 = a^2$ are the points less than a units from (h, k). They satisfy the inequality

$$(x - h)^2 + (y - k)^2 < a^2. \tag{4}$$

They make up the region we call the **interior** of the circle (Fig. 1.50).

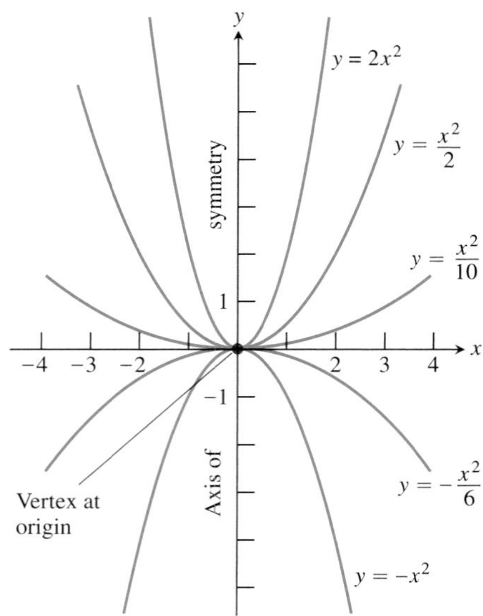

1.51 Besides determining the direction in which the parabola $y = ax^2$ opens, the number a is a scaling factor. The parabola widens as a approaches zero and narrows as a becomes numerically large.

The circle's **exterior** consists of the points that lie more than a units from (h, k). These points satisfy the inequality

$$(x - h)^2 + (y - k)^2 > a^2. \tag{5}$$

EXAMPLE 10

Inequality	Region
$x^2 + y^2 < 1$	Interior of the unit circle
$x^2 + y^2 \leq 1$	Unit circle plus its interior
$x^2 + y^2 > 1$	Exterior of the unit circle
$x^2 + y^2 \geq 1$	Unit circle plus its exterior

Equations for Parabolas

The graph of an equation like $y = 3x^2$ or $y = -5x^2$ that has the form

$$y = ax^2 \tag{6}$$

is a **parabola** whose **axis** (axis of symmetry) is the y-axis. The parabola's **vertex** (point where the parabola and axis cross) lies at the origin. The parabola opens upward if $a > 0$ and downward if $a < 0$. The larger the numerical value of a, the narrower the parabola (Fig. 1.51).

Drawing Lesson

Tip for Drawing Circles: Circle first, axes later

1. The basic shape:

2. The basic shape with axes in different positions:

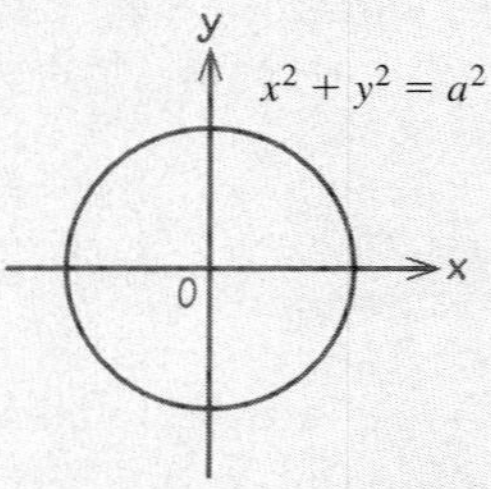

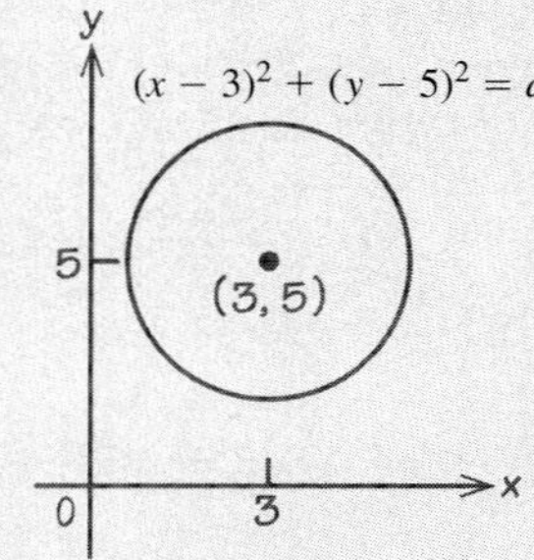

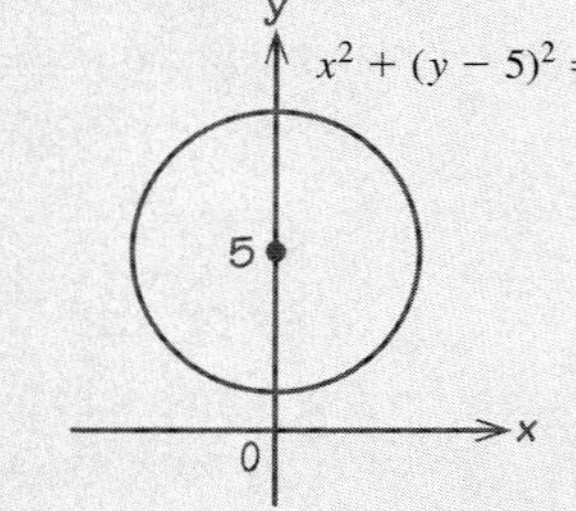

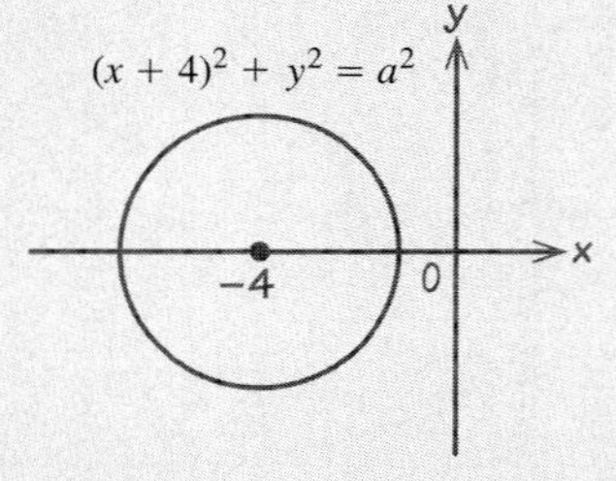

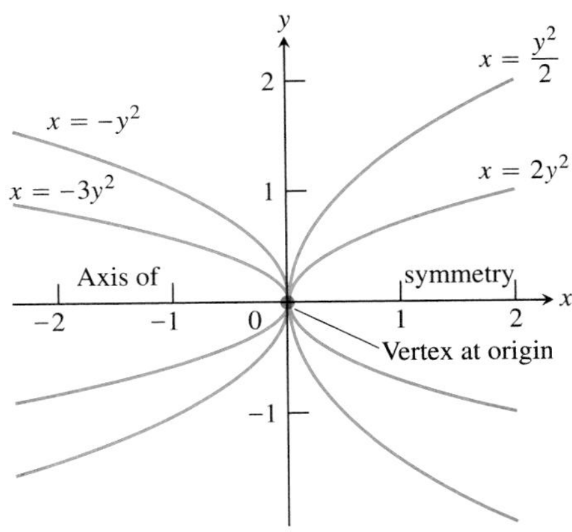

1.52 The parabola $x = ay^2$ is symmetric about the x-axis. It opens to the right if $a > 0$ and to the left if $a < 0$.

If we interchange x and y in the formula $y = ax^2$, we obtain the equation

$$x = ay^2. \tag{7}$$

With the roles of x and y now reversed, the graph is a parabola whose axis is the x-axis and whose vertex lies at the origin (Fig. 1.52).

EXAMPLE 11 The formula $x = y^2$ gives x as a function of y but does *not* give y as a function of x. If we solve for y, we find that $y = \pm\sqrt{x}$. For each positive value of x we get *two* values of y instead of the required single value.

When taken separately, however, the formulas $y = \sqrt{x}$ and $y = -\sqrt{x}$ do define functions of x. Each formula gives exactly one value of y for each possible value of x. The graph of $y = \sqrt{x}$ is the upper half of the parabola $x = y^2$. The graph of $y = -\sqrt{x}$ is the lower half. The two graphs meet at the origin (Fig. 1.53).

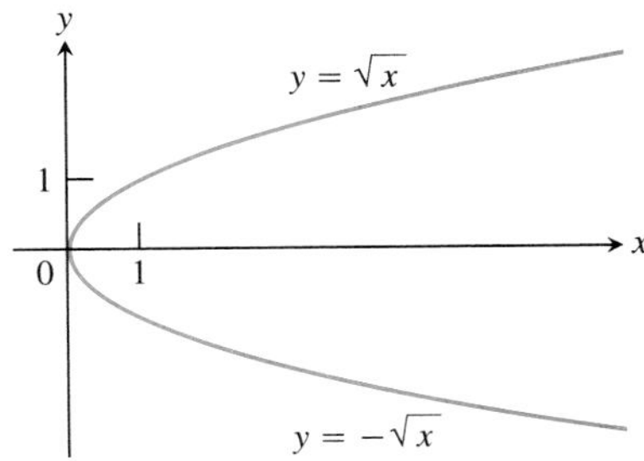

1.53 The graphs of the functions $y = \sqrt{x}$ and $y = -\sqrt{x}$ join at the origin to make the graph of the equation $x = y^2$ (Example 11).

The Equation $y = ax^2 + bx + c$, $a \neq 0$

To shift the parabola $y = ax^2$ horizontally, we rewrite the equation as

$$y = a(x - h)^2. \tag{8}$$

To shift it vertically as well, we change the equation to

$$y = a(x - h)^2 + k. \tag{9}$$

The combined shifts place the vertex at the point (h, k) and the axis along the line $x = h$ (Fig. 1.54).

Normally there would be no point in squaring out the right-hand side of Eq. (9). In this case, however, we can learn something from doing so because the resulting equation, when rearranged, takes the form

$$y = ax^2 + bx + c. \tag{10}$$

This tells us that the graph of every equation of the form $y = ax^2 + bx + c$, $a \neq 0$, is the graph of $y = ax^2$ shifted somewhere else. Why? Because the steps that take us from Eq. (9) to Eq. (10) can be reversed to take us from (10) back to (9). The curve $y = ax^2 + bx + c$ has exactly the same shape and orientation as the curve $y = ax^2$.

The axis of the parabola $y = ax^2 + bx + c$ turns out to be the line $x = -b/(2a)$. The y-intercept is $(0, c)$, obtained by setting $x = 0$.

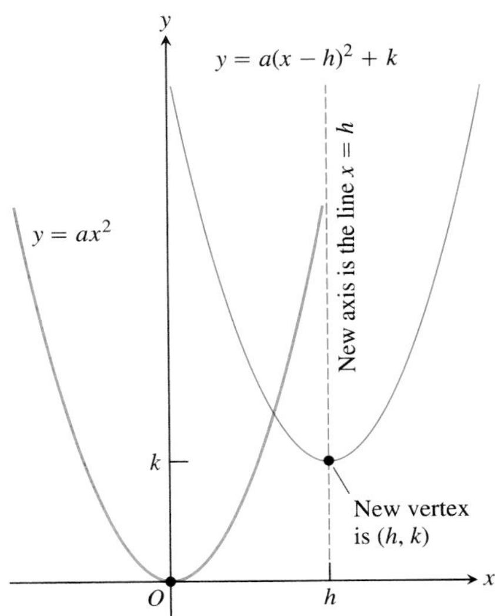

1.54 The parabola $y = ax^2$, $a > 0$, shifted h units to the right and k units up.

The Graph of $y = ax^2 + bx + c$, $a \neq 0$

The graph of $y = ax^2 + bx + c$, $a \neq 0$, is a parabola. The parabola opens upward if $a > 0$ and downward if $a < 0$. The points on its axis, including the vertex, satisfy the equation

$$x = -\frac{b}{2a}. \tag{11}$$

The y-intercept is the point $(0, c)$.

EXAMPLE 12 *Graphing a Parabola.* Sketch the curve $y = -\frac{1}{2}x^2 - x + 4$.

Solution We take the following steps.

STEP 1: *Compare the given equation with the formula $y = ax^2 + bx + c$ to identify a, b, and c.*

$$a = -\frac{1}{2}, \qquad b = -1, \qquad c = 4$$

STEP 2: *Find the direction of opening.* Down, because $a < 0$

STEP 3: *Find the axis and vertex.* The axis of symmetry is the line

$$x = -\frac{b}{2a} = -\frac{(-1)}{2(-1/2)} = -1. \qquad \text{Eq. (11)}$$

The number $x = -1$ is also the x-coordinate of the vertex. We find the y-coordinate of the vertex by substituting $x = -1$ in the parabola's equation.

$$\begin{aligned} y &= -\frac{1}{2}x^2 - x + 4 && \text{Given equation} \\ &= -\frac{1}{2}(-1)^2 - (-1) + 4 && x = -1 \\ &= -\frac{1}{2} + 1 + 4 = \frac{9}{2} \end{aligned}$$

The vertex is $(-1, 9/2)$.

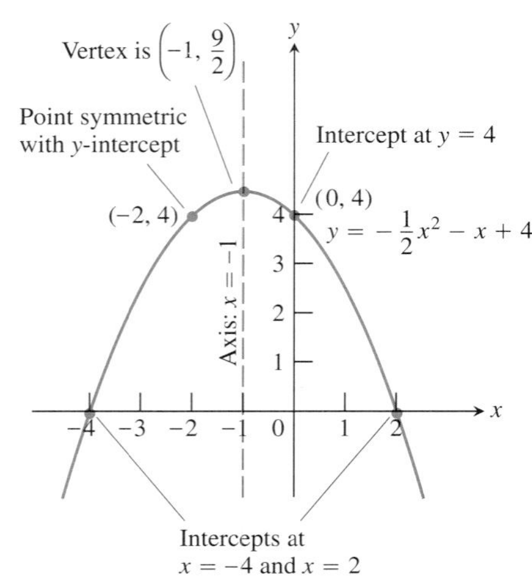

1.55 The parabola in Example 12.

STEP 4: *Find the y-intercept.* $(0, c) = (0, 4)$

STEP 5: *Find the x-intercepts, if any.*

$$\begin{aligned} -\frac{1}{2}x^2 - x + 4 &= 0 && \text{Set } y = 0 \text{ in the parabola's equation} \\ x^2 + 2x - 8 &= 0 && \text{Solve as usual} \\ (x - 2)(x + 4) &= 0 \\ x = 2, \quad x &= -4 \end{aligned}$$

The x-intercepts are $(-4, 0)$ and $(2, 0)$.

STEP 6: *Graph the parabola.* We plot the points, sketch the axis (lightly), and use what we know about symmetry and the direction of opening to complete the sketch (Fig. 1.55).

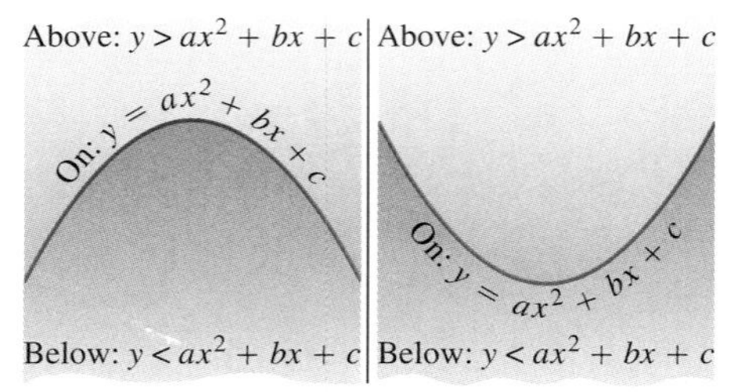

1.56 The inequalities describing the regions above and below the parabola $y = ax^2 + bx + c$, $a \neq 0$.

The Regions Above and Below $y = ax^2 + bx + c$, $a \neq 0$

We can describe the regions into which the parabola separates the plane with the following inequalities (Fig. 1.56).

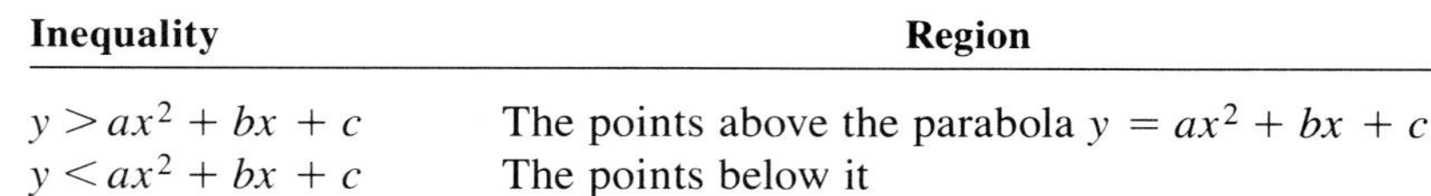

Inequality	Region
$y > ax^2 + bx + c$	The points above the parabola $y = ax^2 + bx + c$
$y < ax^2 + bx + c$	The points below it

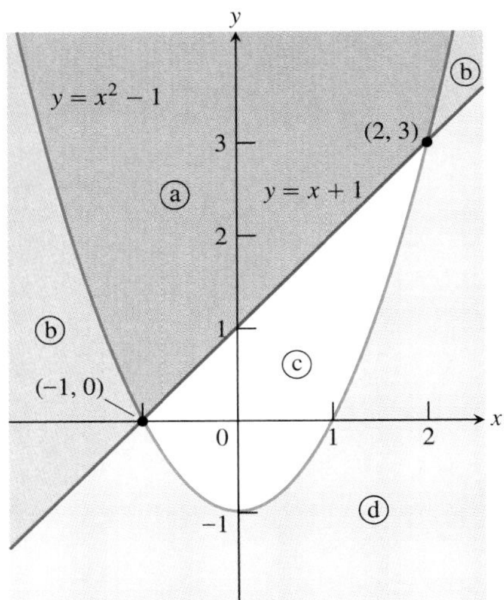

1.57 The curves and regions in Example 13.

EXAMPLE 13 Find the points in which the line $y = x + 1$ crosses the parabola $y = x^2 - 1$. Then graph the line and parabola together and describe the regions defined by the following pairs of inequalities.

a) $y > x + 1$ and $y > x^2 - 1$ **b)** $y > x + 1$ and $y < x^2 - 1$

c) $y < x + 1$ and $y > x^2 - 1$ **d)** $y < x + 1$ and $y < x^2 - 1$

Solution We find the x-coordinates of the points of intersection by solving the equations $y = x + 1$ and $y = x^2 - 1$ simultaneously for x:

$$x^2 - 1 = x + 1 \quad \text{Equate}$$

$$x^2 - x - 2 = 0 \quad \text{Transpose}$$

$$(x + 1)(x - 2) = 0 \quad \text{Factor}$$

$$x = -1, \quad x = 2 \quad \text{Solve}$$

The corresponding y-values (found by substituting in either equation) are $y = 0$ and $y = 3$. The points of intersection are $(-1, 0)$ and $(2, 3)$.

The parabola and line are graphed in Fig. 1.57. The regions defined by the inequalities are these:

Inequalities	Verbal description
a) $y > x + 1$ and $y > x^2 - 1$	The points above the line and above the parabola
b) $y > x + 1$ and $y < x^2 - 1$	The points above the line and below the parabola
c) $y < x + 1$ and $y > x^2 - 1$	The points below the line and above the parabola
d) $y < x + 1$ and $y < x^2 - 1$	The points below the line and below the parabola

Exercises 1.4

1. Figure 1.58 shows the graph of $y = -x^2$ shifted to two new positions. Write equations for the new graphs.

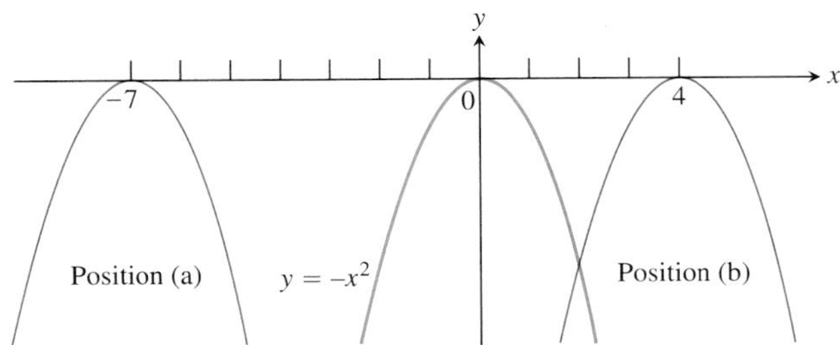

1.58 The parabolas in Exercise 1.

2. Figure 1.59 shows the graph of $y = x^2$ shifted to two new positions. Write equations for the new graphs.

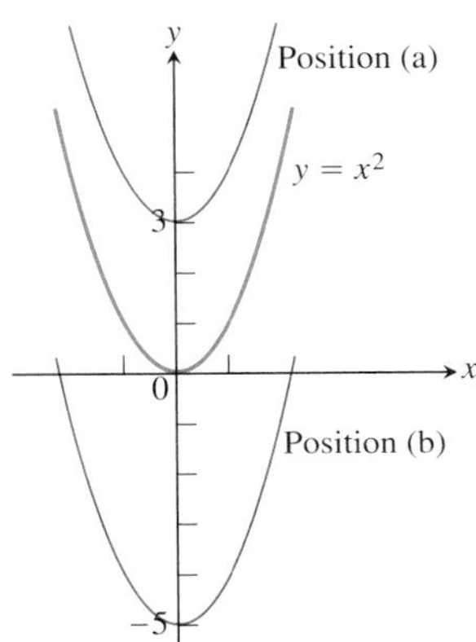

1.59 The parabolas in Exercise 2.

3. Match the equations listed in (a)–(d) to the graphs in Fig. 1.60.

a) $y = (x-1)^2 - 4$ b) $y = (x-2)^2 + 2$
c) $y = (x+2)^2 + 2$ d) $y = (x+3)^2 - 2$

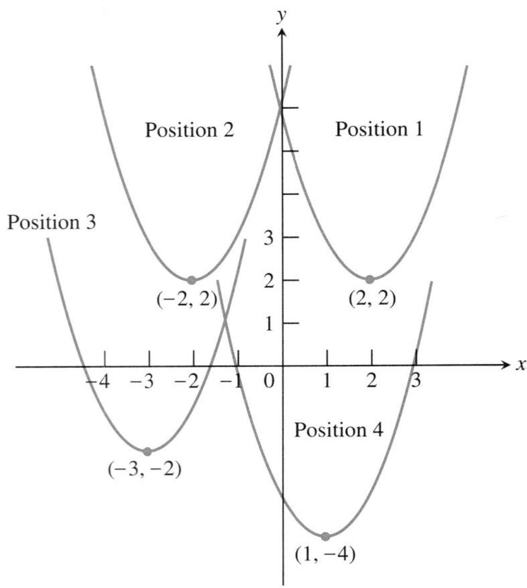

1.60 The parabolas in Exercise 3.

4. Figure 1.61 shows the graph of $y = -x^2$ shifted to four new positions. Write an equation for each new graph.

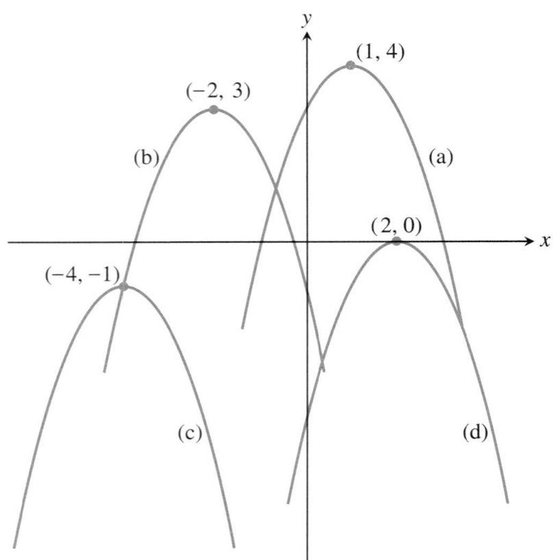

1.61 The parabolas in Exercise 4.

Write equations for the circles in Exercises 5–8.

5.

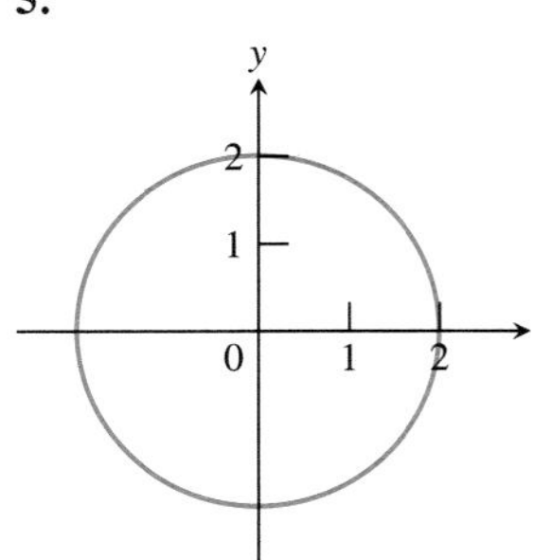

6.

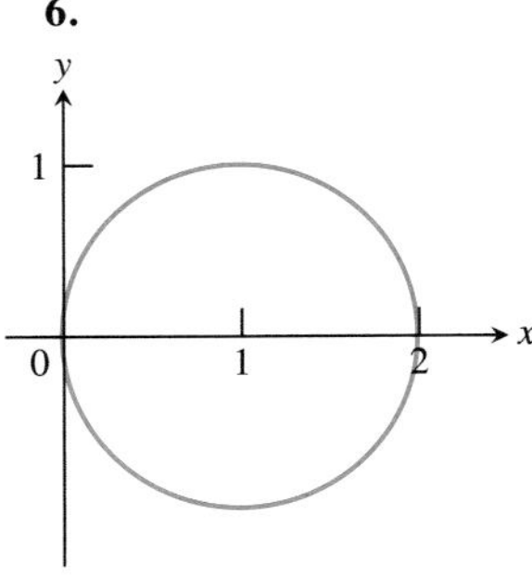

7.

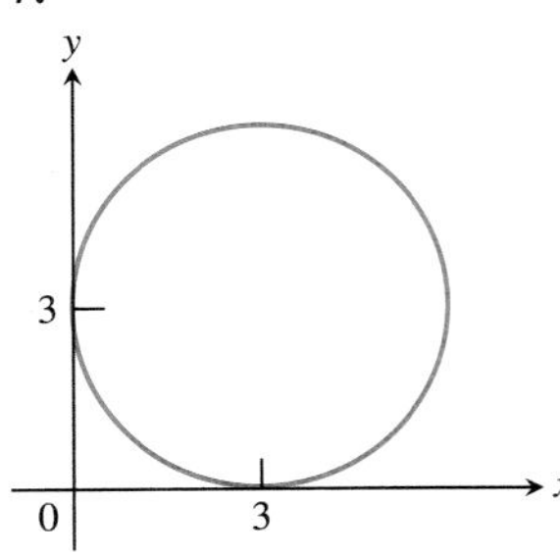

8.

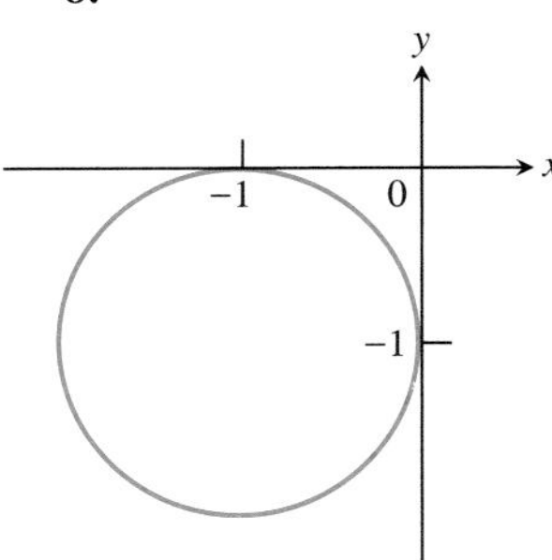

In Exercises 9–14, find an equation for the circle with the given center $C(h, k)$ and radius a. Then sketch the circle in the xy-plane. Include the circle's center in your sketch. Also, label the circle's x- and y-intercepts, if any, with their coordinate pairs.

9. $C(0, 2)$, $a = 2$
10. $C(-3, 0)$, $a = 3$
11. $C(-1, 5)$, $a = 3/2$
12. $C(1, 1)$, $a = \sqrt{2}$
13. $C(-\sqrt{3}, -2)$, $a = 2$
14. $C(3, 1/2)$, $a = 5$

Exercises 15–26 tell how many units and in what directions the graphs of the given equations are to be shifted. Give an equation for the shifted graph in each case. Then sketch the original and shifted graphs together, labeling each graph with its equation. Use the graphs in Fig. 1.28 for reference as needed.

15. $x^2 + y^2 = 49$ Down 3, left 2
16. $x^2 + y^2 = 25$ Up 3, left 4
17. $y = x^3$ Left 1, down 1
18. $y = x^{2/3}$ Right 1, down 1
19. $y = \sqrt{x}$ Left 0.81
20. $y = -\sqrt{x}$ Right 3
21. $y = 2x - 7$ Up 7
22. $y = \frac{1}{2}(x+1) + 5$ Down 5, right 1
23. $x = y^2$ Left 1
24. $x = -3y^2$ Up 2, right 3

25. $y = 1/x$ Up 1, right 1

26. $y = 1/x^2$ Left 2, down 1

In Exercises 27–46, find the function's domain and range. Then graph the function. Use the graphs in Fig. 1.28 for reference as needed.

27. $y = \sqrt{x + 4}$

28. $y = \sqrt{x - 2}$

29. $y = \sqrt{4 - x}$

30. $y = \sqrt{9 - x}$

31. $y = 1 + \sqrt{x - 1}$

32. $y = 1 - \sqrt{x}$

33. $y = (x + 1)^{2/3}$

34. $y = (x - 8)^{2/3}$

35. $y = 1 - x^{2/3}$

36. $y + 4 = x^{2/3}$

37. $y = \sqrt[3]{x - 1} - 1$

38. $y = (x + 2)^{3/2} + 1$

39. $y = \dfrac{1}{x - 2}$

40. $y = \dfrac{1}{x} - 2$

41. $y = \dfrac{1}{x} + 2$

42. $y = \dfrac{1}{x + 2}$

43. $y = \dfrac{1}{(x - 1)^2}$

44. $y = \dfrac{1}{x^2} - 1$

45. $y = \dfrac{1}{x^2} + 1$

46. $y = \dfrac{1}{(x + 1)^2}$

Graph the functions in Exercises 47–50.

47. $y = \sin\left(x + \dfrac{\pi}{2}\right)$

48. $y = \sin\left(x - \dfrac{\pi}{2}\right)$

49. $y = \cos\left(x - \dfrac{\pi}{2}\right)$

50. $y = \cos\left(x + \dfrac{\pi}{2}\right)$

Graph the circles whose equations are given in Exercises 51–56. Label each circle's center and intercepts (if any) with their coordinate pairs. What inequality is satisfied by the coordinates of the points that lie inside the circle?

51. $x^2 + y^2 + 4x - 4y + 4 = 0$

52. $x^2 + y^2 - 8x + 4y + 16 = 0$

53. $x^2 + y^2 - 3y - 4 = 0$

54. $x^2 + y^2 - 4x - (9/4) = 0$

55. $x^2 + y^2 - 4x + 4y = 0$

56. $x^2 + y^2 + 2x = 3$

Graph the parabolas in Exercises 57–64. Label the vertex, axis, and intercepts in each case.

57. $y = x^2 - 2x - 3$

58. $y = x^2 + 4x + 3$

59. $y = -x^2 + 4x$

60. $y = -x^2 + 4x - 5$

61. $y = -x^2 - 6x - 5$

62. $y = 2x^2 - x + 3$

63. $y = \dfrac{1}{2}x^2 + x + 4$

64. $y = -\dfrac{1}{4}x^2 + 2x + 4$

65. Graph the parabola $y = x - x^2$. Then find the domain and range of $f(x) = \sqrt{x - x^2}$.

66. Graph the parabola $y = 3 - 2x - x^2$. Then find the domain and range of $g(x) = \sqrt{3 - 2x - x^2}$.

In Exercises 67 and 68, sketch the regions defined by the given inequalities. Describe each region in words.

67. **a)** $x^2 + y^2 > 1$
    b) $x^2 + y^2 < 4$
    c) the inequalities in (a) and (b) together

68. **a)** $x^2 + y^2 \geq 4$
    b) $x^2 + y^2 \leq 9$
    c) the inequalities in (a) and (b) together

In Exercises 69 and 70, graph the line and parabola together and label their points of intersection. Then identify the regions defined by the pairs of inequalities. Describe each region in words.

69. Line: $y = -x + 3$, Parabola: $y = x^2 + 1$
    a) $y > -x + 3$ and $y > x^2 + 1$
    b) $y > -x + 3$ and $y < x^2 + 1$
    c) $y < -x + 3$ and $y > x^2 + 1$
    d) $y < -x + 3$ and $y < x^2 + 1$

70. Line: $y = x - 1$, Parabola: $y = 1 - x^2$
    a) $y > x - 1$ and $y > 1 - x^2$
    b) $y > x - 1$ and $y < 1 - x^2$
    c) $y < x - 1$ and $y > 1 - x^2$
    d) $y < x - 1$ and $y < 1 - x^2$

In Exercises 71 and 72, graph the two parabolas together and label their points of intersection. Then identify the regions defined by the pairs of inequalities. Describe each region in words.

71. Parabolas: $y = x^2$ and $y = 2 - x^2$
    a) $y > x^2$ and $y > 2 - x^2$
    b) $y > x^2$ and $y < 2 - x^2$
    c) $y < x^2$ and $y > 2 - x^2$
    d) $y < x^2$ and $y < 2 - x^2$

72. Parabolas: $y = 4 - 4x^2$ and $y = x^2 - 1$
    a) $y > 4 - 4x^2$ and $y > x^2 - 1$
    b) $y > 4 - 4x^2$ and $y < x^2 - 1$
    c) $y < 4 - 4x^2$ and $y > x^2 - 1$
    d) $y < 4 - 4x^2$ and $y < x^2 - 1$

73. The line $y = mx$ is shifted horizontally and vertically to make it pass through the point (x_0, y_0). What is the line's new equation? What is special about this equation?

74. The line $y = mx$ is shifted vertically to make it pass through the point $(0, b)$. What is the line's new equation? What is special about this equation?

THE TRANS-ALASKA PIPELINE

The builders of the Trans-Alaska Pipeline used insulated pads to keep the heat from the hot oil in the pipeline from melting the permanently frozen soil beneath. To design the pads, it was necessary to take into account the variation in air temperature throughout the year. The variation was represented in the calculations by a *general sine function* of the form

$$f(x) = A \sin\left(\frac{2\pi}{B}(x - C)\right) + D,$$

where $|A|$ is the *amplitude*, $|B|$ is the *period*, C is the *horizontal shift*, and D is the *vertical shift* (Fig. 1.62).

Figure 1.63 shows how we can use such a function to represent temperature data. The data points in the figure are plots of the mean air temperature for Fairbanks, Alaska, based on records of the National Weather Service from 1941 to 1970. The sine function used to fit the data is

$$f(x) = 37 \sin\left(\frac{2\pi}{365}(x - 101)\right) + 25,$$

where f is temperature in degrees Fahrenheit and x is the number of the day counting from the beginning of the year. The fit is remarkably good.

75. *Temperature in Fairbanks, Alaska.* Find the (a) amplitude, (b) period, (c) horizontal shift, and (d) vertical shift of the general sine function

$$f(x) = 37 \sin\left(\frac{2\pi}{365}(x - 101)\right) + 25.$$

76. *Temperature in Fairbanks, Alaska.* Use the equation in Exercise 75 to approximate the answers to the following questions about the temperature in Fairbanks, Alaska, shown in Fig. 1.63. Assume that the year has 365 days.

a) What are the highest and lowest mean daily temperatures shown?

b) What is the average of the highest and lowest mean daily temperatures shown? Why is this average the vertical shift of the function?

Writing for Your Own Knowledge

Answer the following questions in writing. Some answers will take only a sentence or two; others may require several paragraphs. Some explanations may also call for graphs or sketches.

1. How do you change the equation $y = f(x)$ to shift its graph up or down? Give examples.
2. How do you change the equation $y = f(x)$ to shift its graph to the left or right? Give examples.
3. Describe the steps you would take to graph the circle $x^2 + y^2 + 4x - 6y + 12 = 0$.
4. If a, b, and c are constants, and $a \neq 0$, what can you say about the graph of the equation $y = ax^2 + bx + c$? In particular, how would you go about sketching the curve $y = 2x^2 + 4x$?

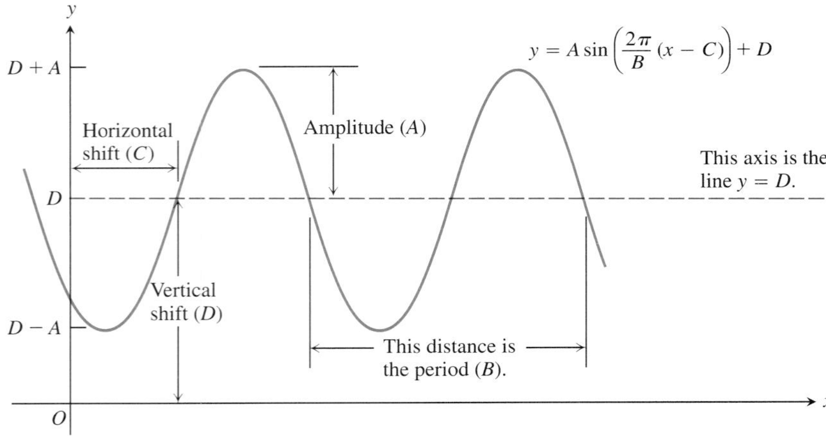

1.62 The general sine curve for A, B, C, and D positive.

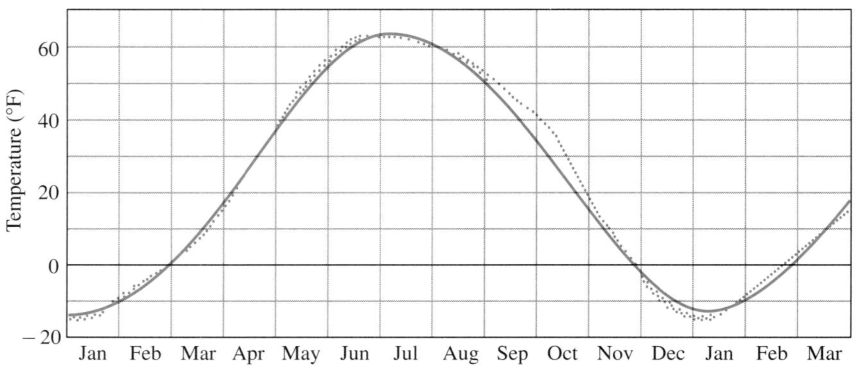

1.63 Normal mean air temperature at Fairbanks, Alaska, plotted as data points. The approximating sine function is

$$f(x) = 37 \sin\left(\frac{2\pi}{365}(x - 101)\right) + 25.$$

(*Source:* "Is the Curve of Temperature Variation a Sine Curve?" by B. M. Lando and C. A. Lando, *The Mathematics Teacher,* 7:6, Fig. 2, p. 535 [September 1977].)

1.5 Calculus and Computation

In this section we look at functions on a scientific calculator, including e^x, $\ln x$, and some of the trigonometric functions. We also discuss how to use a calculator to explore various properties of functions, such as the possibility that two functions are equal or differ by a constant value. We encounter a mysterious pattern (that will be explained later by calculus) and explore the way Fermat wanted to use slopes of lines to define slopes of curves.

Evaluating Functions

Calculators enable us to evaluate most functions in calculus to six or more decimal places with only a few key presses. Calculators work with either algebraic notation or reverse Polish notation. Here are two typical calculations.

EXAMPLE 1 *Algebraic Notation.* To find the sine of 2 radians on a Casio fx-7700G, set the calculator in radian mode and press [SIN] [2] [EXE].

Key	Operation	Display
[SIN]	Choose the function.	SIN
[2]	Enter the input value.	SIN 2
[EXE]	Execute the calculation.	0.9092 97426 8

On another algebraic machine, the appropriate key sequence might be [SIN] [2] [=] or simply [2] [SIN]. There can be quite a bit of variation.

EXAMPLE 2 *Reverse Polish Notation.* To find the sine of 2 radians on an HP 28S, set the calculator in radian mode and press [2] [ENTER] [SIN].

Key	Operation	Display
[2]	Put 2 in the command line.	2
[ENTER]	Enter it in stack level 1.	2
[SIN]	Find the sine of the number in stack level 1.	0.9092 97426 826

Questions of Accuracy

Although machines can calculate only the first few digits of an infinite decimal like

$$\sin 2 = 0.9092\ 97426\ 826\ldots,$$

they give estimates to more decimal places than most printed tables. Calculators are also easier to carry and faster to use than tables.

However, there is something to watch out for. When our inputs require the calculator to do arithmetic with numbers that are very small or very large, the errors associated with rounding and truncation (clipping without rounding) may produce a sizable error in the final result. Sometimes we can avoid round-off and truncation errors by restructuring the calculation. For example, suppose we want to evaluate the quotient

$$Q = \frac{\dfrac{1}{x+h} - \dfrac{1}{x}}{h} \tag{1}$$

when $x = 0.7$ and $h = 10^{-8}$. (We will see why we might want to do this when we get to Chapter 3.) A direct evaluation on one particular calculator gives

$$\begin{aligned} Q &= \frac{1.4285\ 71408\ 8 - 1.4285\ 71429}{10^{-8}} \\ &= -\frac{0.0000\ 00021}{10^{-8}} = -2.1. \end{aligned} \tag{2}$$

The numbers originally in the numerator of Q are precise to 9 digits, but their difference is precise to only 2 digits. We get a bad cancellation and a relatively imprecise answer.

This is not the calculator's fault but rather a consequence of how we structured the calculation. We get a much better result if we combine the fractions in the numerator of Q before we calculate, to get

$$Q = \frac{1}{h}\left(\frac{x-(x+h)}{(x+h)x}\right) = \frac{1}{h}\left(\frac{-h}{(x+h)x}\right) = -\frac{1}{(x+h)x}. \tag{3}$$

Now evaluation gives

$$Q = -\frac{1}{(0.7+10^{-8})(0.7)} = -2.0408\ 16297, \tag{4}$$

which is correct to 10 digits. If we just subtract, as we did in Eq. (2), we lose 8 digits and cannot hope to be anywhere near right.

Occasionally, the errors we encounter are an unavoidable consequence of how a particular calculator works. When we evaluated the tangent of 89.99999° on three popular models, we got three different answers:

Calculator A:	tan 89.99999° = 57295 45
Calculator B:	tan 89.99999° = 57295 77
Calculator C:	tan 89.99999° = 57295 80

Only calculator B returned an answer that was correct in all 7 digits.

When functions lack simple evaluation formulas, calculator designers are forced to generate the function's values with approximations. It is sometimes hard to find an approximation routine that works equally well at all points in a function's domain. A routine that returns accurate results most of the time may have problems when the function begins to take on extreme values, as the tangent does near 90°. There is usually more than one routine available, and choosing among them requires decisions about speed, accuracy, and hardware cost. The designers of calculators A, B, and C obviously chose in different ways.

In this book, we will not ask for calculations that push machines toward the edge of their ability, unless the purpose of the exercise is to reveal the risk of attempting a particular kind of calculation.

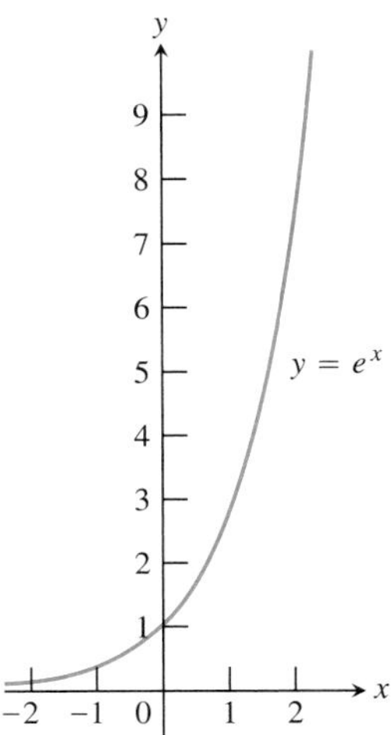

1.64 The graph of $y = e^x$.
Domain: $-\infty < x < \infty$
Range: $y > 0$

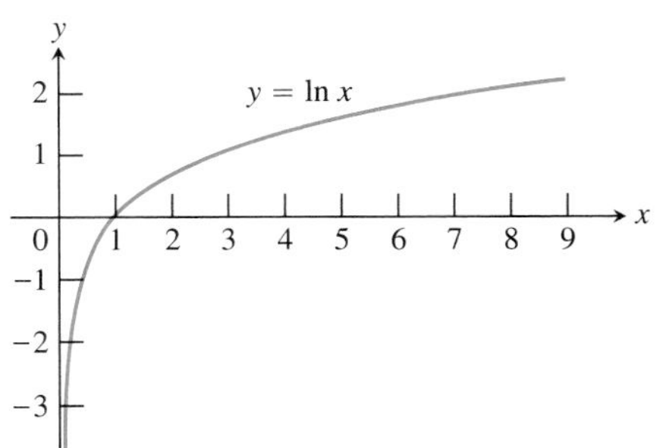

1.65 The graph of $y = \ln x$.
Domain: $x > 0$
Range: $-\infty < y < \infty$

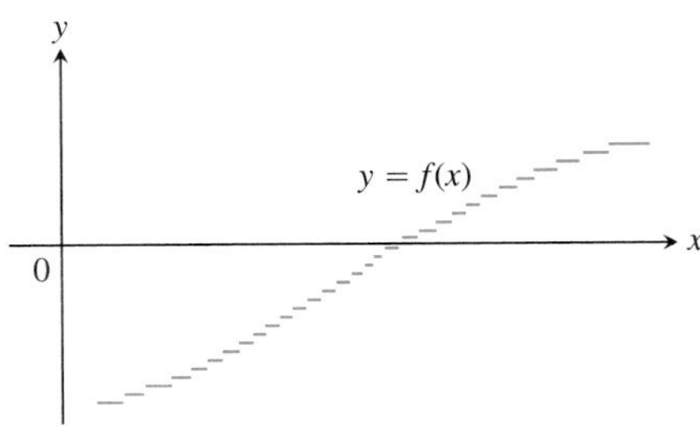

1.66 The graph of f steps across the axis without touching it. Hence, f changes from negative to positive without becoming zero in between. The equation $f(x) = 0$ has no solution.

Exponential and Logarithmic Functions

In addition to having keys for trigonometric functions and functions like x^2, $\sqrt{x}$, and $1/x$, scientific calculators have keys for

e^x	(the exponential function e to the x),
$\ln x$	(the natural logarithm of x),
$\log x$	(the base-10 logarithm of x).

The number e is about 2.7 1828 1828. The graphs of $y = e^x$ and $y = \ln x$ are shown in Figs. 1.64 and 1.65. Since $\log x = (\ln x)/\ln 10$, as we will explain later in the book, the graph of $\log x$ is just a scaled-down version of the graph of $\ln x$. We will study these and a number of other so-called transcendental functions in Chapter 6.

As you look at Figs. 1.64 and 1.65, notice the difference in the rates at which e^x and $\ln x$ grow as x increases. The function e^x grows rapidly—exponentially, in fact (which is where the adverb comes from). As we will see, e^x eventually outgrows any power of x, even $x^{1{,}000{,}000}$, as x increases. In contrast, the natural logarithm $\ln x$ eventually grows more slowly as x increases than any fractional power of x, even $x^{1/1{,}000{,}000}$. As we will see in Chapter 6, the functions e^x and $\ln x$ provide the standards by which we measure the growth rates of other functions.

Solving Equations

Calculus provides the mathematical justification for many of the things we do with a calculator, including the ways we solve equations.

The solutions of an equation $f(x) = 0$ are the x-coordinates of the points where the graph of the equation $y = f(x)$ touches or crosses the x-axis. On a graphing calculator we can try to find these points by displaying the graph of f and reading the coordinates of the points of contact.

At least, that's the idea. But is there really a solution there? Does a curve that crosses the axis really touch the axis as it crosses? Perhaps it steps across the axis instead, without touching it, like the miniature step function in Fig. 1.66.

Also, does a curve that appears to be tangent to the axis really touch it? The function $y = x^2 + 0.0001$ is never zero, but this fact is certainly not revealed by the calculator screen in Fig. 1.67.

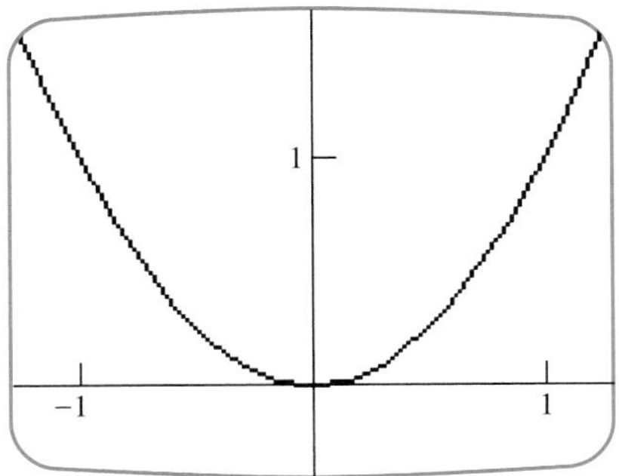

1.67 The graph of $y = x^2 + 0.0001$ appears to pass through the origin on this calculator screen, even though y is never zero. The numerals on the axes, not part of the screen display, were added later to show the picture's scale.

We answer these and other questions about graphs by applying the theorems of calculus, as you will see in the next few chapters. Calculus will tell us when there is a solution (and when there isn't) and how many solutions we may find. It will also furnish us with a first-rate method for calculating solutions to as many decimal places as we please, as we will see in Chapter 3.

Comparing Function Values

In the 1640s, Henry Bond, a British teacher of surveying and navigation, discovered a close agreement between the tables of values of two functions used in navigation. In 1645, in Norwood's *Epitome of Navigation,* he published his conjecture that the two functions were equal. The conjecture became widely known, and in 1666 the mathematician Nicolas Mercator (no relation to the mapmaker) offered a prize to anyone who could settle it.

The conjecture was finally settled by James Gregory in 1668, but with a geometric proof so long that even the genius Edmund Halley (of comet fame) found it nearly too tiresome to read. The first intelligible proof involved calculus and was published by Newton's university mathematics teacher Isaac Barrow in 1669. One of the functions in question was

$$f(x) = \ln\left|\tan\left(\frac{x}{2} + \frac{\pi}{4}\right)\right|. \tag{5}$$

Barrow accomplished his proof by showing that the other function was

$$g(x) = \ln|\sec x + \tan x|, \tag{6}$$

which can be transformed into f with trigonometric identities.

Bond was led to conjecture the equality of the two functions by comparing tables of their values. Today, we can make such comparisons at will with a calculator. If we suspect that two functions f and g are equal or that they differ, say, by some constant value, we can test the possibility by calculating $f(x) - g(x)$ for a number of values of x. If the difference varies from one value of x to another, our suspicion is unfounded. But if the calculated differences are equal, or very nearly so, we may be on to something.

Alternatively, we can graph f and g together with a computer or graphing calculator to see where the graphs may appear to overlap or where they may appear to differ only by a vertical shift. Or we can graph the difference function $f - g$ to see where if anywhere the function appears to have a constant value. Of course, knowing that $f(x) - g(x) = C$ for a few values of x does not prove equality for all values of x. But it makes the possibility worth investigating and gives a target value for C.

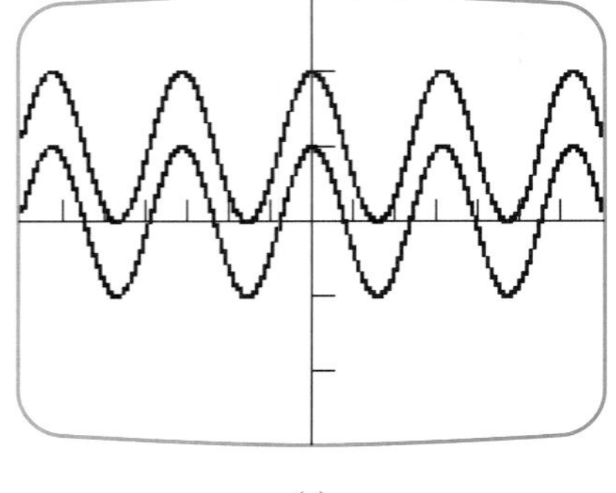

(a)

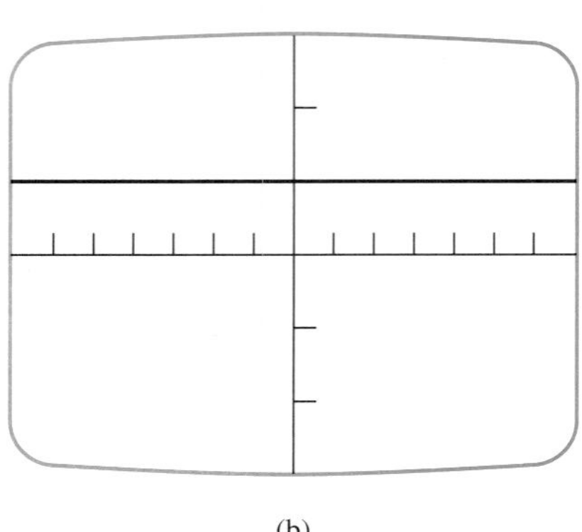

(b)

1.68 (a) The graphs of $f(x) = 2\cos^2 x$ (upper curve) and $g(x) = \cos 2x$ (lower curve) in the window $-7 \le x \le 7$, $-3 \le y \le 3$, on a TI-85 calculator. (b) The difference $f(x) - g(x)$ appears to be constant (Example 3).

EXAMPLE 3 On the calculator screen in Fig. 1.68(a), the graphs of $f(x) = 2\cos^2 x$ and $g(x) = \cos 2x$ appear to be one vertical unit apart. This suggests that $2\cos^2 x = 1 + \cos 2x$ over the interval shown. Does equality really hold for all x in the interval? If so, what about other values of x?

Solution We can gather further evidence that the functions f and g have a constant difference of 1 by graphing the difference $f(x) - g(x)$ (Fig. 1.68b). The graph looks like the horizontal line $y = 1$. The conjectured equality,

$$2\cos^2 x = 1 + \cos 2x, \tag{7}$$

is certainly worth exploring further.

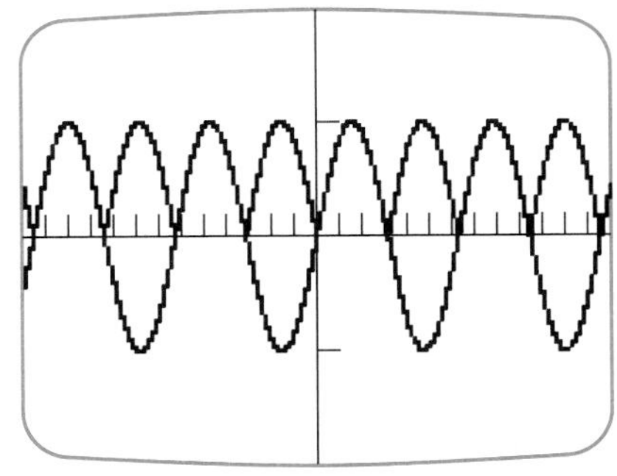

1.69 The graphs of $f(x) = \sin x$ and $g(x) = \sqrt{\sin^2 x}$ in the window $-13 \le x \le 13$, $-2 \le y \le 2$, on a TI-85 calculator. On some intervals the graphs overlap, but on others they do not.

Indeed, Eq. (7) is algebraically equivalent to the trigonometric identity

$$\cos 2x = 2\cos^2 x - 1, \tag{8}$$

which is known to hold for all x.

Just because two functions agree on some intervals does not mean they agree on others, and we have to watch out for this. As a case in point, the graphs of $f(x) = \sin x$ and $g(x) = \sqrt{\sin^2 x}$ in Fig. 1.69 appear to overlap on some intervals but to be mirror images of one another on other intervals. This strongly suggests that $\sqrt{\sin^2 x}$ equals $\sin x$ for some values of x but equals $-\sin x$ for others. What is going on? You may already know the answer. It lies in the notion of absolute value, an idea we will review in the next section.

Pierre de Fermat (1601–1665)

Fermat, a skilled linguist and one of the seventeenth century's greatest mathematicians, refused to publish his work and rarely wrote completed descriptions even for his personal use. His famous "last theorem" (that $a^n = b^n + c^n$ has no positive integer solutions for a, b, and c if n is an integer greater than 2) is known only from a note he jotted in the margin of a book. His name slipped into relative obscurity until the late 1800s, and it was only from a four-volume edition of his works published at the turn of the century that the true importance of his many achievements became clear.

Besides the work in physics and number theory for which he is best known, Fermat found the areas under curves as limits of sums of rectangle areas (as we do today) and developed a method for finding the centroids of shapes bounded by curves in the plane. The standard formula for the first derivative of a polynomial function, the formulas for calculating arc length and for finding the area of a surface of revolution, and the second derivative test for extreme values of functions can all be found in his papers. We will see what these are as the text continues.

Successive Square Roots

Calculators can also reveal interesting behavior on the part of an individual function. If we start with a positive number like $x = 2$ and take the square root repeatedly, here is what we find:

$$\begin{aligned}
x_0 &= 2 & x_7 &= \sqrt{x_6} = 1.0054\ 29901\\
x_1 &= \sqrt{x_0} = 1.4142\ 13562 & x_8 &= \sqrt{x_7} = 1.0027\ 11275\\
x_2 &= \sqrt{x_1} = 1.1892\ 07115 & x_9 &= \sqrt{x_8} = 1.0013\ 54720\\
x_3 &= \sqrt{x_2} = 1.0905\ 07733 & x_{10} &= \sqrt{x_9} = 1.0006\ 77131\\
x_4 &= \sqrt{x_3} = 1.0442\ 73782 & x_{11} &= \sqrt{x_{10}} = 1.0003\ 38508\\
x_5 &= \sqrt{x_4} = 1.0218\ 97149 & x_{12} &= \sqrt{x_{11}} = 1.0001\ 69240\\
x_6 &= \sqrt{x_5} = 1.0108\ 89286 & x_{13} &= \sqrt{x_{12}} = 1.0000\ 84616
\end{aligned}$$

We could continue this further, but the two patterns we want you to see are already emerging. One is that the numbers seem to be approaching the value 1. Indeed they must, as we will see in Chapter 9. The other pattern, less obvious perhaps but more intriguing, is that each keypress divides the decimal part of the number nearly in half. This behavior, too, is explained by calculus, as we will see in Chapter 3.

These two phenomena have nothing to do with the starting number 2. Taking successive square roots of any number greater than 1 brings you ever closer to 1, eventually dividing the decimal part roughly in half with each keypress.

Is This Idea Any Good?

One of the ways Fermat tried to define the slope of a curve at a point P was to run a secant line through P and a nearby point Q and then watch the slope of the secant line as Q approached P (see Fig. 1.70 on the following page). Every time he did this, the secant slopes seemed to approach a value that depended only on the location of P, so he wanted to call this value the slope of the curve at P. Was this a good idea?

To find out, we might try it at a particular point on a particular curve, say at the point $P(0, 0)$ on the curve $y = \sin x$. In the notation of Fig. 1.71 (on the following page), the point Q is the point $(h, \sin h)$. The slope of the secant line is therefore

$$m_{\text{sec}} = \frac{\sin h - 0}{h - 0} = \frac{\sin h}{h}. \tag{9}$$

What happens to the value of this ratio as Q approaches P along the curve?

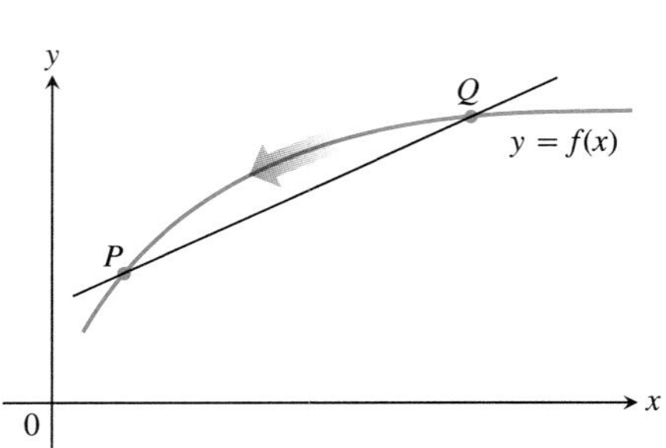

1.70 Fermat wanted to find out whether the slope of the secant PQ would approach a fixed value as Q approached P. If it did, he would call this value the slope of the curve at P.

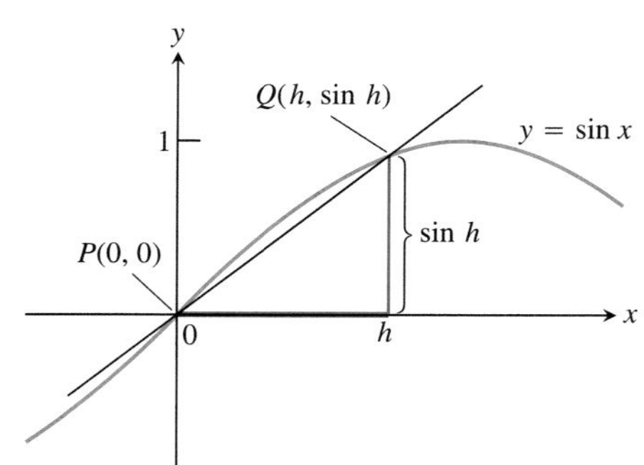

1.71 The slope of secant PQ is rise/run = $(\sin h)/h$.

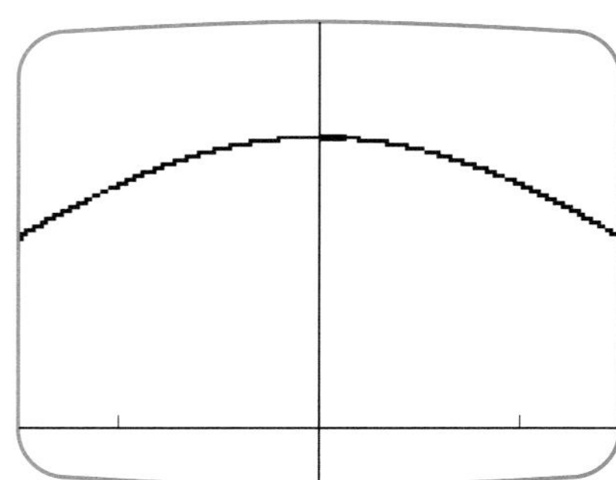

1.72 The function $y = (\sin x)/x$ is not defined at $x = 0$, but this calculator-generated graph for nonzero values of x strongly suggests that the function's values approach 1 as x approaches zero.

To get some idea, we can try graphing the ratio $(\sin h)/h$ with a calculator. We have to name the independent variable x instead of h, but except for this change in notation the resulting graph is the one we want (Fig. 1.72). The graph approaches 1 as x approaches zero from either side, strongly suggesting that $(\sin h)/h$ approaches a limiting value of 1 as h approaches zero. As we will see in Chapter 2, where we will continue our study of limiting values, and in Chapter 3, where we apply what we then know to determining slopes of curves, $(\sin h)/h$ does indeed approach 1 as h approaches zero, and this is precisely the value we should take to be the sine curve's slope at $x = 0$. Fermat was right.

Exercises 1.5

1. a) For how large a value of x can your calculator evaluate e^x?
   b) Calculate e^x for $x = -1, -10, -100$, and -1000. How far to the left of zero can your calculator evaluate e^x without getting 0 or an error message?
2. a) For how large a value of x can your calculator evaluate $\ln x$? How far above the x-axis is the graph of $y = \ln x$ at this point?
   b) The function $y = \ln x$ is defined for all positive values of x. What is the smallest value of x for which your calculator can find $\ln x$? How far below the x-axis is the graph of $y = \ln x$ at this point? How close is the graph to the y-axis there?
3. Graph $y = \sin x$ and estimate the value x^* where the graph first crosses the positive x-axis. To 9 decimal places, $\pi = 3.1415\ 92654$.
4. Graph the function
$$y = 10^{-6}(x - 1000)^3.$$
5. Evaluate the composite function
$$y = e^{(\ln x)}$$
for various values of x. What do you find? (This will be explained in Chapter 6.)
6. Evaluate the composite
$$y = \ln(e^x)$$
for various values of x. What do you find? (This will be explained in Chapter 6.)

In Exercises 7–12, use a grapher or function-table generator to see whether $f(x)$ and $g(x)$ could differ by a constant value on some domain of x-values. If they appear to do so, identify the constant and domain. Then see if you can prove that the functions really do differ by that constant on the domain you identified.

7. $f(x) = \dfrac{x}{x+1}$ and $g(x) = \dfrac{-1}{x+1}$
8. $f(x) = \dfrac{x^2+3}{x^2+1}$ and $g(x) = \dfrac{2}{x^2+1}$
9. $f(x) = \tan x \sin 2x$ and $g(x) = -2\cos^2 x$
10. $f(x) = 2\cos^2 x$ and $g(x) = \cos 2x$
11. $f(x) = \ln 2x$ and $g(x) = \ln x$
12. $f(x) = x$ and $g(x) = \sqrt{x^2}$
13. *Successive Square Roots*
    a) Enter the number 3 into your calculator. Then take the

square root repeatedly, pausing between calculations to read the display. With each new calculation you will find the decimal part of the display approximately halved.

b) Repeat part (a) with other numbers greater than 1.

14. *Continuation of Exercise 13.* One way to describe the halving of the decimal parts of the square roots in Exercise 13 is to say that the number-line distance between 1 and the square root is approximately halved each time. What happens if you start with a positive number that is less than 1 instead of greater than 1? Do successive square roots approach 1 the same way? Try it with $x = 0.5$.

15. *Successive Tenth Roots.* If you have a $\sqrt[x]{\ }$ key or some other key that will enable you to calculate tenth roots, calculate successive tenth roots of 2, pausing to view each new display. What pattern do you see? (This will be explained in Chapter 2.)

16. *Continuation of Exercise 15.* Repeat Exercise 15, starting with 0.5 instead of 2. What pattern do you see now?

17. *A Fast Estimate of $\pi/2$.* Set your calculator in radian mode and enter the number $x_0 = 1$. Then calculate the successive numbers $x_1, x_2, \ldots$ in the following list.

$$x_0 = 1$$
$$x_1 = 1 + \cos 1$$
$$x_2 = x_1 + \cos x_1$$
$$x_3 = x_2 + \cos x_2$$
$$x_4 = x_3 + \cos x_3$$
$$\vdots$$
$$x_n = x_{n-1} + \cos x_{n-1}$$

Formula for generating the sequence

The numbers you calculate will soon begin to repeat at the value $x^* = 1.5707\ 96327$, which is $\pi/2$ to 9 decimal places. Figure 1.73 explains why.

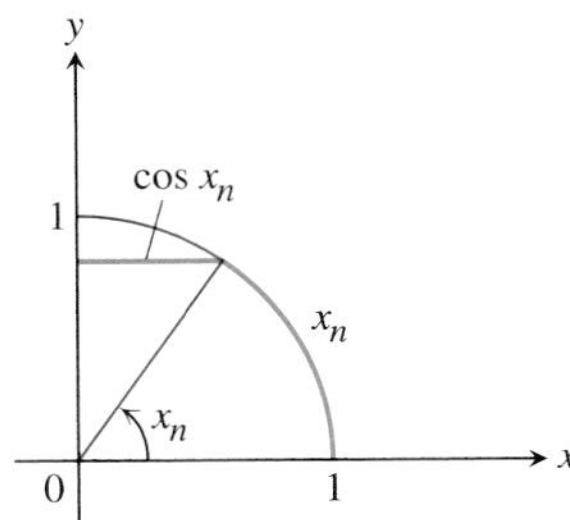

1.73 The length $\pi/2$ of the circular arc is approximated by the length $x_n + \cos x_n$ (blue). See Exercise 17.

18. *Assigning a Value to 0^0.* The rules of exponents tell us that $a^0 = 1$ if a is any number different from zero. They also tell us that $0^n = 0$ if n is any positive number.

If we tried to extend these rules to include the case 0^0, we would get conflicting results. The first rule would say $0^0 = 1$ while the second would say $0^0 = 0$.

We are not dealing with a question of right or wrong here. Neither rule applies as it stands, so there is no contradiction. We could, in fact, define 0^0 to have any value we wanted as long as we could persuade others to agree.

What value would you like 0^0 to have? Here are two examples that might help you to decide. (See Exercise 19 for another example.)

a) *(For calculators with an x^y key.)* Calculate x^x for $x = 0.1$, 0.01, 0.001, and so on as far as your calculator can go. Write down the value you get each time. What pattern do you see?

b) Graph the function $y = x^x$ (as $y = x$ ^ x) for $0 \le x \le 1$. Even though the function is not defined for $x \le 0$, the graph will approach the y-axis from the right. Toward what y-value does it seem to be headed? Zoom in to estimate the value more closely. What do you think it is?

19. *A Reason You Might Want 0^0 to Be Something Other Than 0 or 1.* As the number x increases through positive values, the numbers $1/x$ and $1/(\ln x)$ both approach zero. What happens to the number

$$f(x) = \left(\frac{1}{x}\right)^{1/(\ln x)}$$

as x increases? Here are two ways to find out.

a) Evaluate f for $x = 10, 100, 1000$, and so on, as far as your calculator can reasonably go. What pattern do you see?

b) Graph f over a variety of intervals, including intervals that contain the origin. What do you see? If your calculator has a TRACE option, use it to read y-values along the graph. What do you find? Chapter 6 will explain what is going on.

20. *The Slope of $y = \ln x$ at $x = 1$.* In this exercise we use Fermat's idea to find a numerical candidate for the slope of the curve $y = \ln x$ at the point $P(1, 0)$ where the curve crosses the x-axis (Fig. 1.74). We draw a secant line through P and a point $Q(1 + h, \ln(1 + h))$ nearby. The slope of the secant is

$$\text{Secant slope} = \frac{\ln(1+h) - 0}{(1+h) - 1} = \frac{\ln(1+h)}{h}. \tag{10}$$

We look for a pattern in the value of the slope as h becomes smaller and smaller and Q approaches P along the curve.

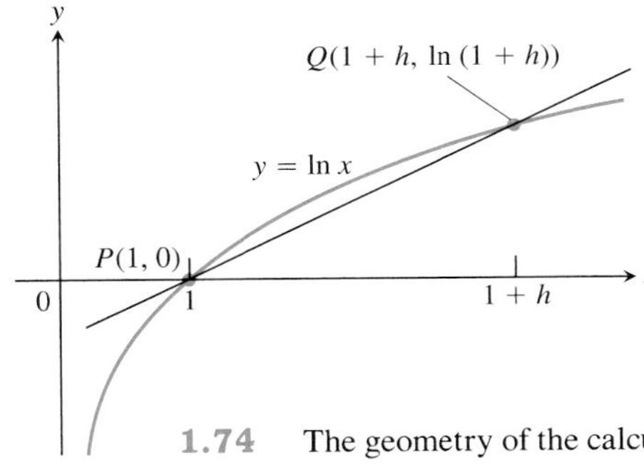

1.74 The geometry of the calculations in Exercise 20.

a) Make a table of values of the secant slope for $h = 0.1$, 0.01, 0.001, and so on as far as your calculator can reasonably go. As far as you can tell, what would be a good value for the curve's slope at $x = 1$?

b) Change h to x in the secant slope formula (Eq. 10) and graph the resulting formula,

$$y = \frac{\ln(1 + x)}{x},$$

as a function of x over intervals containing $x = 0$. Even though the formula is not defined at $x = 0$, the graph will appear to be complete. Where does it appear to cross the y-axis? What do you think the slope of the curve $y = \ln x$ at $x = 1$ should be?

STAIRWAYS

Exercises 21–23 are about the stairway shown in Fig. 1.75. The slope of the stairway can be calculated, from the riser height R and the tread width T, as R/T. The manual from which the drawing was adapted defines a stairway as a stepped footway having a slope not less than 5:16 or $31\frac{1}{4}\%$, and not greater than 9:8 or $112\frac{1}{2}\%$. (The manual goes on to say that below these limits footways become ramps. Above these limits, footways become stepladders.)

21. A common angle for household stairs is 40°. Find the slope of a 40° stairway.
22. If the treads on a 40° stairway are 9 in. wide, about how high are the risers?
23. (An inv or arc key is helpful but not necessary.) To the nearest degree, what are the maximum and minimum angles in Fig. 1.75 allowed by the definition of *stairway?*

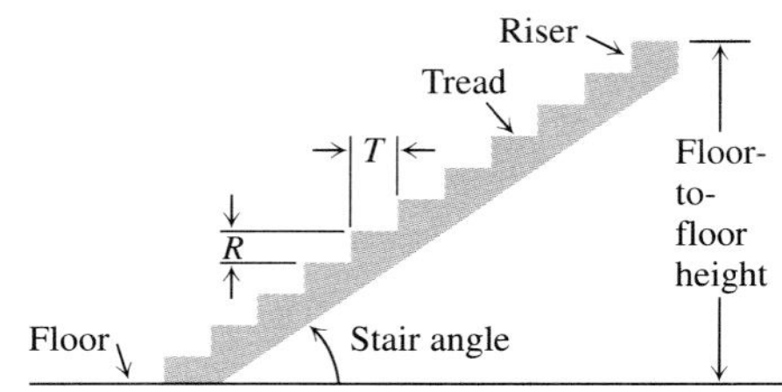

1.75 The stairway in Exercises 21–23.

Writing for Your Own Knowledge

Answer the following questions in writing. Some answers will take only a sentence or two; others may require several paragraphs. Some explanations may also call for graphs or sketches.

1. You suspect that the values of the functions $f(x)$ and $g(x)$ differ by a constant throughout an interval $a \le x \le b$. How would you use a calculator to support or refute this idea?
2. How did Fermat want to define the slope of a curve $y = f(x)$ at a point P on the curve?

EXPLORER PROGRAM

PowerGrapher — Graphs calculator functions.

Makes tables of values of functions and differences of functions.

1.6 *Absolute Values (Magnitudes) and Target Values*

In calculus, we use absolute values to measure differences between numbers, write formulas that define intervals, and control function values.

The Absolute Value Function

The **absolute value function** $y = |x|$ is defined by the formula

$$|x| = \begin{cases} -x, & x < 0 \\ x, & x \ge 0. \end{cases} \tag{1}$$

For example, $|-5| = 5$, $|0| = 0$, and $|3| = 3$. The graph lies along the line $y = -x$ when $x < 0$ and along the line $y = x$ when $x \ge 0$ (Fig. 1.76). The number $|x|$ is the **absolute value** or **magnitude** of x. The vertical bars in $|x|$ are **absolute value bars.**

For any number x,

$$\sqrt{x^2} = |x|. \tag{2}$$

For instance, $\sqrt{(-2)^2} = \sqrt{4} = 2 = |-2|$.

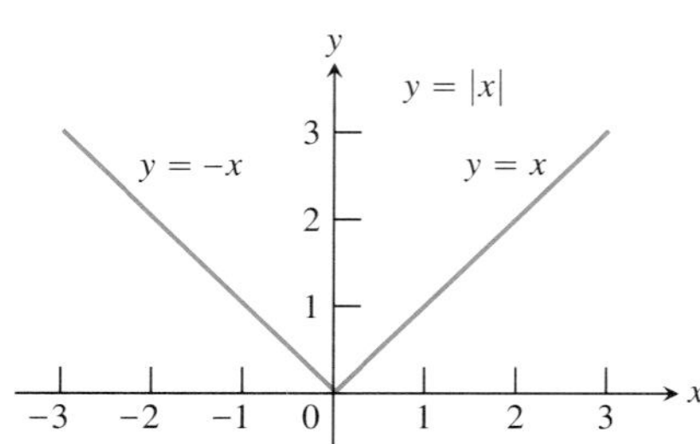

1.76 The absolute value function.

Caution: It is not always true that $\sqrt{x^2} = x$. This equation holds *only if* $x \geq 0$. The appropriate true statement is $\sqrt{x^2} = |x|$.

To solve an equation that contains absolute values, we write equivalent equations without absolute values, then solve as usual.

EXAMPLE 1 Solve the equation $|2x - 3| = 7$.

Solution The equation says that $2x - 3 = \pm 7$, so there are two possibilities:

$$2x - 3 = 7 \qquad 2x - 3 = -7 \qquad \text{Equivalent equations without absolute values}$$

$$2x = 10 \qquad 2x = -4 \qquad \text{Solve as usual.}$$

$$x = 5 \qquad x = -2.$$

The equation $|2x - 3| = 7$ has two solutions: $x = 5$ and $x = -2$.

To graph a formula $y = f(x)$ that contains absolute values, divide the x-axis into intervals on which the absolute values can be removed. Then graph as usual.

EXAMPLE 2 Graph the function

$$f(x) = |x + 1| + |x - 3|.$$

Solution The points where the expressions inside the bars change sign are

$$x = -1 \quad (\text{for } x + 1)$$

$$x = 3 \quad (\text{for } x - 3).$$

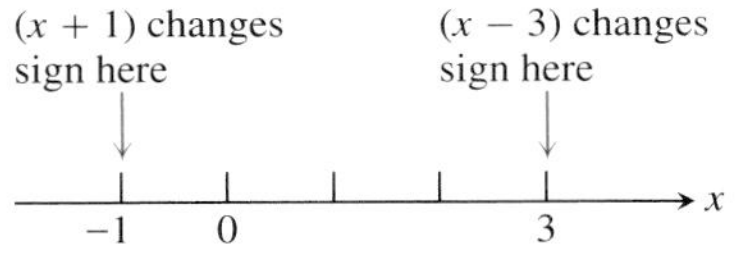

These points divide the x-axis into intervals on which we can write absolute-value-free formulas for $f(x)$:

For $x < -1$: Here, $x + 1 < 0$ and $x - 3 < 0$, so

$$\begin{aligned} f(x) &= |x + 1| + |x - 3| \\ &= -(x + 1) - (x - 3) \\ &= -x - 1 - x + 3 = 2 - 2x \end{aligned}$$

For $-1 \leq x \leq 3$: Here, $x + 1 \geq 0$ and $x - 3 \leq 0$, so

$$\begin{aligned} f(x) &= |x + 1| + |x - 3| \\ &= x + 1 - (x - 3) \\ &= x + 1 - x + 3 = 4 \end{aligned}$$

For $x > 3$: Here, $x + 1 > 0$ and $x - 3 > 0$, so

$$\begin{aligned} f(x) &= |x + 1| + |x - 3| \\ &= x + 1 + x - 3 = 2x - 2 \end{aligned}$$

Thus, $f(x) = |x + 1| + |x - 3|$ is equivalent to

$$f(x) = \begin{cases} 2 - 2x, & x < -1 \\ 4, & -1 \leq x \leq 3 \\ 2x - 2, & x > 3. \end{cases}$$

With the absolute value signs now removed, we can graph f in the usual way (Fig. 1.77).

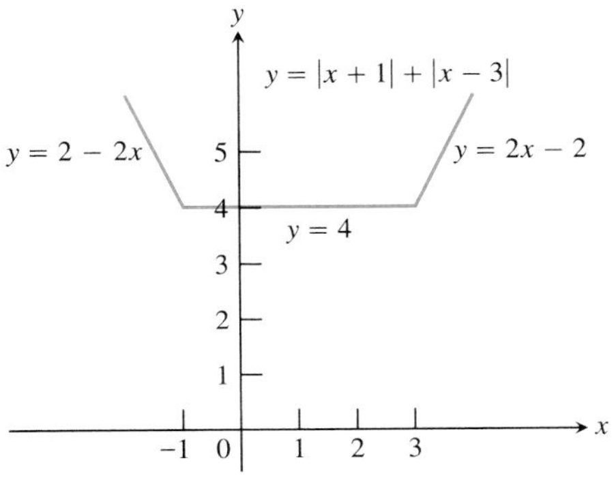

1.77 The graph in Example 2.

When we do arithmetic with absolute values, we can always use the following rules.

Arithmetic with Absolute Values

1. $|-a| = |a|$ A number and its negative have the same absolute value.
2. $|ab| = |a|\,|b|$ The absolute value of a product is the product of the absolute values.
3. $\left|\dfrac{a}{b}\right| = \dfrac{|a|}{|b|}$ The absolute value of a quotient is the quotient of the absolute values.

EXAMPLE 3 **a)** $|-\sin x| = |\sin x|$

b) $|-2(x+5)| = |-2|\,|x+5| = 2|x+5|$

c) $\left|\dfrac{3}{x}\right| = \dfrac{|3|}{|x|} = \dfrac{3}{|x|}$

The absolute value of a sum of two numbers is never larger than the sum of their absolute values. When we put this in symbols, we get the important triangle inequality.

The Triangle Inequality

$$|a+b| \le |a| + |b| \qquad \text{for all numbers } a \text{ and } b \tag{3}$$

The number $|a+b|$ is less than $|a| + |b|$ if a and b have different signs. In all other cases, $|a+b|$ equals $|a| + |b|$.

$$|-3+5| = |2| = 2 < |-3| + |5| = 8$$
$$|3+5| = |8| = 8 = |3| + |5|$$
$$|-3-5| = |-8| = 8 = |-3| + |-5|$$

Notice that absolute value bars in expressions such as $|-3+5|$ also work like parentheses: We do the arithmetic inside *before* we take the absolute value.

Absolute Values and Distance

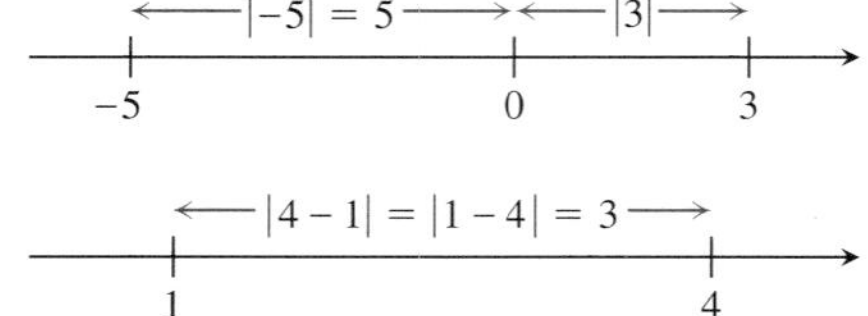

1.78 Absolute values give distances between points on the number line.

The numbers $|a-b|$ and $|b-a|$ are equal because

$$|a-b| = |(-1)(b-a)| = |-1|\,|b-a| = |b-a|. \tag{4}$$

They give the distance between the points a and b on the number line (Fig. 1.78).

Absolute Values and Intervals

The connection between absolute values and distance gives a new way to write formulas for intervals.

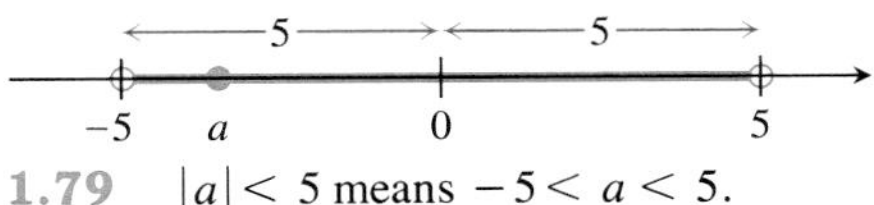

1.79 $|a| < 5$ means $-5 < a < 5$.

The inequality $|a| < 5$ says that the distance from a to the origin is less than 5. This is the same as saying that a lies between -5 and 5 on the number line. In symbols,

$$|a| < 5 \quad \Leftrightarrow \quad -5 < a < 5. \tag{5}$$

The set of numbers a with $|a| < 5$ is the open interval from -5 to 5 (Fig. 1.79).

The general rule is this:

$\Rightarrow$ means "implies" (and is read that way).

$\Leftrightarrow$ means "if and only if." That is, $A \Leftrightarrow B$ means that A implies B and also B implies A.

Relation Between Intervals and Absolute Values

For any positive number D,

$$|a| < D \quad \Leftrightarrow \quad -D < a < D, \tag{6}$$

$$|a| \le D \quad \Leftrightarrow \quad -D \le a \le D. \tag{7}$$

EXAMPLE 4 Describe the interval $-3 < x < 5$ with an absolute value inequality of the form $|x - x_0| < D$.

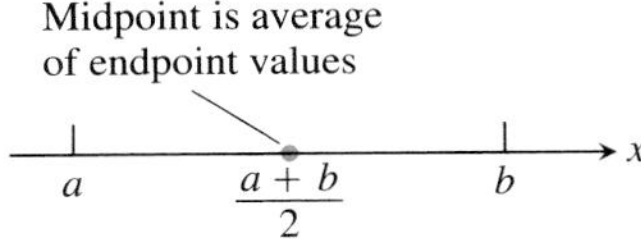

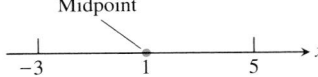

1.80 The midpoint of a finite interval is the average of the endpoint values (Example 4).

Solution We average the endpoint values to find the interval's midpoint:

$$\text{midpoint } x_0 = \frac{-3 + 5}{2} = \frac{2}{2} = 1.$$

The midpoint lies 4 units away from each endpoint (Fig. 1.80). The interval therefore consists of the points that lie within 4 units of the midpoint, or the points x with

$$|x - 1| < 4.$$

EXAMPLE 5 What values of x satisfy the inequality $|x - 5| < 9$?

Solution We rewrite the inequality $|x - 5| < 9$ in stages:

$$|x - 5| < 9$$

$$-9 < x - 5 < 9 \qquad \text{Eq. (6) with } a = x - 5 \text{ and } D = 9$$

$$-9 + 5 < x < 9 + 5 \qquad \text{Adding a number to both sides of an inequality gives an equivalent inequality. Adding 5 here isolates the } x.$$

$$-4 < x < 14.$$

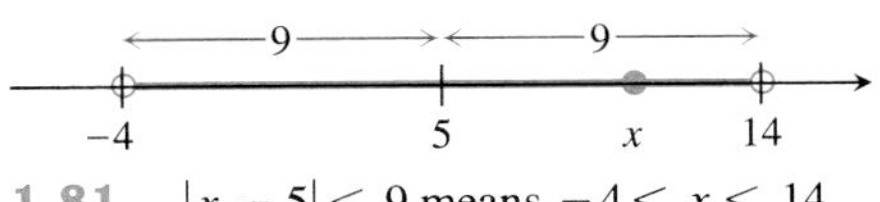

1.81 $|x - 5| < 9$ means $-4 < x < 14$.

The steps we just took are reversible, so the values of x that satisfy the inequality $|x - 5| < 9$ are the numbers in the interval $-4 < x < 14$ (Fig. 1.81). Here 14 is the upper bound on x, and -4 is the lower bound.

The process of finding the interval values of x that satisfy an absolute value inequality is called **solving** the inequality. In Example 5, we solved the inequality $|x - 5| < 9$.

EXAMPLE 6 Solve the inequality $\left|\frac{2x}{3}\right| \le 1$.

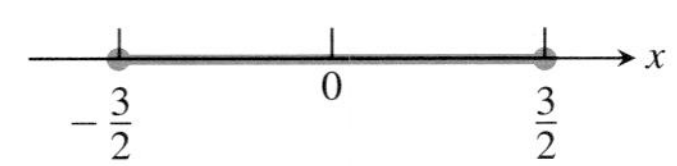

1.82 The inequality $|2x/3| \le 1$ holds on the interval $-3/2 \le x \le 3/2$.

Solution We rewrite the inequality in stages:

$$\left|\frac{2x}{3}\right| \le 1$$

$$-1 \le \frac{2x}{3} \le 1 \qquad \text{Eq. (7) with } a = 2x/3 \text{ and } D = 1$$

$$-3 \le 2x \le 3 \qquad \text{Multiplying both sides of an inequality by a positive number gives an equivalent inequality.}$$

$$-\frac{3}{2} \le x \le \frac{3}{2}. \qquad \text{Dividing both sides of an inequality by a positive number gives an equivalent inequality.}$$

The original inequality holds for x in the interval $-3/2 \le x \le 3/2$ (Fig. 1.82).

EXAMPLE 7 Solve the inequality $\left|5 - \frac{2}{x}\right| < 1$.

Solution Change

$$\left|5 - \frac{2}{x}\right| < 1$$

$$-1 < 5 - \frac{2}{x} < 1 \qquad \text{Eq. (6) with } a = 5 - 2/x \text{ and } D = 1$$

$$-6 < -\frac{2}{x} < -4 \qquad \text{Subtracting a number, in this case 5, from both sides of an inequality gives an equivalent inequality.}$$

$$4 < \frac{2}{x} < 6 \qquad \text{Multiplying both sides of an equality by } -1 \text{ reverses the inequality.}$$

$$2 < \frac{1}{x} < 3 \qquad \text{Divide by 2.}$$

$$\frac{1}{3} < x < \frac{1}{2}. \qquad \text{Take reciprocals. When the numbers involved have the same sign, taking reciprocals reverses an inequality.}$$

The original inequality holds if and only if x lies between 1/3 and 1/ 2.

Keeping Function Outputs near Target Values

We sometimes want the outputs of a function $y = f(x)$ to lie near a particular target value y_0. This need can come about in different ways. A gas station attendant, asked for $5.00 worth of gas, will try to pump the gas to the nearest cent. A mechanic grinding a 3.385-in. cylinder bore will not let the bore exceed this value by more than 0.002 in. A pharmacist making ointments will measure the ingredients to the nearest milligram.

So the question becomes: How accurate do our machines and instruments have to be to keep the outputs within useful bounds? When we express this question with mathematical symbols, we ask: How closely must we control x to keep $y = f(x)$ within an acceptable interval about some particular target value y_0? The following examples address this question.

EXAMPLE 8 *Controlling a Linear Function.* How close to $x_0 = 4$ must we hold x to be sure that $y = 2x - 1$ lies within 2 units of $y_0 = 7$?

Solution We are asked: For what values of x is $|y-7|<2$? To find the answer, we first express $|y-7|$ in terms of x:

$$|y-7| = |(2x-1)-7| = |2x-8|.$$

The question then becomes: What values of x satisfy the inequality $|2x-8|<2$? To find out, we solve the inequality:

$$\begin{aligned} |2x-8| &< 2 \\ -2 < 2x-8 &< 2 \\ 6 < 2x &< 10 \\ 3 < x &< 5. \end{aligned}$$

To keep y within 2 units of $y_0 = 7$, we must keep x within 1 unit of $x_0 = 4$ (Fig. 1.83).

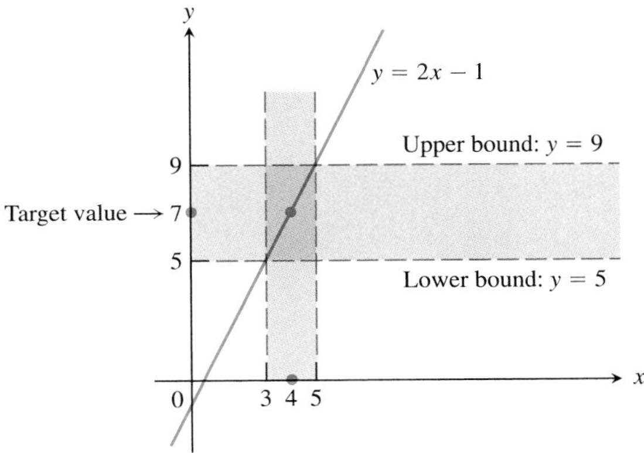

1.83 Keeping x between 3 and 5 will keep $y = 2x - 1$ between $y = 5$ and $y = 9$ (Example 8).

EXAMPLE 9 *Controlling the Area of a Circle.* In what interval about $r_0 = 10$ must we hold r to be sure that $A = \pi r^2$ lies within π square units of $A_0 = 100\pi$?

Solution We want to know the values of r for which $|A - A_0| < \pi$. To find them, we solve the inequality:

$$\begin{aligned} |A - A_0| &< \pi \\ |\pi r^2 - 100\pi| &< \pi \\ -\pi < \pi r^2 - 100\pi &< \pi \\ -1 < r^2 - 100 &< 1 \\ 99 < r^2 &< 101 \\ \sqrt{99} < r &< \sqrt{101}. \end{aligned}$$

For a, b, and c nonnegative, $a < b < c \Leftrightarrow \sqrt{a} < \sqrt{b} < \sqrt{c}$.

The interval of possible radii is the open interval from $r = \sqrt{99} \approx 9.95$ to $r = \sqrt{101} \approx 10.05$ (Fig. 1.84 on the following page).

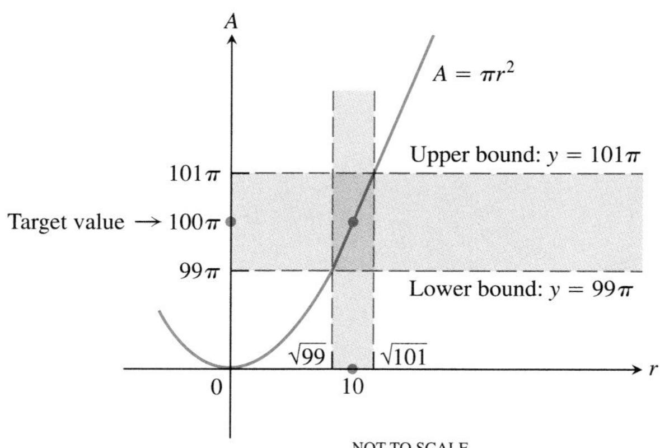

1.84 Keeping r between $\sqrt{99}$ and $\sqrt{101}$ will keep πr^2 between 99π and 101π (Example 9).

EXAMPLE 10 *Why the Stripes on a 1-Liter Kitchen Measuring Cup Are About a Millimeter Wide.* The interior of a typical 1-L measuring cup is a right circular cylinder of radius 6 cm (Fig. 1.85). The volume of water we put in the cup is therefore a function of the level h to which the cup is filled, the formula being

$$V = \pi 6^2 h = 36\pi h.$$

How closely do we have to measure h to measure out 1 L of water (1000 cm^3) with an error of no more than 1% (10 cm^3)?

Solution In terms of V and h, we want to know in what interval to hold values of h to make V satisfy the inequality

$$|V - 1000| = |36\pi h - 1000| \le 10.$$

To find out, we solve the inequality:

$$\begin{aligned} |36\pi h - 1000| &\le 10 \\ -10 \le 36\pi h - 1000 &\le 10 \\ 990 \le 36\pi h &\le 1010 \\ \frac{990}{36\pi} \le h &\le \frac{1010}{36\pi} \\ 8.8 \le h &\le 8.9 \end{aligned}$$

Values found with a calculator

8.8: rounded up, to be safe; 8.9: rounded down, to be safe

The interval in which we should hold h is about 0.1 cm wide (1 mm). With stripes 1 mm wide, we can therefore expect to measure a liter of water with an accuracy of 1%, which is more than enough accuracy for cooking.

Stripes about 1 mm wide

(a)

$r = 6$ cm

h

Liquid volume $V = 36\pi h$

(b)

1.85 A typical 1-L measuring cup (a), modeled in (b) as a right circular cylinder of radius $r = 6$ cm. To get a liter of water to the nearest 1%, how accurately must we measure h? See Example 10.

Why Bother with Target Values?

Although the ability to control the outputs of functions has obvious applications in commercial settings, why do we raise the issue in calculus? It has to do with the notion of limiting value (limit, for short), the key working idea of calculus and the subject of the next chapter.

Suppose we have a function $y = f(x)$ and an interval $y_0 - E < y < y_0 + E$

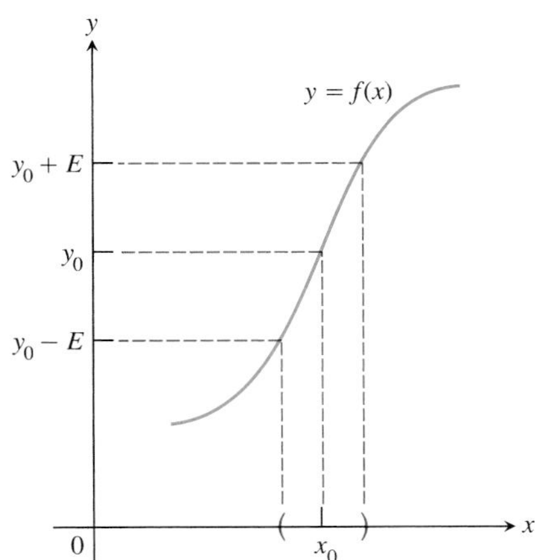

1.86 No matter how small a positive number E is, we can find an interval about x_0 where all the function values lie between $y_0 - E$ and $y_0 + E$.

of y-values about a target value y_0. Further, suppose that we can control the outputs of f so completely that no matter how small E is we can always find an interval centered at x_0 whose function values all lie within the given interval about y_0 (Fig. 1.86). We describe this level of control by saying that y_0 is the limit of the values $f(x)$ as x approaches x_0.

As we will see in Chapter 2, the mathematics we have developed for discussing target values is just what we need for telling when we can expect a function to have a number y_0 as a limit and when we cannot.

Summary: Properties of Inequalities

1. $a < b \quad \Rightarrow \quad a + c < b + c$
2. $a < b \quad \Rightarrow \quad a - c < b - c$
3. $a < b$ and $c > 0 \quad \Rightarrow \quad ac < bc$
4. $a < b$ and $c > 0 \quad \Rightarrow \quad \dfrac{a}{c} < \dfrac{b}{c}$
5. $a < b \quad \Rightarrow \quad -b < -a$
6. $a < b \quad \Rightarrow \quad \dfrac{1}{b} < \dfrac{1}{a}$ Requires a and b both positive or both negative

These properties hold for $\leq$ as well as for $<$.

Exercises 1.6

Find the absolute values in Exercises 1 and 2.

1. **a)** $|2 - 7|$ **b)** $|\sqrt{2} - \sqrt{7}|$ **c)** $|1.1 - 5.2|$

2. **a)** $|-3 - (-5)|$ **b)** $|5 - \sqrt{2}|$ **c)** $|1.4 - 1.9|$

Solve the equations in Exercises 3–8.

3. $|x| = 2$ **4.** $|x - 3| = 7$

5. $|2x + 5| = 4$ **6.** $|1 - y| = 1$

7. $|8 - 3s| = 9$ **8.** $\left|\dfrac{t}{2} - 1\right| = 1$

9. If $2 < x < 6$, which of the following statements about x are true, and which are false?

a) $0 < x < 4$ **b)** $0 < x - 2 < 4$

c) $1 < \dfrac{x}{2} < 3$ **d)** $\dfrac{1}{6} < \dfrac{1}{x} < \dfrac{1}{2}$

e) $1 < \dfrac{6}{x} < 3$ **f)** $|x - 4| < 2$

g) $-6 < -x < 2$ **h)** $-6 < -x < -2$

10. If $-1 < y - 5 < 1$, which of the following statements about y are true, and which are false?

a) $4 < y < 6$ **b)** $|y - 5| < 1$

c) $y > 4$ **d)** $y < 6$

e) $0 < y - 4 < 2$ **f)** $2 < \dfrac{y}{2} < 3$

g) $\dfrac{1}{6} < \dfrac{1}{y} < \dfrac{1}{4}$ **h)** $-6 < y < -4$

In Exercises 11–16, solve each inequality and match it with the interval it determines.

Inequality	Solution Interval
11. $\lvert x + 3\rvert < 1$	**a)** $-2 < x < 1$
12. $\left\lvert\dfrac{x}{2}\right\rvert < 1$	**b)** $-1 < x < 3$
13. $\lvert 1 - x\rvert < 2$	**c)** $-2 < x < 2$
14. $\lvert 2x - 5\rvert \leq 1$	**d)** $-4 < x < 4$
15. $\left\lvert\dfrac{x - 1}{2}\right\rvert < 1$	**e)** $-4 < x < -2$
	f) $2 \leq x \leq 3$
16. $\left\lvert\dfrac{2x + 1}{3}\right\rvert < 1$	**g)** $-2 \leq x \leq 2$

Solve the inequalities in Exercises 17–24.

17. $|y| < 2$ **18.** $|y| \leq 2$

19. $|r-1| \le 2$

20. $|r+2| < 1$

21. $|3s-7| < 2$

22. $|2s+5| < 1$

23. $\left|\frac{t}{2}-1\right| \le 1$

24. $\left|2-\frac{t}{2}\right| < \frac{1}{2}$

Describe the intervals in Exercises 25–28 with inequalities of the form $|x-x_0| < D$. It may help to draw a picture of the interval first.

25. $3 < x < 9$

26. $-3 < x < 9$

27. $-5 < x < 3$

28. $-7 < x < -1$

Each of Exercises 29–34 gives a function $y=f(x)$, a number E, and a target value y_0. In what interval must we hold x in each case to be sure that $y=f(x)$ lies within E units of y_0?

29. $y=x^2, \quad E=1, \quad y_0=100$

30. $y=x^2-5, \quad E=1, \quad y_0=11$

31. $y=\sqrt{x-7}, \quad E=0.1, \quad y_0=4$

32. $y=\sqrt{19-x}, \quad E=1, \quad y_0=3$

33. $y=120/x, \quad E=1, \quad y_0=5$

34. $y=1/(4x), \quad E=1/2, \quad y_0=1$

Each of Exercises 35–42 gives a function $y=f(x)$, a number E, a point x_0, and a target value y_0. In what interval about x_0 must we hold x in each case to be sure that $y=f(x)$ lies within E units of y_0? Describe the interval with an inequality of the form $|x-x_0| < D$.

35. $y=x+1, \quad E=0.5, \quad x_0=3, \quad y_0=4$

36. $y=2x-1, \quad E=1, \quad x_0=-2, \quad y_0=-5$

37. $y=-(x/2)+1, \quad E=1/2, \quad x_0=6, \quad y_0=-2$

38. $y=-2x-2, \quad E=0.2, \quad x_0=-3, \quad y_0=4$

39. $y=mx, \quad E=0.03, \quad x_0=2, \quad y_0=2m$

40. $y=mx, \quad E=c>0, \quad x_0=3, \quad y_0=3m$

41. $y=mx+b, \quad E=0.05, \quad x_0=1, \quad y_0=m+b$

42. $y=mx+b, \quad E=c>0, \quad x_0=1/2, \quad y_0=(m/2)+b$

43. *Grinding Engine Cylinders.* Before contracting to grind engine cylinders to a cross-section area of 9 in^2, you need to know how much deviation from the ideal cylinder diameter of $x_0=3.385$ in. you can allow and still have the area come within 0.01 in^2 of the required 9 in^2. To find out, you let $A=\pi(x/2)^2$ and look for the interval in which you must hold x to make $|A-9| \le 0.01$. What interval do you find?

44. *Manufacturing Electrical Resistors.* Ohm's law for electrical circuits like the one shown in Fig. 1.87 states that $V=RI$. In this equation, V is a constant voltage, I is the current in amperes, and R is the resistance in ohms. Your firm has been asked to supply the resistors for a circuit in which V will be 120 volts and I is to be 5 ± 0.1 amp. In what interval does R have to lie for I to be within 0.1 amp of the target value $I_0=5$?

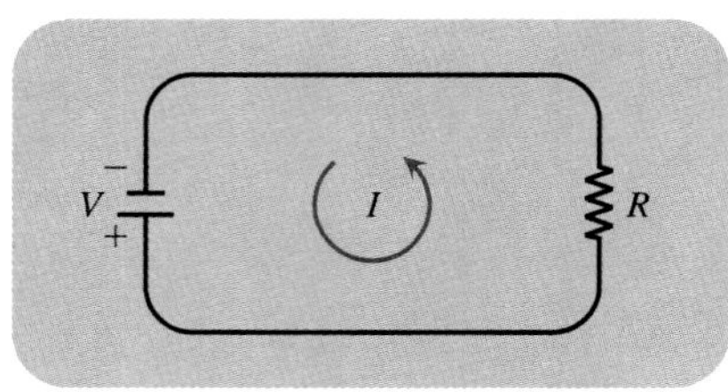

1.87 The circuit in Exercise 44.

45. Match the following equations with the graphs in Fig. 1.88.

a) $y=|x-3|$

b) $y=|x|-3$

c) $y=|x+3|$

d) $y=-|x-3|$

i)
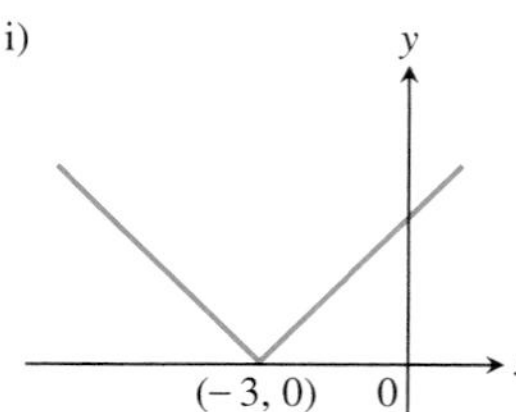

ii)
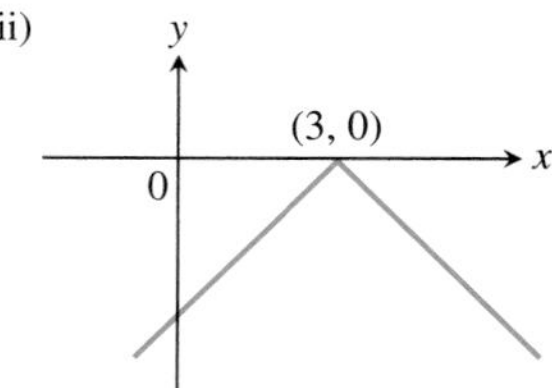

iii)
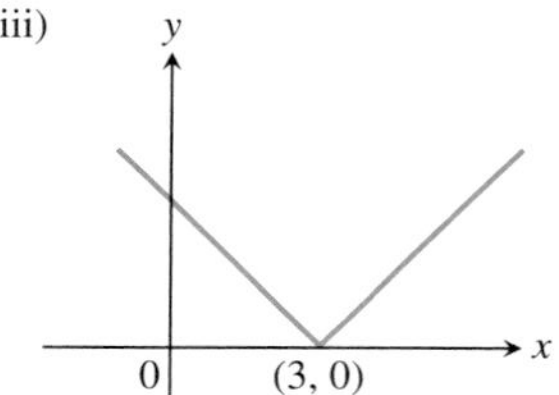

iv)
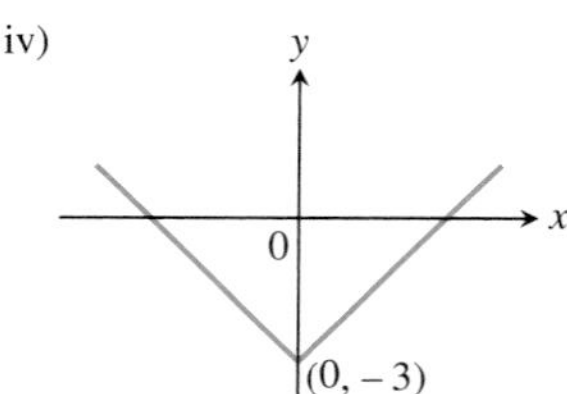

1.88 The graphs for Exercise 45.

46. Match the following equations with the three graphs in Fig. 1.89.

a) $y=|\sin x|$

b) $y=(\sin x+|\sin x|)/2$

c) $y=(|\sin x|-\sin x)/2$

(i)
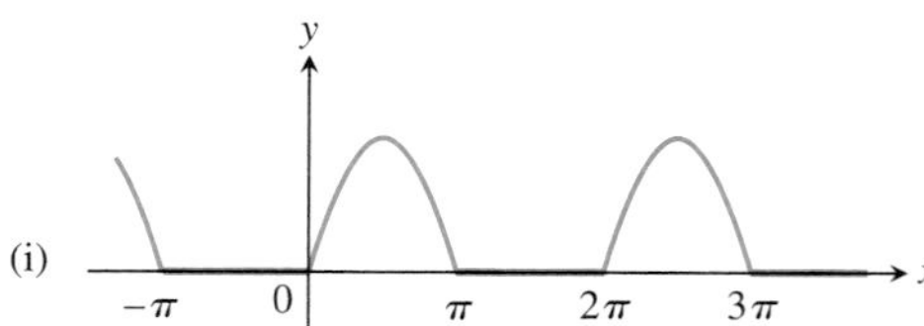

(ii)
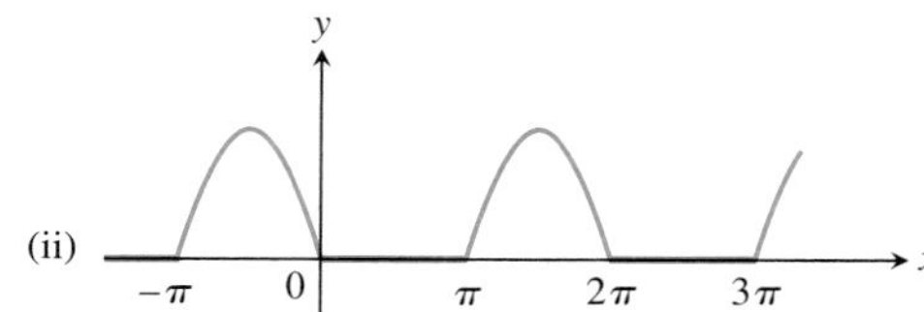

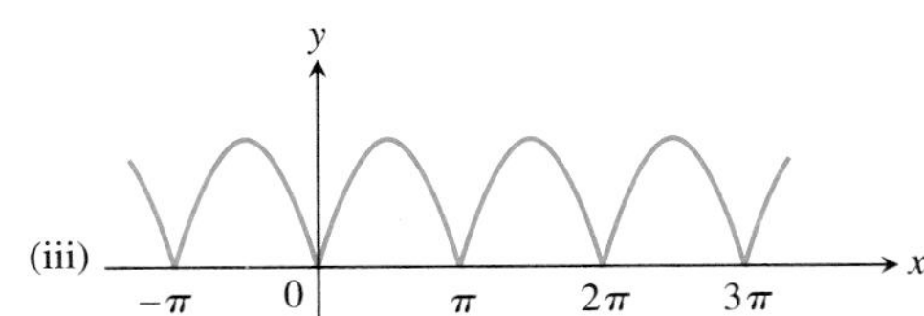

1.89 The graphs for Exercise 46.

Graph the functions in Exercises 47–52.

47. $f(x) = |x + 1| + 2|x - 3|$

48. $g(x) = |x + 2| + |x - 1|$

49. $h(x) = \dfrac{|x|}{x}$

50. $k(x) = \dfrac{|x - 1|}{x - 1}$

51. $f(x) = \dfrac{x - |x|}{2}$

52. $g(x) = \dfrac{x + |x|}{2}$

53. Compare the domains and ranges of the functions $y = \sqrt{x^2}$ and $y = (\sqrt{x})^2$.

54. Find $f(x)$ if $g(x) = \sqrt{x}$ and $(g \circ f)(x) = |x|$.

55. Find $g(x)$ if $f(x) = x^2 + 2x + 1$ and $(g \circ f)(x) = |x + 1|$.

56. Find functions $f(x)$ and $g(x)$ whose composites satisfy the two equations

$$(g \circ f)(x) = |\sin x| \text{ and } (f \circ g)(x) = (\sin \sqrt{x})^2.$$

57. Find the domain and range of

a) $y = \sqrt{4 - |x|}$ b) $y = \sqrt{-|x|}$.

58. a) For what values of x is $|x| - 1$ positive?

b) For what values of x is $|x| - 1$ zero?

c) For what values of x is $|x| - 1$ negative?

d) What are the domain and range of $y = \sqrt{|x| - 1}$?

59. Is it always true that $|-x| = x$? Give reasons for your answer.

60. Is it ever true that $|a| = -a$? Give reasons for your answer.

61. *$\sqrt{\sin^2 x}$ vs. $\sin x$*

a) Graph $y = \sin x$ and $y = \sqrt{\sin^2 x}$ together for $-\pi \le x \le \pi$. For what values of x do the graphs overlap? For what values are the graphs mirror images of one another? Explain.

b) The trigonometric identity

$$\frac{1 - \cos 2x}{2} = \sin^2 x$$

holds for all values of x. For what values of x in the interval $[-\pi, \pi]$ does the equation

$$\sqrt{\frac{1 - \cos 2x}{2}} = \sin x$$

hold? For what values of x in $[-\pi, \pi]$ does the equation

$$\sqrt{\frac{1 - \cos 2x}{2}} = |\sin x|$$

hold?

62. *$\sqrt{\cot^2 x}$ vs. $\cot x$*

a) Graph $y = \cot x$ and $y = \sqrt{\cot^2 x}$ together for $0 < x < \pi$. For what values of x do the graphs overlap? For what values are the graphs mirror images of one another? Explain.

b) The trigonometric identity

$$\cot^2 x = \csc^2 x - 1$$

holds for all values of x. For what values of x in $(0, \pi)$ does the equation

$$\cot x = \sqrt{\csc^2 x - 1}$$

hold? For what values of x in $(0, \pi)$ does the equation

$$|\cot x| = \sqrt{\csc^2 x - 1}$$

hold?

63. Graph the function $y = |(\cos x) - 1|$. What are the function's domain and range?

64. Graph the function

$$y = \frac{1}{|\sin x| + 1}.$$

What are the function's domain and range?

65. *The Best Location for a Factory Assembly Table* (adapted from *Fantastiks of Mathematiks*, by Cliff Sloyer, Janson Publications, Inc., Providence, R.I., 1986). Because of a design change, the parts produced by three machines along a factory aisle (shown here as the x-axis)

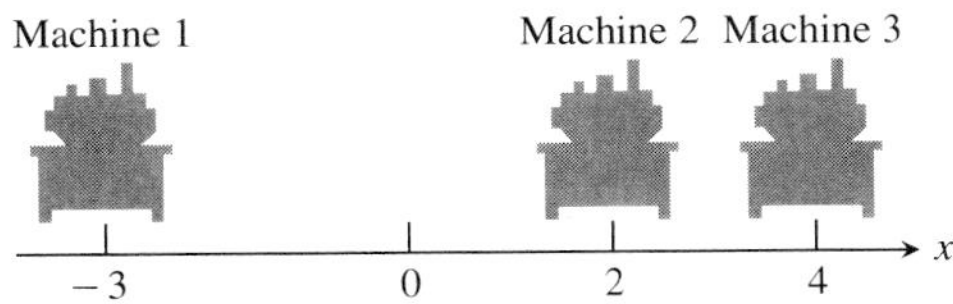

are to go to a nearby table for assembly before they undergo further processing. Each assembly takes one part from each machine and there is a fixed cost per foot for moving each part. As the plant's production engineer, you have been asked to find a location for the assembly table that will keep the total cost of moving the parts at a minimum.

To solve the problem, you let x represent the table's location and look for the value of x that minimizes the sum

$$d(x) = |x + 3| + |x - 2| + |x - 4|$$

of the distances from the table to the three machines. Since the cost of moving the parts to the assembly table is proportional to the total distance the parts travel, any value of x that minimizes d will minimize the cost.

Complete the job now by graphing $d(x)$ to find its smallest value. Then say where you would put the table.

66. *Best Location (Continuation of Exercise 65).* You solved the table location problem in Exercise 65 so well that your manager has asked you to solve a similar problem at a neighboring

plant. This time there are four machines instead of three

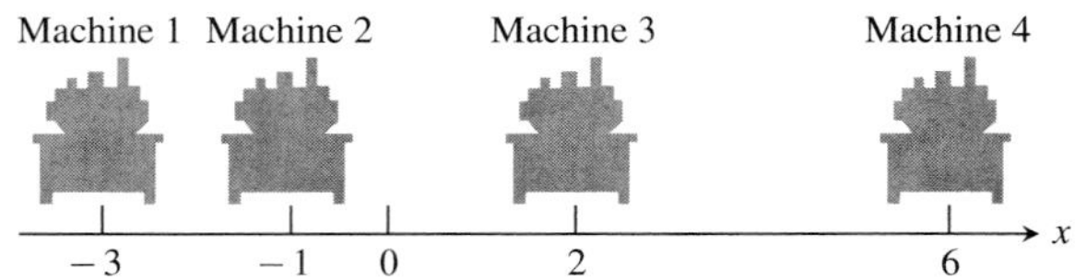

and the cost is proportional to

$$d(x) = |x+3| + |x+1| + |x-2| + |x-6|.$$

Where should the assembly table go now?

67. *Best Location (Continuation of Exercise 66).* As the result of another design change, the assembly in the plant in Exercise 66 is to use twice as many parts from machine 1 as before, and three times as many parts from machine 3 as before. The total cost of moving parts from the four machines to the assembly table is now proportional to the "weighted" distance

$$d(x) = 2|x+3| + |x+1| + 3|x-2| + |x-6|.$$

What is the minimum value of this new function? Where should the table go?

Writing for Your Own Knowledge

Answer the following questions in writing. Some answers will take only a sentence or two; others may require several paragraphs. Some explanations may also call for graphs or sketches.

1. What is a number's absolute value?
2. If a and b are numbers, how are $|-a|$, $|ab|$, $|a/b|$, and $|a+b|$ related to $|a|$ and $|b|$?
3. How do you describe an interval of real numbers with absolute values?
4. Show by example how to restrict the domain of a function to keep the function's outputs near a particular value.

For Your Review

Write brief paragraphs about the following topics and give examples.

The coordinate plane
Increments and slope
Equations for lines
Functions (in general)
Trigonometric functions
Shifts
Circles
Parabolas
Absolute values and intervals
Target values

Practice Exercises

In Exercises 1–16, write equations for the lines described.

1. Passes through (2, 3) with slope −2
2. Passes through (−3, −5) with slope 1
3. Passes through (3, 1) with slope 1/3
4. Passes through (−1, 2) with slope −1/2
5. Passes through (−2, −2) and (1, 3)
6. Passes through (3, 3) and (−2, 5)
7. Has slope −5/4 and y-intercept 7
8. Has slope 1/2 and y-intercept −1
9. Passes through (−8, 10) and has slope 0
10. Passes through (1/2, 10) and has no slope
11. Has y-intercept −4 and x-intercept 3
12. Has y-intercept 5 and x-intercept −2
13. Passes through (6, 0) parallel to the line $2x - y = -2$
14. Passes through (3, 1) parallel to the line $2x - 3y = 7$
15. Passes through (4, −12) perpendicular to the line $4x + 3y = 12$
16. Passes through (0, 1) perpendicular to the line $\sqrt{3}\,x + y = -3$

To be sure you are familiar with the functions in Exercises 17–32, see if you can sketch their graphs from memory. State the function's domain and range with each graph.

17. $y = x^2$ **18.** $y = x^3$ **19.** $y = x^{2/3}$

20. $y = \sqrt{x}$ **21.** $y = \sqrt[3]{x}$ **22.** $y = \dfrac{1}{x}$

23. $y = \dfrac{1}{x^2}$ **24.** $y = x^{3/2}$ **25.** $y = \lfloor x \rfloor$

26. $y = \lceil x \rceil$ **27.** $y = \cos x$ **28.** $y = \sin x$

29. $y = \tan x$ **30.** $y = \cot x$ **31.** $y = \sec x$

32. $y = \csc x$

In Exercises 33–38, say whether the functions are even, odd, or neither.

33. **a)** $y = \cos x$ **b)** $y = -\cos x$ **c)** $y = 1 - \cos x$

34. **a)** $y = \sin x$ **b)** $y = -\sin x$ **c)** $y = 1 - \sin x$

35. **a)** $y = x^2 + 1$ **b)** $y = x$ **c)** $y = x(x^2 + 1)$

36. **a)** $y = x^3$ **b)** $y = -x$ **c)** $y = -x^4$

37. **a)** $y = (\sin x)/x, \quad x \neq 0$ **b)** $y = |x| \sin x$

38. **a)** $y = 3x^5 - 4x^3 + x$ **b)** $y = |3x^5 - 4x^3 + x|$

39. Graph $y = \cos x$ and $y = \lfloor \cos x \rfloor$ together for $0 \le x \le 2\pi$.

40. Graph $y = \cos x$ and $y = \lceil \cos x \rceil$ together for $0 \le x \le 2\pi$.

41. If $f(x)$ is an odd function of x, can you conclude anything about the value of $f(0)$? Give reasons for your answer.

42. If $f(x)$ is an even function of x, can you conclude anything about the function $g(x) = f(x) - 2$? Give reasons for your answer.

Graph the functions in Exercises 43 and 44.

43. $y = \begin{cases} 1, & x \le -2 \\ \dfrac{1}{x+2}, & x > -2 \end{cases}$

44. $y = \begin{cases} \sqrt{-x}, & -4 \le x \le 0 \\ \sqrt{x}, & 0 < x \le 4 \end{cases}$

Write formulas for the functions graphed in Exercises 45 and 46.

45.

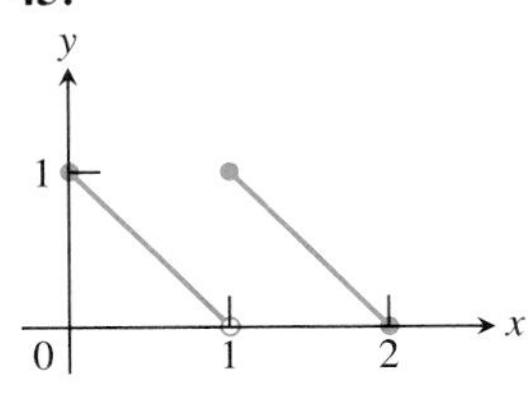

46.

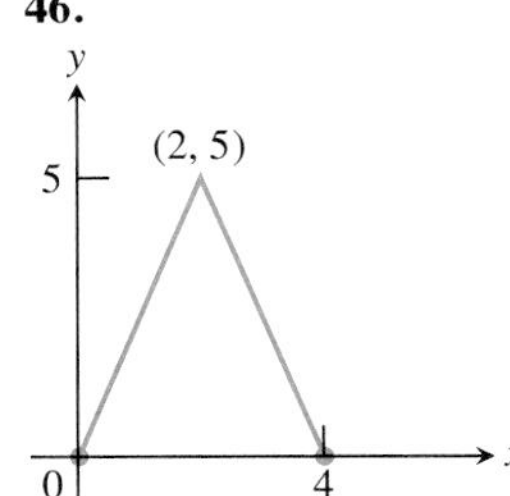

47. Let $f(t) = 1/t$, $g(t) = 1 + t$, $u(t) = \tan t$, and $v(t) = t^2$. Express each of the following functions as a composite involving one or more of f, g, u, and v.

a) $y = \dfrac{1}{1 + t}$ **b)** $y = \dfrac{1}{1 + t^2}$

c) $y = \tan^2 t$ **d)** $y = \sec^2 t$

e) $y = 2 + t$ **f)** $y = 3 + t$

g) $y = \tan(1 + t)$ **h)** $y = \tan\left(1 + \dfrac{1}{t}\right)$

48. Let $f(x) = \sin x$, $g(x) = \sqrt{x}$, $u(x) = x^2$, and $v(x) = x - 0.5$. Express each of the following functions as a composite involving one or more of f, g, u, and v.

a) $y = (\sin x) - 0.5$ **b)** $y = \sqrt{x} - 0.5$

c) $y = \left(\sqrt{x} - 0.5\right)^2$ **d)** $y = x^4$

e) $y = \sin(x - 0.5)$ **f)** $y = |x|$

g) $y = |\sin x|$ **h)** $y = |x| - 0.5$

Exercises 49–54 tell how many units and in what directions the graphs of the given equations are to be shifted. Give an equation for the shifted graph. Then sketch the original and shifted graphs together, labeling each graph with its equation.

49. $y = x^2$ **a)** Down 1, right 2 **b)** Left 2

50. $x = y^2$ **a)** Left 2 **b)** Up 2, right 2

51. $y = \sin x$ **a)** Right $\pi/2$ **b)** Up 1, right π

52. $y = \cos x$ **a)** Left π **b)** Down 1, left $\pi/2$

53. $y = \sqrt{x}$ **a)** Right 2 **b)** Left 2

54. $y = x^3$ **a)** Up 1, right 1 **b)** Left 1

55. The figure below shows the graph of a function $f(x)$. Sketch the graphs of

a) $f(x + 2) - 1$ **b)** $f(x - 1) + 2$.

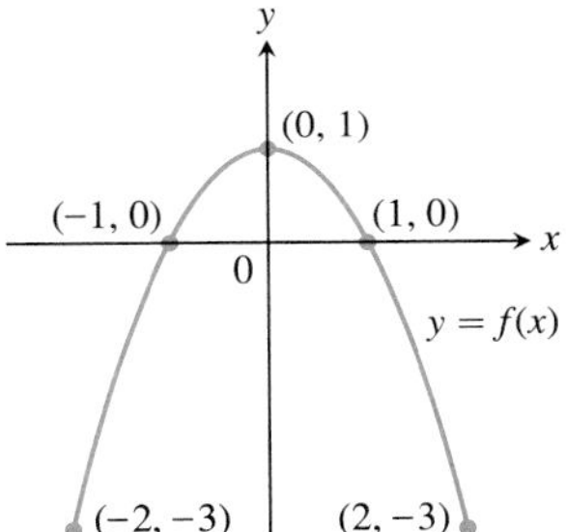

56. The figure below shows the graph of a function $g(x)$. Sketch the graphs of

a) $g(x - 2) + 1$ **b)** $g(x + 1) - 1$.

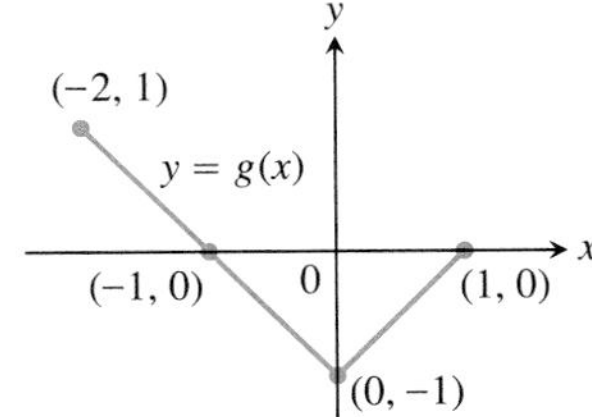

57. The graph of a function $y = f(x)$ in the xy-plane is shifted 5 units to the left and 3 units up. Write an equation for the new graph.

58. The graph of the equation $y - 3 = (x + 7)^2$ is shifted 1 unit to the right and 3 units down. Write an equation for the new graph.

In Exercises 59–62, write an equation for the circle with center (h, k) and radius a.

59. $(h, k) = (1, 1), \quad a = 1$

60. $(h, k) = (2, 0), \quad a = \sqrt{5}$

61. $(h, k) = (2, -3), \quad a = \frac{1}{2}$

62. $(h, k) = (-3, 0), \quad a = 3$

Identify the centers and radii of the circles in Exercises 63–66.

63. $(x-3)^2 + (y+5)^2 = 16$

64. $(x+1)^2 + (y-7)^2 = 121$

65. $x^2 + (y-5)^2 = 2$

66. $(x+4)^2 + y^2 = 3$

Graph the circles in Exercises 67–70. Label each circle's center and intercepts (if any).

67. $x^2 + y^2 - 3x + 3y = 0$

68. $x^2 + y^2 + 2x + 4y = 0$

69. $x^2 + y^2 + 4x - 2y + 3 = 0$

70. $x^2 + y^2 - 5y + 9/4 = 0$

Graph the parabolas in Exercises 71–74. Label the vertex, axis, and intercepts in each case.

71. $y = x^2 - 4x + 3$

72. $y = -x^2 - 4x$

73. $2y = -x^2 + 6x - 9$

74. $3y = x^2 + 6x + 12$

Write inequalities to describe the regions in Exercises 75 and 76.

75. a) The interior of the circle of radius 2 centered at the point $(2, 3)$
 b) The circle in Part (a) plus its interior

76. a) The exterior of the circle of radius 3 centered at the point $(0, 7)$
 b) The circle in Part (a) plus its exterior

77. (a) Graph the line $y = x$ and the parabola $y = -x^2 + 4x$ and label their points of intersection. (b) Shade the points that lie above the line and below the parabola. What inequalities describe these points?

78. (a) Graph the parabolas $y = -x^2 + 2x$ and $y = x^2 - 4$ and label their points of intersection. (b) Shade the points that lie below the first parabola and above the second. What inequalities describe these points?

Solve the equations in Exercises 79–82 for x, s, or t.

79. $|x - 1| = \frac{1}{2}$

80. $|2 - 3x| = 1$

81. $\left|\frac{2s}{5} + 1\right| = 7$

82. $\left|\frac{5-t}{2}\right| = 7$

Solve the inequalities in Exercises 83–86.

83. $|x + 2| \le \frac{1}{2}$

84. $|2x - 7| \le 3$

85. $\left|y - \frac{2}{5}\right| < \frac{3}{5}$

86. $\left|8 - \frac{y}{2}\right| < 1$

Describe the intervals in Exercises 87–90 with inequalities of the form $|x - x_0| < D$ or $|y - y_0| < E$.

87. $3 < x < 11$

88. $-4 < x < 0$

89. $-1 < y < 7$

90. $-1 < y < 6$

Each of Exercises 91–94 gives a function $y = f(x)$, a number E, and a target value y_0. In each case, find the interval of x-values for which $y = f(x)$ lies within E units of y_0. Then describe the interval with an inequality of the form $|x - x_0| < D$.

	$f(x)$	E	y_0
91.	$2x - 3$	2	1
92.	$4 - x$	2	0
93.	$\sqrt{x+2}$	1	4
94.	$\sqrt{\frac{x+1}{2}}$	$\frac{1}{2}$	1

Graph the equations in Exercises 95–100.

95. $y = -|x|$

96. $y = |x - 2|$

97. $y = |x| - 2$

98. $y = |x - 2|/(x - 2)$

99. $y = |x + 2| + x$

100. $y = |x + 2| + |x|$

101. *Controlling the Flow from a Draining Tank.* Torricelli's law says that if you drain a tank like the one in Fig. 1.90, the rate y at which the water runs out is a constant times the square root of the water's depth. As the tank drains, x decreases, and so does y, but y decreases less rapidly than x. The value of the constant depends on the size of the exit valve.

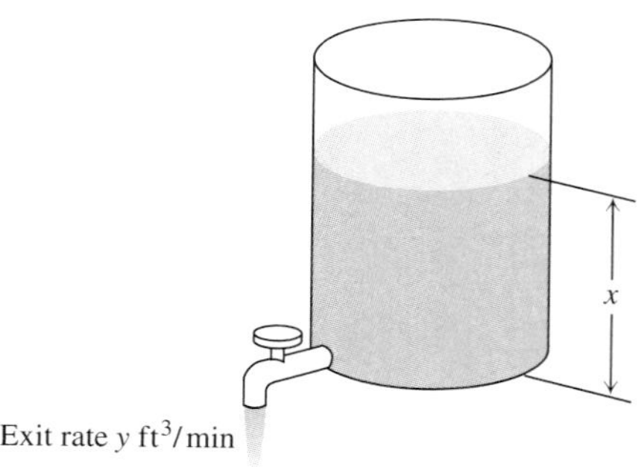

1.90 The tank in Exercise 101.

Suppose that for the tank in question, $y = \sqrt{x}/2$. You are trying to maintain a constant exit rate of $y_0 = 1$ ft^3/min by refilling the tank with a hose from time to time. How deep must you keep the water to keep the rate within 0.2 ft^3/min of $y_0 = 1$? within 0.1 ft^3/min of $y_0 = 1$? In other words, in what interval must you keep x to hold y within 0.2 (or 0.1) units of $y_0 = 1$?

Remark: What if we want to know how long it will take the tank to drain if we do not refill it? We cannot answer such a question with the usual equation time = amount/rate, because the rate changes as the tank drains. We could always open the valve, sit down with a watch, and wait; but with a large tank or a reservoir that might take hours or even days. With calculus, we will be able to find the answer in just a minute or two, as you will see if you do Exercise 59 in Section 4.7.

102. *Dimension Changes in Equipment.* As you probably know, most metals expand when heated and contract when cooled, and people sometimes have to take this into account in their work. Boston and Maine Railroad crews try to lay track at temperatures as close to 65°F as they can, so the track won't expand too much in the summer or shrink too much in the winter. Surveyors have to correct their measurements for temperature when they use steel measuring tapes.

The dimensions of a piece of laboratory equipment are often so critical that the machine shop in which it is made has to be held at the same temperature as the laboratory where the part is to be installed. And, once the piece is installed, the laboratory must continue to be held at that temperature.

A typical aluminum bar that is 10 cm wide at 70°F will be

$$y = 10 + (t - 70) \times 10^{-4}$$

centimeters wide at a nearby temperature t. As t rises above 70, the bar's width increases; as t falls below 70, the bar's width decreases.

Suppose you had a bar like this made for a gravity-wave detector you were building. You need the width of the bar to stay within 0.0005 cm of the ideal 10 cm. How close to 70°F must you maintain the temperature of your laboratory to achieve this? In other words, how close to $t_0 = 70$ must you keep t to be sure that y lies within 0.0005 of $y_0 = 10$?

If you don't think expansion can make a difference, look at these railroad tracks warped by 113° heat in Perugia, Italy. (Source: *The Boston Globe,* July 26, 1988, page 1.)

LIMITS TO POPULATION SIZE

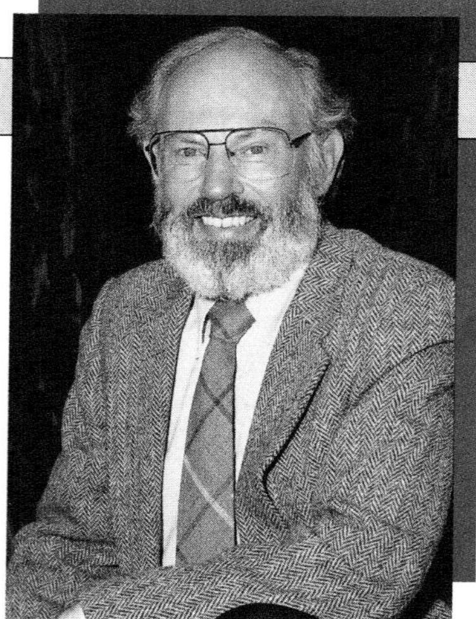

ROLAND LAMBERSON, a mathematician at Humboldt State University, is involved in research that addresses a question on which biologists and economists have disagreed for centuries — "How many is too many?" But overpopulation is hard to define.

Economists argue that additional people produce additional economic resources and a correspondingly higher level of technology. Ecologists and biologists argue that population growth just means more mouths to feed. The underlying question is, "What is the carrying capacity of the environment?" — the upper limit imposed on population size by the environment in which it has to live.

Dr. Lamberson and his colleagues have been trying to answer this question for the northern spotted owl.

Using a mathematical model that varies the initial size of the population but keeps other parameters constant (life span, mating habits, availability of food, number of available nesting sites), they found that the owl population approaches one of two stable levels: 150 pairs for their research area if the initial population is large enough, or zero if the population is not.

The graph here shows the trend in the number of pairs of spotted owls in a 250-year simulation. Each curve was initialized at a different population size. The model assumed that 25% of the landscape was suitable habitat, and that juvenile owls could search 30 sites.

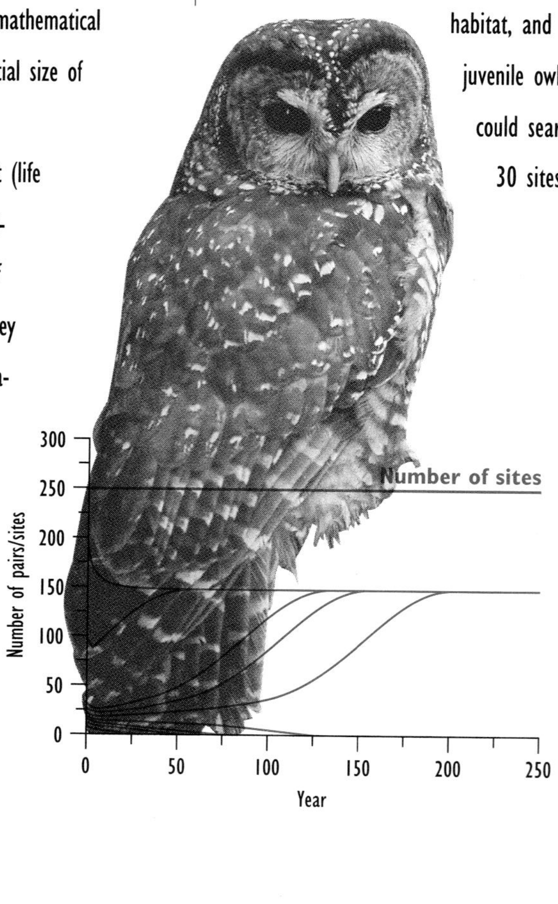

Number of sites
Number of pairs/sites
300
250
200
150
100
50
0
0
50
100
150
200
250
Year

OVERVIEW

This chapter shows how to define and calculate limits of function values.

Calculus is built on the notion of limit. The rules for calculating limits are straightforward and most of the limits we need can be found with a combination of direct substitution and algebra. Proving that the calculation rules always work, however, is a more subtle affair that requires a formal definition of limit. We present this definition in Section 2.5 and show there how it is used to justify the rules.

One of the most important uses of limits in calculus is to test functions for continuity. Continuous functions are widely used in science because they model an enormous range of natural behavior. We will see what makes continuous functions special as the book continues.

2 Limits and Continuity

2.1 Limits of Function Values

A tennis ball falling from the Empire State Building accelerates at first but after four or five seconds reaches a limiting speed we call its terminal speed. The ball then continues on at this speed for its remaining time in the air. A falling leaf reaches its terminal speed more quickly than the ball does, and a falling feather more quickly still. In each case, the resistance of the surrounding air imposes a limit on how fast the object can fall.

When you cough, your windpipe contracts to increase the speed of the air going out. Naturally, there is a limit to how fast the air can go—contract the windpipe a bit and the air speeds up, but contract it too much and the air is choked off.

When a new species is introduced into a region, its population grows rapidly at first but then begins to level off as the members encounter predators and restrictions on food and space. As the days pass, the population, growing ever more slowly, approaches a limiting size, called the carrying capacity of the environment.

These and many other examples convince us that we live in a world of limits. And this is where the calculus comes in. Most of the limits that interest us can be viewed as numerical limits to values of functions, and calculus is the right mathematics for finding the limiting values of functions.

We Live in a World of Limits

There is a limit to how far a cannon can fire a shell. There is a limit to how much an investment can earn in a year. There is a limit to how fast we can stop for a red light. There is a limit to how much weight we can lift and to how long a battery will last. The list is nearly endless.

Examples of Limits

To start off on a slightly different tack, one of the important things to know about a function f is how its outputs will change when the inputs change. If the inputs get closer and closer to some specific value c, for example, will the outputs get closer to some specific value L? If they do, we want to know that because it means we can control the outputs by controlling the inputs, the way we did in Section 1.6.

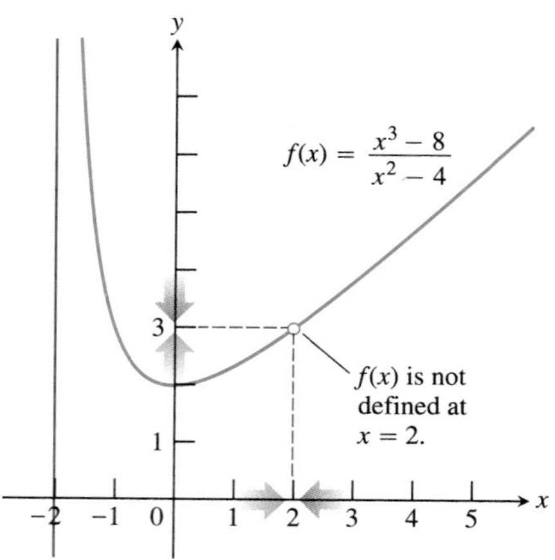

2.1 The values of $f(x) = (x^3 - 8)/(x^2 - 4)$ appear to approach 3 as x approaches 2 (Example 1). The graph has another portion in the third quadrant, not shown here.

EXAMPLE 1 The function

$$f(x) = \frac{x^3 - 8}{x^2 - 4}$$

is not defined at $x = 2$, and we wonder what happens to its values as x approaches this forbidden point. To find out, we make a table of values of f using values of x that approach 2 from either side (Table 2.1) and then graph the function (Fig. 2.1).

TABLE 2.1
Four-place values of $f(x) = (x^3 - 8)/(x^2 - 4)$ as x approaches 2

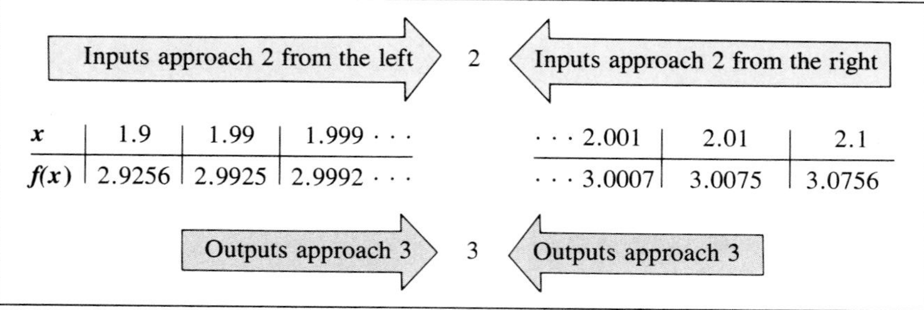

	Inputs approach 2 from the left →			2	← Inputs approach 2 from the right		
x	1.9	1.99	1.999 ···		··· 2.001	2.01	2.1
$f(x)$	2.9256	2.9925	2.9992 ···		··· 3.0007	3.0075	3.0756
		Outputs approach 3 →		3	← Outputs approach 3		

The numerical and graphical evidence suggests that the values of f approach 3 as x approaches 2 from either side.

EXAMPLE 2 The function

$$g(x) = (1 + x)^{1/x}$$

is not defined at $x = 0$, but *is* defined for all values of x greater than zero. It is always a good idea to investigate a function's behavior at the extremes of its domain, so we evaluate g at selected values of x that approach zero from the right (Table 2.2). We also graph the function (Fig. 2.2).

You will notice that the truncated calculator values in Table 2.2 have more decimal places than we can use in graphing. We include them to improve our idea of what the limiting value of g, if it exists, might be. The graph shows the

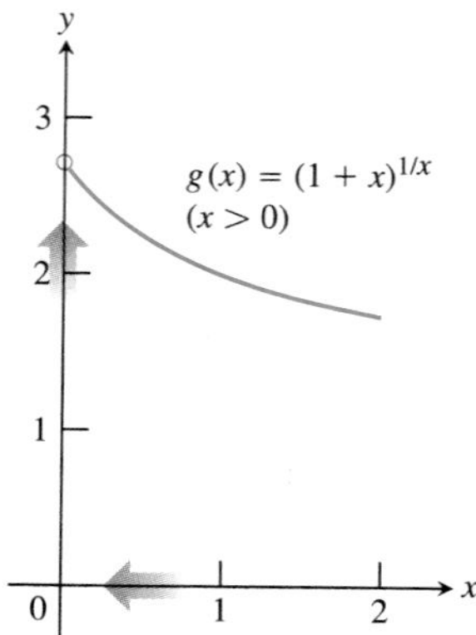

2.2 The values of the function $g(x) = (1 + x)^{1/x}$ for $x > 0$ appear to approach a limiting value of about 2.7 as x approaches zero from the right (Example 2).

TABLE 2.2
Values of $g(x) = (1 + x)^{1/x}$ as x approaches 0 from the right

x	$(1 + x)^{1/x}$ (calculator, truncated)
1.0	2.0
0.5	2.25
0.1	2.5937 42460
0.01	2.7048 13829
0.001	2.7169 23932
0.0000 01	2.7182 80469
1×10^{-8}	2.7182 81814
1×10^{-10}	2.7182 81828

global pattern and reveals the function's behavior in relation to its other values. The table gives the fine details.

The graph suggests that the values of g do approach a limiting value as x approaches zero from the right, and the table suggests that the limit is about 2.71828. As we will see in Chapter 6, this limit is the number e that forms the base of the exponential function $y = e^x$. Its value to 15 places is

$$e = 2.7\ 1828\ 1828\ 45\ 90\ 45.$$

Notice in Examples 1 and 2 that each limit appears to exist even though the function involved is not defined at the value being approached by x. But even if a function is defined at the point x is approaching, it does not mean that the limit has to equal the function value there. The limit may very well be different.

EXAMPLE 3 What happens to the values of the function

$$f(x) = \begin{cases} x, & x \neq 2 \\ 3, & x = 2 \end{cases}$$

as x approaches 2?

Solution The graph of f (Fig. 2.3) consists of the line $y = x$ with the point (2, 2) removed and replaced by the point (2, 3). Even though $f(2)$ now equals 3, the values of f still approach 2 as x approaches 2 from either side.

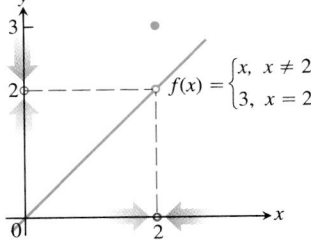

2.3 The graph of

$$f(x) = \begin{cases} x, & x \neq 2 \\ 3, & x = 2. \end{cases}$$

Notice that $f(x) \to 2$ as $x \to 2$ even though $f(2)$ itself is 3.

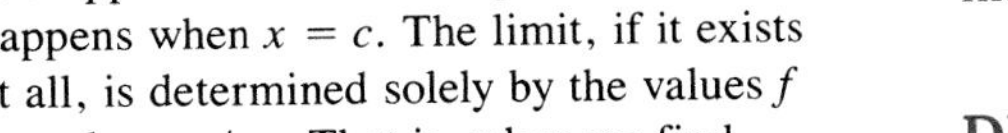

Examples 1–3 illustrate an important point about limits: The limit of a function $f(x)$ as x approaches c *never* depends on what happens when $x = c$. The limit, if it exists at all, is determined solely by the values f has when $x \neq c$. That is, when we find limits, we look at values near c but not equal to c.

An Informal Definition of Limit

To talk effectively about what we have seen in Examples 1–3 and to develop the tools we need to confirm (and sometimes to refute) what graphs and tables seem to say about functions, we need a mathematical language of limits. We develop it in two steps. First, we define the notion of limit informally and learn how to calculate limits. Then, in Section 2.5, we define limit more precisely and examine the mathematics behind our calculations.

DEFINITION

Informal Definition of Limit

If the values of a function $f(x)$ approach the value L as x approaches c, we say that f has **limit** L as x approaches c and write

$$\lim_{x \to c} f(x) = L$$

Read "The limit of f as x approaches c equals L."

Using this mathematical language, we can express the limits found in the previous examples as follows:

$$\lim_{x \to 2} \frac{x^3 - 8}{x^2 - 4} = 3$$

$$\lim_{x \to 0^+} (1 + x)^{1/x} \approx 2.71828$$

$$\lim_{x \to 2} f(x) = 2.$$

The notation $x \to 0^+$ means x is approaching zero *from the right.*

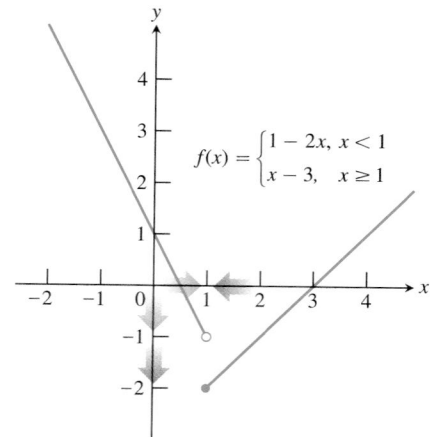

2.4 The function in Example 4.

When Limits Do Not Exist

Unlike the examples just mentioned, there are functions for which a limit does not exist. Before we look at such functions, first notice that the limit in Example 2 is **one-sided,** whereas the limits in Examples 1 and 3 are **two-sided.** A one-sided limit can be either a **right-hand limit** or a **left-hand limit.**

Right-hand:	$\lim_{x\to c^+} f(x)$	The limit of f as x approaches c from the right
Left-hand:	$\lim_{x\to c^-} f(x)$	The limit of f as x approaches c from the left
Two-sided:	$\lim_{x\to c} f(x)$	The limit of f as x approaches c from both sides

EXAMPLE 4 Find $\lim_{x\to 1} f(x)$ for the function

$$f(x) = \begin{cases} 1 - 2x, & x < 1 \\ x - 3, & x \geq 1. \end{cases}$$

Solution We graph the function f in Fig. 2.4. As we can see in the graph,

$$\lim_{x\to 1^-} f(x) = -1 \quad \text{and} \quad \lim_{x\to 1^+} f(x) = -2.$$

The right-hand and left-hand limits of f at 1 differ, so the function has no *single* limiting value as x approaches 1. In this case, we say that $\lim_{x\to 1} f(x)$ does not exist.

Example 4 illustrates the fact that in order for a two-sided limit of a function to exist, it must be unique: It must be the same as both the right-hand limit and the left-hand limit.

Existence of a (Two-sided) Limit

A function $f(x)$ has a limit as x approaches c if and only if the right-hand and left-hand limits at c exist and are equal. In symbols,

$$\lim_{x\to c} f(x) = L \quad \Leftrightarrow \quad \lim_{x\to c^+} f(x) = L \quad \text{and} \quad \lim_{x\to c^-} f(x) = L. \tag{1}$$

The implications in Eq. (1) will be proved formally in Section 2.5, but you can see what is going on if you look at the next examples.

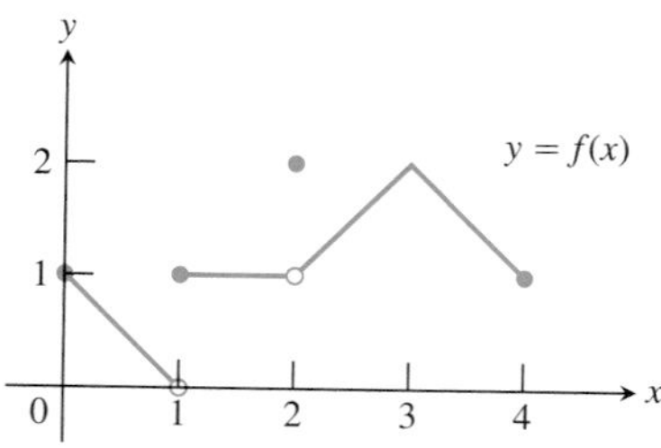

2.5 Example 5 discusses the limit properties of the function $y = f(x)$ graphed here.

EXAMPLE 5 All the following statements about the function $y = f(x)$ graphed in Fig. 2.5 are true.

At $x = 0$: $\lim_{x\to 0^+} f(x) = 1$

At $x = 1$: $\lim_{x\to 1^-} f(x) = 0$ even though $f(1) = 1$,

$\lim_{x\to 1^+} f(x) = 1$,

$f(x)$ has no limit as $x \to 1$ (The right- and left-hand limits at 1 are not equal.)

At $x = 2$: $\lim_{x\to 2^-} f(x) = 1,$

$\lim_{x\to 2^+} f(x) = 1,$

$\lim_{x\to 2} f(x) = 1$ even though $f(2) = 2$

At $x = 3$: $\lim_{x\to 3^-} f(x) = \lim_{x\to 3^+} f(x) = \lim_{x\to 3} f(x) = f(3) = 2$

At $x = 4$: $\lim_{x\to 4^-} f(x) = 1$

At every other point c between 0 and 4, $f(x)$ has a limit as $x \to c$:

$$\lim_{x\to 0.5} f(x) = 0.5, \qquad \lim_{x\to 3.5} f(x) = 1.5, \qquad \text{and so on.}$$

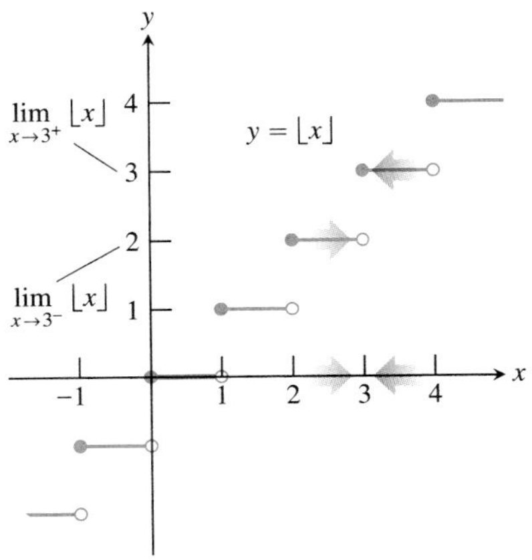

2.6 At each integer, the greatest integer function $y = \lfloor x \rfloor$ has different right-hand and left-hand limits (Example 6).

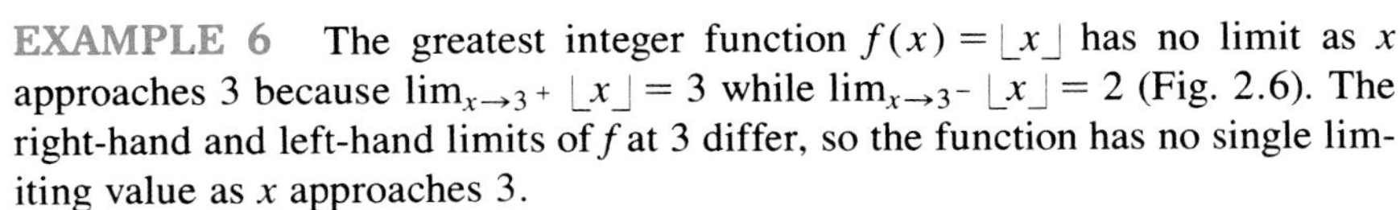

EXAMPLE 6 The greatest integer function $f(x) = \lfloor x \rfloor$ has no limit as x approaches 3 because $\lim_{x\to 3^+} \lfloor x \rfloor = 3$ while $\lim_{x\to 3^-} \lfloor x \rfloor = 2$ (Fig. 2.6). The right-hand and left-hand limits of f at 3 differ, so the function has no single limiting value as x approaches 3.

In general, $\lim_{x\to c} \lfloor x \rfloor$ does not exist if c is an integer. However, if c is any number other than an integer, $\lim_{x\to c^-} \lfloor x \rfloor = \lim_{x\to c^+} \lfloor x \rfloor = \lim_{x\to c} \lfloor x \rfloor = \lfloor c \rfloor$:

$$\lim_{x\to -0.5} \lfloor x \rfloor = \lfloor -0.5 \rfloor = -1, \qquad \lim_{x\to 2.1} \lfloor x \rfloor = \lfloor 2.1 \rfloor = 2, \qquad \text{and so on.}$$

In the examples we have seen so far, the functions that failed to have limits at various points did so because the right-hand and left-hand limits at those points were not equal. The function in the next example fails to have a limit because neither the right-hand limit nor the left-hand limit exists at all.

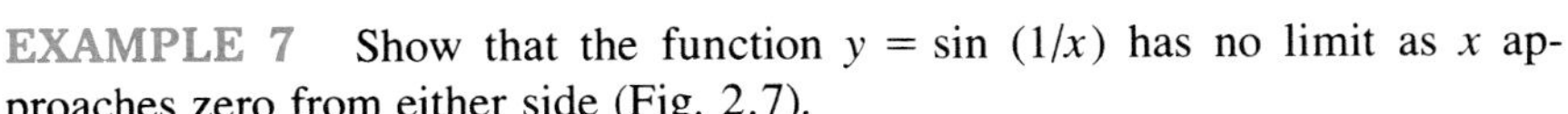

EXAMPLE 7 Show that the function $y = \sin(1/x)$ has no limit as x approaches zero from either side (Fig. 2.7).

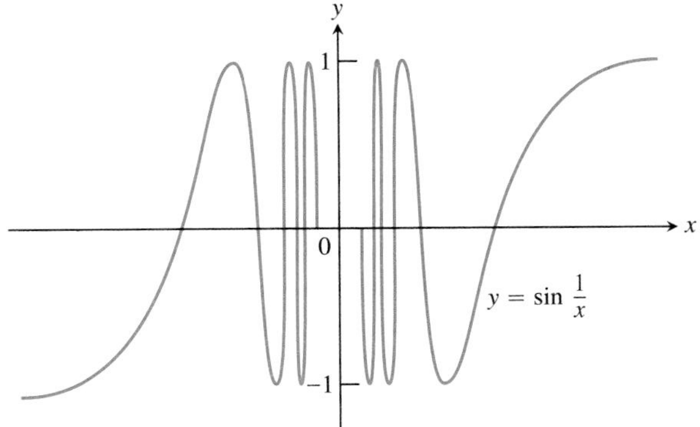

2.7 The function $y = \sin(1/x)$ has neither a right-hand nor a left-hand limit as x approaches zero (Example 7).

Solution As x approaches zero, its reciprocal, $1/x$, becomes infinite and the values of $\sin(1/x)$ cycle repeatedly from -1 to 1. Thus there is no single number L that the function's values all get close to as x approaches zero. This is true even if we restrict x to positive values or to negative values. The function has neither a right-hand limit nor a left-hand limit as x approaches zero.

General Rules for Calculating Limits

In order to find ways to calculate limits of algebraic functions, we need to establish the properties of limits. We first look at the limits of two basic functions: the identity function and the constant function.

EXAMPLE 8 If f is the **identity function** $f(x) = x$, then for any value of c,

$$\lim_{x \to c} f(x) = \lim_{x \to c} x = c.$$

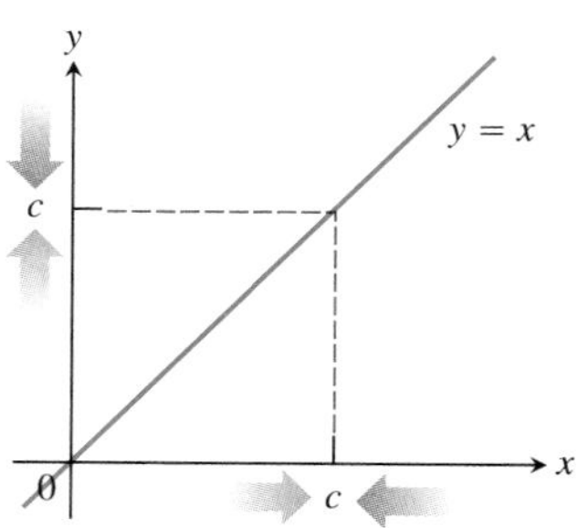

EXAMPLE 9 If f is the **constant function** $f(x) = k$ (the function whose outputs have the constant value k), then for any value of c,

$$\lim_{x \to c} f(x) = \lim_{x \to c} k = k.$$

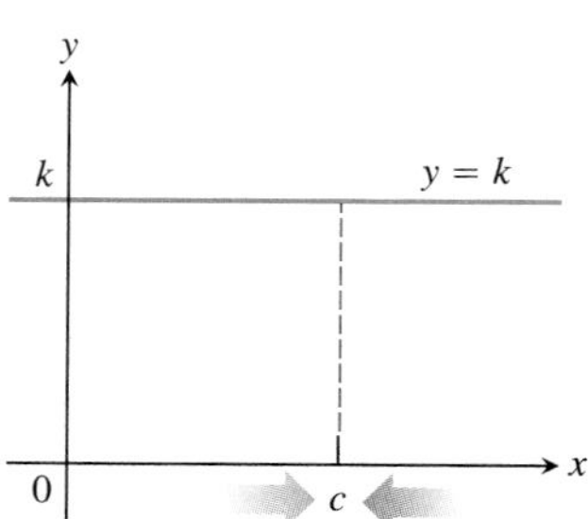

We could now go on to make a huge list of functions and their limits but we would be missing the boat if we did. There is a more constructive way to proceed, as described in the following theorem.

THEOREM 1

Properties of Limits

The following rules hold if $\lim_{x \to c} f(x) = L_1$ and $\lim_{x \to c} g(x) = L_2$. ($L_1$ and L_2 are real numbers.)

1. *Sum Rule:* $\lim_{x \to c} [f(x) + g(x)] = \lim_{x \to c} f(x) + \lim_{x \to c} g(x) = L_1 + L_2$
2. *Difference Rule:* $\lim_{x \to c} [f(x) - g(x)] = \lim_{x \to c} f(x) - \lim_{x \to c} g(x) = L_1 - L_2$
3. *Product Rule:* $\lim_{x \to c} [f(x) \cdot g(x)] = \lim_{x \to c} f(x) \cdot \lim_{x \to c} g(x) = L_1 \cdot L_2$
4. *Constant Multiple Rule:* $\lim_{x \to c} [k \cdot g(x)] = k \lim_{x \to c} g(x) = k \cdot L_2$ (any number k)
5. *Quotient Rule:* $\lim_{x \to c} \dfrac{f(x)}{g(x)} = \dfrac{\lim_{x \to c} f(x)}{\lim_{x \to c} g(x)} = \dfrac{L_1}{L_2}$ if $L_2 \neq 0$

In words, the formulas in Theorem 1 say:

1. The limit of the sum of two functions is the sum of their limits.
2. The limit of the difference of two functions is the difference of their limits.
3. The limit of a product of two functions is the product of their limits.
4. The limit of a constant times a function is the constant times the limit of the function.
5. The limit of a quotient of two functions is the quotient of their limits, provided the denominator does not tend to zero.

We have included a formal proof of Theorem 1 in Appendix 2. Informally, we can paraphrase the theorem in terms that make it seem highly reasonable: When x is close to c, $f(x)$ is close to L_1 and $g(x)$ is close to L_2. Then we naturally expect $f(x) + g(x)$ to be close to $L_1 + L_2$; $f(x) - g(x)$ to be close to $L_1 - L_2$; $f(x) \cdot g(x)$ to be close to $L_1 \cdot L_2$; and $f(x)/g(x)$ to be close to L_1/L_2 if L_2 is not zero.

What keeps this discussion from being a proof is that the word *close* is vague. Phrases like *arbitrarily close to* and *sufficiently close to* might seem at first to improve the argument, but what are really needed are the formal definitions and arguments developed for the purpose by the great European mathematicians of the nineteenth century. You will see what we mean when you read Section 2.5.

In the meantime, here are some examples of what Theorem 1 can do for us.

EXAMPLE 10 We know from Examples 8 and 9 that $\lim_{x\to c} x = c$ and $\lim_{x\to c} k = k$. The various parts of Theorem 1 now let us combine these results to calculate other limits:

a) $\lim_{x\to c} x^2 = \lim_{x\to c} x \cdot x = \lim_{x\to c} x \cdot \lim_{x\to c} x = c \cdot c = c^2$ — Product

b) $\lim_{x\to c} (x^2 + 5) = \lim_{x\to c} x^2 + \lim_{x\to c} 5$ — Sum

$= c^2 + 5$ — From (a)

c) $\lim_{x\to c} 4x^2 = 4 \lim_{x\to c} x^2$ — Constant multiple

$= 4c^2$ — From (a)

d) $\lim_{x\to c} (4x^2 - 3) = \lim_{x\to c} 4x^2 - \lim_{x\to c} 3$ — Difference

$= 4c^2 - 3$ — From (c)

e) $\lim_{x\to c} x^3 = \lim_{x\to c} x^2 \cdot x = c^2 \cdot c = c^3$ — Product and (a)

f) $\lim_{x\to c} (x^3 + 4x^2 - 3) = \lim_{x\to c} x^3 + \lim_{x\to c} (4x^2 - 3)$ — Sum

$= c^3 + 4c^2 - 3$ — From (e) and (d)

g) $\lim_{x\to c} \dfrac{x^3 + 4x^2 - 3}{x^2 + 5} = \dfrac{\lim_{x\to c} (x^3 + 4x^2 - 3)}{\lim_{x\to c} (x^2 + 5)}$ — Quotient

$= \dfrac{c^3 + 4c^2 - 3}{c^2 + 5}$ — From (f) and (b)

Example 10 shows the remarkable power of Theorem 1. From the two simple observations that $\lim_{x \to c} x = c$ and $\lim_{x \to c} k = k$ we can immediately work our way to limits of polynomials and **rational functions** (ratios of polynomials). As in part (f) of Example 10, the limit of any polynomial $f(x)$ as x approaches c is $f(c)$, the number we get when we substitute $x = c$. As in part (g) of Example 10, the limit of the ratio $f(x)/g(x)$ of two polynomials is $f(c)/g(c)$, provided $g(c)$ is not zero.

THEOREM 2

Limits of Polynomials Can Be Found by Substitution

If $f(x) = a_n x^n + a_{n-1} x^{n-1} + \cdots + a_0$ is a polynomial function, and c is any number, then

$$\lim_{x \to c} f(x) = f(c) = a_n c^n + a_{n-1} c^{n-1} + \cdots + a_0. \qquad (2)$$

EXAMPLE 11

a) $\lim_{x \to 3} x^2 (2 - x) = \lim_{x \to 3} (2x^2 - x^3) = 2(3)^2 - (3)^3 = 18 - 27 = -9$

b) Same limit, found another way:

$$\lim_{x \to 3} x^2(2 - x) = \lim_{x \to 3} x^2 \cdot \lim_{x \to 3} (2 - x) = (3)^2 \cdot (2 - 3) = 9 \cdot (-1) = -9.$$

THEOREM 3

The Limit of a Rational Function Can Be Found by Substitution When the Denominator Is Different from Zero

If $f(x)$ and $g(x)$ are polynomials, and c is any number, then

$$\lim_{x \to c} \frac{f(x)}{g(x)} = \frac{f(c)}{g(c)} \qquad \text{provided} \qquad g(c) \neq 0. \qquad (3)$$

EXAMPLE 12

$$\lim_{x \to 2} \frac{x^2 + 2x + 4}{x + 2} = \frac{(2)^2 + 2(2) + 4}{2 + 2} = \frac{12}{4} = 3.$$

In Example 12, we can use Eq. (3) to find the limit of $f(x)/g(x)$ because the value of the denominator $g(x) = x + 2$ is not zero when $x = 2$. In the next example, the denominator *is* zero when $x = 2$, so we cannot apply Eq. (3) directly. We have to rewrite the fraction $f(x)/g(x)$ first.

EXAMPLE 13 *Continuation of Example 1.* Confirm, as suggested by the evidence in Example 1, that

$$\lim_{x \to 2} \frac{x^3 - 8}{x^2 - 4} = 3.$$

Solution The denominator is 0 when $x = 2$, so we cannot calculate the limit of the given rational function by substitution. However, if we factor the numerator and denominator, we can simplify the fraction as

$$\frac{x^3-8}{x^2-4} = \frac{(x-2)(x^2+2x+4)}{(x-2)(x+2)} = \frac{x^2+2x+4}{x+2}. \tag{4}$$

Is it really all right to cancel factors like this? Yes: When we evaluate a limit as $x \to 2$ we are not concerned with what happens *at* $x = 2$, just *close to* $x = 2$. So, $x \neq 2$ when we take this limit.

With the factor $(x - 2)$ out of the way, we can now find the limit by substitution:

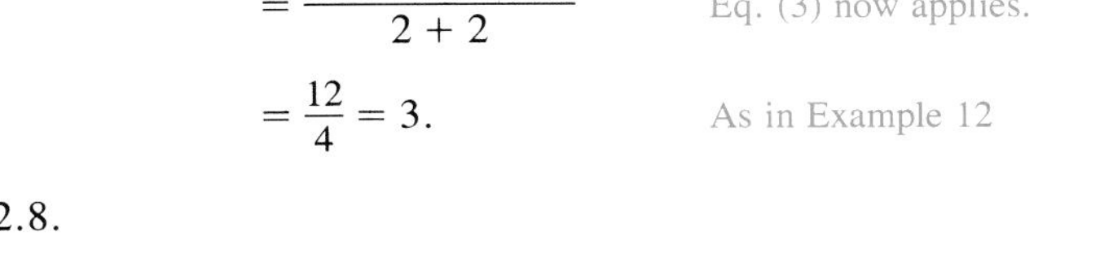

$$\lim_{x\to 2} \frac{x^3-8}{x^2-4} = \lim_{x\to 2} \frac{x^2+2x+4}{x+2} \qquad \text{Eq. (4)}$$

$$= \frac{(2)^2+2(2)+4}{2+2} \qquad \text{Eq. (3) now applies.}$$

$$= \frac{12}{4} = 3. \qquad \text{As in Example 12}$$

See Fig. 2.8.

(a)

(b)

2.8 The functions

$f(x) = (x^3 - 8)/(x^2 - 4)$

and

$g(x) = (x^2 + 2x + 4)/(x + 2)$

differ only at $x = 2$, where f is undefined. Elsewhere, their values and graphs (shown here for $x > -2$) are identical. In particular, they have the same limit as $x \to 2$, a limit that we can find by evaluating g at $x = 2$.

Example 13 illustrates an important fact about finding the limit as $x \to c$ of a rational function where the denominator is 0 when $x = c$: If two functions f and g agree in their values at all but one point c, and if the limit of $g(x)$ as $x \to c$ exists, then the limit of $f(x)$ as $x \to c$ exists and

$$\lim_{x\to c} f(x) = \lim_{x\to c} g(x).$$

In Example 13, we can find the limit of $g(x) = (x^2 + 2x + 4)/(x + 2)$ as $x \to 2$ using substitution. Since $f(x) = (x^3 - 8)/(x^2 - 4)$ and $g(x)$ are identical except at $x = 2$, we also know the limit of $f(x)$ as $x \to 2$.

EXAMPLE 14

$$\lim_{x\to -5} \frac{x^2-25}{3(x+5)}$$

Substitution will not give the limit because $x + 5 = 0$ when $x = -5$.

$$= \lim_{x\to -5} \frac{(x+5)(x-5)}{3(x+5)}$$

We factor the numerator to see if $(x + 5)$ is a factor. It is. We cancel the $(x + 5)$'s, leaving. . .

$$= \lim_{x\to -5} \frac{x-5}{3}$$

. . . an equivalent form whose limit we can now find by substitution.

$$= \frac{-5-5}{3} = -\frac{10}{3}$$

Trigonometric Functions and Square Roots

As we will see in Chapter 3, the limits of trigonometric functions and of composites like square roots of polynomials can be found by substitution at points where they are defined.

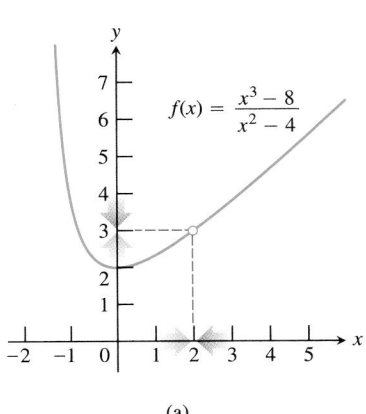

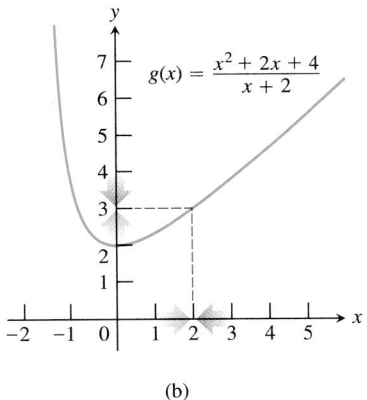

EXAMPLE 15

a) $\lim_{t\to\pi} \dfrac{3+\sin t}{1-\cos t} = \dfrac{3+\sin\pi}{1-\cos\pi} = \dfrac{3+0}{1-(-1)} = \dfrac{3}{2}$

b) $\lim_{x\to 3} \dfrac{\sqrt{3x+7}-\sqrt{7}}{2} = \dfrac{\sqrt{3(3)+7}-\sqrt{7}}{2} = \dfrac{\sqrt{16}-\sqrt{7}}{2} = \dfrac{4-\sqrt{7}}{2}$

Exercises 2.1

In Exercises 1–4, complete the given table and estimate the limit $\lim_{x\to c} f(x)$ suggested by these values.

1. $\lim_{x\to 4} \dfrac{x^2+x-20}{x-4}$

x	3.9	3.99	3.999	4.001	4.01	4.1
$f(x)$						

2. $\lim_{x\to -6} \dfrac{x^2+4x-12}{x+6}$

x	−6.1	−6.01	−6.001	−5.999	−5.99	−5.9
$f(x)$						

3. $\lim_{x\to -1} \dfrac{x^2-1}{|x|-1}$

x	−1.1	−1.01	−1.001	−0.999	−0.99	−0.9
$f(x)$						

4. $\lim_{x\to -2} \dfrac{x^2+3x+2}{2-|x|}$

x	−2.1	−2.01	−2.001	−1.999	−1.99	−1.9
$f(x)$						

In Exercises 5–8, use the graphs to find the limits.

5. $\lim_{x\to 1} f(x)$

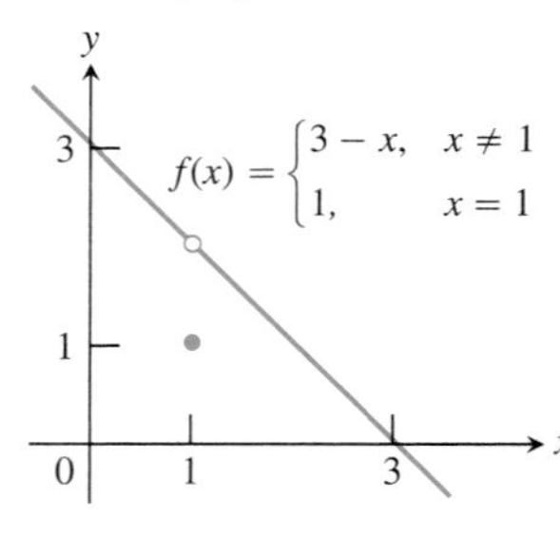

6. $\lim_{x\to -2} f(x)$

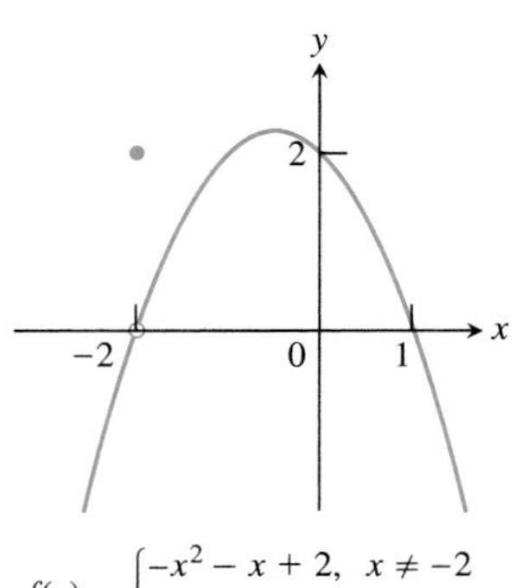

$f(x) = \begin{cases} -x^2 - x + 2, & x \neq -2 \\ 2, & x = -2 \end{cases}$

7. a) $\lim_{x\to 0^+} g(x)$

b) $\lim_{x\to 0^-} g(x)$

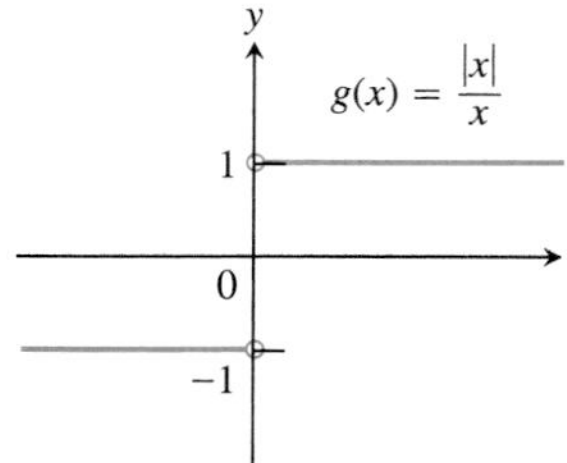

8. a) $\lim_{x\to -2^+} g(x)$

b) $\lim_{x\to -2^-} g(x)$

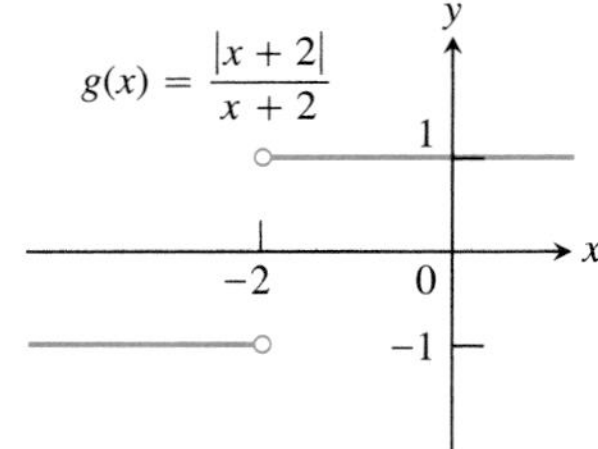

In Exercises 9–12, use the graphs to estimate the limits. (Printed graphs can shift during a press run, so your answers may differ slightly from those in the back of the book.)

9. $\lim_{x\to 0} \dfrac{\sqrt{3x+1}-1}{2x}$

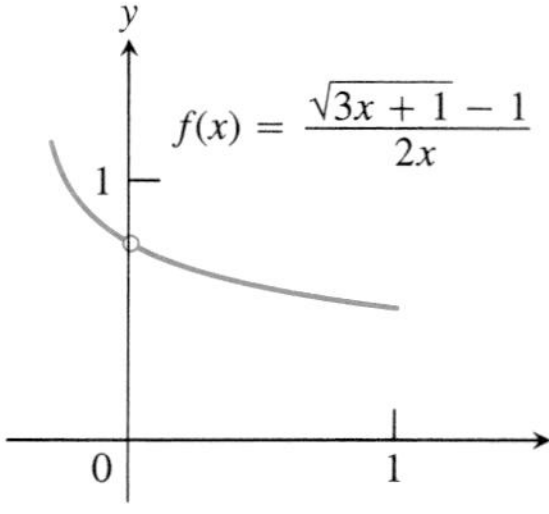

10. $\lim_{x\to 1} \dfrac{x-1}{x-\sqrt[4]{x}}$

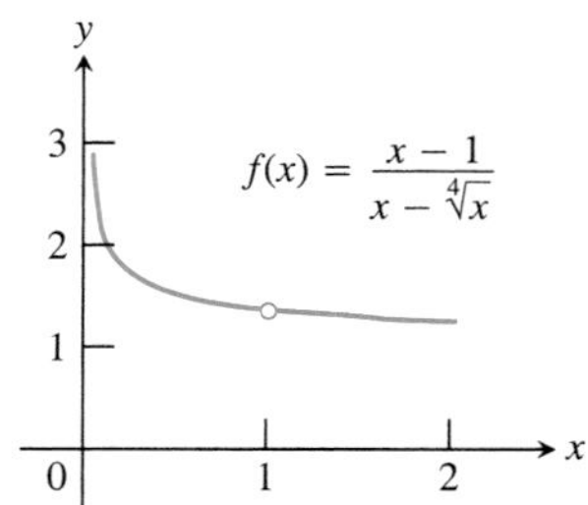

11. $\lim_{x\to 0} \dfrac{3 \tan x}{4x}$

12. $\lim_{x\to 0} \dfrac{5 \cos (x + (\pi/2))}{4x}$

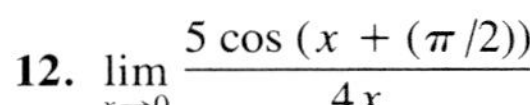

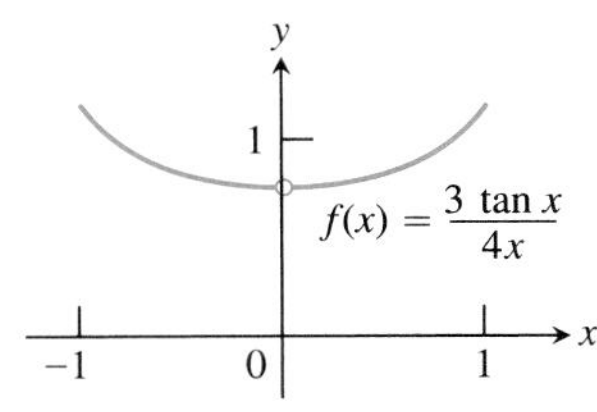

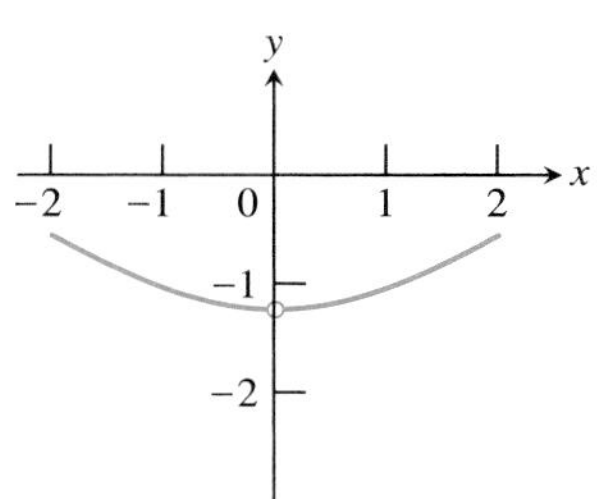

13. Which of the following statements about the function $y = f(x)$ graphed here are true, and which are false?

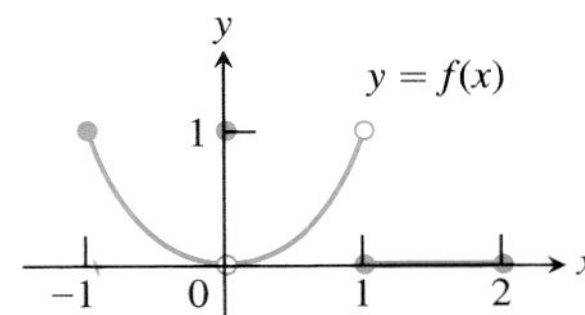

a) $\lim_{x\to -1^+} f(x) = 1$
b) $\lim_{x\to 0^-} f(x) = 0$
c) $\lim_{x\to 0^-} f(x) = 1$
d) $\lim_{x\to 0^-} f(x) = \lim_{x\to 0^+} f(x)$
e) $\lim_{x\to 0} f(x)$ exists
f) $\lim_{x\to 0} f(x) = 0$
g) $\lim_{x\to 0} f(x) = 1$
h) $\lim_{x\to 1} f(x) = 1$
i) $\lim_{x\to 1} f(x) = 0$
j) $\lim_{x\to 2^-} f(x) = 2$

14. Which of the following statements about the function $y = f(x)$ graphed here are true, and which are false?

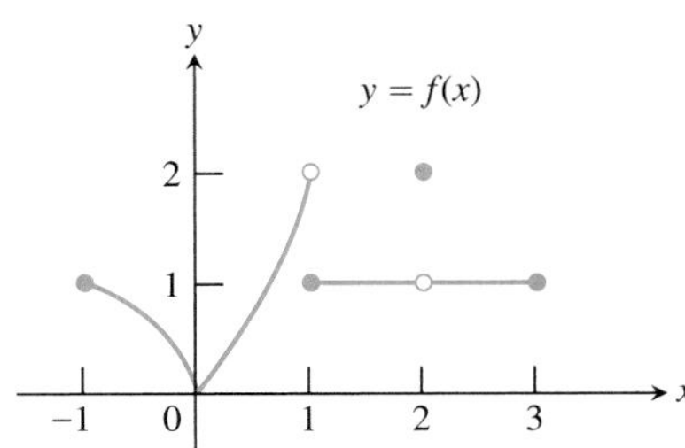

a) $\lim_{x\to -1^+} f(x) = 1$
b) $\lim_{x\to 2} f(x)$ does not exist.
c) $\lim_{x\to 2} f(x) = 2$
d) $\lim_{x\to 1^-} f(x) = 2$
e) $\lim_{x\to 1^+} f(x) = 1$
f) $\lim_{x\to 1} f(x)$ does not exist.
g) $\lim_{x\to 0^+} f(x) = \lim_{x\to 0^-} f(x)$
h) $\lim_{x\to c} f(x)$ exists at every c in the open interval $(-1, 1)$.
i) $\lim_{x\to c} f(x)$ exists at every c in the open interval $(1, 3)$.

15. Let $f(x) = \begin{cases} 3 - x, & x < 2 \\ \dfrac{x}{2} + 1, & x > 2 \end{cases}$

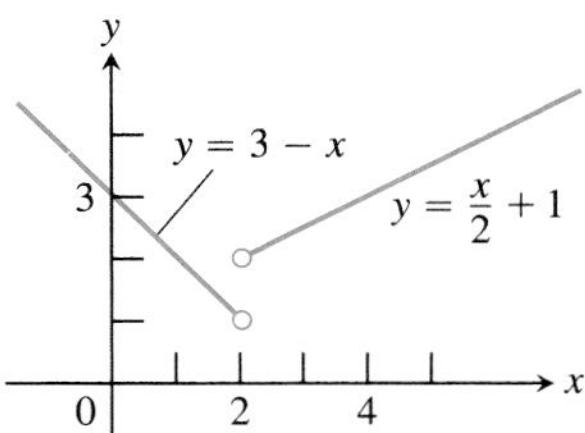

a) Find $\lim_{x\to 2^+} f(x)$ and $\lim_{x\to 2^-} f(x)$.
b) Does $\lim_{x\to 2} f(x)$ exist? If so, what is it? If not, why not?
c) Find $\lim_{x\to 4^-} f(x)$ and $\lim_{x\to 4^+} f(x)$.
d) Does $\lim_{x\to 4} f(x)$ exist? If so, what is it? If not, why not?

16. Let $f(x) = \begin{cases} 3 - x, & x < 2 \\ 2, & x = 2 \\ \dfrac{x}{2}, & x > 2. \end{cases}$

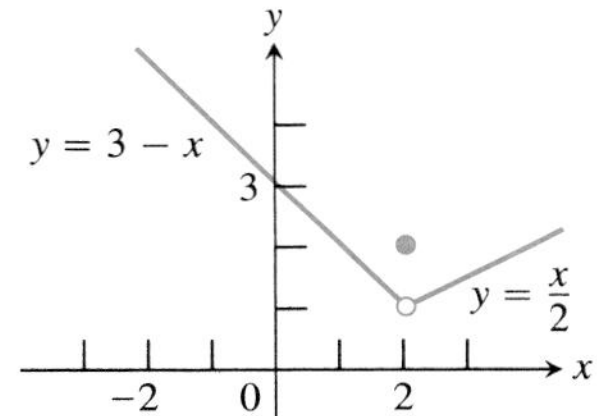

a) Find $\lim_{x\to 2^+} f(x)$, $\lim_{x\to 2^-} f(x)$, and $f(2)$.
b) Does $\lim_{x\to 2} f(x)$ exist? If so, what is it? If not, why not?
c) Find $\lim_{x\to -1^-} f(x)$ and $\lim_{x\to -1^+} f(x)$.
d) Does $\lim_{x\to -1} f(x)$ exist? If so, what is it? If not, why not?

17. **a)** Graph $f(x) = \begin{cases} x^3, & x \neq 1 \\ 0, & x = 1. \end{cases}$
b) Find $\lim_{x\to 1^-} f(x)$ and $\lim_{x\to 1^+} f(x)$.
c) Does $\lim_{x\to 1} f(x)$ exist? If so, what is it? If not, why not?

18. **a)** Graph $f(x) = \begin{cases} 1 - x^2, & x \neq 1 \\ 2, & x = 1. \end{cases}$
b) Find $\lim_{x\to 1^+} f(x)$ and $\lim_{x\to 1^-} f(x)$.
c) Does $\lim_{x\to 1} f(x)$ exist? If so, what is it? If not, why not?

Graph the functions in Exercises 19 and 20. Then answer these questions:

a) What are the domain and range of f?
b) At what points c, if any, in the interior of the domain does $\lim_{x\to c} f(x)$ exist?
c) At what points in the domain does only the left-hand limit exist?
d) At what points in the domain does only the right-hand limit exist?

19. $f(x) = \begin{cases} \sqrt{1-x^2} & \text{if } 0 \le x < 1 \\ 1 & \text{if } 1 \le x < 2 \\ 2 & \text{if } x = 2 \end{cases}$

20. $f(x) = \begin{cases} x & \text{if } -1 \le x < 0, \text{ or } 0 < x \le 1 \\ 1 & \text{if } x = 0 \\ 0 & \text{if } x < -1, \text{ or } x > 1 \end{cases}$

21. Let $f(x) = \begin{cases} 0, & x \le 0 \\ \sin \frac{1}{x}, & x > 0. \end{cases}$

a) Does $\lim_{x\to 0^+} f(x)$ exist? If so, what is it? If not, why not?
b) Does $\lim_{x\to 0^-} f(x)$ exist? If so, what is it? If not, why not?
c) Does $\lim_{x\to 0} f(x)$ exist? If so, what is it? If not, why not?

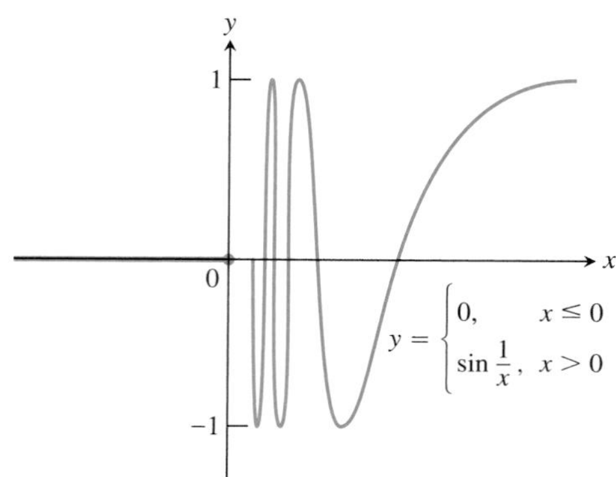

22. Let $f(x) = \begin{cases} 0, & x = 0 \\ x \sin \frac{1}{x}, & x \ne 0. \end{cases}$

a) Does $\lim_{x\to 0^+} f(x)$ exist? If so, what is it? If not, why not?
b) Does $\lim_{x\to 0^-} f(x)$ exist? If so, what is it? If not, why not?
c) Does $\lim_{x\to 0} f(x)$ exist? If so, what is it? If not, why not?

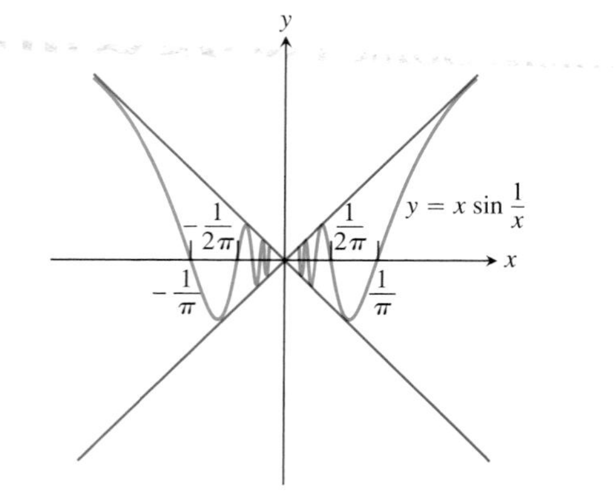

Find the limits in Exercises 23–42. (You may want to visualize your answer by graphing the function using a grapher.)

23. $\lim_{x\to -7} (2x + 5)$

24. $\lim_{x\to 12} (10 - 3x)$

25. $\lim_{x\to 2} (-x^2 + 5x - 2)$

26. $\lim_{x\to -1} (3x^2 - 6x - 1)$

27. $\lim_{x\to 1} (x^3 + 3x^2 - 2x - 17)$

28. $\lim_{x\to -2} (x^3 - 2x^2 + 4x + 8)$

29. $\lim_{x\to 1/3} (3x - 1)$

30. $\lim_{x\to 1/2} x(2 - x)$

31. $\lim_{x\to 0} 5(2x - 1)$

32. $\lim_{x\to -1} 3x(2x - 1)$

33. $\lim_{x\to -1} 3(2x - 1)^2$

34. $\lim_{x\to -4} (x + 3)^{1984}$

35. $\lim_{x\to 2} 5(2x - 1)(x + 1)$

36. $\lim_{x\to 6} 8(x - 5)(x - 7)$

37. $\lim_{x\to 2} \dfrac{x + 3}{x + 6}$

38. $\lim_{x\to 5} \dfrac{4}{x - 7}$

39. $\lim_{x\to -1^+} \dfrac{x + 3}{x^2 + 3x + 1}$

40. $\lim_{x\to 0^+} \dfrac{4 - x}{3 + x^3}$

41. $\lim_{x\to -5} \dfrac{y^2}{5 - y}$

42. $\lim_{y\to 2} \dfrac{y^2 + 5y + 6}{y + 2}$

Find the limits in Exercises 43–52. (You may want to visualize your answer by graphing the function using a grapher.)

43. $\lim_{x\to -3} \sqrt{x + 7}$

44. $\lim_{x\to 0} \sqrt{2x + 3}$

45. $\lim_{x\to 0} \dfrac{3}{\sqrt{3x + 1} + 1}$

46. $\lim_{x\to 0} \dfrac{5}{\sqrt{5x + 4} + 2}$

47. $\lim_{x\to 1.5} 3\lfloor x \rfloor$

48. $\lim_{z\to -0.5} \dfrac{2}{\lfloor z \rfloor}$

49. $\lim_{x\to \pi/4} \sqrt{2} \sin x$

50. $\lim_{x\to \pi/3} \sin x \cos x$

51. $\lim_{x\to 0} \dfrac{x^2 + 5x - 2}{1 - \tan x}$

52. $\lim_{x\to 0} \dfrac{\sin x + \cos x}{1 - x + 2 \cos x}$

Find the limits in Exercises 53–62. (You may want to visualize your answer by graphing the function using a grapher.)

53. $\lim_{x\to 5} \dfrac{x - 5}{x^2 - 25}$

54. $\lim_{x\to -3} \dfrac{x + 3}{x^2 + 4x + 3}$

55. $\lim_{x\to -5} \dfrac{x^2 + 3x - 10}{x + 5}$

56. $\lim_{x\to 2} \dfrac{x^2 - 7x + 10}{x - 2}$

57. $\lim_{t\to 1} \dfrac{t^2 + t - 2}{t^2 - 1}$

58. $\lim_{t\to -1} \dfrac{t^2 + 3t + 2}{t^2 - t - 2}$

59. $\lim_{x\to -2} \dfrac{-2x - 4}{x^3 + 2x^2}$

60. $\lim_{y\to 0} \dfrac{5y^3 + 8y^2}{3y^4 - 16y^2}$

61. $\lim_{u\to 1} \dfrac{u^4 - 1}{u^3 - 1}$

62. $\lim_{v\to 2} \dfrac{v^3 - 8}{v^4 - 16}$

63. Suppose $\lim_{x\to c} f(x) = 5$ and $\lim_{x\to c} g(x) = -2$. Find

a) $\lim_{x\to c} f(x)\, g(x)$

b) $\lim_{x\to c} 2 f(x)\, g(x)$

c) $\lim_{x\to c} (f(x) + 3g(x))$ d) $\lim_{x\to c} \dfrac{f(x)}{f(x) - g(x)}$

64. Suppose $\lim_{x\to 4} f(x) = 0$ and $\lim_{x\to 4} g(x) = -3$. Find

a) $\lim_{x\to 4} (g(x) + 3)$ b) $\lim_{x\to 4} xf(x)$

c) $\lim_{x\to 4} g^2(x)$ d) $\lim_{x\to 4} \dfrac{g(x)}{f(x) - 1}$

65. Suppose $\lim_{x\to b} f(x) = 7$ and $\lim_{x\to b} g(x) = -3$. Find

a) $\lim_{x\to b} (f(x) + g(x))$ b) $\lim_{x\to b} f(x) \cdot g(x)$

c) $\lim_{x\to b} 4g(x)$ d) $\lim_{x\to b} f(x)/g(x)$

66. Suppose that $\lim_{x\to -2} p(x) = 4$, $\lim_{x\to -2} r(x) = 0$, and $\lim_{x\to -2} s(x) = -3$. Find

a) $\lim_{x\to -2} (p(x) + r(x) + s(x))$

b) $\lim_{x\to -2} p(x) \cdot r(x) \cdot s(x)$

c) $\lim_{x\to -2} (-4p(x) + 5r(x))/s(x)$

67. ***Continuation of Exercise 9.*** To find the exact value of the limit of
$$f(x) = \frac{\sqrt{3x + 1} - 1}{2x}$$
as $x \to 0$, first multiply the fraction's numerator and denominator by the quantity $(\sqrt{3x + 1} + 1)$. Then simplify the result to obtain an expression whose limit can be found by substitution. What *is* the limit?

68. Find $\lim_{x\to 0} \dfrac{\sqrt{2x + 3} - \sqrt{3}}{x}$.

(*Hint:* Multiply the fraction's numerator and denominator by $\sqrt{2x + 3} + \sqrt{3}$.)

Use multiplication as in Exercises 67 and 68 to find the limits in Exercises 69 and 70.

69. $\lim_{h\to 0} \dfrac{\sqrt{2 + h} - \sqrt{2}}{h}$ **70.** $\lim_{h\to 0} \dfrac{\sqrt{3h + 7} - \sqrt{7}}{h}$

71. If $\lim_{x\to 1} f(x) = 5$, must f be defined at $x = 1$? If it is, must $f(1) = 5$? Can we conclude *anything* about the values of f at $x = 1$? Explain.

72. If $f(1) = 5$, must $\lim_{x\to 1} f(x)$ exist? If it does, then must $\lim_{x\to 1} f(x) = 5$? Can we conclude *anything* about $\lim_{x\to 1} f(x)$? Explain.

73. Suppose that functions f and g are defined for all values of x and also that $\lim_{x\to 2} (f(x)/g(x)) = 1$. Can $f(2) = 0$? Can $g(2) = 0$? Does it matter what the values of $f(2)$ and $g(2)$ are? Explain.

74. Is it true that we can find $\lim_{x\to c} f(x)$, when it exists, by calculating $\lim_{x\to c^+} f(x)$? Give reasons for your answer.

75. a) Estimate
$$\lim_{x\to 1} x^{1/(x-1)}$$
by taking $x = 1.1, 1.01, 1.001$, and so on as far as your calculator can go. Repeat the process with $x = 0.9, 0.09, 0.009$, and so on. What pattern do you see?

b) Estimate the limit in (a) by graphing $y = x^{1/(x-1)}$ over shorter and shorter intervals containing $x = 1$ and reading the limit from the graph. Use ZOOM and TRACE, if available, to improve your estimate.

76. a) Estimate
$$\lim_{x\to 0} \frac{3^x - 1}{x}$$
by evaluating $f(x) = (3^x - 1)/x$ at $x = 0.1, 0.01, 0.001$, and so on as far as your calculator can go. Repeat the process with $x = -0.1, -0.01, -0.001$, and so on. Where do the values of f seem to be headed?

b) Estimate the limit in (a) by graphing $y = (3^x - 1)/x$ and estimating where the curve jumps over the y-axis. Use ZOOM and TRACE, if available, to improve your estimate.

77. a) Estimate
$$\lim_{x\to 0} \frac{1 - \cos x}{x^2}$$
by evaluating $f(x) = (1 - \cos x)/x^2$ at $x = 0.1, 0.01, 0.001$, and so on as far as your calculator can go. Repeat the process with $x = -0.1, -0.01, -0.001$, and so on. Where do the values of f seem to be headed?

b) Estimate the limit in (a) by graphing $y = (1 - \cos x)/x^2$ and estimating where the curve jumps over the y-axis. Use ZOOM and TRACE, if available, to improve your estimate. (Exercise 43 in Section 2.3 will give an exact value.)

78. a) Estimate
$$\lim_{x\to 0} \frac{\tan 2x}{5x}$$
by evaluating the quotient at $x = 0.1, 0.01, 0.001$, and so on as far as your calculator can go. Repeat the process with $x = -0.1, -0.01, -0.001$, and so on. Where does the quotient seem to be headed?

b) Estimate the limit in (a) by graphing $y = (\tan 2x)/(5x)$ and estimating where the curve jumps over the y-axis. Use ZOOM and TRACE, if available, to improve your estimate. (Example 4 in Section 2.3 will give an exact value.)

Writing for Your Own Knowledge

Answer the following questions in writing. Some answers will take only a sentence or two; others may require several paragraphs. Some explanations may also call for graphs or sketches.

1. How are one-sided and two-sided limits related? How can the relation sometimes be used to determine the existence or nonexistence of a limit?
2. What general rules are available for calculating limits?
3. How do you proceed from knowing that $\lim_{x\to c} x = c$ and $\lim_{x\to c} k = k$ to being able to calculate limits of polynomials and rational functions?
4. What can you say about limits of polynomials and rational functions? of trigonometric functions and square roots?

2.2 Limits Involving Infinity

In this section, we describe what it means for the values of a function to approach infinity and what it means for a function $f(x)$ to have a limit as x approaches infinity. The symbol for infinity (∞) does not represent any real number. We cannot use ∞ in arithmetic in the usual way, but it is convenient to use it to describe the behavior of a function when the values in its domain or range outgrow all finite bounds. For example, when we say "the limit of f as x approaches infinity" we mean the limit of f as x moves increasingly far to the right on the number line. When we say "the limit of f as x approaches negative infinity ($-\infty$)," we mean the limit of f as x moves increasingly far to the left.

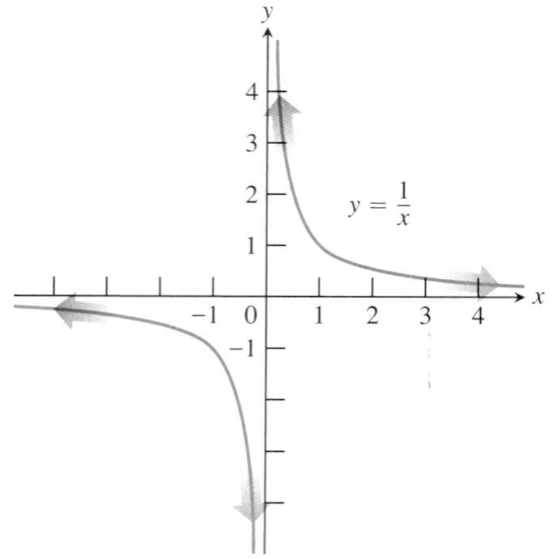

2.9 The graph of $y = 1/x$.

Limits as $x \to \infty$ or $x \to -\infty$

The function $f(x) = 1/x$ is defined for all real numbers except $x = 0$ (Fig. 2.9). As Table 2.3 and Fig. 2.9 suggest,

a) when x is large and positive, $1/x$ is small and positive;
b) when x is small and positive, $1/x$ is large and positive;
c) when x is small and negative, $1/x$ is large and negative;
d) when x is large and negative, $1/x$ is small and negative.

We summarize these facts by writing

a) As $x \to \infty$, $1/x \to 0^+$ — "As x approaches infinity, $1/x$ approaches zero from above."

b) As $x \to 0^+$, $1/x \to \infty$ — "As x approaches zero from the right, $1/x$ approaches infinity."

c) As $x \to 0^-$, $1/x \to -\infty$ — "As x approaches zero from the left, $1/x$ approaches negative infinity."

d) As $x \to -\infty$, $1/x \to 0^-$ — "As x approaches negative infinity, $1/x$ approaches zero from below."

TABLE 2.3
Values of $f(x) = 1/x$ for selected values of x

x	$f(x) = \frac{1}{x}$
⋮	⋮
100000	0.00001
1000	0.001
10	0.1
0.1	10
0.001	1000
⋮	⋮
0	**Undefined**
⋮	⋮
−0.001	−1000
−0.1	−10
−10	−0.1
−1000	−0.001
−100000	−0.00001
⋮	⋮

Calculation Rules for Functions with Finite Limits as $x \to \pm\infty$

Our strategy is again the one that worked so well in Section 2.1. We find the limits of two "basic" functions as $x \to \infty$ and $x \to -\infty$, and then use a theorem about limits of algebraic combinations to find everything else. In Section 2.1, the basic functions were the constant function $y = k$ and the identity function $y = x$. Here, the basic functions are $y = k$ and the reciprocal function $y = 1/x$.

EXAMPLE 1 If f is the constant function $f(x) = k$, then

$$\lim_{x \to \infty} f(x) = \lim_{x \to \infty} k = k$$

$$\lim_{x \to -\infty} f(x) = \lim_{x \to -\infty} k = k.$$

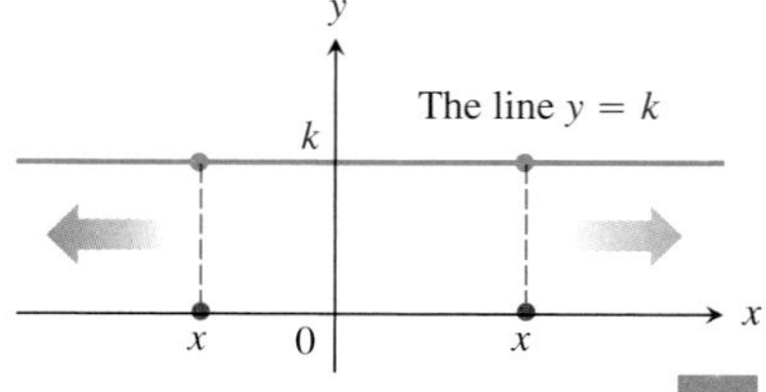

EXAMPLE 2

$$\lim_{x\to\infty} \frac{1}{x} = 0$$

As $x \to \infty$, the graph of $1/x$ gets arbitrarily close to the x-axis: No matter how small a positive number you name, the value of $1/x$ eventually gets smaller.

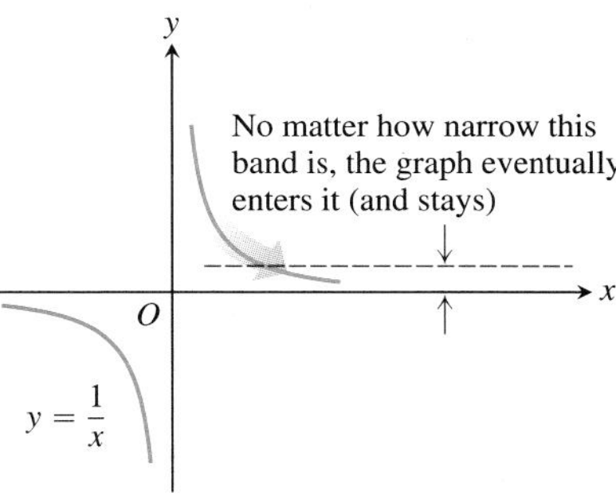

EXAMPLE 3

$$\lim_{x\to -\infty} \frac{1}{x} = 0$$

As $x \to -\infty$, the graph gets arbitrarily close to the x-axis, this time rising toward it from below.

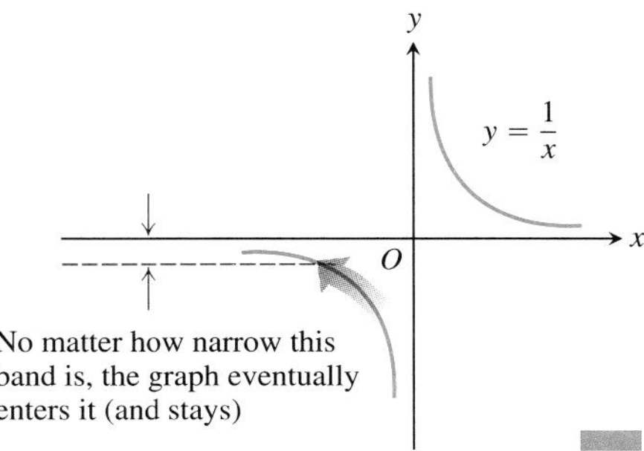

With the following theorem, we can build on these examples to calculate the limits of a wide variety of other functions.

THEOREM 4

Properties of Finite Limits as $x \to \pm\infty$

The following rules hold if

$$\lim_{x\to\pm\infty} f(x) = L_1 \qquad \text{and} \qquad \lim_{x\to\pm\infty} g(x) = L_2$$

and L_1 and L_2 are (finite) real numbers.

1. *Sum Rule:* $\lim_{x\to\pm\infty} (f(x) + g(x)) = L_1 + L_2$
2. *Difference Rule:* $\lim_{x\to\pm\infty} (f(x) - g(x)) = L_1 - L_2$
3. *Product Rule:* $\lim_{x\to\pm\infty} f(x) \cdot g(x) = L_1 \cdot L_2$
4. *Constant Multiple Rule:* $\lim_{x\to\pm\infty} k \cdot g(x) = k \cdot L_2$ (any number k)
5. *Quotient Rule:* $\lim_{x\to\pm\infty} \frac{f(x)}{g(x)} = \frac{L_1}{L_2}$ if $L_2 \neq 0$

These properties are just like the properties in Theorem 1 of the preceding section, and we use them the same way.

EXAMPLE 4

a) $\lim_{x \to \infty} \left(5 + \frac{1}{x}\right) = \lim_{x \to \infty} 5 + \lim_{x \to \infty} \frac{1}{x}$ — Sum Rule

$= 5 + 0 = 5$ — Known values

b) $\lim_{x \to -\infty} \frac{\pi\sqrt{3}}{x^2} = \lim_{x \to -\infty} \pi\sqrt{3} \cdot \frac{1}{x} \cdot \frac{1}{x}$

$= \lim_{x \to -\infty} \pi\sqrt{3} \cdot \lim_{x \to -\infty} \frac{1}{x} \cdot \lim_{x \to -\infty} \frac{1}{x}$ — Product Rule

$= \pi\sqrt{3} \cdot 0 \cdot 0 = 0$ — Known values

Lim $f(x) = \infty$ or lim $f(x) = -\infty$

As suggested by the behavior of $1/x$ as $x \to 0$, we sometimes need to say that function values become arbitrarily large. We can express this as follows:

$$\text{a) } \lim_{x \to c} f(x) = \infty, \quad \text{b) } \lim_{x \to c^+} f(x) = \infty, \quad \text{c) } \lim_{x \to c^-} f(x) = \infty$$

$$\text{d) } \lim_{x \to \infty} f(x) = \infty, \quad \text{e) } \lim_{x \to -\infty} f(x) = \infty. \qquad (1)$$

By saying that the values of $f(x)$ become arbitrarily large, we mean that, given any positive real number B, however large, the values of f will eventually be larger than B. Similarly, we write

$$\text{a) } \lim_{x \to c} f(x) = -\infty, \quad \text{b) } \lim_{x \to c^+} f(x) = -\infty, \quad \text{c) } \lim_{x \to c^-} f(x) = -\infty,$$

$$\text{d) } \lim_{x \to \infty} f(x) = -\infty, \quad \text{e) } \lim_{x \to -\infty} f(x) = -\infty,$$

to say that no matter how far down on the y-axis the negative number $-B$ may lie, the values of f eventually lie below $-B$.

EXAMPLE 5

a) $\lim_{x \to 0^+} \frac{1}{x^{1/3}} = \lim_{x \to 0^+} \left(\frac{1}{x}\right)^{1/3} = \infty$

b) $\lim_{x \to 0^-} \frac{1}{x^{1/3}} = \lim_{x \to 0^-} \left(\frac{1}{x}\right)^{1/3} = -\infty$

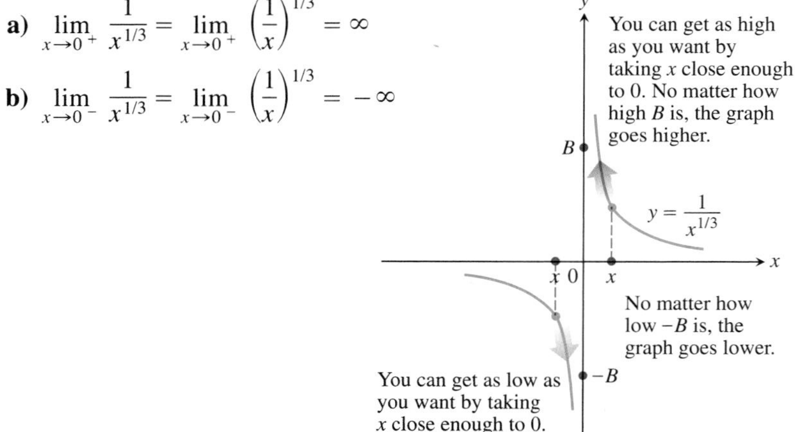

y
You can get as high as you want by taking x close enough to 0. No matter how high B is, the graph goes higher.
B
y = 1/x^{1/3}
x
x 0 x
No matter how low −B is, the graph goes lower.
−B
You can get as low as you want by taking x close enough to 0.

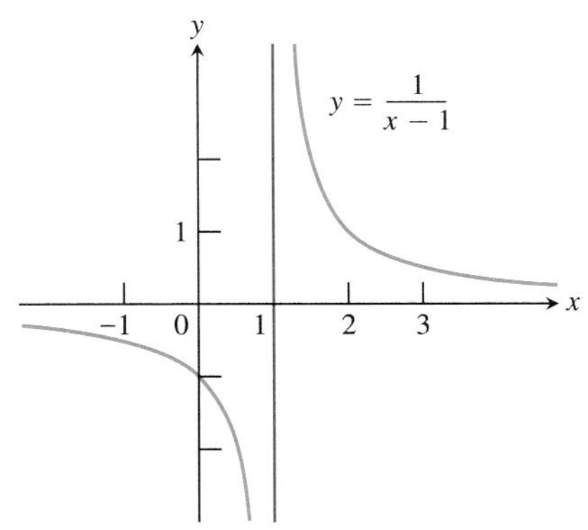

2.10 Near $x = 1$, the function $y = 1/(x-1)$ behaves the way the function $y = 1/x$ behaves near $x = 0$. Its graph is the graph of $y = 1/x$ shifted 1 unit to the right.

EXAMPLE 6

a) $\lim_{x\to 0^+} \frac{1}{x^2} = \infty$

b) $\lim_{x\to 0^-} \frac{1}{x^2} = \infty$

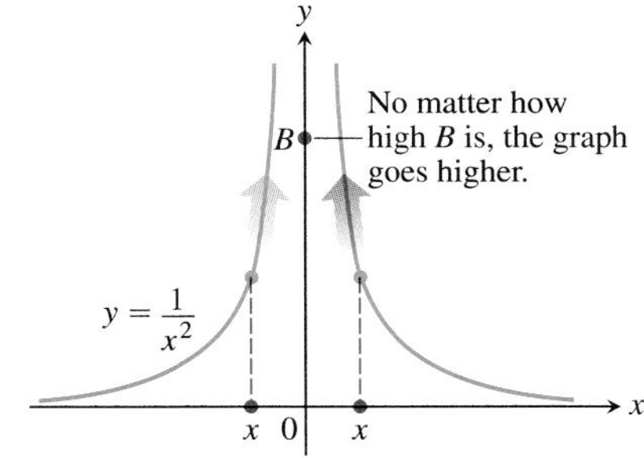

EXAMPLE 7 Find $\lim_{x\to 1^+} \frac{1}{x-1}$ and $\lim_{x\to 1^-} \frac{1}{x-1}$

Solution The idea here is to think about the number $x - 1$. As x approaches 1 from the right, $x - 1$ approaches 0 from above. The reciprocal $1/(x-1)$ stays positive and increases beyond all bounds (Fig. 2.10), so

$$\lim_{x\to 1^+} \frac{1}{x-1} = \infty.$$

On the other hand, if x approaches 1 from the left, $x - 1$ remains negative and approaches 0 from below. Its reciprocal $1/(x-1)$ is negative as well and approaches $-\infty$ (Fig. 2.10), so

$$\lim_{x\to 1^-} \frac{1}{x-1} = -\infty.$$

Limits of Rational Functions as $x \to \pm\infty$

To find the limit of a rational function as $x \to \pm\infty$, when the limit exists, we divide the numerator and denominator by the highest power of x in the denominator. What happens then depends on the degrees of the polynomials involved.

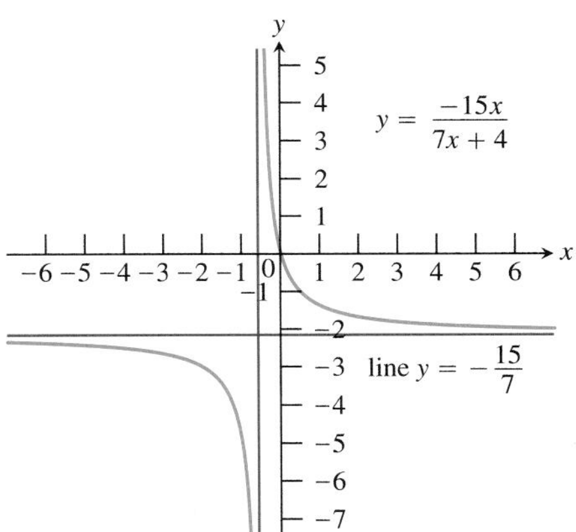

2.11 The graph of the function in Example 8(a). We will study the graphing of rational functions in Chapter 3.

EXAMPLE 8 *Numerator and Denominator of Same Degree*

a) $\lim_{x\to -\infty} \frac{-15x}{7x+4} = \lim_{x\to -\infty} \frac{-15}{7+(4/x)}$ — Divide numerator and denominator by the highest power in the denominator, in this case x.

$= \frac{-15}{7+0}$ — Known values

$= -\frac{15}{7}$ — See Fig. 2.11.

b) $\lim_{x\to\infty} \frac{5x^2+8x-3}{3x^2+2} = \lim_{x\to\infty} \frac{5+(8/x)-(3/x^2)}{3+(2/x^2)}$ — Divide numerator and denominator by x^2.

$= \frac{5+0-0}{3+0}$ — Known values

$= \frac{5}{3}$ — See Fig. 2.12.

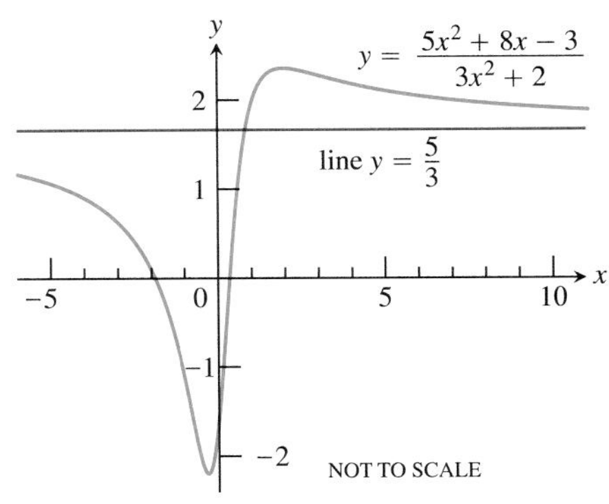

2.12 The function in Example 8(b).

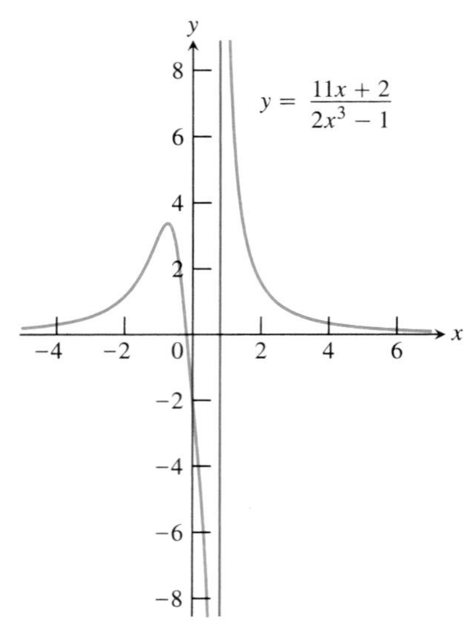

2.13 The graph of the function in Example 9. The graph approaches the x-axis as $|x|$ increases.

The **degree** of the polynomial

$$a_n x^n + a_{n-1} x^{n-1} + \cdots + a_1 x + a_0,$$

$a_n \neq 0$, is n, the largest exponent.

EXAMPLE 9 *Degree of Numerator Less Than Degree of Denominator*

$$\lim_{x \to -\infty} \frac{11x + 2}{2x^3 - 1} = \lim_{x \to -\infty} \frac{(11/x^2) + (2/x^3)}{2 - (1/x^3)}$$ Divide numerator and denominator by x^3.

$$= \frac{0 + 0}{2 - 0}$$ Known values

$$= 0$$ See Fig. 2.13.

EXAMPLE 10 *Degree of Numerator Greater Than Degree of Denominator*

a) $$\lim_{x \to \infty} \frac{2x^2 - 3}{7x + 4} = \lim_{x \to \infty} \frac{2x - (3/x)}{7 + (4/x)}$$ Divide numerator and denominator by x.

$$= \infty$$ As $x \to \infty$, we now have $2x \to \infty$, $(3/x) \to 0$, and $(4/x) \to 0$. Therefore, $[2x - (3/x)] \to \infty$, $[7 + (4/x)] \to 7$, and the ratio $\to \infty$.

b) $$\lim_{x \to -\infty} \frac{2x^2 - 3}{7x + 4} = \lim_{x \to -\infty} \frac{2x - (3/x)}{7 + (4/x)}$$ Divide numerator and denominator by x.

$$= -\infty$$ The numerator now approaches $-\infty$ while the denominator approaches 7, so the ratio $\to -\infty$.

EXAMPLE 11 *Degree of Numerator Greater Than Degree of Denominator*

a) $$\lim_{x \to \infty} \frac{-4x^3 + 7x}{2x^2 - 3x - 10} = \lim_{x \to \infty} \frac{-4x + (7/x)}{2 - (3/x) - (10/x^2)}$$ Divide numerator and denominator by x^2.

$$= -\infty$$ Numerator $\to -\infty$. Denominator $\to 2$. Ratio $\to -\infty$.

b) $$\lim_{x \to -\infty} \frac{-4x^3 + 7x}{2x^2 - 3x - 10} = \lim_{x \to -\infty} \frac{-4x + (7/x)}{2 - (3/x) - (10/x^2)}$$ Divide numerator and denominator by x^2.

$$= \infty$$ Numerator $\to \infty$. Denominator $\to 2$. Ratio $\to \infty$.

Looking at the solutions to Examples 8–11, we see a pattern that can help us devise a quicker way to find limits of rational functions as $x \to \pm\infty$.

1. If the numerator and the denominator have the same degree, the limit is the ratio of the polynomials' leading coefficients (Example 8).
2. If the degree of the numerator is less than the degree of the denominator, the limit is zero (Example 9).
3. If the degree of the numerator is greater than the degree of the denominator, the limit is either $+\infty$ or $-\infty$, depending on the signs assumed by the numerator and denominator as x becomes numerically large (Examples 10 and 11).

So we can find the limit of any rational function in one of two ways: (1) by dividing the numerator and denominator by the highest power of x in the denominator and then calculating the limit, or (2) by inspection using the information in the following summary.

The **leading coefficient** of the polynomial $a_n x^n + a_{n-1} x^{n-1} + \cdots + a_1 x + a_0$, $a_n \neq 0$, is a_n, the coefficient of the highest-powered term.

Summary for Rational Functions

a) If $\deg(f) < \deg(g)$, $\lim_{x \to \pm\infty} \frac{f(x)}{g(x)} = 0.$

b) If $\deg(f) = \deg(g)$, $\lim_{x \to \pm\infty} \frac{f(x)}{g(x)} = \frac{a_n}{b_n}$, the ratio of the leading coefficients of f and g.

c) If $\deg(f) > \deg(g)$, $\lim_{x \to \pm\infty} \frac{f(x)}{g(x)} = \pm\infty$, depending on the signs of numerator and denominator.

Exercises 2.2

Find the limits in Exercises 1–20 (a) as $x \to \infty$ and (b) as $x \to -\infty$. (You may want to visualize your answer by graphing the function using a grapher.)

1. $f(x) = \frac{2}{x} - 3$

2. $g(x) = \pi - \frac{2}{x^2}$

3. $f(x) = \frac{1}{2 + (1/x)}$

4. $g(x) = \frac{1}{8 - (5/x^2)}$

5. $h(x) = \frac{-5 + (7/x)}{3 - (1/x^2)}$

6. $h(x) = \frac{3 - (2/x)}{4 + (\sqrt{2}/x^2)}$

7. $f(x) = \frac{2x + 3}{5x + 7}$

8. $f(x) = \frac{2x^3 + 7}{x^3 - x^2 + x + 7}$

9. $f(x) = \frac{x + 1}{x^2 + 3}$

10. $f(x) = \frac{3x + 7}{x^2 - 2}$

11. $f(x) = \frac{1 - 12x^3}{4x^2 + 12}$

12. $f(x) = \frac{2x^5 + 3}{-x^2 + x}$

13. $g(x) = \frac{3x^2 - 6x}{4x - 8}$

14. $g(x) = \frac{x^4}{x^3 + 1}$

15. $g(x) = \frac{1}{x^3 - 4x + 1}$

16. $g(x) = \frac{10x^5 + x^4 + 31}{x^6}$

17. $h(x) = \frac{7x^3}{x^3 - 3x^2 + 6x}$

18. $h(x) = \frac{9x^4 + x}{2x^4 + 5x^2 - x + 6}$

19. $h(x) = \frac{-2x^3 - 2x + 3}{3x^3 + 3x^2 - 5x}$

20. $h(x) = \frac{-x^4}{x^4 - 7x^3 + 7x^2 + 9}$

The process by which we determine limits of rational functions applies equally well to ratios containing noninteger powers of x: Divide numerator and denominator by the highest power of x in the denominator and proceed from there. Find the limits in Exercises 21–26.

21. $\lim_{x \to \infty} \frac{2\sqrt{2} + x^{-1}}{3x - 7}$

22. $\lim_{x \to \infty} \frac{2 + \sqrt{x}}{2 - \sqrt{x}}$

23. $\lim_{x \to \infty} \frac{2x^{5/3} - x^{1/3} + 7}{x^{8/5} + 3x + \sqrt{x}}$

24. $\lim_{x \to -\infty} \frac{\sqrt[3]{x} - 5x + 3}{2x + x^{2/3} - 4}$

25. $\lim_{x \to -\infty} \frac{\sqrt[3]{x} - \sqrt[5]{x}}{\sqrt[3]{x} + \sqrt[5]{x}}$

26. $\lim_{x \to \infty} \frac{x^{-1} + x^{-4}}{x^{-2} - x^{-3}}$

Find the limits in Exercises 27–38. (You may want to visualize your answer by graphing the function using a grapher.)

27. $\lim_{x \to 0^+} \frac{1}{3x}$

28. $\lim_{x \to 0^+} \frac{5}{2x}$

29. $\lim_{x \to 2^+} \frac{1}{x - 2}$

30. $\lim_{x \to 2^-} \frac{1}{x - 2}$

31. $\lim_{x \to 2^+} \frac{x}{x - 2}$

32. $\lim_{x \to 2^-} \frac{x}{x - 2}$

33. $\lim_{x\to -3^+} \dfrac{x}{x+3}$

34. $\lim_{x\to -3^-} \dfrac{x}{x+3}$

35. a) $\lim_{x\to 0^+} \dfrac{2}{3x^{1/3}}$ **b)** $\lim_{x\to 0^-} \dfrac{2}{3x^{1/3}}$

36. a) $\lim_{x\to 0^+} \dfrac{2}{x^{1/5}}$ **b)** $\lim_{x\to 0^-} \dfrac{2}{x^{1/5}}$

37. $\lim_{x\to 0} \dfrac{4}{x^{2/5}}$

38. $\lim_{x\to 0} \dfrac{1}{x^{2/3}}$

Find the limits in Exercises 39–50. (You may want to visualize your answer by graphing the function using a grapher.)

39. $\lim_{t\to\infty} \dfrac{t^2-2t+3}{2t^2+5t-3}$

40. $\lim_{r\to -\infty} \dfrac{3r}{1-2r^2}$

41. $\lim_{s\to\infty} \left(\dfrac{1}{s^4}+\dfrac{1}{s^2}+1\right)$

42. $\lim_{y\to -\infty} \dfrac{9y^3-7y}{y^3+1}$

43. $\lim_{z\to\infty} \dfrac{z^3-7z+10}{2z^2-7}$

44. $\lim_{x\to\infty} \dfrac{8x^{23}-7x^2+5}{2x^{23}+x^{22}}$

45. $\lim_{t\to\infty} \left(\dfrac{t^2+5}{3t^2-2}\right)-\left(\dfrac{5t-7}{6t+8}\right)$

46. $\lim_{y\to -\infty} \left(\dfrac{y+2}{y+3}-\dfrac{y^3+2}{y^3+3}\right)$

47. $\lim_{x\to -\infty} \left(\dfrac{-x}{x+1}\right)\left(\dfrac{x^2}{5+x^2}\right)$

48. $\lim_{x\to\infty} \left(\dfrac{2}{x}+1\right)\left(\dfrac{5x^2-1}{7x^2}\right)$

49. $\lim_{v\to\infty} \left(\dfrac{1-v^2}{1+2v^2}\right)\left(\dfrac{8v^2+7v}{4v^2}\right)$

50. $\lim_{y\to -\infty} \left(\dfrac{y-3}{y^2-5y+4}\right)\left(\dfrac{y}{y-1}\right)$

In Exercises 51–54, use the graphs to find the values of the limits.

51. $\lim \dfrac{1}{x^2-4}$ as

a) $x\to 2^+$
b) $x\to 2^-$
c) $x\to -2^+$
d) $x\to -2^-$

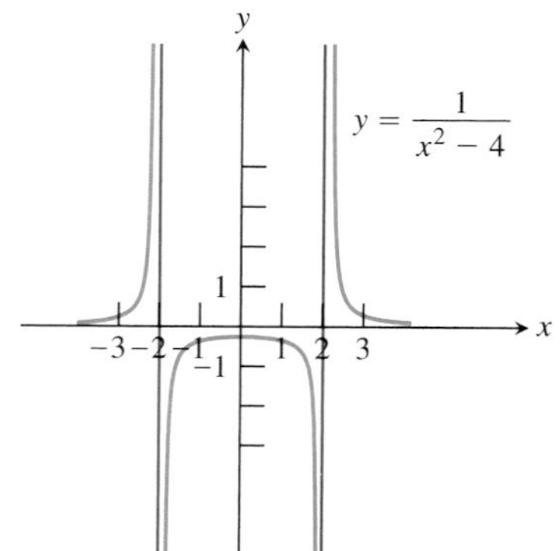

52. $\lim \dfrac{x}{x^2-1}$ as

a) $x\to 1^+$
b) $x\to 1^-$
c) $x\to -1^+$
d) $x\to -1^-$

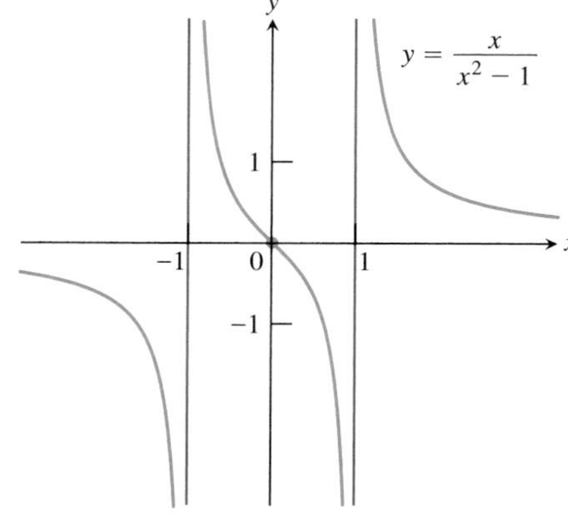

53. $\lim \dfrac{x^2-1}{2x+4}$ as

a) $x\to -2^+$
b) $x\to -2^-$
c) $x\to\infty$
d) $x\to -\infty$

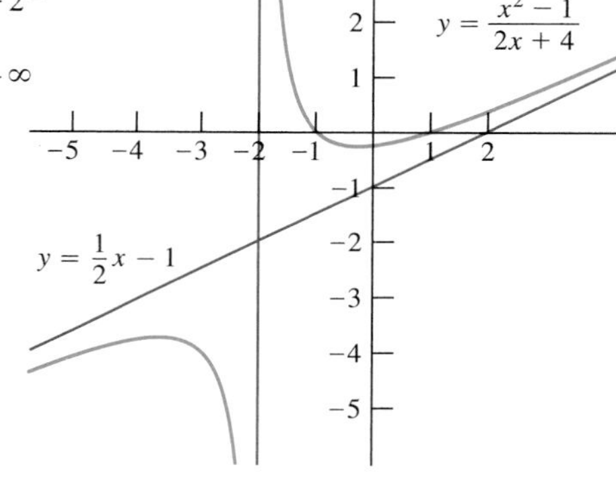

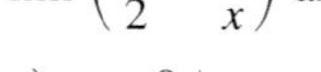

54. $\lim \left(\dfrac{x^2}{2}-\dfrac{1}{x}\right)$ as

a) $x\to 0^+$
b) $x\to 0^-$
c) $x\to \sqrt[3]{2}$
d) $x\to -1$
e) $x\to\infty$
f) $x\to -\infty$

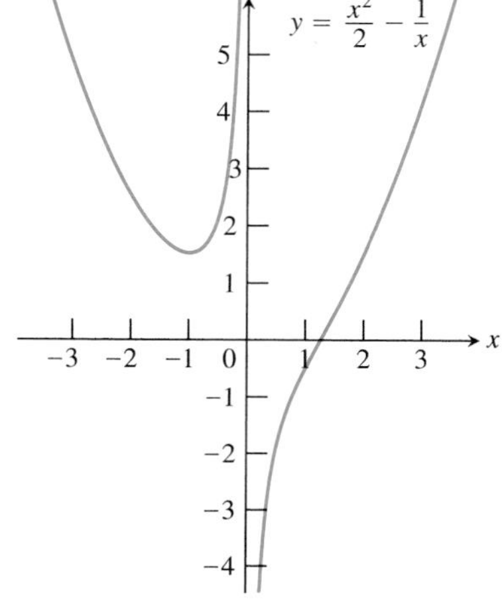

Find the limits in Exercises 55 and 56.

55. a) $\lim_{x\to 0^-} \frac{\lfloor x \rfloor}{x}$ **b)** $\lim_{x\to 0^+} \frac{\lfloor x \rfloor}{x}$

56. a) $\lim_{x\to\infty} \frac{|x|}{|x|+1}$ **b)** $\lim_{x\to -\infty} \frac{x}{|x|}$

In Exercises 57–60, sketch the graph of a function $y = f(x)$ that satisfies the given conditions. No formulas are required—just label the coordinate axes and sketch an appropriate graph. (The answers are not unique, so your graphs may not be exactly like those in the answer section.)

57. $f(0) = 0$, $f(1) = 2$, $f(-1) = -2$, $\lim_{x\to -\infty} f(x) = -1$, and $\lim_{x\to\infty} f(x) = 1$

58. $f(0) = 0$, $\lim_{x\to \pm\infty} f(x) = 0$, $\lim_{x\to 0^+} f(x) = 2$, and $\lim_{x\to 0^-} f(x) = -2$

59. $f(0) = 0$, $\lim_{x\to \pm\infty} f(x) = 0$, $\lim_{x\to 1^-} f(x) = \lim_{x\to -1^+} f(x) = \infty$, $\lim_{x\to 1^+} f(x) = -\infty$, and $\lim_{x\to -1^-} f(x) = -\infty$

60. $f(2) = 1$, $f(-1) = 0$, $\lim_{x\to\infty} f(x) = 0$, $\lim_{x\to 0^+} f(x) = \infty$, $\lim_{x\to 0^-} f(x) = -\infty$, and $\lim_{x\to -\infty} f(x) = 1$

In Exercises 61–64, find a function that satisfies the given conditions and sketch its graph. (The answers here are not unique. Any function that satisfies the conditions is acceptable. Feel free to use formulas defined in pieces if that will help.)

61. $\lim_{x\to\pm\infty} f(x) = 0$, $\lim_{x\to 2^-} f(x) = \infty$, and $\lim_{x\to 2^+} f(x) = \infty$

62. $\lim_{x\to\pm\infty} g(x) = 0$, $\lim_{x\to 3^-} g(x) = -\infty$, and $\lim_{x\to 3^+} g(x) = \infty$

63. $\lim_{x\to -\infty} h(x) = -1$, $\lim_{x\to\infty} h(x) = 1$, $\lim_{x\to 0^-} h(x) = -1$, and $\lim_{x\to 0^+} h(x) = 1$

64. $\lim_{x\to\pm\infty} k(x) = 1$, $\lim_{x\to 1^-} k(x) = \infty$, and $\lim_{x\to 1^+} k(x) = -\infty$

65. For what real value(s) of the exponent p does $\lim_{x\to 0^+} x^p = 0$? 1? ∞? (Experimenting with integer values of p may help you see what is going on.)

66. For what real value(s) of the exponent p does $\lim_{x\to\infty} x^p = 0$? 1? ∞? (Experimenting with integer values of p may help you see what is going on.)

67. Suppose that f is an odd function of x, defined for all values of x. Does knowing that $\lim_{x\to\infty} f(x) = 2$ tell us anything about $\lim_{x\to -\infty} f(x)$? Give reasons for your answer.

68. Suppose f is an even function of x, defined for all values of x. Does knowing that $\lim_{x\to -\infty} f(x) = \pi$ tell us anything about $\lim_{x\to\infty} f(x)$? Give reasons for your answer.

69. Investigate the behavior of

$$f(x) = \left(1 + \frac{1}{x}\right)^x$$

as $x \to \infty$ by taking the following steps.

a) Make a table of values of f for $x = 10, 100, 1000$, and so on. Where do the values of f seem to be headed? Chapter 6 will explain what is going on.

b) Graph f over intervals that start at the origin and move increasingly far to the right. Where do the values of f seem to be headed? Use TRACE and ZOOM, if available, to improve your estimate.

70. *Limits of Ratios of Logarithms.*

a) By taking $x = 10, 100, 1000$, and so on as far as your calculator can go, estimate the value of

$$\lim_{x\to\infty} \frac{\ln(x+1)}{\ln x}.$$

b) Does the 1 in $\ln(x+1)$ really matter? Suppose you have 999 there instead. What do you get for the value of

$$\lim_{x\to\infty} \frac{\ln(x+999)}{\ln x}?$$

c) Estimate the value of

$$\lim_{x\to\infty} \frac{\ln x^2}{\ln x}.$$

d) Estimate the value of

$$\lim_{x\to\infty} \frac{\ln x}{\log x}.$$

The behavior you see here will be explained in Chapter 6.

71. *Continuation of Exercise 70.* To gather further support for your conclusions in parts (a)–(c) in Exercise 70 and to improve your estimate of the numerical value of the limit in part (d), graph the quotients involved over increasingly long intervals of positive x-values. Use TRACE and ZOOM, if available.

72. a) Does

$$\lim_{x\to\infty} \left(\sqrt{x+54} - \sqrt{x}\right)$$

exist? If so, what is it? Try to find out by graphing $f(x) = \sqrt{x+54} - \sqrt{x}$ over increasingly large intervals of x-values.

b) Verify your conclusion in (a) by calculating the limit directly. (*Hint:* Rationalize the expression $\sqrt{x+54} - \sqrt{x}$.)

Writing for Your Own Knowledge

Answer the following questions in writing. Some answers will take only a sentence or two; others may require several paragraphs. Some explanations may also call for graphs or sketches.

1. What general rules are available for calculating finite limits as $x \to \pm\infty$?
2. How do we go from knowing that $\lim_{x\to\pm\infty} k = k$ and $\lim_{x\to\pm\infty} (1/x) = 0$ to being able to calculate limits of rational functions as $x \to \pm\infty$?

3. What do $\lim_{x\to c} f(x) = \infty$ and $\lim_{x\to c} f(x) = -\infty$ mean?
4. What do $\lim_{x\to\infty} f(x) = \infty$, $\lim_{x\to\infty} f(x) = -\infty$, $\lim_{x\to-\infty} f(x) = \infty$, and $\lim_{x\to-\infty} f(x) = -\infty$ mean?
5. What are the rules for finding limits of rational functions as $x \to \pm\infty$?

EXPLORER PROGRAMS

Limit Problems	Provides practice in determining when limits exist and in finding them when they do.
PowerGrapher	Graphs all the functions in this section.

2.3 *The Sandwich Theorem and (sin θ)/θ*

One of the most useful facts in calculus is that when θ is measured in radians, $\lim_{\theta\to 0} (\sin\theta)/\theta = 1$. This beautiful and simple result turns out to be the key to the way we measure the rates at which trigonometric functions change their values, as we will see in Chapter 3.

There is a lot of empirical evidence to suggest that the limit equals 1. Tables of values like those in Table 2.4 show a steady approach toward 1, and graphs like the one in Fig. 2.14 add visual support for this conclusion.

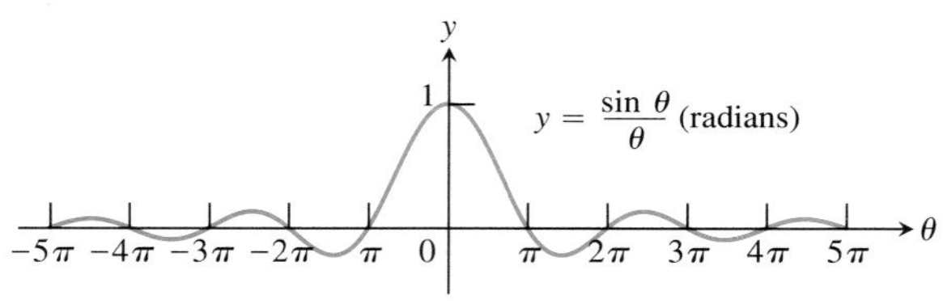

2.14 This computer-generated graph of $f(\theta) = (\sin\theta)/\theta$ appears to cross the y-axis at $y = 1$ even though f is not defined at the origin, a strong indication that $\lim_{\theta\to 0} f(\theta) = 1$.

TABLE 2.4

θ (radians)	sin θ	(sin θ)/θ
0.1	0.0998 33416 65	0.9983 34166 5
0.01	0.0099 99833 334	0.9999 83333 4
0.001	0.0009 99999 8333	0.9999 99833 3
0.0001	0.0000 99999 99983	0.9999 99998 3

But before we build the entire calculus of trigonometric functions on this conclusion, we need to be sure it really holds. Unfortunately, we cannot find the limit by substituting $\theta = 0$. Substitution produces the meaningless form 0/0. So we have to find the limit in a more subtle way. What we do is sandwich the function $(\sin\theta)/\theta$ between 1 and another function that is known to approach 1 as θ approaches zero. This tells us that $(\sin\theta)/\theta$ approaches 1 as well. (We'll see what that other function is in a moment.) The theorem that makes the argument work is the Sandwich Theorem.

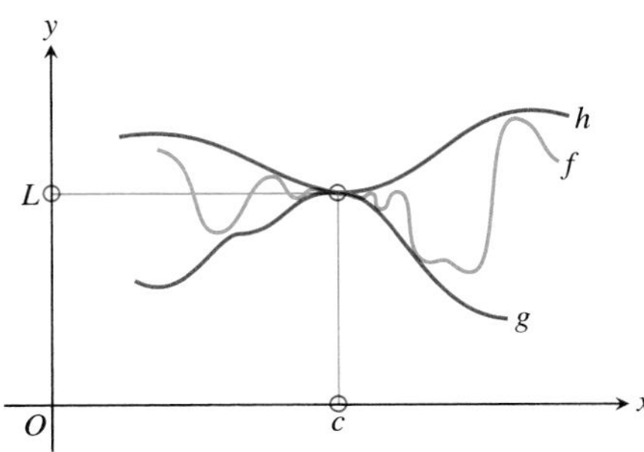

2.15 Functions g and h have limit L as $x \to c$. Since the values of f always lie between the values of g and h, f must have limit L as well.

THEOREM 5

The Sandwich Theorem

Suppose that

$$g(x) \leq f(x) \leq h(x)$$

for all $x \neq c$ in some open interval about c and that

$$\lim_{x \to c} g(x) = \lim_{x \to c} h(x) = L.$$

Then

$$\lim_{x \to c} f(x) = L$$

(Fig. 2.15).

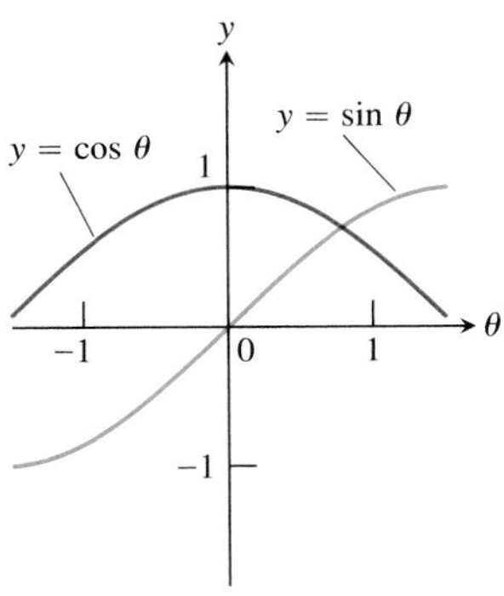

2.16 The sine and cosine of θ near the origin (as functions of radian measure).

Analogous statements hold for one-sided limits. The idea is that if the values of f are sandwiched between the values of two functions that approach L, then the values of f approach L too. We have included a proof in Appendix 2.

To illustrate how the Sandwich Theorem is typically used in limit calculations, we use it first to show that

$$\lim_{\theta \to 0} \sin \theta = 0 \qquad \text{and} \qquad \lim_{\theta \to 0} \cos \theta = 1.$$

These conclusions come as no surprise to anyone who has worked with the sine and cosine functions and has examined their graphs near the origin (Fig. 2.16). But we need these results to argue that $\lim_{\theta \to 0} (\sin \theta)/\theta = 1$. So, in addition to providing practice with the Sandwich Theorem, our first example confirms that these limits are what we need them to be.

EXAMPLE 1 Show that

$$\lim_{\theta \to 0} \sin \theta = 0 \qquad \text{and} \qquad \lim_{\theta \to 0} \cos \theta = 1.$$

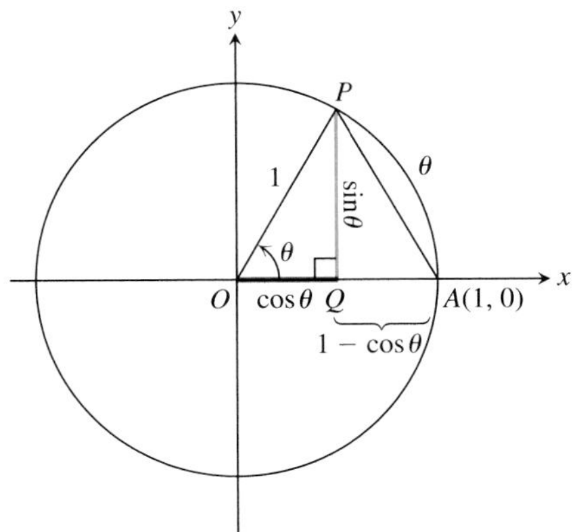

2.17 From the geometry of this figure, drawn for $\theta > 0$, we get an inequality that is the chief step in showing that, as $\theta \to 0$, $\sin \theta \to 0$ and $\cos \theta \to 1$ (Example 1).

Solution We begin by picturing θ as the radian measure of an acute angle in standard position (Fig. 2.17). The circle in the figure is a unit circle, so $|\theta|$ also equals the length of the circular arc AP. The length of the line segment AP is therefore less than $|\theta|$.

Triangle APQ is a right triangle with legs of length

$$QP = |\sin \theta|, \qquad QA = 1 - \cos \theta.$$

From the Pythagorean theorem and the fact that $AP < |\theta|$, we get

$$QP^2 + QA^2 = \sin^2 \theta + (1 - \cos \theta)^2 = (AP)^2 < \theta^2. \tag{1}$$

The terms on the left side of Eq. (1) are both positive, so each is smaller than the sum of the two and hence is less than θ^2:

$$\sin^2 \theta < \theta^2 \qquad \text{and} \qquad (1 - \cos \theta)^2 < \theta^2. \tag{2}$$

By taking square roots we can see this is equivalent to saying that

$$|\sin \theta| < |\theta| \qquad \text{and} \qquad |1 - \cos \theta| < |\theta| \tag{3}$$

or

$$-|\theta| < \sin\theta < |\theta| \quad \text{and} \quad -|\theta| < 1 - \cos\theta < |\theta|. \tag{4}$$

Now let θ approach zero. Since $-|\theta|$ and $|\theta|$ both approach zero, we may apply the Sandwich Theorem to the inequalities in (4) and conclude that $\sin\theta$ and $1 - \cos\theta$ approach zero as θ approaches zero. Since $1 - \cos\theta$ approaches zero, $\cos\theta$ must approach 1, and we have

$$\lim_{\theta\to 0}\sin\theta = 0 \quad \text{and} \quad \lim_{\theta\to 0}\cos\theta = 1.$$

EXAMPLE 2 Building on the results of Example 1, we have

a) $\displaystyle \lim_{x\to 0}\tan x = \lim_{x\to 0}\frac{\sin x}{\cos x}$ $\quad \tan x = \dfrac{\sin x}{\cos x}$

$\displaystyle = \frac{\lim_{x\to 0}\sin x}{\lim_{x\to 0}\cos x}$ $\quad$ Quotient Rule

$\displaystyle = \frac{0}{1} = 0$ $\quad$ Values from Example 1

b) $\displaystyle \lim_{x\to 0}\sec x = \lim_{x\to 0}\frac{1}{\cos x}$ $\quad \sec x = \dfrac{1}{\cos x}$

$\displaystyle = \frac{\lim_{x\to 0} 1}{\lim_{x\to 0}\cos x}$ $\quad$ Quotient Rule

$\displaystyle = \frac{1}{1} = 1$ $\quad$ Known values

Area and Radian Measure

The fraction of a circle's area in a sector whose central angle is θ radians is $\theta/2\pi$. If $\theta = \pi$, the sector contains $\theta/2\pi = \pi/2\pi = 1/2$ of the circle's total area. If $\theta = \pi/2$, the sector contains $\theta/2\pi = (\pi/2)/2\pi = 1/4$ of the circle's total area, and so on.

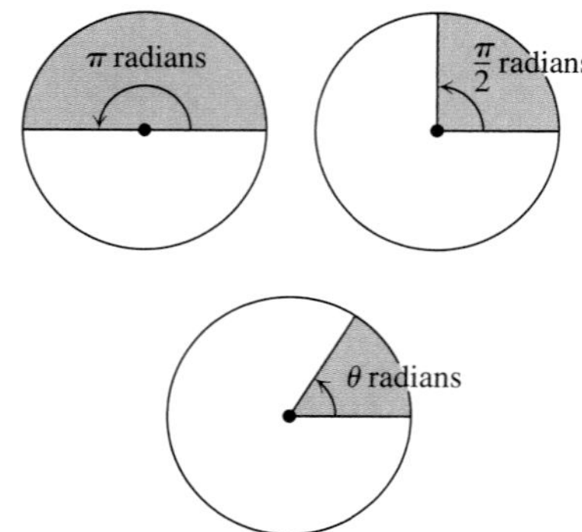

To express the sector's area A in terms of the circle's radius r, we write

$$\begin{aligned} A &= \frac{\theta}{2\pi}\cdot \text{area of entire circle} \\ &= \frac{\theta}{2\pi}\cdot \pi r^2 \\ &= \frac{1}{2}r^2\theta \end{aligned}$$

We now extend the results in Example 1 to show that when θ is measured in radians, $\lim_{\theta\to 0}(\sin\theta)/\theta = 1$. In the proof, we use the formula $A = (1/2)r^2\theta$ for the area of a circular sector (explained in the margin).

THEOREM 6

If θ is measured in radians, then

$$\lim_{\theta\to 0}\frac{\sin\theta}{\theta} = 1. \tag{5}$$

Proof of Theorem 6 Our plan is to establish Eq. (5) by showing that the right-hand and left-hand limits are both 1. We will then know that the two-sided limit is 1 as well.

To show that the right-hand limit is 1, we begin with values of θ that are positive and less than $\pi/2$ (Fig. 2.18). When we compare the areas of ΔOAP, sector OAP, and ΔOAT in the figure, we see that

$$\text{Area } \Delta OAP < \text{area sector } OAP < \text{area } \Delta OAT. \tag{6}$$

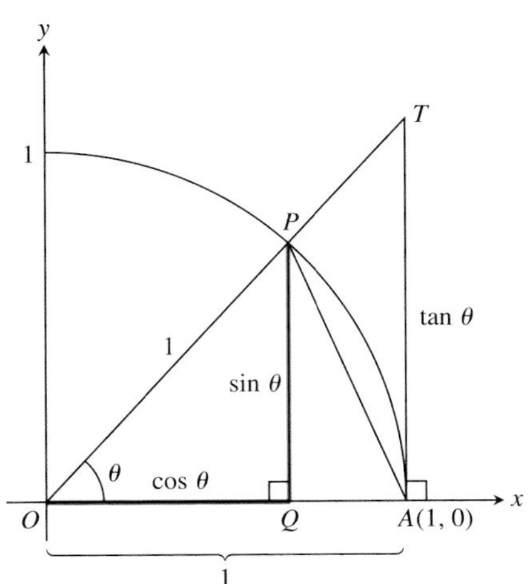

2.18 The figure for the proof of Theorem 6. $TA/OA = \tan\theta$, but $OA = 1$, so $TA = \tan\theta$.

Equation (8) is where the radian measurement comes in: The area of sector OAP is $\theta/2$ if and only if θ is measured in radians.

We can express these areas in terms of θ as follows:

$$\text{Area }\Delta OAP = \frac{1}{2}\text{base} \times \text{height} = \frac{1}{2}(1)(\sin\theta) = \frac{1}{2}\sin\theta \tag{7}$$

$$\text{Area sector }OAP = \frac{1}{2}r^2\theta = \frac{1}{2}(1)^2\theta = \frac{\theta}{2} \tag{8}$$

$$\text{Area }\Delta OAT = \frac{1}{2}\text{base} \times \text{height} = \frac{1}{2}(1)(\tan\theta) = \frac{1}{2}\tan\theta, \tag{9}$$

so that

$$\frac{1}{2}\sin\theta < \frac{1}{2}\theta < \frac{1}{2}\tan\theta. \tag{10}$$

The inequality in (10) will go the same way if we divide all three terms by the positive number $(1/2)\sin\theta$:

$$1 < \frac{\theta}{\sin\theta} < \frac{1}{\cos\theta}. \tag{11}$$

We next take reciprocals in (11), reversing the inequalities:

$$\cos\theta < \frac{\sin\theta}{\theta} < 1. \tag{12}$$

Because $\cos\theta$ approaches 1 as θ approaches 0, the Sandwich Theorem tells us that

$$\lim_{\theta\to 0^+}\frac{\sin\theta}{\theta} = 1. \tag{13}$$

The limit in Eq. (13) is a right-hand limit because we have been dealing with values of θ between 0 and $\pi/2$. But, since the function $(\sin\theta)/\theta$ is even, we obtain the same limit as θ approaches zero from the left. Therefore,

$$\lim_{\theta\to 0}\frac{\sin\theta}{\theta} = 1. \tag{14}$$

■

The equation $\lim_{\theta\to 0}(\sin\theta)/\theta$ holds no matter how θ may be expressed:

$$\lim_{x\to 0}\frac{\sin x}{x} = 1, \quad (\theta = x); \qquad \lim_{x\to 0}\frac{\sin 7x}{7x} = 1; \qquad \lim_{x\to 0}\frac{\sin(2/3)x}{(2/3)x} = 1.$$

As $\theta \to 0$, $x \to 0$ — As $x \to 0$, $7x \to 0$ — As $x \to 0$, $(2/3)x \to 0$

Knowing this helps us calculate related limits involving angles in radian measure.

EXAMPLE 3

$$\lim_{x\to 0}\frac{\sin 2x}{5x} = \lim_{x\to 0}\frac{2}{5}\cdot\frac{\sin 2x}{\frac{2}{5}\cdot 5x}$$

Eq. (5) does not apply. We need to rewrite the fraction by multiplying the numerator and denominator by 2/5.

$$= \frac{2}{5}\lim_{x\to 0}\frac{\sin 2x}{2x}$$

Constant Multiple Rule. Now Eq. (5) applies.

$$= \frac{2}{5}\cdot 1 = \frac{2}{5}$$

■

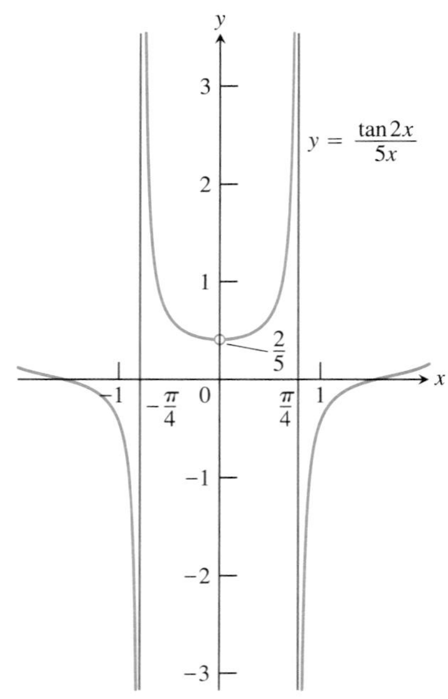

2.19 The graph of $y = (\tan 2x)/5x$ steps across the y-axis at $y = 2/5$ (Example 4).

EXAMPLE 4

$$\lim_{x\to 0}\frac{\tan 2x}{5x} = \lim_{x\to 0}\frac{\sin 2x}{5x}\cdot\frac{1}{\cos 2x} \qquad \tan 2x = \frac{\sin 2x}{\cos 2x}$$

$$= \lim_{x\to 0}\frac{\sin 2x}{5x}\cdot\lim_{x\to 0}\frac{1}{\cos 2x} \qquad \text{Product Rule}$$

$$= \frac{2}{5}\cdot\frac{1}{1} \qquad \text{Values from Examples 3 and 1}$$

$$= \frac{2}{5} \qquad \text{See Fig. 2.19.}$$

Limits as $x \to \pm\infty$

The Sandwich Theorem also holds for limits as $x \to \pm\infty$. Here is a typical application.

EXAMPLE 5 Show that $\lim_{x\to\infty}\frac{\sin x}{x} = 0$.

Solution Writing the quotient as

$$\frac{\sin x}{x} = \frac{1}{x}\cdot\sin x$$

in an attempt to apply the Product Rule does not help because $\lim_{x\to\infty}\sin x$ does not exist. On the other hand, the magnitude of $\sin x$ never exceeds 1, so the decreasing values of $1/x$ should take the product to zero anyway. Indeed, that is just what we find when we apply the Sandwich Theorem. Since

$$-1 \le \sin x \le 1,$$

we have

$$-\frac{1}{x} \le \frac{\sin x}{x} \le \frac{1}{x} \qquad (15)$$

for all positive values of x. Both $-1/x$ and $1/x$ approach zero as $x \to \infty$, so $(\sin x)/x$ approaches zero as well. Figure 2.14, which graphs the quotient as a function of θ instead of x, shows how rapidly the amplitudes of the oscillations die down as the curve moves away from the origin.

Applications

The function $(\sin x)/x$ plays a key role in many scientific fields, and its occurrence in calculus is not an isolated event. It arises in such diverse fields as quantum physics (where it appears in solutions of the wave equation) and electrical engineering (in signal analysis and signal filter design) as well as in the mathematical fields of differential equations and probability theory.

Changing Variables with Substitutions

A change of variable can sometimes turn an unfamiliar expression into one whose limit we know how to find. Here are some examples.

EXAMPLE 6

$$\lim_{x\to\infty}\sin\frac{1}{x} = \lim_{\theta\to 0^+}\sin\theta \qquad \text{Substitute } \theta = 1/x. \text{ Then } \theta\to 0^+ \text{ as } x\to\infty.$$

$$= 0 \qquad \text{Known value}$$

EXAMPLE 7

$$\lim_{y \to -\infty} \left(1 + \frac{2}{y}\right)\left(\cos \frac{1}{y}\right) = \lim_{\theta \to 0^-} (1 + 2\theta)(\cos \theta)$$

Substitute $\theta = 1/y$. Then $\theta \to 0^-$ as $y \to -\infty$.

$$= \lim_{\theta \to 0^-} (1 + 2\theta) \cdot \lim_{\theta \to 0^-} \cos \theta$$

Product Rule

$$= 1 \cdot 1 = 1.$$

Known values

EXAMPLE 8

$$\lim_{t \to (\pi/2)} \frac{\sin\left(t - \frac{\pi}{2}\right)}{t - \frac{\pi}{2}} = \lim_{\theta \to 0} \frac{\sin \theta}{\theta} = 1$$

Set $\theta = t - (\pi/2)$. Then $\theta \to 0$ as $t \to (\pi/2)$.

Exercises 2.3

Find the limits in Exercises 1–26. (You may want to visualize your answer by graphing the function using a grapher.)

1. $\lim_{\theta \to 0} \frac{\sin \sqrt{2}\theta}{\sqrt{2}\theta}$
2. $\lim_{t \to 0} \frac{\sin \pi t}{\pi t}$
3. $\lim_{t \to 0} \frac{\sin 6t}{6t}$
4. $\lim_{s \to 0} \frac{\sin (s/2)}{s/2}$
5. $\lim_{x \to 0} \frac{\sin 2x}{x}$
6. $\lim_{y \to 0} \frac{\sin 3y}{4y}$
7. $\lim_{h \to 0^+} \frac{\tan 2h}{2h}$
8. $\lim_{x \to 0} \frac{\tan 2x}{x}$
9. $\lim_{\theta \to 0^+} \frac{\theta}{\sin \theta}$
10. $\lim_{h \to 0^-} \frac{h}{\sin 3h}$
11. $\lim_{t \to 0} \frac{2t}{\tan t}$
12. $\lim_{r \to 0} \frac{r}{\tan 2r}$
13. $\lim_{x \to 0} \frac{\sin x}{2x^2 - x}$
14. $\lim_{x \to 0} \frac{x^2 - x + \sin x}{2x}$
15. $\lim_{x \to 0} \frac{x + x \cos x}{\sin x \cos x}$
16. $\lim_{x \to 0^+} \frac{3x - \sin x}{x \cos x}$
17. $\lim_{x \to 0^-} x \csc x$
18. $\lim_{x \to 0} 2x \cot x$
19. $\lim_{t \to 0} \frac{\sin (1 - \cos t)}{1 - \cos t}$
20. $\lim_{t \to (\pi/2)} \frac{\tan (t - (\pi/2))}{t - (\pi/2)}$
21. $\lim_{x \to -\pi} \frac{\sin (x + \pi)}{x + \pi}$
22. $\lim_{x \to 0} \frac{3x - \tan 2x}{2x}$
23. $\lim_{\theta \to 0} \frac{\sin \theta}{\sin 2\theta}$
    (*Hint:* Divide numerator and denominator by θ.)
24. $\lim_{x \to 0} \frac{\sin 5x}{\sin 4x}$
    (*Hint:* Divide numerator and denominator by x.)
25. $\lim_{x \to 0} \frac{\tan 2x}{\tan 3x}$
26. $\lim_{y \to 0} \frac{\cot 5y}{\cot 3y}$

Find the limits in Exercises 27–34.

27. $\lim_{x \to \infty} \frac{\sin 2x}{x}$
28. $\lim_{x \to -\infty} \frac{\cos x}{3x}$
29. $\lim_{t \to -\infty} \left(2 + \frac{\sin t}{t}\right)$
30. $\lim_{t \to \infty} \frac{2 - t + \sin t}{t + \cos t}$
31. $\lim_{x \to -\infty} \frac{\cos (1/x)}{1 + (1/x)}$
32. $\lim_{x \to \infty} \left(\frac{3}{x^2} - \sin \frac{1}{x}\right)\left(1 + \cos \frac{1}{x}\right)$
33. $\lim_{y \to \infty} y \sin \frac{1}{y}$
34. $\lim_{t \to \infty} t \tan \frac{2}{t}$

Find the limits in Exercises 35–38.

35. $\lim_{x \to 0^+} \frac{1}{\sin x}$
36. $\lim_{x \to 0^-} \frac{2}{\sin x}$
37. $\lim_{x \to 0^+} \frac{3}{(\cos x) - 1}$
38. $\lim_{x \to 0^-} \frac{x + 2}{1 - \cos x}$

As we mentioned in the text, the Sandwich Theorem also holds for limits as $x \to \pm\infty$. Use this property to find the limits in Exercises 39 and 40.

39. Find $\lim_{x \to \infty} f(x)$ and $\lim_{x \to -\infty} f(x)$ if

$$\frac{2x^2}{x^2 + 1} < f(x) < \frac{2x^2 + 5}{x^2}.$$

40. Find $\lim_{x \to \infty} \lfloor x \rfloor / x$ and $\lim_{x \to -\infty} \lfloor x \rfloor / x$ given that

$$\frac{x - 1}{x} < \frac{\lfloor x \rfloor}{x} \le 1 \qquad (x \ne 0).$$

41. a) It can be shown that the inequalities

$$1-\frac{x^2}{6}<\frac{x \sin x}{2-2\cos x}<1$$

hold for all values of x close to zero. What, if anything, does this tell you about

$$\lim_{x\to 0}\frac{x \sin x}{2-2\cos x}?$$

Give reasons for your answer.

b) Graph $y=1-(x^2/6)$, $y=(x \sin x)/(2-2\cos x)$, and $y=1$ together for $-2\le x\le 2$. Comment on the behavior of the graphs as $x\to 0$.

42. a) Suppose that the inequalities

$$\frac{1}{2}-\frac{x^2}{24}<\frac{1-\cos x}{x^2}<\frac{1}{2}$$

hold for values of x close to zero. (They do, as you will see in Section 9.7.) What, if anything, does this tell you about

$$\lim_{x\to 0}\frac{1-\cos x}{x^2}?$$

Give reasons for your answer.

b) Graph $y=(1/2)-(x^2/24)$, $y=(1-\cos x)/x^2$, and $y=1/2$ together for $-2\le x\le 2$. Comment on the behavior of the graphs as $x\to 0$.

43. Another way to investigate

$$\lim_{x\to 0}\frac{1-\cos x}{x^2}$$

is first to rewrite the fraction by multiplying its numerator and denominator by the quantity $(1+\cos x)$. How does this help? What *is* the limit? Give reasons for your answer.

44. a) Graph

$$f(h)=\frac{\cos h-1}{h}$$

as a function of h for $-15\le h\le 15$. What does the graph suggest about

$$\lim_{h\to 0}\frac{\cos h-1}{h}?$$

b) Confirm the value you found for the limit in (a) by multiplying the numerator and denominator of the fraction $(\cos h-1)/h$ by $(\cos h+1)$ and rewriting the numerator in terms of $\sin h$.

45. Graph $y=(\sin x)/x$, $y=(\sin 2x)/x$, and $y=(\sin 4x)/x$ together over the interval $-2\le x\le 2$. Where does each graph appear to cross the y-axis? Do the graphs really intersect the axis? What would you expect the graphs of $y=(\sin 5x)/x$ and $y=(\sin(-3x))/x$ to do as $x\to 0$? Why? What about the graph of $y=(\sin kx)/x$ for other values of k? Give reasons for your answers.

46. Suppose that $g(x)\le f(x)\le h(x)$ for all $x\ne 2$ and suppose that

$$\lim_{x\to 2} g(x)=\lim_{x\to 2} h(x)=-5.$$

Can we conclude anything about the values of f, g, and h at $x=2$? Could $f(2)=0$? Could $\lim_{x\to 2} f(x)=0$? Give reasons for your answers.

Writing for Your Own Knowledge

Answer the following questions in writing. Some answers will take only a sentence or two; others may require several paragraphs. Some explanations may also call for graphs or sketches.

1. What is the Sandwich Theorem about?
2. What kinds of limits can you calculate now that you know that $\lim_{x\to 0}(\sin x)/x=1$ if x is measured in radians?

EXPLORER PROGRAM

PowerGrapher — Graphs functions singly or together.

2.4 *Continuous Functions*

When Jim Fixx drew the heart rate curve in Fig. 1.3 (reproduced here as Fig. 2.20), he plotted data that came from measurements in the field and fitted the plotted points with an unbroken curve. In doing so, he assumed that the values he was plotting were the values of a continuous function, a function whose outputs varied continuously with the inputs and did not jump from one value to another without taking on the values in between.

Continuous functions are the functions we normally use in the equations that describe numerical relations in the world around us. They are the functions we use to find a cannon's maximum range or a planet's closest approach to the

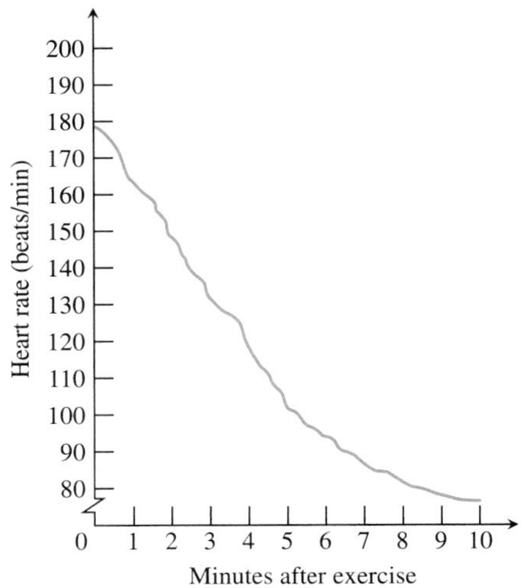

2.20 How the heartbeat returns to a normal rate after running. (Adapted from James F. Fixx's *The Complete Book of Running,* 1977, Random House.)

sun. They are also the functions we use to describe how a body moves through space or how the speed of a chemical reaction changes with time. In fact, so many observable phenomena proceed continuously that throughout the eighteenth and nineteenth centuries it rarely occurred to anyone to look for any other kind of behavior. It came as quite a surprise when the physicists of the 1920s discovered that the vibrating atoms in a hydrogen molecule can oscillate only at discrete energy levels, that light comes in particles, and that, when heated, atoms emit light in discrete frequencies and not in continuous spectra.

The issue of continuity has become one of practical as well as theoretical importance. As scientists, we need to know when continuity is called for, what it is, and how to test for it.

The Definition of Continuity

A function $y = f(x)$ that can be graphed throughout its domain with one continuous motion of the pen (that is, without lifting the pen) is an example of a **continuous function.** At each interior point of the function's domain, like the point c in Fig. 2.21, the function value $f(c)$ is the limit of the function values on either side; that is,

$$f(c) = \lim_{x \to c} f(x).$$

The function value at each endpoint is also the limit of the nearby function values. At the left endpoint a in Fig. 2.21,

$$f(a) = \lim_{x \to a^+} f(x).$$

At the right endpoint b,

$$f(b) = \lim_{x \to b^-} f(x).$$

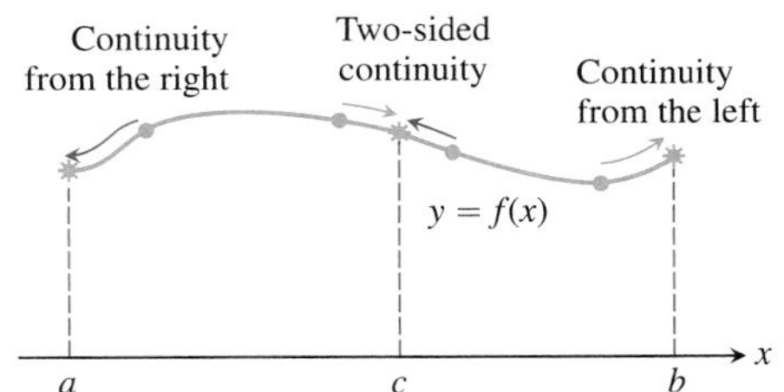

2.21 Continuity at points a, b, and c.

To be specific, let us look at the function in Fig. 2.22, whose limits we investigated in Example 5 of Section 2.1.

EXAMPLE 1 Where is the function f in Fig. 2.22 continuous?

Solution The key to the continuity at any given point of the domain is the relation between the value of f and the value of $\lim f$. At the points of discontinuity, either $\lim_{x \to c} f$ fails to exist or $\lim_{x \to c} f$ does not equal $f(c)$.

At $x = 1$: $\lim_{x \to 1} f$ does not exist.

At $x = 2$: $\lim_{x \to 2} f$ exists but does not equal $f(2)$.

At the points of continuity, the limit of f exists and equals the function's value.

At every interior point c of $[0, 4]$ except $x = 1, 2$: $\lim_{x \to c} f(x) = f(c)$ — For example, $\lim_{x \to 3} f(x) = f(3)$ at $x = 3$.

At the endpoint $x = 0$: $\lim_{x \to 0^+} f(x) = f(0)$

At the endpoint $x = 4$: $\lim_{x \to 4^-} f(x) = f(4)$

In short, f is continuous at every point of its domain except $x = 1$ and $x = 2$, where there are breaks in the graph.

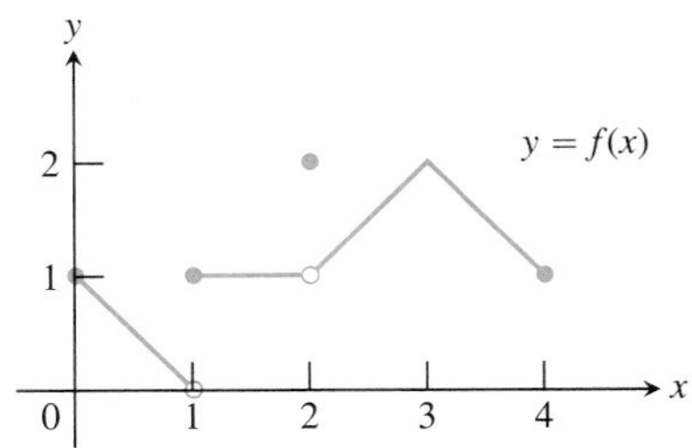

2.22 Continuous except at $x = 1$ and $x = 2$.

We now come to the formal definition of continuity.

DEFINITIONS

Continuity at an interior point

A function $y = f(x)$ is continuous at an interior point c of its domain if

$$\lim_{x \to c} f(x) = f(c). \tag{1}$$

Continuity at an endpoint

A function $y = f(x)$ is continuous at a left endpoint a of its domain if

$$\lim_{x \to a^+} f(x) = f(a). \tag{2}$$

A function $y = f(x)$ is continuous at a right endpoint b of its domain if

$$\lim_{x \to b^-} f(x) = f(b). \tag{3}$$

Continuous function

A function is continuous if it is continuous at each point of its domain.

Discontinuity at a point

If a function f is not continuous at a point c, we say that f is discontinuous at c and call c a point of discontinuity of f.

Continuity at Endpoints

Notice that to see if a function is continuous at a *left endpoint,* you need to find its *right-hand limit* at that point. To see if a function is continuous at a *right endpoint,* you need to find its *left-hand limit* at that point.

How to Test for Continuity at a Point

To test for continuity at a point, we apply the following three steps.

The Continuity Test

A function $y = f(x)$ is continuous at $x = c$ if and only if it meets *all three* of the following conditions.

1. $f(c)$ exists (f is defined at c)
2. $\lim_{x \to c} f(x)$ exists (f has a limit as $x \to c$)
3. $\lim_{x \to c} f(x) = f(c)$ (the limit equals the function value)

To test for continuity at endpoints, use the appropriate one-sided limits.

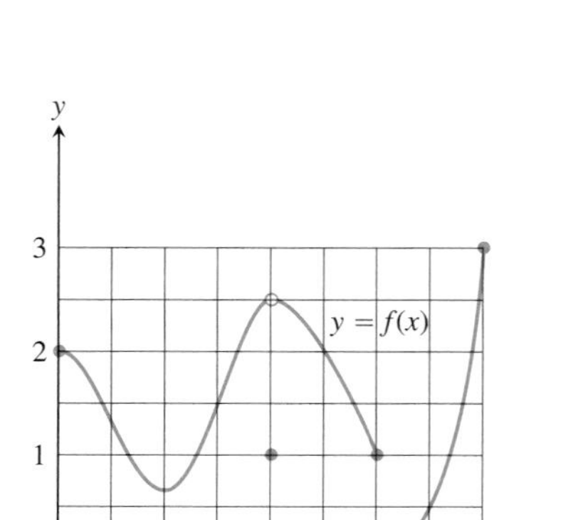

2.23 Continuous at every domain point except $x = 2$ and $x = 3$ (Example 2).

EXAMPLE 2 When applied to the function f in Fig. 2.23, the continuity test gives the following results.

a) f is continuous at $x = 0$ because

1. $f(0)$ exists (it equals 2)
2. $\lim_{x \to 0^+} f(x) = 2$ (f has a limit as $x \to 0^+$)
3. $\lim_{x \to 0^+} f(x) = f(0)$ (the limit equals the function value).

b) f is discontinuous at $x = 2$ because $\lim_{x\to 2} f(x) \neq f(2)$. The function fails Part 3 of the test. The function also fails to be continuous from either the right or the left. The necessary limits exist but do not equal the function's value at $x = 2$.

c) f is discontinuous at $x = 3$ because $\lim_{x\to 3} f(x)$ does not exist. The function fails Part 2 of the test. The function is continuous from the left at $x = 3$ because $\lim_{x\to 3^-} f(x) = f(3) = 1$. But the function is not continuous from the right at $x = 3$ because $\lim_{x\to 3^+} f(x) = 0$ while $f(3) = 1$.

d) f is continuous at the remaining points of its domain. It is continuous at $x = 3.5$, for instance, because

1. $f(3.5)$ exists (it equals 0.5)
2. $\lim_{x\to 3.5} f(x)$ exists (it equals 0.5)
3. the limit equals the function value.

Again, the function is continuous at $x = 4$ because

1. $f(4)$ exists (it equals 3)
2. $\lim_{x\to 4^-} f(x)$ exists (it equals 3)
3. the limit equals the function value.

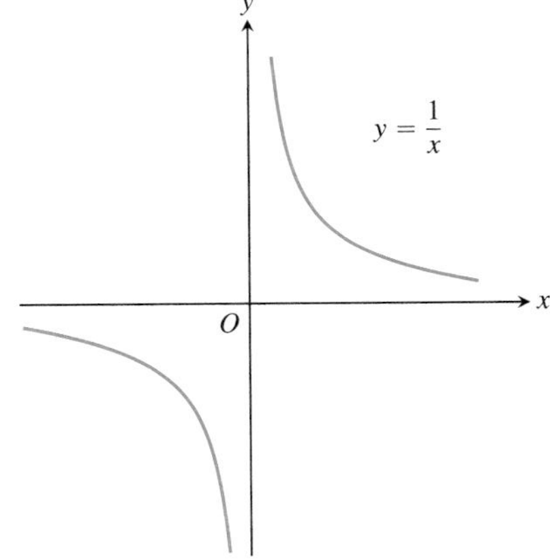

2.24 Discontinuous at the origin (Example 3).

EXAMPLE 3 The function $y = 1/x$ is continuous at every point of its domain. At $x = 0$, where it is not defined, it fails Part 1 of the continuity test; it also fails Part 2. So, $y = 1/x$ is discontinuous at $x = 0$ (Fig. 2.24).

EXAMPLE 4 *Discontinuities of the Greatest Integer Function.* At every integer, the greatest integer function $y = \lfloor x \rfloor$ fails to have a limit and so fails Part 2 of the test (Fig. 2.25).

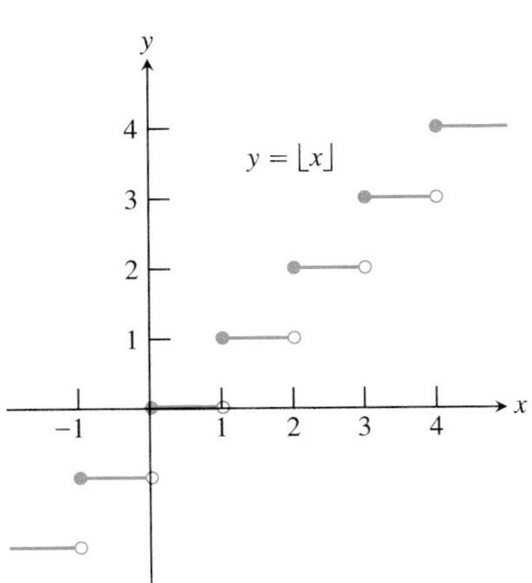

2.25 The greatest integer function is discontinuous at integer values of x (Example 4).

EXAMPLE 5 *Continuity of the Sine and Cosine.* We know that the sine and cosine are continuous at $x = 0$ because

$$\lim_{x\to 0} \sin x = 0 = \sin 0 \quad \text{and} \quad \lim_{x\to 0} \cos x = 1 = \cos 0$$

(limit results from Section 2.3). We will confirm in Chapter 3 that the sine and cosine are continuous at every other point as well.

EXAMPLE 6 *Continuity of Polynomial Functions and Rational Functions.* We saw in Section 2.1 that $\lim_{x\to c} f(x) = f(c)$ for any polynomial function and that if $g(x)$ is also a polynomial function, then $\lim_{x\to c} f(x)/g(x) = f(c)/g(c)$ at every point where the quotient is defined. For instance,

$$f(x) = x^4 + 20 \quad \text{and} \quad g(x) = 5x(x-2)$$

are continuous at every value of x and

$$\frac{f(x)}{g(x)} = \frac{x^4 + 20}{5x(x-2)}$$

is continuous at every value of x except $x = 0$ and $x = 2$, where the denominator is 0.

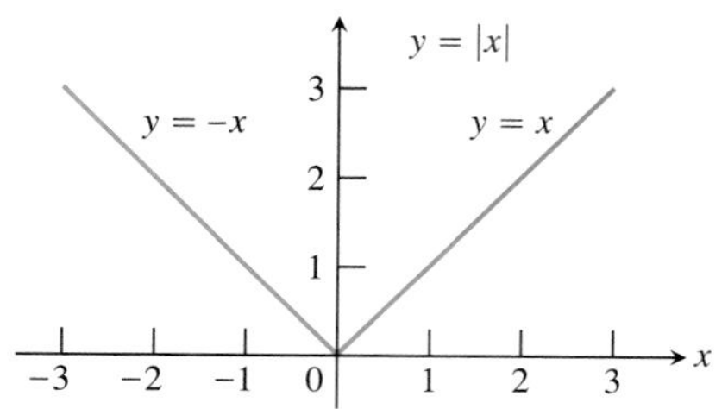

2.26 The sharp corner does not prevent the function from being continuous at the origin (Example 7).

EXAMPLE 7 *Continuity of $y = |x|$.* The function $y = |x|$ is continuous at every value of x (Fig. 2.26). For $x > 0$, it agrees with the continuous (polynomial) function $y = x$. For $x < 0$, it agrees with the function $y = -x$. And, finally, at the origin, $\lim_{x\to 0} |x| = 0 = |0|$.

Algebraic Combinations of Continuous Functions

As you may have guessed, algebraic combinations of continuous functions are continuous at every point at which they are defined.

THEOREM 7

Algebraic Properties of Continuous Functions

If the functions f and g are continuous at $x = c$, then the following combinations are continuous at $x = c$.

1. Sums: $f + g$
2. Differences: $f - g$
3. Products: $f \cdot g$
4. Constant multiples: $k \cdot g$ (any number k)
5. Quotients: f/g (provided $g(c) \neq 0$)

Proof Theorem 7 is a special case of the Limit Property Theorem, Theorem 1 in Section 2.1. If $\lim_{x\to c} f(x) = f(c)$ and $\lim_{x\to c} g(x) = g(c)$, then Theorem 1 tells us that

1. $\lim_{x\to c} [f(x) + g(x)] = f(c) + g(c)$
2. $\lim_{x\to c} [f(x) - g(x)] = f(c) - g(c)$
3. $\lim_{x\to c} f(x)\, g(x) = f(c)\, g(c)$
4. $\lim_{x\to c} kg(x) = kg(c)$ (any number k)
5. $\lim_{x\to c} \dfrac{f(x)}{g(x)} = \dfrac{f(c)}{g(c)}$, provided $g(c) \neq 0$.

In other words, each combination above meets the three requirements of the continuity test at each interior point c of its domain. Similar arguments with right-hand and left-hand limits establish the theorem at endpoints.

EXAMPLE 8 By Theorem 7, the following functions are continuous at every point at which they are defined.

a) $f(x) = 10x - 5x^2 + \dfrac{1}{x^2 + 1}$ — A sum of continuous functions

b) $g(x) = 5x \cos x$ — A constant multiple of a product of continuous functions

c) $\tan x = \dfrac{\sin x}{\cos x}$, $\sec x = \dfrac{1}{\cos x}$

$\cot x = \dfrac{\cos x}{\sin x}$, $\csc x = \dfrac{1}{\sin x}$ Quotients of continuous functions

Removable and Nonremovable Discontinuities

One single type of discontinuity, called a **removable discontinuity,** occurs whenever $\lim_{x\to c} f(x)$ exists but $\lim_{x\to c} f(x) \neq f(c)$. We **remove** the discontinuity by defining (or redefining) $f(c)$ to have the same value as $\lim_{x\to c} f(x)$.

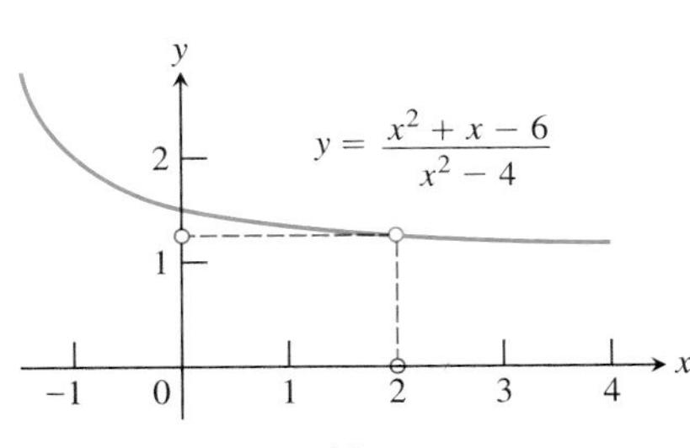

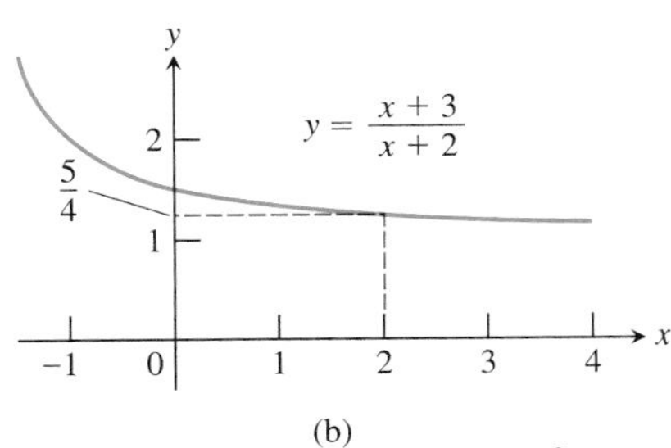

2.27 (a) The graph of $f(x) = \dfrac{x^2+x-6}{x^2-4}$ and (b) the graph of its continuous extension

$$f(x) = \frac{x+3}{x+2} = \begin{cases} \dfrac{x^2+x-6}{x^2-4}, & x \neq 2 \\ \dfrac{5}{4}, & x = 2 \end{cases}$$

(Example 9).

Naming Continuous Extensions

Strictly speaking, when we change a function's domain we should change its name and use different symbols for the function and its continuous extension. But we usually don't bother with this distinction.

EXAMPLE 9 *A Continuous Extension.* The function

$$f(x) = \frac{x^2+x-6}{x^2-4}$$

is not defined at $x = 2$ (or at $x = -2$). Is $x = 2$ a removable discontinuity? If so, how can we extend the function to make it continuous at $x = 2$?

Solution For f to be continuous at $x = 2$, the value of $f(2)$ must equal $\lim_{x\to 2} f(x)$. So, the first questions to answer are does f have a limit at $x = 2$ and, if so, what is it? Working as in Section 2.1, we find that

$$\begin{aligned} \lim_{x\to 2} f(x) &= \lim_{x\to 2} \frac{x^2+x-6}{x^2-4} \\ &= \lim_{x\to 2} \frac{(x-2)(x+3)}{(x-2)(x+2)} \\ &= \lim_{x\to 2} \frac{x+3}{x+2} \\ &= \frac{2+3}{2+2} = \frac{5}{4}. \end{aligned}$$

Defining $f(2)$ to be 5/4 will make $f(2)$ equal to $\lim_{x\to 2} f(x)$. The extended function

$$f(x) = \begin{cases} \dfrac{x^2+x-6}{x^2-4}, & x \neq 2 \\ \dfrac{5}{4}, & x = 2 \end{cases}$$

is continuous at $x = 2$ because $\lim_{x\to 2} f(x)$ equals $f(2)$ (Fig. 2.27).

The removability of a discontinuity of a function at a point $x = c$ requires the existence of $\lim_{x\to c} f(x)$. Without it, there is no way to fulfill the conditions of the continuity test, and the discontinuity is **nonremovable.** The discontinuities of step functions are nonremovable. The functions have different right-hand and left-hand limits at the step points and there is no way to make these limits agree.

Composites of Continuous Functions

All composites of continuous functions are continuous. This means that composites like

$y = \sqrt{x \cos x}$ Composite of $f(x) = x\cos x$ followed by $g(x) = \sqrt{x}$

and

$$y = \tan(2x + 3) \qquad \text{Composite of } f(x) = 2x + 3 \text{ followed by } g(x) = \tan x$$

are continuous at every point at which they are defined. (We will confirm the continuity of $g(x) = \sqrt{x}$ in Chapter 3.) The idea is that if $f(x)$ is continuous at $x = c$ and $g(x)$ is continuous at $x = f(c)$, then $g \circ f$ is continuous at $x = c$, as in the following figure.

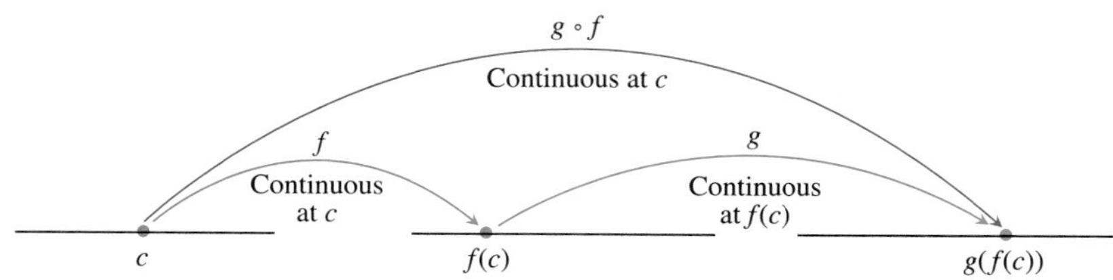

The continuity of composites holds for any finite number of functions. The only requirement is that each function be continuous where it is applied.

THEOREM 8

If f is continuous at c and g is continuous at $f(c)$, then $g \circ f$ is continuous at c.

For an outline of the proof of Theorem 8, see Exercise 6 in Appendix 2.

One of the benefits of knowing that a function is a composite of continuous functions is that, no matter how unfamiliar the expression for the function might be, we can find its limit as x approaches any domain point by evaluating the composite at that point.

EXAMPLE 10 Since $f(x) = \sqrt{x \cos x}$ and $g(x) = \tan(2x + 3)$ are continuous,

$$\lim_{x \to \pi/3} \sqrt{x \cos x} = \sqrt{(\pi/3)\cos(\pi/3)} = \sqrt{\frac{\pi}{3} \cdot \frac{1}{2}} = \sqrt{\frac{\pi}{6}}$$

$$\lim_{x \to -1} \tan(2x + 3) = \tan(-2 + 3) = \tan 1.$$

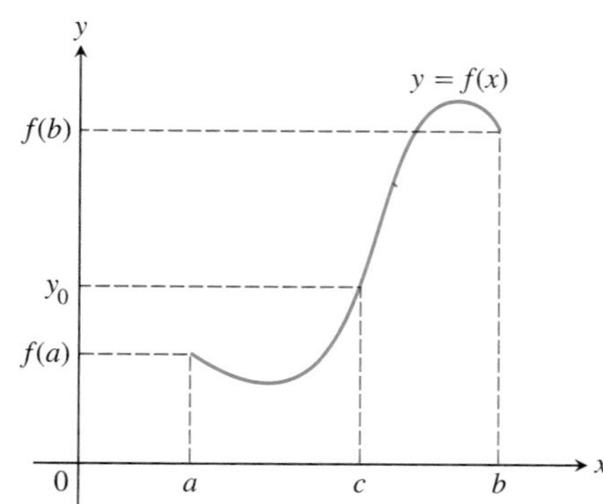

2.28 The Intermediate Value Theorem says that if f is continuous on $[a, b]$ and y_0 is a value between $f(a)$ and $f(b)$, then $y_0 = f(c)$ for some c in $[a, b]$.

The Intermediate Value Property

As we indicated at the beginning of the section, we study continuous functions because they have properties that are useful in mathematics and its applications. One of these properties is the so-called intermediate value property, described in the following theorem.

THEOREM 9

The Intermediate Value Theorem for Continuous Functions

A function $y = f(x)$ that is continuous on a closed interval $[a, b]$ takes on every value between $f(a)$ and $f(b)$ (Fig. 2.28).

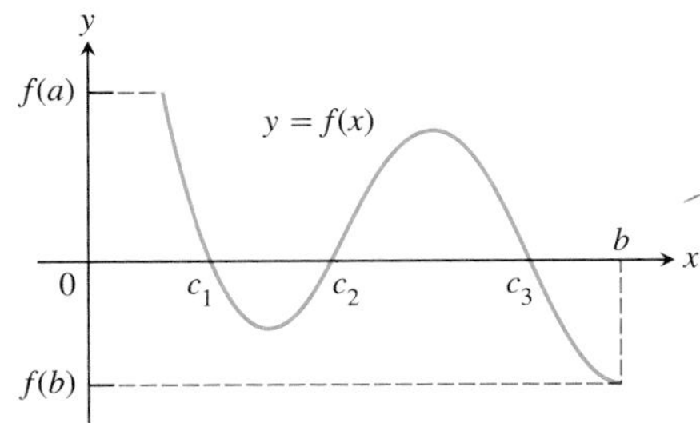

2.29 If f is continuous on $[a, b]$ and $f(a)$ and $f(b)$ differ in sign, then f has at least one zero between a and b. The function f graphed here has three, one at each of c_1, c_2, and c_3.

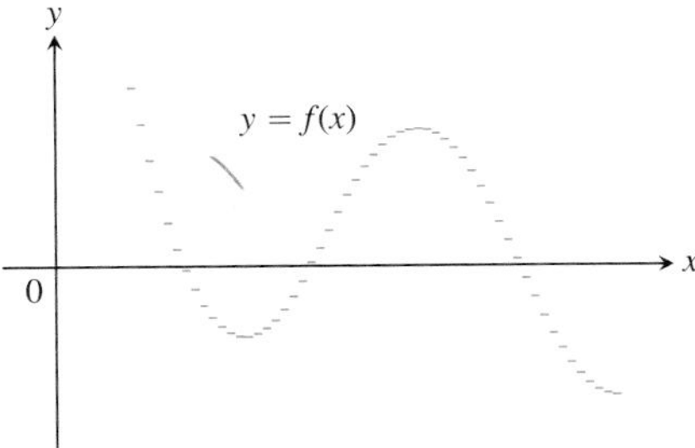

2.30 The graph of a continuous function never steps across the x-axis the way the graph of this step function does.

A Consequence for Graphing: Connectivity Suppose we want to graph a function $y = f(x)$ that is continuous throughout some interval I on the x-axis. Theorem 9 tells us that the graph of f over I will never move from one y-value to another without taking on the y-values in between. The graph of f over I will be **connected:** It will consist of a single, unbroken curve, like the graph of $y = \sin x$. It will not have jumps like the graph of the greatest-integer function or separate branches like the graph of $y = \tan x$.

A Consequence for Root Finding Suppose that $f(x)$ is continuous at every point of a closed interval $[a, b]$ and that $f(a)$ and $f(b)$ differ in sign. Then zero lies between $f(a)$ and $f(b)$, so there is *at least* one number c between a and b where $f(c) = 0$ (Fig. 2.29). In other words, if f is continuous and $f(a)$ and $f(b)$ differ in sign, then the equation $f(x) = 0$ has at least one solution in the open interval (a, b). A point c where $f(c) = 0$ is called a **zero** or **root** of f. Thus, the zeros of f are the points where the graph of f intersects the x-axis.

The observation that there must be at least one zero of f between any point where the graph of f lies above the x-axis and any point where the graph lies below the axis enables us to locate roots of continuous functions by graphing. The graph of a continuous function of x never steps across the x-axis the way the step function in Fig. 2.30 does. When we see the graph of a continuous function cross the x-axis on a computer screen, there really is a root there.

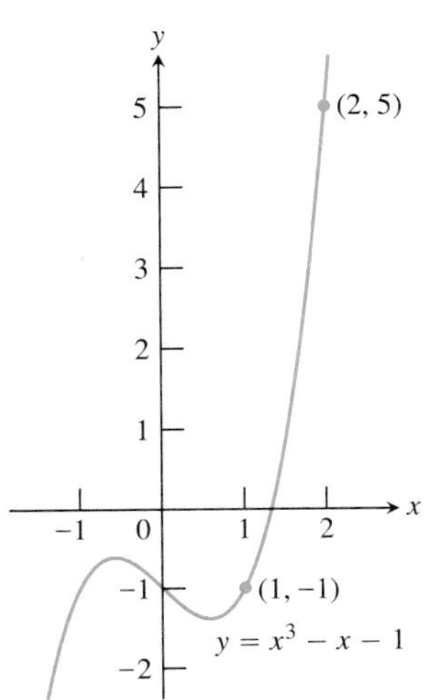

2.31 The graph of $f(x) = x^3 - x - 1$ (Example 11).

EXAMPLE 11 Is any real number exactly 1 less than its cube?

Solution Any such number must satisfy the equation $x = x^3 - 1$ or $x^3 - x - 1 = 0$. Hence, we are looking for a zero value of the function $f(x) = x^3 - x - 1$. By trial we find that $f(1) = -1$ and $f(2) = 5$ and conclude that f has at least one root c between 1 and 2. At this point, $c^3 - c - 1 = 0$, or $c = c^3 - 1$. So, yes, there is a number that is one less than its cube.

The computer-generated graph of f in Fig. 2.31 indicates that the value of c is somewhat closer to 1 than it is to 2. One way to improve this estimate would be to zoom in on c to read its coordinates to more decimal places. Figure 2.32 on the following page shows a typical sequence of steps in such a graphical solution. After six enlargements, the value of c is found to be 1.32472 to 5 decimal places.

Graphical procedures for solving equations and finding zeros of functions, while instructive, are relatively slow. Numerical methods are usually faster, as we will see in Section 3.8.

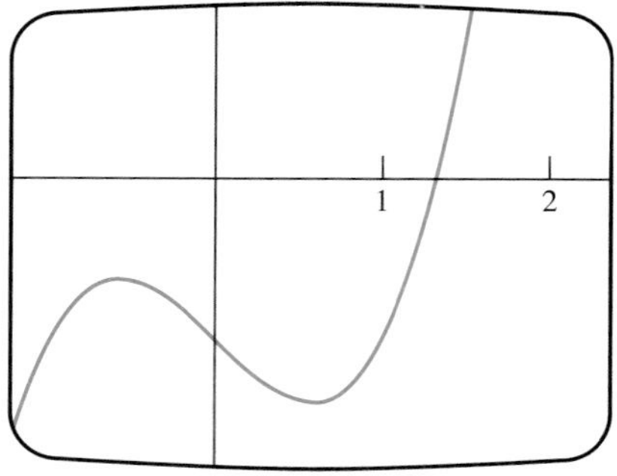

First we make a graph with a relatively large scale. It reveals a root (zero) between $x = 1$ and $x = 2$.

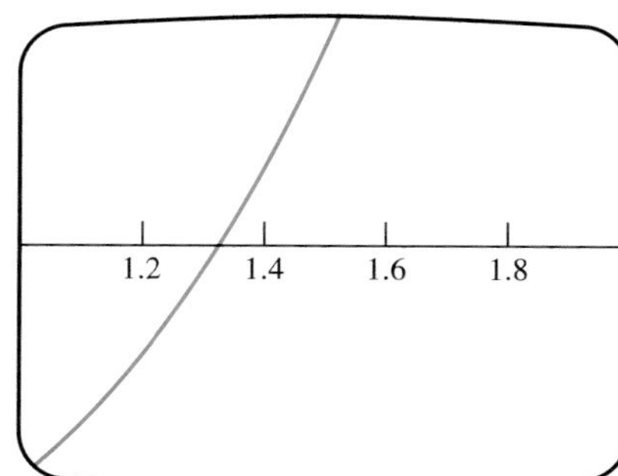

We change the viewing window to $1 \leq x \leq 2, -1 \leq y \leq 1$. We now see that the root lies between 1.3 and 1.4.

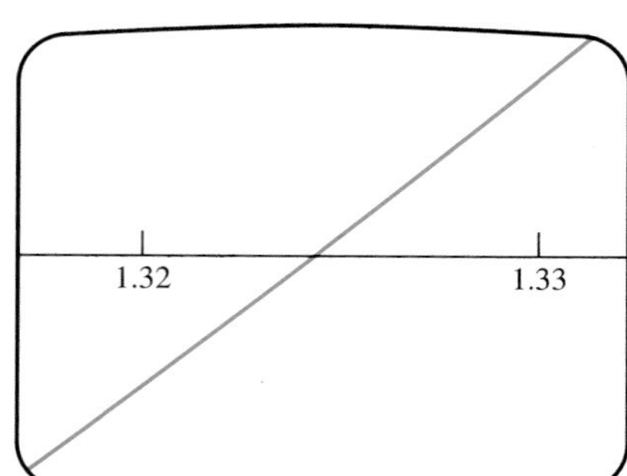

We change the window to $1.3 \leq x \leq 1.35, -0.1 \leq y \leq 0.1$. This shows that the root lies in the interval [1.32, 1.33].

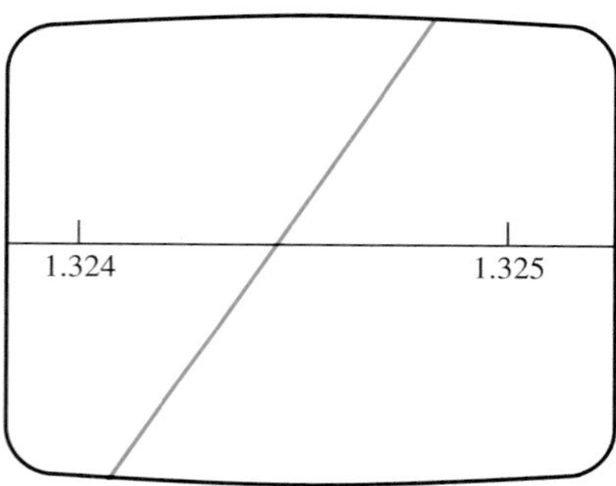

We change the window to $1.32 \leq x \leq 1.33, -0.01 \leq y \leq 0.01$. This shows that the root lies between 1.324 and 1.325.

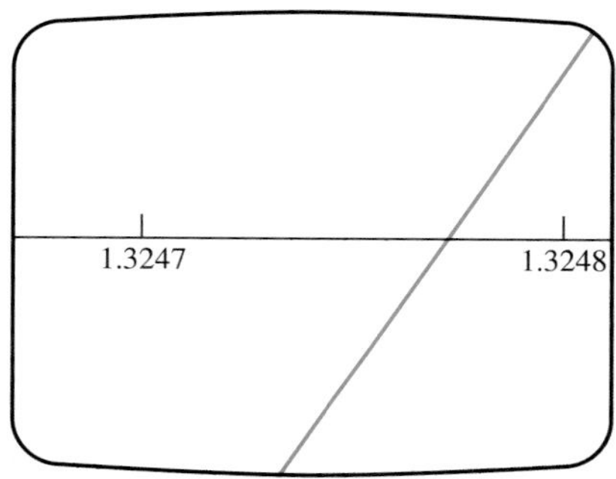

We change the window to $1.324 \leq x \leq 1.325, -0.001 \leq y \leq 0.001$. The root is now seen to lie between 1.3247 and 1.3248.

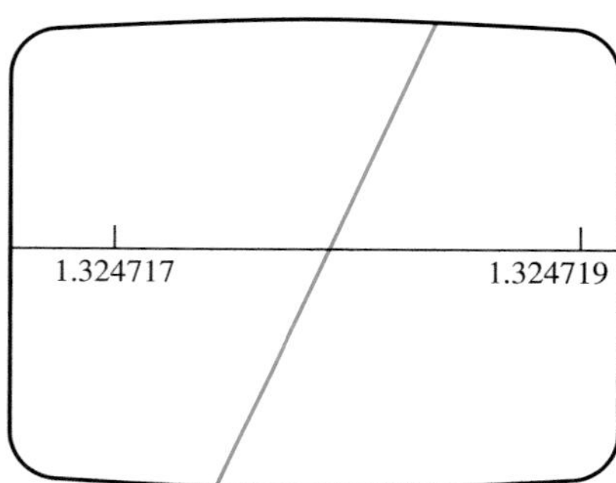

After two more enlargements, we arrive at a screen that shows the root to lie between 1.324717 and 1.324719. To five decimal places, the root is $x = 1.32472$.

2.32 A graphical solution of the equation $x^3 - x - 1 = 0$. We graph the function $f(x) = x^3 - x - 1$ and, with successive screen enlargements, estimate the coordinates of the point where the graph crosses the x-axis.

Continuity vs. Having a Limit

For any function $y = f(x)$ it is important to distinguish between continuity at $x = c$ and having a limit as $x \to c$. The limit is where the function is headed as $x \to c$. Continuity is the property of arriving at the point where $f(x)$ has been heading when x actually gets to c. (Someone is home when you get there, so to speak.)

Finally, remember the test for continuity at a point:

1. Does $f(c)$ exist?
2. Does $\lim_{x \to c} f(x)$ exist?
3. Does $\lim_{x \to c} f(x) = f(c)$?

For f to be continuous at $x = c$, all three answers must be *yes*.

Exercises 2.4

In Exercises 1–4, say whether the function graphed is continuous on the interval $-1 \le x \le 3$. If not, tell where it is not continuous and why.

1. 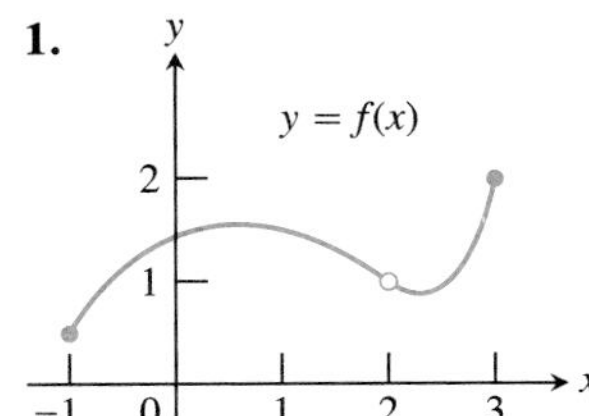

2. 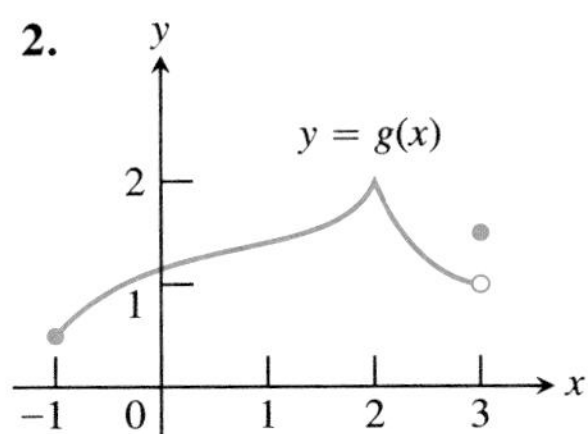

3. 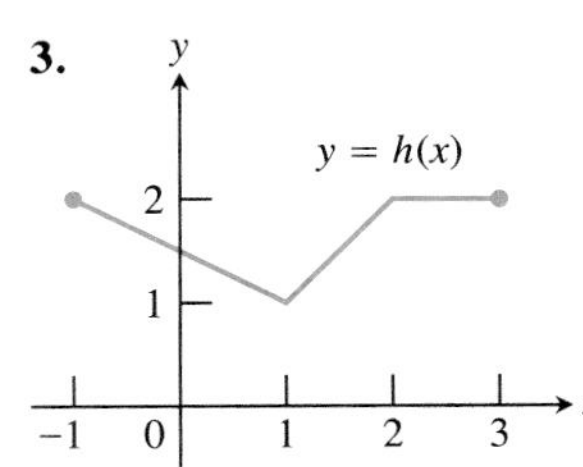

4. 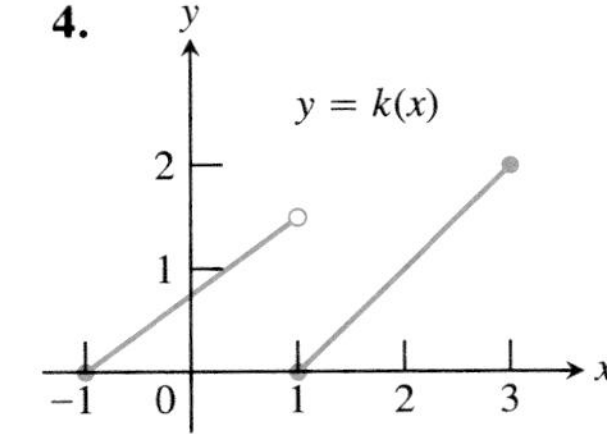

Exercises 5–12 are about the function graphed in Fig. 2.33. Its formula is

$$f(x) = \begin{cases} x^2 - 1, & -1 \le x < 0 \\ 2x, & 0 < x < 1 \\ 1, & x = 1 \\ -2x + 4, & 1 < x < 2 \\ 0, & 2 < x < 3. \end{cases}$$

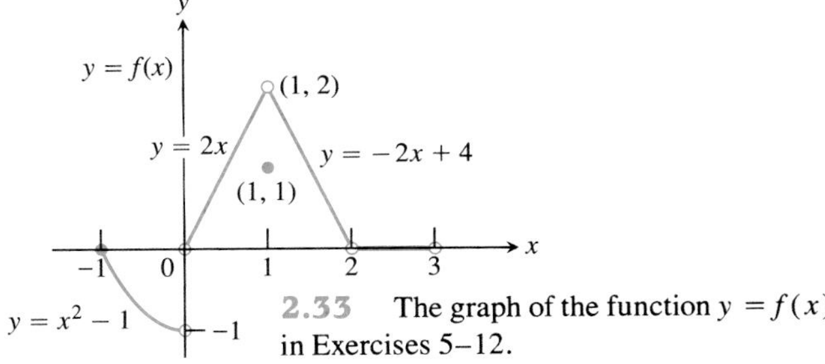

2.33 The graph of the function $y = f(x)$ in Exercises 5–12.

5. a) Does $f(-1)$ exist?
   b) Does $\lim_{x \to -1^+} f(x)$ exist?
   c) Does $\lim_{x \to -1^+} f(x) = f(-1)$?
   d) Is f continuous at $x = -1$?
6. a) Does $f(1)$ exist?
   b) Does $\lim_{x \to 1} f(x)$ exist?
   c) Does $\lim_{x \to 1} f(x) = f(1)$?
   d) Is f continuous at $x = 1$?
7. a) Is f defined at $x = 2$? (Look at the definition of f.)
   b) Is f continuous at $x = 2$?
8. At what values of x is f continuous?
9. a) What is the value of $\lim_{x \to 2} f(x)$?
   b) What value should be assigned to $f(2)$ to make the extended function continuous at $x = 2$?
10. To what new value should $f(1)$ be changed to make the extended function continuous at $x = 1$?
11. Is it possible to extend f to be continuous at $x = 0$? If so, what value should the extended function have there? If not, why not?
12. Is it possible to extend f to be continuous at $x = 3$? If so, what value should the extended function have there? If not, why not?

At which points are the functions in the following exercise in Section 2.1 discontinuous? At which of these points, if any, are the discontinuities removable? not removable? Give reasons for your answers.

13. Exercise 15
14. Exercise 16
15. Exercise 13
16. Exercise 14

Graph the functions in Exercises 17 and 18. At what points are the functions continuous? discontinuous?

17. $f(x) = \begin{cases} 0, & x < 0 \\ 1, & 0 \le x < 1 \\ 0, & 1 < x \end{cases}$

18. $g(x) = \begin{cases} 1, & x < 0 \\ 1 - x^2, & 0 < x \le 1 \\ x, & 1 < x \end{cases}$

Find the points of discontinuity, if any, of the functions in Exercises 19–30.

19. $y = \dfrac{1}{x - 2} - 3x$
20. $y = \dfrac{1}{(x + 2)^2} + 4$
21. $y = \dfrac{x + 1}{x^2 - 4x + 3}$
22. $y = \dfrac{x + 3}{x^2 - 3x - 10}$
23. $y = |x - 1| + \sin x$
24. $y = \dfrac{1}{|x| + 1} - \dfrac{x^2}{2}$
25. $y = \dfrac{\cos x}{x}$
26. $y = \dfrac{x + 2}{\cos x}$
27. $y = \csc 2x$
28. $y = \tan \dfrac{\pi x}{2}$
29. $y = \dfrac{x \tan x}{x^2 + 1}$
30. $y = \dfrac{\sqrt{x^4 + 1}}{1 + \sin^2 x}$
31. Is $f(x) = \begin{cases} (x^2 - 1)/(x - 1), & x \ne 1 \\ 2, & x = 1 \end{cases}$
    continuous at $x = 1$? Explain.

32. Is $f(x) = \begin{cases} \dfrac{\sin^2 3x}{x^2}, & x \neq 0 \\ 9, & x = 0 \end{cases}$

continuous at $x = 0$? Explain.

In Exercises 33–36, find a value of a that makes the function continuous at the given value of x, t, or r.

33. $f(x) = \begin{cases} (x^2 - 1)/(x - 1), & x \neq 1 \\ a, & x = 1 \end{cases}$

34. $g(x) = \begin{cases} (x^2 - 9)/(x + 3), & x \neq -3 \\ a, & x = -3 \end{cases}$

35. $h(t) = \begin{cases} (t^2 + 3t - 10)/(t - 2), & t \neq 2 \\ a, & t = 2 \end{cases}$

36. $f(r) = \begin{cases} (r^2 - 16)/(r^2 - 3r - 4), & r \neq -1, 4 \\ a, & r = 4 \end{cases}$

Show how to extend the functions in Exercises 37–40 to be continuous at every value of x.

37. $f(x) = \dfrac{\sin(x - 2)}{x - 2}$

38. $g(x) = \dfrac{x^3 - x}{x^2 - 1}$

39. $h(x) = \dfrac{\sin 4x}{x}$

40. $f(x) = \dfrac{\tan 3x}{4x}$

Find the limits in Exercises 41–48.

41. $\lim\limits_{x \to \pi} \sin(x - \sin x)$

42. $\lim\limits_{x \to 0} \tan\left(1 - \dfrac{\sin x}{x}\right)$

43. $\lim\limits_{\theta \to 0} \cos\left(\dfrac{\pi\theta}{\sin\theta}\right)$

44. $\lim\limits_{t \to 0} \sin\left(\dfrac{\pi}{2}\cos(\tan t)\right)$

45. $\lim\limits_{y \to 1} \sec(y \sec^2 y - \tan^2 y - 1)$

46. $\lim\limits_{z \to -1} |1 - |z + |z|||$

47. $\lim\limits_{t \to 0} \cos\left(\dfrac{\pi}{\sqrt{19 - 3\sec 2t}}\right)$

48. $\lim\limits_{x \to \pi/6} \sqrt{\csc^2 x + 5\sqrt{3}\tan x}$

49. A continuous function $y = f(x)$ is known to be negative at $x = 0$ and positive at $x = 1$. Why does the equation $f(x) = 0$ have at least one solution between $x = 0$ and $x = 1$? Illustrate with a sketch.

50. Show that the equation $\cos x = x$ has at least one solution. (*Hint:* Show that the equivalent equation $\cos x - x = 0$ has at least one solution.)

51. If $f(x) = x^3 - 8x + 10$, show that there is a value c for which $f(c)$ equals

a) π **b)** $-\sqrt{3}$ **c)** 5,000,000.

52. If $f(x) = (x^3 + x^2)/(x^2 + 1)$, show that there is a value of c for which $f(c)$ equals

a) -2 **b)** $\cos 3$ **c)** 5,000,000.

53. Give an example of a function $f(x)$ that is continuous for all values of x except $x = 2$, where it has a removable discontinuity. Explain how you know that f is discontinuous at $x = 2$, and how you know the discontinuity is removable.

54. Give an example of a function $g(x)$ that is continuous for all values of x except $x = -1$, where it has a nonremovable discontinuity. Explain how you know that g is discontinuous there and why the discontinuity is not removable.

55. If functions $f(x)$ and $g(x)$ are continuous for $0 \le x \le 1$, could $f(x)/g(x)$ possibly be discontinuous at a point of $[0, 1]$? Give reasons for your answer.

56. If the product function $h(x) = f(x) \cdot g(x)$ is continuous at $x = 0$, must $f(x)$ and $g(x)$ be continuous at $x = 0$? Give reasons for your answer.

57. Is it true that a continuous function that is never zero never changes sign? Give reasons for your answer.

58. Is it true that if you stretch a rubber band by moving one end to the right and the other to the left, some point of the band will end up in its original position? Give reasons for your answer.

In Exercises 59–62, graph the function f to see whether it appears to have a continuous extension at the origin. If it does, use TRACE and ZOOM, if available, to find a good candidate for the extended function's value at $x = 0$. If the function does not appear to have a continuous extension, can it be extended to be continuous at the origin from the right or from the left? If so, what do you think the extended function's value should be?

59. $f(x) = \dfrac{10^x - 1}{x}$

60. $f(x) = \dfrac{10^{|x|} - 1}{x}$

61. $f(x) = \dfrac{\sin x}{|x|}$

62. $f(x) = (1 + 2x)^{1/x}$

Writing for Your Own Knowledge

Answer the following questions in writing. Some answers will take only a sentence or two; others may require several paragraphs. Some explanations may also call for graphs or sketches.

1. What is continuity?
2. How do you test for continuity at a point? What if the point is an endpoint of the function's domain?
3. What can be said about algebraic combinations of continuous functions? composites of continuous functions?
4. What does it mean to remove a discontinuity? Can you always do this?
5. What is the intermediate value property? What consequences does it have for graphing and root finding?

EXPLORER PROGRAMS

Continuity	Provides practice with the three-step definition of continuity at a point.
Bisections, Secants, Newton	Approximates roots by any of four methods you select.

2.5 *Defining Limits Formally with Epsilons and Deltas*

We have just spent four sections calculating limits. Our basic tools were the Sandwich Theorem and the theorems that gave the calculation rules for sums, differences, products, and quotients. With these theorems in hand, we started with sensible assumptions about the limits of constant functions and the identity function and worked our way to limits of rational functions. In every case, the calculations were straightforward and the results made sense.

The only problem is that we do not yet know why these theorems are true. The entire calculus depends on these theorems and we haven't a clue about why they hold. If we were to try to prove them now, however, we would soon realize that we never said what a limit really is (except by example) and that the word *approach* in the informal definition of limit is not precise enough to support a successful argument even for a statement as simple as

$$\lim_{x \to x_0} (k) = k \qquad \text{or} \qquad \lim_{x \to x_0} (x) = x_0. \tag{1}$$

To establish these statements and to understand why the limit theorems hold, we need to give the phrase "$f(x)$ approaches L as x approaches c" a numerical description that will enable us to tell exactly when a number is being approached and when it is not. In this section, we develop that description.

As it turns out, the mathematics we need to quantify the notion of approach is the same mathematics we used in Section 1.6 to study target values of functions. There, we had a function $y = f(x)$, a target value y_0, and an upper bound E on the amount of error we could allow the output value y to have. We wanted to know how close we had to keep x to a particular value x_0 so that y would lie within E units of y_0. In symbols, we were asking for a value of D that would make the inequality $|x - x_0| < D$ imply the inequality $|y - y_0| < E$. The number D described the amount by which x could differ from x_0 and still give y-values that approximated y_0 with an error less than E.

In the limit discussions that follow, we use the traditional Greek letters δ (delta) and ϵ (epsilon) in place of the English letters D and E. These are the letters that Cauchy and Weierstrass used in their pioneering work on continuity in the nineteenth century. In their arguments, δ meant "différence" (French for *difference*) and ϵ meant "erreur" (French for *error*).

As you read along, please keep in mind that the purpose of this section is not to calculate limits of particular functions. We already know how to do that. The purpose is to develop a technical definition of limit that is good enough to establish the limit theorems on which our calculations depend.

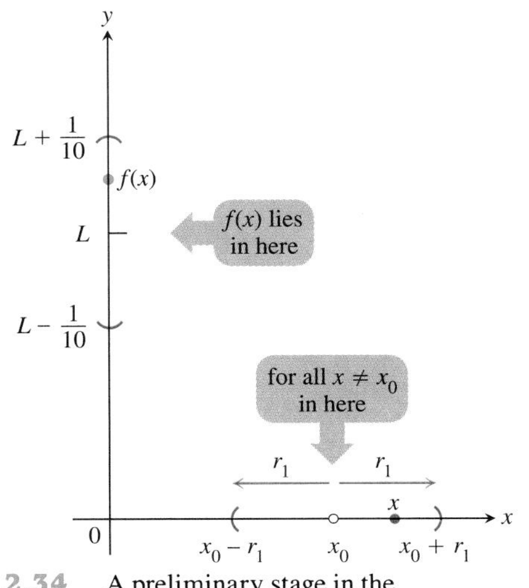

2.34 A preliminary stage in the development of the definition of limit.

The Definition of Limit

Suppose we are watching the values of a function $f(x)$ as x approaches x_0 (without taking on the value x_0 itself). What do we have to know about the values of f to say that they have a particular number L as their limit? What observable pattern in their behavior would guarantee their eventual approach to L?

Certainly we want to be able to say that $f(x)$ stays within one-tenth of a unit of L as soon as x stays within a certain radius r_1 of x_0, as shown in Fig. 2.34. But that in itself is not enough, because as x continues on its course toward x_0, what is to prevent $f(x)$ from jittering about within the interval from $L - 1/10$ to $L + 1/10$ without tending toward L?

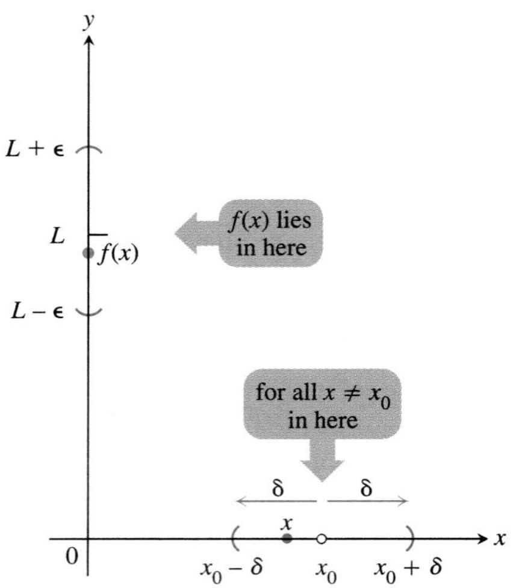

2.35 The relation of δ and ϵ in the definition of limit.

We need to say also that as x continues toward x_0, the number $f(x)$ has to get still closer to L. We might say this by requiring that $f(x)$ lie within 1/100 of a unit of L for all values of x within some smaller radius r_2 of x_0. But this is not enough either. What if $f(x)$ then skips about within the interval from $L - 1/100$ to $L + 1/100$, without heading toward L?

We had better require that $f(x)$ lie within 1/1000 of a unit of L after a while. That is, for all values of x within some still smaller radius r_3 of x_0, all the values of $y = f(x)$ should lie in the interval

$$L - \frac{1}{1000} < y < L + \frac{1}{1000}.$$

This still does not guarantee that $f(x)$ will now move toward L as x approaches x_0. Even if $f(x)$ has not skipped about before, it might start now. We need more.

We need to require that for *every* interval about L, no matter how small, we can find an interval of numbers about x_0 whose f-values all lie within that interval about L. In other words, given any positive radius ϵ about L, there should exist some positive radius δ about x_0 such that for all x within δ units of x_0 (except x_0 itself) the values $y = f(x)$ lie within ϵ units of L (Fig. 2.35). If f satisfies this requirement we will say that

$$\lim_{x \to x_0} f(x) = L.$$

Here, at last, is a mathematical way to say "the closer x gets to x_0, the closer $y = f(x)$ must get to L."

DEFINITION

The **limit** of $f(x)$ as x approaches x_0 is the number L if the following criterion holds:

Given any radius $\epsilon > 0$ about L there exists a radius $\delta > 0$ about x_0 such that for all x

$$0 < |x - x_0| < \delta \quad \text{implies} \quad |f(x) - L| < \epsilon. \tag{2}$$

To return to the notions of error and difference, we might think of machining something like a generator shaft to a close tolerance. We try for diameter L, but since nothing is perfect we must be satisfied to get the diameter $f(x)$ somewhere between $L - \epsilon$ and $L + \epsilon$. The δ is the measure of how accurate our control setting for x must be to guarantee this degree of accuracy in the diameter of the shaft.

Examples: Testing the Definition

Whenever someone proposes a new definition, it is a good idea to see if it gives results that are consistent with past experience. For instance, our experience tells us that as x approaches 1, the number $5x - 3$ approaches $5 - 3 = 2$. If our new definition were to lead to some other result, we would want to throw the definition out and look for another one. The following three examples are included in part to show that the definition in Eq. (2) gives the kinds of results we want.

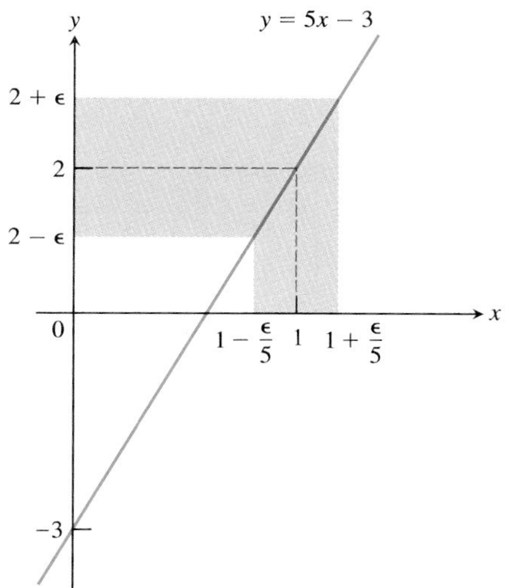

2.36 For the function $f(x) = 5x - 3$, we find that $|x - 1| < \epsilon/5$ will guarantee $|f(x) - 2| < \epsilon$ (Example 1).

EXAMPLE 1 *Testing the Definition.* Show that

$$\lim_{x\to 1} (5x - 3) = 2.$$

Solution In the definition of limit, we set $x_0 = 1, f(x) = 5x - 3$, and $L = 2$. To show that $\lim_{x\to 1} (5x - 3) = 2$, we need to show that for any number $\epsilon > 0$ there exists a number $\delta > 0$ such that for all x

$$0 < |x - 1| < \delta \quad \Rightarrow \quad |(5x - 3) - 2| < \epsilon. \tag{3}$$

To find a suitable value for δ, we solve the ϵ-inequality:

$$\begin{aligned} |(5x - 3) - 2| &< \epsilon \\ |5x - 5| &< \epsilon \\ 5|x - 1| &< \epsilon \\ |x - 1| &< \epsilon/5. \end{aligned}$$

The last line tells us that the original ϵ-inequality, and hence the implication in statement (3), will hold if we choose $\delta = \epsilon/5$ (Fig. 2.36).

The value $\delta = \epsilon/5$ is not the only value that will make the implication in (3) hold. Any smaller positive δ will do as well. The definition does not ask for a "best" δ, just one that will work.

EXAMPLE 2 $\lim_{x\to x_0} x = x_0$. Show that for any number x_0,

$$\lim_{x\to x_0} (x) = x_0.$$

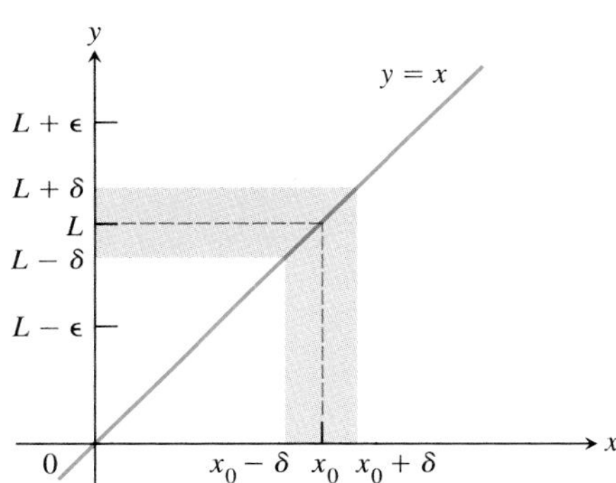

2.37 For the function $f(x) = x$, we find that $|x - x_0| < \delta$ will guarantee $|f(x) - x_0| < \epsilon$ whenever $\delta \le \epsilon$ (Example 2).

Solution In the definition of limit, we set $f(x) = x$ and $L = x_0$. To show that $\lim_{x\to x_0} (x) = x_0$, we must show that for any $\epsilon > 0$ there exists a $\delta > 0$ such that for all x

$$0 < |x - x_0| < \delta \quad \Rightarrow \quad |x - x_0| < \epsilon.$$

The implication will hold if δ is ϵ itself or any smaller positive number (Fig. 2.37).

EXAMPLE 3 *Limits of Constant Functions.* Let $f(x) = k$ be the function whose outputs have the constant value k. Show that for any number x_0,

$$\lim_{x\to x_0} f(x) = \lim_{x\to x_0} k = k.$$

Solution In the definition of limit, we set $f(x) = k$ and $L = k$. To show that $\lim_{x\to x_0} f(x) = k$, we must show that for any $\epsilon > 0$ there exists a $\delta > 0$ such that for all x

$$0 < |x - x_0| < \delta \quad \Rightarrow \quad |k - k| < \epsilon.$$

This implication will hold for any positive δ because $|k - k| = 0$ is less than every positive ϵ for all x (Fig. 2.38).

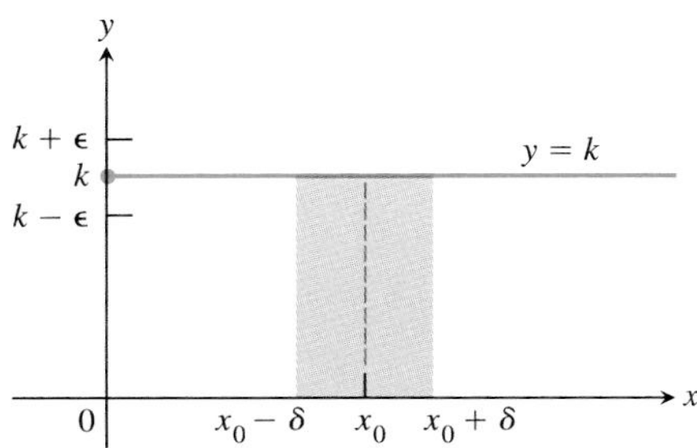

2.38 For the function $f(x) = k$, we find $|f(x) - k| < \epsilon$ for any positive δ (Example 3).

Finding Deltas for Given Epsilons

In Examples 1 and 2, the interval of values about x_0 for which $|f(x) - L|$ was less than ϵ was symmetric about x_0 and we could take δ to be half the length of the interval. When such symmetry is absent, as it usually is, we can take δ to be the distance from x_0 to the interval's nearer endpoint.

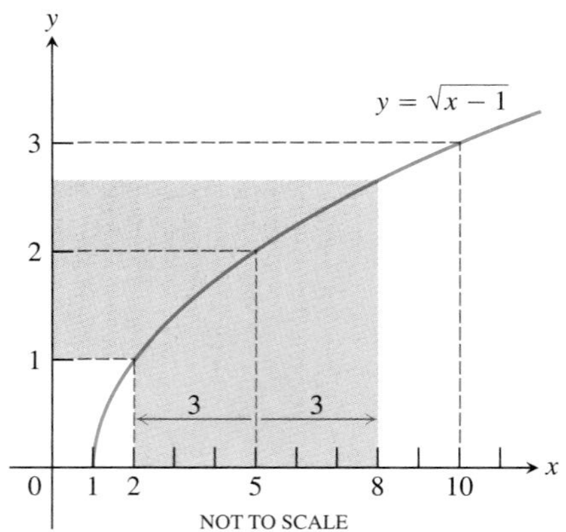

2.39 The function and intervals in Example 4.

EXAMPLE 4 For the limit $\lim_{x\to 5} \sqrt{x-1} = 2$, find a $\delta > 0$ that works for $\epsilon = 1$. That is, find a $\delta > 0$ such that for all x

$$0 < |x - 5| < \delta \quad \Rightarrow \quad |\sqrt{x-1} - 2| < 1. \tag{4}$$

Solution We organize the search into two steps. First we solve the inequality $|\sqrt{x-1} - 2| < 1$ to find an interval (a, b) about $x_0 = 5$ for which the inequality holds. Then we find an interval of radius δ about $x_0 = 5$ that lies inside (a, b). See Fig. 2.39.

STEP 1: We rewrite the inequality $|\sqrt{x-1} - 2| < 1$ in the form $a < x < b$:

$$|\sqrt{x-1} - 2| < 1$$

$$-1 < \sqrt{x-1} - 2 < 1 \qquad \text{Remove absolute value bars.}$$

$$1 < \sqrt{x-1} < 3 \qquad \text{Add 2.}$$

$$1 < x - 1 < 9 \qquad \text{Square.}$$

$$2 < x < 10. \qquad \text{Add 1.}$$

The inequality $|\sqrt{x-1} - 2| < 1$ holds for all x in the interval $2 < x < 10$.

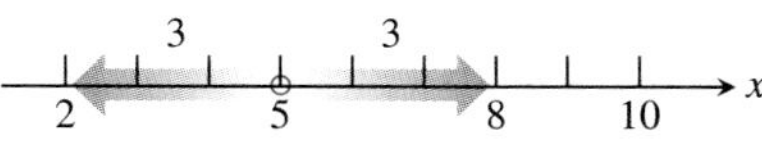

STEP 2: We find a value of δ that places the interval $5 - \delta < x < 5 + \delta$ inside the interval (2, 10). The largest possible value of δ is 3, the distance from $x_0 = 5$ to the nearer endpoint of (2, 10). If δ is 3 or any smaller positive number, the inequality $0 < |x - 5| < \delta$ will automatically place x between 2 and 10 to make $|\sqrt{x-1} - 2| < 1$. In short, for all x

$$0 < |x - 5| < 3 \quad \Rightarrow \quad |\sqrt{x-1} - 2| < 1.$$

How to Find a δ for a Given f, L, x_0, and ϵ

The process of finding a δ such that for all x

$$0 < |x - x_0| < \delta \quad \Rightarrow \quad |f(x) - L| < \epsilon \tag{5}$$

has two steps.

STEP 1: Solve the inequality $|f(x) - L| < \epsilon$ to find an interval $a < x < b$ about x_0 on which the inequality holds.

STEP 2: Find a value of δ that places the interval $x_0 - \delta < x < x_0 + \delta$ inside the interval (a, b). Inequality (5) will hold for all x in this δ-interval.

EXAMPLE 5 For the limit $\lim_{x\to 1/2} (1/x) = 2$, find a δ that works for $\epsilon = 0.01$. That is, find a δ such that for all x

$$0 < \left|x - \frac{1}{2}\right| < \delta \quad \Rightarrow \quad \left|\frac{1}{x} - 2\right| < 0.01. \tag{6}$$

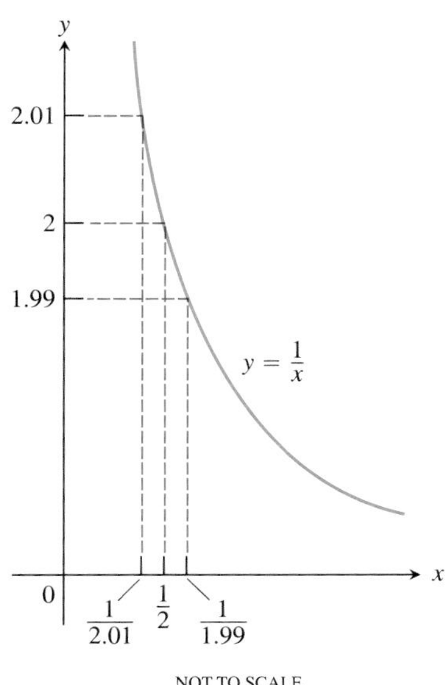

2.40 The graph for Example 5.

Solution As in Example 4, we organize the work into two steps.

STEP 1: *Solve the inequality* $|(1/x) - 2| < 0.01$ *to find the x-values for which it holds.*

$$\left|\frac{1}{x} - 2\right| < 0.01$$

$$-0.01 < \frac{1}{x} - 2 < 0.01 \qquad \text{Remove absolute value bars.}$$

$$1.99 < \frac{1}{x} < 2.01 \qquad \text{Add 2.}$$

$$\frac{1}{2.01} < x < \frac{1}{1.99}. \qquad \text{Take reciprocals.}$$

The inequality $|(1/x) - 2| < 0.01$ holds for all x in the interval from $1/2.01$ up to $1/1.99$ (Fig. 2.40).

STEP 2: *Find a value of* δ *that places the interval* $(1/2) - \delta < x < (1/2) + \delta$ *inside the interval* $(1/2.01,\ 1/1.99)$.

Again, we can take δ to be the distance from x_0 to the nearer endpoint, in this case the distance from $x_0 = 1/2$ to the nearer of the points $1/2.01$ and $1/1.99$. To find out which is nearer, we calculate the distances and compare:

$$\text{Distance from } \frac{1}{2} \text{ to } \frac{1}{2.01}: \qquad \frac{1}{2} - \frac{1}{2.01} = \frac{2.01 - 2}{4.02} = \frac{0.01}{4.02} = \frac{1}{402}$$

$$\text{Distance from } \frac{1}{2} \text{ to } \frac{1}{1.99}: \qquad \frac{1}{1.99} - \frac{1}{2} = \frac{2 - 1.99}{3.98} = \frac{0.01}{3.98} = \frac{1}{398}$$

The smaller of these is $1/402$. If δ has this value (or any smaller positive value), then the inequality $|x - (1/2)| < \delta$ will automatically place x between $1/2.01$ and $1/1.99$ to make $|(1/x) - 2| < 0.01$.

How Limit Theorems Are Proved

Although we will not ask you to prove limit theorems yourself, we want to show a typical proof, if only to support our claim that having a precise definition of limit now makes it possible to prove the limit theorems on which calculus is founded. Our example will be the proof of the Sum Rule for limits (the first part of Theorem 1 from Section 2.1). You can find a proof of the rest of Theorem 1 in Appendix 2.

Theorem 1, Part 1 If $\lim_{x \to x_0} f(x) = L_1$ and $\lim_{x \to x_0} g(x) = L_2$, then $\lim_{x \to x_0} (f(x) + g(x)) = L_1 + L_2$.

Proof To show that $\lim_{x \to x_0} (f(x) + g(x)) = L_1 + L_2$, we must show that for any $\epsilon > 0$ there exists a $\delta > 0$ such that for all x

$$0 < |x - x_0| < \delta \quad \Rightarrow \quad |f(x) + g(x) - (L_1 + L_2)| < \epsilon. \tag{7}$$

Suppose, then, that ϵ is a positive number. The number $\epsilon/2$ is positive, too, and because $\lim_{x \to x_0} f(x) = L_1$ we know that there is a $\delta_1 > 0$ such that for all x

$$0 < |x - x_0| < \delta_1 \quad \Rightarrow \quad |f(x) - L_1| < \frac{\epsilon}{2}. \tag{8}$$

Because $\lim_{x \to x_0} g(x) = L_2$, there is also a $\delta_2 > 0$ such that for all x

$$0 < |x - x_0| < \delta_2 \quad \Rightarrow \quad |g(x) - L_2| < \frac{\epsilon}{2}. \tag{9}$$

Now, either δ_1 equals δ_2 or it doesn't. If δ_1 equals δ_2, the implications in (8) and (9) both hold true for their common value δ. Taken together, (8) and (9) then say that, for all x, $0 < |x - x_0| < \delta$ implies

$$\begin{aligned} |f(x) + g(x) - (L_1 + L_2)| & \\ &= |(f(x) - L_1) + (g(x) - L_2)| \\ &\le |f(x) - L_1| + |g(x) - L_2| && \text{Triangle inequality} \\ &< \frac{\epsilon}{2} + \frac{\epsilon}{2} && \text{The implications in (8) and (9) both hold for } \delta \text{ because } \delta = \delta_1 = \delta_2. \\ &< \epsilon. \end{aligned}$$

If $\delta_1 \ne \delta_2$, let δ be the smaller of δ_1 and δ_2. The implications in (8) and (9) then both hold for all x such that $0 < |x - x_0| < \delta$. As before,

$$|f(x) + g(x) - (L_1 + L_2)| < \epsilon.$$

Either way, we know that given any $\epsilon > 0$ there exists a $\delta > 0$ such that for all x

$$0 < |x - x_0| < \delta \quad \Rightarrow \quad |f(x) + g(x) - (L_1 + L_2)| < \epsilon.$$

According to the ϵ-δ definition of limit, then,

$$\lim_{x \to x_0} (f(x) + g(x)) = L_1 + L_2.$$

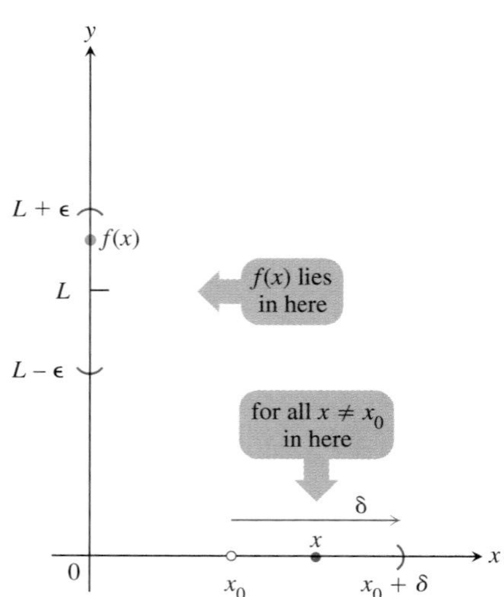

2.41 Diagram for the definition of right-hand limit.

The Relation Between One-sided and Two-sided Limits

The formal definitions of right-hand and left-hand limits go like this:

DEFINITIONS

Right-hand limit: $\lim_{x \to x_0^+} f(x) = L$

The limit of $f(x)$ as x approaches x_0 from the right is the number L if the following criterion holds (Fig. 2.41):

Given any radius $\epsilon > 0$ about L there exists a radius $\delta > 0$ to the right of x_0 such that for all x

$$x_0 < x < x_0 + \delta \quad \Rightarrow \quad |f(x) - L| < \epsilon. \tag{10}$$

Left-hand limit: $\lim_{x \to x_0^-} f(x) = L$

The limit of $f(x)$ as x approaches x_0 from the left is the number L if the following criterion holds (Fig. 2.42):

Given any radius $\epsilon > 0$ about L there exists a radius $\delta > 0$ to the left of x_0 such that for all x

$$x_0 - \delta < x < x_0 \quad \Rightarrow \quad |f(x) - L| < \epsilon. \tag{11}$$

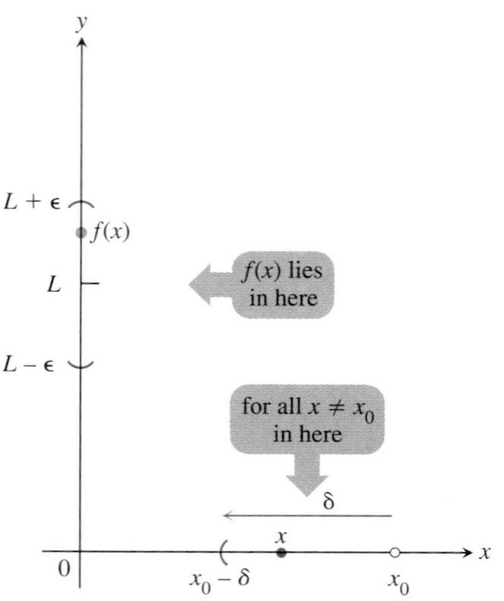

2.42 Diagram for the definition of left-hand limit.

By comparing Eqs. (10) and (11) with Eq. (2), we can see the relation between the one-sided limits just defined and the two-sided limit defined earlier. If we subtract x_0 from the δ-inequalities in Eqs. (10) and (11), they become

$$0 < x - x_0 < \delta \quad \Rightarrow \quad |f(x) - L| < \epsilon \tag{12}$$

and

$$-\delta < x - x_0 < 0 \quad \Rightarrow \quad |f(x) - L| < \epsilon. \tag{13}$$

Together, Eqs. (12) and (13) say the same thing as

$$0 < |x - x_0| < \delta \quad \Rightarrow \quad |f(x) - L| < \epsilon, \tag{14}$$

which is Eq. (2) in the definition of limit. In other words, $f(x)$ has limit L at x_0 if and only if the right-hand and left-hand limits of f at x_0 exist and equal L.

Exercises 2.5

In Exercises 1–8, sketch the interval (a, b) on the x-axis with the point x_0 inside. Then find the largest value of $\delta > 0$ such that $|x - x_0| < \delta$ implies $a < x < b$.

1. $a = 1, \quad b = 7, \quad x_0 = 5$

2. $a = 1, \quad b = 7, \quad x_0 = 2$

3. $a = -7/2, \quad b = -1/2, \quad x_0 = -3$

4. $a = -7/2, \quad b = -1/2, \quad x_0 = -3/2$

5. $a = -5, \quad b = 3, \quad x_0 = 1$

6. $a = -5, \quad b = 3, \quad x_0 = -2$

7. $a = 4/9, \quad b = 4/7, \quad x_0 = 1/2$

8. $a = 2.7591, \quad b = 3.2391, \quad x_0 = 3$

Use the graphs in Exercises 9–14 to find a $\delta > 0$ such that for all x

$$0 < |x - x_0| < \delta \quad \Rightarrow \quad |f(x) - L| < \epsilon.$$

9.

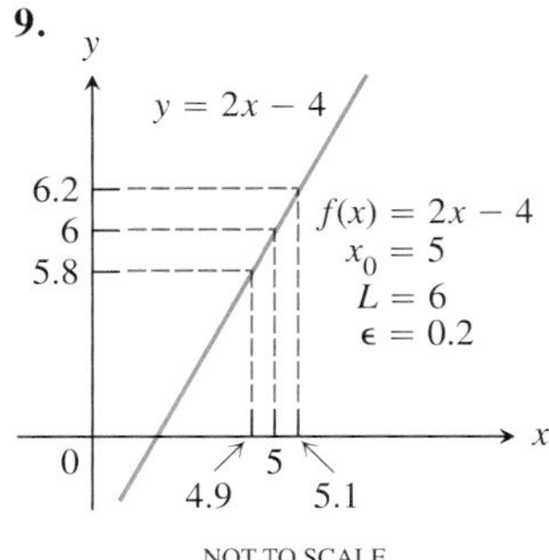

10.

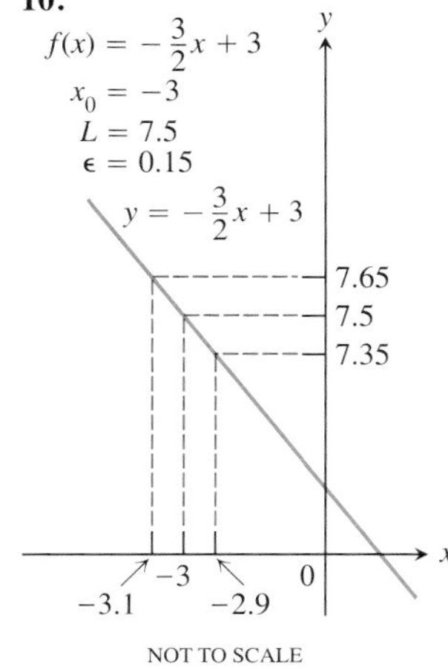

11.

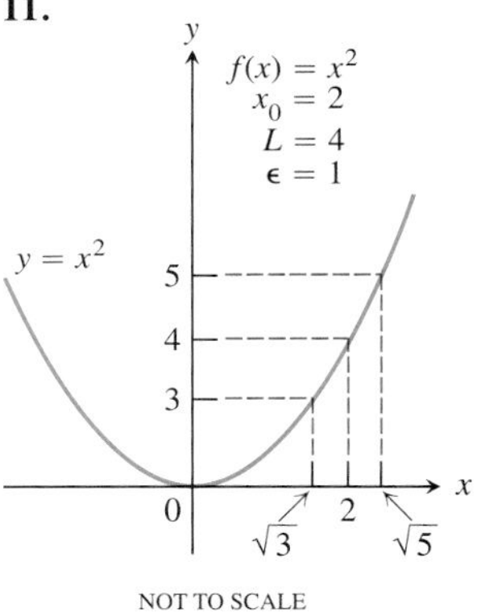

12.

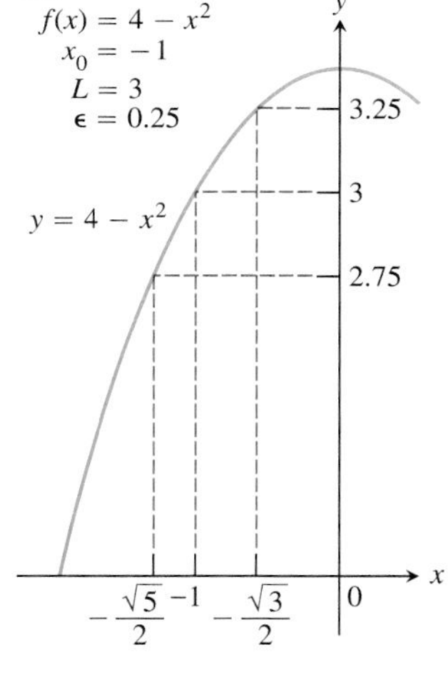

13.

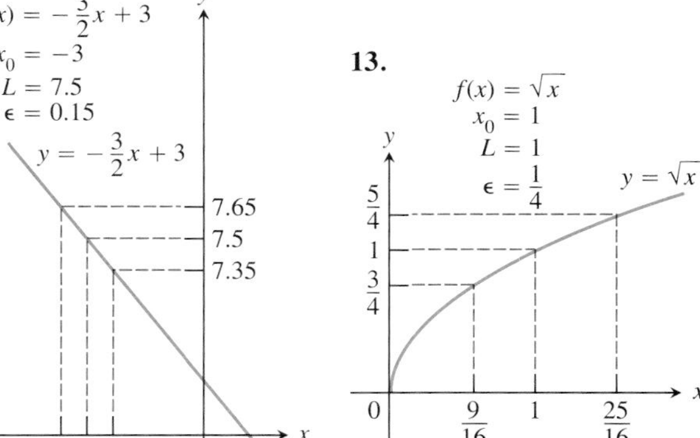

14.

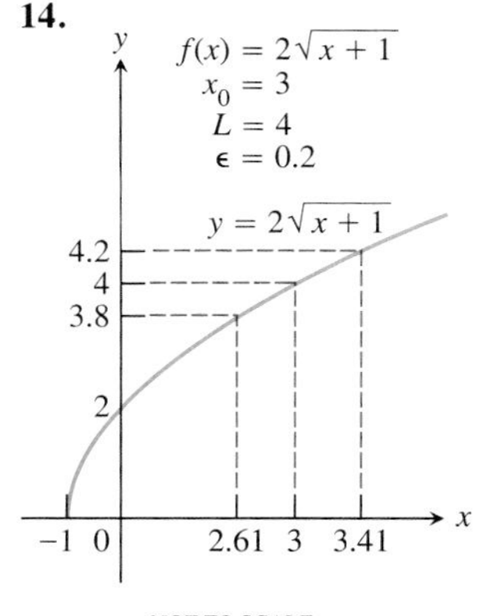

For each function $y = f(x)$ and number $\epsilon > 0$ in Exercises 15–22, find the set of x-values for which $|f(x) - 4| < \epsilon$.

15. $f(x) = x + 1, \quad \epsilon = 0.01$
16. $f(x) = 2x - 2, \quad \epsilon = 0.02$
17. $f(x) = x^2 - 5, \quad \epsilon = 0.05$
18. $f(x) = 4 - x^2, \quad \epsilon = 0.04$
19. $f(x) = \sqrt{19 - x}, \quad \epsilon = 0.03$
20. $f(x) = \sqrt{x + 1}, \quad \epsilon = 0.1$
21. $f(x) = 1/x, \quad \epsilon = 0.1$
22. $f(x) = \dfrac{1}{x - 2}, \quad \epsilon = 0.5$

Each of Exercises 23–32 gives a function $f(x)$, a point x_0, and a positive number ϵ. Find $L = \lim_{x \to x_0} f(x)$. Then find a number $\delta > 0$ such that for all x

$$0 < |x - x_0| < \delta \quad \Rightarrow \quad |f(x) - L| < \epsilon.$$

23. $f(x) = 2x + 3, \quad x_0 = 1, \quad \epsilon = 0.01$
24. $f(x) = 3 - 2x, \quad x_0 = 3, \quad \epsilon = 0.02$
25. $f(x) = 4x - 2, \quad x_0 = 1/2, \quad \epsilon = 0.02$
26. $f(x) = -3x - 2, \quad x_0 = -1, \quad \epsilon = 0.03$
27. $f(x) = \dfrac{x^2 - 4}{x - 2}, \quad x_0 = 2, \quad \epsilon = 0.05$
28. $f(x) = \dfrac{x^2 + 6x + 5}{x + 5}, \quad x_0 = -5, \quad \epsilon = 0.05$
29. $f(x) = \sqrt{x - 7}, \quad x_0 = 11, \quad \epsilon = 0.01$
30. $f(x) = \sqrt{1 - 5x}, \quad x_0 = -3, \quad \epsilon = 0.5$
31. $f(x) = 4/x, \quad x_0 = 2, \quad \epsilon = 0.4$
32. $f(x) = 4/x, \quad x_0 = 1/2, \quad \epsilon = 0.04$

In Exercises 33 and 34, find the largest $\delta > 0$ such that for all x

$$0 < |x - 4| < \delta \quad \Rightarrow \quad |f(x) - 5| < \epsilon.$$

33. $f(x) = 9 - x$; $\epsilon = 0.01, 0.001, 0.0001$, arbitrary $\epsilon > 0$
34. $f(x) = 3x - 7$; $\epsilon = 0.003, 0.0003$, arbitrary $\epsilon > 0$
35. Given $\epsilon > 0$, find an interval $I = (5, 5 + \delta)$, $\delta > 0$, such that if x lies in I then $\sqrt{x - 5} < \epsilon$. What limit is being verified?
36. Given $\epsilon > 0$, find an interval $I = (4 - \delta, 4)$, $\delta > 0$, such that if x lies in I then $\sqrt{4 - x} < \epsilon$. What limit is being verified?
37. Graph the function

$$f(x) = \begin{cases} 4 - 2x, & x < 1, \\ 6x - 4, & x \geq 1. \end{cases}$$

Then, given $\epsilon > 0$, find the largest δ for which $f(x)$ lies between $y = 2 - \epsilon$ and $y = 2 + \epsilon$ for x in the interval $I = (1 - \delta, 1 + \delta)$.

38. Let $f(x) = |x - 5|/(x - 5)$. Find the set of x-values for which

$$1 - \epsilon < f(x) < 1 + \epsilon, \qquad \text{for } \epsilon = 4, 2, 1, \text{ and } 1/2.$$

(*Hint:* First graph f for $x > 5$ and $x < 5$.)

39. Define what it means to say that $\lim_{x \to 2} f(x) = 5$.
40. Define what it means to say that $\lim_{x \to 0} g(x) = k$.
41. *A Wrong Statement About Limits.* Show by example that the following statement is wrong.

    The number L is the limit of $f(x)$ as x approaches x_0 if $f(x)$ gets closer to L as x approaches x_0.

    Explain why the function in your example does not have the given value of L as a limit as $x \to x_0$.

42. *Another Wrong Statement About Limits.* Show by example that the following statement is wrong.

    The number L is the limit of $f(x)$ as x approaches x_0 if, given any $\epsilon > 0$, there exists a value of x for which $|f(x) - L| < \epsilon$.

    Explain why the function in your example does not have the given value of L as a limit as $x \to x_0$.

Writing for Your Own Knowledge

Answer the following questions in writing. Some answers will take only a sentence or two; others may require several paragraphs. Some explanations may also call for graphs or sketches.

1. What does it mean to say that $\lim_{x \to x_0} f(x) = L$?
2. Why bother with ϵ's and δ's?
3. How do you find a δ for a given f, L, x_0, and ϵ?

EXPLORER PROGRAM

Limit Definition	Enables you to work with the definition graphically to choose appropriate δ's for given ϵ's. Also enables you to determine when no such δ exists.

For Your Review

Write brief paragraphs about the following topics and give examples.

General rules for calculating limits
One-sided vs. two-sided limits
Limits of polynomials and rational functions
Finite limits involving infinity
Infinite limits
The Sandwich Theorem and its applications
$\lim_{x\to 0} \frac{\sin x}{x}$
Continuity at an interior point; at an endpoint
Combinations of continuous functions
The Intermediate Value Theorem
Continuity vs. having a limit
The formal definition of limit
Finding a δ for a given $\epsilon > 0$

Practice Exercises

Find the limits in Exercises 1–10.

1. $\lim_{x\to 1} 5x - 4$

2. $\lim_{x\to -3} |7x + 10|$

3. $\lim_{x\to -2} x^2(x + 1)$

4. $\lim_{x\to 3} (x + 2)(x - 5)$

5. $\lim_{x\to -0.5} \sqrt{\frac{x + 2}{x + 1}}$

6. $\lim_{x\to 1.5} \sqrt{\frac{x - 1}{x + 2}}$

7. $\lim_{x\to 3} \frac{x - 9}{x^2}$

8. $\lim_{x\to -1} \frac{x^2 + 1}{3x^2 - 2x + 5}$

9. $\lim_{x\to -2} \left(\frac{x}{x + 1}\right)\left(\frac{3x + 5}{x^2 + x}\right)$

10. $\lim_{x\to 1} \left(\frac{1}{x + 1}\right)\left(\frac{x + 6}{x}\right)\left(\frac{3 - x}{7}\right)$

Find the limits in Exercises 11–14.

11. $\lim_{h\to 0} \frac{1}{2\sqrt{h + 1} + 2}$

12. $\lim_{h\to 0} \frac{1}{\sqrt{7h + 5} + \sqrt{5}}$

13. $\lim_{h\to 0} \frac{\sqrt{h^2 + 4h + 5} - \sqrt{5}}{h}$

14. $\lim_{h\to 0} \frac{\sqrt{5h^2 + 11h + 6} - \sqrt{6}}{h}$

Find the limits in Exercises 15–20.

15. $\lim_{x\to -1} \frac{x^2 - x - 2}{x + 1}$

16. $\lim_{x\to 2} \frac{x^2 - x - 2}{x - 2}$

17. $\lim_{x\to 1} \frac{x^2 - 1}{x - 1}$

18. $\lim_{x\to -5} \frac{x^2 + 3x - 10}{x + 5}$

19. $\lim_{x\to 2} \frac{x - 2}{x^2 + x - 6}$

20. $\lim_{x\to 1} \frac{x^2 - 2x + 1}{x^3 - 2x^2 + x}$

Find the limits in Exercises 21–26.

21. $\lim_{x\to \infty} \frac{2x + 3}{5x + 7}$

22. $\lim_{x\to -\infty} \frac{2x^2 + 3}{5x^2 + 7}$

23. $\lim_{x\to -\infty} \frac{x^2 - 4x + 8}{3x^3}$

24. $\lim_{x\to \infty} \frac{1}{x^2 - 7x + 1}$

25. $\lim_{x\to -\infty} \frac{x^2 - 7x}{x + 1}$

26. $\lim_{x\to \infty} \frac{x^4 + x^3}{12x^3 + 128}$

Find the limits in Exercises 27–34.

27. $\lim_{x\to 3^+} \frac{1}{x - 3}$

28. $\lim_{x\to 3^-} \frac{1}{x - 3}$

29. $\lim_{x\to 0^+} \frac{1}{x^2}$

30. $\lim_{x\to 0^-} \frac{1}{|x|}$

31. a) $\lim_{x\to 0^+} \frac{2}{x^{1/3}}$ **b)** $\lim_{x\to 0^-} \frac{2}{x^{1/3}}$

32. a) $\lim_{x\to 0^+} \frac{8}{x^{1/5}}$ **b)** $\lim_{x\to 0^-} \frac{8}{x^{1/5}}$

33. $\lim_{x\to 0} \frac{1}{3x^{2/3}}$

34. $\lim_{x\to 0} \frac{1}{5x^{4/5}}$

Find the limits in Exercises 35–42.

35. $\lim_{t\to 0} \frac{\sin kt}{t}$ (k constant)

36. $\lim_{t\to 0} \frac{4t}{\sin 2t}$

37. $\lim_{h\to 0} \frac{\sin(\sin h)}{\sin h}$

38. $\lim_{y\to 0} \frac{\cos^2 y - 1}{\cos y - 1}$

39. $\lim_{\theta\to (\pi/2)^-} \frac{4\tan^2\theta + \tan\theta + 1}{\tan^2\theta + 5}$

40. $\lim_{\theta\to 0^+} \frac{1 - 2\cot^2\theta}{5\cot^2\theta - 7\cot\theta - 8}$

41. $\lim_{x\to 0^+} \frac{\sin \lfloor x \rfloor}{x}$

42. $\lim_{x\to 0^+} \frac{\lfloor \sin x \rfloor}{x}$

In Exercises 43 and 44, use the graphs to help find the limits.

43. a) $\lim_{x\to -2^+} \frac{x + 3}{x + 2}$

b) $\lim_{x\to -2^-} \frac{x + 3}{x + 2}$

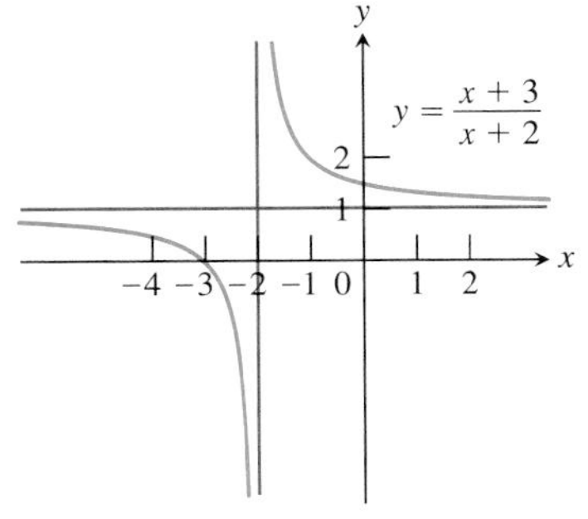

44. **a)** 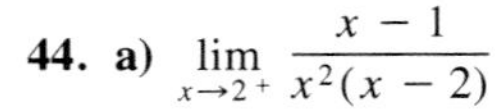 $\lim_{x \to 2^+} \dfrac{x-1}{x^2(x-2)}$

b) 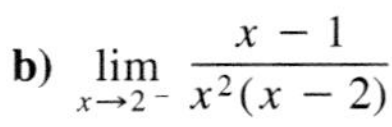 $\lim_{x \to 2^-} \dfrac{x-1}{x^2(x-2)}$

c) $\lim_{x \to 0^+} \dfrac{x-1}{x^2(x-2)}$

d) $\lim_{x \to 0^-} \dfrac{x-1}{x^2(x-2)}$

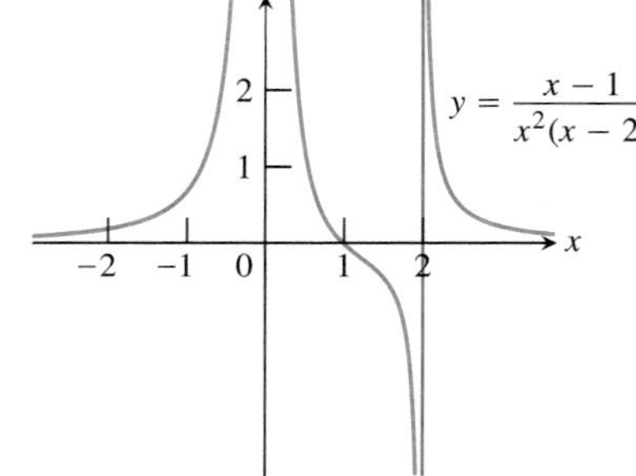

45. When, if ever, does knowing $\lim_{x \to c} f(x)$ help you to find $\lim_{x \to c} 1/f(x)$? Give reasons for your answer.

46. Suppose that $y = f(x)$ is an even function of x. Does knowing that $\lim_{x \to 2} f(x) = 7$ tell you anything about $\lim_{x \to -2} f(x)$? Give reasons for your answer.

47. Does the existence and value of the limit of a function $f(x)$ as x approaches c ever depend on what happens at $x = c$? Explain, and give examples.

48. Once you know $\lim_{x \to c^-} f(x)$ and $\lim_{x \to c^+} f(x)$ at an interior point c of the domain of f, do you then know $\lim_{x \to c} f(x)$? Give reasons for your answer.

49. **a)** Investigate the behavior of $f(x) = x\,(\cos(1/x) - 1)$ as $x \to 0$ and $x \to \infty$. What do you think happens?

b) Use the inequality $-2 \le \cos(1/x) - 1 \le 2$ together with the Sandwich Theorem to confirm your observation about the behavior of f as $x \to 0$. Chapter 6 will explain the behavior of f as $x \to \infty$.

50. *Compound Interest.* If you invest \$100 at a fixed annual rate of 6% and interest is added to your account k times a year, the amount of money you will have when the year is up is

$$A = 100\left(1 + \frac{0.06}{k}\right)^k.$$

If the interest is added quarterly ("compounded quarterly," bankers say), then $k = 4$ and A will be about \$106.14. By the end of the year, you will have earned \$6.14. If the interest is added monthly instead, then $k = 12$ and A will be about \$106.17. You will have earned \$6.17. Suppose that the interest were added daily ($k = 365$) or even more frequently, say, by the hour, by the minute, or even by the second. Would there be any limit to how much your money could earn? Find out by investigating the behavior of the function $y = 100(1 + (0.06/x))^x$ as $x \to \infty$. What do you think is going on? (Chapter 6 will explain.)

51. Suppose that $f(x)$ and $g(x)$ are defined for all x and that $\lim_{x \to c} f(x) = -7$ and $\lim_{x \to c} g(x) = 0$. Find the limit as $x \to c$ of the following functions.

a) $3f(x)$ **b)** $(f(x))^2$ **c)** $f(x) \cdot g(x)$

d) $\dfrac{f(x)}{g(x) - 7}$ **e)** $\cos(g(x))$ **f)** $|f(x)|$

52. Suppose that $f(x)$ and $g(x)$ are defined for all x and that $\lim_{x \to 0} f(x) = 1/2$ and $\lim_{x \to 0} g(x) = \sqrt{2}$. Find the limits as $x \to 0$ of the following functions.

a) $-g(x)$ **b)** $g(x) \cdot f(x)$ **c)** $f(x) + g(x)$

d) $1/f(x)$ **e)** $x + f(x)$ **f)** $\dfrac{f(x) \cdot \sin x}{x}$

53. Use the inequality

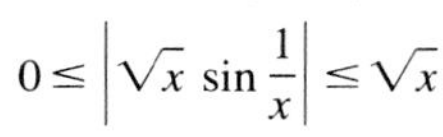

$$0 \le \left|\sqrt{x} \sin \frac{1}{x}\right| \le \sqrt{x}$$

to find $\lim_{x \to 0^+} \sqrt{x} \sin(1/x)$. See Fig. 2.43.

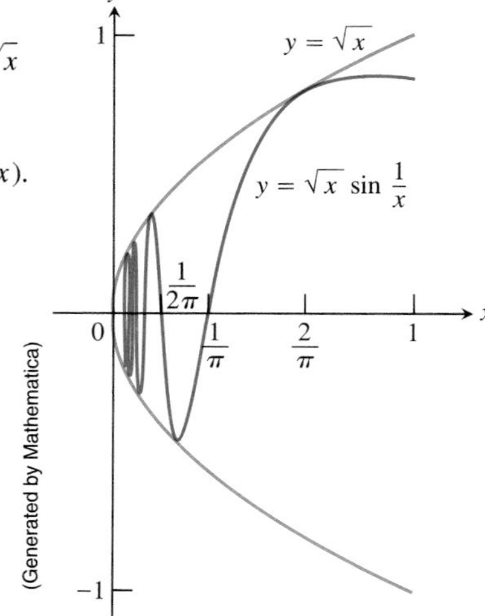

2.43 The graph of $y = \sqrt{x} \sin(1/x)$ (Exercise 53).

54. Use the inequality

$$0 \le \left|x^2 \sin \frac{1}{x}\right| \le x^2$$

to find $\lim_{x \to 0} x^2 \sin(1/x)$. See Fig. 2.44.

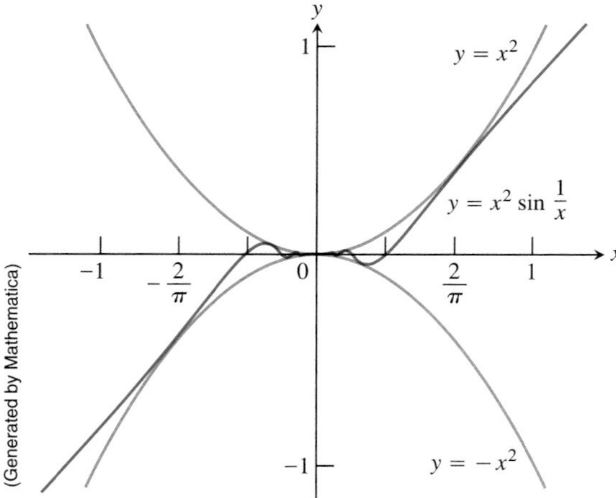

2.44 The graph of $y = x^2 \sin(1/x)$ (Exercise 54).

Use the Sandwich Theorem to find the limits in Exercises 55 and 56.

55. $\lim_{x \to \infty} \dfrac{\sin x}{\sqrt{x}}$

56. $\lim_{x \to \infty} \dfrac{\cos x}{\sqrt{x}}$

Find the limits in Exercises 57 and 58.

57. $\lim_{x \to \infty} \dfrac{x + \sin x}{x}$

58. $\lim_{x \to \infty} \dfrac{x + \sin x}{x + \cos x}$

59. Answer the following questions about the function

$$f(x) = \begin{cases} 1, & x < -1 \\ -x, & -1 < x < 0 \\ 1, & x = 0 \\ -x, & 0 < x < 1 \\ 1, & 1 \le x \end{cases}$$

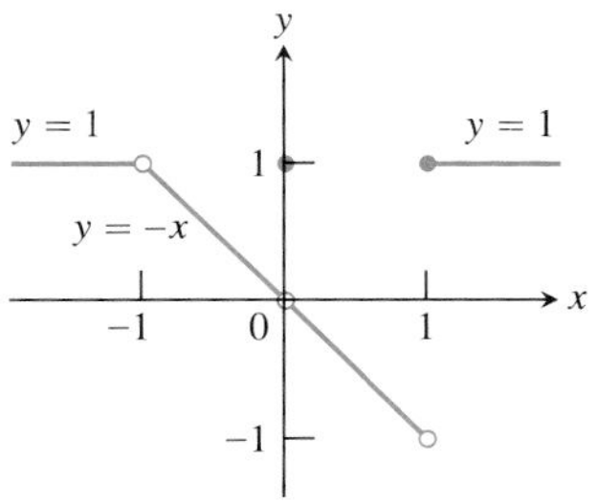

y = 1 y = 1 y = −x

a) Find the right-hand and left-hand limits of f at $x = -1, 0,$ and 1.

b) Does f have a limit as x approaches $-1, 0, 1$? If so, what is it? If not, why not?

c) At what points does f fail to be continuous? Are any of the discontinuities removable? How do you know? How should f be defined or redefined at this point (these points) to make the new function continuous?

60. Repeat the questions in Exercise 59 for the function

$$f(x) = \begin{cases} 0, & x \le -1 \\ |2x|, & -1 < x < 1, \quad x \neq 0 \\ 0, & x = 1 \\ 1, & x > 1 \end{cases}$$

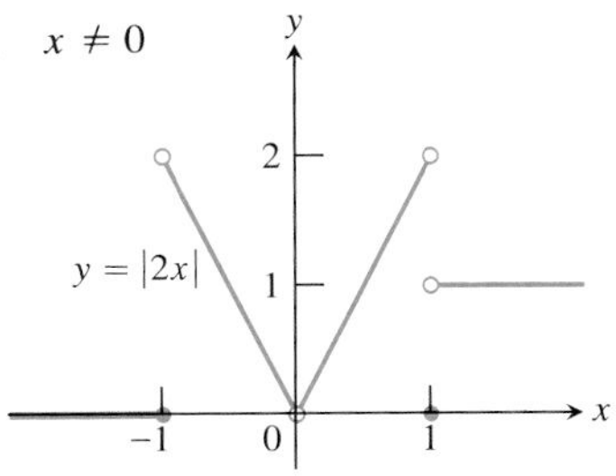

y = |2x|

61. a) Graph the function $f(x) = \begin{cases} -x, & x < 1 \\ x - 1, & x > 1. \end{cases}$

b) Can you extend f to be continuous at $x = 1$? How do you know? If this can be done, what value should the extended function have at $x = 1$? Give reasons for your answers.

62. Repeat Exercise 61 for the function

$$f(x) = \begin{cases} 3x^2, & x < 1 \\ 4 - x^2, & x > 1. \end{cases}$$

63. Is there any value of k that will make

$$g(x) = \begin{cases} \dfrac{x^2 - 2x - 8}{x + 2}, & x \neq -2 \\ k, & x = -2 \end{cases}$$

continuous at $x = -2$? If so, what is it? Give reasons for your answer.

64. Is there any value of k that will make

$$f(x) = \begin{cases} \dfrac{x^2 + 2x - 15,}{x - 3} & x \neq 3 \\ k, & x = 3 \end{cases}$$

continuous at $x = 3$? If so, what is it? Give reasons for your answer.

65. Is there any value of k that will make

$$f(x) = \begin{cases} \dfrac{\sin x}{2x}, & x \neq 0 \\ k, & x = 0 \end{cases}$$

continuous at $x = 0$? If so, what is it? Give reasons for your answer.

66. a) Graph the function

$$f(x) = \begin{cases} \dfrac{x^2}{\sin^2 2x}, & x \neq 0 \\ c, & x = 0. \end{cases}$$

b) Find a value of c that makes f continuous at $x = 0$.

67. If $y = f(x)$ is continuous, with $f(1) = 0$ and $f(2) = 3$, must f take on the value 2.5 at some point between $x = 1$ and $x = 2$? Give reasons for your answer.

68. Are there any values of x for which $x + \cos x = 0$? Give reasons for your answer.

69. Does the equation $\cos x = 2 - x^3$ have a solution? Give reasons for your answer.

70. Show that the equation $x \sin x = 1$ has at least one solution. How many other solutions do you think the equation has? (*Hint:* How many times does the curve $y = x \sin x$ cross the line at $y = 1$?)

THE DEFINITION OF LIMIT

71. Define what it means to say that

$$\lim_{x \to 1} f(x) = 3.$$

72. Define what it means to say that

$$\lim_{x \to 0} \frac{\sin x}{x} = 1.$$

73. The function $f(x) = 2x - 3$ is continuous at $x = 2$. Given a positive number ϵ, how small must δ be for $|x - 2| < \delta$ to imply $|f(x) - 1| < \epsilon$?

74. The function $f(x) = |x|$ is continuous at $x = 0$. Given a positive number ϵ, how small must δ be for $|x - 0| < \delta$ to imply $|f(x) - 0| < \epsilon$?

Each of Exercises 75–82 gives a function $f(x)$, a point x_0, and a positive number ϵ. Find $L = \lim_{x \to x_0} f(x)$. Then find a number $\delta > 0$ such that for all x

$$0 < |x - x_0| < \delta \quad \Rightarrow \quad |f(x) - L| < \epsilon.$$

75. $f(x) = 5x - 10, \quad x_0 = 3, \quad \epsilon = 0.05$

76. $f(x) = 5x - 10, \quad x_0 = 2, \quad \epsilon = 0.05$

77. $f(x) = 5x - 10, \quad x_0 = 1, \quad \epsilon = 0.05$

78. $f(x) = 5x - 10, \quad x_0 = 0, \quad \epsilon = 0.05$

79. $f(x) = \sqrt{x - 5}, \quad x_0 = 9, \quad \epsilon = 1$

80. $f(x) = \sqrt{2x - 3}, \quad x_0 = 2, \quad \epsilon = 1/2$

81. $f(x) = 2/x, \quad x_0 = 2, \quad \epsilon = 0.1$

82. $f(x) = 1/(4x), \quad x_0 = 1/4, \quad \epsilon = 1/20$

AIRBAG SYSTEM DESIGN

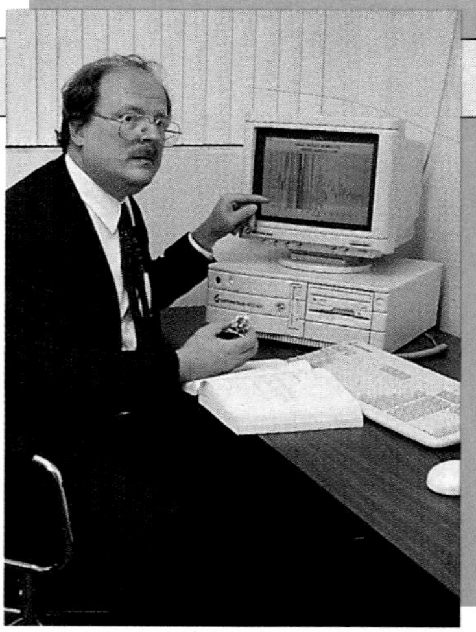

RALPH L. HENSLER directs engineering technology at Breed Technologies, Inc., in Boonton Township, NJ.

Engineers at Breed Technologies design driver and passenger airbag systems and crash pulse sensors. In the event of a sudden shock or deceleration, these are the sensors that initiate or decide against airbag inflation. If you hit a pothole at 6 mi/h, or have a fender bender in a parking lot, you don't want the airbag to inflate. But if you hit a utility pole at 30 mi/h, you do, and in a hurry. In the event of a crash, the driver- and passenger-side airbags must be in place before the occupants have moved 5 in. forward due to the deceleration of the vehicle.

This typically means that the deployment decision (whether to inflate the airbag) must be made within 10 to 40 milliseconds of the onset of the crash. The figure here shows data for a 35 mi/h crash.

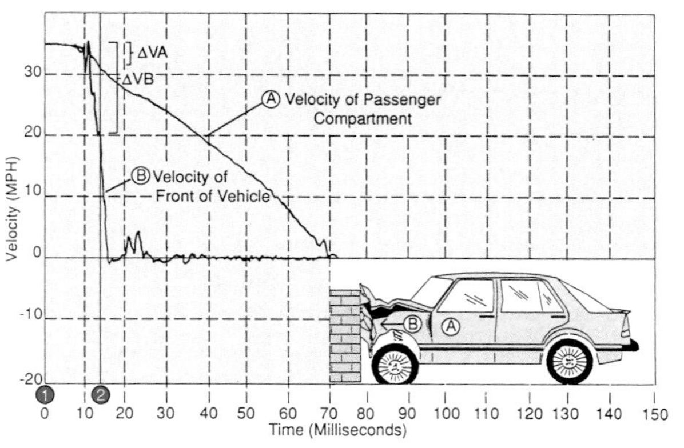

The car hits a barrier at ❶ (time = 0). The initial velocity change ΔVA in the passenger compartment is gradual, so that the information available at ❷ when the decision must be made is limited.

However, the initial velocity change ΔVB at the front of the vehicle is so rapid that more information is available at ❷. Placing one or more velocity-change sensors at the front of the car provides lead time for the deployment decision.

To design a sensor system that will inflate an airbag precisely when it is needed, Hensler's group uses a mathematical model to predict acceleration pulses and sensor responses in different vehicle locations under a variety of crash conditions. The model takes calculus — and about 100 pages of Fortran code — to solve.

OVERVIEW

Derivatives are the functions that measure the rates at which things change. We use them to calculate velocities and accelerations, to predict the effect of flight maneuvers on the heart, to explain why machinery breaks apart when it runs too fast, and to describe how sensitive formulas are to errors in measurement. Now that we can calculate limits, we can find derivatives.

3 Derivatives

3.1 Slopes, Tangent Lines, and Derivatives

This section provides our first view of the role calculus plays in describing how rapidly things change. Our point of departure is the coordinate plane of Descartes and Fermat. The plane is the natural place to draw curves and calculate the slopes of lines and it is from the slopes of lines that we find the slopes of curves. Once we can do that, we can find tangent lines for curves and formulas for rates of change.

Average Rates of Change

We encounter average rates of change in such forms as average speeds (distance traveled divided by elapsed time, say, in miles per hour), growth rates of populations (in percent per year), and average monthly rainfall (in inches per month). The **average rate of change** in a quantity over a period of time is the amount of change divided by the time it takes.

Experimental biologists often want to know the rates at which populations grow under controlled laboratory conditions. Figure 3.1 shows data from a fruit fly–growing experiment, the setting for our first example.

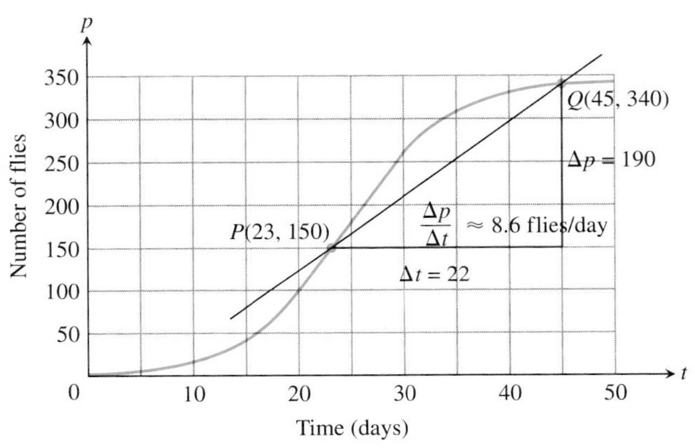

3.1 Growth of a fruit fly population in a controlled experiment. (*Source: Elements of Mathematical Biology* by A. J. Lotka, 1956, Dover, New York, p. 69.)

EXAMPLE 1 *The Average Growth Rate of a Laboratory Population.* The graph in Fig. 3.1 shows how the number of fruit flies (*Drosophila*) grew in a controlled 50-day experiment. The graph was made by counting flies at regular intervals, plotting a point for each count, and drawing a smooth curve through the plotted points.

There were 150 flies on day 23 and 340 flies on day 45. This gave an increase of $340 - 150 = 190$ flies in $45 - 23 = 22$ days. The average rate of change in the population from day 23 to day 45 was therefore

$$\textit{Average rate of change:} \quad \frac{\Delta p}{\Delta t} = \frac{340 - 150}{45 - 23} = \frac{190}{22} \approx 8.6 \text{ flies/day.} \tag{1}$$

The average rate of change in Eq. (1) is also the slope of the secant line through the two points

$$P(23, 150) \quad \text{and} \quad Q(45, 340)$$

on the population curve. (A line through two points on a curve is called a **secant** to the curve.) We can calculate the slope of the secant PQ from the coordinates of P and Q:

$$\textit{Secant slope:} \quad \frac{\Delta p}{\Delta t} = \frac{340 - 150}{45 - 23} = \frac{190}{22} \approx 8.6 \text{ flies/day.} \tag{2}$$

By comparing Eqs. (1) and (2) we can see that the average rate of change in (1) is the same number as the slope in (2), units and all. We can always think of an average rate of change as the slope of a secant line.

In addition to knowing the average rate at which the population grew from day 23 to day 45, we may also want to know how fast the population was growing on day 23 itself. To find out, we can watch the slope of the secant PQ change as we back Q along the curve toward P. Each new position of Q gives a different secant PQ. Figure 3.2 shows four of these secants along with their slopes.

In terms of geometry, what we see as Q approaches P along the curve is this: The secant PQ approaches the tangent line AB that we drew by eye at P (more about tangents in a moment). This means that within the limitations of our drawing, the slopes of the secants approach the slope of the tangent, which we calculate from the coordinates of A and B to be

$$\frac{350 - 0}{35 - 14} = 16.7 \text{ flies/day.}$$

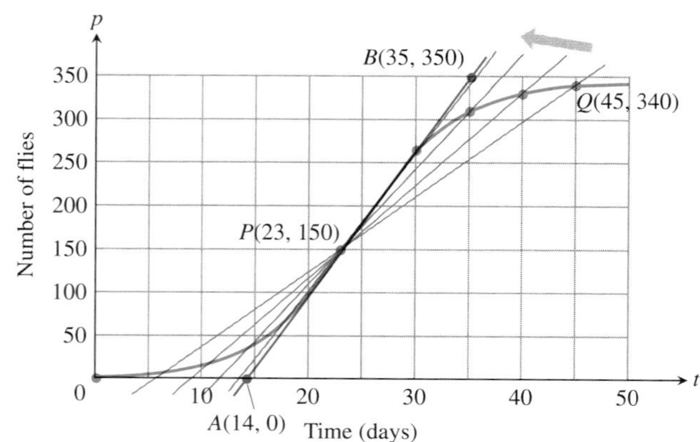

3.2 The positions and slopes of four secants through the point P on the fruit fly graph.

Q	**Slope of $PQ = \Delta p/\Delta t$ (flies/day)**
(45, 340)	$\frac{340 - 150}{45 - 23} \approx 8.6$
(40, 330)	$\frac{330 - 150}{40 - 23} \approx 10.6$
(35, 310)	$\frac{310 - 150}{35 - 23} \approx 13.3$
(30, 265)	$\frac{265 - 150}{30 - 23} \approx 16.4$

Why Find Tangents to Curves?

In mechanics, the tangent determines the direction of a body's motion at every point along its path.

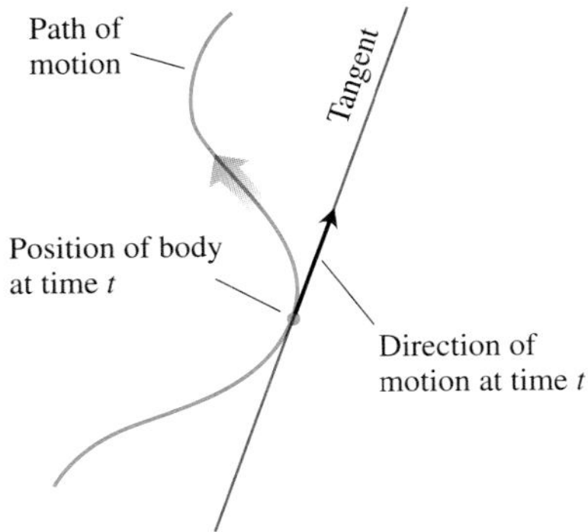

In geometry, the tangents to two curves at a point of intersection determine the angle at which the curves intersect.

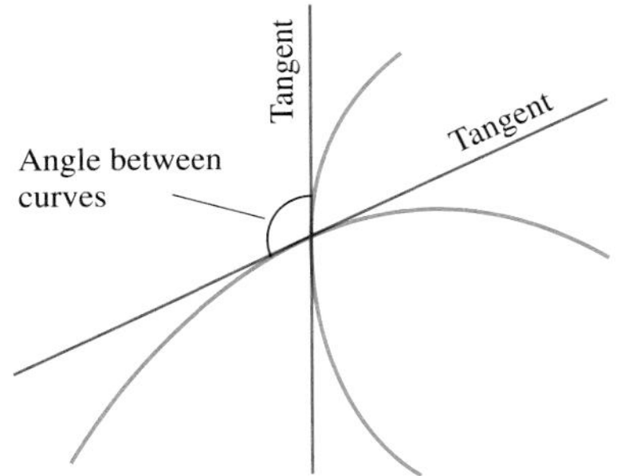

In optics, the tangent determines the angle at which a ray of light enters a curved lens (more about this in Section 3.6). The problem of how to find a tangent to a curve became the dominant mathematical problem of the early seventeenth century and it is hard to overestimate how badly the scientists of the day wanted to know the answer. Descartes went so far as to say that the problem was the most useful and most general problem not only that he knew but that he had any desire to know.

In terms of population change, what we see as Q approaches P is this: The average growth rates for increasingly smaller time intervals approach the slope of the tangent to the curve at P (16.7 flies per day). The slope of the tangent line is therefore the number we take as the rate at which the fly population was changing on day $t = 23$. We call this kind of rate an *instantaneous rate of change* (as opposed to an average rate of change). We'll say more about instantaneous rates in Section 3.3.

Defining Slopes and Tangent Lines

The moral of the fruit fly story would seem to be that we should define the rate at which the value of the function $y = f(x)$ is changing with respect to x at any particular value $x = x_1$ to be the slope of the tangent to the curve $y = f(x)$ at $x = x_1$. But how are we to define the tangent line at an arbitrary point P on the curve and find its slope from the formula $y = f(x)$?

The answer that Fermat finally found in 1629 proved to be one of that century's major contributions to calculus. We still use his method of defining tangents to produce formulas for slopes of curves and rates of change. It goes like this:

1. We start with what we *can* calculate, namely the slope of a secant through P and a point Q nearby on the curve.
2. We find the limiting value of the secant slope (if it exists) as Q approaches P along the curve.
3. We take this number to be the slope of the curve at P and define the tangent to the curve at P to be the line through P with this slope.

EXAMPLE 2 Find the slope of the parabola $y = x^2$ at the point $P(2, 4)$. Then write an equation for the tangent to the parabola at P.

Solution We begin with a secant line through P and a neighboring point Q on the parabola (Fig. 3.3). To find the secant's slope, we need to know the coordinates of Q. Since Q lies a little to the right or left of $P(2, 4)$, we can describe its x-coordinate as $2 + h$, where h is a small increment in x. (Figure 3.3 shows the case $h > 0$, but h could equally well be negative.) The y-coordinate of Q is then

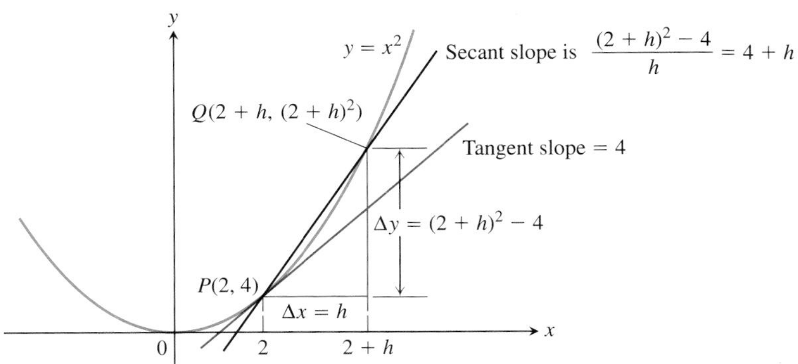

3.3 Diagram for finding the slope of the parabola $y = x^2$ at the point $P(2, 4)$ (Example 2).

$y = x^2 = (2 + h)^2$. In terms of these coordinates, the secant's slope is

$$\text{Secant slope} = \frac{\Delta y}{\Delta x} = \frac{(2+h)^2 - (2)^2}{h} = \frac{4 + 4h + h^2 - 4}{h} = \frac{4h + h^2}{h} = 4 + h.$$

We can divide by h because $h \neq 0$.

We find the limiting value of the secant slope as Q approaches P along the curve. As $Q \to P$, the increment $h \to 0$ and

$$\lim_{Q \to P} (\text{secant slope}) = \lim_{h \to 0} (4 + h) = 4.$$

The slope of the parabola $y = x^2$ at the point P is $m = 4$.

The tangent to the parabola at P is the line through P with slope 4:

Point: $(2, 4)$ Equation: $y - 4 = 4(x - 2)$

Slope: $m = 4$ $y = 4x - 8 + 4$

$y = 4x - 4$

The mathematics we used to find the slope of the parabola $y = x^2$ at $P\,(2, 4)$ will also find the slope of the parabola at any other point. Here is how it works.

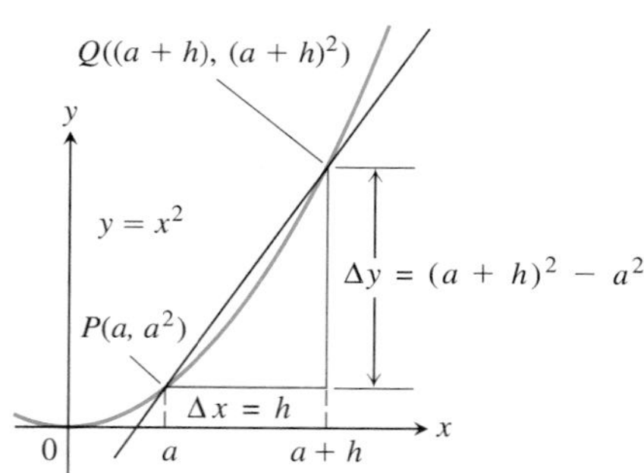

3.4 Diagram for finding the slope of the parabola $y = x^2$ at a general point (Example 3).

EXAMPLE 3 Find the slope of the parabola $y = x^2$ at any point on the curve.

Solution Let $P(a, a^2)$ be the point. In the notation of Fig. 3.4, the slope of the secant line through P and any nearby point $Q(a + h, (a + h)^2)$ is

$$\text{Secant slope} = \frac{\Delta y}{\Delta x} = \frac{(a+h)^2 - a^2}{h} = \frac{a^2 + 2ah + h^2 - a^2}{h} = \frac{2ah + h^2}{h} = 2a + h. \qquad (h \neq 0)$$

As Q approaches P along the curve and $h \to 0$, the limit of the secant slope is

$$\lim_{Q \to P} (\text{secant slope}) = \lim_{h \to 0} (2a + h) = 2a.$$

Since a can be any value of x, we see that the slope at the point (x, x^2) on the parabola is always

$$m = 2x.$$

When $x = 2$, for example, the slope is $m = 2 \cdot 2 = 4$, as in Example 2.

The next example shows how to use the slope formula $m = 2x$ from Example 3 to find equations for tangent lines.

EXAMPLE 4 Find equations for the tangents to the curve $y = x^2$ at the points $(-1/2, 1/4)$ and $(1, 1)$.

Solution We use the slope formula $m = 2x$ from Example 3 to find the point–slope equation for each line.

Tangent at $(-1/2, 1/4)$ Point: $(-1/2, 1/4)$
Slope: $m = 2x = 2(-1/2) = -1$
Equation: $y - 1/4 = -1(x - (-1/2))$
$y - 1/4 = -x - 1/2$
$y = -x - 1/4$

Tangent at $(1, 1)$ Point: $(1, 1)$
Slope: $m = 2x = 2(1) = 2$
Equation: $y - 1 = 2(x - 1)$
$y - 1 = 2x - 2$
$y = 2x - 1$

(See Fig. 3.5.)

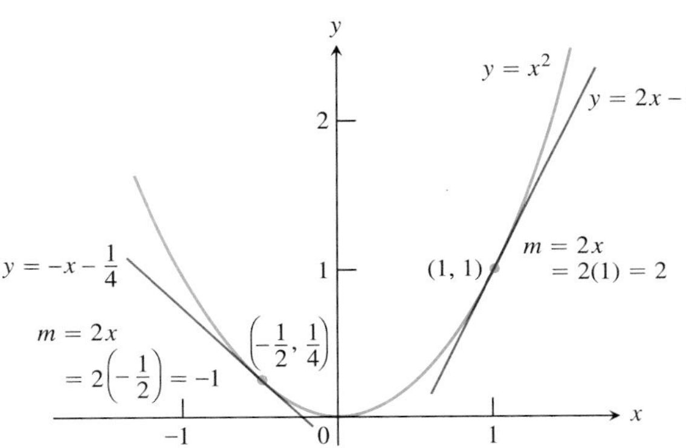

3.5 The tangents in Example 4.

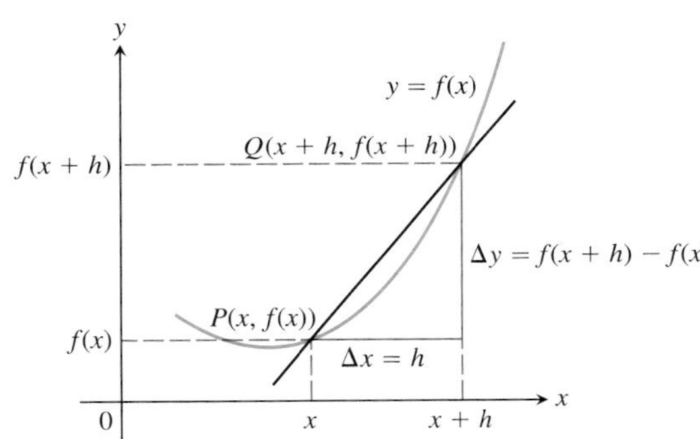

3.6 The slope of the line PQ is $\dfrac{\Delta y}{\Delta x} = \dfrac{f(x+h) - f(x)}{h}$.

The Derivative of a Function

The function $m = 2x$ that gives the slope of the parabola $y = x^2$ at any x is the derivative of the function $y = x^2$.

To find the derivative of an arbitrary function $y = f(x)$ (when the function has one — we'll come back to that), we simply repeat for f the steps we took in Examples 2 and 3 for x^2. We start with an arbitrary point $P(x, f(x))$ on the graph of f, as in Fig. 3.6. The slope of the secant line through P and a nearby point $Q\ (x + h, f(x + h))$ is then

$$\text{Secant slope} = \frac{\Delta y}{\Delta x} = \frac{f(x+h) - f(x)}{h}. \tag{3}$$

The fraction $[f(x + h) - f(x)]/h$ is called a **difference quotient** (or **Fermat's difference quotient**).

The slope of the curve at P is the limit of the secant slope as Q approaches P along the curve. This, in turn, is the limit of the quotient $\Delta y/\Delta x$ as $h \to 0$:

$$\begin{array}{c}\text{Slope of}\\ \text{curve at } P\end{array} = \lim_{Q \to P} \frac{\Delta y}{\Delta x} = \lim_{h \to 0} \frac{f(x+h) - f(x)}{h}. \tag{4}$$

The limit in Eq. (4) is itself a function of x (its value at x may change with each new x). We denote it by f' ("f prime") and call it the derivative of f. ("Derivative" means "derived from"; f' is the function derived from f.) The domain of f' is a subset of the domain of f.

DEFINITION

The **derivative** of a function f is the function f' whose value at x is

$$f'(x) = \lim_{h \to 0} \frac{f(x+h) - f(x)}{h} \quad \text{(if the limit exists).} \qquad (5)$$

If the limit in Eq. (5) exists, we say that f **has a derivative (is differentiable) at x**. If f has a derivative at every point of its domain, we call f **differentiable.** If f is differentiable, we call its graph a **differentiable curve.**

When $f'(x)$ exists for a particular x, it is called the **slope of the curve $y = f(x)$ at x**. The line that passes through the point $P(x, f(x))$ with slope $f'(x)$ is the **tangent to the curve at P**.

The most common notations for the derivative of a function $y = f(x)$, besides $f'(x)$, are

y'	("y prime")	Nice and brief
$\dfrac{dy}{dx}$	("$d\,y\,d\,x$")	Names the variables and has a "d" for derivative
$\dfrac{df}{dx}$	("$d\,f\,d\,x$")	Emphasizes the function's name
$D_x(f)$	("$D\,x$ of f")	Emphasizes the idea that taking the derivative is an operation performed on f
$\dfrac{d}{dx}(f)$	("$d\,dx$ of f")	Ditto

Input: function $y = f(x)$ → Operation $\dfrac{d}{dx}$ → Ouput: derivative $y' = \dfrac{df}{dx}$

3.7 Flow diagram for the operation of taking a derivative with respect to x.

We also read dy/dx as "the derivative of y with respect to x" and df/dx as "the derivative of f with respect to x." See Fig. 3.7.

The Slopes of Lines

We now have two definitions for the slope of a line $y = mx + b$: the number m and, at each point, the derivative of the function $f(x) = mx + b$. Whenever we bring in a new definition, it is a good idea to be sure that the new and old definitions agree on objects to which they both apply. We do this in the next example.

EXAMPLE 5 Show that the derivative of the function $f(x) = mx + b$ is the slope of the line $y = mx + b$.

Solution The idea is to show that the derivative of $f(x) = mx + b$ has the constant value m. To see that this is so, we calculate the limit in Eq. (5) with $f(x) = mx + b$. The calculation takes four steps.

STEP 1: Write out $f(x)$ and $f(x + h)$:

$$f(x) = mx + b$$
$$f(x+h) = m(x+h) + b = mx + mh + b.$$

How to Find a Derivative

The algebraic steps we use to calculate $f'(x)$ directly from the definition are always the same:

1. Write out $f(x)$ and $f(x+h)$.
2. Subtract $f(x)$ from $f(x+h)$.
3. Divide by h.
4. Take the limit as $h \to 0$.

STEP 2: Subtract $f(x)$ from $f(x+h)$:

$$f(x+h) - f(x) = mh.$$

STEP 3: Divide by h:

$$\frac{f(x+h) - f(x)}{h} = \frac{mh}{h} = m \qquad (h \neq 0).$$

STEP 4: Take the limit as $h \to 0$:

$$\lim_{h \to 0} \frac{f(x+h) - f(x)}{h} = \lim_{h \to 0} (m) = m.$$

The derivative of f does indeed have the constant value m.

Typical Derivative Calculations

EXAMPLE 6 Find dy/dx if $y = 1/x$.

Solution We take $f(x) = 1/x$, $f(x+h) = 1/(x+h)$, and form the difference quotient

$$\begin{aligned} \frac{f(x+h) - f(x)}{h} &= \frac{\dfrac{1}{x+h} - \dfrac{1}{x}}{h} \\ &= \frac{1}{h} \cdot \frac{x - (x+h)}{x(x+h)} \\ &= \frac{1}{h} \cdot \frac{-h}{x(x+h)} \\ &= \frac{-1}{x(x+h)} \qquad (h \neq 0). \end{aligned} \tag{6}$$

We then take the limit as $h \to 0$:

$$\frac{dy}{dx} = \lim_{h \to 0} \frac{f(x+h) - f(x)}{h} = \lim_{h \to 0} \frac{-1}{x(x+h)} = \frac{-1}{x(x+0)} = -\frac{1}{x^2}.$$

The derivative of $y = 1/x$ is $y' = -1/x^2$. So at each point x on the graph of $y = 1/x$, the slope is negative and has value $-1/x^2$ (Fig. 3.8).

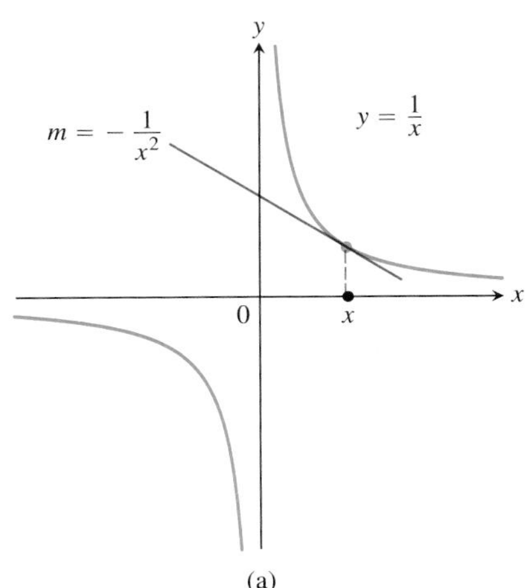

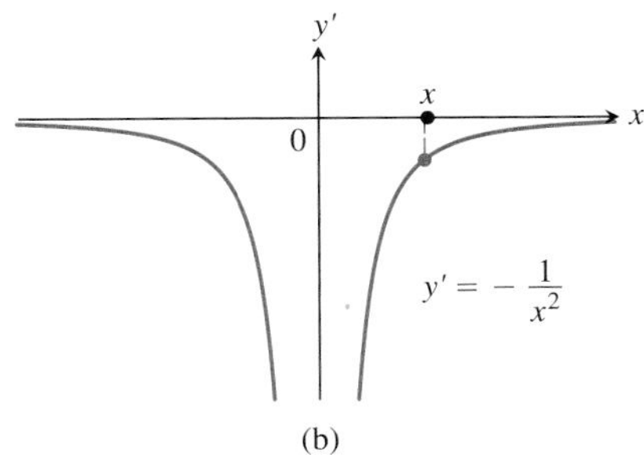

3.8 The graphs of (a) the function $y = 1/x$ and (b) its derivative $y' = -1/x^2$ (Example 6).

EXAMPLE 7 Find $f'(x)$ if $f(x) = x^2 - 2x$.

Solution With $f(x) = x^2 - 2x$ and

$$f(x+h) = (x+h)^2 - 2(x+h) = x^2 + 2hx + h^2 - 2x - 2h$$

we form the difference quotient

$$\begin{aligned} \frac{f(x+h) - f(x)}{h} &= \frac{(x^2 + 2hx + h^2 - 2x - 2h) - (x^2 - 2x)}{h} \\ &= \frac{h^2 + 2hx - 2h}{h} \\ &= h + 2x - 2. \end{aligned}$$

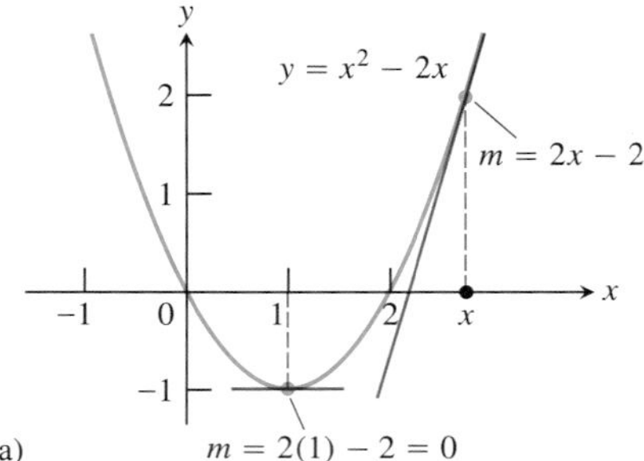

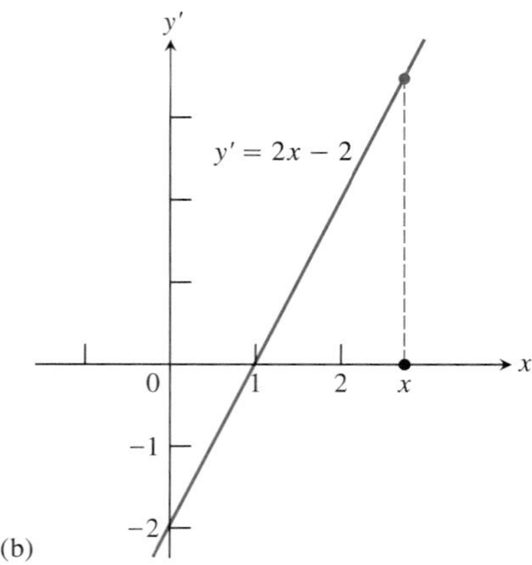

3.9 The graphs of (a) the function $y = x^2 - 2x$ and (b) its derivative. The derivative is zero at the point where the parabola has a horizontal tangent.

We then take the limit as $h \to 0$:

$$f'(x) = \lim_{h\to 0} \frac{f(x+h) - f(x)}{h}$$
$$= \lim_{h\to 0} (h + 2x - 2) = 2x - 2.$$

The derivative of $f(x) = x^2 - 2x$ is $f'(x) = 2x - 2$ (Fig. 3.9).

EXAMPLE 8 Show that the derivative of $y = \sqrt{x}$ is $\dfrac{dy}{dx} = \dfrac{1}{2\sqrt{x}}$ for $x > 0$.

Solution We use Eq. (5) with $f(x+h) = \sqrt{x+h}$ and $f(x) = \sqrt{x}$:

$$\frac{dy}{dx} = \lim_{h\to 0} \frac{f(x+h) - f(x)}{h} = \frac{\sqrt{x+h} - \sqrt{x}}{h}.$$

We cannot divide out the h's this time.

Unfortunately, if we try to calculate the limit by replacing h with 0, the quotient will involve division by 0. We therefore look for an equivalent expression in which this difficulty does not arise. If we rationalize the numerator we get

$$\frac{dy}{dx} = \lim_{h\to 0} \frac{\sqrt{x+h} - \sqrt{x}}{h}$$
$$= \lim_{h\to 0} \frac{\sqrt{x+h} - \sqrt{x}}{h} \cdot \frac{\sqrt{x+h} + \sqrt{x}}{\sqrt{x+h} + \sqrt{x}}$$
$$= \lim_{h\to 0} \frac{(x+h) - x}{h\left(\sqrt{x+h} + \sqrt{x}\right)}$$
$$= \lim_{h\to 0} \frac{h}{h\left(\sqrt{x+h} + \sqrt{x}\right)}$$

Now we can divide out the h's.

$$= \lim_{h\to 0} \frac{1}{\sqrt{x+h} + \sqrt{x}}$$
$$= \frac{1}{\sqrt{x} + \sqrt{x}} = \frac{1}{2\sqrt{x}}.$$

Therefore, the derivative of $y = \sqrt{x}$ is $dy/dx = 1/\left(2\sqrt{x}\right)$, which is positive because $x > 0$. See Fig. 3.10.

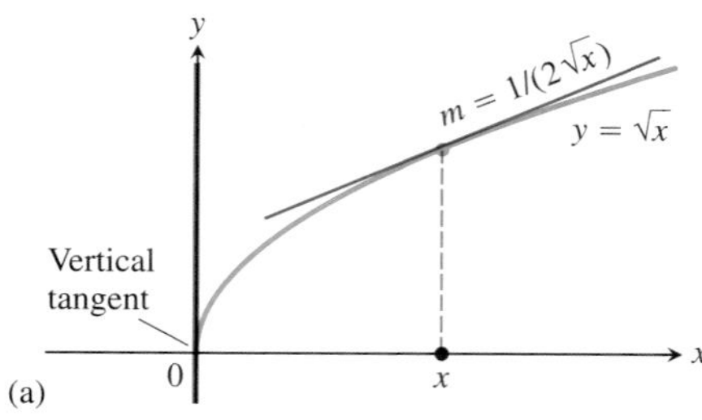

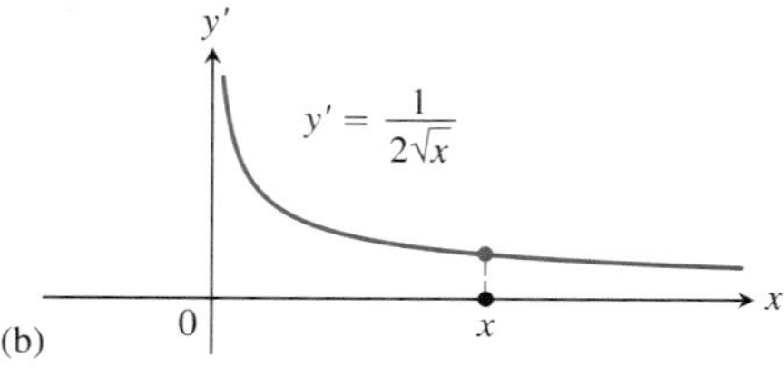

3.10 The graphs of (a) $y = \sqrt{x}$ and (b) $y' = 1/\left(2\sqrt{x}\right)$, $x > 0$ (Example 8). The function is defined at $x = 0$, but its derivative is not.

EXAMPLE 9 Find an equation for the tangent to the curve $y = \sqrt{x}$ at $x = 4$.

Solution The slope at $x = 4$ is the value of the function's derivative there. Example 8 gives $dy/dx = 1/\left(2\sqrt{x}\right)$, so the slope is

$$\left.\frac{1}{2\sqrt{x}}\right|_{x=4} = \frac{1}{2\sqrt{4}} = \frac{1}{4}.$$

The tangent is the line through the point $P\left(4, \sqrt{4}\right) = (4, 2)$ with slope 1/4:

Point: (4, 2) Equation: $y - 2 = \frac{1}{4}(x - 4)$

Slope: $\frac{1}{4}$ $y = \frac{1}{4}x - 1 + 2$

$y = \frac{1}{4}x + 1.$

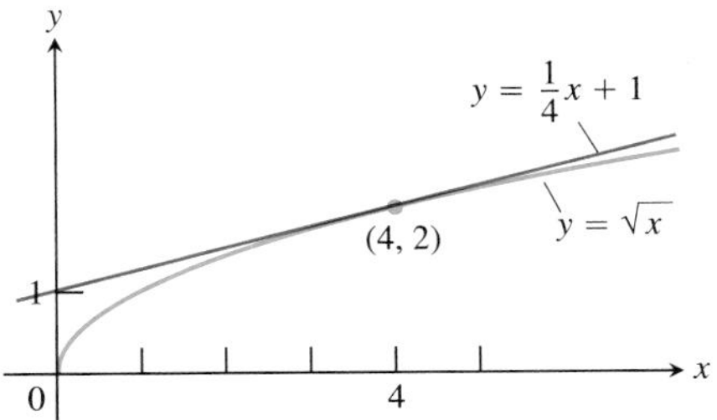

3.11 The curve $y = \sqrt{x}$ and its tangent at (4, 2). The tangent's slope is found by evaluating dy/dx at $x = 4$ (Example 9).

The tangent is the line $y = (1/4)x + 1$ (Fig. 3.11).

Differentiable on a Closed Interval—One-sided Derivatives

A function $y = f(x)$ is **differentiable on a closed interval** $[a, b]$ if it has a derivative at every interior point and if the limits

$$\lim_{h\to 0^+} \frac{f(a+h)-f(a)}{h} \qquad \text{Right-hand derivative at } a$$

$$\lim_{h\to 0^-} \frac{f(b+h)-f(b)}{h} \qquad \text{Left-hand derivative at } b$$

exist at the endpoints. In the right-hand derivative at a, the increment h is positive and $a + h$ approaches a from the right. In the left-hand derivative at b, the increment h is negative and $b + h$ approaches b from the left (Fig. 3.12).

Right-hand and left-hand derivatives may be defined at any point of a function's domain. The usual relation between one-sided and two-sided limits holds for these derivatives. As with limits, if the one-sided derivatives both exist at a point and are not equal, then the derivative does not exist at that point.

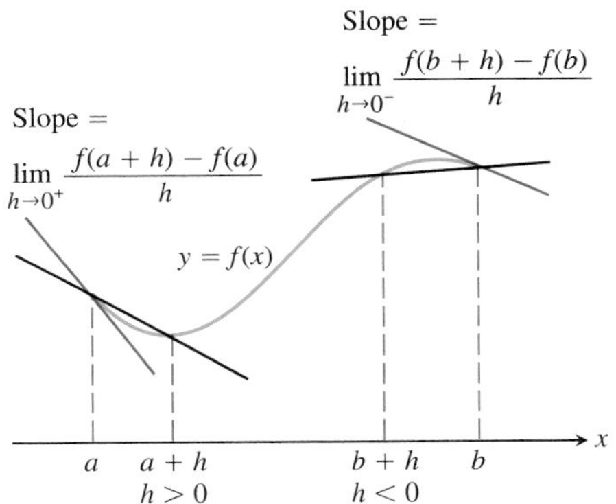

3.12 Derivatives at endpoints are one-sided limits.

EXAMPLE 10 The function $y = |x|$ has no derivative with respect to x at $x = 0$ even though it has a derivative with respect to x everywhere else. To the right of the origin, $|x| = x$ and the slope of the graph is 1 at every point. To the left of the origin, $|x| = -x$ and the slope is -1 at every point (Fig. 3.13). At the origin itself, there can be no derivative because the one-sided derivatives there disagree:

Right-hand derivative of $|x|$ at $x = 0$

$$= \lim_{h\to 0^+} \frac{|0+h|-|0|}{h} \qquad \text{Definition of right-hand derivative}$$

$$= \lim_{h\to 0^+} \frac{|h|}{h}$$

$$= \lim_{h\to 0^+} \frac{h}{h} \qquad |h| = h \text{ when } h > 0$$

$$= \lim_{h\to 0^+} 1 = 1$$

Left-hand derivative of $|x|$ at $x = 0$

$$= \lim_{h\to 0^-} \frac{|0+h|-|0|}{h} \qquad \text{Definition}$$

$$= \lim_{h\to 0^-} \frac{|h|}{h}$$

$$= \lim_{h\to 0^-} \frac{-h}{h} \qquad |h| = -h \text{ when } h < 0$$

$$= \lim_{h\to 0^-} -1 = -1.$$

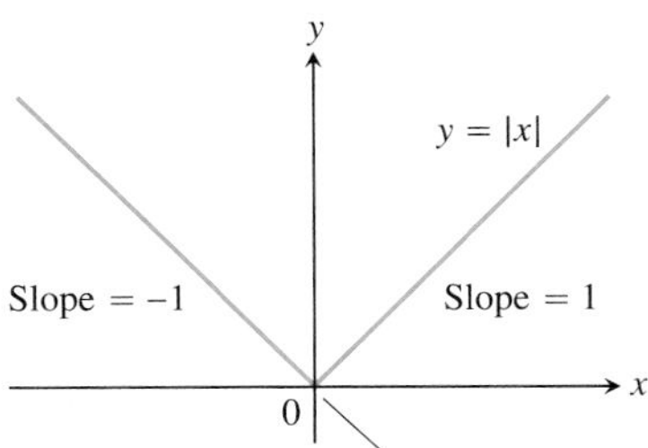

3.13 The absolute value function has a derivative at every point but the origin.

Notice that $y = |x|$ is continuous at $x = 0$ even though it is not differentiable there.

When Does a Function *Not* Have a Derivative at a Point?

A function has a derivative at a point x_0 if the slopes of the secant lines through $P(x_0, f(x_0))$ and a nearby point Q on the graph approach a limit as Q approaches P. Whenever the secants fail to take up a limiting position or become vertical as

How Rough Can the Graph of a Continuous Function Be?

The absolute value function fails to be differentiable at a single point. Using a similar idea, we can use a saw-tooth graph to define a continuous function that fails to have a derivative at infinitely many points.

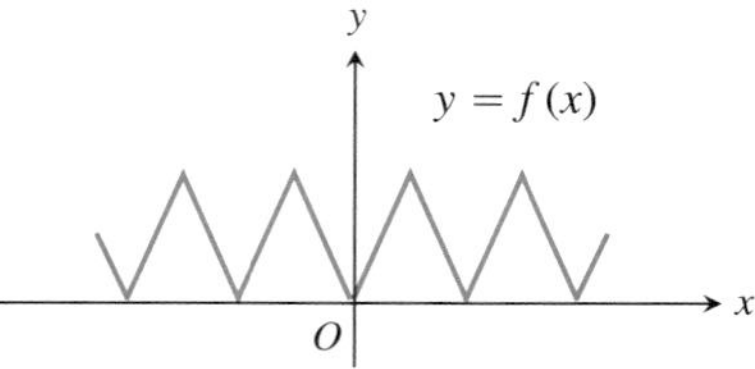

But can a continuous function fail to have a derivative at *every* point?

The answer, surprisingly enough, is yes, as Karl Weierstrass (1815–1897) found in 1872. One of his formulas (there are many like it) was

$$f(x) = \sum_{n=0}^{\infty} \left(\frac{2}{3}\right)^n \cos(9^n \pi x),$$

a formula that expresses f as an infinite sum of cosines with increasingly higher frequencies. By adding wiggles to wiggles infinitely many times, so to speak, the formula produces a graph that is too bumpy in the limit to have a tangent anywhere.

Continuous curves that fail to have a tangent anywhere play a useful role in chaos theory, in part because there is no way to assign a finite length to such a curve. We'll see what length has to do with derivatives when we get to Section 7.4.

Q approaches P, the derivative does not exist. A function whose graph is otherwise smooth will fail to have a derivative at a point where the graph has

1. A *corner* where the one-sided derivatives differ.

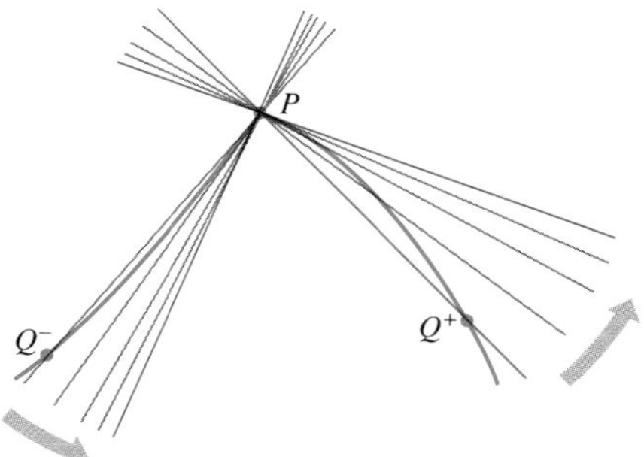

2. A *vertical tangent.* (Here, both one-sided derivatives are infinite.)

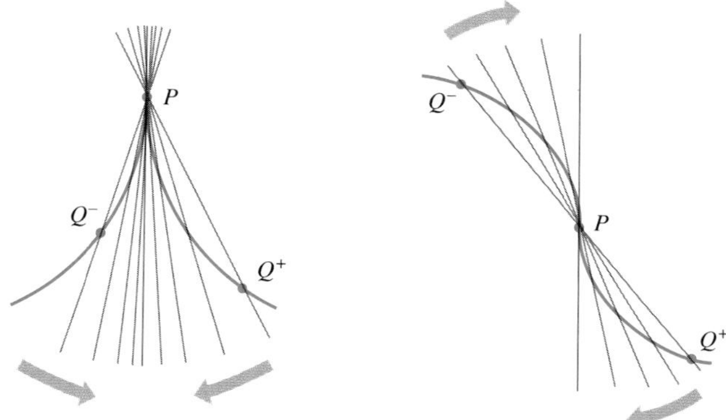

3. A *discontinuity.*

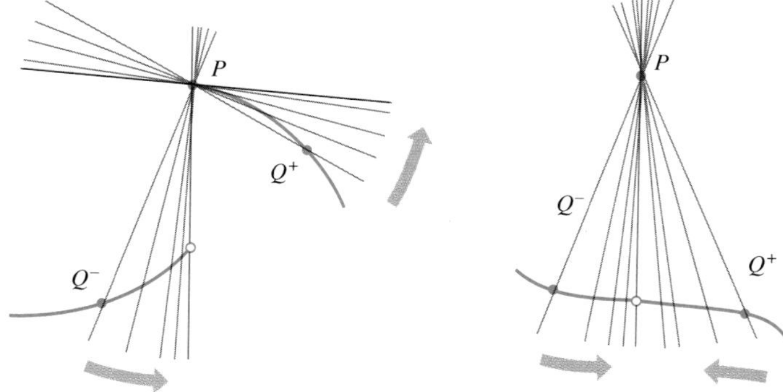

Differentiable Functions Are Continuous

While continuous functions need not be differentiable (as shown in Example 10), differentiable functions must be continuous. That is the content of the following theorem.

THEOREM 1

If f has a derivative at $x = c$, then f is continuous at $x = c$.

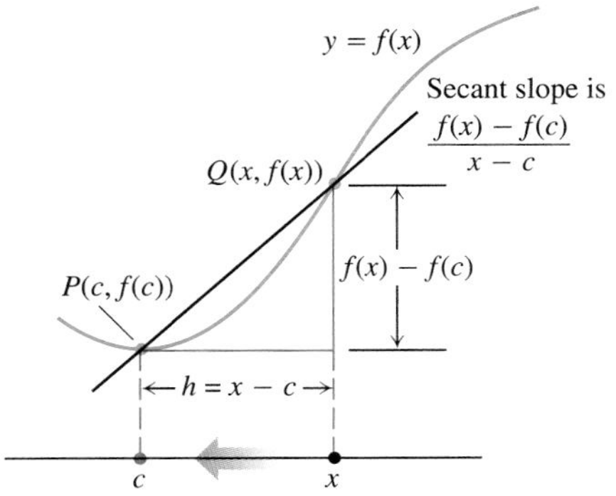

We can restate Theorem 1 in two other equivalent ways:

1. A function is continuous at any point at which it has a derivative.
2. A function can never have a derivative at a point of discontinuity.

So one way to construct functions that are not differentiable is to construct functions that are not continuous.

Proof of Theorem 1 Suppose that f has a derivative at $x = c$. Our task is to show that $\lim_{x\to c} f(x) = f(c)$ or, equivalently, that

$$\lim_{x\to c} [f(x) - f(c)] = 0. \qquad (7)$$

To this end, we let $P(c, f(c))$ be a point on the graph of f and let $Q(x, f(x))$ be a point nearby (Fig. 3.14). The slope of the secant PQ is

$$\text{Secant slope} = \frac{f(x) - f(c)}{x - c}.$$

Derivative of f at c is

$$f'(c) = \lim_{h\to 0} \frac{f(c+h) - f(c)}{h} = \lim_{x\to c} \frac{f(x) - f(c)}{x - c}$$

3.14 The way we write the difference quotient for the derivative of a function f depends on how we label the points involved.

By definition, the derivative of f at c is the limiting value of this slope as Q approaches P along the curve, which means in this case the limit as $x \to c$:

$$f'(c) = \lim_{x\to c} \frac{f(x) - f(c)}{x - c}. \qquad (8)$$

Why should the mere existence of this limit imply that $[f(x) - f(c)] \to 0$ as $x \to c$? Because, with the denominator $x - c$ going to zero, the quotient can have a finite limit only if the numerator goes to zero at the same time. Thus,

$$\begin{aligned} \lim_{x\to c} [f(x) - f(c)] &= \lim_{x\to c} \left[(x - c) \frac{f(x) - f(c)}{x - c} \right] && \text{Divide and multiply by } x - c. \\ &= \lim_{x\to c} (x - c) \cdot \lim_{x\to c} \frac{f(x) - f(c)}{x - c} && \text{Limit Product Rule} \\ &= 0 \cdot f'(c) = 0 && \text{Known values} \end{aligned}$$

■

What Functions Are Differentiable?

Most of the functions we have worked with so far are differentiable. Polynomials are differentiable, as are rational functions and trigonometric functions. Also, composites, sums, differences, products, powers, and quotients of differentiable functions, where defined, are differentiable.

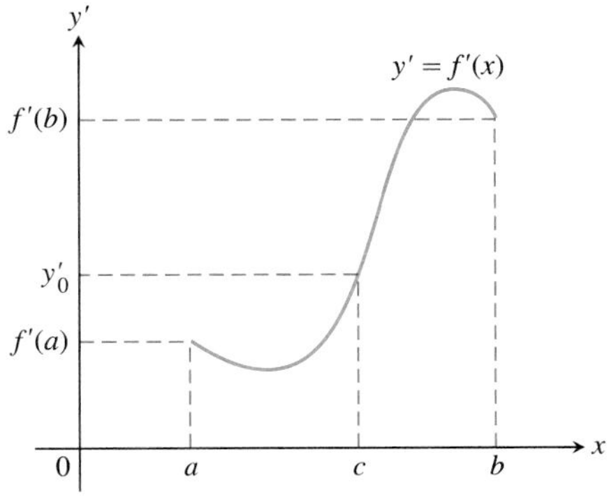

Derivatives Have the Intermediate Value Property

It comes in handy now and then to know that derivatives have the intermediate value property: If f has a derivative at every point of a closed interval $[a, b]$, then f' assumes every value between $f'(a)$ and $f'(b)$ (Fig. 3.15). We will refer to the property briefly in Chapter 4 but will make no attempt to prove it. There are proofs in more advanced texts.

3.15 If $y' = f'(x)$ is the derivative of a function f on $[a, b]$ and if y_0' is a point between $f'(a)$ and $f'(b)$, then $y_0' = f'(c)$ for some c in $[a, b]$.

This property of derivatives allows a partial answer to the question: When is a function defined on an interval the derivative of some other function throughout that interval? The (partial) answer is: Only when it has the intermediate value property. No step functions, for example.

The question of when a function is a derivative is one of the central questions in all calculus, and Newton and Leibniz's answer to this question revolutionized the world of mathematics. We will see what their answer was in Chapter 5.

Exercises 3.1

In Exercises 1–4, use the grid and a straight edge to make a rough estimate of the slope of the curve (in y-units per x-unit) at the points P_1 and P_2. Graphs can shift during a press run, so your estimates may be somewhat different from those in the back of the book.

1.

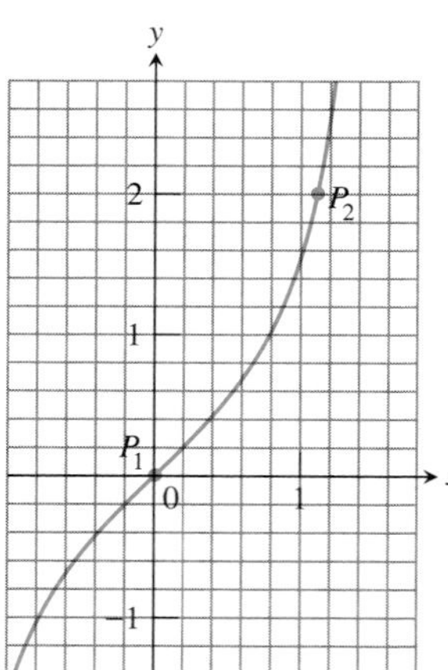

2.

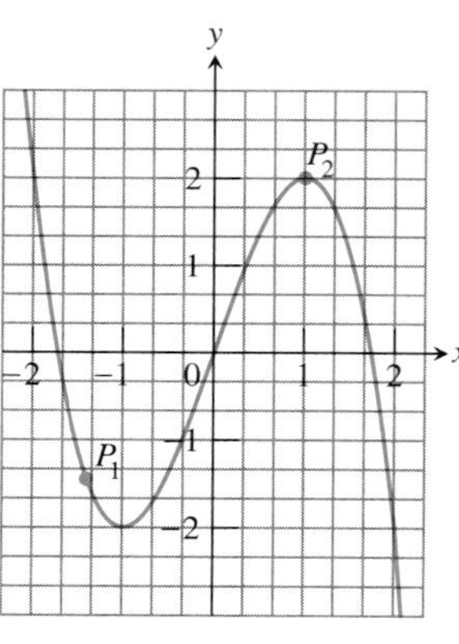

3.

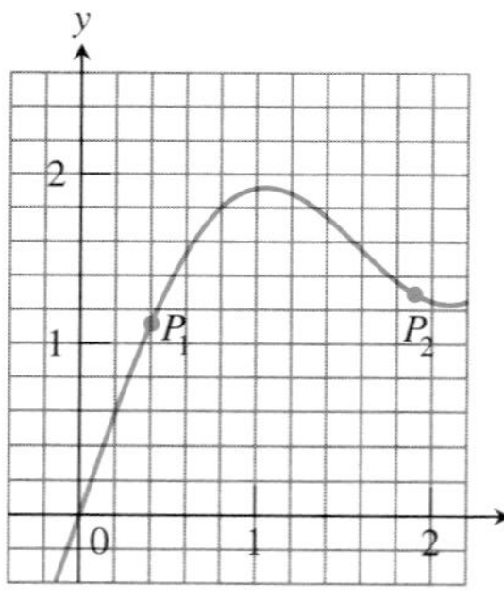

4.

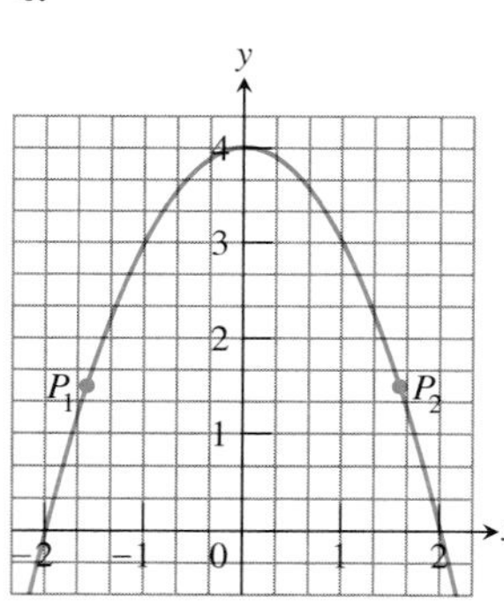

In Exercises 5–20, use the definition of derivative to find $dy/dx = f'(x)$ for the given function. Then find the slope of the curve $y = f(x)$ at $x = 3$.

5. $y = 10 - 3x$

6. $y = 12x - 5$

7. $y = 2x^2 - 5$

8. $y = x^2 - 6x$

9. $y = 2x^2 - 13x + 5$

10. $y = -3x^2 + 4x - 1$

11. $y = \dfrac{2}{x}$

12. $y = \dfrac{1}{x+1}$

13. $y = \dfrac{x}{x+1}$

14. $y = \dfrac{x}{2x+1}$

15. $y = 1 + \sqrt{x}$

16. $y = \sqrt{2x}$

17. $y = \sqrt{x+1}$

18. $y = \sqrt{2x+3}$

19. $y = \dfrac{5}{\sqrt{x-2}}$

20. $y = \dfrac{1}{\sqrt{4-x}}$

In Exercises 21–26, find an equation for the tangent to the curve at the given point. Then sketch the curve and tangent together.

21. $y = 4 - x^2, \quad (-1, 3)$

22. $y = (x - 1)^2 + 1, \quad (1, 1)$

23. $y = 2\sqrt{x}, \quad (1, 2)$

24. $y = \dfrac{1}{x^2}, \quad (-1, 1)$

25. $y = \dfrac{x^3}{8}, \quad (-2, -1)$

26. $y = \dfrac{1}{x^3}, \quad \left(-2, -\dfrac{1}{8}\right)$

In Exercises 27–30,

a) Find the derivative $y' = f'(x)$ of the given function $y = f(x)$.
b) Graph $y = f(x)$ and $y' = f'(x)$ side by side using separate sets of coordinate axes, and answer the following questions.
c) For what values of x, if any, is y' positive? zero? negative?
d) Over what intervals of x-values, if any, does the function $y = f(x)$ increase as x increases? decrease as x increases? How is this related to what you found in (c)? (We will say more about this relationship in Chapter 4.)

27. $y = -x^2$

28. $y = -1/x$

29. $y = x^3/3$

30. $y = x^4/4$

In Exercises 31–36, use the alternate derivative formula

$$f'(c) = \lim_{x \to c} \frac{f(x) - f(c)}{x - c}$$

from the proof of Theorem 1 to find the derivative of f at the given value of c.

31. $f(x) = x^2 - x + 1, \quad c = 1/2$

32. $f(x) = -3x^2 + 7x + 5, \quad c = 2$

33. $f(x) = \dfrac{1}{x+2}, \quad c = -1$

34. $f(x) = \dfrac{1}{(x-1)^2}, \quad c = 2$

35. $f(x) = \dfrac{1}{\sqrt{x}}, \quad c = 9$

36. $f(x) = \dfrac{1}{\sqrt{2x+13}}, \quad c = -2$

Each figure in Exercises 37–42 shows the graph of a function over a particular domain D. At what points do the functions appear to be

a) differentiable?
b) continuous but not differentiable?
c) neither continuous nor differentiable?

37.

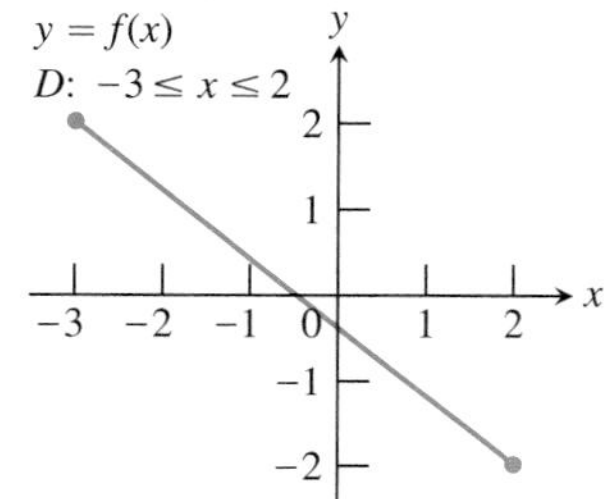

38.

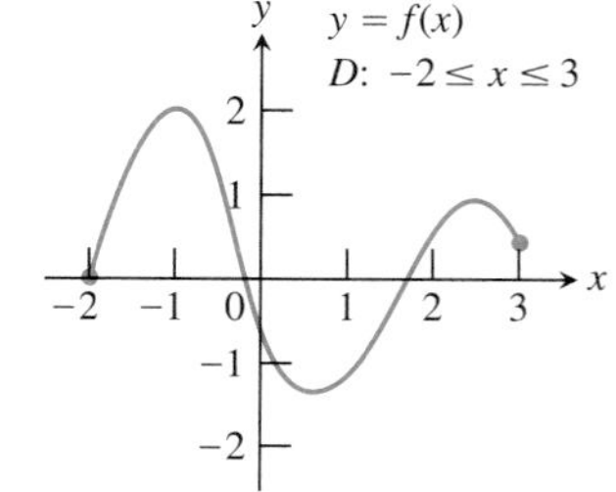

39.

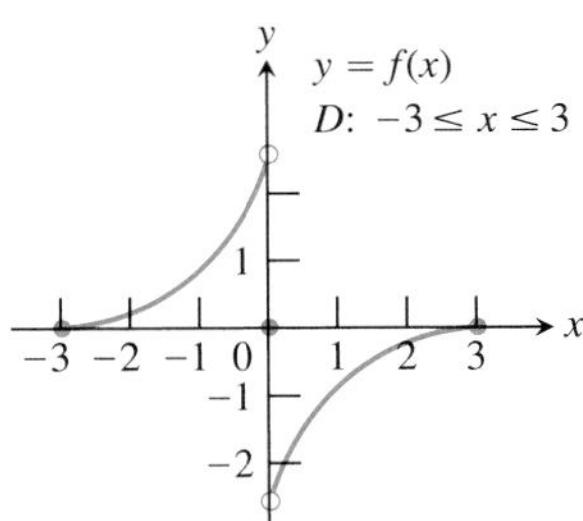

40.

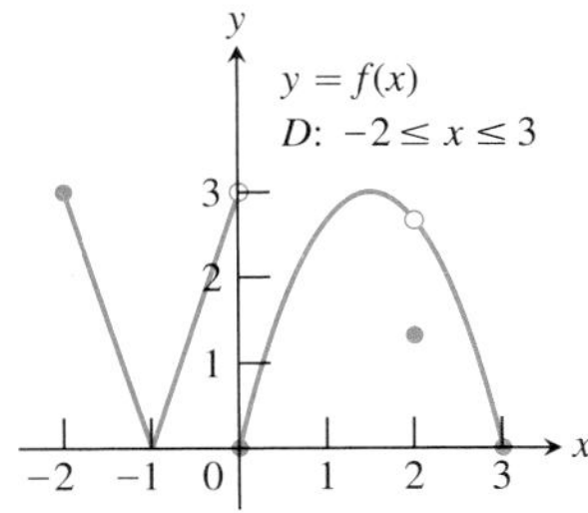

41.

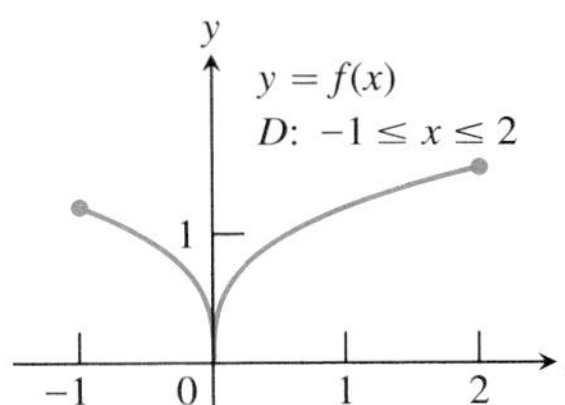

42.

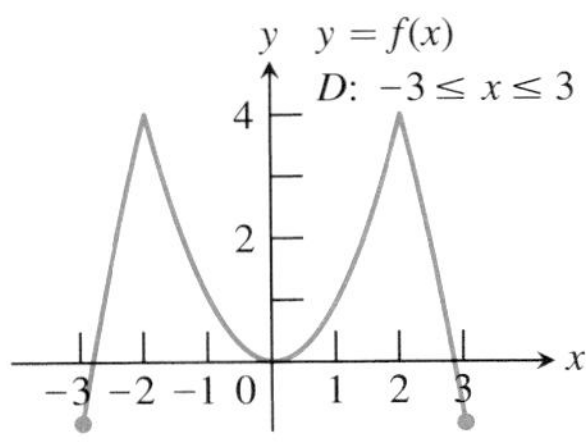

Use right-hand and left-hand derivatives to show that the functions in Exercises 43–46 are not differentiable at the indicated point P.

43.

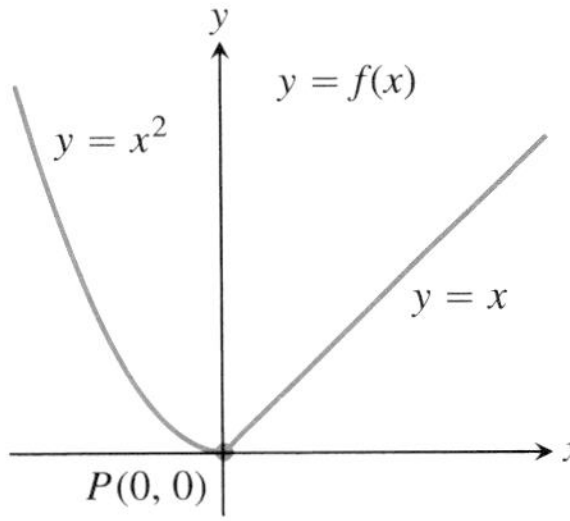

44.

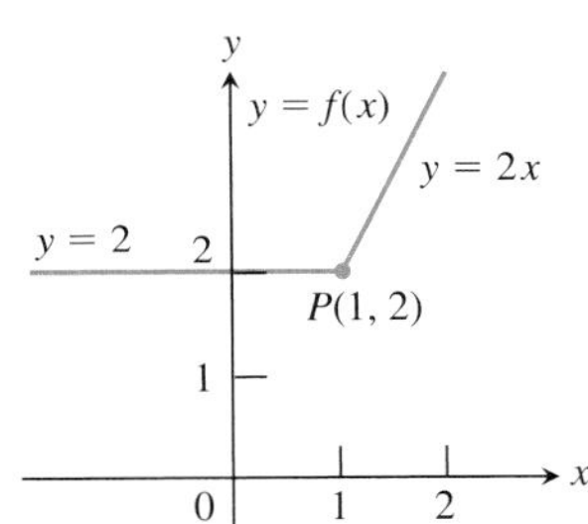

45.

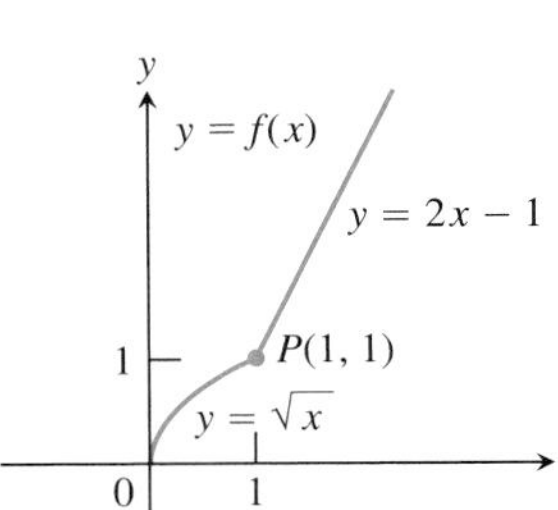

46.

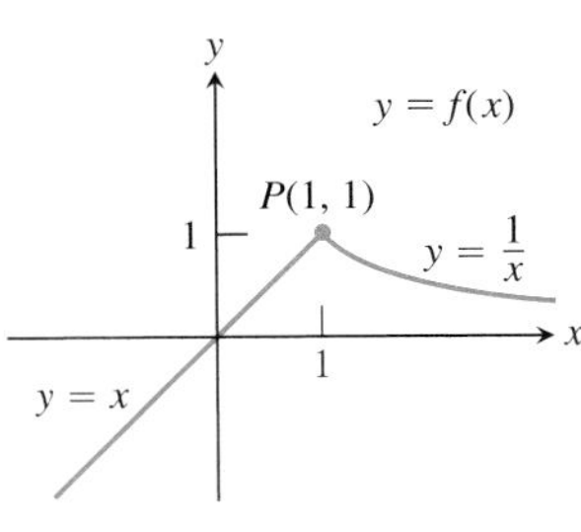

47. Show that the function

$$f(x) = \begin{cases} 0, & -1 \le x < 0 \\ 1, & 0 \le x \le 1 \end{cases}$$

is not the derivative of any function defined on the interval $-1 \le x \le 1$. (*Hint:* Does f have the intermediate value property on the interval? What does the graph look like?)

48. Show that the greatest integer function $y = \lfloor x \rfloor$ is not the derivative of any function throughout the interval $-\infty < x < \infty$.

49. Suppose that the functions $g(t)$ and $h(t)$ are defined for all values of t and that $g(0) = h(0) = 0$. Can $\lim_{t\to 0} (g(t))/(h(t))$ exist? If it does exist, must it be 0? Give reasons for your answers.

50. Does knowing that a function f is differentiable tell us anything about the differentiability of the function $-f$? Give reasons for your answer.

51. Do the two following statements say the same thing about the function $y = f(x)$?

1. f is not continuous at every point of its domain.
2. f is discontinuous at every point of its domain.

Give reasons for your answer. An example or two might help.

52. Do the following two statements say the same thing?

1. Not all functions are differentiable.
2. All functions are not differentiable.

Give reasons for your answer.

Writing for Your Own Knowledge

Answer the following questions in writing. Some answers will take only a sentence or two; others may require several paragraphs. Some explanations may also call for graphs or sketches.

1. What is the difference between average and instantaneous rates of change?
2. How do you define slopes and tangent lines?
3. What is a derivative?
4. When does a function typically not have a derivative at a point?
5. When is a function differentiable on a closed interval?
6. How are continuity and differentiability at a point related?

EXPLORER PROGRAMS

Derivatives	Automatically graphs the derivative of any function you key in.
Secant Lines	Draws secant lines on command and displays their slopes as they change from one position to the next; also draws tangents when they exist.

3.2 Differentiation Rules

Differentiation is the process of calculating a derivative. The goal of this section is to show how to differentiate functions without having to apply the definition each time.

Integer Powers, Multiples, Sums, and Differences

The first differentiation rule is that the derivative of every constant function is zero.

RULE 1

Derivative of a Constant

If c is a constant, then

$$\frac{d}{dx}(c) = 0.$$

EXAMPLE 1 $\frac{d}{dx}(8) = 0, \quad \frac{d}{dx}\left(-\frac{1}{2}\right) = 0, \quad \frac{d}{dx}(\sqrt{3}) = 0$

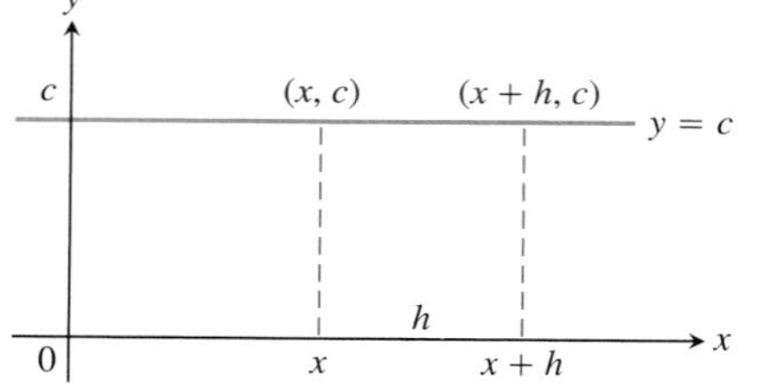

3.16 The rule $(d/dx)(c) = 0$ is another way to say that the values of constant functions never change and that the slope of a horizontal line is zero at every point.

Proof of Rule 1 If $f(x) = c$ is the function with the constant value c (Fig. 3.16), then

$$\frac{d}{dx}(c) = \lim_{h \to 0} \frac{f(x+h) - f(x)}{h} = \lim_{h \to 0} \frac{c - c}{h} = \lim_{h \to 0} \frac{0}{h} = \lim_{h \to 0} 0 = 0.$$

The next rule is about derivatives of positive integer powers of x.

RULE 2

Power Rule for Positive Integer Powers of x

If n is a positive integer, then

$$\frac{d}{dx}(x^n) = nx^{n-1}. \tag{1}$$

To apply the power rule, we subtract 1 from the original exponent (n) and multiply the result by n.

EXAMPLE 2

$$\frac{d}{dx}(x) = \frac{d}{dx}(x^1) = 1 \cdot x^0 = 1 \qquad \frac{d}{dx}(x^4) = 4x^3$$

$$\frac{d}{dx}(x^2) = 2x^1 = 2x \qquad \frac{d}{dx}(x^5) = 5x^4$$

$$\frac{d}{dx}(x^3) = 3x^2$$

Proof of Rule 2 If $f(x) = x^n$, then

$$\frac{d}{dx}(x^n) = \lim_{h\to 0}\frac{f(x+h)-f(x)}{h}$$
$$= \lim_{h\to 0}\frac{(x+h)^n - x^n}{h}.$$

We cannot divide out the h's, so we must rewrite the fraction.

Since n is a positive integer, we can apply the algebra formula

$$a^n - b^n = (a-b)\left[a^{n-1} + a^{n-2}b + \cdots + ab^{n-2} + b^{n-1}\right]$$

with $a = x + h$, $b = x$, and $(a - b) = h$ to change $(x+h)^n - x^n$ into

$$(x+h)^n - x^n = (h)\left[(x+h)^{n-1} + (x+h)^{n-2}(x) + \cdots + (x+h)(x)^{n-2} + (x)^{n-1}\right].$$

Now h is a factor in the numerator.

Rewriting the difference quotient gives

$$\frac{d}{dx}(x^n) = \lim_{h\to 0}\frac{f(x+h)-f(x)}{h} = \lim_{h\to 0}\frac{(x+h)^n - x^n}{h}$$
$$= \lim_{h\to 0}\frac{(h)[(x+h)^{n-1} + (x+h)^{n-2}(x) + \cdots + (x+h)(x)^{n-2} + (x)^{n-1}]}{h}$$
$$= \lim_{h\to 0}[(x+h)^{n-1} + (x+h)^{n-2}(x) + \cdots + (x+h)(x)^{n-2} + (x)^{n-1}]$$

Divide out the h's.

$$= \underbrace{x^{n-1} + x^{n-2}(x) + \cdots + x(x)^{n-2} + (x)^{n-1}}_{n \text{ terms; each term is } x^{n-1}}$$

As $h \to 0$, $(x+h) \to x$

$$= nx^{n-1}.$$

The next rule says that multiplying a differentiable function by a constant multiplies its derivative by the same constant.

RULE 3

The Constant Multiple Rule

If u is a differentiable function of x, and c is a constant, then

$$\frac{d}{dx}(cu) = c\frac{du}{dx}. \qquad (2)$$

In particular, if n is a positive integer, then

$$\frac{d}{dx}(cx^n) = cnx^{n-1}. \qquad (3)$$

Denoting Functions by u and v

The functions we are working with when we need a differentiation formula are likely to be denoted by letters like f and g. When we apply the formula, we do not want to find it using these same letters in some other way. To guard against this, we denote the functions in differentiation rules by letters like u and v that are not likely to be already in use.

EXAMPLE 3

a) $\frac{d}{dx}(3x^2) = \frac{d}{dx}(3 \cdot x^2) = 3 \cdot \frac{d}{dx}(x^2)$ Eq. (3) with $c = 3$

$= 3 \cdot 2x = 6x$

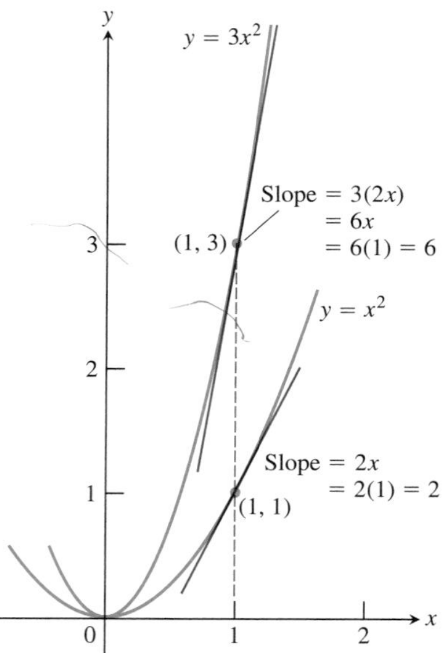

3.17 The graphs of $y = x^2$ and $y = 3x^2$. Tripling the y-coordinates triples the slope (Example 3a).

The formula $(d/dx)(3x^2) = 3 \cdot 2x$ says that if we transform the graph of $y = x^2$ by multiplying each y-coordinate by 3, then we multiply the slope at each point by 3 (Fig. 3.17).

b) $\dfrac{d}{dx}\left(\dfrac{5x^3}{3}\right) = \dfrac{5}{3} \cdot \dfrac{d}{dx}(x^3) = \dfrac{5}{3} \cdot 3x^2 = 5x^2$

EXAMPLE 4 *A Useful Special Case.* The derivative of the negative of any function is the negative of the function's derivative:

$$\frac{d}{dx}(-u) = \frac{d}{dx}(-1 \cdot u)$$

$$= -1 \cdot \frac{d}{dx}(u) \qquad \text{Eq. (2) with } c = -1$$

$$= -\frac{du}{dx}.$$

EXAMPLE 5 *A Useful Special Case.* If c is a constant, then

$$\frac{d}{dx}(cx) = \frac{d}{dx}(cx^1)$$

$$= c \cdot 1 \cdot x^{1-1} \qquad \text{Eq. (3) with } n = 1$$

$$= cx^0 = c.$$

Proof of Rule 3

$$\frac{d}{dx}cu = \lim_{h \to 0} \frac{cu(x+h) - cu(x)}{h} \qquad \text{Derivative definition } f(x) = cu(x)$$

$$= c \lim_{h \to 0} \frac{u(x+h) - u(x)}{h} \qquad \text{Constant Multiple Rule for limits}$$

$$= c\frac{du}{dx} \qquad u \text{ is differentiable.}$$

The next rule says that the derivative of the sum or difference of two differentiable functions is the sum or difference of their derivatives.

The Sum and Difference Rule holds for more than two functions as long as the number of functions involved is finite.

RULE 4

The Sum and Difference Rule

If u and v are differentiable functions of x, then

1. $\dfrac{d}{dx}(u + v) = \dfrac{du}{dx} + \dfrac{dv}{dx}$, **2.** $\dfrac{d}{dx}(u - v) = \dfrac{du}{dx} - \dfrac{dv}{dx}$.

This rule holds only at values of x where both u and v have derivatives.

Example 6 illustrates the fact that we can differentiate any polynomial term by term.

EXAMPLE 6

a) $y = x^4 + 12x$

$$\frac{dy}{dx} = \frac{d}{dx}(x^4) + \frac{d}{dx}(12x)$$
$$= 4x^3 + 12$$

b) $y = \frac{7x^2}{3} - 5$

$$\frac{dy}{dx} = \frac{d}{dx}\left(\frac{7x^2}{3}\right) - \frac{d}{dx}(5)$$
$$= \frac{7}{3} \cdot 2x - 0 = \frac{14}{3}x$$

c) $y = x^3 + 3x^2 - 5x + 1$

$$\frac{dy}{dx} = \frac{d}{dx}(x^3) + \frac{d}{dx}(3x^2) - \frac{d}{dx}(5x) + \frac{d}{dx}(1)$$
$$= 3x^2 + 3 \cdot 2x - 5 + 0$$
$$= 3x^2 + 6x - 5$$

Proof of Rule 4 To prove Part 1, we apply the derivative definition with $f(x) = u(x) + v(x)$:

$$\frac{d}{dx}[u(x) + v(x)] = \lim_{h \to 0} \frac{[u(x+h) + v(x+h)] - [u(x) + v(x)]}{h}$$
$$= \lim_{h \to 0} \left[\frac{u(x+h) - u(x)}{h} + \frac{v(x+h) - v(x)}{h}\right]$$
$$= \lim_{h \to 0} \frac{u(x+h) - u(x)}{h} + \lim_{h \to 0} \frac{v(x+h) - v(x)}{h}$$
$$= \frac{du}{dx} + \frac{dv}{dx}.$$

The proof of Part 2 is similar.

Of particular importance, as we will see in Chapter 4, is any point on a curve $y = f(x)$ where the tangent is horizontal.

EXAMPLE 7 Does the curve $y = x^4 - 2x^2 + 2$ have any horizontal tangents? If so, where?

Solution The horizontal tangents, if any, occur where the slope dy/dx is zero. To find these points, we take the following steps.

STEP 1: Calculate dy/dx.

$$\frac{dy}{dx} = \frac{d}{dx}(x^4 - 2x^2 + 2) = 4x^3 - 4x$$

STEP 2: Solve the equation $\frac{dy}{dx} = 0$ for x.

$$4x^3 - 4x = 0$$
$$4x(x^2 - 1) = 0$$
$$4x = 0 \quad \text{or} \quad x^2 - 1 = 0$$
$$x = 0,\ 1,\ -1$$

The curve $y = x^4 - 2x^2 + 2$ has horizontal tangents at $x = 0$, 1, and -1. The corresponding points on this curve are (0, 2), (1, 1), and $(-1, 1)$. See Fig. 3.18.

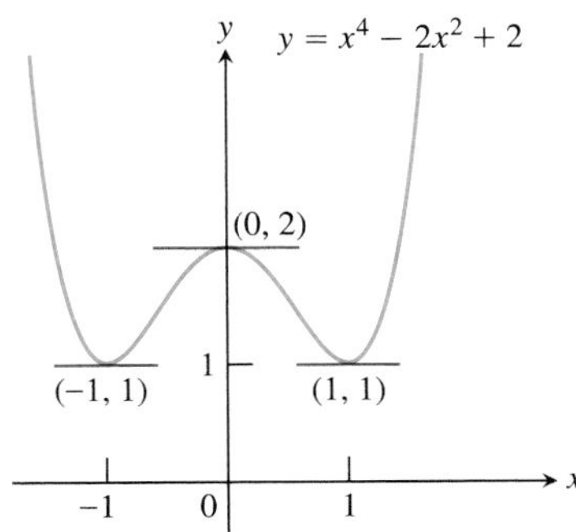

3.18 The curve $y = x^4 - 2x^2 + 2$ and its horizontal tangents (Example 7).

Products

While the derivative of the sum of two functions is the sum of their derivatives, and the derivative of the difference of two functions is the difference of their derivatives, the derivative of the product of two functions is *not* the product of their derivatives. For instance,

$$\frac{d}{dx}(x \cdot x) = \frac{d}{dx}(x^2) = 2x,$$

while

$$\frac{d}{dx}(x) \cdot \frac{d}{dx}(x) = 1 \cdot 1 = 1.$$

The derivative of a product is the sum of *two* products, as we now explain.

You can remember the Product Rule with the phrase "the first times the derivative of the second plus the second times the derivative of the first."

RULE 5

The Product Rule

If u and v are differentiable functions of x, then

$$\frac{d}{dx}(uv) = u\frac{dv}{dx} + v\frac{du}{dx}. \tag{4}$$

As with the Sum and Difference Rule, the Product Rule holds only at values of x where u and v both have derivatives. At such a value of x, the derivative of the product uv is u times the derivative of v plus v times the derivative of u.

EXAMPLE 8 Find the derivative of $y = (x^2 + 1)(x^3 - 5)$.

Solution

$$\begin{aligned}
\frac{dy}{dx} &= \frac{d}{dx}\Big[\underbrace{(x^2+1)}_{u}\cdot\underbrace{(x^3-5)}_{v}\Big] \\
&= \underbrace{(x^2+1)}_{u}\cdot\underbrace{\frac{d}{dx}(x^3-5)}_{\text{derivative of } v} + \underbrace{(x^3-5)}_{v}\cdot\underbrace{\frac{d}{dx}(x^2+1)}_{\text{derivative of } u} \qquad \text{Product Rule} \\
&= (x^2+1)(3x^2) + (x^3-5)(2x) \\
&= 3x^4 + 3x^2 + 2x^4 - 10x \\
&= 5x^4 + 3x^2 - 10x
\end{aligned}$$

The calculations in Example 8 can be done as well (perhaps better) by multiplying out the original expression for y and differentiating the resulting polynomial. We do that now as a check:

$$y = (x^2+1)(x^3-5) = x^5 + x^3 - 5x^2 - 5 \qquad \text{We can use the Sum and Difference Rule.}$$

$$\frac{dy}{dx} = 5x^4 + 3x^2 - 10x.$$

This result agrees with the Product Rule calculation in Example 8.

The second method (multiplying first) is faster in this case, but it is not always possible to multiply the factors involved to produce a simpler expression to differentiate. For functions like $y = x \sin x$ and the function in the next example, the Product Rule *must* be used.

The Product Rule in Prime Notation

When we use primes to denote derivatives with respect to x, the Product Rule

$$\frac{d}{dx}(uv) = u\frac{dv}{dx} + v\frac{du}{dx}$$

becomes

$$(uv)' = uv' + vu'.$$

You may find the latter form easier to remember.

EXAMPLE 9 Let $y = uv$ be the product of the functions u and v, and suppose that

$$u(2) = 3, \qquad u'(2) = -4, \qquad v(2) = 1, \qquad \text{and} \qquad v'(2) = 2.$$

Find $y'(2)$.

Solution From the Product Rule, in the form

$$y' = (uv)' = uv' + vu',$$

we have

$$y'(2) = u(2)v'(2) + v(2)u'(2) = (3)(2) + (1)(-4) = 6 - 4 = 2.$$

Proof of Rule 5

$$\frac{d}{dx}(uv) = \lim_{h\to 0}\frac{u(x+h)v(x+h) - u(x)v(x)}{h}.$$

To change this fraction into an equivalent one that contains difference quotients for the derivatives of u and v, we subtract and add $u(x+h)v(x)$ in the numerator. Then,

$$\begin{aligned}\frac{d}{dx}(uv) &= \lim_{h\to 0}\frac{u(x+h)v(x+h) - u(x+h)v(x) + u(x+h)v(x) - u(x)v(x)}{h} \\ &= \lim_{h\to 0}\left[u(x+h)\frac{v(x+h)-v(x)}{h} + v(x)\frac{u(x+h)-u(x)}{h}\right] \\ &= \lim_{h\to 0} u(x+h)\cdot\lim_{h\to 0}\frac{v(x+h)-v(x)}{h} \\ &\qquad + \lim_{h\to 0} v(x)\cdot\lim_{h\to 0}\frac{u(x+h)-u(x)}{h}.\end{aligned}$$

As $h \to 0$, three things now happen simultaneously:

1. $u(x+h) \to u(x)$ because u, being differentiable at x, is continuous at x.
2. $v(x)$ remains unchanged, having the constant value $v(x)$ (h is changing, but x is not).
3. The two fractions approach the values of dv/dx and du/dx at x.

In short, at each value of x at which u and v are differentiable,

$$\frac{d}{dx}(uv) = u\frac{dv}{dx} + v\frac{du}{dx}.$$

Quotients

Just as the derivative of the product of two differentiable functions is not the product of their derivatives, the derivative of the quotient of two functions is *not* the quotient of their derivatives. What happens instead is this:

RULE 6

The Quotient Rule

If u and v are differentiable functions of x, then at any point where $v \neq 0$,

$$\frac{d}{dx}\left(\frac{u}{v}\right) = \frac{v\dfrac{du}{dx} - u\dfrac{dv}{dx}}{v^2}. \tag{5}$$

As with earlier combination rules, the Quotient Rule holds only at values of x at which u and v both have derivatives.

Using the Quotient Rule

Since order is important in subtraction, be sure you set up the numerator of the Quotient Rule correctly: v times the derivative of u minus u times the derivative of v.

You can remember the Quotient Rule with the phrase "bottom times the derivative of the top minus the top times the derivative of the bottom, all over the bottom squared."

EXAMPLE 10 Find the derivative of $y = \dfrac{x^2 - 1}{x^2 + 1}$.

Solution

$$\frac{dy}{dx} = \frac{d}{dx}\underbrace{\left(\frac{x^2-1}{x^2+1}\right)}_{\frac{u}{v}}$$

$$= \frac{\overbrace{(x^2+1)}^{v}\cdot\overbrace{\frac{d}{dx}(x^2-1)}^{\text{derivative of } u} - \overbrace{(x^2-1)}^{u}\cdot\overbrace{\frac{d}{dx}(x^2+1)}^{\text{derivative of } v}}{\underbrace{(x^2+1)^2}_{v^2}} \qquad \text{Quotient Rule}$$

$$= \frac{(x^2+1)(2x) - (x^2-1)(2x)}{(x^2+1)^2}$$

$$= \frac{2x^3 + 2x - 2x^3 + 2x}{(x^2+1)^2}$$

$$= \frac{4x}{(x^2+1)^2}$$

Proof of Rule 6

$$\frac{d}{dx}\left(\frac{u}{v}\right) = \lim_{h\to 0}\frac{\dfrac{u(x+h)}{v(x+h)} - \dfrac{u(x)}{v(x)}}{h}$$

$$= \lim_{h\to 0}\frac{v(x)u(x+h) - u(x)v(x+h)}{hv(x+h)v(x)}.$$

To change the last fraction into an equivalent one that contains the difference quotients for the derivatives of u and v, we subtract and add $v(x)u(x)$ in the numerator. We then get

$$\frac{d}{dx}\left(\frac{u}{v}\right) = \lim_{h\to 0} \frac{v(x)u(x+h) - v(x)u(x) + v(x)u(x) - u(x)v(x+h)}{hv(x+h)v(x)}$$

$$= \lim_{h\to 0} \frac{v(x)\dfrac{u(x+h)-u(x)}{h} - u(x)\dfrac{v(x+h)-v(x)}{h}}{v(x+h)v(x)}$$

$$= \frac{\lim\limits_{h\to 0} v(x)\cdot \lim\limits_{h\to 0} \dfrac{u(x+h)-u(x)}{h} - \lim\limits_{h\to 0} u(x)\cdot \lim\limits_{h\to 0} \dfrac{v(x+h)-v(x)}{h}}{\lim\limits_{h\to 0} v(x+h)\cdot \lim\limits_{h\to 0} v(x)}$$

$$= \frac{v\dfrac{du}{dx} - u\dfrac{dv}{dx}}{v^2}.$$

Negative Integer Powers of x

The rule for differentiating negative powers of x is the same as the rule for differentiating positive powers of x.

RULE 7

Power Rule for Negative Integer Powers of x

If n is a negative integer and $x \neq 0$, then

$$\frac{d}{dx}(x^n) = nx^{n-1}. \tag{6}$$

EXAMPLE 11

$$\frac{d}{dx}\left(\frac{1}{x}\right) = \frac{d}{dx}(x^{-1}) = (-1)x^{-2} = -\frac{1}{x^2}$$

$$\frac{d}{dx}\left(\frac{4}{x^3}\right) = 4\frac{d}{dx}(x^{-3}) = 4(-3)x^{-4} = -\frac{12}{x^4}$$

Proof of Rule 7 The proof uses the Quotient Rule in a clever way. If n is a negative integer, then $n = -m$ where m is a positive integer. Hence, $x^n = x^{-m} = 1/x^m$ and

$$\frac{d}{dx}(x^n) = \frac{d}{dx}\left(\frac{1}{x^m}\right)$$

$$= \frac{x^m \cdot \dfrac{d}{dx}(1) - 1\cdot\dfrac{d}{dx}(x^m)}{(x^m)^2}$$ Quotient Rule with $u = 1$ and $v = x^m$

$$= \frac{0 - mx^{m-1}}{x^{2m}}$$ Since $m > 0$, $\frac{d}{dx}(x^m) = mx^{m-1}$

$$= -mx^{-m-1}$$

$$= nx^{n-1}.$$ Since $-m = n$

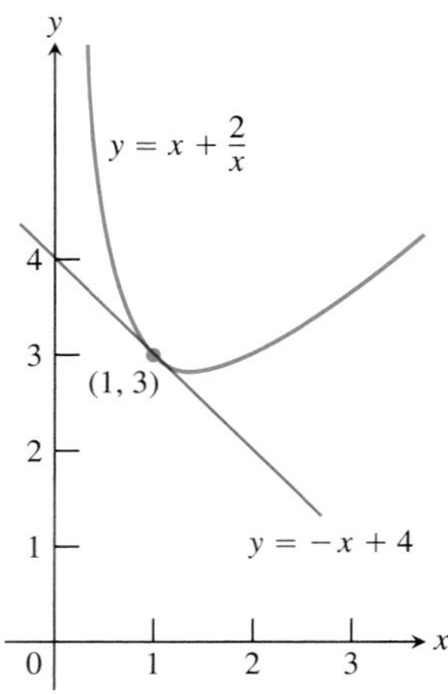

3.19 The tangent to the curve $y = x + (2/x)$ at the point $(1, 3)$ (Example 12). The curve also has a portion in the third quadrant, not shown here. Don't worry about how to sketch graphs like this right now; we'll come to that in Chapter 4.

EXAMPLE 12 Find an equation for the tangent to the curve

$$y = x + \frac{2}{x}$$

at the point $(1, 3)$.

Solution The slope of the curve is

$$\begin{aligned}\frac{dy}{dx} &= \frac{d}{dx}(x) + 2\frac{d}{dx}\left(\frac{1}{x}\right)\\ &= 1 + 2\left(-\frac{1}{x^2}\right) \qquad \text{From Example 11}\\ &= 1 - \frac{2}{x^2}.\end{aligned}$$

The slope at $x = 1$ is

$$\left.\frac{dy}{dx}\right|_{x=1} = \left[1 - \frac{2}{x^2}\right]_{x=1} = \left(1 - \frac{2}{(1)^2}\right) = 1 - 2 = -1.$$

The line through $(1, 3)$ with slope $m = -1$ is

$$\begin{aligned}y - 3 &= (-1)(x - 1) \qquad \text{Point–slope equation}\\ y &= -x + 1 + 3\\ y &= -x + 4.\end{aligned}$$

See Fig. 3.19.

Evaluation Notation

$\left.\frac{dy}{dx}\right|_{x=1}$ means "$\frac{dy}{dx}$ evaluated at $x = 1$."

$\left[1 - \frac{2}{x^2}\right]_{x=1}$ means "$\left[1 - \frac{2}{x^2}\right]$ evaluated at $x = 1$."

Choosing Which Rules to Use

The choice of which rules to use in solving a differentiation problem can make a difference in how much work you have to do. Here is an example.

EXAMPLE 13 Rather than using the Quotient Rule to find the derivative of

$$y = \frac{(x-1)(x^2-2x)}{x^4},$$

expand the numerator and divide by x^4:

$$y = \frac{(x-1)(x^2-2x)}{x^4} = \frac{x^3 - 3x^2 + 2x}{x^4} = x^{-1} - 3x^{-2} + 2x^{-3}.$$

Then use the Sum and Power Rules:

$$\frac{dy}{dx} = -x^{-2} - 3(-2)x^{-3} + 2(-3)x^{-4} = -\frac{1}{x^2} + \frac{6}{x^3} - \frac{6}{x^4}.$$

Notice that

$$\frac{d}{dx}\left(\frac{dy}{dx}\right)$$

does not mean multiplication. It means "the derivative of the derivative."

Second and Higher Order Derivatives

The derivative $y' = dy/dx$ is the **first derivative** of y with respect to x. The first derivative may also be a differentiable function of x. If so, its derivative

$$y'' = \frac{dy'}{dx} = \frac{d}{dx}\left(\frac{dy}{dx}\right) = \frac{d^2y}{dx^2} \tag{7}$$

How to Read the Symbols for Derivatives

y'	(y prime)
y''	(y double prime)
$\frac{d^2y}{dx^2}$	(d squared y dx squared)
y'''	(y triple prime)
$y^{(n)}$	(y super n)

is called the **second derivative** of y with respect to x. If y'' is differentiable, its derivative

$$y''' = \frac{dy''}{dx}$$

is the **third derivative** of y with respect to x. The names continue as you imagine they would, with

$$y^{(n)} = \frac{d}{dx} y^{(n-1)}$$

denoting the ***n*th derivative** of y with respect to x, for any positive integer n.

EXAMPLE 14 The first four derivatives of $y = x^3 - 3x^2 + 2$ are

First derivative:	$y' = 3x^2 - 6x$
Second derivative:	$y'' = 6x - 6$
Third derivative:	$y''' = 6$
Fourth derivative:	$y^{(4)} = 0.$

The function has derivatives of all orders, the fifth and later derivatives all being zero.

Exercises 3.2

In Exercises 1–16, find dy/dx and d^2y/dx^2.

1. $y = -x^2 + 3$

2. $y = x^2 + x + 8$

3. $y = 5x^3 - 3x^5$

4. $y = 3x^7 - 7x^3 + 21x^2$

5. $y = \frac{4x^3}{3} - x$

6. $y = \frac{x^3}{3} + \frac{x^2}{2} + \frac{x}{4}$

7. $y = 3x^{-2}$

8. $y = -2x^{-1}$

9. $y = -\frac{1}{x}$

10. $y = \frac{4}{x^2}$

11. $y = 6x^2 - 10x - 5x^{-2}$

12. $y = 4 - 2x - x^{-3}$

13. $y = \frac{1}{3x^2} - \frac{5}{2x}$

14. $y = \frac{1}{6x^2} + \frac{7}{12x^3}$

15. $y = 9x + 1 + \frac{1}{x}$

16. $y = \frac{12}{x} - \frac{4}{x^3} + \frac{1}{x^4}$

In Exercises 17–22, find dy/dx (a) by applying the Product Rule and (b) by multiplying the factors to produce a sum of simpler terms to differentiate.

17. $y = (3x - 1)(2x + 5)$

18. $y = (5 - x)(4 - 2x)$

19. $y = x^2(x^3 - 1)$

20. $y = (x - 1)(x^2 + x + 1)$

21. $y = x^2\left(x + 5 + \frac{1}{x}\right)$

22. $y = \left(x + \frac{1}{x}\right)\left(x - \frac{1}{x}\right)$

In Exercises 23–30, find $y' = dy/dx$.

23. $y = \frac{2x + 5}{3x - 2}$

24. $y = \frac{2x + 1}{x^2 - 1}$

25. $y = \frac{x^2 - 4}{x + 0.5}$

26. $y = \frac{x^2 - 1}{x^2 + x - 2}$

27. $y = \frac{1}{(x^2 - 1)(x^2 + x + 1)}$

28. $y = \frac{(x + 1)(x + 2)}{(x - 1)(x - 2)}$

29. $y = (1 - x)(1 + x^2)^{-1}$

30. $y = (2x - 7)^{-1}(x + 5)$

In Exercises 31–36, use the fact that

$$\frac{d}{dx}\sqrt{x} = \frac{1}{2\sqrt{x}} \qquad (x > 0)$$

(Section 3.1, Example 8) to find dy/dx.

31. $y = \frac{10}{\sqrt{x} - 4}$

32. $y = \frac{x}{2\sqrt{x} - 7}$

33. $y = \frac{\sqrt{x} - 1}{\sqrt{x} + 1}$

34. $y = \frac{5x + 1}{2\sqrt{x}}$

35. $y = \dfrac{1 + x - 4\sqrt{x}}{x}$

36. $y = 2\left(\dfrac{1}{\sqrt{x}} + \sqrt{x}\right)$

In Exercises 37–40, find dy/dx and d^2y/dx^2.

37. $y = \dfrac{x^3 + 7}{x}$

38. $y = \dfrac{x^2 + 5x - 1}{x^2}$

39. $y = \dfrac{(x - 1)(x^2 + x + 1)}{x^3}$

40. $y = \dfrac{(x^2 + x)(x^2 - x + 1)}{x^4}$

Find all the derivatives of the functions in Exercises 41–44.

41. $y = x^2 - x$

42. $y = \dfrac{x^3}{3} + \dfrac{x^2}{2} - 5$

43. $y = \dfrac{x^4}{2} - \dfrac{3}{2}x^2 - x$

44. $y = \dfrac{x^5}{120}$

In Exercises 45 and 46, find all the derivatives of s with respect to t.

45. $s = 4 - t + t^2 - t^3$

46. $s = 4t^2 - 8t + 1$

In Exercises 47 and 48, find $dr/d\theta$.

47. $r = \dfrac{\theta^2 - 1}{1 - \theta^3}$

48. $r = \dfrac{\theta^2 - 1}{\theta^2 + \theta - 2}$

In Exercises 49 and 50, find dw/dz and d^2w/dz^2.

49. $w = \left(\dfrac{1 + 3z}{3z}\right)(3 - z)$

50. $w = (z + 1)(z - 1)(z^2 + 1)$

In Exercises 51 and 52, find dp/dq and d^2p/dq^2.

51. $p = \left(\dfrac{q^2 + 3}{12q}\right)\left(\dfrac{q^4 - 1}{q^3}\right)$

52. $p = \dfrac{q^2 + 3}{(q - 1)^3 + (q + 1)^3}$

53. Suppose u and v are functions of x that are differentiable at $x = 0$ and that

$$u(0) = 5, \quad u'(0) = -3, \quad v(0) = -1, \quad v'(0) = 2.$$

Find the values of the following derivatives at $x = 0$.

a) $\dfrac{d}{dx}(uv)$ **b)** $\dfrac{d}{dx}\left(\dfrac{u}{v}\right)$ **c)** $\dfrac{d}{dx}\left(\dfrac{v}{u}\right)$ **d)** $\dfrac{d}{dx}(7v - 2u)$

54. Suppose u and v are differentiable functions of x and that

$$u(1) = 2, \quad u'(1) = 0, \quad v(1) = 5, \quad v'(1) = 0.$$

Find the values of the following derivatives at $x = 1$.

a) $\dfrac{d}{dx}(uv)$ **b)** $\dfrac{d}{dx}\left(\dfrac{u}{v}\right)$ **c)** $\dfrac{d}{dx}\left(\dfrac{v}{u}\right)$ **d)** $\dfrac{d}{dx}(7v - 2u)$

In Exercises 55 and 56, find an equation for the tangent to the curve at the given value of x.

55. $y = x - \dfrac{1}{2x}, \quad x = -\dfrac{1}{2}$

56. $y = \dfrac{x}{2} + \dfrac{1}{2x - 4}, \quad x = 3$

57. **a)** Find an equation for the line perpendicular to the tangent to the curve $y = x^3 - 4x + 1$ at the point $(2, 1)$.
b) What is the smallest slope on the curve? At what point on the curve does the curve have this slope?
c) Find equations for the tangents to the curve at the points where the slope of the curve is 8.

58. **a)** Find equations for the horizontal tangents to the curve $y = x^3 - 3x - 2$. Also find equations for the lines that are perpendicular to these tangents at the points of tangency.
b) What is the smallest slope on the curve? At what point on the curve does the curve have this slope? Find an equation for the line that is perpendicular to the curve's tangent at this point.

59. Find the points on the curve $y = 2x^3 - 3x^2 - 12x + 20$ where the tangent is parallel to the x-axis.

60. Find the x- and y-intercepts of the line that is tangent to the curve $y = x^3$ at the point $(-2, -8)$.

61. Find the tangents to *Newton's Serpentine,*

$$y = \frac{4x}{x^2 + 1}$$

at the origin and the point $(1, 2)$.

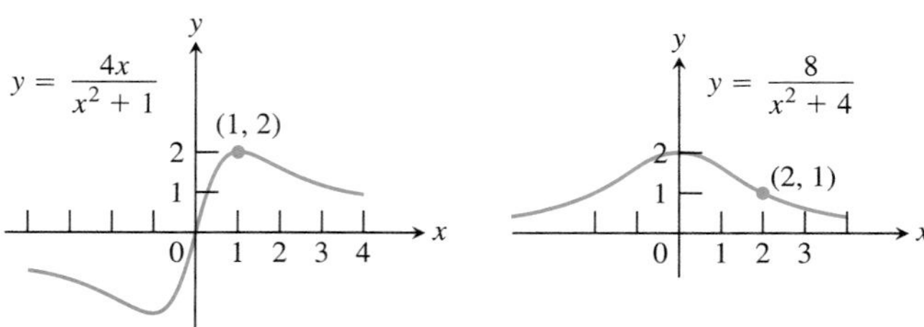

62. Find the tangent to the *Witch of Agnesi*

$$y = \frac{8}{x^2 + 4}$$

at the point $(2, 1)$. There is a story about the name of this curve in the historical note on Agnesi in Chapter 10.

63. **a)** Find an equation for the line that is tangent to the curve $y = x^3 - x$ at the point $(-1, 0)$.
b) Graph the curve and tangent line together. The tangent intersects the curve at another point. Use ZOOM and TRACE, if available, to estimate the point's coordinates.
c) SOLVER Confirm your estimates of the coordinates of the second intersection point by solving the equations for the curve and tangent simultaneously.

64. **a)** Find an equation for the line that is tangent to the curve $y = x^3 - 6x^2 + 5x$ at the origin.
b) Graph the curve and tangent together. The tangent intersects the curve at another point. Use ZOOM and TRACE, if available, to estimate the point's coordinates.

c) Confirm your estimates of the coordinates of the second intersection point by solving the equations for the curve and tangent simultaneously.

When we work with functions of a single variable in mathematics, we normally call the independent variable x and the dependent variable y. Applied fields use many different letters, however. Here are some examples.

65. *Cylinder Pressure.* If the gas in a cylinder is maintained at a constant temperature T, the pressure P is related to the volume V by a formula of the form

$$P = \frac{nRT}{V - nb} - \frac{an^2}{V^2}$$

in which a, b, n, and R are constants. Find dP/dV.

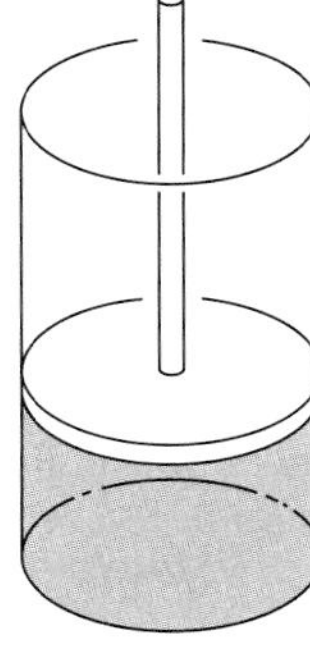

66. *The Body's Reaction to Medicine.* The reaction of the body to a dose of medicine can often be represented by an equation of the form

$$R = M^2\left(\frac{C}{2} - \frac{M}{3}\right),$$

where C is a positive constant and M is the amount of medicine absorbed in the blood. If the reaction is a change in blood pressure, R is measured in millimeters of mercury. If the reaction is a change in temperature, R is measured in degrees, and so on.

Find dR/dM. This derivative, as a function of M, is called the sensitivity of the body to the medicine. In Chapter 4, we will see how to find the amount of medicine to which the body is most sensitive. (*Source: Some Mathematical Models in Biology,* Revised Edition, R. M. Thrall, J. A. Mortimer, K. R. Rebman, R. F. Baum, eds., December 1967, PB-202 364, p. 221; distributed by N.T.I.S., U.S. Department of Commerce.)

67. Figure 3.20 shows the graph of a function $f(x)$ and its derivative $f'(x)$. Which graph is which? Give reasons for your answer.

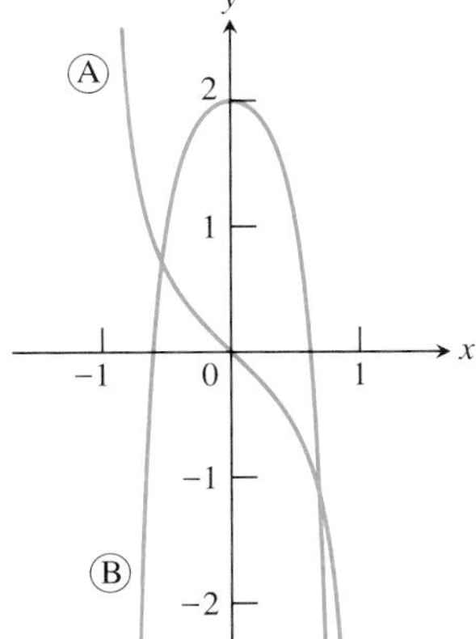

3.20 The graphs for Exercise 67.

68. Figure 3.21 shows the graph of a function $f(x)$ and its first derivative, $f'(x)$. Which graph is which? Give reasons for your answer.

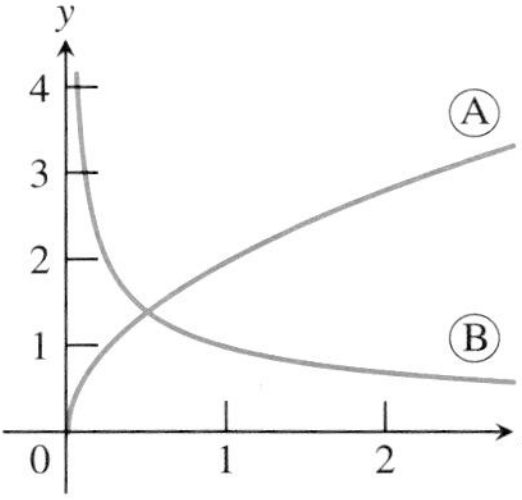

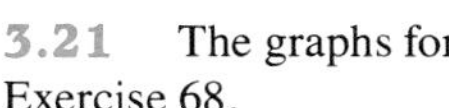

3.21 The graphs for Exercise 68.

69. *Generalizing the Product Rule.* The Product Rule gives the formula

$$\frac{d}{dx}(uv) = u\frac{dv}{dx} + v\frac{du}{dx}$$

for the derivative of the product of two differentiable functions of x. What is the formula for the derivative of uvw, the product of *three* differentiable functions of x? Give reasons for your answer.

70. a) Find $\frac{d}{dx}(x^{3/2})$ by writing $x^{3/2}$ as $x \cdot x^{1/2} = x\sqrt{x}$ and using the Product Rule. Express your answer as a fraction times a fractional power of x.

b) Find $\frac{d}{dx}(x^{5/2})$ for $x > 0$ by writing $x^{5/2}$ as $x^2 \cdot x^{1/2} = x^2\sqrt{x}$ and using the Product Rule. Express your answer as a fraction times a fractional power of x.

c) Find $\frac{d}{dx}(x^{7/2})$, expressing your answer as a fractional power of x.

d) What pattern do you see? Fractional powers are one of the topics of Section 3.6.

71. Write the Sum and Difference Rules and the Quotient Rule using prime notation for the derivatives involved.

72. Replace v in the Sum Rule (Rule 4, Part 1) by $-v$. What does the rule then say? Replace v in the Difference Rule (Rule 4, Part 2) by $-v$. What does the rule then say? What can you conclude about how the Sum and Difference Rules are related?

Writing for Your Own Knowledge

Answer the following questions in writing. Some answers will take only a sentence or two; others may require several paragraphs. Some explanations may also call for graphs or sketches.

1. What are the rules for differentiation? When do they apply?
2. What are higher order derivatives?

EXPLORER PROGRAM

Derivatives	Key in any function $y = f(x)$. The program will automatically graph f and f' together.

3.3 Velocity, Speed, and Other Rates of Change

Derivatives provide the mathematics we need to understand the way things change in the world around us. With derivatives, we can describe the rates at which water reservoirs empty, populations change, rocks fall, the economy changes, and an athlete's blood sugar varies with exercise. We begin with free fall, the kind of fall that takes place in a vacuum near the surface of the earth.

Free Fall

Near the surface of the earth, all bodies fall with the same constant acceleration. The distance a body falls after it is released from rest is a constant multiple of the square of the time elapsed. At least, that is what happens when the body falls in a vacuum, where there is no air to slow it down. The square-of-time rule also holds for dense, heavy objects like rocks, ball bearings, and steel tools during the first few seconds of their fall through air, before their velocities build up to where air resistance begins to matter. When air resistance is absent or insignificant and the only force acting on a falling body is the force of gravity, we call the way the body falls *free fall*.

The equation for the distance an object falls from rest is

$$s = \frac{1}{2}gt^2. \tag{1}$$

In this equation, s is distance, t is time, and g, as we will see in a moment, is the constant acceleration given to an object by the force of gravity.

EXAMPLE 1 The value of g in the equation $s = (1/2)gt^2$ depends on the units used to measure t and s. With t in seconds (the usual unit),

$$g = 32 \text{ ft/sec}^2, \qquad s = \frac{1}{2}(32)t^2 = 16t^2 \text{ ft}$$

$$g = 9.80 \text{ m/sec}^2, \qquad s = \frac{1}{2}(9.80)t^2 = 4.9t^2 \text{ m}.$$

The abbreviation ft/sec^2 is read "feet per second squared" or "feet per second per second," and m/sec^2 is read "meters per second squared."

Figure 3.22 shows the free fall of a heavy ball bearing released from rest at time $t = 0$. During the first 2 sec, the ball falls

$$s(2) = 16(2)^2 = 16 \cdot 4 = 64 \text{ ft}.$$

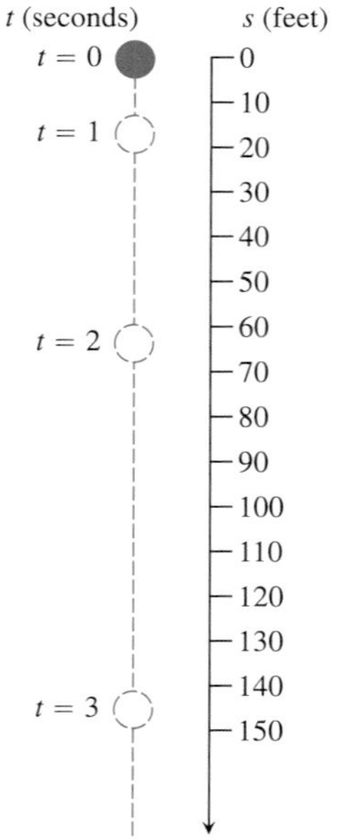

3.22 Distance fallen by a ball bearing released from rest at $t = 0$ sec.

EXAMPLE 2 How long did it take the ball bearing in Fig. 3.22 to fall the first 14.7 m?

Solution The free-fall equation for s in meters and t in seconds is $s = 4.9t^2$ (from Example 1). To find the time it took the ball bearing to cover the first 14.7 m, we substitute $s = 14.7$ and solve for t:

$$14.7 = 4.9t^2$$
$$t^2 = 14.7/4.9 = 3$$
$$t = \sqrt{3}. \qquad \text{Elapsed time increases from } t = 0 \text{ so we ignore the negative root.}$$

It took the ball $t = \sqrt{3}$, or about 1.732 sec, to fall the first 14.7 m.

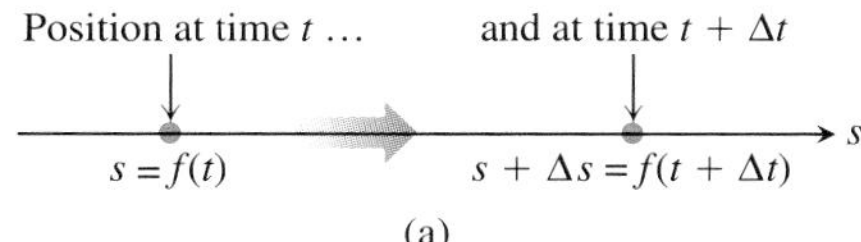

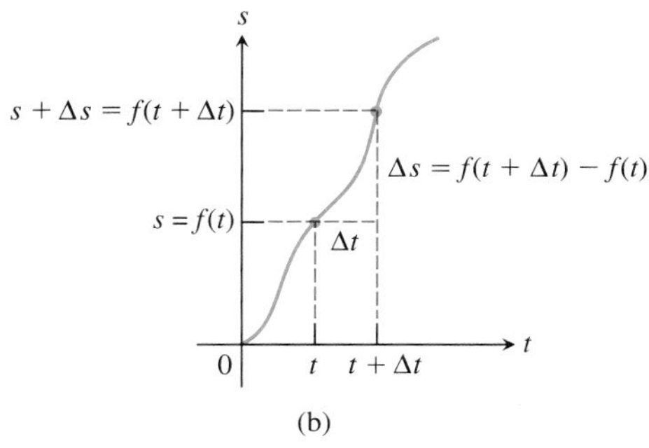

3.23 Two ways to model the positions of a body moving on a coordinate line: (a) on the line itself and (b) in the st-plane. The curve in the st-plane is *not* the actual path of the moving body, but its slope shows the body's velocity at any time t.

Velocity

Suppose we have a body moving along a coordinate line and we know that its position at time t is $s = f(t)$. As the body moves along, it has a velocity at each particular instant and we want to find out what that velocity is. The information we seek must somehow be contained in the formula $s = f(t)$, but how do we find it?

We reason like this: In the interval from any time t to the slightly later time $t + \Delta t$, the body moves from position $s = f(t)$ to position

$$s + \Delta s = f(t + \Delta t) \tag{2}$$

(Fig. 3.23a). The body's net change in position, or **displacement,** for this short time interval is

$$\Delta s = f(t + \Delta t) - f(t). \tag{3}$$

The body's average velocity for the time interval is Δs (change in position) divided by Δt (change in time).

DEFINITION

If a body moving along a line from position $s = f(t)$ to position $s + \Delta s = f(t + \Delta t)$, then the body's **average velocity** for the time interval from t to $t + \Delta t$ is

$$v_{av} = \frac{\text{displacement}}{\text{travel time}} = \frac{\Delta s}{\Delta t} = \frac{f(t + \Delta t) - f(t)}{\Delta t}. \tag{4}$$

To find the body's velocity at the exact instant t, we take the limit of the average velocity over the interval from t to $t + \Delta t$ as the interval gets shorter and shorter and Δt shrinks to zero (Fig. 3.23b). As we now know, this limit is the derivative of s with respect to t.

DEFINITION

Instantaneous velocity (velocity) is the derivative of position with respect to time. If the position function of a body moving along a line is $s = f(t)$, the body's velocity at time t is

$$v = \frac{ds}{dt} = \lim_{\Delta t \to 0} \frac{f(t + \Delta t) - f(t)}{\Delta t}. \tag{5}$$

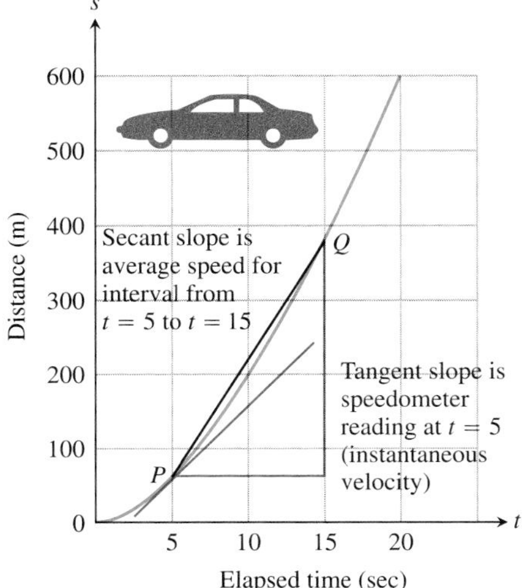

3.24 The time-to-distance data for Example 3.

EXAMPLE 3 Figure 3.24 shows a time-to-distance graph of a 1989 Ford Thunderbird SC. The slope of the secant PQ is the average velocity for the 10-sec interval from $t = 5$ to $t = 15$ sec, in this case 40 m/sec or 144 km/h. The slope of the tangent at P is the speedometer reading at $t = 5$ sec, about 20 m/sec or 72 km/h. The car's top velocity is 235 km/h (146 mph). (*Source: Car and Driver,* March 1989.)

Free-fall equation from Example 1	**Corresponding velocity**
$s = \frac{1}{2}gt^2$	$v = \frac{ds}{dt} = gt$
$s = 16t^2$ ft	$v = 32t$ ft/sec
$s = 4.9t^2$ m	$v = 9.8t$ m/sec

EXAMPLE 4 *Velocity During Free Fall.* The velocity of the falling ball bearing t sec after release is $v = 32t$ ft/sec (Fig. 3.22):

$$\text{At } t = 2: \quad v = 32(2) = 64 \text{ ft/sec}$$
$$\text{At } t = 3: \quad v = 32(3) = 96 \text{ ft/sec.}$$

EXAMPLE 5 A dynamite blast blows a heavy rock straight up with a launch velocity of 160 ft/sec (about 109 mph) (Fig. 3.25a). It reaches a height of $s = 160t - 16t^2$ ft after t sec.

a) How high does the rock go?

b) How fast is the rock traveling when it is 256 ft above the ground on the way up? on the way down?

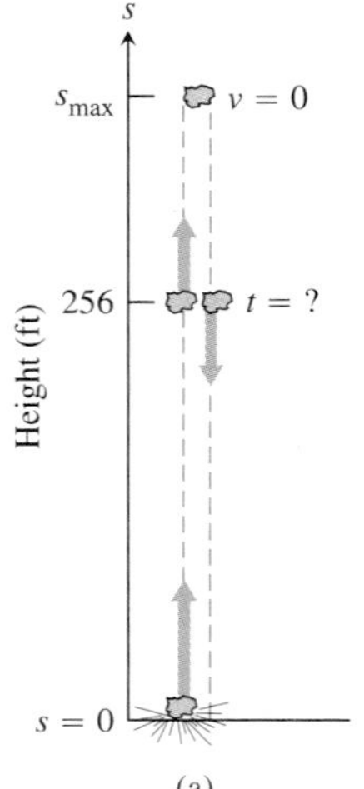

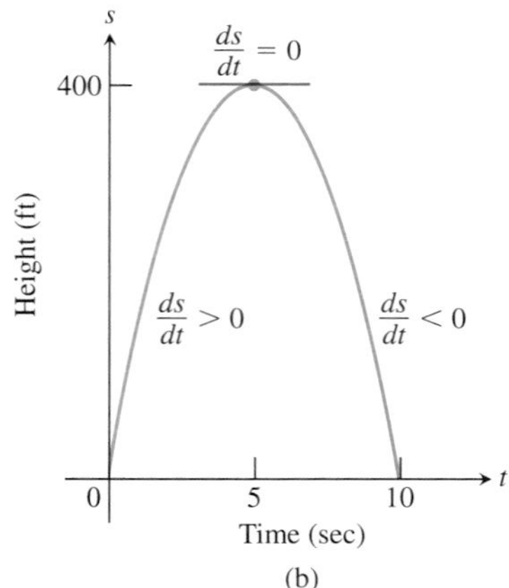

3.25 The graph of the rock's height s as a function of time (Example 5). The curve in (b) is not the path of the rock itself.

Solution

a) The rock reaches its maximum height at the position where its upward velocity is zero. To find this position, we find the value of t at which $v = 0$ and evaluate s at this value of t.

The velocity at time t is

$$v = \frac{ds}{dt} = \frac{d}{dt}(160t - 16t^2) \qquad \text{Velocity is the derivative of position.}$$
$$= 160 - 32t.$$

The velocity is zero when

$$160 - 32t = 0, \qquad \text{or} \qquad t = 5 \text{ sec.}$$

The rock's height at $t = 5$ sec is

$$s_{max} = s(5) = 160(5) - 16(5)^2$$
$$= 800 - 400$$
$$= 400 \text{ ft.}$$

b) To find the rock's velocity at 256 ft on the way up and again on the way down, we find the two values of t for which

$$s(t) = 160t - 16t^2 = 256. \tag{6}$$

To solve Eq. (6) we write

$$16t^2 - 160t + 256 = 0$$
$$16(t^2 - 10t + 16) = 0$$
$$(t - 2)(t - 8) = 0$$
$$t = 2 \text{ sec}, \qquad t = 8 \text{ sec.}$$

The rock is 256 ft above the ground 2 sec after the explosion and again 8 sec after the explosion. The rock's velocities at these times are

$$v(2) = 160 - 32(2) = 160 - 64 = 96 \text{ ft/sec}$$
$$v(8) = 160 - 32(8) = 160 - 256 = -96 \text{ ft/sec.}$$

Why is the downward velocity negative? It has to do with how we set up the coordinate system. Since s measures height from the ground up, changes in s are positive as the rock rises and negative as the rock falls (Fig. 3.25b).

Speed

If we drive to a friend's house and back at 30 mph, say, the speedometer will show 30 on the way over but it will not show -30 on the way back. The speedometer shows only the speed, which is the magnitude of the velocity. Speed measures the rate of progress regardless of direction.

DEFINITION

Speed is the magnitude of velocity. That is, speed $= |v|$.

EXAMPLE 6 When the rock in Example 5 passed the 256-ft mark, its speed was 96 ft/sec on the way up and $|-96| = 96$ ft/sec again on the way down.

EXAMPLE 7 Figure 3.26 shows the velocity $v = f(t)$ of a particle moving on a coordinate line. The particle moves forward for the first 3 seconds, moves backward for the next 2 seconds, stands still for a second, and moves forward again. Notice that the particle achieves its greatest speed at time $t = 4$, while moving backward.

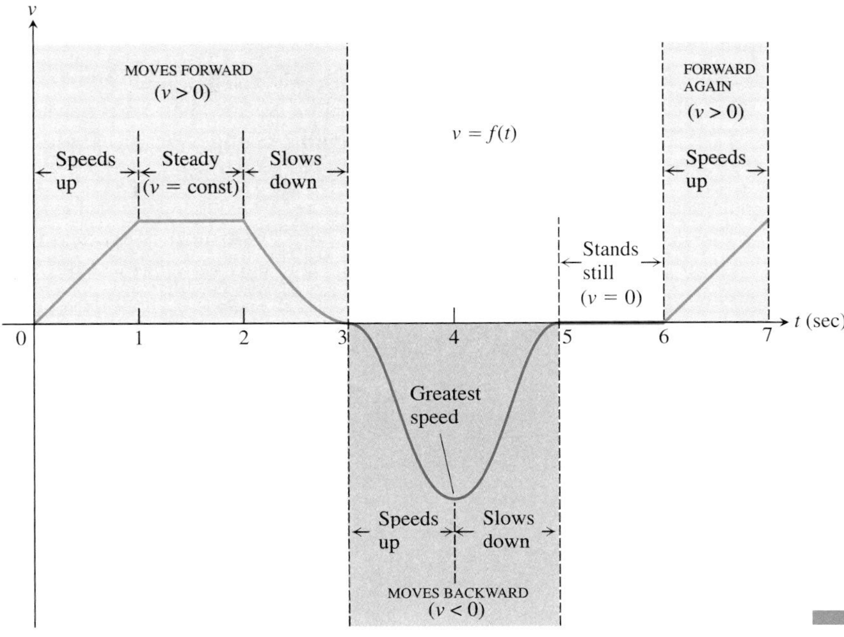

3.26 The velocity graph for Example 7.

Acceleration

In studies of motion along a coordinate line, we usually assume that the body's position function $s = f(t)$ has a second derivative as well as a first. The first derivative gives the body's velocity as a function of time; the second derivative gives the body's acceleration. Thus, velocity is how fast the position is changing and acceleration, the derivative of velocity, is how the fast the velocity is changing. The acceleration tells how quickly the body picks up or loses speed.

DEFINITION

Acceleration is the derivative of velocity. If a body's position at time t is $s = f(t)$, then the body's acceleration at time t is

$$a = \frac{dv}{dt} = \frac{d^2 s}{dt^2}. \tag{7}$$

EXAMPLE 8 The acceleration of the rock in Example 6 is

$$a = \frac{dv}{dt} = \frac{d}{dt}(160 - 32t) = 0 - 32 = -32 \text{ ft/sec}^2.$$

The minus sign confirms that the acceleration is downward, in the negative s direction. Whether the rock is going up or down, it is subject to the same constant downward pull of gravity.

Interpretations of the Derivative $f' = \frac{df}{dx}$

Algebraic Interpretation: f' is the function whose value at x is

$$f'(x) = \lim_{h \to 0} \frac{f(x + h) - f(x)}{h}.$$

Geometric Interpretation: f' is the function whose value at x is the slope of the tangent to the graph of f at x.

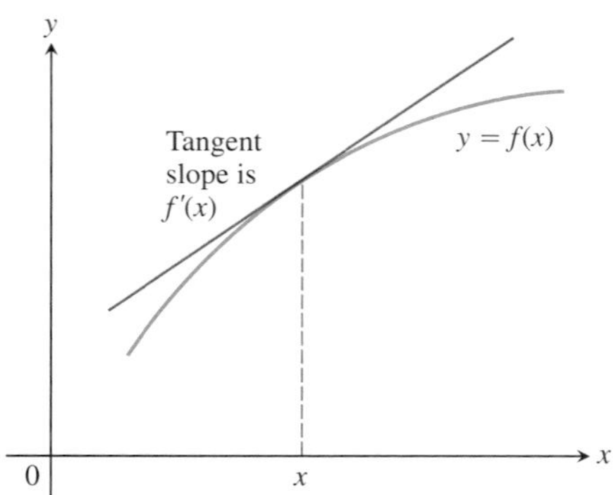

Rate-of-Change Interpretation: f' is the function whose value at x is the instantaneous rate at which f is changing at x.

Other Rates of Change

The language of average and instantaneous rates is appropriate for many other situations.

EXAMPLE 9 The number $g(t)$ of gallons of water in a reservoir at time t (minutes, say) can be regarded as a differentiable function of t. If the water's volume changes by the amount Δg in the interval from time t to time $t + \Delta t$, then

$\frac{\Delta g}{\Delta t}$ (gal/min) = average rate of change in volume for the time interval

$\frac{dg}{dt}$ (gal/min) = instantaneous rate of change in volume at time t.

Although it is natural to think of rates of change in terms of motion and time, there is no need to be so restrictive. Extending our definition of average rate of change in Section 3.1, we can define the average rate of change of any function over an interval in its domain as the change in the function divided by the length of the interval. Likewise, we can then go on to define the instantaneous rate of change as the limit of the average rate of change as the length of the interval goes to zero.

Why Peas Wrinkle

British geneticists have recently discovered that the wrinkling trait comes from an extra piece of DNA that prevents the gene that directs starch synthesis from functioning properly. With the plant's starch conversion impaired, sucrose and water build up in the young seeds. As the seeds mature, they lose much of this water, and the shrinkage leaves them wrinkled.

DEFINITIONS

The **average rate of change** of a function $f(x)$ over the interval from x to $x + h$ is

$$\text{Average rate of change} = \frac{f(x+h) - f(x)}{h}.$$

The **(instantaneous) rate of change** of f at x is the derivative

$$f'(x) = \lim_{h\to 0} \frac{f(x+h) - f(x)}{h},$$

provided the limit exists.

EXAMPLE 10 *Sensitivity to Change.* The Austrian monk Gregor Johann Mendel (1822–1884), working with garden peas and other plants, provided the first scientific explanation of hybridization. His careful records showed that if p (a number between 0 and 1) is the frequency of the gene for smooth skin in peas (dominant) and $(1 - p)$ is the frequency of the gene for wrinkled skin in peas, then the proportion of smooth-skinned peas in the population at large is

$$y = 2p(1 - p) + p^2 = 2p - p^2.$$

The graph of y versus p in Fig. 3.27(a) suggests that the value of y is more sensitive to a change in p when p is small than when p is large. Indeed, this is borne out by the derivative graph in Fig. 3.27(b), which shows that dy/dp is close to 2 when p is near 0 and close to 0 when p is near 1.

We will be able to say more about how sensitive functions are to changes in their variables when we get to Section 3.7.

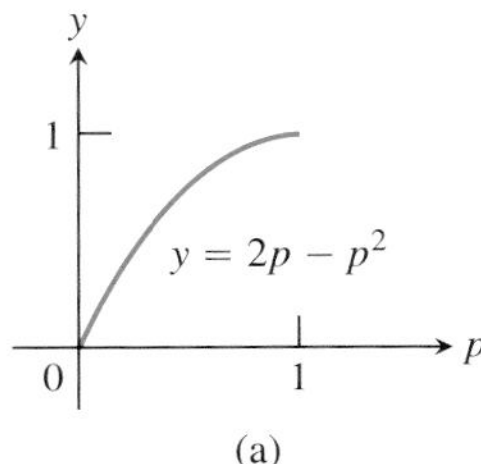

(a)

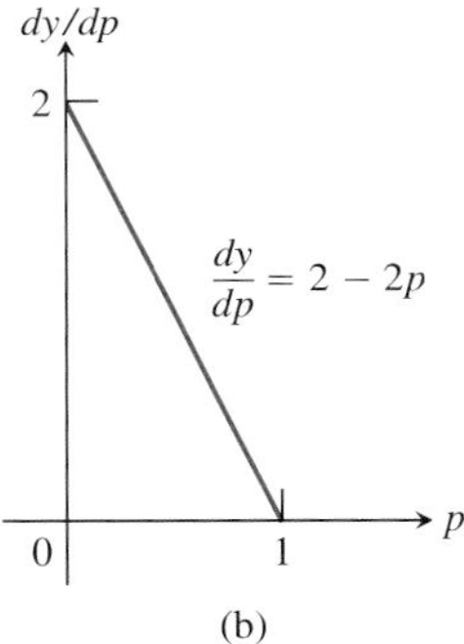

(b)

3.27 (a) The graph of $y = 2p - p^2$, describing the proportion of smooth-skinned peas. (b) The graph of dy/dp.

Derivatives in Economics

Economists often call the derivative of a function the **marginal value** of the function.

EXAMPLE 11 *Marginal Cost.* Suppose it costs a company $c(x)$ dollars to produce x tons of steel in a week. It costs more to produce $x + h$ tons in a week, and the cost difference, divided by h, is the average increase in cost per ton.

$$\frac{c(x+h) - c(x)}{h} = \text{average increase in cost per ton} \tag{8}$$

The limit of the ratio as $h \to 0$ is the marginal cost when x tons of steel are produced.

$$c'(x) = \lim_{h\to 0} \frac{c(x+h) - c(x)}{h} = \text{marginal cost} \tag{9}$$

How are we to interpret this derivative? First of all, it is the slope of the graph of c at the point marked P in Fig. 3.28. But there is more.

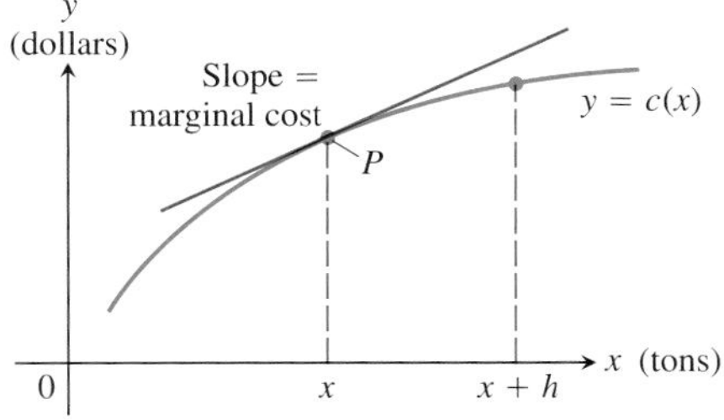

3.28 Weekly steel production: $c(x)$ is the cost of producing x tons in one week.

Figure 3.29 on the following page shows an enlarged view of the curve and its tangent at P. We can see that if the company, currently producing x tons every week, increases its production by one ton, then the additional cost

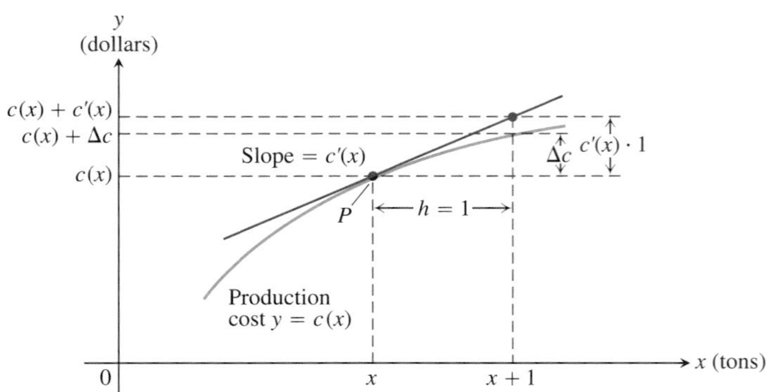

3.29 As weekly steel production increases from x to $x + 1$ tons, the cost curve rises by the amount Δc. The tangent line rises by the amount Slope · run $= c'(x) \cdot 1 = c'(x)$. Since $(\Delta c)/h \approx c'(x)$, we have $\Delta c \approx c'(x)$ when $h = 1$.

$\Delta c = c(x + 1) - c(x)$ of producing that one ton is approximately $c'(x)$. That is,

$$\Delta c \approx c'(x) \qquad \text{when} \qquad h = 1. \tag{10}$$

Herein lies the economic importance of marginal cost: It estimates the cost of producing one unit beyond the present production level.

EXAMPLE 12 *Marginal Cost (continued).* Suppose it costs

$$c(x) = x^3 - 6x^2 + 15x$$

dollars to produce x stoves and your shop is currently producing 10 stoves a day. About how much extra will it cost to produce one more stove a day?

Solution The cost of producing one more stove a day when 10 are produced is about $c'(10)$. Since

$$\begin{aligned} c'(x) &= \frac{d}{dx}(x^3 - 6x^2 + 15x) \\ &= 3x^2 - 12x + 15, \\ c'(10) &= 3(100) - 12(10) + 15 \\ &= 195. \end{aligned}$$

The additional cost will be about \$195 if you produce 11 stoves a day.

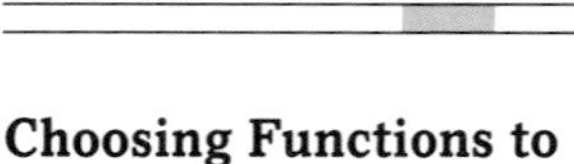

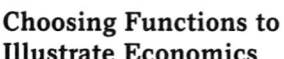

Choosing Functions to Illustrate Economics

In case you are wondering why economists use polynomials of low degree to illustrate complicated phenomena like cost and revenue, here is the rationale: While formulas for real phenomena are rarely available in any given instance, the theory of economics can still provide valuable guidance. The functions about which theory speaks can often be illustrated with low degree polynomials. Cubic polynomials provide a good balance between being easy to work with and being complicated enough to illustrate important points.

EXAMPLE 13 *Marginal Revenue.* If

$$r(x) = x^3 - 3x^2 + 12x$$

gives the dollar revenue from selling x thousand candy bars, the marginal revenue when x thousand are sold is

$$\begin{aligned} r'(x) &= \frac{d}{dx}(x^3 - 3x^2 + 12x) \\ &= 3x^2 - 6x + 12. \end{aligned}$$

As with marginal cost, the marginal revenue function estimates the increase in revenue that will result from selling one additional unit. If you currently sell 10 thousand candy bars a week, you can expect your revenue to increase by about

$$r'(10) = 3(100) - 6(10) + 12 = \$252$$

if you increase sales to 11 thousand bars a week.

Estimating f' from a Graph of f

When we record data in the laboratory or in the field, we usually imagine that we are recording the values of a function $y = f(x)$. We might be recording the pressure in a gas as a function of volume or the size of a population as a function of time. To see what the function looks like, we usually plot the data points and fit them with a curve. Even if we have no formula for the function from which to calculate the derivative $y' = f'(x)$, we can still graph f': We estimate the slopes on the graph of f and plot these slopes. The following examples show how this is done and what we can learn from the graph of f'.

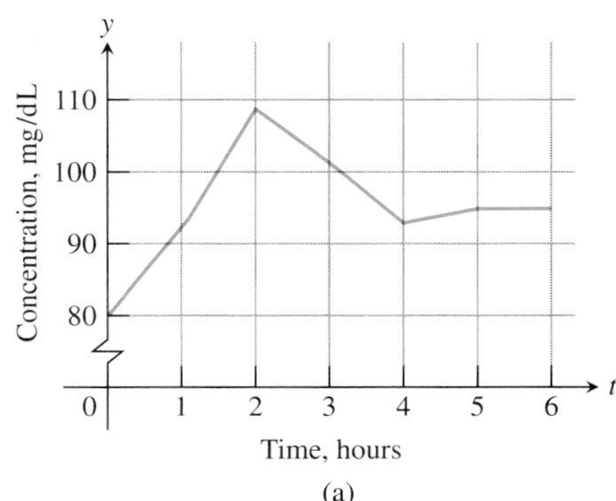

(a)

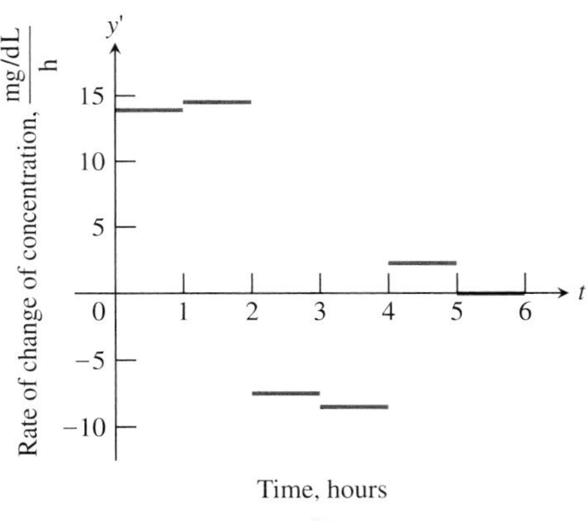

(b)

3.30 (a) The sugar concentration in the blood of a *Daedalus* pilot during a 6-h preflight endurance test. (b) The derivative of the pilot's blood-sugar concentration shows how rapidly the concentration rose and fell during various portions of the test. (*Source: The Daedalus Project: Physiological Problems and Solutions* by Ethan R. Nadel and Steven R. Bussolari, *American Scientist,* Vol. 76, No. 4, July–August 1988, p. 358.)

EXAMPLE 14 On April 23, 1988, the human-powered airplane *Daedalus* flew a record-breaking 119 km from Crete to the island of Santorini in the Aegean Sea, southeast of mainland Greece. During the 6-h endurance tests before the flight, researchers monitored the prospective pilots' blood-sugar concentrations. The concentration graph for one of the athlete-pilots is shown in Fig. 3.30(a), where the concentration in milligrams/deciliter is plotted against time in hours.

The graph is made of line segments connecting data points. The constant slope of each segment gives an estimate of the derivative of the concentration between measurements. We calculated the slopes from the coordinate grid and plotted the derivative as a step function in Fig. 3.30(b). To make the plot for the

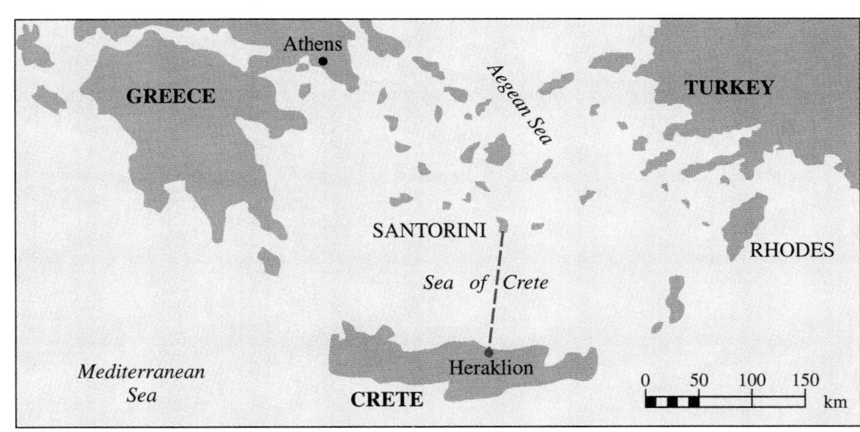

Daedalus's flight path on April 23, 1988.

The *Daedalus* flying over the Sea of Crete on April 23, 1988.

first hour, for instance, we observed that the concentration increased from about 79 mg/dL to 93 mg/dL. The net increase was $\Delta y = 93 - 79 = 14$ mg/dL. Dividing this by $\Delta t = 1$ h gave the rate of change:

$$\frac{\Delta y}{\Delta t} = \frac{14}{1} = 14 \text{ mg/dL per h.}$$

When we have so many data that the graph we get by connecting the data points resembles a smooth curve, we may wish to plot the derivative as a smooth curve. The next example shows how this is done.

EXAMPLE 15 Graph the derivative of the function $y = f(x)$ in Fig. 3.31(a).

Solution We draw a pair of axes, marking the horizontal axis in x-units and the vertical axis in y'-units (Fig. 3.31b). Next we sketch tangents to the graph of f at frequent intervals and use their slopes to estimate the values of $y' = f'(x)$ at these points. We plot the corresponding (x, y') pairs and connect them with a smooth curve.

From the graph of $y' = f'(x)$ we see at a glance

1. where f's rate of change is positive, negative, or zero;
2. the rough size of the growth rate at any x and its size in relation to the size of $f(x)$;
3. where the rate of change itself is increasing or decreasing.

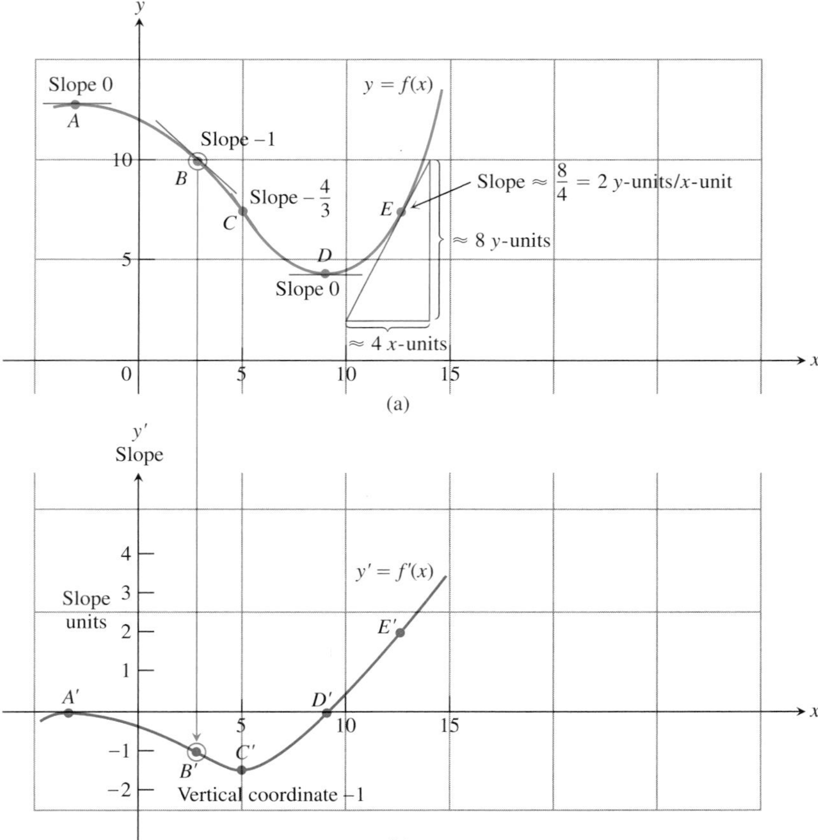

3.31 We made the graph of $y' = f'(x)$ in (b) by plotting slopes from the graph of $y = f(x)$ in (a). The vertical coordinate of B' is the slope at B, and so on. The graph of $y' = f'(x)$ is a visual record of how the slope of f changes with x.

Exercises 3.3

Exercises 1–8 give the position $s = f(t)$ of a body moving along a coordinate line during a time interval $a \le t \le b$, with s in meters and t in seconds.

a) Find the body's displacement and average velocity for the interval.

b) Find the body's speed and acceleration at the beginning and end of the interval.

1. $s = 0.8t^2, \quad 0 \le t \le 10$ (free fall on the moon)
2. $s = 1.86t^2, \quad 0 \le t \le 0.5$ (free fall on Mars)
3. $s = -t^3 + 3t^2 - 2t, \quad 0 \le t \le 2$
4. $s = -t^3 + 3t^2 - 5, \quad 0 \le t \le 2$
5. $s = \dfrac{25}{t^2} - \dfrac{5}{t}, \quad 1 \le t \le 5$
6. $s = \dfrac{25}{t+5}, \quad -4 \le t \le 0$
7. $s = 2t - 4\sqrt{t}, \quad 1 \le t \le 4$
8. $s = 4t\sqrt{t} - t, \quad 1 \le t \le 9$
9. The equations for free fall at the surfaces of Mars and Jupiter (s in meters, t in seconds) are Mars, $s = 1.86t^2$; Jupiter, $s = 11.44t^2$. How long would it take a rock falling from rest to reach a velocity of 16.6 m/sec (about 100 km/h) on each planet?
10. A rock thrown vertically upward from the surface of the moon at a velocity of 24 m/sec (about 86 km/h) reaches a height of $s = 24t - 0.8t^2$ meters in t seconds.
    a) Find the rock's velocity and acceleration at time t. (The acceleration in this case is the acceleration of gravity on the moon.)
    b) How long does it take the rock to reach its highest point?
    c) How high does the rock go?
    d) How long does it take the rock to reach half its maximum height?
    e) How long is the rock aloft?
11. On Earth, in the absence of air, the rock in Exercise 10 would reach a height of $s = 24t - 4.9t^2$ meters in t seconds.
    a) Find the rock's velocity and acceleration at time t.
    b) How long would it take the rock to reach its highest point?
    c) How high would the rock go?
    d) How long would it take the rock to reach half its maximum height?
    e) How long would the rock be aloft?
12. Explorers on a small airless planet used a spring gun to launch a ball bearing vertically upward from the surface at a launch velocity of 15 m/sec. Because the acceleration of gravity at the planet's surface was g_s m/sec^2, the explorers expected the ball bearing to reach a height of $s = 15t - (1/2)g_s t^2$ meters t sec later. The ball bearing reached its maximum height 20 sec after being launched. What was the value of g_s?
13. A 45-caliber bullet fired straight up from the surface of the moon would reach a height of $s = 832t - 2.6t^2$ feet after t seconds. On Earth, in the absence of air, its height would be $s = 832t - 16t^2$ feet after t seconds. How long will the bullet be aloft in each case?
14. When a bactericide was added to a nutrient broth in which bacteria were growing, the bacterium population continued to grow for a while, but then stopped growing and began to decline. The size of the population at time t (hours) was $b = 10^6 + 10^4 t - 10^3 t^2$ (Fig. 3.32). Find the growth rates at (a) $t = 0$; (b) $t = 5$; and (c) $t = 10$ hours.

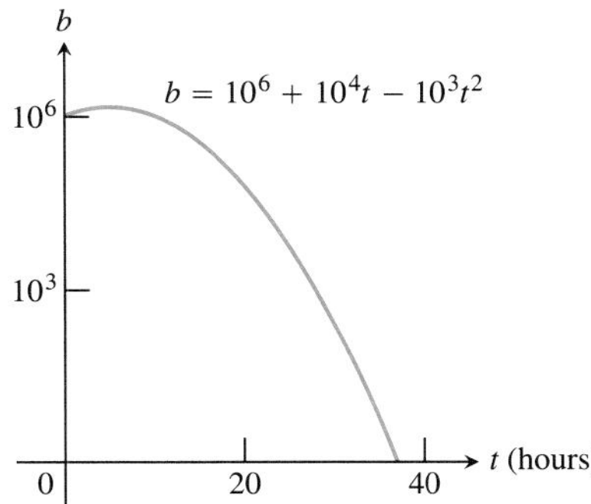

3.32 The graph of the bacterium population in Exercise 14.

15. When the tank in Fig. 3.33 is full, it takes 12 hours to drain it by opening the valve at the bottom. The depth y of fluid in the tank t hours after the valve is opened is given by the formula

$$y = 6\left(1 - \frac{t}{12}\right)^2 \text{ m.}$$

    a) Find the rate dy/dt (m/h) at which the tank is draining at time t.
    b) When is the fluid level in the tank falling fastest? slowest? What are the values of dy/dt at these times?
    c) Graph y and dy/dt together and discuss the behavior of y in relation to the signs and values of dy/dt.

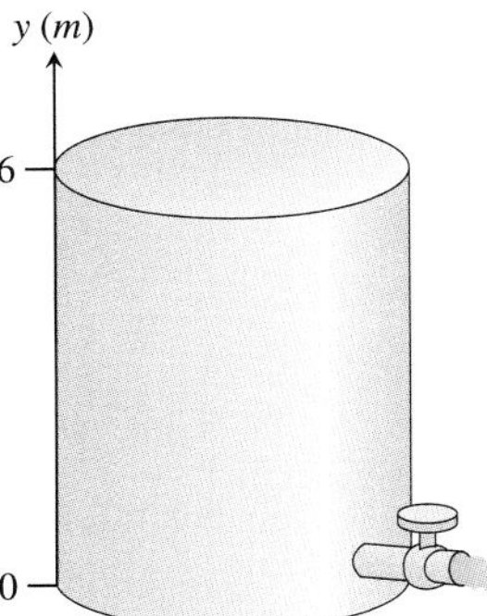

3.33 The tank in Exercise 15.

16. The number of gallons of water in a tank t minutes after the tank has started to drain is $Q(t) = 200(30 - t)^2$. How fast is the water running out at the end of 10 min? What is the average rate at which the water flows out during the first 10 min?

17. *Marginal Cost.* Suppose that the dollar cost of producing x washing machines is $c(x) = 2000 + 100x - 0.1x^2$.

a) Find the average cost per machine of producing the first 100 washing machines.
b) Find the marginal cost when 100 washing machines are produced.
c) Show that the marginal cost when 100 washing machines are produced is approximately the cost of producing one more washing machine after the first 100 have been made, by calculating the latter cost directly.

18. *Marginal Revenue.* Suppose the revenue from selling x custom-made office desks is

$$r(x) = 2000\left(1 - \frac{1}{x+1}\right)$$

dollars.

a) Find the marginal revenue when x desks are produced.
b) Use the function $r'(x)$ to estimate the increase in revenue that will result from increasing production from 5 desks a week to 6 desks a week.
c) Find the limit of $r'(x)$ as $x \to \infty$. How would you interpret this number?

19. The position of a body at time t seconds is $s = t^3 - 6t^2 + 9t$ m. (a) Find the body's acceleration each time the velocity is zero. (b) Find the body's speed each time the acceleration is zero.

20. The velocity of a body is $v = 2t^3 - 9t^2 + 12t - 5$ m/sec at time t. (a) Find the body's speed each time the acceleration is zero. (b) Find the body's velocity each time the acceleration is zero.

21. The accompanying figure shows the velocity $v = ds/dt = f(t)$ (in m/sec) of a body moving along a coordinate line.

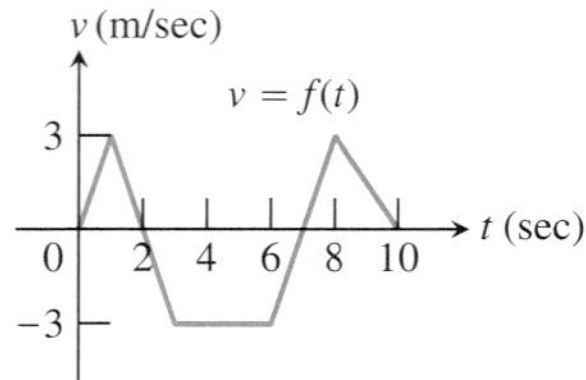

a) When does the body reverse direction?
b) When (approximately) is the body moving at a constant speed?
c) Graph the body's speed.

22. A particle P moves on the number line shown in part (a) of the accompanying figure. Part (b) shows the position of P as a function of time t.

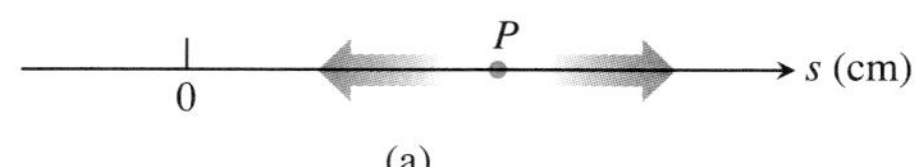

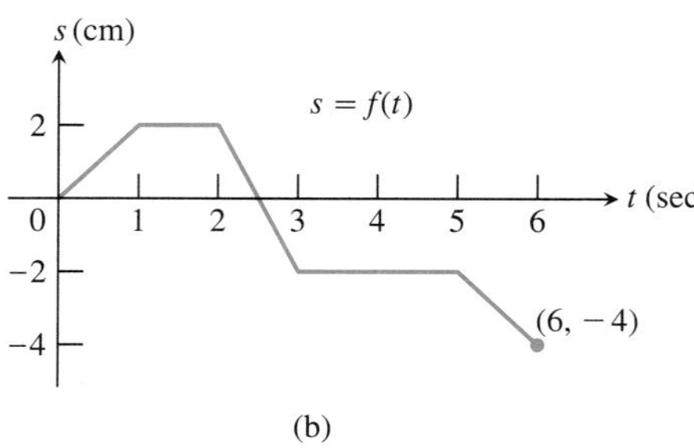

a) When is P moving to the left? moving to the right? standing still?
b) Graph the particle's velocity and speed (where defined).

23. When a model rocket is launched, the propellant burns for a few seconds, accelerating the rocket upward. After burnout, the rocket coasts upward for a while and then begins to fall. A small explosive charge pops out a parachute shortly after the rocket starts down. The parachute slows the rocket to keep it from breaking when it lands.

Figure 3.34 shows velocity data from the flight of a model rocket. Use the data to answer the following.

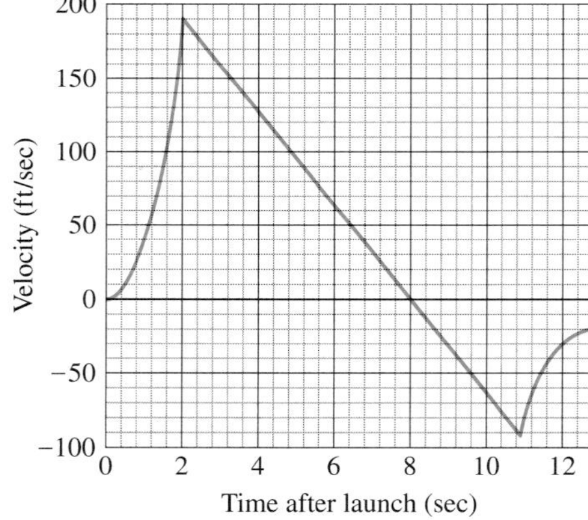

3.34 Velocity of the model rocket in Exercise 23.

a) How fast was the rocket climbing when the engine stopped?
b) For how many seconds did the engine burn?
c) When did the rocket reach its highest point? What was its velocity then?
d) When did the parachute pop out? How fast was the rocket falling then?
e) How long did the rocket fall before the parachute opened?
f) When was the rocket's acceleration greatest?
g) When was the acceleration constant? What was its value then (to the nearest integer)?

24. The accompanying figure shows the velocity $v = f(t)$ of a particle moving on a coordinate line.

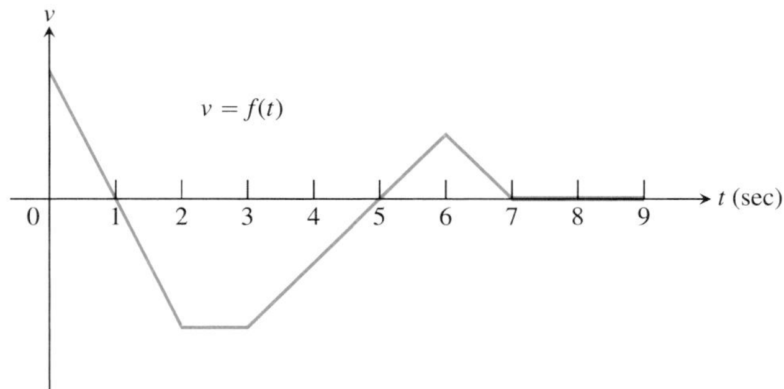

a) When does the particle move forward? move backward? speed up? slow down?
b) When is the particle's acceleration positive? negative? zero?
c) When does the particle move at its greatest speed?
d) When does the particle stand still for more than an instant?

25. *Galileo's Free-fall Formula.* Galileo developed a formula for a body's velocity during free fall by rolling balls from rest down increasingly steep inclined planks and looking for a limiting formula that would predict a ball's behavior when the plank was vertical and the ball fell freely (Fig. 3.35a). He found that, for any given angle of the plank, the ball's velocity t seconds into the motion was a constant multiple of t. That is, the velocity was given by a formula of the form $v = kt$. The value of the constant k depended on the inclination of the plank.

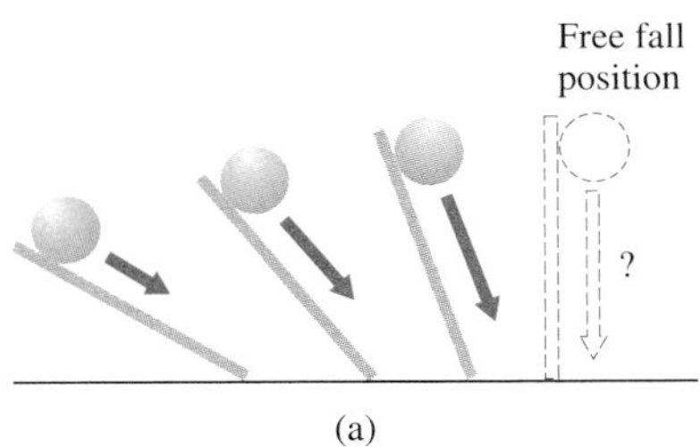

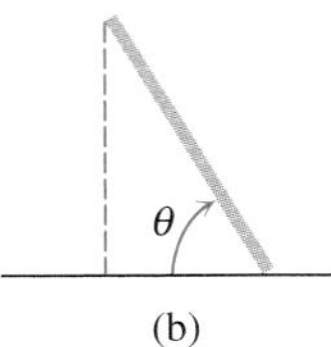

3.35 (a) Galileo's inclined plank experiment, and (b) the angle θ in Exercise 25.

In modern notation (Fig. 3.35b), with distance in meters and time in seconds, what Galileo determined by experiment was that, for any given angle θ, the ball's velocity t seconds into the roll was

$$v = 9.8\ (\sin\theta)t \text{ m/sec.}$$

a) What is the equation for the ball's velocity during free fall?
b) Building on your work in (a), what constant acceleration does a freely falling body experience near the surface of the earth?

26. *Free Fall from the Tower of Pisa.* Had Galileo dropped a cannonball from the tower of Pisa, 179 ft above the ground, the ball's height aboveground t seconds into the fall would have been $s = 179 - 16t^2$.

a) What would have been the ball's velocity, speed, and acceleration at time t?
b) About how long would it have taken the ball to hit the ground?
c) What would have been the ball's velocity at the moment of impact?

Exercises 27 and 28 are about the graphs in Fig. 3.36. The graphs in part (a) show the numbers of rabbits and foxes in a small arctic population. They are plotted as functions of time for 200 days. The number of rabbits increases at first, as the rabbits reproduce. But the foxes prey on the rabbits and, as the number of foxes increases, the rabbit population levels off and then drops. Figure 3.36(b) shows the graph of the derivative of the rabbit population. We made it by plotting slopes, as in Example 15.

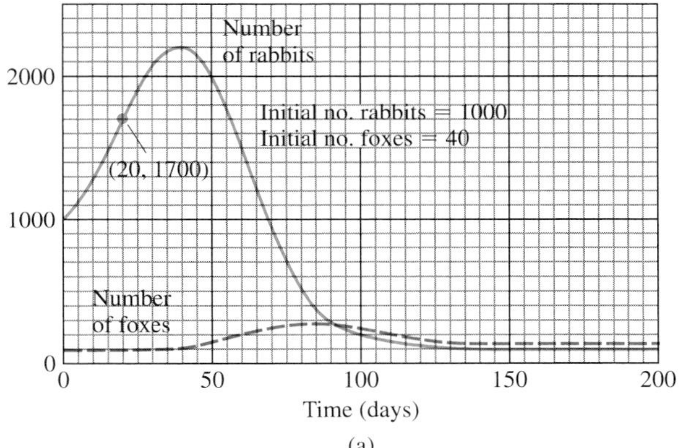

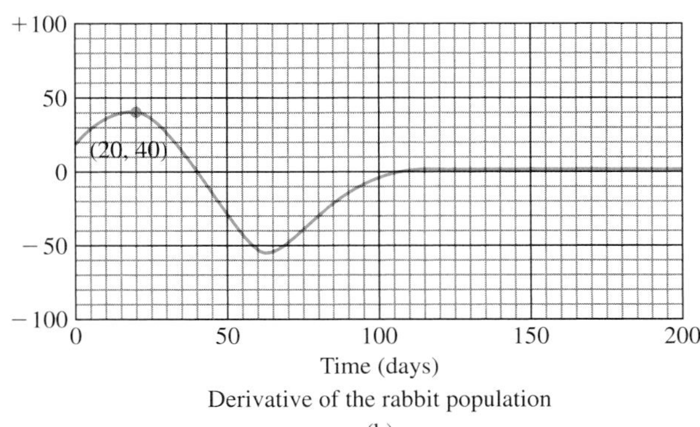

3.36 Rabbits and foxes in an arctic predator-prey food chain. (*Source: Differentiation* by W. U. Walton et al., Project CALC, Education Development Center, Inc., Newton, Mass., 1975, p. 86.)

27. **a)** What is the value of the derivative of the rabbit population in Fig. 3.36 when the number of rabbits is largest? smallest?

b) What is the size of the rabbit population in Fig. 3.36 when its derivative is largest? smallest?

28. In what units should the slopes of the rabbit and fox population curves be measured?

Match the graphs of the functions in Exercises 29–32 with the graphs of the derivatives in the following list:

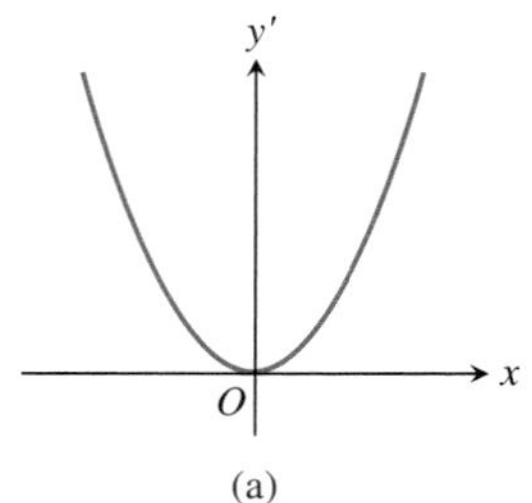

(a)

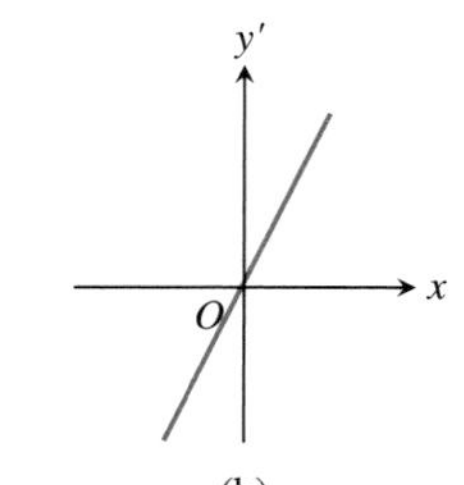

(b)

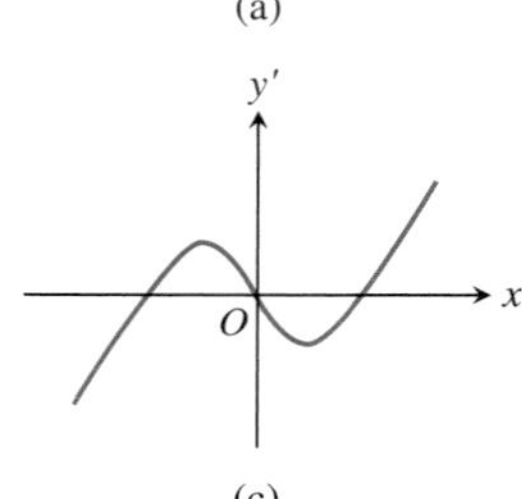

(c)

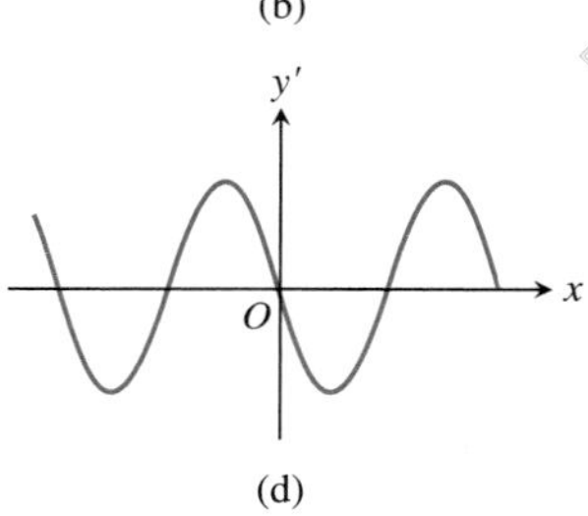

(d)

29.

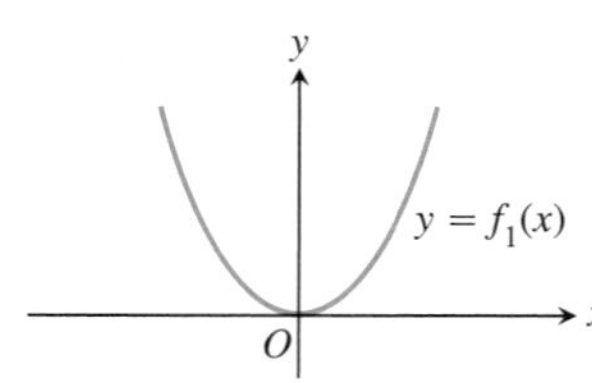

30.

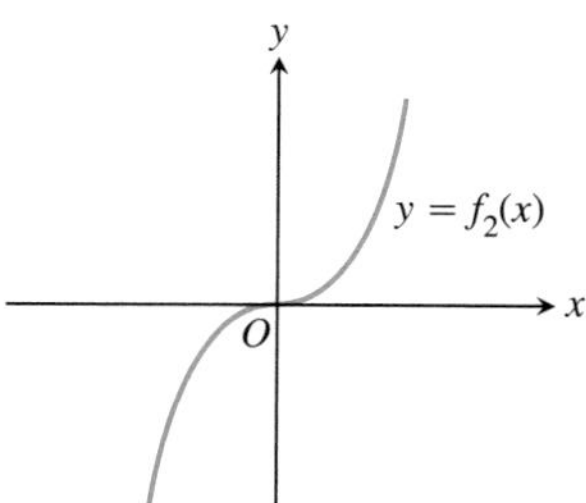

31.

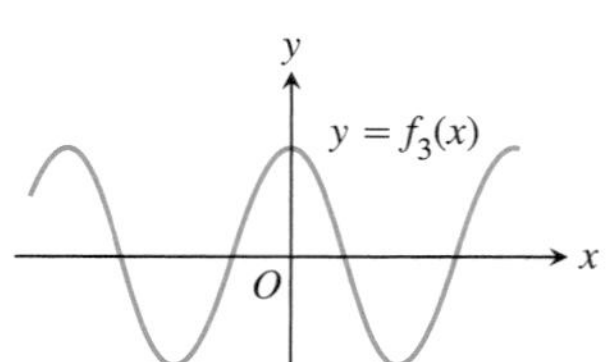

32.

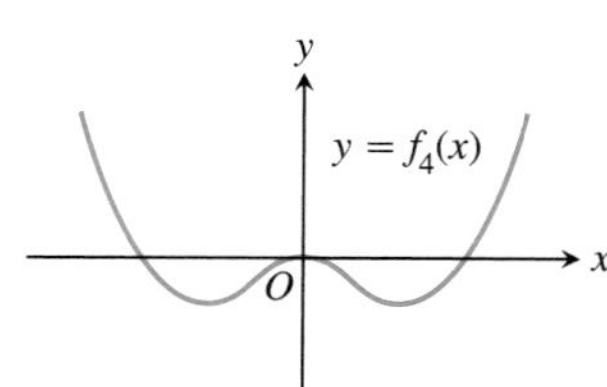

33. The graphs in Fig. 3.37 show the position s, velocity $v = ds/dt$, and acceleration $a = d^2s/dt^2$ of a body moving along a coordinate line as functions of time t. Which graph is which?

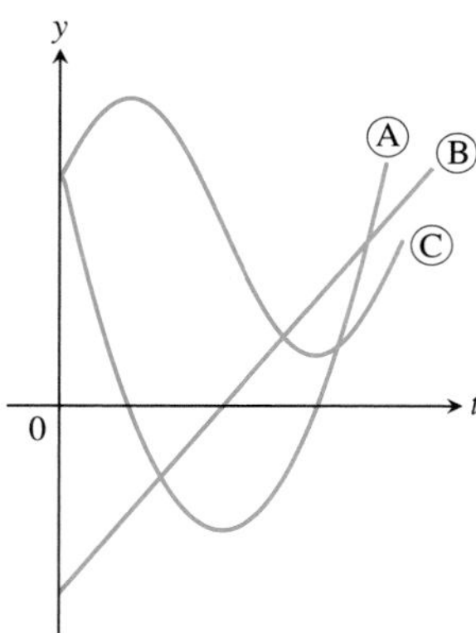

3.37 The graphs for Exercise 33.

Give reasons for your answers.

34. The graphs in Fig. 3.38 show the position s, the velocity $v = ds/dt$, and the acceleration $a = d^2s/dt^2$ of a body moving along the coordinate line as functions of time t. Which graph is which? Give reasons for your answers.

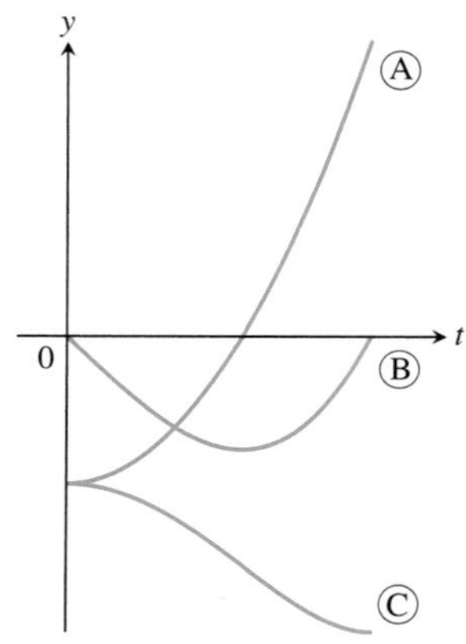

3.38 The graphs for Exercise 34.

35. The graph of the function $y = f(x)$ in the accompanying figure is made of line segments joined end to end.

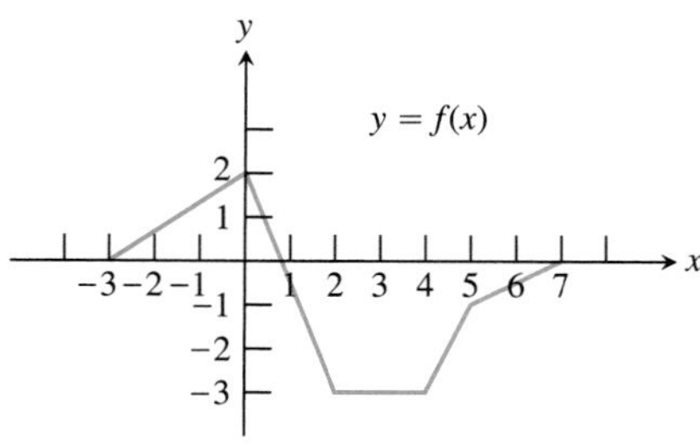

a) Graph the function's derivative (where defined).

b) At what values of x between $x = -3$ and $x = 7$ is the derivative not defined?

36. *Growth in the Economy.* The accompanying graph shows the average annual percentage change $y = f(t)$ in the U.S. gross national product (GNP) for the years 1983–1988. Graph dy/dt (where defined). (*Source: Statistical Abstracts of the United States,* 110th Edition, U.S. Department of Commerce, p. 427.)

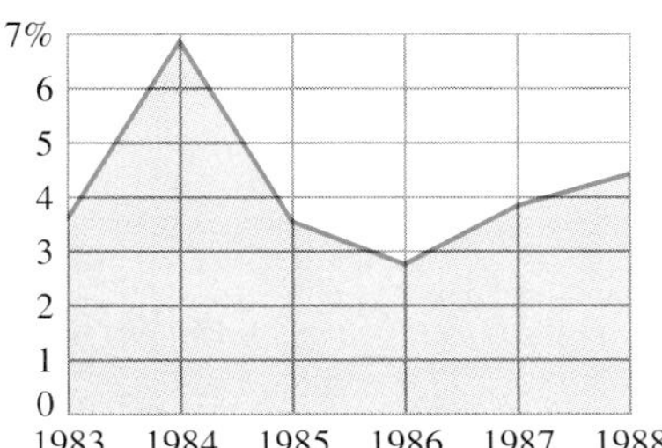

37. *Fruit Flies (Example 1, Section 3.1 continued).* Populations starting out in closed environments grow slowly at first, when there are relatively few members, then more rapidly as the number of reproducing individuals increases and resources are still abundant, then slowly again as the population reaches the carrying capacity of the environment.

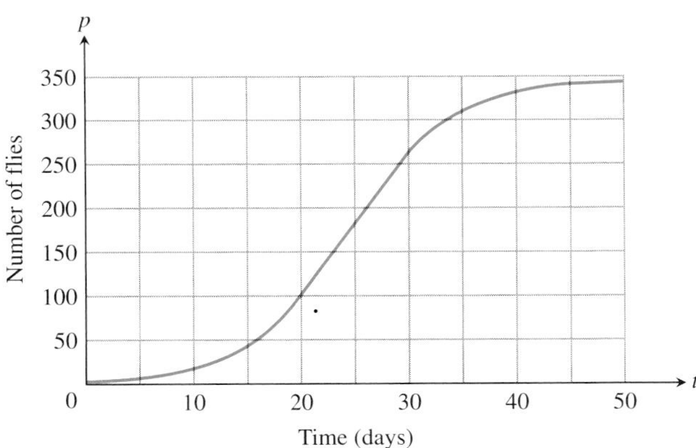

3.39 The graph for Exercise 37.

a) Use the graphical technique of Example 15 to graph the derivative of the fruit fly population introduced in Section 3.1. The graph of the population is reproduced here as Fig. 3.39. What units should be used on the horizontal and vertical axes for the derivative's graph?

b) During what days does the population seem to be increasing fastest? slowest?

38. *Pisa by Parachute.* The accompanying photograph shows Mike McCarthy parachuting from the top of the Tower of Pisa on August 5, 1988. Make a rough sketch to show the shape of the graph of his downward velocity (speed) during the jump.

Mike McCarthy of London jumped from the Tower of Pisa, then opened his parachute in what he said was a world record low-level parachute jump of 179 feet. (*Source: Boston Globe,* Saturday, Aug. 6, 1988.)

Writing for Your Own Knowledge

Answer the following questions in writing. Some answers will take only a sentence or two; others may require several paragraphs. Some explanations may also call for graphs or sketches.

1. What is the difference between average velocity and instantaneous velocity?
2. What are speed and acceleration?
3. What are some typical applications of derivatives?
4. How can you estimate f' from a graph of f?

EXPLORER PROGRAMS

Derivatives	Key in any function $y = f(x)$. The program will graph f and f' together, f and f'' together, or f' and f'' together.
PowerGrapher	Graphs functions and their derivatives in different colors in a common display.

3.4 Derivatives of Trigonometric Functions

Trigonometric functions are important because so many of the phenomena we want information about are periodic (earthquakes, heart rhythms, magnetic fields, weather). A surprising and beautiful theorem from advanced calculus says that every periodic function we are likely to use in mathematical modeling can be written as an algebraic combination of sines and cosines. This, in turn, means that the derivatives that describe the rates at which these periodic functions change can be written as algebraic combinations of the derivatives of the sines and cosines. This section shows how to differentiate sines, cosines, and other trigonometric functions.

The Derivative of the Sine

According to the definition of derivative (Section 3.1), the derivative of the sine is

$$\frac{d}{dx}(\sin x) = \lim_{h\to 0} \frac{\sin(x+h) - \sin x}{h}, \tag{1}$$

a function defined at every point x at which the limit exists. If we graph the quotient

$$y = \frac{\sin(x+h) - \sin x}{h} \tag{2}$$

over the interval $0 \le x \le 2\pi$ for increasingly small positive values of h (Fig. 3.40a), we find that the graphs appear to approach the graph of $\cos x$. We find the same behavior (Fig. 3.40b) for small negative values of h, and we would expect to see this behavior repeated throughout the real line because the sine is periodic. Is all this mere coincidence, or is the derivative of the sine really the cosine?

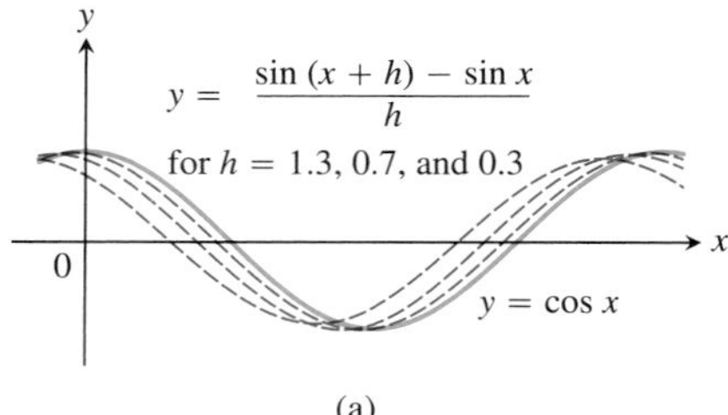

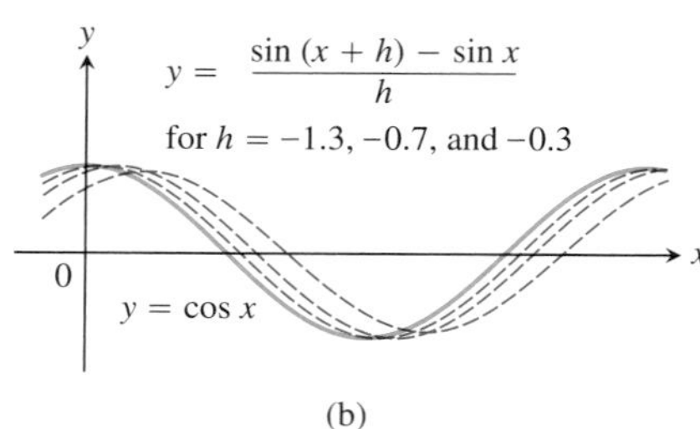

3.40 The graphs of $y = (\sin(x+h) - \sin x)/h$ (a) for $h = 1.3, 0.7$, and 0.3, and (b) for $h = -1.3, -0.7$, and -0.3 approach the graph of $y = \cos x$ as $|h|$ approaches 0.

To find out, we evaluate the limit in Eq. (1). For each value of x, we have

$$\lim_{h\to 0} \frac{\sin(x+h) - \sin x}{h}$$

$$= \lim_{h\to 0} \frac{(\sin x \cos h + \cos x \sin h) - \sin x}{h}$$ $\sin(x+h) = \sin x \cos h + \cos x \sin h$

$$= \lim_{h\to 0} \frac{\sin x(\cos h - 1) + \cos x \sin h}{h}$$ Regroup; factor out $\sin x$.

$$= \lim_{h\to 0}\left(\sin x \cdot \frac{\cos h - 1}{h}\right) + \lim_{h\to 0}\left(\cos x \cdot \frac{\sin h}{h}\right)$$ Limit Sum Rule

$$= \sin x \cdot \lim_{h\to 0} \frac{\cos h - 1}{h} + \cos x \cdot \lim_{h\to 0} \frac{\sin h}{h}$$ Limit Constant Multiple Rule. Only h is changing; x remains fixed as $h \to 0$.

$$= \sin x \cdot 0 + \cos x \cdot 1$$ Section 2.3, Exercise 44 and Eq. (5)

$$= \cos x.$$

Therefore, the derivative of $\sin x$ is $\cos x$.

In case you are still wondering why calculus uses radian measure when the rest of the world seems to use degrees, the answer lies in the argument that the derivative of the sine is the cosine. The derivative of $\sin x$ is $\cos x$ *only* if x is measured in radians. The argument requires that when h is a small increment in x,

$$\lim_{h \to 0} (\sin h)/h = 1.$$

This is true only for radian measure, as we discussed in Section 2.3.

$$\frac{d}{dx}(\sin x) = \cos x. \tag{3}$$

The sine and its derivative obey all the usual differentiation rules.

EXAMPLE 1

a) $y = x^2 - \sin x$: $\quad \dfrac{dy}{dx} = 2x - \dfrac{d}{dx}(\sin x) = 2x - \cos x$ — Difference Rule

b) $y = x^2 \sin x$: $\quad \dfrac{dy}{dx} = x^2 \dfrac{d}{dx}(\sin x) + 2x \sin x = x^2 \cos x + 2x \sin x$ — Product Rule

c) $y = \dfrac{\sin x}{x}$: $\quad \dfrac{dy}{dx} = \dfrac{x \cdot \dfrac{d}{dx}(\sin x) - \sin x \cdot 1}{x^2} = \dfrac{x \cos x - \sin x}{x^2}$ — Quotient Rule

The Derivative of the Cosine

Knowing that the derivative of the sine is the cosine might lead us to suspect that the derivative of the cosine would be the sine, and that is nearly correct. Here is what happens.

When we graph the difference quotient from the definition

$$\frac{d}{dx}(\cos x) = \lim_{h \to 0} \frac{\cos(x+h) - \cos x}{h} \tag{4}$$

over the interval $0 \le x \le 2\pi$ for increasingly small values of $|h|$ (Fig. 3.41), we find that the graphs approach the graph of *minus* the sine. We can confirm this suggested behavior analytically in the following way:

$$\begin{aligned}
\frac{d}{dx}(\cos x) &= \lim_{h \to 0} \frac{\cos(x+h) - \cos x}{h} && \text{Derivative definition} \\
&= \lim_{h \to 0} \frac{(\cos x \cos h - \sin x \sin h) - \cos x}{h} && \cos(x+h) = \cos x \cos h - \sin x \sin h \\
&= \lim_{h \to 0} \frac{\cos x (\cos h - 1) - \sin x \sin h}{h} && \text{Regroup; factor out } \cos x. \\
&= \lim_{h \to 0} \cos x \cdot \frac{\cos h - 1}{h} - \lim_{h \to 0} \sin x \cdot \frac{\sin h}{h} && \text{Limit Difference Rule} \\
&= \cos x \cdot \lim_{h \to 0} \frac{\cos h - 1}{h} - \sin x \cdot \lim_{h \to 0} \frac{\sin h}{h} && \text{Limit Constant Multiple Rule} \\
&= \cos x \cdot 0 - \sin x \cdot 1 && \text{Known values} \\
&= -\sin x.
\end{aligned}$$

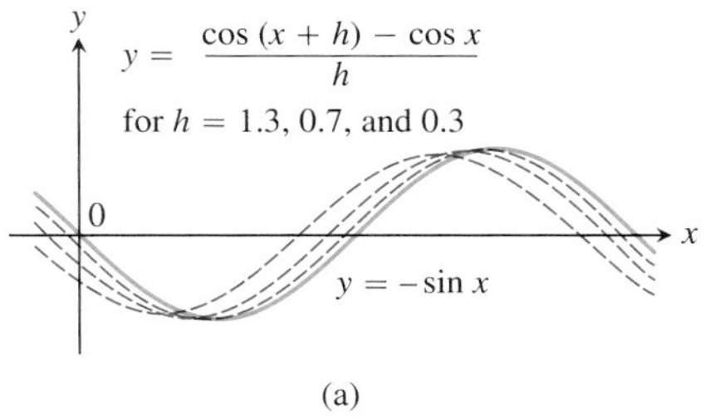

(a)

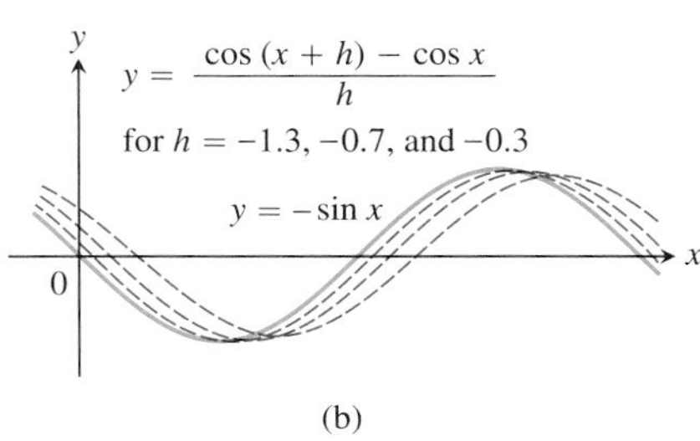

(b)

3.41 The graphs of $y = (\cos(x+h) - \cos x)/h$ (a) for $h = 1.3, 0.7$, and 0.3, and (b) for $h = -1.3, -0.7, -0.3$ approach the graph of $y = -\sin x$ as $|h|$ approaches 0.

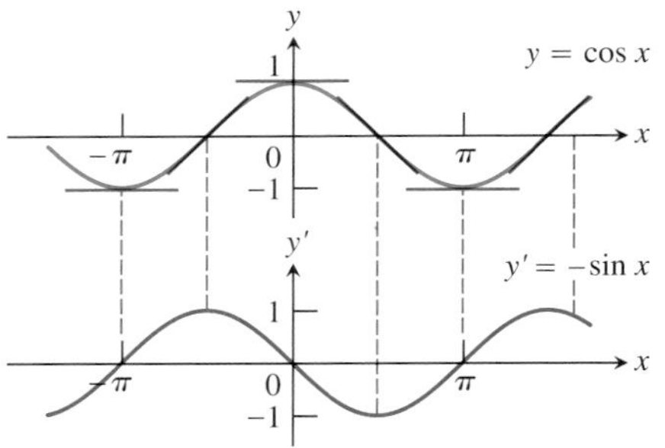

3.42 The curve $y' = -\sin x$ as the graph of the slopes of the tangents to the curve $y = \cos x$. (See Example 15, Section 3.3.)

In short,

$$\frac{d}{dx}(\cos x) = -\sin x. \tag{5}$$

Figure 3.42 shows another way to visualize this result.

EXAMPLE 2

a) $y = 5x + \cos x$

$$\frac{dy}{dx} = \frac{d}{dx}(5x) + \frac{d}{dx}(\cos x) \qquad \text{Sum Rule}$$

$$= 5 - \sin x$$

b) $y = \sin x \cos x$

$$\frac{dy}{dx} = \sin x \frac{d}{dx}(\cos x) + \cos x \frac{d}{dx}(\sin x) \qquad \text{Product Rule}$$

$$= \sin x(-\sin x) + \cos x(\cos x)$$

$$= \cos^2 x - \sin^2 x$$

c) $y = \dfrac{\cos x}{1 - \sin x}$

$$\frac{dy}{dx} = \frac{(1 - \sin x)\frac{d}{dx}(\cos x) - \cos x \frac{d}{dx}(1 - \sin x)}{(1 - \sin x)^2} \qquad \text{Quotient Rule}$$

$$= \frac{(1 - \sin x)(-\sin x) - \cos x(0 - \cos x)}{(1 - \sin x)^2}$$

$$= \frac{1 - \sin x}{(1 - \sin x)^2} \qquad \sin^2 x + \cos^2 x = 1$$

$$= \frac{1}{1 - \sin x}$$

Simple Harmonic Motion

The motion of a body bobbing up and down on the end of a spring is an example of *simple harmonic motion*. The next example describes a case in which there are no opposing forces like air resistance to slow the motion down.

EXAMPLE 3 A body hanging from a spring (Fig. 3.43) is stretched 5 units beyond its rest position and released at time $t = 0$ to bob up and down. Its position at any later time t is

$$s = 5 \cos t.$$

What are its velocity and acceleration at time t?

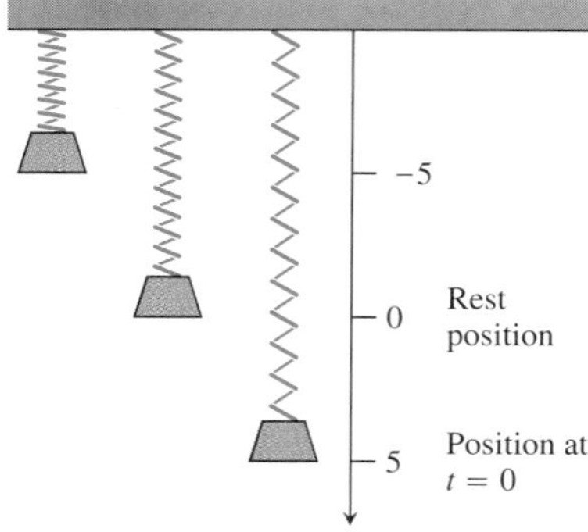

3.43 The body in Example 3.

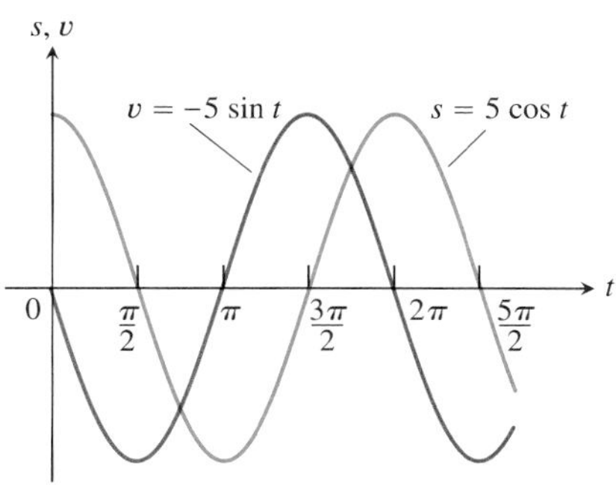

3.44 The graphs of the position and velocity of the body in Example 3.

Solution We have

Position: $s = 5\cos t$

Velocity: $v = \dfrac{ds}{dt} = \dfrac{d}{dt}(5\cos t) = 5\dfrac{d}{dt}(\cos t) = -5\sin t$

Acceleration: $a = \dfrac{dv}{dt} = \dfrac{d}{dt}(-5\sin t) = -5\dfrac{d}{dt}(\sin t) = -5\cos t.$

Here is what we can learn from these equations:

1. As time passes, the body moves up and down between $s = 5$ and $s = -5$ on the s-axis. The amplitude of the motion is 5. The period of the motion is 2π, the period of $\cos t$.
2. The function $\sin t$ attains its greatest magnitude (1) when $\cos t = 0$, as the graphs of the sine and cosine show (Fig. 3.44). Hence, the body's speed, $|v| = 5|\sin t|$, is greatest every time $\cos t = 0$, i.e., every time the body passes its rest position.

   The body's speed is zero when $\sin t = 0$. This occurs at the endpoints of the interval of motion, when $\cos t = \pm 1$.
3. The acceleration, $a = -5\cos t$, is zero only at the rest position, where the cosine is zero. When the body is anywhere else, the spring is either pulling on it or pushing on it. The acceleration is greatest in magnitude at the points farthest from the origin, where $\cos t = \pm 1$.

Jerk

A sudden change in acceleration is called a "jerk." When a ride in a car or a bus is jerky, it is not that the accelerations involved are necessarily large but that the changes in acceleration are abrupt. Jerk is what spills your soft drink. The derivative responsible for jerk is d^3s/dt^3.

DEFINITION

Jerk is the derivative of acceleration. If a body's position at time t is $s = f(t)$, the body's jerk at time t is

$$j = \frac{da}{dt} = \frac{d^3s}{dt^3}. \tag{6}$$

Recent tests have shown that motion sickness comes from accelerations whose changes in magnitude or direction take us by surprise. Keeping an eye on the road helps us to see the changes coming. A driver is less likely to become sick than a passenger reading in the backseat.

EXAMPLE 4

a) The jerk of the constant acceleration of gravity ($g = 32$ ft/sec^2) is zero:

$$j = \frac{d}{dt}(g) = 0.$$

We don't experience motion sickness if we are just sitting around.

b) The jerk of the simple harmonic motion in Example 3 is

$$j = \frac{da}{dt} = \frac{d}{dt}(-5\cos t) = 5\sin t.$$

It has its greatest magnitude when $\sin t = \pm 1$, not at the extremes of the displacement but at the origin, where the acceleration changes direction.

The Derivatives of the Other Basic Functions

Because $\sin x$ and $\cos x$ are differentiable functions of x, the related functions

$$\tan x = \frac{\sin x}{\cos x} \qquad \sec x = \frac{1}{\cos x}$$

$$\cot x = \frac{\cos x}{\sin x} \qquad \csc x = \frac{1}{\sin x}$$

are differentiable at every value of x at which they are defined. Their derivatives, calculated from the quotient rule, are given by the following formulas.

$$\frac{d}{dx}(\tan x) = \sec^2 x \quad (7) \qquad \frac{d}{dx}(\sec x) = \sec x \tan x \quad (8)$$

$$\frac{d}{dx}(\cot x) = -\csc^2 x \quad (9) \qquad \frac{d}{dx}(\csc x) = -\csc x \cot x \quad (10)$$

Notice the minus signs in the equations for the cotangent and cosecant.

To show how a typical calculation goes, we derive Eq. (7). The other derivations are left to you in Exercises 56–58.

EXAMPLE 5 Find dy/dx if $y = \tan x$.

Solution

$$\frac{d}{dx}(\tan x) = \frac{d}{dx}\left(\frac{\sin x}{\cos x}\right) = \frac{\cos x \frac{d}{dx}(\sin x) - \sin x \frac{d}{dx}(\cos x)}{\cos^2 x} \qquad \text{Quotient Rule}$$

$$= \frac{\cos x \cos x - \sin x(-\sin x)}{\cos^2 x}$$

$$= \frac{\cos^2 x + \sin^2 x}{\cos^2 x}$$

$$= \frac{1}{\cos^2 x} = \sec^2 x$$

EXAMPLE 6 Find y'' if $y = \sec x$.

Solution

$$y = \sec x$$

$$y' = \sec x \tan x \quad \text{Eq. 8}$$

$$y'' = \frac{d}{dx}(\sec x \tan x)$$

$$= \sec x \frac{d}{dx}(\tan x) + \tan x \frac{d}{dx}(\sec x) \quad \text{Product Rule}$$

$$= \sec x\,(\sec^2 x) + \tan x\,(\sec x \tan x)$$

$$= \sec^3 x + \sec x \tan^2 x$$

EXAMPLE 7

a) $\frac{d}{dx}(3x + \cot x) = 3 + \frac{d}{dx}(\cot x) = 3 - \csc^2 x$

b) $\frac{d}{dx}\left(\frac{2}{\sin x}\right) = \frac{d}{dx}(2 \csc x) = 2\frac{d}{dx}(\csc x)$

$$= 2(-\csc x \cot x) = -2 \csc x \cot x$$

The Continuity of Trigonometric Functions

Since the six basic trigonometric functions are differentiable, they are also continuous, by Theorem 1, Section 3.1. For each one, $\lim_{x\to c} f(x) = f(c)$ whenever $f(c)$ is defined. This means we can calculate the limits of many algebraic combinations and composites of these functions as $x \to c$ simply by evaluating them at $x = c$.

EXAMPLE 8

$$\lim_{x\to 0} \frac{\sqrt{2 + \sec x}}{\cos(\pi - \tan x)} = \frac{\sqrt{2 + \sec 0}}{\cos(\pi - \tan 0)} = \frac{\sqrt{2 + 1}}{\cos(\pi - 0)} = \frac{\sqrt{3}}{-1} = -\sqrt{3}$$

Exercises 3.4

In Exercises 1–16, find dy/dx.

1. $y = -10x + 3\cos x$

2. $y = 6x^2 - \sin x$

3. $y = 4 + \frac{2}{x} - \cos x$

4. $y = \frac{3}{x} + 5\sin x$

5. $y = \csc x - 4\sqrt{x} + 7$

6. $y = 3x(\sec x + 1)$

7. $y = x^2 \cot x - \frac{1}{x^2}$

8. $y = x\sin x + \cos x$

9. $y = (\sec x + \tan x)(\sec x - \tan x)$

10. $y = \sec x(\sin x + \cos x)$

11. $y = \frac{\cot x}{1 + \cot x}$

12. $y = \frac{\cos x}{1 + \sin x}$

13. $y = \frac{4}{\cos x} + \frac{1}{\tan x}$

14. $y = \frac{\cos x}{x} + \frac{x}{\cos x}$

15. $y = x^2 \sin x + 2x\cos x - 2\sin x$

16. $y = x^2 \cos x - 2x\sin x - 2\cos x$

In Exercises 17–20, find ds/dt.

17. $s = \tan t - t$

18. $s = t^2 - \sec t + 1$

19. $s = \frac{1 + \csc t}{1 - \csc t}$

20. $s = \frac{\sin t}{1 - \cos t}$

In Exercises 21–24, find $dr/d\theta$.

21. $r = 4 - \theta^2 \sin\theta$

22. $r = \theta\sin\theta + \cos\theta$

23. $r = \sec\theta\csc\theta$

24. $r = \sin\theta(1 + \sec\theta)$

In Exercises 25–28, find dp/dq.

25. $p = 5 + \dfrac{1}{\cot q}$ **26.** $p = \cos q\ (1 + \csc q)$

27. $p = \dfrac{\sin q + \cos q}{\cos q}$ **28.** $p = \dfrac{\tan q}{1 + \tan q}$

29. Find y'' if (a) $y = \csc x$, (b) $y = \sec x$.

30. Find $y^{(4)} = d^4y/dx^4$ if (a) $y = -2 \sin x$, (b) $y = 9 \cos x$.

In Exercises 31–34, graph the curves over the given intervals, together with their tangents at the given values of x. Label each curve and tangent with its equation.

31. $y = \sin x, \quad -3\pi/2 \le x \le 2\pi$
$x = -\pi,\ 0,\ 3\pi/2$

32. $y = \tan x, \quad -\pi/2 < x < \pi/2$
$x = -\pi/3,\ 0,\ \pi/3$

33. $y = \sec x, \quad -\pi/2 < x < \pi/2$
$x = -\pi/3,\ \pi/4$

34. $y = 1 + \cos x, \quad -3\pi/2 \le x \le 2\pi$
$x = -\pi/3,\ 3\pi/2$

35. Show that the graphs of $y = \sec x$ and $y = \cos x$ have horizontal tangents at $x = 0$.

36. Show that the graphs of $y = \tan x$ and $y = \cot x$ never have horizontal tangents.

Do the graphs of the functions in Exercises 37–40 have any horizontal tangents in the interval $0 \le x \le 2\pi$? If so, where? If not, why not? You may want to visualize your findings by graphing the functions with a grapher.

37. $y = x + \sin x$ **38.** $y = 2x + \sin x$

39. $y = x + \cos x$ **40.** $y = x + 2 \cos x$

Find the limits in Exercises 41–44.

41. $\lim_{x\to 2} \sin\left(\dfrac{1}{x} - \dfrac{1}{2}\right)$

42. $\lim_{x\to -\pi/6} \sqrt{1 + \cos(\pi \csc x)}$

43. $\lim_{x\to 0} \sec\left(\cos x + \pi \tan\left(\dfrac{\pi}{4 \sec x}\right) - 1\right)$

44. $\lim_{x\to 0} \sin\left(\dfrac{\pi + \tan x}{\tan x - 2 \sec x}\right)$

45. Is there a value of b that will make

$$f(x) = \begin{cases} x + b, & x < 0 \\ \cos x, & x \ge 0 \end{cases}$$

continuous at $x = 0$? If so, what is it? Give reasons for your answer.

46. *Continuation of Exercise 45.* Is there a value of b that will make the function f in Exercise 45 differentiable at $x = 0$? If so, what is it? Give reasons for your answer.

The equations in Exercises 47 and 48 give the position $s = f(t)$ of a body moving on a coordinate line (s in meters, t in seconds). Find the body's velocity, speed, acceleration, and jerk at time $t = \pi/4$ sec.

47. $y = 2 - 2 \sin t$ **48.** $y = \sin t + \cos t$

49. Find all points on the curve $y = \tan x$, $-\pi/2 < x < \pi/2$, where the tangent line is parallel to the line $y = 2x$. Sketch the curve and tangent(s) together, labeling each with its equation.

50. Find all points on the curve $y = \cot x$, $0 < x < \pi$, where the tangent line is parallel to the line $y = -x$. Sketch the curve and tangent(s) together, labeling each with its equation.

In Exercises 51 and 52, find an equation for (a) the tangent to the curve at P and (b) the horizontal tangent to the curve at Q.

51. **52.**

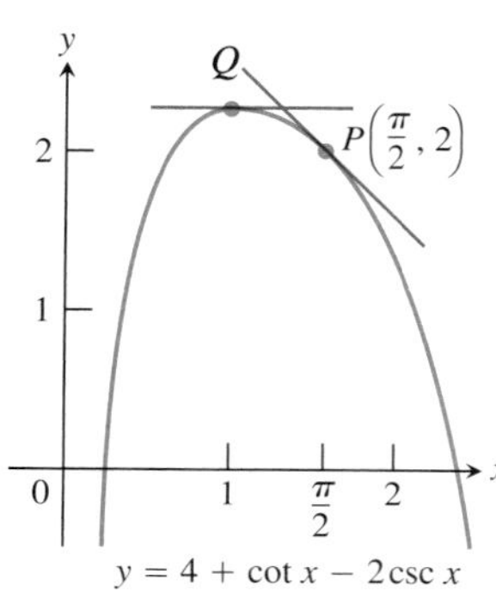

(Generated by Mathematica)

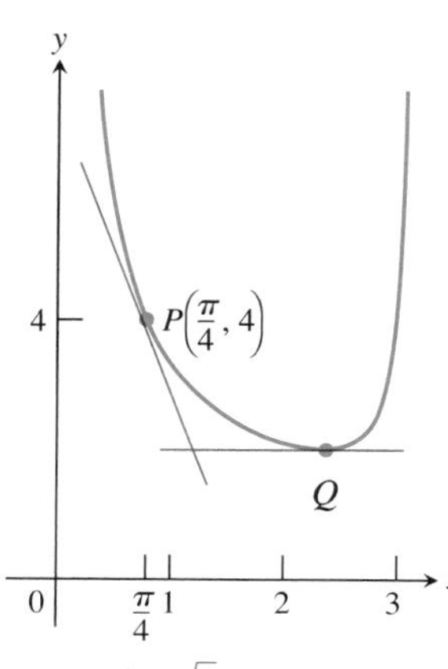

53. Find $\dfrac{d^{999}}{dx^{999}}(\cos x)$.

54. Find $\dfrac{d^{725}}{dx^{725}}(\sin x)$.

55. *Radians vs. Degrees.* What happens if you use degrees instead of radians to calculate

$$\lim_{h\to 0} \frac{\sin h}{h}?$$

To find out, set your calculator in degree mode and make a table of values of $(\sin h)/h$ for $h = 0.1, 0.01, 0.001$, and so on, as far as your calculator can go. Now multiply each entry in the table by $180/\pi$. What do you find? What would the derivative of $\sin x$ be if x were measured in degrees instead of radians? (Look at the derivation of Eq. 3 to find out.)

56. Derive Eq. (8) by writing $\sec x$ as $1/\cos x$ and differentiating with respect to x.

57. Derive Eq. (10) by writing $\csc x$ as $1/\sin x$ and differentiating with respect to x.

58. Derive Eq. (9) by writing $\cot x$ as $(\cos x)/(\sin x)$ and differentiating with respect to x.

59. Graph $y = \tan x$ and its derivative together on $[-\pi/2, \pi/2]$. Then use the graph of the derivative to answer the following questions. Does the graph of the tangent function appear to have a smallest slope? a largest slope? Is the slope ever negative? Give reasons for your answers.

60. Graph $y = \cot x$ and its derivative together for $0 < x < \pi$. Then use the graph of the derivative to answer the following questions. Does the graph of the cotangent function appear to have a smallest slope? a largest slope? Is the slope ever positive? Give reasons for your answers.

Writing for Your Own Knowledge

Answer the following questions in writing. Some answers will take only a sentence or two; others may require several paragraphs. Some explanations may also call for graphs or sketches.

1. What are the derivatives of the six basic trigonometric functions?
2. What does the derivative of the sine function have to do with $\lim_{h\to 0} (\sin h)/h$?
3. Once you know the derivatives of the sine and cosine functions, how can you find the derivatives of the tangent, secant, cotangent, and cosecant functions?
4. What can you say about the continuity of trigonometric functions?
5. What is jerk?

EXPLORER PROGRAMS

Derivatives	Graphs the first and second derivatives of any function you key in.
PowerGrapher	Graphs functions and their derivatives in a common display.

3.5 *The Chain Rule*

We now know how to differentiate $\sin x$ and $x^2 - 4$, but how do we differentiate a composite like $\sin(x^2 - 4)$? The answer is, with the Chain Rule, which is probably the most widely used differentiation rule in mathematics.

EXAMPLE 1 The function $y = 6x - 10 = 2(3x - 5)$ is the composite of the functions $y = 2u$ and $u = 3x - 5$. How are the derivatives of these three functions related?

Solution We have

$$\frac{dy}{dx} = 6, \qquad \frac{dy}{du} = 2, \qquad \frac{du}{dx} = 3.$$

Since $6 = 2 \cdot 3$,

$$\frac{dy}{dx} = \frac{dy}{du} \cdot \frac{du}{dx}.$$

EXAMPLE 2 The function $y = 9x^2 + 6x + 1 = (3x + 1)^2$ is the composite of $y = u^2$ and $u = 3x + 1$. The derivatives involved are

$$\frac{dy}{dx} = \frac{d}{dx}(9x^2 + 6x + 1) = 18x + 6 = 6(3x + 1) = 6u$$

$$\frac{dy}{du} = \frac{d}{du}(u^2) = 2u$$

$$\frac{du}{dx} = \frac{d}{dx}(3x + 1) = 3.$$

Once again, $\dfrac{dy}{dx} = \dfrac{dy}{du} \cdot \dfrac{du}{dx}$.

3.45 When gear A takes x turns, gear B takes u turns, and gear C takes y turns. By comparing circumferences we see that $dy/du = 1/2$ and $du/dx = 3$. What is dy/dx?

EXAMPLE 3 In the gear train in Fig. 3.45, the ratios of the radii of gears A, B, and C are 3:1:2. If gear A turns x times, then gear B turns $u = 3x$ times and gear C turns $y = u/2 = (3/2)x$ times. In terms of derivatives,

$$\frac{dy}{du} = \frac{1}{2} \qquad \text{(C turns at one-half B's rate.)}$$

$$\frac{du}{dx} = 3 \qquad \text{(B turns at 3 times A's rate.)}$$

In this example, too, we can calculate dy/dx by multiplying dy/du by du/dx:

$$\frac{dy}{dx} = \frac{3}{2} = \frac{1}{2} \cdot 3 = \frac{dy}{du} \cdot \frac{du}{dx}.$$

The Chain Rule

The preceding examples all work because the derivative of a composite $f \circ g$ of two differentiable functions is the product of their derivatives. This is the observation we state formally as the Chain Rule. As in Section 1.2, the notation $f \circ g$ ("f of g") denotes the composite of the functions f and g, with f following g. The value of $f \circ g$ at a point x is $(f \circ g)(x) = f(g(x))$.

The Chain Rule (First Form)

Suppose that $f \circ g$ is the composite of the differentiable functions $y = f(u)$ and $u = g(x)$. Then $f \circ g$ is a differentiable function of x whose derivative is

$$(f \circ g)'(x) = f'[g(x)] \cdot g'(x). \qquad (1)$$

See Fig. 3.46.

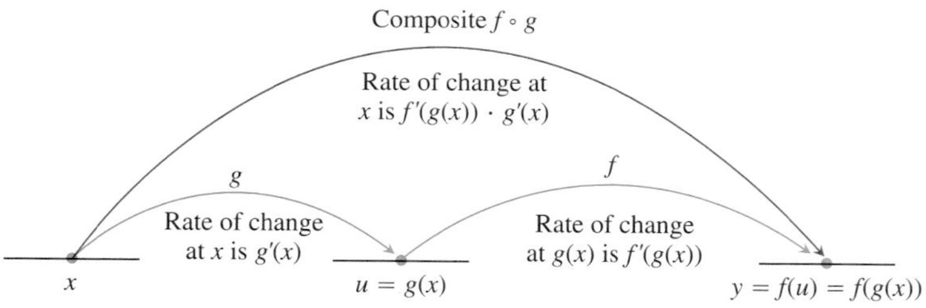

3.46 Rates of change multiply: The derivative of f of g at x is the derivative of f at the point $g(x)$ times the derivative of g at x.

Equation (1) names the functions involved. When we know what the functions are, as we usually do in any particular example, we can get by with writing the Chain Rule a shorter way.

Chain Rule (Shorter Form)

If y is a differentiable function of u, and u is a differentiable function of x, then

$$\frac{dy}{dx} = \frac{dy}{du} \cdot \frac{du}{dx}. \qquad (2)$$

You might think it would be a relatively easy matter to prove the Chain Rule by starting with the derivative definition the way we started the proofs of the Product and Quotient Rules. Unfortunately, this is the way the *hard* proof starts. The (relatively) easy proof begins with an equation in Section 3.7. We have therefore placed the proof of the Chain Rule in Appendix 3, to be read later. We'll direct your attention to it when the time comes.

EXAMPLE 4 Find $(f \circ g)'(x)$ at $x = 2$ if f and g are differentiable functions with $g(2) = 3$, $g'(2) = 4$, and $f'(3) = -5$.

Solution Equation (1) gives

$$\begin{aligned}(f \circ g)'(x) &= f'[g(x)] \cdot g'(x)\\ (f \circ g)'(2) &= f'[g(2)] \cdot g'(2)\\ &= f'(3) \cdot g'(2)\\ &= (-5) \cdot 4 = -20.\end{aligned}$$

EXAMPLE 5 Find dy/dx if $y = \sin(x^2)$.

Solution We take $y = \sin u$ and $u = x^2$ and apply Eq. (2):

$$\begin{aligned}\frac{dy}{dx} &= \frac{dy}{du} \cdot \frac{du}{dx} && \text{Eq. (2)}\\ &= \cos u \cdot \frac{du}{dx} && y = \sin u,\ \frac{dy}{du} = \cos u\\ &= \cos(x^2) \cdot 2x && u = x^2,\ \frac{du}{dx} = 2x\\ &= 2x\cos(x^2).\end{aligned}$$

EXAMPLE 6 Find dy/dx at $x = 0$ if $y = \cos\left(\frac{\pi}{2} - 3x\right)$.

Solution Let $y = \cos u$ and $u = \frac{\pi}{2} - 3x$:

$$\frac{dy}{du} = -\sin u, \qquad \frac{du}{dx} = -3.$$

Then

$$\begin{aligned}\frac{dy}{dx} &= \frac{dy}{du} \cdot \frac{du}{dx} && \text{Eq. (2)}\\ &= -\sin u \cdot (-3)\\ &= 3\sin u\\ &= 3\sin\left(\frac{\pi}{2} - 3x\right) && \text{Substitute } u = \frac{\pi}{2} - 3x.\end{aligned}$$

and

$$\left.\frac{dy}{dx}\right|_{x=0} = 3\sin\left(\frac{\pi}{2}\right) = 3(1) = 3.$$

Integer Powers of Differentiable Functions

The Chain Rule enables us to differentiate powers like $y = \sin^5 x$ and $y = (2x + 1)^{-3}$ because these powers are composites:

$$y = \sin^5 x \quad \text{is} \quad u^5 \quad \text{with} \quad u = \sin x$$
$$y = (2x + 1)^{-3} \quad \text{is} \quad u^{-3} \quad \text{with} \quad u = 2x + 1.$$

If u is any differentiable function of x and $y = u^n$, then the Chain Rule in the form

$$\frac{dy}{dx} = \frac{dy}{du} \cdot \frac{du}{dx}$$

gives

$$\frac{dy}{dx} = \frac{d}{du}(u^n) \cdot \frac{du}{dx}$$
$$= nu^{n-1}\frac{du}{dx}.$$

Differentiating u^n with respect to u itself gives nu^{n-1}.

Power Chain Rule

If u^n is an integer power of a differentiable function $u(x)$, then u^n is differentiable and

$$\frac{d}{dx} u^n = nu^{n-1}\frac{du}{dx}. \tag{3}$$

$\sin^5 x$ is short for $(\sin x)^5$.

EXAMPLE 7

a) $$\frac{d}{dx}\sin^5 x = 5\sin^4 x \frac{d}{dx}(\sin x) = 5\sin^4 x \cos x$$

Eq. (3) with $u = \sin x$, $n = 5$

b) $$\frac{d}{dx}(2x + 1)^{-3} = -3(2x + 1)^{-4}\frac{d}{dx}(2x + 1) = -3(2x + 1)^{-4}(2) = -6(2x + 1)^{-4}$$

Eq. (3) with $u = 2x + 1$, $n = -3$

c) $$\frac{d}{dx}(5x^3 - x^4)^7 = 7(5x^3 - x^4)^6\frac{d}{dx}(5x^3 - x^4) = 7(5x^3 - x^4)^6(5 \cdot 3x^2 - 4x^3) = 7(5x^3 - x^4)^6(15x^2 - 4x^3)$$

Eq. (3) with $u = 5x^3 - x^4$, $n = 7$

d) $$\frac{d}{dx}\left(\frac{1}{3x - 2}\right) = \frac{d}{dx}(3x - 2)^{-1} = -1(3x - 2)^{-2}\frac{d}{dx}(3x - 2) = -1(3x - 2)^{-2}(3) = -\frac{3}{(3x - 2)^2}.$$

Eq. (3) with $u = 3x - 2$, $n = -1$

In part (d) we could also have found the derivative with the Quotient Rule.

TABLE 3.1
Derivative formulas that include the Chain Rule

$$\frac{d}{dx}(u^n) = nu^{n-1}\frac{du}{dx} \qquad (n \text{ an integer})$$
$$\frac{d}{dx}(\sin u) = \cos u \frac{du}{dx}$$
$$\frac{d}{dx}(\cos u) = -\sin u \frac{du}{dx}$$
$$\frac{d}{dx}(\tan u) = \sec^2 u \frac{du}{dx}$$
$$\frac{d}{dx}(\cot u) = -\csc^2 u \frac{du}{dx}$$
$$\frac{d}{dx}(\sec u) = \sec u \tan u \frac{du}{dx}$$
$$\frac{d}{dx}(\csc u) = -\csc u \cot u \frac{du}{dx}$$

Derivative Formulas That Include the Chain Rule

Many of the derivative formulas you will encounter in your scientific work already include the Chain Rule.

If f is a differentiable function of u, and u is a differentiable function of x, then substituting $y = f(u)$ in the Chain Rule formula

$$\frac{dy}{dx} = \frac{dy}{du} \cdot \frac{du}{dx}$$

leads to the formula

$$\frac{d}{dx} f(u) = f'(u)\frac{du}{dx}. \tag{4}$$

When we spell this out for the functions whose derivatives we have studied so far, we get the formulas in Table 3.1.

EXAMPLE 8

$$\frac{d}{dx}\underbrace{\left[\tan\left(\frac{1}{x}\right)\right]}_{f(u)} = \underbrace{\sec^2\left(\frac{1}{x}\right)}_{f'(u)} \cdot \underbrace{\frac{d}{dx}\left(\frac{1}{x}\right)}_{du/dx}$$
$$= \sec^2\left(\frac{1}{x}\right) \cdot \left(-\frac{1}{x^2}\right)$$
$$= -\frac{1}{x^2}\sec^2\left(\frac{1}{x}\right)$$

The "Inside-Outside" Rule

It sometimes helps to think about the Chain Rule the following way. If $y = f(g(x))$, Eq. (2) tells us that

$$\frac{dy}{dx} = f'[g(x)] \cdot g'(x). \tag{5}$$

In words, Eq. (5) says: To find dy/dx, differentiate the "outside" function f and leave the "inside" $g(x)$ alone; then multiply by the derivative of the inside.

EXAMPLE 9

$$\frac{d}{dx}\overset{\text{outside}}{\sin}\underbrace{(x^2 + x)}_{\text{inside}} = \overset{\text{derivative of the outside}}{\cos}\underbrace{(x^2 + x)}_{\text{inside left alone}} \cdot \underbrace{(2x + 1)}_{\text{derivative of the inside}}$$

Repeated Use of the Chain Rule

We sometimes have to use the Chain Rule two or more times to get a job done. Here is an example.

EXAMPLE 10 Find the derivative of

a) $f(x) = \cos^2 3x$ **b)** $g(t) = \tan(5 - \sin 2t)$.

Solution

a)
$$\begin{aligned} f'(x) &= \frac{d}{dx}\cos^2 3x \\ &= \frac{d}{dx}(\cos 3x)^2 \\ &= 2\cos 3x \cdot \frac{d}{dx}(\cos 3x) && \text{Power Chain Rule} \\ &= 2\cos 3x(-\sin 3x)\frac{d}{dx}(3x) && \text{Chain Rule} \\ &= 2\cos 3x(-\sin 3x)(3) \\ &= -6\cos 3x \sin 3x \end{aligned}$$

b)
$$\begin{aligned} g'(t) &= \frac{d}{dt}[\tan(5 - \sin 2t)] \\ &= \sec^2(5 - \sin 2t) \cdot \frac{d}{dt}(5 - \sin 2t) \\ &= \sec^2(5 - \sin 2t) \cdot (-\cos 2t) \cdot \frac{d}{dt}(2t) \\ &= \sec^2(5 - \sin 2t) \cdot (-\cos 2t) \cdot (2) \\ &= -2\cos 2t \sec^2(5 - \sin 2t) \end{aligned}$$

Combining Differentiation Rules

If a function involves a combination of sums, products, quotients, powers, or composites, we may need to combine different rules to find its derivative. Here is an example.

EXAMPLE 11 Find dy/dx for $y = \left(\frac{1-x}{1+x^2}\right)^2$.

Solution

$$\begin{aligned} y &= \left(\frac{1-x}{1+x^2}\right)^2 && u^n \\ \frac{dy}{dx} &= 2\left(\frac{1-x}{1+x^2}\right) \cdot \frac{d}{dx}\left(\frac{1-x}{1+x^2}\right) && nu^{n-1} \cdot \frac{du}{dx} \\ &= 2\left(\frac{1-x}{1+x^2}\right) \cdot \frac{(1+x^2)(-1) - (1-x)(2x)}{(1+x^2)^2} && \text{Quotient Rule} \\ &= \frac{2(1-x)}{1+x^2} \cdot \frac{-1 - x^2 - 2x + 2x^2}{(1+x^2)^2} \\ &= \frac{2(1-x)(x^2 - 2x - 1)}{(1+x^2)^3} \end{aligned}$$

Exercises 3.5

In Exercises 1–14, find dy/dx.

1. $y = 6u - 9, \quad u = \frac{1}{2}x^4$
2. $y = 2u^3, \quad u = 8x - 1$
3. $y = \sin(3x + 1)$
4. $y = \sin(7 - 5x)$
5. $y = \cos(-x/3)$
6. $y = \cos(\sqrt{3}x)$
7. $y = \tan(2x - x^3)$
8. $y = \tan(10x - 5)$
9. $y = \sec(x^2 + \sqrt{2})$
10. $y = \sec(3 - 8x)$
11. $y = -\csc(x^2 + 7x)$
12. $y = \frac{1}{2}\csc(1 - 2x)$
13. $y = 5\cot\left(\frac{2}{x}\right)$
14. $y = \cot\left(\pi - \frac{1}{x}\right)$

In Exercises 15–28, find dy/dx.

15. $y = (2x + 1)^5$
16. $y = (4 - 3x)^9$
17. $y = (x^2 + 1)^{-3}$
18. $y = (x + x^3)^{-2}$
19. $y = \dfrac{1}{5x - 7}$
20. $y = \dfrac{2}{x^2 + 6}$
21. $y = \left(1 - \frac{x}{7}\right)^{-7}$
22. $y = \left(\frac{x}{2} - 1\right)^{-10}$
23. $y = \left(\frac{x^2}{8} + x - \frac{1}{x}\right)^4$
24. $y = \left(\frac{x}{5} + \frac{1}{5x}\right)^5$
25. $y = (\csc x + \cot x)^{-1}$
26. $y = -(\sec x + \tan x)^{-1}$
27. $y = \sin^4 x + \cos^{-2} x$
28. $y = \sin^{-5}x - \cos^3 x$

In Exercises 29–44, use the Chain Rule in combination with other differentiation rules to find the derivative of the function with respect to x.

29. $y = x^5 - 25\sin\left(\frac{x}{5}\right)$
30. $y = 2\cos\left(\frac{x}{2}\right) + \frac{x^2}{4}$
31. $y = x\tan 3x + 7$
32. $y = 2x\sec 2x$
33. $y = \frac{1}{21}(3x - 2)^7 + \left(4 - \frac{1}{2x^2}\right)^{-1}$
34. $y = (5 - 2x)^{-3} + \frac{1}{8}\left(\frac{2}{x} + 1\right)^4$
35. $y = x^3(2x - 5)^4$
36. $y = (1 - x)(3x^2 - 5)^5$
37. $y = (4x + 3)^4(x + 1)^{-3}$
38. $y = (2x - 5)^{-1}(x^2 - 5x)^6$
39. $y = \left(\dfrac{\sin x}{1 + \cos x}\right)^2$
40. $y = \left(\dfrac{1 + \cos x}{\sin x}\right)^{-1}$
41. $f(x) = \left(\dfrac{x}{x - 1}\right)^{-3}$
42. $g(x) = \left(\dfrac{x}{x - 1}\right)^2 - \dfrac{4}{x - 1}$
43. $h(x) = \sin^3 x \tan 4x$
44. $k(x) = \cos^4 x \cot 7x$

In Exercises 45–48, find ds/dt.

45. $s = \cos\left(\frac{\pi}{2} - 3t\right)$
46. $s = \cos(\pi - 4\pi t)$
47. $s = \frac{4}{3\pi}\sin 3t + \frac{4}{5\pi}\cos 5t$
48. $s = \sin\left(\frac{3\pi}{2}t\right) + \cos\left(\frac{7\pi}{4}t\right)$

In Exercises 49–52, find $dr/d\theta$.

49. $r = \tan(2 - \theta)$
50. $r = \sec 2\theta \tan 2\theta$
51. $r = \theta\sin\left(\frac{\theta^2}{2}\right)$
52. $r = \theta^2\cos\left(\frac{1}{\theta}\right)$

In Exercises 53–62, find dy/dt.

53. $y = \sin^2(\pi t - 2)$
54. $y = \sec^2 \pi t$
55. $y = (1 + \cos 2t)^{-4}$
56. $y = (1 + \cot(t/2))^{-2}$
57. $y = \cos(\sin t)$
58. $y = \sin(\sin t)$
59. $y = \sin(\cos(2t - 5))$
60. $y = \cos\left(5\sin\left(\frac{t}{3}\right)\right)$
61. $y = \left(1 + \tan^4\left(\frac{t}{12}\right)\right)^3$
62. $y = \frac{1}{6}\left(1 + \cos^2(7t)\right)^3$

Find y'' in Exercises 63 and 64.

63. $y = \frac{1}{9}\cot(3x - 1)$
64. $y = 9\tan(x/3)$

In Exercises 65–70, find the value of $(f \circ g)'$ at the given value of x.

65. $f(u) = u^5 + 1, \quad u = g(x) = \sqrt{x}, \quad x = 1$
66. $f(u) = 1 - \frac{1}{u}, \quad u = g(x) = \frac{1}{1 - x}, \quad x = -1$
67. $f(u) = \cot\frac{\pi u}{10}, \quad u = g(x) = 5\sqrt{x}, \quad x = 1$
68. $f(u) = u + \frac{1}{\cos^2 u}, \quad u = g(x) = \pi x, \quad x = 1/4$
69. $f(u) = \frac{2u}{u^2 + 1}, \quad u = g(x) = 10x^2 + x + 1, \quad x = 0$
70. $f(u) = \left(\frac{u - 1}{u + 1}\right)^2, \quad u = g(x) = \frac{1}{x^2} - 1, \quad x = -1$

What happens if you can write a function as a composite in different ways? Do you get the same derivative each time? The Chain Rule says you should. Try it with the functions in Exercises 71–74.

71. Find dy/dx if $y = \cos(6x + 2)$ by writing y as a composite with

a) $y = \cos u$ and $u = 6x + 2$
b) $y = \cos 2u$ and $u = 3x + 1$.

72. Find dy/dx if $y = \sin(x^2 + 1)$ by writing y as a composite with

a) $y = \sin(u + 1)$ and $u = x^2$
b) $y = \sin u$ and $u = x^2 + 1$.

73. Find dy/dx if $y = x$ by writing y as the composite of

a) $y = (u/5) + 7$ and $u = 5x - 35$
b) $y = 1 + (1/u)$ and $u = 1/(x - 1)$.

74. Find dy/dx if $y = \sin(\sin(2x))$ by writing y as the composite of

a) $y = \sin u$ and $u = \sin 2x$
b) $y = \sin(\sin u)$ and $u = 2x$.

75. Find ds/dt when $\theta = 3\pi/2$ if $s = \cos\theta$ and $d\theta/dt = 5$.

76. Find dy/dt when $x = 1$ if $y = x^2 + 7x - 5$ and $dx/dt = 1/3$.

77. **a)** Find the tangent to the curve $y = 2\tan(\pi x/4)$ at $x = 1$.
b) What is the smallest value the slope of the curve can ever have on the interval $-\pi/2 < x < \pi/2$? Give reasons for your answer.

78. **a)** Find equations for the tangents to the curves $y = \sin 2x$ and $y = -\sin(x/2)$ at the origin. Is there anything special about how the tangents are related? Give reasons for your answer.
b) Can anything be said about the tangents to the curves $y = \sin mx$ and $y = -\sin(x/m)$ at the origin (m a constant $\neq 0$)? Give reasons for your answer.
c) For a given m, what are the largest values the slopes of the curves $y = \sin mx$ and $y = -\sin(x/m)$ can ever have? Give reasons for your answer.

79. Suppose that functions f and g and their derivatives with respect to x have the following values at $x = 2$ and $x = 3$.

x	$f(x)$	$g(x)$	$f'(x)$	$g'(x)$
2	8	2	1/3	−3
3	3	−4	2π	5

Find the derivatives with respect to x of the following combinations at the given value of x.

a) $2f(x)$ at $x = 2$
b) $f(x) + g(x)$ at $x = 3$
c) $f(x) \cdot g(x)$ at $x = 3$
d) $f(x)/g(x)$ at $x = 2$
e) $f(g(x))$ at $x = 2$
f) $\sqrt{f(x)}$ at $x = 2$
g) $1/g^2(x)$ at $x = 3$
h) $\sqrt{f^2(x) + g^2(x)}$ at $x = 2$

80. Suppose that the functions f and g and their derivatives with respect to x have the following values at $x = 0$ and $x = 1$.

x	$f(x)$	$g(x)$	$f'(x)$	$g'(x)$
0	1	1	5	1/3
1	3	−4	−1/3	−8/3

Find the derivatives with respect to x of the following combinations at the given value of x.

a) $5f(x) - g(x)$, $x = 1$ **b)** $f(x)\,g^3(x)$, $x = 0$
c) $\dfrac{f(x)}{g(x) + 1}$, $x = 1$
d) $f(g(x))$, $x = 0$
e) $g(f(x))$, $x = 0$
f) $(x^{11} + f(x))^{-2}$, $x = 1$
g) $f(x + g(x))$, $x = 0$

81. *Running Machinery Too Fast.* Suppose that a piston is moving straight up and down and that its position at time t seconds is

$$s = A\cos(2\pi bt),$$

with A and b positive. The value of A is the amplitude of the motion, and b is the frequency (number of times the piston moves up and down each second). What effect does doubling the frequency have on the piston's velocity, acceleration, and jerk? (Once you find out, you will know why machinery breaks when you run it too fast.)

82. *Temperatures in Fairbanks, Alaska.* The graph in Fig. 3.47 on the following page shows the average Fahrenheit temperature in Fairbanks, Alaska, during a typical 365-day year. The equation that approximates the temperature on day x is

$$y = 37\sin\left[\frac{2\pi}{365}(x - 101)\right] + 25.$$

a) On what day is the temperature increasing the fastest?
b) About how many degrees per day is the temperature increasing when it is increasing at its fastest?

83. The function $y = \sin x$ completes one period on the interval $[0, 2\pi]$, the function $y = \sin 2x$ completes two periods, the function $y = \sin(x/2)$ completes half a period, and so on (Fig. 3.48 on the following page). Is there any relation between the number of periods $y = \sin mx$ completes on $[0, 2\pi]$ and the slope of the curve $y = \sin mx$ at the origin? Give reasons for your answer.

84. Suppose that $f(x) = x^2$ and $g(x) = |x|$. Then the composites

$$(f \circ g)(x) = |x|^2 = x^2 \quad \text{and} \quad (g \circ f)(x) = |x^2| = x^2$$

are both differentiable at $x = 0$ even though g itself is not differentiable at $x = 0$. Does this contradict the Chain Rule? Explain.

85. Suppose that $u = g(x)$ is differentiable at $x = 1$ and that $y = f(u)$ is differentiable at $u = g(1)$. If the graph of $y = f(g(x))$ has a horizontal tangent at $x = 1$, can we conclude anything about the tangent to the graph of g at $x = 1$ or the tangent to the graph of f at $u = g(1)$? Give reasons for your answer.

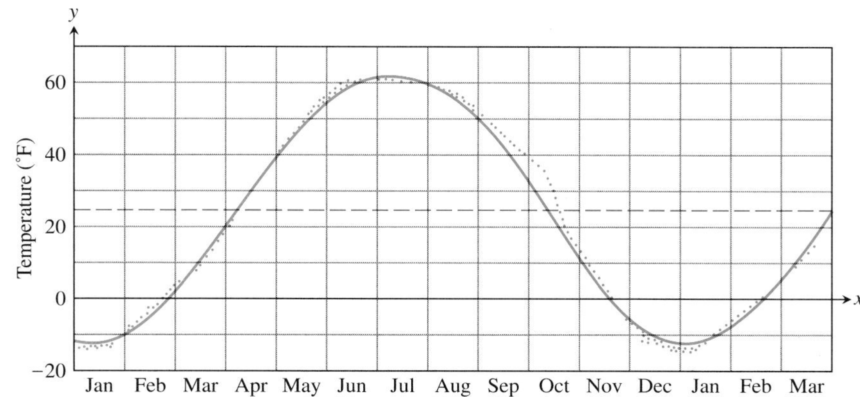

3.47 Normal mean air temperatures at Fairbanks, Alaska, plotted as data points. The approximating sine function is

$$f(x) = 37 \sin\left[\frac{2\pi}{365}(x - 101)\right] + 25.$$

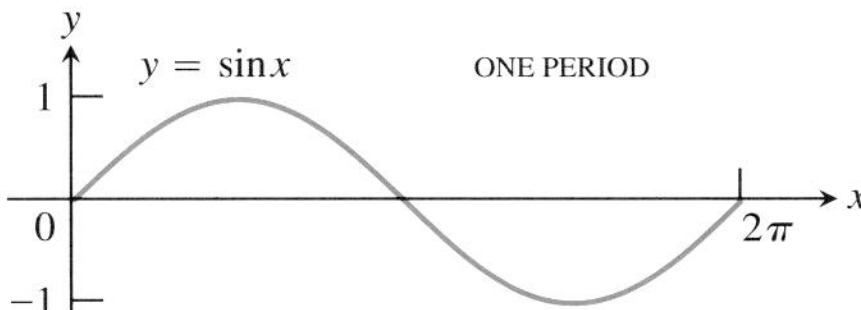

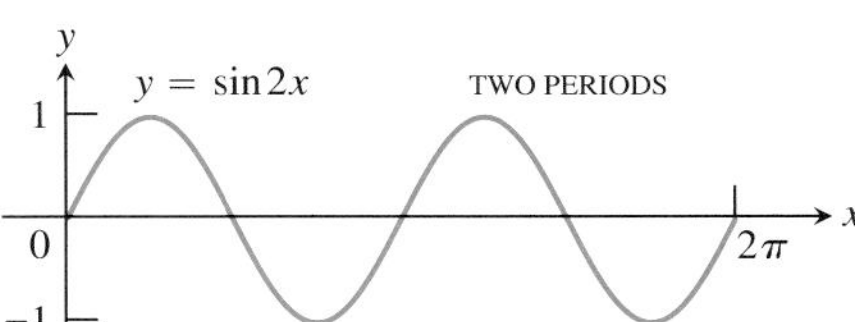

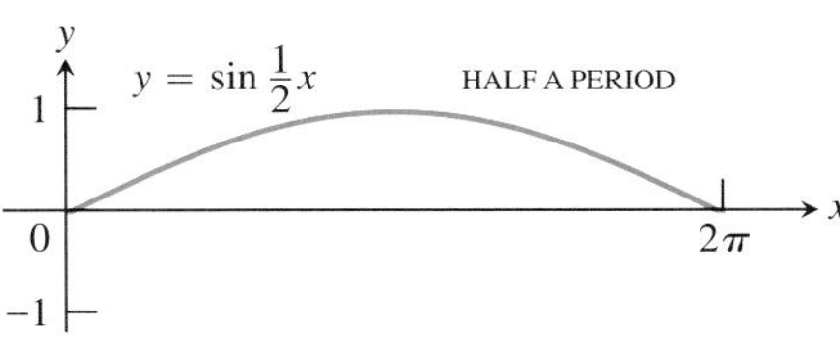

3.48 Periods of $y = \sin mx$ on the interval $[0, 2\pi]$ (Exercise 83).

86. Suppose $u = g(x)$ is differentiable at $x = -5$, $y = f(u)$ is differentiable at $u = g(-5)$, and $(f \circ g)'(-5)$ is negative. What, if anything, can be said about the values of $g'(-5)$ and $f'(g(-5))$?

87. *The Derivative of* $\sin 2x$. Graph the function $y = 2\cos 2x$ for $-2 \le x \le 3.5$. Then, on the same screen, graph

$$y = \frac{\sin 2(x + h) - \sin 2x}{h}$$

for $h = 1.0$, 0.5, and 0.2. Experiment with other values of h, including negative values. What do you see happening as $h \to 0$? Explain this behavior.

88. *The Derivative of* $\cos(x^2)$ Graph $y = -2x \sin(x^2)$ for $-2 \le x \le 3$. Then, on the same screen, graph

$$y = \frac{\cos[(x + h)^2] - \cos(x^2)}{h}$$

for $h = 1.0$, 0.7, and 0.3. Experiment with other values of h. What do you see happening as $h \to 0$? Explain this behavior.

89. As Fig. 3.49 shows, the trigonometric "polynomial"

$$s = f(t) = 0.78540 - 0.63662 \cos 2t - 0.07074 \cos 6t - 0.02546 \cos 10t - 0.01299 \cos 14t$$

gives a good approximation of the sawtooth function $s = g(t)$ on the interval $[-\pi, \pi]$. How well does the derivative of f approximate the derivative of g at the points where dg/dt is defined? To find out, carry out the following steps.

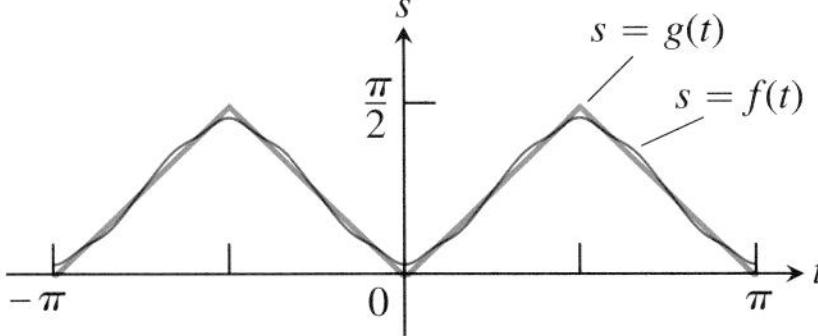

3.49 The approximation of a sawtooth function by a trigonometric "polynomial" (Exercise 89).

a) Graph dg/dt (where defined) over $[-\pi, \pi]$.
b) Find df/dt.
c) Graph df/dt. Where does the approximation of dg/dt by df/dt seem to be best? least good? Approximations by trigonometric polynomials are important in the theories of heat and oscillation, but we must not expect too much of them, as we see in the next exercise.

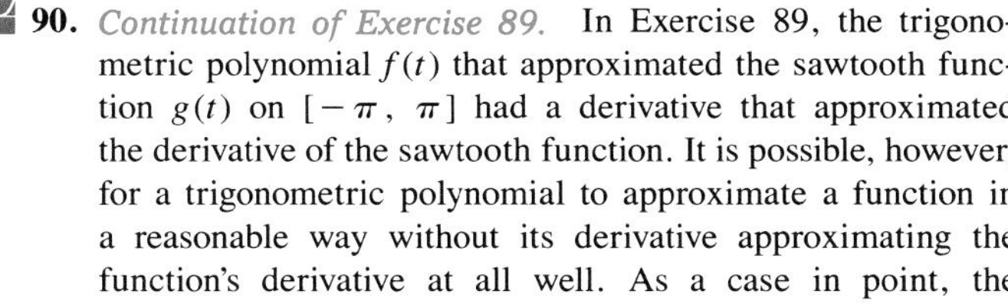

90. *Continuation of Exercise 89.* In Exercise 89, the trigonometric polynomial $f(t)$ that approximated the sawtooth function $g(t)$ on $[-\pi, \pi]$ had a derivative that approximated the derivative of the sawtooth function. It is possible, however, for a trigonometric polynomial to approximate a function in a reasonable way without its derivative approximating the function's derivative at all well. As a case in point, the "polynomial"

$$s = h(t) = 1.2732 \sin 2t + 0.4244 \sin 6t + 0.25465 \sin 10t + 0.18186 \sin 14t + 0.14147 \sin 18t$$

graphed in Fig. 3.50 approximates the step function $s = k(t)$ shown there. Yet the derivative of h is nothing like the derivative of k.

a) Graph dk/dt (where defined) over $[-\pi, \pi]$.
b) Find dh/dt.
c) Graph dh/dt to see how badly the graph fits the graph of dk/dt.

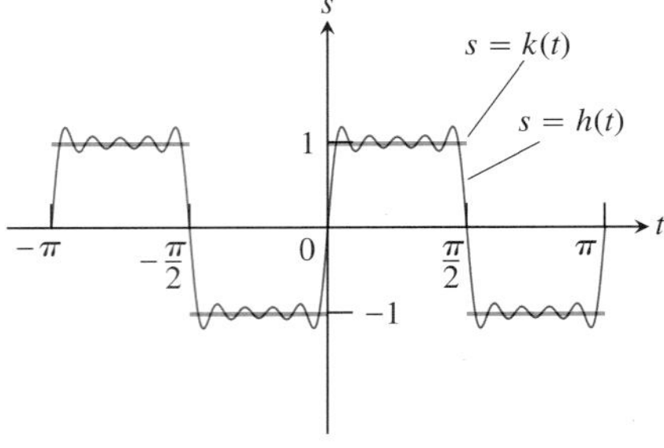

3.50 The approximation of a step function by a trigonometric "polynomial" (Exercise 90).

Writing for Your Own Knowledge

Answer the following questions in writing. Some answers will take only a sentence or two; others may require several paragraphs. Some explanations may also call for graphs or sketches.

1. What is the Chain Rule? When does it apply? How do you use it?
2. What form does the Chain Rule take for integer powers of differentiable functions?

3.6 *Implicit Differentiation and Fractional Powers*

When an equation like $x^3 + y^3 - 15xy = 0$ does not let us solve for y in terms of x conveniently, we can still find dy/dx with a technique called *implicit differentiation*. This section describes the technique and uses it to extend the Power Rule for differentiation to include fractional exponents.

Implicit Differentiation

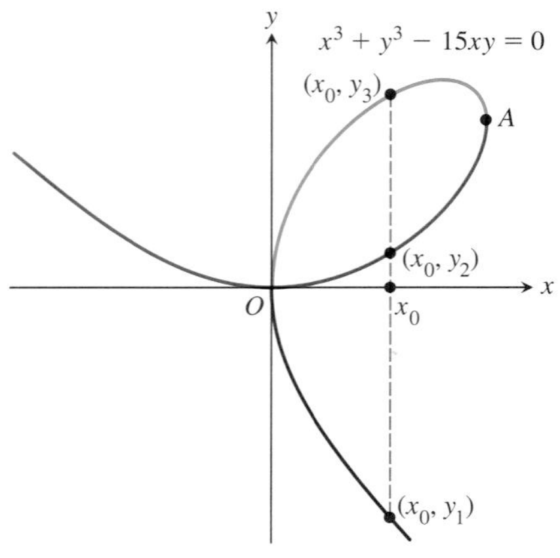

3.51 The curve $x^3 + y^3 - 15xy = 0$ is not the graph of any one function of x. However, the curve can be divided into separate arcs that *are* the graphs of functions of x. This curve, called the folium of Descartes, dates back to 1638.

As you can see in Fig. 3.51, the graph of $x^3 + y^3 - 15xy = 0$ is not the graph of a function of x. The curve gives more than one y-value for some x-values, as we can see from the fact that some vertical lines intersect the curve more than once. However, various parts of the graph *are* the graphs of functions of x. The red curve that comes in to A from the second quadrant, the blue arc OA, and the black curve that runs from O down into the fourth quadrant are all graphs of functions of x. Since the equation $x^3 + y^3 - 15xy = 0$ has defined these functions without furnishing explicit formulas for them in the form $y = f(x)$, we say that the equation has defined the functions **implicitly.**

The equation $x^3 + y^3 - 15xy = 0$ has the form $F(x, y) = 0$, where $F(x, y)$ denotes an expression in the variables x and y. When may we expect the functions defined by such an equation to be differentiable? The answer, from a theorem in advanced mathematics, is when F is continuous (in a sense to be described in Chapter 13) and the first derivatives of F with respect to each variable, with the other variable held fixed, are continuous.

EXAMPLE 1 Find dy/dx if $y^2 = x$.

Solution The equation $y^2 = x$ defines two differentiable functions of x, namely $y = \sqrt{x}$ and $y = -\sqrt{x}$ (Fig. 3.52). We know how to find the derivative of each of these, from Example 8 in Section 3.1. But suppose we knew only that

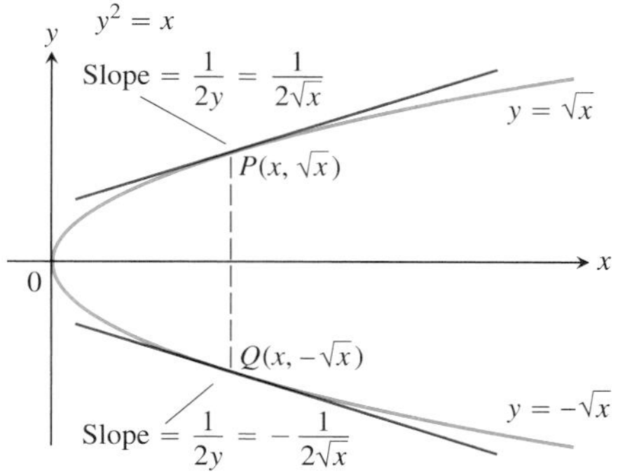

3.52 The equation $y^2 - x = 0$, or $y^2 = x$ as it is usually written, defines two differentiable functions of x on the interval $x \geq 0$. Example 1 shows how to find the derivatives of these functions without solving the equation $y^2 = x$ for y.

the equation $y^2 = x$ defined y as one or more differentiable functions of x without knowing exactly what these functions were. Could we still find dy/dx?

The answer is yes. To find dy/dx we simply differentiate both sides of the equation $y^2 = x$ with respect to x, treating y as a differentiable implicit function of x. When we do this, we get

$$y^2 = x$$

$$2y\frac{dy}{dx} = 1 \qquad \text{The Chain Rule gives } \frac{d}{dx}(y^2) = 2y \cdot \frac{dy}{dx}.$$

$$\frac{dy}{dx} = \frac{1}{2y} \qquad (\text{if } y \neq 0).$$

So we can find dy/dx without solving the equation $y^2 = x$ for y.

How does this compare with what happens when we solve $y^2 = x$ for y first and then differentiate?

With $y = \sqrt{x}$	With $y = -\sqrt{x}$	
$\frac{dy}{dx} = \frac{1}{2\sqrt{x}}$	$\frac{dy}{dx} = -\frac{1}{2\sqrt{x}}$	Section 3.1, Example 8
$= \frac{1}{2y}$	$= \frac{1}{2(-\sqrt{x})}$	
	$= \frac{1}{2y}$	

In both cases, the derivative is given by the formula we obtained without solving for y, so the two methods agree.

EXAMPLE 2 The graph of $F(x, y) = x^2 + y^2 - 1 = 0$ is the unit circle $x^2 + y^2 = 1$. Taken as a whole, the circle is not the graph of any single function of x (Fig. 3.53). Each x in the interval $-1 < x < 1$ gives two values of y, namely $y = \sqrt{1 - x^2}$ and $y = -\sqrt{1 - x^2}$, instead of the required single value.

The upper and lower semicircles are the graphs of the functions $f(x) = \sqrt{1 - x^2}$ and $g(x) = -\sqrt{1 - x^2}$. These functions are differentiable for $|x| < 1$ because they are composites of differentiable functions. The quickest way to find their derivatives, however, is not to differentiate the square root formulas but to differentiate both sides of the original equation, treating y as a differentiable implicit function of x:

$$x^2 + y^2 = 1$$

$$\frac{d}{dx}(x^2) + \frac{d}{dx}(y^2) = \frac{d}{dx}(1) \qquad \text{Sum Rule}$$

$$2x + 2y\frac{dy}{dx} = 0 \qquad \text{Chain Rule}$$

$$\frac{dy}{dx} = -\frac{x}{y} \quad (\text{if } y \neq 0) \qquad \text{Solve for } dy/dx.$$

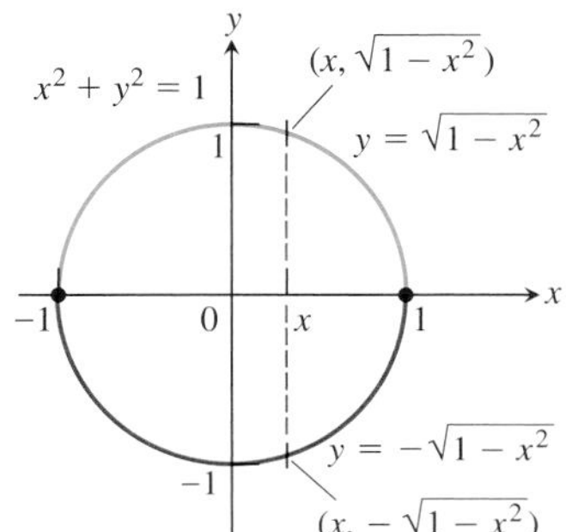

3.53 The two functions defined by the equation $x^2 + y^2 = 1$ are differentiable on the interval $-1 < x < 1$ (Example 2).

This formula for dy/dx is simpler than either of the formulas we would get by differentiating f and g and holds for all points on the curve above or below the x-axis. The formula is also easy to evaluate at any such point. At $(\sqrt{2}/2, \sqrt{2}/2)$, for instance,

$$\frac{dy}{dx} = -\frac{\sqrt{2}/2}{\sqrt{2}/2} = -1.$$

Implicit Differentiation Takes Four Steps

1. Differentiate both sides of the equation with respect to x.
2. Collect the terms with dy/dx on one side of the equation.
3. Factor out dy/dx.
4. Solve for dy/dx by dividing.

To calculate the derivatives of other implicitly defined functions we simply proceed as in Examples 1 and 2: We treat y as a differentiable implicit function of x and apply the already familiar rules of differentiation to differentiate both sides of the defining equation. This procedure is called **implicit differentiation.**

EXAMPLE 3 Find dy/dx if $2y = x^2 + \sin y$.

Solution

$$2y = x^2 + \sin y$$

$$\frac{d}{dx}(2y) = \frac{d}{dx}(x^2) + \frac{d}{dx}(\sin y)$$ Differentiate both sides with respect to x, . . .

$$2\frac{dy}{dx} = 2x + \cos y \frac{dy}{dx}$$ . . . treating y as a function of x.

$$2\frac{dy}{dx} - \cos y \frac{dy}{dx} = 2x$$ Collect terms with dy/dx, . . .

$$(2 - \cos y)\frac{dy}{dx} = 2x$$ . . . and factor out dy/dx.

$$\frac{dy}{dx} = \frac{2x}{2 - \cos y}$$ Solve for dy/dx by dividing.

Lenses, Tangents, and Normal Lines

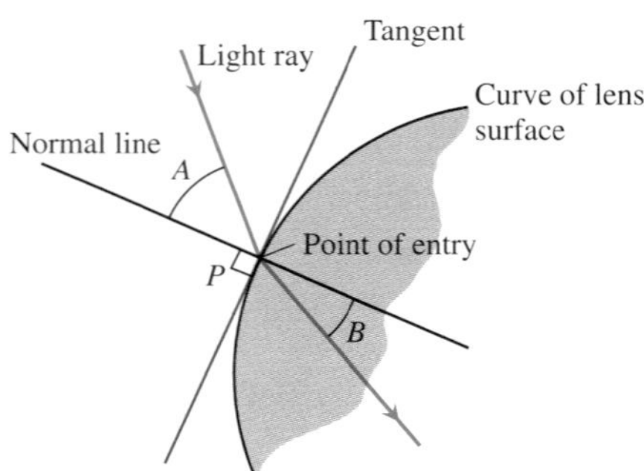

3.54 The profile of a lens, showing the bending (refraction) of a ray of light as it passes through the lens surface.

In the law that describes how light changes direction as it enters a lens, the important angles are the angles the light makes with the line perpendicular to the surface of the lens at the point of entry (angles A and B in Fig. 3.54). This line is called the *normal to the surface* at the point of entry. In a profile view of a lens like the one in Fig. 3.54, the normal is the line perpendicular to the tangent to the profile curve at the point of entry.

DEFINITION

A line is **normal** to a curve at a point if it is perpendicular to the curve's tangent there. The line is called the **normal** to the curve at that point.

EXAMPLE 4 Find the tangent and normal to the curve $x^2 - xy + y^2 = 7$ at the point $(-1, 2)$. (See Fig. 3.55.)

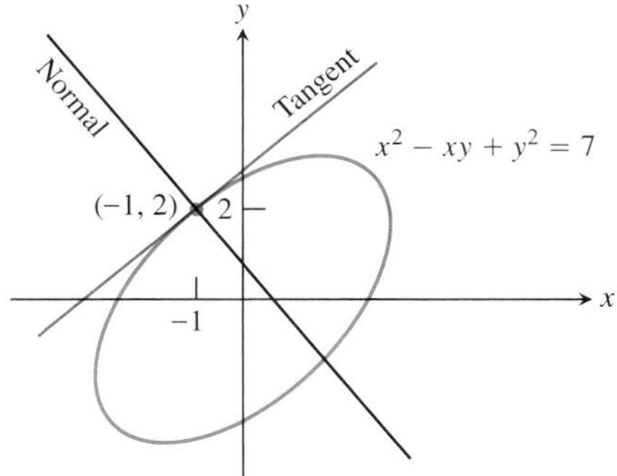

3.55 The graph of $x^2 - xy + y^2 = 7$ is an ellipse. Example 4 shows how to find equations for the tangent and normal lines at the point $(-1, 2)$.

Solution We first use implicit differentiation to find dy/dx:

$$x^2 - xy + y^2 = 7$$

$$\frac{d}{dx}(x^2) - \frac{d}{dx}(xy) + \frac{d}{dx}(y^2) = \frac{d}{dx}(7) \qquad \text{Differentiate both sides with respect to } x, \ldots$$

$$2x - \left(x\frac{dy}{dx} + y\frac{dx}{dx}\right) + 2y\frac{dy}{dx} = 0 \qquad \ldots \text{treating } xy \text{ as a product and } y^2 \text{ as a power.}$$

$$(2y - x)\frac{dy}{dx} = y - 2x \qquad \text{Collect terms.}$$

$$\frac{dy}{dx} = \frac{y - 2x}{2y - x} \qquad \text{Solve for } dy/dx.$$

We then evaluate the derivative at $(x, y) = (-1, 2)$ to obtain

$$\left.\frac{dy}{dx}\right|_{(-1,2)} = \left.\frac{y - 2x}{2y - x}\right|_{(-1,2)} = \frac{2 - 2(-1)}{2(2) - (-1)} = \frac{4}{5}.$$

The slope of the curve at $(-1, 2)$ is $4/5$.

The tangent to the curve at $(-1, 2)$ is the line

$$y - 2 = \frac{4}{5}(x - (-1)) \qquad y - y_0 = m(x - x_0) \text{ with } y_0 = 2,\ m = 4/5,\ x_0 = -1$$

$$= \frac{4}{5}x + \frac{14}{5}.$$

The normal to the curve at $(-1, 2)$ has slope $-5/4$, so its point–slope equation is

$$y - 2 = -\frac{5}{4}(x + 1)$$

$$y = -\frac{5}{4}x + \frac{3}{4}.$$

The Word *Normal*

When analytic geometry was developed in the seventeenth century, European scientists still wrote about their work and ideas in Latin, the one language that all educated Europeans could read and understand. The word *normalis,* which scholars used for "perpendicular" in Latin, became *normal* when they discussed geometry in English.

Using Implicit Differentiation to Find Derivatives of Higher Order

Implicit differentiation can also produce derivatives of higher order. Here is an example.

EXAMPLE 5 Find d^2y/dx^2 if $2x^3 - 3y^2 = 7$.

Solution To start, we differentiate both sides of the equation with respect to x to find $y' = dy/dx$:

$$2x^3 - 3y^2 = 7$$

$$\frac{d}{dx}(2x^3) - \frac{d}{dx}(3y^2) = \frac{d}{dx}(7)$$

$$6x^2 - 6yy' = 0 \tag{1}$$

$$x^2 - yy' = 0$$

$$y' = \frac{x^2}{y} \qquad (\text{if } y \neq 0).$$

Helga von Koch's Snowflake Curve (1904)

Start with an equilateral triangle, calling it Curve 1. On the middle third of each side, build an equilateral triangle pointing outward. Then erase the interiors of the old middle thirds. Call the expanded curve Curve 2. Now put equilateral triangles, again pointing outward, on the middle thirds of the sides of Curve 2. Erase the interiors of the old middle thirds to make Curve 3. Repeat the process, as shown, to define an infinite sequence of plane curves. The limit curve of the sequence is Koch's snowflake curve.

The snowflake curve is too rough to have a tangent at any point. In other words, the equation $F(x, y) = 0$ defining the curve does not define y as a differentiable function of x or x as a differentiable function of y at any point. We will encounter the snowflake curve again when we study length in Section 7.4.

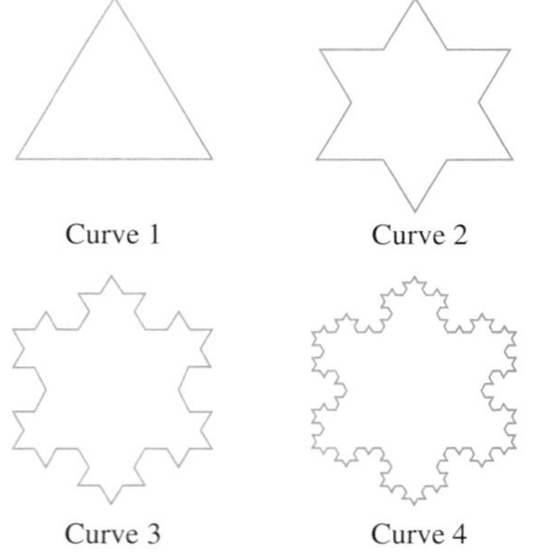

We now apply the Quotient Rule to find y'':

$$\begin{aligned} y'' &= \frac{d}{dx}\left(\frac{x^2}{y}\right) \\ &= \frac{2xy - x^2y'}{y^2} \\ &= \frac{2x}{y} - \frac{x^2}{y^2}y'. \end{aligned} \tag{2}$$

Finally, we substitute $y' = x^2/y$ to express y'' in terms of x and y:

$$y'' = \frac{2x}{y} - \frac{x^2}{y^2}\left(\frac{x^2}{y}\right) = \frac{2x}{y} - \frac{x^4}{y^3} \qquad (\text{if } y \neq 0). \tag{3}$$

Fractional Powers of Differentiable Functions

We know that the Power Rule

$$\frac{d}{dx}u^n = nu^{n-1}\frac{du}{dx} \tag{4}$$

holds when n is an integer. Our goal now is to show that it holds when n is a fraction. We will then be able to differentiate functions like

$$y = x^{4/3} \qquad \text{and} \qquad y = (\cos x)^{-1/5}$$

that were beyond our reach before.

Power Rule for Fractional Exponents

If n is any rational number, then

$$\frac{d}{dx}x^n = nx^{n-1}, \tag{5}$$

provided $x \neq 0$ if $n - 1 < 0$ (i.e., if $n < 1$).

If n is a rational number and u is a differentiable function of x, then u^n is a differentiable function of x and

$$\frac{d}{dx}u^n = nu^{n-1}\frac{du}{dx}, \tag{6}$$

provided $u \neq 0$ if $n < 1$.

In Chapter 6, we will see that the Power Rule holds for *any real* value of n.

The restrictions $x \neq 0$ if $n < 1$ and $u \neq 0$ if $n < 1$ in Eqs. (5) and (6) are there to protect against inadvertent attempts to divide by zero. There is nothing mysterious about these restrictions. They come up quite naturally in practice, as the next example shows.

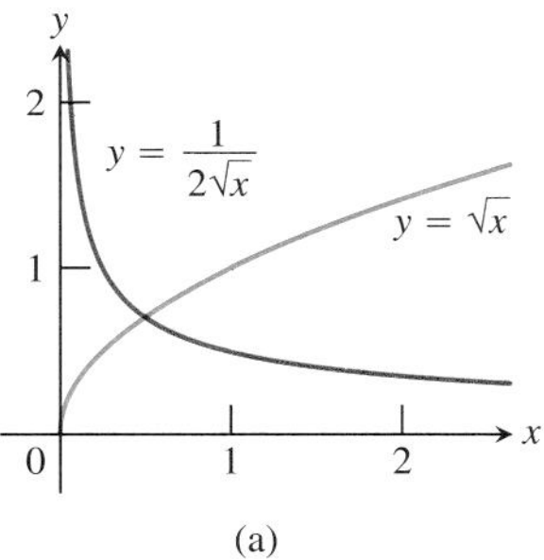

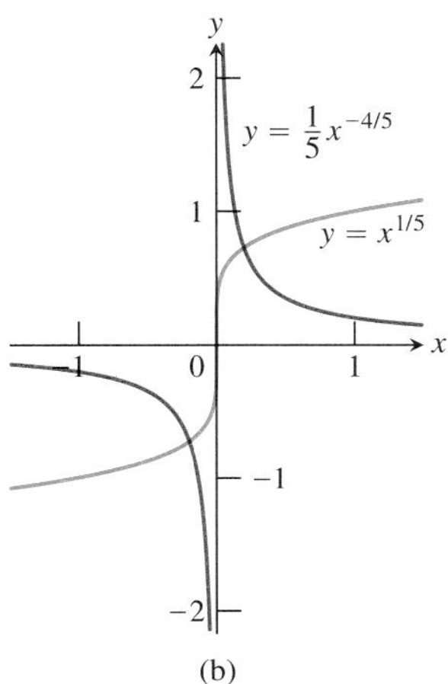

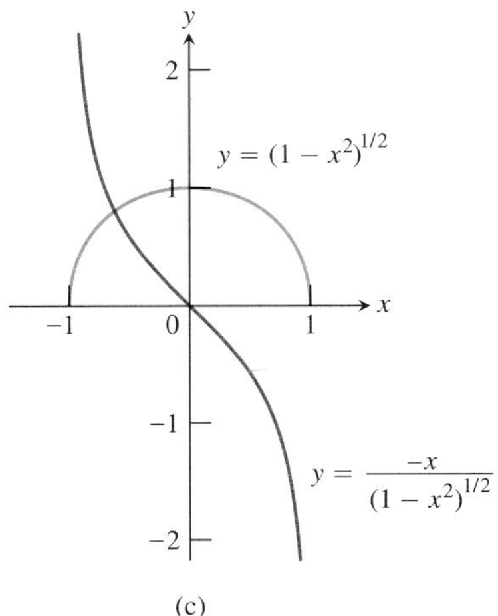

3.56 The graphs of the functions and derivatives in Example 6.

EXAMPLE 6

a) $\frac{d}{dx}(x^{1/2}) = \frac{1}{2}x^{-1/2} = \frac{1}{2\sqrt{x}}$ Eq. (5) with $n = \frac{1}{2}$

function defined for $x \geq 0$; derivative defined only for $x > 0$

b) $\frac{d}{dx}(x^{1/5}) = \frac{1}{5}x^{-4/5}$ Eq. (5) with $n = \frac{1}{5}$

function defined for all x; derivative not defined at $x = 0$

c) $\frac{d}{dx}(1 - x^2)^{1/2} = \frac{1}{2}(1 - x^2)^{-1/2}(-2x)$ Eq. (6) with $u = 1 - x^2$ and $n = \frac{1}{2}$

function defined for $-1 \leq x \leq 1$

$$= \frac{-x}{(1 - x^2)^{1/2}}$$

derivative defined only for $-1 < x < 1$

See Fig. 3.56.

The derivatives of the functions $x^{4/3}$ and $(\cos x)^{-1/5}$ are defined wherever the functions themselves are defined, as we see in the next example.

EXAMPLE 7

a) $\frac{d}{dx}x^{4/3} = \frac{4}{3}x^{1/3}$

b)
$$\frac{d}{dx}(\cos x)^{-1/5} = -\frac{1}{5}(\cos x)^{-6/5}\frac{d}{dx}(\cos x)$$
$$= -\frac{1}{5}(\cos x)^{-6/5}(-\sin x)$$
$$= \frac{1}{5}\sin x\,(\cos x)^{-6/5}$$

Proof of the Power Rule for Fractional Exponents We prove Eq. (5) first and then apply the Chain Rule to get Eq. (6).

To prove Eq. (5), let p and q be integers with $q > 0$ and suppose that $y = x^{p/q}$. Then

$$y^q = x^p.$$

This equation is an algebraic combination of powers of x and y, so the advanced theorem we mentioned at the beginning of the section assures us that y is a differentiable function of x. Since p and q are integers (for which we already have the Power Rule), we can differentiate both sides of the equation implicitly with respect to x and obtain

$$qy^{q-1}\frac{dy}{dx} = px^{p-1}. \tag{7}$$

If $y \neq 0$, we can then divide both sides of Eq. (7) by qy^{q-1} to solve for dy/dx, obtaining

$$\begin{aligned}
\frac{dy}{dx} &= \frac{px^{p-1}}{qy^{q-1}} && \text{Eq. (7) divided by } qy^{q-1} \\
&= \frac{p}{q} \cdot \frac{x^{p-1}}{(x^{(p/q)})^{q-1}} && y = x^{p/q} \text{ because } y^q = x^p \\
&= \frac{p}{q} \cdot \frac{x^{p-1}}{x^{p-p/q}} && \frac{p}{q}(q-1) = p - \frac{p}{q} \\
&= \frac{p}{q} \cdot x^{(p-1)-(p-p/q)} && \text{A law of exponents} \\
&= \frac{p}{q} \cdot x^{(p/q)-1}.
\end{aligned}$$

This proves Eq. (5).

To prove Eq. (6), we let $y = u^{p/q}$ and calculate dy/dx with the Chain Rule:

$$\begin{aligned}
\frac{dy}{dx} &= \frac{dy}{du} \cdot \frac{du}{dx} && \text{Chain Rule} \\
&= \frac{d}{du} u^{(p/q)} \cdot \frac{du}{dx} && y = u^{p/q} \\
&= \frac{p}{q} u^{(p/q)-1} \cdot \frac{du}{dx} && \text{Eq. (5) with } u \text{ in place of } x
\end{aligned}$$

Hence, if $n = p/q$ is any rational number,

$$\frac{d}{dx} u^n = nu^{n-1} \frac{du}{dx},$$

which is what we set out to prove. ▬

Exercises 3.6

Find dy/dx in Exercises 1–16.

1. $y = x^{9/4}$

2. $y = x^{-3/5}$

3. $y = \sqrt[3]{2x}$

4. $y = \sqrt[4]{5x}$

5. $y = 7\sqrt{x+6}$

6. $y = -2\sqrt{x-1}$

7. $y = (2x+5)^{-1/2}$

8. $y = (1-6x)^{2/3}$

9. $y = x(x^2+1)^{1/2}$

10. $y = x(x^2+1)^{-1/2}$

11. $y = 3(\csc x)^{-3/2}$

12. $y = \frac{1}{2}(\sec x)^{-2/5}$

13. $y = (\cos \pi x)^{8/7}$

14. $y = [\sin (x+5)]^{5/4}$

15. $y = \sqrt{1 - \sqrt{x}}$

16. $y = 3(2x^{-1/2}+1)^{-1/3}$

Use implicit differentiation to find dy/dx in Exercises 17–30.

17. $x^2y + xy^2 = 6$

18. $x^3 + y^3 = 18xy$

19. $2xy + y^2 = x + y$

20. $x^3 - xy + y^3 = 1$

21. $x^2(x-y)^2 = x^2 - y^2$

22. $(3xy+7)^2 = 6y$

23. $y^2 = \dfrac{x-1}{x+1}$

24. $x^2 = \dfrac{x-y}{x+y}$

25. $x = \tan y$

26. $x = \sin y$

27. $x + \tan (xy) = 0$

28. $x + \sin y = xy$

29. $y \sin \left(\dfrac{1}{y}\right) = 1 - xy$

30. $y^2 \cos \left(\dfrac{1}{y}\right) = 2x + 2y$

Find $dr/d\theta$ in Exercises 31–34.

31. $\theta^{1/2} + r^{1/2} = 1$

32. $r = 2\theta^{1/2} + \frac{3}{2}\theta^{2/3} + \frac{4}{3}\theta^{3/4}$

33. $\sin (r\theta) = \frac{1}{2}$

34. $\cos r + \cos \theta = r\theta$

In Exercises 35–38, use implicit differentiation to find dy/dx and then d^2y/dx^2.

35. $x^2 + y^2 = 1$

36. $x^{2/3} + y^{2/3} = 1$

37. $y^2 = x^2 + 2x$

38. $y^2 + 2y = 2x + 1$

39. If $x^3 + y^3 = 16$, find the value of d^2y/dx^2 at the point (2, 2).

40. If $xy + y^2 = 1$, find the value of d^2y/dx^2 at the point $(0, -1)$.

In Exercises 41–50, find the lines that are (a) tangent and (b) normal to the curve at the given point.

41. $x^2 + xy - y^2 = 1$, $(2, 3)$

42. $x^2 + y^2 = 25$, $(3, -4)$

43. $x^2y^2 = 9$, $(-1, 3)$

44. $y^2 - 2x - 4y - 1 = 0$, $(-2, 1)$

45. $6x^2 + 3xy + 2y^2 + 17y - 6 = 0$, $(-1, 0)$

46. $x^2 - \sqrt{3}\,xy + 2y^2 = 5$, $(\sqrt{3}, 2)$

47. $2xy + \pi \sin y = 2\pi$, $(1, \pi/2)$

48. $x \sin 2y = y \cos 2x$, $(\pi/4, \pi/2)$

49. $y = 2 \sin(\pi x - y)$, $(1, 0)$

50. $x^2 \cos^2 y - \sin y = 0$, $(0, \pi)$

51. Find the two points where the curve $x^2 + xy + y^2 = 7$ crosses the x-axis, and show that the tangents to the curve at these points are parallel. What is the common slope of these tangents?

52. Find points on the curve $x^2 + xy + y^2 = 7$ (a) where the tangent is parallel to the x-axis and (b) where the tangent is parallel to the y-axis. (In the latter case, dy/dx is not defined, but dx/dy is. What value does dx/dy have at these points?)

53. *The Eight Curve.* Find the slopes of the figure-eight-shaped curve $y^4 = y^2 - x^2$ at the two points shown in Fig. 3.57.

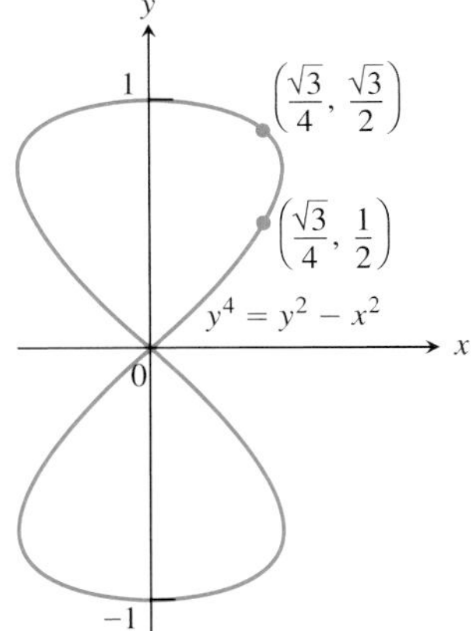

3.57 The eight curve (Exercise 53).

54. *The Cissoid of Diocles (from about 200 B.C.).* Find equations for the tangent and normal lines to the cissoid of Diocles $y^2(2 - x) = x^3$ at (1, 1) (Fig. 3.58).

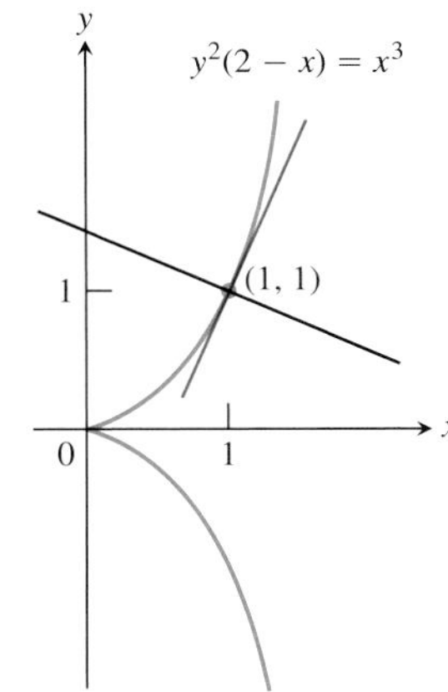

3.58 The cissoid of Diocles (Exercise 54).

55. Which of the following could be true if $f''(x) = x^{-1/3}$?

a) $f(x) = \frac{3}{2}x^{2/3} - 3$
b) $f(x) = \frac{9}{10}x^{5/3} - 7$
c) $f'''(x) = -\frac{1}{3}x^{-4/3}$
d) $f'(x) = \frac{3}{2}x^{2/3} + 6$

56. Is there anything special about the tangents to the curves $2x^2 + 3y^2 = 5$ and $y^2 = x^3$ at the points $(1, \pm 1)$ (Fig. 3.59)? Give reasons for your answer.

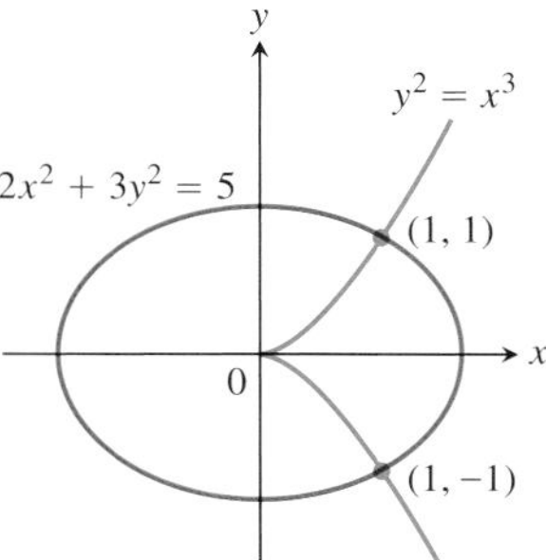

3.59 The curves in Exercise 56.

57. The position of a body moving along a coordinate line at time t is $s = \sqrt{1 + 4t}$, with s in meters and t in seconds. Find the body's velocity and acceleration when $t = 6$ sec.

58. The velocity of a falling body is $v = k\sqrt{s}$ meters per second (k a constant) at the instant the body has fallen s meters from its starting point. What is special about the body's acceleration? Give reasons for your answer.

59. What is the geometry behind the restrictions on the domains of the derivatives in Example 6?

60. a) Given that $x^4 + 4y^2 = 1$, find dy/dx two ways: first by solving for y and differentiating the resulting functions in the usual way, and second by implicit differentiation. Do you get the same result each way?

b) Solve the equation $x^4 + 4y^2 = 1$ for y and graph the resulting functions together to produce a complete graph of the equation $x^4 + 4y^2 = 1$. Then add the graphs of the first derivatives of these functions to your display. Could you have predicted the general behavior of the derivative graphs from looking at the graph of $x^4 + 4y^2 = 1$? Could you have predicted the general behavior of the graph of $x^4 + 4y^2 = 1$ by looking at the derivative graphs? Give reasons for your answers.

61. a) Given that $(x - 2)^2 + y^2 = 4$, find dy/dx two ways: first by solving for y and differentiating the resulting functions with respect to x, and second by implicit differentiation. Do you get the same result each way?

b) Solve the equation $(x - 2)^2 + y^2 = 4$ for y and graph the resulting functions together to produce a complete graph of the equation $(x - 2)^2 + y^2 = 4$. Then add the graphs of the functions' first derivatives to your picture. Could you have predicted the general behavior of the derivative graphs from looking at the graph of $(x - 2)^2 + y^2 = 4$? Could you have predicted the general behavior of the graph of $(x - 2)^2 + y^2 = 4$ by looking at the derivative graphs? Give reasons for your answers.

Writing for Your Own Knowledge

Answer the following questions in writing. Some answers will take only a sentence or two; others may require several paragraphs. Some explanations may also call for graphs or sketches.

1. What is implicit differentiation? When is it called for?
2. What is special about Helga von Koch's snowflake curve?
3. What is meant by the line normal to a curve at a point?
4. How do you find a second derivative by implicit differentiation?
5. What is the power rule for fractional exponents? When does it apply?

3.7 *Linearizations and Differentials*

Sometimes we can approximate complicated functions with simpler ones that give the accuracy we want for specific applications without being so hard to work with. In this section we study the simplest of the useful approximations, called a *linearization*.

We also introduce a new symbol, dx, for an increment in a variable x. This symbol is called the *differential* of x. In the physical sciences, it is used more frequently than Δx. In mathematics, differentials are used to estimate changes in function values, as we will see toward the end of this section.

Linearizations Are Linear Replacement Formulas

As you can see in Fig. 3.60, the tangent to a curve $y = f(x)$ lies close to the curve near the point of tangency. For a brief interval on either side, the y-values

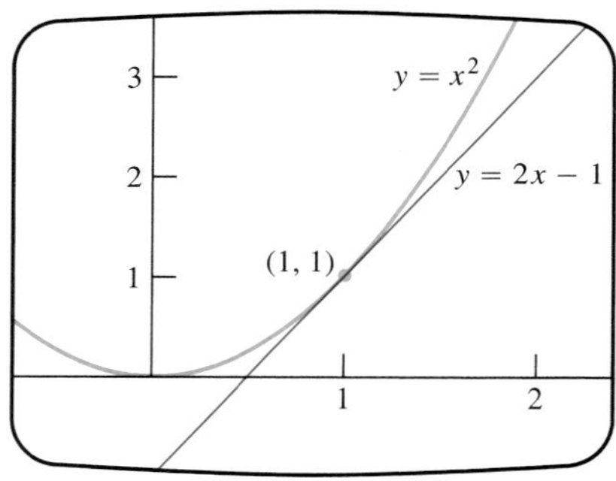

$y = x^2$ and its tangent $y = 2x - 1$ at $(1, 1)$.

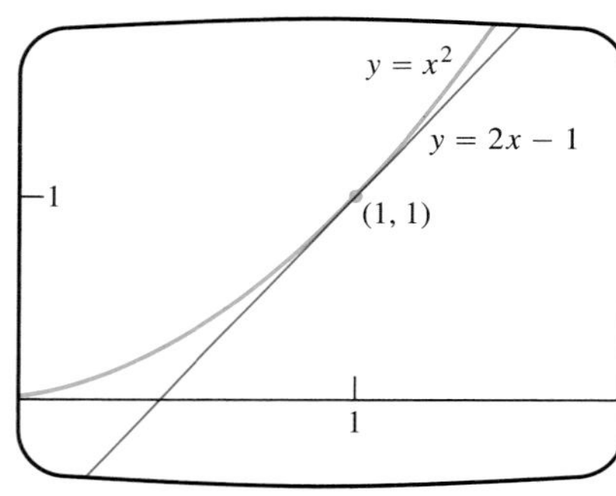

Tangent and curve very close near $(1, 1)$.

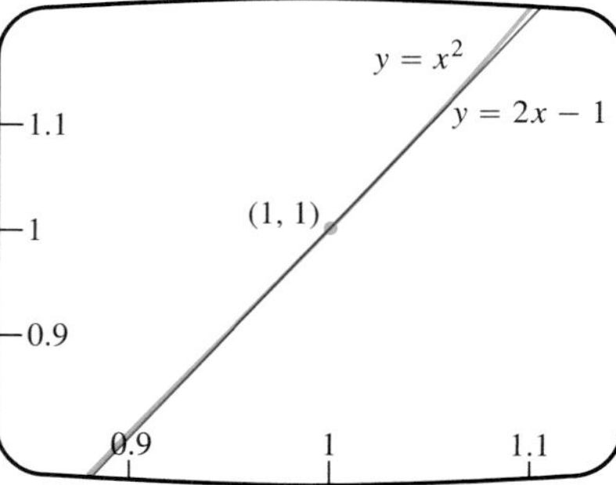

Tangent and curve very close throughout entire x-interval shown.

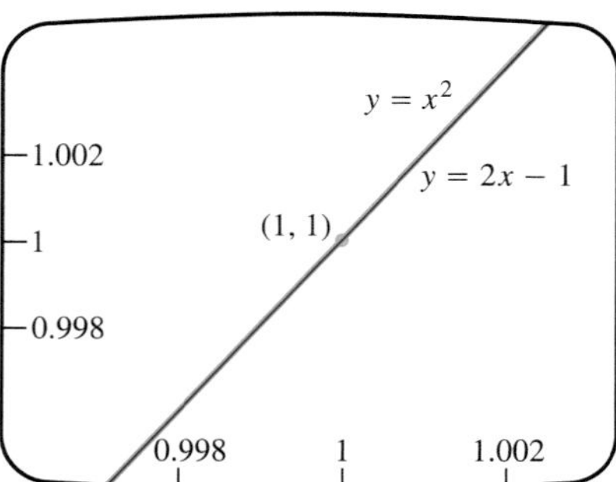

Tangent and curve closer still. Computer screen cannot distinguish tangent from curve on this x-interval.

3.60 The more we magnify the graph of a function near a point where the function is differentiable, the flatter the graph becomes and the more it resembles its tangent. You can see this happening in the four views of the curve $y = x^2$ shown here. As the magnification increases in the vicinity of the point $(1, 1)$, the curve flattens and comes more and more to resemble its tangent line $y = 2x - 1$. Indeed, in the fourth frame, our computer no longer shows any difference between the two.

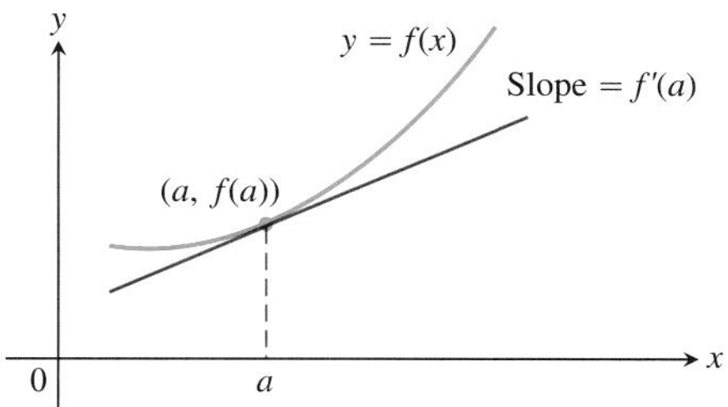

3.61 The equation of the tangent line is $y = f(a) + f'(a)(x - a)$.

along the tangent line give good approximations to the y-values on the curve. Therefore, to simplify the expression for the function near this point, we propose to replace the formula for f over this interval by the formula for its tangent line.

In the notation of Fig. 3.61, the tangent passes through the point $(a, f(a))$ with slope $f'(a)$, so its point–slope equation is

$$y - f(a) = f'(a)(x - a),$$

or

$$y = f(a) + f'(a)(x - a). \tag{1}$$

Thus, the tangent line is the graph of the function

$$L(x) = f(a) + f'(a)(x - a). \tag{2}$$

For as long as the line remains close to the graph of f, $L(x)$ will give a good approximation to $f(x)$.

DEFINITIONS

Linearization and Standard Linear Approximation

If $y = f(x)$ is differentiable at $x = a$, then

$$L(x) = f(a) + f'(a)(x - a) \tag{3}$$

is the **linearization** of f at a. The approximation

$$f(x) \approx L(x)$$

is the **standard linear approximation** of f at a. The **center** of the approximation is at $x = a$.

EXAMPLE 1 Find the linearization of $f(x) = \sqrt{1 + x}$ at $x = 0$.

Solution We evaluate Eq. (3) for $f(x) = \sqrt{1 + x}$ and $a = 0$.

The derivative of f is

$$f'(x) = \frac{1}{2}(1 + x)^{-1/2} = \frac{1}{2\sqrt{1 + x}}.$$

Its value at $x = 0$ is 1/2. We substitute this along with $a = 0$ and $f(0) = 1$ into Eq. (3):

$$L(x) = f(a) + f'(a)(x - a) = 1 + \frac{1}{2}(x - 0) = 1 + \frac{x}{2}.$$

The linearization of $\sqrt{1 + x}$ at $x = 0$ is $L(x) = 1 + \frac{x}{2}$. See Fig. 3.62.

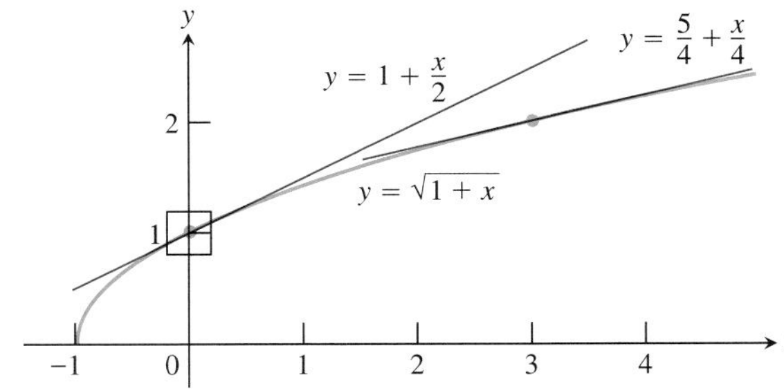

3.62 The graph of $y = \sqrt{1 + x}$ and its linearizations at $x = 0$ and $x = 3$. Figure 3.63 shows a magnified view of the small window about 1 on the y-axis.

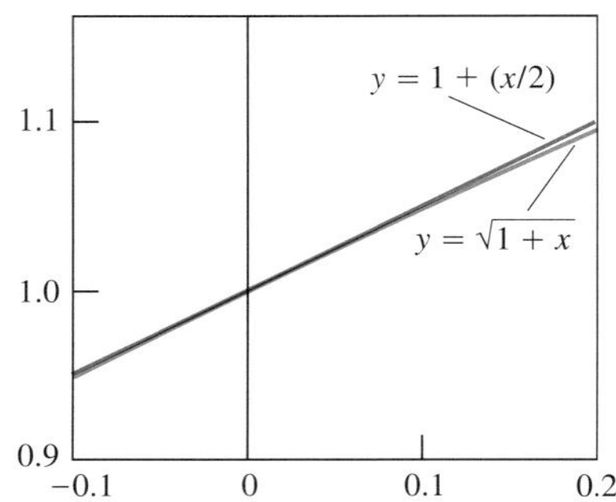

3.63 Magnified view of the window $-0.1 \le x \le 0.2$, $0.9 \le y \le 1.14$ in Fig. 3.62. The graphs of $y = \sqrt{1+x}$ and its linearization $y = 1 + (x/2)$ are so close it is hard to see just how accurate the approximation is. We can readily find out with a calculator, however, as in the text.

In case you are wondering how close the approximation

$$\sqrt{1+x} \approx 1 + \frac{x}{2}$$

really is, we can try a few values with a calculator:

$$\sqrt{1.2} \approx 1 + \frac{0.2}{2} = 1.10, \qquad \text{Accurate to 2 decimals}$$

$$\sqrt{1.05} \approx 1 + \frac{0.05}{2} = 1.025, \qquad \text{Accurate to 3 decimals}$$

$$\sqrt{1.005} \approx 1 + \frac{0.005}{2} = 1.00250. \qquad \text{Accurate to 5 decimals}$$

See Fig. 3.63.

The approximation becomes more accurate as we move toward the center, $x = 0$, and less accurate as we move away from the center. As Fig. 3.62 suggests, the approximation will probably be too crude to be useful if we move out as far, say, as $x = 3$. To approximate $\sqrt{1+x}$ near $x = 3$, we had best find its linearization at $x = 3$.

EXAMPLE 2 Find the linearization of $f(x) = \sqrt{1+x}$ at $x = 3$.

Solution We evaluate Eq. (3) for $f(x) = \sqrt{1+x}$, $f'(x) = 1/(2\sqrt{1+x})$, and $a = 3$. With

$$f(3) = 2, \qquad f'(3) = \frac{1}{2\sqrt{1+3}} = \frac{1}{4}.$$

Eq. (3) gives

$$L(x) = 2 + \frac{1}{4}(x - 3) = 2 + \frac{x}{4} - \frac{3}{4} = \frac{5}{4} + \frac{x}{4}.$$

Thus, near $x = 3$,

$$\sqrt{1+x} \approx \frac{5}{4} + \frac{x}{4}.$$

At $x = 3.2$, this linearization gives

$$\sqrt{1+x} = \sqrt{1+3.2} \approx \frac{5}{4} + \frac{3.2}{4} = 1.250 + 0.800 = 2.050,$$

which differs from $\sqrt{4.2} = 2.04939$ by less than one-thousandth. The linearization from Example 1 gives

$$\sqrt{1+x} = \sqrt{1+3.2} \approx 1 + \frac{3.2}{2} = 1 + 1.6 = 2.6,$$

a result that is off by more than 25%. The linearization at $x = 3$ is clearly the one to use for values of $\sqrt{1+x}$ near 3.

Do not be misled by the calculations here into thinking that whatever we do with a linearization is better done with a calculator. In practice, we would never use a linearization to find the value of a particular square root. That is not what linearizations are for. The utility of the linearizations in Examples 1 and 2 lies in their ability to replace the complicated formula $\sqrt{1+x}$ by a simpler formula. If

Common Linear Approximations for x Numerically Small

$\sin x \approx x$

$\cos x \approx 1$

$\tan x \approx x$

(See Exercises 13 and 14.)

we have to work with $\sqrt{1+x}$ for values of x close to 0 and can tolerate the small amount of error involved, we can safely work with $1 + (x/2)$ instead. Of course, we then need to know just how much error there really is. We shall look at that in a moment but will not have the full answer until Chapter 9.

EXAMPLE 3 The most important linearization for roots and powers is

$$(1+x)^k \approx 1 + kx \qquad (x \approx 0;\ \text{any number } k) \tag{4}$$

(Exercise 22). This approximation, good for values of x sufficiently close to zero, has broad application.

Approximation (x numerically small)	**Source: Eq. (4) with . . .**
$\sqrt{1+x} \approx 1 + \dfrac{x}{2}$	$k = 1/2$
$\dfrac{1}{1-x} = (1-x)^{-1} \approx 1 + (-1)(-x) = 1 + x$	$k = -1$; $-x$ in place of x
$\sqrt[3]{1+5x^4} = (1+5x^4)^{1/3} \approx 1 + \dfrac{1}{3}(5x^4) = 1 + \dfrac{5}{3}x^4$	$k = 1/3$; $5x^4$ in place of x
$\dfrac{1}{\sqrt{1-x^2}} = (1-x^2)^{-1/2} \approx 1 + \left(-\dfrac{1}{2}\right)\left(-x^2\right) = 1 + \dfrac{x^2}{2}$	$k = -1/2$; $-x^2$ in place of x

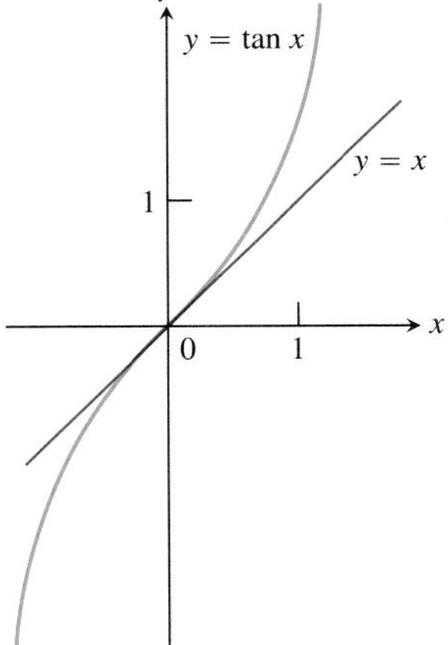

3.64 The linearization of tan x near the origin.

EXAMPLE 4 Find the linearization of $f(x) = \tan x$ at $x = 0$.

Solution We use the equation

$$L(x) = f(a) + f'(a)(x-a)$$

with $f(x) = \tan x$ and $a = 0$. Since

$$f(0) = \tan(0) = 0, \qquad f'(0) = \sec^2(0) = 1,$$

we have $L(x) = 0 + 1(x - 0) = x$. Near $x = 0$, $\tan x \approx x$ (Fig. 3.64).

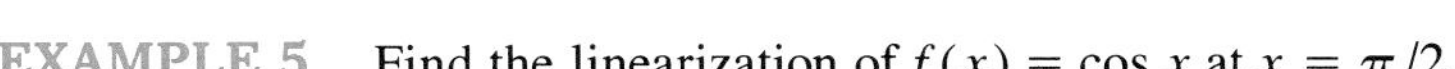

EXAMPLE 5 Find the linearization of $f(x) = \cos x$ at $x = \pi/2$.

Solution We use the equation

$$L(x) = f(a) + f'(a)(x-a)$$

with $f(x) = \cos x$ and $a = \pi/2$. Since

$$f(\pi/2) = \cos(\pi/2) = 0 \qquad \text{and} \qquad f'(\pi/2) = -\sin(\pi/2) = -1,$$

the linearization is

$$L(x) = 0 - 1 \cdot \left(x - \frac{\pi}{2}\right) = -x + \frac{\pi}{2}.$$

Near $x = \pi/2$,

$$\cos x \approx -x + \frac{\pi}{2}.$$

(See Fig. 3.65.)

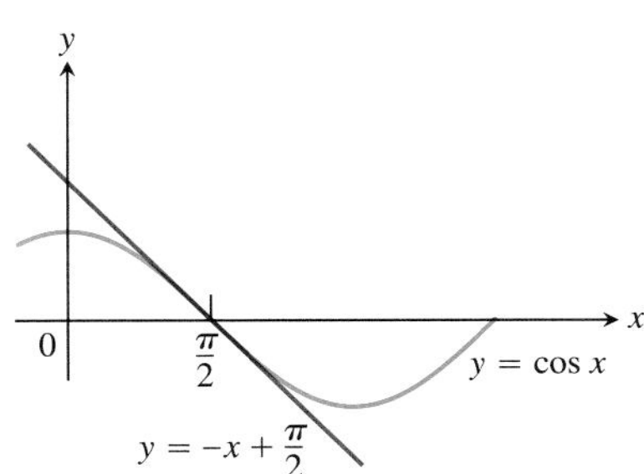

3.65 The graph of $y = \cos x$ and its linearization at $x = \pi/2$. Near $x = \pi/2$, $\cos x \approx -x + (\pi/2)$.

Estimating Change with Differentials

Suppose we know the value of a differentiable function $f(x)$ at a particular x_0 and want to predict how much this value will change if we move to $x_0 + \Delta x$ nearby. If Δx is small, f and its linearization L at x_0 will change by nearly the same amount. Since the values of L are always easier to calculate, calculating the change in L offers a practical way to estimate the change in f.

In the notation of Fig. 3.66, the change in f is

$$\Delta f = f(x_0 + \Delta x) - f(x_0).$$

The corresponding change in $L(x) = f(x_0) + f'(x_0)(x - x_0)$ is

$$\begin{aligned}
\Delta L &= L(x_0 + \Delta x) - L(x_0) \\
&= L(x_0 + \Delta x) - f(x_0) && L(x_0) = f(x_0) \\
&= \overbrace{f(x_0) + f'(x_0)\underbrace{[(x_0 + \Delta x) - x_0]}_{\Delta x}}^{L(x_0+\Delta x)} - f(x_0) && (5) \\
&= f(x_0) + f'(x_0)\,\Delta x - f(x_0) \\
&= f'(x_0)\,\Delta x.
\end{aligned}$$

As you can see, the change in L is just a constant times Δx.

The change $\Delta L = f'(x_0)\,\Delta x$ is usually described in the more suggestive notation

$$df = f'(x_0)\,dx, \tag{6}$$

in which df denotes the change in the linearization of f that results from the change dx in x. We call dx the **differential** of x, and df the corresponding **differential** of f.

If $y = f(x)$ and we divide both sides of the equation $dy = f'(x)\,dx$ by dx, we obtain the familiar equation

$$\frac{df}{dx} = f'(x).$$

This equation now says that we may regard the derivative df/dx as a quotient of differentials. In many calculations, it is convenient to be able to think this way.

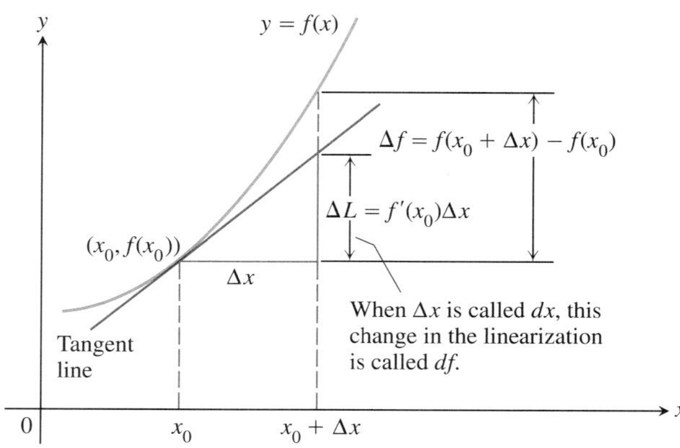

3.66 If Δx is small, the change in the linearization of f is nearly the same as the change in f.

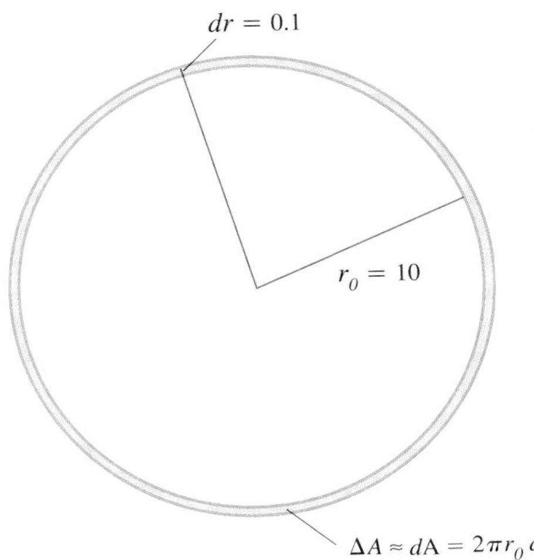

3.67 When dr is small compared with r_0, as it is when $dr = 0.1$ and $r_0 = 10$, the differential $dA = 2\pi r_0\, dr$ gives a good estimate of ΔA (Example 6).

For example, in writing the Chain Rule as

$$\frac{dy}{dx} = \frac{dy}{du} \cdot \frac{du}{dx},$$

we can think of the derivatives on the right as quotients in which the du's cancel to produce the fraction on the left. This gives a quick check on whether we remembered the rule correctly.

EXAMPLE 6 The radius of a circle increases from an initial value of $r_0 = 10$ by an amount $dr = 0.1$ (Fig. 3.67). Estimate the corresponding increase in the circle's area $A = \pi r^2$ by calculating dA. Compare dA with the true change ΔA.

Solution To calculate dA, we apply Eq. (6) to the function $A = \pi r^2$:

$$dA = A'(r_0)\, dr = 2\pi r_0\, dr.$$

We then substitute the values $r_0 = 10$ and $dr = 0.1$:

$$dA = 2\pi(10)(0.1) = 2\pi.$$

The estimated change is 2π square units.

A direct calculation of ΔA gives

$$\Delta A = \pi(10.1)^2 - \pi(10)^2 = (102.01 - 100)\pi = \underbrace{2\pi}_{dA} + \underbrace{0.01\pi}_{\text{error}}.$$

The error in the estimate dA is 0.01π square units. As a percentage of the circle's original area, the error is quite small, as we can see from the following calculation:

$$\frac{\text{error}}{\text{original area}} = \frac{0.01\pi}{100\pi} = 0.01\%.$$

Absolute, Relative, and Percentage Change

What is the difference again between Δf and df? The increment Δf is the change in f; the differential df is the change in the linearization of f. Unlike Δf, the differential df is always simple to calculate, and it gives a good estimate of Δf when the change in x is small.

As we move from x_0 to a nearby point, we can describe the corresponding change in the value of f in three ways:

	True	**Estimate**
Absolute change	Δf	df
Relative change	$\dfrac{\Delta f}{f(x_0)}$	$\dfrac{df}{f(x_0)}$
Percentage change	$\dfrac{\Delta f}{f(x_0)} \times 100$	$\dfrac{df}{f(x_0)} \times 100$

EXAMPLE 7 Estimate the percentage change that will occur in the area of a circle if its radius increases from $r_0 = 10$ units to 10.1 units.

Solution From the preceding table, we have

$$\text{Estimated percentage change} = \frac{dA}{A(r_0)} \times 100.$$

With $dA = 2\pi$ (from Example 6) and $A(r_0) = 100\pi$, the formula gives

$$\frac{dA}{A(r_0)} \times 100 = \frac{2\pi}{100\pi} \times 100 = 2\%.$$

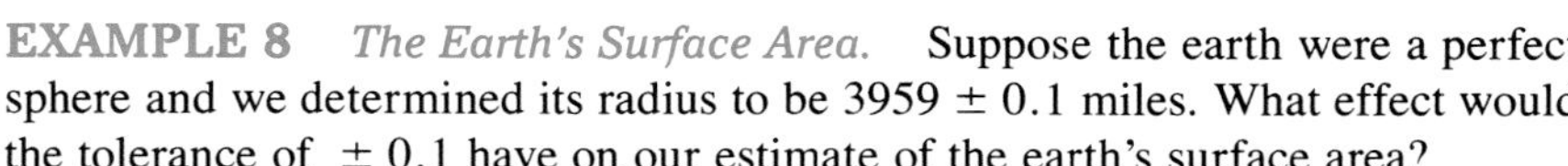

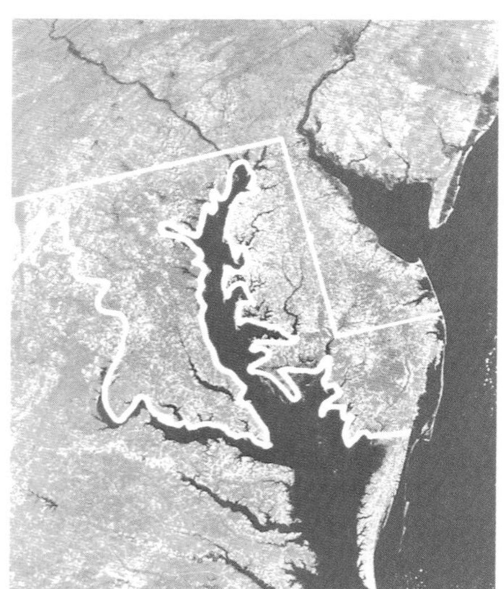

3.68 If we underestimated the radius of the earth by 528 ft during a calculation of the earth's surface area, we would leave out an area the size of the state of Maryland (Example 8).

EXAMPLE 8 *The Earth's Surface Area.* Suppose the earth were a perfect sphere and we determined its radius to be 3959 ± 0.1 miles. What effect would the tolerance of ± 0.1 have on our estimate of the earth's surface area?

Solution The surface area of a sphere of radius r is $S = 4\pi r^2$. The uncertainty in the calculation of S that arises from measuring r with a tolerance of dr miles is about

$$dS = \left(\frac{dS}{dr}\right) dr = 8\pi r\, dr.$$

With $r = 3959$ and $dr = 0.1$,

$$dS = 8\pi(3959)(0.1) = 9950 \text{ mi}^2$$

to the nearest square mile, which is about the area of the state of Maryland (Fig. 3.68). In absolute terms this might seem like a large error. However, 9950 mi^2 is a relatively small error when compared with the calculated surface area of the earth:

$$\frac{dS}{\text{calculated } S} = \frac{9950}{4\pi(3959)^2} \approx \frac{9950}{196{,}961{,}284} \approx 0.005\%.$$

EXAMPLE 9 About how accurately should we measure the radius r of a sphere to calculate the surface area $S = 4\pi r^2$ within 1% of its true value?

Solution We want any inaccuracy in our measurement to be small enough to make the corresponding increment ΔS in the surface area satisfy the inequality

$$|\Delta S| \le \frac{1}{100} S = \frac{4\pi r^2}{100}. \tag{7}$$

We replace ΔS in this inequality with

$$dS = \left(\frac{dS}{dr}\right) dr = 8\pi r\, dr.$$

This gives

$$|8\pi r\, dr| \le \frac{4\pi r^2}{100}, \qquad \text{or} \qquad |dr| \le \frac{1}{8\pi r} \cdot \frac{4\pi r^2}{100} = \frac{1}{2}\frac{r}{100}.$$

We should measure the radius with an error dr that is no more than 0.5% of the true value.

EXAMPLE 10 *Unclogging Arteries.* In the late 1830s, the French physiologist Jean Poiseuille ("pwa-*zoy*") discovered the formula we use today to predict

Angiography: An opaque dye is injected into a partially blocked artery to make the inside visible under x-rays. This reveals the location and severity of the blockage.

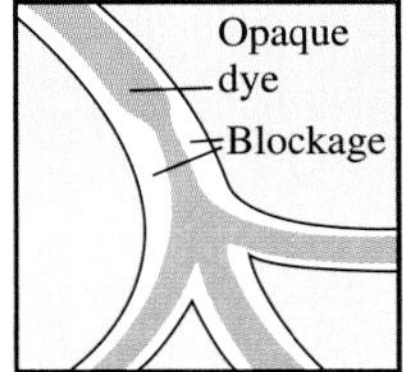

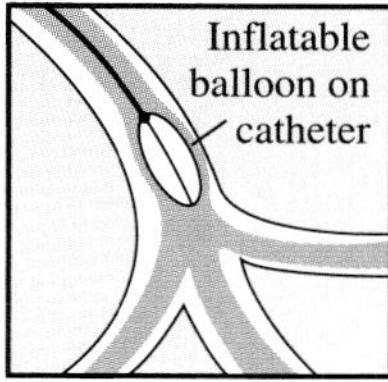

Angioplasty: A balloon-tipped catheter is inflated inside the artery to widen it at the blockage site.

how much the radius of a partially clogged artery has to be expanded to restore normal flow. His formula,

$$V = kr^4, \tag{8}$$

says that the volume V of fluid flowing through a small pipe or tube in a unit of time at a fixed pressure is a constant times the fourth power of the tube's radius r. How will a 10% increase in r affect V?

Solution The differentials of r and V are related by the equation

$$dV = \frac{dV}{dr}\,dr = 4kr^3\,dr.$$

Hence,

$$\frac{dV}{V} = \frac{4kr^3\,dr}{kr^4} = 4\,\frac{dr}{r}. \qquad \text{Dividing by } V = kr^4$$

The relative change in V is four times the relative change in r, so a 10% increase in r will produce a 40% increase in the flow.

Sensitivity

The equation $df = f'(x)\,dx$ tells how sensitive the output of f is to a change in input at different values of x. The larger the value of f' at x, the greater is the effect of a given change dx.

EXAMPLE 11 You want to calculate the height of a bridge from the equation $s = 16t^2$ by timing how long it takes a heavy stone you drop to splash into the water below. How sensitive will your calculation be to a 0.1-sec error in measuring the time?

Solution The size of ds in the equation

$$ds = 32t\,dt$$

depends on how big t is. If $t = 2$ sec, the error caused by $dt = 0.1$ is only

$$ds = 32(2)(0.1) = 6.4 \text{ ft}.$$

Three seconds later, at $t = 5$ sec, the error caused by the same dt is

$$ds = 32(5)(0.1) = 16 \text{ ft}.$$

The Error in the Approximation $\Delta f \approx f'(x_0)\,\Delta x$

How well does $f'(x_0)\,\Delta x$ estimate the true increment $\Delta f = f(x_0 + \Delta x) - f(x_0)$? We measure the error by subtracting one from the other:

$$\begin{aligned}
\text{Approximation error} &= \Delta f - f'(x_0)\,\Delta x \\
&= f(x_0 + \Delta x) - f(x_0) - f'(x_0)\,\Delta x \\
&= \underbrace{\left(\frac{f(x_0 + \Delta x) - f(x_0)}{\Delta x} - f'(x_0)\right)}_{\text{call this part } \epsilon}\Delta x, \qquad (9) \\
&= \epsilon \cdot \Delta x.
\end{aligned}$$

As $\Delta x \to 0$, the difference quotient

$$\frac{f(x_0 + \Delta x) - f(x_0)}{\Delta x}$$

approaches $f'(x_0)$ (remember the definition of $f'(x_0)$), so the quantity in parentheses becomes a very small number (which is why we called it ϵ). In fact, $\epsilon \to 0$ as $\Delta x \to 0$. When Δx is small, the approximation error $\epsilon\,\Delta x$ is smaller still.

$$\underbrace{\Delta f}_{\text{true change}} = \underbrace{f'(x_0)\,\Delta x}_{\text{estimated change}} + \underbrace{\epsilon\,\Delta x}_{\text{error}} \tag{10}$$

While we do not know exactly how small the error is and will not be able to make much progress on this front until Chapter 9, there is something worth noting here, namely the *form* taken by the equation.

If $y = f(x)$ is differentiable at $x = x_0$, and x changes from x_0 to $x_0 + \Delta x$, the change Δy in f is given by an equation of the form

$$\Delta y = f'(x_0)\,\Delta x + \epsilon\,\Delta x \tag{11}$$

in which $\epsilon \to 0$ as $\Delta x \to 0$.

Surprising as it may seem, just knowing the form of Eq. (11) enables us to bring the proof of the Chain Rule to a successful conclusion. You can find out what we mean by turning to Appendix 3.

TABLE 3.2
Formulas for differentials

$$dc = 0$$
$$d(cu) = c\,du$$
$$d(u + v) = du + dv$$
$$d(uv) = u\,dv + v\,du$$
$$d\left(\frac{u}{v}\right) = \frac{v\,du - u\,dv}{v^2}$$
$$d(u^n) = nu^{n-1}\,du$$
$$d(\sin u) = \cos u\,du$$
$$d(\cos u) = -\sin u\,du$$
$$d(\tan u) = \sec^2 u\,du$$
$$d(\cot u) = -\csc^2 u\,du$$
$$d(\sec u) = \sec u \tan u\,du$$
$$d(\csc u) = -\csc u \cot u\,du$$

Derivatives in Differential Notation

Every formula like

$$\frac{d(u + v)}{dx} = \frac{du}{dx} + \frac{dv}{dx}$$

has a corresponding differential formula like

$$d(u + v) = du + dv$$

that comes from multiplying both sides by dx (Table 3.2).

EXAMPLE 12

a) $d(3x^2 - 6) = 6x\,dx$

b) $d(\cos 3x) = (-\sin 3x)\,d(3x) = -3\sin 3x\,dx$

c) $d\left(\dfrac{x}{x + 1}\right) = \dfrac{(x + 1)dx - x\,d(x + 1)}{(x + 1)^2} = \dfrac{x\,dx + dx - x\,dx}{(x + 1)^2} = \dfrac{dx}{(x + 1)^2}$

A differential on one side of an equation always calls for a differential on the other side of the equation. We never have $dy = 3x^2$ but, instead, $dy = 3x^2\,dx$. Likewise, we never have $y' = 3x^2\,dx$.

Exercises 3.7

In Exercises 1–6, find the linearization $L(x)$ of $f(x)$ at $x = a$.

1. $f(x) = x^4$ at $x = 1$
2. $f(x) = x^{-1}$ at $x = 2$
3. $f(x) = x^3 - x$ at $x = 1$
4. $f(x) = x^3 - 2x + 3$ at $x = 2$
5. $f(x) = \sqrt{x}$ at $x = 4$
6. $f(x) = \sqrt{x^2 + 9}$ at $x = -4$

You want linearizations that will replace the functions in Exercises 7–12 over intervals that include the given points x_0. To make your subsequent work as simple as possible, you want to center each linearization not at x_0 but at a nearby integer $x = a$ at which the given function and its derivative are easy to evaluate. What linearization do you use in each case?

7. $f(x) = x^2 + 2x, \quad x_0 = 0.1$
8. $f(x) = x^{-1}, \quad x_0 = 0.6$
9. $f(x) = 2x^2 + 4x - 3, \quad x_0 = -0.9$
10. $f(x) = 1 + x, \quad x_0 = 8.1$
11. $f(x) = \sqrt[3]{x}, \quad x_0 = 8.5$
12. $f(x) = \dfrac{x}{x+1}, \quad x_0 = 1.3$

In Exercises 13–18, find the linearization $L(x)$ of the given function at $x = a$. Then graph f and L together near $x = a$.

13. $f(x) = \sin x$ at $x = 0$
14. $f(x) = \cos x$ at $x = 0$
15. $f(x) = \sin x$ at $x = \pi$
16. $f(x) = \cos x$ at $x = -\pi/2$
17. $f(x) = \tan x$ at $x = \pi/4$
18. $f(x) = \sec x$ at $x = \pi/4$
19. Use the formula $(1 + x)^k \approx 1 + kx$ to find linear approximations of the following functions for values of x near zero.

    a) $f(x) = (1 + x)^2$
    b) $f(x) = \dfrac{1}{(1+x)^5}$
    c) $g(x) = \dfrac{2}{1-x}$
    d) $g(x) = (1 - x)^6$
    e) $h(x) = 3(1 + x)^{1/3}$
    f) $h(x) = \dfrac{1}{\sqrt{1+x}}$

20. *Faster than a Calculator.* Use the approximation $(1 + x)^k \approx 1 + kx$ to estimate

    a) $(1.0002)^{50}$
    b) $\sqrt[3]{1.009}$

21. Find the linearization of $f(x) = \sqrt{x+1} + \sin x$ at $x = 0$. How is it related to the individual linearizations for $\sqrt{x+1}$ and $\sin x$?
22. We know from the Power Rule that the equation

$$\frac{d}{dx}(1+x)^k = k(1+x)^{k-1}$$

holds for every rational number k. In Chapter 6, we will show that it holds for every irrational number as well. Assuming this result for now, verify Eq. (4) by showing that the linearization of $f(x) = (1 + x)^k$ at $x = 0$ is $L(x) = 1 + kx$ for any number k.

23. In Section 1.5, we promised to explain what happened when you used your calculator to take successive square roots of 2. As you may recall, or as you will find if you try it now, each new round of calculation divides the decimal part of the display approximately in half. The explanation comes from the fact that the linearization of $\sqrt{1+x}$ is $1 + (x/2)$. The x is the decimal part of the display $(1.x)$ and each new square root is about $1 + (x/2)$.

    If you have not done so already, enter 2 into your calculator and take repeated square roots to see what happens.

24. If you have not already done so, turn to Section 1.5 and do Exercise 14 there. If you have a key that will enable you to calculate tenth roots, do Exercise 15 as well.

In Exercises 25–30, each function $f(x)$ changes value when x changes from x_0 to $x_0 + dx$. Find

a) the change $\Delta f = f(x_0 + dx) - f(x_0)$;
b) the value of the estimate $df = f'(x_0)\,dx$; and
c) the approximation error $|\Delta f - df|$.

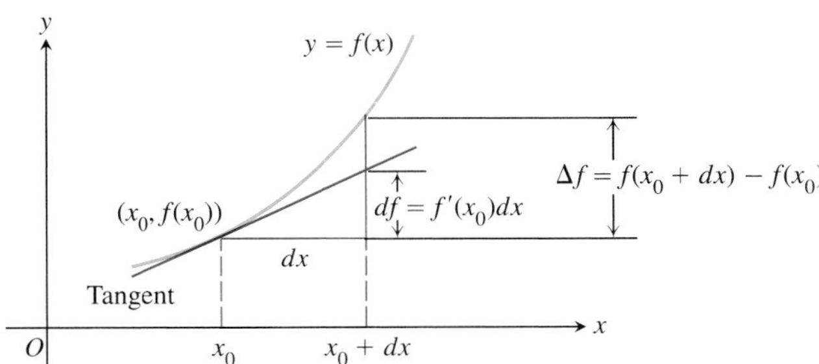

25. $f(x) = x^2 + 2x, \quad x_0 = 0, \quad dx = 0.1$
26. $f(x) = 2x^2 + 4x - 3, \quad x_0 = -1, \quad dx = 0.1$
27. $f(x) = x^3 - x, \quad x_0 = 1, \quad dx = 0.1$
28. $f(x) = x^4, \quad x_0 = 1, \quad dx = 0.1$
29. $f(x) = x^{-1}, \quad x_0 = 0.5, \quad dx = 0.1$
30. $f(x) = x^3 - 2x + 3, \quad x_0 = 2, \quad dx = 0.1$

In Exercises 31–36, write a differential formula that estimates the given change in volume or surface area.

31. The change in the volume $V = (4/3)\pi r^3$ of a sphere when the radius changes from r_0 to $r_0 + dr$.

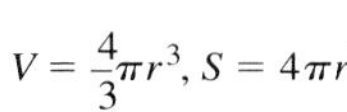

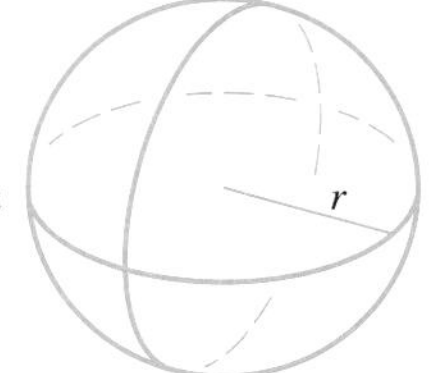

32. The change in the surface area $S = 4\pi r^2$ of a sphere when the radius changes from r_0 to $r_0 + dr$.

33. The change in the volume $V = x^3$ of a cube when the edge lengths change from x_0 to $x_0 + dx$.

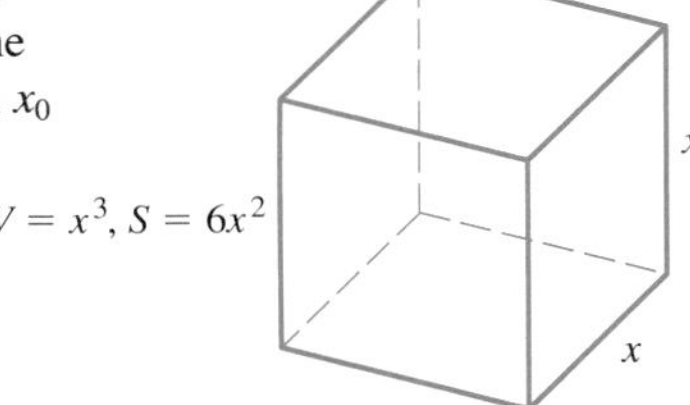

34. The change in the surface area $S = 6x^2$ of a cube when the edge lengths change from x_0 to $x_0 + dx$.

35. The change in the volume $V = \pi r^2 h$ of a right circular cylinder when the radius changes from r_0 to $r_0 + dr$ and the height does not change.

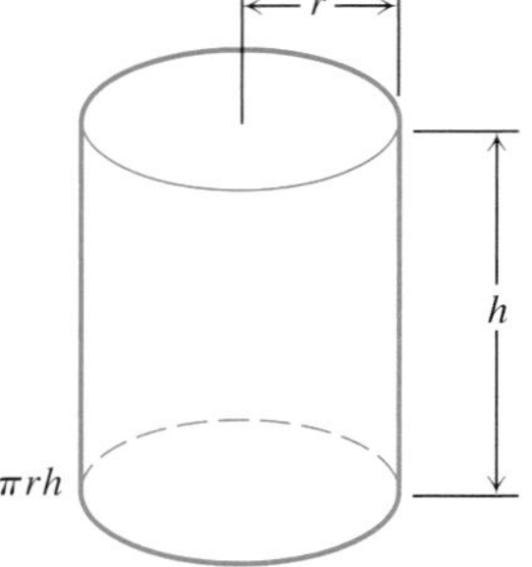

36. The change in the lateral surface area $S = 2\pi rh$ of a right circular cylinder when the height changes from h_0 to $h_0 + dh$ and the radius does not change.

37. The radius of a circle is increased from 2.00 to 2.02 m.
   a) Estimate the resulting change in area.
   b) Express the estimate in (a) as a percentage of the circle's original area.

38. The diameter of a tree was 10 in. During the following year, the circumference grew 2 in. About how much did the tree's diameter grow? the tree's cross-section area?

39. The edge of a cube is measured as 10 cm with an error of 1%. The cube's volume is to be calculated from this measurement. Estimate the percentage error in the volume calculation.

40. About how accurately should you measure the side of a square to be sure of calculating the area within 2% of its true value?

41. The diameter of a sphere is measured as 100 ± 1 cm and the volume is calculated from this measurement. Estimate the percentage error in the volume calculation.

42. Estimate the allowable percentage error in measuring the diameter D of a sphere if the volume is to be calculated correctly to within 3%.

43. The height and radius of a right circular cylinder are equal, so the cylinder's volume is $V = \pi h^3$. The volume is to be calculated from a measurement of h and must be calculated with an error of no more than 1% of the true value. Find approximately the greatest error that can be tolerated in the measurement of h, expressed as a percentage of h.

44. a) About how accurately must the interior diameter of a 10-m-high cylindrical storage tank be measured to calculate the tank's volume to within 1% of its true value?
   b) About how accurately must the tank's exterior diameter be measured to calculate the amount of paint it will take to paint the side of the tank within 5% of the true amount?

45. A manufacturer contracts to mint coins for the federal government. How much variation dr in the radius of the coins can be tolerated if the coins are to weigh within 1/1000 of their ideal weight? Assume that the thickness does not vary.

46. *Continuation of Example 10.* By what percentage should r be increased to increase V by 50%?

47. *Continuation of Example 11.* Show that a 5% error in measuring t will cause about a 10% error in calculating s from the equation $s = 16t^2$.

48. *The Effect of Flight Maneuvers on the Heart.* The amount of work done in a unit of time by the heart's main pumping chamber, the left ventricle, is given by the equation

$$W = PV + \frac{V\delta v^2}{2g},$$

where W is the work, P is the average blood pressure, V is the volume of blood pumped out during the unit of time, δ is the density of the blood, v is the average velocity of the exiting blood, and g is the acceleration of gravity.

When P, V, δ, and v remain constant, W becomes a function of g and the equation takes the simplified form

$$W = a + \frac{b}{g} \qquad (a, b \text{ constant}) \tag{12}$$

As a member of NASA's medical team, you want to know how sensitive W is to apparent changes in g caused by flight maneuvers, and this depends on the initial value of g. As part of your investigation, you decide to compare the effect on W of a given change dg on the moon, where $g = 5.2$ ft/sec^2, with the effect the same change dg would have on Earth, where $g = 32$ ft/sec^2. You use Eq. (12) to find the ratio of dW_{moon} to dW_{Earth}. What do you conclude?

49. Show that the approximation of $\sqrt{1+x}$ by its linearization at the origin (Example 3) must improve as $x \to 0$ by showing that

$$\lim_{x \to 0} \frac{\sqrt{1+x}}{1 + (x/2)} = 1.$$

50. Show that the approximation of $\tan x$ by its linearization at the origin (Example 4) must improve as $x \to 0$ by showing that

$$\lim_{x \to 0} \frac{\tan x}{x} = 1.$$

51. Suppose that the graph of a differentiable function $f(x)$ has a horizontal tangent at $x = a$. Can anything be said about the linearization of f at $x = a$? Give reasons for your answer.

52. *Reading Derivatives from Graphs.* The idea that differentiable curves flatten out when magnified can be used to estimate the values of the derivatives of functions at particular points. We magnify the curve until the portion we see looks like a straight line through the point in question, and then we

use the screen's coordinate grid to read the slope of the curve as the slope of the line it resembles.

a) To see how the process works, try it first with the function $y = x^2$ at $x = 1$. The slope you read should be 2.

b) Then try it with the curve $y = e^x$ at $x = 1$, $x = 0$, and $x = -1$. In each case, compare your estimate of the derivative with the value of e^x at the point. What pattern do you see? Test it with other values of x. Chapter 6 will explain what is going on.

In Exercises 53–64, find *dy*.

53. $y = x^3 - 3\sqrt{x}$

54. $y = x\sqrt{1 - x^2}$

55. $y = \dfrac{2x}{1 + x^2}$

56. $y = \dfrac{2\sqrt{x}}{3(1 + \sqrt{x})}$

57. $2y^{3/2} + xy - x = 0$

58. $xy^2 - 4x^{3/2} - y = 0$

59. $y = \sin(5\sqrt{x})$

60. $y = \cos(x^2)$

61. $y = 4\tan(x^3/3)$

62. $y = \sec(x^2 - 1)$

63. $y = 3\csc(1 - 2\sqrt{x})$

64. $y = 2\cot\left(\dfrac{1}{\sqrt{x}}\right)$

Writing for Your Own Knowledge

Answer the following questions in writing. Some answers will take only a sentence or two; others may require several paragraphs. Some explanations may also call for graphs or sketches.

1. What is a linearization?
2. Why bother with linearization?
3. How do you use differentials to estimate absolute change? relative change? percentage change?
4. How do you express derivatives in differential notation?

EXPLORER PROGRAM

PowerGrapher — Graphs functions and their linearizations together by constructing tangents to curves at points of your choice.

3.8 *Newton's Method*

When exact formulas for solving an equation $f(x) = 0$ are not available, we can turn to numerical techniques from calculus to approximate the solutions we seek. One of these techniques is *Newton's method* or, as it is more accurately called, the *Newton-Raphson method*. It is based on the idea of using tangent lines to replace the graph of $y = f(x)$ near the points where f is zero. Once again, linearization is the key to solving a practical problem.

If you have access to a computer or programmable calculator, you can use the program at the end of this section to do the arithmetic. If not, you can still see how the technique works, and you can work the beginning exercises at the end of the section by hand.

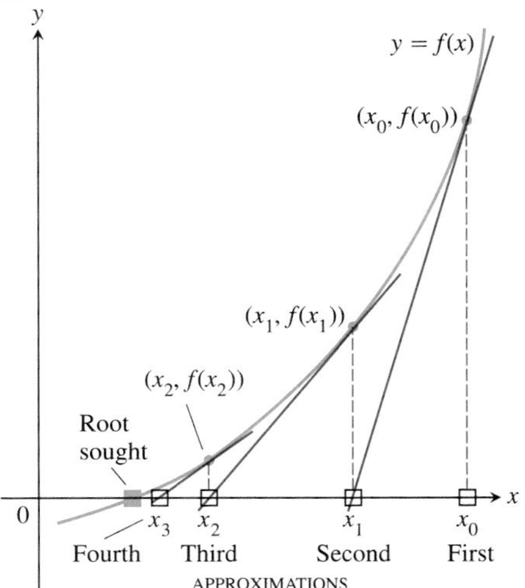

3.69 Newton's method starts with an initial guess x_0 and (under favorable circumstances) improves the guess one step at a time.

The Theory

The goal of Newton's method for estimating a solution of an equation $f(x) = 0$ is to produce a sequence of approximations that approach the solution. We pick the first number x_0 of the sequence. Then, under favorable circumstances, the method does the rest by moving step by step toward a point where the graph of f crosses the x-axis (Fig. 3.69).

The initial estimate, x_0, may be found by graphing or just plain guessing. The method then uses the tangent to the curve $y = f(x)$ at $(x_0, f(x_0))$ to approximate the curve, calling the point where the tangent meets the x-axis x_1. The number x_1 is usually a better approximation to the solution than is x_0. The point x_2 where the tangent to the curve at $(x_1, f(x_1))$ crosses the x-axis is the next approximation in the sequence. We continue on, using each approximation to generate the next, until we are close enough to the root to stop.

We can derive a formula for generating the successive approximations in the

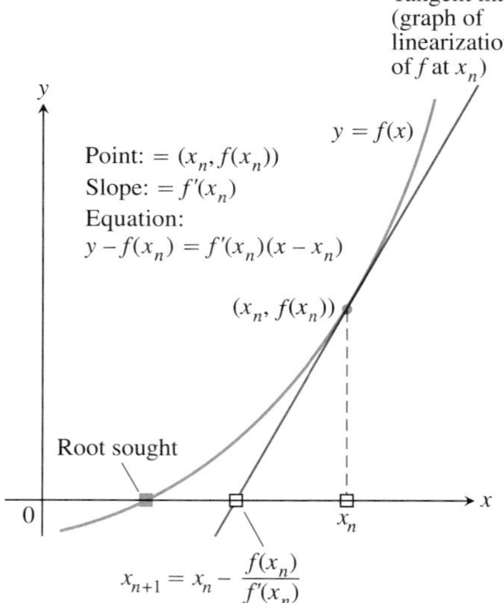

3.70 The geometry of the successive steps of Newton's method. From x_n we go up to the curve and follow the tangent line down to find x_{n+1}.

following way. Given the approximation x_n, the point–slope equation for the tangent to the curve at $(x_n, f(x_n))$ is

$$y - f(x_n) = f'(x_n)(x - x_n) \tag{1}$$

(Fig. 3.70). We find where the tangent crosses the x-axis by setting y equal to 0 in this equation and solving for x, giving, in turn,

$$\begin{aligned} 0 - f(x_n) &= f'(x_n)(x - x_n) && \text{Eq. (1) with } y = 0 \\ -f(x_n) &= f'(x_n)x - f'(x_n)x_n \\ f'(x_n)x &= f'(x_n)x_n - f(x_n) \\ x &= x_n - \frac{f(x_n)}{f'(x_n)}. && \text{Assuming } f'(x_n) \neq 0 \end{aligned} \tag{2}$$

This value of x is the next approximation, x_{n+1}.

The Strategy for Newton's Method

1. Guess a first approximation to a root of the equation $f(x) = 0$. A graph of $y = f(x)$ will help.
2. Use the first approximation to get a second, the second to get a third, and so on, using the formula

$$x_{n+1} = x_n - \frac{f(x_n)}{f'(x_n)}, \qquad (f'(x_n) \neq 0) \tag{3}$$

where $f'(x_n)$ is the derivative of f at x_n.

The Practice

In our first example we find decimal approximations to $\sqrt{2}$ by estimating the positive root of the equation $f(x) = x^2 - 2 = 0$.

EXAMPLE 1 Find the positive root of the equation

$$f(x) = x^2 - 2 = 0.$$

Solution With $f(x) = x^2 - 2$ and $f'(x) = 2x$, Eq. (3) becomes

$$x_{n+1} = x_n - \frac{x_n{}^2 - 2}{2x_n}. \tag{4}$$

To use our calculator efficiently, we rewrite Eq. (4) in a form that uses fewer arithmetic operations:

$$\begin{aligned} x_{n+1} &= x_n - \frac{x_n}{2} + \frac{1}{x_n} \\ &= \frac{x_n}{2} + \frac{1}{x_n}. \end{aligned} \tag{5}$$

The equation

$$x_{n+1} = \frac{x_n}{2} + \frac{1}{x_n} \tag{6}$$

enables us to go from each approximation to the next with just a few keystrokes.

Algorithm and Iteration

It is customary to call a specified sequence of computational steps like the one in Newton's method an *algorithm*. When an algorithm proceeds by repeating a given set of steps over and over, using the answer from the previous step as the input for the next, the algorithm is called *iterative* and each repetition is called an *iteration*. Newton's method is one of the really fast iterative techniques for finding roots.

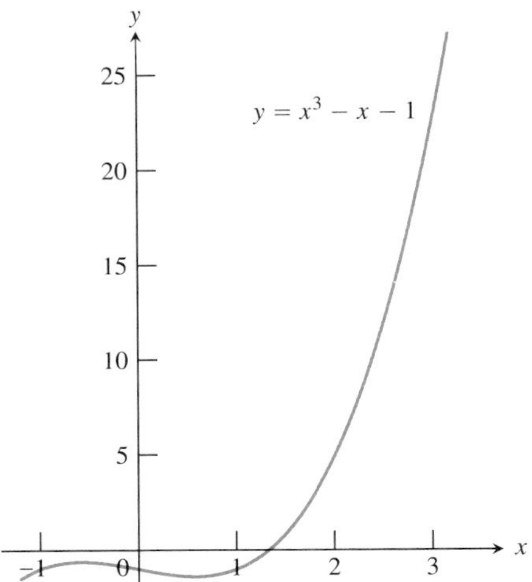

3.71 The graph of $f(x) = x^3 - x - 1$ crosses the x-axis between $x = 1$ and $x = 2$.

With the starting value $x_0 = 1$, we get the results in the first column of the following table. (To 5 decimal places, $\sqrt{2} = 1.41421$.)

	Error	Number of correct figures
$x_0 = 1$	-0.41421	1
$x_1 = 1.5$	$+0.08579$	1
$x_2 = 1.41667$	0.00246	3
$x_3 = 1.41422$	0.00001	5

Newton's method is the method used by most calculators to calculate roots because it converges so fast (more about this later). If the arithmetic in the table in Example 1 had been carried to 13 decimal places instead of 5, then going one step further would have given $\sqrt{2}$ correctly to more than 10 decimal places.

EXAMPLE 2 Find the x-coordinate of the point where the curve $y = x^3 - x$ crosses the horizontal line $y = 1$.

Solution The curve crosses the line when $x^3 - x = 1$ or $x^3 - x - 1 = 0$. When does $f(x) = x^3 - x - 1$ equal zero? The graph of f (Fig. 3.71) shows a single root, located between $x = 1$ and $x = 2$. We apply Newton's method to f with the starting value $x_0 = 1$. The results are displayed in Table 3.3 and Fig. 3.72.

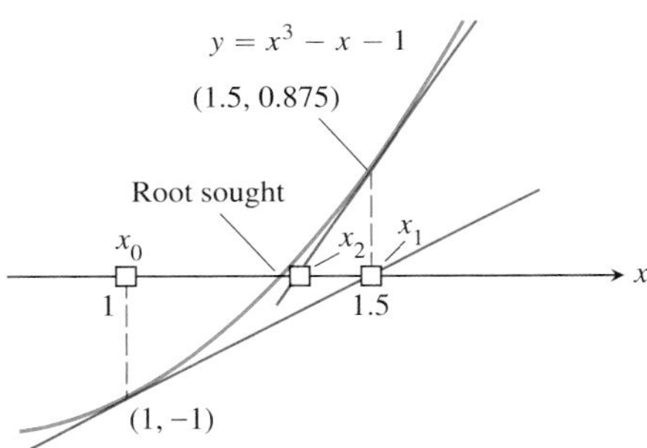

3.72 The first three x-values in Table 3.3.

TABLE 3.3
The result of applying Newton's method to $f(x) = x^3 - x - 1$ with $x_0 = 1$

n	x_n	$f(x_n)$	$f'(x_n)$	$x_{n+1} = x_n - \dfrac{f(x_n)}{f'(x_n)}$
0	1	−1	2	1.5
1	1.5	0.875	5.75	1.3478 26087
2	1.3478 26087	0.1006 82173	4.4499 05482	1.3252 00399
3	1.3252 00399	0.0020 58362	4.2684 68293	1.3247 18174
4	1.3247 18174	0.0000 00924	4.2646 34722	1.3247 17957
5	1.3247 17957	−1.0437E-9	4.2646 32997	1.3247 17957

At $n = 5$ we come to the result $x_6 = x_5 = 1.3247\ 17957$. When $x_{n+1} = x_n$, Eq. (3) shows that $f(x_n) = 0$. We have found a solution of $f(x) = 0$ to 9 decimals.

The equation $x^3 - x - 1 = 0$ is the equation we solved graphically in Section 2.4, Example 11. Notice how much more rapidly and accurately we find the solution here.

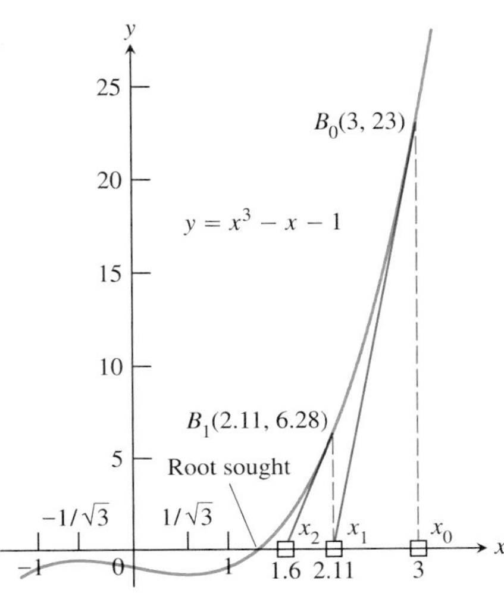

3.73 Any starting value x_0 to the right of $x = 1/\sqrt{3}$ will lead to the root.

In Fig. 3.73, we have indicated that the process in Example 2 might have started at the point $B_0(3, 23)$ on the curve, with $x_0 = 3$. Point B_0 is quite far from the x-axis, but the tangent at B_0 crosses the x-axis at about $(2.11, 0)$, so x_1 is still an improvement over x_0. If we use Eq. (3) repeatedly as before, with

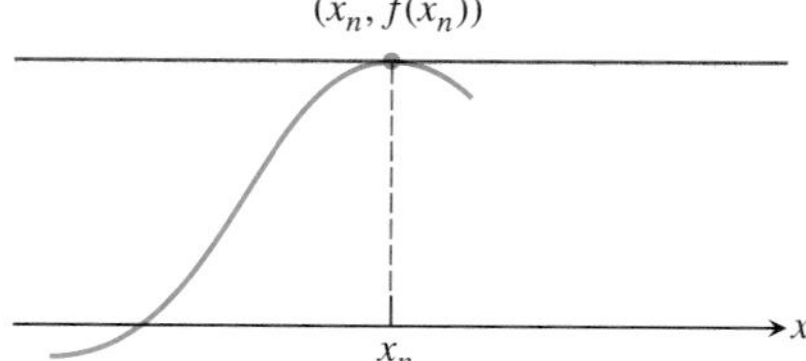

3.74 If $f'(x_n) = 0$, there is no intersection point to define x_{n+1}.

$f(x) = x^3 - x - 1$ and $f'(x) = 3x^2 - 1$, we confirm the 9-place solution $x_6 = x_5 = 1.3247\ 17957$ in six steps.

The curve in Fig. 3.73 has a relative high point at $x = -1/\sqrt{3}$ and a relative low point at $x = +1/\sqrt{3}$. We would not expect good results from Newton's method if we were to start with x_0 between these points, but we can start any place to the right of $x = 1/\sqrt{3}$ and get the answer. It would not be very clever to do so, but we could even begin far to the right of B_0, for example with $x_0 = 10$. It takes a bit longer, but the process still converges to the same answer as before.

Limitations and Strengths

Newton's method fails if it encounters a zero slope, i.e., if $f'(x_n) = 0$ at some stage (Fig. 3.74). If that happens, choose a new starting point. Of course, $f(x) = 0$ and $f'(x) = 0$ may have a common root. To detect whether this is so, we could first find the solutions of $f'(x) = 0$ and check the value of $f(x)$ at such places. Or we could graph f and f' together to look for places where the graphs might cross the x-axis together.

Newton's method does not always converge. For instance, if

$$f(x) = \begin{cases} \sqrt{x - r} & \text{for } x \geq r \\ -\sqrt{r - x} & \text{for } x < r \end{cases} \tag{7}$$

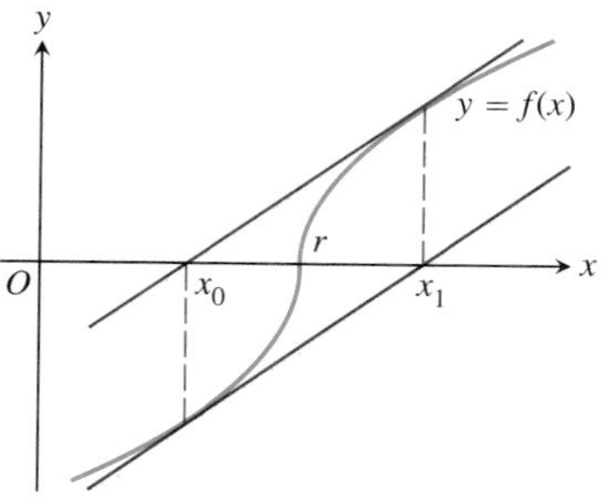

3.75 Newton's method fails to converge.

the graph will be like the one in Fig. 3.75. If we begin with $x_0 = r - h$, we get $x_1 = r + h$, and successive approximations go back and forth between these two values. No amount of iteration brings us closer to the root r than our first guess.

If Newton's method does converge, it converges to a root of $f(x)$. However, the method may converge to a root different from the one we expect if the starting value is not close enough to the root we seek (Fig. 3.76).

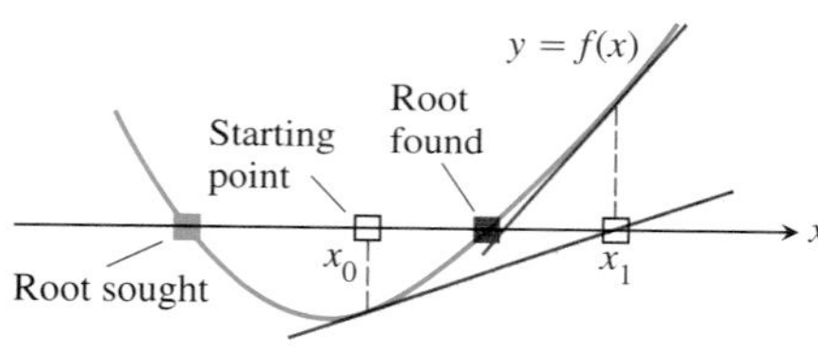

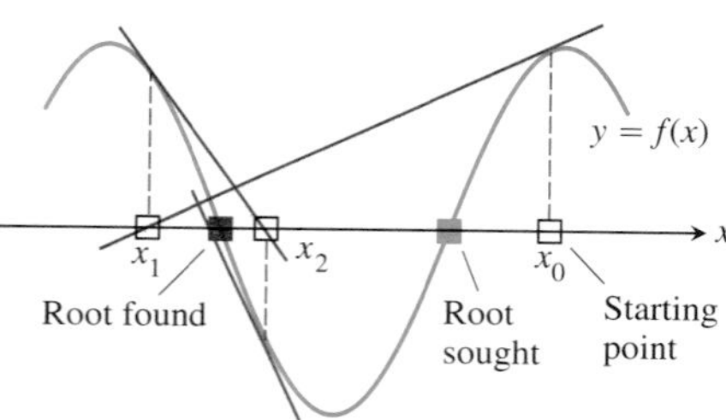

3.76 Newton's method may miss the root you want if you start too far away.

When will Newton's method converge? A result from advanced calculus says that if the inequality

$$\left| \frac{f(x) f''(x)}{[f'(x)]^2} \right| < 1 \tag{8}$$

holds for all values of x in an interval about a root r of f, then the method will converge to r for any starting value x_0 in that interval. This is a *sufficient,* but not a necessary, condition. The method can (and does) converge in some cases when there is no interval about r in which the inequality (Eq. 8) holds. Newton's method will always work if the curve $y = f(x)$ is convex ("bulges") toward the axis in the interval between x_0 and the root sought. See Fig. 3.77.

The speed with which Newton's method converges to a root r is expressed by the advanced calculus formula

$$|r - x_{n+1}| \leq \frac{1}{2} \frac{\max|f''|}{\min|f'|} (r - x_n)^2, \tag{9}$$

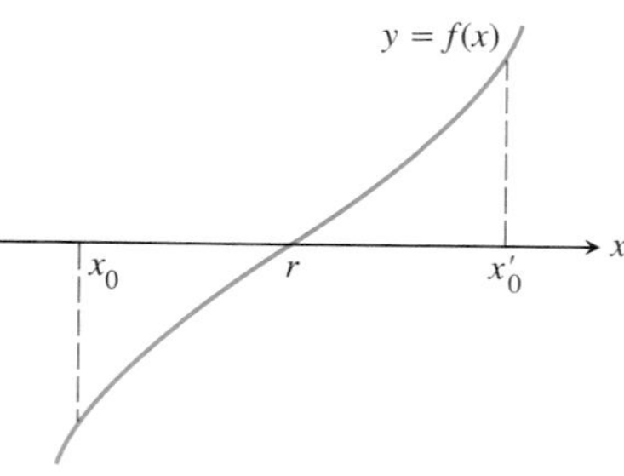

3.77 Newton's method will converge to r from either starting point.

where "max" and "min" refer to the maximum and minimum values of $|f''|$ and $|f'|$ in an interval surrounding r. The formula says that the error at step $n + 1$ is no greater than a constant times the square of the error at step n. That might not seem like much, but think of what it says. If the constant $(1/2)\max|f''|/\min|f'|$ is less than or equal to 1, and $|r - x_n| \leq 10^{-3}$, then $|r - x_{n+1}| \leq 10^{-6}$. *In a single step,* the method takes us to within less than one-millionth of the root. Little wonder that Newton's method, when it applies, is the method of choice for modern computers.

The method will find the root $x = -1$ if x_0 is far enough to the left of $-\sqrt{2}/2$. If x_0 is too close to $-\sqrt{2}/2$, the computer will encounter a zero slope or a value of x_1 too large to handle. There is a zone just to the right of $-\sqrt{2}/2$ where values of x_0 lead to $x = 1$ instead of $x = 0$.

Likewise, selected values of x_0 near $\sqrt{2}/2$ will lead to $x = 1$, $x = 0$, $x = -1$, or no root at all.

Try it.

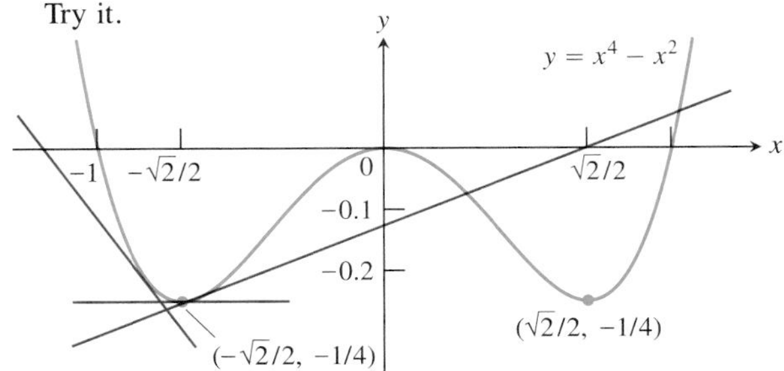

Writing for Your Own Knowledge

Answer the following questions in writing. Some answers will take only a sentence or two; others may require several paragraphs. Some explanations may also call for graphs or sketches.

1. What is Newton's method? What is the theory behind it?
2. What are some of the limitations and strengths of Newton's method?

EXPLORER PROGRAM

Bisections, Secants, Newton	Graphs any function you key in and finds its roots by the method you select.

A Computer Program for Newton's Method

You may already be familiar with BASIC as a programming language, but if you are not you will still be able to follow the next examples. Example 3 describes a program that uses Newton's method to estimate where the graphs of $y = \sin x$ and $y = x^2$ intersect. A quick sketch (Fig. 3.78) shows them to intersect at 0 and again at some point near $x = 1$. That is the point we need Newton's method for. Example 4 shows how to modify the program for other functions.

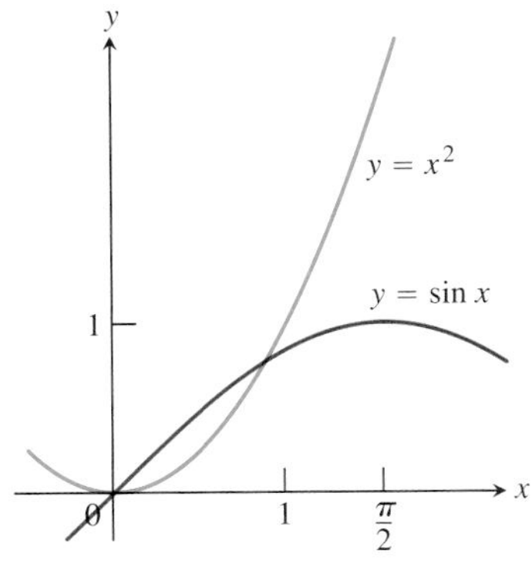

3.78 The curves $y = x^2$ and $y = \sin x$ cross at $x = 0$ and again near $x = 1$. Example 3 uses Newton's method to find this second solution of the equation $\sin x = x^2$.

EXAMPLE 3 Write and run a BASIC program that uses Newton's method to estimate the positive solution of the equation $\sin x = x^2$.

Solution The calculations to be made are these:

1. Start with $x_0 = 1$.
2. We want to make $f(x) = \sin x - x^2$ small, zero if possible; its derivative is $f'(x) = \cos x - 2x$.
3. Given any x_n, the next value of x is

$$x_{n+1} = x_n - \frac{f(x_n)}{f'(x_n)}.$$

For convenience, we label the steps in the program 10, 20, 30, and so on, leaving numbers in between for any additional steps we may wish to include later. The computer does not recognize x^2 unless we write it as x ^ 2, as shown in line 30 of the program that follows. Likewise, 10 ^ (−6) in line 80 is the notation for 10^{-6} in the program. The asterisk (*) in 2 * x indicates multiplication—BASIC does not recognize $2x$ as 2 times x.

Now, let us look again at line 80. We do not know in advance how many iterations may be needed to find a "sufficiently accurate" estimate of the root of $f(x) = 0$, so we arbitrarily tell the computer to stop after it reaches a value of x for which the absolute value of f is less than 10^{-6}. The entire command in line 80 is known as an "IF . . . THEN" conditional. If the condition is satisfied, the machine goes to line 100; but if the condition is not satisfied, the machine proceeds to line 90, which sends it back to line 50 for another round of calculation. Here is the program. Table 3.4 shows what happens when you run the program with the starting value $x = 1$.

PROGRAM		COMMENT
10	INPUT "ENTER A STARTING VALUE ", X	Screen prompt for a starting value.
20	N = 0	We start counting the steps.
30	DEF FNF(X) = SIN(X) − X ^ 2	The function is $F(x) = \sin x - x^2$.
40	DEF FNG(X) = COS(X) − 2*X	We use G for F'.
50	PRINT N; X; FNF(X); FNF(X)/FNG(X)	So we can see the values at each step.
60	X = X − FNF(X)/FNG(X)	The next x will be $x_n - f(x_n)/f'(x_n)$.
70	N = N + 1	Numbers the new x.
80	IF ABS(FNF(X)) < 10 ^ (−6) THEN 100	Conditional command discussed in text.
90	GOTO 50	If the condition ABS(FNF(X)) < 10 ^ (−6) is not yet satisfied, do it again.
100	PRINT N; X; FNF(X); FNF(X)/FNG(X)	Print the final result.
110	END	The program stops only after ABS(FNF(X)) < 10 ^ (−6).

TABLE 3.4
Estimates of the positive solution of $\sin x - x^2 = 0$

n	x_n	$f(x_n)$	$f(x_n)/f'(x_n)$
0	1	−0.1585 29	0.1086 04
1	0.8913 961	−1.6637 21E − 02	1.4411 18E − 02
2	0.8769 848	−2.8818 85E − 04	2.5858 16E − 04
3	0.8767 262	0	0

EXAMPLE 4 To run the program of Example 3 for other functions, you have only to change lines 30 and 40. To estimate where $\cos x$ equals x (Fig. 3.79), you would use

```
30    DEF FNF(X) = X − COS(X)
40    DEF FNG(X) = 1 + SIN(X)
```

Starting the program with $x = 1$ gives the results in Table 3.5.

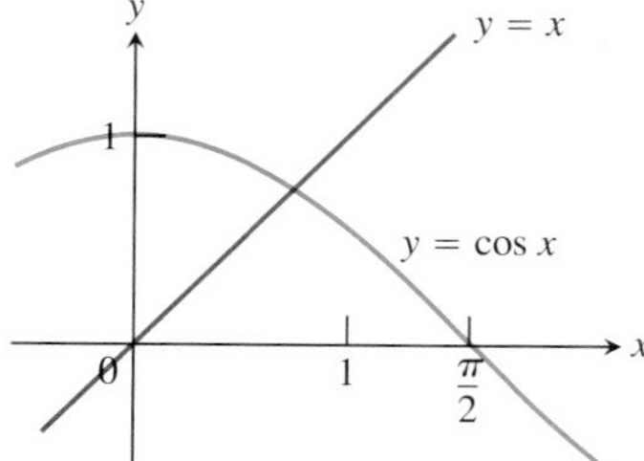

3.79 Example 4 shows how to modify the program in Example 3 to find where $\cos x = x$.

TABLE 3.5
Estimates of the solution of $\cos x = x$

n	x_n	$f(x_n)$	$f(x_n)/f'(x_n)$
0	1	0.4596 977	0.2496 361
1	0.7503 639	0.0189 231	1.1250 99E − 02
2	0.7391 129	4.6372 42E − 05	2.7707 64E − 05
3	0.7390 851	0	0

For Your Review

Write brief paragraphs about the following topics and give examples.

Slopes, tangent lines, and derivatives
Instantaneous vs. average rates of change
Differentiable functions
The following differentiation rules:
- Derivative of a constant
- Power Rule (for powers of x)
- Sum and Difference Rules
- Product Rule
- Quotient Rule

Velocity, speed, and other rates of change
Derivatives of trigonometric functions
The Chain Rule
The Power Chain Rule
Implicit differentiation
Differentiating fractional powers
Linearizations
Differentials
Newton's method

Practice Exercises

In Exercises 1–38, find dy/dx.

1. $y = x^5 - 0.125x^2 + 0.25x$

2. $y = 3 - 0.7x^3 + 0.3x^7$

3. $y = x^3 - 3(x^2 + \pi^2)$

4. $y = x^7 + \sqrt{7}x - \dfrac{1}{\pi + 1}$

5. $y = (x + 1)^2 (x^2 + 2x)$

6. $y = (2x - 5)(4 - x)^{-1}$

7. $y = (x^2 + x + 1)^3$

8. $y = \left(-1 - \dfrac{x}{2} - \dfrac{x^2}{4}\right)^2$

9. $y = \cos(1 - 2x)$

10. $y = \cot \dfrac{2}{x}$

11. $y = 2\tan^2 x - \sec^2 x$

12. $y = \dfrac{1}{\sin^2 x} - \dfrac{2}{\sin x}$

13. $y = \left(\dfrac{\sin x}{\cos x - 1}\right)^2$

14. $y = \left(\dfrac{2\sqrt{x}}{2\sqrt{x} + 1}\right)^2$

15. $y = \sqrt{\dfrac{x^2 + x}{x^2}}$

16. $y = 4x\sqrt{x + \sqrt{x}}$

17. $xy + 2x + 3y = 1$

18. $x^2 + xy + y^2 - 5x = 2$

19. $x^3 + 4xy - 3y^{4/3} = 2x$

20. $5x^{4/5} + 10y^{6/5} = 15$

21. $\sqrt{xy} = 1$

22. $x^2y^2 = 1$

23. $y^2 = \dfrac{x}{x + 1}$

24. $y^2 = \sqrt{\dfrac{1 + x}{1 - x}}$

25. $y^2 = \dfrac{(5x^2 + 2x)^{3/2}}{3}$

26. $y = \dfrac{3}{(5x^2 + 2x)^{3/2}}$

27. $y = (2x + 1)\sqrt{2x + 1}$

28. $y = 20(3x - 4)^{1/4}(3x - 4)^{-1/5}$

29. $y = \csc^5(1 - x)$

30. $y = \sec^7(7x + 7)$

31. $y = \dfrac{1}{2}x^2 \csc \dfrac{2}{x}$

32. $y = 2\sqrt{x} \sin \sqrt{x}$

33. $y = x^{-1/2} \sec 2x$

34. $y = \sqrt{x} \csc(x + 1)$

35. $y = 5 \cot x^2$

36. $y = x^2 \cot 5x$

37. $y = x^2 \sin^2(2x^2)$

38. $y = (3 + \cos^3 3x)^{-1/3}$

In Exercises 39–42, find ds/dt.

39. $s = \dfrac{\sqrt{t}}{1 + \sqrt{t}}$

40. $s = \dfrac{1}{\sqrt{t} - 1}$

41. $s = \left(\dfrac{4t}{t + 1}\right)^{-2}$

42. $s = \dfrac{-1}{15(15t - 1)^3}$

In Exercises 43–46, find $dr/d\theta$.

43. $r = \sqrt{2\theta \sin \theta}$

44. $r = 2\theta\sqrt{\cos \theta}$

45. $r = \sin \sqrt{2\theta}$

46. $r = \sin\left(\theta + \sqrt{\theta + 1}\right)$

47. **a)** Graph the function

$$f(x) = \begin{cases} x^2, & -1 \le x \le 0 \\ -x^2, & 0 \le x \le 1. \end{cases}$$

b) Is f continuous at $x = 0$?

c) Is f differentiable at $x = 0$?

Give reasons for your answers.

48. **a)** Graph the function

$$f(x) = \begin{cases} x, & -1 \leq x < 0 \\ \tan x, & 0 \leq x \leq \pi/4. \end{cases}$$

b) Is f continuous at $x = 0$?
c) Is f differentiable at $x = 0$?

Give reasons for your answers.

49. **a)** Graph the function

$$f(x) = \begin{cases} x, & 0 \leq x \leq 1 \\ 2 - x, & 1 < x \leq 2 \end{cases}$$

b) Is f continuous at $x = 1$?
c) Is f differentiable at $x = 1$?

Give reasons for your answers.

50. For what value or values of the constant m, if any, is

$$f(x) = \begin{cases} \sin 2x, & x \leq 0 \\ mx, & x > 0 \end{cases}$$

a) continuous at $x = 0$?
b) differentiable at $x = 0$?

Give reasons for your answers.

51. Find the points on the curve $y = 2x^3 - 3x^2 - 12x + 20$ where the tangent is

a) perpendicular to the y-axis;
b) parallel to the line $y = \sqrt{2} - 12x$.

52. Show that the tangents to the curve $y = (\pi \sin x)/x$ at $x = \pi$ and $x = -\pi$ meet each other at right angles.

53. Is it true that a tangent to a curve can touch the curve at only one point? Give reasons for your answer.

54. Is a tangent to a curve allowed to cross the curve at the point of tangency? Give reasons for your answer.

55. The position at time $t \geq 0$ of a particle moving along a coordinate line is

$$s = 10 \cos (t + \pi/4).$$

a) What is the particle's starting position ($t = 0$)?
b) What are the points farthest to the left and right of the origin reached by the particle?
c) Find the particle's velocity and acceleration at the points in (b).
d) When does the particle first reach the origin? What are its velocity, speed, and acceleration then?

56. On Earth, you can easily shoot a paper clip 64 ft into the air with a rubber band. In t seconds after firing, the paper clip is $s = 64t - 16t^2$ ft above your hand.

a) How long does it take the paper clip to reach its maximum height? With what velocity does it leave your hand?
b) On the moon, the same force will send the paper clip to a height of $s = 64t - 2.6t^2$ ft in t seconds. About how long will it take the paper clip to reach its maximum height and how high will it go?

57. Figure 3.80 shows a multiflash photograph of two balls falling from rest. The rulers in the figure are marked in centimeters. Use the equation $s = 490t^2$ to answer the following questions.

a) How long did it take the balls to fall the first 160 cm? What was their average velocity for the period?
b) How fast were the balls falling when they reached the 160-cm mark? What was their acceleration then?
c) About how fast was the light flashing (flashes per second)?

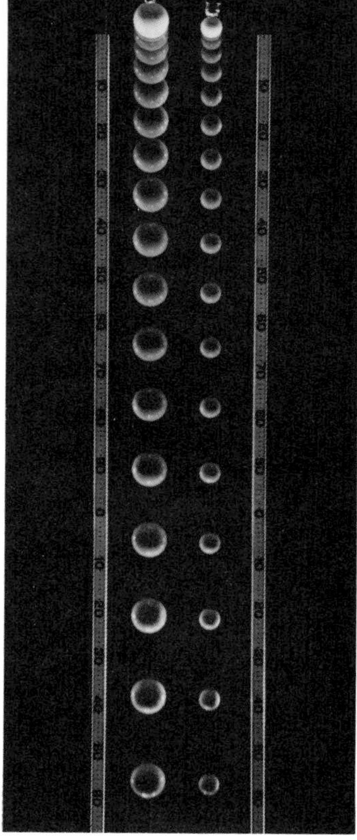

3.80 Two balls falling from rest (Exercise 57).

58. The following data give the coordinates s of a moving body for various values of t. Plot s versus t on coordinate paper and sketch a smooth curve through the given points. Assuming that this smooth curve represents the motion of the body, estimate the velocity at (a) $t = 1.0$; (b) $t = 2.5$; (c) $t = 2.0$.

s (in ft)	10	38	58	70	74	70	58	38	10
t (in sec)	0	0.5	1.0	1.5	2.0	2.5	3.0	3.5	4.0

59. The graphs in Fig. 3.81 show the distance traveled (miles), velocity (mph), and acceleration (mph/sec) for each second of a 2-minute automobile trip. Which graph shows

a) position? **b)** velocity? **c)** acceleration?

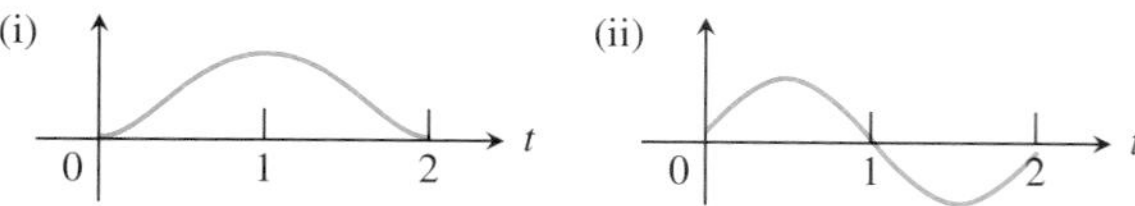

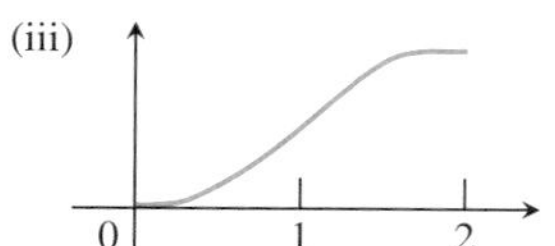

3.81 The graphs for Exercise 59.

60. The graph here shows the position s of a truck traveling on a highway. The truck starts at $t = 0$ and returns 15 hours later at $t = 15$.

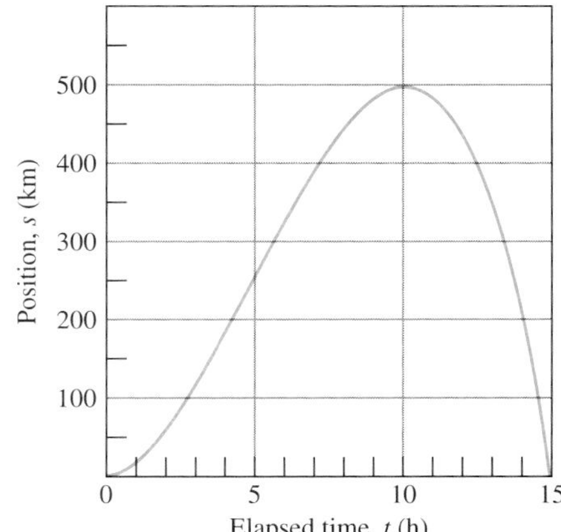

a) Use the technique described at the end of Section 3.3 to graph the truck's velocity $v = ds/dt$ for $0 \le t \le 15$. Then repeat the process, with the velocity curve, to graph the truck's acceleration dv/dt.

b) Suppose $s = 15t^2 - t^3$. Graph ds/dt and d^2s/dt^2 and compare your graphs with those in (a).

61. Use the following information to graph the function $y = f(x)$ for $-1 \le x \le 6$.

i) The graph of f is made of line segments joined end to end.

ii) The graph starts at the point $(-1, 2)$

iii) The derivative of f, where defined, is the step function shown here.

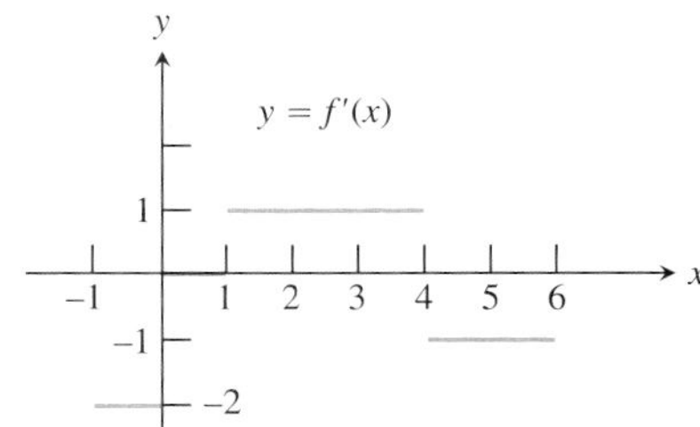

62. Repeat Exercise 61, supposing that the graph starts at $(-1, 0)$ instead of $(-1, 2)$.

63. The accompanying graph suggests that the curve $y = \sin(x - \sin x)$ might have horizontal tangents at the x-axis. Does it?

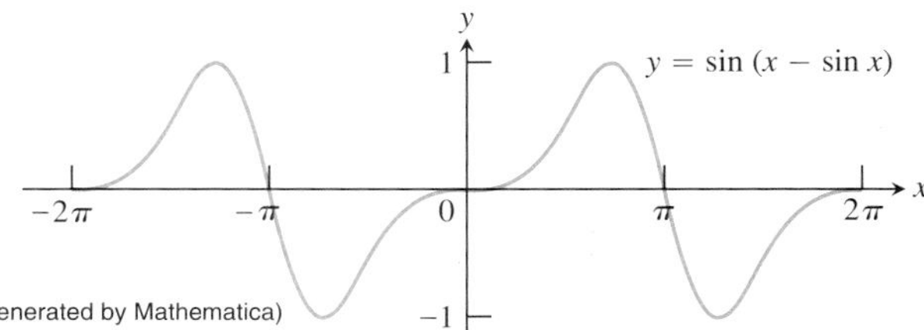

64. The figure shows a boat 1 km offshore, sweeping the shore with a searchlight. The light turns at the constant rate $d\theta/dt = -3/5$ radians per second. (This rate is called the light's *angular velocity*.)

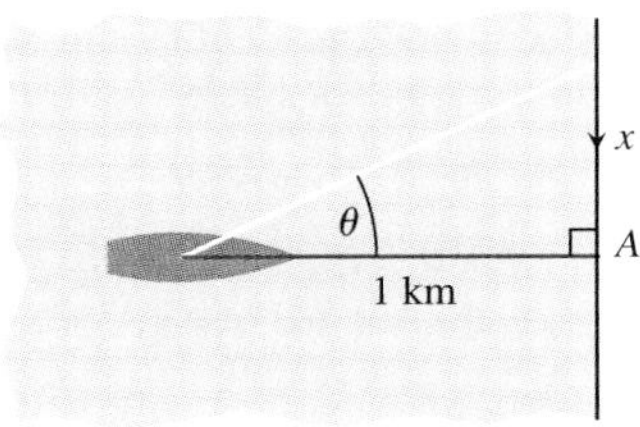

a) Express x (see the figure) in terms of θ.

b) Differentiate both sides of the equation you obtained in (a) with respect to t. Then substitute $d\theta/dt = -3/5$. This will express dx/dt (the rate at which the light moves along the shore) as a function of θ.

c) How fast (m/sec) is the light moving along the shore when it reaches point A?

d) How many revolutions per minute is 0.6 radian per second?

65. Suppose that functions $f(x)$ and $g(x)$ and their first derivatives have the following values at $x = 0$ and $x = 1$.

x	$f(x)$	$g(x)$	$f'(x)$	$g'(x)$
0	1	1	5	1/3
1	3	−4	−1/3	−8/3

Find the first derivatives of the following combinations at the given value of x.

a) $5f(x) - g(x)$, $x = 1$

b) $f(x)g^3(x)$, $x = 0$

c) $\dfrac{f(x)}{g(x)+1}$, $x = 1$

d) $f(g(x))$, $x = 0$

e) $g(f(x))$, $x = 0$

f) $(x + f(x))^{3/2}$, $x = 1$

g) $f(x + g(x))$, $x = 0$

66. Suppose that the function $f(x)$ and its first derivative have the following values at $x = 0$ and $x = 1$.

x	$f(x)$	$f'(x)$
0	9	−2
1	−3	1/5

Find the first derivatives of the following combinations at the given value of x.

a) $\sqrt{x}\,f(x)$, $x = 1$

b) $\sqrt{f(x)}$, $x = 0$

c) $f(\sqrt{x})$, $x = 1$

d) $f(1 - 5\tan x)$, $x = 0$

e) $\dfrac{f(x)}{2 + \cos x}$, $x = 0$

f) $10\sin\left(\dfrac{\pi x}{2}\right) f^2(x)$, $x = 1$

An equation like $\sin^2\theta + \cos^2\theta = 1$ is called an **identity** because it holds for all values of θ. An equation like $\sin\theta = 0.5$ is not an identity because it holds only for selected values of θ, not all. If you differentiate both sides of a trigonometric identity in θ with respect to θ, the resulting new equation will also be an identity.

Differentiate the identities in Exercises 67–70 to show that the resulting equations hold for all θ.

67. $\sin(-\theta) = -\sin\theta$

68. $\cos(-\theta) = \cos\theta$

69. $\sin 2\theta = 2\sin\theta\cos\theta$

70. $\cos 2\theta = \cos^2\theta - \sin^2\theta$

71. Find the value of dy/dt at $t = 0$ if $y = 3\sin 2x$ and $x = t^2 + \pi$.

72. Find the value of ds/du at $u = 2$ if $s = t^2 + 5t$ and $t = (u^2 + 2u)^{1/3}$.

73. Find the value of dw/ds at $s = 0$ if $w = \sin\left(\sqrt{r} - 2\right)$ and $r = 8\sin(s + \pi/6)$.

74. Find the value of dr/dt at $t = 0$ if $r = (\theta^2 + 7)^{1/3}$ and $\theta^2 t + \theta = 1$.

75. Find the points where the tangent to the curve $y = \sqrt{x}$ at $x = 4$ crosses the coordinate axes.

76. What horizontal line crosses the curve $y = \sqrt{x}$ at a 45° angle?

77. The line normal to the curve $y = x^2 + 2x - 3$ at $(1, 0)$ intersects the curve at what other point?

78. Find equations for the tangent and normal to the curve $x + \sqrt{xy} = 6$ at the point $(4, 1)$.

79. Find the points on the curve $y = \tan x$, $-\pi/2 < x < \pi/2$, where the normal is parallel to the line $y = -x/2$. Sketch the curve and normals together, labeling each with its equation.

80. Find equations for the tangent and normal to the curve $y = 1 + \cos x$ at the point $(\pi/2, 1)$. Sketch the curve, tangent, and normal together, labeling each with its equation.

81. Find equations for the tangent and normal to the curve $x^{3/2} + 2y^{3/2} = 17$ at the point $(1, 4)$.

82. Which of the following statements could be true if $f''(x) = x^{1/3}$?

I. $f(x) = \dfrac{9}{28}x^{7/3} + 9$ **II.** $f'(x) = \dfrac{9}{28}x^{7/3} - 2$

III. $f'(x) = \dfrac{3}{4}x^{4/3} + 6$ **IV.** $f(x) = \dfrac{3}{4}x^{4/3} - 4$

a) I only **b)** III only
c) II and IV only **d)** I and III only

83. The designer of a 30-ft-diameter spherical hot-air balloon wishes to suspend the gondola 8 ft below the bottom of the balloon with suspension cables tangent to the surface of the balloon (Fig. 3.82). Two of the cables are shown running from the top edges of the gondola to their points of tangency, $(-12, -9)$ and $(12, -9)$. How wide must the gondola be?

84. *What Determines the Fundamental Frequency of a Vibrating Piano String?* We measure the frequencies at which wires vibrate in cycles (trips back and forth) per second. The unit of measure is a *hertz,* which is 1 cycle per second. Middle A on a piano has a frequency of 440 hertz.

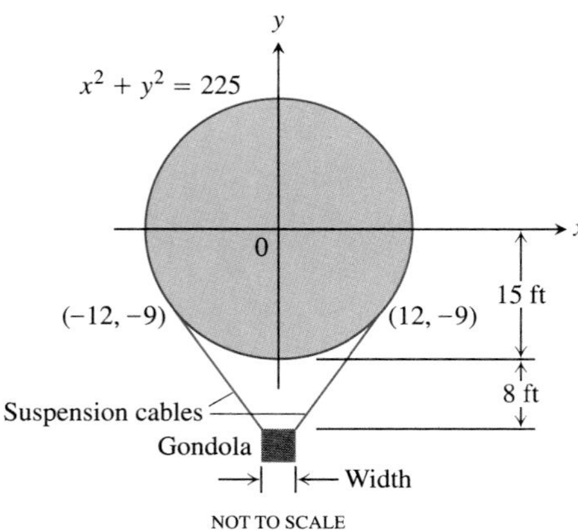

3.82 The balloon and gondola in Exercise 83.

For any given wire, the fundamental frequency y is a function of four variables:

- r: the radius of the wire
- l: the wire's length
- w: the density of the wire (mass/unit volume)
- T: the tension (force) holding the wire taut.

With r and l in centimeters, w in grams per cubic centimeter, and T in dynes (it takes about 100,000 dynes to lift an apple), the fundamental frequency of the wire is

$$y = \frac{1}{2rl}\sqrt{\frac{T}{\pi w}}.$$

If we keep all the variables fixed except one, then y can alternately be thought of as four different functions of one variable, $f(r)$, $g(l)$, $h(w)$, and $k(T)$. How would changing each variable while the others are held fixed affect the string's fundamental frequency? Find out by finding formulas for df/dr, dg/dl, dh/dw, and dk/dT.

85. Find d^2y/dx^2 by implicit differentiation:

a) $x^3 + y^3 = 1$ **b)** $y^2 = 1 - \dfrac{2}{x}$

86. a) By differentiating $x^2 - y^2 = 1$ implicitly, show that $dy/dx = x/y$.

b) Then show that $d^2y/dx^2 = -1/y^3$.

87. Find d^2y/dx^2 if

a) $y = \sqrt{2x + 7}$ **b)** $x^2 + y^2 = 1$

88. If $y^3 + y = 8x - 6$, find d^2y/dx^2 at the point $(1, 1)$.

89. Find the linearizations of

a) $\tan x$ at $x = -\pi/4$ **b)** $\sec x$ at $x = -\pi/4$.

Graph the curves and linearizations together.

90. A useful linear approximation to

$$\frac{1}{1 + \tan x}$$

at $x = 0$ can be obtained by combining the approximations

$$\frac{1}{1+x} \approx 1 - x \quad \text{and} \quad \tan x \approx x$$

to get

$$\frac{1}{1+\tan x} \approx 1 - x.$$

Show this is the usual linear approximation of $1/(1 + \tan x)$.

91. Write a formula that estimates the change that occurs in the volume of a right circular cone when the radius changes from r_0 to $r_0 + dr$ and the height does not change.

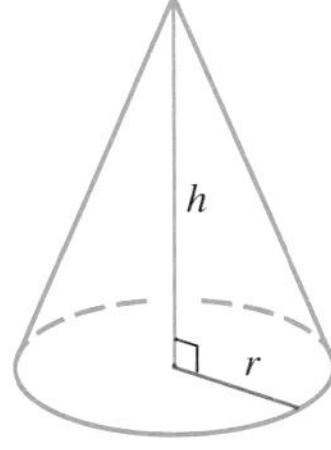

$V = \frac{1}{3}\pi r^2 h$

$S = \pi r \sqrt{r^2 + h^2}$

(Lateral surface area)

92. Write a formula that estimates the change that occurs in the lateral surface area of a cone when the height changes from h_0 to $h_0 + dh$ and the radius does not change.

93. a) How accurately should you measure the edge of a cube to be reasonably sure of calculating the cube's surface area with an error of no more than 2%?

b) Suppose the edge is measured with the accuracy required in (a). About how accurately can the cube's volume be calculated from the edge measurement? To find out, estimate the percentage error in the volume calculation that would result from using the edge measurement.

94. The circumference of a great circle of a sphere is measured as 10 cm with a possible error of 0.4 cm. The measurement is then used to calculate the radius. The radius is then used to calculate the surface area and volume of the sphere. Estimate the percentage errors in the calculated values of (a) the radius, (b) the surface area, and (c) the volume.

95. To find the height of a tree, you measure the angle from the ground to the treetop from a point 100 ft away from the base. The best figure you can get with the equipment at hand is $30° \pm 1°$. About how much error could the tolerance of $\pm 1°$ create in the calculated height? Remember to work in radians.

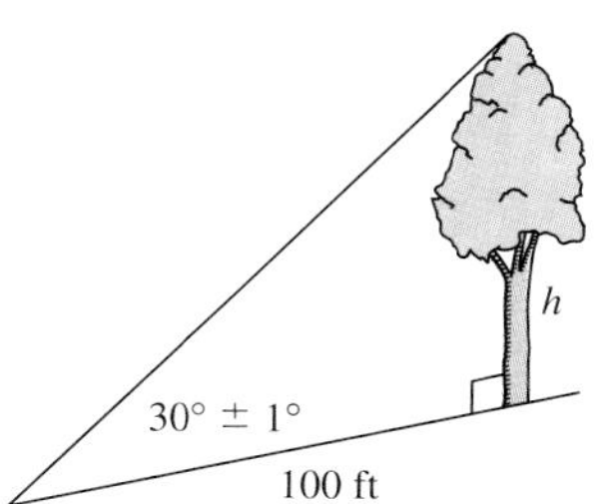

96. To find the height of a lamppost, you stand a 6-ft pole 20 ft from the lamp and measure the length a of its shadow. The figure you get for a is 15 ft, give or take an inch. Calculate the height of the lamppost from the value $a = 15$ and estimate the possible error in the result.

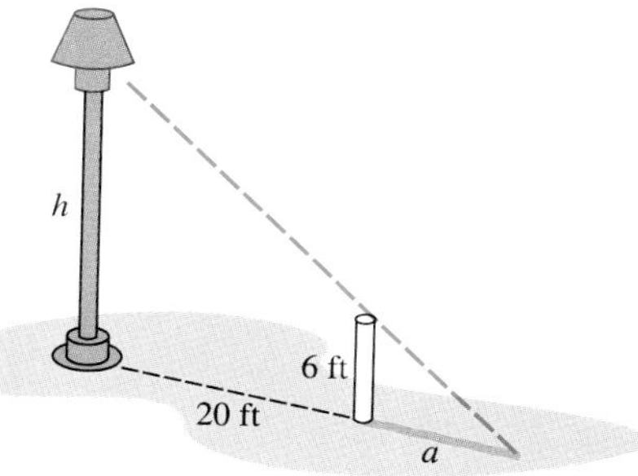

97. Use Newton's method to find to 5 decimal places the point where the curve $y = -x^3 + 3x + 4$ crosses the x-axis.

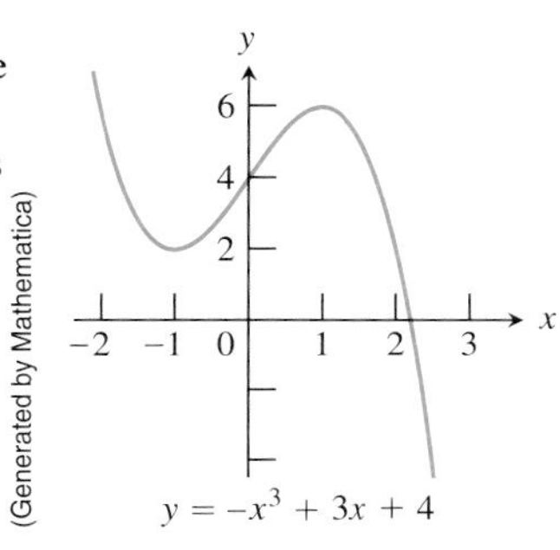

98. Use the Intermediate Value Theorem from Section 2.4 to show that $f(x) = x^4 - x^3 - 75$ has a zero between $x = 3$ and $x = 4$. Then use Newton's method to find the zero to 5 decimal places.

99. Solve the equation $2\cos x - \sqrt{1 + x} = 0$ by using Newton's method to estimate the zero of $f(x) = 2\cos x - \sqrt{1+x}$ to 5 decimal places.

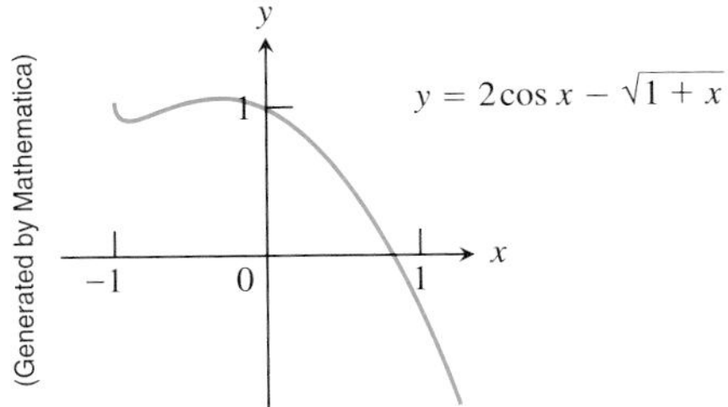

100. Estimate to 5 decimal places the values of r_1 through r_4 in the factorization $8x^4 - 14x^3 - 9x^2 + 11x - 1 = 8(x - r_1) \times (x - r_2)(x - r_3)(x - r_4)$.

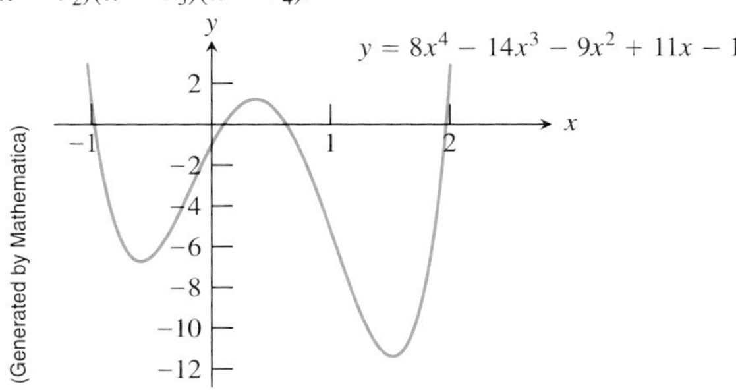

PACKAGING ENGINEERING

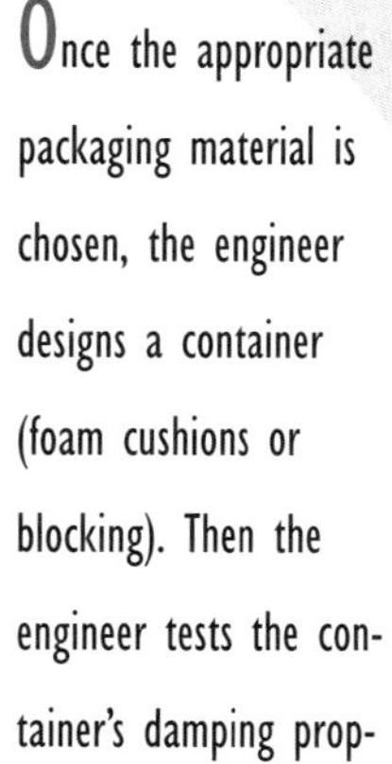

PETER BAGDIGIAN, a packaging engineer at Data General Corporation in Westborough, MA, designs foam pads to keep natural frequencies from reaching a packaged item during transportation.

You may have seen a Memorex® Audio ad of a glass being shattered by sound waves tuned to the glass's natural frequency. Things tend to shake apart when their natural frequencies are in tune with the frequency of an external driving force, like a vibrating railroad car or truck bed. The natural frequencies are specified by the manufacturer.

Once the appropriate packaging material is chosen, the engineer designs a container (foam cushions or blocking). Then the engineer tests the container's damping properties on a random vibration table, which shakes the packaged item back and forth along one direction at frequencies ranging from 2 to 200 Hz (1 Hz (hertz) = 1 cycle/second).

A test is carried out for each major axis of the part. At the same time, an accelerometer measures the effects of the vibration on the packaged item and transmits the data to a computer.

The variables to be controlled are the thickness of the foam packaging and the amount of surface area in contact with the item. These variables are adjusted until the amplitude of the transmitted vibration is minimized or the frequency of the transmitted vibrations is shifted far enough away from all of the natural frequencies to pose no threat.

As you will see in Section 4.5 and in later courses, calculus is the mathematics to use for studying natural frequencies and minimum values.

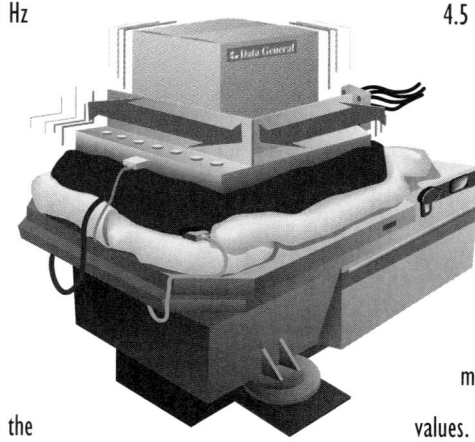

OVERVIEW

This chapter shows how to draw conclusions from derivatives: how to calculate rates that we cannot measure from rates that we can, how to find a function's extreme values, how to determine the shape of a function's graph, and how to find a function when we know only its first derivative and its value at a single point. The key to recovering functions from derivatives is the Mean Value Theorem, a theorem whose corollaries provide the gateway to *integral calculus,* which we will begin in Chapter 5.

4 Applications of Derivatives

4.1 Related Rates of Change

How rapidly will the fluid level inside a vertical cylindrical storage tank drop if we pump the fluid out at the rate of 3000 L/min?

A question like this asks us to calculate a rate that we cannot measure directly from a rate that we can. To do so, we write an equation that relates the variables involved and differentiate it to get an equation that relates the rate we seek to the rate we know.

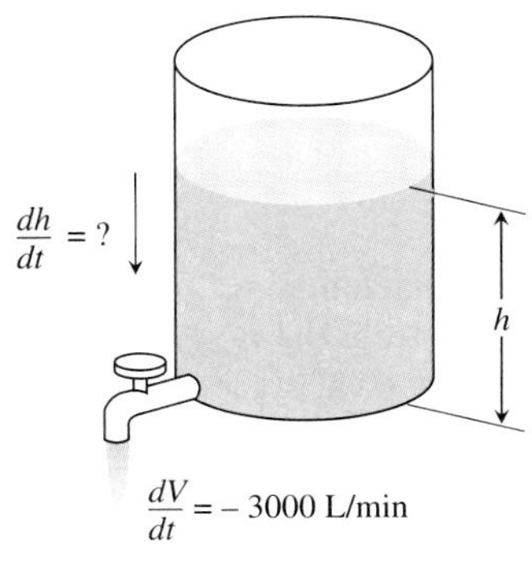

4.1 The cylindrical tank in Example 1.

Reminder

Rates of change are represented by derivatives. If a quantity is increasing, its derivative with respect to time is positive; if a quantity is decreasing, its derivative is negative.

EXAMPLE 1 *Pumping Out a Tank.* How rapidly will the fluid level inside a vertical cylindrical tank drop if we pump the fluid out at the rate of 3000 L/min?

Solution We draw a picture of a partially filled vertical cylindrical tank, calling its radius r and the height of the fluid h (Fig. 4.1). Call the volume of the fluid V.

As time passes, the radius remains constant, but V and h change. We think of V and h as differentiable functions of time and use t to represent time. We are told that

$$\frac{dV}{dt} = -3000.$$ We pump out at the rate of 3000 L/min. The rate is negative because the volume is decreasing.

We are asked to find

$$\frac{dh}{dt}.$$ How fast will the fluid level drop?

To find dh/dt, we first write an equation that relates h to V. The equation depends on the units chosen for V, r, and h. With V in liters and r and h in meters, the appropriate equation is

$$V = 1000\pi r^2 h$$ Fluid volume: $V = \pi r^2 h$

because a cubic meter contains 1000 liters.

Since V and h are differentiable functions of t, we can differentiate both sides of the equation $V = 1000\pi r^2 h$ with respect to t to get an equation that relates dh/dt to dV/dt:

$$\frac{dV}{dt} = 1000\pi r^2 \frac{dh}{dt}. \qquad r \text{ is a constant.} \tag{1}$$

We substitute the known value $dV/dt = -3000$ and solve for dh/dt:

$$\frac{dh}{dt} = \frac{-3000}{1000\pi r^2} = -\frac{3}{\pi r^2}. \qquad \text{The level is decreasing since } dh/dt \text{ is negative.} \tag{2}$$

The fluid level will drop at the rate of $3/\pi r^2$ m/min.

Equation (2) shows how the rate at which the fluid level drops depends on the tank's radius. If r is small, dh/dt will be large; if r is large, dh/dt will be small.

$$\text{If } r = 1 \text{ m:} \quad \frac{dh}{dt} = -\frac{3}{\pi} \approx -0.95 \text{ m/min} = -95 \text{ cm/min}$$

$$\text{If } r = 10 \text{ m:} \quad \frac{dh}{dt} = -\frac{3}{100\pi} \approx -0.0095 \text{ m/min} = -0.95 \text{ cm/min}$$

EXAMPLE 2 *A Rising Balloon.* A hot-air balloon rising straight up from a level field is tracked by a range finder 500 ft from the lift-off point. At the moment the range finder's elevation angle is $\pi/4$, the angle is increasing at the rate of 0.14 rad/min. How fast is the balloon rising at that moment?

Solution We answer the question in six steps.

STEP 1: *Draw a picture and name the variables and constants* (Fig. 4.2): The variables in the picture are

θ = the angle the range finder makes with the ground (radians)

y = the height of the balloon (feet).

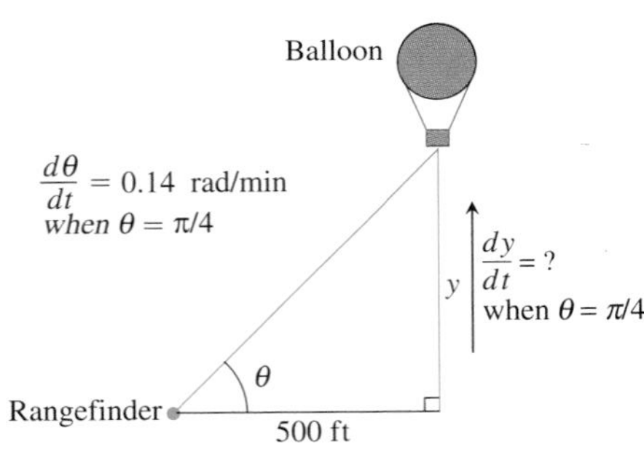

4.2 The balloon in Example 2.

We let t represent time and assume θ and y to be differentiable functions of t.

The one constant in the picture is the distance from the range finder to the lift-off point (500 ft). There is no need to give it a special symbol.

STEP 2: *Write down the additional numerical information:*

$$\frac{d\theta}{dt} = 0.14 \text{ rad/min} \quad \text{when} \quad \theta = \frac{\pi}{4}$$

STEP 3: *Write down what we are asked to find:* We want dy/dt when $\theta = \pi/4$.

STEP 4: *Write an equation that relates the variables y and θ:*

$$\frac{y}{500} = \tan\theta, \quad \text{or} \quad y = 500 \tan\theta$$

STEP 5: *Differentiate with respect to t using the Chain Rule. The result tells how dy/dt (which we want) is related to $d\theta/dt$ (which we know):*

$$\frac{dy}{dt} = 500 \sec^2\theta \, \frac{d\theta}{dt}$$

STEP 6: *Evaluate with $\theta = \pi/4$ and $d\theta/dt = 0.14$ to find dy/dt:*

$$\frac{dy}{dt} = 500(\sqrt{2})^2(0.14) = (1000)(0.14) = 140 \qquad \sec\frac{\pi}{4} = \sqrt{2}$$

At the moment in question, the balloon is rising at the rate of 140 ft/min.

Strategy for Solving Related Rate Problems

1. *Draw a picture and name the variables and constants:* Use t for time. Assume all variables are differentiable functions of t.
2. *Write down the numerical information* (in terms of the symbols you have chosen).
3. *Write down what you are asked to find* (usually a rate, expressed as a derivative).
4. *Write an equation that relates the variables:* You may have to combine two or more equations to get a single equation that relates the variable whose rate you want to the variable whose rate you know.
5. *Differentiate with respect to t:* Then express the rate you want in terms of the rate and variables whose values you know.
6. *Evaluate,* using known values to find the unknown rate.

EXAMPLE 3 *Truck Convoys.* Convoy A is approaching a depot from the east at 60 mi/h while convoy B is moving north away from the depot at 50 mi/h. How fast is the distance between the convoys changing when A is 4 mi from the depot and B is 3 mi from the depot?

Solution We carry out the steps of the basic strategy.

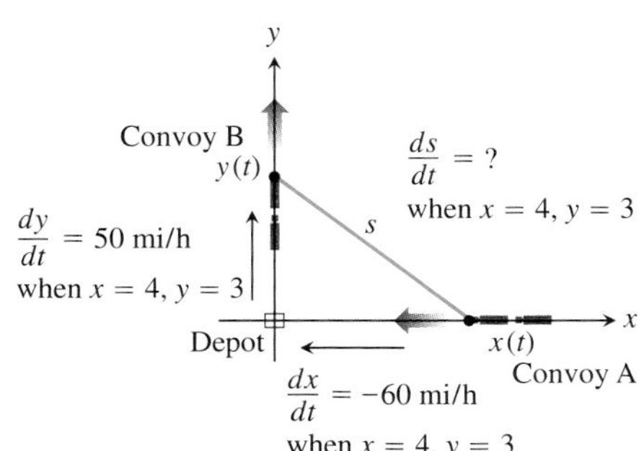

4.3 If you know where the convoys are and how fast they are moving, you can calculate how fast the distance between them is changing (Example 3).

STEP 1: *Picture and variables:* We picture the convoys in the coordinate plane, using the positive x-axis as the highway from the east and the positive y-axis as the highway to the north (Fig. 4.3). We let t represent time and set

$$x = \text{position of convoy A at time } t$$
$$y = \text{position of convoy B at time } t$$
$$s = \text{distance between convoys at time } t.$$

We assume x, y, and s to be differentiable functions of time t.

STEP 2: *Numerical information:* At the time in question,

$$x = 4 \text{ mi}, \qquad y = 3 \text{ mi}, \qquad \frac{dx}{dt} = -60 \text{ mi/h}, \qquad \frac{dy}{dt} = 50 \text{ mi/h}.$$

Notice the minus sign: x is decreasing, so $dx/dt = -60$, not 60.

STEP 3: *To find: ds/dt.*

STEP 4: *How the variables are related:*

$$s^2 = x^2 + y^2 \qquad \text{Pythagorean theorem} \tag{3}$$

STEP 5: *Differentiate with respect to t:*

$$2s\frac{ds}{dt} = 2x\frac{dx}{dt} + 2y\frac{dy}{dt} \qquad \text{Chain Rule}$$

$$\frac{ds}{dt} = \frac{1}{s}\left(x\frac{dx}{dt} + y\frac{dy}{dt}\right)$$

STEP 6: *Evaluate* with $x = 4$, $y = 3$, $s = \sqrt{4^2 + 3^2} = 5$, $\frac{dx}{dt} = -60$, $\frac{dy}{dt} = 50$:

$$\frac{ds}{dt} = \frac{1}{5}[4(-60) + 3(50)]$$

$$= \frac{1}{5}(-240 + 150) = \frac{-90}{5} = -18$$

Since ds/dt is negative at the moment in question, the distance between the convoys is decreasing at the rate of 18 mi/h.

EXAMPLE 4 Water runs into a conical tank at the rate of 9 ft³/min. The tank stands point down and has a height of 10 ft and a base radius of 5 ft. How fast is the water level rising when the water is 6 ft deep?

Solution We carry out the steps of the basic strategy.

STEP 1: *Picture and variables.* We draw a picture of a partially filled conical tank (Fig. 4.4). The variables in the problem are

V = volume (ft³) of water in the tank at time t (min)

x = radius (ft) of the surface of the water at time t

y = depth (ft) of water in the tank at time t.

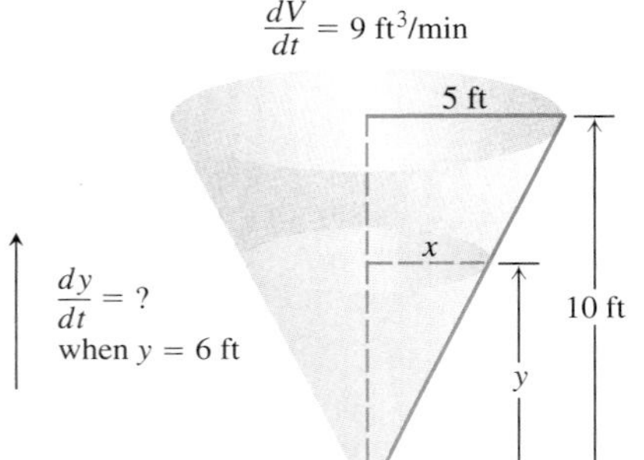

4.4 The conical tank in Example 4.

We assume V, x, and y to be differentiable functions of t. The constants are the dimensions of the tank.

STEP 2: *Numerical information:* At the time in question,

$$y = 6 \text{ ft}, \qquad \frac{dV}{dt} = 9 \text{ ft}^3/\text{min}.$$

STEP 3: *To find:* $\frac{dy}{dt}$.

STEP 4: *How the variables are related:*

$$V = \frac{1}{3}\pi x^2 y \qquad \text{Cone volume formula} \tag{4}$$

This equation involves x as well as V and y. Because no information is given about x and dx/dt at the time in question, we need to eliminate x. Using similar triangles (Fig. 4.4) gives us a way to express x in terms of y:

$$\frac{x}{y} = \frac{5}{10}, \qquad \text{or} \qquad x = \frac{y}{2}.$$

Therefore,

$$V = \frac{1}{3}\pi\left(\frac{y}{2}\right)^2 y = \frac{\pi}{12}y^3. \tag{5}$$

STEP 5: *Differentiate with respect to t:* We differentiate Eq. (5), getting

$$\frac{dV}{dt} = \frac{\pi}{12} \cdot 3y^2 \frac{dy}{dt} = \frac{\pi}{4} y^2 \frac{dy}{dt}. \tag{6}$$

We then solve for dy/dt to express the rate we want (dy/dt) in terms of the rate we know (dV/dt):

$$\frac{dy}{dt} = \frac{4}{\pi y^2} \frac{dV}{dt}.$$

STEP 6: *Evaluate with $y = 6$ and $dV/dt = 9$:*

$$\frac{dy}{dt} = \frac{4}{\pi (6)^2} \cdot 9 = \frac{1}{\pi} \approx 0.32 \text{ ft/min}$$

At the moment in question, the water level is rising at about 0.32 ft/min.

EXAMPLE 5 *Relief from a Heart Attack.* A heart attack victim has been given a blood vessel dilator to lower the pressure against which the heart has to pump. For a short while after the drug is administered, the radii of the affected blood vessels will increase at about 1% per minute. According to Poiseuille's law, $V = kr^4$ (Section 3.7, Example 10), what percentage rate of increase can we expect in the blood flow over the next few minutes (all other things being equal)?

Solution

STEP 1: *Picture and variables:* We really don't need a picture, and the variables r and V are already named. It remains only to assume that r and V are differentiable functions of time t.

STEP 2: *Numerical information:*

$$\frac{dr}{dt} = 0.01\, r = \frac{1}{100} r \qquad r \text{ increases at 1\% of } r \text{ per min.}$$

STEP 3: *To find:* The rate of increase in V expressed as a percentage of V, i.e., the number p such that

$$\frac{dV}{dt} = \frac{p}{100} V.$$

STEP 4: *How the variables are related:* $V = kr^4$.

STEP 5: *Differentiate to find how dV/dt is related to dr/dt:*

$$\frac{dV}{dt} = 4kr^3 \frac{dr}{dt}$$

STEP 6: *Evaluate by substituting $dr/dt = (1/100)\, r$:*

$$\frac{dV}{dt} = 4kr^3 \left(\frac{1}{100} r\right)$$

$$= \frac{4}{100} kr^4 = \frac{4}{100} V \qquad V = kr^4$$

During the next few minutes, the blood flow will increase at $p = 4\%$ per min.

Exercises 4.1

1. Suppose that the radius r and area $A = \pi r^2$ of a circle are differentiable functions of t. Write an equation that relates dA/dt to dr/dt.
2. Suppose that the radius r and surface area $S = 4\pi r^2$ of a sphere are differentiable functions of t. Write an equation that relates dS/dt to dr/dt.
3. The radius r and height h of a right circular cylinder are related to the cylinder's volume V by the formula $V = \pi r^2 h$.
   a) How is dV/dt related to dh/dt if r is constant?
   b) How is dV/dt related to dr/dt if h is constant?
   c) How is dV/dt related to dr/dt and dh/dt if neither r nor h is constant?
4. The radius r and height h of a right circular cone are related to the cone's volume V by the equation $V = (1/3)\pi r^2 h$.
   a) How is dV/dt related to dh/dt if r is constant?
   b) How is dV/dt related to dr/dt if h is constant?
   c) How is dV/dt related to dr/dt and dh/dt if neither r nor h is constant?
5. The area A of a triangle with sides of lengths a and b enclosing an angle of measure θ is
$$A = \frac{1}{2} ab \sin \theta.$$
   a) How is dA/dt related to $d\theta/dt$ if a and b are constant?
   b) How is dA/dt related to $d\theta/dt$ and da/dt if only b is constant?
   c) How is dA/dt related to $d\theta/dt$, da/dt, and db/dt if none of a, b, and θ are constant?
6. The power P (watts) of an electric circuit is related to the circuit's resistance R (ohms) and current i (amperes) by the equation $P = Ri^2$.
   a) How are dP/dt, dR/dt, and di/dt related if none of P, R, and i are constant?
   b) How is dR/dt related to di/dt if P is constant?
7. Let x and y be differentiable functions of t and let $s = \sqrt{x^2 + y^2}$ be the distance between the points $(x, 0)$ and $(0, y)$ in the xy-plane.
   a) How is ds/dt related to dx/dt if y is constant?
   b) How is ds/dt related to dx/dt and dy/dt if neither x nor y is constant?
   c) How is dx/dt related to dy/dt if s is constant?
8. If x, y, and z are the lengths of the edges of a rectangular box, the common length of the box's diagonals is $s = \sqrt{x^2 + y^2 + z^2}$.
   a) Assuming that x, y, and z are differentiable functions of t, how is ds/dt related to dx/dt, dy/dt, and dz/dt?
   b) How is ds/dt related to dy/dt and dz/dt if x is constant?
   c) How are dx/dt, dy/dt, and dz/dt related if s is constant?
9. *Heating a Plate.* When a circular plate of metal is heated in an oven, its radius increases at the rate of 0.01 cm/min. At what rate is the plate's area increasing when the radius is 50 cm?
10. *Changing Voltage.* The voltage V (volts), current I (amperes), and resistance R (ohms) of an electric circuit like the one shown here are related by the equation $V = IR$. Suppose that V is increasing at the rate of 1 volt/sec while I is decreasing at the rate of 1/3 amp/sec. Let t denote time in seconds.
    a) What is the value of dV/dt?
    b) What is the value of dI/dt?
    c) What equation relates dR/dt to dV/dt and dI/dt?
    d) Find the rate at which R is changing when $V = 12$ volts and $I = 2$ amp. Is R increasing, or decreasing?

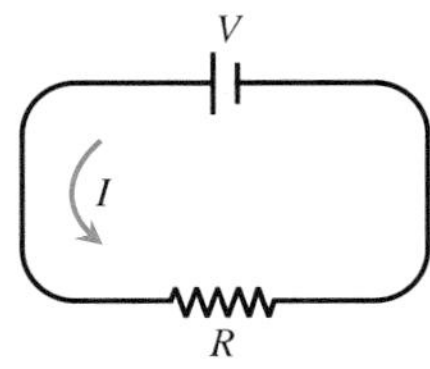

11. *Changing Dimensions in a Rectangle.* The length l of a rectangle is decreasing at the rate of 2 cm/sec while the width w is increasing at the rate of 2 cm/sec. When $l = 12$ cm and $w = 5$ cm, find the rates of change of (a) the area, (b) the perimeter, and (c) the lengths of the diagonals of the rectangle. Which of these quantities are decreasing, and which are increasing?
12. *Changing Dimensions in a Rectangular Box.* Suppose that the edge lengths x, y, and z of a closed rectangular box are changing at the following rates:
$$\frac{dx}{dt} = 1 \text{ m/sec}, \qquad \frac{dy}{dt} = -2 \text{ m/sec}, \qquad \frac{dz}{dt} = 1 \text{ m/sec}.$$
Find the rates at which the box's (a) volume, (b) surface area, and (c) diagonal length $s = \sqrt{x^2 + y^2 + z^2}$ are changing at the instant when $x = 4$, $y = 3$, and $z = 2$.
13. *Commercial Air Traffic.* Two commercial jets at 40,000 ft are flying at 520 mph along straight-line courses that cross at right angles. How fast is the distance between the planes closing when plane A is 5 mi from the intersection point and plane B is 12 mi from the intersection point?

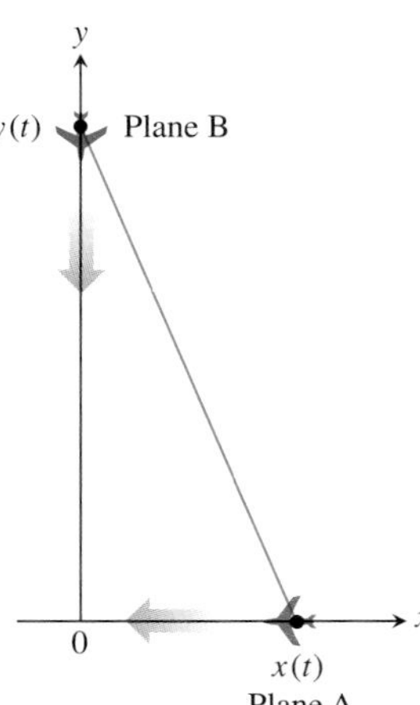

14. *A Sliding Ladder.* A 13-ft ladder is leaning against a house when its base starts to slide away. By the time the base is 12 ft from the house, the base is moving at the rate of 5 ft/sec. How

fast is the top of the ladder sliding down the wall then? How fast is the area of the triangle formed by the ladder, wall, and ground changing?

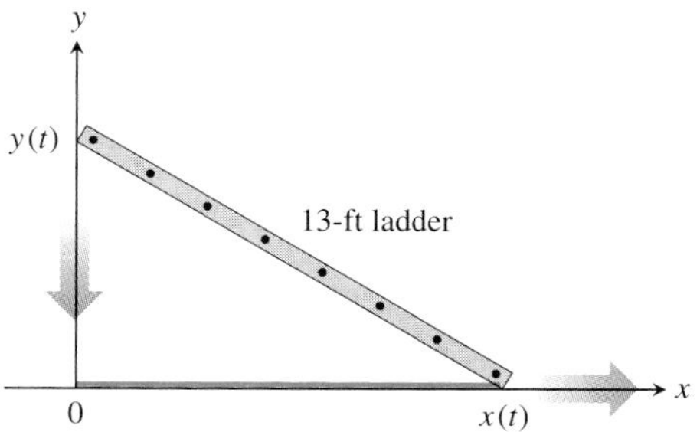

15. *A Shrinking Lollipop.* A spherical Tootsie Roll Pop you are sucking on is giving up volume at a steady rate of 0.08 ml/min. How fast will the radius be decreasing when the Tootsie Roll Pop is 20 mm across?

16. *Boring a Cylinder.* The mechanics at Lincoln Automotive are reboring a 6-in.-deep cylinder to fit a new piston. The machine they are using increases the cylinder's radius one-thousandth of an inch every 3 min. How rapidly is the cylinder volume increasing when the bore (diameter) is 3.800 in.?

17. *A Growing Sand Pile.* Sand falls from a conveyor belt at the rate of 10 m^3/min onto the top of a conical pile. The height of the pile is always three-eighths of the base diameter. How fast are the (a) height and (b) radius changing when the pile is 4 m high? Answer in cm/min.

18. *A Draining Conical Reservoir.* Water is flowing at the rate of 50 m^3/min from a shallow concrete conical reservoir (vertex down) of base radius 45 m and height 6 m. (a) How fast is the water level falling when the water is 5 m deep? (b) How fast is the radius of the water's surface changing then? Answer in cm/min.

19. *A Draining Hemispherical Reservoir.* Water is flowing at the rate of 6 m^3/min from a reservoir shaped like a hemispherical bowl of radius 13 m, shown here in profile. Answer the following questions, given that the volume of water in a hemispherical bowl of radius R is $V = (\pi/3)y^2(3R - y)$ when the water is y units deep.

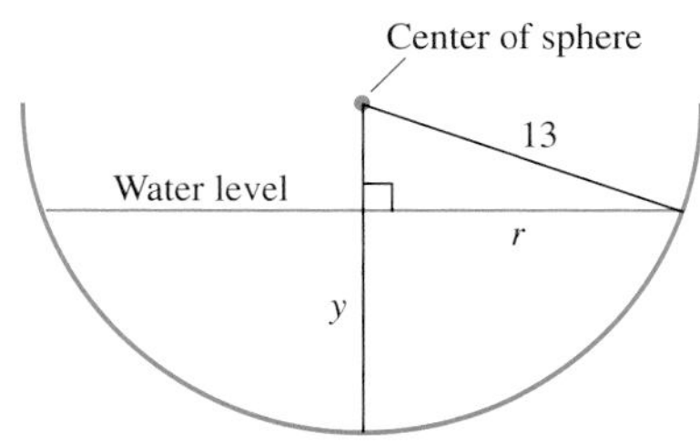

a) At what rate is the water level changing when the water is 8 m deep?

b) What is the radius r of the water's surface when the water is y m deep?

c) At what rate is the radius r changing when the water is 8 m deep?

20. *A Growing Raindrop.* Suppose that a drop of mist is a perfect sphere and that, through condensation, the drop picks up moisture at a rate proportional to its surface area. Show that under these circumstances the drop's radius increases at a constant rate.

21. *The Radius of an Inflating Balloon.* A spherical balloon is inflated with helium at the rate of 100π ft^3/min. How fast is the balloon's radius increasing at the instant the radius is 5 ft? How fast is the surface area increasing?

22. *Hauling in a Dinghy.* A dinghy is pulled toward a dock by a rope from the bow through a ring on the dock 6 ft above the bow. If the rope is hauled in at the rate of 2 ft/sec, how fast is the boat approaching the dock when 10 ft of rope are out?

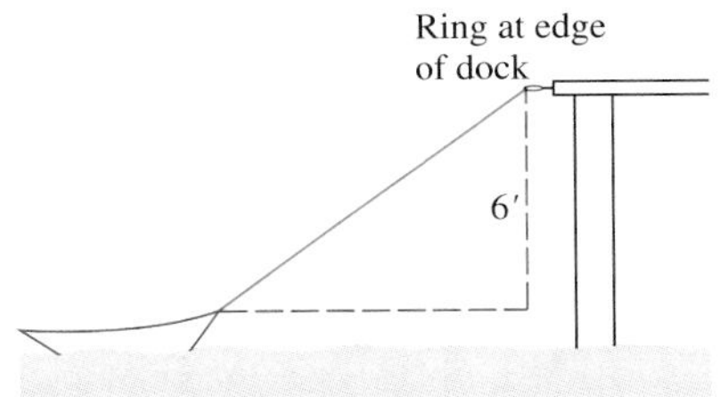

23. *A Balloon and a Bicycle.* A balloon is rising vertically above a level, straight road at a constant rate of 1 ft/sec. Just when the balloon is 65 ft above the ground, a bicycle passes under it, going 17 ft/sec. How fast is the distance between the bicycle and balloon increasing 3 sec later?

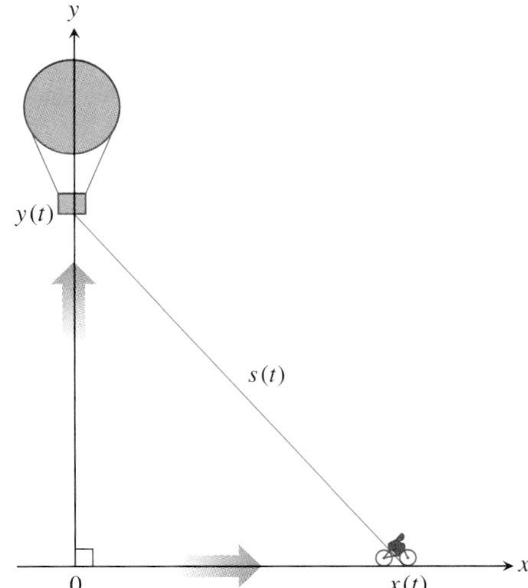

24. *Making Coffee.* Coffee is draining from a conical filter into a cylindrical coffeepot at the rate of 10 in^3/min. (a) How fast is

the level in the pot rising when the coffee in the cone is 5 in. deep? (b) How fast is the level in the cone falling then?

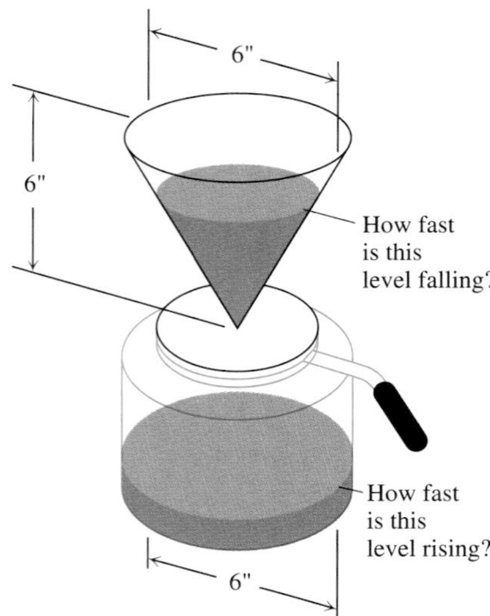

25. *Blood Flow.* Cold water has the effect of contracting the blood vessels in the hands, and the radius of a typical vein might decrease at the rate of 20%/min. According to Poiseuille's law, $V = kr^4$ (see Example 5), at what percentage rate can we expect the volume of blood flowing through that vein to decrease?

26. *Cardiac Output.* In the late 1860s, Adolf Fick, a professor of physiology in the Faculty of Medicine in Würtzberg, Germany, developed the method we use today for measuring how much blood your heart pumps in a minute. Your cardiac output as you read this sentence is probably about 7 liters a minute. At rest it is likely to be a bit under 6 L/min. If you are a trained marathon runner running a marathon, your cardiac output can be as high as 30 L/min.

Your cardiac output can be calculated with the formula

$$y = \frac{Q}{D},$$

where Q is the number of milliliters of CO_2 you exhale in a minute and D is the difference between the CO_2 concentration (ml/L) in the blood pumped to the lungs and the CO_2 concentration in the blood returning from the lungs. With $Q = 233$ ml/min and $D = 97 - 56 = 41$ ml/L,

$$y = \frac{233 \text{ ml/min}}{41 \text{ ml/L}} \approx 5.95 \text{ L/min},$$

close to the 6 L/min that most people have at basal (resting) conditions. (Data courtesy of J. Kenneth Herd, M.D., Quillan College of Medicine, East Tennessee State University.)

Suppose that when $Q = 233$ and $D = 41$, we also know that D is decreasing at the rate of 2 units a minute but that Q remains unchanged. What is happening to the cardiac output?

27. *Moving Along a Parabola.* A particle moves along the parabola $y = x^2$ in the first quadrant in such a way that its x-coordinate (measured in meters) increases at a steady 10 m/sec. How fast is the angle of inclination θ of the line joining the particle to the origin changing when $x = 3$ m?

28. *Moving Along Another Parabola.* A particle moves from right to left along the parabola $y = \sqrt{-x}$ in such a way that its x-coordinate (measured in meters) decreases at the rate of 8 m/sec. How fast is the angle of inclination θ of the line joining the particle to the origin changing when $x = -4$?

29. *Cost, Revenue, and Profit.* A company can manufacture x items at a cost of $c(x)$ dollars, a sales revenue of $r(x)$ dollars, and a profit of $p(x) = r(x) - c(x)$ dollars (everything in thousands). Find dc/dt, dr/dt, and dp/dt for the following values of x and dx/dt.

a) $r(x) = 9x$, $c(x) = x^3 - 6x^2 + 15x$, and $dx/dt = 0.1$ when $x = 2$

b) $r(x) = 70x$, $c(x) = x^3 - 6x^2 + 45/x$, and $dx/dt = 0.05$ when $x = 1.5$

30. *A Moving Shadow.* A man 6 ft tall walks at the rate of 5 ft/sec toward a streetlight that is 16 ft above the ground. At what rate is the tip of his shadow moving? At what rate is the length of his shadow changing when he is 10 ft from the base of the light?

31. *Another Moving Shadow.* A light shines from the top of a pole 50 ft high. A ball is dropped from the same height from a point 30 ft away from the light. How fast is the shadow of the ball moving along the ground 1/2 sec later? (Assume the ball falls a distance $s = 16t^2$ ft in t sec.)

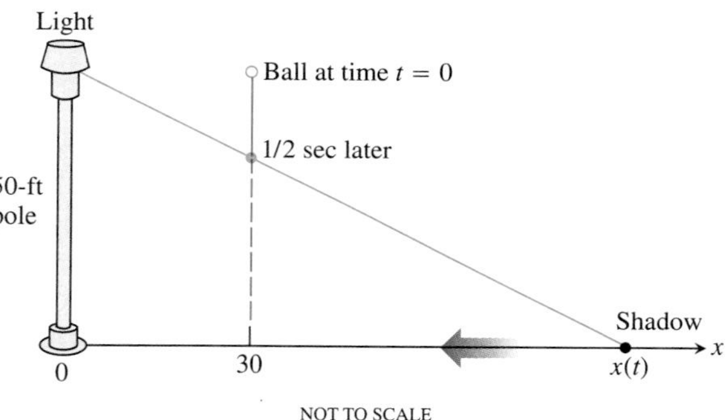

32. *Flying a Kite.* A girl flies a kite at a height of 300 ft, the wind carrying the kite horizontally away from her at a rate of 25 ft/sec. How fast must she let out the string when the kite is 500 ft away from her?

33. *A Melting Ice Layer.* A spherical iron ball 8 in. in diameter is coated with a layer of ice of uniform thickness. If the ice melts at the rate of 10 in³/min, how fast is the thickness of the ice decreasing when it is 2 in. thick? How fast is the outer surface area of ice decreasing?

34. *Highway Patrol.* A highway patrol plane flies 3 mi above a level, straight road at a steady 120 mi/h. The pilot sees an oncoming car and with radar determines that at the instant the line-of-sight distance from plane to car is 5 mi the line-of-sight distance is decreasing at the rate of 160 mi/h. Find the car's speed along the highway.

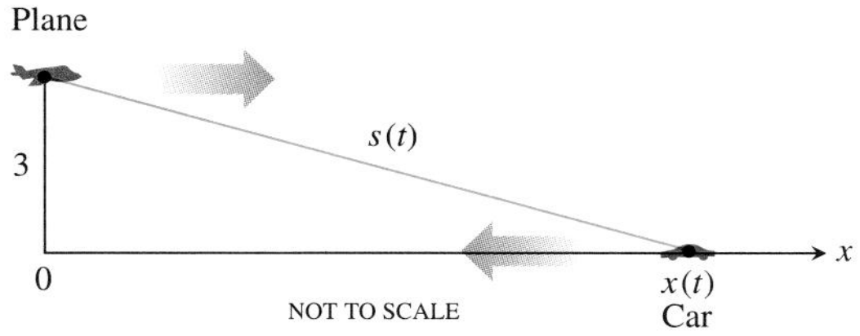

35. *A Building's Shadow.* On a morning of a day when the sun will pass directly overhead, the shadow of an 80-ft building on level ground is 60 ft long. At the moment in question, the angle θ the sun makes with the ground is increasing at the rate of 0.27°/min. At what rate is the shadow decreasing? (Remember to use radians. Express your answer in inches per minute, to the nearest tenth.)

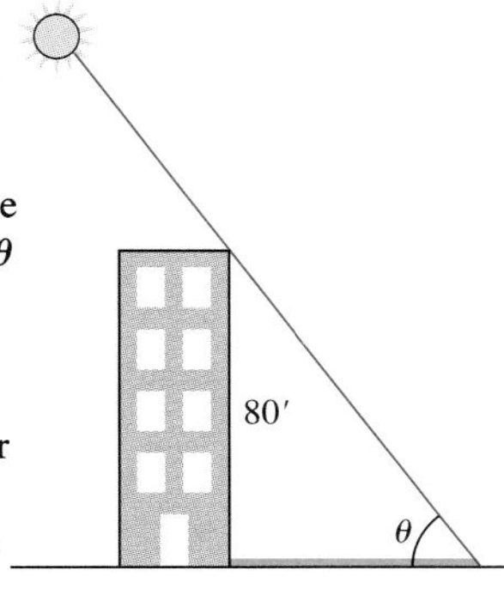

36. *Walkers.* A and B are walking on straight streets that meet at right angles. A approaches the intersection at 2 m/sec; B moves away from the intersection at 1 m/sec. At what rate is the angle θ changing when A is 10 m from the intersection and B is 20 m from the intersection? Express your answer in degrees per second to the nearest degree.

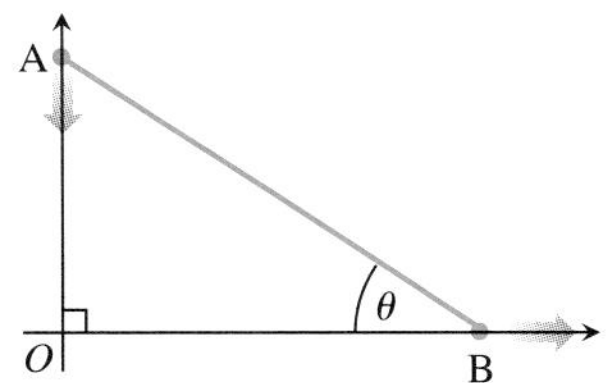

37. *Ships.* Two ships are steaming straight away from a point O along routes that make a 120° angle. Ship A moves at 14 knots (nautical miles per hour; a nautical mile is 2000 yd). Ship B moves at 21 knots. How fast are the ships moving apart when $OA = 5$ and $OB = 3$ nautical miles?

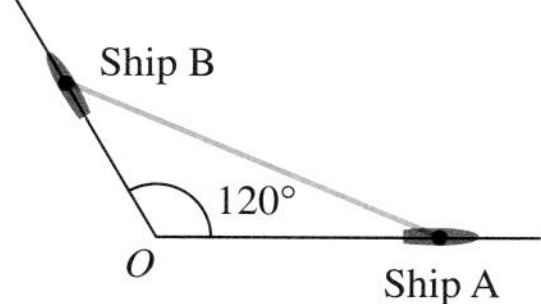

38. *A Second Hand.* At what rate is the distance between the tip of the second hand and the 12 o'clock mark changing when the second hand points to 4 o'clock?

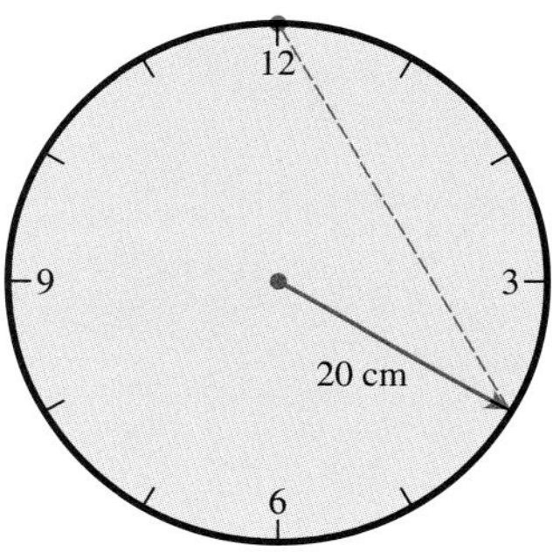

Writing for Your Own Knowledge

Answer the following questions in writing. Some answers will take only a sentence or two; others may require several paragraphs. Some explanations may also call for graphs or sketches.

1. How do you recognize a related rate problem when you see it?
2. How do you solve a related rate problem?

4.2 *Extreme Values of Functions*

In addition to giving information about rates, derivatives help us locate a function's maximum and minimum values. We will see later in the chapter how this enables us to solve a variety of practical problems in mathematics, economics, engineering, and medicine.

Maxima and Minima—Local and Absolute

Figure 4.5 on the following page shows a point c_2 where a function $y = f(x)$ has a maximum value. The curve rises as x approaches c_2 from the left and falls away again as x moves away from c_2 to the right. When we consider more of the curve, however, we see that f has an even larger value at c_4. The maximum value at c_2 is only a local maximum value, not an absolute maximum value.

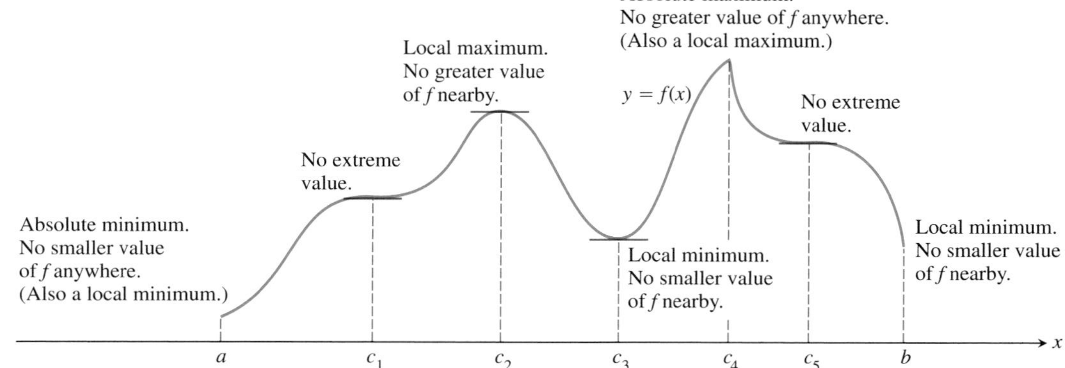

4.5 How to classify maxima and minima.

Relative Maxima and Minima

A function's local maxima and minima are also called its *relative* maxima and minima.

DEFINITIONS

Let c be a point of the domain D of a function f. The number $f(c)$ is

1. a **local maximum value** of f if $f(x) \leq f(c)$ for all domain points x in some open interval I containing c;
2. the **absolute maximum value** of f if $f(x) \leq f(c)$ for all x in D;
3. a **local minimum value** of f if $f(x) \geq f(c)$ for all domain points x in some open interval I containing c;
4. the **absolute minimum value** of f if $f(x) \geq f(c)$ for all x in D.

A function's maximum values (**maxima**) and minimum values (**minima**) are the function's **extreme values (extrema)**. In Fig. 4.5 we see that extreme values can occur not only at interior points but also at the endpoints of the domain D.

In practice, we are usually interested in finding where a function has its absolute maximum or absolute minimum value. But how do we tell if either one exists? Let us first look at a few examples.

EXAMPLE 1 On the closed interval $-\pi/2 \leq x \leq \pi/2$, the cosine takes on an absolute maximum value of 1 (once) and an absolute minimum value of 0 (twice). The sine takes on an absolute maximum value of 1 and an absolute minimum value of -1.

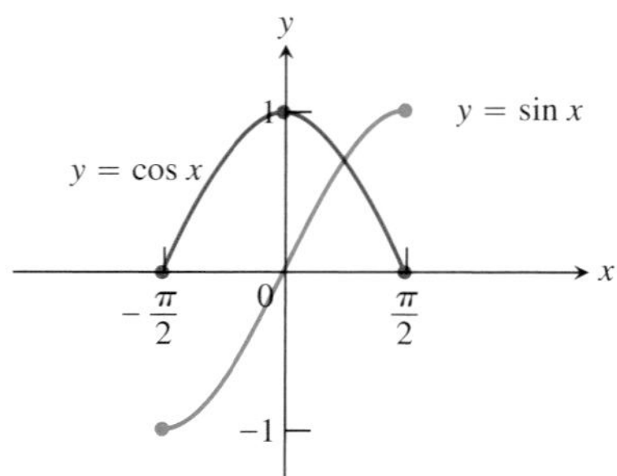

EXAMPLE 2 The function $f(x) = x$, $0 < x < 1$, defined on the open interval (0, 1) has neither an absolute maximum nor an absolute minimum value.

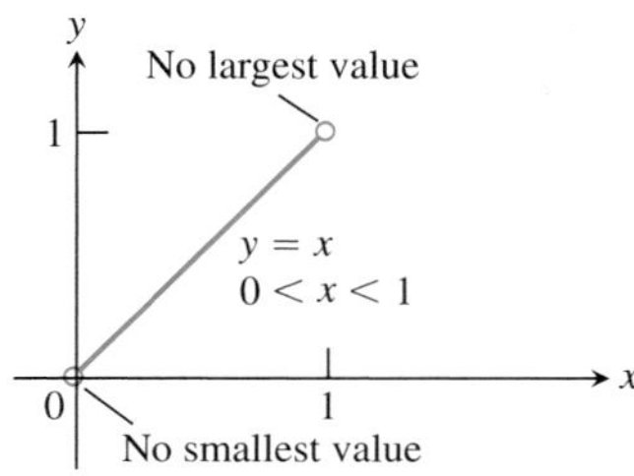

EXAMPLE 3 The function

$$f(x) = \begin{cases} x + 1, & -1 \leq x < 0 \\ 0, & x = 0 \\ x - 1, & 0 < x \leq 1, \end{cases}$$

defined on the closed interval $[-1, 1]$ has neither an absolute maximum nor an absolute minimum value.

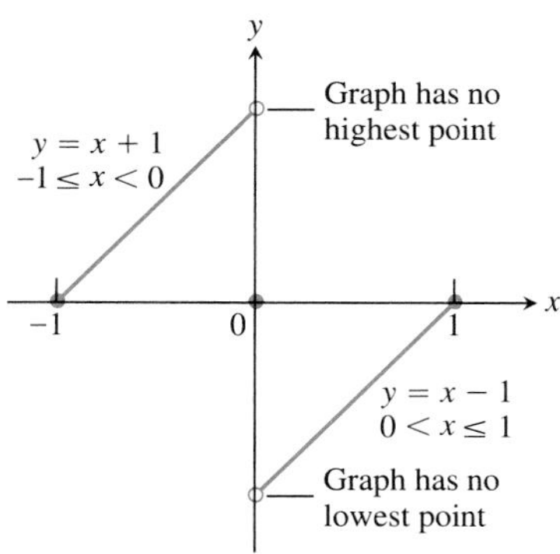

EXAMPLE 4 The function $f(x) = (x - 2)^2$, $0 < x \leq 3$, has an absolute minimum value of 0 but no absolute maximum value.

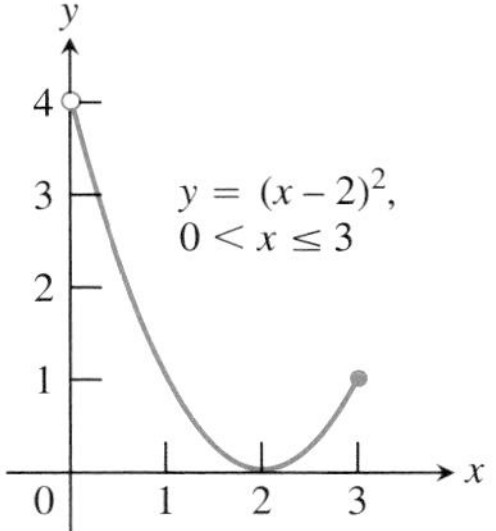

As Examples 1–4 were intended to suggest, continuous functions defined on closed intervals assume absolute maximum and minimum values on those intervals. Discontinuous functions, and functions whose domains are not closed intervals, may or may not assume absolute maximum and minimum values.

THEOREM 1

The Absolute Max-Min Theorem for Continuous Functions

If f is continuous at every point of a closed interval $[a, b]$, then f takes on both an absolute maximum and an absolute minimum value somewhere in $[a, b]$.

The First Derivative Theorem

Theorem 1 is not constructive. It describes circumstances under which we can be sure that extreme values exist but does not say how to find them when they do. That is where derivatives come in. In Fig. 4.5, which shows a variety of local and absolute extreme values, two of the extreme values occur at endpoints of the domain of f, one occurs at a point where f' does not exist, and two occur at interior points were $f' = 0$. This is typical for a function defined on a closed interval. The only places where a function f can ever have an extreme value are

1. interior points where f' is zero;
2. interior points where f' does not exist;
3. endpoints of the function's domain.

Let us look at the first case. The following theorem says that a function's first derivative, when defined, is always zero at an interior point where the function has a local extreme value.

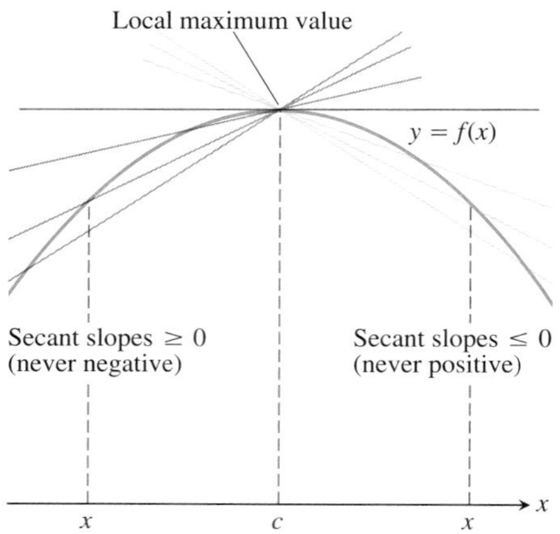

4.6 A curve with a local maximum value. The slope at c, simultaneously the limit of nonpositive numbers and nonnegative numbers, is zero.

THEOREM 2

The First Derivative Theorem for Local Extreme Values

If a function f has a local maximum or a local minimum value at an interior point c of its domain, and if f' is defined at c, then

$$f'(c) = 0.$$

Proof You may not have seen an argument like the one we are about to use, so we will explain its form first. We want to show that $f'(c) = 0$, and our plan is to do that indirectly by showing first that $f'(c)$ cannot be positive and second that $f'(c)$ cannot be negative either. Why does that show $f'(c) = 0$? Because, in the entire real number system, only one number is neither positive nor negative, and that number is zero.

To be specific, suppose f has a local maximum value at $x = c$, so that $f(x) \leq f(c)$ for all values of x near c (Fig. 4.6). Since c is an interior point of f's domain, the limit

$$\lim_{x \to c} \frac{f(x) - f(c)}{x - c} \tag{1}$$

defining $f'(c)$ is two-sided. This means that the right-hand and left-hand limits both exist at $x = c$, and both equal $f'(c)$.

When we examine these limits separately, we find that

$$\lim_{x \to c^+} \frac{f(x) - f(c)}{x - c} \leq 0 \tag{2}$$

because, immediately to the right of c, $f(x) \leq f(c)$ and $x - c > 0$. Similarly,

$$\lim_{x \to c^-} \frac{f(x) - f(c)}{x - c} \geq 0 \tag{3}$$

because, immediately to the left of c, $f(x) \leq f(c)$ and $x - c < 0$.

The inequality in (2) says that $f'(c)$ cannot be greater than zero, whereas (3) says that $f'(c)$ cannot be less than zero. So $f'(c) = 0$.

This proves the theorem for local maximum values. To prove it for local minimum values, simply replace f by $-f$ and run through the argument again. ■

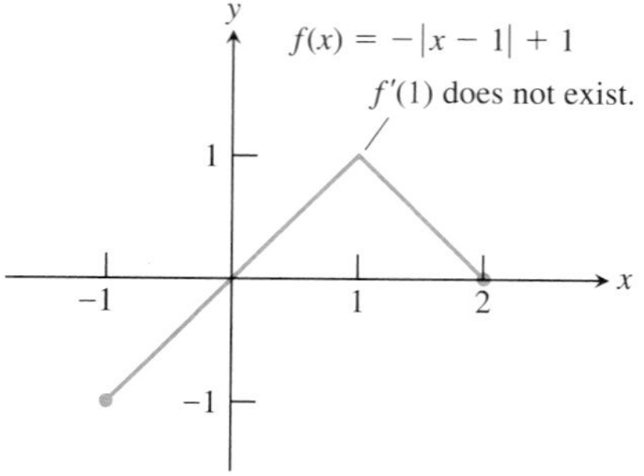

4.7 The function $f(x) = -|x - 1| + 1$, $-1 \leq x \leq 2$, has a local maximum value at an interior point where f' does not exist. It also has local minimum values at the endpoints of its domain.

Theorem 2 says that a function f can have a local extreme value at an interior point where f' exists only if f' is zero at that point. That leaves us only two other kinds of domain points to consider in our quest for extreme values: interior points where f' does not exist and boundary points. Both are real possibilities, as we can see from Fig. 4.7.

The following definition helps us to summarize what we have learned about the locations of extreme values.

DEFINITION

An interior point of the domain of a function f at which f' equals zero or does not exist is a **critical point** of f.

How to Find Absolute Extreme Values on Closed Intervals

To find the absolute maximum and minimum values of a continuous function f on a closed interval:

1. Find the critical points.
2. Evaluate f at the critical points.
3. Evaluate f at the endpoints.
4. Take the largest and smallest of the resulting values.

To sum up, the only points where a function can take on extreme values are critical points and endpoints.

EXAMPLE 5 Find the absolute maximum and minimum values of $f(x) = x^{2/3}$ on the interval $-2 \le x \le 3$.

Solution We evaluate the function at the critical points and endpoints and take the largest and smallest of the resulting values.

The first derivative,

$$y' = \frac{2}{3}x^{-1/3} = \frac{2}{3\sqrt[3]{x}},$$

has no zeros but is undefined at $x = 0$. The values of the function at this one critical point and at the endpoints are

Critical point value: $f(0) = 0$

Endpoint values: $f(-2) = (-2)^{2/3} = [(-2)^2]^{1/3} = 4^{1/3}$

$f(3) = (3)^{2/3} = 9^{1/3}$.

We conclude that the function's absolute maximum value is $9^{1/3} \approx 2.0801$, taken on at the endpoint $x = 3$. The absolute minimum value is 0, taken on at the interior point $x = 0$ (Fig. 4.8).

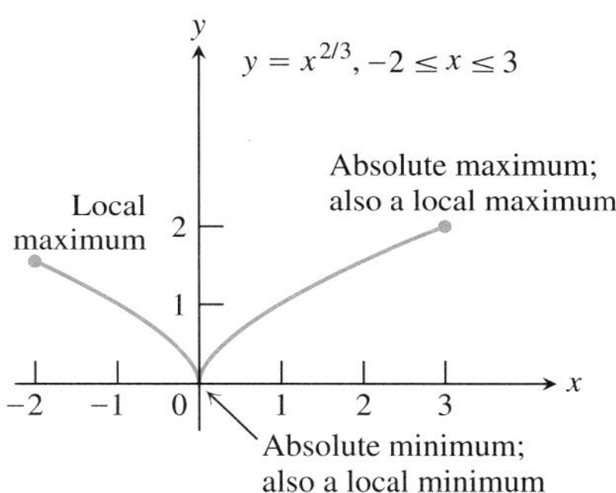

4.8 The extreme values of $y = x^{2/3}$ on the interval $-2 \le x \le 3$ (Example 5).

Not all critical points produce extrema, and there is more to be learned from the graph of the function f in Fig. 4.5 (shown here again as Fig. 4.9). While f assumes local extrema at a, c_2, c_3, c_4, and b, it does not do so at c_1 and c_5 even though $f' = 0$ at these latter points.

The key to the behavior of f at each critical point is the sign of f' in the point's immediate vicinity. As x moves from left to right, the values of f increase where $f' > 0$ and decrease where $f' < 0$, as stated in the following theorem.

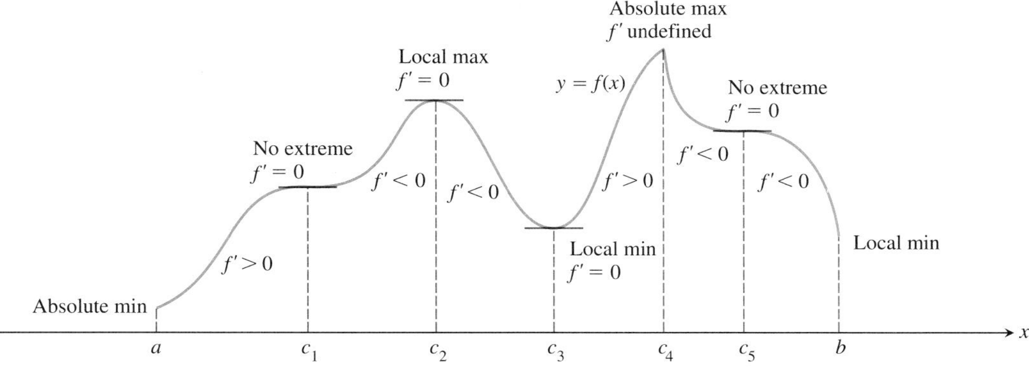

4.9 A function's first derivative tells how the graph rises and falls.

THEOREM 3

The First Derivative Test for Increasing and Decreasing

Suppose that f is continuous on $[a, b]$ and differentiable on (a, b).

1. If $f'(x) > 0$ for all x in (a, b), then f is increasing on $[a, b]$.
2. If $f'(x) < 0$ for all x in (a, b), then f is decreasing on $[a, b]$.

We will see why Theorem 3 holds when we reach Section 4.6. In the meantime, here is what the theorem has to do with the behavior of the function f in Fig. 4.9.

Looking at the points where f has a minimum value, we see that $f' < 0$ on the interval immediately to the left and $f' > 0$ on the interval immediately to the right. (If the point is an endpoint, then there is only the interval on the appropriate side to consider.) This means that the curve is falling (values are decreasing) on the left of the minimum value and rising (values are increasing) on its right. Similarly, looking at the points where f has a maximum value, we see that $f' > 0$ on the interval immediately to the left and $f' < 0$ on the interval immediately to the right. This means that the curve is rising (values are increasing) on the left of the maximum value and falling (values are decreasing) on its right.

These observations lead to the following test for the presence of local extreme values.

THEOREM 4

The First Derivative Test for Local Extreme Values

The following test applies to a continuous function $f(x)$.

At a critical point c:

1. If f' changes from positive to negative at c ($f' > 0$ for $x < c$ and $f' < 0$ for $x > c$), then f has a local maximum value at c.

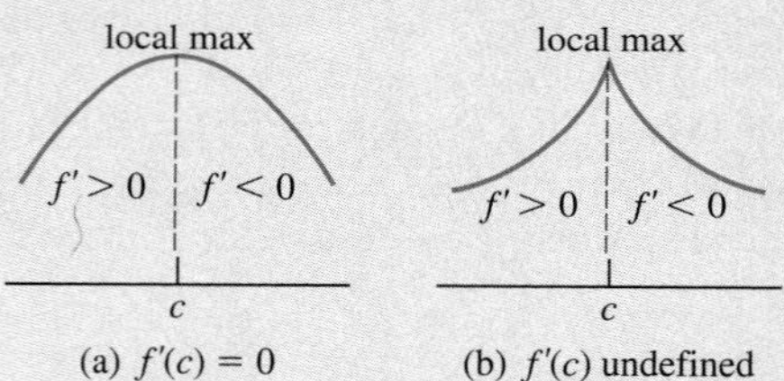

2. If f' changes from negative to positive at c ($f' < 0$ for $x < c$ and $f' > 0$ for $x > c$), then f has a local minimum value at c.

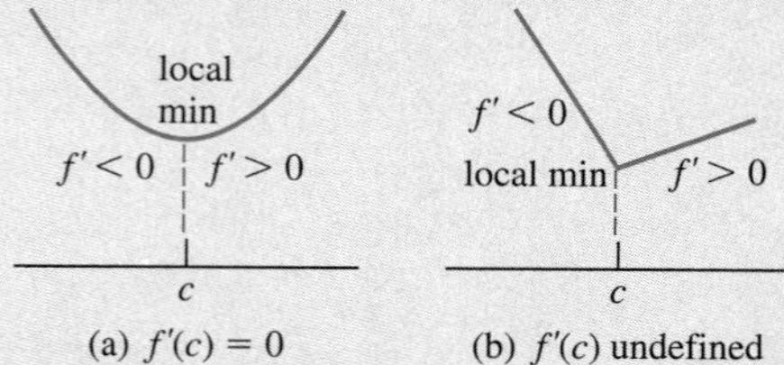

3. If f' does not change sign at c (f' has the same sign on both sides of c), then f has no local extreme value at c.

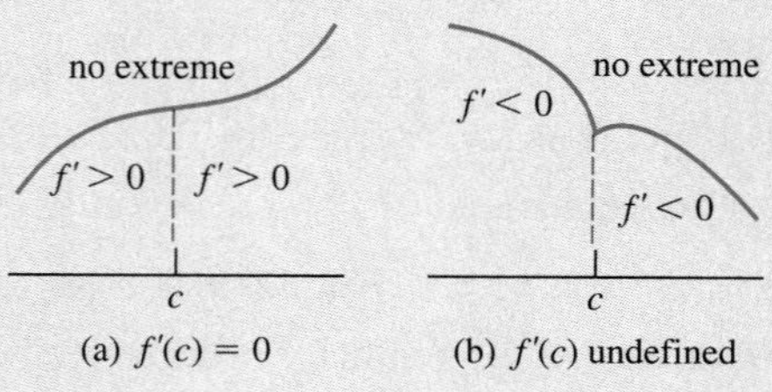

At a left endpoint a:

If $f' < 0$ ($f' > 0$) for $x > a$, then f has a local maximum (minimum) value at a.

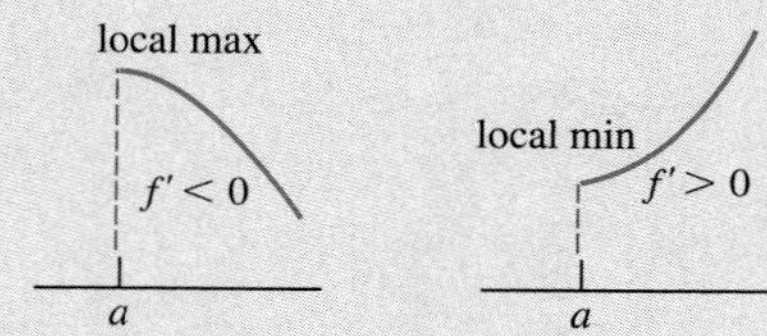

At a right endpoint b:

If $f' < 0$ ($f' > 0$) for $x < b$, then f has a local minimum (maximum) value at b.

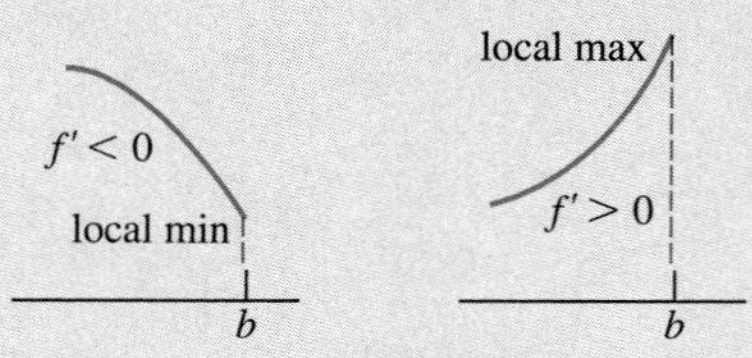

EXAMPLE 6 Find the critical points of

$$f(x) = x^{1/3}(x - 4) = x^{4/3} - 4x^{1/3}.$$

Identify the intervals on which f is increasing and decreasing and find the function's local extreme values.

Solution The function f is defined for all real numbers and is continuous (Fig. 4.10). The first derivative

$$f'(x) = \frac{d}{dx}\left(x^{4/3} - 4x^{1/3}\right) = \frac{4}{3}x^{1/3} - \frac{4}{3}x^{-2/3}$$

$$= \frac{4}{3}x^{-2/3}(x - 1) = \frac{4(x - 1)}{3x^{2/3}}$$

is zero at $x = 1$ and undefined at $x = 0$. There are no endpoints in f's domain, so the critical points, $x = 0$ and $x = 1$, are the only places where f might have an extreme value of any kind.

These critical points divide the x-axis into intervals on which f' is either positive or negative. The sign pattern of f' reveals the behavior of f both between and at the critical points. We can display the information in a picture like the following.

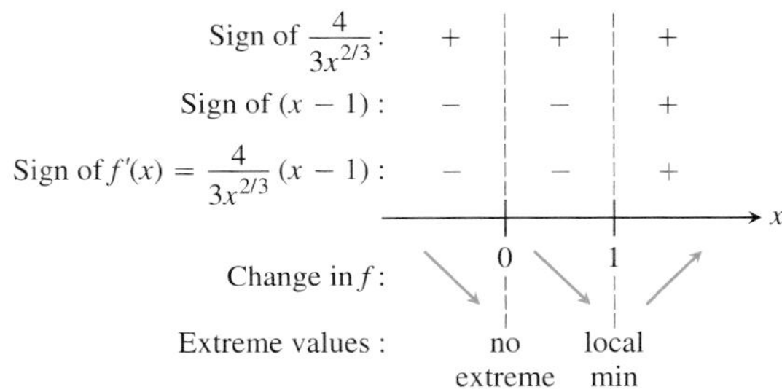

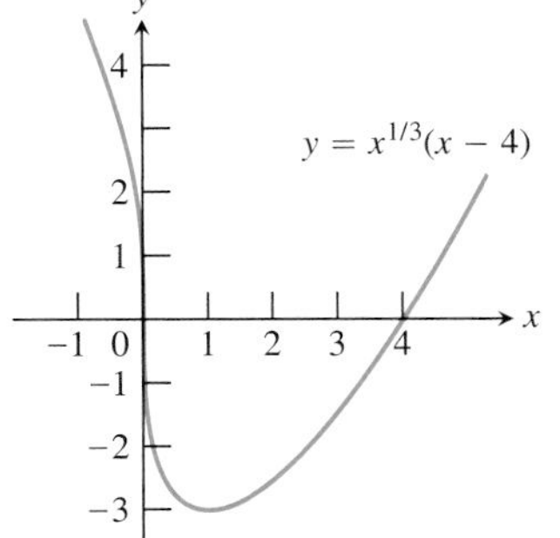

4.10 The graph of $y = x^{1/3}(x - 4)$ (Example 6).

To make the picture, we marked the critical points on the x-axis, noted the sign of each factor of f' on the intervals between the points, and "multiplied" the signs of the factors to find the sign of f'. We then applied Theorem 3 to determine that f decreases (↘) on $(-\infty, 0)$, decreases (↘) on $(0, 1)$, and increases (↗) on $(1, \infty)$. Accordingly, f has no extreme value at $x = 0$ (the graph continues to fall) and f has a local minimum at $x = 1$ (the graph falls on the left and rises on the right). Alternatively, Theorem 4 tells us that f has no extreme at $x = 0$ (f' does not change sign) and that it has a local minimum at $x = 1$ (f' changes from negative to positive). The value of the local minimum, found from the formula for f, is $f(1) = (1)^{1/3}(1 - 4) = -3$. See Fig. 4.10.

EXAMPLE 7 Find the intervals on which

$$g(x) = -x^3 + 12x + 5, \qquad -3 \le x \le 3$$

is increasing and decreasing. Where does the function assume local extreme values, and what are these values?

Solution The function f is continuous on its domain, $[-3, 3]$ (Fig. 4.11 on the following page). The first derivative

$$g'(x) = -3x^2 + 12 = -3(x^2 - 4) = -3(x + 2)(x - 2),$$

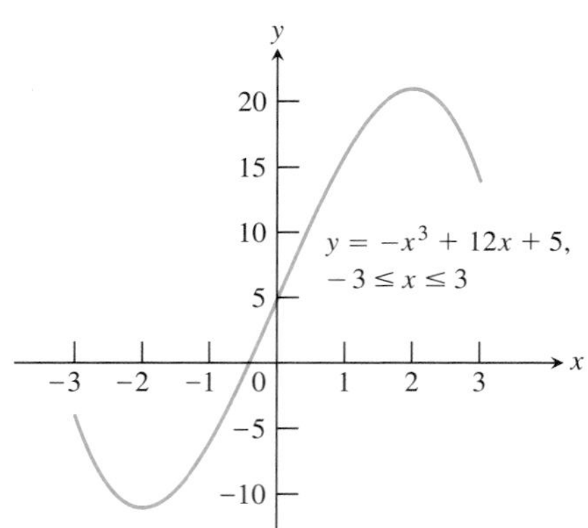

4.11 The graph of
$$g(x) = -x^3 + 12x + 5,$$
$-3 \le x \le 3$ (Example 7).

defined at all points of $[0, 3]$, is zero at $x = -2$ and $x = 2$. These critical points divide the domain of g into intervals on which g' is either positive or negative. We analyze the behavior of g by picturing the sign pattern of g':

	$-3 < x < -2$	$-2 < x < 2$	$2 < x < 3$
Sign of $-3(x+2)$:	+	−	−
Sign of $(x-2)$:	−	−	+
Sign of $g'(x) = -3(x+2)(x-2)$:	−	+	−
Change in $g(x)$:	↘	↗	↘

	-3 (endpoint)	-2	2	3 (endpoint)
Extrema:	local max	local min	local max	local min

We conclude that g has local maxima at $x = -3$ and $x = 2$, and local minima at $x = -2$ and $x = 3$. The corresponding values of $g(x) = -x^3 + 12x + 5$ are

Local maxima: $g(-3) = -4$, $g(2) = 21$

Local minima: $g(-2) = -11$, $g(3) = 14$.

Since g is defined on a closed interval, we also know that $g(-2)$ is the absolute minimum and $g(2)$ is the absolute maximum. Figure 4.11 shows these values in relation to the function's graph.

Exercises 4.2

In Exercises 1–6, determine from the graph whether the function has any absolute extreme values. Then tell how your answer is consistent with Theorem 1.

1.

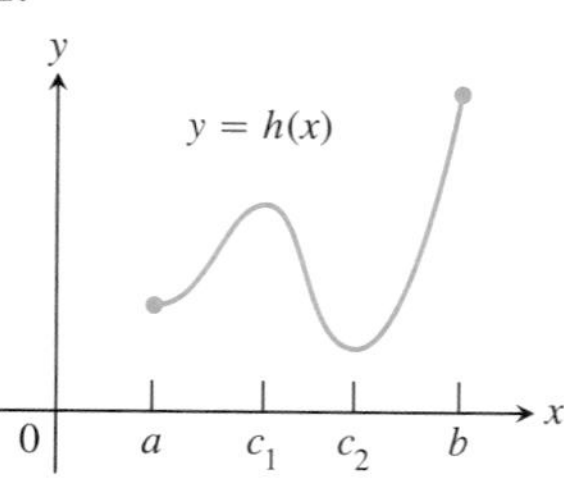

2.

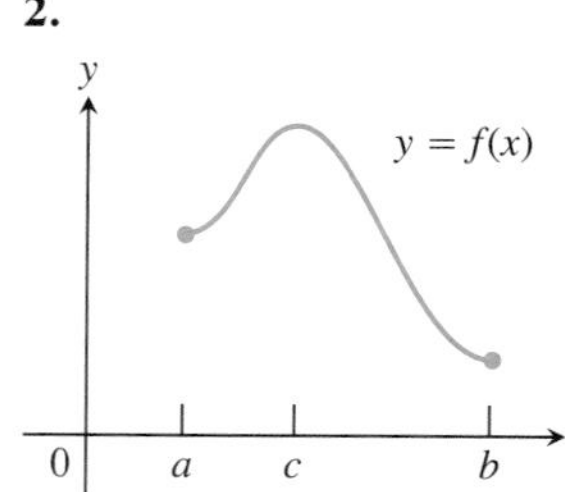

3.

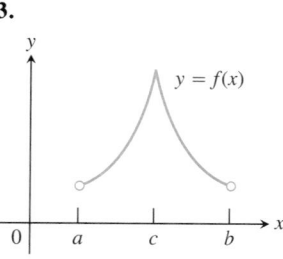

4.

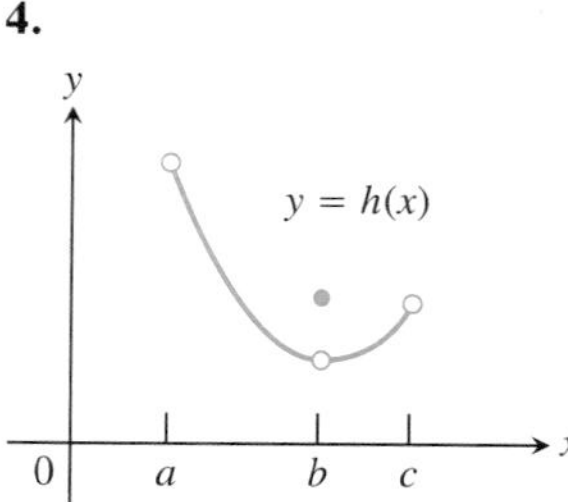

5. **6.**

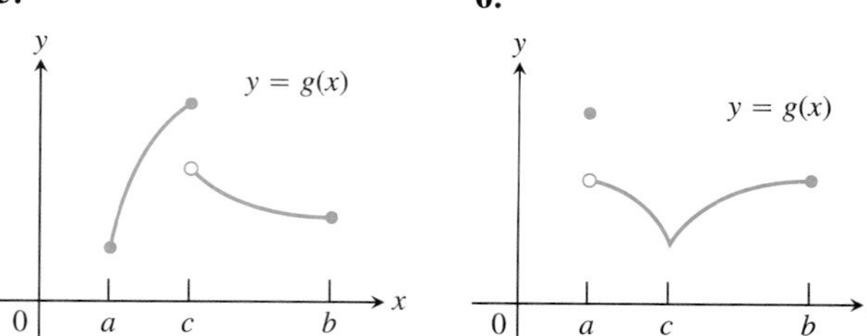

In Exercises 7–22, find the absolute maximum and minimum values of each function on the given interval. Then graph the function. Identify the points on the graph where the absolute extrema occur, and include their coordinates.

7. $f(x) = \frac{2}{3}x - 5, \quad -2 \le x \le 3$

8. $f(x) = -x - 4, \quad -4 \le x \le 1$

9. $f(x) = x^2 - 1, \quad -1 \le x \le 2$

10. $f(x) = 4 - x^2, \quad -3 \le x \le 1$

11. $F(x) = -\frac{1}{x^2}, \quad 0.5 \le x \le 2$

12. $F(x) = -\frac{1}{x}, \quad -2 \le x \le -1$

13. $h(x) = \sqrt[3]{x}, \quad -1 \le x \le 8$

14. $h(x) = -3x^{2/3}, \quad -1 \le x \le 1$

15. $g(x) = \sqrt{4 - x^2}, \quad -2 \le x \le 1$

16. $g(x) = -\sqrt{5 - x^2}, \quad -\sqrt{5} \le x \le 0$

17. $f(\theta) = \sin\theta, \quad -\frac{\pi}{2} \le \theta \le \frac{5\pi}{6}$

18. $f(\theta) = \tan\theta, \quad -\frac{\pi}{3} \le \theta \le \frac{\pi}{4}$

19. $g(x) = \csc x, \quad \frac{\pi}{3} \le x \le \frac{2\pi}{3}$

20. $g(x) = \sec x, \quad -\frac{\pi}{3} \le x \le \frac{\pi}{6}$

21. $f(t) = 2 - |t|, \quad -1 \le t \le 3$

22. $f(t) = |t - 5|, \quad 4 \le t \le 7$

In Exercises 23–26, find the function's absolute maximum and minimum values and say where they are assumed.

23. $f(x) = x^{4/3}, \quad -1 \le x \le 8$

24. $f(x) = x^{5/3}, \quad -1 \le x \le 8$

25. $g(\theta) = \theta^{3/5}, \quad -32 \le \theta \le 1$

26. $h(\theta) = 3\theta^{2/3}, \quad -27 \le \theta \le 8$

Each of Exercises 27–34 gives the first derivative of a function $y = f(x)$. Use the derivative to answer the following questions about the function.

a) What are the critical points of f?
b) On what intervals is f increasing and decreasing?
c) At what points, if any, does f assume local maximum and minimum values?

27. $f'(x) = x(x - 1)$

28. $f'(x) = (x - 1)(x + 2)$

29. $f'(x) = (x - 1)^2(x + 2)$

30. $f'(x) = (x - 1)^2(x + 2)^2$

31. $f'(x) = (x - 1)(x + 2)(x - 3)$

32. $f'(x) = (x - 7)(x + 1)(x + 5)$

33. $f'(x) = x^{-1/3}(x + 2)$

34. $f'(x) = x^{-1/2}(x - 3)$

In Exercises 35–50, use the function's first derivative to find the intervals on which the function is increasing and decreasing. Then identify the function's local extreme values, if there are any, saying where they are assumed and what their values are.

35. $g(t) = -t^2 - 3t + 3$

36. $g(t) = -3t^2 + 9t + 5$

37. $h(x) = -x^3 + 2x^2$

38. $h(x) = 2x^3 - 18x$

39. $f(\theta) = 3\theta^2 - 4\theta^3$

40. $f(\theta) = 6\theta - \theta^3$

41. $f(r) = 3r^3 + 16r$

42. $h(r) = (r + 7)^3$

43. $f(x) = x^4 - 8x^2 + 16$

44. $g(x) = x^4 - 4x^3 + 4x^2$

45. $H(t) = \frac{3}{2}t^4 - t^6$

46. $K(t) = 15t^3 - t^5$

47. $g(x) = x\sqrt{8 - x^2}$

48. $g(x) = x^2\sqrt{5 - x}$

49. $f(x) = \frac{x^2 - 3}{x - 2}, \quad x \ne 2$

50. $f(x) = \frac{x^3}{3x^2 + 1}$

In Exercises 51–54:

a) Find the intervals on which the function is increasing and decreasing.
b) Identify the function's local extrema, saying where each is assumed and what its value is.
c) Graph the function.

51. $f(x) = x^{1/3}(x + 8)$

52. $g(x) = x^{2/3}(x + 5)$

53. $h(x) = x^{1/3}(x^2 - 4)$

54. $k(x) = x^{2/3}(x^2 - 4)$

In Exercises 55–62, identify the function's local extreme values in the given domain and say where they are assumed.

55. $f(x) = 2x - x^2, \quad -\infty < x \le 2$

56. $f(x) = (x + 1)^2, \quad -\infty < x \le 0$

57. $g(x) = x^2 - 4x + 4, \quad 1 \le x < \infty$

58. $g(x) = -x^2 - 6x - 9, \quad -4 \le x < \infty$

59. $f(t) = 12t - t^3, \quad -3 \le t < \infty$

60. $f(t) = t^3 - 3t^2, \quad -\infty < t \le 3$

61. $h(x) = \frac{x^3}{3} - 2x^2 + 4x, \quad 0 \le x < \infty$

62. $k(x) = x^3 + 3x^2 + 3x + 1, \quad -\infty < x \le 0$

In Exercises 63–66, find the function's local extreme values in the given domain and say where they are assumed.

63. $y = x^3 - 6x, \quad -2 \le x \le 2$

64. $y = -x^3 + 6x^2, \quad -1 \le x \le 5$

65. $y = 4x^3 - 3x^4, \quad -1 \le x \le 2$

66. $y = 3x^5 - 5x^2, \quad -1 \le x \le \sqrt{2}$

In Exercises 67–70:

a) Find the local extrema of each function on the given interval and say where they are assumed.
b) Graph the function and its derivative together. Comment on the behavior of f in relation to the signs and values of f'.

67. $f(x) = \frac{x}{2} - 2\sin\frac{x}{2}, \quad 0 \le x \le 2\pi$

68. $f(x) = -2\cos x - \cos^2 x, \quad -\pi \le x \le \pi$

69. $f(x) = \csc^2 x - 2\cot x, \quad 0 < x < \pi$

70. $f(x) = \sec^2 x - 2\tan x, \quad \frac{-\pi}{2} < x < \frac{\pi}{2}$

Use Theorem 4 to show that the functions in Exercises 71 and 72 have local extreme values at the given values of θ, and say which kind of local extreme the function has.

71. $y = 3\cos\frac{\theta}{2}, \quad 0 \le \theta \le 2\pi, \quad$ at $\theta = 0$ and $\theta = 2\pi$

72. $y = 5 \sin \frac{\theta}{2}, \quad 0 \le \theta \le \pi, \quad$ at $\theta = 0$ and $\theta = \pi$

The existence of extreme values can depend as much on a function's domain as it does on the formula or rule that defines the function. Exercises 73 and 74 illustrate this point. In each exercise, find the values of any local maxima and minima the given functions may have on their domains and say where the extrema are assumed. Which, if any, of the extrema are absolute?

73. **a)** $f(x) = x^2 - 4, \quad -2 \le x \le 2$
b) $g(x) = x^2 - 4, \quad -2 \le x < 2$
c) $h(x) = x^2 - 4, \quad -2 < x < 2$
d) $k(x) = x^2 - 4, \quad -2 \le x < \infty$
e) $l(x) = x^2 - 4, \quad 0 < x < \infty$

74. **a)** $f(x) = 2 - 2x^2, \quad -1 \le x \le 1$
b) $g(x) = 2 - 2x^2, \quad -1 < x \le 1$
c) $h(x) = 2 - 2x^2, \quad -1 < x < 1$
d) $k(x) = 2 - 2x^2, \quad -\infty < x \le 1$
e) $l(x) = 2 - 2x^2, \quad -\infty < x < 0$

75. Sketch the graph of a differentiable function $y = f(x)$ through the point $(1, 1)$, if $f'(1) = 0$ and
a) $f'(x) > 0$ for $x < 1$ and $f'(x) < 0$ for $x > 1$;
b) $f'(x) < 0$ for $x < 1$ and $f'(x) > 0$ for $x > 1$;
c) $f'(x) > 0$ for $x \ne 1$;
d) $f'(x) < 0$ for $x \ne 1$.

76. Sketch the graph of a differentiable function $y = f(x)$ that has
a) a local minimum at $(1, 1)$ and a local maximum at $(3, 3)$;
b) a local maximum at $(1, 1)$ and a local minimum at $(3, 3)$;
c) local maxima at $(1, 1)$ and $(3, 3)$;
d) local minima at $(1, 1)$ and $(3, 3)$.

77. As x moves from left to right through the point $c = 2$, is the graph of $f(x) = x^3 - 3x + 2$ rising, or is it falling? Give reasons for your answer.

78. Find the intervals on which the function $f(x) = ax^2 + bx + c$, $a \ne 0$, is increasing and decreasing. Describe the reasoning behind your answer.

79. The function $f(x) = |x|$ has an absolute minimum value at $x = 0$ even though f is not differentiable at $x = 0$. Is this consistent with Theorem 2? Give reasons for your answer.

80. If $f(x)$ has a local maximum value at $x = c$, what can be said about the value of $g(x) = -f(x)$ at $x = c$? Give reasons for your answer.

81. **a)** Show that $g(x) = 1/x$ decreases on every interval in its domain.
b) If the conclusion in (a) is really true, how do you explain the fact that $g(1) = 1$ is actually greater than $g(-1) = -1$?

82. We know how to find the extreme values of a continuous function $f(x)$ by investigating its values at critical points and boundary points. But what if there *are* no critical points or boundary points? What happens then? Do such functions really exist? Give reasons for your answers.

83. Is there any reason to believe that at any given instant there are at least two different points on the earth's equator where the temperatures are the same?

84. Is there any reason to believe that there is always a pair of antipodal points (diametrically opposite points) on the earth's equator where the temperatures are the same?

Writing for Your Own Knowledge

Answer the following questions in writing. Some answers will take only a sentence or two; others may require several paragraphs. Some explanations may also call for graphs or sketches.

1. When you are looking for the extreme values of a function $f(x)$, why is it all right to limit your investigation to the values f takes on at critical points and boundary points?
2. How do you find the absolute extreme values of a continuous function on a closed interval? How do you know if there are any?
3. How can you sometimes use a function's first derivative to identify the function's behavior at the critical points and boundary points of its domain?

EXPLORER PROGRAMS

Derivatives	Graphs functions together with their first derivatives.
PowerGrapher	Graphs all the functions in this section.

4.3 *How y′ and y″ Determine the Shape of a Graph*

In the preceding section, we saw how to use the first derivative to find exactly where a function's graph is rising and falling. In the present section, we see how to use the second derivative to learn how the graph bends as it rises and falls. This tells us the graph's general shape.

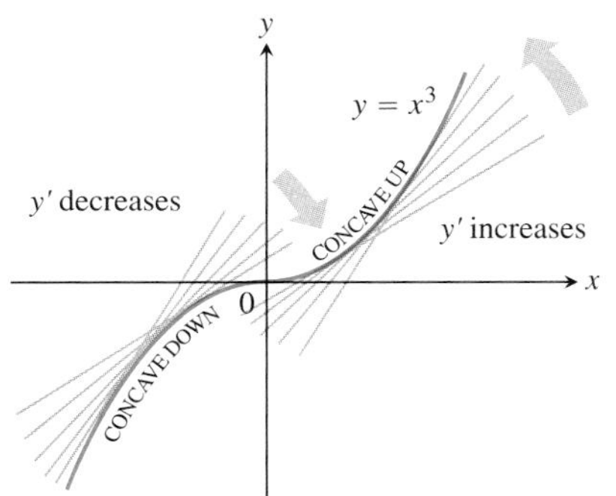

4.12 The graph of $y = x^3$. As x increases, the slopes of the tangents to the curve on $(-\infty, 0)$ are positive and decreasing; the slopes of the tangents to the curve on $(0, \infty)$ are positive and increasing.

Concavity

As you can see in Fig. 4.12, the function $f(x) = x^3$ increases as x increases, but portions of the curve $y = x^3$ increase in different ways. Looking at tangents as we scan from left to right, we see that the slope of the curve decreases on the interval $(-\infty, 0)$ and then increases on the interval $(0, \infty)$. We say that the curve $y = x^3$ is *concave down* on $(-\infty, 0)$, and *concave up* on $(0, \infty)$.

DEFINITION

The graph of a differentiable function $y = f(x)$ is **concave up** on an interval where y' is increasing and **concave down** on an interval where y' is decreasing.

If a function $y = f(x)$ has a second derivative as well as a first, we can apply Theorem 3 from the preceding section to conclude that y' increases if $y'' > 0$ and decreases if $y'' < 0$.

y'' Is the Rate of Change of y'

Remember that since

$$y'' = \frac{d}{dx}(y'),$$

we can think of y'' as a rate of change for y'. That is, y'' tells us how the y'-values are changing.

The Second Derivative Test for Concavity

The graph of $y = f(x)$ is *concave down* on any interval where $y'' < 0$ and *concave up* on any interval where $y'' > 0$.

EXAMPLE 1 The curve $y = x^3$ is concave down on $(-\infty, 0)$, where $y'' = 6x < 0$. It is concave up on $(0, \infty)$, where $y'' = 6x > 0$ (Fig. 4.12).

EXAMPLE 2 The parabola $y = x^2$ is concave up throughout its domain because $y'' = 2$ is always positive (Fig. 4.13).

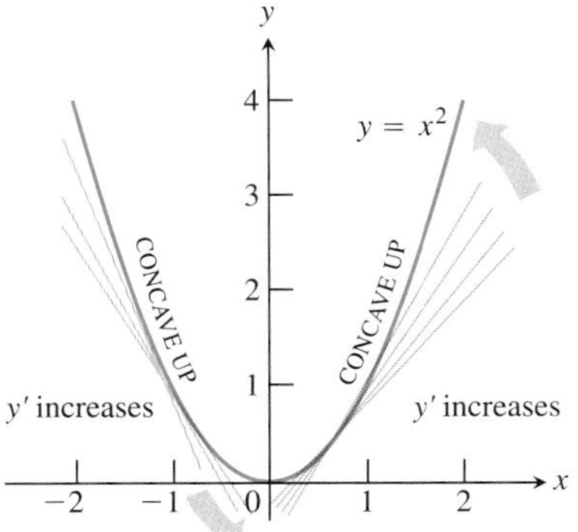

4.13 The graph of $y = x^2$. As x increases, the slopes of the tangents to the curve on $(-\infty, 0)$ are negative and increasing; the slopes of the tangents to the curve on $(0, \infty)$ are positive and increasing.

Points of Inflection

To study the motion of a body moving along a line, we often graph the body's position as a function of time. One reason for doing so is to reveal where the body's acceleration, given by the second derivative, changes sign. On the graph, these are the points where the concavity changes.

DEFINITION

A point where the graph of a function has a tangent line and where the concavity changes is called a **point of inflection.**

Thus a point of inflection on a curve is a point where y'' is positive on one side and negative on the other. At such a point, y'' is either zero (because derivatives have the intermediate value property) or undefined.

On the graph of a twice-differentiable function, $y'' = 0$ at a point of inflection.

EXAMPLE 3 The graph of the simple harmonic motion $s = \cos t$ (Fig. 4.14) changes concavity at $t = \pi/2$ and $t = 3\pi/2$, where the acceleration, $s'' = -\cos t$, is zero.

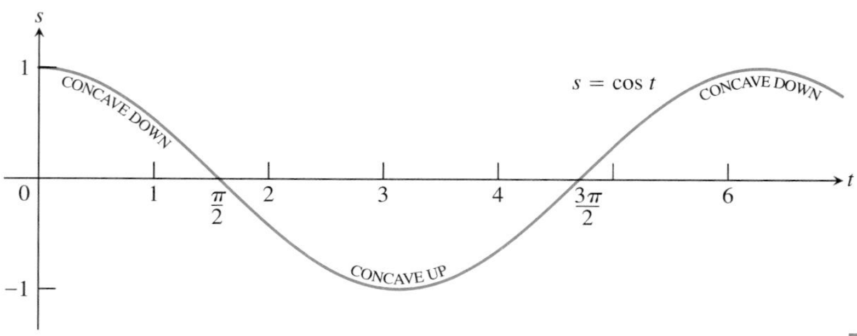

4.14 The motion in Example 3.

EXAMPLE 4 Inflection points have important applications in some areas of economics. Suppose that the function $y = c(x)$ in Fig. 4.15 is the total cost of producing x units of something. The point of inflection at P is then the point at which the marginal cost (the approximate cost of producing one more unit) changes from decreasing to increasing.

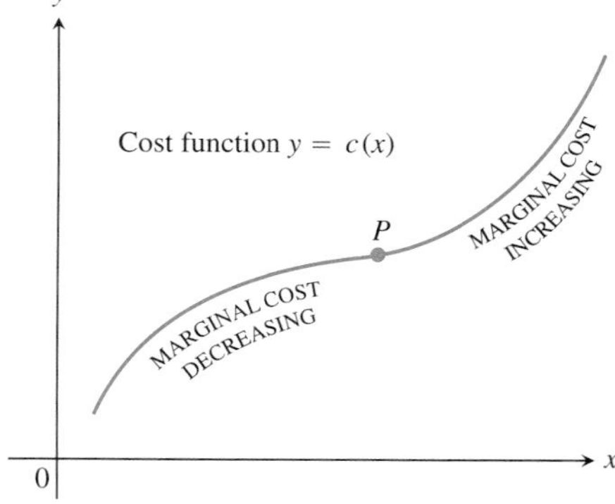

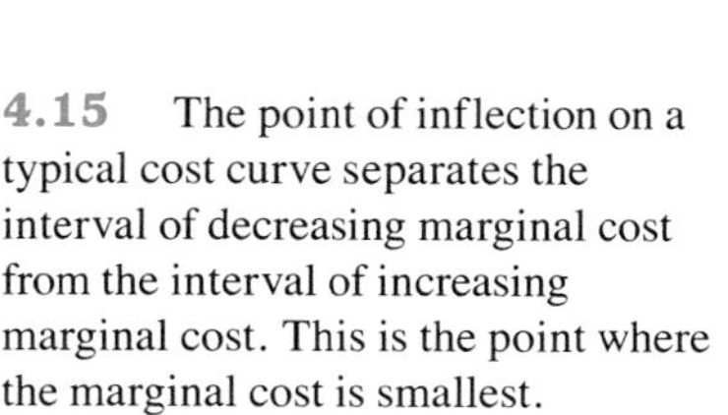

4.15 The point of inflection on a typical cost curve separates the interval of decreasing marginal cost from the interval of increasing marginal cost. This is the point where the marginal cost is smallest.

EXAMPLE 5 *An Inflection Point Where y'' Does Not Exist.* The curve $y = x^{1/3}$ (Fig. 4.16) has a point of inflection at $x = 0$, but y'' does not exist there. The formulas for y' and y'' are

$$y' = \frac{1}{3}x^{-2/3}, \qquad y'' = -\frac{2}{9}x^{-5/3}.$$

The curve is concave up for $x < 0$, where $y'' > 0$ and y' is increasing. It is concave down for $x > 0$, where $y'' < 0$ and y' is decreasing.

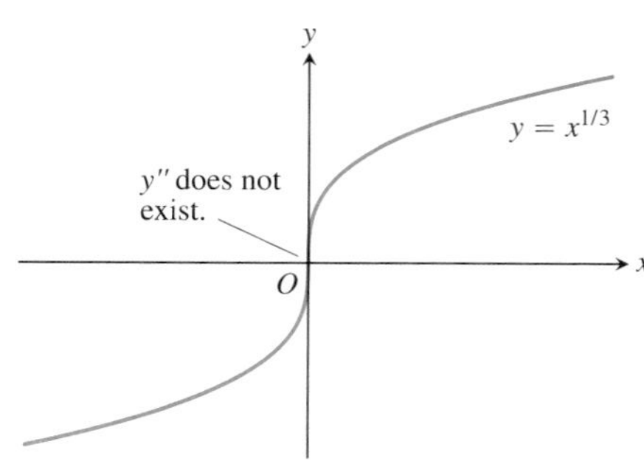

4.16 The graph of $y = x^{1/3}$ shows that a point where y'' fails to exist can be a point of inflection.

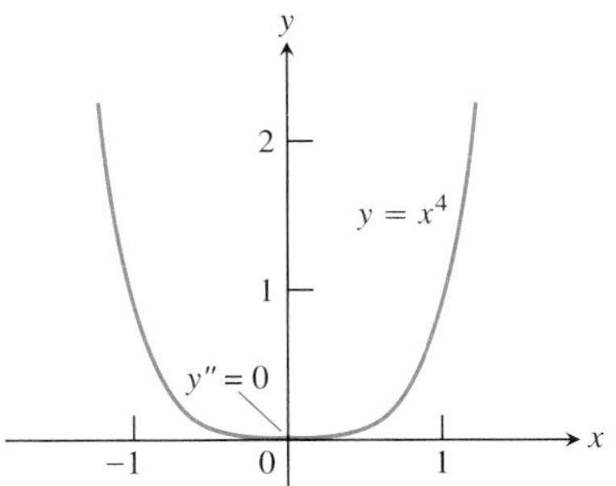

4.17 The graph of $y = x^4$ has no inflection point at the origin, even though $y'' = 0$ there.

It is possible for y'' to be zero at a point that is *not* a point of inflection, and you have to watch out for this.

EXAMPLE 6 *No Inflection Where $y'' = 0$.* The curve $y = x^4$ (Fig. 4.17) has no inflection point at $x = 0$. Even though $y'' = 12x^2$ is zero there, it does not change sign.

A Useful Shortcut—The Second Derivative Test

As you can see in the graphs below, the second derivative can give information about a function's local extreme values. So instead of looking at how the sign of y' changes at a point when $y' = 0$, we can use the following test.

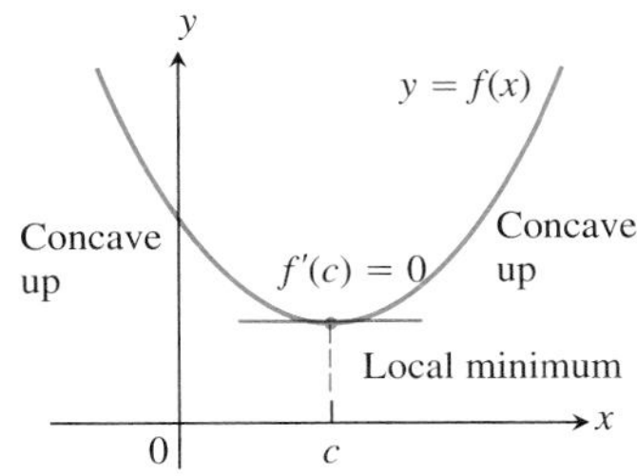

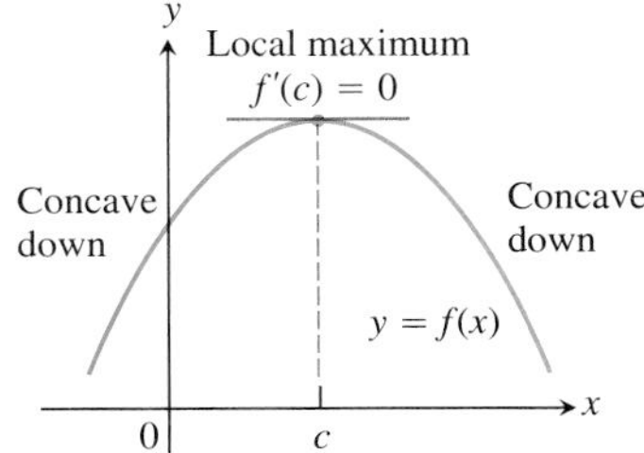

The Second Derivative Test for Local Extreme Values

If $f'(c) = 0$ and $f''(c) < 0$, then f has a local maximum at $x = c$.
If $f'(c) = 0$ and $f''(c) > 0$, then f has a local minimum at $x = c$.

Notice that the test requires us to know y'' only at c itself, and not in an interval about c. This makes the test easy to apply. That's the good news. The bad news is that the test is inconclusive if $y'' = 0$ or if y'' does not exist. When this happens, use the first derivative test for local extreme values.

Testing the Critical Points in Example 7

As a quick test to see if any of the critical points are local extreme values, we could use the second derivative test.

At $x = 3$, $y'' > 0$:
We now know that this point is definitely a local minimum.

At $x = 0$, $y'' = 0$:
Test fails, and so we will need to check the signs of y' to know whether this point is a local extreme value.

Graphing with y' and y''

We now apply what we have learned to sketch the graphs of functions.

EXAMPLE 7 Graph the function

$$y = x^4 - 4x^3 + 10.$$

Solution

STEP 1: *Find y' and y'':*

$$y = x^4 - 4x^3 + 10$$
$$y' = 4x^3 - 12x^2 = 4x^2(x - 3) \qquad \text{Critical points: } x = 0,\ x = 3$$
$$y'' = 12x^2 - 24x = 12x(x - 2) \qquad \text{Possible inflection points: } x = 0,\ x = 2$$

STEP 2: *Rise and fall:* Sketch the sign pattern for y' and use it to describe the behavior of y.

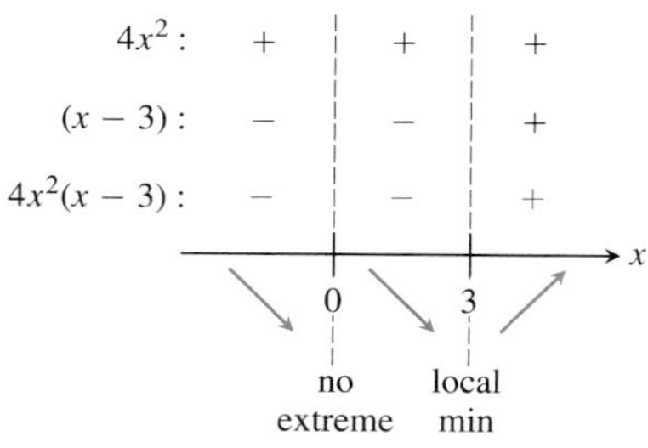

STEP 3: *Concavity:* Sketch the sign pattern for y'' and use it to describe the way the graph bends.

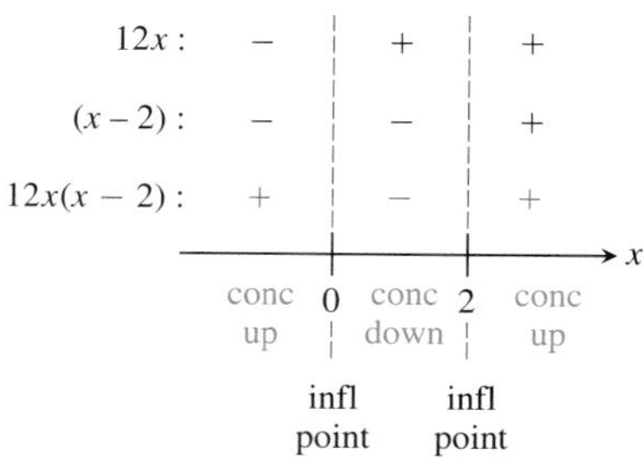

STEP 4: *Summary and general shape:* Summarize the information from Steps 2 and 3. Show the shape over each interval. Then combine the shapes to show the curve's general form.

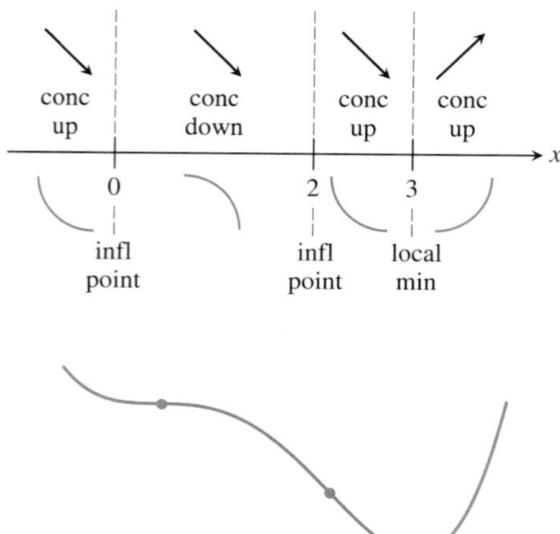

STEP 5: *Specific points and curve:* Plot the curve's intercepts (if convenient) and the points where y' and y'' are zero. Indicate any local extreme values and inflection points. Use the general shape in Step 4 as a guide to sketch the curve. (Plot additional points as needed.)

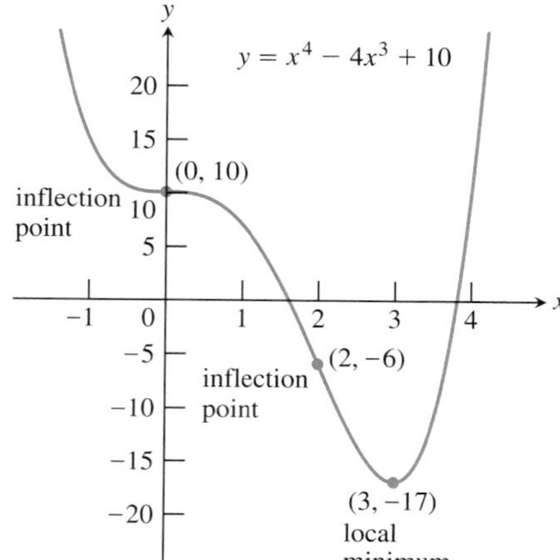

The steps in Example 7 give a general procedure for graphing by hand.

Strategy for graphing $y = f(x)$

1. Find y' and y''.
2. Find the rise and fall of the curve.
3. Determine the concavity of the curve.
4. Make a summary and show the curve's general shape.
5. Plot specific points and sketch the curve.

EXAMPLE 8 Graph

$$y = x^{5/3} - 5x^{2/3}.$$

Solution

STEP 1: *Find y' and y'':*

$$y = x^{5/3} - 5x^{2/3} = x^{2/3}(x - 5)$$

The x-intercepts are at $x = 0$ and $x = 5$.

$$y' = \frac{5}{3}x^{2/3} - \frac{10}{3}x^{-1/3} = \frac{5}{3}x^{-1/3}(x - 2)$$

Critical points: $x = 0$, $x = 2$.

$$y'' = \frac{10}{9}x^{-1/3} + \frac{10}{9}x^{-4/3} = \frac{10}{9}x^{-4/3}(x + 1)$$

Possible inflection points: $x = 0$, $x = -1$.

STEP 2: *Rise and fall:*

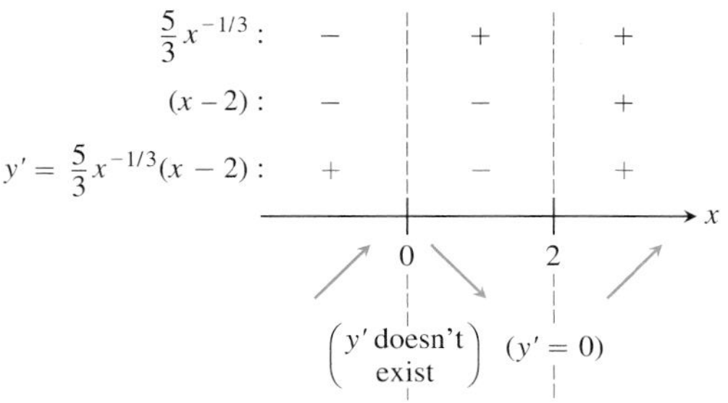

Cusps

The graph of a continuous function has a *cusp* at a point where the tangent is vertical and the concavity is the same on both sides. A cusp can be either a local maximum or a local minimum.

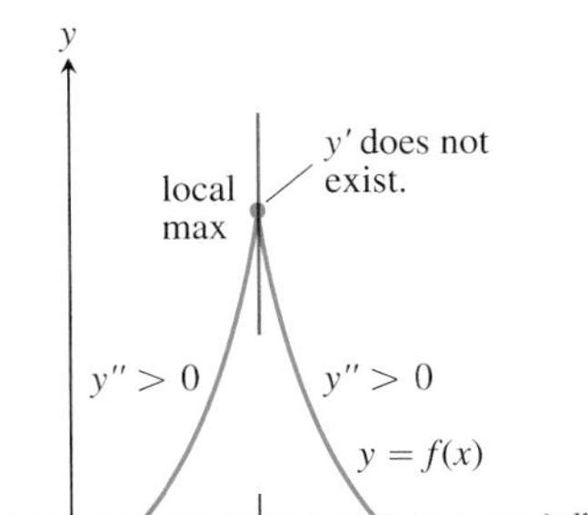

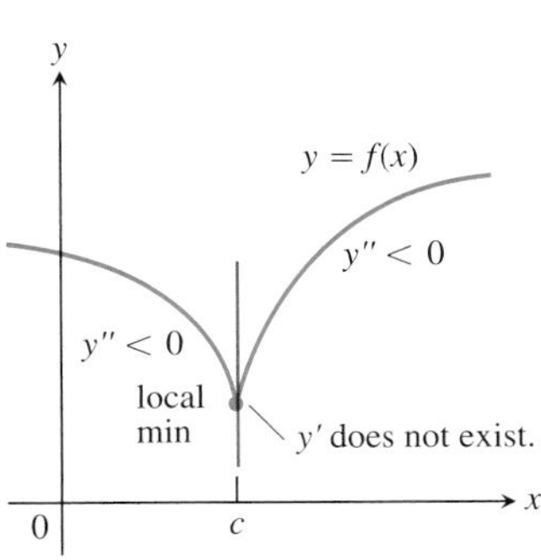

STEP 3: *Concavity:*

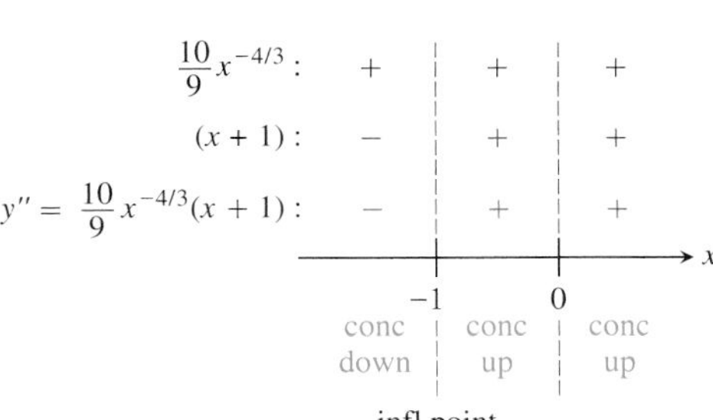

From the sign pattern for y'', we see that there is an inflection point at $x = -1$, but not at $x = 0$. However, knowing that

1. the function $y = x^{5/3} - 5x^{2/3}$ is continuous,
2. y' does not exist at $x = 0$ (Step 2), and
3. the concavity does not change at $x = 0$ (Step 3)

tells us that the graph has a *cusp* at $x = 0$.

STEP 4: *Summary:*

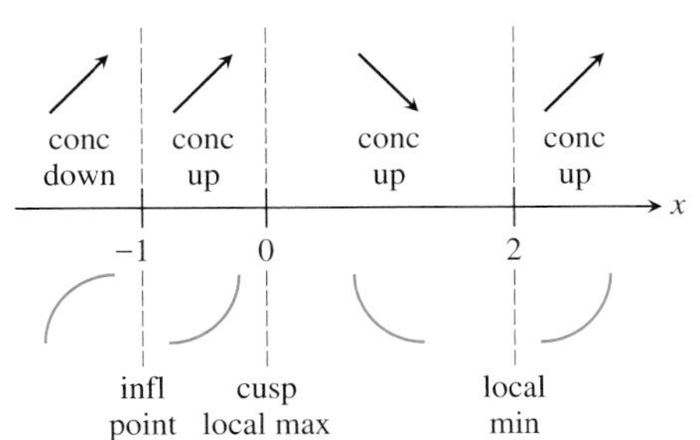

General shape:

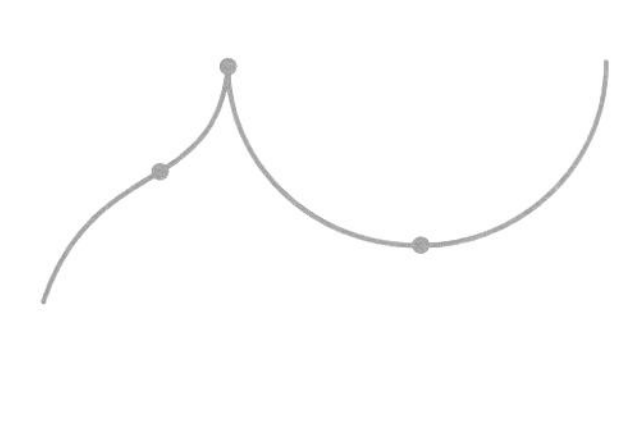

STEP 5: *Specific points and curve:*

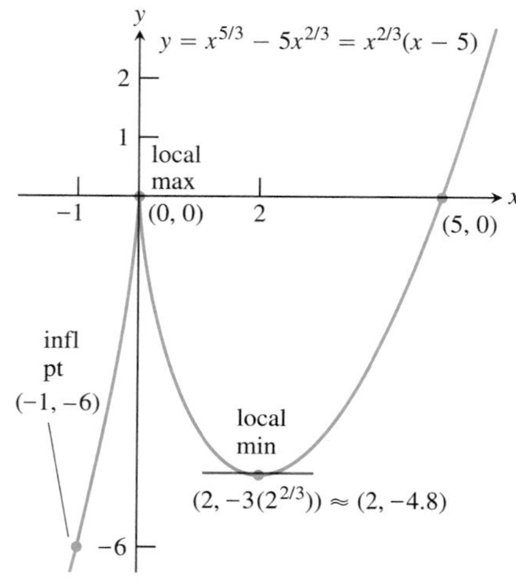

Learning About Functions from Derivatives

Pause for a moment to see how remarkable the conclusions in Examples 7 and 8 really are. In each case, we have been able to recover almost everything we need to know about a differentiable function $y = f(x)$ by examining y'. We can find where the graph rises and falls and where the local extremes are assumed. We can differentiate y' to learn how the graph bends as it passes over the intervals of rise and fall. We can determine the shape of the function's graph. The only information we cannot get from the derivative is how to place the graph in the xy-plane. That requires evaluating the formula for f itself at various points. Or so it would seem. But, as we will see in Section 4.7, even *that* is nearly superfluous. All we really need in addition to y' is the value of f at a single point.

Exercises 4.3

Identify the inflection points and local maxima and minima of the functions graphed in Exercises 1–8. Identify the intervals on which the functions are concave up and concave down.

1. $y = \frac{x^3}{3} - \frac{x^2}{2} - 2x + \frac{1}{3}$

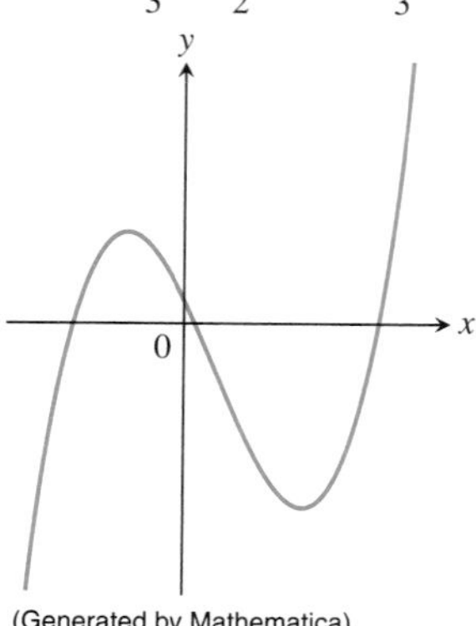

(Generated by Mathematica)

2. $y = \frac{x^4}{4} - 2x^2 + 4$

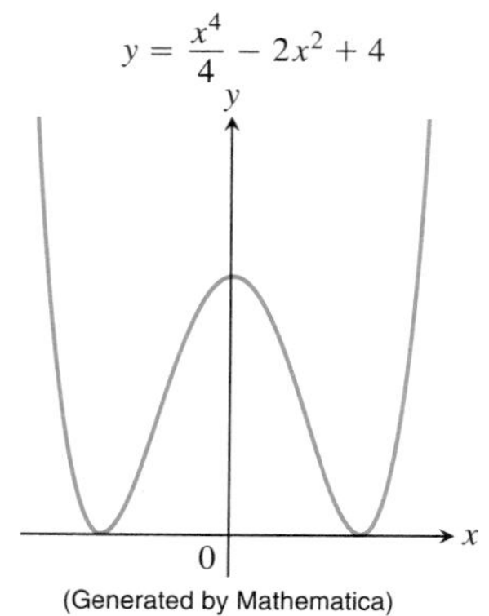

(Generated by Mathematica)

3. $y = \frac{3}{4}(x^2 - 1)^{2/3}$

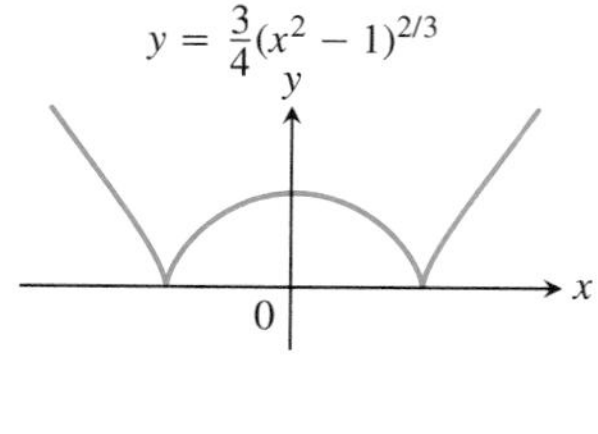

4. $y = \frac{9}{14}x^{1/3}(x^2 - 7)$

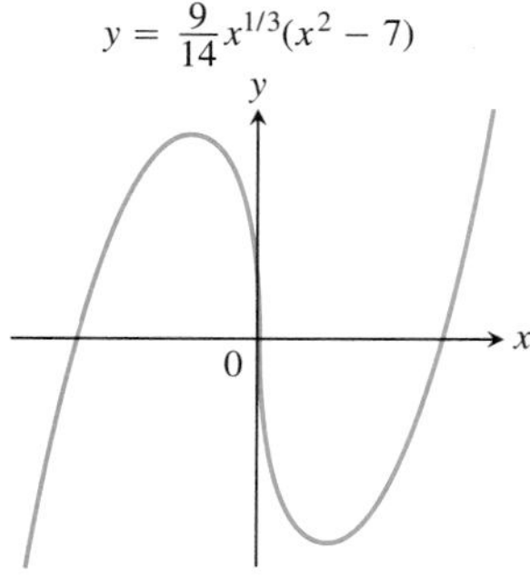

5.

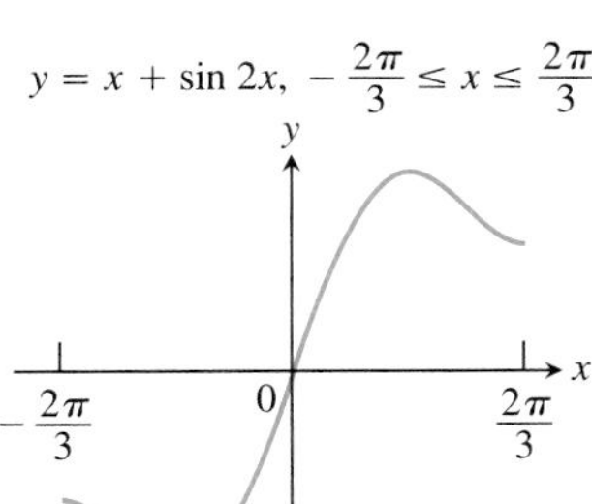

6.

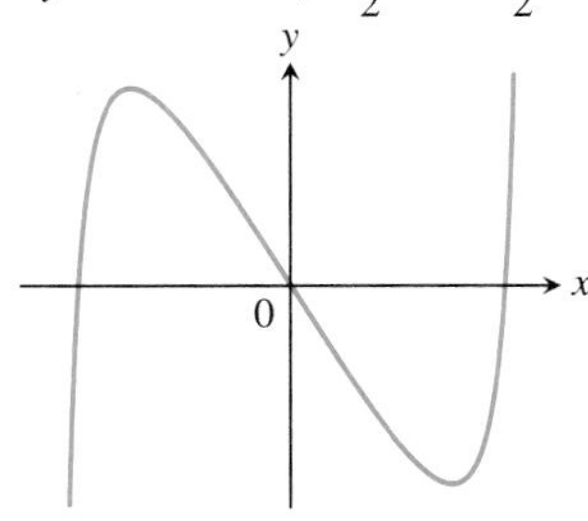

(Generated by Mathematica)

7.

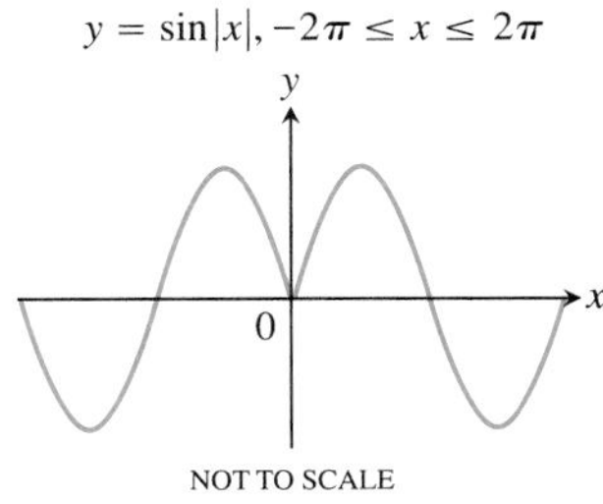

8.

$y = 2\cos x - \sqrt{2}\,x,\ -\pi \le x \le \frac{3\pi}{2}$

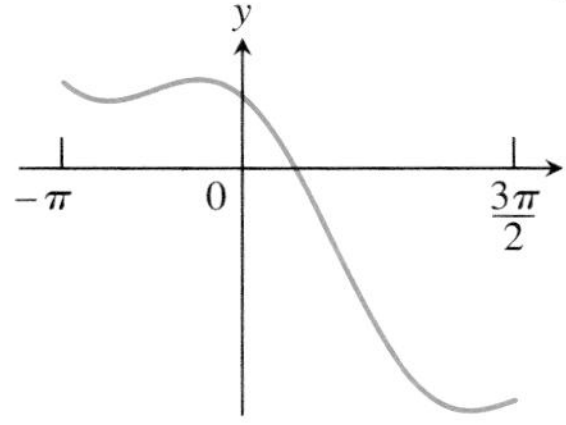

(Generated by Mathematica)

Use the steps of the graphing procedure on page 222 to graph the equations in Exercises 9–44. Include the coordinates of any local extreme points and inflection points in your sketch.

9. $y = x^2 - 4x + 3$

10. $y = 6 - 2x - x^2$

11. $y = x^3 - 3x + 3$

12. $y = x(6 - 2x)^2$

13. $y = -2x^3 + 6x^2 - 3$

14. $y = 1 - 9x - 6x^2 - x^3$

15. $y = (x - 2)^3 + 1$

16. $y = 1 - (x + 1)^3$

17. $y = x^4 - 2x^2 = x^2(x^2 - 2)$

18. $y = -x^4 + 6x^2 - 4 = x^2(6 - x^2) - 4$

19. $y = 4x^3 - x^4 = x^3(4 - x)$

20. $y = x^4 + 2x^3 = x^3(x + 2)$

21. $y = x^5 - 5x^4 = x^4(x - 5)$

22. $y = x\left(\frac{x}{2} - 5\right)^4$

23. $y = -x(x - 5)^4$

24. $y = 5x^2 - 2x^5 = x^2(5 - 2x^3)$

25. $y = x + \sin x,\quad 0 \le x \le 2\pi$

26. $y = x - \sin x,\quad 0 \le x \le 2\pi$

27. $y = 2x + \cot x,\quad 0 < x < \pi$

28. $y = \tan x - 4x,\quad -\pi/2 < x < \pi/2$

29. $y = x^{1/5}$

30. $y = x^{3/5}$

31. $y = x^{2/5}$

32. $y = x^{4/5}$

33. $y = 2x - 3x^{2/3}$

34. $y = 5x^{2/5} - 2x$

35. $y = x^{2/3}\left(\frac{5}{2} - x\right)$

36. $y = x^{2/3}(x - 5)$

37. $y = x\sqrt{8 - x^2}$

38. $y = (2 - x^2)^{3/2}$

39. $y = \dfrac{x^2 - 3}{x - 2},\quad x \ne 2$

40. $y = \dfrac{x^3}{3x^2 + 1}$

41. $y = |x^2 - 1|$

42. $y = |x^2 - 2x|$

43. $y = \sqrt{|x|} = \begin{cases} \sqrt{-x}, & x \le 0 \\ \sqrt{x}, & x > 0 \end{cases}$

44. $y = \sqrt{|x - 4|}$

Each of Exercises 45–66 gives the first derivative of a continuous function $y = f(x)$. Find y'' and then use Steps 2–4 of the graphing procedure on page 222 to sketch the general shape of the graph of f.

45. $y' = 2 + x - x^2$

46. $y' = x^2 - x - 6$

47. $y' = x(x - 3)^2$

48. $y' = x^2(2 - x)$

49. $y' = x(x^2 - 12)$

50. $y' = (x - 1)^2(2x + 3)$

51. $y' = (8x - 5x^2)(4 - x)^2$

52. $y' = (x^2 - 2x)(x - 5)^2$

53. $y' = \sec^2 x,\quad -\frac{\pi}{2} < x < \frac{\pi}{2}$

54. $y' = \tan x,\quad -\frac{\pi}{2} < x < \frac{\pi}{2}$

55. $y' = \cot \frac{\theta}{2},\quad 0 < \theta < 2\pi$

56. $y' = \csc^2 \frac{\theta}{2},\quad 0 < \theta < 2\pi$

57. $y' = \tan^2 \theta - 1,\quad -\frac{\pi}{2} < \theta < \frac{\pi}{2}$

58. $y' = 1 - \cot^2 \theta,\quad 0 < \theta < \pi$

59. $y' = \cos t,\quad 0 \le t \le 2\pi$

60. $y' = \sin t,\quad 0 \le t \le 2\pi$

61. $y' = (x + 1)^{-2/3}$

62. $y' = (x - 2)^{-1/3}$

63. $y' = x^{-2/3}(x - 1)$

64. $y' = x^{-4/5}(x + 1)$

65. $y' = 2|x| = \begin{cases} -2x, & x \le 0 \\ 2x, & x > 0 \end{cases}$

66. $y' = \begin{cases} -x^2, & x \le 0 \\ x^2 & x > 0 \end{cases}$

Velocity and Acceleration. The graphs in Exercises 67 and 68 show the position $s = f(t)$ of a body moving back and forth on a coordinate line. (a) When is the body moving away from the origin? toward the origin? At approximately what times is the (b) velocity equal to zero? (c) acceleration equal to zero? (d) Approximately when is the acceleration positive? negative?

67.

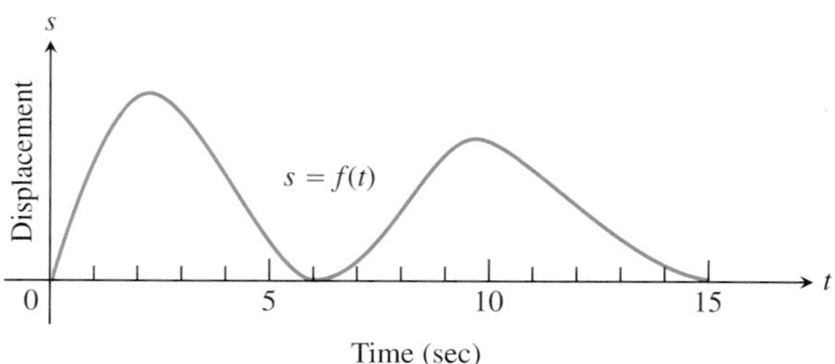

68.

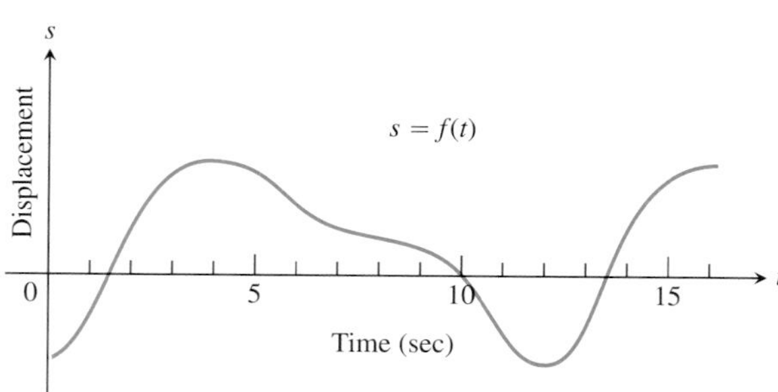

69. *Marginal Cost.* The accompanying graph shows the hypothetical cost $c = f(x)$ of manufacturing x items. At approximately what production level does the marginal cost change from decreasing to increasing?

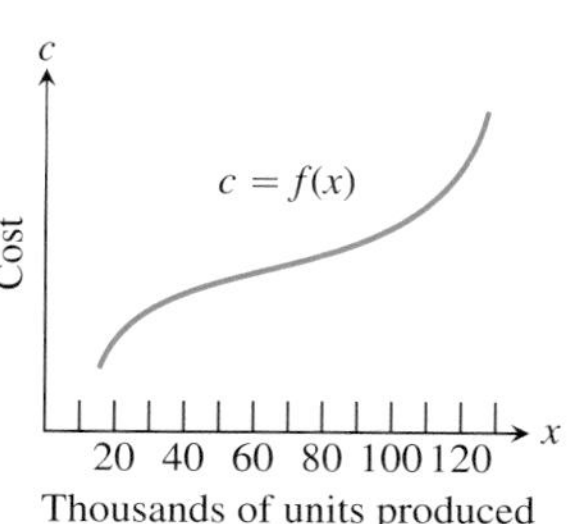

70. The accompanying graph shows the monthly revenue of the Widget Corporation for the last twelve years. During approximately what time intervals was the marginal revenue increasing? decreasing?

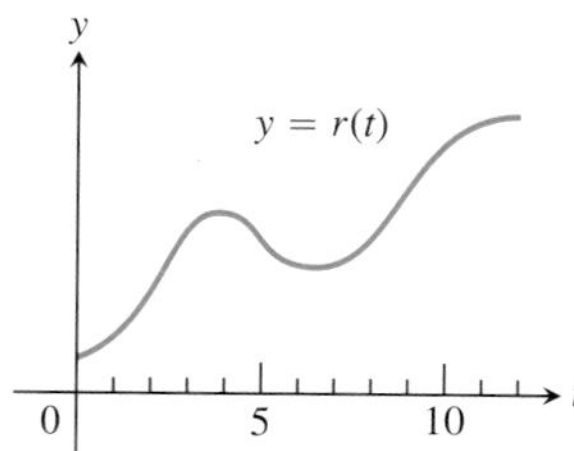

Each of Exercises 71–74 shows the graphs of the first and second derivatives of a function $y = f(x)$. Copy the picture and add to it a sketch of the approximate graph of f, given that the graph passes through the point P.

71.

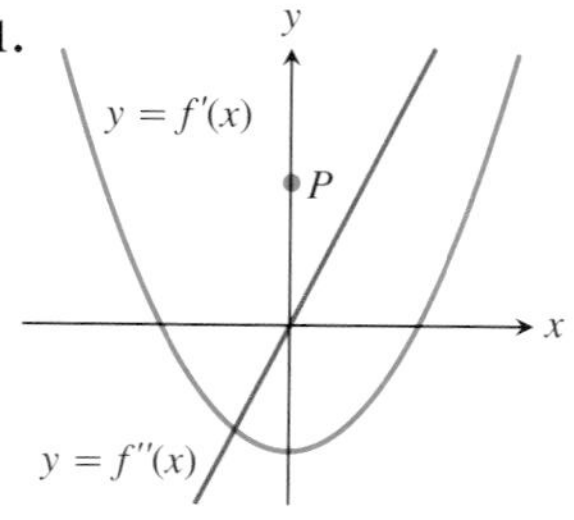

72.

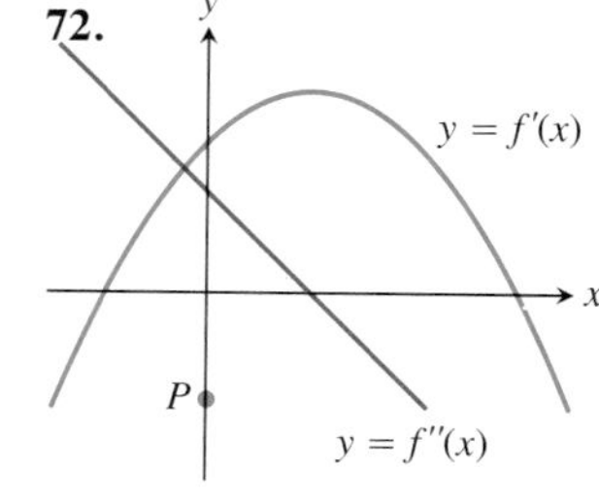

73.

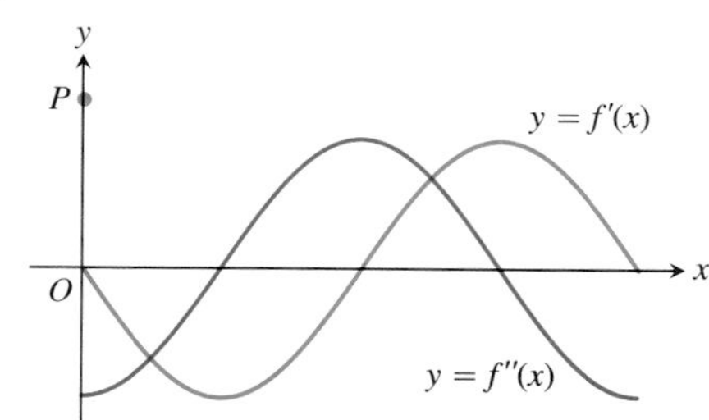

74.

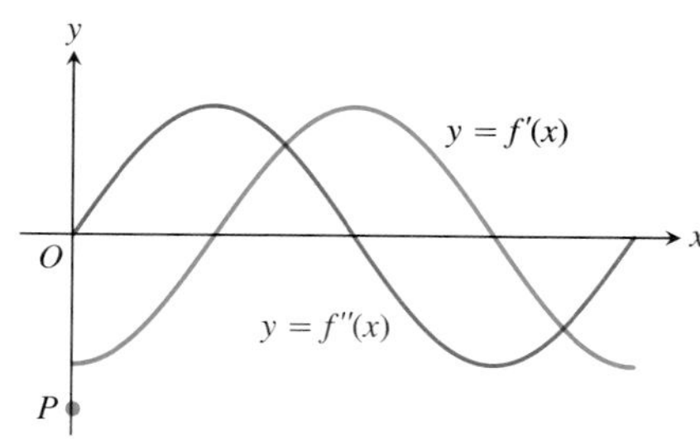

75. If b, c, and d are constants, for what value of b will the curve $y = x^3 + bx^2 + cx + d$ have a point of inflection at $x = 1$? Give reasons for your answer.

76. *Parabolas*

a) Find the coordinates of the vertex of the parabola $y = ax^2 + bx + c$, $a \neq 0$.

b) When is the parabola concave up? concave down? Give reasons for your answers.

77. Can anything be said about the graph of a function $y = f(x)$ that has a continuous second derivative that is never zero? Give reasons for your answer.

78. Is it true that the concavity of the graph of a twice-differentiable function $y = f(x)$ changes every time $f''(x) = 0$? Give reasons for your answer.

79. *Quadratic Curves.* What can you say about the inflection points of a quadratic curve $y = ax^2 + bx + c$, $a \neq 0$? Give reasons for your answer.

80. *Cubic Curves.* What can you say about the inflection points of a cubic curve $y = ax^3 + bx^2 + cx + d$, $a \neq 0$? Give reasons for your answer.

GRAPHER EXERCISES

81. Graph $f(x) = 2x^4 - 4x^2 + 1$ and its first two derivatives together. Comment on the behavior of f in relation to the signs and values of f' and f''.

82. Graph $f(x) = x \cos x$ and its second derivative together for $0 \leq x \leq 2\pi$. Comment on the behavior of the graph of f in relation to the signs and values of f''.

83. a) On a common screen, graph $f(x) = x^3 + kx$ for $k = 0$ and nearby positive and negative values of k. How does the value of k seem to affect the shape of the graph?

b) Find $f'(x)$. As you will see, $f'(x)$ is a quadratic function of x. Find the discriminant of the quadratic (the discriminant of $ax^2 + bx + c$ is $b^2 - 4ac$). For what values of k is the discriminant positive? zero? negative? For what values of k does f' have two zeros? one or no zeros? Now explain what the value of k has to do with the shape of the graph of f.
c) Experiment with other values of k. What appears to happen as $k \to -\infty$? $k \to \infty$?

84. a) On a common screen, graph $f(x) = x^4 + kx^3 + 6x^2$, $-1 \le x \le 4$ for $k = -4$ and some nearby values of k. How does the value of k seem to affect the shape of the graph?
b) Find $f''(x)$. As you will see, $f''(x)$ is a quadratic function of x. What is the discriminant of this quadratic? For what values of k is the discriminant positive? zero? negative? For what values of k does $f''(x)$ have two zeros? one or no zeros? Now explain what the value of k has to do with the shape of the graph of f.

85. a) Graph $y = x^{2/3}(x^2 - 2)$ for $-3 \le x \le 3$. Then use calculus to confirm what the screen shows about concavity, rise, and fall. (Depending on your calculator, you may have to enter $x^{2/3}$ as $(x^2)^{1/3}$ to obtain a plot for negative values of x.)
b) Does the curve have a cusp at $x = 0$, or does it just have a corner with different right-hand and left-hand derivatives?

86. a) Graph $y = 9x^{2/3}(x - 1)$ for $-0.5 \le x \le 1.5$. Then use calculus to confirm what the screen shows about concavity, rise, and fall. What concavity does the curve have to the left of the origin? (Depending on your calculator, you may have to enter $x^{2/3}$ as $(x^2)^{1/3}$ to obtain a plot for negative values of x.)
b) Does the curve have a cusp at $x = 0$, or does it just have a corner with different right-hand and left-hand derivatives?

87. Does the curve $y = x^2 + 3 \sin 2x$ have a horizontal tangent near $x = -3$? Give reasons for your answer.

88. *Linearizations at Inflection Points.* Linearizations fit particularly well at points of inflection. You will see what we mean if you graph the following examples.
a) $f(x) = \sin x$ and its linearization $L(x) = x$ at $x = 0$
b) *Newton's serpentine.* $f(x) = 4x/(x^2 + 1)$ and its linearization $L(x) = 4x$ at $x = 0$
c) *Newton's serpentine.* $f(x) = 4x/(x^2 + 1)$ and its linearization $L(x) = -(x/2) + 3\sqrt{3}/2$ at the point $(\sqrt{3}, \sqrt{3})$

Writing for Your Own Knowledge

Answer the following questions in writing. Some answers will take only a sentence or two; others may require several paragraphs. Some explanations may also call for graphs or sketches.

1. When is a curve concave up? concave down? How do you test for concavity?
2. What is an inflection point? How do you locate inflection points? What real-world interpretation do inflection points have?
3. What is the second derivative test for extreme values?
4. How do you tell when the graph of a continuous function has a cusp?
5. How do y' and y'' determine the shape of a function's graph?

EXPLORER PROGRAMS

Derivatives	Graphs the first and second derivatives of functions you key in.
PowerGrapher	Graphs all the functions in this section. Draws tangents to graphs.

4.4 *Graphs of Rational Functions—Asymptotes and Dominant Terms*

In Section 4.3, we analyzed the graphs of polynomial functions by studying first and second derivatives. To understand the graphs of rational functions, we need the additional notions of asymptote and dominant term.

Horizontal and Vertical Asymptotes

If the distance between the graph of a function and some fixed line approaches zero as the graph moves increasingly far from the origin, we say that the graph approaches the line asymptotically and that the line is an *asymptote* of the graph.

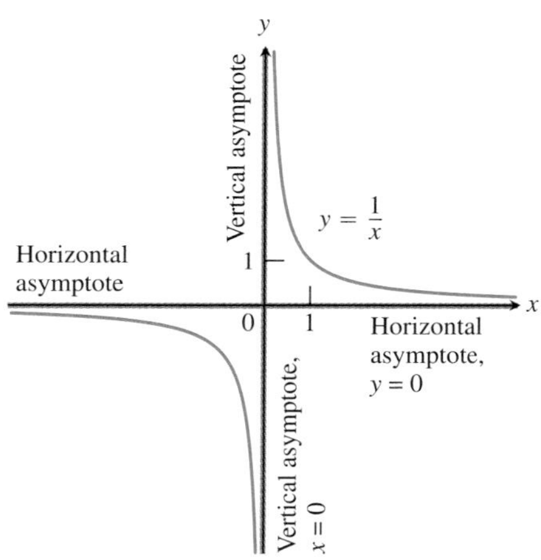

4.18 The coordinate axes are asymptotes of both branches of the hyperbola $y = 1/x$.

EXAMPLE 1 The coordinate axes are asymptotes of the curve $y = 1/x$ (Fig. 4.18). The x-axis is an asymptote of the curve on the right because

$$\lim_{x\to\infty} \frac{1}{x} = 0$$

and on the left because

$$\lim_{x\to-\infty} \frac{1}{x} = 0.$$

The y-axis is an asymptote of the curve both above and below because

$$\lim_{x\to0^+} \frac{1}{x} = \infty \qquad \text{and} \qquad \lim_{x\to0^-} \frac{1}{x} = -\infty.$$

Notice that the denominator is zero at $x = 0$ and the function is undefined.

DEFINITIONS

A line $y = b$ is a **horizontal asymptote** of the graph of a function $y = f(x)$ if either

$$\lim_{x\to\infty} f(x) = b \qquad \text{or} \qquad \lim_{x\to-\infty} f(x) = b.$$

A line $x = a$ is a **vertical asymptote** of the graph if either

$$\lim_{x\to a^+} f(x) = \pm\infty \qquad \text{or} \qquad \lim_{x\to a^-} f(x) = \pm\infty.$$

Vertical Asymptotes of Rational Functions

For rational functions reduced to lowest terms (all common factors canceled from numerator and denominator), the vertical asymptotes occur where the denominator is zero.

EXAMPLE 2 The curves

$$y = \sec x = \frac{1}{\cos x} \qquad \text{and} \qquad y = \tan x = \frac{\sin x}{\cos x}$$

have vertical asymptotes at odd-integer multiples of $\pi/2$, where $\cos x = 0$ (Fig. 4.19). The graphs of

$$y = \csc x = \frac{1}{\sin x} \qquad \text{and} \qquad y = \cot x = \frac{\cos x}{\sin x}$$

have vertical asymptotes at integer multiples of π, where $\sin x = 0$ (Fig. 4.20 on the following page).

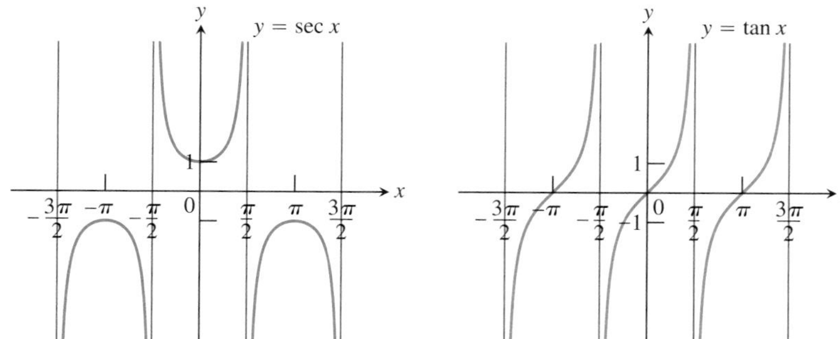

4.19 The graphs of $\sec x$ and $\tan x$ (Example 2).

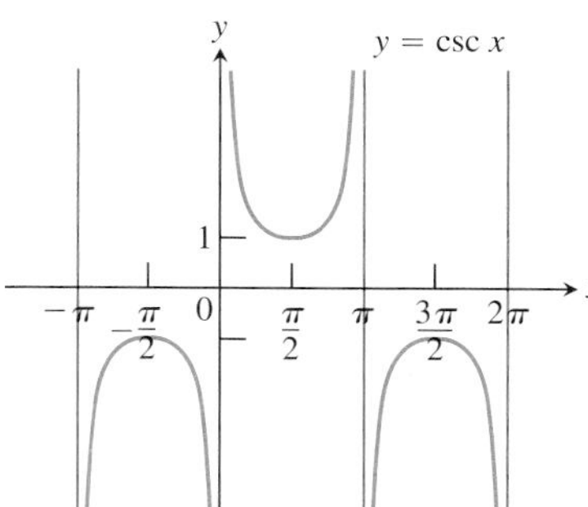

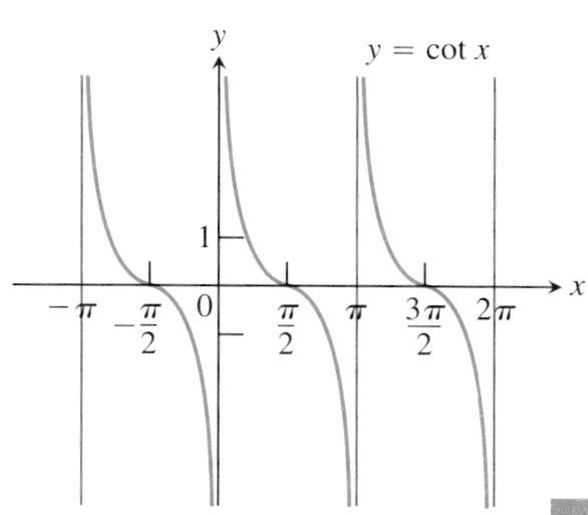

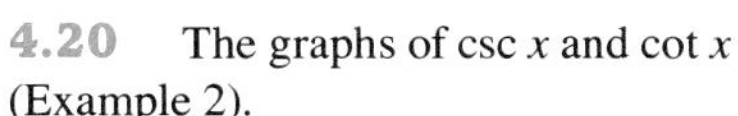

4.20 The graphs of csc x and cot x (Example 2).

EXAMPLE 3 Find the asymptotes of the curve

$$y = \frac{x+3}{x+2}.$$

Solution The asymptotes are quickly revealed if we divide $(x + 2)$ into $(x + 3)$:

$$\begin{array}{r} 1 \\ x+2\overline{)\,x+3} \\ \underline{x+2} \\ 1 \end{array}$$

This enables us to rewrite the formula for y as

$$y = 1 + \frac{1}{x+2}.$$

This lets us analyze the graph in terms of shifts.

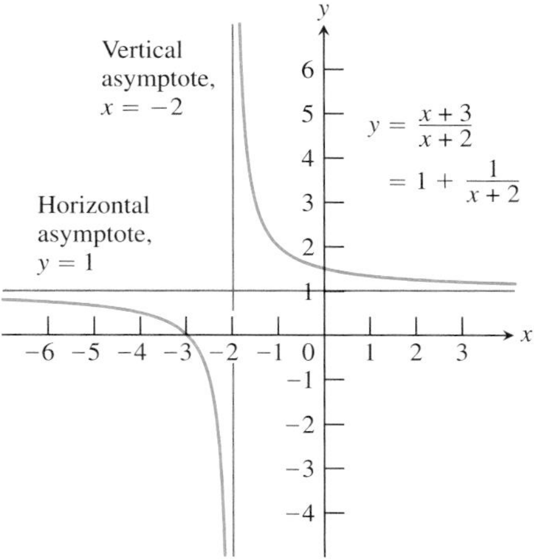

4.21 The lines $y = 1$ and $x = -2$ are asymptotes of the curve $y = (x + 3)/(x + 2)$ (Example 3).

From this we see that the curve in question is the graph of $y = 1/x$ shifted 1 unit up and 2 units to the left. Instead of being the x- and y-axes, the asymptotes are now the lines $y = 1$ and $x = -2$ (Fig. 4.21). We can confirm the vertical asymptote by noticing that the denominator $x + 2$ is 0 at $x = -2$. Also, applying the horizontal asymptote definition gives

$$\lim_{x\to\infty}\left(1 + \frac{1}{x+2}\right) = 1 \quad \text{and} \quad \lim_{x\to-\infty}\left(1 + \frac{1}{x+2}\right) = 1.$$

EXAMPLE 4 Find the asymptotes of the curve

$$y = -\frac{8}{x^2-4}.$$

Solution The line $y = 0$ is an asymptote on the right because $y \to 0$ as $x \to +\infty$, and again on the left because $y \to 0$ as $x \to -\infty$ (Fig. 4.22). We expect this symmetry because the function is even.

The lines $x = 2$ and $x = -2$ are vertical asymptotes because $x^2 - 4 = 0$ at $x = \pm 2$. As $x \to 2$ or $x \to -2$, the function values become infinite. There are no other asymptotes because y has a finite limit at every other point.

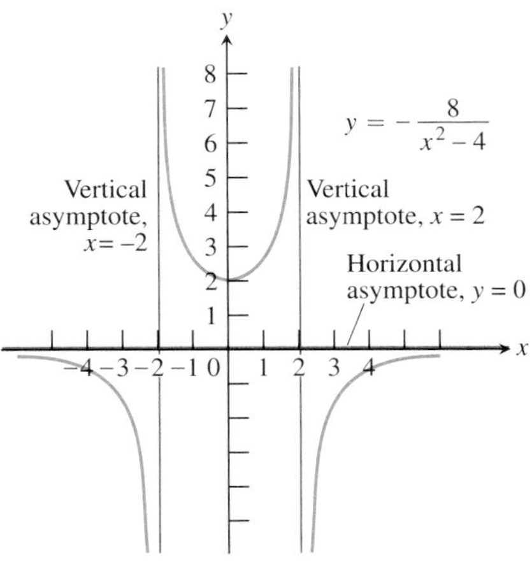

4.22 The graph of $y = -8/(x^2 - 4)$. Notice that the curve approaches the x-axis from only one side. Asymptotes do not have to be two-sided.

Oblique Asymptotes

If the degree of the numerator of a rational function is one greater than the degree of the denominator, the graph has an **oblique asymptote,** that is, a linear asymptote that is neither vertical nor horizontal.

EXAMPLE 5 Find the asymptotes of the curve

$$y = \frac{x^2 - 3}{2x - 4}.$$

Solution To find the asymptotes, oblique and otherwise, we divide $(2x - 4)$ into $(x^2 - 3)$:

$$\begin{array}{r} \frac{x}{2} + 1 \\ 2x - 4 \,\overline{)\, x^2 - 3} \\ \underline{x^2 - 2x} \\ 2x - 3 \\ \underline{2x - 4} \\ 1 \end{array}$$

This tells us that

$$y = \frac{x^2 - 3}{2x - 4} = \underbrace{\frac{x}{2} + 1}_{\text{linear}} + \underbrace{\frac{1}{2x - 4}}_{\substack{\text{a remainder} \\ \text{that goes to 0} \\ \text{as } x \to \pm\infty}}. \qquad (1)$$

From this representation we see that the line $y = (x/2) + 1$ is an asymptote of the curve:

$$\underbrace{\left(\frac{x^2 - 3}{2x - 4}\right) - \left(\frac{x}{2} + 1\right)}_{\substack{\text{vertical distance between} \\ \text{curve and line}}} = \frac{1}{2x - 4} \to 0 \quad \text{as} \quad x \to \pm\infty.$$

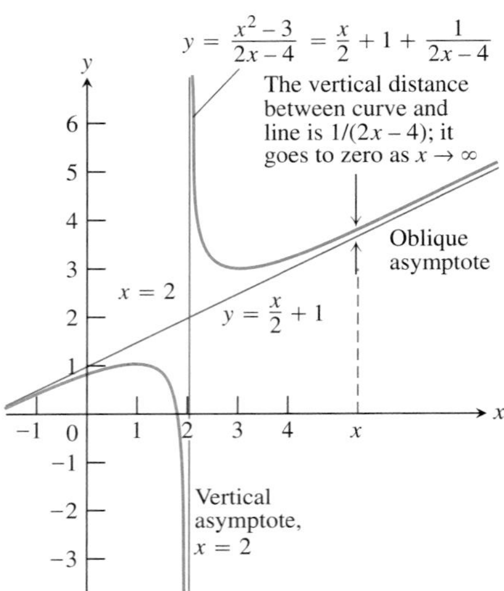

4.23 The graph of $y = (x^2 - 3)/(2x - 4)$ (Example 5).

Equation (1) also reveals the presence of a vertical asymptote at $x = 2$ where the denominator is zero (Fig. 4.23).

Graphing with Asymptotes and Dominant Terms

Of all the observations we can make quickly about the function

$$y = \frac{x^2 - 3}{2x - 4}$$

in Example 5, probably the most useful is that

$$\frac{x^2 - 3}{2x - 4} = \frac{x}{2} + 1 + \frac{1}{2x - 4}. \qquad \text{Obtained by dividing as in Eq. (1)}$$

This tells us immediately that

$$y \approx \frac{x}{2} + 1 \qquad \text{for } x \text{ numerically large}$$

$$y \approx \frac{1}{2x - 4} \qquad \text{for } x \text{ close to 2.}$$

If we want to know quickly how the function "goes," this is the way to find out. It goes like $y = (x/2) + 1$ when x is numerically large and like $y = 1/(2x - 4)$ when x is close to 2.

We say that $(x/2) + 1$ **dominates** when x is numerically large and that $1/(2x - 4)$ dominates when x is close to 2.

Dominant terms like these are the key to predicting the function's behavior over different portions of the x-axis.

EXAMPLE 6 For the function

$$y = \frac{x+3}{x+2} = 1 + \frac{1}{x+2}, \qquad \text{Example 3}$$

$$y \approx 1 \quad \text{for } |x| \text{ large,} \qquad y \approx \frac{1}{x+2} \quad \text{for } x \text{ near } -2. \tag{2}$$

See Fig. 4.21.

When combined with information about symmetry and derivatives, asymptotes and dominant terms give us the guidance we need to graph rational functions effectively.

EXAMPLE 7 Graph the function

$$y = \frac{x^3 + 1}{x}.$$

Solution We find out all we can about dominant terms, asymptotes, rise, fall, and concavity. Then we draw the graph.

STEP 1: *Find any dominant terms:* We divide x into $x^3 + 1$ to express the function as

$$y = x^2 + \frac{1}{x}. \tag{3}$$

This tells us that

$$y \approx x^2, \qquad |x| \text{ large} \qquad \text{and} \qquad y \approx \frac{1}{x}, \qquad x \text{ near } 0.$$

STEP 2: *Asymptotes:* Equation (3) reveals the curve's asymptotes:

$$x = 0 \qquad \text{Vertical asymptote}$$

STEP 3: *Rise and fall:* The first derivative,

$$y' = 2x - \frac{1}{x^2} = \frac{2x^3 - 1}{x^2}, \qquad \text{From Eq. (3)}$$

is undefined at $x = 0$ and zero when

$$2x - \frac{1}{x^2} = 0$$

$$2x^3 - 1 = 0$$

$$x^3 = \frac{1}{2}$$

$$x = \frac{1}{\sqrt[3]{2}} \approx 0.8.$$

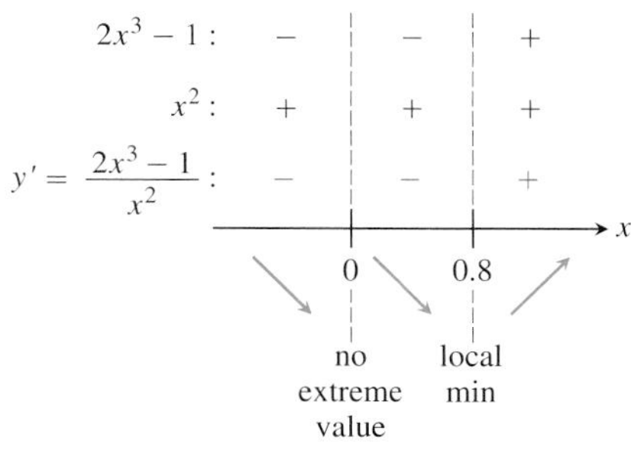

$2x^3 - 1$:	−	−	+
x^2:	+	+	+
$y' = \frac{2x^3-1}{x^2}$:	−	−	+

x: 0, 0.8

0: no extreme value; 0.8: local min

Strategy for Graphing Rational Functions

1. Find the dominant terms.
2. Find the asymptotes.
3. Determine rise and fall.
4. Determine the concavity.
5. Make a summary and show the curve's general shape.
6. Plot points and dominant terms, and sketch the curve.

STEP 4: *Concavity:* The second derivative,

$$y'' = 2 + \frac{2}{x^3} = \frac{2x^3 + 2}{x^3},$$

is undefined at $x = 0$ and zero when

$$2 + \frac{2}{x^3} = 0$$

$$2x^3 + 2 = 0$$

$$x^3 = -1$$

$$x = -1.$$

	$x < -1$	$-1 < x < 0$	$x > 0$
$2x^3 + 2$:	−	+	+
x^3:	−	−	+
$y'' = \frac{2x^3+2}{x^3}$:	+	−	+
	conc up	conc down	conc up

$x = -1$: infl point; $x = 0$: infl point

STEP 5: *Summary:* *General shape:*

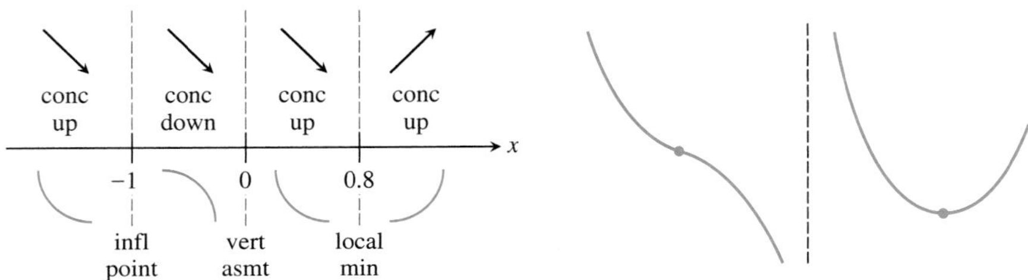

STEP 6: *Points, dominant terms, and curve:* Plot the curve's intercepts (if convenient), mark any horizontal tangents, and graph the dominant terms.

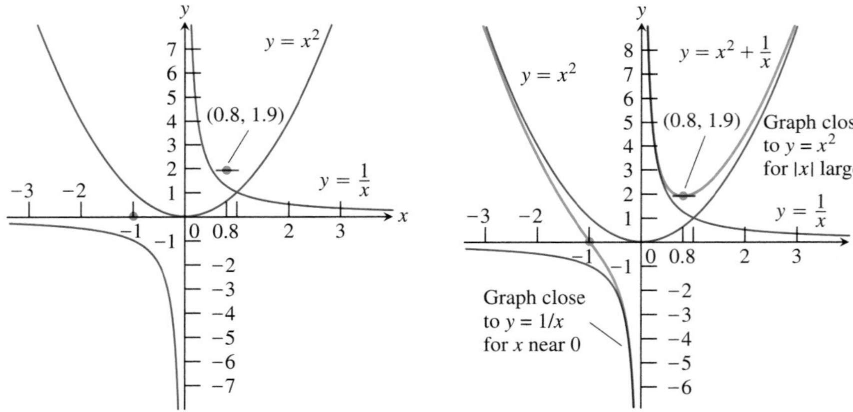

Then sketch a curve that fits these, using the general shape in Step 5 as a guide. In making the sketch, take advantage of any symmetries the graph may have (none, in this particular case). The graph is symmetric with respect to the y-axis if the function is even. It is symmetric with respect to the origin if the function is odd.

Exercises 4.4

Use the graphing procedure on page 232 to graph the functions in Exercises 1–28. Include the graphs and equations of the asymptotes and dominant terms.

1. $y = \dfrac{1}{x - 1}$

2. $y = \dfrac{1}{x + 1}$

3. $y = \dfrac{1}{2x + 4}$

4. $y = \dfrac{-3}{x - 3}$

5. $y = \dfrac{x + 3}{x + 2}$

6. $y = \dfrac{2x}{x + 1}$

7. $y = \dfrac{3x + 1}{2x - 1}$

8. $y = \dfrac{x - 4}{x - 5}$

9. $y = \dfrac{x^2 - 1}{x}$

10. $y = \dfrac{x^2 + 4}{2x}$

11. $y = \dfrac{x^4 + 1}{x^2}$

12. $y = \dfrac{x^3 + 1}{x^2}$

13. $y = \dfrac{1}{x^2 - 1}$

14. $y = \dfrac{x^2}{x^2 - 1}$

15. $y = -\dfrac{x^2 - 2}{x^2 - 1}$

16. $y = \dfrac{x^2 - 4}{x^2 - 2}$

17. $y = \dfrac{x^2}{x - 1}$

18. $y = -\dfrac{x^2}{x + 1}$

19. $y = \dfrac{x^2 - 4}{x - 1}$

20. $y = -\dfrac{x^2 - 4}{x + 1}$

21. $y = \dfrac{x^2 - x + 1}{x - 1}$

22. $y = -\dfrac{x^2 - x + 1}{x - 1}$

23. $y = \dfrac{-x^2 + 2x - 2}{x - 1}$

24. $y = \dfrac{x^2 + x - 6}{2x - 2}$

25. $y = \dfrac{x}{x^2 - 1}$

26. $y = \dfrac{x - 1}{x^2(x - 2)}$

27. $y = \dfrac{8}{x^2 + 4}$ (Agnesi's witch)

28. $y = \dfrac{4x}{x^2 + 4}$ (Newton's serpentine)

Graph the functions in Exercises 29–32.

29. $y = \dfrac{x}{\sqrt{4 - x^2}}$

30. $y = \dfrac{-1}{\sqrt{4 - x^2}}$

31. $y = x^{2/3} + \dfrac{1}{x^{1/3}}$

32. $y = 2\sqrt{x} + \dfrac{2}{\sqrt{x}} - 3$

Graph the functions in Exercises 33 and 34.

33. $y = \sin\left(\dfrac{\pi}{x^2 + 1}\right)$

34. $y = -\cos\left(\dfrac{\pi}{x^2 + 1}\right)$

Each of the functions in Exercises 35–38 is given as the sum or difference of two terms. First graph the terms (with the same set of axes). Then, using these graphs as guides, sketch in the graph of the function.

35. $y = \sec x + \dfrac{1}{x}, \quad -\dfrac{\pi}{2} < x < \dfrac{\pi}{2}$

36. $y = \sec x - \dfrac{1}{x^2}, \quad -\dfrac{\pi}{2} < x < \dfrac{\pi}{2}$

37. $y = \tan x + \dfrac{1}{x^2}, \quad -\dfrac{\pi}{2} < x < \dfrac{\pi}{2}$

38. $y = \dfrac{1}{x} - \tan x, \quad -\dfrac{\pi}{2} < x < \dfrac{\pi}{2}$

39. The word *asymptote* derives from an old Greek word for "never touching." In practice, however, a curve may cross one of its asymptotes a finite number of times or even infinitely often, as does the curve $y = 2 + (\sin x)/x$, $x > 0$, graphed here.

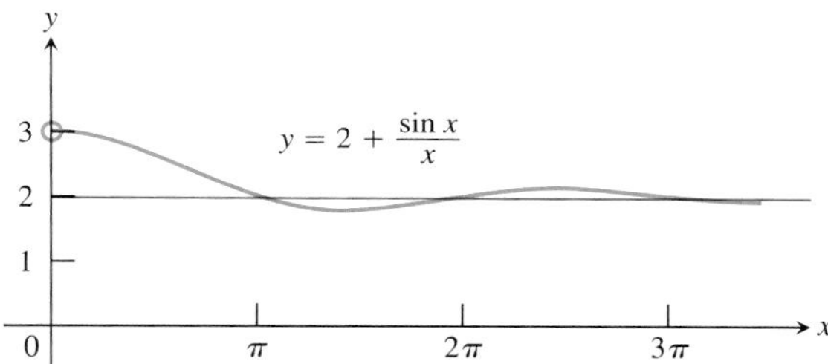

Show that the slope of the curve nevertheless approaches the slope of the asymptote as $x \to \infty$.

40. *Symmetry*

a) Suppose that an odd function is known to be increasing for $x > 0$. What can be said of its behavior for $x < 0$?

b) Suppose that an even function is known to be increasing on the interval $-\infty < x < 0$. What can be said about its behavior for $x > 0$?

41. Suppose that $f(x)$ and $g(x)$ are polynomials in x and that $\lim_{x\to\infty} (f(x)/g(x)) = 2$. Can you conclude anything about $\lim_{x\to-\infty} (f(x)/g(x))$? Give reasons for your answer.

42. Suppose that $f(x)$ and $g(x)$ are polynomials in x. Can the graph of $f(x)/g(x)$ have an asymptote if $g(x)$ is never zero? Give reasons for your answer.

GRAPHER EXERCISES

Graph the functions in Exercises 43–46. What asymptotes do the graphs have? Why are the asymptotes located where they are?

43. $y = -\dfrac{x^2 - 4}{x + 1}$

44. $y = \dfrac{x^2 + x - 6}{2x - 2}$

45. $y = \dfrac{x^3 - x^2 - 1}{x^2 - 1}$

46. $y = \dfrac{x^3 - 2x^2 + x + 1}{x - x^2}$

Graph the functions in Exercises 47–52 together with their dominant terms. Comment on the relation of the graphs of the dominant terms to the graphs of the functions.

47. $y = x^3 + \dfrac{3}{x}$

48. $y = x^3 - \dfrac{3}{x}$

49. $y = 2\sin x + \dfrac{1}{x}$

50. $y = 2\cos x - \dfrac{1}{x}$

51. $y = \dfrac{x^2}{2} + 3\sin 2x$

52. $y = (x-1)^{11} + 2\sin 2\pi x$

Graph the functions in Exercises 53 and 54. Then answer the following questions.

a) How does the graph behave as $x \to 0^+$? $x \to 0^-$?
b) How does the graph behave as $x \to \pm\infty$?
c) How does the graph behave at $x = 1$ and $x = -1$?

Give reasons for your answers.

53. $y = \dfrac{3}{2}\left(x - \dfrac{1}{x}\right)^{2/3}$

54. $y = \dfrac{3}{2}\left(\dfrac{x}{x-1}\right)^{2/3}$

Every time we have examined the graph of a rational function $f(x)/g(x)$, the graph has had a vertical asymptote at each zero of g. But that need not be the case, as the functions in Exercises 55 and 56 show. In each exercise, carry out the following steps.

a) Graph the function.
b) Find the zeros of the function's denominator. Why does the function have a vertical asymptote at one zero but not the other?
c) Find an equation for the graph's oblique asymptote and add that asymptote to your picture.

55. $y = \dfrac{x^3 - 3x^2 + 3x - 1}{x^2 + x - 2}$

56. $y = \dfrac{x^3 + x - 2}{x - x^2}$

57. Graph the function

$$y = -\frac{x^3 - 2}{x^2 + 1}$$

over the following intervals.

a) $-9 \le x \le 9$
b) $-90 \le x \le 90$
c) $-900 \le x \le 900$

The graph in (a) should be good. The graph in (b) may indicate some activity near the origin but will not show what. The graph in (c) will look just like the graph of the line $y = -x$. Why?

58. Graph the function $y = x^{2/3}/(x^2 - 1)$ over the interval $-2 \le x \le 2$. The curve will appear to be concave down between $x = -1$ and $x = 1$, with no sign of a cusp at the origin. Zoom in on the origin and watch the true shape of the graph emerge. Why do you think the cusp fails to appear in the first view of the graph?

Writing for Your Own Knowledge

Answer the following questions in writing. Some answers will take only a sentence or two; others may require several paragraphs. Some explanations may also call for graphs or sketches.

1. How do you locate the vertical asymptotes of a rational function?
2. When does a rational function have an oblique (linear) asymptote? How do you find the asymptote?
3. What is the general procedure for sketching the graph of a rational function?

EXPLORER PROGRAM

PowerGrapher	Graphs functions together, so you can graph a function along with its dominant terms.

4.5 *Optimization*

To optimize something means to maximize or minimize some aspect of it. What is the size of the most profitable production run? What is the least expensive shape for an oil can? What is the stiffest beam we can cut from a 12-inch log? In the mathematical models in which we use functions to describe the things that interest us, we usually answer such questions by finding the greatest or smallest value of some particular function, using the techniques of Sections 4.2 and 4.3.

Examples from Business and Industry

EXAMPLE 1 *Metal Fabrication.* An open-top box is to be made by cutting small congruent squares from the corners of a 12-by-12-in. sheet of tin and

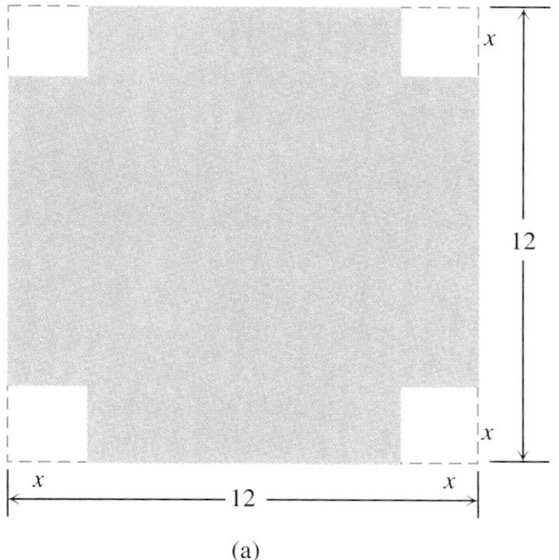

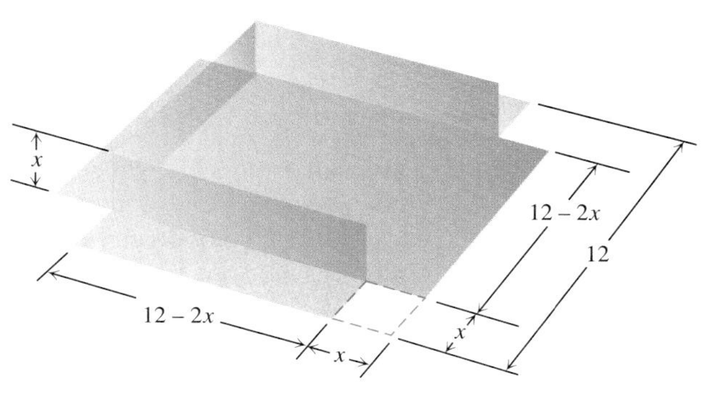

4.24 An open box made by cutting the corners from a square sheet of tin.

bending up the sides. How large should the squares cut from the corners be to make the box hold as much as possible?

Solution We start with a picture, the way we do when we solve a problem in related rates (Fig. 4.24). In the figure, the corner squares are x inches on a side. The volume of the box is a function of this variable:

$$V(x) = x(12 - 2x)^2 = 144x - 48x^2 + 4x^3. \qquad V = lwh$$

Since the sides of the sheet of tin are only 12 in. long, $x \leq 6$ and the domain of V is the interval $0 \leq x \leq 6$.

A graph of V (Fig. 4.25) suggests a minimum value of 0 at $x = 0$ and $x = 6$ and a maximum near $x = 2$. To learn more, we examine the first derivative of V with respect to x:

$$\frac{dV}{dx} = 144 - 96x + 12x^2 = 12(12 - 8x + x^2) = 12(2 - x)(6 - x).$$

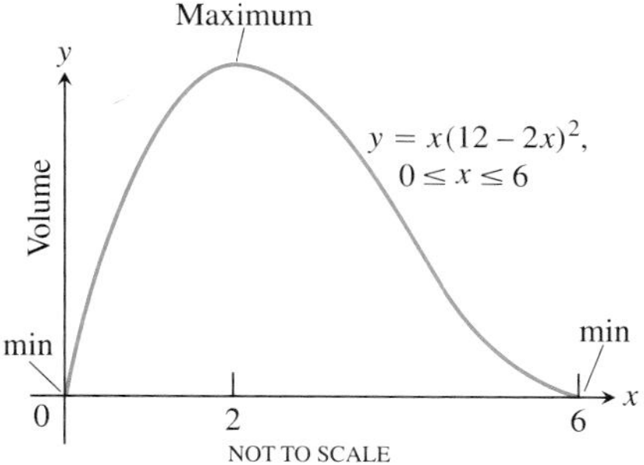

4.25 The volume of the box in Fig. 4.24 graphed as a function of x.

Of the two zeros, $x = 2$ and $x = 6$, only $x = 2$ lies in the interior of the function's domain and makes the critical-point list. The values of V at this one critical point and two endpoints are

Critical point value: $V(2) = 128$

Endpoint values: $V(0) = 0, \quad V(6) = 0.$

The maximum volume is 128 in^3. The cut-out squares should be 2 in. on a side.

EXAMPLE 2 *Product Design.* You have been asked to design a 1-L oil can shaped like a right circular cylinder. What dimensions will use the least material?

Solution We picture the can as a right circular cylinder with height h and diameter $2r$ (Fig. 4.26). If r and h are measured in centimeters and the volume is expressed as 1000 cm^3, then r and h are related by the equation

$$\pi r^2 h = 1000. \qquad 1\text{ L} = 1000\text{ cm}^3 \qquad (1)$$

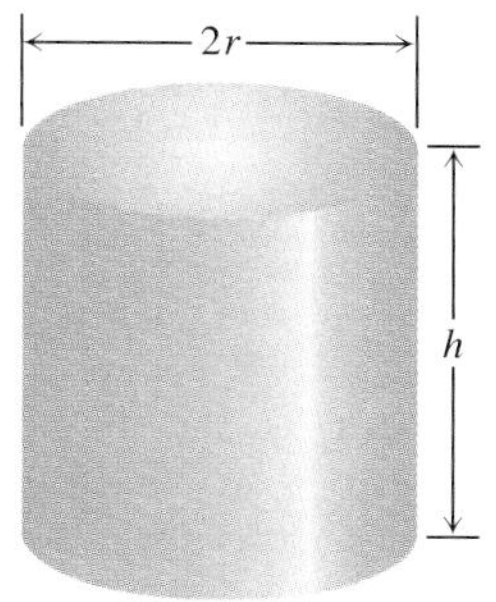

4.26 This 1-L can uses the least material when $h = 2r$ (Example 2).

How shall we interpret the phrase "least material"? One possibility is to ignore the thickness of the material and the waste in manufacturing. Then we ask for dimensions r and h that make the total surface area

$$A = \underbrace{2\pi r^2}_{\substack{\text{cylinder}\\ \text{ends}}} + \underbrace{2\pi rh}_{\substack{\text{cylinder}\\ \text{wall}}} \tag{2}$$

as small as possible while satisfying the constraint $\pi r^2 h = 1000$. (Exercise 18 describes one way we might take waste into account.)

What kind of oil can do we expect? Not a tall, thin one like a 6-ft pipe, nor a short, wide one like a covered pizza pan. We expect something in between.

We are not quite ready to find critical points because Eq. (2) gives A as a function of two variables and our procedure calls for A to be a function of a single variable. However, Eq. (1) can be solved to express either r or h in terms of the other.

Solving for h is easier, so we take

$$h = \frac{1000}{\pi r^2}. \tag{3}$$

This changes the formula for A to

$$A = 2\pi r^2 + 2\pi rh = 2\pi r^2 + 2\pi r \frac{1000}{\pi r^2} = 2\pi r^2 + \frac{2000}{r}. \tag{4}$$

Our mathematical goal is to find the minimum value of A on the open interval $r > 0$. Since A is differentiable throughout its domain, and its domain has no endpoints, it can have a minimum value only where its first derivative is zero.

$$A = 2\pi r^2 + \frac{2000}{r}$$

$$\frac{dA}{dr} = 4\pi r - \frac{2000}{r^2} \qquad \text{Find } dA/dr.$$

$$4\pi r - \frac{2000}{r^2} = 0 \qquad \text{Set it equal to 0.}$$

$$4\pi r^3 = 2000 \qquad \text{Solve for } r.$$

$$r = \sqrt[3]{\frac{500}{\pi}} \qquad \text{Critical point}$$

So something happens at $r = \sqrt[3]{500/\pi}$, but what?

If the domain of A were a closed interval, we could find out by evaluating A at this critical point and the endpoints and comparing the results. But the domain is not a closed interval so we must learn what is happening at $r = \sqrt[3]{500/\pi}$ by determining the shape of A's graph. We can do this by investigating the second derivative, d^2A/dr^2:

$$\frac{dA}{dr} = 4\pi r - \frac{2000}{r^2}$$

$$\frac{d^2A}{dr^2} = 4\pi + \frac{4000}{r^3}.$$

The second derivative is positive throughout the domain of A. The value of A at $r = \sqrt[3]{500/\pi}$ is therefore an absolute minimum because the graph of A is concave up (Fig. 4.27).

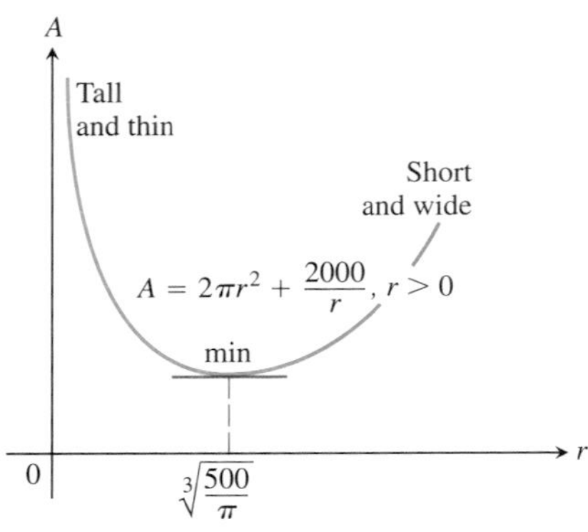

4.27 The graph of $A = 2\pi r^2 + 2000/r$ is concave up.

When

$$r = \sqrt[3]{500/\pi},$$

$$h = \frac{1000}{\pi r^2} = 2\sqrt[3]{500/\pi} = 2r. \qquad \text{After some arithmetic} \qquad (5)$$

Equation (5) tells us that the most efficient can has its height equal to its diameter. With a calculator we find

$$r \approx 5.42 \text{ cm}, \qquad h \approx 10.84 \text{ cm}.$$

Strategy for Solving Max-Min Problems

1. *Draw a picture.* Label the parts that are important in the problem.
2. *Write an equation.* Write an equation for the quantity whose maximum or minimum you want. If you can, express the quantity as a function of a single variable, say $y = f(x)$. This may require some algebra and the use of information from the statement of the problem. Note the domain in which the values of x are to be found.
3. *Test the critical points and endpoints.* List the values of f at these points. If f has an absolute maximum or minimum on its domain, it will appear on the list. You may have to examine the signs of f' or f'' to decide whether a given value represents a maximum, a minimum, or neither.

Examples from Mathematics

EXAMPLE 3 *Products of Numbers.* Find two positive numbers whose sum is 20 and whose product is as large as possible.

Solution If one number is x, the other is $(20 - x)$. Their product is

$$f(x) = x(20 - x) = 20x - x^2.$$

We want the value or values of x that make $f(x)$ as large as possible. The domain of f is the closed interval $0 \le x \le 20$.

We evaluate f at the critical points and endpoints. The first derivative,

$$f'(x) = 20 - 2x,$$

is defined at every point of the interval $0 \le x \le 20$ and is zero only at $x = 10$. Listing the values of f at this one critical point and the endpoints gives

Critical point value: $f(10) = 20(10) - (10)^2 = 100$

Endpoint values: $f(0) = 0, \quad f(20) = 0.$

We conclude that the maximum value is $f(10) = 100$. The corresponding numbers are $x = 10$ and $(20 - 10) = 10$ (Fig. 4.28).

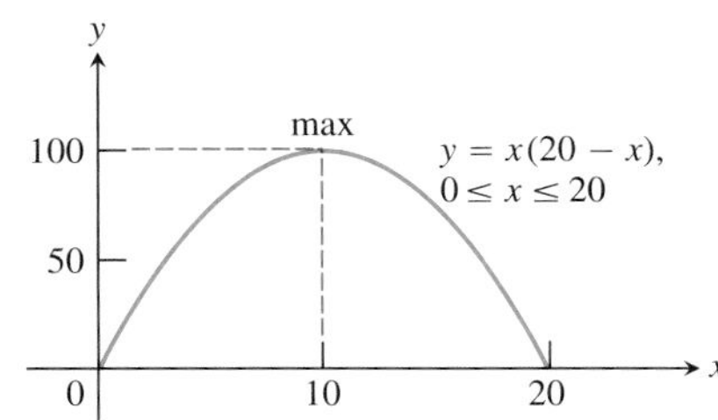

4.28 The product of x and $(20 - x)$ reaches a maximum value of 100 when $x = 10$ (Example 3).

EXAMPLE 4 *Geometry.* A rectangle is to be inscribed in a semicircle of radius 2. What is the largest area the rectangle can have, and what are its dimensions?

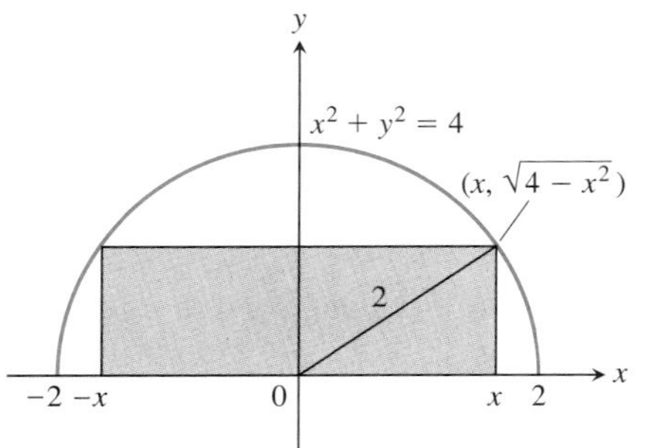

4.29 The rectangle and semicircle in Example 4.

Solution To describe the dimensions of the rectangle, we place the circle and rectangle in the coordinate plane (Fig. 4.29). The length, height, and area of the rectangle can then be expressed in terms of the position x of the lower right-hand corner:

Length: $2x$
Height: $\sqrt{4 - x^2}$
Area: $2x \cdot \sqrt{4 - x^2}$.

Notice that the values of x are to be found in the interval $0 \leq x \leq 2$, where the selected corner of the rectangle lies.

Our mathematical goal is now to find the absolute maximum value of the continuous function

$$A(x) = 2x\sqrt{4 - x^2}$$

on the domain $[0, 2]$. We do this by examining the values of A at the critical points and endpoints.

The derivative

$$\frac{dA}{dx} = \frac{-2x^2}{\sqrt{4 - x^2}} + 2\sqrt{4 - x^2}$$

is not defined when $x = 2$ and is equal to zero when

$$\frac{-2x^2}{\sqrt{4 - x^2}} + 2\sqrt{4 - x^2} = 0$$

$$-2x^2 + 2(4 - x^2) = 0 \qquad \text{Multiply both sides by } \sqrt{4 - x^2}.$$

$$8 - 4x^2 = 0$$

$$x^2 = 2$$

$$x = \pm\sqrt{2}.$$

Of the two zeros, $x = \sqrt{2}$ and $x = -\sqrt{2}$, only $x = \sqrt{2}$ lies in the interior of A's domain and makes the critical-point list. The values of A at the endpoints and at this one critical point are

Critical point value: $A(\sqrt{2}) = 2\sqrt{2}\sqrt{4 - 2} = 4$
Endpoint values: $A(0) = 0, \quad A(2) = 0.$

The area has a maximum value of 4 when the rectangle is $x = \sqrt{2}$ units high and $2x = 2\sqrt{2}$ units long.

Cost and Revenue Examples in Economics

Here we want to point out two of the many places where calculus makes a contribution to economic theory. The first has to do with the relationship between profit, revenue (money received), and cost.

Suppose that

$r(x) =$ the revenue from selling x items
$c(x) =$ the cost of producing the x items
$p(x) = r(x) - c(x) =$ the profit from selling x items.

The marginal revenue and cost at this production level (x items) are

$$\frac{dr}{dx} = \text{marginal revenue}$$

$$\frac{dc}{dx} = \text{marginal cost.}$$

The first observation is about the relationship of p to these derivatives.

FIRST OBSERVATION

Maximum profit (if any) occurs at a production level at which marginal revenue equals marginal cost.

Proof We assume that $r(x)$ and $c(x)$ are differentiable for all $x > 0$, so if $p(x) = r(x) - c(x)$ has a maximum value, it occurs at a production level at which $p'(x) = 0$. Since $p'(x) = r'(x) - c'(x)$, $p'(x) = 0$ implies

$$r'(x) - c'(x) = 0 \qquad \text{or} \qquad r'(x) = c'(x).$$

This concludes the proof (Fig. 4.30). ■

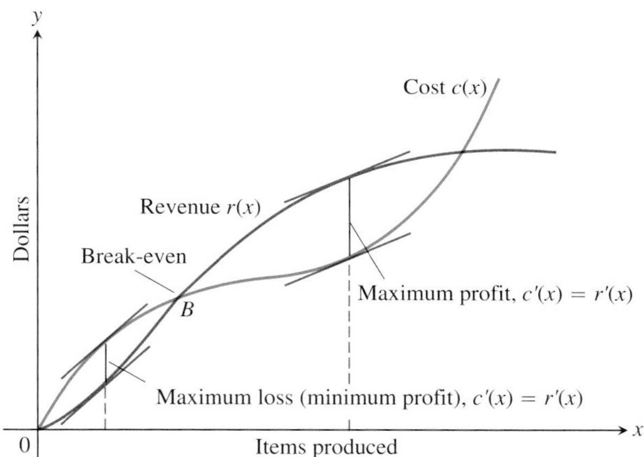

4.30 The graph of a typical cost function starts concave down and later turns concave up. It crosses the revenue curve at the break-even point B. To the left of B, the company operates at a loss. To the right, the company operates at a profit, with the maximum profit occurring where $c'(x) = r'(x)$. Farther to the right, cost exceeds revenue (perhaps because of a combination of market saturation and rising labor and material costs) and product levels become unprofitable again.

What guidance do we get from this observation? We know that a production level at which $p'(x) = 0$ need not be a level of maximum profit. It might be a level of minimum profit, for example. But if we are making financial projections for our company, we should look for production levels at which marginal cost seems to equal marginal revenue. If there is a most profitable production level, it will be one of these.

EXAMPLE 5 Suppose that

$$r(x) = 9x \qquad \text{and} \qquad c(x) = x^3 - 6x^2 + 15x,$$

where x represents thousands of units. Is there a production level that maximizes profit? If so, what is it?

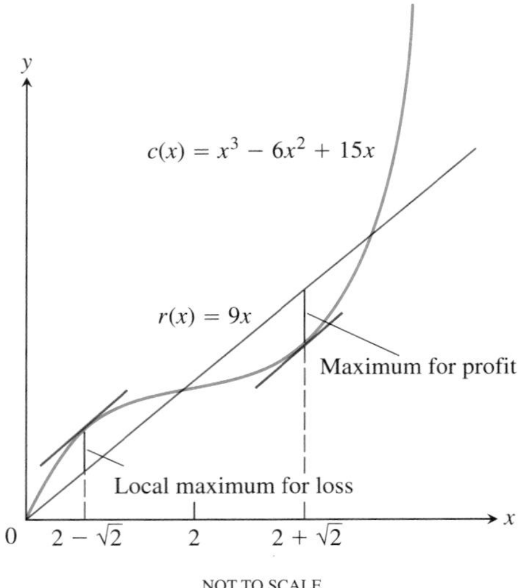

4.31 The cost and revenue curves for Example 5.

Solution

$$
\begin{aligned}
r(x) &= 9x, \qquad c(x) = x^3 - 6x^2 + 15x && \text{Find } r'(x) \text{ and } c'(x).\\
r'(x) &= 9, \qquad c'(x) = 3x^2 - 12x + 15 &&\\
3x^2 - 12x + 15 &= 9 && \text{Set them equal.}\\
3x^2 - 12x + 6 &= 0 && \text{Rearrange.}\\
x^2 - 4x + 2 &= 0 &&\\
x &= \frac{4 \pm \sqrt{16 - 4 \cdot 2}}{2} && \text{Solve for } x \text{ with the quadratic formula.}\\
&= \frac{4 \pm 2\sqrt{2}}{2}\\
&= 2 \pm \sqrt{2}
\end{aligned}
$$

The possible production levels for maximum profit are $x = 2 + \sqrt{2}$ thousand units and $x = 2 - \sqrt{2}$ thousand units. A quick glance at the graphs in Fig. 4.31 or at the corresponding values of r and c shows $x = 2 + \sqrt{2}$ to be a point of maximum profit and $x = 2 - \sqrt{2}$ to be a local maximum for loss.

Another way to look for optimal production levels is to look for levels that minimize the average cost of the units produced. The next observation helps us to find them.

SECOND OBSERVATION

The production level (if any) at which average cost is smallest is a level at which the average cost equals the marginal cost.

Proof We start with

$$c(x) = \text{cost of producing } x \text{ items}, \; x > 0,$$

$$\frac{c(x)}{x} = \text{average cost of producing } x \text{ items},$$

assumed differentiable.

If the average cost can be minimized, it will be at a production level at which

$$
\begin{aligned}
\frac{d}{dx}\left(\frac{c(x)}{x}\right) &= 0\\
\frac{xc'(x) - c(x)}{x^2} &= 0 && \text{Quotient Rule}\\
xc'(x) - c(x) &= 0 && \text{Multiplied by } x^2\\
\underbrace{c'(x)}_{\text{marginal cost}} &= \underbrace{\frac{c(x)}{x}}_{\text{average cost}}.
\end{aligned}
$$

This completes the proof.

Again we have to be careful about what the second observation does and does not say. It does not say that there is a production level of minimum average cost, but it does say where to look to see if there is one. Look for production levels at which average cost and marginal cost are equal. Then check to see if any of them gives a minimum average cost.

EXAMPLE 6 Suppose $c(x) = x^3 - 6x^2 + 15x$ (x in thousands of units). Is there a production level that minimizes average cost? If so, what is it?

Solution We look for levels at which average cost equals marginal cost.

Cost: $c(x) = x^3 - 6x^2 + 15x$

Marginal cost: $c'(x) = 3x^2 - 12x + 15$

Average cost: $\dfrac{c(x)}{x} = x^2 - 6x + 15$

$$3x^2 - 12x + 15 = x^2 - 6x + 15 \qquad \text{MC = AC}$$
$$2x^2 - 6x = 0$$
$$2x(x - 3) = 0$$
$$x = 0 \quad \text{or} \quad x = 3$$

Since $x > 0$, the only production level that might minimize average cost is $x = 3$ thousand units.

We check the derivatives:

$$\frac{c(x)}{x} = x^2 - 6x + 15 \qquad \text{Average cost}$$
$$\frac{d}{dx}\left(\frac{c(x)}{x}\right) = 2x - 6$$
$$\frac{d^2}{dx^2}\left(\frac{c(x)}{x}\right) = 2 > 0.$$

The second derivative is positive, so $x = 3$ gives an absolute minimum.

Modeling Discrete Phenomena with Differentiable Functions

In case you are wondering how we can use differentiable functions $c(x)$ and $r(x)$ to describe the cost and revenue that come from producing a number of items x that can only be an integer, here is the rationale.

When x is large, we can reasonably fit the cost and revenue data with smooth curves $c(x)$ and $r(x)$ that are defined not only at integer values of x but at the values in between. Once we have these differentiable functions, which are supposed to behave like the real cost and revenue when x is an integer, we can apply calculus to draw conclusions about their values. We then translate these mathematical conclusions into inferences about the real world that we hope will have predictive value. When they do, as is the case with the economic theory here, we say that the functions give a good model of reality.

What do we do when our calculus tells us that the best production level is a value of x that isn't an integer, as it did in Example 5 when it said that $x = 2 + \sqrt{2}$ thousand units would be the production level for maximum profit? The answer is to use the nearest convenient integer. For $x = 2 + \sqrt{2}$ thousand, we might use 3414, or perhaps 3410 or 3420 if we ship in boxes of 10.

Exercises 4.5

If you have a grapher, this is a good place to use it. We have included some specific grapher exercises but there is something to be learned from graphing in most of the other exercises as well.

Whenever you are maximizing or minimizing a function of a single variable, we urge you to graph it over the domain that is appropriate to the problem you are solving. The graph will provide insight before you calculate and will furnish a visual context for understanding your answer.

1. The sum of two nonnegative numbers is 20. Find the numbers (a) if the sum of their squares is to be as large as possible; as small as possible; (b) if one number plus the square root of the other is to be as large as possible; as small as possible.

2. What is the largest possible area for a right triangle whose hypotenuse is 5 cm long?

3. What is the smallest perimeter possible for a rectangle whose area is 16 in^2?

4. Show that among all rectangles with an 8-ft perimeter, the one with the largest area is a square.

5. The figure shown here shows a rectangle inscribed in an isosceles right triangle whose hypotenuse is 2 units long.

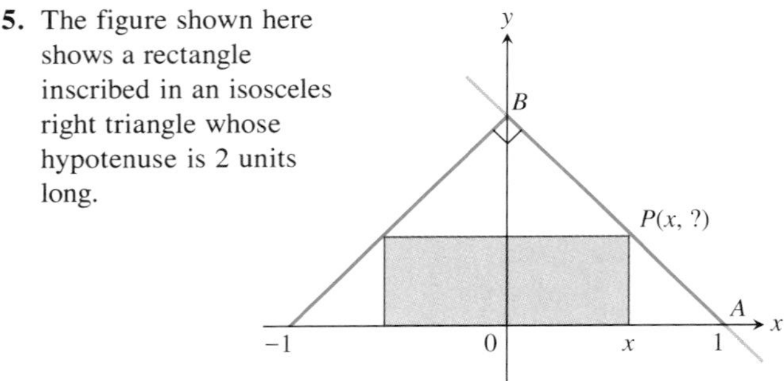

a) Express the y-coordinate of P in terms of x. (You might start by writing an equation for the line AB.)

b) Express the area of the rectangle in terms of x.

c) What is the largest area the rectangle can have?

6. A rectangle has its base on the x-axis and its upper two vertices on the parabola $y = 12 - x^2$. What is the largest area the rectangle can have?

7. You are planning to make an open rectangular box from an 8-by-15-in. piece of cardboard by cutting squares from the corners and folding up the sides. What are the dimensions of the box of largest volume you can make this way?

8. You are planning to close off a corner of the first quadrant with a line segment 20 units long running from $(a, 0)$ to $(0, b)$. Show that the area of the triangle enclosed by the segment is largest when $a = b$.

9. A rectangular plot of farmland will be bounded on one side by a river and on the other three sides by a single-strand electric fence. With 800 m of wire at your disposal, what is the largest area you can enclose?

10. A 216-m^2 rectangular pea patch is to be enclosed by a fence and divided into two equal parts by another fence parallel to one of the sides. What dimensions for the outer rectangle will require the smallest total length of fence? How much fence will be needed?

11. *The Lightest Steel Holding Tank.* Your iron works has contracted to design and build a 500-ft^3, square-based, open-top, rectangular steel holding tank for a paper company. The tank is to be made by welding $\frac{1}{2}$-in.-thick stainless steel plates together along their edges. As the production engineer, your job is to find dimensions for the base and height that will make the tank weigh as little as possible. What dimensions do you tell the shop to use?

12. *Catching Rainwater.* An 1125-ft^3 open-top rectangular tank with a square base x ft on a side and y ft deep is to be built with its top flush with the ground to catch runoff water. The costs associated with the tank involve not only the material from which the tank is made but also an excavation charge proportional to the product xy. If the total cost is

$$c = 5(x^2 + 4xy) + 10xy,$$

what values of x and y will minimize it?

13. You are designing a poster to contain 50 in^2 of printing with margins of 4 in. each at top and bottom and 2 in. at each side. What overall dimensions will minimize the amount of paper used?

14. The height of an object moving vertically is given by

$$s = -16t^2 + 96t + 112,$$

with s in feet and t in seconds. Find (a) the object's velocity when $t = 0$, (b) its maximum height, and (c) its velocity when $s = 0$.

15. Two sides of a triangle have lengths a and b, and the angle between them is θ. What value of θ will maximize the triangle's area? (*Hint:* $A = (1/2)ab \sin \theta$.)

16. Find the largest possible value of $s = 2x + y$ if x and y are side lengths in a right triangle whose hypotenuse is $\sqrt{5}$ units long.

17. What are the dimensions of the lightest open-top right circular cylindrical can that will hold a volume of 1000 cm^3? Compare the result here with the result in Example 2.

18. You are designing 1000-cm^3 right circular cylindrical cans whose manufacture will take waste into account. There is no waste in cutting the aluminum for the sides, but the tops and bottoms of radius r will be cut from squares that measure $2r$ units on a side. The total amount of aluminum used up by each can will therefore be

$$A = 8r^2 + 2\pi rh$$

rather than the $A = 2\pi r^2 + 2\pi rh$ in Example 2. In Example 2 the ratio of h to r for the most economical cans was 2 to 1. What is the ratio now?

19. a) The U.S. Postal Service will accept a box for domestic shipment only if the sum of its length and girth (distance around) does not exceed 108 in. What dimensions will give a box with a square end the largest possible volume?

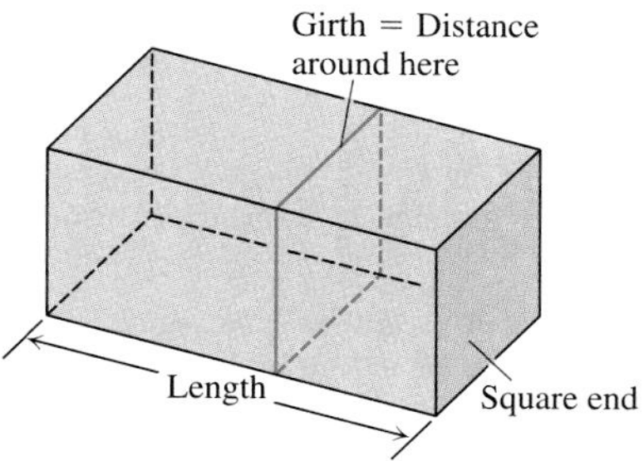

b) Graph the volume of a 108-in. box (length plus girth equals 108 in.) as a function of its length, and compare what you see with your answer in (a).

20. *Conclusion of the Sonobuoy Problem (Exercise 22, Section 3.8)*

a) Show that the value of x that minimizes the square of the distance, and hence the distance, between two points (x, x^2) and $(2, -1/2)$ in Fig. 4.32 is a solution of the equation $x = 1/(x^2 + 1)$.

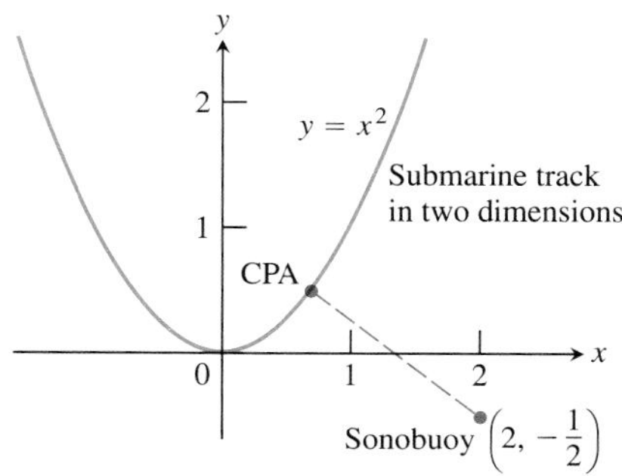

4.32 The submarine track and sonobuoy in Exercise 20. CPA = closest point of approach.

b) Graph the function $f(x) = x - (1/(x^2 + 1))$.

c) If you did not already do so in Section 3.8, solve the equation $x = 1/(x^2 + 1)$ to 5 decimal places.

21. Compare the answers to the following two construction problems.

a) A rectangular sheet of perimeter 36 cm and dimensions x cm by y cm is to be rolled into the cylinder in Fig. 4.33(a). What values of x and y give the largest volume?

b) The rectangular sheet of perimeter 36 cm and dimensions x by y is to be revolved about one of the sides of length y to sweep out the cylinder in Fig. 4.33(b). What values of x and y give the largest volume?

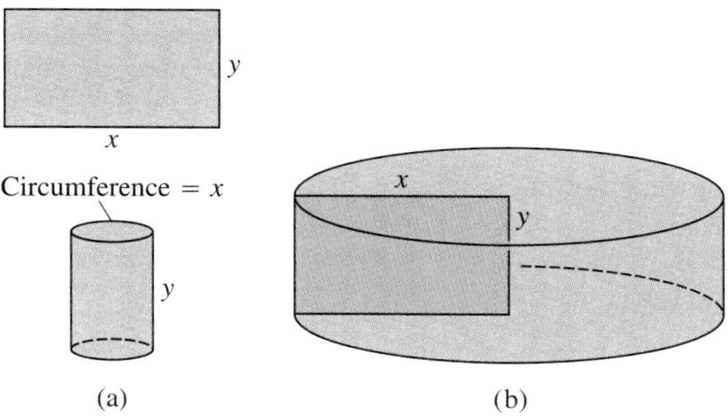

4.33 The rectangular sheet and cylinders in Exercise 21.

22. A right triangle whose hypotenuse is $\sqrt{3}$ m long is revolved about one of its legs to generate a right circular cone. Find the radius, height, and volume of the cone of greatest volume that can be made this way.

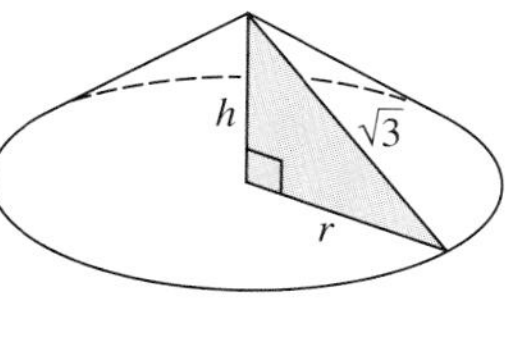

23. What value of a makes $f(x) = x^2 + (a/x)$ have (a) a local minimum of $x = 2$; (b) a point of inflection at $x = 1$?

24. Show that $f(x) = x^2 + (a/x)$ cannot have a local maximum for any value of a.

25. What values of a and b make

$$f(x) = x^3 + ax^2 + bx$$

have (a) a local maximum at $x = -1$ and a local minimum at $x = 3$; (b) a local minimum at $x = 4$ and a point of inflection at $x = 1$?

26. Find the volume of the largest right circular cone that can be inscribed in a sphere of radius 3.

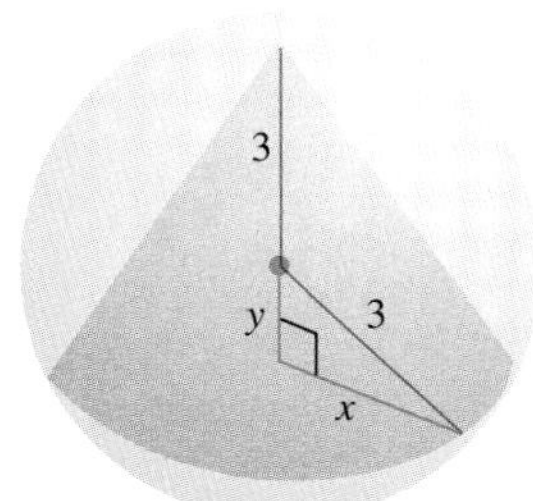

27. *The Strength of a Beam.* The strength S of a rectangular beam is proportional to its width times the square of its depth.

a) Find the dimensions of the strongest beam that can be cut from a 12-in.-diameter cylindrical log.

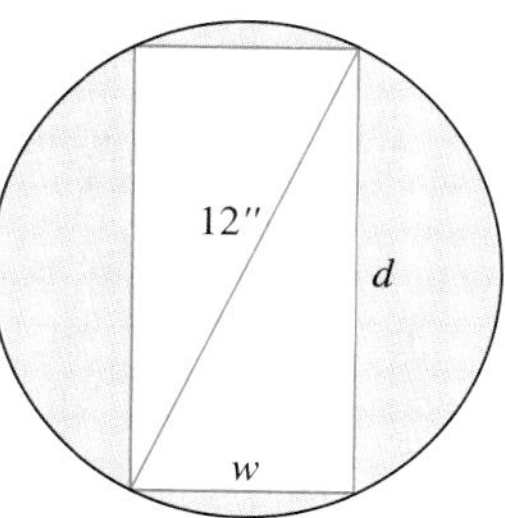

b) Graph S as a function of the beam's width w, assuming the proportionality constant to be $k = 1$. Reconcile what you see with your answer in (a).

c) On the same screen, or on a separate screen, graph S as a function of the beam's depth d, again taking $k = 1$. Compare the graphs with one another and with your answer in (a). What would be the effect of changing to some other value of k? Try it.

28. *The Stiffness of a Beam.* The stiffness S of a rectangular beam is proportional to its width times the cube of its depth.

a) Find the dimensions of the stiffest beam that can be cut from a 12-in.-diameter log.

b) Graph S as a function of the beam's width w, assuming the proportionality constant to be $k = 1$. Reconcile what you see with your answer in (a).

c) On the same screen, or on a separate screen, graph S as a function of the beam's depth d, again taking $k = 1$. Compare the graphs with one another and with your answer in (a). What would be the effect of changing to some other value of k? Try it.

29. Suppose that at any given time t (sec) the current i (amp) in an alternating current circuit is $i = 2 \cos t + 2 \sin t$. What is the peak current for this circuit (largest magnitude)?

30. A small frictionless cart, attached to the wall by a spring, is pulled 10 cm from its rest position and released at time $t = 0$ to roll back and forth for 4 sec. Its position at time t is $s = 10 \cos \pi t$.

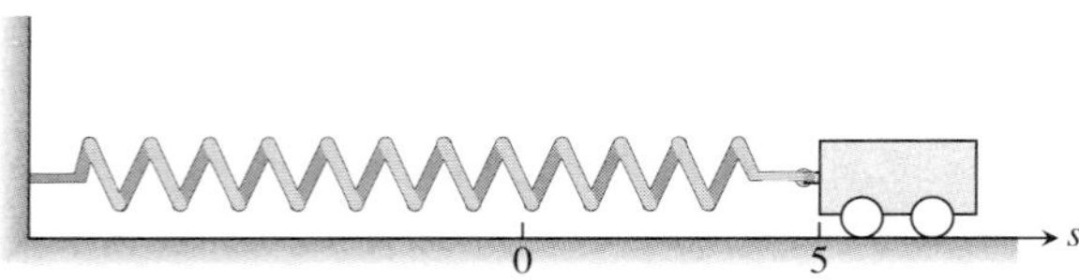

a) What is the cart's maximum speed? When is the cart moving that fast? Where is it then? What is the magnitude of the acceleration then?

b) Where is the cart when the magnitude of the acceleration is greatest? What is the cart's speed then?

31. **a)** The function $y = \cot x - \sqrt{2} \csc x$ has an absolute maximum value on the interval $0 < x < \pi$. Find it.

b) Graph the function and compare what you see with your answer in (a).

32. **a)** The function $y = \tan x + 3 \cot x$ has an absolute minimum value on the interval $0 < x < \pi/2$. Find it.

b) Graph the function and compare what you see with your answer in (a).

33. How close does the curve $y = \sqrt{x}$ come to the point $(3/2, 0)$? (*Hint:* If you minimize the *square* of the distance, you can avoid square roots.)

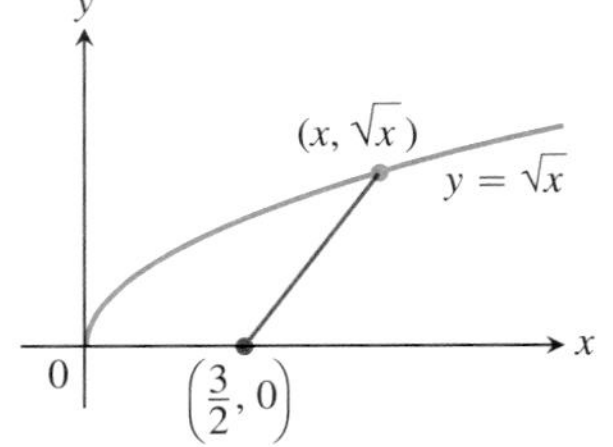

34. How close does the semicircle $y = \sqrt{16 - x^2}$ come to the point $(1, \sqrt{3})$?

35. Is the function $f(x) = x^2 - x + 1$ ever negative? Explain.

36. You have been asked to determine whether the function $f(x) = 3 + 4 \cos x + \cos 2x$ is ever negative.

a) Explain why you need consider values of x only in the interval $[0, 2\pi]$.

b) Is f ever negative? Explain.

37. Two masses hanging side by side from springs have positions $s_1 = 2 \sin t$ and $s_2 = \sin 2t$, respectively.

a) At what times in the interval $0 < t$ do the masses pass each other? (*Hint:* $\sin 2t = 2 \sin t \cos t$.)

b) When in the interval $0 \le t \le 2\pi$ is the vertical distance between the masses the greatest? What is this distance? (*Hint:* $\cos 2t = 2 \cos^2 t - 1$.)

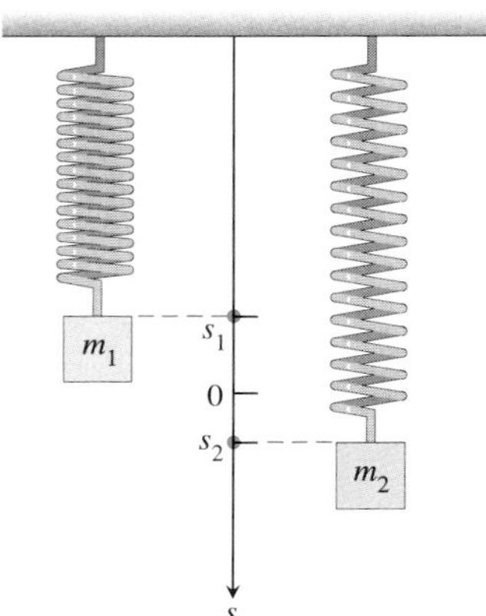

38. The positions of two particles on the s-axis are $s_1 = \sin t$ and $s_2 = \sin (t + \pi/3)$.

a) At what time(s) in the interval $0 \le t \le 2\pi$ do the particles meet?

b) What is the farthest apart the particles ever get?

c) When in the interval $0 \le t \le 2\pi$ is the distance between the particles changing the fastest?

39. The trough below is to be made to the dimensions shown. Only the angle θ can be varied. What value of θ will maximize the trough's volume?

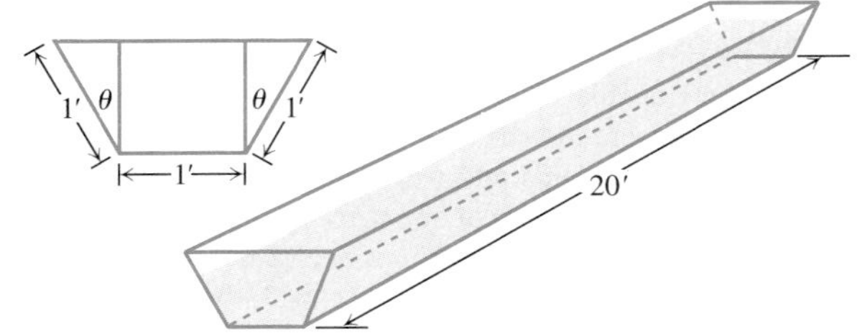

40. A rectangular sheet of $8\frac{1}{2}$-by-11-in. paper shown on the following page is placed on a flat surface, and one of the corners is placed on the opposite longer edge. The other corners are held in their original positions. With all four corners now held fixed, the paper is smoothed flat. The problem is to make the length of the crease as small as possible. Call the length L.

a) Try it with paper.

b) Show that $L^2 = 2x^3/(2x - 8.5)$.

c) What value of x minimizes L^2?

d) Find the minimum value of L to the nearest tenth of an inch.

e) Graph L as a function of x and compare what you see with your answer in (d).

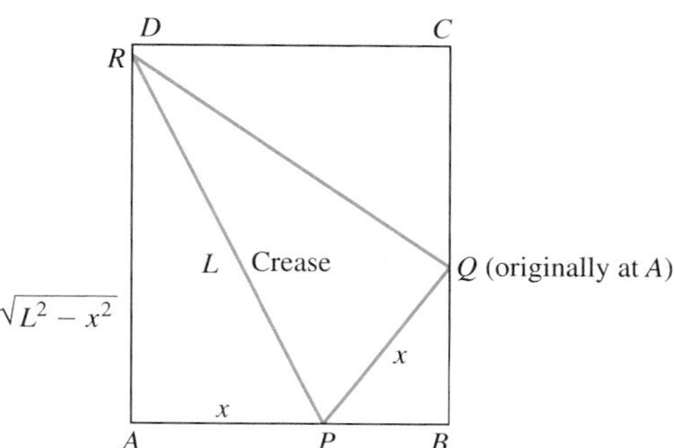

41. Fermat's principle in optics states that light always travels from one point to another along a path that minimizes the travel time. Figure 4.34 shows light from a source A reflected by a plane mirror to a receiver at point B. Show that for the light to obey Fermat's principle, the angle of incidence must equal the angle of reflection. (This result can also be derived without calculus. There is a purely geometric argument, which you may prefer.)

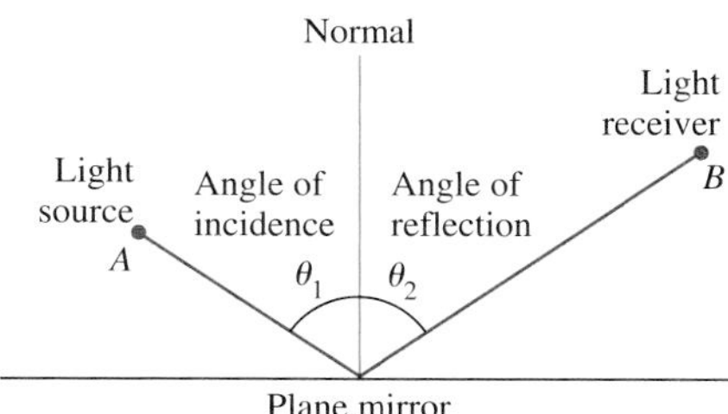

4.34 In studies of light reflection, the angles of incidence and reflection are measured from the line normal to the reflecting surface. Exercise 41 asks you to show that if light obeys Fermat's "least-time" principle, then $\theta_1 = \theta_2$.

42. Let $f(x)$ and $g(x)$ be the differentiable functions graphed here. Point c is the point where the vertical distance between the curves is the greatest. Is there anything special about the tangents to the two curves at c? Give reasons for your answer.

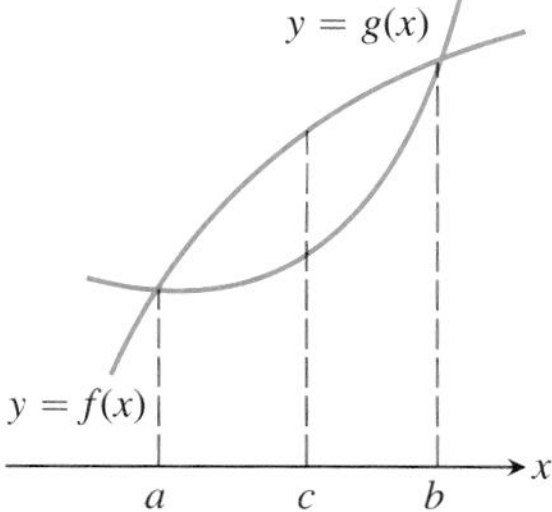

43. *Tin Pest.* Metallic tin, when kept below 13°C for a while, becomes brittle and crumbles to a gray powder. Tin objects eventually crumble to this gray powder spontaneously if kept in a cold climate for years. The Europeans who saw the tin organ pipes in their churches crumble away years ago called the change *tin pest* because it seemed to be contagious. And indeed it was, for the gray powder is a catalyst for its own formation.

A *catalyst* for a chemical reaction is a substance that controls the rate of the reaction without undergoing any permanent change in itself. An *autocatalytic reaction* is one whose product is a catalyst for its own formation. Such a reaction may proceed slowly at first if the amount of catalyst present is small and slowly again at the end, when most of the original substance is used up. But in between, when both the substance and its catalyst product are abundant, the reaction proceeds at a faster pace.

In some cases it is reasonable to assume that the rate $v = dx/dt$ of the reaction is proportional both to the amount of the original substance present and to the amount of product. That is, v may be considered to be a function of x alone, and

$$v = kx(a - x) = kax - kx^2,$$

where

x = the amount of product
a = the amount of substance at the beginning
k = a positive constant.

At what value of x does the rate v have a maximum? What is the maximum value of v?

44. Suppose that at time $t \geq 0$ the position of a particle moving on the x-axis is $x = (t - 1)(t - 4)^4$.

a) When is the particle at rest?

b) During what time interval does the particle move to the left?

c) What is the fastest the particle goes while moving to the left?

d) Graph x as a function of t for $0 \leq t \leq 6$. Graph dx/dt over the same interval, in another color if possible. Compare the graphs with one another and with your answers in (a)–(c).

45. *How We Cough*

a) When we cough, the trachea (windpipe) contracts to increase the velocity of the air going out. This raises the questions of how much it should contract to maximize the velocity and whether it really contracts that much when we cough.

Under reasonable assumptions about the elasticity of the tracheal wall and about how the air near the wall is slowed by friction, the average flow velocity v can be modeled by the equation

$$v = c(r_0 - r)r^2 \text{ cm/sec} \qquad \frac{r_0}{2} \leq r \leq r_0,$$

where r_0 is the rest radius of the trachea in centimeters and c is a positive constant whose value depends in part on the length of the trachea.

Show that v is greatest when $r = (2/3)r_0$, that is, when the trachea is about 33% contracted. The remarkable fact is that x-ray photographs confirm that the trachea contracts about this much during a cough.

b) Take r_0 to be 0.5 and c to be 1, and graph v over the interval $0 \le r \le 0.5$. Compare what you see to the claim that v is at a maximum when $r = (2/3)r_0$.

46. *Sensitivity to Medicine (Continuation of Exercise 66, Section 3.2).* Find the amount of medicine to which the body is most sensitive by finding the value of M that maximizes the derivative dR/dM, where

$$R = M^2\left(\frac{C}{2} - \frac{M}{3}\right)$$

and C is a constant.

BUSINESS

47. It costs you c dollars each to manufacture and distribute backpacks. If the backpacks sell at x dollars each, the number sold is given by $n = a/(x - c) + b(100 - x)$, where a and b are certain positive constants. What selling price will bring a maximum profit?

48. You operate a tour service that offers the following rates:

a) \$200 per person if 50 people (the minimum number to book the tour) go on the tour.

b) For each additional person, up to a maximum of 80 people total, everyone's charge is reduced by \$2.

It costs \$6000 (a fixed cost) plus \$32 per person to conduct the tour. How many people does it take to maximize your profit?

49. *The Best Quantity to Order.* One of the formulas for inventory management says that the average weekly cost of ordering, paying for, and holding merchandise is

$$A(q) = \frac{km}{q} + cm + \frac{hq}{2},$$

where q is the quantity you order when things run low (shoes, radios, brooms, or whatever the item might be), k is the cost of placing an order (the same, no matter how often you order), c is the cost of one item (a constant), m is the number of items sold each week (a constant), and h is the weekly holding cost per item (a constant that takes into account things such as space, utilities, insurance, and security). Your job, as the inventory manager for your store, is to find the quantity that will minimize $A(q)$. What is it? (The formula you get for the answer is called the *Wilson lot size formula.*)

50. *Continuation of Exercise 49.* Shipping costs sometimes depend on order size. When they do, it is more realistic to replace k by $k + bq$, the sum of k and a constant multiple of q. What is the most economical quantity to order now?

ECONOMICS

51. Show that if $r(x) = 6x$ and $c(x) = x^3 - 6x^2 + 15x$ are your revenue and cost functions, then the best you can do is break even (have revenue equal cost).

52. Suppose $c(x) = x^3 - 20x^2 + 20{,}000x$ is the cost of manufacturing x items. Find a production level that will minimize the average cost of making x items.

Writing for Your Own Knowledge

Answer the following questions in writing. Some answers will take only a sentence or two; others may require several paragraphs. Some explanations may also call for graphs or sketches.

1. How do you solve a typical optimization problem?
2. What does calculus have to say about production levels that maximize profit?
3. What does calculus have to say about production levels that minimize cost?
4. What is the rationale for modeling discrete phenomena with differentiable functions?

EXPLORER PROGRAM

PowerGrapher	Evaluates functions at multiple points in an interval, enabling you to make informed guesses about zeros and extremes. Graphs functions singly or together.

4.6 *The Mean Value Theorem*

If the graphs of two functions start at the same point and the functions have the same rate of change at every point, do the graphs have to be identical? It is hard to imagine how they could be anything else. It is equally hard to see how to proceed with a proof. If f and g are the functions, we know that $f(x_0) = g(x_0)$ at some initial point x_0 and that

$$\lim_{h\to 0} \frac{f(x+h) - f(x)}{h} = \lim_{h\to 0} \frac{g(x+h) - g(x)}{h}$$

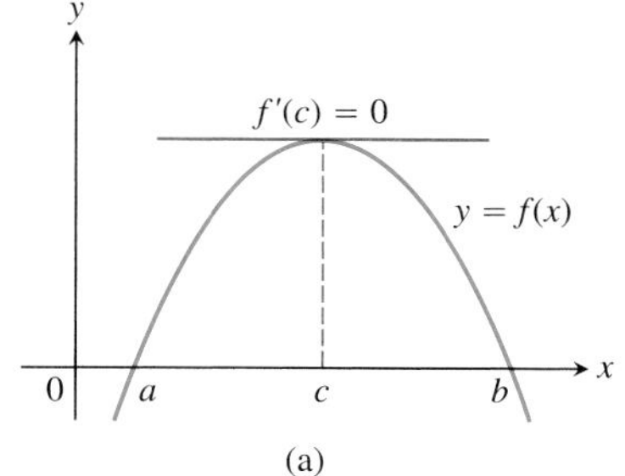

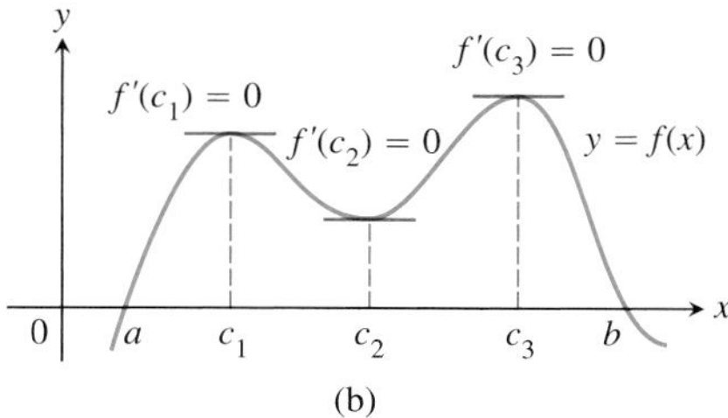

4.35 Rolle's theorem says that a smooth curve has at least one horizontal tangent between any two points where it crosses the x-axis. It may have just one (a), or it may have more (b).

at every x. But how are we to conclude the equality of f and g from this information? It is not at all obvious.

The fact that f must equal g under these circumstances can be derived, as we will see, from the Mean Value Theorem. The theorem is usually proved by appealing to a special case, called Rolle's theorem.

Rolle's Theorem

There is strong geometric evidence that between any two points where a smooth curve crosses the x-axis there is a point on the curve where the tangent is horizontal. A 300-year-old theorem of Michel Rolle (1652–1719) assures us that this is indeed the case.

THEOREM 5

Rolle's Theorem

Suppose that $y = f(x)$ is continuous at every point of the closed interval $[a, b]$ and differentiable at every point of its interior (a, b). If

$$f(a) = f(b) = 0,$$

then there is at least one number c between a and b at which

$$f'(c) = 0.$$

See Fig. 4.35.

Proof We know from Section 4.2 that a continuous function defined on a closed interval assumes absolute maximum and minimum values on the interval. The question is, where? There are only three places to look:

1. At interior points where f' is zero
2. At interior points where f' does not exist
3. At the endpoints of the function's domain, in this case a and b

By hypothesis, f has a derivative at every interior point. That rules out (2), leaving us with interior points where $f' = 0$ and with the two endpoints a and b.

If either the maximum or the minimum occurs at a point c inside the interval, then $f'(c) = 0$ by Theorem 2 in Section 4.2, and we have found a point for Rolle's theorem.

If both maximum and minimum are at a or b, then f is constant, $f' = 0$, and c can be taken anywhere in the interval. This completes the proof. ■

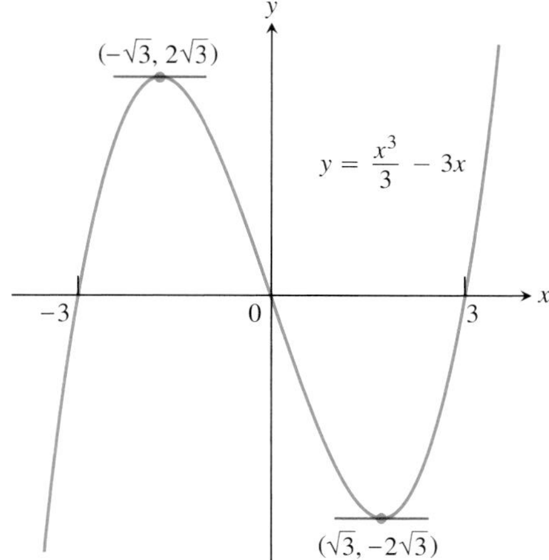

4.36 As predicted by Rolle's theorem, this smooth curve has horizontal tangents between the points where it crosses the x-axis (Example 1).

EXAMPLE 1 The polynomial function

$$f(x) = \frac{x^3}{3} - 3x$$

graphed in Fig. 4.36 is continuous at every point of $[-3, 3]$ and differentiable at every point of $(-3, 3)$. Since $f(-3) = f(3) = 0$, Rolle's theorem says that f' must be zero at least once in the open interval between $a = -3$ and $b = 3$. In fact, $f'(x) = x^2 - 3$ is zero twice in this interval, once at $x = -\sqrt{3}$ and again at $x = \sqrt{3}$.

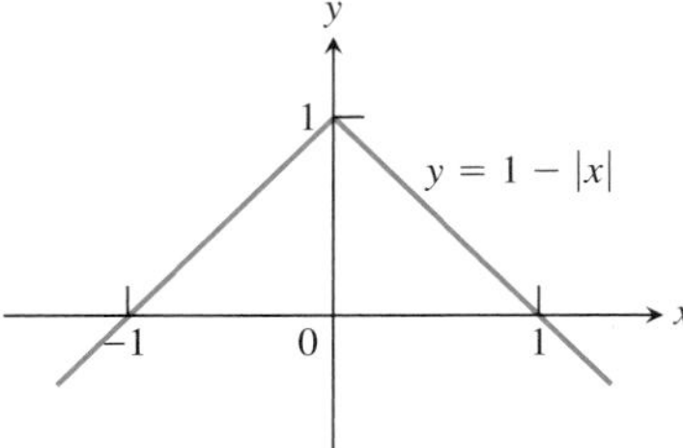

4.37 This curve with a corner has no horizontal tangent between the points where it crosses the x-axis (Example 2).

EXAMPLE 2 As the function $f(x) = 1 - |x|$ shows (Fig. 4.37), the differentiability of f is essential to Rolle's theorem. If we allow even one interior point where f is not differentiable, its graph may fail to have a horizontal tangent.

The Mean Value Theorem

The Mean Value Theorem is a slanted version of Rolle's theorem. See Fig. 4.38. The figure shows the graph of a differentiable function f defined on an interval $a \le x \le b$. There is a point on the curve where the tangent is parallel to the chord AB. In Rolle's theorem, the line AB is the x-axis and $f'(c) = 0$. Here the line AB is a chord joining the endpoints of the curve above a and b, and $f'(c)$ is the slope of the chord.

When the French mathematician Michel Rolle published his theorem in 1691, his goal was to show that between every two zeros of a polynomial function there always lies a zero of the polynomial we now know to be the function's derivative. (The modern version of the theorem is not restricted to polynomials.)

Rolle distrusted the new methods of calculus, however, and spent a great deal of time and energy denouncing their use and attacking l'Hôpital's all too popular (he felt) calculus book. It is ironic that Rolle is known today only for his inadvertent contribution to a field he tried to suppress.

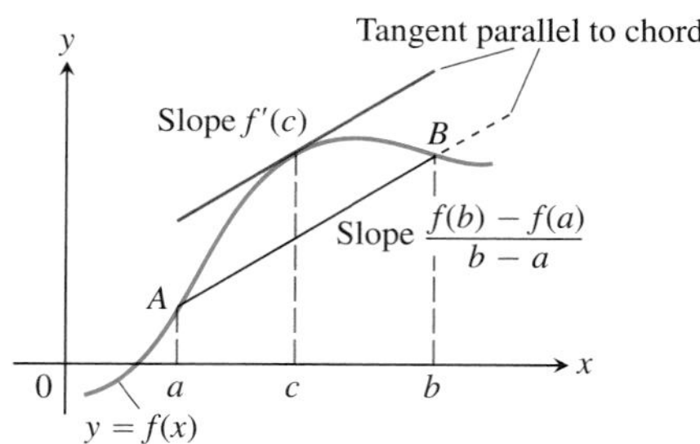

4.38 Geometrically, the Mean Value Theorem says that somewhere between A and B the curve has at least one tangent parallel to chord AB.

THEOREM 6

The Mean Value Theorem

If $y = f(x)$ is continuous at every point of the closed interval $[a, b]$ and differentiable at every point of its interior (a, b), then there is at least one number c between a and b at which

$$\frac{f(b) - f(a)}{b - a} = f'(c). \tag{1}$$

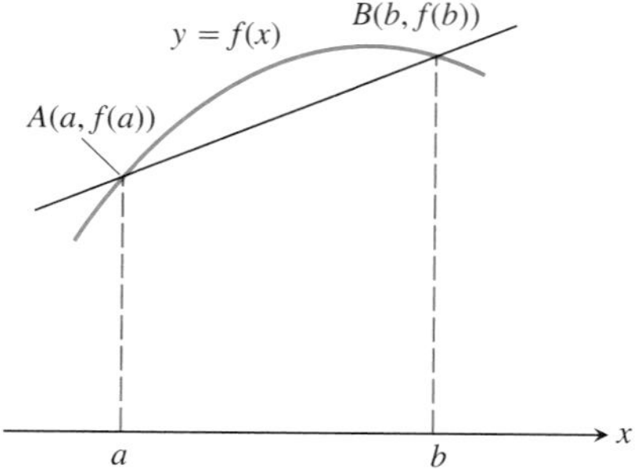

4.39 The graph of f and the chord AB over the interval $a \le x \le b$.

Proof The figure we get when we graph f over $[a, b]$ and draw the line through the endpoints $A\,(a, f(a))$ and $B\,(b, f(b))$ (Fig. 4.39) resembles the one we drew for Rolle's theorem. The difference is that the line AB need not be the x-axis because $f(a)$ and $f(b)$ may not be zero. We cannot apply Rolle's theorem directly to f, but we can apply it to the function that measures the vertical distance between the graph of f and the line AB. This, it turns out, will tell us what we want to know about the derivative of f.

The line AB is the graph of the function

$$g(x) = f(a) + \frac{f(b) - f(a)}{b - a}(x - a) \tag{2}$$

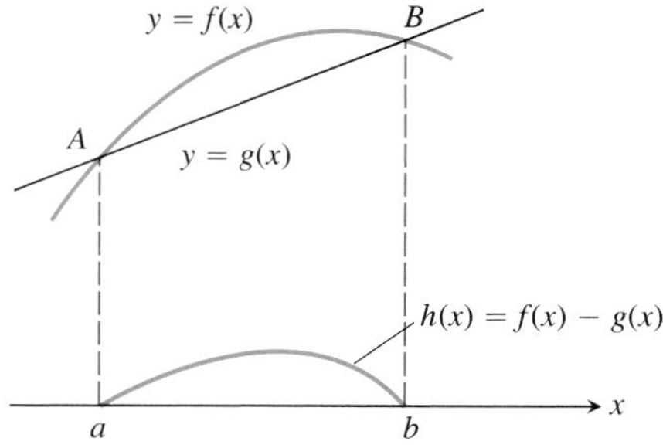

4.40 The chord AB in Fig. 4.39 is the graph of the function $g(x)$. The function $h(x) = f(x) - g(x)$ gives the vertical distance between the graphs of f and g at x.

(point–slope equation), and the formula for the vertical distance between the graphs of f and g at x is

$$h(x) = f(x) - g(x) = f(a) - \frac{f(b) - f(a)}{b - a}(x - a). \tag{3}$$

Figure 4.40 shows the graphs of f, g, and h together.

The function h satisfies the hypotheses of Rolle's theorem on the interval $[a, b]$. It is continuous on $[a, b]$ and differentiable in (a, b) because f and g are. Both $h(a)$ and $h(b)$ are zero because the graphs of f and g pass through A and B.

Therefore $h' = 0$ at some point c between a and b. To see what this says about f', we differentiate both sides of Eq. (3) with respect to x and set $x = c$. This gives

$$h'(x) = f'(x) - \frac{f(b) - f(a)}{b - a} \qquad \text{Derivative of Eq. (3) . . .}$$

$$h'(c) = f'(c) - \frac{f(b) - f(a)}{b - a} \qquad \text{. . . with } x = c$$

$$0 = f'(c) - \frac{f(b) - f(a)}{b - a} \qquad h'(c) = 0$$

$$f'(c) = \frac{f(b) - f(a)}{b - a}, \qquad \text{Rearranged}$$

which is what we set out to prove. ■

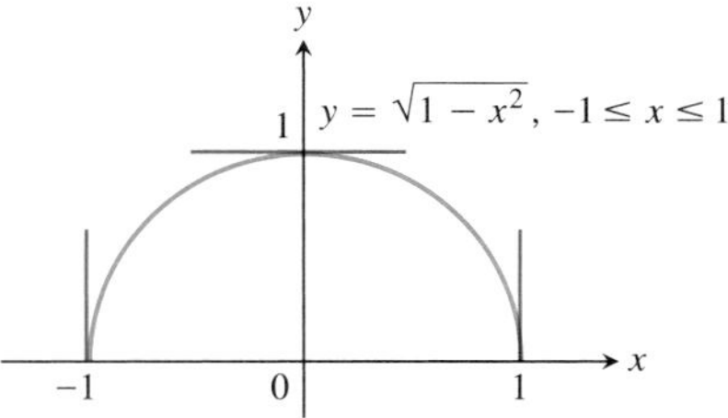

4.41 The function $f(x) = \sqrt{1 - x^2}$ satisfies the hypotheses (and conclusion) of the Mean Value Theorem on the interval $[-1, 1]$ even though f is not differentiable at the interval's endpoints.

Notice that the hypotheses of the Mean Value Theorem do not require f to be differentiable at either a or b. Continuity at a and b is enough (Fig. 4.41).

If $f'(x)$ is continuous on $[a, b]$, then the Max-Min Theorem for continuous functions in Section 4.2 tells us that f' has an absolute maximum value max f' and an absolute minimum value min f' on the interval. Since the number $f'(c)$ can neither exceed max f' nor be less than min f', the equation

$$\frac{f(b) - f(a)}{b - a} = f'(c) \tag{4}$$

gives us the inequality

$$\min f' \le \frac{f(b) - f(a)}{b - a} \le \max f'. \tag{5}$$

The importance of the Mean Value Theorem lies in the estimates that sometimes come from Eq. (5) and in the mathematical conclusions that come from Eq. (4), a few of which we will see in a moment.

We usually do not know any more about the number c than the theorem tells us, which is that c exists. In a few cases we can satisfy our curiosity about the identity of c, as in the next example. Keep in mind, however, that our ability to identify c is the exception rather than the rule. The importance of the theorem lies elsewhere.

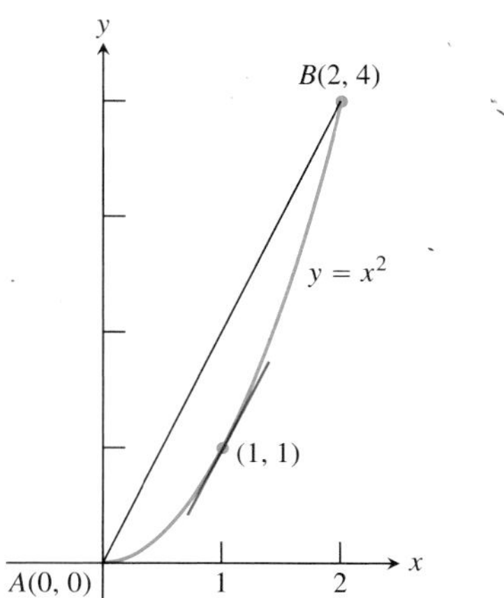

4.42 As we find in Example 3, $c = 1$ is where the tangent is parallel to the chord.

EXAMPLE 3 The function $f(x) = x^2$ (Fig. 4.42) is continuous for $0 \le x \le 2$ and differentiable for $0 < x < 2$. Since $f(0) = 0$ and $f(2) = 4$, the Mean Value Theorem says that at some point c in the interval, the derivative $f'(x) = 2x$ must have the value $(4 - 0)/(2 - 0) = 2$. In this (exceptional) case we can identify c by solving the equation $2c = 2$ to get $c = 1$. ■

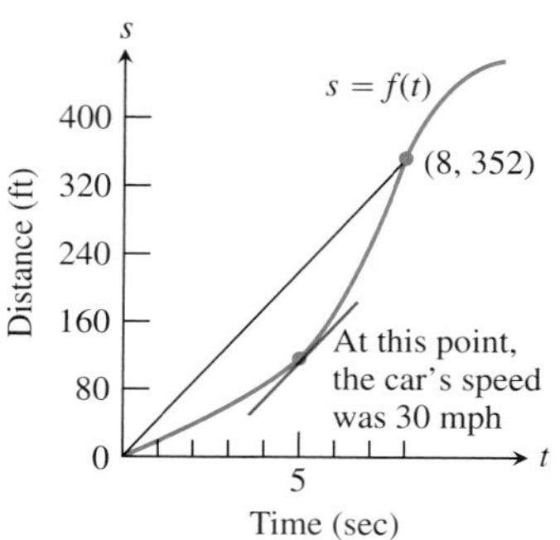

4.43 Distance vs. elapsed time for the car in Example 4.

Physical Interpretations

If we think of the number $(f(b) - f(a))/(b - a)$ as the average change in f over $[a, b]$ and $f'(c)$ as an instantaneous change, then the Mean Value Theorem says that at some interior point the instantaneous change must equal the average change over the entire interval.

EXAMPLE 4 If a car accelerating from zero takes 8 sec to go 352 ft, its average velocity for the 8-sec interval is $352/8 = 44$ ft/sec. At some point during the acceleration, the Mean Value Theorem says, the speedometer must read exactly 30 mph (44 ft/sec) (Fig. 4.43).

Corollaries

We know that the derivative of a constant function is zero. The Mean Value Theorem's first corollary provides the converse: The only functions with zero derivatives are constant functions.

COROLLARY 1

Functions with Zero Derivatives Are Constant Functions

If $f'(x) = 0$ for all x in an interval I, then $f(x) = C$ for all x in I, where C is a constant.

Proof We want to show that f has a constant value on I. We do so by showing that if x_1 and x_2 are any two points in I, then $f(x_1) = f(x_2)$.

Suppose that x_1 and x_2 are two points in I, numbered from left to right so that $x_1 < x_2$. Then f satisfies the hypotheses of the Mean Value Theorem on $[x_1, x_2]$: It is differentiable at every point of $[x_1, x_2]$, and hence continuous at every point as well. Therefore,

$$\frac{f(x_2) - f(x_1)}{x_2 - x_1} = f'(c)$$

at some point c between x_1 and x_2. Since $f' = 0$ throughout I, this equation translates successively into

$$\frac{f(x_2) - f(x_1)}{x_2 - x_1} = 0, \quad f(x_2) - f(x_1) = 0, \quad \text{and} \quad f(x_1) = f(x_2).$$

If the graphs of two functions start at the same point and the functions have the same rate of change at every point, do the graphs have to be identical? This is the question with which we began the present section, and the next corollary provides the answer.

COROLLARY 2

Functions with the Same Derivative Differ Only by a Constant

If $f'(x) = g'(x)$ at each point of an interval I, then $f(x) = g(x) + C$ for all x in I, where C is a constant.

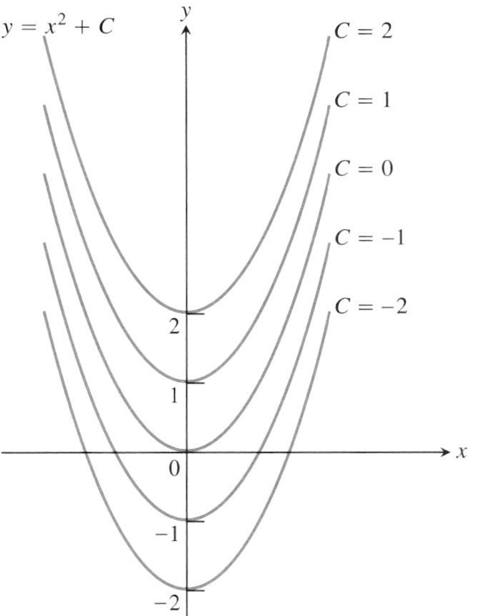

4.44 From a geometric point of view, Corollary 2 of the Mean Value Theorem says that the graphs of functions with identical derivatives can differ only by a vertical shift. The graphs of the functions with derivative $2x$ are the parabolas $y = x^2 + C$, shown here for selected values of C.

Proof Since $f'(x) = g'(x)$ at each point of I, the derivative of the difference function $h = f - g$ at each point is

$$h'(x) = f'(x) - g'(x) = 0.$$

Thus, $h(x) = C$ on I (Corollary 1). That is, $f(x) - g(x) = C$ on I, so $f(x) = g(x) + C$. ■

Corollary 2 says that two functions can have identical rates of change throughout an interval only if their values on the interval differ by a constant. For instance, we know that the derivative of x^2 is $2x$. Therefore, any other function with derivative $2x$ on an interval must have the formula $x^2 + C$ for some value of C. No other functions can have $2x$ as their derivative (Fig. 4.44). In Section 4.7, we will see the importance of this observation.

Corollary 2 now answers our original question about graphs of differentiable functions. If f and g have the same rate of change, then f and g differ by a constant. But if $f(x_0) = g(x_0)$ as well, then the constant is zero and $f(x) = g(x)$ for all x.

The final corollary is the first derivative test for increasing and decreasing. In Section 4.2 we called it Theorem 3, and now we can prove it using the Mean Value Theorem.

COROLLARY 3

f Increases When $f' > 0$ and Decreases When $f' < 0$

Suppose that f is continuous at each point of $[a, b]$ and differentiable at each point of (a, b). If $f' > 0$ at each point of (a, b), then f increases throughout $[a, b]$. If $f' < 0$ at each point of (a, b), then f decreases throughout $[a, b]$.

To prove the corollary, we need definitions of increasing and decreasing.

DEFINITIONS

Let f be a real-valued function defined for all x in a domain of real numbers D.

1. f **increases** on D if $x_1 < x_2 \Rightarrow f(x_1) < f(x_2)$.
2. f **decreases** on D if $x_1 < x_2 \Rightarrow f(x_2) < f(x_1)$.

Proof of Corollary 3 Let x_1 and x_2 be any two numbers in $[a, b]$ with $x_1 < x_2$. Apply the Mean Value Theorem to f on $[x_1, x_2]$. It says that

$$f(x_2) - f(x_1) = f'(c)(x_2 - x_1) \tag{6}$$

for some c between x_1 and x_2. The sign of the right-hand side of Eq. (6) is the same as the sign of $f'(c)$ because $x_2 - x_1$ is positive. Therefore, $f(x_2) > f(x_1)$ if $f'(x)$ is positive on (a, b) (f is increasing) and $f(x_2) < f(x_1)$ if $f'(x)$ is negative on (a, b) (f is decreasing). ■

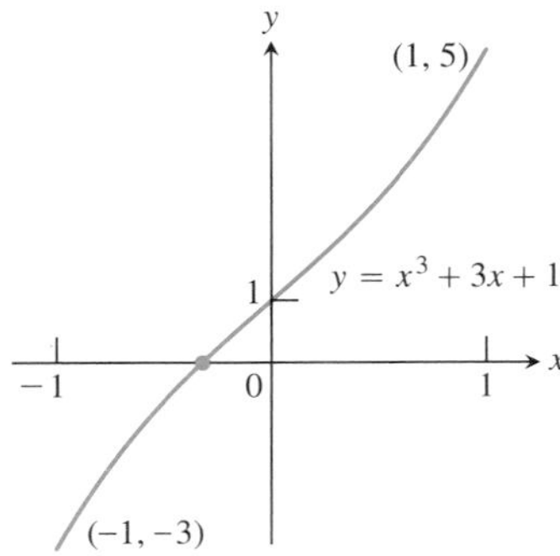

4.45 The only real zero of the polynomial $y = x^3 + 3x + 1$ is the one shown here between -1 and 0 (Example 5).

Solving Equations

When we solve equations numerically, we usually want to know beforehand how many solutions to look for in a given interval. With the help of Corollary 1 we can sometimes find out.

Suppose, for example, that

1. f is continuous on $[a, b]$ and differentiable on (a, b);
2. $f(a)$ and $f(b)$ have opposite signs;
3. $f' > 0$ on (a, b) or $f' < 0$ on (a, b).

Then f has exactly one zero between a and b: It cannot have more than one because it is either increasing on $[a, b]$ or decreasing on $[a, b]$. Yet it has at least one, by the Intermediate Value Theorem of Section 2.4.

EXAMPLE 5 The function $f(x) = x^3 + 3x + 1$ is continuous and differentiable on $[-1, 1]$, the values $f(-1) = -3$ and $f(1) = 5$ have opposite signs, and $f'(x) = 3x^2 + 3$ is always positive. The equation $x^3 + 3x + 1 = 0$ therefore has exactly one solution in $[-1, 1]$ (Fig. 4.45).

Exercises 4.6

Find the value or values of c that satisfy the equation

$$\frac{f(b) - f(a)}{b - a} = f'(c)$$

in the conclusion of the Mean Value Theorem for the functions and intervals in Exercises 1–4.

1. $f(x) = x^2 + 2x - 1, \quad [0, 1]$

2. $f(x) = x^{2/3}, \quad [0, 1]$

3. $f(x) = x + \dfrac{1}{x}, \quad \left[\dfrac{1}{2}, 2\right]$

4. $f(x) = \sqrt{x - 1}, \quad [1, 3]$

Which of the functions in Exercises 5–8 satisfy the hypotheses of the Mean Value Theorem on the given interval, and which do not? Give reasons for your answers.

5. $f(x) = x^{2/3}, \quad [-1, 8]$

6. $f(x) = x^{4/5}, \quad [0, 1]$

7. $f(x) = \sqrt{x(1 - x)}, \quad [0, 1]$

8. $f(x) = \begin{cases} \dfrac{\sin x}{x}, & -\pi \le x < 0 \\ 0, & x = 0 \end{cases}$

9. *Speeding.* A trucker handed in a ticket at a tollbooth, showing that the truck had covered 161 mi in 2 h. Show that at some place along the road the trucker was going 80 mi/h.

10. *Temperature Change.* It took 20 sec for a thermometer to rise from 10°F to 212°F when it was taken from a freezer and placed in boiling water. Show that somewhere along the way the mercury was rising at exactly 10.1°F/sec.

11. *Triremes.* Classical accounts tell us that a 170-oar trireme like the one shown here once covered 184 nautical miles in 24 hours. Show that at some point during this feat the trireme's speed exceeded 7.5 knots (nautical miles per hour).

12. *A Marathon.* A marathoner ran the 26.2-mi New York Marathon course in 2.2 h. Show that at least twice, the marathoner was running at exactly 11 mi/h.

Show that the equations in Exercises 13–22 have exactly one solution on the given interval.

13. $x^4 + 3x + 1 = 0, \quad [-2, -1]$

14. $-x^3 - 3x + 1 = 0, \quad [0, 1]$

15. $x - \dfrac{2}{x} = 0, \quad [1, 3]$

16. $x^3 + \dfrac{4}{x^2} + 7 = 0, \quad (-\infty, 0)$

17. $\sqrt{x} + \sqrt{1+x} - 4 = 0, \quad (0, \infty)$

18. $\dfrac{1}{1-x} + \sqrt{1+x} - 3.1 = 0, \quad (-1, 1)$

19. $x + \sin^2\left(\dfrac{x}{3}\right) - 8 = 0, \quad (-\infty, \infty)$

20. $2x - \cos x + \sqrt{2} = 0, \quad (-\infty, \infty)$

21. $\sec x - \dfrac{1}{x^3} + 5 = 0, \quad (0, \pi/2)$

22. $\tan x - \cot x - x = 0, \quad (0, \pi/2)$

23. **a)** Plot the zeros of each polynomial on a line together with the zeros of its first derivative:
   i) $y = x^2 - 4$ **ii)** $y = x^2 + 8x + 15$
   iii) $y = x^3 - 3x^2 + 4 = (x+1)(x-2)^2$
   iv) $y = x^3 - 33x^2 + 216x = x(x-9)(x-24)$
   What pattern do you see?

   b) Use Rolle's theorem to prove that between every two zeros of $x^n + a_{n-1}x^{n-1} + \cdots + a_1x + a_0$ there lies a zero of
   $$nx^{n-1} + (n-1)a_{n-1}x^{n-2} + \cdots + a_1.$$

24. The function
$$f(x) = \begin{cases} x, & 0 \le x < 1 \\ 0, & x = 1 \end{cases}$$
is zero at $x = 0$ and $x = 1$ and differentiable on $(0, 1)$, but its derivative on $(0, 1)$ is never zero. How can this be? Doesn't Rolle's theorem say the derivative has to be zero somewhere in $(0, 1)$? Give reasons for your answer.

25. Suppose that f is differentiable on $[0, 1]$ and that its derivative is never zero. Show that $f(0) \neq f(1)$.

26. Show that $|\sin b - \sin a| \le |b - a|$ for any numbers a and b.

27. Suppose that f is differentiable on $[a, b]$ and that $f(b) < f(a)$. Can you then say anything about the values of f' on $[a, b]$?

28. Suppose that f and g are differentiable on $[a, b]$ and that $f(a) = g(a)$ and $f(b) = g(b)$. Show that there is at least one point between a and b where the tangents to the graphs of f and g are parallel.

Make the estimates in Exercises 29 and 30 by applying the inequality
$$\min f' \le \frac{f(b) - f(a)}{b - a} \le \max f'.$$

29. Suppose that $f'(x) = 1/(1 + x^4 \cos x)$ for $0 \le x \le 0.1$ and that $f(0) = 1$. Estimate $f(0.1)$.

30. Suppose that $f'(x) = 1/(1 - x^4)$ for $0 \le x \le 0.1$ and that $f(0) = 2$. Estimate $f(0.1)$.

31. *A Surprising Graph.* Graph the function
$$f(x) = \sin x \sin(x + 2) - \sin^2(x + 1).$$
What does the graph do? Why does the function behave this way? Give reasons for your answers.

32. Suppose that $f(-1) = 3$ and that $f'(x) = 0$ for all x. Must $f(x) = 3$ for all x? Give reasons for your answer.

33. Suppose that $f(0) = 5$ and that $f'(x) = 2$ for all x. Must $f(x) = 2x + 5$ for all x? Give reasons for your answer.

34. Suppose that $f'(x) = 2x$ for all x. Find $f(2)$ if
   a) $f(0) = 0$ **b)** $f(1) = 0$ **c)** $f(-2) = 3$.

Writing for Your Own Knowledge

Answer the following questions in writing. Some answers will take only a sentence or two; others may require several paragraphs. Some explanations may also call for graphs or sketches.

1. What does Rolle's theorem say? How is Rolle's theorem a special case of the Mean Value Theorem?
2. How does the Mean Value Theorem relate average change to instantaneous change?
3. How does the Mean Value Theorem sometimes enable us to estimate function values?
4. What does the Mean Value Theorem tell us about functions with positive derivatives? functions with negative derivatives? functions with zero derivatives? functions with identical derivatives?
5. What consequence does the corollary about increasing and decreasing functions sometimes have for root finding?

4.7 *Antiderivatives, Differential Equations, and Modeling*

One of the early accomplishments of calculus was predicting the future position of a moving body from one of its known locations and a formula for its velocity function. Today we view this as one of a number of occasions on which we recover a function from one of its known values and a formula for its rate of change. It is a routine process today, thanks to calculus, to calculate a factory's future output from its present output and its production rate or to predict a population's future size from its present size and its growth rate.

The process of finding a function from one of its known values and its derivative $f(x)$ has two steps. The first is to find a formula that gives all the functions that could possibly have f as a derivative. These functions are called *antiderivatives of* f, and the formula that gives them all is called the *general antiderivative of* f. The second step is then to use the known function value to select the particular antiderivative we want.

Finding a formula that gives all of a function's antiderivatives might seem like an impossible task, or at least to require a little magic, but this is not the case at all. It turns out that if we can find even one of a function's antiderivatives, then we can find them all, thanks to Corollary 2 of the Mean Value Theorem.

The present section shows how to "reverse" known differentiation formulas to find general antiderivatives and uses this technique to solve differential equations. It closes with a brief discussion of mathematical modeling, the process by which we use mathematics to learn about reality.

Finding Antiderivatives

As we mentioned in the introduction, a function $F(x)$ is an **antiderivative** of a function $f(x)$ over an interval I if $F'(x) = f(x)$ at every point of I. Once we have found one antiderivative F of f, Corollary 2 of the Mean Value Theorem tells us that all others are given by the formula

$$y = F(x) + C.$$

We call $F(x) + C$ the **general antiderivative** of f over the interval I. Each particular antiderivative of f is given by this formula for some value of C. The constant C is called the **arbitrary constant** in the formula. Thus once we have a particular antiderivative F of f, the general antiderivative of f is F plus an arbitrary constant.

In the examples that follow, the interval I will be the natural domain of f unless we say otherwise.

The use of the letters F and f is conventional in this context, even though F and f are pronounced the same way in normal speech. To distinguish between the two, we recommend saying "cap eff" for F and "little eff" for f.

We can find many of the antiderivatives we need in scientific work by reversing derivative formulas we already know.

EXAMPLE 1

Function $f(x)$	**General antiderivative $F(x) + C$**	**Reversed derivative formula**
$\cos x$	$\sin x + C$	$\frac{d}{dx}(\sin x) = \cos x$
$\cos 2x$	$\frac{\sin 2x}{2} + C$	$\frac{d}{dx}\left(\frac{\sin 2x}{2}\right) = \cos 2x$
$3x^2$	$x^3 + C$	$\frac{d}{dx}(x^3) = 3x^2$
$\frac{1}{2\sqrt{x}}$	$\sqrt{x} + C$	$\frac{d}{dx}(\sqrt{x}) = \frac{1}{2\sqrt{x}}$
$\frac{1}{x^2}$	$-\frac{1}{x} + C$	$\frac{d}{dx}\left(-\frac{1}{x}\right) = \frac{1}{x^2}$

Table 4.1 lists some useful general rules and the examples that follow show how to apply these rules when finding antiderivatives.

TABLE 4.1
General rules

Function	General Antiderivative	Source
1. $k\frac{du}{dx}$ (k constant)	$ku + C$	Constant Multiple Rule
2. $\frac{du}{dx} + \frac{dv}{dx}$	$u + v + C$	Sum Rule
3. $\frac{du}{dx} - \frac{dv}{dx}$	$u - v + C$	Difference Rule
4. x^n $(n \neq -1)$	$\frac{x^{n+1}}{n+1} + C$	Power Rule
5. $\sin kx$	$-\frac{\cos kx}{k} + C$	Chain Rule
6. $\cos kx$	$\frac{\sin kx}{k} + C$	Chain Rule

EXAMPLE 2 *We Can Find Antiderivatives Term by Term.*

Function	General antiderivative	Source
$10x$	$5x^2 + C$	Constant Multiple and Power Rules . . .
$10x - x^2$	$5x^2 - \frac{x^3}{3} + C$	. . . along with the Difference Rule . . .
$10x - x^2 + 2$	$5x^2 - \frac{x^3}{3} + 2x + C$	. . . and Sum Rule

EXAMPLE 3 *Fractional Powers Are Handled Like Integer Powers.*

Function	General antiderivative	Source
$\sqrt{x} = x^{1/2}$	$\frac{x^{3/2}}{3/2} + C = \frac{2}{3}x^{3/2} + C$	Power Rule with $n = 1/2$
$\frac{1}{\sqrt{x}} = x^{-1/2}$	$\frac{x^{1/2}}{1/2} + C = 2x^{1/2} + C$	Power Rule with $n = -1/2$

EXAMPLE 4 *The k in Rules 5 and 6 Can Be Any Nonzero Number.*

Function	General antiderivative	Source
$6 \sin 3x$	$6 \cdot \frac{-\cos 3x}{3} + C = -2 \cos 3x + C$	Rule 5 with $k = 3$
$5 \cos \frac{x}{2}$	$5 \cdot \frac{\sin (x/2)}{1/2} + C = 10 \sin \frac{x}{2} + C$	Rule 6 with $k = \frac{1}{2}$
$\cos 2\pi x$	$\frac{\sin 2\pi x}{2\pi} + C$	Rule 6 with $k = 2\pi$

Differential Equations and Initial Value Problems

When we observe the real world, we are usually noticing change and wanting to predict the future behavior of a function from the way we see its current values changing. The problem of finding a function y of x when we know its derivative

$$\frac{dy}{dx} = f(x) \tag{1}$$

and its value y_0 at a particular point or time x_0 is called an **initial value problem.** We solve such a problem in two steps. First we find the general antiderivative of f,

$$y = F(x) + C. \tag{2}$$

Then we use the **initial condition** that $y = y_0$ when $x = x_0$ to find the right value for C.

Equation (1) is called a **differential equation** because it contains a derivative. A more complicated differential equation might involve y on the right-hand side as well as x:

$$\frac{dy}{dx} = 2xy^2. \tag{3}$$

It might also involve higher order derivatives:

$$\frac{d^2y}{dx^2} - \frac{dy}{dx} + 5y = 3. \tag{4}$$

For now, we will steer away from such complications.

In the language of differential equations, the general antiderivative $y = F(x) + C$ of a function $f(x)$ is called the **general solution** of the equation $dy/dx = f(x)$. We **solve** the differential equation by finding its general solution. We solve an initial value problem by first solving the differential equation and then using the initial condition to find the **particular solution** we want.

EXAMPLE 5 *Finding a Body's Velocity from Its Acceleration and Initial Velocity.* The acceleration of gravity near the surface of the earth is 9.8 m/sec^2. This means that the velocity v of a body falling freely in a vacuum changes at the rate of

$$\frac{dv}{dt} = 9.8 \text{ m/sec}^2.$$

If the body is dropped from rest, what will its velocity be t seconds after it is released?

Solution In mathematical terms, we want to solve the initial value problem that consists of

The differential equation: $\dfrac{dv}{dt} = 9.8$

The initial condition: $v = 0$ when $t = 0$.

To solve it, we first use what we know about antiderivatives to find the general solution of the differential equation $dv/dt = 9.8$:

$$v = 9.8t + C. \qquad \text{Reversed derivative formula: } \frac{d}{dt}(9.8t) = 9.8$$

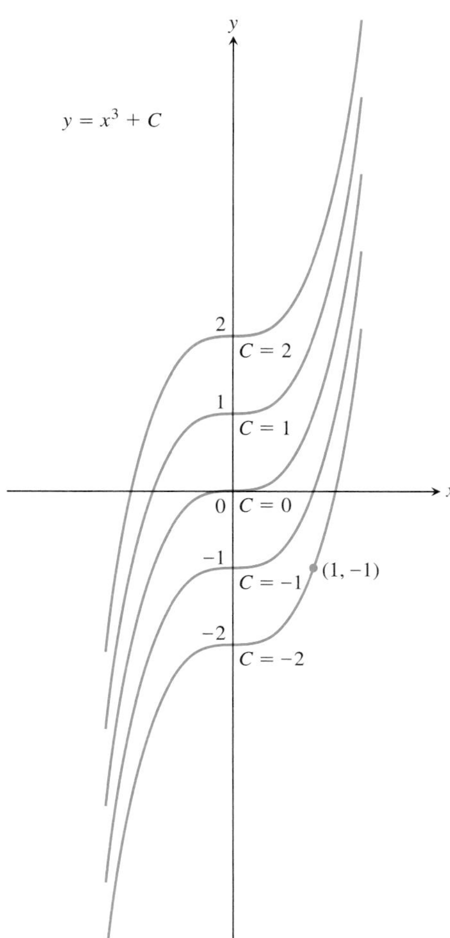

4.46 The curves $y = x^3 + C$ fill the coordinate plane without overlapping. In Example 6 we identify the curve $y = x^3 - 2$ as the one that passes through the given point $(1, -1)$.

Then we use the initial condition to find the right value of C for this particular problem:

$$\begin{aligned} v &= 9.8t + C \\ 0 &= 9.8(0) + C \qquad v = 0 \text{ when } t = 0 \\ C &= 0. \end{aligned}$$

The body's velocity t seconds after release is $v = 9.8t$ m/sec.

EXAMPLE 6 *Finding a Curve from Its Slope Function and a Point.* Find the curve whose slope at the point (x, y) is $3x^2$ if the curve is required to pass through the point $(1, -1)$.

Solution In mathematical language, we are asked to solve the initial value problem that consists of

The differential equation: $\dfrac{dy}{dx} = 3x^2$

The initial condition: $y = -1$ when $x = 1$.

To solve it, we first use what we know about antiderivatives to find the general solution of the differential equation:

$$y = x^3 + C. \qquad \text{Reverse derivative formula: } \frac{d}{dx}(x^3) = 3x^2$$

Then we substitute $x = 1$ and $y = -1$ to find C:

$$y = x^3 + C \qquad -1 = (1)^3 + C \qquad C = -2.$$

The curve we want is $y = x^3 - 2$ (Fig. 4.46).

EXAMPLE 7 *Finding a Cost Function from the Marginal Cost and an Initial Cost.* Suppose that the marginal cost of manufacturing an item when x thousand items are produced is

$$\frac{dc}{dx} = 10 + 3\sqrt{x}$$

thousand dollars and that the cost of producing 4 thousand items is 60 thousand dollars. What will it cost to produce 9 thousand items?

Solution We have

The differential equation: $\dfrac{dc}{dx} = 10 + 3\sqrt{x}$

The initial condition: $c = 60$ when $x = 4$.

The general solution of the differential equation is

$$\begin{aligned} c &= 10x + 3\frac{x^{3/2}}{3/2} + C \qquad \text{Power Rule with } n = \frac{1}{2} \\ &= 10x + 2x^{3/2} + C. \end{aligned}$$

We substitute $x = 4$, $c = 60$ to find the right value for C:

$$60 = 10(4) + 2(4)^{3/2} + C$$
$$60 = 40 + 2(8) + C$$
$$C = 60 - 40 - 16 = 4.$$

The cost of producing x thousand items is therefore

$$c = 10x + 2x^{3/2} + 4.$$

The cost of producing 9 thousand items is

$$c = 90 + 2(9)^{3/2} + 4 = 94 + 2(27) = 148$$

thousand dollars.

Some problems require us to solve two or more differential equations in a row.

EXAMPLE 8 *Finding a Projectile's Height from Its Acceleration, Initial Velocity, and Initial Position.* A heavy projectile is fired straight up from a platform 3 m above the ground, with an initial velocity of 160 m/sec. Assume that the only force affecting the projectile during its flight is from gravity, which produces a downward acceleration of 9.8 m/sec^2. Find an equation for the projectile's height as a function of time t if $t = 0$ when the projectile is fired. How high above the ground is the projectile 3 sec after firing?

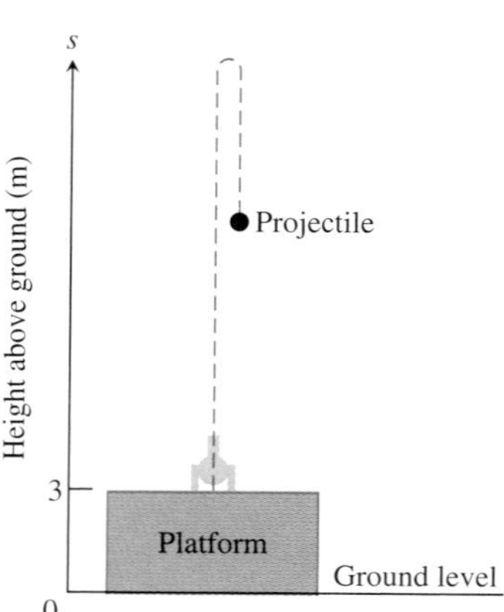

4.47 The sketch for modeling the projectile motion in Example 8.

Solution To model the problem, we draw a figure (Fig. 4.47) and let s denote the projectile's height above the ground at time t. We assume s to be a twice-differentiable function of t and represent the projectile's velocity and acceleration with the derivatives

$$v = \frac{ds}{dt} \quad \text{and} \quad a = \frac{dv}{dt} = \frac{d^2s}{dt^2}.$$

Since gravity acts in the negative s direction (the direction of decreasing s in our model), the initial value problem to solve is

Differential equation: $a = \dfrac{dv}{dt} = -9.8$

Initial conditions: $v = 160$ and $s = 3$ when $t = 0$.

We find v from the differential equation $dv/dt = -9.8$:

$$v = -9.8t + C_1 \qquad \text{General antiderivative of } -9.8$$
$$\frac{ds}{dt} = -9.8t + C_1 \qquad v = \frac{ds}{dt}$$

From this differential equation we find s:

$$s = -4.9t^2 + C_1t + C_2. \qquad \text{General antiderivative of } -9.8t + C_1$$

The values of C_1 and C_2 are determined by the initial conditions:

$$C_1 = v(0) = 160, \qquad C_2 = s(0) = 3.$$

This completes the formula for s as a function of t:

$$s = -4.9t^2 + 160t + 3.$$

To find the projectile's height 3 sec into the flight, we set $t = 3$ in the formula for s. The height is

$$s = -4.9(3)^2 + 160(3) + 3 = 438.9 \text{ m}.$$

When we find a function from its first derivative, we have one arbitrary constant, as in Examples 5–7. When we find a function from its second derivative, we have to deal with two constants, one from each "antidifferentiation," as in Example 8. To find a function from its third derivative would require us to find the values of three constants, and so on. In each case, the values of the constants are determined by the problem's initial conditions. Each time we find an antiderivative, we need an initial condition to tell us the value of C.

Sketching Solution Curves

The graph of a solution of a differential equation is called a **solution curve.** The curves $y = x^3 + C$ in Fig. 4.46 are solution curves of the differential equation $dy/dx = 3x^2$. When we cannot find explicit formulas for the solution curves of an equation $dy/dx = f(x)$ (that is, we cannot find an antiderivative of f), we may still be able to find their general shape by examining derivatives.

EXAMPLE 9 Sketch the solutions of the differential equation

$$y' = \frac{1}{x^2 + 1}.$$

Solution

STEP 1: *y' and y'':* As in Section 4.3, the curve's general shape is determined by y' and y''. We already know y':

$$y' = \frac{1}{x^2 + 1}.$$

We find y'' by differentiation, in the usual way:

$$y'' = \frac{d}{dx}(y') = \frac{d}{dx}\left(\frac{1}{x^2 + 1}\right) = \frac{-2x}{(x^2 + 1)^2}.$$

STEP 2: *Rise and fall:* The domain of y' is $(-\infty, \infty)$. There are no critical points, so the solution curves have no cusps or extrema. The curves rise from left to right because $y' > 0$. At $x = 0$, the curves have slope 1.

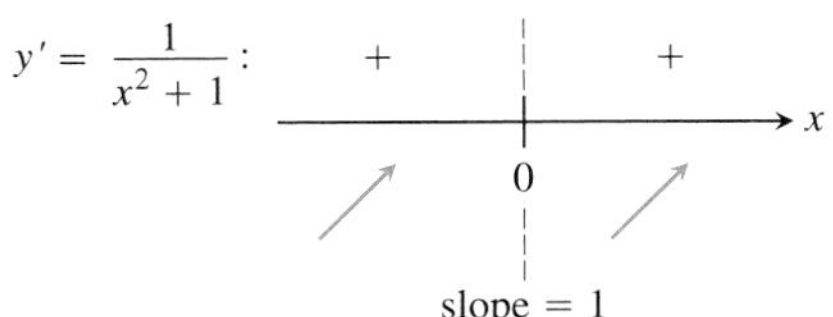

STEP 3: *Concavity:* The second derivative changes from $(+)$ to $(-)$ at $x = 0$, so the curves all have an inflection point at $x = 0$.

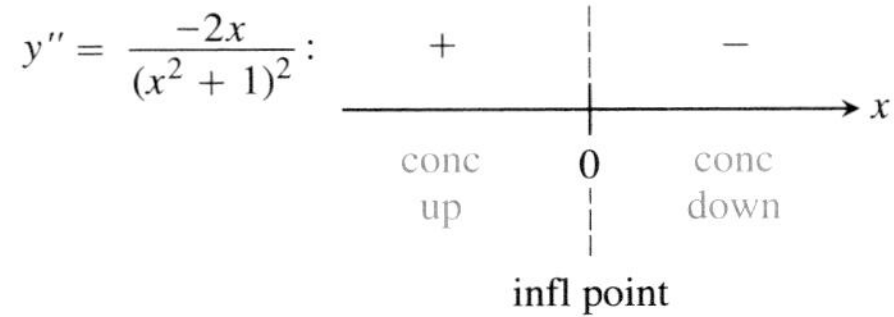

STEP 4: *Summary:*

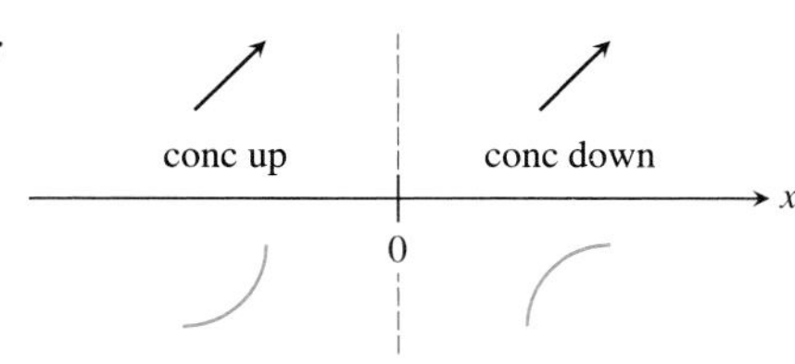

General shape:

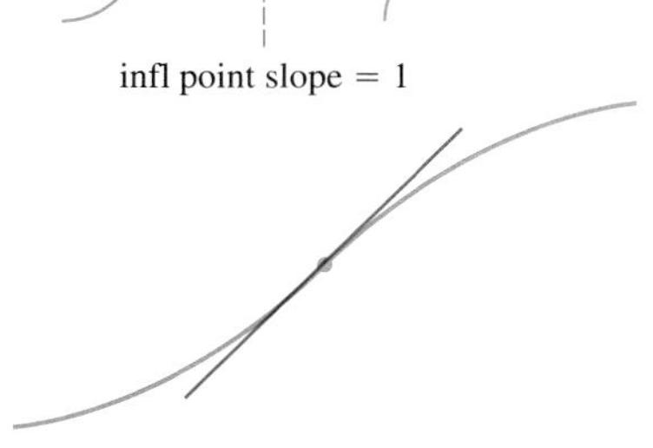

The first derivative tells us still more:

$$\lim_{x \to \pm\infty} y' = \lim_{x \to \pm\infty} \frac{1}{x^2 + 1} = 0,$$

so the curves level off as $x \to \pm\infty$.

STEP 5: *Specific points and solution curves:* We plot an assortment of points on the y-axis where we know the curves' slope (it is 1 at $x = 0$), mark tangents with that slope for guidance, and sketch "parallel" curves of the right general shape.

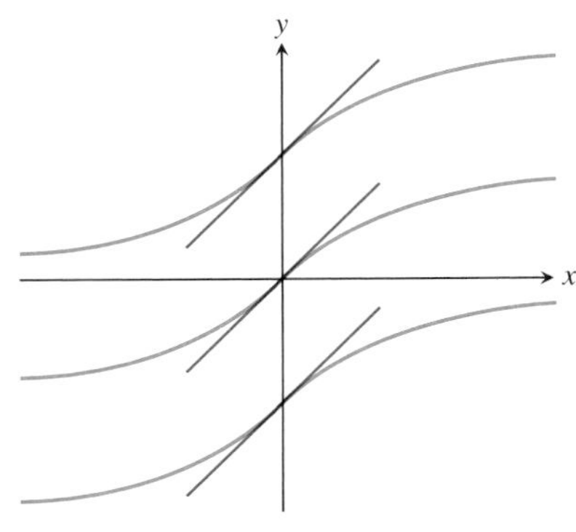

EXAMPLE 10 Sketch the solution of the initial value problem

Differential equation: $y' = \dfrac{1}{x^2 + 1}$

Initial condition: $y = 0$ when $x = 0$.

Solution We find the solution's general shape (Example 9) and sketch the solution curve that passes through the point (0, 0) (Fig. 4.48).

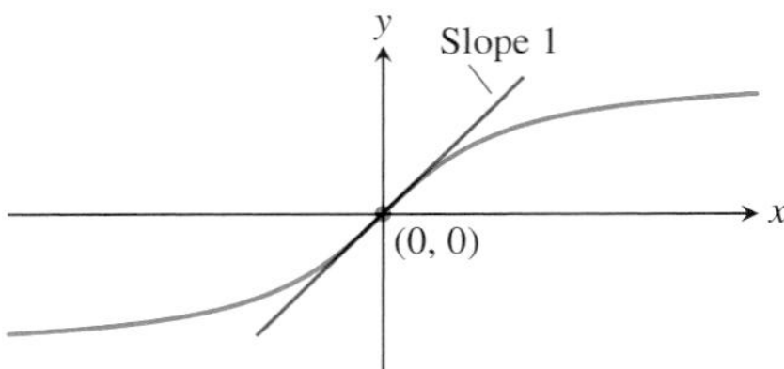

4.48 The solution curve in Example 10.

The technique we have learned for sketching solutions is particularly helpful when we are faced with an equation $dy/dx = f(x)$ that involves a function whose antiderivatives have no elementary formula. The antiderivatives of the function $f(x) = 1/(x^2 + 1)$ in Example 9 do have an elementary formula, as we will see in Chapter 6, but the antiderivatives of $g(x) = \sqrt{1 + x^4}$ do not. To solve the equation $dy/dx = \sqrt{1 + x^4}$, we must proceed either graphically or numerically.

Mathematical Modeling

The development of a mathematical model usually takes four steps: First we observe something in the real world (a ball bearing falling from rest or the trachea contracting during a cough, for example) and construct a system of mathematical variables and relationships that imitate some of its important features. We build a mathematical metaphor for what we see. Next we apply (usually) existing mathematics to the variables and relationships in the model to draw conclusions about them. After that we translate the mathematical conclusions into information about the system under study. Finally we check the information against observation to see if the model has predictive value. We also investigate the possibility that the model applies to other systems. The really good models are the ones that lead to conclusions that are consistent with observation, that have predictive value and broad application, and that are not too hard to use.

The natural cycle of mathematical imitation, deduction, interpretation, and comparison is shown in the diagrams on the following page.

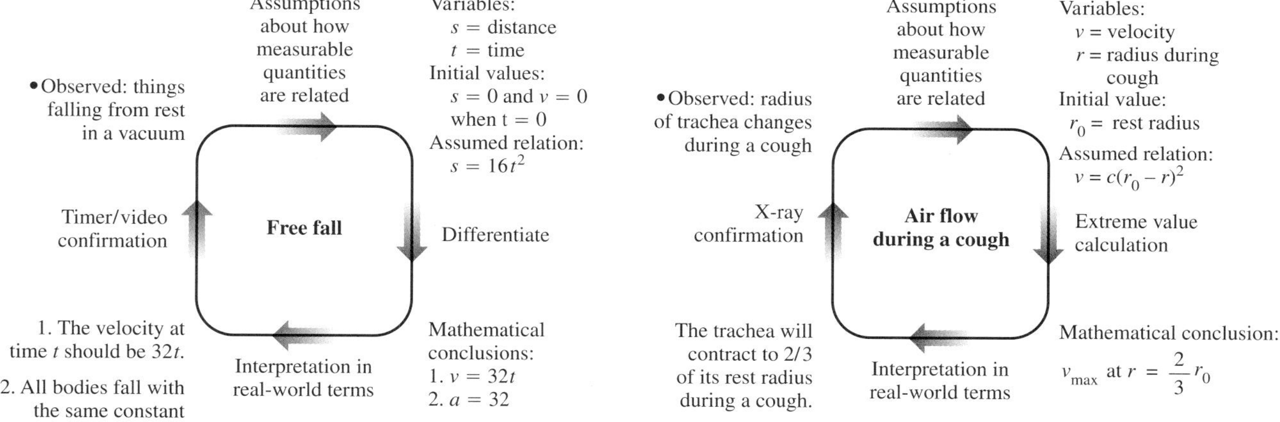

• Observed: things falling from rest in a vacuum
Assumptions about how measurable quantities are related
Variables: s = distance, t = time
Initial values: s = 0 and v = 0 when t = 0
Assumed relation: s = 16t²
Timer/video confirmation
Free fall
Differentiate
1. The velocity at time t should be 32t.
2. All bodies fall with the same constant acceleration: 32 ft/sec².
Interpretation in real-world terms
Mathematical conclusions:
1. v = 32t
2. a = 32
• Observed: radius of trachea changes during a cough
Assumptions about how measurable quantities are related
Variables: v = velocity, r = radius during cough
Initial value: r₀ = rest radius
Assumed relation: v = c(r₀ − r)²
X-ray confirmation
Air flow during a cough
Extreme value calculation
The trachea will contract to 2/3 of its rest radius during a cough.
Interpretation in real-world terms
Mathematical conclusion: v_max at r = (2/3)r₀

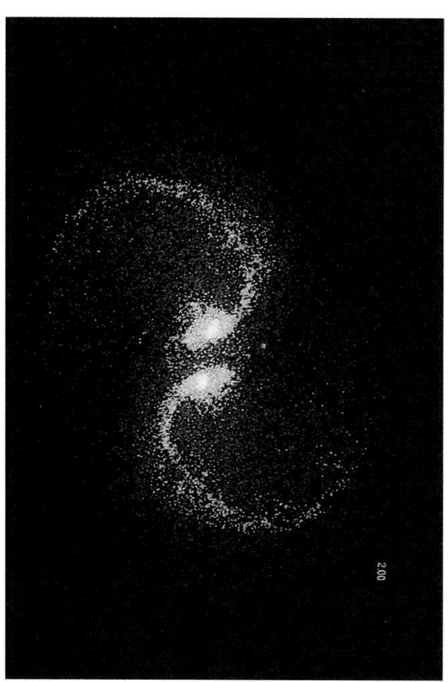
200

Computer Simulation

When a system we want to study is complicated, we can sometimes experiment first to see how the system behaves under different circumstances. But if this is not possible (the experiments might be expensive, time-consuming, or dangerous), we might run a series of simulated experiments on a computer — experiments that behave like the real thing, without the disadvantages. Thus we might model the effects of atomic war, the effect of waiting a year longer to harvest trees, the effect of crossing particular breeds of cattle, or the effect of reducing atmospheric ozone by 1%, all without having to pay the consequences or wait to see how things work out.

We also bring computers in when the model we want to use has too many calculations to be practical any other way. NASA's space flight models are run on computers — they have to be to generate course corrections on time. If you want to model the behavior of galaxies that contain billions and billions of stars, a computer offers the only possible way. One of the most spectacular computer simulations in recent years, carried out by Alar Toomre at MIT, explained a peculiar galactic shape that was not consistent with our previous ideas about how galaxies are formed. The galaxies had acquired their odd shapes, Toomre concluded, by passing through one another.

Models in Biology

You may have noticed that we haven't mentioned models in biology yet. The reason is that most mathematical models of life processes use either exponential functions or logarithms, functions that will not make their formal appearance until Chapter 6. Typical of the models we will study there is the model for unchecked bacterial growth. The basic assumption is that at any time t the rate dy/dt at which the population is changing is proportional to the number $y(t)$ of bacteria present. If the population's original size is y_0, this leads to the initial value problem

Differential equation: $\dfrac{dy}{dt} = ky$

Initial condition: $y = y_0$ when $t = 0$.

As you will see, the solution turns out to be $y = y_0 e^{kt}$, so the modeling cycle looks like this:

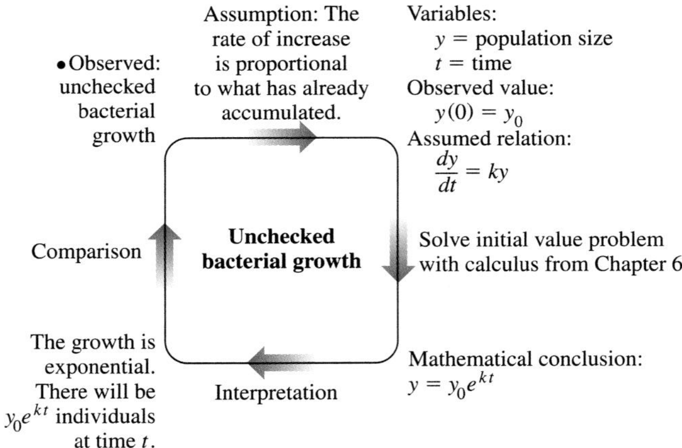

This model is one of the really good models we talked about earlier, because it applies to so many of the phenomena we want to forecast and understand: cell growth, heat transfer, radioactive decay, the flow of electrical current, and the accumulation of capital by compound interest, to mention only a few. We will see how all of this works by the time we are through with Chapter 6.

Exercises 4.7

Find the general antiderivatives of the functions in Exercises 1–18. Do as many as you can mentally.

1. **a)** $2x$ **b)** x^2 **c)** $x^2 - 2x + 1$

2. **a)** $6x$ **b)** x^7 **c)** $x^7 - 6x + 8$

3. **a)** $-3x^{-4}$ **b)** x^{-4} **c)** $x^{-4} + 2x + 3$

4. **a)** $2x^{-3}$ **b)** $\frac{x^{-3}}{2} + x^2$ **c)** $-x^{-3} + x - 1$

5. **a)** $\frac{1}{x^2}$ **b)** $\frac{5}{x^2}$ **c)** $2 - \frac{5}{x^2}$

6. **a)** $-\frac{2}{x^3}$ **b)** $\frac{1}{2x^3}$ **c)** $x^3 - \frac{1}{x^3}$

7. **a)** $\frac{3}{2}\sqrt{x}$ **b)** $\frac{1}{2\sqrt{x}}$ **c)** $\sqrt{x} + \frac{1}{\sqrt{x}}$

8. **a)** $\frac{4}{3}\sqrt[3]{x}$ **b)** $\frac{1}{3\sqrt[3]{x}}$ **c)** $\sqrt[3]{x} + \frac{1}{\sqrt[3]{x}}$

9. **a)** $\frac{2}{3}x^{-1/3}$ **b)** $\frac{1}{3}x^{-2/3}$ **c)** $-\frac{1}{3}x^{-4/3}$

10. **a)** $\frac{1}{2}x^{-1/2}$ **b)** $-\frac{1}{2}x^{-3/2}$ **c)** $-\frac{3}{2}x^{-5/2}$

11. **a)** $-\pi \sin \pi x$ **b)** $3 \sin x$ **c)** $\sin \pi x - 3 \sin 3x$

12. **a)** $\pi \cos \pi x$ **b)** $\frac{\pi}{2} \cos \frac{\pi x}{2}$ **c)** $\cos \frac{\pi x}{2} + \pi \cos x$

13. **a)** $\sec^2 x$ **b)** $\frac{2}{3} \sec^2 \frac{x}{3}$ **c)** $-\sec^2 \frac{3x}{2}$

14. **a)** $\csc^2 x$ **b)** $-\frac{3}{2} \csc^2 \frac{3x}{2}$ **c)** $1 - 8 \csc^2 2x$

15. **a)** $\csc x \cot x$ **b)** $-\csc 5x \cot 5x$ **c)** $-\pi \csc \frac{\pi x}{2} \cot \frac{\pi x}{2}$

16. **a)** $\sec x \tan x$ **b)** $4 \sec 3x \tan 3x$ **c)** $\sec \frac{\pi x}{2} \tan \frac{\pi x}{2}$

17. $(\sin x - \cos x)^2$ (*Hint:* $2 \sin x \cos x = \sin 2x$)

18. $(1 + 2 \cos x)^2$ (*Hint:* $2 \cos^2 x = 1 + \cos 2x$)

19. Suppose that $1 - \sqrt{x}$ is an antiderivative of $f(x)$ and that $x + 2$ is an antiderivative of $g(x)$. Find the *general* antiderivatives of the following functions.

a) $f(x)$ **b)** $g(x)$
c) $-f(x)$ **d)** $-g(x)$
e) $f(x) + g(x)$ **f)** $3f(x) - 2g(x)$
g) $x + f(x)$ **h)** $g(x) - 4$

20. Repeat Exercise 19, assuming that e^x is an antiderivative of $f(x)$ and that $x \sin x$ is an antiderivative of $g(x)$.

21. Which of the following graphs shows the solution of the initial value problem

$$\frac{dy}{dx} = 2x, \quad y = 4 \text{ when } x = 1?$$

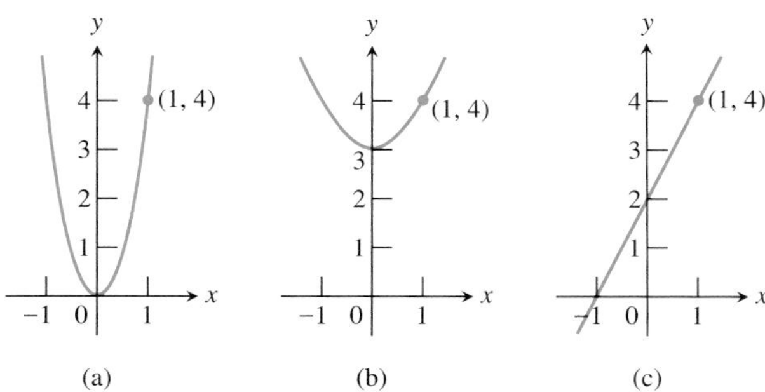

Give reasons for your answer.

22. Which of the following graphs shows the solution of the initial value problem

$$\frac{dy}{dx} = -x, \quad y = 1 \text{ when } x = -1?$$

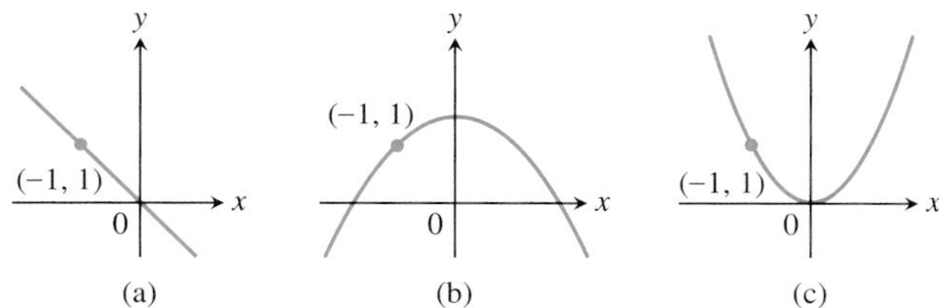

Give reasons for your answer.

Solve the initial value problems in Exercises 23–42.

23. $\dfrac{dy}{dx} = 2x - 7, \quad y = 0$ when $x = 2$

24. $\dfrac{dy}{dx} = 10 - x, \quad y = -1$ when $x = 0$

25. $\dfrac{dy}{dx} = \dfrac{1}{x^2} + x, \quad x > 0; \quad y = 1$ when $x = 2$

26. $\dfrac{dy}{dx} = 9x^2 - 4x + 5, \quad y = 0$ when $x = -1$

27. $\dfrac{dy}{dx} = 3\sqrt{x}, \quad y = 4$ when $x = 9$

28. $\dfrac{dy}{dx} = \dfrac{1}{2\sqrt{x}}, \quad y = 0$ when $x = 4$

29. $\dfrac{ds}{dt} = 1 + \cos t, \quad s = 4$ when $t = 0$

30. $\dfrac{ds}{dt} = \cos t + \sin t, \quad s = 1$ when $t = \pi$

31. $\dfrac{dr}{d\theta} = -\pi \sin \pi\theta, \quad r = 0$ when $\theta = 0$

32. $\dfrac{dr}{d\theta} = \cos \pi\theta, \quad r = 1$ when $\theta = 0$

33. $\dfrac{dv}{dt} = \dfrac{1}{2} \sec t \tan t, \quad v = 1$ when $t = 0$

34. $\dfrac{dv}{dt} = 8t + \csc^2 t, \quad v = -7$ when $t = \dfrac{\pi}{2}$

35. $\dfrac{d^2y}{dx^2} = 2 - 6x, \quad \dfrac{dy}{dx} = 4$ and $y = 1$ when $x = 0$

36. $\dfrac{d^2y}{dx^2} = 0, \quad \dfrac{dy}{dx} = 2$ and $y = 0$ when $x = 0$

37. $\dfrac{d^2r}{dt^2} = \dfrac{2}{t^3}, \quad \dfrac{dr}{dt} = 1$ and $r = 1$ when $t = 1$

38. $\dfrac{d^2s}{dt^2} = \dfrac{3t}{8}, \quad \dfrac{ds}{dt} = 3$ and $s = 4$ when $t = 4$

39. $\dfrac{d^3y}{dx^3} = 6; \quad \dfrac{d^2y}{dx^2} = -8, \quad \dfrac{dy}{dx} = 0$, and $y = 5$ when $x = 0$

40. $\dfrac{d^3\theta}{dt^3} = 0; \quad \dfrac{d^2\theta}{dt^2} = -2, \quad \dfrac{d\theta}{dt} = -\dfrac{1}{2}$, and $\theta = \sqrt{2}$ when $t = 0$

41. $y^{(4)} = -\sin t + \cos t; \quad y''' = 7, \ y'' = -1, \ y' = -1$, and $y = 0$ when $t = 0$

42. $y^{(4)} = -\cos x + 8 \sin 2x; \quad y''' = 0, \ y'' = 1, \ y' = 1$, and $y = 3$ when $x = 0$

Exercises 43–46 give the velocity $v = ds/dt$ and initial position of a body moving along a coordinate line. Find the body's position at time t.

43. $v = 9.8t + 5, \quad s = 10$ when $t = 0$

44. $v = 32t - 2, \quad s = 4$ when $t = 1/2$

45. $v = \sin \pi t, \quad s = 0$ when $t = 0$

46. $v = \dfrac{2}{\pi} \cos \dfrac{2t}{\pi}, \quad s = 1$ when $t = \pi^2$

Exercises 47–50 give the acceleration $a = d^2s/dt^2$, initial velocity, and initial position of a body moving on a coordinate line. Find the body's position at time t.

47. $a = 32, \quad v = 20$ and $s = 5$ when $t = 0$

48. $a = 9.8, \quad v = -3$ and $s = 0$ when $t = 0$

49. $a = -4 \sin 2t, \quad v = 2$ and $s = -3$ when $t = 0$

50. $a = \dfrac{9}{\pi^2} \cos \dfrac{3t}{\pi}, \quad v = 0$ and $s = -1$ when $t = 0$

51. Find the curve in the xy-plane that passes through the point (9, 4) and whose slope at each point is $3\sqrt{x}$.

52. **a)** Find a function $y = f(x)$ with the following properties:

i) $\dfrac{d^2y}{dx^2} = 6x$

ii) Its graph in the xy-plane passes through the point (0, 1) and has a horizontal tangent there.

b) How many functions like this are there? How do you know? Give reasons for your answer.

53. *Revenue from Marginal Revenue.* Suppose that the marginal revenue when x thousand units are sold is

$$\frac{dr}{dx} = 3x^2 - 6x + 12$$

dollars per unit. Find the revenue function $r(x)$ if $r(0) = 0$.

54. *Cost from Marginal Cost.* Suppose that the marginal cost of manufacturing an item when x thousand items are produced is

$$\frac{dc}{dx} = 3x^2 - 12x + 15$$

dollars per item. Find the cost function $c(x)$ if $c(0) = 400$.

55. On the moon the acceleration of gravity is 1.6 m/sec^2. If a rock is dropped into a crevasse, how fast will it be going just before it hits bottom 30 sec later?

56. A rocket lifts off the surface of Earth with a constant acceleration of 20 m/sec^2. How fast will the rocket be going 1 min later?

57. With approximately what velocity do you enter the water if you dive from a 10-m platform? (Use $g = 9.8$ m/sec^2.)

58. The acceleration of gravity near the surface of Mars is 3.72 m/sec^2. If a rock is blasted straight up from the surface with an initial velocity of 93 m/sec (about 208 mph), how high does it go? (*Hint:* When is the velocity zero?)

59. *How Long Will It Take a Tank to Drain?* If we open a valve to drain the water from a cylindrical tank, the water will flow fast when the tank is full but slow down as the tank drains. It turns out that the rate at which the water level drops is proportional to the square root of the water's depth. In the notation of the accompanying figure, this means that

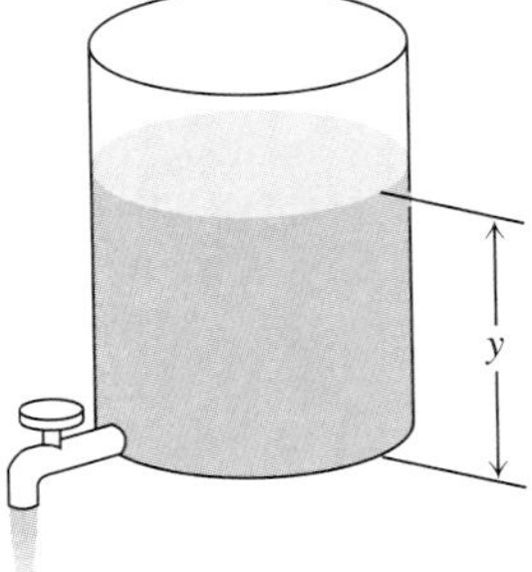

$$\frac{dy}{dt} = -k\sqrt{y}. \qquad (5)$$

The value of k depends on the acceleration of gravity, the shape of the hole, the fluid, and the cross-section areas of the tank and drain hole. Equation (5) has a minus sign because y decreases with time. To solve Eq. (5), rewrite it as

$$\frac{1}{\sqrt{y}}\frac{dy}{dt} = -k \qquad (6)$$

and carry out the following steps.

a) Find the general antiderivative of each side of Eq. (6).
b) Set the antiderivatives in (a) equal and combine their arbitrary constants into a single arbitrary constant. (Nothing is achieved by having two when one will do.) This will give an equation that relates y directly to t.
c) Suppose t is measured in minutes and $k = 1/10$. Find y as a function of t if $y = 9$ ft when $t = 0$. How long does it take the tank to drain if the water is 9 ft deep to start with?

60. *Stopping a Car in Time.* You are driving along a highway at a steady 60 mph (88 ft/sec) when you see an accident ahead and slam on the brakes. What constant deceleration is required to stop your car in 242 ft? To find out, carry out the following steps.

STEP 1: Solve the initial value problem

Differential equation: $\dfrac{d^2s}{dt^2} = -k \quad (k \text{ constant})$

Initial conditions: $\dfrac{ds}{dt} = 88$ and $s = 0$ when $t = 0$.

Measuring time and distance from when the brakes are applied

STEP 2: Find the value of t that makes $ds/dt = 0$. (The answer will involve k.)

STEP 3: Find the value of k that makes $s = 242$ for the value of t you found in Step 2.

61. *The Hammer and the Feather.* When *Apollo 15* astronaut David Scott dropped a hammer and a feather on the moon to demonstrate that in a vacuum all bodies fall with the same (constant) acceleration, he dropped them from about 4 ft above the ground. The television footage of the event shows the hammer and feather falling more slowly than on Earth, where, in a vacuum, they would have taken only half a second to fall the 4 ft. How long did it take the hammer and feather to fall 4 ft on the moon? To find out, solve the following initial value problem for s as a function of t. Then find the value of t that makes s equal 0.

Differential equation: $\dfrac{d^2s}{dt^2} = -5.2 \text{ ft/sec}^2$

Initial conditions: $\dfrac{ds}{dt} = 0$ and $s = 4$ when $t = 0$

62. *Height Above Ground*

a) Find a formula for the height s of an object released from rest to fall freely from s_0 units above the surface of a planet where the acceleration of gravity is g length-units/sec^2 by solving the following initial value problem.

Differential equation: $\dfrac{d^2s}{dt^2} = -g$

Initial conditions: $\dfrac{ds}{dt} = 0$ and $s = s_0$ when $t = 0$

b) On Mars, $g = 1.86$ m/sec^2. If you drop a hammer from an elevation of 4 ft (1.22 m), how long does it take to hit the ground?

63. *Finding Displacement from an Antiderivative of Velocity*

a) Suppose that the velocity of a body moving along the s-axis is

$$\frac{ds}{dt} = v = 9.8t - 3.$$

1) Find the body's displacement from $t = 1$ to $t = 3$ given that $s = 5$ when $t = 0$.

2) Find the body's displacement from $t = 1$ to $t = 3$ given that $s = -2$ when $t = 0$.

3) Now find the body's displacement from $t = 1$ to $t = 3$ given that $s = s_0$ when $t = 0$.

b) Suppose the position s of a body moving along a coordinate line is a differentiable function of time t. Is it true that once you know an antiderivative of the velocity function ds/dt you can find the body's displacement from $t = a$ to $t = b$ even if you do not know the body's exact position at either of those times? Give reasons for your answer.

64. *Uniqueness of Solutions.* Are the solutions of initial value problems unique? That is, if differentiable functions $y = F(x)$ and $y = G(x)$ both solve the initial value problem

Differential equation: $\dfrac{dy}{dx} = f(x)$

Initial condition: $y = y_0$ when $x = x_0$

must $F(x) = G(x)$ for every x? Give reasons for your answer.

Use the technique described in Example 9 to sketch the solutions of the differential equations in Exercises 65–68. Then solve the equations to check on how well you did.

65. $\dfrac{dy}{dx} = 2x$

66. $\dfrac{dy}{dx} = -2x + 2$

67. $\dfrac{dy}{dx} = 1 - 3x^2$

68. $\dfrac{dy}{dx} = x^2$

Use the technique described in Examples 9 and 10 to sketch some of the solutions of the initial value problems in Exercises 69–72.

69. $\dfrac{dy}{dx} = \dfrac{1}{\sqrt{1 - x^2}}, \quad -1 < x < 1; \quad y = 0$ when $x = 0$

70. $\dfrac{dy}{dx} = \sqrt{1 + x^4}, \quad y = 1$ when $x = 0$

71. $\dfrac{dy}{dx} = \dfrac{1}{x^2 + 1} - 1, \quad y = 1$ when $x = 0$

72. $\dfrac{dy}{dx} = \dfrac{x}{x^2 + 1}, \quad y = 0$ when $x = 0$

Writing for Your Own Knowledge

Answer the following questions in writing. Some answers will take only a sentence or two; others may require several paragraphs. Some explanations may also call for graphs or sketches.

1. What is an antiderivative? a general antiderivative?
2. How does knowing one of a function's antiderivatives help you find the others?
3. How do you find antiderivatives?
4. How can you solve an initial value problem
$$\frac{dy}{dx} = f(x), \quad y = y_0 \text{ when } x = x_0$$
when you know an antiderivative of $f(x)$?
5. How can you sometimes sketch the solution curves of a differential equation $dy/dx = f(x)$ when you cannot find an antiderivative of f?

EXPLORER PROGRAM

Slope Fields — Graphs solutions of the initial value problem $y' = f(x, y)$, $y(x_0) = y_0$. You can see the effect of changing x_0 and y_0 by graphing different solutions together.

For Your Review

Write brief paragraphs about the following topics and give examples.

How to recognize and solve related rate problems
Local and absolute maxima and minima of functions
  Definitions
  Relation to continuity
  Relation to first and second derivatives
The first derivative test for increasing and decreasing
How y' and y'' determine the shape of a function's graph
Graphing rational functions
Optimization
Maximizing profit and minimizing average cost in economics
Rolle's theorem
The Mean Value Theorem
  Statement
  Geometric interpretation
  Corollaries
Finding antiderivatives
Differential equations and initial value problems
Sketching solutions of differential equations and initial value problems
Mathematical modeling

Practice Exercises

1. The total surface area S of a right circular cylinder is related to the base radius r and height h by the equation $S = 2\pi r^2 + 2\pi rh$.
   a) How is dS/dt related to dr/dt if h is constant?
   b) How is dS/dt related to dh/dt if r is constant?
   c) How is dS/dt related to dr/dt and dh/dt if neither r nor h is constant?
   d) How is dr/dt related to dh/dt if S is constant?
2. The lateral surface area S of a right circular cone is related to the base radius r and height h by the equation $S = \pi r\sqrt{r^2 + h^2}$.
   a) How is dS/dt related to dr/dt if h is constant?
   b) How is dS/dt related to dh/dt if r is constant?
   c) How is dS/dt related to dr/dt and dh/dt if neither r nor h is constant?
3. The radius of a circle is changing at the rate of $-2/\pi$ m/sec. At what rate is the circle's area changing when $r = 10$ m?
4. The volume of a cube is increasing at the rate of 1200 cm³/min at the instant its edges are 20 cm long. At what rate are the edges changing at that instant?
5. If two resistors of R_1 and R_2 ohms are connected in parallel in an electric circuit to make an R-ohm resistor, the value of R can be found from the equation

$$\frac{1}{R} = \frac{1}{R_1} + \frac{1}{R_2}.$$

If R_1 is decreasing at the rate of 1 ohm/sec and R_2 is increasing at the rate of 0.5 ohm/sec, at what rate is R changing when $R_1 = 75$ ohms and $R_2 = 50$ ohms?

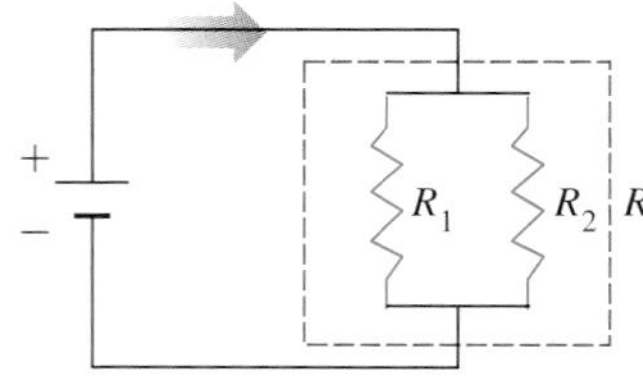

6. The impedance Z (ohms) in a series circuit is related to the resistance R (ohms) and reactance X (ohms) by the equation $Z = \sqrt{R^2 + X^2}$. If R is increasing at 3 ohms/sec and X is decreasing at 2 ohms/sec, at what rate is Z changing when $R = 10$ ohms and $X = 20$ ohms?
7. The coordinates of a particle moving in the metric xy-plane are differentiable functions of time t with $dx/dt = -1$ m/sec and $dy/dt = -5$ m/sec. How fast is the particle approaching the origin as it passes through the point (5, 12)?
8. A particle moves along the curve $y = x^{3/2}$ in the first quadrant in such a way that its distance from the origin increases at the rate of 11 units per second. Find dx/dt when $x = 3$.
9. Water drains from the conical tank shown here at the rate of 5 ft³/min. (a) What is the relation between the variables h and r in the figure? (b) How fast is the water level dropping when $h = 6$ ft?

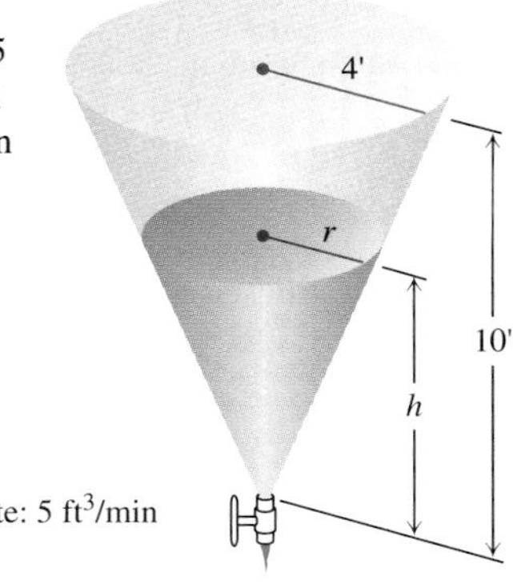

10. Two cars are approaching an intersection along straight highways that cross at right angles, car A moving at 36 mph and car B at 50 mph. At what rate is the straight-line distance between the cars changing when car A is 5 mi and car B is 12 mi from the intersection?

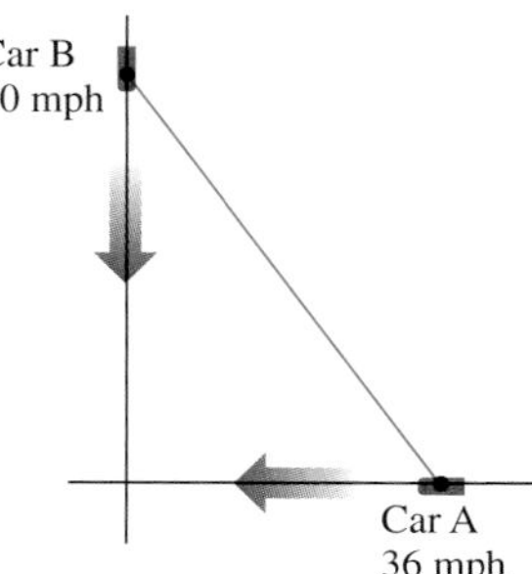

11. You are videotaping a race from a stand 132 ft from the track, following a car that is traveling at 180 mph (264 ft/sec). How fast will your camera angle θ be changing when the car is right in front of you? a half-second later?

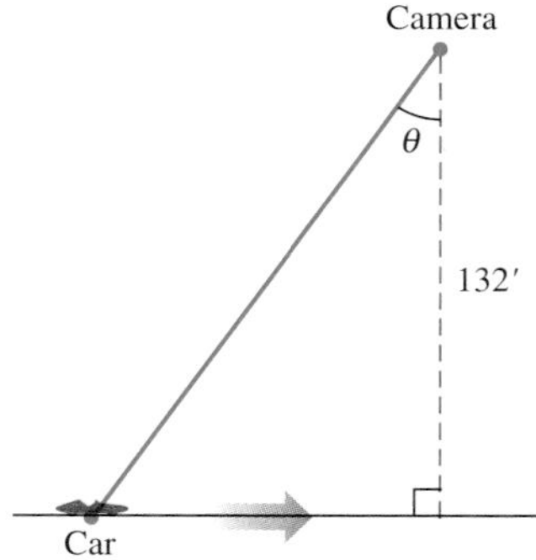

12. As television cable is pulled from a large spool to be strung from the telephone poles along a street, it unwinds from the spool in layers of constant radius. If the truck pulling the cable moves at a steady 6 ft/sec (a touch over 4 mph), use the equa-

tion $s = r\theta$ to find how fast (rad/sec) the spool is turning when the layer of radius 1.2 ft is being unwound.

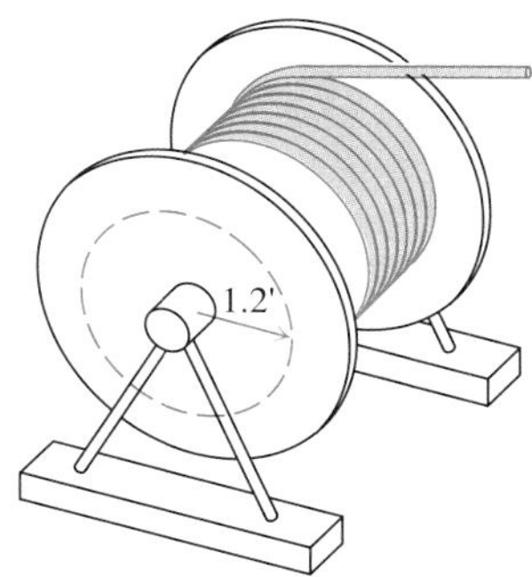

13. Does $f(x) = x^3 + 2x + \tan x$ have any local maximum or minimum values? Give reasons for your answer.

14. Does $g(x) = \csc x + 2 \cot x$ have any local maximum values? Give reasons for your answer.

15. a) Show that $g(t) = \sin^2 t - 3t$ decreases on every interval in its domain.
    b) How many solutions does the equation $\sin^2 t - 3t = 5$ have? Give reasons for your answer.

16. a) Show that $y = \tan \theta$ increases on every interval in its domain.
    b) If the conclusion in (a) is really correct, how do you explain the fact that $\tan(\pi) = 0$ is less than $\tan(\pi/4) = 1$?

17. Is it true that a discontinuous function cannot have both an absolute maximum and an absolute minimum value on a closed interval? Give reasons for your answer.

18. Can you conclude anything about the extreme values of a continuous function on an open interval? on a half-open interval? Give reasons for your answer.

19. The greatest integer function $f(x) = \lfloor x \rfloor$, defined for all values of x, assumes a local maximum value of 0 at each point of $[0, 1)$. Could any of these local maximum values also be local minimum values of f? Give reasons for your answer.

20. a) Give an example of a differentiable function f whose first derivative is zero at some point c even though f has neither a local maximum nor local minimum at c.
    b) How is this consistent with Theorem 2 in Section 4.2? Give reasons for your answer.

Graph the curves in Exercises 21–30.

21. $y = x^2 - (x^3/6)$
22. $y = x^3 - 3x^2 + 3$
23. $y = -x^3 + 6x^2 - 9x + 3$
24. $y = (1/8)(x^3 + 3x^2 - 9x - 27)$
25. $y = x^3(8 - x)$
26. $y = x^2(2x^2 - 9)$
27. $y = x - 3x^{2/3}$
28. $y = x^{1/3}(x - 4)$
29. $y = x\sqrt{3 - x}$
30. $y = x\sqrt{4 - x^2}$

Each of Exercises 31–36 gives the first derivative of a function $y = f(x)$. (a) At what points, if any, does the graph of f have a local maximum, local minimum, or inflection point? (b) Sketch the general shape of the graph.

31. $y' = 16 - x^2$
32. $y' = x^2 - x - 6$
33. $y' = 6x(x + 1)(x - 2)$
34. $y' = x^2(6 - 4x)$
35. $y' = x^4 - 2x^2$
36. $y' = 4x^2 - x^4$

Each of the graphs in Exercises 37 and 38 is the graph of the position function $s = f(t)$ of a body moving on a coordinate line (t represents time). At approximately what times (if any) is each body's (a) velocity equal to zero? (b) acceleration equal to zero? During approximately what time intervals does the body move (c) forward? (d) backward?

37.
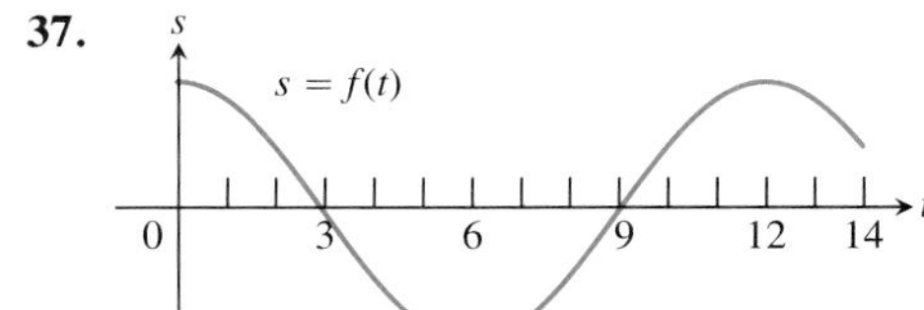

38.
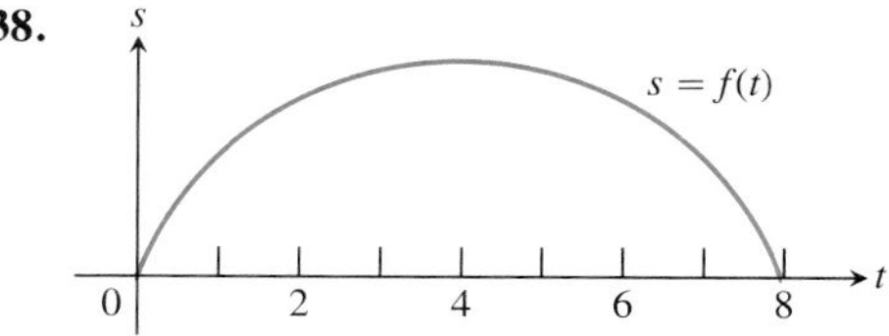

39. At which of the five points on the graph of $y = f(x)$ shown here (a) are y' and y'' both negative? (b) is y' negative and y'' positive?

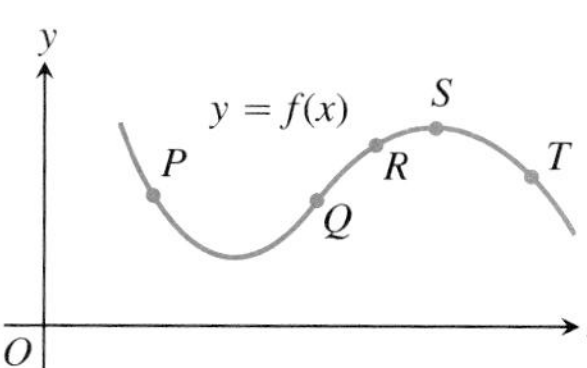

40. On approximately what day did the growth rate of the fruit fly population of Fig. 3.39, page 151, change from increasing to decreasing?

In Exercises 41–44, graph each function. Then use the function's first derivative to explain what you see.

41. $y = x^{2/3} + (x - 1)^{1/3}$
42. $y = x^{2/3} + (x - 1)^{2/3}$
43. $y = x^{1/3} + (x - 1)^{1/3}$
44. $y = x^{2/3} - (x - 1)^{1/3}$

Sketch the graphs of the functions in Exercises 45–52.

45. $y = \dfrac{x + 1}{x - 3}$
46. $y = \dfrac{2x}{x + 5}$
47. $y = \dfrac{x^2 + 1}{x}$
48. $y = \dfrac{x^2 - x + 1}{x}$
49. $y = \dfrac{x^3 + 2}{2x}$
50. $y = \dfrac{x^4 - 1}{x^2}$

51. $y = \dfrac{x^2 - 4}{x^2 - 3}$

52. $y = \dfrac{x^2}{x^2 - 4}$

Using the graphs of the dominant terms as a guide, sketch the graphs of the equations in Exercises 53 and 54.

53. $y = \csc x - \dfrac{1}{x^2}, \quad 0 < x < \pi$

54. $y = \tan x - \dfrac{2}{x}, \quad -\dfrac{\pi}{2} < x < 0$

55. Use the following information to find the values of a, b, and c in the formula $f(x) = (x + a)/(bx^2 + cx + 2)$.

i) The values of a, b, and c are either 0 or 1.
ii) The graph of f passes through the point $(-1, 0)$.
iii) The line $y = 1$ is an asymptote of the graph of f.

56. For what value or values of the constant k will the curve $y = x^3 + kx^2 + 3x - 4$ have exactly one horizontal tangent?

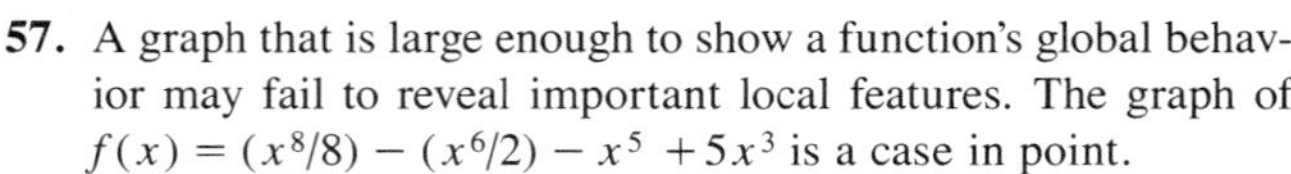

57. A graph that is large enough to show a function's global behavior may fail to reveal important local features. The graph of $f(x) = (x^8/8) - (x^6/2) - x^5 + 5x^3$ is a case in point.

a) Graph f over the interval $-2.5 \le x \le 2.5$. Where does the graph appear to have local extreme values or points of inflection?

b) Now factor $f'(x)$ and show that f has a local maximum at $x = \sqrt[3]{5} \approx 1.70998$ and local minima at $x = \pm\sqrt{3} \approx \pm 1.73205$.

c) Zoom in on the graph to find a viewing window that shows the presence of the extreme values at $x = \sqrt[3]{5}$ and $x = \sqrt{3}$.

The moral here is that without calculus the existence of two of the three extreme values would probably have gone unnoticed. On any normal graph of the function, the values would lie close enough together to fall within the dimensions of a single pixel on the screen.

(*Source: Uses of Technology in the Mathematics Curriculum* by Benny Evans and Jerry Johnson, Oklahoma State University, published in 1990 under National Science Foundation Grant USE-8950044.)

58. *Continuation of Exercise 57.*

a) Graph $f(x) = (x^8/8) - (2/5)x^5 - 5x - (5/x^2) + 11$ over the interval $-2 \le x \le 2$. Where does the graph appear to have local extreme values or points of inflection?

b) Show that f has a local maximum value at $x = \sqrt[7]{5} \approx 1.2585$ and a local minimum value at $x = \sqrt[3]{2} \approx 1.2599$.

c) Zoom in to find a viewing window that shows the presence of the extreme values at $x = \sqrt[7]{5}$ and $x = \sqrt[3]{2}$.

59. The sum of two nonnegative numbers is 36. Find the numbers if (a) the difference of their square roots is to be as large as possible, (b) the sum of their square roots is to be as large as possible.

60. Find the largest product you can get from two nonnegative numbers whose sum is 36. What are the numbers?

61. If the perimeter of the circular sector shown here is 100 ft, what values of r and s will give the sector its greatest area?

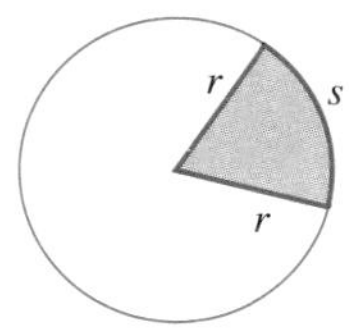

62. An isosceles triangle has its vertex at the origin and its base parallel to the x-axis with the vertices above the axis on the curve $y = 27 - x^2$. Find the largest area the triangle can have.

63. Find the dimensions of the largest open storage bin with a square base and vertical sides that can be made from 108 ft^2 of sheet steel. (Neglect the thickness of the steel and assume there is no waste.)

64. A customer has asked you to design an open-top rectangular stainless steel vat. It is to have a square base and a volume of 32 ft^3, to be welded from quarter-inch plate, and to weigh no more than necessary. What dimensions do you recommend?

65. Find the height and radius of the largest right circular cylinder that can be put in a sphere of radius $\sqrt{3}$.

66. The figure below shows two right circular cones, one upside down inside the other. The two bases are parallel, and the vertex of the smaller cone lies at the center of the larger cone's base. What values of r and h will give the smaller cone the largest possible volume?

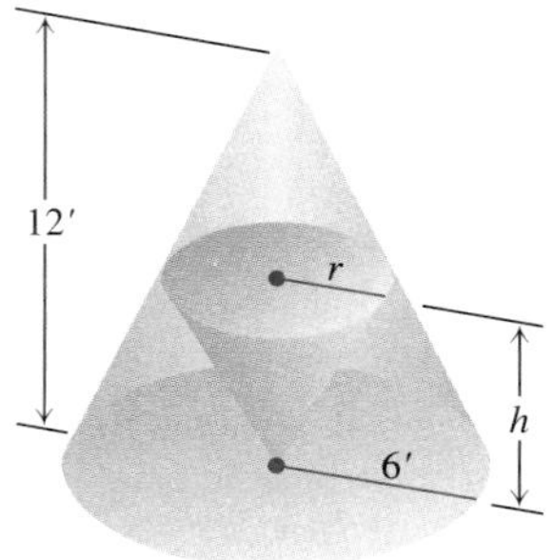

67. A drilling rig 12 mi offshore is to be connected by a pipe to a refinery onshore, 20 mi down the coast from the rig. If underwater pipe costs \$50,000 per mile and land-based pipe costs \$30,000 per mile, what values of x and y give the least expensive connection?

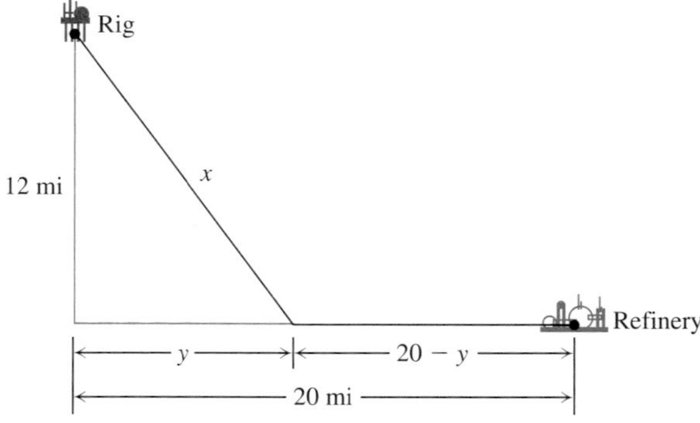

68. An athletic field is to be built in the shape of a rectangle x units long capped by semicircular regions of radius r at the two ends. The field is to be bounded by a 400-m racetrack. What values of x and r give the rectangle the largest possible area?

69. Your company can manufacture x hundred grade A tires and y hundred grade B tires a day, where $0 \le x \le 4$ and

$$y = \frac{40 - 10x}{5 - x}.$$

Your profit on grade A tires is twice your profit on grade B tires. Find the most profitable number of each kind of tire to make.

70. Suppose a manufacturer can sell x items a week for a revenue of $r = 200x - 0.01x^2$ cents, and it costs $c = 50x + 20{,}000$ cents to make x items. Is there a most profitable number of items to make each week? If so, what is it? Explain.

71. **a)** Show that the equation $x^4 + 2x - 2 = 0$ has exactly one solution on $[0, 1]$.

b) Find the solution to five decimal places graphically.

c) SOLVER Find the solution to 5 places numerically.

72. What is the most f can increase on $[0, 6]$ if $f'(x) \le 2$ for all x?

73. The formula $F(x) = 3x + C$ gives a different function for each value of C. All of these functions, however, have the same derivative with respect to x, namely $F'(x) = 3$. Are these the only differentiable functions whose derivative is 3? Could there be any others? Give reasons for your answers.

74. Show that

$$\frac{d}{dx}\left(\frac{x}{x+1}\right) = \frac{d}{dx}\left(-\frac{1}{x+1}\right)$$

even though

$$\frac{x}{x+1} \ne -\frac{1}{x+1}.$$

Doesn't this contradict Corollary 2 of the Mean Value Theorem? Give reasons for your answer.

75. Find the general antiderivatives of the following functions.

a) 0 **b)** x **c)** x^{10}
d) x^{-5} **e)** $x^{4/3}$ **f)** $x^{-3/7}$
g) $\sin x$ **h)** $\sec^2 x$ **i)** $\sec x \tan x$

76. Find the general antiderivatives of the following functions.

a) 1 **b)** x^2 **c)** x^{-2}
d) $x^{3/4}$ **e)** $x^{-1/2}$ **f)** $x^{-7/3}$
g) $\cos x$ **h)** $-\csc^2 x$ **i)** $-\csc x \cot x$

Find the general antiderivatives of the functions in Exercises 77–92.

77. $3x^2 + 5x - 7$

78. $\dfrac{1}{x^2} + x + 1$

79. $\sqrt{x} + \dfrac{1}{\sqrt{x}}$

80. $\sqrt[3]{x} + \sqrt[4]{x}$

81. $\sqrt{5}\cos\sqrt{5}\,x + 8\sin\dfrac{x}{2}$

82. $\cos\dfrac{3x}{2} - \sin \pi x$

83. $\sqrt{t} + 5\cos 2t$

84. $\sin 2t - 2\sin t + 1$

85. $3\sec^2 x - \dfrac{1}{x^2}$

86. $9 - 4\csc^2 2x$

87. $\sec\dfrac{\theta}{3}\tan\dfrac{\theta}{3} + 5$

88. $\theta - \csc 2\theta \cot 2\theta$

89. $\tan^2 x$ (*Hint:* $\tan^2 x = \sec^2 x - 1$)

90. $\cot^2 x$ (*Hint:* $\cot^2 x = \csc^2 x - 1$)

91. $2\sin^2 x$ (*Hint:* $2\sin^2 x = 1 - \cos 2x$)

92. $\cos^2 x - \sin^2 x$ (*Hint:* $\cos^2 x - \sin^2 x = \cos 2x$)

Solve the initial value problems in Exercises 93–98.

93. $\dfrac{dy}{dx} = 1 + x + \dfrac{x^2}{2}, \quad y = 1$ when $x = 0$

94. $\dfrac{dy}{dx} = 4x^3 - 21x^2 + 14x - 7, \quad y = 1$ when $x = 1$

95. $\dfrac{dy}{dx} = \dfrac{x^2 + 1}{x^2}, \quad y = -1$ when $x = 1$

96. $\dfrac{dy}{dx} = \left(x + \dfrac{1}{x}\right)^2, \quad y = 1$ when $x = 1$

97. $\dfrac{d^2y}{dx^2} = -\sin x, \quad y = 0$ and $\dfrac{dy}{dx} = 1$ when $x = 0$

98. $\dfrac{d^2y}{dx^2} = \cos x, \quad y = -1$ and $\dfrac{dy}{dx} = 0$ when $x = 0$

99. Does any function $y = f(x)$ satisfy all of the following conditions? If so, what is it? If not, why not? Explain.

i) $d^2y/dx^2 = 0$ for all x
ii) $dy/dx = 1$ when $x = 0$
iii) $y = 0$ when $x = 0$

100. Find an equation for the curve in the xy-plane that passes through the point $(1, -1)$ if its slope at x is always $3x^2 + 2$.

101. You sling a shovelful of dirt up from the bottom of a 17-ft hole with an initial velocity of 32 ft/sec. Is that enough speed to get the dirt out of the hole, or had you better duck? Give reasons for your answer.

102. The acceleration of a particle moving along a coordinate line is $d^2s/dt^2 = 2 + 6t$ m/sec². At $t = 0$, the velocity is 4 m/sec. Find the velocity as a function of t. Then find how far the particle moves during the first second of its trip, from $t = 0$ to $t = 1$.

103. Suppose that $f(1) = g(1)$ and that $f'(x) = g'(x)$ for all x. How must f and g be related? Give reasons for your answer.

104. Suppose that $f(1) = -1$, that $g(1) = 3$, and that $f'(x) = g'(x)$ for all x. How must f and g be related? Give reasons for your answer.

Sketch the solutions of the initial value problems in Exercises 105 and 106.

105. $\dfrac{dy}{dx} = 4 - \sqrt{x^2 + 3}, \quad y = 0$ when $x = 0$

106. $\dfrac{dy}{dx} = \sqrt{x^2 + 1} - 1, \quad y = 1$ when $x = 0$

MEASURING CARDIAC OUTPUT

DR. MARK C. RICK and his colleagues at the internationally renowned Alamo Pintado Equine Medical Center in Los Olivos, CA, routinely monitor cardiac output during operations that require gas anesthesia.

A horse's cardiac output (number of liters the heart pumps per minute) is one of the vital-sign measurements that provide guidance to anesthesiologists and surgeons during the course of an operation. The accompanying photograph (taken by Dr. Rick) shows Drs. Linda Lauper, Douglas Herthel, and John Moody during the final stages of leg-ligament surgery on a young Arabian horse.

Operations requiring cardiac monitoring might involve the removal of a bone chip from a joint, repairing a broken leg, abdominal exploration (why has the horse been losing weight in recent weeks?), or reproductive surgery.

Tooth removal and tumor removal requiring more than 20 or 30 minutes of general anesthesia would also go on the cardiac monitor.

Breeders and trainers may some day measure the cardiac outputs of prospective racehorses to see if they will be good racers.

Most animals do not have cardiac disease to the extent that people do, and the measurements of cardiac output in people tend more to be associated with assessing heart damage and measuring loss of heart function (Section 5.1).

5 Integration

OVERVIEW

The formula $d = rt$ (distance equals rate times time) for calculating distance traveled can be used only when the rate does not vary over the given time interval. If the rate does vary, we have to find the distance some other way. One way is to partition the time interval into short time intervals on which the rate remains fairly constant, use the formula $d = rt$ to make a reasonable estimate for each interval, and then add the results to estimate the distance for the entire trip. The more finely we partition the time interval, the better the estimate will be.

As the present chapter explains, the idea of estimating a final result by summing a finite number of close estimates made with a standard formula is the key to measuring all sorts of things. The new calculation formulas to which these summations lead, called integrals, are the formulas with which we find surface area, mass, the length of a space vehicle's trajectory, the future size of a population, and the amount of work it takes to move an object against a force that varies with time or position.

The mathematics of integrals is called *integral calculus.* Our shift from derivatives to finite sums and integrals may seem abrupt at this point, but the two are closely connected. The nature of the connection is the most important idea in the chapter, and its discovery by Leibniz and Newton still constitutes one of the greatest technical advances of modern times.

5.1 Estimating with Finite Sums

This section shows how practical questions can lead in a natural way to approximation by finite sums.

Distance Traveled

Suppose we know the velocity function $v = ds/dt = f(t)$ m/sec of a car moving down a highway and want to know how far the car will travel in the time interval $a \le t \le b$. If we know an antiderivative F of f, we can find the car's position function $s = F(t) + C$ and calculate the distance traveled as the difference between the car's positions at times $t = a$ and $t = b$ (as in Section 4.7, Exercise 63).

If we do not know an antiderivative of $v = f(t)$, we can approximate the answer with a sum in the following way. We partition $[a, b]$ into short time intervals *on each of which v is fairly constant.* Since velocity is the rate at which the car is traveling, we approximate the distance traveled on each time interval with the formula

$$\text{Distance} = \text{rate} \times \text{time} = f(t) \cdot \Delta t$$

and add the results across $[a, b]$. To be specific, suppose the partitioned interval looks like this

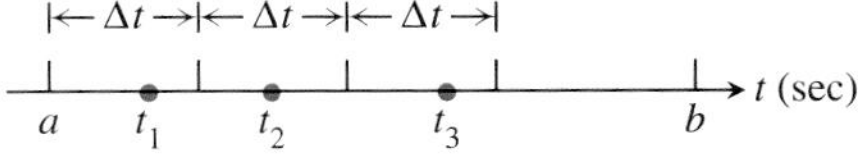

with the subintervals all of length Δt. Let t_1 be a point in the first subinterval. If the interval is short enough so the rate is almost constant, the car will move about $f(t_1)\,\Delta t$ m during that interval. If t_2 is a point in the second interval, the car will move an additional $f(t_2)\,\Delta t$ m during that interval, and so on. The sum of these products approximates the total distance S traveled from $t = a$ to $t = b$. If we use n subintervals, then

$$S \approx f(t_1)\,\Delta t + f(t_2)\,\Delta t + \cdots + f(t_n)\,\Delta t. \tag{1}$$

Let's try this on the projectile in Example 8, Section 4.7. The projectile was fired straight into the air. Its velocity t sec into the flight was $v = f(t) = 160 - 9.8t$ and it rose 435.9 m from a height of 3 m to a height of 438.9 m during the first 3 sec of flight.

EXAMPLE 1 The velocity function of a projectile fired straight into the air is $f(t) = 160 - 9.8t$. Use the summation technique just described to estimate how far the projectile rises during the first 3 sec. How close do the sums come to the exact figure of 435.9 m?

Solution We explore the results for different numbers of intervals and different choices of evaluation points.

3 subintervals of length 1, *with f evaluated at left-hand endpoints:*

With f evaluated at $t = 0$, 1, and 2, we have

$$\begin{aligned} S &\approx f(t_1)\,\Delta t + f(t_2)\,\Delta t + f(t_3)\,\Delta t \qquad \text{Eq. (1)} \\ &\approx [160 - 9.8(0)](1) + [160 - 9.8(1)](1) + [160 - 9.8(2)](1) \\ &\approx 450.6. \end{aligned}$$

3 subintervals of length 1, *with f evaluated at right-hand endpoints:*

With f evaluated at $t = 1$, 2, and 3, we have

$$\begin{aligned} S &\approx f(t_1)\,\Delta t + f(t_2)\,\Delta t + f(t_3)\,\Delta t \qquad \text{Eq. (1)} \\ &\approx [160 - 9.8(1)](1) + [160 - 9.8(2)](1) + [160 - 9.8(3)](1) \\ &\approx 421.2. \end{aligned}$$

With 6 subintervals of length 1/2, we get

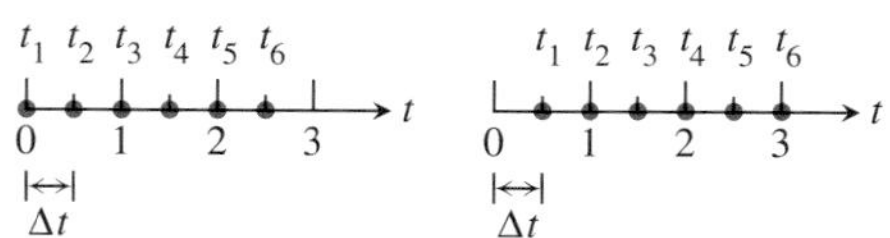

Using left-hand endpoints: $S \approx 443.25$.

Using right-hand endpoints: $S \approx 428.55$.

These six-interval estimates are somewhat closer than the three-interval estimates. The results improve as the subintervals get shorter.

As we can see in Table 5.1, the left-endpoint sums approach the true value 435.9 from above while the right-endpoint sums approach it from below. The true value lies between these upper and lower sums. The magnitude of the error in the closest entries is 0.23, a small percentage of the true value.

Error magnitude = |true value − calculated value|

$$\text{Error percentage} = \frac{0.23}{435.9} \approx 0.05\%.$$

TABLE 5.1
Travel-distance estimates

Number of Subintervals	Length of Each Subinterval	Left-Endpoint Sum	Right-Endpoint Sum
3	1	450.6	421.2
6	0.5	443.25	428.55
12	0.25	439.58	432.23
24	0.125	437.74	434.06
48	0.0625	436.82	434.98
96	0.03125	436.36	435.44
192	0.015625	436.13	435.67

It would be safe to conclude from the table's last entries that the projectile rose about 436 m during its first 3 sec of flight.

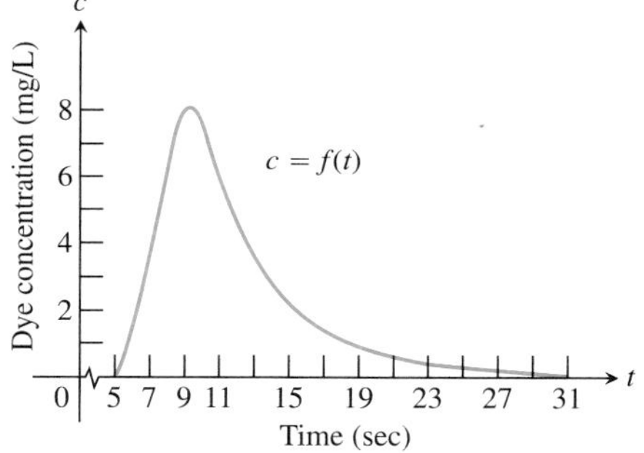

5.1 The dye concentrations from Table 5.2, plotted and fitted with a smooth curve. Time is measured with $t = 0$ at the time of injection. The dye concentrations are zero at the beginning, while the dye passes through the lungs. They then rise to a maximum at about $t = 9$ sec and taper to zero by $t = 31$ sec.

Area and Cardiac Output

The number of liters of blood your heart pumps in a minute is called your *cardiac output.* For a person at rest, the rate might be 5 or 6 liters per minute. During strenuous exercise the rate might be as high as 30 liters per minute. It might also be altered significantly by disease.

Instead of measuring a patient's cardiac output with exhaled carbon dioxide, as in Exercise 26 in Section 4.1, a doctor may prefer to use the dye-dilution technique described here. You inject 5 to 10 mg of dye in a main vein near the heart. The dye is drawn into the right side of the heart and pumped through the lungs and out the left side of the heart into the aorta, where its concentration can be measured every few seconds as the blood flows past. The data in Table 5.2 and the plot in Fig. 5.1 show the response of a healthy, resting patient to an injection of 5.6 mg of dye.

To calculate the patient's cardiac output we divide the amount of dye by the area under the dye concentration curve and multiply the result by 60:

$$\text{Cardiac output} = \frac{\text{amount of dye}}{\text{area under curve}} \times 60. \tag{2}$$

TABLE 5.2
Dye-dilution data

Seconds After Injection t	Dye Concentration (adjusted for recirculation) c	Seconds After Injection t	Dye Concentration (adjusted for recirculation) c
5	0	19	0.91
7	3.8	21	0.57
9	8.0	23	0.36
11	6.1	25	0.23
13	3.6	27	0.14
15	2.3	29	0.09
17	1.45	31	0

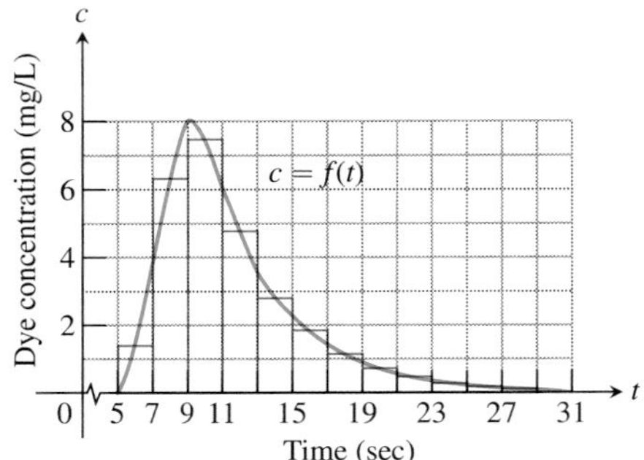

5.2 The region under the concentration curve of Fig. 5.1 is approximated with rectangles. We ignore the portion from $t = 29$ to $t = 31$; its concentration is negligible.

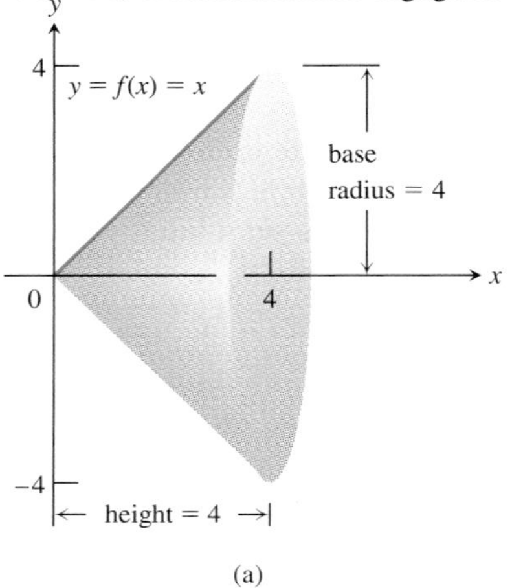

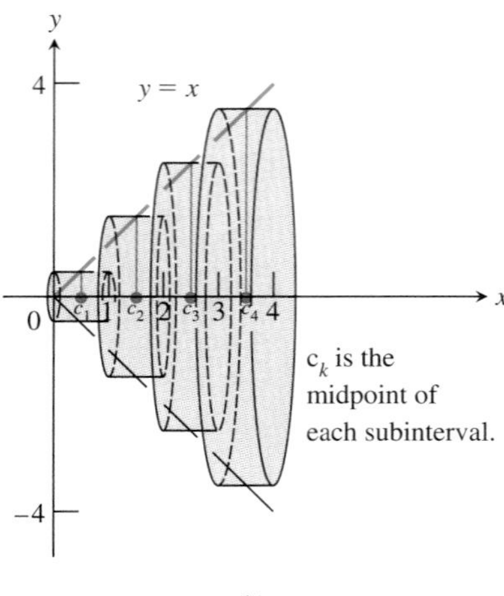

5.3 Approximating a solid cone with cylindrical slabs (Example 3). In calculating each cylinder's volume, let $r = f(x)$ and $h = \Delta x = 1$.

You can see why the formula works if you check the units in which the various quantities are measured. The amount of dye is in milligrams and the area is in (milligrams/liter) × seconds, which gives cardiac output in liters/minute:

$$\frac{\text{mg}}{\frac{\text{mg}}{\text{L}}\cdot\text{sec}}\cdot\frac{\text{sec}}{\text{min}} = \text{mg}\cdot\frac{\text{L}}{\text{mg}\cdot\text{sec}}\cdot\frac{\text{sec}}{\text{min}} = \frac{\text{L}}{\text{min}}.$$

In the example that follows, we estimate the area under the concentration curve in Fig. 5.1 and find the patient's cardiac output.

EXAMPLE 2 Find the cardiac output of the patient whose data appear in Table 5.2 and Fig. 5.1.

Solution We know the amount of dye to use in Eq. (2) (it is 5.6 mg), so all we need is the area under the concentration curve. None of the area formulas we know can be used for this irregularly shaped region. But we can get a good estimate of this area by approximating the region between the curve and the t-axis with rectangles and adding the areas of the rectangles (Fig. 5.2). Each rectangle omits some of the area under the curve but includes area from outside the curve, which compensates. In Fig. 5.2 each rectangle has a base 2 units long and a height that is equal to the height of the curve above the midpoint of the base. The rectangle's height acts as a sort of average value of the function over the time interval on which the rectangle stands. After reading rectangle heights from the curve, we multiply each rectangle's height and base to find its area, and then get the following estimate:

$$\begin{aligned}\text{Area under the curve} &\approx \text{sum of rectangle areas}\\ &\approx f(6)\cdot 2 + f(8)\cdot 2 + f(10)\cdot 2 + \cdots + f(28)\cdot 2\\ &\approx (1.2)(2) + (6.8)(2) + (7.4)(2) + \cdots + (0.1)(2)\\ &\approx (27.9)(2) = 55.8 \text{ mg}\cdot\text{sec/L}. \qquad (3)\end{aligned}$$

Dividing this figure into the dye concentration and multiplying by 60 gives a corresponding estimate of the cardiac output:

$$\text{Cardiac output} \approx \frac{\text{dye concentration}}{\text{area estimate}} \times 60 = \frac{5.6}{55.8} \times 60 = 6.02 \text{ L/min}.$$

The patient's cardiac output is about 6.02 L/min.

Notice the mathematical similarity between Examples 1 and 2. In each case, we have a function $f(t)$ defined on a closed interval and estimate what we need to know with a sum of function values multiplied by interval lengths. We can use similar sums to estimate volumes.

Volume

Here are two examples of how we can use finite sums to estimate volumes.

EXAMPLE 3 Estimate the volume of a solid right circular cone of height 4 and base radius 4.

Solution We picture the cone (Fig. 5.3a) as if its surface were generated by revolving the line segment that is the graph of the function $f(x) = x$, $0 \le x \le 4$

about the x-axis. We partition the interval from $x = 0$ to $x = 4$ on the x-axis into 4 subintervals of length $\Delta x = 1$. Using each subinterval as an axis, we construct a solid right circular cylinder whose radius is the height of the graph of f above the interval's midpoint (Fig. 5.3b). We then add the cylinders' volumes to estimate the volume of the cone.

We calculate the volume of each cylinder with the geometry formula $V = \pi r^2 h$. The sum S of the four cylinders' volumes is

$$\begin{aligned} S &= \pi [f(c_1)]^2 \Delta x + \pi [f(c_2)]^2 \Delta x + \pi [f(c_3)]^2 \Delta x + \pi [f(c_4)]^2 \Delta x \\ &= \pi (c_1)^2 \cdot 1 + \pi (c_2)^2 \cdot 1 + \pi (c_3)^2 \cdot 1 + \pi (c_4)^2 \cdot 1 \\ &= \pi\left[\left(\frac{1}{2}\right)^2 + \left(\frac{3}{2}\right)^2 + \left(\frac{5}{2}\right)^2 + \left(\frac{7}{2}\right)^2\right] \\ &= \frac{\pi}{4}(1 + 9 + 25 + 49) = \frac{\pi}{4}(84) = 21\pi . \end{aligned}$$

This compares favorably with the cone's true volume,

$$V = \frac{1}{3}\pi r^2 h = \frac{1}{3}\pi (4)^2 (4) = \frac{64}{3}\pi \approx 21.3\pi .$$

The magnitude of the error between S and V is only a small percentage of the true volume V:

$$\text{Error percentage} = \frac{|V - S|}{V} = \frac{|(64/3)\pi - 21\pi|}{(64/3)\pi} = \frac{|64 - 63|}{64} = \frac{1}{64} \approx 1.6\%.$$

As you will see in the exercises, the estimates get even better if we use more subintervals.

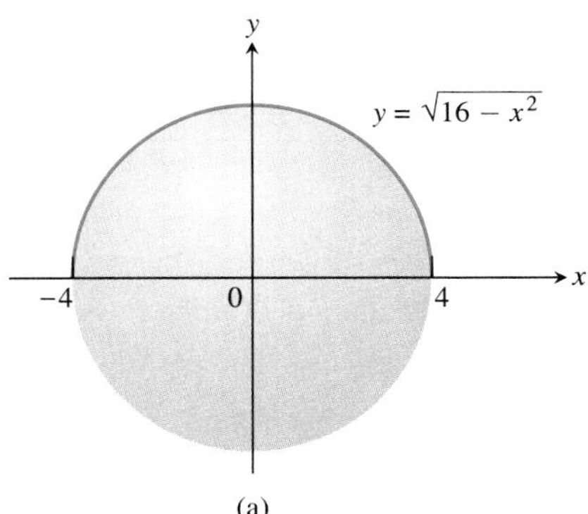

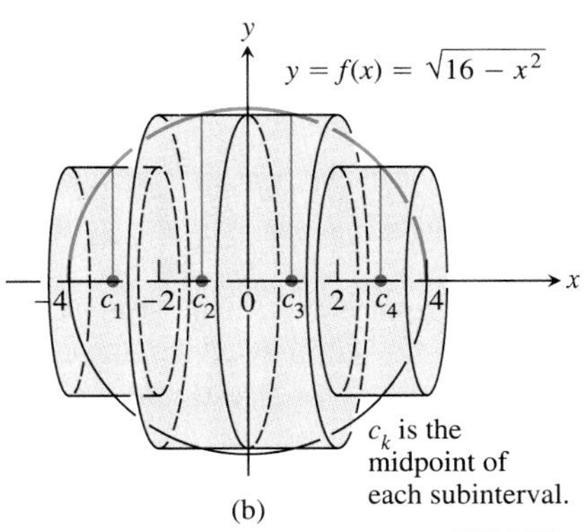

5.4 (a) The semicircle $y = \sqrt{16 - x^2}$ revolved about the x-axis to outline a solid sphere. (b) The sphere approximated with cylindrical slabs (Example 4). In calculating each cylinder's volume, let $r = f(x) = \sqrt{16 - x^2}$ and $h = \Delta x = 2$.

EXAMPLE 4 Estimate the volume of a solid sphere of radius 4.

Solution We picture the sphere as if its surface were generated by revolving the semicircle that is the graph of the function $f(x) = \sqrt{16 - x^2}$ about the x-axis (Fig. 5.4a). We partition the interval $-4 \le x \le 4$ into 4 subintervals of length $\Delta x = 2$. Around each subinterval, we construct a right circular cylinder whose radius is the curve's height above the interval's midpoint (Fig. 5.4b). We add the cylinder's volumes to estimate the volume of the sphere.

As in Example 3, we calculate the cylinders' volumes with the formula $V = \pi r^2 h$. The sum S of the four cylinders' volumes is

$$\begin{aligned} S &= \pi [f(c_1)]^2 \Delta x + \pi [f(c_2)]^2 \Delta x + \pi [f(c_3)]^2 \Delta x + \pi [f(c_4)]^2 \Delta x \\ &= \pi \left[\sqrt{16 - c_1^2}\right]^2 \cdot 2 + \pi \left[\sqrt{16 - c_2^2}\right]^2 \cdot 2 \\ &\quad + \pi \left[\sqrt{16 - c_3^2}\right]^2 \cdot 2 + \pi \left[\sqrt{16 - c_4^2}\right]^2 \cdot 2 \\ &= 2\pi[(16 - (-3)^2) + (16 - (-1)^2) + (16 - (1)^2) + (16 - (3)^2)] \\ &= 2\pi(7 + 15 + 15 + 7) = 2\pi(44) = 88\pi . \end{aligned}$$

This overestimates the sphere's true volume,

$$V = \frac{4}{3}\pi r^3 = \frac{4}{3}\pi (4)^3 = \frac{256}{3}\pi \approx 85.3\pi ,$$

by only about 3%:

$$\text{Error percentage} = \frac{|V - S|}{V} = \frac{|(256/3)\pi - 88\pi|}{(256/3)\pi} = \frac{1}{32} \approx 3\%.$$

With more subintervals, the approximation would have been even better.

The Average Value of a Positive Function

To find the average of a finite set of values, we add them and divide by the number of values added. But what happens if we want to find the average of an infinite number of values? For example, what is the average value of the function $f(x) = x^2$ on the interval $[0, 1]$? To see what this kind of "continuous" average might mean, imagine that we are pollsters sampling the function. We pick random x's between 0 and 1, square them, and average the squares. As we take larger samples, we expect this average to approach some number, which seems reasonable to call the *average of f over* $[0, 1]$.

A look at the graph suggests that the average square should be less than 1/2, because there are more x's with squares less than 1/2 than there are with squares greater than 1/2. If we had a computer to generate random numbers, we could carry out the sampling experiment described above, but it is much easier to estimate the average value with a finite sum.

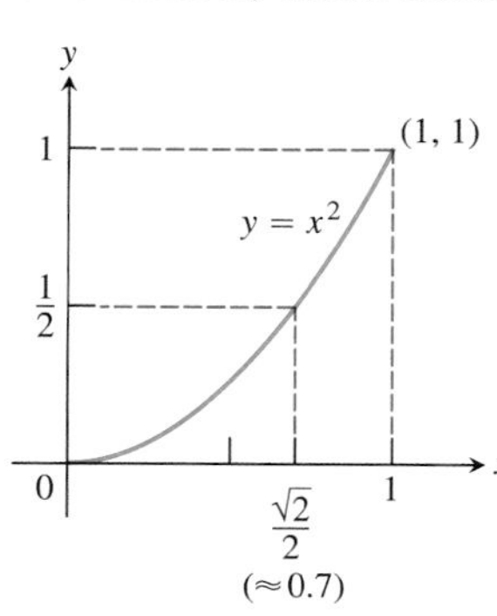

EXAMPLE 5 Estimate the average value of the function $f(x) = x^2$ on the interval $[0, 1]$.

Solution We first look at the graph of $y = x^2$ and partition the interval $[0, 1]$ into 5 subintervals of length $\Delta x = 1/5$.

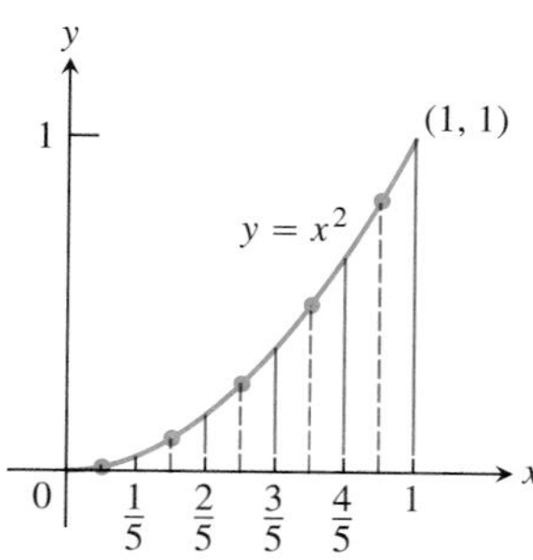

It appears that a good estimate for the average square on each subinterval is the square of the midpoint of the subinterval. Since the subintervals all have the same width, we can average these five estimates to get a final estimate for the average value over $[0, 1]$.

$$\text{Average value} \approx \frac{\left(\frac{1}{10}\right)^2 + \left(\frac{3}{10}\right)^2 + \left(\frac{5}{10}\right)^2 + \left(\frac{7}{10}\right)^2 + \left(\frac{9}{10}\right)^2}{5}$$

$$\approx \frac{1}{5} \cdot \frac{1 + 9 + 25 + 49 + 81}{100} = \frac{165}{500} = 0.33$$

We will be able to show later that the true average value is 1/3, so our estimate is very close.

You will notice that the calculation in Example 5 is very similar to the area calculation in Example 2. In fact, what we have really done in Example 5 is estimate the area of the region between the graph of $y = x^2$ and the x-axis on the interval [0, 1]. We can use the idea of area to give a definition of average value that does not depend on an imaginary sampling experiment:

DEFINITION

Let $y = f(x)$ be a positive continuous function defined on a closed interval I. The **average value** of f on I, denoted by **av(*f*)** ("average of f") is the value of f defined by the equation

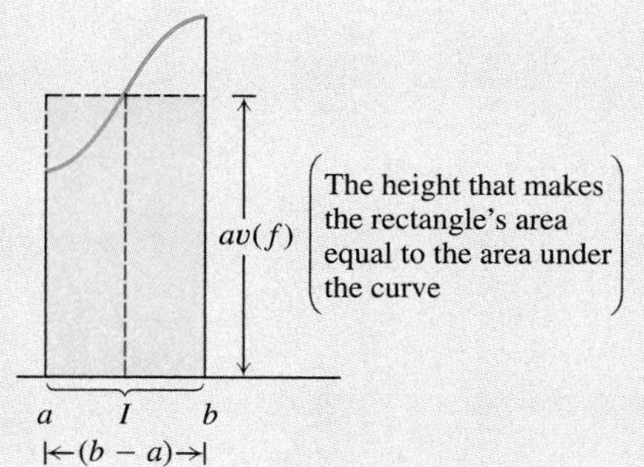

$$\text{av}(f)\cdot(\text{length of } I) = \begin{pmatrix}\text{area under the}\\ \text{curve } y = f(x)\end{pmatrix}. \tag{4}$$

In short,

$$\text{av}(f) = \frac{\text{area under the curve}}{\text{length of the interval}}. \tag{5}$$

Of course, we have to know how to define the area under a curve $y = f(x)$ for the definition to make sense. We will take care of this matter as the chapter continues. In the meantime, we can work with specific functions and familiar geometric shapes.

EXAMPLE 6 Find the average value of $f(x) = \sqrt{9 - x^2}$ on $[-3, 3]$. Approximately where does the function assume this value? Graph the function and sketch a rectangle with base $[-3, 3]$ and height av(f).

Solution The graph of f over $[-3, 3]$ is a semicircle of radius 3 (Fig. 5.5). The area between it and the x-axis is $\pi r^2/2 = \pi(3)^2/2 = 9\pi/2$. The length of $[-3, 3]$ is 6. Hence, the average value of f over $[-3, 3]$ is

$$\text{av}(f) = \frac{\text{area}}{\text{interval length}} = \frac{9\pi/2}{6} = \frac{9\pi}{12} = \frac{3\pi}{4} \approx 2.4. \qquad \text{Eq. (5)}$$

We find where f assumes this value by solving the equation $f(x) = 3\pi/4$ for x:

$$\sqrt{9 - x^2} = \frac{3\pi}{4}$$

$$9 - x^2 = \frac{9\pi^2}{16}$$

$$x^2 = 9 - \frac{9\pi^2}{16}$$

$$x = \pm\sqrt{9 - \frac{9\pi^2}{16}} \approx \pm 1.9.$$

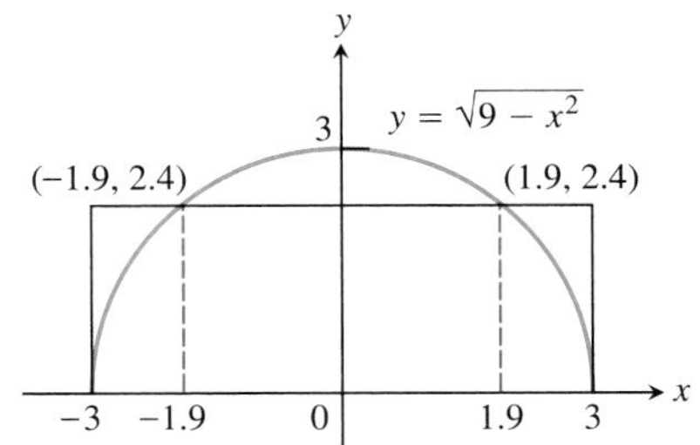

5.5 The curve and rectangle in Example 6.

To sum up, the average value of $f(x) = \sqrt{9 - x^2}$ on $[-3, 3]$ is about 2.4. The function assumes this value at two points, $x \approx \pm 1.9$.

We add to the sketch in Fig. 5.5 a rectangle on $[-3, 3]$ whose top passes through the semicircle directly above these points.

Conclusion

Examples 1, 2, and 5 describe instances in which sums of function values multiplied by interval lengths provide approximations that are good enough to answer practical questions. Examples 3 and 4 show how similar sums provide good approximations to volumes. You will find additional examples in the exercises that follow.

As you will recall, the distance approximations in Example 1 improved as the intervals involved became shorter and more numerous. We knew this because we had already found the exact answer with an antiderivative back in Section 4.7. If we had made our partitions of the time interval in Example 1 still finer (that is, more numerous and shorter), would the sums have approached the exact answer as a limit? Is the connection between the sums and the antiderivative in this case just a coincidence? Could we have calculated the area in Example 2 and the volumes in Examples 3 and 4 with antiderivatives as well? As we will see, the answers are "yes, they would have," "no, it is not a coincidence," and "yes, we could have."

Exercises 5.1

1. The table below shows the velocity of a model train engine moving along a track for 10 sec. Estimate the distance traveled by the engine using 10 subintervals of length 1 with (a) left-endpoint values and (b) right-endpoint values.

Time (sec)	Velocity (in./sec)	Time (sec)	Velocity (in./sec)
0	0	6	11
1	12	7	6
2	22	8	2
3	10	9	6
4	5	10	0
5	13		

2. You are sitting on the bank of a tidal river watching the incoming tide carry a bottle upstream. You record the velocity of the flow every five minutes for an hour, with the results shown in the table to the right. About how far upstream did the bottle travel during that hour? Find an estimate using 12 subintervals of length 5 with (a) left-endpoint values and (b) right-endpoint values.

Time (min)	Velocity (m/sec)	Time (min)	Velocity (m/sec)
0	1	35	1.2
5	1.2	40	1.0
10	1.7	45	1.8
15	2.0	50	1.5
20	1.8	55	1.2
25	1.6	60	0
30	1.4		

3. You and a companion are about to drive a twisty stretch of dirt road in a car whose speedometer works but whose odometer (mileage counter) is broken. To find out how long this particular stretch of road is, you record the car's velocity at 10-sec intervals, with the results shown in the table at the top of the next column. Estimate the length of the road (a) using left-endpoint values and (b) using right-endpoint values.

Time (sec)	Velocity (converted to ft/sec) (30 mi/h = 44 ft/sec)	Time (sec)	Velocity (converted to ft/sec) (30 mi/h = 44 ft/sec)
0	0	70	15
10	44	80	22
20	15	90	35
30	35	100	44
40	30	110	30
50	44	120	35
60	35		

4. The table below gives data for the velocity of a vintage sports car accelerating from 0 to 142 mi/h in 36 sec (10 thousandths of an hour).

Time (h)	Velocity (mi/h)	Time (h)	Velocity (mi/h)
0.0	0	0.006	116
0.001	40	0.007	125
0.002	62	0.008	132
0.003	82	0.009	137
0.004	96	0.010	142
0.005	108		

a) Use rectangles to estimate how far the car traveled during the 36 sec it took to reach 142 mi/h.

b) Roughly how many seconds did it take the car to reach the halfway point? About how fast was the car going then?

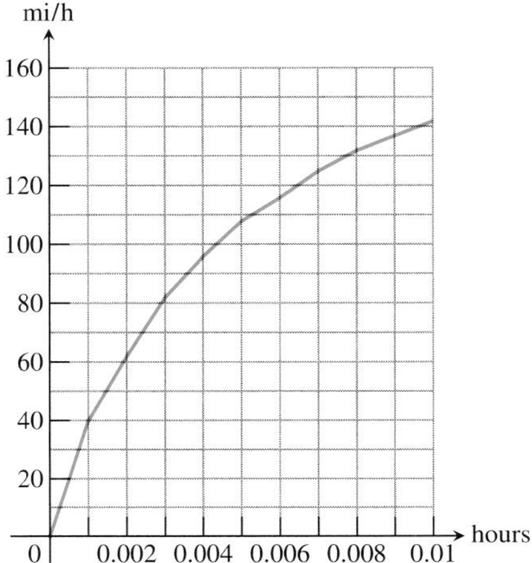

5. The table at the top of the next column gives dye concentrations for a dye-dilution cardiac-output determination like the one in Example 2. The amount of dye injected in this case was 5 mg instead of 5.6 mg. Use rectangles to estimate the area under the dye concentration curve and then go on to estimate the patient's cardiac output.

Seconds After Injection t	Dye Concentration (adjusted for recirculation) c
2	0
4	0.6
6	1.4
8	2.7
10	3.7
12	4.1
14	3.8
16	2.9
18	1.7
20	1.0
22	0.5
24	0

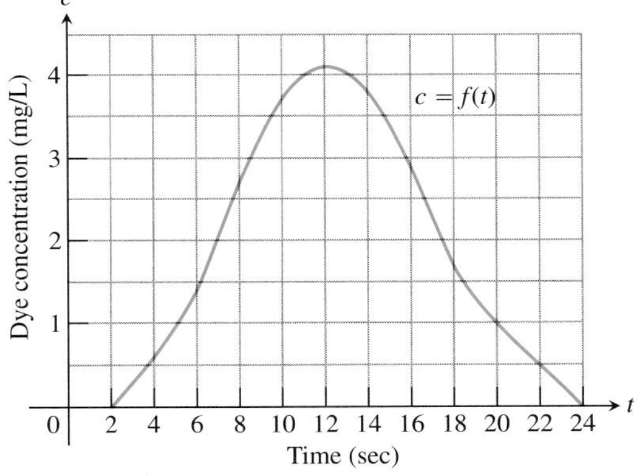

6. The table below gives dye concentrations for a cardiac-output determination like the one in Example 2. The amount of dye injected in this case was 10 mg. Plot the data and connect the data points with a smooth curve. Estimate the area under the curve and calculate the cardiac output from this estimate.

Seconds After Injection t	Dye Concentration (adjusted for recirculation) c	Seconds After Injection t	Dye Concentration (adjusted for recirculation) c
0	0	16	7.9
2	0	18	7.8
4	0.1	20	6.1
6	0.6	22	4.7
8	2.0	24	3.5
10	4.2	26	2.1
12	6.3	28	0.7
14	7.5	30	0

7. *Continuation of Example 3.* If you estimate the volume of the cone with two subintervals instead of four, the estimate is somewhat small, but still not bad, especially for a quick estimate. What do you get for the sum of the volumes of the two approximating cylinders?

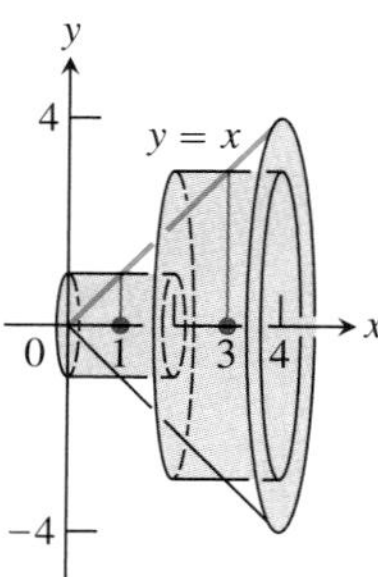

8. *Continuation of Example 3.* Partition [0, 4] into eight subintervals instead of four. Construct a right circular cylinder around each interval, using the height of the curve $f(x) = x$ above the interval's midpoint as the radius. Then add the volumes of the eight cylinders to estimate the volume of the cone. What estimate do you get?

9. To estimate the volume of a solid cone of height 6 and base radius 2, imagine it to be the cone whose lateral surface is traced out by revolving the graph of $f(x) = x/3$, $0 \le x \le 6$ about the x-axis. Partition the interval $0 \le x \le 6$ into three subintervals of length 2, and approximate the cone with solid cylinders whose radii are the heights of the graph of f above the midpoints of these subintervals.

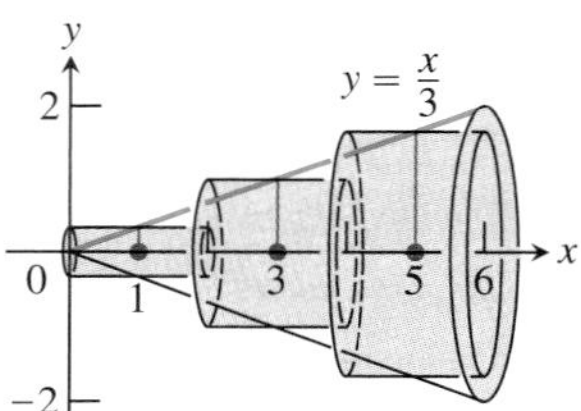

a) Add the cylinders' volumes to get an estimate S for the volume V of the cone.
b) Express the magnitude of the error $|V - S|$ as a percentage of V to the nearest percent.

10. *Continuation of Exercise 9.* Approximate the cone's volume V using six subintervals of length 1 instead of three subintervals of length 2.

a) What is the sum S of the cylinders' volumes now?
b) Express the magnitude of the error $|V - S|$ as a percentage of V to the nearest percent.

11. *Continuation of Example 4.* Suppose we use only two cylinders to estimate the volume V of the sphere in Example 4, as shown in the figure here.

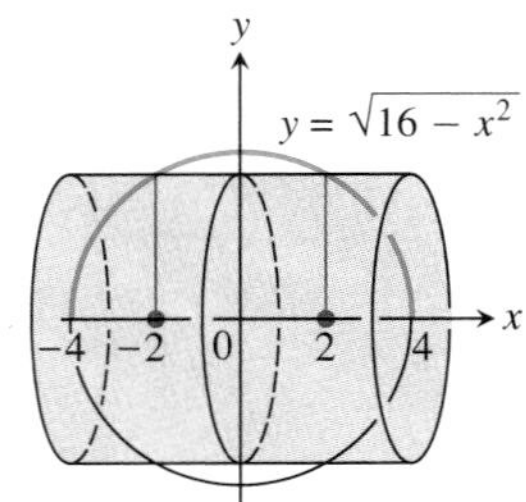

a) Find the sum S of the volumes of the cylinders.
b) Express $|V - S|$ as a percentage of V to the nearest percent.

12. *Continuation of Example 4.* Approximate the volume V of the sphere by partitioning [−4, 4] into eight subintervals and using eight cylinders instead of four. The radius of each cylinder is the height of the semicircle above the midpoint of the interval around which it is constructed.

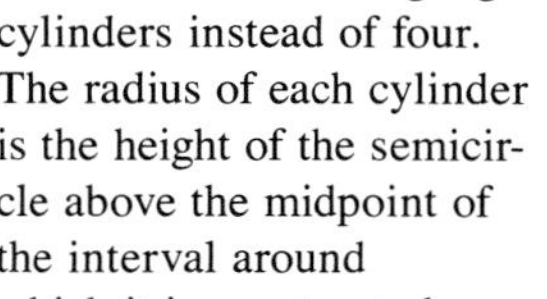

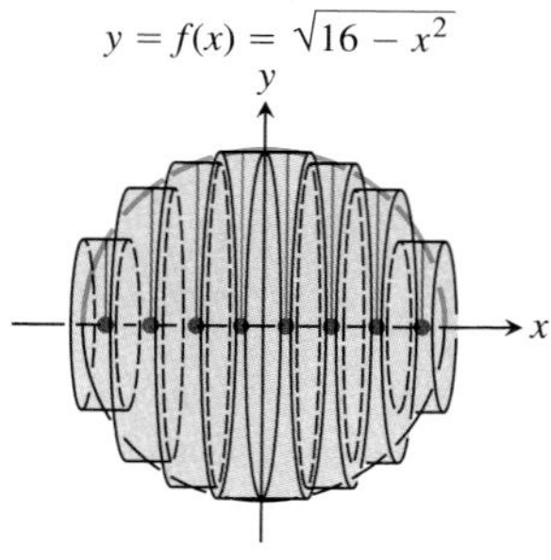

a) Find the sum S of the cylinders' volumes.
b) Express $|V - S|$ as a percentage of V to the nearest percent.

13. Estimate the volume V of a sphere of radius 6 by partitioning a diameter into six subintervals of length 2 and constructing a solid circular cylinder around each subinterval.

a) Find the sum S of the cylinders' volumes.
b) Express $|V - S|$ as a percentage of V to the nearest percent.

14. *Continuation of Exercise 13.* Estimate the sphere's volume V by approximating the sphere with twelve cylinders instead of six.

a) Find the sum S of the cylinders' volumes.
b) Express $|V - S|$ as a percentage of V to the nearest percent.

15. A hemispherical reservoir of radius 8 m is filled with water to a depth of 4 m. Estimate the water's volume by approximating the water with (a) two and (b) four solid cylinders. As we will see in Chapter 7, the water's volume is $V = 320\pi/3$ m^3. For each estimate S, find the error percentage of V to the nearest percent.

16. A hemispherical bowl of radius 5 m is filled with water to a depth of 4 m.

a) Estimate the water's volume by approximating the water with four solid cylinders.
b) The water's volume is $V = 176\pi/3$ m^3. For your estimate S, express $|V - S|$ as a percentage of V to the nearest percent.

17. A rectangular swimming pool is 30 ft wide and 50 ft long. The table below shows the depth $h(x)$ of the water at 5-ft intervals from one end of the pool to the other. Estimate the volume of water in the pool using (a) left-endpoint values of h; (b) right-endpoint values of h.

Position x ft	Depth $h(x)$ ft	Position x ft	Depth $h(x)$ ft
0	6.0	30	11.5
5	8.2	35	11.9
10	9.1	40	12.3
15	9.9	45	12.7
20	10.5	50	13.0
25	11.0		

18. The nose section of a rocket is a paraboloid obtained by revolving the curve $y = \sqrt{x}$, $0 \le x \le 5$, about the x-axis, where x is measured in ft.

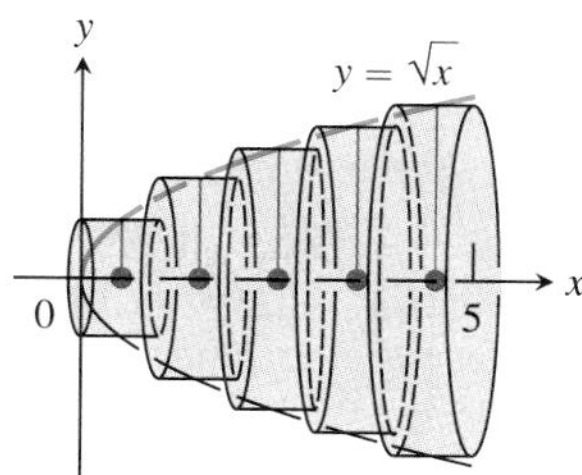

a) Estimate the volume of the section by partitioning [0, 5] into five subintervals and constructing a cylinder on each interval of radius equal to the height of the curve $y = \sqrt{x}$ above the interval's midpoint. Use S to denote the sum of the cylinders' volumes.

b) As you will see in Section 5.4, Exercise 68, the volume of the nose section is $V = 25\pi/2$ ft³. Find $|V - S|$ as a percentage of V to the nearest percent.

In Exercises 19–22, use a finite sum to estimate the average value of f on the given interval by partitioning the interval into four subintervals of equal length and evaluating f at the subinterval midpoints.

19. $f(x) = x^3$ on $[0, 2]$

20. $f(x) = 1/x$ on $[1, 9]$

21. $f(t) = (1/2) + \sin^2 \pi t$ on $[0, 2]$

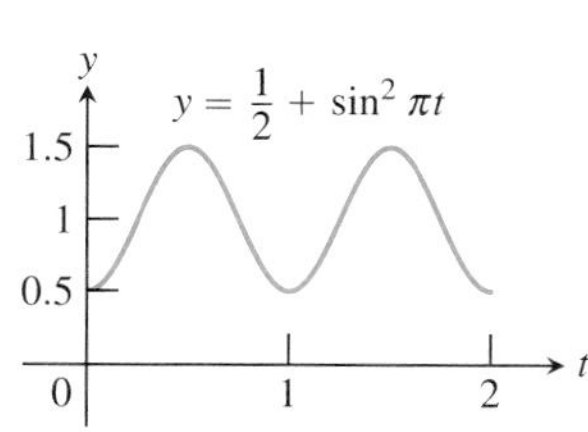

22. $f(t) = 1 - \left(\cos \frac{\pi t}{4}\right)^4$ on $[0, 4]$

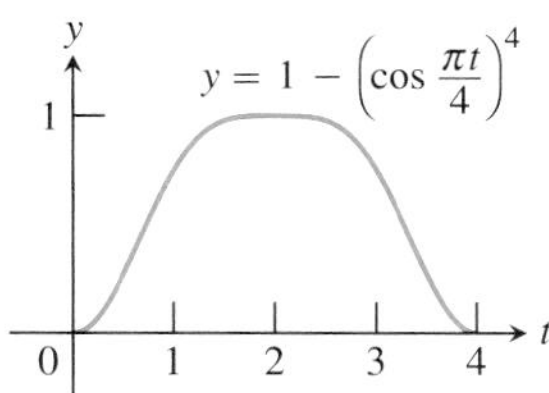

In Exercises 23–26, use the definition of average value in terms of area to find the average value of the function on the given interval.

23. $f(x) = \begin{cases} 2x + 2, & -1 \le x \le 1 \\ -x + 5, & 1 < x \le 5 \end{cases}$

on $[-1, 5]$

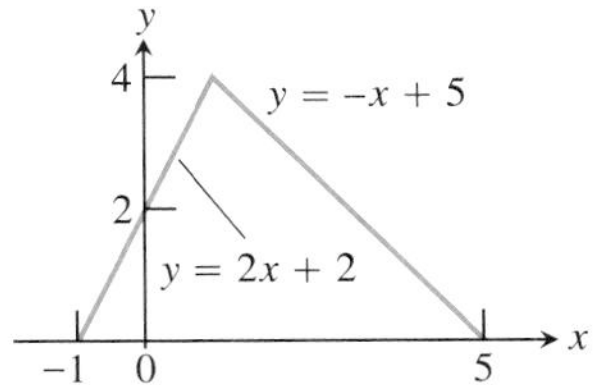

24. $f(x) = \begin{cases} x + 4, & -4 \le x \le -1 \\ -x + 2, & -1 < x \le 2 \end{cases}$

on $[-4, 2]$

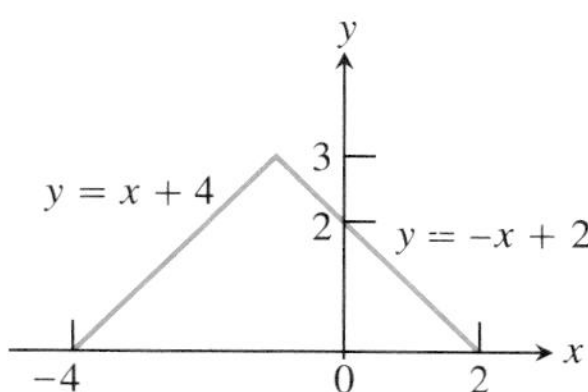

25. $f(t) = 1 - \sqrt{1 - t^2}$ on $[-1, 1]$

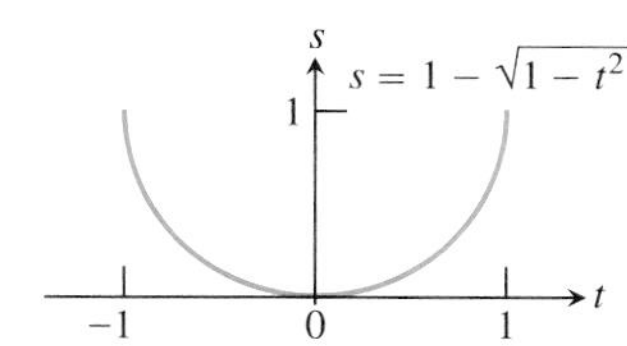

26. $f(t) = \begin{cases} 6 - \sqrt{9 - t^2}, & -3 \le t < 0 \\ \sqrt{9 - t^2}, & 0 \le t \le 3 \end{cases}$

on $[-3, 3]$

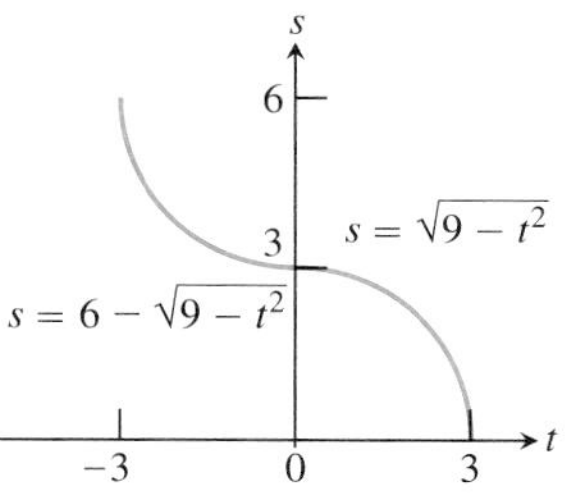

27. If you average 30 mi/h on a 150-mi trip and then return over the same 150 mi at the rate of 50 mi/h, what is your average speed for the trip? Give reasons for your answer. (*Source:* David H. Pleacher, *The Mathematics Teacher,* Vol. 85, No. 6, pp. 445–446, September 1992.)

28. A dam released 1000 m³ of water at 10 m³/min and then released another 1000 m³ at 20 m³/min. What was the average rate at which the water was released? Give reasons for your answer.

Writing for Your Own Knowledge

Answer the following questions in writing. Some answers will take only a sentence or two; others may require several paragraphs. Some explanations may also call for graphs or sketches.

1. How can you sometimes estimate quantities like distance traveled, area, and volume with finite sums? Why might you want to do so?
2. How do you find the average value of a positive continuous function over an interval in its domain?

5.2 Riemann Sums and Definite Integrals

In the preceding section, we estimated distances, areas, volumes, and average values with finite sums. The terms in the sums were obtained by multiplying selected function values by the lengths of intervals. In this section, we say what it means for sums like these to approach a limit as the intervals involved become more numerous and shorter. We begin by introducing a compact notation for sums that contain large numbers of terms.

Sigma Notation for Finite Sums

We use the capital Greek letter Σ ("sigma") to write an abbreviation for the sum

$$f(t_1)\,\Delta t + f(t_2)\,\Delta t + \cdots + f(t_n)\,\Delta t \tag{1}$$

as

$$\sum_{k=1}^{n} f(t_k)\,\Delta t. \tag{2}$$

"The sum from k equals 1 to n of f of t_k times delta t."

When we write a sum this way, we say that we have written it in sigma notation.

DEFINITIONS

Sigma Notation for Finite Sums

The symbol $\sum_{k=1}^{n} a_k$ denotes the sum $a_1 + a_2 + \cdots + a_n$. The a's are the **terms** of the sum: a_1 is the first term, a_2 is the second term, a_k is the **kth term,** and a_n is the nth and last term. The variable k is the **index of summation.** The values of k run through the integers from 1 to n. The number 1 is the **lower limit of summation;** the number n is the **upper limit of summation.**

EXAMPLE 1

The Sum in Sigma Notation	The Sum Written Out—One Term for Each Value of k	The Value of the Sum
$\sum_{k=1}^{5} k$	$1 + 2 + 3 + 4 + 5$	15
$\sum_{k=1}^{3} (-1)^k k$	$(-1)^1(1) + (-1)^2(2) + (-1)^3(3)$	$-1 + 2 - 3 = -2$
$\sum_{k=1}^{2} \frac{k}{k+1}$	$\frac{1}{1+1} + \frac{2}{2+1}$	$\frac{1}{2} + \frac{2}{3} = \frac{7}{6}$

The lower limit of summation does not have to be 1; it can be any integer.

EXAMPLE 2 Express the sum $1 + 3 + 5 + 7 + 9$ in sigma notation.

Solution

Starting with $k = 2$: $1 + 3 + 5 + 7 + 9 = \sum_{k=2}^{6} (2k - 3)$

Starting with $k = -3$: $1 + 3 + 5 + 7 + 9 = \sum_{k=-3}^{1} (2k + 7)$

Notice that the formula generating the terms changes with the lower limit of summation, but the terms generated remain the same. It is often simplest to begin with $k = 0$ or $k = 1$.

Starting with $k = 0$: $1 + 3 + 5 + 7 + 9 = \sum_{k=0}^{4} (2k + 1)$

Starting with $k = 1$: $1 + 3 + 5 + 7 + 9 = \sum_{k=1}^{5} (2k - 1)$

Algebra with Finite Sums

We can use the following rules whenever we work with finite sums.

Algebra Rules for Finite Sums

1. *Sum Rule:* $\sum_{k=1}^{n} (a_k + b_k) = \sum_{k=1}^{n} a_k + \sum_{k=1}^{n} b_k$
2. *Difference Rule:* $\sum_{k=1}^{n} (a_k - b_k) = \sum_{k=1}^{n} a_k - \sum_{k=1}^{n} b_k$
3. *Constant Multiple Rule:* $\sum_{k=1}^{n} ca_k = c \cdot \sum_{k=1}^{n} a_k$ (Any number c)
4. *Constant Value Rule:* $\sum_{k=1}^{n} c = n \cdot c$ (c is any constant value)

There are no surprises in this list, but the formal proofs require mathematical induction (Appendix 4).

EXAMPLE 3

a) $\sum_{k=1}^{n} (3k - k^2) = 3 \sum_{k=1}^{n} k - \sum_{k=1}^{n} k^2$ — Difference Rule and Constant Multiple Rule

b) $\sum_{k=1}^{n} (-a_k) = \sum_{k=1}^{n} (-1) \cdot a_k = -1 \cdot \sum_{k=1}^{n} a_k = -\sum_{k=1}^{n} a_k$ — Constant Multiple Rule

c) $\sum_{k=1}^{3} (k + 4) = \sum_{k=1}^{3} k + \sum_{k=1}^{3} 4$ — Sum Rule

$= (1 + 2 + 3) + (3 \cdot 4)$ — Constant Value Rule

$= 6 + 12 = 18$

Sum Formula for Positive Integers

Over the years people have discovered a variety of formulas for the values of finite sums. The most famous of these are the formula for the sum of the first n integers (Gauss discovered it at age 5) and the formulas for the sums of the squares and cubes of the first n integers.

The first n integers: $$\sum_{k=1}^{n} k = \frac{n(n+1)}{2} \tag{3}$$

The first n squares: $$\sum_{k=1}^{n} k^2 = \frac{n(n+1)(2n+1)}{6} \tag{4}$$

The first n cubes: $$\sum_{k=1}^{n} k^3 = \left(\frac{n(n+1)}{2}\right)^2 \tag{5}$$

EXAMPLE 4 Evaluate $\sum_{k=1}^{4} (k^2 - 3k)$.

Solution We can use the algebra rules and known formulas to evaluate the sum without writing out the terms.

$$\sum_{k=1}^{4} (k^2 - 3k) = \sum_{k=1}^{4} k^2 - 3\sum_{k=1}^{4} k$$ Difference Rule and Constant Multiple Rule

$$= \frac{4(4+1)(8+1)}{6} - 3\left(\frac{4(4+1)}{2}\right)$$ Eqs. (4) and (3) with $n = 4$

$$= 30 - 30 = 0$$

Riemann Sums

The approximating sums in Section 5.1 are all examples of a more general kind of sum called a *Riemann* (*ree*-mahn) *sum.* The functions in the examples had only nonnegative values, but the more general notion has no such restriction. Given an arbitrary continuous function $y = f(x)$ on an interval $[a, b]$ (Fig. 5.6), we partition the interval $[a, b]$ into n subintervals by choosing $n - 1$ points, say $x_1, x_2, \ldots, x_{n-1}$, between a and b subject only to the condition that

$$a < x_1 < x_2 < \cdots < x_{n-1} < b. \tag{6}$$

To make the notation consistent, we usually denote a by x_0 and b by x_n. The set

$$P = \{x_0, x_1, \ldots, x_n\} \tag{7}$$

is then called a **partition** of $[a, b]$.

The partition P defines n closed **subintervals**

$$[x_0, x_1], [x_1, x_2], \ldots, [x_{n-1}, x_n]. \tag{8}$$

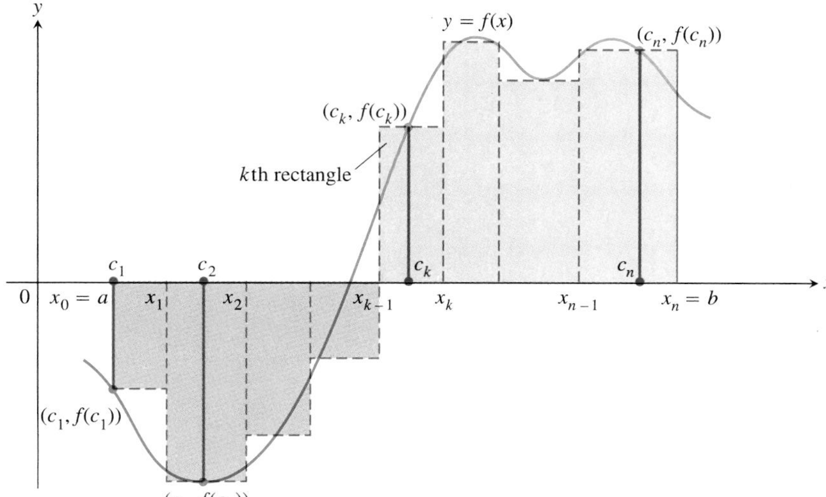

5.6 The graph of a typical function $y = f(x)$ over a closed interval $[a, b]$. The rectangles approximate the region between the graph of the function and the x-axis.

The typical closed subinterval $[x_{k-1}, x_k]$ is called the ***k*th subinterval** of P.

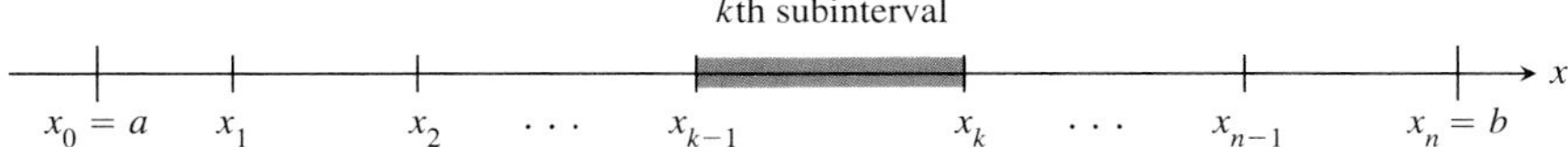

The length of the kth subinterval is $\Delta x_k = x_k - x_{k-1}$.

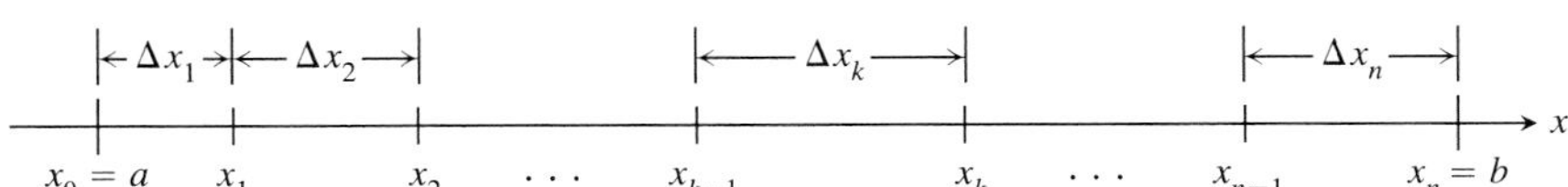

On each subinterval we stand a vertical rectangle that reaches from the x-axis to the curve $y = f(x)$. The exact height of the rectangle does not matter as long as its top or base touches the curve at some point $(c_k, f(c_k))$ where $x_{k-1} \leq c_k \leq x_k$. See Fig. 5.6 again.

If $f(c_k)$ is positive, the number $f(c_k)\,\Delta x_k$ = height × base is the area of the rectangle. If $f(c_k)$ is negative, then $f(c_k)\,\Delta x_k$ is the negative of the area. In any case, we add the n products $f(c_k)\,\Delta x_k$ to form the sum

$$S_P = \sum_{k=1}^{n} f(c_k)\,\Delta x_k. \tag{9}$$

This sum, which depends on P and the choice of the numbers c_k, is called a **Riemann sum for *f* on the interval [*a*, *b*],** after German mathematician Georg Friedrich Bernhard Riemann (1826–1866), who studied the limits of such sums.

EXAMPLE 5 Three Riemann sums for $f(x) = x^2 - 2x - 1$ on $[1, 4]$:

a) Partition (Fig. 5.7a on the following page): $P = \{1, 2, 3, 4\}$

Subinterval lengths: $\Delta x_k = 1$

Choice of c_k: Midpoints of subintervals:

$c_1 = 1.5,\ c_2 = 2.5,\ c_3 = 3.5$

Corresponding Riemann sum:

$$\begin{aligned}\sum_{k=1}^{3} f(c_k)\,\Delta x_k &= \sum_{k=1}^{3}\left[c_k{}^2 - 2c_k - 1\right]\cdot 1\\ &= \sum_{k=1}^{3}\left[c_k{}^2 - 2c_k - 1\right]\\ &= \left[(1.5)^2 - 2(1.5) - 1\right] + \left[(2.5)^2 - 2(2.5) - 1\right] + \left[(3.5)^2 - 2(3.5) - 1\right]\\ &= -1.75 + 0.25 + 4.25 = 2.75\end{aligned}$$

b) Partition (Fig. 5.7b): $P = \{1, 1.5, 2, 2.5, 3, 3.5, 4\}$
Subinterval lengths: $\Delta x_k = 0.5$
Choice of c_k: Left-hand endpoints:
$c_1 = 1,\ c_2 = 1.5,\ c_3 = 2$
$c_4 = 2.5,\ c_5 = 3,\ c_6 = 3.5$

Corresponding Riemann sum:

$$\begin{aligned}\sum_{k=1}^{6} f(c_k)\,\Delta x_k &= \sum_{k=1}^{6}\left[c_k{}^2 - 2c_k - 1\right]\cdot(0.5)\\ &= 0.5\cdot\sum_{k=1}^{6}\left[c_k{}^2 - 2c_k - 1\right]\\ &= 0.5\cdot(-2 - 1.75 - 1 + 0.25 + 2 + 4.25)\\ &= 0.5\cdot(1.75) = 0.875\end{aligned}$$

c) Partition (Fig. 5.7c): $P = \{1, 1.5, 2, 2.5, 3, 3.5, 4\}$
Subinterval lengths: $\Delta x_k = 0.5$
Choice of c_k: Right-hand endpoints:
$c_1 = 1.5,\ c_2 = 2,\ c_3 = 2.5,$
$c_4 = 3,\ c_5 = 3.5,\ c_6 = 4$

Corresponding Riemann sum:

$$\begin{aligned}\sum_{k=1}^{6} f(c_k)\,\Delta x_k &= \sum_{k=1}^{6}\left[c_k{}^2 - 2c_k - 1\right]\cdot(0.5)\\ &= 0.5\cdot\sum_{k=1}^{6}\left[c_k{}^2 - 2c_k - 1\right]\\ &= 0.5\cdot(-1.75 - 1 + 0.25 + 2 + 4.25 + 7)\\ &= 0.5\cdot(10.75) = 5.375\end{aligned}$$

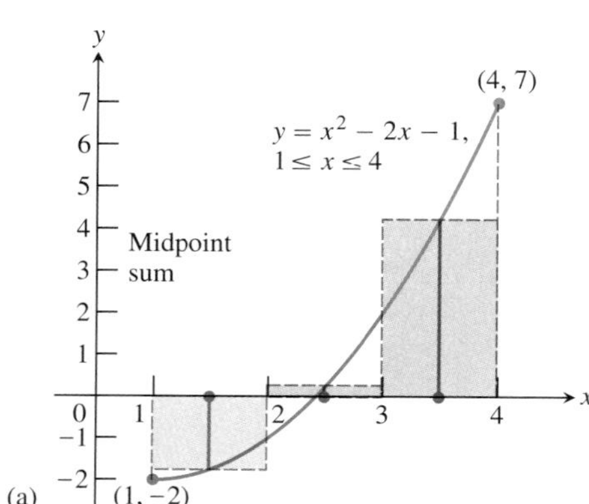

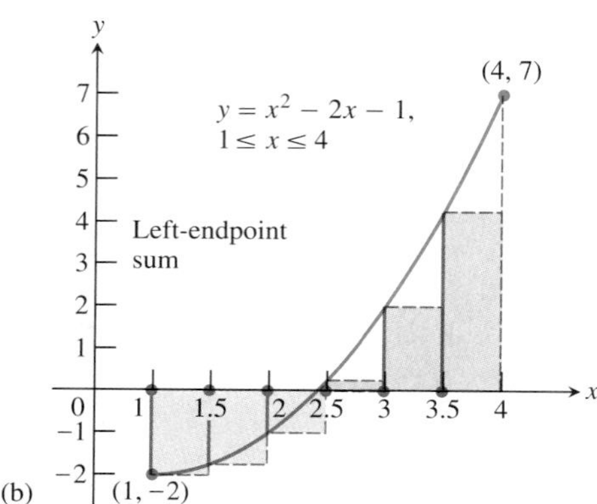

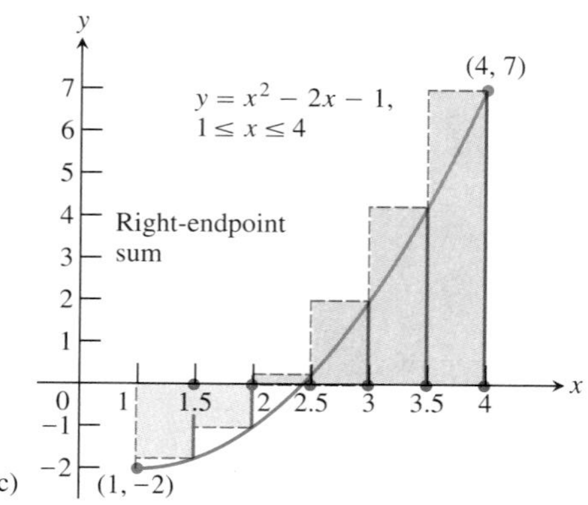

5.7 The approximating rectangles in Example 5.

As the partitions of $[a, b]$ become finer, the rectangles whose bases are the subintervals defined by the partition approximate the region between the x-axis and the graph of f with increasing accuracy (Fig. 5.8). So we expect the associated Riemann sums to have a limiting value. To test this expectation, we need to develop a numerical way to say that partitions become finer and to determine whether the corresponding sums have a limit. We accomplish this with the following definitions.

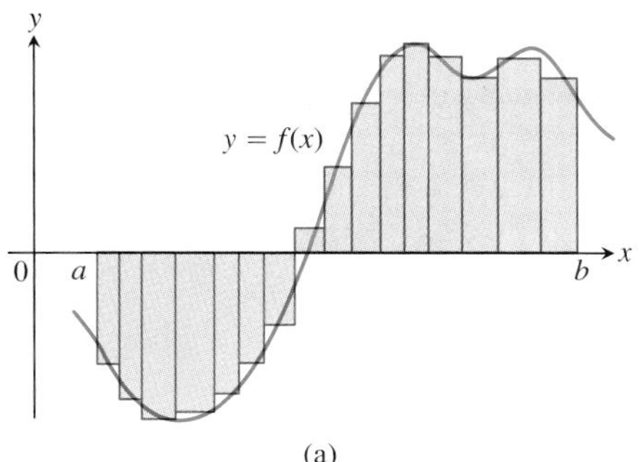

(a)

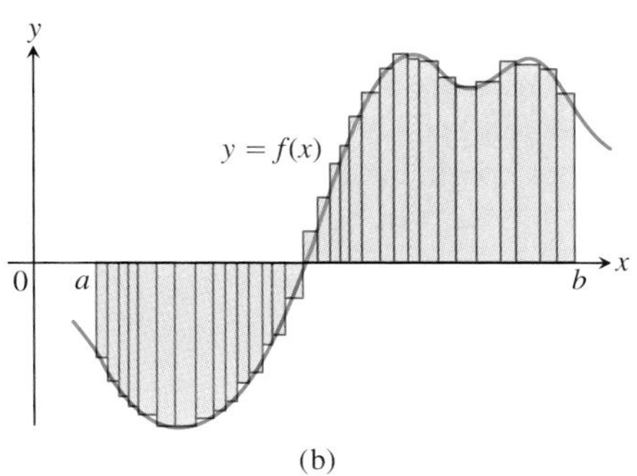

(b)

5.8 The curve of Fig. 5.6 with rectangles from finer partitions of $[a, b]$. Finer partitions create more rectangles with shorter bases.

The **norm** of a partition P is the partition's longest subinterval length. It is denoted by

$$\|P\| \qquad \text{(read "the norm of } P\text{")}.$$

The way to say that successive partitions of an interval become finer is to say that the norms of these partitions approach zero.

EXAMPLE 6 The set $P = \{0, 0.2, 0.6, 1, 1.5, 2\}$ is a partition of $[0, 2]$. There are five subintervals of P: $[0, 0.2]$, $[0.2, 0.6]$, $[0.6, 1]$, $[1, 1.5]$, and $[1.5, 2]$.

$|\leftarrow \Delta x_1 \rightarrow|\leftarrow \Delta x_2 \rightarrow|\leftarrow \Delta x_3 \rightarrow|\leftarrow \Delta x_4 \rightarrow|\leftarrow \Delta x_5 \rightarrow|$

0 0.2 0.6 1 1.5 2 x

The lengths of the subintervals are $\Delta x_1 = 0.2$, $\Delta x_2 = 0.4$, $\Delta x_3 = 0.4$, $\Delta x_4 = 0.5$, and $\Delta x_5 = 0.5$. The longest subinterval length is 0.5, so the norm of the partition is $\|P\| = 0.5$. As you can see, there are two subintervals of this length.

DEFINITION

The Definite Integral as a Limit of Riemann Sums

Let $f(x)$ be a function defined on a closed interval $[a, b]$. We say that the **limit** of the Riemann sums $\sum_{k=1}^{n} f(c_k)\,\Delta x_k$ on $[a, b]$ as $\|P\| \to 0$ is the number I if the following condition is satisfied:

Given any positive number ϵ, there exists a positive number δ such that for every partition P of $[a, b]$

$$\|P\| < \delta \quad \text{implies} \quad \left| \sum_{k=1}^{n} f(c_k)\,\Delta x_k - I \right| < \epsilon \tag{10}$$

for any choice of the numbers c_k in the subintervals $[x_{k-1}, x_k]$.

If the limit exists, we write

$$\lim_{\|P\| \to 0} \sum_{k=1}^{n} f(c_k)\,\Delta x_k = I. \tag{11}$$

We call I the **definite integral** of f over $[a, b]$, we say that f is **integrable** over $[a, b]$, and we say that the Riemann sums of f on $[a, b]$ approach the number I.

We usually write I as $\int_a^b f(x)\,dx$, which is read "the integral of f from a to b." Thus, if the limit exists,

$$\lim_{\|P\| \to 0} \sum_{k=1}^{n} f(c_k)\,\Delta x_k = \int_a^b f(x)\,dx. \tag{12}$$

The amazing fact is that despite the variety in the Riemann sums $\Sigma f(c_k)\Delta x_k$ as the partitions change and the arbitrary choice of c_k's in the intervals of each new partition, the sums always have the same limit as $\|P\| \to 0$ as long as f is continuous. The need to establish the existence of this limit became clear as the nineteenth century progressed, and it was finally established when Riemann proved the following theorem in 1854. You can find a current version of Riemann's proof of this theorem in most advanced calculus books.

THEOREM 1

The Existence of Definite Integrals

All continuous functions are integrable. That is, if a function $y = f(x)$ is continuous on an interval $[a, b]$, then its definite integral over $[a, b]$ exists.

Theorem 1 says nothing about how to *calculate* definite integrals. Except for a few special cases, that takes another theorem, which we will discuss in Section 5.4. Also, Theorem 1 speaks only about continuous functions. Many discontinuous functions are integrable as well, but we will not deal with this here.

Terminology and Notation

There is a fair amount of terminology to learn in connection with definite integrals.

The symbol $\int$ is an **integral sign.** Leibniz chose it because it resembled the S in the German word for *summation*. When we find the value of $\int_a^b f(x)\,dx$, we say that we have **evaluated the integral** and that we have **integrated** f from a to b. We call $[a, b]$ the **interval of integration.** The numbers a and b are the **limits of integration,** a being the **lower limit of integration** and b the **upper limit of integration.** The function f is the **integrand** of the integral. The variable x is the **variable of integration.**

While the integral of f from a to b is usually denoted by $\int_a^b f(x)\,dx$, the value of a definite integral of a function over any particular interval depends on the function and not on the letter we choose to represent its independent variable. If we decide to use t or u instead of x, we write the integral as

$$\int_a^b f(t)\,dt \qquad \text{or} \qquad \int_a^b f(u)\,du \qquad \text{instead of} \qquad \int_a^b f(x)\,dx.$$

But, no matter how we write the integral, it is still the same number, defined as a limit of Riemann sums.

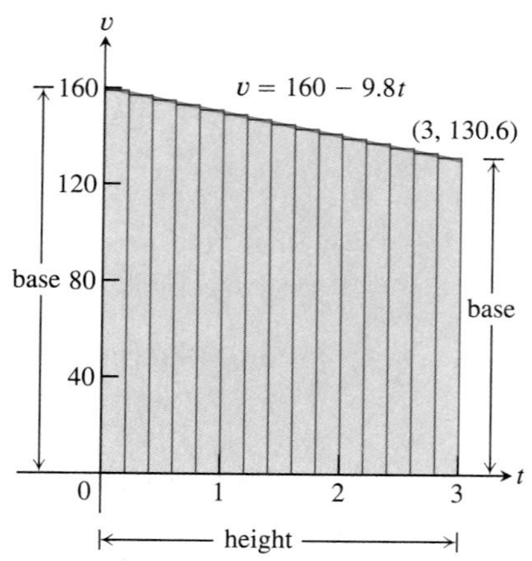

5.9 Rectangles for a Riemann sum of the velocity function $f(t) = 160 - 9.8t$ over the interval $[0, 3]$.

Areas Under the Graphs of Nonnegative Functions

The sums we used to estimate the height of the projectile in Example 1 of Section 5.1 were Riemann sums for the projectile's velocity function

$$v = f(t) = 160 - 9.8t \tag{13}$$

on the interval $[0, 3]$. We can see from Fig. 5.9 how the associated rectangles approximate the trapezoid between the t-axis and the curve $v = 160 - 9.8t$. As the norm of the partition goes to zero, the rectangles fit the trapezoid with increasing accuracy and the sum of the areas they enclose approaches the trapezoid's area, which is

$$\text{Trapezoid area} = h \cdot \frac{b_1 + b_2}{2} = 3 \cdot \frac{160 + 130.6}{2} = 435.9. \tag{14}$$

This confirms our suspicion that the sums we were constructing in Section 5.1 approached a limit of 435.9. Since the limit of these sums is also the integral of f from 0 to 3, we now know the value of the integral as well—

$$\int_0^3 (160 - 9.8t)\, dt = \text{trapezoid area} = 435.9.$$

We can exploit the connection between integrals and area in two ways. When we know a formula for the area of the region between the x-axis and the graph of a continuous nonnegative function $y = f(x)$, we can use it to evaluate the function's integral. When we do not know the region's area, we can use the function's integral to define and calculate the area.

DEFINITION

Let $f(x)$ be a continuous function whose values are nonnegative for $a \leq x \leq b$. The **area** of the region between the graph of f and the interval $[a, b]$ is the integral of f from a to b.

$$\text{Area} = \int_a^b f(x)\, dx \qquad (15)$$

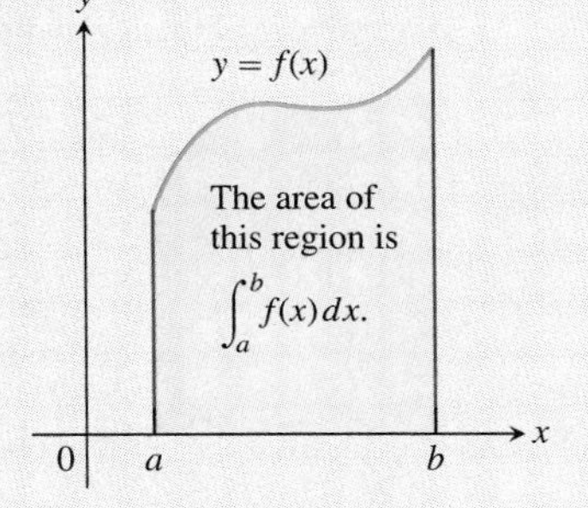

Whenever we make a new definition, as we have here, the question of consistency becomes an issue. Does the definition that we have just developed for nonstandard shapes give correct results for standard shapes? The answer is yes, but the proof is complicated and we will not go into it.

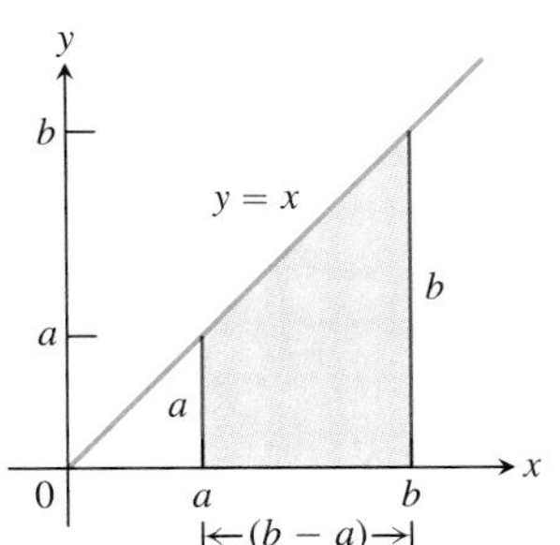

5.10 The region in Example 7.

EXAMPLE 7 *Using an Area to Evaluate a Definite Integral.* Evaluate

$$\int_a^b x\, dx, \qquad 0 < a < b.$$

Solution We sketch the region under the curve $y = x$, $a \leq x \leq b$ (Fig. 5.10), and see that it is a trapezoid with height $(b - a)$ and bases a and b. The value of the integral is the area of this trapezoid:

$$\int_a^b x\, dx = (b - a) \cdot \frac{a + b}{2} = \frac{b^2}{2} - \frac{a^2}{2}. \qquad (16)$$

Thus,

$$\int_1^3 x\, dx = \frac{(3)^2}{2} - \frac{(1)^2}{2} = \frac{9}{2} - \frac{1}{2} = 4,$$

$$\int_{\sqrt{2}}^{\sqrt{3}} x\, dx = \frac{(\sqrt{3})^2}{2} - \frac{(\sqrt{2})^2}{2} = \frac{3}{2} - \frac{2}{2} = \frac{1}{2},$$

and so on.

Notice that $x^2/2$ is an antiderivative of x, further evidence of a connection between antiderivatives and summation.

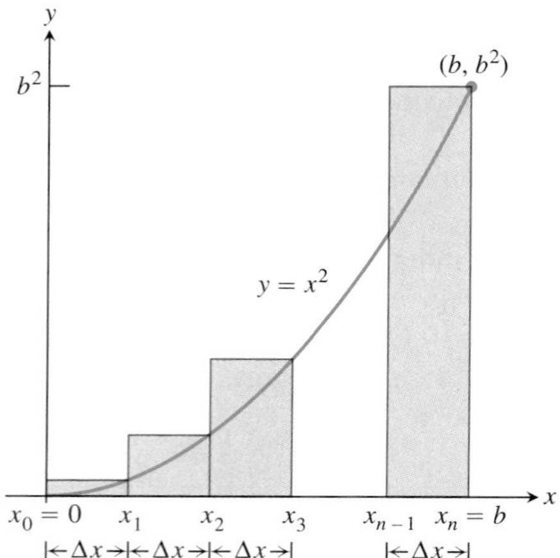

5.11 The rectangles of the Riemann sums in Example 8.

EXAMPLE 8 *Using a Definite Integral to Find an Area.* Find the area of the region between the parabola $y = x^2$ and the x-axis on the interval $[0, b]$.

Solution We evaluate the integral for the area as a limit of Riemann sums.

We begin by sketching the region (a nonstandard shape) (Fig. 5.11) and partitioning $[0, b]$ into n subintervals of length $\Delta x = (b - 0)/n = b/n$. The points of the partition are

$$x_0 = 0,\ x_1 = \Delta x,\ x_2 = 2\Delta x,\ \cdots,\ x_{n-1} = (n-1)\Delta x,\ x_n = n\Delta x = b.$$

We are free to choose the c_k's any way we please. We choose each c_k to be the right-hand endpoint of its subinterval, a choice that leads to manageable arithmetic. Thus, $c_1 = x_1$, $c_2 = x_2$, and so on. The rectangles defined by these choices (from left to right) have areas

$$\begin{aligned} f(c_1)\,\Delta x &= f(\Delta x)\Delta x = (\Delta x)^2\,\Delta x = (1^2)(\Delta x)^3 \\ f(c_2)\,\Delta x &= f(2\Delta x)\Delta x = (2\Delta x)^2\,\Delta x = (2^2)(\Delta x)^3 \\ &\vdots \\ f(c_n)\,\Delta x &= f(n\Delta x)\Delta x = (n\Delta x)^2\,\Delta x = (n^2)(\Delta x)^3. \end{aligned}$$

The sum of these areas is

$$\begin{aligned} S_n &= \sum_{k=1}^{n} f(c_k)\,\Delta x \\ &= \sum_{k=1}^{n} k^2(\Delta x)^3 \\ &= (\Delta x)^3 \sum_{k=1}^{n} k^2 && (\Delta x)^3 \text{ is a constant.} \\ &= \frac{b^3}{n^3}\cdot\frac{n(n+1)(2n+1)}{6} && \Delta x = b/n, \text{ and Eq. (4)} \\ &= \frac{b^3}{6}\cdot\frac{(n+1)(2n+1)}{n^2} \\ &= \frac{b^3}{6}\cdot\frac{2n^2+3n+1}{n^2} \\ &= \frac{b^3}{6}\cdot\left(2+\frac{3}{n}+\frac{1}{n^2}\right). \end{aligned} \tag{17}$$

We can now use the definition of definite integral

$$\int_a^b f(x)\,dx = \lim_{\|P\|\to 0} \sum_{k=1}^{n} f(c_k)\,\Delta x \qquad \text{Eq. (12)}$$

to find the area under the parabola from $x = 0$ to $x = b$ as

$$\begin{aligned} \int_0^b x^2\,dx &= \lim_{n\to\infty} S_n && \text{In this example, } \|P\|\to 0 \text{ is equivalent to } n\to\infty. \\ &= \lim_{n\to\infty} \frac{b^3}{6}\cdot\left(2+\frac{3}{n}+\frac{1}{n^2}\right) && \text{Eq. (17)} \\ &= \frac{b^3}{6}\cdot(2+0+0) = \frac{b^3}{3}. \end{aligned}$$

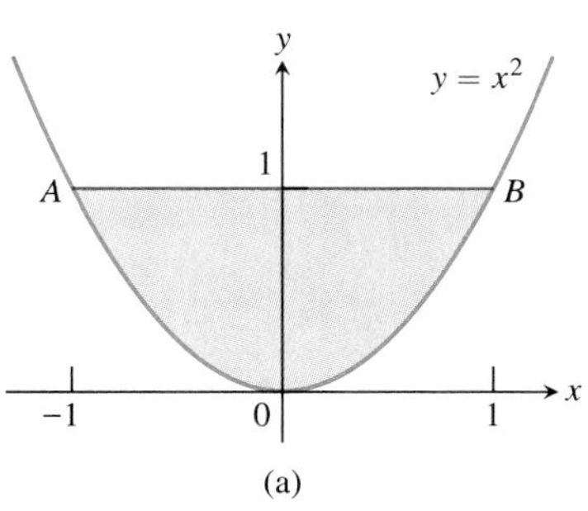

(a)

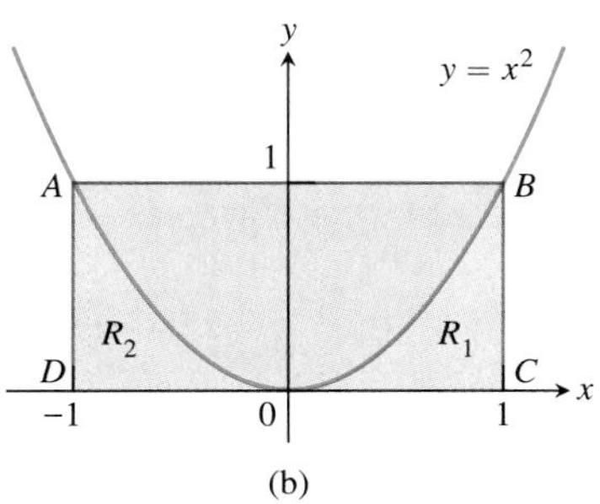

(b)

5.12 The regions and rectangle in Example 9.

With different values of b, we get

$$\int_0^1 x^2\,dx = \frac{1^3}{3} = \frac{1}{3}, \qquad \int_0^{1.5} x^2\,dx = \frac{(1.5)^3}{3} = \frac{3.375}{3} = 1.125,$$

and so on.

EXAMPLE 9 Find the area of the shaded region in Fig. 5.12(a).

Solution We drop perpendiculars from A and B to the x-axis to make a rectangle (Fig. 5.12b) and subtract the areas of regions R_1 and R_2 from the area of the rectangle.

$$\text{Area of } R_1 = \int_0^1 x^2\,dx = \frac{(1)^3}{3} = \frac{1}{3} \qquad \text{Value from Example 8}$$

$$\text{Area of } R_2 = \text{Area of } R_1 = \frac{1}{3} \qquad \text{The symmetry of the parabola gives congruence.}$$

$$\text{Area of } ABCD = 2 \cdot 1 = 2 \qquad \text{base} \times \text{height}$$

$$\text{Area of shaded region} = 2 - \frac{1}{3} - \frac{1}{3} = \frac{4}{3}.$$

Constant Functions

Another kind of integral we can evaluate directly from the definition is the integral of a constant function $f(x) = c$ over a closed interval $[a, b]$. No matter how the c_k's are chosen,

$$\begin{aligned}
\sum_{k=1}^{n} f(c_k)\Delta x_k &= \sum_{k=1}^{n} c \cdot \Delta x_k && f(c_k) \text{ always equals } c. \\
&= c \cdot \sum_{k=1}^{n} \Delta x_k && \text{Constant Multiple Rule for Sums} \\
&= c(b - a). && \sum_{k=1}^{n} \Delta x_k = \text{length of interval } [a, b] = b - a
\end{aligned}$$

Since the sums all have the value $c(b - a)$, their limit, the integral, does too.

If $f(x)$ has the constant value c on $[a, b]$, then

$$\int_a^b f(x)\,dx = \int_a^b c\,dx = c(b - a) \tag{18}$$

EXAMPLE 10

a) $\displaystyle\int_{-1}^{4} 3\,dx = 3(4 - (-1)) = (3)(5) = 15$

$\displaystyle\int_{-1}^{4} 3\,dx = (3)(5) = 15$ = area of rectangle

y
y = 3
−1 0 4 x

b) $\int_{-1}^{4} (-3)\, dx = -3(4-(-1)) = (-3)(5) = -15$

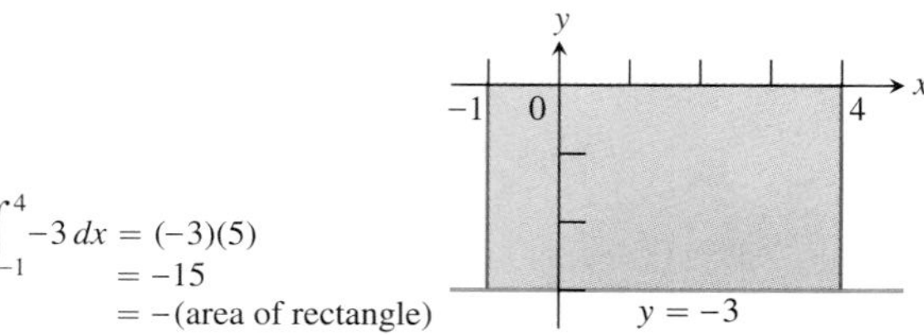

Exercises 5.2

Write the sums in Exercises 1–6 without sigma notation. Then evaluate them.

1. $\sum_{k=1}^{2} \frac{6k}{k+1}$

2. $\sum_{k=1}^{3} \frac{k-1}{k}$

3. $\sum_{k=1}^{4} \cos k\pi$

4. $\sum_{k=1}^{5} \sin k\pi$

5. $\sum_{k=1}^{3} (-1)^{k+1} \sin \frac{\pi}{k}$

6. $\sum_{k=1}^{4} (-1)^{k} \cos k\pi$

7. Which of the following express $1+2+4+8+16+32$ in sigma notation?

 a) $\sum_{k=1}^{6} 2^{k-1}$ b) $\sum_{k=0}^{5} 2^{k}$ c) $\sum_{k=-1}^{4} 2^{k+1}$

8. Which of the following express $1-2+4-8+16-32$ in sigma notation?

 a) $\sum_{k=1}^{6} (-2)^{k-1}$ b) $\sum_{k=0}^{5} (-1)^{k} 2^{k}$

 c) $\sum_{k=-2}^{3} (-1)^{k+1} 2^{k+2}$

9. Which formula is not equivalent to the other two?

 a) $\sum_{k=2}^{4} \frac{(-1)^{k-1}}{k-1}$ b) $\sum_{k=0}^{2} \frac{(-1)^{k}}{k+1}$ c) $\sum_{k=-1}^{1} \frac{(-1)^{k}}{k+2}$

10. Which formula is not equivalent to the other two?

 a) $\sum_{k=1}^{4} (k-1)^2$ b) $\sum_{k=-1}^{3} (k+1)^2$

 c) $\sum_{k=-3}^{-1} k^2$

Express the sums in Exercises 11–16 in sigma notation. The form of your answer will depend on your choice of the lower limit of summation.

11. $1+2+3+4+5+6$

12. $1+4+9+16$

13. $\frac{1}{2}+\frac{1}{4}+\frac{1}{8}+\frac{1}{16}$

14. $2+4+6+8+10$

15. $1-\frac{1}{2}+\frac{1}{3}-\frac{1}{4}+\frac{1}{5}$

16. $-\frac{1}{5}+\frac{2}{5}-\frac{3}{5}+\frac{4}{5}-\frac{5}{5}$

17. Suppose that $\sum_{k=1}^{n} a_k = -5$ and $\sum_{k=1}^{n} b_k = 6$. Find the values of

 a) $\sum_{k=1}^{n} 3a_k$ b) $\sum_{k=1}^{n} \frac{b_k}{6}$

 c) $\sum_{k=1}^{n} (a_k + b_k)$ d) $\sum_{k=1}^{n} (a_k - b_k)$

 e) $\sum_{k=1}^{n} (b_k - 2a_k)$

18. Suppose that $\sum_{k=1}^{n} a_k = 0$ and $\sum_{k=1}^{n} b_k = 1$. Find the values of

 a) $\sum_{k=1}^{n} 8a_k$ b) $\sum_{k=1}^{n} 250b_k$

 c) $\sum_{k=1}^{n} (a_k + 1)$ d) $\sum_{k=1}^{n} (b_k - 1)$

Use the algebra rules on p. 283 and the formulas in Eqs. (3)–(5) to evaluate the sums in Exercises 19–28.

19. a) $\sum_{k=1}^{10} k$ b) $\sum_{k=1}^{10} k^2$ c) $\sum_{k=1}^{10} k^3$

20. a) $\sum_{k=1}^{13} k$ b) $\sum_{k=1}^{13} k^2$ c) $\sum_{k=1}^{13} k^3$

21. $\sum_{k=1}^{7} (-2k)$

22. $\sum_{k=1}^{5} \frac{\pi k}{15}$

23. $\sum_{k=1}^{6} (3-k^2)$

24. $\sum_{k=1}^{6} (k^2-5)$

25. $\sum_{k=1}^{5} k(3k+5)$

26. $\sum_{k=1}^{7} k(2k+1)$

27. $\sum_{k=1}^{5} \frac{k^3}{225} + \left(\sum_{k=1}^{5} k\right)^3$

28. $\left(\sum_{k=1}^{7} k\right)^2 - \sum_{k=1}^{7} \frac{k^3}{4}$

In Exercises 29–32, graph each function $f(x)$ over the given interval. Partition the interval into four subintervals of equal length. Then add to your sketch the rectangles associated with the Riemann sum $\sum_{k=1}^{4} f(c_k)\,\Delta x_k$, given that c_k is the (a) left-hand endpoint, (b) right-hand endpoint, (c) midpoint of the kth subinterval. (Make a separate sketch for each set of rectangles.)

29. $f(x) = x^2 - 1, \quad [0, 2]$

30. $f(x) = -x^2, \quad [0, 1]$

31. $f(x) = \sin x, \quad [-\pi, \pi]$

32. $f(x) = \sin x + 1, \quad [-\pi, \pi]$

33. Find the norm of the partition $P = \{0, 1.2, 1.5, 2.3, 2.6, 3\}$.

34. Find the norm of the partition $P = \{-2, -1.6, -0.5, 0, 0.8, 1\}$.

Express the limits in Exercises 35–42 as definite integrals.

35. $\lim_{\|P\|\to 0} \sum_{k=1}^{n} c_k^2\,\Delta x_k$, where P is a partition of $[0, 2]$

36. $\lim_{\|P\|\to 0} \sum_{k=1}^{n} 2c_k^3\,\Delta x_k$, where P is a partition of $[-1, 0]$

37. $\lim_{\|P\|\to 0} \sum_{k=1}^{n} (c_k^2 - 3c_k)\Delta x_k$, where P is a partition of $[-7, 5]$

38. $\lim_{\|P\|\to 0} \sum_{k=1}^{n} \left(\frac{1}{c_k}\right)\Delta x_k$, where P is a partition of $[1, 4]$

39. $\lim_{\|P\|\to 0} \sum_{k=1}^{n} \frac{1}{1 - c_k}\,\Delta x_k$, where P is a partition of $[2, 3]$

40. $\lim_{\|P\|\to 0} \sum_{k=1}^{n} \sqrt{4 - c_k^2}\,\Delta x_k$, where P is a partition of $[0, 1]$

41. $\lim_{\|P\|\to 0} \sum_{k=1}^{n} (\sec c_k)\,\Delta x_k$, where P is a partition of $[-\pi/4, 0]$

42. $\lim_{\|P\|\to 0} \sum_{k=1}^{n} (\tan c_k)\,\Delta x_k$, where P is a partition of $[0, \pi/4]$

In Exercises 43–50, graph the integrands and use areas to evaluate the integrals.

43. $\int_{-2}^{4} \left(\frac{x}{2} + 3\right) dx$

44. $\int_{1/2}^{3/2} (-2x + 4)\, dx$

45. $\int_{-3}^{3} \sqrt{9 - x^2}\, dx$

46. $\int_{-4}^{0} \sqrt{16 - x^2}\, dx$

47. $\int_{-2}^{1} |x|\, dx$

48. $\int_{-1}^{1} (1 - |x|)\, dx$

49. $\int_{-1}^{1} (2 - |x|)\, dx$

50. $\int_{-1}^{1} \left(1 + \sqrt{1 - x^2}\right) dx$

Use the results of Examples 7 and 8 to evaluate the integrals in Exercises 51–62.

51. $\int_{1}^{\sqrt{2}} x\, dx$

52. $\int_{0.5}^{2.5} x\, dx$

53. $\int_{\pi}^{2\pi} \theta\, d\theta$

54. $\int_{\sqrt{2}}^{5\sqrt{2}} r\, dr$

55. $\int_{0}^{\sqrt[3]{7}} x^2\, dx$

56. $\int_{0}^{0.3} s^2\, ds$

57. $\int_{0}^{1/2} t^2\, dt$

58. $\int_{0}^{\pi/2} \theta^2\, d\theta$

59. $\int_{a}^{2a} x\, dx$

60. $\int_{a}^{\sqrt{3}a} x\, dx$

61. $\int_{0}^{\sqrt[3]{b}} x^2\, dx$

62. $\int_{0}^{3b} x^2\, dx$

Find the areas of the shaded regions in Exercises 63–**68.**

63.

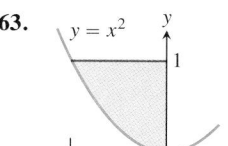

64.

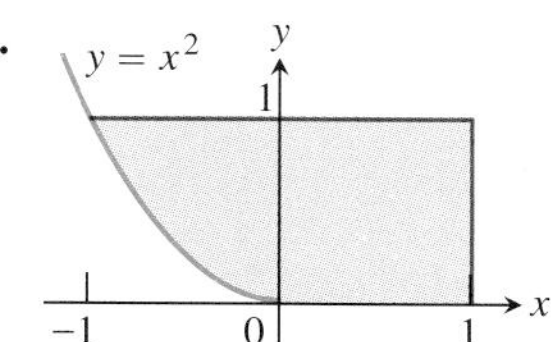

65.

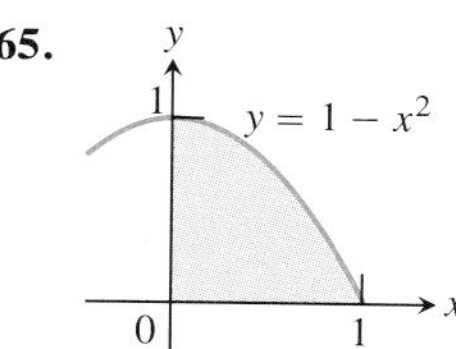

66.

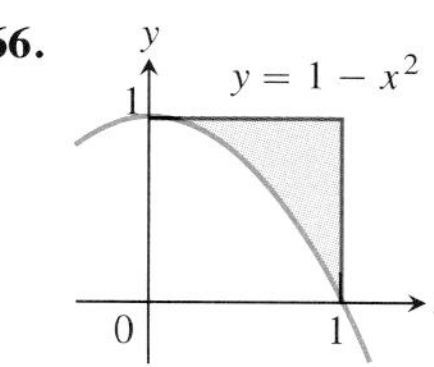

67.

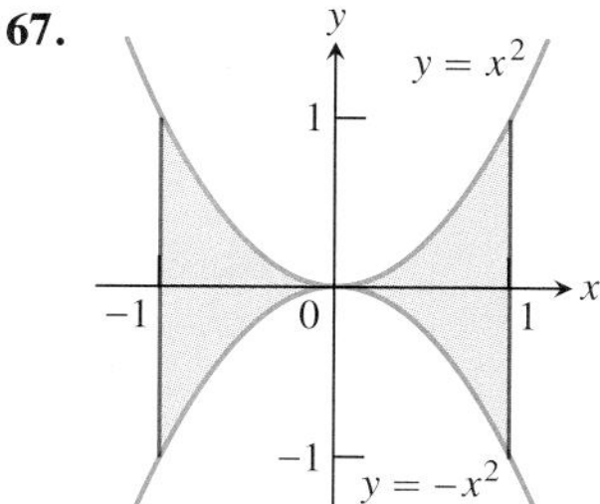

68.

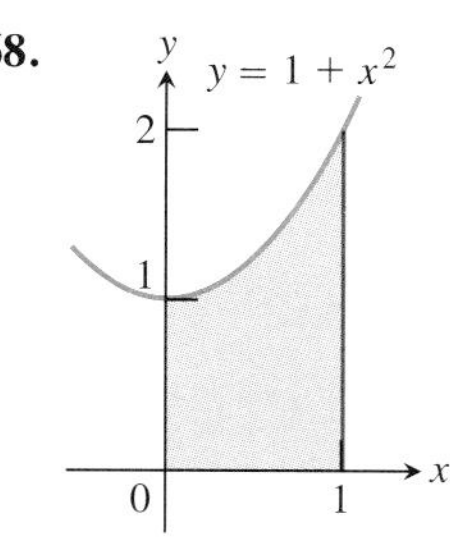

Evaluate the integrals in Exercises 69–74.

69. $\int_{-2}^{1} 5\, dx$

70. $\int_{3}^{7} (-20)\, dx$

71. $\int_{0}^{3} (-160)\, dt$

72. $\int_{-4}^{-1} \frac{\pi}{2}\, d\theta$

73. $\int_{-2.1}^{3.4} 0.5\, ds$

74. $\int_{\sqrt{2}}^{\sqrt{18}} \sqrt{2}\, dr$

Use areas to evaluate the integrals in Exercises 75–78.

75. $\int_{0}^{b} x\, dx, \quad b > 0$

76. $\int_{0}^{b} 4x\, dx, \quad b > 0$

77. $\int_{a}^{b} 2s\, ds, \quad 0 < a < b$

78. $\int_{a}^{b} 3t\, dt, \quad 0 < a < b$

In Exercises 79–82, use a definite integral to find the area of the region between the given curve and the x-axis on the interval $[0, b]$, as in Example 8.

79. $y = 3x^2$

80. $y = \pi x^2$

81. $y = 2x$

82. $y = \frac{x}{2} + 1$

If you have access to a program that draws rectangles associated with Riemann sums, use it to draw rectangles associated with Riemann sums that converge to the integrals in Exercises 83–88. Use $n = 4$, 10, 20, and 50 subintervals of equal length in each case.

83. $\int_0^1 (1 - x)\, dx = \frac{1}{2}$

84. $\int_0^1 (x^2 + 1)\, dx = \frac{4}{3}$

85. $\int_{-\pi}^{\pi} \cos x\, dx = 0$

86. $\int_0^{\pi/4} \sec^2 x\, dx = 1$

87. $\int_{-1}^{1} |x|\, dx = 1$

88. $\int_1^2 \frac{1}{x}\, dx$ (The integral's value is ln 2.)

Writing for Your Own Knowledge

Answer the following questions in writing. Some answers will take only a sentence or two; others may require several paragraphs. Some explanations may also call for graphs or sketches.

1. What is sigma notation? What advantage does it offer?
2. What rules are available for calculating with sigma notation?
3. What is a Riemann sum? Why might you consider such a sum?
4. What is the norm of a partition of a closed interval?
5. What is the definite integral of a function f over a closed interval $[a, b]$? When can you be sure that it exists?
6. How can you sometimes use definite integrals to define areas of nonstandard shapes?
7. How can you sometimes use area formulas from geometry to evaluate definite integrals?

EXPLORER PROGRAM

Riemann Sums	Draws rectangles for upper-endpoint and lower-endpoint Riemann sums.

5.3 *Basic Properties, Area, and the Mean Value Theorem for Integrals*

This section describes rules that reduce the work of evaluating integrals, examines the relationship between the integrals of arbitrary continuous functions and area, and takes a fresh look at the notion of average value.

Properties of Definite Integrals

We can sometimes lessen the work of evaluating integrals by applying one or more of the rules in Table 5.3.

Rule 1 extends the definition of definite integral to allow for the case $a = b$. Rule 2 extends the definition of definite integral to allow for the case $b < a$. Rules 3 and 4 are like the analogous rules for limits and antiderivatives. Once we know the integrals of two functions, we automatically know the integrals of various algebraic combinations of these functions. Rules 3 and 4 enable us to integrate sums and differences of functions term by term. For any constants $c_1, \ldots, c_n$, regardless of sign, and functions $f_1(x), \ldots, f_n(x)$, integrable on $[a, b]$,

$$\int_a^b (c_1 f_1(x) + \cdots + c_n f_n(x))\, dx = c_1 \int_a^b f_1(x)\, dx + \cdots + c_n \int_a^b f_n(x)\, dx. \tag{1}$$

The proof, omitted, comes from mathematical induction.

TABLE 5.3
Rules for working with definite integrals

The following rules hold when the necessary integrals exist.

1. *Zero:*	$\int_a^a f(x)\,dx = 0$	(A definition)
2. *Order of integration:*	$\int_b^a f(x)\,dx = -\int_a^b f(x)\,dx$	(Also a definition)
3. *Constant multiples:*	$\int_a^b kf(x)\,dx = k\int_a^b f(x)\,dx$	(Any number k)
	$\int_a^b -f(x)\,dx = -\int_a^b f(x)\,dx$	$(k = -1)$
4. *Sums and differences:*	$\int_a^b (f(x) + g(x))\,dx = \int_a^b f(x)\,dx + \int_a^b g(x)\,dx$	
	$\int_a^b (f(x) - g(x))\,dx = \int_a^b f(x)\,dx - \int_a^b g(x)\,dx$	
5. *Additivity:*	$\int_a^b f(x)\,dx + \int_b^c f(x)\,dx = \int_a^c f(x)\,dx.$	

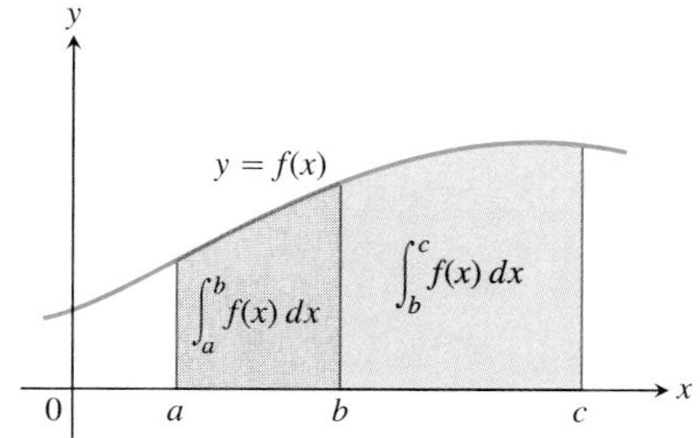

5.13 Additivity for definite integrals:

$$\int_a^b f(x)\,dx + \int_b^c f(x)\,dx = \int_a^c f(x)\,dx$$

$$\int_b^c f(x)\,dx = \int_a^c f(x)\,dx - \int_a^b f(x)\,dx$$

Figure 5.13 illustrates Rule 5 with a positive function, but the rule applies to any integrable function.

EXAMPLE 1 Suppose that f, g, and h are integrable and that

$$\int_{-1}^{1} f(x)\,dx = 5, \qquad \int_{1}^{4} f(x)\,dx = -2, \qquad \int_{-1}^{1} h(x)\,dx = 7.$$

Then

1. $\int_4^1 f(x)\,dx = -\int_1^4 f(x)\,dx = -(-2) = 2$ Rule 2

2. $\int_{-1}^{1} [2f(x) + 3h(x)]\,dx = 2\int_{-1}^{1} f(x)\,dx + 3\int_{-1}^{1} h(x)\,dx$

$= 2(5) + 3(7) = 31$ Rules 3 and 4

3. $\int_{-1}^{1} [f(x) - h(x)]\,dx = 5 - 7 = -2$ Rule 4

4. $\int_{-1}^{4} f(x)\,dx = \int_{-1}^{1} f(x)\,dx + \int_{1}^{4} f(x)\,dx$

$= 5 + (-2) = 3.$ Rule 5

In Section 5.2 we learned to evaluate three general integrals:

$$\int_a^b c\,dx = c(b-a) \qquad \text{(Any constant } c) \tag{2}$$

$$\int_a^b x\,dx = \frac{b^2}{2} - \frac{a^2}{2} \qquad (0 < a < b) \tag{3}$$

$$\int_0^b x^2\,dx = \frac{b^3}{3} \qquad (b > 0). \tag{4}$$

The rules in Table 5.3 enable us to build on these results.

EXAMPLE 2 Evaluate $\displaystyle\int_0^2 \left(\frac{t^2}{4} - 7t + 5\right) dt.$

Solution

$$\begin{aligned}\int_0^2 \left(\frac{t^2}{4} - 7t + 5\right) dt &= \frac{1}{4}\int_0^2 t^2\,dt - 7\int_0^2 t\,dt + \int_0^2 5\,dt && \text{Sum, Difference, and Constant Multiple Rules}\\ &= \frac{1}{4}\left(\frac{(2)^3}{3}\right) - 7\left(\frac{(2)^2}{2} - \frac{(0)^2}{2}\right) + 5(2-0) && \text{Eqs. (2)–(4)}\\ &= \frac{2}{3} - 14 + 10 = -\frac{10}{3}\end{aligned}$$

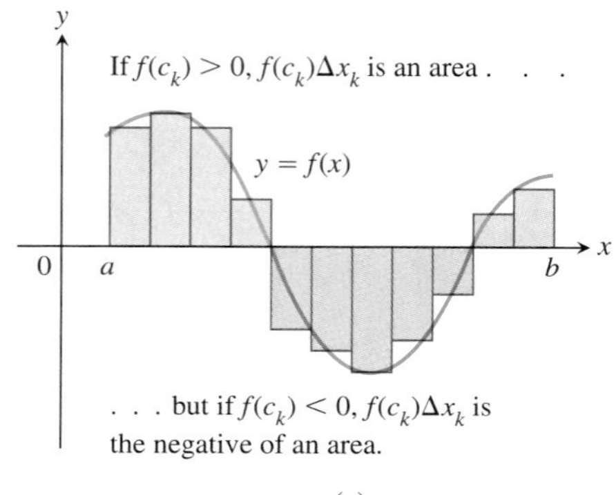

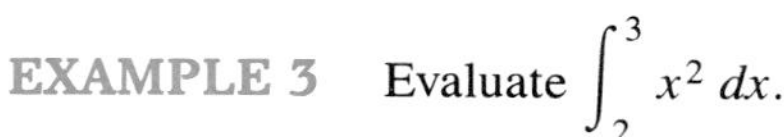

EXAMPLE 3 Evaluate $\displaystyle\int_2^3 x^2\,dx.$

Solution We cannot apply Eq. (4) directly because the lower limit of integration is different from 0. We can, however, use the Additivity Rule to express $\int_2^3 x^2\,dx$ as a difference of two integrals that *can* be evaluated with Eq. (4):

$$\begin{aligned}\int_0^2 x^2\,dx + \int_2^3 x^2\,dx &= \int_0^3 x^2\,dx && \text{Additivity}\\ \int_2^3 x^2\,dx &= \int_0^3 x^2\,dx - \int_0^2 x^2\,dx && \text{Solve for } \textstyle\int_2^3 x^2\,dx.\\ &= \frac{(3)^3}{3} - \frac{(2)^3}{3} && \text{Eq. (4) now applies.}\\ &= \frac{27}{3} - \frac{8}{3} = \frac{19}{3}\end{aligned}$$

In Section 5.4, we will see how to evaluate $\int_2^3 x^2\,dx$ in a more direct way.

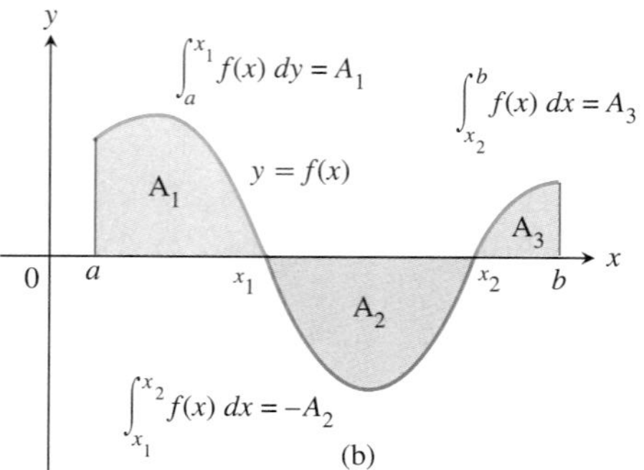

5.14 (a) The Riemann sums are algebraic sums of areas and so is the integral to which they converge. (b) The value of the integral of f from a to b is

$$\int_a^b f(x)\,dx = \int_a^{x_1} f(x)\,dx + \int_{x_1}^{x_2} f(x)\,dx + \int_{x_2}^{b} f(x)\,dx = A_1 - A_2 + A_3.$$

Integrals and Area

If an integrable function $y = f(x)$ has both positive and negative values on an interval $[a, b]$, then the Riemann sums for f on $[a, b]$ add the areas of the rectangles that lie above the x-axis to the negatives of the areas of the rectangles that lie below it (Fig. 5.14). The resulting cancellation reduces the sums, so their limiting value is a number whose magnitude is less than the total area between the curve and the x-axis. The value of the integral is the area above the axis minus the area below the axis.

This means that we must take special care in finding areas by integration.

How to Find the Area of the Region Between a Curve $y = f(x)$, $a \le x \le b$, and the x-Axis

1. Partition $[a, b]$ with the zeros of f.
2. Integrate f over each subinterval.
3. Add the absolute values of the integrals.

EXAMPLE 4 Find the area of the region between the curve $y = 4 - x^2$, $0 \le x \le 3$, and the x-axis.

Solution The x-intercept of the curve partitions $[0, 3]$ into subintervals on which $f(x) = 4 - x^2$ has the same sign (Fig. 5.15). To find the area of the region between the graph of f and the x-axis, we integrate f over each subinterval and add the absolute values of the results.

Integral over $[0, 2]$:

$$\int_0^2 (4 - x^2)\,dx = \int_0^2 4\,dx - \int_0^2 x^2\,dx \qquad \text{Difference Rule}$$

$$= 4(2 - 0) - \frac{(2)^3}{3} \qquad \text{Eqs. (2) and (4)}$$

$$= 8 - \frac{8}{3} = \frac{16}{3}$$

Integral over $[2, 3]$:

$$\int_2^3 (4 - x^2)\,dx = \int_2^3 4\,dx - \int_2^3 x^2\,dx \qquad \text{Difference Rule}$$

$$= 4(3 - 2) - \left(\frac{(3)^3}{3} - \frac{(2)^3}{3}\right) \qquad \text{Eq. (2) and Example 3}$$

$$= 4 - \frac{19}{3} = -\frac{7}{3}$$

The region's area: $\quad \text{Area} = \dfrac{16}{3} + \left|-\dfrac{7}{3}\right| = \dfrac{23}{3}.$

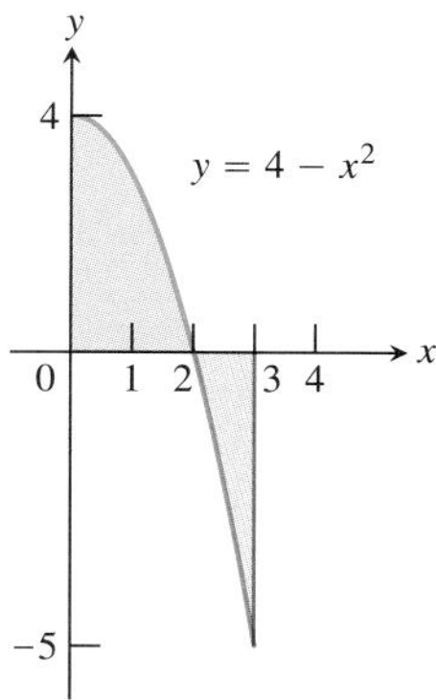

5.15 Part of the region in Example 4 lies below the x-axis.

The Average Value of an Arbitrary Continuous Function

In Section 5.1 we introduced the average value of a positive continuous function as a representative height for the function's graph. We are now ready to define average value without requiring f to be positive, and to show that every continuous function assumes its average value at least once.

We start once again with the idea from arithmetic that the average of n numbers is the sum of the numbers divided by n. For a continuous function f on a closed interval $[a, b]$ there may be infinitely many values to consider, but we can sample them in an orderly way. We partition $[a, b]$ into n subintervals of equal length (the length is $\Delta x = (b - a)/n$) and evaluate f at a point c_k in each subinterval (Fig. 5.16). The average of the n sampled values is

$$\frac{f(c_1) + f(c_2) + \cdots + f(c_n)}{n} = \frac{1}{n} \cdot \sum_{k=1}^{n} f(c_k) \qquad \text{The sum in sigma notation}$$

$$= \frac{\Delta x}{b - a} \cdot \sum_{k=1}^{n} f(c_k) \qquad \Delta x = \frac{b - a}{n}$$

$$= \frac{1}{b - a} \cdot \underbrace{\sum_{k=1}^{n} f(c_k)\,\Delta x}_{\text{a Riemann sum for } f \text{ on } [a,\, b]} \tag{5}$$

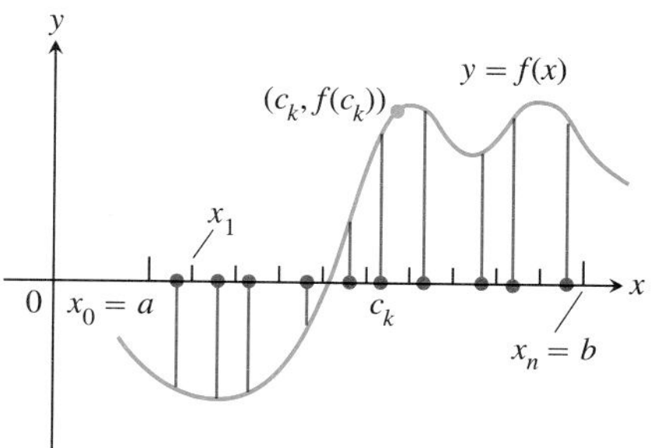

5.16 A sample of values of a function on an interval $[a, b]$.

Thus, the average of the sampled values is always $1/(b - a)$ times a Riemann sum for f on $[a, b]$. As we increase the size of the sample and let the norm of the partition approach zero, the average of the sampled values must approach $(1/(b - a)) \int_a^b f(x)\,dx$. We are led by this remarkable fact to the following definition.

DEFINITION

If f is integrable on $[a, b]$ its **average (mean) value** on $[a, b]$ is

$$\text{av}(f) = \frac{1}{b - a}\int_a^b f(x)\,dx. \tag{6}$$

If f happens to be positive, the integral in Eq. (6) gives the area under the graph of f and the new definition of average gives the same result as the old one. The advantage of the new definition is that it includes functions with negative values.

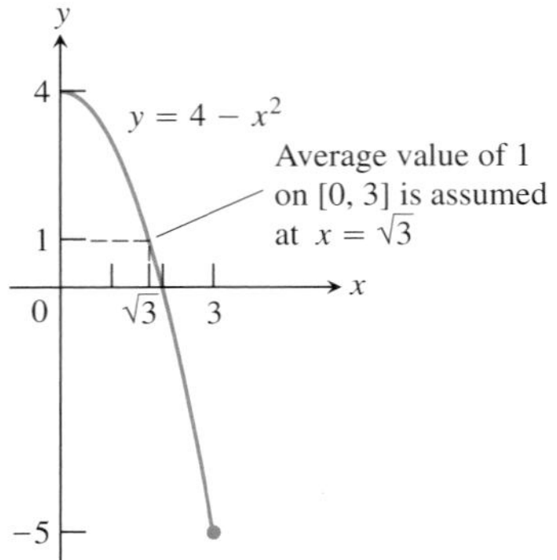

5.17 The average value of $f(x) = 4 - x^2$ on $[0, 3]$ occurs at $x = \sqrt{3}$ (Example 5).

EXAMPLE 5 Find the average value of $f(x) = 4 - x^2$ on $[0, 3]$. Does f actually take on this value at some point in the given domain?

Solution

$$\text{av}(f) = \frac{1}{b - a}\int_a^b f(x)\,dx \qquad \text{Definition, Eq. (6)}$$

$$= \frac{1}{3 - 0}\int_0^3 (4 - x^2)\,dx = \frac{1}{3}\left(\int_0^3 4\,dx - \int_0^3 x^2\,dx\right)$$

$$= \frac{1}{3}\left(4(3 - 0) - \frac{(3)^3}{3}\right) = \frac{1}{3}(12 - 9) = 1$$

The average value of $f(x) = 4 - x^2$ over the interval $[0, 3]$ is 1. The function assumes this value when $4 - x^2 = 1$ or $x = \pm\sqrt{3}$. Since one of these points, $x = \sqrt{3}$, lies in $[0, 3]$, the function does assume its average value in the given domain (Fig. 5.17).

The Mean Value Theorem for Definite Integrals

The statement that a continuous function on a closed interval assumes its average value at least once in the interval is known as the Mean Value Theorem for Definite Integrals.

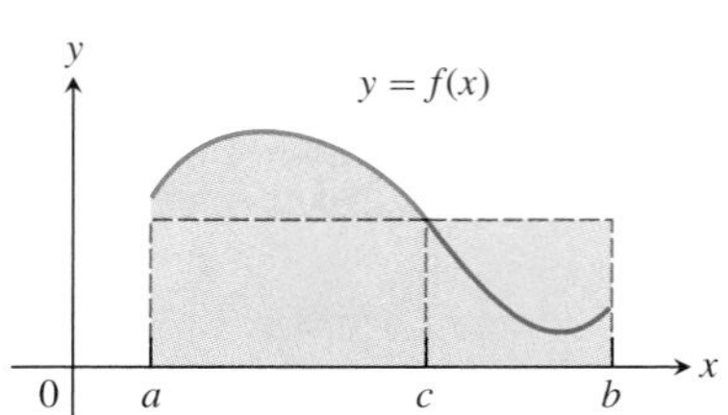

5.18 Theorem 2 for a positive function: At some point c in $[a, b]$,

$$f(c)\cdot(b - a) = \int_a^b f(x)\,dx.$$

THEOREM 2

The Mean Value Theorem for Definite Integrals

If f is continuous on $[a, b]$, then at some point c in $[a, b]$,

$$f(c) = \frac{1}{b - a}\int_a^b f(x)\,dx. \tag{7}$$

(Fig. 5.18).

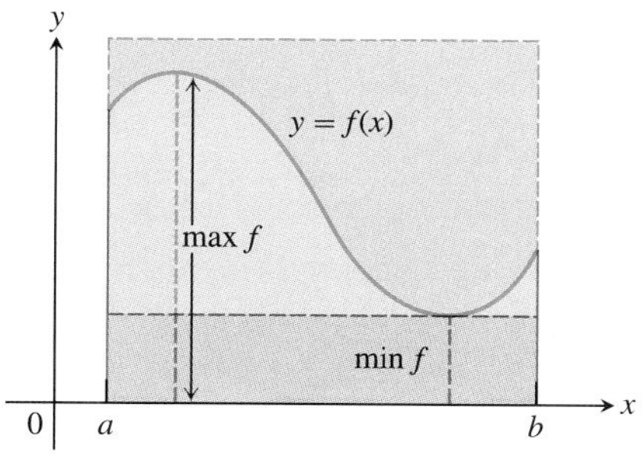

Area of red rectangle = $\min f \cdot (b - a)$

Area under the curve = $\int_a^b f(x)\,dx$

Area of largest rectangle = $\max f \cdot (b - a)$

5.19 The Max-Min Inequality for a positive function:

$$\min f \cdot (b - a) \le \int_a^b f(x)\,dx \le \max f \cdot (b - a)$$

In Example 5, we found a point where f assumed its average value by setting $f(x)$ equal to the calculated average value and solving the resulting equation for x. But this does not prove that such a point will always exist. It proves only that it existed in Example 5. To prove Theorem 2, we need a more general argument, and we can get it from the following inequality.

The Max-Min Inequality for Definite Integrals

If $\max f$ and $\min f$ are the maximum and minimum values of f on $[a, b]$, then

$$\min f \cdot (b - a) \le \int_a^b f(x)\,dx \le \max f \cdot (b - a). \tag{8}$$

The Max-Min Inequality says that the integral of f over $[a, b]$ is never smaller than the minimum value of f times the length of $[a, b]$ and never larger than the maximum value of f times the length of $[a, b]$. In other words, $\min f \cdot (b - a)$ is a **lower bound** for the value of the integral and $\max f \cdot (b - a)$ is an **upper bound** for the value of the integral (Fig. 5.19).

If we divide both sides of Eq. (8) by $(b - a)$, we get

$$\min f \le \frac{1}{b - a}\int_a^b f(x)\,dx \le \max f. \tag{9}$$

If f is continuous, the Intermediate Value Theorem for Continuous Functions (Theorem 9, Section 2.4) says that f must assume every value between $\min f$ and $\max f$. It must therefore assume the value $(1/(b - a)) \int_a^b f(x)\,dx$ somewhere in $[a, b]$. Thus, at some point c in $[a, b]$, $f(c)$ equals $(1/(b - a)) \int_a^b f(x)\,dx$, the mean value on $[a, b]$.

The continuity of f is important here. A discontinuous function can step over its average value (Fig. 5.20).

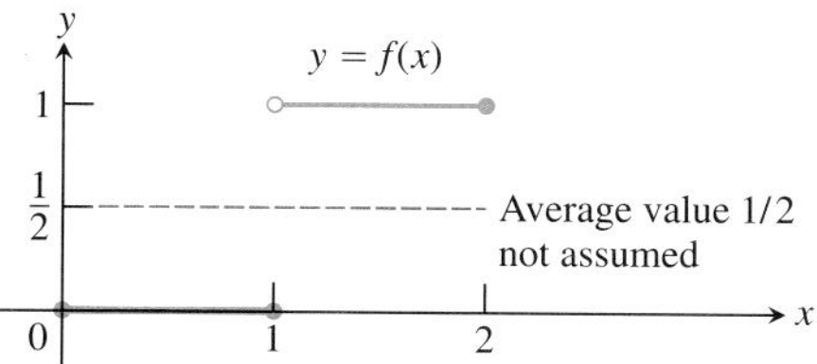

5.20 A discontinuous function need not assume its average value.

What else can we learn from Theorem 2 and the Max-Min Inequality? Here are some examples.

EXAMPLE 6 Show that if f is continuous on $[a, b]$ and if

$$\int_a^b f(x)\,dx = 0,$$

then $f(x) = 0$ at least once in $[a, b]$.

Solution The average value of f on $[a, b]$ is

$$\text{av}(f) = \frac{1}{b - a}\int_a^b f(x)\,dx = \frac{1}{b - a} \cdot 0 = 0.$$

By Theorem 2, f assumes this value at some point c in $[a, b]$. ■

EXAMPLE 7 Show that the value of

$$\int_0^1 \sqrt{1 + \cos x}\,dx$$

cannot possibly be 2.

Solution The maximum value of $\sqrt{1+\cos x}$ on $[0, 1]$ is $\sqrt{1+1} = \sqrt{2}$, so

$$\int_0^1 \sqrt{1+\cos x}\, dx \le \max \sqrt{1+\cos x} \cdot (1-0) \le \sqrt{2} \cdot 1 = \sqrt{2}.$$

From Eq. (8) with $f(x) = \sqrt{1+\cos x}$, $a = 0$, $b = 1$

The integral cannot exceed $\sqrt{2}$, so it cannot possibly equal 2.

Domination

A function $f(x)$ **dominates** a function $g(x)$ on $[a, b]$ if $f(x) \ge g(x)$ for all x in $[a, b]$. What interests us here is that if f and g are integrable and f dominates g then the integral of f dominates the integral of g.

The Domination Inequality for Definite Integrals

If $f(x) \ge g(x)$ on $[a, b]$, then

$$\int_a^b f(x)\, dx \ge \int_a^b g(x)\, dx. \tag{10}$$

EXAMPLE 8 Use the inequality $\cos x \ge (1 - x^2/2)$, which holds for all x, to find a lower bound for the value of $\int_0^1 \cos x\, dx$.

Solution

$$\int_0^1 \cos x\, dx \ge \int_0^1 \left(1 - \frac{x^2}{2}\right) dx$$

Eq. (10) with $f(x) = \cos x$ and $g(x) = 1 - (x^2/2)$

$$\ge \int_0^1 1\, dx - \frac{1}{2}\int_0^1 x^2\, dx$$

$$\ge 1 \cdot (1-0) - \frac{1}{2} \cdot \frac{(1)^3}{3} = \frac{5}{6} \approx 0.83.$$

The value of the integral is at least 5/6.

Exercises 5.3

1. Suppose that f and g are continuous and that

$$\int_1^2 f(x)\, dx = -4, \quad \int_1^5 f(x)\, dx = 6, \quad \int_1^5 g(x)\, dx = 8.$$

Use the rules in Table 5.3 to find

a) $\int_2^2 g(x)\, dx$ **b)** $\int_5^1 g(x)\, dx$

c) $\int_1^2 3f(x)\, dx$ **d)** $\int_2^5 f(x)\, dx$

e) $\int_1^5 [f(x) - g(x)]\, dx$ **f)** $\int_1^5 [4f(x) - g(x)]\, dx$

2. Suppose that f and h are continuous and that

$$\int_1^9 f(x)\, dx = -1, \quad \int_7^9 f(x)\, dx = 5, \quad \int_7^9 h(x)\, dx = 4.$$

Use the rules in Table 5.3 to find

a) $\int_1^9 -2f(x)\, dx$ **b)** $\int_7^9 [f(x) + h(x)]\, dx$

c) $\displaystyle\int_7^9 [2f(x) - 3h(x)]\,dx$ d) $\displaystyle\int_9^1 f(x)\,dx$

e) $\displaystyle\int_1^7 f(x)\,dx$ f) $\displaystyle\int_9^7 [h(x) - f(x)]\,dx$

3. Suppose that $\int_1^2 f(x)\,dx = 5$. Find

a) $\displaystyle\int_1^2 f(u)\,du$ b) $\displaystyle\int_1^2 f(z)\,dz$

c) $\displaystyle\int_2^1 f(t)\,dt$ d) $\displaystyle\int_1^2 [-f(x)]\,dx$

4. Suppose that $\int_{-3}^0 g(t)\,dt = \sqrt{2}$. Find

a) $\displaystyle\int_0^{-3} g(t)\,dt$ b) $\displaystyle\int_{-3}^0 g(u)\,du$

c) $\displaystyle\int_{-3}^0 [-g(x)]\,dx$ d) $\displaystyle\int_{-3}^0 \frac{g(r)}{\sqrt{2}}\,dr$

5. Suppose that f is continuous and that $\int_0^3 f(z)\,dz = 3$ and $\int_0^4 f(z)\,dz = 7$. Find

a) $\displaystyle\int_3^4 f(z)\,dz$ b) $\displaystyle\int_4^3 f(z)\,dz$

6. Suppose that h is continuous and that $\int_{-1}^1 h(r)\,dr = 0$ and $\int_{-1}^3 h(r)\,dr = 6$. Find

a) $\displaystyle\int_1^3 h(r)\,dr$ b) $\displaystyle -\int_3^1 h(r)\,dr$

Evaluate the integrals in Exercises 7–18.

7. $\displaystyle\int_3^1 7\,dx$ **8.** $\displaystyle\int_0^{-2} \sqrt{2}\,dx$

9. $\displaystyle\int_0^2 5x\,dx$ **10.** $\displaystyle\int_3^5 \frac{x}{8}\,dx$

11. $\displaystyle\int_0^2 (2x - 3)\,dx$ **12.** $\displaystyle\int_0^{\sqrt{2}} \left(x - \sqrt{2}\right)dx$

13. $\displaystyle\int_2^1 \left(1 + \frac{x}{2}\right)dx$ **14.** $\displaystyle\int_3^0 (2x - 3)\,dx$

15. $\displaystyle\int_1^2 3x^2\,dx$ **16.** $\displaystyle\int_{1/2}^1 24x^2\,dx$

17. $\displaystyle\int_0^2 (3x^2 + x - 5)\,dx$ **18.** $\displaystyle\int_1^0 (3x^2 + x - 5)\,dx$

In Exercises 19–22, find the total shaded area.

19.

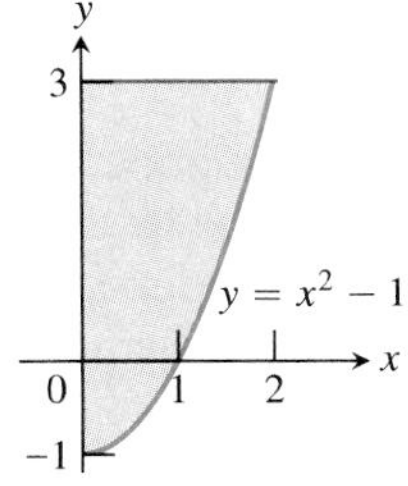

20.

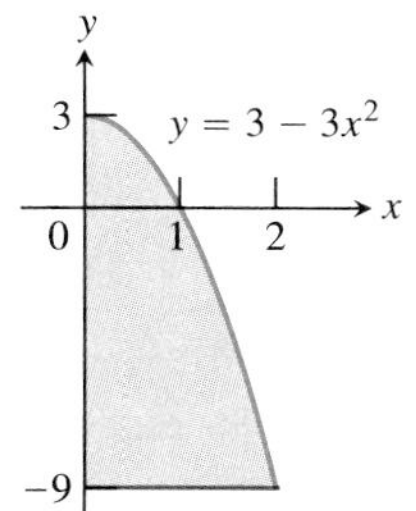

21.

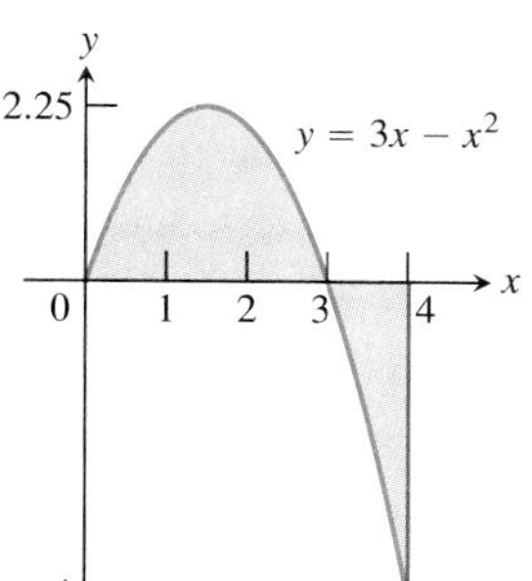

22.

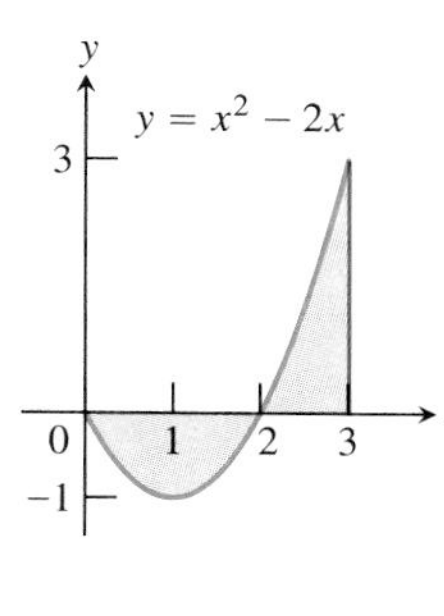

In Exercises 23–26, (a) graph the function over the given interval. Next, (b) integrate the function over the interval. Then, (c) find the area of the region between the graph and the x-axis.

23. $y = x^2 - 6x + 8, \quad [0, 3]$

24. $y = -x^2 + 5x - 4, \quad [0, 2]$

25. $y = 2x - x^2, \quad [0, 3]$ **26.** $y = x^2 - 4x, \quad [0, 5]$

In Exercises 27–34, graph the function and find its average value over the given interval. At what point or points in the given interval does the function assume its average value?

27. $f(x) = x^2 - 1$ on $\left[0, \sqrt{3}\right]$

28. $f(x) = -\dfrac{x^2}{2}$ on $[0, 3]$

29. $f(x) = -3x^2 - 1$ on $[0, 1]$

30. $f(x) = 3x^2 - 3$ on $[0, 1]$

31. $f(t) = \sin t$ on $[0, 2\pi]$

32. $f(\theta) = \tan\theta$ on $\left[\dfrac{-\pi}{4}, \dfrac{\pi}{4}\right]$

33. $g(x) = |x| - 1$ on **a)** $[-1, 1]$, **b)** $[1, 3]$, and **c)** $[-1, 3]$

34. $h(x) = -|x|$ on **a)** $[-1, 0]$, **b)** $[0, 1]$, and **c)** $[-1, 1]$

35. Use the Max-Min Inequality (Eq. 8) to find upper and lower bounds for the value of

$$\int_0^1 \frac{1}{1 + x^2}\,dx.$$

36. *Continuation of Exercise 35.* Use the Max-Min Inequality to find upper and lower bounds for

$$\int_0^{0.5} \frac{1}{1 + x^2}\,dx \quad \text{and} \quad \int_{0.5}^1 \frac{1}{1 + x^2}\,dx.$$

Add these to arrive at an improved estimate of

$$\int_0^1 \frac{1}{1 + x^2}\,dx.$$

37. Show that the value of $\int_0^1 \sin(x^2)\,dx$ cannot possibly be 2.

38. Show that the value of $\int_0^1 \sqrt{x + 8}\,dx$ lies between $2\sqrt{2} \approx 2.8$ and 3.

39. Suppose that f is continuous and that $\int_1^2 f(x)\,dx = 4$. Show that $f(x) = 4$ at least once on $[1, 2]$.

40. Suppose that f and g are continuous on $[a, b]$ and that $\int_a^b (f(x) - g(x))\,dx = 0$. Show that $f(x) = g(x)$ at least once in $[a, b]$.

41. *Integrals of Nonnegative Functions.* Use the Max-Min Inequality (Eq. 8) to show that if f is integrable then

$$f(x) \geq 0 \quad \text{on} \quad [a, b] \quad \Rightarrow \quad \int_a^b f(x)\,dx \geq 0.$$

42. *Integrals of Nonpositive Functions.* Show that if f is integrable then

$$f(x) \leq 0 \quad \text{on} \quad [a, b] \quad \Rightarrow \quad \int_a^b f(x)\,dx \leq 0.$$

43. Use the inequality $\sin x \leq x$, which holds for $x \geq 0$, to find an upper bound for the value of $\int_0^1 \sin x\,dx$.

44. The inequality $\sec x \geq 1 + (x^2/2)$ holds on $(-\pi/2, \pi/2)$. Use it to find a lower bound for the value of $\int_0^1 \sec x\,dx$.

45. If $\text{av}(f)$ really is a typical value of the integrable function $f(x)$ on $[a, b]$, then the number $\text{av}(f)$ should have the same integral over $[a, b]$ that f does. Does it? That is, does

$$\int_a^b \text{av}(f)\,dx = \int_a^b f(x)\,dx?$$

Give reasons for your answer.

46. It would be nice if average values of integrable functions obeyed the following rules on an interval $[a, b]$:

a) $\text{av}(f + g) = \text{av}(f) + \text{av}(g)$
b) $\text{av}(kf) = k\,\text{av}(f)$ (any number k)
c) $\text{av}(f) \leq \text{av}(g)$ if $f(x) \leq g(x)$ on $[a, b]$.

Do these rules ever hold? Give reasons for your answers.

Writing for Your Own Knowledge

Answer the following questions in writing. Some answers will take only a sentence or two; others may require several paragraphs. Some explanations may also call for graphs or sketches.

1. What are the rules for integrating sums, differences, and constant multiples of integrable functions?
2. How do you find the area of the region between the graph of a continuous function $f(x)$, $a \leq x \leq b$, and the x-axis?
3. What does finding a function's average value have to do with integration?
4. What bounds can you place on the value of a continuous function's integral?
5. How does the inequality $f(x) \geq g(x)$ carry over to the integrals of f and g?

5.4 *The Fundamental Theorem of Calculus*

This section presents the Fundamental Theorem of Calculus. The first part of the theorem says that the definite integral of a continuous function is a differentiable function of its upper limit of integration and tells us what the value of that derivative is. The second part says that the definite integral of a continuous function from a to b can be found from any one of the function's antiderivatives F as the number $F(b) - F(a)$. The discovery by Newton and Leibniz of these astonishing connections between integration and differentiation started the mathematical development that fueled the scientific revolution for the next 200 years and constitutes what is still regarded as the most important computational discovery in the history of the world.

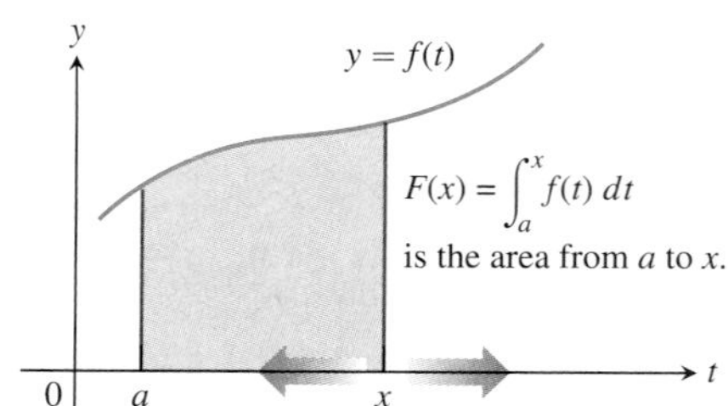

5.21 With a fixed, the shaded region and its area then depend on the value of x.

Part 1 of the Fundamental Theorem

If f is an integrable function, its integral from a fixed number a to another number x defines a function F whose value at x is

$$F(x) = \int_a^x f(t)\,dt. \tag{1}$$

If f were nonnegative and x lay to the right of a, then $F(x)$ would be the area under the graph of f from a to x (Fig. 5.21). Even though x is an integral's upper limit of integration, the function F is simply another real-valued function of a real variable. For each value of x there is a well defined numerical output $F(x)$.

Equation (1) gives an important way to define new functions and to describe solutions of differential equations (more about this later). The reason for mentioning Eq. (1) now, however, is the connection it makes between integrals and derivatives. For if f is any continuous function whatever, then F is a differentiable function of x whose derivative is f itself. At every value of x,

$$\frac{d}{dx}F(x) = \frac{d}{dx}\int_a^x f(t)\,dt = f(x). \tag{2}$$

This conclusion is beautiful, powerful, deep, and surprising, and Eq. (2) may well be the most important equation in mathematics. It says that the differential equation $dF/dx = f$ has a solution for every continuous function f. It says that every continuous function f is the derivative of some other function, namely $\int_a^x f(t)\,dt$. It says that every continuous function has an antiderivative. And it says that the processes of integration and differentiation are inverses of one another.

Equation (2) constitutes the first part of the Fundamental Theorem of Calculus.

THEOREM 3

The Fundamental Theorem of Calculus, Part 1

If f is continuous on $[a, b]$ then $F(x) = \int_a^x f(t)\,dt$ has a derivative at every point of $[a, b]$ and

$$\frac{dF}{dx} = \frac{d}{dx}\int_a^x f(t)\,dt = f(x). \tag{3}$$

Proof We prove Theorem 3 by applying the definition of derivative directly to the function $F(x)$. This means writing out Fermat's difference quotient,

$$\frac{F(x+h) - F(x)}{h}, \tag{4}$$

and showing that its limit as $h \to 0$ is the number $f(x)$.

When we replace $F(x + h)$ and $F(x)$ by their defining integrals, the numerator in Eq. (4) becomes

$$F(x+h) - F(x) = \int_a^{x+h} f(t)\,dt - \int_a^x f(t)\,dt. \tag{5}$$

The Additivity Rule for integrals (Table 5.10 in Section 5.3) simplifies the right-hand side to

$$\int_x^{x+h} f(t)\,dt \tag{6}$$

(Fig. 5.22 on the following page), so that Eq. (4) becomes

$$\begin{aligned}\frac{F(x+h) - F(x)}{h} &= \frac{1}{h}[F(x+h) - F(x)]\\ &= \frac{1}{h}\int_x^{x+h} f(t)\,dt.\end{aligned} \tag{7}$$

According to the Mean Value Theorem for Definite Integrals (Theorem 2 in the preceding section), the value of the last expression in Eq. (7) is one of the

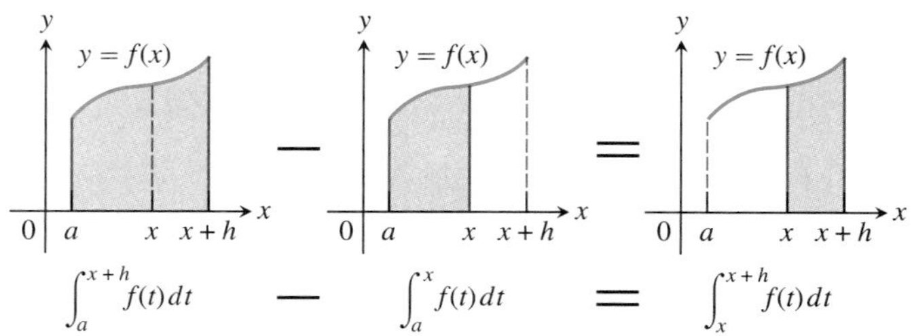

5.22 Equations (5) and (6) for a positive function.

values taken on by f in the interval joining x and $x+h$. That is, for some number c in this interval,

$$\frac{1}{h}\int_x^{x+h} f(t)\,dt = f(c). \tag{8}$$

We can therefore find out what happens to $(1/h)$ times the integral as $h \to 0$ by watching what happens to $f(c)$ as $h \to 0$.

What does happen to $f(c)$ as $h \to 0$? As $h \to 0$, the endpoint $x+h$ approaches x, pushing c ahead of it like a bead on a wire:

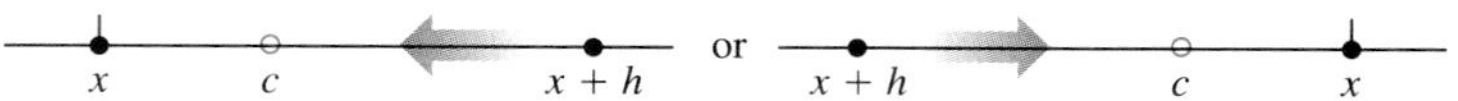

So c approaches x, and, since f is continuous at x, $f(c)$ approaches $f(x)$:

$$\lim_{h\to 0} f(c) = f(x). \tag{9}$$

Going back to the beginning, then, we have

$$\begin{aligned}
\frac{dF}{dx} &= \lim_{h\to 0}\frac{F(x+h)-F(x)}{h} && \text{Definition of derivative}\\
&= \lim_{h\to 0}\frac{1}{h}\int_x^{x+h} f(t)\,dt && \text{Eq. (7)}\\
&= \lim_{h\to 0} f(c) && \text{Eq. (8)}\\
&= f(x). && \text{Eq. (9)}
\end{aligned}$$

This concludes the proof.

EXAMPLE 1

$$\frac{d}{dx}\int_{-\pi}^{x} \cos t\,dt = \cos x \qquad \text{Eq. (3) with } f(t) = \cos t$$

$$\frac{d}{dx}\int_0^x \frac{1}{1+t^2}\,dt = \frac{1}{1+x^2} \qquad \text{Eq. (3) with } f(t) = \frac{1}{1+t^2}$$

EXAMPLE 2 Find dy/dx if

$$y = \int_1^{x^2} \cos t\,dt.$$

Solution Notice that the upper limit of integration is not x but x^2. To find dy/dx we must therefore treat y as the composite of

$$y = \int_1^u \cos t\, dt \quad \text{and} \quad u = x^2$$

and apply the Chain Rule:

$$\begin{aligned}
\frac{dy}{dx} &= \frac{dy}{du} \cdot \frac{du}{dx} && \text{Chain Rule} \\
&= \frac{d}{du}\int_1^u \cos t\, dt \cdot \frac{du}{dx} && \text{Substitute the formula for } y. \\
&= \cos u \cdot \frac{du}{dx} && \text{Eq. (3) with } f(t) = \cos t \\
&= \cos x^2 \cdot 2x && u = x^2 \\
&= 2x \cos x^2. && \text{Usual form}
\end{aligned}$$

EXAMPLE 3 Express the solution of the following initial value problem in terms of an integral.

Differential equation: $\dfrac{dy}{dx} = \tan x$

Initial condition: $y = 5$ when $x = 1$

Solution The function

$$F(x) = \int_1^x \tan t\, dt$$

is an antiderivative of $\tan x$. Hence the general solution of the equation is

$$y = \int_1^x \tan t\, dt + C.$$

As always, the initial conditions determine the right value for C:

$$\begin{aligned}
5 &= \int_1^1 \tan t\, dt + C && y = 5 \text{ when } x = 1 \\
5 &= 0 + C && (10) \\
C &= 5.
\end{aligned}$$

The solution of the initial value problem is

$$y = \int_1^x \tan t\, dt + 5.$$

How did we know where to start integrating when we constructed $F(x)$? We could have started anywhere, but the best value to start with is the initial value of x (in this case $x = 1$). Then the integral will be zero when we apply the initial condition (as it was in Eq. 10) and C will automatically be the initial value of y.

The Evaluation of Definite Integrals

We now come to the second part of the Fundamental Theorem of Calculus, the part that describes how to evaluate definite integrals.

THEOREM 4

The Fundamental Theorem of Calculus, Part 2

If f is continuous at every point of $[a, b]$ and F is any antiderivative of f on $[a, b]$, then

$$\int_a^b f(x)\,dx = F(b) - F(a). \tag{11}$$

Theorem 4 says that to evaluate the definite integral of a continuous function f from a to b, all we need do is find an antiderivative F of f and calculate the number $F(b) - F(a)$. The existence of the antiderivative is assured by the first part of the Fundamental Theorem.

Proof of Theorem 4 To prove Theorem 4, we use the fact that functions with identical derivatives differ only by a constant. We already know one function whose derivative equals f, namely,

$$G(x) = \int_a^x f(t)\,dt.$$

Therefore, if F is any other such function, then

$$F(x) = G(x) + C \tag{12}$$

throughout $[a, b]$ for some constant C. When we use Eq. (12) to calculate $F(b) - F(a)$, we find that

$$\begin{aligned} F(b) - F(a) &= [G(b) + C] - [G(a) + C] = G(b) - G(a) \\ &= \int_a^b f(t)\,dt - \int_a^a f(t)\,dt \\ &= \int_a^b f(t)\,dt - 0 = \int_a^b f(t)\,dt. \end{aligned}$$

This establishes Eq. (11) and concludes the proof. ∎

Part 2 of the Fundamental Theorem reduces the problem of evaluating definite integrals of continuous functions to one of finding and evaluating antiderivatives. We no longer have to evaluate integrals by finding limits of Riemann sums. As for finding the necessary antiderivatives, there is no need to worry. We will get better at that as we learn more calculus. There are also good numerical methods for approximating the values of integrals, as we will see in Section 5.7.

Notation

The usual notation for the number $F(b) - F(a)$ is $F(x)]_a^b$ or $[F(x)]_a^b$, depending on whether F has one or more terms. This notation provides a compact "recipe" for the evaluation.

Write $F(x)]_a^b$ for $F(b) - F(a)$ when $F(x)$ has a single term.

Write $[F(x)]_a^b$ for $F(b) - F(a)$ when $F(x)$ has more than one term.

EXAMPLE 4

a) $$\int_0^{\pi} \cos x\,dx = \sin x\Big]_0^{\pi} = \sin \pi - \sin 0 = 0 - 0 = 0$$

an antiderivative of $\cos x$

b) $\displaystyle\int_{-\pi/4}^{0} \sec x \tan x\, dx = \sec x\Big]_{-\pi/4}^{0} = \sec 0 - \sec\left(-\frac{\pi}{4}\right) = 1 - \sqrt{2}$

an antiderivative of $\sec x \tan x$

an antiderivative of $(3/2)\sqrt{x} - 4/x^2$

c) $$\int_1^4 \left(\frac{3}{2}\sqrt{x} - \frac{4}{x^2}\right) dx = \left[x^{3/2} + \frac{4}{x}\right]_1^4 = \left[(4)^{3/2} + \frac{4}{4}\right] - \left[(1)^{3/2} + \frac{4}{1}\right]$$
$$= [8 + 1] - [5] = 4.$$

How to Evaluate $\int_a^b f(x)\, dx$

1. Find an antiderivative F of f. Any antiderivative will do, so pick the simplest one you can.
2. Calculate the number $F(b) - F(a)$. This number will be $\int_a^b f(x)\, dx$.

Theorem 4 explains the formulas we derived for the integrals of x and x^2 in Section 5.3. We can now see that without any restriction whatever on the signs of a and b,

$$\int_a^b x\, dx = \frac{x^2}{2}\Big]_a^b = \frac{b^2}{2} - \frac{a^2}{2} \qquad \text{Because } x^2/2 \text{ is an antiderivative of } x \qquad (13)$$

$$\int_a^b x^2\, dx = \frac{x^3}{3}\Big]_a^b = \frac{b^3}{3} - \frac{a^3}{3} \qquad \text{Because } x^3/3 \text{ is an antiderivative of } x^2 \qquad (14)$$

EXAMPLE 5 Find the area of the region between the x-axis and the graph of $f(x) = x^3 - x^2 - 2x,\ -1 \le x \le 2$.

Solution First find the zeros of f. Since

$$f(x) = x^3 - x^2 - 2x = x(x^2 - x - 2) = x(x + 1)(x - 2),$$

the zeros are $x = 0,\ -1$, and 2 (Fig. 5.23). The zeros partition $[-1, 2]$ into two subintervals: $[-1, 0]$, on which $f \ge 0$ and $[0, 2]$, on which $f \le 0$. We integrate f over each subinterval and add the absolute values of the calculated values.

Integral over $[-1, 0]$: $$\int_{-1}^{0} (x^3 - x^2 - 2x)\, dx = \left[\frac{x^4}{4} - \frac{x^3}{3} - x^2\right]_{-1}^{0} = 0 - \left[\frac{1}{4} + \frac{1}{3} - 1\right] = \frac{5}{12}$$

Integral over $[0, 2]$: $$\int_0^2 (x^3 - x^2 - 2x)\, dx = \left[\frac{x^4}{4} - \frac{x^3}{3} - x^2\right]_0^2 = \left[4 - \frac{8}{3} - 4\right] - 0 = -\frac{8}{3}$$

Enclosed area: Total enclosed area $= \dfrac{5}{12} + \left|-\dfrac{8}{3}\right| = \dfrac{37}{12}$

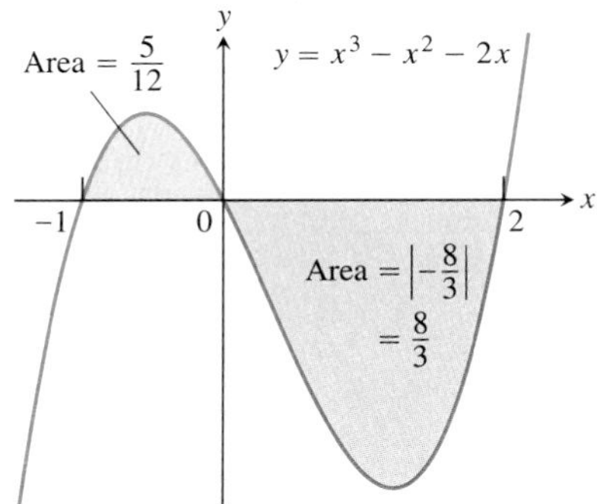

5.23 The region between the curve $y = x^3 - x^2 - 2x$ and the x-axis (Example 5).

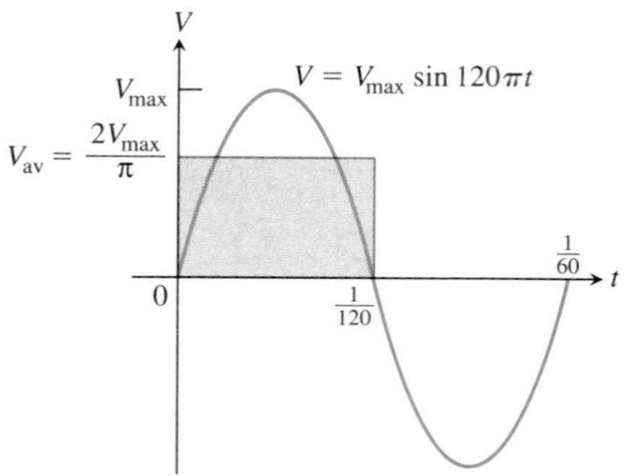

5.24 The graph of the household voltage $V = V_{max} \sin 120\pi t$ over a full cycle. Its average value over a half-cycle is $2V_{max}/\pi$. Its average value over a full cycle is zero.

EXAMPLE 6 *Household Electricity.* We model the voltage in our home wiring with the sine function

$$V = V_{max} \sin 120\pi t,$$

which expresses the voltage V in volts as a function of time t in seconds. The function runs through 60 cycles each second (its frequency is 60 hertz, or 60 Hz). The positive number V_{max} ("vee max") is the **peak voltage.**

The average value of V over a half-cycle (duration 1/120 sec; see Fig. 5.24) is

$$\begin{aligned} V_{av} &= \frac{1}{(1/120) - 0} \int_0^{1/120} V_{max} \sin 120\pi t \, dt \\ &= 120V_{max} \left[-\frac{1}{120\pi} \cos 120\pi t \right]_0^{1/120} \\ &= \frac{V_{max}}{\pi} \left[-\cos \pi + \cos 0 \right] \\ &= \frac{2V_{max}}{\pi}. \end{aligned}$$

The average value of the voltage over a full cycle, as we can see from Fig. 5.24, is zero. (Also see Exercise 57.) If we measured the voltage with a standard moving-coil galvanometer, the meter would read zero.

To measure the voltage effectively, we use an instrument that measures the square root of the average value of the square of the voltage, namely

$$V_{rms} = \sqrt{(V^2)_{av}}. \tag{15}$$

The subscript "rms" (read the letters separately) stands for "root mean square." Since the average value of $V^2 = (V_{max})^2 \sin^2 120\pi t$ over a cycle is

$$(V^2)_{av} = \frac{1}{(1/60) - 0} \int_0^{1/60} (V_{max})^2 \sin^2 120\pi t \, dt = \frac{(V_{max})^2}{2}, \tag{16}$$

(Exercise 58), the rms voltage is

$$V_{rms} = \sqrt{\frac{(V_{max})^2}{2}} = \frac{V_{max}}{\sqrt{2}}. \tag{17}$$

The values given for household currents and voltages are always rms values. Thus, "115 volts ac" means that the rms voltage is 115. The peak voltage,

$$V_{max} = \sqrt{2}\, V_{rms} = \sqrt{2} \cdot 115 \approx 163 \text{ volts},$$

obtained from Eq. (17), is considerably higher.

EXAMPLE 7 *Cost from Marginal Cost.* The fixed cost of starting a manufacturing run and producing the first 10 units is \$200. After that the marginal cost at x units output is

$$\frac{dc}{dx} = \frac{1000}{x^2}.$$

Find the total cost of producing the first 100 units.

Solution If $c(x)$ is the cost of x units, then

$$\underbrace{c(100)}_{\substack{\text{cost of}\\ \text{100 units}}} = \underbrace{200}_{\substack{\text{startup}\\ \text{first 10}}} + \underbrace{c(100) - c(10)}_{\substack{\text{cost of units}\\ \text{11–100}}}$$

$$= 200 + \int_{10}^{100} \frac{dc}{dx}\,dx$$

$$= 200 + \int_{10}^{100} \frac{1000}{x^2}\,dx \qquad \frac{dc}{dx} = \frac{1000}{x^2}$$

$$= 200 + 1000 \int_{10}^{100} \frac{1}{x^2}\,dx$$

$$= 200 + 1000\left[-\frac{1}{x}\right]_{10}^{100} = 200 + 1000\left[-\frac{1}{100} + \frac{1}{10}\right]$$

$$= 200 - 10 + 100 = 290.$$

The total cost of producing the first 100 units is \$290.

Exercises 5.4

Evaluate the integrals in Exercises 1–24.

1. $\int_{-2}^{0} (2x + 5)\,dx$
2. $\int_{-3}^{4} \left(5 - \frac{x}{2}\right) dx$
3. $\int_{0}^{4} \left(3x - \frac{x^3}{4}\right) dx$
4. $\int_{-2}^{2} (x^3 - 2x + 3)\,dx$
5. $\int_{0}^{1} (x^2 + \sqrt{x})\,dx$
6. $\int_{0}^{5} x^{3/2}\,dx$
7. $\int_{1}^{32} x^{-6/5}\,dx$
8. $\int_{-2}^{-1} \frac{2}{x^2}\,dx$
9. $\int_{0}^{\pi} \sin x\,dx$
10. $\int_{0}^{\pi} (1 + \cos x)\,dx$
11. $\int_{0}^{\pi/3} 2\sec^2 x\,dx$
12. $\int_{\pi/6}^{5\pi/6} \csc^2 x\,dx$
13. $\int_{\pi/4}^{3\pi/4} \csc\theta\cot\theta\,d\theta$
14. $\int_{0}^{\pi/3} 4\sec u\tan u\,du$
15. $\int_{\pi/2}^{0} \frac{1 + \cos 2t}{2}\,dt$
16. $\int_{-\pi/3}^{\pi/3} \frac{1 - \cos 2t}{2}\,dt$
17. $\int_{-\pi/2}^{\pi/2} (8y^2 + \sin y)\,dy$
18. $\int_{-\pi/3}^{-\pi/4} \left(4\sec^2 t + \frac{\pi}{t^2}\right) dt$
19. $\int_{1}^{-1} (r + 1)^2\,dr$
20. $\int_{-\sqrt{3}}^{\sqrt{3}} (t + 1)(t^2 + 4)\,dt$
21. $\int_{\sqrt{2}}^{1} \left(\frac{u^7}{2} - \frac{1}{u^5}\right) du$
22. $\int_{1/2}^{1} \left(\frac{1}{v^3} - \frac{1}{v^4}\right) dv$
23. $\int_{1}^{\sqrt{2}} \frac{s^2 + \sqrt{s}}{s^2}\,ds$
24. $\int_{9}^{4} \frac{1 - \sqrt{u}}{\sqrt{u}}\,du$

In Exercises 25–30, find the total area of the region between the curve and the x-axis.

25. $y = -x^2 - 2x, \quad -3 \le x \le 2$
26. $y = 3x^2 - 3, \quad -2 \le x \le 2$
27. $y = x^3 - 3x^2 + 2x, \quad 0 \le x \le 2$
28. $y = x^3 - 4x, \quad -2 \le x \le 2$
29. $y = x^{1/3}, \quad -1 \le x \le 8$
30. $y = x^{1/3} - x, \quad -1 \le x \le 8$

Find the areas of the shaded regions in Exercises 31–34.

31.

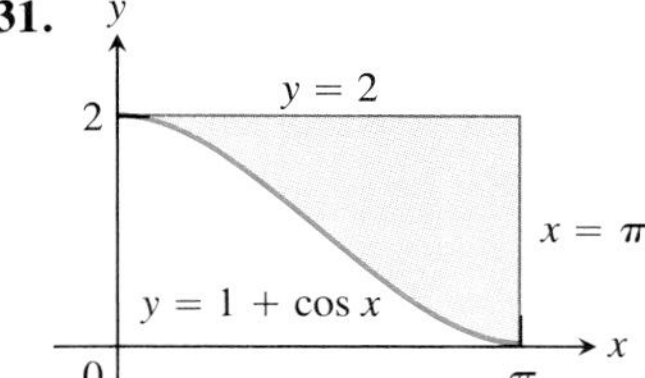

32.

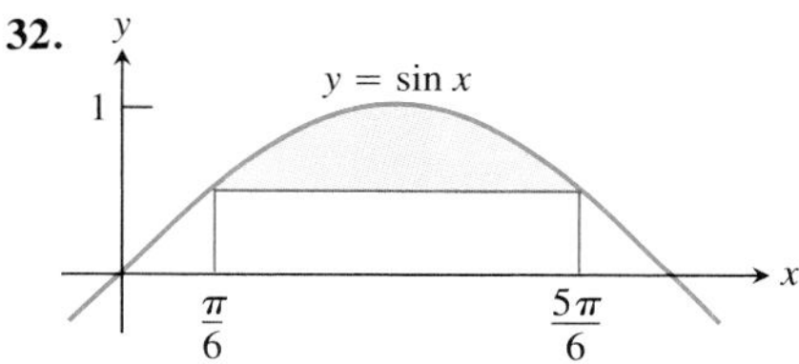

33.

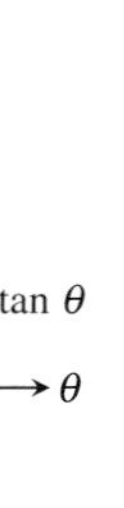

34.

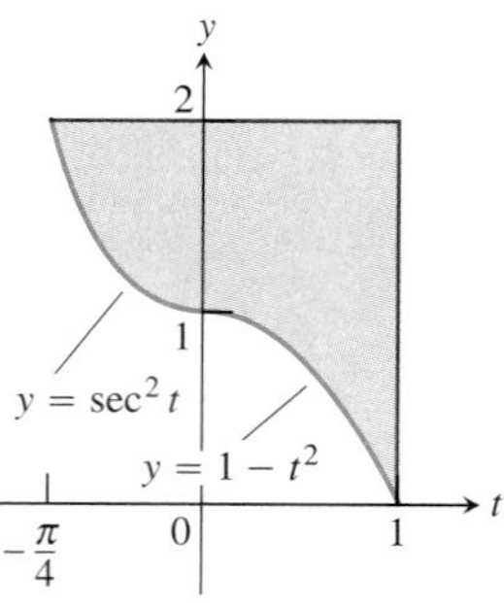

Find the derivatives in Exercises 35–38 (a) by evaluating the integral and differentiating the result and (b) by differentiating the integral directly.

35. $\dfrac{d}{dx}\displaystyle\int_0^{\sqrt{x}} \cos t\, dt$

36. $\dfrac{d}{dx}\displaystyle\int_1^{\sin x} 3t^2\, dt$

37. $\dfrac{d}{dt}\displaystyle\int_0^{t^4} \sqrt{u}\, du$

38. $\dfrac{d}{d\theta}\displaystyle\int_0^{\tan\theta} \sec^2 y\, dy$

Find dy/dx in Exercises 39–44.

39. $y = \displaystyle\int_0^x \sqrt{1 + t^2}\, dt$

40. $y = \displaystyle\int_1^x \frac{1}{t}\, dt, \quad x > 0$

41. $y = \displaystyle\int_0^{\sqrt{x}} \sin(t^2)\, dt$

42. $y = \displaystyle\int_0^{x^2} \cos\sqrt{t}\, dt$

43. $y = \displaystyle\int_0^{\sin x} \frac{dt}{\sqrt{1 - t^2}}, \quad |x| < \frac{\pi}{2}$

44. $y = \displaystyle\int_0^{\tan x} \frac{dt}{1 + t^2}$

Each of the following functions solves one of the initial value problems in Exercises 45–48. Which function solves which problem? Give brief reasons for your answers.

a) $y = \displaystyle\int_1^x \frac{1}{t}\, dt - 3$

b) $y = \displaystyle\int_0^x \sec t\, dt + 4$

c) $y = \displaystyle\int_{-1}^x \sec t\, dt + 4$

d) $y = \displaystyle\int_\pi^x \frac{1}{t}\, dt - 3$

45. $\dfrac{dy}{dx} = \dfrac{1}{x}, \; y(\pi) = -3$

46. $y' = \sec x, \; y(-1) = 4$

47. $y' = \sec x, \; y(0) = 4$

48. $y' = \dfrac{1}{x}, \; y(1) = -3$

Express the solutions of the initial value problems in Exercises 49–52 in terms of integrals.

49. $\dfrac{dy}{dx} = \sec x, \quad y = 3 \quad \text{when} \quad x = 2$

50. $\dfrac{dy}{dx} = \sqrt{1 + x^2}, \quad y = -2 \quad \text{when} \quad x = 1$

51. $\dfrac{ds}{dt} = f(t), \quad s = s_0 \quad \text{when} \quad t = t_0$

52. $\dfrac{dv}{dt} = g(t), \quad v = v_0 \quad \text{when} \quad t = t_0$

53. Show that if k is a positive constant, then the area between the x-axis and one arch of the curve $y = \sin kx$ is $2/k$.

54. *Archimedes' Area Formula for Parabolas.* Archimedes (287–212 B.C.), inventor, military engineer, physicist, and the greatest mathematician of classical times in the Western world, discovered that the area under a parabolic arch like the one shown here is two-thirds the base times the height.

a) Use an integral to find the area under the arch

$$y = 6 - x - x^2, \quad -3 \le x \le 2.$$

b) Find the height of the arch. (Where does y have its maximum value?)

c) Show that the area is two-thirds the base times the height.

d) Graph the parabolic arch $y = h - (4h/b^2)x^2$, $-b/2 \le x \le b/2$, assuming that h and b are positive. Then use calculus to find the area of the region enclosed between the arch and the x-axis.

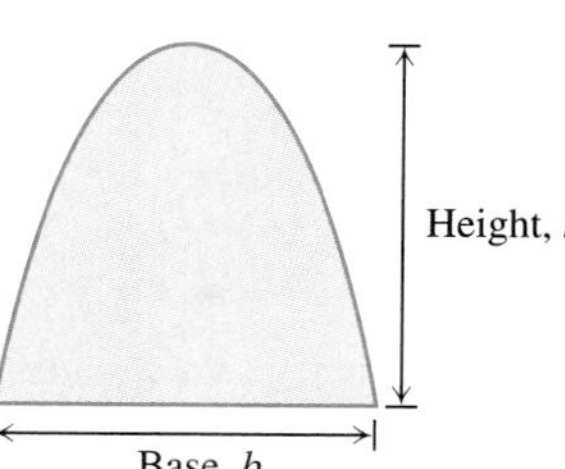

55. Suppose that f is the differentiable function graphed here and that the position at time t (sec) of a particle moving along a coordinate axis is

$$s = \int_0^t f(x)\, dx$$

meters. Use the graph to answer the following questions. Give reasons for your answers.

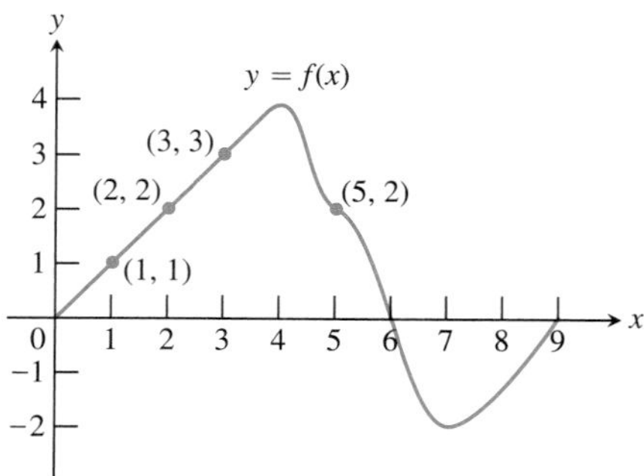

a) What is the particle's velocity at time $t = 5$?

b) Is the acceleration of the particle at time $t = 5$ positive, or negative?

c) What is the particle's position at time $t = 3$?

d) At what time during the first 9 sec does s have its largest value?

e) Approximately when is the acceleration zero?

f) When is the particle moving toward the origin? away from the origin?

g) On which side of the origin does the particle lie at time $t = 9$?

56. Suppose that g is the differentiable function graphed here

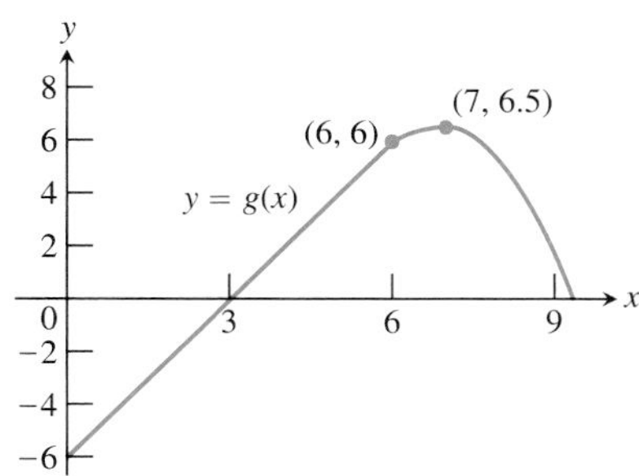

and that the position at time t (sec) of a particle moving along a coordinate axis is

$$s = \int_0^t g(x)\,dx$$

meters. Use the graph to answer the following questions. Give reasons for your answers.

a) What is the particle's velocity at $t = 3$?
b) Is the acceleration at time $t = 3$ positive, or negative?
c) What is the particle's position at $t = 3$?
d) When does the particle pass through the origin?
e) When is the acceleration zero?
f) When is the particle moving away from the origin? toward the origin?
g) On which side of the origin does the particle lie at $t = 9$?

57. *Continuation of Example 6*

a) Show by evaluating the integral in the expression

$$\frac{1}{(1/60) - 0}\int_0^{1/60} V_{\max} \sin 120\pi t\,dt$$

that the average value of $V = V_{\max} \sin 120\pi t$ over a full cycle is zero. (Remember that $V_{\max}$ is a constant.)

b) The circuit that runs your electric stove is rated 240 volts rms. What is the peak value of the allowable voltage?

58. Verify Eq. (16) by showing that

$$\int_0^{1/60} \left(V_{\max}\right)^2 \sin^2 120\pi t\,dt = \frac{\left(V_{\max}\right)^2}{120}.$$

(Remember, $V_{\max}$ is a constant and $\sin^2\theta = (1 - \cos 2\theta)/2$.)

59. *Cost from Marginal Cost.* The marginal cost of printing a poster when x posters have been printed is

$$\frac{dc}{dx} = \frac{1}{2\sqrt{x}}$$

dollars. Find (a) $c(100) - c(1)$, the cost of printing posters 2–100; (b) $c(400) - c(100)$, the cost of printing posters 101–400.

60. *Revenue from Marginal Revenue.* Suppose that a company's marginal revenue from the manufacture and sale of egg beaters is

$$\frac{dr}{dx} = 2 - 2/(x + 1)^2,$$

where r is measured in thousands of dollars and x in thousands of units. How much money should the company expect from a production run of $x = 3$ thousand egg beaters? To find out, integrate the marginal revenue from $x = 0$ to $x = 3$, given that $-1/(x + 1)$ is an antiderivative of $1/(x + 1)^2$. In the next section, we will see why this latter relationship holds.

AVERAGE DAILY INVENTORY

Average value is used in economics to study such things as average daily inventory. If $I(t)$ is the number of radios, tires, shoes, or whatever product a firm has on hand on day t (we call I an **inventory function**), the average value of I over a time period $[0, T]$ is called the firm's average daily inventory for the period.

$$\textbf{Average daily inventory} = \text{av}(I) = \frac{1}{T}\int_0^T I(t)\,dt.$$

If h is the dollar cost of holding one item per day, the product $\text{av}(I)\cdot h$ is the **average daily holding cost** for the period.

61. As a wholesaler, Tracey Burr Distributors receives a shipment of 1200 cases of chocolate bars every 30 days. TBD sells the chocolate to retailers at a steady rate, and t days after a shipment arrives, its inventory of cases on hand is $I(t) = 1200 - 40t$, $0 \le t \le 30$. What is TBD's average daily inventory for the 30-day period? What is its average daily holding cost if the cost of holding one case is 3¢ a day?

62. Rich Wholesale Foods, a manufacturer of cookies, stores its cases of cookies in an air conditioned warehouse for shipment every 14 days. Rich tries to keep 600 cases on reserve to meet occasional peaks in demand, so a typical 14-day inventory function is $I(t) = 600 + 600t$, $0 \le t \le 14$. The daily holding cost for each case is 4 cents per day. Find Rich's average daily inventory and average daily holding cost.

63. Solon Container receives 450 drums of plastic pellets every 30 days. The inventory function (drums on hand as a function of days) is $I(t) = 450 - t^2/2$. Find the average daily inventory. If the holding cost for one drum is 2¢ per day, find the average daily holding cost.

64. Mitchell Mailorder receives a shipment of 600 cases of athletic socks every 60 days. The number of cases on hand t days after the shipment arrives is $I(t) = 600 - 20\sqrt{15t}$. Find the average daily inventory. If the holding cost for one case is 1/2¢ per day, find the average daily holding cost.

65. *Continuation of Section 5.1, Example 3.* The approximating sums for the volume of the cone in Example 3 of Section 5.1 were Riemann sums for the integral

$$\int_0^4 \pi x^2\,dx.$$

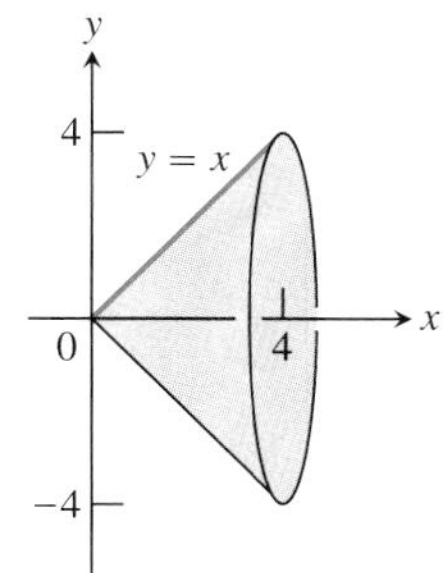

Calculate the cone's volume by evaluating this integral.

66. Find the volume of a solid right circular cone of height h and base radius r by evaluating the integral

$$\int_0^h \pi \left(\frac{r}{h}x\right)^2 dx.$$

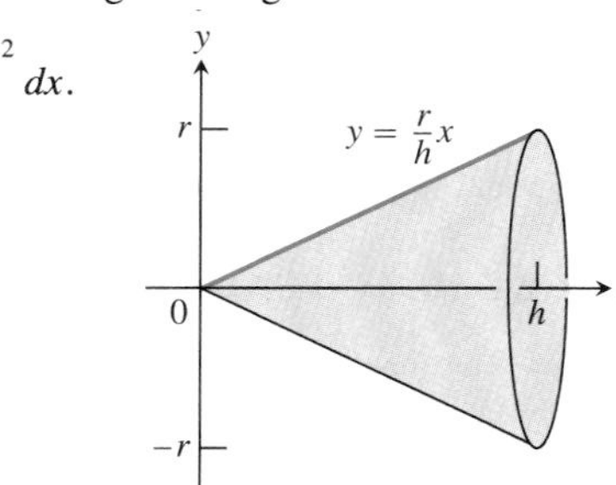

67. *Continuation of Section 5.1, Example 4.* The approximating sums for the volume of the sphere in Example 4 in Section 5.1 were Riemann sums for the integral

$$\int_0^4 \pi \left(\sqrt{16 - x^2}\,\right)^2 dx.$$

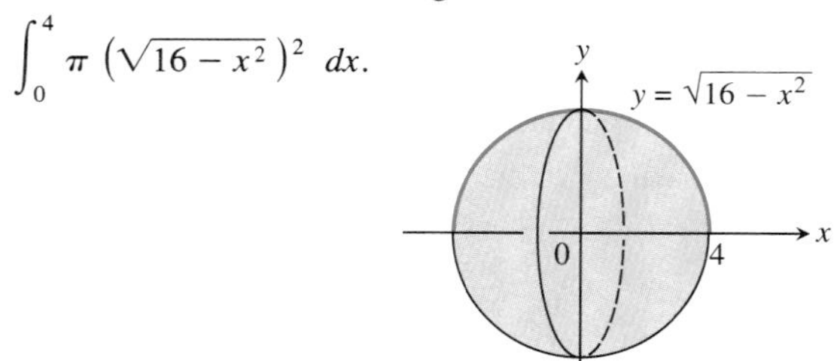

Evaluate this integral to find the volume of the sphere.

68. *Continuation of Section 5.1, Exercise 18.* The approximating sums for the volume of the nose section of the rocket in Exercise 18 of Section 5.1 were Riemann sums for the integral

$$\int_0^5 \pi \left(\sqrt{x}\right)^2 dx.$$

Find the volume of the nose section by evaluating this integral.

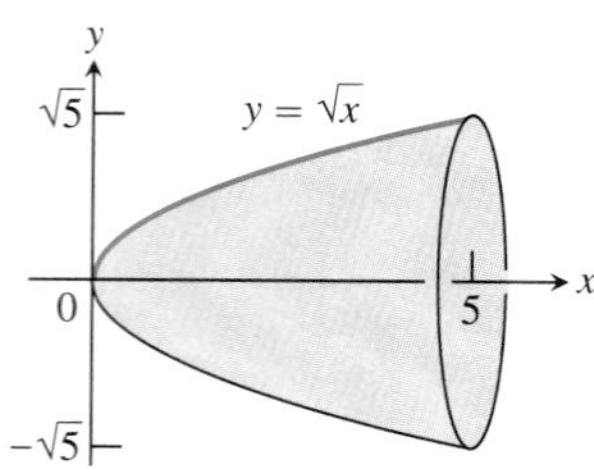

69. Suppose $\int_1^x f(t)\,dt = x^2 - 2x + 1$. Find $f(x)$.

70. Find $f(4)$ if $\int_0^x f(t)\,dt = x \cos \pi x$.

71. Find the linearization of

$$f(x) = 2 - \int_2^{x+1} \frac{9}{1+t}\,dt$$

at $x = 1$.

72. Find the linearization of

$$g(x) = 3 + \int_1^{x^2} \sec(t-1)\,dt$$

at $x = -1$.

73. Suppose that f has a positive derivative for all values of x and that $f(1) = 0$. Which of the following statements must be true of the function

$$g(x) = \int_0^x f(t)\,dt?$$

Give reasons for your answers.

a) g is a differentiable function of x.
b) g is a continuous function of x.
c) The graph of g has a horizontal tangent at $x = 1$.
e) g has a local minimum at $x = 1$.
f) The graph of g has an inflection point at $x = 1$.
g) The graph of dg/dx crosses the x-axis at $x = 1$.

74. Suppose that f has a negative derivative for all values of x and that $f(1) = 0$. Which of the following statements must be true of the function

$$h(x) = \int_0^x f(t)\,dt?$$

Give reasons for your answers.

a) h is a twice-differentiable function of x.
b) h and dh/dx are both continuous.
c) The graph of h has a horizontal tangent at $x = 1$.
d) h has a local maximum at $x = 1$.
e) h has a local minimum at $x = 1$.
f) The graph of h has an inflection point at $x = 1$.
g) The graph of dh/dx crosses the x-axis at $x = 1$.

If you have access to a grapher that can graph a function $f(x)$ and its integral $F(x) = \int_0^x f(t)\,dt$ together, try it on the functions in Exercises 75–78. Watch how the slopes of the curves $y = \int_0^x f(t)\,dt$ match the graphs of the integrands. We know that

i) if F has a relative maximum at $x = c$, then $f(c) = 0$,
ii) F increases on any interval where $f > 0$,
iii) F decreases on any interval where $f < 0$.

Look for these relationships in the graphs and describe what you find in each case.

75. $f(x) = \sin x$

76. $f(x) = x \cos \pi x$

77. $f(x) = x^2 - 4$

78. $f(x) = x^3 - 4x^2 + 3x$

Writing for Your Own Knowledge

Answer the following questions in writing. Some answers will take only a sentence or two; others may require several paragraphs. Some explanations may also call for graphs or sketches.

1. What is the Fundamental Theorem of Calculus?

2. Why is the Fundamental Theorem of Calculus so important?

3. If f is continuous, how can you express the solution of the initial value problem

Differential equation: $\frac{dy}{dx} = f(x)$

Initial condition: $y = y_0$ when $x = x_0$

in terms of a definite integral?

EXPLORER PROGRAMS

Derivatives	Graphs $f(x)$ and $\int_a^x f(t)\,dt$ together for your choice of f and a.
PowerGrapher	Graphs functions together.

5.5 *Indefinite Integrals*

Because antiderivatives make it possible to evaluate definite integrals with arithmetic, we will work with antiderivatives a great deal. We therefore need a notation that makes antiderivatives easier to describe and work with. This section introduces the notation and shows how to use it.

The Indefinite Integral of a Function

We call the set of all antiderivatives of a function the indefinite integral of the function, according to the following definition.

DEFINITIONS

If the function f is a derivative, then the set of all antiderivatives of f is called the **indefinite integral** of f, denoted by the symbols

$$\int f(x)\,dx.$$

As in definite integrals, the symbol $\int$ is called an **integral sign.** The function f is the **integrand** of the integral and x is the **variable of integration.**

Since every continuous function has an antiderivative, every continuous function has an indefinite integral.

Once we have found an antiderivative $F(x)$ of a function $f(x)$, the other antiderivatives of f differ from F only by a constant (Corollary 2 of the Mean Value Theorem). We indicate this in the new notation by writing

$$\int f(x)\,dx = F(x) + C. \quad (1)$$

The constant C is called the **constant of integration** or the **arbitrary constant,** and Eq. (1) is read, "The indefinite integral of f with respect to x is $F(x) + C$." When we find $F(x) + C$, we say that we have **evaluated** the indefinite integral.

How to evaluate $\int f(x)\,dx$

STEP 1: Find an antiderivative $F(x)$ of $f(x)$.

STEP 2: Add C (the constant of integration). Then

$$\int f(x)\,dx = F(x) + C.$$

EXAMPLE 1

$$\int x^8\,dx = \frac{x^9}{9} + C$$

The constant of integration (C)

An antiderivative of x^8 ($\frac{x^9}{9}$)

TABLE 5.4
Integration formulas

1. $\int x^n \, dx = \frac{x^{n+1}}{n+1} + C \qquad (n \neq -1)$

2. $\int \sin kx \, dx = -\frac{\cos kx}{k} + C$

3. $\int \cos kx \, dx = \frac{\sin kx}{k} + C$

4. $\int \sec^2 x \, dx = \tan x + C$

5. $\int \csc^2 x \, dx = -\cot x + C$

6. $\int \sec x \tan x \, dx = \sec x + C$

7. $\int \csc x \cot x \, dx = -\csc x + C$

The formulas for general antiderivatives in Section 4.7 translate into the formulas for evaluating indefinite integrals listed in Table 5.4.

In case you are wondering why the integrals of the tangent, cotangent, secant, and cosecant are not listed here, the answer is that the usual formulas for them require logarithms. We know that these functions do have indefinite integrals on intervals where they are continuous, but we will have to wait until Chapters 6 and 8 to see what the integrals are.

EXAMPLE 2 *Selected Integrals from Table 5.4*

a) $\int x^5 \, dx = \frac{x^6}{6} + C$ — Formula 1

b) $\int \sin 2x \, dx = -\frac{\cos 2x}{2} + C$ — Formula 2 with $k = 2$

c) $\int \cos \frac{x}{2} \, dx = \int \cos \frac{1}{2} x \, dx = \frac{\sin (1/2)x}{1/2} + C$ — Formula 3 with $k = 1/2$

$$= 2 \sin \frac{x}{2} + C$$

How to Check an Integration

The formulas in Table 5.4 hold because, in each case, the derivative of the function $F(x) + C$ on the right is the integrand $f(x)$ on the left. Finding an integral formula can sometimes be a difficult task, but *checking* an integral formula, once found, is relatively easy: Differentiate the right-hand side. If the derivative is the integrand, the formula is correct; otherwise it is wrong.

EXAMPLE 3

CORRECT:

$$\int x \cos x \, dx = x \sin x + \cos x + C$$

Reason: The derivative of the right-hand side is the integrand:

$$\frac{d}{dx}(x \sin x + \cos x + C) = x \cos x + \sin x - \sin x + 0 = x \cos x.$$

WRONG:

$$\int x \cos x \, dx = x \sin x + C$$

Reason: The derivative of the right-hand side is not the integrand:

$$\frac{d}{dx}(x \sin x + C) = x \cos x + \sin x + 0 \neq x \cos x.$$

Do not worry about where the (correct) integral formula in Example 3 comes from right now. There is a nice technique in Chapter 8 for evaluating integrals like this.

Rules of Algebra

Among the things we know about antiderivatives are these:

1. The general antiderivative of a derivative dF/dx is $F(x) + C$.
2. When we differentiate an antiderivative of a function $f(x)$ with respect to x, we get f back again.
3. A function is an antiderivative of a constant multiple kf of a function f if and only if it is k times an antiderivative of f.
4. In particular, a function is an antiderivative of $-f$ if and only if it is the negative of an antiderivative of f.
5. A function is an antiderivative of a sum $f(x) + g(x)$ if and only if it is the sum of an antiderivative of f and an antiderivative of g.
6. A function is an antiderivative of a difference $f(x) - g(x)$ if and only if it is an antiderivative of f minus an antiderivative of g.

These observations can be expressed very nicely in the notation of indefinite integrals (Table 5.5).

TABLE 5.5
Rules for indefinite integrals

1.	$\int \frac{dF}{dx}\, dx = F(x) + C$	
2.	$\frac{d}{dx}\int f(x)\, dx = f(x)$	
3.	$\int kf(x)\, dx = k\int f(x)\, dx$	Provided k is a constant. Does not work if k varies with x.
4.	$\int -f(x)\, dx = -\int f(x)\, dx$	Special case of Rule 3
5.	$\int [f(x) + g(x)]\, dx = \int f(x)\, dx + \int g(x)\, dx$	
6.	$\int [f(x) - g(x)]\, dx = \int f(x)\, dx - \int g(x)\, dx$	

EXAMPLE 4

$$\int \cos x\, dx = \int \frac{d}{dx}(\sin x)\, dx = \sin x + C \qquad \text{Rule 1 with } F(x) = \sin x$$

EXAMPLE 5

$$\frac{d}{dx}\int \tan x\, dx = \tan x \qquad \text{Rule 2 with } f(x) = \tan x$$

We know this even without knowing how to evaluate the integral.

EXAMPLE 6 *Rewriting the Constant of Integration.*

$$\begin{aligned}
\int 8\sqrt[3]{x}\, dx &= 8\int x^{1/3}\, dx && \text{Table 5.5, Rule 3, with } k = 8,\ f(x) = x^{1/3}\\
&= 8\left(\frac{x^{4/3}}{4/3} + C\right) && \text{Table 5.4, Formula 1}\\
&= 8\left(\frac{3}{4}x^{4/3} + C\right) && \text{First form}\\
&= 6x^{4/3} + 8\,C\\
&= 6\,x^{4/3} + C' && \text{Shorter form}\\
&= 6\,x^{4/3} + C && \text{Usual form — no prime}
\end{aligned}$$

What about all the different forms in Example 6? Each one of them gives all the antiderivatives of $f(x) = 8\sqrt[3]{x}$, so each answer is correct. But the least complicated of the three, and the usual choice, is

$$\int 8\sqrt[3]{x}\, dx = 6x^{4/3} + C.$$

After you become proficient with the formulas and rules of integration, you will probably want to go from $\int kf(x)\,dx = k\int f(x)\,dx$ directly to $\int kf(x)\,dx = kF(x) + C$, as we did here.

EXAMPLE 7

$$\int (-5\sec x \tan x)\, dx = -5\sec x + C \qquad \text{Table 5.5, Rule 3, and Table 5.4, Formula 6}$$

EXAMPLE 8 *Term-by-term Integration.* Evaluate

$$\int (x^2 - 2x + 5)\, dx.$$

Solution If we recognize that $(x^3/3) - x^2 + 5x$ is an antiderivative of $x^2 - 2x + 5$, we can evaluate the integral immediately as

$$\int (x^2 - 2x + 5) = \frac{x^3}{3} - x^2 + 5x + C. \tag{2}$$

But what if we do not recognize the antiderivative? The answer is to evaluate the integral one term at a time, using the sum and difference rules in Table 5.12:

$$\begin{aligned}
\int (x^2 - 2x + 5)\, dx &= \int x^2\, dx - \int 2x\, dx + \int 5\, dx\\
&= \frac{x^3}{3} + C_1 - x^2 + C_2 + 5x + C_3.
\end{aligned} \tag{3}$$

What do we do with all the constants of integration? Equation (3) certainly gives all the antiderivatives of $x^2 - 2x + 5$. But it is more complicated than it needs to be to do this. If we were to combine C_1, C_2, and C_3 into a single arbitrary constant $C = C_1 + C_2 + C_3$, the formula would simplify to

$$\frac{x^3}{3} - x^2 + 5x + C \tag{4}$$

and still give all the antiderivatives there are, as we saw in Eq. (2). For this reason we recommend that when you integrate term by term you go right to the simplified form.

Term-by-term Integration

When we integrate an expression term by term, we combine the constants of integration into a single arbitrary constant at the end.

Write

$$\int (x^2 - 2x + 5)\,dx = \int x^2\,dx - \int 2x\,dx + \int 5\,dx = \frac{x^3}{3} - x^2 + 5x + C.$$

Find the simplest antiderivative you can for each part, then add the arbitrary constant C at the end.

The Integrals of $\sin^2 x$ and $\cos^2 x$

We can sometimes use trigonometric identities to transform unfamiliar integrals into integrals we know how to evaluate. Among the examples you should know about, important because of how frequently they arise in applications, are the integral formulas for $\sin^2 x$ and $\cos^2 x$.

EXAMPLE 9

$$\begin{aligned}\int \sin^2 x\,dx &= \int \frac{1 - \cos 2x}{2}\,dx && \text{Because } \sin^2 x = \frac{1 - \cos 2x}{2}\\ &= \frac{1}{2}\int (1 - \cos 2x)\,dx = \frac{1}{2}\int dx - \frac{1}{2}\int \cos 2x\,dx\\ &= \frac{1}{2}x - \frac{1}{2}\frac{\sin 2x}{2} + C = \frac{x}{2} - \frac{\sin 2x}{4} + C\end{aligned}$$

EXAMPLE 10

$$\begin{aligned}\int \cos^2 x\,dx &= \int \frac{1 + \cos 2x}{2}\,dx && \cos^2 x = \frac{1 + \cos 2x}{2}\\ &= \frac{x}{2} + \frac{\sin 2x}{4} + C && \text{As in Example 9, but with a sign change}\end{aligned}$$

Solving Initial Value Problems with Indefinite Integrals

As you know, we solve initial value problems with antiderivatives. We now look at the solutions in the language of indefinite integration. The first example is based on Example 5 in Section 4.7. You need not look back, however, unless you are interested in the modeling that gave rise to the problem. The solution we give here is mathematically self-contained.

EXAMPLE 11 *Finding Velocity from Its Acceleration and Initial Velocity.* As a function of elapsed time t, the velocity v of a body falling from rest in a vacuum near the surface of the earth satisfies

Differential equation: $\dfrac{dv}{dt} = 9.8$ — The acceleration is 9.8 m/sec².

Initial condition: $v = 0$ when $t = 0$. — The velocity is 0 at the start.

Find v as a function of t.

Solution We find the general solution of the differential equation by integrating both sides of it with respect to t:

$$\frac{dv}{dt} = 9.8 \qquad \text{Differential equation}$$

$$\int \frac{dv}{dt}\,dt = \int 9.8\,dt \qquad \text{Integral equation}$$

$$v + C_1 = 9.8t + C_2 \qquad \text{Integrals evaluated}$$

$$v = 9.8t + C_2 - C_1 \qquad \text{Solved for } v$$

$$v = 9.8t + C. \qquad \text{Arbitrary constants combined as one}$$

This last equation tells us that the body's velocity t seconds into the fall is $9.8t + C$ m/sec for some value of C. What value? We find out from the initial condition:

$$v = 9.8t + C$$

$$0 = 9.8(0) + C \qquad v = 0 \text{ when } t = 0$$

$$C = 0.$$

Conclusion: The body's velocity t seconds into the fall is

$$v = 9.8t + 0 = 9.8t \text{ m/sec.}$$

In the next example we have to integrate a second derivative twice to find the function we are after. The first integration,

$$\int \frac{d^2y}{dx^2}\,dx = \frac{dy}{dx} + C, \qquad (5)$$

gives the function's first derivative. The second integration gives the function.

EXAMPLE 12 Solve the following initial value problem for y as a function of x:

Differential equation: $\dfrac{d^2y}{dx^2} = 6x - \pi^2 \cos \pi x$

Initial conditions: $\dfrac{dy}{dx} = 0$ and $y = 2$ when $x = 1$

Solution We integrate the differential equation with respect to x to find dy/dx:

$$\int \frac{d^2y}{dx^2}\,dx = \int (6x - \pi^2 \cos \pi x)\,dx$$

$$\frac{dy}{dx} = 6 \cdot \frac{x^2}{2} - \pi^2 \cdot \frac{\sin \pi x}{\pi} + C_1 \qquad \text{Constants of integration combined as } C_1$$

$$= 3x^2 - \pi \sin \pi x + C_1.$$

We apply the first initial condition to find C_1:

$$0 = 3(1)^2 - \pi \sin \pi + C_1 \qquad \frac{dy}{dx} = 0 \text{ when } x = 1$$

$$C_1 = -3 + \pi(0) = -3.$$

This completes the formula for dy/dx:

$$\frac{dy}{dx} = 3x^2 - \pi \sin \pi x - 3.$$

We integrate dy/dx with respect to x to find y:

$$\int \frac{dy}{dx}\, dx = \int (3x^2 - \pi \sin \pi x - 3)\, dx$$

$$y = 3 \cdot \frac{x^3}{3} - \pi \cdot \left(-\frac{\cos \pi x}{\pi}\right) - 3x + C_2 \qquad \text{Constants of integration combined as } C_2$$

$$= x^3 + \cos \pi x - 3x + C_2.$$

We apply the second initial condition to find C_2:

$$2 = (1)^3 + \cos \pi - 3(1) + C_2 \qquad y = 2 \text{ when } x = 1$$

$$2 = 1 - 1 - 3 + C_2$$

$$C_2 = 5.$$

This completes the formula for y as a function of x:

$$y = x^3 + \cos \pi x - 3x + 5.$$

Exercises 5.5

Evaluate the integrals in Exercises 1–38. You can check your answers by differentiating.

1. $\int (x + 1)\, dx$

2. $\int (5 - 6x)\, dx$

3. $\int \left(3t^2 + \frac{t}{2}\right) dt$

4. $\int \left(\frac{t^2}{2} + 4t^3\right) dt$

5. $\int (2x^3 - 5x + 7)\, dx$

6. $\int (1 - x^2 - 3x^5)\, dx$

7. $\int \left(\frac{1}{x^2} - x^2 - \frac{1}{3}\right) dx$

8. $\int \left(\frac{1}{5} - \frac{2}{x^3} + 2x\right) dx$

9. $\int x^{-1/3}\, dx$

10. $\int x^{-5/4}\, dx$

11. $\int (\sqrt{x} + \sqrt[3]{x})\, dx$

12. $\int \left(\frac{\sqrt{x}}{2} + \frac{2}{\sqrt{x}}\right) dx$

13. $\int \left(8y - \frac{2}{y^{1/4}}\right) dy$

14. $\int \left(\frac{1}{7} - \frac{1}{y^{5/4}}\right) dy$

15. $\int 2x\left(1 - x^{-3}\right) dx$

16. $\int x^{-3}(x + 1)\, dx$

17. $\int \frac{t\sqrt{t} + \sqrt{t}}{t^2}\, dt$

18. $\int \frac{4 + \sqrt{t}}{t^3}\, dt$

19. $\int (-2 \cos t)\, dt$

20. $\int (-5 \sin t)\, dt$

21. $\int \sin \frac{\theta}{3}\, d\theta$

22. $\int 3 \cos 5\theta\, d\theta$

23. $\int (-3 \csc^2 x)\, dx$

24. $\int \left(-\frac{\sec^2 x}{3}\right) dx$

25. $\int \frac{\csc \theta \cot \theta}{2}\, d\theta$

26. $\int \frac{2}{5} \sec \theta \tan \theta\, d\theta$

27. $\int (4 \sec x \tan x - 2 \sec^2 x)\, dx$

28. $\int \frac{1}{2}(\csc^2 x - \csc x \cot x)\, dx$

29. $\int (\sin 2x - \csc^2 x)\, dx$

30. $\int (2 \cos 2x - 3 \sin 3x)\, dx$

31. $\int 4 \sin^2 y \, dy$

32. $\int \frac{\cos^2 y}{7} \, dy$

33. $\int \frac{1 + \cos 4t}{2} \, dt$

34. $\int \frac{1 - \cos 6t}{2} \, dt$

35. $\int (1 + \tan^2 \theta) \, d\theta$
(*Hint:* $1 + \tan^2 \theta = \sec^2 \theta$)

36. $\int (2 + \tan^2 \theta) \, d\theta$

37. $\int \cot^2 x \, dx$
(*Hint:* $1 + \cot^2 x = \csc^2 x$)

38. $\int (1 - \cot^2 x) \, dx$

Show that the integral formulas in Exercises 39–44 are correct by showing that the derivatives of the right-hand sides are the integrands of the integrals on the left-hand sides. In Section 5.6, we will see where formulas like these come from.

39. $\int (7x - 2)^3 \, dx = \frac{(7x - 2)^4}{28} + C$

40. $\int (3x + 5)^{-2} \, dx = -\frac{(3x + 5)^{-1}}{3} + C$

41. $\int \sec^2 \pi x \, dx = \frac{\tan \pi x}{\pi} + C$

42. $\int \csc^2 \frac{x}{5} \, dx = -5 \cot \frac{x}{5} + C$

43. $\int \frac{1}{(x + 1)^2} \, dx = -\frac{1}{x + 1} + C$

44. $\int \frac{1}{(x + 1)^2} \, dx = \frac{x}{x + 1} + C$

45. Right, or wrong? Say which for each formula and give a brief reason for each answer.

a) $\int x \sin x \, dx = \frac{x^2}{2} \sin x + C$

b) $\int x \sin x \, dx = -x \cos x + C$

c) $\int x \sin x \, dx = -x \cos x + \sin x + C$

46. Right, or wrong? Say which for each formula and give a brief reason for each answer.

a) $\int \tan \theta \sec^2 \theta \, d\theta = \frac{\sec^3 \theta}{3} + C$

b) $\int \tan \theta \sec^2 \theta \, d\theta = \frac{1}{2} \tan^2 \theta + C$

c) $\int \tan \theta \sec^2 \theta \, d\theta = \frac{1}{2} \sec^2 \theta + C$

47. Right, or wrong? Say which for each formula and give a brief reason for each answer.

a) $\int (2x + 1)^2 \, dx = \frac{(2x + 1)^3}{3} + C$

b) $\int 3(2x + 1)^2 \, dx = (2x + 1)^3 + C$

c) $\int 6(2x + 1)^2 \, dx = (2x + 1)^3 + C$

48. Right, or wrong? Say which for each formula and give a brief reason for each answer.

a) $\int \sqrt{2x + 1} \, dx = \sqrt{x^2 + x + C}$

b) $\int \sqrt{2x + 1} \, dx = \sqrt{x^2 + x} + C$

c) $\int \sqrt{2x + 1} \, dx = \frac{1}{3} \left(\sqrt{2x + 1}\right)^3 + C$

Solve the initial value problems in Exercises 49–56.

49. Differential equation: $\frac{dy}{dx} = 3\sqrt{x}$
Initial condition: $y = 4$ when $x = 9$

50. Differential equation: $\frac{dy}{dx} = \frac{1}{2\sqrt{x}}$
Initial condition: $y = 0$ when $x = 4$

51. Differential equation: $\frac{dy}{dt} = -\pi \sin \pi t$
Initial condition: $y = 0$ when $t = 0$

52. Differential equation: $\frac{dy}{dt} = \frac{1}{2} \sec t \tan t$
Initial condition: $y = 1$ when $t = 0$

53. Differential equation: $\frac{d^2y}{dx^2} = 0$
Initial conditions: $\frac{dy}{dx} = 2$ and $y = 1$ when $x = -2$

54. Differential equation: $\frac{d^2y}{dx^2} = \frac{2}{x^3}$
Initial conditions: $\frac{dy}{dx} = -1$ and $y = 7/2$ when $x = 1/2$

55. Differential equation: $\frac{d^3y}{dx^3} = 6 + \sin x$
Initial conditions: $\frac{d^2y}{dx^2} = -1$, $\frac{dy}{dx} = -5$, and
$y = 2$ when $x = 0$

56. Differential equation: $\frac{d^3y}{dx^3} = -\cos x$
Initial conditions: $\frac{d^2y}{dx^2} = 0$, $\frac{dy}{dx} = 1/\pi$, and
$y = 2$ when $x = -\pi$

When we use the language of integration (instead of antidifferentiation) to describe how we solve differential equations, we often call the solution curves **integral curves.** They are the same curves, but we use a different vocabulary to talk about them. Exercises 57–60 show integral curves of differential equations. In each exercise, find an equation for the curve through the labeled point.

57.

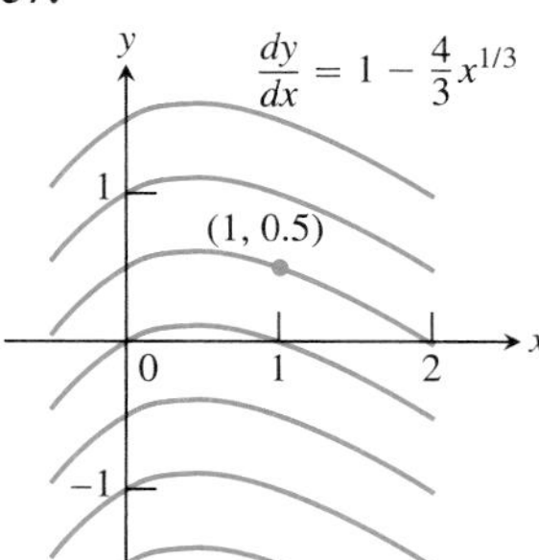

58.

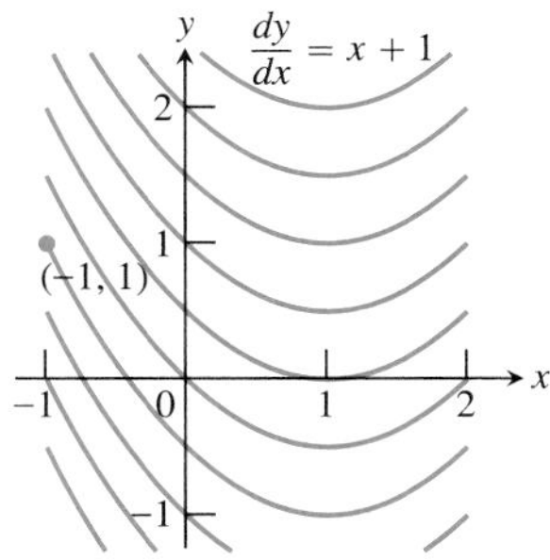

59.

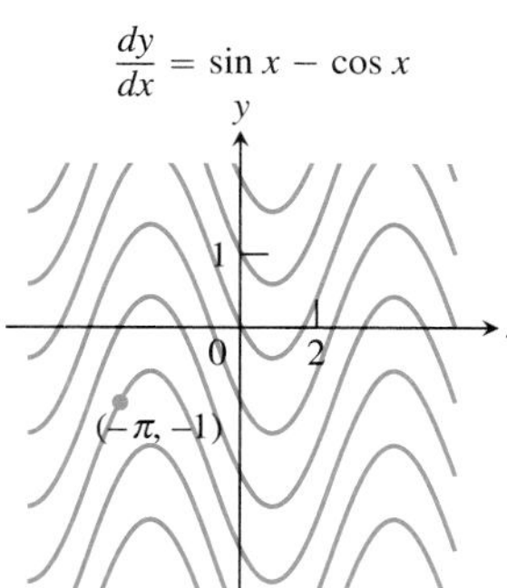

60.

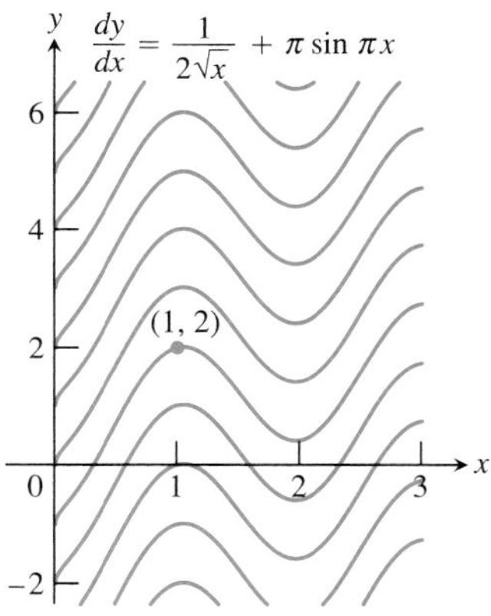

61. *Motion Along a Coordinate Line.* A particle moves on a coordinate line with acceleration $a = d^2s/dt^2 = 15\sqrt{t} - (3/\sqrt{t})$, subject to the conditions that $ds/dt = 4$ and $s = 0$ when $t = 1$. Find

a) the velocity $v = ds/dt$ in terms of t,
b) the position s in terms of t.

62. *Stopping a Motorcycle.* The State of Illinois Cycle Rider Safety Program requires riders to be able to brake from 30 mph (44 ft/sec) to 0 in 45 ft. What constant deceleration does it take to do that? To find out, carry out these steps:

STEP 1: Solve the following initial value problem. The answer will involve k.

Differential equation: $\frac{d^2s}{dt^2} = -k$

Initial conditions: $ds/dt = 44$ and $s = 0$ when $t = 0$

STEP 2: Find the time t^* when $ds/dt = 0$. The answer will still involve k.

STEP 3: Solve the equation $s(t^*) = 45$ for k.

63. *Motion with Constant Acceleration.* The standard equation for the position s of a body moving with a constant acceleration a along a coordinate line is

$$s = \frac{a}{2}t^2 + v_0t + s_0, \tag{6}$$

where v_0 and s_0 are the body's velocity and position at time $t = 0$. Derive this equation by solving the initial value problem

Differential equation: $\frac{d^2s}{dt^2} = a$

Initial conditions: $\frac{ds}{dt} = v_0$ and $s = s_0$ when $t = 0$

64. *(Continuation of Exercise 63) Free Fall Near the Surface of a Planet.* For free fall near the surface of a planet where the acceleration of gravity has a constant magnitude of g length-units/sec^2, Eq. (6) takes the form

$$s = -\frac{1}{2}gt^2 + v_0t + s_0. \tag{7}$$

The equation has a minus sign because, in the coordinate system shown here, the acceleration acts downward, in the direction of decreasing s. The velocity v_0 is positive if the object is rising at time $t = 0$, and negative if the object is falling.

Instead of using the result of Exercise 63, you can derive Eq. (7) directly by solving an appropriate initial value problem. What initial value problem? Solve it to be sure you have the right one, explaining the solution steps as you go along.

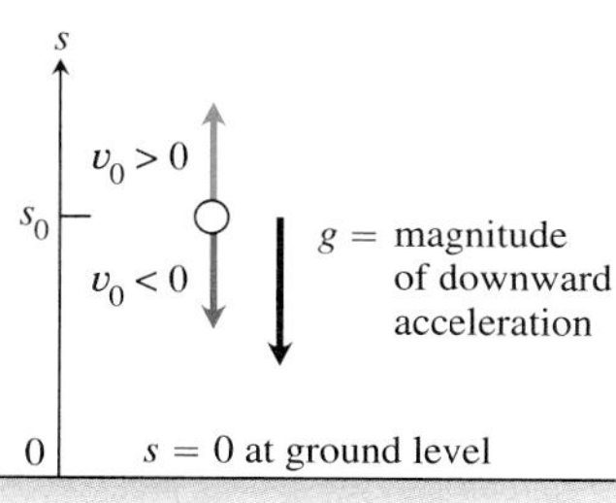

Writing for Your Own Knowledge

Answer the following questions in writing. Some answers will take only a sentence or two; others may require several paragraphs. Some explanations may also call for graphs or sketches.

1. What is an indefinite integral?
2. How do you find indefinite integrals of sums, differences, and constant multiples of functions whose indefinite integrals you already know?
3. How can you sometimes use a trigonometric identity to transform an unfamiliar integral into one you know how to evaluate?

EXPLORER PROGRAM

Slope Fields — Graphs solutions of the initial value problem $dy/dx = f(x, y)$, $y = y_0$ when $x = x_0$. You can see the effect of changing x_0 and y_0 by graphing integral curves together.

5.6 Integration by Substitution—Running the Chain Rule Backward

A change of variable can often turn an unfamiliar integral into one we can evaluate. The method for doing this is called the substitution method of integration. It is one of the principal methods for evaluating integrals. This section shows how and why the method works.

The Generalized Power Rule in Integral Form

When u is a differentiable function of x and n is a rational number different from -1, the Chain Rule tells us that

$$\frac{d}{dx}\left(\frac{u^{n+1}}{n+1}\right) = u^n \frac{du}{dx}. \tag{1}$$

This same equation, from another point of view, says that $u^{n+1}/(n+1)$ is one of the antiderivatives of $u^n(du/dx)$. The set of all antiderivatives of $u^n(du/dx)$ is therefore

$$\int \left(u^n \frac{du}{dx}\right) dx = \frac{u^{n+1}}{n+1} + C. \tag{2}$$

The integral on the left-hand side of this equation is usually written in the simpler "differential" form,

$$\int u^n \, du, \tag{3}$$

obtained by treating the dx's as differentials that cancel. Combining Eqs. (2) and (3) then gives the following rule.

If u is any differentiable function,

$$\int u^n \, du = \frac{u^{n+1}}{n+1} + C, \qquad (n \neq -1). \tag{4}$$

In deriving Eq. (4) we assumed u to be a differentiable function of the variable x, but the name of the variable does not matter and does not appear in the final formula. We could have represented the variable with θ, t, y, or any other letter. Equation (4) says that whenever we can cast an integral in the form

$$\int u^n \, du, \qquad (n \neq -1)$$

with u a differentiable function and du its differential, we can evaluate the integral as $\left[u^{n+1}/(n+1)\right] + C$.

EXAMPLE 1 Evaluate $\int (x+2)^5 \, dx$.

Solution We can put the integral in the form

$$\int u^n \, du$$

by substituting

$$u = x + 2 \quad \text{with} \quad n = 5$$

$$du = d(x + 2) = \frac{d}{dx}(x + 2) \cdot dx = 1 \cdot dx = dx.$$

Then $\int (x + 2)^5\, dx = \int u^5\, du$ $\qquad u = x + 2,\ du = dx$

$= \dfrac{u^6}{6} + C$ $\qquad$ Integrate, using Eq. (4) with $n = 5$.

$= \dfrac{(x + 2)^6}{6} + C.$ $\qquad$ Replace u by $x + 2$.

EXAMPLE 2

$\int \sqrt{1 + y^2} \cdot 2y\, dy = \int u^{1/2}\, du$ $\qquad$ Let $u = 1 + y^2$, $du = 2y\, dy$.

$= \dfrac{u^{(1/2) + 1}}{(1/2) + 1} + C$ $\qquad$ Integrate, using Eq. (4) with $n = 1/2$.

$= \dfrac{2}{3} u^{3/2} + C$ $\qquad$ Simpler form

$= \dfrac{2}{3}(1 + y^2)^{3/2} + C$ $\qquad$ Replace u by $1 + y^2$.

EXAMPLE 3 *Adjusting the Integrand by a Constant.*

$\int \sqrt{4t - 1}\, dt = \int u^{1/2} \cdot \dfrac{1}{4}\, du$ $\qquad$ Let $u = 4t - 1$, $du = 4\, dt$, $\frac{1}{4}\, du = dt$.

$= \dfrac{1}{4} \int u^{1/2}\, du$ $\qquad$ With the $\frac{1}{4}$ out front, the integral is now in standard form.

$= \dfrac{1}{4} \cdot \dfrac{u^{3/2}}{3/2} + C$ $\qquad$ Integrate, using Eq. (4) with $n = 1/2$.

$= \dfrac{1}{6} u^{3/2} + C$ $\qquad$ Simpler form

$= \dfrac{1}{6}(4t - 1)^{3/2} + C$ $\qquad$ Replace u by $4t - 1$.

Sines and Cosines

If u is a differentiable function of x, then $\sin u$ is a differentiable function of x. The Chain Rule gives the derivative of $\sin u$ as

$$\frac{d}{dx} \sin u = \cos u \frac{du}{dx}. \tag{5}$$

From another point of view, however, this same equation says that $\sin u$ is one of the antiderivatives of the product $\cos u \cdot (du/dx)$. The set of all antiderivatives of the product is therefore

$$\int \left(\cos u \frac{du}{dx}\right) dx = \sin u + C. \tag{6}$$

A formal cancellation of the dx's in the integral on the left leads to the following rule.

If u is a differentiable function, then

$$\int \cos u \, du = \sin u + C. \tag{7}$$

Equation (7) says that whenever we can cast an integral in the form

$$\int \cos u \, du,$$

we can integrate with respect to u in the usual way to evaluate the integral as $\sin u + C$.

EXAMPLE 4

$$\int \cos(7\theta + 5)\, d\theta = \int \cos u \cdot \frac{1}{7}\, du$$

Let $u = 7\theta + 5$, $du = 7\, d\theta$, $\frac{1}{7}\, du = d\theta$.

$$= \frac{1}{7}\int \cos u \, du$$

With $\frac{1}{7}$ out front, the integral is now in standard form.

$$= \frac{1}{7}\sin u + C$$

Integrate with respect to u.

$$= \frac{1}{7}\sin(7\theta + 5) + C$$

Replace u by $7\theta + 5$.

The companion formula for the integral of $\sin u$ when u is a differentiable function is

---

$$\int \sin u \, du = -\cos u + C. \tag{8}$$

EXAMPLE 5

$$\int x^2 \sin(x^3)\, dx = \int \sin(x^3) \cdot x^2\, dx$$

$$= \int \sin u \cdot \frac{1}{3}\, du$$

Let $u = x^3$, $du = 3x^2\, dx$, $\frac{1}{3}\, du = x^2\, dx$.

$$= \frac{1}{3}\int \sin u \, du$$

$$= \frac{1}{3}(-\cos u) + C$$

Integrate with respect to u.

$$= -\frac{1}{3}\cos(x^3) + C$$

Replace u by x^3.

The Chain Rule formulas for the derivatives of the tangent, cotangent, secant, and cosecant of a differentiable function u lead to the following integrals.

$$\int \sec^2 u\, du = \tan u + C \qquad (9)$$

$$\int \csc^2 u\, du = -\cot u + C \qquad (10)$$

$$\int \sec u \tan u\, du = \sec u + C \qquad (11)$$

$$\int \csc u \cot u\, du = -\csc u + C \qquad (12)$$

In each formula, u is a differentiable function of a real variable. Each formula can be checked by differentiating the right-hand side with respect to that variable. In each case, the Chain Rule applies to produce the integrand on the left.

EXAMPLE 6

$$\int \frac{1}{\cos^2 2\theta}\, d\theta = \int \sec^2 2\theta\, d\theta \qquad \sec 2\theta = \frac{1}{\cos 2\theta}$$

$$= \int \sec^2 u \cdot \frac{1}{2}\, du \qquad \text{Let } u = 2\theta,\ du = 2\, d\theta,\ d\theta = \tfrac{1}{2}\, du.$$

$$= \frac{1}{2}\int \sec^2 u\, du$$

$$= \frac{1}{2}\tan u + C \qquad \text{Integrate, using Eq. (9).}$$

$$= \frac{1}{2}\tan 2\theta + C \qquad \text{Replace } u \text{ by } 2\theta.$$

Check:

$$\frac{d}{d\theta}\left(\frac{1}{2}\tan 2\theta + C\right) = \frac{1}{2}\cdot\frac{d}{d\theta}\left(\tan 2\theta\right) + 0$$

$$= \frac{1}{2}\cdot\left(\sec^2 2\theta \cdot \frac{d}{d\theta}(2\theta)\right) \qquad \text{Chain Rule}$$

$$= \frac{1}{2}\cdot \sec^2 2\theta \cdot 2 = \frac{1}{\cos^2 2\theta}$$

The Substitution Method of Integration

The substitutions in the preceding examples are all instances of the following general rule.

$$\int f(g(x))\cdot g'(x)\, dx = \int f(u)\, du \qquad \text{1. Substitute } u = g(x),\ du = g'(x)\, dx.$$

$$= F(u) + C \qquad \text{2. Evaluate by finding an antiderivative } F(u) \text{ of } f(u). \text{ (Any one will do.)}$$

$$= F(g(x)) + C \qquad \text{3. Replace } u \text{ by } g(x).$$

These three steps are the steps of the substitution method of integration.

The Substitution Method of Integration

Take these steps to evaluate the integral

$$\int f(g(x))g'(x)\,dx$$

when f and g' are continuous functions:

STEP 1: Substitute $u = g(x)$ and $du = g'(x)\,dx$ to obtain the integral

$$\int f(u)\,du.$$

STEP 2: Integrate with respect to u.

STEP 3: Replace u by $g(x)$ in the result.

The method works because $F(g(x))$ is an antiderivative of $f(g(x)) \cdot g'(x)$ whenever F is an antiderivative of f:

$$\begin{aligned} \frac{d}{dx}F(g(x)) &= F'(g(x)) \cdot g'(x) && \text{Chain Rule} \\ &= f(g(x)) \cdot g'(x) && \text{Because } F' = f \end{aligned}$$

EXAMPLE 7

$$\begin{aligned} \int (x^2 + 2x - 3)^2(x + 1)\,dx &= \int u^2 \cdot \frac{1}{2}\,du && \begin{aligned} \text{Let } u &= x^2 + 2x - 3, \\ du &= 2x\,dx + 2\,dx \\ &= 2(x + 1)\,dx, \\ \tfrac{1}{2}\,du &= (x + 1)\,dx. \end{aligned} \\ &= \frac{1}{2}\int u^2\,du \\ &= \frac{1}{2} \cdot \frac{u^3}{3} + C = \frac{1}{6}u^3 + C && \text{Integrate with respect to } u. \\ &= \frac{1}{6}(x^2 + 2x - 3)^3 + C && \text{Replace } u. \end{aligned}$$

EXAMPLE 8

$$\begin{aligned} \int \sin^4 t \cos t\,dt &= \int u^4\,du && \begin{aligned} \text{Let } u &= \sin t, \\ du &= \cos t\,dt. \end{aligned} \\ &= \frac{u^5}{5} + C && \text{Integrate with respect to } u. \\ &= \frac{\sin^5 t}{5} + C && \text{Replace } u. \end{aligned}$$

The success of the substitution method depends on our finding a substitution that will change an integral we cannot evaluate directly into one that we can. If our first substitution fails, we can try to simplify the integrand further with an additional substitution or two. (You will see what we mean if you do Exercises 73 and 74.) Alternatively, we can start afresh. There can be more than one good way to start, as in the next example.

EXAMPLE 9 Evaluate

$$\int \frac{2z\,dz}{\sqrt[3]{z^2 + 1}}.$$

Solution We can use the substitution method of integration as an exploratory tool: Substitute for the most troublesome part of the integrand and see how things work out. For the integral here, we might try $u = z^2 + 1$ or we might even press our luck and take u to be the entire cube root. Here is what happens in each case.

SOLUTION 1: Substitute $u = z^2 + 1$.

$$\int \frac{2z\,dz}{\sqrt[3]{z^2+1}} = \int \frac{du}{u^{1/3}} \qquad \begin{aligned}\text{Let } u &= z^2+1,\\ du &= 2z\,dz.\end{aligned}$$

$$= \int u^{-1/3}\,du \qquad \text{In the form } \textstyle\int u^n\,du.$$

$$= \frac{u^{2/3}}{2/3} + C \qquad \text{Integrate with respect to } u.$$

$$= \frac{3}{2}u^{2/3} + C$$

$$= \frac{3}{2}(z^2+1)^{2/3} + C \qquad \text{Replace } u \text{ by } z^2+1.$$

SOLUTION 2: Substitute $u = \sqrt[3]{z^2+1}$ instead.

$$\int \frac{2z\,dz}{\sqrt[3]{z^2+1}} = \int \frac{3u^2\,du}{u} \qquad \begin{aligned}\text{Let } u &= \sqrt[3]{z^2+1},\\ u^3 &= z^2+1,\\ 3u^2\,du &= 2z\,dz.\end{aligned}$$

$$= 3\int u\,du$$

$$= 3\cdot\frac{u^2}{2} + C \qquad \text{Integrate with respect to } u.$$

$$= \frac{3}{2}(z^2+1)^{2/3} + C \qquad \text{Replace } u \text{ by } (z^2+1)^{1/3}.$$

Substitution in Definite Integrals

There are two methods for evaluating a definite integral by substitution, and they both work well. One is to find the corresponding indefinite integral by substitution and use one of the resulting antiderivatives to evaluate the definite integral by the Fundamental Theorem. The other is to use the following formula.

Substitution in Definite Integrals

The formula

$$\int_a^b f(g(x))\cdot g'(x)\,dx = \int_{g(a)}^{g(b)} f(u)\,du \tag{13}$$

How to use it

Substitute $u = g(x)$, $du = g'(x)\,dx$, and integrate from $g(a)$ to $g(b)$.

To use the formula, make the same u-substitution you would use to evaluate the corresponding indefinite integral. Then integrate with respect to u from the value u has at $x = a$ to the value u has at $x = b$.

EXAMPLE 10 Evaluate $\displaystyle\int_{-1}^{1} 3x^2\sqrt{x^3+1}\,dx$.

Solution We have two choices:

METHOD 1: Transform the integral as an indefinite integral, integrate, change back to x, and use the original x-limits.

$$\int 3x^2\sqrt{x^3+1}\,dx = \int \sqrt{u}\,du \qquad \text{Let } u = x^3+1,\ du = 3x^2\,dx.$$

$$= \frac{2}{3}u^{3/2} + C \qquad \text{Integrate with respect to } u.$$

$$= \frac{2}{3}(x^3+1)^{3/2} + C \qquad \text{Replace } u \text{ by } x^3+1.$$

$$\int_{-1}^{1} 3x^2\sqrt{x^3+1}\,dx = \frac{2}{3}(x^3+1)^{3/2}\Big]_{-1}^{1} \qquad \text{Use the integral just found, with limits of integration for } x.$$

$$= \frac{2}{3}\left[((1)^3+1)^{3/2} - ((-1)^3+1)^{3/2}\right]$$

$$= \frac{2}{3}\left[2^{3/2} - 0^{3/2}\right] = \frac{2}{3}\left[2\sqrt{2}\right] = \frac{4\sqrt{2}}{3}$$

METHOD 2: Transform the integral and evaluate the transformed integral with the transformed limits given by Eq. (13).

$$\int_{-1}^{1} 3x^2\sqrt{x^3+1}\,dx$$

$$= \int_0^2 \sqrt{u}\,du \qquad \begin{array}{l}\text{Let } u = x^3+1,\ du = 3x^2\,dx.\\ \text{When } x = -1,\ u = (-1)^3+1 = 0.\\ \text{When } x = 1,\ u = (1)^3+1 = 2.\end{array}$$

$$= \frac{2}{3}u^{3/2}\Big]_0^2 \qquad \text{Evaluate the new definite integral.}$$

$$= \frac{2}{3}\left[2^{3/2} - 0^{3/2}\right] = \frac{2}{3}\left[2\sqrt{2}\right] = \frac{4\sqrt{2}}{3}$$

Which method is better—transforming the integral, integrating, and transforming back to use the original limits of integration, or evaluating the transformed integral with transformed limits? In Example 10, the second method seems easier, but that is not always the case. As a rule, it is best to know both methods and to use whichever one seems better at the time.

Here is another example of evaluating a transformed integral with transformed limits.

EXAMPLE 11

$$\int_{\pi/4}^{\pi/2} \cot\theta\,\csc^2\theta\,d\theta = \int_1^0 u\cdot(-du) \qquad \begin{array}{l}\text{Let } u = \cot\theta,\ du = -\csc^2\theta\,d\theta\\ \qquad\qquad -du = \csc^2\theta\,d\theta.\\ \text{When } \theta = \pi/4,\ u = \cot(\pi/4) = 1.\\ \text{When } \theta = \pi/2,\ u = \cot(\pi/2) = 0.\end{array}$$

$$= -\int_1^0 u\,du$$

$$= -\left[\frac{u^2}{2}\right]_1^0 = -\left[\frac{(0)^2}{2} - \frac{(1)^2}{2}\right] = \frac{1}{2}$$

Exercises 5.6

Evaluate the indefinite integrals in Exercises 1–10 by using the given substitutions to reduce the integrals to standard form.

1. $\int \sin 3x\, dx,\ u = 3x$

2. $\int x \sin(2x^2)\, dx,\ u = 2x^2$

3. $\int \sec 2t \tan 2t\, dt,\ u = 2t$

4. $\int \left(1 - \cos\frac{t}{2}\right)^2 \sin\frac{t}{2}\, dt,\ u = 1 - \cos\frac{t}{2}$

5. $\int 28(7x - 2)^{-5}\, dx,\ u = 7x - 2$

6. $\int x^3(x^4 - 1)^2\, dx,\ u = x^4 - 1$

7. $\int \frac{9r^2\, dr}{\sqrt{1 - r^3}},\ u = 1 - r^3$

8. $\int 12(y^4 + 4y^2 + 1)^2 (y^3 + 2y)\, dy,\ u = y^4 + 4y^2 + 1$

9. $\int \csc^2 2\theta \cot 2\theta\, d\theta,$

   a) Using $u = \cot 2\theta$ b) Using $u = \csc 2\theta$

10. $\int \frac{dx}{\sqrt{5x + 8}}$

   a) Using $u = 5x + 8$ b) Using $u = \sqrt{5x + 8}$

Evaluate the integrals in Exercises 11–40.

11. $\int \sqrt{3 - 2s}\, ds$

12. $\int (2x + 1)^3\, dx$

13. $\int \frac{1}{\sqrt{5s + 4}}\, ds$

14. $\int \frac{3\, dx}{(2 - x)^2}$

15. $\int \theta \sqrt[4]{1 - \theta^2}\, d\theta$

16. $\int 8\theta \sqrt[3]{\theta^2 - 1}\, d\theta$

17. $\int 3y\sqrt{7 - 3y^2}\, dy$

18. $\int \frac{4y\, dy}{\sqrt{2y^2 + 1}}$

19. $\int \cos(3z + 4)\, dz$

20. $\int \sin(8z - 5)\, dz$

21. $\int \sec^2(3x + 2)\, dx$

22. $\int \sec^2\left(\frac{x}{4}\right) dx$

23. $\int \sin^5\frac{x}{3} \cos\frac{x}{3}\, dx$

24. $\int \tan^7\frac{x}{2} \sec^2\frac{x}{2}\, dx$

25. $\int r^2\left(\frac{r^3}{18} - 1\right)^5 dr$

26. $\int r^4\left(7 - \frac{r^5}{10}\right)^3 dr$

27. $\int x^{1/2} \sin(x^{3/2} + 1)\, dx$

28. $\int x^{1/3} \sin(x^{4/3} - 8)\, dx$

29. $\int \sec\left(v + \frac{\pi}{2}\right) \tan\left(v + \frac{\pi}{2}\right) dv$

30. $\int \csc\left(\frac{v - \pi}{2}\right) \cot\left(\frac{v - \pi}{2}\right) dv$

31. $\int \frac{\sin(2t + 1)}{\cos^2(2t + 1)}\, dt$

32. $\int \frac{6\cos t}{(2 + \sin t)^3}\, dt$

33. $\int \sqrt{\cot y} \csc^2 y\, dy$

34. $\int \frac{\sec z \tan z}{\sqrt{\sec z}}\, dz$

35. $\int \frac{3}{x^2}\left(1 - \frac{1}{x}\right)^3 dx$

36. $\int \frac{\left(1 + \sqrt{x}\right)^3}{\sqrt{x}}\, dx$

37. $\int \frac{1}{t^2} \cos\left(\frac{1}{t} - 1\right) dt$

38. $\int \frac{1}{\sqrt{t}} \cos\left(\sqrt{t} + 3\right) dt$

39. $\int (s^3 + 2s^2 - 5s + 5)(3s^2 + 4s - 5)\, ds$

40. $\int (\theta^4 - 2\theta^2 + 8\theta - 2)(\theta^3 - \theta + 2)\, d\theta$

Evaluate the integrals in Exercises 41–62.

41. a) $\int_0^3 \sqrt{y + 1}\, dy$ b) $\int_{-1}^0 \sqrt{y + 1}\, dy$

42. a) $\int_0^1 r\sqrt{1 - r^2}\, dr$ b) $\int_{-1}^1 r\sqrt{1 - r^2}\, dr$

43. a) $\int_0^{\pi/4} \tan x \sec^2 x\, dx$ b) $\int_{-\pi/4}^0 \tan x \sec^2 x\, dx$

44. a) $\int_0^{\pi} 3\cos^2 x \sin x\, dx$ b) $\int_{2\pi}^{3\pi} 3\cos^2 x \sin x\, dx$

45. a) $\int_0^1 t^3(1 + t^4)^3\, dt$ b) $\int_{-1}^1 t^3(1 + t^4)^3\, dt$

46. a) $\int_0^{\sqrt{7}} t(t^2 + 1)^{1/3}\, dt$ b) $\int_{-\sqrt{7}}^0 t(t^2 + 1)^{1/3}\, dt$

47. a) $\int_{-1}^1 \frac{5r}{(4 + r^2)^2}\, dr$ b) $\int_0^1 \frac{5r}{(4 + r^2)^2}\, dr$

48. a) $\int_0^1 \frac{10\sqrt{v}}{(1 + v^{3/2})^2}\, dv$ b) $\int_1^4 \frac{10\sqrt{v}}{(1 + v^{3/2})^2}\, dv$

49. a) $\int_0^{\sqrt{3}} \frac{4x}{\sqrt{x^2 + 1}}\, dx$ b) $\int_{-\sqrt{3}}^{\sqrt{3}} \frac{4x}{\sqrt{x^2 + 1}}\, dx$

50. a) $\int_0^1 \frac{x^3}{\sqrt{x^4 + 9}}\, dx$ b) $\int_{-1}^0 \frac{x^3}{\sqrt{x^4 + 9}}\, dx$

51. a) $\int_0^{\pi/6} (1 - \cos 3t) \sin 3t\, dt$

   b) $\int_{\pi/6}^{\pi/3} (1 - \cos 3t) \sin 3t\, dt$

52. **a)** $\displaystyle\int_{-\pi/2}^{0}\left(2+\tan\frac{t}{2}\right)\sec^2\frac{t}{2}\,dt$

b) $\displaystyle\int_{-\pi/2}^{\pi/2}\left(2+\tan\frac{t}{2}\right)\sec^2\frac{t}{2}\,dt$

53. **a)** $\displaystyle\int_{0}^{2\pi}\frac{\cos z}{\sqrt{4+3\sin z}}\,dz$ **b)** $\displaystyle\int_{-\pi}^{\pi}\frac{\cos z}{\sqrt{4+3\sin z}}\,dz$

54. **a)** $\displaystyle\int_{-\pi/2}^{0}\frac{\sin w}{(3+2\cos w)^2}\,dw$ **b)** $\displaystyle\int_{0}^{\pi/2}\frac{\sin w}{(3+2\cos w)^2}\,dw$

55. $\displaystyle\int_{0}^{1}\sqrt{t^5+2t}\,(5t^4+2)\,dt$

56. $\displaystyle\int_{1}^{4}\frac{dy}{2\sqrt{y}\,\left(1+\sqrt{y}\right)^2}$

57. $\displaystyle\int_{0}^{\pi/6}\cos^{-3}2\theta\sin 2\theta\,d\theta$

58. $\displaystyle\int_{\pi}^{3\pi/2}\tan^{-5}\left(\frac{\theta}{6}\right)\sec^2\left(\frac{\theta}{6}\right)d\theta$

59. $\displaystyle\int_{0}^{\pi}5(5-4\cos t)^{1/4}\sin t\,dt$

60. $\displaystyle\int_{0}^{\pi/4}(1-\sin 2t)^{3/2}\cos 2t\,dt$

61. $\displaystyle\int_{0}^{1}(4y-y^2+4y^3+1)^{-2/3}(12y^2-2y+4)\,dy$

62. $\displaystyle\int_{0}^{1}(y^3+6y^2-12y+9)^{-1/2}(y^2+4y-4)\,dy$

Find the total areas of the shaded regions in Exercises 63–66.

63

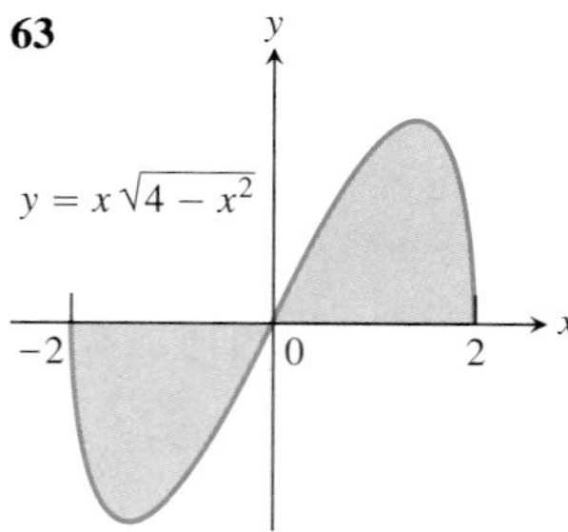

64.

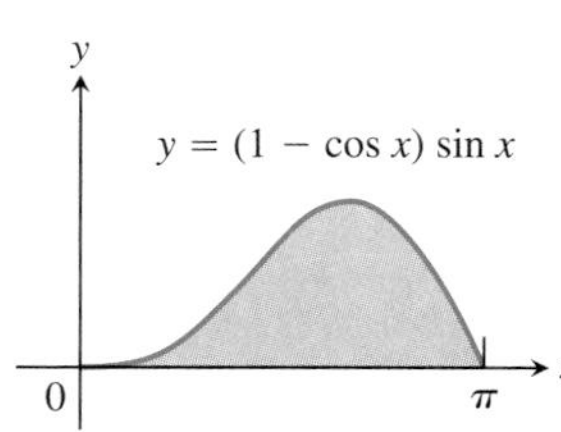

65.

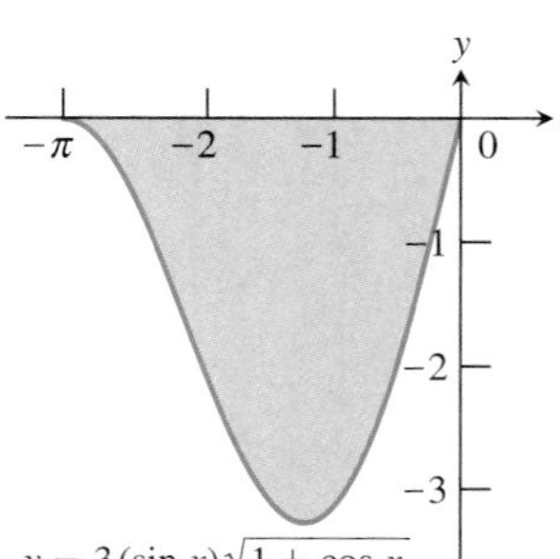

66.

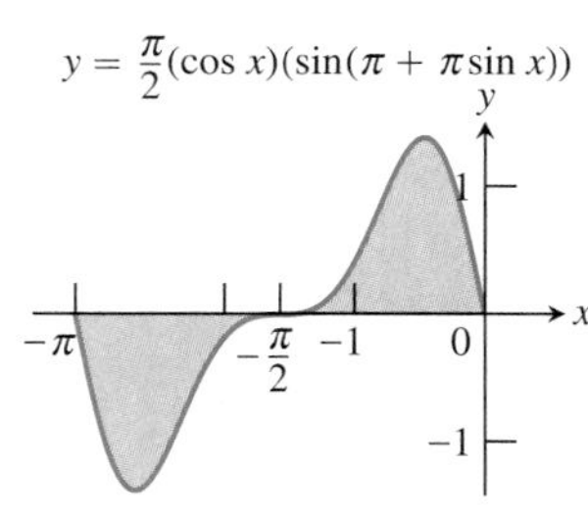

67. It looks as if we can integrate $2\sin x\cos x$ with respect to x in three different ways:

a) $\displaystyle\int 2\sin x\cos x\,dx = \int 2u\,du \qquad u=\sin x,$

$\displaystyle = u^2 + C_1 = \sin^2 x + C_1;$

b) $\displaystyle\int 2\sin x\cos x\,dx = \int -2u\,du \qquad u=\cos x,$

$\displaystyle = -u^2 + C_2 = -\cos^2 x + C_2;$

c) $\displaystyle\int 2\sin x\cos x\,dx = \int \sin 2x\,dx \qquad 2\sin x\cos x = \sin 2x$

$\displaystyle = -\frac{\cos 2x}{2} + C_3.$

Can all three integrations be correct? Give reasons for your answer.

68. The substitution $u = \tan x$ gives

$$\int \sec^2 x\tan x\,dx = \int u\,du = \frac{u^2}{2} + C = \frac{\tan^2 x}{2} + C.$$

The substitution $u = \sec x$ gives

$$\int \sec^2 x\tan x\,dx = \int u\,du = \frac{u^2}{2} + C = \frac{\sec^2 x}{2} + C.$$

Can both integrations be correct? Give reasons for your answer.

Solve the initial value problems in Exercises 69–72.

69. $\displaystyle\frac{ds}{dt} = 24t(3t^2-1)^3, \quad s=0 \text{ when } t=0$

70. $\displaystyle\frac{dy}{dx} = 4x(x^2+8)^{-1/3}, \quad y=0 \text{ when } x=0$

71. $\displaystyle\frac{ds}{dt} = 6\sin(t+\pi), \quad s=0 \text{ when } t=0$

72. $\displaystyle\frac{d^2s}{dt^2} = -4\sin\left(2t-\frac{\pi}{2}\right), \quad \frac{ds}{dt} = 100 \text{ and } s=0 \text{ when } t=0$

SIMPLIFYING INTEGRALS STEP BY STEP

If you do not know what substitution to make, try reducing the integral step by step, using a trial substitution to simplify the integral a bit and then another to simplify it some more. You will see what we mean if you try the sequences of substitutions in Exercises 73 and 74.

73. $\displaystyle\int_{0}^{\pi/4}\frac{18\tan^2 x\sec^2 x}{(2+\tan^3 x)^2}\,dx$

a) $u = \tan x$, followed by $v = u^3$, then by $w = 2 + v$
b) $u = \tan^3 x$, followed by $v = 2 + u$
c) $u = 2 + \tan^3 x$

74. $\displaystyle\int \sqrt{1+\sin^2(x-1)}\,\sin(x-1)\cos(x-1)\,dx$

a) $u = x - 1$, followed by $v = \sin u$, then by $w = 1 + v^2$
b) $u = \sin(x-1)$, followed by $v = 1 + u^2$
c) $u = 1 + \sin^2(x-1)$

Writing for Your Own Knowledge

Answer the following questions in writing. Some answers will take only a sentence or two; others may require several paragraphs. Some explanations may also call for graphs or sketches.

1. How can you sometimes evaluate indefinite integrals by substitution?
2. How does the substitution method work for definite integrals?
3. How is the substitution method of integration related to the Chain Rule for differentiation?

5.7 *Numerical Integration*

As we have seen, the ideal way to evaluate a definite integral $\int_a^b f(x)\,dx$ is to find a formula $F(x)$ for one of the antiderivatives of $f(x)$ and calculate the number $F(b) - F(a)$. But some antiderivatives are hard to find, and still others, like the antiderivatives of $(\sin x)/x$ and $\sqrt{1 + x^4}$, have no elementary formulas. We do not mean merely that no one has yet succeeded in finding elementary formulas for the antiderivatives of $(\sin x)/x$ and $\sqrt{1 + x^4}$. We mean it has been proved that no such formulas exist.

Whatever the reason, when we cannot evaluate a definite integral with an antiderivative, we turn to numerical methods such as the trapezoidal rule and Simpson's rule, described in this section.

The Trapezoidal Rule

When we cannot find a workable antiderivative for a function f that we have to integrate, we partition the interval of integration, replace f by a closely fitting polynomial on each subinterval, integrate the polynomials, and add the results to approximate the integral of f. The higher the degrees of the polynomials for a given partition, the better the results. For a given degree, the finer the partition, the better the results, until we reach limits imposed by round-off and truncation errors.

The polynomials do not need to be of high degree to be effective. Even line segments (graphs of polynomials of degree 1) give good approximations if we use enough of them. To see why, suppose we partition the domain $[a, b]$ of f into n subintervals of length $h = (b - a)/n$ and join the corresponding points on the curve with line segments (Fig. 5.25). The vertical lines from the ends of the segments to the partition points create a collection of trapezoids that approximate

The length $h = (b - a)/n$ is called the **step size.**

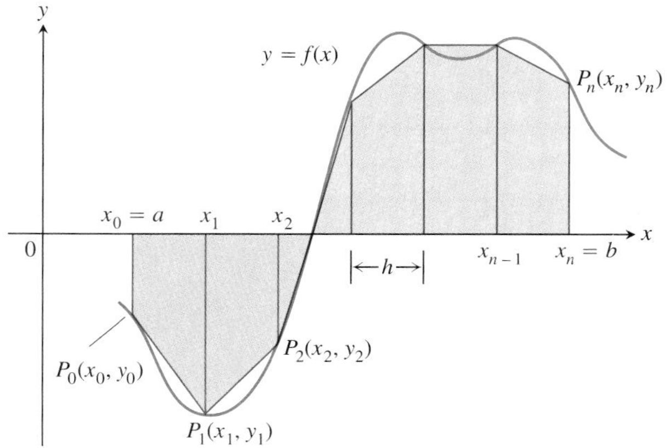

5.25 The trapezoidal rule approximates short stretches of the curve $y = f(x)$ with line segments. To estimate the integral of f from a to b, we add the "signed" areas of the trapezoids made by joining the ends of the segments to the x-axis.

the region between the curve and the x-axis. We add the areas of the trapezoids, counting area above the x-axis as positive and area below the axis as negative. The sum of the "signed" areas is

$$T = \frac{1}{2}(y_0 + y_1)h + \frac{1}{2}(y_1 + y_2)h + \cdots + \frac{1}{2}(y_{n-2} + y_{n-1})h + \frac{1}{2}(y_{n-1} + y_n)h$$

$$= h\left(\frac{1}{2}y_0 + y_1 + y_2 + \cdots + y_{n-1} + \frac{1}{2}y_n\right)$$

$$= \frac{h}{2}(y_0 + 2y_1 + 2y_2 + \cdots + 2y_{n-1} + y_n), \tag{1}$$

where

$$y_0 = f(a), \quad y_1 = f(x_1), \quad \ldots, \quad y_{n-1} = f(x_{n-1}), \quad y_n = f(b).$$

The trapezoidal rule says: Use T to estimate the integral of f from a to b.

The Trapezoidal Rule

To approximate $\int_a^b f(x)\,dx$, use

$$T = \frac{h}{2}(y_0 + 2y_1 + 2y_2 + \cdots + 2y_{n-1} + y_n) \tag{2}$$

(for n subintervals of length $h = (b - a)/n$ and $y_k = f(x_k)$).

EXAMPLE 1 Use the trapezoidal rule with $n = 4$ to estimate

$$\int_1^2 x^2\,dx.$$

Compare the estimate with the exact value of the integral.

TABLE 5.6

x	$y = x^2$
1	1
$\frac{5}{4}$	$\frac{25}{16}$
$\frac{6}{4}$	$\frac{36}{16}$
$\frac{7}{4}$	$\frac{49}{16}$
2	4

Solution To find the trapezoidal approximation, we divide the interval of integration into four subintervals of equal length and list the values of $y = x^2$ at the endpoints and partition points (see Table 5.6). We then evaluate Eq. (2) with $n = 4$ and $h = 1/4$:

$$T = \frac{h}{2}(y_0 + 2y_1 + 2y_2 + 2y_3 + y_4)$$

$$= \frac{1}{8}\left(1 + 2\left(\frac{25}{16}\right) + 2\left(\frac{36}{16}\right) + 2\left(\frac{49}{16}\right) + 4\right) = \frac{75}{32} = 2.34375.$$

The exact value of the integral is

$$\int_1^2 x^2\,dx = \frac{x^3}{3}\bigg]_1^2 = \frac{8}{3} - \frac{1}{3} = \frac{7}{3} = 2.\overline{3}.$$

The approximation is a slight overestimate. Each trapezoid contains slightly more than the corresponding strip under the curve (Fig. 5.26).

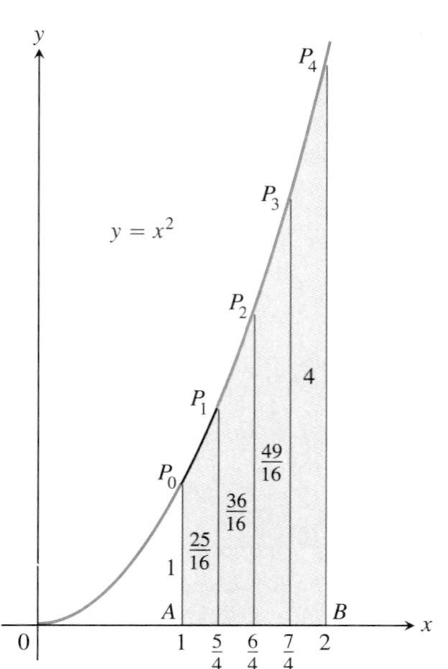

5.26 The trapezoidal approximation of the area under the graph of $y = x^2$ from $x = 1$ to $x = 2$ is a slight overestimate.

Controlling the Error in the Trapezoidal Approximation

Pictures suggest that the magnitude of the error

$$E_T = \int_a^b f(x)\,dx - T \tag{3}$$

in the trapezoidal approximation will decrease as the **step size** h decreases, because the trapezoids fit the curve better as their number increases. A theorem from advanced calculus assures us that this will be the case if f has a continuous second derivative.

The Error Estimate for the Trapezoidal Rule

If f'' is continuous and M is any upper bound for the values of $|f''|$ on $[a, b]$, then

$$|E_T| \leq \frac{b-a}{12} h^2 M. \tag{4}$$

Although theory tells us there will always be a smallest safe value of M, in practice we can hardly ever find it. Instead, we find the best value we can and go on from there to estimate $|E_T|$. This may seem sloppy, but it works. To make $|E_T|$ small for a given M, we make h small.

EXAMPLE 2 Find an upper bound for the error in the approximation found in Example 1 for the value of

$$\int_1^2 x^2\, dx.$$

Solution We first find an upper bound M for the magnitude of the second derivative of $f(x) = x^2$ on the interval $1 \leq x \leq 2$. Since $f''(x) = 2$ for all x, we may safely take $M = 2$. With $b - a = 1$ and $h = 1/4$, Eq. (4) gives

$$|E_T| \leq \frac{b-a}{12} h^2 M = \frac{1}{12}\left(\frac{1}{4}\right)^2 (2) = \frac{1}{96}.$$

This is precisely what we find when we subtract $T = 75/32$ from $\int_1^2 x^2\, dx = 7/3$, since $|7/3 - 75/32| = |-1/96|$. Here our estimate gave the error's magnitude *exactly,* but this is exceptional.

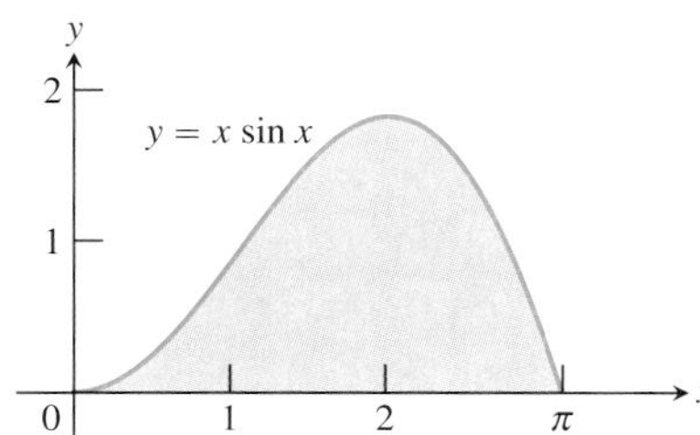

5.27 With $n = 10$ subintervals, the trapezoidal rule estimates the area under the curve with a relative error of about 4%. With $n = 100$ subintervals, the relative error is about 0.04% (Example 3).

EXAMPLE 3 Find an upper bound for the error incurred in estimating

$$\int_0^{\pi} x \sin x\, dx$$

with the trapezoidal rule with $n = 10$ steps (Fig. 5.27).

Solution With $a = 0$, $b = \pi$, and $h = (b - a)/n = \pi/10$, Eq. (4) gives

$$|E_T| \leq \frac{b-a}{12} h^2 M = \frac{\pi}{12}\left(\frac{\pi}{10}\right)^2 M = \frac{\pi^3}{1200} M.$$

The number M can be any upper bound for the magnitude of the second derivative of $f(x) = x \sin x$ on $[0, \pi]$. A routine calculation gives

$$f''(x) = 2\cos x - x \sin x,$$

so

$$\begin{aligned}|f''(x)| &= |2\cos x - x\sin x| \\ &\le |2\cos x| + |-x\sin x| && \text{Triangle inequality: } |a+b| \le |a| + |b| \\ &\le |2|\,|\cos x| + |-x|\,|\sin x| \\ &\le 2\,|\cos x| + |x|\,|\sin x| \\ &\le 2\cdot 1 + \pi\cdot 1 = 2 + \pi && |\cos x| \text{ and } |\sin x| \text{ never exceed 1, and } 0 \le x \le \pi\end{aligned}$$

We can safely take $M = 2 + \pi$. Therefore,

$$|E_T| \le \frac{\pi^3}{1200}M = \frac{\pi^3(2+\pi)}{1200} < 0.133. \qquad \text{Rounded up to be safe}$$

The absolute error is no greater than 0.133.

For greater accuracy, we would not try to improve M but would take more steps. With $n = 100$ steps, for example, $h = \pi/100$ and

$$|E_T| \le \frac{\pi}{12}\left(\frac{\pi}{100}\right)^2 M = \frac{\pi^3(2+\pi)}{120{,}000} < 0.00133 = 1.33 \times 10^{-3}.$$

EXAMPLE 4 As we will see in Chapter 6, the value of ln 2 can be calculated from the integral

$$\ln 2 = \int_1^2 \frac{1}{x}\,dx.$$

How many subintervals (steps) should be used in the trapezoidal rule to approximate the integral with an error of magnitude less than 10^{-4}?

Solution To determine n, the number of subintervals, we use Eq. (4) with

$$b - a = 2 - 1 = 1, \qquad h = \frac{b-a}{n} = \frac{1}{n},$$

$$\begin{aligned}f''(x) &= \frac{d^2}{dx^2}(x^{-1}) \\ &= 2x^{-3} = \frac{2}{x^3}.\end{aligned}$$

Then

$$\left|E_T\right| \le \frac{b-a}{12}h^2 \max\left|f''(x)\right| = \frac{1}{12}\left(\frac{1}{n}\right)^2 \max\left|\frac{2}{x^3}\right|,$$

where max refers to the interval [1, 2].

This is one of the rare cases where we can find the exact value of $\max|f''|$. On [1, 2], $y = 2/x^3$ decreases steadily from a maximum of $y = 2$ to a minimum of $y = 1/4$ (Fig. 5.28). Therefore,

$$|E_T| \le \frac{1}{12}\left(\frac{1}{n}\right)^2 \cdot 2 = \frac{1}{6n^2}.$$

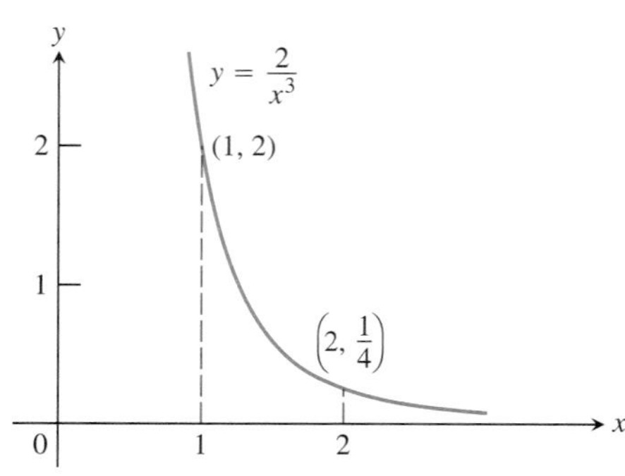

5.28 The continuous function $y = 2/x^3$ has its maximum value on [1, 2] at $x = 1$ (Example 4).

The error's absolute value will therefore be less than 10^{-4} if

$$\frac{1}{6n^2} < 10^{-4},$$

$$\frac{10^4}{6} < n^2, \qquad \text{Multiply both sides by } 10^4 n^2.$$

$$\frac{100}{\sqrt{6}} < |n|, \qquad \text{Square roots of both sides}$$

$$\frac{100}{\sqrt{6}} < n, \qquad n \text{ is positive}$$

$$40.83 < n. \qquad \text{Rounded up, to be safe}$$

The first integer beyond 40.83 is $n = 41$. With $n = 41$ subintervals we can guarantee calculating ln 2 with an error of magnitude less than 10^{-4}. Any larger n will work, too.

Simpson's One-Third Rule

The idea of using the formula

$$A = \frac{h}{3}(y_0 + 4y_1 + y_2)$$

to estimate the area under a curve is known as Simpson's one-third rule. But the rule was in use long before Thomas Simpson (1720–1761) was born. It is another of history's beautiful quirks that one of the ablest mathematicians of eighteenth-century England is remembered not for his successful texts and his contributions to mathematical analysis but for a rule that was never his, that he never laid claim to, and that bears his name only because he happened to mention it in a book he wrote.

Simpson's Rule

Simpson's rule for approximating $\int_a^b f(x)\,dx$ is based on approximating f with quadratic polynomials instead of linear polynomials. We approximate the graph of f with parabolic arcs instead of line segments (Fig. 5.29).

The integral of the quadratic polynomial $y = Ax^2 + Bx + C$ in Fig. 5.30 from $x = -h$ to $x = h$ is

$$\int_{-h}^{h} (Ax^2 + Bx + C)\,dx = \frac{h}{3}(y_0 + 4y_1 + y_2) \tag{5}$$

(Appendix 5). Simpson's rule follows from partitioning $[a, b]$ into an even number of subintervals of equal length h, applying Eq. (5) to successive interval pairs, and adding the results.

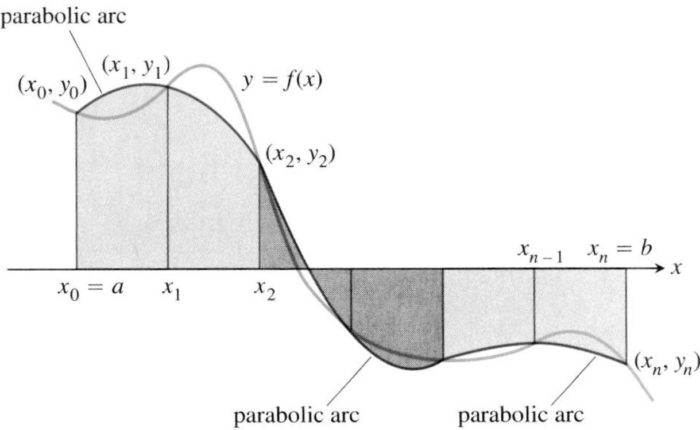

5.29 Simpson's rule approximates short stretches of curve with parabolic arcs.

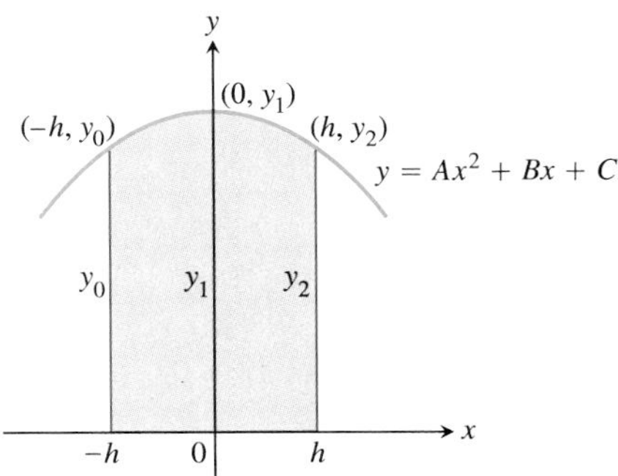

5.30 By integrating from $-h$ to h, we find the shaded area to be

$$\frac{h}{3}\left(y_0 + 4y_1 + y_2\right).$$

Simpson's Rule

To approximate $\int_a^b f(x)\,dx$, use

$$S = \frac{h}{3}(y_0 + 4y_1 + 2y_2 + 4y_3 + \cdots + 2y_{n-2} + 4y_{n-1} + y_n). \tag{6}$$

The y's are the values of f at the partition points

$x_0 = a,\quad x_1 = a + h,\quad x_2 = a + 2h,\quad \ldots,\quad x_{n-1} = a + (n-1)h,\quad b = x_n.$

The number n is even, and $h = (b - a)/n$.

Error Control for Simpson's Rule

The magnitude of the Simpson's rule error,

$$E_S = \int_a^b f(x)\,dx - S, \tag{7}$$

decreases with the step size, as we would expect from our experience with the trapezoidal rule. The inequality for controlling the Simpson's rule error, however, assumes f to have a continuous fourth derivative instead of merely a continuous second derivative. The formula, once again from advanced calculus, is this:

The Error Estimate for Simpson's Rule

If $f^{(4)}$ is continuous and M is any upper bound for the values of $|f^{(4)}|$ on $[a, b]$, then

$$|E_S| \le \frac{b-a}{180} h^4 M. \tag{8}$$

As with the trapezoidal rule, we can almost never find the smallest possible value of M. We just find the best value we can and go on from there to estimate $|E_S|$.

EXAMPLE 5 Use Simpson's rule with $n = 4$ to approximate

$$\int_0^1 5x^4\,dx.$$

What estimate does Eq. (8) give for the error in the approximation?

Solution Again we have chosen an integral whose exact value we can calculate directly:

$$\int_0^1 5x^4\,dx = x^5\Big]_0^1 = 1.$$

To find the Simpson approximation, we partition the interval of integration into four subintervals and evaluate $f(x) = 5x^4$ at the partition points (Table 5.7).

TABLE 5.7

x	$y = 5x^4$
0	0
$\frac{1}{4}$	$\frac{5}{256}$
$\frac{2}{4}$	$\frac{80}{256}$
$\frac{3}{4}$	$\frac{405}{256}$
1	5

We then evaluate Eq. (6) with $n = 4$ and $h = 1/4$:

$$S = \frac{h}{3}(y_0 + 4y_1 + 2y_2 + 4y_3 + y_4)$$

$$= \frac{1}{12}\left(0 + 4\left(\frac{5}{256}\right) + 2\left(\frac{80}{256}\right) + 4\left(\frac{405}{256}\right) + 5\right) \approx 1.00260.$$

To estimate the error, we first find an upper bound M for the magnitude of the fourth derivative of $f(x) = 5x^4$ on the interval $0 \le x \le 1$. Since the fourth derivative has the constant value $f^{(4)}(x) = 120$, we may safely take $M = 120$. With $b - a = 1$ and $h = 1/4$, Eq. (8) then gives

$$|E_S| \le \frac{b-a}{180} h^4 M = \frac{1}{180}\left(\frac{1}{4}\right)^4 (120) = \frac{1}{384} < 0.00261.$$

Calculus and Computation

Here is another example of calculus having something to say about computation. It is a straightforward matter to implement the trapezoidal rule and Simpson's rule on a computer. But that in itself is not enough. We need to know how many steps to take to achieve the accuracy we want, and the guidance for *that* comes from calculus.

Which Rule Gives Better Results?

The answer lies in the error-control formulas for the two rules:

$$|E_T| \le \frac{b-a}{12} h^2 M, \qquad |E_S| \le \frac{b-a}{180} h^4 M. \tag{9}$$

The M's of course mean different things, the first being an upper bound on $|f''|$ and the second an upper bound on $|f^{(4)}|$. But there is more. The factor $(b - a)/180$ in the Simpson formula is one-fifteenth of the factor $(b - a)/12$ in the trapezoidal formula. More important still, the Simpson formula has an h^4 while the trapezoidal formula has only an h^2. If h is one-tenth, then h^2 is one-hundredth but h^4 is only one ten-thousandth. If both M's are 1, for example, and $b - a = 1$, then, with $h = 1/10$,

$$|E_T| \le \frac{1}{12}\left(\frac{1}{10}\right)^2 \cdot 1 \le \frac{1}{1200}, \tag{10}$$

while

$$|E_S| \le \frac{1}{180}\left(\frac{1}{10}\right)^4 \cdot 1 \le \frac{1}{1{,}800{,}000} = \frac{1}{1500} \cdot \frac{1}{1200}. \tag{11}$$

For roughly the same amount of computational effort, we get better accuracy with Simpson's rule—at least in this case.

The h^2 versus h^4 is the key. If h is less than 1, then h^4 can be significantly smaller than h^2. On the other hand, if h equals 1, there is no difference between h^2 and h^4. If h is greater than 1, the value of h^4 may be significantly larger than the value of h^2. In the latter two cases, the error-control formulas offer little help. We have to go back to the geometry of the curve $y = f(x)$ to see whether trapezoids or parabolas, if either, are going to give the results we want.

Working with Numerical Data

The next example shows how we can use Simpson's rule to estimate the integral of a function from values measured in the laboratory or in the field even when we have no formula for the function. We can use the trapezoidal rule the same way.

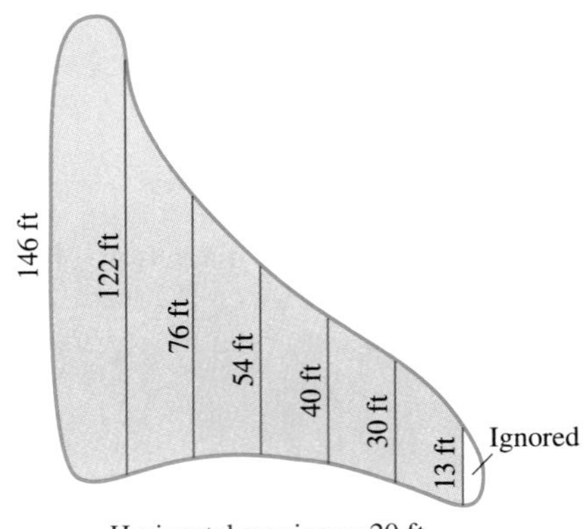

5.31 The swamp in Example 6.

EXAMPLE 6 A town wants to drain and fill a small polluted swamp (Fig. 5.31). The swamp averages 5 ft deep. About how many cubic yards of dirt will it take to fill the area after the swamp is drained?

Solution To calculate the volume of the swamp, we estimate the surface area and multiply by 5. To estimate the area, we use Simpson's rule with $h = 20$ ft and the y's equal to the distances measured across the swamp, as shown in Fig. 5.31.

$$S = \frac{h}{3}(y_0 + 4y_1 + 2y_2 + 4y_3 + 2y_4 + 4y_5 + y_6)$$

$$= \frac{20}{3}(146 + 488 + 152 + 216 + 80 + 120 + 13) = 8100.$$

The volume is about $(8100)(5) = 40{,}500\ \text{ft}^3$ or $1500\ \text{yd}^3$.

Round-off Errors

Although decreasing the step size h reduces the error in the Simpson and trapezoidal approximations in theory, it may fail to do so in practice. When h is very small, say $h = 10^{-5}$, the round-off errors in the arithmetic required to evaluate S and T may accumulate to such an extent that the error formulas no longer describe what is going on. Shrinking h below a certain size can actually make things worse. While this will not be an issue in the present book, you should consult a text on numerical analysis for alternative methods if you are having problems with round-off.

Exercises 5.7

The instructions for the integrals in Exercises 1–10 have two parts, one for the trapezoidal rule and one for Simpson's rule.

I. *Using the trapezoidal rule*

a) Estimate the integral with $n = 4$ steps and use Eq. (4) to find an upper bound for $|E_T|$.

b) Evaluate the integral directly, and use Eq. (3) to find $|E_T|$.

c) Use the formula $(|E_T|/\text{True value}) \times 100$ to express $|E_T|$ as a percentage of the integral's true value.

II. *Using Simpson's rule*

a) Estimate the integral with $n = 4$ steps and use Eq. (8) to find an upper bound for $|E_S|$.

b) Evaluate the integral directly and use Eq. (7) to find $|E_S|$.

c) Use the formula $(|E_S|/\text{True value}) \times 100$ to express $|E_S|$ as a percentage of the integral's true value.

1. $\int_1^2 x\,dx$

2. $\int_1^3 (2x - 1)\,dx$

3. $\int_{-1}^1 (x^2 + 1)\,dx$

4. $\int_{-2}^0 (x^2 - 1)\,dx$

5. $\int_0^2 (t^3 + t)\,dt$

6. $\int_{-1}^1 (t^3 + 1)\,dt$

7. $\int_1^2 \frac{1}{s^2}\,ds$

8. $\int_2^4 \frac{1}{(s-1)^2}\,ds$

9. $\int_0^\pi \sin t\,dt$

10. $\int_0^1 \sin \pi t\,dt$

In Exercises 11–14, use the tabulated values of the integrand to estimate the integral with (a) the trapezoidal rule and (b) Simpson's rule with $n = 8$ steps. Then (c) find the integral's exact value and the approximation error E_T or E_S, as appropriate, from Eqs. (3) and (7).

11. $\int_0^1 x\sqrt{1 - x^2}\,dx$

x	$x\sqrt{1-x^2}$
0	0.0
0.125	0.12402
0.25	0.24206
0.375	0.34763
0.5	0.43301
0.625	0.48789
0.75	0.49608
0.875	0.42361
1.0	0

12. $\displaystyle\int_0^3 \frac{\theta}{\sqrt{16+\theta^2}}\,d\theta$

θ	$\theta/\sqrt{16+\theta^2}$
0	0
0.375	0.09334
0.75	0.18429
1.125	0.27075
1.5	0.35112
1.875	0.42443
2.25	0.49026
2.625	0.58466
3.0	0.6

13. $\displaystyle\int_{-\pi/2}^{\pi/2} \frac{3\cos t}{(2+\sin t)^2}\,dt$

t	$(3\cos t)/(2+\sin t)^2$
−1.57080	0.0
−1.17810	0.99138
−0.78540	1.26906
−0.39270	1.05961
0	0.75
0.39270	0.48821
0.78540	0.28946
1.17810	0.13429
1.57080	0

14. $\displaystyle\int_{\pi/4}^{\pi/2} (\csc^2 y)\sqrt{\cot y}\,dy$

y	$(\csc^2 y)\sqrt{\cot y}$
0.78540	0.5
0.88357	1.51606
0.98175	1.18237
1.07992	0.93998
1.17810	0.75402
1.27627	0.60145
1.37445	0.46364
1.47262	0.31688
1.57080	0

In Exercises 15–26, use Eqs. (4) and (8), as appropriate, to estimate the minimum number of subintervals needed to approximate the integrals with an error of magnitude less than 10^{-4} by (a) the trapezoidal rule and (b) Simpson's rule. (The integrals in Exercises 15–22 are the integrals from Exercises 1–8.)

15. $\displaystyle\int_1^2 x\,dx$

16. $\displaystyle\int_1^3 (2x-1)\,dx$

17. $\displaystyle\int_{-1}^1 (x^2+1)\,dx$

18. $\displaystyle\int_{-2}^0 (x^2-1)\,dx$

19. $\displaystyle\int_0^2 (t^3+t)\,dt$

20. $\displaystyle\int_{-1}^1 (t^3+1)\,dt$

21. $\displaystyle\int_1^2 \frac{1}{s^2}\,ds$

22. $\displaystyle\int_2^4 \frac{1}{(s-1)^2}\,ds$

23. $\displaystyle\int_0^3 \sqrt{x+1}\,dx$

24. $\displaystyle\int_0^3 \frac{1}{\sqrt{x+1}}\,dx$

25. $\displaystyle\int_0^2 \sin(x+1)\,dx$

26. $\displaystyle\int_{-1}^1 \cos(x+\pi)\,dx$

27. As the fish-and-game warden of your township, you are responsible for stocking the town pond with fish before fishing season. The average depth of the pond is 20 ft. You plan to start the season with one fish per 1000 ft^3. You intend to have at least 25% of the opening day's fish population left at the end of the season. What is the maximum number of licenses the town can sell if the average seasonal catch is 20 fish per license?

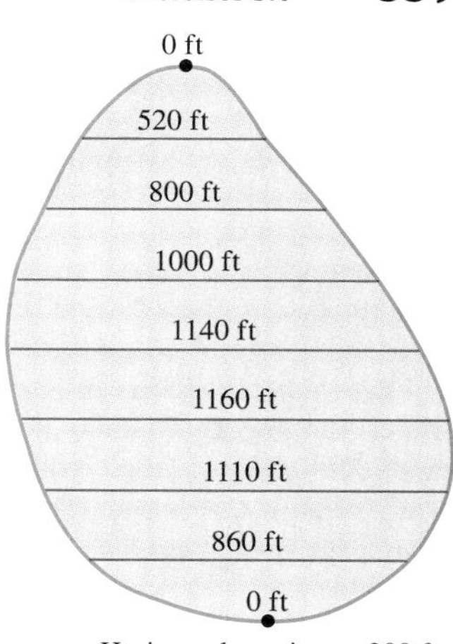

Horizontal spacing = 200 ft

28. A vehicle's aerodynamic drag is determined in part by its cross-section area and, all other things being equal, engineers try to make this area as small as possible. Use Simpson's rule to estimate the cross-section area of the body of James Worden's solar-powered Solectria car at M.I.T. from the diagram below.

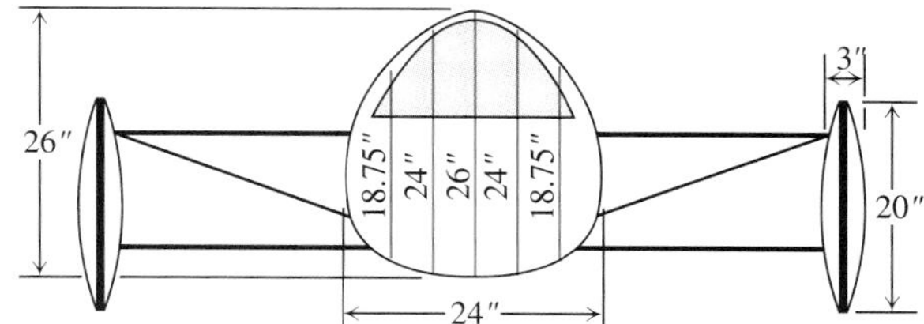

Solectria solar cars are produced by Solectron Corp., Arlington, MA.

ELECTRIC ENERGY CONSUMPTION

The Louisiana Power and Light Company tries to forecast the demand for electricity throughout the day so that it can have enough generators on line at any given time to carry the load. Boilers take a while to fire up, so the company has to know in advance what the load is going to be if service is not to be interrupted. Like all power companies, Louisiana Power measures electrical demand in kilowatt-hours (KWH on your electric bill). A 1500-watt space heater, running for 10 hours, for instance, uses 15,000 watt-hours or 15 kilowatt-hours of electricity. A kilowatt, like a horsepower, is a unit of power. A kilowatt-hour is a unit of energy, and energy is what Louisiana Power, despite its name, sells.

Table 5.8 and the graph in Fig. 5.32 show the results of a 1984 residential-load study of Louisiana Power residential customers with electric heating, for typical weekdays and weekend days in January. A typical customer used 56.60 kwh on a weekday that January and 53.46 kwh on a weekend day. At the time of the study, 56.60 kwh cost a customer $3.40.

TABLE 5.8
Residential electric loads (Exercises 29 and 30)

Hour of Day	Weekday kw	Weekend kw
1	1.88	1.69
2	1.88	1.64
3	2.02	1.63
4	2.02	1.73
5	2.25	1.80
6	2.76	1.97
7	3.60	2.25
8	3.66	2.68
9	3.05	3.05
10	2.70	3.05
11	2.38	2.88
12	2.17	2.55
13	2.02	2.25
14	1.82	1.95
15	1.72	1.87
16	1.77	1.83
17	1.97	1.90
18	2.43	2.17
19	2.68	2.46
20	2.75	2.52
21	2.65	2.50
22	2.40	2.57
23	2.21	2.40
24	1.90	2.22

29. Find the weekday energy consumption of a typical residential customer by using the trapezoidal rule to estimate the area under the weekday power curve. To save time, you might try using only the data for the even-numbered hours or the data for the odd-numbered hours. How close do you come to Louisiana Power's own estimate if you do that? (If you use the even-numbered hours, be sure to count hour 2 twice so that you cover a complete 24-h period. If you use odd-numbered hours, use hour 1 twice.)

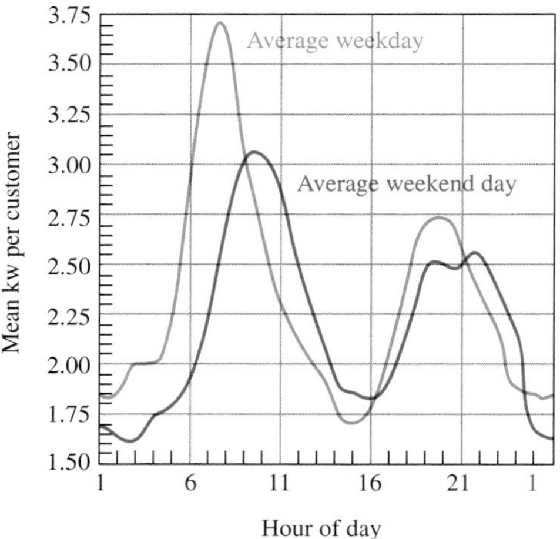

5.32 Louisiana Power and Light Company's 1984 residential-load profile of residential customers with electric heating, averaged days for January. The curves plot kilowatts against hours. The areas under the curves give kilowatt-hours. See Table 5.8 for data.

30. *Continuation of Exercise 29.* Use the trapezoidal rule to find the daily weekend energy consumption.

31. *Polynomials of Low Degree.* The magnitude of the error in the trapezoidal approximation of $\int_a^b f(x)\,dx$ is

$$|E_T| = \frac{b-a}{12} h^2 |f''(c)|,$$

where c is some point (usually unidentified) in (a, b). If f is a linear function of x, then $f''(c) = 0$, so $E_T = 0$ and T gives the exact value of the integral for any value of h. This is no surprise, really, for if f is linear, the line segments approximating the graph of f fit the graph exactly. The surprise comes with Simpson's rule. The magnitude of the error in Simpson's rule is

$$|E_S| = \frac{b-a}{180} h^4 |f^{(4)}(c)|,$$

where once again c lies in (a, b). If f is a polynomial of degree less than four, then $f^{(4)} = 0$ no matter what c is, so $E_S = 0$ and S gives the integral's exact value—even if we use only two steps. As a case in point, use Simpson's rule with $n = 2$ to estimate

$$\int_0^2 x^3\,dx.$$

Compare your answer with the integral's exact value.

32. *Usable Values of the Sine-Integral Function.* The sine-integral function,

$$\mathrm{Si}(x) = \int_0^x \frac{\sin t}{t}\,dt, \qquad \text{"Sine integral of } x\text{"}$$

is one of the many functions in engineering whose formulas cannot be simplified. There is no elementary formula for the antiderivative of $(\sin t)/t$. The values of $\mathrm{Si}(x)$, however, are readily estimated by numerical integration.

Although the notation does not show it explicitly, the function being integrated is

$$f(t) = \begin{cases} \dfrac{\sin t}{t}, & t \neq 0, \\ 1, & t = 0, \end{cases}$$

the continuous extension of $(\sin t)/t$ to the interval $[0, x]$. The function has derivatives of all orders at every point of its domain. Its graph is smooth (Fig. 5.33) and you can expect good results from Simpson's rule.

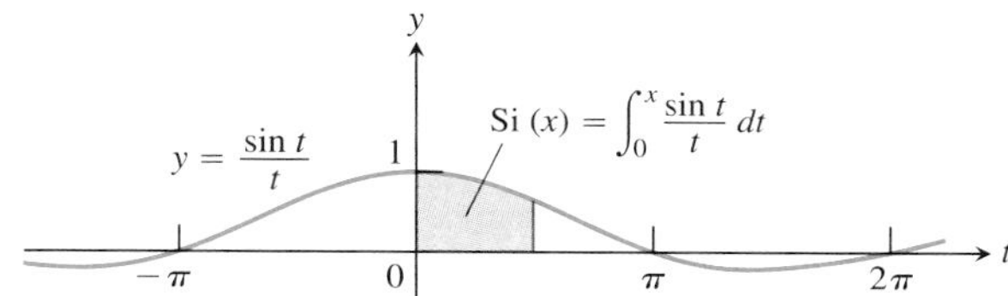

5.33 The continuous extension of $y = (\sin t)/t$. The sine-integral function $\mathrm{Si}(x)$ is the subject of Exercise 32.

a) Use the fact that $|f^{(4)}| \leq 1$ on $[0, \pi/2]$ to give an upper bound for the error that will occur if

$$\mathrm{Si}\left(\frac{\pi}{2}\right) = \int_0^{\pi/2} \frac{\sin t}{t}\,dt$$

is estimated by Simpson's rule with $n = 4$.

b) Estimate $\mathrm{Si}(\pi/2)$ by Simpson's rule with $n = 4$.

c) Express the error bound you found in (a) as a percentage of the value you found in (b).

33. *Continuation of Example 3.* The error bounds in Eqs. (4) and (8) are "worst case" estimates, and the trapezoidal and Simpson rules are often more accurate than the bounds suggest. The trapezoidal-rule estimate of

$$\int_0^{\pi} x \sin x\,dx$$

in Example 3 is a case in point.

a) Use the trapezoidal rule with $n = 10$ to approximate the value of the integral. The table to the right gives the necessary y values.

x	$x \sin x$
0	0
$(0.1)\pi$	0.09708
$(0.2)\pi$	0.36932
$(0.3)\pi$	0.76248
$(0.4)\pi$	1.19513
$(0.5)\pi$	1.57079
$(0.6)\pi$	1.79270
$(0.7)\pi$	1.77912
$(0.8)\pi$	1.47727
$(0.9)\pi$	0.87372
π	0

b) Find the magnitude of the difference between π, the integral's value, and your approximation in (a). You will find the difference to be considerably less than the upper bound of 0.133 calculated with $n = 10$ in Example 3.

c) The upper bound of 0.133 for $|E_T|$ in Example 3 could have been improved somewhat by having a better bound for

$$|f''(x)| = |2\cos x - x \sin x|$$

on $[0, \pi]$. The upper bound we used was $2 + \pi$. Graph f'' over $[0, \pi]$ and use TRACE or ZOOM to improve this upper bound.

Use the improved upper bound as M in Eq. (4) to make an improved estimate of $|E_T|$. Notice that the trapezoidal-rule approximation in (a) is also better than this improved estimate would suggest.

34. *Continuation of Exercise 33.*

a) Show that the fourth derivative of $f(x) = x \sin x$ is

$$f^{(4)}(x) = -4\cos x + x \sin x.$$

Find an upper bound M for the values of $|f^{(4)}|$ on $[0, \pi]$.

b) Use the value of M from (a) together with Eq. (8) to obtain an upper bound for the magnitude of the error in estimating the value of

$$\int_0^{\pi} x \sin x\,dx$$

with Simpson's rule with $n = 10$ steps.

c) Use the data in Table 5.16 to estimate $\int_0^{\pi} x \sin x\,dx$ with Simpson's rule with $n = 10$ steps.

d) To five decimal places, find the magnitude of the difference between your estimate in (c) and the integral's true value, π. You will find the magnitude to be considerably less than the upper bound obtained with Eq. (8) in (b).

You are planning to use Simpson's rule to estimate the values of the integrals in Exercises 35 and 36. Before proceeding, you turn to Eq. (8) to determine the step size h needed to assure the accuracy you want. What happens? Can this be avoided by using the trapezoidal rule and Eq. (4) instead? Give reasons for your answers.

35. $\displaystyle\int_0^4 x^{3/2}\,dx$ **36.** $\displaystyle\int_0^1 x^{5/2}\,dx$

NUMERICAL INTEGRATOR

As we mentioned at the beginning of the section, the definite integrals of many continuous functions cannot be evaluated with the Fundamental Theorem of Calculus because their antiderivatives lack elementary formulas. Numerical integration offers a practical way to estimate the values of these so-called *nonelementary integrals.* If your calculator or computer has a numerical integration routine, try it on the integrals in Exercises 37–40.

37. $\displaystyle\int_0^1 \sqrt{1 + x^4}\,dx$ A nonelementary integral that came up in Newton's research

38. $\displaystyle\int_0^{\pi/2} \frac{\sin x}{x}\,dx$ The integral from Exercise 32. To avoid division by zero, you may have to start the integration at a small positive number like 10^{-6} instead of 0.

39. $\int_0^{\pi/2} \sin(x^2)\,dx$ An integral associated with the diffraction of light

40. $\int_0^{\pi/2} 40\sqrt{1 - 0.64\cos^2 t}\,dt$ The length of the ellipse $(x^2/25) + (y^2/9) = 1$

Writing for Your Own Knowledge

Answer the following questions in writing. Some answers will take only a sentence or two; others may require several paragraphs. Some explanations may also call for graphs or sketches.

1. You are collaborating to produce a short "how-to" manual for numerical integration, and are writing about the trapezoidal rule. (a) What will you say about the rule itself and how to use it? how to achieve accuracy? (b) What would you say if you were writing about Simpson's rule instead?
2. How would you compare the relative merits of Simpson's rule and the trapezoidal rule?

EXPLORER PROGRAM

Integral Evaluation	Evaluates $\int_a^b f(x)\,dx$ by the trapezoidal rule, Simpson's rule, and Romberg's accelerated version of the trapezoidal rule.

For Your Review

Write brief paragraphs about the following topics and give examples.

Estimating with finite sums
Sigma notation for finite sums
Algebra with finite sums
Partitions and norms
The definite integral as a limit of Riemann sums
Properties of definite integrals
Definite integrals and area
The average value of a continuous function
The Mean Value Theorem for Definite Integrals
The Max-Min Inequality for definite integrals
The domination inequality for definite integrals
The Fundamental Theorem of Calculus
Indefinite integrals
Rules of algebra for indefinite integrals
Integration by substitution
 a) for indefinite integrals
 b) for definite integrals
The trapezoidal rule
Simpson's rule

Practice Exercises

1. The accompanying figure shows the graph of the velocity (ft/sec) of a model rocket for the first 8 sec after launch. The rocket accelerated straight up for the first 2 sec and then coasted to reach its maximum height at $t = 8$ sec.

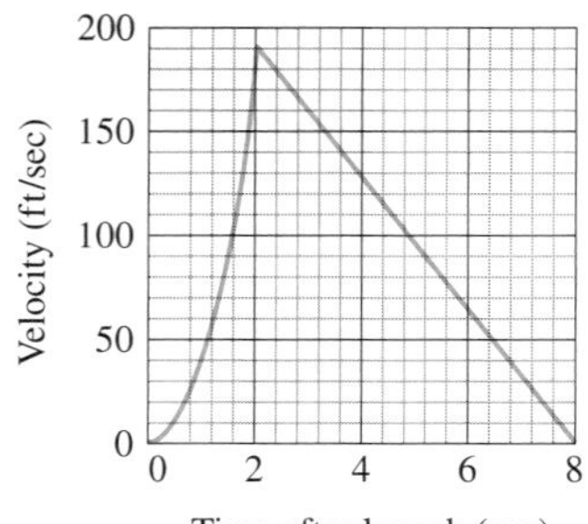

Assuming that the rocket was launched from ground level, about how high did it go? (This is the same rocket as the one in Section 3.3, Exercise 23, but you do not need to do Exercise 23 to do the exercise here.)

2. The accompanying figure shows the velocity (m/sec) of a body moving along the s-axis during the time interval from $t = 0$ to $t = 10$ sec. About how far did the body travel during those 10 seconds?

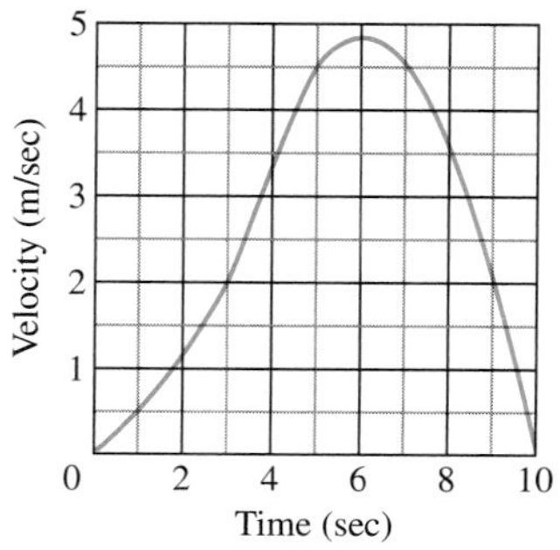

3. Suppose that $\sum_{k=1}^{10} a_k = -2$ and $\sum_{k=1}^{10} b_k = 25$. Find the value of

a) $\sum_{k=1}^{10} \frac{a_k}{4}$ b) $\sum_{k=1}^{10} (b_k - 3a_k)$

c) $\sum_{k=1}^{10} (a_k + b_k - 1)$ d) $\sum_{k=1}^{10} \left(\frac{5}{2} - b_k\right)$

4. Suppose that $\sum_{k=1}^{20} a_k = 0$ and $\sum_{k=1}^{20} b_k = 7$. Find the values of

a) $\sum_{k=1}^{20} 3a_k$ b) $\sum_{k=1}^{20} (a_k + b_k)$

c) $\sum_{k=1}^{4} \left(\frac{1}{2} - \frac{2b_k}{7}\right)$ d) $\sum_{k=1}^{20} (a_k - 2)$

In Exercises 5–8, express each limit as a definite integral. Then evaluate the integral to find the value of the limit. In each case, P is a partition of the given interval and the numbers c_k are chosen from the subintervals of P.

5. $\lim_{\|P\|\to 0} \sum_{k=1}^{n} (2c_k - 1)^{-1/2} \Delta x_k$, where P is a partition of $[1, 5]$.

6. $\lim_{\|P\|\to 0} \sum_{k=1}^{n} c_k(c_k{}^2 - 1)^{1/3} \Delta x_k$, where P is a partition of $[1, 3]$.

7. $\lim_{\|P\|\to 0} \sum_{k=1}^{n} \left(\cos\left(\frac{c_k}{2}\right)\right) \Delta x_k$, where P is a partition of $[-\pi, 0]$.

8. $\lim_{\|P\|\to 0} \sum_{k=1}^{n} (\sin c_k)(\cos c_k) \Delta x_k$, where P is a partition of $[0, \pi/2]$.

9. If $\int_{-2}^{2} 3f(x)\,dx = 12$, $\int_{-2}^{5} f(x)\,dx = 6$, and $\int_{-2}^{5} g(x)\,dx = 2$, find the values of the following:

a) $\int_{-2}^{2} f(x)\,dx$ b) $\int_{2}^{5} f(x)\,dx$

c) $\int_{5}^{-2} g(x)\,dx$ d) $\int_{-2}^{5} (-\pi g(x))\,dx$

e) $\int_{-2}^{5} \left(\frac{f(x) + g(x)}{5}\right) dx$

10. If $\int_0^2 f(x)\,dx = \pi$, $\int_0^2 7g(x)\,dx = 7$ and $\int_0^1 g(x)\,dx = 2$, find the values of the following:

a) $\int_{0}^{2} g(x)\,dx$ b) $\int_{1}^{2} g(x)\,dx$

c) $\int_{2}^{0} f(x)\,dx$ d) $\int_{0}^{2} \sqrt{2}\,f(x)\,dx$

e) $\int_{0}^{2} (g(x) - 3f(x))\,dx$

In Exercises 11–14, find the total area of the region between the graph of f and the x-axis.

11. $f(x) = x^2 - 4x + 3, \quad 0 \le x \le 3$

12. $f(x) = 1 - (x^2/4), \quad -2 \le x \le 3$

13. $f(x) = 5 - 5x^{2/3}, \quad -1 \le x \le 8$

14. $f(x) = 1 - \sqrt{x}, \quad 0 \le x \le 4$

15. Show that the function $y = x^2 + \int_1^x \frac{1}{t}\,dt + 1$ solves the initial value problem.

Differential equation: $\frac{d^2y}{dx^2} = 2 - \frac{1}{x^2}$

Initial conditions: $\frac{dy}{dx} = 3$ and $y = 2$ when $x = 1$

16. Show that the function $y = \int_0^x \left(1 + 2\sqrt{\sec t}\right) dt$ solves the initial value problem.

Differential equation: $\frac{d^2y}{dx^2} = \sqrt{\sec x}\tan x$

Initial conditions: $\frac{dy}{dx} = 3$ and $y = 0$ when $x = 0$

Express the solutions of the initial value problems in Exercises 17 and 18 in terms of integrals.

17. Differential equation: $\frac{dy}{dx} = \frac{\sin x}{x}$

Initial condition: $y = -3$ when $x = 5$

18. Differential equation: $\frac{dy}{dx} = \sqrt{2 - \sin^2 x}$

Initial condition: $y = 2$ when $x = -1$

Evaluate the integrals in Exercises 19–40.

19. $\int (x^3 + 5x - 7)\,dx$

20. $\int \left(8t^3 - \frac{t^2}{2} + t\right) dt$

21. $\int \left(3\sqrt{t} + \frac{4}{t^2}\right) dt$

22. $\int \left(\frac{1}{2\sqrt{t}} - \frac{3}{t^4}\right) dt$

23. $\int \frac{r\,dr}{(r^2 + 5)^2}$

24. $\int \frac{6r^2\,dr}{\left(r^3 - \sqrt{2}\right)^3}$

25. $\int 3\theta\sqrt{2 - \theta^2}\,d\theta$

26. $\int \frac{\theta^2}{9\sqrt{73 + \theta^3}}\,d\theta$

27. $\int x^3(1 + x^4)^{-1/4}\,dx$

28. $\int (2 - x)^{3/5}\,dx$

29. $\int \sec^2 \frac{s}{10}\,ds$

30. $\int \csc^2 \pi s\,ds$

31. $\int \csc\sqrt{2}\theta \cot\sqrt{2}\theta\,d\theta$

32. $\int \sec\frac{\theta}{3}\tan\frac{\theta}{3}\,d\theta$

33. $\int \sin^2 \frac{x}{4}\,dx$

34. $\int \cos^2 \frac{x}{2}\,dx$

35. $\int 2(\cos x)^{-1/2}\sin x\,dx$

36. $\int (\tan x)^{-3/2}\sec^2 x\,dx$

37. $\int (2\theta + 1 + 2\cos(2\theta + 1))\, d\theta$

38. $\int \left(\frac{1}{\sqrt{2\theta - \pi}} + 2\sec^2(2\theta - \pi)\right) d\theta$

39. $\int \left(t - \frac{2}{t}\right)\left(t + \frac{2}{t}\right) dt$

40. $\int \frac{(t+1)^2 - 1}{t^4}\, dt$

Evaluate the integrals in Exercises 41–64.

41. $\int_{-1}^{1} (3x^2 - 4x + 7)\, dx$

42. $\int_{0}^{1} (8s^3 - 12s^2 + 5)\, ds$

43. $\int_{1}^{2} \frac{4}{v^2}\, dv$

44. $\int_{1}^{27} x^{-4/3}\, dx$

45. $\int_{1}^{4} \frac{dt}{t\sqrt{t}}$

46. $\int_{0}^{2} 3\sqrt{4x+1}\, dx$

47. $\int_{0}^{1} \frac{36\, dx}{(2x+1)^3}$

48. $\int_{1}^{2} \left(w + \frac{1}{w^2}\right) dw$

49. $\int_{1/8}^{1} x^{-1/3}(1 - x^{2/3})^{3/2}\, dx$

50. $\int_{0}^{1/2} x^3(1 + 9x^4)^{-3/2}\, dx$

51. $\int_{0}^{\pi} \sin 5r\, dr$

52. $\int_{0}^{\pi} \cos 5t\, dt$

53. $\int_{0}^{\pi/3} \sec^2\theta\, d\theta$

54. $\int_{\pi/4}^{3\pi/4} \csc^2 x\, dx$

55. $\int_{\pi}^{3\pi} \cot^2\frac{x}{6}\, dx$

56. $\int_{0}^{\pi} \tan^2\frac{\theta}{3}\, d\theta$

57. $\int_{-\pi/3}^{0} \sec x \tan x\, dx$

58. $\int_{\pi/4}^{3\pi/4} \csc z \cot z\, dz$

59. $\int_{0}^{\pi/2} 5(\sin x)^{3/2}\cos x\, dx$

60. $\int_{-1}^{1} 2x\sin(1 - x^2)\, dx$

61. $\int_{-\pi/2}^{\pi/2} 15\sin^4 3x\cos 3x\, dx$

62. $\int_{0}^{2\pi/3} \cos^{-4}\left(\frac{x}{2}\right)\sin\left(\frac{x}{2}\right) dx$

63. $\int_{0}^{\pi/2} \frac{3\sin x\cos x}{\sqrt{1 + 3\sin^2 x}}\, dx$

64. $\int_{0}^{\pi/4} \frac{\sec^2 x}{(1 + 7\tan x)^{2/3}}\, dx$

65. Find the average value of $f(x) = mx + b$
   a) over $[-1, 1]$
   b) over $[-k, k]$

66. Find the average value of
   a) $y = \sqrt{3x}$ over $[0, 3]$
   b) $y = \sqrt{ax}$ over $[0, a]$

67. Let f be a function that is differentiable on $[a, b]$. In Chapter 3 we defined the average rate of change of f on $[a, b]$ to be

$$\frac{f(b) - f(a)}{b - a}$$

and the instantaneous rate of change of f at x to be $f'(x)$. In this chapter we defined the average value of a function. For the new definition of average to be consistent with the old one, we should have

$$\frac{f(b) - f(a)}{b - a} = \text{average value of } f' \text{ on } [a, b].$$

Show that this is the case.

68. Is it true that the average value of an integrable function over an interval of length 2 is half the function's integral over the interval? Give reasons for your answer.

69. Is it true that every function $y = f(x)$ that is differentiable on $[a, b]$ is itself the derivative of some function on $[a, b]$? Give reasons for your answer.

70. Suppose that $F(x)$ is an antiderivative of $f(x) = \sqrt{1 + x^4}$. Express $\int_0^1 \sqrt{1 + x^4}\, dx$ in terms of F and give a reason for your answer.

71. Find dy/dx if $y = \int_x^1 \sqrt{1 + t^2}\, dt$. Explain the main steps in your calculation.

72. Find dy/dx if $y = \int_{\cos x}^{0} (1/(1 - t^2))\, dt$. Explain the main steps in your calculation.

73. *A New Parking Lot.* To meet the demand for parking, your town has allocated the area shown here. As the town engineer, you have been asked by the town council to find out if the lot can be built for \$11,000. The cost to clear the land will be \$0.10 a square foot, and the lot will cost \$2.00 a square foot to pave. Can the job be done for \$11,000?

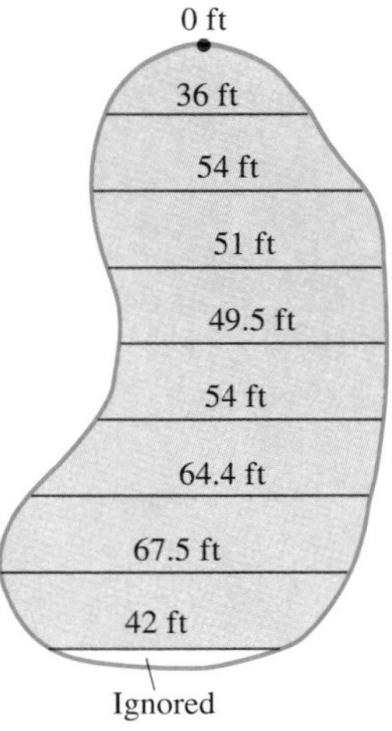

74. The design of a new airplane requires a gasoline tank of constant cross-section area in each wing. A scale drawing of a cross section is shown here. The tank must hold 5000 lb of gasoline that weighs 42 lb/ft³. Estimate the length of the tank.

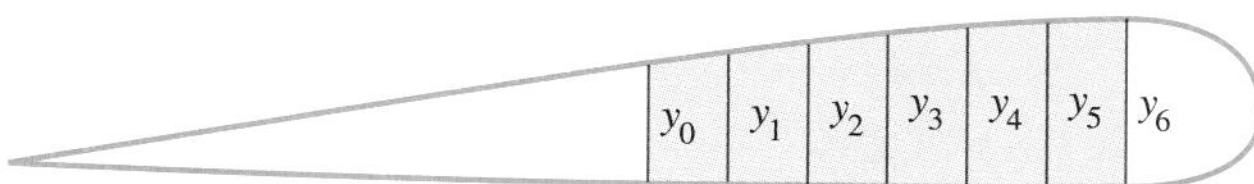

$y_0 = 1.5$ ft, $y_1 = 1.6$ ft, $y_2 = 1.8$ ft, $y_3 = 1.9$ ft,
$y_4 = 2.0$ ft, $y_5 = y_6 = 2.1$ ft Horizontal spacing = 1 ft

75. According to the error-bound formula for Simpson's rule, how many subintervals should you use to be sure of estimating the value of

$$\ln 3 = \int_1^3 \frac{1}{x}\,dx$$

by Simpson's rule with an error of no more than 10^{-4} in absolute value? (Remember that for Simpson's rule, the number of subintervals has to be even.)

76. A brief calculation shows that if $0 \le x \le 1$, then the second derivative of $f(x) = \sqrt{1 + x^4}$ lies between 0 and 8. Based on this, about how many subdivisions would you need to estimate the integral of f from 0 to 1 with an error no greater than 10^{-3} in absolute value using the trapezoidal rule?

77. A direct calculation shows that

$$\int_0^{\pi} 2\sin^2 x\,dx = \pi.$$

How close do you come to this value by using the trapezoidal rule with $n = 6$? Simpson's rule with $n = 6$? Try them and find out.

78. You are planning to use Simpson's rule to estimate the value of the integral

$$\int_1^2 f(x)\,dx$$

with an error magnitude less than 10^{-5}. You have determined that $|f^{(4)}(x)| \le 3$ throughout the interval of integration. How many subintervals should you use to assure the required accuracy? (Remember that for Simpson's rule the number has to be even.)

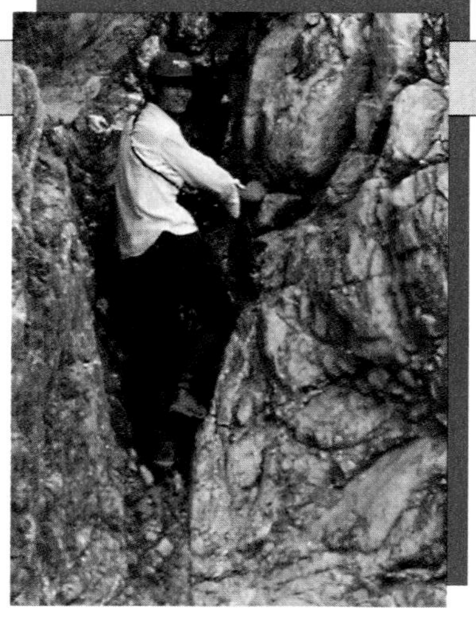

JIAN LIN, a scientist at the Woods Hole Oceanographic Institution, studies the forces that drive the earth's tectonic plates.

Earth's solid outer crust (the lithosphere) is broken into rigid plates that grind against one another as they are moved by slow currents in the liquid rock below. The problem, of course, is that the plates do not move smoothly, and tend to stick along their boundaries (called "fault" lines) as the forces build up. They can sometimes stick for years before breaking free to release colossal amounts of energy in a few jolting seconds.

We experience the energy releases as earthquakes and measure the energy released on a logarithmic scale devised by Charles F. Richter (Section 6.3). Most of the one million or so earthquakes that occur every year are too small to be felt. The largest ones, however, which measure 8.0 or more on the Richter scale, can create tidal waves, change the courses of rivers, and level cities.

Dr. Lin's model of the earth's movements uses computer calculations that are based on calculus to simulate the physical forces that determine how the earth moves. The predictions of the model are compared with relief data collected at sea.

Shown here is a data-based computer image of the Atlantis Transform Fault along the boundary of two of the tectonic plates that make up the floor of the mid-Atlantic Ocean. The deepest parts of the transform valley are more than 6 km below sea level. The vertical relief from the top to the bottom of the valley is more than 4 km, and is shown at three-times vertical exaggeration. The red vertical bars in the top right-hand corner are an imaging artifact.

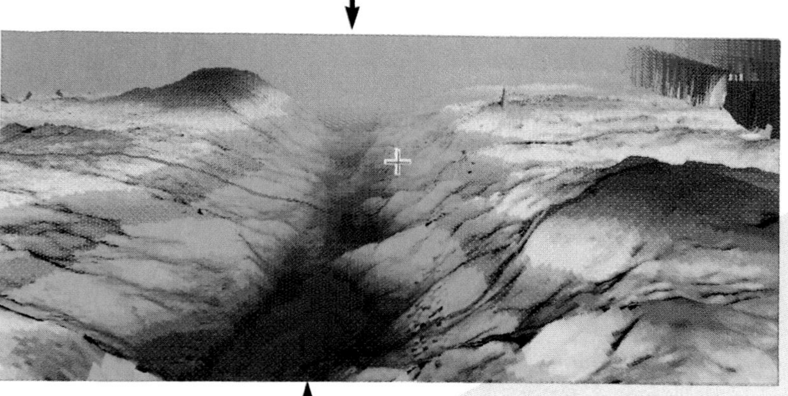

OVERVIEW

Many of the functions in mathematics and science are inverses of one another. The functions ln x and e^x are probably the most famous function–inverse pair but others are nearly as important. The trigonometric functions, when suitably restricted, have useful inverses and there are other pairs of logarithmic and exponential functions. Less widely known are the hyperbolic functions and their inverses, functions that arise when we study hanging cables, heat flow, and the friction encountered by objects falling through the air. We describe all of these functions in this chapter and look at the kinds of problems they were designed to solve.

6 Transcendental Functions

6.1 Exponential Functions and the Derivative of e^x

In this section, we introduce exponential functions and begin our study of the world's most useful exponential function, $y = e^x$.

Exponential Functions

In algebra, we learned how to raise a positive number a to a rational power. For example, $3^{2/3}$ is defined as $\sqrt[3]{3^2}$ or $\sqrt[3]{9}$, which is about 2.08. Thus, we know how to find any rational power of 3, such as 3^{-1}, 3^6, $3^{7/5}$, $3^{-1/2}$, and $3^{1.4}$. But how do we define and calculate a positive number raised to an irrational power, such as $3^{\sqrt{2}}$?

We do so by looking at the successive rational numbers in the decimal representation of $\sqrt{2}$, which is $\sqrt{2} = 1.4142\ 13562\ 37\ \ldots$. Starting with 1, these numbers are

$$1,\quad 1.4,\quad 1.41,\quad 1.414,\quad 1.4142,\quad 1.41421,\ \ldots$$

and so on. It seems reasonable to assume that the closer these numbers come to $\sqrt{2}$, the closer 3 raised to these numbers will come to a number we can call $3^{\sqrt{2}}$. In other words, since

$$1,\quad 1.4,\quad 1.41,\quad 1.414,\quad 1.4142,\quad 1.41421,\ \ldots \rightarrow \sqrt{2},$$

we should have

$$3^1,\quad 3^{1.4},\quad 3^{1.41},\quad 3^{1.414},\quad 3^{1.4142},\quad 3^{1.41421},\ \ldots \rightarrow 3^{\sqrt{2}}.$$

It can be shown that this is indeed the case. As suggested by the calculator values in Table 6.1, $3^{\sqrt{2}} = 4.7288\ 04\ \ldots$.

We can raise 3 to any other irrational number x the same way: Raise 3 to successively closer finite decimal approximations of x and define 3^x to be the number approached by these powers. It can be shown, using advanced theorems

TABLE 6.1
How the decimal representation of $\sqrt{2}$ defines $3^{\sqrt{2}}$

r	3^r
1.0	3
1.4	4.6555 367
1.41	4.7069 650
1.414	4.7276 950
1.4142	4.7287 339
1.4142 1	4.7287 859
1.4142 13	4.7288 015
1.4142 135	4.7288 041
⋮	⋮
$\sqrt{2}$	$3^{\sqrt{2}}$

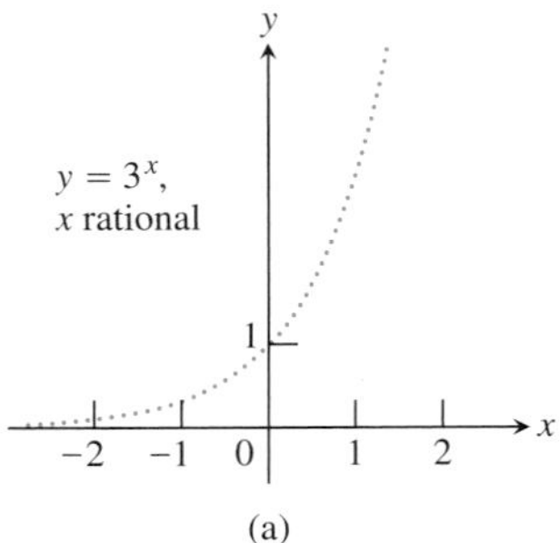

(a)

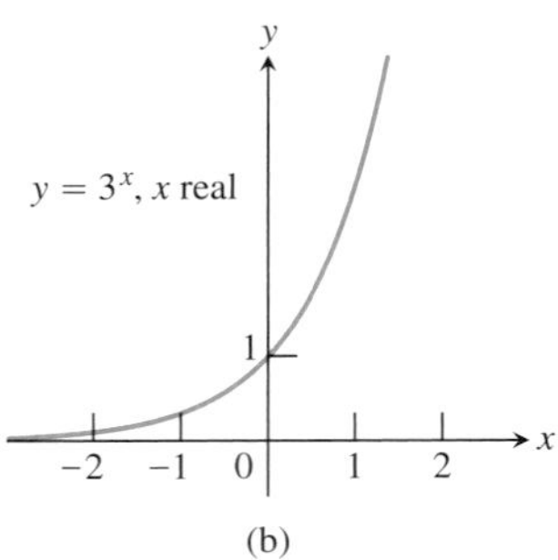

(b)

6.1 (a) Plotting $f(x) = 3^x$ for rational values of x gives a graph with gaps at the irrational values of x, as suggested here. (b) We define $f(x) = 3^x$ for irrational values of x by filling in the holes.

about real numbers, that the newly defined irrational powers of 3 fit together with the rational powers of 3 to make a continuous function $y = 3^x$. Figure 6.1 shows what is going on geometrically.

The function $y = 3^x$ is one of a family of functions called exponential functions. We will describe an alternative way to define exponential functions in Section 6.4.

DEFINITION

For any constant $a > 0$, the continuous function f defined by the equation

$$f(x) = a^x$$

is the **exponential function to the base *a*.** The positive number a is the **base** of the function.

Figure 6.2 shows the graph of $y = a^x$ for various positive values of a. The only constant exponential function is $y = 1^x$. The other exponential functions either increase or decrease. Their range is $(0, \infty)$ and their graphs all have the x-axis as a horizontal asymptote. As the graphs in the figure suggest, the values of exponential functions *are always positive*. They have the following limits as $x \to \pm\infty$.

If $0 < a < 1$: $\lim_{x\to\infty} a^x = 0$, $\lim_{x\to-\infty} a^x = \infty$

If $a > 1$: $\lim_{x\to\infty} a^x = \infty$, $\lim_{x\to-\infty} a^x = 0$

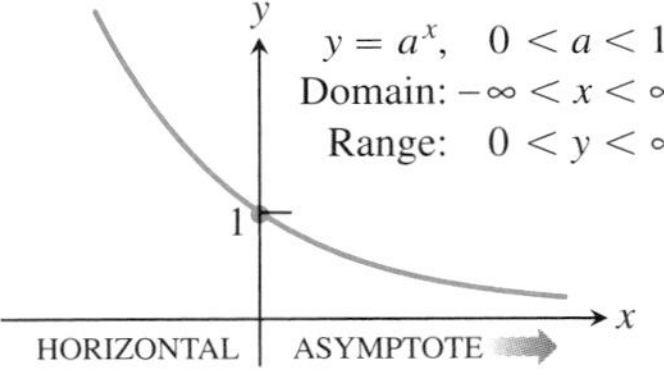

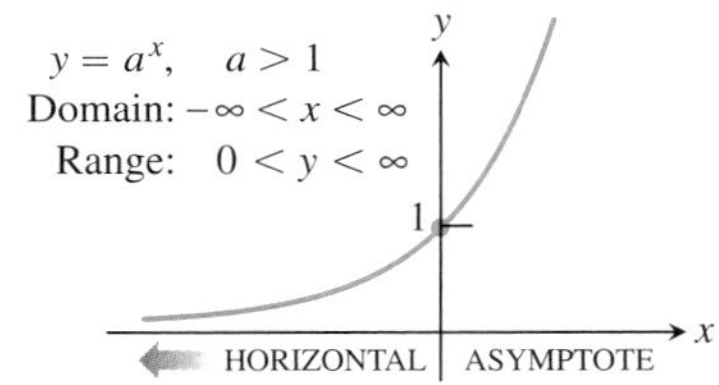

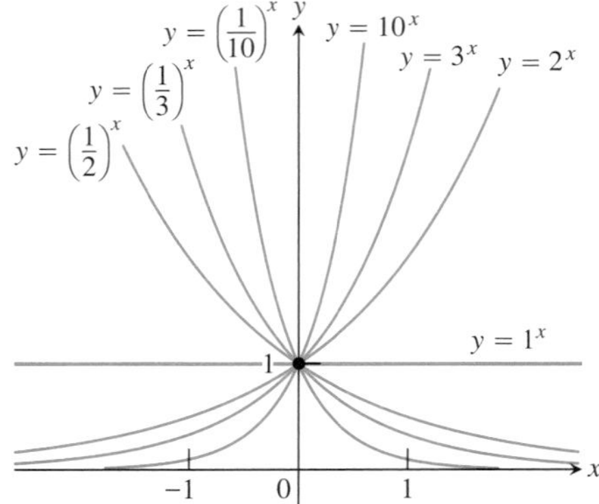

6.2 Exponential functions decrease if $0 < a < 1$ and increase if $a > 1$.

Exponential functions obey the usual laws of exponents (Table 6.2).

TABLE 6.2
Laws of exponents

If $a > 0$ and $b > 0$ the following equations hold for all real numbers x and y.

1. $a^x \cdot a^y = a^{x+y}$

2. $\dfrac{a^x}{a^y} = a^{x-y}$

$\dfrac{1}{a^y} = a^{-y}$ The special case $x = 0$

3. $(a^x)^y = (a^y)^x = a^{xy}$

4. $a^x \cdot b^x = (ab)^x$

5. $\left(\dfrac{a}{b}\right)^x = \dfrac{a^x}{b^x}$

EXAMPLE 1

1. $3^{1.1} \cdot 3^{0.7} = 3^{1.1+0.7} = 3^{1.8}$
2. $\dfrac{(\sqrt{10})^3}{\sqrt{10}} = (\sqrt{10})^{3-1} = (\sqrt{10})^2 = 10$
3. $\left(5^{\sqrt{2}}\right)^{\sqrt{2}} = 5^{\sqrt{2}\cdot\sqrt{2}} = 5^2 = 25$
4. $7^\pi \cdot 8^\pi = (56)^\pi$
5. $\left(\dfrac{4}{9}\right)^{1/2} = \dfrac{4^{1/2}}{9^{1/2}} = \dfrac{2}{3}$

The Exponential Function e^x

When we apply the definition of derivative to $f(x) = a^x$, we see that the derivative is a numerical multiple of a^x itself:

$$\begin{aligned}
\frac{d}{dx}(a^x) &= \lim_{h\to 0}\frac{a^{x+h}-a^x}{h} && \text{Derivative definition}\\
&= \lim_{h\to 0}\frac{a^x\cdot a^h - a^x}{h} && a^{x+h}=a^x\cdot a^h\\
&= \lim_{h\to 0} a^x\cdot\frac{a^h-1}{h} && \text{Factoring out } a^x\\
&= a^x\cdot\lim_{h\to 0}\frac{a^h-1}{h} && a^x \text{ remains constant as } h\to 0\\
&= \underbrace{\left(\lim_{h\to 0}\frac{a^h-1}{h}\right)}_{\text{a fixed number } L}\cdot a^x. && (1)
\end{aligned}$$

Thus,

$$\frac{d}{dx}(a^x) = L\cdot a^x,$$

where

$$L = \lim_{h\to 0}\frac{a^h-1}{h}. \qquad (2)$$

It can be proved that this limit exists. To estimate its value, we can graph $y = (a^h - 1)/h$ as a function of h to see where the graph approaches the y-axis as $h \to 0$. Figure 6.3 shows the graphs for $a = 2$, 2.5, and 3, and for one other value we will discuss in a moment. The value of L is approximately 0.69 if $a = 2$, 0.92 if $a = 2.5$, and 1.10 if $a = 3$. Accordingly,

$$\begin{aligned}
\frac{d}{dx}(2^x) &\approx (0.69)\,2^x,\\
\frac{d}{dx}\left(2.5^x\right) &\approx (0.92)\,2.5^x, && (3)\\
\frac{d}{dx}\left(3^x\right) &\approx (1.10)\,3^x.
\end{aligned}$$

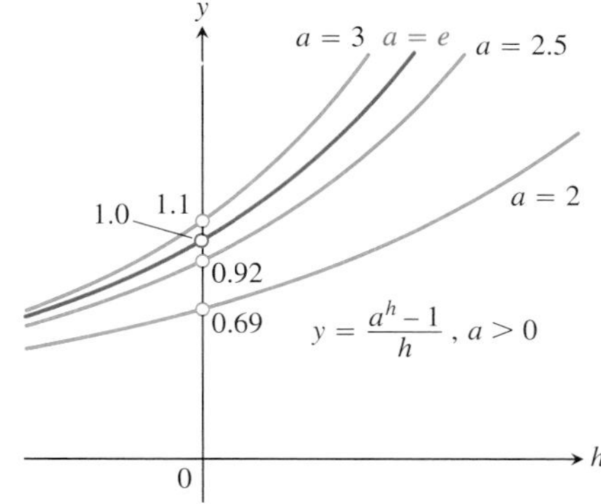

6.3 The position of the curve $y = (a^h - 1)/h$, $a > 0$, varies continuously with a.

The good news is that we now have some idea of the values of these derivatives. The bad news is that the multipliers accumulate as we continue to differentiate. For instance,

$$\begin{aligned}
&\frac{d}{dx}(2^x) \approx (0.69)\,2^x,\\
&\frac{d^2}{dx^2}(2^x) \approx (0.69)\frac{d}{dx}(2^x) \approx (0.69)^2 \cdot 2^x,\\
&\quad\vdots\\
&\frac{d^n}{dx^n}(2^x) \approx (0.69)^n \cdot 2^x.
\end{aligned} \tag{4}$$

Another look at Fig. 6.3 suggests a way to avoid this problem. For $a = 2.5$, the graph of $y = (a^h - 1)/h$ steps across the y-axis at about 0.92. For $a = 3$, the graph steps across at about 1.1. Thus at some value of a between 2.5 and 3, the graph should step across the axis at $y = 1$. For this particular value of a, which we call e, the limit in Eq. (2) is 1 and the exponential function is its own derivative.

DEFINITION

The number $\boldsymbol{e}$ is the value of a that satisfies the equation

$$\lim_{h\to 0} \frac{a^h - 1}{h} = 1, \tag{5}$$

so that

$$\frac{d}{dx}(e^x) = 1 \cdot e^x = e^x. \tag{6}$$

To 15 decimal places,

$$e = 2.7\ 1828\ 1828\ 45\ 90\ 45$$

This layout makes the number easier to remember.

The fact that e^x is its own derivative makes e^x the exponential function of choice in calculus. In applied fields, it is the primary function for describing the natural processes of growth and decay, as we will see in this section and again in Section 6.5.

The Chain Rule extends Eq. (6) in the usual way to a more general form.

If u is a differentiable function of x, then

$$\frac{d}{dx}(e^u) = e^u \frac{du}{dx}. \tag{7}$$

EXAMPLE 2

a) $\frac{d}{dx}(e^{5x}) = e^{5x} \cdot \frac{d}{dx}(5x) = 5e^{5x}$ — Eq. (7) with $u = 5x$

b) $\frac{d}{dx}(e^{kx}) = e^{kx} \cdot \frac{d}{dx}(kx) = ke^{kx}$ — Eq. (7) with $u = kx$, any number k

c) $\frac{d}{dx}(e^{-x}) = -e^{-x}$ — Eq. (7) with $u = -1x$

d) $\frac{d}{dx}(e^{x^2}) = e^{x^2} \cdot \frac{d}{dx}(x^2) = 2xe^{x^2}$ — Eq. (7) with $u = x^2$

e) $\frac{d}{dx} e^{\sin x} = e^{\sin x} \cdot \frac{d}{dx}(\sin x) = e^{\sin x} \cdot \cos x$ — Eq. (7) with $u = \sin x$

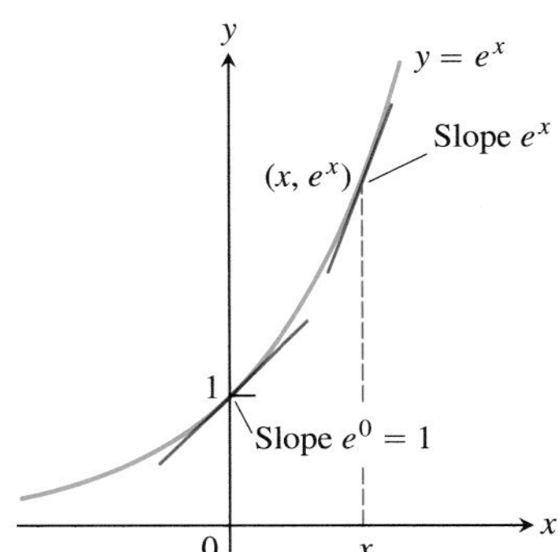

6.4 At each x, the slope of the curve $y = e^x$ is e^x.

The Geometric Significance of $\lim_{h\to 0} \frac{a^h - 1}{h}$

You may have noticed that the graph of each of the functions $f(x) = a^x$ passes through the point (0, 1) with a different slope. And what is this slope? It is none other than

$$f'(0) = \lim_{h\to 0} \frac{a^{0+h} - a^0}{h} = \lim_{h\to 0} \frac{a^h - 1}{h}, \tag{8}$$

the limit at the end of Eq. (1). Thus, Eq. (1) can be reinterpreted to say that if $f(x) = a^x$, then

$$f'(x) = f'(0) \cdot f(x). \tag{9}$$

The derivative of $y = a^x$ is a^x multiplied by the slope at the point where the graph crosses the y-axis. The graph of e^x crosses the y-axis with slope 1, so e^x is its own derivative (Fig. 6.4).

Exponential Change

In many instances in science, some positive quantity increases or decreases at a rate that at any given time t is proportional to the amount that is present at time t. In Section 6.5 we will show that in these instances the amount can be represented by an equation of the form $y = y_0 e^{kt}$, where y_0 is the amount initially present at time $t = 0$.

The equation

$$y = y_0 e^{kt} \tag{10}$$

is called the **law of exponential change.**

EXAMPLE 3 *The Growth of a Cell.* In an ideal environment, the mass m of a cell will grow exponentially, at least early on. Nutrients pass quickly through the cell wall, and growth is limited only by the metabolism within the cell, which in turn depends on the mass of participating molecules. If we make the reasonable assumption that, at each instant of time, the cell's growth rate is proportional to the mass that has already been accumulated, then

$$m = m_0 e^{kt},$$

where m_0 is the initial mass of the cell. There are limitations, of course, and in any particular case we would expect this equation to provide reliable information only for values of m below a certain size.

EXAMPLE 4 *The Incidence of a Disease.* One model for the way diseases spread assumes that the rate at which the number y of infected people changes is proportional to y itself. The more infected people there are, the faster the disease will spread. The fewer there are, the slower it will spread. If y_0 is the number of infected people at time $t = 0$, then the number of infected people at any time in the near future will be about

$$y = y_0 e^{kt}.$$

If $k = 0.3$ and there are $y_0 = 25{,}000$ infected people right now, then in 2 years the number of people infected will be

$$y = 25{,}000\, e^{(0.3)2} = 25{,}000\, e^{0.6} \approx 45{,}553.$$

Suppose we want to use the equation $y = y_0 e^{kt}$ from Example 4 to answer questions about the course of a particular disease. To be specific, suppose that a worldwide eradication program is reducing the number y of cases at the rate of 20% a year. There are 10,000 recorded cases today, and we want to know how many years it will take to lower the number to 1000.

Starting with the equation $y = y_0 e^{kt}$, there are three things to find:

1. The value of y_0,
2. The value of k,
3. The value of t that makes $y = 1000$.

If we start counting time from today, then $y = 10{,}000$ when $t = 0$, so $y_0 = 10{,}000$. Our equation is

$$y = 10{,}000\, e^{kt}. \tag{11}$$

That was perfectly straightforward, but we encounter a problem when we now try to determine k. The available information tells us that when $t = 1$ (i.e., when one year has passed) the number of cases will be 80% of its present value, or 8000. Hence,

$$10{,}000\, e^{k(1)} = 8000, \qquad \text{Eq. (11) with } t = 1,\ y = 8000$$

so that

$$e^k = 0.8.$$

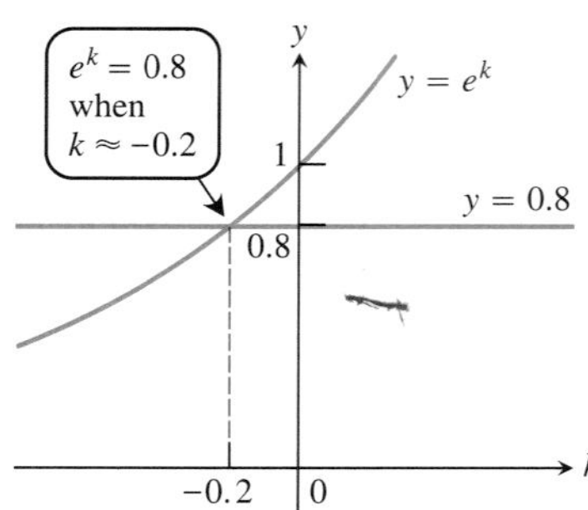

6.5 A graphical estimate of the value of k that makes $e^k = 0.8$.

How do we solve this equation for k?

One way would be to graph the equation $y = e^k$ as a function of k and find the value of k where the graph crosses the horizontal line $y = 0.8$ (Fig. 6.5). This would reveal k to be about -0.2. We could then find the value of t that makes $y = 1000$ by solving the following equation for t:

$$10{,}000\, e^{-0.2t} = 1000 \qquad \text{Eq. (11) with } k = -0.2,\ y = 1000$$

or

$$e^{-0.2t} = 0.1$$

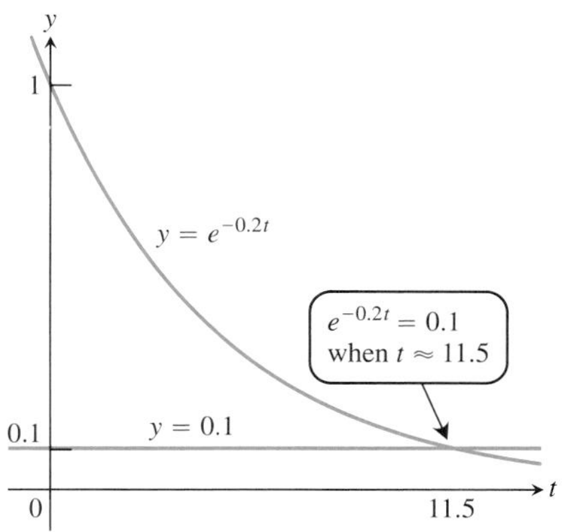

6.6 A graphical estimate of the solution of the equation $e^{-0.2t} = 0.1$ for t.

Once again we could work graphically to find the value of t where the graph of $y = e^{-0.2t}$ as a function of t crosses the line $y = 0.1$ (Fig. 6.6). This would reveal t to be about 11.5. The number of cases would thus be seen to drop to 1000 in about 11.5 years.

This is not a bad estimate, but it is not a particularly good one either. As we will see in Section 6.5, we have overestimated the time by more than a year. We could go back and draw more accurate graphs, but we would be missing the point if we did. We really need a faster way to solve the equation

$$e^x = y$$

for x. This is the reverse of the usual situation in which we need to find a function's output for a given input. Here, we need to find the input that produces a given output. Given y, we need to *reverse* (more properly, *invert*) the function $y = e^x$ to find x as a function of y. As you might guess, not every function can be inverted, but e^x and many others can, as we will see in the next section.

Once we know how to invert the function $y = e^x$, we will be able to solve an equation like $e^k = 0.8$ for k. We will also see how all exponential functions are related to one another. And, finally, we will see new meaning in the number

$$\lim_{h\to 0} \frac{a^h - 1}{h}.$$

Exercises 6.1

In Exercises 1–6, sketch the given curves together in the appropriate coordinate plane and label each curve with its equation.

1. $y = 2^x$, $y = 4^x$, $y = 3^{-x}$, $y = (1/5)^x$

2. $y = 3^x$, $y = 8^x$, $y = 2^{-x}$, $y = (1/4)^x$

3. $y = 2^{-t}$ and $y = -2^t$

4. $y = 3^{-t}$ and $y = -3^t$

5. $y = e^x$ and $y = 1/e^x$

6. $y = -e^x$ and $y = -e^{-x}$

In each of Exercises 7–10, sketch the shifted exponential curves together with their common horizontal asymptote. Label the curves and asymptotes with their equations.

7. $y = 2^x - 1$ and $y = 2^{-x} - 1$

8. $y = 3^x + 2$ and $y = 3^{-x} + 2$

9. $y = 1 - e^x$ and $y = 1 - e^{-x}$

10. $y = -1 - e^x$ and $y = -1 - e^{-x}$

Find the limits in Exercises 11–16.

11. a) $\lim_{x\to\infty} (1.01)^x$ **b)** $\lim_{x\to-\infty} (1.01)^x$

12. a) $\lim_{x\to\infty} (0.99)^x$ **b)** $\lim_{x\to-\infty} (0.99)^x$

13. $\lim_{x\to\infty} (4 + e^{-x})$

14. $\lim_{x\to\infty} (0.2 - 3^{-x})$

15. $\lim_{t\to\infty} \dfrac{3}{2 + 3e^{-t}}$

16. $\lim_{t\to\infty} \dfrac{\pi}{5 - e^{-t}}$

Use the laws of exponents to simplify the expressions in Exercises 17–26.

17. $16^2 \cdot 16^{-1.75}$

18. $9^{1/3} \cdot 9^{1/6}$

19. $\dfrac{4^{4.2}}{4^{3.7}}$

20. $\dfrac{3^{5/3}}{3^{2/3}}$

21. $\left(25^{1/8}\right)^4$

22. $\left(13^{\sqrt{2}}\right)^{\sqrt{2}/2}$

23. $2^{\sqrt{3}} \cdot 7^{\sqrt{3}}$

24. $\left(\sqrt{3}\right)^{1/2} \cdot \left(\sqrt{12}\right)^{1/2}$

25. $\left(\dfrac{2}{\sqrt{2}}\right)^4$

26. $\left(\dfrac{\sqrt{6}}{3}\right)^2$

In Exercises 27–58, find the derivative of y with respect to x, t, or θ, as appropriate.

27. $y = e^{-5x}$

28. $y = e^{100x}$

29. $y = e^{2x/3}$

30. $y = e^{-4x/5}$

31. $y = e^{x+\sqrt{2}}$

32. $y = e^{x-\pi}$

33. $y = e^{3x^2}$

34. $y = e^{-x^2/2}$

35. $y = e^{5t^2 - 7t}$

36. $y = e^{4t + t^2}$

37. $y = 2e^{\tan\theta}$

38. $y = 7e^{\sec 4\theta}$

39. $y = xe^x$

40. $y = -3te^t$

41. $y = xe^x - e^x$

42. $y = (1 + 2x)\, e^{-2x}$

43. $y = (6x^2 + 6x + 3)\, e^{2x}$

44. $y = (9x^2 - 6x + 2)\, e^{3x}$

45. $y = 2t\, e^{\sqrt{t}}$

46. $y = t^2\, e^{2/t}$

47. $y = \dfrac{e^x}{e^{-x} + 1}$

48. $y = \dfrac{e^{-x}}{e^x + 1}$

49. $y = (\cos\theta - 1)\, e^{\cos\theta}$

50. $y = (\sin\theta - 1)\, e^{\sin\theta}$

51. $y = \frac{e^{t}}{2}(\sin t + \cos t)$

52. $y = \frac{e^{-t}}{2}(\sin t - \cos t)$

53. $y = \frac{e^{-x}}{5}(2\sin 2x - \cos 2x)$

54. $y = \frac{e^{2x}}{13}(2\sin 3x - 3\cos 3x)$

55. $y = \frac{ax-1}{a^2}e^{ax}$ (a constant)

56. $y = \frac{ax+1}{a^2}e^{-ax}$ (a constant)

57. $y = \frac{e^{2\theta}}{e^{2\theta}+1}$

58. $y = \frac{e^{\theta}}{1-e^{2\theta}}$

In Exercises 59 and 60, find the absolute maximum and minimum value of the function on the given interval.

59. $y = \sqrt{x}\, e^{-x}$, $[0, 1]$

60. $y = x^2 e^{-x}$, $[-1, 2]$

Use Steps 1–5 of the graphing procedure on p. 222 to graph the curves in Exercises 61 and 62.

61. $y = e^{-x^2/2}$

62. $y = 7xe^{x}$ (For the purposes of your sketch, $7/e \approx 2.5$ and $14/e^2 \approx 2$.)

63. Where does the periodic function $f(x) = 2\, e^{\sin(x/2)}$ take on its extreme values and what are these values?

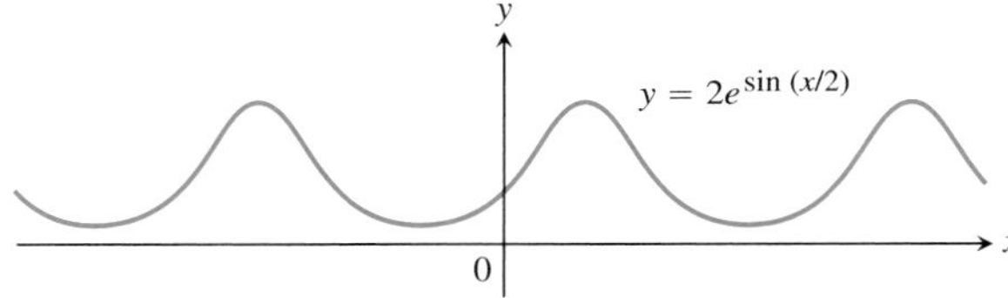

64. Where does the periodic function $f(x) = 1 - e^{(1+\cos\pi x)}$ take on its extreme values and what are these values?

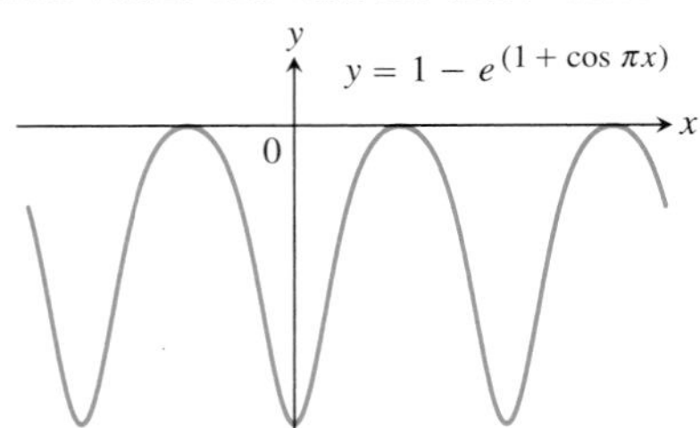

Find the absolute maxima and minima of the functions in Exercises 65–68 and say where they are assumed.

65. $f(x) = e^{x/(x^2+1)}$

66. $g(x) = e^{x/\sqrt{x^4+1}}$

67. $h(t) = e^{t\sqrt{4-t^2}}$

68. $k(t) = e^{\sqrt{3-2t-t^2}}$

69. Write an equation that says that the rate at which the number y of yeast cells in a laboratory experiment is growing at time t is proportional to the number of yeast cells present at time t.

70. Write an equation that says that the rate at which the amount of money A in a savings account is growing at time t is proportional to the amount of money present at time t.

71. Write an equation that says that the rate at which the pressure p in a leaking tire is changing at time t is proportional to the pressure at time t.

72. Write an equation that says that the rate at which the number y of radioactive atoms in a sample of carbon is changing at time t is proportional to the number of radioactive atoms present at time t.

73. Find the linearization of $f(x) = e^{x}$ at $x = 0$.

74. Find the linearization of $f(x) = x + e^{4x}$ at $x = 0$.

75. *Approximating* $2^{\sqrt{3}}$. The decimal representation

$$\sqrt{3} = 1.7320\ 50807\ 57\ \ldots$$

generates the beginning terms of a sequence of rational numbers with limit $\sqrt{3}$. Raise 2 to each of these numbers (as many as your calculator permits) to generate the beginning terms of a sequence of rational powers of 2 with limit $2^{\sqrt{3}}$. Organize your work in a function table like Table 6.1.

76. *Approximating* $5^{\sqrt{0.3}}$. The decimal representation

$$\sqrt{0.3} = 0.5477\ 22557\ 505\ \ldots$$

generates the beginning terms of a sequence of rational numbers with limit $\sqrt{0.3}$. Raise 5 to each of these numbers (as many as your calculator permits) to generate the beginning terms of a sequence of rational powers of 5 with limit $5^{\sqrt{0.3}}$. Organize your work in a table like Table 6.1.

77. **a)** How are the derivative of $f(x) = 4^{x}$ and the number

$$L = \lim_{h\to 0}\frac{4^h - 1}{h}$$

related? Give reasons for your answer.

b) What is the approximate value of L?

78. **a)** How are the derivative of $g(x) = (0.5)^{x}$ and the number

$$L = \lim_{h\to 0}\frac{(0.5)^h - 1}{h}$$

related? Give reasons for your answer.

b) What is the approximate value of L?

79. Estimate the value of t where the graph of $y = e^{t}$ crosses the line $y = 2$.

80. Estimate the value of k where the graph of $y = e^{k}$ crosses the line $y = 1/2$.

81. **a)** Graph $h(x) = xe^{-x^2/2}$ together with its first derivative for $-4 \le x \le 4$. Comment on the behavior of h in relation to the signs and values of h'.

b) Where does the graph of h appear to have inflection points? How are these points related to the behavior of h'?

82. **a)** Graph $f(x) = x^2e^{x}$ together with its first derivative for $-4 \le x \le 1$. Comment on the behavior of f in relation to the signs and values of f'.

b) Where does the graph of f appear to have inflection points? How are these points related to the behavior of f'?

Writing for Your Own Knowledge

Answer the following questions in writing. Some answers will take only a sentence or two; others may require several paragraphs. Some explanations may also call for graphs or sketches.

1. How can the decimal representation of an irrational number x be used to define and estimate the value of a number like 3^x?
2. How is the derivative of $f(x) = a^x$ $(a > 0)$ related to the limit $L = \lim_{h \to 0} (a^h - 1)/h$? What is the geometric significance of this limit?
3. What is special about the exponential function $f(x) = e^x$?
4. What is the law of exponential change?

EXPLORER PROGRAM

PowerGrapher	Graphs functions and their first derivatives in a common display.

6.2 *Inverse Functions and Their Derivatives*

As we saw at the end of the preceding section, we need to invert some of the functions we have been working with. In this section, we say what it means for functions to be inverses of one another and look at what this says about the formulas, graphs, and derivatives of function–inverse pairs.

One-to-One Functions

As you know, a function is a rule that assigns a value from its range to each point in its domain. Some functions assign the same value to more than one point. The squares of -1 and 1 are both 1, and the sines of $\pi/3$ and $2\pi/3$ are both 1/2. Other functions never assume a given value more than once. The square roots and cubes of different numbers are always different. A function that has distinct values at distinct points is called one-to-one.

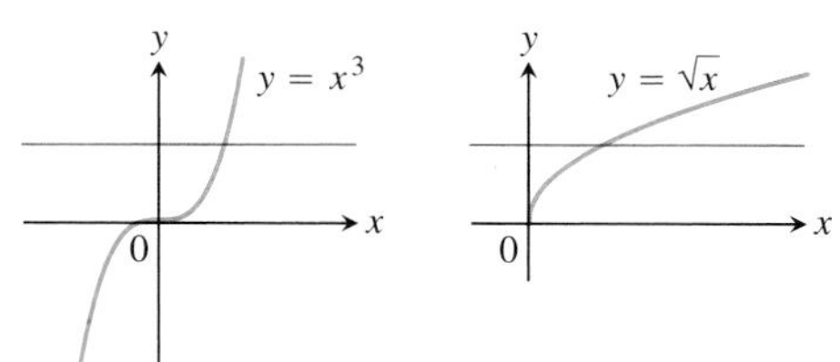

One-to-one: Graph meets each horizontal line at most once.

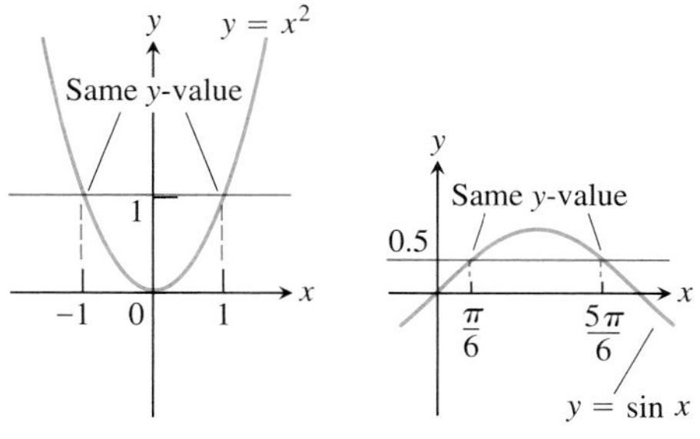

Not one-to-one: Graph meets one or more horizontal lines more than once.

6.7 Using the horizontal line test, we see that $y = \sqrt{x}$ and $y = x^3$ are one-to-one, but $y = x^2$ and $y = \sin x$ are not.

DEFINITION

A function $f(x)$ is **one-to-one** on a domain D if $f(x_1) \neq f(x_2)$ whenever $x_1 \neq x_2$.

EXAMPLE 1 $f(x) = \sqrt{x}$ is one-to-one on any domain of nonnegative numbers because $\sqrt{x_1} \neq \sqrt{x_2}$ whenever $x_1 \neq x_2$.

EXAMPLE 2 $g(x) = \sin x$ *is not* one-to-one on the interval $[0, \pi]$ because $\sin(\pi/6) = \sin(5\pi/6)$. The sine *is* one-to-one on $[0, \pi/2]$, however, because sines of angles in the first quadrant are distinct.

The graph of a one-to-one function $y = f(x)$ can intersect a given horizontal line at most once. If it intersected the line more than once it would assume the same y-value more than once, and therefore not be one-to-one (Fig. 6.7).

The Horizontal Line Test

A function $y = f(x)$ is one-to-one if and only if its graph intersects each horizontal line at most once.

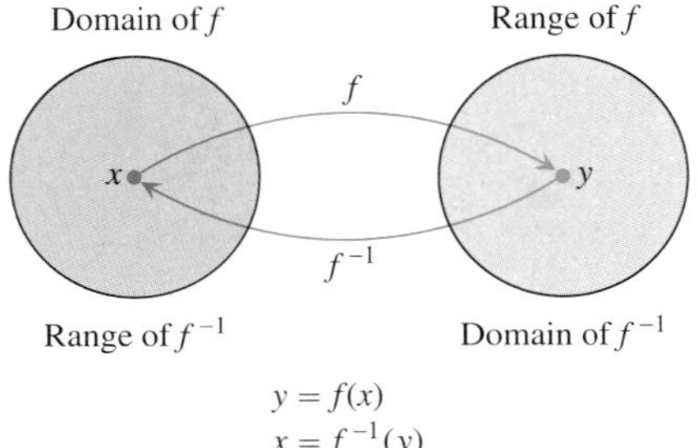

6.8 The inverse of a function f sends each output back to the input from which it came.

Inverses

Since each output of a one-to-one function comes from just one input, a one-to-one function can be reversed to send the outputs back to the inputs from which they came. The function defined by reversing a one-to-one function f is called the **inverse** of f. The symbol for the inverse of f is $\boldsymbol{f^{-1}}$, read "f inverse" (Fig. 6.8). The -1 in f^{-1} is *not* an exponent: $f^{-1}(x)$ does not mean $1/f(x)$.

As Fig. 6.8 suggests, the result of composing f and f^{-1} in either order is the **identity function,** the function that assigns each number to itself. This gives a way to test whether two functions f and g are inverses of one another. Compute $f \circ g$ and $g \circ f$. If $(f \circ g)(x) = (g \circ f)(x) = x$, then f and g are inverses of one another; otherwise they are not. If f cubes every number in its domain, g had better take cube roots or it isn't the inverse of f.

What Functions Have Inverses?

A function has an inverse if and only if it is one-to-one. This means, for example, that increasing functions have inverses and decreasing functions have inverses (Exercises 41 and 42). Functions with positive derivatives have inverses because they increase throughout their domains (Corollary 3 of the Mean Value Theorem, Section 4.6). Similarly, because they decrease throughout their domains, functions with negative derivatives have inverses.

How is the graph of the inverse of a function related to the graph of the function? If the function is increasing, say, its graph rises from left to right, like the graph in Fig. 6.9(a). To read the graph, we start at the point x on the x-axis, go up to the graph, and then move over to the y-axis to read the value of y. If we start with y and want to find the x from which it came, we reverse the process (Fig. 6.9b).

The graph of f is already the graph of f^{-1}, although the latter graph is not drawn in the usual way with the domain axis horizontal and the range axis vertical. The input–output pairs are reversed. To display the graph in the usual way, we have to reverse the pairs by reflecting the graph in the 45° line $y = x$ (Fig. 6.9c) and interchanging the letters x and y (Fig. 6.9d). This puts the independent

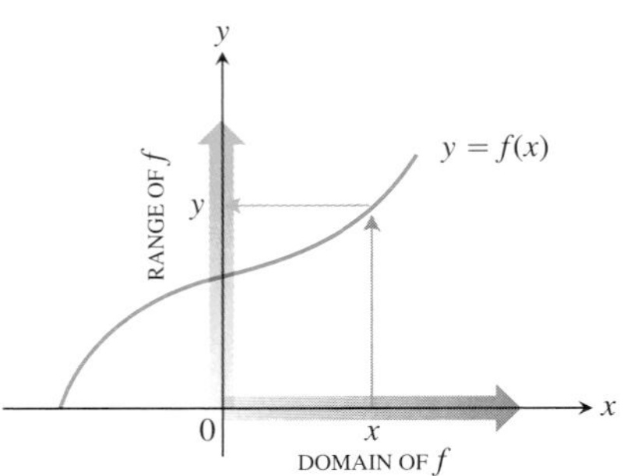

(a) To find the value of f at x, we start at x and go up to the curve and over to the y-axis.

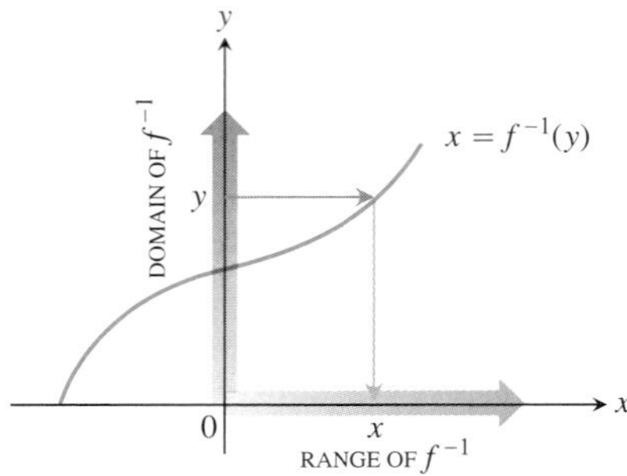

(b) The graph of f is also the graph of f^{-1}. To find the x that gave y, we start at y and go over to the curve and down to the x-axis. The domain of f^{-1} is the range of f. The range of f^{-1} is the domain of f.

6.9 The graph of $f^{-1}(x)$.

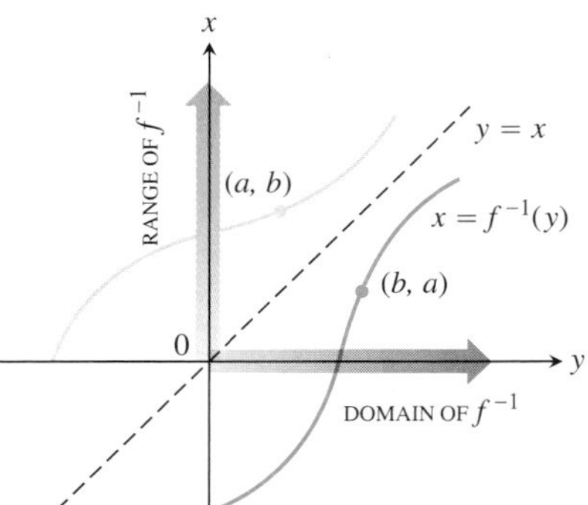

(c) To draw the graph of f^{-1} in the usual way, we reflect it in the line $y = x$.

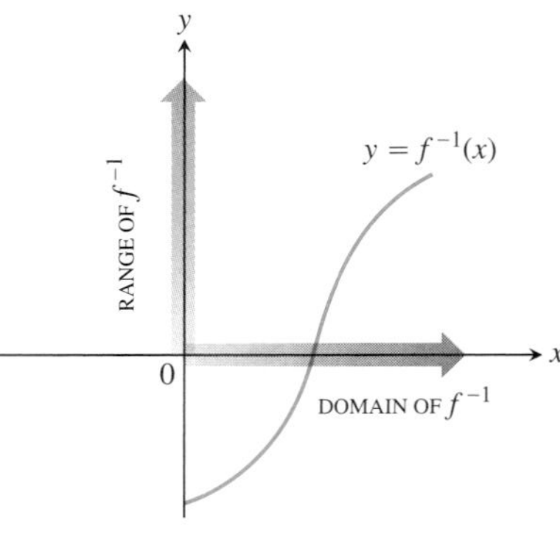

(d) Then we interchange the letters x and y. We now have a normal–looking graph of f^{-1} as a function of x.

How to Express f^{-1} as a Function of x

STEP 1: Solve the equation $y = f(x)$ for x in terms of y.

STEP 2: Interchange x and y. The resulting formula will be $y = f^{-1}(x)$.

variable, now called x, on the horizontal axis and the dependent variable, now called y, on the vertical axis.

Notice that the graphs of f and f^{-1} are symmetric about the line $y = x$. This is to be expected because the input–output pairs (a, b) of f have been reversed to produce the input–output pairs (b, a) of f^{-1}. The points (a, b) and (b, a) are symmetric about the line $y = x$.

The pictures in Fig. 6.9 tell us how to express f^{-1} as a function of x, which is stated at the left.

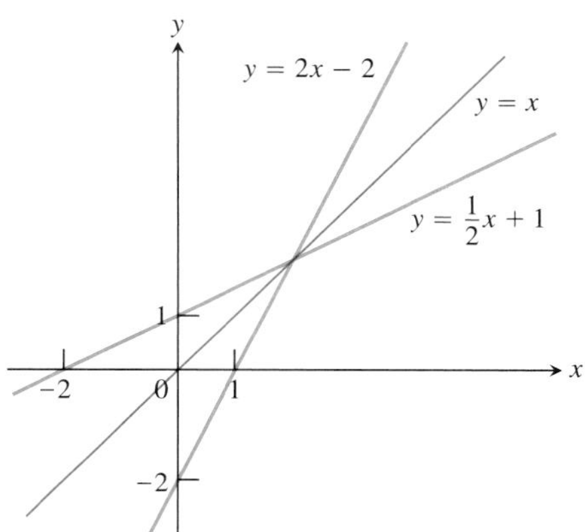

6.10 Graphing the functions $f(x) = (1/2)x + 1$ and $f^{-1}(x) = 2x - 2$ together shows the graphs' symmetry with respect to the line $y = x$.

EXAMPLE 3 Find the inverse of $y = \frac{1}{2}x + 1$, expressed as a function of x.

Solution

STEP 1: Solve for x in terms of y:
$$y = \frac{1}{2}x + 1$$
$$2y = x + 2$$
$$x = 2y - 2$$

STEP 2: Interchange x and y: $y = 2x - 2$

The inverse of the function $f(x) = (1/2)x + 1$ is the function $f^{-1}(x) = 2x - 2$. To check, we verify that both composites give the identity function:

$$f^{-1}(f(x)) = 2\left(\frac{1}{2}x + 1\right) - 2 = x + 2 - 2 = x,$$

$$f(f^{-1}(x)) = \frac{1}{2}(2x - 2) + 1 = x - 1 + 1 = x.$$

See Fig. 6.10.

EXAMPLE 4 Find the inverse of the function $y = x^2$, $x \geq 0$, expressed as a function of x.

Solution

STEP 1: Solve for x in terms of y:
$$y = x^2$$
$$\sqrt{y} = \sqrt{x^2} = x \qquad \sqrt{x^2} = x \text{ because } x \geq 0$$

STEP 2: Interchange x and y: $y = \sqrt{x}$

The inverse of the function $y = x^2$, $x \geq 0$, is the function $y = \sqrt{x}$. See Fig. 6.11.

Notice that, unlike the restricted function $y = x^2$, $x \geq 0$, the unrestricted function $y = x^2$ is not one-to-one and therefore has no inverse.

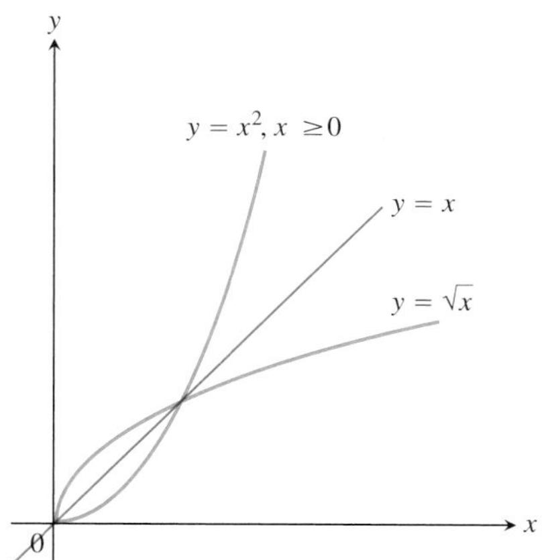

6.11 The functions $y = \sqrt{x}$ and $y = x^2$, $x \geq 0$, are inverses of one another.

Derivatives of Inverses of Differentiable Functions

If we calculate the derivatives of $f(x) = (1/2)x + 1$ and its inverse $f^{-1}(x) = 2x - 2$ from Example 3, we see that

$$\frac{d}{dx}f(x) = \frac{d}{dx}\left(\frac{1}{2}x + 1\right) = \frac{1}{2}$$

$$\frac{d}{dx}f^{-1}(x) = \frac{d}{dx}(2x - 2) = 2.$$

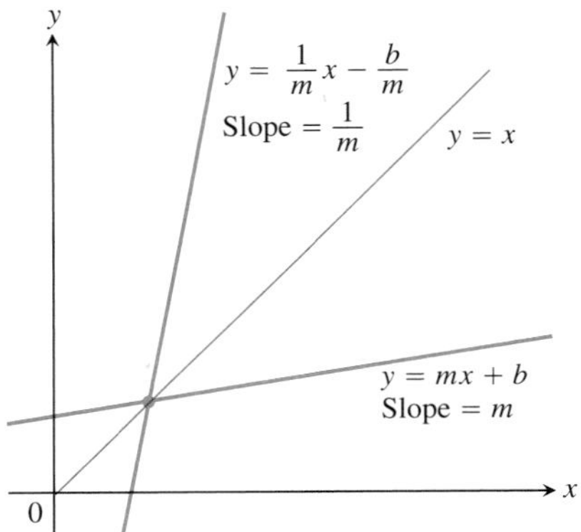

6.12 The slopes of nonvertical lines reflected across the line $y = x$ are reciprocals of one another.

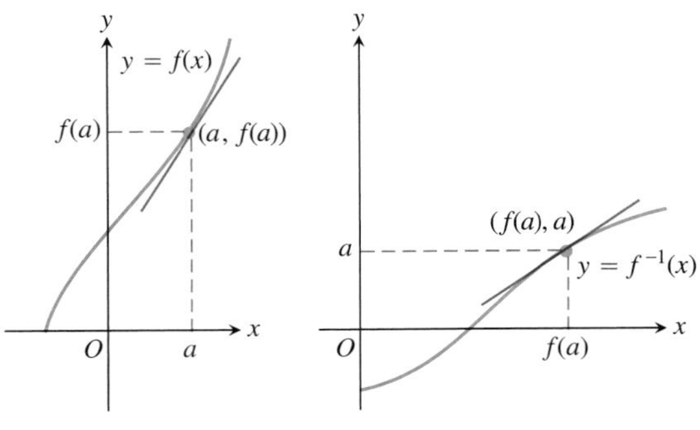

The slopes are reciprocal: $\left.\frac{df^{-1}}{dx}\right|_{f(a)} = \frac{1}{\left.\frac{df}{dx}\right|_{a}}$

6.13 The graphs of inverse functions have reciprocal slopes at corresponding points.

The derivatives are reciprocals of one another. The graph of f is the line $y = (1/2)x + 1$, and the graph of f^{-1} is the line $y = 2x - 2$ (Fig. 6.10). Their slopes are reciprocals of one another.

This is not a special case. Reflecting any nonhorizontal or nonvertical line across the line $y = x$ always inverts the line's slope. If the original line has slope $m \neq 0$ (Fig. 6.12), the reflected line has slope $1/m$ (Exercise 38).

The reciprocal relation between the slopes of graphs of inverses holds for other functions as well. If the slope of $y = f(x)$ at the point $(a, f(a))$ is $f'(a) \neq 0$, then the slope of $y = f^{-1}(x)$ at the corresponding point $(f(a), a)$ is $1/f'(a)$ (Fig. 6.13). Thus, the derivative of f^{-1} at $f(a)$ equals the reciprocal of the derivative of f at a. As you might imagine, we have to impose some mathematical conditions on f to be sure this conclusion holds. The usual conditions, from advanced calculus, are stated in Theorem 1.

THEOREM 1

The Derivative Rule for Inverses

If f is differentiable at every point of an interval I and df/dx is never zero on I, then f^{-1} is differentiable at every point of the interval $f(I)$. The value of df^{-1}/dx at any particular point $f(a)$ is the reciprocal of the value of df/dx at a:

$$\left(\frac{df^{-1}}{dx}\right)_{x = f(a)} = \frac{1}{\left(\frac{df}{dx}\right)_{x = a}} \qquad (1)$$

Equation (1) tells how each derivative is to be evaluated. When we do not need to be told, we can get along with the shorter form

$$\frac{df^{-1}}{dx} = \frac{1}{\frac{df}{dx}}. \qquad (2)$$

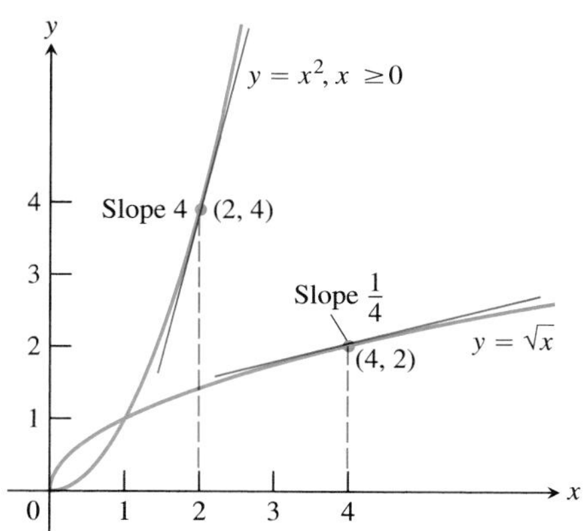

6.14 The derivative of $f^{-1}(x) = \sqrt{x}$ at the point (4, 2) is the reciprocal of the derivative of $f(x) = x^2$ at (2, 4).

EXAMPLE 5 For $f(x) = x^2$, $x \geq 0$, and its inverse $f^{-1}(x) = \sqrt{x}$ (Fig. 6.14), we have

$$\frac{df}{dx} = \frac{d}{dx}(x^2) = 2x \qquad \text{and} \qquad \frac{df^{-1}}{dx} = \frac{d}{dx}\sqrt{x} = \frac{1}{2\sqrt{x}}, \quad x > 0.$$

The point (4, 2) is the mirror image of the point (2, 4) across the line $y = x$.

$$\text{At the point } (2, 4): \qquad \frac{df}{dx} = 2x = 2(2) = 4.$$

$$\text{At the point } (4, 2): \qquad \frac{df^{-1}}{dx} = \frac{1}{2\sqrt{x}} = \frac{1}{2\sqrt{4}} = \frac{1}{4} = \frac{1}{\frac{df}{dx}}.$$

Equation (1) sometimes enables us to find specific values of df^{-1}/dx without knowing a formula for f^{-1}.

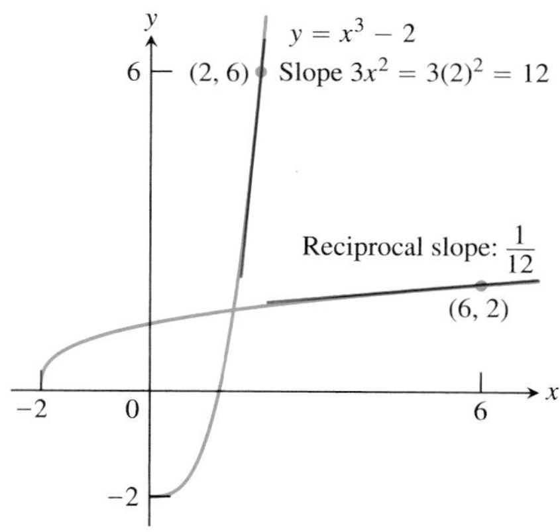

6.15 The derivative of $f(x) = x^3 - 2$ at $x = 2$ tells us the derivative of f^{-1} at $x = 6$.

EXAMPLE 6 For $f(x) = x^3 - 2$, find the value of df^{-1}/dx at $x = 6 = f(2)$ without finding a formula for $f^{-1}(x)$.

Solution

$$\left(\frac{df^{-1}}{dx}\right)_{x=6} = \left(\frac{df^{-1}}{dx}\right)_{x=f(2)}$$

$$= \frac{1}{\left(\frac{df}{dx}\right)_{x=2}} \qquad \text{Eq. (1) with } a = 2$$

$$= \frac{1}{(3x^2)_{x=2}} \qquad \frac{df}{dx} = \frac{d}{dx}(x^3 - 2) = 3x^2$$

$$= \frac{1}{3(2)^2} = \frac{1}{12}.$$

See Fig. 6.15.

Exercises 6.2

Which of the functions graphed in Exercises 1–6 are one-to-one and which are not?

1.

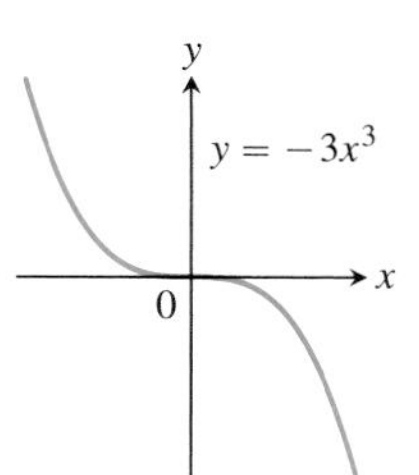

2.

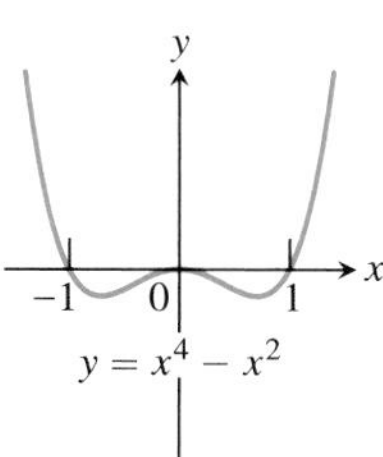

3.

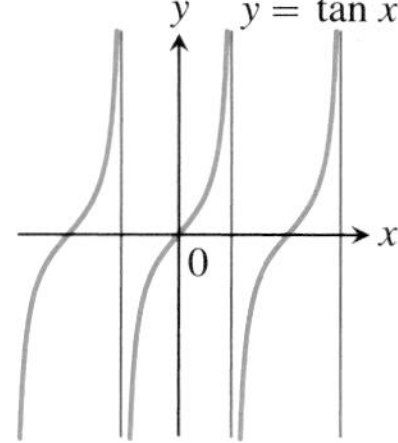

4.

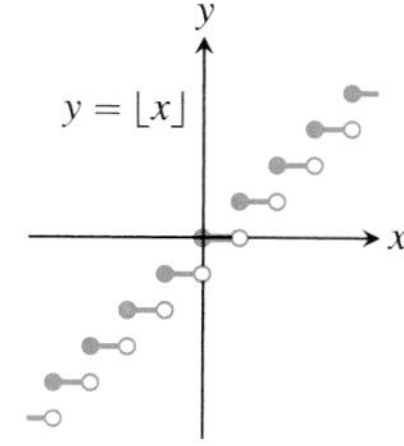

5.

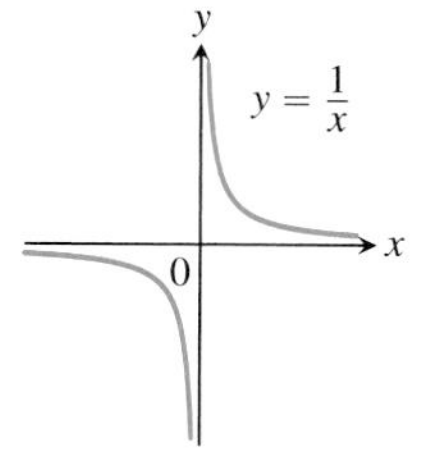

6.

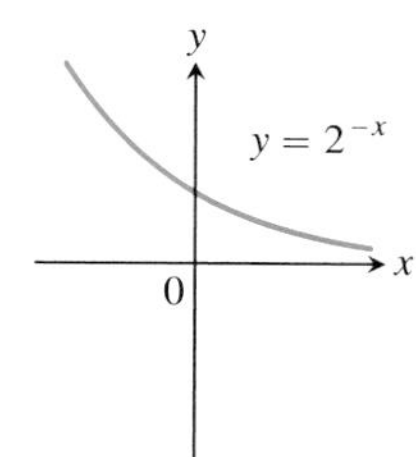

Each of Exercises 7–12 gives a formula for a function $y = f(x)$ and shows the graphs of f and f^{-1}. Find a formula for $f^{-1}(x)$ in each case.

7. $f(x) = x^2 + 1,\ x \geq 0$

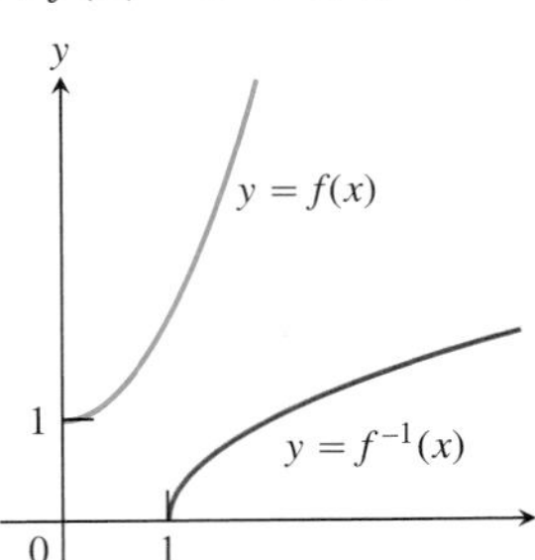

8. $f(x) = x^2,\ x \leq 0$

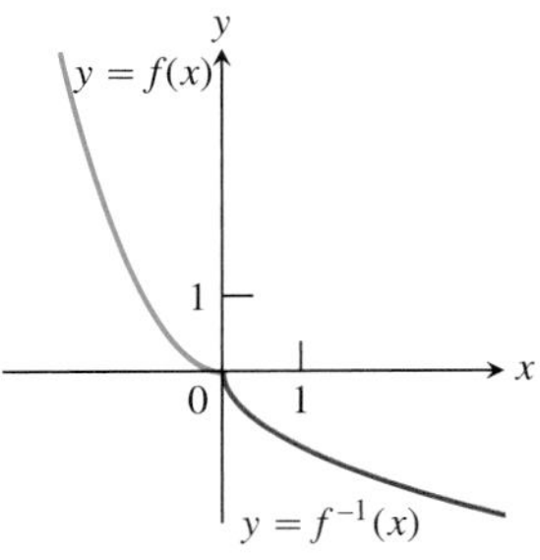

9. $f(x) = x^3 - 1$

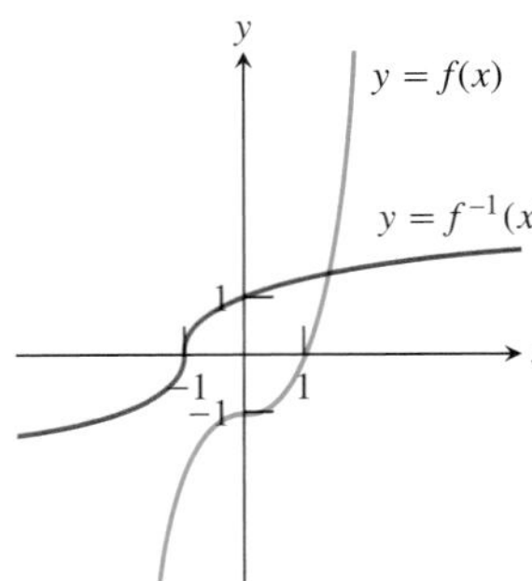

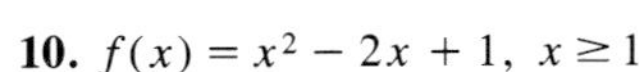

10. $f(x) = x^2 - 2x + 1,\ x \geq 1$

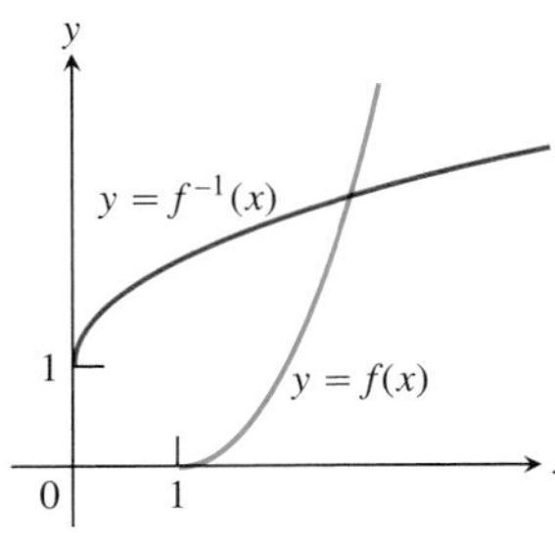

11. $f(x) = (x + 1)^2,\ x \geq -1$

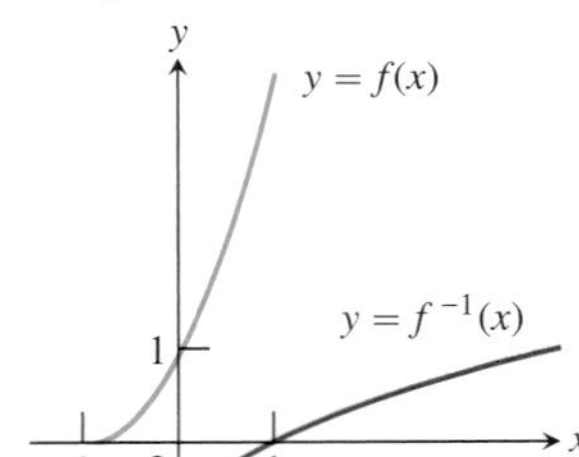

12. $f(x) = x^{2/3},\ x \geq 0$

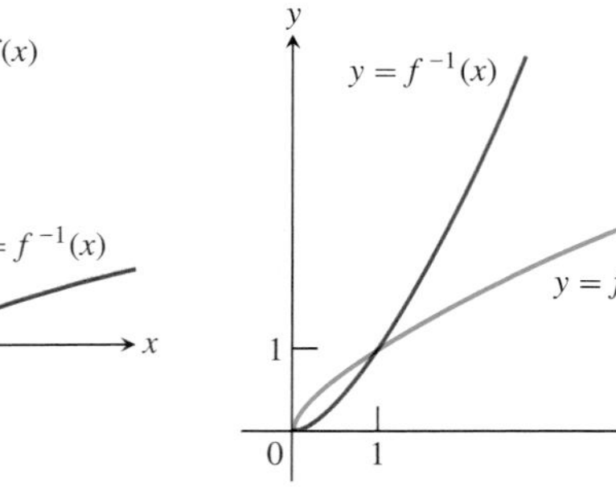

Each of Exercises 13–18 shows the graph of a function $y = f(x)$. Copy the graph and draw in the line $y = x$. Then use the fact that the graphs of f and f^{-1} are symmetric with respect to the line $y = x$ to sketch the graph of f^{-1}, using the same axes. (It is not necessary to find a formula for $f^{-1}(x)$.) In each case, identify the domain and range of f^{-1}.

13.

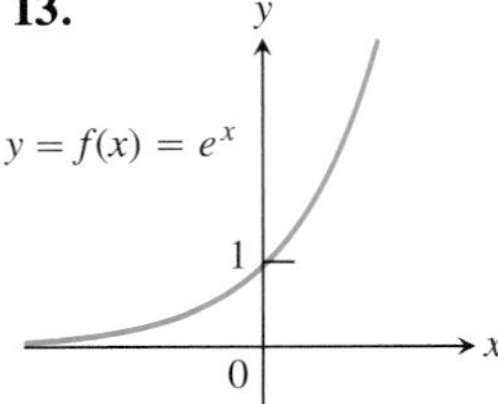

14.

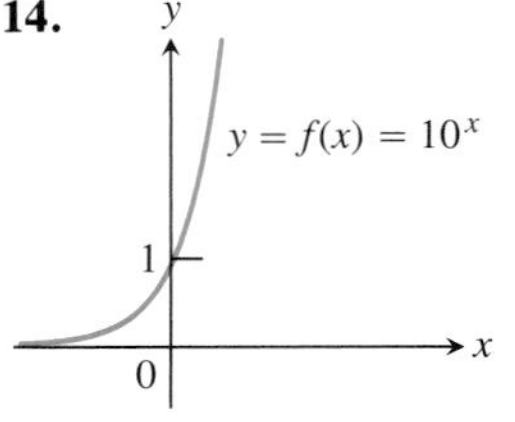

15.

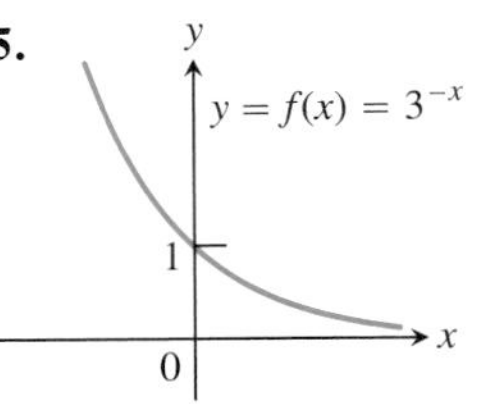

16.

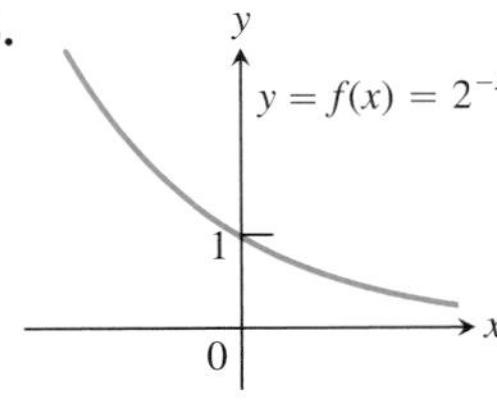

17.

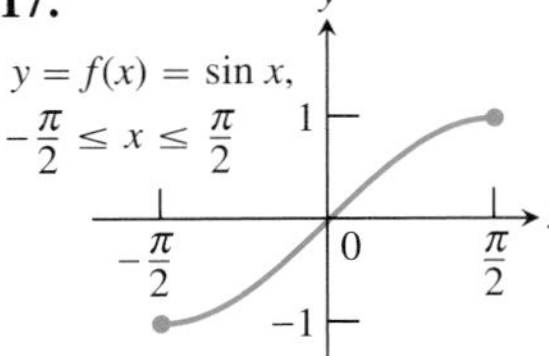

18.

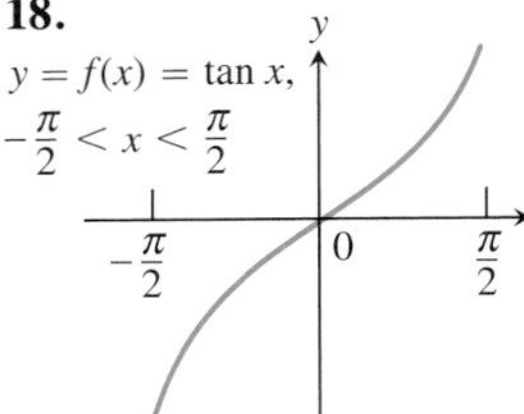

Each of Exercises 19–24 gives a formula for a function $y = f(x)$. In each case, find $f^{-1}(x)$ and identify the domain and range of f^{-1}. As a check, show that $f(f^{-1}(x)) = f^{-1}(f(x)) = x$.

19. $f(x) = x^5$

20. $f(x) = x^4,\quad x \geq 0$

21. $f(x) = x^3 + 1$

22. $f(x) = (1/2)x - 7/2$

23. $f(x) = 1/x^2,\quad x > 0$

24. $f(x) = 1/x^3,\quad x \neq 0$

In Exercises 25–28:

a) Find $f^{-1}(x)$.
b) Graph f and f^{-1} together.
c) Evaluate df/dx at $x = a$ and df^{-1}/dx at $x = f(a)$ to show that at these points $df^{-1}/dx = 1/(df/dx)$.

25. $f(x) = 2x + 3,\quad a = -1$

26. $f(x) = 5 - 4x,\quad a = 1/2$

27. $f(x) = (1/5)x + 7,\quad a = -1$

28. $f(x) = 2x^2,\quad x \geq 0,\quad a = 5$

29. **a)** Show that $f(x) = x^3$ and $g(x) = \sqrt[3]{x}$ are inverses of one another.
b) Graph f and g over an x-interval large enough to show the graphs intersecting at $(1, 1)$ and $(-1, -1)$. Be sure the picture shows the required symmetry in the line $y = x$.
c) Find the slopes of the tangents to the graphs of f and g at $(1, 1)$ and $(-1, -1)$ (four tangents in all).
d) What lines are tangent to the curves at the origin?

30. **a)** Show that $h(x) = x^3/4$ and $k(x) = (4x)^{1/3}$ are inverses of one another.
b) Graph h and k over an x-interval large enough to show the graphs intersecting at $(2, 2)$ and $(-2, -2)$. Be sure the picture shows the required symmetry about the line $y = x$.
c) Find the slopes of the tangents to the graphs of h and k at $(2, 2)$ and $(-2, -2)$.
d) What lines are tangent to the curves at the origin?

31. Let $f(x) = x^3 - 3x^2 - 1,\ x \geq 2$. Find the value of df^{-1}/dx at the point $x = -1 = f(3)$.

32. Let $f(x) = x^2 - 4x - 5,\ x > 2$. Find the value of df^{-1}/dx at the point $x = 0 = f(5)$.

33. Suppose that the differentiable function $y = f(x)$ has an inverse, and that the graph of f passes through the point (2, 4) and has a slope of 1/3 there. Find the value of df^{-1}/dx at $x = 4$.

34. Suppose that the differentiable function $y = g(x)$ has an inverse, and that the graph of g passes through the origin with slope 2. Find the slope of the graph of g^{-1} at the origin.

35. **a)** Graph the function $f(x) = \sqrt{1 - x^2}$, $0 \le x \le 1$. What symmetry does the graph have?
b) Show that f is its own inverse. (Remember that $\sqrt{x^2} = x$ if $x \ge 0$.)

36. **a)** Graph the function $f(x) = 1/x$. What symmetry does the graph have?
b) Show that f is its own inverse.

37. **a)** Find the inverse of the function $f(x) = mx$, where m is a constant different from zero.
b) What can you conclude about the inverse of a function $y = f(x)$ whose graph is a line through the origin with a nonzero slope m?

38. Show that the graph of the inverse of $f(x) = mx + b$, where m and b are constants and $m \ne 0$, is a line with slope $1/m$ and y-intercept $-b/m$.

39. **a)** Find the inverse of $f(x) = x + 1$. Graph f and its inverse together. Add the line $y = x$ to your sketch, drawing it with dashes or dots for contrast.
b) Find the inverse of $f(x) = x + b$ (b constant). How is the graph of f^{-1} related to the graph of f?
c) What can you conclude about the inverses of functions whose graphs are lines parallel to the line $y = x$?

40. **a)** Find the inverse of $f(x) = -x + 1$. Graph the line $y = -x + 1$ together with the line $y = x$. At what angle do the lines intersect?
b) Find the inverse of $f(x) = -x + b$ (b constant). What angle does the line $y = -x + b$ make with the line $y = x$?
c) What can you conclude about the inverses of functions whose graphs are lines perpendicular to the line $y = x$?

41. *Increasing Functions.* As we saw in Section 4.6, a function $f(x)$ *increases* on a domain D of real numbers if, throughout D, $x_1 < x_2 \Rightarrow f(x_1) < f(x_2)$. Show that if $f(x)$ increases on D then f is one-to-one on D.

42. *Decreasing Functions.* As we saw in Section 4.6, a function $f(x)$ *decreases* on a domain D of real numbers if, throughout D, $x_1 < x_2 \Rightarrow f(x_1) > f(x_2)$. Show that if $f(x)$ decreases on D then f is one-to-one on D.

43. If $f(x)$ is one-to-one, can anything be said about $g(x) = -f(x)$? Give reasons for your answer.

44. If $f(x)$ is one-to-one and $f(x)$ is never 0, can anything be said about $h(x) = 1/f(x)$? Give reasons for your answer.

45. Suppose that the range of g lies in the domain of f so that the composite $f \circ g$ is defined. If f and g are one-to-one, can anything be said about $f \circ g$? Give reasons for your answer.

46. If a composite $f \circ g$ is one-to-one, must g be one-to-one? Give reasons for your answer.

Writing for Your Own Knowledge

Answer the following questions in writing. Some answers will take only a sentence or two; others may require several paragraphs. Some explanations may also call for graphs or sketches.

1. What functions have inverses?
2. How do you know if two functions f and g are inverses of one another?
3. What symmetry do you expect to see in the graphs of a function and its inverse?
4. How can you sometimes express the inverse of a function $f(x)$ as a function of x?
5. Under what circumstances can you be sure that the inverse of a differentiable function is differentiable? How are the derivatives of f and f^{-1} related?

EXPLORER PROGRAM

Picard's Fixed Point	An equation solver that also enables you to toggle between the graphs of a function and of its inverse.

6.3

Logarithmic Functions and the Derivative of ln x

The inverse of the exponential function e^x is called the natural logarithm function, $y = \ln x$. In this section, we study the natural logarithm both as a differentiable function and as a device for simplifying calculations. As we will learn in the process, every exponential function a^x is a numerical power of e^x and every logarithmic function is a numerical multiple of $\ln x$. Thus, we can learn nearly everything we need to know about exponentials and logarithms by studying the functions $y = e^x$ and $y = \ln x$.

The Natural Logarithm

Since $f(x) = e^x$ is one-to-one, we know that it has an inverse. We call this inverse the natural logarithm function.

DEFINITION

The **natural logarithm function** $y = \ln x$ is the inverse of the exponential function $y = e^x$.

Typical 2-Place Values of ln x

x	$\ln x$
0	undefined
0.05	−3.00
0.5	−0.69
1	0
2	0.69
3	1.10
4	1.39
10	2.30

We obtain the graph of $y = \ln x$ by reflecting the graph of $y = e^x$ across the line $y = x$ (Fig. 6.16). The domain of $\ln x$ (range of e^x) is the set of positive real numbers. The range of $\ln x$ (domain of e^x) is the set of all real numbers. The graph of $\ln x$ crosses the x-axis at $(1, 0)$, so $\ln 1 = 0$. Also,

$$\lim_{x \to 0^+} \ln x = -\infty \quad \text{and} \quad \lim_{x \to \infty} \ln x = \infty. \tag{1}$$

Because e^x and $\ln x$ are inverses of one another, composing them in either order gives the identity function. This gives two useful equations.

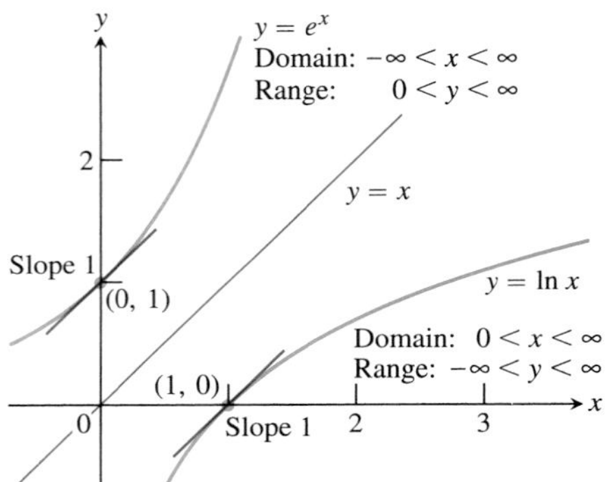

6.16 The function $y = e^x$ and its inverse, $y = \ln x$.

The Inverse Equations for e^x and ln x

$$e^{\ln x} = x \qquad (x > 0) \tag{2}$$

$$\ln (e^x) = x \qquad (\text{any } x) \tag{3}$$

EXAMPLE 1

a) $e^{\ln (x^2+1)} = x^2 + 1$

b) $e^{3 \ln 2} = (e^{\ln 2})^3 = (2)^3 = 8$

c) $e^{x + \ln 2} = e^x \cdot e^{\ln 2} = e^x \cdot 2 = 2e^x$

d) $e^{-\ln x} = \dfrac{1}{e^{\ln x}} = \dfrac{1}{x}$

e) $\ln e^3 = 3$

f) $\ln \sqrt{e} = \ln (e^{1/2}) = \dfrac{1}{2}$

g) $\ln e^{-1/x} = -\dfrac{1}{x}$

h) $\ln e^{\sin x} = \sin x$

Useful Operating Rules

1. To remove logarithms from an equation, exponentiate both sides.
2. To remove exponentials from an equation, take the logarithm of both sides.

   Exponentiation works because

$$e^a = e^b \quad \Leftrightarrow \quad a = b.$$

Taking logarithms works because, for positive numbers a and b,

$$\ln a = \ln b \quad \Leftrightarrow \quad a = b.$$

EXAMPLE 2 Solve $\ln y = 3t + 5$ for y.

Solution

$$\begin{aligned} \ln y &= 3t + 5 \\ e^{\ln y} &= e^{3t+5} && \text{Exponentiate both sides} \\ y &= e^{3t+5} && \text{Eq. (2)} \end{aligned}$$

EXAMPLE 3 Solve the equation $e^{2k} = 10$ for k.

Solution

$$\begin{aligned} e^{2k} &= 10 \\ \ln e^{2k} &= \ln 10 && \text{Take logarithms of both sides} \\ 2k &= \ln 10 && \text{Eq. (3)} \\ k &= \tfrac{1}{2} \ln 10 \approx 1.1513 && \text{Calculator} \end{aligned}$$

In the late 1500s, a Scottish baron, John Napier, invented a device called the *logarithm* that simplified arithmetic by replacing multiplication by addition. The equation that accomplished this was

$$\ln ax = \ln a + \ln x.$$

To multiply two positive numbers a and x, you looked up their logarithms in a table, added the logarithms, found the sum in the body of the table, and read the table backward to find the product ax.

Having the table was the key, of course, and Napier spent the last 20 years of his life working on a table he never finished (while the astronomer Tycho Brahe waited in vain for the information he needed to speed his calculations). The table was completed after Napier's death (and Brahe's) by Napier's friend Henry Briggs in London. Base 10 logarithms subsequently became known as Briggs's logarithms (what else?) and some books on navigation still refer to them this way.

Napier also invented an artillery piece that could hit a cow a mile away. Horrified by the weapon's accuracy, he stopped production and suppressed the cannon's design.

As Example 3 suggests, we normally find numerical values of ln x with a calculator. There is also an integral formula for ln x, which we will investigate in Section 6.4.

Properties of Logarithms

Like the base 10 logarithm you may have studied before, the natural logarithm has the following arithmetic properties.

TABLE 6.3
Properties of natural logarithms

For any numbers $x > 0$ and $y > 0$,

1. *Product Rule:*	$\ln xy = \ln x + \ln y$	
2. *Quotient Rule:*	$\ln \frac{x}{y} = \ln x - \ln y$	
3. *Reciprocal Rule:*	$\ln \frac{1}{y} = -\ln y$	Rule 2 with $x = 1$
4. *Power Rule:*	$\ln x^y = y \ln x$	

With the help of the inverse equations (Eqs. 2 and 3), we can derive these properties from the laws of exponents in Table 6.2, Section 6.1. The derivations are outlined in Exercises 109–112.

EXAMPLE 4

a) $\ln 6 = \ln (2 \cdot 3) = \ln 2 + \ln 3$ Product

b) $\ln 4 - \ln 5 = \ln \frac{4}{5} = \ln 0.8$ Quotient

c) $\ln \frac{1}{8} = -\ln 8$ Reciprocal

$= -\ln 2^3 = -3 \ln 2$ Power

EXAMPLE 5

a) $\ln 4 + \ln \sin x = \ln (4 \sin x)$ Product

b) $\ln \frac{x+1}{2x-3} = \ln (x+1) - \ln (2x-3)$ Quotient

c) $\ln \sec x = \ln \frac{1}{\cos x} = -\ln \cos x$ Reciprocal

d) $\ln \sqrt[3]{x+1} = \ln (x+1)^{1/3} = \frac{1}{3} \ln (x+1)$ Power

The Derivative of $y = \ln x$

Theorem 1 in Section 6.2 tells us that the natural logarithm function is differentiable because it is the inverse of a differentiable function whose derivative is never zero. Knowing this, we can calculate what the derivative of the logarithm must be:

$$
\begin{aligned}
y &= \ln x \\
e^y &= x && \text{Exponentiate both sides.} \\
\frac{d}{dx}(e^y) &= \frac{d}{dx}(x) && \text{Take the derivative of both sides.} \\
e^y \frac{dy}{dx} &= 1 && \text{Chain Rule: } \frac{d}{dx}(e^u) = e^u \frac{du}{dx} \\
\frac{dy}{dx} &= \frac{1}{e^y} && \text{We can divide by } e^y \text{ because } e^y \text{ is never zero.} \\
\frac{dy}{dx} &= \frac{1}{x} && \text{Replacing } e^y \text{ by } x.
\end{aligned}
$$

In short,

$$\frac{d}{dx}(\ln x) = \frac{1}{x}. \tag{4}$$

The Chain Rule extends Eq. (4) to a more general form.

If $u > 0$ is a differentiable function of x, then

$$\frac{d}{dx}(\ln u) = \frac{1}{u} \cdot \frac{du}{dx}. \tag{5}$$

EXAMPLE 6

$$
\begin{aligned}
\frac{d}{dx}[\ln(x^2+3)] &= \frac{1}{x^2+3} \cdot \frac{d}{dx}(x^2+3) && \text{Eq. (5) with } u = x^2+3 \\
&= \frac{2x}{x^2+3}
\end{aligned}
$$

Logarithmic Differentiation

The derivatives of positive functions given by formulas that involve products, quotients, and powers can often be found more quickly if we take the natural logarithm of both sides before differentiating. This enables us to use the rules in Table 6.3 to simplify the formulas before differentiating. The process, called **logarithmic differentiation,** is illustrated in the next example.

How to Differentiate $y = f(x)$, $(y > 0)$ by Logarithmic Differentiation

1. Take logs of both sides and simplify.
2. Differentiate.
3. Solve for dy/dx.
4. Substitute for y.

EXAMPLE 7 Find dy/dx if $y = \dfrac{(x^2+1)(x+3)^{1/2}}{x-1}$, $\quad x > 1$.

Solution We take the natural logarithm of both sides and simplify the result with the rules in Table 6.3:

$$
\begin{aligned}
\ln y &= \ln \frac{(x^2+1)(x+3)^{1/2}}{x-1} \\
&= \ln (x^2+1)(x+3)^{1/2} - \ln (x-1) && \text{Quotient Rule} \\
&= \ln (x^2+1) + \ln (x+3)^{1/2} - \ln (x-1) && \text{Product Rule} \\
&= \ln (x^2+1) + \frac{1}{2}\ln (x+3) - \ln (x-1). && \text{Power Rule}
\end{aligned}
$$

We then take derivatives of both sides with respect to x, using Eq. (5) on the left.

$$\frac{1}{y}\frac{dy}{dx} = \frac{1}{x^2+1}\cdot 2x + \frac{1}{2}\cdot\frac{1}{x+3} - \frac{1}{x-1}.$$

Next we solve for dy/dx:

$$\frac{dy}{dx} = y\left(\frac{2x}{x^2+1} + \frac{1}{2x+6} - \frac{1}{x-1}\right).$$

Finally, we substitute for y:

$$\frac{dy}{dx} = \frac{(x^2+1)(x+3)^{1/2}}{x-1}\left(\frac{2x}{x^2+1} + \frac{1}{2x+6} - \frac{1}{x-1}\right).$$

Base a Logarithms

As we saw in Section 6.1, if a is any positive number other than 1, the base a exponential function $f(x) = a^x$ is one-to-one. It therefore has an inverse. We call the inverse the base a logarithm function.

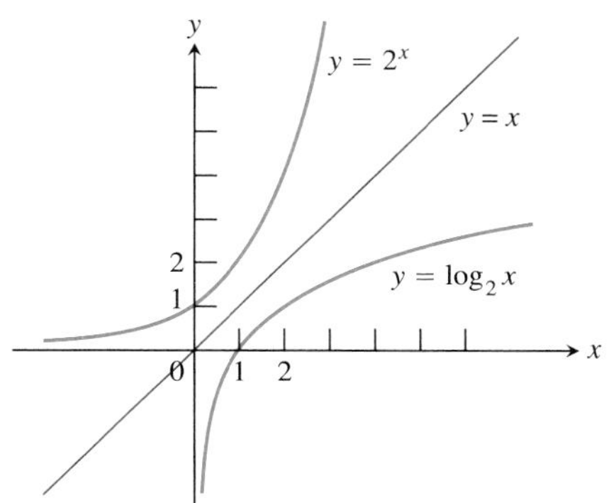

6.17 The graph of 2^x and its inverse, $\log_2 x$.

DEFINITION

The **base *a* logarithm function** $y = \log_a x$ is the inverse of the function $y = a^x$ $(a > 0,\ a \neq 1)$.

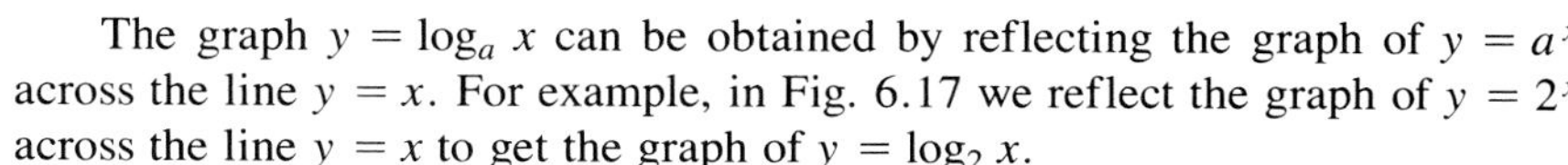

The graph $y = \log_a x$ can be obtained by reflecting the graph of $y = a^x$ across the line $y = x$. For example, in Fig. 6.17 we reflect the graph of $y = 2^x$ across the line $y = x$ to get the graph of $y = \log_2 x$.

Since $\log_a x$ and a^x are inverses of one another, composing them in either order gives the identity function.

The Inverse Equations for a^x and $\log_a x$

$$a^{\log_a(x)} = x \qquad (x > 0) \qquad (6)$$

$$\log_a(a^x) = x \qquad (\text{any } x) \qquad (7)$$

EXAMPLE 8

a) $\log_2(2^5) = 5$

b) $\log_{10}(10^{-7}) = -7$

c) $2^{\log_2(3)} = 3$

d) $10^{\log_{10}(4)} = 4$

The Evaluation of $\log_a x$

The evaluation of $\log_a x$ is simplified by the observation that $\log_a x$ is a numerical multiple of $\ln x$.

We use this equation to evaluate $\log_a x$.

$$\log_a x = \frac{1}{\ln a}\cdot \ln x = \frac{\ln x}{\ln a} \qquad (8)$$

We can derive Eq. (8) from Eq. (6):

$$a^{\log_a(x)} = x \qquad \text{Eq. (6)}$$

$$\ln a^{\log_a(x)} = \ln x \qquad \text{Take the natural logarithm of both sides.}$$

$$\log_a(x) \cdot \ln a = \ln x \qquad \text{The Power Rule in Table 6.3}$$

$$\log_a x = \frac{\ln x}{\ln a} \qquad \text{Solve for } \log_a x.$$

TABLE 6.4
Properties of base a logarithms

For any numbers $x > 0$ and $y > 0$,

1. *Product Rule:*
   $\log_a xy = \log_a x + \log_a y$
2. *Quotient Rule:*
   $\log_a \frac{x}{y} = \log_a x - \log_a y$
3. *Reciprocal Rule:*
   $\log_a \frac{1}{y} = -\log_a y$
4. *Power Rule:*
   $\log_a x^y = y \log_a x$

EXAMPLE 9

$$\log_{10} 2 = \frac{\ln 2}{\ln 10} \approx \frac{0.69315}{2.30259} \approx 0.30103$$

The arithmetic properties of $\log_a x$ are the same as the ones for $\ln x$ (Table 6.4). These rules can be proved by dividing the corresponding rules for the natural logarithm function by $\ln a$. For example,

$$\ln xy = \ln x + \ln y \qquad \text{Rule 1 for natural logarithms . . .}$$

$$\frac{\ln xy}{\ln a} = \frac{\ln x}{\ln a} + \frac{\ln y}{\ln a} \qquad \text{. . . divided by } \ln a \text{ . . .}$$

$$\log_a xy = \log_a x + \log_a y \qquad \text{. . . gives Rule 1 for base } a \text{ logarithms.}$$

The Derivative of $\log_a u$

To find the derivative of a base a logarithm, we first convert it to a natural logarithm. If u is a positive differentiable function of x, then

$$\frac{d}{dx}(\log_a u) = \frac{d}{dx}\left(\frac{\ln u}{\ln a}\right) = \frac{1}{\ln a}\frac{d}{dx}(\ln u) = \frac{1}{\ln a} \cdot \frac{1}{u}\frac{du}{dx}.$$

$$\frac{d}{dx}(\log_a u) = \frac{1}{\ln a} \cdot \frac{1}{u}\frac{du}{dx} \tag{9}$$

A work crew surveying a collapsed portion of I-880 in Oakland, CA. The damage was caused by a major earthquake that hit the Bay Area in October 1989.

EXAMPLE 10

$$\frac{d}{dx}\log_{10}(3x+1) = \frac{1}{\ln 10} \cdot \frac{1}{3x+1}\frac{d}{dx}(3x+1) = \frac{3}{(\ln 10)(3x+1)}$$

Base 10 Logarithms (Optional)

Base 10 logarithms, often called **common logarithms,** appear in many scientific formulas. For example, earthquake intensity is often reported on the logarithmic **Richter scale.** Here the formula is

$$\text{Magnitude } R = \log_{10}\left(\frac{a}{T}\right) + B, \tag{10}$$

where a is the amplitude of the ground motion in microns at the receiving station, T is the period of the seismic wave in seconds, and B is an empirical factor that allows for the weakening of the seismic wave with increasing distance from the epicenter of the earthquake.

EXAMPLE 11 For an earthquake 10,000 km from the receiving station, $B = 6.8$. If the recorded vertical ground motion is $a = 10$ microns and the period is $T = 1$ sec, the earthquake's magnitude is

$$R = \log_{10}\left(\frac{10}{1}\right) + 6.8 = 1 + 6.8 = 7.8.$$

An earthquake of this magnitude does great damage near its epicenter.

Most Foods Are Acidic (pH $<$ 7).

Food	pH Value
Bananas	4.5–4.7
Grapefruit	3.0–3.3
Oranges	3.0–4.0
Limes	1.8–2.0
Milk	6.3–6.6
Soft drinks	2.0–4.0
Spinach	5.1–5.7

The **pH scale** for measuring the acidity of a solution is a base 10 logarithmic scale. The pH value (hydrogen potential) of the solution is the common logarithm of the reciprocal of the solution's hydronium ion concentration, $[H_3O^+]$:

$$\text{pH} = \log_{10}\frac{1}{[H_3O^+]} = -\log_{10}[H_3O^+]. \tag{11}$$

The hydronium ion concentration is measured in moles per liter. Vinegar has a pH of 3, distilled water a pH of 7, seawater a pH of 8.15, and household ammonia a pH of 12. The total scale ranges from about 0.1 for normal hydrochloric acid to 14 for a normal (1 N) solution of sodium hydroxide.

Another example of the use of common logarithms is the **decibel** or db ("dee bee") **scale** for measuring loudness. If I is the **intensity** of sound in watts per square meter, the decibel level of the sound is

$$\textbf{Sound level} = 10\log_{10}(I \times 10^{12})\text{ db}. \tag{12}$$

If you ever wondered why doubling the power of your audio amplifier increases the sound level by only a few decibels, Eq. (12) provides the answer. As the following example shows, doubling I adds only about 3 db.

Typical Sound Levels

Threshold of hearing	0 db
Rustle of leaves	10 db
Average whisper	20 db
Quiet automobile	50 db
Ordinary conversation	65 db
Pneumatic drill 10 feet away	90 db
Threshold of pain	120 db

EXAMPLE 12 Doubling I in Eq. (12) adds about 3 db. Writing log for $\log_{10}$ (a common practice), we have

$$\begin{aligned} \text{Sound level with } I \text{ doubled} &= 10\log(2I \times 10^{12}) && \text{Eq. (12) with } 2I \text{ for } I \\ &= 10\log(2 \cdot I \times 10^{12}) \\ &= 10\log 2 + 10\log(I \times 10^{12}) \\ &= \text{original sound level} + 10\log 2 \\ &\approx \text{original sound level} + 3. && \log_{10} 2 \approx 0.30 \end{aligned}$$

The Function $y = a^x$ and Its Derivative

Even though common logarithms have useful applications in calculus, we are mainly interested in $\ln x$ and its inverse e^x. Just as every logarithmic function is a numerical multiple of $\ln x$, every exponential function a^x is a numerical power of e^x.

If $a > 0$, and x is any number, then $a^x > 0$ and a^x lies in the domain of $\ln x$. Equation (2) then tells us that

$$\begin{aligned} a^x &= e^{\ln(a^x)} && \text{Eq. (2) with } a^x \text{ in place of } x \\ &= e^{x\ln a}. && \text{Power Rule for logarithms} \end{aligned} \tag{13}$$

Many calculators use the equation $a^x = e^{x \ln a}$ to evaluate noninteger powers of a and for this reason have trouble when a is negative. We know to evaluate $(-2)^{4/3}$ as $(16)^{1/3} \approx 2.5198$. But the calculator attempts to evaluate it as $e^{(4/3)\ln(-2)}$ and cannot succeed because $\ln(-2)$ is undefined.

$$a^x = e^{x \ln a} \quad (a > 0) \tag{14}$$

Equation (14) reveals that a^x is e^x raised to the power $\ln a$:

$$a^x = e^{x \ln a} = (e^x)^{\ln a} \tag{15}$$

Whenever we have to work with a^x, we can work with $e^{x \ln a}$ instead (if we want). In particular, Eq. (14) enables us to express the derivative of a^x as

$$\begin{aligned} \frac{d}{dx}(a^x) &= \frac{d}{dx}(e^{x \ln a}) && \text{Eq. (14)} \\ &= e^{x \ln a} \cdot \frac{d}{dx}(x \ln a) && \text{Chain Rule for } e^u \\ &= a^x \cdot \frac{d}{dx}(x \ln a) && e^{x \ln a} = a^x \\ &= a^x \ln a. && \ln a \text{ is a constant.} \end{aligned}$$

In short,

$$\frac{d}{dx}(a^x) = a^x \ln a. \tag{16}$$

In Section 6.1, we saw that

$$\frac{d}{dx}(a^x) = a^x \cdot \lim_{h \to 0} \frac{a^h - 1}{h}. \tag{17}$$

By comparing Eqs. (16) and (17), we can now understand the value of the limit on the right. It is $\ln a$, the natural logarithm of a:

$$\lim_{h \to 0} \frac{a^h - 1}{h} = \ln a. \tag{18}$$

Equation (16) also comes in a more general form, based on the Chain Rule.

If $a > 0$ and u is a differentiable function of x, then

$$\frac{d}{dx}(a^u) = (a^u \ln a)\frac{du}{dx}. \tag{19}$$

EXAMPLE 13

a) $\dfrac{d}{dx} 3^x = 3^x \ln 3$

b) $\dfrac{d}{dx} 3^{-x} = (3^{-x} \ln 3) \dfrac{d}{dx}(-x) = -3^{-x} \ln 3$

c) $\dfrac{d}{dx} 3^{\sin x} = (3^{\sin x} \ln 3) \dfrac{d}{dx}(\sin x) = 3^{\sin x} (\ln 3) \cos x$

The Power Rule for Differentiation (Arbitrary Real Exponents)

Now that we have Eq. (14), we can prove the Power Rule for differentiation in its final form:

$$\begin{aligned} x^n &= e^{n \ln x} && \text{Eq. (14)} \\ \frac{d}{dx}(x^n) &= \frac{d}{dx}(e^{n \ln x}) && \text{Derivative of both sides} \\ &= e^{n \ln x} \cdot \frac{d}{dx}(n \ln x) && \text{Chain Rule for } e^u \\ &= x^n \cdot \frac{n}{x} \\ &= n x^{n-1}. \end{aligned}$$

As long as $x > 0$,

$$\frac{d}{dx}(x^n) = n x^{n-1}. \qquad (20)$$

The Chain Rule extends Eq. (20) to the Power Rule's final form.

Power Rule (Arbitrary Real Exponents)

If u is a positive differentiable function of x, and n is any real number, then

$$\frac{d}{dx}(u^n) = nu^{n-1}\frac{du}{dx}. \qquad (21)$$

EXAMPLE 14

$$\frac{d}{dx}x^{\sqrt{2}} = \sqrt{2}x^{\sqrt{2}-1} \qquad (x > 0)$$

$$\frac{d}{dx}(\sin x)^{\pi} = \pi(\sin x)^{\pi - 1}\cos x \qquad (\sin x > 0)$$

Derivatives of Other Power Functions

If u and v are positive differentiable functions of x, we can differentiate u^v by writing it as $e^{v \ln u}$.

EXAMPLE 15 Find dy/dx if $y = x^x$, $x > 0$.

Solution The rule

$$\frac{d}{dx}(a^x) = a^x \ln a$$

does not apply here because it requires the base a to be constant. The rule

$$\frac{d}{dx}(x^n) = n x^{n-1}$$

does not apply either, because it requires the exponent n to be constant. In $y = x^x$, both the base and the exponent vary with x. To solve this problem, we

We could also differentiate $y = x^x$ using logarithmic differentiation.

first write x^x as a power of e:

$$y = x^x = e^{x \ln x}. \qquad \text{Eq. (14) with } a = x$$

We then differentiate both sides, using the Chain Rule on the right:

$$\begin{aligned} y &= e^{x \ln x} \\ \frac{dy}{dx} &= \frac{d}{dx}(e^{x \ln x}) \\ &= e^{x \ln x}\left(\frac{d}{dx}(x \ln x)\right) && \text{Chain Rule} \\ &= e^{x \ln x}\left(x \cdot \frac{1}{x} + 1 \cdot \ln x\right) && \text{Product Rule} \\ &= e^{x \ln x}(1 + \ln x) \\ &= x^x(1 + \ln x). \end{aligned}$$

Exercises 6.3

Find simpler expressions for the numbers in Exercises 1–4.

1. a) $e^{\ln 7.2}$ b) $e^{-\ln x^2}$ c) $e^{\ln x - \ln y}$
2. a) $e^{\ln (x^2 + y^2)}$ b) $e^{-\ln 0.3}$ c) $e^{\ln \pi x - \ln 2}$
3. a) $2 \ln \sqrt{e}$ b) $\ln (\ln e^e)$ c) $\ln (e^{-x^2 - y^2})$
4. a) $\ln (e^{\sec \theta})$ b) $\ln (e^{(e^x)})$ c) $\ln (e^{2 \ln x})$

In Exercises 5–10, solve for y in terms of t or x, as appropriate.

5. $\ln y = 2t + 4$
6. $\ln y = -t + 5$
7. $\ln (y - 40) = 5t$
8. $\ln (1 - 2y) = t$
9. $\ln (y - 1) - \ln 2 = x + \ln x$
10. $\ln (y^2 - 1) - \ln (y + 1) = \ln (\sin x)$

In Exercises 11 and 12, solve for k.

11. a) $e^{2k} = 4$ b) $100e^{10k} = 200$ c) $e^{k/1000} = a$
12. a) $e^{5k} = \frac{1}{4}$ b) $80e^k = 1$ c) $e^{(\ln 0.8)k} = 0.8$

In Exercises 13 and 14, solve for t.

13. a) $e^{-0.3t} = 27$ b) $e^{kt} = \frac{1}{2}$ c) $e^{(\ln 0.2)t} = 0.4$
14. a) $e^{-0.01t} = 1000$ b) $e^{kt} = \frac{1}{10}$ c) $e^{(\ln 2)t} = \frac{1}{2}$
15. Express the following logarithms in terms of ln 2 and ln 3.
    a) $\ln 0.75$ b) $\ln (4/9)$ c) $\ln (1/2)$
    d) $\ln \sqrt[3]{9}$ e) $\ln 3\sqrt{2}$ f) $\ln \sqrt{13.5}$
16. Express the following logarithms in terms of ln 5 and ln 7.
    a) $\ln (1/125)$ b) $\ln 9.8$ c) $\ln 7\sqrt{7}$
    d) $\ln 1225$ e) $\ln 0.056$
    f) $(\ln 35 + \ln (1/7))/(\ln 25)$

Use the properties of logarithms to simplify the expressions in Exercises 17 and 18.

17. a) $\ln \sin \theta - \ln \left(\frac{\sin \theta}{5}\right)$
    b) $\ln (3x^2 - 9x) + \ln \left(\frac{1}{3x}\right)$
    c) $\frac{1}{2} \ln (4t^4) - \ln 2$
18. a) $\ln \sec \theta + \ln \cos \theta$
    b) $\ln (8x + 4) - 2 \ln 2$
    c) $3 \ln \sqrt[3]{t^2 - 1} - \ln (t + 1)$

In Exercises 19–40, find the derivative of y with respect to x, t, or θ, as appropriate.

19. $y = \ln 5x$
20. $y = \ln (x/5)$
21. $y = \ln (t^2)$
22. $y = \ln (t^{3/2})$
23. $y = \ln \frac{3}{x}$
24. $y = \ln \frac{10}{x}$
25. $y = \ln (\theta + 1)$
26. $y = \ln (2\theta + 2)$
27. $y = \frac{x^4}{4} \ln x - \frac{x^4}{16}$
28. $y = \frac{x^3}{3} \ln x - \frac{x^3}{9}$
29. $y = t (\ln t)^2$
30. $y = t\sqrt{\ln t}$
31. $y = \frac{\ln t}{t}$
32. $y = \frac{1 + \ln t}{t}$
33. $y = \frac{\ln x}{1 + \ln x}$
34. $y = \frac{x \ln x}{1 + \ln x}$
35. $y = \ln (3te^{-t})$
36. $y = \ln (2e^{-t} \sin t)$
37. $y = \ln \left(\frac{e^\theta}{1 + e^\theta}\right)$
38. $y = \ln \left(\frac{\sqrt{\theta}}{1 + \sqrt{\theta}}\right)$

39. $y = \ln(\csc\theta + \cot\theta)$

40. $y = \ln(\sec\theta + \tan\theta)$

In Exercises 41–52, use logarithmic differentiation to find the derivative of y with respect to the given independent variable.

41. $y = \sqrt{x(x+1)}$

42. $y = \sqrt{e^{2x}(x^2+1)}$

43. $y = \sqrt{\dfrac{t}{t+1}}$

44. $y = \sqrt{\dfrac{1}{t(t+1)}}$

45. $y = \sqrt{\theta+3}\,\sin\theta$

46. $y = (\tan\theta)\sqrt{2\theta+1}$

47. $y = t(t+1)(t+2)$

48. $y = \dfrac{1}{t(t+1)(t+2)}$

49. $y = \dfrac{\theta+5}{\theta\cos\theta}$

50. $y = \dfrac{\theta\sin\theta}{\sqrt{\sec\theta}}$

51. $y = \dfrac{x\sqrt{x^2+1}}{(x+1)^{2/3}}$

52. $y = \sqrt{\dfrac{(x+1)^{10}}{(2x+1)^5}}$

Simplify the expressions in Exercises 53 and 54.

53. a) $5^{\log_5 7}$ b) $8^{\log_8 \sqrt{2}}$ c) $1.3^{\log_{1.3} 75}$
d) $\log_4 16$ e) $\log_3 \sqrt{3}$ f) $\log_4\left(\dfrac{1}{4}\right)$

54. a) $2^{\log_2 3}$ b) $10^{\log_{10}(1/2)}$ c) $\pi^{\log_\pi 7}$
d) $\log_{11} 121$ e) $\log_{121} 11$ f) $\log_3\left(\dfrac{1}{9}\right)$

Solve the equations in Exercises 55–58 for x.

55. $3^{\log_3(7)} + 2^{\log_2(5)} = 5^{\log_5(x)}$

56. $8^{\log_8(3)} - e^{\ln 5} = x^2 - 7^{\log_7(3x)}$

57. $3^{\log_3(x^2)} = 5e^{\ln x} - 3\cdot 10^{\log_{10}(2)}$

58. $\ln e + 4^{-2\log_4(x)} = \dfrac{1}{x}\log_{10}(100)$

In Exercises 59–66, find the derivative of y with respect to the given independent variable.

59. $y = \log_2 5\theta$

60. $y = \log_3(1 + \theta\ln 3)$

61. $y = \log_4 x + \log_4 x^2$

62. $y = \log_{25} e^x - \log_5 \sqrt{x}$

63. $y = \log_2 r\cdot\log_4 r$

64. $y = \log_3 r\cdot\log_9 r$

65. $y = \log_3\left(\left(\dfrac{x+1}{x-1}\right)^{\ln 3}\right)$

66. $y = \log_5\sqrt{\left(\dfrac{7x}{3x+2}\right)^{\ln 5}}$

In Exercises 67–76, find the derivative of y with respect to the given independent variable.

67. $y = 2^x$

68. $y = 8^x$

69. $y = 3^{-x}$

70. $y = 9^{-x}$

71. $y = 5^{\sqrt{s}}$

72. $y = 2^{(s^2)}$

73. $y = 7^{\sec\theta}\ln 7$

74. $y = 3^{\tan\theta}\ln 3$

75. $y = 2^{\sin 3t}$

76. $y = 5^{-\cos 2t}$

Find the limits in Exercises 77 and 78.

77. a) $\displaystyle\lim_{h\to 0}\frac{2^h-1}{h}$ b) $\displaystyle\lim_{h\to 0}\frac{5^h-1}{h}$

78. a) $\displaystyle\lim_{t\to 0}\frac{\pi^t-1}{t}$ b) $\displaystyle\lim_{\theta\to 0}\frac{(0.5)^\theta-1}{\theta}$

In Exercises 79–84, find the derivative of y with respect to the given independent variable.

79. $y = x^\pi$

80. $y = x^{\ln 2}$

81. $y = t^{3-\sqrt{2}}$

82. $y = t^{1-e}$

83. $y = (\cos\theta)^{\sqrt{2}}$

84. $y = (\ln\theta)^\pi$

In Exercises 85–90, find the derivative of y with respect to the given independent variable.

85. $y = (x+1)^x$

86. $y = x^{(x+1)}$

87. $y = \left(\sqrt{t}\right)^t$

88. $y = t^{\sqrt{t}}$

89. $y = (\sin x)^x$

90. $y = x^{\sin x}$

91. Find the absolute maximum value of $f(x) = x^2\ln(1/x)$, and say where it is assumed.

92. Locate and identify the absolute extreme values of
a) $\ln(\cos x)$ on $[-\pi/4, \pi/3]$.
b) $\cos(\ln x)$ on $[1/2, 2]$.

Use the graphing procedure of Section 4.3 to graph the equations in Exercises 93 and 94. Include the coordinates of any local extreme points and points of inflection in your sketch.

93. $y = x^2\ln x$

94. $y = x\ln x$

95. *Blood pH.* The pH of human blood normally falls between 7.37 and 7.44. Find the corresponding bounds for $[H_3O^+]$.

96. *Brain Fluid pH.* The cerebrospinal fluid in the brain has a hydronium ion concentration of about $[H_3O^+] = 4.8 \times 10^{-8}$ moles per liter. What is the pH?

97. *Audio Amplifiers.* By what factor k do you have to multiply the intensity I of the sound from your audio amplifier to add 10 db to the sound level?

98. *Audio Amplifiers.* You multiplied the intensity of the sound of your audio system by a factor of 10. By how many decibels did this increase the sound level?

99. *Continuation of Section 6.1, Example 4.* In Example 4, a program to eradicate a disease was reducing the number of cases by 20% per year. There were currently 10,000 cases, and we wanted to know how long it would take to get the number down to 1000. Starting with the equation $y = 10{,}000\,e^{kt}$, we first needed to know the value of k. Then, given k we wanted to find the value of t that made $10{,}000\,e^{kt}$ equal 1000. This meant solving

$$e^k = 0.8 \tag{1}$$

for k (by graphing, we estimated k at -0.2) and then solving

$$e^{-0.2t} = 1000 \tag{2}$$

for t. By graphing, we estimated t to be about 11.5 years.

Logarithms enable us to solve Eqs. (1) and (2) more accurately, and without graphing.

a) Solve $e^k = 0.8$ for k.
b) Using the value of k found in (a), solve the equation $10{,}000\, e^{kt} = 1000$ for t. About how long will it take to reduce the number of cases of the disease to 1000?

100. Most scientific calculators have keys for $\log_{10} x$ and $\ln x$. To find logarithms to other bases, we use the equation $\log_a x = (\ln x)/(\ln a)$.

To find $\log_2 x$, find $\ln x$ and divide by $\ln 2$: $\log_2 5 = \dfrac{\ln 5}{\ln 2} \approx 2.3219.$

To find $\ln x$ given $\log_2 x$, multiply by $\ln 2$: $\ln 5 = \log_2 5 \cdot \ln 2 \approx 1.6094.$

Find the following logarithms to five decimal places.

a) $\log_3 8$
b) $\log_7 0.5$
c) $\log_{20} 17$
d) $\log_{0.5} 7$
e) $\ln x$, given that $\log_{10} x = 2.3$
f) $\ln x$, given that $\log_2 x = 1.4$
g) $\ln x$, given that $\log_2 x = -1.5$
h) $\ln x$, given that $\log_{10} x = -0.7$

101. In Section 2.2, Exercise 70(c), you discovered that

$$\lim_{x\to\infty} \frac{\ln (x^2)}{\ln x} \approx 2.$$

Explain this result.

102. In Section 2.2, Exercise 70(d), you discovered that

$$\lim_{x\to\infty} \frac{\ln x}{\log x} \approx 2.30.$$

Explain this result.

103. *The Derivative of* $\ln kx$. Could $y = \ln 2x$ and $y = \ln 3x$ possibly have the same derivative at each point? (Differentiate them to find out.) What about $y = \ln kx$, for other positive values of the constant k? Give reasons for your answer.

104. *Conversion Factors.*

a) Show that the equation for converting base 10 logarithms to base 2 logarithms is

$$\log_2 x = \frac{\ln 10}{\ln 2} \log_{10} x.$$

b) Show that the equation for converting base a logarithms to base b logarithms is

$$\log_b x = \frac{\ln a}{\ln b} \log_a x.$$

105. The equation $x^2 = 2^x$ has three solutions: $x = 2$, $x = 4$, and one other. Estimate the third solution as accurately as you can by graphing.

106. Could $x^{\ln 2}$ possibly be the same as $2^{\ln x}$ for $x > 0$? Graph the two functions and explain what you see.

107. Graph $f(x) = x^e \cdot e^{-x}$ and its first derivative together for $0 \le x \le 7$. Comment on the behavior of f in relation to the signs and values of f'.

108. Graph $g(x) = e^x - x^e$ and its first derivative together for $0 \le x \le 4$. Comment on the behavior of g in relation to the signs and values of g'.

THE LOGARITHM ARITHMETIC RULES

Exercises 109–112 are about the derivations of the rules in Table 6.3.

109. Explain why Rule 3 is a special case of Rule 2.

110. How does Rule 1 read when x is replaced by the number x/y? How is the new formula related to Rule 2? What does this say about the relationship between Rules 1 and 2? Do we need to prove both Rule 1 and Rule 2, or is proving one of them enough? Explain.

111. Here is an outline of a proof of Rule 1. Give reasons for steps (a)–(c).

$$\begin{aligned} \ln xy &= \ln (e^{\ln x} \cdot e^{\ln y}) && \text{(a)}\\ &= \ln (e^{\ln x + \ln y}) && \text{(b)}\\ &= \ln x + \ln y && \text{(c)} \end{aligned}$$

112. Here is an outline of a proof of Rule 4. Give reasons for steps (a)–(c).

$$\begin{aligned} \ln x^y &= \ln (e^{\ln x})^y && \text{(a)}\\ &= \ln (e^{y \ln x}) && \text{(b)}\\ &= y \ln x && \text{(c)} \end{aligned}$$

Writing for Your Own Knowledge

Answer the following questions in writing. Some answers will take only a sentence or two; others may require several paragraphs. Some explanations may also call for graphs or sketches.

1. What is the natural logarithm function? What arithmetic properties does it have? What is its derivative?
2. What other logarithms are there? How are they related to natural logarithms? How do you find their derivatives?
3. How are all exponential functions related to the function $f(x) = e^x$? How do you find their derivatives?
4. If a is a positive number, what is the value of $\lim_{h\to 0} ((a^h - 1)/h)$?
5. If u is a positive differentiable function of x, how do you find $d(u^n)/dx$ if n is an arbitrary real number?
6. If u and v are positive differentiable functions of x, how do you find $d(u^v)/dx$?

EXPLORER PROGRAM

PowerGrapher	Graphs all of the functions in this section (after you express them in terms of e^x and $\ln x$).

6.4 Exponential and Logarithmic Integrals; $\ln x = \int_1^x \frac{1}{t}\,dt$

The derivative formulas from the preceding sections have companion integral formulas, which we list in Table 6.5.

TABLE 6.5
Integration formulas

1.	$\int e^u\,du = e^u + C$	(1)
2.	$\int a^u\,du = \frac{a^u}{\ln a} + C$	(2)
3.	$\int \frac{1}{u}\,du = \ln\lvert u\rvert + C$	(3)

The only surprise in Table 6.5 is the presence of the absolute value bars in the formula for the integral of $1/u$. We need them, and they arise in the following way.

If u is a positive differentiable function of x, then $\ln u$ is defined, and reversing the formula

$$\frac{d}{dx}(\ln u) = \frac{1}{u}\cdot\frac{du}{dx} \tag{4}$$

gives

$$\int \frac{1}{u}\,du = \ln u + C, \qquad u > 0. \tag{5}$$

If u is negative instead of positive, we can rewrite

$$\int \frac{1}{u}\,du \qquad \text{as} \qquad \int \frac{1}{(-u)}\,d(-u). \tag{6}$$

With $-u$ *positive* (because $u < 0$), we then have

$$\int \frac{1}{(-u)}\,d(-u) = \ln(-u) + C. \qquad -u \text{ for } u \text{ in Eq. (5)} \tag{7}$$

So,

$$\int \frac{1}{u}\,du = \begin{cases} \ln u + C, & \text{if } u > 0 \\ \ln(-u) + C, & \text{if } u < 0. \end{cases} \tag{8}$$

Either way, the answer is $\ln\lvert u\rvert + C$, so

$$\int \frac{1}{u}\,du = \ln\lvert u\rvert + C. \tag{9}$$

This is what we have in Eq. (3).

EXAMPLE 1

a)
$$\begin{aligned}
\int e^{3x}\,dx &= \int e^u\cdot\frac{1}{3}\,du && u = 3x,\ \tfrac{1}{3}\,du = dx \\
&= \frac{1}{3}\int e^u\,du \\
&= \frac{1}{3}e^u + C && \text{Eq. (1)} \\
&= \frac{1}{3}e^{3x} + C && \text{Replace } u \text{ by } 3x.
\end{aligned}$$

b)
$$\begin{aligned}
\int_0^{\ln 2} e^{3x}\,dx &= \frac{1}{3}e^{3x}\Big]_0^{\ln 2} && \text{Antiderivative from Part (a)} \\
&= \frac{1}{3}[e^{3\ln 2} - e^0] \\
&= \frac{1}{3}[e^{\ln 8} - 1] && 3\ln 2 = \ln 2^3 = \ln 8 \\
&= \frac{1}{3}[8 - 1] = \frac{7}{3} && (e^{\ln 8} = 8)
\end{aligned}$$

EXAMPLE 2

$$\int_0^{\pi/2} e^{\sin x} \cos x \, dx = \int_0^1 e^u \, du \qquad \begin{array}{l} u = \sin x,\ du = \cos x\, dx \\ \text{When } x = 0,\ u = \sin 0 = 0. \\ \text{When } x = \pi/2,\ u = \sin(\pi/2) = 1. \end{array}$$

$$= e^u \Big]_0^1 = e^1 - e^0 = e - 1$$

EXAMPLE 3 Solve the following initial value problem for y as a function of t.

Differential equation: $\quad e^y \dfrac{dy}{dt} = 2t, \qquad t > \sqrt{3}$

Initial condition: $\quad y = 0 \quad \text{when} \quad t = 2$

Solution We integrate both sides of the differential equation with respect to t, obtaining

$$e^y = t^2 + C. \qquad \int \left(e^y \frac{dy}{dt}\right) dt = \int \frac{d}{dt}(e^y)\, dt = e^y$$

Next, we use the initial condition to determine C:

$$e^0 = (2)^2 + C, \qquad y = 0 \quad \text{when} \quad t = 2$$
$$C = 1 - 4 = -3$$

This completes the formula for e^y:

$$e^y = t^2 - 3. \tag{10}$$

To solve for y, we take logarithms of both sides:

$$\begin{aligned} \ln(e^y) &= \ln(t^2 - 3), \\ y &= \ln(t^2 - 3). \end{aligned} \tag{11}$$

Notice that the solution is valid for $t > \sqrt{3}$.

EXAMPLE 4

a) $\displaystyle\int 8^x \, dx = \frac{8^x}{\ln 8} + C \qquad$ Eq. (2) with $a = 8$ and $u = x$

b) $\displaystyle\int 5^{\cos x} \sin x \, dx = -\int 5^u \, du \qquad$ $u = \cos x,\ du = -\sin x\, dx$

$$= -\frac{5^u}{\ln 5} + C \qquad \text{Eq. (2) with } a = 5$$

$$= -\frac{5^{\cos x}}{\ln 5} + C \qquad u = \cos x$$

EXAMPLE 5

$$\int \frac{4 \cos \theta \, d\theta}{1 + 2 \sin \theta} = \int \frac{2\, du}{u} \qquad u = 1 + 2\sin\theta,\ du = 2\cos\theta\, d\theta$$

$$= 2 \ln |u| + C$$

$$= 2 \ln |1 + 2 \sin \theta| + C \qquad u = 1 + 2\sin\theta$$

EXAMPLE 6

$$\int_{-1}^{2} \frac{2x\,dx}{x^2 - 7} = \int_{-6}^{-3} \frac{du}{u} \qquad u = x^2 - 7,\ du = 2x\,dx$$

When $x = -1$, $u = (-1)^2 - 7 = -6$.
When $x = 2$, $u = (2)^2 - 7 = -3$.

$$= \ln |u| \Big]_{-6}^{-3}$$

$$= \ln |-3| - \ln |-6| = \ln 3 - \ln 6$$

$$= \ln (3/6) = \ln (1/2) = -\ln 2$$

EXAMPLE 7

$$\int \frac{\ln 7x}{x}\,dx = \int u\,du \qquad u = \ln 7x,\ du = d(\ln 7x) = \frac{1}{7x} \cdot d(7x) = \frac{1}{7x} \cdot 7\,dx = \frac{dx}{x}$$

$$= \frac{u^2}{2} + C$$

$$= \frac{(\ln 7x)^2}{2} + C \qquad u = \ln 7x$$

EXAMPLE 8

$$\int \frac{\log_2 x}{x}\,dx = \int \frac{\ln x}{\ln 2} \cdot \frac{dx}{x} \qquad \log_2 x = \frac{\ln x}{\ln 2}$$

$$= \frac{1}{\ln 2} \int u\,du \qquad u = \ln x,\ du = \frac{1}{x}\,dx$$

$$= \frac{1}{\ln 2} \cdot \frac{u^2}{2} + C$$

$$= \frac{(\ln x)^2}{2 \ln 2} + C \qquad u = \ln x$$

The Integrals of $\tan x$ and $\cot x$

Equation (3) shows how to integrate the tangent and cotangent functions (at last). For the tangent,

$$\int \tan x\,dx = \int \frac{\sin x}{\cos x}\,dx = \int \frac{-du}{u} \qquad u = \cos x,\ du = -\sin x\,dx$$

$$= -\int \frac{du}{u} = -\ln |u| + C \qquad \text{Eq. (3)}$$

$$= -\ln |\cos x| + C \qquad \text{Replace } u \text{ by } \cos x.$$

$$= \ln \left|\frac{1}{\cos x}\right| + C \qquad -\ln a = \ln \frac{1}{a}$$

$$= \ln |\sec x| + C.$$

The calculation for the cotangent is similar:

$$\int \cot x\,dx = \int \frac{\cos x}{\sin x}\,dx = \int \frac{du}{u} \qquad u = \sin x,\ du = \cos x\,dx$$

$$= \ln |u| + C = \ln |\sin x| + C.$$

The general formulas are these:

$$\int \tan u \, du = -\ln|\cos u| + C = \ln|\sec u| + C. \tag{12}$$

$$\int \cot u \, du = \ln|\sin u| + C = -\ln|\csc u| + C. \tag{13}$$

EXAMPLE 9

$$\int_0^{\pi/6} \tan 2x \, dx = \int_0^{\pi/3} \tan u \cdot \frac{du}{2}$$

$u = 2x$, $(du/2) = dx$
When $x = 0$, $u = 2(0) = 0$.
When $x = \pi/6$, $u = 2(\pi/6) = \pi/3$.

$$= \frac{1}{2}\int_0^{\pi/3} \tan u \, du$$

$$= \frac{1}{2} \ln|\sec u|\Big]_0^{\pi/3}$$ Eq. (12)

$$= \frac{1}{2}(\ln 2 - \ln 1) = \frac{1}{2}\ln 2$$

The Integral Formula for ln x

According to Eq. (3), if $x > 0$ then

$$\int_1^x \frac{1}{t}\,dt = \ln|t|\Big]_1^x = \ln|x| - \ln 1 = \ln x - 0 = \ln x. \tag{14}$$

Turning this around gives

$$\ln x = \int_1^x \frac{1}{t}\,dt, \qquad x > 0. \tag{15}$$

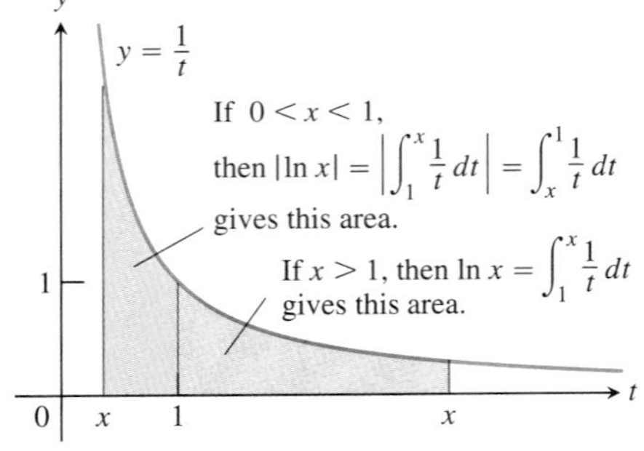

y
$y = \frac{1}{t}$
If $0 < x < 1$,
then $|\ln x| = \left|\int_1^x \frac{1}{t}\,dt\right| = \int_x^1 \frac{1}{t}\,dt$
gives this area.
If $x > 1$, then $\ln x = \int_1^x \frac{1}{t}\,dt$
gives this area.
1
0
x
1
x
t

6.18 $|\ln x|$ as an area.

This formula offers a practical way to estimate values of $\ln x$. For instance,

$$\ln 2 = \int_1^2 \frac{1}{t}\,dt. \tag{16}$$

Simpson's rule gives excellent results.

Equation (15) enables us to interpret $\ln x$ as an area if $x > 1$, and to interpret $|\ln x|$ as an area if $0 < x < 1$ (Fig. 6.18).

An Alternative Development of Exponentials and Logarithms

An alternative development of exponential and logarithmic functions introduces the equation

$$\ln x = \int_1^x \frac{1}{t}\,dt, \qquad x > 0 \tag{17}$$

at the beginning rather than the end. It proceeds directly from Part 1 of the Fundamental Theorem of Calculus to Eq. (17) as the *definition* of $\ln x$.

Starting with Eq. (17), we then see immediately that $\ln(1) = 0$ and that the first and second derivatives of $\ln x$ are $1/x$ and $-1/x^2$, respectively. This gives us complete information about the graph of $\ln x$, as in Chapter 4.

We then derive the arithmetic properties of $\ln x$ by looking at derivatives. For instance, the functions $\ln ax$ and $\ln x$, having the same derivative with respect to x, must differ by a constant, so that

$$\ln ax = \ln x + C. \tag{18}$$

Substituting $x = 1$ into this equation gives $\ln a = 0 + C$, which shows that C equals $\ln a$. Therefore,

$$\ln ax = \ln x + \ln a. \tag{19}$$

The function $\ln x$, $x > 0$, having a positive derivative, is one-to-one and therefore has an inverse, $\ln^{-1} x$. We define e to be the number $\ln^{-1} 1$. Then, after proving $\ln^{-1} ax = (\ln^{-1} a)^x$, we derive the equation $e^x = \ln^{-1} x$. After that it is smooth sailing again. We define a^x, $a > 0$, as $e^{x \ln a}$, and $\log_a x$ as the inverse of a^x.

The approach we have taken in the present book (exponentials first) and the approach we have just outlined ($\ln x$ first) both work well. One builds on our past experience with exponential functions. The other builds on our recent experience with the fundamental theorem.

Exercises 6.4

Evaluate the integrals in Exercises 1–20.

1. $\int (e^{3x} + 5e^{-x})\,dx$

2. $\int (2e^x - 3e^{-2x})\,dx$

3. $\int_{\ln 2}^{\ln 3} e^x\,dx$

4. $\int_{-\ln 2}^{0} e^{-x}\,dx$

5. $\int 8e^{(x+1)}\,dx$

6. $\int 2e^{(2x-1)}\,dx$

7. $\int_{\ln 4}^{\ln 9} e^{x/2}\,dx$

8. $\int_{0}^{\ln 16} e^{x/4}\,dx$

9. $\int \frac{e^{\sqrt{r}}}{\sqrt{r}}\,dr$

10. $\int \frac{e^{-\sqrt{r}}}{\sqrt{r}}\,dr$

11. $\int 2t\,e^{-t^2}\,dt$

12. $\int t^3 e^{(t^4)}\,dt$

13. $\int \frac{e^{1/x}}{x^2}\,dx$

14. $\int \frac{e^{-1/x^2}}{x^3}\,dx$

15. $\int_0^{\pi/4} (1 + e^{\tan\theta}) \sec^2\theta\,d\theta$

16. $\int_{\pi/4}^{\pi/2} (1 + e^{\cot\theta}) \csc^2\theta\,d\theta$

17. $\int e^{\sec \pi t} \sec \pi t \tan \pi t\,dt$

18. $\int e^{\csc(\pi + t)} \csc(\pi + t) \cot(\pi + t)\,dt$

19. $\int_{\ln(\pi/6)}^{\ln(\pi/2)} 2e^v \cos e^v\,dv$

20. $\int_0^{\sqrt{\ln \pi}} 2x\,e^{x^2} \cos(e^{x^2})\,dx$

Evaluate the integrals in Exercises 21–28.

21. $\int 5^x\,dx$

22. $\int (1.3)^x\,dx$

23. $\int_0^1 2^{-\theta}\,d\theta$

24. $\int_{-2}^{0} 5^{-\theta}\,d\theta$

25. $\int_1^{\sqrt{2}} x2^{(x^2)}\,dx$

26. $\int_1^4 \frac{2^{\sqrt{x}}}{\sqrt{x}}\,dx$

27. $\int_0^{\pi/2} 7^{\cos t} \sin t\,dt$

28. $\int_0^{\pi/4} \left(\frac{1}{3}\right)^{\tan t} \sec^2 t\,dt$

Evaluate the integrals in Exercises 29–50.

29. $\int_{-3}^{-2} \frac{dx}{x}$

30. $\int_{-9}^{-4} \frac{dx}{2x}$

31. $\int \frac{dx}{2x-5}$

32. $\int \frac{dx}{7x+8}$

33. $\int_{-1}^{0} \frac{3\,dt}{3t-2}$

34. $\int_{-1}^{0} \frac{dt}{2t+3}$

35. $\int \frac{2x\,dx}{x^2-25}$

36. $\int \frac{8x\,dx}{4x^2-5}$

37. $\int_0^{\pi} \frac{\sin\theta}{(\cos\theta)-2}\,d\theta$

38. $\int_0^{\pi/3} \frac{4\sin\theta}{1-4\cos\theta}\,d\theta$

39. $\int \frac{\ln x}{3x}\,dx$

40. $\int \frac{(\ln x)^2}{7x}\,dx$

41. $\int \frac{4}{x(\ln x)^2}\,dx$

42. $\int \frac{(\ln x)^{2/3}}{x}\,dx$

43. $\int_{-1}^{1} \frac{e^r}{1+e^r}\,dr$

44. $\int_0^{\ln 4} \frac{2e^s}{1+2e^s}\,ds$

45. $\int 5\tan\frac{\theta}{2}\,d\theta$

46. $\int 2\cot\frac{\theta}{3}\,d\theta$

47. $\int_{-1/2}^{-1/4} \pi\cot\pi x\,dx$

48. $\int_{5/6}^{1} \pi\tan\pi x\,dx$

49. $\int_{1/2}^{2/3} \tan\frac{\pi t}{2}\,dt$

50. $\int_2^3 \cot\frac{\pi t}{12}\,dt$

Evaluate the integrals in Exercises 51–58.

51. $\int \frac{\log_7 x}{x}\,dx$

52. $\int \frac{\log_5 x}{x}\,dx$

53. $\int_{1/10}^{10} \frac{\log_{10}(10x)}{x}\,dx$

54. $\int_0^9 \frac{2\log_{10}(x+1)}{x+1}\,dx$

55. $\int_0^2 \frac{[\log_2(x+2)]^2}{x+2}\,dx$

56. $\int_2^3 \frac{\sqrt{\log_2(x-1)}}{x-1}\,dx$

57. $\int \frac{dx}{x\log_{10} x}$

58. $\int \frac{dx}{x(\log_8 x)^2}$

Evaluate the integrals in Exercises 59–62.

59. $\int 3x^{\sqrt{3}}\,dx$

60. $\int x^{\sqrt{2}-1}\,dx$

61. $\int_0^3 (\sqrt{2}+1)\,x^{\sqrt{2}}\,dx$

62. $\int_1^e x^{(\ln 2)-1}\,dx$

Evaluate the integrals in Exercises 63–66.

63. $\int_1^{\ln x} \frac{1}{t}\,dt, \quad x>1$

64. $\int_1^{e^x} \frac{1}{t}\,dt$

65. $\int_1^{1/x} \frac{1}{t}\,dt, \quad x>0$

66. $\frac{1}{\ln a}\int_1^x \frac{1}{t}\,dt, \quad x>0$

Solve the initial value problems in Exercises 67–72.

67. Differential equation: $\frac{dy}{dx} = 1 + \frac{1}{x}, \quad x>0$

Initial condition: $y = 3$ when $x = 1$

68. Differential equation: $\frac{dy}{dx} = \frac{2x}{x^2+3}$

Initial condition: $y = \ln 2$ when $x = 1$

69. Differential equation: $\frac{dy}{dt} = e^t \sin(e^t - 2)$

Initial condition: $y = 0$ when $t = \ln 2$

70. Differential equation: $\frac{dy}{dt} = e^{-t}\sec^2(\pi e^{-t})$

Initial condition: $y = 2/\pi$ when $t = \ln 4$

71. Differential equation: $\frac{d^2y}{d\theta^2} = \sec^2\theta, \quad -\frac{\pi}{2} < \theta < \frac{\pi}{2}$

Initial conditions: $y = 0$ and $\frac{dy}{d\theta} = 1$ when $\theta = 0$

72. Differential equation: $\frac{d^2y}{d\theta^2} = \csc^2\theta, \quad 0 < \theta < \pi$

Initial conditions: $y = \frac{\pi}{2}$ and $\frac{dy}{d\theta} = 1$ when $\theta = \frac{\pi}{2}$

73. Find the area of the region between the curve $y = 2x/(1+x^2)$ and the interval $-2 \le x \le 2$ of the x-axis.

74. Find the area of the region between the curve $y = 2^{1-x}$ and the interval $-1 \le x \le 1$ of the x-axis.

75. ***Linearization of*** $\ln x$. Instead of approximating $\ln x$ near $x = 1$, we approximate $\ln(1+x)$ near $x = 0$. We get a simpler formula that way:

$$\ln(1+x) \approx x.$$

a) Show that the linearization of $f(x) = \ln(x+1)$ at $x = 0$ is $L(x) = x$.

b) Find the linearization of $g(x) = \ln x$ at $x = 1$.

c) Graph $f(x) = \ln(x+1)$ and $L(x) = x$ together for $0 \le x \le 0.1$. Where does the approximation of f by L seem to be best? Least good? Estimate to five decimal places the maximum error that you would incur if you were to replace $\ln(x+1)$ by x on this interval.

76. *Estimating Values of* $\ln x$ *with Simpson's Rule.* Although linearizations are good for replacing the logarithmic function over short intervals, when it comes to estimating *particular* values of $\ln x$, Simpson's rule is better.

As a case in point, the values of $\ln(1.2)$ and $\ln(0.8)$ to five places are

$$\ln(1.2) = 0.18232, \quad \ln(0.8) = -0.22314.$$

Estimate $\ln(1.2)$ and $\ln(0.8)$ first with the formula

$$\ln(1+x) \approx x.$$

Then use Simpson's rule with $n = 2$. (Impressive, isn't it?)

77. A body moves along a coordinate line with acceleration $d^2s/dt^2 = 4/(4-t)^2$. When $t = 0$, the body's velocity is 2 m/sec. Find the total distance traveled by the body from time $t = 1$ to $t = 2$ sec.

78. Show that, for any number $a > 1$,

$$\int_1^a \ln x\,dx + \int_0^{\ln a} e^y\,dy = a\ln a$$

(see Fig. 6.19).

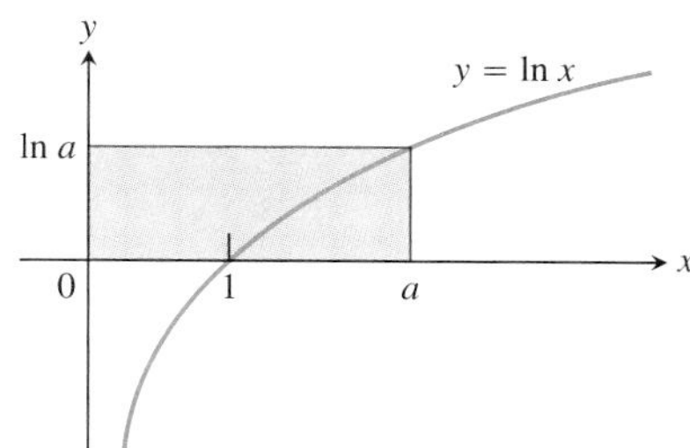

6.19 Figure for Exercise 78.

79. **a)** Show that $\int \ln x\, dx = x \ln x - x + C$.
b) Find the average value of $\ln x$ over $[1, e]$.

80. Find the average value of $f(x) = 1/x$ on $[1, 2]$.

Writing for Your Own Knowledge

Answer the following questions in writing. Some answers will take only a sentence or two; others may require several paragraphs. Some explanations may also call for graphs or sketches.

1. If $f(x)$ is differentiable and never zero for $a \le x \le b$, what is the value of
$$\int_a^b \frac{f'(x)}{f(x)}\, dx?$$
2. How do you integrate exponential functions?
3. How do you integrate the tangent and cotangent functions?
4. How can you estimate values of $\ln x$ with an integral?

EXPLORER PROGRAMS

Bisections, Secants, Newton	Solves equations numerically.
PowerGrapher	Graphs all functions in this section (after you rewrite them in terms of e^x and $\ln x$).

6.5 Growth and Decay

The Law of Exponential Change

To set the stage once again, suppose we are interested in a quantity y (velocity, temperature, electrical current, whatever) that increases or decreases at a rate that at any given time t is proportional to the amount present. If we also know the amount present at time $t = 0$, call it y_0, we can find y as a function of t by solving the initial value problem

$$\text{Differential equation:} \quad \frac{dy}{dt} = ky, \qquad (1)$$
$$\text{Initial condition:} \quad y = y_0 \quad \text{when} \quad t = 0.$$

If y is positive and increasing, then k is positive, and we use Eq. (1) to say that the rate of growth is proportional to what has already been accumulated. If y is positive and decreasing, then k is negative, and we use Eq. (1) to say that the rate of decay is proportional to the amount still left.

We see right away that the constant function $y = 0$ is a solution of Eq. (1). To find the nonzero solutions, we divide Eq. (1) by y:

$$\frac{1}{y} \cdot \frac{dy}{dt} = k$$
$$\ln|y| = kt + C \qquad \text{Integrate with respect to } t;\ \int (1/u)\,du = \ln|u| + C.$$
$$|y| = e^{kt+C} \qquad \text{Exponentiate.}$$
$$|y| = e^C \cdot e^{kt} \qquad e^{a+b} = e^a \cdot e^b$$
$$y = \pm e^C e^{kt} \qquad \text{If } |y| = r, \text{ then } y = \pm r.$$
$$y = Ae^{kt}. \qquad A \text{ is a more convenient name for } \pm e^C.$$

By allowing A to take on the value 0 in addition to all possible values $\pm e^C$, we can include the solution $y = 0$ in the formula.

We find the right value of A for the initial value problem by solving for A when $y = y_0$ and $t = 0$:

$$y_0 = Ae^{k \cdot 0} = A.$$

The solution of the initial value problem is therefore $y = y_0 e^{kt}$.

The Law of Exponential Change

$$y = y_0 e^{kt} \tag{2}$$

Growth: $k > 0$ Decay: $k < 0$

The number k is the **rate constant** of the equation.

The derivation of Eq. (2) explains why the only functions that are their own derivatives are constant multiples of the exponential function. The equation $dy/dt = y$ is Eq. (1) with $k = 1$. With $k = 1$, the solutions are all given by the formula $y = y_0 e^t$.

Population Growth

Strictly speaking, the number of individuals in a population (of people, plants, foxes, or bacteria, for example) is a discontinuous function of time because it takes on discrete values. However, as soon as the number of individuals becomes large enough, it may safely be described with a continuous or even differentiable function. If we assume that the proportion of reproducing individuals remains constant and assume a constant fertility, then at any instant t the birth rate is proportional to the number $y(t)$ of individuals present. If, further, we neglect departures, arrivals, and deaths, the growth rate dy/dt will be the same as the birth rate ky. In other words, $dy/dt = ky$, so that $y = y_0 e^{kt}$. As with all kinds of growth, there may be limitations imposed by the surrounding environment, but we will not go into these here.

EXAMPLE 1 Let us return to the disease eradication example (Example 4) from Section 6.1. We supposed that in the course of any given year the number y of cases worldwide is reduced by 20%. There are 10,000 known cases today, and we want to know how long it will be before the number of cases is reduced to 1000.

Solution As before, we use the equation $y = y_0 e^{kt}$, and there are three things to find:

1. the value of y_0,
2. the value of k,
3. the value of t that makes $y = 1000$.

STEP 1: *The value of* y_0. We are free to count time beginning anywhere we want. If we count from today, then $y = 10{,}000$ when $t = 0$, so $y_0 = 10{,}000$. Our equation is now

$$y = 10{,}000\, e^{kt}. \tag{3}$$

So far, this is no different from what we did in Section 6.1. What is new is the way we determine the values of k and t in the next two steps. In Section 6.1 we had to resort to graphical solutions. But now we can use logarithms, and to better effect.

STEP 2: *The value of k.* When $t = 1$ year, the number of cases will be 80% of its present value, or 8000. Hence,

$$10{,}000\, e^{k \cdot 1} = 8000 \qquad \text{Eq. (3) with } t = 1 \text{ and } y = 8000$$
$$e^k = 0.8$$
$$\ln (e^k) = \ln 0.8 \qquad \text{Take logarithms of both sides.}$$
$$k = \ln 0.8.$$

At any given time t, therefore,

$$y = 10{,}000\, e^{(\ln 0.8)t}. \tag{4}$$

STEP 3: *The value of t that makes* $y = 1000$. We set y in Eq. (4) equal to 1000 and solve for t:

$$10{,}000\, e^{(\ln 0.8)t} = 1000$$
$$e^{(\ln 0.8)t} = 0.1$$
$$(\ln 0.8)t = \ln 0.1 \qquad \text{Logs of both sides}$$
$$t = \frac{\ln 0.1}{\ln 0.8} \approx 10.32 \text{ years.}$$

It will take a little more than 10 years to reduce the number of cases to 1000.

Continuously Compounded Interest

If you invest an amount A_0 of money at a fixed annual interest rate r (expressed as a decimal) and if interest is added to your account k times a year, it turns out that the amount of money you will have at the end of t years is

$$A_t = A_0 \left(1 + \frac{r}{k}\right)^{kt}. \tag{5}$$

The interest might be added ("compounded," bankers say) monthly ($k = 12$), weekly ($k = 52$), daily ($k = 365$), or even more frequently, say by the hour or by the minute. But there is still a limit to how much you will earn that way, and the limit is

$$\lim_{k \to \infty} A_t = \lim_{k \to \infty} A_0 \left(1 + \frac{r}{k}\right)^{kt} = A_0\, e^{rt}. \tag{6}$$

The resulting formula for the amount of money in your account after t years is $A(t) = A_0\, e^{rt}$.

Finding the limit

$$\lim_{k \to \infty} A_0 \left(1 + \frac{r}{k}\right)^{kt}$$

in Eq. (6) involves what is called an indeterminate form. In Section 6.6, you will see how to find limits of this type. Then in Exercise 57 of Section 6.6, you will be asked to verify that the limit in Eq. (6) is $A_0\, e^{rt}$.

The Continuous Compound Interest Formula

$$A(t) = A_0\, e^{rt} \tag{7}$$

Interest paid according to this formula is said to be **compounded continuously.** The number r is called the **continuous interest rate.**

EXAMPLE 2 Suppose you deposit \$621 in a bank account that pays 6% compounded continuously. How much money will you have 8 years later?

Solution We use Eq. (7) with $A_0 = 621$, $r = 0.06$, and $t = 8$:

$$A(8) = 621\, e^{(0.06)(8)} = 621\, e^{0.48} = 1003.58 \qquad \text{Nearest cent}$$

Had the bank paid interest quarterly ($k = 4$ in Eq. (5)), the amount in your account would have been \$1000.01. Thus the effect of continuous compounding, as compared with quarterly compounding, has been an addition of \$3.57. A bank might decide it would be worth this additional amount to be able to advertise, "We compound interest every second, night and day—better yet, we compound the interest continuously."

Radioactivity

When an atom emits some of its mass as radiation, the remainder of the atom reforms to make an atom of some new element. This process of radiation and change is called **radioactive decay,** and an element whose atoms go spontaneously through this process is called **radioactive.** Thus, radioactive carbon-14 decays into nitrogen; radium, through a number of intervening radioactive steps, decays into lead.

For radon-222 gas, t is measured in days and $k = 0.18$. For radium-226, which used to be painted on watch dials to make them glow at night (a dangerous practice), t is measured in years and $k = 4.3 \times 10^{-2}$. The decay of radium in the earth's crust is the source of the radon we sometimes find in our basements.

Experiments have shown that at any given time the rate at which a radioactive element decays (as measured by the number of nuclei that change per unit time) is approximately proportional to the number of radioactive nuclei present. Thus, the decay of a radioactive element is described by the equation $dy/dt = -ky$, $k > 0$. If y_0 is the number of radioactive nuclei present at time zero, the number still present at any later time t will be $y = y_0\, e^{-kt}$.

It is conventional to use $-k\ (k > 0)$ here instead of $k\ (k < 0)$ to emphasize that y is decreasing.

Radioactive Decay Equation

$$y = y_0\, e^{-kt}, \qquad k > 0 \tag{8}$$

EXAMPLE 3 *Half-life.* The **half-life** of a radioactive element is the time required for half of the radioactive nuclei present in a sample to decay. It is a remarkable fact that the half-life is a constant that does not depend on the number of radioactive nuclei initially present in the sample.

To see why, let y_0 be the number of radioactive nuclei initially present in the sample. Then the number y present at any later time t will be $y = y_0\, e^{-kt}$. We seek the value of t at which the number of radioactive nuclei present equals half the original number:

$$y_0\, e^{-kt} = \frac{1}{2} y_0$$

$$e^{-kt} = \frac{1}{2}$$

$$-kt = \ln \frac{1}{2} = -\ln 2 \qquad \text{Reciprocal Rule for logarithms}$$

$$t = \frac{\ln 2}{k}$$

This value of t is the half-life of the element. It depends only on the value of k; the number y_0 does not enter in.

$$\text{Half-life} = \frac{\ln 2}{k} \qquad (9)$$

EXAMPLE 4 *Polonium-210.* The effective radioactive lifetime of polonium-210 is so short we measure it in days rather than years. The number of radioactive atoms remaining after t days in a sample that starts with y_0 radioactive atoms is

$$y = y_0\, e^{-4.95 \times 10^{-3} t}.$$

Find the element's half-life.

Solution

$$\begin{aligned} \text{Half-life} &= \frac{\ln 2}{k} && \text{Eq. (9)} \\ &= \frac{\ln 2}{4.95 \times 10^{-3}} && \text{The } k \text{ from polonium's decay equation} \\ &\approx 140 \text{ days} \end{aligned}$$

EXAMPLE 5 *Carbon-14.* People who do carbon-14 dating use a figure of 5700 years for its half-life (more about carbon-14 dating in the exercises). Find the age of a sample in which 10% of the radioactive nuclei originally present have decayed.

Solution We use the decay equation $y = y_0\, e^{-kt}$. There are two things to find:

1. the value of k,
2. the value of t when $y_0\, e^{-kt} = 0.9\, y_0$, or $e^{-kt} = 0.9$ (90% of the radioactive nuclei still present)

STEP 1: *The value of k.* We use the half-life equation:

$$k = \frac{\ln 2}{\text{half-life}} = \frac{\ln 2}{5700} \qquad (\text{about } 1.2 \times 10^{-4})$$

STEP 2: *The value of t that makes $e^{-kt} = 0.9$.*

$$\begin{aligned} e^{-kt} &= 0.9 \\ e^{-(\ln 2/5700)t} &= 0.9 \\ -\frac{\ln 2}{5700}\, t &= \ln 0.9 && \text{Logs of both sides} \\ t &= -\frac{5700 \ln 0.9}{\ln 2} \approx 866 \text{ years.} \end{aligned}$$

The sample is about 866 years old.

Carbon-14 Dating

The half-lives of radioactive elements can sometimes be used to date events from the Earth's past. The ages of rocks more than 2 billion years old have been measured by the extent of the radioactive decay of uranium (half-life 4.5 billion years!). In a living organism, the ratio of radioactive carbon, carbon-14, to ordinary carbon stays fairly constant during the lifetime of the organism, being approximately equal to the ratio in the organism's surroundings at the time. After the organism's death, however, no new carbon is ingested, and the proportion of carbon-14 in the organism's remains decreases as the carbon-14 decays. Since the half-life of carbon-14 is known to be about 5700 years, it is possible to estimate the age of organic remains by comparing the proportion of carbon-14 they contain with the proportion assumed to have been in the organism's environment at the time it lived. Archeologists have dated shells (which contain $CaCO_3$), seeds, and wooden artifacts this way. The estimate of 15,500 years for the age of the cave paintings at Lascaux, France, is based on carbon-14 dating. After generations of controversy, the Shroud of Turin, long believed by many to be the burial cloth of Christ, was shown by carbon-14 dating in 1988 to have been made after 1200 A.D.

Heat Transfer: Newton's Law of Cooling

Soup left in a tin cup cools to the temperature of the surrounding air. A hot silver ingot immersed in water cools to the temperature of the surrounding water. In situations like these, the rate at which an object's temperature is changing at any given time is roughly proportional to the difference between its temperature and the temperature of the surrounding medium. This observation is called **Newton's law of cooling,** although it applies to warming as well, and there is an equation for it.

If T is the temperature of the object at time t, and T_S is the surrounding temperature, then

$$\frac{dT}{dt} = -k(T - T_S). \tag{10}$$

If we substitute y for $(T - T_S)$ then

$$\begin{aligned} \frac{dy}{dt} &= \frac{d}{dt}(T - T_S) = \frac{dT}{dt} - \frac{d}{dt}(T_S) \\ &= \frac{dT}{dt} - 0 \qquad T_S \text{ is a constant.} \\ &= \frac{dT}{dt} \end{aligned} \tag{11}$$

In terms of y, Eq. (10) therefore reads

$$\frac{dy}{dt} = -ky, \tag{12}$$

and we know that the solution to this differential equation is

$$y = y_0\, e^{-kt}.$$

Thus,

$$T - T_S = (T_0 - T_S)e^{-kt}, \tag{13}$$

where T_0 is the value of T at time zero.

Newton's Law of Cooling

$$T = T_S + (T_0 - T_S)e^{-kt} \tag{14}$$

EXAMPLE 6 A hard-boiled egg at 98°C is put in a sink of 18°C water. After 5 minutes, the egg's temperature is 38°C. Assuming that the water has not warmed appreciably, how much longer will it take the egg to reach 20°C?

Solution We find how long it would take the egg to cool from 98°C to 20°C and subtract the 5 minutes that have already elapsed.

According to Eq. (14), the egg's temperature t minutes after it is put in the sink is

$$T = 18 + (98 - 18)e^{-kt} = 18 + 80e^{-kt}.$$

To find k, we use the information that $T = 38$ when $t = 5$:

$$38 = 18 + 80e^{-5k}$$

$$e^{-5k} = \frac{1}{4}$$

$$-5k = \ln\frac{1}{4} = -\ln 4$$

$$k = \frac{1}{5}\ln 4 = 0.2\ln 4 \qquad \text{(about 0.28).}$$

The egg's temperature at time t is $T = 18 + 80e^{-(0.2\ln 4)t}$. Now find the time t when $T = 20$:

$$20 = 18 + 80e^{-(0.2\ln 4)t}$$

$$80e^{-(0.2\ln 4)t} = 2$$

$$e^{-(0.2\ln 4)t} = \frac{1}{40}$$

$$-(0.2\ln 4)t = \ln\frac{1}{40} = -\ln 40$$

$$t = \frac{\ln 40}{0.2\ln 4} \approx 13 \text{ min.}$$

The egg's temperature will reach 20°C about 13 min after it is put in water to cool. Since it took 5 min to reach 38° C, it will take about 8 min more to reach 20°C.

Exercises 6.5

The answers to most of the following exercises are in terms of logarithms and exponentials. A calculator can be helpful, enabling you to express the answers in decimal form.

1. *Human Evolution Continues.* The analysis of tooth shrinkage by C. Loring Brace and colleagues at the University of Michigan's Museum of Anthropology indicates that human tooth size is continuing to decrease and that the evolutionary process did not come to a halt some 30,000 years ago as many scientists contend. In northern Europeans, for example, tooth size reduction now has a rate of 1% per 1000 years.

a) If t represents time in years and y represents tooth size, use the condition that $y = 0.99y_0$ when $t = 1000$ to find the value of k in the equation $y = y_0 e^{kt}$. Then use this value of k to answer the following questions.

b) In about how many years will human teeth be 90% of their present size?

c) What will be our descendants' tooth size 20,000 years from now (as a percentage of our present tooth size)?

(Source: *LSA Magazine,* Spring 1989, Vol. 12, No. 2, p. 19, Ann Arbor, MI.)

2. *Atmospheric Pressure.* The earth's atmospheric pressure p is often modeled by assuming that the rate dp/dh at which p changes with the altitude h above sea level is proportional to p. Suppose that the pressure at sea level is 1013 millibars (about 14.7 pounds per square inch) and that the pressure at an altitude of 20 km is 90 millibars.

a) Solve the initial value problem

Differential equation: $dp/dh = kp$ (k a constant)

Initial condition: $p = p_0$ when $h = 0$

to express p in terms of h. Determine the values of p_0 and k from the given altitude–pressure data.

b) What is the atmospheric pressure at $h = 50$ km?

c) At what altitude does the pressure equal 900 millibars?

3. *First Order Chemical Reactions.* In some chemical reactions, the rate at which the amount of a substance changes with time is proportional to the amount present. For the change of δ-glucono lactone into gluconic acid, for example,

$$\frac{dy}{dt} = -0.6y$$

when t is measured in hours. If there are 100 grams of δ-glucono lactone present when $t = 0$, how many grams will be left after the first hour?

4. *The Inversion of Sugar.* The processing of raw sugar has a step called "inversion" that changes the sugar's molecular structure. Once the process has begun, the rate of change of the amount of raw sugar is proportional to the amount of raw sugar remaining. If 1000 kg of raw sugar reduces to 800 kg of raw sugar during the first 10 hours, how much raw sugar will remain after another 14 hours?

5. *Working Underwater.* The intensity $L(x)$ of light x feet beneath the surface of the ocean satisfies the differential equation

$$\frac{dL}{dx} = -kL.$$

As a diver, you know from experience that diving to 18 ft in the Caribbean Sea cuts the intensity in half. You cannot work without artificial light when the intensity falls below one-tenth of the surface value. About how deep can you expect to work without artificial light?

6. *Voltage in a Discharging Capacitor.* Suppose that electricity is draining from a capacitor at a rate that is proportional to the voltage V across its terminals and that, if t is measured in seconds,

$$\frac{dV}{dt} = -\frac{1}{40}V.$$

Solve this equation for V, using V_0 to denote the value of V when $t = 0$. How long will it take the voltage to drop to 10% of its original value?

7. *Cholera Bacteria.* Suppose that the bacteria in a colony can grow unchecked, by the law of exponential change. The colony starts with 1 bacterium and doubles every half hour. How many bacteria will the colony contain at the end of 24 h? (Under favorable laboratory conditions, the number of cholera bacteria can double every 30 min. In an infected person, many bacteria are destroyed, but this example helps explain why a person who feels well in the morning may be dangerously ill by evening.)

8. *Growth of Bacteria.* A colony of bacteria is grown under ideal conditions in a laboratory so that the population increases exponentially with time. At the end of 3 h there are 10,000 bacteria. At the end of 5 h there are 40,000. How many bacteria were present initially?

9. *The Incidence of a Disease (Continuation of Example 1).* Suppose that in any given year the number of cases can be reduced by 25% instead of 20%.

   a) How long will it take to reduce the number of cases to 1000?
   b) How long will it take to eradicate the disease, that is, reduce the number of cases to less than 1?

10. *The U.S. Population.* The Museum of Science in Boston displays a running total of the U.S. population. On May 11, 1993, the total was increasing at the rate of 1 person every 14 sec. The displayed population figure for 3:45 P.M. that day was 257,313,431.

   a) Assuming exponential growth at a constant rate, find the rate constant for the population's growth (people per 365-day year).
   b) At this rate, what will the U.S. population be at 3:45 P.M. Boston time on April 10, 2001?

11. *Oil Depletion.* Suppose the amount of oil pumped from one of the canyon wells in Whittier, California, decreases at the continuous rate of 10% per year. When will the well's output fall to one-fifth of its present value?

12. *Continuous Price Discounting.* To encourage buyers to place 100-unit orders, your firm's sales department applies a continuous discount that makes the unit price a function $p(x)$ of the number of units x ordered. The discount decreases the price at the rate of \$0.01 per unit ordered. The price per unit for a 100-unit order is $p(100) = \$20.09$.

   a) Find $p(x)$ by solving the following initial value problem:

   Differential equation: $\dfrac{dp}{dx} = -\dfrac{1}{100}p,$

   Initial condition: $p(100) = 20.09.$

   b) Find the unit price $p(10)$ for a 10-unit order and the unit price $p(90)$ for a 90-unit order.
   c) The sales department has asked you to find out if it is discounting so much that the firm's revenue, $r(x) = x \cdot p(x)$, will actually be less for a 100-unit order than, say, for a 90-unit order. Reassure them by showing that r has its maximum value at $x = 100$.
   d) Graph the revenue function $r(x) = xp(x)$ for $0 \le x \le 200$.

13. *Continuously Compounded Interest.* You have just placed A_0 dollars in a bank account that pays 4% interest, compounded continuously.

   a) How much money will you have in the account in 5 years?
   b) How long will it take your money to double? to triple?

14. *John Napier's Question.* John Napier (1550–1617), the Scottish laird who invented logarithms, was the first person to answer the question: What happens if you invest an amount of money at 100% interest, compounded continuously?

   a) What does happen?
   b) How long does it take to triple your money?
   c) How much can you earn in a year?

   Give reasons for your answers.

15. *Benjamin Franklin's Will.* The Franklin Technical Institute of Boston owes its existence to a provision in a codicil to Benjamin Franklin's will. In part the codicil reads:

> I wish to be useful even after my Death, if possible, in forming and advancing other young men that may be serviceable to their Country in both Boston and Philadelphia. To this end I devote Two thousand Pounds Sterling, which I give, one thousand thereof to the Inhabitants of the Town of Boston in Massachusetts, and the other thousand to the

> inhabitants of the City of Philadelphia, in Trust and for the Uses, Interests and Purposes hereinafter mentioned and declared.

Franklin's plan was to lend money to young apprentices at 5% interest with the provision that each borrower should pay each year along

> . . . with the yearly Interest, one tenth part of the Principal, which sums of Principal and Interest shall be again let to fresh Borrowers. . . . If this plan is executed and succeeds as projected without interruption for one hundred Years, the Sum will then be one hundred and thirty-one thousand Pounds of which I would have the Managers of the Donation to the Inhabitants of the Town of Boston, then lay out at their discretion one hundred thousand Pounds in Public Works. . . . The remaining thirty-one thousand Pounds, I would have continued to be let out on Interest in the manner above directed for another hundred Years. . . . At the end of this second term if no unfortunate accident has prevented the operation the sum will be Four Millions and Sixty-one Thousand Pounds.

It was not always possible to find as many borrowers as Franklin had planned, but the managers of the trust did the best they could. At the end of 100 years from the reception of the Franklin gift, in January 1894, the fund had grown from 1000 pounds to almost exactly 90,000 pounds. In 100 years the original capital had multiplied about 90 times instead of the 131 times Franklin had imagined.

What rate of interest, compounded continuously for 100 years, would have multiplied Benjamin Franklin's original capital by 90?

16. *Continuation of Exercise 15.* In Benjamin Franklin's estimate that the original 1000 pounds would grow to 131,000 in 100 years, he was using an annual rate of 5% and compounding once each year. What rate of interest per year when compounded continuously for 100 years would multiply the original amount by 131?

17. *Radon-222.* The decay equation for radon-222 gas is $y = y_0 e^{-0.18t}$, with t in days. About how long will it take the radon in a sealed sample of air to fall to 90% of its original value?

18. *Polonium-210.* The half-life of polonium is 140 days, but your sample will not be useful to you after 95% of the radioactive nuclei present on the day the sample arrives has disintegrated. For about how many days after the sample arrives will you be able to use the polonium?

19. *The Mean Life of a Radioactive Nucleus.* Physicists using the radioactivity equation $y = y_0 e^{-kt}$ call the number $1/k$ the *mean life* of a radioactive nucleus. The mean life of a radon nucleus is about $1/0.18 = 5.6$ days. The mean life of a carbon-14 nucleus is more than 8000 years. Show that 95% of the radioactive nuclei originally present in a sample will disintegrate within three mean lifetimes, i.e., by time $t = 3/k$. Thus, the mean life of a nucleus gives a quick way to estimate how long the radioactivity of a sample will last.

20. *Californium-252.* What costs $27 million per gram and can be used to treat brain cancer, analyze coal for its sulfur content, and detect explosives in luggage? The answer is Californium-252, a radioactive isotope so rare that only 8 g of it have been made in the western world since its discovery by Glenn Seaborg in 1950. The half-life of the isotope is 2,645 years—long enough for a useful service life and short enough to have a high radioactivity per unit mass. One microgram of the isotope releases 170 million neutrons per second.

a) What is the value of k in the decay equation for this isotope?
b) What is the isotope's mean life? (See Exercise 19.)
c) How long will it take 95% of a sample's radioactive nuclei to disintegrate?

21. *Cooling Soup.* Suppose that a cup of soup cooled from 90°C to 60°C after 10 minutes in a room whose temperature was 20°C. Use Newton's law of cooling to answer the following questions.

a) How much longer would it take the soup to cool to 35°C?
b) Instead of being left to stand in the room, the cup of 90°C soup is put in a freezer whose temperature is −15°C. How long will it take the soup to cool from 90°C to 35°C?

22. *A Beam of Unknown Temperature.* An aluminum beam was brought from the outside cold into a machine shop where the temperature was held at 65°. After 10 minutes, the beam had warmed to 35°F and after another 10 minutes it was 50°F. Use Newton's law of cooling to estimate the beam's initial temperature.

23. *Surrounding Medium of Unknown Temperature.* A pan of warm water (46°C) was put in a refrigerator. Ten minutes later, the water's temperature was 39°C; 10 minutes after that, it was 33°C. Use Newton's law of cooling to estimate how cold the refrigerator was.

24. *Silver Cooling in Air.* The temperature of an ingot of silver is 60°C above room temperature right now. Twenty minutes ago, it was 70°C above room temperature. How far above room temperature will the silver be

a) 15 minutes from now?
b) Two hours from now?
c) When will the silver be 10°C above room temperature?

25. *The Age of Crater Lake.* The charcoal from a tree killed in the volcanic eruption that formed Crater Lake in Oregon contained 44.5% of the carbon-14 found in living matter. About how old is Crater Lake?

26. *The Sensitivity of Carbon-14 Dating to Measurement.* To see the effect of a relatively small error in the estimate of the amount of carbon-14 in a sample being dated, consider this hypothetical situation:

a) A fossilized bone found in central Illinois in the year 2000 A.D. contains 17% of its original carbon-14 content. Estimate the year the animal died.
b) Repeat (a) assuming 18% instead of 17%.
c) Repeat (a) assuming 16% instead of 17%.

27. *Art Forgery.* A painting attributed to Vermeer (1632–1675), which should contain no more than 96.2% of its original carbon-14, contains 99.5% instead. About how old is the forgery?

Writing for Your Own Knowledge

Answer the following questions in writing. Some answers will take only a sentence or two; others may require several paragraphs. Some explanations may also call for graphs or sketches.

1. What is the law of exponential change? Where does it come from?
2. What does it mean for interest to be compounded continuously?
3. What is the half-life of a radioactive element? Why might we want to know a radioactive element's half-life?
4. What is Newton's law of cooling?

EXPLORER PROGRAM

PowerGrapher — Graphs exponential functions.

6.6 *L'Hôpital's Rule*

In the late seventeenth century, John Bernoulli discovered a rule for calculating limits of fractions whose numerators and denominators both approach zero. The rule is known today as **l'Hôpital's rule,** after Guillaume Francois Antoine de l'Hôpital (1661–1704), Marquis de St. Mesme, a French nobleman who wrote the first introductory differential calculus text, where the rule first appeared in print.

Indeterminate Quotients

If functions $f(x)$ and $g(x)$ are both zero at $x = a$, then $\lim_{x\to a} f(x)/g(x)$ cannot be found by substituting $x = a$. The substitution produces 0/0, a meaningless expression known as an **indeterminate form.** Our experience so far has been that limits that lead to indeterminate forms may or may not be hard to find. It took a lot of work to find $\lim_{x\to 0} (\sin x)/x$ in Section 2.3. But we have had remarkable success with the limit

$$f'(a) = \lim_{x\to a} \frac{f(x) - f(a)}{x - a}$$

from which we calculate derivatives, which always produces 0/0. L'Hôpital's rule enables us to draw on our success with derivatives to evaluate limits that lead to indeterminate forms.

THEOREM 2

L'Hôpital's Rule (First Form)

Suppose that $f(a) = g(a) = 0$, that $f'(a)$ and $g'(a)$ exist, and that $g'(a) \neq 0$. Then

$$\lim_{x\to a} \frac{f(x)}{g(x)} = \frac{f'(a)}{g'(a)}. \tag{1}$$

Proof Working backward from $f'(a)$ and $g'(a)$, which are themselves limits, we have

$$\frac{f'(a)}{g'(a)} = \frac{\displaystyle\lim_{x\to a} \frac{f(x)-f(a)}{x-a}}{\displaystyle\lim_{x\to a} \frac{g(x)-g(a)}{x-a}} = \lim_{x\to a} \frac{\dfrac{f(x)-f(a)}{x-a}}{\dfrac{g(x)-g(a)}{x-a}}$$

$$= \lim_{x\to a} \frac{f(x)-f(a)}{g(x)-g(a)}$$

$$= \lim_{x\to a} \frac{f(x)-0}{g(x)-0}$$

$$= \lim_{x\to a} \frac{f(x)}{g(x)}.$$

■

EXAMPLE 1

Caution: To apply l'Hôpital's rule to f/g, divide the derivative of f by the derivative of g. Do not fall into the trap of taking the derivative of f/g. The quotient to use is f'/g', not $(f/g)'$.

a) $\displaystyle\lim_{x\to 0} \frac{3x - \sin x}{x} = \frac{3 - \cos x}{1}\bigg|_{x=0} = 2$

b) $\displaystyle\lim_{x\to 0} \frac{\sqrt{1+x} - 1}{x} = \frac{\dfrac{1}{2\sqrt{1+x}}}{1}\Bigg|_{x=0} = \frac{1}{2}$

c) $\displaystyle\lim_{x\to 0} \frac{x - \sin x}{x^3} = \frac{1 - \cos x}{3x^2}\bigg|_{x=0} = ?$ Still $\frac{0}{0}$ ■

What can we do about the limit in Example 1(c)? A stronger form of l'Hôpital's rule says that whenever the rule gives 0/0 we can apply it again, repeating the process until we get a different result. With this stronger rule we get

$$\lim_{x\to 0} \frac{x - \sin x}{x^3} = \lim_{x\to 0} \frac{1 - \cos x}{3x^2} \qquad \text{Still } \tfrac{0}{0}\text{; apply the rule again.}$$

$$= \lim_{x\to 0} \frac{\sin x}{6x} \qquad \text{Still } \tfrac{0}{0}\text{; apply the rule again.}$$

$$= \lim_{x\to 0} \frac{\cos x}{6} = \frac{1}{6}. \qquad \text{A different result. Stop.}$$

THEOREM 3

L'Hôpital's Rule (Stronger Form)

Suppose that $f(a) = g(a) = 0$ and that f and g are differentiable on an open interval containing a. Suppose also that $g'(x) \neq 0$ if $x \neq a$. Then

$$\lim_{x\to a} \frac{f(x)}{g(x)} = \lim_{x\to a} \frac{f'(x)}{g'(x)}, \tag{2}$$

if the limit on the right exists (or is ∞ or $-\infty$).

A Misnamed Rule and the First Differential Calculus Text

In 1694 John Bernoulli agreed to accept a retainer of 300 pounds per year from his former student l'Hôpital to solve problems for him and keep him up to date on calculus. One of the problems was the so-called 0/0 problem, which Bernoulli solved as agreed. When l'Hôpital published his notes on calculus in book form in 1696, the 0/0 rule appeared as a theorem. L'Hôpital acknowledged his debt to Bernoulli and, to avoid claiming authorship of the book's entire contents, had the book published anonymously. Bernoulli nevertheless accused l'Hôpital of plagiarism, an accusation inadvertently supported after l'Hôpital's death in 1704 by the publisher's promotion of the book as l'Hôpital's. By 1721, Bernoulli, a man so jealous he once threw his son Daniel out of the house for accepting a mathematics prize from the French Academy of Sciences, claimed to have been the author of the entire work. As puzzling and fickle as ever, history accepted Bernoulli's claim (until recently), but still named the rule after l'Hôpital.

EXAMPLE 2

$$\lim_{x\to 0}\frac{\sqrt{1+x}-1-(x/2)}{x^2} \qquad \frac{0}{0}$$

$$= \lim_{x\to 0}\frac{(1/2)(1+x)^{-1/2}-(1/2)}{2x} \qquad \text{Still } \frac{0}{0}$$

$$= \lim_{x\to 0}\frac{-(1/4)(1+x)^{-3/2}}{2} = -\frac{1}{8} \qquad \text{Not } \frac{0}{0}\text{; limit is found.}$$

When you apply l'Hôpital's rule, look for a change from 0/0 to something else. This is where the limit is revealed.

EXAMPLE 3

$$\lim_{x\to 0}\frac{1-\cos x}{x+x^2} \qquad \frac{0}{0}$$

$$= \lim_{x\to 0}\frac{\sin x}{1+2x} = \frac{0}{1} = 0 \qquad \text{Not } \frac{0}{0}\text{; limit is found.}$$

If we continue to differentiate in an attempt to apply l'Hôpital's rule once more, we get

$$\lim_{x\to 0}\frac{1-\cos x}{x+x^2} = \lim_{x\to 0}\frac{\sin x}{1+2x} = \lim_{x\to 0}\frac{\cos x}{2} = \frac{1}{2},$$

which is wrong.

EXAMPLE 4

$$\lim_{x\to 0^+}\frac{\sin x}{x^2} \qquad \frac{0}{0}$$

$$= \lim_{x\to 0^+}\frac{\cos x}{2x} = \infty \qquad \text{Not } \frac{0}{0}\text{; limit is found.}$$

L'Hôpital's rule also applies to quotients that lead to the indeterminate form ∞/∞. If $f(x)$ and $g(x)$ both approach infinity as $x \to a$, then

$$\lim_{x\to a}\frac{f(x)}{g(x)} = \lim_{x\to a}\frac{f'(x)}{g'(x)},$$

provided the latter limit exists. The a here may itself be either finite or infinite.

EXAMPLE 5

a) $$\lim_{x\to(\pi/2)^-}\frac{\tan x}{1+\tan x} \qquad \frac{\infty}{\infty}$$

$$= \lim_{x\to(\pi/2)^-}\frac{\sec^2 x}{\sec^2 x} = \lim_{x\to(\pi/2)^-} 1 = 1$$

b) $$\lim_{x\to\infty}\frac{x-2x^2}{3x^2+5} = \lim_{x\to\infty}\frac{1-4x}{6x} = \lim_{x\to\infty}\frac{-4}{6} = -\frac{2}{3}$$

Indeterminate Products and Differences

We can sometimes handle the indeterminate forms $0 \cdot \infty$ and $\infty - \infty$ by using algebra to get $0/0$ or ∞/∞ instead. Here again, we do not mean to suggest that there is a number $0 \cdot \infty$ or $\infty - \infty$ any more than we mean to suggest that there is a number $0/0$ or ∞/∞. These forms are not numbers but descriptions of function behavior.

EXAMPLE 6

$$\lim_{x \to 0^+} x \cot x \qquad 0 \cdot \infty;\text{ rewrite } x \cot x.$$

$$= \lim_{x \to 0^+} x \cdot \frac{1}{\tan x} \qquad \cot x = \frac{1}{\tan x}$$

$$= \lim_{x \to 0^+} \frac{x}{\tan x} \qquad \text{Now } \frac{0}{0}$$

$$= \lim_{x \to 0^+} \frac{1}{\sec^2 x} = \frac{1}{1} = 1$$

EXAMPLE 7 Find $\lim_{x \to 0} \left(\frac{1}{\sin x} - \frac{1}{x} \right)$.

Solution If $x \to 0^+$, then $\sin x \to 0^+$ and

$$\frac{1}{\sin x} - \frac{1}{x} \to \infty - \infty.$$

Similarly, if $x \to 0^-$, then $\sin x \to 0^-$ and

$$\frac{1}{\sin x} - \frac{1}{x} \to -\infty - (-\infty) = -\infty + \infty.$$

Neither form reveals what happens in the limit. To find out, we first combine the fractions,

$$\frac{1}{\sin x} - \frac{1}{x} = \frac{x - \sin x}{x \sin x}, \qquad \text{Common denominator is } x \sin x.$$

and then apply l'Hôpital's rule to the result:

$$\lim_{x \to 0} \left(\frac{1}{\sin x} - \frac{1}{x} \right) = \lim_{x \to 0} \frac{x - \sin x}{x \sin x} \qquad \frac{0}{0}$$

$$= \lim_{x \to 0} \frac{1 - \cos x}{\sin x + x \cos x} \qquad \text{Still } \frac{0}{0}$$

$$= \lim_{x \to 0} \frac{\sin x}{2 \cos x - x \sin x} = \frac{0}{2} = 0$$

Indeterminate Powers

Limits that lead to the indeterminate forms 1^∞, 0^0, ∞^0, and 0^∞ can sometimes be handled by taking logarithms first. We use l'Hôpital's rule to find the limit of the logarithm and then exponentiate to find the original function behavior.

Flowchart 6.1
L'Hôpital's rule

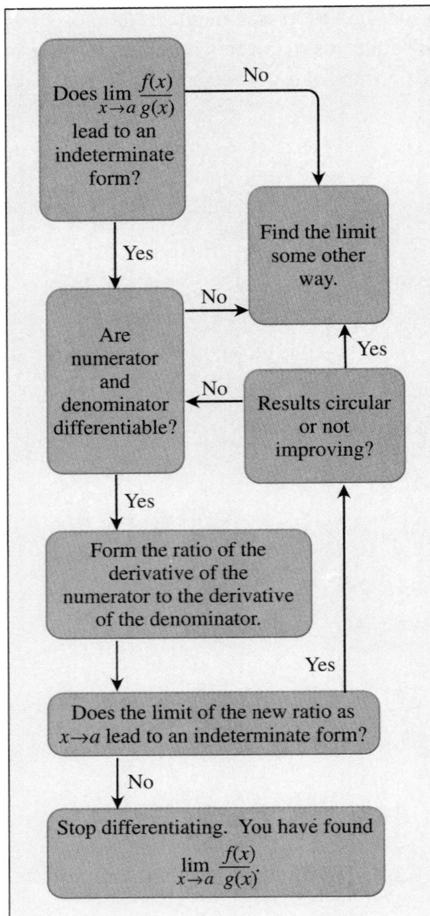

If $\lim_{x\to a} \ln f(x) = L$, then

$$\lim_{x\to a} f(x) = \lim_{x\to a} e^{\ln f(x)} = e^L. \tag{3}$$

Here, a may be either finite or infinite.

EXAMPLE 8 Show that $\lim_{x\to 0^+} (1+x)^{1/x} = e$.

Solution The limit leads to the indeterminate form 1^∞. We let $f(x) = (1+x)^{1/x}$ and find $\lim_{x\to 0^+} \ln f(x)$. Since

$$\begin{aligned}\ln f(x) &= \ln (1+x)^{1/x}\\ &= \frac{1}{x}\ln(1+x),\end{aligned}$$

l'Hôpital's rule now applies to give

$$\begin{aligned}\lim_{x\to 0^+} \ln f(x) &= \lim_{x\to 0^+} \frac{\ln(1+x)}{x} \qquad \frac{0}{0}\\ &= \lim_{x\to 0^+} \frac{\frac{1}{1+x}}{1}\\ &= \frac{1}{1} = 1.\end{aligned}$$

Therefore,

$$\lim_{x\to 0^+} (1+x)^{1/x} = \lim_{x\to 0^+} f(x) = \lim_{x\to 0^+} e^{\ln f(x)} = e^1 = e.$$

EXAMPLE 9 Find $\lim_{x\to\infty} x^{1/x}$.

Solution The limit leads to the form ∞^0. We let $f(x) = x^{1/x}$ and find $\lim_{x\to\infty} \ln f(x)$. Since

$$\begin{aligned}\ln f(x) &= \ln x^{1/x}\\ &= \frac{\ln x}{x},\end{aligned}$$

l'Hôpital's rule gives

$$\begin{aligned}\lim_{x\to\infty} \ln f(x) &= \lim_{x\to\infty} \frac{\ln x}{x} \qquad \frac{\infty}{\infty}\\ &= \lim_{x\to\infty} \frac{1/x}{1}\\ &= \frac{0}{1} = 0.\end{aligned}$$

Therefore,

$$\lim_{x\to\infty} x^{1/x} = \lim_{x\to\infty} f(x) = \lim_{x\to\infty} e^{\ln f(x)} = e^0 = 1.$$

Exercises 6.6

Use l'Hôpital's rule to find the limits in Exercises 1–36.

1. $\lim_{x \to 2} \frac{x-2}{x^2-4}$

2. $\lim_{x \to -5} \frac{x^2-25}{x+5}$

3. $\lim_{t \to -3} \frac{t^3-4t+15}{t^2-t-12}$

4. $\lim_{t \to 1} \frac{t^3-1}{4t^3-t-3}$

5. $\lim_{x \to \infty} \frac{5x^2-3x}{7x^2+1}$

6. $\lim_{x \to \infty} \frac{x-8x^2}{12x^2+5x}$

7. $\lim_{t \to 0} \frac{\sin t^2}{t}$

8. $\lim_{t \to 0} \frac{\sin 5t}{t}$

9. $\lim_{x \to 0} \frac{8x^2}{\cos x - 1}$

10. $\lim_{x \to 0} \frac{\sin x - x}{x^3}$

11. $\lim_{\theta \to \pi/2} \frac{2\theta - \pi}{\cos(2\pi - \theta)}$

12. $\lim_{\theta \to -\pi/3} \frac{3\theta + \pi}{\sin(\theta + (\pi/3))}$

13. $\lim_{\theta \to \pi/2} \frac{1 - \sin\theta}{1 + \cos 2\theta}$

14. $\lim_{x \to 1} \frac{x-1}{\ln x - \sin \pi x}$

15. $\lim_{x \to 0} \frac{x^2}{\ln(\sec x)}$

16. $\lim_{x \to \pi/2} \frac{\ln(\csc x)}{(x - (\pi/2))^2}$

17. $\lim_{t \to 0} \frac{t(1-\cos t)}{t - \sin t}$

18. $\lim_{t \to 0} \frac{t \sin t}{1 - \cos t}$

19. $\lim_{x \to (\pi/2)^-} \left(x - \frac{\pi}{2}\right) \sec x$

20. $\lim_{x \to (\pi/2)^-} \left(\frac{\pi}{2} - x\right) \tan x$

21. $\lim_{\theta \to 0} \frac{3^{\sin\theta} - 1}{\theta}$

22. $\lim_{\theta \to 0} \frac{(1/2)^{\theta} - 1}{\theta}$

23. $\lim_{x \to 0} \frac{x2^x}{2^x - 1}$

24. $\lim_{x \to 0} \frac{(x+1)2^x}{2^x - 1}$

25. $\lim_{x \to \infty} \frac{\ln(x+1)}{\log_2 x}$

26. $\lim_{x \to \infty} \frac{\log_2 x}{\log_3(x+3)}$

27. $\lim_{x \to 0^+} \frac{\ln(x^2+2x)}{\ln x}$

28. $\lim_{x \to 0^+} \frac{\ln(e^x - 1)}{\ln x}$

29. $\lim_{y \to 0} \frac{\sqrt{5y+25} - 5}{y}$

30. $\lim_{y \to 0} \frac{\sqrt{ay+a^2} - a}{y}, \quad a > 0$

31. $\lim_{x \to \infty} (\ln 2x - \ln(x+1))$

32. $\lim_{x \to 0^+} (\ln x - \ln \sin x)$

33. $\lim_{x \to 0^+} \left(\frac{1}{x} - \frac{1}{\sin x}\right)$

34. $\lim_{x \to 0^+} \left(\frac{3x+1}{x} - \frac{1}{\sin x}\right)$

35. $\lim_{x \to 1^+} \left(\frac{1}{x-1} - \frac{1}{\ln x}\right)$

36. $\lim_{x \to 0^+} (\csc x - \cot x + \cos x)$

Find the limits in Exercises 37–46.

37. $\lim_{x \to 1^+} x^{1/(1-x)}$

38. $\lim_{x \to 1^+} x^{1/(x-1)}$

39. $\lim_{x \to \infty} (\ln x)^{1/x}$

40. $\lim_{x \to e^+} (\ln x)^{1/(x-e)}$

41. $\lim_{x \to 0^+} x^{-1/\ln x}$

42. $\lim_{x \to \infty} x^{1/\ln x}$

43. $\lim_{x \to \infty} (1+2x)^{1/(2 \ln x)}$

44. $\lim_{x \to 0} (e^x + x)^{1/x}$

45. $\lim_{x \to 0^+} x^x$

46. $\lim_{x \to 0^+} \left(1 + \frac{1}{x}\right)^x$

L'Hôpital's rule does not help with the limits in Exercises 47–50. Try it—you just keep on cycling. Find the limits some other way.

47. $\lim_{x \to \infty} \frac{\sqrt{9x+1}}{\sqrt{x+1}}$

48. $\lim_{x \to 0^+} \frac{\sqrt{x}}{\sqrt{\sin x}}$

49. $\lim_{x \to (\pi/2)^-} \frac{\sec x}{\tan x}$

50. $\lim_{x \to 0^+} \frac{\cot x}{\csc x}$

51. Which one is correct and which one is wrong? Give reasons for your answers.

 a) $\lim_{x \to 3} \frac{x-3}{x^2-3} = \lim_{x \to 3} \frac{1}{2x} = \frac{1}{6}$

 b) $\lim_{x \to 3} \frac{x-3}{x^2-3} = \frac{0}{6} = 0$

52. Which one is correct and which one is wrong? Give reasons for your answers.

 a) $\lim_{x \to 0} \frac{x^2-2x}{x^2-\sin x} = \lim_{x \to 0} \frac{2x-2}{2x-\cos x}$
 $= \lim_{x \to 0} \frac{2}{2+\sin x} = \frac{2}{2+0} = 1$

 b) $\lim_{x \to 0} \frac{x^2-2x}{x^2-\sin x} = \lim_{x \to 0} \frac{2x-2}{2x-\cos x} = \frac{-2}{0-1} = 2$

53. Only one of these calculations is correct. Which one? Why are the others wrong? Give reasons for your answers.

 a) $\lim_{x \to 0^+} x \ln x = 0 \cdot (-\infty) = 0$

 b) $\lim_{x \to 0^+} x \ln x = 0 \cdot (-\infty) = -\infty$

 c) $\lim_{x \to 0^+} x \ln x = \lim_{x \to 0^+} \frac{\ln x}{(1/x)} = \frac{-\infty}{\infty} = -1$

 d) $\lim_{x \to 0^+} x \ln x = \lim_{x \to 0^+} \frac{\ln x}{(1/x)}$
 $= \lim_{x \to 0^+} \frac{(1/x)}{(-1/x^2)} = \lim_{x \to 0^+} (-x) = 0$

54. Let

$$f(x) = \begin{cases} x+2, & x \neq 0 \\ 0, & x = 0 \end{cases}$$

$$g(x) = \begin{cases} x+1, & x \neq 0 \\ 0, & x = 0. \end{cases}$$

Show that

$$\lim_{x\to 0} \frac{f'(x)}{g'(x)} = 1 \quad \text{but that} \quad \lim_{x\to 0} \frac{f(x)}{g(x)} = 2.$$

Doesn't this contradict l'Hôpital's rule? Give reasons for your answers.

55. Find a value of c that makes the function

$$f(x) = \begin{cases} \dfrac{9x - 3\sin 3x}{5x^3}, & x \neq 0 \\ c, & x = 0 \end{cases}$$

continuous at $x = 0$. Explain why your value of c works.

56. Find a value of c that makes the function

$$g(\theta) = \begin{cases} \dfrac{(\tan\theta)^2}{\sin(4\theta^2/\pi)}, & \theta \neq 0 \\ c, & \theta = 0 \end{cases}$$

continuous from the right at $\theta = 0$. Explain why your value of c works.

57. *The Continuous Compound Interest Formula.* In deriving the formula $A(t) = A_0 e^{rt}$ in Section 6.5, we claimed that

$$\lim_{k\to\infty} A_0\left(1 + \frac{r}{k}\right)^{kt} = A_0 e^{rt}.$$

This equation will hold if

$$\lim_{k\to\infty} \left(1 + \frac{r}{k}\right)^{kt} = e^{rt},$$

and this, in turn, will hold if

$$\lim_{k\to\infty} \left(1 + \frac{r}{k}\right)^{k} = e^{r}.$$

As you can see, the limit leads to the indeterminate form 1^∞. Verify the limit using l'Hôpital's rule.

58. *Determining the Value of e.*

a) Show that

$$\lim_{x\to\infty} \left(1 + \frac{1}{x}\right)^{x} = e.$$

b) See how close you can come to

$$e = 2.7\ 1828\ 1828\ 45\ 90\ 45$$

by evaluating $f(x) = (1 + (1/x))^x$ for $x = 10, 10^2, 10^3, \ldots$ and so on. You can expect the approximations to approach e at first, but on some calculators they will move away again as round-off errors take their toll.

c) If you have a grapher, you may prefer to do part (b) by graphing $f(x) = (1 + (1/x))^x$ for large values of x, using TRACE to display the coordinates along the graph. Again, you may expect to find decreasing accuracy as x increases, and, beyond $x = 10^{10}$ or so, erratic behavior.

59. This exercise explores the difference between the limit

$$\lim_{x\to\infty} \left(1 + \frac{1}{x^2}\right)^{x}$$

and the limit

$$\lim_{x\to\infty} \left(1 + \frac{1}{x}\right)^{x} = e,$$

studied in Exercise 58.

a) Graph

$$f(x) = \left(1 + \frac{1}{x^2}\right)^{x} \quad \text{and} \quad g(x) = \left(1 + \frac{1}{x}\right)^{x}$$

together for $x \geq 0$. How does the behavior of f compare with that of g? Estimate the value of $\lim_{x\to\infty} f(x)$.

b) Confirm your estimate of $\lim_{x\to\infty} f(x)$ by calculating it with l'Hôpital's rule.

60. a) If you did not do so in Section 3.4, estimate the value of

$$\lim_{h\to 0} \frac{\cos h - 1}{h^2}$$

by graphing $f(h) = (\cos h - 1)/h^2$ near $h = 0$ or by making a table of values for f with $h = 1, 0.1, 0.01, \ldots$ and so on (as far as your calculator can go).

b) Then confirm your estimate by finding the limit with l'Hôpital's rule.

61. a) Estimate the value of

$$\lim_{x\to\infty} \left(x - \sqrt{x^2 + x}\right)$$

by graphing $f(x) = x - \sqrt{x^2 + x}$ over a suitably large interval of x-values.

b) Now confirm your estimate by finding the limit with l'Hôpital's rule. As the first step, multiply $f(x)$ by the fraction $\left(x + \sqrt{x^2 + x}\right)/\left(x + \sqrt{x^2 + x}\right)$ and simplify the new numerator.

62. Estimate the value of

$$\lim_{x\to 2} \frac{x^2 - 4}{\sqrt{x^2 + 5} - 3}$$

by graphing. Then confirm your estimate with l'Hôpital's rule.

63. Estimate the value of

$$\lim_{x\to 1} \frac{2x^2 - (3x + 1)\sqrt{x} + 2}{x - 1}$$

by graphing. Then confirm your estimate with l'Hôpital's rule.

64. a) Estimate the value of

$$\lim_{x\to 1} \frac{(x - 1)^2}{x\ln x - x - \cos\pi x}$$

by graphing $f(x) = (x - 1)^2/(x \ln x - x - \cos \pi x)$ near $x = 1$. Then confirm your estimate with l'Hôpital's rule.

b) Graph f for $0 \leq x \leq 11$. You will find the graph interesting.

Writing for Your Own Knowledge

Answer the following questions in writing. Some answers will take only a sentence or two; others may require several paragraphs. Some explanations may also call for graphs or sketches.

1. What is l'Hôpital's rule? Why might you want to use it?

2. Once you start using l'Hôpital's rule, how do you know when to stop?
3. How can you sometimes use l'Hôpital's rule to find limits that lead to indeterminate products and differences?
4. How can you sometimes use l'Hôpital's rule to find limits that lead to indeterminate powers?

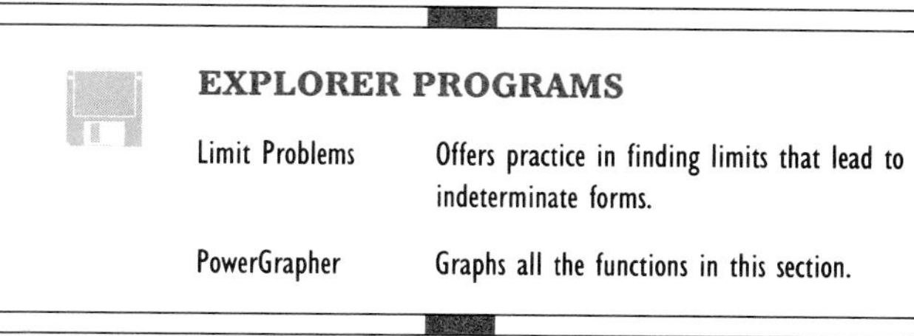

EXPLORER PROGRAMS
Limit Problems
Offers practice in finding limits that lead to indeterminate forms.
PowerGrapher
Graphs all the functions in this section.

6.7 *Relative Rates of Growth*

This section shows how to compare the rates at which functions of x grow as x becomes large and introduces the so-called little-oh and big-oh notation sometimes used to describe the results of these comparisons. We restrict our attention to functions whose values eventually become and remain positive as $x \to \infty$. Functions with negative values can be compared by taking absolute values first.

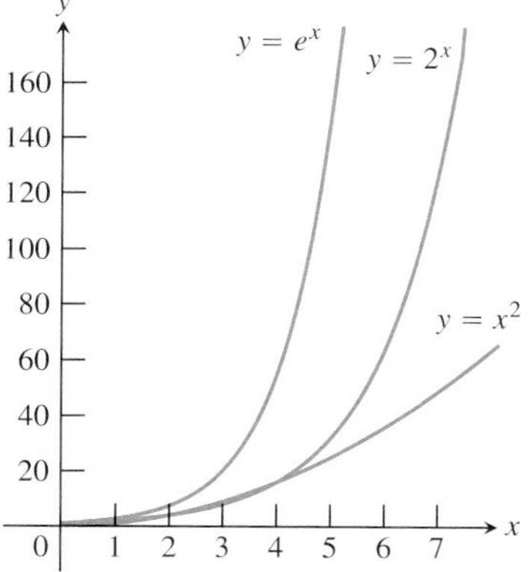

6.20 The graphs of e^x, 2^x, and x^2.

6.21 Scale drawings of the graphs of e^x and $\ln x$.

Relative Rates of Growth

You may have noticed that exponential functions like 2^x and e^x seem to grow more rapidly as x gets large than the polynomials and rational functions we graphed in Chapter 4. These exponentials certainly grow more rapidly than x itself, and you can see 2^x outgrowing x^2 as x increases in Fig. 6.20. In fact, as $x \to \infty$, the functions 2^x and e^x grow faster than any power of x, even $x^{1{,}000{,}000}$ (Exercise 13).

To get a feeling for how rapidly the values of $y = e^x$ grow with increasing x, think of graphing the function on a large blackboard, with the axes scaled in centimeters. At $x = 1$ cm, the graph is $e^1 \approx 3$ cm above the x-axis. At $x = 6$ cm, the graph is $e^6 \approx 403$ cm ≈ 4 m high (it is about to go through the ceiling if it hasn't done so already). At $x = 10$ cm, the graph is $e^{10} \approx 22{,}026$ cm ≈ 220 m high, higher than most buildings. At $x = 24$ cm, the graph is more than halfway to the moon, and at $x = 43$ cm from the origin, the graph is high enough to reach past the sun's closest stellar neighbor, the red dwarf star Proxima Centauri:

$$\begin{aligned} e^{43} &\approx 4.7 \times 10^{18} \text{ cm} \\ &= 4.7 \times 10^{13} \text{ km} \\ &\approx 1.57 \times 10^{8} \text{ light-seconds} \qquad \text{In a vacuum, light travels at 300,000 km/sec.} \\ &\approx 5.0 \text{ light-years} \end{aligned} \tag{1}$$

The distance to Proxima Centauri is about 4.22 light-years. Yet with $x = 43$ cm from the origin, the graph is still less than 2 feet to the right of the y-axis.

In contrast, logarithmic functions like $y = \log_2 x$ and $y = \ln x$ grow more slowly as $x \to \infty$ than any positive power of x (Exercise 15). With axes scaled in centimeters, you have to go nearly 5 light-years out on the x-axis to find a point where the graph of $y = \ln x$ is even $y = 43$ cm high. See Fig. 6.21.

These important comparisons of exponential, polynomial, and logarithmic functions can be made precise by defining what it means for a function $f(x)$ to grow faster than a function $g(x)$ as $x \to \infty$.

DEFINITION

Rates of Growth as $x \to \infty$ (Positive Functions)

1. f **grows faster than** g as $x \to \infty$ if

$$\lim_{x\to\infty} \frac{f(x)}{g(x)} = \infty \tag{2}$$

or, equivalently, if

$$\lim_{x\to\infty} \frac{g(x)}{f(x)} = 0. \tag{3}$$

2. If f grows faster than g as $x \to \infty$, we also say that g **grows slower than** f as $x \to \infty$.
3. f and g **grow at the same rate** as $x \to \infty$ if

$$\lim_{x\to\infty} \frac{f(x)}{g(x)} = L \neq 0. \qquad L \text{ finite and not zero} \tag{4}$$

According to these definitions, $y = 2x$ does not grow faster than $y = x$. The two functions grow at the same rate because

$$\lim_{x\to\infty} \frac{2x}{x} = \lim_{x\to\infty} 2 = 2,$$

which is a finite, nonzero limit. The reason for this apparent disregard of common sense is that we want "f grows faster than g" to mean that for large x-values, g is negligible when compared with f.

EXAMPLE 1 e^x grows faster than x^2 as $x \to \infty$ because

$$\underbrace{\lim_{x\to\infty} \frac{e^x}{x^2}}_{\infty/\infty} = \underbrace{\lim_{x\to\infty} \frac{e^x}{2x}}_{\infty/\infty} = \lim_{x\to\infty} \frac{e^x}{2} = \infty. \qquad \text{Using l'Hôpital's rule twice}$$

EXAMPLE 2

a) 3^x grows faster than 2^x as $x \to \infty$ because

$$\lim_{x\to\infty} \frac{3^x}{2^x} = \lim_{x\to\infty} \left(\frac{3}{2}\right)^x = \infty.$$

b) As part (a) suggests, exponential functions with different bases never grow at the same rate as $x \to \infty$. If $a > b > 0$, then a^x grows faster than b^x. Since $(a/b) > 1$,

$$\lim_{x\to\infty} \frac{a^x}{b^x} = \lim_{x\to\infty} \left(\frac{a}{b}\right)^x = \infty.$$

EXAMPLE 3 x^2 grows faster than $\ln x$ as $x \to \infty$ because

$$\lim_{x\to\infty} \frac{x^2}{\ln x} = \lim_{x\to\infty} \frac{2x}{1/x} = \lim_{x\to\infty} 2x^2 = \infty. \qquad \text{l'Hôpital's rule}$$

EXAMPLE 4 $\ln x$ grows slower than x as $x \to \infty$ because

$$\lim_{x\to\infty} \frac{\ln x}{x} = \lim_{x\to\infty} \frac{1/x}{1} \qquad \text{l'Hôpital's rule}$$

$$= \lim_{x\to\infty} \frac{1}{x} = 0.$$

EXAMPLE 5 In contrast to exponential functions, logarithmic functions with different bases a and b always grow at the same rate as $x \to \infty$:

$$\lim_{x\to\infty} \frac{\log_a x}{\log_b x} = \lim_{x\to\infty} \frac{\ln x/\ln a}{\ln x/\ln b} = \frac{\ln b}{\ln a}.$$

The limiting ratio is always finite and never zero.

If f grows at the same rate as g as $x \to \infty$, and g grows at the same rate as h as $x \to \infty$, then f grows at the same rate as h as $x \to \infty$. The reason is that

$$\lim_{x\to\infty} \frac{f}{g} = L_1 \qquad \text{and} \qquad \lim_{x\to\infty} \frac{g}{h} = L_2$$

together imply

$$\lim_{x\to\infty} \frac{f}{h} = \lim_{x\to\infty} \frac{f}{g} \cdot \frac{g}{h} = L_1 L_2.$$

If L_1 and L_2 are finite and nonzero, then so is $L_1 L_2$.

EXAMPLE 6 Show that $\sqrt{x^2+5}$ and $(2\sqrt{x}-1)^2$ grow at the same rate as $x \to \infty$.

Solution We show that the functions grow at the same rate by showing that they both grow at the same rate as the function x:

$$\lim_{x\to\infty} \frac{\sqrt{x^2+5}}{x} = \lim_{x\to\infty} \sqrt{1+\frac{5}{x^2}} = 1,$$

$$\lim_{x\to\infty} \frac{(2\sqrt{x}-1)^2}{x} = \lim_{x\to\infty} \left(\frac{2\sqrt{x}-1}{\sqrt{x}}\right)^2 = \lim_{x\to\infty} \left(2-\frac{1}{\sqrt{x}}\right)^2 = 4.$$

Order and Oh-Notation

Here we introduce the "little-oh" and "big-oh" notation invented by number theorists a hundred years ago and now commonplace in mathematical analysis and computer science.

DEFINITION

A function f is **of smaller order than** g as $x \to \infty$ if $\lim_{x\to\infty} \frac{f(x)}{g(x)} = 0$. We indicate this by writing $f = o(g)$ ("f is little-oh of g").

Notice that saying $f = o(g)$ as $x \to \infty$ is another way to say that f grows slower than g as $x \to \infty$.

EXAMPLE 7

$$\ln x = o(x) \text{ as } x \to \infty \quad \text{because} \quad \lim_{x\to\infty} \frac{\ln x}{x} = 0$$

$$x^2 = o(x^3 + 1) \text{ as } x \to \infty \quad \text{because} \quad \lim_{x\to\infty} \frac{x^2}{x^3 + 1} = 0$$

If $f(x)/g(x)$ fails to approach zero as $x \to \infty$ but the ratio remains bounded, we say that f is at most the order of g as $x \to \infty$. What we mean, exactly, is that $f(x)/g(x)$ stays less than or equal to some integer M for x sufficiently large.

DEFINITION

A function f is **of at most the order of** g as $x \to \infty$ if there is a positive integer M for which

$$\frac{f(x)}{g(x)} \le M,$$

for x sufficiently large. We indicate this by writing $\boldsymbol{f = O(g)}$ ("f is big-oh of g").

EXAMPLE 8

$$x + \sin x = O(x) \text{ as } x \to \infty \quad \text{because} \quad \frac{x + \sin x}{x} \le 2 \text{ for } x \text{ sufficiently large.}$$

EXAMPLE 9

$$e^x + x^2 = O(e^x) \text{ as } x \to \infty \quad \text{because} \quad \frac{e^x + x^2}{e^x} \to 1 \text{ as } x \to \infty,$$

$$x = O(e^x) \text{ as } x \to \infty \quad \text{because} \quad \frac{x}{e^x} \to 0 \text{ as } x \to \infty.$$

If you look at the definitions again, you will see that $f = o(g)$ implies $f = O(g)$. Also, if f and g grow at the same rate, then $f = O(g)$ and $g = O(f)$ (Exercise 21).

Sequential vs. Binary Search

Computer scientists sometimes measure the efficiency of an algorithm by counting the number of steps a computer must take to make the algorithm do something. There can be significant differences in how efficiently algorithms perform, even if they are designed to accomplish the same task. These differences are often described in big-oh notation. Here is an example.

Webster's Third New International Dictionary lists about 26,000 words that begin with the letter a. One way to look up a word, or to learn it is not there, is to read through the list one word at a time until you either find the word or determine that it is not there. This method, called sequential search, makes no particular use of the words' alphabetical arrangement. You can be sure of getting an answer, but it might take 26,000 steps.

Another way to find the word or to learn it is not there is to go straight to the middle of the list (give or take a few words). If you do not find the word, then go to the middle of the half that contains it and forget about the half that does not. (You know which half contains it because you know the list is ordered alphabetically.) This method eliminates roughly 13,000 words in a single step. If you do not find the word on the second try, then jump to the middle of the half that contains it. Continue this way until you have either found the word or divided the list in half so many times there are no words left. How many times do you have to divide the list to find the word or learn that it is not there? At most 15, because

$$(26{,}000/2^{15}) < 1.$$

That certainly beats a possible 26,000 steps.

For a list of length n, a sequential search algorithm takes on the order of n steps to find a word or determine that it is not in the list. A binary search, as the second algorithm is called, takes on the order of $\log_2 n$ steps. The reason is that if $2^{m-1} < n \leq 2^m$, then $m - 1 < \log_2 n \leq m$, and the number of bisections required to narrow the list to one word will be at most $m = \lceil \log_2 n \rceil$, the integer ceiling for $\log_2 n$.

Big-oh notation provides a compact way to say all this. The number of steps in a sequential search of an ordered list is $O(n)$; the number of steps in a binary search is $O(\log_2 n)$. In our example, there is a big difference between the two (26,000 vs. 15), and the difference can only increase with n because n grows faster than $\log_2 n$ as $n \to \infty$.

To find an item in a list of length n:

A sequential search takes $O(n)$ steps.

A binary search takes $O(\log_2 n)$ steps.

Exercises 6.7

1. Which of the following functions grow faster than e^x as $x \to \infty$? Which grow at the same rate as e^x? Which grow slower?

   a) $x + 3$ b) $x^3 + \sin^2 x$
   c) $\sqrt{x}$ d) 4^x
   e) $(3/2)^x$ f) $e^{x/2}$
   g) $e^x/2$ h) $\log_{10} x$

2. Which of the following functions grow faster than e^x as $x \to \infty$? Which grow at the same rate as e^x? Which grow slower?

   a) $10x^4 + 30x + 1$ b) $x \ln x - x$
   c) $\sqrt{1 + x^4}$ d) $(5/2)^x$
   e) e^{-x} f) xe^x
   g) $e^{\cos x}$ h) e^{x-1}

3. Which of the following functions grow faster than x^2 as $x \to \infty$? Which grow at the same rate as x^2? Which grow slower?

   a) $x^2 + 4x$ b) $x^5 - x^2$
   c) $\sqrt{x^4 + x^3}$ d) $(x + 3)^2$
   e) $x \ln x$ f) 2^x
   g) $x^3 e^{-x}$ h) $8x^2$

4. Which of the following functions grow faster than x^2 as $x \to \infty$? Which grow at the same rate as x^2? Which grow slower?

   a) $x^2 + \sqrt{x}$ b) $10x^2$
   c) $x^2 e^{-x}$ d) $\log_{10}(x^2)$
   e) $x^3 - x^2$ f) $(1/10)^x$
   g) $(1.1)^x$ h) $x^2 + 100x$

5. Which of the following functions grow faster than $\ln x$ as $x \to \infty$? Which grow at the same rate as $\ln x$? Which grow slower?

a) $\log_3 x$ b) $\ln 2x$
c) $\ln \sqrt{x}$ d) $\sqrt{x}$
e) x f) $5 \ln x$
g) $1/x$ h) e^x

6. Which of the following functions grow faster than $\ln x$ as $x \to \infty$? Which grow at the same rate as $\ln x$? Which grow slower?

a) $\log_2 (x^2)$ b) $\log_{10} 10x$
c) $1/\sqrt{x}$ d) $1/x^2$
e) $x - 2 \ln x$ f) e^{-x}
g) $\ln (\ln x)$ h) $\ln (2x + 5)$

7. Order the following functions from slowest growing to fastest growing as $x \to \infty$.

a) e^x b) x^x c) $(\ln x)^x$ d) $e^{x/2}$

8. Order the following functions from slowest growing to fastest growing as $x \to \infty$.

a) 2^x b) x^2 c) $(\ln 2)^x$ d) e^x

9. Show that $\sqrt{10x + 1}$ and $\sqrt{x + 1}$ grow at the same rate as $x \to \infty$ by showing that they both grow at the same rate as $\sqrt{x}$ as $x \to \infty$.

10. Show that $\sqrt{x^4 + x}$ and $\sqrt{x^4 - x^3}$ grow at the same rate as $x \to \infty$ by showing that they both grow at the same rate as x^2 as $x \to \infty$.

11. True, or false? As $x \to \infty$,

a) $x = o(x)$ b) $x = o(x + 5)$
c) $x = O(x + 5)$ d) $x = O(2x)$
e) $e^x = o(e^{2x})$ f) $x + \ln x = O(x)$
g) $\ln x = o(\ln 2x)$ h) $\sqrt{x^2 + 5} = O(x)$

12. True, or false? As $x \to \infty$,

a) $\frac{1}{x + 3} = O\left(\frac{1}{x}\right)$ b) $\frac{1}{x} + \frac{1}{x^2} = O\left(\frac{1}{x}\right)$
c) $\frac{1}{x} - \frac{1}{x^2} = o\left(\frac{1}{x}\right)$ d) $2 + \cos x = O(2)$
e) $e^x + x = O(e^x)$ f) $x \ln x = o(x^2)$
g) $\ln (\ln x) = O(\ln x)$ h) $\ln (x) = o(\ln (x^2 + 1))$

13. Show that e^x grows faster as $x \to \infty$ than x^n for any positive integer n, even $x^{1,000,000}$. (*Hint:* What is the nth derivative of x^n?)

14. *The Function e^x Outgrows Any Polynomial.* Show that e^x grows faster as $x \to \infty$ than any polynomial

$$a_n x^n + a_{n-1} x^{n-1} + \cdots + a_1 x + a_0.$$

15. a) Show that $\ln x$ grows slower as $x \to \infty$ than $x^{1/n}$ for any positive integer n, even $x^{1/1,000,000}$.

b) Although the values of $x^{1/1,000,000}$ eventually overtake the values of $\ln x$, you have to go way out on the x-axis before this happens. Find a value of x greater than 1 for which $x^{1/1,000,000} > \ln x$. You might start by observing that when $x > 1$ the equation $\ln x = x^{1/1,000,000}$ is equivalent to the equation $\ln (\ln x) = (\ln x)/1,000,000$.

c) Even $x^{1/10}$ takes a long time to overtake $\ln x$. Experiment with a calculator to find the value of x at which the graphs of $x^{1/10}$ and $\ln x$ cross, or, equivalently, at which $\ln x = 10 \ln (\ln x)$. Bracket the crossing point between powers of 10 and then close in by successive halving.

d) *(Continuation of Part c).* The value of x at which $\ln x = 10 \ln (\ln x)$ is too far out for some graphers and root finders to identify. Try it on the equipment available to you and see what happens.

16. *The Function $\ln x$ Grows Slower Than Any Polynomial.* Show that $\ln x$ grows slower as $x \to \infty$ than any nonconstant polynomial.

17. a) Suppose you have three different algorithms for solving the same problem and each algorithm takes a number of steps that is of the order of one of the functions listed here:

$$n \log_2 n, \quad n^{3/2}, \quad n(\log_2 n)^2.$$

Which of the algorithms is the most efficient in the long run? Give reasons for your answer.

b) Graph the functions in Part (a) together to get a sense of how rapidly each one grows.

18. Repeat Exercise 17 for the functions

$$n, \quad \sqrt{n} \log_2 n, \quad (\log_2 n)^2.$$

19. Suppose you are looking for an item in an ordered list one million items long. How many steps might it take to find that item with a sequential search? A binary search?

20. You are looking for an item in an ordered list 450,000 items long (the length of *Webster's Third New International Dictionary*). How many steps might it take to find the item with a sequential search? A binary search?

21. Show that if functions $f(x)$ and $g(x)$ grow at the same rate as $x \to \infty$, then $f = O(g)$ and $g = O(f)$.

22. What do the conclusions we drew in Section 2.2 about the limits of rational functions tell us about the relative growth rates of polynomials as $x \to \infty$? (See the summary at the end of Section 2.2.)

23. When is a polynomial $f(x)$ of smaller order than a polynomial $g(x)$ as $x \to \infty$? Give reasons for your answer.

24. When is a polynomial $f(x)$ of at most the order of a polynomial $g(x)$ as $x \to \infty$? Give reasons for your answer.

25. a) If you did Exercise 70 in Section 2.2, you found that

$$\lim_{x \to \infty} \frac{\ln (x + 1)}{\ln x} = 1 \quad \text{and} \quad \lim_{x \to \infty} \frac{\ln (x + 999)}{\ln x} = 1.$$

Use l'Hôpital's rule to explain these results.

b) Show that the value of

$$\lim_{x \to \infty} \frac{\ln (x + a)}{\ln x}$$

is the same no matter what value you assign to the constant a. What does this say about the relative rates at which the functions $f(x) = \ln (x + a)$ and $g(x) = \ln x$ grow?

26. *Simpson's Rule and the Trapezoidal Rule.* The definitions in the present section can be made more general by lifting the restriction that $x \to \infty$ and considering limits as $x \to a$ for any real number a. Show that the error E_S in the Simpson's rule approximation of a definite integral is $O(h^4)$ as $h \to 0$ while the error E_T in the trapezoidal rule approximation is $O(h^2)$. This gives another way to explain the relative accuracies of the two approximation methods.

Writing for Your Own Knowledge

Answer the following questions in writing. Some answers will take only a sentence or two; others may require several paragraphs. Some explanations may also call for graphs or sketches.

1. How do you compare growth rates of functions?
2. What roles do the functions e^x and $\ln x$ play in growth comparisons?
3. What is oh-notation?
4. Which is more efficient—a sequential search or a binary search?

EXPLORER PROGRAM

PowerGrapher	Graphs most functions. (Enter $\log_a x$ as $(\ln x)/(\ln a)$.)

6.8 *Inverse Trigonometric Functions*

Inverse trigonometric functions arise in problems that require finding angles from side measurements in triangles. They also provide useful antiderivatives for a wide variety of functions and appear in solutions to differential equations that arise in mathematics, engineering, and physics. This section shows how these functions are defined, graphed, and evaluated.

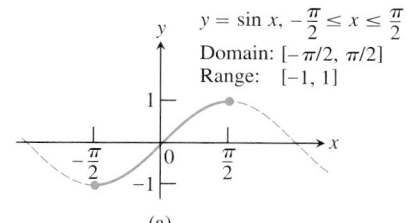

$y = \sin x,\ -\frac{\pi}{2} \le x \le \frac{\pi}{2}$
Domain: $[-\pi/2, \pi/2]$
Range: $[-1, 1]$

(a)

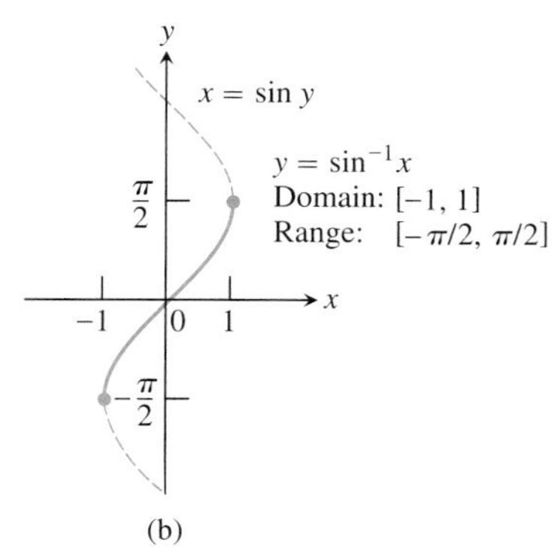

6.22 The graphs of (a) $y = \sin x$, $-\pi/2 \le x \le \pi/2$, and (b) its inverse, $y = \sin^{-1} x$. The graph of $\sin^{-1} x$, obtained by reflection across the line $y = x$, is a portion of the curve $x = \sin y$.

The Arc Sine

The function $y = \sin x$ is not one-to-one. It repeats the same values after every interval of length 2π. The restricted function

$$y = \sin x, \quad -\pi/2 \le x \le \pi/2,$$

however, is one-to-one (Fig. 6.22). We denote its inverse by

$$y = \sin^{-1} x. \tag{1}$$

This equation is read as "y equals the **arc sine** of x" or "y equals arc sin x." It is sometimes written as $y = \arcsin x$.

For every value of x in $[-1, 1]$, $y = \sin^{-1} x$ is the number in $[-\pi/2, \pi/2]$ whose sine is x. Thus,

$$\sin^{-1}(-1) = -\frac{\pi}{2} \qquad \text{because } \sin\left(-\frac{\pi}{2}\right) = -1,$$

$$\sin^{-1} 0 = 0 \qquad \text{because } \sin 0 = 0,$$

$$\sin^{-1} 1 = \frac{\pi}{2} \qquad \text{because } \sin \frac{\pi}{2} = 1.$$

We can find other values of $\sin^{-1} x$ by drawing reference right triangles and using the definition $\sin y$ = side opposite/hypotenuse.

Caution: The -1 in $\sin^{-1} x$ means "inverse," not reciprocal. The *reciprocal* of $\sin x$ is $(\sin x)^{-1} = 1/\sin x = \csc x$.

EXAMPLE 1 Common values of $\sin^{-1} x$.

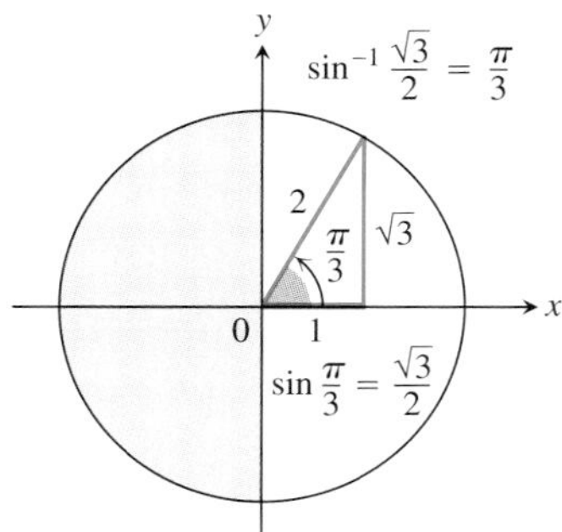

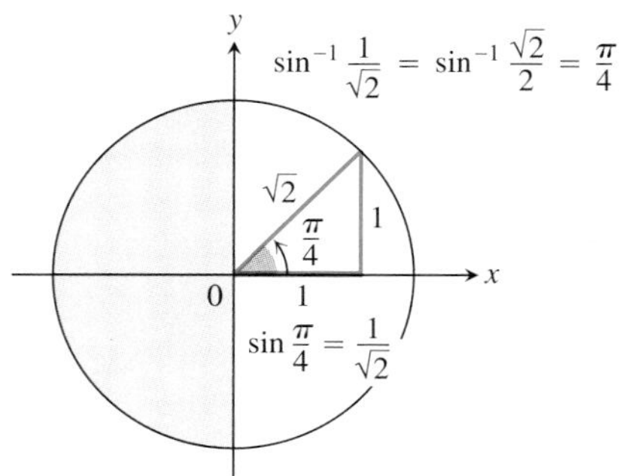

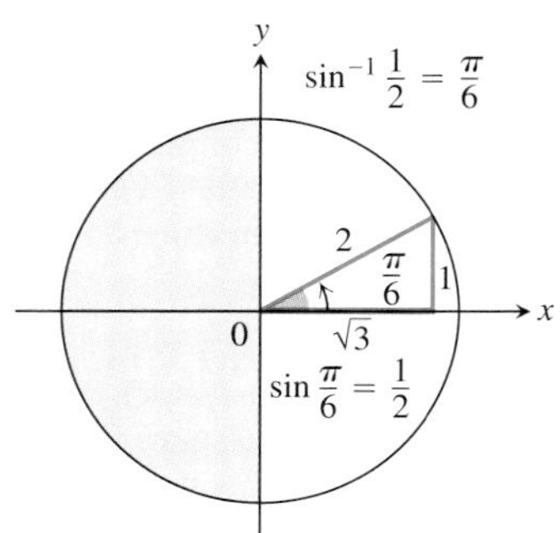

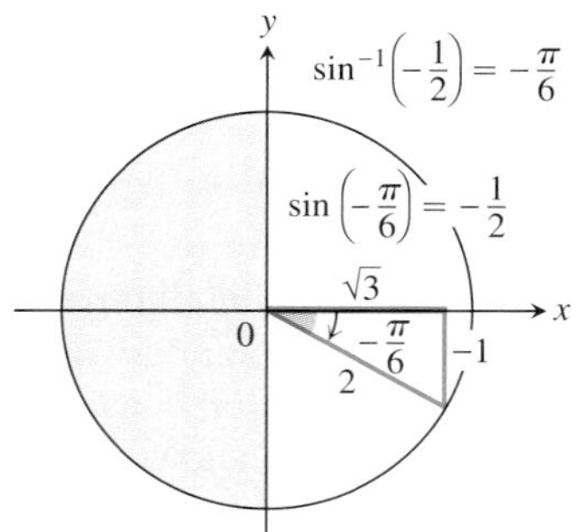

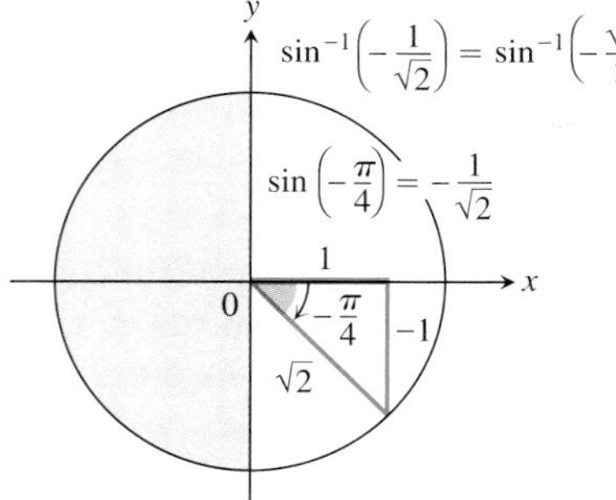

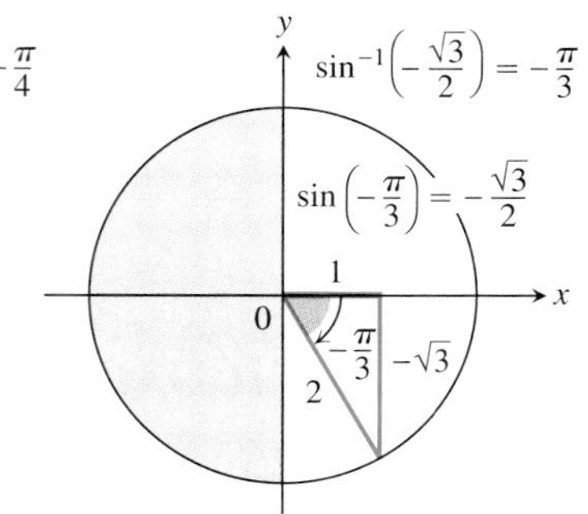

The angles come from the first and fourth quadrants because the range of the arc sine is $[-\pi/2, \pi/2]$.

The graph of $\sin^{-1} x$ (Fig. 6.22) is symmetric about the origin (it lies along the graph of $x = \sin y$), so the arc sine is an odd function of x:

$$\sin^{-1}(-x) = -\sin^{-1} x. \tag{2}$$

The Arc Cosine

Like the sine, the cosine (Fig. 6.23) is not one-to-one. The restricted function

$$y = \cos x,\ 0 \le x \le \pi,$$

however, is one-to-one. We call its inverse,

$$y = \cos^{-1} x, \tag{3}$$

the **arc cosine** of x. For every value of x in $[-1, 1]$, $\cos^{-1} x$ is the number in $[0, \pi]$ whose cosine is x. Notice that the range of $\cos^{-1} x$ is not the same as the range of $\sin^{-1} x$. Arc sines come from $[-\pi/2, \pi/2]$. Arc cosines come from $[0, \pi]$.

From the graphs in Fig. 6.23 we can see that $\cos^{-1}(-1) = \pi$, $\cos^{-1} 0 = \pi/2$, and $\cos^{-1} 1 = 0$. We can find other values of $\cos^{-1} x$ using reference right triangles and the definition $\cos y$ = side adjacent/hypotenuse.

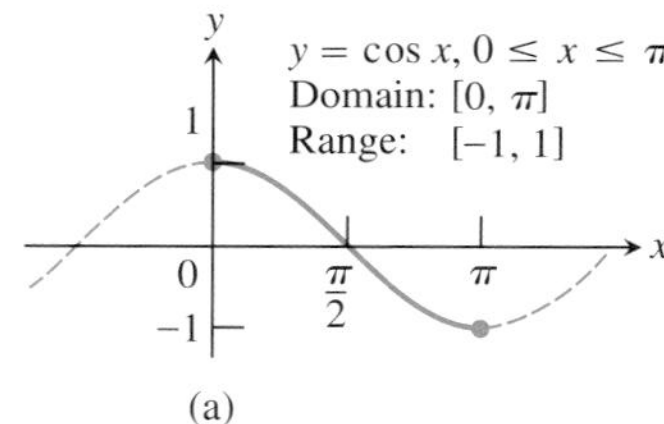

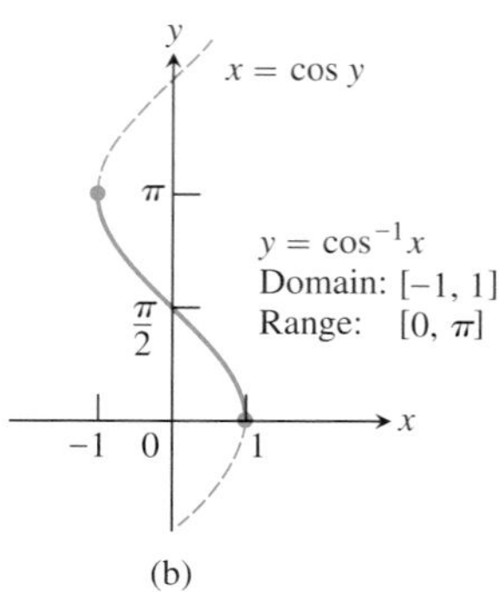

6.23 The graphs of (a) $y = \cos x$, $0 \le x \le \pi$, and (b) its inverse, $y = \cos^{-1} x$. The graphs of $\cos^{-1} x$, obtained by reflection across the line $y = x$, is a portion of the curve $x = \cos y$.

EXAMPLE 2 Common values of $\cos^{-1} x$.

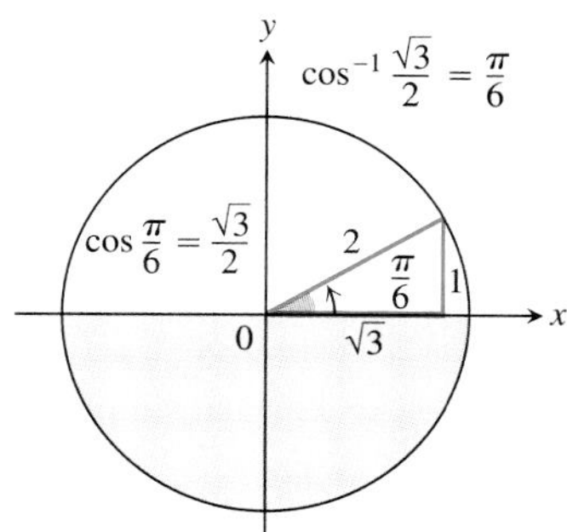

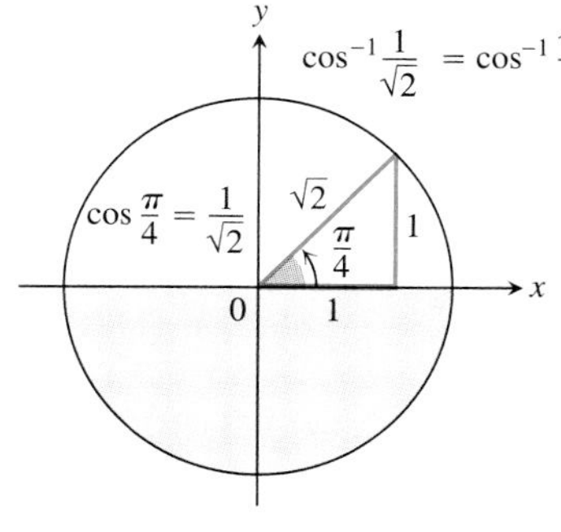

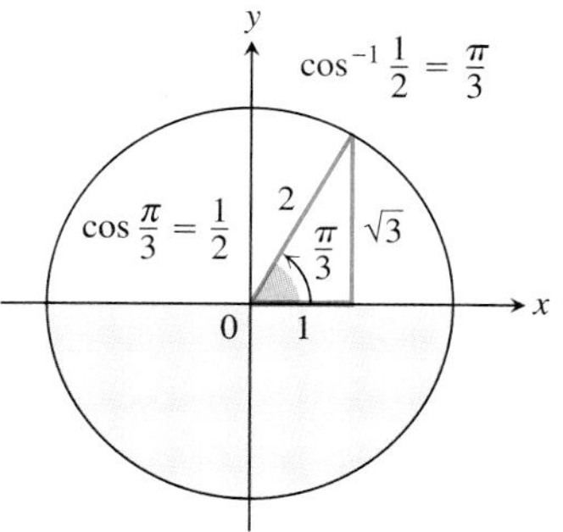

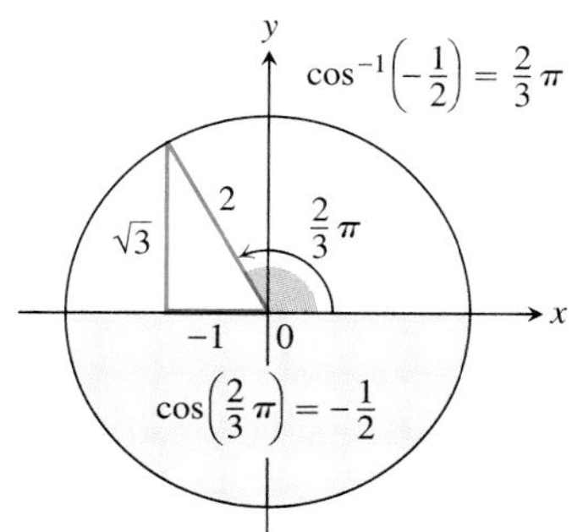

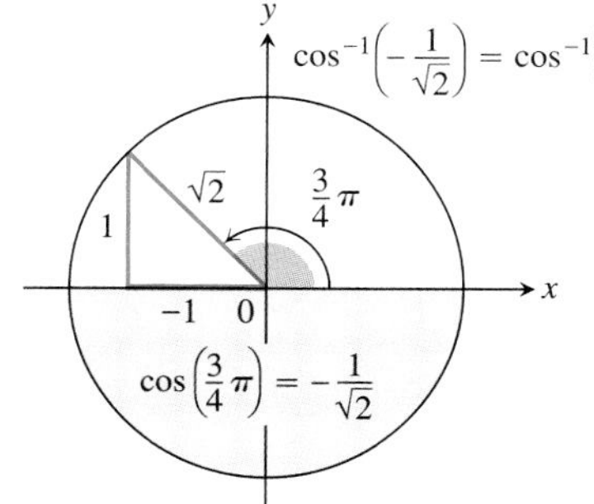

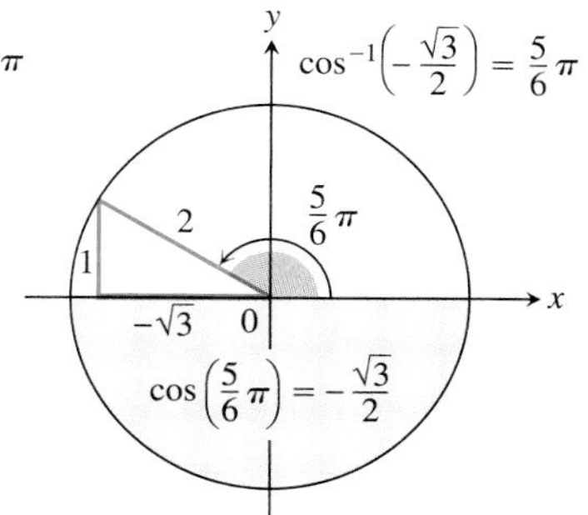

The angles come from the first and second quadrants because the range of the arc cosine is $[0, \pi]$.

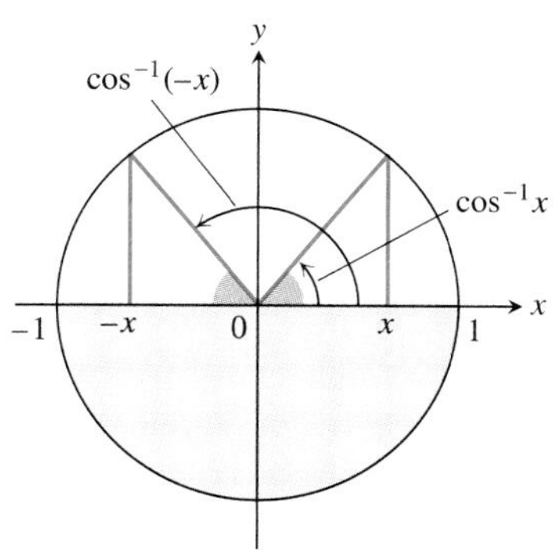

6.24 $\cos^{-1}x + \cos^{-1}(-x) = \pi$

As we can see from Fig. 6.24, the arc cosine of x satisfies the identity

$$\cos^{-1} x + \cos^{-1} (-x) = \pi, \tag{4}$$

or

$$\cos^{-1}(-x) = \pi - \cos^{-1} x. \tag{5}$$

And we can see from the triangle in Fig. 6.25 that for $x > 0$,

$$\sin^{-1} x + \cos^{-1} x = \pi/2. \tag{6}$$

Equation (6) holds for the other values of x in $[-1, 1]$ as well, but we cannot conclude this from the triangle in Fig. 6.25. It is, however, a consequence of Eqs. (2) and (5).

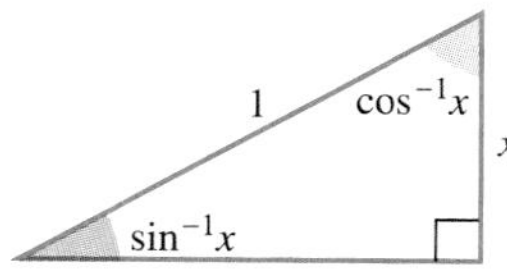

6.25 In this figure, $\sin^{-1}x + \cos^{-1}x = \pi/2$.

The Arc Tangent

The arc tangent function

$$y = \tan^{-1} x \tag{7}$$

is the inverse of the restricted function

$$y = \tan x, \quad -\pi/2 < x < \pi/2 \tag{8}$$

(Fig. 6.26 on the following page). For every real value of x, $y = \tan^{-1} x$ is the angle between $-\pi/2$ and $\pi/2$ whose tangent is x.

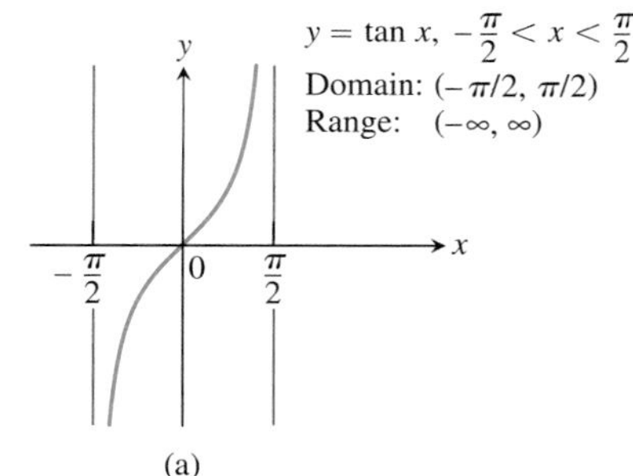

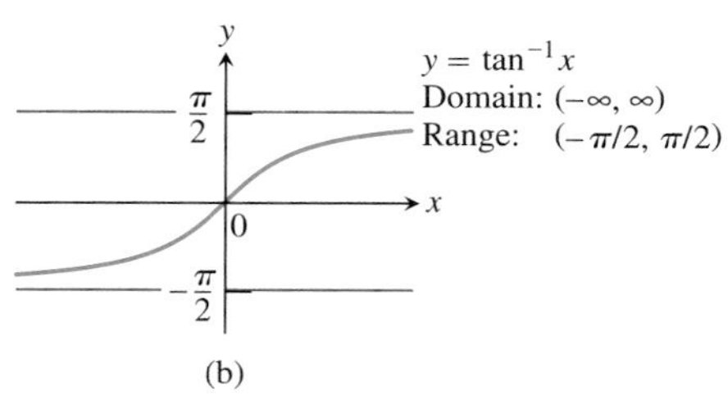

6.26 The graphs of (a) $y = \tan x$, $-\pi/2 < x < \pi/2$, and (b) its inverse, $y = \tan^{-1} x$.

The graph of $\tan^{-1} x$ is symmetric about the origin. Like the arc sine, the arc tangent is an odd function of x:

$$\tan^{-1}(-x) = -\tan^{-1} x. \tag{9}$$

From Fig. 6.26 we can see that $\tan^{-1} x$ has the same sign as x and that $\tan^{-1} 0 = 0$. Other values can be found from right triangles using the definition $\tan y$ = side opposite/side adjacent.

EXAMPLE 3 Common values of $\tan^{-1} x$.

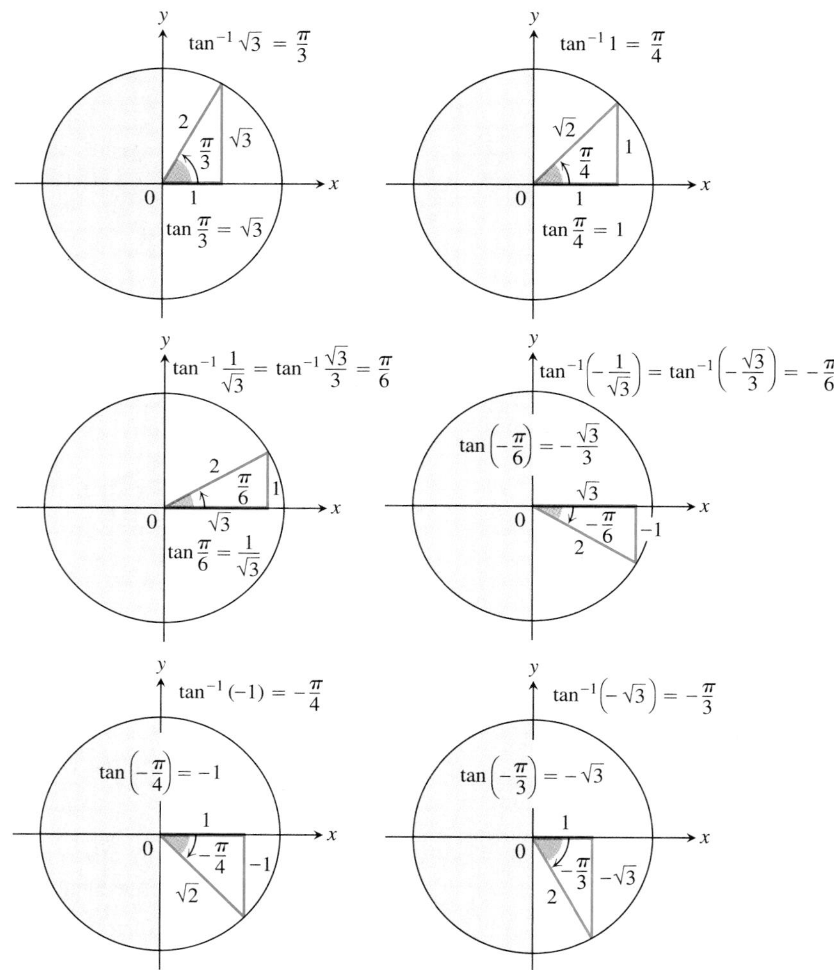

The angles come from the first and fourth quadrants because the range of the arc tangent is $(-\pi/2, \pi/2)$.

The Arc Secant, Arc Cosecant, and Arc Cotangent

The inverses of the restricted functions

$$y = \sec x, \quad 0 \le x \le \pi, \quad x \ne \pi/2, \tag{10}$$

$$y = \csc x, \quad -\pi/2 \le x \le \pi/2, \quad x \ne 0, \tag{11}$$

$$y = \cot x, \quad 0 < x < \pi, \tag{12}$$

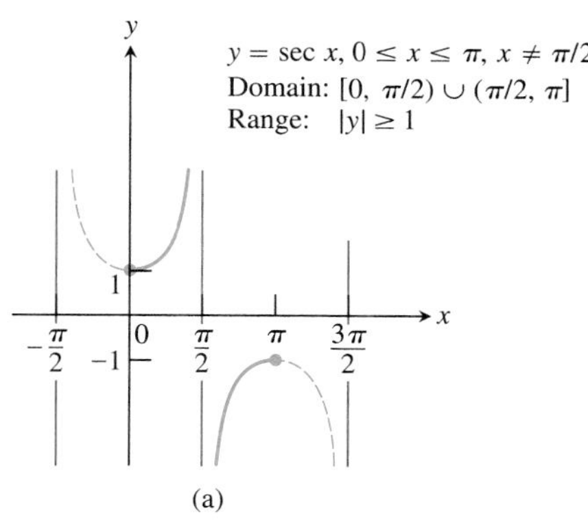

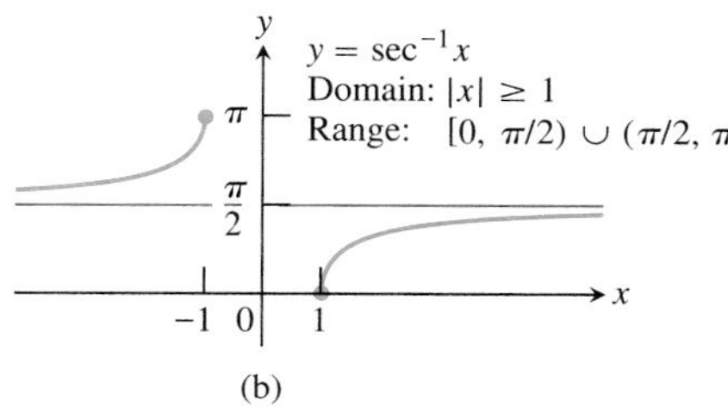

6.27 The graphs of (a) $y = \sec x$, $0 \le x \le \pi$, $x \ne \pi/2$, and (b) its inverse, $y = \sec^{-1} x$.

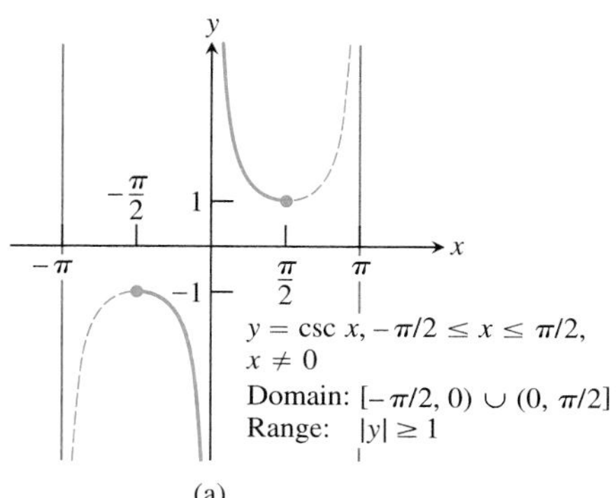

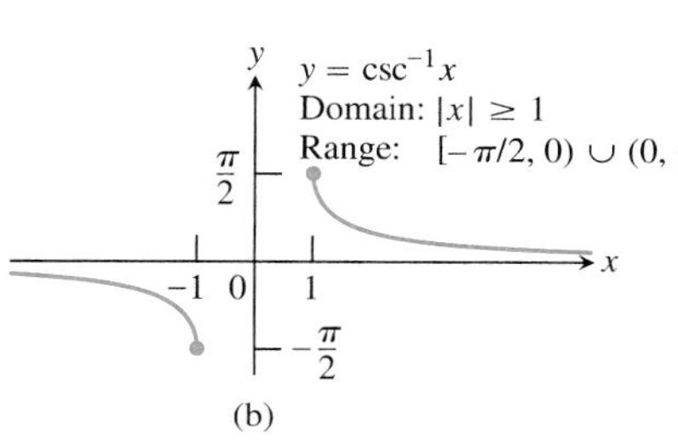

6.28 The graphs of (a) $y = \csc x$, $-\pi/2 \le x \le \pi/2$, $x \ne 0$, and (b) $y = \csc^{-1} x$.

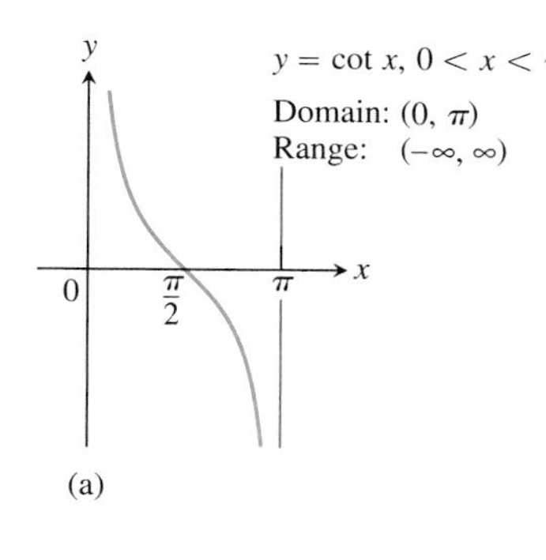

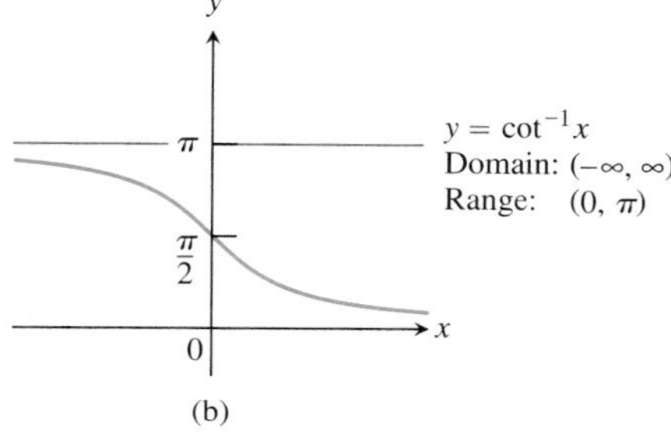

6.29 The graphs of (a) $y = \cot x$, $0 < x < \pi$, and (b) its inverse, $y = \cot^{-1} x$.

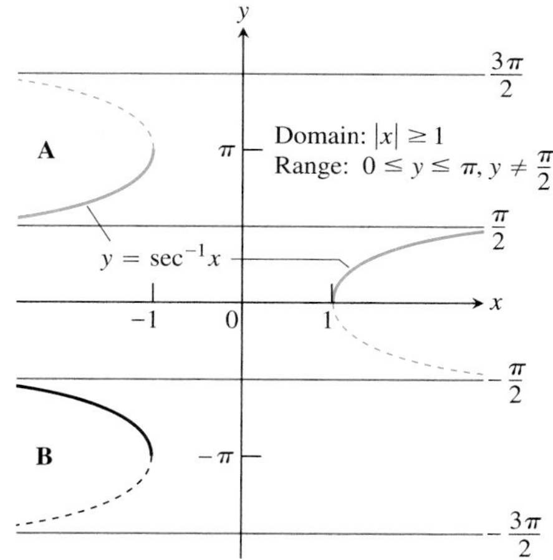

6.30 There are two logical choices for the left-hand branch of $y = \sec^{-1} x$. With choice **A**, Eq. (13) holds, but the formula for the derivative of the arc secant is complicated by absolute value bars. Choice **B** leads to a simpler derivative formula, but Eq. (13) no longer holds. The more frequent choice is **A**, the choice we have made.

are the functions graphed in Figs. 6.27–6.29. They are chosen this way to satisfy the following relationships.

$$\sec^{-1} x = \cos^{-1}(1/x) \tag{13}$$

$$\csc^{-1} x = \sin^{-1}(1/x) \tag{14}$$

$$\cot^{-1} x = \pi/2 - \tan^{-1} x \tag{15}$$

We can use these relationships to find values of $\sec^{-1} x$, $\csc^{-1} x$, and $\cot^{-1} x$ on calculators that give only $\cos^{-1} x$, $\sin^{-1} x$, and $\tan^{-1} x$. As in Examples 1–3, we can also find a few of the more common values of $\sec^{-1} x$, $\csc^{-1} x$, and $\cot^{-1} x$ using reference right triangles.

Warning: There is no general agreement about how to define $\sec^{-1} x$ for negative values of x. We chose angles in the second quadrant between $\pi/2$ and π. This choice makes $\sec^{-1} x = \cos^{-1}(1/x)$, which matches $\sec x = 1/\cos x$. It also makes $\sec^{-1} x$ an increasing function of x. Some tables choose $\sec^{-1} x$ to lie in the third quadrant, between $-\pi/2$ and $-\pi$ (Fig. 6.30). This has the advantage of simplifying the formula for the derivative (our formula needs absolute value signs) but the third-quadrant values fail to satisfy the equation $\sec^{-1} x = \cos^{-1}(1/x)$.

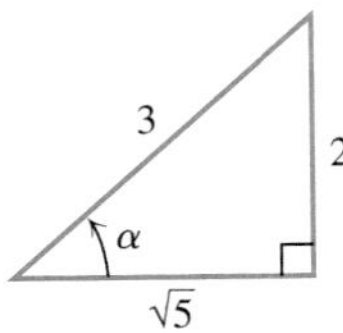

6.31 If $\alpha = \sin^{-1}(2/3)$, then the values of the other basic trigonometric functions of α can be read from this triangle (Example 4).

EXAMPLE 4 Find $\cos\alpha$, $\tan\alpha$, $\sec\alpha$, $\csc\alpha$, and $\cot\alpha$ if

$$\alpha = \sin^{-1}\frac{2}{3}. \qquad (16)$$

Solution Equation (16) says that $\sin\alpha = \frac{2}{3}$.

We picture α as an angle in a right triangle with opposite side 2 and hypotenuse 3 (Fig. 6.31). The length of the remaining side is

$$\sqrt{(3)^2 - (2)^2} = \sqrt{9-4} = \sqrt{5}. \qquad \text{Pythagorean theorem}$$

We add this information to the figure and then read the values we want from the completed triangle:

$$\cos\alpha = \frac{\sqrt{5}}{3}, \quad \tan\alpha = \frac{2}{\sqrt{5}}, \quad \sec\alpha = \frac{3}{\sqrt{5}}, \quad \csc\alpha = \frac{3}{2}, \quad \cot\alpha = \frac{\sqrt{5}}{2}.$$

The "Arc" in Arc Sine and Arc Cosine

In case you are wondering about the "arc," look at the accompanying figure. It gives a geometric interpretation of $y = \sin^{-1}x$ and $y = \cos^{-1}x$ for angles in the first quadrant. For a unit circle, the equation $s = r\theta$ becomes $s = \theta$, so central angles and the arcs they subtend have the same measure. If $x = \sin y$, then, in addition to being the angle whose sine is x, y is also the length of arc on the unit circle that subtends an angle whose sine is x. So we call y "the arc whose sine is x." When angles were measured by intercepted arc length, as they once were, this was a natural way to speak. Today it can sound a bit strange, but the language has stayed with us. The arc cosine has a similar interpretation.

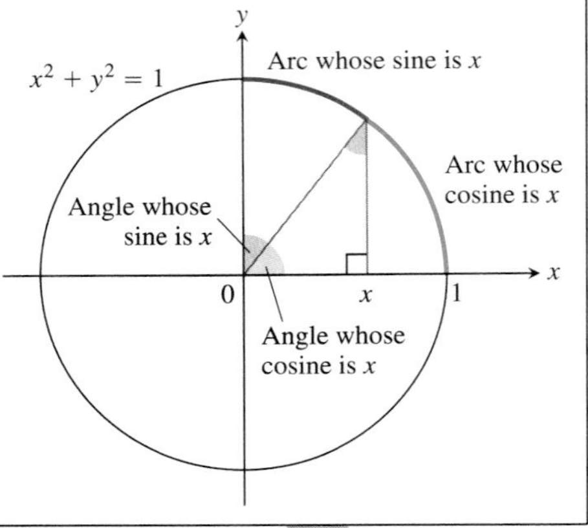

EXAMPLE 5 Find $\cot\left(\sec^{-1}\left(-\frac{2}{\sqrt{3}}\right) + \csc^{-1}(-2)\right)$.

Solution We work from inside out, using reference triangles to exhibit ratios and angles.

STEP 1: Negative values of the secant come from second-quadrant angles:

$$\sec^{-1}\left(-\frac{2}{\sqrt{3}}\right) = \sec^{-1}\left(\frac{2}{-\sqrt{3}}\right) = \frac{5\pi}{6}.$$

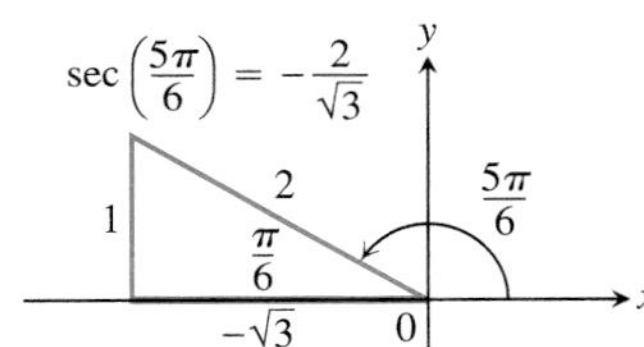

STEP 2: Negative values of the cosecant come from fourth-quadrant angles:

$$\csc^{-1}(-2) = \csc^{-1}\left(\frac{2}{-1}\right) = -\frac{\pi}{6}.$$

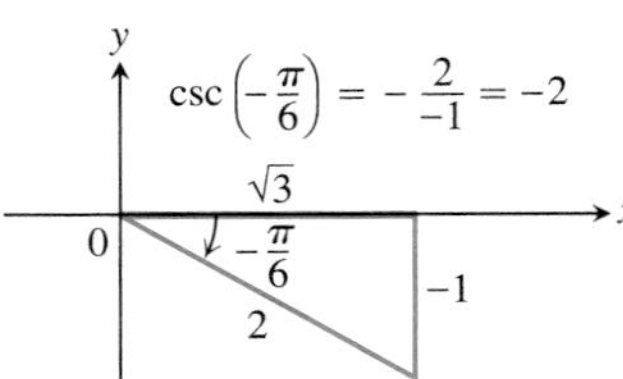

STEP 3:

$$\cot\left(\sec^{-1}\left(-\frac{2}{\sqrt{3}}\right) + \csc^{-1}(-2)\right) = \cot\left(\frac{5\pi}{6} - \frac{\pi}{6}\right) = \cot\left(\frac{2\pi}{3}\right) = -\frac{1}{\sqrt{3}}$$

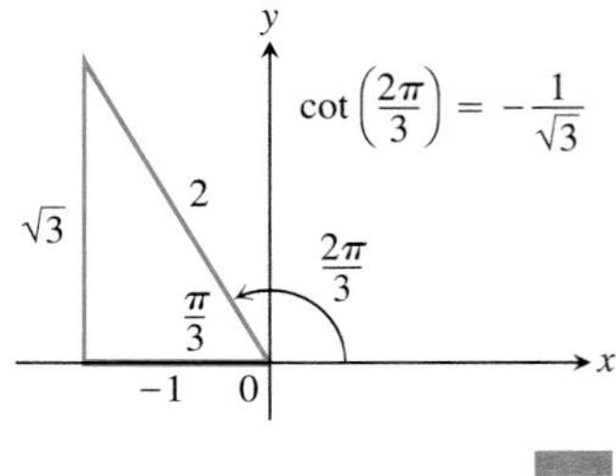

EXAMPLE 6 Find $\sec\left(\tan^{-1}\dfrac{x}{3}\right)$.

$\tan\theta = \frac{x}{3}$

$\sec\theta = \frac{\sqrt{x^2+9}}{3}$

Solution We let $\theta = \tan^{-1}(x/3)$ (to give the angle a name) and picture θ in a right triangle with

$$\tan\theta = \text{opposite/adjacent} = x/3.$$

The length of the triangle's hypotenuse is

$$\sqrt{3^2 + x^2} = \sqrt{x^2+9}.$$

Thus,

$$\sec\left(\tan^{-1}\frac{x}{3}\right) = \sec\theta = \frac{\sqrt{x^2+9}}{3}. \qquad \sec\theta = \frac{\text{hypotenuse}}{\text{adjacent}}$$

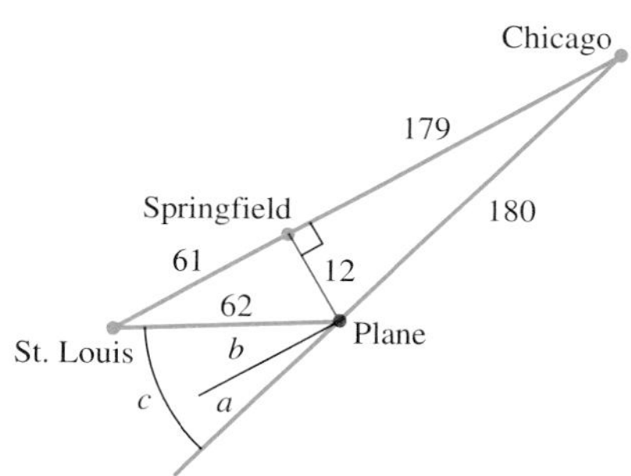

6.32 Diagram for drift correction (Example 7), with distances rounded to the nearest mile (drawing not to scale).

EXAMPLE 7 *Drift Correction.* During an airplane flight from Chicago to St. Louis the navigator determines that the plane is 12 mi off course, as shown in Fig. 6.32. Find the angle a for a course parallel to the original, correct course, the angle b, and the correction angle $c = a + b$.

Solution

$$a = \sin^{-1}\frac{12}{180} \approx 0.067 \text{ radian} \approx 3.8°,$$

$$b = \sin^{-1}\frac{12}{62} \approx 0.195 \text{ radian} \approx 11.2°,$$

$$c = a + b \approx 15°.$$

Exercises 6.8

Use reference triangles like those in Examples 1–3 to find the angles in Exercises 1–12.

1. a) $\tan^{-1} 1$ b) $\tan^{-1}(-\sqrt{3})$ c) $\tan^{-1}\left(\frac{1}{\sqrt{3}}\right)$
2. a) $\tan^{-1}(-1)$ b) $\tan^{-1}\sqrt{3}$ c) $\tan^{-1}\left(\frac{-1}{\sqrt{3}}\right)$
3. a) $\sin^{-1}\left(\frac{-1}{2}\right)$ b) $\sin^{-1}\left(\frac{1}{\sqrt{2}}\right)$ c) $\sin^{-1}\left(\frac{-\sqrt{3}}{2}\right)$
4. a) $\sin^{-1}\left(\frac{1}{2}\right)$ b) $\sin^{-1}\left(\frac{-1}{\sqrt{2}}\right)$ c) $\sin^{-1}\left(\frac{\sqrt{3}}{2}\right)$
5. a) $\cos^{-1}\left(\frac{1}{2}\right)$ b) $\cos^{-1}\left(\frac{-1}{\sqrt{2}}\right)$ c) $\cos^{-1}\left(\frac{\sqrt{3}}{2}\right)$
6. a) $\cos^{-1}\left(\frac{-1}{2}\right)$ b) $\cos^{-1}\left(\frac{1}{\sqrt{2}}\right)$ c) $\cos^{-1}\left(\frac{-\sqrt{3}}{2}\right)$
7. a) $\sec^{-1}(-\sqrt{2})$ b) $\sec^{-1}\left(\frac{2}{\sqrt{3}}\right)$ c) $\sec^{-1}(-2)$
8. a) $\sec^{-1}\sqrt{2}$ b) $\sec^{-1}\left(\frac{-2}{\sqrt{3}}\right)$ c) $\sec^{-1} 2$
9. a) $\csc^{-1}\sqrt{2}$ b) $\csc^{-1}\left(\frac{-2}{\sqrt{3}}\right)$ c) $\csc^{-1} 2$
10. a) $\csc^{-1}(-\sqrt{2})$ b) $\csc^{-1}\left(\frac{2}{\sqrt{3}}\right)$ c) $\csc^{-1}(-2)$
11. a) $\cot^{-1}(-1)$ b) $\cot^{-1}\sqrt{3}$ c) $\cot^{-1}\left(\frac{-1}{\sqrt{3}}\right)$
12. a) $\cot^{-1} 1$ b) $\cot^{-1}(-\sqrt{3})$ c) $\cot^{-1}\left(\frac{1}{\sqrt{3}}\right)$
13. Given that $\alpha = \sin^{-1}(5/13)$, find $\cos\alpha$, $\tan\alpha$, $\sec\alpha$, $\csc\alpha$, and $\cot\alpha$.

14. Given that $\alpha = \tan^{-1}(4/3)$, find $\sin\alpha$, $\cos\alpha$, $\sec\alpha$, $\csc\alpha$, and $\cot\alpha$.

15. Given that $\alpha = \sec^{-1}\left(-\sqrt{5}\right)$, find $\sin\alpha$, $\cos\alpha$, $\tan\alpha$, $\csc\alpha$, and $\cot\alpha$.

16. Given that $\alpha = \sec^{-1}\left(-\sqrt{13}/2\right)$, find $\sin\alpha$, $\cos\alpha$, $\tan\alpha$, $\csc\alpha$, and $\cot\alpha$.

Evaluate the expressions in Exercises 17–28.

17. $\sin\left(\cos^{-1}\dfrac{\sqrt{2}}{2}\right)$

18. $\sec\left(\cos^{-1}\dfrac{1}{2}\right)$

19. $\tan\left(\sin^{-1}\left(-\dfrac{1}{2}\right)\right)$

20. $\cot\left(\sin^{-1}\left(-\dfrac{\sqrt{3}}{2}\right)\right)$

21. $\csc\left(\sec^{-1}2\right) + \cos\left(\tan^{-1}\left(-\sqrt{3}\right)\right)$

22. $\tan\left(\sec^{-1}1\right) + \sin\left(\csc^{-1}(-2)\right)$

23. $\sin\left(\sin^{-1}\left(-\dfrac{1}{2}\right) + \cos^{-1}\left(-\dfrac{1}{2}\right)\right)$

24. $\cot\left(\sin^{-1}\left(-\dfrac{1}{2}\right) - \sec^{-1}2\right)$

25. $\sec\left(\tan^{-1}1 + \csc^{-1}1\right)$

26. $\sec\left(\cot^{-1}\sqrt{3} + \csc^{-1}(-1)\right)$

27. $\sec^{-1}\left(\sec\left(-\dfrac{\pi}{6}\right)\right)$ (The answer is *not* $-\pi/6$.)

28. $\cot^{-1}\left(\cot\left(-\dfrac{\pi}{4}\right)\right)$ (The answer is *not* $-\pi/4$.)

Evaluate the expressions in Exercises 29–40.

29. $\sec\left(\tan^{-1}\dfrac{x}{2}\right)$

30. $\sec\left(\tan^{-1}2x\right)$

31. $\tan\left(\sec^{-1}3y\right)$

32. $\tan\left(\sec^{-1}\dfrac{y}{5}\right)$

33. $\cos\left(\sin^{-1}x\right)$

34. $\tan\left(\cos^{-1}x\right)$

35. $\sin\left(\tan^{-1}\sqrt{x^2-2x}\right),\ x \ge 2$

36. $\sin\left(\tan^{-1}\dfrac{x}{\sqrt{x^2+1}}\right)$

37. $\cos\left(\sin^{-1}\dfrac{2y}{3}\right)$

38. $\cos\left(\sin^{-1}\dfrac{y}{5}\right)$

39. $\sin\left(\sec^{-1}\dfrac{x}{4}\right)$

40. $\sin\left(\sec^{-1}\dfrac{\sqrt{x^2+4}}{x}\right)$

Find the limits in Exercises 41–48. (If in doubt, look at the function's graph.)

41. $\lim\limits_{x\to 1^-} \sin^{-1}x$

42. $\lim\limits_{x\to -1^+} \cos^{-1}x$

43. $\lim\limits_{x\to\infty} \tan^{-1}x$

44. $\lim\limits_{x\to -\infty} \tan^{-1}x$

45. $\lim\limits_{x\to\infty} \sec^{-1}x$

46. $\lim\limits_{x\to -\infty} \sec^{-1}x$

47. $\lim\limits_{x\to\infty} \csc^{-1}x$

48. $\lim\limits_{x\to -\infty} \csc^{-1}x$

49. You are sitting in a classroom next to the wall looking at the blackboard at the front of the room. The blackboard is 12 ft long and starts 3 ft from the wall you are sitting next to. Show that your viewing angle is

$$\alpha = \cot^{-1}\frac{x}{15} - \cot^{-1}\frac{x}{3}$$

if you are x ft from the front wall.

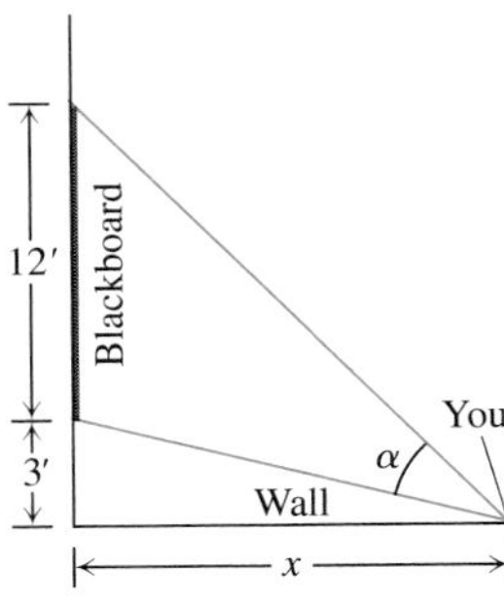

50. The slant height of the cone shown here is 3 m. How large should the indicated angle be to maximize the cone's volume?

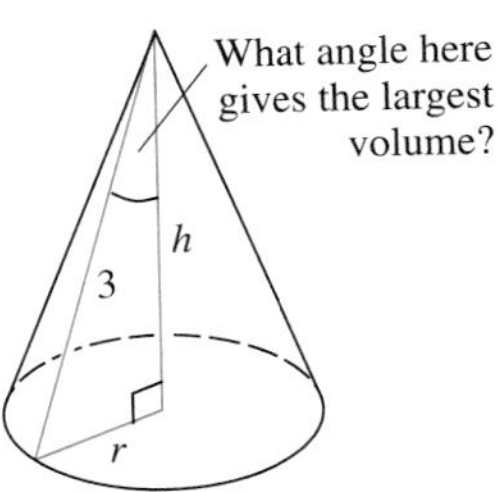

51. Find the angle α.

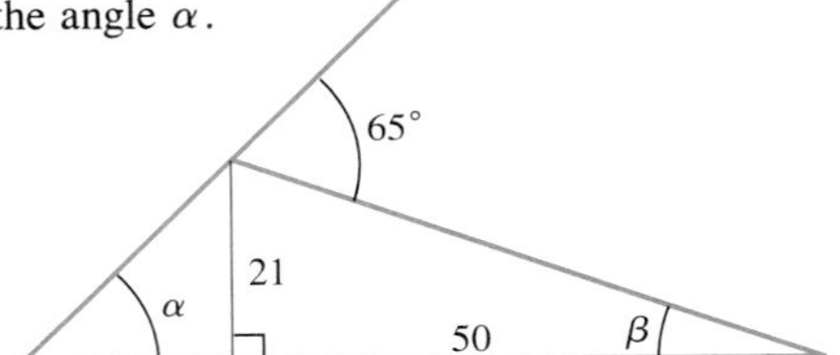

52. Here is an informal proof that $\tan^{-1}1 + \tan^{-1}2 + \tan^{-1}3 = \pi$. Explain what is going on.

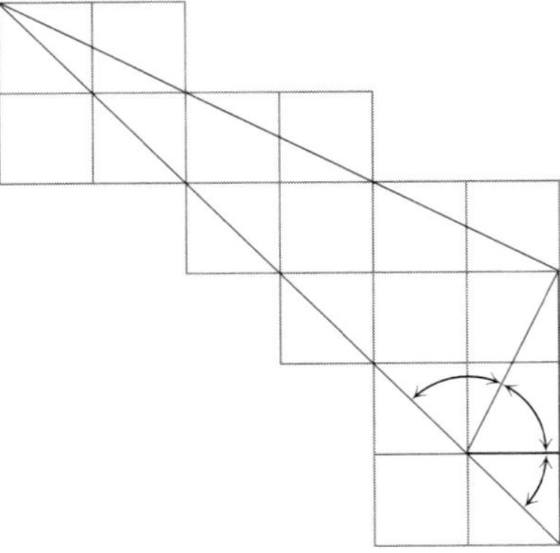

53. Find the values of

a) $\sec^{-1}1.5$ **b)** $\csc^{-1}(-1.5)$ **c)** $\cot^{-1}2$

54. Find the values of

a) $\sec^{-1}(-3)$ **b)** $\csc^{-1}1.7$ **c)** $\cot^{-1}(-2)$

Which of the expressions in Exercises 55–58 are defined and which are not? Give reasons for your answers.

55. a) $\tan^{-1} 2$ **b)** $\cos^{-1} 2$

56. a) $\csc^{-1} \frac{1}{2}$ **b)** $\csc^{-1} 2$

57. a) $\sec^{-1} 0$ **b)** $\sin^{-1} \sqrt{2}$

58. a) $\cot^{-1} \left(-\frac{1}{2}\right)$ **b)** $\cos^{-1}(-5)$

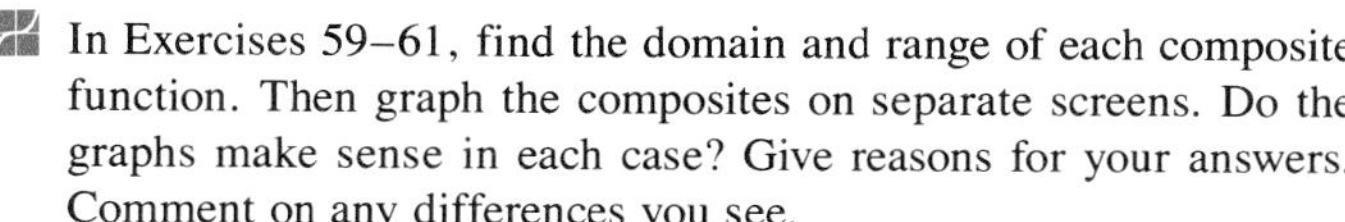

In Exercises 59–61, find the domain and range of each composite function. Then graph the composites on separate screens. Do the graphs make sense in each case? Give reasons for your answers. Comment on any differences you see.

59. a) $y = \tan^{-1}(\tan x)$ **b)** $y = \tan(\tan^{-1} x)$

60. a) $y = \sin^{-1}(\sin x)$ **b)** $y = \sin(\sin^{-1} x)$

61. a) $y = \cos^{-1}(\cos x)$ **b)** $y = \cos(\cos^{-1} x)$

62. Graph $y = \sec(\sec^{-1} x) = \sec(\cos^{-1}(1/x))$. Explain what you see.

Writing for Your Own Knowledge

Answer the following questions in writing. Some answers will take only a sentence or two; others may require several paragraphs. Some explanations may also call for graphs or sketches.

1. How are the inverse trigonometric functions defined?
2. How can you sometimes use reference right triangles to find values of inverse trigonometric functions?
3. How can you find values of $\sec^{-1} x$, $\csc^{-1} x$, and $\cot^{-1} x$ using a calculator's keys for $\cos^{-1} x$, $\sin^{-1} x$, and $\tan^{-1} x$?

EXPLORER PROGRAM

PowerGrapher — Graphs functions singly or together.

6.9 Derivatives of Inverse Trigonometric Functions; Integrals

Inverse trigonometric functions provide antiderivatives for a variety of functions that arise in mathematics, engineering, and physics. In this section we find the derivatives of the inverse trigonometric functions (Table 6.6) and discuss related integrals.

TABLE 6.6
Derivatives of the inverse trigonometric functions

1. $\dfrac{d(\sin^{-1} u)}{dx} = \dfrac{du/dx}{\sqrt{1-u^2}}, \quad |u| < 1$

2. $\dfrac{d(\tan^{-1} u)}{dx} = \dfrac{du/dx}{1+u^2}$

3. $\dfrac{d(\sec^{-1} u)}{dx} = \dfrac{du/dx}{|u|\sqrt{u^2-1}}, \quad |u| > 1$

4. $\dfrac{d(\cos^{-1} u)}{dx} = -\dfrac{du/dx}{\sqrt{1-u^2}}, \quad |u| < 1$

5. $\dfrac{d(\cot^{-1} u)}{dx} = -\dfrac{du/dx}{1+u^2}$

6. $\dfrac{d(\csc^{-1} u)}{dx} = \dfrac{-du/dx}{|u|\sqrt{u^2-1}}, \quad |u| > 1$

EXAMPLE 1

a) $$\frac{d}{dx}\sin^{-1}(x^2) = \frac{1}{\sqrt{1-(x^2)^2}} \cdot \frac{d}{dx}(x^2) = \frac{2x}{\sqrt{1-x^4}}$$

b) $$\frac{d}{dx}\tan^{-1}\sqrt{x+1} = \frac{1}{1+\left(\sqrt{x+1}\right)^2} \cdot \frac{d}{dx}\left(\sqrt{x+1}\right)$$
$$= \frac{1}{x+2} \cdot \frac{1}{2\sqrt{x+1}} = \frac{1}{2\sqrt{x+1}(x+2)}$$

c) $$\frac{d}{dx}\sec^{-1}(-3x) = \frac{1}{|-3x|\sqrt{(-3x)^2-1}} \cdot \frac{d}{dx}(-3x)$$
$$= \frac{-3}{|3x|\sqrt{9x^2-1}} = \frac{-1}{|x|\sqrt{9x^2-1}}.$$

EXAMPLE 2

$$\int_0^1 \frac{e^{\tan^{-1} x}}{1+x^2}\,dx = \int_0^{\pi/4} e^u\,du \qquad u = \tan^{-1} x,\quad du = \frac{dx}{1+x^2},\quad u(0) = 0,\quad u(1) = \pi/4$$
$$= e^u\Big]_0^{\pi/4} = e^{\pi/4} - 1$$

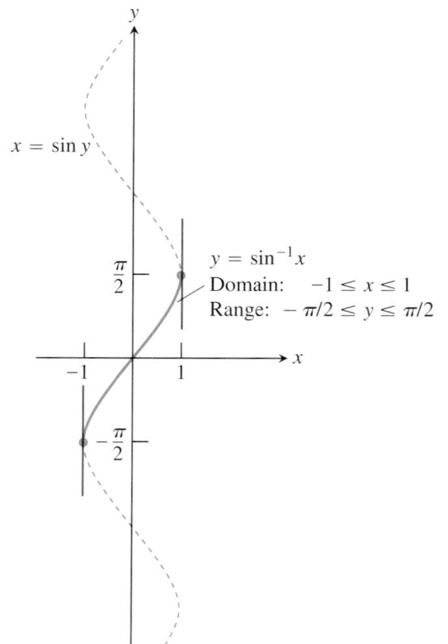

6.33 The graph of $y = \sin^{-1} x$ has vertical tangents at $x = -1$ and $x = 1$.

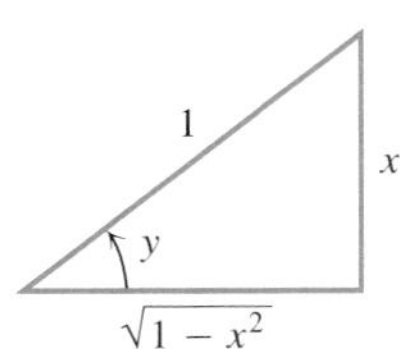

6.34 In the reference right triangle above,

$$\sin y = \frac{x}{1} = x,$$

$$\cos y = \frac{\sqrt{1-x^2}}{1} = \sqrt{1-x^2}.$$

We derive Formulas 1 and 3 from Table 6.6. The derivation of Formula 2 is similar. Formulas 4–6 can be derived from Formulas 1–3 by differentiating appropriate identities (Exercises 83–85).

The Derivative of $y = \sin^{-1} u$

We know that the function $x = \sin y$ is differentiable in the interval $-\pi/2 < y < \pi/2$ and that its derivative, the cosine, is positive there. Theorem 1 in Section 6.2 therefore assures us that the inverse function $y = \sin^{-1} x$ is differentiable throughout the interval $-1 < x < 1$. We cannot expect it to be differentiable at $x = 1$ or $x = -1$ because the tangents to the graph are vertical at these points (see Fig. 6.33).

We find the derivative of $y = \sin^{-1} x$ as follows:

$$\sin y = x \qquad y = \sin^{-1} x \iff \sin y = x$$

$$\frac{d}{dx}(\sin y) = 1 \qquad \text{Derivative of both sides with respect to } x$$

$$\cos y \frac{dy}{dx} = 1 \qquad \text{Chain Rule}$$

$$\frac{dy}{dx} = \frac{1}{\cos y} \qquad \text{We can divide because } \cos y > 0 \text{ for } -\pi/2 < y < \pi/2.$$

$$= \frac{1}{\sqrt{1-x^2}} \qquad \text{Fig. 6.34}$$

The derivative of $y = \sin^{-1} x$ with respect to x is

$$\frac{d}{dx}(\sin^{-1} x) = \frac{1}{\sqrt{1-x^2}}. \tag{1}$$

If u is a differentiable function of x with $|u| < 1$, we apply the Chain Rule

$$\frac{dy}{dx} = \frac{dy}{du} \cdot \frac{du}{dx}$$

to $y = \sin^{-1} u$ to obtain

$$\frac{d}{dx}(\sin^{-1} u) = \frac{1}{\sqrt{1-u^2}} \frac{du}{dx}, \qquad |u| < 1. \tag{2}$$

The Derivative of $y = \sec^{-1} u$

We find the derivative of $y = \sec^{-1} x$, $|x| > 1$, in a similar way.

$$\sec y = x \qquad y = \sec^{-1} x \iff \sec y = x$$

$$\frac{d}{dx}(\sec y) = 1 \qquad \text{Derivative of both sides with respect to } x$$

$$\sec y \tan y \frac{dy}{dx} = 1 \qquad \text{Chain Rule}$$

$$\frac{dy}{dx} = \frac{1}{\sec y \tan y} \qquad \text{Since } |x| > 1,\ y \text{ lies in } (0, \pi/2) \cup (\pi/2, \pi) \text{ and } \sec y \tan y \neq 0.$$

$$= \pm \frac{1}{x\sqrt{x^2-1}} \qquad \text{Fig. 6.35}$$

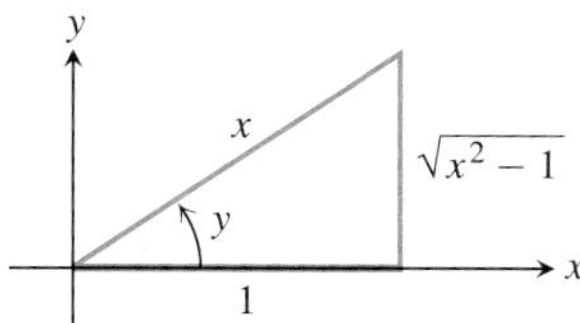

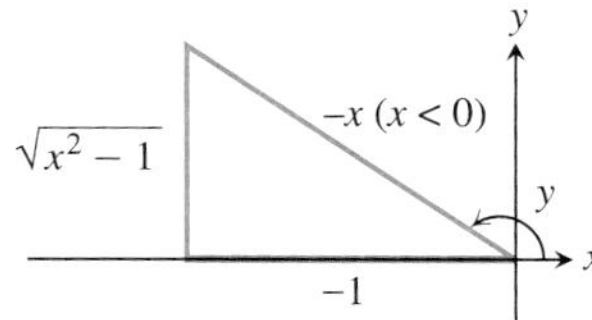

6.35 In both quadrants, $\sec y = x/1 = x$. In the first quadrant,

$$\tan y = \sqrt{x^2-1}/1 = \sqrt{x^2-1}.$$

In the second quadrant,

$$\tan y = \sqrt{x^2-1}/(-1) = -\sqrt{x^2-1}.$$

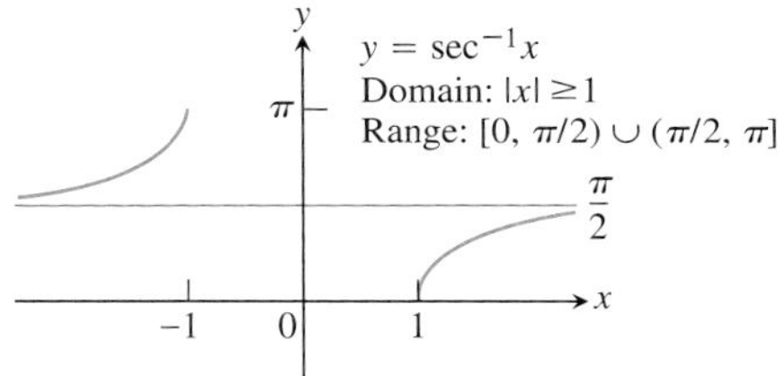

6.36 The slope of the curve $y = \sec^{-1} x$ is positive for both $x < -1$ and $x > 1$.

What do we do about the sign? A glance at Fig. 6.36 shows that for $|x| > 1$ the slope of the graph of $y = \sec^{-1} x$ is always positive. Therefore,

$$\frac{d}{dx}(\sec^{-1} x) = \begin{cases} \dfrac{1}{x\sqrt{x^2-1}} & \text{if } x > 1, \\ -\dfrac{1}{x\sqrt{x^2-1}} & \text{if } x < -1. \end{cases} \tag{3}$$

With absolute values, we can write Eq. (3) as a single formula:

$$\frac{d}{dx}(\sec^{-1} x) = \frac{1}{|x|\sqrt{x^2-1}}, \qquad |x| > 1. \tag{4}$$

If u is a differentiable function of x with $|u| > 1$, we can then apply the Chain Rule to obtain

$$\frac{d}{dx}(\sec^{-1} u) = \frac{1}{|u|\sqrt{u^2-1}}\frac{du}{dx}, \qquad |u| > 1. \tag{5}$$

Integration Formulas

The derivative formulas in Table 6.6 yield three useful integration formulas in Table 6.7.

TABLE 6.7
Integrals evaluated with inverse trigonometric functions

The following formulas hold for any constant $a \neq 0$.

1. $\displaystyle\int \frac{du}{\sqrt{a^2-u^2}} = \sin^{-1}\left(\frac{u}{a}\right) + C$ (Valid for $u^2 < a^2$) (6)

2. $\displaystyle\int \frac{du}{a^2+u^2} = \frac{1}{a}\tan^{-1}\left(\frac{u}{a}\right) + C$ (Valid for all u) (7)

3. $\displaystyle\int \frac{du}{u\sqrt{u^2-a^2}} = \frac{1}{a}\sec^{-1}\left|\frac{u}{a}\right| + C$ (Valid for $u^2 > a^2$) (8)

The derivative formulas in Table 6.6 have $a = 1$, but in most integrations $a \neq 1$, and the formulas in Table 6.7 are more useful. They are readily verified by differentiating the functions on the right-hand sides.

EXAMPLE 3

a) $$\int_{\sqrt{2}/2}^{\sqrt{3}/2} \frac{dx}{\sqrt{1-x^2}} = \sin^{-1}(x)\Big]_{\sqrt{2}/2}^{\sqrt{3}/2}$$
$$= \sin^{-1}\left(\frac{\sqrt{3}}{2}\right) - \sin^{-1}\left(\frac{\sqrt{2}}{2}\right) = \frac{\pi}{3} - \frac{\pi}{4} = \frac{\pi}{12}$$

b) $$\int_0^1 \frac{dx}{1+x^2} = \tan^{-1}(x)\Big]_0^1 = \tan^{-1}(1) - \tan^{-1}(0) = \frac{\pi}{4} - 0 = \frac{\pi}{4}$$

c) $$\int_{2/\sqrt{3}}^{\sqrt{2}} \frac{dx}{x\sqrt{x^2-1}} = \sec^{-1}(x)\Big]_{2/\sqrt{3}}^{\sqrt{2}} = \frac{\pi}{4} - \frac{\pi}{6} = \frac{\pi}{12}$$

EXAMPLE 4

a) $\displaystyle\int \frac{dx}{\sqrt{9-x^2}} = \int \frac{dx}{\sqrt{(3)^2-x^2}} = \sin^{-1}\left(\frac{x}{3}\right) + C$ — Eq. (6) with $a = 3$, $u = x$

b) $\displaystyle\int \frac{dx}{\sqrt{3-4x^2}} = \frac{1}{2}\int \frac{du}{\sqrt{a^2-u^2}}$ — $a = \sqrt{3}$, $u = 2x$, and $du/2 = dx$

$$= \frac{1}{2}\sin^{-1}\left(\frac{u}{a}\right) + C \qquad \text{Eq. (6)}$$

$$= \frac{1}{2}\sin^{-1}\left(\frac{2x}{\sqrt{3}}\right) + C$$

For more information about completing the square, see Appendix 1 and Section 1.4, Example 8.

EXAMPLE 5 Evaluate $\displaystyle\int \frac{dx}{\sqrt{4x-x^2}}$.

Solution The expression $\sqrt{4x-x^2}$ does not match any of the formulas in Table 6.7, so we first rewrite $4x - x^2$ by completing the square:

$$4x - x^2 = -(x^2 - 4x) = -(x^2 - 4x + 4) + 4 = 4 - (x-2)^2.$$

Then we substitute $a = 2$, $u = x - 2$, and $du = dx$ to get

$$\int \frac{dx}{\sqrt{4x-x^2}} = \int \frac{dx}{\sqrt{4-(x-2)^2}}$$

$$= \int \frac{du}{\sqrt{a^2-u^2}} \qquad a = 2,\ u = x - 2,\ \text{and } du = dx$$

$$= \sin^{-1}\left(\frac{u}{a}\right) + C \qquad \text{Eq. (6)}$$

$$= \sin^{-1}\left(\frac{x-2}{2}\right) + C$$

EXAMPLE 6

a) $\displaystyle\int \frac{dx}{10+x^2} = \frac{1}{\sqrt{10}}\tan^{-1}\left(\frac{x}{\sqrt{10}}\right) + C$ — Eq. (7) with $a = \sqrt{10}$, $u = x$

b) $\displaystyle\int \frac{dx}{7+3x^2} = \frac{1}{\sqrt{3}}\int \frac{du}{a^2+u^2}$ — $a = \sqrt{7}$, $u = \sqrt{3}x$, and $du/\sqrt{3} = dx$

$$= \frac{1}{\sqrt{3}} \cdot \frac{1}{a}\tan^{-1}\left(\frac{u}{a}\right) + C \qquad \text{Eq. (7)}$$

$$= \frac{1}{\sqrt{3}} \cdot \frac{1}{\sqrt{7}}\tan^{-1}\left(\frac{\sqrt{3}x}{\sqrt{7}}\right) + C$$

$$= \frac{1}{\sqrt{21}}\tan^{-1}\left(\frac{\sqrt{3}x}{\sqrt{7}}\right) + C$$

EXAMPLE 7 Evaluate $\displaystyle\int \frac{dx}{4x^2+4x+2}$.

Solution We complete the square on the binomial $4x^2 + 4x$:

$$4x^2 + 4x + 2 = 4(x^2 + x) + 2 = 4\left(x^2 + x + \frac{1}{4}\right) + 2 - \frac{4}{4}$$
$$= 4\left(x + \frac{1}{2}\right)^2 + 1 = (2x + 1)^2 + 1.$$

Then we substitute $a = 1$, $u = 2x + 1$, and $du/2 = dx$ to get

$$\int \frac{dx}{4x^2 + 4x + 2} = \int \frac{dx}{(2x + 1)^2 + 1}$$
$$= \frac{1}{2}\int \frac{du}{u^2 + a^2} \qquad a = 1,\ u = 2x + 1,\ \text{and } du/2 = dx$$
$$= \frac{1}{2} \cdot \frac{1}{a} \tan^{-1}\left(\frac{u}{a}\right) \qquad \text{Eq. (7)}$$
$$= \frac{1}{2} \tan^{-1}(2x + 1) + C \qquad a = 1,\ u = 2x + 1$$

EXAMPLE 8 Evaluate $\displaystyle\int \frac{dx}{x\sqrt{4x^2 - 5}}$.

Solution

$$\int \frac{dx}{x\sqrt{4x^2 - 5}} = \int \frac{\frac{du}{2}}{\frac{u}{2}\sqrt{u^2 - a^2}} \qquad u = 2x,\ x = u/2,\ dx = du/2,\ a = \sqrt{5}$$
$$= \int \frac{du}{u\sqrt{u^2 - a^2}} \qquad \text{The 2's cancel.}$$
$$= \frac{1}{a} \sec^{-1}\left|\frac{u}{a}\right| + C \qquad \text{Eq. (8)}$$
$$= \frac{1}{\sqrt{5}} \sec^{-1}\left(\frac{2|x|}{\sqrt{5}}\right) + C \qquad a = \sqrt{5},\ u = 2x$$

EXAMPLE 9 Evaluate $\displaystyle\int \frac{dx}{\sqrt{e^{2x} - 6}}$.

Solution

$$\int \frac{dx}{\sqrt{e^{2x} - 6}} = \int \frac{du/u}{\sqrt{u^2 - a^2}} \qquad u = e^x,\ du = e^x\,dx,\ dx = du/e^x = du/u,\ a = \sqrt{6}$$
$$= \int \frac{du}{u\sqrt{u^2 - a^2}}$$
$$= \frac{1}{a} \sec^{-1}\left|\frac{u}{a}\right| + C \qquad \text{Eq. (8)}$$
$$= \frac{1}{\sqrt{6}} \sec^{-1}\left|\frac{e^x}{\sqrt{6}}\right| + C$$
$$= \frac{1}{\sqrt{6}} \sec^{-1}\left(\frac{e^x}{\sqrt{6}}\right) + C$$

Exercises 6.9

In Exercises 1–22, find the derivative of y with respect to the appropriate variable.

1. $y = \cos^{-1}(x^2)$
2. $y = \cos^{-1}(1/x)$
3. $y = \sin^{-1}\sqrt{2}\,t$
4. $y = \sin^{-1}(1 - t)$
5. $y = \sec^{-1}(2s + 1)$
6. $y = \sec^{-1} 5s$
7. $y = \csc^{-1}(x^2 + 1), \quad x > 0$
8. $y = \csc^{-1}\dfrac{x}{2}$
9. $y = \sec^{-1}\dfrac{1}{t}, \quad 0 < t < 1$
10. $y = \sin^{-1}\dfrac{3}{t^2}$
11. $y = \cot^{-1}\sqrt{t}$
12. $y = \cot^{-1}\sqrt{t - 1}$
13. $y = \ln(\tan^{-1} x)$
14. $y = \tan^{-1}(\ln x)$
15. $y = \csc^{-1}(e^t)$
16. $y = \cos^{-1}(e^{-t})$
17. $y = s\sqrt{1 - s^2} + \cos^{-1} s$
18. $y = \sqrt{s^2 - 1} - \sec^{-1} s$
19. $y = \tan^{-1}\sqrt{x^2 - 1} + \csc^{-1} x, \quad x > 1$
20. $y = \cot^{-1}\dfrac{1}{x} - \tan^{-1} x$
21. $y = x \sin^{-1} x + \sqrt{1 - x^2}$
22. $y = \ln(x^2 + 4) - x \tan^{-1}\left(\dfrac{x}{2}\right)$

Verify the integration formulas in Exercises 23–26.

23. $\displaystyle\int \frac{\tan^{-1} x}{x^2}\,dx = \ln x - \frac{1}{2}\ln(1 + x^2) - \frac{\tan^{-1} x}{x} + C$
24. $\displaystyle\int x^3 \cos^{-1} 5x\,dx = \frac{x^4}{4}\cos^{-1} 5x + \frac{5}{4}\int \frac{x^4\,dx}{\sqrt{1 - 25x^2}}$
25. $\displaystyle\int (\sin^{-1} x)^2\,dx = x(\sin^{-1} x)^2 - 2x + 2\sqrt{1 - x^2}\sin^{-1} x + C$
26. $\displaystyle\int \ln(a^2 + x^2)\,dx = x\ln(a^2 + x^2) - 2x + 2a\tan^{-1}\frac{x}{a} + C$

Evaluate the integrals in Exercises 27–50.

27. $\displaystyle\int \frac{dx}{\sqrt{9 - x^2}}$
28. $\displaystyle\int \frac{dx}{\sqrt{1 - 4x^2}}$
29. $\displaystyle\int \frac{dx}{17 + x^2}$
30. $\displaystyle\int \frac{dx}{9 + 3x^2}$
31. $\displaystyle\int \frac{dx}{x\sqrt{25x^2 - 2}}$
32. $\displaystyle\int \frac{dx}{x\sqrt{5x^2 - 4}}$
33. $\displaystyle\int_0^1 \frac{4\,ds}{\sqrt{4 - s^2}}$
34. $\displaystyle\int_0^{3\sqrt{2}/4} \frac{ds}{\sqrt{9 - 4s^2}}$
35. $\displaystyle\int_0^2 \frac{dt}{8 + 2t^2}$
36. $\displaystyle\int_{-2}^2 \frac{dt}{4 + 3t^2}$
37. $\displaystyle\int_{-1}^{-\sqrt{2}/2} \frac{dy}{y\sqrt{4y^2 - 1}}$
38. $\displaystyle\int_{-2/3}^{-\sqrt{2}/3} \frac{dy}{y\sqrt{9y^2 - 1}}$
39. $\displaystyle\int \frac{3\,dr}{\sqrt{1 - 4(r - 1)^2}}$
40. $\displaystyle\int \frac{6\,dr}{\sqrt{4 - (r + 1)^2}}$
41. $\displaystyle\int \frac{dx}{2 + (x - 1)^2}$
42. $\displaystyle\int \frac{dx}{1 + (3x + 1)^2}$
43. $\displaystyle\int \frac{dx}{(2x - 1)\sqrt{(2x - 1)^2 - 4}}$
44. $\displaystyle\int \frac{dx}{(x + 3)\sqrt{(x + 3)^2 - 25}}$
45. $\displaystyle\int_{-\pi/2}^{\pi/2} \frac{2\cos\theta\,d\theta}{1 + (\sin\theta)^2}$
46. $\displaystyle\int_{\pi/6}^{\pi/4} \frac{\csc^2 x\,dx}{1 + (\cot x)^2}$
47. $\displaystyle\int_0^{\ln\sqrt{3}} \frac{e^x\,dx}{1 + e^{2x}}$
48. $\displaystyle\int_1^{e^{\pi/4}} \frac{4\,dt}{t(1 + \ln^2 t)}$
49. $\displaystyle\int \frac{y\,dy}{\sqrt{1 - y^4}}$
50. $\displaystyle\int \frac{\sec^2 y\,dy}{\sqrt{1 - \tan^2 y}}$

Evaluate the integrals in Exercises 51–60.

51. $\displaystyle\int \frac{dx}{\sqrt{-x^2 + 4x - 3}}$
52. $\displaystyle\int \frac{dx}{\sqrt{2x - x^2}}$
53. $\displaystyle\int_{-1}^0 \frac{6\,dt}{\sqrt{3 - 2t - t^2}}$
54. $\displaystyle\int_{1/2}^1 \frac{6\,dt}{\sqrt{3 + 4t - 4t^2}}$
55. $\displaystyle\int \frac{dy}{y^2 - 2y + 5}$
56. $\displaystyle\int \frac{dy}{y^2 + 6y + 10}$
57. $\displaystyle\int_1^2 \frac{8\,dx}{x^2 - 2x + 2}$
58. $\displaystyle\int_2^4 \frac{2\,dx}{x^2 - 6x + 10}$
59. $\displaystyle\int \frac{dx}{(x + 1)\sqrt{x^2 + 2x}}$
60. $\displaystyle\int \frac{dx}{(x - 2)\sqrt{x^2 - 4x + 3}}$

Evaluate the integrals in Exercises 61–68.

61. $\displaystyle\int \frac{e^{\sin^{-1} x}\,dx}{\sqrt{1 - x^2}}$
62. $\displaystyle\int \frac{e^{\cos^{-1} x}\,dx}{\sqrt{1 - x^2}}$
63. $\displaystyle\int \frac{(\sin^{-1} x)^2\,dx}{\sqrt{1 - x^2}}$
64. $\displaystyle\int \frac{\sqrt{\tan^{-1} x}\,dx}{1 + x^2}$
65. $\displaystyle\int \frac{dy}{(\tan^{-1} y)(1 + y^2)}$
66. $\displaystyle\int \frac{dy}{(\sin^{-1} y)\sqrt{1 - y^2}}$
67. $\displaystyle\int_1^{\sqrt{2}} \frac{\sec^2(\sec^{-1} x)\,dx}{x\sqrt{x^2 - 1}}$
68. $\displaystyle\int_1^2 \frac{\cos(\sec^{-1} x)\,dx}{x\sqrt{x^2 - 1}}$

Find the limits in Exercises 69–72.

69. $\displaystyle\lim_{x\to 0} \frac{\sin^{-1} 5x}{x}$
70. $\displaystyle\lim_{x\to 1^+} \frac{\sqrt{x^2 - 1}}{\sec^{-1} x}$
71. $\displaystyle\lim_{x\to\infty} x\tan^{-1}\frac{2}{x}$
72. $\displaystyle\lim_{x\to 0} \frac{2\tan^{-1} 3x}{7x^2}$

73. *Continuation of Exercise 49, Section 6.8.* You want to move your chair to a position along the wall that will maximize your viewing angle α. About how far from the front of the room should you sit?

74. What value of x maximizes θ in the angle shown here? How large is θ at that point? Begin by showing that $\theta = \pi - \cot^{-1} x - \cot^{-1} (2 - x)$.

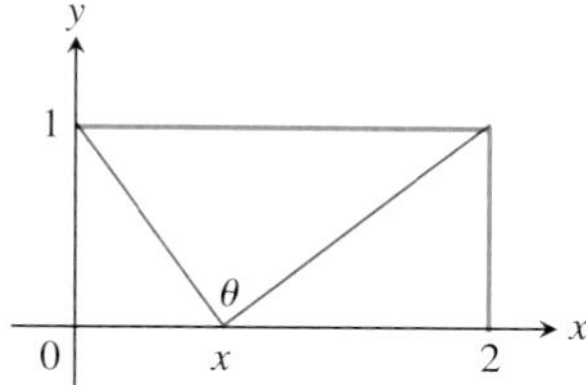

Solve the initial value problems in Exercises 75–78.

75. Differential equation: $\dfrac{dy}{dx} = \dfrac{1}{\sqrt{1 - x^2}}$

Initial condition: $y = 0$ when $x = 0$

(This is the initial value problem whose solution was sketched in Section 4.7, Exercise 71.)

76. Differential equation: $\dfrac{dy}{dx} = \dfrac{1}{x^2 + 1} - 1$

Initial condition: $y = 1$ when $x = 0$

(This is the initial value problem whose solution was sketched in Section 4.7, Exercise 73.)

77. Differential equation: $\dfrac{dy}{dx} = \dfrac{1}{x\sqrt{x^2 - 1}}, \quad x > 1$

Initial condition: $y = \pi$ when $x = 2$

78. Differential equation: $\dfrac{dy}{dx} = \dfrac{1}{1 + x^2} - \dfrac{2}{\sqrt{1 - x^2}}$

Initial condition: $y = 2$ when $x = 0$

79. Can the integrations in (a) and (b) both be correct? Explain.

a) $\displaystyle\int \frac{dx}{\sqrt{1 - x^2}} = \sin^{-1} x + C$

b) $\displaystyle\int \frac{dx}{\sqrt{1 - x^2}} = -\int -\frac{dx}{\sqrt{1 - x^2}} = -\cos^{-1} x + C$

80. Can the integrations in (a) and (b) both be correct? Explain.

a) $\displaystyle\int \frac{dx}{\sqrt{1 - x^2}} = -\int -\frac{dx}{\sqrt{1 - x^2}} = -\cos^{-1} x + C$

b) $\displaystyle\int \frac{dx}{\sqrt{1 - x^2}} = \int \frac{-du}{\sqrt{1 - (-u)^2}}$ $\quad x = -u,\ dx = -du$

$\displaystyle = \int \frac{-du}{\sqrt{1 - u^2}}$

$= \cos^{-1} u + C$

$= \cos^{-1}(-x) + C$ $\quad u = -x$

81. What is special about the functions

$$f(x) = \sin^{-1} \frac{x - 1}{x + 1}, \quad x \geq 0, \quad \text{and} \quad g(x) = 2 \tan^{-1} \sqrt{x}?$$

Explain.

82. What is special about the functions

$$f(x) = \sin^{-1} \frac{1}{\sqrt{x^2 + 1}} \quad \text{and} \quad g(x) = \tan^{-1} \frac{1}{x}?$$

Explain.

83. Use the identity

$$\cos^{-1} u = \frac{\pi}{2} - \sin^{-1} u$$

to derive the formula for the derivative of $\cos^{-1} u$ in Table 6.6 from the formula for the derivative of $\sin^{-1} u$.

84. Use the identity

$$\cot^{-1} u = \frac{\pi}{2} - \tan^{-1} u$$

to derive the formula for the derivative of $\cot^{-1} u$ in Table 6.6 from the formula for the derivative of $\tan^{-1} u$.

85. Use the identity

$$\csc^{-1} u = \frac{\pi}{2} - \sec^{-1} u$$

to derive the formula for the derivative of $\csc^{-1} u$ in Table 6.6 from the formula for the derivative of $\sec^{-1} u$.

86. Derive the formula

$$\frac{dy}{dx} = \frac{1}{1 + x^2}$$

for the derivative of $y = \tan^{-1} x$ by differentiating both sides of the equivalent equation $\tan y = x$.

87. Graph $f(x) = \sin^{-1} x$ together with its first two derivatives. Comment on the behavior of f and the shape of its graph in relation to the signs and values of f' and f''.

88. Graph $f(x) = \tan^{-1} x$ together with its first two derivatives. Comment on the behavior of f and the shape of its graph in relation to the signs and values of f' and f''.

Writing for Your Own Knowledge

Answer the following questions in writing. Some answers will take only a sentence or two; others may require several paragraphs. Some explanations may also call for graphs or sketches.

1. What are the derivatives of the inverse trigonometric functions? How do the domains of the derivatives compare with the domains of the functions?
2. What are the three standard integration formulas associated with the derivatives of the inverse trigonometric functions? Why three and not six?
3. How do substitution and completing the square broaden the application of the integration formulas in Table 6.7?

EXPLORER PROGRAMS

Derivatives	Graphs functions and their derivatives.
PowerGrapher	Graphs all functions in this section.

6.10 Hyperbolic Functions

Every function f that is defined on an interval centered at the origin can be written in a unique way as the sum of one even function and one odd function. The decomposition is

$$f(x) = \underbrace{\frac{f(x)+f(-x)}{2}}_{\text{even part}} + \underbrace{\frac{f(x)-f(-x)}{2}}_{\text{odd part}}.$$

If we write e^x this way, we get

$$e^x = \underbrace{\frac{e^x + e^{-x}}{2}}_{\text{even part}} + \underbrace{\frac{e^x - e^{-x}}{2}}_{\text{odd part}}.$$

The notation $\cosh x$ is often read "kosh x," rhyming with either "gosh x" or "gauche x," and $\sinh x$ is pronounced as if spelled "cinch x" or "shine x."

The even and odd parts of e^x, called the hyperbolic cosine and hyperbolic sine of x, respectively, are useful in their own right. They describe the motions of waves in elastic solids, the shapes of hanging electric power lines, and the temperature distributions in metal cooling fins. The center line of the Gateway Arch to the West in St. Louis is a weighted hyperbolic cosine curve.

Definitions and Identities

The hyperbolic cosine and hyperbolic sine functions are defined by the first two equations in Table 6.8. The table also lists the definitions of the hyperbolic tangent, cotangent, secant, and cosecant. As we will see, the hyperbolic functions bear a number of similarities to the trigonometric functions after which they are named. (See Exercise 74 as well.)

Identities

Hyperbolic functions satisfy the identities in Table 6.9. Except for differences in sign, these are identities we already know for trigonometric functions.

TABLE 6.8
The six basic hyperbolic functions (See Fig. 6.37 for graphs.)

Hyperbolic cosine of x:	$\cosh x = \dfrac{e^x + e^{-x}}{2}$
Hyperbolic sine of x:	$\sinh x = \dfrac{e^x - e^{-x}}{2}$
Hyperbolic tangent:	$\tanh x = \dfrac{\sinh x}{\cosh x} = \dfrac{e^x - e^{-x}}{e^x + e^{-x}}$
Hyperbolic cotangent:	$\coth x = \dfrac{\cosh x}{\sinh x} = \dfrac{e^x + e^{-x}}{e^x - e^{-x}}$
Hyperbolic secant:	$\operatorname{sech} x = \dfrac{1}{\cosh x} = \dfrac{2}{e^x + e^{-x}}$
Hyperbolic cosecant:	$\operatorname{csch} x = \dfrac{1}{\sinh x} = \dfrac{2}{e^x - e^{-x}}$

TABLE 6.9
Identities for hyperbolic functions

$$\sinh 2x = 2 \sinh x \cosh x$$

$$\cosh 2x = \cosh^2 x + \sinh^2 x$$

$$\cosh^2 x = \frac{\cosh 2x + 1}{2}$$

$$\sinh^2 x = \frac{\cosh 2x - 1}{2}$$

$$\cosh^2 x - \sinh^2 x = 1$$

$$\tanh^2 x = 1 - \operatorname{sech}^2 x$$

$$\coth^2 x = 1 + \operatorname{csch}^2 x$$

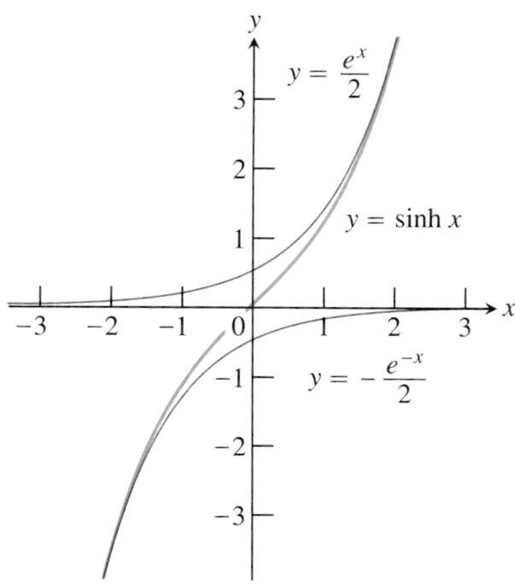

(a) The hyperbolic sine and its component exponentials.

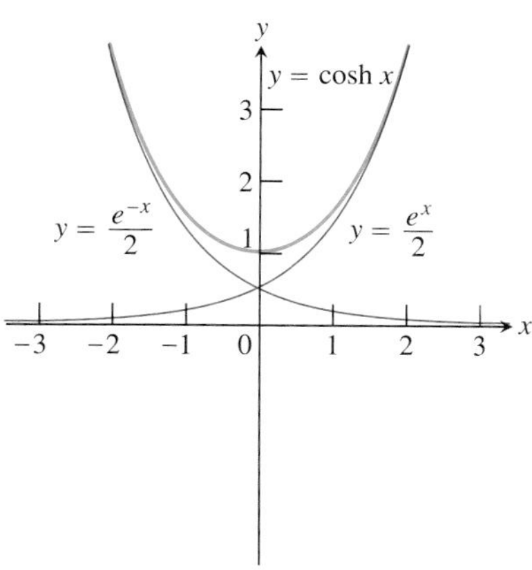

(b) The hyperbolic cosine and its component exponentials.

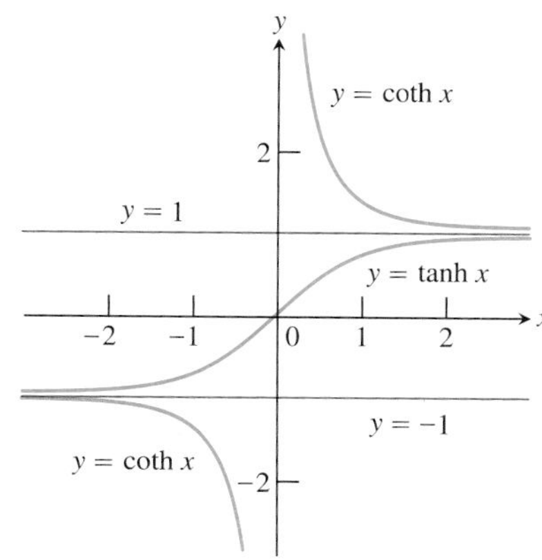

(c) The graphs of $y = \tanh x$ and $y = \coth x = 1/\tanh x$.

6.37 The graphs of the six hyperbolic functions.

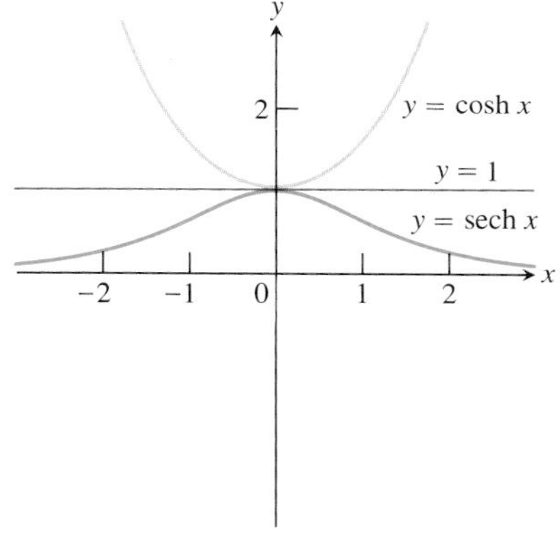

(d) The graphs of $y = \cosh x$ and $y = \operatorname{sech} x = 1/\cosh x$.

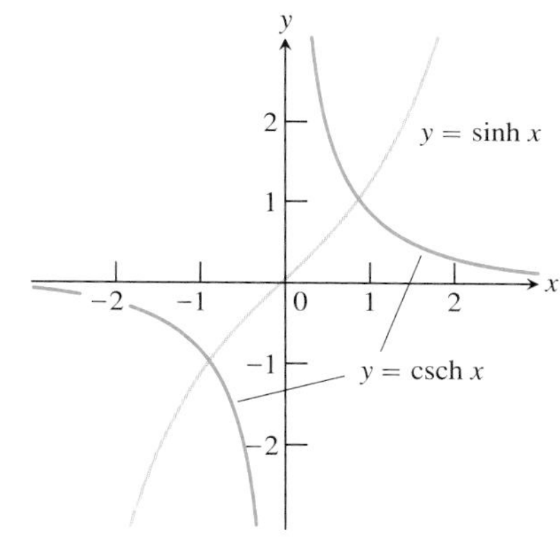

(e) The graphs of $y = \sinh x$ and $y = \operatorname{csch} x = 1/\sinh x$.

TABLE 6.10
Derivatives of hyperbolic functions

$$\frac{d}{dx}(\sinh u) = \cosh u \frac{du}{dx}$$

$$\frac{d}{dx}(\cosh u) = \sinh u \frac{du}{dx}$$

$$\frac{d}{dx}(\tanh u) = \operatorname{sech}^2 u \frac{du}{dx}$$

$$\frac{d}{dx}(\coth u) = -\operatorname{csch}^2 u \frac{du}{dx}$$

$$\frac{d}{dx}(\operatorname{sech} u) = -\operatorname{sech} u \tanh u \frac{du}{dx}$$

$$\frac{d}{dx}(\operatorname{csch} u) = -\operatorname{csch} u \coth u \frac{du}{dx}$$

Derivatives and Integrals

The six hyperbolic functions, being rational combinations of the differentiable functions e^x and e^{-x}, have derivatives at every point at which they are defined (Table 6.10). Again, there are similarities with trigonometric functions. The derivative formulas in Table 6.10 lead to the integral formulas in Table 6.11 (on the following page).

EXAMPLE 1

$$\frac{d}{dt}\left(\tanh \sqrt{1+t^2}\right) = \operatorname{sech}^2 \sqrt{1+t^2} \cdot \frac{d}{dt}\left(\sqrt{1+t^2}\right)$$

$$= \frac{t}{\sqrt{1+t^2}} \operatorname{sech}^2 \sqrt{1+t^2}$$

TABLE 6.11
Integral formulas for hyperbolic functions

$$\int \sinh u\, du = \cosh u + C$$

$$\int \cosh u\, du = \sinh u + C$$

$$\int \operatorname{sech}^2 u\, du = \tanh u + C$$

$$\int \operatorname{csch}^2 u\, du = -\coth u + C$$

$$\int \operatorname{sech} u \tanh u\, du = -\operatorname{sech} u + C$$

$$\int \operatorname{csch} u \coth u\, du = -\operatorname{csch} u + C$$

EXAMPLE 2

$$\int \coth 5x\, dx = \int \frac{\cosh 5x}{\sinh 5x}\, dx = \frac{1}{5}\int \frac{du}{u} \qquad u = \sinh 5x,\ du = 5\cosh 5x\, dx$$

$$= \frac{1}{5}\ln|u| + C = \frac{1}{5}\ln|\sinh 5x| + C$$

EXAMPLE 3

$$\int_0^1 \sinh^2 x\, dx = \int_0^1 \frac{\cosh 2x - 1}{2}\, dx \qquad \text{Table 6.9}$$

$$= \frac{1}{2}\int_0^1 (\cosh 2x - 1)\, dx = \frac{1}{2}\left[\frac{\sinh 2x}{2} - x\right]_0^1$$

$$= \frac{\sinh 2}{4} - \frac{1}{2} \approx 0.40672$$

As in Example 3, hyperbolic functions are usually evaluated with a calculator. Use the [hyp], [cos], [sin], and [tan] keys, or [e^x].

EXAMPLE 4

$$\int_0^{\ln 2} 4e^x \sinh x\, dx = \int_0^{\ln 2} 4e^x \frac{e^x - e^{-x}}{2}\, dx = \int_0^{\ln 2} (2e^{2x} - 2)\, dx$$

$$= [e^{2x} - 2x]_0^{\ln 2} = (e^{2\ln 2} - 2\ln 2) - (1 - 0)$$

$$= 4 - 2\ln 2 - 1$$

$$\approx 1.6137$$

The Inverse Hyperbolic Functions

$\sinh^{-1}$ is read "the arc hyperbolic sine of x" or "the inverse hyperbolic sine of x."

We use the inverses of the six basic hyperbolic functions in integration. Since $d(\sinh^{-1} x)/dx = \cosh x > 0$, the hyperbolic sine is an increasing function of x. We denote its inverse by

$$y = \sinh^{-1} x. \tag{1}$$

For every value of x in the interval $-\infty < x < \infty$, the value of $y = \sinh^{-1} x$ is the number whose hyperbolic sine is x. The graphs of $y = \sinh x$ and $y = \sinh^{-1} x$ are shown in Fig. 6.38(a).

The function $y = \cosh x$ is not one-to-one, as we can see from the graph in Fig. 6.37. But the restricted function $y = \cosh x$, $x \geq 0$, is one-to-one and therefore has an inverse, denoted by

$$y = \cosh^{-1} x. \tag{2}$$

For every value of $x \geq 1$, $y = \cosh^{-1} x$ is the number in the interval $0 \leq y < \infty$ whose hyperbolic cosine is x. The graphs of $y = \cosh x$, $x \geq 0$, and $y = \cosh^{-1} x$ are shown in Fig. 6.38(b).

Like $y = \cosh x$, the function $y = \operatorname{sech} x = 1/\cosh x$ fails to be one-to-one, but its restriction to nonnegative values of x does have an inverse, denoted by

$$y = \operatorname{sech}^{-1} x. \tag{3}$$

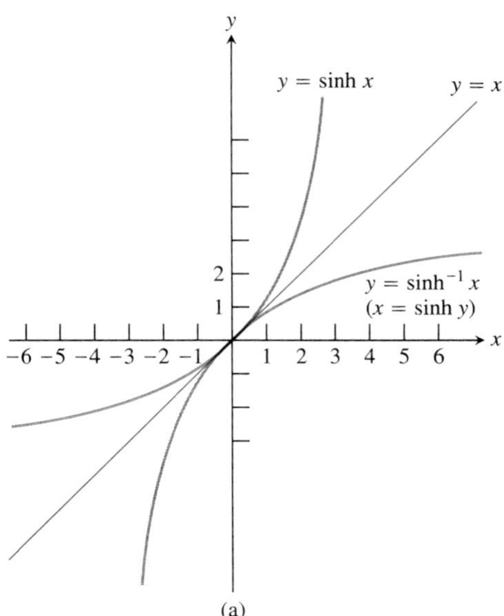

(a)

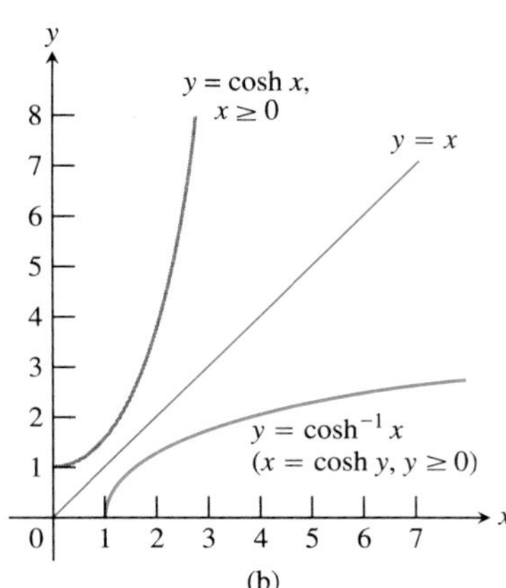

(b)

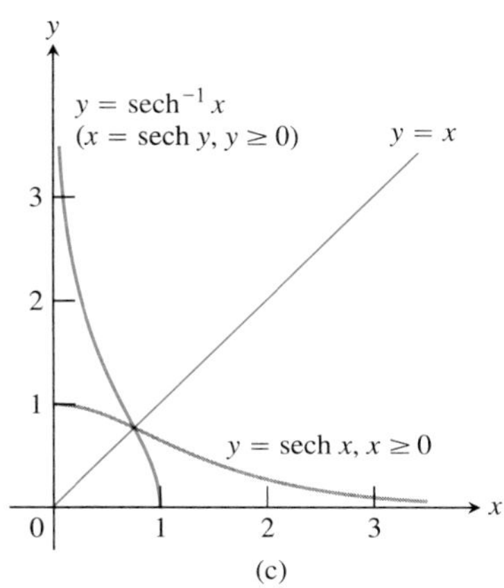

(c)

6.38 The graphs of the inverse hyperbolic sine, cosine, and secant of x. Notice the symmetries about the line $y = x$.

For every value of x in the interval $(0, 1]$, $y = \operatorname{sech}^{-1} x$ is the nonnegative number whose hyperbolic secant is x. The graphs of $y = \operatorname{sech} x$, $x \geq 0$, and $y = \operatorname{sech}^{-1} x$ are shown in Fig. 6.38(c).

The hyperbolic tangent, cotangent, and cosecant are one-to-one on their domains and therefore have inverses, denoted by

$$y = \tanh^{-1} x, \qquad y = \coth^{-1} x, \qquad y = \operatorname{csch}^{-1} x. \tag{4}$$

These functions are graphed in Fig. 6.39.

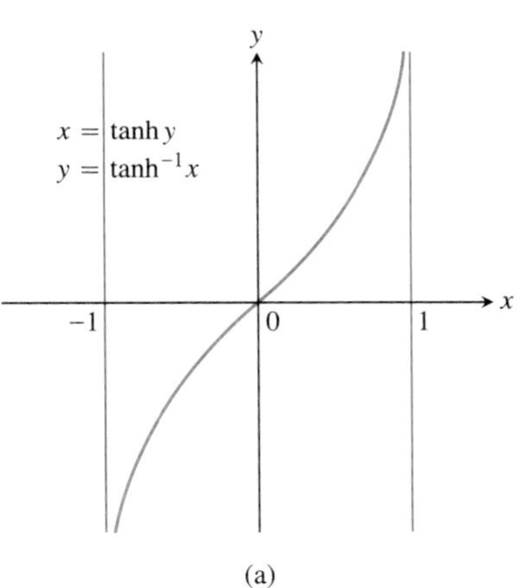

(a)

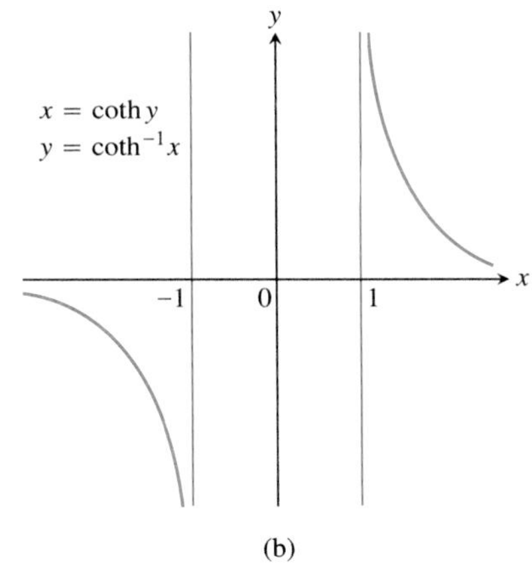

(b)

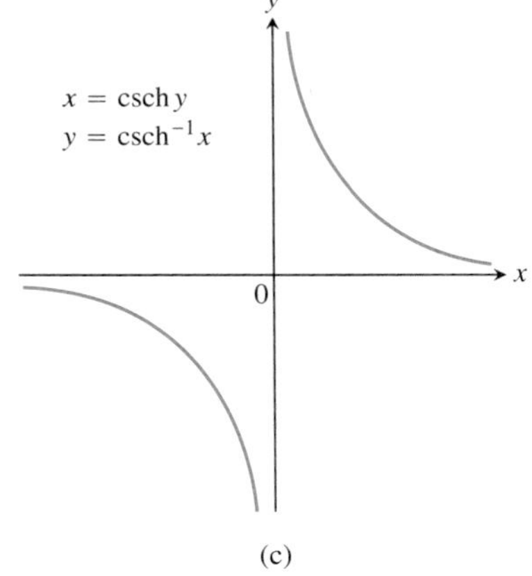

(c)

6.39 The graphs of the inverse hyperbolic tangent, cotangent, and cosecant of x.

TABLE 6.12
Identities for inverse hyperbolic functions

$\operatorname{sech}^{-1} x = \cosh^{-1} \dfrac{1}{x}$
$\operatorname{csch}^{-1} x = \sinh^{-1} \dfrac{1}{x}$
$\coth^{-1} x = \tanh^{-1} \dfrac{1}{x}$

Useful Identities

We use the identities in Table 6.12 to calculate the values of $\operatorname{sech}^{-1} x$, $\operatorname{csch}^{-1} x$, and $\coth^{-1} x$ on calculators that give only $\cosh^{-1} x$, $\sinh^{-1} x$, and $\tanh^{-1} x$.

Derivatives and Integrals

The chief use of inverse hyperbolic functions lies in integrations that reverse the derivative formulas in Table 6.13 (on the following page).

TABLE 6.13
Derivatives of inverse hyperbolic functions

$$\frac{d(\sinh^{-1}u)}{dx} = \frac{1}{\sqrt{1+u^2}}\frac{du}{dx}$$

$$\frac{d(\cosh^{-1}u)}{dx} = \frac{1}{\sqrt{u^2-1}}\frac{du}{dx}, \quad u>1$$

$$\frac{d(\tanh^{-1}u)}{dx} = \frac{1}{1-u^2}\frac{du}{dx}, \quad |u|<1$$

$$\frac{d(\coth^{-1}u)}{dx} = \frac{1}{1-u^2}\frac{du}{dx}, \quad |u|>1$$

$$\frac{d(\operatorname{sech}^{-1}u)}{dx} = \frac{-du/dx}{u\sqrt{1-u^2}}, \quad 0<u<1$$

$$\frac{d(\operatorname{csch}^{-1}u)}{dx} = \frac{-du/dx}{|u|\sqrt{1+u^2}}, \quad u\neq 0$$

The restrictions $|u|<1$ and $|u|>1$ on the derivative formulas for $\tanh^{-1}u$ and $\coth^{-1}u$ come from the natural restrictions on the values of these functions. (See Figs. 6.39a and b.) The distinction between $|u|<1$ and $|u|>1$ becomes important when we convert the derivative formulas into integral formulas. If $|u|<1$, the integral of $1/(1-u^2)$ is $\tanh^{-1}u + C$. If $|u|>1$, the integral is $\coth^{-1}u + C$.

EXAMPLE 5 Show that if u is a differentiable function of x whose values are greater than 1, then

$$\frac{d}{dx}(\cosh^{-1}u) = \frac{1}{\sqrt{u^2-1}}\frac{du}{dx}.$$

Solution First we find the derivative of $y = \cosh^{-1}x$ for $x>1$:

$$y = \cosh^{-1}x$$

$$x = \cosh y \qquad \text{Equivalent equation}$$

$$1 = \sinh y \frac{dy}{dx} \qquad \text{Differentiation with respect to } x$$

$$\frac{dy}{dx} = \frac{1}{\sinh y} = \frac{1}{\sqrt{\cosh^2 y - 1}} \qquad \text{Since } x>1,\ y>0 \text{ and } \sinh y>0$$

$$= \frac{1}{\sqrt{x^2-1}} \qquad \cosh y = x$$

In short, $\dfrac{d}{dx}(\cosh^{-1}x) = \dfrac{1}{\sqrt{x^2-1}}$.

The Chain Rule gives the final result:

$$\frac{d}{dx}(\cosh^{-1}u) = \frac{1}{\sqrt{u^2-1}}\frac{du}{dx}.$$

With appropriate substitutions, the derivative formulas in Table 6.13 lead to the integration formulas in Table 6.14.

TABLE 6.14
Integrals leading to inverse hyperbolic functions

1. $$\int \frac{du}{\sqrt{a^2+u^2}} = \sinh^{-1}\left(\frac{u}{a}\right) + C, \quad a>0$$

2. $$\int \frac{du}{\sqrt{u^2-a^2}} = \cosh^{-1}\left(\frac{u}{a}\right) + C, \quad u>a>0$$

3. $$\int \frac{du}{a^2-u^2} = \begin{cases} \dfrac{1}{a}\tanh^{-1}\left(\dfrac{u}{a}\right) + C & \text{if } u^2<a^2 \\ \dfrac{1}{a}\coth^{-1}\left(\dfrac{u}{a}\right) + C & \text{if } u^2>a^2 \end{cases}$$

4. $$\int \frac{du}{u\sqrt{a^2-u^2}} = -\frac{1}{a}\operatorname{sech}^{-1}\left(\frac{u}{a}\right) + C, \quad 0<u<a$$

5. $$\int \frac{du}{u\sqrt{a^2+u^2}} = -\frac{1}{a}\operatorname{csch}^{-1}\left|\frac{u}{a}\right| + C$$

As in Example 6, inverse hyperbolic functions are usually evaluated with a calculator. On calculators without inv and hyp keys, we use formulas that express the inverse hyperbolic functions as combinations of natural logarithms. We have included these in Table 6.15 in the exercises.

EXAMPLE 6 Evaluate $\int_0^1 \frac{2\,dx}{\sqrt{3+4x^2}}$.

Solution The indefinite integral is

$$\int \frac{2\,dx}{\sqrt{3+4x^2}} = \int \frac{du}{\sqrt{a^2+u^2}} \qquad u = 2x,\ du = 2\,dx,\ a = \sqrt{3}$$

$$= \sinh^{-1}\left(\frac{u}{a}\right) + C \qquad \text{Formula from Table 6.14}$$

$$= \sinh^{-1}\left(\frac{2x}{\sqrt{3}}\right) + C.$$

Therefore,

$$\int_0^1 \frac{2\,dx}{\sqrt{3+4x^2}} = \sinh^{-1}\left(\frac{2x}{\sqrt{3}}\right)\Big]_0^1 = \sinh^{-1}\left(\frac{2}{\sqrt{3}}\right) - \sinh^{-1}(0)$$

$$= \sinh^{-1}\left(\frac{2}{\sqrt{3}}\right) - 0 \approx 0.98665.$$

Exercises 6.10

Exercises 1 and 2 give values for sinh x and cosh x respectively. In each case, use the definitions and the identity $\cosh^2 x - \sinh^2 x = 1$ to find the values of the remaining five hyperbolic functions.

1. $\sinh x = -\frac{3}{4}$
2. $\cosh x = \frac{17}{15}, \quad x > 0$

Rewrite the expressions in Exercises 3–6 in terms of exponentials and simplify the results as much as you can.

3. $2\cosh(\ln x)$
4. $\sinh(2\ln x)$
5. $(\sinh x + \cosh x)^4$
6. $\ln(\cosh x + \sinh x) + \ln(\cosh x - \sinh x)$

In Exercises 7–18, find the derivative of y with respect to the appropriate variable.

7. $y = 6\sinh\frac{x}{3}$
8. $y = \frac{1}{2}\sinh(2x+1)$
9. $y = 2\sqrt{t}\tanh\sqrt{t}$
10. $y = t^2\tanh\frac{1}{t}$
11. $y = \ln(\sinh z)$
12. $y = \ln(\cosh z)$
13. $y = \operatorname{sech}\theta\,(1 - \ln\operatorname{sech}\theta)$
14. $y = \operatorname{csch}\theta\,(1 - \ln\operatorname{csch}\theta)$
15. $y = \ln\cosh v - \frac{1}{2}\tanh^2 v$
16. $y = \ln\sinh v - \frac{1}{2}\coth^2 v$
17. $y = (x^2+1)\operatorname{sech}(\ln x)$
(*Hint:* Before differentiating, express in terms of exponentials and simplify.)
18. $y = (4x^2 - 1)\operatorname{csch}(\ln 2x)$

In Exercises 19–30, find the derivative of y with respect to the appropriate variable.

19. $y = \sinh^{-1}\sqrt{x}$
20. $y = \cosh^{-1} 2\sqrt{x+1}$
21. $y = (1-\theta)\tanh^{-1}\theta$
22. $y = (\theta^2 + 2\theta)\tanh^{-1}(\theta+1)$
23. $y = (1-t)\coth^{-1}\sqrt{t}$
24. $y = (1-t^2)\coth^{-1} t$
25. $y = \cos^{-1} x - x\operatorname{sech}^{-1} x$
26. $y = \ln x + \sqrt{1-x^2}\operatorname{sech}^{-1} x$
27. $y = \operatorname{csch}^{-1}\left(\frac{1}{2}\right)^{\theta}$
28. $y = \operatorname{csch}^{-1} 2^{\theta}$
29. $y = \sinh^{-1}(\tan x)$
30. $y = \cosh^{-1}(\sec x), \quad 0 < x < \pi/2$

Verify the integration formulas in Exercises 31–34.

31. **a)** $\int \operatorname{sech} x\,dx = \tan^{-1}(\sinh x) + C$

 b) $\int \operatorname{sech} x\,dx = \sin^{-1}(\tanh x) + C$
32. $\int x\operatorname{sech}^{-1} x\,dx = \frac{x^2}{2}\operatorname{sech}^{-1} x - \frac{1}{2}\sqrt{1-x^2} + C$
33. $\int x\coth^{-1} x\,dx = \frac{x^2-1}{2}\coth^{-1} x + \frac{x}{2} + C$
34. $\int \tanh^{-1} x\,dx = x\tanh^{-1} x + \frac{1}{2}\ln(1-x^2) + C$

Evaluate the integrals in Exercises 35–44.

35. $\int \sinh 2x\, dx$

36. $\int \sinh \frac{x}{5}\, dx$

37. $\int 6 \cosh \left(\frac{x}{2} - \ln 3\right) dx$

38. $\int 4 \cosh (3x - \ln 2)\, dx$

39. $\int \tanh \frac{x}{7}\, dx$

40. $\int \coth \frac{\theta}{\sqrt{3}}\, d\theta$

41. $\int \operatorname{sech}^2 \left(x - \frac{1}{2}\right) dx$

42. $\int \operatorname{csch}^2 (5 - x)\, dx$

43. $\int \frac{\operatorname{sech} \sqrt{t} \tanh \sqrt{t}\, dt}{\sqrt{t}}$

44. $\int \frac{\operatorname{csch} (\ln t) \coth (\ln t)\, dt}{t}$

Evaluate the integrals in Exercises 45–54.

45. $\int_{\ln 2}^{\ln 4} \coth x\, dx$

46. $\int_0^{\ln 2} \tanh 2x\, dx$

47. $\int_{-\ln 4}^{-\ln 2} 2e^{\theta} \cosh \theta\, d\theta$

48. $\int_0^{\ln 2} 4e^{-\theta} \sinh \theta\, d\theta$

49. $\int_{-\pi/4}^{\pi/4} \cosh (\tan \theta) \sec^2 \theta\, d\theta$

50. $\int_0^{\pi/2} 2 \sinh (\sin \theta) \cos \theta\, d\theta$

51. $\int_1^2 \frac{\cosh (\ln t)}{t}\, dt$

52. $\int_1^4 \frac{8 \cosh \sqrt{x}}{\sqrt{x}}\, dx$

53. $\int_{-\ln 2}^{0} \cosh^2 \left(\frac{x}{2}\right) dx$

54. $\int_0^{\ln 10} 4 \sinh^2 \left(\frac{x}{2}\right) dx$

EVALUATING INVERSE HYPERBOLIC FUNCTIONS AND RELATED INTEGRALS

When hyperbolic function keys are not available on a calculator, it is still possible to evaluate the inverse hyperbolic functions by expressing them as logarithms as shown in the table below.

$$\sinh^{-1} x = \ln \left(x + \sqrt{x^2 + 1}\right), \quad -\infty < x < \infty$$

$$\cosh^{-1} x = \ln \left(x + \sqrt{x^2 - 1}\right), \quad x \ge 1$$

$$\tanh^{-1} x = \frac{1}{2} \ln \frac{1 + x}{1 - x}, \quad |x| < 1$$

$$\operatorname{sech}^{-1} x = \ln \left(\frac{1 + \sqrt{1 - x^2}}{x}\right), \quad 0 < x \le 1$$

$$\operatorname{csch}^{-1} x = \ln \left(\frac{1}{x} + \frac{\sqrt{1 + x^2}}{|x|}\right), \quad x \ne 0$$

$$\coth^{-1} x = \frac{1}{2} \ln \frac{x + 1}{x - 1}, \quad |x| > 1$$

Use the formulas in the table at lower left to express the numbers in Exercises 55–60 in terms of natural logarithms.

55. $\sinh^{-1} (-5/12)$

56. $\cosh^{-1} (5/3)$

57. $\tanh^{-1} (-1/2)$

58. $\coth^{-1} (5/4)$

59. $\operatorname{sech}^{-1} (3/5)$

60. $\operatorname{csch}^{-1} \left(-1/\sqrt{3}\right)$

Evaluate the integrals in Exercises 61–68 in terms of (a) inverse hyperbolic functions; (b) natural logarithms.

61. $\int_0^{2\sqrt{3}} \frac{dx}{\sqrt{4 + x^2}}$

62. $\int_0^{1/3} \frac{6\, dx}{\sqrt{1 + 9x^2}}$

63. $\int_{5/4}^{2} \frac{dx}{1 - x^2}$

64. $\int_0^{1/2} \frac{dx}{1 - x^2}$

65. $\int_{1/5}^{3/13} \frac{dx}{x\sqrt{1 - 16x^2}}$

66. $\int_1^2 \frac{dx}{x\sqrt{4 + x^2}}$

67. $\int_0^{\pi} \frac{\cos x\, dx}{\sqrt{1 + \sin^2 x}}$

68. $\int_1^e \frac{dx}{x\sqrt{1 + (\ln x)^2}}$

69. *Even and Odd.* Show that if a function f is defined on an interval symmetric about the origin (so that f is defined at $-x$ whenever it is defined at x), then

$$f(x) = \frac{f(x) + f(-x)}{2} + \frac{f(x) - f(-x)}{2}. \qquad (5)$$

Then show that $(f(x) + f(-x))/2$ is even and that $(f(x) - f(-x))/2$ is odd.

70. *Continuation of Exercise 69.* Equation (5) simplifies considerably if f itself is (a) even or (b) odd. What are the new equations? Give reasons for your answers.

71. *Skydiving.* If a body of mass m falling from rest under the action of gravity encounters an air resistance proportional to the square of the velocity, then the body's velocity t seconds into the fall satisfies the differential equation

$$m \frac{dv}{dt} = mg - kv^2,$$

where k is a constant that depends on the body's aerodynamic properties and the density of the air. (We assume that the fall is short enough so that the variation in the air's density will not affect the outcome.)

a) Show that

$$v = \sqrt{\frac{mg}{k}} \tanh \left(\sqrt{\frac{gk}{m}}\, t\right)$$

satisfies the differential equation and the initial condition that $v = 0$ when $t = 0$.

b) Find the body's *limiting velocity,* $\lim_{t\to\infty} v$.

c) For a 160-lb skydiver ($mg = 160$), and with time in seconds and distance in feet, a typical value for k is 0.005. What is the diver's limiting velocity?

Skydivers can vary their limiting velocities by changing the amount of body area opposing the fall. Their velocities can vary from 95 to 180 miles per hour.

72. *Accelerations Whose Magnitudes Are Proportional to Displacement.* Suppose that the position of a body moving along a coordinate line at time t is

a) $s = a \cos kt + b \sin kt$,
b) $s = a \cosh kt + b \sinh kt$.

Show in both cases the acceleration d^2s/dt^2 is proportional to s but that in the first case it is directed toward the origin while in the second case it is directed away from the origin.

73. *Tractor Trailers and the Tractrix.* When a tractor trailer turns into a cross street or driveway, its rear wheels follow a curve like the one shown here. (This is why the rear wheels sometimes ride up over the curb.)

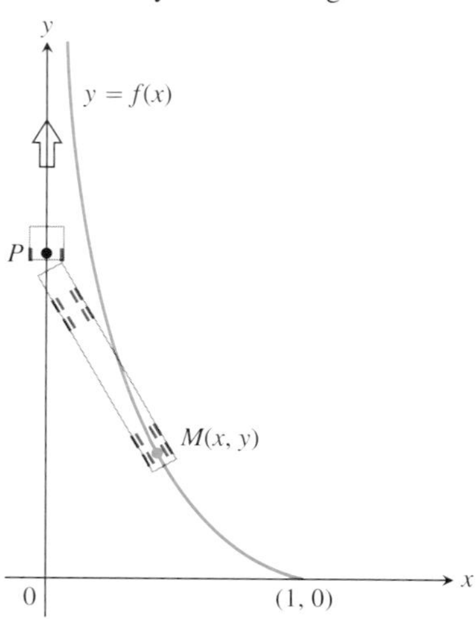

We can find an equation for the curve if we picture the rear wheels as a mass M at the point $(1, 0)$ on the x-axis attached by a rod of unit length to a point P representing the cab at the origin. As the point P moves up the y-axis, it drags M along behind it. The curve traced by M, called a *tractrix* from the Latin word *tractum* for "drag," can be shown to be the graph of the function $y = f(x)$ that solves the initial value problem

Differential equation: $\dfrac{d}{dx} = -\dfrac{1}{x\sqrt{1-x^2}} + \dfrac{x}{\sqrt{1-x^2}}$,

Initial condition: $y = 0$ when $x = 1$.

Solve the initial value problem to find an equation for the curve. (You need an inverse hyperbolic function.)

74. *The Hyperbolic in Hyperbolic Functions.* In case you are wondering where the name *hyperbolic* comes from, here is the answer: Just as $x = \cos u$ and $y = \sin u$ are identified with points (x, y) on the unit circle, the functions $x = \cosh u$ and $y = \sinh u$ are identified with points (x, y) on the right-hand branch of the unit hyperbola, $x^2 - y^2 = 1$ (Fig. 6.40).

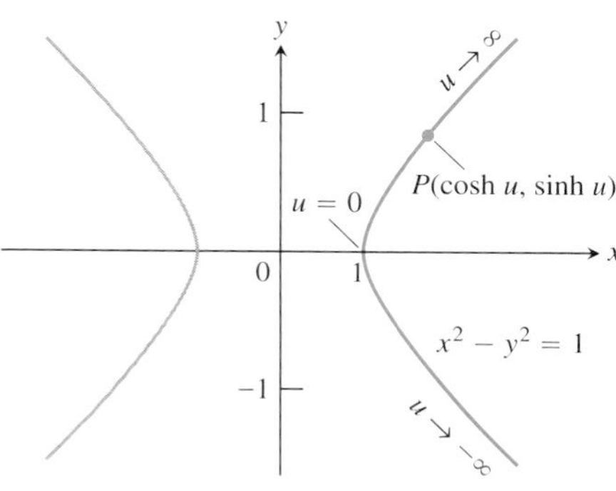

6.40 Since $\cosh^2 u - \sinh^2 u = 1$, the point $(\cosh u, \sinh u)$ lies on the right-hand branch of the hyperbola $x^2 - y^2 = 1$ for every value of u (Exercise 74).

Another analogy between hyperbolic and circular functions is that the variable u in the coordinates $(\cosh u, \sinh u)$ for the points of the right-hand branch of the hyperbola $x^2 - y^2 = 1$ is twice the area of the sector AOP pictured in Fig. 6.41. To see why this is so, carry out the following steps.

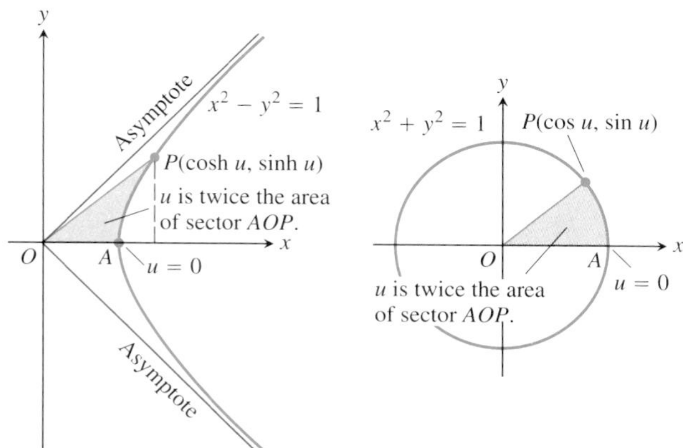

6.41 One of the analogies between hyperbolic and circular functions is revealed by these two diagrams (Exercise 74).

a) Show that the area $A(u)$ of sector AOP is given by the formula

$$A(u) = \frac{1}{2}\cosh u \sinh u - \int_1^{\cosh u} \sqrt{x^2 - 1}\, dx.$$

b) Differentiate both sides of the equation in (a) with respect to u to show that

$$A'(u) = \frac{1}{2}.$$

c) Solve this last equation for $A(u)$. What is the value of $A(0)$? What is the value of the constant of integration C in your solution? With C determined, what does your solution say about the relationship of u to $A(u)$?

Writing for Your Own Knowledge

Answer the following questions in writing. Some answers will take only a sentence or two; others may require several paragraphs. Some explanations may also call for graphs or sketches.

1. In what way are $\cosh x$ and $\sinh x$ the even and odd parts of e^x?
2. What are the six basic hyperbolic functions? Comment on their domains, ranges, and graphs. What are some of the identities relating them?
3. What are the derivatives of the hyperbolic functions? What are the corresponding integral formulas? What similarities do you find here with the six basic trigonometric functions?
4. How are the inverse hyperbolic functions defined? Comment on their domains, ranges, and graphs. How can you find values of $\operatorname{sech}^{-1} x$, $\operatorname{csch}^{-1} x$, and $\coth^{-1} x$ using a calculator's keys for $\cosh^{-1} x$, $\sinh^{-1} x$, and $\tanh^{-1} x$?
5. What integrals lead naturally to inverse hyperbolic functions?
6. If you did Exercise 74, explain the "hyperbolic" in hyperbolic function.

EXPLORER PROGRAM

PowerGrapher	Graphs hyperbolic functions as combinations of exponentials, and graphs inverse hyperbolic functions as logarithms.

6.11 *First Order Differential Equations*

In Section 6.5 we derived the law of exponential change, $y = y_0 e^{kt}$, as the solution of the initial value problem $dy/dt = ky$, $y = y_0$ when $t = 0$. As we saw, this problem models population growth, radioactive decay, heat transfer, and a great many other phenomena. In the present section, we study initial value problems based on the equation $dy/dx = f(x, y)$, in which f is a function of both the independent and dependent variables. The applications of this equation, a generalization of $dy/dt = ky$ (think of t as x), are broader still.

First Order Differential Equations

A **first order** differential equation is a relation

$$\frac{dy}{dx} = f(x, y) \qquad (1)$$

in which $f(x, y)$ is a function of two variables defined on a region in the xy-plane. A **solution** of Eq. (1) is a differentiable function $y = y(x)$ defined on an interval of x-values (perhaps infinite) such that

$$\frac{d}{dx} y(x) = f(x, y(x))$$

on that interval. The initial condition that $y = y_0$ when $x = x_0$ (i.e., $y(x_0) = y_0$) amounts to requiring the solution curve $y = y(x)$ to pass through the point (x_0, y_0).

EXAMPLE 1 The equation

$$\frac{dy}{dx} = 1 - \frac{y}{x}$$

is a first order differential equation in which $f(x, y) = 1 - (y/x)$.

EXAMPLE 2 Show that the function

$$y = \frac{1}{x} + \frac{x}{2}$$

is a solution of the initial value problem

$$\frac{dy}{dx} = 1 - \frac{y}{x}, \qquad y(2) = \frac{3}{2}.$$

Solution The given function satisfies the initial condition because

$$y(2) = \left(\frac{1}{x} + \frac{x}{2}\right)_{x=2} = \frac{1}{2} + \frac{2}{2} = \frac{3}{2}.$$

To show that it satisfies the differential equation, we show that the two sides of the equation agree when we substitute $(1/x) + (x/2)$ for y.

On the left: $$\frac{dy}{dx} = \frac{d}{dx}\left(\frac{1}{x} + \frac{x}{2}\right) = -\frac{1}{x^2} + \frac{1}{2}$$

On the right: $$1 - \frac{y}{x} = 1 - \frac{1}{x}\left(\frac{1}{x} + \frac{x}{2}\right)$$

$$= 1 - \frac{1}{x^2} - \frac{1}{2} = -\frac{1}{x^2} + \frac{1}{2}$$

The function $y = (1/x) + (x/2)$ satisfies both the differential equation and the initial condition, which is what we needed to show.

Separable Equations

We sometimes write $y' = f(x, y)$ for $dy/dx = f(x, y)$.

The equation $y' = f(x, y)$ is **separable** if f can be expressed as a product of a function of x and a function of y. The differential equation then has the form

$$\frac{dy}{dx} = g(x)h(y). \tag{2}$$

If $h(y) \neq 0$, we can **separate the variables** by dividing both sides by h and multiplying both sides by dx, obtaining

$$\frac{1}{h(y)}\, dy = g(x)\, dx. \tag{3}$$

This groups the y-terms with dy on the left and the x-terms with dx on the right. We then integrate both sides, obtaining

$$\int \frac{1}{h(y)}\, dy = \int g(x)\, dx. \tag{4}$$

The integrated equation provides the solutions we seek by expressing y either explicitly or implicitly as a function of x, up to an arbitrary constant.

EXAMPLE 3 Solve the differential equation

$$\frac{dy}{dx} = (1 + y^2)\, e^x.$$

Solution Since $1 + y^2$ is never zero, we can solve the equation by separating the variables.

$$\frac{dy}{dx} = (1 + y^2)\, e^x$$

$$dy = (1 + y^2)\, e^x\, dx \qquad \text{Treat } dy/dx \text{ as a quotient of differentials and multiply both sides by } dx.$$

$$\frac{dy}{1 + y^2} = e^x\, dx \qquad \text{Divide by } (1 + y^2).$$

$$\int \frac{dy}{1 + y^2} = \int e^x\, dx \qquad \text{Integrate both sides.}$$

$$\tan^{-1} y = e^x + C \qquad C \text{ represents the combined constants of integration.}$$

The equation $\tan^{-1} y = e^x + C$ gives y as an implicit function of x. In this case, we can solve for y as an explicit function of x by taking the tangent of both sides:

$$\tan(\tan^{-1} y) = \tan(e^x + C)$$

$$y = \tan(e^x + C).$$

Linear First Order Equations

A first order differential equation that can be written in the form

$$\frac{dy}{dx} + P(x)y = Q(x), \tag{5}$$

where P and Q are functions of x is a **linear** first order equation. Equation (5) is the equation's **standard form.**

EXAMPLE 4 Put the following equation in standard form.

$$x\frac{dy}{dx} = x^2 + 3y, \qquad x > 0$$

Solution

$$x\frac{dy}{dx} = x^2 + 3y$$

$$\frac{dy}{dx} = x + \frac{3}{x}y \qquad \text{Divide by } x.$$

$$\frac{dy}{dx} - \frac{3}{x}y = x \qquad \text{Standard form with } P(x) = -3/x \text{ and } Q(x) = x$$

Notice that $P(x)$ is $-3/x$, not $+3/x$. The standard form is $y' + P(x)y = Q(x)$, so the minus sign is part of the formula for $P(x)$.

EXAMPLE 5 The equation

$$\frac{dy}{dx} = ky$$

with which we modeled bacterial growth, radioactive decay, and temperature change in Section 6.5 is a linear first order equation. Its standard form is

$$\frac{dy}{dx} - ky = 0. \qquad P(x) = -k \text{ and } Q(x) = 0$$

We solve the equation

$$\frac{dy}{dx} + P(x)y = Q(x) \tag{6}$$

by multiplying both sides by a positive function $v(x)$ that transforms the left hand side into the derivative of the product $v(x) \cdot y$. We will show how to find v in a moment, but first we want to show how, once found, it provides the solution we seek. Here is why multiplying by v works:

$$\frac{dy}{dx} + P(x)y = Q(x)$$ Original equation is in standard form.

$$v(x)\frac{dy}{dx} + P(x)v(x)y = v(x)\,Q(x)$$ Multiply by $v(x)$.

$$\frac{d}{dx}(v(x) \cdot y) = v(x)\,Q(x)$$ $v(x)$ is chosen to make $v\frac{dy}{dx} + Pvy = \frac{d}{dx}(v \cdot y)$

We call $v(x)$ an **integrating factor** for Eq. (6) because its presence makes the equation integrable.

$$v\,(x) \cdot y = \int v(x)\,Q(x)\,dx$$ Integrate with respect to x.

$$y = \frac{1}{v(x)}\int v(x)\,Q(x)\,dx \tag{7}$$ Solve for y.

Equation (7) expresses the solution of Eq. (6) in terms of $v(x)$ and $Q(x)$.

Why doesn't the formula for $P(x)$ appear in the solution as well? It does, but indirectly, in the construction of the positive function $v(x)$. We have

$$\frac{d}{dx}(vy) = v\frac{dy}{dx} + Pvy$$ Condition imposed on v

$$v\frac{dy}{dx} + y\frac{dv}{dx} = v\frac{dy}{dx} + Pvy$$ Product Rule for derivatives

$$y\frac{dv}{dx} = Pvy$$ The terms $v\frac{dy}{dx}$ cancel.

This last equation will hold if

$$\frac{dv}{dx} = Pv$$

$$\frac{dv}{v} = P\,dx$$ Variables separated

$$\int \frac{dv}{v} = P\,dx$$ Integrate both sides.

$$\ln v = \int P\,dx$$ Since $v > 0$, we do not need absolute value signs in $\ln v$.

$$e^{\ln v} = e^{\int P\,dx}$$ Exponentiate both sides to solve for v.

$$v = e^{\int P\,dx} \tag{8}$$

From this, we see that any function v that satisfies Eq. (8) will enable us to solve Eq. (6) with the formula in Eq. (7). We do not need the most general possible v, only one that will work. Therefore, it will do no harm to simplify our lives by choosing the simplest possible antiderivative of P for $\int P\,dx$.

THEOREM 4

The solution of the equation

$$\frac{dy}{dx} + P(x)y = Q(x) \tag{9}$$

is

$$y = \frac{1}{v(x)} \int v(x)\,Q(x)\,dx, \tag{10}$$

where

$$v(x) = e^{\int P(x)\,dx}. \tag{11}$$

In the formula for v, we do not need the most general antiderivative of $P(x)$. Any antiderivative will do.

EXAMPLE 6 Solve the equation $x\dfrac{dy}{dx} = x^2 + 3y, \quad x > 0.$

How to Solve a Linear First Order Equation

1. Put it in standard form.
2. Find an antiderivative of $P(x)$.
3. Find $v(x) = e^{\int P(x)\,dx}$.
4. Use Eq. (10) to find y.

Solution We solve the equation in four steps.

STEP 1: *Put the equation in standard form to identify P and Q.*

$$\frac{dy}{dx} - \frac{3}{x}y = x, \qquad P(x) = -\frac{3}{x}, \qquad Q(x) = x. \qquad \text{Example 4}$$

STEP 2: *Find an antiderivative of P(x) (any one will do):*

$$\int P(x)\,dx = \int -\frac{3}{x}\,dx = -3\int \frac{1}{x}\,dx = -3\ln|x| = -3\ln x \qquad (x > 0).$$

STEP 3: *Find the integrating factor v(x):*

$$v(x) = e^{\int P(x)\,dx} = e^{-3\ln x} = e^{\ln x^{-3}} = \frac{1}{x^3}. \qquad \text{Eq. (11)}$$

STEP 4: *Find the solution:*

$$\begin{aligned}
y &= \frac{1}{v(x)} \int v(x)Q(x)\,dx && \text{Eq. (10)}\\
&= \frac{1}{(1/x^3)} \int \left(\frac{1}{x^3}\right)(x)\,dx && \text{Values from steps 1–3}\\
&= x^3 \cdot \int \frac{1}{x^2}\,dx\\
&= x^3\left(-\frac{1}{x} + C\right) && \text{Don't forget the } C \ldots\\
&= -x^2 + Cx^3 && \ldots \text{it provides part of the answer.}
\end{aligned}$$

The solution is $y = -x^2 + Cx^3, \quad x > 0.$

EXAMPLE 7 Solve the equation

$$xy' = x^2 + 3y, \quad x > 0,$$

given the initial condition $y(1) = 2$.

Solution We first solve the differential equation (Example 6), obtaining

$$y = -x^2 + Cx^3, \qquad x > 0.$$

We then use the initial condition to find the right value for C:

$$\begin{aligned} y &= -x^2 + Cx^3 \\ 2 &= -(1)^2 + C(1)^3 \qquad y = 2 \text{ when } x = 1 \\ C &= 2 + (1)^2 = 3. \end{aligned}$$

The solution of the initial value problem is the function $y = -x^2 + 3x^3$. ■

Resistance Proportional to Velocity

In some cases it makes sense to assume that, other forces being absent, the resistance encountered by a moving object, like a car coasting to a stop, is proportional to the object's velocity. The slower the object moves, the less its forward progress is resisted by the air through which it passes. We can describe this in mathematical terms if we picture the object as a mass m moving along a coordinate line with position s and velocity v at time t. The resisting force opposing the motion is mass $\times$ acceleration $= m(dv/dt)$, and we can write

$$m\frac{dv}{dt} = -kv \qquad (k > 0) \tag{12}$$

to say that the force decreases in proportion to velocity. If we rewrite (12) as

$$\frac{dv}{dt} + \frac{k}{m}v = 0, \qquad \text{Standard form} \tag{13}$$

and let v_0 denote the object's velocity at time $t = 0$, we can apply Theorem 4 to arrive at the solution

$$v = v_0\, e^{-(k/m)t} \tag{14}$$

(Exercise 34).

What can we learn from Eq. (14)? For one thing, we can see that if m is something large, like the mass of a 20,000-ton ore boat in Lake Erie, it will take a long time for the velocity to approach zero. For another, we can integrate the equation to find s as a function of t.

Suppose a body is coasting to a stop and the only force acting on it is a resistance proportional to its speed. How far will it coast? To find out, we start with Eq. (14) and solve the initial value problem

$$\frac{ds}{dt} = v_0\, e^{-(k/m)t}, \qquad s(0) = 0.$$

Integrating with respect to t gives

$$s = -\frac{v_0 m}{k} e^{-(k/m)t} + C. \tag{15}$$

Substituting $s = 0$ when $t = 0$ gives

$$0 = -\frac{v_0 m}{k} + C \qquad \text{and} \qquad C = \frac{v_0 m}{k}.$$

The body's position at time t is therefore

$$s(t) = -\frac{v_0 m}{k} e^{-(k/m)t} + \frac{v_0 m}{k} = \frac{v_0 m}{k}(1 - e^{-(k/m)t}). \tag{16}$$

To find how far the body will coast, we find the limit of $s(t)$ as $t \to \infty$. Since $-(k/m) < 0$, we know that $e^{-(k/m)t} \to 0$ as $t \to \infty$ so that

$$\lim_{t\to\infty} s(t) = \lim_{t\to\infty} \frac{v_0 m}{k}(1 - e^{-(k/m)t}) = \frac{v_0 m}{k}(1 - 0) = \frac{v_0 m}{k}. \tag{17}$$

Thus,

$$\text{Distance coasted} = \frac{v_0 m}{k}. \tag{18}$$

This is an ideal figure, of course. Only in mathematics can time stretch to infinity. The number $v_0\, m/k$ is only an upper bound (albeit a useful one). It is true to life in one respect, at least—if m is large, it will take a lot of energy to stop the body. That is why ocean liners have to be docked by tugboats. Any liner of conventional design entering a slip with enough speed to steer would smash into the pier before it could stop.

Weight vs. Mass

Weight is the force that results from gravity pulling on a mass. The two are related by the equation in Newton's second law,

Weight = mass × acceleration.

To convert mass to weight, multiply by the acceleration of gravity. To convert weight to mass, divide by the acceleration of gravity. In the English system, where weight is measured in pounds, mass is measured in **slugs.** Thus,

Pounds = slugs × 32

and

Pounds/32 = slugs.

A skater weighing 192 lb has a mass of

192/32 = 6 slugs.

EXAMPLE 8 For a 192-lb ice skater, the k in Eq. (14) is about 1/3 slug/sec and $m = 192/32 = 6$ slugs. How long will it take the skater to coast from 11 ft/sec (7.5 mph) to 1 ft/sec? How far will the skater coast before coming to a complete stop?

Solution We answer the first question by solving Eq. (14) for t:

$$\begin{aligned} 11e^{-t/18} &= 1 && \text{Eq. (14) with } k = 1/3,\ m = 6,\ v_0 = 11,\ v = 1 \\ e^{-t/18} &= 1/11 \\ -t/18 &= \ln(1/11) = -\ln 11 \\ t &= 18 \ln 11 \approx 43 \text{ sec.} \end{aligned}$$

We answer the second question with Eq. (18):

$$\text{Distance coasted} = \frac{v_0 m}{k} = \frac{11 \cdot 6}{1/3} = 198 \text{ ft.}$$

RL Circuits

The diagram in Fig. 6.42 represents an electrical circuit whose total resistance is a constant R ohms and whose self-inductance, shown as a coil, is L henries, also a constant. There is a switch whose terminals at a and b can be closed to connect a constant electrical source of V volts.

Ohm's law, $V = RI$, has to be modified for such a circuit. The modified form is

$$L\frac{di}{dt} + Ri = V, \tag{19}$$

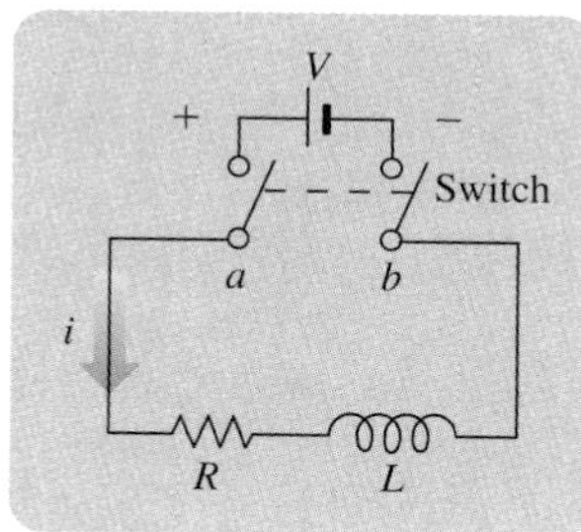

6.42 The RL circuit in Example 9.

where i is the intensity of the current in amperes and t is the time in seconds. By solving this equation, we can predict how the current will flow after the switch is closed.

EXAMPLE 9 The switch in the RL circuit in Fig. 6.42 is closed at time $t = 0$. How will the current flow as a function of time?

Solution Equation (19) is a linear first order differential equation for i as a function of t. Its standard form is

$$\frac{di}{dt} + \frac{R}{L}i = \frac{V}{L}, \tag{20}$$

and the corresponding solution, from Theorem 4, given that $i = 0$ when $t = 0$, is

$$i = \frac{V}{R} - \frac{V}{R}e^{-(R/L)t} \tag{21}$$

(Exercise 42). Since R and L are positive, $-(R/L)$ is negative and $e^{-(R/L)t} \to 0$ as $t \to \infty$. Thus,

$$\lim_{t\to\infty} i = \lim_{t\to\infty}\left(\frac{V}{R} - \frac{V}{R}e^{-(R/L)t}\right) = \frac{V}{R} - \frac{V}{R}\cdot 0 = \frac{V}{R}. \tag{22}$$

At any given time, the current is theoretically less than V/R, but as time passes the current approaches the **steady state value** V/R. According to the equation

$$L\frac{di}{dt} + Ri = V,$$

$I = V/R$ is the current that will flow in the circuit if either $L = 0$ (no inductance) or $di/dt = 0$ (steady current, $i =$ constant) (Fig. 6.43).

Equation (21) expresses the solution of Eq. (20) as the sum of two terms: a **steady state solution** V/R and a **transient solution** $-(V/R)\,e^{-(R/L)t}$ that tends to zero as $t \to \infty$.

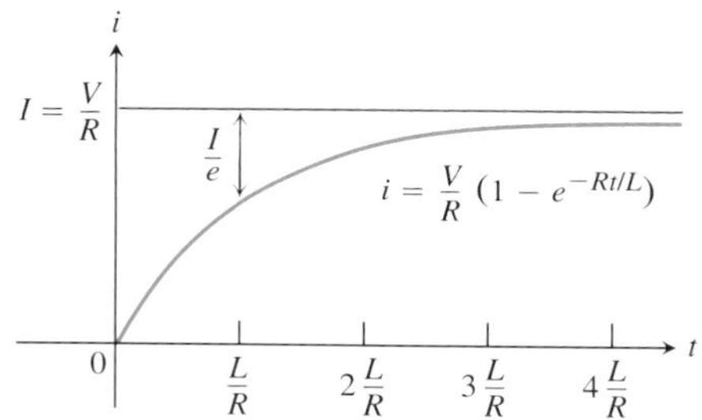

6.43 The growth of the current in the RL circuit in Example 9. I is the current's steady-state value. The number $t = L/R$ is the time constant of the circuit. The current gets to within 5% of its steady-state value in 3 time constants (Exercise 41).

Exercises 6.11

In Exercises 1 and 2, show that each function $y = f(x)$ is a solution of the accompanying differential equation.

1. $2y' + 3y = e^{-x}$

a) $y = e^{-x}$
b) $y = e^{-x} + e^{-(3/2)x}$
c) $y = e^{-x} + Ce^{-(3/2)x}$

2. $y' = y^2$

a) $y = -\dfrac{1}{x}$ **b)** $y = -\dfrac{1}{x+3}$ **c)** $y = -\dfrac{1}{x+C}$

In Exercises 3 and 4, show that the function $y = f(x)$ is a solution of the given differential equation.

3. $y = \dfrac{1}{x}\displaystyle\int_1^x \frac{e^t}{t}\,dt,\quad x^2y' + xy = e^x$

4. $y = \dfrac{1}{\sqrt{1+x^4}}\displaystyle\int_1^x \sqrt{1+t^4}\,dt,\quad y' + \dfrac{2x^3}{1+x^4}y = 1$

In Exercises 5–8, show that each function is a solution of the given initial value problem.

	Differential equation	Initial condition	Solution candidate
5.	$y' + y = \dfrac{2}{1+4e^{2x}}$	$y(-\ln 2) = \dfrac{\pi}{2}$	$y = e^{-x}\tan^{-1}(2e^x)$
6.	$y' = e^{-x^2} - 2xy$	$y(2) = 0$	$y = (x-2)e^{-x^2}$
7.	$xy' + y = -\sin x,\quad x > 0$	$y\left(\dfrac{\pi}{2}\right) = 0$	$y = \dfrac{\cos x}{x}$
8.	$x^2y' = xy - y^2,\quad x > 1$	$y(e) = e$	$y = \dfrac{x}{\ln x}$

Solve the differential equations in Exercises 9–14.

9. $2\sqrt{xy}\,\dfrac{dy}{dx} = 1, \quad x, y > 0$

10. $\dfrac{dy}{dx} = x^2\sqrt{y}, \quad y > 0$

11. $\dfrac{dy}{dx} = e^{x-y}$

12. $\dfrac{dy}{dx} = \dfrac{2x^2+1}{xe^y}, \quad x > 0$

13. $\sec x\,\dfrac{dy}{dx} = e^{y+\sin x}$

14. $\sqrt{x}\,\dfrac{dy}{dx} = e^{y+\sqrt{x}}, \quad x > 0$

Solve the differential equations in Exercises 15–24.

15. $e^x\,\dfrac{dy}{dx} + 2e^x y = 1$

16. $2\,\dfrac{dy}{dx} - y = e^{x/2}$

17. $xy' + 3y = \dfrac{\sin x}{x^2}, \quad x > 0$

18. $e^{2x}y' + 2e^{2x}y = 2x$

19. $(t-1)^3\dfrac{ds}{dt} + 4(t-1)^2 s = t+1, \quad t > 1$

20. $(t+1)\dfrac{ds}{dt} + 2s = 3(t+1) + \dfrac{1}{(t+1)^2}, \quad t > -1$

21. $\sin\theta\,\dfrac{dr}{d\theta} + (\cos\theta)r = \tan\theta, \quad 0 < \theta < \pi/2$

22. $\tan\theta\,\dfrac{dr}{d\theta} + r = \sin^2\theta, \quad 0 < \theta < \pi/2$

23. $\cosh x\,\dfrac{dy}{dx} + (\sinh x)y = e^{-x}$

24. $\sinh x\,\dfrac{dy}{dx} + 3(\cosh x)y = \cosh x \sinh x$

Solve the initial value problems in Exercises 25–30 for y as a function of x.

Differential equation	Initial condition
25. $\dfrac{dy}{dt} + 2y = t$	$y(0) = 1$
26. $t\dfrac{dy}{dt} + 2y = t^3, \quad t > 0$	$y(2) = 1$
27. $\theta\dfrac{dy}{d\theta} + y = \sin\theta, \quad \theta > 0$	$y(\pi/2) = 1$
28. $\theta\dfrac{dy}{d\theta} - 2y = \theta^3\sec\theta\tan\theta, \quad \theta > 0$	$y(\pi/3) = 2$
29. $(x+1)\dfrac{dy}{dx} - 2(x^2+x)y = \dfrac{e^{x^2}}{x+1}, \quad x > -1$	$y(0) = 5$
30. $\dfrac{dy}{dx} + xy = x$	$y(0) = -6$

31. Is either of the following equations correct? Give reasons for your answers.

a) $x\displaystyle\int \frac{1}{x}\,dx = x\ln|x| + C$

b) $x\displaystyle\int \frac{1}{x}\,dx = x\ln|x| + Cx$

32. Is either of the following equations correct? Give reasons for your answers.

a) $\dfrac{1}{\cos x}\displaystyle\int \cos x\,dx = \tan x + C$

b) $\dfrac{1}{\cos x}\displaystyle\int \cos x\,dx = \tan x + \frac{C}{\cos x}$

33. What do you get when you use Theorem 4 to solve the following initial value problem for y as a function of t?

$$\frac{dy}{dt} = ky \qquad (k \text{ constant}), \quad y(0) = y_0$$

34. Use Theorem 4 to solve the following initial value problem for v as a function of t.

$$\frac{dv}{dt} + \frac{k}{m}v = 0 \quad (k \text{ and } m \text{ positive constants}), \quad v(0) = v_0$$

35. *Blood Sugar.* If glucose is fed intravenously at a constant rate, the change in the overall concentration $c(t)$ of glucose in the blood with respect to time may be described by the differential equation

$$\frac{dc}{dt} = \frac{G}{100V} - kc.$$

In this equation, G, V, and k are positive constants, G being the rate at which glucose is admitted, in milligrams per minute, and V the volume of blood in the body, in liters (around 5 liters for an adult). The concentration $c(t)$ is measured in milligrams per centiliter. The term $-kc$ is included because the glucose is assumed to be changing continually into other molecules at a rate proportional to its concentration.

a) Solve the equation for $c(t)$, using c_0 to denote $c(0)$.
b) Find the steady-state concentration, $\lim_{t\to\infty} c(t)$.

36. *Continuous Compounding.* You have \$1000 with which to open an account and plan to add \$1000 per year. All funds in the account will earn 10% interest per year compounded continuously. If the added deposits are also credited to your account continuously, the number of dollars x in your account at time t (years) will satisfy the initial value problem

$$\frac{dx}{dt} = 1000 + 0.10x, \qquad x(0) = 1000.$$

a) Solve the initial value problem for x as a function of t.
b) About how many years will it take for the amount in your account to reach \$100,000?

RESISTANCE PROPORTIONAL TO VELOCITY

37. For a 145-lb cyclist on a 15-lb bicycle on level ground, the k in Eq. (14) is about 1/5 slug/sec and $m = 160/32 = 5$ slugs. The cyclist starts coasting at 22 ft/sec (15 mph).

a) About how far will the cyclist coast before reaching a complete stop?

b) To the nearest second, about how long will it take the cyclist's speed to drop to 1 ft/sec?

38. For a 56,000-ton Iowa class battleship, $m = 1{,}750{,}000$ slugs and the k in Eq. (14) might be 3000 slugs/sec. Suppose the battleship loses power when it is moving at a speed of 22 ft/sec (13.2 knots).

a) About how far will the ship coast before it stops?

b) About how long will it take the ship's speed to drop to 1 ft/sec?

RL CIRCUITS

39. *Current in a Closed RL Circuit.* How many seconds after the switch in an RL circuit is closed will it take the current i to reach half of its steady-state value? Notice that the time depends only on R and L and not on how much voltage is applied.

40. *Current in an Open RL Circuit.* If the switch is thrown open after the current in an RL circuit has built up to its steady-state value, the decaying current (graphed here) obeys the equation

$$L\frac{di}{dt} + Ri = 0, \tag{23}$$

which is Eq. (19) with $V = 0$.

a) Solve Eq. (23) to express i as a function of t.

b) How long after the switch is thrown will it take the current to fall to half its original value?

c) What is the value of the current when $t = L/R$? (The significance of this time is explained in the next exercise.)

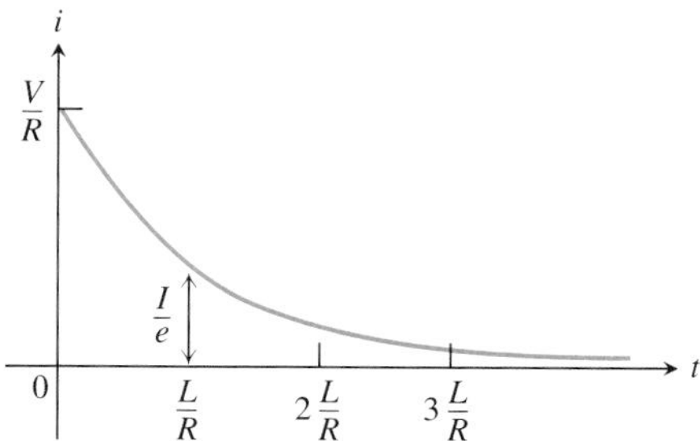

41. *Time Constants.* Engineers call the number L/R the *time constant* of the RL circuit in Fig. 6.42. The significance of the time constant is that the current will reach 95% of its final value within 3 time constants of the time the switch is closed (Fig. 6.43). Thus, the time constant gives a built-in measure of how rapidly an individual circuit will reach equilibrium.

a) Find the value of i in Eq. (21) that corresponds to $t = 3L/R$ and show that it is about 95% of the steady-state value $I = V/R$.

b) Approximately what percentage of the steady-state current will be flowing in the circuit 2 time constants after the switch is closed (i.e., when $t = 2L/R$)?

42. (Derivation of Eq. (21) in Example 9)

a) Use Theorem 4 to show that the solution of the equation

$$\frac{di}{dt} + \frac{R}{L}i = \frac{V}{L}$$

is

$$i = \frac{V}{R} + Ce^{-(R/L)t}.$$

b) Then use the initial condition $i(0) = 0$ to determine the value of C. This will complete the derivation of Eq. (21).

c) Show that both $i = V/R$ and $i = Ce^{-(R/L)t}$ are solutions of Eq. (21) in their own right.

MIXTURE PROBLEMS

A chemical in a liquid solution (or dispersed in a gas) runs into a container holding the liquid (or the gas) with, possibly, a specified amount of the chemical dissolved as well. The mixture is kept uniform by stirring and flows out of the container at a known rate. In this process it is often important to know the concentration of the chemical in the container at any given time. The differential equation describing the process is based on the formula

$$\begin{pmatrix}\text{rate of change of}\\ \text{amount in container}\end{pmatrix} = \begin{pmatrix}\text{rate at which}\\ \text{chemical arrives}\end{pmatrix} - \begin{pmatrix}\text{rate at which}\\ \text{chemical departs.}\end{pmatrix} \tag{24}$$

If $y(t)$ is the amount of chemical in the container at time t and $V(t)$ is the total volume of liquid in the container at time t, then the departure rate of the chemical at time t is

$$\begin{aligned}\text{departure rate} &= \frac{y(t)}{V(t)}\cdot(\text{outflow rate})\\ &= \begin{pmatrix}\text{concentration in}\\ \text{container at time } t\end{pmatrix}\cdot(\text{outflow rate}).\end{aligned} \tag{25}$$

Accordingly, Eq. (24) becomes

$$\frac{dy}{dt} = (\text{chemical's arrival rate}) - \frac{y(t)}{V(t)}\cdot(\text{outflow rate}). \tag{26}$$

If, say, y is measured in pounds, V in gallons, and t in minutes, the units in Eq. (26) are

$$\frac{\text{pounds}}{\text{min}} = \frac{\text{pounds}}{\text{min}} - \frac{\text{pounds}}{\text{gal}}\cdot\frac{\text{gal}}{\text{min}}. \tag{27}$$

43. A tank initially contains 100 gal of brine in which 50 lb of salt are dissolved. A brine containing 2 lb/gal of salt runs into the tank at the rate of 5 gal/min. The mixture is kept uniform by stirring and flows out of the tank at the rate of 4 gal/min.

a) At what rate (lb/min) does salt enter the tank at time t?

b) What is the volume of brine in the tank at time t?

c) At what rate (lb/min) does salt leave the tank at time t?

d) Write down and solve the initial value problem describing the mixing process.

e) Find the concentration of salt in the tank 25 min after the process starts.

44. In an oil refinery a storage tank contains 2000 gal of gasoline that initially has 100 lb of an additive dissolved in it. In preparation for winter weather, gasoline containing 2 lb of additive per gallon is pumped into the tank at a rate of 40 gal/min. The well-mixed solution is pumped out at the rate of 45 gal/min. Find the amount of additive in the tank 20 minutes after the process starts.

45. A tank contains 100 gal of fresh water. A solution containing 1 lb/gal of soluble lawn fertilizer runs into the tank at the rate of 1 gal/min, and the mixture is pumped out of the tank at the rate of 3 gal/min. Find the maximum amount of fertilizer in the tank and the time required to reach the maximum.

46. An executive conference room of a corporation contains 4500 cubic feet of air initially free of carbon monoxide. Starting at time $t = 0$, cigarette smoke containing 4 percent carbon monoxide is blown into the room at the rate of 0.3 ft^3/min. A ceiling fan keeps the air in the room well circulated and the air leaves the room at the same rate of 0.3 ft^3/min. Find the time when the concentration of carbon monoxide in the room reaches 0.01 percent.

Writing for Your Own Knowledge

Answer the following questions in writing. Some answers will take only a sentence or two; others may require several paragraphs. Some explanations may also call for graphs or sketches.

1. What is a first order differential equation? When is a function a solution of such an equation?
2. How do you solve separable first order differential equations?
3. How do you solve linear first order differential equations?
4. What are some typical applications of first order differential equations?
5. How are an object's weight and mass related?

EXPLORER PROGRAM

Slope Fields	Graphs solutions of the initial value problem $y' = f(x, y)$, $y = y_0$ when $x = x_0$, for your choice of f, x_0, and y_0.

For Your Review

Write brief paragraphs about the following topics and give examples.

Defining exponential functions
The derivative of a^x and the limit $\lim_{h\to 0} (a^h - 1)/h$
The function e^x
Inverses of functions
Derivatives of inverses of differentiable functions
The function $\ln x$ and its derivative
The inverse equations for $\ln x$ and e^x
Arithmetic properties of $\ln x$
Logarithmic differentiation
The function $\log_a x$
  Definition
  Evaluation
  Arithmetic properties
  Derivative
The inverse equations for a^x and $\log_a x$
Base 10 logarithms
The function $y = a^x$ and its derivative
Differentiating arbitrary real powers of x
Derivatives of other power functions
Integrals involving exponential and logarithmic functions
The integral formula for $\ln x$
The law of exponential change
  The incidence of disease
  Population growth
  Continuous compound interest
  Radioactive decay
  Newton's law of cooling
Relative rates of growth
Big-oh and little-oh notation
Inverse trigonometric functions
  Definitions
  Graphs
  Evaluation
  Derivatives
Integrals leading to inverse trigonometric functions
Hyperbolic functions
  Definitions
  Graphs
  Identities
  Derivatives
Integrals leading to hyperbolic functions
Inverse hyperbolic functions
  Definitions
  Graphs
  Derivatives
Integrals leading to inverse hyperbolic functions
Separable first order differential equations
Linear first order differential equations
Typical initial value problems

Practice Exercises

In Exercises 1–22, find the derivative of y with respect to the appropriate independent variable.

1. $y = 10e^{-x/5}$
2. $y = \sqrt{2}\, e^{\sqrt{2}x}$
3. $y = \frac{1}{4}xe^{4x} - \frac{1}{16}e^{4x}$
4. $y = x^2 e^{-2/x}$
5. $y = \ln (\sin^2 \theta)$
6. $y = \ln (\sec^2 \theta)$
7. $y = \log_2 (x^2/2)$
8. $y = \log_5 (3x - 7)$
9. $y = 8^{-t}$
10. $y = 9^{2t}$
11. $y = 5x^{3.6}$
12. $y = \sqrt{2}\, x^{-\sqrt{2}}$
13. $y = (x + 2)^{x+2}$
14. $y = 2 (\ln x)^{x/2}$
15. $y = \sin^{-1} \sqrt{1 - u^2}, \quad 0 < u < 1$
16. $y = \sin^{-1} \left(\frac{1}{\sqrt{v}}\right), \quad v > 1$
17. $y = z \sec^{-1} z - \sqrt{z^2 - 1}, \quad z > 1$
18. $y = z \cos^{-1} z - \sqrt{1 - z^2}$
19. $y = t \tan^{-1} t - \frac{1}{2} \ln t$
20. $y = (1 + t^2) \cot^{-1} 2t$
21. $y = 2\sqrt{x - 1} \sec^{-1} \sqrt{x}$
22. $y = \csc^{-1} (\sec \theta), \quad 0 < \theta < \pi/2$

Use logarithmic differentiation to find dy/dx in Exercises 23–26.

23. $y = \dfrac{2(x^2 + 1)}{\sqrt{\cos 2x}}$
24. $y = \sqrt[10]{\dfrac{3x + 4}{2x - 4}}$
25. $y = \left(\dfrac{(x + 5)(x - 1)}{(x - 2)(x + 3)}\right)^5, \quad x > 2$
26. $y = \dfrac{2x\, 2^x}{\sqrt{x^2 + 1}}$

Verify the integration formulas in Exercises 27 and 28.

27. $\int \tan^{-1} t\, dt = t \tan^{-1} t - \frac{1}{2} \ln (1 + t^2) + C$
28. $\int \sec^{-1} \theta\, d\theta = \theta \sec^{-1} \theta - \ln \left(\theta + \sqrt{\theta^2 - 1}\right) + C, \quad \theta > 1$

Evaluate the integrals in Exercises 29–48.

29. $\int e^x \sin (e^x)\, dx$
30. $\int e^t \cos (3e^t - 2)\, dt$
31. $\int e^x \sec^2 (e^x - 7)\, dx$
32. $\int e^y \csc (e^y + 1) \cot (e^y + 1)\, dy$
33. $\int \sec^2 (x)\, e^{\tan x}\, dx$
34. $\int \csc^2 x\, e^{\cot x}\, dx$
35. $\int_{-1}^{1} \dfrac{dx}{3x - 4}$
36. $\int_{1}^{e} \dfrac{\sqrt{\ln x}}{x}\, dx$
37. $\int_{0}^{\pi} \tan \dfrac{x}{3}\, dx$
38. $\int_{1/6}^{1/4} 2 \cot \pi x\, dx$
39. $\int_{0}^{4} \dfrac{2t}{t^2 - 25}\, dt$
40. $\int_{-\pi/2}^{\pi/6} \dfrac{\cos t}{1 - \sin t}\, dt$
41. $\int \dfrac{\tan (\ln v)}{v}\, dv$
42. $\int \dfrac{dv}{v \ln v}$
43. $\int \dfrac{(\ln x)^{-3}}{x}\, dx$
44. $\int \dfrac{\ln (x - 5)}{x - 5}\, dx$
45. $\int \dfrac{1}{r} \csc^2 (1 + \ln r)\, dr$
46. $\int \dfrac{\cos (1 - \ln v)}{v}\, dv$
47. $\int x 3^{x^2}\, dx$
48. $\int 2^{\tan x} \sec^2 x\, dx$

Evaluate the integrals in Exercises 49–62.

49. $\int_{1}^{7} \dfrac{3}{x}\, dx$
50. $\int_{1}^{32} \dfrac{1}{5x}\, dx$
51. $\int_{1}^{4} \left(\dfrac{x}{8} + \dfrac{1}{2x}\right) dx$
52. $\int_{1}^{8} \left(\dfrac{2}{3x} - \dfrac{8}{x^2}\right) dx$
53. $\int_{-2}^{-1} e^{-(x+1)}\, dx$
54. $\int_{-\ln 2}^{0} e^{2w}\, dw$
55. $\int_{0}^{\ln 5} e^r (3e^r + 1)^{-3/2}\, dr$
56. $\int_{0}^{\ln 9} e^\theta (e^\theta - 1)^{1/2}\, d\theta$
57. $\int_{1}^{e} \dfrac{1}{x} (1 + 7 \ln x)^{-1/3}\, dx$
58. $\int_{e}^{e^2} \dfrac{1}{x\sqrt{\ln x}}\, dx$
59. $\int_{1}^{3} \dfrac{(\ln (v + 1))^2}{v + 1}\, dv$
60. $\int_{2}^{4} (1 + \ln t)\, t \ln t\, dt$
61. $\int_{1}^{8} \dfrac{\log_4 \theta}{\theta}\, d\theta$
62. $\int_{1}^{e} \dfrac{8 \ln 3 \log_3 \theta}{\theta}\, d\theta$

Evaluate the integrals in Exercises 63–76.

63. $\int_{-3/4}^{3/4} \dfrac{6\, dx}{\sqrt{9 - 4x^2}}$
64. $\int_{-3/4}^{3/4} \dfrac{6\, dx}{\sqrt{4 - 25x^2}}$
65. $\int_{-2}^{2} \dfrac{3\, dt}{4 + 3t^2}$
66. $\int_{\sqrt{3}}^{3} \dfrac{dt}{3 + t^2}$
67. $\int \dfrac{dy}{y\sqrt{4y^2 - 1}}$
68. $\int \dfrac{24\, dy}{y\sqrt{y^2 - 16}}$
69. $\int_{\sqrt{2}/3}^{2/3} \dfrac{dy}{|y| \sqrt{9y^2 - 1}}$
70. $\int_{-2/\sqrt{5}}^{-\sqrt{6}/\sqrt{5}} \dfrac{dy}{|y| \sqrt{5y^2 - 3}}$
71. $\int \dfrac{dx}{\sqrt{-2x - x^2}}$
72. $\int \dfrac{dx}{\sqrt{-x^2 + 4x - 1}}$
73. $\int_{-2}^{-1} \dfrac{2\, dv}{v^2 + 4v + 5}$
74. $\int_{-1}^{1} \dfrac{3\, dv}{4v^2 + 4v + 4}$
75. $\int \dfrac{dt}{(t + 1)\sqrt{t^2 + 2t - 8}}$
76. $\int \dfrac{dt}{(3t + 1)\sqrt{9t^2 + 6t}}$

In Exercises 77–82, solve for y.

77. $3^y = 2^{y+1}$

78. $4^{-y} = 3^{y+2}$

79. $9e^{2y} = x^2$

80. $3^y = 3 \ln x$

81. $\ln (y - 1) = x + \ln y$

82. $\ln (10 \ln y) = \ln 5x$

Find the limits in Exercises 83–94.

83. $\lim_{x \to 0} \dfrac{10^x - 1}{x}$

84. $\lim_{\theta \to 0} \dfrac{3^\theta - 1}{\theta}$

85. $\lim_{x \to 0} \dfrac{2^{\sin x} - 1}{e^x - 1}$

86. $\lim_{x \to 0} \dfrac{2^{-\sin x} - 1}{e^x - 1}$

87. $\lim_{x \to 0} \dfrac{5 - 5 \cos x}{e^x - x - 1}$

88. $\lim_{x \to 0} \dfrac{4 - 4e^x}{xe^x}$

89. $\lim_{t \to 0} \dfrac{t - \ln (1 + 2t)}{t^2}$

90. $\lim_{x \to 4} \dfrac{\sin^2 (\pi x)}{e^{x-4} + 3 - x}$

91. $\lim_{t \to 0^+} \left(\dfrac{e^t}{t} - \dfrac{1}{t}\right)$

92. $\lim_{y \to 0^+} e^{-1/y} \ln y$

93. $\lim_{x \to \infty} \left(1 + \dfrac{3}{x}\right)^x$

94. $\lim_{x \to 0^+} \left(1 + \dfrac{3}{x}\right)^x$

95. The function $f(x) = e^x + x$, being differentiable and one-to-one, has a differentiable inverse $f^{-1}(x)$. Find the value of df^{-1}/dx at the point $f(\ln 2)$.

96. Find the inverse of the function $f(x) = 1 + (1/x)$, $x \neq 0$. Then show that $f^{-1}(f(x)) = f(f^{-1}(x)) = x$ and that

$$\left.\frac{df^{-1}}{dx}\right|_{f(x)} = \frac{1}{f'(x)}.$$

In Exercises 97 and 98, find the absolute maximum and minimum values of each function on the given interval.

97. $y = x \ln 2x - x, \quad \left[\dfrac{1}{2e}, \dfrac{e}{2}\right]$

98. $y = 10x (2 - \ln x), \quad (0, e^2]$

99. A particle is traveling upward and to the right along the curve $y = \ln x$. Its x-coordinate is increasing at the rate $(dx/dt) = \sqrt{x}$ m/sec. At what rate is the y-coordinate changing at the point $(e^2, 2)$?

100. A girl is sliding down a slide shaped like the curve $y = 9e^{-x/3}$ in the accompanying figure. Her y-coordinate is changing at the rate $dy/dt = (-1/4)\sqrt{9 - y}$ ft/sec. At approximately what rate is her x-coordinate changing when she reaches the bottom of the slide at $x = 9$ ft? (Take e^3 to be 20 and round your answer to the nearest ft/sec.)

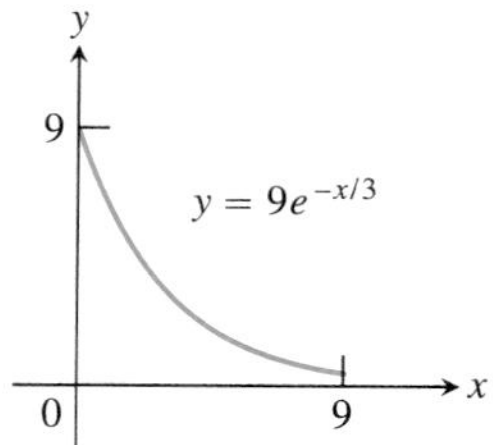

101. The rectangle shown below left has one side on the positive y-axis, one side on the positive x-axis, and its upper right-hand vertex on the curve $y = e^{-x^2}$. What dimensions give the rectangle its largest area, and what is that area?

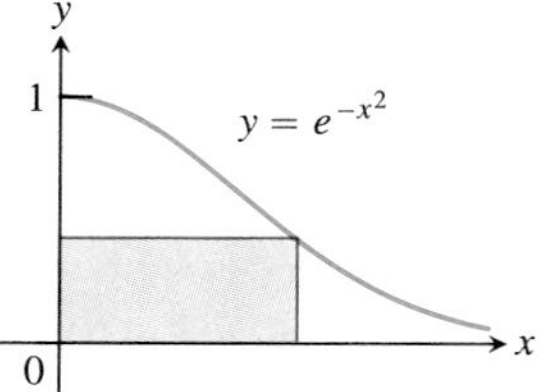

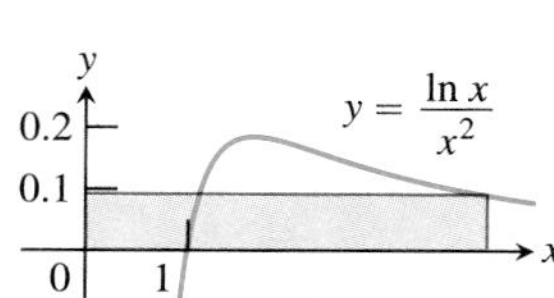

102. The rectangle shown above right has one side on the positive y-axis, one side on the positive x-axis, and its upper right-hand vertex on the curve $y = (\ln x)/x^2$. What dimensions give the rectangle its largest area, and what is that area?

103. A round underwater transmission cable consists of a core of copper wires surrounded by nonconducting insulation. If x denotes the ratio of the radius of the core to the thickness of the insulation, it is known that the speed of the transmission signal is given by the equation $v = x^2 \ln (1/x)$. If the radius of the core is 1 cm, what insulation thickness h will allow the greatest transmission speed?

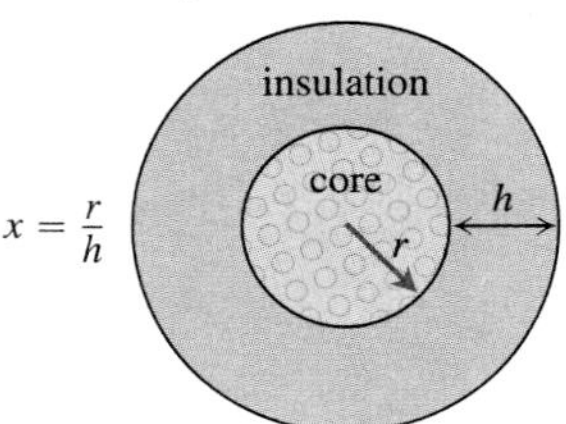

104. Show that $\ln x$ is always less than $\sqrt{x}$.

105. What can be said about the function g if

$$\int_1^x g(t)\, dt = x \ln x + \sqrt{x} + 7?$$

Give reasons for your answer.

106. a) Find df/dx if

$$f(x) = \int_1^{e^x} \frac{2 \ln t}{t}\, dt.$$

b) Find $f(0)$.

c) What can you conclude about the graph of f? Give reasons for your answer.

107. The functions $f(x) = \ln 5x$ and $g(x) = \ln 3x$ differ by a constant. What constant? Give reasons for your answer.

108. The quotient $(\log_4 x)/(\log_2 x)$ has a constant value. What value? Give reasons for your answer.

109. **$\log_x (2)$ vs. $\log_2 (x)$.** How does $f(x) = \log_x (2)$ compare with $g(x) = \log_2 (x)$? Here is one way to find out:

a) Use the equation $\log_a b = (\ln b)/(\ln a)$ to express $f(x)$ and $g(x)$ in terms of natural logarithms.

b) Graph f and g together. Comment on the behavior of f in relation to the signs and values of g.

c) At what points do the graphs of f and g appear to cross? Confirm this algebraically.

110. The graph of $f(x) = \sqrt{x} - \ln x$ has one inflection point.

a) It is hard to find the inflection point by graphing. Try it.
b) Find the inflection point using calculus.

111. What is the age of a sample of charcoal in which 90% of the carbon-14 originally present has decayed?

112. *Cooling a Pie.* A deep-dish apple pie, whose internal temperature was 220°F when removed from the oven, was set out on a breezy 40°F porch to cool. Fifteen minutes later, the pie's internal temperature was 180°F. How long did it take the pie to cool from there to 70°F?

113. Does f grow faster, slower, or at the same rate as g as $x \to \infty$? Give reasons for your answers.

a) $f(x) = \log_2 x, \quad g(x) = \log_3 x$
b) $f(x) = x, \quad g(x) = x + \dfrac{1}{x}$
c) $f(x) = x/100, \quad g(x) = xe^{-x}$
d) $f(x) = x, \quad g(x) = \tan^{-1} x$
e) $f(x) = \csc^{-1} x, \quad g(x) = 1/x$
f) $f(x) = \sinh x, \quad g(x) = e^x$

114. Does f grow faster, slower, or at the same rate as g as $x \to \infty$? Give reasons for your answers.

a) $f(x) = 3^{-x}, \quad g(x) = 2^{-x}$
b) $f(x) = \ln 2x, \quad g(x) = \ln x^2$
c) $f(x) = 10x^3 + 2x^2, \quad g(x) = e^x$
d) $f(x) = \tan^{-1}(1/x), \quad g(x) = 1/x$
e) $f(x) = \sin^{-1}(1/x), \quad g(x) = 1/x^2$
f) $f(x) = \operatorname{sech} x, \quad g(x) = e^{-x}$

115. True, or false? Give reasons for your answers.

a) $\dfrac{1}{x^2} + \dfrac{1}{x^4} = O\left(\dfrac{1}{x^2}\right)$ b) $\dfrac{1}{x^2} + \dfrac{1}{x^4} = O\left(\dfrac{1}{x^4}\right)$
c) $x = o(x + \ln x)$ d) $\ln(\ln x) = o(\ln x)$
e) $\tan^{-1} x = O(1)$ f) $\cosh x = O(e^x)$

116. True, or false? Give reasons for your answers.

a) $\dfrac{1}{x^4} = O\left(\dfrac{1}{x^2} + \dfrac{1}{x^4}\right)$ b) $\dfrac{1}{x^4} = o\left(\dfrac{1}{x^2} + \dfrac{1}{x^4}\right)$
c) $\ln x = o(x + 1)$ d) $\ln 2x = O(\ln x)$
e) $\sec^{-1} x = O(1)$ f) $\sinh x = O(e^x)$

117. The figure here shows an informal proof that

$$\tan^{-1}\frac{1}{2} + \tan^{-1}\frac{1}{3} = \frac{\pi}{4}.$$

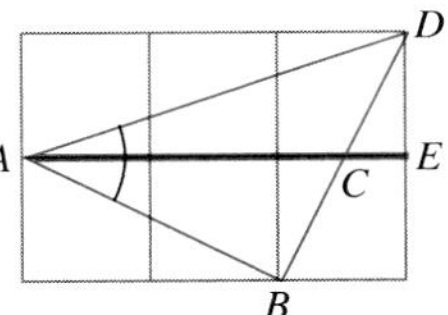

How does the argument go? (*Source:* "Behold! Sums of Arctan" by Edward M. Harris, *The College Mathematics Journal,* Vol. 18, No. 2, March 1987, p. 141.)

118. Graph $f(x) = \tan^{-1} x + \tan^{-1}(1/x)$ for $-5 \le x \le 5$. Then use calculus to explain what you see. How would you expect f to behave beyond the interval $[-5, 5]$? Give reasons for your answer.

119. Use the accompanying figure to show that

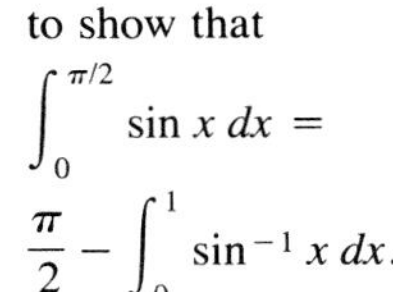

$$\int_0^{\pi/2} \sin x\, dx = \frac{\pi}{2} - \int_0^1 \sin^{-1} x\, dx.$$

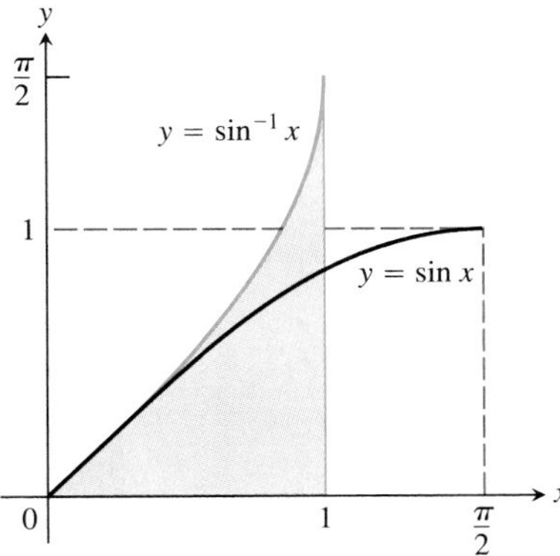

120. *Transport Through a Cell Membrane.* Under some conditions the result of the movement of a dissolved substance across a cell's membrane is described by the equation

$$\frac{dy}{dt} = k\frac{A}{V}(c - y).$$

In this equation, y is the concentration of the substance inside the cell and dy/dt is the rate with which y changes over time. The letters k, A, V, and c stand for constants, k being the *permeability coefficient* (a property of the membrane), A the surface area of the membrane, V the cell's volume, and c the concentration of the substance outside the cell. The equation says that the rate at which the concentration changes within the cell is proportional to the difference between it and the outside concentration.

a) Solve the equation for $y(t)$, using y_0 to denote $y(0)$.
b) Find the steady-state concentration, $\lim_{t\to\infty} y(t)$.

(Based on *Some Mathematical Models in Biology* by R. M. Thrall, J. A. Mortimer, K. R. Rebman, R. F. Baum, Eds., Revised Edition, December 1967, PB-202 364, pp. 101–103; distributed by N.T.I.S., U.S. Department of Commerce.)

Solve the initial value problems in Exercises 121–124.

	Differential equation	Initial condition
121.	$\dfrac{dy}{dx} = e^{-x-y-2}$	$y(0) = -2$
122.	$\dfrac{dy}{dx} = -\dfrac{y \ln y}{1 + x^2}$	$y(0) = e^2$
123.	$(x + 1)\dfrac{dy}{dx} + 2y = x, \quad x > -1$	$y(0) = 1$
124.	$x\dfrac{dy}{dx} + 2y = x^2 + 1, \quad x > 0$	$y(1) = 1$

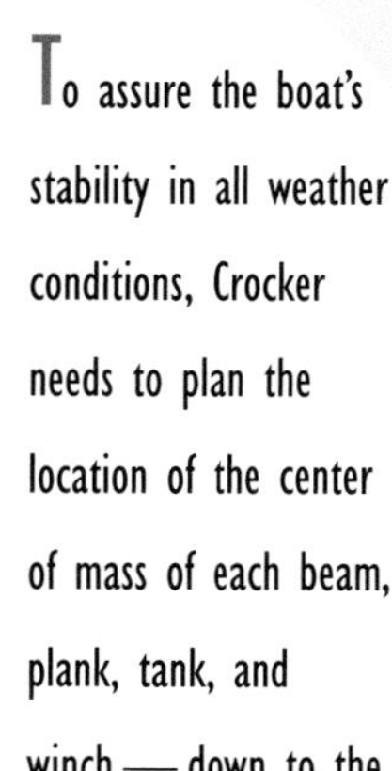

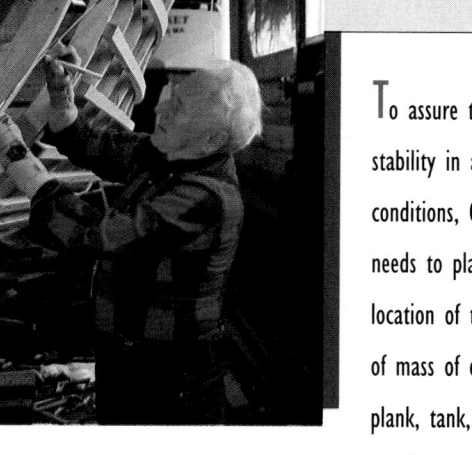

STURGIS CROCKER, owner of Crocker's Boatyard in Manchester, MA, needs to consider seaworthiness, comfort, beauty, speed, and safety each time he builds a boat.

He must think about practicality as well, weighing the advantages of each building material (strength, water tightness, reduced maintenance, resistance to rot) against the disadvantages (brittleness, inflammability, propensity to corrode, excessive cost). Designing a beautiful and safe boat requires both experience and judgment. It also requires a great deal of calculation.

To assure the boat's stability in all weather conditions, Crocker needs to plan the location of the center of mass of each beam, plank, tank, and winch — down to the last nut-and-bolt assembly. He must even calculate the center of mass of the point. He also needs to find the boat's displacement (the weight of the water displaced by the floating boat) and the boat's prismatic coefficient (a predictor of hull performance).

The prismatic coefficient is the ratio of the volume of displacement to the volume of a prism whose height equals the boat's waterline length and whose base equals the area of the boat's largest submerged cross section. The best sailboats today have prismatic coefficients between 0.51 and 0.54.

You will see how calculations like these are carried out in Sections 7.7 and 7.8.

7 Applications of Integration

OVERVIEW

Many things we want to know can be calculated with integrals: the areas between curves, the volumes and surface areas of solids, the lengths of curves, the amount of work it takes to pump liquids from below ground, the forces against floodgates, the coordinates of the points where solid objects will balance. We define all of these as limits of Riemann sums of continuous functions on closed intervals and evaluate these limits with calculus.

There is a pattern to how we define the integrals in applications, a pattern that, once learned, enables us to define new integrals whenever we need them. We look at specific applications first, then examine the pattern and show how it leads to integrals in new situations.

7.1 Areas Between Curves

This section shows how to find the areas of regions in the coordinate plane by integrating the functions that define the regions' boundaries.

The Basic Formula as a Limit of Riemann Sums

Suppose we want to find the area of a region that is bounded above by the curve $y = f(x)$, below by the curve $y = g(x)$, and on the left and right by the lines $x = a$ and $x = b$ (Fig. 7.1). The region might accidentally have a shape whose area we could find with geometry, but if f and g are arbitrary continuous functions we usually have to find the area with an integral.

To see what the integral should be, we first approximate the region with n vertical rectangles based on a partition $P = \{x_0, x_1, \ldots, x_n\}$ of $[a, b]$ (Fig. 7.2). The area of the kth rectangle (Fig. 7.3) is

$$\Delta A_k = \text{height} \times \text{width} = [f(c_k) - g(c_k)]\,\Delta x_k.$$

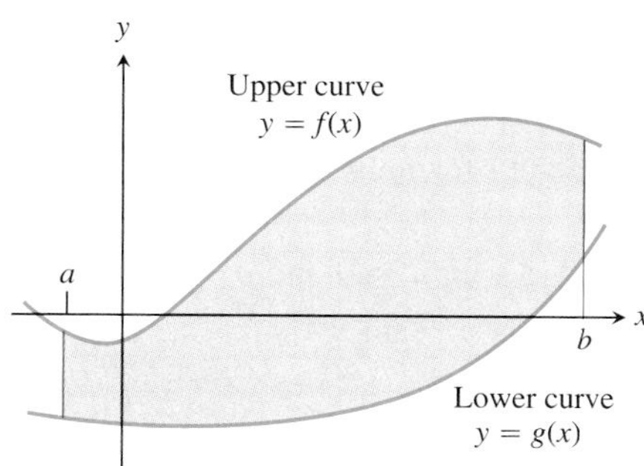

7.1 The region between $y = f(x)$ and $y = g(x)$ and the lines $x = a$ and $x = b$.

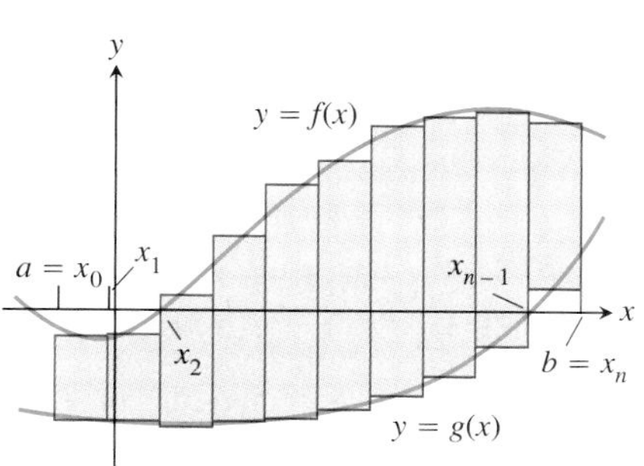

7.2 We approximate the region with rectangles perpendicular to the x-axis.

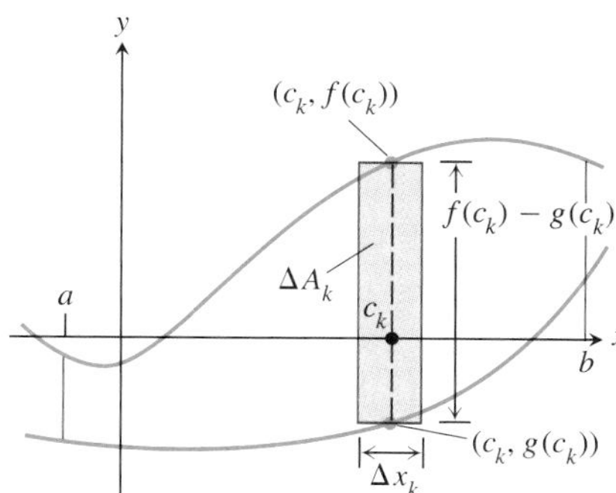

7.3 ΔA_k = area of kth rectangle
$f(c_k) - g(c_k)$ = height
Δx_k = width

We then approximate the area of the region by adding the areas of the n rectangles:

$$A \approx \sum_{k=1}^{n} \Delta A_k = \sum_{k=1}^{n} [f(c_k) - g(c_k)]\,\Delta x_k \qquad \text{(Riemann sum).} \qquad (1)$$

As $\|P\| \to 0$ the sums on the right approach the limit $\int_a^b [f(x) - g(x)]\,dx$ because f and g are continuous. We take the area of the region to be the value of this integral. That is,

$$A = \lim_{\|P\| \to 0} \sum_{k=1}^{n} [f(c_k) - g(c_k)]\,\Delta x_k = \int_a^b [f(x) - g(x)]\,dx. \qquad (2)$$

DEFINITION

If f and g are continuous with $f(x) \geq g(x)$ throughout $[a, b]$, then the **area** of the region between the curves $y = f(x)$ and $y = g(x)$ from a to b is the integral of $[f - g]$ from a to b:

$$A = \int_a^b [f(x) - g(x)]\,dx. \qquad (3)$$

To apply Eq. (3) we take the following steps:

How to Find the Area Between Two Curves

1. *Graph the curves and draw a representative rectangle.* This reveals which curve is f (upper curve) and which is g (lower curve). It also helps find the limits of integration if you do not already know them.
2. *Find the limits of integration.*
3. *Write a formula for $f(x) - g(x)$.* Simplify it if you can.
4. *Integrate $[f(x) - g(x)]$ from a to b.* The number you get is the area.

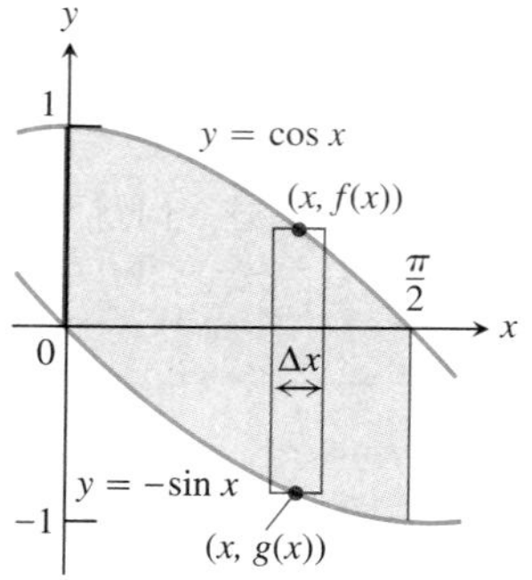

7.4 The region in Example 1 with a typical approximating rectangle.

EXAMPLE 1 Find the area between $y = \cos x$ and $y = -\sin x$ from 0 to $\pi/2$.

Solution

STEP 1: We sketch the curves and a vertical rectangle (Fig. 7.4). The upper curve is $y = \cos x$, so $f(x) = \cos x$ in the area formula. The lower curve is $y = -\sin x$, so $g(x) = -\sin x$.

STEP 2: The limits of integration are already given: $a = 0$ and $b = \pi/2$.

STEP 3: $f(x) - g(x) = \cos x - (-\sin x) = \cos x + \sin x$

STEP 4: $A = \int_0^{\pi/2} (\cos x + \sin x)\,dx = \Big[\sin x - \cos x\Big]_0^{\pi/2}$

$= [1 - 0] - [0 - 1] = 2$

The area of the given region is 2.

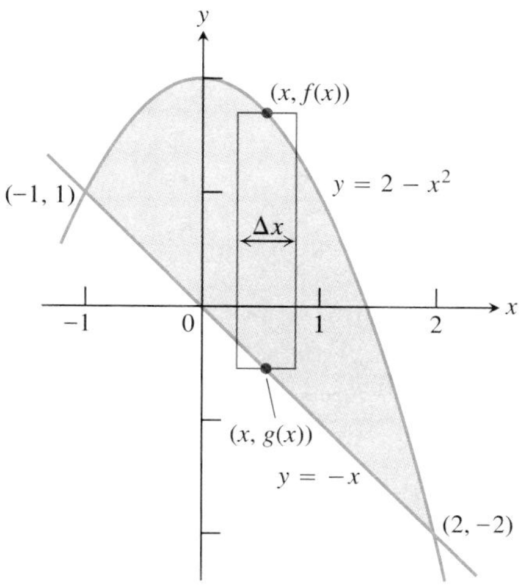

7.5 The region in Example 2 with a typical approximating rectangle.

Curves That Intersect

When a region is determined by curves that intersect, the intersection points give the limits of integration.

EXAMPLE 2 Find the area of the region enclosed by the parabola $y = 2 - x^2$ and the line $y = -x$.

Solution

STEP 1: Sketch the curves and a vertical rectangle (Fig. 7.5). Identifying the upper and lower curves, we take $f(x) = 2 - x^2$ and $g(x) = -x$. The x-coordinates of the intersection points are the limits of integration.

STEP 2: We find the limits of integration with respect to x by solving the equations $y = 2 - x^2$ and $y = -x$ simultaneously for x:

$$
\begin{aligned}
2 - x^2 &= -x && \text{Equate } f(x) \text{ and } g(x).\\
x^2 - x - 2 &= 0 && \text{Rewrite.}\\
(x+1)(x-2) &= 0 && \text{Factor.}\\
x = -1, \qquad x &= 2. && \text{Solve.}
\end{aligned}
$$

The region runs from $x = -1$ on the left to $x = 2$ on the right. The limits of integration are $a = -1$ and $b = 2$.

STEP 3:

$$
\begin{aligned}
f(x) - g(x) &= (2 - x^2) - (-x) = 2 - x^2 + x && \text{Rearrangement a matter of taste}\\
&= 2 + x - x^2
\end{aligned}
$$

STEP 4:

$$
\begin{aligned}
\int_a^b [f(x) - g(x)]\,dx &= \int_{-1}^{2} (2 + x - x^2)\,dx = \left[2x + \frac{x^2}{2} - \frac{x^3}{3}\right]_{-1}^{2}\\
&= \left(4 + \frac{4}{2} - \frac{8}{3}\right) - \left(-2 + \frac{1}{2} + \frac{1}{3}\right)\\
&= 6 + \frac{3}{2} - \frac{9}{3} = \frac{9}{2}
\end{aligned}
$$

The area of the region is 9/2.

Boundaries with Changing Formulas

If the formula for a bounding curve changes at one or more points, we partition the region into subregions that correspond to the formula changes and apply Eq. (2) as before.

EXAMPLE 3 Find the area of the region in the first quadrant that is bounded above by $y = \sqrt{x}$ and below by the x-axis and the line $y = x - 2$.

Solution

STEP 1: The sketch (Fig. 7.6 on the following page) shows that the region's upper boundary is the graph of $f(x) = \sqrt{x}$. The lower boundary changes from $g(x) = 0$ for $0 \le x \le 2$ to $g(x) = x - 2$ for $2 \le x \le 4$ (there is agreement at $x = 2$). We partition the region at $x = 2$ into subregions A and B and sketch a representative rectangle for each subregion.

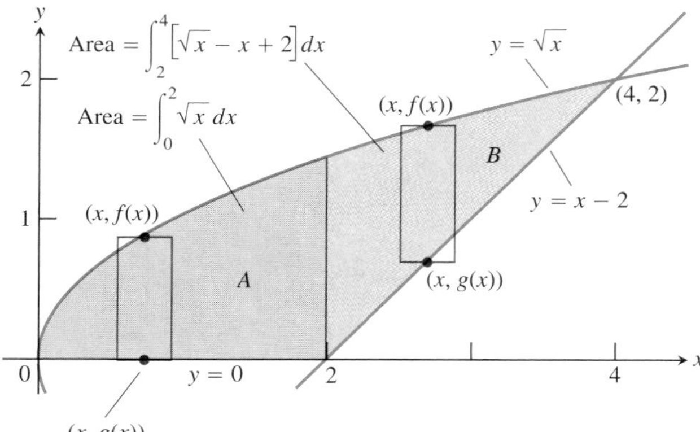

7.6 When the formula for a bounding curve changes, the area integral changes to match (Example 3).

STEP 2: The limits of integration for region A are $a = 0$ and $b = 2$. The left-hand limit for region B is $a = 2$. To find the right-hand limit, we solve the equations $y = \sqrt{x}$ and $y = x - 2$ simultaneously for x:

$$\sqrt{x} = x - 2 \qquad \text{Equate } f(x) \text{ and } g(x).$$
$$x = (x-2)^2 = x^2 - 4x + 4 \qquad \text{Square both sides.}$$
$$x^2 - 5x + 4 = 0 \qquad \text{Rewrite.}$$
$$(x-1)(x-4) = 0 \qquad \text{Factor.}$$
$$x = 1, \qquad x = 4 \qquad \text{Solve.}$$

Only the value $x = 4$ satisfies the equation $\sqrt{x} = x - 2$. The value $x = 1$ is an extraneous root introduced by squaring. The right-hand limit is $b = 4$.

STEP 3: For $0 \le x \le 2$: $\quad f(x) - g(x) = \sqrt{x} - 0 = \sqrt{x}$

For $2 \le x \le 4$: $\quad f(x) - g(x) = \sqrt{x} - (x - 2) = \sqrt{x} - x + 2$

STEP 4: We add the area of subregions A and B to find the total area:

$$\text{Total area} = \underbrace{\int_0^2 \sqrt{x}\,dx}_{\text{area of } A} + \underbrace{\int_2^4 \left(\sqrt{x} - x + 2\right) dx}_{\text{area of } B}$$
$$= \left[\frac{2}{3}x^{3/2}\right]_0^2 + \left[\frac{2}{3}x^{3/2} - \frac{x^2}{2} + 2x\right]_2^4$$
$$= \frac{2}{3}(2)^{3/2} - 0 + \left(\frac{2}{3}(4)^{3/2} - 8 + 8\right) - \left(\frac{2}{3}(2)^{3/2} - 2 + 4\right)$$
$$= \frac{2}{3}(8) - 2 = \frac{10}{3}.$$

The area of the region is 10/3.

Integration with Respect to y

If a region's bounding curves are described by functions of y, the approximating rectangles are horizontal instead of vertical and the basic formula has y's in it instead of x's.

For regions like these

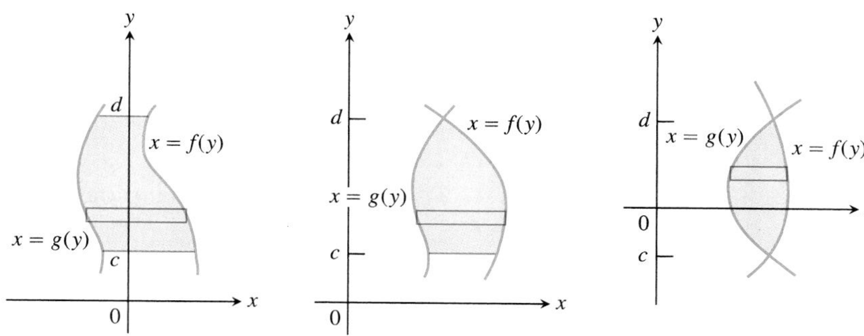

In Eq. (4), f always denotes the right-hand curve and g the left-hand curve, so $f(y) - g(y)$ is nonnegative.

use the formula

$$A = \int_c^d [f(y) - g(y)]\, dy. \tag{4}$$

EXAMPLE 4 Find the area of the region in Example 3 by integrating with respect to y.

Solution

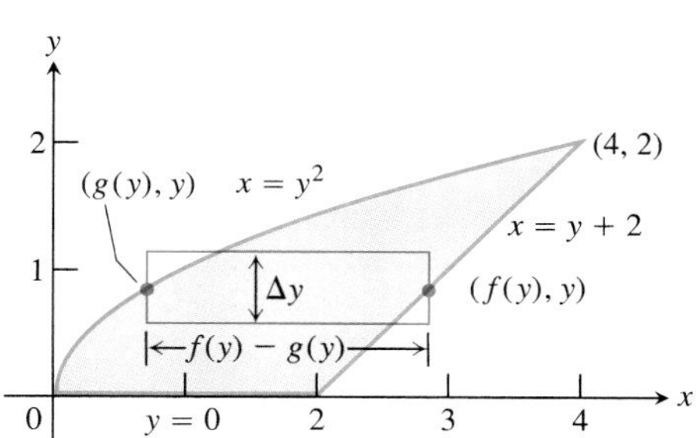

7.7 It takes two integrations to find the area of this region if we integrate with respect to x. It takes only one if we integrate with respect to y (Example 4).

STEP 1: We sketch the region and a typical *horizontal* rectangle based on a partition of an interval of y-values (Fig. 7.7). The region's right-hand boundary is the line $x = y + 2$, so $f(y) = y + 2$. The left-hand boundary is the curve $x = y^2$, so $g(y) = y^2$.

STEP 2: The lower limit of integration is $y = 0$. We find the upper limit by solving the equations $x = y + 2$ and $x = y^2$ simultaneously for y:

$$y + 2 = y^2 \qquad \text{Equate } f(y) = y + 2 \text{ and } g(y) = y^2.$$
$$y^2 - y - 2 = 0 \qquad \text{Rewrite.}$$
$$(y + 1)(y - 2) = 0 \qquad \text{Factor.}$$
$$y = -1, \quad y = 2 \qquad \text{Solve.}$$

The upper limit of integration is $b = 2$. (The value $y = -1$ gives a point of intersection *below* the x-axis.)

STEP 3: $f(y) - g(y) = y + 2 - y^2 = 2 + y - y^2$ Rearrangement a matter of taste

STEP 4:

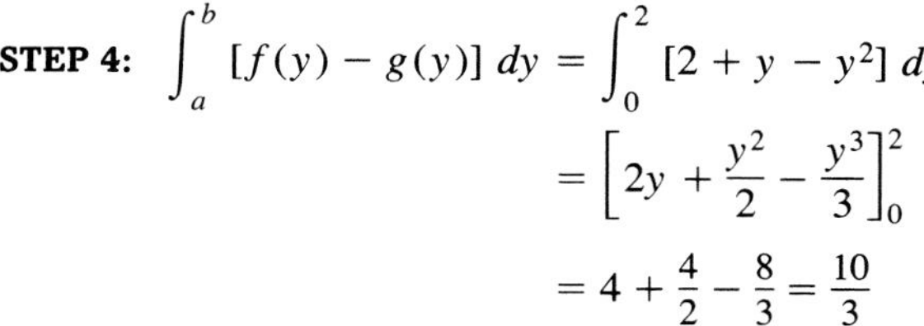

$$\int_a^b [f(y) - g(y)]\, dy = \int_0^2 [2 + y - y^2]\, dy$$
$$= \left[2y + \frac{y^2}{2} - \frac{y^3}{3}\right]_0^2$$
$$= 4 + \frac{4}{2} - \frac{8}{3} = \frac{10}{3}$$

The area of the region is 10/3. This is the result of Example 3, found with less work.

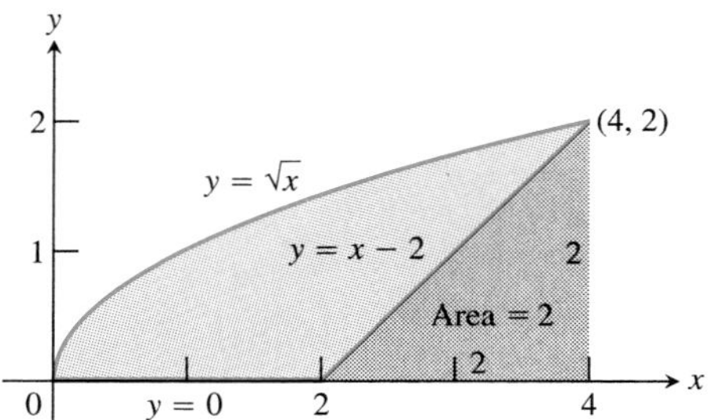

7.8 The area of the blue region is the area under the parabola $y = \sqrt{x}$ minus the area of the triangle.

Combining Integrals with Formulas from Geometry

Sometimes the fastest way to find the area of a region is to combine calculus and geometry.

EXAMPLE 5 *The Area of the Region in Example 3 Found the Fastest Way.* Find the area of the region in Example 3.

Solution The area we want is the area between the curve $y = \sqrt{x}$, $0 \le x \le 4$, and the x-axis, *minus* the area of a triangle with base 2 and height 2 (Fig. 7.8):

$$\begin{aligned}\text{Area} &= \int_0^4 \sqrt{x}\,dx - \frac{1}{2}(2)(2)\\ &= \frac{2}{3}x^{3/2}\Big]_0^4 - 2\\ &= \frac{2}{3}(8) - 0 - 2 = \frac{10}{3}.\end{aligned}$$

Moral of Examples 3–5: It is sometimes easier to find the area between two curves by integrating with respect to y instead of x. Also, it may help to combine geometry and calculus. After sketching the region, take a moment to determine the best way to proceed.

Exercises 7.1

Find the areas of the shaded regions in Exercises 1–12.

1.

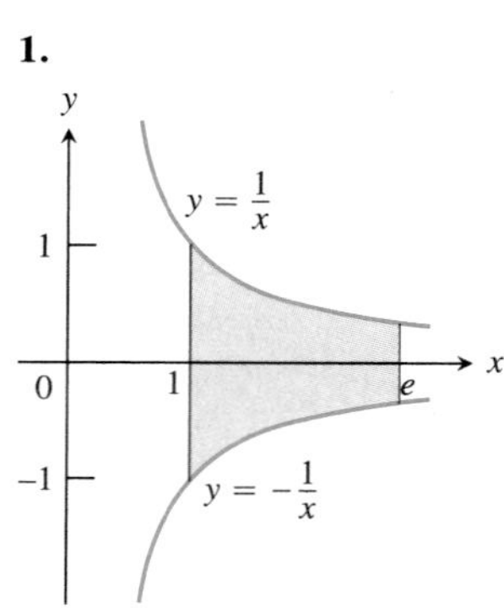

2.

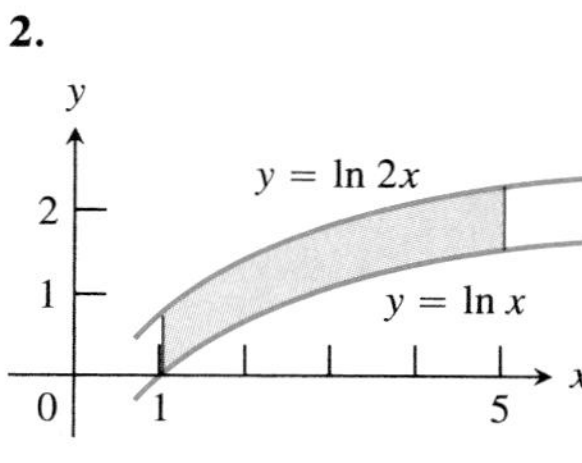

5.

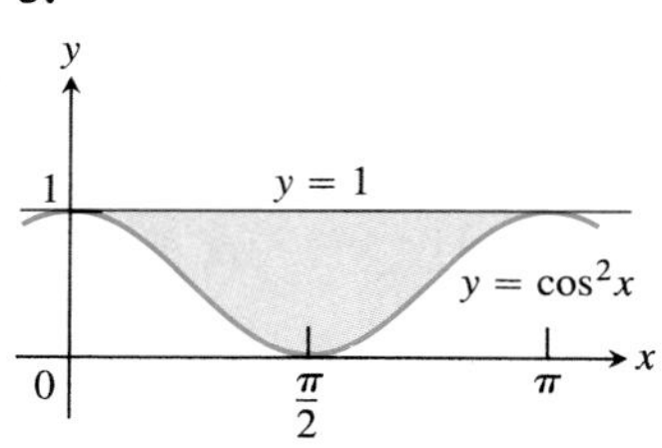

6.

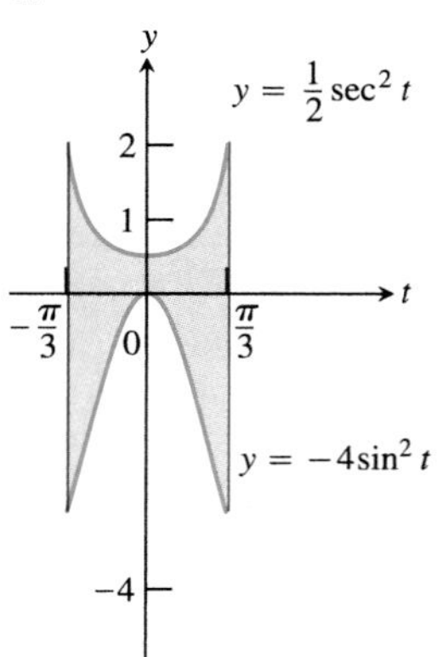

3.

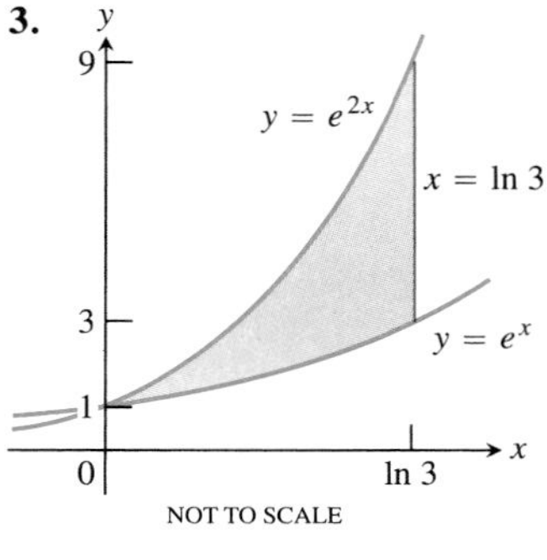

4.

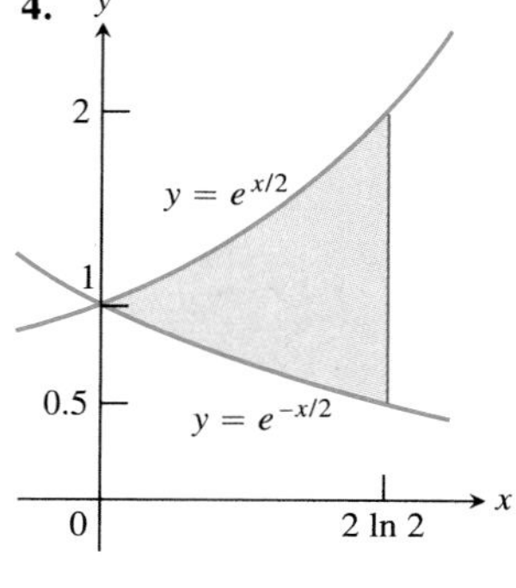

7.

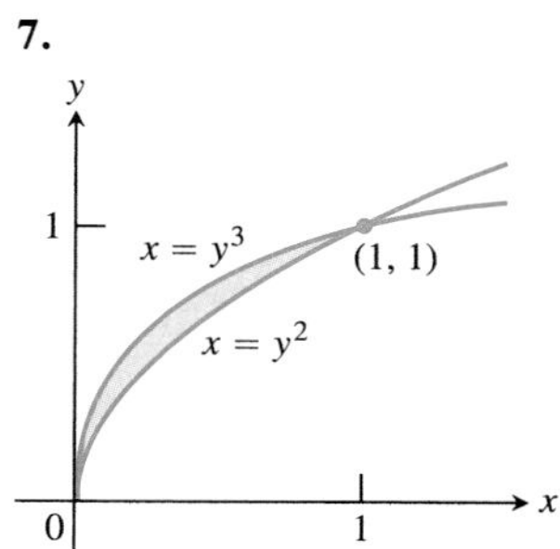

8.

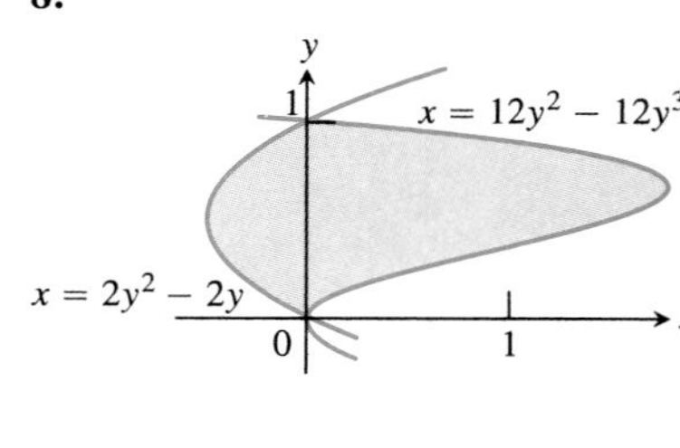

9.
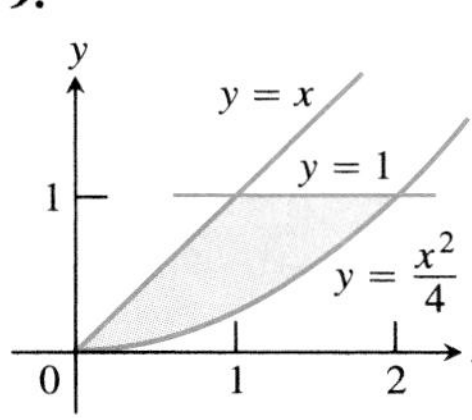

10.
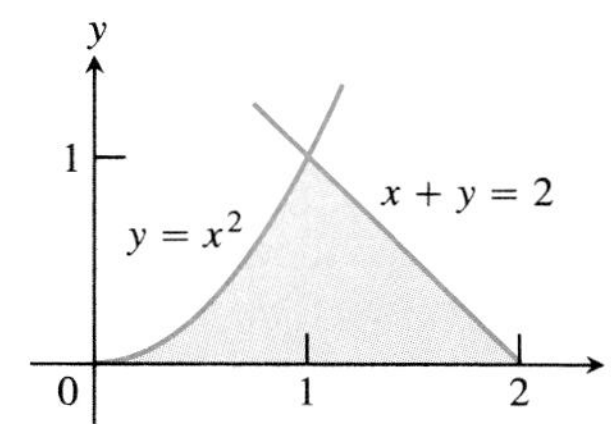

11.
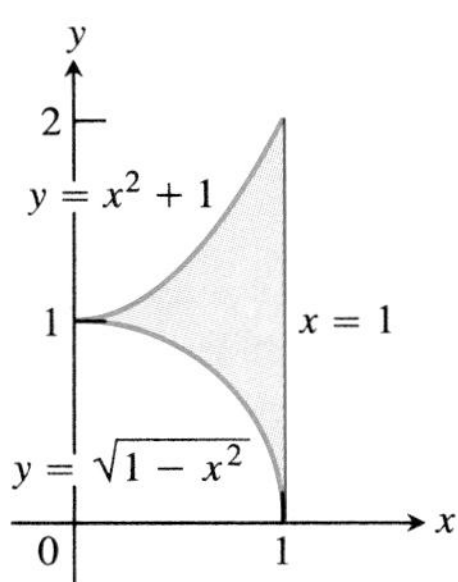

12.
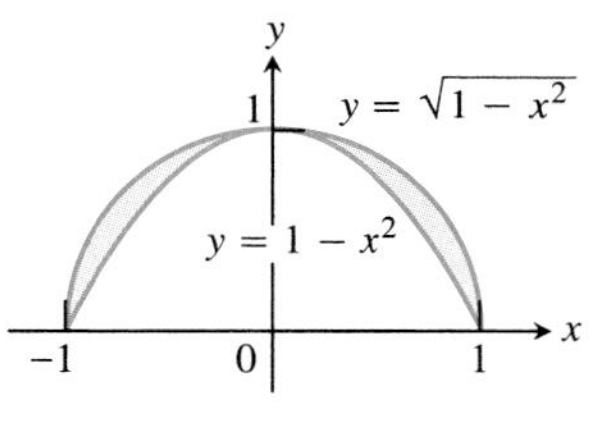

Find the areas of the regions enclosed by the lines and curves in Exercises 13–18.

13. $y = x^2 - 2$ and $y = 2$

14. $y = 2x - x^2$ and $y = -3$

15. $y = x^4$ and $y = 8x$

16. $y = x^2 - 2x$ and $y = x$

17. $y = x^2$ and $y = -x^2 + 4x$

18. $y = 7 - 2x^2$ and $y = x^2 + 4$

Find the areas of the regions enclosed by the lines and curves in Exercises 19–24.

19. $x = 2y^2$, $x = 0$, and $y = 3$

20. $x = y^2$ and $x = y + 2$

21. $y^2 - 4x = 4$ and $4x - y = 16$

22. $x - y^2 = 0$ and $x + 2y^2 = 3$

23. $x + y^2 = 0$ and $x + 3y^2 = 2$

24. $x - y^{2/3} = 0$ and $x + y^4 = 2$

Find the areas of the regions enclosed by the curves in Exercises 25–28.

25. $4x^2 + y = 4$ and $x^4 - y = 1$

26. $x^3 - y = 0$ and $3x^2 - y = 4$

27. $x + 4y^2 = 4$ and $x + y^4 = 1$

28. $x + y^2 = 3$ and $4x + y^2 = 0$

Find the areas of the regions enclosed by the lines and curves in Exercises 29–36.

29. $y = 2 \sin x$ and $y = \sin 2x$, $0 \le x \le \pi$

30. $y = 8 \cos x$ and $y = \sec^2 x$, $-\pi/3 \le x \le \pi/3$

31. $y = \cos(\pi x/2)$ and $y = 1 - x^2$

32. $y = \sin(\pi x/2)$ and $y = x$

33. $y = \sec^2 x$, $y = \tan^2 x$, $x = -\pi/4$, and $x = \pi/4$

34. $x = \tan^2 y$ and $x = -\tan^2 y$, $-\pi/4 \le y \le \pi/4$

35. $x = 3 \sin y \sqrt{\cos y}$ and $x = 0$, $0 \le y \le \pi/2$

36. $y = \sec^2(\pi x/3)$ and $y = x^{1/3}$, $-1 \le x \le 1$

In Exercises 37–40, find the total shaded area.

37.
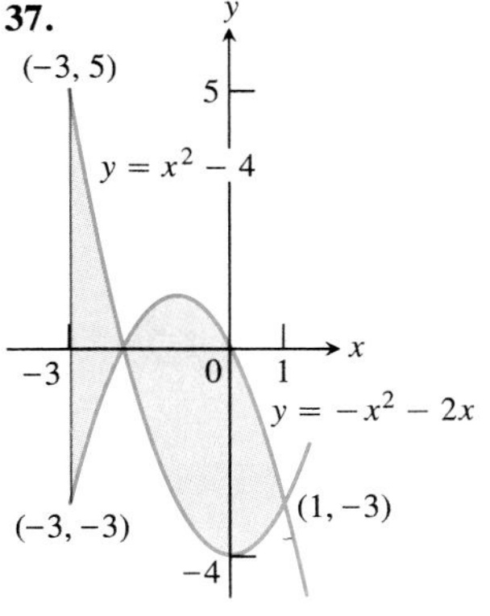

38.
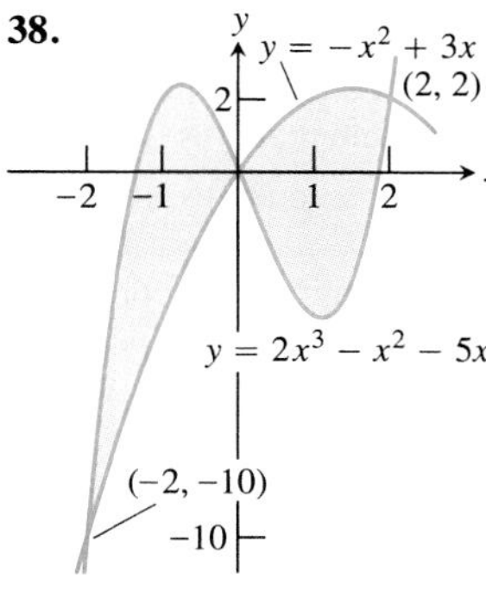

39.
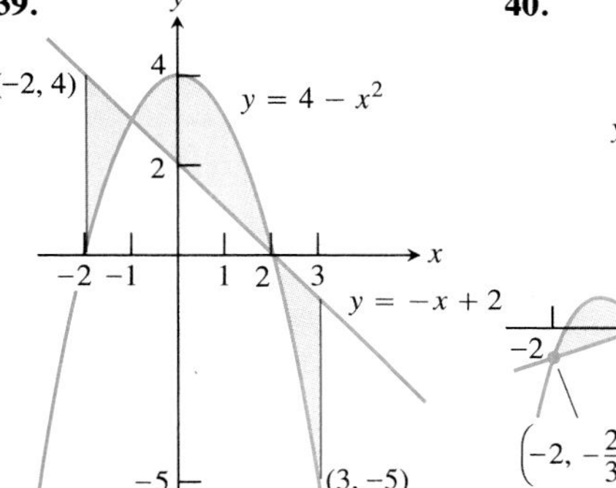

40.
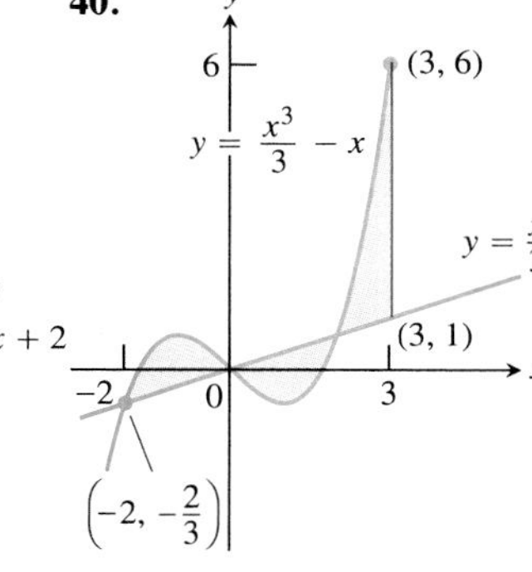

41. Find the area of the propeller shaped region enclosed by the curve $x - y^3 = 0$ and the line $x - y = 0$.

42. Find the area of the propeller shaped region enclosed by the curves $x - y^{1/3} = 0$ and $x - y^{1/5} = 0$.

43. Find the area of the small "triangular" region in the first quadrant enclosed by the curve $y = 1/x$ and the lines $y = x$ and $x = 2$.

44. Find the area of the "triangular" region enclosed by the line $x = 1/e$ and the curves $y = 1/x$ and $y = (\ln x)/x$.

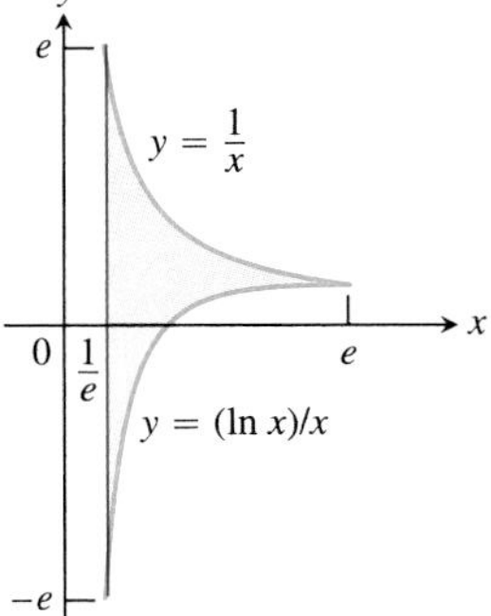

45. The region bounded below by the parabola $y = x^2$ and above by the line $y = 4$ is to be partitioned into two subsections of equal area by cutting across it with the horizontal line $y = c$.

 a) Sketch the region and draw a line $y = c$ across it that looks about right. In terms of c, what are the coordinates of the points where the line and parabola intersect? Add them to your figure.

 b) Find c by integrating with respect to y. (This puts c in the limits of integration.)

 c) Find c by integrating with respect to x. (This puts c into the integrand as well.)

46. The accompanying figure shows triangle AOC inscribed in the region cut from the parabola $y = x^2$ by the line $y = a^2$. Find the limit of the ratio of the area of the triangle to the area of the parabolic region as a approaches zero.

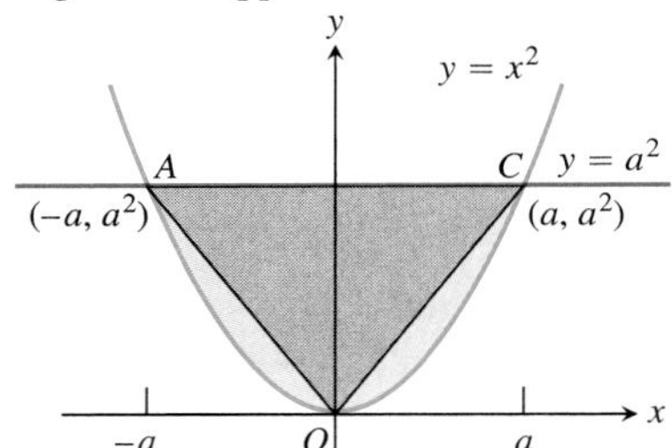

47. Which of the following integrals, if either, calculates the area of the shaded region shown here? Give reasons for your answer.

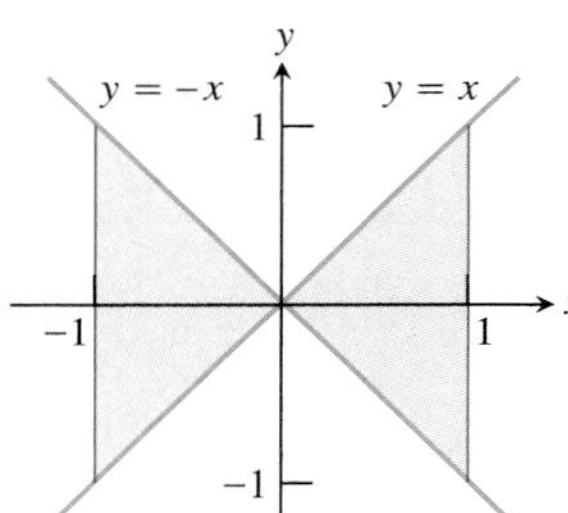

 a) $\int_{-1}^{1} (x - (-x))\, dx = \int_{-1}^{1} 2x\, dx$

 b) $\int_{-1}^{1} (-x - (x))\, dx = \int_{-1}^{1} -2x\, dx$

48. True, sometimes true, or never true? The area of the region between the graphs of the continuous functions $y = f(x)$ and $y = g(x)$ and the vertical lines $x = a$ and $x = b$ $(a < b)$ is

$$\int_a^b [f(x) - g(x)]\, dx.$$

Give reasons for your answer.

Writing for Your Own Knowledge

Answer the following questions in writing. Some answers will take only a sentence or two; others may require several paragraphs. Some explanations may also call for graphs or sketches.

1. How do you define the area of the region between the curves $y = f(x)$ and $y = g(x)$ from $x = a$ to $x = b$ if f and g are continuous and $f(x) \geq g(x)$ throughout $[a, b]$?
2. How do you find the area of a region determined by curves that intersect?
3. How do you find the area of a region if the formula for a bounding curve changes at one or more points?

EXPLORER PROGRAM

PowerGrapher	Enables you to portray regions in the plane by graphing functions together.

7.2 Volumes of Solids of Revolution—Disks and Washers

Solids generated by revolving plane regions about axes are **solids of revolution.** Threaded spools are solids of revolution; so are hand weights and billiard balls. These solids have volumes we can find with geometry. But, likely as not, we will want to find the volume of a blimp instead, or to predict the weight of a part that will be turned on a lathe. In cases like these, formulas from geometry are of little help and we turn to calculus for the answers.

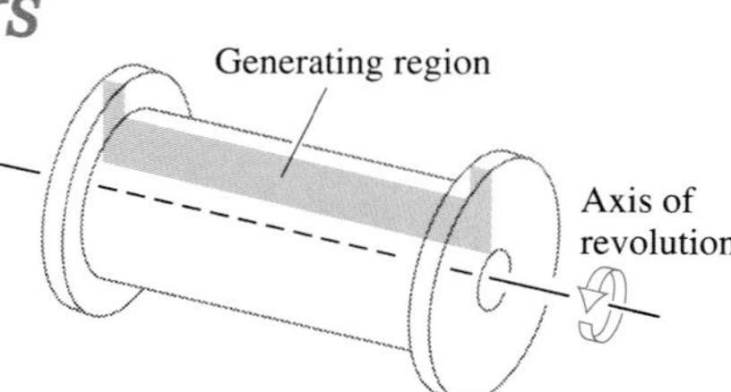

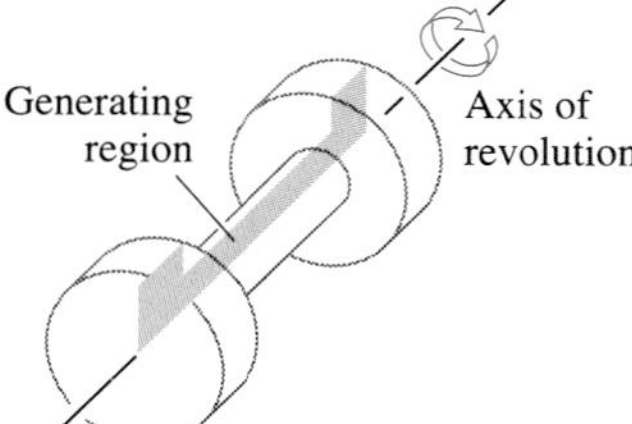

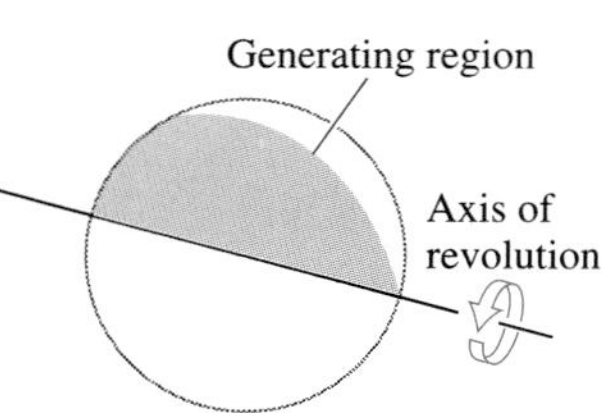

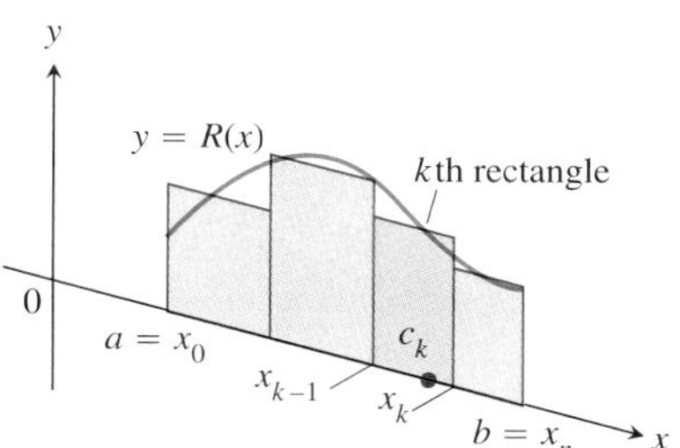

7.9 The first step in developing an integral to calculate the volume of a solid of revolution is to approximate the generating region with rectangles.

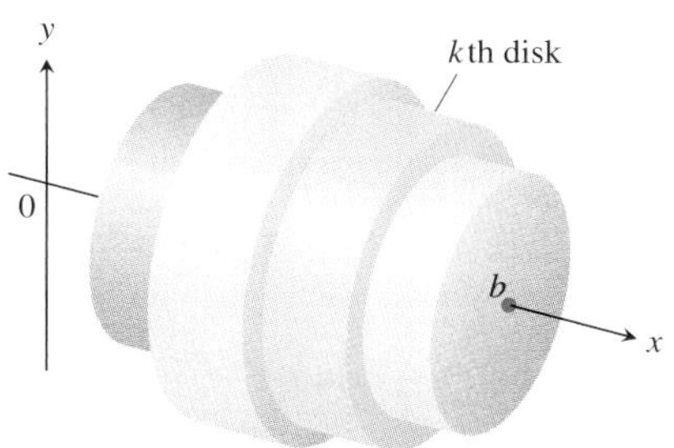

7.10 The rectangles revolve around the x-axis to generate solid disks whose volumes, when added, approximate the volume of the solid.

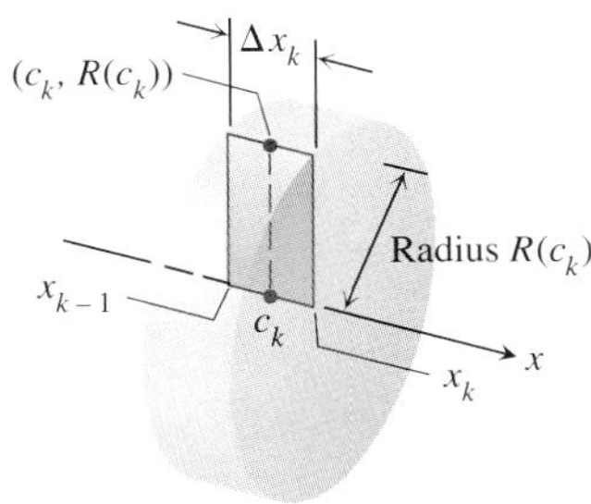

7.11 Enlarged view of the kth disk from Fig. 7.10. Its volume is

base area × thickness $= \pi [R(c_k)]^2 \times \Delta x_k$.

The Disk Method

If we can set things up so that the axis of revolution is the x-axis and the region is the region of the plane between the x-axis and the graph of a continuous function $y = R(x)$, $a \leq x \leq b$, we can calculate the volume of the solid as follows.

We approximate the region with n vertical rectangles based on a partition P of $[a, b]$ (Fig. 7.9). We then imagine the rectangles to be revolved along with the region about the x-axis. Each rectangle generates a solid disk (Fig. 7.10), and the disks, taken together, approximate the solid.

A typical disk (Fig. 7.11) is a right circular cylinder with height (in the figure, thickness) Δx_k and radius $R(c_k)$. The volume of the kth disk is

$$\Delta V_k = \pi \times (\text{radius})^2 \times \text{thickness} = \pi [R(c_k)]^2 \, \Delta x_k. \tag{1}$$

We approximate the volume of the solid by adding the volumes of the n disks:

$$V \approx \sum_{k=1}^{n} \Delta V_k = \sum_{k=1}^{n} \pi [R(c_k)]^2 \, \Delta x_k. \qquad \text{A Riemann sum} \tag{2}$$

We take the limit of this sum as $\|P\| \to 0$ to find the volume V of the solid:

$$V = \lim_{\|P\| \to 0} \sum_{k=1}^{n} \pi [R(c_k)]^2 \, \Delta x_k = \int_a^b \pi [R(x)]^2 \, dx. \tag{3}$$

DEFINITION

Volume of a Solid of Revolution (Rotation About the x-Axis)

The **volume** of the solid generated by revolving the region between the x-axis and the graph of a continuous function $y = R(x)$, $a \leq x \leq b$, about the x-axis is

$$V = \int_a^b \pi (\text{radius})^2 \, dx = \int_a^b \pi [R(x)]^2 \, dx. \tag{4}$$

EXAMPLE 1 The region between the curve $y = \sqrt{x}$, $0 \leq x \leq 4$, and the x-axis is revolved about the x-axis to generate the solid in Fig. 7.12 (on the following page). Find its volume.

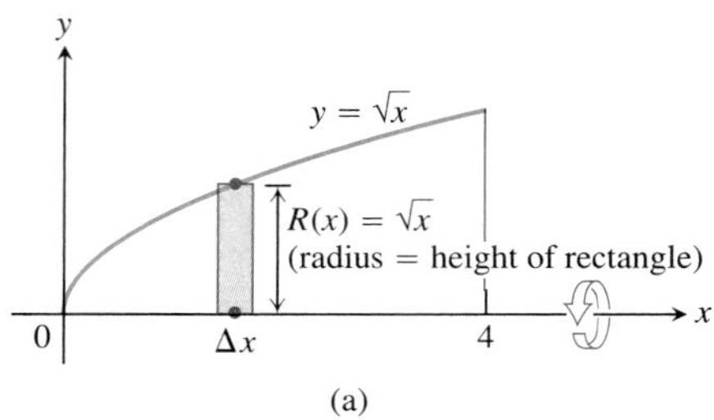

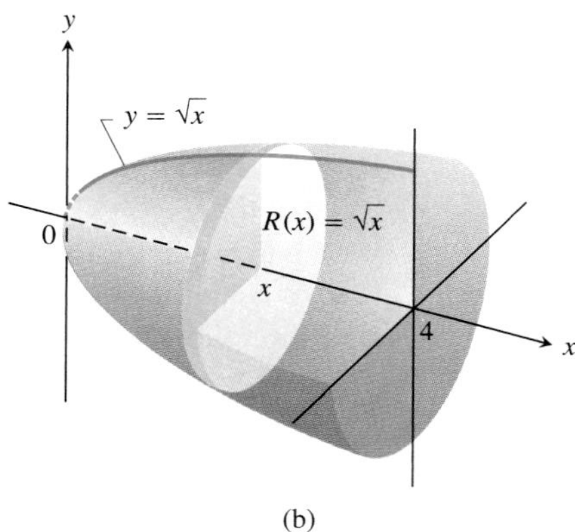

7.12 (a) The region with a typical approximating rectangle, and (b) the solid in Example 1.

Solution

$$V = \int_a^b \pi [R(x)]^2\, dx \qquad \text{Eq. (4)}$$

$$= \int_0^4 \pi \left[\sqrt{x}\right]^2 dx \qquad R(x) = \sqrt{x}$$

$$= \pi \int_0^4 x\, dx = \pi \left.\frac{x^2}{2}\right]_0^4 = \pi \frac{(4)^2}{2} = 8\pi$$

How to Find Volumes by the Disk Method

1. Draw the region and sketch a thin rectangle across the region *perpendicular* to the axis of revolution.
2. Determine the radius function R (the height of the rectangle gives R). Then square the expression for R.
3. Multiply by π.
4. Integrate to find the volume.

EXAMPLE 2 Find the volume generated by revolving the region bounded by $y = \sqrt{x}$ and the lines $y = 1$ and $x = 4$ about the line $y = 1$.

Solution We sketch this region, a typical approximating rectangle, and the generated solid (Fig. 7.13). The volume is

$$V = \int_1^4 \pi [R(x)]^2\, dx \qquad \text{Eq. (4)}$$

$$= \int_1^4 \pi \left[\sqrt{x} - 1\right]^2 dx \qquad R(x) = \sqrt{x} - 1$$

$$= \pi \int_1^4 \left[x - 2\sqrt{x} + 1\right] dx$$

$$= \pi \left[\frac{x^2}{2} - 2 \cdot \frac{2}{3} x^{3/2} + x\right]_1^4 = \frac{7\pi}{6}.$$

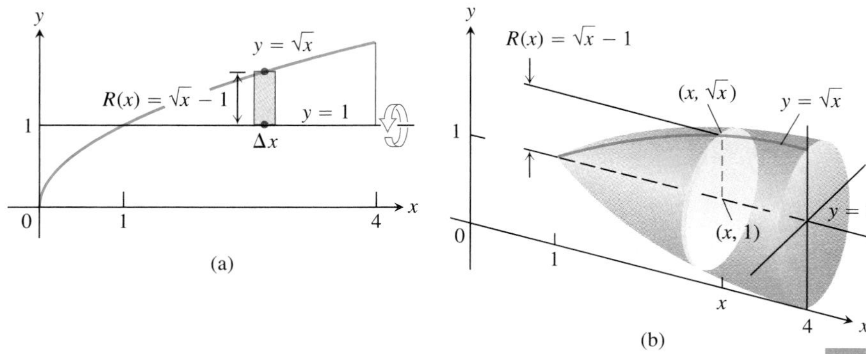

7.13 (a) The region with a typical approximating rectangle, and (b) the solid in Example 2.

To find the volume of a solid generated by revolving the region between the y-axis and a curve $x = R(y)$, $c \le y \le d$, about the y-axis, we use Eq. (4) with x replaced by y.

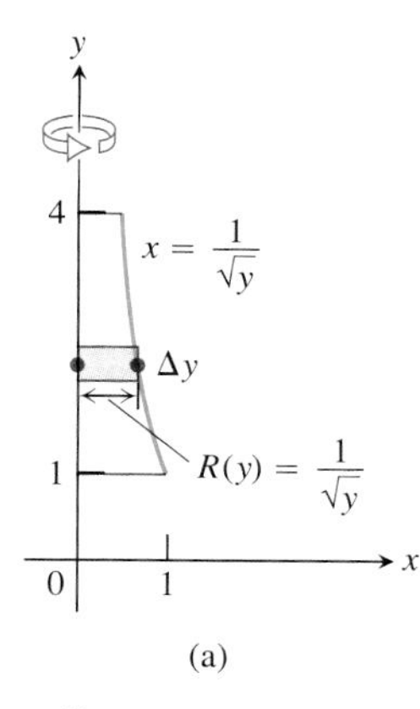

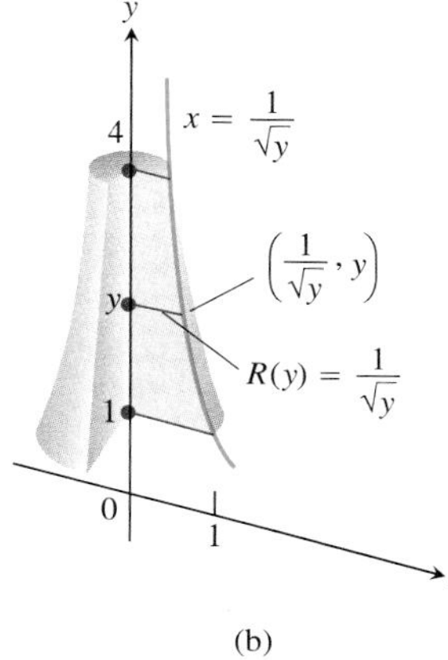

7.14 (a) The region with a typical approximating rectangle, and (b) the solid in Example 3.

Volume of a Solid of Revolution (Rotation About the y-Axis)

$$V = \int_c^d \pi\,(\text{radius})^2\, dy = \int_c^d \pi\,[R(y)]^2\, dy \tag{5}$$

EXAMPLE 3 Find the volume of the solid generated by revolving the region between the y-axis and the curve $x = 1/\sqrt{y}$, $1 \le y \le 4$, about the y-axis (Fig. 7.14).

Solution

$$\begin{aligned} V &= \int_1^4 \pi\,[R(y)]^2\, dy && \text{Eq. (5)} \\ &= \int_1^4 \pi\left[\frac{1}{\sqrt{y}}\right]^2 dy && R(y) = \frac{1}{\sqrt{y}} \\ &= \pi \int_1^4 \frac{1}{y}\, dy = \pi \ln y\Big]_1^4 \\ &= \pi \ln 4 - 0 = 2\pi \ln 2 \end{aligned}$$

EXAMPLE 4 Find the volume of the solid generated by revolving the region between the parabola $x = y^2 + 1$ and the line $x = 3$ about the line $x = 3$.

Solution We sketch the region, a typical approximating rectangle, and the generated solid (Fig. 7.15). The y-coordinates of the intersection points are $y = -\sqrt{2}$ and $y = \sqrt{2}$. The volume is

$$\begin{aligned} V &= \int_{-\sqrt{2}}^{\sqrt{2}} \pi\,[R(y)]^2\, dy && \text{Eq. (5)} \\ &= \int_{-\sqrt{2}}^{\sqrt{2}} \pi\,[2 - y^2]^2\, dy && R(y) = 3 - (y^2 + 1) = 2 - y^2 \\ &= \pi \int_{-\sqrt{2}}^{\sqrt{2}} [4 - 4y^2 + y^4]\, dy \\ &= \pi\left[4y - \frac{4}{3}y^3 + \frac{y^5}{5}\right]_{-\sqrt{2}}^{\sqrt{2}} = \frac{64\pi\sqrt{2}}{15}. \end{aligned}$$

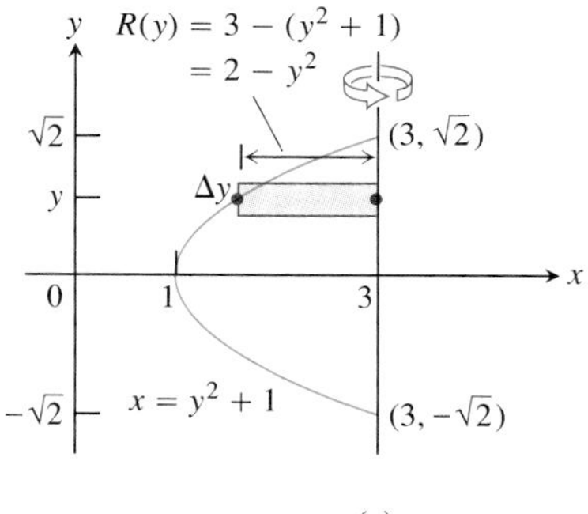

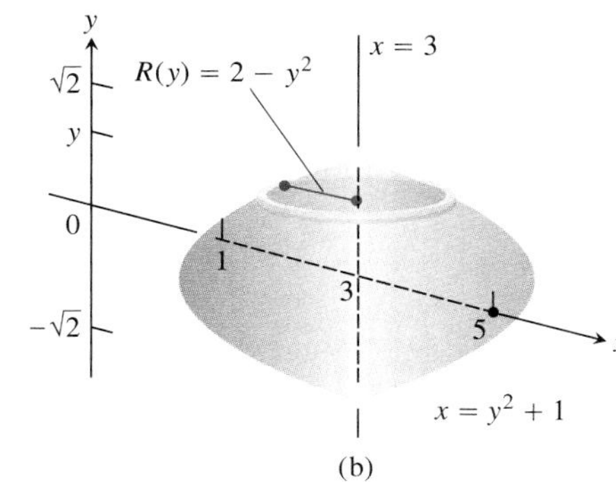

7.15 (a) The region with an approximating rectangle, and (b) the generated solid in Example 4.

The Washer Method

If the region we revolve to generate a solid does not border on the axis of revolution,

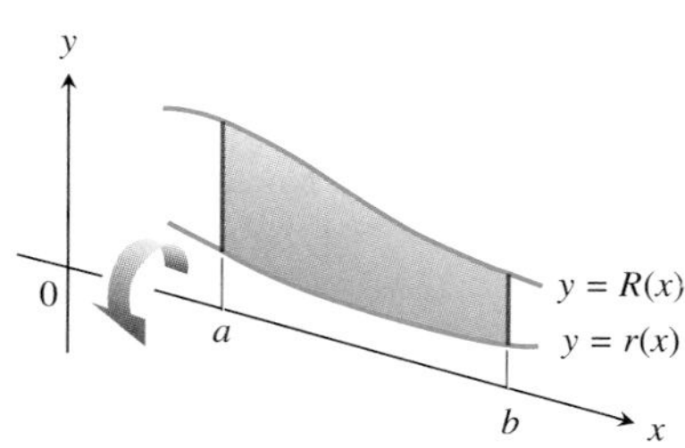

. . . the solid has a hole in it.

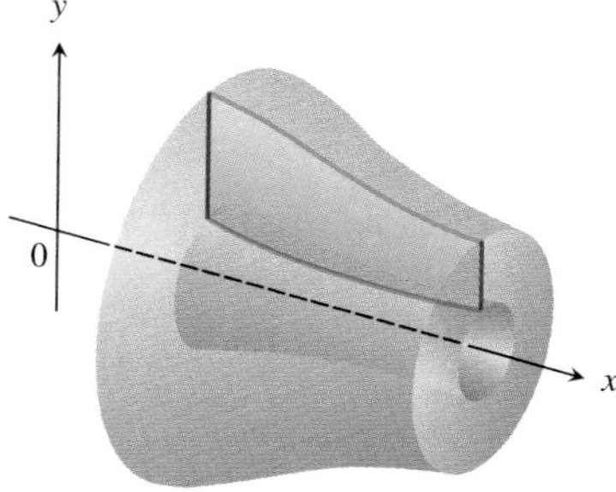

The cross sections perpendicular to the axis of revolution are washers instead of disks.

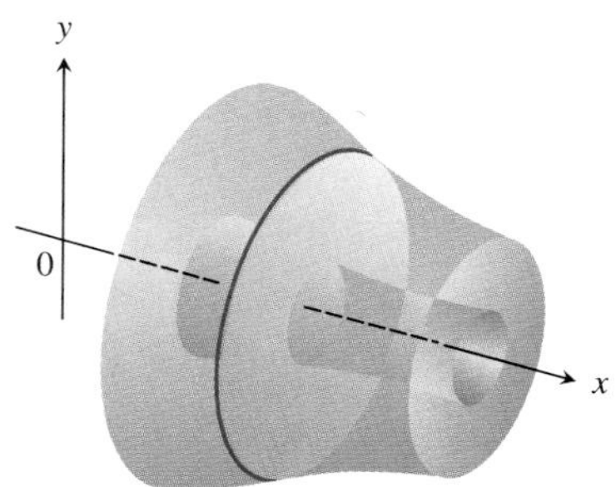

If we fill in the hole, the volume is

$$\int_a^b \pi [R(x)]^2\, dx.$$

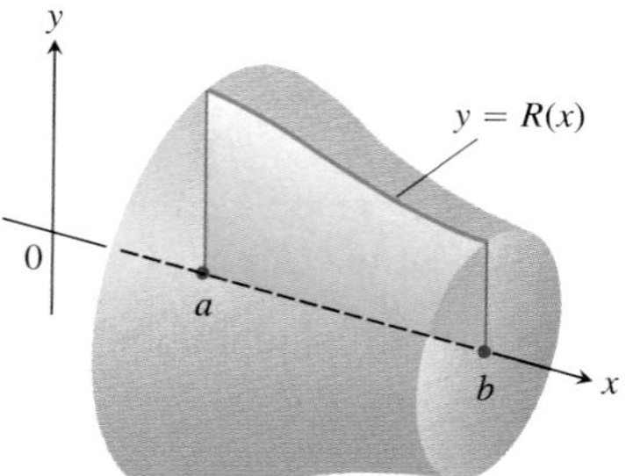

Hole filled in

The volume of the hole itself is

$$\int_a^b \pi [r(x)]^2\, dx.$$

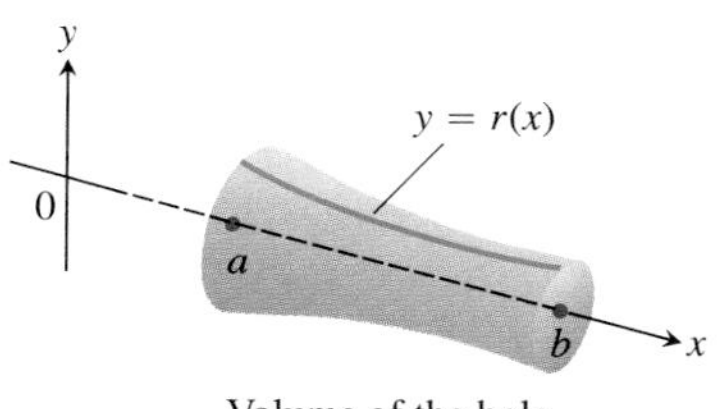

Volume of the hole

The volume of the original solid is therefore

(volume with hole filled in) − (volume of hole)

$$= \int_a^b \pi \left([R(x)]^2 - [r(x)]^2\right) dx.$$

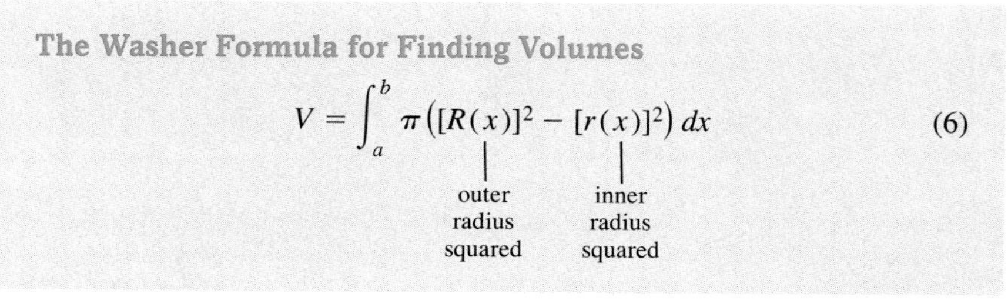

The Washer Formula for Finding Volumes

$$V = \int_a^b \pi \left([R(x)]^2 - [r(x)]^2\right) dx \tag{6}$$

outer radius squared — inner radius squared

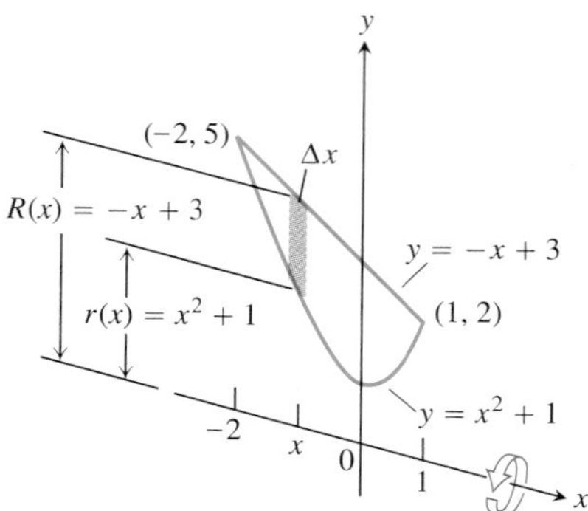

7.16 The region bounded by the curve $y = x^2 + 1$ and the line $y = -x + 3$ with a thin rectangle perpendicular to the axis of revolution.

Notice that the function integrated in Eq. (6) is $\pi(R^2 - r^2)$, not $\pi(R - r)^2$. Also notice that Eq. (6) gives the disk-method formula if $r(x)$ is zero throughout $[a, b]$. Thus, the disk method is a special case of the washer method.

EXAMPLE 5 The region bounded by the curve $y = x^2 + 1$ and the line $y = -x + 3$ is revolved about the x-axis to generate a solid. Find the volume of the solid.

Solution

STEP 1: Draw the region and sketch a thin rectangle across it perpendicular to the axis of revolution (the orange rectangle in Fig. 7.16). Since the width of the rectangle is Δx, we integrate with respect to x.

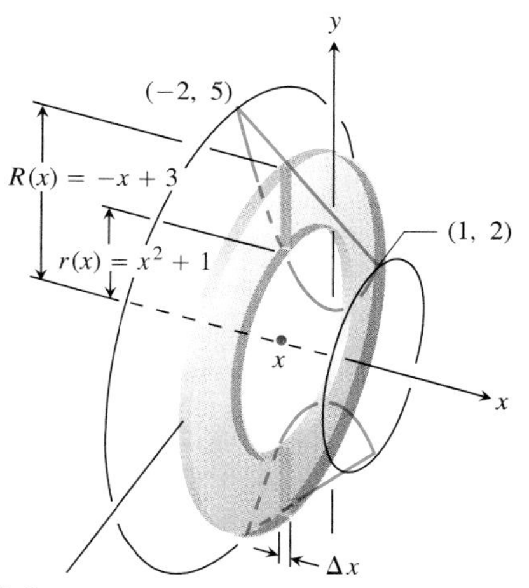

Washer
Thickness: Δx
Outer radius: $R(x) = -x + 3$
Inner radius: $r(x) = x^2 + 1$

7.17 The inner and outer radii of the washer swept out by the rectangle in Fig. 7.16.

STEP 2: Find the limits of integration by finding the x-coordinates of the intersection points.

$$\begin{aligned} x^2 + 1 &= -x + 3 \\ x^2 + x - 2 &= 0 \\ (x + 2)(x - 1) &= 0 \\ x = -2, \quad & x = 1 \end{aligned}$$

STEP 3: Find the outer and inner radii of the washer that would be swept out by the rectangle if it were revolved about the x-axis along with the region. (We drew the washer in Fig. 7.17, but in your own work you need not do that.) These radii are the distances of the two ends of the rectangle from the axis of revolution.

$$\text{Outer radius:} \quad R(x) = -x + 3$$
$$\text{Inner radius:} \quad r(x) = x^2 + 1$$

STEP 4: Evaluate the volume integral.

$$V = \int_a^b \pi\left([R(x)]^2 - [r(x)]^2\right) dx \qquad \text{Eq. (6)}$$
$$= \int_{-2}^{1} \pi((-x + 3)^2 - (x^2 + 1)^2)\, dx \qquad \text{Values from Steps 2 and 3}$$
$$= \int_{-2}^{1} \pi(8 - 6x - x^2 - x^4)\, dx \qquad \text{Expressions squared and combined}$$
$$= \pi\left[8x - 3x^2 - \frac{x^3}{3} - \frac{x^5}{5}\right]_{-2}^{1} = \frac{117\pi}{5}$$

The volume of the solid is $117\pi/5$.

How to Find Volumes by the Washer Method

1. Draw the region and sketch a thin rectangle across the region *perpendicular* to the axis of revolution. Determine whether the integration will be with respect to x or to y.
2. Find the limits of integration.
3. Find the inner and outer radii of the washer swept out by the rectangle.
4. Integrate to find the volume.

To find the volume of a solid generated by revolving a region about the y-axis, we use the steps listed above but integrate with respect to y instead of x.

EXAMPLE 6 The region bounded by the parabola $y = x^2$ and the line $y = 2x$ in the first quadrant is revolved about the y-axis to generate a solid. Find the volume of the solid.

Solution

STEP 1: We draw the region and sketch a rectangle across it perpendicular to the y-axis. The width of the rectangle is Δy, so we integrate with respect to y (Fig. 7.18 on the following page).

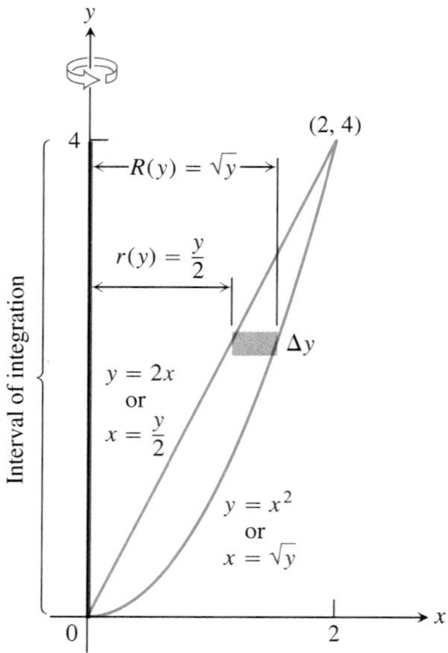

7.18 The region, limits of integration, and radii in Example 6.

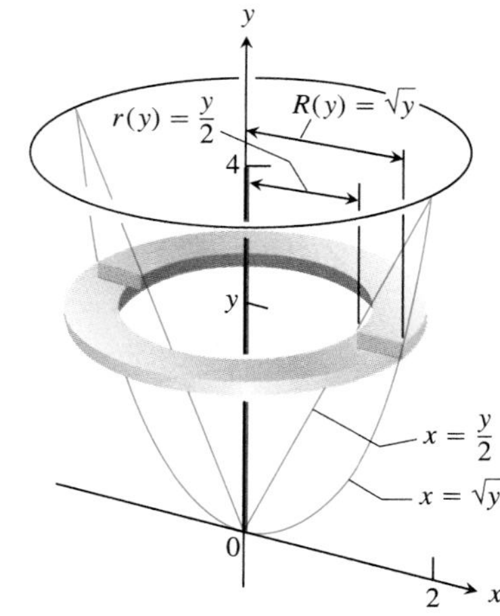

7.19 The washer swept out by the rectangle in Fig. 7.18.

STEP 2: The line and parabola intersect at $y = 0$ and $y = 4$, so the limits of integration are $c = 0$ and $d = 4$.

STEP 3: The radii of the washer swept out by the rectangle (Figs. 7.18 and 7.19) are $R(y) = \sqrt{y}$ and $r(y) = y/2$.

STEP 4:

$$V = \int_c^d \pi\left([R(y)]^2 - [r(y)]^2\right) dy \qquad \text{Eq. (6) with } y \text{ in place of } x$$

$$= \int_0^4 \pi\left(\left[\sqrt{y}\right]^2 - \left[\frac{y}{2}\right]^2\right) dy \qquad \text{Values from Steps 2 and 3}$$

$$= \pi \int_0^4 \left(y - \frac{y^2}{4}\right) dy = \pi \left[\frac{y^2}{2} - \frac{y^3}{12}\right]_0^4 = \frac{8}{3}\pi$$

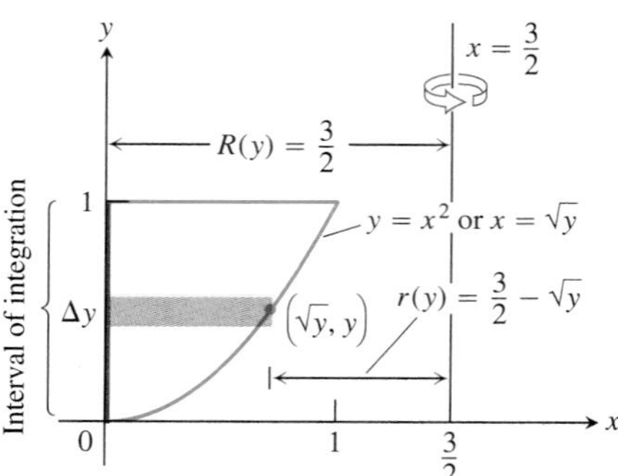

7.20 The region, limits of integration, and radii in Example 7.

EXAMPLE 7 The region in the first quadrant enclosed by the parabola $y = x^2$, the y-axis, and the line $y = 1$ is revolved about the line $x = 3/2$ to generate a solid. Find the volume of the solid.

Solution

STEP 1: We draw the region and sketch a rectangle across it perpendicular to the y-axis (Fig. 7.20). The width of the triangle is Δy, so we integrate with respect to y.

STEP 2: The limits of integration are $y = 0$ to $y = 1$.

STEP 3: The radii of the washer swept out by the rectangle (Figs. 7.20 and 7.21) are $R(y) = 3/2$ and $r(y) = (3/2) - \sqrt{y}$.

STEP 4:

$$V = \int_c^d \pi\left([R(y)]^2 - [r(y)]^2\right) dy \qquad \text{Eq. (6) with } y \text{ in place of } x$$

$$= \int_0^1 \pi\left(\left[\frac{3}{2}\right]^2 - \left[\frac{3}{2} - \sqrt{y}\right]^2\right) dy$$

$$= \pi \int_0^1 \left(3\sqrt{y} - y\right) dy = \pi \left[2y^{3/2} - \frac{y^2}{2}\right]_0^1 = \frac{3\pi}{2}$$

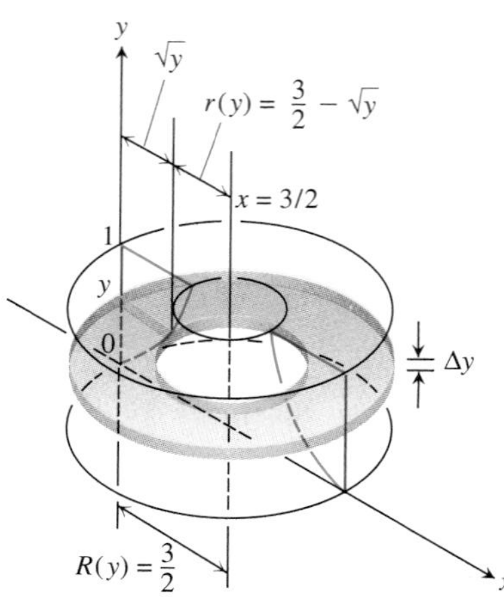

7.21 The washer swept out by the rectangle in Fig. 7.20.

Exercises 7.2

In Exercises 1–8, find the volume of the solid generated by revolving the shaded region about the given axes.

1. About the x-axis

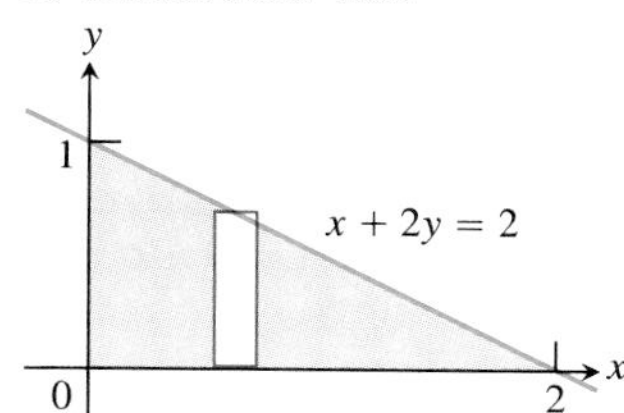

2. About the y-axis

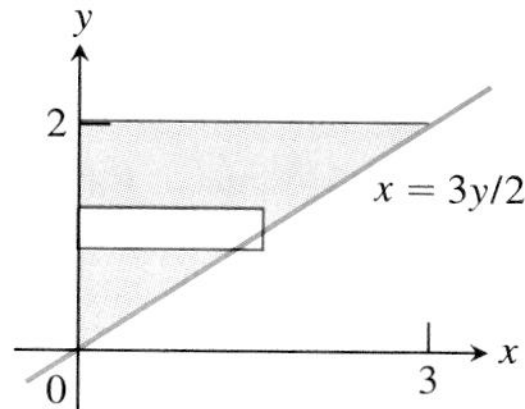

3. About the y-axis

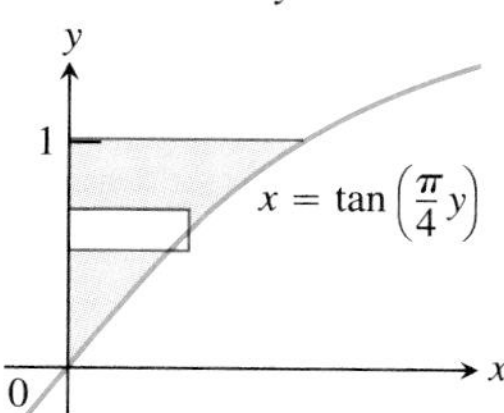

4. About the x-axis

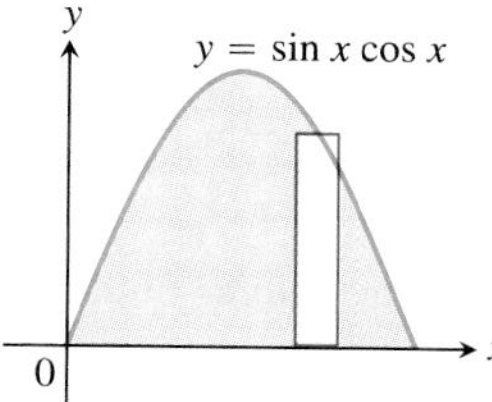

5. About the x-axis

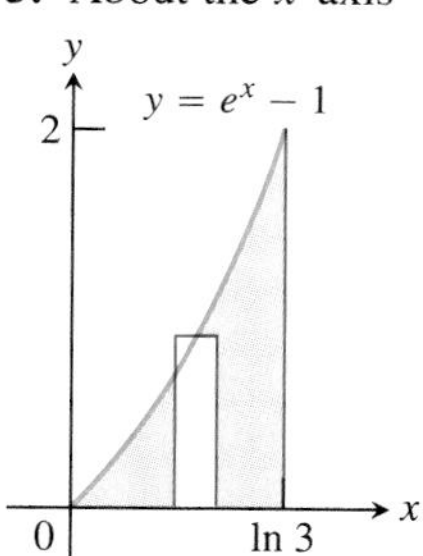

6. About the y-axis

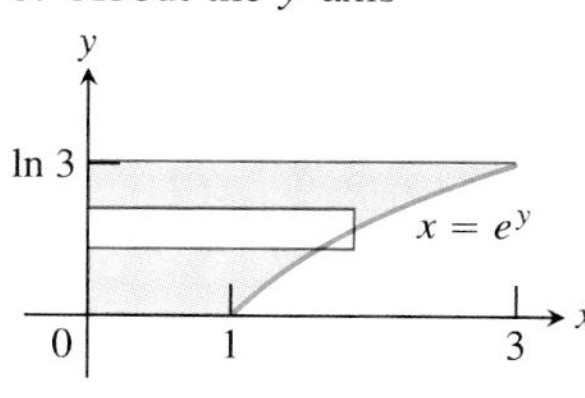

7. About the y-axis

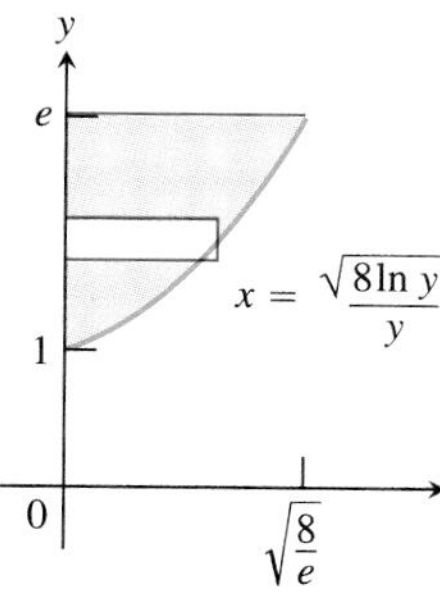

8. About the x-axis

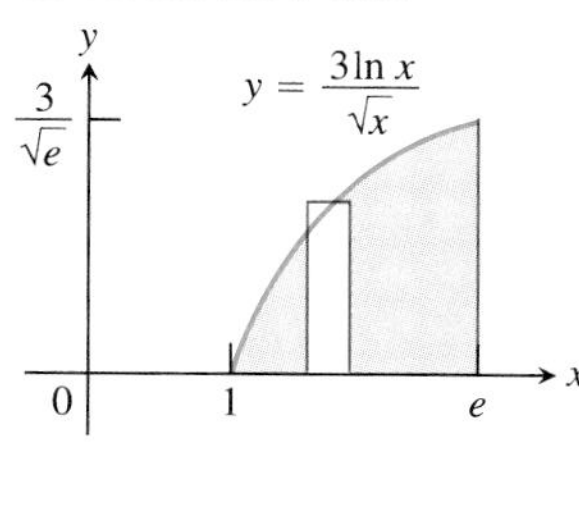

Find the volumes of the solids generated by revolving the regions bounded by the lines and curves in Exercises 9–14 about the x-axis.

9. $y = x^2, \quad y = 0, \quad x = 2$

10. $y = x^3, \quad y = 0, \quad x = 2$

11. $y = \sqrt{9 - x^2}, \quad y = 0$

12. $y = x - x^2, \quad y = 0$

13. $y = \sqrt{\cos x}, \quad 0 \le x \le \pi/2, \quad y = 0, \quad x = 0$

14. $y = \sec x, \quad y = 0, \quad x = -\pi/4, \quad x = \pi/4$

In Exercises 15 and 16, find the volume of the solid generated by revolving the region about the given axis.

15. The region in the first quadrant bounded above by the line $y = 1$, below by the curve $y = \tan x$, and on the left by the y-axis, about the line $y = 1$

16. The region in the first quadrant bounded above by the line $y = 2$, below by the curve $y = 2 \sin x$, $0 \le x \le \pi/2$, and on the left by the y-axis, about the line $y = 2$

Find the volumes of the solids generated by revolving the regions bounded by the lines and curves in Exercises 17–22 about the y-axis.

17. $x = \sqrt{5}\, y^2, \quad x = 0, \quad y = -1, \quad y = 1$

18. $x = y^{3/2}, \quad x = 0, \quad y = 2$

19. $x = \sqrt{2 \sin 2y}, \quad 0 \le y \le \pi/2, \quad x = 0$

20. $x = \sqrt{\cos(\pi y/4)}, \quad -2 \le y \le 0, \quad x = 0$

21. $x = 2/\sqrt{y + 1}, \quad x = 0, \quad y = 0, \quad y = 3$

22. $x = \sqrt{2y/(y^2 + 1)}, \quad x = 0, \quad y = 1$

In Exercises 23 and 24, find the volume of the solid generated by revolving each region about the given axis.

23. The region in the first quadrant that is bounded above by the line $y = 2 \ln 2$, on the left by the line $x = 1$, and on the right by the curve $x = e^{y/2}$, about the line $x = 1$

24. The region in the first quadrant that is bounded above by the curve $x = e^y - 1$, below by the x-axis, and on the right by the line $x = 2$, about the line $x = 2$

Find the volumes of the solids generated by revolving the regions bounded by the lines and curves in Exercises 25–32 about the x-axis.

25. $y = x, \quad y = 1, \quad x = 0$

26. $y = 2x, \quad y = x, \quad x = 1$

27. $y = 2\sqrt{x}, \quad y = 2, \quad x = 0$

28. $y = -\sqrt{x}, \quad y = -2, \quad x = 4$

29. $y = x^2 + 1, \quad y = x + 3$

30. $y = 4 - x^2, \quad y = 2 - x$

31. $y = \sec x, \quad y = \sqrt{2}, \quad -\pi/4 \le x \le \pi/4$

32. $y = \sec x, \quad y = \tan x, \quad x = 0, \quad x = 1$

In Exercises 33 and 34, find the volume of the solid generated by revolving each region about the given axis.

33. The region in the first quadrant bounded above by the curve $y = \tan(x/2)$, $0 \le x \le \pi/2$, below by the x-axis, and on the right by the line $x = \pi/2$, about the line $y = 1$

34. The region in the first quadrant bounded above by the curve $y = 2 \sin x$, $0 \le x \le \pi$, and below by the x-axis, about the line $y = 2$

In Exercises 35–40, find the volume of the solid generated by revolving each region about the y-axis.

35. The region enclosed by the triangle with vertices $(1, 0)$, $(2, 1)$, and $(1, 1)$

36. The region enclosed by the triangle with vertices $(0, 1)$, $(1, 0)$, and $(1, 1)$

37. The region in the first quadrant bounded above by the parabola $y = x^2$, below by the x-axis, and on the right by the line $x = 2$

38. The region bounded above by the curve $y = \sqrt{x}$ and below by the line $y = x$

39. The region in the first quadrant bounded on the left by the circle $x^2 + y^2 = 3$, on the right by the line $x = \sqrt{3}$, and above by the line $y = \sqrt{3}$

40. The region bounded on the left by the line $x = 4$ and on the right by the circle $x^2 + y^2 = 25$

In Exercises 41 and 42, find the volume of the solid generated by revolving each region about the given axis.

41. The region in the first quadrant bounded above by the curve $y = x^2$, below by the x-axis, and on the right by the line $x = 1$, about the line $x = -1$

42. The region in the second quadrant bounded above by the curve $y = -x^3$, below by the x-axis, and on the left by the line $x = -1$, about the line $x = -2$

Find the volumes of the solids generated by revolving the shaded regions in Exercises 43–46 about the indicated axes.

43. The x-axis

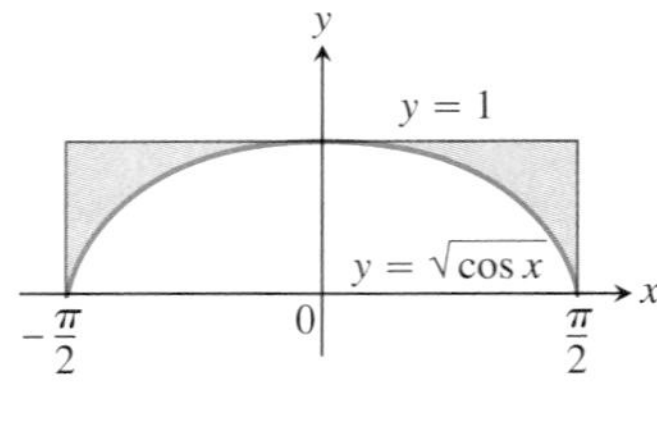

44. The x-axis

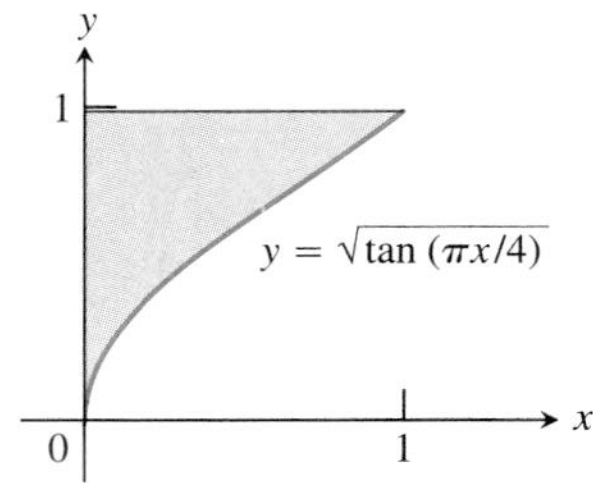

45. **a)** The x-axis
b) The y-axis
c) The line $x = 1$

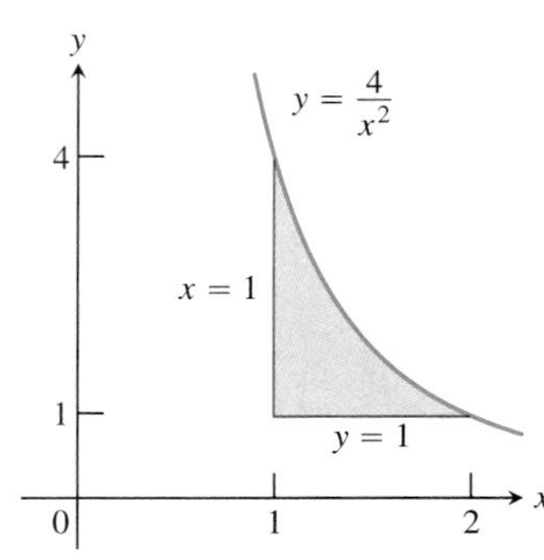

46. **a)** The x-axis
b) The y-axis
c) The line $y = 1$

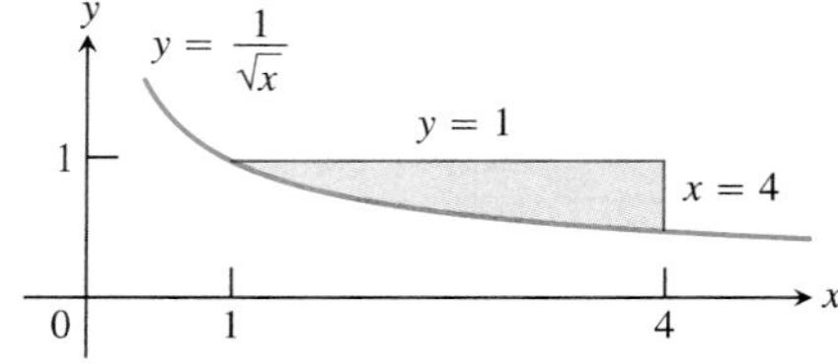

47. Find the volume of the solid generated by revolving the region bounded by $y = \sqrt{x}$ and the lines $y = 2$ and $x = 0$ about
a) the x-axis
b) the y-axis
c) the line $y = 2$
d) the line $x = 4$.

48. Find the volume of the solid generated by revolving the triangular region bounded by the lines $y = 2x$, $y = 0$, and $x = 1$ about
a) the line $x = 1$
b) the line $x = 2$.

49. Find the volume of the solid generated by revolving the region bounded by the parabola $y = x^2$ and the line $y = 1$ about
a) the line $y = 1$
b) the line $y = 2$
c) the line $y = -1$.

50. By integration, find the volume of the solid generated by revolving the triangular region with vertices $(0, 0)$, $(b, 0)$, $(0, h)$ about
a) the x-axis
b) the y-axis.

51. *Designing a Wok.* You are designing a wok frying pan that will be shaped like a spherical bowl with handles. A bit of experimentation at home persuades you that you can get one that holds about 3 L if you make it 9 cm deep and give the sphere a radius of 16 cm. To be sure, you picture the wok as a solid of revolution, as shown here, and calculate its volume with an integral. To the nearest cubic centimeter, what volume do you really get? (1 L = 1000 cm^3)

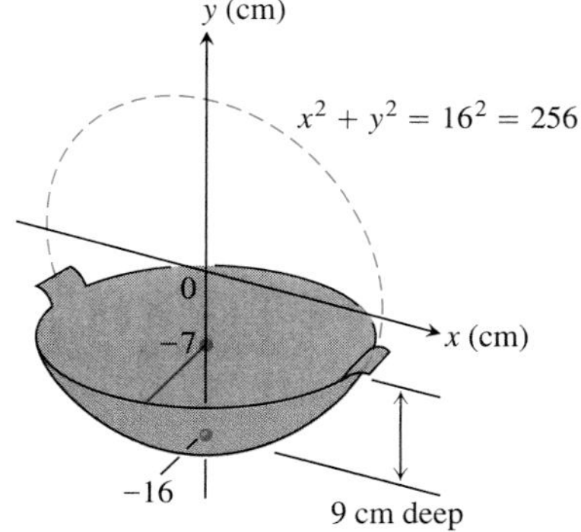

52. *Designing a Plumb Bob.* Having been asked to design a brass plumb bob that will weigh in the neighborhood of 190 g, you decide to shape it like the solid of revolution shown here. Find the plumb bob's volume. If you specify a brass that weighs 8.5 g/cm^3, how much will the plumb bob weigh (to the nearest gram)?

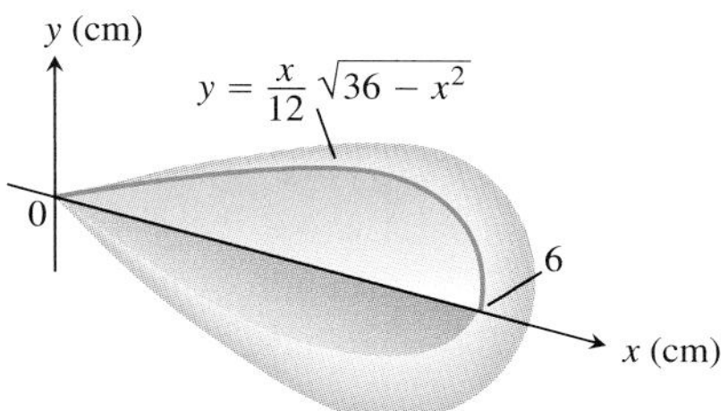

53. The arch $y = \sin x$, $0 \le x \le \pi$, is revolved about the line $y = c$, $0 \le c \le 1$, to generate the solid in Fig. 7.22.

a) Find the value of c that minimizes the volume of the solid. What is the minimum value?

b) What value of c in $[0, 1]$ maximizes the volume of the solid.

c) Graph the solid's volume as a function of c, first for $0 \le c \le 1$ and then on a larger domain. What happens to the volume of the solid as c moves away from $[0, 1]$? Does this make sense physically? Give reasons for your answer.

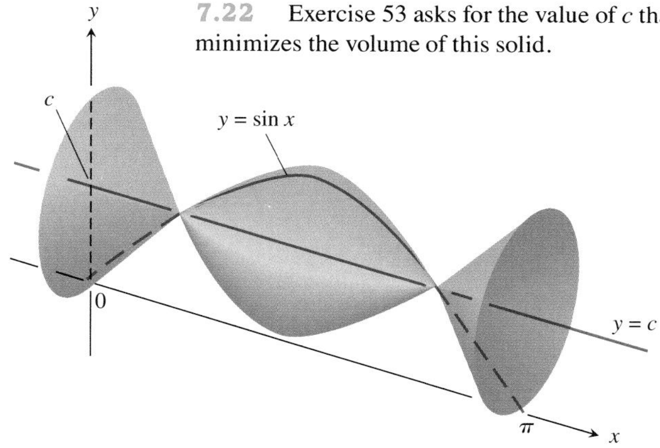

7.22 Exercise 53 asks for the value of c that minimizes the volume of this solid.

54. *An Auxiliary Fuel Tank.* You are designing an auxiliary fuel tank that will fit under a helicopter's fuselage to extend its range. After some experimentation at your drawing board, you decide to shape the tank like the surface generated by revolving the curve $y = 1 - (x^2/16)$, $-4 \le x \le 4$, about the x-axis (dimensions in feet).

a) How many cubic feet of fuel will the tank hold (to the nearest cubic foot)?

b) A cubic foot holds 7.481 gal. If the helicopter gets 2 mi to the gallon, how many additional miles will the helicopter be able to fly once the tank is installed (to the nearest mile)?

55. Let $A(t)$ be the area of the region in the first quadrant enclosed by the coordinate axes, the curve $y = e^{-x}$, and the line $x = t > 0$. Let $V(t)$ be the volume of the solid generated by revolving the region about the x-axis. Find the following limits.

a) $\lim_{t \to \infty} A(t)$

b) $\lim_{t \to \infty} V(t)/A(t)$

c) $\lim_{t \to 0^+} V(t)/A(t)$

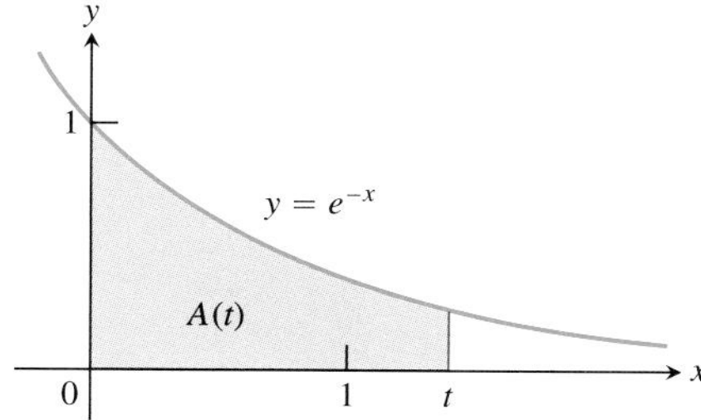

56. *Testing the Consistency of the Calculus Definition of Volume.* The volume formulas in this section are all consistent with the standard formulas from geometry.

a) As a case in point, show that if you revolve the region enclosed by the semicircle $y = \sqrt{a^2 - x^2}$ and the x-axis about the x-axis to generate a solid sphere, the disk method for volume will give $(4/3)\pi a^3$ just as it should.

b) Use calculus to show that the volume of a right circular cone of height h and base radius r is $(1/3)\pi r^2 h$.

Writing for Your Own Knowledge

Answer the following questions in writing. Some answers will take only a sentence or two; others may require several paragraphs. Some explanations may also call for graphs or sketches.

1. What is a solid of revolution?
2. How do you find the volume of a solid of revolution by the disk method?
3. How do you find the volume of a solid of revolution by the washer method?
4. How are the disk and washer methods related?

EXPLORER PROGRAM

PowerGrapher	Enables you to portray regions in the plane by graphing their bounding curves.

7.3 Cylindrical Shells—An Alternative to Washers

If the rectangular strips that approximate a region being revolved about an axis run parallel to the axis instead of perpendicular to it, they sweep out cylindrical shells (Fig. 7.23). Shells are sometimes more convenient than washers because they lead to a volume formula that does not require squaring.

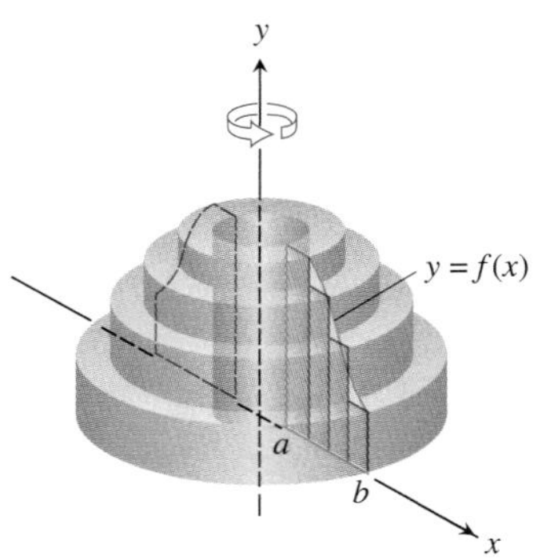

7.23 A solid of revolution approximated by cylindrical shells.

The Shell Formula

Suppose we revolve the tinted region in Fig. 7.24 about the y-axis to generate a solid. To estimate the volume of the solid, we can approximate the region with rectangles based on a partition P of the interval $[a, b]$ over which the region stands. The typical approximating rectangle is Δx_k units wide by $f(c_k)$ units high, where c_k is the midpoint of the rectangle's base. A formula from geometry tells us that the volume of the shell swept out by the rectangle is

$$\Delta V_k = 2\pi \times \text{average shell radius} \times \text{shell height} \times \text{thickness},$$

which, in our case, is

$$\Delta V_k = 2\pi \times c_k \times f(c_k) \times \Delta x_k. \tag{1}$$

We approximate the volume of the solid by adding the volumes of the shells swept out by the n rectangles based on P:

$$V \approx \sum_{k=1}^{n} \Delta V_k = \sum_{k=1}^{n} 2\pi\, c_k\, f(c_k)\, \Delta x_k. \qquad \text{A Riemann sum} \tag{2}$$

The limit of this sum as $\|P\| \to 0$ gives the volume of the solid:

$$V = \lim_{\|P\| \to 0} \sum_{k=1}^{n} 2\pi\, c_k\, f(c_k)\, \Delta x_k = \int_a^b 2\pi x\, f(x)\, dx. \tag{3}$$

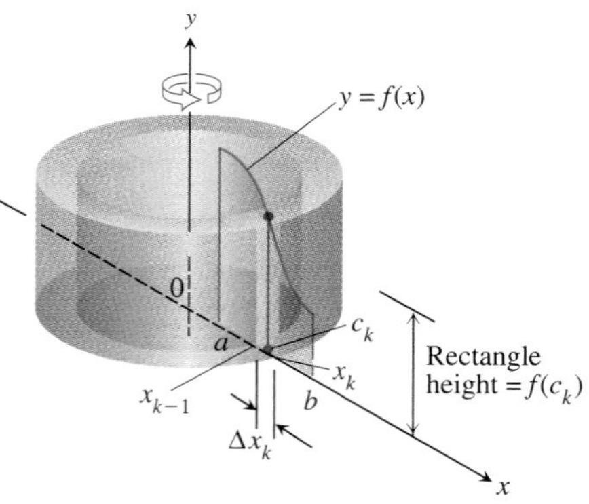

7.24 The shell swept out by the kth rectangle.

The Shell Formula for Revolution About the y-Axis

The volume of the solid generated by revolving the region between the x-axis and the graph of a continuous function $y = f(x)$, $a \le x \le b$, about the y-axis is

$$V = \int_a^b 2\pi \begin{pmatrix}\text{shell}\\ \text{radius}\end{pmatrix} \begin{pmatrix}\text{shell}\\ \text{height}\end{pmatrix} dx = \int_a^b 2\pi x\, f(x)\, dx. \tag{4}$$

EXAMPLE 1 The region bounded by the curve $y = \sqrt{x}$, the x-axis, and the line $x = 4$ is revolved about the y-axis to generate a solid. Find the volume of the solid.

Solution

STEP 1: Sketch the region and a thin rectangle across it parallel to the axis of revolution (Fig. 7.25). Label the rectangle's height (shell height), width (shell thickness), and distance from the axis of revolution (shell radius). The width of

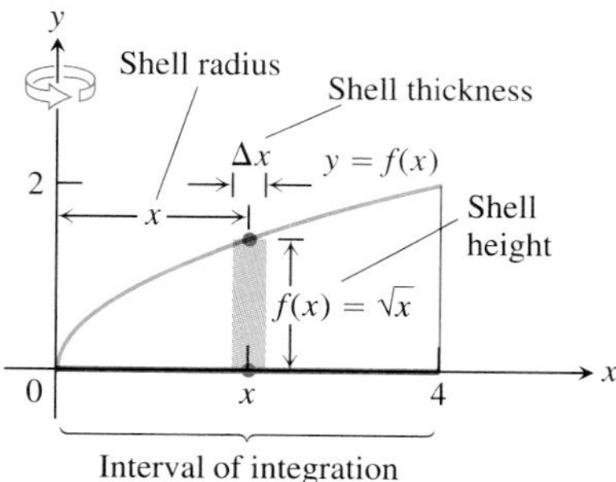

7.25 The region, shell dimensions, and interval of integration in Example 1.

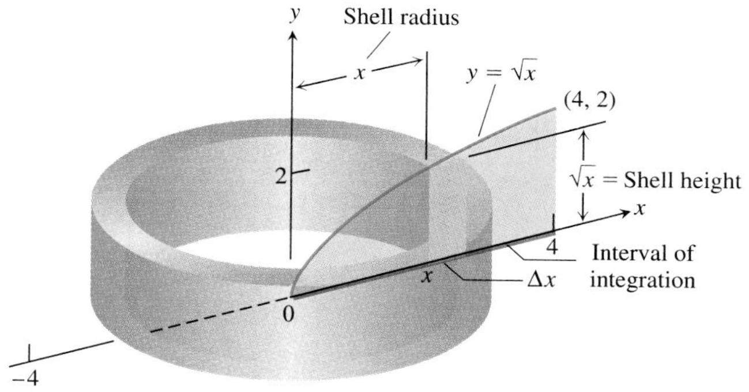

7.26 The shell swept out by the rectangle in Fig. 7.25.

One way to remember Eq. (4) is to imagine cutting and unrolling a cylindrical shell to get a (nearly) rectangular solid.

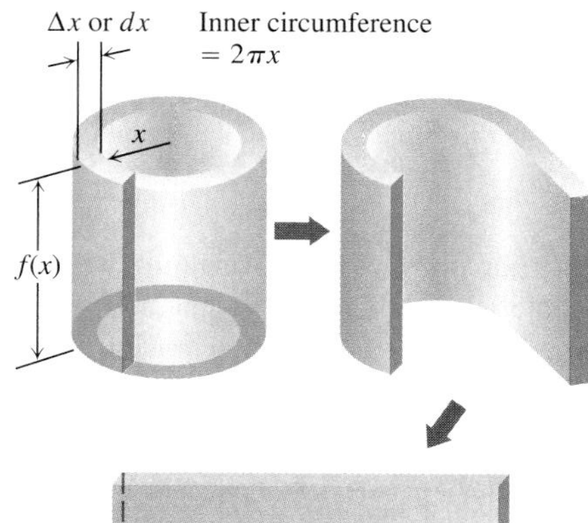

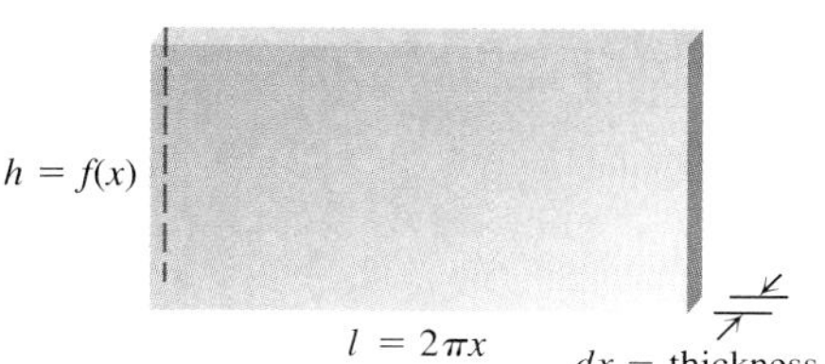

Almost a rectangular solid
$V \approx$ length × height × thickness
$\approx 2\pi x \cdot f(x) \cdot dx$

the rectangle is Δx, so we integrate with respect to x. (We drew the shell in Fig. 7.26, but you need not do that.)

STEP 2: Identify the limits of integration: x runs from $a = 0$ to $b = 4$.

STEP 3: Integrate to find the volume.

$$V = \int_a^b 2\pi \begin{pmatrix}\text{shell}\\ \text{radius}\end{pmatrix}\begin{pmatrix}\text{shell}\\ \text{height}\end{pmatrix} dx \qquad \text{Eq. (4)}$$

$$= \int_0^4 2\pi (x)(\sqrt{x})\, dx \qquad \text{Values from Steps 1 and 2}$$

$$= 2\pi \int_0^4 x^{3/2}\, dx = 2\pi \left[\frac{2}{5}x^{5/2}\right]_0^4 = \frac{128\pi}{5}$$

The volume is $128\pi/5$.

Equation (4) is for vertical axes of revolution. If we use a horizontal axis, we have to replace the x's with y's.

The Shell Formula for Revolution About the x-Axis

$$V = \int_c^d 2\pi \begin{pmatrix}\text{shell}\\ \text{radius}\end{pmatrix}\begin{pmatrix}\text{shell}\\ \text{height}\end{pmatrix} dy = \int_c^d 2\pi y\, f(y)\, dy \qquad (5)$$

EXAMPLE 2 The region bounded by the curve $y = \sqrt{x}$, the x-axis, and the line $x = 4$ is revolved about the x-axis to generate a solid. Find the volume of the solid.

Solution

STEP 1: Sketch the region and a thin rectangle across it parallel to the axis of revolution (Fig. 7.27 on the following page). Label the rectangle's length (shell height), width (shell thickness), and distance from the axis of revolution (shell radius). The width of the rectangle is Δy, so we integrate with respect to y. (We drew the shell in Fig. 7.28 on the following page, but you need not do that.)

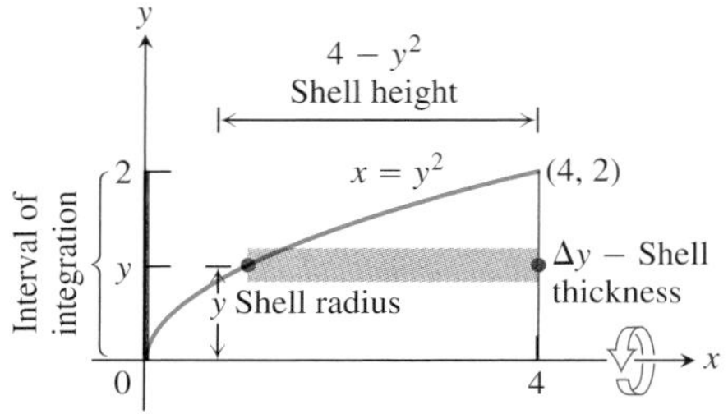

7.27 The region, shell dimensions, and interval of integration in Example 2.

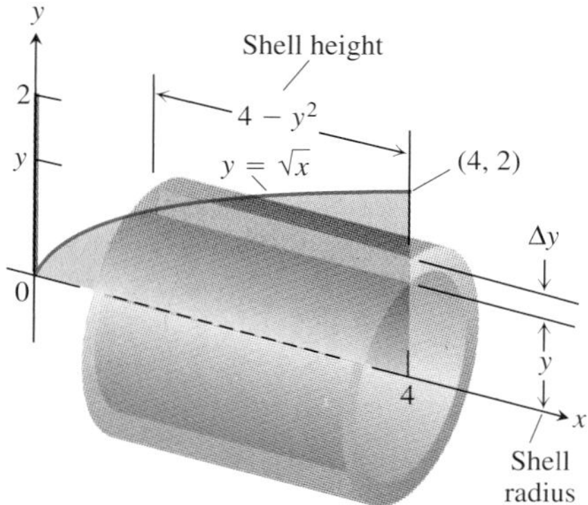

7.28 The shell swept out by the rectangle in Fig. 7.27.

STEP 2: Identify the limits of integration: y runs from $c = 0$ to $d = 2$.

STEP 3: Integrate to find the volume.

$$\begin{aligned} V &= \int_c^d 2\pi \begin{pmatrix}\text{shell}\\ \text{radius}\end{pmatrix} \begin{pmatrix}\text{shell}\\ \text{height}\end{pmatrix} dy && \text{Eq. (5)} \\ &= \int_0^2 2\pi (y)(4 - y^2)\, dy && \text{Values from Steps 1 and 2} \\ &= 2\pi \left[2y^2 - \frac{y^4}{4} \right]_0^2 = 8\pi \end{aligned}$$

This agrees with the disk method of calculation in Section 7.2, Example 1.

How to Use the Shell Method

Regardless of the position of the axis of revolution (horizontal or vertical), the steps for implementing the shell method are these:

1. Draw a thin rectangle across the region *parallel* to the axis of revolution. Label the rectangle's height or length (shell height), width (shell thickness), and distance from the axis of revolution (shell radius).
2. Identify the limits of integration.
3. Integrate the product 2π(shell radius)(shell height) with respect to the appropriate variable (x or y) to find the volume.

In the next example, the axis of revolution is the vertical line $x = 2$.

EXAMPLE 3 The region in the first quadrant bounded by the parabola $y = x^2$, the y-axis, and the line $y = 1$ is revolved about the line $x = 2$ to generate a solid. Find the volume of the solid.

Solution

STEP 1: Draw a thin rectangle across the region parallel to the axis of revolution (the line $x = 2$) (Fig. 7.29). Label the rectangle's height (shell height), width (shell thickness), and distance from the axis of revolution (shell radius). The rectangle's width is Δx, so we integrate with respect to x. (We drew the shell in Fig. 7.30, but you need not do that.)

STEP 2: The limits of integration: x runs from $a = 0$ to $b = 1$.

STEP 3:

$$\begin{aligned} V &= \int_a^b 2\pi \begin{pmatrix}\text{shell}\\ \text{radius}\end{pmatrix} \begin{pmatrix}\text{shell}\\ \text{height}\end{pmatrix} dx && \text{Eq. (4)} \\ &= \int_0^1 2\pi (2 - x)(1 - x^2)\, dx && \text{Values from Steps 1 and 2} \\ &= 2\pi \int_0^1 (2 - x - 2x^2 + x^3)\, dx \\ &= \frac{13\pi}{6} \end{aligned}$$

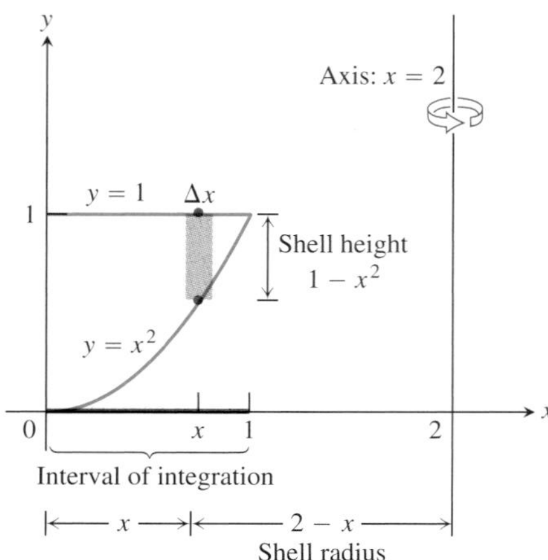

7.29 The region, shell dimensions, and interval of integration in Example 3.

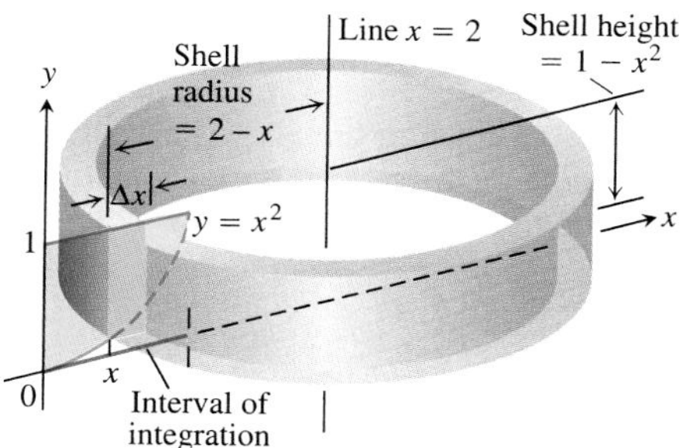

7.30 The shell swept out by the rectangle in Fig. 7.29.

Table 7.1 summarizes the washer and shell methods for the solid generated by revolving the region bounded by $y = x$ and $y = x^2$ about the coordinate axes. For this particular region, both methods work well for both axes of revolution. But this is not always the case. When a region is revolved about the y-axis, for example, and washers are used, we must integrate with respect to y. However it may not be possible to express the integrand in terms of y. In such a case, the shell method allows us to integrate with respect to x instead.

TABLE 7.1
Washers versus shells

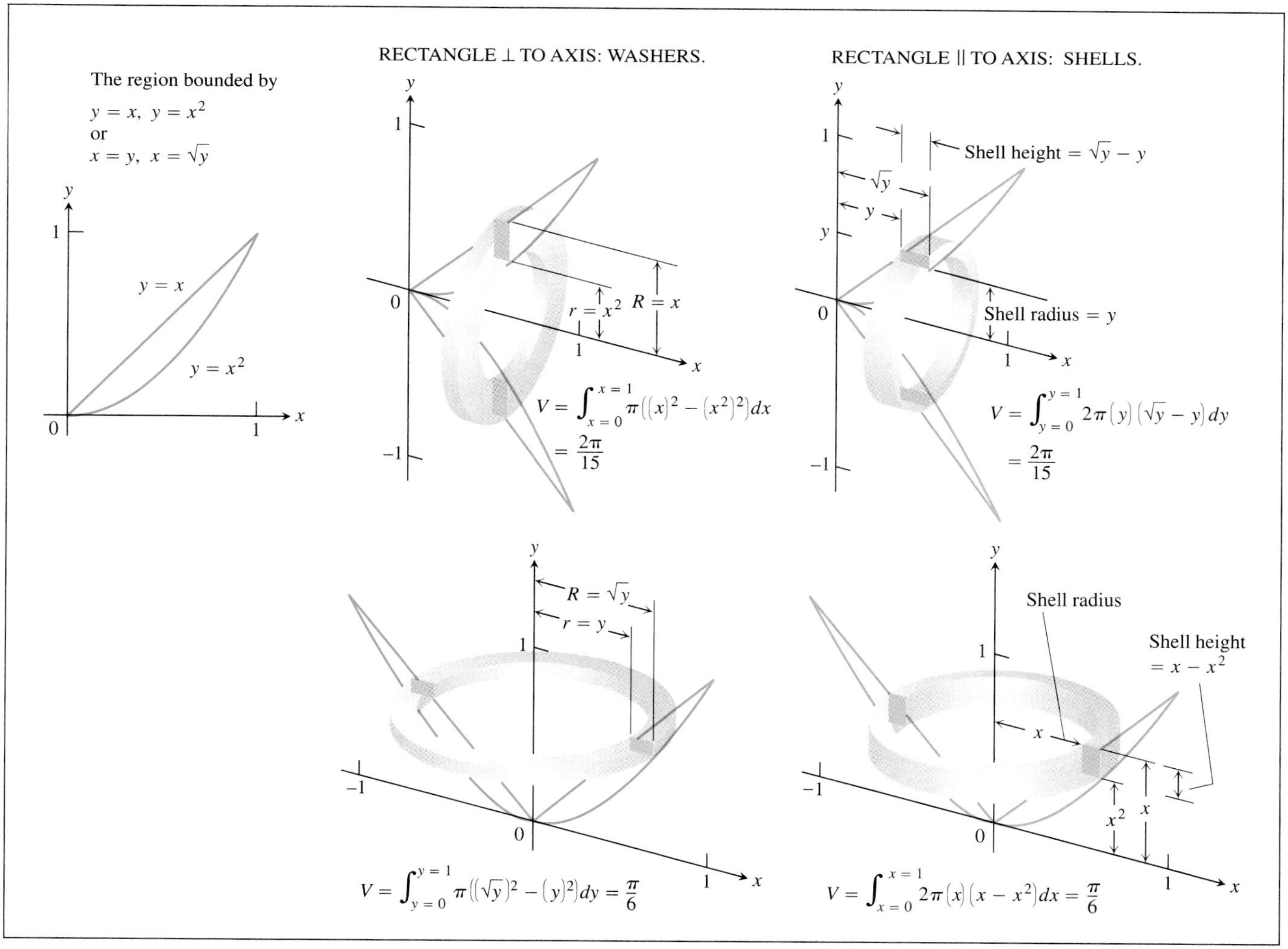

The region bounded by
$y = x,\ y = x^2$
or
$x = y,\ x = \sqrt{y}$

RECTANGLE ⊥ TO AXIS: WASHERS.

RECTANGLE || TO AXIS: SHELLS.

Revolution about the x-axis, washers: $r = x^2$, $R = x$

$$V = \int_{x=0}^{x=1} \pi\left((x)^2 - (x^2)^2\right)dx = \frac{2\pi}{15}$$

Revolution about the x-axis, shells: Shell height $= \sqrt{y} - y$, Shell radius $= y$

$$V = \int_{y=0}^{y=1} 2\pi(y)(\sqrt{y} - y)\,dy = \frac{2\pi}{15}$$

Revolution about the y-axis, washers: $R = \sqrt{y}$, $r = y$

$$V = \int_{y=0}^{y=1} \pi\left((\sqrt{y})^2 - (y)^2\right)dy = \frac{\pi}{6}$$

Revolution about the y-axis, shells: Shell radius $= x$, Shell height $= x - x^2$

$$V = \int_{x=0}^{x=1} 2\pi(x)(x - x^2)\,dx = \frac{\pi}{6}$$

Exercises 7.3

In Exercises 1–8, use the shell method to find the volumes of the solids generated by revolving the shaded region about the indicated axis.

1.

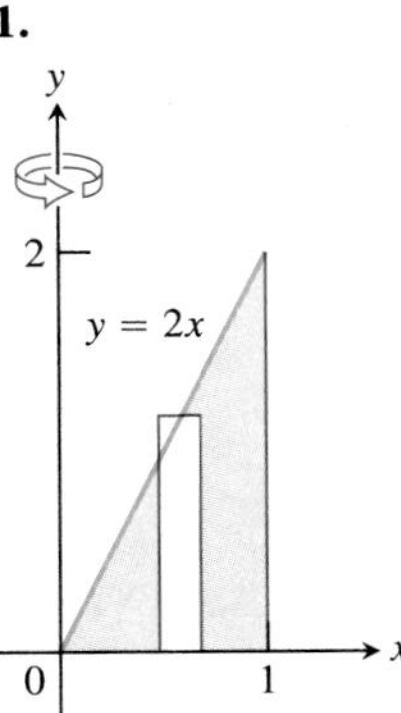

2.

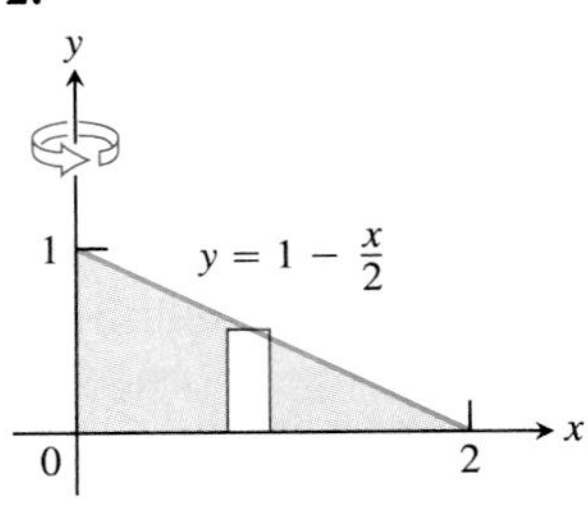

3.

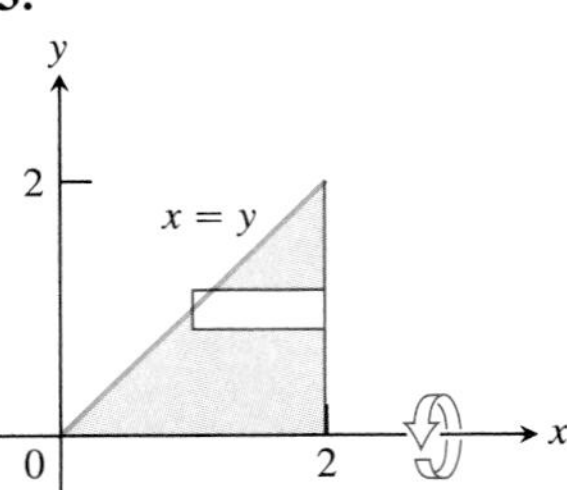

4.

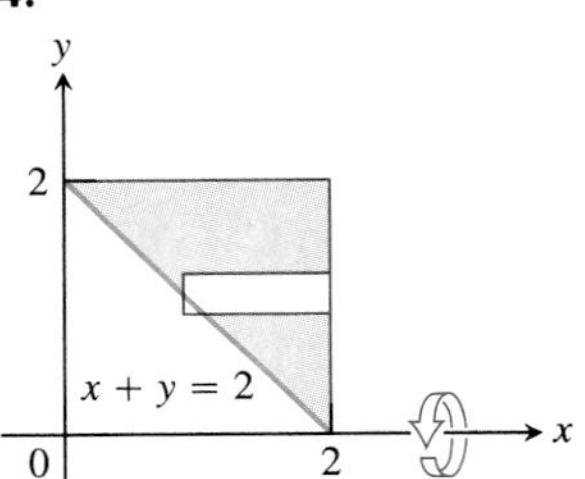

5.

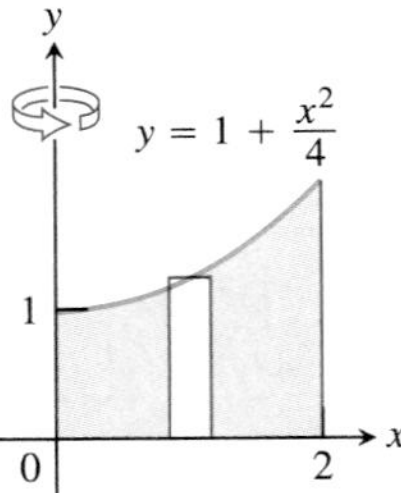

6.

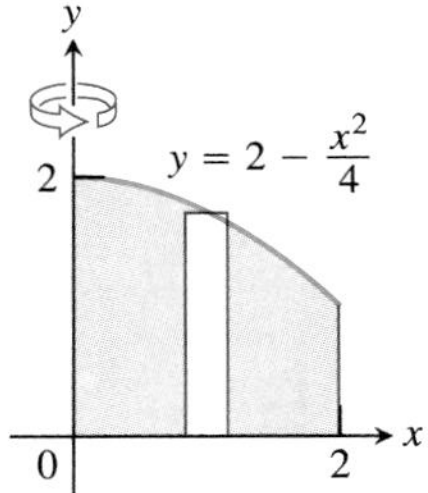

7.

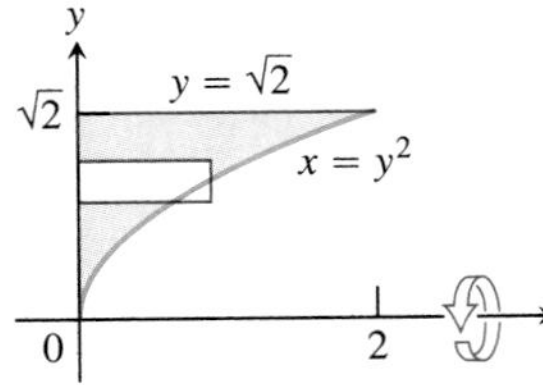

8.

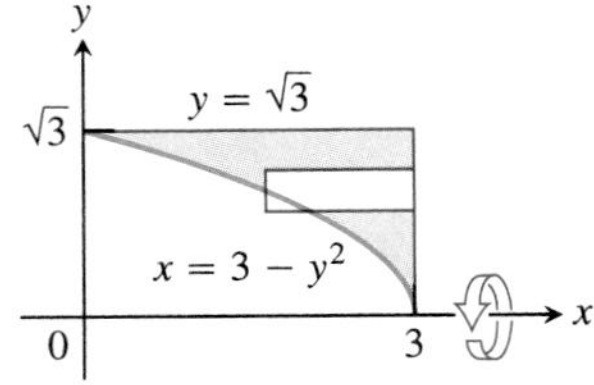

Use the shell method to find the volumes of the solids generated by revolving the regions bounded by the curves and lines in Exercises 9–14 about the y-axis.

9. $y = x, \quad y = -x/2, \quad x = 2$ **10.** $y = 2x, \quad y = x/2, \quad x = 1$

11. $y = x^2, \quad y = 2 - x, \quad x = 0$

12. $y = 2 - x^2, \quad y = x^2, \quad x = 0$

13. $y = 1/x, \quad y = 0, \quad x = 1/2, \quad x = 2$

14. $y = 1/x^2, \quad y = 0, \quad x = 1/2, \quad x = 2$

Use the shell method to find the volumes of the solids generated by revolving the regions bounded by the curves and lines in Exercises 15–22 about the x-axis.

15. $x = \sqrt{y}, \quad x = -y, \quad y = 2$

16. $x = y^2, \quad x = -y, \quad y = 2$

17. $x = 2y - y^2, \quad x = 0$ **18.** $x = 2y - y^2, \quad x = y$

19. $y = x, \quad y = -x, \quad y = 1$

20. $y = x, \quad y = 2x, \quad y = 2$

21. $y = \sqrt{x}, \quad y = 0, \quad y = x - 2$

22. $y = \sqrt{x}, \quad y = 0, \quad y = 2 - x$

In Exercises 23–32, use the shell method to find the volumes of the solids generated by revolving the shaded regions about the indicated axes.

23. The y-axis

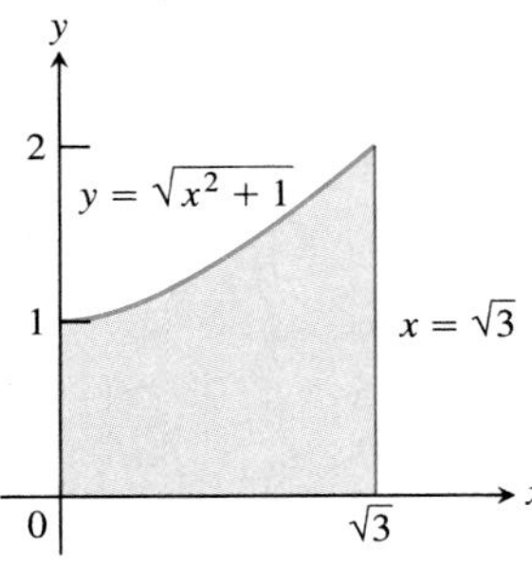

24. The y-axis

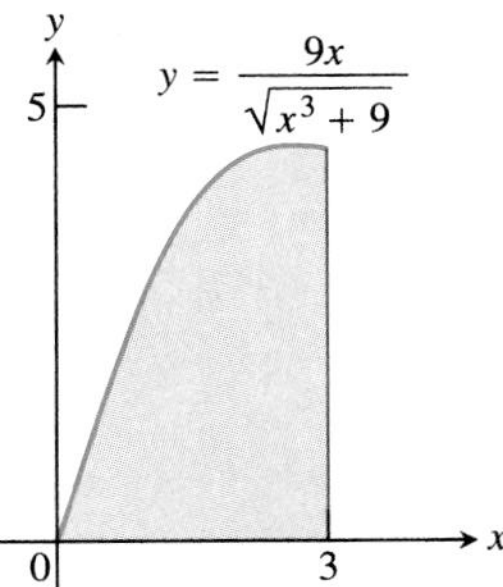

25. The y-axis

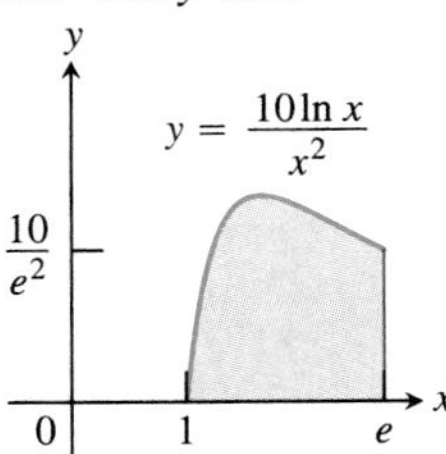

26. The y-axis

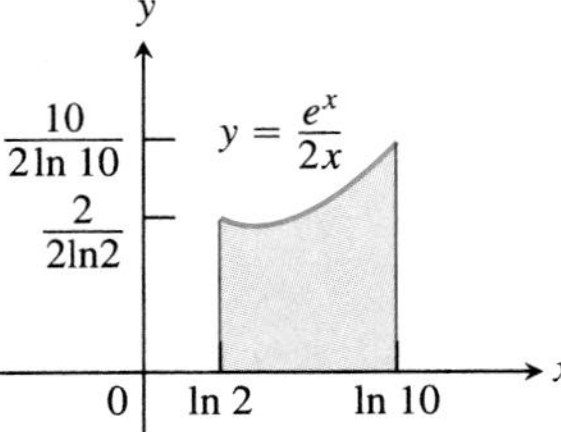

27. The x-axis

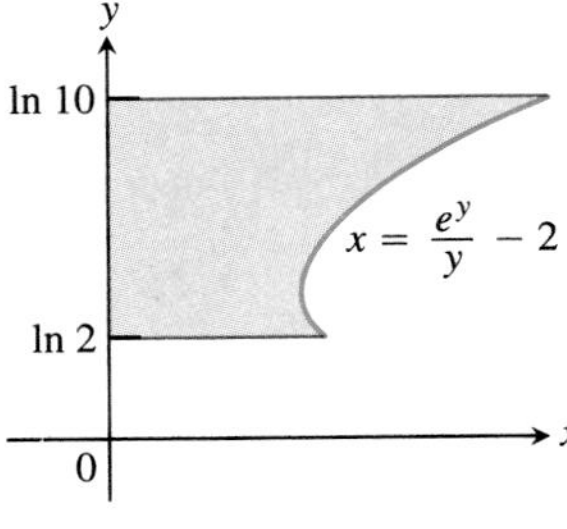

28. The x-axis

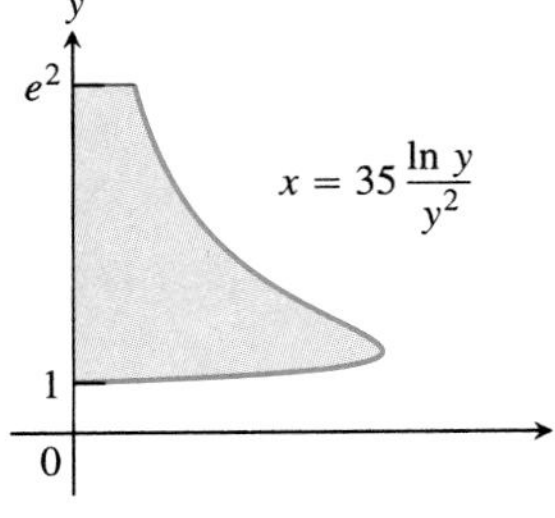

29. a) The x-axis b) The line $y = 1$
c) The line $y = 8/5$ d) The line $y = -2/5$

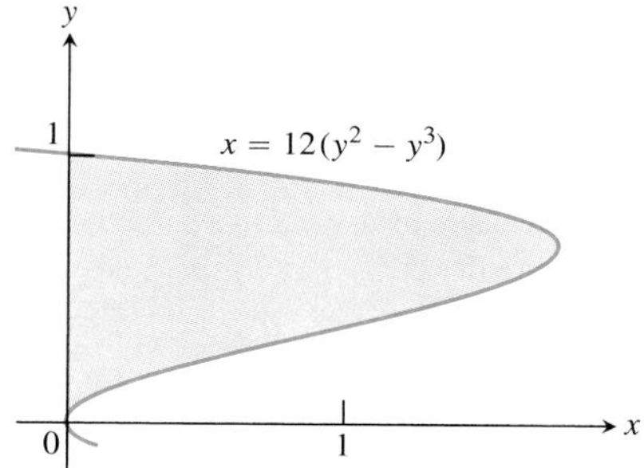

30. a) The x-axis
b) The line $y = 2$
c) The line $y = 5$
d) The line $y = -5/8$

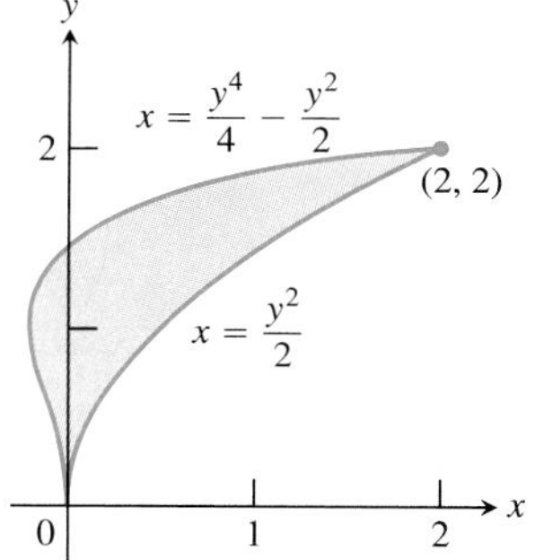

31. a) The y-axis
b) The line $x = 2$
c) The line $x = -3$

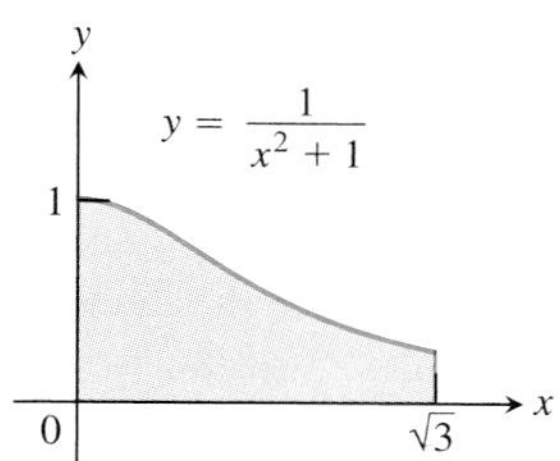

32. a) The y-axis
b) The line $x = \sqrt{2}/2$
c) The line $x = -2$

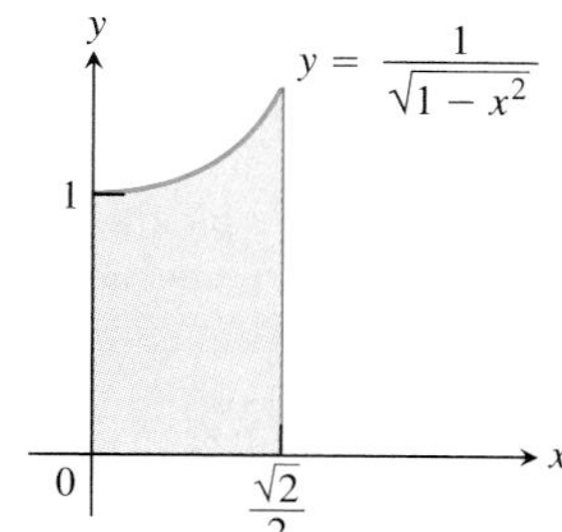

In Exercises 33–40, find the volumes of the solids generated by revolving the regions about the given axes.

33. The triangle with vertices (1, 1), (1, 2), and (2, 2) about (a) the x-axis; (b) the y-axis; (c) the line $x = 10/3$; (d) the line $y = 1$

34. The region in the first quadrant bounded by the curve $x = y - y^3$ and the y-axis about (a) the x-axis; (b) the line $y = 1$

35. The region in the first quadrant bounded by $x = y - y^3$, $x = 1$, and $y = 1$ about (a) the x-axis; (b) the y-axis; (c) the line $x = 1$; (d) the line $y = 1$

36. The triangular region bounded by the lines $2y = x + 4$, $y = x$, and $x = 0$ about (a) the x-axis; (b) the y-axis; (c) the line $x = 4$; (d) the line $y = 8$

37. The region in the first quadrant bounded by $y = x^3$ and $y = 4x$ about (a) the x-axis; (b) the line $y = 8$

38. The region bounded by $y = \sqrt{x}$ and $y = x^2/8$ about (a) the x-axis; (b) the y-axis

39. The region bounded by $y = 2x - x^2$ and $y = x$ about (a) the y-axis; (b) the line $x = 1$

40. The region bounded by $y = \sqrt{x}$, $y = 2$, $x = 0$ about (a) the x-axis; (b) the y-axis; (c) the line $x = 4$; (d) the line $y = 2$

41. The region in the first quadrant that is bounded above by the curve $y = 1/\sqrt{x}$, on the left by the line $x = 1/4$, and below by the line $y = 1$, is revolved about the x-axis to generate a solid. Find the volume of the solid by (a) the washer method; (b) the shell method.

42. The region in Exercise 41 is revolved about the y-axis to generate a solid. Find the volume of the solid by (a) the washer method; (b) the shell method.

43. Let $f(x) = \begin{cases} (\sin x)/x, & 0 < x \le \pi \\ 1, & x = 0. \end{cases}$

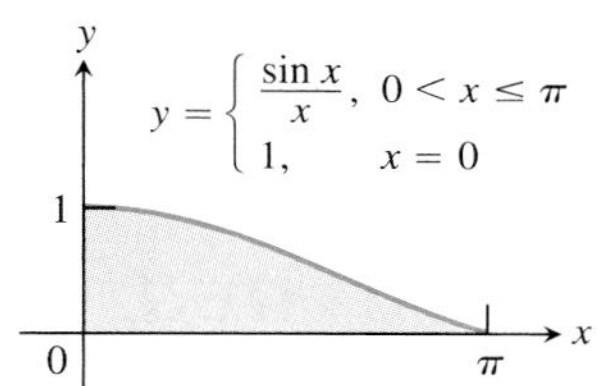

a) Show that $xf(x) = \sin x$, $0 \le x \le \pi$.
b) Find the volume of the solid generated by revolving the shaded region about the y-axis.

44. Let $g(x) = \begin{cases} (\tan x)/x, & 0 < x \le \pi/3 \\ 1, & x = 0. \end{cases}$

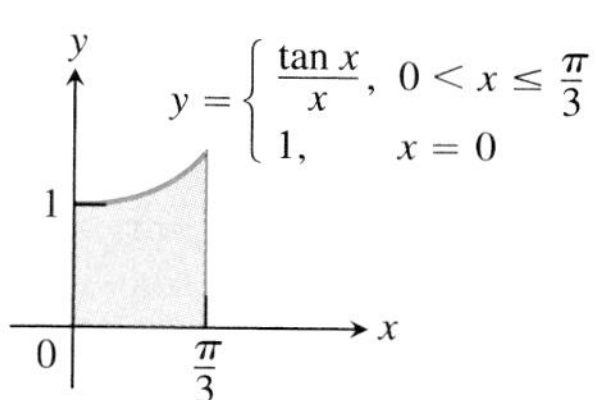

a) Show that $xg(x) = \tan x$, $0 \le x \le \pi/3$.
b) Find the volume of the solid generated by revolving the shaded region about the y-axis.

45. The region shown here is to be revolved about the x-axis to generate a solid. Which of the methods (disk, washer, shell) could you use to find the volume of the solid? How many integrals would be required in each case? Explain.

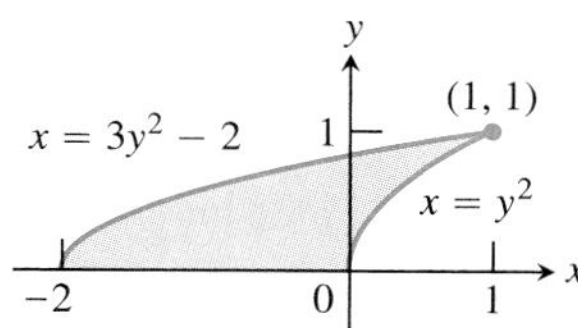

46. The region shown here is to be revolved about the y-axis to generate a solid. Which of the methods (disk, washer, shell) could you use to find the volume of the solid? How many integrals would be required in each case? Give reasons for your answers.

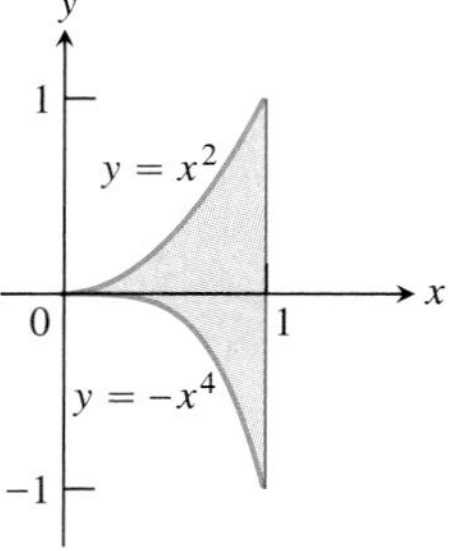

Writing for Your Own Knowledge

Answer the following questions in writing. Some answers will take only a sentence or two; others may require several paragraphs. Some explanations may also call for graphs or sketches.

1. What is the shell method for calculating volumes of solids of revolution?
2. Why might you want to use the shell method instead of the disk or washer methods?

EXPLORER PROGRAM

PowerGrapher — Enables you to portray regions in the plane by graphing their bounding curves.

7.4 *Curve Length and Surface Area*

When you jump rope, the rope sweeps out a surface in space around you, a surface called a surface of revolution. As you can imagine, the area of this surface depends on the rope's length and how far away each segment of the rope swings. This section shows how to calculate the lengths of smooth plane curves and how the area of a surface of revolution can be calculated from the length and reach of the curve that generates it.

The Basic Length Formula

Suppose the curve whose length we want to find is the graph of the function $y = f(x)$ from $x = a$ to $x = b$. We partition $[a, b]$ in the usual way and connect the corresponding points on the curve with line segments (Fig. 7.31). The line segments, taken together, form a polygonal path that approximates the curve. If we can find a formula for the sum of the lengths of these line segments, we will have a formula for approximating the length of the curve.

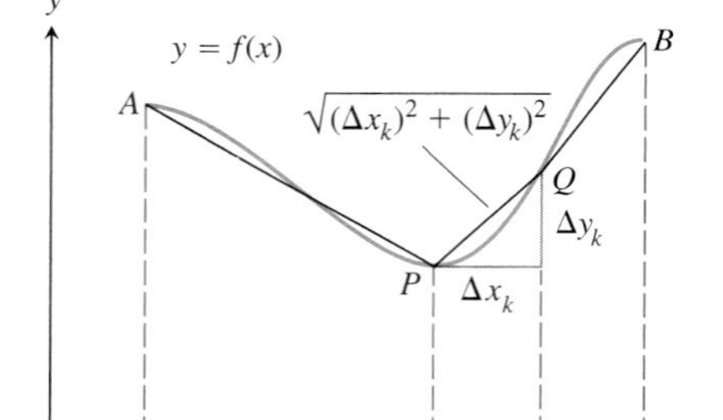

7.31 A typical segment PQ of a polygonal path approximating the curve AB.

The length of a typical line segment PQ (shown in the figure) is

$$\sqrt{(\Delta x_k)^2 + (\Delta y_k)^2}. \tag{1}$$

The length of the curve is therefore approximated by the sum

$$\sum_{k=1}^{n} \sqrt{(\Delta x_k)^2 + (\Delta y_k)^2}. \tag{2}$$

We expect the approximation to improve as the partition of $[a, b]$ becomes finer, and we would like to show that the sums in (2) approach a calculable limit as the norm of the partition goes to zero. To show this, we rewrite the sum in (2) in a form to which we can apply the Integral Existence Theorem from Section 5.2. Our starting point is the Mean Value Theorem for derivatives.

Suppose that f has a derivative that is continuous at every point of $[a, b]$ (we call such a function **smooth** on $[a, b]$ and call its graph a **smooth curve**).

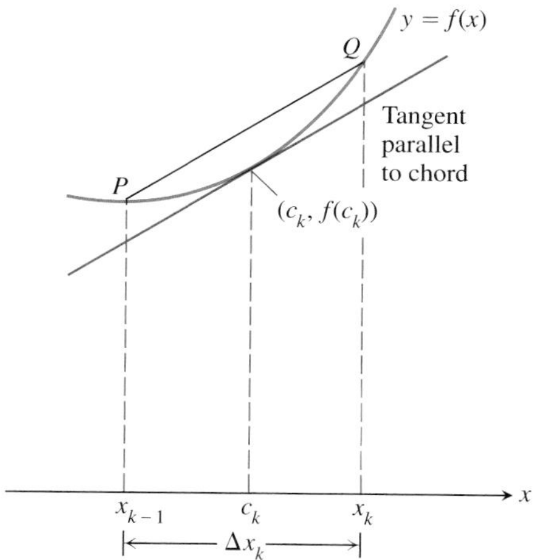

7.32 Enlargement of the arc PQ in Fig. 7.31.

Then, by the Mean Value Theorem, there is a point $(c_k, f(c_k))$ on the curve between P and Q where the tangent is parallel to the segment PQ (Fig. 7.32). At this point

$$f'(c_k) = \frac{\Delta y_k}{\Delta x_k}, \qquad \text{or} \qquad \Delta y_k = f'(c_k)\Delta x_k.$$

With this substitution for Δy_k, the sums in (2) take the form

$$\sum_{k=1}^{n} \sqrt{(\Delta x_k)^2 + (f'(c_k)\Delta x_k)^2} = \sum_{k=1}^{n} \sqrt{1 + (f'(c_k))^2}\,\Delta x_k. \qquad \text{A Riemann sum} \tag{3}$$

Because $\sqrt{1 + (f'(x))^2}$ is continuous on $[a, b]$, the limit of the sums on the right as the norm of the partition goes to zero is $\int_a^b \sqrt{1 + (f'(x))^2}\,dx$. We define the length of the curve to be the value of this integral.

DEFINITION

If f is smooth on $[a, b]$, the **length** of the curve $y = f(x)$ from a to b is the number

$$L = \int_a^b \sqrt{1 + \left(\frac{dy}{dx}\right)^2}\,dx. \tag{4}$$

EXAMPLE 1 Find the length of the curve

$$y = \frac{4\sqrt{2}}{3}x^{3/2} - 1, \qquad 0 \le x \le 1.$$

Solution We use Eq. (4) with $a = 0$, $b = 1$, and

$$y = \frac{4\sqrt{2}}{3}x^{3/2} - 1,$$

$$\frac{dy}{dx} = \frac{4\sqrt{2}}{3}\cdot\frac{3}{2}x^{1/2} = 2\sqrt{2}x^{1/2},$$

$$\left(\frac{dy}{dx}\right)^2 = \left(2\sqrt{2}x^{1/2}\right)^2 = 8x.$$

The length of the curve from $x = 0$ to $x = 1$ is

$$L = \int_0^1 \sqrt{1 + \left(\frac{dy}{dx}\right)^2}\,dx = \int_0^1 \sqrt{1 + 8x}\,dx \qquad \text{Eq. (4) with } a = 0,\ b = 1$$

$$= \frac{2}{3}\cdot\frac{1}{8}(1 + 8x)^{3/2}\Big]_0^1 = \frac{13}{6}. \qquad \text{Let } u = 1 + 8x, \text{ integrate, and replace } u \text{ by } 1 + 8x.$$

Dealing with Discontinuities in dy/dx

At a point on a curve where dy/dx fails to exist, dx/dy may exist and we may be able to find the curve's length by expressing x as a function of y and applying the following analogue of Eq. (4):

Formula for the Length of a Smooth Curve $x = g(y)$ from $y = c$ to $y = d$

$$L = \int_c^d \sqrt{1 + \left(\frac{dx}{dy}\right)^2}\, dy \tag{5}$$

EXAMPLE 2 Find the length of the curve $y = (x/2)^{2/3}$ from $x = 0$ to $x = 2$.

Solution The derivative

$$\frac{dy}{dx} = \frac{2}{3}\left(\frac{x}{2}\right)^{-1/3} \cdot \frac{1}{2} = \frac{1}{3}\left(\frac{2}{x}\right)^{1/3}$$

is not defined at $x = 0$, so we cannot find the curve's length with Eq. (4).

We therefore rewrite the equation to express x in terms of y:

$$y = \left(\frac{x}{2}\right)^{2/3}$$

$$y^{3/2} = \frac{x}{2} \qquad \text{Raise both sides to the power 3/2.}$$

$$x = 2y^{3/2}. \qquad \text{Solve for } x.$$

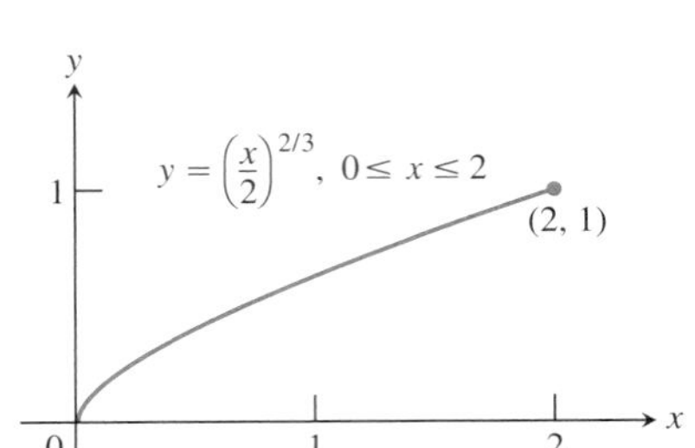

7.33 The graph of $y = (x/2)^{2/3}$ from $x = 0$ to $x = 2$ is also the graph of $x = 2y^{3/2}$ from $y = 0$ to $y = 1$.

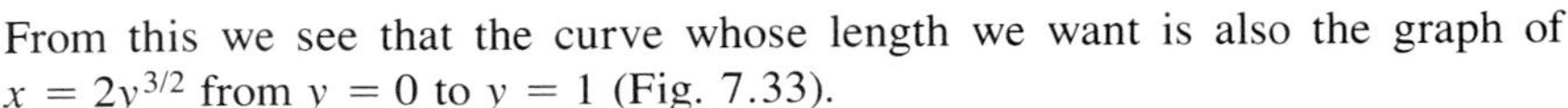

From this we see that the curve whose length we want is also the graph of $x = 2y^{3/2}$ from $y = 0$ to $y = 1$ (Fig. 7.33).

The derivative

$$\frac{dx}{dy} = 2 \cdot \frac{3}{2} y^{1/2} = 3y^{1/2}$$

is continuous on $[0, 1]$. We may therefore use Eq. (5) to find the curve's length:

$$L = \int_c^d \sqrt{1 + \left(\frac{dx}{dy}\right)^2}\, dy = \int_0^1 \sqrt{1 + 9y}\, dy \qquad \text{Eq. (5) with } c = 0,\ d = 1$$

$$= \frac{1}{9} \cdot \frac{2}{3}(1 + 9y)^{3/2}\Big]_0^1 \qquad \text{Let } u = 1 + 9y,\ du/9 = dy, \text{ integrate, and substitute back.}$$

$$= \frac{2}{27}\left(10\sqrt{10} - 1\right) \approx 2.27.$$

Curves with Infinite Length

As you may recall from Section 3.6, Helga von Koch's snowflake curve K is the limit curve of an infinite sequence $C_1, C_2, \ldots, C_n, \ldots$ of "triangular" polygonal curves. Figure 7.34 shows the first four curves in the sequence. Each time we introduce a new vertex in the construction process, it remains as a vertex in all subsequent curves and becomes a point on the limit curve K. This means that each of the C's is itself a polygonal approximation of K—the endpoints of its sides all belonging to K. The length of K should therefore be the limit of the lengths of the curves C_n. At least, that is what it should be if we apply the definition of length we developed for smooth curves.

Curve 1 Curve 2 Curve 3 Curve 4

7.34 The first four polygonal approximations in the construction of Helga von Koch's snowflake.

What, then, is the limit of the lengths of the curves C_n? If the original equilateral triangle C_1 has sides of length 1, the total length of C_1 is 3. To make C_2 from C_1, we replace each side of C_1 by four segments, each of which is one-third as long as the original side. The total length of C_2 is therefore 3(4/3). To get the length of C_3, we multiply by 4/3 again. We do so again to get the length of C_4. By the time we get to C_n, we have a curve of length $3(4/3)^{n-1}$.

Curve Number	1	2	3	. . .	n	. . .
Length	3	$3\left(\frac{4}{3}\right)$	$3\left(\frac{4}{3}\right)^2$	. . .	$3\left(\frac{4}{3}\right)^{n-1}$	. . .

The length of C_{10} is nearly 40 and the length of C_{100} is greater than 7,000,000,000,000. The lengths grow too rapidly to have a finite limit. Therefore the snowflake curve has no length, or, if you prefer, infinite length.

What went wrong? Nothing. The formulas we derived for length are for the graphs of smooth functions, curves that are smooth enough to have a continuously turning tangent at every point. Helga von Koch's snowflake curve is too rough for that, and our derivative-based formulas do not apply.

Benoit Mandelbrot's theory of fractals has proved to be a rich source of curves with infinite length, curves that when magnified prove to be as rough and varied as they looked before magnification. Like coastlines on an ocean, such curves cannot be smoothed out by magnification (Fig. 7.35).

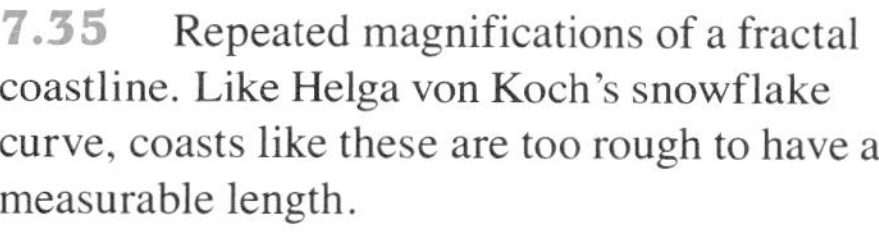
7.35 Repeated magnifications of a fractal coastline. Like Helga von Koch's snowflake curve, coasts like these are too rough to have a measurable length.

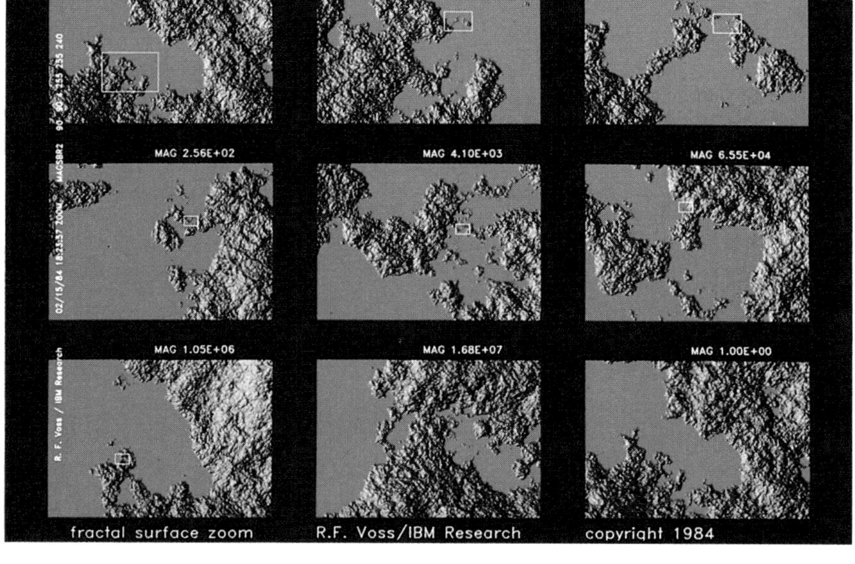

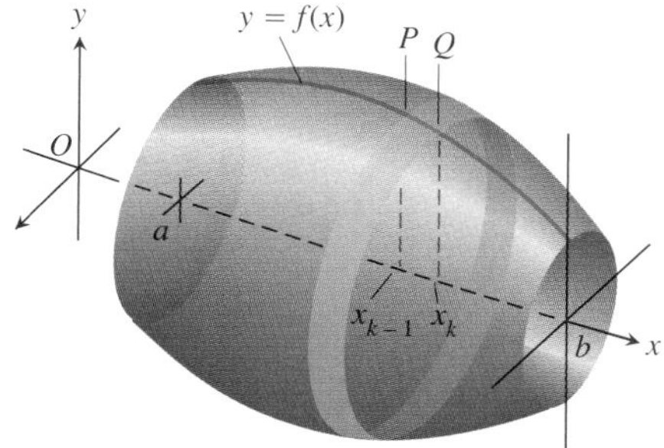

7.36 The surface generated by revolving the graph of a nonnegative function $y = f(x)$, $a \le x \le b$, about the x-axis. The surface is a union of bands like the one swept out by the arc PQ.

Areas of Surfaces of Revolution

Suppose we want to find the area of the surface swept out by revolving the graph of a nonnegative function $y = f(x)$, $a \le x \le b$, about the x-axis. We partition $[a, b]$ in the usual way and use the points in the partition to divide the graph into short arcs. Figure 7.36 shows a typical arc PQ and the band it sweeps out as part of the graph of f.

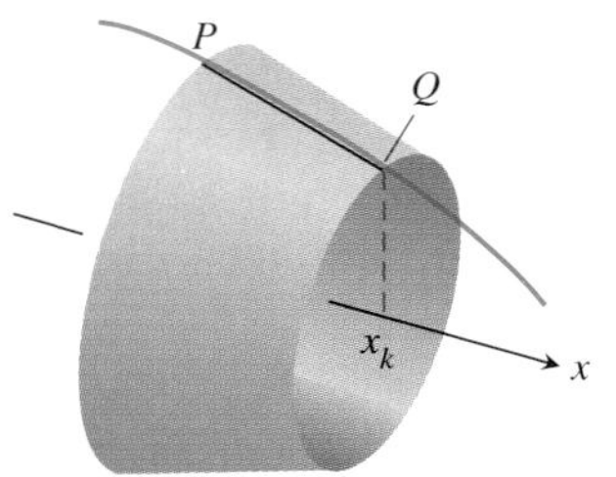

7.37 The line segment joining P and Q sweeps out a frustum of a cone.

As the arc PQ revolves about the x-axis, the line segment joining P and Q sweeps out part of a cone whose axis lies along the x-axis (magnified view in Fig. 7.37). A piece of a cone like this is called a frustum of the cone, *frustum* being Latin for "piece." The surface area of the frustum approximates the surface area of the band swept out by the arc PQ.

The surface area of a frustum of a cone (see Fig. 7.38) is 2π times the average of the base radii times the slant height:

$$\text{Frustum surface area} = 2\pi \cdot \frac{r_1 + r_2}{2} \cdot L = \pi(r_1 + r_2)\, L. \tag{6}$$

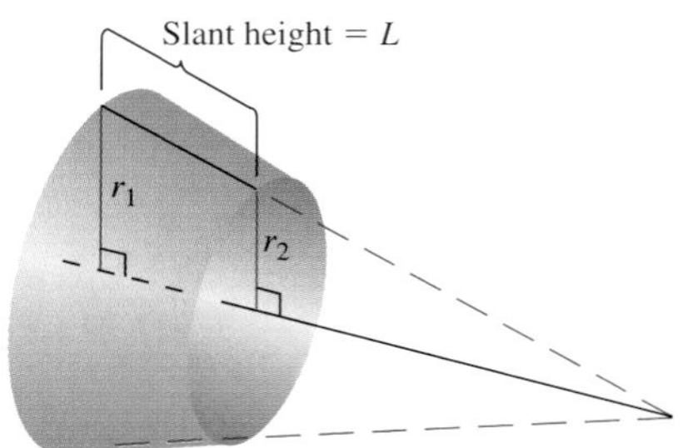

7.38 The important dimensions of the frustum in Fig. 7.37.

For the frustum swept out by the segment PQ (Fig. 7.39), this works out to be

$$\text{Frustum surface area} = \pi(f(x_{k-1}) + f(x_k))\sqrt{(\Delta x_k)^2 + (\Delta y_k)^2}. \tag{7}$$

The area of the original surface, being the sum of the areas of the bands swept out by arcs like arc PQ, is approximated by the frustum area sum

$$\sum_{k=1}^{n} \pi(f(x_{k-1}) + f(x_k))\sqrt{(\Delta x_k)^2 + (\Delta y_k)^2}. \tag{8}$$

We expect the approximation to improve as the partition of $[a, b]$ becomes finer, and we would like to show that the sums in Eq. (8) approach a calculable limit as the norm of the partition goes to zero.

To show this, we try to rewrite the sum in Eq. (8) as the Riemann sum of some function over the interval from a to b. As in the calculation of arc length, we begin by appealing to the Mean Value Theorem for derivatives.

If f is smooth, then, by the Mean Value Theorem, there is a point $(c_k, f(c_k))$ on the curve between P and Q where the tangent is parallel to the segment PQ (Fig. 7.40). At this point,

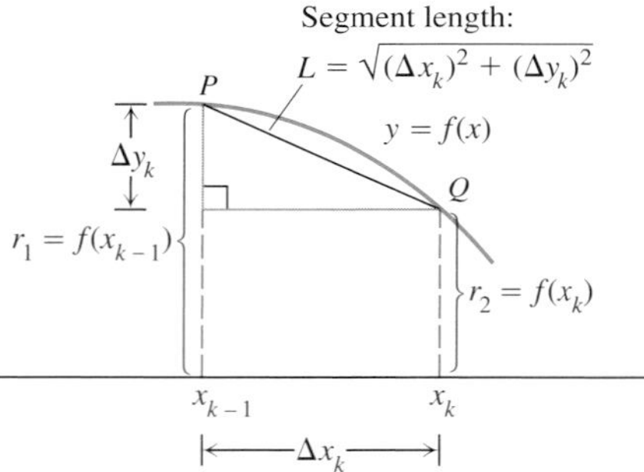

7.39 Dimensions associated with the arc and segment PQ.

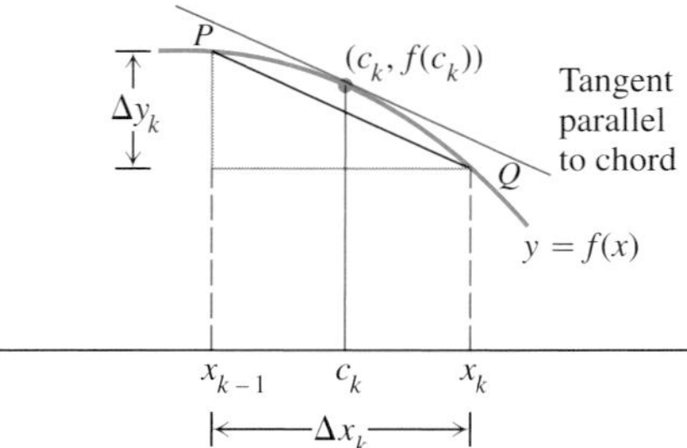

7.40 If f is smooth, the Mean Value Theorem guarantees the existence of a point on arc PQ where the tangent is parallel to segment PQ.

With this substitution for Δy_k, the sums in Eq. (8) take the form

$$\sum_{k=1}^{n} \pi(f(x_{k-1}) + f(x_k))\sqrt{(\Delta x_k)^2 + (f'(c_k)\Delta x_k)^2}$$

$$= \sum_{k=1}^{n} \pi(f(x_{k-1}) + f(x_k))\sqrt{1 + (f'(c_k))^2}\,\Delta x_k. \tag{9}$$

At this point there is both good news and bad.

The bad news is that the sums in Eq. (9) are not the Riemann sums of any function because the points x_{k-1}, x_k, and c_k are not the same and there is no way to make them the same. The good news is that this does not matter. A theorem called Bliss's theorem, from advanced calculus, assures us that as the norm of the subdivision of $[a, b]$ goes to zero, the sums in Eq. (9) converge to

$$\int_a^b 2\pi f(x)\sqrt{1 + (f'(x))^2}\, dx \tag{10}$$

just the way we want them to. We therefore define this integral to be the area of the surface swept out by the graph of f from a to b.

DEFINITION

The Surface Area Formula for Revolution About the x-axis

If the function $f(x) \geq 0$ is smooth throughout $[a, b]$, the **area** of the surface generated by revolving the curve $y = f(x)$ about the x-axis is

$$S = \int_a^b 2\pi y \sqrt{1 + \left(\frac{dy}{dx}\right)^2}\, dx. \tag{11}$$

The square root in Eq. (11) is the same one that appears in the formula for the length of the generating curve.

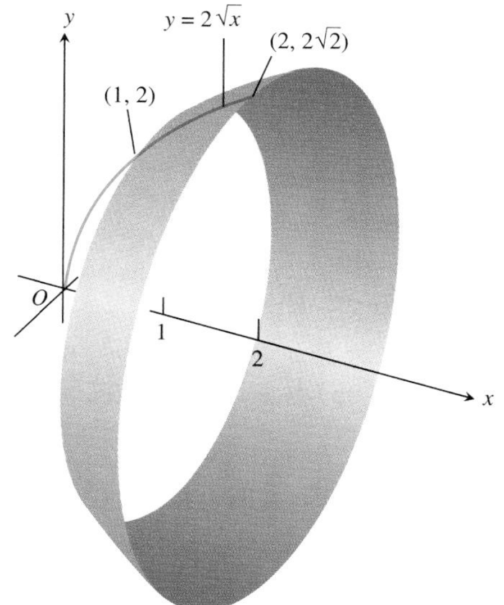

7.41 Example 3 calculates the area of this surface.

EXAMPLE 3 Find the area of the surface generated by revolving the curve $y = 2\sqrt{x}$, $1 \leq x \leq 2$, about the x-axis (Fig. 7.41).

Solution We evaluate the formula

$$S = \int_a^b 2\pi y \sqrt{1 + \left(\frac{dy}{dx}\right)^2}\, dx \qquad \text{Eq. (11)}$$

with

$$a = 1, \qquad b = 2, \qquad y = 2\sqrt{x}, \qquad \frac{dy}{dx} = \frac{1}{\sqrt{x}},$$

$$\sqrt{1 + \left(\frac{dy}{dx}\right)^2} = \sqrt{1 + \left(\frac{1}{\sqrt{x}}\right)^2} = \sqrt{1 + \frac{1}{x}} = \sqrt{\frac{x+1}{x}} = \frac{\sqrt{x+1}}{\sqrt{x}}.$$

With these substitutions,

$$S = \int_1^2 2\pi \cdot 2\sqrt{x}\,\frac{\sqrt{x+1}}{\sqrt{x}}\, dx = 4\pi \int_1^2 \sqrt{x+1}\, dx$$

$$= 4\pi \cdot \frac{2}{3}(x+1)^{3/2}\Big]_1^2 = \frac{8\pi}{3}\left(3\sqrt{3} - 2\sqrt{2}\right).$$

The surface area is $8\pi\left(3\sqrt{3} - 2\sqrt{2}\right)/3$, or about 19.84 square units.

Equation (11) is for revolution about the x-axis. To find the area of the surface generated by revolving the curve about the y-axis, we use the formula with the x and y interchanged.

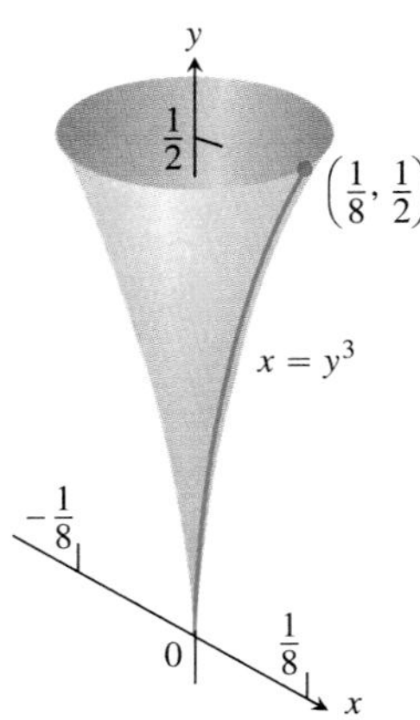

7.42 The surface generated by revolving the curve $x = y^3$, $0 \le y \le 1/2$, about the y-axis could be the design for a champagne glass (Example 4).

The Surface Area Formula for Revolution About the y-axis

If the function $x = g(y) \ge 0$ is smooth throughout $[c, d]$, the area of the surface generated by revolving the curve $x = g(y)$ about the y-axis is

$$S = \int_c^d 2\pi x \sqrt{1 + \left(\frac{dx}{dy}\right)^2}\, dy. \qquad (12)$$

EXAMPLE 4 Find the area of the surface generated by revolving the curve $x = y^3$, $0 \le y \le 1/2$, about the y-axis (Fig. 7.42).

Solution

$$\begin{aligned}
S &= \int_c^d 2\pi x \sqrt{1 + \left(\frac{dx}{dy}\right)^2}\, dy && \text{Eq. (12)}\\
&= \int_0^{1/2} 2\pi y^3 \sqrt{1 + (3y^2)^2}\, dy && x = y^3 \text{ and } dx/dy = 3y^2\\
&= 2\pi \int_0^{1/2} y^3 \sqrt{1 + 9y^4}\, dy\\
&= \frac{2\pi}{36} \int_1^{25/16} \sqrt{u}\, du && u = 1 + 9y^4,\ du/36 = y^3\, dy\\
&= \frac{\pi}{18}\left[\frac{2}{3}u^{3/2}\right]_1^{25/16} = \frac{\pi}{27}\left[\frac{125}{64} - 1\right] = \frac{61\pi}{1728} \approx 0.1109
\end{aligned}$$

As with arc-length calculations, even the simplest curves can provide a workout.

Exercises 7.4

Set up, but do not evaluate, integrals for the lengths of the curves in Exercises 1–6.

1. $y = x^2, \quad -1 \le x \le 2$

2. $y = \tan x, \quad -\pi/3 \le x \le 0$

3. $x = \sin y, \quad 0 \le y \le \pi$

4. $x = \sqrt{1 - y^2}, \quad -1/2 \le y \le 1/2$

5. $y = \int_0^x \tan t\, dt, \quad 0 \le x \le \pi/6$

6. $x = \int_0^y \sqrt{\sec^2 t - 1}\, dt, \quad -\pi/3 \le y \le \pi/4$

Set up, but do not evaluate, integrals for the areas of the surfaces generated by revolving the curves in Exercises 7–12 about the given axes.

7. $y = \tan x, \quad -\pi/4 \le x \le \pi/4; \quad x$-axis

8. $y = x^2, \quad 0 \le x \le 2; \quad x$-axis

9. $xy = 1, \quad 1 \le y \le 2; \quad y$-axis

10. $x = \sin y, \quad 0 \le y \le \pi; \quad y$-axis

11. $x^{1/2} + y^{1/2} = 3$ from $(4, 1)$ to $(1, 4)$; x-axis

12. $y + 2\sqrt{y} = x, \quad 1 \le y \le 2; \quad y$-axis

Find the lengths of the curves in Exercises 13–24. If you have a grapher, you may want to graph these curves to see what they look like.

13. $y = (1/3)(x^2 + 2)^{3/2}$ from $x = 0$ to $x = 3$

14. $y = x^{3/2}$ from $x = 0$ to $x = 4$

15. $x = (y^3/3) + 1/(4y)$ from $y = 1$ to $y = 3$
(*Hint:* $1 + (dx/dy)^2$ is a perfect square.)

16. $x = (y^{3/2}/3) - y^{1/2}$ from $y = 1$ to $y = 9$
(*Hint:* $1 + (dx/dy)^2$ is a perfect square.)

17. $x = (y^4/4) + 1/(8y^2)$ from $y = 1$ to $y = 2$
(*Hint:* $1 + (dx/dy)^2$ is a perfect square.)

18. $x = (y^3/6) + 1/(2y)$ from $y = 2$ to $y = 3$
(*Hint:* $1 + (dx/dy)^2$ is a perfect square.)

19. $y = (3/4)x^{4/3} - (3/8)x^{2/3} + 5, \quad 1 \le x \le 8$

20. $y = (x^3/3) + x^2 + x + 1/(4x + 4), \quad 0 \le x \le 2$

21. $y = (x^2/8) - \ln x, \quad$ from $\quad x = 4$ to $x = 8$

22. $x = (y/4)^2 - 2 \ln (y/4), \quad 4 \le y \le 12$

23. $x = \int_0^y \sqrt{\sec^4 t - 1}\, dt, \quad -\pi/4 \le y \le \pi/4$

24. $y = \int_{-2}^x \sqrt{3t^4 - 1}\, dt, \quad -2 \le x \le -1$

25. Find the length of the curve $y = \sqrt{1 - x^2}, \quad -1/2 \le x \le 1/2$.

26. Find the length of the curve $y = \sqrt{4 - x^2}, \quad -1 \le x \le \sqrt{3}$.

27. Find a curve through the point (0, 1) whose length from $x = 0$ to $x = 1$ is

$$L = \int_0^1 \sqrt{1 + e^{2x}}\, dx.$$

28. Find a curve through the point (1, 0) whose length from $x = 1$ to $x = 2$ is

$$L = \int_1^2 \sqrt{1 + \frac{1}{x^2}}\, dx.$$

29. Find the lateral (side) surface area of the cone generated by revolving the line segment $y = x/2$, $0 \le x \le 4$, about the x-axis. Check your answer with the geometry formula

$$\text{Lateral surface area} = \frac{1}{2} \times \text{base circumference} \times \text{slant height}.$$

30. Find the lateral surface area of the cone generated by revolving the line segment $y = x/2$, $0 \le x \le 4$ about the y-axis. Check your answer with the geometry formula

$$\text{Lateral surface area} = \frac{1}{2} \times \text{base circumference} \times \text{slant height}.$$

31. Find the surface area of the cone frustum generated by revolving the line segment $y = (x/2) + (1/2)$, $1 \le x \le 3$, about the x-axis. Check your result with the geometry formula

$$\text{Frustum surface area} = \pi(r_1 + r_2) \times \text{slant height}$$

(Eq. 6 in the text).

32. Find the surface area of the cone frustum generated by revolving the line segment $y = (x/2) + (1/2)$, $1 \le x \le 3$, about the y-axis. Check your result with the geometry formula

$$\text{Frustum surface area} = \pi(r_1 + r_2) \times \text{slant height}$$

(Eq. 6 in the text).

Find the areas of the surfaces generated by revolving the curves in Exercises 33–40 about the indicated axes. If you have a grapher, you may want to graph these curves to see what they look like.

33. $y = x^3/9, \quad 0 \le x \le 2, \quad x$-axis

34. $y = \sqrt{x}, \quad 3/4 \le x \le 15/4, \quad x$-axis

35. $y = \sqrt{2x - x^2}, \quad 0.5 \le x \le 1.5, \quad x$-axis

36. $y = \sqrt{x + 1}, \quad 1 \le x \le 5, \quad x$-axis

37. $x = y^3/3, \quad 0 \le y \le 1, \quad y$-axis

38. $x = (1/3)y^{3/2} - y^{1/2}, \quad 1 \le y \le 3, \quad y$-axis

39. $x = 2\sqrt{4 - y}, \quad 0 \le y \le 15/4, \quad y$-axis

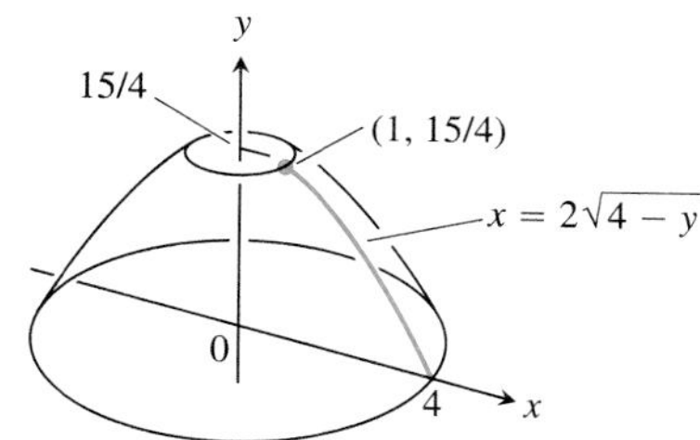

40. $x = \sqrt{2y - 1}, \quad 5/8 \le y \le 1, \quad y$-axis

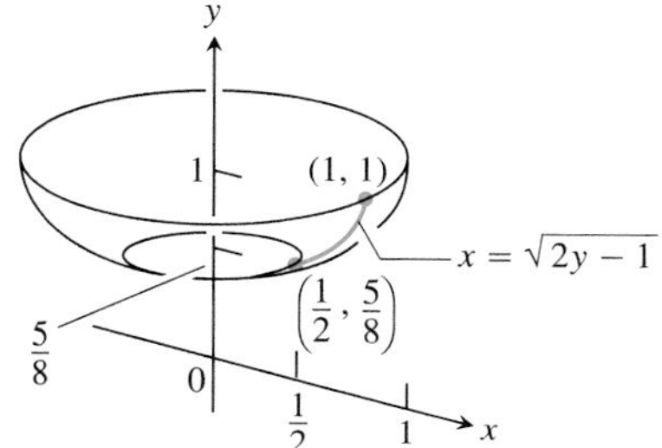

41. *Testing the Definition of Length.* As you know, the perimeter of a circle of radius a is $2\pi a$. Show that the calculus definition of length leads to the same result by using Eq. (4) to show that the length of the quarter circle shown here is $\pi a/2$.

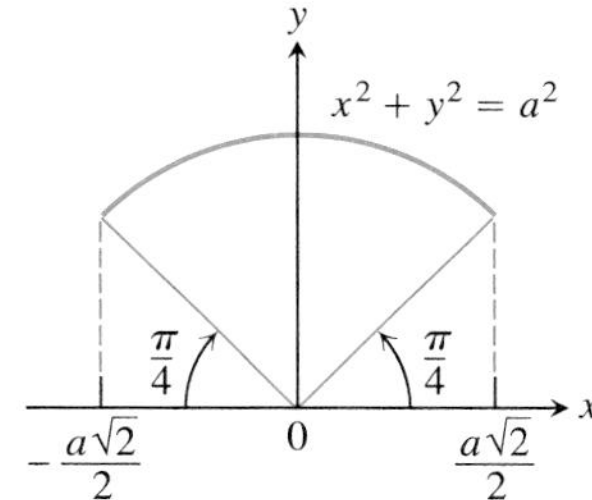

42. *Testing the Definition of Length.* The Pythagorean theorem gives $\sqrt{a^2 + b^2}$ for the length of line segment OP. Show that the calculus definition of length leads to the same result by using Eq. (4) to find the length of the curve $y = (b/a)x$, $0 \le x \le a$.

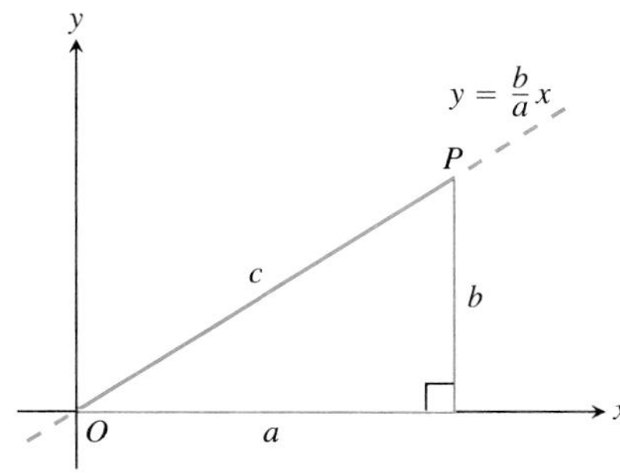

43. *Testing the Definition of Surface Area.* Show that the surface area of a sphere of radius a is still $4\pi a^2$ by using Eq. (11) to find the area of the surface generated by revolving the curve $y = \sqrt{a^2 - x^2}$, $-a \le x \le a$, about the x-axis.

44. *Testing the Definition of Surface Area.* The lateral (side) surface area of a cone of height h and base radius r should be $\pi r\sqrt{r^2 + h^2}$, the semiperimeter of the base times the slant height. Show that this is still the case by finding the area of the surface generated by revolving the line segment $y = (r/h)x$, $0 \le x \le h$, about the x-axis. (See diagram below at left.)

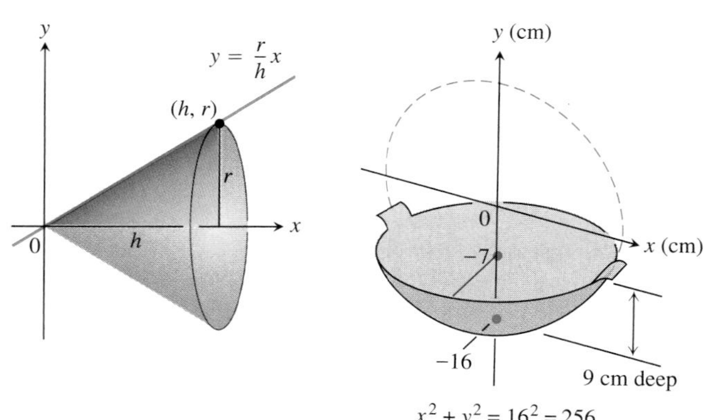

45. *Enameling Woks.* Your company decided to put out a deluxe version of the successful wok you designed in Section 7.2, Exercise 51. The plan is to coat it inside with white enamel and outside with blue enamel. Each enamel will be sprayed on 0.5 mm thick before baking. (See diagram above at right.) Your manufacturing department wants to know how much enamel to have on hand for a production run of 5000 woks. What do you tell them? (Neglect waste and unused material and give your answer in liters. Remember that 1 cm^3 = 1 mL so 1 L = 1000 cm^3.)

46. *Slicing Bread.* Did you know that if you cut a spherical loaf of bread into slices of equal width, each slice will have the same amount of crust? To see why, suppose the semicircle $y = \sqrt{r^2 - x^2}$ shown here is revolved about the x-axis to generate a sphere. Let AB be an arc of the semicircle that lies above an interval of length h on the x-axis. Show that the area swept out by AB does not depend on the location of the interval. (It does depend on the length of the interval.)

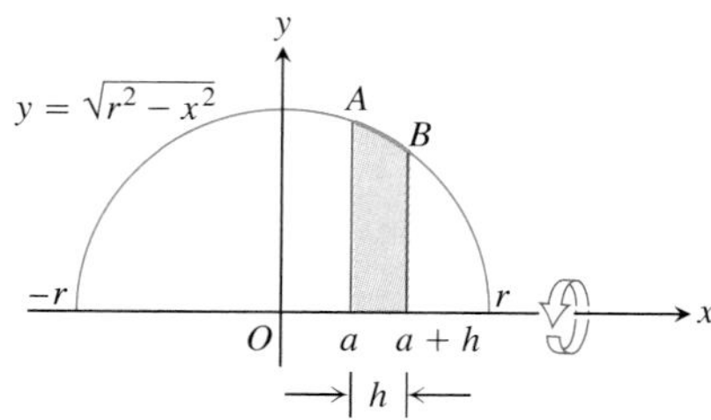

47. The shaded band shown below left is cut from a sphere of radius R by parallel planes h units apart. Show that the surface area of the band is $2\pi Rh$.

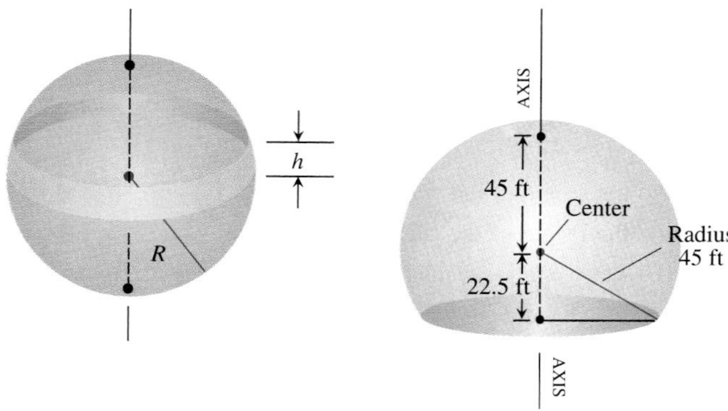

48. Above right is a schematic drawing of the 90-ft dome used by the U.S. National Weather Service to house radar in Bozeman, Mont.

a) How much outside surface is there to paint (not counting the bottom)?

b) Express the answer to the nearest square foot.

NUMERICAL INTEGRATION

You may have wondered why so many of the curves we have been working with have unusual formulas. The reason is that the square root $\sqrt{1 + (dy/dx)^2}$ that appears in the integrals for length and surface area almost never leads to a function whose antiderivative we can find. In fact, the square root itself is a well-known source of nonelementary integrals. Most integrals for length and surface area have to be evaluated numerically, as in Exercises 49–54.

49. Your metal fabrication company is bidding for a contract to make sheets of corrugated iron roofing like the one shown here. The cross sections of the corrugated sheets are to conform to the curve

$$y = \sin \frac{3\pi}{20}x, \quad 0 \le x \le 20 \text{ in.}$$

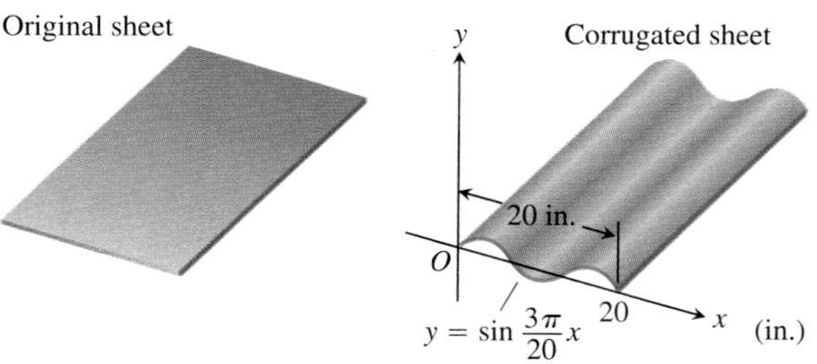

If the roofing is to be stamped from flat sheets by a process that does not stretch the material, how wide should the original material be? To find out, use numerical integration to approximate the length of the sine curve to two decimal places.

50. Your engineering firm is bidding for the contract to construct the tunnel shown here. The tunnel is 300 ft long and 50 ft wide at the base. The cross section is shaped like one arch of the curve $y = 25\cos(\pi x/50)$. Upon completion, the tunnel's inside surface (excluding the roadway) will be treated with a waterproof sealer that costs \$1.75 per square foot to apply. How much will it cost to apply the sealer? (*Hint:* Use numerical integration to find the length of the cosine curve.)

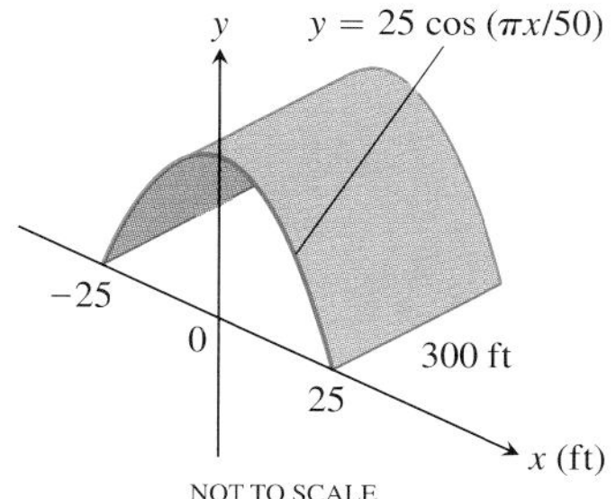

Find, to two decimal places, the areas of the surfaces generated by revolving the curves in Exercises 51–54 about the x-axis.

51. $y = \sin x, \quad 0 \le x \le \pi$

52. $y = x^2/4, \quad 0 \le x \le 2$

53. $y = x + \sin 2x, \quad -2\pi/3 \le x \le 2\pi/3$ (the curve in Section 4.3, Exercise 5)

54. $y = \dfrac{x}{12}\sqrt{36 - x^2}$, $0 \le x \le 6$ (the surface of the plumb bob in Section 7.2, Exercise 52)

HANGING CABLES AND HYPERBOLIC COSINES

It can be shown that clotheslines, chains, telephone lines, and electric power cables that are strung from one support to another hang in the shape of a hyperbolic cosine curve (Fig. 7.43). In contrast, the cables of suspension bridges, which support a uniform load per horizontal foot, hang in parabolas. Hyperbolic cosine curves are sometimes called **chain curves** or **catenaries,** the latter deriving from the Latin *catena,* for "chain."

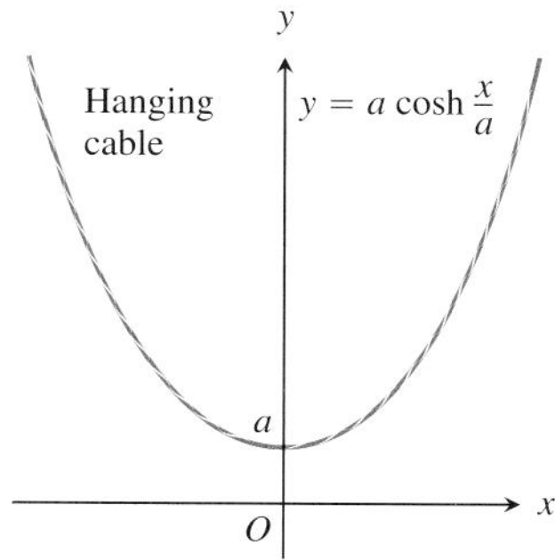

7.43 A hanging cable typically has this shape.

55. Find the length of the curve $y = 10\cosh(x/10)$ from $x = -10\ln 10$ to $x = 10\ln 10$.

56. Find the length of the curve $y = (1/2)\cosh 2x$ from $x = 0$ to $x = \ln\sqrt{5}$.

57. *A Minimal Surface.* It can be shown that, of all smooth curves joining the points A and B in Fig. 7.44, the catenary $y = 4\cosh(x/4)$ generates the surface of least area. If you made a rigid wire frame of the end-circles through A and B and dipped them in a soap film solution, the surface spanning the circles would be the one generated by the catenary. Find the area of the surface generated by revolving the curve $y = 4\cosh(x/4)$, $-\ln 16 \le x \le \ln 81$ about the x-axis (Fig. 7.44).

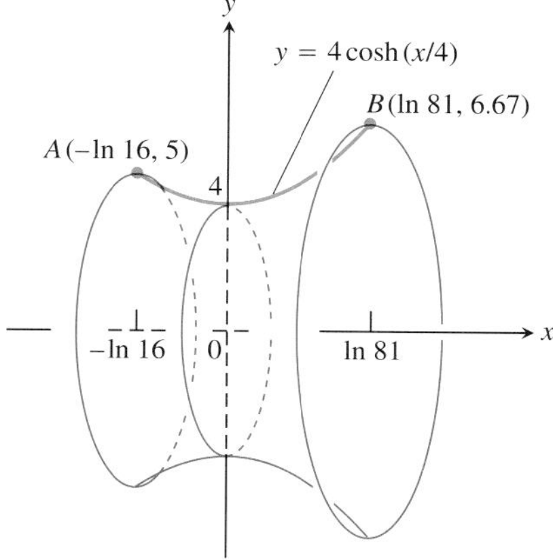

7.44 The minimal surface in Exercise 57.

58. Find the area of the surface generated by revolving the curve $y = 2\cosh(x/2)$, $0 \le x \le \ln 8$, about the x-axis.

Writing for Your Own Knowledge

Answer the following questions in writing. Some answers will take only a sentence or two; others may require several paragraphs. Some explanations may also call for graphs or sketches.

1. How do you calculate the length of a smooth curve?
2. Does every curve have a length?
3. How do you calculate the area of a surface of revolution? What conditions do you want the generating curve to satisfy?

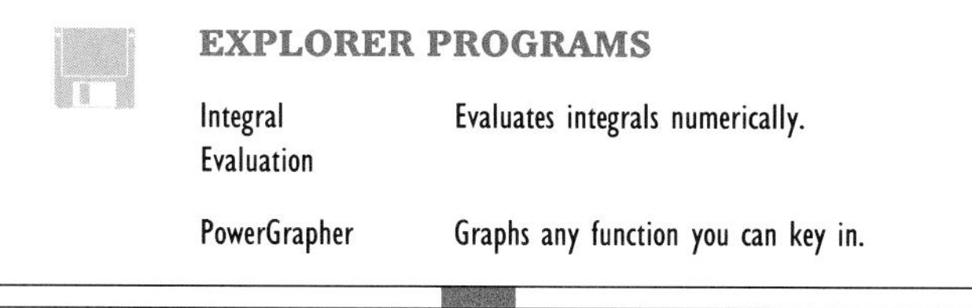

EXPLORER PROGRAMS

Integral Evaluation	Evaluates integrals numerically.
PowerGrapher	Graphs any function you can key in.

7.5 Work

In everyday life, *work* means an activity that requires muscular or mental effort. In science, the term refers specifically to a force acting on a body and the body's subsequent displacement. This section shows how to calculate work. The applications run from compressing railroad car springs and emptying subterranean tanks to forcing electrons together and lifting satellites into orbit.

Work Done by a Constant Force

When a body moves a distance d along a straight line as a result of being acted on by a force of constant magnitude F in the direction of motion, the **work** W done by the force on the body is F times d:

$$W = Fd \qquad \text{(Constant-force formula for work).} \tag{1}$$

Right away we can see a considerable difference between what we are used to calling work and what this formula says work is. If you push a car down the street, you will be doing work on the car, both by your own reckoning and by Eq. (1). But if you push against the car and the car does not move, Eq. (1) says you will do no work on the car, even if you push for an hour.

From Eq. (1) we see that the unit of work in any system is the unit of force multiplied by the unit of distance. In SI units (SI stands for *Système International* or International System), the unit of force is a newton, the unit of distance is a meter, and the unit of work is a newton-meter (N · m). This combination appears so often it has a special name, the **joule.** In the British system, the unit of work is the foot-pound, a unit frequently used by engineers.

Joules

The joule, abbreviated J and pronounced "jewel," is named after the English physicist James Prescott Joule (1818–1889). The defining equation is

$$1 \text{ joule} = (1 \text{ newton})(1 \text{ meter}).$$

In symbols, 1 J = 1 N · m.

It takes a force of about 1 N to lift an apple from a table. If you lift it 1 m you have done about 1 J of work on the apple. If you then eat the apple you will have consumed about 80 food calories, the heat equivalent of nearly 335,000 joules. If this energy were directly useful for mechanical work, it would enable you to lift 335,000 more apples up 1 m.

EXAMPLE 1 If you jack up the side of a 2000-lb car 1.25 ft to change a tire (you have to apply a constant vertical force of about 1000 lb) you will perform $1000 \times 1.25 = 1250$ ft-lb of work on the car. In SI units, you have applied a force of 4448 N through a distance of 0.381 m to do $4448 \times 0.381 \approx 1695$ J of work.

Work Done by a Variable Force

If the force you apply varies along the way, as it will if you are lifting a leaking bucket or compressing a spring, the formula $W = Fd$ has to be replaced by an integral formula that takes the variation in F into account.

Suppose that the force performing the work acts along a line that we can model with the x-axis and that its magnitude F is a continuous function of the position. We want to find the work done over the interval from $x = a$ to $x = b$. We partition $[a, b]$ in the usual way and choose an arbitrary point c_k in each subinterval $[x_{k-1}, x_k]$. If the subinterval is short enough, F, being continuous, will not vary much from x_{k-1} to x_k. The amount of work done across the interval will be about $F(c_k)$ times the distance Δx_k, the same as it would be if F were constant and we could apply Eq. (1). The total work done from a to b is therefore approximated by the Riemann sum

$$\sum_{k=1}^{n} F(c_k)\,\Delta x_k. \tag{2}$$

We expect the approximation to improve as the norm of the partition goes to zero, so we define the work done by the force from a to b to be the integral of F from a to b.

DEFINITION

The **work** done by a variable force $F(x)$ directed along the x-axis from $x = a$ to $x = b$ is

$$W = \int_a^b F(x)\,dx. \tag{3}$$

The units of the integral are joules if F is in Newtons and x is in meters, and foot-pounds if F is in pounds and x in feet.

EXAMPLE 2 The work done by a force of $F(x) = 1/x^2$ N along the x-axis from $x = 1$ m to $x = 10$ m is

$$W = \int_1^{10} \frac{1}{x^2}\,dx = -\frac{1}{x}\bigg]_1^{10} = -\frac{1}{10} + 1 = 0.9 \text{ J.}$$

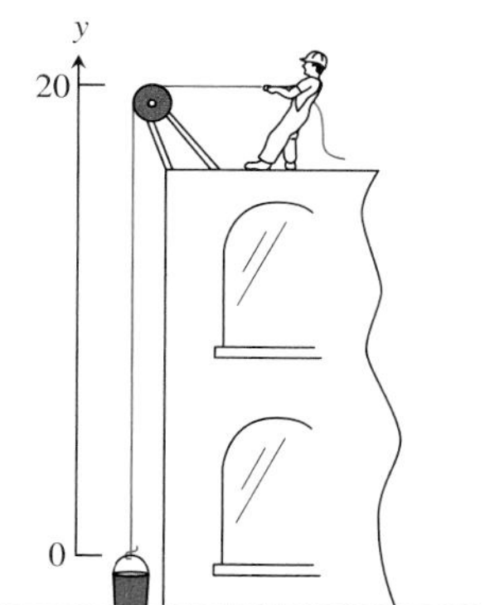

7.45 The leaky bucket in Example 3.

EXAMPLE 3 A leaky 5-lb bucket is lifted from the ground into the air by pulling in 20 ft of rope at a constant speed (Fig. 7.45). The rope weighs 0.08 lb/ft. The bucket starts with 2 gal of water (16 lb) and leaks at a constant rate. It finishes draining just as it reaches the top. How much work was spent

a) lifting the water alone;

b) lifting the water and bucket together;

c) lifting the water, bucket, and rope?

Solution

a) *The water alone.* The force required to lift the water is equal to the water's weight, which varies steadily from 16 to 0 lb over the 20-ft lift. When the bucket is x ft off the ground, the water weighs

$$F(x) = 16\left(\frac{20 - x}{20}\right) = 16\left(1 - \frac{x}{20}\right) = 16 - \frac{4x}{5} \text{ lb.}$$

original weight of water (16); proportion left at elevation x $\left(\frac{20-x}{20}\right)$

The work done is

$$W = \int_a^b F(x)\,dx \qquad \text{Use Eq. (3) for variable forces.}$$

$$= \int_0^{20} \left(16 - \frac{4x}{5}\right) dx = \left[16x - \frac{2x^2}{5}\right]_0^{20} = 320 - 160 = 160 \text{ ft} \cdot \text{lb.}$$

b) *The water and bucket together.* According to Eq. (1), it takes $5 \times 20 = 100$ ft · lb to lift a 5-lb weight 20 ft. Therefore

$$160 + 100 = 260 \text{ ft} \cdot \text{lb}$$

of work were spent lifting the water and bucket together.

c) *The water, bucket, and rope.* Now the total weight at level x is

$$F(x) = \underbrace{\left(16 - \frac{4x}{5}\right)}_{\substack{\text{variable} \\ \text{weight} \\ \text{of water}}} + \underbrace{5}_{\substack{\text{constant} \\ \text{weight of} \\ \text{bucket}}} + \underbrace{\overset{\text{lb/ft}}{(0.08)}(20 - \overset{\text{ft}}{x})}_{\substack{\text{weight of rope} \\ \text{paid out at} \\ \text{elevation } x}}.$$

The work lifting the rope is

$$\text{Work on rope} = \int_0^{20} (0.08)(20 - x)\,dx = \int_0^{20} (1.6 - 0.08x)\,dx$$

$$= \Big[1.6x - 0.04x^2\Big]_0^{20} = 32 - 16 = 16 \text{ ft} \cdot \text{lb}.$$

The total work for the water, bucket, and rope combined is

$$160 + 100 + 16 = 276 \text{ ft} \cdot \text{lb}.$$

Hooke's Law for Springs: $F = kx$

Hooke's law says that the force it takes to stretch or compress a spring x length units from its natural (unstressed) length is proportional to x. In symbols,

$$F = kx. \tag{4}$$

The constant k, measured in force units per unit length, is a characteristic of the spring, called the **force constant** (or spring constant) of the spring. Hooke's law (Eq. 4) gives good results as long as the force doesn't distort the metal in the spring. We assume that the forces in this section are too small to do that.

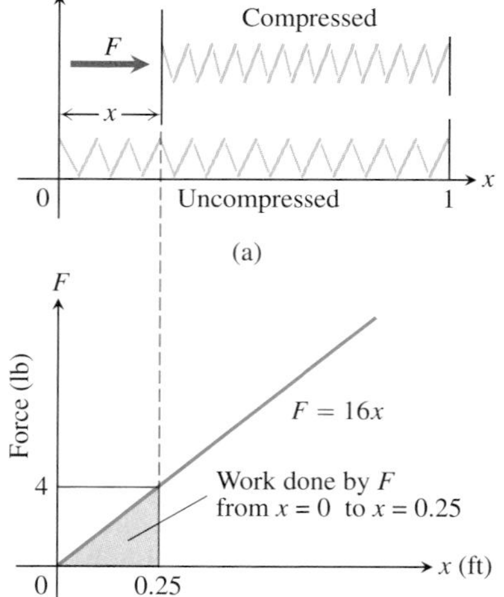

7.46 The force F needed to hold a spring under compression increases linearly as the spring is compressed.

EXAMPLE 4 Find the work required to compress a spring from its natural length of 1 ft to a length of 0.75 ft if the force constant is $k = 16$ lb/ft.

Solution We picture the uncompressed spring laid out along the x-axis with its movable end at the origin and its fixed end at $x = 1$ ft (Fig. 7.46). This enables us to describe the force required to compress the spring from 0 to x with the formula $F = 16x$. To compress the spring from 0 to 0.25 ft, the force must increase from

$$F(0) = 16 \cdot 0 = 0 \text{ lb} \qquad \text{to} \qquad F(0.25) = 16 \cdot 0.25 = 4 \text{ lb}.$$

The work done by F over this interval is

$$W = \int_0^{0.25} 16x\,dx = 8x^2\Big]_0^{0.25} = 0.5 \text{ ft} \cdot \text{lb}. \qquad \text{Eq. (3) with } a = 0,\ b = 0.25,\ F(x) = 16x$$

EXAMPLE 5 A spring has a natural length of 1 m. A force of 24 N stretches the spring to a length of 1.8 m.

a) Find the force constant k.

b) How much work will it take to stretch the spring 2 m beyond its natural length?

c) How far will a 45-N force stretch the spring?

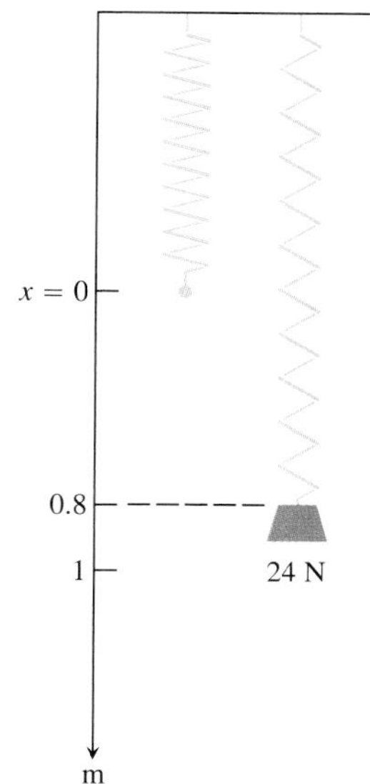

7.47 A 24-N weight stretches this spring 0.8 m beyond its unstressed length.

Solution

a) *The force constant.* We find the force constant from Eq. (4). A force of 24 N stretches the spring 0.8 m, so

$$24 = k(0.8) \qquad \text{Eq. (4) with } F = 24,\ x = 0.8$$
$$k = 24/0.8 = 30 \text{ N/m}.$$

b) *The work to stretch the spring* 2 m. We imagine the unstressed spring hanging along the x-axis with its free end at $x = 0$ (Fig. 7.47). The force required to stretch the spring x m beyond its natural length is the force required to pull the free end of the spring x units from the origin. Hooke's law with $k = 30$ says that this force is

$$F(x) = 30x.$$

The work done by F on the spring from $x = 0$ m to $x = 2$ m is

$$W = \int_0^2 30x\,dx = 15x^2\Big]_0^2 = 60 \text{ J}.$$

c) *How far will a* 45-N *force stretch the spring?* We substitute $F = 45$ in the equation $F = 30x$ to find

$$45 = 30x, \qquad \text{or} \qquad x = 1.5 \text{ m}.$$

A 45-N force will stretch the spring 1.5 m. No calculus is required to find this.

Pumping Liquids from Containers

How much work does it take to pump all or part of the liquid from a container? To find out, we imagine lifting the liquid out one thin horizontal slab at a time and applying the equation $W = Fd$ to each slab. We then evaluate the integral this leads to as the slabs become thinner and more numerous. The integral we get each time depends on the weight of the liquid and the dimensions of the container, but the way we find the integral is always the same. The next examples show what to do.

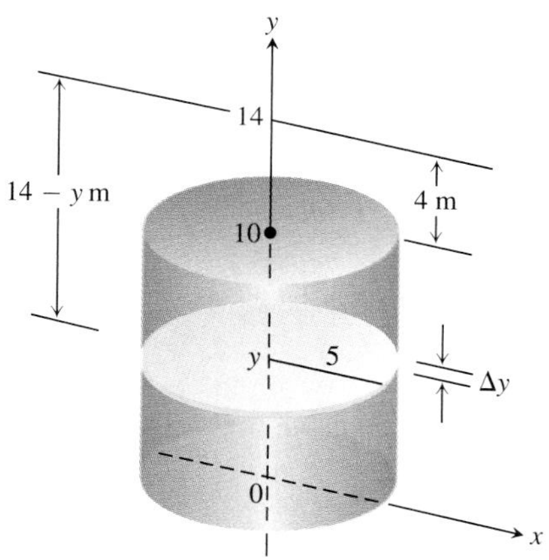

7.48 To find the work it takes to pump the water from a tank, think of lifting the water one thin slab at a time.

EXAMPLE 6 How much work does it take to pump the water from a full upright circular cylindrical tank of radius 5 m and height 10 m to a level 4 m above the top of the tank?

Solution We draw the tank (Fig. 7.48), add coordinate axes, and imagine the water divided into thin horizontal slabs by planes perpendicular to the y-axis at the points of a partition P of the interval $[0, 10]$.

The typical slab between the planes at y and $y + \Delta y$ has a volume of

$$\Delta V = \pi(\text{radius})^2(\text{thickness}) = \pi(5)^2\,\Delta y = 25\pi\,\Delta y \text{ m}^3.$$

The force F required to lift the slab is equal to its weight,

$$F = 9800\,\Delta V \qquad \text{Water weighs 9800 N/m}^3$$
$$= 9800\,(25\pi\,\Delta y) = 245{,}000\pi\,\Delta y \text{ N}.$$

The distance through which F must act is about $(14 - y)$ m, so the work

How to Find Work Done During Pumping

1. Draw a figure with a coordinate system.
2. Find the weight F of a thin horizontal slab of liquid.
3. Find the work ΔW it takes to lift the slab to its destination.
4. Integrate the work expression from the base to the surface of the liquid.

done lifting the slab is about

$$\Delta W = \text{force} \times \text{distance} = 245{,}000\pi(14 - y)\,\Delta y \text{ J.}$$

The work it takes to lift all the water is approximately

$$W \approx \sum_{0}^{10} \Delta W = \sum_{0}^{10} 245{,}000\pi(14 - y)\,\Delta y \text{ J.}$$

This is a Riemann sum for the function $245{,}000\pi(14 - y)$ over the interval $0 \le y \le 10$. The work of pumping the tank dry is the limit of these sums as $\|P\| \to 0$:

$$W = \int_0^{10} 245{,}000\pi(14 - y)\,dy = 245{,}000\pi \int_0^{10} (14 - y)\,dy$$

$$= 245{,}000\pi\left[14y - \frac{y^2}{2}\right]_0^{10} = 245{,}000\pi\,[90]$$

$$\approx 69{,}272{,}118 \approx 69.3 \times 10^6 \text{ J.}$$

A 1-horsepower output motor rated at 746 J/sec could empty the tank in a little less than 26 h.

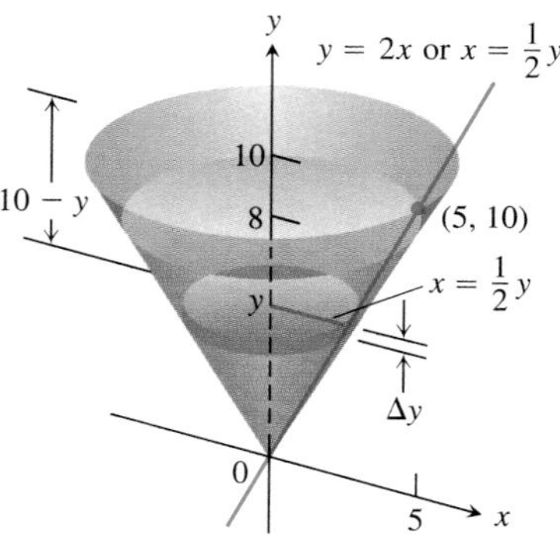

7.49 The olive oil in Example 7.

EXAMPLE 7 The conical tank in Fig. 7.49 is filled to within 2 ft of the top with olive oil weighing 57 lb/ft^3. How much work does it take to pump the oil to the rim of the tank?

Solution We imagine the oil divided into thin slabs by planes perpendicular to the y-axis at the points of a partition of the interval $[0, 8]$.

The typical slab between the planes at y and $y + \Delta y$ has a volume of about

$$\Delta V = \pi(\text{radius})^2(\text{thickness}) = \pi\left(\frac{1}{2}y\right)^2 \Delta y = \frac{\pi}{4}y^2\,\Delta y \text{ ft}^3.$$

The force $F(y)$ required to lift this slab is equal to its weight,

$$F(y) = 57\,\Delta V = \frac{57\pi}{4}y^2\,\Delta y \text{ lb.}$$

Weight = weight per unit volume × volume

The distance through which $F(y)$ must act to lift this slab to the level of the rim of the cone is about $(10 - y)$ ft, so the work done lifting the slab is about

$$\Delta W = \frac{57\pi}{4}(10 - y)\,y^2\,\Delta y \text{ ft} \cdot \text{lb.}$$

The work done lifting all the slabs from $y = 0$ to $y = 8$ to the rim is approximately

$$W \approx \sum_{0}^{8} \frac{57\pi}{4}(10 - y)\,y^2\,\Delta y \text{ ft} \cdot \text{lb.}$$

This is a Riemann sum for the function $(57\pi/4)(10 - y)y^2$ on the interval from $y = 0$ to $y = 8$. The work of pumping the oil to the rim is the limit of these sums as the norm of the partition goes to zero.

$$W = \int_0^8 \frac{57\pi}{4}(10 - y)\,y^2\,dy = \frac{57\pi}{4}\int_0^8 (10y^2 - y^3)\,dy$$

$$= \frac{57\pi}{4}\left[\frac{10y^3}{3} - \frac{y^4}{4}\right]_0^8 \approx 30{,}561 \text{ ft} \cdot \text{lb}$$

Exercises 7.5

1. The workers in Example 3 changed to a larger bucket that held 5 gal (40 lb) of water, but the new bucket had an even larger leak so that it, too, was empty by the time it reached the top. Assuming that the water leaked out at a steady rate, how much work was done lifting the water? (Do not include the rope and bucket.)

2. The bucket in Example 3 is hauled up twice as fast so that there is still 1 gal (8 lb) of water left when the bucket reaches the top. How much work is done lifting the water this time? (Do not include the rope and bucket.)

3. A mountain climber is about to haul up a 50-m length of hanging rope. How much work will it take if the rope weighs 0.624 N/m?

4. It took 1800 J of work to stretch a spring from its natural length of 2 m to a length of 5 m. Find the spring's force constant.

5. An electric elevator with a motor at the top has a multistrand cable weighing 4.5 lb/ft. When the car is at the first floor, 180 ft of cable are paid out, and effectively 0 ft are out when the car is at the top floor. How much work does the motor do just lifting the cable when it takes the car from the first floor to the top?

6. A bag of sand originally weighing 144 lb was lifted at a constant rate. As it rose, sand also leaked out at a constant rate. The sand was half gone by the time the bag had been lifted 18 ft. How much work was done lifting the sand this far? (Neglect the weight of the bag and lifting equipment.)

7. A force of 2 N will stretch a rubber band 2 cm (0.02 m). Assuming Hooke's law applies, how far will a 4-N force stretch the rubber band? How much work does it take to stretch the rubber band this far?

8. If a force of 90 N stretches a spring 1 m beyond its natural length, how much work does it take to stretch the spring 5 m beyond its natural length?

9. *Subway Car Springs.* It takes a force of 21,714 lb to compress a coil spring assembly on a New York City Transit Authority subway car from its free height of 8 in. to its fully compressed height of 5 in.

   a) What is the assembly's spring constant?

   b) How much work does it take to compress the assembly the first half inch? the second half inch?

   (Data courtesy of Bombardier, Inc., Mass Transit Division, for spring assemblies in subway cars delivered to the New York City Transit Authority from 1985 to 1987.)

10. A bathroom scale is compressed 1/16 in. when a 150-lb person stands on it. Assuming the scale behaves like a spring that obeys Hooke's Law, how much does someone who compresses the scale 1/8 in. weigh? How much work is done compressing the scale 1/8 in.?

The Weight of Water

Because of variations in the earth's gravitational field, the weight of a cubic foot of water at sea level can vary from about 62.26 lb at the equator to as much as 62.59 lb near the poles, a variation of about 0.5%. A cubic foot that weighs about 62.4 lb in Melbourne and New York City will weigh 62.5 lb in Juneau and Stockholm. While 62.4 is a typical figure and a common textbook value, there is considerable variation.

11. The rectangular tank shown here, with its top at ground level, is used to catch runoff water. Assume that the water weighs 62.4 lb/ft^3.

    a) How much work does it take to empty the tank by pumping the water back to ground level once the tank is full?

    b) If the water is pumped to ground level with a (5/11)-hp motor (work output 250 ft · lb/sec), how long will it take to empty the full tank?

    c) Show that the pump in part (b) will lower the water level 10 ft (halfway) during the first 25 min of pumping.

    d) What are the answers to parts (a) and (b) in a location where water weighs 62.26 lb/ft^3? 62.59 lb/ft^3?

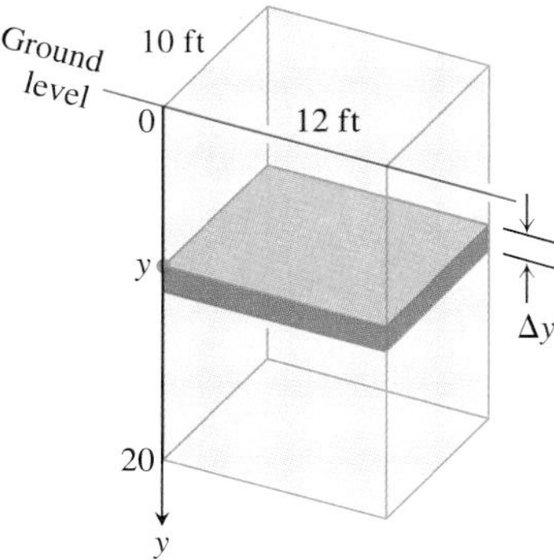

12. The rectangular cistern (storage tank for rain water) shown below has its top 10 ft below ground level. The cistern, currently full, is to be emptied for inspection by pumping its contents to ground level.

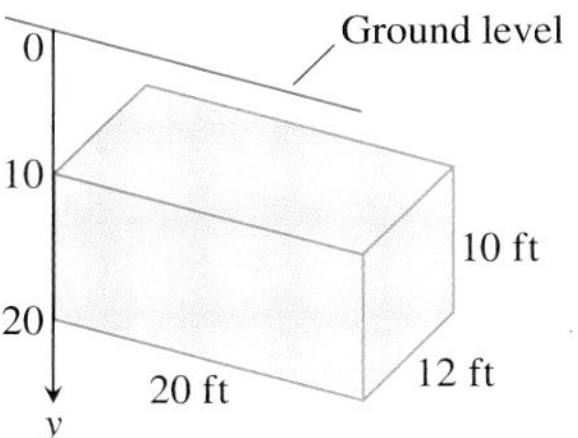

a) How much work will it take to empty the cistern?
b) How long will it take a (1/2)-hp pump, rated at 275 ft · lb/sec, to pump the tank dry?
c) How long will it take the pump in part (b) to empty the tank halfway? (It will be less than half the time required to empty the tank completely.)
d) What are the answers to parts (a)–(c) in a location where water weighs 62.26 lb/ft^3? 62.59 lb/ft^3?

13. How much work would it take to pump the water from the tank in Example 6 to the level of the top of the tank (instead of 4 m higher)?

14. Suppose that instead of being full the tank in Example 6 is only half full. How much work does it take to pump the remaining water to a level 4 m above the top of the tank?

15. A vertical right circular cylindrical tank measures 30 ft high and 20 ft in diameter. It is full of kerosene weighing 51.2 lb/ft^3. How much work does it take to pump the kerosene to the level of the top of the tank?

16. The cylindrical tank shown below left can be filled by pumping water from a lake 15 ft below the bottom of the tank. There are two ways to go about it. One is to pump the water through a hose attached to a valve in the bottom of the tank. The other is to attach the hose to the rim of the tank and let the water pour in. Which way will be faster? Give reasons for your answer.

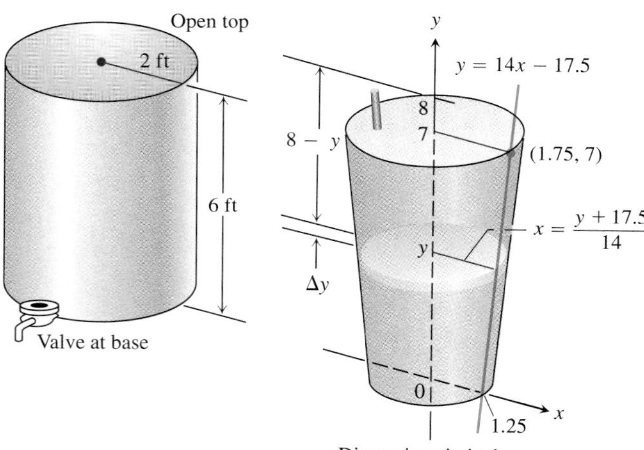

17. The truncated conical container shown above right is full of strawberry milkshake that weighs (4/9) oz/in^3. As you can see, the container is 7 in. deep, 2.5 in. across at the base, and 3.5 in. across at the top (a standard size at *Brigham's* in Boston). The straw sticks up an inch above the top. About how much work does it take to suck up the milkshake through the straw (neglecting friction)? Answer in inch-ounces.

18. a) Suppose the conical container in Example 7 contained milk (weighing 64.5 lb/ft^3) instead of olive oil. How much work would it have taken to pump the contents to the rim?
b) How much work would it have taken to pump the oil in Example 7 to a level 3 ft above the cone's rim?

19. To design the interior surface of a huge stainless steel tank, you revolve the curve $y = x^2$, $0 \le x \le 4$, about the y-axis. The container, with dimensions in meters, is to be filled with seawater, which weighs 10,000 N/m^3. How much work will it take to empty the tank by pumping the water to the tank's top?

20. We model pumping from spherical containers the way we do from other containers, with the axis of integration along the vertical axis of the sphere. Use the figure below to find how much work it takes to empty a full hemispherical water reservoir of radius 5 m by pumping the water to a height of 4 m above the top of the reservoir. Water weighs 9800 N/m^3.

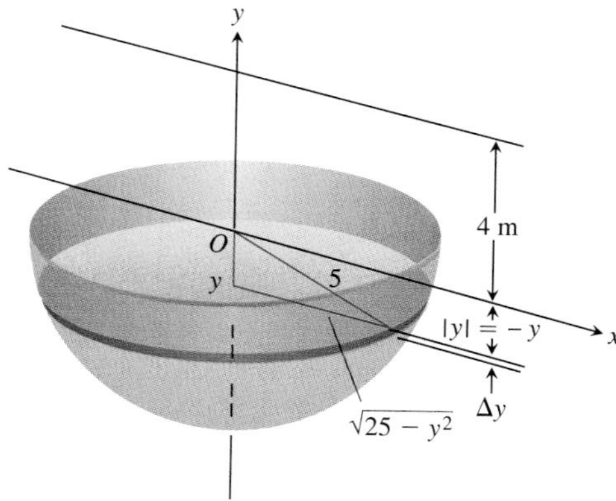

21. You are in charge of the evacuation and repair of the storage tank shown here. The tank is a hemisphere of radius 10 ft and is full of benzene weighing 56 lb/ft^3. A firm you contacted says it can empty the tank for 1/2¢ per foot-pound of work. Find the work required to empty the tank by pumping the benzene to an outlet 2 ft above the top of the tank. If you have $5000 budgeted for the job, can you afford to hire the firm?

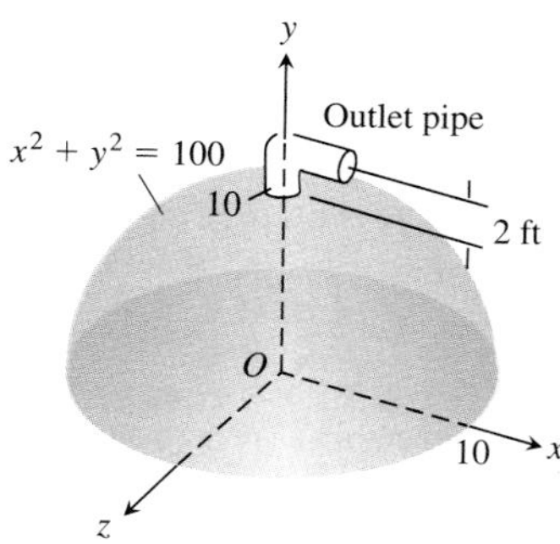

22. Your town has decided to drill a well to increase its water supply. As the town engineer, you have determined that a water tower will be necessary to provide the pressure needed for distribution, and you have designed the system in Fig. 7.50. The water is to be pumped from a 300-ft well through a vertical 4-in. pipe into the base of a cylindrical tank 20 ft in diameter and 25 ft high. The base of the tank will be 60 ft above ground. The pump is a 3-hp pump, rated at 1650 ft · lb/sec.

How long will it take to fill the tank the first time? (Include the time it takes to fill the pipe.) Assume water weighs 62.4 lb/ft³.

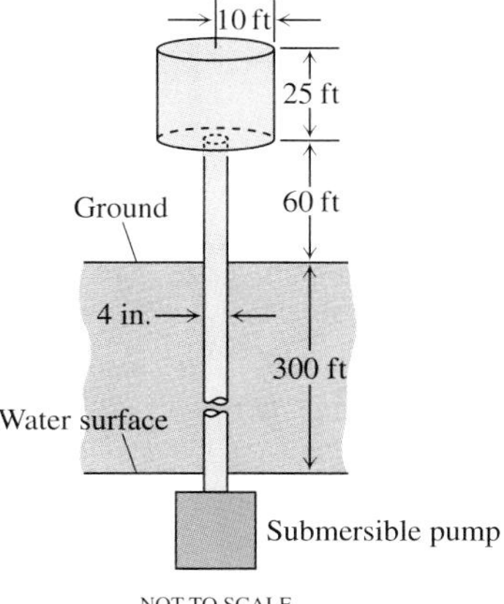

7.50 The water tower and well in Exercise 22.

23. *Putting a Satellite in Orbit.* The strength of the earth's gravitational field varies with the distance r from the earth's center, and the magnitude of the gravitational force experienced by a satellite of mass m during and after launch is

$$F(r) = \frac{mMG}{r^2}.$$

Here, $M = 5.975 \times 10^{24}$ kg is the earth's mass, $G = 6.6720 \times 10^{-11}$ Nm²kg⁻² is the universal gravitational constant, and r is measured in meters. The work it takes to lift a 1000-kg satellite from the earth's surface to a circular orbit 35,780 km above the earth's center is therefore given by the integral

$$\text{Work} = \int_{6,370,000}^{35,780,000} \frac{1000\,MG}{r^2}\,dr \text{ joules.}$$

Evaluate the integral. The lower limit of integration is the earth's radius in meters at the launch site. (This calculation does not take into account energy spent lifting the launch vehicle or energy spent bringing the satellite to orbit velocity.)

24. *Forcing Electrons Together.* Two electrons r meters apart repel each other with a force of

$$F = \frac{23 \times 10^{-29}}{r^2} \text{ newtons.}$$

a) Suppose one electron is held fixed at the point $(1, 0)$ on the x-axis (units in meters). How much work does it take to move a second electron along the x-axis from the point $(-1, 0)$ to the origin?

b) Suppose an electron is held fixed at each of the points $(-1, 0)$ and $(1, 0)$. How much work does it take to move a third electron along the x-axis from $(5, 0)$ to $(3, 0)$?

Writing for Your Own Knowledge

Answer the following questions in writing. Some answers will take only a sentence or two; others may require several paragraphs. Some explanations may also call for graphs or sketches.

1. What is work? What units are used to measure it?
2. In theory, how do you calculate the work done by a variable force?
3. How do you calculate the work done in compressing a spring?
4. How do you calculate the work done in pumping a liquid from a container?

7.6 Fluid Pressures and Fluid Forces

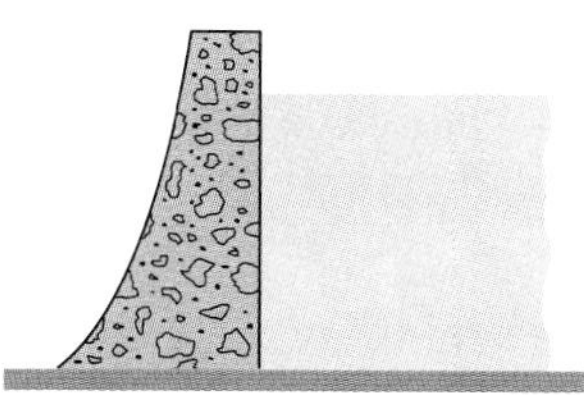

7.51 To withstand the increasing pressure, dams are built thicker as they go down.

We make dams thicker at the bottom than at the top (Fig. 7.51) because the pressure against them increases with depth. It is a remarkable fact that the pressure at any point on a dam depends only on how far below the surface the point is and not on how much the surface of the dam happens to be tilted at that point. The pressure, in pounds per square foot at a point h feet below the surface, is always $62.4h$. The number 62.4 is the weight-density of water in pounds per cubic foot.

The formula, pressure $= 62.4h$, makes sense when you think of the units involved:

$$\frac{\text{lb}}{\text{ft}^2} = \frac{\text{lb}}{\text{ft}^3} \times \text{ft}. \tag{1}$$

As you can see, this equation depends only on units and not on what fluid is involved. The pressure h feet below the surface of any fluid is the fluid's weight-density times h.

Weight-Density

A fluid's **weight-density** is its weight per unit volume. Typical values (lb/ft^3) are:

Gasoline	42
Mercury	849
Milk	64.5
Molasses	100
Olive oil	57
Seawater	64
Water	62.4

The Pressure-Depth Equation

In a fluid that is standing still, the pressure p at depth h is the fluid's weight-density w times h:

$$p = wh. \tag{2}$$

In this section we use the equation $p = wh$ to derive a formula for the total force exerted by a fluid against all or part of a vertical or horizontal containing wall.

The Constant-Depth Formula for Fluid Force

In a container of fluid with a flat horizontal base, the total force exerted by the fluid against the base can be calculated by multiplying the area of the base by the pressure at the base. We can do this because total force equals force per unit area (pressure) times area. (See Fig. 7.52.) If F, p, and A are the total force, pressure, and area, then

$$\begin{aligned} F &= \text{total force} = \text{force per unit area} \times \text{area} \\ &= \text{pressure} \times \text{area} = p\,A \\ &= wh\,A. \qquad\qquad p = wh \text{ from Eq. (2)} \end{aligned}$$

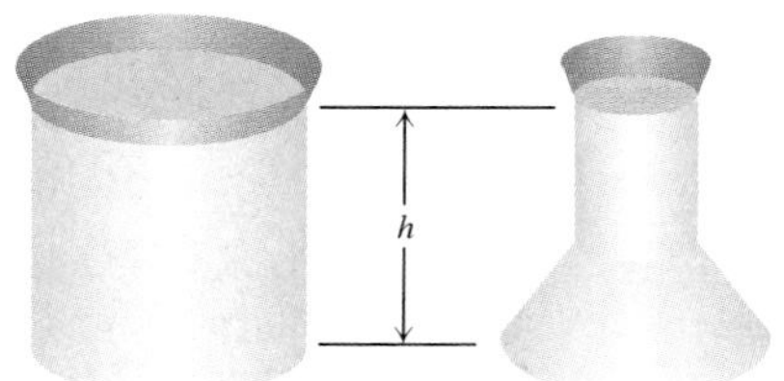

7.52 These containers are filled with water to the same depth and have the same base area. The total force is therefore the same on the bottom of each container. The containers' shapes do not matter here.

Fluid Force on a Constant-Depth Surface

$$F = p\,A = wh\,A \tag{3}$$

EXAMPLE 1 *The Great Molasses Flood.* At 1:00 P.M. on January 15, 1919, an unusually warm day, a 90-ft-high, 90-ft-diameter cylindrical metal tank in which the Puritan Distilling Company was storing molasses at the corner of Foster and Commercial streets in Boston's North End exploded. The molasses flooded into the streets, 30 ft deep, trapping pedestrians and horses, knocking down buildings, and oozing into homes. It was eventually tracked all over town and even made its way into the suburbs (on trolley cars and people's shoes). It took weeks to clean up.

Given that the molasses weighed 100 lb/ft^3, what was the total force exerted by the molasses against the bottom of the tank at the time it blew? Assuming the tank was full, we can find out from Eq. (3):

$$\text{Total force} = wh\,A = (100)(90)(\pi(45)^2) \approx 57{,}255{,}526 \text{ lb.}$$

How about the force against the walls of the tank? For example, what was the total force against the bottom foot-wide band of tank wall (Fig. 7.53)?

The area of the band was

$$A = \pi\,d\,h = \pi(90)(1) = 90\pi \text{ ft}^2.$$

The tank was 90 ft deep, so the pressure near the bottom was about

$$p = wh = (100)(90) = 9000 \text{ lb/ft}^2.$$

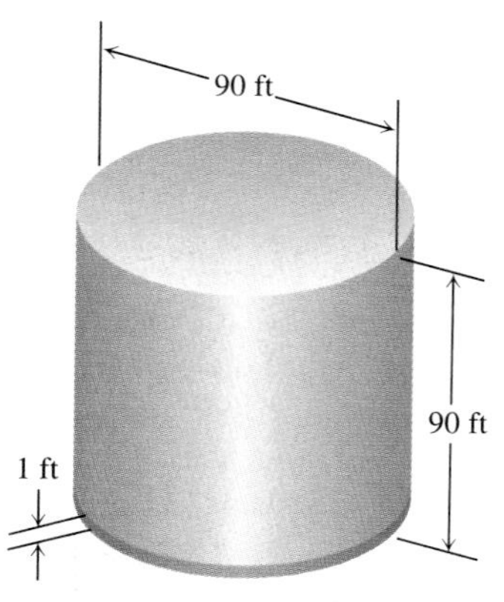

7.53 Schematic drawing of the molasses tank in Example 1. How much force did the lowest foot of the vertical wall have to withstand when the tank was full? It takes an integral to find out. Notice that the proportions of the tank were ideal.

Therefore the total force against the band was about

$$F = whA = (9000)(90\pi) \approx 2{,}544{,}690 \text{ lb}.$$

But this is not exactly right. The top of the band was 89 ft below the surface, not 90, and the pressure there was less. To find out exactly what the force on the band was, we need to take into account the variation of the pressure across the band.

The Variable-Depth Formula

Suppose we want to know the force exerted by a fluid against one side of a vertical plate submerged in a fluid of weight-density w. To find it, we model the plate as a region extending from $y = a$ to $y = b$ below the x-axis in the xy-plane (Fig. 7.54). We partition $[a, b]$ in the usual way and imagine the region to be cut into thin horizontal strips by planes perpendicular to the y-axis at the partition points. The typical strip from y to $y + \Delta y$ is Δy units wide by $L(y)$ units long. We assume $L(y)$ to be a continuous function of y.

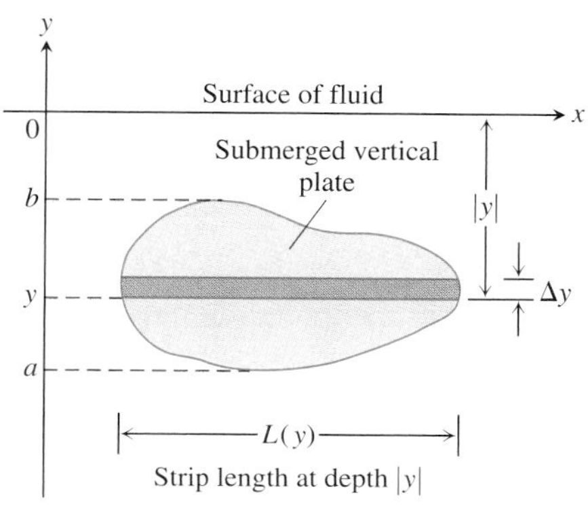

7.54 The force exerted by a fluid against one side of a horizontal strip $|y|$ units beneath the surface is about ΔF = pressure × area = $w|y| \times L(y)\Delta y$. The plate shown here is flat, but it might have been curved instead, like the vertical wall of a cylindrical tank. Whatever the case, the strip length $L(y)$ is measured along the surface of the plate.

The pressure varies across the strip from top to bottom, just as it did in the molasses tank. But if the strip is narrow enough, the pressure will remain close to its bottom-edge value $w|y|$. The total force exerted by the fluid against one side of the strip will therefore be about

$$\begin{aligned}\Delta F &= (\text{pressure along bottom edge}) \times (\text{area}) \\ &= w|y| \times L(y)\,\Delta y. \qquad (4)\end{aligned}$$

The force against the entire plate wall will be about

$$\sum_a^b \Delta F = \sum_a^b w|y|L(y)\,\Delta y. \qquad (5)$$

The sum on the right-hand side of Eq. (5) is a Riemann sum for the continuous function $w|y|L(y)$ on $[a, b]$. We expect the approximations to improve as the norm of the partition goes to zero, so we define the total force against the plate wall to be the limit of these sums as the norm goes to zero.

DEFINITION

The Integral for Fluid Force

Suppose a submerged vertical plate runs from depth $|a|$ up to a depth $|b|$ in a fluid of weight density w, as in Fig. 7.54. Suppose also that at depth $|y|$ the plate is $L(y)$ units wide, as measured along the plate. Then the total force exerted by the fluid against one side of the plate is

$$F = \int_a^b w|y|L(y)\,dy. \qquad (6)$$

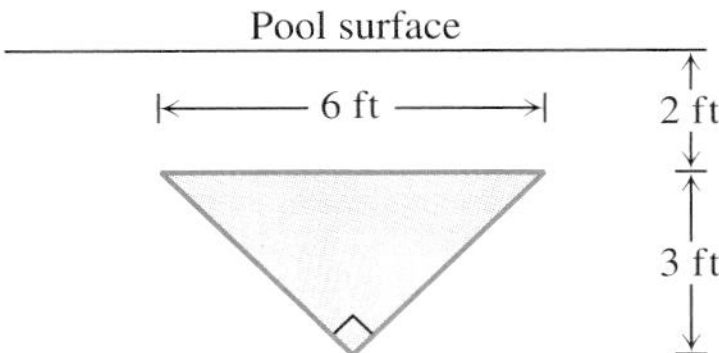

7.55 The plate in Example 2.

EXAMPLE 2 A flat isosceles right triangular plate with base 6 ft and height 3 ft is submerged vertically, base up, 2 ft below the surface of a swimming pool (Fig. 7.55). Find the force exerted by the water against one side of the plate.

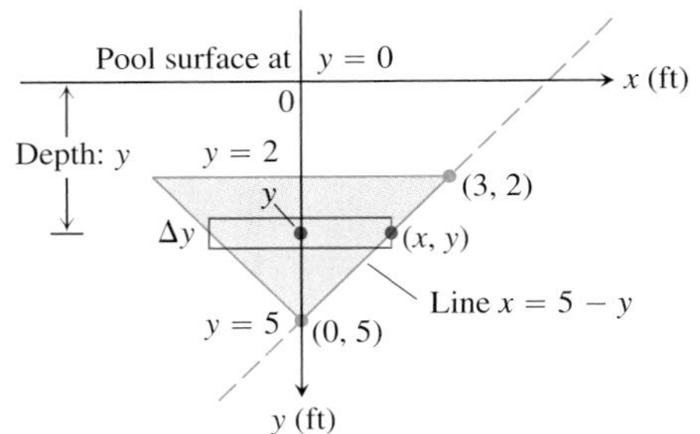

7.56 To find the force on one side of the submerged plate in Fig. 7.55, we can use a coordinate system like the one here (Example 2).

Solution We establish a coordinate system to work in by running the x-axis along the surface of the liquid and running the y-axis downward along the axis of symmetry of the plate (Fig. 7.56). (We will look at another coordinate system in the next example and two others in Exercises 3 and 4.) This places the top edge of the plate along the line $y = 2$ and the bottom vertex at the point $(0, 5)$. Since the plate's base is 6 units long, it extends 3 units to the right of the y-axis, to the point $(3, 2)$.

To find the width of the plate at a typical depth y, we first find an equation for the line of the plate's right-hand edge. The line passes through $(3, 2)$ and $(0, 5)$ so its slope is

$$m = \frac{\Delta y}{\Delta x} = \frac{5-2}{0-3} = -1.$$

(Don't be put off by the negative slope—the coordinate system is upside down.) The line's y-intercept is 5, so its equation is

$$y = mx + b = -x + 5. \tag{7}$$

If we let x denote the width of the right-hand half of the triangle at depth y, then

$$x = 5 - y \qquad \text{Eq. (7) solved for } x$$

and the total width is

$$L(y) = 2x = 2(5 - y).$$

The force exerted by the water against one side of the plate is therefore

$$\begin{aligned} F &= \int_a^b w \cdot y \cdot L(y)\, dy && \text{Eq. (6)} \\ &= \int_2^5 62.4 \cdot y \cdot 2(5 - y)\, dy && \text{For water, } w = 62.4 \\ &= 124.8 \int_2^5 (5y - y^2)\, dy \\ &= 124.8 \left[\frac{5}{2}y^2 - \frac{1}{3}y^3\right]_2^5 = 1684.8 \text{ lb.} \end{aligned}$$

A coordinate system with the positive y-axis pointing down is not always the most convenient one to use. It is sometimes better to put the origin at the bottom of the plate instead of at the fluid's surface and have the y-axis point up. This changes the factor y in the integrand to some other expression for the depth, but the rest of the integral remains the same. The next expression finds the force in Example 2 with this kind of coordinate system.

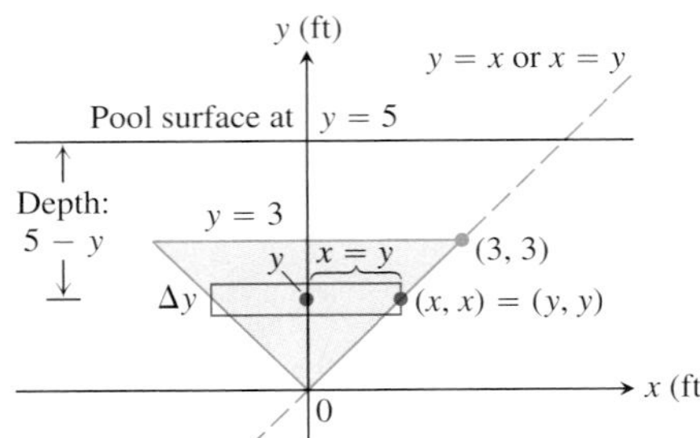

7.57 Example 3 calculates the fluid force in Example 2 using this more convenient coordinate system.

EXAMPLE 3 Find the force exerted by the water on one side of the plate in Example 2 using the coordinate system in Fig. 7.57.

Solution With the origin at the bottom vertex of the plate and the y-axis running upward along the plate's axis of symmetry, the surface of the pool lies along the line $y = 5$ and the top edge of the plate lies along the line $y = 3$. This places the right-hand vertex of the plate at $(3, 3)$. The line of the plate's right-hand edge, being the line through $(0, 0)$ and $(3, 3)$, is now the line $y = x$. The width of a thin strip at level y is now

$$L(y) = 2x = 2y.$$

The depth of the strip beneath the surface is $(5 - y)$. The force exerted by the water against one side of the plate is therefore

$$\begin{aligned}
F &= \int_a^b w \cdot \begin{pmatrix}\text{strip}\\ \text{depth}\end{pmatrix} \cdot L(y)\,dy && \text{Eq. (6), modified}\\
&= \int_0^3 62.4 \cdot (5 - y) \cdot 2y\,dy\\
&= 124.8 \int_0^3 (5y - y^2)\,dy\\
&= 124.8\left[\frac{5}{2}y^2 - \frac{y^3}{3}\right]_0^3 = 1684.8 \text{ lb.}
\end{aligned}$$

How to Find Fluid Force

Whatever coordinate system you use, you can find the fluid force against one side of a submerged vertical plate or wall by taking these steps:

1. Find expressions for the length and depth of a typical thin horizontal strip.
2. Multiply their product by the fluid's weight-density w and integrate over the interval of depths occupied by the plate or wall.

It is sometimes more natural to put the origin of the coordinate system at the bottom of the plate instead of at the fluid's surface.

EXAMPLE 4 We can now calculate exactly the force exerted by the molasses against the bottom 1-ft band of the Puritan Distilling Company's storage tank when the tank was full.

The tank was a right circular cylindrical tank 90 ft high and 90 ft in diameter. Using a coordinate system with the origin at the bottom of the tank and the y-axis pointing up (Fig. 7.58), we find that the typical horizontal strip at level y has

Strip depth: $(90 - y)$,

Strip length: $\pi \times \text{tank diameter} = 90\pi$.

The force against the band is therefore

$$\begin{aligned}
\text{Force} &= \int_0^1 w\,(\text{depth})(\text{length})\,dy = \int_0^1 100(90 - y)(90\pi)\,dy && \text{For molasses, } w = 100\\
&= 9000\pi \int_0^1 (90 - y)\,dy \approx 2{,}530{,}553 \text{ lb.}
\end{aligned}$$

As expected, the force is slightly less than the constant-depth estimate following Example 1.

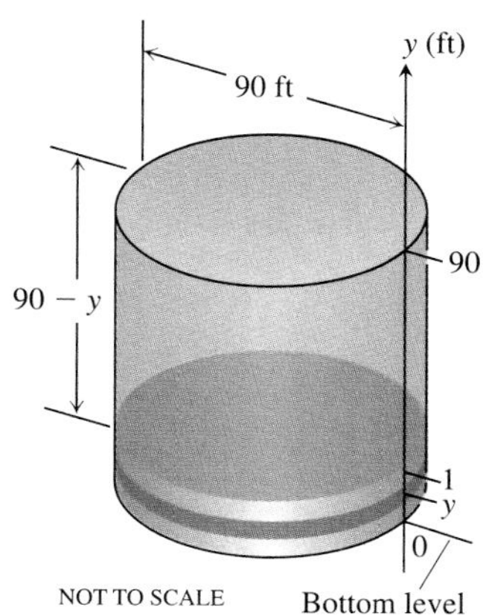

7.58 The molasses tank with the coordinate origin at the bottom (Example 4).

Exercises 7.6

The weight-densities of the fluids in the following exercises can be found in the table on page 480.

1. What was the total fluid force against the cylindrical inside wall of the molasses tank in Example 1 when the tank was full? half full?

2. What was the total fluid force against the bottom 1-ft band of the inside wall of the molasses tank in Example 1 when the tank was half full?

3. Calculate the fluid force on one side of the plate in Example 2 using the coordinate system shown here.

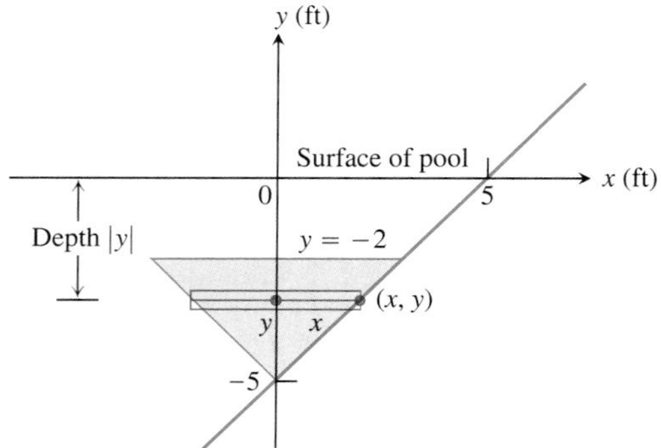

4. Calculate the fluid force on one side of the plate in Example 2 using the coordinate system shown here.

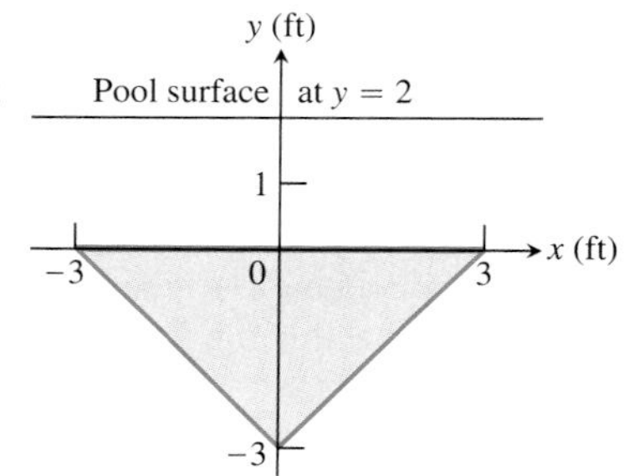

5. The plate in Example 2 is lowered another 2 ft into the water. What is the fluid force on one side of the plate now?

6. The plate in Example 2 is raised to put its top edge at the surface of the pool. What is the fluid force on one side of the plate now?

7. The isosceles triangular plate shown here is submerged vertically 1 ft below the surface of a freshwater lake.
   a) Find the fluid force against one face of the plate.
   b) What would be the fluid force on one side of the plate if the water were seawater instead of freshwater?

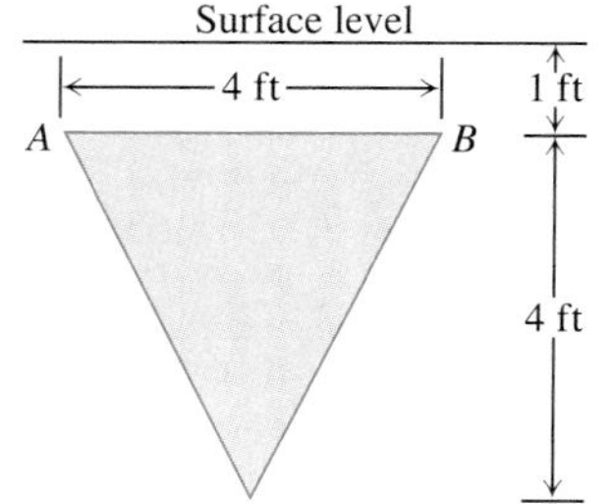

8. The plate in Exercise 7 is revolved 180° about line AB so that part of the plate sticks out of the lake, as shown here. What force does the water exert on one face of the plate now?

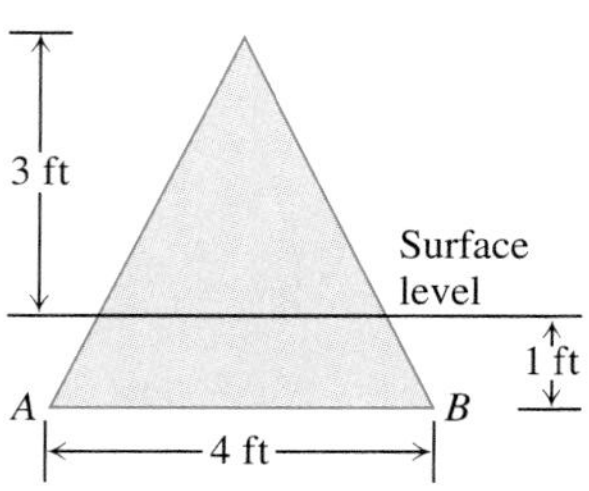

9. The vertical ends of a watering trough are isosceles triangles like the one shown here (dimensions in feet).
   a) Find the fluid force against the ends when the trough is full.
   b) How many inches do you have to lower the water level in the trough to cut the fluid force on the ends in half? (Answer to the nearest half inch.)
   c) Does it matter how long the trough is? Give reasons for your answer.

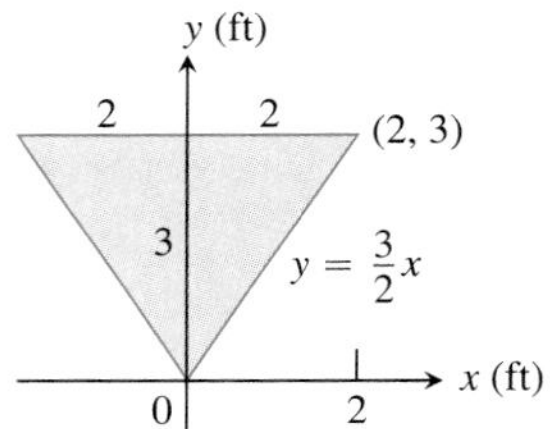

10. The vertical ends of a watering trough are squares 3 ft on a side.
    a) Find the fluid force against the ends when the trough is full.
    b) How many inches do you have to lower the water level in the trough to reduce the fluid force by 25%?
    c) Does it matter how long the trough is? Give reasons for your answer.

11. The viewing portion of the rectangular glass window in a typical fish tank at the New England Aquarium in Boston is 63 in. wide and runs from 0.5 in. below the water's surface to 33.5 in. below the surface. Find the fluid force against this portion of the window. The weight-density of seawater is 64 lb/ft^3. (In case you were wondering, the glass is 3/4 in. thick and the tank walls extend 4 in. above the water to keep the fish from jumping out.)

12. A horizontal rectangular freshwater fish tank of interior dimensions $2 \times 2 \times 4$ ft (shown on the following page) is filled to within 2 in. of the top.
    a) Find the fluid force against each side and end of the tank.
    b) If the tank is sealed and stood on end (without spilling), so that one of the square ends is the base, what does that do to the fluid force on the rectangular sides?

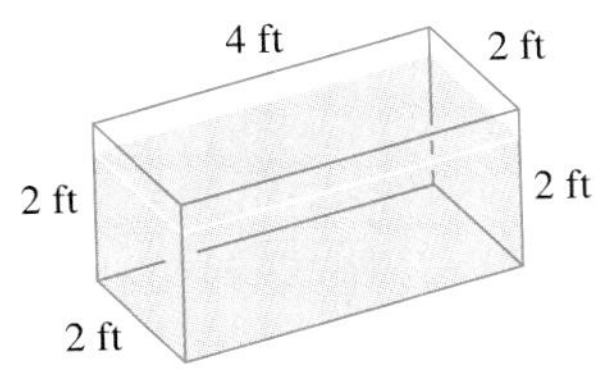

13. A rectangular milk carton measures $3.75 \times 3.75 \times 7.75$ in. Find the force of the milk on one side when the carton is full.

14. A standard olive oil can measures 5.75 by 3.5 by 10 in. Find the fluid force against the base and each side of the can when the can is full.

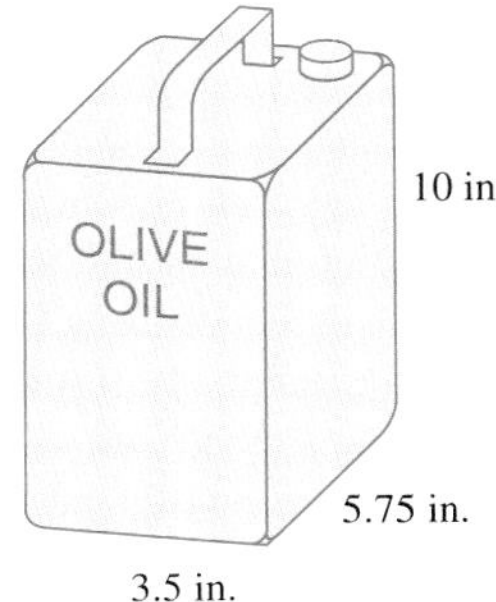

15. The semicircular plate shown here sticks straight down into fresh water with its diameter along the surface. Find the force exerted by the water on one side of the plate.

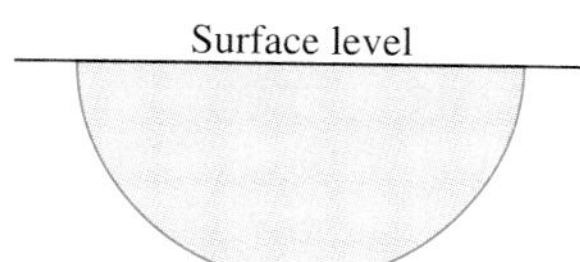

Submerged 2-ft diameter vertical plate

16. A tank truck hauls milk in a 6-ft diameter horizontal right circular cylindrical tank. How much force does the milk exert on each end of the tank when the tank is half full?

17. The cubical metal tank shown here has a parabolic gate, held in place by bolts and designed to withstand a fluid force of 160 lb without rupturing. The liquid you plan to store has a weight-density of 50 lb/ft^3.

a) What is the fluid force on the gate when the liquid is 2 ft deep?

b) What is the maximum height to which the container can be filled without exceeding its design limitation?

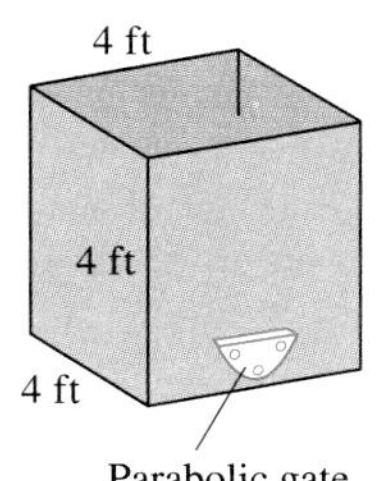

Parabolic gate

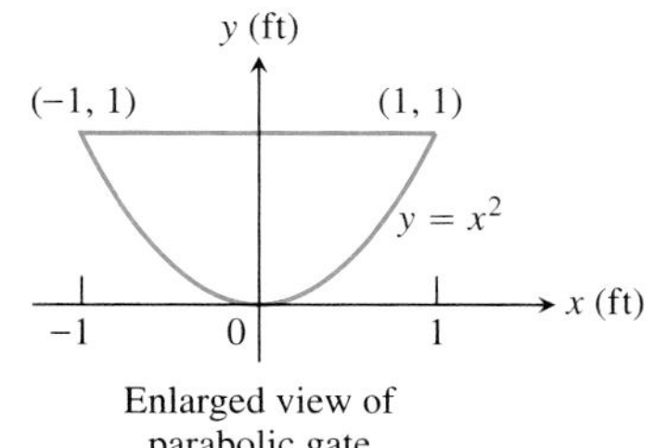

Enlarged view of parabolic gate

18. The rectangular tank shown here has a 1 ft $\times$ 1 ft square window 1 ft above the base. The window is designed to withstand a fluid force of 312 lb without cracking.

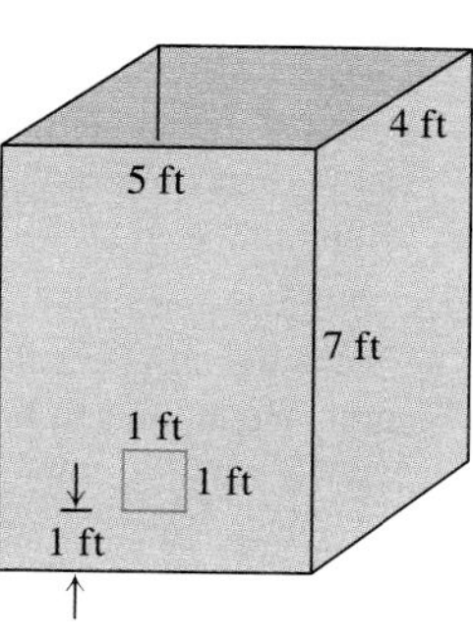

a) What fluid force will the window have to withstand if the tank is filled with water to a depth of 3 ft?

b) To what level can the tank be filled with water without exceeding the window's design limitation?

19. The end plates of the trough shown below were designed to withstand a fluid force of 6667 lb. How many cubic feet of water can the tank hold without exceeding this limitation?

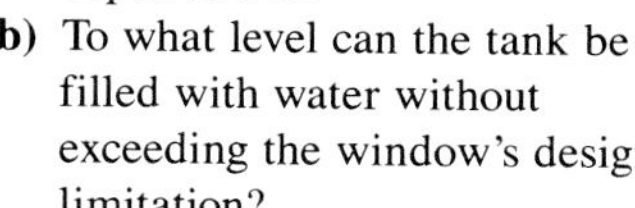

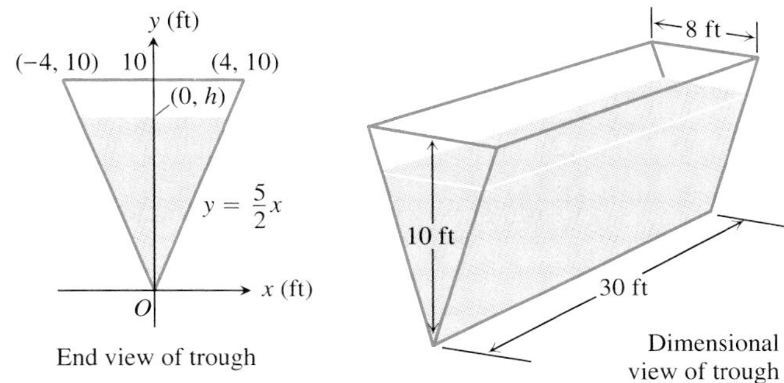

End view of trough

Dimensional view of trough

20. Water is running into the rectangular swimming pool shown below at the rate of 1000 ft^3/h.

a) Find the fluid force against the triangular drain plate after 9 h of filling.

b) The drain plate is designed to withstand a fluid force of 520 lb. How high can you fill the pool without exceeding this limitation?

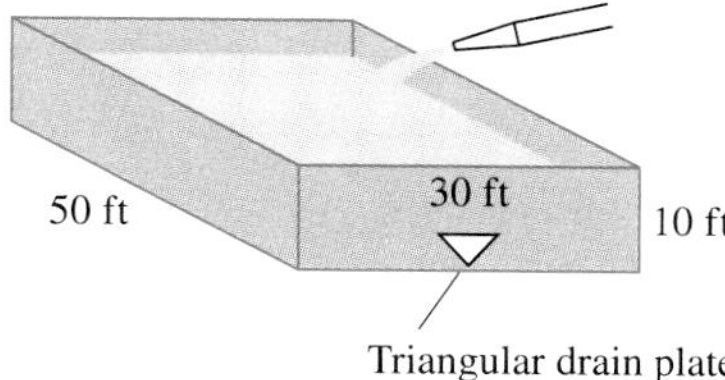

Triangular drain plate

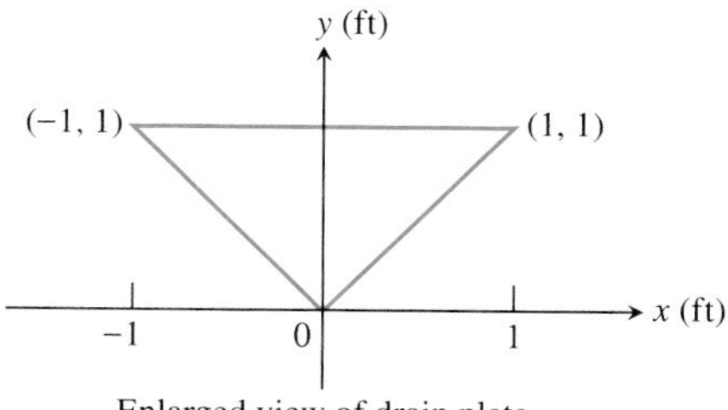

Enlarged view of drain plate

21. A vertical rectangular plate a units long by b units wide is submerged in a fluid of weight density w with its long edges parallel to the fluid's surface. Find the average value of the pressure along the vertical dimension of the plate. Explain your answer.

22. *Continuation of Exercise 21.* Show that the force exerted by the fluid on one side of the plate is the average value of the pressure (found in Exercise 21) times the area of the plate.

Writing for Your Own Knowledge

Answer the following questions in writing. Some answers will take only a sentence or two; others may require several paragraphs. Some explanations may also call for graphs or sketches.

1. How do you find the force exerted by a fluid against the (horizontal) base of a container? against one side of a flat, horizontal submerged plate?
2. How do you use the formula for the fluid force on a constant-depth surface to derive a formula for the force exerted by a fluid against one side of a submerged vertical plate or wall?

7.7 Centers of Mass

Many structures and mechanical systems behave as if their masses were concentrated at a single point called the center of mass (Fig. 7.59). It is important to know how to locate this point, and doing so is basically a mathematical enterprise. For the moment we deal with one- and two-dimensional objects. Three-dimensional objects are best done with the multiple integrals of Chapter 14.

Masses Along a Line

We develop our mathematical model in stages. The first stage is to imagine masses m_1, m_2, and m_3 on a rigid x-axis supported by a fulcrum at the origin.

x_1 O x_2 x_3 x

m_1 m_2 m_3

Fulcrum at origin

The resulting system might balance, or it might not. It depends on how large the masses are and how they are arranged.

Each mass m_k exerts a downward force $m_k g$ equal to the magnitude of the mass times the acceleration of gravity. Each of these forces has a tendency to turn the axis about the origin, the way you turn a seesaw. This turning effect, called a **torque,** is measured by multiplying the force $m_k g$ by the signed distance x_k from the point of application to the origin. Masses to the left of the origin exert negative (counterclockwise) torque. Masses to the right of the origin exert positive (clockwise) torque.

The sum of the torques measures the tendency of a system to rotate about the origin. This sum is called the **system torque.**

$$\text{System torque} = m_1 g x_1 + m_2 g x_2 + m_3 g x_3 \tag{1}$$

The system will balance if and only if its net torque is zero.

If we factor out the g in Eq. (1), we see that the system torque is

$$g(m_1 x_1 + m_2 x_2 + m_3 x_3). \tag{2}$$

a feature of the environment (pointing to g); a feature of the system (pointing to $m_1x_1 + m_2x_2 + m_3x_3$)

Thus the torque is the product of the gravitational acceleration g, which is a feature of the environment in which the system happens to reside, and the number

Mass vs. Weight

Weight is the force that results from gravity pulling on a mass. If an object of mass m is placed in a location where the acceleration of gravity is g, the object's weight there is

$$F = mg$$

(as in Newton's second law).

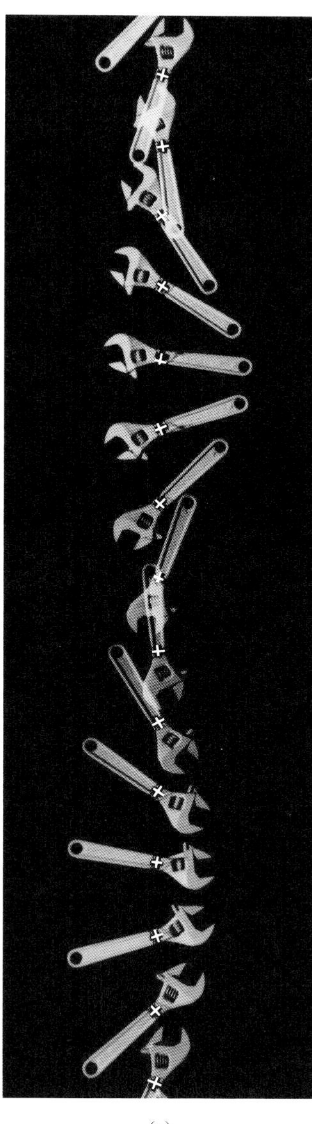

(a)

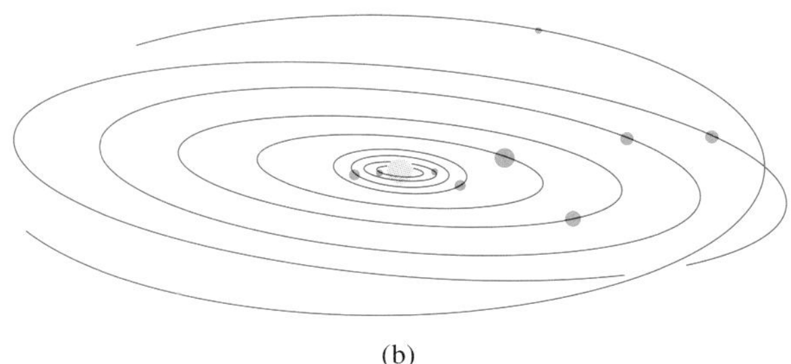

(b)

(c)

(d)

7.59 (a) The motion of this wrench gliding on ice seems haphazard until we notice that the wrench is simply turning about its center of mass as the center glides in a straight line. (b) The planets, asteroids, and comets of our solar system revolve about their collective center of mass. (It lies inside the sun.) (c) This rock balances because its center of mass lies directly above the point where the rock touches the ground. (d) These acrobats stay in place because their collective center of mass lies directly above the wire.

$(m_1x_1 + m_2x_2 + m_3x_3)$, which is a feature of the system itself, a constant that stays the same no matter where the system is placed.

The number $(m_1x_1 + m_2x_2 + m_3x_3)$ is called the **moment of the system about the origin.**

$$M_O = \text{Moment of system about origin } = \sum m_k\, x_k \qquad (3)$$

(We shift to sigma notation here to allow for sums with more terms. For $\sum m_k x_k$, read "summation m_k times x_k.")

We usually want to know where to place the fulcrum to make the system balance, that is, at what point $\bar{x}$ to place it to make the torque zero.

x_1 O x_2 $\bar{x}$ x_3 x

m_1 m_2 m_3

Special location for balance

The torque of each mass about the fulcrum in this special location is

$$\text{Torque of } m_k \text{ about } \bar{x} = \begin{pmatrix}\text{signed distance}\\ \text{of } m_k \text{ from } \bar{x}\end{pmatrix} \cdot \begin{pmatrix}\text{downward}\\ \text{force}\end{pmatrix}$$
$$= (x_k - \bar{x}) \cdot m_k g. \qquad (4)$$

When we write the equation that says that the sum of these torques is zero, we get an equation we can solve for $\bar{x}$:

$$\sum (x_k - \bar{x})m_k g = 0 \qquad \text{Sum of the torques equals zero}$$

$$g \sum (x_k - \bar{x})m_k = 0 \qquad \text{Constant Multiple Rule for Sums}$$

$$\sum (m_k x_k - \bar{x} m_k) = 0 \qquad g \text{ divided out, } m_k \text{ distributed}$$

$$\sum m_k x_k - \sum \bar{x} m_k = 0 \qquad \text{Difference Rule for Sums}$$

$$\sum m_k x_k = \bar{x} \sum m_k \qquad \text{Rearranged, Constant Multiple Rule again}$$

$$\bar{x} = \frac{\sum m_k x_k}{\sum m_k}. \qquad \text{Solved for } \bar{x}$$

This last equation tells us to find $\bar{x}$ by dividing the system's moment about the origin by the system's total mass:

$$\bar{x} = \frac{\sum x_k m_k}{\sum m_k} = \frac{\text{system moment about origin}}{\text{system mass}}. \tag{5}$$

The point $\bar{x}$ is called the system's **center of mass.**

Wires and Thin Rods

In many applications, we want to know the center of mass of a rod or a thin strip of metal. In cases like these where we can model the distribution of mass with a continuous function, the summation signs in our formulas become integrals in a manner we now describe.

Imagine a long, thin strip lying along the x-axis from $x = a$ to $x = b$ and cut into small pieces of mass Δm_k by a partition of the interval $[a, b]$.

x_k x a Δm_k b

Each piece is Δx units long and lies approximately x_k units from the origin. Now observe three things.

First, the strip's center of mass $\bar{x}$ is nearly the same as that of the system of point masses we would get by attaching each mass Δm_k to the point x_k:

$$\bar{x} \approx \frac{\text{system moment}}{\text{system mass}}. \tag{6}$$

Second, the moment of each piece of the strip about the origin is approximately $x_k \Delta m_k$, so the system moment is approximately the sum of the $x_k \Delta m_k$:

$$\text{system moment} \approx \sum x_k \Delta m_k. \tag{7}$$

Third, if the density of the strip at x_k is $\delta(x_k)$, expressed in terms of mass per unit length, and δ is continuous, then Δm_k is approximately equal to $\delta(x_k)\Delta x$ (mass per unit length times length):

$$\Delta m_k \approx \delta(x_k)\Delta x. \tag{8}$$

Density

A material's density is its mass per unit volume. In practice, however, we tend to use units we can conveniently measure. For wires, rods, and narrow strips we use mass per unit length. For flat sheets and plates we use mass per unit area.

Combining these three observations gives

$$\bar{x} \approx \frac{\text{system moment}}{\text{system mass}} \approx \frac{\sum x_k \Delta m_k}{\sum \Delta m_k} \approx \frac{\sum x_k\, \delta(x_k)\Delta x}{\sum \delta(x_k)\Delta x}. \tag{9}$$

The sum in the last numerator in Eq. (9) is a Riemann sum for the continuous function $x\delta(x)$ over the closed interval $[a, b]$. The sum in the denominator is a Riemann sum for the function $\delta(x)$ over this interval. We expect the approximations in (9) to improve as the strip is partitioned more finely and are led to the equation

$$\bar{x} = \frac{\int_a^b x\delta(x)\, dx}{\int_a^b \delta(x)\, dx}. \tag{10}$$

This is the formula we use to find $\bar{x}$.

Moment, Mass, and Center of Mass of a Thin Rod or Strip Along the x-Axis

Moment about the origin: $$M_O = \int_a^b x\delta(x)\, dx \tag{11a}$$

Mass: $$M = \int_a^b \delta(x)\, dx \tag{11b}$$

Center of mass: $$\bar{x} = \frac{M_O}{M} \tag{11c}$$

Equation (11c) says that to find the center of mass of a rod or a thin strip, we divide its moment about the origin by its mass.

EXAMPLE 1 *Strips and Rods of Constant Density.* Show that the center of mass of a straight, thin strip or rod of constant density lies halfway between its two ends.

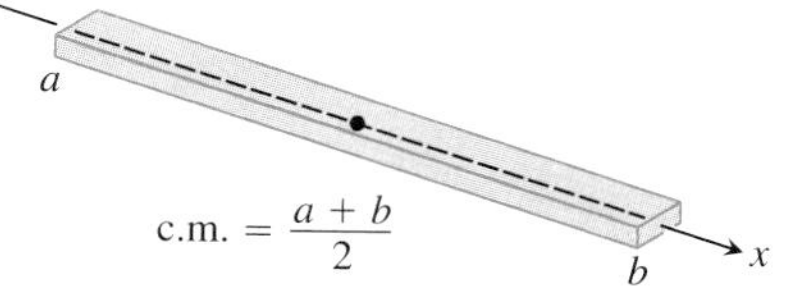

7.60 The center of mass of a straight, thin rod or strip of constant density lies halfway between its ends.

Solution We model the strip as a portion of the x-axis from $x = a$ to $x = b$ (Fig. 7.60). Our goal is to show that $\bar{x} = (a + b)/2$, the point halfway between a and b.

The key is the density's having a constant value. This enables us to regard the function $\delta(x)$ in the integrals in Eqs. (11) as a constant (call it δ), with the result that

$$M_O = \int_a^b \delta x\, dx = \delta \int_a^b x\, dx = \delta\left[\frac{1}{2}x^2\right]_a^b = \frac{\delta}{2}(b^2 - a^2),$$

$$M = \int_a^b \delta\, dx = \delta \int_a^b dx = \delta\Big[x\Big]_a^b = \delta(b - a),$$

$$\bar{x} = \frac{M_O}{M} = \frac{\frac{\delta}{2}(b^2 - a^2)}{\delta(b - a)} = \frac{a + b}{2}.$$

The δ's cancel in the formula for $\bar{x}$.

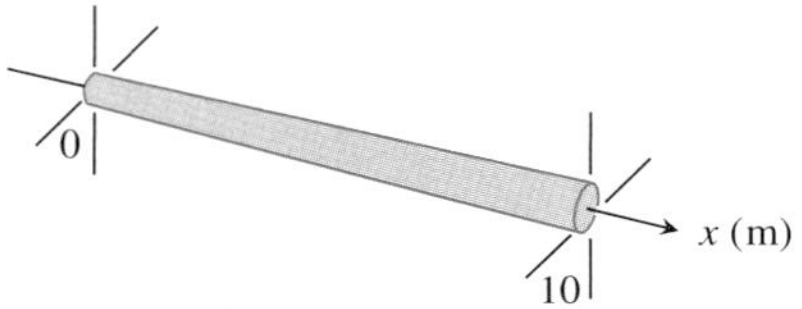

7.61 We can treat a rod of variable thickness as a rod of variable density. See Example 2.

EXAMPLE 2 *A Variable Density.* The 10-m-long rod in Fig. 7.61 thickens from left to right so that its density, instead of being constant, is $\delta(x) = 1 + (x/10)$ kg/m. Find the rod's center of mass.

Solution The rod's moment about the origin (Eq. 11a) is

$$M_O = \int_0^{10} x\delta(x)\,dx = \int_0^{10} x\left(1 + \frac{x}{10}\right) dx = \int_0^{10} \left(x + \frac{x^2}{10}\right) dx$$

$$= \left[\frac{x^2}{2} + \frac{x^3}{30}\right]_0^{10} = 50 + \frac{100}{3} = \frac{250}{3}\text{ kg}\cdot\text{m}.$$

The units of a moment are mass × length.

The rod's mass (Eq. 11b) is

$$M = \int_0^{10} \delta(x)\,dx = \int_0^{10} \left(1 + \frac{x}{10}\right) dx = \left[x + \frac{x^2}{20}\right]_0^{10} = 10 + 5 = 15\text{ kg}.$$

The center of mass (Eq. 11c) is located at the point

$$\bar{x} = \frac{M_O}{M} = \frac{250}{3} \cdot \frac{1}{15} = \frac{50}{9} \approx 5.56\text{ m}.$$

Masses Distributed over a Plane Region

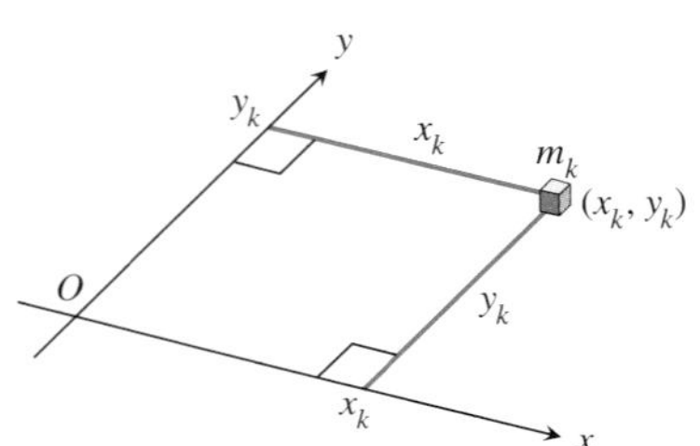

7.62 Each mass m_k has a moment about each axis.

Suppose we have a finite collection of masses located in the coordinate plane, the mass m_k being located at the point (x_k, y_k) (see Fig. 7.62). The total mass of the system is

$$\text{System mass:} \qquad M = \sum m_k.$$

Each mass m_k has a moment about each axis. Its moment about the x-axis is $m_k y_k$, and its moment about the y-axis is $m_k x_k$. The moments of the entire system about the two axes are

$$\text{Moment about } x\text{-axis:} \qquad M_x = \sum m_k y_k,$$

$$\text{Moment about } y\text{-axis:} \qquad M_y = \sum m_k x_k.$$

The x-coordinate of the system's center of mass is defined to be

$$\bar{x} = \frac{M_y}{M} = \frac{\sum m_k x_k}{\sum m_k}. \tag{12}$$

With this choice of $\bar{x}$, as in the one-dimensional case, the system balances about the line $x = \bar{x}$ (Fig. 7.63).

The y-coordinate of the system's center of mass is defined to be

$$\bar{y} = \frac{M_x}{M} = \frac{\sum m_k y_k}{\sum m_k}. \tag{13}$$

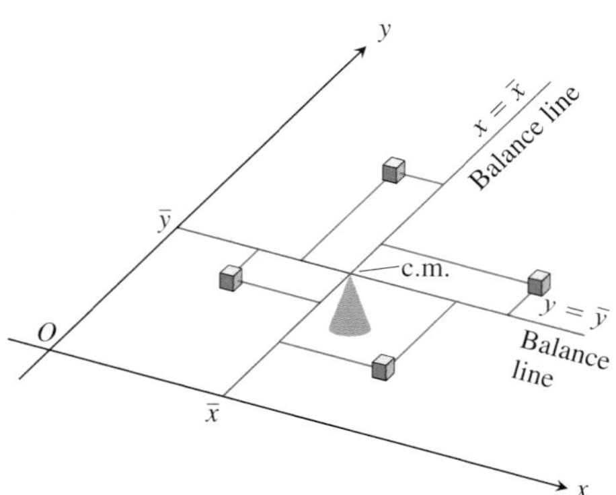

7.63 A two-dimensional array of masses balances on its center of mass.

With this choice of $\bar{y}$, the system balances about the line $y = \bar{y}$ as well. The torques exerted by the masses about the line $y = \bar{y}$ cancel out. Thus, as far as balance is concerned, the system behaves as if all its mass were at the single point $(\bar{x}, \bar{y})$. We call this point the system's center of mass.

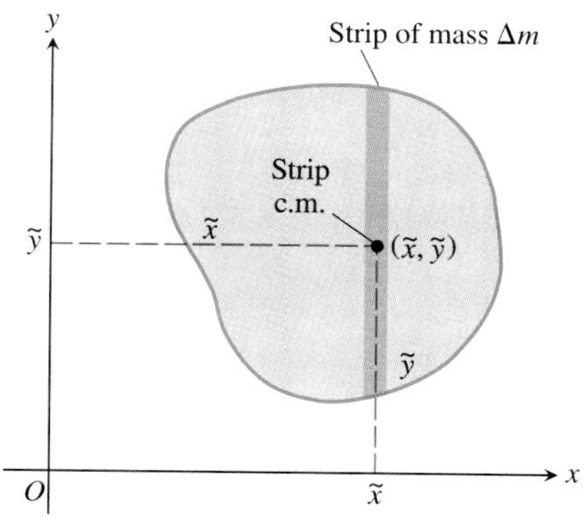

7.64 A plate cut into thin strips parallel to the y-axis. The moment exerted by a typical strip about each axis is the moment its mass Δm would exert if concentrated at the strip's center of mass $(\tilde{x}, \tilde{y})$.

The symbol ~ over the x and y is a *tilde,* pronounced to rhyme with "Hilda." Thus $\tilde{x}$ is read "x tilde."

Thin, Flat Plates

In many applications, we need to find the center of mass of a thin, flat plate: a disk of aluminum, say, or a triangular sheet of steel. In such cases we assume the distribution of mass to be continuous, and the formulas we use to calculate $\bar{x}$ and $\bar{y}$ contain integrals instead of finite sums. The integrals arise in the following way.

Imagine the plate occupying a region in the xy-plane, cut into thin strips parallel to one of the axes (in Fig. 7.64, the y-axis). The center of mass of a typical strip is $(\tilde{x}, \tilde{y})$. We treat the strip's mass Δm as if it were concentrated at $(\tilde{x}, \tilde{y})$. The moment of the strip about the y-axis is then $\tilde{x}\,\Delta m$. The moment of the strip about the x-axis is $\tilde{y}\,\Delta m$. Equations (12) and (13) then become

$$\bar{x} = \frac{M_y}{M} = \frac{\sum \tilde{x}\,\Delta m}{\sum \Delta m}, \qquad \bar{y} = \frac{M_x}{M} = \frac{\sum \tilde{y}\,\Delta m}{\sum \Delta m}. \tag{14}$$

As in the one-dimensional case, the sums in the numerator and denominator are Riemann sums for integrals and approach these integrals as limiting values as the strips into which the plate is cut become narrower and narrower. We write these integrals symbolically as

$$\bar{x} = \frac{\int \tilde{x}\,dm}{\int dm} \quad \text{and} \quad \bar{y} = \frac{\int \tilde{y}\,dm}{\int dm}. \tag{15}$$

Moments, Mass, and Center of Mass of a Thin Plate Covering a Region in the xy-Plane

Moment about the x-axis: $\quad M_x = \int \tilde{y}\,dm$

Moment about the y-axis: $\quad M_y = \int \tilde{x}\,dm \qquad (16)$

Mass: $\quad M = \int dm$

Center of mass: $\quad \bar{x} = \dfrac{M_y}{M}, \quad \bar{y} = \dfrac{M_x}{M}$

To evaluate these integrals, we picture the plate in the coordinate plane and sketch a strip of mass parallel to one of the coordinate axes. We then express the strip's mass dm and the coordinates $(\tilde{x}, \tilde{y})$ of the strip's center of mass in terms of x or y. Finally, we integrate $\tilde{y}\,dm$, $\tilde{x}\,dm$, and dm between limits of integration determined by the plate's location in the plane.

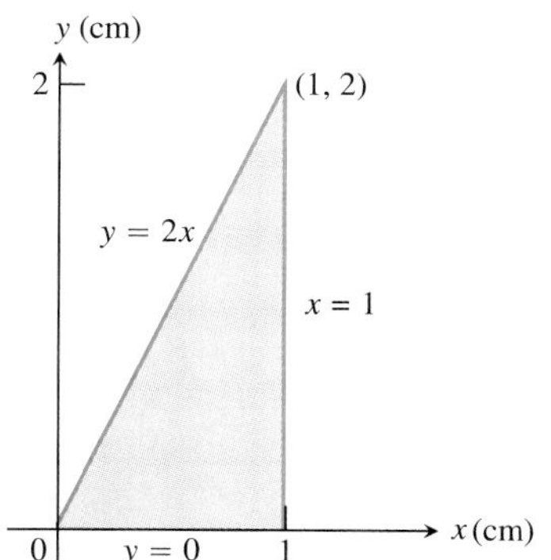

7.65 The plate in Example 3.

EXAMPLE 3 The triangular plate shown in Fig. 7.65 has a constant density of $\delta = 3$ g/cm^2. Find (a) the plate's moment M_y about the y-axis, (b) the plate's mass M, and (c) the x-coordinate of the plate's center of mass.

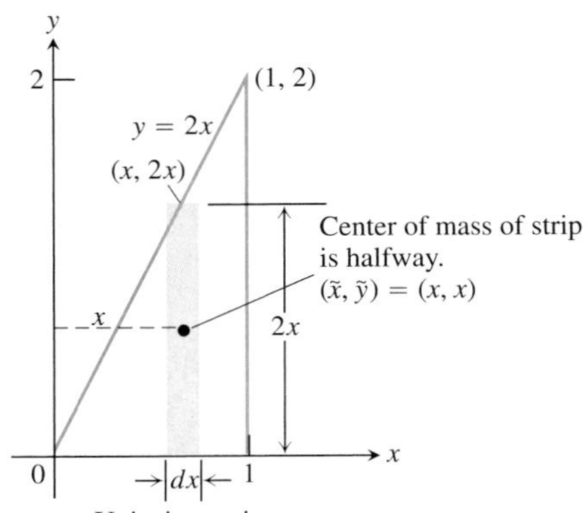

7.66 Modeling the plate in Example 3 with vertical strips.

Solution

METHOD 1: *Vertical strips* (Fig. 7.66).

a) The moment M_y: The typical vertical strip has center of mass (c.m.): $(\tilde{x}, \tilde{y}) = (x, x)$,

length: $2x$, area: $dA = 2x\,dx$,

width: dx, mass: $dm = \delta\,dA = 3 \cdot 2x\,dx = 6x\,dx$,

distance of c.m. from y-axis: $\tilde{x} = x$.

The moment of the strip about the y-axis is

$$\tilde{x}\,dm = x \cdot 6x\,dx = 6x^2\,dx.$$

The moment of the plate about the y-axis is therefore

$$M_y = \int \tilde{x}\,dm = \int_0^1 6x^2\,dx = 2x^3\Big]_0^1 = 2\text{ g}\cdot\text{cm}.$$

b) The plate's mass:

$$M = \int dm = \int_0^1 6x\,dx = 3x^2\Big]_0^1 = 3\text{ g}.$$

c) The x-coordinate of the plate's center of mass:

$$\bar{x} = \frac{M_y}{M} = \frac{2\text{ g}\cdot\text{cm}}{3\text{ g}} = \frac{2}{3}\text{ cm}.$$

By a similar computation we could find M_x and $\bar{y} = M_x/M$.

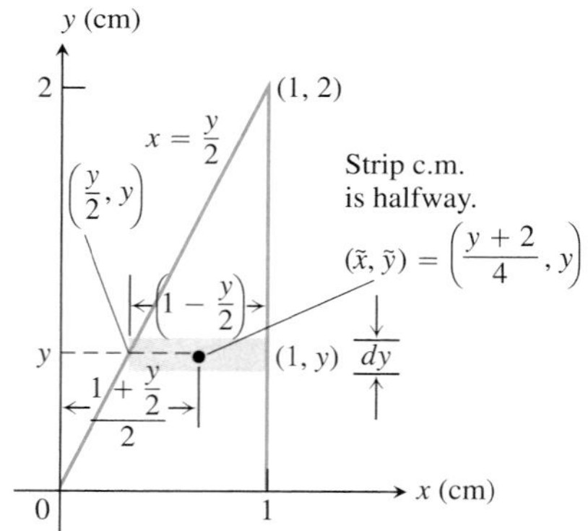

7.67 Modeling the plate in Example 3 with horizontal strips.

METHOD 2: *Horizontal strips* (Fig. 7.67)

a) The moment M_y: The y-coordinate of the center of mass of a typical horizontal strip is y (see the figure), so

$$\tilde{y} = y.$$

The x-coordinate is the x-coordinate of the point halfway across the triangle. This makes it the average of $y/2$ (the strip's left-hand x-value) and 1 (the strip's right-hand x-value):

$$\tilde{x} = \frac{(y/2) + 1}{2} = \frac{y}{4} + \frac{1}{2} = \frac{y+2}{4}.$$

We also have:

length: $1 - \dfrac{y}{2} = \dfrac{2-y}{2}$,

width: dy,

area: $dA = \dfrac{2-y}{2}\,dy$,

mass: $dm = \delta\,dA = 3 \cdot \dfrac{2-y}{2}\,dy$,

distance of c.m. to y-axis: $\tilde{x} = \dfrac{y+2}{4}$.

The moment of the strip about the y-axis is

$$\tilde{x}\,dm = \frac{y+2}{4} \cdot 3 \cdot \frac{2-y}{2}\,dy = \frac{3}{8}(4-y^2)\,dy.$$

The moment of the plate about the y-axis is

$$M_y = \int \tilde{x}\,dm = \int_0^2 \frac{3}{8}(4-y^2)\,dy = \frac{3}{8}\left[4y - \frac{y^3}{3}\right]_0^2 = \frac{3}{8}\left(\frac{16}{3}\right) = 2\text{ g} \cdot \text{cm}.$$

b) The plate's mass:

$$M = \int dm = \int_0^2 \frac{3}{2}(2-y)\,dy = \frac{3}{2}\left[2y - \frac{y^2}{2}\right]_0^2 = \frac{3}{2}(4-2) = 3\text{ g}.$$

c) The x-coordinate of the plate's center of mass:

$$\bar{x} = \frac{M_y}{M} = \frac{2\text{ g} \cdot \text{cm}}{3\text{ g}} = \frac{2}{3}\text{ cm}.$$

By a similar computation, we could find M_x and $\bar{y}$.

How to Find a Plate's Center of Mass

1. Picture the plate in the xy-plane.
2. Sketch a strip of mass parallel to one of the coordinate axes and find its dimensions.
3. Find the strip's mass dm and center of mass $(\tilde{x}, \tilde{y})$.
4. Integrate $\tilde{y}\,dm$, $\tilde{x}\,dm$, and dm to find M_x, M_y, and M.
5. Divide the moments by the mass to calculate $\bar{x}$ and $\bar{y}$.

If the distribution of mass in a thin, flat plate has an axis of symmetry, the center of mass will lie on this axis. If there are two axes of symmetry, the center of mass will lie at their intersection. These facts often help to simplify our work.

EXAMPLE 4 Find the center of mass of a thin plate of constant density δ covering the region bounded above by the parabola $y = 4 - x^2$ and below by the x-axis (Fig. 7.68).

Solution Since the plate is symmetric about the y-axis and its density is constant, the distribution of mass is symmetric about the y-axis and the center of mass lies on the y-axis. This means that $\bar{x} = 0$. It remains to find $\bar{y} = M_x/M$.

A trial calculation with horizontal strips (Fig. 7.68a) leads to an inconvenient integration:

$$M_x = \int_0^4 2\delta y\sqrt{4-y}\,dy.$$

We therefore model the distribution of mass with vertical strips instead (Fig. 7.68b). The typical vertical strip has

center of mass (c.m.): $(\tilde{x}, \tilde{y}) = \left(x, \dfrac{4-x^2}{2}\right)$,

length: $4 - x^2$,

width: dx,

area: $dA = (4-x^2)\,dx$,

mass: $dm = \delta\,dA = \delta(4-x^2)\,dx$,

distance from c.m. to x-axis: $\tilde{y} = \dfrac{4-x^2}{2}$.

The moment of the strip about the x-axis is

$$\tilde{y}\,dm = \frac{4-x^2}{2} \cdot \delta(4-x^2)\,dx = \frac{\delta}{2}(4-x^2)^2\,dx.$$

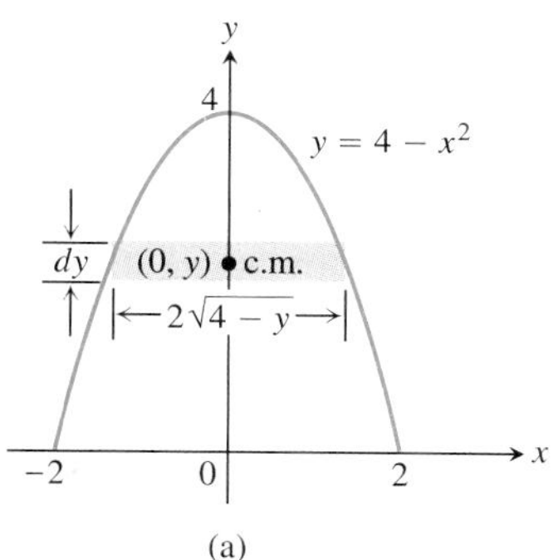

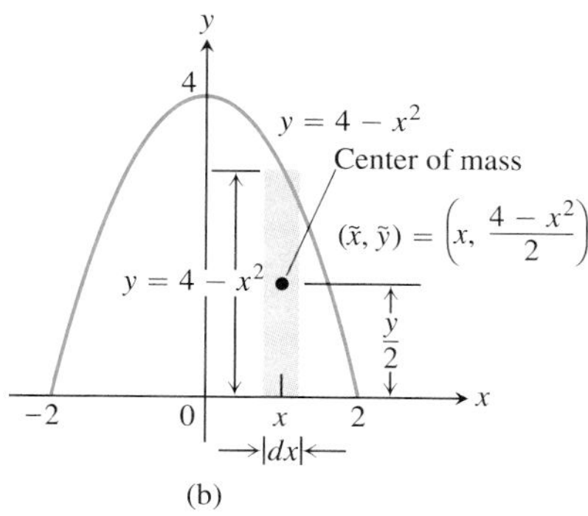

7.68 Modeling the plate in Example 4 with (a) horizontal strips leads to an inconvenient integration, so we model with (b) vertical strips instead.

The moment of the plate about the x-axis is

$$M_x = \int \tilde{y}\, dm = \int_{-2}^{2} \frac{\delta}{2}(4 - x^2)^2\, dx$$
$$= \frac{\delta}{2}\int_{-2}^{2} (16 - 8x^2 + x^4)\, dx = \frac{256}{15}\,\delta. \tag{17}$$

The mass of the plate is

$$M = \int dm = \int_{-2}^{2} \delta\,(4 - x^2)\, dx = \frac{32}{3}\,\delta. \tag{18}$$

Therefore,

$$\bar{y} = \frac{M_x}{M} = \frac{\frac{256}{15}\,\delta}{\frac{32}{3}\,\delta} = \frac{8}{5}.$$

The plate's center of mass is the point

$$(\bar{x}, \bar{y}) = \left(0, \frac{8}{5}\right).$$

EXAMPLE 5 *Variable Density.* Find the center of mass of the plate in Example 4 if the density at the point (x, y) is $\delta = 2x^2$, twice the square of the distance from the point to the y-axis.

Solution The mass distribution is still symmetric about the y-axis, so $\bar{x} = 0$. With $\delta = 2x^2$, Eqs. (17) and (18) become

$$M_x = \int \tilde{y}\, dm = \int_{-2}^{2} \frac{\delta}{2}(4 - x^2)^2\, dx = \int_{-2}^{2} x^2(4 - x^2)^2\, dx$$
$$= \int_{-2}^{2} (16x^2 - 8x^4 + x^6)\, dx = \frac{2048}{105}, \tag{17'}$$

$$M = \int dm = \int_{-2}^{2} \delta(4 - x^2)\, dx = \int_{-2}^{2} 2x^2(4 - x^2)\, dx$$
$$= \int_{-2}^{2} (8x^2 - 2x^4)\, dx = \frac{256}{15}. \tag{18'}$$

Therefore,

$$\bar{y} = \frac{M_x}{M} = \frac{2048}{105} \cdot \frac{15}{256} = \frac{8}{7}.$$

The plate's new center of mass is

$$(\bar{x}, \bar{y}) = \left(0, \frac{8}{7}\right).$$

Centroids

When the density function is constant, it cancels out of the numerator and denominator of the formulas for $\bar{x}$ and $\bar{y}$. (This happened in nearly every example in this section.) Thus, when the density is constant, the location of the center of mass is a feature of the geometry of the object and not of the material from which it is made. In such cases engineers may call the center of mass the **centroid** of the shape, as in "Find the centroid of a triangle or a solid cone." To do so, just set δ equal to 1 and proceed to find $\bar{x}$ and $\bar{y}$ as before, by dividing moments by masses.

Exercises 7.7

1. Two children are balancing on a seesaw. The 80-lb child is 5 ft from the fulcrum. How far from the fulcrum is the 100-lb child?

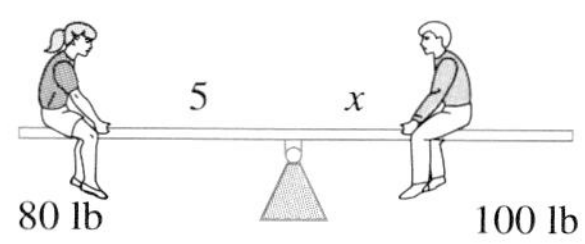

2. The ends of two thin steel rods of equal length are welded together to make a right-angled frame. Locate the frame's center of mass. (*Hint:* Where is the center of mass of each rod?)

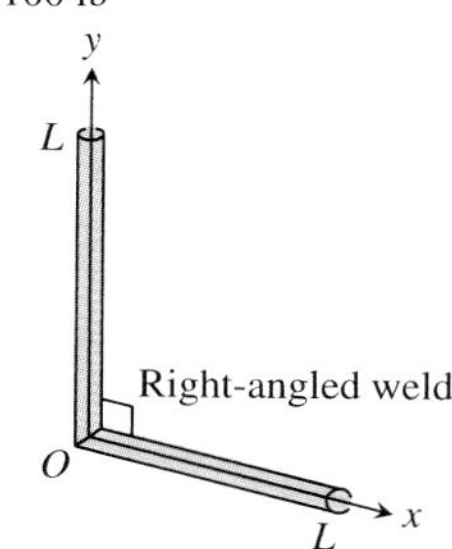

Exercises 3–10 give density functions of thin rods lying along various intervals of the x-axis. Use Eqs. (11a–c) to find each rod's moment about the origin, mass, and center of mass.

3. $\delta(x) = 4, \quad 0 \le x \le 2$

4. $\delta(x) = 4, \quad 1 \le x \le 3$

5. $\delta(x) = 1 + (x/3), \quad 0 \le x \le 3$

6. $\delta(x) = 2 - (x/4), \quad 0 \le x \le 4$

7. $\delta(x) = 1 + (1/x), \quad 1 \le x \le 4$

8. $\delta(x) = (2/x) + (1/x^2), \quad 0.5 \le x \le 1$

9. $\delta(x) = \begin{cases} 2 - x, & 0 \le x \le 1 \\ x, & 1 \le x \le 2 \end{cases}$

10. $\delta(x) = \begin{cases} x + 1, & 0 \le x \le 1 \\ 2, & 1 \le x \le 2 \end{cases}$

In Exercises 11–22, find the center of mass of a thin plate of constant density δ covering the given region.

11. The region bounded by the parabola $y = x^2$ and the line $y = 4$

12. The region bounded by the parabola $y = 25 - x^2$ and the x-axis

13. The region bounded by the parabola $y = x - x^2$ and the line $y = -x$

14. The region enclosed by the parabolas $y = x^2 - 3$ and $y = -2x^2$

15. The region bounded by the y-axis and the curve $x = y - y^3$, $0 \le y \le 1$

16. The region bounded by the parabola $x = y^2 - y$ and the line $y = x$

17. The region bounded by the x-axis and the curve $y = \cos x$, $-\pi/2 \le x \le \pi/2$

18. The region between the x-axis and the curve $y = \sec x$, $-\pi/4 \le x \le \pi/4$

19. The region bounded by the parabolas $y = 2x^2 - 4x$ and $y = 2x - x^2$

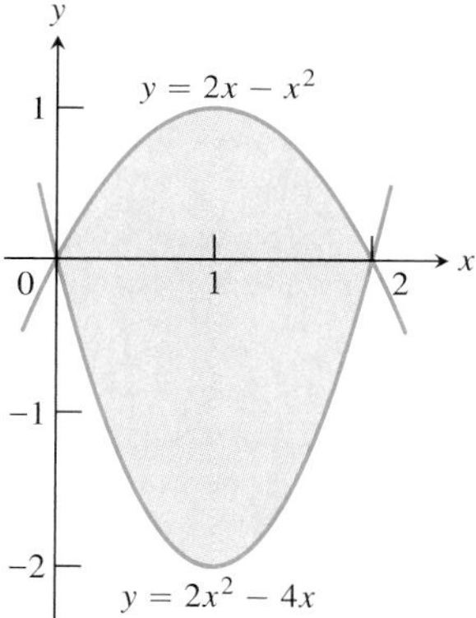

20. **a)** The region cut from the first quadrant by the circle $x^2 + y^2 = 9$

b) The region bounded by the x-axis and the semicircle $y = \sqrt{9 - x^2}$

Compare your answer with the answer in (a).

21. The "triangular" region in the first quadrant between the circle $x^2 + y^2 = 9$ and the lines $x = 3$ and $y = 3$. (*Hint:* Use geometry to find the area.)

22. The region bounded above by the curve $y = 1/x^3$, below by the curve $y = -1/x^3$, and on the left and right by the lines $x = 1$ and $x = a > 1$. Also, find $\lim_{a \to \infty} \bar{x}$.

23. **a)** Find the centroid of the region between the curve $y = 1/x$ and the x-axis from $x = 1$ to $x = 2$.

b) Find the centroid's coordinates to two decimal places. Then sketch the region and show the centroid in your sketch.

24. a) Find the center of mass of a thin plate of constant density covering the region bounded by the curves $y = 1/(1+x^2)$ and $y = -1/(1+x^2)$ and by the lines $x = 0$ and $x = 1$.

b) Find the coordinates of the center of mass to two decimal places. Then show the location of the center of mass in a sketch of the region.

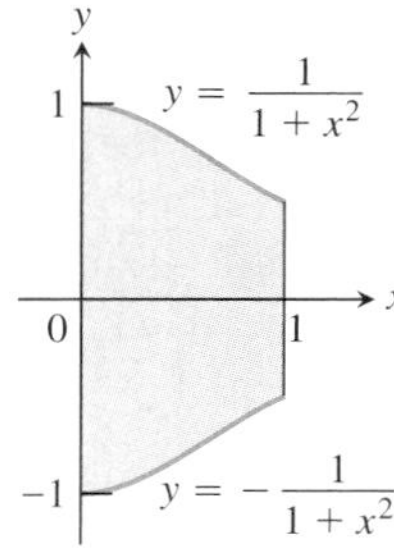

25. Find the center of mass of a thin plate covering the region between the x-axis and the curve $y = 2/x^2$, $1 \le x \le 2$, if the plate's density at the point (x, y) is $\delta(x) = x^3$.

26. Find the center of mass of a thin plate covering the region bounded below by the parabola $y = x^2$ and above by the line $y = x$ if the plate's density at the point (x, y) is $\delta(x) = 12x$.

27. The region bounded by the curves $y = \pm 4/\sqrt{x}$ and the lines $x = 1$ and $x = 4$ is revolved about the y-axis to generate a solid.

a) Find the volume of the solid.

b) Find the center of mass of a thin plate covering the region if the plate's density at the point (x, y) is $\delta(x) = 2/\sqrt{x}$.

c) Find the coordinates of the plate's center of mass to two decimal places. Then sketch the plate and show the center of mass in your sketch.

28. The region between the curve $y = 2/x$ and the x-axis from $x = 1/2$ to $x = 4$ is revolved about the x-axis to generate a solid.

a) Find the volume of the solid.

b) Find the center of mass of a thin plate covering the region if the plate's density at the point (x, y) is $\delta(x) = x$.

c) Find the coordinates of the plate's center of mass to two decimal places. Then sketch the plate and show the center of mass in your sketch.

CENTROIDS OF TRIANGLES

It can be shown that the centroid of a triangle lies at the intersection of the medians, one third of the way from the midpoint of each side toward the opposite vertex. Use this fact to find the centroids of the triangles whose vertices appear in Exercises 29–32. (*Hint:* Sketch each triangle first.)

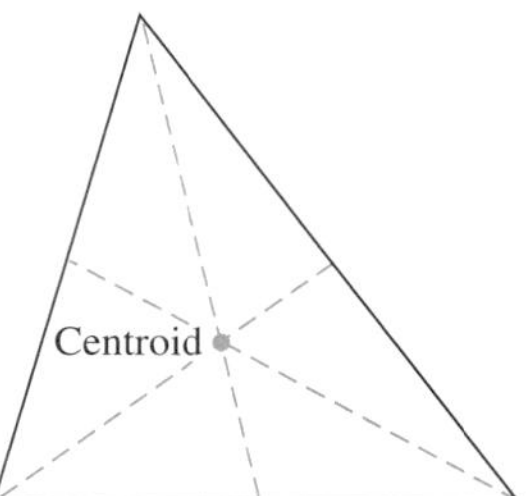

29. $(-1, 0)$, $(1, 0)$, $(0, 3)$

30. $(0, 0)$, $(1, 0)$, $(0, 1)$

31. $(0, 0)$, $(a, 0)$, $(0, a)$; $a > 0$

32. $(0, 0)$, $(a, 0)$, $(0, b)$; $a, b > 0$

PAPPUS'S THEOREMS

In the third century A.D., an Alexandrian Greek named Pappus discovered two formulas that relate centroids to surfaces and solids of revolution. The formulas stated below provide shortcuts to a number of otherwise lengthy calculations.

Pappus's Theorem for Volumes

If a plane region is revolved once about a line in the plane that does not cut through the region's interior, then the volume of the solid it generates equals the region's area times the distance traveled by the region's centroid during the revolution. If ρ is the distance from the axis of revolution to the centroid, then

$$V = 2\pi \rho A. \tag{1}$$

Pappus's Theorem for Surface Areas

If an arc of a smooth plane curve is revolved once about a line in the plane that does not cut through the arc's interior, then the area of the surface generated by the arc equals the length of the arc times the distance traveled by the arc's centroid during the revolution. If ρ is the distance from the axis of revolution to the centroid, then

$$S = 2\pi \rho L. \tag{2}$$

EXAMPLE The volume of the solid torus (doughnut) generated by revolving a circular disk of radius a about an axis in its plane at a distance $b \ge a$ from its center is

$$V = 2\pi \rho A = 2\pi (b)(\pi a^2) = 2\pi^2 ba^2.$$

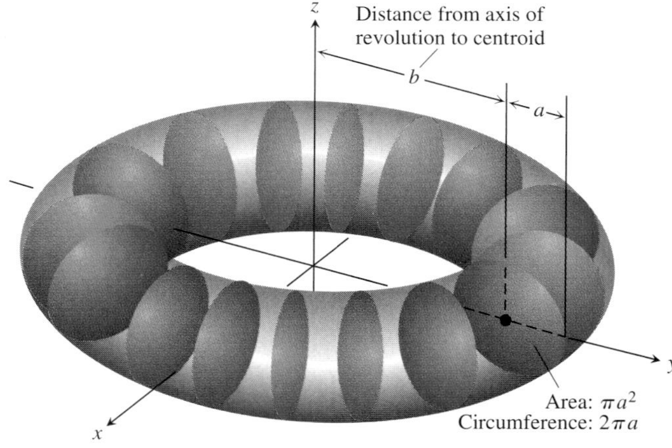

The surface of the torus is generated by the disk's bounding circle. The surface area of the torus is the product of the circumference of the circle and the distance traveled by the centroid:

$$S = 2\pi \rho L = 2\pi (b)(2\pi a) = 4\pi^2 ba.$$

33. The square region with vertices (0, 2), (2, 0), (4, 2) and (2, 4) is revolved about the x-axis to generate a solid. Find the volume and surface area of the solid.

34. Use a theorem of Pappus to find the volume generated by revolving about the line $x = 5$ the triangular region bounded by the coordinate axes and the line $2x + y = 6$. (The centroid of a triangle lies at the intersection of the medians, one third of the way from the midpoint of each side toward the opposite vertex.)

35. Find the volume of the torus generated by revolving the circle $(x - 2)^2 + y^2 = 1$ about the y-axis.

36. Use the theorems of Pappus to find the lateral surface area and the volume of a right circular cone.

37. Use Pappus's surface area theorem and the fact that the surface area of a sphere of radius a is $4\pi a^2$ to find the centroid of the semicircle $y = \sqrt{a^2 - x^2}$.

38. As found in Exercise 37, the centroid of the semicircle $y = \sqrt{a^2 - x^2}$ lies at the point $(0, 2a/\pi)$. Find the area of the surface swept out by revolving the semicircle about the line $y = a$.

Writing for Your Own Knowledge

Answer the following questions in writing. Some answers will take only a sentence or two; others may require several paragraphs. Some explanations may also call for graphs or sketches.

1. How are an object's mass and weight related?
2. When a finite number of masses are distributed along a coordinate line, what is the system's
   a) torque about the origin?
   b) moment about the origin?
   c) center of mass?
3. How do you find the center of mass of a thin rod or strip of material along the x-axis?
4. How do you find the center of mass of a thin plate covering a finite region of the xy-plane?
5. What is a centroid?

7.8 *The Basic Pattern and Other Modeling Applications*

There is a pattern to what we have been doing in the preceding sections. In each section we wanted to measure something that was modeled or described by one or more continuous functions. In Section 7.1 it was the area between the graphs of two continuous functions. In Section 7.2 it was the volume of a solid. In Section 7.5 it was the work done by a force whose magnitude was a continuous function, and so on. In each case we responded by partitioning the interval on which the function or functions were defined and approximating what we wanted to measure with Riemann sums over the interval. We then used the integral defined by the limit of the Riemann sums to define and calculate what we wanted to measure. Table 7.2 (on the following page) shows the pattern.

Literally thousands of things in biology, chemistry, economics, engineering, finance, geology, medicine, and other fields (the list would fill pages) are modeled and calculated by exactly this process.

In this section we review the process and look at a few more of the integrals it leads to.

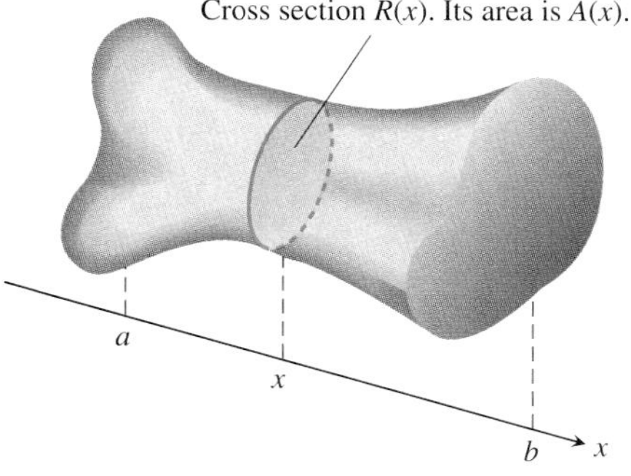

7.69 If the area $A(x)$ of the cross section $R(x)$ is a continuous function of x, we can find the volume of the solid by integrating $A(x)$ from a to b.

Volumes of Arbitrary Solids: Slicing

From the areas of regions with curved boundaries we can calculate the volumes of cylinders with curved bases by multiplying base area by height. From the volumes of such cylinders, we can calculate the volumes of other new solids.

Suppose we want to find the volume of a solid like the one shown in Fig. 7.69. The solid lies between planes perpendicular to the x-axis at $x = a$ and $x = b$. Each cross section of the solid by a plane perpendicular to the x-axis is a region whose area we know how to find. Specifically, at each point x in the closed interval $[a, b]$ the cross section of the solid is a region $R(x)$ whose area is $A(x)$. This makes A a real-valued function of x. If it is also a continuous function of x, we can use it to define and calculate the volume of the solid as an integral in the following way.

TABLE 7.2
The phases of developing an integral to calculate something

Phase I	Phase 2	Phase 3
We describe or model something we want to measure in terms of one or more continuous functions defined on a closed interval $[a, b]$.	We partition $[a, b]$ into subintervals of length Δx_k and choose a point c_k in each subinterval. We approximate what we want to measure with a finite sum. We identify the sum as a Riemann sum of a continuous function over $[a, b]$.	The approximations improve as the norm of the partition goes to zero. The Riemann sums approach a limiting integral. We use the integral to define and calculate what we originally wanted to measure.
The area between the curves $y = f(x)$, $y = g(x)$ on $[a, b]$ when $f(x) \geq g(x)$	$\sum [f(c_k) - g(c_k)]\, \Delta x_k$	$A = \lim_{\|P\| \to 0} \sum [f(c_k) - g(c_k)]\, \Delta x_k$ $= \int_a^b [f(x) - g(x)]\, dx$
The volume of the solid defined by revolving the curve $y = R(x)$, $a \leq x \leq b$, about the x-axis 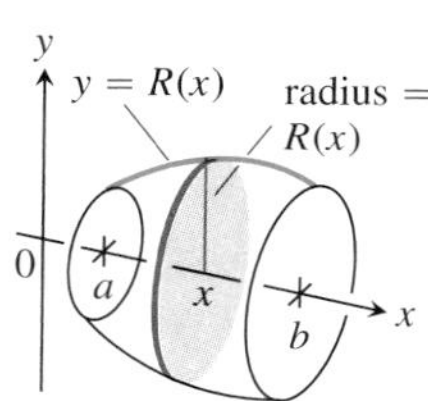	$\sum \pi [R(c_k)]^2\, \Delta x_k$	$V = \lim_{\|P\| \to 0} \sum \pi [R(c_k)]^2\, \Delta x_k$ $= \int_a^b \pi [R(x)]^2\, dx$
The work done by a continuous variable force of magnitude $F(x)$ directed along the x-axis from a to b 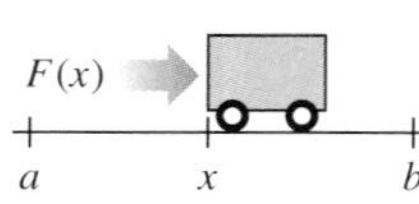	$\sum F(c_k)\, \Delta x_k$	$W = \lim_{\|P\| \to 0} \sum F(c_k)\, \Delta x_k$ $= \int_a^b F(x)\, dx$

We partition the interval $[a, b]$ along the x-axis in the usual manner and slice the solid, as we would a loaf of bread, by planes perpendicular to the x-axis at the partition points. The kth slice, the one between the planes at x_{k-1} and x_k, has approximately the same volume as the cylinder between these two planes based on the region $R(x_k)$ (Fig. 7.70). The volume of this cylinder is

$$\begin{aligned} V_k &= \text{base area} \times \text{height} \\ &= A(x_k) \times (\text{distance between the planes at } x_{k-1} \text{ and } x_k) \\ &= A(x_k)\Delta x_k. \end{aligned} \tag{1}$$

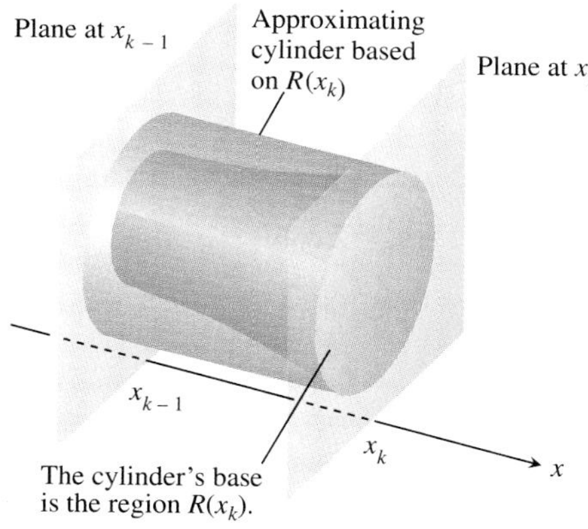

7.70 Enlarged view of the slice of the solid between the planes at x_{k-1} and x_k and its approximating cylinder.

The volume of the solid is therefore approximated by the cylinder volume sum

$$\sum_{k=1}^{n} A(x_k)\Delta x_k. \tag{2}$$

This is a Riemann sum for the function $A(x)$ on $[a, b]$. We expect the approximations from these sums to improve as the norm of the partition of $[a, b]$ goes to zero, so we define their limiting integral to be the volume of the solid.

DEFINITION

The **volume** of a solid of known integrable cross-section area $A(x)$ from $x = a$ to $x = b$ is the integral of A from a to b:

$$V = \int_a^b A(x)\,dx. \tag{3}$$

To apply Eq. (3), we take the following steps.

How to Find Volumes by the Method of Slicing

1. Sketch the solid and a typical cross section.
2. Find a formula for $A(x)$.
3. Find the limits of integration.
4. Integrate $A(x)$ to find the volume.

EXAMPLE 1 A pyramid 3 m high has a square base that is 3 m on a side. The cross section of the pyramid perpendicular to the altitude x m down from the vertex is a square x m on a side. Find the volume of the pyramid.

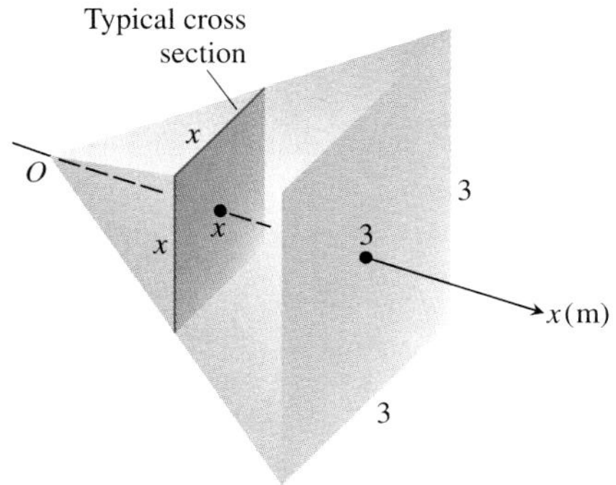

7.71 The cross sections of the pyramid in Example 1 are squares.

Solution

STEP 1: *A sketch.* We draw the pyramid with its altitude along the x-axis and its vertex at the origin and include a typical cross section (Fig. 7.71).

STEP 2: *A formula for A(x).* The cross section at x is a square x meters on a side, so its area is

$$A(x) = x^2.$$

STEP 3: *The limits of integration.* The squares go from $x = 0$ to $x = 3$.

STEP 4: *The volume.*

$$V = \int_a^b A(x)\,dx = \int_0^3 x^2\,dx = \left.\frac{x^3}{3}\right]_0^3 = 9.$$

The volume is 9 m^3. ∎

EXAMPLE 2 A curved wedge is cut from a cylinder of radius 3 by two planes. One plane is perpendicular to the axis of the cylinder. The second plane crosses the first plane at a 45° angle at the center of the cylinder. Find the volume of the wedge.

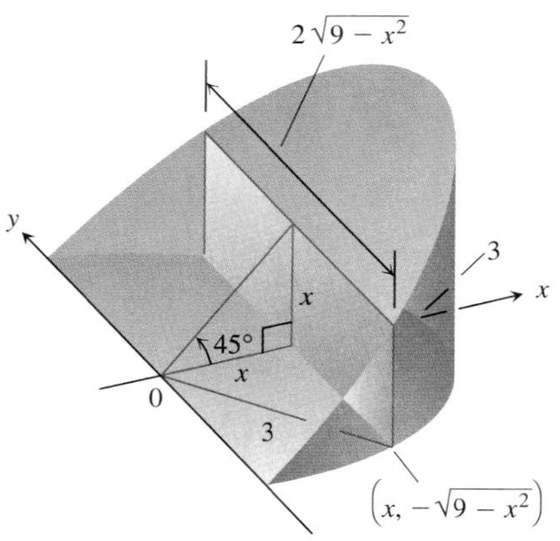

7.72 The wedge of Example 2, sliced perpendicular to the x-axis. The cross sections are rectangles.

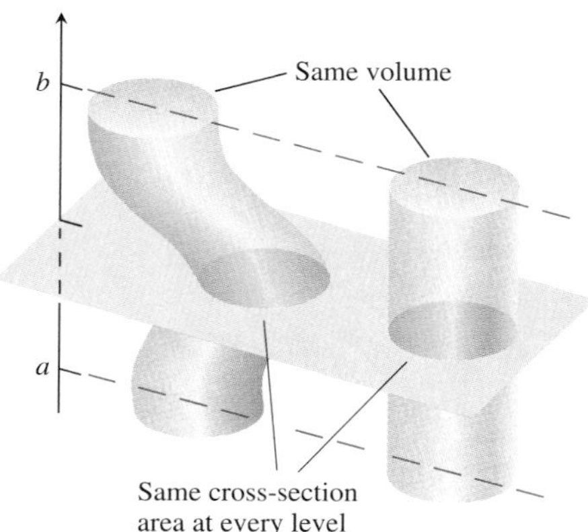

7.73 *Cavalieri's theorem:* These solids have the same volume. You can illustrate this yourself with stacks of coins.

Bonaventura Cavalieri (1598–1647)

Cavalieri, a student of Galileo's, discovered that if two plane regions can be arranged to lie over the same interval of the x-axis in such a way that they have identical vertical cross sections at every point, then the regions have the same area. The theorem (and a letter of recommendation from Galileo) were enough to win Cavalieri a chair at the University of Bologna in 1629. The solid geometry version in Example 3, which Cavalieri

(continued)

Solution

STEP 1: *A sketch.* We draw the wedge and sketch a typical cross section perpendicular to the x-axis (Fig. 7.72).

STEP 2: *The formula for A(x).* The cross section at x is a rectangle of area

$$A(x) = (\text{height})(\text{width}) = (x)\left(2\sqrt{9-x^2}\right) = 2x\sqrt{9-x^2}.$$

STEP 3: *The limits of integration.* The rectangles run from $x = 0$ to $x = 3$.

STEP 4: *The volume.*

$$\begin{aligned} V &= \int_a^b A(x)\,dx = \int_0^3 2x\sqrt{9-x^2}\,dx \\ &= -\frac{2}{3}(9-x^2)^{3/2}\Big]_0^3 = 0 + \frac{2}{3}(9)^{3/2} \\ &= 18. \end{aligned}$$

Let $u = 9 - x^2$, $du = -2x\,dx$, integrate, and substitute back.

EXAMPLE 3 *Cavalieri's Theorem.* Cavalieri's theorem says that solids with equal altitudes and identical parallel cross sections have the same volume (Fig. 7.73). We can see this immediately from Eq. (3) because the cross-section area function $A(x)$ is the same in each case.

Displacement vs. Distance Traveled

If a body moves along a coordinate line without changing direction, we can calculate the total distance it travels by integrating its velocity function, as we did in Chapter 5. If the body changes direction one or more times during the trip, we need to integrate the body's *speed* (velocity's absolute value) to find the total distance traveled. Integrating the velocity will only give the body's *displacement,* the difference between its initial and final positions on the line.

To see why, partition the time interval $a \le t \le b$ into subintervals in the usual way and let Δt_k denote the length of the kth interval. If Δt_k is small enough, the body's velocity $v(t)$ will not change much from t_{k-1} to t_k and the right-hand endpoint value $v(t_k)$ will give a good approximation of the velocity throughout the interval. Accordingly, the change in the body's position coordinate during the kth time interval will be about

$$v(t_k)\Delta t_k. \tag{4}$$

The change will be positive if $v(t_k)$ is positive and negative if $v(t_k)$ is negative.

In either case, the distance traveled during the kth interval will be about

$$|v(t_k)|\Delta t_k. \tag{5}$$

The total trip distance will be approximately

$$\sum_{k=1}^{n} |v(t_k)|\Delta t_k. \tag{6}$$

The sum in Eq. (6) is a Riemann sum for the speed $|v(t)|$ on the interval $[a, b]$. We expect the approximations to improve as the norm of the partition of $[a, b]$ goes to zero. It therefore looks as if we should be able to calculate the total distance traveled by the body by integrating the body's speed from a to b. In practice, this turns out to be the right thing to do. The mathematical model predicts the distance correctly every time.

Bonaventura Cavalieri (*continued*)

never proved, was given his name by later geometers.

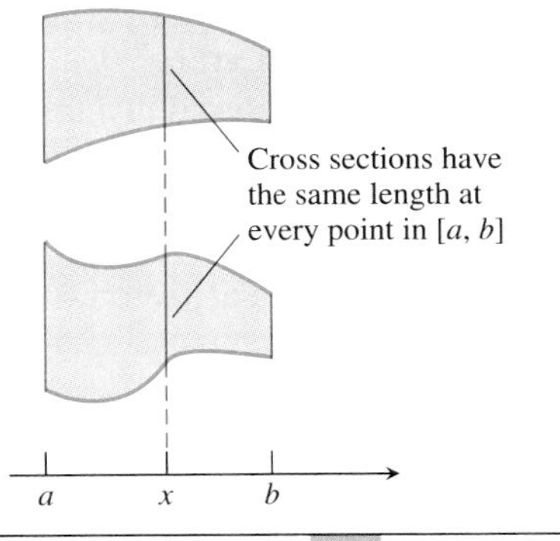

$$\text{Distance traveled} = \int_a^b |v(t)|\,dt \tag{7}$$

If we wish to predict how far up or down the line from its initial position a body will end up when a trip is over, we integrate v instead of its absolute value.

To see why, let $s(t)$ be the body's position at time t and let F be an antiderivative of v. Then

$$s(t) = F(t) + C$$

for some constant C. The shift in the body's position **(displacement)** caused by the trip from $t = a$ to $t = b$ is

$$s(b) - s(a) = (F(b) + C) - (F(a) + C) = F(b) - F(a) = \int_a^b v(t)\,dt. \tag{8}$$

$$\text{Displacement} = \int_a^b v(t)\,dt \tag{9}$$

EXAMPLE 4 The velocity of a body moving along a line from $t = 0$ to $t = 3\pi/2$ sec was

$$v(t) = 5\cos t \text{ m/sec}.$$

Find the total distance traveled and the body's displacement.

Solution

$$\begin{aligned}
\text{Distance traveled} &= \int_0^{3\pi/2} |5\cos t|\,dt \qquad \text{Distance is the integral of speed.}\\
&= \int_0^{\pi/2} 5\cos t\,dt + \int_{\pi/2}^{3\pi/2} (-5\cos t)\,dt\\
&= 5\sin t\Big]_0^{\pi/2} - 5\sin t\Big]_{\pi/2}^{3\pi/2}\\
&= 5(1-0) - 5(-1-1) = 5 + 10 = 15 \text{ m}
\end{aligned}$$

$$\begin{aligned}
\text{Displacement} &= \int_0^{3\pi/2} 5\cos t\,dt \qquad \text{Displacement is the integral of velocity.}\\
&= 5\sin t\Big]_0^{3\pi/2} = 5(-1) - 5(0) = -5 \text{ m}
\end{aligned}$$

During the trip, the body traveled 5 m forward and 10 m backward for a total distance of 15 m. This displaced the body 5 m to the left (Fig. 7.74).

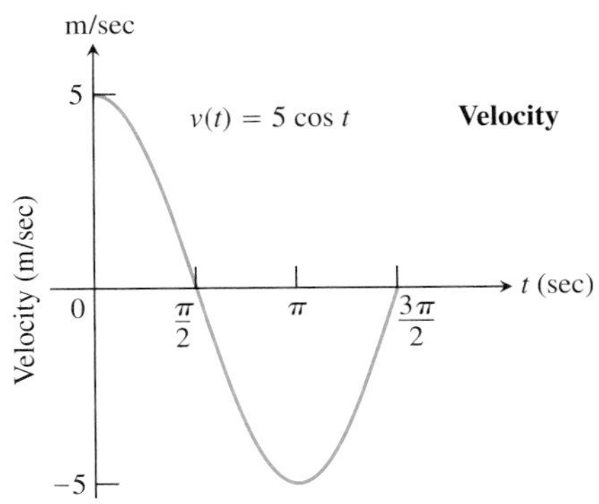

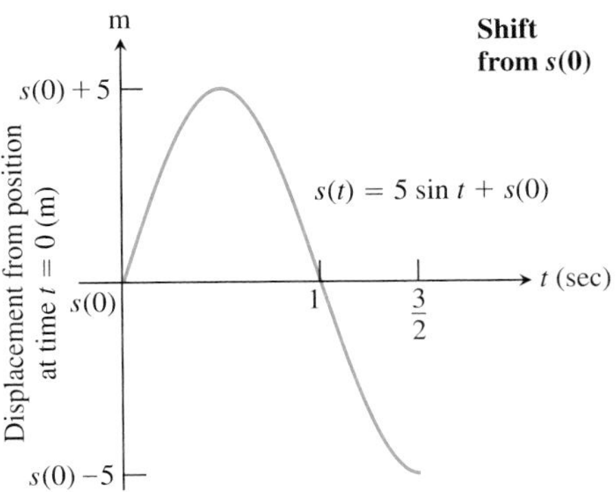

7.74 The position and velocity of the body in Example 4. The velocity is positive at first, and the corresponding displacement is positive. But the body stops at $t = \pi/2$ and reverses direction. By time $t = 3\pi/2$, the body has moved 5 m to the left of where it started.

Delesse's Rule

As you may know, the sugar in an apple starts turning into starch as soon as the apple is picked, and the longer the apple sits around, the starchier it becomes. You can tell fresh apples from stale by both flavor and consistency.

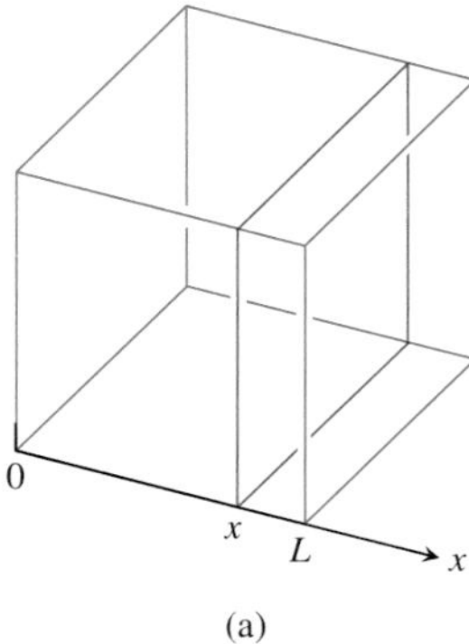

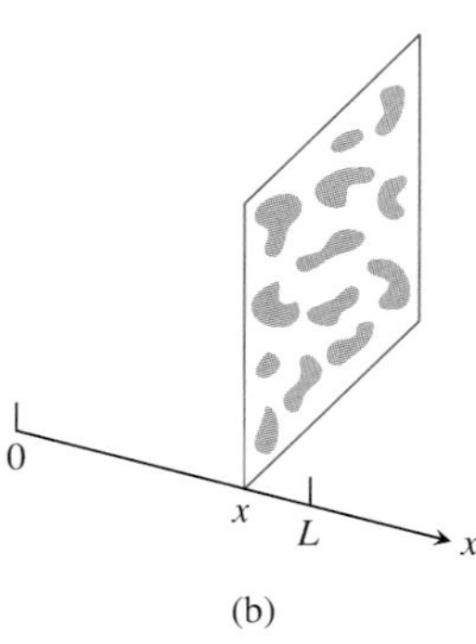

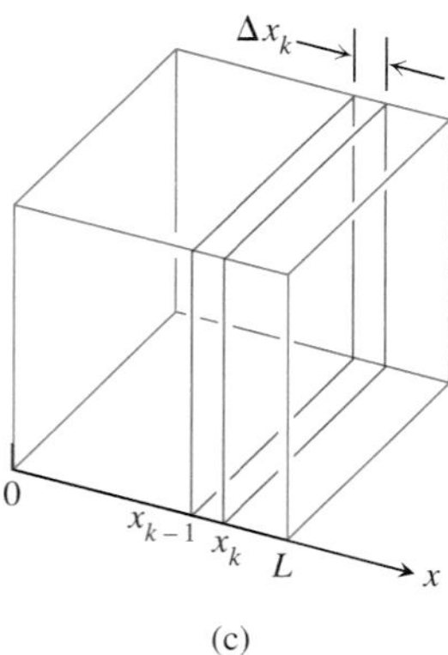

7.75 The steps leading to Delesse's rule: (a) a slice through a sample cube; (b) the granular material in the slice; (c) the slab between consecutive slices determined by a subdivision of $[0, L]$.

To find out how much starch is in a given apple, we can look at a thin slice under a microscope. The cross sections of the starch granules will show up clearly, and it is easy to estimate the proportion of the viewing area they occupy. This two-dimensional proportion will be the same as the three-dimensional proportion of uncut starch granules in the apple itself. The apparently magical equality of these proportions was first discovered by a French geologist, Achille Ernest Delesse, in the 1840s. Its explanation lies in the notion of average value.

Suppose we want to find the proportion of some granular material in a solid and that the sample we have chosen to analyze is a cube whose edges have length L. We picture the cube with an x-axis along one edge and imagine slicing the cube with planes perpendicular to points of the interval $[0, L]$ (Fig. 7.75). Call the proportion of the area of the slice at x occupied by the granular material of interest (starch, in our apple example) $r(x)$ and assume r is a continuous function of x.

Now partition the interval $[0, L]$ into subintervals in the usual way. Imagine the cube sliced into thin slices by planes at the subdivision points. The length Δx_k of the kth subinterval is the distance between the planes at x_{k-1} and x_k. If the planes are close enough together, the sections cut from the grains by the planes will resemble cylinders with bases in the plane at x_k. The proportion of granular material between the planes will therefore be about the same as the proportion of cylinder base area in the plane at x_k, which in turn will be about $r(x_k)$. Thus the amount of granular material in the slab between the two planes will be about

$$(\text{Proportion}) \times (\text{slab volume}) = r(x_k)L^2\,\Delta x_k. \tag{10}$$

The amount of granular material in the entire sample cube will be about

$$\sum_{k=1}^{n} r(x_k)L^2\,\Delta x_k. \tag{11}$$

This sum is a Riemann sum for the function $r(x)L^2$ over the interval $[0, L]$. We expect the approximations by sums like these to improve as the norm of the subdivision of $[0, L]$ goes to zero and therefore expect the integral

$$\int_a^b r(x)L^2\,dx \tag{12}$$

to give the amount of granular material in the sample cube.

We can obtain the proportion of granular material in the sample by dividing this amount by the cube's volume L^3. If we have chosen our sample well, this will also be the proportion of granular material in the solid from which the sample was taken. Putting it all together, we get

$$\begin{aligned}
\begin{matrix}\text{Proportion of granular}\\ \text{material in solid}\end{matrix} &= \begin{matrix}\text{Proportion of granular}\\ \text{material in the sample cube}\end{matrix}\\
&= \frac{\int_0^L r(x)L^2\,dx}{L^3} = \frac{L^2\int_0^L r(x)\,dx}{L^3} = \frac{1}{L}\int_0^L r(x)\,dx \qquad (13)\\
&= \text{average value of } r(x) \text{ over } [0, L]\\
&= \text{proportion of area occupied by granular material in a typical cross section.}
\end{aligned}$$

> **Delesse's Rule**
>
> Achille Ernest Delesse was a mid-nineteenth-century mining engineer interested in determining the composition of rocks. To find out how much of a particular mineral a rock contained, he cut it through, polished an exposed face, and covered the face with transparent waxed paper, trimmed to size. He then traced on the paper the exposed portions of the mineral that interested him. After weighing the paper, he cut out the mineral traces and weighed them. The ratio of the weights gave not only the proportion of the surface occupied by the mineral but, more important, the proportion of the entire rock occupied by the mineral. This rule is still used by petroleum geologists today. A two-dimensional analogue of it is used to determine the porosities of the ceramic filters that extract organic molecules in chemistry laboratories and screen out microbes in water purifiers.

This is Delesse's rule. Once we have found $\bar{r}$, the average of $r(x)$ over $[0, L]$, we have found the proportion of granular material in the solid.

In practice, $\bar{r}$ is found by averaging over a number of cross sections. There are several things to watch out for in the process. In addition to the possibility that the granules cluster in ways that make representative samples difficult to find, there is the possibility that we might not recognize a granule's trace for what it is. Some cross sections of normal red blood cells look like disks and ovals, while others look surprisingly like dumbbells. We do not want to dismiss the dumbbells as experimental error the way one research group did a few years ago.

Useless Integrals

Some of the integrals we get from forming Riemann sums do what we want, but others do not. It all depends on how we choose to model the problems we want to solve. Some choices are good; others are not. Here is an example.

We use the surface area formula

$$S = \int_a^b 2\pi f(x) \sqrt{1 + \left(\frac{df}{dx}\right)^2}\, dx \qquad (14)$$

because it has predictive value and always gives results consistent with information from other sources. In other words, the model we used to derive the formula (Fig. 7.76) was a good one.

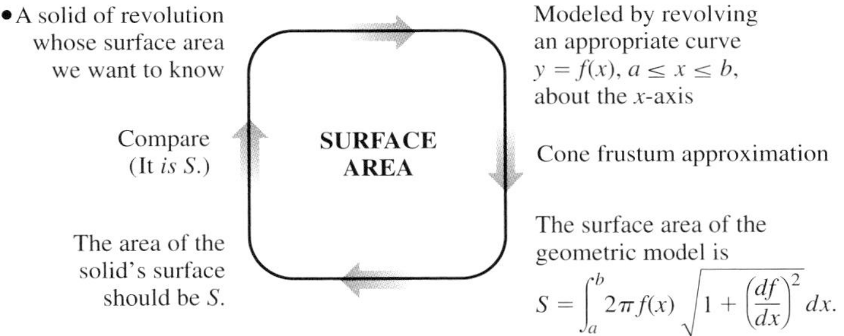

7.76 The modeling cycle for surface area.

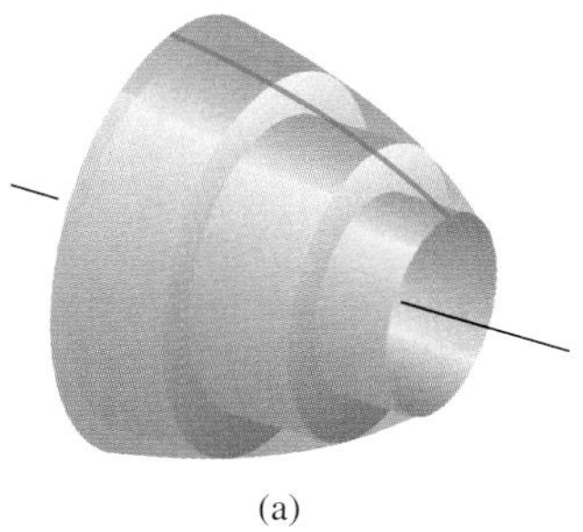

(a)

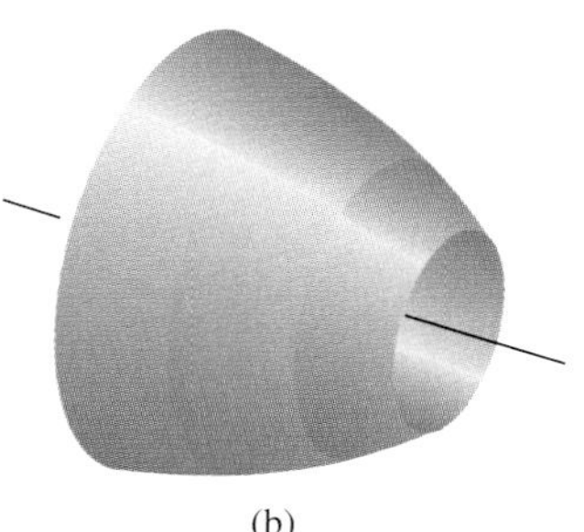

(b)

7.77 Why not use (a) cylindrical bands instead of (b) conical bands to approximate surface area?

Why not find the surface area by approximating with cylindrical bands instead of conical bands, as suggested in Fig. 7.77? The Riemann sums we get this way converge just as nicely as the ones based on conical bands, and the resulting integral is simpler. Instead of Eq. (14), we get

$$S = \int_a^b 2\pi f(x)\, dx. \qquad (15)$$

After all, we might argue, we used cylinders to derive good volume formulas, so why not use them again to derive surface area formulas?

The answer is that the formula in Eq. (15) has no predictive value and almost never gives results consistent with other calculations. The comparison step in the modeling process fails if we use this formula.

There is a moral here: Just because we end up with a nice-looking integral does not mean it will do what we want. Constructing an integral is not enough—we have to test it too (Exercises 29 and 30).

Exercises 7.8

THE METHOD OF SLICING

Find the volumes of the solids in Exercises 1–10.

1. The solid lies between planes perpendicular to the x-axis at $x = 0$ and $x = 4$. The cross sections perpendicular to the axis on the interval $0 \le x \le 4$ are squares whose diagonals run from the parabola $y = -\sqrt{x}$ to the parabola $y = \sqrt{x}$.

2. The solid lies between planes perpendicular to the x-axis at $x = -1$ and $x = 1$. The cross sections perpendicular to the x-axis are circular disks whose diameters run from the parabola $y = x^2$ to the parabola $y = 2 - x^2$.

3. The solid lies between planes perpendicular to the x-axis at $x = -1$ and $x = 1$. The cross sections perpendicular to the axis between these planes are vertical squares whose base edges run from the semicircle $y = -\sqrt{1 - x^2}$ to the semicircle $y = \sqrt{1 - x^2}$.

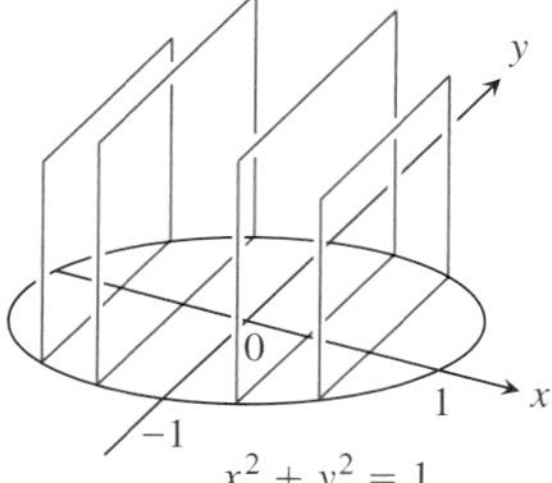

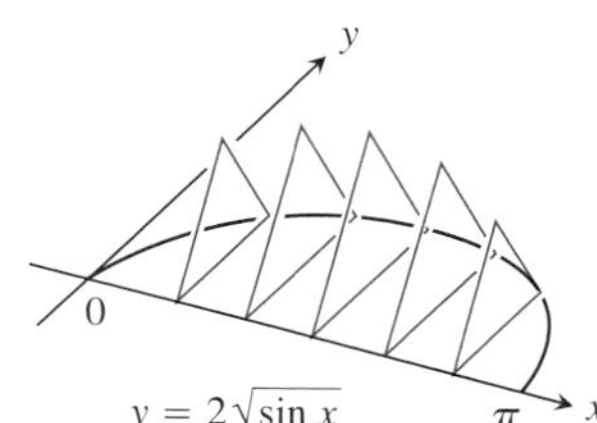

4. The base of the solid is the region between the curve $y = 2\sqrt{\sin x}$ and the interval $[0, \pi]$ on the x-axis. The cross sections perpendicular to the x-axis are

   a) vertical equilateral triangles with bases running from the x-axis to the curve.

   b) vertical squares with bases running from the x-axis to the curve.

5. The solid lies between planes perpendicular to the x-axis at $x = -\pi/3$ and $x = \pi/3$. The cross sections perpendicular to the x-axis are

   a) circular disks with diameters running from the curve $y = \tan x$ to the curve $y = \sec x$;

   b) vertical squares whose base edges run from the curve $y = \tan x$ to the curve $y = \sec x$.

6. The solid lies between planes perpendicular to the x-axis at $x = -1$ and $x = 1$. The cross sections perpendicular to the x-axis between these planes are squares whose diagonals run from the semicircle $y = -\sqrt{1 - x^2}$ to the semicircle $y = \sqrt{1 - x^2}$. (The length of a square's diagonal is $\sqrt{2}$ times the length of its sides.)

7. The solid lies between planes perpendicular to the x-axis at $x = -1$ and $x = 1$. The cross sections perpendicular to the x-axis are

   a) circles whose diameters stretch from the curve $y = -1/\sqrt{1 + x^2}$ to the curve $y = 1/\sqrt{1 + x^2}$;

   b) vertical squares whose base edges run from the curve $y = -1/\sqrt{1 + x^2}$ to the curve $y = 1/\sqrt{1 + x^2}$.

8. The solid lies between planes perpendicular to the x-axis at $x = -\sqrt{2}/2$ and $x = \sqrt{2}/2$. The cross sections are

   a) circles whose diameters stretch from the x-axis to the curve $y = 2/\sqrt[4]{1 - x^2}$.

   b) squares whose diagonals stretch from the x-axis to the curve $y = 2/\sqrt[4]{1 - x^2}$.

9. The solid lies between planes perpendicular to the x-axis at $x = 0$ and $x = 2$. The cross sections perpendicular to the x-axis are circular disks with diameters running from the x-axis up to the parabola $y = \sqrt{5}x^2$.

10. The base of the solid is the disk $x^2 + y^2 \le 1$. The cross sections by planes perpendicular to the y-axis between $y = -1$ and $y = 1$ are isosceles right triangles with one leg in the disk.

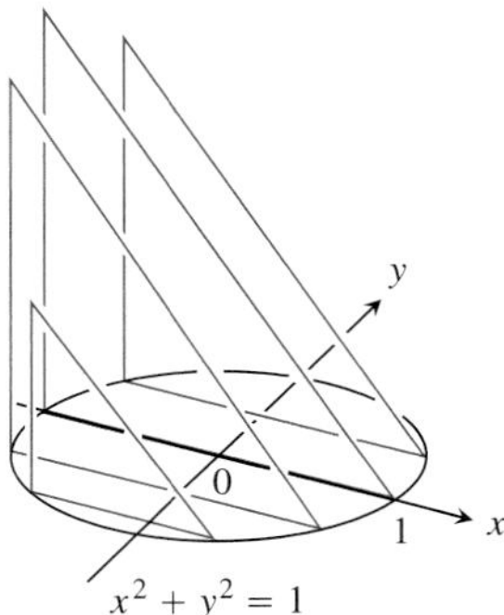

CAVALIERI'S THEOREM

11. *A Twisted Solid.* A square of side length s lies in a plane perpendicular to a line L. One vertex of the square lies on L. As this square moves a distance h along L, the square turns one revolution about L to generate a corkscrew-like column with square cross sections.

    a) Find the volume of the column.

    b) What will the volume be if the square turns twice instead of once? Give reasons for your answer.

12. A solid lies between planes perpendicular to the x-axis at $x = 0$ and $x = 12$. The cross sections by planes perpendicular to the x-axis are circular disks whose diameters run from the line $y = x/2$ to the line $y = x$. Explain why the solid has the same volume as a right circular cone with base radius 3 and height 12.

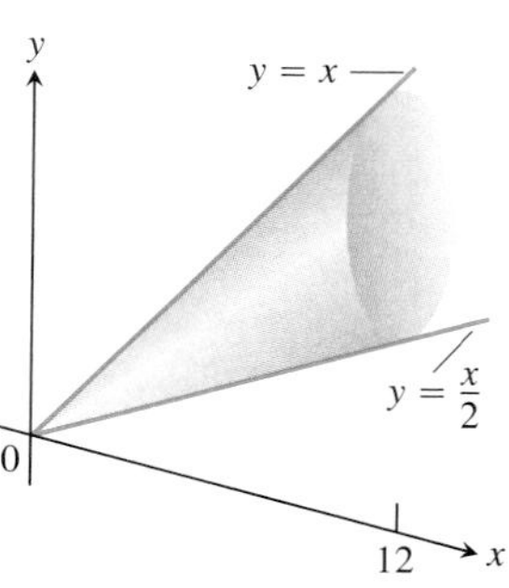

13. *Cavalieri's Original Theorem.* Prove Cavalieri's original theorem (marginal note, pages 500–501) assuming that each region is bounded above and below by the graphs of continuous functions.

14. *The Volume of a Hemisphere (A Classical Application of Cavalieri's Theorem).* Derive the formula $V = (2/3)\pi R^3$ for the volume of a hemisphere of radius R by comparing its cross sections with the cross sections of a solid right circular cylinder of radius R and height R from which a solid right circular cone of base radius R and height R has been removed.

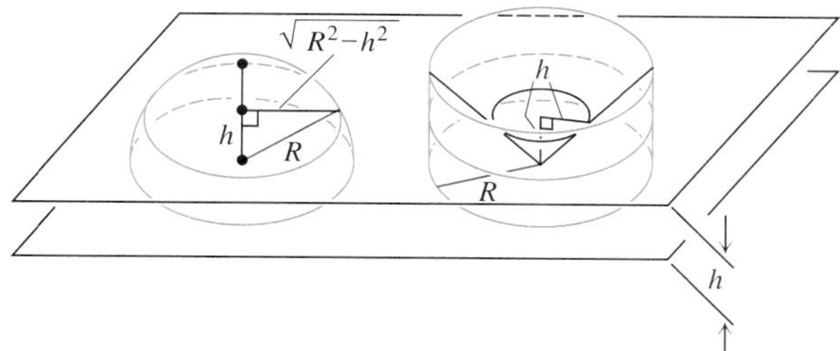

DISTANCE AND DISPLACEMENT

In Exercises 15–22, the function $v(t)$ is the velocity in meters per second of a body moving along a coordinate line. (a) Graph v to see where it is positive and negative. Then find (b) the total distance traveled by the body during the given time interval and (c) the body's displacement.

15. $v(t) = 5\cos t, \quad 0 \le t \le 2\pi$

16. $v(t) = \sin \pi t, \quad 0 \le t \le 2$

17. $v(t) = 6\sin 3t, \quad 0 \le t \le \pi/2$

18. $v(t) = 4\cos 2t, \quad 0 \le t \le \pi$

19. $v(t) = 49 - 9.8t, \quad 0 \le t \le 10$

20. $v(t) = 8 - 1.6t, \quad 0 \le t \le 10$

21. $v(t) = 6t^2 - 18t + 12 = 6(t-1)(t-2), \quad 0 \le t \le 2$

22. $v(t) = 6t^2 - 18t + 12 = 6(t-1)(t-2), \quad 0 \le t \le 3$

23. The function $s = (1/3)t^3 - 3t^2 + 8t$ gives the position of a body moving on the horizontal s-axis at time $t \ge 0$ (s in meters, t in seconds).
    a) Show that the body is moving to the right at time $t = 0$.
    b) When does the particle move to the left?
    c) What is the particle's position at time $t = 3$?
    d) When $t = 3$, what is the total distance the particle has traveled?
    e) Graph s as a function of t and comment on the relationship of the graph to the body's motion.

24. The function $s = -t^3 + 6t^2 - 9t$ gives the position of a body moving on the horizontal s-axis at time $t \ge 0$ (s in meters, t in seconds).
    a) Show that the particle is moving to the left at $t = 0$.
    b) When does the particle move to the right?
    c) Does the particle ever move to the right of the origin? Give reasons for your answer.
    d) What is the particle's position at time $t = 3$?
    e) What is the total distance the particle has traveled by the time $t = 3$?
    f) Graph s as a function of t and comment on the relationship of the graph to the body's motion.

25. Here are the velocity graphs of two bodies moving on a coordinate line. Find the total distance traveled and the body's displacement for the given time interval.

(a)

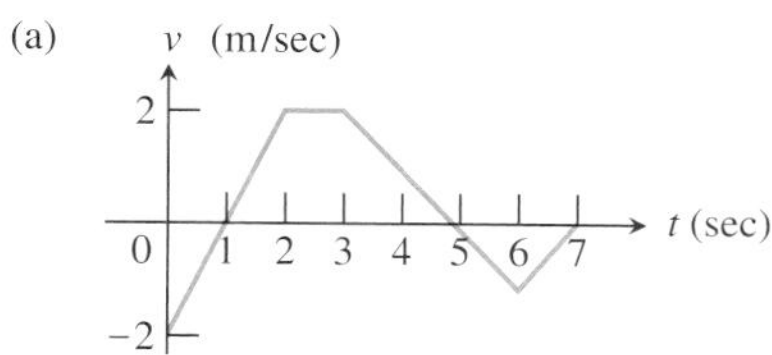

(b)

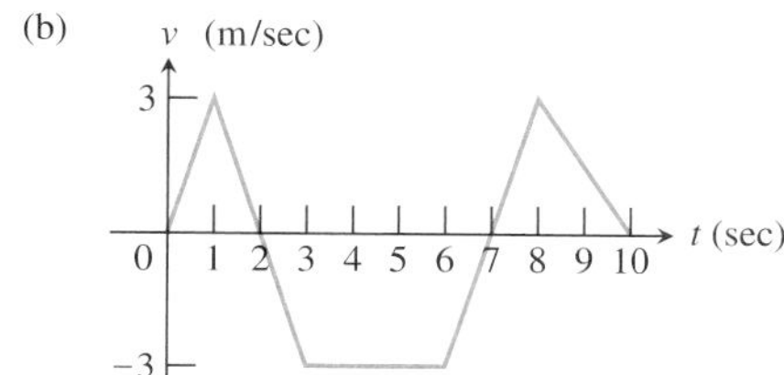

26. The table below shows the velocity of a model train engine moving back and forth on a track for 10 sec. Use Simpson's rule to find the resulting displacement and total distance traveled.

Time (sec)	Velocity (in. per sec)	Time (sec)	Velocity (in. per sec)
0	0	6	−11
1	12	7	−6
2	22	8	2
3	10	9	6
4	−5	10	0
5	−13		

DELESSE'S RULE

27. The photograph below shows a grid superimposed on the polished face of a piece of granite. Use the grid and Delesse's rule to estimate the proportion of shrimp-colored granular material in the rock.

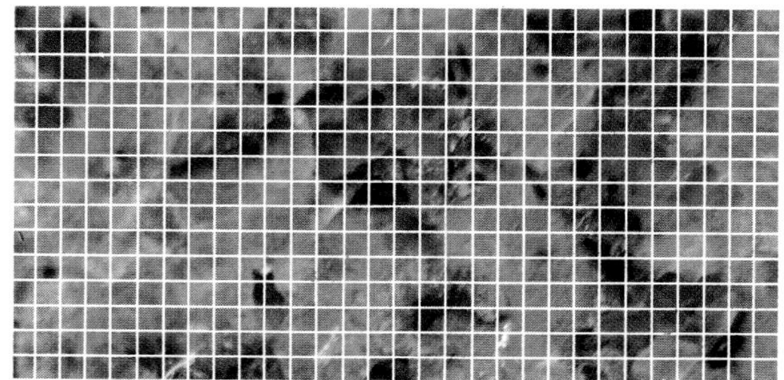

28. The photograph below shows a grid superimposed on a microscopic view of a stained section of human lung tissue. The clear spaces between the cells are cross sections of the lung's air sacks (called *aveolae* — accent on the second syllable). Use the grid and Delesse's rule to estimate the proportion of air space in the lung.

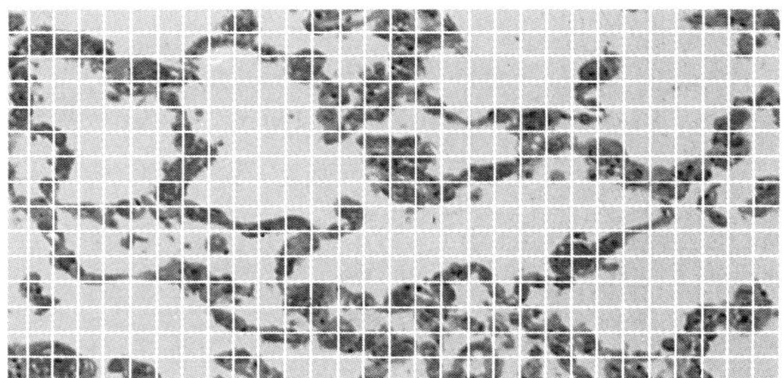

MODELING SURFACE AREA

29. *Modeling Surface Area.* The lateral surface area of the cone swept out by revolving the line segment $y = x/\sqrt{3}$, $0 \le x \le \sqrt{3}$, about the x-axis should be (1/2)(base circumference)(slant height) $= (1/2)(2\pi)(2) = 2\pi$. What do you get if you use Eq. (15) with $f(x) = x/\sqrt{3}$?

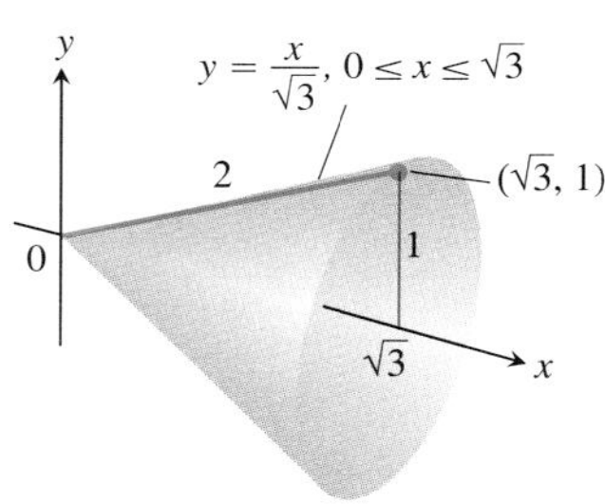

30. *Modeling Surface Area.* The only surface for which Eq. (15) gives the area we want is a cylinder. Show that Eq. (15) gives $S = 2\pi rh$ for the cylinder swept out by revolving the line segment $y = r$, $0 \le x \le h$, about the x-axis.

31. *A Sailboat's Displacement.* To find the volume of water displaced by a sailboat, the common practice is to partition the waterline into 10 subintervals of equal length, measure the cross section area $A(x)$ of the submerged portion of the hull at each partition point, and then use Simpson's rule to estimate the integral of $A(x)$ from one end of the water line to the other. The table in the next column lists the area measurements at "Stations" 0 through 10, as the partition points are called, for the cruising sloop *Pipedream* (Fig. 7.78). The common subinterval length (distance between consecutive stations) is $h = 2.54$ ft (about 2′ 6 1/2″ — chosen for the convenience of the builder).

a) Estimate *Pipedream's* displacement volume to the nearest cubic foot.

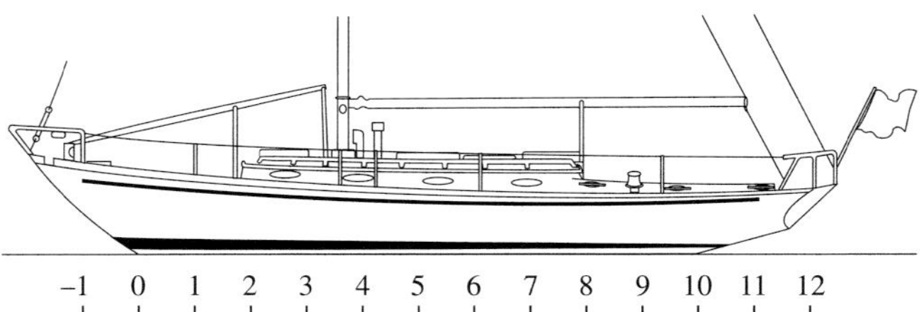

7.78 Stations along the waterline of the sloop *Pipedream*.

Station	Area (ft²)
0	0
1	1.07
2	3.84
3	7.82
4	12.20
5	15.18
6	16.14
7	14.00
8	9.21
9	3.24
10	0

b) The figures in the table above are for seawater, which weighs 64 lb/ft³. How many pounds of water does *Pipedream* displace? (Displacement is given in pounds for small craft, and long tons [1 long ton = 2,240 lb] for larger vessels.)

(Data from *Skene's Elements of Yacht Design,* Francis S. Kinney, Dodd, Mead & Company, Inc. 1962)

32. *Prismatic Coefficients (Continuation of Exercise 31).* A boat's prismatic coefficient is the ratio of the displacement volume to the volume of a prism whose height equals the boat's waterline length and whose base equals the area of the boat's largest submerged cross section. The best sailboats have prismatic coefficients between 0.51 and 0.54. Find *Pipedream's* prismatic coefficient, given a waterline length of 25.4 ft and a largest submerged cross section area of 16.14 ft² (at Station 6).

Writing for Your Own Knowledge

Answer the following questions in writing. Some answers will take only a sentence or two; others may require several paragraphs. Some explanations may also call for graphs or sketches.

1. What are the phases of developing an integral to define or calculate something?
2. How do you find volumes by the method of slicing?
3. What is Cavalieri's theorem?
4. What is the difference between displacement and distance traveled? How are they related to a moving body's velocity function?
5. What is Delesse's rule?

For Your Review

Write brief paragraphs about the following topics and give examples.

Areas of regions bounded by curves
Volumes of solids of revolution
  Disks
  Washers
  Cylindrical shells
The length of a curve
The area of a surface of revolution
Work done
  by a constant force
  by a variable force
  in compressing a spring
  in pumping a liquid from a container
The force exerted by a liquid
  on a constant-depth surface
  against one side of a submerged vertical plate or wall
The center of mass
  of a system consisting of a finite number of masses
    placed along a rigid axis
  of a thin straight rod or strip
  of a thin plate covering a region of the xy-plane
The phases of developing an integral to calculate something
Finding volumes of arbitrary solids
Cavalieri's theorem
Displacement vs. distance traveled
Delesse's rule

Practice Exercises

Find the areas of the regions enclosed by the curves and lines in Exercises 1–14.

1. $y = x, \quad y = 1/x^2, \quad x = 2$

2. $y = x, \quad y = 1/\sqrt{x}, \quad x = 2$

3. $\sqrt{x} + \sqrt{y} = 1, \quad x = 0, \quad y = 0$

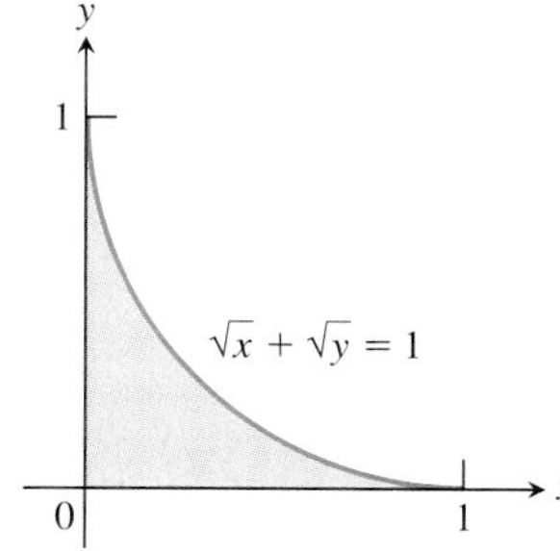

4. $x^3 + \sqrt{y} = 1, \quad x = 0, \quad y = 0, \quad \text{for} \quad 0 \le x \le 1$

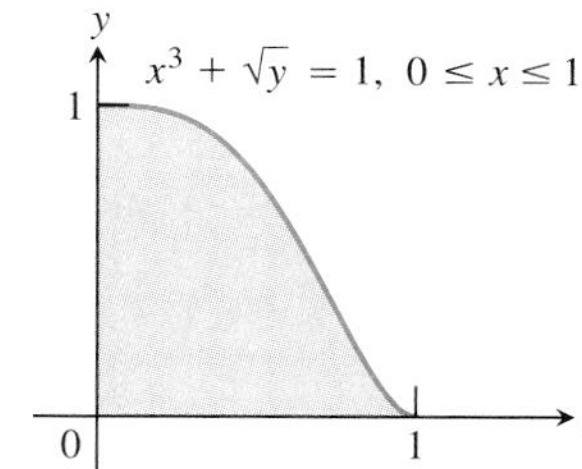

5. $x = 2y^2, \quad x = 0, \quad y = 3$

6. $x = 4 - y^2, \quad x = 0$

7. $y^2 = 4x, \quad y = 4x - 2$

8. $y^2 = 4x + 4, \quad y = 4x - 16$

9. $y = \sin x, \quad y = x, \quad 0 \le x \le \pi/4$

10. $y = |\sin x|, \quad y = 1, \quad -\pi/2 \le x \le \pi/2$

11. $y = 2 \sin x, \quad y = \sin 2x, \quad 0 \le x \le \pi$

12. $y = 8 \cos x, \quad y = \sec^2 x, \quad -\pi/3 \le x \le \pi/3$

13. The "triangular" region bounded on the left by $x + y = 2$, on the right by $y = x^2$, and above by $y = 2$

14. The "triangular" region bounded on the left by $y = \sqrt{x}$, on the right by $y = 6 - x$, and below by $y = 1$

Find the areas of the shaded regions in Exercises 15 and 16.

15.

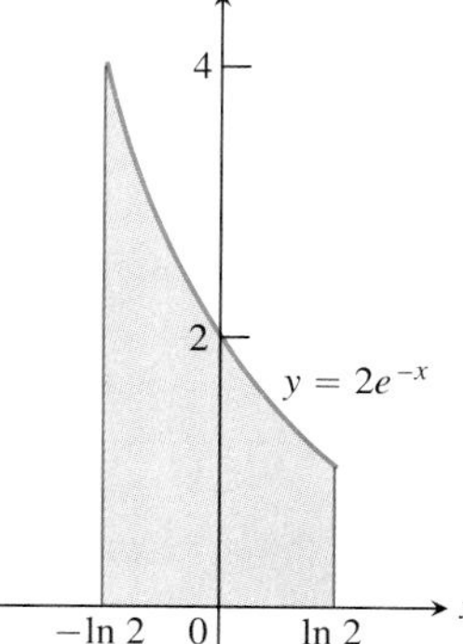

16.

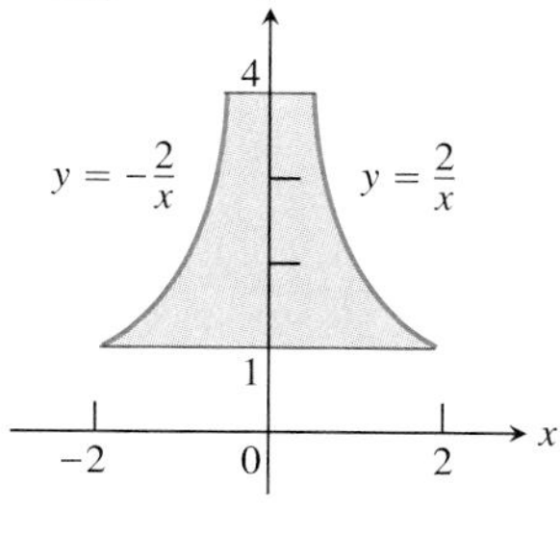

In Exercises 17–24, find the volume of the solid generated by revolving the regions about the given axes.

17. The region in the second quadrant bounded above by the line $y = 4$, below by the parabola $y = 4x^2$, and on the right by the

y-axis, about (a) the y-axis; (b) the line $x = -1$; (c) the x-axis; (d) the line $y = 4$

18. The region in the first quadrant bounded above by the curve $y^2 = 4x$ and below by the line $y = x$, about (a) the x-axis; (b) the y-axis; (c) the line $x = 4$; (d) the line $y = 4$

19. The region enclosed by the x-axis, the curve $y = 3x^4$, and the lines $x = \pm 1$, about (a) the x-axis; (b) the line $y = 3$; (c) the y-axis

20. The region bounded on the left by the parabola $x = y^2 + 1$ and on the right by the line $x = 5$, about (a) the line $x = 5$; (b) the y-axis; (c) the x-axis

21. The region in the first quadrant bounded above by the line $y = \sqrt{3}$, on the left by the y-axis, and below by the curve $y = \tan x$, $0 \le x \le \pi/3$, about (a) the x-axis; (b) the line $y = \sqrt{3}$

22. The region in the first quadrant bounded above by the curve $y = \cot x$, $\pi/4 \le x \le \pi/2$, on the left by the line $x = \pi/4$, and below by the x-axis, about (a) the x-axis; (b) the line $y = 1$

23. The region enclosed by the curve $y = 1/\sqrt{x}$, the x-axis, and the lines $x = 1$ and $x = 16$, about (a) the x-axis; (b) the line $y = 1$

24. The region enclosed by the curve $y = e^{x+1}$, the x-axis, the y-axis, and the line $x = -1$, about (a) the x-axis; (b) the line $y = e$

25. A round hole of radius $\sqrt{3}$ ft is bored through the center of a sphere of radius 2 ft. Find the volume cut out.

26. The profile of a football resembles the ellipse shown here. Find the volume of the football to the nearest cubic inch.

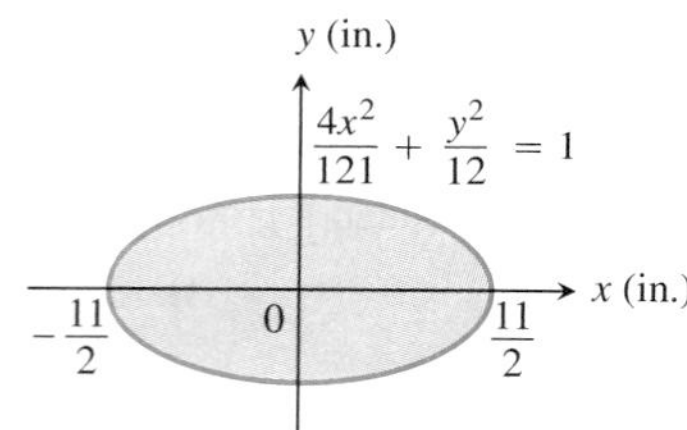

Find the lengths of the curves in Exercises 27–30.

27. $x = y^3/12 + (1/y)$, $1 \le y \le 2$

28. $x = y^{2/3}$, $1 \le y \le 8$

29. $y = x^2 - (1/8)\ln x$, $1 \le x \le 4$

30. $y = e^x + (1/4)e^{-x}$, $0 \le x \le \ln 3$

In Exercises 31–34, find the areas of the surfaces generated by revolving the curves about the given axes.

31. $y = \sqrt{2x + 1}$, $0 \le x \le 3$, x-axis

32. $y = x^3/3$, $0 \le x \le 1$, x-axis

33. $x = \sqrt{4y - y^2}$, $1 \le y \le 2$, y-axis

34. $x = \sqrt{y}$, $2 \le y \le 6$, y-axis

35. A rock climber is about to haul up 100 N (about 22.5 lb) of equipment that has been hanging beneath her on 40 m of rope that weighs 0.8 newton per meter. How much work will it take? (*Hint:* Solve for the rope and equipment separately; then add.)

36. You drove an 800-gal tank truck from the base of Mt. Washington to the summit and discovered on arrival that the tank was only half full. You started with a full tank, climbed at a steady rate, and accomplished the 4750-ft elevation change in 50 min. Assuming that the water leaked out at a steady rate, how much work was spent in carrying water to the top? Do not count the work done in getting yourself and the truck there. Water weighs 8 lb/U.S. gal.

37. If a force of 20 lb is required to hold a spring 1 ft beyond its unstressed length, how much work does it take to stretch the spring this far? an additional foot?

38. A force of 200 N will stretch a garage-door spring 0.8 m beyond its unstressed length. How far will a 300-N force stretch the spring? How much work does it take to stretch the spring this far?

39. A reservoir, shaped like a right circular cone point down, 20 ft across the top and 8 ft deep, is full of water. How much work does it take to pump the water to a level 6 ft above the top?

40. *Continuation of Exercise 39.* The reservoir is filled to a depth of 5 ft, and the water is to be pumped to the same level as the top. How much work does it take?

41. The vertical triangular plate shown here is the end plate of a triangular watering trough full of water. How much force does the water exert against the plate?

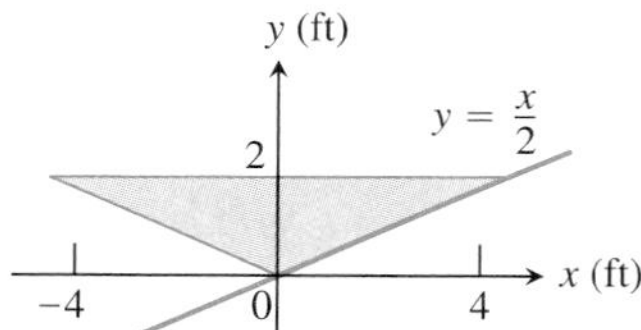

42. The vertical trapezoidal plate shown here is the end plate of a trough of maple syrup weighing 75 lb/ft³. How much force does the syrup exert against the end of the trough when the syrup is 10 in. deep?

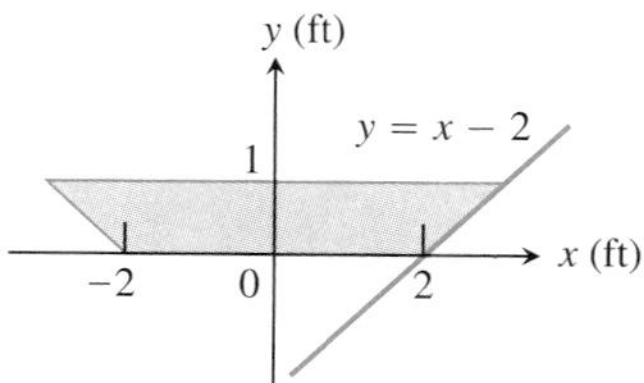

43. A flat vertical gate in the face of a fresh water dam is shaped like the parabolic region between the curve $y = 4x^2$ and the line $y = 4$, with measurements in feet. The top of the gate lies 5 ft below the surface of the water. How much force does the water exert against the gate? (Use $w = 62.4$ lb/ft³).

44. You plan to store mercury ($w = 849$ lb/ft^3) in a vertical right circular cylindrical tank of radius 1 ft whose interior side wall can withstand a total fluid force of 40,000 lb. About how many cubic feet of mercury can you store in the tank at any one time?

45. Find the centroid of a thin, flat plate covering the region enclosed by the parabolas $y = 2x^2$ and $y = 3 - x^2$.

46. Find the centroid of a thin, flat plate covering the region enclosed by the x-axis, the lines $x = 2$ and $x = -2$, and the parabola $y = x^2$.

47. Find the centroid of a thin, flat plate covering the "triangular" region in the first quadrant bounded by the y-axis, the parabola $y = x^2/4$, and the line $y = 4$.

48. Find the centroid of a thin, flat plate covering the region enclosed by the parabola $y^2 = x$ and the line $x = 2y$.

49. A thin plate covers the region enclosed by the x-axis, the curve $y = 1/(1 + x^2)$, and the lines $x = \pm 1$. Find the center of mass if the plate's density at the point (x, y) is $\delta(x) = |x|$.

50. A thin plate covers the region enclosed by the x-axis, the curve $y = 1/\sqrt{1 - x^2}$, and the lines $x = \pm 4/5$. Find the center of mass if the plate's density at the point (x, y) is $\delta(x) = |x|$.

Find the volumes of the solids in Exercises 51–56.

51. The solid lies between planes perpendicular to the x-axis at $x = 0$ and $x = 1$. The cross sections perpendicular to the x-axis between these planes are circular disks whose diameters run from the parabola $y = x^2$ to the parabola $y = \sqrt{x}$.

52. The base of the solid is the region in the first quadrant between the line $y = x$ and the parabola $y = 2\sqrt{x}$. The cross sections of the solid perpendicular to the x-axis are equilateral triangles whose bases stretch from the line to the curve.

53. The solid lies between planes perpendicular to the x-axis at $x = \pi/4$ and $x = 5\pi/4$. The cross sections between these planes are circular disks whose diameters run from the curve $y = 2\cos x$ to the curve $y = 2\sin x$.

54. The solid lies between planes perpendicular to the x-axis at $x = 0$ and $x = 6$. The cross sections between these planes are squares whose bases run from the x-axis up to the curve $x^{1/2} + y^{1/2} = \sqrt{6}$.

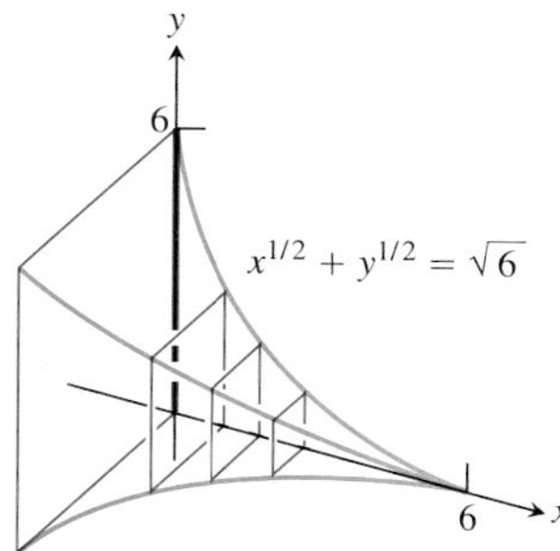

55. The solid lies between planes perpendicular to the x-axis at $x = 0$ and $x = 4$. The cross sections of the solid perpendicular to the x-axis between these planes are circular disks whose diameters run from the curve $x^2 = 4y$ to the curve $y^2 = 4x$.

56. The base of the solid is the region bounded by the parabola $y^2 = 4x$, and the line $x = 1$ in the xy-plane. Each cross section perpendicular to the x-axis is an equilateral triangle with one edge in the plane. (The triangles all lie on the same side of the plane.)

In Exercises 57–60, the function $v = f(t)$ is the velocity (m/sec) of a body moving along a coordinate line. Find (a) the total distance the body travels during the given time interval and (b) the body's displacement.

57. $v = t^2 - 8t + 12, \quad 0 \le t \le 6$

58. $v = t^3 - 3t^2 + 2t, \quad 0 \le t \le 2$

59. $v = 5\cos t, \quad 0 \le t \le 3\pi/2$

60. $v = -\pi \sin \pi t, \quad 0 \le t \le 3/2$

STEPHEN S. MORSE, a virologist at The Rockefeller University in New York City, works in a field that studies the way viral diseases spread within a population. The dissemination of a viral disease like influenza, hepatitis, rabies, yellow fever, or AIDS can involve many factors.

One general factor is the disease's so-called reproductive rate — the average number R_0 of secondary infections produced when you put one infected host in a totally susceptible population. According to the R_0 model devised by Robert May and Roy Anderson, if $R_0 < 1$, the disease will die off. If $R_0 > 1$, the disease has the potential to spread, and many other factors then come into play. If the disease is too virulent, for example, it may kill its host before it can spread to another.

Another factor is the rate at which a virus can mutate to produce a form that can evade or break down a host's immune system. Still another is the availability of alternate hosts (for example, bats, dogs, and raccoons for rabies).

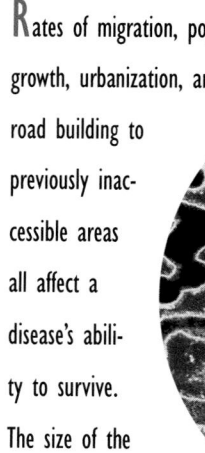

Rates of migration, population growth, urbanization, and road building to previously inaccessible areas all affect a disease's ability to survive. The size of the susceptible population is important as well. To maintain measles you need a human host population of 300,000 or so.

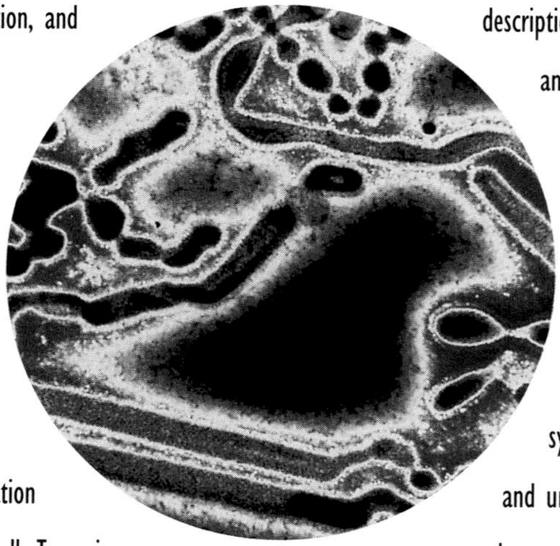

To eradicate smallpox, it was not necessary to vaccinate the entire world population — 80% was enough. Diseases also interact with one another. A person infected by one disease may become more susceptible to a second. And, if the second disease is more virulent, it may kill the host before the first disease can move on to someone else. It gets complicated.

As you can imagine, the mathematical description of the relationships among all the rates involved can lead to large systems of differential equations. These systems resemble the systems of equations and unknowns in algebra, except that now the unknowns involve functions and we must solve for these functions by integration.

OVERVIEW

We have seen how integrals arise in modeling real phenomena and in measuring objects in the world around us, and we know in theory how integrals are evaluated with antiderivatives. The more sophisticated our models become, however, the more involved our integrals become. We need to know how to change these more involved integrals into forms we can work with. The goal of this chapter is to show how to change unfamiliar integrals into integrals we can recognize, find in a table, or evaluate with a computer.

8 Techniques of Integration

8.1 Basic Integration Formulas

As we saw in Section 5.5, we evaluate an indefinite integral by finding an antiderivative of the integrand and adding an arbitrary constant. Table 8.1 shows the basic forms of the integrals we have evaluated so far. There is a more extensive table at the back of the book; we will discuss it in Section 8.5.

TABLE 8.1
Basic integration formulas

1. $\int du = u + C$

2. $\int k\,du = ku + C \qquad \text{(any number } k)$

3. $\int (du + dv) = \int du + \int dv$

4. $\int u^n\,du = \dfrac{u^{n+1}}{n+1} + C \qquad (n \neq -1)$

5. $\int \dfrac{du}{u} = \ln|u| + C$

6. $\int \sin u\,du = -\cos u + C$

7. $\int \cos u\,du = \sin u + C$

8. $\int \sec^2 u\,du = \tan u + C$

9. $\int \csc^2 u\,du = -\cot u + C$

10. $\int \sec u \tan u\,du = \sec u + C$

11. $\int \csc u \cot u\,du = -\csc u + C$

12. $\int \tan u\,du = -\ln|\cos u| + C = \ln|\sec u| + C$

13. $\int \cot u\,du = \ln|\sin u| + C = -\ln|\csc u| + C$

14. $\int e^u\,du = e^u + C$

15. $\int a^u\,du = \dfrac{a^u}{\ln a} + C \qquad (a > 0,\ a \neq 1)$

16. $\int \dfrac{du}{\sqrt{a^2 - u^2}} = \sin^{-1}\left(\dfrac{u}{a}\right) + C$

17. $\int \dfrac{du}{a^2 + u^2} = \dfrac{1}{a}\tan^{-1}\left(\dfrac{u}{a}\right) + C$

18. $\int \dfrac{du}{u\sqrt{u^2 - a^2}} = \dfrac{1}{a}\sec^{-1}\left|\dfrac{u}{a}\right| + C$

Algebraic Procedures

We often have to rewrite an integral to match it to a standard formula.

EXAMPLE 1 *A Simplifying Substitution.* Evaluate $\displaystyle\int \frac{2x-9}{\sqrt{x^2-9x+1}}\,dx$.

Solution

$$\begin{aligned}\int \frac{2x-9}{\sqrt{x^2-9x+1}}\,dx &= \int \frac{du}{\sqrt{u}} && u = x^2-9x+1,\quad du = 2x\,dx - 9\,dx = (2x-9)\,dx\\ &= \int u^{-1/2}\,du \\ &= \frac{u^{(-1/2)+1}}{(-1/2)+1} + C && \text{Table 8.1, Formula 4, with } n = -1/2\\ &= 2u^{1/2} + C\\ &= 2\sqrt{x^2-9x+1} + C\end{aligned}$$

EXAMPLE 2 *Completing the Square.* Evaluate $\displaystyle\int \frac{dx}{\sqrt{8x-x^2}}$.

Solution We complete the square to write the radicand as

$$\begin{aligned}8x - x^2 &= -(x^2-8x) = -(x^2-8x+16-16)\\ &= -(x^2-8x+16)+16 = 16-(x-4)^2.\end{aligned}$$

Then

$$\begin{aligned}\int \frac{dx}{\sqrt{8x-x^2}} &= \int \frac{dx}{\sqrt{16-(x-4)^2}}\\ &= \int \frac{du}{\sqrt{a^2-u^2}} && a = 4,\ u = (x-4),\quad du = dx\\ &= \sin^{-1}\left(\frac{u}{a}\right) + C && \text{Table 8.1, Formula 16}\\ &= \sin^{-1}\left(\frac{x-4}{4}\right) + C.\end{aligned}$$

EXAMPLE 3 *Expanding a Power and Using a Trigonometric Identity.* Evaluate $\displaystyle\int (\sec x + \tan x)^2\,dx$.

Solution We expand the integrand and get

$$(\sec x + \tan x)^2 = \sec^2 x + 2\sec x\tan x + \tan^2 x.$$

The first two terms on the right-hand side of this equation are old friends; we can integrate them at once. How about $\tan^2 x$? There is an identity that connects it with $\sec^2 x$:

$$\tan^2 x + 1 = \sec^2 x, \qquad \tan^2 x = \sec^2 x - 1.$$

We replace $\tan^2 x$ by $\sec^2 x - 1$ and get

$$\begin{aligned}\int (\sec x + \tan x)^2\,dx &= \int (\sec^2 x + 2\sec x\tan x + \sec^2 x - 1)\,dx\\ &= 2\int \sec^2 x\,dx + 2\int \sec x \tan x\,dx - \int 1\,dx\\ &= 2\tan x + 2\sec x - x + C.\end{aligned}$$

EXAMPLE 4 *Eliminating a Square Root.* Evaluate $\int_0^{\pi/4} \sqrt{1+\cos 4x}\,dx$.

Solution We use the identity

$$\cos^2\theta = \frac{1+\cos 2\theta}{2}, \quad \text{or} \quad 1+\cos 2\theta = 2\cos^2\theta.$$

With $\theta = 2x$, this becomes

$$1 + \cos 4x = 2\cos^2 2x.$$

Hence,

$$\begin{aligned}\int_0^{\pi/4} \sqrt{1+\cos 4x}\,dx &= \int_0^{\pi/4} \sqrt{2}\sqrt{\cos^2 2x}\,dx\\ &= \sqrt{2}\int_0^{\pi/4} |\cos 2x|\,dx && \sqrt{u^2} = |u|\\ &= \sqrt{2}\int_0^{\pi/4} \cos 2x\,dx && \text{On } [0, \pi/4],\ \cos 2x \ge 0 \text{ so } |\cos 2x| = \cos 2x.\\ &= \sqrt{2}\left[\frac{\sin 2x}{2}\right]_0^{\pi/4}\\ &= \sqrt{2}\left[\frac{1}{2} - 0\right] = \frac{\sqrt{2}}{2}\end{aligned}$$

EXAMPLE 5 *Reducing an Improper Fraction.* Evaluate $\int \frac{3x^2 - 7x}{3x+2}\,dx$.

Solution The integrand is an improper fraction (degree of numerator greater than or equal to degree of denominator). To integrate it, we divide first, getting a quotient plus a remainder that is a proper fraction:

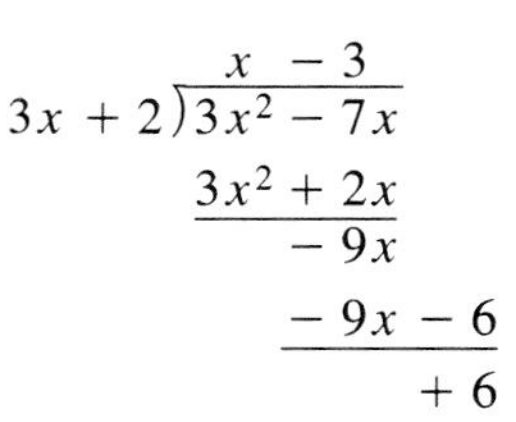

$$\frac{3x^2-7x}{3x+2} = x - 3 + \frac{6}{3x+2}.$$

Therefore,

$$\int \frac{3x^2-7x}{3x+2}\,dx = \int\left(x - 3 + \frac{6}{3x+2}\right)dx = \frac{x^2}{2} - 3x + 2\ln|3x+2| + C.$$

Reducing an improper fraction by long division (Example 5) does not always lead to an expression we can integrate directly. We will see what to do about that in Section 8.3.

EXAMPLE 6 *Separating a Fraction.* Evaluate $\int \frac{3x+2}{\sqrt{1-x^2}}\,dx$.

Solution We first separate the integrand to get

$$\int \frac{3x+2}{\sqrt{1-x^2}}\,dx = 3\int \frac{x\,dx}{\sqrt{1-x^2}} + 2\int \frac{dx}{\sqrt{1-x^2}}.$$

In the first of these new integrals we substitute

$$u = 1 - x^2, \qquad du = -2x\,dx, \qquad \text{and} \qquad x\,dx = -\frac{1}{2}\,du.$$

$$\begin{aligned} 3\int \frac{x\,dx}{\sqrt{1-x^2}} &= 3\int \frac{(-1/2)\,du}{\sqrt{u}} = -\frac{3}{2}\int u^{-1/2}\,du \\ &= -\frac{3}{2}\cdot\frac{u^{1/2}}{1/2} + C_1 = -3\sqrt{1-x^2} + C_1. \end{aligned}$$

The second of the new integrals is a standard form,

$$2\int \frac{dx}{\sqrt{1-x^2}} = 2\sin^{-1} x + C_2.$$

Combining these results and renaming $C_1 + C_2$ as C gives

$$\int \frac{3x+2}{\sqrt{1-x^2}}\,dx = -3\sqrt{1-x^2} + 2\sin^{-1} x + C.$$

EXAMPLE 7 *Multiplying by a Form of 1.* Evaluate $\int \sec x\,dx$.

Solution

$$\begin{aligned} \int \sec x\,dx &= \int (\sec x)(1)\,dx = \int \sec x \cdot \frac{\sec x + \tan x}{\sec x + \tan x}\,dx \\ &= \int \frac{\sec^2 x + \sec x \tan x}{\sec x + \tan x}\,dx \\ &= \int \frac{du}{u} \qquad \begin{aligned} u &= \sec x + \tan x \\ du &= (\sec^2 x + \sec x \tan x)\,dx \end{aligned} \\ &= \ln|u| + C = \ln|\sec x + \tan x| + C \end{aligned}$$

With cosecants and cotangents in place of secants and tangents, the method of Example 7 leads to a companion formula for the integral of the cosecant (Exercise 79).

TABLE 8.2
The secant and cosecant integrals

1. $\int \sec u\,du = \ln|\sec u + \tan u| + C$
2. $\int \csc u\,du = -\ln|\csc u + \cot u| + C$

Procedures for Matching Integrals to Basic Formulas

Procedure	Example
Making a simplifying substitution	$\dfrac{2x-9}{\sqrt{x^2-9x+1}}\,dx = \dfrac{du}{\sqrt{u}}$
Completing the square	$\sqrt{8x-x^2} = \sqrt{16-(x-4)^2}$
Using a trigonometric identity	$(\sec x + \tan x)^2 = \sec^2 x + 2\sec x \tan x + \tan^2 x$ $= \sec^2 x + 2\sec x\tan x + (\sec^2 x - 1)$ $= 2\sec^2 x + 2\sec x \tan x - 1$
Eliminating a square root	$\sqrt{1+\cos 4x} = \sqrt{2\cos^2 2x} = \sqrt{2}\,\lvert\cos 2x\rvert$
Reducing an improper fraction	$\dfrac{3x^2-7x}{3x+2} = x - 3 + \dfrac{6}{3x+2}$
Separating a fraction	$\dfrac{3x+2}{\sqrt{1-x^2}} = \dfrac{3x}{\sqrt{1-x^2}} + \dfrac{2}{\sqrt{1-x^2}}$
Multiplying by a form of 1	$\sec x = \sec x \cdot \dfrac{\sec x + \tan x}{\sec x + \tan x}$ $= \dfrac{\sec^2 x + \sec x \tan x}{\sec x + \tan x}$

Exercises 8.1

Evaluate the integrals in Exercises 1–32 by using appropriate integration formulas.

1. $\displaystyle\int \frac{16x\,dx}{\sqrt{8x^2+1}}$

2. $\displaystyle\int \frac{3\cos x\,dx}{\sqrt{1+3\sin x}}$

3. $\displaystyle\int 3\sqrt{\sin v}\cos v\,dv$

4. $\displaystyle\int \cot^3 y\csc^2 y\,dy$

5. $\displaystyle\int_0^1 \frac{16x\,dx}{8x^2+2}$

6. $\displaystyle\int_0^{\sqrt{\pi/3}} 4z\tan(z^2)\,dz$

7. $\displaystyle\int \frac{dx}{\sqrt{x}\left(\sqrt{x}+1\right)}$

8. $\displaystyle\int \frac{dx}{\sqrt{x}\,(x+1)}$

9. $\displaystyle\int \cot(3-7x)\,dx$

10. $\displaystyle\int \csc(\pi x - 1)\,dx$

11. $\displaystyle\int e^{\theta}\csc(e^{\theta}+1)\,d\theta$

12. $\displaystyle\int \frac{\cot(3+\ln x)}{x}\,dx$

13. $\displaystyle\int \sec\frac{t}{3}\,dt$

14. $\displaystyle\int x\sec(x^2-5)\,dx$

15. $\displaystyle\int \csc(s-\pi)\,ds$

16. $\displaystyle\int \frac{1}{\theta^2}\csc\frac{1}{\theta}\,d\theta$

17. $\displaystyle\int_0^{\sqrt{\ln 2}} 2xe^{x^2}\,dx$

18. $\displaystyle\int_{\pi/2}^{\pi} \sin(y)e^{\cos y}\,dy$

19. $\displaystyle\int e^{\tan v}\sec^2 v\,dv$

20. $\displaystyle\int \frac{e^{\sqrt{t}}\,dt}{\sqrt{t}}$

21. $\displaystyle\int 3^{x+1}\,dx$

22. $\displaystyle\int \frac{2^{\ln x}}{x}\,dx$

23. $\displaystyle\int \frac{2^{\sqrt{w}}\,dw}{2\sqrt{w}}$

24. $\displaystyle\int 10^{2\theta}\,d\theta$

25. $\displaystyle\int \frac{9\,du}{1+9u^2}$

26. $\displaystyle\int \frac{4\,dx}{1+(2x+1)^2}$

27. $\displaystyle\int_0^{1/6} \frac{dx}{\sqrt{1-9x^2}}$

28. $\displaystyle\int_0^1 \frac{dt}{\sqrt{4-t^2}}$

29. $\displaystyle\int \frac{2s\,ds}{\sqrt{1-s^4}}$

30. $\displaystyle\int \frac{2\,dx}{x\sqrt{1-4\ln^2 x}}$

31. $\displaystyle\int \frac{6\,dx}{x\sqrt{25x^2-1}}$

32. $\displaystyle\int \frac{dr}{r\sqrt{r^2-9}}$

Evaluate the integrals in Exercises 33–38.

33. $\displaystyle\int \frac{dx}{\sqrt{-x^2-2x+3}}$

34. $\displaystyle\int \frac{dx}{\sqrt{4x-4x^2}}$

35. $\int \frac{8\,dt}{t^2 + 2t + 65}$

36. $\int \frac{d\theta}{\theta^2 + 2\theta + 3}$

37. $\int \frac{7\,dx}{(x-1)\sqrt{x^2 - 2x - 48}}$

38. $\int \frac{dx}{(2x+1)\sqrt{4x^2 + 4x}}$

Evaluate the integrals in Exercises 39–42.

39. $\int (\sec x + \cot x)^2\,dx$

40. $\int (\csc x - \tan x)^2\,dx$

41. $\int (\csc x - \sec x)(\sin x + \cos x)\,dx$

42. $\int (\csc x + \sec x)(\tan x + \cot x)\,dx$

Evaluate the integrals in Exercises 43–50.

43. $\int_0^{2\pi} \sqrt{\frac{1 - \cos x}{2}}\,dx$

44. $\int_0^{\pi} \sqrt{1 - \cos 2x}\,dx$

45. $\int_{\pi/2}^{\pi} \sqrt{1 + \cos 2t}\,dt$

46. $\int_{-\pi}^{0} \sqrt{1 + \cos t}\,dt$

47. $\int_{-\pi}^{0} \sqrt{1 - \cos^2 \theta}\,d\theta$

48. $\int_{\pi/2}^{\pi} \sqrt{1 - \sin^2 \theta}\,d\theta$

49. $\int_{-\pi/4}^{\pi/4} \sqrt{1 + \tan^2 y}\,dy$

50. $\int_{-\pi/4}^{0} \sqrt{\sec^2 y - 1}\,dy$

Evaluate the integrals in Exercises 51–60.

51. $\int \frac{x}{x+1}\,dx$

52. $\int \frac{x^2}{x^2+1}\,dx$

53. $\int_{\sqrt{2}}^{3} \frac{2x^3}{x^2 - 1}\,dx$

54. $\int_{-1}^{3} \frac{4x^2 - 7}{2x + 3}\,dx$

55. $\int \frac{4t^3 - t^2 + 16t}{t^2 + 4}\,dt$

56. $\int \frac{2\theta^3 - 7\theta^2 + 7\theta}{2\theta - 5}\,d\theta$

57. $\int \frac{1 - x}{\sqrt{1 - x^2}}\,dx$

58. $\int \frac{x + 2\sqrt{x - 1}}{2x\sqrt{x - 1}}\,dx$

59. $\int_0^{\pi/4} \frac{1 + \sin x}{\cos^2 x}\,dx$

60. $\int_0^{1/2} \frac{2 - 8x}{1 + 4x^2}\,dx$

Evaluate the integrals in Exercises 61–66.

61. $\int \frac{1}{1 + \sin x}\,dx$

62. $\int \frac{1}{1 + \cos x}\,dx$

63. $\int \frac{1}{\sec \theta + \tan \theta}\,d\theta$

64. $\int \frac{1}{\csc \theta + \cot \theta}\,d\theta$

65. $\int \frac{1}{1 - \sec x}\,dx$

66. $\int \frac{1}{1 - \csc x}\,dx$

67. **a)** Evaluate $\int \cos^3 \theta\,d\theta$. (*Hint:* $\cos^2 \theta = 1 - \sin^2 \theta$.)
b) Evaluate $\int \cos^5 \theta\,d\theta$.
c) Without actually evaluating the integral, explain how you would evaluate $\int \cos^9 \theta\,d\theta$.

68. **a)** Evaluate $\int \sin^3 \theta\,d\theta$. (*Hint:* $\sin^2 \theta = 1 - \cos^2 \theta$)
b) Evaluate $\int \sin^5 \theta\,d\theta$.
c) Evaluate $\int \sin^7 \theta\,d\theta$.
d) Without actually evaluating the integral, explain how you would evaluate $\int \sin^{13} \theta\,d\theta$.

69. **a)** Express $\int \tan^3 \theta\,d\theta$ in terms of $\int \tan \theta\,d\theta$. Then evaluate $\int \tan^3 \theta\,d\theta$. (*Hint:* $\tan^2 \theta = \sec^2 \theta - 1$)
b) Express $\int \tan^5 \theta\,d\theta$ in terms of $\int \tan^3 \theta\,d\theta$.
c) Express $\int \tan^7 \theta\,d\theta$ in terms of $\int \tan^5 \theta\,d\theta$.
d) Express $\int \tan^{2k+1} \theta\,d\theta$, where k is a positive integer, in terms of $\int \tan^{2k-1} \theta\,d\theta$.

70. **a)** Express $\int \cot^3 \theta\,d\theta$ in terms of $\int \cot \theta\,d\theta$. Then evaluate $\int \cot^3 \theta\,d\theta$. (*Hint:* $\cot^2 \theta = \csc^2 \theta - 1$)
b) Express $\int \cot^5 \theta\,d\theta$ in terms of $\int \cot^3 \theta\,d\theta$.
c) Express $\int \cot^7 \theta\,d\theta$ in terms of $\int \cot^5 \theta\,d\theta$.
d) Express $\int \cot^{2k+1} \theta\,d\theta$, where k is a positive integer, in terms of $\int \cot^{2k-1} \theta\,d\theta$.

71. Find the area of the region bounded above by $y = 2 \cos x$ and below by $y = \sec x$, $-\pi/4 \le x \le \pi/4$.

72. Find the area of the "triangular" region that is bounded from above and below by the curves $y = \csc x$ and $y = \sin x$, $\pi/6 \le x \le \pi/2$, and on the left by the line $x = \pi/6$.

73. Find the volume of the solid generated by revolving the region in Exercise 71 about the x-axis.

74. Find the volume of the solid generated by revolving the region in Exercise 72 about the x-axis.

75. Find the length of the curve $y = \ln(\cos x)$, $0 \le x \le \pi/3$.

76. Find the length of the curve $y = \ln(\sec x)$, $0 \le x \le \pi/4$.

77. Find the centroid of the region bounded by the x-axis, the curve $y = \sec x$, and the lines $x = -\pi/4$, $x = \pi/4$.

78. Find the centroid of the region that is bounded by the x-axis, the curve $y = \csc x$, and the lines $x = \pi/6$, $x = 5\pi/6$.

79. *The Integral of* $\csc x$. Repeat the derivation in Example 7, using cofunctions, to show that

$$\int \csc x\,dx = -\ln|\csc x + \cot x| + C.$$

80. Show that the integral

$$\int \left((x^2 - 1)(x + 1)\right)^{-2/3} dx$$

can be evaluated with any of the following substitutions:

a) $u = 1/(x + 1)$
b) $u = ((x - 1)/(x + 1))^k$ for $k = 1, 1/2, 1/3, -1/3, -2/3$, and -1
c) $u = \tan^{-1} x$
d) $u = \tan^{-1} \sqrt{x}$
e) $u = \tan^{-1}((x - 1)/2)$
f) $u = \cos^{-1} x$
g) $u = \cosh^{-1} x$

What is the value of the integral? (From "Problems and Solutions," *College Mathematics Journal*, Vol. 21, No. 5, Nov. 1990, pp. 425–426.)

Writing for Your Own Knowledge

Answer the following questions in writing. Some answers will take only a sentence or two; others may require several paragraphs. Some explanations may also call for graphs or sketches.

1. What basic integration formulas do you know?
2. What procedures do you know for matching integrals to basic formulas?
3. What are the indefinite integrals of the secant and cosecant functions?
4. (For those who have done Exercises 67 and 68) How do you integrate odd positive integer powers of (a) $\cos\theta$? (b) $\sin\theta$?

8.2 *Integration by Parts*

Integration by parts is a technique used mainly for simplifying integrals of the form

$$\int f(x)\, g(x)\, dx \tag{1}$$

in which f can be differentiated repeatedly and g can be integrated repeatedly without difficulty. The integral

$$\int xe^{x}\, dx$$

is such an integral because $f(x) = x$ can be differentiated twice to become zero and $g(x) = e^{x}$ can be integrated repeatedly without difficulty. Integration by parts also applies to integrals like

$$\int e^{x} \sin x\, dx,$$

in which each part of the integrand appears again after repeated differentiation or integration.

In this section, we describe integration by parts and show how to apply it.

The Formula

The formula for integration by parts comes from the Product Rule,

$$\frac{d}{dx}(uv) = u\frac{dv}{dx} + v\frac{du}{dx}.$$

In its differential form, the rule becomes

$$d(uv) = u\, dv + v\, du,$$

which is then written as

$$u\, dv = d(uv) - v\, du$$

and integrated to give the following formula.

The Integration-by-Parts Formula

$$\int u\, dv = uv - \int v\, du. \tag{2}$$

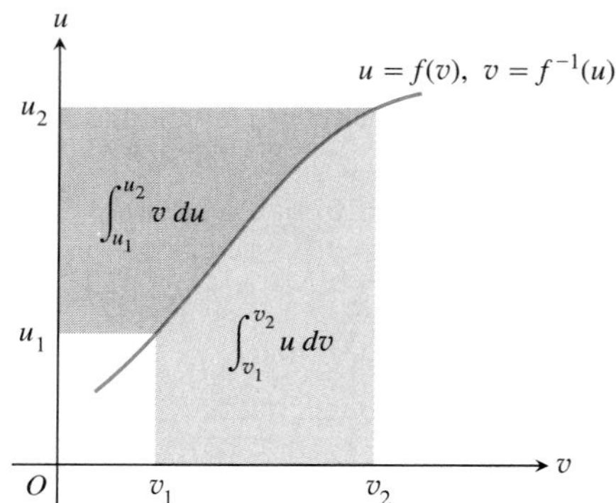

8.1 The area of the blue region, $\int_{v_1}^{v_2} u\,dv$, equals the area of the large rectangle, $u_2 v_2$, minus the areas of the small rectangle, $u_1 v_1$, and the gray region, $\int_{u_1}^{u_2} v\,du$. In symbols,

$$\int_{v_1}^{v_2} u\,dv = (u_2 v_2 - u_1 v_1) - \int_{u_1}^{u_2} v\,du.$$

When and How to Use Integration by Parts

When: If substitution doesn't work, try integration by parts.

How: Start with an integral of the form

$$\int f(x)\,g(x)\,dx.$$

Match this with an integral of the form

$$\int u\,dv$$

by choosing dv to be part of the integrand including dx and possibly $f(x)$ or $g(x)$.

Guideline for choosing u and dv: The formula

$$\int u\,dv = uv - \int v\,du$$

gives a new integral on the right side of the equation. If the new integral is more complex than the original one, try a different choice for u and dv.

The integration-by-parts formula expresses one integral, $\int u\,dv$, in terms of a second integral, $\int v\,du$. With a proper choice of u and v, the second integral may be easier to evaluate than the first. This is the reason for the importance of the formula. When faced with an integral we cannot handle, we can replace it by one with which we might have more success.

The equivalent formula for definite integrals is

$$\int_{v_1}^{v_2} u\,dv = (u_2 v_2 - u_1 v_1) - \int_{u_1}^{u_2} v\,du. \tag{3}$$

Figure 8.1 shows how the different parts of the formula may be interpreted as areas.

EXAMPLE 1 Find $\int x \cos x\,dx$.

Solution We use the formula $\int u\,dv = uv - \int v\,du$ with

$$u = x, \qquad dv = \cos x\,dx,$$
$$du = dx, \qquad v = \sin x. \qquad \text{Simplest antiderivative of } \cos x.$$

Then

$$\int x \cos x\,dx = x \sin x - \int \sin x\,dx = x \sin x + \cos x + C.$$

Before we go on to new examples, let's look at the choices available in Example 1.

EXAMPLE 2 *Example 1 Revisited.* To apply integration by parts to

$$\int x \cos x\,dx = \int u\,dv$$

we have four possible choices:

1. Let $u = 1$ and $dv = x \cos x\,dx$.
2. Let $u = x$ and $dv = \cos x\,dx$.
3. Let $u = x \cos x$ and $dv = dx$.
4. Let $u = \cos x$ and $dv = x\,dx$.

Let's examine these one at a time.

Choice 1 won't do because we don't know how to integrate $dv = x \cos x\,dx$ to get v.

Choice 2 works well, as we saw in Example 1.

Choice 3 leads to

$$u = x \cos x, \qquad dv = dx,$$
$$du = \cos x - x \sin x, \qquad v = x,$$

and the new integral

$$\int v\,du = \int (x \cos x - x^2 \sin x)\,dx.$$

This is worse than the integral we started with.

Choice 4 leads to

$$u = \cos x, \qquad dv = x\,dx,$$
$$du = -\sin x, \qquad v = x^2/2,$$

so the new integral is

$$\int v\,du = -\int \frac{x^2}{2} \sin x\,dx.$$

This, too, is worse.

Summary. Keep in mind that the object is to go from the given integral $\int u\,dv$ to a new integral $\int v\,du$ that is simpler. Integration by parts does not always work, so we can't always achieve the goal.

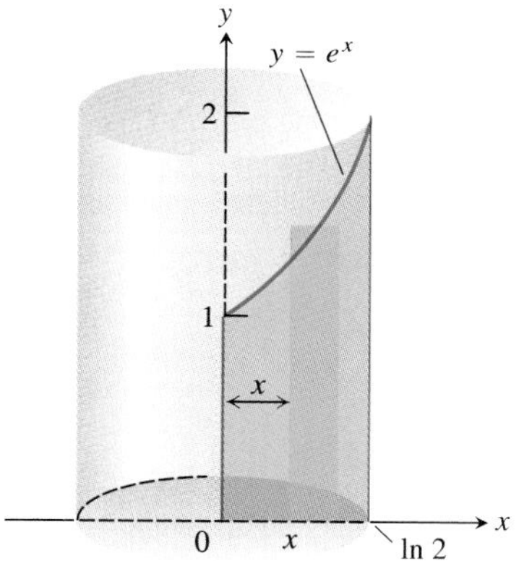

8.2 The solid in Example 3.

EXAMPLE 3 Find the volume of the solid generated by revolving about the y-axis the region in the first quadrant enclosed by the coordinate axes, the curve $y = e^x$ and the line $x = \ln 2$ (Fig. 8.2).

Solution Using the method of cylindrical shells, we find

$$V = \int_a^b 2\pi x\, f(x)\,dx \qquad \text{The shell volume formula}$$
$$= 2\pi \int_0^{\ln 2} x\, e^x\,dx.$$

To evaluate the integral, we use the formula $\int u\,dv = uv - \int v\,du$ with

$$u = x, \qquad dv = e^x\,dx$$
$$du = dx, \qquad v = e^x. \qquad \text{Simplest antiderivative of } e^x$$

Then

$$\int x\,e^x\,dx = x\,e^x - \int e^x\,dx,$$

so

$$\int_0^{\ln 2} x\,e^x\,dx = x\,e^x\Big]_0^{\ln 2} - \int_0^{\ln 2} e^x\,dx$$
$$= \left[\ln 2\, e^{\ln 2} - 0\right] - \left[e^x\right]_0^{\ln 2}$$
$$= 2 \ln 2 - [2 - 1]$$
$$= 2 \ln 2 - 1.$$

The solid's volume is therefore

$$V = 2\pi \int_0^{\ln 2} x\,e^x\,dx = 2\pi(2 \ln 2 - 1).$$

Integration by parts can be useful even when the integrand has only a single factor. For example, we can use this method to find $\int \ln x\, dx$ (next example) or $\int \cos^{-1} x\, dx$ (Exercise 43).

EXAMPLE 4 Find $\int \ln x\, dx$.

Solution Since $\int \ln x\, dx$ can be written as $\int \ln x \cdot 1\, dx$, we use the formula $\int u\, dv = uv - \int v\, du$ with

$$u = \ln x \quad \text{Simplifies when differentiated} \qquad dv = dx \quad \text{Easy to integrate}$$

$$du = \frac{1}{x}\, dx \qquad\qquad v = x. \quad \text{Simplest antiderivative}$$

Then

$$\int \ln x\, dx = x \ln x - \int x \cdot \frac{1}{x}\, dx = x \ln x - \int dx = x \ln x - x + C.$$

Repeated Use

Sometimes we have to use integration by parts more than once to obtain an answer.

EXAMPLE 5 Find $\displaystyle\int x^2 e^x\, dx$.

Solution We use the formula $\displaystyle\int u\, dv = uv - \int v\, du$ with

$$u = x^2, \qquad dv = e^x\, dx, \qquad v = e^x, \quad du = 2x\, dx.$$

This gives

$$\int x^2 e^x\, dx = x^2 e^x - 2 \int x e^x\, dx.$$

It takes a second integration by parts to find the integral on the right. As in Example 3, its value is $xe^x - e^x + C'$. Hence

$$\int x^2 e^x\, dx = x^2 e^x - 2xe^x + 2e^x + C.$$

Solving for the Unknown Integral

Integrals like the one in the next example occur in electrical engineering. Their evaluation requires two integrations by parts, followed by solving for the unknown integral.

EXAMPLE 6 Find $\displaystyle\int e^x \cos x\, dx$.

Solution We first use the formula $\displaystyle\int u\, dv = uv - \int v\, du$ with

$$u = e^x, \qquad dv = \cos x\, dx, \qquad v = \sin x, \qquad du = e^x\, dx.$$

Then

$$\int e^x \cos x\,dx = e^x \sin x - \int e^x \sin x\,dx. \tag{4}$$

The second integral is like the first, except it has $\sin x$ in place of $\cos x$. To evaluate it, we use integration by parts with

$$u = e^x, \qquad dv = \sin x\,dx, \qquad v = -\cos x, \qquad du = e^x\,dx.$$

Then

$$\begin{aligned}\int e^x \cos x\,dx &= e^x \sin x - \left(-e^x \cos x - \int (-\cos x)(e^x\,dx)\right)\\ &= e^x \sin x + e^x \cos x - \int e^x \cos x\,dx.\end{aligned}$$

The unknown integral now appears on both sides of the equation. Combining the two expressions gives

$$2\int e^x \cos x\,dx = e^x \sin x + e^x \cos x + C.$$

Dividing by 2 and renaming the constant of integration gives

$$\int e^x \cos x\,dx = \frac{e^x \sin x + e^x \cos x}{2} + C'.$$

The choice of $u = e^x$ and $dv = \sin x\,dx$ in the second integration may have seemed arbitrary but it wasn't. In theory, we could have chosen $u = \sin x$ and $dv = e^x\,dx$. Doing so, however, would have turned Eq. (4) into

$$\begin{aligned}\int e^x \cos x\,dx &= e^x \sin x - \left(e^x \sin x - \int e^x \cos x\,dx\right)\\ &= \int e^x \cos x\,dx.\end{aligned}$$

The resulting identity is correct, but useless. *Moral:* Once you have decided on what to differentiate and integrate in circumstances like these, stick with them. General formulas for the integrals of $e^{ax} \cos bx$ and the closely related $e^{ax} \sin bx$ can be found in the integral table at the end of this book.

Tabular Integration

We have seen that integrals of the form $\int f(x)\,g(x)\,dx$, in which f can be differentiated repeatedly to become zero and g can be integrated repeatedly without difficulty, are natural candidates for integration by parts. However, if many repetitions are required, the calculations can be cumbersome. In situations like this, there is a way to organize the calculations that saves a great deal of work. It is called **tabular integration** and is illustrated in the following examples.

EXAMPLE 7 Find $\int x^2 e^x\,dx$ by tabular integration.

Solution With $f(x) = x^2$ and $g(x) = e^x$, we list

$f(x)$ and its derivatives		$g(x)$ and its integrals
x^2	$(+)$	e^x
$2x$	$(-)$	e^x
2	$(+)$	e^x
0		e^x.

We add the products of the functions connected by the arrows, with the middle sign changed, to obtain

$$\int x^2 e^x \, dx = x^2 e^x - 2xe^x + 2e^x + C.$$

EXAMPLE 8 Find $\int x^3 \sin x \, dx$ by tabular integration.

Solution With $f(x) = x^3$ and $g(x) = \sin x$, we list

$f(x)$ and its derivatives		$g(x)$ and its integrals
x^3	$(+)$	$\sin x$
$3x^2$	$(-)$	$-\cos x$
$6x$	$(+)$	$-\sin x$
6	$(-)$	$\cos x$
0		$\sin x$.

Again we add the products of the functions connected by the arrows, with every other sign changed, to obtain

$$\int x^3 \sin x \, dx = -x^3 \cos x + 3x^2 \sin x + 6x \cos x - 6 \sin x + C.$$

Exercises 8.2

Evaluate the integrals in Exercises 1–30.

1. $\int x \sin \frac{x}{2} \, dx$
2. $\int \theta \cos \pi\theta \, d\theta$
3. $\int t^2 \cos t \, dt$
4. $\int x^2 \sin x \, dx$
5. $\int_1^2 x \ln x \, dx$
6. $\int_1^e x^3 \ln x \, dx$
7. $\int \tan^{-1} y \, dy$
8. $\int \sin^{-1} y \, dy$
9. $\int x \sec^2 x \, dx$
10. $\int 4x \sec^2 2x \, dx$
11. $\int x^3 e^x \, dx$
12. $\int p^4 e^{-p} \, dp$
13. $\int (x^2 - 5x)e^x \, dx$
14. $\int (r^2 + r + 1)e^r \, dr$
15. $\int x^5 e^x \, dx$
16. $\int t^2 e^{4t} \, dt$
17. $\int_0^{\pi/2} \theta^2 \sin 2\theta \, d\theta$
18. $\int_0^{\pi/2} x^3 \cos 2x \, dx$

19. $\int_{2/\sqrt{3}}^{2} t \sec^{-1} t\, dt$

20. $\int_{0}^{1/\sqrt{2}} 2x \sin^{-1}(x^2)\, dx$

21. $\int e^{\theta} \sin \theta\, d\theta$

22. $\int e^{-y} \cos y\, dy$

23. $\int e^{2x} \cos 3x\, dx$

24. $\int e^{-2x} \sin 2x\, dx$

25. $\int e^{\sqrt{3s+9}}\, ds$

26. $\int_{0}^{1} x\sqrt{1-x}\, dx$

27. $\int_{0}^{\pi/3} x \tan^2 x\, dx$

28. $\int \ln(x + x^2)\, dx$

29. $\int \sin(\ln x)\, dx$

30. $\int z(\ln z)^2\, dz$

31. Find the area of the region enclosed by the curve $y = x \sin x$ and the x-axis for (a) $0 \le x \le \pi$, (b) $\pi \le x \le 2\pi$, (c) $2\pi \le x \le 3\pi$. (d) What pattern do you see here? What is the area between the curve and the x-axis for $n\pi \le x \le (n+1)\pi$, n an arbitrary positive integer? Give reasons for your answer.

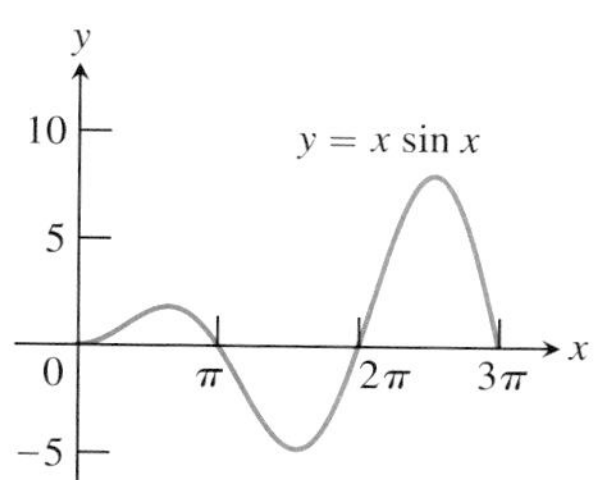

32. Find the area of the region enclosed by the curve $y = x^2 \ln x$ and the x-axis for $1 \le x \le e$.

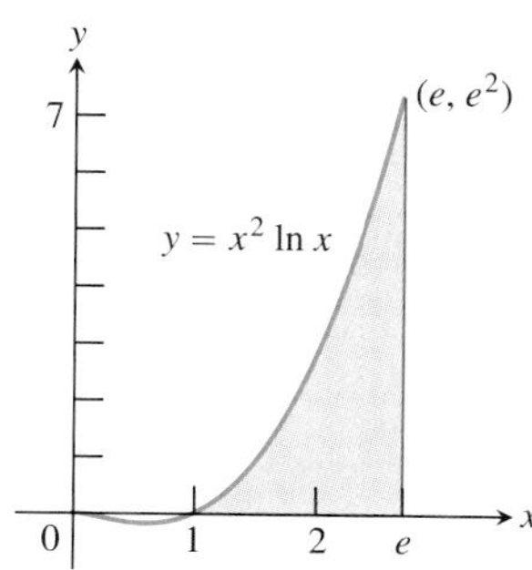

33. Find the volume of the solid generated by revolving the region in the first quadrant bounded by the coordinate axes, the curve $y = e^x$, and the line $x = \ln 2$ about the line $x = \ln 2$.

34. Find the volume of the solid generated by revolving the region in the first quadrant bounded by the coordinate axes, the curve $y = e^{-x}$, and the line $x = 1$ (a) about the y-axis, (b) about the line $x = 1$.

35. Find the volume of the solid generated by revolving the region in the first quadrant bounded by the coordinate axes and the curve $y = \cos x$, $0 \le x \le \pi/2$, about (a) the y-axis, (b) the line $x = \pi/2$.

36. Find the volume of the solid generated by revolving the region bounded by the x-axis and the curve $y = x \sin x$, $0 \le x \le \pi$, about (a) the y-axis, (b) the line $x = \pi$. (See Exercise 31 for a graph.)

37. a) Find the centroid of a thin plate of constant density covering the region in the first quadrant enclosed by the curve $y = x^2 e^x$, the x-axis, and the line $x = 1$.
b) Find the coordinates of the centroid to two decimal places. Show the center of mass in a rough sketch of the plate.

38. a) Find the centroid of a thin plate of constant density covering the region enclosed by the curve $y = \ln x$, the x-axis, and the line $x = e$.
b) Find the coordinates of the centroid to two decimal places. Show the centroid in a rough sketch of the plate.

39. Find the moment about the y-axis of a thin plate of density $\delta = 1 + x$ covering the region bounded by the x-axis and the curve $y = \sin x$, $0 \le x \le \pi$.

40. Although we usually drop the constant of integration in determining v as $\int dv$ in integration by parts, choosing the constant to be different from zero can occasionally be helpful. As a case in point, evaluate

$$\int x \tan^{-1} x\, dx,$$

with $u = \tan^{-1} x$ and $v = (x^2/2) + C$, and find a value of C that simplifies the resulting formula.

41. A retarding force, symbolized by the dashpot in the accompanying figure, slows the motion of the weighted spring so that the mass's position at time t is

$$y = 2e^{-t} \cos t, \quad t \ge 0.$$

a) Find the average value of y over the interval $0 \le t \le 2\pi$.
b) Graph y over the interval $0 \le t \le 2\pi$. Copy the graph and mark the average value of y as a point on the y-axis.

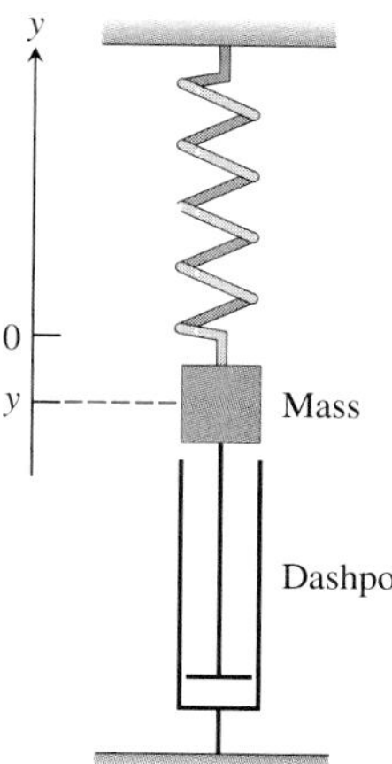

42. In a mass-spring-dashpot system like the one in Exercise 41, the mass's position at time t is

$$y = 4e^{-t}(\sin t - \cos t), \quad t \ge 0.$$

a) Find the average value of y over the interval $0 \le t \le 2\pi$.
b) Graph y over the interval $0 \le t \le 2\pi$. Copy the graph and mark the average value of y as a point on the y-axis.

INTEGRATING INVERSES OF FUNCTIONS

One way to integrate $f^{-1}(x)$ (when f^{-1} is differentiable) is to use the formula

$$\int u\,dv = uv - \int v\,du$$

with $u = f^{-1}(x)$ and $dv = dx$ to rewrite the integral of f^{-1} as

$$\int f^{-1}(x)\,dx = xf^{-1}(x) - \int x\left(\frac{d}{dx}f^{-1}(x)\right)dx. \qquad (5)$$

Use Eq. (5) to evaluate the following integrals. In each case, check your work by differentiating your answer with respect to x.

43. $\int \cos^{-1} x\,dx$

44. $\int \sec^{-1} x\,dx$

45. $\int \sinh^{-1} x\,dx$

46. $\int \cosh^{-1} x\,dx$

47. $\int \tanh^{-1} x\,dx$

48. $\int \operatorname{sech}^{-1} x\,dx$

Writing for Your Own Knowledge

Answer the following questions in writing. Some answers will take only a sentence or two; others may require several paragraphs. Some explanations may also call for graphs or sketches.

1. What is the formula for integration by parts? Where does it come from? Why might you want to use it?
2. When applying the formula for integration by parts, how do you choose the u and dv?
3. How can you apply integration by parts to an integral of the form $\int f(x)\,dx$?
4. What is tabular integration?

8.3 Partial Fractions

A theorem from advanced algebra (mentioned later in more detail) says that every rational function, no matter how complicated, can be rewritten as a sum of simpler fractions, which we can integrate with techniques we already know. For instance,

$$\frac{5x-3}{x^2-2x-3} = \frac{2}{x+1} + \frac{3}{x-3}, \qquad (1)$$

so we can integrate the rational function on the left by integrating the fractions on the right instead.

The method for rewriting rational functions this way is called the **method of partial fractions.** In this particular case, it consists of finding constants A and B such that

$$\frac{5x-3}{x^2-2x-3} = \frac{A}{x+1} + \frac{B}{x-3}. \qquad (2)$$

(Pretend for a moment that we do not know that $A = 2$ and $B = 3$ will work.) We call the fractions $A/(x+1)$ and $B/(x-3)$ **partial fractions** because their denominators are only part of the original denominator $x^2 - 2x - 3$. We call A and B **undetermined coefficients** until proper values for them have been found.

To find A and B, we first clear Eq. (2) of fractions, obtaining

$$5x - 3 = A(x-3) + B(x+1) = (A+B)x - 3A + B.$$

This will be an identity in x if and only if the coefficients of like powers of x on the two sides are equal:

$$A + B = 5, \qquad -3A + B = -3.$$

Solving these equations simultaneously gives $A = 2$ and $B = 3$.

EXAMPLE 1 *Two Distinct Linear Factors in the Denominator.* Find

$$\int \frac{5x - 3}{(x + 1)(x - 3)}\,dx.$$

Solution From the discussion above,

$$\begin{aligned}\int \frac{5x - 3}{(x + 1)(x - 3)}\,dx &= \int \frac{2}{x + 1}\,dx + \int \frac{3}{x - 3}\,dx \\ &= 2\ln|x + 1| + 3\ln|x - 3| + C.\end{aligned}$$

EXAMPLE 2 *A Repeated Linear Factor in the Denominator.* Express

$$\frac{6x + 7}{(x + 2)^2}$$

as a sum of partial fractions.

How to Evaluate Undetermined Coefficients

1. Clear the given equation of fractions.
2. Equate the coefficients of like terms (powers of x).
3. Solve the resulting equations for the coefficients.

Solution Since the denominator has a repeated linear factor, $(x + 2)^2$, we must express the fraction in the form

$$\frac{6x + 7}{(x + 2)^2} = \frac{A}{x + 2} + \frac{B}{(x + 2)^2}. \tag{3}$$

Clearing Eq. (3) of fractions gives

$$6x + 7 = A(x + 2) + B = Ax + (2A + B).$$

Matching coefficients of like terms gives $A = 6$ and

$$7 = 2A + B = 12 + B, \qquad \text{or} \qquad B = -5.$$

Hence,
$$\frac{6x + 7}{(x + 2)^2} = \frac{6}{x + 2} - \frac{5}{(x + 2)^2}.$$

EXAMPLE 3 *An Improper Fraction.* Express

$$\frac{2x^3 - 4x^2 - x - 3}{x^2 - 2x - 3}$$

as a sum of partial fractions.

Solution First we divide the denominator into the numerator to get a polynomial plus a proper fraction. Then we write the proper fraction as a sum of partial fractions. Long division gives

$$\begin{array}{r} 2x \phantom{{}- 4x^2 - x - 3} \\ x^2 - 2x - 3 \,\big)\, \overline{2x^3 - 4x^2 - x - 3} \\ \underline{2x^3 - 4x^2 - 6x} \phantom{{}- 3} \\ 5x - 3 \end{array}$$

Hence,

$$\begin{aligned}\frac{2x^3 - 4x^2 - x - 3}{x^2 - 2x - 3} &= 2x + \frac{5x - 3}{x^2 - 2x - 3} && \text{Result of the division} \\ &= 2x + \frac{2}{x + 1} + \frac{3}{x - 3}. && \text{Proper fraction expanded as in Example 1}\end{aligned}$$

A quadratic polynomial is **irreducible** if it cannot be written as the product of two linear terms with real coefficients.

EXAMPLE 4 *An Irreducible Quadratic Factor in the Denominator.* Express

$$\frac{-2x+4}{(x^2+1)(x-1)^2}$$

as a sum of partial fractions.

Solution The denominator has an irreducible quadratic factor as well as a repeated linear factor, so we write

$$\frac{-2x+4}{(x^2+1)(x-1)^2} = \frac{Ax+B}{x^2+1} + \frac{C}{x-1} + \frac{D}{(x-1)^2}. \tag{4}$$

Notice the numerator over x^2+1: For quadratic factors, we use first-degree numerators, not constant numerators. Clearing the equation of fractions gives

$$\begin{aligned} -2x+4 &= (Ax+B)(x-1)^2 + C(x-1)(x^2+1) + D(x^2+1) \\ &= (A+C)x^3 + (-2A+B-C+D)x^2 \\ &\quad + (A-2B+C)x + (B-C+D). \end{aligned}$$

Equating coefficients of like terms gives

Coefficients of x^3: $0 = A + C$

Coefficients of x^2: $0 = -2A + B - C + D$

Coefficients of x^1: $-2 = A - 2B + C$

Coefficients of x^0: $4 = B - C + D$

We solve these equations simultaneously to find the values of A, B, C, and D:

$-4 = -2A, \quad A = 2$ — Subtract fourth equation from second

$C = -A = -2$ — From the first equation

$B = 1$ — $A = 2$ and $C = -2$ in third equation

$D = 4 - B + C = 1.$ — From the fourth equation

We substitute these values into Eq. (4), obtaining

$$\frac{-2x+4}{(x^2+1)(x-1)^2} = \frac{2x+1}{x^2+1} - \frac{2}{x-1} + \frac{1}{(x-1)^2}.$$

EXAMPLE 5 Evaluate $\displaystyle\int \frac{-2x+4}{(x^2+1)(x-1)^2}\,dx.$

Solution We expand the integrand by partial fractions, as in Example 4, and integrate the terms of the expansion:

$$\begin{aligned} \int \frac{-2x+4}{(x^2+1)(x-1)^2}\,dx &= \int \left(\frac{2x+1}{x^2+1} - \frac{2}{x-1} + \frac{1}{(x-1)^2}\right) dx \qquad \text{Example 4} \\ &= \int \left(\frac{2x}{x^2+1} + \frac{1}{x^2+1} - \frac{2}{x-1} + \frac{1}{(x-1)^2}\right) dx \\ &= \ln(x^2+1) + \tan^{-1} x - 2\ln|x-1| - \frac{1}{x-1} + C. \end{aligned}$$

Cases Discussed So Far

Proper fraction		*Decomposition*
$\dfrac{\text{numerator}}{(x+p)(x+q)}$	=	$\dfrac{A}{(x+p)}+\dfrac{B}{(x+q)}$
$\dfrac{\text{numerator}}{(x+p)^2}$	=	$\dfrac{A}{(x+p)}+\dfrac{B}{(x+p)^2}$
$\dfrac{\text{numerator}}{(x^2+p)(x+q)^2}$	=	$\dfrac{Ax+B}{x^2+p}+\dfrac{C}{x+q}+\dfrac{D}{(x+q)^2}$

General Description of the Method

Success in writing a rational function $f(x)/g(x)$ as a sum of partial fractions depends on two things:

1. *The degree of $f(x)$ must be less than the degree of $g(x)$.* (If it isn't, divide and work with the remainder term.)
2. *We must know the factors of $g(x)$.* (In theory, any polynomial with real coefficients can be written as a product of real linear factors and real quadratic factors. In practice, the factors may be hard to find.)

A theorem from advanced algebra says that when these two conditions are met, we may write $f(x)/g(x)$ as the sum of partial fractions by taking these steps.

The Method of Partial Fractions ($f(x)/g(x)$ *Proper*)

STEP 1: Let $x-r$ be a linear factor of $g(x)$. Suppose $(x-r)^m$ is the highest power of $x-r$ that divides $g(x)$. Then assign the sum of m partial fractions to this factor, as follows:

$$\frac{A_1}{x-r}+\frac{A_2}{(x-r)^2}+\cdots+\frac{A_m}{(x-r)^m}.$$

Do this for each distinct linear factor of $g(x)$.

STEP 2: Let x^2+px+q be a quadratic factor of $g(x)$. Suppose

$$(x^2+px+q)^n$$

is the highest power of this factor that divides $g(x)$. Then to this factor assign the sum of the n partial fractions:

$$\frac{B_1x+C_1}{x^2+px+q}+\frac{B_2x+C_2}{(x^2+px+q)^2}+\cdots+\frac{B_nx+C_n}{(x^2+px+q)^n}.$$

Do this for each distinct quadratic factor of $g(x)$ that cannot be factored into linear factors with real coefficients.

STEP 3: Set the original fraction $f(x)/g(x)$ equal to the sum of all these partial fractions. Clear the resulting equation of fractions and arrange the terms in decreasing powers of x.

STEP 4: Equate the coefficients of corresponding powers of x and solve the resulting equations for the undetermined coefficients.

Exercises 8.3

Expand the quotients in Exercises 1–8 by partial fractions.

1. $\dfrac{5x-13}{(x-3)(x-2)}$
2. $\dfrac{5x-7}{x^2-3x+2}$
3. $\dfrac{x+4}{(x+1)^2}$
4. $\dfrac{2x+2}{x^2-2x+1}$
5. $\dfrac{x+1}{x^2(x-1)}$
6. $\dfrac{z}{z^3-z^2-6z}$
7. $\dfrac{x^2+8}{x^2-5x+6}$
8. $\dfrac{x^4+9}{x^4+9x^2}$

Evaluate the integrals in Exercises 9–36.

9. $\int \frac{dx}{1-x^2}$

10. $\int \frac{dx}{x^2+2x}$

11. $\int \frac{x+4}{x^2+5x-6}\,dx$

12. $\int \frac{2x+1}{x^2-7x+12}\,dx$

13. $\int_4^8 \frac{y\,dy}{y^2-2y-3}$

14. $\int_{1/2}^1 \frac{y+4}{y^2+y}\,dy$

15. $\int \frac{dt}{t^3+t^2-2t}$

16. $\int \frac{x+3}{2x^3-8x}\,dx$

17. $\int_0^1 \frac{x^3\,dx}{x^2+2x+1}$

18. $\int_{-1}^0 \frac{x^3\,dx}{x^2-2x+1}$

19. $\int \frac{dx}{(x^2-1)^2}$

20. $\int \frac{x^2\,dx}{(x-1)(x^2+2x+1)}$

21. $\int \frac{(x-2)^2\tan^{-1}(2x)-12x^3-3x}{(4x^2+1)(x-2)^2}\,dx$

22. $\int \frac{(x+1)^2\tan^{-1}(3x)+9x^3+x}{(9x^2+1)(x+1)^2}\,dx$

23. $\int \frac{4x^2\,dx}{4x^2+9}$

24. $\int \frac{18x^3+8x-2}{9x^2+4}\,dx$

25. $\int \frac{y^4+y^2-1}{y^3+y}\,dy$

26. $\int \frac{-8y^3+2y^2+1}{2y^2+1}\,dy$

27. $\int_0^1 \frac{dx}{(x+1)(x^2+1)}$

28. $\int_1^{\sqrt{3}} \frac{3t^2+t+4}{t^3+t}\,dt$

29. $\int \frac{\theta^4+2\theta}{\theta^2+4}\,d\theta$

30. $\int \frac{9x^3+1}{9x^2+1}\,dx$

31. $\int \frac{y^2+2y+1}{(y^2+1)^2}\,dy$

32. $\int \frac{8x^2+8x+2}{(4x^2+1)^2}\,dx$

33. $\int \frac{2s+2}{(s^2+1)(s-1)^3}\,ds$

34. $\int \frac{s^4+81}{s(s^2+9)^2}\,ds$

35. $\int \frac{2\theta^3+5\theta^2+8\theta+4}{(\theta^2+2\theta+2)^2}\,d\theta$

36. $\int \frac{\theta^4-4\theta^3+2\theta^2-3\theta+1}{(\theta^2+1)^3}\,d\theta$

Evaluate the integrals in Exercises 37–44.

37. $\int \frac{e^t\,dt}{e^{2t}+3e^t+2}$

38. $\int \frac{e^{4t}+2e^{2t}-e^t}{e^{2t}+1}\,dt$

39. $\int \frac{\cos y\,dy}{\sin^2 y+\sin y-6}$

40. $\int \frac{\sin\theta\,d\theta}{\cos^2\theta+\cos\theta-2}$

41. $\int \frac{1-\sqrt{x}}{1+\sqrt{x}}\,dx$

42. $\int \frac{d\theta}{\sqrt{\theta}+\sqrt[3]{\theta}}$

43. $\int t\ln(t+5)\,dt$

44. $\int \ln(r^2+1)\,dr$

In Exercises 45–47, find the volume of the solid generated by revolving the shaded region about the indicated axis.

45. The x-axis

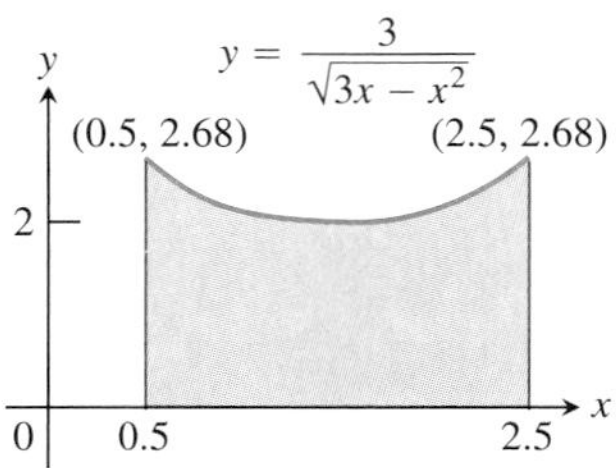

46. The y-axis

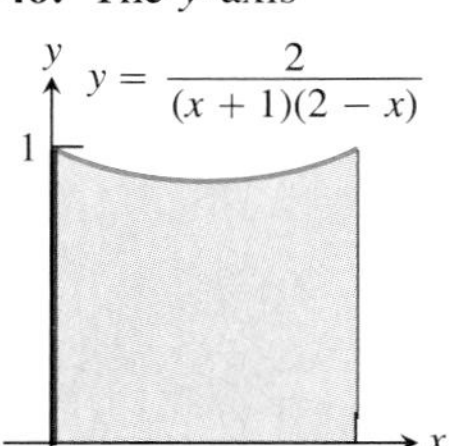

47. The x-axis

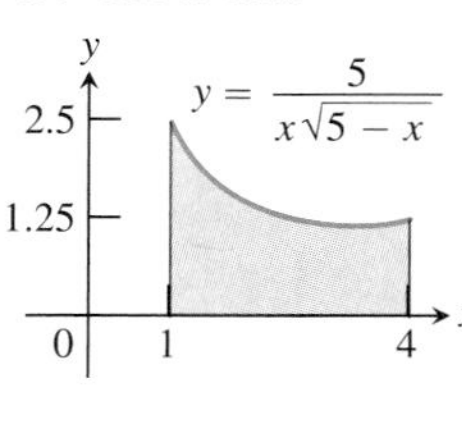

48. Find the length of the curve $y=\ln(1-x^2)$, $0\le x\le 1/2$.

49. Find, to two decimal places, the x-coordinate of the centroid of the region in the first quadrant bounded by the x-axis, the curve $y=\tan^{-1}x$, and the line $x=\sqrt{3}$.

50. Find the x-coordinate of the centroid of this region to two decimal places.

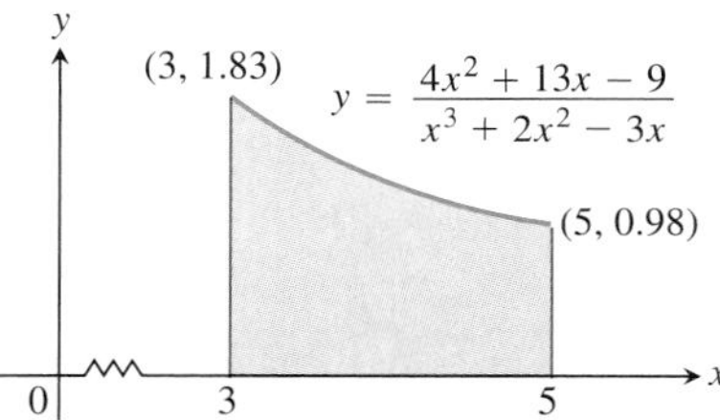

51. *Social Diffusion.* Sociologists sometimes use the phrase "social diffusion" to describe the way information spreads through a population. The information might be a rumor, a cultural fad, or news about a technical innovation. In a sufficiently large population, the number of people x who have the information is treated as a differentiable function of time t, and the rate of diffusion, dx/dt, is assumed to be proportional to the number of people who have the information times the number of people who do not. This leads to the equation

$$\frac{dx}{dt}=kx(N-x),$$

where N is the number of people in the population.

Suppose t is in days, $k=1/250$, and two people start a rumor at time $t=0$ in a population of $N=1000$ people.

a) Find x as a function of t.

b) When will half the population have heard the rumor? (This is when the rumor will be spreading the fastest.)

52. *Second-order Chemical Reactions.* Many chemical reactions are the result of the interaction of two molecules that undergo a change to produce a new product. The rate of the reaction typically depends on the concentrations of the two kinds of molecules. If a is the amount of substance A and b is the amount of substance B at time $t = 0$, and if x is the amount of product at time t, then the rate of formation of x may be given by the differential equation

$$\frac{dx}{dt} = k(a - x)(b - x),$$

or

$$\frac{1}{(a - x)(b - x)} \frac{dx}{dt} = k,$$

where k is a constant for the reaction. Integrate both sides of this equation to obtain a relation between x and t

a) if $a = b$, and
b) if $a \neq b$. Assume in each case that $x = 0$ when $t = 0$.

Solve the initial value problems in Exercises 53–56 for x as a function of t.

53. Differential equation: $(t^2 - 3t + 2)\frac{dx}{dt} = 1 \quad (t > 2)$

Initial condition: $x = 0$ when $t = 3$

54. Differential equation: $(3t^4 + 4t^2 + 1)\frac{dx}{dt} = 2\sqrt{3}$

Initial condition: $x = -\pi\sqrt{3}/4$ when $t = 1$

55. Differential equation: $(t^2 + 2t)\frac{dx}{dt} = 2x + 2 \quad (t, x > 0)$

Initial condition: $x = 1$ when $t = 1$

56. Differential equation: $(t + 1)\frac{dx}{dt} = x^2 + 1 \quad (t > -1)$

Initial condition: $x = \pi/4$ when $t = 0$

57. *An Integral Connecting π to the Approximation 22/7.*

a) Evaluate $\int_0^1 \frac{x^4(x - 1)^4}{x^2 + 1}\, dx$.

b) How good is the approximation $\pi \approx 22/7$? Find out by expressing $(\pi - 22/7)$ as a percentage of π.

Writing for Your Own Knowledge

Answer the following questions in writing. Some answers will take only a sentence or two; others may require several paragraphs. Some explanations may also call for graphs or sketches.

1. What is the goal of the method of partial fractions?
2. When the degree of $f(x)$ is less than the degree of $g(x)$, how do you write the rational function $f(x)/g(x)$ as a sum of partial fractions if $g(x)$
   a) is a product of distinct linear factors?
   b) consists of a repeated linear factor?
   c) contains an irreducible quadratic factor?
3. What do you do if $f(x)/g(x)$ is not a proper fraction?

8.4 *Trigonometric Substitutions*

Trigonometric substitutions enable us to replace the binomials $a^2 + x^2$, $a^2 - x^2$, and $x^2 - a^2$ by single squared terms and thereby transform a number of integrals containing square roots into integrals we can evaluate directly.

Three Basic Substitutions

The most common substitutions are $x = a \tan\theta$, $x = a \sin\theta$, and $x = a \sec\theta$. They come from the reference right triangles in Fig. 8.3 (on the following page).

With $x = a \tan\theta$,

$$a^2 + x^2 = a^2 + a^2\tan^2\theta = a^2(1 + \tan^2\theta) = a^2\sec^2\theta. \tag{1}$$

With $x = a \sin\theta$,

$$a^2 - x^2 = a^2 - a^2\sin^2\theta = a^2(1 - \sin^2\theta) = a^2\cos^2\theta. \tag{2}$$

With $x = a \sec\theta$,

$$x^2 - a^2 = a^2\sec^2\theta - a^2 = a^2(\sec^2\theta - 1) = a^2\tan^2\theta. \tag{3}$$

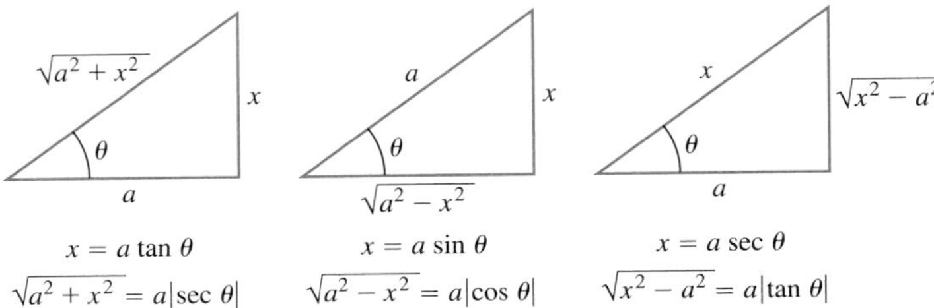

8.3 Reference triangles for trigonometric substitutions that change binomials into single squared terms.

Trigonometric Substitutions

1. $x = a\tan\theta$ replaces $a^2 + x^2$ by $a^2\sec^2\theta$,
2. $x = a\sin\theta$ replaces $a^2 - x^2$ by $a^2\cos^2\theta$,
3. $x = a\sec\theta$ replaces $x^2 - a^2$ by $a^2\tan^2\theta$.

We want any substitution we use in an integration to be reversible so that we can change back to the original variable afterward. For example, if $x = a\tan\theta$, we want to be able to set $\theta = \tan^{-1}(x/a)$ after the integration takes place. If $x = a\sin\theta$, we want to be able to set $\theta = \sin^{-1}(x/a)$ when we're done, and similarly for $x = a\sec\theta$.

As we know from Section 6.8, the functions in these substitutions have inverses only for selected values of θ (Fig. 8.4). For reversibility,

$$x = a\tan\theta \quad \text{requires} \quad \theta = \tan^{-1}\left(\frac{x}{a}\right) \quad \text{with} \quad -\frac{\pi}{2} < \theta < \frac{\pi}{2},$$

$$x = a\sin\theta \quad \text{requires} \quad \theta = \sin^{-1}\left(\frac{x}{a}\right) \quad \text{with} \quad -\frac{\pi}{2} \le \theta \le \frac{\pi}{2},$$

$$x = a\sec\theta \quad \text{requires} \quad \theta = \sec^{-1}\left(\frac{x}{a}\right) \quad \text{with} \quad \begin{cases} 0 \le \theta < \dfrac{\pi}{2} & \text{if } \dfrac{x}{a} \ge 1, \\ \dfrac{\pi}{2} < \theta \le \pi & \text{if } \dfrac{x}{a} \le -1. \end{cases}$$

To simplify calculations with the substitution $x = a\sec\theta$, we will restrict its use to integrals in which $(x/a) \ge 1$. This will place θ in $[0, \pi/2)$ and make $\tan\theta \ge 0$. We will then have $\sqrt{x^2 - a^2} = \sqrt{a^2\tan^2\theta} = |a\tan\theta| = a\tan\theta$, free of absolute values, provided $a > 0$.

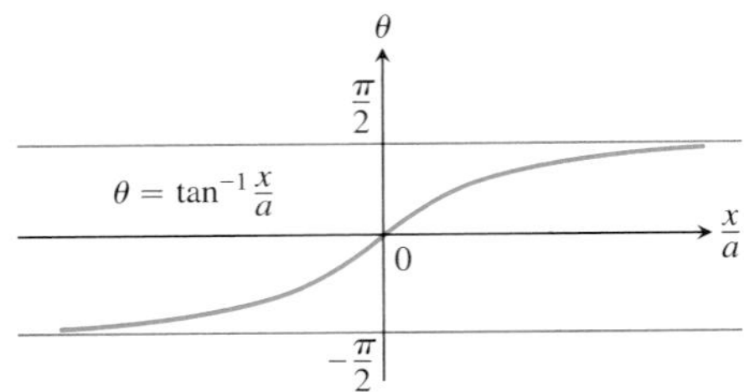

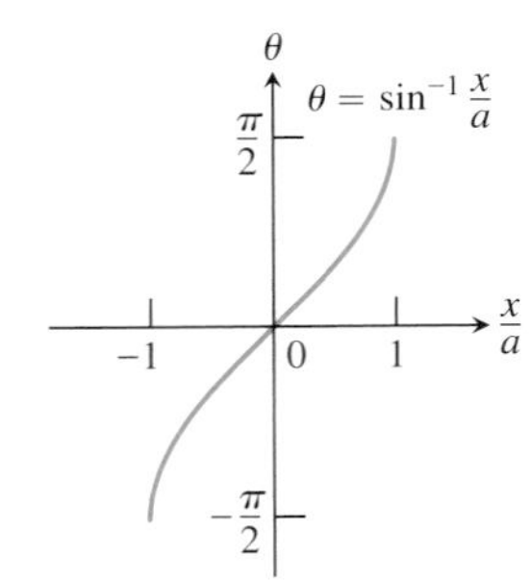

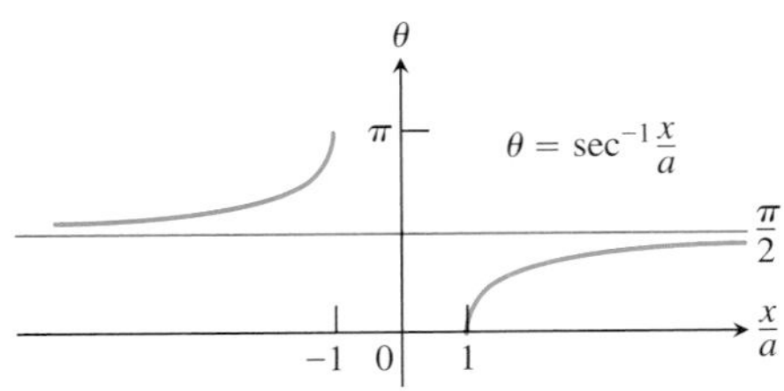

8.4 The arc tangent, arc sine, and arc secant of x/a, graphed as functions of x/a.

EXAMPLE 1 Evaluate $\displaystyle\int \frac{dx}{\sqrt{4 + x^2}}$.

Solution We set

$$x = 2\tan\theta, \qquad dx = 2\sec^2\theta\, d\theta, \qquad -\frac{\pi}{2} < \theta < \frac{\pi}{2},$$

$$4 + x^2 = 4 + 4\tan^2\theta = 4(1 + \tan^2\theta) = 4\sec^2\theta.$$

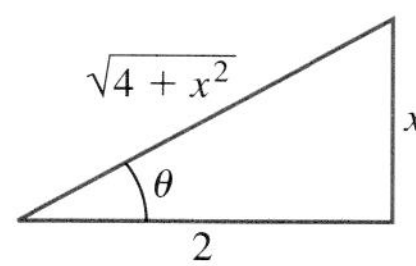

8.5 Reference triangle for $x = 2\tan\theta$ (Example 1):

$$\tan\theta = \frac{x}{2}$$

and

$$\sec\theta = \frac{\sqrt{4+x^2}}{2}$$

Then

$$\begin{aligned}
\int \frac{dx}{\sqrt{4+x^2}} &= \int \frac{2\sec^2\theta\,d\theta}{\sqrt{4\sec^2\theta}} = \int \frac{\sec^2\theta\,d\theta}{|\sec\theta|} && \sqrt{\sec^2\theta} = |\sec\theta| \\
&= \int \sec\theta\,d\theta && \sec\theta > 0 \text{ for } -\frac{\pi}{2} < \theta < \frac{\pi}{2} \\
&= \ln|\sec\theta + \tan\theta| + C \\
&= \ln\left|\frac{\sqrt{4+x^2}}{2} + \frac{x}{2}\right| + C && \text{From Fig. 8.5} \\
&= \ln\left|\sqrt{4+x^2} + x\right| + C'. && \text{Taking } C' = C - \ln 2
\end{aligned}$$

Notice how we expressed $\ln|\sec\theta + \tan\theta|$ in terms of x: We drew a reference triangle for the original substitution $x = 2\tan\theta$ (Fig. 8.5) and read the ratios from the triangle.

EXAMPLE 2 Evaluate $\displaystyle\int \frac{x^2\,dx}{\sqrt{9-x^2}}$.

Solution To replace $9 - x^2$ by a single squared term, we set

$$x = 3\sin\theta, \qquad dx = 3\cos\theta\,d\theta, \qquad -\frac{\pi}{2} < \theta < \frac{\pi}{2},$$

$$9 - x^2 = 9(1 - \sin^2\theta) = 9\cos^2\theta.$$

Then

$$\begin{aligned}
\int \frac{x^2\,dx}{\sqrt{9-x^2}} &= \int \frac{9\sin^2\theta \cdot 3\cos\theta\,d\theta}{|3\cos\theta|} \\
&= 9\int \sin^2\theta\,d\theta && \cos\theta > 0 \text{ for } -\frac{\pi}{2} < \theta < \frac{\pi}{2} \\
&= 9\int \frac{1-\cos 2\theta}{2}\,d\theta \\
&= \frac{9}{2}\left(\theta - \frac{\sin 2\theta}{2}\right) + C \\
&= \frac{9}{2}(\theta - \sin\theta\cos\theta) + C && \sin 2\theta = 2\sin\theta\cos\theta \\
&= \frac{9}{2}\left(\sin^{-1}\frac{x}{3} - \frac{x}{3}\cdot\frac{\sqrt{9-x^2}}{3}\right) + C && \text{Fig. 8.6} \\
&= \frac{9}{2}\sin^{-1}\frac{x}{3} - \frac{x}{2}\sqrt{9-x^2} + C.
\end{aligned}$$

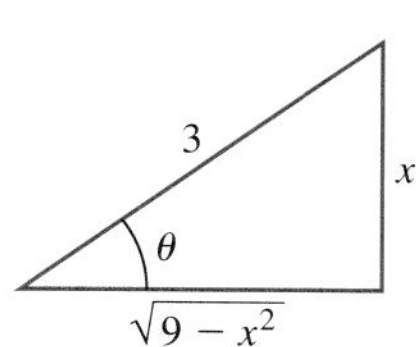

8.6 Reference triangle for $x = 3\sin\theta$ (Example 2):

$$\sin\theta = \frac{x}{3}$$

and

$$\cos\theta = \frac{\sqrt{9-x^2}}{3}$$

EXAMPLE 3 Evaluate $\displaystyle\int \frac{dx}{\sqrt{25x^2-4}}, \quad x > \frac{2}{5}$.

Solution We first rewrite the radical as

$$\sqrt{25x^2-4} = \sqrt{25\left(x^2 - \frac{4}{25}\right)} = 5\sqrt{x^2 - \left(\frac{2}{5}\right)^2}$$

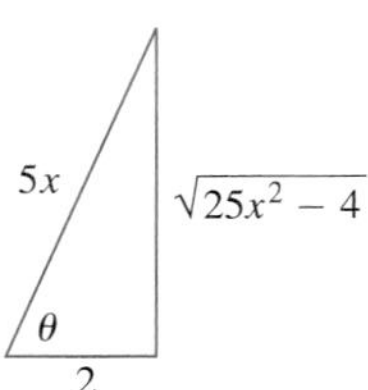

8.7 If $x = (2/5)\sec\theta$, $0 \le \theta \le \pi/2$, then $\theta = \sec^{-1}(5x/2)$ and we can read the values of the other trigonometric functions of θ from this right triangle.

to put the radicand in the form $x^2 - a^2$. We then substitute

$$x = \frac{2}{5}\sec\theta, \qquad dx = \frac{2}{5}\sec\theta\tan\theta\,d\theta,$$

$$x^2 - \left(\frac{2}{5}\right)^2 = \frac{4}{25}\sec^2\theta - \frac{4}{25} = \frac{4}{25}(\sec^2\theta - 1) = \frac{4}{25}\tan^2\theta,$$

$$\sqrt{x^2 - \left(\frac{2}{5}\right)^2} = \frac{2}{5}\tan\theta.$$

With these substitutions, we have

$$\int \frac{dx}{\sqrt{25x^2-4}} = \int \frac{dx}{5\sqrt{x^2-(4/25)}} = \int \frac{(2/5)\sec\theta\tan\theta\,d\theta}{5\cdot(2/5)\tan\theta}$$

$$= \frac{1}{5}\int \sec\theta\,d\theta = \frac{1}{5}\ln|\sec\theta + \tan\theta| + C$$

$$= \frac{1}{5}\ln\left|\frac{5x}{2} + \frac{\sqrt{25x^2-4}}{2}\right| + C \qquad \text{Fig. 8.7}$$

A trigonometric substitution can sometimes help us to evaluate an integral containing an integer power of a quadratic binomial, as in the next example.

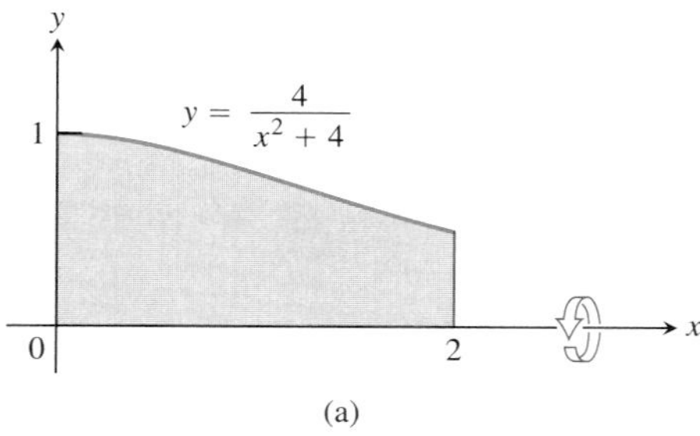

(a)

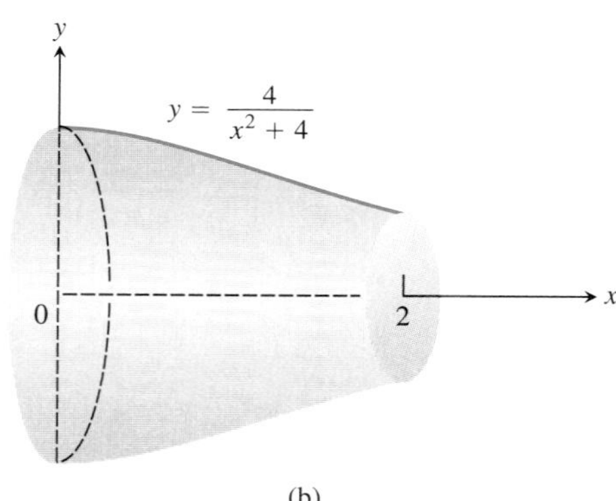

(b)

8.8 The region (a) and solid (b) in Example 4.

EXAMPLE 4 Find the volume of the solid generated by revolving about the x-axis the region bounded by the curve $y = 4/(x^2+4)$, the x-axis, and the lines $x = 0$ and $x = 2$.

Solution We sketch the region (Fig. 8.8) and use the disk method (Section 7.2):

$$V = \int_0^2 \pi[R(x)]^2\,dx = 16\pi\int_0^2 \frac{dx}{(x^2+4)^2}. \qquad R(x) = \frac{4}{x^2+4}$$

To evaluate the integral, we set

$$x = 2\tan\theta, \qquad dx = 2\sec^2\theta\,d\theta, \qquad \theta = \tan^{-1}\frac{x}{2},$$

$$x^2 + 4 = 4\tan^2\theta + 4 = 4(\tan^2\theta + 1) = 4\sec^2\theta$$

(Fig. 8.9). With these substitutions,

$$V = 16\pi\int_0^2 \frac{dx}{(x^2+4)^2}$$

$$= 16\pi\int_0^{\pi/4} \frac{2\sec^2\theta\,d\theta}{(4\sec^2\theta)^2} \qquad \theta = 0 \text{ when } x = 0;\ \theta = \pi/4 \text{ when } x = 2$$

$$= 16\pi\int_0^{\pi/4} \frac{2\sec^2\theta\,d\theta}{16\sec^4\theta} = \pi\int_0^{\pi/4} 2\cos^2\theta\,d\theta$$

$$= \pi\int_0^{\pi/4}(1+\cos 2\theta)\,d\theta = \pi\left[\theta + \frac{\sin 2\theta}{2}\right]_0^{\pi/4} \qquad 2\cos^2\theta = 1 + \cos 2\theta$$

$$= \pi\left[\frac{\pi}{4} + \frac{1}{2}\right] \approx 4.04.$$

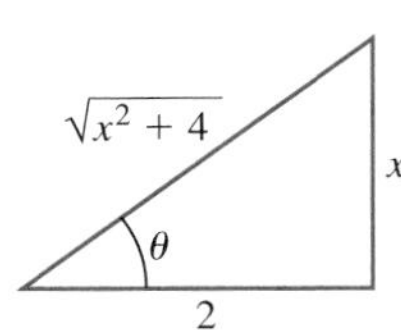

8.9 Reference triangle for $x = 2\tan\theta$ (Example 4).

Exercises 8.4

Evaluate the integrals in Exercises 1–28.

1. $\int \frac{dy}{\sqrt{9+y^2}}$

2. $\int \frac{3\,dy}{\sqrt{1+9y^2}}$

3. $\int \frac{x^3\,dx}{\sqrt{x^2+4}}$

4. $\int \frac{dx}{x^2\sqrt{x^2+1}}$

5. $\int \frac{8\,dw}{w^2\sqrt{4-w^2}}$

6. $\int \frac{\sqrt{9-w^2}}{w^2}\,dw$

7. $\int \sqrt{25-t^2}\,dt$

8. $\int \sqrt{1-9t^2}\,dt$

9. $\int \frac{dx}{x^2\sqrt{x^2-1}}, \quad x>1$

10. $\int \frac{2\,dx}{x^3\sqrt{x^2-1}}, \quad x>1$

11. $\int \frac{dx}{\sqrt{4x^2-49}}, \quad x>\frac{7}{2}$

12. $\int \frac{5\,dx}{\sqrt{25x^2-9}}, \quad x>\frac{3}{5}$

13. $\int_1^e \frac{dy}{y\sqrt{1+(\ln y)^2}}$

14. $\int_0^{\ln 4} \frac{e^t\,dt}{\sqrt{e^{2t}+9}}$

15. $\int_0^{3\sqrt{2}} \frac{4x^2\,dx}{(1-x^2)^{3/2}}$

16. $\int_0^1 \frac{dx}{(4-x^2)^{3/2}}$

17. $\int \frac{dx}{(x^2-1)^{3/2}}, \quad x>1$

18. $\int \frac{x^2\,dx}{(x^2-1)^{5/2}}, \quad x>1$

19. $\int_0^1 (1+t^2)^{-3/2}\,dt$

20. $\int_{\ln(3/4)}^{\ln(4/3)} \frac{e^t\,dt}{(1+e^{2t})^{3/2}}$

21. $\int \frac{(1-x^2)^{3/2}}{x^6}\,dx$

22. $\int \frac{(1-x^2)^{1/2}}{x^4}\,dx$

23. $\int \frac{\sqrt{y^2-49}}{y}\,dy, \quad y>7$

24. $\int \frac{\sqrt{y^2-25}}{y^3}\,dy, \quad y>5$

25. $\int \frac{8\,dx}{(4x^2+1)^2}$

26. $\int \frac{6\,dt}{(9t^2+1)^2}$

27. $\int \frac{v^2\,dv}{(1-v^2)^{5/2}}$

28. $\int \frac{(1-r^2)^{5/2}}{r^8}\,dr$

Use trigonometric substitutions in Exercises 29–32 to evaluate the integrals. (The answers should look familiar.)

29. $\int \frac{dx}{x\sqrt{x^2-1}}$

30. $\int \frac{dx}{1+x^2}$

31. $\int \frac{x\,dx}{\sqrt{x^2-1}}$

32. $\int \frac{dx}{\sqrt{1-x^2}}$

33. Find the area of the shaded region.

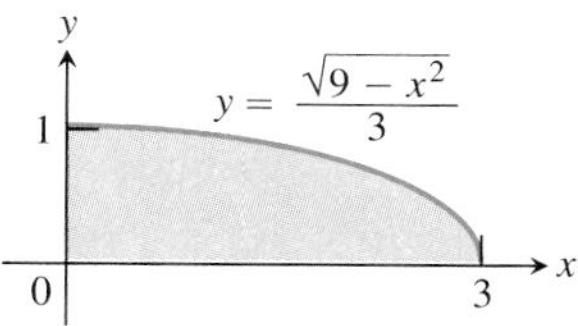

34. Find the volume of the solid generated by revolving about the x-axis the region in the first quadrant enclosed by the coordinate axes, the curve $y = 2/(1+x^2)$, and the line $x = 1$.

Solve the initial value problems in Exercises 35 and 36.

35. $x\frac{dy}{dx} = \sqrt{x^2-4}, \quad x \ge 2, \quad y = 0$ when $x = 2$

36. $\sqrt{x^2-9}\,\frac{dy}{dx} = 1, \quad x>3, \quad y = \ln 3$ when $x = 5$

THE SUBSTITUTION $z = \tan(x/2)$

The substitution

$$z = \tan\frac{x}{2} \tag{1}$$

reduces the problem of integrating a rational expression in $\sin x$ and $\cos x$ to a problem of integrating a rational function of z. This in turn can be integrated by partial fractions. Thus the substitution (1) is a powerful tool. It is cumbersome, however, and is used only when simpler methods fail.

Figure 8.10 shows how $\tan(x/2)$ expresses a rational function of $\sin x$ and $\cos x$. To see the effect of the substitution, we calculate

$$\cos x = 2\cos^2\left(\frac{x}{2}\right) - 1 = \frac{2}{\sec^2(x/2)} - 1$$

$$= \frac{2}{1+\tan^2(x/2)} - 1 = \frac{2}{1+z^2} - 1,$$

$$\cos x = \frac{1-z^2}{1+z^2}, \tag{2}$$

and

$$\sin x = 2\sin\frac{x}{2}\cos\frac{x}{2} = 2\frac{\sin(x/2)}{\cos(x/2)}\cdot\cos^2\left(\frac{x}{2}\right)$$

$$= 2\tan\frac{x}{2}\cdot\frac{1}{\sec^2(x/2)} = \frac{2\tan(x/2)}{1+\tan^2(x/2)},$$

$$\sin x = \frac{2z}{1+z^2}. \tag{3}$$

Finally, $x = 2\tan^{-1} z$, so

$$dx = \frac{2\,dz}{1+z^2}. \tag{4}$$

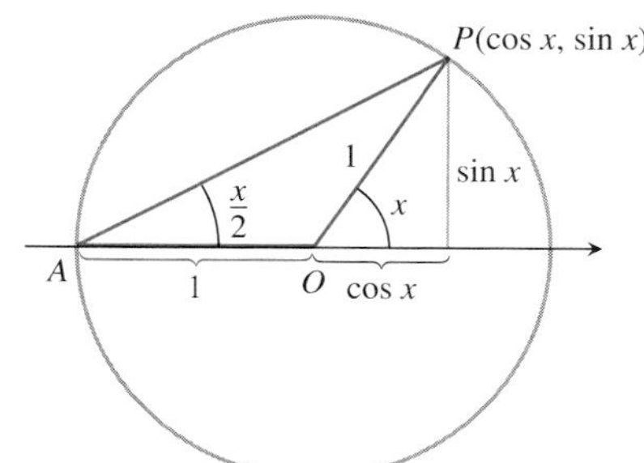

8.10 From this figure, we can read the relation

$$\tan\frac{x}{2} = \frac{\sin x}{1+\cos x}$$

EXAMPLE

a) $$\int \frac{1}{1+\cos x}\,dx = \int \frac{1+z^2}{2}\,\frac{2\,dz}{1+z^2}$$

$$= \int dz = z + C = \tan\left(\frac{x}{2}\right) + C$$

b) $$\int \frac{1}{2+\sin x}\,dx = \int \frac{1+z^2}{2+2z+2z^2}\,\frac{2\,dz}{1+z^2}$$

$$= \int \frac{dz}{z^2+z+1} = \int \frac{dz}{(z+(1/2))^2+3/4}$$

$$= \int \frac{du}{u^2+a^2}$$

$$= \frac{1}{a}\tan^{-1}\left(\frac{u}{a}\right) + C$$

$$= \frac{2}{\sqrt{3}}\tan^{-1}\frac{2z+1}{\sqrt{3}} + C$$

$$= \frac{2}{\sqrt{3}}\tan^{-1}\frac{1+2\tan(x/2)}{\sqrt{3}} + C$$

Use the substitutions in Eqs. (1)–(4) to evaluate the integrals in Exercises 37–44. Integrals like these arise in calculating the average angular velocity of the output shaft of a universal joint when the input and output shafts are not aligned.

37. $\int \frac{dx}{1-\sin x}$

38. $\int \frac{dx}{1+\sin x+\cos x}$

39. $\int_0^{\pi/2} \frac{dx}{1+\sin x}$

40. $\int_{\pi/3}^{\pi/2} \frac{dx}{1-\cos x}$

41. $\int_0^{\pi/2} \frac{d\theta}{2+\cos\theta}$

42. $\int_{\pi/2}^{2\pi/3} \frac{\cos\theta\,d\theta}{\sin\theta\cos\theta+\sin\theta}$

43. $\int \frac{dt}{\sin t-\cos t}$

44. $\int \frac{\cos t\,dt}{1-\cos t}$

Writing for Your Own Knowledge

Answer the following questions in writing. Some answers will take only a sentence or two; others may require several paragraphs. Some explanations may also call for graphs or sketches.

1. What substitutions are sometimes used to change quadratic binomials into single squared terms? Why might you want to make such a change?
2. What restrictions can you place on the variables involved in the three basic trigonometric substitutions to make sure the substitutions are reversible?

8.5 Integral Tables

As you know, the basic techniques of integration are substitution and integration by parts. We apply these techniques to transform unfamiliar integrals into integrals whose forms we recognize or can find in a table. But where do the integrals in the tables come from? They come from applying substitutions and integration by parts. We could derive them all from scratch if we had to but having the table saves us the trouble of repeating laborious calculations. When an integral matches an integral in the table, or can be changed into one of the tabulated integrals with some appropriate combination of algebra, trigonometry, substitution, and calculus, we have a ready-made solution for the problem at hand. The examples and exercises of this section show how the formulas in integral tables are derived and used. The emphasis is on use. The integration formulas at the back of this book are stated in terms of constants a, b, c, m, n, and so on. These constants can usually assume any real value and need not be integers. Occasional limitations on their values are stated with the formulas. Formula 5 requires $n \neq -1$, for example, and Formula 11 requires $n \neq -2$.

The formulas also assume that the constants do not take on values that require dividing by zero or taking even roots of negative numbers. For example, Formula 8 assumes $a \neq 0$, and Formula 13(a) cannot be used unless b is negative.

EXAMPLE 1 Find $\int x(2x+5)^{-1}\,dx$.

Solution We use Formula 8 (not 7, which requires $n \neq -1$):

$$\int x(ax+b)^{-1}\,dx = \frac{x}{a} - \frac{b}{a^2}\ln|ax+b| + C.$$

With $a = 2$ and $b = 5$, we have

$$\int x(2x+5)^{-1}\,dx = \frac{x}{2} - \frac{5}{4}\ln|2x+5| + C.$$

EXAMPLE 2 Find $\displaystyle\int \frac{dx}{x\sqrt{2x+4}}$.

Solution We use Formula 13(b):

$$\int \frac{dx}{x\sqrt{ax+b}} = \frac{1}{\sqrt{b}}\ln\left|\frac{\sqrt{ax+b}-\sqrt{b}}{\sqrt{ax+b}+\sqrt{b}}\right| + C, \qquad \text{if } b > 0.$$

With $a = 2$ and $b = 4$, we have

$$\int \frac{dx}{x\sqrt{2x+4}} = \frac{1}{\sqrt{4}}\ln\left|\frac{\sqrt{2x+4}-\sqrt{4}}{\sqrt{2x+4}+\sqrt{4}}\right| + C$$

$$= \frac{1}{2}\ln\left|\frac{\sqrt{2x+4}-2}{\sqrt{2x+4}+2}\right| + C.$$

Formula 13(a), which requires $b < 0$, would not have been appropriate here. It *is* appropriate, however, in the next example.

EXAMPLE 3 Find $\displaystyle\int \frac{dx}{x\sqrt{2x-4}}$.

Solution We use Formula 13(a):

$$\int \frac{dx}{x\sqrt{ax+b}} = \frac{2}{\sqrt{-b}}\tan^{-1}\sqrt{\frac{ax+b}{-b}} + C, \qquad \text{if } b < 0.$$

With $a = 2$ and $b = -4$, we have

$$\int \frac{dx}{x\sqrt{2x-4}} = \frac{2}{\sqrt{-(-4)}}\tan^{-1}\sqrt{\frac{2x-4}{-(-4)}} + C = \tan^{-1}\sqrt{\frac{x-2}{2}} + C.$$

EXAMPLE 4 Find $\displaystyle\int \frac{dx}{x^2\sqrt{2x-4}}$.

Solution We begin with Formula 15:

$$\int \frac{dx}{x^2\sqrt{ax+b}} = -\frac{\sqrt{ax+b}}{bx} - \frac{a}{2b}\int \frac{dx}{x\sqrt{ax+b}} + C.$$

With $a = 2$ and $b = -4$, we have

$$\int \frac{dx}{x^2\sqrt{2x-4}} = -\frac{\sqrt{2x-4}}{-4x} + \frac{2}{2\cdot 4}\int \frac{dx}{x\sqrt{2x-4}} + C.$$

We then use Formula 13(a) to evaluate the integral on the right (Example 3) to obtain

$$\int \frac{dx}{x^2\sqrt{2x-4}} = \frac{\sqrt{2x-4}}{4x} + \frac{1}{4}\tan^{-1}\sqrt{\frac{x-2}{2}} + C.$$

EXAMPLE 5 Find $\int x \sin^{-1} x\, dx$.

Solution We use Formula 99:

$$\int x^n \sin^{-1} ax\, dx = \frac{x^{n+1}}{n+1}\sin^{-1} ax - \frac{a}{n+1}\int \frac{x^{n+1}\,dx}{\sqrt{1-a^2x^2}}, \qquad n \neq -1.$$

With $n = 1$ and $a = 1$, we have

$$\int x \sin^{-1} x\, dx = \frac{x^2}{2}\sin^{-1} x - \frac{1}{2}\int \frac{x^2\,dx}{\sqrt{1-x^2}}.$$

The integral on the right is found in the table as Formula 33:

$$\int \frac{x^2}{\sqrt{a^2-x^2}}\,dx = \frac{a^2}{2}\sin^{-1}\left(\frac{x}{a}\right) - \frac{1}{2}x\sqrt{a^2-x^2} + C.$$

With $a = 1$,

$$\int \frac{x^2\,dx}{\sqrt{1-x^2}} = \frac{1}{2}\sin^{-1} x - \frac{1}{2}x\sqrt{1-x^2} + C.$$

The combined result is

$$\begin{aligned}\int x \sin^{-1} x\, dx &= \frac{x^2}{2}\sin^{-1} x - \frac{1}{2}\left(\frac{1}{2}\sin^{-1} x - \frac{1}{2}x\sqrt{1-x^2}\right) + C \\ &= \left(\frac{x^2}{2} - \frac{1}{4}\right)\sin^{-1} x + \frac{1}{4}x\sqrt{1-x^2} + C.\end{aligned}$$

Reduction Formulas

The time required for repeated integrations by parts can sometimes be shortened by applying formulas like

$$\int \tan^n x\, dx = \frac{1}{n-1}\tan^{n-1} x - \int \tan^{n-2} x\, dx, \tag{1}$$

$$\int (\ln x)^n\, dx = x(\ln x)^n - n\int (\ln x)^{n-1}\, dx, \tag{2}$$

$$\begin{aligned}\int \sin^n x \cos^m x\, dx = &-\frac{\sin^{n-1} x \cos^{m+1} x}{m+n} + \\ &\frac{n-1}{m+n}\int \sin^{n-2} x \cos^m x\, dx \qquad (n \neq -m).\end{aligned} \tag{3}$$

Formulas like these are called **reduction formulas** because they replace an integral containing some power of a function with an integral of the same form with the power reduced. By applying such a formula repeatedly, we can eventually express the original integral in terms of a power low enough to be evaluated directly.

EXAMPLE 6 Find $\int \tan^5 x\, dx$.

Solution We apply Eq. (1) with $n = 5$ to get

$$\int \tan^5 x\, dx = \frac{1}{4}\tan^4 x - \int \tan^3 x\, dx.$$

We then apply Eq. (1) again, with $n = 3$, to evaluate the remaining integral:

$$\int \tan^3 x\, dx = \frac{1}{2}\tan^2 x - \int \tan x\, dx = \frac{1}{2}\tan^2 x + \ln|\cos x| + C.$$

The combined result is

$$\int \tan^5 x\, dx = \frac{1}{4}\tan^4 x - \frac{1}{2}\tan^2 x - \ln|\cos x| + C.$$

As their form suggests, reduction formulas are derived by integration by parts.

EXAMPLE 7 *Deriving a Reduction Formula.* Show that for any positive integer n,

$$\int (\ln x)^n\, dx = x(\ln x)^n - n\int (\ln x)^{n-1}\, dx.$$

Solution We use the integration by parts formula

$$\int u\, dv = uv - \int v\, du$$

with

$$u = (\ln x)^n, \qquad du = n(\ln x)^{n-1}\frac{dx}{x}, \qquad dv = dx, \qquad v = x,$$

to obtain

$$\int (\ln x)^n\, dx = x(\ln x)^n - n\int (\ln x)^{n-1}\, dx.$$

Sometimes two reduction formulas come into play.

EXAMPLE 8 Find $\int \sin^2 x \cos^3 x\, dx$.

Solution 1 We apply Eq. (3) with $n = 2$ and $m = 3$ to get

$$\begin{aligned}\int \sin^2 x \cos^3 x\, dx &= -\frac{\sin x \cos^4 x}{2+3} + \frac{1}{2+3}\int \sin^0 x \cos^3 x\, dx \\ &= -\frac{\sin x \cos^4 x}{5} + \frac{1}{5}\int \cos^3 x\, dx.\end{aligned}$$

We can evaluate the remaining integral with Formula 61 (another reduction formula):

$$\int \cos^n ax\, dx = \frac{\cos^{n-1} ax \sin ax}{na} + \frac{n-1}{n}\int \cos^{n-2} ax\, dx.$$

With $n = 3$ and $a = 1$, we have

$$\int \cos^3 x\, dx = \frac{\cos^2 x \sin x}{3} + \frac{2}{3}\int \cos x\, dx$$

$$= \frac{\cos^2 x \sin x}{3} + \frac{2}{3}\sin x + C.$$

The combined result is

$$\int \sin^2 x \cos^3 x\, dx = -\frac{\sin x \cos^4 x}{5} + \frac{1}{5}\left(\frac{\cos^2 x \sin x}{3} + \frac{2}{3}\sin x + C\right)$$

$$= -\frac{\sin x \cos^4 x}{5} + \frac{\cos^2 x \sin x}{15} + \frac{2}{15}\sin x + C'.$$

Solution 2 Equation (3) corresponds to Formula 68 in the table, but there is another formula we might use, namely Formula 69. With $a = 1$, Formula 69 gives

$$\int \sin^n x \cos^m x\, dx = \frac{\sin^{n+1} x \cos^{m-1} x}{m+n} + \frac{m-1}{m+n}\int \sin^n x \cos^{m-2} x\, dx.$$

In our case, $n = 2$ and $m = 3$, so that

$$\int \sin^2 x \cos^3 x\, dx = \frac{\sin^3 x \cos^2 x}{5} + \frac{2}{5}\int \sin^2 x \cos x\, dx$$

$$= \frac{\sin^3 x \cos^2 x}{5} + \frac{2}{5}\left(\frac{\sin^3 x}{3}\right) + C$$

$$= \frac{\sin^3 x \cos^2 x}{5} + \frac{2}{15}\sin^3 x + C.$$

As you can see, it is faster to use Formula 69, but we often cannot tell beforehand how things will work out. Do not spend a lot of time looking for the "best" formula. Just find one that will work and forge ahead.

Notice also that Formulas 68 (Solution 1) and 69 (Solution 2) lead to different-looking answers. That is often the case with trigonometric integrals, and is no cause for concern. The results are equivalent, and we may use whichever one we please.

Nonelementary Integrals

The development of computers and calculators that find antiderivatives by symbolic manipulation has led to a renewed interest in determining which antiderivatives can be expressed as finite combinations of elementary functions (the functions we have been studying) and which cannot. Integrals of functions that do not have elementary antiderivatives are called **nonelementary** integrals. They require infinite series (Chapter 9) or numerical methods for their evaluation. Examples of the latter include the error function

$$\operatorname{erf}(x) = \frac{2}{\sqrt{\pi}}\int_0^x e^{-t^2}\, dt$$

and integrals such as

$$\int \sin x^2\,dx \qquad \text{and} \qquad \int \sqrt{1+x^4}\,dx$$

that arise in engineering and physics. These and a number of others, such as

$$\int \frac{e^x}{x}\,dx, \qquad \int e^{(e^x)}\,dx, \qquad \int \frac{1}{\ln x}\,dx, \qquad \int \ln(\ln x)\,dx, \qquad \int \frac{\sin x}{x}\,dx,$$

$$\int \sqrt{1-k^2\sin^2 x}\,dx, \qquad 0<k<1,$$

look so easy they tempt us to try them just to see how they turn out. It can be proved, however, that there is no way to express these integrals as finite combinations of elementary functions. The same applies to integrals that can be changed into these by substitution. The integrands all have antiderivatives — they are, after all, continuous — but none of the antiderivatives is elementary.

None of the integrals you are asked to evaluate in the present chapter falls into this category, but you may encounter nonelementary integrals from time to time in your other work.

A General Procedure for Indefinite Integration

While there is no surefire way to evaluate all indefinite integrals, the procedure in Flowchart 8.1 may help.

FLOWCHART 8.1 Procedure for indefinite integration

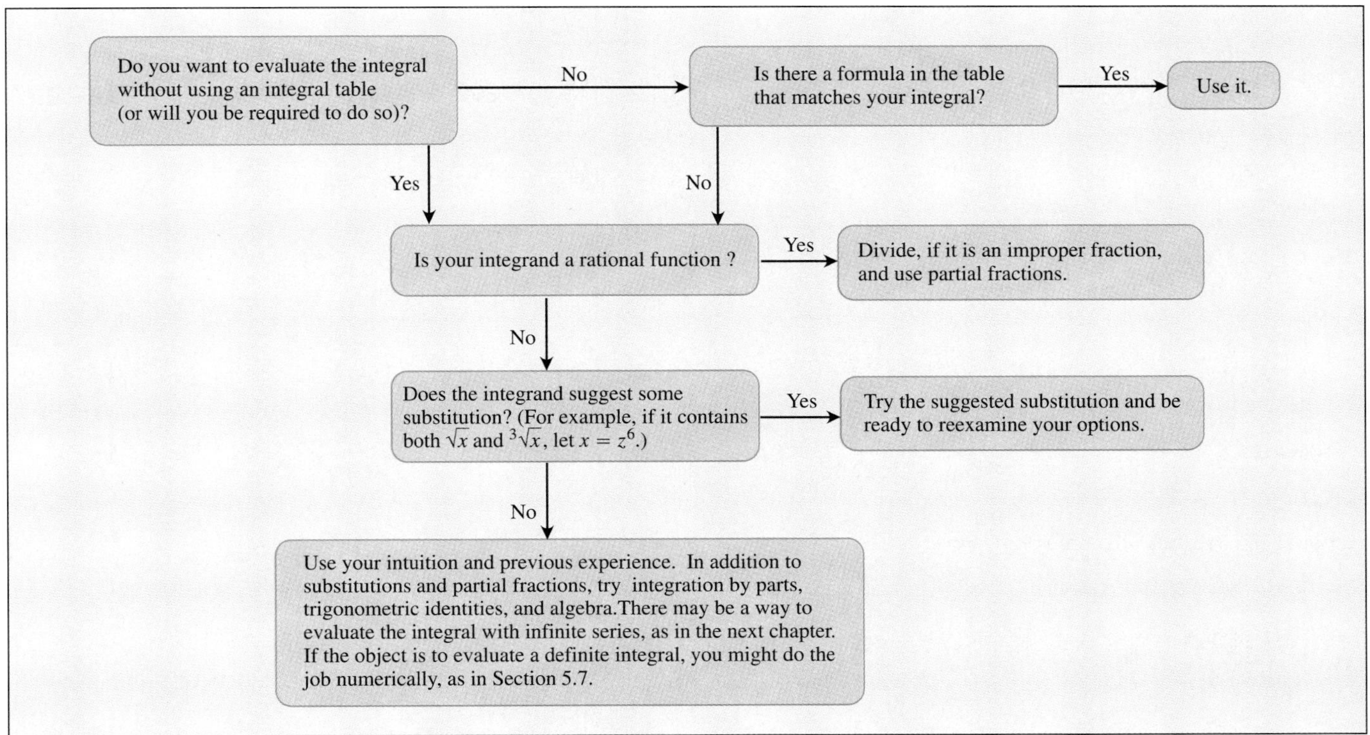

Exercises 8.5

For this exercise set, use the table of integrals at the back of the book.

Evaluate the integrals in Exercises 1–22.

1. $\int \frac{dx}{x\sqrt{x-3}}$

2. $\int \frac{dx}{x\sqrt{x+4}}$

3. $\int \frac{x\,dx}{\sqrt{x-2}}$

4. $\int \frac{x\,dx}{(2x+3)^{3/2}}$

5. $\int x\sqrt{2x-3}\,dx$

6. $\int x(7x+5)^{2/3}\,dx$

7. $\int \frac{\sqrt{9-4x}}{x^2}\,dx$

8. $\int \frac{x^2}{\sqrt{9-4x}}\,dx$

9. $\int x\sqrt{4x-x^2}\,dx$

10. $\int \frac{\sqrt{x-x^2}}{x}\,dx$

11. $\int \frac{dx}{x\sqrt{7+x^2}}$

12. $\int \frac{dx}{x\sqrt{7-x^2}}$

13. $\int \frac{\sqrt{4-x^2}}{x}\,dx$

14. $\int \frac{\sqrt{x^2-4}}{x}\,dx$

15. $\int \sqrt{25-p^2}\,dp$

16. $\int q^2\sqrt{25-q^2}\,dq$

17. $\int \frac{r^2}{\sqrt{4-r^2}}\,dr$

18. $\int \frac{ds}{\sqrt{s^2-2}}$

19. $\int \frac{d\theta}{5+4\sin 2\theta}$

20. $\int \frac{d\theta}{4+5\sin 2\theta}$

21. $\int e^{2t}\cos 3t\,dt$

22. $\int e^{-3t}\sin 4t\,dt$

Evaluate the integrals in Exercises 23–30.

23. $\int x\cos^{-1}x\,dx$

24. $\int x\sin^{-1}x\,dx$

25. $\int \frac{ds}{(9-s^2)^2}$

26. $\int \frac{d\theta}{(2-\theta^2)^2}$

27. $\int \frac{\sqrt{4x+9}}{x^2}\,dx$

28. $\int \frac{\sqrt{9x-4}}{x^2}\,dx$

29. $\int \frac{\sqrt{3t-4}}{t}\,dt$

30. $\int \frac{\sqrt{3t+9}}{t}\,dt$

Evaluate the integrals in Exercises 31–34.

31. $\int x^2\tan^{-1}x\,dx$

32. $\int \frac{\tan^{-1}x}{x^2}\,dx$

33. $\int \frac{x^3+x+1}{(x^2+1)^2}\,dx$

34. $\int \frac{x^2+6x}{(x^2+3)^2}\,dx$

In Exercises 35–44, use a substitution to change the integral into one you can find in the table. Then evaluate the integral.

35. $\int \sin^{-1}\sqrt{x}\,dx$

36. $\int \frac{\cos^{-1}\sqrt{x}}{\sqrt{x}}\,dx$

37. $\int \frac{\sqrt{x}}{\sqrt{1-x}}\,dx$

38. $\int \frac{\sqrt{2-x}}{\sqrt{x}}\,dx$

39. $\int \cot t\sqrt{1-\sin^2 t}\,dt$

40. $\int \frac{dt}{\tan t\sqrt{4-\sin^2 t}}$

41. $\int \frac{dy}{y\sqrt{3+(\ln y)^2}}$

42. $\int \frac{\cos\theta\,d\theta}{\sqrt{5+\sin^2\theta}}$

43. $\int \frac{3\,dr}{\sqrt{9r^2-1}}$

44. $\int \frac{3\,dy}{\sqrt{1+9y^2}}$

Use reduction formulas to evaluate the integrals in Exercises 45–70.

45. $\int \sin^5 2x\,dx$

46. $\int \sin^5\frac{\theta}{2}\,d\theta$

47. $\int 8\cos^4 2\pi t\,dt$

48. $\int 3\cos^5 3y\,dy$

49. $\int \sin 3x\cos 2x\,dx$

50. $\int \sin 2x\cos 3x\,dx$

51. $\int 8\sin 4t\sin\frac{t}{2}\,dt$

52. $\int \sin\frac{t}{3}\sin\frac{t}{6}\,dt$

53. $\int \cos\frac{\theta}{3}\cos\frac{\theta}{4}\,d\theta$

54. $\int \cos\frac{\theta}{2}\cos 7\theta\,d\theta$

55. $\int \sin^2 2\theta\cos^3 2\theta\,d\theta$

56. $\int 9\sin^3\theta\cos^{3/2}\theta\,d\theta$

57. $\int 2\sin^2 t\cos^{-4} t\,dt$

58. $\int \sin^{-2} y\cos^5 y\,dy$

59. $\int 4\tan^3 2x\,dx$

60. $\int \tan^4\left(\frac{x}{2}\right)dx$

61. $\int 8\cot^4 t\,dt$

62. $\int 4\cot^3 2t\,dt$

63. $\int 2\sec^3 \pi x\,dx$

64. $\int \frac{1}{2}\csc^3\frac{x}{2}\,dx$

65. $\int 3\sec^4 3x\,dx$

66. $\int \csc^4\frac{\theta}{3}\,d\theta$

67. $\int \csc^5 x\,dx$

68. $\int \sec^5 x\,dx$

69. $\int 16x^3(\ln x)^2\,dx$

70. $\int (\ln x)^3\,dx$

Although integer powers of x times e^x and other exponentials can be integrated by tabular integration (Section 8.2), they can also be evaluated with reduction formulas. Use table Formulas 103–106 to evaluate the integrals in Exercises 71–78.

71. $\int x e^{3x}\,dx$

72. $\int x e^{-2x}\,dx$

73. $\int x^3 e^{x/2}\,dx$

74. $\int x^2 e^{\pi x}\,dx$

75. $\int x^2 2^x\,dx$

76. $\int x^2 2^{-x}\,dx$

77. $\int x \pi^x\,dx$

78. $\int x 2^{\sqrt{2}x}\,dx$

Evaluate the integrals in Exercises 79–82 by making a trigonometric substitution and then applying a reduction formula.

79. $\int_0^1 2\sqrt{x^2+1}\,dx$

80. $\int_0^{\sqrt{3}/2} \frac{dy}{(1-y^2)^{5/2}}$

81. $\int_1^2 \frac{(r^2-1)^{3/2}}{r}\,dr$

82. $\int_0^{1/\sqrt{3}} \frac{dt}{(t^2+1)^{7/2}}$

In Exercises 83–86, use a substitution to change the integral into one you can evaluate with a reduction formula. Then evaluate the integral.

83. $\int e^t \sec^3(e^t - 1)\,dt$

84. $\int \frac{\csc^3\sqrt{\theta}}{\sqrt{\theta}}\,d\theta$

85. $\int \cos^{-1}\sqrt{x}\,dx$

86. $\int \tan^{-1}\sqrt{y}\,dy$

Exercises 87–94 refer to formulas in the table of integrals at the back of the book.

87. Derive Formula 9 by using the substitution $u = ax + b$ to evaluate

$$\int \frac{x}{(ax+b)^2}\,dx.$$

88. Derive Formula 17 by using a trigonometric substitution to evaluate

$$\int \frac{dx}{(a^2+x^2)^2}.$$

89. Derive Formula 29 by using a trigonometric substitution to evaluate

$$\int \sqrt{a^2-x^2}\,dx.$$

90. Derive Formula 46 by using a trigonometric substitution to evaluate

$$\int \frac{dx}{x^2\sqrt{x^2-a^2}}.$$

91. Derive Formula 80 by evaluating

$$\int x^n \sin ax\,dx$$

by integration by parts.

92. Derive Formula 110 by evaluating

$$\int x^n (\ln ax)^m\,dx$$

by integration by parts.

93. Derive Formula 99 by evaluating

$$\int x^n \sin^{-1} ax\,dx$$

by integration by parts.

94. Derive Formula 101 by evaluating

$$\int x^n \tan^{-1} ax\,dx$$

by integration by parts.

95. Find the area of the surface generated by revolving the curve $y = \sqrt{x^2+2}$, $0 \le x \le \sqrt{2}$, about the x-axis.

96. Find the length of the curve $y = x^2$, $0 \le x \le \sqrt{3}/2$.

97. Find the centroid of the region cut from the first quadrant by the curve $y = 1/\sqrt{x+1}$ and the line $x = 3$.

98. A thin plate of constant density $\delta = 1$ occupies the region enclosed by the curve $y = 36/(2x+3)$ and the line $x = 3$ in the first quadrant. Find the moment of the plate about the y-axis.

99. Use the integral table and a calculator to find to two decimal places the area of the surface generated by revolving the curve $y = x^2$, $-1 \le x \le 1$, about the x-axis.

100. The head of your firm's accounting department has asked you to find a formula she can use in a computer program to calculate the year-end inventory of gasoline in the company's tanks. A typical tank is shaped like a right circular cylinder of radius r and length L, mounted horizontally, as shown here. The data come to the accounting office as depth measurements taken with a vertical measuring stick marked in centimeters.

a) Show, in the notation of the figure here, that the volume of gasoline that fills the tank to a depth d is

$$V = 2L\int_{-r}^{-r+d} \sqrt{r^2-y^2}\,dy.$$

b) Evaluate the integral.

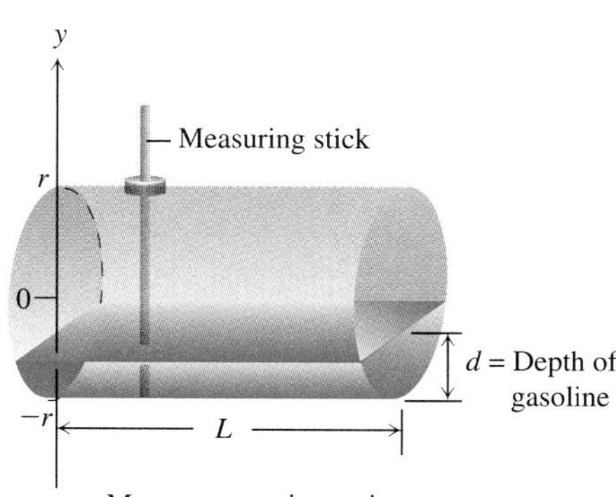

Measurements in centimeters

101. What is the largest value

$$\int_a^b \sqrt{x - x^2}\, dx$$

can have for any a and b? Give reasons for your answer.

102. What is the largest value

$$\int_a^b x\sqrt{2x - x^2}\, dx$$

can have for any a and b? Give reasons for your answer.

Writing for Your Own Knowledge

Answer the following questions in writing. Some answers will take only a sentence or two; others may require several paragraphs. Some explanations may also call for graphs or sketches.

1. What is a reduction formula?
2. How are reduction formulas typically derived?
3. How are some of the other formulas in integral tables derived?
4. How are integral tables used?
5. Why bother with integral tables?
6. Can you expect to find every integral you want in an integral table?

8.6 *Improper Integrals*

Up to now, we have required our definite integrals to have two properties. First, that the domain of integration, from a to b, be finite. Second, that the range of the integrand be finite on this domain. In practice, however, we frequently encounter problems that fail to meet one or both of these conditions. As an example of an infinite domain, we might want to consider the area under the curve $y = (\ln x)/x^2$ from $x = 1$ to $x = \infty$ (Fig. 8.11a). As an example of an infinite range, we might want to consider the area under the curve $y = 1/\sqrt{x}$ between $x = 0$ and $x = 1$ (Fig. 8.11b). We treat both examples in the same reasonable way. We ask, "What is the integral when the domain is slightly less?" and examine the answer as the domain increases to the limit. We do the finite case, and then see what happens as we approach infinity.

(a)

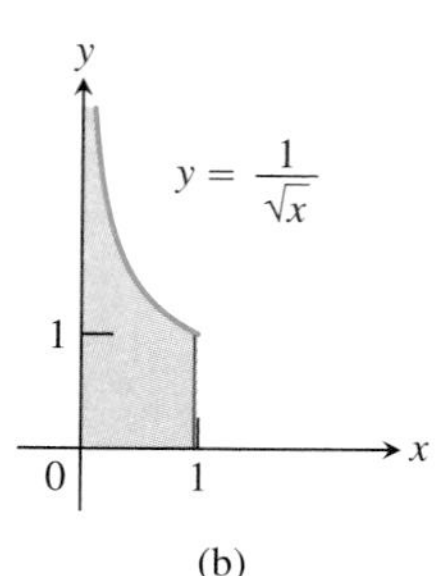

(b)

8.11 Are the areas under these infinite curves finite? See Examples 1 and 2.

EXAMPLE 1 Is the area under the curve $y = (\ln x)/x^2$ from $x = 1$ to $x = \infty$ finite? If so, what is it?

Solution We find the area under the curve from $x = 1$ to $x = b$ and examine the limit as $b \to \infty$. If the limit is finite, we take it to be the area under the infinite curve (Fig. 8.12). The area from 1 to b is

$$\int_1^b \frac{\ln x}{x^2}\, dx = \left[(\ln x)\left(-\frac{1}{x}\right)\right]_1^b - \int_1^b \left(-\frac{1}{x}\right)\left(\frac{1}{x}\right) dx$$

Integration by parts with $u = \ln x$, $dv = dx/x^2$, $du = dx/x$, $v = -1/x$

$$= -\frac{\ln b}{b} - \left[\frac{1}{x}\right]_1^b$$

$$= -\frac{\ln b}{b} - \frac{1}{b} + 1.$$

The limit of the area as $b \to \infty$ is

$$\lim_{b\to\infty}\left[-\frac{\ln b}{b} - \frac{1}{b} + 1\right] = -\left[\lim_{b\to\infty}\frac{\ln b}{b}\right] - 0 + 1$$

$$= -\left[\lim_{b\to\infty}\frac{1/b}{1}\right] + 1 = 0 + 1 = 1.$$

l'Hôpital's rule

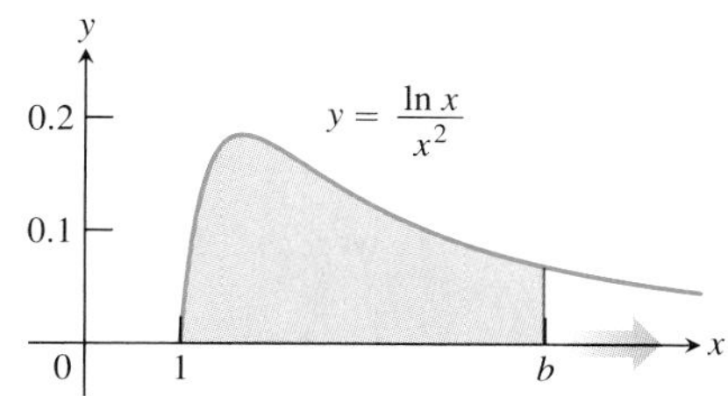

8.12 The area under this curve is $\lim_{b\to\infty} \int_1^b ((\ln x)/x^2)\, dx$ (Example 1).

In integral notation, the area under the infinite curve from 1 to ∞ is

$$\int_1^\infty \frac{\ln x}{x^2}\, dx = \lim_{b\to\infty} \int_1^b \frac{\ln x}{x^2}\, dx = 1.$$

EXAMPLE 2 Is the area under the curve $y = 1/\sqrt{x}$ from $x = 0$ to $x = 1$ finite? If so, what is it?

Solution We find the area under the curve from a to 1 and examine the limit as $a \to 0^+$. If the limit is finite, we take it to be the area under the infinite curve (Fig. 8.13). The area from a to 1 is

$$\int_a^1 \frac{1}{\sqrt{x}}\, dx = 2\sqrt{x}\Big]_a^1 = 2 - 2\sqrt{a}.$$

The limit as $a \to 0^+$ is

$$\lim_{a\to 0^+} (2 - 2\sqrt{a}) = 2 - 0 = 2.$$

In integral notation, the area under the infinite curve from 0 to 1 is

$$\int_0^1 \frac{1}{\sqrt{x}}\, dx = \lim_{a\to 0^+} \int_a^1 \frac{1}{\sqrt{x}}\, dx = 2.$$

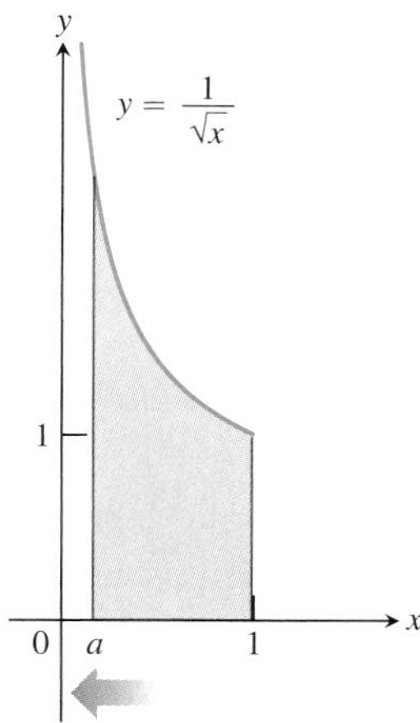

8.13 The area under this curve is $\lim_{a\to 0^+} \int_a^1 (1/\sqrt{x})\, dx$ (Example 2).

Improper Integrals

The integrals for the areas in Examples 1 and 2 are improper integrals.

DEFINITION

Integrals with infinite limits of integration and integrals of functions that become infinite at a point within the interval of integration are **improper integrals.** When the limits involved exist, we evaluate such integrals with the following definitions:

1. If f is continuous on $[a, \infty)$, then

$$\int_a^\infty f(x)\, dx = \lim_{b\to\infty} \int_a^b f(x)\, dx. \tag{1}$$

2. If f is continuous on $(-\infty, b]$, then

$$\int_{-\infty}^b f(x)\, dx = \lim_{a\to-\infty} \int_a^b f(x)\, dx. \tag{2}$$

3. If f is continuous on $(a, b]$ then

$$\int_a^b f(x)\, dx = \lim_{c\to a^+} \int_c^b f(x)\, dx. \tag{3}$$

4. If f is continuous on $[a, b)$, then

$$\int_a^b f(x)\, dx = \lim_{c\to b^-} \int_a^c f(x)\, dx. \tag{4}$$

In each case, if the limit is finite we say that the improper integral **converges** and that the limit is the **value** of the improper integral. If the limit fails to exist the improper integral **diverges.**

Example 1 illustrates Part 1 of the definition:

$$\int_1^\infty \frac{\ln x}{x^2}\,dx = \lim_{b\to\infty}\int_a^b \frac{\ln x}{x^2}\,dx = 1$$

Infinite upper limit of integration

Example 2 illustrates Part 3 of the definition:

$$\int_0^1 \frac{1}{\sqrt{x}}\,dx = \lim_{a\to 0^+}\int_a^b \frac{1}{\sqrt{x}}\,dx = 2$$

Integrand becomes infinite at lower limit of integration.

In each case, the integral converges. The integral in the next example diverges.

EXAMPLE 3 *A Divergent Improper Integral.* Investigate the convergence of

$$\int_0^1 \frac{1}{1-x}\,dx.$$

Solution The integrand $f(x) = 1/(1-x)$ is continuous on $[0, 1)$ but becomes infinite as $x \to 1^-$ (Fig. 8.14). We evaluate the integral as

$$\lim_{b\to 1^-}\int_0^b \frac{1}{1-x}\,dx = \lim_{b\to 1^-}\Big[-\ln|1-x|\Big]_0^b$$

$$= \lim_{b\to 1^-}[-\ln(1-b)+0] = \infty.$$

The limit is infinite, so the integral diverges.

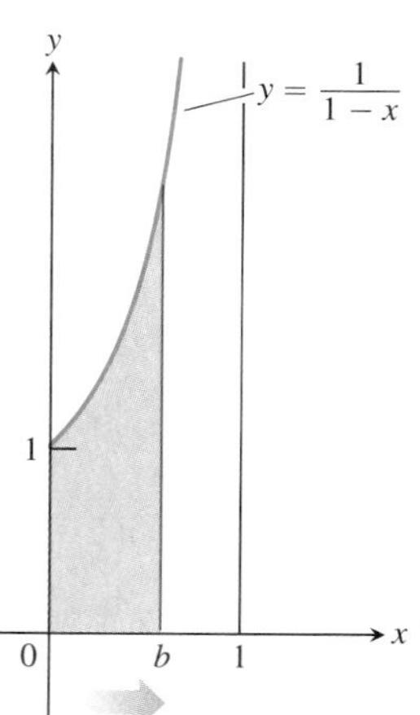

8.14 If the limit exists $\int_0^1 (1/(1-x))\,dx = \lim_{b\to 1^-}\int_0^b (1/(1-x))\,dx$ (Example 3).

The list in the preceding definition extends in a natural way to integrals with both limits of integration being infinite. We will examine this case later in the section. The list also extends to integrals of functions that become infinite at an interior point d of the interval of integration. In this case, we define the integral from a to b to be the sum of the integrals from a to d and d to b.

DEFINITION

If f becomes infinite at an interior point d of $[a, b]$, then

$$\int_a^b f(x)\,dx = \int_a^d f(x)\,dx + \int_d^b f(x)\,dx. \tag{5}$$

The integral from a to b **converges** if the integrals from a to d and d to b both converge. Otherwise, the integral from a to b **diverges.**

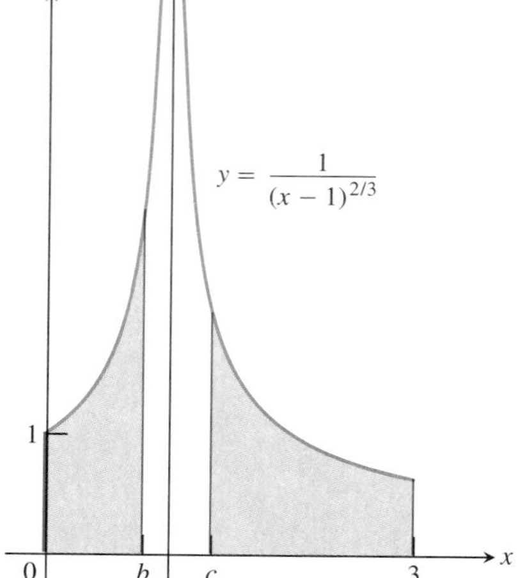

8.15 Example 4 investigates the convergence of $\int_0^3 (1/(x-1)^{2/3})\,dx$.

EXAMPLE 4 *Infinite at an Interior Point.* Investigate the convergence of

$$\int_0^3 \frac{dx}{(x-1)^{2/3}}.$$

Solution The integrand $f(x) = 1/(x-1)^{2/3}$ becomes infinite at $x = 1$ but is continuous on $[0, 1)$ and $(1, 3]$ (Fig. 8.15). The convergence of the integral over $[0, 3]$ depends on the integrals from 0 to 1 and 1 to 3. On $[0, 1]$ we have

$$\int_0^1 \frac{dx}{(x-1)^{2/3}} = \lim_{b\to 1^-}\int_0^b \frac{dx}{(x-1)^{2/3}}$$

$$= \lim_{b\to 1^-}[3(b-1)^{1/3} - 3(0-1)^{1/3}] = 3.$$

On [1, 3] we have

$$\int_1^3 \frac{dx}{(x-1)^{2/3}} = \lim_{c\to 1^+} \int_c^3 \frac{dx}{(x-1)^{2/3}}$$
$$= \lim_{c\to 1^+} [3\,(3-1)^{1/3} - 3\,(c-1)^{1/3}] = 3\sqrt[3]{2}.$$

Both limits are finite, so the integral of f from 0 to 3 converges and its value is $3 + 3\sqrt[3]{2}$.

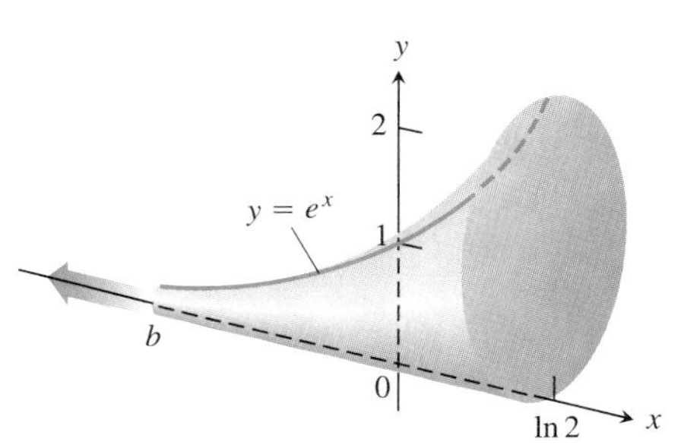

8.16 The calculation in Example 5 shows that this infinite horn has a finite volume.

EXAMPLE 5 The cross sections of the solid horn in Fig. 8.16 perpendicular to the x-axis are circular disks with diameters reaching from the x-axis to the curve $y = e^x$, $-\infty < x \le \ln 2$. Find the volume of the horn.

Solution The area of a typical cross section is

$$A(x) = \pi\,(\text{radius})^2 = \pi\left(\frac{1}{2}y\right)^2 = \frac{\pi}{4}e^{2x}.$$

We define the volume of the horn to be the limit as $b \to -\infty$ of the volume of the portion from b to ln 2. As in Section 7.8 (the method of slicing), the volume of this portion is

$$V = \int_b^{\ln 2} A(x)\,dx = \int_b^{\ln 2} \frac{\pi}{4}e^{2x}\,dx = \frac{\pi}{8}e^{2x}\Big]_b^{\ln 2}$$
$$= \frac{\pi}{8}(e^{\ln 4} - e^{2b}) = \frac{\pi}{8}(4 - e^{2b}).$$

As $b \to -\infty$, $e^{2b} \to 0$ and $V \to (\pi/8)(4-0) = \pi/2$. The volume of the horn is $\pi/2$.

EXAMPLE 6 Evaluate $\displaystyle\int_2^\infty \frac{x+3}{(x-1)(x^2+1)}\,dx.$

Solution

$$\int_2^\infty \frac{x+3}{(x-1)(x^2+1)}\,dx = \lim_{b\to\infty} \int_2^b \frac{x+3}{(x-1)(x^2+1)}\,dx$$
$$= \lim_{b\to\infty} \int_2^b \left(\frac{2}{x-1} - \frac{2x+1}{x^2+1}\right) dx \qquad \text{Partial fractions}$$
$$= \lim_{b\to\infty} \Big[2\ln(x-1) - \ln(x^2+1) - \tan^{-1}x\Big]_2^b$$
$$= \lim_{b\to\infty} \left[\ln\frac{(x-1)^2}{x^2+1} - \tan^{-1}x\right]_2^b \qquad \text{Combine the logarithms.}$$
$$= \lim_{b\to\infty} \left[\ln\left(\frac{(b-1)^2}{b^2+1}\right) - \tan^{-1}b\right] - \ln\left(\frac{1}{5}\right) + \tan^{-1}2$$
$$= 0 - \frac{\pi}{2} + \ln 5 + \tan^{-1}2 \approx 1.1458$$

Notice that we combined the logarithms in the antiderivative *before* we calculated the limit as $b \to \infty$. Had we not done so, we would have encountered the indeterminate form

$$\lim_{b\to\infty} (2\ln(b-1) - \ln(b^2+1)) = \infty - \infty.$$

The way to evaluate the indeterminate form, of course, is to combine the logarithms, so we would have arrived at the same answer in the end. But our original route was shorter.

Integrals from $-\infty$ to ∞

In the mathematics underlying studies of light, electricity, and sound we encounter integrals with two infinite limits of integration. The next definition addresses the convergence of such integrals.

DEFINITION

If f is continuous on $(-\infty, \infty)$ and if $\int_{-\infty}^{a} f(x)\,dx$ and $\int_{a}^{\infty} f(x)\,dx$ both converge, we say that $\int_{-\infty}^{\infty} f(x)\,dx$ **converges** and define its value to be

$$\int_{-\infty}^{\infty} f(x)\,dx = \int_{-\infty}^{a} f(x)\,dx + \int_{a}^{\infty} f(x)\,dx. \tag{6}$$

If either or both of the integrals on the right-hand side of this equation diverge, the integral of f from $-\infty$ to ∞ **diverges.**

It can be shown that the choice of a in Eq. (6) is unimportant. We can evaluate or determine the convergence of $\int_{-\infty}^{\infty} f(x)\,dx$ with any convenient choice.

The integral of f from $-\infty$ to ∞ need not equal $\lim_{b\to\infty} \int_{-b}^{b} f(x)\,dx$, which may exist even if $\int_{-\infty}^{\infty} f(x)\,dx$ does not converge (Exercise 71).

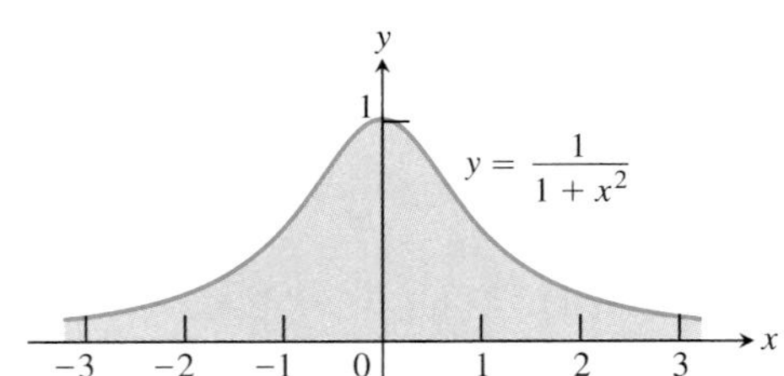

8.17 The area under this "doubly" infinite curve is finite (Example 7).

EXAMPLE 7

$$\int_{-\infty}^{\infty} \frac{dx}{1+x^2} = \int_{-\infty}^{0} \frac{dx}{1+x^2} + \int_{0}^{\infty} \frac{dx}{1+x^2} \qquad \text{Eq. (6) with } a = 0$$

$$= \lim_{b\to-\infty} \Big[\tan^{-1} x\Big]_b^0 + \lim_{c\to\infty} \Big[\tan^{-1} x\Big]_0^c$$

$$= \lim_{b\to-\infty} \Big[\tan^{-1} 0 - \tan^{-1} b\Big] + \lim_{c\to\infty} \Big[\tan^{-1} c - \tan^{-1} 0\Big]$$

$$= 0 - \left(-\frac{\pi}{2}\right) + \frac{\pi}{2} - 0 = \pi.$$

We interpret the integral as the area of the infinite region between the curve $y = 1/(1+x^2)$ and the x-axis (Fig. 8.17).

The Integral $\int_1^{\infty} dx/x^p$

The convergence of the integral $\int_1^{\infty} dx/x^p$ depends on p. The next example illustrates this with $p = 1$ and $p = 2$.

EXAMPLE 8 Investigate the convergence of

$$\int_1^{\infty} \frac{dx}{x} \quad \text{and} \quad \int_1^{\infty} \frac{dx}{x^2}.$$

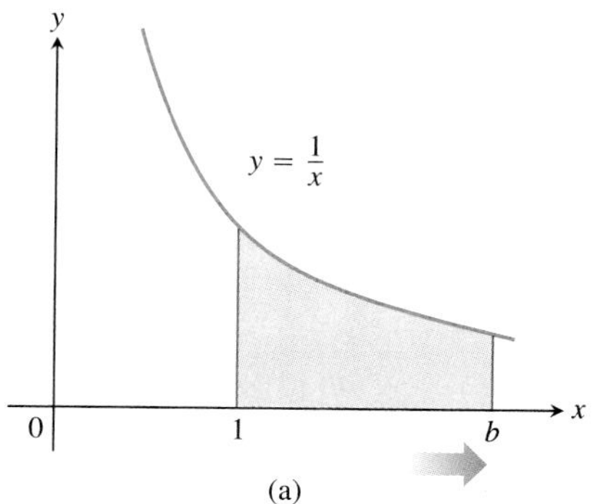

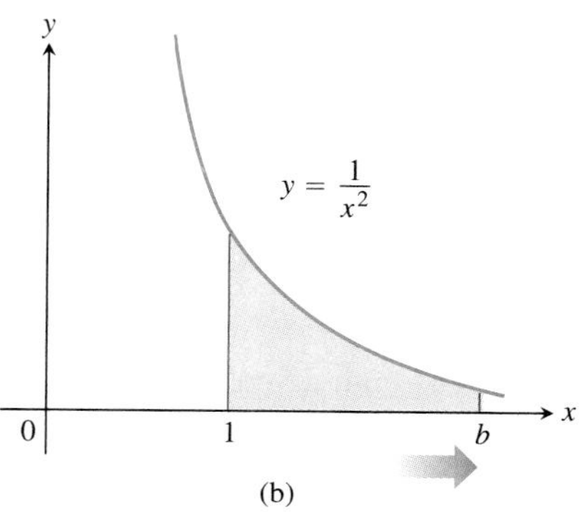

8.18 One of these limits is finite; the other isn't (Example 8).

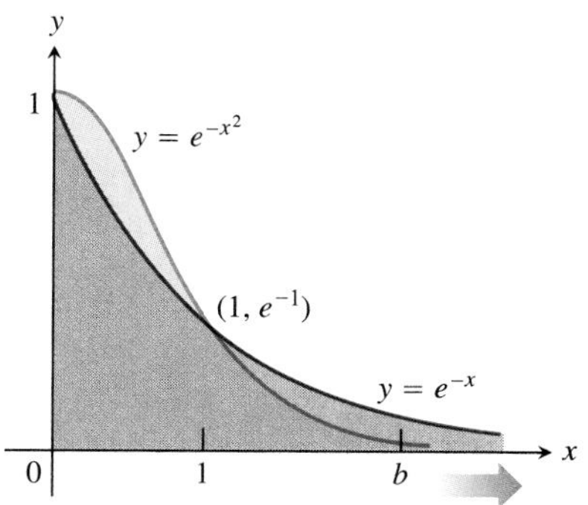

8.19 The graph of e^{-x^2} lies below the graph of e^{-x} for $x > 1$ (Example 9).

Solution The functions involved are continuous on $[1, \infty)$ and their graphs both approach the x-axis as $x \to \infty$ (Fig. 8.18), so it is reasonable to think that the areas under these infinite curves might be finite. In the first case,

$$\int_1^\infty \frac{dx}{x} = \lim_{b\to\infty} \int_1^b \frac{dx}{x} = \lim_{b\to\infty} (\ln b - \ln 1) = \infty,$$

so the integral diverges. In the second case,

$$\int_1^\infty \frac{dx}{x^2} = \lim_{b\to\infty} \int_1^b \frac{dx}{x^2} = \lim_{b\to\infty} \left(-\frac{1}{b} + 1\right) = 1,$$

so the integral converges and its value is 1.

Generally, $\int_1^\infty dx/x^p$ converges if $p > 1$ and diverges if $p \le 1$ (Exercise 63).

Tests for Convergence and Divergence

When an improper integral cannot be evaluated directly (the usual case in practice) we turn to the two-step procedure of first establishing the fact of convergence and then approximating the integral numerically. The principal tests for convergence are the direct comparison and limit comparison tests.

EXAMPLE 9 Investigate the convergence of $\displaystyle\int_1^\infty e^{-x^2}\,dx$.

Solution By definition,

$$\int_1^\infty e^{-x^2}\,dx = \lim_{b\to\infty} \int_1^b e^{-x^2}\,dx.$$

We cannot evaluate the latter integral directly because it is nonelementary. But we *can* show that its limit as $b \to \infty$ is finite. We know that $\int_1^b e^{-x^2}\,dx$ is an increasing function of b. Therefore either it becomes infinite as $b \to \infty$ or it has a finite limit as $b \to \infty$. It does not become infinite: For every value of $b \ge 1$ we have $e^{-x^2} \le e^{-x}$ (Fig. 8.19), so that

$$\int_1^b e^{-x^2}\,dx \le \int_1^b e^{-x}\,dx = -e^{-b} + e^{-1} < e^{-1} \approx 0.36788.$$

Hence

$$\int_1^\infty e^{-x^2}\,dx = \lim_{b\to\infty} \int_1^b e^{-x^2}\,dx$$

converges to some definite finite value. We do not know exactly what the value is except that it is something less than 0.37.

The comparison of e^{-x^2} and e^{-x} in Example 9 is a special case of the following test.

THEOREM 1

Direct Comparison Test

If f and g are continuous on $[a, \infty)$ and if $0 \le f(x) \le g(x)$ for all $x \ge a$, then $\int_a^\infty f(x)\,dx$ converges if $\int_a^\infty g(x)\,dx$ converges.

Notice that under the same hypotheses we can conclude that the integral of g diverges if the integral of f diverges. If the integral of g converged, the integral of f would have to converge, too.

EXAMPLE 10

a) $\int_1^\infty e^{-2x}\,dx$ converges because $e^{-2x} < e^{-x}$ on $[1, \infty)$ and $\int_1^\infty e^{-x}\,dx$ converges.

b) $\displaystyle\int_1^\infty \frac{1}{\sqrt{x^2 - 0.1}}\,dx$ diverges because $\displaystyle\frac{1}{\sqrt{x^2 - 0.1}} \ge \frac{1}{x}$ on $[2, \infty)$ and $\displaystyle\int_1^\infty \frac{1}{x}\,dx$ diverges.

THEOREM 2

Limit Comparison Test

If the positive functions f and g are continuous on $[a, \infty)$ and if

$$\lim_{x\to\infty} \frac{f(x)}{g(x)} = L \qquad (0 < L < \infty),$$

then $\int_a^\infty f(x)\,dx$ and $\int_a^\infty g(x)\,dx$ both converge or both diverge.

In the language of Section 6.7, Theorem 2 says that if two functions grow at the same rate as $x \to \infty$, then their integrals from a to ∞ behave alike: they both converge or both diverge. This does not mean that their integrals have the same value, however, as the next example shows.

EXAMPLE 11 Compare

$$\int_1^\infty \frac{dx}{x^2} \quad \text{and} \quad \int_1^\infty \frac{dx}{1 + x^2}$$

with the limit comparison test.

Solution With $f(x) = 1/x^2$ and $g(x) = 1/(1 + x^2)$, we have

$$\lim_{x\to\infty} \frac{f(x)}{g(x)} = \lim_{x\to\infty} \frac{1/x^2}{1/(1 + x^2)}$$

$$= \lim_{x\to\infty} \frac{1 + x^2}{x^2} = \lim_{x\to\infty} \left(\frac{1}{x^2} + 1\right) = 0 + 1 = 1,$$

a positive finite limit (Fig. 8.20). Therefore, $\displaystyle\int_1^\infty \frac{dx}{1 + x^2}$ converges because $\displaystyle\int_1^\infty \frac{dx}{x^2}$ converges.

The integrals converge to different values, however.

$$\int_1^\infty \frac{dx}{x^2} = 1, \qquad \text{Example 8}$$

and

$$\int_1^\infty \frac{dx}{1 + x^2} = \lim_{b\to\infty} \int_1^b \frac{dx}{1 + x^2} = \lim_{b\to\infty} [\tan^{-1} b - \tan^{-1} 1] = \frac{\pi}{2} - \frac{\pi}{4} = \frac{\pi}{4}.$$

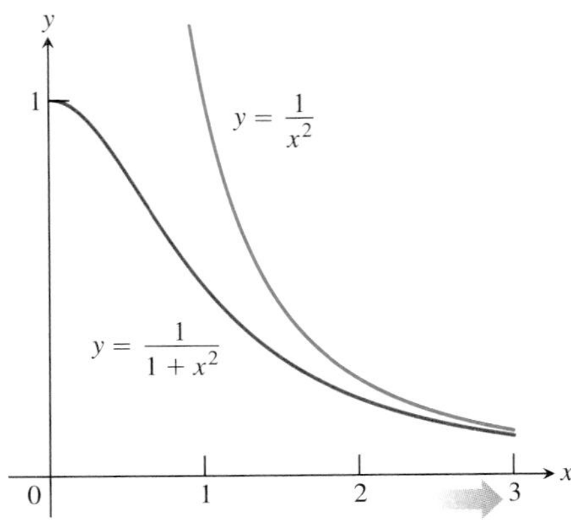

8.20 The functions in Example 11.

EXAMPLE 12

$$\int_1^\infty \frac{3}{e^x + 5}\,dx \qquad \text{converges because} \qquad \int_1^\infty \frac{1}{e^x}\,dx \quad \text{converges}$$

and

$$\lim_{x\to\infty} \frac{1/e^x}{3/(e^x+5)} = \lim_{x\to\infty} \frac{e^x+5}{3e^x} = \lim_{x\to\infty}\left(\frac{1}{3} + \frac{5}{3e^x}\right) = \frac{1}{3} + 0 = \frac{1}{3},$$

a positive finite limit. As far as the convergence of the improper integral is concerned, $3/(e^x + 5)$ behaves like $1/e^x$.

Types of Improper Integrals Discussed in This Section

Infinite limits of integration

1. Upper limit

$$\int_1^\infty \frac{\ln x}{x^2}\,dx = \lim_{b\to\infty} \int_1^b \frac{\ln x}{x^2}\,dx$$

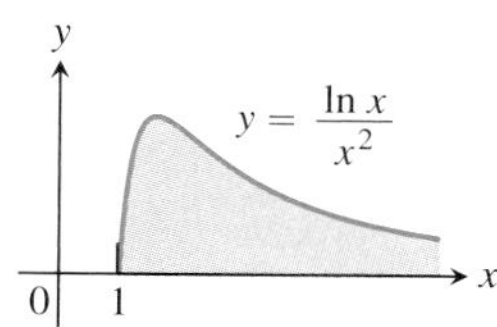

2. Lower limit

$$\int_{-\infty}^0 \frac{dx}{1+x^2} = \lim_{a\to-\infty} \int_a^0 \frac{dx}{1+x^2}$$

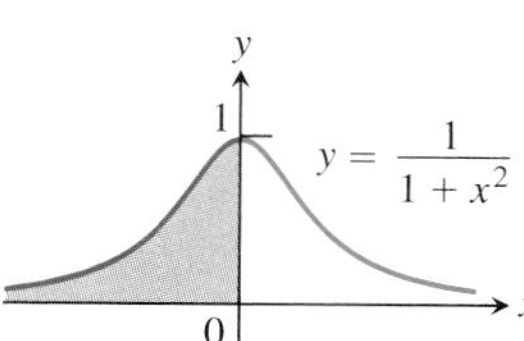

3. Both limits

$$\int_{-\infty}^\infty \frac{dx}{1+x^2} = \lim_{b\to-\infty} \int_b^0 \frac{dx}{1+x^2} + \lim_{c\to\infty} \int_0^c \frac{dx}{1+x^2}$$

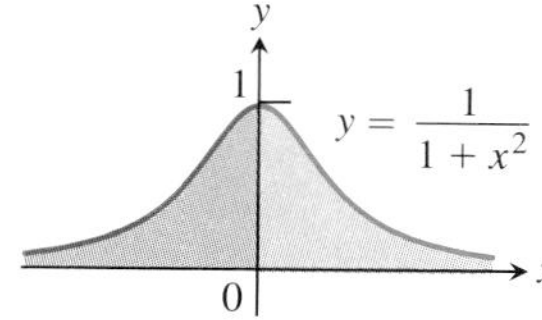

Integrand becomes infinite

4. Upper endpoint

$$\int_0^1 \frac{dx}{(x-1)^{2/3}} = \lim_{b\to1^-} \int_0^b \frac{dx}{(x-1)^{2/3}}$$

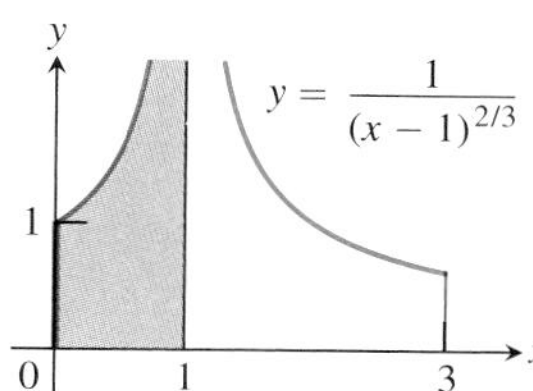

5. Lower endpoint

$$\int_1^3 \frac{dx}{(x-1)^{2/3}} = \lim_{d\to1^+} \int_d^3 \frac{dx}{(x-1)^{2/3}}$$

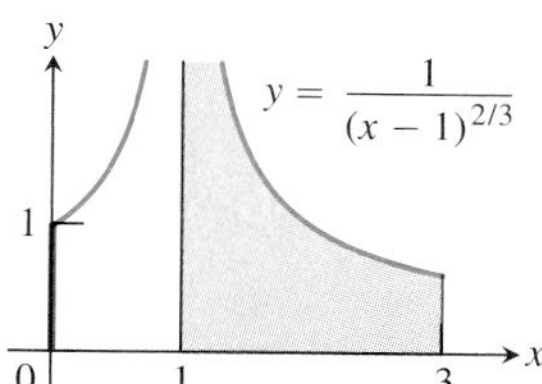

6. Interior point

$$\int_0^3 \frac{dx}{(x-1)^{2/3}} = \int_0^1 \frac{dx}{(x-1)^{2/3}} + \int_1^3 \frac{dx}{(x-1)^{2/3}}$$

Exercises 8.6

Evaluate the integrals in Exercises 1–30 without using tables.

1. $\int_0^{\infty} \frac{dx}{x^2+1}$

2. $\int_1^{\infty} \frac{dx}{x^{1.001}}$

3. $\int_{-\infty}^{-2} \frac{2\,dx}{x^2-1}$

4. $\int_{-\infty}^{2} \frac{2\,dx}{x^2+4}$

5. $\int_0^{4} \frac{dx}{\sqrt{4-x}}$

6. $\int_0^{1} \frac{dx}{\sqrt{1-x^2}}$

7. $\int_0^{1} \frac{dr}{r^{0.999}}$

8. $\int_0^{1} \frac{\theta+1}{\sqrt{\theta^2+2\theta}}\,d\theta$

9. $\int_{-1}^{1} \frac{dx}{x^{2/3}}$

10. $\int_{-8}^{1} \frac{dx}{x^{1/3}}$

11. $\int_{-\infty}^{\infty} \frac{2x\,dx}{(x^2+1)^2}$

12. $\int_{-\infty}^{\infty} \frac{x\,dx}{(x^2+4)^{3/2}}$

13. $\int_0^{\infty} \frac{dv}{(1+v^2)(1+\tan^{-1} v)}$

14. $\int_0^{\infty} \frac{16\tan^{-1} x}{1+x^2}\,dx$

15. $\int_{-\infty}^{1} \frac{8r^3\,dr}{(r^4+1)^2}$

16. $\int_{-\infty}^{0} \theta e^{\theta}\,d\theta$

17. $\int_0^{2} \frac{ds}{\sqrt{4-s^2}}$

18. $\int_0^{1} \frac{4r\,dr}{\sqrt{1-r^4}}$

19. $\int_1^{2} \frac{ds}{s\sqrt{s^2-1}}$

20. $\int_2^{4} \frac{dt}{t\sqrt{t^2-4}}$

21. $\int_{-1}^{4} \frac{dx}{\sqrt{|x|}}$

22. $\int_0^{2} \frac{dx}{\sqrt{|x-1|}}$

23. $\int_{-\infty}^{\infty} e^{-|x|}\,dx$

24. $\int_{-\infty}^{\infty} 2xe^{-x^2}\,dx$

25. $\int_0^{1} x\ln x\,dx$

26. $\int_0^{1} (-\ln x)\,dx$

27. $\int_2^{\infty} \frac{2}{v^2-v}\,dv$

28. $\int_2^{\infty} \frac{2\,dt}{t^2-1}$

29. $\int_{-1}^{\infty} \frac{d\theta}{\theta^2+5\theta+6}$

30. $\int_0^{\infty} \frac{dx}{(x+1)(x^2+1)}$

In Exercises 31–60, use integration, the direct comparison test, or the limit comparison test to test the integrals for convergence. If more than one method applies, use whatever method you prefer.

31. $\int_0^{\pi/2} \tan\theta\,d\theta$

32. $\int_0^{\pi/2} \cot\theta\,d\theta$

33. $\int_0^{\pi} \frac{\sin\theta\,d\theta}{\sqrt{\pi-\theta}}$

34. $\int_{-\pi/2}^{\pi/2} \frac{\cos\theta\,d\theta}{(\pi-2\theta)^{1/3}}$

35. $\int_0^{\ln 2} x^{-2}e^{-1/x}\,dx$

36. $\int_0^{1} \frac{e^{-\sqrt{x}}}{\sqrt{x}}\,dx$

37. $\int_0^{\pi} \frac{dt}{\sqrt{t}+\sin t}$

38. $\int_0^{1} \frac{dt}{t-\sin t}$ *Hint:* $t \geq \sin t$ for $t \geq 0$

39. $\int_0^{2} \frac{dx}{1-x^2}$

40. $\int_0^{2} \frac{dx}{1-x}$

41. $\int_{-1}^{1} \ln|x|\,dx$

42. $\int_{-1}^{1} -x\ln|x|\,dx$

43. $\int_1^{\infty} \frac{dx}{x^3+1}$

44. $\int_4^{\infty} \frac{dx}{\sqrt{x}-1}$

45. $\int_2^{\infty} \frac{dv}{\sqrt{v-1}}$

46. $\int_0^{\infty} \frac{d\theta}{1+e^{\theta}}$

47. $\int_0^{\infty} \frac{dx}{\sqrt{x^6+1}}$

48. $\int_2^{\infty} \frac{dx}{\sqrt{x^2-1}}$

49. $\int_1^{\infty} \frac{\sqrt{x}+1}{x^2}\,dx$

50. $\int_2^{\infty} \frac{x\,dx}{\sqrt{x^4-1}}$

51. $\int_{\pi}^{\infty} \frac{2+\cos x}{x}\,dx$

52. $\int_{\pi}^{\infty} \frac{1+\sin x}{x^2}\,dx$

53. $\int_4^{\infty} \frac{2\,dt}{t^{3/2}-1}$

54. $\int_2^{\infty} \frac{1}{\ln x}\,dx$

55. $\int_1^{\infty} \frac{e^x}{x}\,dx$

56. $\int_{e^e}^{\infty} \ln(\ln x)\,dx$

57. $\int_1^{\infty} \frac{1}{\sqrt{e^x-x}}\,dx$

58. $\int_1^{\infty} \frac{1}{e^x-2^x}\,dx$

59. $\int_{-\infty}^{\infty} \frac{dx}{\sqrt{x^4+1}}$

60. $\int_{-\infty}^{\infty} \frac{dx}{e^x+e^{-x}}$

61. *Estimating the Value of a Convergent Improper Integral Whose Domain Is Infinite.*

a) Show that

$$\int_3^{\infty} e^{-3x}\,dx = \frac{1}{3}e^{-9} < 0.000042,$$

and hence that $\int_3^{\infty} e^{-x^2}\,dx < 0.000042$. Explain why this means that $\int_0^{\infty} e^{-x^2}\,dx$ can be replaced by $\int_0^{3} e^{-x^2}\,dx$ without introducing an error of magnitude greater than 0.000042.

b) NUMERICAL INTEGRATOR. Evaluate this last integral numerically.

62. *The Infinite Paint Can or Gabriel's Horn.* As Example 8 shows, the integral $\int_1^{\infty} (dx/x)$ diverges. This means that the integral

$$\int_1^{\infty} 2\pi\frac{1}{x}\sqrt{1+\frac{1}{x^4}}\,dx,$$

which measures the *surface area* of the solid of revolution traced out by revolving the curve $y = 1/x$, $1 \leq x$, about the x-axis, diverges also. By comparing the two integrals, we see that, for every finite value $b > 1$,

$$\int_1^b 2\pi \frac{1}{x}\sqrt{1+\frac{1}{x^4}}\,dx > 2\pi \int_1^b \frac{1}{x}\,dx.$$

However, the integral

$$\int_1^\infty \pi\left(\frac{1}{x}\right)^2 dx$$

for the *volume* of the solid converges. (a) Calculate it. (b) This solid of revolution is sometimes described as a can that does not hold enough paint to cover its own interior. Think about that for a moment. It is common sense that a finite amount of paint cannot cover an infinite surface. But if we fill the horn with paint (a finite amount), then we *will* have covered an infinite surface. Explain the apparent contradication.

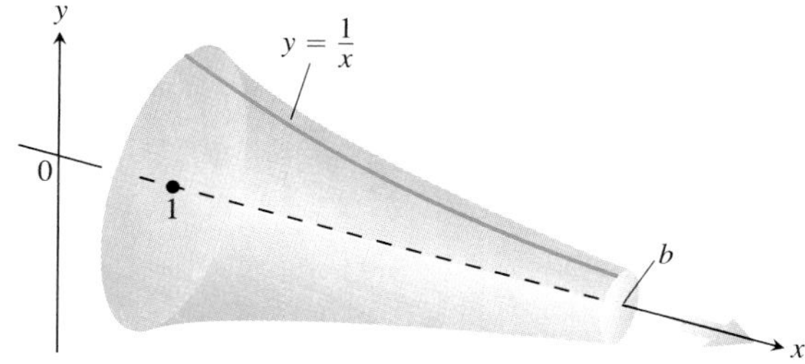

63. Show that $\displaystyle\int_1^\infty \frac{dx}{x^p} = \frac{1}{p-1}$ when $p > 1$

but that the integral is infinite when $p < 1$. Example 8 shows what happens when $p = 1$.

64. Find the values of p for which each integral converges:

a) $\displaystyle\int_1^2 \frac{dx}{x(\ln x)^p}$, **b)** $\displaystyle\int_2^\infty \frac{dx}{x(\ln x)^p}$.

Exercises 65–68 are about the infinite region in the first quadrant between the curve $y = e^{-x}$ and the x-axis.

65. Find the area of the region.

66. Find the centroid of the region.

67. Find the volume swept out by revolving the region about the y-axis.

68. Find the volume swept out by revolving the region about the x-axis.

69. Find the area of the region that lies between the curves $y = \sec x$ and $y = \tan x$ for $0 \le x \le \pi/2$.

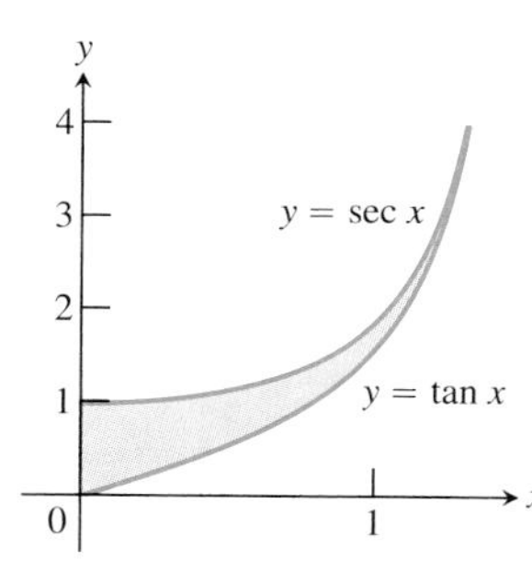

70. The region in Exercise 69 is revolved about the x-axis to generate a solid.

a) Find the volume of the solid.

b) Use the inequalities

$$\int_0^{\pi/2} \sec^2 x\,dx \le \int_0^{\pi/2} \sqrt{1+\sec^4 x}\,dx$$

and

$$\int_0^{\pi/2} \sec x \tan x\,dx \le \int_0^{\pi/2} \sqrt{1+\sec^2 x \tan^2 x}\,dx$$

to show that the inner and outer surfaces of the solid have infinite area.

71. $\displaystyle\int_{-\infty}^{\infty} f(x)\,dx$ ***may not equal*** $\displaystyle\lim_{b\to\infty}\int_{-b}^{b} f(x)\,dx$. Show that

$$\int_0^\infty \frac{2x\,dx}{x^2+1}$$

diverges and hence that

$$\int_{-\infty}^\infty \frac{2x\,dx}{x^2+1}$$

diverges. Then show that

$$\lim_{b\to\infty}\int_{-b}^{b} \frac{2x\,dx}{x^2+1} = 0.$$

72. Here is an argument that ln 3 equals $\infty - \infty$. Where does the argument go wrong? Give reasons for your answer.

$$\begin{aligned}
\ln 3 &= \ln 1 + \ln 3 = \ln 1 - \ln\frac{1}{3}\\
&= \lim_{b\to\infty}\ln\left(\frac{b-2}{b}\right) - \ln\frac{1}{3}\\
&= \lim_{b\to\infty}\left[\ln\frac{x-2}{x}\right]_3^b\\
&= \lim_{b\to\infty}\left[\ln(x-2) - \ln x\right]_3^b\\
&= \lim_{b\to\infty}\int_3^b\left(\frac{1}{x-2} - \frac{1}{x}\right)dx\\
&= \int_3^\infty\left(\frac{1}{x-2} - \frac{1}{x}\right)dx\\
&= \int_3^\infty \frac{1}{x-2}\,dx - \int_3^\infty \frac{1}{x}\,dx\\
&= \lim_{b\to\infty}\Big[\ln(x-2)\Big]_3^b - \lim_{b\to\infty}\Big[\ln x\Big]_3^b\\
&= \infty - \infty.
\end{aligned}$$

73. Is the following calculation correct? Give reasons for your answer.

$$\int_{-1}^3 \frac{1}{x^2}\,dx = -\frac{1}{x}\bigg]_{-1}^3 = -\frac{1}{3} + \frac{1}{-1} = -\frac{4}{3}$$

Writing for Your Own Knowledge

Answer the following questions in writing. Some answers will take only a sentence or two; others may require several paragraphs. Some explanations may also call for graphs or sketches.

1. What is an improper integral?
2. How are the values of various types of improper integrals defined?
3. What can you say about the convergence and divergence of the integral $\int_1^\infty (dx/x^p)$?
4. What tests are available for determining the convergence and divergence of improper integrals that cannot be evaluated directly?

For Your Review

Write brief paragraphs about the following topics and give examples.

Changing integrals into standard forms
Integration by parts
Partial fractions
Trigonometric substitutions
Reduction formulas
A general strategy for evaluating indefinite integrals
Improper integrals

Practice Exercises

Evaluate the integrals in Exercises 1–70.

1. $\int x\sqrt{4x^2-9}\,dx$
2. $\int 6x\sqrt{3x^2+5}\,dx$
3. $\int x(2x+1)^{1/2}\,dx$
4. $\int x(1-x)^{-1/2}\,dx$
5. $\int \frac{x\,dx}{\sqrt{8x^2+1}}$
6. $\int \frac{x\,dx}{\sqrt{9-4x^2}}$
7. $\int \frac{y\,dy}{25+y^2}$
8. $\int \frac{y^3\,dy}{4+y^4}$
9. $\int \frac{t^3\,dt}{\sqrt{9-4t^4}}$
10. $\int \frac{2t\,dt}{t^4+1}$
11. $\int z^{2/3}(z^{5/3}+1)^{2/3}\,dz$
12. $\int z^{-1/5}(1+z^{4/5})^{-1/2}\,dz$
13. $\int \frac{\sin 2\theta\,d\theta}{(1-\cos 2\theta)^2}$
14. $\int \frac{\cos\theta\,d\theta}{(1+\sin\theta)^{1/2}}$
15. $\int \frac{\sin t}{3+4\cos t}\,dt$
16. $\int \frac{\cos 2t}{1+\sin 2t}\,dt$
17. $\int \sin 2x\, e^{\cos 2x}\,dx$
18. $\int \sec x\tan x\, e^{\sec x}\,dx$
19. $\int e^\theta \sin e^\theta \cos^2(e^\theta)\,d\theta$
20. $\int e^\theta \sec^2(e^\theta)\,d\theta$
21. $\int 2^{x-1}\,dx$
22. $\int 5^{x\sqrt{2}}\,dx$
23. $\int \frac{dv}{v\ln v}$
24. $\int \frac{dv}{v(2+\ln v)}$
25. $\int \frac{dx}{(x^2+1)(2+\tan^{-1}x)}$
26. $\int \frac{\sin^{-1}x}{\sqrt{1-x^2}}\,dx$
27. $\int \frac{2\,dx}{\sqrt{1-4x^2}}$
28. $\int \frac{dx}{\sqrt{49-x^2}}$
29. $\int \frac{dt}{\sqrt{16-9t^2}}$
30. $\int \frac{dt}{\sqrt{9-4t^2}}$
31. $\int \frac{dt}{9+t^2}$
32. $\int \frac{dt}{1+25t^2}$
33. $\int \frac{4\,dx}{5x\sqrt{25x^2-16}}$
34. $\int \frac{6\,dx}{x\sqrt{4x^2-9}}$
35. $\int \frac{dx}{\sqrt{4x-x^2}}$
36. $\int \frac{dx}{\sqrt{4x-x^2-3}}$
37. $\int \frac{dy}{y^2-4y+8}$
38. $\int \frac{dt}{t^2+4t+5}$
39. $\int \frac{dx}{(x-1)\sqrt{x^2-2x}}$
40. $\int \frac{dv}{(v+1)\sqrt{v^2+2v}}$
41. $\int \sin^2 x\,dx$
42. $\int \cos^2 3x\,dx$
43. $\int \sin^3\frac{\theta}{2}\,d\theta$
44. $\int \sin^3\theta\cos^2\theta\,d\theta$
45. $\int \tan^3 2t\,dt$
46. $\int 6\sec^4 t\,dt$
47. $\int \frac{dx}{2\sin x\cos x}$
48. $\int \frac{2\,dx}{\cos^2 x-\sin^2 x}$
49. $\int_{\pi/4}^{\pi/2} \sqrt{\csc^2 y-1}\,dy$
50. $\int_{\pi/4}^{3\pi/4} \sqrt{\cot^2 t+1}\,dt$

51. $\int_0^{\pi} \sqrt{1 - \cos^2 2x}\, dx$ **52.** $\int_0^{2\pi} \sqrt{1 - \sin^2 \frac{x}{2}}\, dx$

53. $\int_{-\pi/2}^{\pi/2} \sqrt{1 - \cos 2t}\, dt$ **54.** $\int_{\pi}^{2\pi} \sqrt{1 + \cos 2t}\, dt$

55. $\int \frac{x^2}{x^2 + 4}\, dx$ **56.** $\int \frac{x^3}{9 + x^2}\, dx$

57. $\int \frac{4x^2 + 3}{2x - 1}\, dx$ **58.** $\int \frac{2x}{x - 4}\, dx$

59. $\int \frac{2y - 1}{y^2 + 4}\, dy$ **60.** $\int \frac{y + 4}{y^z + 1}\, dy$

61. $\int \frac{t + 2}{\sqrt{4 - t^2}}\, dt$ **62.** $\int \frac{2t^2 + \sqrt{1 - t^2}}{t\sqrt{1 - t^2}}\, dt$

63. $\int \sqrt{1 + \sin x}\, dx$ **64.** $\int \sqrt{1 - \sin x}\, dx$

65. $\int \frac{\tan x\, dx}{\tan x + \sec x}$ **66.** $\int \frac{\cot x}{\cot x + \csc x}\, dx$

67. $\int \sec (5 - 3x)\, dx$ **68.** $\int x \csc (x^2 + 3)\, dx$

69. $\int \cot \left(\frac{x}{4}\right) dx$ **70.** $\int \tan (2x - 7)\, dx$

Evaluate the integrals in Exercises 71–80.

71. $\int x\sqrt{1 - x}\, dx$ **72.** $\int 3x\sqrt{2x + 1}\, dx$

73. $\int \ln (x + 1)\, dx$ **74.** $\int x^2 \ln x\, dx$

75. $\int \tan^{-1} 3x\, dx$ **76.** $\int \cos^{-1} \left(\frac{x}{2}\right) dx$

77. $\int \frac{\ln x}{x}\, dx$ **78.** $\int e^x \cos 2x\, dx$

79. $\int (x + 1)^2 e^x\, dx$ **80.** $\int x^2 \sin (1 - x)\, dx$

Evaluate the integrals in Exercises 81–100.

81. $\int \frac{x\, dx}{x^2 - 3x + 2}$ **82.** $\int \frac{x\, dx}{x^2 + 4x + 3}$

83. $\int \frac{dx}{x(x + 1)^2}$ **84.** $\int \frac{x + 1}{x^2(x - 1)}\, dx$

85. $\int \frac{\sin \theta\, d\theta}{\cos^2 \theta + \cos \theta - 2}$ **86.** $\int \frac{\cos \theta\, d\theta}{\sin^2 \theta + \sin \theta - 6}$

87. $\int \frac{3x^2 + 4x + 4}{x^3 + x}\, dx$ **88.** $\int \frac{4x\, dx}{x^3 + 4x}$

89. $\int \frac{v + 3}{2v^3 - 8v}\, dv$ **90.** $\int \frac{(3v - 7)\, dv}{(v - 1)(v - 2)(v - 3)}$

91. $\int \frac{dt}{t^4 + 4t^2 + 3}$ **92.** $\int \frac{t\, dt}{t^4 - t^2 - 2}$

93. $\int \frac{x^3 + x^2}{x^2 + x - 2}\, dx$ **94.** $\int \frac{x^3 + 1}{x^3 - x}\, dx$

95. $\int \frac{x^3 + 4x^2}{x^2 + 4x + 3}\, dx$

96. $\int \frac{2x^3 + x^2 - 21x + 24}{x^2 + 2x - 8}\, dx$

97. $\int \frac{dx}{x(3\sqrt{x + 1})}$ **98.** $\int \frac{dx}{x\left(1 + \sqrt[3]{x}\right)}$

99. $\int \frac{ds}{e^s - 1}$ **100.** $\int \frac{ds}{\sqrt{e^s + 1}}$

Evaluate the integrals in Exercises 101–12.

101. $\int \sqrt{z^2 + 1}\, dz$ **102.** $\int (16 + z^2)^{-3/2}\, dz$

103. $\int \frac{dy}{\sqrt{25 + y^2}}$ **104.** $\int \frac{dy}{\sqrt{25 + 9y^2}}$

105. $\int \frac{dx}{x^2\sqrt{1 - x^2}}$ **106.** $\int \frac{x^3\, dx}{\sqrt{1 - x^2}}$

107. $\int \frac{x^2\, dx}{\sqrt{1 - x^2}}$ **108.** $\int \sqrt{4 - x^2}\, dx$

109. $\int \frac{dx}{\sqrt{x^2 - 9}}$ **110.** $\int \frac{12\, dx}{(x^2 - 1)^{3/2}}$

111. $\int \frac{\sqrt{w^2 - 1}}{w}\, dw$ **112.** $\int \frac{\sqrt{z^2 - 16}}{z}\, dz$

Evaluate the integrals in Exercises 113–22.

113. $\int_0^3 \frac{dx}{\sqrt{9 - x^2}}$ **114.** $\int_0^1 \ln x\, dx$

115. $\int_{-1}^1 \frac{dy}{y^{2/3}}$ **116.** $\int_{-2}^{\infty} \frac{d\theta}{(\theta + 1)^{3/5}}$

117. $\int_3^{\infty} \frac{2\, du}{u^2 - 2u}$ **118.** $\int_1^{\infty} \frac{3v - 1}{4v^2 - v}\, dv$

119. $\int_0^{\infty} x^2 e^{-x}\, dx$ **120.** $\int_{-\infty}^0 x e^{3x}\, dx$

121. $\int_{-\infty}^{\infty} \frac{dx}{4x^2 + 9}$ **122.** $\int_{-\infty}^{\infty} \frac{4\, dx}{x^2 + 16}$

Which of the integrals in Exercises 123–28 converge and which diverge?

123. $\int_6^{\infty} \frac{d\theta}{\sqrt{\theta^2 + 1}}$ **124.** $\int_0^{\infty} e^{-u} \cos u\, du$

125. $\int_1^{\infty} \frac{\ln z}{z}\, dz$ **126.** $\int_1^{\infty} \frac{e^{-t}}{\sqrt{t}}\, dt$

127. $\int_{-\infty}^{\infty} \frac{dx}{e^x + e^{-x}}$ **128.** $\int_{-\infty}^{\infty} \frac{dx}{x^2(1 + e^x)}$

Evaluate the integrals in Exercises 129–94. The integrals are listed in random order.

129. $\int \frac{x\,dx}{1+\sqrt{x}}$

130. $\int \frac{x^3+2}{4-x^2}\,dx$

131. $\int \frac{dx}{x(x^2+1)^2}$

132. $\int \frac{\cos\sqrt{x}}{\sqrt{x}}\,dx$

133. $\int \frac{dx}{\sqrt{-2x-x^2}}$

134. $\int \frac{(t-1)\,dt}{\sqrt{t^2-2t}}$

135. $\int \frac{du}{\sqrt{1+u^2}}$

136. $\int e^t \cos e^t\,dt$

137. $\int \frac{2-\cos x+\sin x}{\sin^2 x}\,dx$

138. $\int \frac{\sin^2\theta}{\cos^2\theta}\,d\theta$

139. $\int \frac{9\,dv}{81-v^4}$

140. $\int \frac{\cos x\,dx}{1+\sin^2 x}$

141. $\int \theta\cos(2\theta+1)\,d\theta$

142. $\int_2^\infty \frac{dx}{(x-1)^2}$

143. $\int \frac{x^3\,dx}{x^2-2x+1}$

144. $\int \frac{d\theta}{\sqrt{1+\sqrt{\theta}}}$

145. $\int \frac{2\sin\sqrt{x}\,dx}{\sqrt{x}\sec\sqrt{x}}$

146. $\int \frac{x^5\,dx}{x^4-16}$

147. $\int \frac{dy}{\sin y\cos y}$

148. $\int \frac{d\theta}{\theta^2-2\theta+4}$

149. $\int \frac{\tan x}{\cos^2 x}\,dx$

150. $\int \frac{dr}{(r+1)\sqrt{r^2+2r}}$

151. $\int \frac{(r+2)\,dr}{\sqrt{-r^2-4r}}$

152. $\int \frac{y\,dy}{4+y^4}$

153. $\int \frac{\sin 2\theta\,d\theta}{(1+\cos 2\theta)^2}$

154. $\int \frac{dx}{(x^2-1)^2}$

155. $\int_{\pi/4}^{\pi/2} \sqrt{1+\cos 4x}\,dx$

156. $\int (15)^{2x+1}\,dx$

157. $\int \frac{x\,dx}{\sqrt{2-x}}$

158. $\int \frac{\sqrt{1-v^2}}{v^2}\,dv$

159. $\int \frac{dy}{y^2-2y+2}$

160. $\int \ln\sqrt{x-1}\,dx$

161. $\int \theta^2\tan(\theta^3)\,d\theta$

162. $\int \frac{x\,dx}{\sqrt{8-2x^2-x^4}}$

163. $\int \frac{z+1}{z^2(z^2+4)}\,dz$

164. $\int x^3 e^{(x^2)}\,dx$

165. $\int \frac{t\,dt}{\sqrt{9-4t^2}}$

166. $\int_0^{\pi/10} \sqrt{1+\cos 5\theta}\,d\theta$

167. $\int \frac{\cot\theta\,d\theta}{1+\sin^2\theta}$

168. $\int \frac{\tan^{-1}x}{x^2}\,dx$

169. $\int \frac{\tan\sqrt{y}}{2\sqrt{y}}\,dy$

170. $\int \frac{e^t\,dt}{e^{2t}+3e^t+2}$

171. $\int \frac{\theta^2\,d\theta}{4-\theta^2}$

172. $\int \frac{1-\cos 2x}{1+\cos 2x}\,dx$

173. $\int e^x(\cos e^x)\,dx$

174. $\int \frac{\cos x\,dx}{\sin^3 x-\sin x}$

175. $\int \sin\frac{x}{2}\cos\frac{x}{2}\,dx$

176. $\int \frac{x^2-x+2}{(x^2+2)^2}\,dx$

177. $\int \frac{e^t\,dt}{1+e^t}$

178. $\int \tan^3 t\,dt$

179. $\int_1^\infty \frac{\ln y}{y^3}\,dy$

180. $\int \frac{3+\sec^2 x+\sin x}{\tan x}\,dx$

181. $\int \frac{\cot v\,dv}{\ln\sin v}$

182. $\int \frac{dx}{(2x-1)\sqrt{x^2-x}}$

183. $\int e^{\ln\sqrt{x}}\,dx$

184. $\int e^\theta\sqrt{3+4e^\theta}\,d\theta$

185. $\int \frac{\sin 5t\,dt}{1+(\cos 5t)^2}$

186. $\int \frac{dv}{\sqrt{e^{2v}-1}}$

187. $\int (27)^{3\theta+1}\,d\theta$

188. $\int x^5\sin x\,dx$

189. $\int \frac{dr}{1+\sqrt{r}}$

190. $\int \frac{4x^3-20x}{x^4-10x^2+9}\,dx$

191. $\int \frac{8\,dy}{y^3(y+2)}$

192. $\int \frac{(t+1)\,dt}{(t^2+2t)^{2/3}}$

193. $\int \frac{8\,dm}{m\sqrt{49m^2-4}}$

194. $\int \frac{dt}{t(1+\ln t)\sqrt{(\ln t)(2+\ln t)}}$

Evaluate the integrals in Exercises 195–98 (a) without using a trigonometric substitution; (b) using a trigonometric substitution.

195. $\int \frac{y\,dy}{\sqrt{16-y^2}}$

196. $\int \frac{x\,dx}{\sqrt{4+x^2}}$

197. $\int \frac{x\,dx}{4-x^2}$

198. $\int \frac{t\,dt}{\sqrt{4t^2-1}}$

199. Find the length of the curve

$$y=\int_0^x \sqrt{\cos 2t}\,dt$$

from $x=0$ to $x=\pi/4$.

200. Find the area of the region that is bounded below by the curve $y=\sec x$, $-\pi/3\le x\le\pi/3$, and above by the line $y=2$.

201. Find the volume of the solid generated by revolving the shaded region shown here about the y-axis.

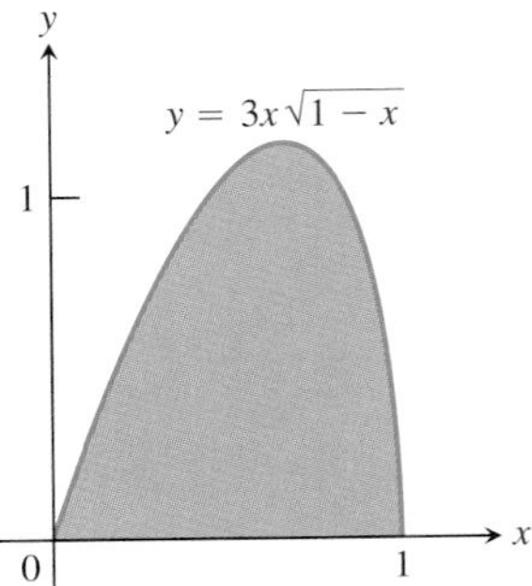

202. Find the centroid of the region in the first quadrant that is bounded below by the x-axis, above by the curve $y = \ln x$, and on the right by the line $x = e$.

203. The region in the first quadrant enclosed by the coordinate axes, the curve $y = e^x$, and the line $x = 1$ is revolved about the y-axis to generate a solid. Find the volume of the solid.

204. The region in the first quadrant that is bounded above by the curve $y = e^x - 1$, below by the x-axis, and on the right by the line $x = \ln 2$ is revolved about the line $x = \ln 2$ to generate a solid. Find the volume of the solid.

205. Find the volume of the solid generated by revolving the shaded region about

a) the x-axis **b)** the line $y = 1$

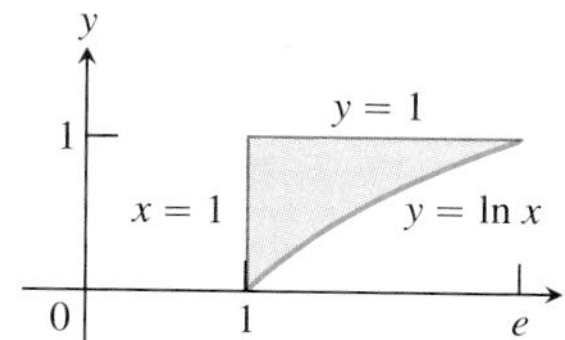

206. *Autocatalytic Reactions.* The equation describing the autocatalytic reaction in Section 4.5, Exercise 43, can be written as $dx/dt = kx(a - x)$. Read Exercise 43 for background (there is no need to do the exercise). Then solve the differential equation above to find x as a function of t, assuming that $x = a/10$ when $t = 0$.

207. The region between the curve

$$y = f(x) = \begin{cases} 0, & x = 0 \\ x \ln x, & 0 < x \le 2 \end{cases}$$

is revolved about the x-axis to generate the solid shown here.

a) Show that f is continuous at $x = 0$.
b) Find the volume of the solid.

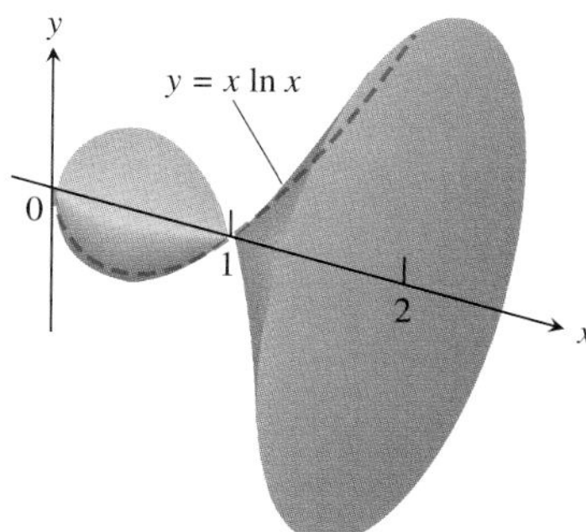

208. The infinite region bounded by the coordinate axes and the curve $y = -\ln x$ in the first quadrant is revolved about the x-axis to generate a solid. Find the volume of the solid.

209. Find the centroid of the region enclosed by the curves $y = \pm(1 - x^2)^{-1/2}$ and the lines $x = 0$ and $x = 1$.

210. Without evaluating either integral, show why

$$2\int_{-1}^{1} \sqrt{1 - x^2}\,dx = \int_{-1}^{1} \frac{dx}{\sqrt{1 - x^2}}.$$

(*Source:* Peter A. Lindstrom, *Mathematics Magazine*, Vol. 45, No. 1, January 1972, p. 47.)

211. *The Length of an Astroid.* The graph of the equation $x^{2/3} + y^{2/3} = 1$ is one of a family of curves called *astroids* (not "asteroids") because of their starlike appearance (Fig. 8.21). Find the length of this particular astroid.

212. *The Surface Generated by an Astroid.* Find the area of the surface generated by revolving the curve in Fig. 8.21 about the x-axis.

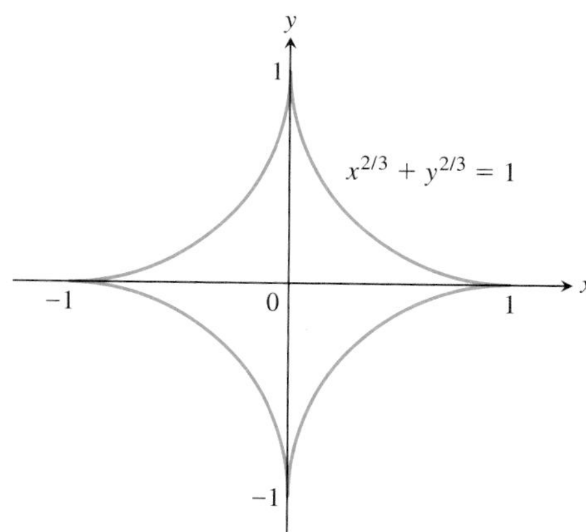

8.21 The astroid in Exercises 211 and 212.

213. Find a curve through the origin whose length is

$$\int_0^4 \sqrt{1 + \frac{1}{4x}}\,dx.$$

214. a) Graph the function $f(x) = e^{(x - e^x)}$, $-5 \le x \le 3$.
b) Show that $\int_{-\infty}^{\infty} f(x)\,dx$ converges and find the integral's value.

RED TAPE

G. R. BOYNTON, a political scientist at the University of Iowa, has followed the federal government's war on red tape since it was first declared by President Gerald Ford in 1975.

Red tape refers to the laws that are passed by Congress and the rules needed to say what the laws mean in specific situations. When a new law is passed, that adds to the red tape. When a situation changes, new rules interpreting the law are required, adding to the red tape. The important point is understanding why the simplest solution — just pass fewer laws — won't work.

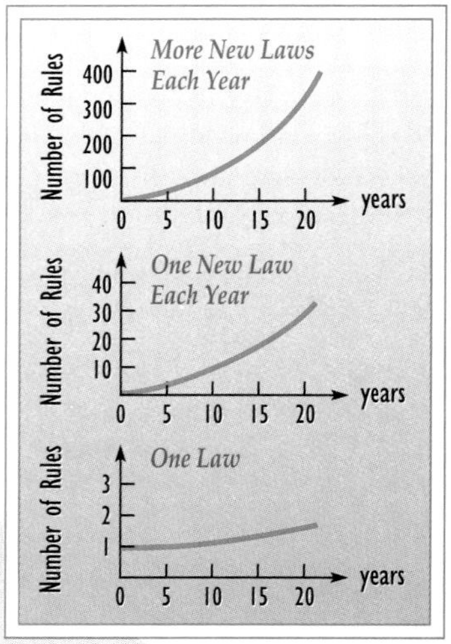

The three graphs show what happens when the number of laws passed increases each year, when the number of new laws passed is the same from year to year, and when no new laws are being passed.

Here is how it works. Each year, we start with last year's laws, add some new laws, and interpret a percentage of older laws.

Suppose that every year we pass 100 new laws and reinterpret 5% of the laws that are two years old or older.

Starting with 100 laws this year would generate the numbers of rules in the following table:

Year	New Laws	From Last Year	From Interpretation	On the Books at Year End
1	100	0	0	100
2	100	100	0	200
3	100	200	0	200
4	100	305	10	415
5	100	415	15	530
•				
•				
•				
10	100	1196	53	1349

Ten years from now there would be not 1000 but 1349 rules on the books. In 20 years there would be 3326. The real culprit is that 5%, which adds a geometric component to an otherwise arithmetic series. Even if no new laws were passed after year 1, there would be 145 rules on the books 10 years later. But we don't do that. Each year, we pass more laws than the year before — bad news for the twenty-first-century Americans.

9 Infinite Series

OVERVIEW

In this chapter we develop one of the most remarkable formulas in all of mathematics, a formula that enables us to express many functions as "infinite polynomials" and at the same time tells how much error we will incur if we truncate those polynomials to make them finite. In addition to providing effective polynomial approximations of differentiable functions, these infinite polynomials (called power series) have many other uses. They provide an efficient way to evaluate nonelementary integrals and they solve differential equations that give insight into heat flow, vibration, chemical diffusion, and signal transmission. What you will learn here sets the stage for the roles played by series of functions of all kinds in science and mathematics.

9.1 Sequences

Informally, a sequence is any list (or ordered collection) of things, but in this chapter the things will usually be numbers. We have seen sequences before, such as the sequence $S_2, S_4, S_6, \ldots, S_{2n}, \ldots$ of approximations generated by Simpson's rule and the sequence $C_1, C_2, \ldots, C_n, \ldots$ of polygons that converge to Helga von Koch's snowflake curve. These sequences have limits, but many sequences, such as the sequence $1, 2, 3, \ldots, n, \ldots$ of positive integers, do not.

Definitions and Notation

We can list the integer multiples of 3 by assigning each multiple a position:

$$\begin{array}{cccc} 1 & 2 & 3 \ldots & n \ldots \\ \downarrow & \downarrow & \downarrow & \downarrow \\ 3 & 6 & 9 & 3n \end{array}$$

The first number is 3, the second 6, the third 9, and so on. The assignment is a function that assigns $3n$ to the nth place. And that is the basic idea for constructing sequences. There is a function that tells us where each item is to be placed.

DEFINITION

A **sequence (infinite sequence)** is a function whose domain is the set of positive integers.

Sequences are defined the way other functions are, some typical rules being

$$a(n) = n - 1, \qquad a(n) = 1 - \frac{1}{n}, \qquad a(n) = \frac{\ln n}{n^2}. \tag{1}$$

9.1 The sequences of Example 1 are graphed here in two different ways: by plotting the numbers a_n on a horizontal axis and by plotting the points (n, a_n) in the coordinate plane.

The terms $a_n = n - 1$ eventually surpass every integer, so the sequence $\{a_n\}$ diverges, . . .

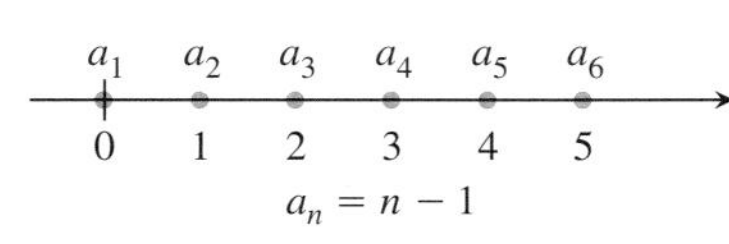

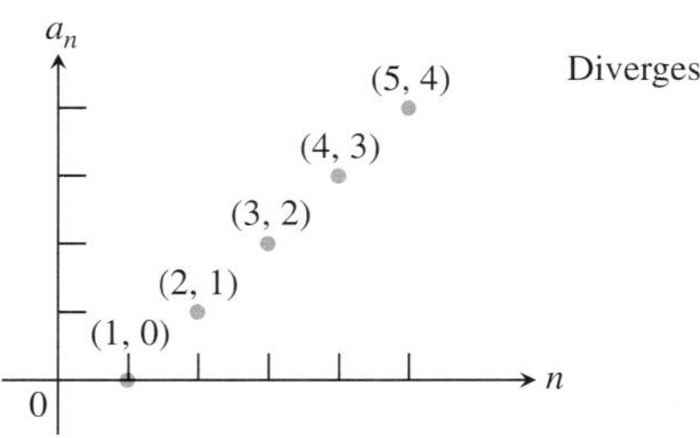

. . . but the terms $a_n = 1/n$ decrease steadily and get arbitrarily close to 0 as n increases, so the sequence $\{a_n\}$ converges to 0.

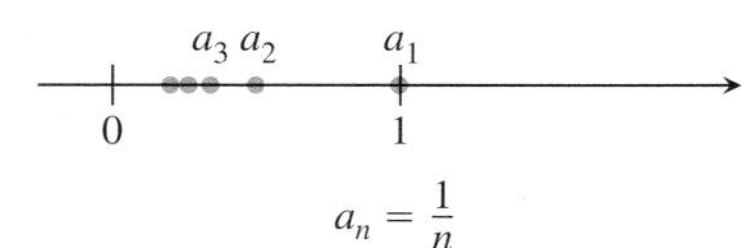

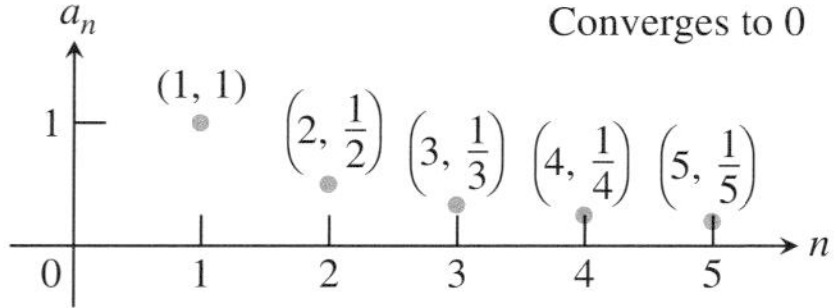

The terms $a_n = (-1)^{n+1}(1/n)$ alternate in sign but still converge to 0.

a_2 a_4 a_5 a_3 a_1

0 1

$a_n = (-1)^{n+1}\frac{1}{n}$

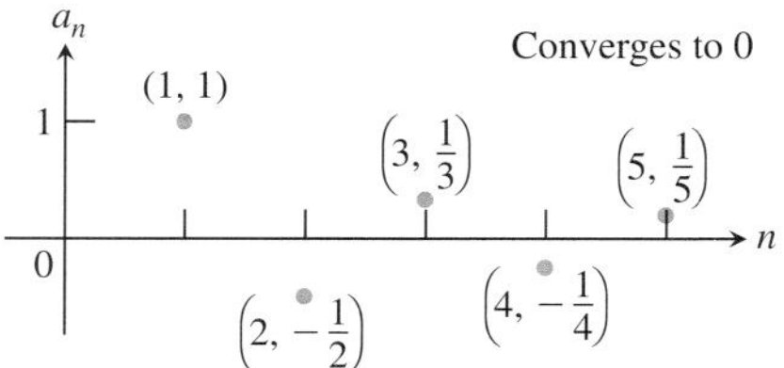

The terms $a_n = (n - 1)/n$ approach 1 steadily and get arbitrarily close as n increases, so the sequence $\{a_n\}$ converges to 1.

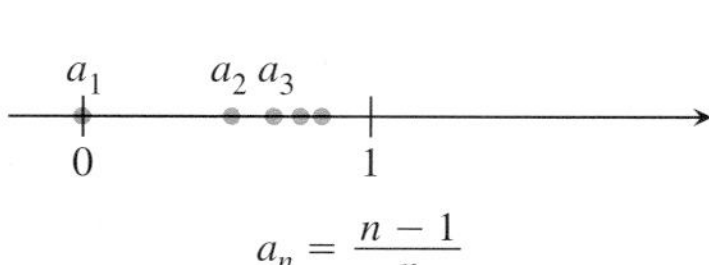

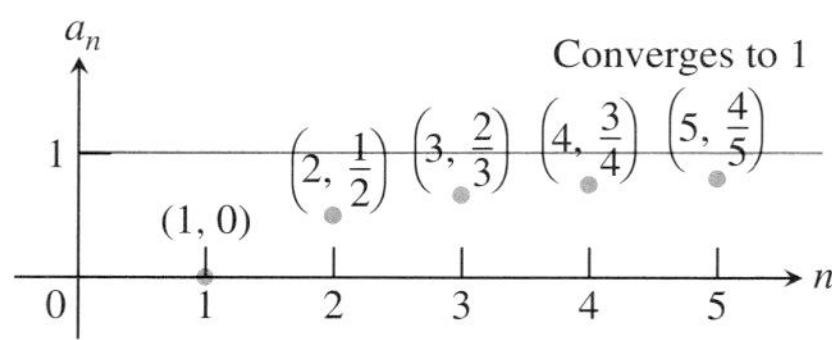

The terms $a_n = (-1)^{n+1}[(n - 1)/n]$ alternate in sign. The positive terms approach 1. But the negative terms approach -1 as n increases, so the sequence $\{a_n\}$ diverges.

a_6 a_4 a_2 a_1 a_3 a_5

-1 0 1

$a_n = (-1)^{n+1}\left(\frac{n-1}{n}\right)$

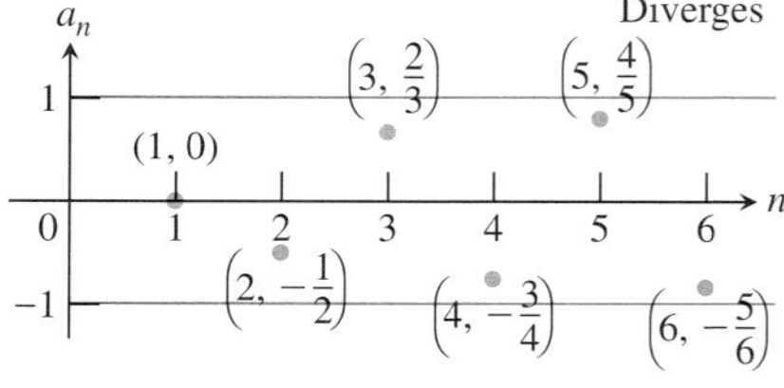

The terms in the sequence of constants $a_n = 3$ have the same value for all n, so the sequence $\{a_n\}$ converges to 3.

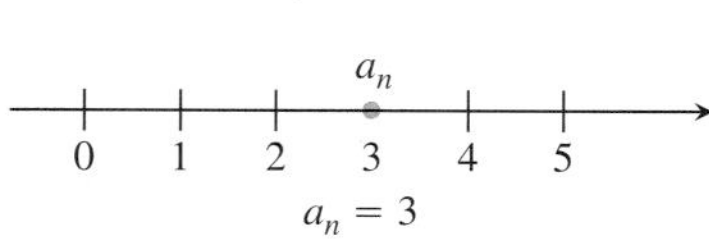

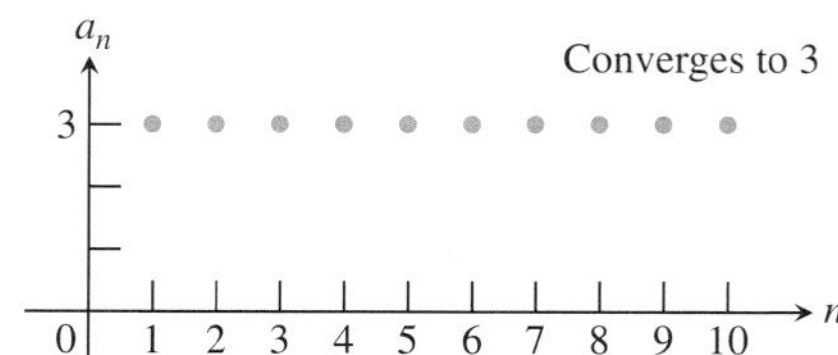

The number $a(n)$ is the **nth term** of the sequence, or the **term with index n**. If $a(n) = (n-1)/n$, we have

First term	Second term	Third term	nth term
$a(1) = 0$	$a(2) = \frac{1}{2}$,	$a(3) = \frac{2}{3}$, . . . ,	$a(n) = \frac{n-1}{n}$, . . .

(2)

If we use the subscript notation a_n for $a(n)$, we have

$$a_1 = 0, \quad a_2 = \frac{1}{2}, \quad a_3 = \frac{2}{3}, \quad \ldots, \quad a_n = \frac{n-1}{n}, \quad \ldots \tag{3}$$

To describe sequences, we often write the first few terms and the nth term.

Notation

We usually denote the sequence $a_1, a_2, \ldots, a_n, \ldots$ by $\{a_n\}$ ("the sequence a sub n"). The second sequence in Example 1 is $\{1/n\}$ ("the sequence 1 over n"); the last sequence is $\{3\}$ ("the sequence 3").

EXAMPLE 1

Sequence	Formula for nth term
$0, 1, 2, \ldots, n-1, \ldots$	$a_n = n - 1$
$1, \frac{1}{2}, \frac{1}{3}, \ldots, \frac{1}{n}, \ldots$	$a_n = \frac{1}{n}$
$1, -\frac{1}{2}, \frac{1}{3}, -\frac{1}{4}, \ldots, (-1)^{n+1}\frac{1}{n}, \ldots$	$a_n = (-1)^{n+1}\frac{1}{n}$
$0, \frac{1}{2}, \frac{2}{3}, \frac{3}{4}, \ldots, \frac{n-1}{n}, \ldots$	$a_n = \frac{n-1}{n}$
$0, -\frac{1}{2}, \frac{2}{3}, -\frac{3}{4}, \ldots, (-1)^{n+1}\left(\frac{n-1}{n}\right), \ldots$	$a_n = (-1)^{n+1}\left(\frac{n-1}{n}\right)$
$3, 3, 3, \ldots, 3, \ldots$	$a_n = 3$

Convergence and Divergence

As Fig. 9.1 shows, the sequences of Example 1 exhibit different kinds of behavior. The sequences $\{1/n\}$, $\{(-1)^{n+1}(1/n)\}$, and $\{(n-1)/n\}$ each appear to approach single limiting values as n increases, and $\{3\}$ is already at its limiting value from the very first. On the other hand, terms of $\{(-1)^{n+1}(n-1)/n\}$ accumulate near two different values, -1 and 1, while the terms of $\{n-1\}$ become increasingly large and do not accumulate anywhere.

We distinguish sequences that approach a unique limiting value as n increases from those that do not.

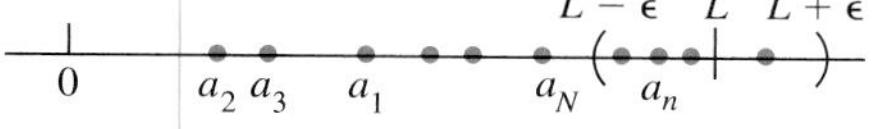

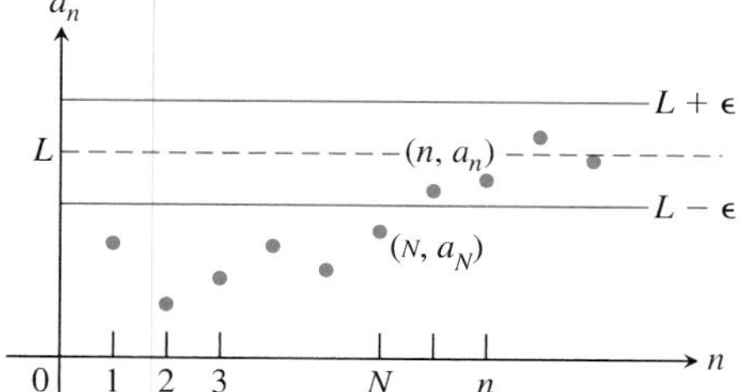

9.2 $a_n \to L$ if L is a horizontal asymptote of the sequence of points $\{(n, a_n)\}$. In this figure, all the a_n's after a_N lie within ϵ of L.

DEFINITIONS

The sequence $\{a_n\}$ **converges** to the number L if to every positive number ϵ there corresponds an integer N such that for all n

$$n > N \quad \Rightarrow \quad |a_n - L| < \epsilon. \tag{4}$$

If no such limit exists, we say that $\{a_n\}$ **diverges.**

If $\{a_n\}$ converges to L, we write $\lim_{n\to\infty} a_n = L$ or $a_n \to L$, and call L the **limit** of the sequence (Fig. 9.2).

A **tail** of a sequence is the collection of terms whose indices are greater than or equal to some integer N. Another way to say that $a_n \to L$ is to say that every ϵ-interval about L contains a tail of the sequence. Convergence or divergence has nothing to do with how a sequence begins. It depends only on how the tails behave.

All numerical and graphical evidence indicates that the sequence

$$1, \frac{1}{2}, \frac{1}{3}, \frac{1}{4}, \ldots, \frac{1}{n}, \ldots$$

converges to 0 (Fig. 9.1), and we would expect the definition of convergence to affirm this observation. It does, as the next example shows.

EXAMPLE 2 *Testing the Definition.* Show that $\{1/n\}$ converges to 0.

Solution We set $a_n = 1/n$ and $L = 0$ in the definition of convergence. To show that $1/n \to 0$, we must show that for any $\epsilon > 0$ there exists an integer N such that for all n

$$n > N \quad \Rightarrow \quad \left|\frac{1}{n} - 0\right| < \epsilon \qquad \text{Eq. (4) with } a_n = 1/n \text{ and } L = 0$$

or, more simply, that for all n

$$n > N \quad \Rightarrow \quad \frac{1}{n} < \epsilon. \tag{5}$$

This is equivalent to saying that $n > N \Rightarrow n > 1/\epsilon$, so any $N \geq 1/\epsilon$ will suffice. For example, if $\epsilon = 1/10$, we use $N = 10$, and so on.

A similar argument could be used to show that if k is any number then $\{k\}$ converges to k.

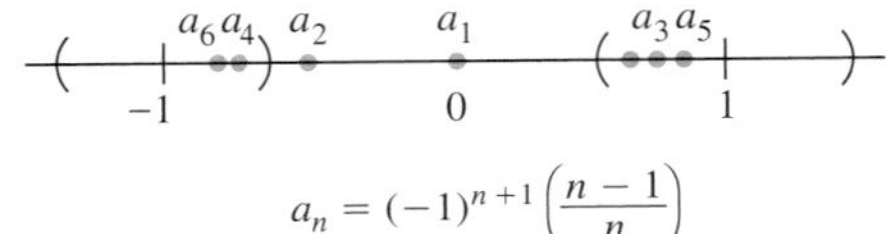

Neither the ϵ-interval about 1 nor the ϵ-interval about −1 contains a complete tail of the sequence.

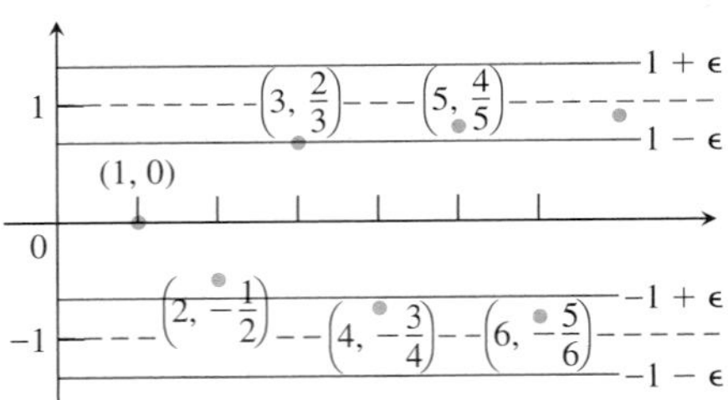

9.3 The sequence $\{(-1)^{n+1}(n-1)/n\}$ diverges.

EXAMPLE 3 Show that $\{(-1)^{n+1}(n-1)/n\}$ diverges.

Solution Take a positive ϵ smaller than 1 so that the bands shown in Fig. 9.3 about the lines $y = 1$ and $y = -1$ do not overlap. Any $\epsilon < 1$ will do. Convergence to 1 would require every point of the graph beyond a certain index N to lie inside the upper band, but this will never happen. As soon as a point (n, a_n) lies in the upper band, every alternate point starting with $(n+1, a_{n+1})$ lies in the lower band. Hence the sequence cannot converge to 1. Likewise, it cannot converge to −1. On the other hand, because the terms of the sequence get alternately closer to 1 and −1, they never accumulate near any other value. Therefore, the sequence diverges.

Example 3 illustrates the fact that a sequence cannot converge to two different limits. If a sequence converges, its limit is unique.

Recursive Definitions

So far, we have calculated each a_n directly from the value of n. But sequences are often defined **recursively** by giving

1. The value(s) of the initial term or terms, and
2. A rule, called a **recursion formula,** for calculating any later term from terms that precede it.

Recursion formulas arise regularly in computer programs and numerical routines for solving differential equations.

Factorial Notation

The notation $n!$ ("n factorial") means the product $1 \cdot 2 \cdot 3 \cdot \cdots \cdot n$ of the integers from 1 to n. Notice that $(n+1)! = (n+1) \cdot n!$. Thus, $4! = 1 \cdot 2 \cdot 3 \cdot 4 = 24$ and $5! = 1 \cdot 2 \cdot 3 \cdot 4 \cdot 5 = 5 \cdot 4! = 120$. We also define $0!$ to be 1. Factorials grow even faster than exponentials, as the following table suggests.

n	e^n (rounded)	$n!$
1	3	1
5	148	120
10	22,026	3,628,800
20	4.8×10^8	2.4×10^{18}

EXAMPLE 4 *Sequences Constructed Recursively*

a) The statements $a_1 = 1$ and $a_n = a_{n-1} + 1$ define the sequence $1, 2, 3, \ldots, n, \ldots$ of positive integers. With $a_1 = 1$, we have $a_2 = a_1 + 1 = 2$, $a_3 = a_2 + 1 = 3$, and so on.

b) The statements $a_1 = 1$ and $a_n = n \cdot a_{n-1}$ define the sequence $1, 2, 6, 24, \ldots, n!, \ldots$ of factorials. With $a_1 = 1$, we have $a_2 = 2 \cdot a_1 = 2$, $a_3 = 3 \cdot a_2 = 6$, $a_4 = 4 \cdot a_3 = 24$, and so on.

c) The statements $a_1 = 1$, $a_2 = 1$, and $a_{n+1} = a_n + a_{n-1}$ define the sequence $1, 1, 2, 3, 5, \ldots$ of **Fibonacci numbers.** With $a_1 = 1$ and $a_2 = 1$, we have $a_3 = 1 + 1 = 2$, $a_4 = 2 + 1 = 3$, $a_5 = 3 + 2 = 5$, and so on.

Subsequences

If the terms of one sequence appear within another sequence in their given order, we call the first sequence a **subsequence** of the second.

EXAMPLE 5 *Subsequences of the Sequence of Positive Integers*

a) The sequence of even integers: $2, 4, 6, \ldots, 2n, \ldots$

b) The sequence of odd integers: $1, 3, 5, \ldots, 2n - 1, \ldots$

c) The sequence of primes: $2, 3, 5, 7, 11, \ldots$

Subsequences are important for two reasons. First, if a sequence $\{a_n\}$ converges to a limit L, then all subsequences of $\{a_n\}$ also converge to L. If we know a sequence converges, it may be quicker for us to find or estimate its limit by choosing a rapidly converging subsequence. The second reason is related to the first: If any subsequence of the original sequence diverges, or if two subsequences have different limits, then the original sequence diverges. We know that the sequence $\{(-1)^{n-1}\}$ diverges because the subsequence $1, 1, 1, \ldots$ of odd-numbered terms converges to 1 while the subsequence $-1, -1, -1, \ldots$ of even-numbered terms converges to -1, which is a different limit.

Useful Theorems

The study of sequences would be cumbersome if we had to answer every question about convergence by applying the definition. Three theorems make this largely unnecessary. The first is the sequence version of Theorem 1 in Chapter 2.

THEOREM 1

The following rules hold if $\lim_{n\to\infty} a_n = A$ and $\lim_{n\to\infty} b_n = B$ (A and B real numbers)

1. *Sum Rule:* $\lim_{n\to\infty} (a_n + b_n) = A + B$
2. *Difference Rule:* $\lim_{n\to\infty} (a_n - b_n) = A - B$
3. *Product Rule:* $\lim_{n\to\infty} (a_n \cdot b_n) = A \cdot B$
4. *Constant Multiple Rule:* $\lim_{n\to\infty} (k \cdot b_n) = k \cdot B$ (Any number k)
5. *Quotient Rule:* $\lim_{n\to\infty} \dfrac{a_n}{b_n} = \dfrac{A}{B}$ if $B \neq 0$

By combining Theorem 1 with Example 2, we can proceed immediately to

$$\lim_{n\to\infty}\left(-\frac{1}{n}\right) = -1\cdot\lim_{n\to\infty}\frac{1}{n} = -1\cdot 0 = 0,$$

$$\lim_{n\to\infty}\left(\frac{n-1}{n}\right) = \lim_{n\to\infty}\left(1-\frac{1}{n}\right) = \lim_{n\to\infty}1 - \lim_{n\to\infty}\frac{1}{n} = 1-0 = 1,$$

$$\lim_{n\to\infty}\frac{5}{n^2} = 5\cdot\lim_{n\to\infty}\frac{1}{n}\cdot\lim_{n\to\infty}\frac{1}{n} = 5\cdot 0\cdot 0 = 0,$$

$$\lim_{n\to\infty}\frac{4-7n^6}{n^6+3} = \lim_{n\to\infty}\frac{(4/n^6)-7}{1+(3/n^6)} = \frac{0-7}{1+0} = -7.$$

One consequence of Theorem 1 is that every nonzero multiple of a divergent sequence $\{a_n\}$ diverges. For, suppose $\{ca_n\}$ were to converge for some number $c \neq 0$. Then $(1/c)\{ca_n\} = \{a_n\}$ would converge by the Constant Multiple Rule—but it does not.

The next theorem is the sequence version of the Sandwich Theorem.

THEOREM 2

The Sandwich Theorem for Sequences

If $a_n \le b_n \le c_n$ holds for all n beyond some index N, and if $\lim_{n\to\infty} a_n = \lim_{n\to\infty} c_n = L$, then $\lim_{n\to\infty} b_n = L$ also.

An immediate consequence of Theorem 2 is that, if $|b_n| \le c_n$ and $c_n \to 0$, then $b_n \to 0$ because $-c_n \le b_n \le c_n$. We use this fact in the next example.

EXAMPLE 6 Since $1/n \to 0$, we know that

a) $\dfrac{\cos n}{n} \to 0$ because $\left|\dfrac{\cos n}{n}\right| = \dfrac{|\cos n|}{n} \le \dfrac{1}{n}$;

b) $\dfrac{1}{2^n} \to 0$ because $\dfrac{1}{2^n} \le \dfrac{1}{n}$;

c) $(-1)^n\dfrac{1}{n} \to 0$ because $\left|(-1)^n\dfrac{1}{n}\right| \le \dfrac{1}{n}$.

The application of Theorems 1 and 2 is broadened by a theorem stating that applying a continuous function to a convergent sequence produces a convergent sequence. We state the theorem without proof.

THEOREM 3

If $a_n \to L$ and if f is a function that is continuous at L and defined at all a_n, then $f(a_n) \to f(L)$.

EXAMPLE 7 Show that $\sqrt{(n+1)/n} \to 1$.

Solution We know that $(n+1)/n \to 1$. Taking $f(x) = \sqrt{x}$ and $L = 1$ in Theorem 3 gives $\sqrt{(n+1)/n} \to \sqrt{1} = 1$.

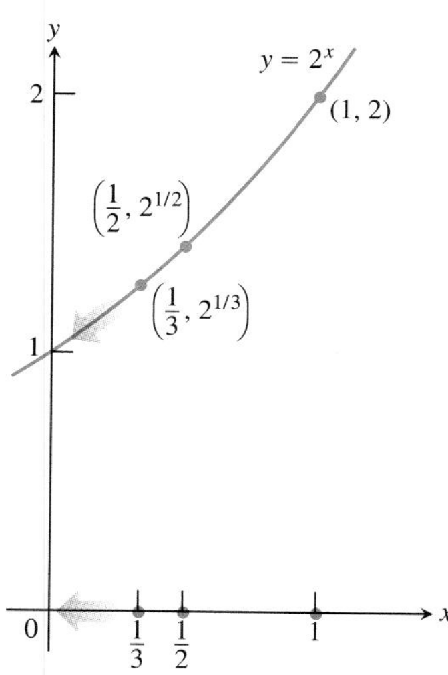

9.4 As $n \to \infty$, $x = 1/n \to 0$ and $y = 2^{1/n} \to 2^0 = 1$ (Example 8).

EXAMPLE 8 Show that $2^{1/n} \to 1$ (Fig. 9.4).

Solution We know that $1/n \to 0$. Taking $f(x) = 2^x$ and $L = 0$ in Theorem 3 therefore gives $2^{1/n} \to 2^0 = 1$. Some sample values are shown at the right.

n	$2^{1/n}$
1	2
2	1.4142 13562
4	1.1892 07115
10	1.0717 73463
100	1.0069 55555
1000	1.0006 93387
10000	1.0000 69317

In Section 1.5, we saw that entering 2 in a calculator and pressing the square root key repeatedly produces a succession of numbers that approach 1. The result of Example 8 now tells us why. The number 2 and its successive square roots form a subsequence 2, $2^{1/2}$, $2^{1/4}$, $2^{1/8}$, . . . of $\{2^{1/n}\}$. The latter sequence converges to 1, so the subsequence does, too. Notice that the subsequence was constructed recursively, each term after 2 being the square root of the one before it. With $a_1 = 2$, the recursion formula is $a_n = \sqrt{a_{n-1}}$.

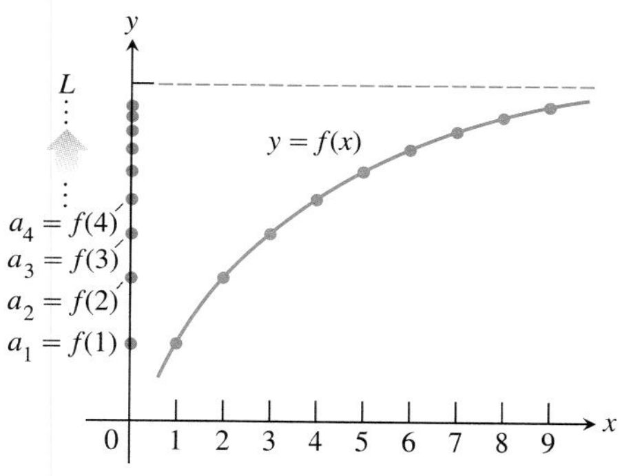

9.5 If $\lim_{x\to\infty} f(x) = L$ then $f(n) \to L$.

THEOREM 4

Suppose $a_n = f(n)$ for every positive integer n. If $\lim_{x\to\infty} f(x) = L$, then $\lim_{n\to\infty} a_n = L$ (Fig. 9.5).

This means that under favorable conditions we can find the limit of a sequence $\{a_n\}$ by treating n as a continuous real variable and applying what we know about finding limits of real-valued functions.

EXAMPLE 9 Investigate the convergence of the sequence whose nth term is $a_n = (\ln n)/n$.

Solution The function $f(x) = (\ln x)/x$ is defined for all $x \geq 1$ and agrees with the given sequence at positive integer values of x. Therefore, $\lim_{n\to\infty} (\ln n)/n$ will equal $\lim_{x\to\infty} (\ln x)/x$ if the latter exists. A single application of l'Hôpital's rule shows that

$$\lim_{x\to\infty} f(x) = \lim_{x\to\infty} \frac{\ln x}{x} = \lim_{x\to\infty} \frac{1/x}{1} = \frac{0}{1} = 0.$$

We apply Theorem 4 to conclude that

$$\lim_{n\to\infty} \frac{\ln n}{n} = \lim_{x\to\infty} f(x) = 0.$$

There was really no need to change n to x before applying l'Hôpital's rule in Example 9. We obtain the same result by differentiation with respect to n:

$$\lim_{n\to\infty} \frac{\ln n}{n} = \lim_{n\to\infty} \frac{1/n}{1} = \frac{0}{1} = 0.$$

EXAMPLE 10 Investigate the convergence of the sequence whose nth term is $a_n = 2^n/5n$.

Solution By l'Hôpital's rule,

$$\lim_{n\to\infty} a_n = \lim_{n\to\infty} \frac{2^n}{5n} = \lim_{n\to\infty} \frac{2^n \cdot \ln 2}{5} = \infty.$$

The sequence diverges.

Limits That Arise Frequently

The limits in Table 9.1 arise frequently. The first limit is from Example 9. The others are derived in Appendix 6.

TABLE 9.1

1. $\lim_{n\to\infty} \frac{\ln n}{n} = 0$
2. $\lim_{n\to\infty} \sqrt[n]{n} = 1$
3. $\lim_{n\to\infty} x^{1/n} = 1 \quad (x > 0)$
4. $\lim_{n\to\infty} x^n = 0 \quad (|x| < 1)$
5. $\lim_{n\to\infty} \left(1 + \frac{x}{n}\right)^n = e^x \quad (\text{Any } x)$
6. $\lim_{n\to\infty} \frac{x^n}{n!} = 0 \quad (\text{Any } x)$

In formulas (3)–(6), x remains fixed as $n \to \infty$.

EXAMPLE 11 *Limits from Table 9.1*

1. $\frac{\ln (n^2)}{n} = \frac{2 \ln n}{n} \to 2 \cdot 0 = 0$ — Formula 1
2. $\sqrt[n]{n^2} = n^{2/n} = (n^{1/n})^2 \to (1)^2 = 1$ — Formula 2
3. $\sqrt[n]{3n} = 3^{1/n}(n^{1/n}) \to 1 \cdot 1 = 1$ — Formula 3 with $x = 3$, and Formula 2
4. $\left(-\frac{1}{2}\right)^n \to 0$ — Formula 4 with $x = -\frac{1}{2}$
5. $\left(\frac{n-2}{n}\right)^n = \left(1 + \frac{-2}{n}\right)^n \to e^{-2}$ — Formula 5 with $x = -2$
6. $\frac{100^n}{n!} \to 0$ — Formula 6 with $x = 100$

Exercises 9.1

Each of Exercises 1–4 gives a formula for the nth term a_n of a sequence $\{a_n\}$. Find the values of a_1, a_2, a_3, and a_4.

1. $a_n = \frac{1-n}{n^2}$
2. $a_n = \frac{1}{n!}$
3. $a_n = \frac{(-1)^{n+1}}{2n-1}$
4. $a_n = 2 + (-1)^n$

In Exercises 5–12, find a formula for the nth term of the sequence.

5. The sequence $1, -1, 1, -1, 1, \ldots$ 1's with alternating signs
6. The sequence $-1, 1, -1, 1, -1, \ldots$ 1's with alternating signs
7. The sequence $1, -4, 9, -16, 25, \ldots$ the squares of the positive integers, with alternating signs
8. The sequence $1, -\frac{1}{4}, \frac{1}{9}, -\frac{1}{16}, \frac{1}{25}, \ldots$ reciprocals of squares of the positive integers, with alternating signs
9. The sequence $0, 3, 8, 15, 24, \ldots$ squares of the positive integers diminished by 1
10. The sequence $-3, -2, -1, 0, 1, \ldots$ integers beginning with -3
11. The sequence $1, 5, 9, 13, 17, \ldots$ every other odd positive integer
12. The sequence $2, 6, 10, 14, 18, \ldots$ every other even positive integer

Each of Exercises 13–18 gives the first term or two of a sequence along with a recursion formula for the remaining terms. Write out the first ten terms of the sequence.

13. $a_1 = 1, \quad a_{n+1} = a_n + (1/2^n)$
14. $a_1 = 1, \quad a_{n+1} = a_n/(n+1)$
15. $a_1 = 2, \quad a_{n+1} = (-1)^{n+1} a_n/2$
16. $a_1 = -2, \quad a_{n+1} = na_n/(n+1)$
17. $a_1 = a_2 = 1, \quad a_{n+2} = a_{n+1} + a_n$
18. $a_1 = 2, \quad a_2 = -1, \quad a_{n+2} = a_{n+1}/a_n$

Which of the sequences $\{a_n\}$ in Exercises 19–70 converge and which diverge? Find the limit of each convergent sequence.

19. $a_n = 2 + (0.1)^n$
20. $a_n = \frac{n + (-1)^n}{n}$

21. $a_n = \frac{1-2n}{1+2n}$

22. $a_n = \frac{2n+1}{1-3\sqrt{n}}$

23. $a_n = \frac{1-5n^4}{n^4+8n^3}$

24. $a_n = \frac{n+3}{n^2+5n+6}$

25. $a_n = \frac{n^2-2n+1}{n-1}$

26. $a_n = \frac{1-n^3}{70-4n^2}$

27. $a_n = 1 + (-1)^n$

28. $a_n = (-1)^n\left(1 - \frac{1}{n}\right)$

29. $a_n = \left(\frac{n+1}{2n}\right)\left(1 - \frac{1}{n}\right)$

30. $a_n = \left(2 - \frac{1}{2^n}\right)\left(3 + \frac{1}{2^n}\right)$

31. $a_n = \frac{(-1)^{n+1}}{2n-1}$

32. $a_n = \left(-\frac{1}{2}\right)^n$

33. $a_n = \frac{\sin n}{n}$

34. $a_n = \frac{\sin^2 n}{2^n}$

35. $a_n = \sqrt{\frac{2n}{n+1}}$

36. $a_n = \sin\left(\frac{\pi}{2} + \frac{1}{n}\right)$

37. $a_n = \tan^{-1} n$

38. $a_n = \ln n - \ln(n+1)$

39. $a_n = \frac{n}{2^n}$

40. $a_n = \frac{3^n}{n^3}$

41. $a_n = \frac{\ln(n+1)}{\sqrt{n}}$

42. $a_n = \frac{\ln n}{\ln 2n}$

43. $a_n = 8^{1/n}$

44. $a_n = (0.03)^{1/n}$

45. $a_n = \left(1 + \frac{7}{n}\right)^n$

46. $a_n = \left(1 - \frac{1}{n}\right)^n$

47. $a_n = \frac{1}{(0.9)^n}$

48. $a_n = n\pi \cos n\pi$

49. $a_n = \sqrt[n]{10n}$

50. $a_n = \sqrt[n]{n^2}$

51. $a_n = \left(\frac{3}{n}\right)^{1/n}$

52. $a_n = (n+4)^{1/(n+4)}$

53. $a_n = \frac{\ln n}{n^{1/n}}$

54. $a_n = \sqrt[n]{4^n n}$

55. $a_n = \left(\frac{1}{3}\right)^n + \frac{1}{\sqrt{2^n}}$

56. $a_n = \sqrt[n]{3^{2n+1}}$

57. $a_n = \frac{n!}{n^n}$ (*Hint:* Compare the quotient with $1/n$.)

58. $a_n = \frac{(-4)^n}{n!}$

59. $a_n = \left(\frac{1}{n}\right)^{1/\ln n}$

60. $a_n = \frac{n!}{2^n \cdot 3^n}$

61. $a_n = \frac{n!}{10^{6n}}$

62. $a_n = \frac{3^n \cdot 6^n}{2^{-n} \cdot n!}$

63. $a_n = \tanh n$

64. $a_n = \sinh(\ln n)$

65. $a_n = \ln\left(1 + \frac{1}{n}\right)^n$

66. $a_n = \left(\frac{n}{n+1}\right)^n$

67. $a_n = \frac{1}{n}\int_1^n \frac{1}{x}\,dx$

68. $a_n = \int_1^n \frac{1}{x^p}\,dx, \quad p > 1$

69. $a_n = \frac{n^2}{2n-1}\sin\frac{1}{n}$

70. $a_n = n\left(1 - \cos\frac{1}{n}\right)$

71. Which of the following statements are true and which are false? Give reasons for your answers.

a) If a sequence does not converge then it diverges.
b) If a sequence $\{a_n\}$ does not converge, then $a_n \to \infty$.
c) Many convergent sequences converge to two different limits.
d) Every subsequence of a convergent sequence must converge.
e) Every subsequence of a divergent sequence must diverge.

72. Which of the following statements are true and which are false? Give reasons for your answers.

a) The term-by-term sum of two convergent sequences never diverges.
b) The term-by-term sum of two divergent sequences never converges.
c) No constant multiple of a divergent sequence can converge.
d) No constant multiple of a convergent sequence can diverge.
e) The term-by-term product of a convergent sequence and a divergent sequence must diverge.

In Exercises 73–76, experiment with a calculator to identify a value of N that will make the inequality hold for $n > N$.

73. $|\sqrt[n]{0.5} - 1| < 10^{-3}$

74. $|\sqrt[n]{n} - 1| < 10^{-3}$

75. $(0.9)^n < 10^{-3}$

76. $2^n/n! < 10^{-7}$

77. If you invest an amount of money A_0 at a fixed annual interest rate r and interest is added to your account every month, the amount you have after n months is

$$A_n = A_0\left(1 + \frac{r}{12}\right)^n.$$

a) Does $\{A_n\}$ converge?
b) Find the first 10 terms of the sequence if $A_0 = 1000$ and $r = 0.02583$ (one of the rates offered by Wells Fargo Bank in 1993).

78. According to a front-page article in the December 15, 1992, issue of *The Wall Street Journal*, Ford Motor Company now uses about $7\frac{1}{4}$ hours of labor to produce stampings for the average vehicle, down from an estimated 15 hours in 1980. The Japanese need only about $3\frac{1}{2}$ hours.

Ford's improvement since 1980 represents an average decrease of 6% per year. If that rate continues, then n years from now Ford will use about

$$S_n = 7.25(0.94)^n$$

hours of labor to produce stampings for the average vehicle. Assuming that the Japanese continue to spend $3\frac{1}{2}$ hours per vehicle, how many more years will it take Ford to catch up? Find out two ways:

a) Find the first term of the sequence $\{S_n\}$ that is less than or equal to 3.5.

b) Graph $f(x) = 7.25(0.94)^x$ and use TRACE to find where the graph crosses the line $y = 3.5$.

RECURSIVELY DEFINED SEQUENCES

79. The first term of a sequence is $x_1 = 1$. Each succeeding term is the sum of all those before it:

$$x_n = x_1 + x_2 + \cdots + x_{n-1}.$$

Write out enough early terms to deduce a general formula for x_n that holds for $n \geq 2$.

80. The first term of a sequence is $x_1 = 3$. Each succeeding term is the sum of all those before it:

$$x_n = x_1 + x_2 + \cdots + x_{n-1}.$$

Write out enough early terms to deduce a general formula for x_n that holds for $n \geq 2$.

81. *Sequences Generated by Newton's Method.* Newton's method, applied to a differentiable function $f(x)$, begins with a starting value x_0 and constructs from it a sequence of numbers $\{x_n\}$ that under favorable circumstances converges to a zero of f. The recursion formula for the sequence is

$$x_{n+1} = x_n - \frac{f(x_n)}{f'(x_n)}.$$

Do the following sequences converge? If so, to what value? In each case, begin by identifying the function f that generates the sequence.

a) $x_0 = 1, \quad x_{n+1} = x_n - \dfrac{x_n{}^2 - 2}{2x_n} = \dfrac{x_n}{2} + \dfrac{1}{x_n}$

b) $x_0 = 1, \quad x_{n+1} = x_n - \dfrac{\tan x_n - 1}{\sec^2 x_n}$

c) $x_0 = 1, \quad x_{n+1} = x_n - 1$

82. Newton's method uses the formula $x_{n+1} = (x_n + a/x_n)/2$ to generate a sequence of approximations to the positive solution of the equation $x^2 - a = 0$, $a > 0$. Starting with $x_0 = 1$ and $a = 3$, calculate the successive terms of the sequence until you have approximated $\sqrt{3}$ as accurately as your calculator permits.

83. *A Recursive Definition of $\pi/2$.* If you start with $x_1 = 1$ and define the subsequent terms of $\{x_n\}$ by the rule $x_n = x_{n-1} + \cos x_{n-1}$, you generate a sequence that converges rapidly to $\pi/2$. (a) Try it. (b) Use the accompanying figure to explain why the convergence is so rapid.

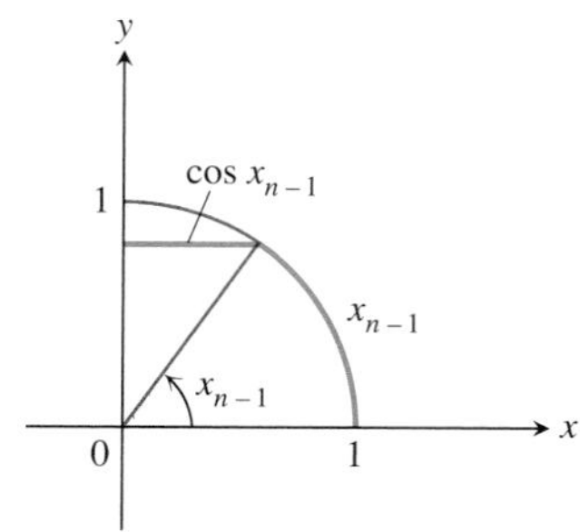

84. *A Recursive Solution of the Equation $\cos x = x$.* If you start with $x_0 = 1$ and define the subsequent terms of $\{x_n\}$ by the rule $x_n = \cos x_{n-1}$, you generate a sequence that converges to a solution of the equation $\cos x = x$. (a) Try it. (b) Use the accompanying figure to explain what is going on.

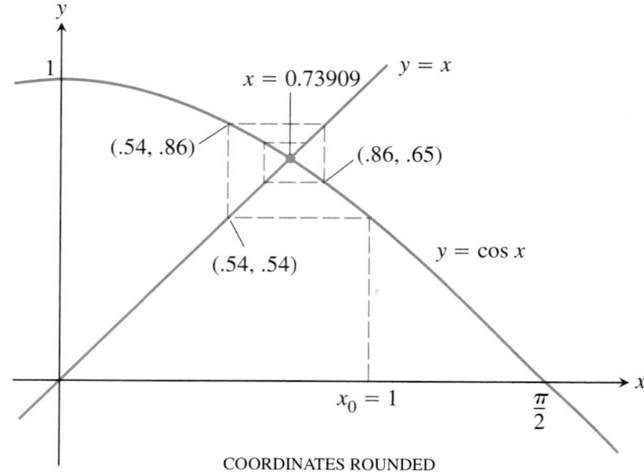

Writing for Your Own Knowledge

Answer the following questions in writing. Some answers will take only a sentence or two; others may require several paragraphs. Some explanations may also call for graphs or sketches.

1. Must a sequence have a limit? Can it have more than one limit?
2. How do you define a sequence of numbers recursively? How else might you define a sequence of numbers?
3. What is factorial notation?
4. What uses can be found for subsequences?
5. What theorems are available for finding limits of sequences?
6. What six limits are likely to arise in your later work?

EXPLORER PROGRAM

Sequences and Series	Generates terms of one or two sequences and graphs them. You may define sequences recursively or by giving formulas for nth terms. Enables you to look for graphical and numerical evidence of convergence or divergence.

9.2 Infinite Series

In mathematics and science we often write functions as infinite polynomials, such as

$$\frac{1}{1-x} = 1 + x + x^2 + x^3 + \cdots + x^n + \cdots, \qquad |x| < 1,$$

(we will see the importance of doing so as the chapter continues). For any allowable value of x, we evaluate the polynomial as an infinite sum of constants, a sum we call an *infinite series*. The goal of this section and the next three is to familiarize ourselves with infinite series.

Series and Partial Sums

We begin by asking how to assign meaning to an expression like

$$1 + \frac{1}{2} + \frac{1}{4} + \frac{1}{8} + \frac{1}{16} + \cdots.$$

The way to do so is not to try to add all the terms at once (we cannot) but rather to add the terms one at a time from the beginning and look for a pattern in how these partial sums grow. When we do this, we find the following.

Partial sum		Value
first:	$s_1 = 1$	$2 - 1$
second:	$s_2 = 1 + \frac{1}{2}$	$2 - \frac{1}{2}$
third:	$s_3 = 1 + \frac{1}{2} + \frac{1}{4}$	$2 - \frac{1}{4}$
$\vdots$	$\vdots$	$\vdots$
nth:	$s_n = 1 + \frac{1}{2} + \frac{1}{4} + \cdots + \frac{1}{2^{n-1}}$	$2 - \frac{1}{2^{n-1}}$

Indeed there is a pattern. The partial sums form a sequence whose nth term is

$$s_n = 2 - \frac{1}{2^{n-1}},$$

and this sequence converges to 2. We say

"the sum of the infinite series $1 + \frac{1}{2} + \frac{1}{4} + \cdots + \frac{1}{2^{n-1}} + \cdots$ is 2."

Is the sum of any finite number of terms in this series equal to 2? No. Can we actually add an infinite number of terms one by one? No. But we can still define their sum by defining it to be the limit of the sequence of partial sums as $n \to \infty$, in this case 2 (Fig. 9.6). Our knowledge of sequences and limits enables us to break away from the confines of finite sums.

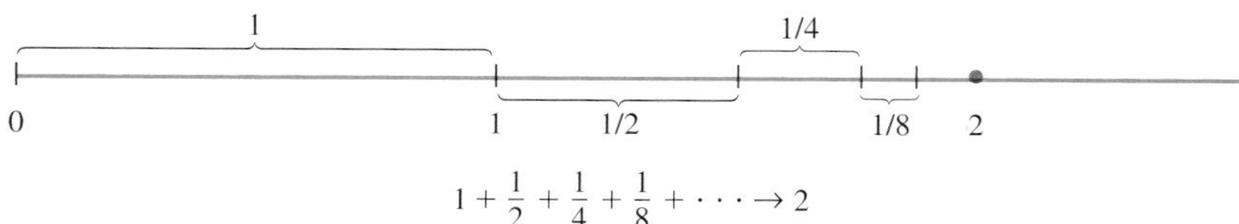

9.6 As the lengths 1, 1/2, 1/4, 1/8, . . . are added one by one, the sum approaches 2.

DEFINITIONS

Given a sequence of numbers $\{a_n\}$, an expression of the form

$$a_1 + a_2 + a_3 + \cdots + a_n + \cdots \tag{1}$$

is an **infinite series.** The number a_n is the ***n*th term** of the series. The sequence $\{s_n\}$ defined by

$$\begin{aligned} s_1 &= a_1 \\ s_2 &= a_1 + a_2 \\ &\vdots \\ s_n &= a_1 + a_2 + \cdots + a_n = \sum_{k=1}^{n} a_k \\ &\vdots \end{aligned} \tag{2}$$

is the **sequence of partial sums** of the series, the number s_n being the ***n*th partial sum.** If the sequence of partial sums converges to a limit L, we say that the series **converges** and that its **sum** is L. In this case, we also write

$$a_1 + a_2 + \cdots + a_n + \cdots = \sum_{n=1}^{\infty} a_n = L. \tag{3}$$

If the sequence of partial sums of the series does not converge, we say that the series **diverges.**

Suggestions for Reading Sigma Notation

$\sum_{n=1}^{\infty} a_n$ "The sum from $n = 1$ to ∞ of a sub n"

$\sum a_n$ "The sum of a sub n" or "Summation a sub n"

When we begin to study a given series $a_1 + a_2 + \cdots + a_n + \cdots$, we might not know whether it converges or diverges. In either case, it is convenient to use sigma notation to write the series as

$$\sum_{n=1}^{\infty} a_n, \qquad \sum_{k=1}^{\infty} a_k, \qquad \text{or} \qquad \sum a_n.$$

Geometric Series

Geometric series are series of the form

$$a + ar + ar^2 + \cdots + ar^{n-1} + \cdots = \sum_{n=1}^{\infty} ar^{n-1} \tag{4}$$

in which a and r are fixed real numbers and $a \neq 0$. The **ratio** r can be positive, as in

$$1 + \frac{1}{2} + \frac{1}{4} + \cdots + \left(\frac{1}{2}\right)^{n-1} + \cdots, \tag{5}$$

or negative, as in

$$1 - \frac{1}{3} + \frac{1}{9} - \cdots + \left(-\frac{1}{3}\right)^{n-1} + \cdots. \tag{6}$$

If $r = 1$, the nth partial sum of the geometric series in (4) is

$$s_n = a + a(1) + a(1)^2 + \cdots + a(1)^{n-1} = na,$$

and the series diverges because $\lim_{n\to\infty} s_n = \pm\infty$, depending on the sign of a. If $r \neq 1$, we can determine the convergence or divergence of the series in the following way:

$$s_n = a + ar + ar^2 + \cdots + ar^{n-1}$$

$$rs_n = ar + ar^2 + \cdots + ar^{n-1} + ar^n \qquad \text{Multiply } s_n \text{ by } r.$$

$$s_n - rs_n = a - ar^n \qquad \text{Subtract } rs_n \text{ from } s_n. \text{ Most of the terms on the right cancel.}$$

$$s_n(1 - r) = a(1 - r^n) \qquad \text{Factor.}$$

$$s_n = \frac{a(1 - r^n)}{1 - r}, \qquad (r \neq 1) \qquad \text{We can solve for } s_n \text{ if } r \neq 1.$$

If $|r| < 1$, then $r^n \to 0$ as $n \to \infty$ (as in Section 9.1) and $s_n \to a/(1 - r)$. If $|r| > 1$, then $|r^n| \to \infty$ and the series diverges.

Equation (7) holds *only* if the summation begins with $n = 1$.

If $|r| < 1$, the geometric series $a + ar + ar^2 + \cdots + ar^{n-1} + \cdots$ converges to $a/(1 - r)$:

$$\sum_{n=1}^{\infty} ar^{n-1} = \frac{a}{1 - r}, \qquad |r| < 1. \tag{7}$$

If $|r| \geq 1$, the geometric series diverges.

EXAMPLE 1 Find the sum of the geometric series

$$\frac{1}{9} + \frac{1}{27} + \frac{1}{81} + \cdots.$$

Solution This is the series with $a = 1/9$ and $r = 1/3$, so

$$\frac{1}{9} + \frac{1}{27} + \frac{1}{81} + \cdots = \sum_{n=1}^{\infty} \frac{1}{9}\left(\frac{1}{3}\right)^{n-1} = \frac{1/9}{1 - (1/3)} \qquad \text{Eq. (7) with } a = 1/9,\ r = 1/3$$

$$= \frac{1/9}{2/3} = \frac{3}{2} \cdot \frac{1}{9} = \frac{1}{6}.$$

EXAMPLE 2 Find the sum of the geometric series

$$4 - 2 + 1 - \frac{1}{2} + \frac{1}{4} - \cdots.$$

Solution This is the geometric series with $a = 4$ and $r = -1/2$, so

$$4 - 2 + 1 - \frac{1}{2} + \frac{1}{4} - \cdots = \sum_{n=1}^{\infty} 4\left(-\frac{1}{2}\right)^{n-1} = \frac{4}{1 - (-1/2)} \qquad \text{Eq. (7) with } a = 4,\ r = -1/2$$

$$= \frac{4}{3/2} = \frac{8}{3}.$$

EXAMPLE 3 You drop a ball from a meters above a flat surface. Each time the ball hits the surface after falling a distance h, it rebounds a distance rh, where r is positive but less than 1. Find the total distance the ball travels up and down (Fig. 9.7 on the following page).

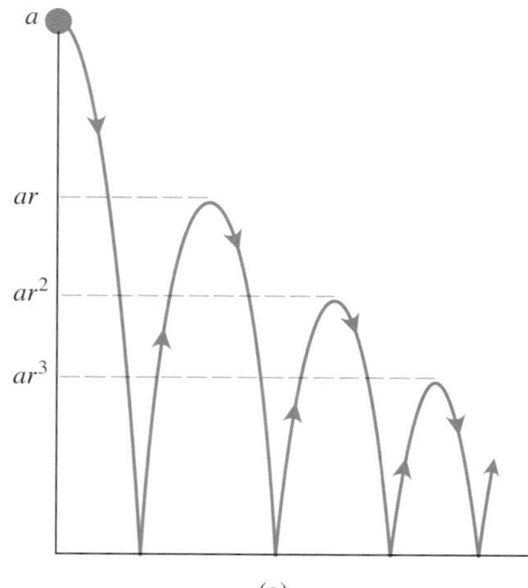

(a)

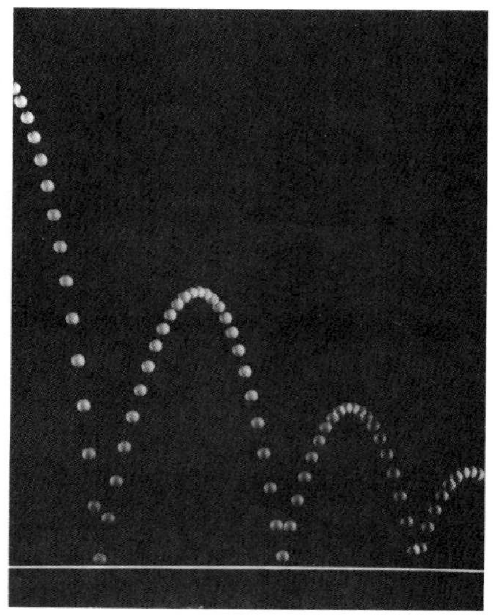

(b)

9.7 (a) Example 3 shows how to use a geometric series to calculate the total vertical distance traveled by a bouncing ball if the height of each rebound is reduced by the factor r. (b) A stroboscopic photo of a bouncing ball.

Solution The total distance is

$$s = a + 2ar + \underbrace{2ar^2 + 2ar^3 + \cdots}_{\text{This sum is } 2ar/(1-r).} = a + \frac{2ar}{1-r} = a\frac{1+r}{1-r}.$$

If $a = 6$ m and $r = 2/3$, for instance, the distance is

$$s = 6 \cdot \frac{1 + (2/3)}{1 - (2/3)} = 6\left(\frac{5/3}{1/3}\right) = 30 \text{ m.}$$

Repeating Decimals

Geometric series explain why repeating decimals represent rational numbers.

EXAMPLE 4 Express the repeating decimal 5.23 23 23 . . . as the ratio of two integers.

Solution

$$5.23\ 23\ 23 \ldots = 5 + \frac{23}{100} + \frac{23}{(100)^2} + \frac{23}{(100)^3} + \cdots$$

$$= 5 + \frac{23}{100}\underbrace{\left(1 + \frac{1}{100} + \left(\frac{1}{100}\right)^2 + \cdots\right)}_{1/(1-0.01)} \qquad a = 1,\ r = 1/100$$

$$= 5 + \frac{23}{100}\left(\frac{1}{0.99}\right) = 5 + \frac{23}{99} = \frac{518}{99}.$$

Telescoping Series

Unfortunately, formulas like the one we found for the sum of a convergent geometric series are rare and we usually have to settle for an estimate of a series' sum (more about this later). The next example, however, is another of those rare cases in which we can find the sum exactly.

EXAMPLE 5 Find the sum of the series $\displaystyle\sum_{n=1}^{\infty} \frac{1}{n(n+1)}$.

Solution We look for a pattern in the sequence of partial sums that might lead us to a formula for s_k. The key formula here, as in the integration

$$\int \frac{dx}{x(x+1)} = \int \frac{dx}{x} - \int \frac{dx}{x+1},$$

is partial fractions. The observation that

$$\frac{1}{k(k+1)} = \frac{1}{k} - \frac{1}{k+1} \tag{8}$$

permits us to write the partial sum

$$\sum_{n=1}^{k} \frac{1}{n(n+1)} = \frac{1}{1 \cdot 2} + \frac{1}{2 \cdot 3} + \cdots + \frac{1}{k \cdot (k+1)}$$

as

$$s_k = \left(\frac{1}{1} - \frac{1}{2}\right) + \left(\frac{1}{2} - \frac{1}{3}\right) + \cdots + \left(\frac{1}{k} - \frac{1}{k+1}\right). \tag{9}$$

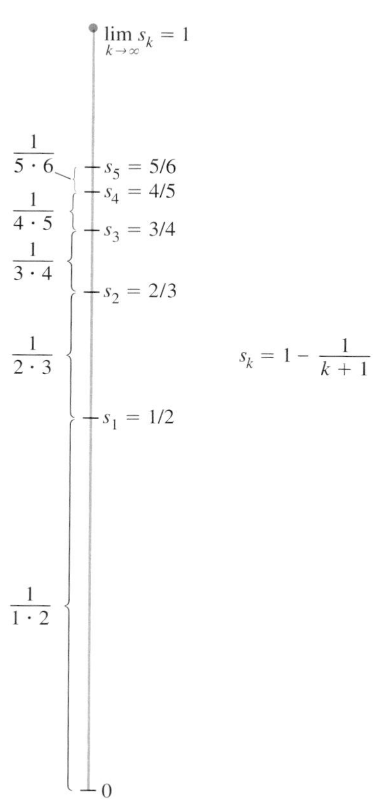

9.8 The partial sums of the series in Example 5.

We call the series in Example 5 a telescoping series because it collapses like an old hand-held telescope.

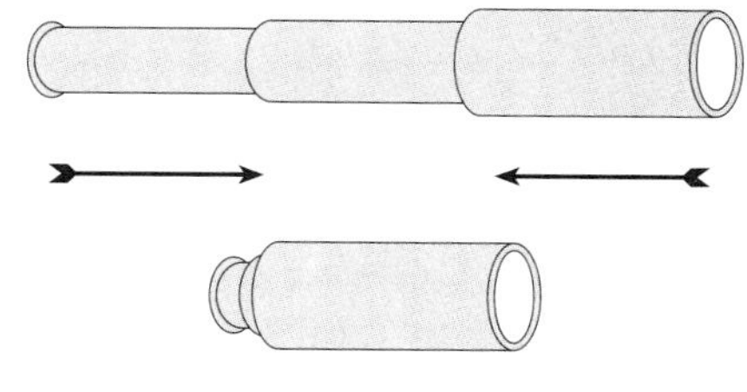

Caution: Theorem 5 *does not* say that $\Sigma\, a_n$ converges if $a_n \to 0$. It is possible for a series to diverge even when $a_n \to 0$.

Removing parentheses and canceling the terms of opposite sign collapses the sum to

$$s_k = 1 - \frac{1}{k+1}. \tag{10}$$

We then see that $s_k \to 1$ as $k \to \infty$. The series converges, and its sum is 1 (Fig. 9.8).

$$\sum_{n=1}^{\infty} \frac{1}{n(n+1)} = 1.$$

Divergent Series

Geometric series with $|r| \geq 1$ are not the only series to diverge.

EXAMPLE 6 The series

$$\sum_{n=1}^{\infty} n^2 = 1 + 4 + 9 + \cdots + n^2 + \cdots$$

diverges because the partial sums grow beyond every number L. After $n = 1$, the partial sum $s_n = 1 + 4 + 9 + \cdots + n^2$ is greater than n^2.

EXAMPLE 7 The series

$$\sum_{n=1}^{\infty} \frac{n+1}{n} = \frac{2}{1} + \frac{3}{2} + \frac{4}{3} + \cdots + \frac{n+1}{n} + \cdots$$

diverges because the partial sums eventually outgrow every preassigned number. Each term is greater than 1, so the sum of n terms is greater than n.

EXAMPLE 8 The geometric series $\Sigma_{n=1}^{\infty} (-1)^{n+1}$ diverges because its partial sums alternate between 1 and 0:

$$s_1 = (-1)^2 = 1,$$
$$s_2 = (-1)^2 + (-1)^3 = 1 - 1 = 0,$$
$$s_3 = (-1)^2 + (-1)^3 + (-1)^4 = 1 - 1 + 1 = 1,$$

and so on.

The nth-Term Test for Divergence

One of the things true of any convergent series $\Sigma_{n=1}^{\infty} a_n$ is that $\lim_{n\to\infty} a_n = 0$. To see why, let S represent the series' sum and $s_n = a_1 + a_2 + \cdots + a_n$ the nth partial sum. When n is large, both s_n and s_{n-1} are close to S, so their difference, a_n, is close to zero. More formally,

$$a_n = s_n - s_{n-1} \to S - S = 0. \qquad \text{Difference Rule for sequences}$$

THEOREM 5

If $\sum_{n=1}^{\infty} a_n$ converges then $a_n \to 0$.

EXAMPLE 9 The partial sums of the series

$$1 + \underbrace{\frac{1}{2} + \frac{1}{2}}_{2 \text{ terms}} + \underbrace{\frac{1}{4} + \frac{1}{4} + \frac{1}{4} + \frac{1}{4}}_{4 \text{ terms}} + \cdots + \underbrace{\frac{1}{2^n} + \frac{1}{2^n} + \cdots + \frac{1}{2^n}}_{2^n \text{ terms}} + \cdots$$

$$= 1 + 1 + 1 + \cdots + 1 + \cdots$$

can be made larger than any positive integer. Therefore, the series diverges even though its terms form a sequence that converges to 0.

What Theorem 5 *does* say is that if $\{a_n\}$ diverges or if $\{a_n\}$ converges to any number other than zero then $\Sigma\, a_n$ diverges.

The *n*th-Term Test for Divergence

$\sum_{n=1}^{\infty} a_n$ diverges if $\lim_{n\to\infty} a_n$ either fails to exist or is different from zero.

When we apply the *n*th-Term Test to the series in Examples 6, 7, and 8, we find that

$\sum_{n=1}^{\infty} n^2$ diverges because $n^2 \to \infty$,

$\sum_{n=1}^{\infty} \frac{n+1}{n}$ diverges because $\frac{n+1}{n} \to 1$,

$\sum_{n=1}^{\infty} (-1)^{n+1}$ diverges because $\lim_{n\to\infty} (-1)^{n+1}$ does not exist.

EXAMPLE 10 Determine whether each series converges or diverges. If it converges, find its sum.

a) $\sum_{n=1}^{\infty} \frac{n}{2n+5}$ **b)** $\sum_{n=1}^{\infty} \frac{5(-1)^n}{4^n}$

Solution

a) $\lim_{n\to\infty} \frac{n}{2n+5} = \frac{1}{2} \neq 0$. The series diverges by the *n*th-Term Test.

b) This is a geometric series with $a = -5/4$ and $r = -1/4$. It converges to

$$\frac{a}{1-r} = \frac{-5/4}{1+(1/4)} = -1.$$

Whenever we have two convergent series, we can add them term by term, subtract them term by term, and multiply them by constants to make new convergent series.

THEOREM 6

If $\Sigma\, a_n = A$ and $\Sigma\, b_n = B$ are convergent series, then

1. *Sum Rule:* $\sum (a_n + b_n) = \sum a_n + \sum b_n = A + B$
2. *Difference Rule:* $\sum (a_n - b_n) = \sum a_n - \sum b_n = A - B$
3. *Constant Multiple Rule:* $\sum ka_n = k \sum a_n = kA$ (Any number k)

As corollaries of Theorem 6 we have

1. Every nonzero constant multiple of a divergent series diverges.
2. If $\Sigma\, a_n$ converges and $\Sigma\, b_n$ diverges then $\Sigma\, (a_n + b_n)$ and $\Sigma\, (a_n - b_n)$ both diverge.

We omit the proofs.

EXAMPLE 11 Find the sums of the following series.

a)
$$\sum_{n=1}^{\infty} \frac{3^{n-1}-1}{6^{n-1}} = \sum_{n=1}^{\infty} \left(\frac{1}{2^{n-1}} - \frac{1}{6^{n-1}}\right)$$
$$= \sum_{n=1}^{\infty} \frac{1}{2^{n-1}} - \sum_{n=1}^{\infty} \frac{1}{6^{n-1}} \qquad \text{Difference Rule}$$
$$= \frac{1}{1-(1/2)} - \frac{1}{1-(1/6)} \qquad \text{Geometric series with } a = 1 \text{ and } r = 1/2,\ 1/6$$
$$= 2 - \frac{6}{5} = \frac{4}{5}$$

b)
$$\sum_{n=1}^{\infty} \frac{4}{2^{n-1}} = 4 \sum_{n=1}^{\infty} \frac{1}{2^{n-1}} \qquad \text{Constant Multiple Rule}$$
$$= 4\left(\frac{1}{1-(1/2)}\right) \qquad \text{Geometric series with } a = 1,\ r = 1/2$$
$$= 8$$

Adding and Deleting Terms

Adding a finite number of terms to a series or deleting a finite number of terms from a series does not alter convergence or divergence. If the original series converged, so will the new series (but the sum will probably be different). If the original series diverged, so will the new series. For instance,

$$\sum_{n=1}^{\infty} \frac{1}{5^{n-1}} = 1 + \frac{1}{5} + \left(\sum_{n=3}^{\infty} \frac{1}{5^{n-1}}\right) \text{ and } \sum_{n=3}^{\infty} \frac{1}{5^{n-1}} = \left(\sum_{n=1}^{\infty} \frac{1}{5^{n-1}}\right) - 1 - \frac{1}{5}. \tag{11}$$

In each case, the series on the left and right converge, albeit to different sums. The series on the right and left sides of the next equation both diverge:

$$\sum_{n=1}^{\infty} n = 1 + 2 + 3 + \left(\sum_{n=4}^{\infty} n\right). \tag{12}$$

Reindexing

As long as we preserve the order of its terms, we can reindex any series without altering its convergence. To raise the starting value of the index h units, replace the n in the formula for a_n by $n - h$:

$$\sum_{n=1}^{\infty} a_n = \sum_{n=1+h}^{\infty} a_{n-h} = a_1 + a_2 + a_3 + \cdots.$$

To lower the starting value of the index h units, replace the n in the formula for a_n by $n + h$:

$$\sum_{n=1}^{\infty} a_n = \sum_{n=1-h}^{\infty} a_{n+h} = a_1 + a_2 + a_3 + \cdots.$$

It works like translation.

EXAMPLE 12 We can write the geometric series that starts with

$$1 + \frac{1}{2} + \frac{1}{4} + \cdots$$

as

$$\sum_{n=0}^{\infty} \frac{1}{2^n}, \quad \sum_{n=5}^{\infty} \frac{1}{2^{n-5}}, \quad \text{or even} \quad \sum_{n=-4}^{\infty} \frac{1}{2^{n+4}}.$$

The partial sums remain the same no matter which indexing we choose.

We usually give preference to indexings that lead to simple expressions.

Exercises 9.2

In Exercises 1–6, find a formula for the nth partial sum of each series and use it to find the series' sum if the series converges.

1. $2 + \frac{2}{3} + \frac{2}{9} + \frac{2}{27} + \cdots + \frac{2}{3^{n-1}} + \cdots$

2. $\frac{9}{100} + \frac{9}{100^2} + \frac{9}{100^3} + \cdots + \frac{9}{100^n} + \cdots$

3. $1 - \frac{1}{2} + \frac{1}{4} - \frac{1}{8} + \cdots + (-1)^{n-1}\frac{1}{2^{n-1}} + \cdots$

4. $1 - 2 + 4 - 8 + \cdots + (-1)^{n-1}2^{n-1} + \cdots$

5. $\frac{1}{2 \cdot 3} + \frac{1}{3 \cdot 4} + \frac{1}{4 \cdot 5} + \cdots + \frac{1}{(n+1)(n+2)} + \cdots$

6. $\frac{5}{1 \cdot 2} + \frac{5}{2 \cdot 3} + \frac{5}{3 \cdot 4} + \cdots + \frac{5}{n(n+1)} + \cdots$

In Exercises 7–14, write out the first few terms of each series to show how the series starts. Then find the sum of the series.

7. $\sum_{n=0}^{\infty} \frac{(-1)^n}{4^n}$

8. $\sum_{n=2}^{\infty} \frac{1}{4^n}$

9. $\sum_{n=1}^{\infty} \frac{7}{4^n}$

10. $\sum_{n=0}^{\infty} (-1)^n \frac{5}{4^n}$

11. $\sum_{n=0}^{\infty} \left(\frac{5}{2^n} + \frac{1}{3^n}\right)$

12. $\sum_{n=0}^{\infty} \left(\frac{5}{2^n} - \frac{1}{3^n}\right)$

13. $\sum_{n=0}^{\infty} \left(\frac{1}{2^n} + \frac{(-1)^n}{5^n}\right)$

14. $\sum_{n=0}^{\infty} \left(\frac{2^{n+1}}{5^n}\right)$

Use partial fractions to find the sum of each series in Exercises 15–18.

15. $\sum_{n=1}^{\infty} \frac{4}{(4n-3)(4n+1)}$

16. $\sum_{n=1}^{\infty} \frac{6}{(2n-1)(2n+1)}$

17. $\sum_{n=1}^{\infty} \frac{40n}{(2n-1)^2(2n+1)^2}$

18. $\sum_{n=1}^{\infty} \frac{2n+1}{n^2(n+1)^2}$

Which series in Exercises 19–38 converge and which diverge? Give reasons for your answers. If a series converges, find its sum.

19. $\sum_{n=0}^{\infty} \left(\frac{1}{\sqrt{2}}\right)^n$

20. $\sum_{n=1}^{\infty} \ln \frac{1}{n}$

21. $\sum_{n=1}^{\infty} (-1)^{n+1} \frac{3}{2^n}$

22. $\sum_{n=1}^{\infty} (\sqrt{2})^n$

23. $\sum_{n=0}^{\infty} \cos n\pi$

24. $\sum_{n=0}^{\infty} \frac{\cos n\pi}{5^n}$

25. $\sum_{n=0}^{\infty} e^{-2n}$

26. $\sum_{n=1}^{\infty} \frac{n^2+1}{n}$

27. $\sum_{n=1}^{\infty} (-1)^{n+1} n$

28. $\sum_{n=1}^{\infty} \frac{2}{10^n}$

29. $\sum_{n=0}^{\infty} \frac{2^n-1}{3^n}$

30. $\sum_{n=1}^{\infty} \left(1-\frac{1}{n}\right)^n$

31. $\sum_{n=0}^{\infty} \frac{n!}{1000^n}$

32. $\sum_{n=0}^{\infty} \frac{1}{x^n}, \quad |x|>1$

33. $\sum_{n=1}^{\infty} \ln\left(\frac{n}{n+1}\right)$

34. $\sum_{n=1}^{\infty} \ln\left(\frac{n}{2n+1}\right)$

35. $\sum_{n=1}^{\infty} \left(\frac{1}{\sqrt{n}} - \frac{1}{\sqrt{n+1}}\right)$

36. $\sum_{n=1}^{\infty} \left(\frac{1}{2^{1/n}} - \frac{1}{2^{1/(n+1)}}\right)$

37. $\sum_{n=1}^{\infty} \left(\frac{1}{\ln(n+2)} - \frac{1}{\ln(n+1)}\right)$

38. $\sum_{n=1}^{\infty} (\tan^{-1}(n) - \tan^{-1}(n+1))$

The series in Exercises 39–42 are geometric series. In each case, write out the first few terms of the series to find a and r. Then express the inequality $|r|<1$ in terms of x and find the values of x for which the inequality holds and the series converges.

39. $\frac{1}{1+x} = \sum_{n=0}^{\infty} (-1)^n x^n$

40. $\frac{1}{1+x^2} = \sum_{n=0}^{\infty} (-1)^n x^{2n}$

41. $\frac{6}{3-x} = \sum_{n=0}^{\infty} 3\left(\frac{x-1}{2}\right)^n$

42. $\frac{3+\sin x}{8+2\sin x} = \sum_{n=0}^{\infty} \frac{(-1)^n}{2}\left(\frac{1}{3+\sin x}\right)^n$

Express each of the numbers in Exercises 43–50 as the ratio of two integers.

43. $0.\overline{23} = 0.23\ 23\ 23\ldots$

44. $0.\overline{234} = 0.234\ 234\ 234\ldots$

45. $0.\overline{7} = 0.7777\ldots$

46. $0.\overline{d} = 0.dddd\ldots,$ where d is a digit

47. $0.0\overline{6} = 0.06666\ldots$

48. $1.\overline{414} = 1.414\ 414\ 414\ldots$

49. $1.24\overline{123} = 1.24\ 123\ 123\ 123\ldots$

50. $3.\overline{142857} = 3.142857\ 142857\ldots$

51. A ball is dropped from a height of 4 m. Each time it strikes the pavement after falling from a height of h m it rebounds to a height of $0.75h$ m. Find the total distance the ball travels up and down.

52. *Continuation of Exercise 51.* Find the total number of seconds the ball in Exercise 51 is traveling. (*Hint:* The formula $s = 4.9t^2$ gives $t = \sqrt{s/4.9}$.)

53. The series in Exercise 5 can also be written as

$$\sum_{n=1}^{\infty} \frac{1}{(n+1)(n+2)} \quad \text{and} \quad \sum_{n=-1}^{\infty} \frac{1}{(n+3)(n+4)}.$$

Write it as a sum beginning with (a) $n=-2$, (b) $n=0$, (c) $n=5$.

54. The series in Exercise 6 can also be written as

$$\sum_{n=1}^{\infty} \frac{5}{n(n+1)} \quad \text{and} \quad \sum_{n=0}^{\infty} \frac{5}{(n+1)(n+2)}.$$

Write it as a sum beginning with (a) $n=-1$, (b) $n=3$, (c) $n=20$.

55. The accompanying figure shows the first five of a sequence of squares. The outermost square has an area of 4 m². Each of the other squares is obtained by joining the midpoints of the sides of the square before it. Find the sum of the areas of all the squares.

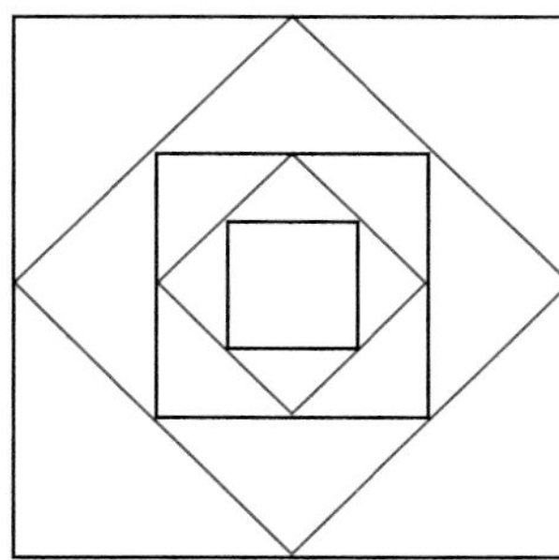

56. The accompanying figure shows the first three rows and part of the fourth row of a sequence of rows of semicircles. There are 2^n semicircles in the nth row, each of radius $1/2^n$. Find the sum of the areas of all the semicircles.

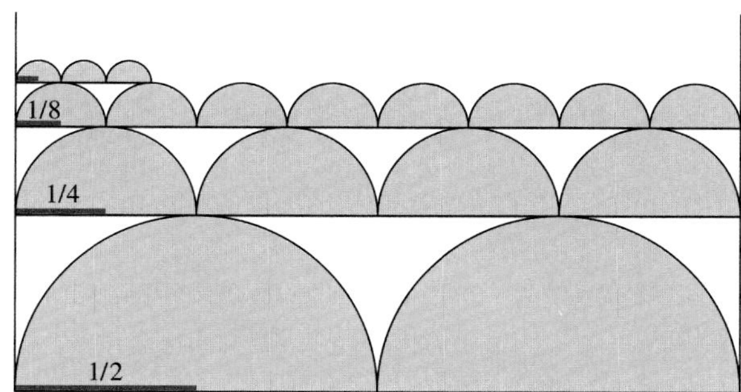

57. *Helga von Koch's Snowflake Curve.* Helga von Koch's snowflake (p. 172) is a curve of infinite length that encloses a

region of finite area. To see why this is so, suppose the curve is generated by starting with an equilateral triangle whose sides have length 1.

a) Find the length L_n of the nth curve C_n and show that $\lim_{n\to\infty} L_n = \infty$.
b) Find the area A_n of the region enclosed by C_n and calculate $\lim_{n\to\infty} A_n$.

58. Make up an infinite series of nonzero terms that converges to

a) 1 b) -3 c) 0.

59. Show by example that $\Sigma\,(a_n/b_n)$ may diverge even though $\Sigma\, a_n$ and $\Sigma\, b_n$ converge and no b_n equals 0.

60. Find convergent geometric series $A = \Sigma\, a_n$ and $B = \Sigma\, b_n$ that illustrate the fact that $\Sigma\, a_n b_n$ may converge without being equal to AB.

61. Show by example that $\Sigma\,(a_n/b_n)$ may converge to something other than A/B even when $A = \Sigma\, a_n$, $B = \Sigma\, b_n \neq 0$, and no b_n equals 0.

62. Is it possible for $\Sigma(a_n + b_n)$ to converge if $\Sigma\, a_n$ and $\Sigma\, b_n$ both diverge? Give reasons for your answer.

63. If $\Sigma\, a_n$ converges and $a_n > 0$ for all n, can anything be said about $\Sigma\,(1/a_n)$? Give reasons for your answer.

Writing for Your Own Knowledge

Answer the following questions in writing. Some answers will take only a sentence or two; others may require several paragraphs. Some explanations may also call for graphs or sketches.

1. What is a geometric series? How can you tell when it converges?
2. Show by example how to express a repeating decimal as a rational number.
3. Show by example how to find the sum of a telescoping series.
4. How are the two following statements related?

   a) $\Sigma\, a_n$ converges
   b) $a_n \to 0$

   How does the relationship sometimes help you to determine the divergence of the series? Can it help you to prove convergence?
5. What can be said about term-by-term sums and differences of convergent series? about constant multiples of convergent series?

EXPLORER PROGRAM

Sequences and Series	Enables you to look for numerical and graphical indications of convergence and divergence of a sequence or series. Also plots the initial terms of a series and the series' partial sums in a common graph. You may define your sequence or the terms of your series either recursively or by giving a formula for the nth term.

9.3 *Series with Nonnegative Terms—Comparison and Integral Tests*

Given a series $\Sigma\, a_n$, we have two questions:

1. Does the series converge?
2. If it converges, what is its sum?

Much of the rest of this chapter is devoted to answering the first question. But as a practical matter, the second question is just as important, and we will return to it later.

In this section and the next we study series that do not have negative terms. The reason for this restriction is that the partial sums of these series form nondecreasing sequences, and nondecreasing sequences *that are bounded from above* always converge. To show that a series of nonnegative terms converges, we need only show that there is some number beyond which the partial sums never go.

It may first seem to be a drawback that this approach establishes the fact of convergence without producing the sum of the series in question. Surely it would be better to compute sums of series directly from formulas for their partial sums. But in most cases such formulas are not available, and in their absence we have to turn instead to the two-step procedure of first establishing convergence and then approximating the sum.

Nondecreasing Sequences

Suppose that $\Sigma\, a_n$ is an infinite series and that $a_n \geq 0$ for every n. Then, when we calculate the partial sums s_1, s_2, s_3, and so on, we see that each one is greater than or equal to its predecessor because $s_{n+1} = s_n + a_n$:

$$s_1 \leq s_2 \leq s_3 \leq \cdots \leq s_n \leq s_{n+1} \leq \cdots. \tag{1}$$

DEFINITION

A sequence $\{s_n\}$ with the property that $s_n \leq s_{n+1}$ for every n is a **nondecreasing** sequence.

There are two kinds of nondecreasing sequences — those that surpass every finite bound and those that do not.

DEFINITIONS

A sequence $\{s_n\}$ is **bounded from above** if there exists a number M such that $s_n \leq M$ for all n. In this case, the number M is an **upper bound** for the sequence. If no number less than M is an upper bound for the sequence, M is the **least upper bound** for the sequence.

EXAMPLE 1 If $s_n = n/(n+1)$ then 1 is an upper bound for $\{s_n\}$ and so is any number greater than 1. No number smaller than 1 is an upper bound for $\{s_n\}$, so 1 is the least upper bound. ■

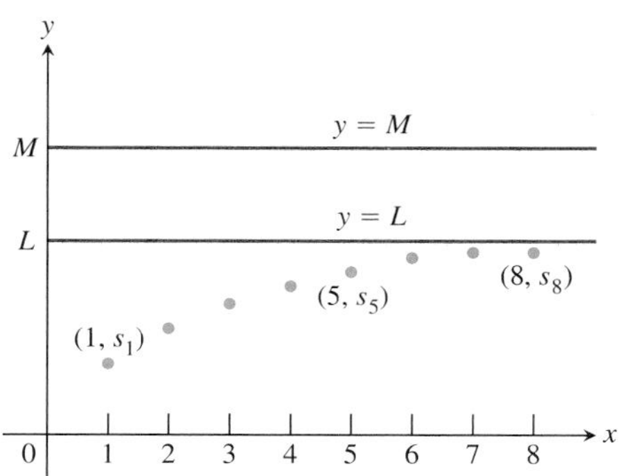

9.9 If the terms of a nondecreasing sequence have an upper bound M, they have a limit $L \leq M$.

A nondecreasing sequence that is bounded from above always has a least upper bound, but we will not prove this fact. Instead, we prove that if L is the least upper bound, then the sequence converges to L. The following argument shows why L is the limit.

Suppose we plot the points $(1, s_1)$, $(2, s_2)$, . . . , (n, s_n) in the xy-plane. If M is an upper bound of the sequence, all these points will lie on or below the line $y = M$ (Fig. 9.9). The line $y = L$ is the lowest such line. None of the points (n, s_n) lies above $y = L$, but some do lie above any lower line $y = L - \epsilon$, if ϵ is a positive number. The sequence converges to L because

a) $s_n \leq L$ for *all* values of n and

b) given any $\epsilon > 0$, there exists at least one integer N for which $s_N > L - \epsilon$.

The fact that $\{s_n\}$ is a nondecreasing sequence tells us further that

$$s_n \geq s_N > L - \epsilon \qquad \text{for all } n \geq N.$$

This means that *all* the numbers s_n beyond the Nth number lie within ϵ of L. This is precisely the condition for L to be the limit of the sequence s_n.

The facts for nondecreasing sequences are summarized in the following theorem. A similar result holds for nonincreasing sequences (Exercise 59).

THEOREM 7

The Nondecreasing Sequence Theorem

A nondecreasing sequence converges if and only if its terms are bounded from above. If all the terms are less than or equal to M, then the limit of the sequence is less than or equal to M as well.

Since the partial sums s_n of a series $\Sigma\, a_n$ of nonnegative terms form a nondecreasing sequence, Theorem 7 tells us that an infinite series of nonnegative terms must converge if its partial sums are bounded from above.

COROLLARY 1

A series $\Sigma\, a_n$ of nonnegative terms converges if and only if its partial sums are bounded from above.

The question, of course, is how to find out in any particular instance whether the s_n's have an upper bound. Sometimes we can show that the s_n's are bounded from above by showing that each one is less than or equal to the corresponding partial sum of a series that is already known to converge. The next example shows how this can happen.

EXAMPLE 2 The series

$$\sum_{n=0}^{\infty} \frac{1}{n!} = 1 + \frac{1}{1!} + \frac{1}{2!} + \frac{1}{3!} + \cdots \tag{2}$$

converges because its terms are all positive and less than or equal to the corresponding terms of

$$1 + \sum_{n=0}^{\infty} \frac{1}{2^n} = 1 + 1 + \frac{1}{2} + \frac{1}{2^2} + \cdots. \tag{3}$$

To see how this relationship leads to an upper bound for the partial sums of $\Sigma_{n=0}^{\infty}\,(1/(n!))$, let

$$s_n = 1 + \frac{1}{1!} + \frac{1}{2!} + \cdots + \frac{1}{n!}$$

and observe that, for each n,

$$s_n \le 1 + 1 + \frac{1}{2} + \frac{1}{2^2} + \cdots + \frac{1}{2^n} < 1 + \sum_{n=0}^{\infty} \frac{1}{2^n} = 1 + \frac{1}{1 - (1/2)} = 3.$$

Thus the partial sums of $\Sigma_{n=0}^{\infty}\,(1/(n!))$ are all less than 3, so $\Sigma_{n=0}^{\infty}\,(1/(n!))$ converges.

The fact that 3 is an upper bound for the partial sums of $\Sigma_{n=0}^{\infty}\,(1/(n!))$ does not mean that the series converges to 3. As we will see in Section 9.7, the series converges to e.

Notice that the nth-Term Test for divergence does not detect the divergence of the harmonic series. The nth term, $1/n$, goes to zero but the series still diverges.

EXAMPLE 3 *The Harmonic Series.* The series

$$\sum_{1}^{\infty} \frac{1}{n} = 1 + \frac{1}{2} + \frac{1}{3} + \cdots + \frac{1}{n} + \cdots$$

is called the **harmonic series.** It diverges because there is no upper bound for its partial sums. To see why, group the terms of the series in the following way:

$$1 + \frac{1}{2} + \underbrace{\left(\frac{1}{3} + \frac{1}{4}\right)}_{> \frac{2}{4} = \frac{1}{2}} + \underbrace{\left(\frac{1}{5} + \frac{1}{6} + \frac{1}{7} + \frac{1}{8}\right)}_{> \frac{4}{8} = \frac{1}{2}} + \underbrace{\left(\frac{1}{9} + \frac{1}{10} + \cdots + \frac{1}{16}\right)}_{> \frac{8}{16} = \frac{1}{2}} + \cdots.$$

The sum of the first two terms is 1.5. The sum of the next two terms is $1/3 + 1/4$, which is greater than $1/4 + 1/4 = 1/2$. The sum of the next four terms is $1/5 + 1/6 + 1/7 + 1/8$, which is greater than $1/8 + 1/8 + 1/8 + 1/8 = 1/2$. The sum of the next eight terms is $1/9 + 1/10 + 1/11 + 1/12 + 1/13 + 1/14 + 1/15 + 1/16$, which is greater than $8/16 = 1/2$. The sum of the next 16 terms is greater than $16/32 = 1/2$, and so on. In general, the sum of 2^n terms ending with $1/2^{n+1}$ is greater than $2^n/2^{n+1} = 1/2$. The sequence of partial sums is not bounded: If $n = 2^k$, the partial sum s_n is greater than $k/2$. The harmonic series diverges.

Nicole Oresme (1320–1382)

The argument we use to show the divergence of the harmonic series was devised more than 600 years ago by the French theologian, mathematician, physicist, and bishop Nicole Oresme (pronounced "or-*rem*"). Oresme was a vigorous opponent of astrology, a dynamic preacher, an adviser of princes, a friend of King Charles V, a popularizer of science, and a skillful translator of Latin into French.

The Direct Comparison Test for Convergence

We established the convergence of the series in Example 2 by comparing it with a series that was already known to converge. This is typical of a procedure called the Direct Comparison Test for convergence of series of nonnegative terms.

Direct Comparison Test for Series of Nonnegative Terms

Let $\Sigma\, a_n$ be a series with no negative terms.

a) Test for convergence. $\Sigma\, a_n$ converges if there is a convergent series $\Sigma\, c_n$ with $a_n \le c_n$ for all $n > N$, for some positive integer N.

b) Test for divergence. $\Sigma\, a_n$ diverges if there is a divergent series of nonnegative terms $\Sigma\, d_n$ with $a_n \ge d_n$ for all $n > N$, for some positive integer N.

In part (a), the partial sums of the series $\Sigma\, a_n$ are bounded above by

$$M = a_1 + a_2 + \cdots + a_N + \sum_{n=N+1}^{\infty} c_n .$$

They therefore form a nondecreasing sequence with a limit $L \le M$.

In part (b), the partial sums for $\Sigma\, a_n$ are not bounded from above. If they were, the partial sums for $\Sigma\, d_n$ would be bounded by

$$M' = d_1 + d_2 + \cdots + d_N + \sum_{n=N+1}^{\infty} a_n$$

and $\Sigma\, d_n$ would have to converge instead of diverge.

To apply the Direct Comparison Test to a series, we do not have to include the early terms of the series. We can start the test with any index N, provided we include all the terms of the series being tested from there on.

EXAMPLE 4 Does the following series converge?

$$5 + \frac{2}{3} + 1 + \frac{1}{7} + \frac{1}{2} + \frac{1}{3!} + \frac{1}{4!} + \cdots + \frac{1}{k!} + \cdots$$

Solution We ignore the first four terms and compare the remaining terms with the terms of the convergent geometric series $\Sigma_{n=1}^{\infty} 1/2^n$. We see that

$$\frac{1}{2} + \frac{1}{3!} + \frac{1}{4!} + \cdots \leq \frac{1}{2} + \frac{1}{4} + \frac{1}{8} + \cdots.$$

Therefore, the original series converges by the Direct Comparison Test.

To apply the Direct Comparison Test, we need to have on hand a list of series we already know about. Here is what we know so far:

Convergent series	Divergent series
Geometric series with $\lvert r \rvert < 1$	Geometric series with $\lvert r \rvert \geq 1$
Telescoping series like $\sum_{n=1}^{\infty} \frac{1}{n(n+1)}$	The harmonic series $\sum_{n=1}^{\infty} \frac{1}{n}$
The series $\sum_{n=0}^{\infty} \frac{1}{n!}$	Any series $\Sigma\, a_n$ for which $\lim_{n\to\infty} a_n$ does not exist or $\lim_{n\to\infty} a_n \neq 0$

The next test will add more series to these lists.

The Integral Test

We introduce the Integral Test with a series that is related to the harmonic series, but in which the nth term is $1/n^2$ instead of $1/n$.

EXAMPLE 5 Does the following series converge?

$$\sum_{n=1}^{\infty} \frac{1}{n^2} = 1 + \frac{1}{4} + \frac{1}{9} + \frac{1}{16} + \cdots + \frac{1}{n^2} + \cdots \tag{4}$$

Solution We determine the convergence of $\Sigma_{n=1}^{\infty} (1/n^2)$ by comparing it with $\int_1^{\infty} (1/x^2)\, dx$. To carry out the comparison, we think of the terms of the series as values of the function $f(x) = 1/x^2$ and interpret these values as the areas of rectangles under the curve $y = 1/x^2$.

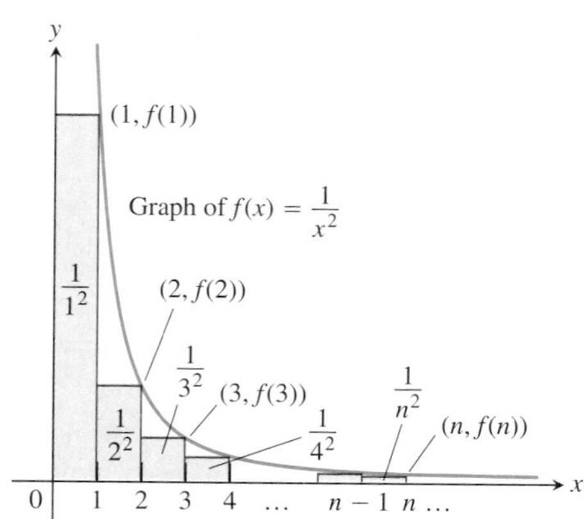

9.10 Figure for the area comparisons in Example 5.

As Fig. 9.10 shows,

$$\begin{aligned} s_n &= \frac{1}{1^2} + \frac{1}{2^2} + \frac{1}{3^2} + \cdots + \frac{1}{n^2} \\ &= f(1) + f(2) + f(3) + \cdots + f(n) \\ &< f(1) + \int_1^n \frac{1}{x^2}\, dx \\ &< 1 + \int_1^{\infty} \frac{1}{x^2}\, dx \\ &< 1 + 1 = 2. \end{aligned}$$

As in Section 8.5, Example 8, $\int_1^{\infty} (1/x^2)\, dx = 1$.

Thus the partial sums of $\Sigma_{n=1}^{\infty} 1/n^2$ are bounded from above (by 2) and the series converges. The sum of the series is known to be $\pi^2/6 \approx 1.64493$.

Caution: The series and integral need not have the same value in the convergent case. As we saw in Example 5, $\Sigma_{n=1}^{\infty}(1/n^2) = \pi^2/6$ while $\int_1^{\infty}(1/x^2)\,dx = 1$.

Integral Test

Let $a_n = f(n)$ where $f(x)$ is a continuous, positive, decreasing function of x for all $x \geq 1$. Then the series $\Sigma_{n=1}^{\infty} a_n$ and the integral $\int_1^{\infty} f(x)\,dx$ both converge or both diverge.

Proof We start with the assumption that f is a decreasing function with $f(n) = a_n$ for every n. This leads us to observe that the rectangles in Fig. 9.11(a), which have areas $a_1, a_2, \ldots, a_n$, collectively enclose more area than that under the curve $y = f(x)$ from $x = 1$ to $x = n + 1$. That is,

$$\int_1^{n+1} f(x)\,dx \leq a_1 + a_2 + \cdots + a_n.$$

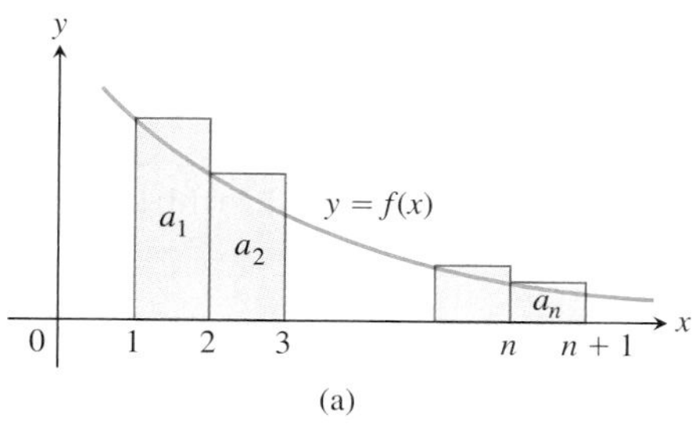

(a)

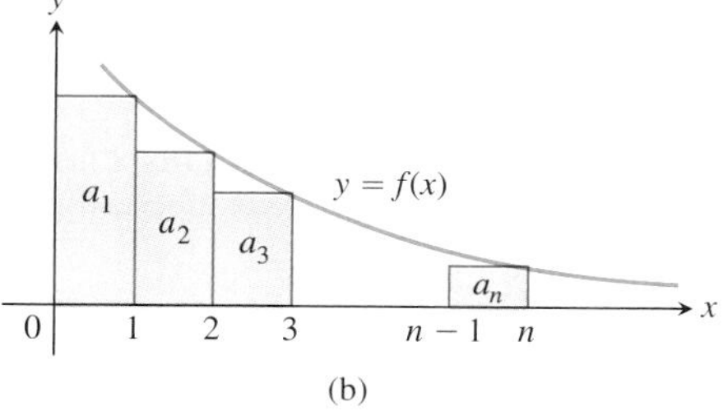

(b)

9.11 Subject to the conditions of the Integral Test, the series $\Sigma_{n=1}^{\infty} a_n$ and the integral $\int_1^{\infty} f(x)\,dx$ both converge or both diverge.

In Fig. 9.11(b) the rectangles have been faced to the left instead of to the right. If we momentarily disregard the first rectangle, of area a_1, we see that

$$a_2 + a_3 + \cdots + a_n \leq \int_1^{n} f(x)\,dx.$$

If we include a_1, we have

$$a_1 + a_2 + \cdots + a_n \leq a_1 + \int_1^{n} f(x)\,dx.$$

Combining these results gives

$$\int_1^{n+1} f(x)\,dx \leq a_1 + a_2 + \cdots + a_n \leq a_1 + \int_1^{n} f(x)\,dx. \tag{5}$$

If the integral $\int_1^{\infty} f(x)\,dx$ is finite, the right-hand inequality shows that $\Sigma\, a_n$ is also finite. But if $\int_1^{\infty} f(x)\,dx$ is infinite, then the left-hand inequality shows that the series is also infinite.

Hence the series and the integral are both finite or both infinite. ∎

EXAMPLE 6 *The p-series.* Show that if p is a real constant, then the ***p*-series**

$$\sum_{n=1}^{\infty} \frac{1}{n^p} = \frac{1}{1^p} + \frac{1}{2^p} + \frac{1}{3^p} + \cdots + \frac{1}{n^p} + \cdots \tag{6}$$

converges if $p > 1$ and diverges if $p \leq 1$.

Solution If $p > 1$, then $f(x) = 1/x^p$ is a positive decreasing function of x. Since

$$\int_1^{\infty} \frac{1}{x^p}\,dx = \int_1^{\infty} x^{-p}\,dx = \lim_{b\to\infty}\left[\frac{x^{-p+1}}{-p+1}\right]_1^b$$

$$= \frac{1}{1-p}\lim_{b\to\infty}\left(\frac{1}{b^{p-1}} - 1\right)$$

$$= \frac{1}{1-p}(0-1) = \frac{1}{p-1},$$

$b^{p-1} \to \infty$ as $b \to \infty$ because $p - 1 > 0$.

the series converges by the Integral Test.

If $p = 1$, we have the (divergent) harmonic series

$$1 + \frac{1}{2} + \frac{1}{3} + \cdots + \frac{1}{n} + \cdots.$$

If $p < 1$, the terms of the p-series are greater than the corresponding terms of the divergent harmonic series, so the p-series diverges by the Direct Comparison Test.

We have convergence for $p > 1$ but divergence for every other value of p.

The Limit Comparison Test

We now present a more powerful form of the Direct Comparison Test, known as the Limit Comparison Test. It is particularly handy for series in which a_n is a rational function of n.

EXAMPLE 7 Do the following series converge, or diverge?

a) $\displaystyle\sum_{n=2}^{\infty} \frac{2n}{n^2 - n + 1}$ **b)** $\displaystyle\sum_{n=2}^{\infty} \frac{2n^3 + 100n^2 + 1000}{(1/8)n^6 - n + 2}$

Solution In determining convergence or divergence, only the tails matter. And when n is very large, the highest powers of n in numerator and denominator are what matter the most. So in (a), we reason this way:

$$a_n = \frac{2n}{n^2 - n + 1}$$

behaves approximately like $2n/n^2 = 2/n$, and, by comparing it with $\Sigma\ 1/n$, we guess that $\Sigma\ a_n$ diverges. In (b), we reason that a_n will behave approximately like $2n^3/(1/8)n^6 = 16/n^3$ and, by comparing it with $\Sigma\ 1/n^3$, a p-series with $p = 3$, we guess that the series converges.

To be more precise, in (a) we take

$$a_n = \frac{2n}{n^2 - n + 1} \qquad \text{and} \qquad d_n = \frac{1}{n}$$

and look at the ratio

$$\frac{a_n}{d_n} = \frac{2n^2}{n^2 - n + 1} = \frac{2}{1 - \left(\frac{1}{n}\right) + \left(\frac{1}{n^2}\right)}.$$

As $n \to \infty$, the limit is 2: $\lim\ (a_n/d_n) = 2$.

This means, in particular, that if we take $\epsilon = 1$ in the definition of limit there is an integer N such that a_n/d_n is within 1 unit of this limit for all $n \geq N$:

$$2 - 1 \leq a_n/d_n \leq 2 + 1 \qquad \text{for} \quad n \geq N.$$

Thus $a_n \geq d_n$ for $n \geq N$. By the Direct Comparison Test, $\Sigma\ a_n$ diverges because $\Sigma\ d_n$ diverges.

In (b), if we let $c_n = 1/n^3$, we can show that $\lim\ (a_n/c_n) = 16$.

Taking $\epsilon = 1$ in the definition of limit, we can conclude that there is an index N' such that a_n/c_n is between 15 and 17 when $n \geq N'$. Since $\Sigma\ c_n$ converges, so also does $\Sigma\ 17c_n$ and thus $\Sigma\ a_n$.

Our rough guesswork led to successful choices of comparison series. We make this more precise in the following Limit Comparison Test.

Limit Comparison Test

a) Test for convergence. If $a_n \geq 0$ for $n \geq N$ and there is a convergent series $\Sigma\, c_n$ such that $c_n > 0$ and

$$\lim \frac{a_n}{c_n} < \infty, \tag{7}$$

then $\Sigma\, a_n$ converges.

b) Test for divergence. If $a_n \geq 0$ for $n \geq N$ and there is a divergent series $\Sigma\, d_n$ such that $d_n > 0$ and

$$\lim \frac{a_n}{d_n} > 0 \quad \text{or} \quad \lim \frac{a_n}{d_n} = \infty, \tag{8}$$

then $\Sigma\, a_n$ diverges.

A slightly more restrictive version of the Limit Comparison Test combines parts (a) and (b) in the following way.

The Simplified Limit Comparison Test is the one we use most often.

Simplified Limit Comparison Test

If the terms of the two series $\Sigma\, a_n$ and $\Sigma\, b_n$ are positive for $n \geq N$, and the limit of a_n/b_n is finite and positive, then both series converge or both diverge.

EXAMPLE 8 Which of the following series converge and which diverge?

a) $\dfrac{3}{4} + \dfrac{5}{9} + \dfrac{7}{16} + \dfrac{9}{25} + \cdots = \displaystyle\sum_{n=1}^{\infty} \frac{2n+1}{(n+1)^2}$

b) $\dfrac{101}{3} + \dfrac{102}{10} + \dfrac{103}{29} + \cdots = \displaystyle\sum_{n=1}^{\infty} \frac{100+n}{n^3+2}$

c) $\dfrac{1}{1} + \dfrac{1}{3} + \dfrac{1}{7} + \cdots = \displaystyle\sum_{n=1}^{\infty} \frac{1}{2^n - 1}$

Solution

a) Let $a_n = (2n+1)/(n^2+2n+1)$ and $d_n = 1/n$. Then

$$\sum d_n \text{ diverges} \quad \text{and} \quad \lim \frac{a_n}{d_n} = \lim \frac{2n^2+n}{n^2+2n+1} = 2,$$

so $\Sigma\, a_n$ diverges.

b) Let $a_n = (100+n)/(n^3+2)$. When n is large, this ought to compare with $n/n^3 = 1/n^2$, so we let $c_n = 1/n^2$ and apply the Limit Comparison Test:

$$\sum c_n \text{ converges} \quad \text{and} \quad \lim \frac{a_n}{c_n} = \lim \frac{n^3+100n^2}{n^3+2} = 1,$$

so $\Sigma\, a_n$ converges.

c) Let $a_n = 1/(2^n - 1)$ and $c_n = 1/2^n$. (We reason that $2^n - 1$ behaves like 2^n when n is large.) Then

$$\frac{a_n}{c_n} = \frac{2^n}{2^n - 1} = \frac{1}{1 - (1/2)^n} \to 1 \quad \text{as} \quad n \to \infty.$$

Because $\Sigma\, c_n$ converges, we conclude that $\Sigma\, a_n$ does also.

Exercises 9.3

Which of the series in Exercises 1–54 converge and which diverge? Give reasons for your answers. (When checking your answers, remember there may be more than one way to determine a series' convergence or divergence.)

1. $\sum_{n=1}^{\infty} \frac{1}{10^n}$ **2.** $\sum_{n=1}^{\infty} e^{-n}$ **3.** $\sum_{n=1}^{\infty} \frac{n}{n+1}$

4. $\sum_{n=1}^{\infty} \frac{5}{n+1}$ **5.** $\sum_{n=1}^{\infty} \frac{3}{\sqrt{n}}$ **6.** $\sum_{n=1}^{\infty} \frac{3}{n+\sqrt{n}}$

7. $\sum_{n=1}^{\infty} \frac{\sin^2 n}{2^n}$ **8.** $\sum_{n=1}^{\infty} \frac{1+\cos n}{n^2}$ **9.** $\sum_{n=1}^{\infty} -\frac{1}{8^n}$

10. $\sum_{n=1}^{\infty} \frac{-8}{n}$ **11.** $\sum_{n=2}^{\infty} \frac{\ln n}{n}$ **12.** $\sum_{n=1}^{\infty} \frac{1}{n\sqrt{n}}$

13. $\sum_{n=1}^{\infty} \frac{2^n}{3^n}$ **14.** $\sum_{n=0}^{\infty} \frac{-2}{n+1}$ **15.** $\sum_{n=1}^{\infty} \frac{1}{1+\ln n}$

16. $\sum_{n=1}^{\infty} \frac{1}{2n-1}$ **17.** $\sum_{n=1}^{\infty} \frac{2^n}{n+1}$ **18.** $\sum_{n=1}^{\infty} \left(\frac{n}{3n+1}\right)^n$

19. $\sum_{n=1}^{\infty} \frac{1}{\sqrt{n^3+2}}$ **20.** $\sum_{n=1}^{\infty} \frac{n}{n^2+1}$ **21.** $\sum_{n=2}^{\infty} \frac{\sqrt{n}}{\ln n}$

22. $\sum_{n=2}^{\infty} \frac{\ln n}{\sqrt{n}}$ **23.** $\sum_{n=3}^{\infty} \frac{1}{\ln(\ln n)}$ **24.** $\sum_{n=2}^{\infty} \frac{1}{(\ln n)^2}$

25. $\sum_{n=1}^{\infty} \frac{(\ln n)^2}{n^3}$ **26.** $\sum_{n=1}^{\infty} \frac{(\ln n)^3}{n^3}$ **27.** $\sum_{n=1}^{\infty} \frac{1}{n\sqrt[n]{n}}$

28. $\sum_{n=1}^{\infty} \frac{\sqrt[n]{n}}{n^2}$ **29.** $\sum_{n=1}^{\infty} \left(1+\frac{1}{n}\right)^n$ **30.** $\sum_{n=1}^{\infty} \frac{\sqrt{n}}{n^2+1}$

31. $\sum_{n=1}^{\infty} \frac{1-n}{n \cdot 2^n}$ **32.** $\sum_{n=1}^{\infty} \frac{n+2^n}{n^2\, 2^n}$ **33.** $\sum_{n=1}^{\infty} \frac{1}{(\ln 2)^n}$

34. $\sum_{n=1}^{\infty} \frac{1}{(\ln 3)^n}$ **35.** $\sum_{n=1}^{\infty} \frac{1}{3^{n-1}+1}$ **36.** $\sum_{n=1}^{\infty} \frac{3^{n-1}+1}{3^n}$

37. $\sum_{n=1}^{\infty} \sin\frac{1}{n}$ **38.** $\sum_{n=1}^{\infty} \tan\frac{1}{n}$ **39.** $\sum_{n=1}^{\infty} n \sin\frac{1}{n}$

40. $\sum_{n=1}^{\infty} n \tan\frac{1}{n}$ **41.** $\sum_{n=1}^{\infty} \frac{8\tan^{-1} n}{1+n^2}$ **42.** $\sum_{n=2}^{\infty} \frac{1}{n\sqrt{n^2-1}}$

43. $\sum_{n=1}^{\infty} \frac{10n+1}{n(n+1)(n+2)}$ **44.** $\sum_{n=3}^{\infty} \frac{5n^3-3n}{n^2(n-2)(n^2+5)}$

45. $\sum_{n=1}^{\infty} \frac{\tan^{-1} n}{n^{1.1}}$ **46.** $\sum_{n=1}^{\infty} \frac{\sec^{-1} n}{n^{1.3}}$

47. $\sum_{n=3}^{\infty} \frac{(1/n)}{(\ln n)\sqrt{\ln^2 n - 1}}$ **48.** $\sum_{n=1}^{\infty} \frac{1}{n(1+\ln^2 n)}$

49. $\sum_{n=1}^{\infty} \frac{2}{1+e^n}$ **50.** $\sum_{n=1}^{\infty} \frac{e^n}{1+e^{2n}}$

51. $\sum_{n=1}^{\infty} \operatorname{sech} n$ **52.** $\sum_{n=1}^{\infty} \operatorname{csch} n$

53. $\sum_{n=1}^{\infty} \frac{\coth n}{n^2}$ **54.** $\sum_{n=1}^{\infty} \frac{\tanh n}{n^2}$

55. a) Draw illustrations like those in Figs. 9.10 and 9.11 to show that the partial sums of the harmonic series satisfy the inequalities

$$\ln(n+1) = \int_1^{n+1} \frac{1}{x}\,dx \le 1 + \frac{1}{2} + \cdots + \frac{1}{n}$$
$$\le 1 + \int_1^n \frac{1}{x}\,dx = 1 + \ln n$$

b) There is absolutely no empirical evidence for the divergence of the harmonic series even though we know it diverges. The partial sums just grow too slowly. To see what we mean, suppose you had started with $s_1 = 1$ the day the universe was formed, thirteen billion years ago, and added a new term every *second*. About how large would the partial sum s_n be today, assuming a 365-day year?

56. Are there any values of x for which $\Sigma_{n=1}^{\infty}\,(1/(nx))$ converge? Give reasons for your answer.

57. Is it true that if $\Sigma_{n=1}^{\infty}\, a_n$ is a divergent series of positive numbers then there is also a divergent series $\Sigma_{n=1}^{\infty}\, b_n$ of positive numbers with $b_n < a_n$ for every n? Is there a "smallest" divergent series of positive numbers? Give reasons for your answers.

58. If $\Sigma_{n=1}^{\infty}\, a_n$ is a convergent series of nonnegative numbers, can anything be said about the series $\Sigma_{n=1}^{\infty}\,(a_n/n)$?

59. *Nonincreasing Sequences.* A sequence of numbers $\{s_n\}$ in which $s_n \ge s_{n+1}$ for every n is called a **nonincreasing sequence.** A sequence $\{s_n\}$ is bounded from below if there is a finite constant M with $M \le s_n$ for every n. Such a number M is called a lower bound for the sequence. Deduce from Theorem 7 that a nonincreasing sequence that is bounded from below converges, and that a nonincreasing sequence that is not bounded from below diverges.

60. *The Cauchy Condensation Test.* The Cauchy condensation test says: Let $\{a_n\}$ be a nonincreasing sequence ($a_n \geq a_{n+1}$ for all n) of positive terms that converges to 0. Then $\Sigma\, a_n$ converges if and only if $\Sigma\, 2^n a_{2^n}$ converges. For example, $\Sigma\,(1/n)$ diverges because $\Sigma\, 2^n \cdot (1/2^n) = \Sigma\, 1$ diverges.

Use the Cauchy condensation test to show that

a) $\displaystyle\sum_{n=2}^{\infty} \frac{1}{n \ln n}$ diverges,

b) $\displaystyle\sum_{n=1}^{\infty} \frac{1}{n^p}$ converges if $p > 1$ and diverges if $p \leq 1$.

61. *Logarithmic p-series*

a) Show that

$$\int_2^{\infty} \frac{dx}{x(\ln x)^p} \qquad (p \text{ a positive constant})$$

converges if and only if $p > 1$.

b) What implications does the fact in (a) have for the convergence of the series

$$\sum_{n=2}^{\infty} \frac{1}{n\,(\ln n)^p}?$$

Give reasons for your answer.

62. *Continuation of Exercise 61.* Use the result in Exercise 61 to determine which of the following series converge and which diverge. Support your answer in each case.

a) $\displaystyle\sum_{n=2}^{\infty} \frac{1}{n(\ln n)}$ b) $\displaystyle\sum_{n=2}^{\infty} \frac{1}{n(\ln n)^{1.01}}$

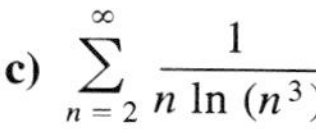

c) $\displaystyle\sum_{n=2}^{\infty} \frac{1}{n \ln (n^3)}$ d) $\displaystyle\sum_{n=2}^{\infty} \frac{1}{n(\ln n)^3}$

Writing for Your Own Knowledge

Answer the following questions in writing. Some answers will take only a sentence or two; others may require several paragraphs. Some explanations may also call for graphs or sketches.

1. What are the basic facts about nondecreasing sequences of numbers?
2. What do nondecreasing sequences of positive numbers have to do with the convergence of infinite series of nonnegative terms?
3. What tests are available for determining the convergence of infinite series of positive terms?

EXPLORER PROGRAM

Sequences and Series	Generates terms of one or two sequences and graphs them while you watch. You may define the sequences recursively or by giving formulas for their nth terms. Enables you to look for graphical and numerical evidence of convergence or divergence.

9.4 *Series with Nonnegative Terms — Ratio and Root Tests*

Convergence tests that depend on comparing a series with another series or an integral are called *extrinsic* tests. They are useful, but there are reasons to look for tests that do not require comparison. As a practical matter, we may not be able to find the series or function we need to make a comparison work. And, in principle, all the information about a given series should be contained in its own terms. We therefore turn our attention to *intrinsic* tests — tests that depend only on the series at hand.

The Ratio Test

The first intrinsic test, the Ratio Test, measures the rate of growth (or decline) of a series by examining the ratio a_{n+1}/a_n. For a geometric series, this rate is a constant, and the series converges if and only if its ratio is less than 1 in absolute value. But even if the ratio is not constant, we may be able to find a geometric series for comparison, as in Example 1.

EXAMPLE 1 Let $a_1 = 1$ and define a_{n+1} to be $a_{n+1} = \dfrac{n}{2n+1}\, a_n$.

Does the series $\Sigma\, a_n$ converge?

The series in Example 1 converges rapidly, as the following computer data suggest.

n	s_n
5	1.5607 5
10	1.5705 5
15	1.5707 89894
20	1.5707 96149
25	1.5707 96322
30	1.5707 96327
35	1.5707 96327

Solution We begin by writing a few terms of the series:

$$a_1 = 1, \qquad a_2 = \frac{1}{3}a_1 = \frac{1}{3}, \qquad a_3 = \frac{2}{5}a_2 = \frac{1\cdot 2}{3\cdot 5}, \qquad a_4 = \frac{3}{7}a_3 = \frac{1\cdot 2\cdot 3}{3\cdot 5\cdot 7}.$$

Each term is somewhat less than 1/2 the term before it, because $n/(2n+1)$ is less than 1/2. Therefore the terms of the series are less than or equal to the terms of the geometric series

$$1 + \left(\frac{1}{2}\right) + \left(\frac{1}{4}\right) + \cdots + \left(\frac{1}{2}\right)^{n-1} + \cdots,$$

which converges to 2. So our series also converges, and its sum is less than 2. The computer data in the margin show how quickly the sequence of partial sums approaches its limit, $\pi/2$.

In proving the Ratio Test, we will make a comparison with an appropriate geometric series as in Example 1, but when we *apply* it there is no need for comparison.

The Ratio Test

Let $\Sigma\, a_n$ be a series with positive terms, and suppose that

$$\lim_{n\to\infty} \frac{a_{n+1}}{a_n} = \rho.$$

Then

a) the series *converges* if $\rho < 1$,

b) the series *diverges* if $\rho > 1$,

c) the series *may converge or it may diverge* if $\rho = 1$. (The test provides no information.)

Proof

a) $\rho < 1$**.** Let r be a number between ρ and 1. Then the number $\epsilon = r - \rho$ is positive. Since

$$\frac{a_{n+1}}{a_n} \to \rho,$$

a_{n+1}/a_n must lie within ϵ of ρ when n is large enough, say for all $n > N$. In particular,

$$\frac{a_{n+1}}{a_n} < \rho + \epsilon = r, \qquad \text{when } n > N.$$

That is,

$$\begin{aligned} a_{N+1} &< ra_N, \\ a_{N+2} &< ra_{N+1} < r^2 a_N, \\ a_{N+3} &< ra_{N+2} < r^3 a_N, \\ &\vdots \\ a_{N+m} &< ra_{N+m-1} < r^m a_N. \end{aligned}$$

These inequalities show that the terms of our series, after the Nth term, approach zero more rapidly than the terms in a geometric series with ratio

$r < 1$. More precisely, consider the series $\Sigma\, c_n$, where $c_n = a_n$ for $n = 1, 2, \ldots, N$ and $c_{N+1} = ra_N$, $c_{N+2} = r^2 a_N, \ldots, c_{N+m} = r^m a_N, \ldots$. Now $a_n \le c_n$ for all n, and

$$\begin{aligned}\sum_{n=1}^{\infty} c_n &= a_1 + a_2 + \cdots + a_{N-1} + a_N + ra_N + r^2 a_N + \cdots \\ &= a_1 + a_2 + \cdots + a_{N-1} + a_N(1 + r + r^2 + \cdots).\end{aligned}$$

The geometric series $1 + r + r^2 + \cdots$ converges because $|r| < 1$, so $\Sigma\, c_n$ converges. Since $a_n \le c_n$, $\Sigma\, a_n$ also converges.

b) $\boldsymbol{\rho > 1}$**.** From some index M on,

$$\frac{a_{n+1}}{a_n} > 1 \qquad \text{and} \qquad a_M < a_{M+1} < a_{M+2} < \cdots.$$

The terms of the series do not approach zero as n becomes infinite, and the series diverges by the nth-Term Test.

c) $\boldsymbol{\rho = 1}$**.** The two series

$$\sum_{n=1}^{\infty} \frac{1}{n} \qquad \text{and} \qquad \sum_{n=1}^{\infty} \frac{1}{n^2}$$

show that some other test for convergence must be used when $\rho = 1$.

For $\displaystyle\sum_{n=1}^{\infty} \frac{1}{n}$: $\quad \dfrac{a_{n+1}}{a_n} = \dfrac{1/(n+1)}{1/n} = \dfrac{n}{n+1} \to 1.$

For $\displaystyle\sum_{n=1}^{\infty} \frac{1}{n^2}$: $\quad \dfrac{a_{n+1}}{a_n} = \dfrac{1/(n+1)^2}{1/n^2} = \left(\dfrac{n}{n+1}\right)^2 \to 1^2 = 1.$

In both cases $\rho = 1$, yet the first series diverges while the second converges.

The Ratio Test is often effective when the terms of a series contain factorials of expressions involving n or expressions raised to the nth power.

EXAMPLE 2 Investigate the convergence of the following series.

a) $\displaystyle\sum_{n=1}^{\infty} \frac{n!n!}{(2n)!}$ **b)** $\displaystyle\sum_{n=1}^{\infty} \frac{4^n n!n!}{(2n)!}$ **c)** $\displaystyle\sum_{n=0}^{\infty} \frac{2^n + 5}{3^n}$

Solution

a) If $a_n = n!n!/(2n)!$, then $a_{n+1} = (n+1)!(n+1)!/(2n+2)!$, and

$$\begin{aligned}\frac{a_{n+1}}{a_n} &= \frac{(n+1)!(n+1)!(2n)!}{n!n!(2n+2)(2n+1)(2n)!} \\ &= \frac{(n+1)(n+1)}{(2n+2)(2n+1)} = \frac{n+1}{4n+2} \to \frac{1}{4}.\end{aligned}$$

The series converges because $\rho = 1/4$ is less than 1.

b) If $a_n = 4^n n!n!/(2n)!$, then

$$\begin{aligned}\frac{a_{n+1}}{a_n} &= \frac{4^{n+1}(n+1)!(n+1)!}{(2n+2)(2n+1)(2n)!} \cdot \frac{(2n)!}{4^n n!n!} \\ &= \frac{4(n+1)(n+1)}{(2n+2)(2n+1)} = \frac{2(n+1)}{2n+1} \to 1.\end{aligned}$$

Because the limit is $\rho = 1$, we cannot decide from the Ratio Test alone whether the series converges or diverges. However, when we notice that $a_{n+1}/a_n = (2n+2)/(2n+1)$, we conclude that a_{n+1} is always greater than a_n because $(2n+2)/(2n+1)$ is always greater than 1. Therefore, all terms are greater than or equal to $a_1 = 2$, and the nth term does not approach zero as $n \to \infty$. By the nth-Term Test, the series diverges.

c) For the series $\sum_{n=0}^{\infty} (2^n + 5)/3^n$,

$$\frac{a_{n+1}}{a_n} = \frac{(2^{n+1}+5)/3^{n+1}}{(2^n+5)/3^n} = \frac{1}{3} \cdot \frac{2^{n+1}+5}{2^n+5} = \frac{1}{3} \cdot \left(\frac{2+5\cdot 2^{-n}}{1+5\cdot 2^{-n}}\right) \to \frac{1}{3} \cdot \frac{2}{1} = \frac{2}{3}.$$

The series converges because $\rho = 2/3$ is less than 1.

This does *not* mean that 2/3 is the sum of the series. In fact,

$$\sum_{n=0}^{\infty} \frac{2^n+5}{3^n} = \sum_{n=0}^{\infty} \left(\frac{2}{3}\right)^n + \sum_{n=0}^{\infty} \frac{5}{3^n} = \frac{1}{1-(2/3)} + \frac{5}{1-(1/3)} = \frac{21}{2}.$$

The nth-Root Test

We return to the question "Does $\Sigma\, a_n$ converge?" When there is a simple formula for a_n, we can try one of the tests we already have. But consider the following:

EXAMPLE 3 Let $a_n = f(n)/2^n$, where

$$f(n) = \begin{cases} n, & n \text{ odd}, \\ 1, & n \text{ even}. \end{cases}$$

Does $\sum_{n=1}^{\infty} a_n$ converge?

Solution We write out several terms of the series:

$$\sum_{n=1}^{\infty} a_n = \frac{1}{2^1} + \frac{1}{2^2} + \frac{3}{2^3} + \frac{1}{2^4} + \frac{5}{2^5} + \frac{1}{2^6} + \frac{7}{2^7} + \cdots$$
$$= \frac{1}{2} + \frac{1}{4} + \frac{3}{8} + \frac{1}{16} + \frac{5}{32} + \frac{1}{64} + \frac{7}{128} + \cdots.$$

Clearly, this is not a geometric series. The nth term approaches zero as $n \to \infty$, so we do not know if the series diverges. The Integral Test does not look promising. The Ratio Test produces

$$\frac{a_{n+1}}{a_n} = \frac{1}{2}\frac{f(n+1)}{f(n)} = \begin{cases} \dfrac{1}{2n}, & n \text{ odd}, \\[2ex] \dfrac{n+1}{2}, & n \text{ even}. \end{cases}$$

As $n \to \infty$, the ratio alternates between small and large and has no limit.

A test that will answer the question (affirmatively—yes, the series converges) is the nth-Root Test. To apply it, we consider the following:

$$\sqrt[n]{a_n} = \sqrt[n]{\frac{f(n)}{2^n}} = \frac{\sqrt[n]{f(n)}}{2} = \begin{cases} \dfrac{\sqrt[n]{n}}{2}, & n \text{ odd}, \\[2ex] \dfrac{1}{2}, & n \text{ even}. \end{cases}$$

Therefore,

$$\frac{1}{2} \le \sqrt[n]{a_n} \le \frac{\sqrt[n]{n}}{2}.$$

Since $\sqrt[n]{n} \to 1$ as $n \to \infty$ (Limit 2 in Table 9.1), we have $\lim_{n\to\infty} \sqrt[n]{a_n} = 1/2$ by the Sandwich Theorem. Because this limit is less than 1, the nth-Root Test tells us that the series converges, as we will now see.

The nth-Root Test

Let $\Sigma\, a_n$ be a series with $a_n \geq 0$ for $n \geq N$, and suppose that $\sqrt[n]{a_n} \to \rho$ as $n \to \infty$. Then

a) the series *converges* if $\rho < 1$,

b) the series *diverges* if $\rho > 1$,

c) the test is *not conclusive* if $\rho = 1$.

Proof

a) $\boldsymbol{\rho < 1}$**.** Choose an $\epsilon > 0$ so small that $\rho + \epsilon < 1$. Since $\sqrt[n]{a_n} \to \rho$, the terms $\sqrt[n]{a_n}$ eventually get closer than ϵ to ρ. In other words, there exists an index $M \geq N$ such that

$$\sqrt[n]{a_n} < \rho + \epsilon \qquad \text{when } n \geq M.$$

Then it is also true that

$$a_n < (\rho + \epsilon)^n \qquad \text{for } n \geq M.$$

Now, $\Sigma_{n=M}^{\infty} (\rho + \epsilon)^n$, a geometric series with ratio $(\rho + \epsilon) < 1$, converges. By comparison, $\Sigma_{n=M}^{\infty}\, a_n$ converges, from which it follows that

$$\sum_{n=1}^{\infty} a_n = a_1 + \cdots + a_{M-1} + \sum_{n=M}^{\infty} a_n$$

converges.

b) $\boldsymbol{\rho > 1}$**.** For all indices beyond some integer M, we have $\sqrt[n]{a_n} > 1$, so that $a_n > 1$ for $n > M$. The terms of the series do not converge to zero. The series diverges by the nth-Term Test.

c) $\boldsymbol{\rho = 1}$**.** The series $\Sigma_{n=1}^{\infty} (1/n)$ and $\Sigma_{n=1}^{\infty} (1/n^2)$ show that the test is not conclusive when $\rho = 1$. The first series diverges and the second converges, but in both cases $\sqrt[n]{a_n} \to 1$.

EXAMPLE 4 Which of the following series converges and which diverges?

a) $\displaystyle\sum_{n=1}^{\infty} \frac{n^2}{2^n}$ **b)** $\displaystyle\sum_{n=1}^{\infty} \frac{2^n}{n^2}$

Solution

a) $\displaystyle\sum_{n=1}^{\infty} \frac{n^2}{2^n}$ converges because $\displaystyle\sqrt[n]{\frac{n^2}{2^n}} = \frac{\sqrt[n]{n^2}}{\sqrt[n]{2^n}} = \frac{\left(\sqrt[n]{n}\right)^2}{2} \to \frac{1}{2} < 1.$

b) $\displaystyle\sum_{n=1}^{\infty} \frac{2^n}{n^2}$ diverges because $\displaystyle\sqrt[n]{\frac{2^n}{n^2}} = \frac{2}{\left(\sqrt[n]{n}\right)^2} \to \frac{2}{1} = 2 > 1.$

Exercises 9.4

Which of the series in Exercises 1–26 converge and which diverge? Give reasons for your answers. (When checking your answers, remember there may be more than one way to determine a series' convergence or divergence.)

1. $\sum_{n=1}^{\infty} \frac{n^2}{2^n}$

2. $\sum_{n=1}^{\infty} n^2 e^{-n}$

3. $\sum_{n=1}^{\infty} n! e^{-n}$

4. $\sum_{n=1}^{\infty} \frac{n!}{10^n}$

5. $\sum_{n=1}^{\infty} \frac{n^{10}}{10^n}$

6. $\sum_{n=1}^{\infty} \left(\frac{n-2}{n}\right)^n$

7. $\sum_{n=1}^{\infty} \frac{2+(-1)^n}{1.25^n}$

8. $\sum_{n=1}^{\infty} \frac{(-2)^n}{3^n}$

9. $\sum_{n=1}^{\infty} \left(1-\frac{3}{n}\right)^n$

10. $\sum_{n=1}^{\infty} \left(1-\frac{1}{3n}\right)^n$

11. $\sum_{n=1}^{\infty} \frac{\ln n}{n^3}$

12. $\sum_{n=1}^{\infty} \frac{(\ln n)^n}{n^n}$

13. $\sum_{n=1}^{\infty} \left(\frac{1}{n}-\frac{1}{n^2}\right)$

14. $\sum_{n=1}^{\infty} \left(\frac{1}{n}-\frac{1}{n^2}\right)^n$

15. $\sum_{n=1}^{\infty} \frac{\ln n}{n}$

16. $\sum_{n=1}^{\infty} \frac{n \ln n}{2^n}$

17. $\sum_{n=1}^{\infty} \frac{(n+1)(n+2)}{n!}$

18. $\sum_{n=1}^{\infty} e^{-n}(n^3)$

19. $\sum_{n=1}^{\infty} \frac{(n+3)!}{3!\,n!\,3^n}$

20. $\sum_{n=1}^{\infty} \frac{n 2^n (n+1)!}{3^n n!}$

21. $\sum_{n=1}^{\infty} \frac{n!}{(2n+1)!}$

22. $\sum_{n=1}^{\infty} \frac{n!}{n^n}$

23. $\sum_{n=2}^{\infty} \frac{n}{(\ln n)^n}$

24. $\sum_{n=2}^{\infty} \frac{n}{(\ln n)^{(n/2)}}$

25. $\sum_{n=1}^{\infty} \frac{n! \ln n}{n(n+2)!}$

26. $\sum_{n=1}^{\infty} \frac{3^n}{n^3 2^n}$

Which of the series $\sum_{n=1}^{\infty} a_n$ defined by the formulas in Exercises 27–38 converge and which diverge? Give reasons for your answers.

27. $a_1 = 2, \quad a_{n+1} = \frac{1+\sin n}{n} a_n$

28. $a_1 = 1, \quad a_{n+1} = \frac{1+\tan^{-1} n}{n} a_n$

29. $a_1 = \frac{1}{3}, \quad a_{n+1} = \frac{3n-1}{2n+5} a_n$

30. $a_1 = 3, \quad a_{n+1} = \frac{n}{n+1} a_n$

31. $a_1 = 2, \quad a_{n+1} = \frac{2}{n} a_n$

32. $a_1 = 5, \quad a_{n+1} = \frac{\sqrt[n]{n}}{2} a_n$

33. $a_1 = 1, \quad a_{n+1} = \frac{+\ln n}{n} a_n$

34. $a_1 = \frac{1}{2}, \quad a_{n+1} = \frac{n+\ln n}{n+10} a_n$

35. $a_1 = \frac{1}{3}, \quad a_{n+1} = \sqrt[n]{a_n}$

36. $a_1 = \frac{1}{2}, \quad a_{n+1} = \left(a_n\right)^{n+1}$

37. $a_n = \frac{2^n n! n!}{(2n)!}$

38. $a_n = \frac{(3n)!}{n!(n+1)!(n+2)!}$

Which of the series in Exercises 39–42 converge and which diverge? Give reasons for your answers.

39. $\sum_{n=1}^{\infty} \frac{(n!)^n}{(n^n)^2}$

40. $\sum_{n=1}^{\infty} \frac{n^n}{n!}$

41. $\sum_{n=1}^{\infty} \frac{n^n}{2^{(n^2)}}$

42. $\sum_{n=1}^{\infty} \frac{n^n}{(2^n)^2}$

43. Neither the Ratio nor the nth-Root Test helps with p-series. Try them on $\sum_{n=1}^{\infty} (1/n^p)$ and show that both tests fail to provide information about convergence.

44. Show that neither the Ratio Test nor the nth-Root Test provides information about the convergence of $\sum_{n=2}^{\infty} 1/(\ln n)^p$ (p constant).

Writing for Your Own Knowledge

Answer the following questions in writing. Some answers will take only a sentence or two; others may require several paragraphs. Some explanations may also call for graphs or sketches.

1. What is the Ratio Test?
2. What is the nth-Root Test?
3. Do the Ratio and nth-Root Tests always give the information you need to determine convergence?

EXPLORER PROGRAM

Sequences and Series	Generates terms of one or two sequences and graphs them. You may define the sequences recursively or by giving formulas for their nth terms. Enables you to look for graphical and numerical evidence of convergence or divergence.

9.5 Alternating Series and Absolute Convergence

A series in which the terms are alternately positive and negative is an **alternating series.** Here are three examples:

$$1-\frac{1}{2}+\frac{1}{3}-\frac{1}{4}+\frac{1}{5}-\cdots+\frac{(-1)^{n+1}}{n}+\cdots \tag{1}$$

$$-2+1-\frac{1}{2}+\frac{1}{4}-\frac{1}{8}+\cdots+\frac{(-1)^{n}4}{2^{n}}+\cdots \tag{2}$$

$$1-2+3-4+5-6+\cdots+(-1)^{n+1}n+\cdots \tag{3}$$

Series (1), called the **alternating harmonic series,** converges, as we will see in a moment. Series (2), a geometric series with ratio $r=-1/2$, converges to $-2/[1+(1/2)]=-4/3$. Series (3) diverges because the nth term does not approach zero.

We prove the convergence of the alternating harmonic series by applying the Alternating Series Theorem.

THEOREM 8

The Alternating Series Theorem (Leibniz's Theorem)

The series

$$\sum_{n=1}^{\infty}(-1)^{n+1}a_n=a_1-a_2+a_3-a_4+\cdots \tag{4}$$

converges if all three of the following conditions are satisfied:

1. The a_n's are all positive.
2. $a_n \geq a_{n+1}$ for all n.
3. $a_n \to 0$.

Proof If n is an even integer, say $n=2m$, then the sum of the first n terms is

$$\begin{aligned} s_{2m} &= (a_1-a_2)+(a_3-a_4)+\cdots+(a_{2m-1}-a_{2m}) \\ &= a_1-(a_2-a_3)-(a_4-a_5)-\cdots-(a_{2m-2}-a_{2m-1})-a_{2m}. \end{aligned} \tag{5}$$

The first equality shows that s_{2m} is the sum of m nonnegative terms, since each term in parentheses is positive or zero. Hence $s_{2m+2} \geq s_{2m}$, and the sequence $\{s_{2m}\}$ is nondecreasing. The second equality shows that $s_{2m} \leq a_1$. Since $\{s_{2m}\}$ is nondecreasing and bounded from above, it has a limit, say

$$\lim_{m\to\infty} s_{2m}=L. \tag{6}$$

If n is an odd integer, say $n=2m+1$, then the sum of the first n terms is $s_{2m+1}=s_{2m}+a_{2m+1}$. Since $a_n \to 0$,

$$\lim_{m\to\infty} a_{2m+1}=0$$

and, as $m\to\infty$,

$$s_{2m+1}=s_{2m}+a_{2m+1}\to L+0=L. \tag{7}$$

When we combine the results of (6) and (7), we get $\lim_{n\to\infty} s_n=L$. ∎

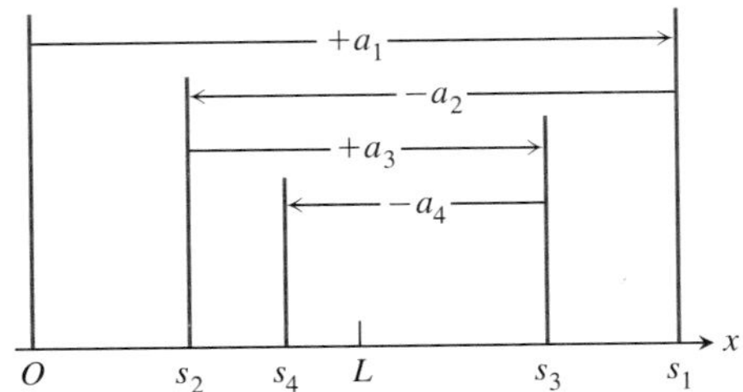

9.12 The partial sums of an alternating series that satisfies the hypotheses of Theorem 8 straddle the limit.

EXAMPLE 1 The alternating harmonic series

$$\sum_{n=1}^{\infty} (-1)^{n+1} \frac{1}{n} = 1 - \frac{1}{2} + \frac{1}{3} - \frac{1}{4} + \cdots$$

satisfies the three requirements of Theorem 8; it therefore converges.

We can use a graphical interpretation of the partial sums to gain insight into the way an alternating series converges to its limit L when the three conditions of Theorem 8 are satisfied. Starting from the origin of the x-axis (Fig. 9.12), we lay off the positive distance $s_1 = a_1$. To find the point corresponding to $s_2 = a_1 - a_2$, we back up a distance equal to a_2. Since $a_2 \le a_1$, we do not back up any farther than O at most. Next we go forward a distance a_3 and mark the point corresponding to $s_3 = a_1 - a_2 + a_3$. Since $a_3 \le a_2$, we go forward by an amount no greater than the previous backward step; that is, $s_3 \le s_1$. We continue in this seesaw fashion, backing up or going forward as the signs in the series demand. But each forward or backward step is shorter than (or at most the same size as) the preceding step, because $a_{n+1} \le a_n$. And since the nth term approaches zero as n increases, the size of step we take forward or backward gets smaller and smaller. We oscillate across the limit L, and the amplitude of oscillation approaches zero. The even-numbered partial sums $s_2, s_4, s_6, \ldots, s_{2m}$ increase toward L; the odd-numbered sums $s_1, s_3, s_5, \ldots, s_{2m+1}$ decrease toward L. The limit L lies between any two successive sums s_n and s_{n+1} and hence differs from s_n by an amount less than a_{n+1}.

Because

$$|L - s_n| < a_{n+1} \qquad \text{for every } n, \tag{8}$$

we can make useful estimates of the sums of convergent alternating series.

THEOREM 9

The Alternating Series Estimation Theorem

If the alternating series $\sum_{n=1}^{\infty} (-1)^{n+1} a_n$ satisfies the three conditions of Theorem 8, then

$$s_n = a_1 - a_2 + \cdots + (-1)^{n+1} a_n$$

approximates the sum L of the series with an error whose absolute value is less than a_{n+1}, the numerical value of the first unused term. Furthermore, the remainder, $L - s_n$, has the same sign as the first unused term.

We leave the determination of the sign of the remainder for Exercise 51.

EXAMPLE 2 We first try Theorem 9 on a series whose sum we know:

$$\sum_{n=0}^{\infty} (-1)^n \frac{1}{2^n} = 1 - \frac{1}{2} + \frac{1}{4} - \frac{1}{8} + \frac{1}{16} - \frac{1}{32} + \frac{1}{64} - \frac{1}{128} \;\Big|\; + \frac{1}{256} - \cdots.$$

The theorem says that if we truncate the series after the eighth term, we throw away a total that is positive and less than 1/256. The sum of the first eight terms is 0.6640 625. The sum of the series is

$$\frac{1}{1-(-1/2)}=\frac{1}{3/2}=\frac{2}{3}.$$

The difference, $(2/3) - 0.6640\ 625 = 0.0026\ 04166\ 6. . .$, is positive and less than $(1/256) = 0.0039\ 0625$.

Absolute Convergence

DEFINITION

A series $\Sigma\, a_n$ **converges absolutely** (is **absolutely convergent**) if the corresponding series of absolute values, $\Sigma|a_n|$, converges.

The geometric series

$$1-\frac{1}{2}+\frac{1}{4}-\frac{1}{8}+\cdots$$

converges absolutely because the corresponding series of absolute values

$$1+\frac{1}{2}+\frac{1}{4}+\frac{1}{8}+\cdots$$

converges. The alternating harmonic series does not converge absolutely. The corresponding series of absolute values is the (divergent) harmonic series.

DEFINITION

A series that converges but does not converge absolutely **converges conditionally.**

The alternating harmonic series converges conditionally.

Absolute convergence is important because, first, we have many good tests for convergence of series of positive terms. Second, if a series converges absolutely, then it converges. That is the thrust of the next theorem.

THEOREM 10

The Absolute Convergence Theorem

If $\Sigma_{n=1}^{\infty} |a_n|$ converges, then $\Sigma_{n=1}^{\infty} a_n$ converges.

Proof For each n,

$$-|a_n| \le a_n \le |a_n|, \qquad \text{so} \qquad 0 \le a_n + |a_n| \le 2|a_n|.$$

If $\Sigma_{n=1}^{\infty} |a_n|$ converges, then $\Sigma_{n=1}^{\infty} 2|a_n|$ converges and, by the Direct

Comparison Test, the nonnegative series $\Sigma_{n=1}^{\infty}(a_n + |a_n|)$ converges. The equality $a_n = (a_n + |a_n|) - |a_n|$ now lets us express $\Sigma_{n=1}^{\infty} a_n$ as the difference of two convergent series:

$$\sum_{n=1}^{\infty} a_n = \sum_{n=1}^{\infty} (a_n + |a_n| - |a_n|) = \sum_{n=1}^{\infty} (a_n + |a_n|) - \sum_{n=1}^{\infty} |a_n|.$$

Therefore, $\Sigma_{n=1}^{\infty} a_n$ converges. ■

We can rephrase Theorem 10 to say that *every absolutely convergent series converges*. However, the converse statement is false. Many convergent series do not converge absolutely. The convergence of many series depends on the series' having infinitely many positive and negative terms arranged in a particular order.

EXAMPLE 3 For $\displaystyle\sum_{n=1}^{\infty} (-1)^{n+1}\frac{1}{n^2} = 1 - \frac{1}{4} + \frac{1}{9} - \frac{1}{16} + \cdots$, the corresponding series of absolute values is the convergent series

$$\sum_{n=1}^{\infty} \frac{1}{n^2} = 1 + \frac{1}{4} + \frac{1}{9} + \frac{1}{16} + \cdots.$$

The original series converges because it converges absolutely. ■

EXAMPLE 4 For $\displaystyle\sum_{n=1}^{\infty} \frac{\sin n}{n^2} = \frac{\sin 1}{1} + \frac{\sin 2}{4} + \frac{\sin 3}{9} + \cdots$, the corresponding series of absolute values is

$$\sum_{n=1}^{\infty} \left|\frac{\sin n}{n^2}\right| = \frac{|\sin 1|}{1} + \frac{|\sin 2|}{4} + \cdots,$$

which converges by comparison with $\Sigma_{n=1}^{\infty}(1/n^2)$ because $|\sin n| \le 1$ for every n. The original series converges absolutely; therefore it converges. ■

Alternating p-series

When p is a positive constant, the sequence $\{1/n^p\}$ is a decreasing sequence with limit zero. Therefore the alternating p-series

$$\sum_{n=1}^{\infty} \frac{(-1)^{n-1}}{n^p} = 1 - \frac{1}{2^p} + \frac{1}{3^p} - \frac{1}{4^p} + \cdots, \qquad p > 0$$

converges.

For $p > 1$, the series converges absolutely. For $0 < p \le 1$, the series converges conditionally.

Conditional convergence: $\quad 1 - \dfrac{1}{\sqrt{2}} + \dfrac{1}{\sqrt{3}} - \dfrac{1}{\sqrt{4}} + \cdots$

Absolute convergence: $\quad 1 - \dfrac{1}{2^{3/2}} + \dfrac{1}{3^{3/2}} - \dfrac{1}{4^{3/2}} + \cdots$

Preview of Power Series

In the next section we take up the subject of power series, series in which the nth term is a constant times x^n. We investigate the convergence of such series with the Ratio Test or nth-Root Test, as in the next example.

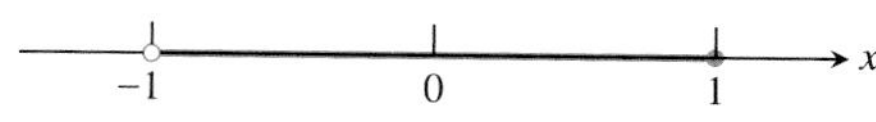

9.13 The interval of convergence of the series

$$\sum_{n=1}^{\infty} (-1)^{n-1} \frac{x^n}{n}$$

(Example 5). The series converges absolutely in the interior of the interval and conditionally at the interval's right-hand endpoint. This is typical of power series, as we will see in Section 9.6.

EXAMPLE 5 Find all values of x for which the series

$$x - \frac{x^2}{2} + \frac{x^3}{3} - \frac{x^4}{4} + \cdots + (-1)^{n-1}\frac{x^n}{n} + \cdots$$

converges.

Solution The series converges absolutely for all values of x for which

$$\lim_{n\to\infty} \sqrt[n]{\left|(-1)^{n-1}\frac{x^n}{n}\right|} = \lim_{n\to\infty} \frac{|x|}{\sqrt[n]{n}} = |x|$$

is less than 1 (Root Test).

At $x = 1$, the series is the alternating harmonic series, which converges. At $x = -1$, the series is the negative of the harmonic series and diverges. For $|x| > 1$, the nth term of the series does not approach zero, and the series diverges. Hence the series converges for $-1 < x \le 1$ (Fig. 9.13). ■

TABLE 9.2
Tests for convergence and divergence

Test	Series	Convergence	Divergence	Comment
Geometric Series	$\sum_{n=1}^{\infty} ar^{n-1}$	$\|r\| < 1$	$\|r\| \ge 1$	$S = \frac{a}{1-r}$
nth-Term	$\sum_{n=1}^{\infty} a_n$	Gives no information	$\lim_{n\to\infty} a_n$ does not exist, or $\neq 0$	$a_n \to 0$ does not imply convergence
Partial Sum	$\sum_{n=1}^{\infty} a_n, \quad a_n \ge 0$	$\{s_n\}$ bounded from above	$\{s_n\}$ unbounded	
Direct Comparison	$\sum_{n=1}^{\infty} a_n, \quad a_n \ge 0$	$a_n \le c_n$ for $n \ge N$ and $\Sigma\, c_n$ converges	$0 \le d_n \le a_n$ for $n \ge N$ and $\Sigma\, d_n$ diverges	
Integral	$\sum_{n=1}^{\infty} a_n, \quad a_n = f(n) > 0,$ $f(x)$ continuous and decreasing	$\int_1^{\infty} f(x)\,dx$ converges	$\int_1^{\infty} f(x)\,dx$ diverges	Convergence (divergence) of integral implies convergence (divergence) of sum.
Limit Comparison	$\sum_{n=1}^{\infty} a_n, \quad a_n \ge 0$	$\lim_{n\to\infty} \frac{a_n}{c_n} < \infty$ and $\Sigma\, c_n$ converges	$\lim_{n\to\infty} \frac{a_n}{d_n} > 0$ and $\Sigma\, d_n$ diverges	
Simplified Limit Comparison	$\sum_{n=1}^{\infty} a_n, \quad a_n > 0$	$0 < \lim_{n\to\infty} \frac{a_n}{b_n} < \infty$ and $\Sigma\, b_n$ converges	$0 < \lim_{n\to\infty} \frac{a_n}{b_n} < \infty$ and $\Sigma\, b_n$ diverges	
Ratio	$\sum_{n=1}^{\infty} a_n, \quad a_n > 0$	$\lim_{n\to\infty} \left\|\frac{a_{n+1}}{a_n}\right\| < 1$	$\lim_{n\to\infty} \left\|\frac{a_{n+1}}{a_n}\right\| > 1$	Inconclusive if $\lim = 1$
Root	$\sum_{n=1}^{\infty} a_n, \quad a_n \ge 0$	$\lim_{n\to\infty} \sqrt[n]{a_n} < 1$	$\lim_{n\to\infty} \sqrt[n]{a_n} > 1$	Inconclusive if $\lim = 1$
Alternating Series	$\sum_{n=1}^{\infty} (-1)^{n+1} a_n, \quad a_n > 0$	$a_n \ge a_{n+1}$ and $a_n \to 0$		$\|L - s_n\| < a_{n+1}$

Exercises 9.5

Which of the alternating series in Exercises 1–10 converge and which diverge? Give reasons for your answers.

1. $\sum_{n=1}^{\infty} (-1)^{n+1} \frac{1}{n^2}$

2. $\sum_{n=1}^{\infty} (-1)^{n+1} \frac{1}{n^{3/2}}$

3. $\sum_{n=1}^{\infty} (-1)^{n+1} \left(\frac{n}{10}\right)^n$

4. $\sum_{n=1}^{\infty} (-1)^{n+1} \frac{10^n}{n^{10}}$

5. $\sum_{n=2}^{\infty} (-1)^{n+1} \frac{1}{\ln n}$

6. $\sum_{n=1}^{\infty} (-1)^{n+1} \frac{\ln n}{n}$

7. $\sum_{n=2}^{\infty} (-1)^{n+1} \frac{\ln n}{\ln n^2}$

8. $\sum_{n=1}^{\infty} (-1)^{n} \ln\left(1 + \frac{1}{n}\right)$

9. $\sum_{n=1}^{\infty} (-1)^{n+1} \frac{\sqrt{n}+1}{n+1}$

10. $\sum_{n=1}^{\infty} (-1)^{n+1} \frac{3\sqrt{n+1}}{\sqrt{n}+1}$

Which of the series in Exercises 11–42 converge absolutely, which converge, and which diverge? Give reasons for your answers.

11. $\sum_{n=1}^{\infty} (-1)^{n+1} (0.1)^n$

12. $\sum_{n=1}^{\infty} (-1)^{n+1} \frac{(0.1)^n}{n}$

13. $\sum_{n=1}^{\infty} (-1)^{n} \frac{1}{\sqrt{n}}$

14. $\sum_{n=1}^{\infty} \frac{(-1)^n}{1+\sqrt{n}}$

15. $\sum_{n=1}^{\infty} (-1)^{n+1} \frac{n}{n^3+1}$

16. $\sum_{n=1}^{\infty} (-1)^{n+1} \frac{n!}{2^n}$

17. $\sum_{n=1}^{\infty} (-1)^{n} \frac{1}{n+3}$

18. $\sum_{n=1}^{\infty} (-1)^{n} \frac{\sin n}{n^2}$

19. $\sum_{n=1}^{\infty} (-1)^{n+1} \frac{3+n}{5+n}$

20. $\sum_{n=2}^{\infty} (-1)^{n} \frac{1}{\ln (n^3)}$

21. $\sum_{n=1}^{\infty} (-1)^{n+1} \frac{1+n}{n^2}$

22. $\sum_{n=1}^{\infty} \frac{(-2)^{n+1}}{n+5^n}$

23. $\sum_{n=1}^{\infty} (-1)^{n} n^2 (2/3)^n$

24. $\sum_{n=1}^{\infty} (-1)^{n+1} \left(\sqrt[n]{10}\right)$

25. $\sum_{n=1}^{\infty} (-1)^{n} \frac{\tan^{-1} n}{n^2+1}$

26. $\sum_{n=2}^{\infty} (-1)^{n+1} \frac{1}{n \ln n}$

27. $\sum_{n=1}^{\infty} (-1)^{n} \frac{n}{n+1}$

28. $\sum_{n=1}^{\infty} (-1)^{n} \frac{\ln n}{n - \ln n}$

29. $\sum_{n=1}^{\infty} \frac{(-100)^n}{n!}$

30. $\sum_{n=1}^{\infty} (-5)^{-n}$

31. $\sum_{n=1}^{\infty} \frac{(-1)^{n-1}}{n^2+2n+1}$

32. $\sum_{n=2}^{\infty} (-1)^{n} \left(\frac{\ln n}{\ln n^2}\right)^n$

33. $\sum_{n=1}^{\infty} \frac{\cos n\pi}{n\sqrt{n}}$

34. $\sum_{n=1}^{\infty} \frac{\cos n\pi}{n}$

35. $\sum_{n=1}^{\infty} \frac{(-1)^n (n+1)^n}{(2n)^n}$

36. $\sum_{n=1}^{\infty} \frac{(-1)^{n+1} (n!)^2}{(2n)!}$

37. $\sum_{n=1}^{\infty} (-1)^{n} \frac{(2n)!}{2^n n! n}$

38. $\sum_{n=1}^{\infty} (-1)^{n} \frac{(n!)^2 3^n}{(2n+1)!}$

39. $\sum_{n=1}^{\infty} (-1)^{n} \left(\sqrt{n+1} - \sqrt{n}\right)$

40. $\sum_{n=1}^{\infty} (-1)^{n} \left(\sqrt{n^2+n} - n\right)$

41. $\sum_{n=1}^{\infty} (-1)^{n} \operatorname{sech} n$

42. $\sum_{n=1}^{\infty} (-1)^{n} \operatorname{csch} n$

In Exercises 43–46, estimate the magnitude of the error involved in using the sum of the first four terms to approximate the sum of the entire series.

43. $\sum_{n=1}^{\infty} (-1)^{n+1} \frac{1}{n}$

44. $\sum_{n=1}^{\infty} (-1)^{n+1} \frac{1}{10^n}$

45. $\sum_{n=1}^{\infty} (-1)^{n+1} \frac{(0.01)^n}{n}$ As you will see in Section 9.8, the sum is ln (1.01).

46. $\frac{1}{1+t} = \sum_{n=0}^{\infty} (-1)^n t^n, \quad 0 < t < 1$

Approximate the sums in Exercises 47 and 48 with an error of magnitude less than 5×10^{-6}.

47. $\sum_{n=0}^{\infty} (-1)^{n} \frac{1}{(2n)!}$ As you will see in Section 9.7, the sum is cos 1, the cosine of 1 radian.

48. $\sum_{n=0}^{\infty} (-1)^{n} \frac{1}{n!}$ As you will see in Section 9.7, the sum is e^{-1}.

49. **a)** The series

$$\frac{1}{3} - \frac{1}{2} + \frac{1}{9} - \frac{1}{4} + \frac{1}{27} - \frac{1}{8} + \cdots + \frac{1}{3^n} - \frac{1}{2^n} + \cdots$$

does not meet one of the conditions of Theorem 8. Which one?

b) Find the sum of the series in (a).

50. The limit L of an alternating series that satisfies the conditions of Theorem 8 lies between the values of any two consecutive partial sums. This suggests using the average

$$\frac{s_n + s_{n+1}}{2} = s_n + \frac{1}{2}(-1)^{n+2} a_{n+1}$$

to estimate L. Compute

$$s_{20} + \frac{1}{2} \cdot \frac{1}{21}$$

as an approximation to the sum of the alternating harmonic series. The exact sum is $\ln 2 \approx 0.69315$.

51. *The Sign of the Remainder of an Alternating Series That Satisfies the Conditions of Theorem 8* Prove the assertion in Theorem 9 that whenever an alternating series satisfying the conditions of Theorem 8 is approximated with one of its partial sums, the remainder (sum of the unused terms) has the same sign as the first unused term. (*Hint:* Group the remainder's terms in consecutive pairs.)

52. Show that the sum of the first $2n$ terms of the series

$$1 - \frac{1}{2} + \frac{1}{2} - \frac{1}{3} + \frac{1}{3} - \frac{1}{4} + \frac{1}{4} - \frac{1}{5} + \frac{1}{5} - \frac{1}{6} + \cdots$$

is the same as the sum of the first n terms of the series

$$\frac{1}{1 \cdot 2} + \frac{1}{2 \cdot 3} + \frac{1}{3 \cdot 4} + \frac{1}{4 \cdot 5} + \frac{1}{5 \cdot 6} + \cdots.$$

Do these series converge? What is the sum of the first $2n + 1$ terms of the first series? If the series converge, what is their sum? Give reasons for your answers.

53. Which of the following statements are true and which are false? Give reasons for your answers.

a) Some alternating series converge and some do not.
b) Convergent series converge absolutely.
c) Conditionally convergent series never converge absolutely.
d) Series of positive terms never converge conditionally.

Writing for Your Own Knowledge

Answer the following questions in writing. Some answers will take only a sentence or two; others may require several paragraphs. Some explanations may also call for graphs or sketches.

1. What is an alternating series?
2. What does Leibniz's theorem say about the convergence of alternating series?
3. How can you sometimes estimate the error involved in approximating the sum of an alternating series with one of the series' partial sums?
4. What does it mean for $\sum_{n=1}^{\infty} a_n$ to be absolutely convergent? conditionally convergent?
5. How are convergence and absolute convergence related?
6. What tests are now available for determining the convergence and divergence of infinite series?

EXPLORER PROGRAM

Sequences and Series	Generates terms of one or two sequences and graphs them. You may define the sequences recursively or by giving formulas for their nth terms. Enables you to look for graphical and numerical evidence of convergence or divergence.

9.6 *Power Series*

Now that we can test infinite series for convergence we can study the infinite polynomials mentioned at the beginning of Section 9.2. We call these polynomials power series because they are defined as infinite series of powers of some variable, in our case x. Like polynomials, power series can be added, subtracted, multiplied, differentiated, and integrated to give new power series.

Power Series and Convergence

We begin with the formal definition.

DEFINITION

A **power series** is a series of the form

$$\sum_{n=0}^{\infty} c_n x^n = c_0 + c_1 x + c_2 x^2 + \cdots + c_n x^n + \cdots \qquad (1)$$

or

$$\sum_{n=0}^{\infty} c_n (x-a)^n = c_0 + c_1 (x-a) + c_2 (x-a)^2 + \cdots + c_n (x-a)^n + \cdots \qquad (2)$$

in which the **center** a and the **coefficients** $c_0, c_1, c_2, \ldots, c_n, \ldots$ are constants.

Equation (1) is the special case obtained by taking $a = 0$ in Eq. (2).

EXAMPLE 1 Taking all the coefficients to be 1 in Eq. (1) gives what we call the geometric power series

$$\sum_{n=0}^{\infty} x^n = 1 + x + x^2 + \cdots + x^n + \cdots.$$

This is the geometric series with first term 1 and ratio x. It converges to $1/(1-x)$ when $|x| < 1$. We express this fact by writing

$$\frac{1}{1-x} = 1 + x + x^2 + \cdots + x^n + \cdots, \qquad -1 < x < 1. \tag{3}$$

So far, we have used Eq. (3) as a formula for the sum of the series on the right. We now change the focus: We think of the partial sums of the series on the right as polynomials $P_n(x)$ that approximate the function on the left. For values of x near zero, we need take only a few terms of the series to get a good approximation. As we move toward $x = 1$, or -1, we must take more terms. Figure 9.14 shows the graphs of $f(x) = 1/(1-x)$, and the approximating polynomials $y_n = P_n(x)$ for $n = 0, 1, 2$, and 8.

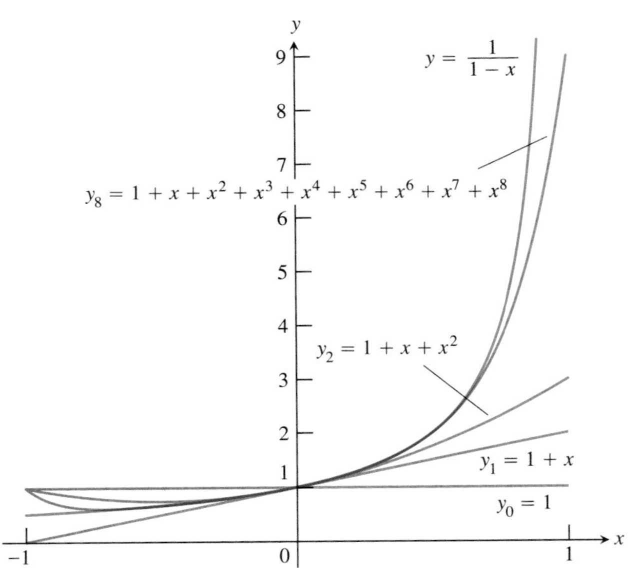

9.14 The graphs of $f(x) = 1/(1-x)$ and four of its polynomial approximations (Example 1).

EXAMPLE 2 The power series

$$1 - \frac{1}{2}(x-2) + \frac{1}{4}(x-2)^2 + \cdots + \left(-\frac{1}{2}\right)^n (x-2)^n + \cdots \tag{4}$$

matches Eq. (2) with $a = 2$, $c_0 = 1$, $c_1 = -1/2$, $c_2 = 1/4, \ldots, c_n = (-1/2)^n$. This is a geometric series with first term 1 and ratio $r = -\frac{x-2}{2}$. The series converges for $\left|\frac{x-2}{2}\right| < 1$ or $0 < x < 4$. The sum is

$$\frac{1}{1-r} = \frac{1}{1 + \frac{x-2}{2}} = \frac{2}{x},$$

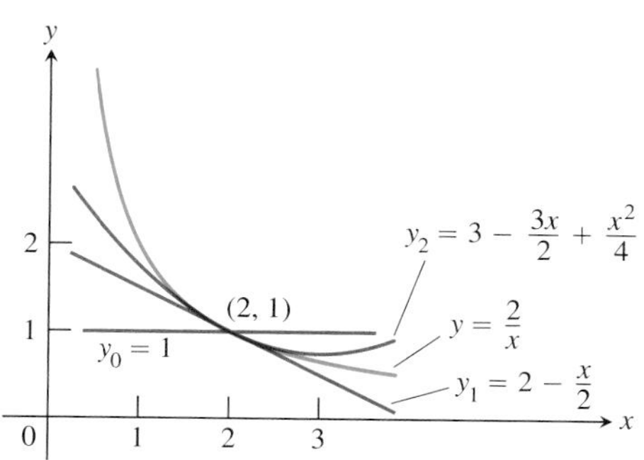

9.15 The graphs of $f(x) = 2/x$ and its first three polynomial approximations (Example 2).

so

$$\frac{2}{x} = 1 - \frac{(x-2)}{2} + \frac{(x-2)^2}{4} - \cdots + \left(-\frac{1}{2}\right)^n (x-2)^n + \cdots, \qquad 0 < x < 4.$$

Series (4) generates useful polynomial approximations of $f(x) = 2/x$ for values of x near 2:

$$P_0(x) = 1,$$

$$P_1(x) = 1 - \frac{1}{2}(x-2) = 2 - \frac{x}{2},$$

$$P_2(x) = 1 - \frac{1}{2}(x-2) + \frac{1}{4}(x-2)^2 = 3 - \frac{3x}{2} + \frac{x^2}{4},$$

and so on (Fig. 9.15).

EXAMPLE 3 For what values of x do the following power series converge?

a) $\displaystyle\sum_{n=1}^{\infty} (-1)^{n-1} \frac{x^n}{n} = x - \frac{x^2}{2} + \frac{x^3}{3} - \cdots$

b) $\displaystyle\sum_{n=1}^{\infty} (-1)^{n-1} \frac{x^{2n-1}}{2n-1} = x - \frac{x^3}{3} + \frac{x^5}{5} - \cdots$

c) $\displaystyle\sum_{n=0}^{\infty} \frac{x^n}{n!} = 1 + x + \frac{x^2}{2!} + \frac{x^3}{3!} + \cdots$

d) $\displaystyle\sum_{n=0}^{\infty} n!\, x^n = 1 + x + 2!\, x^2 + 3!\, x^3 + \cdots$

Solution Apply the Ratio Test to the series $\Sigma\, |u_n|$, where u_n is the nth term of the series in question.

a) $\displaystyle\left|\frac{u_{n+1}}{u_n}\right| = \frac{n}{n+1}|x| \to |x|$. The series converges absolutely for $|x| < 1$. It diverges if $|x| > 1$ because the nth term does not converge to zero. At $x = 1$, we get the alternating harmonic series $1 - 1/2 + 1/3 - 1/4 + \cdots$, which converges. At $x = -1$ we get $-1 - 1/2 - 1/3 - 1/4 - \cdots$, which is the negative of the harmonic series; it diverges. Series (a) converges for $-1 < x \le 1$ and diverges elsewhere.

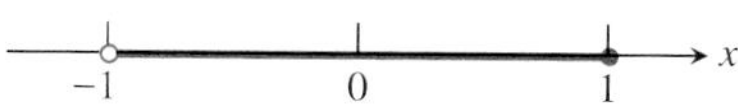

b) $\displaystyle\left|\frac{u_{n+1}}{u_n}\right| = \frac{2n-1}{2n+1}x^2 \to x^2$. The series converges absolutely for $x^2 < 1$. It diverges for $x^2 > 1$ because the nth term does not converge to zero. At $x = 1$ the series becomes $1 - 1/3 + 1/5 - 1/7 + \cdots$, which converges by the Alternating Series Theorem. It also converges at $x = -1$ because it again is an alternating series that satisfies the conditions for convergence. The value at $x = -1$ is the negative of the value at $x = 1$. Series (b) converges for $-1 \le x \le 1$ and diverges elsewhere.

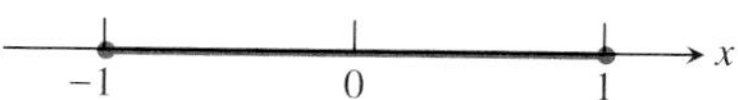

c) $\left|\frac{u_{n+1}}{u_n}\right| = \left|\frac{x^{n+1}}{(n+1)!} \cdot \frac{n!}{x^n}\right| = \frac{|x|}{n+1} \to 0$ for every x. The series converges absolutely for all x.

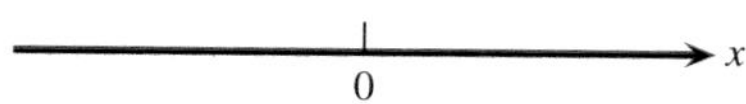

d) $\left|\frac{u_{n+1}}{u_n}\right| = \left|\frac{(n+1)!x^{n+1}}{n!x^n}\right| = (n+1)|x| \to \infty$ unless $x = 0$. The series diverges for all values of x except $x = 0$.

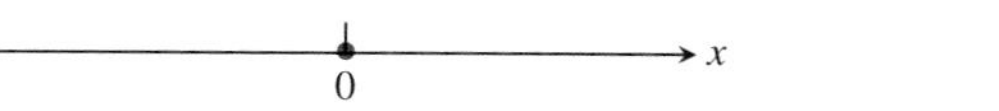

Example 3 illustrates how we usually test a power series for convergence, and the kinds of results we'll get.

How to Test a Power Series for Convergence

STEP 1 Use the Ratio Test (or nth Root Test) to find the interval where the series converges absolutely. Ordinarily, this is an open interval

$$|x - a| < h \quad \text{or} \quad a - h < x < a + h.$$

In some instances, as in Example 3(c), the series converges for all values of x. These instances are not uncommon. In rare cases, the series may converge only at a single point, as in Example 3(d).

STEP 2: If the interval of absolute convergence is finite, test for convergence or divergence at each of the two endpoints, as in Example 2 and Examples 3(a) and (b). Neither the Ratio Test nor the nth-Root Test helps at these points. Use a Comparison Test, the Integral Test, or the Alternating Series Theorem.

STEP 3: If the interval of absolute convergence is $a - h < x < a + h$, the series diverges (it does not even converge conditionally) for $|x - a| > h$, because the nth term does not approach zero for those values of x.

To simplify the notation, the next theorem deals with the convergence of series of the form $\Sigma\, a_n x^n$. For series of the form $\Sigma\, a_n(x - a)^n$ we can replace $x - a$ by x' and apply the results to the series $\Sigma\, a_n\,(x')^n$.

THEOREM 11

The Convergence Theorem for Power Series

If

$$\sum_{n=0}^{\infty} a_n x^n = a_0 + a_1 x + a_2 x^2 + \cdots \qquad (5)$$

converges for $x = c \neq 0$, then it converges absolutely for all $|x| < |c|$. If the series diverges for $x = d$, then it diverges for all $|x| > |d|$.

Proof Suppose the series

$$\sum_{n=0}^{\infty} a_n c^n \tag{6}$$

converges. Then $\lim_{n\to\infty} a_n c^n = 0$. Hence, there is an integer N such that $|a_n c^n| < 1$ for all $n \geq N$. That is,

$$|a_n| < \frac{1}{|c|^n} \qquad \text{for } n \geq N. \tag{7}$$

Now take any x such that $|x| < |c|$ and consider

$$|a_0| + |a_1 x| + \cdots + |a_{N-1} x^{N-1}| + |a_N x^N| + |a_{N+1} x^{N+1}| + \cdots .$$

There are only a finite number of terms prior to $|a_N x^N|$, and their sum is finite. Starting with $|a_N x^N|$ and beyond, the terms are less than

$$\left|\frac{x}{c}\right|^N + \left|\frac{x}{c}\right|^{N+1} + \left|\frac{x}{c}\right|^{N+2} + \cdots \tag{8}$$

because of (7). But the series in (8) is a geometric series with ratio $r = |x/c|$, which is less than 1, since $|x| < |c|$. Hence the series (8) converges, so the original series (6) converges absolutely. This proves the first half of the theorem.

The second half of the theorem follows from the first. If the series diverges at $x = d$ and converges at a value x_0 with $|x_0| > |d|$, we may take $c = x_0$ in the first half of the theorem and conclude that the series converges absolutely at d. But the series cannot converge absolutely and diverge at one and the same time. Hence, if it diverges at d, it diverges for all $|x| > |d|$. ∎

The Radius and Interval of Convergence

The examples we have looked at, and the theorem we just proved, lead to the conclusion that a power series behaves in one of the following three ways.

Possible Behavior of $\Sigma\, c_n (x - a)^n$

1. There is a positive number h such that the series diverges for $|x - a| > h$ but converges absolutely for $|x - a| < h$. The series may or may not converge at either of the endpoints $x = a - h$ and $x = a + h$.
2. The series converges absolutely for every x ($h = \infty$).
3. The series converges at $x = a$ and diverges elsewhere ($h = 0$).

In case 1, the set of points at which the series converges is a finite interval, called the **interval of convergence.** We know from past examples that the interval may be open, half-open, or closed, depending on the particular series. But no matter which kind of interval it is, h is called the **radius of convergence** of the series, and $a + h$ is the least upper bound of the set of points at which the series converges. The convergence is absolute at every point in the interior of the interval. If a power series converges absolutely for all values of x, we say that its radius of convergence is infinite. If it converges only at $x = a$, the radius of convergence is zero.

Term-by-Term Differentiation of Power Series

A theorem from advanced calculus says that a power series can be differentiated term by term at each interior point of its interval of convergence.

A Word of Caution

Term-by-term differentiation might not work for other kinds of series. For example, the trigonometric series

$$\sum_{n=1}^{\infty} \frac{\sin(n!x)}{n^2}$$

converges for all x. But if we differentiate term by term we get the series

$$\sum_{n=1}^{\infty} \frac{n!\cos(n!x)}{n^2},$$

which diverges for all x.

THEOREM 12

The Term-by-Term Differentiation Theorem

If $\Sigma\, c_n(x-a)^n$ converges for $a-h<x<a+h$ for some $h>0$, it defines a function f:

$$f(x)=\sum_{n=0}^{\infty} c_n(x-a)^n, \qquad a-h<x<a+h.$$

Such a function f has derivatives of all orders inside the interval of convergence. We can obtain the derivatives by differentiating the original series term by term:

$$f'(x)=\sum_{n=0}^{\infty} n\,c_n(x-a)^{n-1},$$

$$f''(x)=\sum_{n=0}^{\infty} n(n-1)\,c_n(x-a)^{n-2},$$

and so on. Each of these derived series converges at every interior point of the interval of convergence of the original series.

EXAMPLE 4 Identify the function

$$f(x)=\sum_{n=0}^{\infty}\frac{(-1)^n x^{2n+1}}{2n+1}=x-\frac{x^3}{3}+\frac{x^5}{5}-\cdots, \qquad -1\le x\le 1.$$

Solution We differentiate the original series term by term and get

$$f'(x)=\sum_{n=0}^{\infty}\frac{(2n+1)(-1)^n x^{2n}}{2n+1}=\sum_{n=0}^{\infty}(-1)^n x^{2n}=1-x^2+x^4-x^6+\cdots,$$

converging for $-1<x<1$.

This is a geometric series with first term 1 and ratio $-x^2$, so

$$f'(x)=\frac{1}{1-(-x^2)}=\frac{1}{1+x^2}.$$

We can now integrate $f'(x)=1/(1+x^2)$ to get

$$\int f'(x)\,dx=\int\frac{dx}{1+x^2}=\tan^{-1}x+C.$$

The series for $f(x)$ is zero when $x=0$, so $C=0$. Hence

$$f(x)=x-\frac{x^3}{3}+\frac{x^5}{5}-\frac{x^7}{7}+\cdots=\tan^{-1}x, \qquad -1\le x\le 1. \tag{9}$$

The function is the restriction of $\tan^{-1}x$ to the interval $[-1, 1]$.

Notice that the original series in Example 4 converges at both endpoints of the original interval of convergence, but the differentiated series converges only inside the interval. This is all the theorem guarantees.

Term-by-Term Integration of Power Series

Another advanced theorem states that a power series can be integrated term by term throughout its interval of convergence.

THEOREM 13

The Term-by-Term Integration Theorem

If $\Sigma\, c_n\,(x-a)^n$ converges when $a-h<x<a+h$ for some $h>0$ and

$f(x)=\sum_{n=0}^{\infty} c_n\,(x-a)^n$ for $a-h<x<a+h$, then the infinite series $\sum_{n=0}^{\infty} c_n \dfrac{(x-a)^{n+1}}{n+1}$ converges for $a-h<x<a+h$ and

$$\int f(x)\,dx=\sum_{n=0}^{\infty} c_n \frac{(x-a)^{n+1}}{n+1}+C \qquad \text{for} \qquad a-h<x<a+h.$$

EXAMPLE 5 The series

$$\frac{1}{1+t}=1-t+t^2-t^3\cdots$$

converges on the open interval $-1<t<1$. Therefore,

$$\begin{aligned}\ln(1+x)&=\int_0^x \frac{1}{1+t}\,dt=t-\frac{t^2}{2}+\frac{t^3}{3}-\frac{t^4}{4}+\cdots\Big]_0^x\\ &=x-\frac{x^2}{2}+\frac{x^3}{3}-\frac{x^4}{4}+\cdots, \qquad -1<x<1.\end{aligned}$$

As we know, the latter series also converges at $x=1$, but that was not guaranteed by the theorem.

Multiplication of Power Series

Still another advanced theorem states that absolutely converging power series can be multiplied term by term.

THEOREM 14

The Series Multiplication Theorem for Power Series

If both $\Sigma\, a_n\, x^n$ and $\Sigma\, b_n\, x^n$ converge absolutely for $|x|<h$, and

$$c_n=a_0\,b_n+a_1\,b_{n-1}+a_2\,b_{n-2}+\cdots+a_{n-1}\,b_1+a_n\,b_0=\sum_{k=0}^{n} a_k b_{n-k}, \tag{10}$$

then the series $\Sigma\, c_n\, x^n$ converges absolutely for $|x|<h$, and

$$(\Sigma\, a_n\, x^n)\cdot(\Sigma\, b_n\, x^n)=\Sigma\, c_n\, x^n. \tag{11}$$

EXAMPLE 6 Multiply the geometric series

$$\sum_{n=0}^{\infty} x^n = 1 + x + x^2 + \cdots + x^n + \cdots = \frac{1}{1-x}, \qquad \text{for } |x| < 1,$$

by itself to get the power series for $1/(1-x)^2$, for $|x| < 1$.

Solution Let

$$A(x) = \sum_{n=0}^{\infty} a_n x^n = 1 + x + x^2 + \cdots + x^n + \cdots = 1/(1-x)$$

$$B(x) = \sum_{n=0}^{\infty} b_n x^n = 1 + x + x^2 + \cdots + x^n + \cdots = 1/(1-x)$$

and

$$c_n = \underbrace{a_0 b_n + a_1 b_{n-1} + \cdots + a_k b_{n-k} + \cdots + a_n b_0}_{n+1 \text{ terms}}$$

$$= \underbrace{1 + 1 + \cdots + 1}_{n+1 \text{ ones}} = n + 1.$$

Then, by the series multiplication theorem,

$$A(x) \cdot B(x) = \sum_{n=0}^{\infty} c_n x^n = \sum_{n=0}^{\infty} (n+1)\, x^n$$

$$= 1 + 2x + 3x^2 + 4x^3 + \cdots + (n+1)\, x^n + \cdots$$

is the series for $1/(1-x)^2$. The series all converge absolutely for $|x| < 1$.

Exercises 9.6

Each of Exercises 1–32 gives a formula for the nth term of a series. (a) Find the series' radius and interval of convergence. For what values of x does the series converge (b) absolutely; (c) conditionally?

1. x^n **2.** $(x+5)^n$ **3.** $(-1)^n (4x+1)^n$

4. $\dfrac{(3x-2)^n}{n}$ **5.** $\dfrac{(x-2)^n}{10^n}$ **6.** $(2x)^n$

7. $\dfrac{nx^n}{n+2}$ **8.** $\dfrac{(-1)^n (x+2)^n}{n}$ **9.** $\dfrac{x^n}{n\sqrt{n}\,3^n}$

10. $\dfrac{(x-1)^n}{\sqrt{n}}$ **11.** $\dfrac{(-1)^n x^n}{n!}$ **12.** $\dfrac{3^n x^n}{n!}$

13. $\dfrac{x^{2n+1}}{n!}$ **14.** $\dfrac{(2x+3)^{2n+1}}{n!}$ **15.** $\dfrac{x^n}{\sqrt{n^2+3}}$

16. $\dfrac{(-1)^n x^n}{\sqrt{n^2+3}}$ **17.** $\dfrac{n(x+3)^n}{5^n}$ **18.** $\dfrac{nx^n}{4^n(n^2+1)}$

19. $\dfrac{\sqrt{n}\, x^n}{3^n}$ **20.** $\sqrt[n]{n}\,(2x+5)^n$ **21.** $\left(1+\dfrac{1}{n}\right)^n x^n$

22. $(\ln n)x^n$ **23.** $n^n x^n$ **24.** $n!(x-4)^n$

25. $\dfrac{(-1)^{n+1}(x+2)^n}{n2^n}$ **26.** $(-2)^n (n+1)(x-1)^n$

27. $\dfrac{x^n}{n(\ln n)^2}$ Get the information you need about $\sum 1/(n(\ln n)^2)$ from Section 9.3, Exercise 61.

28. $\dfrac{x^n}{n \ln n}$ Get the information you need about $\sum 1/(n \ln n)$ from Section 9.3, Exercise 60.

29. $\dfrac{(4x-5)^{2n+1}}{n^{3/2}}$ **30.** $\dfrac{(3x+1)^{n+1}}{2n+2}$

31. $\dfrac{(x+\pi)^n}{\sqrt{n}}$ **32.** $\dfrac{\left(x-\sqrt{2}\right)^{2n+1}}{2^n}$

In Exercises 33–38, find the series' interval of convergence and, within this interval, the sum of the series as a function of x.

33. $\displaystyle\sum_{n=0}^{\infty} \frac{(x-1)^{2n}}{4^n}$ **34.** $\displaystyle\sum_{n=0}^{\infty} \frac{(x+1)^{2n}}{9^n}$ **35.** $\displaystyle\sum_{n=0}^{\infty} \left(\frac{\sqrt{x}}{2}-1\right)^n$

36. $\displaystyle\sum_{n=0}^{\infty} (\ln x)^n$ **37.** $\displaystyle\sum_{n=0}^{\infty} \left(\frac{x^2+1}{3}\right)^n$ **38.** $\displaystyle\sum_{n=0}^{\infty} \left(\frac{x^2-1}{2}\right)^n$

39. For what values of x does the series

$$1 - \frac{1}{2}(x-3) + \frac{1}{4}(x-3)^2 + \cdots + \left(-\frac{1}{2}\right)^n (x-3)^n + \cdots$$

converge? What is its sum? What series do you get if you differentiate the given series term by term? For what values of x does the new series converge? What is its sum?

40. If you integrate the series in Exercise 39 term by term, what new series do you get? For what values of x does the new series converge and what is another name for its sum?

41. The series for $\tan x$,

$$\tan x = x + \frac{x^3}{3} + \frac{2x^5}{15} + \frac{17x^7}{315} + \frac{62x^9}{2835} + \cdots,$$

converges for $-\pi/2 < x < \pi/2$.

a) Find the first five terms of the series for $\ln|\sec x|$. For what values of x should the series converge?

b) Find the first five terms of the series for $\sec^2 x$. For what values of x should this series converge?

c) Check your result in (b) by squaring the series given for $\sec x$ in Exercise 42.

42. The series for $\sec x$,

$$\sec x = 1 + \frac{x^2}{2} + \frac{5}{24}x^4 + \frac{61}{720}x^6 + \frac{277}{8064}x^8 + \cdots,$$

converges for $-\pi/2 < x < \pi/2$.

a) Find the first five terms of a power series for the function $\ln|\sec x + \tan x|$. For what values of x should the series converge?

b) Find the first four terms of a series for $\sec x \tan x$. For what values of x should the series converge?

c) Check your result in (b) by multiplying the series for $\sec x$ by the series given for $\tan x$ in Exercise 41.

43. *Uniqueness of Convergent Power Series*

a) Show that if two power series $\sum_{n=0}^{\infty} a_n x^n$ and $\sum_{n=0}^{\infty} b_n x^n$ are convergent and equal for all values of x in an open interval $(-c, c)$, then $a_n = b_n$ for every n. (*Hint:* Let $f(x) = \sum_{n=0}^{\infty} a_n x^n = \sum_{n=0}^{\infty} b_n x^n$. Differentiate term by term to show that a_n and b_n both equal $f^{(n)}(0)/(n!)$.)

b) Show that if $\sum_{n=0}^{\infty} a_n x^n = 0$ for all x in an open interval $(-c, c)$, then $a_n = 0$ for every n.

44. *The Sum of the Series $\sum_{n=0}^{\infty} (n^2/2^n)$.* To find the sum of this series, express $1/(1-x)$ as a geometric series, differentiate both sides of the resulting equation with respect to x, multiply both sides of the result by x, differentiate again, multiply by x again, and set x equal to $1/2$. What do you get? (*Source:* David E. Dobbs' letter to the editor, *Illinois Mathematics Teacher,* Vol. 33, Issue 4, 1982, p. 27.)

45. *Convergence at Endpoints.* Show by examples that the convergence of a power series at an endpoint of its interval of convergence may be either conditional or absolute.

46. Make up a power series whose interval of convergence is

a) $(-3, 3)$ **b)** $(-2, 0)$ **c)** $(1, 5)$.

47. Differentiate the series

$$f(x) = \sum_{n=0}^{\infty} \frac{x^n}{n!} = 1 + x + \frac{x^2}{2!} + \frac{x^3}{3!} + \cdots$$

from Example 3(c) term by term. What must f be? For what values of x does the differentiated series converge? Give reasons for your answers.

48. Integrate the series

$$g(x) = \sum_{n=0}^{\infty} (-1)^n x^n = 1 - x + x^2 - x^3 + \cdots$$

term by term. By what other name is this integral known? For what values of x does the integrated series converge? Give reasons for your answers.

Writing for Your Own Knowledge

Answer the following questions in writing. Some answers will take only a sentence or two; others may require several paragraphs. Some explanations may also call for graphs or sketches.

1. What is a power series?
2. How do you test power series for convergence? What kinds of results are possible?
3. What are the basic facts about

   a) term-by-term differentiation of power series?
   b) term-by-term integration of power series?
   c) multiplication of power series?

9.7 *Taylor and Maclaurin Series*

This section shows how to find power series called Taylor series and how to control the errors involved in using the partial sums of these series to approximate the functions the series represent. As a special case, we will see how to control the errors in linearizations. Taylor series enable us to extend the domains of functions to include complex numbers. We will go into this briefly at the end of the section.

DEFINITIONS

Let f be a function with derivatives of all orders throughout some interval containing a as an interior point. Then the **Taylor series generated by f at a is**

$$\sum_{k=0}^{\infty} \frac{f^{(k)}(a)}{k!}(x-a)^k = f(a) + f'(a)(x-a) + \frac{f''(a)}{2!}(x-a)^2 + \cdots + \frac{f^{(n)}(a)}{n!}(x-a)^n + \cdots. \tag{1}$$

The **Maclaurin series generated by f** is

$$\sum_{k=0}^{\infty} \frac{f^{(k)}(0)}{k!}x^k = f(0) + f'(0)x + \frac{f''(0)}{2!}x^2 + \cdots + \frac{f^{(n)}(0)}{n!}x^n + \cdots, \tag{2}$$

the Taylor series generated by f at $a = 0$.

Once we have found the Taylor series generated by a function f at a particular a, we can apply the usual tests to find where the series converges: usually in some interval $(a - h, a + h)$ or for all x. When the series does converge, we ask, "Does it converge to $f(x)$?" For most of the functions we are interested in, we are not yet equipped to answer this question. For the function $f(x) = 1/x$, however, we can answer the question, as the next example shows.

EXAMPLE 1 Find the Taylor series generated by $f(x) = 1/x$ at $a = 2$. Where, if anywhere, does the series converge to $1/x$?

Solution We need to find $f(2)$, $f'(2)$, $f''(2)$, ... Taking derivatives we get

$$\begin{aligned}
f(x) &= x^{-1}, & f(2) &= 2^{-1} = \frac{1}{2}, \\
f'(x) &= -x^{-2}, & f'(2) &= -\frac{1}{2^2}, \\
f''(x) &= 2!\,x^{-3}, & \frac{f''(2)}{2!} &= 2^{-3} = \frac{1}{2^3}, \\
f'''(x) &= -3!\,x^{-4}, & \frac{f'''(2)}{3!} &= -\frac{1}{2^4}, \\
&\ \vdots & &\ \vdots \\
f^{(n)}(x) &= (-1)^n n!\,x^{-(n+1)}, & \frac{f^{(n)}(2)}{n!} &= \frac{(-1)^n}{2^{n+1}}.
\end{aligned}$$

The Taylor series is

$$\begin{aligned}
f(2) + f'(2)(x-2) &+ \frac{f''(2)}{2!}(x-2)^2 + \frac{f'''(2)}{3!}(x-2)^3 + \cdots + \frac{f^{(n)}(2)}{n!}(x-2)^n + \cdots \\
&= \frac{1}{2} - \frac{(x-2)}{2^2} + \frac{(x-2)^2}{2^3} - \cdots + (-1)^n\frac{(x-2)^n}{2^{n+1}} + \cdots.
\end{aligned}$$

This is a geometric series with first term 1/2 and ratio $r = -(x-2)/2$. It converges absolutely for $|x-2| < 2$ and its sum is

$$\frac{1/2}{1+(x-2)/2} = \frac{1}{2+(x-2)} = \frac{1}{x}.$$

In this example the Taylor series generated by $f(x) = 1/x$ at $a = 2$ converges to $1/x$ for $|x-2| < 2$ or $0 < x < 4$.

Taylor Polynomials

The linearization of a differentiable function f at a point a is the polynomial

$$P_1(x) = f(a) + f'(a)(x-a).$$

If f has derivatives of higher order at a, then it has higher order polynomial approximations as well, one for each available derivative. These polynomials are called the Taylor polynomials of f.

We speak of a Taylor polynomial of *order n* rather than *degree n* because $f^{(n)}(a)$ may be zero. The first two Taylor polynomials of $\cos x$ at $x = 0$, for example, are $P_0(x) = 1$ and $P_1(x) = 1$. The first-order polynomial has degree zero, not one.

DEFINITION

Let f be a function with derivatives of order k for $k = 1, 2, \ldots, N$ in some interval containing a as an interior point. Then for any integer n from 0 through N, the **Taylor polynomial of order n** generated by f at a is the polynomial

$$P_n(x) = f(a) + f'(a)(x-a) + \frac{f''(a)}{2!}(x-a)^2 + \cdots + \frac{f^{(k)}(a)}{k!}(x-a)^k + \cdots + \frac{f^{(n)}(a)}{n!}(x-a)^n. \quad (3)$$

Special Property of Taylor Polynomials

What is so special about Taylor polynomials? We answer by looking for polynomials whose values at $x = a$ are equal to $f(a)$ and whose derivatives at $x = a$ are $f'(a)$, $f''(a)$, and so on. With that object in mind, we start with a polynomial of order n in powers of $(x-a)$ with undetermined coefficients $c_0, c_1, c_2, \ldots, c_n$:

$$P(x) = c_0 + c_1(x-a) + c_2(x-a)^2 + c_3(x-a)^3 + \cdots + c_n(x-a)^n. \quad (4)$$

Its derivatives of order $1, 2, \ldots, n$ are

$$\begin{aligned}
P'(x) &= c_1 + 2c_2(x-a) + 3c_3(x-a)^2 + \cdots + nc_n(x-a)^{n-1} \\
P''(x) &= 2c_2 + (3)(2)c_3(x-a) + \cdots + n(n-1)c_n(x-a)^{n-2} \\
P'''(x) &= (3!)c_3 + \cdots + n(n-1)(n-2)c_n(x-a)^{n-3} \\
&\vdots \\
P^{(n)}(x) &= (n!)c_n
\end{aligned}$$

When we substitute $x = a$, the terms with $(x-a)$ become 0. We also want $P(a) = f(a)$, $P'(a) = f'(a)$, $P''(a) = f''(a)$, . . . , $P^{(n)}(a) = f^{(n)}(a)$. This leads to

$$P(a) = f(a) = c_0, \qquad P'(a) = f'(a) = c_1,$$
$$P''(a) = f''(a) = (2!)c_2, \qquad P'''(a) = f'''(a) = (3!)c_3,$$
$$\vdots$$
$$P^{(n)}(a) = f^{(n)}(a) = (n!)c_n.$$

From these equations we see that

$$c_0 = f(a), \quad c_1 = f'(a), \quad c_2 = \frac{f''(a)}{2!}, \quad c_3 = \frac{f'''(a)}{3!}, \quad \ldots, \quad c_n = \frac{f^{(n)}(a)}{n!}.$$

Substituting these values for $c_0, c_1, \ldots, c_n$ in Eq. (4) gives the Taylor polynomial $P_n(x)$ in Eq. (3). The special property of the Taylor polynomials is this:

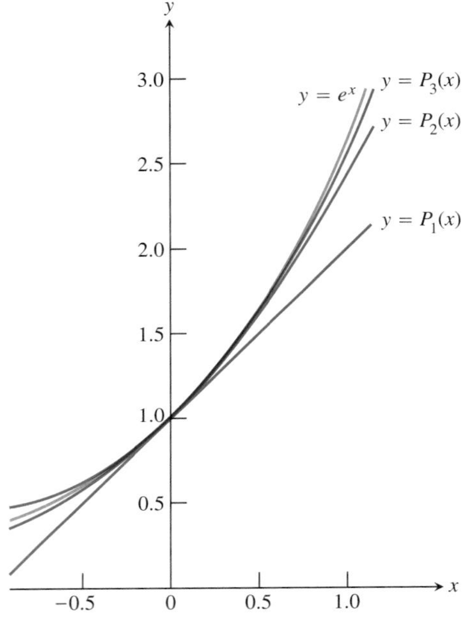

9.16 The graph of $f(x) = e^x$ and its Taylor polynomials $P_1(x) = 1 + x$, $P_2(x) = 1 + x + (x^2/2!)$, and $P_3(x) = 1 + x + (x^2/2!) + (x^3/3!)$. Notice the close agreement near the center $x = 0$.

The Taylor polynomial of order n and its first n derivatives have the same values that f and its first n derivatives have at $x = a$.

A function with derivatives of all orders at $x = a$ generates Taylor polynomials of all orders at $x = a$.

EXAMPLE 2 Find the Taylor polynomials generated by $f(x) = e^x$ at $a = 0$.

Solution Expressed in terms of x, the given function and its derivatives are

$$f(x) = e^x, \qquad f'(x) = e^x, \qquad \ldots, \qquad f^{(n)}(x) = e^x,$$

so

$$f(0) = e^0 = 1, \qquad f'(0) = 1, \qquad \ldots, \qquad f^{(n)}(0) = 1,$$

and

$$P_n(x) = 1 + x + \frac{x^2}{2!} + \frac{x^3}{3!} + \cdots + \frac{x^{(n)}}{n!}.$$

See Fig. 9.16.

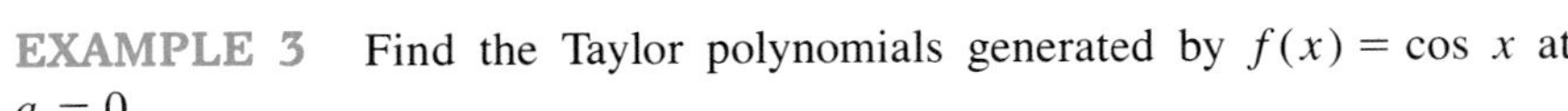

EXAMPLE 3 Find the Taylor polynomials generated by $f(x) = \cos x$ at $a = 0$.

Solution The cosine and its derivatives are

$$f(x) = \cos x, \qquad f'(x) = -\sin x,$$
$$f''(x) = -\cos x, \qquad f^{(3)}(x) = \sin x,$$
$$\vdots \qquad\qquad \vdots$$
$$f^{(2n)}(x) = (-1)^n \cos x, \qquad f^{(2n+1)}(x) = (-1)^{n+1} \sin x.$$

When $x = 0$, the cosines are 1 and the sines are 0, so

$$f^{(2n)}(0) = (-1)^n, \qquad f^{(2n+1)}(0) = 0.$$

Notice that the Taylor polynomials of orders $2n$ and $2n + 1$ are identical:

$$P_{2n}(x) = P_{2n+1}(x) = 1 - \frac{x^2}{2!} + \frac{x^4}{4!} - \cdots + (-1)^n \frac{x^{2n}}{(2n)!}.$$

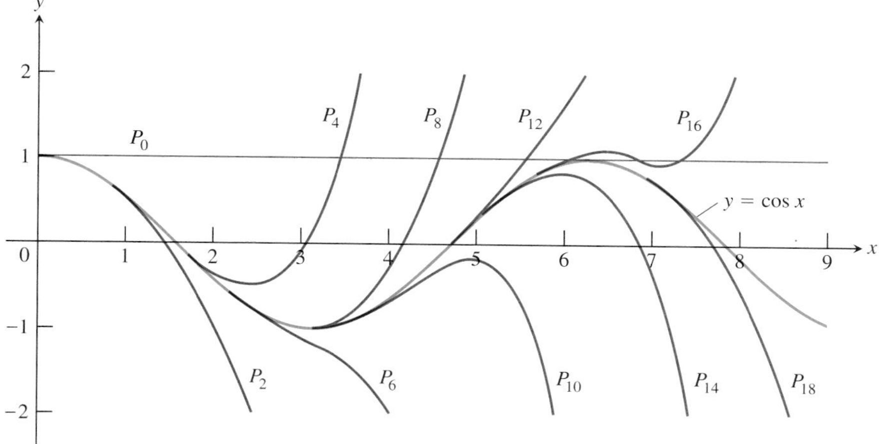

9.17 The polynomials

$$P_{2n}(x) = \sum_{k=0}^{n} [(-1)^k x^{2k}/(2k)!]$$

converge to $\cos x$ as $n \to \infty$. Notice how we can deduce the behavior of $\cos x$ arbitrarily far away solely from knowing the values of the cosine and its derivatives at $a = 0$.

Figure 9.17 shows how well these polynomials approximate $y = \cos x$ near $x = 0$. Only the right-hand portions of the graphs are shown because the graphs are symmetric about the y-axis.

Taylor's Theorem with Remainder

The preceding examples involved Taylor polynomials of order n for $n = 0, 1, 2, \ldots$. As $n \to \infty$, the Taylor polynomials become the partial sums of the Taylor series generated by f at a. The next theorem helps us find out whether the series actually converges to f.

THEOREM 15

Taylor's Theorem

If f and its first n derivatives $f', f'', \ldots, f^{(n)}$ are continuous on $[a, b]$ or on $[b, a]$, and $f^{(n)}$ is differentiable on (a, b) or on (b, a), then there exists a number c between a and b such that

$$f(b) = f(a) + f'(a)(b - a) + \frac{f''(a)}{2!}(b - a)^2 + \cdots + \frac{f^{(n)}(a)}{n!}(b - a)^n + \frac{f^{(n+1)}(c)}{(n+1)!}(b - a)^{n+1}.$$

We prove the theorem assuming $a < b$. The proof for $a > b$ is nearly the same.

Proof (for $a < b$) The Taylor polynomial

$$P_n(x) = f(a) + f'(a)(x - a) + \frac{f''(a)}{2!}(x - a)^2 + \cdots + \frac{f^{(n)}(a)}{n!}(x - a)^n$$

and its first n derivatives match the function f and its first n derivatives at $x = a$. We do not disturb that matching if we add another term of the form $K(x - a)^{n+1}$, where K is any constant, because such a term and its first n

derivatives are all equal to zero at $x = a$. The new function

$$\phi_n(x) = P_n(x) + K(x - a)^{n+1}$$

and its first n derivatives still agree with f and its first n derivatives at $x = a$.

We now choose the particular value of K that makes the curve $y = \phi_n(x)$ agree with the original curve $y = f(x)$ at $x = b$. In symbols,

$$f(b) = P_n(b) + K(b - a)^{n+1}, \qquad \text{or} \qquad K = \frac{f(b) - P_n(b)}{(b - a)^{n+1}}. \tag{5}$$

With K defined by Eq. (5), the function

$$F(x) = f(x) - \phi_n(x) \tag{6}$$

measures the difference between the original function f and the approximating function ϕ_n for each x in $[a, b]$.

We now use Rolle's theorem. First, because $F(a) = F(b) = 0$ and both F and F' are continuous on $[a, b]$, we know that

$$F'(c_1) = 0 \qquad \text{for some } c_1 \text{ in } (a, b).$$

Next, because $F'(a) = F'(c_1) = 0$ and both F' and F'' are continuous on $[a, c_1]$, we know that

$$F''(c_2) = 0 \qquad \text{for some } c_2 \text{ in } (a, c_1).$$

Rolle's theorem, applied successively to F'', F''', . . . , $F^{(n-1)}$ implies the existence of

$$\begin{aligned} &c_3 \text{ in } (a, c_2) && \text{such that } F'''(c_3) = 0, \\ &c_4 \text{ in } (a, c_3) && \text{such that } F^{(4)}(c_4) = 0, \\ &\quad\vdots && \\ &c_n \text{ in } (a, c_{n-1}) && \text{such that } F^{(n)}(c_n) = 0. \end{aligned}$$

Finally, because $F^{(n)}$ is continuous on $[a, c_n]$ and differentiable on (a, c_n), and $F^{(n)}(a) = F^{(n)}(c_n) = 0$, Rolle's theorem implies that there is a number c_{n+1} in (a, c_n) such that

$$F^{(n+1)}(c_{n+1}) = 0. \tag{7}$$

If we differentiate $F(x) = f(x) - P_n(x) - K(x - a)^{n+1}$ a total of $n + 1$ times, we get

$$F^{(n+1)}(x) = f^{(n+1)}(x) - 0 - (n + 1)!\,K. \tag{8}$$

Equations (7) and (8) together give

$$K = \frac{f^{(n+1)}(c)}{(n + 1)!} \qquad \text{for some number } c = c_{n+1} \text{ in } (a, b). \tag{9}$$

Equations (5) and (9) give

$$f(b) = P_n(b) + \frac{f^{(n+1)}(c)}{(n + 1)!}(b - a)^{n+1}.$$

This concludes the proof. ▬

When we apply Taylor's theorem, we usually want to hold a fixed and treat b as an independent variable. Taylor's formula is easier to use in circumstances like these if we change b to x. Here is how the theorem reads with this change.

Taylor's Formula

If f has derivatives of all orders in an open interval I containing a, then for each positive integer n and for each x in I,

$$f(x) = f(a) + f'(a)(x-a) + \frac{f''(a)}{2!}(x-a)^2 + \cdots + \frac{f^{(n)}(a)}{n!}(x-a)^n + R_n(x), \tag{10}$$

where

$$R_n(x) = \frac{f^{(n+1)}(c)}{(n+1)!}(x-a)^{n+1} \quad \text{for some } c \text{ between } a \text{ and } x. \tag{11}$$

When we state Taylor's theorem this way, it says that for each x in I,

$$f(x) = P_n(x) + R_n(x). \tag{12}$$

Pause for a moment to think about how remarkable this equation is. For any value of n we want, the equation gives both a polynomial approximation of f of that order and a formula for the error involved in using that approximation over the interval I.

Equation (10) is called **Taylor's formula.** The function $R_n(x)$ is called the **remainder of order n** or the **error term** for the approximation of f by $P_n(x)$ over I. If $R_n(x) \to 0$ as $n \to \infty$ for all x in I, we say that the Taylor series generated by f at $x = a$ **converges** to f on I and we write

$$f(x) = \sum_{k=0}^{\infty} \frac{f^{(k)}(a)}{k!}(x-a)^k. \tag{13}$$

EXAMPLE 4 *The Maclaurin Series for e^x.* Show that the Taylor series generated by $f(x) = e^x$ at $x = 0$ converges to $f(x)$ for every real value of x.

Solution The function has derivatives of all orders throughout the interval $-\infty < x < \infty$. Equations (10) and (11) with $f(x) = e^x$ and $a = 0$ give

$$e^x = 1 + x + \frac{x^2}{2!} + \cdots + \frac{x^n}{n!} + R_n(x), \quad \text{Polynomial from Example 2}$$

and

$$R_n(x) = \frac{e^c}{(n+1)!}x^{n+1} \quad \text{for some } c \text{ between 0 and } x.$$

Since e^x is an increasing function of x, e^c lies between $e^0 = 1$ and e^x. When x is negative, so is c, and $e^c < 1$. When x is zero, $e^x = 1$ and $R_n(x) = 0$. When x is positive, so is c, and $e^c < e^x$. Thus,

$$|R_n(x)| \le \frac{|x|^{n+1}}{(n+1)!} \qquad \text{when } x \le 0,$$

and

$$|R_n(x)| < e^x \frac{x^{n+1}}{(n+1)!} \qquad \text{when } x > 0.$$

Finally, because

$$\lim_{n\to\infty} \frac{x^{n+1}}{(n+1)!} = 0 \qquad \text{for every } x, \qquad \text{Section 9.1}$$

$\lim_{n\to\infty} R_n(x) = 0$, and the series converges to e^x for every x.

$$e^x = \sum_{k=0}^{\infty} \frac{x^k}{k!} = 1 + x + \frac{x^2}{2!} + \cdots + \frac{x^k}{k!} + \cdots. \tag{14}$$

Estimating the Remainder

It is often possible to estimate $R_n(x)$ as we did in Example 4. This method of estimation is so convenient that we state it as a theorem for future reference.

THEOREM 16

The Remainder Estimation Theorem

If there are positive constants M and r such that $|f^{(n+1)}(t)| \le Mr^{n+1}$ for all t between a and x, inclusive, then the remainder term $R_n(x)$ in Taylor's theorem satisfies the inequality

$$|R_n(x)| \le M \frac{r^{n+1}|x-a|^{n+1}}{(n+1)!}.$$

If these conditions hold for every n and all the other conditions of Taylor's theorem are satisfied by f, then the series converges to $f(x)$.

In the simplest examples, we can take $r = 1$ provided f and all its derivatives are bounded in magnitude by some constant M. But if $f(x) = 2\cos(3x)$, each time we differentiate we get a factor of 3 and r needs to be greater than 1. In this particular case, we can take $r = 3$ along with $M = 2$.

We are now ready to look at some examples of how the Remainder Estimation Theorem and Taylor's theorem can be used together to settle questions of convergence. As you will see, they can also be used to determine the accuracy with which a function is approximated by one of its Taylor polynomials.

EXAMPLE 5 *The Maclaurin Series for* $\sin x$*.* Show that the Maclaurin series for $\sin x$ converges to $\sin x$ for all x.

Solution The function and its derivatives are

$$\begin{aligned} f(x) &= \sin x, & f'(x) &= \cos x, \\ f''(x) &= -\sin x, & f'''(x) &= -\cos x, \\ &\vdots & &\vdots \\ f^{(2k)}(x) &= (-1)^k \sin x, & f^{(2k+1)}(x) &= (-1)^k \cos x, \end{aligned}$$

so

$$f^{(2k)}(0) = 0 \qquad \text{and} \qquad f^{(2k+1)}(0) = (-1)^k.$$

The series has only odd-power terms and, for $n = 2k + 1$, Taylor's theorem gives

$$\sin x = x - \frac{x^3}{3!} + \frac{x^5}{5!} - \cdots + \frac{(-1)^k x^{2k+1}}{(2k+1)!} + R_{2k+1}(x).$$

All the derivatives of $\sin x$ have absolute values less than or equal to 1, so we can apply the Remainder Estimation Theorem with $M = 1$ and $r = 1$ to obtain

$$|R_{2k+1}(x)| \le 1 \cdot \frac{|x|^{2k+2}}{(2k+2)!}.$$

Since $\left(|x|^{2k+2}/(2k+2)!\right) \to 0$ as $k \to \infty$, whatever the value of x, $R_{2k+1}(x) \to 0$, and the Maclaurin series for $\sin x$ converges to $\sin x$ for every x.

$$\sin x = \sum_{k=0}^{\infty} \frac{(-1)^k x^{2k+1}}{(2k+1)!} = x - \frac{x^3}{3!} + \frac{x^5}{5!} - \frac{x^7}{7!} + \cdots. \tag{15}$$

Who Invented Taylor Series?

Brook Taylor (1685–1731) did not invent Taylor series, and Maclaurin series were not developed by Colin Maclaurin (1698–1746). James Gregory was already working with Taylor series when Taylor was only a few years old, and he published the Maclaurin series for $\tan x$, $\sec x$, $\tan^{-1} x$, and $\sec^{-1} x$ ten years before Maclaurin was born. Nicolaus Mercator discovered the Maclaurin series for $\ln(1 + x)$ at about the same time.

Taylor was unaware of Gregory's work when he published his book *Methodus incrementorum directa et inversa* in 1715, containing what we now call Taylor series. Maclaurin quoted Taylor's work in a calculus book he wrote in 1742. The book popularized series representations of functions and although Maclaurin never claimed to have discovered them, Taylor series centered at $a = 0$ became known as Maclaurin series. History evened things up in the end. Maclaurin, a brilliant mathematician, was the original discoverer of the rule for solving systems of equations that we call Cramer's rule.

EXAMPLE 6 *The Maclaurin Series for* cos *x.* Show that the Maclaurin series for $\cos x$ converges to $\cos x$ for every value of x.

Solution We add the remainder term to the Taylor polynomial for $\cos x$ in Example 3 to obtain Taylor's formula for $\cos x$ with $n = 2k$:

$$\cos x = 1 - \frac{x^2}{2!} + \frac{x^4}{4!} - \cdots + (-1)^k \frac{x^{2k}}{(2k)!} + R_{2k}(x).$$

Because the derivatives of the cosine have absolute value less than or equal to 1, the Remainder Estimation Theorem with $M = 1$ and $r = 1$ gives

$$|R_{2k}(x)| \le 1 \cdot \frac{|x|^{2k+1}}{(2k+1)!}.$$

For every value of x, $R_{2k} \to 0$ as $k \to \infty$. Therefore, the series converges to $\cos x$ for every value of x.

$$\cos x = \sum_{k=0}^{\infty} \frac{(-1)^k x^{2k}}{(2k)!} = 1 - \frac{x^2}{2!} + \frac{x^4}{4!} - \frac{x^6}{6!} + \cdots. \tag{16}$$

EXAMPLE 7 *Finding a Maclaurin Series by Substitution.* Find the Maclaurin series for $\cos 2x$.

Solution We can find the Maclaurin series for $\cos 2x$ by substituting $2x$ for x in the Maclaurin series for $\cos x$:

$$\cos 2x = \sum_{k=0}^{\infty} \frac{(-1)^k (2x)^{2k}}{(2k)!} = 1 - \frac{(2x)^2}{2!} + \frac{(2x)^4}{4!} - \frac{(2x)^6}{6!} + \cdots \qquad \text{Eq. (16) with } 2x \text{ for } x$$

$$= 1 - \frac{2^2 x^2}{2!} + \frac{2^4 x^4}{4!} - \frac{2^6 x^6}{6!} + \cdots$$

$$= \sum_{k=0}^{\infty} (-1)^k \frac{4^k x^{2k}}{(2k)!}.$$

Eq. (16) holds for $-\infty < x < \infty$, implying that it holds for $-\infty < 2x < \infty$, so the newly created series converges for all x. Exercise 57 explains why the series is in fact the Maclaurin series for $\cos 2x$.

EXAMPLE 8 *Finding a Maclaurin Series by Multiplication.* Find the Maclaurin series for $x \sin x$.

Solution We can find the Maclaurin series for $x \sin x$ by multiplying the Maclaurin series for $\sin x$ (Eq. 15) by x:

$$x \sin x = x\left(x - \frac{x^3}{3!} + \frac{x^5}{5!} - \frac{x^7}{7!} + \cdots\right)$$

$$= x^2 - \frac{x^4}{3!} + \frac{x^6}{5!} - \frac{x^8}{7!} + \cdots.$$

The new series converges for all x because the series for $\sin x$ converges for all x. Exercise 57 explains why the series is the Maclaurin series for $x \sin x$.

Truncation Error

The Maclaurin series for e^x converges to e^x for all x. But we still need to decide how many terms to use to approximate e^x to a given degree of accuracy. We get this information from the Remainder Estimation Theorem.

EXAMPLE 9 Calculate e with an error of less than 10^{-6}.

Solution We can use the result of Example 4 with $x = 1$ to write

$$e = 1 + 1 + \frac{1}{2!} + \cdots + \frac{1}{n!} + R_n(1),$$

with

$$R_n(1) = e^c \frac{1}{(n+1)!} \qquad \text{for some } c \text{ between 0 and 1.}$$

For the purposes of this example, we assume that we know that $e < 3$. Hence, we are certain that

$$\frac{1}{(n+1)!} < R_n(1) < \frac{3}{(n+1)!}$$

because $1 < e^c < 3$ for $0 < c < 1$.

By experiment we find that $1/9! > 10^{-6}$, while $3/10! < 10^{-6}$. Thus we should take $(n+1)$ to be at least 10, or n to be at least 9. With an error of less than 10^{-6},

$$e = 1 + 1 + \frac{1}{2} + \frac{1}{3!} + \cdots + \frac{1}{9!} \approx 2.7182\ 82.$$

EXAMPLE 10 For what values of x can we replace $\sin x$ by $x - (x^3/3!)$ with an error of magnitude no greater than 3×10^{-4}?

Solution Here we can take advantage of the fact that the Maclaurin series for $\sin x$ is an alternating series for every nonzero value of x. According to the Alternating Series Estimation Theorem (Section 9.5), the error in truncating

$$\sin x = x - \frac{x^3}{3!} \,\Big|\, + \frac{x^5}{5!} - \cdots$$

after $(x^3/3!)$ is no greater than

$$\left|\frac{x^5}{5!}\right| = \frac{|x|^5}{120}.$$

Therefore the error will be less than or equal to 3×10^{-4} if

$$\frac{|x|^5}{120} < 3 \times 10^{-4} \qquad \text{or} \qquad |x| < \sqrt[5]{360 \times 10^{-4}} \approx 0.514.$$

Rounded down, to be safe

The Alternating Series Estimation Theorem tells us something that the Remainder Estimation Theorem does not: namely, that the estimate $x - (x^3/3!)$ for $\sin x$ is an underestimate when x is positive because then $x^5/120$ is positive.

Figure 9.18 shows the graph of $\sin x$, along with the graphs of a number of its approximating Taylor polynomials. The graph of $P_3(x) = x - (x^3/3!)$ is almost indistinguishable from the sine curve when $-1 \le x \le 1$.

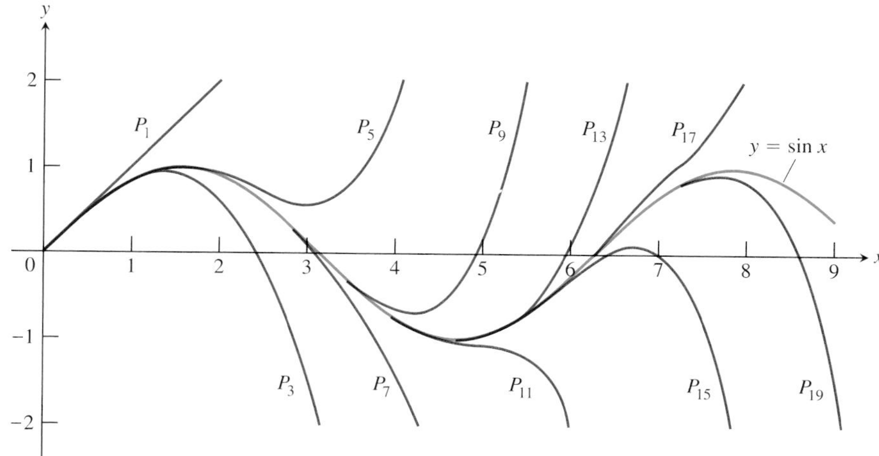

9.18 The polynomials

$$P_{2n+1}(x) = \sum_{k=0}^{n} \frac{(-1)^k x^{2k+1}}{(2k+1)!}$$

converge to $\sin x$ as $n \to \infty$.

You might wonder how the estimate given by the Remainder Estimation Theorem compares with the one just obtained from the Alternating Series Estimation Theorem. If we write

$$\sin x = x - \frac{x^3}{3!} + R_3,$$

then the Remainder Estimation Theorem gives

$$|R_3| \leq 1 \cdot \frac{|x|^4}{4!} = \frac{|x|^4}{24},$$

which is not very good. But if we recognize that $x - (x^3/3!) = 0 + x + 0x^2 - (x^3/3!) + 0x^4$ is the Taylor polynomial of order 4 as well as of order 3, then we have

$$\sin x = x - \frac{x^3}{3!} + 0 + R_4,$$

and the Remainder Estimation Theorem with $M = r = 1$ gives

$$|R_4| \leq 1 \cdot \frac{|x|^5}{5!} = \frac{|x|^5}{120}.$$

This is what we had from the Alternating Series Estimation Theorem.

Combining Taylor Series

On common intervals of convergence, Taylor series can be added, subtracted, and multiplied by constants just as other series can, and the results are once again Taylor series. The Taylor series for $f(x) + g(x)$ is the sum of the Taylor series for $f(x)$ and $g(x)$ because the nth derivative of $f + g$ is $f^{(n)} + g^{(n)}$, and so on. Thus we obtain the Maclaurin series for $(1 + \cos 2x)/2$ by adding 1 to the Maclaurin series for $\cos 2x$ and dividing the combined results by 2, and the Maclaurin series for $\sin x + \cos x$ is the term-by-term sum of the Maclaurin series for $\sin x$ and $\cos x$.

$e^{i\theta} = \cos\theta + i\sin\theta$

As you may recall, a complex number is a number of the form $a + bi$, where a and b are real numbers and $i = \sqrt{-1}$. If we substitute $x = i\theta$ (θ real) in the Maclaurin series for e^x and use the relations

$$i^2 = -1, \qquad i^3 = i^2 i = -i, \qquad i^4 = i^2 i^2 = 1, \qquad i^5 = i^4 i = i,$$

and so on, to simplify the result, we obtain

$$\begin{aligned} e^{i\theta} &= 1 + \frac{i\theta}{1!} + \frac{i^2\theta^2}{2!} + \frac{i^3\theta^3}{3!} + \frac{i^4\theta^4}{4!} + \frac{i^5\theta^5}{5!} + \frac{i^6\theta^6}{6!} + \cdots \\ &= \left(1 - \frac{\theta^2}{2!} + \frac{\theta^4}{4!} - \frac{\theta^6}{6!} + \cdots\right) + i\left(\theta - \frac{\theta^3}{3!} + \frac{\theta^5}{5!} - \cdots\right) = \cos\theta + i\sin\theta. \end{aligned} \tag{17}$$

This does not *prove* that $e^{i\theta} = \cos\theta + i\sin\theta$ because we have not yet defined what it means to raise e to an imaginary power. But it does say how we ought to define $e^{i\theta}$ to be consistent with other things we know.

One of the amazing consequences of Euler's formula is the equation

$$e^{i\pi} = -1.$$

When written in the form $e^{i\pi} + 1 = 0$, this equation combines the five most important constants in mathematics.

DEFINITION

For any real number θ, $e^{i\theta} = \cos\theta + i\sin\theta$. (18)

Equation (18), called **Euler's formula,** enables us to define e^{a+bi} to be $e^a \cdot e^{bi}$ for any complex number $a + bi$.

Exercises 9.7

In Exercises 1–8, find the Taylor polynomials of orders 0, 1, 2, and 3 generated by f at a.

1. $f(x) = \ln x, \quad a = 1$

2. $f(x) = \ln(1 + x), \quad a = 0$

3. $f(x) = 1/x, \quad a = 2$

4. $f(x) = 1/(x + 2), \quad a = 0$

5. $f(x) = \sin x, \quad a = \pi/4$

6. $f(x) = \cos x, \quad a = \pi/4$

7. $f(x) = \sqrt{x}, \quad a = 4$

8. $f(x) = \sqrt{x + 4}, \quad a = 0$

Use substitution (as in Example 7) to find the Maclaurin series of the functions in Exercises 9–16.

9. e^{-5x}

10. $e^{x/2}$

11. $\sin 3x$

12. $\sin \dfrac{x}{2}$

13. $7 \cos(-x)$

14. $5 \cos \pi x$

15. $\cos \sqrt{x}$

16. $\cos\left(x^{3/2}/\sqrt{2}\right)$

Find Maclaurin series for the functions in Exercises 17–26.

17. xe^x

18. $x^2 \sin x$

19. $\dfrac{\sin x}{x}$

20. $\dfrac{e^x - 1}{x}$

21. $\dfrac{x^2}{2} - 1 + \cos x$

22. $\sin x - x + \dfrac{x^3}{3!}$

23. $\cos^2 x \quad$ (*Hint:* $\cos^2 x = (1 + \cos 2x)/2$)

24. $\sin^2 x$

25. $\cosh x = (e^x + e^{-x})/2$

26. $\sinh x = (e^x - e^{-x})/2$

QUADRATIC APPROXIMATIONS

Write out Taylor's formula (Eq. 10) with $n = 2$ and $a = 0$ for the functions in Exercises 27–32. This will give you the quadratic approximations of these functions at $x = 0$ and the associated error terms.

27. $e^{\tan x}$

28. $e^{\sin x}$

29. $\ln(\cos x)$

30. $\dfrac{1}{\sqrt{1 - x^2}}$

31. $\sinh x$

32. $\cosh x$

33. Use the Taylor series generated by e^x at $x = a$ to show that

$$e^x = e^a\left[1 + (x - a) + \frac{(x - a)^2}{2!} + \cdots\right].$$

34. *Continuation of Exercise 33.* Find the Taylor series generated by e^x at $a = 1$. Compare your answer with the formula in Exercise 33.

35. For approximately what values of x can you replace $\sin x$ by $x - (x^3/6)$ with an error of magnitude no greater than 5×10^{-4}? Give reasons for your answer.

36. If $\cos x$ is replaced by $1 - (x^2/2)$ and $|x| < 0.5$, what estimate can be made of the error? Does $1 - (x^2/2)$ tend to be too large, or too small? Give reasons for your answer.

37. How close is the approximation $\sin x = x$ when $|x| < 10^{-3}$? For which of these values of x is $x < \sin x$?

38. The estimate $\sqrt{1 + x} = 1 + (x/2)$ is used when x is small. Estimate the error when $|x| < 0.01$.

39. The approximation $e^x = 1 + x + (x^2/2)$ is used when x is small. Use the Remainder Estimation Theorem to estimate the error when $|x| < 0.1$.

40. *Continuation of Exercise 39.* When $x < 0$, the series for e^x is an alternating series. Use the Alternating Series Estimation Theorem to estimate the error that results from replacing e^x by $1 + x + (x^2/2)$ when $-0.1 < x < 0$. Compare your estimate with the one you obtained in Exercise 39.

Each of the series in Exercises 41 and 42 is the value of the Maclaurin series of a function $f(x)$ at some point. What function and what point? What is the sum of the series?

41. $(0.1) - \dfrac{(0.1)^3}{3!} + \dfrac{(0.1)^5}{5!} - \cdots + \dfrac{(-1)^k(0.1)^{2k+1}}{(2k + 1)!} + \cdots$

42. $1 - \dfrac{\pi^2}{4^2 \cdot 2!} + \dfrac{\pi^4}{4^4 \cdot 4!} - \cdots + \dfrac{(-1)^k(\pi)^{2k}}{4^{2k} \cdot (2k!)} - \cdots$

43. Differentiate the Maclaurin series for $\sin x$, $\cos x$, and e^x term by term and compare your results with the Maclaurin series for $\cos x$, $\sin x$, and e^x, respectively.

44. Integrate the Maclaurin series for $\sin x$, $\cos x$, and e^x term by term and compare your results with the Maclaurin series for $\cos x$, $\sin x$, and e^x, respectively.

45. Multiply the Maclaurin series for $2 \cos x$ and $\sin x$ together to find the first five nonzero terms of the product series. Confirm that this is the beginning of the Maclaurin series for $\sin 2x$.

46. Multiply the Maclaurin series for e^x and $\cos x$ together to find the first five nonzero terms of the Maclaurin series for $e^x \cos x$.

47. a) Use the Maclaurin series for $\sin x$ and the Alternating Series Estimation Theorem to show that

$$1 - \frac{x^2}{6} < \frac{\sin x}{x} < 1, \quad x \neq 0.$$

b) Graph $f(x) = (\sin x)/x$ together with the functions $y = 1 - (x^2/6)$ and $y = 1$ for $-5 \le x \le 5$. Comment on the relationships among the graphs.

48. a) Use the Maclaurin series for $\cos x$ and the Alternating Series Estimation Theorem to show that

$$\frac{1}{2}-\frac{x^2}{24}<\frac{1-\cos x}{x^2}<\frac{1}{2}, \quad x \neq 0.$$

(This is the inequality in Section 2.3, Exercise 42.)

b) Graph $f(x)=(1-\cos x)/x^2$ together with $y=(1/2)-(x^2/24)$ and $y=1/2$ for $-9 \leq x \leq 9$. Comment on the relationships among the graphs.

49. Use the identity $\sin^2 x=(1-\cos 2x)/2$ to obtain a power series for $\sin^2 x$. Then differentiate this series to obtain a series for $2 \sin x \cos x$. Check that this is the series for $\sin 2x$.

50. *A Convergent Taylor Series That Converges to its Generating Function Only at its Center.* It can be shown (though not simply) that the function f defined by the rule

$$f(x)=\begin{cases}0 & \text{if } x=0 \\ e^{-1/x^2} & \text{if } x \neq 0\end{cases}$$

has derivatives of all orders at $x=0$ (Fig. 9.19) and that $f^{(n)}(0)=0$ for all n.

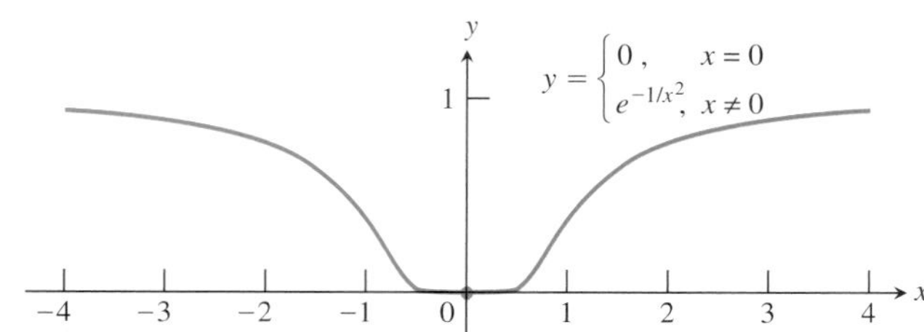

9.19 The graph of the continuous extension of $y=e^{-1/x^2}$ is so flat at the origin that all of its derivatives there are zero (Exercise 50).

a) Use the fact that $f^{(n)}(0)=0$ for all n to find the Maclaurin series generated by f. At what values of x does the series converge? At what values of x does the series converge to $f(x)$?

b) Write out Taylor's formula (Eq. 10) for f, taking $a=0$ and assuming $x \neq 0$. What does the formula tell you about the value of $R_n(x)$?

51. Use Eq. (18) to write the following powers of e in the form $a+bi$.

a) $e^{-i\pi}$ **b)** $e^{i\pi/4}$ **c)** $e^{-i\pi/2}$

52. *Euler's Identities.* Use Eq. (18) to show that

$$\cos\theta=\frac{e^{i\theta}+e^{-i\theta}}{2} \quad \text{and} \quad \sin\theta=\frac{e^{i\theta}-e^{-i\theta}}{2i}.$$

53. Establish the equations in Exercise 52 by combining the formal Maclaurin series for $e^{i\theta}$ and $e^{-i\theta}$.

54. Show that

a) $\cosh i\theta=\cos\theta$, **b)** $\sinh i\theta=i\sin\theta$.

55. By multiplying the Maclaurin series for e^x and $\sin x$, find the terms through x^5 of the Maclaurin series for $e^x \sin x$. This series is the imaginary part of the series for

$$e^x \cdot e^{ix}=e^{(1+i)x}.$$

Use this fact to check your answer. For what values of x should the series for $e^x \sin x$ converge?

56. When a and b are real, we define $e^{(a+ib)x}$ with the equation

$$e^{(a+ib)x}=e^{ax}\cdot e^{ibx}=e^{ax}(\cos bx+i\sin bx).$$

Differentiate the right-hand side of this equation to show that

$$\frac{d}{dx}e^{(a+ib)x}=(a+ib)e^{(a+ib)x}.$$

Thus the familiar rule $(d/dx)e^{kx}=ke^{kx}$ holds for k complex as well as real.

57. *The Maclaurin Series Generated by $f(x)=\Sigma_{n=0}^{\infty} a_n x^n$ is $\Sigma_{n=0}^{\infty} a_n x^n$.* A function defined by a power series $\Sigma_{n=0}^{\infty} a_n x^n$ with a radius of convergence $c>0$ has a Maclaurin series that converges to the function at every point of $(-c, c)$. Show this by showing that the Maclaurin series generated by $f(x)=\Sigma_{n=0}^{\infty} a_n x^n$ is the series $\Sigma_{n=0}^{\infty} a_n x^n$ itself.

An immediate consequence of this is that series like

$$x\sin x=x^2-\frac{x^4}{3!}+\frac{x^6}{5!}-\frac{x^8}{7!}+\cdots$$

and

$$x^2 e^x=x^2+x^3+\frac{x^4}{2!}+\frac{x^5}{3!}+\cdots,$$

obtained by multiplying Maclaurin series by powers of x, as well as series obtained by integration and differentiation of convergent power series, are themselves the Maclaurin series generated by the functions they represent.

58. Suppose that the series $f(x)=\Sigma_{n=0}^{\infty} a_n(x-a)^n$ converges for $|x-a|<h$. Must the coefficients a_n be the same as those in the Taylor series generated by f at a? Give reasons for your answer.

Writing for Your Own Knowledge

Answer the following questions in writing. Some answers will take only a sentence or two; others may require several paragraphs. Some explanations may also call for graphs or sketches.

1. What is a Taylor series? a Maclaurin series?
2. What are Taylor polynomials? What is special about them?
3. What does Taylor's theorem say?
4. What is Taylor's formula?
5. How do you measure the accuracy with which a (sufficiently differentiable) function is approximated over an interval by one of its Taylor polynomials?
6. What are the Maclaurin series for e^x, $\sin x$, and $\cos x$? For what values of x does each series converge?

9.8 Calculations with Taylor Series

This section introduces the binomial series for estimating powers and roots and shows how series are sometimes used to evaluate nonelementary integrals and solve initial value problems.

The Binomial Series for Powers and Roots

The Maclaurin series generated by $f(x) = (1 + x)^m$, when m is constant, is

$$1 + mx + \frac{m(m-1)}{2!}x^2 + \frac{m(m-1)(m-2)}{3!}x^3 + \cdots + \frac{m(m-1)(m-2)\cdots(m-k+1)}{k!}x^k + \cdots. \quad (1)$$

This series, called the **binomial series,** converges absolutely for $|x| < 1$. To derive the series, we first list the function and its derivatives:

$$\begin{aligned} f(x) &= (1+x)^m, \\ f'(x) &= m(1+x)^{m-1}, \\ f''(x) &= m(m-1)(1+x)^{m-2}, \\ f'''(x) &= m(m-1)(m-2)(1+x)^{m-3}, \\ &\vdots \\ f^{(k)}(x) &= m(m-1)(m-2)\cdots(m-k+1)(1+x)^{m-k}. \end{aligned}$$

We then evaluate these at $x = 0$ and substitute in the Maclaurin series formula to obtain the series in (1).

If m is an integer greater than or equal to zero, the series stops after $(m + 1)$ terms because the coefficients from $k = m + 1$ on are zero.

If m is not a positive integer or zero, the series is infinite and converges for $|x| < 1$. To see why, let u_k be the term involving x^k. Then apply the Ratio Test for absolute convergence to see that

$$\left|\frac{u_{k+1}}{u_k}\right| = \left|\frac{m-k}{k+1}x\right| \to |x| \qquad \text{as } k \to \infty. \quad (2)$$

Our derivation of the binomial series shows only that it is generated by $(1 + x)^m$ and converges for $|x| < 1$. The derivation does not show that the series converges to $(1 + x)^m$. It does, but we assume that part without proof.

For $-1 < x < 1$,

$$(1+x)^m = 1 + \sum_{k=1}^{\infty} \binom{m}{k} x^k, \quad (3)$$

where

$$\binom{m}{1} = m, \qquad \binom{m}{2} = \frac{m(m-1)}{2!},$$

and

$$\binom{m}{k} = \frac{m(m-1)(m-2)\cdots(m-k+1)}{k!} \qquad \text{for } k \geq 3.$$

EXAMPLE 1 Show that when $m = -1$, Eq. (3) gives the geometric series

$$\frac{1}{1+x} = 1 - x + x^2 - x^3 + \cdots + (-1)^k x^k + \cdots. \tag{4}$$

Solution When $m = -1$,

$$\binom{-1}{1} = -1, \qquad \binom{-1}{2} = \frac{-1(-2)}{2!} = 1,$$

and

$$\binom{-1}{k} = \frac{-1(-2)(-3)\cdots(-1-k+1)}{k!} = (-1)^k\left(\frac{k!}{k!}\right) = (-1)^k.$$

With these coefficient values, Eq. (3) becomes

$$(1+x)^{-1} = 1 + \sum_{k=1}^{\infty}(-1)^k x^k = 1 - x + x^2 - x^3 + \cdots + (-1)^k x^k + \cdots,$$

which is Eq. (4).

Evaluating Nonelementary Integrals

Maclaurin series are often used to express nonelementary integrals in terms of series.

EXAMPLE 2 Express $\int \sin x^2\, dx$ as a power series.

Solution From the series for $\sin x$ we obtain

$$\sin x^2 = x^2 - \frac{x^6}{3!} + \frac{x^{10}}{5!} - \frac{x^{14}}{7!} + \frac{x^{18}}{9!} - \cdots.$$

Therefore,

$$\int \sin x^2\, dx = C + \frac{x^3}{3} - \frac{x^7}{7\cdot 3!} + \frac{x^{11}}{11\cdot 5!} - \frac{x^{15}}{15\cdot 7!} + \frac{x^{19}}{19\cdot 9!} - \cdots.$$

EXAMPLE 3 Estimate $\int_0^1 \sin x^2\, dx$ with an error of less than 0.001.

Solution From the indefinite integral in Example 3,

$$\int_0^1 \sin x^2\, dx = \frac{1}{3} - \frac{1}{7\cdot 3!} + \frac{1}{11\cdot 5!} - \frac{1}{15\cdot 7!} + \frac{1}{19\cdot 9!} - \cdots.$$

The series alternates, and we find by experiment that

$$\frac{1}{11\cdot 5!} \approx 0.0007\ 6$$

is the first term to be numerically less than 0.001. The sum of the preceding two terms gives

$$\int_0^1 \sin x^2\, dx \approx \frac{1}{3} - \frac{1}{42} \approx 0.310.$$

With two more terms we could estimate

$$\int_0^1 \sin x^2\, dx \approx 0.3102\ 68$$

with an error of less than 10^{-6}, and with only one term beyond that we have

$$\int_0^1 \sin x^2\, dx \approx \frac{1}{3} - \frac{1}{42} + \frac{1}{1320} - \frac{1}{75600} + \frac{1}{6894720} \approx 0.3102\ 68303,$$

with an error of less than 10^{-9}. To guarantee this accuracy with the error formula for the trapezoidal rule would require using about 13,000 subintervals.

Arctangents

In Section 9.6, Example 4, we found a series for $\tan^{-1} x$ by differentiating to get

$$\frac{d}{dx} \tan^{-1} x = \frac{1}{1 + x^2} = 1 - x^2 + x^4 - x^6 + \cdots$$

and integrating to get

$$\tan^{-1} x = x - \frac{x^3}{3} + \frac{x^5}{5} - \frac{x^7}{7} + \cdots.$$

However, we did not prove the term-by-term integration theorem on which this conclusion depended. We now derive the series again by integrating both sides of the finite formula

We take this route instead of finding the Maclaurin series directly because the formulas for the higher order derivatives of $\tan^{-1} x$ are unmanageable.

$$\frac{1}{1 + t^2} = 1 - t^2 + t^4 - t^6 + \cdots + (-1)^n t^{2n} + \frac{(-1)^{n+1} t^{2n+2}}{1 + t^2}, \qquad (5)$$

in which the last term comes from adding the remaining terms as a geometric series with first term $a = t^{2n+2}$ and ratio $r = -t^2$. Integrating both sides of Eq. (5) from $t = 0$ to $t = x$ gives

$$\tan^{-1} x = x - \frac{x^3}{3} + \frac{x^5}{5} - \frac{x^7}{7} + \cdots + (-1)^n \frac{x^{2n+1}}{2n+1} + R(n, x),$$

where

$$R(n, x) = \int_0^x \frac{(-1)^{n+1} t^{2n+2}}{1 + t^2}\, dt.$$

The denominator of the integrand is greater than or equal to 1; hence

$$|R(n, x)| \le \int_0^{|x|} t^{2n+2}\, dt = \frac{|x|^{2n+3}}{2n+3}.$$

If $|x| \le 1$, the right side of this inequality approaches zero as $n \to \infty$. Therefore $\lim_{n\to\infty} R(n, x) = 0$ if $|x| \le 1$ and

$$\tan^{-1} x = \sum_{n=0}^{\infty} \frac{(-1)^n x^{2n+1}}{2n+1}, \qquad |x| \le 1.$$

$$\tan^{-1} x = x - \frac{x^3}{3} + \frac{x^5}{5} - \frac{x^7}{7} + \cdots, \qquad |x| \le 1 \qquad (6)$$

When we put $x = 1$ and $\tan^{-1} 1 = \pi/4$ in Eq. (6), we get **Leibniz's formula:**

$$\frac{\pi}{4} = 1 - \frac{1}{3} + \frac{1}{5} - \frac{1}{7} + \frac{1}{9} - \cdots + \frac{(-1)^n}{2n+1} + \cdots.$$

This series converges too slowly to be a useful source of decimal approximations of π. It is better to use a formula like

$$\pi = 48 \tan^{-1} \frac{1}{18} + 32 \tan^{-1} \frac{1}{57} - 20 \tan^{-1} \frac{1}{239}, \tag{7}$$

which uses values of x closer to zero.

Power Series Solutions of Initial Value Problems

When we cannot find a relatively simple expression for the solution of an initial value problem, we try to get information about the solution in other ways. One way is to try to find a power series representation for the solution. If we can do so, we immediately have a source of polynomial approximations of the solution, which may be all that we really need. The next example deals with the initial value problem

$$\frac{dy}{dx} - y = 0, \qquad y = 3 \quad \text{when} \quad x = 0. \tag{8}$$

We know from Chapter 7 that the solution is $y = 3e^x$. Example 4 shows how, not knowing this, we could solve the problem with power series.

EXAMPLE 4 Find a power series solution of the initial value problem

$$\frac{dy}{dx} - y = 0, \qquad y = 3 \quad \text{when} \quad x = 0 \tag{9}$$

Solution We assume that there is a solution of the form

$$y = a_0 + a_1 x + a_2 x^2 + \cdots + a_{n-1} x^{n-1} + a_n x^n + \cdots. \tag{10}$$

Our goal is to find what the coefficients a_k have to be to make the series and its first derivative

$$\frac{dy}{dx} = a_1 + 2a_2 x + 3a_3 x^2 + \cdots + n a_n x^{n-1} + \cdots \tag{11}$$

satisfy the given differential equation and initial condition (9). The series for $(dy/dx) - y$ is the difference of the series in Eqs. (11) and (10):

$$\begin{aligned} \frac{dy}{dx} - y &= (a_1 - a_0) + (2a_2 - a_1)x + (3a_3 - a_2)x^2 + \cdots \\ &\quad + (na_n - a_{n-1})x^{n-1} + \cdots. \end{aligned} \tag{12}$$

If y and its first derivative are to satisfy the equation $(dy/dx) - y = 0$, then the coefficients of the individual powers of x on the right-hand side of Eq. (12) must all be zero (power series representations are unique, as you saw if you did Exercise 43 in Section 9.6):

$$a_1 - a_0 = 0, \qquad 2a_2 - a_1 = 0, \qquad 3a_3 - a_2 = 0, \tag{13}$$

and, in general,

$$na_n - a_{n-1} = 0. \tag{14}$$

We also see from Eq. (10) that $y = a_0$ when $x = 0$, which means that $a_0 = 3$ (that being the initial condition). Therefore,

$$a_0 = 3, \qquad a_1 = a_0 = 3, \qquad a_2 = \frac{a_1}{2} = \frac{3}{2},$$

$$a_3 = \frac{a_2}{3} = \frac{3}{3 \cdot 2} = \frac{3}{3!}, \quad \ldots \quad a_n = \frac{a_{n-1}}{n} = \frac{3}{n!} \quad \ldots$$

Substituting these coefficient values into the equation for y (Eq. 10) gives

$$\begin{aligned} y &= 3 + 3x + 3\frac{x^2}{2} + 3\frac{x^3}{3!} + \cdots + 3\frac{x^n}{n!} + \cdots \\ &= 3\underbrace{\left(1 + x + \frac{x^2}{2} + \frac{x^3}{3!} + \cdots + \frac{x^n}{n!} + \cdots\right)}_{\text{the Maclaurin series for } e^x} \\ &= 3e^x. \end{aligned}$$

The solution of the initial value problem is $y = 3e^x$.

EXAMPLE 5 Solve the initial value problem

$$\frac{dy}{dx} - y = x, \qquad y = 1 \quad \text{when} \quad x = 0. \tag{15}$$

Solution We assume that there is a solution of the form

$$y = a_0 + a_1 x + a_2 x^2 + \cdots + a_{n-1}x^{n-1} + a_n x^n + \cdots \tag{16}$$

and deduce, as in Example 4, that

$$\begin{aligned} \frac{dy}{dx} - y = {} & (a_1 - a_0) + (2a_2 - a_1)x + (3a_3 - a_2)x^2 + \cdots \\ & + (na_n - a_{n-1})x^{n-1} + \cdots. \end{aligned} \tag{17}$$

For this series to equal x, the coefficients must satisfy the equations

$$\begin{aligned} a_1 - a_0 &= 0, && \text{Constant terms} \\ 2a_2 - a_1 &= 1, && \text{Coefficients of } x \\ 3a_3 - a_2 &= 0, && \text{Coefficients of } x^2 \\ &\vdots && \vdots \\ na_n - a_{n-1} &= 0, && \text{Coefficients of } x^{n-1} \\ &\vdots && \vdots \end{aligned}$$

We can also see from Eq. (16) that $y = a_0$ when $x = 0$, so that $a_0 = 1$ (this being the initial condition). Putting it all together, we have

$$a_0 = 1, \qquad a_1 = a_0 = 1, \qquad a_2 = \frac{1 + a_1}{2} = \frac{1+1}{2} = \frac{2}{2},$$

$$a_3 = \frac{a_2}{3} = \frac{2}{3 \cdot 2} = \frac{2}{3!}, \quad \ldots \quad a_n = \frac{a_{n-1}}{n} = \frac{2}{n!} \quad \ldots$$

Substituting these coefficient values into the equation for y (Eq. 16) gives

$$\begin{aligned} y &= 1 + x + 2 \cdot \frac{x^2}{2} + 2 \cdot \frac{x^3}{3!} + \cdots + 2 \cdot \frac{x^n}{n!} + \cdots \\ &= 1 + x + 2 \underbrace{\left(\frac{x^2}{2} + \frac{x^3}{3!} + \cdots + \frac{x^n}{n!} + \cdots \right)}_{\text{the Maclaurin series for } e^x - 1 - x} \\ &= 1 + x + 2\,(e^x - 1 - x) = 2e^x - 1 - x. \end{aligned}$$

The solution of the initial value problem is $y = 2e^x - 1 - x$.

Frequently Used Maclaurin Series

$$\frac{1}{1-x} = 1 + x + x^2 + \cdots + x^n + \cdots = \sum_{n=0}^{\infty} x^n, \qquad |x| < 1$$

$$\frac{1}{1+x} = 1 - x + x^2 - \cdots + (-x)^n + \cdots = \sum_{n=0}^{\infty} (-1)^n x^n, \qquad |x| < 1$$

$$e^x = 1 + x + \frac{x^2}{2!} + \cdots + \frac{x^n}{n!} + \cdots = \sum_{n=0}^{\infty} \frac{x^n}{n!}, \qquad |x| < \infty$$

$$\sin x = x - \frac{x^3}{3!} + \frac{x^5}{5!} - \cdots + (-1)^n \frac{x^{2n+1}}{(2n+1)!} + \cdots = \sum_{n=0}^{\infty} \frac{(-1)^n x^{2n+1}}{(2n+1)!}, \qquad |x| < \infty$$

$$\cos x = 1 - \frac{x^2}{2!} + \frac{x^4}{4!} - \cdots + (-1)^n \frac{x^{2n}}{(2n)!} + \cdots = \sum_{n=0}^{\infty} \frac{(-1)^n x^{2n}}{(2n)!}, \qquad |x| < \infty$$

$$\ln(1+x) = x - \frac{x^2}{2} + \frac{x^3}{3} - \cdots + (-1)^{n-1} \frac{x^n}{n} + \cdots = \sum_{n=1}^{\infty} \frac{(-1)^{n-1} x^n}{n}, \qquad -1 < x \le 1$$

$$\ln \frac{1+x}{1-x} = 2 \tanh^{-1} x = 2\left(x + \frac{x^3}{3} + \frac{x^5}{5} + \cdots + \frac{x^{2n+1}}{2n+1} + \cdots \right) = 2 \sum_{n=0}^{\infty} \frac{x^{2n+1}}{2n+1}, \qquad |x| < 1$$

$$\tan^{-1} x = x - \frac{x^3}{3} + \frac{x^5}{5} - \cdots + (-1)^n \frac{x^{2n+1}}{2n+1} + \cdots = \sum_{n=0}^{\infty} \frac{(-1)^n x^{2n+1}}{2n+1}, \qquad |x| \le 1$$

Binomial Series

$$\begin{aligned} (1+x)^m &= 1 + mx + \frac{m(m-1)x^2}{2!} + \frac{m(m-1)(m-2)x^3}{3!} + \cdots + \frac{m(m-1)(m-2)\cdots(m-k+1)x^k}{k!} + \cdots \\ &= 1 + \sum_{k=1}^{\infty} \binom{m}{k} x^k, \qquad |x| < 1, \end{aligned}$$

where $\displaystyle \binom{m}{1} = m, \qquad \binom{m}{2} = \frac{m(m-1)}{2!}, \qquad \binom{m}{k} = \frac{m(m-1)\cdots(m-k+1)}{k!}$ for $k \ge 3$.

NOTE: It is customary to define $\binom{m}{0}$ to be 1 and to take $x^0 = 1$ (even in the usually excluded case where $x = 0$) to write the binomial series compactly. If m is a *positive integer,* the series terminates at x^m, and the result converges for all x.

Exercises 9.8

Find the first four terms of the binomial series for the functions in Exercises 1–10.

1. $(1+x)^{1/2}$
2. $(1+x)^{1/3}$
3. $(1+3x)^{1/3}$
4. $(1-2x)^{1/2}$
5. $\left(1+\frac{x}{2}\right)^{-2}$
6. $\left(1-\frac{x}{2}\right)^{-2}$
7. $(1+x^3)^{-1/2}$
8. $(1+x^2)^{-1/3}$
9. $\left(1+\frac{1}{x}\right)^{1/2}$
10. $\left(1-\frac{2}{x}\right)^{1/3}$

Find the binomial series for the functions in Exercises 11–14.

11. $(1+x)^4$
12. $(1+x^2)^3$
13. $(1-2x)^3$
14. $\left(1-\frac{x}{2}\right)^4$

In Exercises 15–22, use series to estimate the integrals' values with an error of magnitude less than 10^{-3}. (The answer section gives the integrals' values rounded to 5 decimal places.)

15. $\int_0^{0.2} \sin x^2\, dx$
16. $\int_0^{0.1} \tan^{-1} x\, dx$
17. $\int_0^{0.1} x^2 e^{-x^2}\, dx$
18. $\int_0^{0.1} \frac{\tan^{-1} x}{x}\, dx$
19. $\int_0^{0.4} \frac{1-e^{-x}}{x}\, dx$
20. $\int_0^{0.1} \frac{\ln(1+x)}{x}\, dx$
21. $\int_0^{0.1} \frac{1}{\sqrt{1+x^4}}\, dx$
22. $\int_0^{0.25} \sqrt[3]{1+x^2}\, dx$

Use series to approximate the values of the integrals in Exercises 23–26 with an error of magnitude less than 10^{-8}. (The answer section gives the integrals' values rounded to 10 decimal places.)

23. $\int_0^{0.1} \frac{\sin x}{x}\, dx$
24. $\int_0^{0.1} e^{-x^2}\, dx$
25. $\int_0^{0.1} \sqrt{1+x^4}\, dx$
26. $\int_0^{1} \frac{1-\cos x}{x^2}\, dx$

27. Replace x by $-x$ in the Maclaurin series for $\ln(1+x)$ to obtain a series for $\ln(1-x)$. Then subtract this from the Maclaurin series for $\ln(1+x)$ to show that for $|x|<1$.
$$\ln\frac{1+x}{1-x} = 2\left(x+\frac{x^3}{3}+\frac{x^5}{5}+\cdots\right).$$
28. How many terms of the Maclaurin series for $\ln(1+x)$ should you add to be sure of calculating $\ln(1.1)$ with an error of magnitude less than 10^{-8}? Give reasons for your answer.
29. According to the Alternating Series Estimation Theorem, how many terms of the Maclaurin series for $\tan^{-1} 1$ would you have to add to be sure of finding $\pi/4$ with an error of magnitude less than 10^{-3}? Give reasons for your answer.
30. Show that the Maclaurin series for $f(x)=\tan^{-1} x$ diverges for $|x|>1$.
31. About how many terms of the Maclaurin series for $\tan^{-1} x$ would you have to use to evaluate each term on the right-hand side of the equation
$$\pi = 48\tan^{-1}\frac{1}{18} + 32\tan^{-1}\frac{1}{57} - 20\tan^{-1}\frac{1}{239}$$
with an error of magnitude less than 10^{-6}? In contrast, the convergence of $\sum_{n=1}^{\infty}(1/n^2)$ to $\pi^2/6$ is so slow that even 50 terms will not yield two-place accuracy.
32. Integrate the first three nonzero terms of the Maclaurin series for $\tan t$ from 0 to x to obtain the first three nonzero terms of the Maclaurin series for $\ln\sec x$.
33. **a)** Use the binomial series and the fact that
$$\frac{d}{dx}\sin^{-1} x = (1-x^2)^{-1/2}$$
to generate the first four nonzero terms of the Maclaurin series for $\sin^{-1} x$. What is the radius of convergence?
b) Use your result in (a) to find the first five nonzero terms of the Maclaurin series for $\cos^{-1} x$.
34. **a)** Find the first four nonzero terms of the Maclaurin series for
$$\sinh^{-1} x = \int_0^x \frac{dt}{\sqrt{1+t^2}}.$$
b) Use the first *three* terms of the series in (a) to estimate $\sinh^{-1} 0.25$. Give an upper bound for the magnitude of the estimation error.
35. Obtain the Maclaurin series for $1/(1+x)^2$ from the series for $-1/(1+x)$.
36. Use the Maclaurin series for $1/(1-x^2)$ to obtain a series for $2x/(1-x^2)^2$.

Use power series to solve the initial value problems in Exercises 37–46 given that $y=y_0$ when $x=0$.

37. $\frac{dy}{dx}+y=0,\quad y_0=1$
38. $\frac{dy}{dx}-y=0,\quad y_0=-3$
39. $\frac{dy}{dx}-y=1,\quad y_0=0$
40. $\frac{dy}{dx}+y=1,\quad y_0=2$
41. $\frac{dy}{dx}-2y=0,\quad y_0=1$
42. $\frac{dy}{dx}+2y=0,\quad y_0=3$
43. $\frac{dy}{dx}-y=x,\quad y_0=0$
44. $\frac{dy}{dx}-y=3x,\quad y_0=-1$
45. $\frac{dy}{dx}+y=x,\quad y_0=0$
46. $\frac{dy}{dx}+y=2x,\quad y_0=-1$

Writing for Your Own Knowledge

Answer the following questions in writing. Some answers will take only a sentence or two; others may require several paragraphs. Some explanations may also call for graphs or sketches.

1. What is the binomial series for $(1 + x)^m$? When is the series finite? infinite? What is the infinite series' interval of convergence?
2. How can you sometimes use power series to evaluate nonelementary indefinite integrals?
3. How can you sometimes use power series to estimate the values of definite integrals?
4. What are the Maclaurin series for $1/(1 + x)$ and $1/(1 - x)$? What is each series' interval of convergence?
5. What are the Maclaurin series for $\ln(1 + x)$ and $\tan^{-1} x$? What is each series' interval of convergence?
6. How can you sometimes use power series to solve initial value problems?

For Your Review

Write brief paragraphs about the following topics and give examples.

Sequences
Geometric series
The nth-Term Test
The Direct Comparison Test
The Integral Test
The Limit Comparison Test
The Ratio Test
The Root Test
Alternating series
Absolute convergence
Power series
Term-by-term integration and differentiation of power series
Taylor and Maclaurin series
Taylor's formula and remainder estimation
The use of series to evaluate nonelementary integrals
The use of power series to solve initial value problems

Practice Exercises

Which of the sequences $\{a_n\}$ whose nth terms appear in Exercises 1–16 converge and which diverge? Find the limit of each convergent sequence.

1. $a_n = 1 + \dfrac{(-1)^n}{n}$
2. $a_n = \dfrac{1 - (-1)^n}{\sqrt{n}}$
3. $a_n = \dfrac{1 - 2^n}{2^n}$
4. $a_n = 1 + (0.9)^n$
5. $a_n = \sin \dfrac{n\pi}{2}$
6. $a_n = \sin n\pi$
7. $a_n = \dfrac{\ln(n^2)}{n}$
8. $a_n = \dfrac{\ln(2n + 1)}{n}$
9. $a_n = \dfrac{n + \ln n}{n}$
10. $a_n = \dfrac{n}{n + \ln n}$
11. $a_n = \left(\dfrac{n + 5}{n}\right)^n$
12. $a_n = \left(\dfrac{n - 5}{n}\right)^n$
13. $a_n = \sqrt[n]{\dfrac{3^n}{n}}$
14. $a_n = \left(\dfrac{3}{n}\right)^{1/n}$
15. $a_n = \dfrac{(n + 1)!}{n!}$
16. $a_n = \dfrac{(-4)^n}{n!}$

Find the sums of the series in Exercises 17–22.

17. $\displaystyle\sum_{n=3}^{\infty} \frac{1}{(2n - 3)(2n - 1)}$
18. $\displaystyle\sum_{n=2}^{\infty} \frac{-2}{n(n + 1)}$
19. $\displaystyle\sum_{n=1}^{\infty} \frac{9}{(3n - 1)(3n + 2)}$
20. $\displaystyle\sum_{n=3}^{\infty} \frac{-8}{(4n - 3)(4n + 1)}$
21. $\displaystyle\sum_{n=0}^{\infty} e^{-n}$
22. $\displaystyle\sum_{n=1}^{\infty} (-1)^n \frac{3}{4^n}$

Which of the series in Exercises 23–38 converge absolutely, which converge conditionally, and which diverge? Give reasons for your answers.

23. $\displaystyle\sum_{n=1}^{\infty} \frac{1}{\sqrt{n}}$
24. $\displaystyle\sum_{n=1}^{\infty} \frac{-5}{n}$
25. $\displaystyle\sum_{n=1}^{\infty} \frac{(-1)^n}{\sqrt{n}}$
26. $\displaystyle\sum_{n=1}^{\infty} \frac{1}{2n^3}$
27. $\displaystyle\sum_{n=1}^{\infty} \frac{(-1)^n}{\ln(n + 1)}$
28. $\displaystyle\sum_{n=2}^{\infty} \frac{1}{n(\ln n)^2}$
29. $\displaystyle\sum_{n=1}^{\infty} \frac{\ln n}{n^3}$
30. $\displaystyle\sum_{n=3}^{\infty} \frac{\ln n}{\ln(\ln n)}$
31. $\displaystyle\sum_{n=1}^{\infty} \frac{(-1)^n}{n\sqrt{n^2 + 1}}$
32. $\displaystyle\sum_{n=1}^{\infty} \frac{(-1)^n 3n^2}{n^3 + 1}$
33. $\displaystyle\sum_{n=1}^{\infty} \frac{n + 1}{n!}$
34. $\displaystyle\sum_{n=1}^{\infty} \frac{(-1)^n(n^2 + 1)}{2n^2 + n - 1}$
35. $\displaystyle\sum_{n=1}^{\infty} \frac{(-3)^n}{n!}$
36. $\displaystyle\sum_{n=1}^{\infty} \frac{2^n 3^n}{n^n}$
37. $\displaystyle\sum_{n=1}^{\infty} \frac{1}{\sqrt{n(n + 1)(n + 2)}}$
38. $\displaystyle\sum_{n=2}^{\infty} \frac{1}{n\sqrt{n^2 - 1}}$

Each of Exercises 39–46 gives a formula for the nth term of an infinite series. (a) Find the series' radius and interval of convergence. For what values of x does the series converge (b) absolutely; (c) conditionally?

39. $\dfrac{(x+4)^n}{n3^n}$

40. $\dfrac{(x-1)^{2n-2}}{(2n-1)!}$

41. $\dfrac{(-1)^{n-1}(3x-1)^n}{n^2}$

42. $\dfrac{n+1}{2n+1}\dfrac{(2x+1)^n}{2^n}$

43. $\dfrac{x^n}{n^n}$

44. $\dfrac{x^n}{\sqrt{n}}$

45. $\dfrac{(n+1)\,x^{2n-1}}{3^n}$

46. $\dfrac{(-1)^n(x-1)^{2n+1}}{2n+1}$

47. a) Show that the series

$$\sum_{n=1}^{\infty}\left(\sin\frac{1}{2n}-\sin\frac{1}{2n+1}\right)$$

converges.

b) Estimate the magnitude of the error involved in using the sum of the sines through sin (1/40) to approximate the sum of the series. Is the approximation too large, or too small? Give reasons for your answer.

48. a) Show that the series $\sum_{n=1}^{\infty}\left(\tan\frac{1}{2n}-\tan\frac{1}{2n+1}\right)$ converges.

b) Estimate the magnitude of the error involved in using the sum of the tangents through $-\tan(1/41)$ to approximate the sum of the series. Is the approximation too large, or too small? Give reasons for your answer.

Each of the series in Exercises 49–54 is the value of the Maclaurin series of a function $f(x)$ at a particular point. What function and what point? What is the sum of the series?

49. $1-\dfrac{1}{4}+\dfrac{1}{16}-\cdots+(-1)^n\dfrac{1}{4^n}+\cdots$

50. $\dfrac{2}{3}-\dfrac{4}{18}+\dfrac{8}{81}-\cdots+(-1)^{n-1}\dfrac{2^n}{n3^n}+\cdots$

51. $\pi-\dfrac{\pi^3}{3!}+\dfrac{\pi^5}{5!}-\cdots+(-1)^n\dfrac{\pi^{2n+1}}{(2n+1)!}+\cdots$

52. $1-\dfrac{\pi^2}{9\cdot 2!}+\dfrac{\pi^4}{81\cdot 4!}-\cdots+(-1)^n\dfrac{\pi^{2n}}{3^{2n}(2n)!}+\cdots$

53. $1+\ln 2+\dfrac{(\ln 2)^2}{2!}+\cdots+\dfrac{(\ln 2)^n}{n!}+\cdots$

54. $\dfrac{1}{\sqrt{3}}-\dfrac{1}{9\sqrt{3}}+\dfrac{1}{45\sqrt{3}}-\cdots+(-1)^{n-1}\dfrac{1}{(2n-1)(\sqrt{3})^{2n-1}}+\cdots$

In Exercises 55 and 56, find the first four nonzero terms of the Taylor series generated by f at a.

55. $f(x)=\sqrt{3+x^2}$ at $a=-1$

56. $f(x)=1/(1-x)$ at $a=2$

Find Maclaurin series for the functions in Exercises 57–64.

57. $\dfrac{1}{1-2x}$

58. $\dfrac{1}{1+x^3}$

59. $\sin\pi x$

60. $\sin\dfrac{2x}{3}$

61. $\cos(x^{5/2})$

62. $\cos\sqrt{5x}$

63. $e^{(\pi x/2)}$

64. e^{-x^2}

Use series to approximate the values of the integrals in Exercises 65 and 66 with an error of magnitude less than 10^{-8}. (The answer section gives the integrals' values rounded to 10 decimal places.)

65. $\displaystyle\int_0^{1/2} e^{-x^3}\,dx$

66. $\displaystyle\int_0^{1/2}\frac{\tan^{-1}x}{x}\,dx$

Determine the convergence or divergence of the series in Exercises 67–70. Give reasons for your answers.

67. $\displaystyle\sum_{n=1}^{\infty}\ln\left(\frac{n}{n+1}\right)$

68. $\displaystyle\sum_{n=1}^{\infty}\ln\left(\frac{n+1}{n}\right)$

69. $\displaystyle\sum_{n=1}^{\infty}\left(1-\frac{1}{n}\right)^n$

70. $\displaystyle\sum_{n=1}^{\infty}\frac{n!}{n^n}$

71. If $\Sigma_{n=1}^{\infty}a_n$ and $\Sigma_{n=1}^{\infty}b_n$ are convergent series of nonnegative numbers, can anything be said about $\Sigma_{n=1}^{\infty}a_n b_n$? Give reasons for your answer.

72. If $\Sigma_{n=1}^{\infty}a_n$ and $\Sigma_{n=1}^{\infty}b_n$ are divergent series of nonnegative numbers, can anything be said about $\Sigma_{n=1}^{\infty}a_n b_n$? Give reasons for your answer.

Use power series to solve the initial value problems in Exercises 73–76 given that $y=y_0$ when $x=0$.

73. $\dfrac{dy}{dx}+y=0,\quad y_0=-1$

74. $\dfrac{dy}{dx}+y=1,\quad y_0=0$

75. $\dfrac{dy}{dx}-y=x,\quad y_0=1$

76. $\dfrac{dy}{dx}-y=-x,\quad y_0=2$

R. L. (BEN) BRUNGRABER of Benson Woodworking, Alstead, NH, and **LEONARD J. MORSE-FORTIER** at the Massachusetts Institute of Technology are both structural engineers who currently collaborate on designs for timber structures and are prepared to consult on anything from computer modeling to suspension bridges.

The graceful form of a suspension bridge is a familiar and, for many, appealing sight. The drape of the main cables has a lot to do with derivatives, based on the mechanics of load carrying in the main cables.

The slope of the main cable at any point along the span is described by the first derivative of its vertical position and reveals the degree to which the cable is carrying vertical load. The greater the vertical component of tension, the steeper the cable slope and the larger the magnitude of its first derivative.

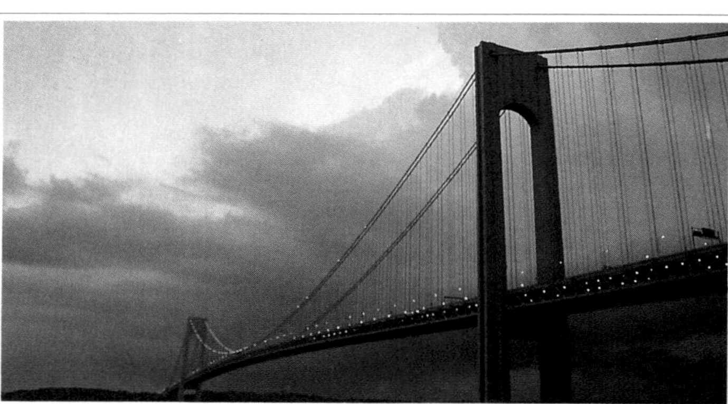

The change in load along the main cable is related to the change in slope, which is the second derivative of the cable's vertical position. Since the evenly spaced vertical hangers in a suspension bridge each carry the same load, the second derivative of the main cable's shape is constant. This makes the main cable assume a parabolic shape.

Bridge designers and builders use their knowledge of the final resting shape of the main cables throughout the analysis and construction process. For really long bridges, other issues affect the final cable configuration as well. For instance, the towers of the Verrazano-Narrows Bridge in New York City are nearly a foot farther apart at the top than they are at the water line, reflecting the intervening curvature of the earth.

10 Conic Sections, Parametrized Curves, and Polar Coordinates

OVERVIEW

The study of motion has been important since ancient times, and calculus provides the mathematics we need to describe it. In this chapter, we extend our ability to analyze motion by showing how to track the position of a moving body as a function of time. We begin with equations for conic sections, since these are the paths traveled by planets, satellites, and other bodies (even electrons) whose motions are driven by inverse square forces. As we will see in Chapter 12, once we know that the path of a moving body is a conic section, we immediately have information about the body's velocity and the force that drives it. Planetary motion is best described in polar coordinates (another of Newton's inventions, although James Bernoulli usually gets the credit), so we also investigate curves, derivatives, and integrals in this new coordinate system.

10.1 Conic Sections and Quadratic Equations

This section shows how the conic sections from Greek geometry are described today as the graphs of quadratic equations in the coordinate plane. The Greeks of Plato's time described these curves as the curves formed by cutting a double cone with a plane (Fig. 10.1); hence the name *conic section*.

Circles

DEFINITIONS

A **circle** is the set of points in a plane whose distance from a given fixed point in the plane is constant. The fixed point is the **center** of the circle; the constant distance is the **radius.**

The standard-form equations for circles are these:

Equations for circles in the xy-plane are derived from the distance formula

$$d = \sqrt{(x_2 - x_1)^2 + (y_2 - y_1)^2}.$$

See Section 1.4.

Circles

Circle of radius a centered at the origin:

$x^2 + y^2 = a^2$

Circle of radius a centered at the point (h, k):

$(x - h)^2 + (y - k)^2 = a^2$

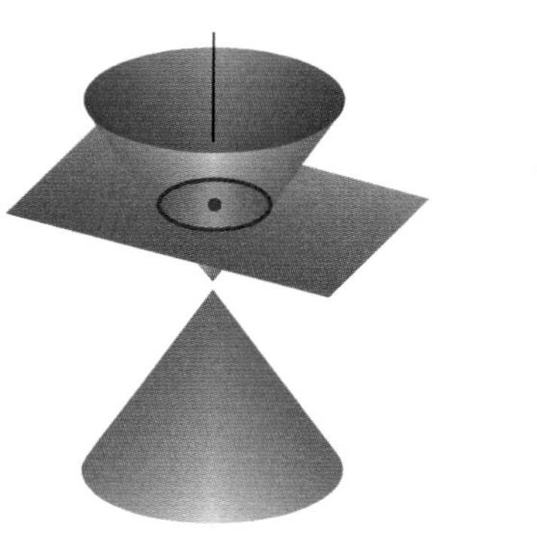

Circle: plane perpendicular to cone axis

Ellipse

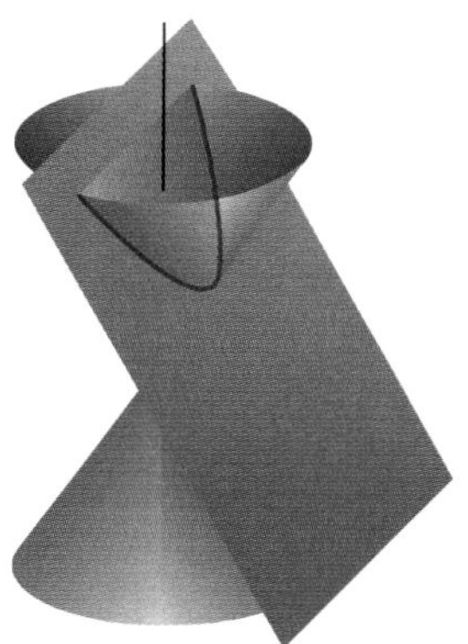

Parabola: plane parallel to side of cone

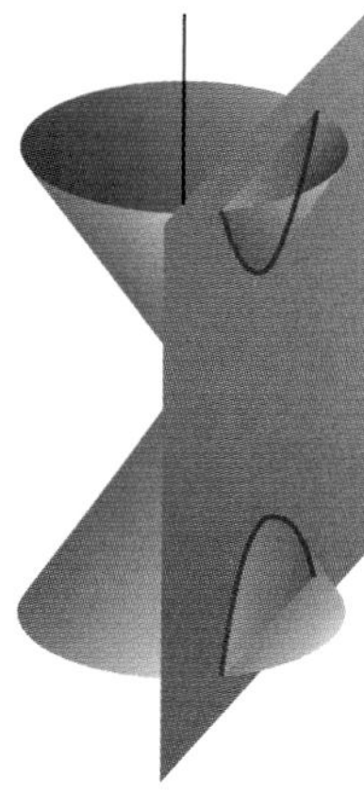

Hyperbola: plane parallel to cone axis

(a)

10.1 The standard conic sections (a) are the curves in which a plane cuts a double cone. Hyperbolas come in two parts, called *branches*. The point and lines obtained by passing the plane through the cone's vertex (b) are *degenerate* conic sections.

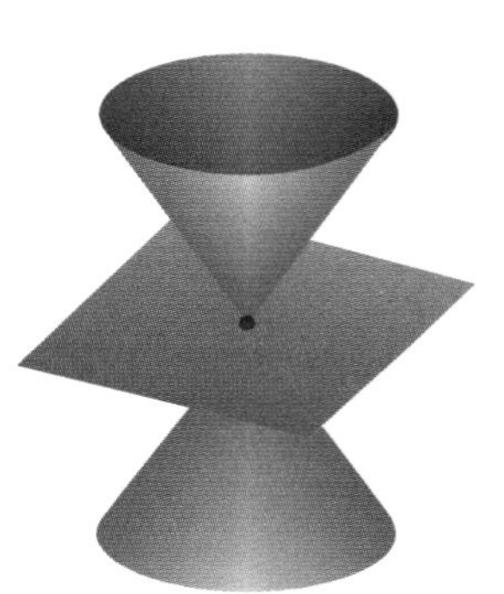

Point: plane through cone vertex only

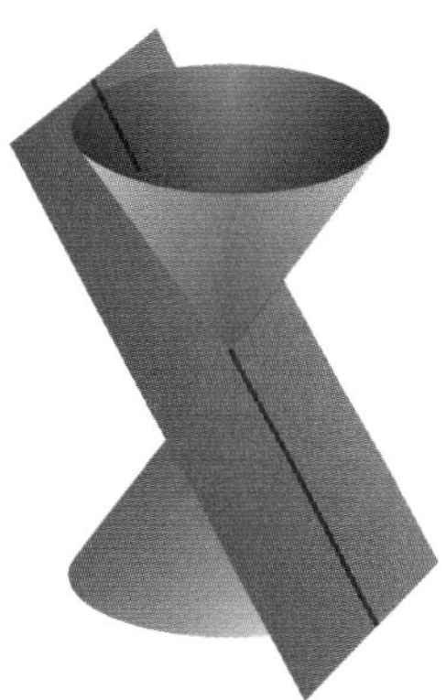

Single line: plane tangent to cone

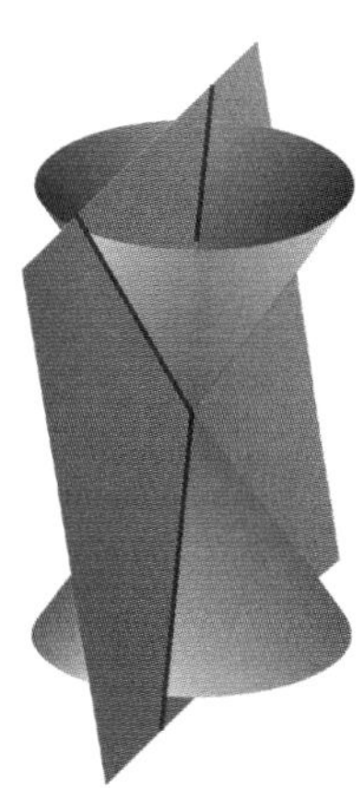

Pair of intersecting lines

(b)

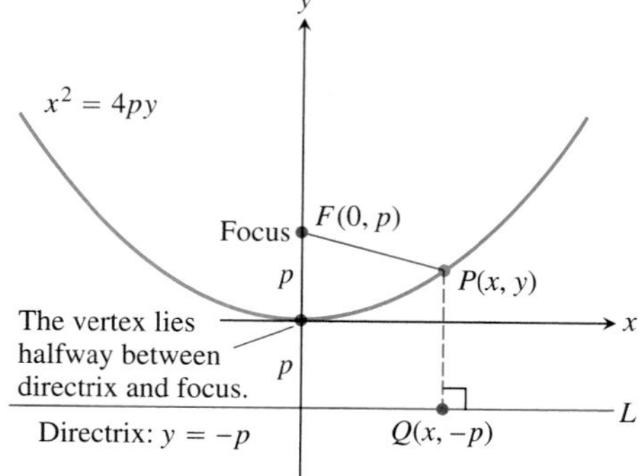

10.2 The parabola $x^2 = 4py$.

Parabolas

DEFINITIONS

A set that consists of all the points in a plane equidistant from a given fixed point and a given fixed line in the plane is a **parabola.** The fixed point is the **focus** of the parabola. The fixed line is the **directrix.**

If the focus F lies on the directrix L, the parabola is the line through F perpendicular to L. We consider this to be a degenerate case and assume henceforth that F does not lie on L.

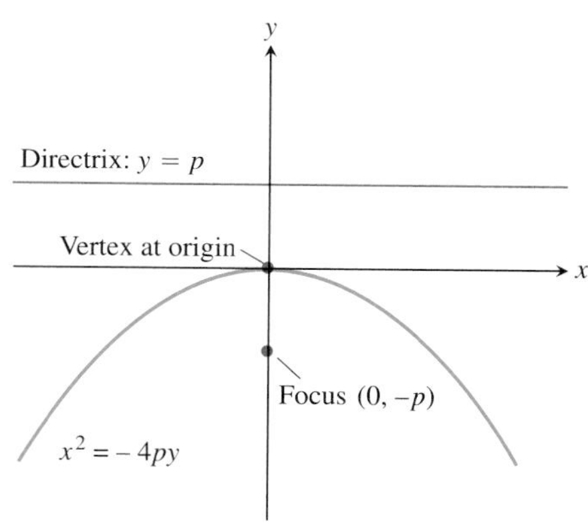

10.3 The parabola $x^2 = -4py$.

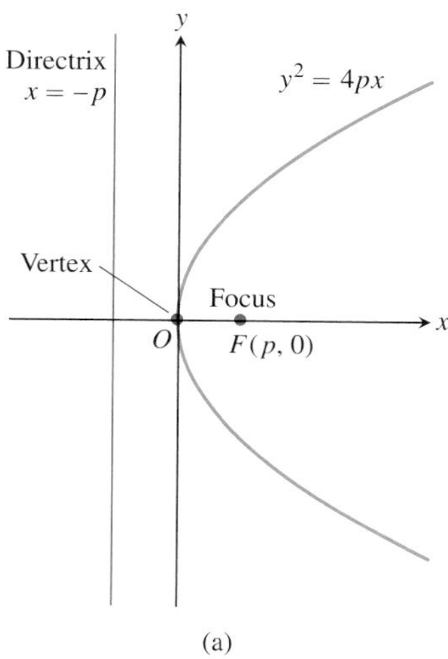

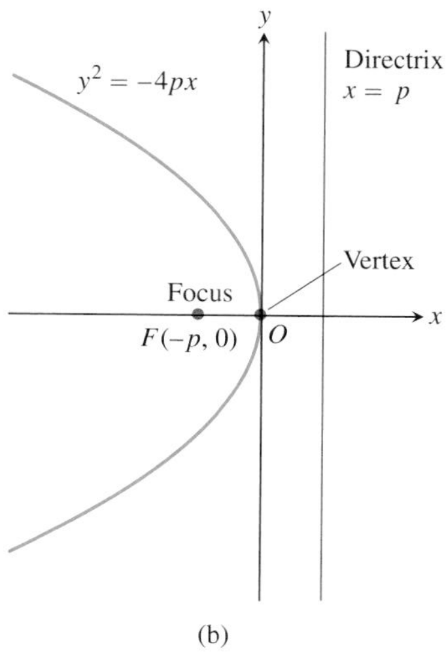

10.4 (a) The parabola $y^2 = 4px$. (b) The parabola $y^2 = -4px$.

A parabola has its simplest equation when its focus and directrix straddle one of the coordinate axes. For example, suppose that the focus lies at the point $F(0, p)$ on the positive y-axis and that the directrix is the line $y = -p$ (Fig. 10.2). In the notation of the figure, a point $P(x, y)$ lies on the parabola if and only if $PF = PQ$. From the distance formula,

$$PF = \sqrt{(x-0)^2 + (y-p)^2} = \sqrt{x^2 + (y-p)^2},$$
$$PQ = \sqrt{(x-x)^2 + (y-(-p))^2} = \sqrt{(y+p)^2}. \qquad (1)$$

When we equate these expressions, square, and simplify, we get

$$y = \frac{x^2}{4p} \quad \text{or} \quad x^2 = 4py. \qquad \text{Standard form} \qquad (2)$$

These equations reveal the parabola's symmetry about the y-axis. We call the y-axis the **axis** of the parabola (short for "axis of symmetry").

The point where a parabola crosses its axis is the **vertex.** The vertex of the parabola $x^2 = 4py$ lies at the origin (Fig. 10.2). The positive number p is the parabola's **focal length.**

If the parabola opens downward, with its focus at $(0, -p)$ and its directrix the line $y = p$, then Eqs. (2) become

$$y = -\frac{x^2}{4p} \quad \text{and} \quad x^2 = -4py \qquad (3)$$

(Fig. 10.3). We obtain similar equations for parabolas opening to the right or to the left (Fig. 10.4 and Table 10.1).

TABLE 10.1
Standard-form equations for parabolas with vertices at the origin ($p > 0$)

Equation	Focus	Directrix	Axis	Opens
$x^2 = 4py$	$(0, p)$	$y = -p$	y-axis	Up
$x^2 = -4py$	$(0, -p)$	$y = p$	y-axis	Down
$y^2 = 4px$	$(p, 0)$	$x = -p$	x-axis	To the right
$y^2 = -4px$	$(-p, 0)$	$x = p$	x-axis	To the left

EXAMPLE 1 Find the focus and directrix of the parabola $y^2 = 10x$.

Solution We find the value of p in the standard equation $y^2 = 4px$:

$$4p = 10, \quad \text{so} \quad p = \frac{10}{4} = \frac{5}{2}.$$

Then we find the focus and directrix for this value of p:

Focus: $(p, 0) = \left(\frac{5}{2}, 0\right)$

Directrix: $x = -p$ or $x = -\frac{5}{2}$.

As in Section 1.4, the horizontal and vertical shift formulas can be applied to the equations in Table 10.1 to give equations for a variety of parabolas in other locations (see Exercises 47, 48, and 53–56).

Ellipses

DEFINITIONS

An **ellipse** is the set of points in a plane whose distances from two fixed points in the plane have a constant sum. The two fixed points are the **foci** of the ellipse.

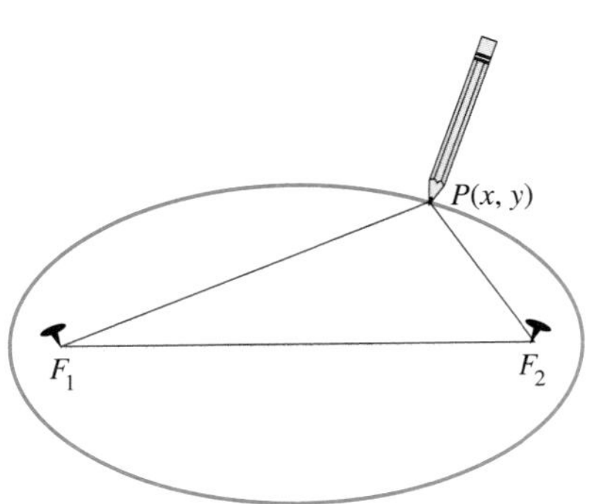

10.5 How to draw an ellipse.

The quickest way to construct an ellipse uses the definition. Put a loop of string around two tacks F_1 and F_2, pull the string taut with a pencil point P, and move the pencil around to trace a closed curve (Fig. 10.5). The curve is an ellipse because the sum $PF_1 + PF_2$, being the length of the loop minus the distance between the tacks, remains constant. The ellipse's foci lie at F_1 and F_2.

DEFINITIONS

The line through the foci of an ellipse is the ellipse's **focal axis.** The point on the axis halfway between the foci is the **center.** The points where the focal axis and ellipse cross are the ellipse's **vertices.**

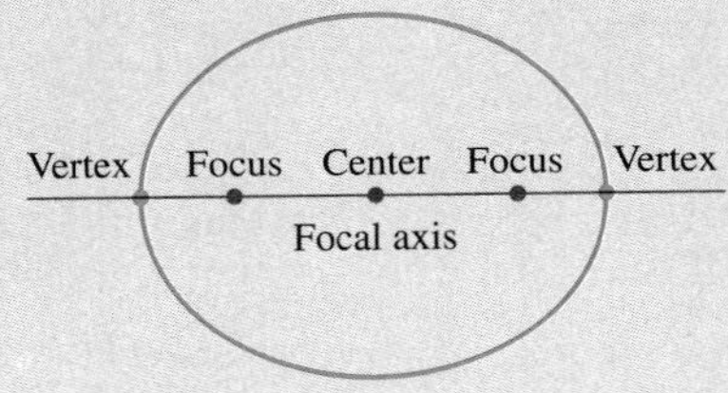

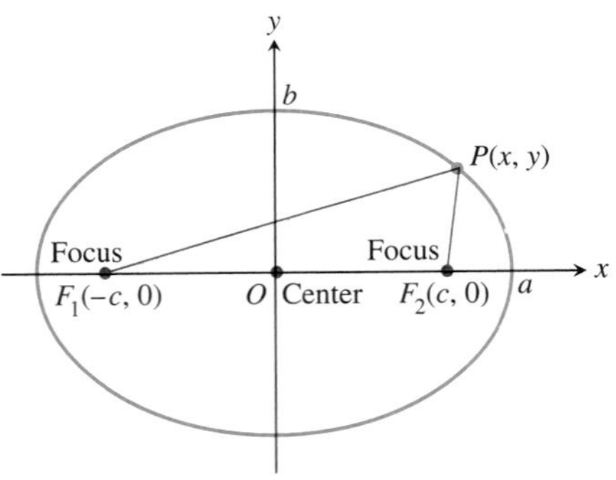

10.6 The ellipse defined by the equation $PF_1 + PF_2 = 2a$ is the graph of the equation $(x^2/a^2) + (y^2/b^2) = 1$.

If the foci are $F_1(-c, 0)$ and $F_2(c, 0)$ (Fig. 10.6), and $PF_1 + PF_2$ is denoted by $2a$, then the coordinates of a point P on the ellipse satisfy the equation

$$\sqrt{(x+c)^2 + y^2} + \sqrt{(x-c)^2 + y^2} = 2a. \tag{4}$$

To simplify this equation, we move the second radical to the right-hand side, square, isolate the remaining radical, and square again, obtaining

$$\frac{x^2}{a^2} + \frac{y^2}{a^2 - c^2} = 1. \tag{5}$$

Since $PF_1 + PF_2$ is greater than the length F_1F_2 (triangle inequality for triangle PF_1F_2), the number $2a$ is greater than $2c$. Accordingly, $a > c$ and the number $a^2 - c^2$ in Eq. (5) is positive.

The algebraic steps leading to Eq. (5) can be reversed to show that every point P whose coordinates satisfy an equation of this form with $0 < c < a$ also satisfies the equation $PF_1 + PF_2 = 2a$. A point therefore lies on the ellipse if and only if its coordinates satisfy Eq. (5).

If

$$b = \sqrt{a^2 - c^2}, \tag{6}$$

Drawing Lesson

How to Graph the Ellipse $\frac{x^2}{a^2} + \frac{y^2}{b^2} = 1$

1 Mark the points $(\pm a, 0)$ and $(0, \pm b)$ with line segments perpendicular to the coordinate axes.

2 Use the segments as tangent lines to guide your drawing.

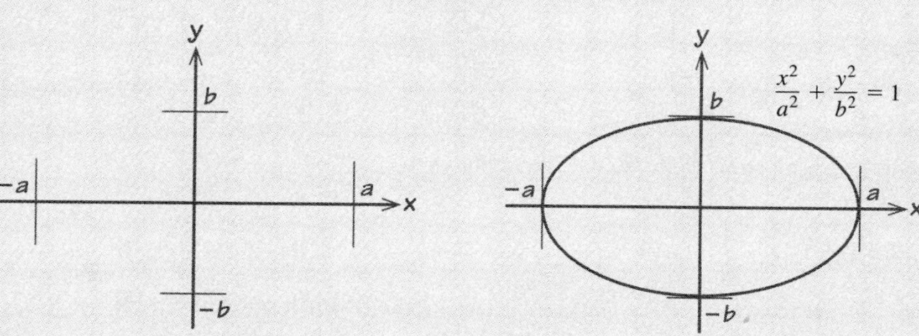

then $a^2 - c^2 = b^2$ and Eq. (6) takes the form

$$\frac{x^2}{a^2} + \frac{y^2}{b^2} = 1. \tag{7}$$

Equation (7) reveals that this ellipse is symmetric with respect to the origin and both coordinate axes. It lies inside the rectangle bounded by the lines $x = \pm a$ and $y = \pm b$. It crosses the axes at the points $(\pm a, 0)$ and $(0, \pm b)$. The tangents at these points are perpendicular to the axes because

$$\frac{dy}{dx} = -\frac{b^2 x}{a^2 y} \qquad \text{Obtained from Eq. (7) by implicit differentiation}$$

is zero if $x = 0$ and infinite if $y = 0$. These observations are the basis of the drawing lesson.

The Major and Minor Axes of an Ellipse

The **major axis** of the ellipse in Eq. (7) is the line segment of length $2a$ joining the points $(\pm a, 0)$. The **minor axis** is the line segment of length $2b$ joining the points $(0, \pm b)$. The number a itself is the **semimajor axis,** the number b the **semiminor axis.** The number c, found from Eq. (6) as

$$c = \sqrt{a^2 - b^2}, \tag{8}$$

is the **center-to-focus distance** of the ellipse.

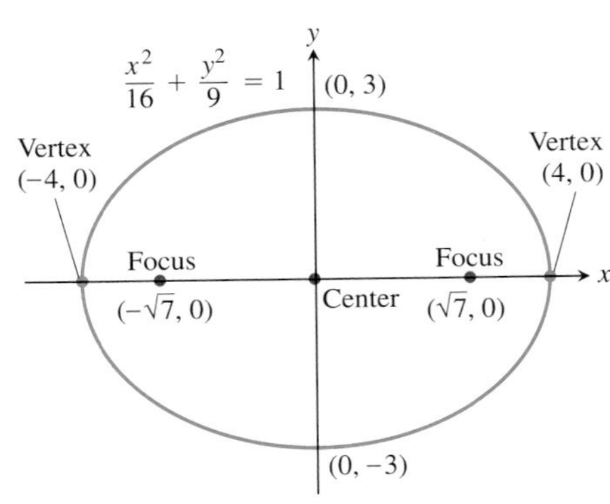

10.7 Major axis is horizontal (Example 2).

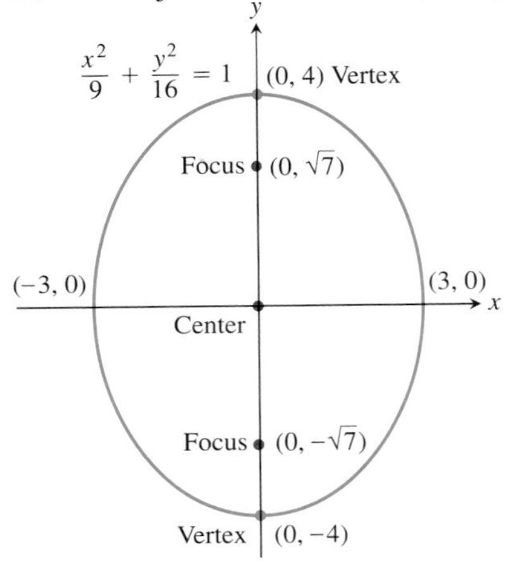

10.8 Major axis is vertical (Example 3).

EXAMPLE 2 *Major Axis Horizontal.* The ellipse

$$\frac{x^2}{16} + \frac{y^2}{9} = 1 \tag{9}$$

(Fig. 10.7) has

Semimajor axis: $a = \sqrt{16} = 4$, Semiminor axis: $b = \sqrt{9} = 3$
Center-to-focus distance: $c = \sqrt{16 - 9} = \sqrt{7}$
Foci: $(\pm c, 0) = (\pm \sqrt{7}, 0)$
Vertices: $(\pm a, 0) = (\pm 4, 0)$
Center: $(0, 0)$.

EXAMPLE 3 *Major Axis Vertical.* The ellipse

$$\frac{x^2}{9} + \frac{y^2}{16} = 1, \tag{10}$$

obtained by interchanging x and y in Eq. (9), has its major axis vertical instead of horizontal (Fig. 10.8). With a^2 still equal to 16 and b^2 equal to 9, we have

Semimajor axis: $a = \sqrt{16} = 4$, Semiminor axis: $b = \sqrt{9} = 3$
Center-to-focus distance: $c = \sqrt{16 - 9} = \sqrt{7}$
Foci: $(0, \pm c) = (0, \pm \sqrt{7})$
Vertices: $(0, \pm a) = (0, \pm 4)$
Center: $(0, 0)$.

There is never any cause for confusion in analyzing equations like (9) and (10). We simply find the intercepts on the coordinate axes; then we know which way the major axis runs because it is the longer of the two axes. The center always lies at the origin and the foci lie on the major axis.

Standard-Form Equations for Ellipses Centered at the Origin

Foci on the x-axis: $\frac{x^2}{a^2} + \frac{y^2}{b^2} = 1 \quad (a > b)$

Center-to-focus distance: $c = \sqrt{a^2 - b^2}$
Foci: $(\pm c, 0)$
Vertices: $(\pm a, 0)$

Foci on the y-axis: $\frac{x^2}{b^2} + \frac{y^2}{a^2} = 1 \quad (a > b)$

Center-to-focus distance: $c = \sqrt{a^2 - b^2}$
Foci: $(0, \pm c)$
Vertices: $(0, \pm a)$

In each case, a is the semimajor axis and b is the semiminor axis.

Hyperbolas

DEFINITIONS

A **hyperbola** is the set of points in a plane whose distances from two fixed points in the plane have a constant difference. The two fixed points are the **foci** of the hyperbola.

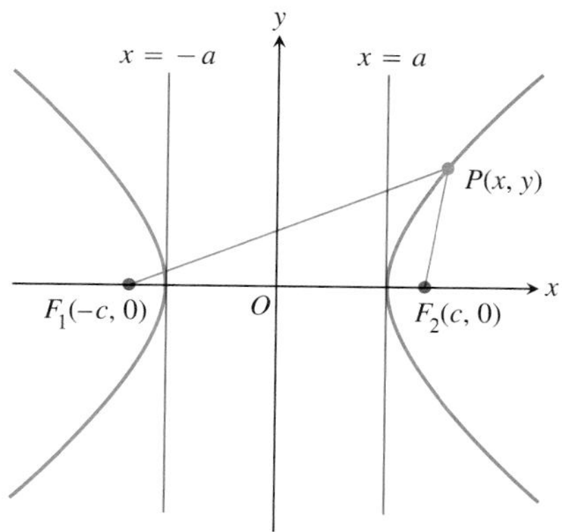

10.9 Hyperbolas have two branches. For points on the right-hand branch of the hyperbola shown here, $PF_1 - PF_2 = 2a$. For points on the left-hand branch, $PF_2 - PF_1 = 2a$.

If the foci are $F_1(-c, 0)$ and $F_2(c, 0)$ (Fig. 10.9) and the constant difference is $2a$, then a point (x, y) lies on the hyperbola if and only if

$$\sqrt{(x+c)^2 + y^2} - \sqrt{(x-c)^2 + y^2} = \pm 2a. \tag{11}$$

To simplify this equation, we move the second radical to the right-hand side, square, isolate the remaining radical, and square again, obtaining

$$\frac{x^2}{a^2} + \frac{y^2}{a^2 - c^2} = 1. \tag{12}$$

So far, this looks just like the equation for an ellipse. But now $a^2 - c^2$ is negative because $2a$, being the difference of two sides of triangle PF_1F_2, is less than $2c$, the third side.

The algebraic steps leading to Eq. (12) can be reversed to show that every point P whose coordinates satisfy an equation of this form with $0 < a < c$ also satisfies Eq. (11). A point therefore lies on the hyperbola if and only if its coordinates satisfy Eq. (12).

If we let b denote the positive square root of $c^2 - a^2$,

$$b = \sqrt{c^2 - a^2}, \tag{13}$$

then $a^2 - c^2 = -b^2$ and Eq. (12) takes the more compact form

$$\frac{x^2}{a^2} - \frac{y^2}{b^2} = 1. \tag{14}$$

The differences between Eq. (14) and the equation for an ellipse (Eq. 7) are the minus sign and the new relation

$$c^2 = a^2 + b^2. \qquad \text{From Eq. (13)} \tag{15}$$

Like the ellipse, the hyperbola is symmetric with respect to the origin and coordinate axes. It crosses the x-axis at the points $(\pm a, 0)$. The tangents at these points are vertical because

$$\frac{dy}{dx} = \frac{b^2x}{a^2y} \qquad \text{Obtained from Eq. (14) by implicit differentiation}$$

is infinite when $y = 0$. The hyperbola has no y-intercepts; in fact, no part of the curve lies between the lines $x = -a$ and $x = a$.

DEFINITIONS

The line through the foci of a hyperbola is the hyperbola's **focal axis.** The point on the axis halfway between the foci is the hyperbola's **center.** The points where the focal axis and hyperbola cross are the hyperbola's **vertices.**

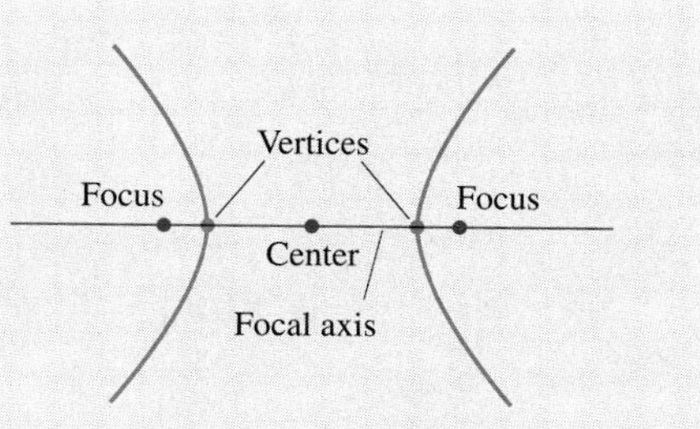

Asymptotes of Hyperbolas—Graphing

The hyperbola

$$\frac{x^2}{a^2} - \frac{y^2}{b^2} = 1 \tag{16}$$

has two asymptotes, the lines

$$y = \pm \frac{b}{a} x. \tag{17}$$

The asymptotes give us the guidance we need to graph hyperbolas quickly. (See the drawing lesson.) The fastest way to find the equations of the asymptotes is to replace the 1 in Eq. (16) by 0 and solve the new equation for y:

$$\underbrace{\frac{x^2}{a^2} - \frac{y^2}{b^2} = 1}_{\text{hyperbola}} \Rightarrow \underbrace{\frac{x^2}{a^2} - \frac{y^2}{b^2} = 0}_{0\text{ for }1} \Rightarrow \underbrace{y = \pm \frac{b}{a} x.}_{\text{asymptotes}} \tag{18}$$

Standard-Form Equations for Hyperbolas Centered at the Origin

Foci on the x-axis: $\dfrac{x^2}{a^2} - \dfrac{y^2}{b^2} = 1$

Center-to-focus distance: $c = \sqrt{a^2 + b^2}$
Foci: $(\pm c, 0)$
Vertices: $(\pm a, 0)$
Asymptotes: $\dfrac{x^2}{a^2} - \dfrac{y^2}{b^2} = 0$ or $y = \pm \dfrac{b}{a} x$

Foci on the y-axis: $\dfrac{y^2}{a^2} - \dfrac{x^2}{b^2} = 1$

Center-to-focus distance: $c = \sqrt{a^2 + b^2}$
Foci: $(0, \pm c)$
Vertices: $(0, \pm a)$
Asymptotes: $\dfrac{y^2}{a^2} - \dfrac{x^2}{b^2} = 0$ or $y = \pm \dfrac{a}{b} x$

Notice the difference in the asymptote equations (b/a in the first, a/b in the second).

Drawing Lesson

How to Graph the Hyperbola $\dfrac{x^2}{a^2} - \dfrac{y^2}{b^2} = 1$

1 Mark the points $(\pm a, 0)$ and $(0, \pm b)$ with line segments and complete the rectangle they determine.

2 Sketch the asymptotes by extending the rectangle's diagonals.

3 Use the rectangle and asymptotes to guide your drawing.

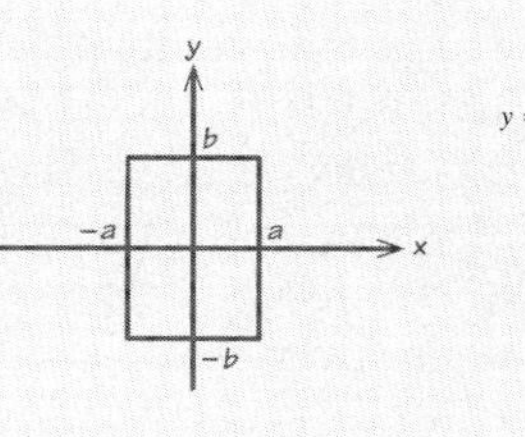

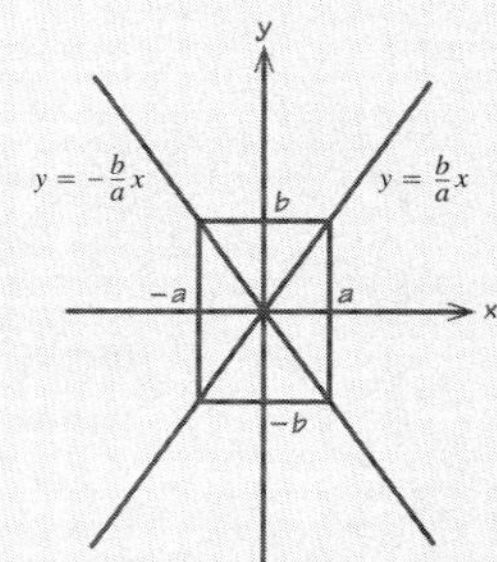

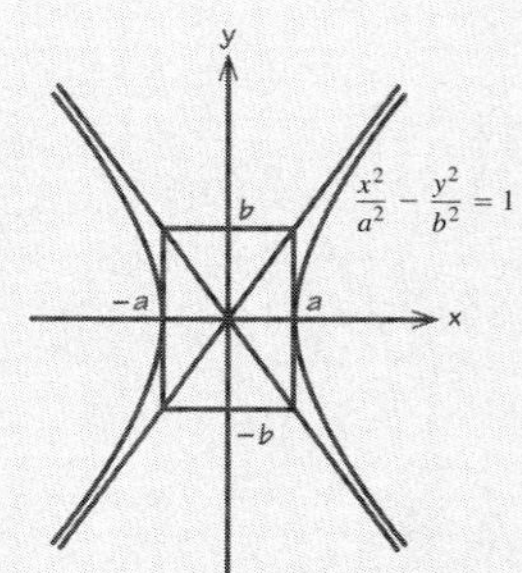

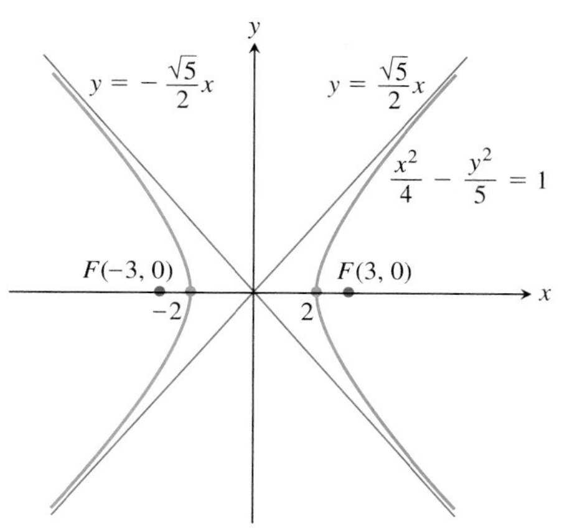

10.10 The hyperbola in Example 4.

EXAMPLE 4 *Foci on the x-axis.* The equation

$$\frac{x^2}{4} - \frac{y^2}{5} = 1 \tag{19}$$

is Eq. (14) with $a^2 = 4$ and $b^2 = 5$ (Fig. 10.10). We have

Center-to-focus distance: $c = \sqrt{a^2 + b^2} = \sqrt{4 + 5} = 3$

Foci: $(\pm c, 0) = (\pm 3, 0)$, Vertices: $(\pm a, 0) = (\pm 2, 0)$

Center: $(0, 0)$

Asymptotes: $\frac{x^2}{4} - \frac{y^2}{5} = 0$ or $y = \pm \frac{\sqrt{5}}{2} x.$

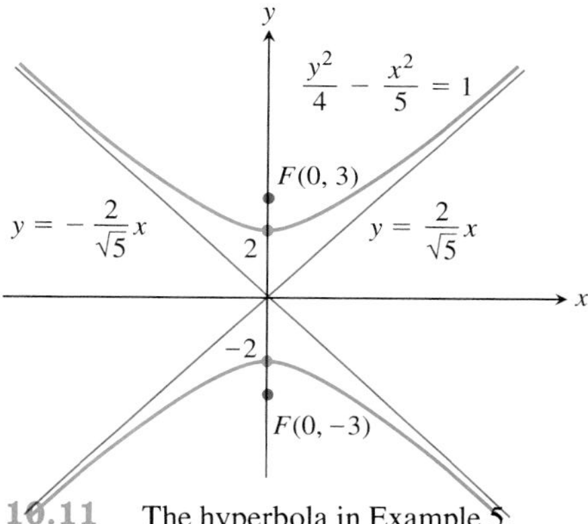

10.11 The hyperbola in Example 5.

EXAMPLE 5 *Foci on the y-axis.* The hyperbola

$$\frac{y^2}{4} - \frac{x^2}{5} = 1, \tag{20}$$

obtained by interchanging x and y in Eq. (19), has its vertices on the y-axis instead of the x-axis (Fig. 10.11). With a^2 still equal to 4 and b^2 equal to 5, we have

Center-to-focus distance: $c = \sqrt{a^2 + b^2} = \sqrt{4 + 5} = 3$

Foci: $(0, \pm c) = (0, \pm 3)$, Vertices: $(0, \pm a) = (0, \pm 2)$

Center: $(0, 0)$

Asymptotes: $\frac{y^2}{4} - \frac{x^2}{5} = 0$ or $y = \pm \frac{2}{\sqrt{5}} x.$

Classifying Conic Sections by Eccentricity: The Focus–Directrix Equation

Although the center-to-focus distance c does not appear in the equation

$$\frac{x^2}{a^2} + \frac{y^2}{b^2} = 1 \quad (a > b),$$

we can still determine the value of c from the equation $c = \sqrt{a^2 - b^2}$. If we fix a and vary c over the interval $0 \le c \le a$, the resulting ellipses will vary in shape (Fig. 10.12). They are circles if $c = 0$ (so that $a = b$) and flatten as c increases. If $c = a$, the foci and vertices overlap and the ellipse degenerates into a line segment.

We use the ratio of c to a to describe the various shapes the ellipse can take. We call this ratio the ellipse's eccentricity.

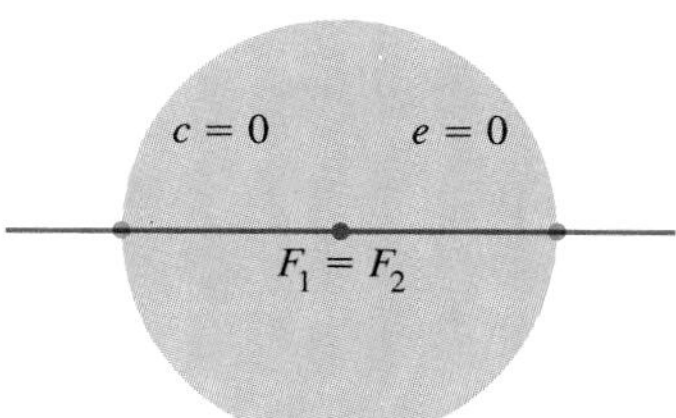

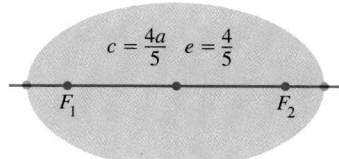

10.12 The ellipse changes from a circle to a line segment as c increases from 0 to a.

DEFINITION

The **eccentricity** of the ellipse $(x^2/a^2) + (y^2/b^2) = 1$ $(a > b)$ is

$$e = \frac{c}{a} = \frac{\sqrt{a^2 - b^2}}{a}. \tag{21}$$

TABLE 10.2
Eccentricities of planetary orbits

Mercury	0.21	Saturn	0.06
Venus	0.01	Uranus	0.05
Earth	0.02	Neptune	0.01
Mars	0.09	Pluto	0.25
Jupiter	0.05		

The planets in the solar system revolve around the sun in elliptical orbits with the sun at one focus. Most of the orbits are nearly circular, as can be seen from the eccentricities in Table 10.2. Pluto has a fairly eccentric orbit, with $e = 0.25$, as does Mercury, with $e = 0.21$. Other members of the solar system have orbits that are even more eccentric. Icarus, an asteroid about 1 mile wide that revolves around the sun every 409 Earth days, has an orbital eccentricity of 0.83 (Fig. 10.13).

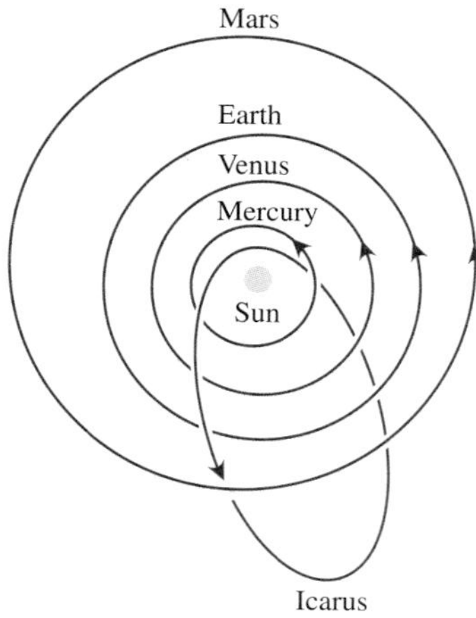

10.13 The orbit of the asteroid Icarus is highly eccentric. Earth's orbit is so nearly circular that its foci lie inside the sun.

EXAMPLE 6 The orbit of Halley's comet is an ellipse 36.18 astronomical units long by 9.12 astronomical units wide. (One *astronomical unit* (AU) is 149,597,870 km, the semimajor axis of Earth's orbit.) Its eccentricity is

$$e = \frac{\sqrt{a^2 - b^2}}{a} = \frac{\sqrt{(36.18/2)^2 - (9.12/2)^2}}{(36.18/2)} = \frac{\sqrt{(18.09)^2 - (4.56)^2}}{18.09} \approx 0.97.$$

Whereas a parabola has one focus and one directrix, each ellipse has two foci and two directrices. These are the lines perpendicular to the major axis at distances $\pm a/e$ from the center. The parabola has the property that

$$PF = 1 \cdot PD \tag{22}$$

for any point P on it, where F is the focus and D is the point nearest P on the directrix. For an ellipse, it can be shown that the equations that replace (22) are

$$PF_1 = e \cdot PD_1, \qquad PF_2 = e \cdot PD_2. \tag{23}$$

Here, e is the eccentricity, P is any point on the ellipse, F_1 and F_2 are the foci, and D_1 and D_2 are the points on the directrices nearest P (Fig. 10.14).

In each equation in (23) the directrix and focus must correspond; that is, if we use the distance from P to F_1, we must also use the distance from P to the directrix at the same end of the ellipse. The directrix $x = -a/e$ corresponds to $F_1(-c, 0)$, and the directrix $x = a/e$ corresponds to $F_2(c, 0)$.

The eccentricity of a hyperbola is also $e = c/a$, only in this case c equals $\sqrt{a^2 + b^2}$ instead of $\sqrt{a^2 - b^2}$. In contrast to the eccentricity of an ellipse, the eccentricity of a hyperbola is always greater than 1.

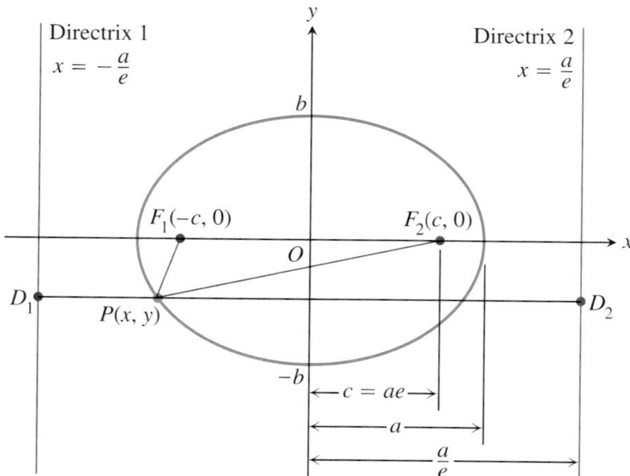

10.14 The foci and directrices of the ellipse $(x^2/a^2) + (y^2/b^2) = 1$. Directrix 1 corresponds to focus F_1, and directrix 2 to focus F_2.

Halley's Comet

Edmund Halley (1656–1742; pronounced *haw*-ley), British biologist, geologist, sea captain, pirate, spy, Antarctic voyager, astronomer, adviser on fortifications, company founder and director, and author of the first actuarial mortality tables, was also the mathematician who pushed and harried Newton into writing his *Principia*. Despite his accomplishments, Halley is known today chiefly as the man who calculated the orbit of the great comet of 1682: "wherefore if according to what we have already said [the comet] should return again about the year 1758, candid posterity will not refuse to acknowledge that this was first discovered by an Englishman." Indeed, candid posterity did not refuse—ever since the comet's return in 1758, it has been known as Halley's comet.

Last seen rounding the sun during the winter and spring of 1985–86, the comet is due to return in the year 2062. A recent study indicates that the comet has made about 2000 cycles so far with about the same number to go before the sun erodes it away completely.

DEFINITION

The **eccentricity** of the hyperbola $(x^2/a^2) - (y^2/b^2) = 1$ is

$$e = \frac{c}{a} = \frac{\sqrt{a^2+b^2}}{a}. \tag{24}$$

In both ellipse and hyperbola, the eccentricity is the ratio of the distance between the foci to the distance between the vertices (because $c/a = 2c/2a$).

$$\text{Eccentricity} = \frac{\text{distance between foci}}{\text{distance between vertices}} \tag{25}$$

In an ellipse, the foci are closer together than the vertices and the ratio is less than 1. In a hyperbola, the foci are farther apart than the vertices and the ratio is greater than 1.

EXAMPLE 7 Find the eccentricity of the hyperbola $9x^2 - 16y^2 = 144$.

Solution We divide both sides of the hyperbola's equation by 144 to put it in standard form, obtaining

$$\frac{9x^2}{144} - \frac{16y^2}{144} = 1 \quad \text{and} \quad \frac{x^2}{16} - \frac{y^2}{9} = 1.$$

With $a^2 = 16$ and $b^2 = 9$, we find that $c = \sqrt{a^2+b^2} = \sqrt{16+9} = 5$, so

$$e = \frac{c}{a} = \frac{5}{4}.$$

As with the ellipse, it can be shown that the lines $x = \pm a/e$ act as directrices for the hyperbola and that

$$PF_1 = e \cdot PD_1 \quad \text{and} \quad PF_2 = e \cdot PD_2. \tag{26}$$

Here P is any point on the hyperbola, F_1 and F_2 are the foci, and D_1 and D_2 are the points nearest P on the directrices (Fig. 10.15).

To complete the picture, we define the eccentricity of a parabola to be $e = 1$. Equations (22), (23), and (26) then have the common form $PF = e \cdot PD$.

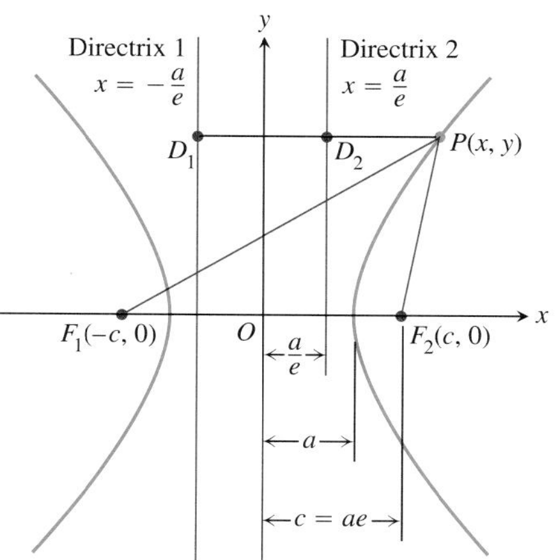

10.15 The foci and directrices of the hyperbola $(x^2/a^2) - (y^2/b^2) = 1$. No matter where P lies on the hyperbola, $PF_1 = e \cdot PD_1$ and $PF_2 = e \cdot PD_2$.

DEFINITION

The **eccentricity** of a parabola is $e = 1$.

The "focus–directrix" equation $PF = e \cdot PD$ unites the parabola, ellipse, and hyperbola in the following way. Suppose that the distance PF of a point P from a fixed point F (the focus) is a constant multiple of its distance from a fixed line (the directrix). That is, suppose

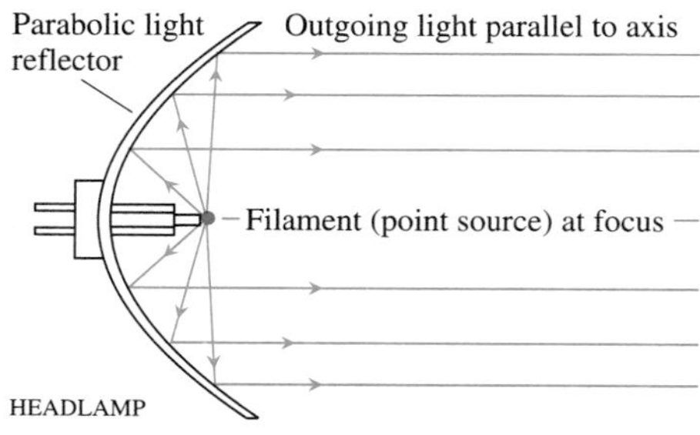

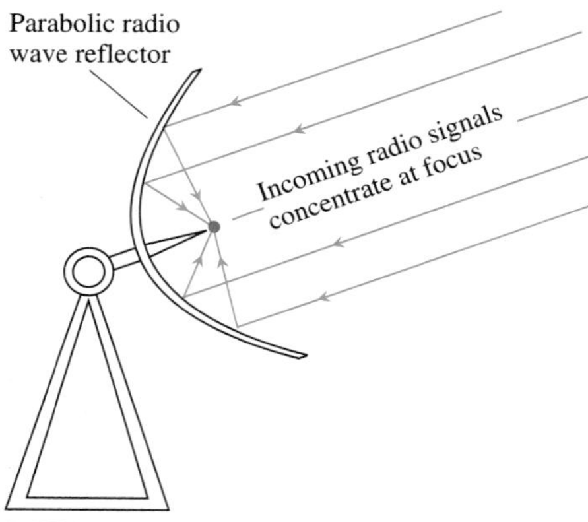

10.16 Two of the many uses of parabolic reflectors.

Statuary Hall in the U.S. Capitol building is elliptical. A person standing at one focus can carry on a whispered conversation with someone at the other focus even when the room is noisy.

$$PF = e \cdot PD, \tag{27}$$

where e is the constant of proportionality. Then the path traced by P is

a) a *parabola* if $e = 1$,

b) an *ellipse* of eccentricity e if $e < 1$, and

c) a *hyperbola* of eccentricity e if $e > 1$.

Equation (27) may not look like much to get excited about. There are no coordinates in it and when we try to translate it into coordinate form it translates in different ways, depending on the size of e. At least, that is what happens in Cartesian coordinates. However, in polar coordinates, as we will see in Section 10.7, the equation $PF = e \cdot PD$ translates into a single equation regardless of the size of e, an equation so simple that it has been the equation of choice for astronomers and space scientists for nearly 300 years.

Reflective Properties

The chief applications of parabolas involve their use as reflectors of light and radio waves. Rays originating at a parabola's focus are reflected out of the parabola parallel to the parabola's axis (Fig. 10.16 and Exercise 42). This property is used by flashlight, headlight, and spotlight reflectors and by microwave broadcast antennas to direct radiation from point sources into narrow beams. Conversely, electromagnetic waves arriving parallel to a parabolic reflector's axis are directed toward the reflector's focus. This property is used to intensify signals picked up by radio telescopes and television satellite dishes, to focus the arriving light in telescopes, and to concentrate sunlight in solar heaters.

If an ellipse is revolved about its major axis to generate a surface (the surface is called an *ellipsoid*), and the interior is silvered to produce a mirror, light from one focus will be reflected to the other focus (Fig. 10.17). Ellipsoids reflect sound the same way, and this property is used to construct *whispering galleries,* rooms in which a person standing at one focus can hear a whisper from the other focus. Statuary Hall in the U.S. Capitol building is a whispering gallery. Ellipsoids also appear in instruments used to study aircraft noise in wind tunnels (sound at one focus can be received at the other focus with relatively little interference from other sources).

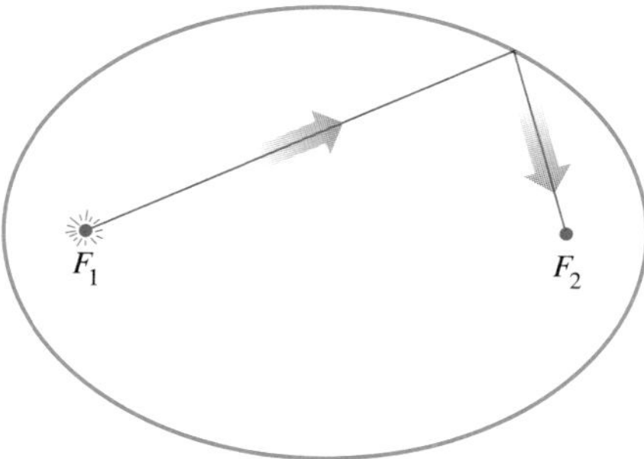

10.17 An elliptical mirror (shown here in profile) reflects light from one focus to the other.

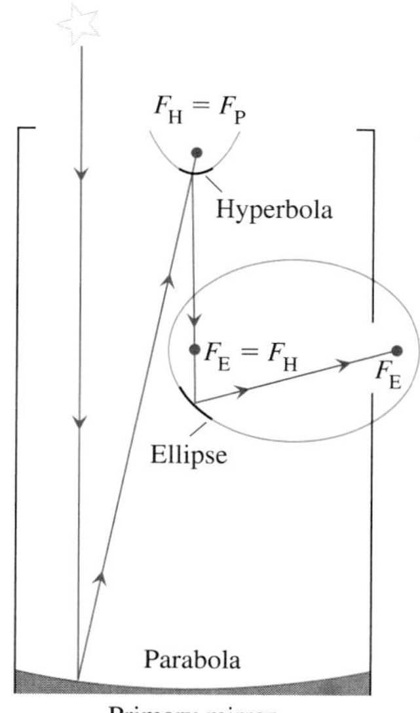

10.18 Schematic drawing of a reflecting telescope.

Light directed toward one focus of a hyperbolic mirror is reflected toward the other focus. This property of hyperbolas is combined with the reflective properties of parabolas and ellipses in designing modern telescopes. In Fig. 10.18 starlight reflects off a primary parabolic mirror toward the mirror's focus F_P. It is then reflected by a small hyperbolic mirror, whose focus is $F_H = F_P$, toward the second focus of the hyperbola, $F_E = F_H$. Since this focus is shared by an ellipse, the light is reflected by the elliptical mirror to the ellipse's second focus to be seen by an observer.

As recent experience with NASA's Hubble space telescope shows, the mirrors have to be nearly perfect to focus properly. The aberration causing the malfunction in Hubble's primary mirror amounts to about half a wavelength of visible light, no more than 1/50 the width of a human hair.

Other Applications

Water pipes are sometimes designed with elliptical cross sections to allow for expansion when the water freezes. The triggering mechanisms in some lasers are elliptical, and stones on a beach become more and more elliptical as they are ground down by waves. There are also applications of ellipses to fossil formation. The ellipsolith, once thought to be a separate species, is now known to be an elliptically deformed nautilus.

Hyperbolic paths arise in Einstein's theory of relativity and form the basis for the (unrelated) LORAN radio navigation system. (LORAN is short for "long range navigation.") Hyperbolas also form the basis for a new system the Burlington Northern Railroad has developed for using synchronized electronic signals from satellites to track freight trains. Computers aboard Burlington Northern locomotives in Minnesota have been able to track trains to within one mile per hour of their speed and to within 150 feet of their actual location.

Exercises 10.1

Match the parabolas in Exercises 1–4 with the following equations:

$$x^2 = 2y, \quad x^2 = -6y, \quad y^2 = 8x, \quad y^2 = -4x.$$

Then find the parabola's focus and directrix.

1.

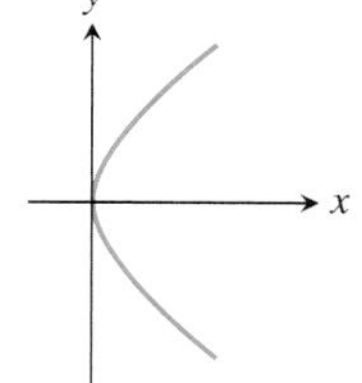

2.

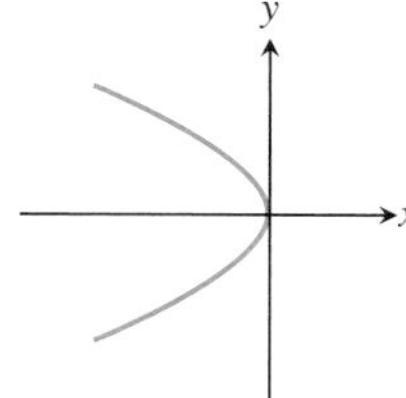

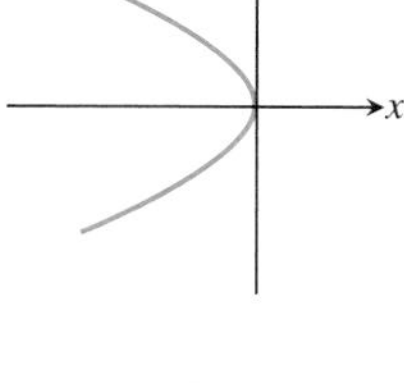

3.

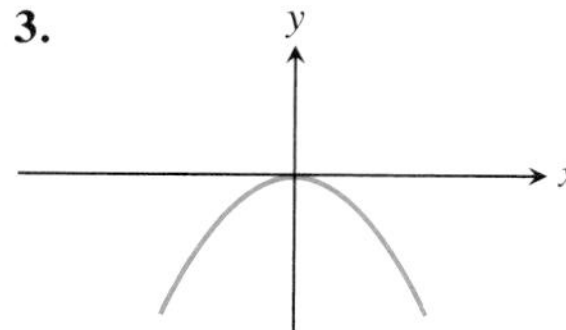

4.

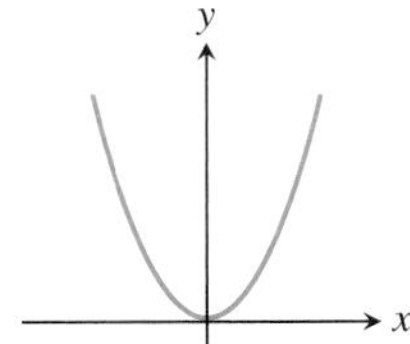

Match the conic sections in Exercises 5–8 with the following equations:

$$\frac{x^2}{4} + \frac{y^2}{9} = 1, \quad \frac{x^2}{2} + y^2 = 1,$$

$$\frac{y^2}{4} - x^2 = 1, \quad \frac{x^2}{4} - \frac{y^2}{9} = 1.$$

Then find the conic section's focus, eccentricity, and directrices. If the conic section is a hyperbola, find its asymptotes as well.

5.

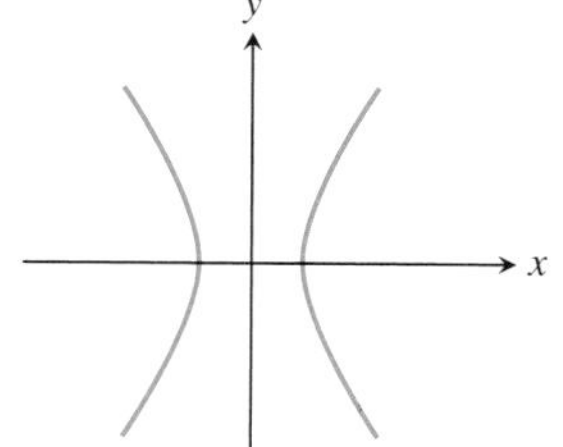

6.

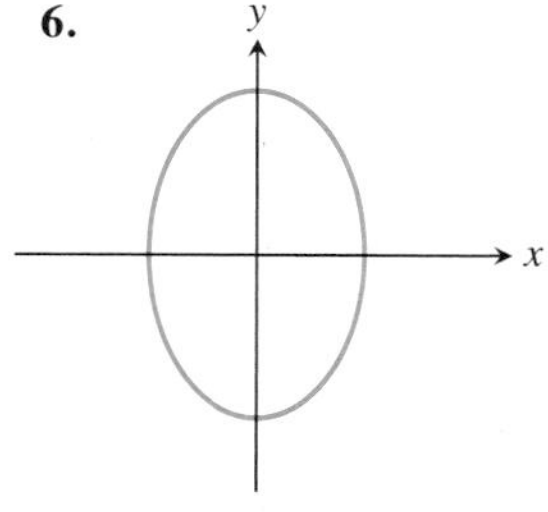

7. **8.**

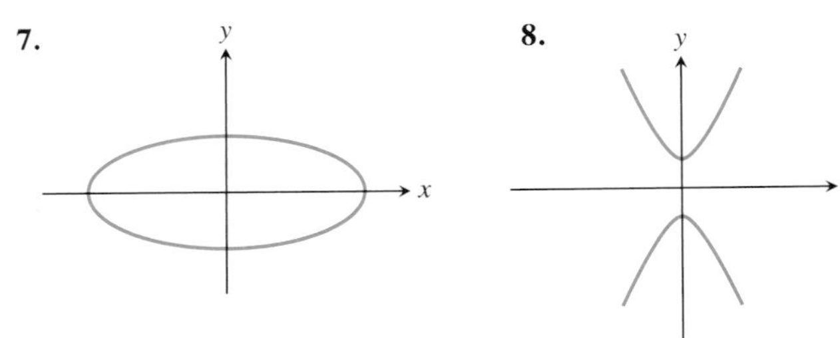

Exercises 9–16 give equations of parabolas. Find each parabola's focus and directrix. Then sketch the parabola. Include the focus and directrix in your sketch.

9. $y^2 = 12x$ **10.** $x^2 = 6y$ **11.** $x^2 = -8y$

12. $y^2 = -2x$ **13.** $y = 4x^2$ **14.** $y = -8x^2$

15. $x = -3y^2$ **16.** $x = 2y^2$

Exercises 17–24 give equations for ellipses. Put each equation in standard form and find the ellipse's eccentricity. Then sketch the ellipse. Include the foci in your sketch.

17. $16x^2 + 25y^2 = 400$ **18.** $7x^2 + 16y^2 = 112$

19. $2x^2 + y^2 = 2$ **20.** $2x^2 + y^2 = 4$

21. $3x^2 + 2y^2 = 6$ **22.** $9x^2 + 10y^2 = 90$

23. $6x^2 + 9y^2 = 54$ **24.** $169x^2 + 25y^2 = 4225$

Exercises 25–32 give equations for hyperbolas. Put each equation in standard form and find the hyperbola's eccentricity and asymptotes. Then sketch the hyperbola. Include the asymptotes and foci in your sketch.

25. $x^2 - y^2 = 1$ **26.** $9x^2 - 16y^2 = 144$

27. $y^2 - x^2 = 8$ **28.** $y^2 - x^2 = 4$

29. $8x^2 - 2y^2 = 16$ **30.** $y^2 - 3x^2 = 3$

31. $8y^2 - 2x^2 = 16$ **32.** $64x^2 - 36y^2 = 2304$

33. *Archimedes' Formula for the Volume of a Parabolic Solid.* The region enclosed by the parabola $y = (4h/b^2)x^2$ and the line $y = h$ is revolved about the y-axis to generate the solid shown here. Show that the volume of the solid is 3/2 the volume of the corresponding cone.

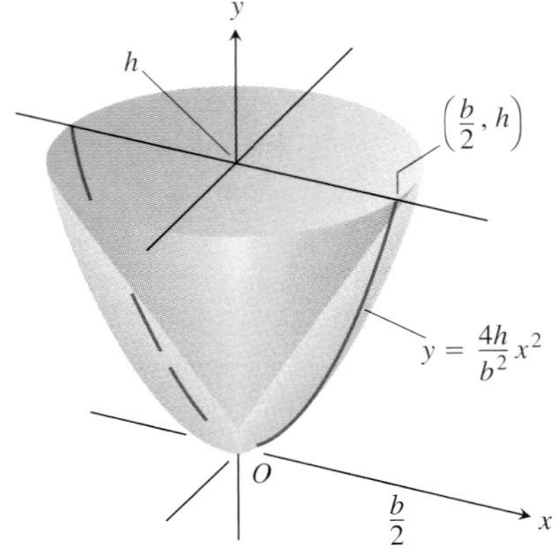

34. *Suspension Bridge Cables Hang in Parabolas.* The suspension bridge cable shown here supports a uniform load of w pounds per horizontal foot. It can be shown that if H is the horizontal tension of the cable at the origin, then the curve of the cable satisfies the equation

$$\frac{dy}{dx} = \frac{w}{H}x.$$

Show that the cable hangs in a parabola by solving this differential equation subject to the initial condition that $y = 0$ when $x = 0$.

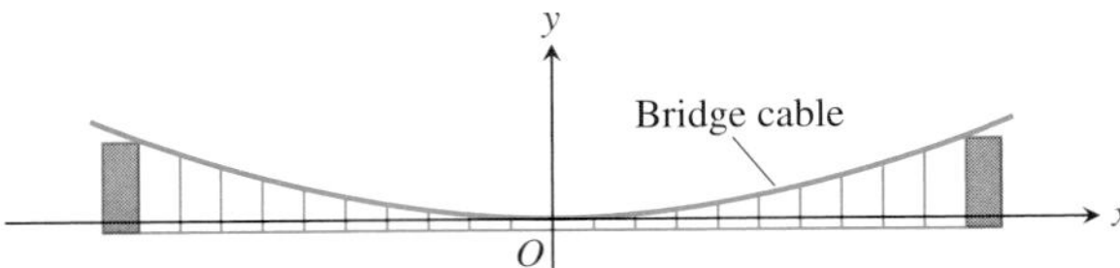

35. Find the dimensions of the rectangle of largest area that can be inscribed in the ellipse $x^2 + 4y^2 = 4$ with its sides parallel to the coordinate axes. What is the area of the rectangle?

36. Find the volume of the solid generated by revolving the region enclosed by the ellipse $9x^2 + 4y^2 = 36$ about the (a) x-axis, (b) y-axis.

37. The "triangular" region in the first quadrant bounded by the x-axis, the line $x = 4$, and the hyperbola $9x^2 - 4y^2 = 36$ is revolved about the x-axis to generate a solid. Find the volume of the solid.

38. The region bounded on the left by the y-axis, on the right by the hyperbola $x^2 - y^2 = 1$, and above and below by the lines $y = \pm 3$ is revolved about the y-axis to generate a solid. Find the volume of the solid.

39. Draw an ellipse of eccentricity 4/5. Explain your procedure.

40. Draw the orbit of Pluto to scale. Explain your procedure.

41. The circular waves in the photograph below were made by touching the surface of a ripple tank, first at A and then at B. As the waves expanded, their point of intersection appeared to trace a hyperbola. Did it really do that?

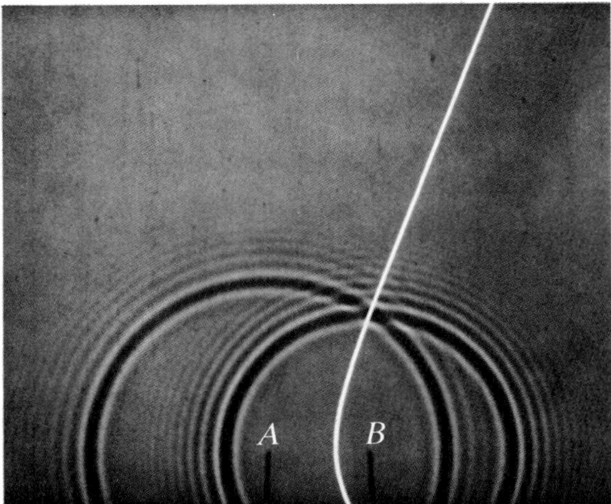

The expanding waves in Exercise 41.

To find out, we can model the waves with circles centered at A and B.

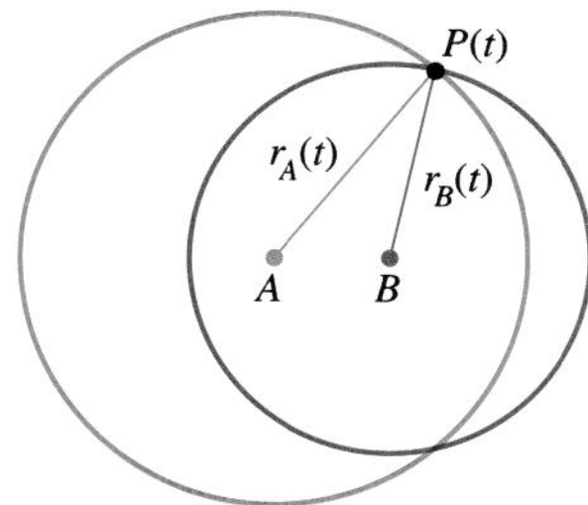

At time t, the point P is $r_A(t)$ units from A and $r_B(t)$ units from B. Since the radii of the circles increase at a constant rate, the rate at which the waves are traveling is

$$\frac{dr_A}{dt} = \frac{dr_B}{dt}.$$

Conclude from this equation that $r_A - r_B$ has a constant value, so that P must lie on a hyperbola with foci at A and B.

42. *The Reflective Property of Parabolas.* The figure below shows a typical point $P(x_0, y_0)$ on the parabola $y^2 = 4px$. The line L is tangent to the parabola at P. The parabola's focus lies at $F(p, 0)$. The ray L' extending from P to the right is parallel to the x-axis. We show that light from F to P will be reflected out along L' by showing that β equals α. Establish this equality by taking the following steps.

1. Show that $\tan\beta = 2p/y_0$.
2. Show that $\tan\phi = y_0/(x_0 - p)$.
3. Use the identity

$$\tan\alpha = \frac{\tan\phi - \tan\beta}{1 + \tan\phi\,\tan\beta}$$

to show that $\tan\alpha = 2p/y_0$.

Since α and β are both acute, $\tan\beta = \tan\alpha$ implies $\beta = \alpha$.

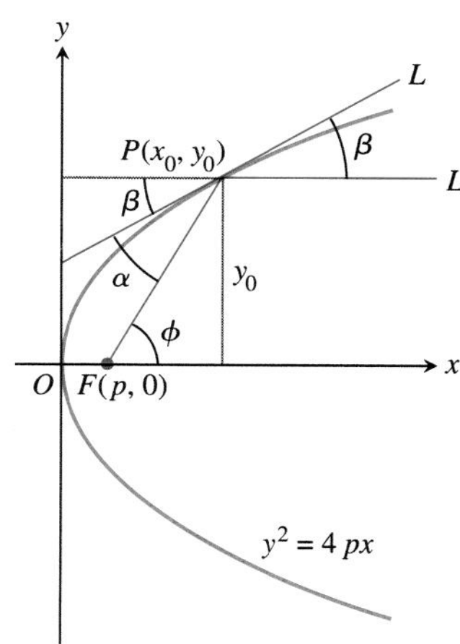

43. If lines are drawn parallel to the coordinate axes through a point P on the parabola $y^2 = kx$ $(k > 0)$, the parabola partitions the rectangular region bounded by the lines and the coordinate axes into two smaller regions, A and B.

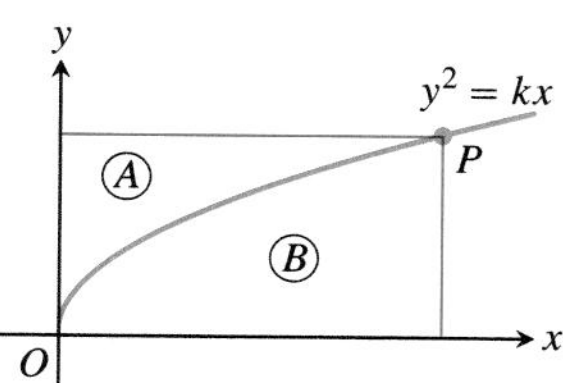

If the two smaller regions are revolved about the y-axis, show that they generate solids whose volumes have the ratio 4:1.

44. *Continuation of Exercise 43.* Find the ratio of the volumes of the solids generated by revolving regions A and B about the x-axis.

45. *How the Astronomer Kepler Used String to Draw Parabolas.* Kepler's method for drawing a parabola (with more modern tools) requires a string the length of a T square and a table whose edge can serve as the parabola's directrix. Pin one end of the string to the point where you want the focus to be and the other end to the upper end of the T square. Then, holding the string taut against the T square with a pencil, slide the T square along the table's edge. As the T square moves, the pencil will trace a parabola. Why?

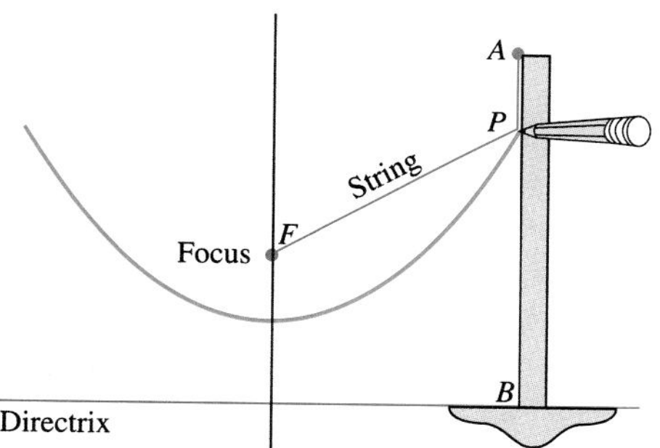

46. *Construction of a Hyperbola.* The following diagrams appeared (unlabeled) in Ernest J. Eckert, "Constructions Without Words," *Mathematics Magazine,* Vol. 66, No. 2, April 1993, p. 113. Explain the constructions.

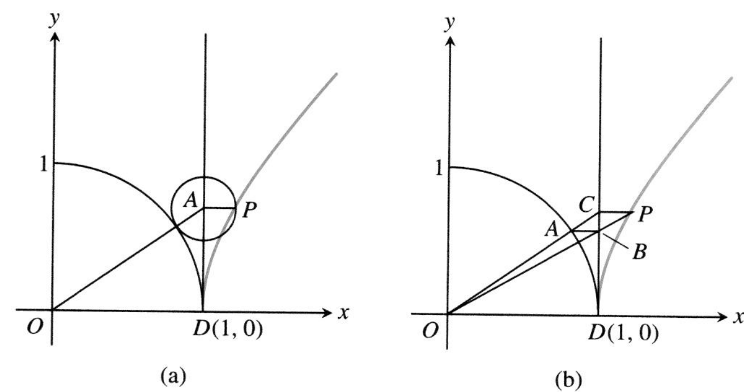

SHIFTING CONIC SECTIONS

47. The parabola $y^2 = 8x$ is shifted down 2 units and right 1 unit to generate the parabola $(y + 2)^2 = 8(x - 1)$. (a) Find the new parabola's vertex, focus, and directrix. (b) Plot the new vertex, focus, and directrix, and sketch in the parabola.

48. The parabola $x^2 = -4y$ is shifted left 1 unit and up 3 units to generate the parabola $(x + 1)^2 = -4(y - 3)$. (a) Find the new parabola's vertex, focus, and directrix. (b) Plot the new vertex, focus and directrix, and sketch in the parabola.

49. The ellipse $(x^2/16) + (y^2/9) = 1$ is shifted 4 units to the right and 3 units up to generate the ellipse

$$\frac{(x-4)^2}{16} + \frac{(y-3)^2}{9} = 1.$$

(a) Find the foci, vertices, and center of the new ellipse. (b) Plot the new foci, vertices, and center, and sketch in the new ellipse.

50. The ellipse $(x^2/9) + (y^2/25) = 1$ is shifted 3 units to the left and 2 units down to generate the ellipse

$$\frac{(x+3)^2}{9} + \frac{(y+2)^2}{25} = 1.$$

(a) Find the foci, vertices, and center of the new ellipse. (b) Plot the new foci, vertices, and center, and sketch in the new ellipse.

51. The hyperbola $(x^2/16) - (y^2/9) = 1$ is shifted 2 units to the right to generate the hyperbola

$$\frac{(x-2)^2}{16} - \frac{y^2}{9} = 1.$$

(a) Find the center, foci, vertices, and asymptotes of the new hyperbola. (b) Plot the new center, foci, vertices, and asymptotes, and sketch in the hyperbola.

52. The hyperbola $(y^2/4) - (x^2/5) = 1$ is shifted 2 units down to generate the hyperbola

$$\frac{(y+2)^2}{4} - \frac{x^2}{5} = 1.$$

(a) Find the center, foci, vertices, and asymptotes of the new hyperbola. (b) Plot the new center, foci, vertices, and asymptotes, and sketch in the hyperbola.

Exercises 53–56 give equations for parabolas and tell how many units up or down and to the right or left each parabola is to be shifted. Find an equation for the new parabola, and find the new vertex, focus, and directrix.

53. $y^2 = 4x$, left 2, down 3

54. $y^2 = -12x$, right 4, up 3

55. $x^2 = 8y$, right 1, down 7

56. $x^2 = 6y$, left 3, down 2

Exercises 57–60 give equations for ellipses and tell how many units up or down and to the right or left each ellipse is to be shifted. Find an equation for the new ellipse, and find the new foci, vertices, and center.

57. $\frac{x^2}{6} + \frac{y^2}{9} = 1$, left 2, down 1

58. $\frac{x^2}{2} + y^2 = 1$, right 3, up 4

59. $\frac{x^2}{3} + \frac{y^2}{2} = 1$, right 2, up 3

60. $\frac{x^2}{16} + \frac{y^2}{25} = 1$, left 4, down 5

Exercises 61–64 give equations for hyperbolas and tell how many units up or down and to the right or left each hyperbola is to be shifted. Find an equation for the new hyperbola, and find the new center, foci, vertices, and asymptotes.

61. $\frac{x^2}{4} - \frac{y^2}{5} = 1$, right 2, up 2

62. $\frac{x^2}{16} - \frac{y^2}{9} = 1$, left 5, down 1

63. $y^2 - x^2 = 1$, left 1, down 1

64. $\frac{y^2}{3} - x^2 = 1$, right 1, up 3

Find the center, foci, and vertices of the conic sections in Exercises 65–72. If the conic section is a hyperbola, find the asymptotes.

65. $x^2 + 5y^2 + 4x = 1$

66. $9x^2 + 6y^2 + 36y = 0$

67. $x^2 + 2y^2 - 2x - 4y = -1$

68. $4x^2 + y^2 + 8y - 2y = -1$

69. $x^2 - y^2 - 2x + 4y = 4$

70. $x^2 - y^2 + 4x - 6y = 6$

71. $2x^2 - y^2 + 6y = 3$

72. $y^2 - 4x^2 + 16x = 24$

Writing for Your Own Knowledge

Answer the following questions in writing. Some answers will take only a sentence or two; others may require several paragraphs. Some explanations may also call for graphs or sketches.

1. What is a parabola? What are the standard equations for parabolas with vertices at the origin? How do you find the focus and directrix of such parabolas?
2. What is an ellipse? What are the standard equations for ellipses centered at the origin? How do you find the foci and vertices of such ellipses?
3. How do you sketch the ellipse $(x^2/a^2) + (y^2/b^2) = 1$?
4. What is a hyperbola? What are the standard equations for hyperbolas centered at the origin? How do you find the foci, vertices, and asymptotes of such hyperbolas?
5. How do you sketch the hyperbola $(x^2/a^2) - (y^2/b^2) = 1$?
6. How are an ellipse's shape and eccentricity related?
7. How do you classify conic sections by eccentricity?
8. What equation unites the parabola, ellipse, and hyperbola?
9. What reflective properties do conic sections have?

10.2 The Graphs of Quadratic Equations in x and y; Rotations About the Origin

In this section, we examine one of the most amazing results in analytic geometry, which is that the Cartesian graph of any equation

$$Ax^2 + Bxy + Cy^2 + Dx + Ey + F = 0, \tag{1}$$

in which A, B, and C are not all zero, is nearly always a conic section. The exceptions are the cases in which there is no graph at all or the graph consists of two parallel lines. It is conventional to call all graphs of Eq. (1), curved or not, **quadratic curves.**

The Cross-Product Term

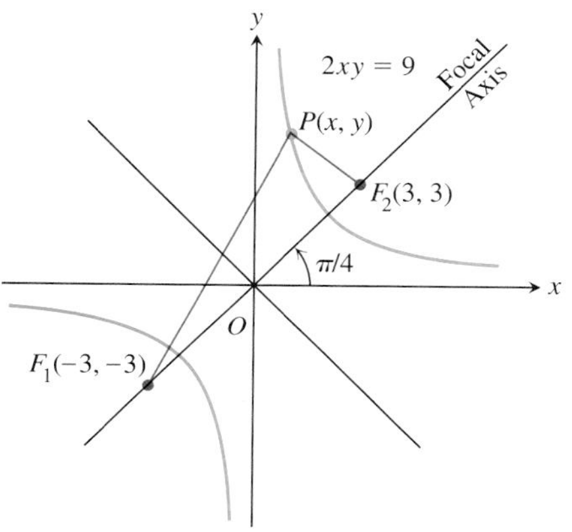

10.19 The focal axis of the hyperbola $2xy = 9$ makes an angle of $\pi/4$ radians with the positive x-axis.

You may have noticed that the term Bxy did not appear in the equations for the conic sections in Section 10.1. This happened because the axes of the conic sections ran parallel to (in fact, coincided with) the coordinate axes.

To see what happens when the parallelism is absent, let us write an equation for a hyperbola with $a = 3$ and foci at $F_1(-3, -3)$ and $F_2(3, 3)$ (Fig. 10.19). The equation $|PF_1 - PF_2| = 2a$ becomes $|PF_1 - PF_2| = 2(3) = 6$ and

$$\sqrt{(x+3)^2 + (y+3)^2} - \sqrt{(x-3)^2 + (y-3)^2} = \pm 6.$$

When we transpose one radical, square, solve for the radical that still appears, and square again, the equation reduces to

$$2xy = 9, \tag{2}$$

a case of Eq. (1) in which the cross-product term is present. The asymptotes of the hyperbola in Eq. (2) are the x- and y-axes, and the focal axis makes an angle of $\pi/4$ radians with the positive x-axis. As in this example, the cross-product term is present in Eq. (1) only when the axes of the conic are tilted.

Rotating the Coordinate Axes to Eliminate the Cross-Product Term

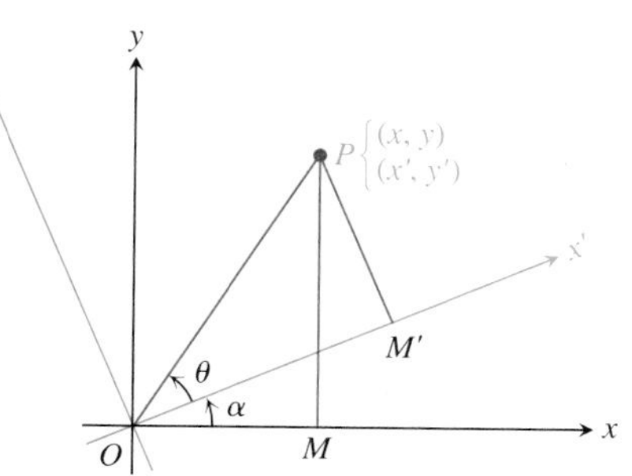

10.20 A counterclockwise rotation through angle α about the origin.

To eliminate the xy-term from the equation of a conic, we rotate the coordinate axes to eliminate the "tilt" in the axes of the conic. The equations for the rotations we use are derived in the following way. In the notation of Fig. 10.20, which shows a counterclockwise rotation about the origin through an angle α,

$$\begin{aligned} x &= OM = OP\cos(\theta+\alpha) = OP\cos\theta\cos\alpha - OP\sin\theta\sin\alpha, \\ y &= MP = OP\sin(\theta+\alpha) = OP\cos\theta\sin\alpha + OP\sin\theta\cos\alpha. \end{aligned} \tag{3}$$

Since

$$OP\cos\theta = OM' = x' \quad \text{and} \quad OP\sin\theta = M'P = y', \tag{4}$$

the equations in (3) reduce to the following.

Equations for Rotating Coordinate Axes

$$\begin{aligned} x &= x'\cos\alpha - y'\sin\alpha \\ y &= x'\sin\alpha + y'\cos\alpha \end{aligned} \tag{5}$$

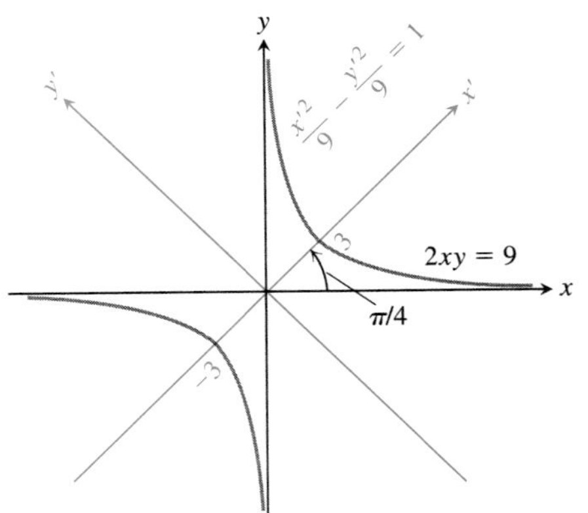

10.21 The hyperbola in Example 1.

EXAMPLE 1 The x- and y-axes are rotated through an angle of $\pi/4$ radians about the origin. Find an equation for the hyperbola $2xy = 9$ in the new coordinates.

Solution Since $\cos \pi/4 = \sin \pi/4 = 1/\sqrt{2}$, we substitute

$$x = \frac{x' - y'}{\sqrt{2}}, \qquad y = \frac{x' + y'}{\sqrt{2}}$$

from Eqs. (5) into the equation $2xy = 9$ and obtain

$$2\left(\frac{x' - y'}{\sqrt{2}}\right)\left(\frac{x' + y'}{\sqrt{2}}\right) = 9$$

$$x'^2 - y'^2 = 9$$

$$\frac{x'^2}{9} - \frac{y'^2}{9} = 1.$$

See Fig. 10.21.

If we apply Eqs. (5) to the quadratic equation (1), we obtain a new quadratic equation

$$A'x'^2 + B'x'y' + C'y'^2 + D'x' + E'y' + F' = 0. \tag{6}$$

The new and old coefficients are related by the equations

$$\begin{aligned} A' &= A\cos^2\alpha + B\cos\alpha\sin\alpha + C\sin^2\alpha \\ B' &= B\cos 2\alpha + (C - A)\sin 2\alpha \\ C' &= A\sin^2\alpha - B\sin\alpha\cos\alpha + C\cos^2\alpha \\ D' &= D\cos\alpha + E\sin\alpha \\ E' &= -D\sin\alpha + E\cos\alpha \\ F' &= F. \end{aligned} \tag{7}$$

These equations show, among other things, that if we start with an equation for a curve in which the cross-product term is present ($B \neq 0$), we can find a rotation angle α that produces an equation in which no cross-product term appears ($B' = 0$). To find α, we set $B' = 0$ in the second equation in (7) and solve the resulting equation,

$$B\cos 2\alpha + (C - A)\sin 2\alpha = 0,$$

for α. In practice, this means determining α from one of the two equations

$$\cot 2\alpha = \frac{A - C}{B} \qquad \text{or} \qquad \tan 2\alpha = \frac{B}{A - C}. \tag{8}$$

EXAMPLE 2 The coordinate axes are to be rotated through an angle α to produce an equation for the curve

$$2x^2 + \sqrt{3}\,xy + y^2 - 10 = 0$$

that has no cross-product term. Find α and the new equation. Identify the curve.

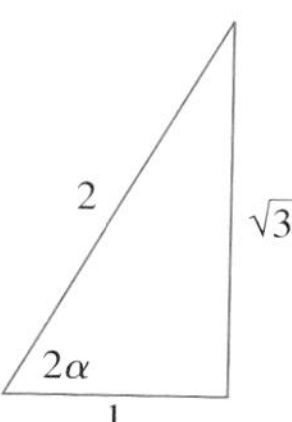

10.22 This triangle identifies $2\alpha = \cot^{-1}(1/\sqrt{3})$ as $\pi/3$ (Example 2).

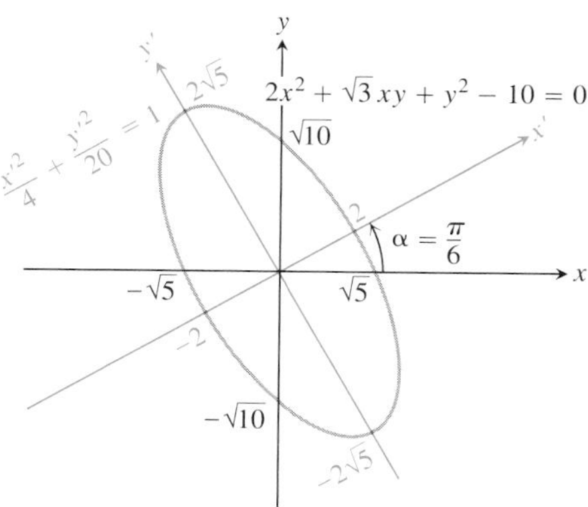

10.23 The conic section in Example 2.

Solution The equation $2x^2 + \sqrt{3}\,xy + y^2 - 10 = 0$ has $A = 2$, $B = \sqrt{3}$, and $C = 1$. We substitute these values into Eq. (8) to find α:

$$\cot 2\alpha = \frac{A - C}{B} = \frac{2-1}{\sqrt{3}} = \frac{1}{\sqrt{3}}.$$

From the right triangle in Fig. 10.22, we see that one appropriate choice of angle is $2\alpha = \pi/3$, so we take $\alpha = \pi/6$. Substituting $\alpha = \pi/6$, $A = 2$, $B = \sqrt{3}$, $C = 1$, $D = E = 0$, and $F = -10$ into Eqs. (7) gives

$$A' = \frac{5}{2}, \qquad B' = 0, \qquad C' = \frac{1}{2}, \qquad D' = E' = 0, \qquad F' = -10.$$

Equation (6) then gives

$$\frac{5}{2}x'^2 + \frac{1}{2}y'^2 - 10 = 0, \qquad \text{or} \qquad \frac{x'^2}{4} + \frac{y'^2}{20} = 1.$$

The curve is an ellipse with foci on the new y'-axis (Fig. 10.23).

Possible Graphs of Quadratic Equations

We now return to the graph of the general quadratic equation.

Since axes may always be rotated to eliminate the cross-product term, there is no loss of generality in assuming that this has been done and that our equation has the form

$$Ax^2 + Cy^2 + Dx + Ey + F = 0. \tag{9}$$

Equation (9) represents

a) a *circle* if $A = C \neq 0$ (special cases: the graph is a point or there is no graph at all);

b) a *parabola* if Eq. (9) is quadratic in one variable and linear in the other;

c) an *ellipse* if A and C are both positive or both negative (special cases: a single point or no graph at all);

d) a *hyperbola* if A and C have opposite signs (special case: a pair of intersecting lines);

e) a *straight line* if A and C are zero and at least one of D and E is different from zero;

f) *one or two straight lines* if the left-hand side of Eq. (9) can be factored into the product of two linear factors.

See Table 10.3 (on page 649) for examples.

The Discriminant Test

We do not need to eliminate the xy-term from the equation

$$Ax^2 + Bxy + Cy^2 + Dx + Ey + F = 0 \tag{10}$$

to tell what kind of conic section the equation represents. If this is the only information we want, we can apply the following test instead.

As we have seen, if $B \neq 0$, then rotating the coordinate axes through an angle α that satisfies the equation

$$\cot 2\alpha = \frac{A - C}{B} \tag{11}$$

will change Eq. (10) into an equivalent form

$$A'x'^2 + C'y'^2 + D'x' + E'y' + F' = 0 \tag{12}$$

without a cross-product term.

Now, the graph of Eq. (12) is a (real or degenerate)

a) *parabola* if A' or $C' = 0$; that is, if $A'C' = 0$;

b) *ellipse* if A' and C' have the same sign; that is, if $A'C' > 0$;

c) *hyperbola* if A' and C' have opposite signs; that is, if $A'C' < 0$.

It can also be verified from Eqs. (7) that for any rotation of axes,

$$B^2 - 4AC = B'^2 - 4A'C'. \tag{13}$$

This means that the quantity $B^2 - 4AC$ is not changed by a rotation. But when we rotate through the angle α given by Eq. (11), B' becomes zero, so

$$B^2 - 4AC = -4A'C'.$$

Since the curve is a parabola if $A'C' = 0$, an ellipse if $A'C' > 0$, and a hyperbola if $A'C' < 0$, the curve must be a parabola if $B^2 - 4AC = 0$, an ellipse if $B^2 - 4AC < 0$, and a hyperbola if $B^2 - 4AC > 0$. The number $B^2 - 4AC$ is called the **discriminant** of Eq. (10).

The Discriminant Test

With the understanding that occasional degenerate cases may arise, the quadratic curve $Ax^2 + Bxy + Cy^2 + Dx + Ey + F = 0$ is

a) a **parabola** if $B^2 - 4AC = 0$,

b) an **ellipse** if $B^2 - 4AC < 0$,

c) a **hyperbola** if $B^2 - 4AC > 0$.

EXAMPLE 3

a) $3x^2 - 6xy + 3y^2 + 2x - 7 = 0$ represents a parabola because

$$B^2 - 4AC = (-6)^2 - 4 \cdot 3 \cdot 3 = 36 - 36 = 0.$$

b) $x^2 + xy + y^2 - 1 = 0$ represents an ellipse because

$$B^2 - 4AC = (1)^2 - 4 \cdot 1 \cdot 1 = -3 < 0.$$

c) $xy - y^2 - 5y + 1 = 0$ represents a hyperbola because

$$B^2 - 4AC = (1)^2 - 4(0)(-1) = 1 > 0.$$

TABLE 10.3
Examples of quadratic curves

$Ax^2 + Bxy + Cy^2 + Dx + Ey + F = 0$

	A	*B*	*C*	*D*	*E*	*F*	Equation	Remarks
Circle	1		1			−4	$x^2 + y^2 = 4$	$A = C$; $F < 0$
Parabola			1	−9			$y^2 = 9x$	Quadratic in y, linear in x
Ellipse	4		9			−36	$4x^2 + 9y^2 = 36$	A, C have same sign, $A \neq C$; $F < 0$
Hyperbola	1		−1			−1	$x^2 - y^2 = 1$	A, C have opposite signs
One line (still a conic section)	1						$x^2 = 0$	y-axis
Intersecting lines (still a conic section)		1		1	−1	−1	$xy + x - y - 1 = 0$	Factors to $(x - 1)(y + 1) = 0$, so $x = 1$, $y = -1$
Parallel lines (not a conic section)	1			−3		2	$x^2 - 3x + 2 = 0$	Factors to $(x - 1)(x - 2) = 0$, so $x = 1$, $x = 2$
Point	1		1				$x^2 + y^2 = 0$	The origin
No graph	1					1	$x^2 = -1$	No graph

Exercises 10.2

Use the discriminant $B^2 - 4AC$ to decide whether the equations in Exercises 1–16 represent parabolas, ellipses, or hyperbolas.

1. $x^2 - 3xy + y^2 - x = 0$
2. $3x^2 - 18xy + 27y^2 - 5x + 7y = -4$
3. $3x^2 - 7xy + \sqrt{17}\,y^2 = 1$
4. $2x^2 - \sqrt{15}\,xy + 2y^2 + x + y = 0$
5. $x^2 + 2xy + y^2 + 2x - y + 2 = 0$
6. $2x^2 - y^2 + 4xy - 2x + 3y = 6$
7. $x^2 + 4xy + 4y^2 - 3x = 6$
8. $x^2 + y^2 + 3x - 2y = 10$
9. $xy + y^2 - 3x = 5$
10. $3x^2 + 6xy + 3y^2 - 4x + 5y = 12$
11. $3x^2 - 5xy + 2y^2 - 7x - 14y = -1$
12. $2x^2 - 4.9xy + 3y^2 - 4x = 7$
13. $x^2 - 3xy + 3y^2 + 6y = 7$
14. $25x^2 + 21xy + 4y^2 - 350x = 0$
15. $6x^2 + 3xy + 2y^2 + 17y + 2 = 0$
16. $3x^2 + 12xy + 12y^2 + 435x - 9y + 72 = 0$

In Exercises 17–26, rotate the coordinate axes to change the given equation into an equation that has no cross-product (xy) term. Then identify the graph of the equation. (The new equations will vary with the size and direction of the rotation you use.)

17. $xy = 2$
18. $x^2 + xy + y^2 = 1$
19. $3x^2 + 2\sqrt{3}\,xy + y^2 - 8x + 8\sqrt{3}\,y = 0$
20. $x^2 - \sqrt{3}\,xy + 2y^2 = 1$
21. $x^2 - 2xy + y^2 = 2$
22. $3x^2 - 2\sqrt{3}\,xy + y^2 = 1$
23. $\sqrt{2}\,x^2 + 2\sqrt{2}\,xy + \sqrt{2}\,y^2 - 8x + 8y = 0$
24. $xy - y - x + 1 = 0$
25. $3x^2 + 2xy + 3y^2 = 19$
26. $3x^2 + 4\sqrt{3}\,xy - y^2 = 7$

The conic sections in Exercises 17–26 were chosen to have rotation angles that were "nice" in the sense that once we knew $\cot 2\alpha$ or $\tan 2\alpha$ we could identify 2α and find $\sin \alpha$ and $\cos \alpha$ from familiar triangles. The conic sections encountered in practice may not have such nice rotation angles, and we may have to use a calculator to determine α from the value of $\cot 2\alpha$ or $\tan 2\alpha$.

In Exercises 27–32, use a calculator to find an angle α through which the coordinate axes can be rotated to change the given equation into a quadratic equation that has no cross-product term. Then find $\sin \alpha$ and $\cos \alpha$ to 2 decimal places and use Eqs. (7) to find the coefficients of the new equation to the nearest decimal place. In each case, say whether the conic section is an ellipse, a hyperbola, or a parabola.

27. $x^2 - xy + 3y^2 + x - y - 3 = 0$

28. $2x^2 + xy - 3y^2 + 3x - 7 = 0$

29. $x^2 - 4xy + 4y^2 - 5 = 0$

30. $2x^2 - 12xy + 18y^2 - 49 = 0$

31. $3x^2 + 5xy + 2y^2 - 8y - 1 = 0$

32. $2x^2 + 7xy + 9y^2 + 20x - 86 = 0$

33. What effect does a 90° rotation about the origin have on the equations of the following conic sections? Give the new equation in each case.

a) The ellipse $(x^2/a^2) + (y^2/b^2) = 1 \quad (a > b)$
b) The hyperbola $(x^2/a^2) - (y^2/b^2) = 1$
c) The circle $x^2 + y^2 = a^2$
d) The line $y = mx$
e) The line $y = mx + b$

34. What effect does a 180° rotation about the origin have on the equations of the following conic sections? Give the new equation in each case.

a) The ellipse $(x^2/a^2) + (y^2/b^2) = 1 \quad (a > b)$
b) The hyperbola $(x^2/a^2) - (y^2/b^2) = 1$
c) The circle $x^2 + y^2 = a^2$
d) The line $y = mx$
e) The line $y = mx + b$

35. *The Hyperbola $xy = a$.* The hyperbola $xy = 1$ is one of many hyperbolas of the form $xy = a$ that appear in science and mathematics.

a) Rotate the coordinate axes through an angle of 45° to change the equation $xy = 1$ into an equation with no xy-term. What is the new equation?
b) Do the same for the equation $xy = a$.

36. Find the eccentricity of the hyperbola $xy = 2$.

37. Can anything be said about the graph of the equation $Ax^2 + Bxy + Cy^2 + Dx + Ey + F = 0$ if $AC < 0$? Give reasons for your answer.

38. Does any nondegenerate conic section $Ax^2 + Bxy + Cy^2 + Dx + Ey + F = 0$ have all of the following properties?

1. It is symmetric with respect to the origin.
2. It passes through the point $(1, 0)$.
3. It is tangent to the line $y = 1$ at the point $(-2, 1)$.

Give reasons for your answer.

39. Show that the equation $x^2 + y^2 = a^2$ becomes $x'^2 + y'^2 = a^2$ for every choice of the angle α in the rotation equations (5).

40. Show that rotating the axes through an angle of $\pi/4$ radians will eliminate the xy-term from Eq. (1) whenever $A = C$.

Writing for Your Own Knowledge

Answer the following questions in writing. Some answers will take only a sentence or two; others may require several paragraphs. Some explanations may also call for graphs or sketches.

1. What is a quadratic curve?
2. What are the equations for rotating coordinate axes?
3. How do you rotate the coordinate axes to eliminate the cross-product term from the equation of a quadratic curve?
4. What graphs can a quadratic equation in x and y have?
5. How can you tell what kind of graph to expect from a quadratic equation?

EXPLORER PROGRAM

Conic Sections	Shows how the coefficients in the equation $Ax^2 + Bxy + Cy^2 + Dx + Ey + F = 0$ change as the conic section it describes is rotated in the xy-plane.

10.3 Parametrizations of Curves

When the path of a particle moving in the plane looks like the curve in Fig. 10.24, we cannot hope to describe it with a Cartesian formula that expresses y directly in terms of x or x directly in terms of y. Instead, we express each of the particle's coordinates as a function of time t and describe the path with a pair of equations, $x = f(t)$ and $y = g(t)$. For studying motion, equations like these are preferable to a Cartesian formula because they tell us the particle's position at any time t.

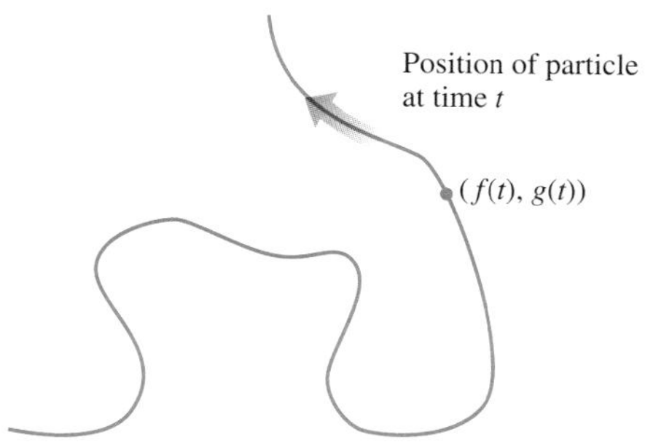

10.24 The path traced by a particle moving in the xy-plane is not always the graph of a function of x or a function of y.

DEFINITIONS

If x and y are given as continuous functions

$$x = f(t), \qquad y = g(t) \tag{1}$$

over an interval of t-values, then the set of points $(x, y) = (f(t), g(t))$ defined by these equations is a **curve** in the coordinate plane. The equations are **parametric equations** for the curve. The variable t is a **parameter** for the curve and its domain I is the **parameter interval.** If I is a closed interval, $a \leq t \leq b$, the point $(f(a), g(a))$ is the **initial point** of the curve and $(f(b), g(b))$ is the **terminal point** of the curve. When we give parametric equations and a parameter interval for a curve in the plane, we say that we have **parametrized** the curve. The equations and interval constitute a **parametrization** of the curve.

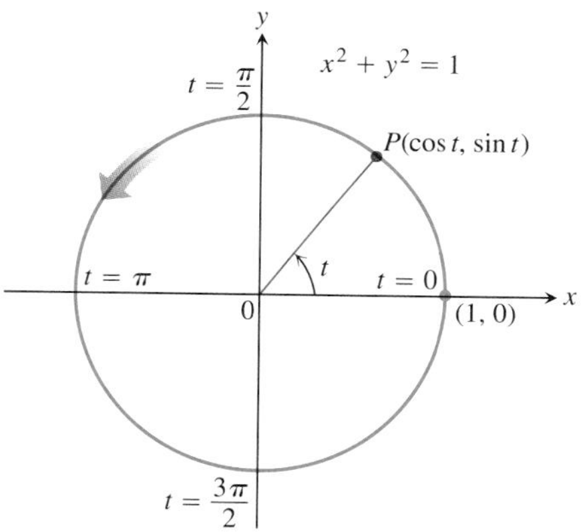

10.25 The equations $x = \cos t$, $y = \sin t$ describe motion on the circle $x^2 + y^2 = 1$. The arrow shows the direction of increasing t (Example 1).

In many applications t denotes time, but it might instead denote an angle (as in some of the following examples) or the distance a particle has traveled along its path from its starting point (as it sometimes will when we later study motion).

EXAMPLE 1 *The Circle $x^2 + y^2 = 1$.* The equations and parameter interval

$$x = \cos t, \qquad y = \sin t, \qquad 0 \leq t \leq 2\pi,$$

describe the position $P(x, y)$ of a particle that moves counterclockwise around the circle $x^2 + y^2 = 1$ as t increases (Fig. 10.25).

We know that the point lies on this circle for every value of t because

$$x^2 + y^2 = \cos^2 t + \sin^2 t = 1.$$

But how much of the circle does the point $P(x, y)$ actually traverse? The parameter t is the radian measure of the angle that radius OP makes with the positive x-axis. The particle starts at $(1, 0)$, moves up and to the left as t approaches $\pi/2$, and continues around the circle to stop again at $(1, 0)$ when $t = 2\pi$. The particle traces the circle exactly once.

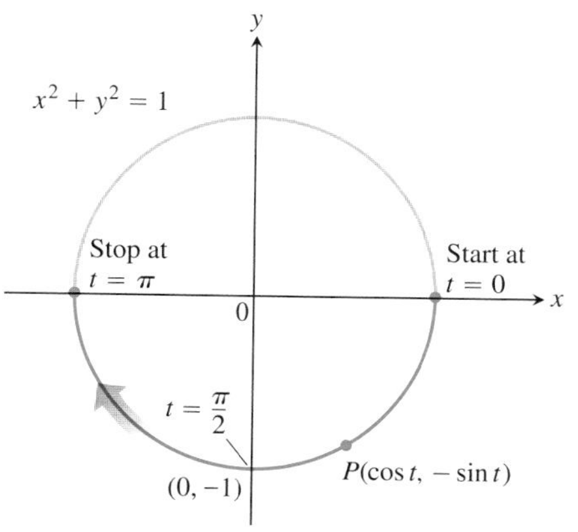

10.26 The point $P(\cos t, -\sin t)$ moves clockwise as t increases from 0 to π (Example 2).

EXAMPLE 2 *A Semicircle.* The equations and parameter interval

$$x = \cos t, \qquad y = -\sin t, \qquad 0 \leq t \leq \pi,$$

describe the position $P(x, y)$ of a particle that moves clockwise around the circle $x^2 + y^2 = 1$ as t increases from 0 to π.

We know that the point P lies on this circle for all t because its coordinates satisfy the circle's equation. How much of the circle does the particle traverse? To find out, we track the motion as t runs from 0 to π. As in Example 1, the particle starts at $(1, 0)$. But now as t increases, y becomes negative, decreasing to -1 when $t = \pi/2$ and then increasing back to 0 as t approaches π. The motion stops at $t = \pi$ with only the lower half of the circle covered (Fig. 10.26).

EXAMPLE 3 *Half a Parabola.* The position $P(x, y)$ of a particle moving in the xy-plane is given by the equations and parameter interval

$$x = \sqrt{t}, \qquad y = t, \qquad t \geq 0.$$

Identify the path traced by the particle and describe the motion.

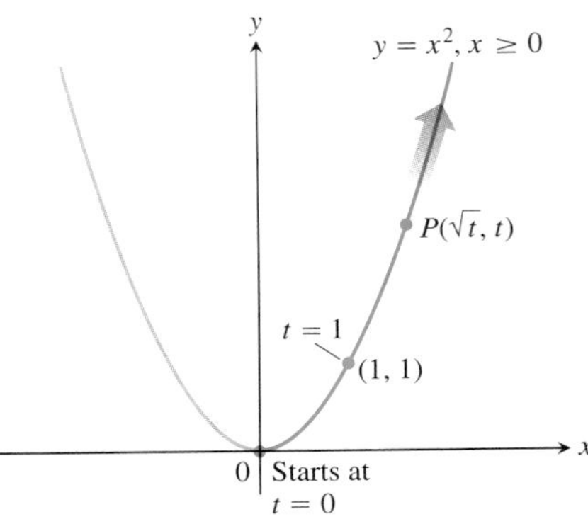

10.27 The equations $x = \sqrt{t}$, $y = t$ and interval $t \geq 0$ describe the motion of a particle that traces the right-hand half of the parabola $y = x^2$ (Example 3).

Solution We try to identify the path by eliminating t between the equations $x = \sqrt{t}$ and $y = t$. With any luck, this will produce a recognizable algebraic relation between x and y. We find that

$$y = t = \left(\sqrt{t}\right)^2 = x^2.$$

This means that the particle's position coordinates satisfy the equation $y = x^2$, so the particle moves along the parabola $y = x^2$.

It would be a mistake, however, to conclude that the particle's path is the entire parabola $y = x^2$—it is only half the parabola. The particle's x-coordinate is never negative. The particle starts at $(0, 0)$ when $t = 0$ and rises into the first quadrant as t increases (Fig. 10.27).

EXAMPLE 4 *An Entire Parabola.* The position $P(x, y)$ of a particle moving in the xy-plane is given by the equations and parameter interval

$$x = t, \qquad y = t^2, \qquad -\infty < t < \infty.$$

Identify the particle's path and describe the motion.

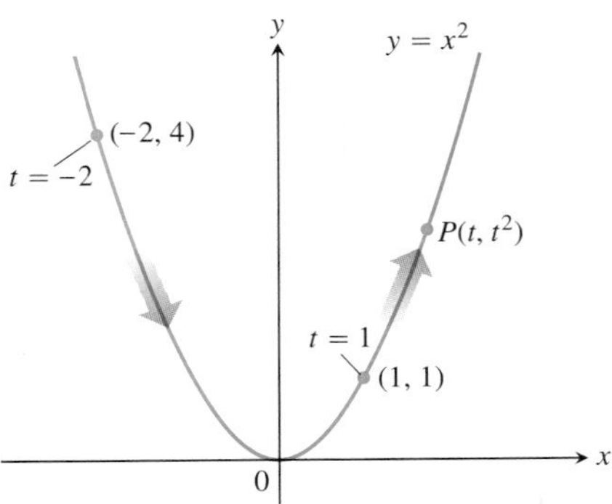

10.28 The path defined by $x = t$, $y = t^2$, $-\infty < t < \infty$ is the entire parabola $y = x^2$ (Example 4).

Solution We identify the path by eliminating t between the equations $x = t$ and $y = t^2$, obtaining

$$y = (t)^2 = x^2.$$

The particle's position coordinates satisfy the equation $y = x^2$, so the particle moves along this curve.

In contrast to Example 3, the particle now traverses the entire parabola. As t increases from $-\infty$ to ∞, the particle comes down the left-hand side, passes through the origin, and moves up the right-hand side (Fig. 10.28).

As Example 4 illustrates, any curve $y = f(x)$ has the parametrization $x = t$, $y = f(t)$. This is so simple we usually do not use it, but the point of view is occasionally helpful.

EXAMPLE 5 *A Parametrization of the Ellipse $x^2/a^2 + y^2/b^2 = 1$.* Describe the motion of a particle whose position $P(x, y)$ at time t is given by

$$x = a \cos t, \qquad y = b \sin t, \qquad 0 \leq t \leq 2\pi.$$

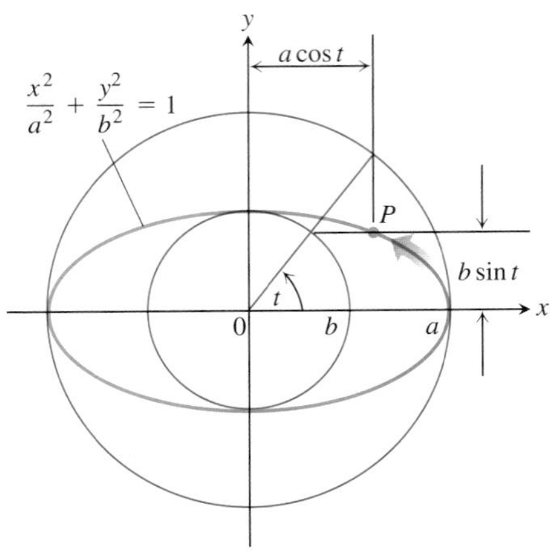

10.29 The coordinates of P are $x = a \cos t$, $y = b \sin t$ (Example 5).

Solution We find a Cartesian equation for the particle's coordinates by eliminating t between the equations

$$\cos t = \frac{x}{a}, \qquad \sin t = \frac{y}{b}.$$

We accomplish this with the identity $\cos^2 t + \sin^2 t = 1$, which yields

$$\left(\frac{x}{a}\right)^2 + \left(\frac{y}{b}\right)^2 = 1, \qquad \text{or} \qquad \frac{x^2}{a^2} + \frac{y^2}{b^2} = 1.$$

The particle's coordinates (x, y) satisfy the equation $(x^2/a^2) + (y^2/b^2) = 1$, so the particle moves along this ellipse. When $t = 0$, the particle's coordinates are

$$x = a \cos(0) = a, \qquad y = b \sin(0) = 0,$$

so the motion starts at $(a, 0)$. As t increases, the particle rises and moves toward the left, moving counterclockwise. It traverses the ellipse once, returning to its starting position $(a, 0)$ at time $t = 2\pi$ (Fig. 10.29).

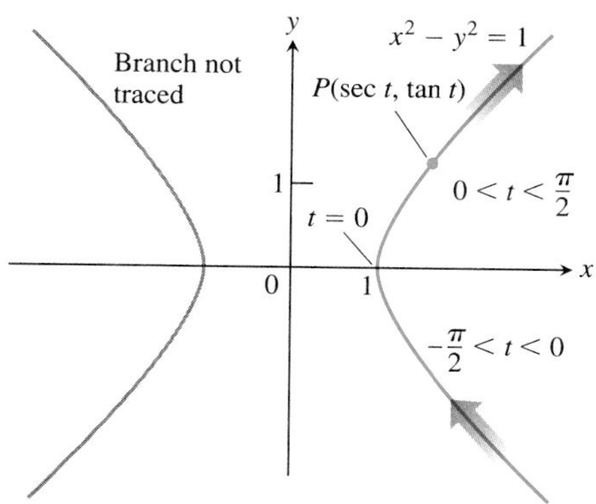

10.30 The equations $x = \sec t$, $y = \tan t$ and interval $-\pi/2 < t < \pi/2$ describe the right-hand branch of the hyperbola $x^2 - y^2 = 1$ (Example 7).

EXAMPLE 6 *A Parametrization of the Circle $x^2 + y^2 = a^2$.* The equations and parameter interval

$$x = a \cos t, \qquad y = a \sin t, \qquad 0 \le t \le 2\pi,$$

obtained by taking $b = a$ in Example 5, describe the circle $x^2 + y^2 = a^2$.

EXAMPLE 7 *A Parametrization of the Right-hand Branch of the Hyperbola $x^2 - y^2 = 1$.* Describe the motion of the particle whose position $P(x, y)$ at time t is given by

$$x = \sec t, \qquad y = \tan t, \qquad -\frac{\pi}{2} < t < \frac{\pi}{2}.$$

Solution We find a Cartesian equation for the coordinates of P by eliminating t between the equations

$$\sec t = x, \qquad \tan t = y.$$

We accomplish this with the identity $\sec^2 t - \tan^2 t = 1$, which yields

$$x^2 - y^2 = 1.$$

Since the particle's coordinates (x, y) satisfy the equation $x^2 - y^2 = 1$, the motion takes place somewhere on this hyperbola. As t runs between $-\pi/2$ and $\pi/2$, $x = \sec t$ remains positive and $y = \tan t$ runs between $-\infty$ and ∞, so P traverses the hyperbola's right-hand branch. It comes in along the branch's lower half as $t \to 0^-$, reaches $(1, 0)$ at $t = 0$, and moves out into the first quadrant as t increases toward $\pi/2$ (Fig. 10.30).

Huygens's Clock

The problem with a pendulum clock whose bob swings in a circular arc is that the frequency of the swing depends on the amplitude of the swing. The wider the swing, the longer it takes the bob to return to center.

This does not happen if the bob can be made to swing in a cycloid. In 1673, Christiaan Huygens (1629–1695), the Dutch mathematician, physicist, and astronomer who discovered the rings of Saturn, driven by a need to make accurate determinations of longitude at sea, designed a pendulum clock whose bob would swing in a cycloid. He hung the bob from a fine wire constrained by guards that caused it to draw up as it swung away from center. How were the guards shaped? They were cycloids, too.

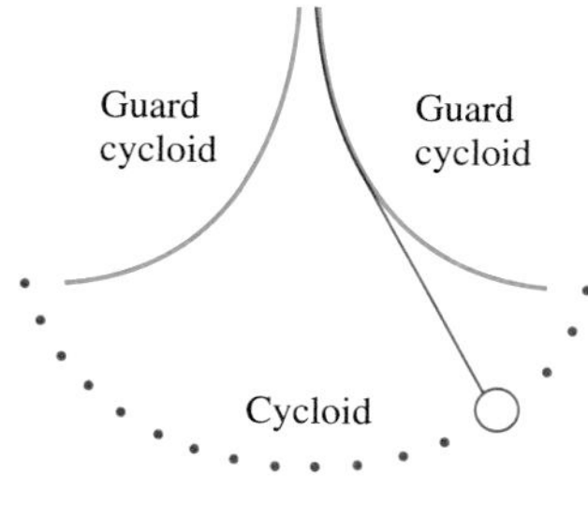

EXAMPLE 8 *Cycloids.* A wheel of radius a rolls along a horizontal straight line. Find parametric equations for the path traced by a point P on the wheel's circumference. The path is called a **cycloid.**

Solution We take the line to be the x-axis, mark a point P on the wheel, start the wheel with P at the origin, and roll the wheel to the right. As parameter, we use the angle t through which the wheel turns, measured in radians. Figure 10.31 shows the wheel a short while later, when its base lies at units from the origin. The wheel's center C lies at (at, a) and the coordinates of P are

$$x = at + a \cos \theta, \qquad y = a + a \sin \theta. \tag{2}$$

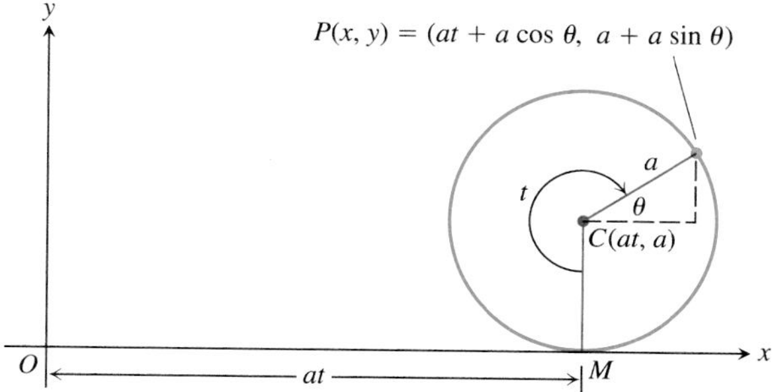

10.31 The position of $P(x, y)$ on the rolling wheel at time t (Example 8).

The Witch of Agnesi

Although l'Hôpital wrote the first text on differential calculus, the first text to include differential and integral calculus along with analytic geometry, infinite series, and differential equations was written in the 1740s by the Italian mathematician Maria Gaetana Agnesi (1718–1799). Agnesi, a gifted scholar and linguist whose Latin essay defending higher education for women was published when she was only nine years old, was a well-published scientist by age 20 and an honorary faculty member of the University of Bologna by age 30.

Today, Agnesi is remembered chiefly for a bell-shaped curve called *the witch of Agnesi*. This name, found only in English texts, is the result of a mistranslation. Agnesi's own name for the curve was *versiera* or "turning curve." John Colson, a noted Cambridge mathematician who felt Agnesi's text so important that he learned Italian to translate it "for the benefit of British youth" (he particularly had in mind young women, for whom he hoped Agnesi would be a role model), probably confused versiera with *avversiera,* which means "wife of the devil" and translates into "witch." You can find out more about the witch by doing Exercise 27.

To express θ in terms of t, we observe that $t + \theta = 3\pi/2$, so that

$$\theta = \frac{3\pi}{2} - t. \tag{3}$$

This makes

$$\cos\theta = \cos\left(\frac{3\pi}{2} - t\right) = -\sin t, \qquad \sin\theta = \sin\left(\frac{3\pi}{2} - t\right) = -\cos t. \tag{4}$$

The equations we seek are

$$x = at - a\sin t, \qquad y = a - a\cos t. \tag{5}$$

These are usually written with the a factored out:

$$x = a(t - \sin t), \qquad y = a(1 - \cos t). \tag{6}$$

Figure 10.32 shows the first arch of the cycloid and part of the next.

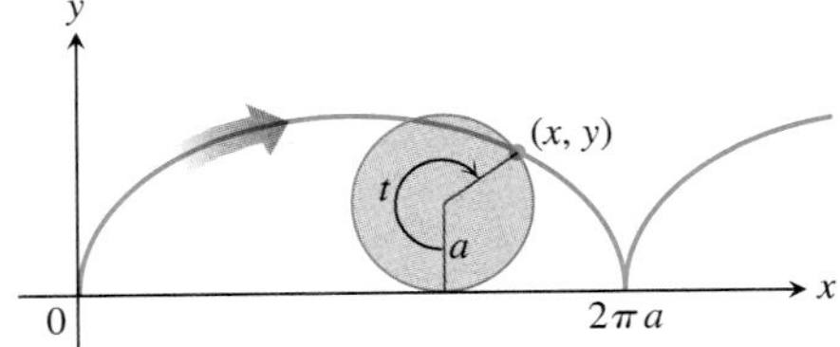

10.32 The cycloid $x = a(t - \sin t)$, $y = a(1 - \cos t)$, for $t \geq 0$.

Standard Parametrizations

Circle $x^2 + y^2 = a^2$:

$$x = a\cos t$$
$$y = a\sin t$$
$$0 \leq t \leq 2\pi$$

Ellipse $\dfrac{x^2}{a^2} + \dfrac{y^2}{b^2} = 1$:

$$x = a\cos t$$
$$y = b\sin t$$
$$0 \leq t \leq 2\pi$$

Cycloid generated by a circle of radius a:

$$x = a(t - \sin t),$$
$$y = a(1 - \cos t)$$

Exercises 10.3

Exercises 1–24 give parametric equations and parameter intervals for the motion of a particle in the xy-plane. Identify the particle's path by finding a Cartesian equation for it. Graph the Cartesian equation. (The graphs will vary with the equation used.) Indicate the portion of the graph traced by the particle and the direction of motion.

1. $x = \cos t, \quad y = \sin t, \quad 0 \leq t \leq \pi$
2. $x = \cos 2t, \quad y = \sin 2t, \quad 0 \leq t \leq \pi$
3. $x = \sin[2\pi(1 - t)], \quad y = \cos[2\pi(1 - t)], \quad 0 \leq t \leq 1$
4. $x = \cos(\pi - t), \quad y = \sin(\pi - t), \quad 0 \leq t \leq \pi$
5. $x = 4\cos t, \quad y = 2\sin t, \quad 0 \leq t \leq 2\pi$
6. $x = 4\sin t, \quad y = 2\cos t, \quad 0 \leq t \leq \pi$
7. $x = 4\cos t, \quad y = 5\sin t, \quad 0 \leq t \leq \pi$
8. $x = 4\sin t, \quad y = 5\cos t, \quad 0 \leq t \leq 2\pi$
9. $x = 3t, \quad y = 9t^2, \quad -\infty < t < \infty$

10. $x = -\sqrt{t}, \quad y = t, \quad t \geq 0$

11. $x = t, \quad y = \sqrt{t}, \quad t \geq 0$

12. $x = \sec^2 t - 1, \quad y = \tan t, \quad -\pi/2 < t < \pi/2$

13. $x = -\sec t, \quad y = \tan t, \quad -\pi/2 < t < \pi/2$

14. $x = \csc t, \quad y = \cot t, \quad 0 < t < \pi$

15. $x = 2t - 5, \quad y = 4t - 7, \quad -\infty < t < \infty$

16. $x = 1 - t, \quad y = 1 + t, \quad -\infty < t < \infty$

17. $x = t, \quad y = 1 - t, \quad 0 \leq t \leq 1$

18. $x = 3 - 3t, \quad y = 2t, \quad 0 \leq t \leq 1$

19. $x = t, \quad y = \sqrt{1 - t^2}, \quad -1 \leq t \leq 0$

20. $x = t, \quad y = \sqrt{4 - t^2}, \quad 0 \leq t \leq 2$

21. $x = t^2, \quad y = \sqrt{t^4 + 1}, \quad t \geq 0$

22. $x = \sqrt{t + 1}, \quad y = \sqrt{t}, \quad t \geq 0$

23. $x = -\cosh t, \quad y = \sinh t, \quad -\infty < t < \infty$

24. $x = 2 \sinh t, \quad y = 2 \cosh t, \quad -\infty < t < \infty$

25. Find parametric equations and a parameter interval for the motion of a particle that starts at $(a, 0)$ and traces the circle $x^2 + y^2 = a^2$

a) once clockwise,
b) once counterclockwise,
c) twice clockwise,
d) twice counterclockwise.

(There are many ways to do these, so your answers may not be the same as the ones in the back of the book.)

26. Find parametric equations and a parameter interval for the motion of a particle that starts at $(a, 0)$ and traces the ellipse $(x^2/a^2) + (y^2/b^2) = 1$

a) once clockwise,
b) once counterclockwise,
c) twice clockwise,
d) twice counterclockwise.

(As in Exercise 25, there are many correct answers.)

27. *The Witch of Maria Agnesi.* The bell-shaped witch of Maria Agnesi can be constructed in the following way. Start with a circle of radius 1, centered at the point $(0, 1)$, as shown in the accompanying figure. Choose a point A on the line $y = 2$ and connect it to the origin with a line segment. Call the point where the segment crosses the circle B. Let P be the point where the vertical line through A crosses the horizontal line through B. The witch is the curve traced by P as A moves along the line $y = 2$. Find parametric equations and a parameter interval for the witch by expressing the coordinates of P in terms of t, the radian measure of the angle that segment OA makes with the positive x-axis. The following equalities (which you may assume) will help.

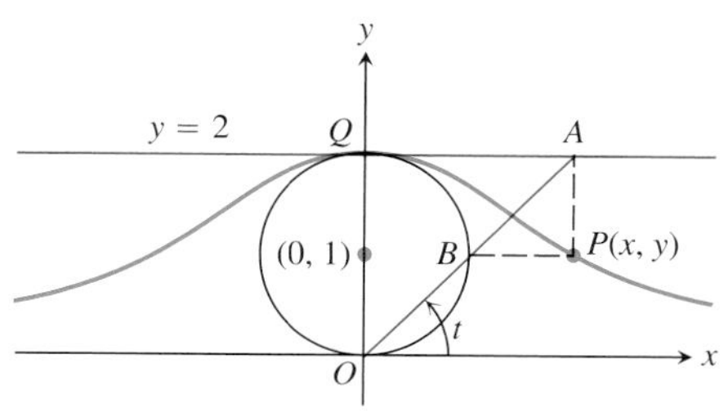

1. $x = AQ$
2. $y = 2 - AB \sin t$
3. $AB \cdot OA = (AQ)^2$

28. *The Involute of a Circle.* If a string wound around a fixed circle is unwound while held taut in the plane of the circle, its end P traces an *involute* of the circle. In Fig. 10.33, the circle in question is the circle $x^2 + y^2 = 1$ and the tracing point starts at $(1, 0)$. The unwound portion of the string is tangent to the circle at Q, and t is the radian measure of the angle from the positive x-axis to segment OQ. Derive parametric equations for the involute by expressing the coordinates x and y of P in terms of t for $t \geq 0$.

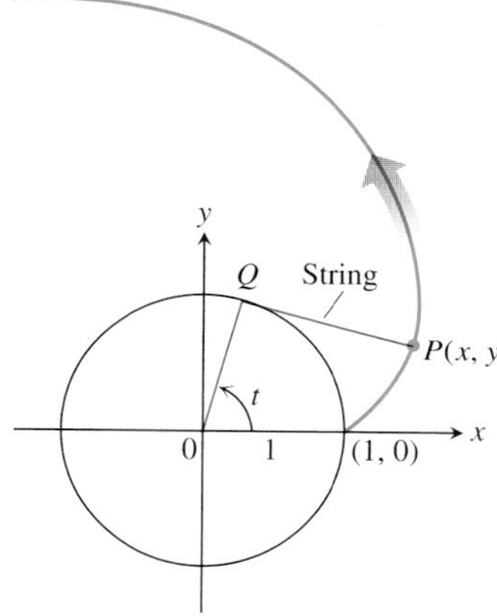

10.33 The involute of a circle of radius 1 (Exercise 28).

29. Find the point on the parabola $x = t, \ y = t^2, \ -\infty < t < \infty$, closest to the point $(2, 1/2)$. (*Hint:* Minimize the square of the distance as a function of t.)

30. Find the point on the ellipse $x = 2 \cos t, \ y = \sin t, \ 0 \leq t \leq 2\pi$ closest to the point $(3/4, 0)$. (*Hint:* Minimize the square of the distance as a function of t.)

31. *Parametrizations of Lines in the Plane (Fig. 10.34)*

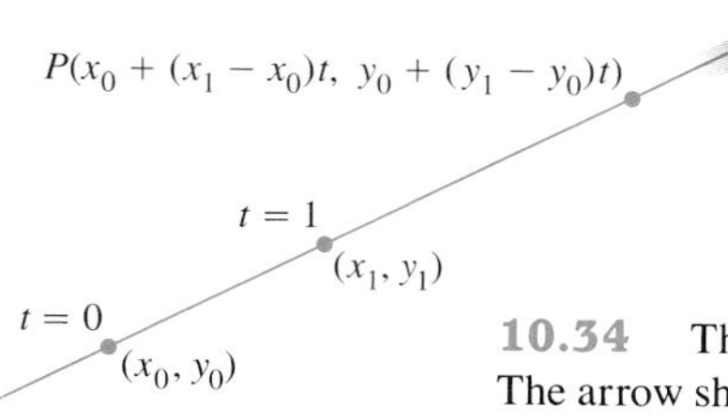

10.34 The line in Exercise 31. The arrow shows the direction of increasing t.

a) Show that the equations and parameter interval $x = x_0 + (x_1 - x_0)t, \ y = y_0 + (y_1 - y_0)t, \ -\infty < t < \infty$, describe the line through the points (x_0, y_0) and (x_1, y_1).
b) Using the same parameter interval, write parametric equations for the line through a point (x_1, y_1) and the origin.
c) Using the same parameter interval, write parametric equations for the line through $(-1, 0)$ and $(0, 1)$.

If you have a parametric equation grapher, graph the following equations over the given intervals.

32. *Ellipse.* $x = 4\cos t$, $y = 2\sin t$, over

a) $0 \le t \le 2\pi$, **b)** $0 \le t \le \pi$, **c)** $-\pi/2 \le t \le \pi/2$.

33. *Hyperbola Branch.* $x = \sec t$ (enter as $1/\cos(t)$), $y = \tan t$ (enter as $\sin(t)/\cos(t)$), over

a) $-1.5 \le t \le 1.5$, **b)** $-0.5 \le t \le 0.5$, **c)** $-0.1 \le t \le 0.1$.

34. *Parabola.* $x = 2t + 3$, $y = t^2 - 1$, $-2 \le t \le 2$

35. *Cycloid.* $x = t - \sin t$, $y = 1 - \cos t$, over

a) $0 \le t \le 2\pi$, **b)** $0 \le t \le 4\pi$, **c)** $\pi \le t \le 3\pi$.

36. *Astroid.* $x = \cos^3 t$, $y = \sin^3 t$, over

a) $0 \le t \le 2\pi$, **b)** $-\pi/2 \le t \le \pi/2$.

37. *A Nice Curve (a Deltoid)*
$x = 2\cos t + \cos 2t$, $y = 2\sin t - \sin 2t$, $0 \le t \le 2\pi$

What happens if you replace 2 with -2 in the equations for x and y? Graph the new equations and find out.

38. *An Even Nicer Curve*
$x = 3\cos t + \cos 3t$, $y = 3\sin t - \sin 3t$, $0 \le t \le 2\pi$

What happens if you replace 3 with -3 in the equations for x and y? Graph the new equations and find out.

39. *Projectile Motion.* Graph
$x = (64\cos\alpha)t$, $y = -16t^2 + (64\sin\alpha)t$, $0 \le t \le 4\sin\alpha$

for the following firing angles.

a) $\alpha = \pi/4$ **b)** $\alpha = \pi/6$ **c)** $\alpha = \pi/3$
d) $\alpha = \pi/2$ (watch out—here it comes!)

40. *Three Beautiful Curves*

a) *Epicycloid:*
$x = 9\cos t - \cos 9t$, $y = 9\sin t - \sin 9t$, $0 \le t \le 2\pi$

b) *Hypocycloid:*
$x = 8\cos t + 2\cos 4t$, $y = 8\sin t - 2\sin 4t$, $0 \le t \le 2\pi$

c) *Hypotrochoid:*
$x = \cos t + 5\cos 3t$, $y = 6\cos t - 5\sin 3t$, $0 \le t \le 2\pi$

Writing for Your Own Knowledge

Answer the following questions in writing. Some answers will take only a sentence or two; others may require several paragraphs. Some explanations may also call for graphs or sketches.

1. What is a parametrized curve?
2. How can you sometimes find a Cartesian equation for the path of a particle whose motion is described parametrically? Can you expect an exact match between the Cartesian equation's graph and the path of motion?
3. What is a cycloid?

EXPLORER PROGRAM

PowerGrapher	Traces the curves for $x(t)$, $y(t)$, and $P(x, y)$ in side-by-side displays as t increases through the parameter interval. Also graphs $P(x, y)$ in a separate display.
	Graphs different sets of parametric equations in a common display.

10.4 Calculus with Parametrized Curves

This section shows how to find slopes, lengths, and surface areas associated with parametrized curves.

Slopes of Parametrized Curves

DEFINITIONS

A parametrized curve $x = f(t)$, $y = g(t)$ is said to be **differentiable at $t = t_0$** if f and g are differentiable at $t = t_0$. The curve is **differentiable** if it is differentiable at every parameter value. The curve is **smooth** if f' and g' are continuous and not simultaneously zero.

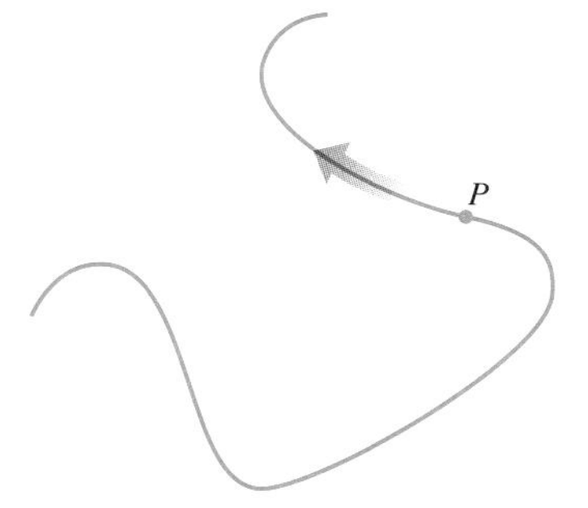

10.35 When dx/dt, dy/dt, and dy/dx exist at a point P on a parametrized curve, they are related by the equation

$$\frac{dy}{dt} = \frac{dy}{dx} \cdot \frac{dx}{dt}.$$

At a point on a differentiable parametrized curve where y is also a differentiable function of x, the derivatives dx/dt, dy/dt, and dy/dx are related by the Chain Rule equation

$$\frac{dy}{dt} = \frac{dy}{dx} \cdot \frac{dx}{dt} \tag{1}$$

(Fig. 10.35). If $dx/dt \neq 0$, we may divide both sides of this equation by dx/dt to solve for dy/dx.

Formula for Finding dy/dx from dy/dt and dx/dt $(dx/dt \neq 0)$

$$\frac{dy}{dx} = \frac{dy/dt}{dx/dt} \tag{2}$$

EXAMPLE 1 Find the tangent to the right-hand hyperbola branch

$$x = \sec t, \qquad y = \tan t, \qquad -\frac{\pi}{2} < t < \frac{\pi}{2},$$

at the point $(\sqrt{2}, 1)$, where $t = \pi/4$ (Fig. 10.36).

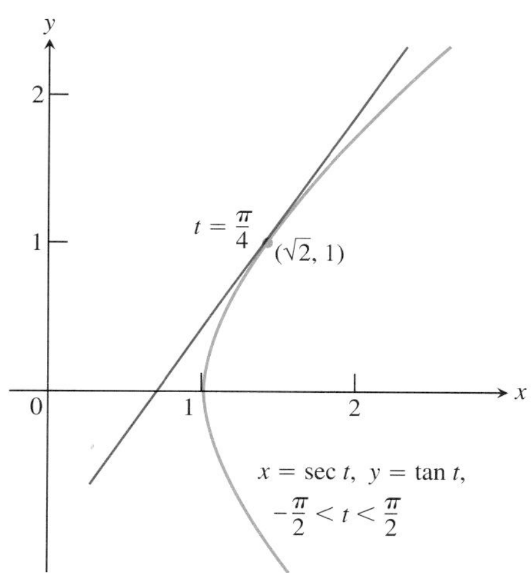

10.36 The hyperbola branch in Example 1.

Solution The slope of the curve at t is

$$\frac{dy}{dx} = \frac{dy/dt}{dx/dt} = \frac{\sec^2 t}{\sec t \tan t} = \frac{\sec t}{\tan t}. \qquad \text{Eq. (2)}$$

Setting t equal to $\pi/4$ gives

$$\left.\frac{dy}{dx}\right|_{t=\pi/4} = \frac{\sec(\pi/4)}{\tan(\pi/4)} = \frac{\sqrt{2}}{1} = \sqrt{2}.$$

The point–slope equation of the tangent is

$$\begin{aligned} y - y_0 &= m(x - x_0) \\ y - 1 &= \sqrt{2}\left(x - \sqrt{2}\right) \\ y &= \sqrt{2}\,x - 2 + 1 \\ y &= \sqrt{2}\,x - 1. \end{aligned}$$

The Parametric Formula for d^2y/dx^2

If the parametric equations for a curve define y as a twice-differentiable function of x, we may calculate d^2y/dx^2 as a function of t in the following way:

$$\frac{d^2y}{dx^2} = \frac{d}{dx}(y') = \frac{dy'/dt}{dx/dt}. \qquad \text{Eq. (2) with } y \text{ replaced by } y'$$

Formula for Finding d^2y/dx^2 from dx/dt and $y' = dy/dx$ $(dx/dt \neq 0)$

$$\frac{d^2y}{dx^2} = \frac{dy'/dt}{dx/dt} \tag{3}$$

Notice the lack of symmetry in Eq. (3). To find d^2y/dx^2, we divide the derivative of y' by the derivative of x, not by the derivative of x'.

How to Express d^2y/dx^2 in Terms of t

STEP 1: Express $y' = dy/dt$ in terms of t.

STEP 2: Find dy'/dt.

STEP 3: Divide dy'/dt by dx/dt. The quotient is d^2y/dx^2.

EXAMPLE 2 Find d^2y/dx^2 if $x = t - t^2$ and $y = t - t^3$.

Solution

STEP 1: *Express y' in terms of t:*

$$y' = \frac{dy}{dx} = \frac{dy/dt}{dx/dt} = \frac{1 - 3t^2}{1 - 2t} \qquad \text{Eq. (2) with } x = t - t^2,\ y = t - t^3$$

STEP 2: *Differentiate y' with respect to t:*

$$\frac{dy'}{dt} = \frac{d}{dt}\left(\frac{1 - 3t^2}{1 - 2t}\right) = \frac{2 - 6t + 6t^2}{(1 - 2t)^2}$$

STEP 3: *Divide dy'/dt by dx/dt.* Since

$$\frac{dx}{dt} = \frac{d}{dt}(t - t^2) = 1 - 2t, \qquad x = t - t^2$$

we have

$$\frac{d^2y}{dx^2} = \frac{dy'/dt}{dx/dt} \qquad \text{Eq. (3)}$$

$$= \frac{2 - 6t + 6t^2}{(1 - 2t)^2} \cdot \frac{1}{1 - 2t}$$

$$= \frac{2 - 6t + 6t^2}{(1 - 2t)^3}.$$

Lengths of Parametrized Curves

A derivation similar to the one in Section 7.4 leads to the following formula for the length of a smooth parametrized curve $x = f(t)$, $y = g(t)$, $a \le t \le b$.

Length

If a smooth curve $x = f(t)$, $y = g(t)$, $a \le t \le b$, is traversed exactly once as t increases from a to b, the curve's length is

$$L = \int_a^b \sqrt{\left(\frac{dx}{dt}\right)^2 + \left(\frac{dy}{dt}\right)^2}\, dt. \tag{4}$$

The length formulas in Section 7.4 are special cases of Eq. (4) (Exercises 31 and 32).

What if there are two different parametrizations for a curve whose length we want to find—does it matter which one we use? The answer, from advanced calculus, is no, as long as the parametrization we choose meets the conditions preceding Eq. (4).

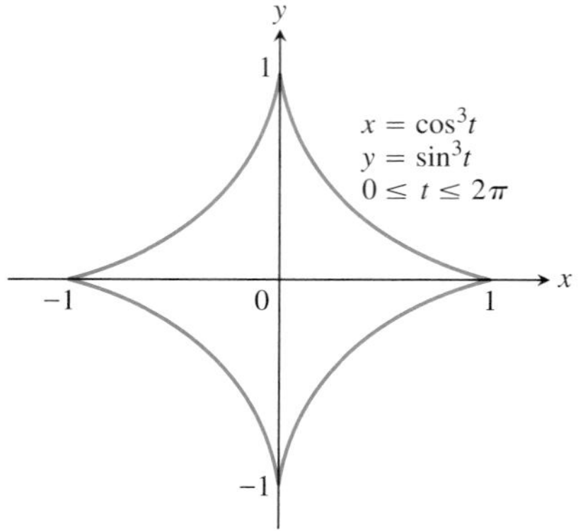

10.37 The astroid in Example 3.

EXAMPLE 3 Find the length of the astroid (Fig. 10.37)

$$x = \cos^3 t, \qquad y = \sin^3 t, \qquad 0 \le t \le 2\pi.$$

Solution Because of the curve's symmetry with respect to the coordinate axes, its length is four times the length of the first-quadrant portion. We have

$$x = \cos^3 t, \qquad y = \sin^3 t$$

$$\left(\frac{dx}{dt}\right)^2 = [3\cos^2 t(-\sin t)]^2 = 9\cos^4 t \sin^2 t$$

$$\left(\frac{dy}{dt}\right)^2 = [3\sin^2 t(\cos t)]^2 = 9\sin^4 t \cos^2 t$$

$$\begin{aligned}\sqrt{\left(\frac{dx}{dt}\right)^2 + \left(\frac{dy}{dt}\right)^2} &= \sqrt{9\cos^2 t \sin^2 t\underbrace{(\cos^2 t + \sin^2 t)}_{1}} \\ &= \sqrt{9\cos^2 t \sin^2 t} \\ &= 3|\cos t \sin t| \\ &= 3\cos t \sin t. \qquad \cos t \sin t \geq 0 \text{ for } 0 \leq t \leq \pi/2\end{aligned}$$

Therefore,

$$\begin{aligned}\text{Length of first-quadrant portion} &= \int_0^{\pi/2} 3\cos t \sin t \, dt \\ &= \frac{3}{2}\int_0^{\pi/2} \sin 2t \, dt \qquad \cos t \sin t = (1/2)\sin 2t \\ &= -\frac{3}{4}\cos 2t\Big]_0^{\pi/2} = \frac{3}{2}.\end{aligned}$$

The length of the astroid is four times this: $4(3/2) = 6$.

The Area of a Surface of Revolution

For smooth parametrized curves, the length formula in Eq. (4) leads to the following formulas for surfaces of revolution. The derivations are similar to the derivations of the Cartesian formulas in Section 7.4.

Surface Area

If a smooth curve $x = f(t)$, $y = g(t)$, $a \leq t \leq b$, is traversed exactly once as t increases from a to b, then the areas of the surfaces generated by revolving the curve about the coordinate axes are as follows.

1. Revolution about the x-axis ($y \geq 0$): $$S = \int_a^b 2\pi y \sqrt{\left(\frac{dx}{dt}\right)^2 + \left(\frac{dy}{dt}\right)^2}\, dt \qquad (5)$$

2. Revolution about the y-axis ($x \geq 0$): $$S = \int_a^b 2\pi x \sqrt{\left(\frac{dx}{dt}\right)^2 + \left(\frac{dy}{dt}\right)^2}\, dt \qquad (6)$$

As with length, we can calculate surface area from any convenient parametrization that meets the stated criteria.

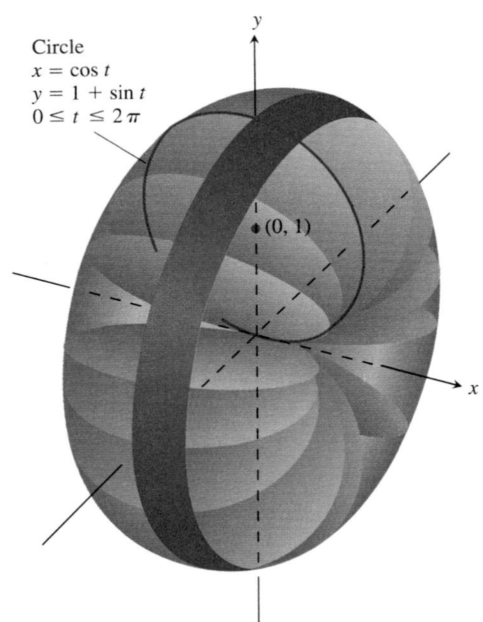

10.38 The surface in Example 4.

EXAMPLE 4 The standard parametrization of the circle of radius 1 centered at the point (0, 1) in the xy-plane is

$$x = \cos t, \qquad y = 1 + \sin t, \qquad 0 \le t \le 2\pi.$$

Use this parametrization to find the area of the surface swept out by revolving the circle about the x-axis (Fig. 10.38).

Solution We evaluate the formula

$$S = \int_a^b 2\pi y \sqrt{\left(\frac{dx}{dt}\right)^2 + \left(\frac{dy}{dt}\right)^2}\, dt \qquad \text{Eq. (5), for revolution about the } x\text{-axis}$$

$$= \int_0^{2\pi} 2\pi (1 + \sin t) \underbrace{\sqrt{(-\sin t)^2 + (\cos t)^2}}_{1}\, dt$$

$$= 2\pi \int_0^{2\pi} (1 + \sin t)\, dt$$

$$= 2\pi \Big[t - \cos t \Big]_0^{2\pi} = 4\pi^2.$$

Exercises 10.4

In Exercises 1–12, find an equation for the line tangent to the curve at the point defined by the given value of t. Also, find the value of d^2y/dx^2 at this point.

1. $x = 2\cos t, \quad y = 2\sin t; \quad t = \pi/4$
2. $x = \sin 2\pi t, \quad y = \cos 2\pi t; \quad t = -1/6$
3. $x = 4\sin t, \quad y = 2\cos t; \quad t = \pi/4$
4. $x = \cos t, \quad y = \sqrt{3}\cos t; \quad t = 2\pi/3$
5. $x = t, \quad y = \sqrt{t}; \quad t = 1/4$
6. $x = \sec^2 t - 1, \quad y = \tan t; \quad t = -\pi/4$
7. $x = \sec t, \quad y = \tan t; \quad t = \pi/6$
8. $x = -\sqrt{t+1}, \quad y = \sqrt{3t}; \quad t = 3$
9. $x = 2t^2 + 3, \quad y = t^4; \quad t = -1$
10. $x = 1/t, \quad y = -2 + \ln t; \quad t = 1$
11. $x = t - \sin t, \quad y = 1 - \cos t; \quad t = \pi/3$
12. $x = \cos t, \quad y = 1 + \sin t; \quad t = \pi/2$

Assuming that the equations in Exercises 13–16 define x and y implicitly as differentiable functions $x = f(t)$, $y = g(t)$, find the slope of the curve $x = f(t)$, $y = g(t)$ at the given value of t.

13. $x^2 - 2tx + 2t^2 = 4, \quad 2y^3 - 3t^2 = 4, \quad t = 2$
14. $x = \sqrt{5 - \sqrt{t}}, \quad y(t-1) = \ln y, \quad t = 1$
15. $x + 2x^{3/2} = t^2 + t, \quad y\sqrt{t+1} + 2t\sqrt{y} = 4, \quad t = 0$
16. $x \sin t + 2x = t, \quad t \sin t - 2t = y, \quad t = \pi$

Find the lengths of the curves in Exercises 17–22.

17. $x = \cos t, \quad y = t + \sin t, \quad 0 \le t \le \pi$
18. $x = t^3, \quad y = 3t^2/2, \quad 0 \le t \le \sqrt{3}$
19. $x = t^2/2, \quad y = (2t+1)^{3/2}/3, \quad 0 \le t \le 4$
20. $x = (2t+3)^{3/2}/3, \quad y = t + t^2/2, \quad 0 \le t \le 3$
21. $x = 8\cos t + 8t\sin t,$ $y = 8\sin t - 8t\cos t,$ $0 \le t \le \pi/2$
22. $x = \ln(\sec t + \tan t) - \sin t,$ $y = \cos t,$ $0 \le t \le \pi/3$ (See Fig. 10.39)

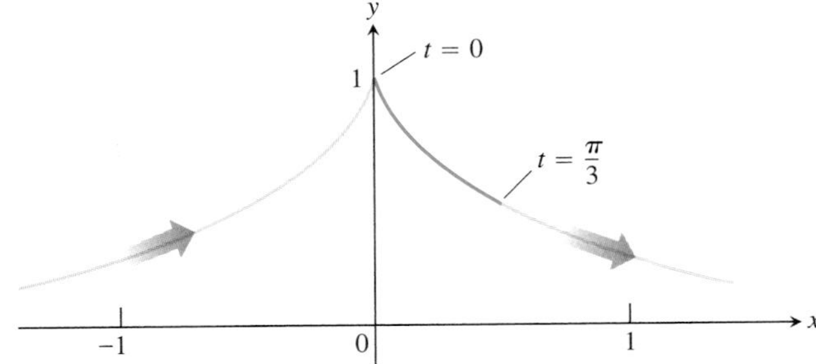

10.39 The curve in Exercise 22 is a portion of a curve that covers the entire x-axis as t runs between $-\pi/2$ and $\pi/2$. The arrows show the direction of increasing t.

Find the areas of the surfaces generated by revolving the curves in Exercises 23–26 about the indicated axes.

23. $x = \cos t, \quad y = 2 + \sin t, \quad 0 \le t \le 2\pi$; x-axis

24. $x = (2/3)t^{3/2}, \quad y = 2\sqrt{t}, \quad 0 \le t \le \sqrt{3}$; y-axis

25. $x = t + \sqrt{2}, \quad y = (t^2/2) + \sqrt{2}t, \quad -\sqrt{2} \le t \le \sqrt{2}$; y-axis

26. $x = \ln(\sec t + \tan t) - \sin t, \quad y = \cos t, \quad 0 \le t \le \pi/3$; x-axis

27. *A Cone Frustum.* The line segment joining the points (0, 1) and (2, 2) is revolved about the x-axis to generate a frustum of a cone. Find the surface area of the frustum using the equations $x = 2t, \quad y = t + 1, \quad 0 \le t \le 1$. Check your result with the geometry formula: Area $= \pi(r_1 + r_2)$(slant height).

28. *A Cone.* The line segment joining the origin to the point (h, r) is revolved about the x-axis to generate a cone of height h and base radius r. Find the cone's surface area with the parametric equations $x = ht, \quad y = rt, \quad 0 \le t \le 1$. Check your result with the geometry formula: Area $= \pi(r)$(slant height).

29. *Length Is Independent of Parametrization.* To illustrate the fact that the numbers we get for length do not depend on the way we parametrize our curves (except for the mild restrictions mentioned earlier), calculate the length of the semicircle $y = \sqrt{1 - x^2}$ with these two different parametrizations:

a) $x = \cos 2t, \quad y = \sin 2t, \quad 0 \le t \le \pi/2$

b) $x = \sin \pi t, \quad y = \cos \pi t, \quad -1/2 \le t \le 1/2$

30. *Elliptic Integrals.* The length of the ellipse

$$x = a \cos t, \quad y = b \sin t, \quad 0 \le t \le 2\pi$$

turns out to be

$$\text{Length} = 4a \int_0^{\pi/2} \sqrt{1 - e^2 \cos^2 t}\, dt,$$

where e is the ellipse's eccentricity. The integral in this formula, called an *elliptic integral,* is nonelementary except when $e = 0$ or 1.

a) Use the Trapezoidal Rule with $n = 10$ to estimate the length of the ellipse when $a = 1$ and $e = 1/2$.

b) Use the fact that the absolute value of the second derivative of $f(t) = \sqrt{1 - e^2 \cos^2 t}$ is less than 1, to find an upper bound for the error in the estimate you obtained in (a).

31. As mentioned in Section 10.3, the graph of a function $y = f(x)$ over an interval $[a, b]$ automatically has the parametrization

$$x = x, \quad y = f(x), \quad a \le x \le b.$$

The parameter, in this case, is x itself.

Show that for this parametrization the parametric length formula

$$L = \int_a^b \sqrt{\left(\frac{dx}{dt}\right)^2 + \left(\frac{dy}{dt}\right)^2}\, dt$$

reduces to the Cartesian formula

$$L = \int_a^b \sqrt{1 + \left(\frac{dy}{dx}\right)^2}\, dx$$

derived in Section 7.4. This will show that the Cartesian formula is a special case of the parametric formula.

32. *Continuation of Exercise 31.* Show that the Cartesian formula

$$L = \int_c^d \sqrt{1 + \left(\frac{dx}{dy}\right)^2}\, dy$$

for the length of the curve $x = g(y), \ c \le y \le d$ (Section 7.4, Eq. 5), is a special case of the parametric length formula

$$L = \int_a^b \sqrt{\left(\frac{dx}{dt}\right)^2 + \left(\frac{dy}{dt}\right)^2}\, dt.$$

The curves drawn by computer in Exercises 33 and 34 are called *Bowditch curves* or *Lissajous figures.* In each case, find the point in the interior of the first quadrant where the tangent to the curve is horizontal and find the equations of the two tangents at the origin.

33. **34.**

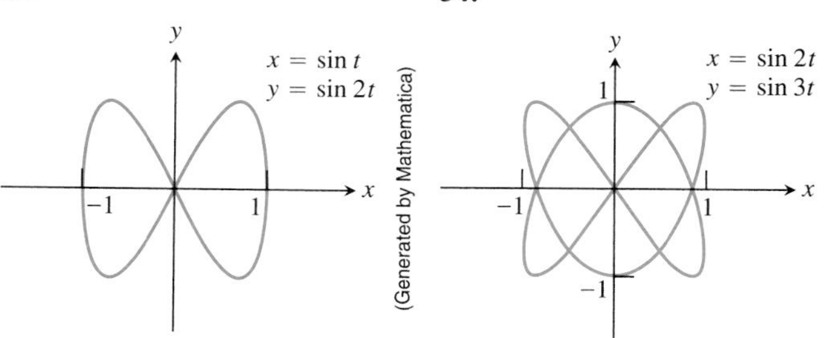

Graph the parametric curves in Exercises 35–41 over parameter intervals of your choice. The curves are Bowditch curves (Lissajous figures), the general formula being

$$x = a \sin(mt + d), \qquad y = b \sin nt,$$

with m and n integers.

35. $x = \sin 2t, \quad y = \sin t$

36. $x = \sin 3t, \quad y = \sin 4t$

37. $x = \sin t, \quad y = \sin 4t$

38. $x = \sin t, \quad y = \sin 5t$

39. $x = \sin 3t, \quad y = \sin 5t$

40. $x = \sin(3t + \pi/2), \quad y = \sin 5t$

41. $x = \sin(3t + \pi/4), \quad y = \sin 5t$

Writing for Your Own Knowledge

Answer the following questions in writing. Some answers will take only a sentence or two; others may require several paragraphs. Some explanations may also call for graphs or sketches.

1. How can you sometimes find the slope at a point of a parametrized curve?

2. If a curve in the plane is given by parametric equations $x = f(t), y = g(t)$ that are sufficiently differentiable, how can you sometimes find d^2y/dx^2?

3. How do you find the length of a smooth parametrized curve?
4. How do you find the area of a surface generated by revolving a smooth parametrized curve about one of the coordinate axes?

EXPLORER PROGRAM

PowerGrapher	Traces the curves for $x(t)$, $y(t)$, and $P(x, y)$ in side-by-side displays as t increases through the parameter interval. Also graphs $P(x, y)$ in a separate display.
	Graphs different sets of parametric equations in a common display.

10.5 Polar Coordinates

In this section, we study polar coordinates and their relation to Cartesian coordinates. While a point in the plane has just one pair of Cartesian coordinates, it has infinitely many pairs of polar coordinates. This has interesting consequences for graphing, as we will see in the next section.

Definition of Polar Coordinates

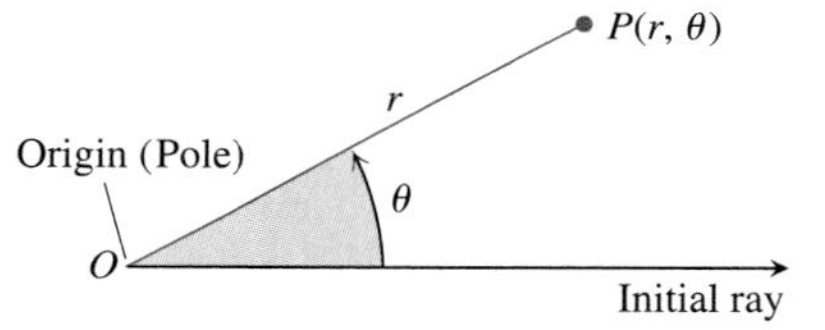

10.40 To define polar coordinates for the plane, we start with an origin called the pole, and an initial ray.

To define polar coordinates, we first fix an **origin** O (called the **pole**) and an **initial ray** from O (Fig. 10.40). Then each point P can be located by assigning to it a **polar coordinate pair** (r, θ) in which r gives the directed distance from O to P and θ gives the directed angle from the initial ray to ray OP:

Polar Coordinates

$$P(r, \theta) \tag{1}$$

Directed distance from O to P (for r); Directed angle from initial ray to OP (for θ)

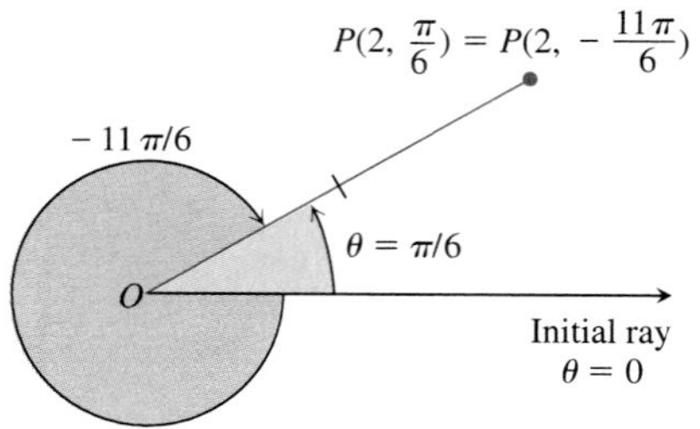

10.41 Polar coordinates are not unique.

As in trigonometry, θ is positive when measured counterclockwise and negative when measured clockwise. The angle associated with a given point is not unique. For instance, the point 2 units from the origin along the ray $\theta = \pi/6$ has polar coordinates $r = 2$, $\theta = \pi/6$. It also has coordinates $r = 2$, $\theta = -11\pi/6$ (Fig. 10.41).

Negative Values of r

There are occasions when we wish to allow r to be negative. That is why we use directed distance in (1). The point $P\,(2, 7\pi/6)$ can be reached by turning $7\pi/6$ rad counterclockwise from the initial ray and going forward 2 units (Fig. 10.42). It can also be reached by turning $\pi/6$ rad counterclockwise from the initial ray and going *backward* 2 units. So the point also has polar coordinates $r = -2$, $\theta = \pi/6$.

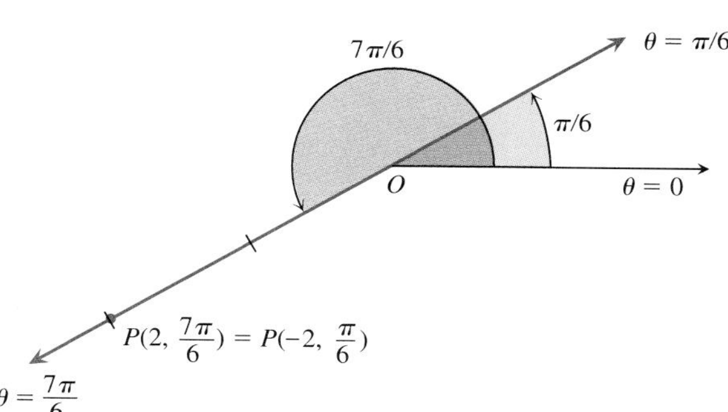

10.42 Polar coordinates can have negative r-values.

EXAMPLE 1 Find all the polar coordinates of the point $P\,(2,\ \pi/6)$.

Solution We sketch the initial ray of the coordinate system, draw the ray from the origin that makes an angle of $\pi/6$ rad with the initial ray, and mark the point $(2,\ \pi/6)$ (Fig. 10.43). We then find the angles for the other coordinate pairs of P in which $r = 2$ and $r = -2$.

For $r = 2$, the complete list of angles is

$$\frac{\pi}{6},\quad \frac{\pi}{6} \pm 2\pi,\quad \frac{\pi}{6} \pm 4\pi,\quad \frac{\pi}{6} \pm 6\pi,\quad \ldots. \tag{2}$$

For $r = -2$, the angles are

$$-\frac{5\pi}{6},\quad -\frac{5\pi}{6} \pm 2\pi,\quad -\frac{5\pi}{6} \pm 4\pi,\quad -\frac{5\pi}{6} \pm 6\pi,\quad \ldots. \tag{3}$$

The corresponding coordinate pairs of P are

$$\left(2,\ \frac{\pi}{6} + 2n\pi\right), \qquad n = 0,\ \pm 1,\ \pm 2,\ \ldots \tag{4}$$

and

$$\left(-2,\ -\frac{5\pi}{6} + 2n\pi\right), \qquad n = 0,\ \pm 1,\ \pm 2,\ \ldots. \tag{5}$$

When $n = 0$, the formulas give $(2,\ \pi/6)$ and $(-2,\ -5\pi/6)$. When $n = 1$, they give $(2,\ 13\pi/6)$ and $(-2,\ 7\pi/6)$, and so on.

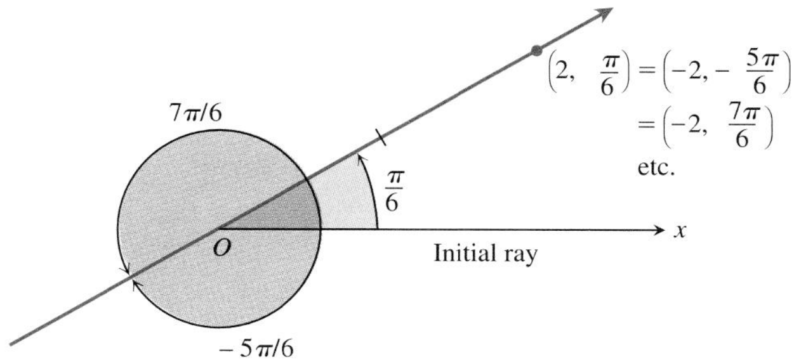

10.43 The point $P(2,\ \pi/6)$ has infinitely many polar coordinate pairs.

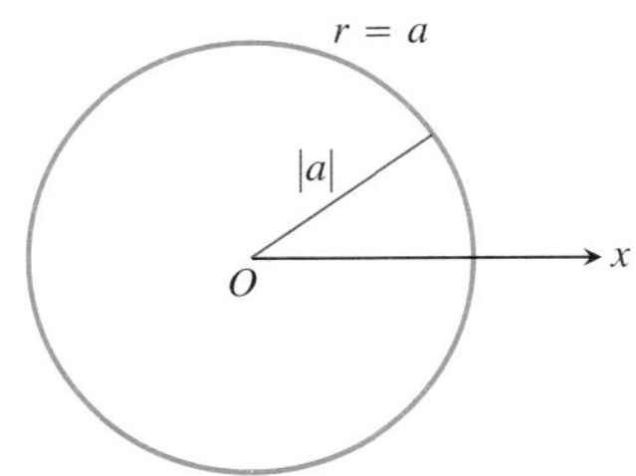

10.44 The polar equation for this circle is $r = a$.

Elementary Coordinate Equations and Inequalities

If we hold r fixed at a constant nonzero value $r = a$, then the point $P(r, \theta)$ lies $|a|$ units from the origin. As θ varies over any interval of length 2π radians, P traces a circle of radius $|a|$ centered at the origin (Fig. 10.44).

Circle of Radius $|a|$ Centered at the Origin

$$r = a \tag{6}$$

EXAMPLE 2 The equation $r = 1$ is an equation for the circle of radius 1 centered at the origin. So is the equation $r = -1$.

If we hold θ fixed at a constant value $\theta = \theta_0$ and let r run between $-\infty$ and ∞, the point $P(r, \theta)$ traces the line through the origin that makes an angle of measure θ_0 with the initial ray.

Equation for Lines Through the Origin

$$\theta = \theta_0 \tag{7}$$

EXAMPLE 3 One equation for the line in Fig. 10.43 is $\theta = \pi/6$. The equations $\theta = 7\pi/6$ and $\theta = -5\pi/6$ are also equations for this line.

Equations of the form $r = a$ and $\theta = \theta_0$ can be combined to define regions, segments, and rays.

EXAMPLE 4 Graph the sets of points whose polar coordinates satisfy the following conditions.

a) $1 \le r \le 2$ and $0 \le \theta \le \dfrac{\pi}{2}$

b) $-3 \le r \le 2$ and $\theta = \dfrac{\pi}{4}$

c) $r \le 0$ and $\theta = \dfrac{\pi}{4}$

d) $\dfrac{2\pi}{3} \le \theta \le \dfrac{3\pi}{4}$ (no restriction on r)

Solution The graphs are shown in Fig. 10.45.

(a)

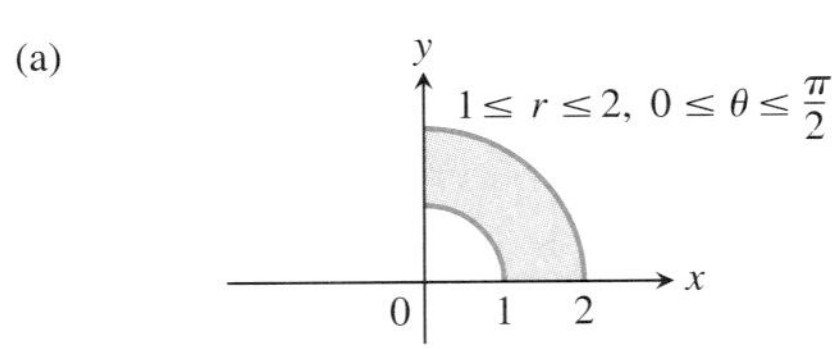

(b)

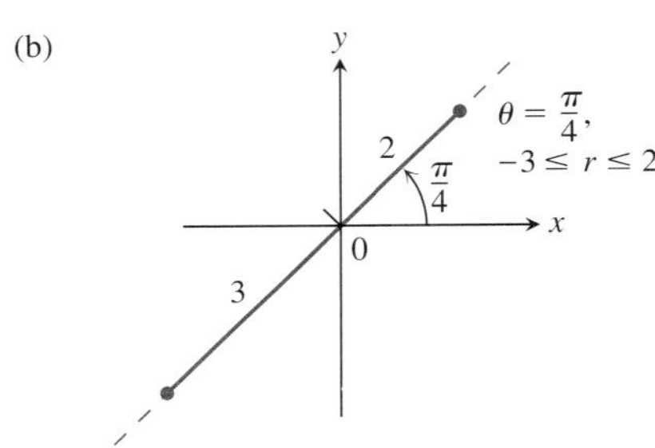

(c)

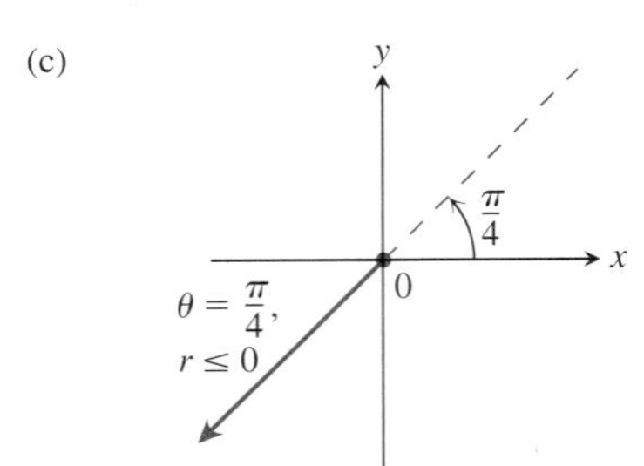

(d)

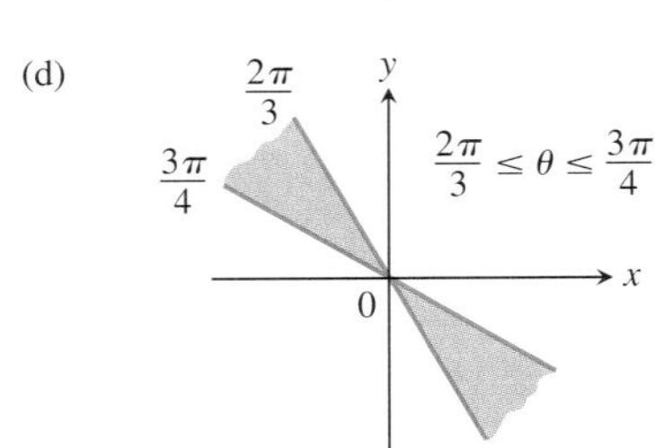

10.45 The graphs of typical inequalities in r and θ (Example 4).

Cartesian Versus Polar Coordinates

When we use both polar and Cartesian coordinates in a plane, we place the two origins together and take the initial polar ray as the positive x-axis. The ray $\theta = \pi/2$, $r > 0$, becomes the positive y-axis (Fig. 10.46). The two coordinate systems are then related by the following equations.

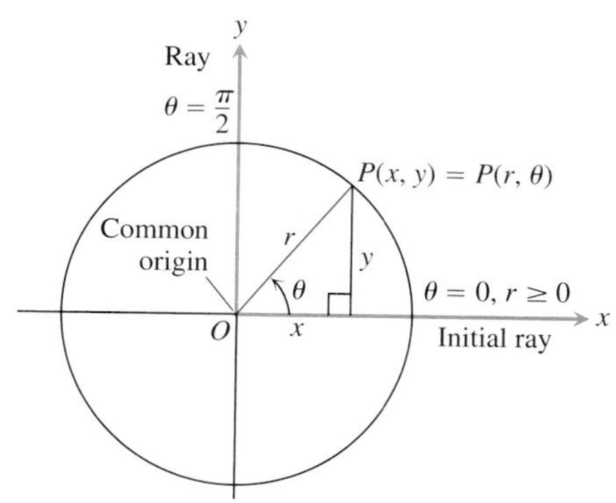

10.46 The usual way to relate polar and Cartesian coordinates.

Equations Relating Polar and Cartesian Coordinates

$$x = r\cos\theta, \qquad y = r\sin\theta, \qquad x^2 + y^2 = r^2, \qquad \frac{y}{x} = \tan\theta \tag{8}$$

We use Eqs. (8) to rewrite polar equations in Cartesian form and vice versa.

EXAMPLE 5

Polar equation	Cartesian equivalent
$r\cos\theta = 2$	$x = 2$
$r^2\cos\theta\sin\theta = 4$	$xy = 4$
$r^2\cos^2\theta - r^2\sin^2\theta = 1$	$x^2 - y^2 = 1$
$r = 1 + 2r\cos\theta$	$y^2 - 3x^2 - 4x - 1 = 0$
$r = 1 - \cos\theta$	$x^4 + y^4 + 2x^2y^2 + 2x^3 + 2xy^2 - y^2 = 0$

With some curves, we are better off with polar coordinates; with others, we aren't.

EXAMPLE 6 Find a polar equation for the circle $x^2 + (y-3)^2 = 9$ (Fig. 10.47).

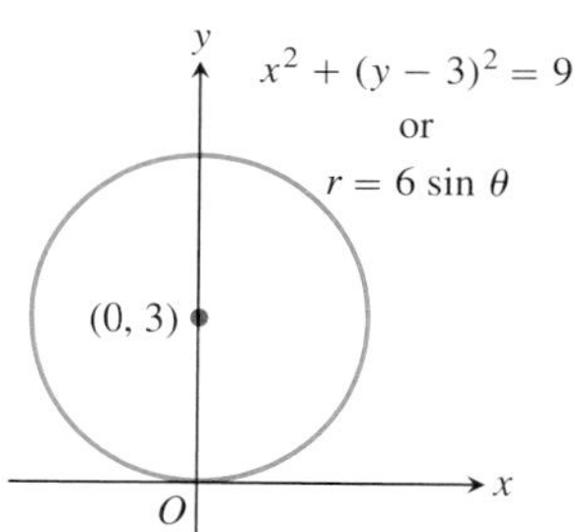

10.47 The circle in Example 6.

Solution

$$\begin{aligned} x^2 + y^2 - 6y + 9 &= 9 && \text{Expand } (y-3)^2. \\ x^2 + y^2 - 6y &= 0 && \text{The 9's cancel.} \\ r^2 - 6r\sin\theta &= 0 && x^2 + y^2 = r^2 \\ r - 6\sin\theta &= 0 && r \neq 0\text{, so we can divide both sides by } r. \\ r &= 6\sin\theta \end{aligned}$$

We will say more about polar equations of conic sections in Section 10.7.

EXAMPLE 7 Replace the following polar equations by equivalent Cartesian equations, and identify their graphs.

a) $r\cos\theta = -4$

b) $r^2 = 4r\cos\theta$

c) $r = \dfrac{4}{2\cos\theta - \sin\theta}$

Solution We use the substitutions $r\cos\theta = x$, $r\sin\theta = y$, $r^2 = x^2 + y^2$.

a) $r\cos\theta = -4$

The Cartesian equation: $r\cos\theta = -4$
$x = -4$

The graph: Vertical line through $x = -4$ on the x-axis

b) $r^2 = 4r \cos \theta$

The Cartesian equation:

$$r^2 = 4r \cos \theta$$
$$x^2 + y^2 = 4x$$
$$x^2 - 4x + y^2 = 0$$
$$x^2 - 4x + 4 + y^2 = 4 \quad \text{Completing the square}$$
$$(x-2)^2 + y^2 = 4$$

The graph: Circle, radius 2, center $(h, k) = (2, 0)$

c) $r = \dfrac{4}{2 \cos \theta - \sin \theta}$

The Cartesian equation:

$$r(2 \cos \theta - \sin \theta) = 4$$
$$2r \cos \theta - r \sin \theta = 4$$
$$2x - y = 4$$
$$y = 2x - 4$$

The graph: Line, slope $m = 2$, y-intercept $b = -4$

Exercises 10.5

NOTE: *All angles are in radians.*

1. Which polar coordinate pairs label the same point?

a) $(3, 0)$ **b)** $(-3, 0)$ **c)** $(-3, \pi)$
d) $(-3, 2\pi)$ **e)** $(2, 2\pi/3)$ **f)** $(2, -2\pi/3)$
g) $(2, 7\pi/3)$ **h)** $(-2, \pi/3)$ **i)** $(2, -\pi/3)$
j) $(2, \pi/3)$ **k)** $(-2, -\pi/3)$ **l)** $(-2, 2\pi/3)$
m) (r, θ) **n)** $(r, \theta + \pi)$ **o)** $(-r, \theta + \pi)$
p) $(-r, \theta)$

2. Find the Cartesian coordinates of the points whose polar coordinates are given in parts (a)–(l) of Exercise 1.

3. Plot the following points (given in polar coordinates). Then find all the polar coordinates of each point.

a) $(2, \pi/2)$ **b)** $(2, 0)$
c) $(-2, \pi/2)$ **d)** $(-2, 0)$

4. Plot the following points (given in polar coordinates). Then find all the polar coordinates of each point.

a) $(3, \pi/4)$ **b)** $(-3, \pi/4)$
c) $(3, -\pi/4)$ **d)** $(-3, -\pi/4)$

5. Find the Cartesian coordinates of the following points (given in polar coordinates).

a) $(\sqrt{2}, \pi/4)$ **b)** $(1, 0)$
c) $(0, \pi/2)$ **d)** $(-\sqrt{2}, \pi/4)$
e) $(-3, 5\pi/6)$ **f)** $(5, \tan^{-1}(4/3))$
g) $(-1, 7\pi)$ **h)** $(2\sqrt{3}, 2\pi/3)$

6. Find all polar coordinates of the origin.

Graph the sets of points whose polar coordinates satisfy the equations and inequalities in Exercises 7–22.

7. $r = 2$ **8.** $0 \le r \le 2$
9. $r \ge 1$ **10.** $1 \le r \le 2$
11. $0 \le \theta \le \pi/6, \quad r \ge 0$ **12.** $\theta = 2\pi/3, \quad r \le -2$
13. $\theta = \pi/3, \quad -1 \le r \le 3$
14. $\theta = 11\pi/4, \quad r \ge -1$
15. $\theta = \pi/2, \quad r \ge 0$ **16.** $\theta = \pi/2, \quad r \le 0$
17. $0 \le \theta \le \pi, \quad r = 1$
18. $0 \le \theta \le \pi, \quad r = -1$
19. $\pi/4 \le \theta \le 3\pi/4, \quad 0 \le r \le 1$
20. $-\pi/4 \le \theta \le \pi/4, \quad -1 \le r \le 1$
21. $-\pi/2 \le \theta \le \pi/2, \quad 1 \le r \le 2$
22. $0 \le \theta \le \pi/2, \quad 1 \le |r| \le 2$

Replace the polar equations in Exercises 23–46 by equivalent Cartesian equations. Then describe or identify the graph.

23. $r \cos \theta = 2$ **24.** $r \sin \theta = -1$
25. $r \sin \theta = 0$ **26.** $r \cos \theta = 0$
27. $r = 4 \csc \theta$ **28.** $r = -3 \sec \theta$
29. $r \cos \theta + r \sin \theta = 1$ **30.** $r \sin \theta = r \cos \theta$
31. $r^2 = 1$ **32.** $r^2 = 4r \sin \theta$
33. $r = \dfrac{5}{\sin \theta - 2 \cos \theta}$ **34.** $r^2 \sin 2\theta = 2$

35. $r = \cot\theta \csc\theta$

36. $r = 4\tan\theta \sec\theta$

37. $r = \csc\theta\, e^{r\cos\theta}$

38. $r\sin\theta = \ln r + \ln\cos\theta$

39. $r^2 + 2r^2\cos\theta\sin\theta = 1$

40. $\cos^2\theta = \sin^2\theta$

41. $r^2 = -4r\cos\theta$

42. $r^2 = -6\,r\sin\theta$

43. $r = 8\sin\theta$

44. $r = 3\cos\theta$

45. $r = 2\cos\theta + 2\sin\theta$

46. $r = 2\cos\theta - \sin\theta$

Replace the Cartesian equations in Exercises 47–60 by equivalent polar equations.

47. $x = 7$

48. $y = 1$

49. $x = y$

50. $x - y = 3$

51. $x^2 + y^2 = 4$

52. $x^2 - y^2 = 1$

53. $\dfrac{x^2}{9} + \dfrac{y^2}{4} = 1$

54. $xy = 2$

55. $y^2 = 4x$

56. $x^2 + xy + y^2 = 1$

57. $x^2 + (y - 2)^2 = 4$

58. $(x - 5)^2 + y^2 = 25$

59. $(x - 3)^2 + (y + 1)^2 = 4$

60. $(x + 2)^2 + (y - 5)^2 = 16$

61. *Vertical and Horizontal Lines.* (a) Show that every vertical line in the xy-plane has a polar equation of the form $r = a\sec\theta$. (b) What is the analogous equation for horizontal lines in the xy-plane? Give reasons for your answer.

Writing for Your Own Knowledge

Answer the following questions in writing. Some answers will take only a sentence or two; others may require several paragraphs. Some explanations may also call for graphs or sketches.

1. What are polar coordinates? How many pairs of polar coordinates can a point have?
2. What are some typical regions defined by numerical inequalities involving r and θ?
3. What equations enable you to change back and forth between polar and Cartesian coordinates? Why might you want to make such a change?
4. What are some typical polar equations for lines and curves in the plane?

10.6 *Polar Graphs*

This section describes techniques for graphing equations in polar coordinates.

Symmetry

Figure 10.48 illustrates the standard polar coordinate tests for symmetry.

Symmetry Tests for Polar Graphs

1. *Symmetry about the x-axis:* If the point (r, θ) lies on the graph, the point $(r, -\theta)$ or $(-r, \pi - \theta)$ lies on the graph (Fig. 10.48a).
2. *Symmetry about the* y-axis: If the point (r, θ) lies on the graph, the point $(r, \pi - \theta)$ or $(-r, -\theta)$ lies on the graph (Fig. 10.48b).
3. *Symmetry about the origin:* If the point (r, θ) lies on the graph, the point $(-r, \theta)$ or $(r, \theta + \pi)$ lies on the graph (Fig. 10.48c).

10.48 Three tests for symmetry.

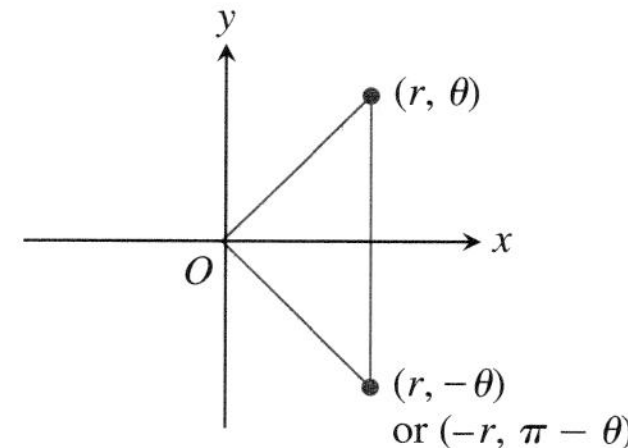

About the x-axis
(a)

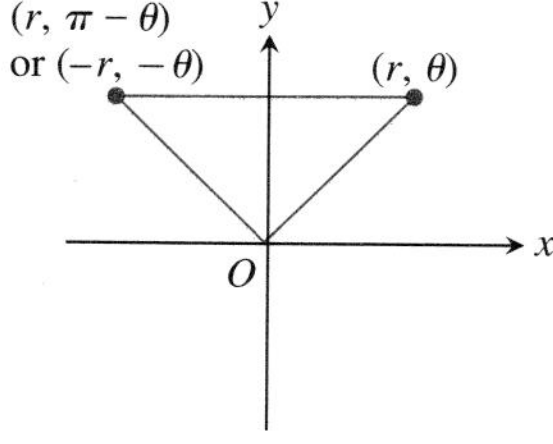

About the y-axis
(b)

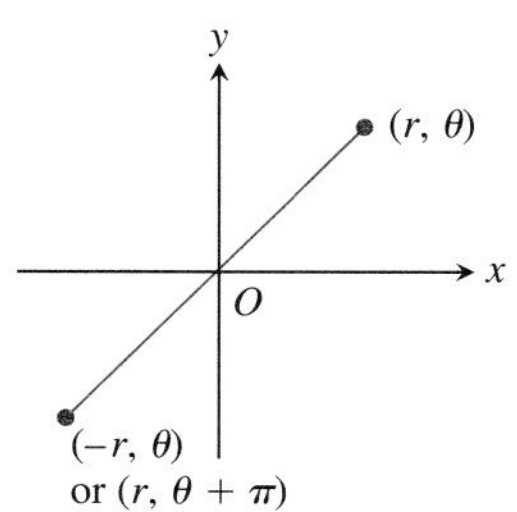

About the origin
(c)

Slope

The slope of a polar curve $r = f(\theta)$ is not given by the derivative $r' = df/d\theta$, but by a different formula. To see why, and what the formula is, think of the graph of f as the graph of the parametric equations

$$x = r\cos\theta = f(\theta)\cos\theta, \qquad y = r\sin\theta = f(\theta)\sin\theta. \tag{1}$$

If f is a differentiable function of θ, then so are x and y and, when $dx/d\theta \neq 0$, we may calculate dy/dx from the parametric formula

$$\frac{dy}{dx} = \frac{dy/d\theta}{dx/d\theta} \qquad \text{Section 10.4, Eq. (2) with } t = \theta$$

$$= \frac{\dfrac{d}{d\theta}(f(\theta)\cdot\sin\theta)}{\dfrac{d}{d\theta}(f(\theta)\cdot\cos\theta)}$$

$$= \frac{\dfrac{df}{d\theta}\sin\theta + f(\theta)\cos\theta}{\dfrac{df}{d\theta}\cos\theta - f(\theta)\sin\theta} \qquad \text{Product Rule for Derivatives}$$

Slope of the Curve $r = f(\theta)$

$$\left.\frac{dy}{dx}\right|_{(r,\,\theta)} = \frac{f'(\theta)\sin\theta + f(\theta)\cos\theta}{f'(\theta)\cos\theta - f(\theta)\sin\theta}, \tag{2}$$

provided $dx/d\theta \neq 0$ at (r, θ).

If the curve $r = f(\theta)$ passes through the origin at $\theta = \theta_0$, then $f(\theta_0) = 0$, and Eq. (2) gives

$$\left.\frac{dy}{dx}\right|_{(0,\,\theta_0)} = \frac{f'(\theta_0)\sin\theta_0}{f'(\theta_0)\cos\theta_0} = \tan\theta_0. \tag{3}$$

If the graph of $r = f(\theta)$ passes through the origin at the value $\theta = \theta_0$, the slope of the curve there is $\tan\theta_0$. The reason we say "slope at $(0, \theta_0)$" and not just "slope at the origin" is that a polar curve may pass through the origin more than once, with different slopes at different θ-values. This is not the case in our first example, however.

EXAMPLE 1 *A Cardioid.* Graph the curve $r = 1 - \cos\theta$.

Solution The curve is symmetric about the x-axis because

$$\begin{aligned} (r, \theta) \text{ on the graph} \quad &\Rightarrow \quad r = 1 - \cos\theta \\ &\Rightarrow \quad r = 1 - \cos(-\theta) \qquad \cos\theta = \cos(-\theta) \\ &\Rightarrow \quad (r, -\theta) \text{ on the graph.} \end{aligned}$$

As θ increases from 0 to π, $\cos\theta$ decreases from 1 to -1, and $r = 1 - \cos\theta$ increases from a minimum value of 0 to a maximum value of 2. As θ continues on from π to 2π, $\cos\theta$ increases from -1 back to 1 and r decreases from 2 back to 0. The curve starts to repeat when $\theta = 2\pi$ because the cosine has period 2π.

θ	$r = 1 - \cos\theta$
0	0
$\frac{\pi}{3}$	$\frac{1}{2}$
$\frac{\pi}{2}$	1
$\frac{2\pi}{3}$	$\frac{3}{2}$
π	2

(a)

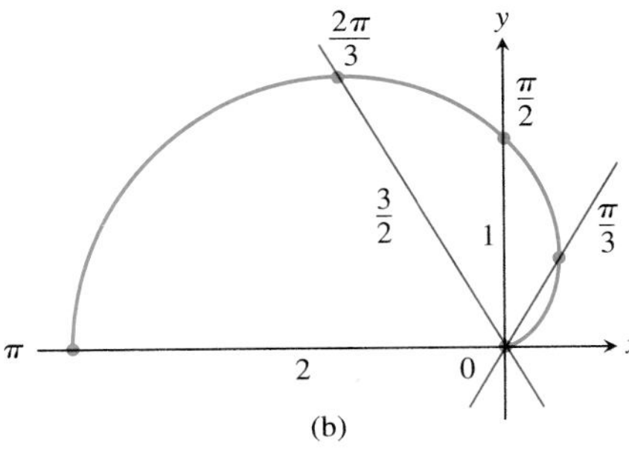

(b)

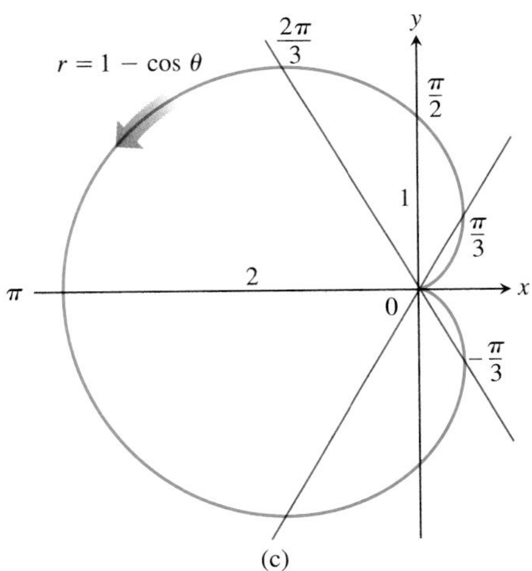

(c)

10.49 The steps in graphing the cardioid $r = 1 - \cos\theta$ (Example 1). The arrow shows the direction of increasing θ.

The curve leaves the origin with slope $\tan(0) = 0$ and returns to the origin with slope $\tan(2\pi) = 0$.

We make a table of values from $\theta = 0$ to $\theta = \pi$, plot the points, draw a smooth curve through them with a horizontal tangent at the origin, and reflect the curve across the x-axis to complete the graph (Fig. 10.49). The curve is called a *cardioid* because of its heart shape.

EXAMPLE 2 Graph the curve $r^2 = 4\cos\theta$.

Solution Although $\cos\theta$ has period 2π, the equation $r^2 = 4\cos\theta$ requires $\cos\theta \geq 0$, so we get the entire graph by running θ from $-\pi/2$ to $\pi/2$. The curve is symmetric about the x-axis because

$$\begin{aligned} (r, \theta) \text{ on the graph} \quad &\Rightarrow \quad r^2 = 4\cos\theta \\ &\Rightarrow \quad r^2 = 4\cos(-\theta) \qquad \cos\theta = \cos(-\theta) \\ &\Rightarrow \quad (r, -\theta) \text{ on the graph.} \end{aligned}$$

The curve is also symmetric about the origin because

$$\begin{aligned} (r, \theta) \text{ on the graph} \quad &\Rightarrow \quad r^2 = 4\cos\theta \\ &\Rightarrow \quad (-r)^2 = 4\cos\theta \\ &\Rightarrow \quad (-r, \theta) \text{ on the graph.} \end{aligned}$$

Together, these two symmetries imply symmetry about the y-axis.

The curve passes through the origin when $\theta = -\pi/2$ and $\theta = \pi/2$. It has a vertical tangent both times because $\tan\theta$ is infinite.

For each value of θ in the interval between $-\pi/2$ and $\pi/2$, the formula $r^2 = 4\cos\theta$ gives two values of r:

$$r = \pm 2\sqrt{\cos\theta}.$$

We make a short table of values, plot the corresponding points, and use information about symmetry and tangents to guide us in connecting the points with a smooth curve (Fig. 10.50).

θ	$\cos\theta$	$r = \pm 2\sqrt{\cos\theta}$
0	1	± 2
$\pm\frac{\pi}{6}$	$\frac{\sqrt{3}}{2}$	± 1.9
$\pm\frac{\pi}{4}$	$\frac{1}{\sqrt{2}}$	± 1.7
$\pm\frac{\pi}{3}$	$\frac{1}{2}$	± 1.4
$\pm\frac{\pi}{2}$	0	0

(a)

$r^2 = 4\cos\theta$

Loop for $r = -2\sqrt{\cos\theta}$, $-\frac{\pi}{2} \leq \theta \leq \frac{\pi}{2}$

Loop for $r = 2\sqrt{\cos\theta}$, $-\frac{\pi}{2} \leq \theta \leq \frac{\pi}{2}$

(b)

10.50 The graph of $r^2 = 4\cos\theta$ (Example 2). The arrows show the direction of increasing θ. The values of r in the table were found with a calculator and rounded.

Steps for Faster Graphing

STEP 1: First graph $r = f(\theta)$ in the *Cartesian* $r\theta$-plane (that is, plot the values of θ on a horizontal axis and the corresponding values of r along a vertical axis).

STEP 2: Then use the Cartesian graph as a "table" and guide to sketch the *polar* coordinate graph.

Faster Graphing

One way to graph a polar equation $r = f(\theta)$ is to make a table of (r, θ) values, plot the corresponding points, and connect them in order of increasing θ. This can work well if there are enough points to reveal all the loops and dimples in the graph. Here we describe another method of graphing that is usually quicker and more reliable. The steps are listed in the sidelight.

This method is better than simple point plotting because the Cartesian graph, even when hastily drawn, shows at a glance where r is positive, negative, and nonexistent, as well as where r is increasing and decreasing. As examples, we graph $r = 1 + \cos(\theta/2)$ and $r^2 = \sin 2\theta$.

EXAMPLE 3 Graph the curve

$$r = 1 + \cos\frac{\theta}{2}.$$

Solution We first graph r as a function of θ in the Cartesian $r\theta$-plane. Since the cosine has period 2π, we must let θ run from 0 to 4π to produce the entire graph (Fig. 10.51a). The arrows from the θ-axis to the curve give radii for graphing $r = 1 + \cos(\theta/2)$ in the polar plane (Fig. 10.51b).

EXAMPLE 4 *A Lemniscate.* Graph the curve $r^2 = \sin 2\theta$.

Solution Here we begin by plotting r^2 (not r) as a function of θ in the Cartesian $r^2\theta$-plane, treating r^2 as a variable that may have negative as well as positive values (Fig. 10.52a). We pass from there to the graph of $r = \pm\sqrt{\sin 2\theta}$ in the $r\theta$-plane (Fig. 10.52b) and then draw the polar graph (Fig. 10.52c). The graph in Fig. 10.52(b) "covers" the final polar graph in Fig. 10.52(c) twice. We could have managed with either loop alone, with the two upper halves, or with the two lower halves. The double covering does no harm, however, and we learn a little more about the behavior of the function this way.

Finding the Points Where Curves Intersect

The fact that we can represent a point in different ways in polar coordinates makes extra care necessary in deciding when a point lies on the graph of a polar equation and in determining the points in which polar graphs intersect. The problem is that a point of intersection may satisfy the equation of one curve with polar coordinates that are different from the ones with which it satisfies the equation of another curve. Thus, solving the equations of two curves simultaneously may not identify all their points of intersection. The only sure way to identify all the points of intersection is to graph the equations.

EXAMPLE 5 Show that the point $(2, \pi/2)$ lies on the curve $r = 2\cos 2\theta$.

Solution It may seem at first that the point $(2, \pi/2)$ does not lie on the curve because substituting the given coordinates into the equation gives

$$2 = 2\cos 2\left(\frac{\pi}{2}\right) = 2\cos\pi = -2,$$

which is not a true equality. The magnitude is right, but the sign is wrong. This suggests looking for a pair of coordinates for the given point in which r is nega-

Drawing Lesson

How to Use Cartesian Graphs to Draw Polar Graphs

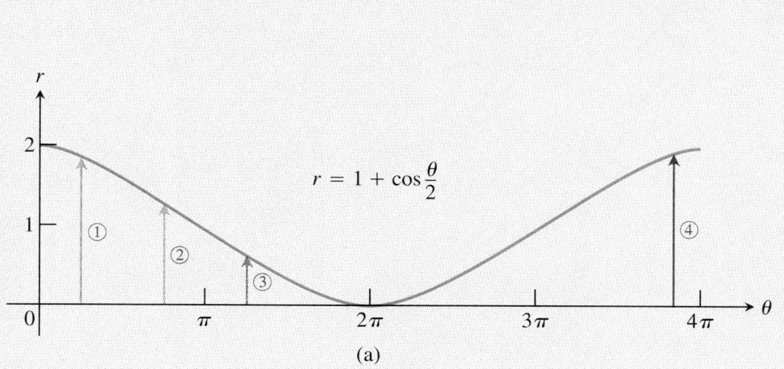

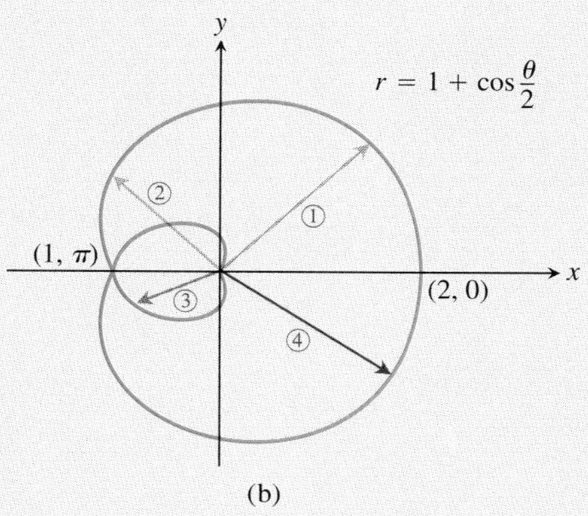

10.51 (a) The graph of $r = 1 + \cos(\theta/2)$ in the Cartesian $r\theta$-plane gives the radii for the graph in the polar $r\theta$-plane (b).

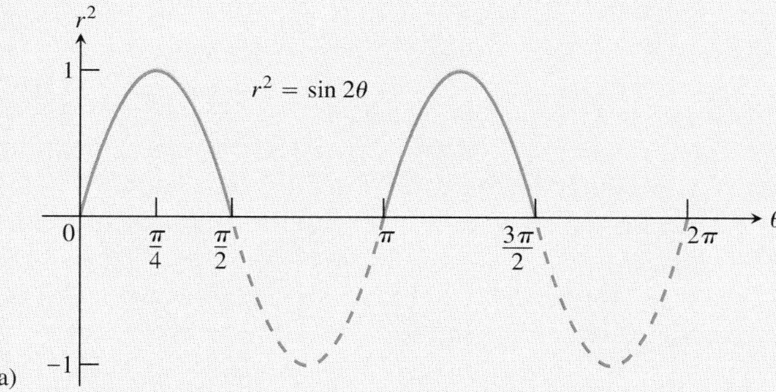

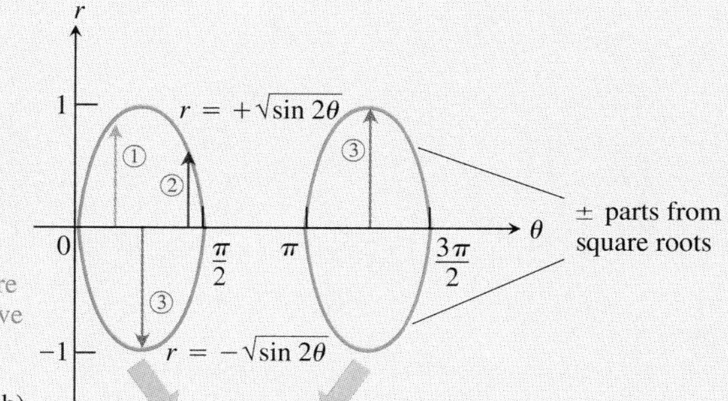

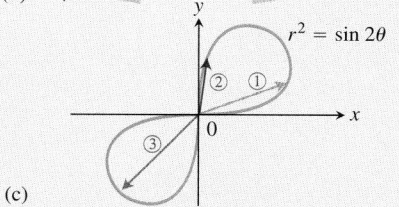

10.52 (a) The graph of $r^2 = \sin 2\theta$ in the Cartesian $r^2\theta$-plane includes negative values of the dependent variable r^2 as well as positive values.
(b) When we graph r vs. θ in the Cartesian $r\theta$-plane, we ignore the points where r is imaginary but plot + and − parts from the points where r^2 is positive.
(c) In the polar $r\theta$-plane, the radii from the previous sketch cover the final graph twice.

tive, for example, $(-2, -(\pi/2))$. If we try these in the equation $r = 2\cos 2\theta$, we find

$$-2 = 2\cos 2\left(-\frac{\pi}{2}\right) = 2(-1) = -2,$$

and the equation is satisfied. The point $(2, \pi/2)$ does lie on the curve. ■

EXAMPLE 6 Find the points of intersection of the curves

$$r^2 = 4\cos\theta \qquad \text{and} \qquad r = 1 - \cos\theta.$$

Solution In Cartesian coordinates, we can always find the points where two curves cross by solving their equations simultaneously. In polar coordinates, the story is different. Simultaneous solution may reveal some intersection points without revealing others. In this example, simultaneous solution reveals only two of the four intersection points. The others are found by graphing. (Also, see Exercise 39.)

If we substitute $\cos\theta = r^2/4$ in the equation $r = 1 - \cos\theta$, we get

$$r = 1 - \cos\theta = 1 - \frac{r^2}{4}$$

$$4r = 4 - r^2$$

$$r^2 + 4r - 4 = 0$$

$$r = -2 \pm 2\sqrt{2}. \qquad \text{Quadratic Formula}$$

The value $r = -2 - 2\sqrt{2}$ has too large an absolute value to belong to either curve. The values of θ corresponding to $r = -2 + 2\sqrt{2}$ are

$$\begin{aligned}
\theta &= \cos^{-1}(1 - r) && \text{From } r = 1 - \cos\theta \\
&= \cos^{-1}\left(1 - \left(2\sqrt{2} - 2\right)\right) && \text{Set } r = 2\sqrt{2} - 2. \\
&= \cos^{-1}\left(3 - 2\sqrt{2}\right) \\
&= \pm 80°. && \text{Rounded to the nearest degree}
\end{aligned}$$

We have thus identified two intersection points: $(r, \theta) = \left(2\sqrt{2} - 2, \pm 80°\right)$.

If we graph the equations $r^2 = 4\cos\theta$ and $r = 1 - \cos\theta$ together (Fig. 10.53), as we can now do by combining the graphs in Figs. 10.49 and 10.50, we see that the curves also intersect at the point $(2, \pi)$ and the origin. Why weren't the r-values of these points revealed by the simultaneous solution? The answer is that the points $(0, 0)$ and $(2, \pi)$ are not on the curves "simultaneously." They are not reached at the same value of θ. On the curve $r = 1 - \cos\theta$, the point $(2, \pi)$ is reached when $\theta = \pi$. On the curve $r^2 = 4\cos\theta$, it is reached when $\theta = 0$, where it is identified not by the coordinates $(2, \pi)$, which do not satisfy the equation, but by the coordinates $(-2, 0)$, which do. Similarly, the cardioid reaches the origin when $\theta = 0$, but the curve $r^2 = 4\cos\theta$ reaches the origin when $\theta = \pi/2$.

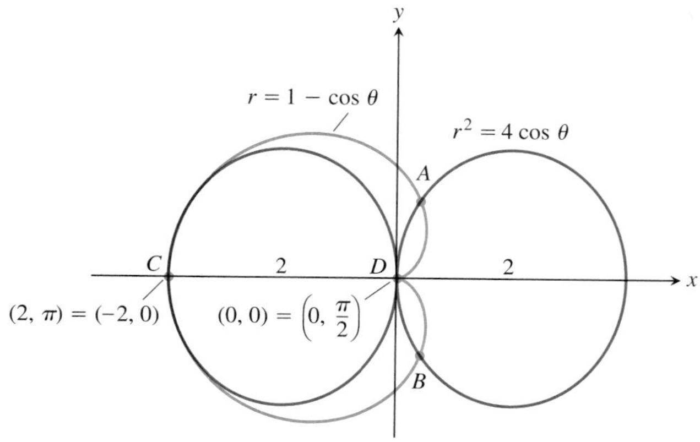

10.53 The four points of intersection of the curves $r = 1 - \cos\theta$ and $r^2 = 4\cos\theta$ (Example 6). Only A and B were found by simultaneous solution. The other two were disclosed by graphing.

Exercises 10.6

Identify the symmetries of the curves in Exercises 1–12. Then sketch the curves.

1. $r = 1 + \cos\theta$
2. $r = 2 - 2\cos\theta$
3. $r = 1 - \sin\theta$
4. $r = 1 + \sin\theta$
5. $r = 2 + \sin\theta$
6. $r = 1 + 2\sin\theta$
7. $r = \sin(\theta/2)$
8. $r = \cos(\theta/2)$
9. $r^2 = \cos\theta$
10. $r^2 = \sin\theta$
11. $r^2 = -\sin\theta$
12. $r^2 = -\cos\theta$

Sketch the curves in Exercises 13 and 14.

13. $r = \theta$
14. $r = -\theta$

Use Eq. (2) to find the slopes of the curves in Exercises 15–18 at the given points. Sketch the curves along with their tangents at these points.

15. *Cardioid.* $r = -1 + \cos\theta;\quad \theta = \pm\pi/2$
16. *Cardioid.* $r = -1 + \sin\theta;\quad \theta = 0, \pi$
17. *Four-Leaved Rose.* $r = \sin 2\theta;\ \theta = \pm\pi/4,\ \pm 3\pi/4$
18. *Four-Leaved Rose.* $r = \cos 2\theta;\ \theta = 0,\ \pm\pi/2,\ \pi$

Graph the lemniscates in Exercises 19–22. What symmetries do these curves have?

19. $r^2 = 4\cos 2\theta$
20. $r^2 = 4\sin 2\theta$
21. $r^2 = -\sin 2\theta$
22. $r^2 = -\cos 2\theta$

Graph the limaçons in Exercises 23–26. Limaçon ("*lee*-ma-sahn") is Old French for "snail." You will understand the name when you graph the limaçons in Exercise 23. Equations for limaçons have the form $r = a \pm b\cos\theta$ or $r = a \pm b\sin\theta$. There are four basic shapes.

23. *Limaçons with an Inner Loop*
    a) $r = \frac{1}{2} + \cos\theta$
    b) $r = \frac{1}{2} + \sin\theta$
24. *Cardioids*
    a) $r = 1 - \cos\theta$
    b) $r = -1 + \sin\theta$
25. *Dimpled Limaçons*
    a) $r = \frac{3}{2} + \cos\theta$
    b) $r = \frac{3}{2} - \sin\theta$
26. *Oval Limaçons*
    a) $r = 2 + \cos\theta$
    b) $r = -2 + \sin\theta$
27. Sketch the region defined by the inequality $0 \le r \le 2 - 2\cos\theta$.
28. Sketch the region defined by the inequality $0 \le r^2 \le \cos\theta$.
29. Show that the point $(2, 3\pi/4)$ lies on the curve $r = 2\sin 2\theta$.
30. Show that $(1/2, 3\pi/2)$ lies on the curve $r = -\sin(\theta/3)$.

Find the points of intersection of the pairs of curves in Exercises 31–38.

31. $r = 1 + \cos\theta,\quad r = 1 - \cos\theta$
32. $r = 1 + \sin\theta,\quad r = 1 - \sin\theta$
33. $r = 2\sin\theta,\quad r = 2\sin 2\theta$
34. $r = \cos\theta,\quad r = 1 - \cos\theta$
35. $r = \sqrt{2},\quad r^2 = 4\sin\theta$
36. $r^2 = \sqrt{2}\sin\theta,\quad r^2 = \sqrt{2}\cos\theta$
37. $r = 1,\quad r^2 = 2\sin 2\theta$
38. $r^2 = \sqrt{2}\cos 2\theta,\quad r^2 = \sqrt{2}\sin 2\theta$
39. *Continuation of Example 6.* The simultaneous solution of the equations

$$r^2 = 4\cos\theta \tag{4}$$

$$r = 1 - \cos\theta \tag{5}$$

in the text did not reveal the points $(0, 0)$ and $(2, \pi)$ in which their graphs intersected.

   a) We could have found the point $(2, \pi)$, however, by replacing the (r, θ) in Eq. (4) by the equivalent $(-r, \theta + \pi)$ to obtain

$$\begin{aligned} r^2 &= 4\cos\theta \\ (-r)^2 &= 4\cos(\theta + \pi) \\ r^2 &= -4\cos\theta. \end{aligned} \tag{6}$$

   Solve Eqs. (5) and (6) simultaneously to show that $(2, \pi)$ is a common solution. (This will still not reveal that the graphs intersect at $(0, 0)$.)

   b) The origin is still a special case. (It often is.) Here is one way to handle it: Set $r = 0$ in Eqs. (4) and (5) and solve each equation for a corresponding value of θ. Since $(0, \theta)$ is the origin for *any* θ, this will show that both curves pass through the origin even if they do so for different θ-values.

40. If a curve has any two of the symmetries listed at the beginning of the section, can anything be said about its having or not having the third symmetry? Give reasons for your answer.

Find the points of intersection of the pairs of curves in Exercises 41–44.

41. $r^2 = \sin 2\theta,\quad r^2 = \cos 2\theta$
42. $r = 1 + \cos\frac{\theta}{2},\quad r = 1 - \sin\frac{\theta}{2}$
43. $r = 1,\quad r = 2\sin 2\theta$
44. $r = 1,\quad r^2 = 2\sin 2\theta$
45. *A Rose Within a Rose.* Graph the equation $r = 1 - 2\sin 3\theta$.
46. *The Nephroid of Freeth.* Graph the nephroid of Freeth:

$$r = 1 + 2\sin\frac{\theta}{2}.$$

47. *Roses.* Graph the roses $r = \cos m\theta$ for $m = 1/3, 2, 3$, and 7.
48. *Spirals.* Polar coordinates are just the thing for defining spirals. Graph the following spirals:
    a) *A logarithmic spiral:* $r = e^{\theta/10}$
    b) *A hyperbolic spiral:* $r = 8/\theta$
    c) *Equilateral hyperbola:* $r = \pm 10/\sqrt{\theta}$ (Try using different colors for the two branches.)

Writing for Your Own Knowledge

Answer the following questions in writing. Some answers will take only a sentence or two; others may require several paragraphs. Some explanations may also call for graphs or sketches.

1. What tests are available for determining symmetry in graphs of polar equations?
2. How can you find the slope of a curve $r = f(\theta)$ (when f is a differentiable function of θ)?
3. How does the formula for the slope of the curve $r = f(\theta)$ simplify when you calculate slopes at the origin?
4. How can Cartesian graphs sometimes help you in drawing polar graphs?
5. What is involved in finding the points in which the graphs of two polar equations intersect?

EXPLORER PROGRAM

PowerGrapher	Graphs equations of the form $r = f(\theta)$ singly or together in a common display.

10.7 *Polar Equations for Conic Sections*

Polar coordinates are important in astronomy and astronautical engineering because the ellipses, parabolas, and hyperbolas along which satellites, moons, planets, and comets move can all be described with one basic equation. We develop that equation here.

Lines

Suppose the perpendicular from the origin to line L meets L at the point $P_0(r_0, \theta_0)$, with $r_0 \geq 0$ (Fig. 10.54). Then, if $P(r, \theta)$ is any other point on L, the points P, P_0, and O are the vertices of a right triangle, from which we can read the relation

$$\frac{r_0}{r} = \cos(\theta - \theta_0) \tag{1}$$

or

$$r\cos(\theta - \theta_0) = r_0. \tag{2}$$

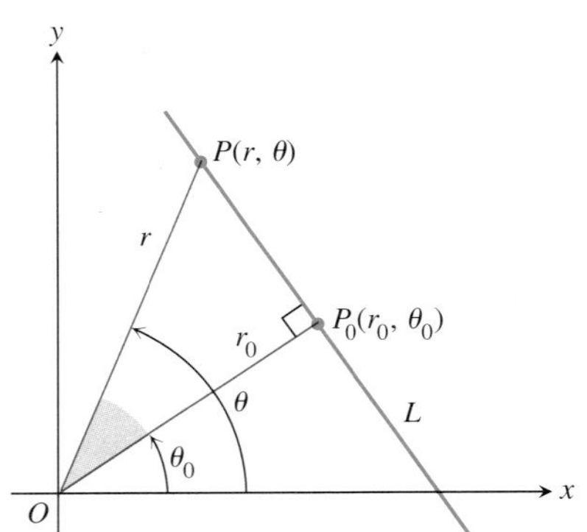

10.54 We can obtain a polar equation for line L by reading the relation $r_0/r = \cos(\theta - \theta_0)$ from triangle OP_0P.

The Standard Polar Equation for Lines

If the point $P_0(r_0, \theta_0)$ is the foot of the perpendicular from the origin to the line L, and $r_0 \geq 0$, then an equation for L is

$$r\cos(\theta - \theta_0) = r_0. \tag{3}$$

EXAMPLE 1 The standard polar equation for the line shown here is

$$r\cos\left(\theta - \frac{\pi}{3}\right) = 2.$$

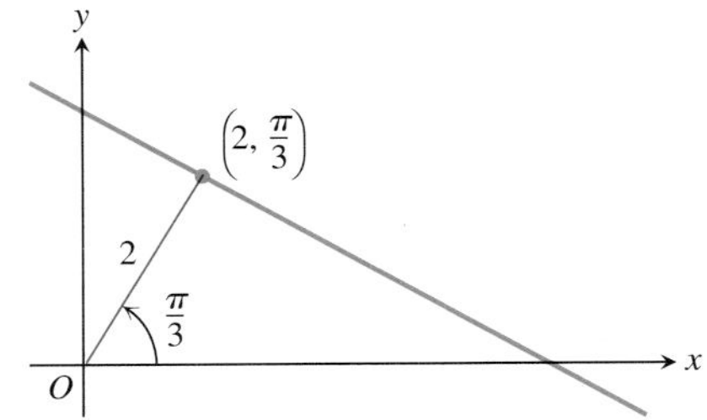

The Law of Cosines

$a^2 = b^2 + c^2 - 2bc \cos A$

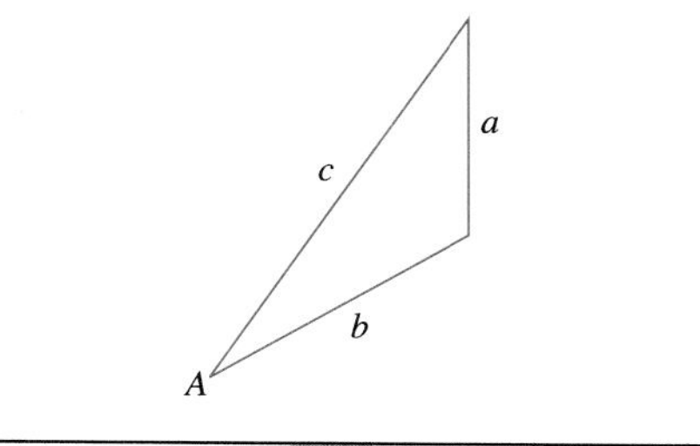

EXAMPLE 2 Use the identity $\cos(A - B) = \cos A \cos B + \sin A \sin B$ to find a Cartesian equation for the line in Example 1.

Solution

$$r \cos\left(\theta - \frac{\pi}{3}\right) = 2$$

$$r\left(\cos\theta \cos\frac{\pi}{3} + \sin\theta \sin\frac{\pi}{3}\right) = 2$$

$$\frac{1}{2} r \cos\theta + \frac{\sqrt{3}}{2} r \sin\theta = 2$$

$$\frac{1}{2} x + \frac{\sqrt{3}}{2} y = 2$$

$$x + \sqrt{3}\, y = 4$$

Circles

To find a polar equation for the circle of radius a centered at $P_0(r_0, \theta_0)$, we let $P(r, \theta)$ be a point on the circle and apply the Law of Cosines to triangle OP_0P (Fig. 10.55). This gives

$$a^2 = r_0^2 + r^2 - 2r_0 r \cos(\theta - \theta_0). \tag{4}$$

If the circle passes through the origin, then $r_0 = a$ and Eq. (4) simplifies to

$$a^2 = a^2 + r^2 - 2ar \cos(\theta - \theta_0) \qquad \text{Eq. (4) with } r_0 = a$$

$$r^2 = 2ar \cos(\theta - \theta_0)$$

$$r = 2a \cos(\theta - \theta_0). \tag{5}$$

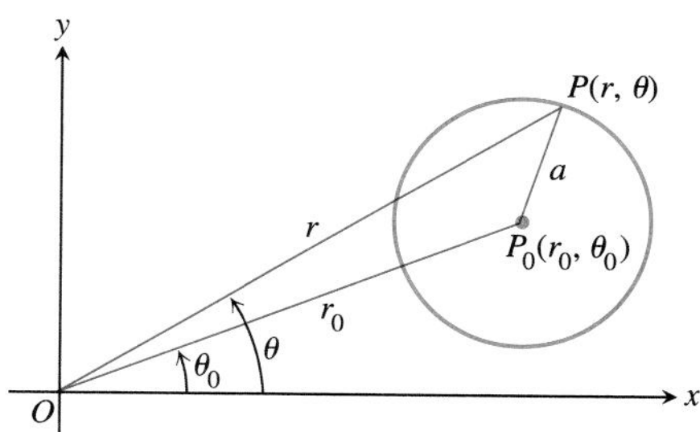

10.55 We can get a polar equation for this circle by applying the Law of Cosines to triangle OP_0P.

If the circle's center lies on the positive x-axis, $\theta_0 = 0$ and Eq. (5) becomes

$$r = 2a \cos\theta. \tag{6}$$

If the center lies on the positive y-axis, $\theta = \pi/2$, $\cos(\theta - \pi/2) = \sin\theta$, and Eq. (5) becomes

$$r = 2a \sin\theta. \tag{7}$$

Equations for circles through the origin centered on the negative x- and y-axes can be obtained from Eqs. (6) and (7) by replacing r with $-r$.

Polar Equations for Circles Through the Origin Centered on the x- and y-axes, Radius a

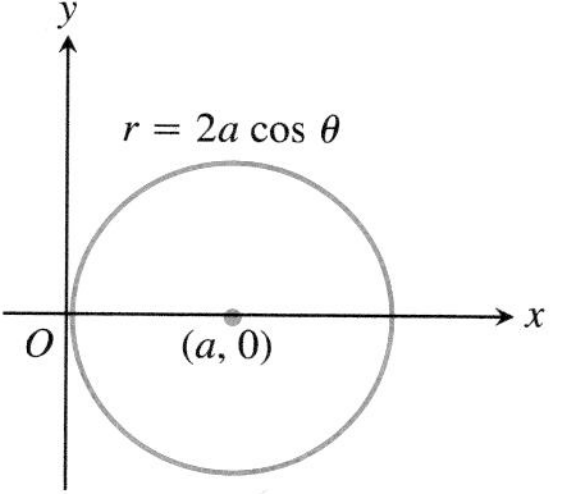

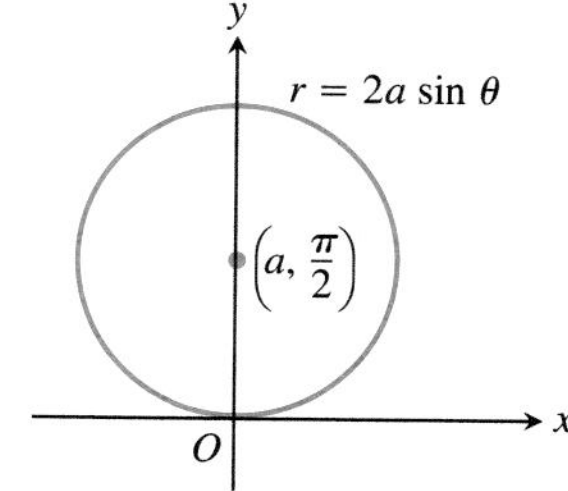

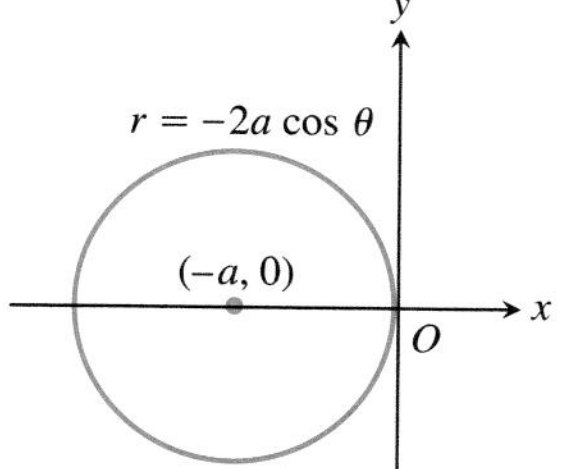

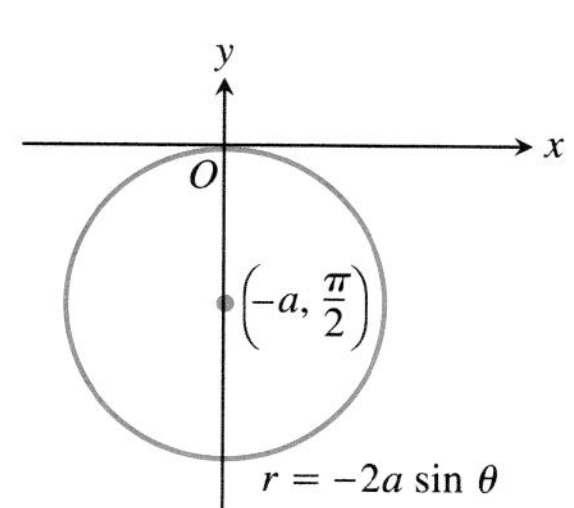

EXAMPLE 3 *Circles Through the Origin*

Radius	Center (polar coordinates)	Equation
3	$(3, 0)$	$r = 6\cos\theta$
2	$(2, \pi/2)$	$r = 4\sin\theta$
1/2	$(-1/2, 0)$	$r = -\cos\theta$
1	$(-1, \pi/2)$	$r = -2\sin\theta$

Ellipses, Parabolas, and Hyperbolas Unified

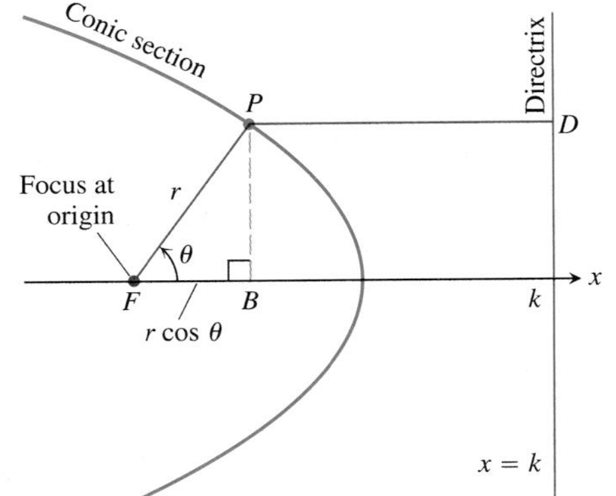

10.56 If a conic section is put in this position, then $PF = r$ and $PD = k - r\cos\theta$.

To find polar equations for ellipses, parabolas, and hyperbolas, we place one focus at the origin and the corresponding directrix to the right of the origin along the vertical line $x = k$ (Fig. 10.56). This makes

$$PF = r \tag{8}$$

and

$$PD = k - FB = k - r\cos\theta. \tag{9}$$

The conic's focus–directrix equation $PF = e \cdot PD$ then becomes

$$r = e(k - r\cos\theta), \tag{10}$$

which can be solved for r to obtain

$$r = \frac{ke}{1 + e\cos\theta}. \tag{11}$$

This equation represents an ellipse if $0 < e < 1$, a parabola if $e = 1$, and a hyperbola if $e > 1$. And there we have it—ellipses, parabolas, and hyperbolas all with the same basic equation.

EXAMPLE 4 *Typical Conics from Eq.* (11)

$e = \frac{1}{2}$: ellipse $\quad r = \frac{k}{2 + \cos\theta}$

$e = 1$: parabola $\quad r = \frac{k}{1 + \cos\theta}$

$e = 2$: hyperbola $\quad r = \frac{2k}{1 + 2\cos\theta}$

You may see variations of Eq. (11) from time to time, depending on the location of the directrix. If the directrix is the line $x = -k$ to the left of the origin (the origin is still a focus), we replace Eq. (11) by

$$r = \frac{ke}{1 - e\cos\theta}. \tag{12}$$

The denominator now has a $(-)$ instead of a $(+)$. If the directrix is either of the lines $y = k$ or $y = -k$, the equations we get have sines in them instead of cosines, as shown in Table 10.4.

TABLE 10.4
Equations for conic sections ($e > 0$)

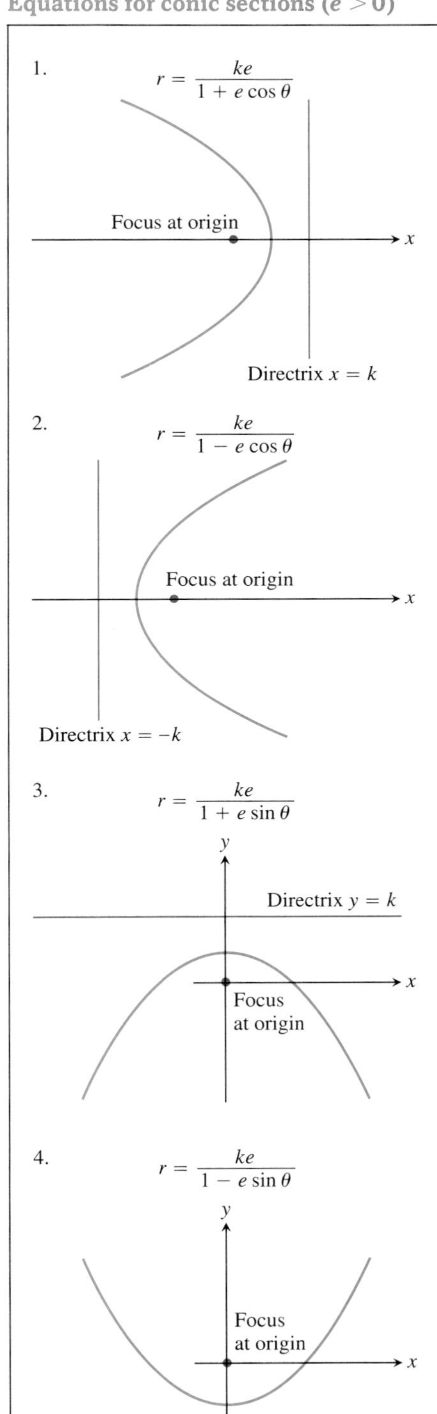

EXAMPLE 5 Find an equation for the hyperbola with eccentricity 3/2 and directrix $x = 2$.

Solution We use Eq. (1) in Table 10.4 with $k = 2$ and $e = 3/2$ to get

$$r = \frac{2(3/2)}{1 + (3/2)\cos\theta} \quad \text{or} \quad r = \frac{6}{2 + 3\cos\theta}.$$

EXAMPLE 6 Find the directrix of the parabola

$$r = \frac{25}{10 + 10\cos\theta}.$$

Solution We divide the numerator and denominator by 10 to put the equation in standard form:

$$r = \frac{5/2}{1 + \cos\theta}.$$

This is the equation

$$r = \frac{ke}{1 + e\cos\theta}$$

with $k = 5/2$ and $e = 1$. The equation of the directrix is $x = 5/2$.

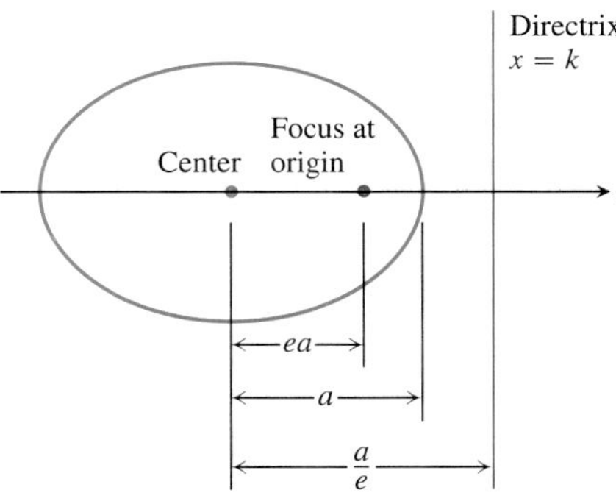

10.57 In an ellipse with semimajor axis a, the focus–directrix distance is $k = (a/e) - ea$, so $ke = a(1 - e^2)$.

From the ellipse diagram in Fig. 10.57, we see that k is related to the eccentricity e and the semimajor axis a by the equation

$$k = \frac{a}{e} - ea. \tag{13}$$

From this, we find that $ke = a(1 - e^2)$. Replacing ke in Eq. (11) by $a(1 - e^2)$ gives the standard polar equation for an ellipse.

Ellipse with Eccentricity *e* and Semimajor Axis *a*

$$r = \frac{a(1 - e^2)}{1 + e\cos\theta} \tag{14}$$

Notice that when $e = 0$, Eq. (14) becomes $r = a$, which represents a circle.

Equation (14) is the starting point for calculating planetary orbits.

EXAMPLE 7 Find a polar equation for an ellipse with semimajor axis 39.44 AU (astronomical units) and eccentricity 0.25. This is the approximate size of Pluto's orbit around the sun.

Solution We use Eq. (14) with $a = 39.44$ and $e = 0.25$ to find

$$r = \frac{39.44(1 - (0.25)^2)}{1 + 0.25\cos\theta} = \frac{147.9}{4 + \cos\theta}.$$

At its point of closest approach (perihelion), Pluto is

$$r = \frac{147.9}{4 + 1} = 29.58 \text{ AU}$$

from the sun. At its most distant point (aphelion), Pluto is

$$r = \frac{147.9}{4 - 1} = 49.3 \text{ AU}$$

from the sun (Fig. 10.58).

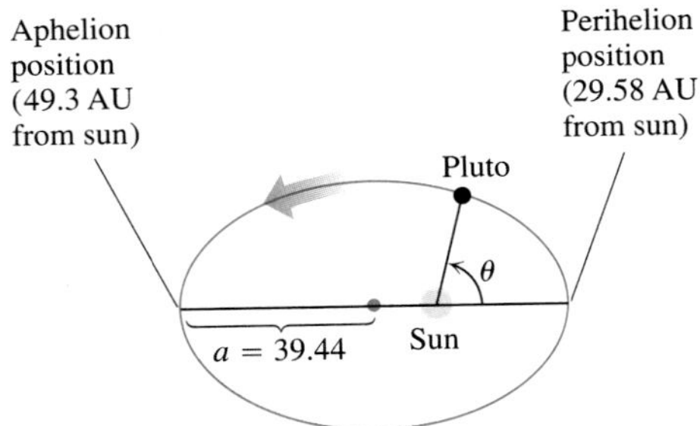

10.58 The orbit of Pluto (Example 7).

EXAMPLE 8 Find the distance from one focus of the ellipse in Example 7 to the associated directrix.

Solution We use Eq. (13) with $a = 39.44$ and $e = 0.25$ to find

$$k = 39.44\left(\frac{1}{0.25} - 0.25\right) = 147.9 \text{ AU}.$$

Exercises 10.7

Find polar and Cartesian equations for the lines in Exercises 1–4.

1.

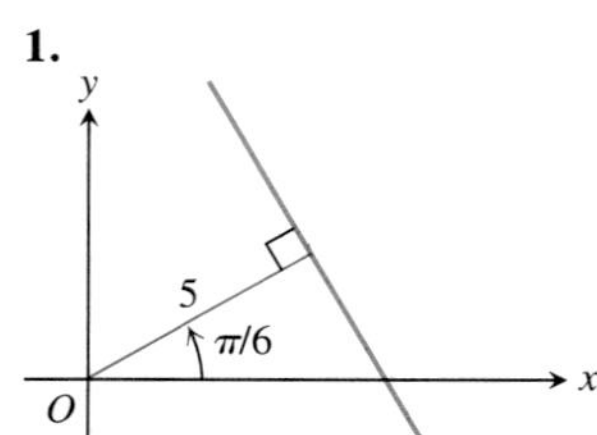

2.

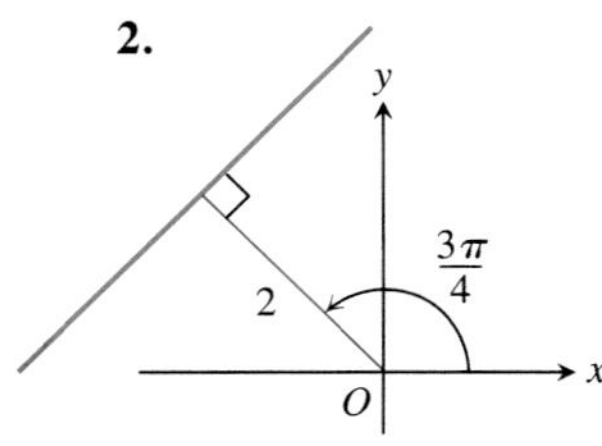

3. **4.**

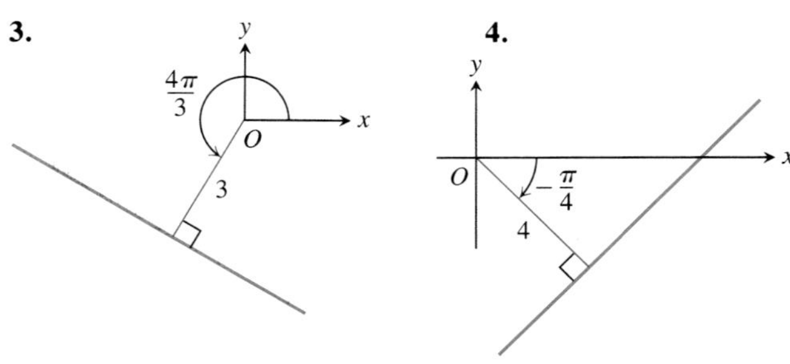

Sketch the lines in Exercises 5–8 and find Cartesian equations for them.

5. $r\cos\left(\theta - \frac{\pi}{4}\right) = \sqrt{2}$

6. $r\cos\left(\theta + \frac{3\pi}{4}\right) = 1$

7. $r\cos\left(\theta - \frac{2\pi}{3}\right) = 3$

8. $r\cos\left(\theta + \frac{\pi}{3}\right) = 2$

Find polar equations for the circles in Exercises 9–12.

9.

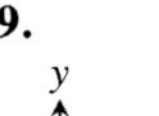

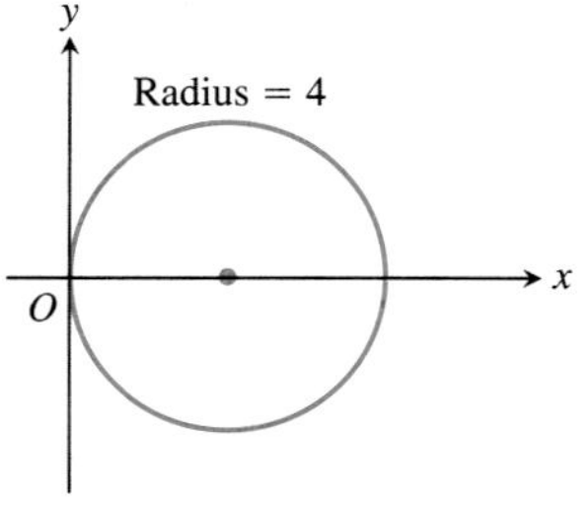

10.

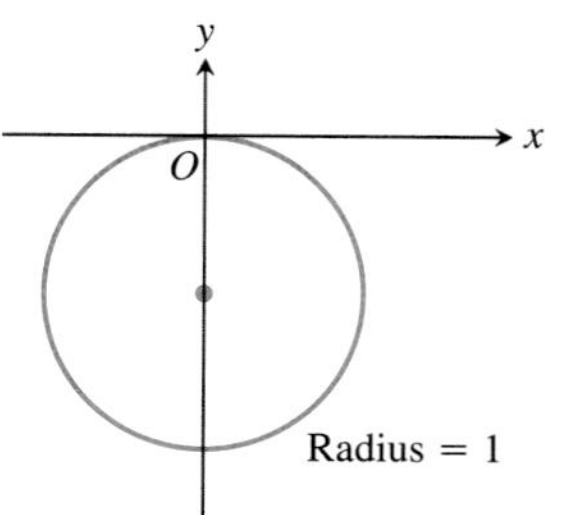

11.

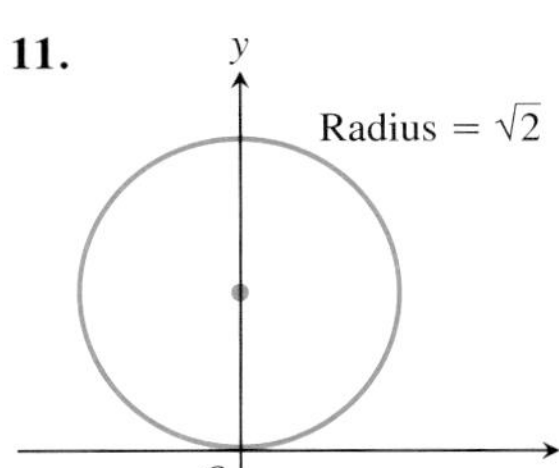

12.

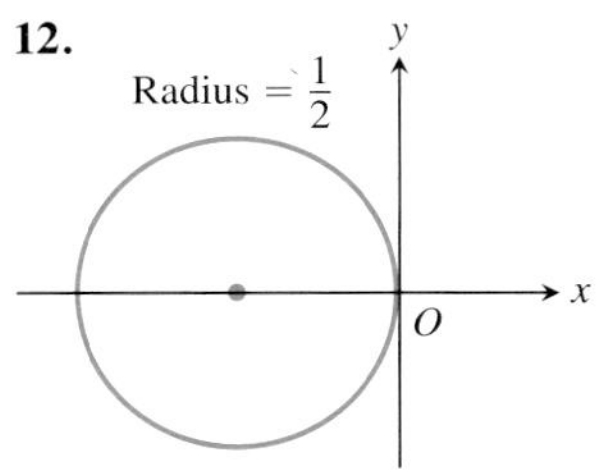

Sketch the circles in Exercises 13–16. Give polar coordinates for their centers and identify their radii.

13. $r = 4 \cos \theta$

14. $r = 6 \sin \theta$

15. $r = -2 \cos \theta$

16. $r = -8 \sin \theta$

Find polar equations for the circles in Exercises 17–24. Sketch each circle in the coordinate plane and label it with both its Cartesian and polar equations.

17. $(x - 6)^2 + y^2 = 36$

18. $(x + 2)^2 + y^2 = 4$

19. $x^2 + (y - 5)^2 = 25$

20. $x^2 + (y + 7)^2 = 49$

21. $x^2 + 2x + y^2 = 0$

22. $x^2 - 16x + y^2 = 0$

23. $x^2 + y^2 + y = 0$

24. $x^2 + y^2 - \frac{4}{3}y = 0$

Exercises 25–32 give the eccentricities of conic sections with one focus at the origin, along with the directrix corresponding to that focus. Find a polar equation for each conic section.

25. $e = 1, \quad x = 2$

26. $e = 1, \quad y = 2$

27. $e = 2, \quad x = 4$

28. $e = 5, \quad y = -6$

29. $e = 1/2, \quad x = 1$

30. $e = 1/4, \quad x = -2$

31. $e = 1/5, \quad y = -10$

32. $e = 1/3, \quad y = 6$

Sketch the parabolas and ellipses in Exercises 33–40. Include the directrix that corresponds to the focus at the origin. Label the vertices with appropriate polar coordinates. Label the centers of the ellipses as well.

33. $r = \dfrac{1}{1 + \cos \theta}$

34. $r = \dfrac{6}{2 + \cos \theta}$

35. $r = \dfrac{25}{10 - 5 \cos \theta}$

36. $r = \dfrac{4}{2 - 2 \cos \theta}$

37. $r = \dfrac{400}{16 + 8 \sin \theta}$

38. $r = \dfrac{12}{3 + 3 \sin \theta}$

39. $r = \dfrac{8}{2 - 2 \sin \theta}$

40. $r = \dfrac{4}{2 - \sin \theta}$

Sketch the regions defined by the inequalities in Exercises 41 and 42.

41. $0 \le r \le 2 \cos \theta$

42. $-3 \cos \theta \le r \le 0$

43. *Perihelion and Aphelion.* A planet travels about its sun in an ellipse whose semimajor axis has length a.

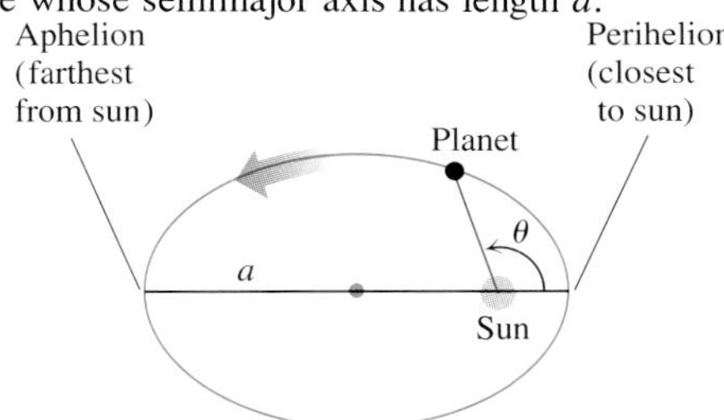

a) Show that $r = a(1 - e)$ when the planet is closest to the sun and that $r = a(1 + e)$ when the planet is farthest from the sun.

b) Use the data in the table below to find how close each planet in our solar system comes to the sun and how far away each planet gets from the sun.

44. *Planetary Orbits.* In Example 7, we found a polar equation for the orbit of Pluto. Use the data in the table below to find polar equations for the orbits of the other planets.

Planet	Semimajor Axis (astronomical units)	Eccentricity
Mercury	0.3871	0.2056
Venus	0.7233	0.0068
Earth	1.000	0.0167
Mars	1.524	0.0934
Jupiter	5.203	0.0484
Saturn	9.539	0.0543
Uranus	19.18	0.0460
Neptune	30.06	0.0082
Pluto	39.44	0.2481

45. a) Find Cartesian equations for the curves $r = 4 \sin \theta$ and $r = \sqrt{3} \sec \theta$.

b) Sketch the curves together and label their points of intersection in both Cartesian and polar coordinates.

46. Repeat Exercise 45 for $r = 8 \cos \theta$ and $r = 2 \sec \theta$.

47. Find a polar equation for the parabola with focus $(0, 0)$ and directrix the line $r \cos \theta = 4$.

48. Find a polar equation for the parabola whose focus lies at the origin and whose directrix is the line $r \cos (\theta - \pi/2) = 2$.

49. a) *The Space Engineer's Formula for Eccentricity.* The space engineer's formula for the eccentricity of an elliptical orbit is

$$e = \frac{r_{max} - r_{min}}{r_{max} + r_{min}},$$

where r is the distance from the space vehicle to the focus of the ellipse along which it travels. Why does the formula work?

b) *Drawing Ellipses with String.* You have a string with a knot in each end that can be pinned to a drawing board.

The string is 10 in. long from the center of one knot to the center of the other. How far apart should the pins be to use the method illustrated in Fig. 10.5 (Section 10.1) to draw an ellipse of eccentricity 0.2? The resulting ellipse would resemble the orbit of Mercury.

50. *Halley's Comet*

a) Write an equation for the orbit of Halley's comet in a coordinate system in which the sun lies at the origin and the other focus lies on the negative x-axis, scaled in astronomical units.

b) How close does the comet come to the sun in astronomical units? in kilometers?

c) What is the farthest the comet gets from the sun in astronomical units? in kilometers?

Graph the lines and conic sections in Exercises 51–60.

51. $r = 3 \sec(\theta - \pi/3)$

52. $r = 4 \sec(\theta + \pi/6)$

53. $r = 4 \sin \theta$

54. $r = -2 \cos \theta$

55. $r = 8/(4 + \cos \theta)$

56. $r = 8/(4 + \sin \theta)$

57. $r = 1/(1 - \sin \theta)$

58. $r = 1/(1 + \cos \theta)$

59. $r = 1/(1 + 2 \sin \theta)$

60. $r = 1/(1 + 2 \cos \theta)$

Writing for Your Own Knowledge

Answer the following questions in writing. Some answers will take only a sentence or two; others may require several paragraphs. Some explanations may also call for graphs or sketches.

Explain the standard polar equations for the following conic sections.

1. Lines
2. Circles through the origin and centered on the coordinate axes
3. Ellipses, parabolas, and hyperbolas with one focus at the origin

EXPLORER PROGRAM

PowerGrapher — Graphs all conic sections in polar coordinates.

10.8 *Integration in Polar Coordinates*

This section shows how to calculate areas of plane regions, lengths of curves, and areas of surfaces of revolution in polar coordinates.

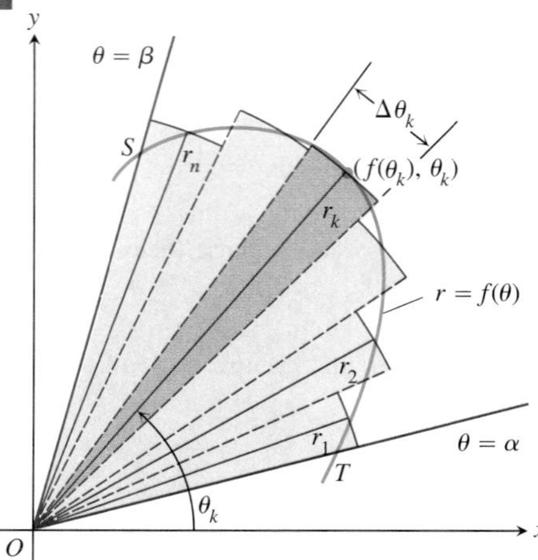

10.59 To derive a formula for the area of region OTS, we approximate the region with fan-shaped circular sectors.

Area in the Plane

The region OTS in Fig. 10.59 is bounded by the rays $\theta = \alpha$ and $\theta = \beta$ and the curve $r = f(\theta)$. We approximate the region with n nonoverlapping fan-shaped circular sectors based on a partition P of angle TOS. The typical sector has radius $r_k = f(\theta_k)$ and central angle of radian measure $\Delta\theta_k$. Its area is

$$A_k = \frac{1}{2} r_k^2 \,\Delta\theta_k = \frac{1}{2}\left(f(\theta_k)\right)^2 \Delta\theta_k. \tag{1}$$

The area of region OTS is approximately

$$\sum_{k=1}^{n} A_k = \sum_{k=1}^{n} \frac{1}{2}\left(f(\theta_k)\right)^2 \Delta\theta_k. \tag{2}$$

If f is continuous, we expect the approximations to improve as $\|P\| \to 0$, and we are led to the following formula for the region's area:

$$\begin{aligned} A &= \lim_{\|P\|\to 0} \sum_{k=1}^{n} \frac{1}{2}\left(f(\theta_k)\right)^2 \Delta\theta_k \\ &= \int_{\alpha}^{\beta} \frac{1}{2}\left(f(\theta)\right)^2 d\theta. \end{aligned} \tag{3}$$

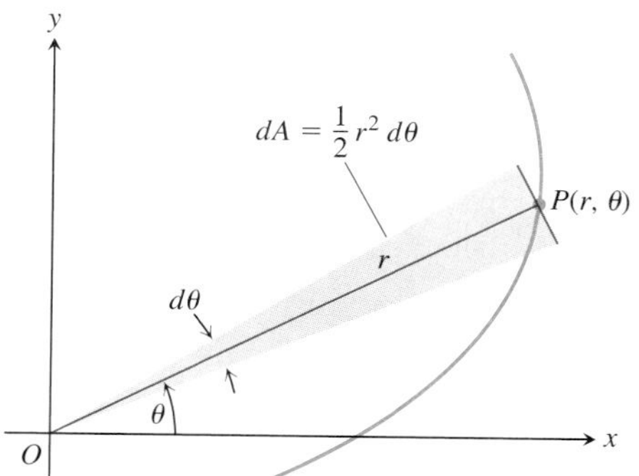

10.60 The area differential dA.

Area of the Fan-shaped Region Between the Origin and the Curve $r = f(\theta)$, $\alpha \le \theta \le \beta$

$$A = \int_{\alpha}^{\beta} \frac{1}{2} r^2\,d\theta. \tag{4}$$

This is the integral of the **area differential** (Fig. 10.60)

$$dA = \frac{1}{2} r^2\,d\theta. \tag{5}$$

EXAMPLE 1 Find the area of the region enclosed by the cardioid $r = 2(1 + \cos\theta)$.

Solution We graph the cardioid (Fig. 10.61) and determine that the radius OP sweeps out the region exactly once as θ runs from 0 to 2π. The area is therefore

$$\begin{aligned}
\int_{\theta=0}^{\theta=2\pi} \frac{1}{2} r^2\,d\theta &= \int_0^{2\pi} \frac{1}{2}\cdot 4(1+\cos\theta)^2\,d\theta \\
&= \int_0^{2\pi} 2(1 + 2\cos\theta + \cos^2\theta)\,d\theta \\
&= \int_0^{2\pi} \left(2 + 4\cos\theta + 2\,\frac{1+\cos 2\theta}{2}\right) d\theta \\
&= \int_0^{2\pi} (3 + 4\cos\theta + \cos 2\theta)\,d\theta \\
&= \left[3\theta + 4\sin\theta + \frac{\sin 2\theta}{2}\right]_0^{2\pi} \\
&= 6\pi - 0 = 6\pi.
\end{aligned}$$

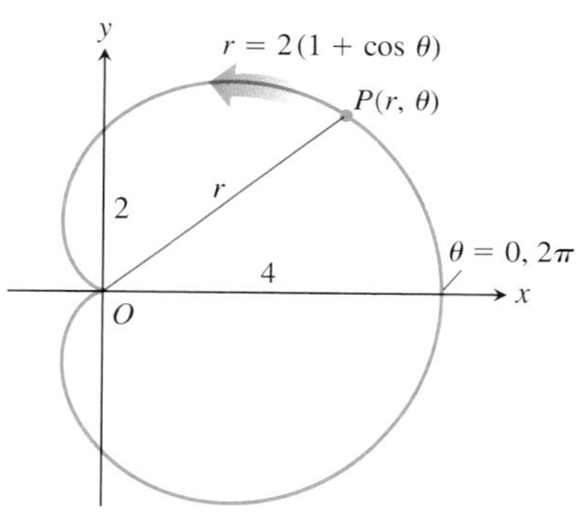

10.61 The cardioid in Example 1.

EXAMPLE 2 Find the area inside the smaller loop of the limaçon

$$r = 2\cos\theta + 1.$$

Solution After sketching the curve (Fig. 10.62), we see that the smaller loop is traced out by the point (r, θ) as θ increases from $\theta = 2\pi/3$ to $\theta = 4\pi/3$. Since the curve is symmetric about the x-axis (the equation is unaltered when we replace θ by $-\theta$), we may calculate the area of the shaded half of the inner loop by integrating from $\theta = 2\pi/3$ to $\theta = \pi$. The area we seek will be twice the resulting integral:

$$A = 2\int_{2\pi/3}^{\pi} \frac{1}{2} r^2\,d\theta = \int_{2\pi/3}^{\pi} r^2\,d\theta.$$

Since

$$\begin{aligned}
r^2 = (2\cos\theta + 1)^2 &= 4\cos^2\theta + 4\cos\theta + 1 \\
&= 4\cdot\frac{1+\cos 2\theta}{2} + 4\cos\theta + 1 \\
&= 2 + 2\cos 2\theta + 4\cos\theta + 1 \\
&= 3 + 2\cos 2\theta + 4\cos\theta,
\end{aligned}$$

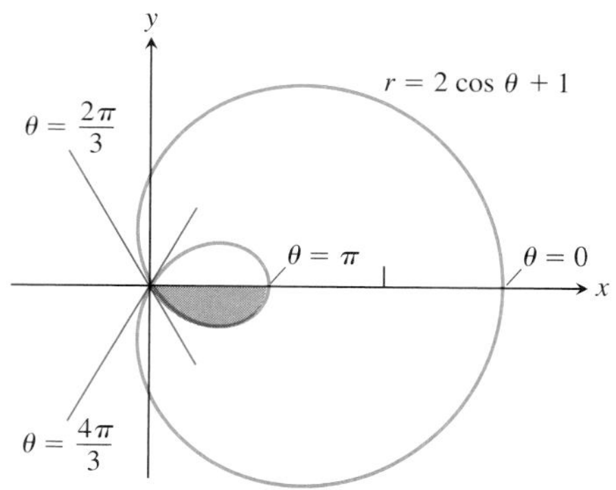

10.62 The limaçon in Example 2.

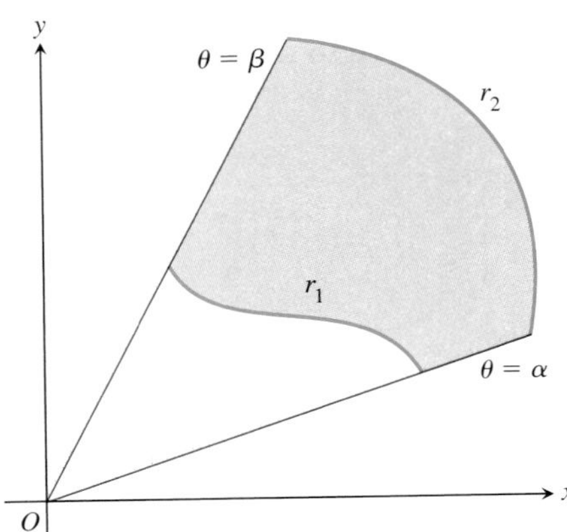

10.63 The area of the shaded region is calculated by subtracting the area of the region between r_1 and the origin from the area of the region between r_2 and the origin.

we have

$$A = \int_{2\pi/3}^{\pi} (3 + 2\cos 2\theta + 4\cos\theta)\,d\theta$$
$$= \Big[3\theta + \sin 2\theta + 4\sin\theta\Big]_{2\pi/3}^{\pi}$$
$$= (3\pi) - \left(2\pi - \frac{\sqrt{3}}{2} + 4\cdot\frac{\sqrt{3}}{2}\right) = \pi - \frac{3\sqrt{3}}{2}.$$

To find the area of a region like the one in Fig. 10.63, which lies between two polar curves from $\theta = \alpha$ to $\theta = \beta$, we subtract the integral of $(1/2)r_1^2\,d\theta$ from the integral of $(1/2)r_2^2\,d\theta$. This leads to the following formula.

Area of the Region $0 \le r_1(\theta) \le r \le r_2(\theta)$, $\alpha \le \theta \le \beta$

$$A = \int_{\alpha}^{\beta} \frac{1}{2} r_2^2\,d\theta - \int_{\alpha}^{\beta} \frac{1}{2} r_1^2\,d\theta = \int_{\alpha}^{\beta} \frac{1}{2}(r_2^2 - r_1^2)\,d\theta \tag{6}$$

EXAMPLE 3 Find the area of the region that lies inside the circle $r = 1$ and outside the cardioid $r = 1 - \cos\theta$.

Solution We sketch the region to determine its boundaries and find the limits of integration (Fig. 10.64). The outer curve is $r_2 = 1$, the inner curve is $r_1 = 1 - \cos\theta$, and θ runs from $-\pi/2$ to $\pi/2$. The area, from Eq. (6), is

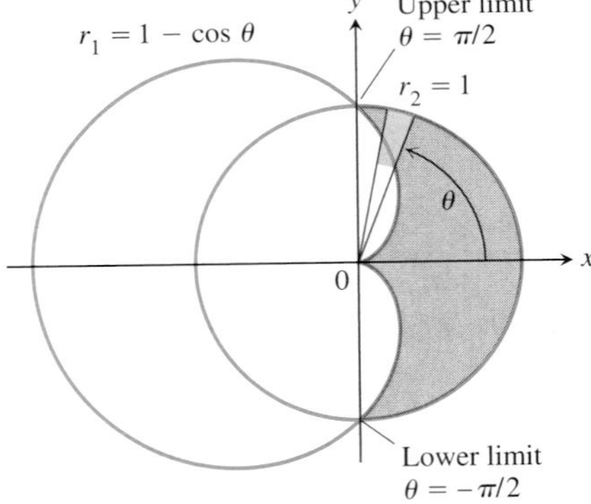

10.64 The region and limits of integration in Example 3.

$$A = \int_{-\pi/2}^{\pi/2} \frac{1}{2}(r_2^2 - r_1^2)\,d\theta$$
$$= 2\int_{0}^{\pi/2} \frac{1}{2}(r_2^2 - r_1^2)\,d\theta \qquad \text{Symmetry}$$
$$= \int_{0}^{\pi/2} (1 - (1 - 2\cos\theta + \cos^2\theta))\,d\theta$$
$$= \int_{0}^{\pi/2} (2\cos\theta - \cos^2\theta)\,d\theta = \int_{0}^{\pi/2} \left(2\cos\theta - \frac{1 + \cos 2\theta}{2}\right) d\theta$$
$$= \left[2\sin\theta - \frac{\sin 2\theta}{4} - \frac{\theta}{2}\right]_0^{\pi/2} = 2 - \frac{\pi}{4}.$$

The Length of a Curve

We can obtain a polar coordinate formula for the length of a curve $r = f(\theta)$, $\alpha \le \theta \le \beta$, by parametrizing the curve as

$$x = r\cos\theta = f(\theta)\cos\theta, \qquad y = r\sin\theta = f(\theta)\sin\theta, \qquad \alpha \le \theta \le \beta. \tag{7}$$

The parametric length formula, Eq. (4) from Section 10.4, then gives the length as

$$L = \int_{\alpha}^{\beta} \sqrt{\left(\frac{dx}{d\theta}\right)^2 + \left(\frac{dy}{d\theta}\right)^2}\,d\theta. \tag{8}$$

This equation becomes

$$L = \int_{\alpha}^{\beta} \sqrt{r^2 + \left(\frac{dr}{d\theta}\right)^2}\, d\theta \tag{9}$$

when Eqs. (7) are substituted for x and y (Exercise 35).

Length of a Curve

If $r = f(\theta)$ has a continuous first derivative for $\alpha \le \theta \le \beta$ and if the point $P(r, \theta)$ traces the curve $r = f(\theta)$ exactly once as θ runs from α to β, then the length of the curve is

$$L = \int_{\alpha}^{\beta} \sqrt{r^2 + \left(\frac{dr}{d\theta}\right)^2}\, d\theta. \tag{10}$$

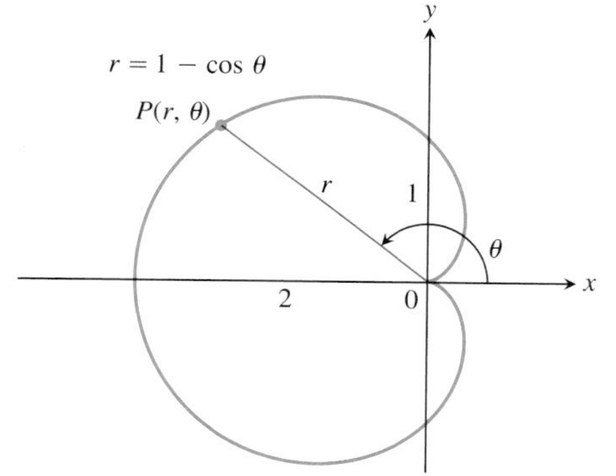

10.65 Example 4 calculates the length of this cardioid.

EXAMPLE 4 Find the length of the cardioid $r = 1 - \cos\theta$.

Solution We sketch the cardioid to determine the limits of integration (Fig. 10.65). The point $P(r, \theta)$ traces the curve once, counterclockwise as θ runs from 0 to 2π, so these are the values we take for α and β.

With

$$r = 1 - \cos\theta, \qquad \frac{dr}{d\theta} = \sin\theta,$$

we have

$$\begin{aligned} r^2 + \left(\frac{dr}{d\theta}\right)^2 &= (1 - \cos\theta)^2 + (\sin\theta)^2 \\ &= 1 - 2\cos\theta + \underbrace{\cos^2\theta + \sin^2\theta}_{1} = 2 - 2\cos\theta \end{aligned}$$

and

$$\begin{aligned} L &= \int_{\alpha}^{\beta} \sqrt{r^2 + \left(\frac{dr}{d\theta}\right)^2}\, d\theta = \int_0^{2\pi} \sqrt{2 - 2\cos\theta}\, d\theta \\ &= \int_0^{2\pi} \sqrt{4\sin^2\frac{\theta}{2}}\, d\theta \qquad 1 - \cos\theta = 2\sin^2\frac{\theta}{2} \\ &= \int_0^{2\pi} 2\left|\sin\frac{\theta}{2}\right| d\theta \\ &= \int_0^{2\pi} 2\sin\frac{\theta}{2}\, d\theta \qquad \sin\frac{\theta}{2} \ge 0 \quad \text{for} \quad 0 \le \theta \le 2\pi \\ &= \left[-4\cos\frac{\theta}{2}\right]_0^{2\pi} = 4 + 4 = 8. \end{aligned}$$

The Area of a Surface of Revolution

To derive the polar coordinate formulas for surface area, we parametrize the curve $r = f(\theta)$, $\alpha \le \theta \le \beta$, with Eqs. (7) and substitute into Eqs. (5) and (6) from Section 10.4.

Area of a Surface of Revolution

If $r = f(\theta)$ has a continuous first derivative for $\alpha \le \theta \le \beta$ and if the point $P(r, \theta)$ traces the curve $r = f(\theta)$ exactly once as θ runs from α to β, then the areas of the surfaces generated by revolving the curve about the x- and y-axes are given by the following formulas:

1. Revolution about the x-axis ($y \ge 0$):

$$S = \int_{\alpha}^{\beta} 2\pi r \sin\theta \sqrt{r^2 + \left(\frac{dr}{d\theta}\right)^2}\, d\theta \qquad (11)$$

2. Revolution about the y-axis ($x \ge 0$):

$$S = \int_{\alpha}^{\beta} 2\pi r \cos\theta \sqrt{r^2 + \left(\frac{dr}{d\theta}\right)^2}\, d\theta \qquad (12)$$

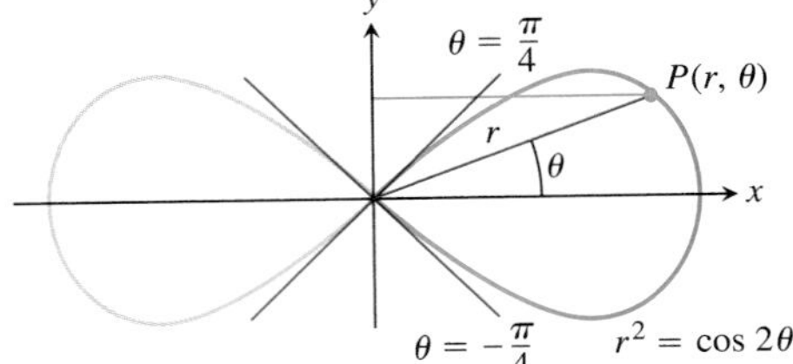

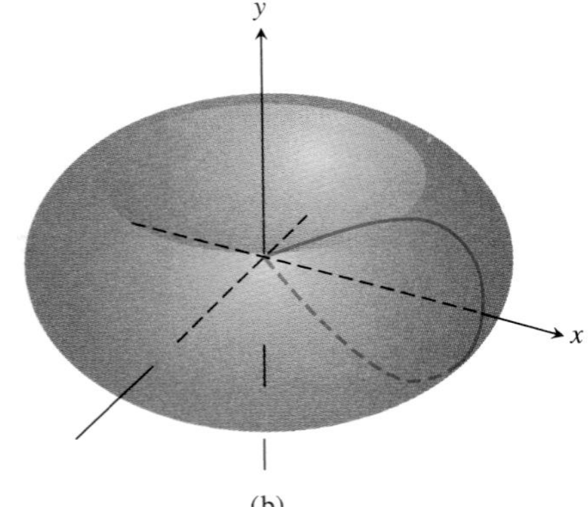

10.66 The right-hand half of a lemniscate (a) is revolved about the y-axis to generate a surface (b), whose area is calculated in Example 5.

EXAMPLE 5 Find the area of the surface generated by revolving the right-hand loop of the lemniscate $r^2 = \cos 2\theta$ about the y-axis.

Solution We sketch the loop to determine the limits of integration (Fig. 10.66). The point $P(r, \theta)$ traces the curve once, counterclockwise as θ runs from $-\pi/4$ to $\pi/4$, so these are the values we take for α and β.

We evaluate the area integrand in Eq. (11) in stages. First,

$$2\pi r \cos\theta \sqrt{r^2 + \left(\frac{dr}{d\theta}\right)^2} = 2\pi \cos\theta \sqrt{r^4 + \left(r\frac{dr}{d\theta}\right)^2}. \qquad (13)$$

Next, $r^2 = \cos 2\theta$, so

$$2r\frac{dr}{d\theta} = -2\sin 2\theta$$

$$r\frac{dr}{d\theta} = -\sin 2\theta$$

$$\left(r\frac{dr}{d\theta}\right)^2 = \sin^2 2\theta.$$

Finally, $r^4 = (r^2)^2 = \cos^2 2\theta$, so the square root on the right-hand side of Eq. (13) simplifies to

$$\sqrt{r^4 + \left(r\frac{dr}{d\theta}\right)^2} = \sqrt{\cos^2 2\theta + \sin^2 2\theta} = 1.$$

All together, we have

$$\begin{aligned} S &= \int_{\alpha}^{\beta} 2\pi r \cos\theta \sqrt{r^2 + \left(\frac{dr}{d\theta}\right)^2}\, d\theta \qquad \text{Eq. (11)} \\ &= \int_{-\pi/4}^{\pi/4} 2\pi \cos\theta \cdot (1)\, d\theta \\ &= 2\pi \Big[\sin\theta\Big]_{-\pi/4}^{\pi/4} \\ &= 2\pi\left[\frac{\sqrt{2}}{2} + \frac{\sqrt{2}}{2}\right] = 2\pi\sqrt{2}. \end{aligned}$$

Exercises 10.8

Find the areas of the shaded regions in Exercises 1–4.

1.

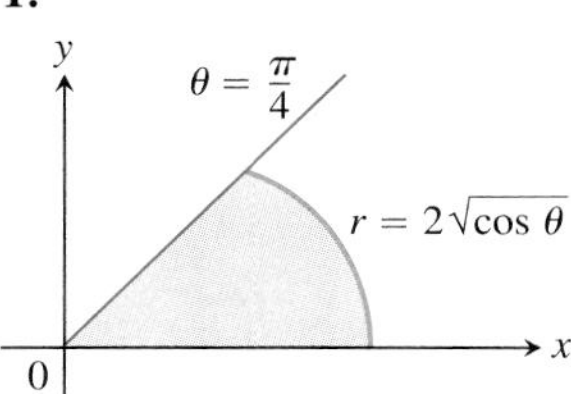

2.

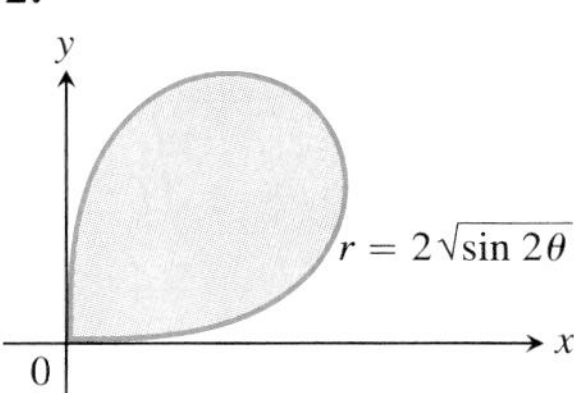

3.

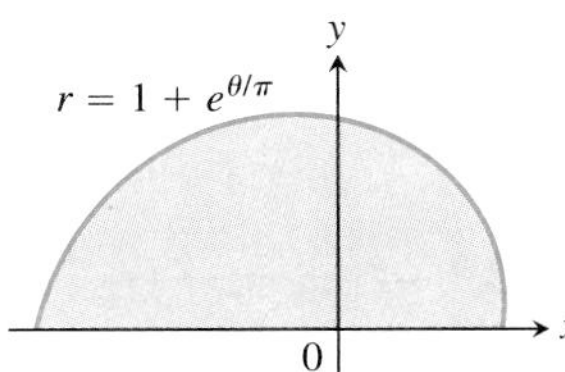

4.

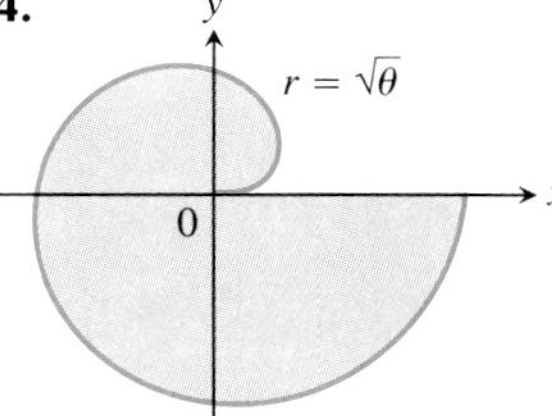

Find the areas of the regions in Exercises 5–20.

5. Inside the oval limaçon $r = 4 + 2 \cos \theta$

6. Inside the cardioid $r = a(1 + \cos \theta), \quad a > 0$

7. Inside one leaf of the four-leaved rose $r = \cos 2\theta$

8. Inside the lemniscate $r^2 = 2a^2 \cos 2\theta, \quad a > 0$

9. Inside one loop of the lemniscate $r^2 = 4 \sin 2\theta$

10. Inside the six-leaved rose $r^2 = 2 \sin 3\theta$ (Fig. 10.67)

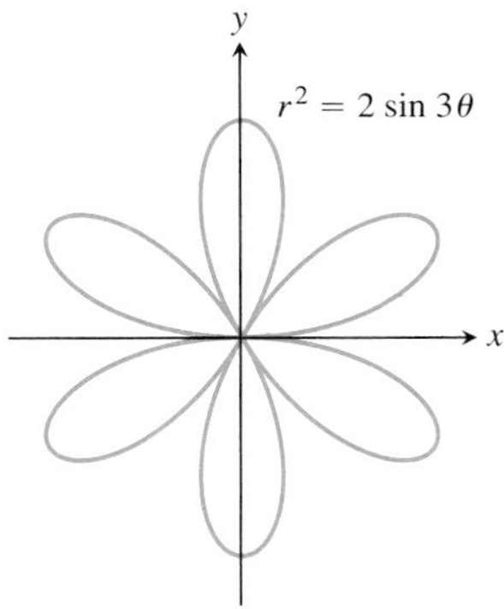

10.67 The rose in Exercise 10.

11. Shared by the circles $r = 2 \cos \theta$ and $r = 2 \sin \theta$

12. Shared by the circles $r = 1$ and $r = 2 \sin \theta$

13. Shared by the circle $r = 2$ and the cardioid $r = 2(1 - \cos \theta)$

14. Shared by the cardioids $r = 2(1 + \cos \theta)$ and $r = 2(1 - \cos \theta)$

15. Inside the lemniscate $r^2 = 6 \cos 2\theta$ and outside the circle $r = \sqrt{3}$

16. Inside the circle $r = 3a \cos \theta$ and outside the cardioid $r = a(1 + \cos \theta), a > 0$

17. Inside the circle $r = -2 \cos \theta$ and outside the circle $r = 1$

18. **a)** Inside the outer loop of the limaçon $r = 2 \cos \theta + 1$

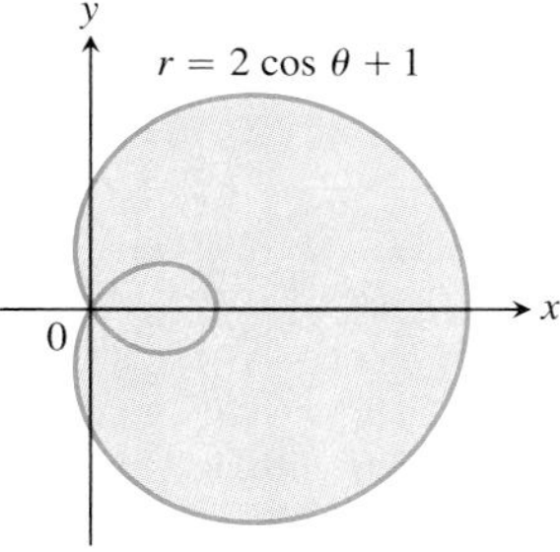

b) Inside the outer loop and outside the inner loop

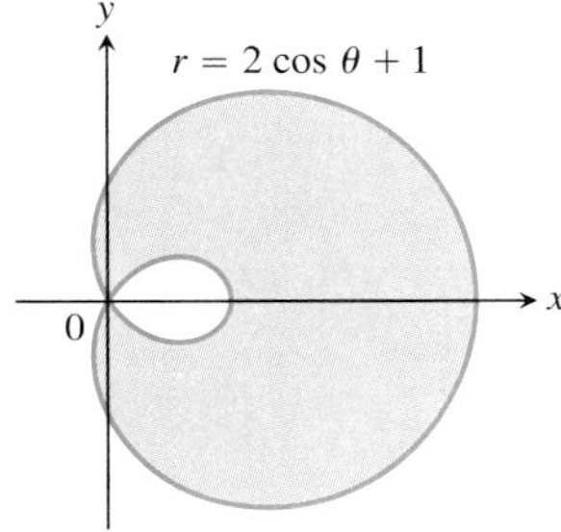

19. Inside the circle $r = 6$ above the line $r = 3 \csc \theta$

20. Inside the lemniscate $r^2 = 6 \cos 2\theta$ to the right of the line $r = (3/2)\sec \theta$.

21. **a)** Find the area of the shaded region in Fig. 10.68.

b) It looks as if the graph of $r = \tan \theta, \ -\pi/2 < \theta < \pi/2$, could be asymptotic to the lines $x = 1$ and $x = -1$. Is it? Give reasons for your answer.

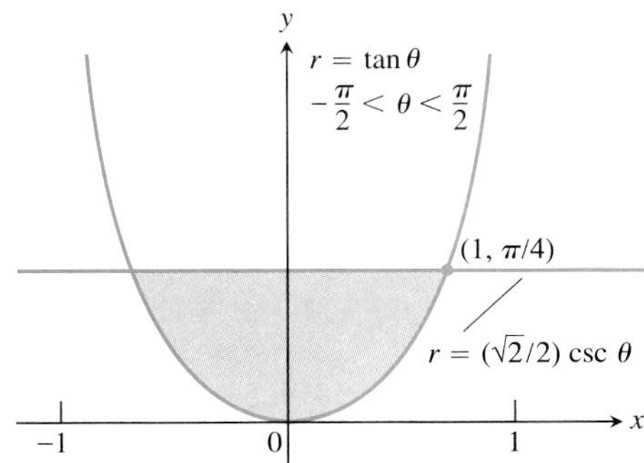

10.68 The region in Exercise 21.

22. The area of the region that lies inside the cardioid curve $r = \cos \theta + 1$ and outside the circle $r = \cos \theta$ is not

$$\frac{1}{2}\int_0^{2\pi} [(\cos \theta + 1)^2 - \cos^2 \theta]\, d\theta = \pi.$$

Why not? What *is* the area? Give reasons for your answers.

Find the lengths of the curves in Exercises 23–29.

23. The spiral $r = \theta^2, \quad 0 \le \theta \le \sqrt{5}$

24. The spiral $r = e^{\theta}/\sqrt{2}, \quad 0 \le \theta \le \pi$

25. The cardioid $r = 1 + \cos\theta$

26. The curve $r = a\sin^2(\theta/2), \quad 0 \le \theta \le \pi, \quad a > 0$

27. The curve $r = \cos^3(\theta/3), \quad 0 \le \theta \le \pi/4$

28. The curve $r = \sqrt{1 + \sin 2\theta}, \quad 0 \le \theta \le \pi\sqrt{2}$

29. The curve $r = \sqrt{1 + \cos 2\theta}, \quad 0 \le \theta \le \pi\sqrt{2}$

30. *Circumferences of Circles.* As usual, when faced with a new formula, it is a good idea to try it on familiar objects to be sure it gives results consistent with past experience. Use the length formula in Eq. (10) to calculate the circumferences of the following circles ($a > 0$):

a) $r = a$ **b)** $r = a\cos\theta$ **c)** $r = a\sin\theta$

Find the areas of the surfaces generated by revolving the curves in Exercises 31–34 about the indicated axes.

31. $r = \sqrt{\cos 2\theta}, \quad 0 \le \theta \le \pi/4, \quad y$-axis

32. $r = \sqrt{2}e^{\theta/2}, \quad 0 \le \theta \le \pi/2, \quad x$-axis

33. $r^2 = \cos 2\theta, \quad x$-axis

34. $r = 2a\cos\theta, \ a > 0, \quad y$-axis

35. *The Length of the Curve $r = f(\theta)$, $\alpha \le \theta \le \beta$.* Assuming that the necessary derivatives are continuous, show how the substitutions

$$x = f(\theta)\cos\theta, \qquad y = f(\theta)\sin\theta$$

(Eqs. 7 in the text) transform

$$L = \int_{\alpha}^{\beta} \sqrt{\left(\frac{dx}{d\theta}\right)^2 + \left(\frac{dy}{d\theta}\right)^2}\, d\theta$$

into

$$L = \int_{\alpha}^{\beta} \sqrt{r^2 + \left(\frac{dr}{d\theta}\right)^2}\, d\theta.$$

36. *Average Value.* If f is continuous, the average value of the polar coordinate r over the curve $r = f(\theta)$, $\alpha \le \theta \le \beta$, with respect to θ is given by the formula

$$r_{\text{av}} = \frac{1}{\beta - \alpha}\int_{\alpha}^{\beta} f(\theta)\, d\theta.$$

Use this formula to find the average value of r with respect to θ over the following curves ($a > 0$).

a) The cardioid $r = a(1 - \cos\theta)$

b) The circle $r = a$

c) The circle $r = a\cos\theta, \quad -\pi/2 \le \theta \le \pi/2$

37. **$r = 2f(\theta)$ *vs.* $r = f(\theta)$**

a) Can anything be said about the relative lengths of the curves $r = f(\theta)$, $\alpha \le \theta \le \beta$, and $r = 2f(\theta)$, $\alpha \le \theta \le \beta$?

b) Can anything be said about the areas of the surfaces generated by revolving the curves in (a) about the coordinate axes?

(Assume that Eqs. 10–12 apply.)

Writing for Your Own Knowledge

Answer the following questions in writing. Some answers will take only a sentence or two; others may require several paragraphs. Some explanations may also call for graphs or sketches.

1. How do you find the area of a region defined by the polar coordinate inequalities $0 \le r_1(\theta) \le r_2(\theta)$, $\alpha \le \theta \le \beta$?
2. How do you find the length of a smooth curve $r = f(\theta)$, $\alpha \le \theta \le \beta$?
3. How can you sometimes find the area of the surface swept out by revolving a curve $r = f(\theta)$, $\alpha \le \theta \le \beta$, about one of the coordinate axes?

EXPLORER PROGRAM

PowerGrapher — Graphs curves in polar coordinates in color.

For Your Review

Write brief paragraphs about the following topics and give examples.

Defining conic sections
- **a)** with planes and cones
- **b)** in terms of distance

Standard-form equations for
- **a)** parabolas
- **b)** ellipses
- **c)** hyperbolas

Eccentricities of ellipses, parabolas, and hyperbolas

The equation $PF = e \cdot PD$

Eliminating the xy-term from the equation
$Ax^2 + Bxy + Cy^2 + Dx + Ey + F = 0$

The discriminant test for quadratic equations in x and y

Parametrizations of plane curves

Cycloids

Finding dy/dx and d^2y/dx^2 from a curve's parametrization

The parametric formulas for
- **a)** length of a curve
- **b)** surface area

Polar coordinates
Relations between polar and Cartesian coordinates
Symmetry tests in polar coordinates
Typical curves in polar coordinates
Graphing in polar coordinates

Polar equations for
- **a)** lines
- **b)** circles
- **c)** parabolas, ellipses, and hyperbolas

Finding, in polar coordinates,
- **a)** the area of a plane region
- **b)** the length of a curve
- **c)** the area of a surface of revolution

Practice Exercises

Sketch the parabolas in Exercises 1–4. Include the focus and directrix in each sketch.

1. $x^2 = -4y$

2. $x^2 = 2y$

3. $y^2 = 3x$

4. $y^2 = -(8/3)x$

Find the eccentricities of the ellipses and hyperbolas in Exercises 5–8. Sketch each conic section. Include the foci, vertices, and asymptotes (as appropriate) in your sketch.

5. $16x^2 + 7y^2 = 112$

6. $x^2 + 2y^2 = 4$

7. $3x^2 - y^2 = 3$

8. $5y^2 - 4x^2 = 20$

Exercises 9–14 give equations for conic sections and tell how many units up or down and to the right or left each curve is to be shifted. Find an equation for the new conic section and find the new foci, vertices, centers, and asymptotes, as appropriate. If the curve is a parabola, find the new directrix as well.

9. $x^2 = -12y$, right 2, up 3

10. $y^2 = 10x$, left 1/2, down 1

11. $\dfrac{x^2}{9} + \dfrac{y^2}{25} = 1$, left 3, down 5

12. $\dfrac{x^2}{169} + \dfrac{y^2}{144} = 1$, right 5, up 12

13. $\dfrac{y^2}{8} - \dfrac{x^2}{2} = 1$, right 2, up $2\sqrt{2}$

14. $\dfrac{x^2}{36} - \dfrac{y^2}{64} = 1$, left 10, down 3

Identify the conic sections in Exercises 15–22 and find their foci, vertices, centers, and asymptotes (as appropriate). If the curve is a parabola, find its directrix as well.

15. $x^2 - 4x - 4y^2 = 0$

16. $4x^2 - y^2 + 4y = 8$

17. $y^2 - 2y + 16x = -49$

18. $x^2 - 2x + 8y = -17$

19. $9x^2 + 16y^2 + 54x - 64y = -1$

20. $25x^2 + 9y^2 - 100x + 54y = 44$

21. $x^2 + y^2 - 2x - 2y = 0$

22. $x^2 + y^2 + 4x + 2y = 1$

What conic sections or degenerate cases do the equations in Exercises 23–28 represent? Give a reason for your answer in each case.

23. $x^2 + xy + y^2 + x + y + 1 = 0$

24. $x^2 + 4xy + 4y^2 + x + y + 1 = 0$

25. $x^2 + 3xy + 2y^2 + x + y + 1 = 0$

26. $x^2 + 2xy - 2y^2 + x + y + 1 = 0$

27. $x^2 - 2xy + y^2 = 0$

28. $x^2 - 3xy + 4y^2 = 0$

Identify the conic sections in Exercises 29–32. Then rotate the coordinate axes to find a new equation for the conic section that has no cross-product term. (The new equations will vary with the size and direction of the rotations used.)

29. $2x^2 + xy + 2y^2 - 15 = 0$

30. $3x^2 + 2xy + 3y^2 = 19$

31. $x^2 + 2\sqrt{3}\,xy - y^2 + 4 = 0$

32. $x^2 - 3xy + y^2 = 5$

33. Find the volume of the solid generated by revolving the region enclosed by the ellipse $9x^2 + 4y^2 = 36$ about (a) the x-axis, (b) the y-axis.

34. The "triangular" region in the first quadrant bounded by the x-axis, the line $x = 4$, and the hyperbola $9x^2 - 4y^2 = 36$ is revolved about the x-axis to generate a solid. Find the volume of the solid.

Exercises 35–40 give parametric equations and parameter intervals for the motion of a particle in the xy-plane. Identify the particle's path by finding a Cartesian equation for it. Graph the Cartesian equation and indicate the direction of motion and the portion traced by the particle.

35. $x = t/2, \quad y = t + 1; \quad -\infty < t < \infty$

36. $x = \sqrt{t}, \quad y = 1 - \sqrt{t}; \quad t \geq 0$

37. $x = (1/2) \tan t, \quad y = (1/2) \sec t; \quad -\pi/2 < t < \pi/2$

38. $x = -2 \cos t, \quad y = 2 \sin t; \quad 0 \leq t \leq \pi$

39. $x = -\cos t, \quad y = \cos^2 t; \quad 0 \leq t \leq \pi$

40. $x = 4 \cos t, \quad y = 9 \sin t; \quad 0 \leq t \leq 2\pi$

41. Find parametric equations and a parameter interval for the motion of a particle in the xy-plane that traces the ellipse $16x^2 + 9y^2 = 144$ once counterclockwise. (There are many ways to do this, so your answer may not be the same as the one in the back of the book.)

42. Find parametric equations and a parameter interval for the motion of a particle that starts at the point $(-2, 0)$ in the xy-plane and traces the circle $x^2 + y^2 = 4$ three times clockwise. (There are many ways to do this.)

In Exercises 43 and 44, find an equation for the line in the xy-plane that is tangent to the curve at the point corresponding to the given value of t. Also, find the value of d^2y/dx^2 at this point.

43. $x = (1/2)\tan t, \quad y = (1/2)\sec t; \quad t = \pi/3$

44. $x = 1 + 1/t^2, \quad y = 1 - 3/t; \quad t = 2$

Find the lengths of the curves in Exercises 45 and 46.

45. $x = e^{2t} - \dfrac{t}{8}, \quad y = e^t; \quad 0 \le t \le \ln 2$

46. The closed loop in Fig. 10.69.

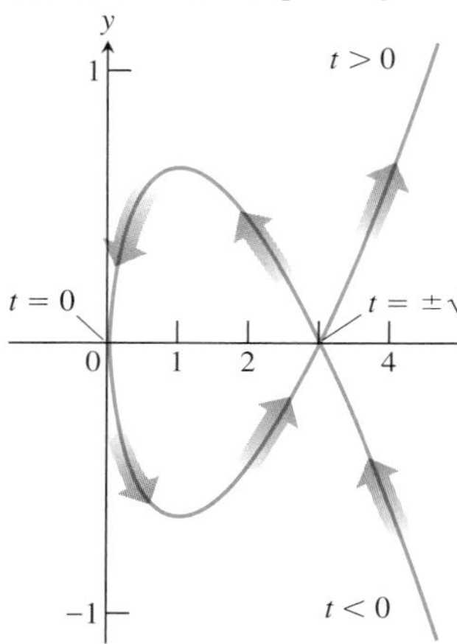

10.69 Exercise 46 refers to the curve $x = t^2$, $y = (t^3/3) - t$ shown here. The loop starts at $t = -\sqrt{3}$ and ends at $t = \sqrt{3}$.

Find the areas of the surfaces generated by revolving the curves in Exercises 47 and 48 about the indicated axes.

47. $x = t^2/2, \quad y = 2t, \quad 0 \le t \le \sqrt{5}; \quad x\text{-axis}$

48. $x = t^2 + 1/(2t), \quad y = 4\sqrt{t}, \quad 1/\sqrt{2} \le t \le 1; \quad y\text{-axis}$

Sketch the regions defined by the polar coordinate inequalities in Exercises 49 and 50.

49. $0 \le r \le 6 \cos \theta$

50. $-4 \sin \theta \le r \le 0$

Match each graph in Exercises 51–58 with the appropriate equation (a) – (l). There are more equations than graphs, so some equations will not be matched.

a) $r = \cos 2\theta$

b) $r \cos \theta = 1$

c) $r = \dfrac{6}{1 - 2 \cos \theta}$

d) $r = \sin 2\theta$

e) $r = \theta$

f) $r^2 = \cos 2\theta$

g) $r = 1 + \cos \theta$

h) $r = 1 - \sin \theta$

i) $r = \dfrac{2}{1 - \cos \theta}$

j) $r^2 = \sin 2\theta$

k) $r = -\sin \theta$

l) $r = 2 \cos \theta + 1$

51. Four-leaved rose

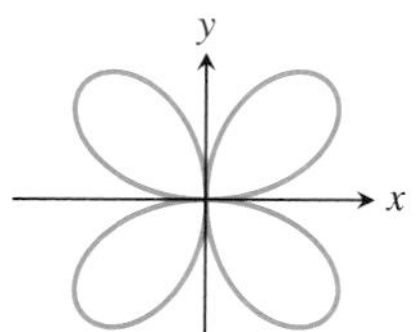

52. Spiral

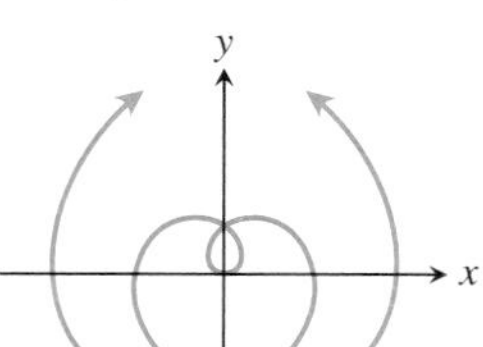

53. Limaçon

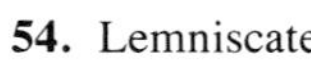

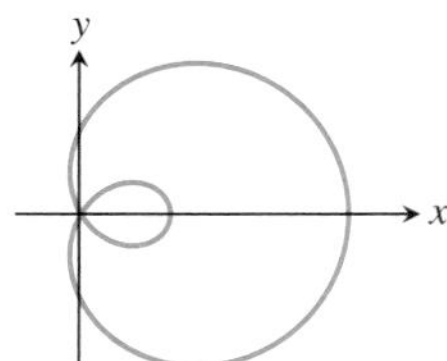

54. Lemniscate

55. Circle

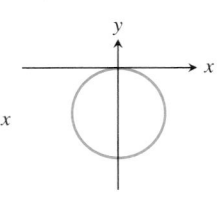

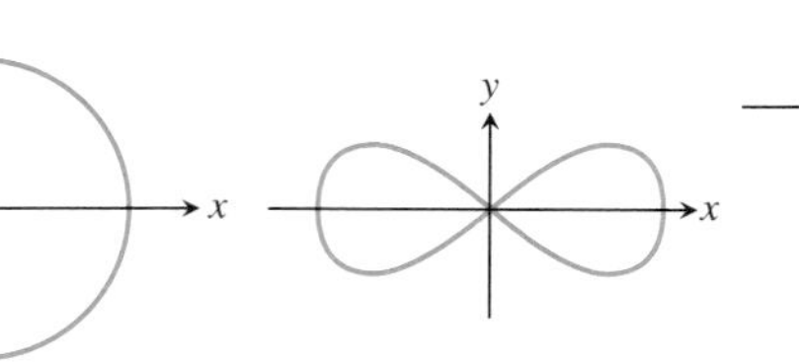

56. Cardioid

57. Parabola

58. Lemniscate

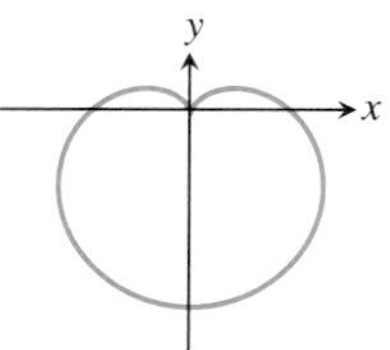

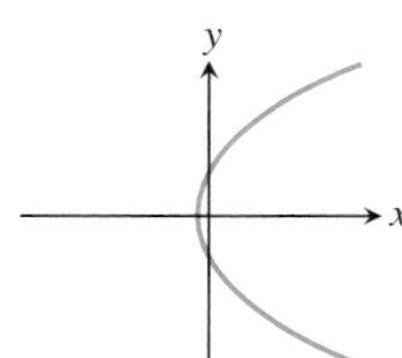

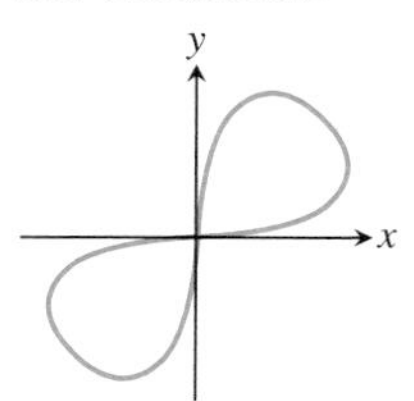

Find the points of intersection of the curves given by the polar coordinate equations in Exercises 59–66.

59. $r = \sin \theta, \quad r = 1 + \sin \theta$

60. $r = \cos \theta, \quad r = 1 - \cos \theta$

61. $r = 1 + \cos \theta, \quad r = 1 - \cos \theta$

62. $r = 1 + \sin \theta, \quad r = 1 - \sin \theta$

63. $r = 1 + \sin \theta, \quad r = -1 + \sin \theta$

64. $r = 1 + \cos \theta, \quad r = -1 + \cos \theta$

65. $r = \sec \theta, \quad r = 2 \sin \theta$

66. $r = -2 \csc \theta, \quad r = -4 \cos \theta$

In Exercises 67 and 68, find equations for the lines that are tangent to the polar coordinate curves at the origin.

67. The lemniscate $r^2 = \cos 2\theta$

68. The limaçon $r = 2 \cos \theta + 1$

69. Find polar coordinate equations for the lines that are tangent to the tips of the petals of the four-leaved rose $r = \sin 2\theta$.

70. Find polar coordinate equations for the lines that are tangent to the cardioid $r = 1 + \sin \theta$ at the points where it crosses the x-axis.

Sketch the lines in Exercises 71–76. Also, find a Cartesian equation for each line.

71. $r \cos\left(\theta + \dfrac{\pi}{3}\right) = 2\sqrt{3}$

72. $r \cos\left(\theta - \dfrac{3\pi}{4}\right) = \dfrac{\sqrt{2}}{2}$

73. $r = 2 \sec \theta$

74. $r = -\sqrt{2} \sec \theta$

75. $r = -(3/2) \csc \theta$

76. $r = \left(3\sqrt{3}\right) \csc \theta$

Find polar equations for the circles in Exercises 77–80. Sketch each circle in the coordinate plane and label it with both its Cartesian and polar equations.

77. $x^2 + y^2 + 5y = 0$

78. $x^2 + y^2 - 2y = 0$

79. $x^2 + y^2 - 3x = 0$

80. $x^2 + y^2 + 4x = 0$

Find Cartesian equations for the circles in Exercises 81–84. Sketch each circle in the coordinate plane and label it with both its Cartesian and polar equations.

81. $r = -4 \sin \theta$

82. $r = 3\sqrt{3} \sin \theta$

83. $r = 2\sqrt{2} \cos \theta$

84. $r = -6 \cos \theta$

Sketch the conic sections whose polar coordinate equations are given in Exercises 85–88. Give polar coordinates for the vertices and, in the case of ellipses, for the centers as well.

85. $r = \dfrac{2}{1 + \cos \theta}$

86. $r = \dfrac{8}{2 + \cos \theta}$

87. $r = \dfrac{6}{1 - 2 \cos \theta}$

88. $r = \dfrac{12}{3 + \sin \theta}$

Exercises 89–92 give the eccentricities of conic sections with one focus at the origin of the polar coordinate plane, along with the directrix for that focus. Find a polar equation for each conic section.

89. $e = 2, \quad r \cos \theta = 2$

90. $e = 1, \quad r \cos \theta = -4$

91. $e = 1/2, \quad r \sin \theta = 2$

92. $e = 1/3, \quad r \sin \theta = -6$

Find the areas of the regions in the polar coordinate plane described in Exercises 93–96.

93. Enclosed by the limaçon $r = 2 - \cos \theta$

94. Enclosed by one leaf of the three-leaved rose $r = \sin 3\theta$

95. Inside the "figure eight" $r = 1 + \cos 2\theta$ and outside the circle $r = 1$

96. Inside the cardioid $r = 2(1 + \sin \theta)$ and outside the circle $r = 2 \sin \theta$

Find the lengths of the curves given by the polar coordinate equations in Exercises 97–100.

97. $r = -1 + \cos \theta$

98. $r = 2 \sin \theta + 2 \cos \theta, \quad 0 \le \theta \le \pi/2$

99. $r = 8 \sin^3 (\theta/3), \quad 0 \le \theta \le \pi/4$

100. $r = \sqrt{1 + \cos 2\theta}, \quad -\pi/2 \le \theta \le \pi/2$

Find the areas of the surfaces generated by revolving the polar coordinate curves in Exercises 101 and 102 about the indicated axes.

101. $r = \sqrt{\cos 2\theta}, \quad 0 \le \theta \le \pi/4, \quad x\text{-axis}$

102. $r^2 = \sin 2\theta, \quad y\text{-axis}$

103. A ripple tank is made by bending a strip of tin around the perimeter of an ellipse for the wall of the tank and soldering a flat bottom onto this. An inch or two of water is put in the tank and you drop a marble into it, right at one focus of the ellipse. Ripples radiate outward through the water, reflect from the strip around the edge of the tank, and a few seconds later a drop of water spurts up at the second focus. Why?

104. *LORAN.* A radio signal was sent simultaneously from towers *A* and *B*, located several hundred miles apart on the northern California coast. A ship offshore received the signal from *A* 1400 microseconds before receiving the signal from *B*. Assuming that the signals traveled at the rate of 980 ft/microsecond, what can be said about the location of the ship relative to the two towers?

105. On a level plane, at the same instant, you hear the sound of a rifle and that of the bullet hitting the target. What can be said about your location relative to the rifle and target?

106. *Archimedes Spirals.* The graph of an equation of the form $r = a\theta$, where a is a nonzero constant, is called an **Archimedes spiral.** Is there anything special about the widths between the successive turns of such a spiral?

107. a) Show that the equations $x = r \cos \theta$, $y = r \sin \theta$ transform the polar equation

$$r = \frac{k}{1 + e \cos \theta}$$

into the Cartesian equation

$$(1 - e^2)x^2 + y^2 + 2kex - k^2 = 0.$$

b) Then apply the criteria of Section 10.2 to show that

$$\begin{aligned} e = 0 &\Rightarrow \text{circle} \\ 0 < e < 1 &\Rightarrow \text{ellipse} \\ e = 1 &\Rightarrow \text{parabola} \\ e > 1 &\Rightarrow \text{hyperbola.} \end{aligned}$$

108. *A Satellite Orbit.* A satellite is in an orbit that passes over the North and South Poles of the earth. When it is over the South Pole it is at the highest point of its orbit, 1000 miles above the earth's surface. Above the North Pole it is at the lowest point of its orbit, 300 miles above the earth's surface.

a) Assuming that the orbit is an ellipse with one focus at the center of the earth, find its eccentricity. (Take the diameter of the earth to be 8000 miles.)

b) Using the north–south axis of the earth as the x-axis and the center of the earth as origin, find a polar equation for the orbit.

SPIN CASTING MIRRORS

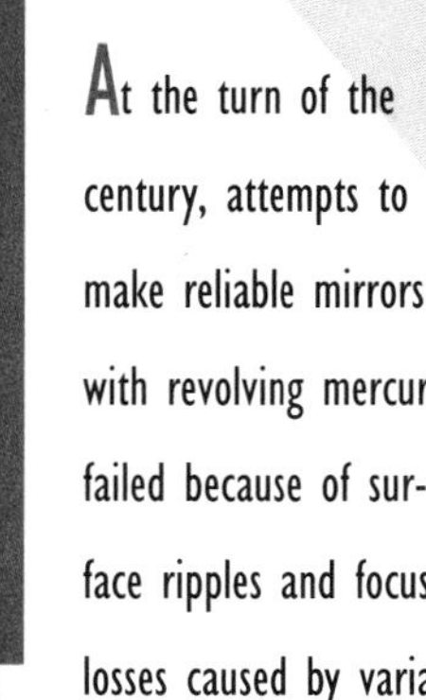

ROGER ANGEL, an astronomer at the Steward Observation Mirror Laboratory in Tucson, AZ, is creating new "windows" for looking at the universe. These windows are actually giant telescope mirrors made by spin casting glass, a procedure pioneered by Angel.

When a circular pan of liquid is rotated about its vertical axis, the surface of the liquid does not stay flat. Instead, it assumes the shape of a paraboloid of revolution (Section 11.6), exactly what is needed for the primary mirror of a reflecting telescope.

At the turn of the century, attempts to make reliable mirrors with revolving mercury failed because of surface ripples and focus losses caused by variations in the speed of rotation.

Today, these difficulties can be overcome with synchronous motors that are driven by oscillator-stabilized power supplies and checked against constant clocks.

Using the same idea, astronomer Angel has used a large spinning turntable heated to 1180°C to cast borosilicate glass blanks for mirrors more than 20 ft in diameter. Spincast mirrors can be made thicker (stiffer) and hollow while traditionally cast mirrors are solid. They weigh only a fifth as much (10 tons vs. 50 tons), and cost less.

Spincast mirrors also adjust faster to changes in external temperatures and their shorter focal lengths permit the use of compact telescope structures that are less expensive to house and less likely to flex in the wind.

11 Vectors and Analytic Geometry in Space

OVERVIEW

This chapter introduces vectors and coordinate systems for space. Just as the coordinate plane is the natural place to study functions of a single variable, coordinate space is the place to study functions of two or three variables.

Equations in three variables define surfaces in space the way equations in two variables define curves in the plane. We use such surfaces to graph functions (not in this chapter, but later), define regions, bound solids, describe walls of containers, and so on. We use them to do all the things we do in the plane, but stepped up one dimension.

Once in space, we can model motion in three dimensions and track the positions of moving bodies with vectors. We can also calculate the directions and magnitudes of velocities and accelerations and predict the effects of forces. As we will see in the next chapter, coordinates and vectors make a powerful combination. Coordinates tell us where a moving body is, and vectors tell us what is happening to it.

11.1 Vectors in the Plane

Some of the things we measure are determined by their magnitudes. To record mass, length, or time, for example, we need only write down a number and name an appropriate unit of measure. But we need more than that to describe a force, displacement, or velocity, for these quantities have direction as well as magnitude. To describe a force, we need to record the direction in which it acts as well as how large it is. To describe a body's displacement, we have to say in what direction it moved as well as how far it moved. To describe a body's velocity, we have to know where the body is headed as well as how fast it is going.

Quantities that have direction as well as magnitude are usually represented by arrows that point in the direction of the action and whose lengths give the magnitude of the action in terms of a suitably chosen unit. When we describe these arrows abstractly, as directed line segments, we call them *vectors.*

DEFINITIONS

A **vector** in the plane is a directed line segment. Two vectors are **equal** or **the same** if they have the same length and direction.

The arrows we use to draw vectors are understood to represent the same vector if they have the same length and point the same way.

In print, vectors are usually represented by single boldface roman letters, as in **v** ("vector **v**"). The vector defined by the directed line segment from point A to point B, however, is written as $\overrightarrow{AB}$ ("vector AB"). In handwritten work it is customary to draw arrows above letters representing vectors. Thus the equation $\mathbf{v} = \overrightarrow{AB}$ in print would appear as $\vec{v} = \overrightarrow{AB}$ when written by hand.

EXAMPLE 1 The arrows shown here have the same length and direction. They therefore represent the same vector, and we write

$$\overrightarrow{AB} = \overrightarrow{CD} = \overrightarrow{OP} = \overrightarrow{EF}.$$

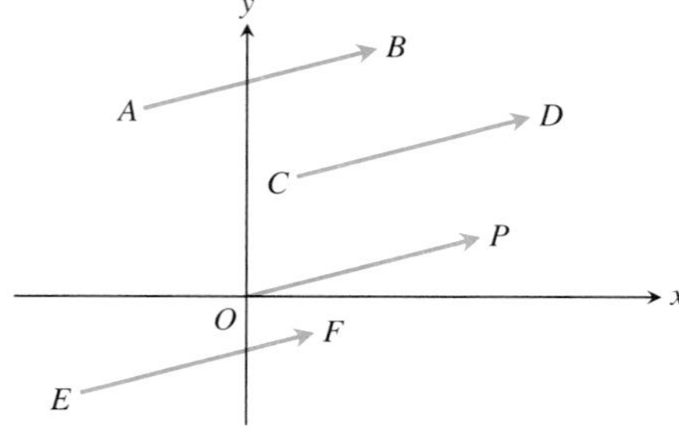

Scalars and Scalar Multiples

We scale vectors by multiplying them by real numbers. To double a vector's length, we multiply the vector by 2. To increase its length 50%, we multiply by 1.5. To reverse a vector's direction and double its length at the same time, we multiply by -2.

If c is a number and **v** a vector, the direction of $c\mathbf{v}$ agrees with **v** if c is positive and is opposite to that of **v** if c is negative (Fig. 11.1). Since real numbers work like scaling factors in this context, we call them **scalars.** We call multiples like $c\mathbf{v}$ **scalar multiples** of **v**.

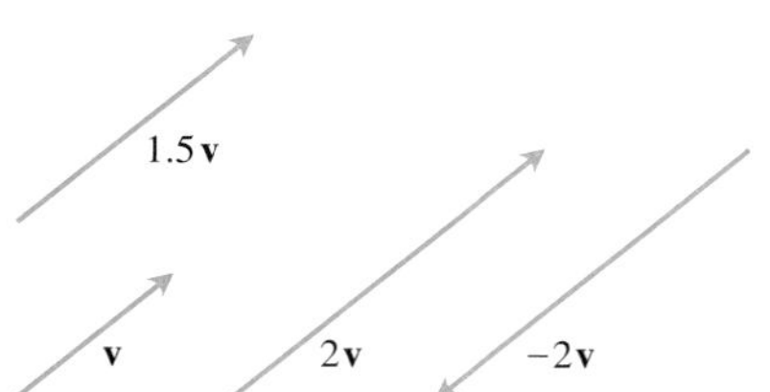

11.1 Scalar multiples of **v**.

Geometric Addition: The Parallelogram Law

Two vectors $\mathbf{v}_1$ and $\mathbf{v}_2$ may be added by drawing a representative of $\mathbf{v}_1$, say from A to B as in Fig. 11.2, and a representative of $\mathbf{v}_2$ starting from the terminal point of $\mathbf{v}_1$. In Fig. 11.2, $\mathbf{v}_2 = \overrightarrow{BC}$. The sum $\mathbf{v}_1 + \mathbf{v}_2$ is then the vector from the initial point A of $\mathbf{v}_1$ to the terminal point C of $\mathbf{v}_2$. That is, if

$$\mathbf{v}_1 = \overrightarrow{AB} \qquad \text{and} \qquad \mathbf{v}_2 = \overrightarrow{BC},$$

then

$$\mathbf{v}_1 + \mathbf{v}_2 = \overrightarrow{AB} + \overrightarrow{BC} = \overrightarrow{AC}.$$

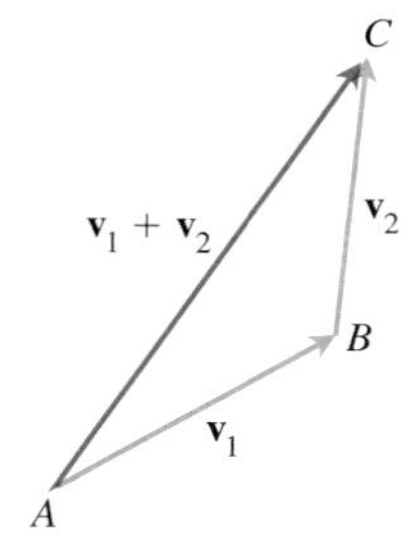

11.2 The sum of $\mathbf{v}_1$ and $\mathbf{v}_2$.

This description of addition is called the **Parallelogram Law of Addition** because $\mathbf{v}_1 + \mathbf{v}_2$ is given by the diagonal of the parallelogram determined by $\mathbf{v}_1$ and $\mathbf{v}_2$ (Fig. 11.3).

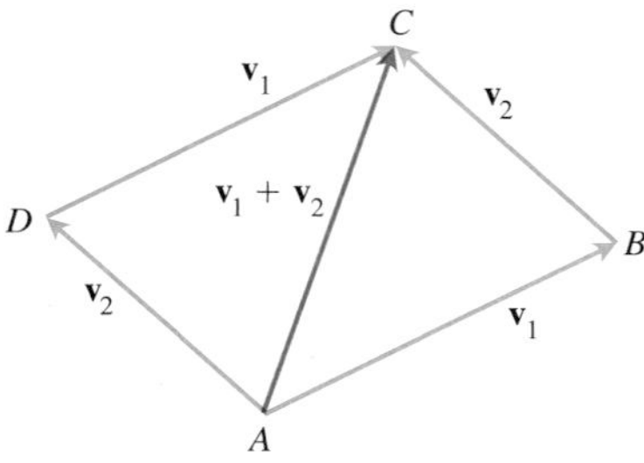

11.3 The Parallelogram Law of Addition. Quadrilateral $ABCD$ is a parallelogram because opposite sides have equal lengths. The law was used by Aristotle to describe the combined action of two forces.

Components

Whenever a vector **v** can be written as a sum $\mathbf{v} = \mathbf{v}_1 + \mathbf{v}_2$, the vectors $\mathbf{v}_1$ and $\mathbf{v}_2$ are said to be **components** of **v**. We also say that we have **represented** or **resolved v** in terms of $\mathbf{v}_1$ and $\mathbf{v}_2$.

The most common algebra of vectors is based on representing each vector in terms of components parallel to the coordinate axes and writing each component as an appropriate multiple of a **basic** vector of unit length. The basic vector in the positive x direction is the vector **i** from (0, 0) to (1, 0). The basic vector in the positive y direction is the vector **j** from (0, 0) to (0, 1). Then $a\mathbf{i}$, a being a scalar, represents a vector of length $|a|$ parallel to the x-axis, pointing to the right if $a > 0$ and to the left if $a < 0$. Similarly, $b\mathbf{j}$ is a vector of length $|b|$ parallel to the

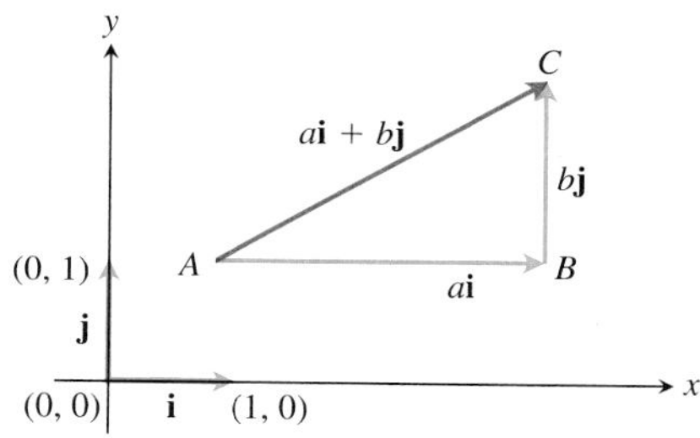

11.4 The basic vectors $\mathbf{i}$ and $\mathbf{j}$. Any vector $\overrightarrow{AC}$ in the plane can be expressed as a scalar multiple of $\mathbf{i}$ plus a scalar multiple of $\mathbf{j}$.

y-axis, pointing up if $b > 0$ and down if $b < 0$. Figure 11.4 shows a vector $\mathbf{v} = \overrightarrow{AC}$ resolved into its $\mathbf{i}$- and $\mathbf{j}$-components as $\mathbf{v} = a\,\mathbf{i} + b\,\mathbf{j}$.

DEFINITIONS

If $\mathbf{v} = a\,\mathbf{i} + b\,\mathbf{j}$, the vectors $a\,\mathbf{i}$ and $b\,\mathbf{j}$ are the **vector components** of $\mathbf{v}$ in the directions of $\mathbf{i}$ and $\mathbf{j}$. We call $a\,\mathbf{i}$ the **horizontal** or ***x*-component** and $b\,\mathbf{j}$ the **vertical** or ***y*-component.** The numbers a and b are the **scalar components** of $\mathbf{v}$ in the directions of $\mathbf{i}$ and $\mathbf{j}$.

Components enable us to define the equality of vectors algebraically.

DEFINITION

Equality of Vectors (Algebraic Definition)

$$a\,\mathbf{i} + b\,\mathbf{j} = a'\,\mathbf{i} + b'\,\mathbf{j} \quad \Leftrightarrow \quad a = a' \text{ and } b = b'. \tag{1}$$

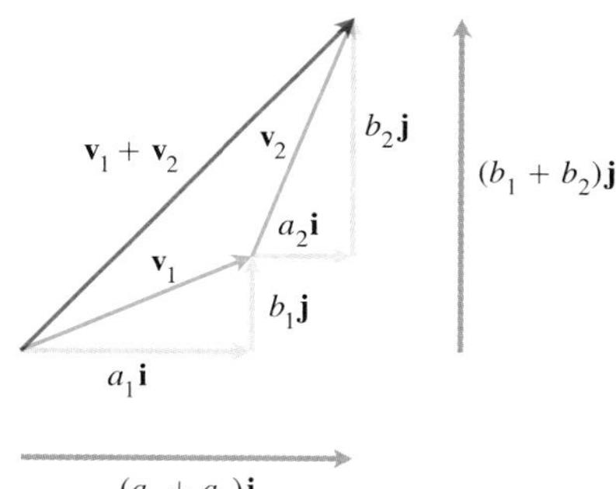

11.5 If $\mathbf{v}_1 = a_1\,\mathbf{i} + b_1\,\mathbf{j}$ and $\mathbf{v}_2 = a_2\,\mathbf{i} + b_2\,\mathbf{j}$, then $\mathbf{v}_1 + \mathbf{v}_2 = (a_1 + a_2)\,\mathbf{i} + (b_1 + b_2)\,\mathbf{j}$.

Vectors are equal precisely when their scalar components in the directions of $\mathbf{i}$ and $\mathbf{j}$ are equal.

Algebraic Addition

Vectors may be added algebraically by adding their corresponding scalar components, as shown in Fig. 11.5.

If $\mathbf{v}_1 = a_1\,\mathbf{i} + b_1\,\mathbf{j}$, and $\mathbf{v}_2 = a_2\,\mathbf{i} + b_2\,\mathbf{j}$, then

$$\mathbf{v}_1 + \mathbf{v}_2 = (a_1 + a_2)\,\mathbf{i} + (b_1 + b_2)\,\mathbf{j}. \tag{2}$$

EXAMPLE 2

$$(2\,\mathbf{i} - 4\,\mathbf{j}) + (5\,\mathbf{i} + 3\,\mathbf{j}) = (2 + 5)\,\mathbf{i} + (-4 + 3)\,\mathbf{j} = 7\,\mathbf{i} - \mathbf{j}.$$

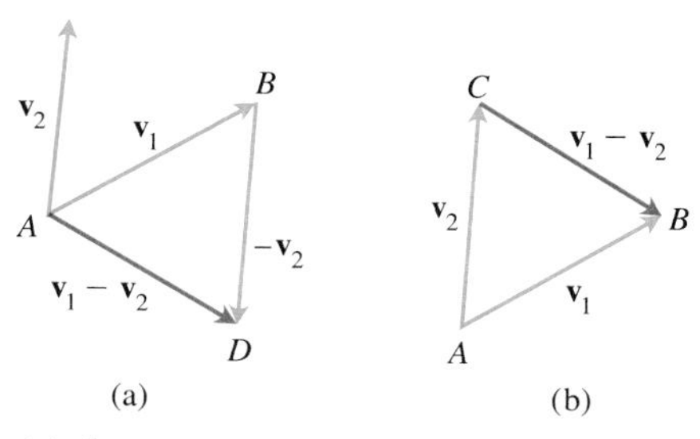

11.6 Two ways to draw $\mathbf{v}_1 - \mathbf{v}_2$: (a) as $\mathbf{v}_1 + (-\mathbf{v}_2)$ and (b) as the vector from the tip of $\mathbf{v}_2$ to the tip of $\mathbf{v}_1$.

Subtraction

The negative of a vector $\mathbf{v}$ is the vector $-\mathbf{v}$ that has the same length as $\mathbf{v}$ but points in the opposite direction. To subtract a vector $\mathbf{v}_2$ from a vector $\mathbf{v}_1$, we add $-\mathbf{v}_2$ to $\mathbf{v}_1$. This may be done geometrically by drawing $-\mathbf{v}_2$ from the tip of $\mathbf{v}_1$ and then drawing the vector from the initial point of $\mathbf{v}_1$ to the tip of $-\mathbf{v}_2$, as shown in Fig. 11.6(a), where

$$\overrightarrow{AD} = \overrightarrow{AB} + \overrightarrow{BD} = \mathbf{v}_1 + (-\mathbf{v}_2) = \mathbf{v}_1 - \mathbf{v}_2.$$

Another way to draw $\mathbf{v}_1 - \mathbf{v}_2$ is to draw $\mathbf{v}_1$ and $\mathbf{v}_2$ with a common initial point and then draw $\mathbf{v}_1 - \mathbf{v}_2$ as the vector from the tip of $\mathbf{v}_2$ to the tip of $\mathbf{v}_1$. This is illustrated in Fig. 11.6(b), where

$$\overrightarrow{CB} = \overrightarrow{CA} + \overrightarrow{AB} = -\mathbf{v}_2 + \mathbf{v}_1 = \mathbf{v}_1 - \mathbf{v}_2.$$

Thus, $\overrightarrow{CB}$ is the vector that when added to $\mathbf{v}_2$ gives $\mathbf{v}_1$:

$$\overrightarrow{CB} + \mathbf{v}_2 = (\mathbf{v}_1 - \mathbf{v}_2) + \mathbf{v}_2 = \mathbf{v}_1.$$

In terms of components,

$$\mathbf{v}_1 - \mathbf{v}_2 = (a_1 - a_2)\,\mathbf{i} + (b_1 - b_2)\,\mathbf{j}. \quad (3)$$

Corresponding scalar components are subtracted.

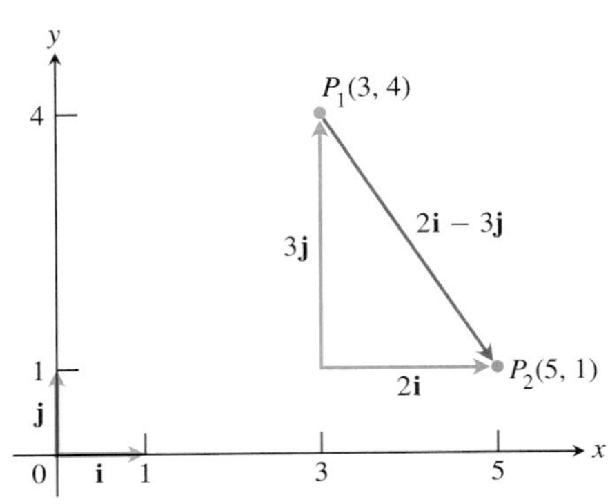

11.7 Diagram for $\overrightarrow{P_1P_2}$ (Example 4).

EXAMPLE 3

$$(6\,\mathbf{i} + 2\,\mathbf{j}) - (3\,\mathbf{i} - 5\,\mathbf{j}) = (6 - 3)\,\mathbf{i} + (2 - (-5))\,\mathbf{j} = 3\,\mathbf{i} + 7\,\mathbf{j}.$$

We find the components of the vector from a point $P_1(x_1, y_1)$ to a point $P_2(x_2, y_2)$ by subtracting the components of $\overrightarrow{OP_1} = x_1\,\mathbf{i} + y_1\,\mathbf{j}$ from the components of $\overrightarrow{OP_2} = x_2\,\mathbf{i} + y_2\,\mathbf{j}$.

The vector from $P_1(x_1, y_1)$ to $P_2(x_2, y_2)$ is

$$\overrightarrow{P_1P_2} = (x_2 - x_1)\,\mathbf{i} + (y_2 - y_1)\,\mathbf{j}. \quad (4)$$

EXAMPLE 4 The vector from P_1 (3, 4) to P_2 (5, 1) (Fig. 11.7) is

$$\overrightarrow{P_1P_2} = (5 - 3)\,\mathbf{i} + (1 - 4)\,\mathbf{j} = 2\,\mathbf{i} - 3\,\mathbf{j}.$$

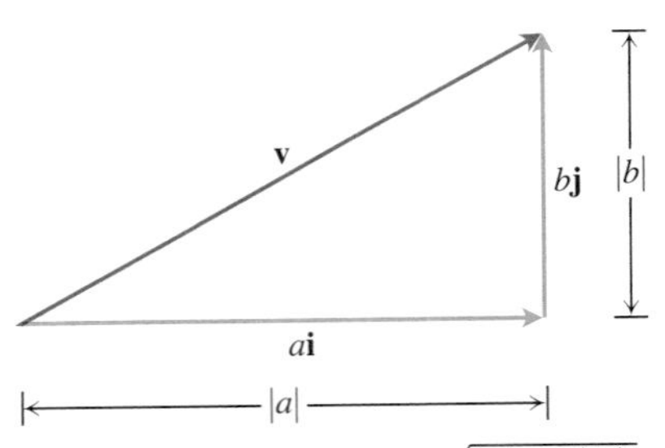

11.8 The length of **v** is $\sqrt{|a|^2 + |b|^2} = \sqrt{a^2 + b^2}$.

Magnitude

The **magnitude** or **length** of $\mathbf{v} = a\,\mathbf{i} + b\,\mathbf{j}$ is $|\mathbf{v}| = \sqrt{a^2 + b^2}$. We arrive at this number by applying the Pythagorean theorem to the right triangle determined by **v** and its two vector components (Fig. 11.8).

Magnitude or Length

$$|\mathbf{v}| = |a\,\mathbf{i} + b\,\mathbf{j}| = \sqrt{a^2 + b^2} \quad (5)$$

The Symbol for Magnitude

The bars in $|\mathbf{v}|$ (read "the magnitude of **v**") are the same bars we use for the magnitude (absolute value) of a real number.

EXAMPLE 5 You push a loaded supermarket cart by applying a 20-lb force **F** that makes a 30° angle with the horizontal. Resolve **F** into its x- and y-components. (The x-component is the effective force in the direction of motion. The y-component just adds weight to the cart.)

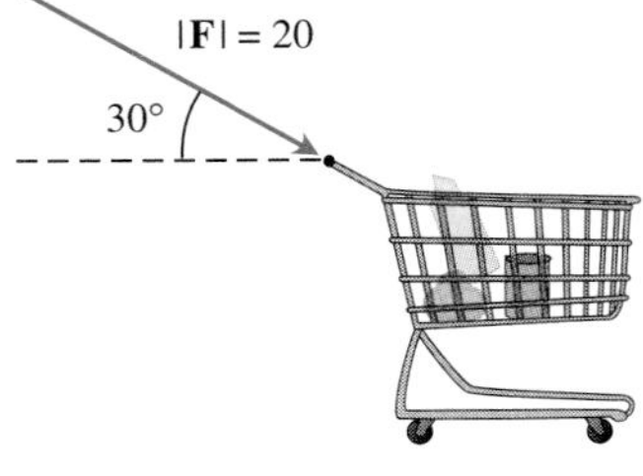

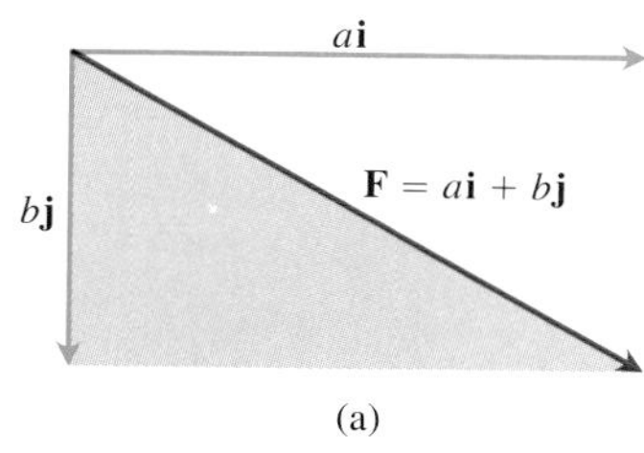

(a)

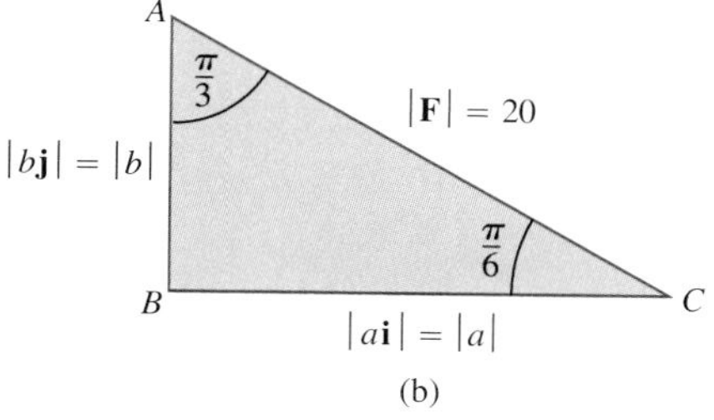

(b)

11.9 (a) The horizontal and vertical components of the vector **F** in Example 5. (b) The right triangle determined by **F** and its components.

Solution We draw a vector triangle for $\mathbf{F} = a\,\mathbf{i} + b\,\mathbf{j}$ and its components along with the right triangle determined by their magnitudes (Fig. 11.9). The triangle is a 30-60-90 triangle, so $|a| = 10\sqrt{3}$ and $|b| = 10$. The x-component of **F** is $10\sqrt{3}\,\mathbf{i}$. The y-component is $-10\,\mathbf{j}$ (negative because it points down). That is, $\mathbf{F} = 10\sqrt{3}\,\mathbf{i} - 10\,\mathbf{j}$.

Scalar Multiplication

Scalar multiplication can be accomplished component by component.

If c is a scalar and $\mathbf{v} = a\,\mathbf{i} + b\,\mathbf{j}$ is a vector, then

$$c\,\mathbf{v} = c(a\,\mathbf{i} + b\,\mathbf{j}) = (ca)\,\mathbf{i} + (cb)\,\mathbf{j}. \tag{6}$$

The length of $c\,\mathbf{v}$ is $|c|$ times the length of $\mathbf{v}$:

$$\begin{aligned} |c\,\mathbf{v}| &= |(ca)\,\mathbf{i} + (cb)\,\mathbf{j}| && \text{Eq. (6)} \\ &= \sqrt{(ca)^2 + (cb)^2} && \text{Eq. (5) with } ca \text{ and } cb \text{ in place of } a \text{ and } b \\ &= \sqrt{c^2(a^2 + b^2)} \\ &= \sqrt{c^2}\sqrt{a^2 + b^2} \\ &= |c|\,|\mathbf{v}|. \end{aligned}$$

If c is a scalar and $\mathbf{v}$ is a vector, then $|c\,\mathbf{v}| = |c|\,|\mathbf{v}|$. (7)

EXAMPLE 6 If $c = -2$ and $\mathbf{v} = -3\,\mathbf{i} + 4\,\mathbf{j}$, then

$$|\mathbf{v}| = |-3\,\mathbf{i} + 4\,\mathbf{j}| = \sqrt{(-3)^2 + (4)^2} = \sqrt{9 + 16} = \sqrt{25} = 5$$

$$\begin{aligned} |-2\,\mathbf{v}| &= |(-2)(-3\,\mathbf{i} + 4\,\mathbf{j})| = |6\,\mathbf{i} - 8\,\mathbf{j}| = \sqrt{(6)^2 + (-8)^2} = \sqrt{36 + 64} \\ &= \sqrt{100} = 10 = |-2|\,5 = |c|\,|\mathbf{v}|. \end{aligned}$$

The Zero Vector

The **zero vector** is the vector

$$\mathbf{0} = 0\,\mathbf{i} + 0\,\mathbf{j}. \tag{8}$$

Unit Vectors

Any vector whose length is 1 is a **unit vector.** The vectors **i** and **j** are unit vectors.

$$|\mathbf{i}| = |1\,\mathbf{i} + 0\,\mathbf{j}| = \sqrt{1^2 + 0^2} = 1, \qquad |\mathbf{j}| = |0\,\mathbf{i} + 1\,\mathbf{j}| = \sqrt{0^2 + 1^2} = 1.$$

In handwritten work it is common to denote unit vectors with small "hats," as in û (pronounced "*u* hat"). In hat notation, **i** and **j** become $\hat{\imath}$ and $\hat{\jmath}$.

If **u** is the unit vector obtained by rotating **i** through an angle θ in the positive direction, then (Fig. 11.10) **u** has a horizontal component $\cos\theta$ and a vertical component $\sin\theta$, so that

$$\mathbf{u} = (\cos\theta)\,\mathbf{i} + (\sin\theta)\,\mathbf{j}. \tag{9}$$

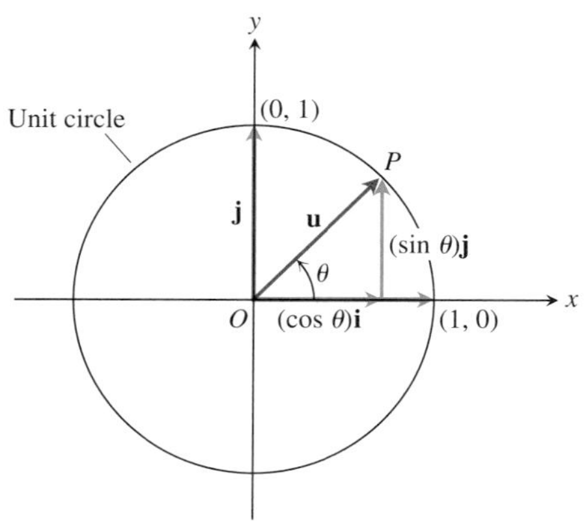

11.10 The unit vector that makes an angle of measure θ with the positive x-axis. Every unit vector has the form

$$\mathbf{u} = (\cos\theta)\,\mathbf{i} + (\sin\theta)\,\mathbf{j}$$

for some θ.

As θ varies from 0 to 2π, the point P in Fig. 11.10 traces the circle $x^2 + y^2 = 1$ counterclockwise. This takes in all possible directions, so every unit vector in the plane is given by Eq. (9) for some value of θ.

Direction as a Vector

It is common in subjects like electricity and magnetism, which use vectors a great deal, to define the direction of a nonzero vector $\mathbf{v}$ to be the unit vector obtained by dividing $\mathbf{v}$ by its own length.

DEFINITION

If $\mathbf{v} \neq \mathbf{0}$, the **direction** of $\mathbf{v}$ is $\dfrac{\mathbf{v}}{|\mathbf{v}|}$. (10)

The vector $\mathbf{v}/|\mathbf{v}|$ really is a unit vector:

$$\text{Length of } \frac{\mathbf{v}}{|\mathbf{v}|} = \left|\frac{\mathbf{v}}{|\mathbf{v}|}\right| = \left|\frac{1}{|\mathbf{v}|}\cdot\mathbf{v}\right|$$

$$= \frac{1}{|\mathbf{v}|}|\mathbf{v}| \qquad \text{Eq. (7) with } c = \frac{1}{|\mathbf{v}|}$$

$$= 1.$$

The zero vector, having no length, so to speak, has no direction either.

It is also common practice to call $\mathbf{v}/|\mathbf{v}|$ a unit vector in the direction of $\mathbf{v}$.

Any nonzero vector can be expressed in terms of its length and direction by using the equation

$$\mathbf{v} = |\mathbf{v}|\cdot\frac{\mathbf{v}}{|\mathbf{v}|} = (\text{length of } \mathbf{v})\cdot(\text{direction of } \mathbf{v}). \qquad (11)$$

EXAMPLE 7 Express $\mathbf{v} = 3\,\mathbf{i} - 4\,\mathbf{j}$ in terms of its length and direction.

Solution Length of $\mathbf{v}$: $|\mathbf{v}| = \sqrt{(3)^2 + (-4)^2} = \sqrt{9 + 16} = 5$

Direction of $\mathbf{v}$: $\dfrac{\mathbf{v}}{|\mathbf{v}|} = \dfrac{3\,\mathbf{i} - 4\,\mathbf{j}}{5} = \dfrac{3}{5}\mathbf{i} - \dfrac{4}{5}\mathbf{j}$

$$\mathbf{v} = 3\,\mathbf{i} - 4\,\mathbf{j} = \underbrace{5}_{\text{length of } \mathbf{v}}\underbrace{\left(\tfrac{3}{5}\mathbf{i} - \tfrac{4}{5}\mathbf{j}\right)}_{\text{direction of } \mathbf{v}}$$

See Fig. 11.11.

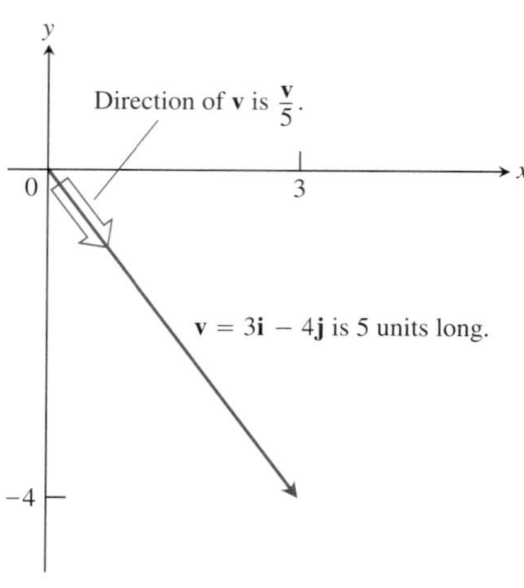

11.11 The vectors in Example 7.

It follows from the definition of direction that vectors $\mathbf{A}$ and $\mathbf{B}$ have the same direction precisely when

$$\frac{\mathbf{A}}{|\mathbf{A}|} = \frac{\mathbf{B}}{|\mathbf{B}|} \quad \text{or} \quad \mathbf{A} = \frac{|\mathbf{A}|}{|\mathbf{B}|}\mathbf{B}. \qquad (12)$$

Thus, if **A** and **B** have the same direction, then **A** is a positive scalar multiple of **B**. Conversely, if $\mathbf{A} = k\,\mathbf{B}$, $k > 0$, then

$$\frac{\mathbf{A}}{|\mathbf{A}|} = \frac{k\mathbf{B}}{|k\mathbf{B}|} = \frac{k}{|k|}\frac{\mathbf{B}}{|\mathbf{B}|} = \frac{k}{k}\frac{\mathbf{B}}{|\mathbf{B}|} = \frac{\mathbf{B}}{|\mathbf{B}|}. \tag{13}$$

Therefore, two nonzero vectors **A** and **B** point in the same direction precisely when **A** is a positive scalar multiple of **B**.

We say that two nonzero vectors **A** and **B** have **opposite** directions if their directions are negatives of one another:

$$\frac{\mathbf{A}}{|\mathbf{A}|} = -\frac{\mathbf{B}}{|\mathbf{B}|}. \tag{14}$$

It follows that **A** and **B** have opposite directions precisely when **A** is a negative scalar multiple of **B**.

EXAMPLE 8

a) Same direction:

$\mathbf{A} = 3\,\mathbf{i} - 4\,\mathbf{j}$ and $\mathbf{B} = \frac{3}{2}\mathbf{i} - 2\,\mathbf{j} = \frac{1}{2}\mathbf{A}$ — **B** is a positive scalar multiple of **A**.

b) Opposite directions:

$\mathbf{A} = 3\,\mathbf{i} - 4\,\mathbf{j}$ and $\mathbf{B} = -9\,\mathbf{i} + 12\,\mathbf{j} = -3\,\mathbf{A}$ — **B** is a negative scalar multiple of **A**.

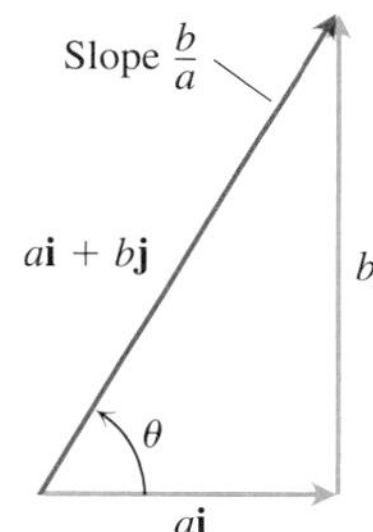

11.12 If $a \neq 0$, the vector $a\,\mathbf{i} + b\,\mathbf{j}$ has slope $b/a = \tan\theta$.

Slopes, Tangents, and Normals

Two vectors are **parallel** if they are nonzero scalar multiples of one another or, equivalently, if the line segments representing them are parallel. Similarly, a vector is parallel to a line if the segments that represent the vector are parallel to the line. The **slope** of a vector that is not parallel to the y-axis is the slope shared by the lines parallel to the vector. Thus, if $a \neq 0$, the vector $\mathbf{v} = a\,\mathbf{i} + b\,\mathbf{j}$ has a well-defined slope, which can be calculated from the components of **v** as the number b/a (Fig. 11.12).

A vector is **tangent** or **normal** to a differentiable curve at a point if it is parallel or normal to the line that is tangent to the curve at the point. The next example shows how to find such vectors.

EXAMPLE 9 Find unit vectors tangent and normal to the curve

$$y = \frac{x^3}{2} + \frac{1}{2}$$

at the point (1, 1).

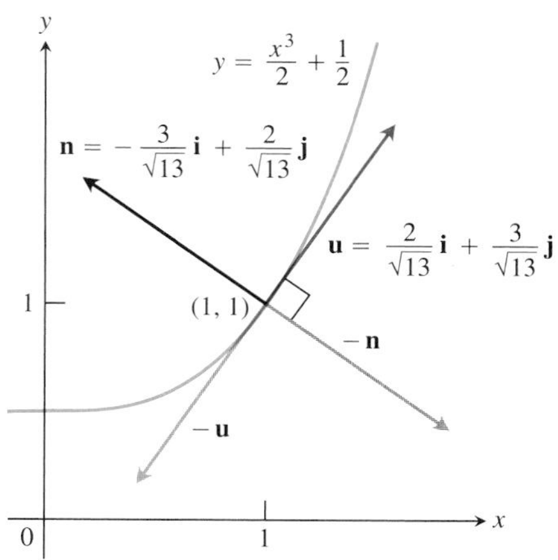

11.13 The unit tangent and normal vectors at the point (1, 1) on the curve $y = (x^3/2) + 1/2$.

Solution We find the unit vectors that are parallel and normal to the curve's tangent line at (1, 1) (Fig. 11.13).

The slope of the line tangent to the curve at (1, 1) is

$$y' = \left.\frac{3x^2}{2}\right|_{x=1} = \frac{3}{2}.$$

We look for a unit vector with this slope. The vector $\mathbf{v} = 2\,\mathbf{i} + 3\,\mathbf{j}$ has slope 3/2, as does every nonzero multiple of $\mathbf{v}$. To find a multiple of $\mathbf{v}$ that is a unit vector, we divide $\mathbf{v}$ by $|\mathbf{v}| = \sqrt{2^2 + 3^2} = \sqrt{13}$, obtaining

$$\mathbf{u} = \frac{\mathbf{v}}{|\mathbf{v}|} = \frac{2}{\sqrt{13}}\mathbf{i} + \frac{3}{\sqrt{13}}\mathbf{j}.$$

The vector $\mathbf{u}$ is tangent to the curve at (1, 1) because it has the same slope as $\mathbf{v}$. Of course, the vector

$$-\mathbf{u} = -\frac{2}{\sqrt{13}}\mathbf{i} - \frac{3}{\sqrt{13}}\mathbf{j},$$

which points in the opposite direction, is also tangent to the curve at (1, 1). Without some additional requirement, there is no reason to prefer one of these vectors to the other.

If $\mathbf{v} = a\,\mathbf{i} + b\,\mathbf{j}$, then $\mathbf{p} = -b\,\mathbf{i} + a\,\mathbf{j}$ and $\mathbf{q} = b\,\mathbf{i} - a\,\mathbf{j}$ are perpendicular to $\mathbf{v}$ because their slopes are both $-a/b$, the negative reciprocal of $\mathbf{v}$'s slope.

To find unit vectors normal to the curve at (1, 1), we look for unit vectors whose slopes are the negative reciprocal of the slope of $\mathbf{u}$. This is quickly done by interchanging the scalar components of $\mathbf{u}$ and changing the sign of one of them. We obtain

$$\mathbf{n} = -\frac{3}{\sqrt{13}}\mathbf{i} + \frac{2}{\sqrt{13}}\mathbf{j} \quad \text{and} \quad -\mathbf{n} = \frac{3}{\sqrt{13}}\mathbf{i} - \frac{2}{\sqrt{13}}\mathbf{j}.$$

Again, either one will do. The vectors have opposite directions but both are normal to the curve at the point (1, 1).

Exercises 11.1

1. The vectors **A, B,** and **C** shown here lie in a plane. Copy them on a sheet of paper. Then, by arranging the vectors head to tail, as in Figs. 11.2 and 11.6, sketch
   - **a)** $\mathbf{A} + \mathbf{B}$
   - **b)** $\mathbf{A} + \mathbf{B} + \mathbf{C}$
   - **c)** $\mathbf{A} - \mathbf{B}$
   - **d)** $\mathbf{A} - \mathbf{C}$

2. The vectors **A**, **B**, and **C** shown here lie in a plane. Copy them on a sheet of paper. Then, by arranging the vectors head to tail, as in Figs. 11.2 and 11.6, sketch
   - **a)** $\mathbf{A} - \mathbf{B}$
   - **b)** $\mathbf{A} - \mathbf{B} + \mathbf{C}$
   - **c)** $2\mathbf{A} - \mathbf{B}$
   - **d)** $\mathbf{A} + \mathbf{B} + \mathbf{C}$

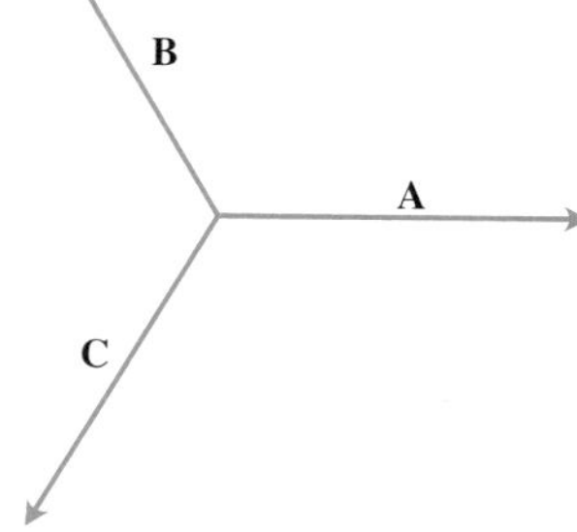

3. Vectors $\mathbf{u}$ and $\mathbf{w}$ are determined by the sides of parallelogram $ABDC$ as shown, and P is the midpoint of the diagonal AD. Express $\overrightarrow{DA}$ and $\overrightarrow{DP}$ in terms of $\mathbf{u}$ and $\mathbf{w}$.

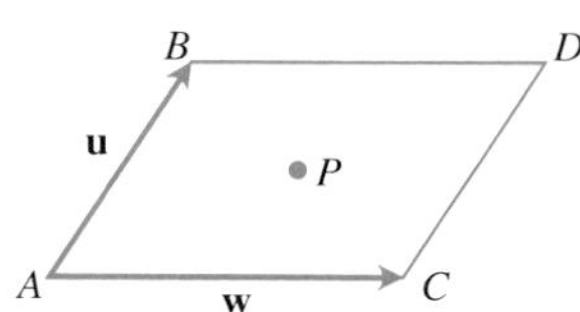

4. *Continuation of Exercise 3.* Express $\overrightarrow{BD} + \overrightarrow{CD}$ in terms of $\mathbf{u}$ and $\mathbf{w}$.

5. Vectors $\mathbf{u}$, $\mathbf{v}$, and $\mathbf{w}$ are determined by the sides of triangle ABC as shown.
   - **a)** Express $\mathbf{w}$ in terms of $\mathbf{u}$ and $\mathbf{v}$.
   - **b)** Express $\mathbf{v}$ in terms of $\mathbf{u}$ and $\mathbf{w}$.

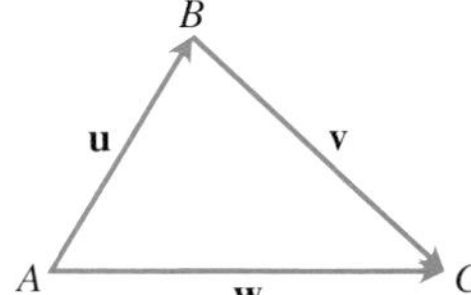

6. *Continuation of Exercise 5.* If P is the midpoint of side BC, express **c** in terms of **v**.

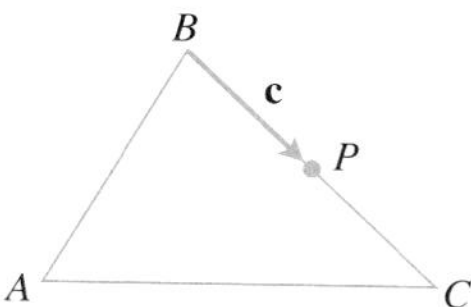

7. Vectors **u** and **w** are determined by the sides of triangle ABC as shown, and P is the midpoint of side BC. Express **a** in terms of **u** and **w**.

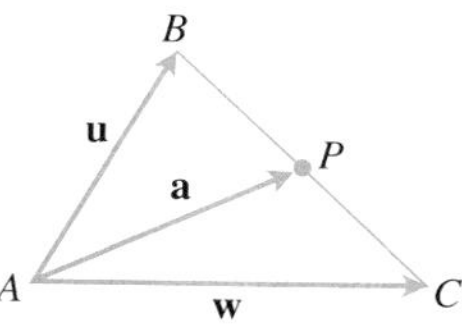

8. Vectors **u**, **v**, and **w** are determined by the sides of triangle ABC as shown, and Q and P are the midpoints of sides AB and BC. Express $\overrightarrow{QP}$ in terms of (a) **u** and **v**, (b) **w**.

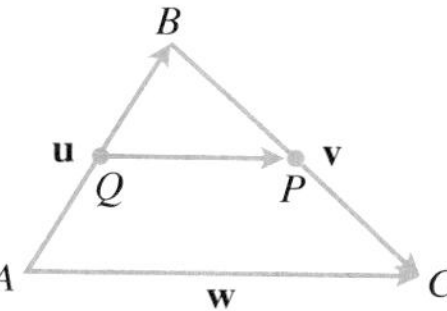

Write the sums and differences in Exercises 9–14 in the form $a\,\mathbf{i} + b\,\mathbf{j}$.

9. $(2\,\mathbf{i} - 7\,\mathbf{j}) + (\mathbf{i} + 6\,\mathbf{j})$

10. $\left(\sqrt{3}\,\mathbf{i} - 3\,\mathbf{j}\right) + 6\,\mathbf{i}$

11. $(-2\,\mathbf{i} + 6\,\mathbf{j}) - 2(\mathbf{i} + \mathbf{j}) + 3\,\mathbf{i} - 4\,\mathbf{j}$

12. $3\left(\frac{\mathbf{i}}{2} - \frac{\mathbf{j}}{3}\right) - \frac{1}{2}(5\,\mathbf{i} - 2\,\mathbf{j})$

13. $2((\ln 2)\,\mathbf{i} + \mathbf{j}) - ((\ln 8)\,\mathbf{i} + \pi\,\mathbf{j})$

14. $\left(\mathbf{i} + \sqrt{2}\,\mathbf{j}\right) - 7(\mathbf{i} - \mathbf{j}) - \sqrt{2}(2\,\mathbf{i} + \mathbf{j})$

Express the vectors in Exercises 15–18 in the form $a\,\mathbf{i} + b\,\mathbf{j}$.

15. $\overrightarrow{P_1P_2}$ if P_1 is the point (1, 3) and P_2 is the point (2, −1)

16. $\overrightarrow{OP_3}$ if O is the origin and P_3 is the midpoint of the vector $\overrightarrow{P_1P_2}$ joining $P_1(2, -1)$ and $P_2(-4, 3)$

17. The vector from the point $A(2, 3)$ to the origin

18. The sum of the vectors $\overrightarrow{AB}$ and $\overrightarrow{CD}$, given the four points $A(1, -1)$, $B(2, 0)$, $C(-1, 3)$, and $D(-2, 2)$

Sketch the vectors in Exercises 19–22 and express each vector in the form $a\,\mathbf{i} + b\,\mathbf{j}$.

19. The unit vectors $\mathbf{u} = (\cos\theta)\,\mathbf{i} + (\sin\theta)\,\mathbf{j}$ for $\theta = \pi/6$ and $\theta = 2\pi/3$. Include the circle $x^2 + y^2 = 1$ in your sketch.

20. The unit vectors $\mathbf{u} = (\cos\theta)\,\mathbf{i} + (\sin\theta)\,\mathbf{j}$ for $\theta = -\pi/4$ and $\theta = -3\pi/4$. Include the circle $x^2 + y^2 = 1$ in your sketch.

21. The unit vector obtained by rotating **j** counterclockwise $3\pi/4$ rad about the origin

22. The unit vector obtained by rotating **j** clockwise $2\pi/3$ rad about the origin

23. You are pulling on a suitcase with a force **F** (pictured here) whose magnitude is $|\mathbf{F}| = 10$ lb. Find the x- and y-components of **F**.

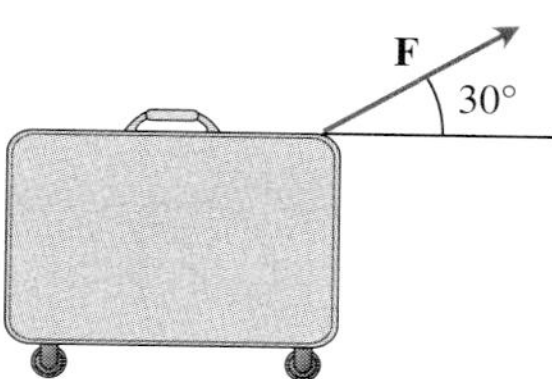

24. A kite string exerts a 12-lb pull $(|\mathbf{F}| = 12)$ on a kite and makes a 45° angle with the horizontal. Find the horizontal and vertical components of **F**.

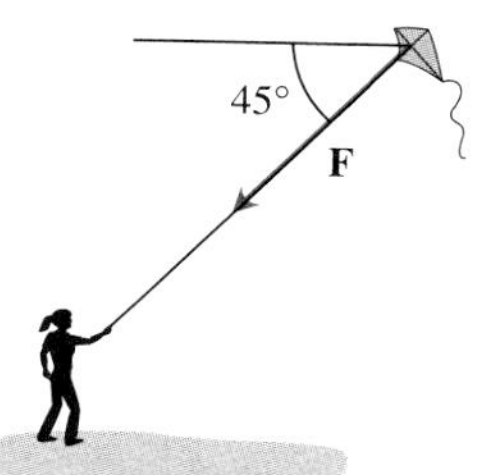

25. A dinghy being towed by a rope that is angled 20° up from the horizontal exerts a pull of 100 lb along the rope $(|\mathbf{F}| = 100)$. Find the horizontal and vertical components of **F** to the nearest decimal place.

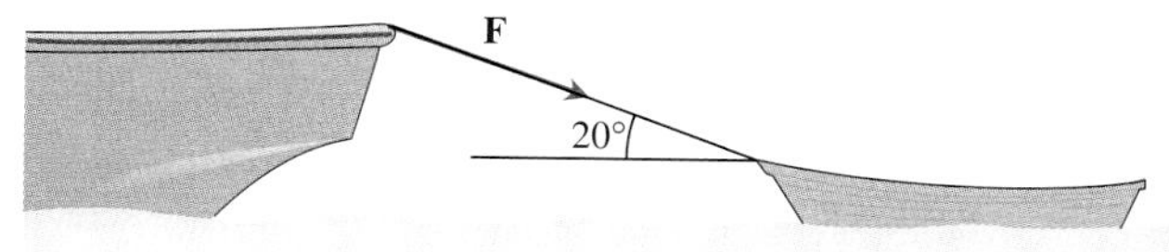

26. You push against a car with an 80-lb force $(|\mathbf{F}| = 80)$ at a slight downward angle of 10°. Find the horizontal and vertical components of **F** to the nearest decimal place.

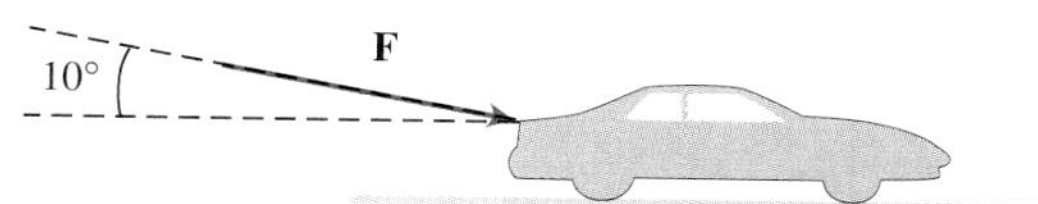

Use Eq. (11) to express the vectors in Exercises 27–32 as products of their lengths and directions.

27. $\mathbf{i} + \mathbf{j}$

28. $2\,\mathbf{i} - 3\,\mathbf{j}$

29. $\sqrt{3}\,\mathbf{i} + \mathbf{j}$

30. $-2\,\mathbf{i} + 3\,\mathbf{j}$

31. $5\,\mathbf{i} + 12\,\mathbf{j}$

32. $-5\,\mathbf{i} - 12\,\mathbf{j}$

33. Show that $\mathbf{A} = -4\,\mathbf{i} + 6\,\mathbf{j}$ and $\mathbf{B} = 2\,\mathbf{i} - 3\,\mathbf{j}$ have opposite directions. Sketch **A** and **B** together.

34. Show that $\mathbf{A} = 3\,\mathbf{i} + 6\,\mathbf{j}$ and $\mathbf{B} = (3/2)\,\mathbf{i} + 3\,\mathbf{j}$ have the same direction. Sketch **A** and **B** together.

35. Find a vector 2 units long in the direction of $\mathbf{A} = -\mathbf{i} - \mathbf{j}$.

36. Find a vector 5 units long in the direction opposite to the direction of $\mathbf{A} = (3/5)\,\mathbf{i} + (4/5)\,\mathbf{j}$.

In Exercises 37–42, find the unit vectors that are tangent and normal to the curve at the given point (four vectors in all). Show the curve and vectors together in a sketch.

37. $y = x^2$, $(2, 4)$

38. $y = e^x$, $(\ln 2, 2)$

39. $x^2 + 2y^2 = 6$, $(2, 1)$

40. $4x^2 + y^2 = 16$, $(\sqrt{2}, -2\sqrt{2})$

41. $y = \tan^{-1} x$, $(1, \pi/4)$

42. $y = \sin^{-1} x$, $(\sqrt{2}/2, \pi/4)$

43. Let **v** be a vector in the plane not parallel to the y-axis. How is the slope of $-\mathbf{v}$ related to the slope of **v**? Give reasons for your answer.

44. Is it true that the zero vector is the only vector whose length is zero? Give reasons for your answer.

Writing for Your Own Knowledge

Answer the following questions in writing. Some answers will take only a sentence or two; others may require several paragraphs. Some explanations may also call for graphs or sketches.

1. How do you add and subtract vectors geometrically? algebraically?
2. What is a vector's magnitude? How can you express a nonzero vector in terms of its magnitude and direction?
3. What is scalar multiplication? How can you interpret it geometrically? When are two vectors parallel?
4. How do you find unit vectors that are tangent and normal to a curve at a point where the curve is differentiable?

11.2 Cartesian (Rectangular) Coordinates and Vectors in Space

Our goal now is to describe the three-dimensional Cartesian coordinate system and learn our way around in space. This means defining distance, practicing with the arithmetic of vectors (the rules are the same as in the plane but with an extra term), and making connections between sets of points and equations and inequalities.

Cartesian Coordinates

To locate points in space, we use three mutually perpendicular coordinate axes, arranged as in Fig. 11.14. The axes Ox, Oy, and Oz shown there make a *right-handed* coordinate frame. When you hold your right hand so that the fingers curl from the positive x-axis toward the positive y-axis, your thumb points along the positive z-axis.

The Cartesian coordinates (x, y, z) of a point P in space are the numbers at which the planes through P perpendicular to the axes cut the axes.

Points on the x-axis have y- and z-coordinates equal to zero. That is, they have coordinates of the form $(x, 0, 0)$. Similarly, points on the y-axis have coordinates of the form $(0, y, 0)$. Points on the z-axis have coordinates of the form $(0, 0, z)$.

The points in a plane perpendicular to the x-axis all have the same x-coordinate, this being the number at which that plane cuts the x-axis. Similarly, the points in a plane perpendicular to the y-axis have a common y-coordinate and the points in a plane perpendicular to the z-axis have a common z-coordinate. To write equations for these planes, we name the common coordinate's value. The plane $x = 2$ is the plane perpendicular to the x-axis at $x = 2$. The plane $y = 3$ is the plane perpendicular to the y-axis at $y = 3$. The plane $z = 5$ is the plane perpendicular to the z-axis at $z = 5$. Figure 11.15 shows the planes $x = 2$, $y = 3$, and $z = 5$, together with their intersection point $(2, 3, 5)$.

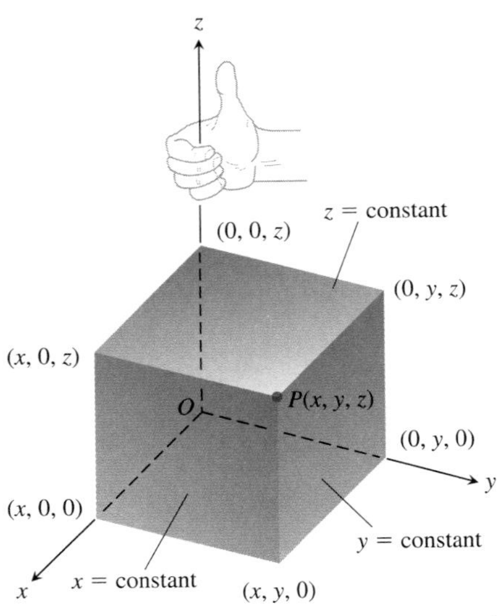

11.14 The Cartesian coordinate system is right-handed.

Cartesian coordinates for space are also called *rectangular coordinates* because the axes that define them meet at right angles.

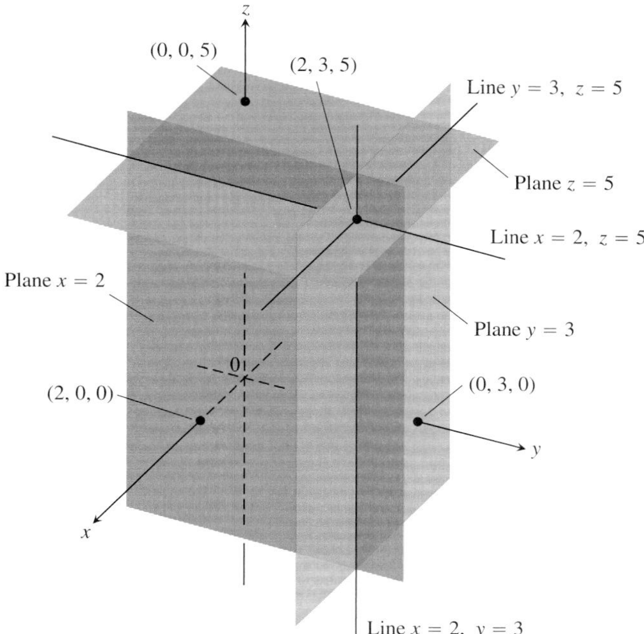

11.15 The planes $x = 2$, $y = 3$, and $z = 5$ determine three lines through the point (2, 3, 5).

The planes $x = 2$ and $y = 3$ in Fig. 11.15 intersect in a line parallel to the z-axis. This line is described by the *pair* of equations $x = 2$, $y = 3$. A point (x, y, z) lies on the line if and only if $x = 2$ and $y = 3$. Similarly, the line of intersection of the planes $y = 3$ and $z = 5$ is described by the equation pair $y = 3$, $z = 5$. This line runs parallel to the x-axis. The line of intersection of the planes $x = 2$ and $z = 5$, parallel to the y-axis, is described by the equation pair $x = 2$, $z = 5$.

The planes determined by the coordinate axes are the ***xy*-plane,** whose standard equation is $z = 0$; the ***yz*-plane**, whose standard equation is $x = 0$; and the ***xz*-plane,** whose standard equation is $y = 0$. They meet at the **origin** $(0, 0, 0)$ (Fig. 11.16).

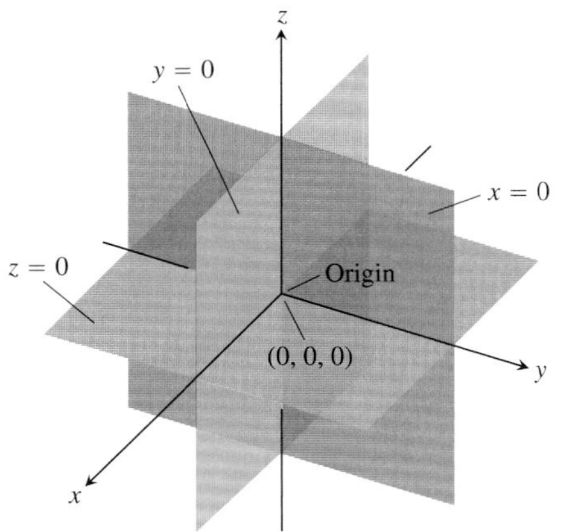

11.16 The planes $x = 0$, $y = 0$, and $z = 0$ divide space into eight octants.

The three **coordinate planes** $x = 0$, $y = 0$, and $z = 0$ divide space into eight cells called **octants.** The octant in which the point coordinates are all positive is called the **first octant;** there is no conventional numbering for the other seven octants.

In the following examples, we match coordinate equations and inequalities with the sets of points they define in space.

EXAMPLE 1

Defining equations and inequalities	Verbal description
$z \geq 0$	The half-space consisting of the points on and above the xy-plane.
$x = -3$	The plane perpendicular to the x-axis at $x = -3$. This plane lies parallel to the yz-plane and 3 units behind it.

(continued)

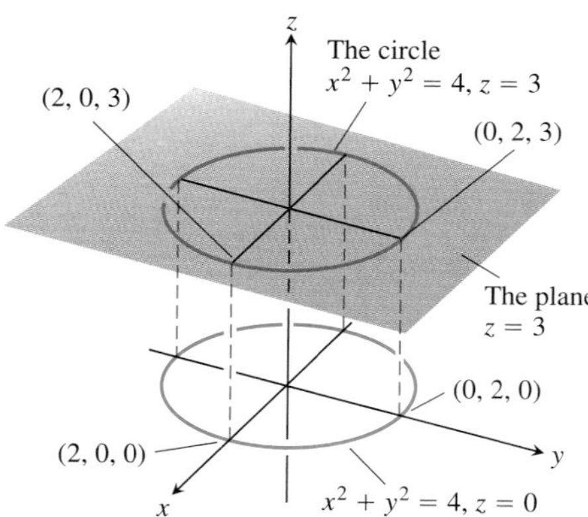

11.17 The circle $x^2 + y^2 = 4$, $z = 3$.

Defining equations and inequalities	Verbal description
$z = 0, x \leq 0, y \geq 0$	The second quadrant of the xy-plane.
$x \geq 0, y \geq 0, z \geq 0$	The first octant.
$-1 \leq y \leq 1$	The slab between the planes $y = -1$ and $y = 1$ (planes included).
$y = -2, z = 2$	The line in which the planes $y = -2$ and $z = 2$ intersect. Alternatively, the line through the point $(0, -2, 2)$ parallel to the x-axis.

EXAMPLE 2 What points $P(x, y, z)$ satisfy the equations

$$x^2 + y^2 = 4 \quad \text{and} \quad z = 3?$$

Solution The points lie in the horizontal plane $z = 3$ and, in this plane, make up the circle $x^2 + y^2 = 4$. We call this set of points "the circle $x^2 + y^2 = 4$ in the plane $z = 3$" or, more simply, "the circle $x^2 + y^2 = 4$, $z = 3$" (Fig. 11.17).

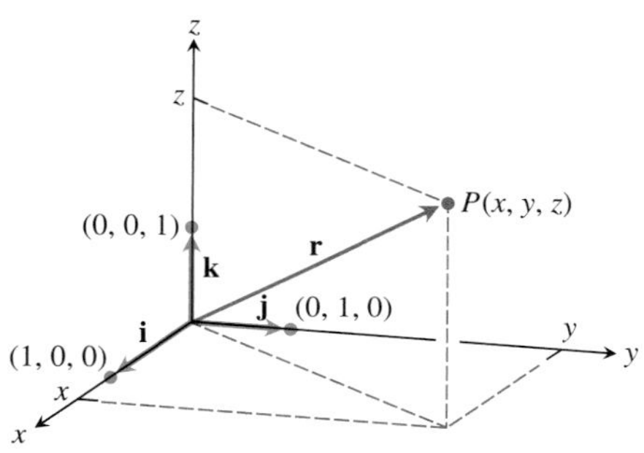

11.18 The position vector of a point in space.

Vectors in Space

The sets of equivalent directed line segments we use to represent forces, displacements, and velocities in space are called vectors, just as in the plane. The same rules of addition, subtraction, and scalar multiplication apply.

The vectors represented by the directed line segments from the origin to the points (1, 0, 0), (0, 1, 0), and (0, 0, 1) are the **basic vectors** (Fig. 11.18). We denote them by **i**, **j**, and **k**. The **position vector r** from the origin O to the typical point $P(x, y, z)$ is

$$\mathbf{r} = \overrightarrow{OP} = x\,\mathbf{i} + y\,\mathbf{j} + z\,\mathbf{k}. \tag{1}$$

Addition, Subtraction, and Scalar Multiplication for Vectors in Space

For any vectors $\mathbf{A} = a_1\,\mathbf{i} + a_2\,\mathbf{j} + a_3\,\mathbf{k}$ and $\mathbf{B} = b_1\,\mathbf{i} + b_2\,\mathbf{j} + b_3\,\mathbf{k}$, and for any scalar c,

$$\begin{aligned}\mathbf{A} + \mathbf{B} &= (a_1 + b_1)\,\mathbf{i} + (a_2 + b_2)\,\mathbf{j} + (a_3 + b_3)\,\mathbf{k}\\ \mathbf{A} - \mathbf{B} &= (a_1 - b_1)\,\mathbf{i} + (a_2 - b_2)\,\mathbf{j} + (a_3 - b_3)\,\mathbf{k}\\ c\,\mathbf{A} &= (ca_1)\,\mathbf{i} + (ca_2)\,\mathbf{j} + (ca_3)\,\mathbf{k}.\end{aligned}$$

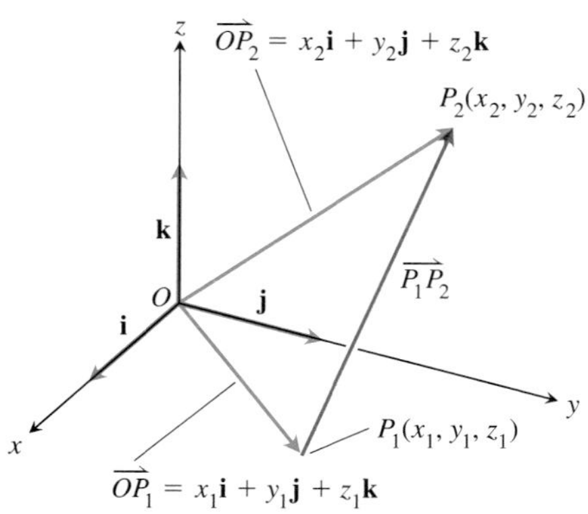

11.19 The vector from P_1 to P_2 is $\overrightarrow{P_1P_2} = (x_2 - x_1)\,\mathbf{i} + (y_2 - y_1)\,\mathbf{j} + (z_2 - z_1)\,\mathbf{k}$.

The Vector Between Two Points

We can express the vector $\overrightarrow{P_1P_2}$ from the point $P_1(x_1, y_1, z_1)$ to the point $P_2(x_2, y_2, z_2)$ in terms of the coordinates of P_1 and P_2 because (Fig. 11.19)

$$\begin{aligned}\overrightarrow{P_1P_2} &= \overrightarrow{OP_2} - \overrightarrow{OP_1}\\ &= (x_2\,\mathbf{i} + y_2\,\mathbf{j} + z_2\,\mathbf{k}) - (x_1\,\mathbf{i} + y_1\,\mathbf{j} + z_1\,\mathbf{k})\\ &= (x_2 - x_1)\,\mathbf{i} + (y_2 - y_1)\,\mathbf{j} + (z_2 - z_1)\,\mathbf{k}.\end{aligned} \tag{2}$$

The vector from $P_1(x_1, y_1, z_1)$ to $P_2(x_2, y_2, z_2)$ is

$$\overrightarrow{P_1P_2} = (x_2 - x_1)\,\mathbf{i} + (y_2 - y_1)\,\mathbf{j} + (z_2 - z_1)\,\mathbf{k}. \tag{3}$$

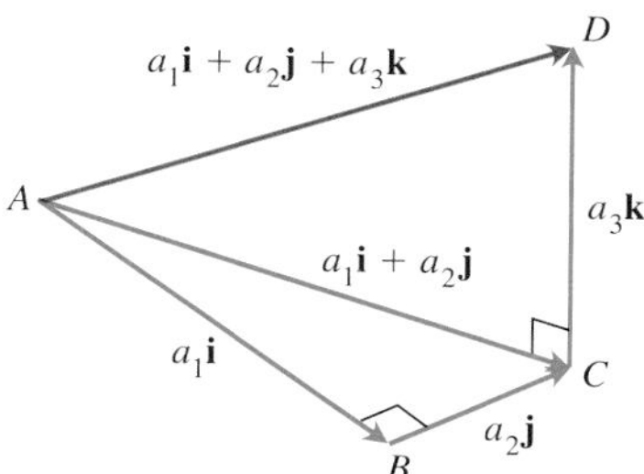

11.20 We find the length of $\overrightarrow{AD}$ by applying the Pythagorean theorem to the right triangles *ABC* and *ACD*.

Magnitude and Direction

As always, the important features of a vector are its magnitude and direction. We find a formula for the magnitude (length) of $a_1\,\mathbf{i} + a_2\,\mathbf{j} + a_3\,\mathbf{k}$ by applying the Pythagorean theorem to the right triangles in Fig. 11.20. From triangle *ABC*,

$$|\overrightarrow{AC}| = \sqrt{a_1^2 + a_2^2}$$

and from triangle *ACD*

$$|a_1\,\mathbf{i} + a_2\,\mathbf{j} + a_3\,\mathbf{k}| = |\overrightarrow{AD}| = \sqrt{|\overrightarrow{AC}|^2 + |\overrightarrow{CD}|^2} = \sqrt{a_1^2 + a_2^2 + a_3^2}.$$

The **magnitude (length)** of $\mathbf{A} = a_1\,\mathbf{i} + a_2\,\mathbf{j} + a_3\,\mathbf{k}$ is

$$|\mathbf{A}| = |a_1\,\mathbf{i} + a_2\,\mathbf{j} + a_3\,\mathbf{k}| = \sqrt{a_1^2 + a_2^2 + a_3^2}. \tag{4}$$

EXAMPLE 3 The length of $\mathbf{A} = \mathbf{i} - 2\,\mathbf{j} + 3\,\mathbf{k}$ is

$$|\mathbf{A}| = \sqrt{(1)^2 + (-2)^2 + (3)^2} = \sqrt{1 + 4 + 9} = \sqrt{14}.$$

If we multiply $\mathbf{A} = a_1\,\mathbf{i} + a_2\,\mathbf{j} + a_3\,\mathbf{k}$ by a scalar c, the length of $c\mathbf{A}$ is $|c|$ times the length of $\mathbf{A}$, as in the plane. The reason is the same, as well:

$$\begin{aligned} c\,\mathbf{A} &= ca_1\,\mathbf{i} + ca_2\,\mathbf{j} + ca_3\,\mathbf{k}, \\ |c\,\mathbf{A}| &= \sqrt{(ca_1)^2 + (ca_2)^2 + (ca_3)^2} = \sqrt{c^2a_1^2 + c^2a_2^2 + c^2a_3^2} \\ &= |c|\sqrt{a_1^2 + a_2^2 + a_3^2} = |c||\mathbf{A}|. \end{aligned} \tag{5}$$

EXAMPLE 4 If $\mathbf{A}$ is the vector of Example 3, then the length of

$$2\,\mathbf{A} = 2(\mathbf{i} - 2\,\mathbf{j} + 3\,\mathbf{k}) = 2\,\mathbf{i} - 4\,\mathbf{j} + 6\,\mathbf{k}$$

is

$$\begin{aligned} \sqrt{(2)^2 + (-4)^2 + (6)^2} &= \sqrt{4 + 16 + 36} = \sqrt{56} \\ &= \sqrt{4 \cdot 14} = 2\sqrt{14} = 2|\mathbf{A}|. \end{aligned}$$

As with vectors in the plane, vectors of length 1 are called **unit vectors.** The vectors $\mathbf{i}$, $\mathbf{j}$, and $\mathbf{k}$ are unit vectors because

$$\begin{aligned} |\mathbf{i}| &= |1\,\mathbf{i} + 0\,\mathbf{j} + 0\,\mathbf{k}| = \sqrt{1^2 + 0^2 + 0^2} = 1, \\ |\mathbf{j}| &= |0\,\mathbf{i} + 1\,\mathbf{j} + 0\,\mathbf{k}| = \sqrt{0^2 + 1^2 + 0^2} = 1, \\ |\mathbf{k}| &= |0\,\mathbf{i} + 0\,\mathbf{j} + 1\,\mathbf{k}| = \sqrt{0^2 + 0^2 + 1^2} = 1. \end{aligned}$$

The direction of a nonzero vector $\mathbf{A}$ is the unit vector obtained by dividing $\mathbf{A}$ by its length.

$$\text{The **direction** of } \mathbf{A} \text{ is } \frac{\mathbf{A}}{|\mathbf{A}|}. \qquad (\mathbf{A} \neq \mathbf{0}) \tag{6}$$

As in the plane, we use the equation

$$\mathbf{A} = |\mathbf{A}| \cdot \frac{\mathbf{A}}{|\mathbf{A}|} \tag{7}$$

to express a nonzero vector as a product of its length and direction.

EXAMPLE 5 Express $\mathbf{A} = \mathbf{i} - 2\,\mathbf{j} + 3\,\mathbf{k}$ as a product of its length and direction.

Solution

$$\begin{aligned}
\mathbf{A} &= |\mathbf{A}| \cdot \frac{\mathbf{A}}{|\mathbf{A}|} && \text{Eq. (7)} \\
&= \sqrt{14} \cdot \frac{\mathbf{i} - 2\,\mathbf{j} + 3\,\mathbf{k}}{\sqrt{14}} && \text{From Example 3} \\
&= \sqrt{14}\left(\frac{1}{\sqrt{14}}\mathbf{i} - \frac{2}{\sqrt{14}}\mathbf{j} + \frac{3}{\sqrt{14}}\mathbf{k}\right) = (\text{length of } \mathbf{A}) \cdot (\text{direction of } \mathbf{A})
\end{aligned}$$

EXAMPLE 6 Find a unit vector $\mathbf{u}$ in the direction of the vector from $P_1(1, 0, 1)$ to $P_2(3, 2, 0)$.

Solution To find the direction of $\overrightarrow{P_1P_2}$, we divide $\overrightarrow{P_1P_2}$ by its length:

$$\overrightarrow{P_1P_2} = (3 - 1)\,\mathbf{i} + (2 - 0)\,\mathbf{j} + (0 - 1)\,\mathbf{k} = 2\,\mathbf{i} + 2\,\mathbf{j} - \mathbf{k}$$

$$|\overrightarrow{P_1P_2}| = \sqrt{(2)^2 + (2)^2 + (-1)^2} = \sqrt{4 + 4 + 1} = \sqrt{9} = 3$$

$$\mathbf{u} = \frac{\overrightarrow{P_1P_2}}{|\overrightarrow{P_1P_2}|} = \frac{2\,\mathbf{i} + 2\,\mathbf{j} - \mathbf{k}}{3} = \frac{2}{3}\mathbf{i} + \frac{2}{3}\mathbf{j} - \frac{1}{3}\mathbf{k}.$$

EXAMPLE 7 Find a vector 6 units long in the direction of $\mathbf{A} = 2\,\mathbf{i} + 2\,\mathbf{j} - \mathbf{k}$.

Solution The vector we want is

$$6\frac{\mathbf{A}}{|\mathbf{A}|} = 6\frac{2\,\mathbf{i} + 2\,\mathbf{j} - \mathbf{k}}{\sqrt{2^2 + 2^2 + (-1)^2}} = 6\frac{2\,\mathbf{i} + 2\,\mathbf{j} - \mathbf{k}}{3} = 4\,\mathbf{i} + 4\,\mathbf{j} - 2\,\mathbf{k}.$$

Distance in Space

The distance between two points P_1 and P_2 in space is the length of $\overrightarrow{P_1P_2}$.

The Distance Between $P_1(x_1, y_1, z_1)$ and $P_2(x_2, y_2, z_2)$

$$|\overrightarrow{P_1P_2}| = \sqrt{(x_2 - x_1)^2 + (y_2 - y_1)^2 + (z_2 - z_1)^2} \tag{8}$$

EXAMPLE 8 The distance between $P_1(2, 1, 5)$ and $P_2(-2, 3, 0)$ is

$$\begin{aligned}|\overrightarrow{P_1P_2}| &= \sqrt{(-2-2)^2 + (3-1)^2 + (0-5)^2} \\ &= \sqrt{16+4+25} \\ &= \sqrt{45} = 3\sqrt{5}.\end{aligned}$$

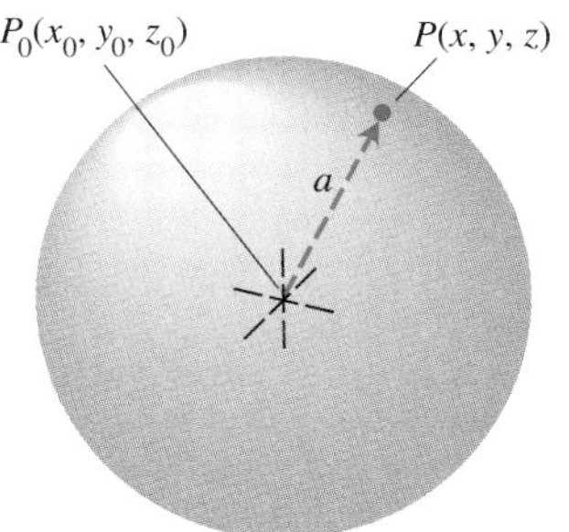

11.21 The standard equation of the sphere of radius a centered at (x_0, y_0, z_0) is

$$(x-x_0)^2 + (y-y_0)^2 + (z-z_0)^2 = a^2.$$

Spheres

We use Eq. (8) to write equations for spheres (Fig. 11.21). Since a point $P(x, y, z)$ lies on the sphere of radius a centered at $P_0(x_0, y_0, z_0)$ precisely when it lies a units from P_0, it lies on the sphere if and only if $|\overrightarrow{P_0P}| = a$ or

$$(x-x_0)^2 + (y-y_0)^2 + (z-z_0)^2 = a^2.$$

The Standard Equation for the Sphere of Radius a and Center (x_0, y_0, z_0)

$$(x-x_0)^2 + (y-y_0)^2 + (z-z_0)^2 = a^2 \tag{9}$$

EXAMPLE 9 Find the center and radius of the sphere $x^2 + y^2 + z^2 + 3x - 4z + 1 = 0$.

Solution We find the center and radius of a sphere the way we find the center and radius of a circle: Complete the squares on the x-, y-, and z-terms as necessary and write each quadratic as a squared linear expression. Then, from the equation in standard form, read off the center and radius. For the sphere here we have

$$\begin{gathered}x^2 + y^2 + z^2 + 3x - 4z + 1 = 0 \\ (x^2 + 3x \quad) + y^2 + (z^2 - 4z \quad) = -1 \\ \left(x^2 + 3x + \left(\frac{3}{2}\right)^2\right) + y^2 + \left(z^2 - 4z + \left(\frac{-4}{2}\right)^2\right) = -1 + \left(\frac{3}{2}\right)^2 + \left(\frac{-4}{2}\right)^2 \\ \left(x + \frac{3}{2}\right)^2 + y^2 + (z-2)^2 = -1 + \frac{9}{4} + 4 = \frac{21}{4}.\end{gathered}$$

This is Eq. (9) with $x_0 = -3/2$, $y_0 = 0$, $z_0 = 2$, and $a = \sqrt{21}/2$. The center is $(-3/2, 0, 2)$. The radius is $\sqrt{21}/2$.

EXAMPLE 10 *Sets Bounded by Spheres or Portions of Spheres*

Defining equations and inequalities	Description
a) $x^2 + y^2 + z^2 < 4$	The interior of the sphere $x^2 + y^2 + z^2 = 4$.
b) $x^2 + y^2 + z^2 \leq 4$	The solid ball bounded by the sphere $x^2 + y^2 + z^2 = 4$. Alternatively, the sphere $x^2 + y^2 + z^2 = 4$ together with its interior.
c) $x^2 + y^2 + z^2 > 4$	The exterior of the sphere $x^2 + y^2 + z^2 = 4$.
d) $x^2 + y^2 + z^2 = 4$, $z \leq 0$	The lower hemisphere cut from the sphere $x^2 + y^2 + z^2 = 4$ by the xy-plane (the plane $z = 0$).

Drawing Lesson

How to Draw Three-dimensional Objects to Look Three-dimensional

1 Break lines. When one line passes behind another, break it to show that it doesn't touch and that part of it is hidden.

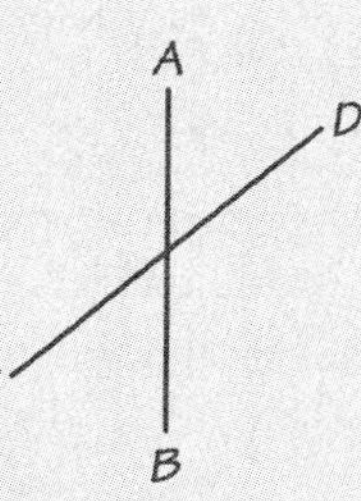

Intersecting

CD behind *AB*

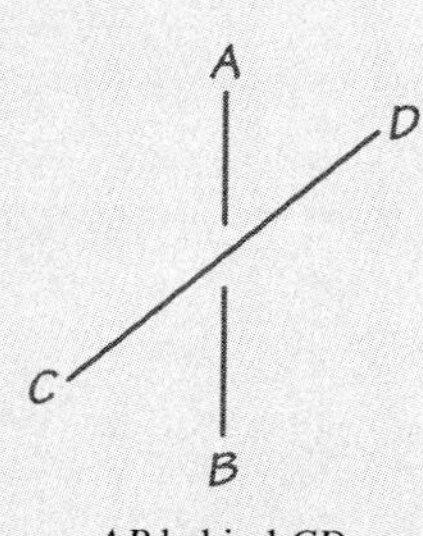

AB behind *CD*

2 Make the angle between the positive x-axis and the positive y-axis large enough.

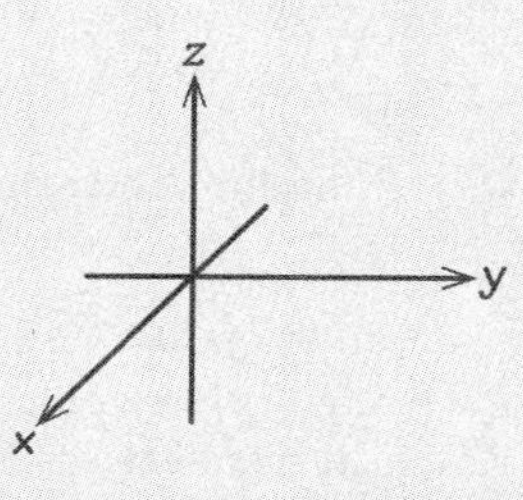

This

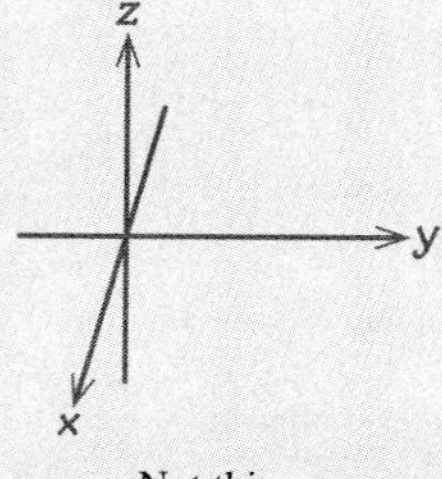

Not this

3 Draw planes parallel to the coordinate planes as if they were rectangles with sides parallel to the coordinate axes.

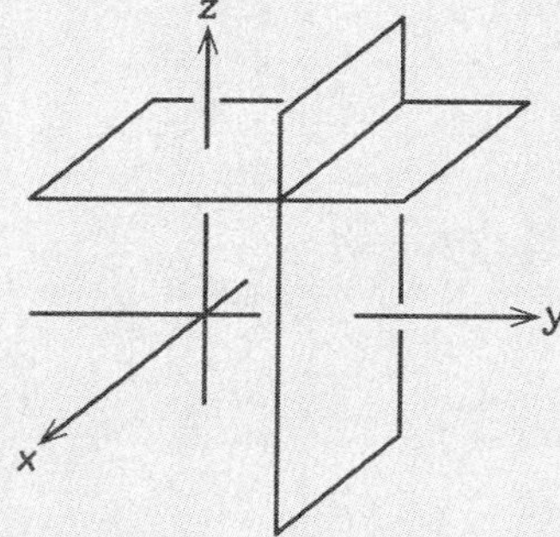

4 Dash or omit hidden portions of lines. Don't let the line touch the boundary of the parallelogram that represents the plane, unless the line lies in the plane.

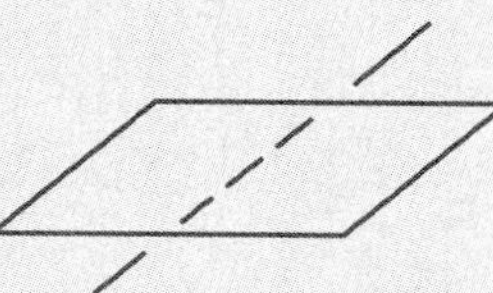
Line below plane

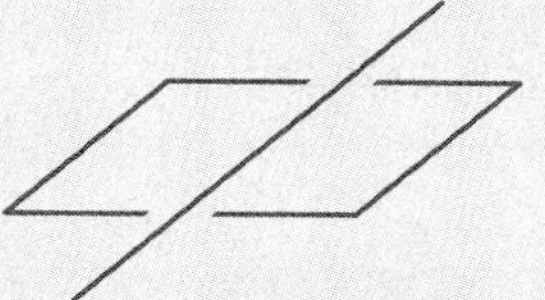
Line above plane

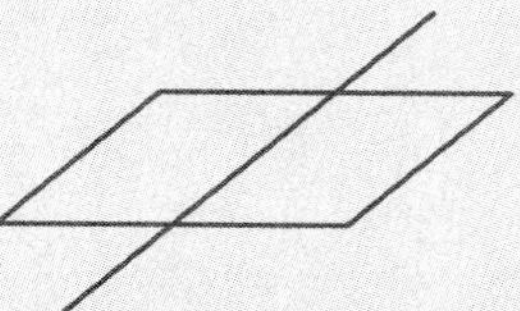
Line *in* plane

5 Spheres: Draw the sphere first (outline and equator); draw axes, if any, later. Use line breaks and dashed lines.

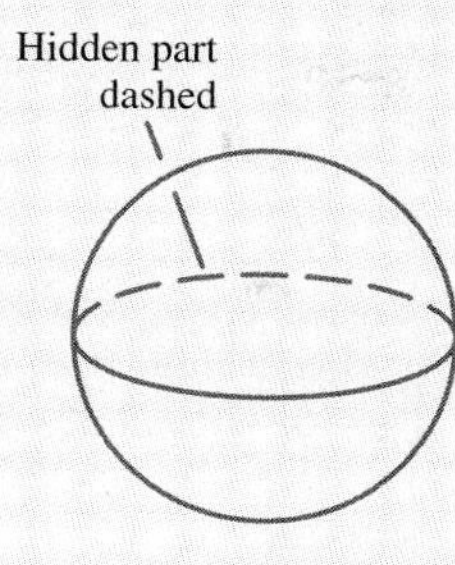

Sphere first

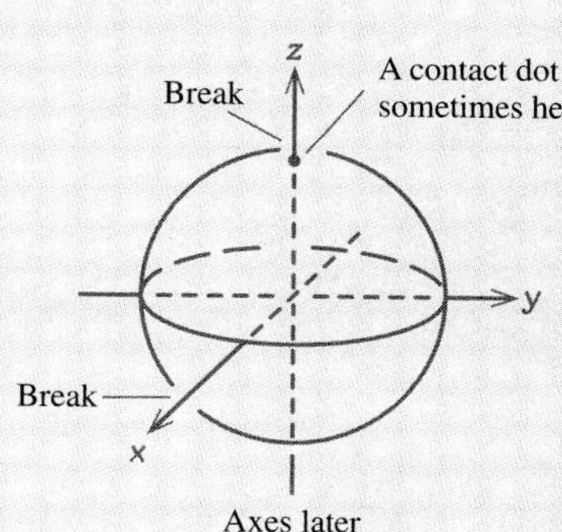

Axes later

6 A general rule for perspective: Draw the object as if it lies some distance away, below, and to your left.

Advice ignored

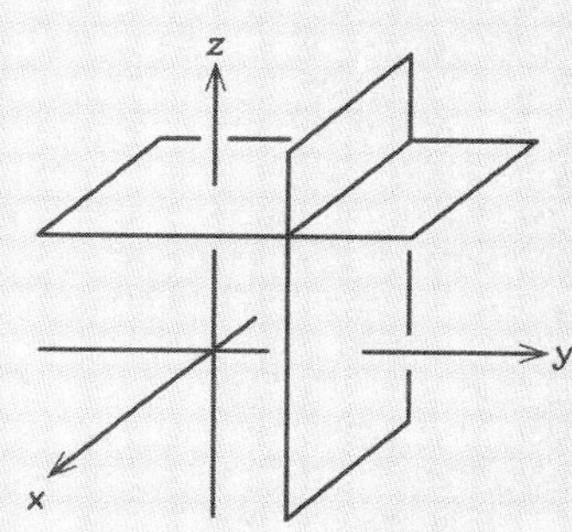

Advice followed

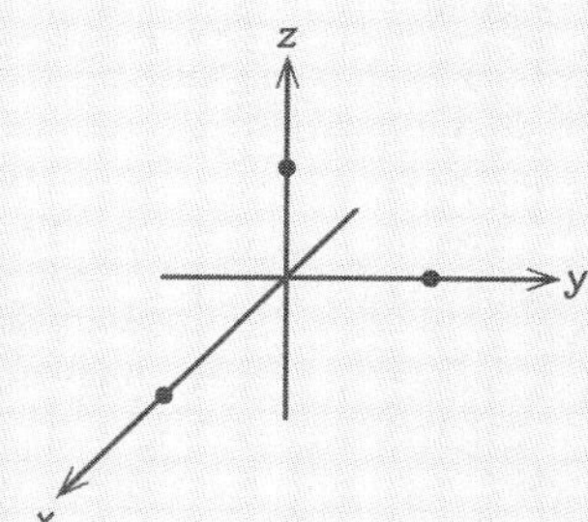

(a)

(b)

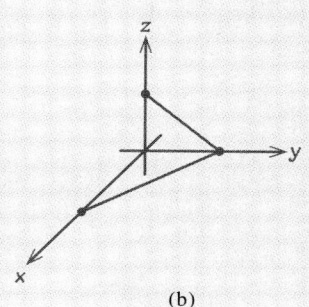

7 To draw a plane that crosses all three coordinate axes, follow the steps shown here: (a) Sketch the axes and mark the intercepts. (b) Connect the intercepts to form two sides of a parallelogram. (c) Complete the parallelogram and enlarge it by drawing lines parallel to its sides. (d) Darken the exposed parts, break hidden lines, and, if desired, dash hidden portions of the axes. You may wish to erase the smaller parallelogram at this point.

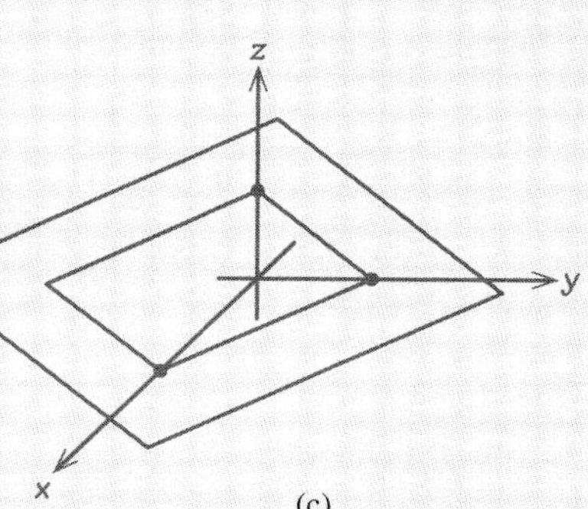

(c)

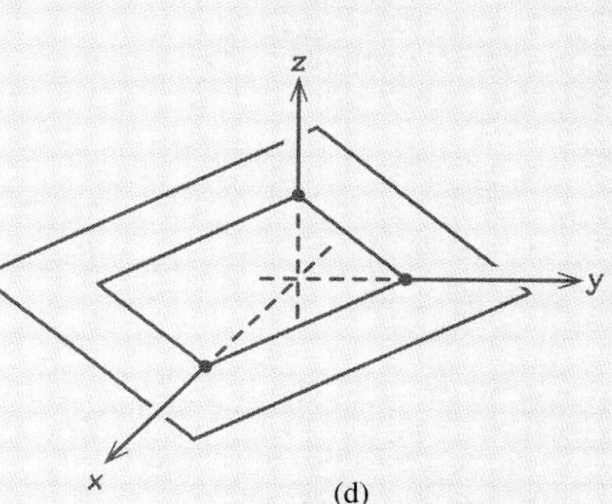

(d)

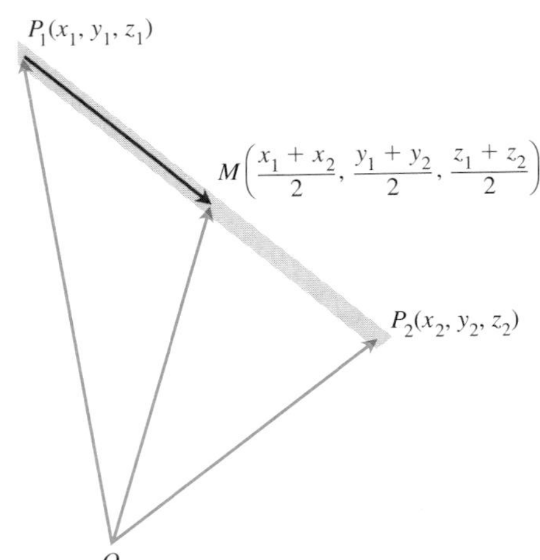

11.22 The coordinates of the midpoint are the averages of the coordinates of P_1 and P_2.

Midpoints of Line Segments

The coordinates of the midpoint M of the line segment joining two points $P_1(x_1, y_1, z_1)$ and $P_2(x_2, y_2, z_2)$ are found by averaging the coordinates of P_1 and P_2:

$$M = \left(\frac{x_1 + x_2}{2}, \frac{y_1 + y_2}{2}, \frac{z_1 + z_2}{2}\right). \tag{10}$$

To see why, observe that these coordinates are the scalar components of the position vector $\overrightarrow{OM}$ (Fig. 11.22) and that

$$\begin{aligned} \overrightarrow{OM} &= \overrightarrow{OP_1} + \frac{1}{2}(\overrightarrow{P_1P_2}) = \overrightarrow{OP_1} + \frac{1}{2}(\overrightarrow{OP_2} - \overrightarrow{OP_1}) \\ &= \frac{1}{2}(\overrightarrow{OP_1} + \overrightarrow{OP_2}) \\ &= \frac{x_1 + x_2}{2}\mathbf{i} + \frac{y_1 + y_2}{2}\mathbf{j} + \frac{z_1 + z_2}{2}\mathbf{k}. \end{aligned}$$

EXAMPLE 11 The midpoint of the segment joining $P_1(3, -2, 0)$ and $P_2(7, 4, 4)$ is

$$\left(\frac{3+7}{2}, \frac{-2+4}{2}, \frac{0+4}{2}\right) = (5, 1, 2).$$

Exercises 11.2

In Exercises 1–12, give a geometric description of the set of points in space whose coordinates satisfy the given pairs of equations.

1. $x = 2, \quad y = 3$
2. $x = -1, \quad z = 0$
3. $y = 0, \quad z = 0$
4. $x = 1, \quad y = 0$
5. $x^2 + y^2 = 4, \quad z = 0$
6. $x^2 + y^2 = 4, \quad z = -2$
7. $x^2 + z^2 = 4, \quad y = 0$
8. $y^2 + z^2 = 1, \quad x = 0$
9. $x^2 + y^2 + z^2 = 1, \quad x = 0$
10. $x^2 + y^2 + z^2 = 25, \quad y = -4$
11. $x^2 + y^2 + (z + 3)^2 = 25, \quad z = 0$
12. $x^2 + (y - 1)^2 + z^2 = 4, \quad y = 0$

In Exercises 13–18, describe the sets of points in space whose coordinates satisfy the given inequalities or combinations of equations and inequalities.

13. a) $x \geq 0, \quad y \geq 0, \quad z = 0$
    b) $x \geq 0, \quad y \leq 0, \quad z = 0$
14. a) $0 \leq x \leq 1$
    b) $0 \leq x \leq 1, \quad 0 \leq y \leq 1$
    c) $0 \leq x \leq 1, \quad 0 \leq y \leq 1, \quad 0 \leq z \leq 1$
15. a) $x^2 + y^2 + z^2 \leq 1$
    b) $x^2 + y^2 + z^2 > 1$
16. a) $x^2 + y^2 \leq 1, \quad z = 0$
    b) $x^2 + y^2 \leq 1, \quad z = 3$
    c) $x^2 + y^2 \leq 1$, no restriction on z
17. a) $x^2 + y^2 + z^2 = 1, \quad z \geq 0$
    b) $x^2 + y^2 + z^2 \leq 1, \quad z \geq 0$
18. a) $x = y, \quad z = 0$
    b) $x = y$, no restriction on z

In Exercises 19–28, describe the given set with a single equation or with a pair of equations.

19. The plane perpendicular to the
    a) x-axis at $(3, 0, 0)$
    b) y-axis at $(0, -1, 0)$
    c) z-axis at $(0, 0, -2)$
20. The plane through the point $(3, -1, 2)$ perpendicular to the
    a) x-axis b) y-axis c) z-axis
21. The plane through the point $(3, -1, 1)$ parallel to the
    a) xy-plane b) yz-plane c) xz-plane
22. The circle of radius 2 centered at $(0, 0, 0)$ and lying in the
    a) xy-plane b) yz-plane c) xz-plane
23. The circle of radius 2 centered at $(0, 2, 0)$ and lying in the
    a) xy-plane b) yz-plane c) plane $y = 2$
24. The circle of radius 1 centered at $(-3, 4, 1)$ and lying in a plane parallel to the
    a) xy-plane b) yz-plane c) xz-plane

25. The line through the point (1, 3, −1) parallel to the
   a) x-axis b) y-axis c) z-axis

26. The set of points in space equidistant from the origin and the point (0, 2, 0)

27. The circle in which the plane through the point (1, 1, 3) perpendicular to the z-axis meets the sphere of radius 5 centered at the origin

28. The set of points in space that lie 2 units from the point (0, 0, 1) and, at the same time, 2 units from the point (0, 0, −1)

Write inequalities to describe the sets in Exercises 29–34.

29. The slab bounded by the planes $z = 0$ and $z = 1$ (planes included)

30. The solid cube in the first octant bounded by the coordinate planes and the planes $x = 2$, $y = 2$, and $z = 2$

31. The half-space consisting of the points on and below the xy-plane

32. The upper hemisphere of the sphere of radius 1 centered at the origin

33. The (a) interior and (b) exterior of the sphere of radius 1 centered at the point (1, 1, 1)

34. The closed region bounded by the spheres of radius 1 and radius 2 centered at the origin. (*Closed* means the spheres are to be included. Had we wanted the spheres left out, we would have asked for the *open* region bounded by the spheres. This is analogous to the way we use "closed" and "open" to describe intervals: "closed" means endpoints included, "open" means endpoints left out. Closed sets include boundaries; open sets leave them out.)

In Exercises 35–44, express each vector as a product of its length and direction.

35. $2\mathbf{i} + \mathbf{j} - 2\mathbf{k}$

36. $3\mathbf{i} - 6\mathbf{j} + 2\mathbf{k}$

37. $\mathbf{i} + 4\mathbf{j} - 8\mathbf{k}$

38. $9\mathbf{i} - 2\mathbf{j} + 6\mathbf{k}$

39. $5\mathbf{k}$

40. $-4\mathbf{j}$

41. $\frac{3}{5}\mathbf{i} + \frac{4}{5}\mathbf{k}$

42. $\frac{1}{\sqrt{2}}\mathbf{i} - \frac{1}{\sqrt{2}}\mathbf{k}$

43. $\frac{1}{\sqrt{6}}\mathbf{i} - \frac{1}{\sqrt{6}}\mathbf{j} - \frac{1}{\sqrt{6}}\mathbf{k}$

44. $\frac{\mathbf{i}}{\sqrt{3}} + \frac{\mathbf{j}}{\sqrt{3}} + \frac{\mathbf{k}}{\sqrt{3}}$

In Exercises 45–50, find

a) the distance between points P_1 and P_2,
b) the direction of $\overrightarrow{P_1P_2}$,
c) the midpoint of line segment P_1P_2.

45. $P_1(1, 1, 1)$, $P_2(3, 3, 0)$

46. $P_1(-1, 1, 5)$, $P_2(2, 5, 0)$

47. $P_1(1, 4, 5)$, $P_2(4, -2, 7)$

48. $P_1(3, 4, 5)$, $P_2(2, 3, 4)$

49. $P_1(0, 0, 0)$, $P_2(2, -2, -2)$

50. $P_1(5, 3, -2)$, $P_2(0, 0, 0)$

51. Find the vectors whose lengths and directions are given. Try to do the calculations without writing.

Length	Direction
a) 2	$\mathbf{i}$
b) $\sqrt{3}$	$-\mathbf{k}$
c) $\frac{1}{2}$	$\frac{3}{5}\mathbf{j} + \frac{4}{5}\mathbf{k}$
d) 7	$\frac{6}{7}\mathbf{i} - \frac{2}{7}\mathbf{j} + \frac{3}{7}\mathbf{k}$

52. Find the vectors whose lengths and directions are given. Try to do the calculations without writing.

Length	Direction
a) 7	$-\mathbf{j}$
b) $\sqrt{2}$	$-\frac{3}{5}\mathbf{i} - \frac{4}{5}\mathbf{k}$
c) $\frac{13}{12}$	$\frac{3}{13}\mathbf{i} - \frac{4}{13}\mathbf{j} - \frac{12}{13}\mathbf{k}$
d) $a > 0$	$\frac{1}{\sqrt{2}}\mathbf{i} + \frac{1}{\sqrt{3}}\mathbf{j} - \frac{1}{\sqrt{6}}\mathbf{k}$

53. Find a vector of magnitude 7 in the direction of $\mathbf{A} = 12\mathbf{i} - 5\mathbf{k}$.

54. Find a vector $\sqrt{5}$ units long in the direction of $\mathbf{A} = \mathbf{i} + \mathbf{j} + \mathbf{k}$.

55. Find a vector 5 units long in the direction opposite to the direction of $\mathbf{A} = 2\mathbf{i} - 3\mathbf{j} + 6\mathbf{k}$.

56. Find a vector of magnitude 3 in the direction opposite to the direction of $\mathbf{A} = (1/2)\mathbf{i} - (1/2)\mathbf{j} - (1/2)\mathbf{k}$.

SPHERES AND DISTANCE

Find the centers and radii of the spheres in Exercises 57–60.

57. $(x + 2)^2 + y^2 + (z - 2)^2 = 8$

58. $\left(x + \frac{1}{2}\right)^2 + \left(y + \frac{1}{2}\right)^2 + \left(z + \frac{1}{2}\right)^2 = \frac{21}{4}$

59. $(x - \sqrt{2})^2 + (y - \sqrt{2})^2 + (z + \sqrt{2})^2 = 2$

60. $x^2 + \left(y + \frac{1}{3}\right)^2 + \left(z - \frac{1}{3}\right)^2 = \frac{29}{9}$

Find equations for the spheres whose centers and radii are given in Exercises 61–64.

	Center	Radius
61.	(1, 2, 3)	$\sqrt{14}$
62.	(0, −1, 5)	2
63.	(−2, 0, 0)	$\sqrt{3}$
64.	(0, −7, 0)	7

Find the centers and radii of the spheres in Exercises 65–68.

65. $x^2 + y^2 + z^2 + 4x - 4z = 0$

66. $x^2 + y^2 + z^2 - 6y + 8z = 0$

67. $2x^2 + 2y^2 + 2z^2 + x + y + z = 9$

68. $3x^2 + 3y^2 + 3z^2 + 2y - 2z = 9$

69. Find a formula for the distance from the point $P(x, y, z)$ to the
 a) x-axis b) y-axis c) z-axis

70. Find a formula for the distance from the point $P(x, y, z)$ to the
 a) xy-plane b) yz-plane c) xz-plane

Writing for Your Own Knowledge

Answer the following questions in writing. Some answers will take only a sentence or two; others may require several paragraphs. Some explanations may also call for graphs or sketches.

1. What is the rectangular coordinate system for space?
2. How do you write equations for planes parallel to the coordinate planes? lines parallel to the coordinate axes?
3. What sets are described by numerical inequalities in x, y, and z?
4. How do you
 a) find the vector from one point to another?
 b) write a vector in terms of its length and direction?
 c) measure distance in space?
 d) write equations for spheres?
 e) find a sphere's center and radius from its equation?
 f) find the midpoint of a line segment?
5. What inequalities describe the regions bounded by a sphere in space?

11.3 Dot Products

We now introduce the dot product of two vectors, the first of two methods we will learn for multiplying vectors together. Our motivation is the need to calculate the work done by a constant force in displacing a mass. If we represent the force and displacement as vectors, we can calculate the work by finding their dot product. Dot products are called *scalar products* because the result of the multiplication is a scalar, not a vector. Cross products, which we study in the next section, are vectors.

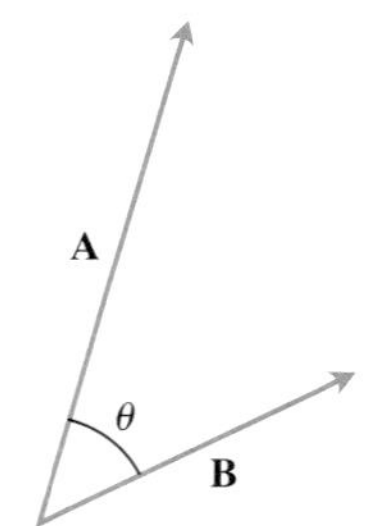

11.23 $\mathbf{A} \cdot \mathbf{B}$ is the number $|\mathbf{A}||\mathbf{B}| \cos \theta$.

DEFINITION

The **scalar product** $\mathbf{A} \cdot \mathbf{B}$ ("$\mathbf{A}$ dot $\mathbf{B}$") or **dot product** of two vectors $\mathbf{A}$ and $\mathbf{B}$ is the number

$$\mathbf{A} \cdot \mathbf{B} = |\mathbf{A}||\mathbf{B}| \cos \theta, \tag{1}$$

where θ measures the smaller angle made by $\mathbf{A}$ and $\mathbf{B}$ when their initial points coincide (as in Fig. 11.23).

In words, the scalar product of $\mathbf{A}$ and $\mathbf{B}$ is the length of $\mathbf{A}$ times the length of $\mathbf{B}$ times the cosine of the angle between $\mathbf{A}$ and $\mathbf{B}$. The product is a scalar, not a vector. It is called the dot product because of the dot in the notation $\mathbf{A} \cdot \mathbf{B}$.

From Eq. (1) we see that the scalar product of two vectors is positive when the angle between them is acute, negative when the angle is obtuse.

Since the angle a vector $\mathbf{A}$ makes with itself is zero, and $\cos 0 = 1$,

$$\mathbf{A} \cdot \mathbf{A} = |\mathbf{A}|\,|\mathbf{A}| \cos 0 = |\mathbf{A}|\,|\mathbf{A}|(1) = |\mathbf{A}|^2, \qquad \text{or} \qquad |\mathbf{A}| = \sqrt{\mathbf{A} \cdot \mathbf{A}}. \tag{2}$$

Calculation

To calculate $\mathbf{A} \cdot \mathbf{B}$ from the components of $\mathbf{A}$ and $\mathbf{B}$, we let

$$\mathbf{A} = a_1\,\mathbf{i} + a_2\,\mathbf{j} + a_3\,\mathbf{k},$$
$$\mathbf{B} = b_1\,\mathbf{i} + b_2\,\mathbf{j} + b_3\,\mathbf{k},$$

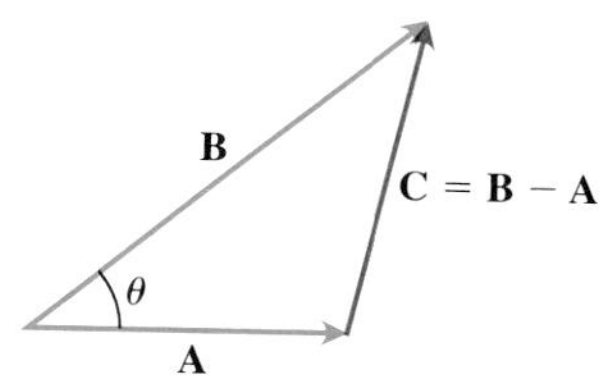

11.24 We obtain Eq. (3) by applying the law of cosines to a triangle whose sides represent **A**, **B**, and **C** = **B** − **A**.

and

$$\mathbf{C} = \mathbf{B} - \mathbf{A} = (b_1 - a_1)\,\mathbf{i} + (b_2 - a_2)\,\mathbf{j} + (b_3 - a_3)\,\mathbf{k}.$$

Then we apply the law of cosines to a triangle whose sides represent **A**, **B**, and **C** (Fig. 11.24) and obtain

$$|\mathbf{C}|^2 = |\mathbf{A}|^2 + |\mathbf{B}|^2 - 2|\mathbf{A}||\mathbf{B}|\cos\theta,$$

$$|\mathbf{A}||\mathbf{B}|\cos\theta = \frac{|\mathbf{A}|^2 + |\mathbf{B}|^2 - |\mathbf{C}|^2}{2}.$$

The left side of this equation is $\mathbf{A} \cdot \mathbf{B}$. We evaluate the right side by applying Eq. (4) of Section 11.2 to find $|\mathbf{A}|$, $|\mathbf{B}|$, and $|\mathbf{C}|$. The resulting cancellations give

$$\mathbf{A} \cdot \mathbf{B} = a_1 b_1 + a_2 b_2 + a_3 b_3. \qquad (3)$$

Thus, to find the scalar product of two given vectors we multiply their corresponding **i**, **j**, and **k** components and add the results.

Solving Eq. (1) for θ gives a formula for finding angles between vectors.

The angle between two nonzero vectors **A** and **B** is

$$\theta = \cos^{-1}\left(\frac{\mathbf{A} \cdot \mathbf{B}}{|\mathbf{A}||\mathbf{B}|}\right). \qquad (4)$$

Since the values of the arc cosine lie in $[0, \pi]$, Eq. (4) automatically gives the smaller of the two angles made by **A** and **B**.

EXAMPLE 1 Find the angle between $\mathbf{A} = \mathbf{i} - 2\,\mathbf{j} - 2\,\mathbf{k}$ and $\mathbf{B} = 6\,\mathbf{i} + 3\,\mathbf{j} + 2\,\mathbf{k}$.

Solution We use Eq. (4):

$$\mathbf{A} \cdot \mathbf{B} = (1)(6) + (-2)(3) + (-2)(2) = 6 - 6 - 4 = -4$$

$$|\mathbf{A}| = \sqrt{(1)^2 + (-2)^2 + (-2)^2} = \sqrt{9} = 3$$

$$|\mathbf{B}| = \sqrt{(6)^2 + (3)^2 + (2)^2} = \sqrt{49} = 7,$$

$$\theta = \cos^{-1}\left(\frac{\mathbf{A} \cdot \mathbf{B}}{|\mathbf{A}||\mathbf{B}|}\right) \qquad \text{Eq. (4)}$$

$$= \cos^{-1}\left(\frac{-4}{(3)(7)}\right) = \cos^{-1}\left(-\frac{4}{21}\right) \approx 1.76 \text{ rad} \qquad \text{About } 101°$$

Laws of Multiplication

From the equation $\mathbf{A} \cdot \mathbf{B} = a_1b_1 + a_2b_2 + a_3b_3$, we can see right away that

$$\mathbf{A} \cdot \mathbf{B} = \mathbf{B} \cdot \mathbf{A}. \qquad (5)$$

In other words, scalar multiplication is commutative. We can also see from Eq. (3) that if c is any number, then

$$(c\mathbf{A}) \cdot \mathbf{B} = \mathbf{A} \cdot (c\mathbf{B}) = c(\mathbf{A} \cdot \mathbf{B}). \tag{6}$$

If $\mathbf{C} = c_1\,\mathbf{i} + c_2\,\mathbf{j} + c_3\,\mathbf{k}$ is any third vector, then

$$\begin{aligned} \mathbf{A} \cdot (\mathbf{B} + \mathbf{C}) &= a_1(b_1 + c_1) + a_2(b_2 + c_2) + a_3(b_3 + c_3) \\ &= (a_1b_1 + a_2b_2 + a_3b_3) + (a_1c_1 + a_2c_2 + a_3c_3) \\ &= \mathbf{A} \cdot \mathbf{B} + \mathbf{A} \cdot \mathbf{C}. \end{aligned}$$

Hence scalar products obey the distributive law:

$$\mathbf{A} \cdot (\mathbf{B} + \mathbf{C}) = \mathbf{A} \cdot \mathbf{B} + \mathbf{A} \cdot \mathbf{C}. \tag{7}$$

If we combine this with the commutative law, Eq. (5), it is also evident that

$$(\mathbf{A} + \mathbf{B}) \cdot \mathbf{C} = \mathbf{A} \cdot \mathbf{C} + \mathbf{B} \cdot \mathbf{C}. \tag{8}$$

Equations (7) and (8) together permit us to multiply sums of vectors by the familiar laws of algebra. For example,

$$(\mathbf{A} + \mathbf{B}) \cdot (\mathbf{C} + \mathbf{D}) = \mathbf{A} \cdot \mathbf{C} + \mathbf{A} \cdot \mathbf{D} + \mathbf{B} \cdot \mathbf{C} + \mathbf{B} \cdot \mathbf{D}. \tag{9}$$

Orthogonal Vectors

Vectors whose scalar product is zero are said to be *orthogonal*. If neither $|\mathbf{A}|$ nor $|\mathbf{B}|$ is zero, then $\mathbf{A} \cdot \mathbf{B} = |\mathbf{A}||\mathbf{B}| \cos\theta$ is zero if and only if $\cos\theta$ is zero, or θ equals $\pi/2$. Hence, for the vectors we are dealing with, "orthogonal" means "perpendicular."

DEFINITION

Vectors $\mathbf{A}$ and $\mathbf{B}$ are **orthogonal** if $\mathbf{A} \cdot \mathbf{B} = 0$. (10)

EXAMPLE 2 $\mathbf{A} = 3\,\mathbf{i} - 2\,\mathbf{j} + \mathbf{k}$ and $\mathbf{B} = 2\,\mathbf{j} + 4\,\mathbf{k}$ are orthogonal because

$$\mathbf{A} \cdot \mathbf{B} = (3)(0) + (-2)(2) + (1)(4) = 0.$$

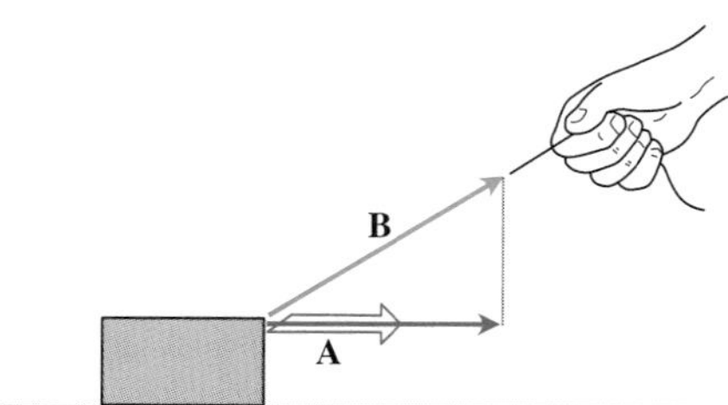

11.25 We may pull on the box with force **B** to move the box in the direction of **A**. The effective force in this direction is represented by the vector projection of **B** onto **A**.

Vector Projections and Scalar Components

The vector we get by projecting a vector **B** onto the line through a vector **A** is called the **vector projection of B onto A,** sometimes denoted

$\text{proj}_{\mathbf{A}}\,\mathbf{B}$ ("the vector projection of **B** onto **A**").

If **B** represents a force, then the vector projection of **B** onto **A** gives the effective force in the direction of **A** (Fig. 11.25).

If the angle between **B** and **A** is acute, the length of the vector projection of **B** onto **A** is $|\mathbf{B}| \cos\theta$. If the angle is obtuse, its cosine is negative and the length

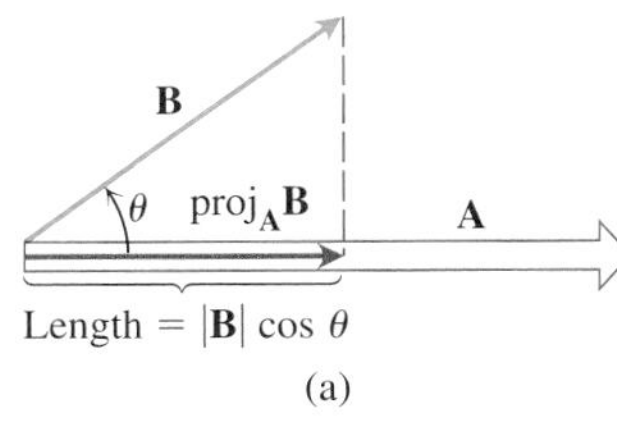

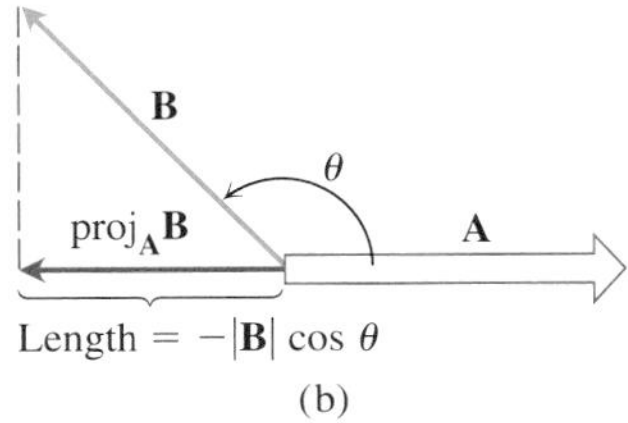

11.26 (a) When θ is acute, the length of the vector projection of **B** onto **A** is $|\mathbf{B}| \cos \theta$, the scalar component of **B** in the direction of **A**. (b) When θ is obtuse, the scalar component of **B** in the direction of **A** is negative and the length of the vector projection of **B** onto **A** is $-|\mathbf{B}| \cos \theta$.

of $\text{proj}_{\mathbf{A}}\,\mathbf{B}$ is $-|\mathbf{B}| \cos \theta$. In either case, the number $|\mathbf{B}| \cos \theta$ itself is called the **scalar component of B in the direction of A** (Fig. 11.26).

The scalar component of **B** in the direction of **A** can be found by dividing both sides of the equation $\mathbf{A} \cdot \mathbf{B} = |\mathbf{A}||\mathbf{B}| \cos \theta$ by $|\mathbf{A}|$. This gives

$$|\mathbf{B}| \cos \theta = \frac{\mathbf{A} \cdot \mathbf{B}}{|\mathbf{A}|} = \mathbf{B} \cdot \frac{\mathbf{A}}{|\mathbf{A}|}. \tag{11}$$

The vector projection of **B** onto **A** is the scalar component of **B** in the direction of **A** times the direction of **A**. If the angle between **A** and **B** is acute, the vector projection has length $|\mathbf{B}| \cos \theta$ and direction $\mathbf{A}/|\mathbf{A}|$. If the angle is obtuse, the vector projection has length $-|\mathbf{B}| \cos \theta$ and direction $-\mathbf{A}/|\mathbf{A}|$. In either case,

$$\text{proj}_{\mathbf{A}}\,\mathbf{B} = (|\mathbf{B}| \cos \theta) \frac{\mathbf{A}}{|\mathbf{A}|}. \tag{12}$$

Equations (11) and (12) together give a useful way to calculate $\text{proj}_{\mathbf{A}}\,\mathbf{B}$:

$$\begin{aligned} \text{proj}_{\mathbf{A}}\,\mathbf{B} &= (|\mathbf{B}| \cos \theta) \frac{\mathbf{A}}{|\mathbf{A}|} && \text{Eq. (12)} \\ &= \left(\frac{\mathbf{A} \cdot \mathbf{B}}{|\mathbf{A}|}\right) \frac{\mathbf{A}}{|\mathbf{A}|} && \text{Eq. (11)} \\ &= \frac{\mathbf{A} \cdot \mathbf{B}}{\mathbf{A} \cdot \mathbf{A}} \mathbf{A}. && |\mathbf{A}|^2 = \mathbf{A} \cdot \mathbf{A} \end{aligned} \tag{13}$$

$$\text{proj}_{\mathbf{A}}\,\mathbf{B} = \frac{\mathbf{A} \cdot \mathbf{B}}{\mathbf{A} \cdot \mathbf{A}} \mathbf{A} \tag{14}$$

Equation (11) says that the scalar component of **B** in the direction of **A** can be obtained by "dotting" **B** with the direction of **A**.

EXAMPLE 3 Find the vector projection of $\mathbf{B} = 6\,\mathbf{i} + 3\,\mathbf{j} + 2\,\mathbf{k}$ onto $\mathbf{A} = \mathbf{i} - 2\,\mathbf{j} - 2\,\mathbf{k}$ and the scalar component of **B** in the direction of **A**.

Solution We find $\text{proj}_{\mathbf{A}}\,\mathbf{B}$ from Eq. (14):

$$\begin{aligned} \text{proj}_{\mathbf{A}}\,\mathbf{B} &= \frac{\mathbf{A} \cdot \mathbf{B}}{\mathbf{A} \cdot \mathbf{A}} \mathbf{A} = \frac{6 - 6 - 4}{1 + 4 + 4}(\mathbf{i} - 2\,\mathbf{j} - 2\,\mathbf{k}) \\ &= -\frac{4}{9}(\mathbf{i} - 2\,\mathbf{j} - 2\,\mathbf{k}) = -\frac{4}{9}\mathbf{i} + \frac{8}{9}\mathbf{j} + \frac{8}{9}\mathbf{k}. \end{aligned}$$

We find the scalar component of **B** in the direction of **A** from Eq. (11):

$$\begin{aligned} |\mathbf{B}| \cos \theta &= \mathbf{B} \cdot \frac{\mathbf{A}}{|\mathbf{A}|} = (6\,\mathbf{i} + 3\,\mathbf{j} + 2\,\mathbf{k}) \cdot \left(\frac{1}{3}\mathbf{i} - \frac{2}{3}\mathbf{j} - \frac{2}{3}\mathbf{k}\right) \\ &= 2 - 2 - \frac{4}{3} = -\frac{4}{3}. \end{aligned}$$

Writing a Vector as a Sum of Orthogonal Vectors

In mechanics, we often want to express a vector **B** as a sum of a vector $\mathbf{B}_1$ parallel to a vector **A** and a vector $\mathbf{B}_2$ orthogonal to **A** (Fig. 11.27). We can do this by writing **B** as a sum of its vector projection on **A** plus whatever is left over. The leftover part will automatically be orthogonal to **A**.

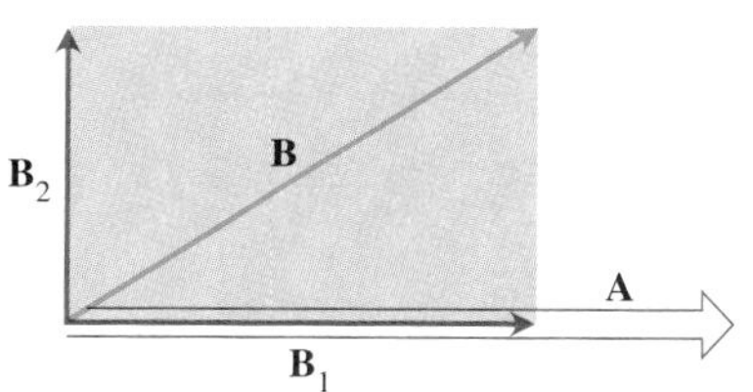

11.27 The vector **B** as the sum of vectors parallel and orthogonal to **A**.

Where Vectors Came From

Although Aristotle used vectors to describe the effects of forces, the idea of resolving vectors into geometric components parallel to the coordinate axes came from Descartes. The algebra of vectors we use today was developed simultaneously and independently in the 1870s by Josiah Willard Gibbs (1839–1903), a mathematical physicist at Yale University, and by the English mathematical physicist Oliver Heaviside (1850–1925), the Heaviside of Heaviside layer fame. The works of Gibbs and Heaviside grew out of more complicated mathematical theories developed some years earlier by the Irish mathematician William Hamilton (1805–1865) and the German linguist, physicist, and geometer Hermann Grassman (1809–1877).

Formula for Writing B as a Vector Parallel to A Plus a Vector Orthogonal to A

$$\mathbf{B} = \underbrace{\frac{\mathbf{A}\cdot\mathbf{B}}{\mathbf{A}\cdot\mathbf{A}}\mathbf{A}}_{\substack{\mathbf{B}_1 \\ \text{parallel to } \mathbf{A}}} + \underbrace{\left(\mathbf{B} - \frac{\mathbf{A}\cdot\mathbf{B}}{\mathbf{A}\cdot\mathbf{A}}\mathbf{A}\right)}_{\substack{\mathbf{B}_2 \\ \text{orthogonal to } \mathbf{A}}} \tag{15}$$

The vector $\mathbf{B}_1$, being the vector projection of $\mathbf{B}$ onto $\mathbf{A}$, is parallel to $\mathbf{A}$, while $\mathbf{B}_2$ can be seen to be orthogonal to $\mathbf{A}$ because $\mathbf{A}\cdot\mathbf{B}_2$ is zero:

$$\mathbf{A}\cdot\mathbf{B}_2 = \mathbf{A}\cdot\left(\mathbf{B} - \frac{\mathbf{A}\cdot\mathbf{B}}{\mathbf{A}\cdot\mathbf{A}}\mathbf{A}\right) = \mathbf{A}\cdot\mathbf{B} - \frac{\mathbf{A}\cdot\mathbf{B}}{\mathbf{A}\cdot\mathbf{A}}\mathbf{A}\cdot\mathbf{A} = \mathbf{A}\cdot\mathbf{B} - \mathbf{A}\cdot\mathbf{B} = 0. \tag{16}$$

EXAMPLE 4 Express $\mathbf{B} = 2\,\mathbf{i} + \mathbf{j} - 3\,\mathbf{k}$ as the sum of a vector parallel to $\mathbf{A} = 3\,\mathbf{i} - \mathbf{j}$ and a vector orthogonal to $\mathbf{A}$.

Solution We use Eq. (15). With

$$\mathbf{A}\cdot\mathbf{B} = 6 - 1 = 5 \quad \text{and} \quad \mathbf{A}\cdot\mathbf{A} = 9 + 1 = 10,$$

Eq. (15) gives

$$\begin{aligned}\mathbf{B} = \frac{\mathbf{A}\cdot\mathbf{B}}{\mathbf{A}\cdot\mathbf{A}}\mathbf{A} + \left(\mathbf{B} - \frac{\mathbf{A}\cdot\mathbf{B}}{\mathbf{A}\cdot\mathbf{A}}\mathbf{A}\right) &= \frac{5}{10}(3\,\mathbf{i} - \mathbf{j}) + \left(2\,\mathbf{i} + \mathbf{j} - 3\,\mathbf{k} - \frac{5}{10}(3\,\mathbf{i} - \mathbf{j})\right) \\ &= \left(\frac{3}{2}\mathbf{i} - \frac{1}{2}\mathbf{j}\right) + \left(\frac{1}{2}\mathbf{i} + \frac{3}{2}\mathbf{j} - 3\,\mathbf{k}\right).\end{aligned}$$

Check: The first vector in the sum is parallel to $\mathbf{A}$ because it is $(1/2)\,\mathbf{A}$. The second vector in the sum is orthogonal to $\mathbf{A}$ because

$$\left(\frac{1}{2}\mathbf{i} + \frac{3}{2}\mathbf{j} - 3\,\mathbf{k}\right)\cdot(3\,\mathbf{i} - \mathbf{j}) = \frac{3}{2} - \frac{3}{2} = 0.$$

Lines in the Plane. Distances from Points to Lines

Dot products give a new understanding of the equations we write for lines in the xy-plane and a quick way to find distances from points to lines.

Suppose L is a line through the point $P_0(x_0, y_0)$ perpendicular to a vector $\mathbf{N} = A\,\mathbf{i} + B\,\mathbf{j}$ (Fig. 11.28). Then a point $P(x, y)$ lies on L if and only if

$$\mathbf{N}\cdot\overrightarrow{P_0P} = 0 \quad \text{or} \quad A(x - x_0) + B(y - y_0) = 0. \tag{17}$$

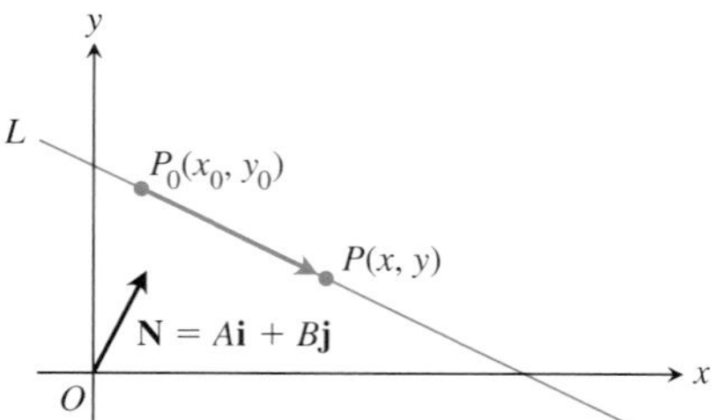

11.28 A point $P(x, y)$ lies on the line through P_0 perpendicular to $\mathbf{N}$ if and only if $\mathbf{N}\cdot\overrightarrow{P_0P} = 0$.

When rearranged, the second equation becomes

$$Ax + By = Ax_0 + By_0. \tag{18}$$

Line Through $P(x_0, y_0)$ Normal (Perpendicular) to $\mathbf{N} = A\,\mathbf{i} + B\,\mathbf{j}$

$$A(x - x_0) + B(y - y_0) = 0 \tag{19}$$

or

$$Ax + By = C, \quad \text{where} \quad C = Ax_0 + By_0 \tag{20}$$

Notice how the components of $\mathbf{N}$ become coefficients in the equation $Ax + By = C$.

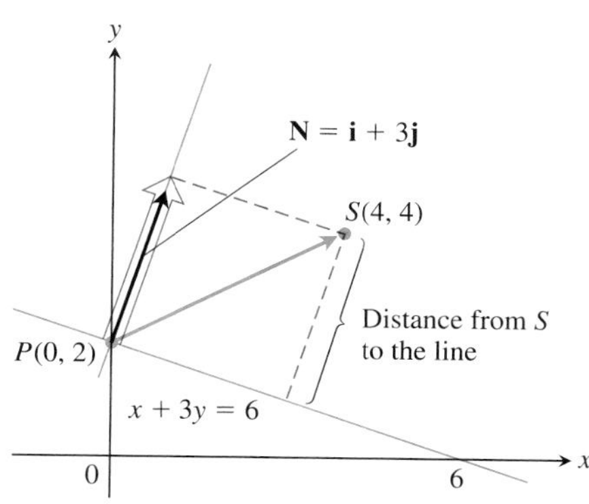

11.29 The distance from S to the line is the length of the vector projection of $\overrightarrow{PS}$ onto $\mathbf{N}$ (Example 6).

How to Find the Distance from a Point to a Line

To find the distance d from a point S to the line L: $Ax + By = C$, find

1. a point P on L,
2. $\overrightarrow{PS}$,
3. the direction of $\mathbf{N} = A\,\mathbf{i} + B\,\mathbf{j}$.

Then $d = \left|\overrightarrow{PS} \cdot \dfrac{\mathbf{N}}{|\mathbf{N}|}\right|$.

EXAMPLE 5 Find the line through $P_0(3, 5)$ perpendicular to $\mathbf{N} = \mathbf{i} + 2\,\mathbf{j}$.

Solution We use Eqs. (20) with $A = 1$, $B = 2$, and $C = (1)(3) + (2)(5) = 13$ to get

$$x + 2y = 13.$$

EXAMPLE 6 Find the distance from the point $S(4, 4)$ to the line L: $x + 3y = 6$.

Solution We find a point P on the line and calculate the distance as the length of the vector projection of $\overrightarrow{PS}$ onto a vector $\mathbf{N}$ perpendicular to the line (Fig. 11.29). Any point on the line will do for P and we can find $\mathbf{N}$ from the coefficients of $x + 3y = 6$ as $\mathbf{N} = \mathbf{i} + 3\,\mathbf{j}$. With $P = (0, 2)$, say, we then have

$$\overrightarrow{PS} = (4 - 0)\,\mathbf{i} + (4 - 2)\,\mathbf{j} = 4\,\mathbf{i} + 2\,\mathbf{j},$$

$$\text{distance from } S \text{ to } L = |\text{proj}_{\mathbf{N}}\,\overrightarrow{PS}| = \left|\overrightarrow{PS} \cdot \frac{\mathbf{N}}{|\mathbf{N}|}\right|$$

$$= \left|(4\,\mathbf{i} + 2\,\mathbf{j}) \cdot \frac{\mathbf{i} + 3\,\mathbf{j}}{\sqrt{(1)^2 + (3)^2}}\right| = \frac{4 + 6}{\sqrt{10}} = \sqrt{10}.$$

Work

As we mentioned at the beginning of the section, the work done by a constant force $\mathbf{F}$ when the point of application undergoes a displacement $\overrightarrow{PQ}$ (Fig. 11.30) is defined to be the dot product of $\mathbf{F}$ with $\overrightarrow{PQ}$.

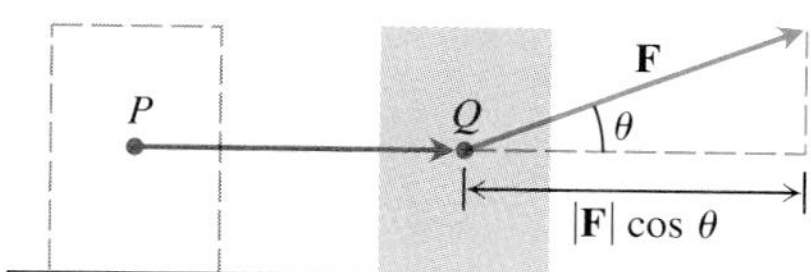

11.30 The work done by a constant force $\mathbf{F}$ during a displacement $\overrightarrow{PQ}$ is $(|\mathbf{F}|\cos\theta)|\overrightarrow{PQ}|$.

DEFINITION

The **work** done by a constant force $\mathbf{F}$ acting through a displacement $\overrightarrow{PQ}$ is

$$\text{Work} = \mathbf{F} \cdot \overrightarrow{PQ} = |\mathbf{F}||\overrightarrow{PQ}| \cos\theta. \qquad (21)$$

Work

The standard units of work are the foot-pound and newton-meter, both force–distance units. The newton-meter is usually called a *joule*. For more about the notion of work and the units involved, read the first few paragraphs of Section 7.5.

EXAMPLE 7 If $|\mathbf{F}| = 40$ N (newtons), $|\overrightarrow{PQ}| = 3$ m, and $\theta = 60°$, the work done by $\mathbf{F}$ in acting from P to Q is

$$\begin{aligned} \text{Work} &= |\mathbf{F}||\overrightarrow{PQ}| \cos\theta && \text{Eq. (21)} \\ &= (40)(3)\cos 60° && \text{Given values} \\ &= (120)(1/2) \\ &= 60 \text{ J (joules)} \end{aligned}$$

We will encounter more interesting work problems in Chapter 15 when we can find the work done by a variable force along a path in space.

Exercises 11.3

In Exercises 1–12, find $\mathbf{A} \cdot \mathbf{B}$, $|\mathbf{A}|$, $|\mathbf{B}|$, the cosine of the angle between $\mathbf{A}$ and $\mathbf{B}$, the scalar component of $\mathbf{B}$ in the direction of $\mathbf{A}$, and the vector projection of $\mathbf{B}$ onto $\mathbf{A}$.

1. $\mathbf{A} = 2\,\mathbf{i} - 4\,\mathbf{j} + \sqrt{5}\,\mathbf{k}, \quad \mathbf{B} = -2\,\mathbf{i} + 4\,\mathbf{j} - \sqrt{5}\,\mathbf{k}$
2. $\mathbf{A} = (3/5)\,\mathbf{i} + (4/5)\,\mathbf{k}, \quad \mathbf{B} = 5\,\mathbf{i} + 12\,\mathbf{j}$
3. $\mathbf{A} = 10\,\mathbf{i} + 11\,\mathbf{j} - 2\,\mathbf{k}, \quad \mathbf{B} = 3\,\mathbf{j} + 4\,\mathbf{k}$
4. $\mathbf{A} = 2\,\mathbf{i} + 10\,\mathbf{j} - 11\,\mathbf{k}, \quad \mathbf{B} = 2\,\mathbf{i} + 2\,\mathbf{j} + \mathbf{k}$
5. $\mathbf{A} = -2\,\mathbf{i} + 7\,\mathbf{j}, \quad \mathbf{B} = \mathbf{k}$
6. $\mathbf{A} = \dfrac{1}{\sqrt{2}}\mathbf{i} + \dfrac{1}{\sqrt{3}}\mathbf{j} + \dfrac{1}{\sqrt{6}}\mathbf{k}, \quad \mathbf{B} = \dfrac{1}{\sqrt{2}}\mathbf{j} - \mathbf{k}$
7. $\mathbf{A} = 5\,\mathbf{j} - 3\,\mathbf{k}, \quad \mathbf{B} = \mathbf{i} + \mathbf{j} + \mathbf{k}$
8. $\mathbf{A} = \mathbf{i} + \mathbf{k}, \quad \mathbf{B} = \mathbf{i} + \mathbf{j} + \mathbf{k}$
9. $\mathbf{A} = 3\,\mathbf{i} + 2\,\mathbf{j}, \quad \mathbf{B} = 5\,\mathbf{j} + \mathbf{k}$
10. $\mathbf{A} = 3\,\mathbf{i} - 2\,\mathbf{j} - \mathbf{k}, \quad \mathbf{B} = -2\,\mathbf{j}$
11. $\mathbf{A} = -\mathbf{i} + \mathbf{j}, \quad \mathbf{B} = \sqrt{2}\,\mathbf{i} + \sqrt{3}\,\mathbf{j} + 2\,\mathbf{k}$
12. $\mathbf{A} = -5\,\mathbf{i} + \mathbf{j}, \quad \mathbf{B} = 2\,\mathbf{i} + \sqrt{17}\,\mathbf{j} + 10\,\mathbf{k}$
13. Write the vector $\mathbf{B} = 3\,\mathbf{j} + 4\,\mathbf{k}$ as the sum of a vector parallel to $\mathbf{A} = \mathbf{i} + \mathbf{j}$ and a vector orthogonal to $\mathbf{A}$.
14. Write $\mathbf{B} = \mathbf{j} + \mathbf{k}$ as the sum of a vector parallel to $\mathbf{A} = \mathbf{i} + \mathbf{j}$ and a vector orthogonal to $\mathbf{A}$.
15. Write $\mathbf{B} = 8\,\mathbf{i} + 4\,\mathbf{j} - 12\,\mathbf{k}$ as the sum of a vector parallel to $\mathbf{A} = \mathbf{i} + 2\,\mathbf{j} - \mathbf{k}$ and a vector orthogonal to $\mathbf{A}$.
16. $\mathbf{B} = \mathbf{i} + (\mathbf{j} + \mathbf{k})$ is already the sum of a vector parallel to $\mathbf{i}$ and a vector orthogonal to $\mathbf{i}$. If you use Eq. (15) with $\mathbf{A} = \mathbf{i}$, do you get $\mathbf{B}_1 = \mathbf{i}$ and $\mathbf{B}_2 = \mathbf{j} + \mathbf{k}$? Try it and find out.

In Exercises 17–20, find an equation for the line in the xy-plane that passes through the given point perpendicular to the given vector. Then sketch the line. Include the vector in your sketch as a vector starting at the origin (as in Fig. 11.28).

17. $P(2, 1), \quad \mathbf{i} + 2\,\mathbf{j}$
18. $P(-1, 2), \quad -2\,\mathbf{i} - \mathbf{j}$
19. $P(-2, -7), \quad -2\,\mathbf{i} + \mathbf{j}$
20. $P(11, 10), \quad 2\,\mathbf{i} - 3\,\mathbf{j}$

In Exercises 21–24, find the distance in the xy-plane from the point to the line.

21. $S(2, 8), \quad x + 3y = 6$
22. $S(0, 0), \quad x + 3y = 6$
23. $S(2, 1), \quad x + y = 1$
24. $S(1, 3), \quad y = -2x$
25. Find the distance between the parallel lines $3x + 2y = 5$ and $3x + 2y = 7$.
26. Find the distance between the parallel lines $4x - 3y = 1$ and $4x - 3y = -19$.
27. Show that the vectors
$$\mathbf{A} = \frac{1}{\sqrt{3}}(\mathbf{i} - \mathbf{j} + \mathbf{k}), \quad \mathbf{B} = \frac{1}{\sqrt{2}}(\mathbf{j} + \mathbf{k}),$$
$$\mathbf{C} = \frac{1}{\sqrt{6}}(-2\,\mathbf{i} - \mathbf{j} + \mathbf{k})$$
are orthogonal to one another.
28. Find the vector projections of $\mathbf{D} = \mathbf{i} + \mathbf{j} + \mathbf{k}$ on the vectors $\mathbf{A}$, $\mathbf{B}$, and $\mathbf{C}$ of Exercise 27. Then show that $\mathbf{D}$ is the sum of these vector projections.
29. a) Use the fact that $\mathbf{u} \cdot \mathbf{v} = |\mathbf{u}|\,|\mathbf{v}| \cos\theta$ to show that the inequality $|\mathbf{u} \cdot \mathbf{v}| \le |\mathbf{u}|\,|\mathbf{v}|$ for any vectors $\mathbf{u}$ and $\mathbf{v}$.
    b) Under what circumstances, if any, does $|\mathbf{u} \cdot \mathbf{v}|$ equal $|\mathbf{u}|\,|\mathbf{v}|$? Give reasons for your answer.
30. Copy the axes and vector shown here. Then shade in the points (x, y) for which $(x\,\mathbf{i} + y\,\mathbf{j}) \cdot \mathbf{v} \le 0$. Justify your answer.

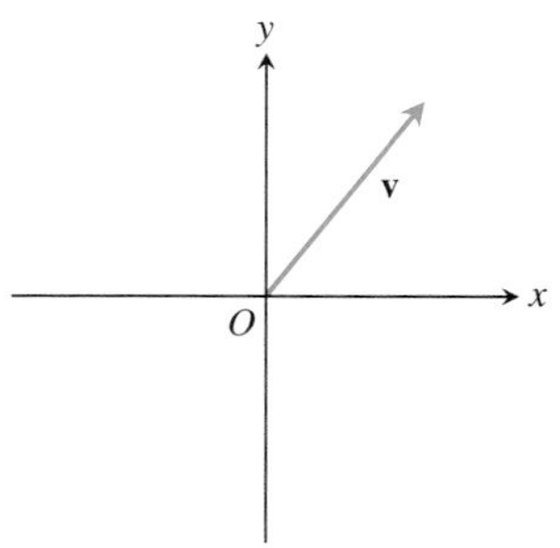

31. If $\mathbf{u}_1$ and $\mathbf{u}_2$ are orthogonal unit vectors and $\mathbf{v} = a\,\mathbf{u}_1 + b\,\mathbf{u}_2$, find $\mathbf{v} \cdot \mathbf{u}_1$.
32. *Cancellation in Dot Products.* In real-number multiplication, if $ab_1 = ab_2$ and a is not zero, we can cancel the a and conclude that $b_1 = b_2$. Does the same rule hold for vector multiplication: If $\mathbf{A} \cdot \mathbf{B}_1 = \mathbf{A} \cdot \mathbf{B}_2$ and $\mathbf{A} \ne 0$, can you conclude that $\mathbf{B}_1 = \mathbf{B}_2$? Give reasons for your answer.
33. *Sums and Differences.* In the accompanying figure, it looks as if $\mathbf{v}_1 + \mathbf{v}_2$ and $\mathbf{v}_1 - \mathbf{v}_2$ are orthogonal. Is this mere coincidence, or are there circumstances under which we may expect the sum of two vectors to be orthogonal to their difference? Give reasons for your answer.

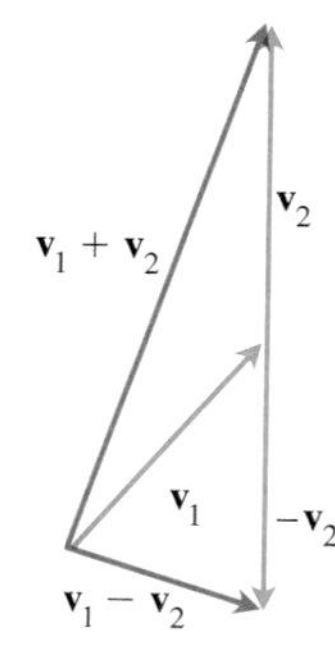

34. Suppose that AB is the diameter of a circle with center O and that C is a point on one of the two arcs joining A and B. Show that $\overrightarrow{CA}$ and $\overrightarrow{CB}$ are orthogonal.

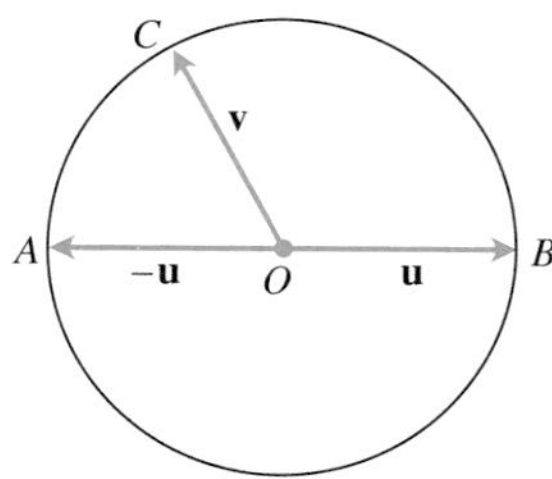

35. Show that the diagonals of a rhombus (parallelogram with sides of equal length) are perpendicular.

36. Show that squares are the only rectangles with perpendicular diagonals.

37. Prove the fact, often exploited by carpenters, that a parallelogram is a rectangle if and only if its diagonals are equal in length.

38. Show that the indicated diagonal of the parallelogram determined by vectors **u** and **v** bisects the angle between **u** and **v** if $|\mathbf{u}| = |\mathbf{v}|$.

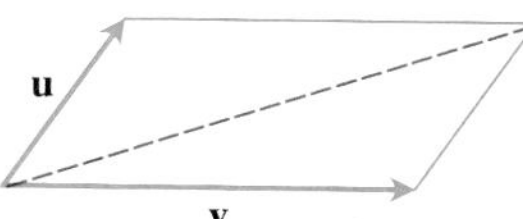

39. The accompanying figure shows a pyramid $OABCD$ with a square base whose sides are 1 unit long. The pyramid's height is also 1 unit, and the point D stands directly above the midpoint of the diagonal OB. Find the angle between $\overrightarrow{OB}$ and $\overrightarrow{OD}$.

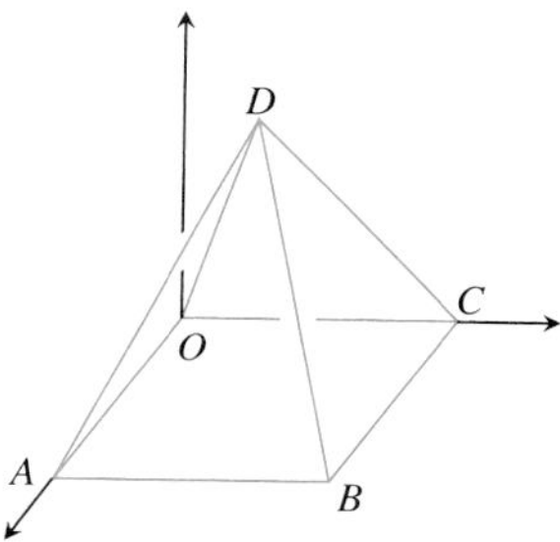

40. *Direction Angles.* The direction angles α, β, and γ of a vector $\mathbf{v} = a\,\mathbf{i} + b\,\mathbf{j} + c\,\mathbf{k}$ are defined as follows:

α is the angle between **v** and the positive x-axis $(0 \le \alpha \le \pi)$,
β is the angle between **v** and the positive y-axis $(0 \le \beta \le \pi)$,
γ is the angle between **v** and the positive z-axis $(0 \le \gamma \le \pi)$.

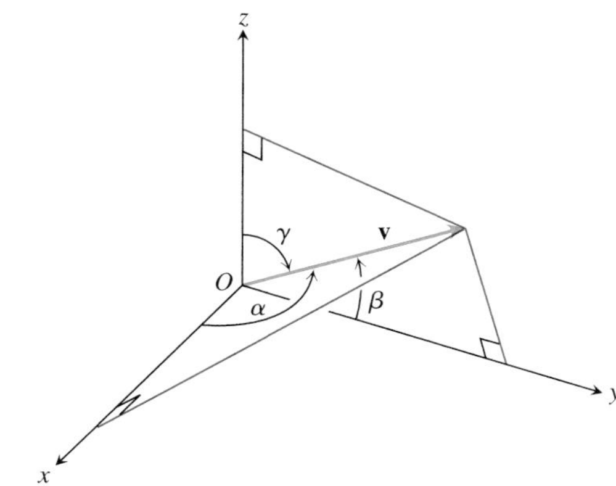

Show that

$$\cos\alpha = \frac{a}{|\mathbf{v}|}, \quad \cos\beta = \frac{b}{|\mathbf{v}|}, \quad \cos\gamma = \frac{c}{|\mathbf{v}|},$$

and $\cos^2\alpha + \cos^2\beta + \cos^2\gamma = 1$.

Find the angles between the vectors in Exercises 41–44 to the nearest hundredth of a radian.

41. $\mathbf{A} = 2\,\mathbf{i} + \mathbf{j}, \quad \mathbf{B} = \mathbf{i} + 2\,\mathbf{j} - \mathbf{k}$

42. $\mathbf{A} = 2\,\mathbf{i} - 2\,\mathbf{j} + \mathbf{k}, \quad \mathbf{B} = 3\,\mathbf{i} + 4\,\mathbf{k}$

43. $\mathbf{A} = \sqrt{3}\,\mathbf{i} - 7\,\mathbf{j}, \quad \mathbf{B} = \sqrt{3}\,\mathbf{i} + \mathbf{j} - 2\,\mathbf{k}$

44. $\mathbf{A} = \mathbf{i} + \sqrt{2}\,\mathbf{j} - \sqrt{2}\,\mathbf{k}, \quad \mathbf{B} = -\mathbf{i} + \mathbf{j} + \mathbf{k}$

Find the angles in Exercises 45–48 to the nearest hundredth of a radian.

45. The interior angles of the triangle ABC whose vertices are $A(-1, 0, 2)$, $B(2, 1, -1)$, and $C(1, -2, 2)$

46. The angle between $\mathbf{A} = 2\,\mathbf{i} + 2\,\mathbf{j} + \mathbf{k}$ and $\mathbf{B} = 2\,\mathbf{i} + 10\,\mathbf{j} - 11\,\mathbf{k}$

47. The angle between the diagonal of a cube and the diagonal of one of its faces. (*Hint:* Use a cube whose edges represent **i**, **j**, and **k**.)

48. The angle between the diagonal of a cube and one of the edges it meets at a vertex

WORK

49. Find the work done by a force $\mathbf{F} = 5\,\mathbf{k}$ (magnitude 5 N) in moving an object along the line from the origin to the point (1, 1, 1) (distance in meters).

50. The Union Pacific's *Big Boy* locomotive could pull 6000-ton trains with a tractive effort (pull) of 602,148 N (135,375 lb). At this level of effort, about how much work did *Big Boy* do on the (approximately straight) 605-km journey from San Francisco to Los Angeles?

51. How much work does it take to slide a crate 20 m along a loading dock by pulling on it with a 200-N force at an angle of 30° from the horizontal?

52. The wind passing over a boat's sail exerted a 1000-lb-magnitude force **F** as shown in Fig. 11.31. How much work did the wind perform in moving the boat forward 1 mi? Answer in foot-pounds.

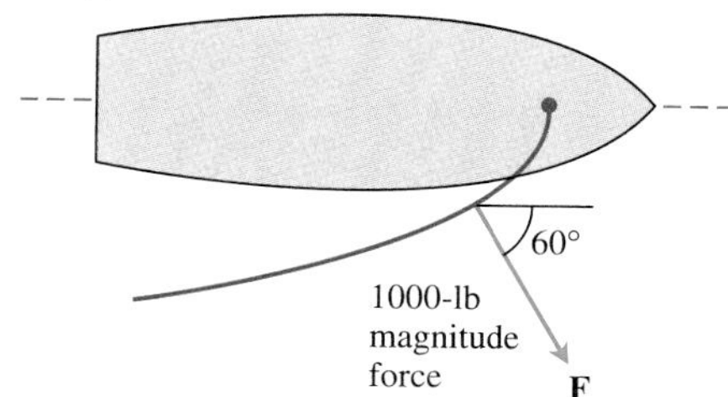

11.31 The boat in Exercise 52.

ANGLES BETWEEN LINES

The acute angle between two intersecting lines that do not cross at right angles is the same as the acute angle determined by the vectors normal to the lines (Fig. 11.32 on the following page). Use this fact to find the acute angles between the lines in Exercises 53–56.

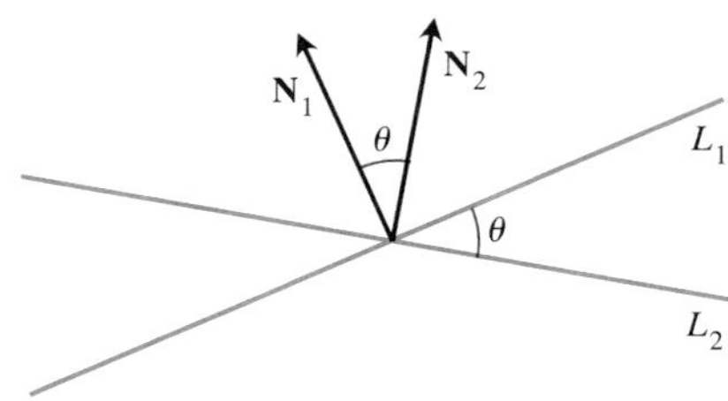

11.32 The acute angle between lines L_1 and L_2 is the same as the acute angle determined by the normal vectors $\mathbf{N}_1$ and $\mathbf{N}_2$ (Exercises 53–56).

53. $3x + y = 5, \quad 2x - y = 4$

54. $y = \sqrt{3}\,x - 1, \quad y = -\sqrt{3}\,x + 2$

55. $\sqrt{3}\,x - y = -2, \quad x - \sqrt{3}\,y = 1$

56. $x + \sqrt{3}\,y = 1, \quad (1 - \sqrt{3})x + (1 + \sqrt{3})y = 8$

In Exercises 57 and 58, find the angles between the lines to the nearest hundredth of a radian.

57. $3x - 4y = 3, \quad x - y = 7$

58. $12x + 5y = 1, \quad 2x - 2y = 3$

ANGLES BETWEEN DIFFERENTIABLE CURVES

The angles between two differentiable curves at a point of intersection are the angles between the curves' tangent lines at these points. Find the angles between the curves in Exercises 59–62. (You will not need a calculator.)

59. $y = (3/2) - x^2, \quad y = x^2$ (two points of intersection)

60. $x = (3/4) - y^2, \quad x = y^2 - (3/4)$ (two points of intersection)

61. $y = x^3, \quad x = y^2$ (two points of intersection)

62. $y = -x^2, \quad y = \sqrt[3]{x}$ (two points of intersection)

Writing for Your Own Knowledge

Answer the following questions in writing. Some answers will take only a sentence or two; others may require several paragraphs. Some explanations may also call for graphs or sketches.

1. What is the scalar product of two vectors?
2. What can you accomplish with scalar products?
3. How can you find the distance from a point to a line in the xy-plane?

11.4 *Cross Products*

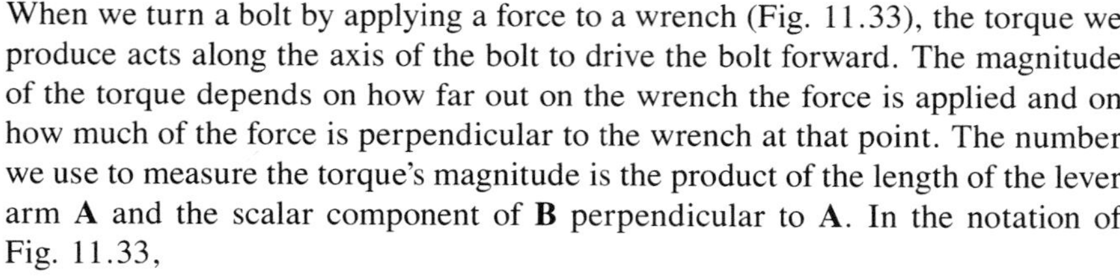

When we turn a bolt by applying a force to a wrench (Fig. 11.33), the torque we produce acts along the axis of the bolt to drive the bolt forward. The magnitude of the torque depends on how far out on the wrench the force is applied and on how much of the force is perpendicular to the wrench at that point. The number we use to measure the torque's magnitude is the product of the length of the lever arm $\mathbf{A}$ and the scalar component of $\mathbf{B}$ perpendicular to $\mathbf{A}$. In the notation of Fig. 11.33,

$$\text{Magnitude of the torque vector} = |\mathbf{A}||\mathbf{B}| \sin\theta.$$

If we let $\mathbf{n}$ be a unit vector along the axis of the bolt in the direction of the torque, then the complete description of the torque vector is

$$\text{Torque vector} = \mathbf{n}\,|\mathbf{A}||\mathbf{B}| \sin\theta.$$

In mathematics, we call $\mathbf{n}\,|\mathbf{A}||\mathbf{B}| \sin\theta$ the vector product of $\mathbf{A}$ and $\mathbf{B}$.

Vector products are widely used to describe the effects of forces in studies of electricity, magnetism, fluid mechanics, and planetary motion. This section presents the mathematical properties of vector products that account for their use in these fields.

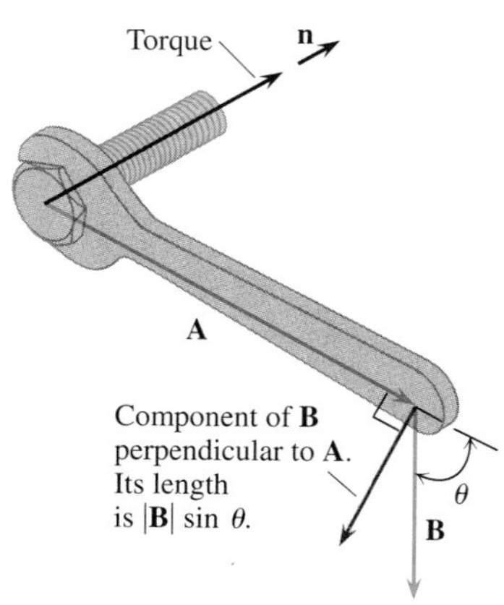

11.33 The torque vector describes the tendency of the force $\mathbf{B}$ to drive the bolt forward.

The Vector Product of Two Vectors in Space

When we define vector products in mathematics, we start with two nonzero vectors $\mathbf{A}$ and $\mathbf{B}$ in space without requiring them to have any particular physical interpretation. If $\mathbf{A}$ and $\mathbf{B}$ are not parallel, they determine a plane. We select a unit vector $\mathbf{n}$ perpendicular to the plane by the **right-hand rule.** This means we choose $\mathbf{n}$ to be the unit (normal) vector that points the way your right thumb

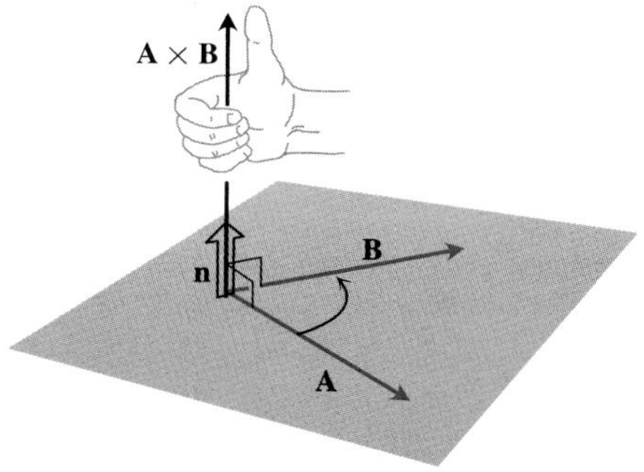

11.34 The construction of **A** × **B**.

points when your fingers curl through the angle θ from **A** to **B** (Fig. 11.34). We then define the **vector product A × B** ("**A** cross **B**") to be

$$\mathbf{A} \times \mathbf{B} = \mathbf{n}\, |\mathbf{A}||\mathbf{B}| \sin \theta. \tag{1}$$

The vector **A** × **B** is orthogonal to both **A** and **B** because it is a scalar multiple of **n**.

Since the sines of 0 and π are both zero in Eq. (1), it makes sense to define the vector product of two parallel nonzero vectors to be **0**. This is consistent with the torque interpretation. If the force **B** in Fig. 11.33 is parallel to the wrench, meaning that we are trying to turn the bolt by pushing or pulling straight along the handle of the wrench, the torque produced is **0**.

If one or both of **A** and **B** is zero, we define **A** × **B** to be zero. This way, the cross product of two vectors **A** and **B** is zero if and only if **A** and **B** are parallel or one or both of them is zero.

Nonzero vectors **A** and **B** are parallel if and only if **A** × **B** = **0**.

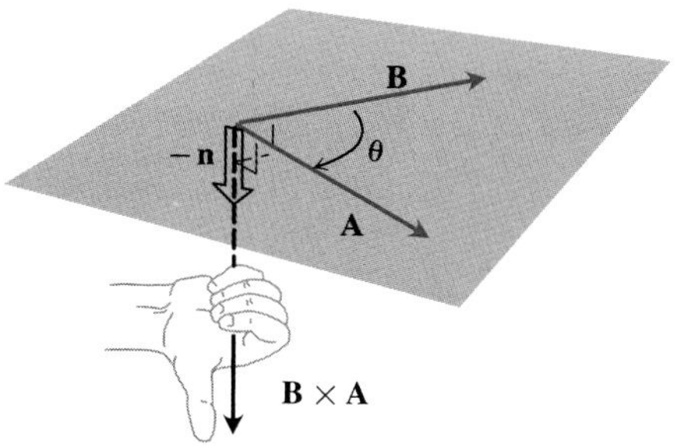

11.35 The construction of **B** × **A**.

The vector product of **A** and **B** is often called the **cross product** of **A** and **B** because of the cross in the notation **A** × **B**.

A × B Versus B × A

Reversing the order of the factors in a nonzero cross product reverses the direction of the resulting vector. When the fingers of our right hand curl through the angle θ from **B** to **A**, our thumb points the opposite way and the unit vector we choose in forming **B** × **A** is the negative of the one we choose in forming **A** × **B** (Fig. 11.35). Thus, for all vectors **A** and **B**,

$$\mathbf{B} \times \mathbf{A} = -(\mathbf{A} \times \mathbf{B}). \tag{2}$$

Unlike the dot product, the cross product is not commutative.

When we apply the definition to calculate the pairwise cross products of **i**, **j**, and **k**, we find (Fig. 11.36)

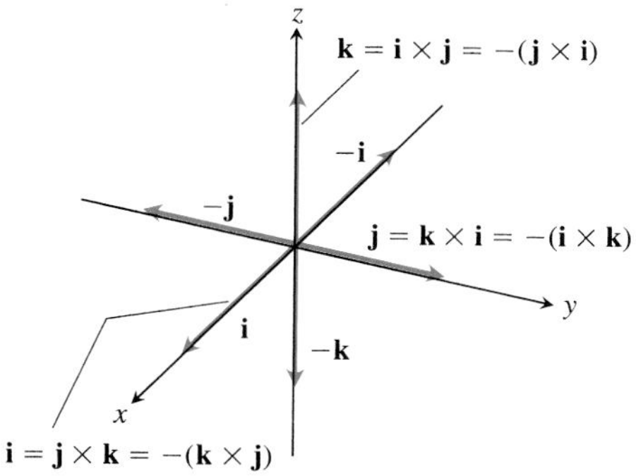

11.36 The pairwise cross products of **i**, **j**, and **k**.

$$\begin{aligned} \mathbf{i} \times \mathbf{j} &= -(\mathbf{j} \times \mathbf{i}) = \mathbf{k} \\ \mathbf{j} \times \mathbf{k} &= -(\mathbf{k} \times \mathbf{j}) = \mathbf{i} \\ \mathbf{k} \times \mathbf{i} &= -(\mathbf{i} \times \mathbf{k}) = \mathbf{j} \end{aligned} \tag{3}$$

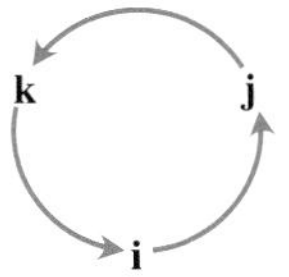

Diagram for recalling these products

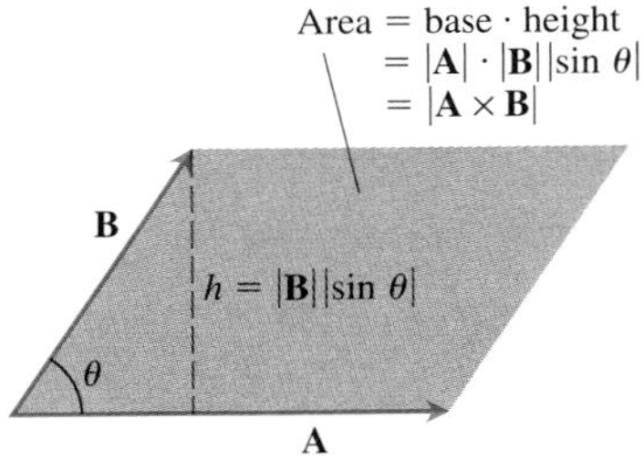

11.37 The parallelogram determined by **A** and **B**.

and

$$\mathbf{i} \times \mathbf{i} = \mathbf{j} \times \mathbf{j} = \mathbf{k} \times \mathbf{k} = \mathbf{0}.$$

Because $\mathbf{n}$ is a unit vector, the magnitude of $\mathbf{A} \times \mathbf{B}$ is

$$|\mathbf{A} \times \mathbf{B}| = |\mathbf{n}||\mathbf{A}||\mathbf{B}| \sin \theta = |\mathbf{A}||\mathbf{B}| \sin \theta. \tag{4}$$

This is the area of the parallelogram determined by $\mathbf{A}$ and $\mathbf{B}$ (Fig. 11.37), $|\mathbf{A}|$ being the base and $|\mathbf{B}| \sin \theta$ the height.

The Magnitude of a Torque

Equation (4) is the equation we use to calculate magnitudes of torques.

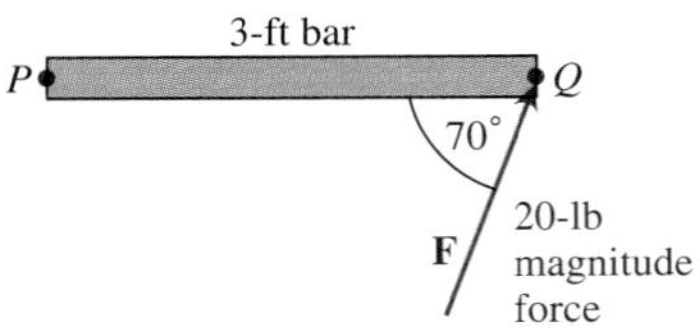

11.38 The magnitude of the torque exerted by **F** about P is about 56.4 ft-lb (Example 1).

EXAMPLE 1 The magnitude of the torque exerted by force $\mathbf{F}$ about the pivot point P in Fig. 11.38 is

$$\begin{aligned} |\overrightarrow{PQ} \times \mathbf{F}| &= |\overrightarrow{PQ}||\mathbf{F}| \sin 70^\circ \qquad \text{Eq. (4)} \\ &\approx (3)(20)(0.94) \\ &\approx 56.4 \text{ ft-lb.} \end{aligned}$$

The Associative and Distributive Laws

As a rule, cross-product multiplication is not associative because $(\mathbf{A} \times \mathbf{B}) \times \mathbf{C}$ lies in the plane of $\mathbf{A}$ and $\mathbf{B}$ whereas $\mathbf{A} \times (\mathbf{B} \times \mathbf{C})$ lies in the plane of $\mathbf{B}$ and $\mathbf{C}$. However, the **Scalar Distributive Law**,

$$(r\mathbf{A}) \times (s\mathbf{B}) = (rs)\mathbf{A} \times \mathbf{B} \tag{5}$$

does hold, as do the **Vector Distributive Laws**,

$$\mathbf{A} \times (\mathbf{B} + \mathbf{C}) = \mathbf{A} \times \mathbf{B} + \mathbf{A} \times \mathbf{C} \tag{6}$$

and

$$(\mathbf{B} + \mathbf{C}) \times \mathbf{A} = \mathbf{B} \times \mathbf{A} + \mathbf{C} \times \mathbf{A}. \tag{7}$$

As a special case of Eq. (5) we have

$$(-\mathbf{A}) \times \mathbf{B} = \mathbf{A} \times (-\mathbf{B}) = -(\mathbf{A} \times \mathbf{B}). \tag{8}$$

The Scalar Distributive Law can be verified by applying Eq. (1) to the products on both sides of Eq. (5) and comparing the results. The Vector Distributive Law in Eq. (6) is not easy to prove, and we will assume it here. Equation (7) follows from Eq. (6): multiply both sides of Eq. (6) by -1 and reverse the orders of the products.

The Determinant Formula for $\mathbf{A} \times \mathbf{B}$

Our next objective is to calculate $\mathbf{A} \times \mathbf{B}$ from the components of $\mathbf{A}$ and $\mathbf{B}$.

Suppose

$$\mathbf{A} = a_1\mathbf{i} + a_2\mathbf{j} + a_3\mathbf{k}, \qquad \mathbf{B} = b_1\mathbf{i} + b_2\mathbf{j} + b_3\mathbf{k}.$$

Determinants

(For more information, see Appendix 7.)

$$\begin{vmatrix} a & b \\ c & d \end{vmatrix} = ad - bc$$

EXAMPLE

$$\begin{vmatrix} 2 & 1 \\ -4 & 3 \end{vmatrix} = (2)(3) - (1)(-4)$$

$$= 6 + 4 = 10$$

$$\begin{vmatrix} a_1 & a_2 & a_3 \\ b_1 & b_2 & b_3 \\ c_1 & c_2 & c_3 \end{vmatrix}$$

$$= a_1\begin{vmatrix} b_2 & b_3 \\ c_2 & c_3 \end{vmatrix} - a_2\begin{vmatrix} b_1 & b_3 \\ c_1 & c_3 \end{vmatrix} + a_3\begin{vmatrix} b_1 & b_2 \\ c_1 & c_2 \end{vmatrix}$$

EXAMPLE

$$\begin{vmatrix} -5 & 3 & 1 \\ 2 & 1 & 1 \\ -4 & 3 & 1 \end{vmatrix}$$

$$= (-5)\begin{vmatrix} 1 & 1 \\ 3 & 1 \end{vmatrix} - (3)\begin{vmatrix} 2 & 1 \\ -4 & 1 \end{vmatrix} + (1)\begin{vmatrix} 2 & 1 \\ -4 & 3 \end{vmatrix}$$

$$= -5(1 - 3) - 3(2 + 4) + 1(6 + 4)$$
$$= 10 - 18 + 10 = 2$$

Then the distributive laws and the rules for multiplying **i**, **j**, and **k** tell us that

$$\begin{aligned}\mathbf{A} \times \mathbf{B} &= (a_1\,\mathbf{i} + a_2\,\mathbf{j} + a_3\,\mathbf{k}) \times (b_1\,\mathbf{i} + b_2\,\mathbf{j} + b_3\,\mathbf{k}) \\ &= a_1 b_1\,\mathbf{i} \times \mathbf{i} + a_1 b_2\,\mathbf{i} \times \mathbf{j} + a_1 b_3\,\mathbf{i} \times \mathbf{k} \\ &\quad + a_2 b_1\,\mathbf{j} \times \mathbf{i} + a_2 b_2\,\mathbf{j} \times \mathbf{j} + a_2 b_3\,\mathbf{j} \times \mathbf{k} \\ &\quad + a_3 b_1\,\mathbf{k} \times \mathbf{i} + a_3 b_2\,\mathbf{k} \times \mathbf{j} + a_3 b_3\,\mathbf{k} \times \mathbf{k} \\ &= (a_2 b_3 - a_3 b_2)\,\mathbf{i} - (a_1 b_3 - a_3 b_1)\,\mathbf{j} + (a_1 b_2 - a_2 b_1)\,\mathbf{k}.\end{aligned} \tag{9}$$

The terms at the end of Eq. (9) are the same as the terms in the expansion of the symbolic determinant

$$\begin{vmatrix} \mathbf{i} & \mathbf{j} & \mathbf{k} \\ a_1 & a_2 & a_3 \\ b_1 & b_2 & b_3 \end{vmatrix}.$$

We therefore have the following rule.

If $\mathbf{A} = a_1\,\mathbf{i} + a_2\,\mathbf{j} + a_3\,\mathbf{k}$ and $\mathbf{B} = b_1\,\mathbf{i} + b_2\,\mathbf{j} + b_3\,\mathbf{k}$, then

$$\mathbf{A} \times \mathbf{B} = \begin{vmatrix} \mathbf{i} & \mathbf{j} & \mathbf{k} \\ a_1 & a_2 & a_3 \\ b_1 & b_2 & b_3 \end{vmatrix}. \tag{10}$$

EXAMPLE 2 Find $\mathbf{A} \times \mathbf{B}$ and $\mathbf{B} \times \mathbf{A}$ if

$$\mathbf{A} = 2\,\mathbf{i} + \mathbf{j} + \mathbf{k}, \qquad \mathbf{B} = -4\,\mathbf{i} + 3\,\mathbf{j} + \mathbf{k}.$$

Solution

$$\mathbf{A} \times \mathbf{B} = \begin{vmatrix} \mathbf{i} & \mathbf{j} & \mathbf{k} \\ 2 & 1 & 1 \\ -4 & 3 & 1 \end{vmatrix} = \begin{vmatrix} 1 & 1 \\ 3 & 1 \end{vmatrix}\mathbf{i} - \begin{vmatrix} 2 & 1 \\ -4 & 1 \end{vmatrix}\mathbf{j} + \begin{vmatrix} 2 & 1 \\ -4 & 3 \end{vmatrix}\mathbf{k} \qquad \text{Eq. (9)}$$

$$= -2\,\mathbf{i} - 6\,\mathbf{j} + 10\,\mathbf{k}$$

$$\mathbf{B} \times \mathbf{A} = -(\mathbf{A} \times \mathbf{B}) = 2\,\mathbf{i} + 6\,\mathbf{j} - 10\,\mathbf{k} \qquad \text{Eq. (2)}$$

EXAMPLE 3 Find a vector perpendicular to the plane of $P(1, -1, 0)$, $Q(2, 1, -1)$, and $R(-1, 1, 2)$.

Solution The vector $\overrightarrow{PQ} \times \overrightarrow{PR}$ is perpendicular to the plane because it is perpendicular to both vectors. In terms of components,

$$\overrightarrow{PQ} = (2 - 1)\,\mathbf{i} + (1 + 1)\,\mathbf{j} + (-1 - 0)\,\mathbf{k} = \mathbf{i} + 2\,\mathbf{j} - \mathbf{k}$$

$$\overrightarrow{PR} = (-1 - 1)\,\mathbf{i} + (1 + 1)\,\mathbf{j} + (2 - 0)\,\mathbf{k} = -2\,\mathbf{i} + 2\,\mathbf{j} + 2\,\mathbf{k}$$

$$\overrightarrow{PQ} \times \overrightarrow{PR} = \begin{vmatrix} \mathbf{i} & \mathbf{j} & \mathbf{k} \\ 1 & 2 & -1 \\ -2 & 2 & 2 \end{vmatrix} = \begin{vmatrix} 2 & -1 \\ 2 & 2 \end{vmatrix}\mathbf{i} - \begin{vmatrix} 1 & -1 \\ -2 & 2 \end{vmatrix}\mathbf{j} + \begin{vmatrix} 1 & 2 \\ -2 & 2 \end{vmatrix}\mathbf{k}$$

$$= 6\,\mathbf{i} + 6\,\mathbf{k}.$$

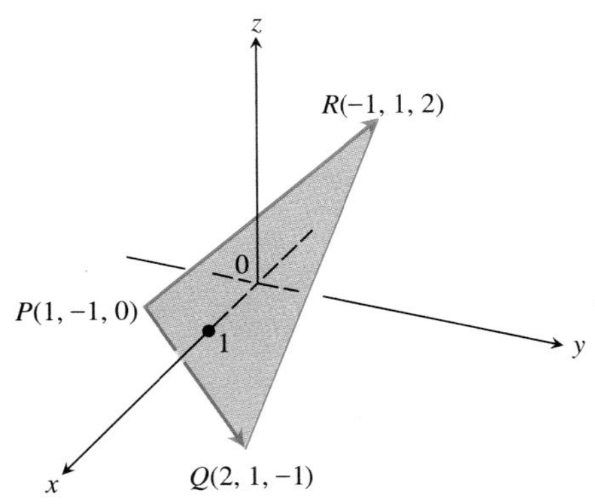

11.39 The area of triangle PQR is half of $|\overrightarrow{PQ} \times \overrightarrow{PR}|$ (Example 4).

EXAMPLE 4 Find the area of the triangle with vertices $P(1, -1, 0)$, $Q(2, 1, -1)$, and $R(-1, 1, 2)$ (Fig. 11.39).

Solution The area of the parallelogram determined by P, Q, and R is

$$\begin{aligned} |\overrightarrow{PQ} \times \overrightarrow{PR}| &= |6\,\mathbf{i} + 6\,\mathbf{k}| \qquad \text{Values from Example 3} \\ &= \sqrt{(6)^2 + (6)^2} = \sqrt{2 \cdot 36} = 6\sqrt{2}. \end{aligned}$$

The triangle's area is half of this, or $3\sqrt{2}$.

EXAMPLE 5 Find a unit vector perpendicular to the plane of $P(1, -1, 0)$, $Q(2, 1, -1)$, and $R(-1, 1, 2)$.

Solution Since $\overrightarrow{PQ} \times \overrightarrow{PR}$ is perpendicular to the plane, its direction $\mathbf{n}$ is a unit vector perpendicular to the plane. Taking values from Examples 3 and 4,

$$\mathbf{n} = \frac{\overrightarrow{PQ} \times \overrightarrow{PR}}{|\overrightarrow{PQ} \times \overrightarrow{PR}|} = \frac{6\,\mathbf{i} + 6\,\mathbf{k}}{6\sqrt{2}} = \frac{1}{\sqrt{2}}\mathbf{i} + \frac{1}{\sqrt{2}}\mathbf{k}.$$

The Triple Scalar or Box Product

The product $(\mathbf{A} \times \mathbf{B}) \cdot \mathbf{C}$ is called the **triple scalar product** of $\mathbf{A}$, $\mathbf{B}$, and $\mathbf{C}$ (in that order). As you can see from the formula

$$|(\mathbf{A} \times \mathbf{B}) \cdot \mathbf{C}| = |\mathbf{A} \times \mathbf{B}||\mathbf{C}||\cos\theta|, \tag{11}$$

the absolute value of the product is the volume of the parallelepiped (parallelogram-sided box) determined by $\mathbf{A}$, $\mathbf{B}$, and $\mathbf{C}$ (Fig. 11.40). The number $|\mathbf{A} \times \mathbf{B}|$ is the area of the base parallelogram. The number $|\mathbf{C}||\cos\theta|$ is the parallelepiped's height. Because of this geometry, $(\mathbf{A} \times \mathbf{B}) \cdot \mathbf{C}$ is also called the **box product** of $\mathbf{A}$, $\mathbf{B}$, and $\mathbf{C}$.

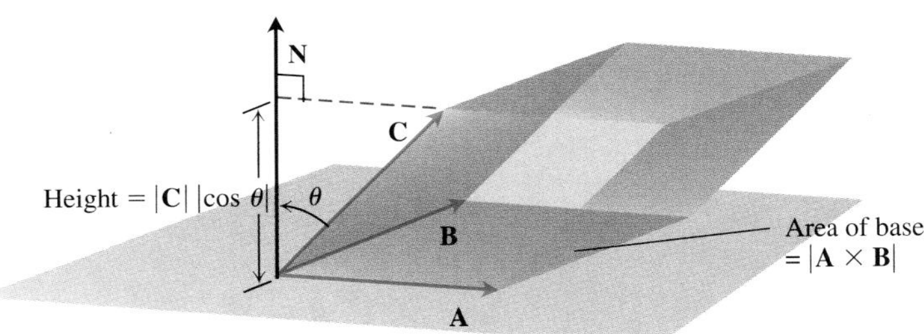

11.40 The number $|(\mathbf{A} \times \mathbf{B}) \cdot \mathbf{C}|$ is the volume of a parallelepiped.

By treating the planes of $\mathbf{B}$ and $\mathbf{C}$ and of $\mathbf{C}$ and $\mathbf{A}$ as the base planes of the parallelepiped determined by $\mathbf{A}$, $\mathbf{B}$, and $\mathbf{C}$, we see that

$$(\mathbf{A} \times \mathbf{B}) \cdot \mathbf{C} = (\mathbf{B} \times \mathbf{C}) \cdot \mathbf{A} = (\mathbf{C} \times \mathbf{A}) \cdot \mathbf{B}. \tag{12}$$

The dot and cross may be interchanged in a triple scalar product without altering its value.

Since the dot product is commutative, Eq. (12) also gives

$$(\mathbf{A} \times \mathbf{B}) \cdot \mathbf{C} = \mathbf{A} \cdot (\mathbf{B} \times \mathbf{C}). \tag{13}$$

The triple scalar product can be evaluated as a determinant:

$$\mathbf{A}\cdot(\mathbf{B}\times\mathbf{C}) = \mathbf{A}\cdot\left[\begin{vmatrix} b_2 & b_3 \\ c_2 & c_3 \end{vmatrix}\mathbf{i} - \begin{vmatrix} b_1 & b_3 \\ c_1 & c_3 \end{vmatrix}\mathbf{j} + \begin{vmatrix} b_1 & b_2 \\ c_1 & c_2 \end{vmatrix}\mathbf{k}\right]$$

$$= a_1\begin{vmatrix} b_2 & b_3 \\ c_2 & c_3 \end{vmatrix} - a_2\begin{vmatrix} b_1 & b_3 \\ c_1 & c_3 \end{vmatrix} + a_3\begin{vmatrix} b_1 & b_2 \\ c_1 & c_2 \end{vmatrix}$$

$$= \begin{vmatrix} a_1 & a_2 & a_3 \\ b_1 & b_2 & b_3 \\ c_1 & c_2 & c_3 \end{vmatrix}$$

$$\mathbf{A}\cdot(\mathbf{B}\times\mathbf{C}) = (\mathbf{A}\times\mathbf{B})\cdot\mathbf{C} = \begin{vmatrix} a_1 & a_2 & a_3 \\ b_1 & b_2 & b_3 \\ c_1 & c_2 & c_3 \end{vmatrix} \tag{14}$$

EXAMPLE 6 Find the volume of the box (parallelepiped) determined by $\mathbf{A} = \mathbf{i} + 2\mathbf{j} - \mathbf{k}$, $\mathbf{B} = -2\mathbf{i} + 3\mathbf{k}$, and $\mathbf{C} = 7\mathbf{j} - 4\mathbf{k}$.

Solution

$$\mathbf{A}\cdot(\mathbf{B}\times\mathbf{C}) = \begin{vmatrix} 1 & 2 & -1 \\ -2 & 0 & 3 \\ 0 & 7 & -4 \end{vmatrix} = \begin{vmatrix} 0 & 3 \\ 7 & -4 \end{vmatrix} - 2\begin{vmatrix} -2 & 3 \\ 0 & -4 \end{vmatrix} - \begin{vmatrix} -2 & 0 \\ 0 & 7 \end{vmatrix}$$

$$= -21 - 16 + 14 = -23.$$

The volume is $|\mathbf{A}\cdot(\mathbf{B}\times\mathbf{C})| = 23$.

Exercises 11.4

In Exercises 1–8, find the length and direction (when defined) of $\mathbf{A}\times\mathbf{B}$ and $\mathbf{B}\times\mathbf{A}$.

1. $\mathbf{A} = 2\mathbf{i} - 2\mathbf{j} - \mathbf{k}$, $\mathbf{B} = \mathbf{i} - \mathbf{k}$
2. $\mathbf{A} = 2\mathbf{i} + 3\mathbf{j}$, $\mathbf{B} = -\mathbf{i} + \mathbf{j}$
3. $\mathbf{A} = 2\mathbf{i} - 2\mathbf{j} + 4\mathbf{k}$, $\mathbf{B} = -\mathbf{i} + \mathbf{j} - 2\mathbf{k}$
4. $\mathbf{A} = \mathbf{i} + \mathbf{j} - \mathbf{k}$, $\mathbf{B} = \mathbf{0}$
5. $\mathbf{A} = 2\mathbf{i}$, $\mathbf{B} = -3\mathbf{j}$
6. $\mathbf{A} = \mathbf{i}\times\mathbf{j}$, $\mathbf{B} = \mathbf{j}\times\mathbf{k}$
7. $\mathbf{A} = -8\mathbf{i} - 2\mathbf{j} - 4\mathbf{k}$, $\mathbf{B} = 2\mathbf{i} + 2\mathbf{j} + \mathbf{k}$
8. $\mathbf{A} = \frac{3}{2}\mathbf{i} - \frac{1}{2}\mathbf{j} + \mathbf{k}$, $\mathbf{B} = \mathbf{i} + \mathbf{j} + 2\mathbf{k}$

In Exercises 9–14, sketch the coordinate axes and then include the vectors $\mathbf{A}$, $\mathbf{B}$, and $\mathbf{A}\times\mathbf{B}$ as vectors starting at the origin.

9. $\mathbf{A} = \mathbf{i}$, $\mathbf{B} = \mathbf{j}$
10. $\mathbf{A} = \mathbf{i} - \mathbf{k}$, $\mathbf{B} = \mathbf{j}$
11. $\mathbf{A} = \mathbf{i} - \mathbf{k}$, $\mathbf{B} = \mathbf{j} + \mathbf{k}$
12. $\mathbf{A} = 2\mathbf{i} - \mathbf{j}$, $\mathbf{B} = \mathbf{i} + 2\mathbf{j}$
13. $\mathbf{A} = \mathbf{i} + \mathbf{j}$, $\mathbf{B} = \mathbf{i} - \mathbf{j}$
14. $\mathbf{A} = \mathbf{j} + 2\mathbf{k}$, $\mathbf{B} = \mathbf{i}$

In Exercises 15–18:

a) Find the area of the triangle determined by the points P, Q, and R.
b) Find a unit vector perpendicular to plane PQR.

15. $P(1, -1, 2)$, $Q(2, 0, -1)$, $R(0, 2, 1)$
16. $P(1, 1, 1)$, $Q(2, 1, 3)$, $R(3, -1, 1)$
17. $P(2, -2, 1)$, $Q(3, -1, 2)$, $R(3, -1, 1)$
18. $P(-2, 2, 0)$, $Q(0, 1, -1)$, $R(-1, 2, -2)$
19. Let $\mathbf{A} = 5\mathbf{i} - \mathbf{j} + \mathbf{k}$, $\mathbf{B} = \mathbf{j} - 5\mathbf{k}$, $\mathbf{C} = -15\mathbf{i} + 3\mathbf{j} - 3\mathbf{k}$. Which vectors, if any, are (a) perpendicular, (b) parallel? Give reasons for your answers.
20. Let $\mathbf{A} = \mathbf{i} + 2\mathbf{j} - \mathbf{k}$, $\mathbf{B} = -\mathbf{i} + \mathbf{j} + \mathbf{k}$, $\mathbf{C} = \mathbf{i} + \mathbf{k}$, $\mathbf{D} = -(\pi/2)\mathbf{i} - \pi\mathbf{j} + (\pi/2)\mathbf{k}$. Which vectors, if any, are (a) perpendicular, (b) parallel? Give reasons for your answers.

In Exercises 21 and 22, find the magnitude of the torque exerted by **F** on the bolt at P if $|\overrightarrow{PQ}| = 8$ in. and $|\mathbf{F}| = 30$ lb. Answer in foot-pounds.

21.

22.

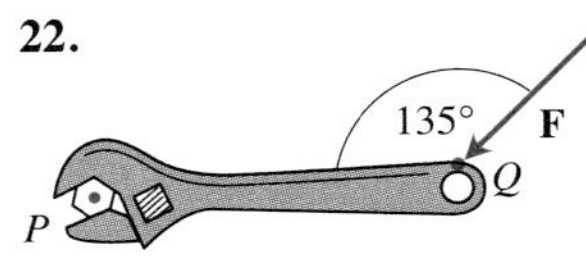

In Exercises 23–26, verify that $(\mathbf{A} \times \mathbf{B}) \cdot \mathbf{C} = (\mathbf{B} \times \mathbf{C}) \cdot \mathbf{A} = (\mathbf{C} \times \mathbf{A}) \cdot \mathbf{B}$ and find the volume of the parallelepiped (box) determined by **A**, **B**, and **C**.

	A	**B**	**C**
23.	$2\mathbf{i}$	$2\mathbf{j}$	$2\mathbf{k}$
24.	$\mathbf{i} - \mathbf{j} + \mathbf{k}$	$2\mathbf{i} + \mathbf{j} - 2\mathbf{k}$	$-\mathbf{i} + 2\mathbf{j} - \mathbf{k}$
25.	$2\mathbf{i} + \mathbf{j}$	$2\mathbf{i} - \mathbf{j} + \mathbf{k}$	$\mathbf{i} + 2\mathbf{k}$
26.	$\mathbf{i} + \mathbf{j} - 2\mathbf{k}$	$-\mathbf{i} - \mathbf{k}$	$2\mathbf{i} + 4\mathbf{j} - 2\mathbf{k}$

27. If A, B, and C are points in space such that $\overrightarrow{AB} \times \overrightarrow{AC} = 2\mathbf{i} - 4\mathbf{j} + 4\mathbf{k}$, what is the area of triangle ABC? Give reasons for your answer.

28. What is $\mathbf{u} \cdot (\mathbf{u} \times \mathbf{v})$? Give reasons for your answer.

29. Given nonzero vectors **A**, **B**, and **C**, use dot-product and cross-product notation, as appropriate, to describe the following.

a) The vector projection of **A** onto **B**
b) A vector orthogonal to **A** and **B**
c) A vector orthogonal to $\mathbf{A} \times \mathbf{B}$ and **C**
d) The volume of the parallelepiped determined by **A**, **B**, and **C**

30. Given nonzero vectors **A**, **B**, and **C**, use dot-product and cross-product notation to describe the following.

a) A vector orthogonal to $\mathbf{A} \times \mathbf{B}$ and $\mathbf{A} \times \mathbf{C}$
b) A vector orthogonal to $\mathbf{A} + \mathbf{B}$ and $\mathbf{A} - \mathbf{B}$
c) A vector of length $|\mathbf{A}|$ in the direction of **B**
d) The area of the parallelogram determined by **A** and **C**

31. *Cancellation in Cross Products.* If $\mathbf{A} \times \mathbf{B} = \mathbf{A} \times \mathbf{C}$ and $\mathbf{A} \neq \mathbf{0}$, then does $\mathbf{B} = \mathbf{C}$? Give reasons for your answer.

32. *Double Cancellation.* If $\mathbf{A} \neq \mathbf{0}$, and if $\mathbf{A} \times \mathbf{B} = \mathbf{A} \times \mathbf{C}$ and $\mathbf{A} \cdot \mathbf{B} = \mathbf{A} \cdot \mathbf{C}$, then does $\mathbf{B} = \mathbf{C}$? Give reasons for your answers.

AREAS IN THE PLANE

To find the area of a parallelogram in a plane, picture the plane as the xy-plane in space. Then write vectors for a pair of adjacent sides (their **k**-components will be zero) and calculate the magnitude of their cross product.

Find the areas of the parallelograms whose vertices are given in Exercises 33–36.

33. $A(1, 0)$, $B(0, 1)$, $C(-1, 0)$, $D(0, -1)$

34. $A(0, 0)$, $B(7, 3)$, $C(9, 8)$, $D(2, 5)$

35. $A(-1, 2)$, $B(2, 0)$, $C(7, 1)$, $D(4, 3)$

36. $A(-6, 0)$, $B(1, -4)$, $C(3, 1)$, $D(-4, 5)$

Find the areas of the triangles whose vertices are given in Exercises 37–40.

37. $A(0, 0)$, $B(-2, 3)$, $C(3, 1)$

38. $A(-1, -1)$, $B(3, 3)$, $C(2, 1)$

39. $A(-5, 3)$, $B(1, -2)$, $C(6, -2)$

40. $A(-6, 0)$, $B(10, -5)$, $C(-2, 4)$

41. Find a formula for the area of the triangle in the xy-plane with vertices at $(0, 0)$, (a_1, a_2), and (b_1, b_2). Explain your work.

Writing for Your Own Knowledge

Answer the following questions in writing. Some answers will take only a sentence or two; others may require several paragraphs. Some explanations may also call for graphs or sketches.

1. What is the vector product of two vectors? What are its geometric and physical interpretations?
2. What can you say about $\mathbf{A} \times \mathbf{B}$ vs. $\mathbf{B} \times \mathbf{A}$?
3. How can you find the areas of triangles and parallelograms in space?
4. How do you evaluate cross products from scalar components?
5. How can you find a unit vector perpendicular to a plane?
6. How can you find the volume of the parallelepiped determined by three vectors in space?

11.5 Lines and Planes in Space

This section shows how to use scalar and vector products to write equations for lines, line segments, and planes in space.

Equations for Lines and Line Segments

Suppose L is a line in space that passes through a point $P_0(x_0, y_0, z_0)$ and lies parallel to a vector $\mathbf{v} = A\,\mathbf{i} + B\,\mathbf{j} + C\,\mathbf{k}$. Then L is the set of all points $P(x, y, z)$

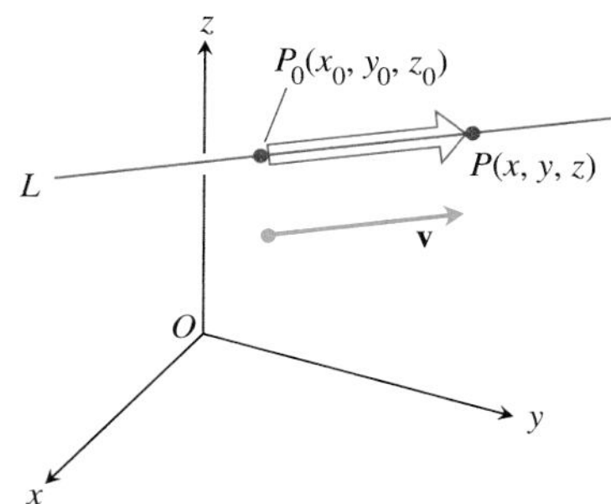

11.41 A point P lies on the line through P_0 parallel to $\mathbf{v}$ if and only if $\overrightarrow{P_0P}$ is a scalar multiple of $\mathbf{v}$.

for which the vector $\overrightarrow{P_0P}$ is parallel to $\mathbf{v}$ (Fig. 11.41). That is, P lies on L if and only if

$$\overrightarrow{P_0P} = t\,\mathbf{v} \tag{1}$$

for some number t, $-\infty < t < \infty$.

If we write Eq. (1) in terms of $\mathbf{i}$-, $\mathbf{j}$-, and $\mathbf{k}$- components and equate the corresponding components of the two sides, we get three equations involving the parameter t:

$$(x - x_0)\,\mathbf{i} + (y - y_0)\,\mathbf{j} + (z - z_0)\,\mathbf{k} = t(A\,\mathbf{i} + B\,\mathbf{j} + C\mathbf{k}), \qquad \text{Eq. (1) expanded}$$

$$x - x_0 = t\,A, \qquad y - y_0 = t\,B, \qquad z - z_0 = t\,C. \qquad \text{Components equated}$$

When rearranged, these last three equations give us the standard parametrization of the line for the parameter interval $-\infty < t < \infty$.

Standard Parametrization of the Line Through $P_0(x_0, y_0, z_0)$ Parallel to $\mathbf{v} = A\,\mathbf{i} + B\,\mathbf{j} + C\,\mathbf{k}$

$$x = x_0 + t\,A, \qquad y = y_0 + t\,B, \qquad z = z_0 + t\,C, \qquad -\infty < t < \infty \tag{2}$$

We rarely use any t-interval other than $(-\infty, \infty)$ to parametrize a line, so we call the equations in (2) the **standard parametric equations** for the line through P_0 parallel to $\mathbf{v}$. When we want parametric equations for this line, these are the ones we produce, the interval $(-\infty, \infty)$ being understood.

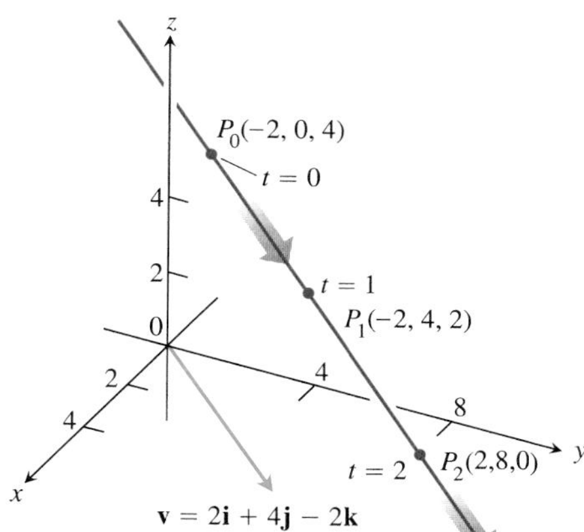

11.42 Selected points and parameter values on the line $x = -2 + 2t$, $y = 4t$, $z = 4 - 2t$. The arrows show the direction of increasing t (Example 1).

EXAMPLE 1 Find parametric equations for the line through $(-2, 0, 4)$ parallel to $\mathbf{v} = 2\,\mathbf{i} + 4\,\mathbf{j} - 2\,\mathbf{k}$ (Fig. 11.42).

Solution With $P_0(x_0, y_0, z_0)$ equal to $(-2, 0, 4)$ and $A\,\mathbf{i} + B\,\mathbf{j} + C\,\mathbf{k}$ equal to $2\,\mathbf{i} + 4\,\mathbf{j} - 2\,\mathbf{k}$, Eqs. (2) become

$$x = -2 + 2t, \qquad y = 4t, \qquad z = 4 - 2t.$$

EXAMPLE 2 Find parametric equations for the line through $P(-3, 2, -3)$ and $Q(1, -1, 4)$.

Solution The vector

$$\begin{aligned}\overrightarrow{PQ} &= (1 - (-3))\,\mathbf{i} + (-1 - 2)\,\mathbf{j} + (4 - (-3))\,\mathbf{k} \\ &= 4\,\mathbf{i} - 3\,\mathbf{j} + 7\,\mathbf{k}\end{aligned}$$

is parallel to the line, and Eqs. (2) with $(x_0, y_0, z_0) = (-3, 2, -3)$ give

$$x = -3 + 4t, \qquad y = 2 - 3t, \qquad z = -3 + 7t. \tag{3}$$

We could have chosen $Q(1, -1, 4)$ as the "base point" and written

$$x = 1 + 4t, \qquad y = -1 - 3t, \qquad z = 4 + 7t \tag{4}$$

as equations for the line. The parametrizations in (3) and (4) place you at different points for a given value of t, but each set of equations covers the line completely as t runs from $-\infty$ to ∞.

Notice that parametrizations of lines are not unique.

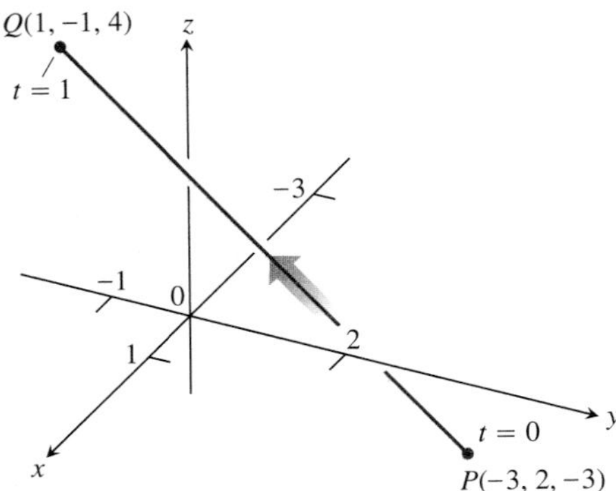

11.43 Example 3 derives a parametrization of the line segment joining P and Q. The arrow shows the direction of increasing t.

To parametrize a line segment joining two points, we first parametrize the line through the points. We then find the t-values for the endpoints and restrict t to lie in the closed interval bounded by these values. The line equations together with this added restriction parametrize the segment.

EXAMPLE 3 Parametrize the line segment joining the points $P(-3, 2, -3)$ and $Q(1, -1, 4)$ (Fig. 11.43).

Solution We begin with equations for the line through P and Q, taking them, in this case, from Example 2:

$$x = -3 + 4t, \qquad y = 2 - 3t, \qquad z = -3 + 7t. \tag{5}$$

We observe that the point

$$(x, y, z) = (-3 + 4t,\ 2 - 3t,\ -3 + 7t)$$

passes through $P(-3, 2, -3)$ at $t = 0$ and $Q(1, -1, 4)$ at $t = 1$. We add the restriction $0 \le t \le 1$ to Eqs. (5) to parametrize the segment:

$$x = -3 + 4t, \qquad y = 2 - 3t, \qquad z = -3 + 7t, \qquad 0 \le t \le 1.$$

The Distance from a Point to a Line in Space

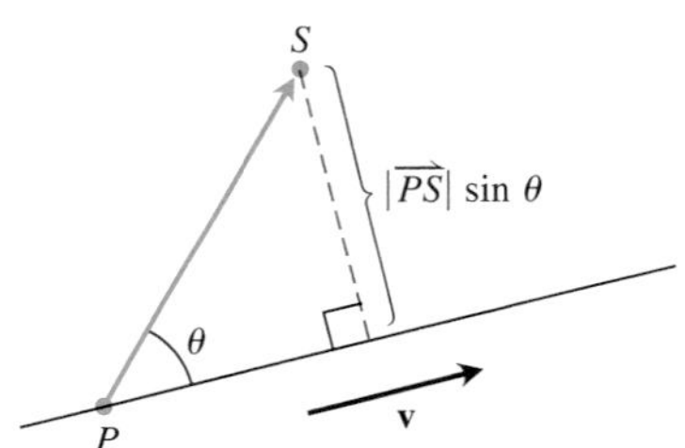

11.44 The distance from S to the line through P parallel to $\mathbf{v}$ is $|\overrightarrow{PS}| \sin\theta$, where θ is the angle between $\overrightarrow{PS}$ and $\mathbf{v}$.

To find the distance from a point S to a line L that passes through a point P parallel to a vector $\mathbf{v}$, we find the length of the component of $\overrightarrow{PS}$ normal to the line (Fig. 11.44). In the notation of Fig. 11.44, the length is

$$|\overrightarrow{PS}| \sin\theta = |\overrightarrow{PS}| \frac{|\overrightarrow{PS} \times \mathbf{v}|}{|\overrightarrow{PS}|\,|\mathbf{v}|} \qquad |\overrightarrow{PS}|\,|\mathbf{v}| \sin\theta = |\overrightarrow{PS} \times \mathbf{v}|$$

$$= \frac{|\overrightarrow{PS} \times \mathbf{v}|}{|\mathbf{v}|}. \tag{6}$$

Distance from a Point S to a Line Through P Parallel to v

$$d = \frac{|\overrightarrow{PS} \times \mathbf{v}|}{|\mathbf{v}|} \tag{7}$$

EXAMPLE 4 Find the distance from the point $S(1, 1, 5)$ to the line

$$L: \qquad x = 1 + t, \quad y = 3 - t, \quad z = 2t.$$

Solution We see from the equations for L that L passes through $P(1, 3, 0)$ parallel to $\mathbf{v} = \mathbf{i} - \mathbf{j} + 2\mathbf{k}$. With

$$\overrightarrow{PS} = (1 - 1)\mathbf{i} + (1 - 3)\mathbf{j} + (5 - 0)\mathbf{k} = -2\mathbf{j} + 5\mathbf{k}$$

and

$$\overrightarrow{PS} \times \mathbf{v} = \begin{vmatrix} \mathbf{i} & \mathbf{j} & \mathbf{k} \\ 0 & -2 & 5 \\ 1 & -1 & 2 \end{vmatrix} = \mathbf{i} + 5\mathbf{j} + 2\mathbf{k},$$

Eq. (7) gives

$$d = \frac{|\overrightarrow{PS} \times \mathbf{v}|}{|\mathbf{v}|} = \frac{\sqrt{1 + 25 + 4}}{\sqrt{1 + 1 + 4}} = \frac{\sqrt{30}}{\sqrt{6}} = \sqrt{5}.$$

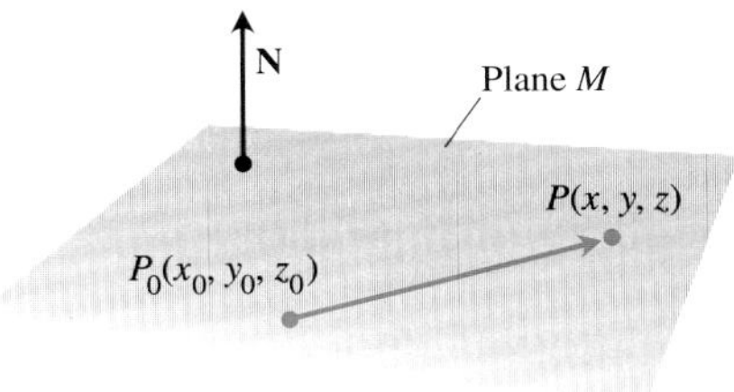

11.45 The standard equation for a plane in space is defined in terms of a vector normal to the plane: A point P lies in the plane through P_0 normal to $\mathbf{N}$ if and only if $\mathbf{N}\cdot\overrightarrow{P_0P} = 0$.

Equations for Planes

Suppose a plane M passes through a point $P_0(x_0, y_0, z_0)$ and is normal (perpendicular) to the nonzero vector $\mathbf{N} = A\,\mathbf{i} + B\,\mathbf{j} + C\,\mathbf{k}$. Then M consists of all points $P(x, y, z)$ for which $\overrightarrow{P_0P}$ is orthogonal to $\mathbf{N}$ (Fig. 11.45). That is, P lies on M if and only if

$$\begin{aligned} \mathbf{N}\cdot\overrightarrow{P_0P} &= 0 \\ (A\mathbf{i} + B\mathbf{j} + C\mathbf{k})\cdot[(x - x_0)\,\mathbf{i} + (y - y_0)\,\mathbf{j} + (z - z_0)\,\mathbf{k}] &= 0 \\ A(x - x_0) + B(y - y_0) + C(z - z_0) &= 0 \\ Ax + By + Cz &= Ax_0 + By_0 + Cz_0. \end{aligned} \tag{8}$$

Plane Through $P_0(x_0, y_0, z_0)$ Normal to $\mathbf{N} = A\,\mathbf{i} + B\,\mathbf{j} + C\,\mathbf{k}$

$$A(x - x_0) + B(y - y_0) + C(z - z_0) = 0 \tag{9}$$

or

$$Ax + By + Cz = D, \quad \text{where} \quad D = Ax_0 + By_0 + Cz_0 \tag{10}$$

Notice how the components of $\mathbf{N}$ become coefficients in the equation $Ax + By + Cz = D$, just the way they did for lines in the plane.

EXAMPLE 5 Find an equation for the plane through $P_0(-3, 0, 7)$ perpendicular to $\mathbf{N} = 5\,\mathbf{i} + 2\,\mathbf{j} - \mathbf{k}$.

Solution

$$5(x - (-3)) + 2(y - 0) + (-1)(z - 7) = 0 \qquad \text{Eq. (10) with the given } \mathbf{N} \text{ and } P_0$$

$$5x + 15 + 2y - z + 7 = 0$$

$$5x + 2y - z = -22$$

EXAMPLE 6 Find the plane through $A(0, 0, 1)$, $B(2, 0, 0)$, and $C(0, 3, 0)$.

Solution We find a vector normal to the plane and use it with one of the points (it does not matter which one) to write an equation for the plane.

The cross product

$$\overrightarrow{AB}\times\overrightarrow{AC} = \begin{vmatrix} \mathbf{i} & \mathbf{j} & \mathbf{k} \\ 2 & 0 & -1 \\ 0 & 3 & -1 \end{vmatrix} = 3\,\mathbf{i} + 2\,\mathbf{j} + 6\,\mathbf{k}$$

is normal to the plane. We substitute the components of this vector and the coordinates of the point $(0, 0, 1)$ into Eq. (9) to get

$$3x + 2y + 6z = 6$$

as an equation for the plane.

EXAMPLE 7 Find the point where the line

$$x = \frac{8}{3} + 2t, \qquad y = -2t, \qquad z = 1 + t$$

meets the plane $3x + 2y + 6z = 6$.

Solution The point

$$\left(\frac{8}{3} + 2t,\ -2t,\ 1 + t\right)$$

lies in the plane if its coordinates satisfy the equation of the plane; that is, if

$$3\left(\frac{8}{3} + 2t\right) + 2(-2t) + 6(1 + t) = 6$$
$$8 + 6t - 4t + 6 + 6t = 6$$
$$8t = -8$$
$$t = -1.$$

The point of intersection is

$$(x, y, z)\Big|_{t=-1} = \left(\frac{8}{3} - 2,\ 2,\ 1 - 1\right) = \left(\frac{2}{3},\ 2,\ 0\right).$$

How to Find the Distance from a Point to a Plane

To find the distance from a point S to a plane $Ax + By + Cz = D$, find

1. a point P on the plane,
2. $\overrightarrow{PS}$,
3. the direction of $\mathbf{N} = A\,\mathbf{i} + B\,\mathbf{j} + C\,\mathbf{k}$.

Then calculate the distance as

$$d = \left|\overrightarrow{PS} \cdot \frac{\mathbf{N}}{|\mathbf{N}|}\right|.$$

EXAMPLE 8 Find the distance from $S(1, 1, 3)$ to the plane $3x + 2y + 6z = 6$.

Solution We use the same approach we used in Section 11.3 to find the distance from a point to a line: We find a point P in the plane and calculate the length of the vector projection of $\overrightarrow{PS}$ onto a vector $\mathbf{N}$ normal to the plane (Fig. 11.46).

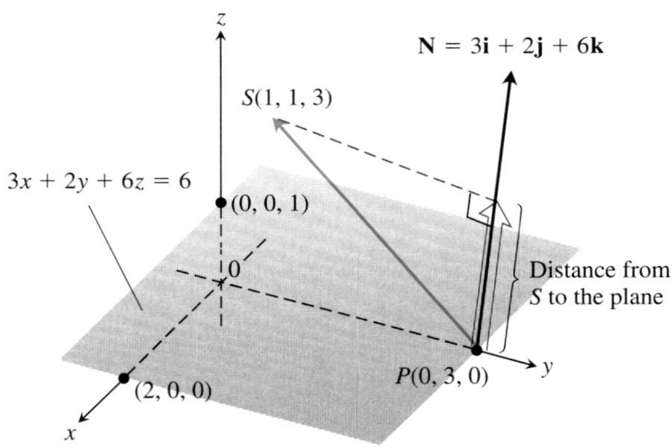

11.46 The distance from S to the plane is the length of the vector projection of $\overrightarrow{PS}$ onto $\mathbf{N}$ (Example 8).

The coefficients in the equation $3x + 2y + 6z = 6$ give

$$\mathbf{N} = 3\,\mathbf{i} + 2\,\mathbf{j} + 6\,\mathbf{k}.$$

The points on the plane easiest to find from the plane's equation are the intercepts. If we take P to be the y-intercept $(0, 3, 0)$, then

$$\overrightarrow{PS} = (1 - 0)\,\mathbf{i} + (1 - 3)\,\mathbf{j} + (3 - 0)\,\mathbf{k}$$
$$= \mathbf{i} - 2\,\mathbf{j} + 3\,\mathbf{k},$$
$$|\mathbf{N}| = \sqrt{(3)^2 + (2)^2 + (6)^2} = \sqrt{49} = 7.$$

The distance from S to the plane is

$$\begin{aligned} d &= \left| \overrightarrow{PS} \cdot \frac{\mathbf{N}}{|\mathbf{N}|} \right| \\ &= \left| (\mathbf{i} - 2\,\mathbf{j} + 3\,\mathbf{k}) \cdot \left(\frac{3}{7}\mathbf{i} + \frac{2}{7}\mathbf{j} + \frac{6}{7}\mathbf{k} \right) \right| \\ &= \left| \frac{3}{7} - \frac{4}{7} + \frac{18}{7} \right| = \frac{17}{7}. \end{aligned}$$

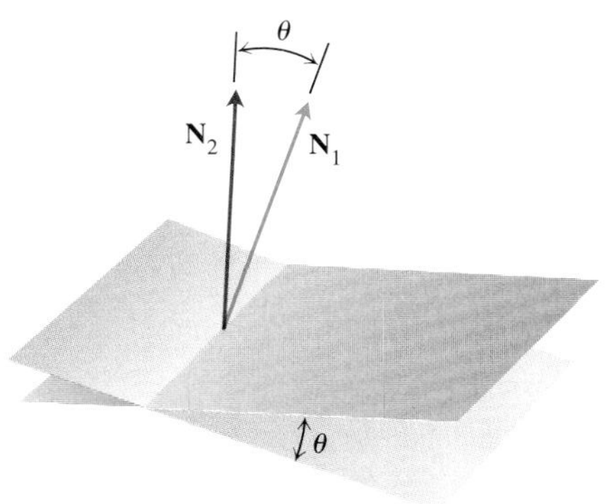

11.47 The angle between two planes is obtained from the angle between their normals.

Angles Between Planes; Lines of Intersection

The angle between two intersecting planes is defined to be the (acute) angle made by their normal vectors (Fig. 11.47).

EXAMPLE 9 Find the angle between the planes $3x - 6y - 2z = 15$ and $2x + y - 2z = 5$.

Solution The vectors

$$\mathbf{N}_1 = 3\,\mathbf{i} - 6\,\mathbf{j} - 2\,\mathbf{k} \qquad \mathbf{N}_2 = 2\,\mathbf{i} + \mathbf{j} - 2\,\mathbf{k}$$

are normals to the planes. The angle between them is

$$\begin{aligned} \theta &= \cos^{-1}\left(\frac{\mathbf{N}_1 \cdot \mathbf{N}_2}{|\mathbf{N}_1||\mathbf{N}_2|} \right) && \text{Eq. (4), Section 11.3} \\ &= \cos^{-1}\frac{4}{21} \\ &\approx 1.38 \text{ rad} && \text{About } 79^\circ \end{aligned}$$

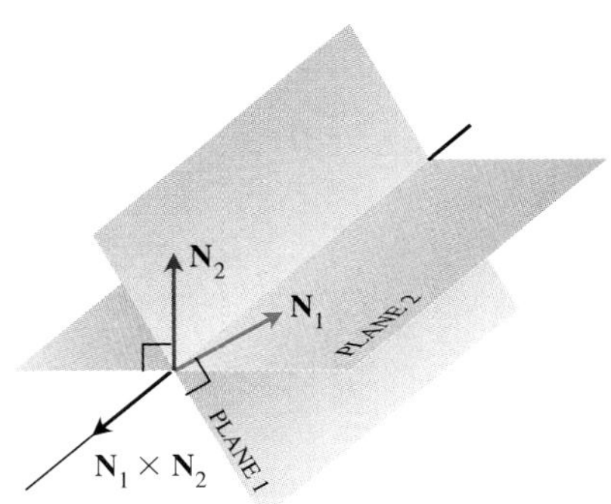

11.48 How the line of intersection of two planes is related to the planes' normal vectors (Example 10).

EXAMPLE 10 Find a vector parallel to the line of intersection of the planes $3x - 6y - 2z = 15$ and $2x + y - 2z = 5$.

Solution The line of intersection of two planes is perpendicular to the planes' normal vectors $\mathbf{N}_1$ and $\mathbf{N}_2$ (Fig. 11.48), and therefore parallel to $\mathbf{N}_1 \times \mathbf{N}_2$. Turning this around, $\mathbf{N}_1 \times \mathbf{N}_2$ is a vector parallel to the planes' line of intersection. In our case,

$$\mathbf{N}_1 \times \mathbf{N}_2 = \begin{vmatrix} \mathbf{i} & \mathbf{j} & \mathbf{k} \\ 3 & -6 & -2 \\ 2 & 1 & -2 \end{vmatrix} = 14\,\mathbf{i} + 2\,\mathbf{j} + 15\,\mathbf{k}.$$

Any nonzero scalar multiple of $\mathbf{N}_1 \times \mathbf{N}_2$ will do as well.

EXAMPLE 11 Find parametric equations for the line in which the planes $3x - 6y - 2z = 15$ and $2x + y - 2z = 5$ intersect.

Solution We find a vector parallel to the line and a point on the line and use Eqs. (2).

Example 10 identifies $\mathbf{v} = 14\,\mathbf{i} + 2\,\mathbf{j} + 15\,\mathbf{k}$ as a vector parallel to the line. To find a point on the line, we can take any point common to the two planes. Substituting $z = 0$ in the plane equations and solving for x and y simultaneously gives the point $(3, -1, 0)$. The line is

$$x = 3 + 14t, \qquad y = -1 + 2t, \qquad z = 15t.$$

Exercises 11.5

Find parametric equations for the lines in Exercises 1–12.

1. The line through the point $P(3, -4, -1)$ parallel to the vector $\mathbf{i} + \mathbf{j} + \mathbf{k}$
2. The line through $P(1, 2, -1)$ and $Q(-1, 0, 1)$
3. The line through $P(-2, 0, 3)$ and $Q(3, 5, -2)$
4. The line through $P(1, 2, 0)$ and $Q(1, 1, -1)$
5. The line through the origin parallel to the vector $2\mathbf{j} + \mathbf{k}$
6. The line through the point $(3, -2, 1)$ parallel to the line $x = 1 + 2t$, $y = 2 - t$, $z = 3t$
7. The line through $(1, 1, 1)$ parallel to the z-axis
8. The line through $(2, 4, 5)$ perpendicular to the plane $3x + 7y - 5z = 21$
9. The line through $(0, -7, 0)$ perpendicular to the plane $x + 2y + 2z = 13$
10. The line through $(2, 3, 0)$ perpendicular to the vectors $\mathbf{A} = \mathbf{i} + 2\mathbf{j} + 3\mathbf{k}$ and $\mathbf{B} = 3\mathbf{i} + 4\mathbf{j} + 5\mathbf{k}$
11. The x-axis
12. The z-axis

Find parametrizations for the line segments joining the points in Exercises 13–20. Draw coordinate axes and sketch each segment, indicating the direction of increasing t for your parametrization.

13. $(0, 0, 0)$, $(1, 1, 3/2)$
14. $(0, 0, 0)$, $(1, 0, 0)$
15. $(1, 0, 0)$, $(1, 1, 0)$
16. $(1, 1, 0)$, $(1, 1, 1)$
17. $(0, 1, 1)$, $(0, -1, 1)$
18. $(0, 2, 0)$, $(3, 0, 0)$
19. $(2, 0, 2)$, $(0, 2, 0)$
20. $(1, 0, -1)$, $(0, 3, 0)$

Find equations for the planes in Exercises 21–26.

21. The plane through $P_0(0, 2, -1)$ normal to $\mathbf{N} = 3\mathbf{i} - 2\mathbf{j} - \mathbf{k}$
22. The plane through $(1, -1, 3)$ parallel to the plane $3x + y + z = 7$
23. The plane through $(1, 1, -1)$, $(2, 0, 2)$, and $(0, -2, 1)$
24. The plane through $(2, 4, 5)$, $(1, 5, 7)$, and $(-1, 6, 8)$
25. The plane through $P_0(2, 4, 5)$ perpendicular to the line
$$x = 5 + t, \quad y = 1 + 3t, \quad z = 4t$$
26. The plane through $A(1, -2, 1)$ perpendicular to the vector from the origin to A
27. Find an equation for the plane that contains both the point $(1, 2, 3)$ and the line $x = 3t - 1$, $y = 6$, $z = t + 2$.
28. Find an equation for the plane that contains the intersecting lines
$$L_1:\ x = 3t - 1, \quad y = t + 1, \quad z = t - 1, \quad -\infty < t < \infty$$
$$L_2:\ x = 5s - 1, \quad y = 2s + 1, \quad z = -s - 1, \quad -\infty < s < \infty$$
29. Use Eqs. (2) to generate a parametrization of the line through $P(2, -4, 7)$ parallel to $\mathbf{v}_1 = 2\mathbf{i} - \mathbf{j} + 3\mathbf{k}$. Then generate another parametrization of the line using the point $P_2(-2, -2, 1)$ and the vector $\mathbf{v}_2 = -\mathbf{i} + (1/2)\mathbf{j} - (3/2)\mathbf{k}$.
30. Use Eq. (9) to generate an equation for the plane through $P_1(4, 1, 5)$ normal to $\mathbf{N}_1 = \mathbf{i} - 2\mathbf{j} + \mathbf{k}$. Then generate another equation for the same plane using the point $P_2(3, -2, 0)$ and the normal vector $\mathbf{N}_2 = -\sqrt{2}\,\mathbf{i} + 2\sqrt{2}\,\mathbf{j} - \sqrt{2}\,\mathbf{k}$.

In Exercises 31–36, find the distance from the point to the line.

31. $(0, 0, 12)$; $x = 4t$, $y = -2t$, $z = 2t$
32. $(0, 0, 0)$; $x = 5 + 3t$, $y = 5 + 4t$, $z = -3 - 5t$
33. $(2, 1, 3)$; $x = 2 + 2t$, $y = 1 + 6t$, $z = 3$
34. $(2, 1, -1)$; $x = 2t$, $y = 1 + 2t$, $z = 2t$
35. $(3, -1, 4)$; $x = 4 - t$, $y = 3 + 2t$, $z = -5 + 3t$
36. $(-1, 4, 3)$; $x = 10 + 4t$, $y = -3$, $z = 4t$

In Exercises 37–42, find the distance from the point to the plane.

37. $(2, -3, 4)$, $x + 2y + 2z = 13$
38. $(0, 0, 0)$, $3x + 2y + 6z = 6$
39. $(0, 1, 1)$, $4y + 3z = -12$
40. $(2, 2, 3)$, $2x + y + 2z = 4$
41. $(0, -1, 0)$, $2x + y + 2z = 4$
42. $(1, 0, -1)$, $-4x + y + z = 4$

In Exercises 43–46, find the point in which the line meets the plane.

43. $x = 1 - t$, $y = 3t$, $z = 1 + t$; $2x - y + 3z = 6$
44. $x = 2$, $y = 3 + 2t$, $z = -2 - 2t$; $6x + 3y - 4z = -12$
45. $x = 1 + 2t$, $y = 1 + 5t$, $z = 3t$; $x + y + z = 2$
46. $x = -1 + 3t$, $y = -2$, $z = 5t$; $2x - 3z = 7$

Find the angles between the planes in Exercises 47 and 48 (calculator not needed).

47. $x + y = 1$, $2x + y - 2z = 2$
48. $5x + y - z = 10$, $x - 2y + 3z = -1$

Use a calculator to find the acute angles between the planes in Exercises 49–52 to the nearest hundredth of a radian.

49. $2x + 2y + 2z = 3$, $2x - 2y - z = 5$
50. $x + y + z = 1$, $z = 0$ (the xy-plane)
51. $2x + 2y - z = 3$, $x + 2y + z = 2$
52. $4y + 3z = -12$, $3x + 2y + 6z = 6$

Find parametrizations for the lines in which the planes in Exercises 53–56 intersect.

53. $x + y + z = 1$, $x + y = 2$
54. $3x - 6y - 2z = 3$, $2x + y - 2z = 2$
55. $x - 2y + 4z = 2$, $x + y - 2z = 5$
56. $5x - 2y = 11$, $4y - 5z = -17$

57. Find the points in which the line $x = 1 + 2t$, $y = -1 - t$, $z = 3t$ meets the coordinate planes. Describe the reasoning behind your answer.

58. Find equations for the line in the plane $z = 3$ that makes an angle of $\pi/6$ rad with $\mathbf{i}$ and an angle of $\pi/3$ rad with $\mathbf{j}$. Describe the reasoning behind your answer.

59. Is the line $x = 1 - 2t$, $y = 2 + 5t$, $z = -3t$ parallel to the plane $2x + y - z = 8$? Give reasons for your answer.

60. How can you tell when two planes $A_1x + B_1y + C_1z = D_1$ and $A_2x + B_2y + C_2z = D_2$ are parallel? perpendicular? Give reasons for your answer.

In Exercises 61 and 62, find the plane determined by the intersecting lines.

61. $L1$: $x = -1 + t$, $y = 2 + t$, $z = 1 - t$, $-\infty < t < \infty$

$L2$: $x = 1 - 4s$, $y = 1 + 2s$, $z = 2 - 2s$, $-\infty < s < \infty$

62. $L1$: $x = t$, $y = 3 - 3t$, $z = -2 - t$, $-\infty < t < \infty$

$L2$: $x = 1 + s$, $y = 4 + s$, $z = -1 + s$, $-\infty < s < \infty$

Given two lines in space, they are either parallel, or they intersect, or they are skew (imagine, for example, the flight paths of two planes in the sky). Exercises 63 and 64 each give three lines. In each exercise, determine whether the lines, taken two at a time, are parallel, intersect, or are skew.

63. $L1$: $x = 3 + 2t$, $y = -1 + 4t$, $z = 2 - t$, $-\infty < t < \infty$

$L2$: $x = 1 + 4s$, $y = 1 + 2s$, $z = -3 + 4s$, $-\infty < s < \infty$

$L3$: $x = 3 + 2r$, $y = 2 + r$, $z = -2 + 2r$, $-\infty < r < \infty$

64. $L1$: $x = 1 + 2t$, $y = -1 - t$, $z = 3t$, $-\infty < t < \infty$

$L2$: $x = 2 - s$, $y = 3s$, $z = 1 + s$, $-\infty < s < \infty$

$L3$: $x = 5 + 2r$, $y = 1 - r$, $z = 8 + 3r$, $-\infty < r < \infty$

Writing for Your Own Knowledge

Answer the following questions in writing. Some answers will take only a sentence or two; others may require several paragraphs. Some explanations may also call for graphs or sketches.

1. How do you write equations for lines in space? for the line segment joining two points?
2. How do you find the distance from a point to a line in space?
3. How do you find an equation for the plane
   a) through a given point normal to a given vector?
   b) through three noncollinear points?
4. How do you find the distance from a point to a plane?
5. How do you find the angles between intersecting planes?
6. How do you find equations for the line in which two planes intersect?

11.6 *Surfaces in Space*

Just as we call the graph of an equation $F(x, y) = 0$ in the plane a curve, we call the graph of the equation $F(x, y, z) = 0$ in space a **surface.** We use surfaces to describe boundaries of solids, to model the membranes across which fluids flow, to describe plates over which electrical charges are distributed, and to define the walls of containers that are subjected to pressures of various kinds. We will see some of these applications in the chapters to come.

Our goal in the present section is to become acquainted with the surfaces most commonly used in the theory and applications of the calculus of functions of more than one variable. This means finding out what the surfaces look like, what their equations are, and how to draw them.

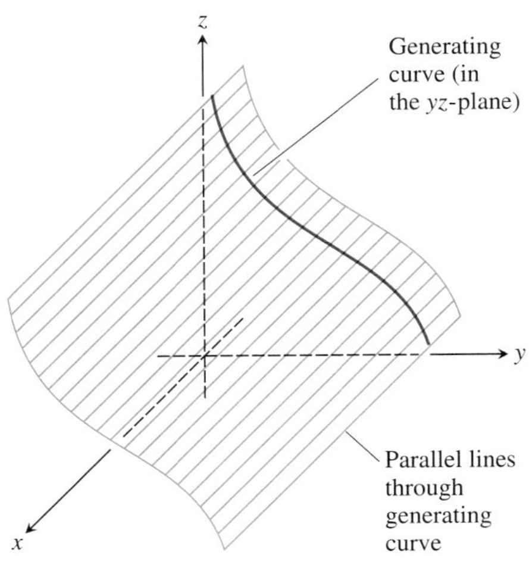

Cylinders

Besides planes, the simplest surfaces to draw are cylinders.

DEFINITIONS

A **cylinder** is a surface composed of all the lines parallel to a given line that pass through a given plane curve. The curve is the **generating curve** for the cylinder. (See diagram at the left.)

In solid geometry, *cylinder* usually means *circular cylinder,* but we now allow cylinders to have cross sections of any kind. The cross sections of the cylinder in the first example are parabolas, not circles.

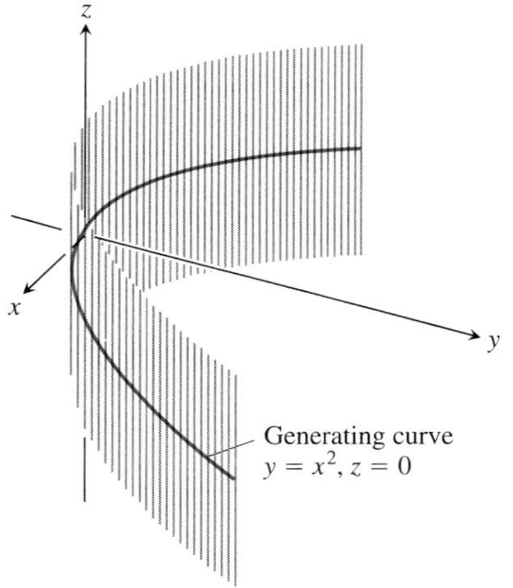

11.49 The cylinder of lines passing through the parabola $y = x^2$ in the xy-plane parallel to the z-axis (Example 1).

EXAMPLE 1 *The Parabolic Cylinder* $y = x^2$. Find an equation for the cylinder made by the lines parallel to the z-axis that pass through the parabola $y = x^2$, $z = 0$ (Fig. 11.49).

Solution Suppose that the point $P_0(x_0, x_0^2, 0)$ lies on the parabola $y = x^2$ in the xy-plane. Then, for any value of z, the point $Q(x_0, x_0^2, z)$ will lie on the cylinder because it lies on the line $x = x_0$, $y = x_0^2$ through P_0 parallel to the z-axis. Conversely, any point $Q(x_0, x_0^2, z)$ whose y-coordinate is the square of its x-coordinate lies on the cylinder because it lies on the line $x = x_0$, $y = x_0^2$ through P_0 parallel to the z-axis (Fig. 11.50).

Regardless of the value of z, therefore, the points on the surface are the points whose coordinates satisfy the equation $y = x^2$. This makes $y = x^2$ an equation for the cylinder. Because of this, we call the cylinder "the cylinder $y = x^2$."

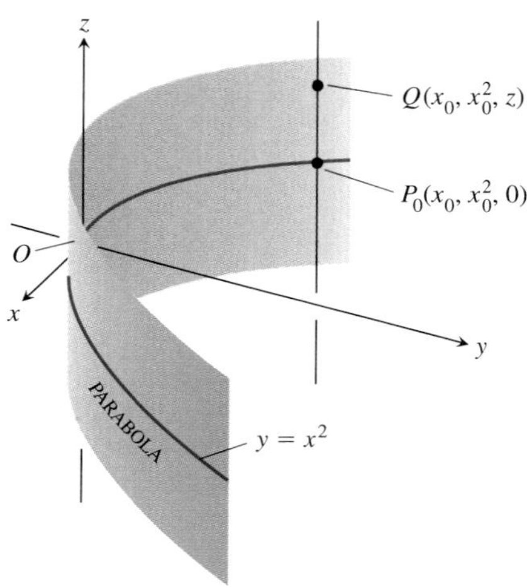

11.50 Every point of the cylinder in Fig. 11.49 has coordinates of the form (x_0, x_0^2, z). We call the cylinder "the cylinder $y = x^2$."

As Example 1 suggests, any curve $f(x, y) = c$ in the xy-plane defines a cylinder parallel to the z-axis whose equation is also $f(x, y) = c$. The equation $x^2 + y^2 = 1$ defines the circular cylinder made by the lines parallel to the z-axis that pass through the circle $x^2 + y^2 = 1$ in the xy-plane. The equation $x^2 + 4y^2 = 9$ defines the elliptical cylinder made by the lines parallel to the z-axis that pass through the ellipse $x^2 + 4y^2 = 9$ in the xy-plane.

In a similar way, any curve $g(x, z) = c$ in the xz-plane defines a cylinder parallel to the y-axis whose space equation is also $g(x, z) = c$. Any curve $h(y, z) = c$ defines a cylinder parallel to the x-axis whose space equation is also $h(y, z) = c$. An equation in any two of the three Cartesian coordinates defines a cylinder parallel to the axis of the third coordinate. See Figs. 11.51 and 11.52.

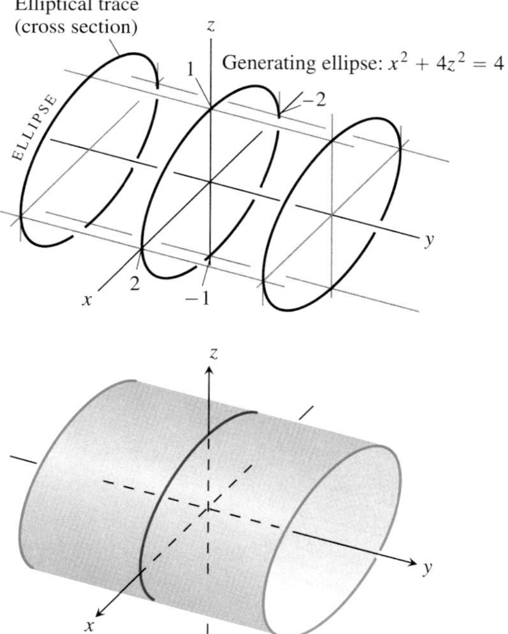

11.51 The elliptic cylinder $x^2 + 4z^2 = 4$ is made of lines parallel to the y-axis and passing through the ellipse $x^2 + 4z^2 = 4$ in the xz-plane. The cross sections or "traces" of the cylinder in planes perpendicular to the y-axis are ellipses congruent to the generating ellipse. The cylinder extends along the entire y-axis, but we can draw only a finite portion of it.

Drawing Lesson

How to Draw Cylinders Parallel to the Coordinate Axes

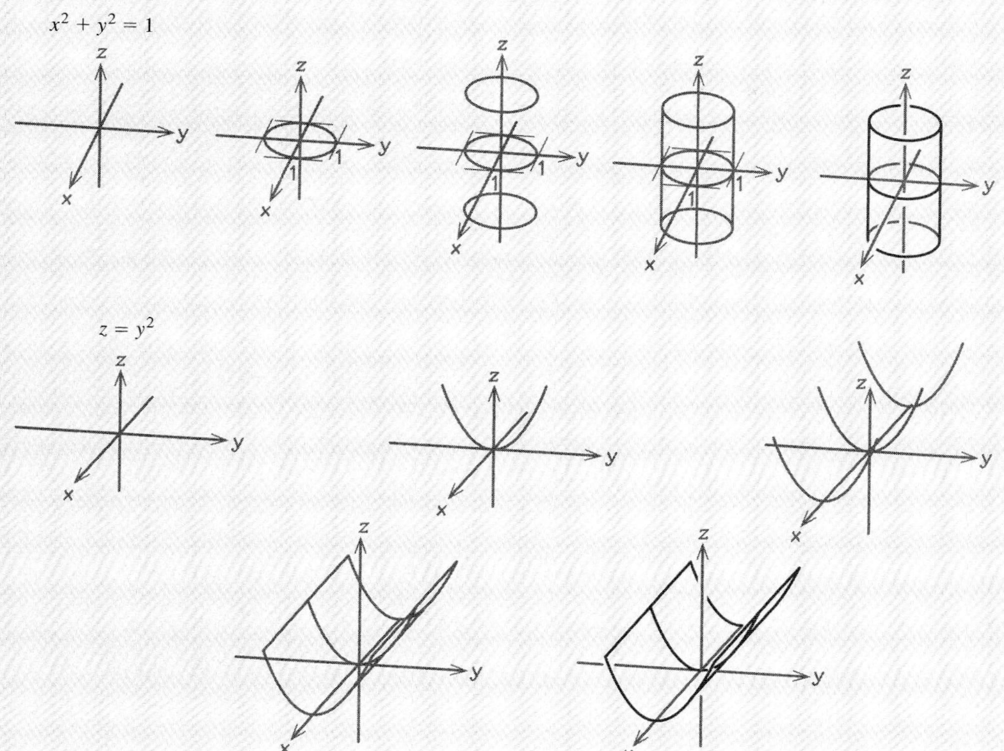

1 Sketch all three coordinate axes *very lightly*.

2 Sketch the trace of the cylinder in the coordinate plane of the two variables that appear in the cylinder's equation. Sketch *very lightly*.

3 Sketch traces in parallel planes on either side (again, lightly).

4 Add parallel outer edges to give the shape definition.

5 If more definition is required, darken the parts of the lines that are exposed to view. Leave the hidden parts light. Use line breaks when you can.

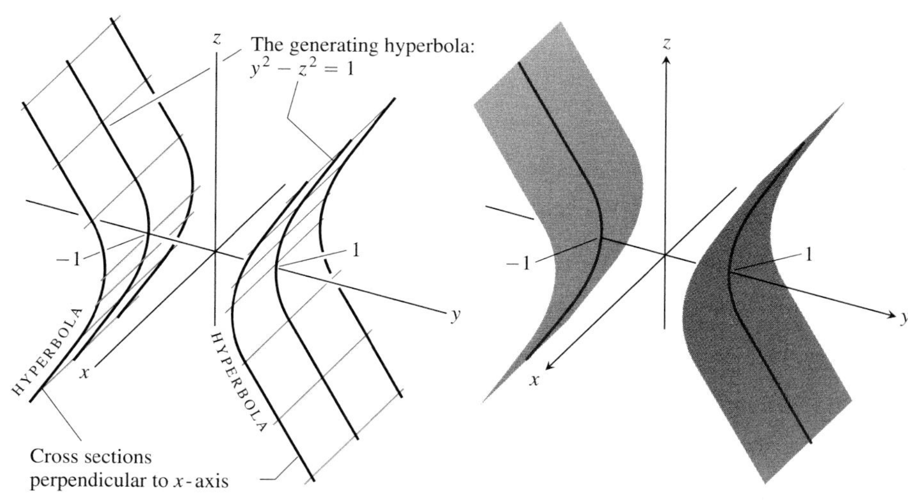

11.52 The hyperbolic cylinder $y^2 - z^2 = 1$ is made of lines parallel to the x-axis and passing through the hyperbola $y^2 - z^2 = 1$ in the yz-plane. The cross sections or "traces" of the cylinder in planes perpendicular to the x-axis are hyperbolas congruent to the generating hyperbola.

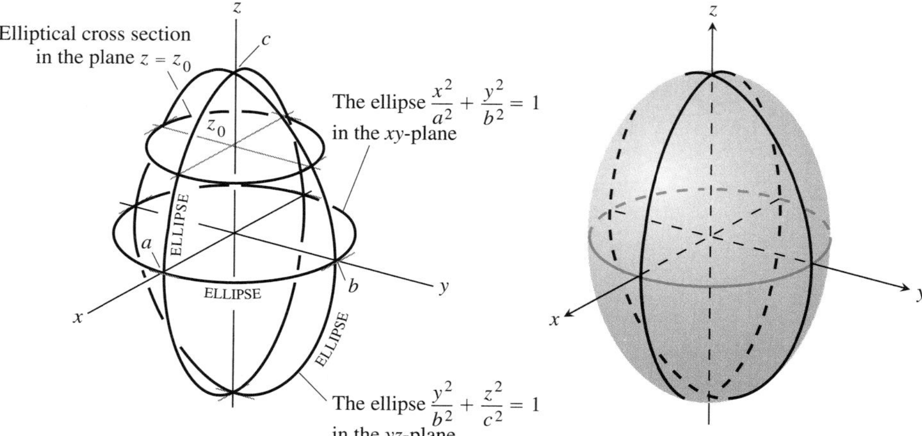

11.53 The ellipsoid

$$\frac{x^2}{a^2} + \frac{y^2}{b^2} + \frac{z^2}{c^2} = 1$$

in Example 2.

Quadric Surfaces

The cylinders in Figs. 11.50–11.52 are all **quadric surfaces,** surfaces whose equations combine quadratic terms with linear terms and constants. The examples that follow describe the other important quadric surfaces: ellipsoids (these include spheres), paraboloids, cones, and hyperboloids. The numbers a, b, and c that appear in the equations for these surfaces are assumed to be positive.

EXAMPLE 2 The **ellipsoid**

$$\frac{x^2}{a^2} + \frac{y^2}{b^2} + \frac{z^2}{c^2} = 1 \qquad (1)$$

(Fig. 11.53) cuts the coordinate axes at $(\pm a, 0, 0)$, $(0, \pm b, 0)$, and $(0, 0, \pm c)$. It lies within the rectangular box defined by the inequalities $|x| \leq a$, $|y| \leq b$, and $|z| \leq c$. The surface is symmetric with respect to each of the coordinate planes because the variables in the defining equation are squared.

The curves in which the three coordinate planes cut the surface are ellipses. For example,

$$\frac{x^2}{a^2} + \frac{y^2}{b^2} = 1 \qquad \text{when} \qquad z = 0.$$

The section cut from the surface by the plane $z = z_0$, $|z_0| < c$, is the ellipse

$$\frac{x^2}{a^2(1 - (z_0/c)^2)} + \frac{y^2}{b^2(1 - (z_0/c)^2)} = 1. \qquad (2)$$

If any two of the semiaxes a, b, and c are equal, the surface is an ellipsoid of revolution. If all three are equal, the surface is a sphere.

EXAMPLE 3 The **elliptic paraboloid**

$$\frac{x^2}{a^2} + \frac{y^2}{b^2} = \frac{z}{c} \qquad (3)$$

is symmetric with respect to the planes $x = 0$ and $y = 0$ (Fig. 11.54). The only intercept on the axes is the origin. Except for this point, the surface lies above the xy-plane because z is positive whenever either x or y is different from zero.

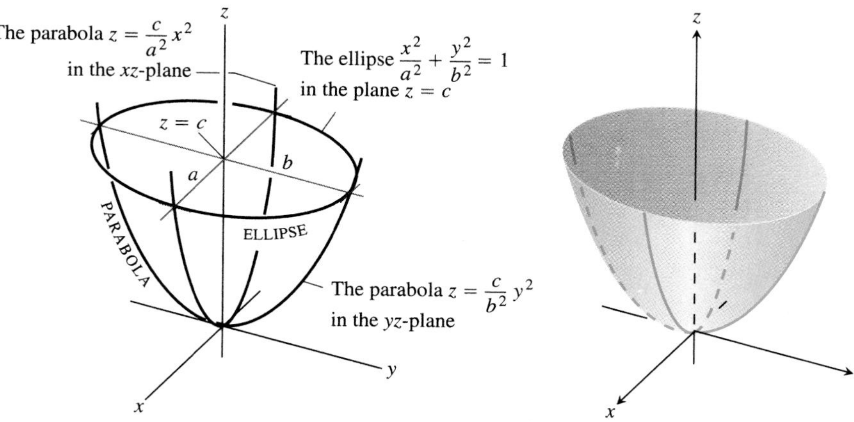

11.54 The elliptic paraboloid $(x^2/a^2) + (y^2/b^2) = z/c$ in Example 3, shown for $c > 0$. The cross sections perpendicular to the z-axis above the xy-plane are ellipses. The cross sections in the planes that contain the z-axis are parabolas.

The sections cut by the coordinate planes are

$$x = 0: \quad \text{the parabola } z = \frac{c}{b^2}y^2$$

$$y = 0: \quad \text{the parabola } z = \frac{c}{a^2}x^2 \tag{4}$$

$$z = 0: \quad \text{the point } (0, 0, 0).$$

Each plane $z = z_0$ above the xy-plane cuts the surface in the ellipse

$$\frac{x^2}{a^2} + \frac{y^2}{b^2} = \frac{z_0}{c}.$$

EXAMPLE 4 The **circular paraboloid** or **paraboloid of revolution**

$$\frac{x^2}{a^2} + \frac{y^2}{a^2} = \frac{z}{c} \tag{5}$$

is obtained by taking $b = a$ in Eq. (3) for the elliptic paraboloid. The cross sections of the surface by planes perpendicular to the z-axis are circles centered on the z-axis. The cross sections by planes containing the z-axis are congruent parabolas with a common focus at the point $(0, 0, a^2/4c)$.

Shapes cut from circular paraboloids are used for antennas in radio telescopes, satellite trackers, and microwave radio links (Fig. 11.55).

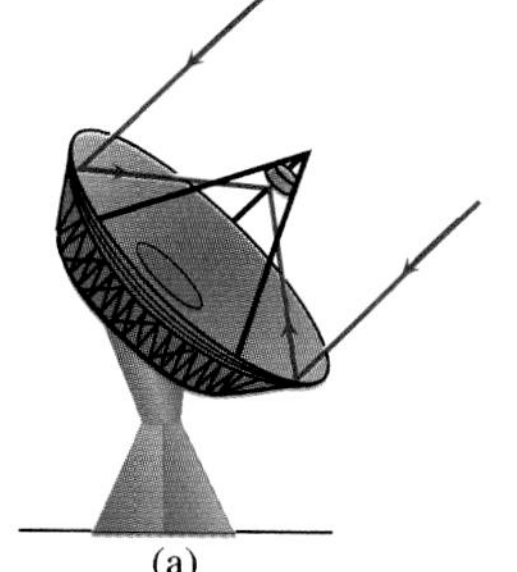

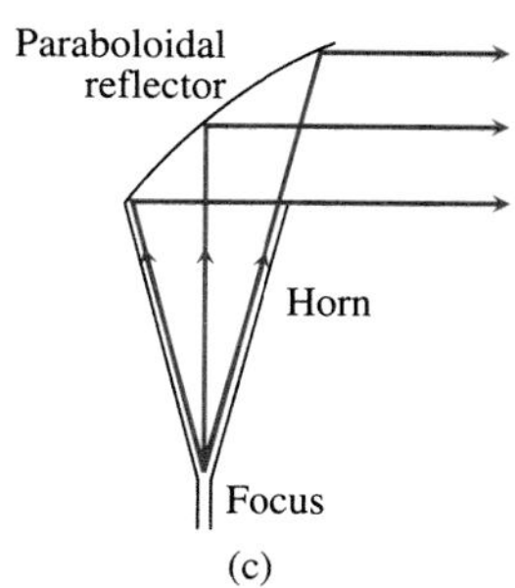

11.55 Many antennas are shaped like pieces of paraboloids of revolution. (a) Radio telescopes use the same principles as optical telescopes. (b) A "rectangular-cut" radar reflector. (c) The profile of a horn antenna in a microwave radio link.

EXAMPLE 5 The **elliptic cone**

$$\frac{x^2}{a^2} + \frac{y^2}{b^2} = \frac{z^2}{c^2} \tag{6}$$

is symmetric with respect to the three coordinate planes (Fig. 11.56 on the following page). The sections cut by the coordinate planes are

$$x = 0: \quad \text{the lines } z = \pm\frac{c}{b}y \tag{7}$$

$$y = 0: \quad \text{the lines } z = \pm\frac{c}{a}x \tag{8}$$

$$z = 0: \quad \text{the point } (0, 0, 0).$$

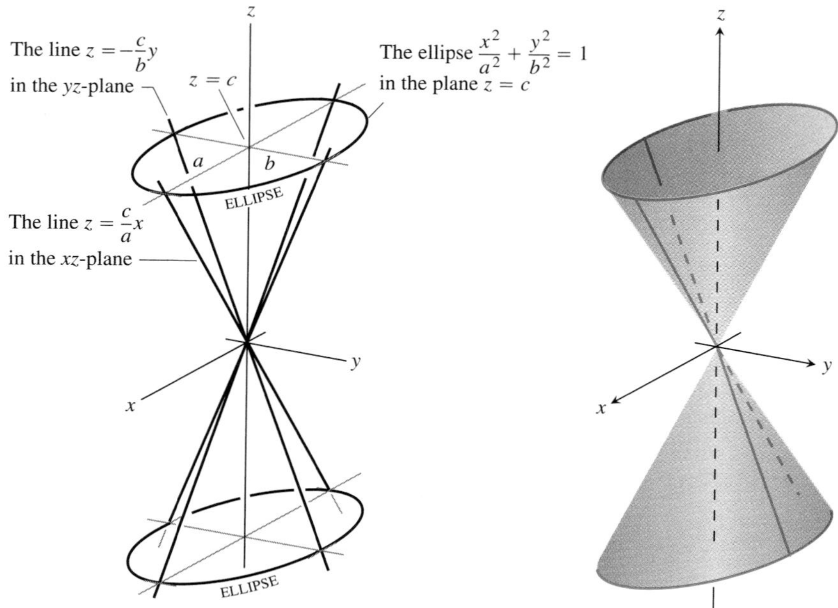

11.56 The elliptic cone $(x^2/a^2) + (y^2/b^2)$ z^2/c^2 in Example 5. Planes perpendicular to the z-axis cut the cone in ellipses above and below the xy-plane. Vertical planes that contain the z-axis cut it in pairs of intersecting lines.

The sections cut by planes $z = z_0$ above and below the xy-plane are ellipses whose centers lie on the z-axis and whose vertices lie on the lines in Eqs. (7) and (8).

If $a = b$, the cone is a right circular cone.

EXAMPLE 6 The **hyperboloid of one sheet**

$$\frac{x^2}{a^2} + \frac{y^2}{b^2} - \frac{z^2}{c^2} = 1 \tag{9}$$

is symmetric with respect to each of the three coordinate planes (Fig. 11.57).

Part of the hyperbola $\frac{x^2}{a^2} - \frac{z^2}{c^2} = 1$ in the xz-plane

z

$z = c$

The ellipse $\frac{x^2}{a^2} + \frac{y^2}{b^2} = 2$ in the plane $z = c$

$b\sqrt{2}$

$a\sqrt{2}$

ELLIPSE

The ellipse $\frac{x^2}{a^2} + \frac{y^2}{b^2} = 1$ in the xy-plane

HYPERBOLA

b

y

a

ELLIPSE

HYPERBOLA

x

Part of the hyperbola $\frac{y^2}{b^2} - \frac{z^2}{c^2} = 1$ in the yz-plane

ELLIPSE

11.57 The hyperboloid $(x^2/a^2) + (y^2/b^2) - (z^2/c^2) = 1$ in Example 6. Planes perpendicular to the z-axis cut it in ellipses. Vertical planes containing the z-axis cut it in hyperbolas.

The sections cut out by the coordinate planes are

$$\begin{aligned} x = 0&: \quad \text{the hyperbola } \frac{y^2}{b^2} - \frac{z^2}{c^2} = 1 \\ y = 0&: \quad \text{the hyperbola } \frac{x^2}{a^2} - \frac{z^2}{c^2} = 1 \\ z = 0&: \quad \text{the ellipse } \frac{x^2}{a^2} + \frac{y^2}{b^2} = 1. \end{aligned} \tag{10}$$

The plane $z = z_0$ cuts the surface in an ellipse with center on the z-axis and vertices on one of the hyperbolas in (10).

The surface is connected, meaning that it is possible to travel from one point on it to any other without leaving the surface. For this reason, it is said to have *one* sheet, in contrast to the hyperboloid in the next example, which has two sheets.

If $a = b$, the hyperboloid is a surface of revolution.

EXAMPLE 7 The **hyperboloid of two sheets**

$$\frac{z^2}{c^2} - \frac{x^2}{a^2} - \frac{y^2}{b^2} = 1 \tag{11}$$

is symmetric with respect to the three coordinate planes (Fig. 11.58). The plane $z = 0$ does not intersect the surface; in fact, for a horizontal plane to intersect the surface, we must have $|z| \geq c$. The hyperbolic sections

$$x = 0: \quad \frac{z^2}{c^2} - \frac{y^2}{b^2} = 1, \qquad y = 0: \quad \frac{z^2}{c^2} - \frac{x^2}{a^2} = 1,$$

have their vertices and foci on the z-axis. The surface is separated into two portions, one above the plane $z = c$ and the other below the plane $z = -c$. This accounts for its name.

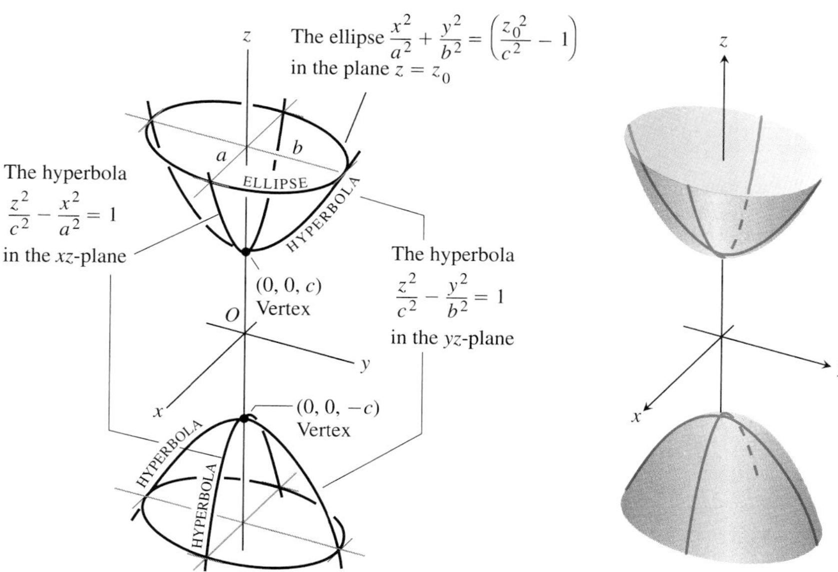

11.58 The hyperboloid $(z^2/c^2) - (x^2/a^2) - (y^2/b^2) = 1$ in Example 7. Planes perpendicular to the z-axis above and below the vertices cut it in ellipses. Vertical planes containing the z-axis cut it in hyperbolas.

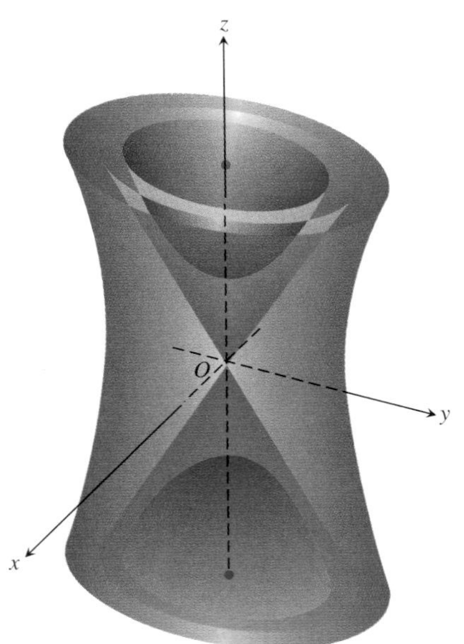

11.59 Both hyperboloids are asymptotic to the cone (Example 7).

Equations (9) and (11) have different numbers of negative terms. The number in each case is the same as the number of sheets of the hyperboloid. If we compare with Eq. (6), we see that replacing the 1 on the right side of either Eq. (9) or (11) by 0 gives the equation of a cone. If we replace the 1 on the right side of either Eq. (9) or Eq. (11) by 0, we obtain the equation

$$\frac{x^2}{a^2} + \frac{y^2}{b^2} - \frac{z^2}{c^2} = 0$$

for an elliptic cone (Eq. 6). The hyperboloids are asymptotic to this cone (Fig. 11.59) in the same way that the hyperbolas

$$\frac{x^2}{a^2} - \frac{y^2}{b^2} = \pm 1$$

are asymptotic to the lines

$$\frac{x^2}{a^2} - \frac{y^2}{b^2} = 0$$

in the xy-plane.

EXAMPLE 8 The **hyperbolic paraboloid**

$$\frac{y^2}{b^2} - \frac{x^2}{a^2} = \frac{z}{c} \tag{12}$$

has symmetry with respect to the planes $x = 0$ and $y = 0$ (Fig. 11.60). The sections in these planes are

$$x = 0: \quad \text{the parabola } z = \frac{c}{b^2}y^2, \tag{13}$$

$$y = 0: \quad \text{the parabola } z = -\frac{c}{a^2}x^2. \tag{14}$$

In the plane $x = 0$, the parabola opens upward from the origin. The parabola in the plane $y = 0$ opens downward.

If we cut the surface by a plane $z = z_0 > 0$, the section is a hyperbola,

$$\frac{y^2}{b^2} - \frac{x^2}{a^2} = \frac{z_0}{c}, \tag{15}$$

11.60 The hyperbolic paraboloid $(y^2/b^2) - (x^2/a^2) = z/c$ in Example 8. The cross sections in planes perpendicular to the z-axis above and below the xy-plane are hyperbolas. The cross sections in planes perpendicular to the other axes are parabolas.

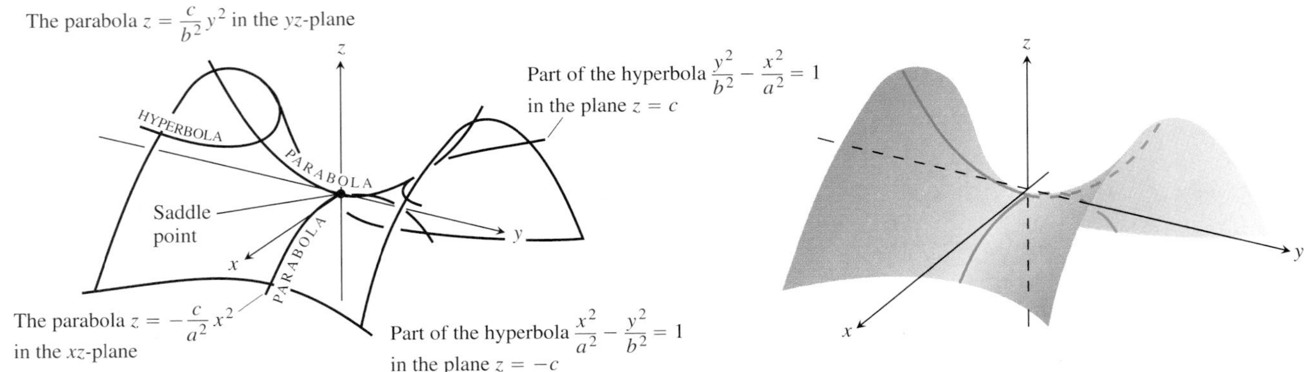

with its focal axis parallel to the y-axis and its vertices on the parabola in (13). If z_0 is negative, the focal axis is parallel to the x-axis and the vertices lie on the parabola in (14).

Near the origin, the surface is shaped like a saddle. To a person traveling along the surface in the yz-plane, the origin looks like a minimum. To a person traveling in the xz-plane, the origin looks like a maximum. Such a point is called a **minimax** or **saddle point** of a surface.

Drawing Lesson

How to Draw Quadric Surfaces

$$x^2 + \frac{y^2}{4} + z^2 = 1 \qquad\qquad z = 4 - x^2 - y^2$$

1 Lightly sketch the three coordinate axes.

2 Decide on a scale and mark the intercepts on the axes.

3 Sketch cross sections in the coordinate planes and in a few parallel planes, but don't clutter the picture. Use tangent lines as guides.

4 If more is required, darken the parts exposed to view. Leave the rest light. Use line breaks when you can.

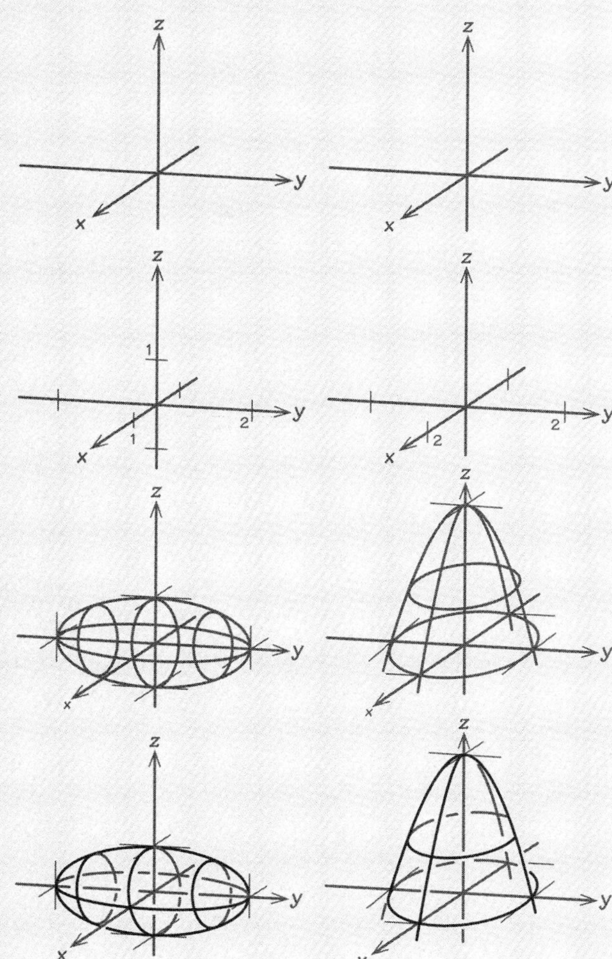

Exercises 11.6

In Exercises 1–12, match the equation with the surface it defines. Also, identify each surface by type (paraboloid, ellipsoid, etc.) The surfaces are labeled (a)–(l).

1. $x^2 + y^2 + 4z^2 = 10$
2. $z^2 + 4y^2 - 4x^2 = 4$
3. $9y^2 + z^2 = 16$
4. $y^2 + z^2 = x^2$
5. $x = y^2 - z^2$
6. $x = -y^2 - z^2$
7. $x^2 + 2z^2 = 8$
8. $z^2 + x^2 - y^2 = 1$
9. $x = z^2 - y^2$
10. $z = -4x^2 - y^2$
11. $x^2 + 4z^2 = y^2$
12. $9x^2 + 4y^2 + 2z^2 = 36$

(a)

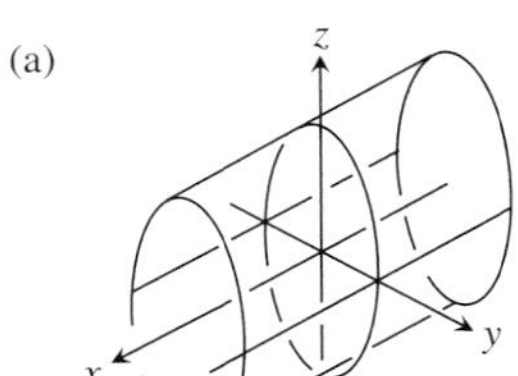

(b)

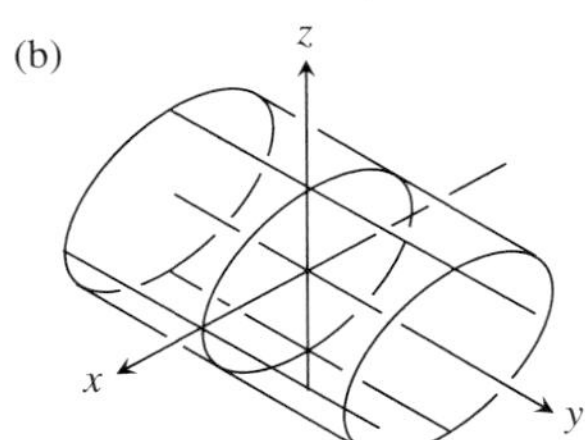

(c)

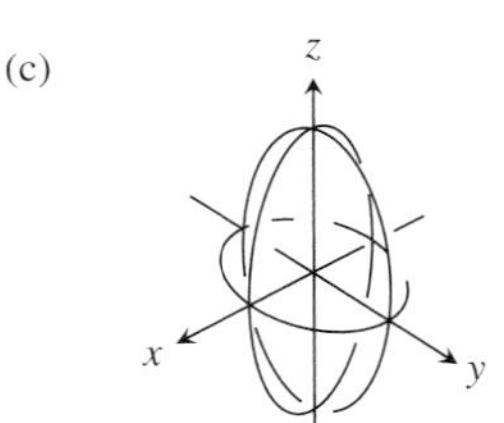

(d)

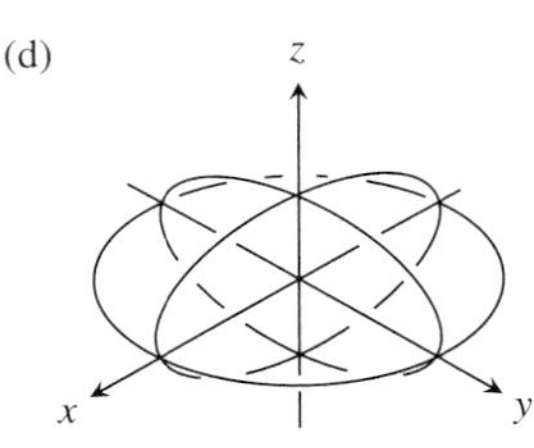

(e)

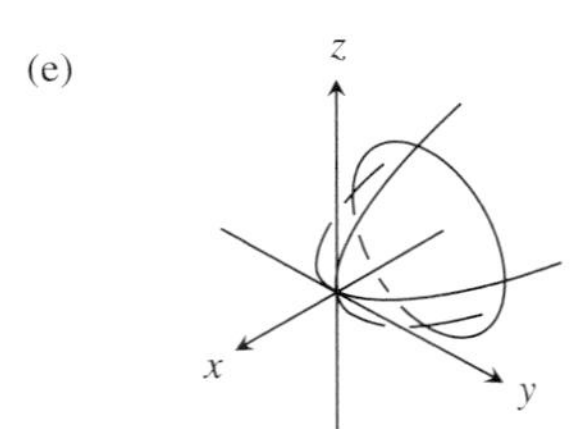

(f)

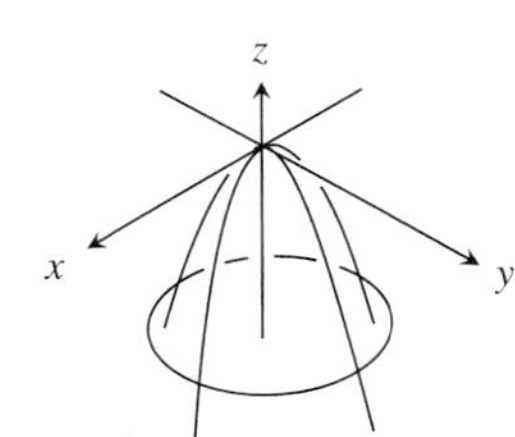

(g)

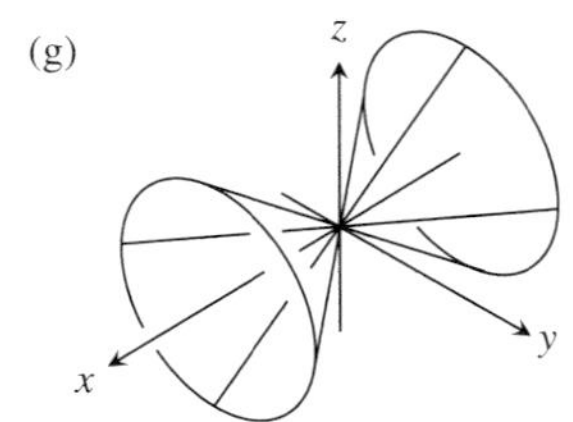

(h)

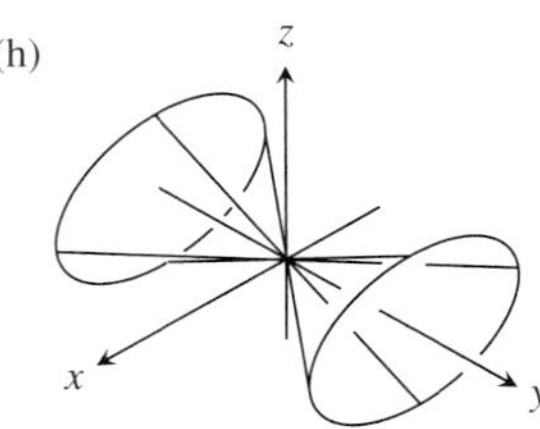

(i)

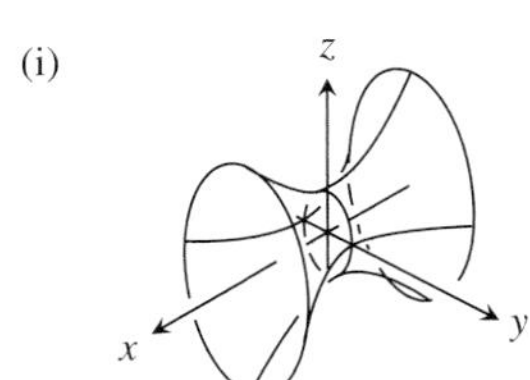

(j)

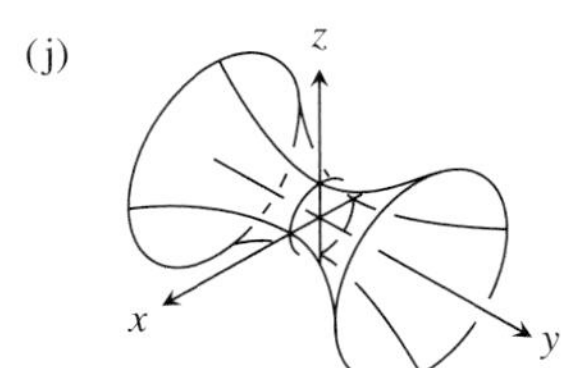

(k)

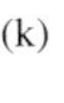

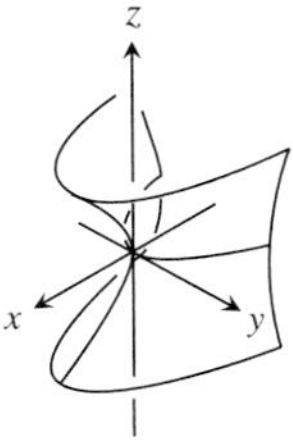

(l)

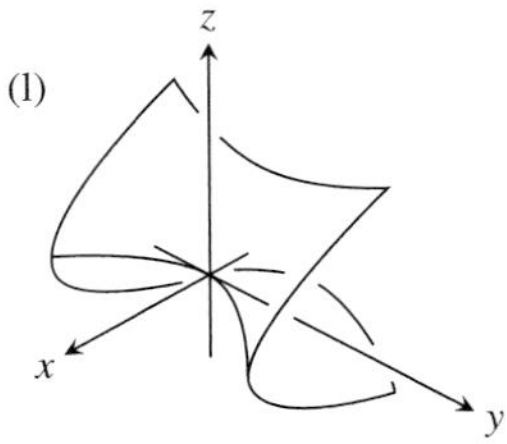

Sketch the surfaces in Exercises 13–76.

CYLINDERS

13. $x^2 + y^2 = 4$
14. $x^2 + z^2 = 4$
15. $z = y^2 - 1$
16. $x = y^2$
17. $x^2 + 4z^2 = 16$
18. $4x^2 + y^2 = 36$
19. $z^2 - y^2 = 1$
20. $yz = 1$

ELLIPSOIDS

21. $9x^2 + y^2 + z^2 = 9$
22. $4x^2 + 4y^2 + z^2 = 16$
23. $4x^2 + 9y^2 + 4z^2 = 36$
24. $9x^2 + 4y^2 + 36z^2 = 36$

PARABOLOIDS

25. $z = x^2 + 4y^2$
26. $z = x^2 + 9y^2$
27. $z = 8 - x^2 - y^2$
28. $z = 18 - x^2 - 9y^2$
29. $x = 4 - 4y^2 - z^2$
30. $y = 1 - x^2 - z^2$

CONES

31. $x^2 + y^2 = z^2$
32. $y^2 + z^2 = x^2$
33. $4x^2 + 9z^2 = 9y^2$
34. $9x^2 + 4y^2 = 36z^2$

HYPERBOLOIDS

35. $x^2 + y^2 - z^2 = 1$
36. $y^2 + z^2 - x^2 = 1$
37. $(y^2/4) + (z^2/9) - (x^2/4) = 1$
38. $(x^2/4) + (y^2/4) - (z^2/9) = 1$
39. $z^2 - x^2 - y^2 = 1$
40. $(y^2/4) - (x^2/4) - z^2 = 1$
41. $x^2 - y^2 - (z^2/4) = 1$
42. $(x^2/4) - y^2 - (z^2/4) = 1$

HYPERBOLIC PARABOLOIDS

43. $y^2 - x^2 = z$
44. $x^2 - y^2 = z$

ASSORTED

45. $x^2 + y^2 + z^2 = 4$
46. $4x^2 + 4y^2 = z^2$
47. $z = 1 + y^2 - x^2$
48. $y^2 - z^2 = 4$
49. $y = -(x^2 + z^2)$
50. $z^2 - 4x^2 - 4y^2 = 4$

51. $16x^2 + 4y^2 = 1$

52. $z = x^2 + y^2 + 1$

53. $x^2 + y^2 - z^2 = 4$

54. $x = 4 - y^2$

55. $x^2 + z^2 = y$

56. $z^2 - (x^2/4) - y^2 = 1$

57. $x^2 + z^2 = 1$

58. $4x^2 + 4y^2 + z^2 = 4$

59. $16y^2 + 9z^2 = 4x^2$

60. $z = x^2 - y^2 - 1$

61. $9x^2 + 4y^2 + z^2 = 36$

62. $4x^2 + 9z^2 = y^2$

63. $x^2 + y^2 - 16z^2 = 16$

64. $z^2 + 4y^2 = 9$

65. $z = -(x^2 + y^2)$

66. $y^2 - x^2 - z^2 = 1$

67. $x^2 - 4y^2 = 1$

68. $z = 4x^2 + y^2 - 4$

69. $4y^2 + z^2 - 4x^2 = 4$

70. $z = 1 - x^2$

71. $x^2 + y^2 = z$

72. $(x^2/4) + y^2 - z^2 = 1$

73. $yz = 1$

74. $36x^2 + 9y^2 + 4z^2 = 36$

75. $9x^2 + 16y^2 = 4z^2$

76. $4z^2 - x^2 - y^2 = 4$

77. **a)** Express the area A of the cross section cut from the ellipsoid

$$x^2 + \frac{y^2}{4} + \frac{z^2}{9} = 1$$

by the plane $z = c$ as a function of c. (The area of an ellipse with semiaxes a and b is πab.)

b) Use slices perpendicular to the z-axis to find the volume of the ellipsoid in (a).

c) Now find the volume of the ellipsoid

$$\frac{x^2}{a^2} + \frac{y^2}{b^2} + \frac{z^2}{c^2} = 1.$$

Does your formula give the volume of a sphere of radius a if $a = b = c$?

78. The barrel shown at the top of the next column is shaped like an ellipsoid with equal pieces cut from the ends by planes perpendicular to the z-axis. The cross sections perpendicular to the z-axis are circular. The barrel is $2h$ units high, its midsection radius is R, and its end radii are both r. Find a formula for the barrel's volume. Then check two things. First, suppose the sides of the barrel are straightened to turn the barrel into a cylinder of radius R and height $2h$. Does your formula give the cylinder's volume? Second, suppose $r = 0$ and $h = R$ so the barrel is a sphere. Does your formula give the sphere's volume?

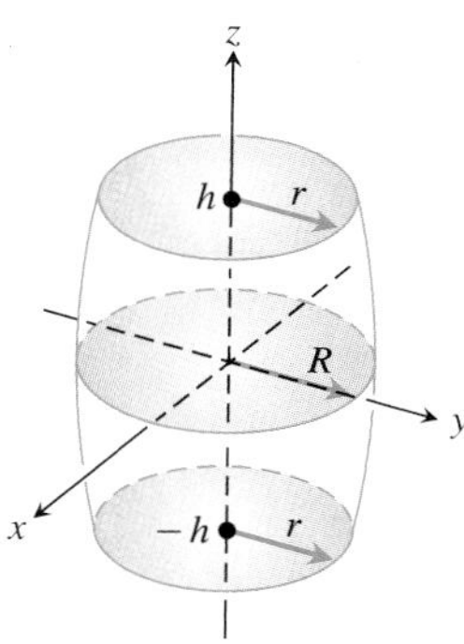

If you have access to a 3-D computer grapher, try graphing the surfaces in Exercises 79–85.

79. $z = y^2$

80. $z = 1 - y^2$

81. $z = x^2 + y^2$

82. $z = x^2 + 2y^2$

83. $z = \sqrt{1 - x^2}$ (upper half of a circular cylinder)

84. $z = \sqrt{1 - (y^2/4)}$ (upper half of an elliptical cylinder)

85. $z = \sqrt{x^2 + 2y^2 + 4}$ (one sheet of an elliptic hyperboloid)

Writing for Your Own Knowledge

Answer the following questions in writing. Some answers will take only a sentence or two; others may require several paragraphs. Some explanations may also call for graphs or sketches.

1. What is a cylinder?

2. Describe

a) an ellipsoid
b) an elliptic paraboloid
c) a paraboloid of revolution
d) an elliptic cone
e) a hyperboloid of one sheet
f) a hyperboloid of two sheets
g) a hyperbolic paraboloid

EXPLORER PROGRAM

3D Grapher	Graphs equations of the form $z = f(x, y)$.

11.7 *Cylindrical and Spherical Coordinates*

This section introduces two new coordinate systems for space: cylindrical coordinates and spherical coordinates. Cylindrical coordinates provide simple equations for circular cylinders whose axes lie along the z-axis and for planes that contain the z-axis. Spherical coordinates provide simple equations for spheres centered at the origin and for single cones at the origin whose axes lie along the z-axis. If your work involves these shapes, these may be the best coordinate systems to use.

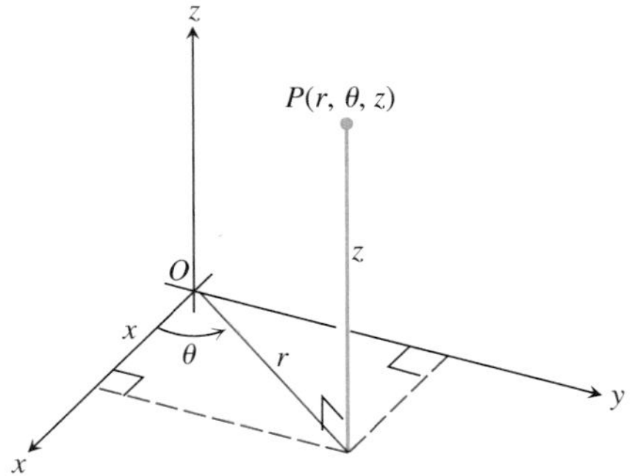

11.61 The cylindrical coordinates of a point in space are r, θ, and z.

Cylindrical Coordinates

We obtain cylindrical coordinates for space by combining polar coordinates in the xy-plane with the usual z-axis. This assigns to every point in space one or more coordinate triples of the form (r, θ, z), as shown in Fig. 11.61.

Cylindrical coordinates represent a point P in space by ordered triples (r, θ, z) in which

1. r and θ are polar coordinates for the vertical projection of P on the xy-plane,
2. z is the rectangular vertical coordinate.

The values of x, y, r, and θ in rectangular and cylindrical coordinates are related by the usual equations:

Equations Relating Rectangular (x, y, z) and Cylindrical (r, θ, z) Coordinates

$$\begin{gathered} x = r\cos\theta, \qquad y = r\sin\theta, \qquad z = z \\ r^2 = x^2 + y^2, \qquad \tan\theta = y/x \end{gathered} \tag{1}$$

In cylindrical coordinates, the equation $r = a$ describes not just a circle in the xy-plane but an entire cylinder about the z-axis (Fig. 11.62). The z-axis is given by $r = 0$. The equation $\theta = \theta_0$ describes the plane that contains the z-axis and makes an angle θ_0 with the positive x-axis. And, just as in rectangular coordinates, the equation $z = z_0$ describes a plane perpendicular to the z-axis.

EXAMPLE 1 What points satisfy the equations

$$r = 2, \qquad \theta = \frac{\pi}{4}\,?$$

Solution These points make up the line in which the cylinder $r = 2$ cuts the portion of the plane $\theta = \pi/4$ where r is positive (Fig. 11.63). This is the line through the point $(2, \pi/4, 0)$ parallel to the z-axis.

EXAMPLE 2 Sketch the surface $r = 1 + \cos\theta$.

Solution The equation involves only r and θ; the coordinate variable z is missing. Therefore, the surface is a cylinder of lines that pass through the cardioid $r = 1 + \cos\theta$ in the $r\theta$-plane and lie parallel to the z-axis. The rules for sketching the cylinder are the same as always: sketch the x-, y-, and z-axes, draw a few perpendicular cross sections, connect the cross sections with parallel lines, and darken the exposed parts (Fig. 11.64).

EXAMPLE 3 Find a Cartesian equation for the surface $z = r^2$ and identify the surface.

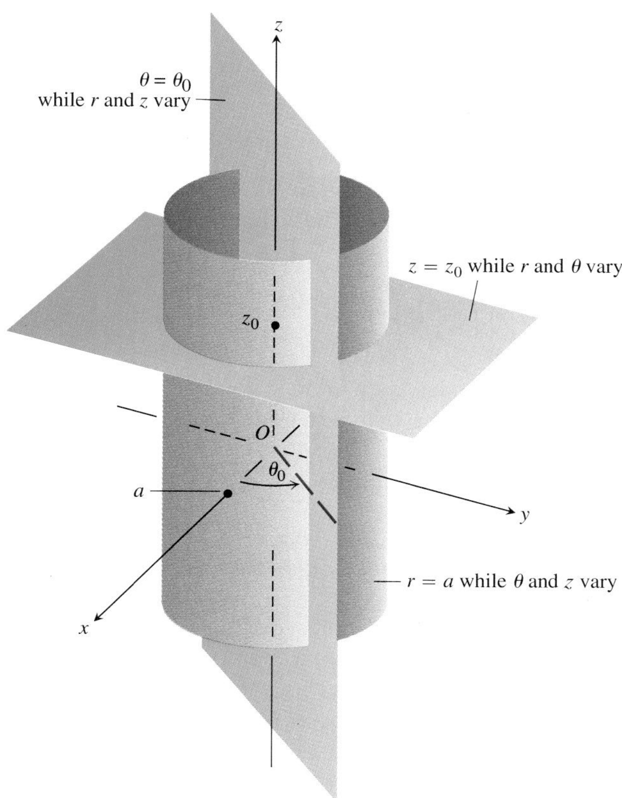

11.62 Constant-coordinate equations in cylindrical coordinates yield cylinders and planes.

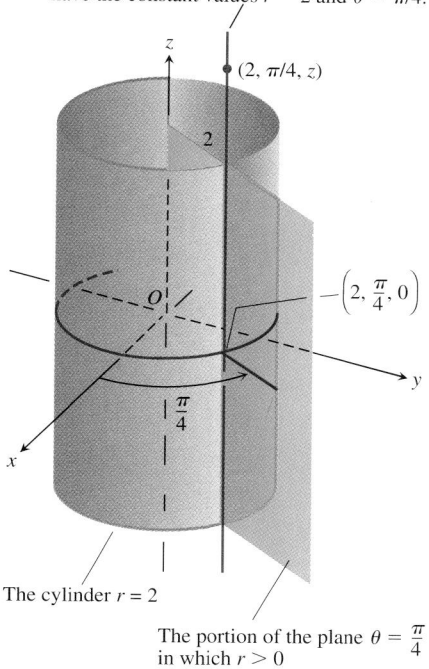

Along this line, z varies while r and θ have the constant values $r = 2$ and $\theta = \pi/4$.

$(2, \pi/4, z)$

$\left(2, \frac{\pi}{4}, 0\right)$

The cylinder $r = 2$

The portion of the plane $\theta = \frac{\pi}{4}$ in which $r > 0$

11.63 The points whose first two cylindrical coordinates are $r = 2$ and $\theta = \pi/4$ form a line parallel to the z-axis (Example 1).

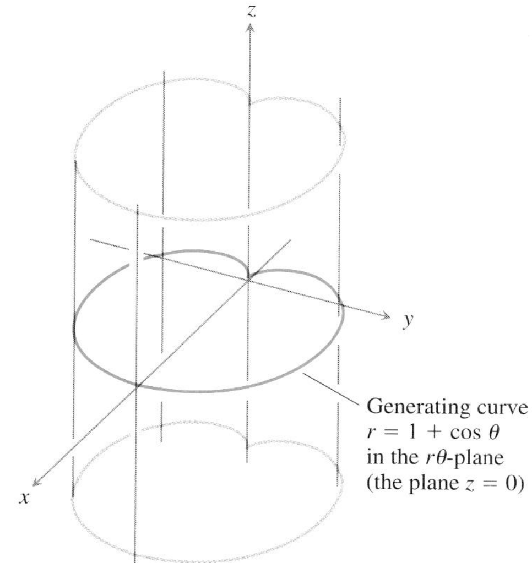

11.64 The cylindrical coordinate equation $r = 1 + \cos\theta$ defines a cylinder in space whose cross sections perpendicular to the z-axis are cardioids (Example 2).

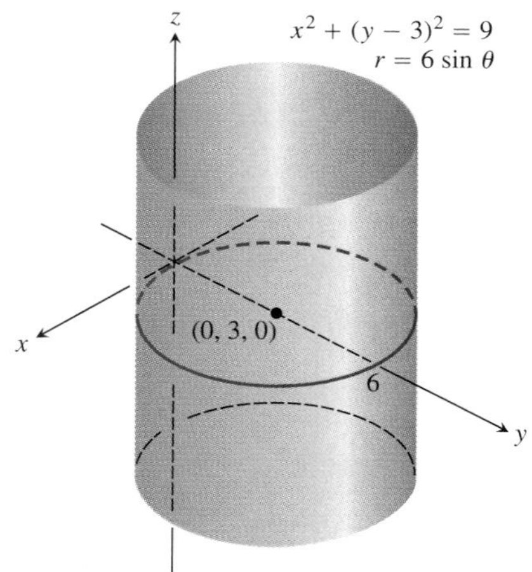

11.65 The cylinder in Example 5.

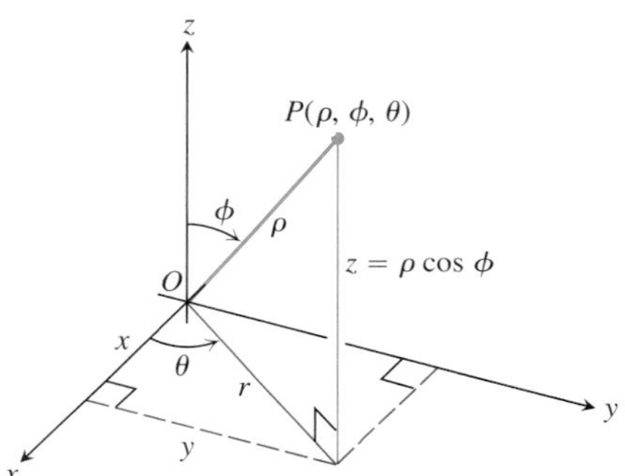

11.66 The spherical coordinates ρ, ϕ, and θ and their relation to x, y, z, and r.

A few books give spherical coordinates in the order (ρ, θ, ϕ), with the θ and ϕ reversed. Watch out for this when you read elsewhere.

Solution From Eqs. (1) we have $z = r^2 = x^2 + y^2$. The surface is the circular paraboloid $x^2 + y^2 = z$.

EXAMPLE 4 Find an equation for the circular cylinder $4x^2 + 4y^2 = 9$ in cylindrical coordinates.

Solution The cylinder consists of the points whose distance from the z-axis is $\sqrt{x^2 + y^2} = 3/2$. The corresponding equation in cylindrical coordinates is $r = 3/2$.

EXAMPLE 5 Find an equation for the cylinder $x^2 + (y - 3)^2 = 9$ in cylindrical coordinates (Fig. 11.65).

Solution The equation for the cylinder in cylindrical coordinates is the same as the polar equation for the cylinder's base in the xy-plane:

$$r = 6 \sin \theta.$$

Spherical Coordinates

Spherical coordinates locate points in space with two angles and a distance, as shown in Fig. 11.66.

The first coordinate, $\rho = |\overrightarrow{OP}|$, is the point's distance from the origin. Unlike r, the variable ρ is never negative. The second coordinate, ϕ, is the angle $\overrightarrow{OP}$ makes with the positive z-axis. It is required to lie in the interval $[0, \pi]$. The third coordinate is the angle θ from cylindrical coordinates.

Spherical coordinates represent a point P in space by ordered triples (ρ, ϕ, θ) in which

1. ρ is the distance from P to the origin,
2. ϕ is the angle $\overrightarrow{OP}$ makes with the positive z-axis $(0 \le \phi \le \pi)$,
3. θ is the angle from cylindrical coordinates.

The equation $\rho = a$ describes the sphere of radius a centered at the origin (Fig. 11.67). The equation $\phi = \phi_0$ describes a single cone whose vertex lies at the origin and whose axis lies along the z-axis. (We broaden our interpretation to include the xy-plane as the cone $\phi = \pi/2$.) If ϕ_0 is greater than $\pi/2$, the cone $\phi = \phi_0$ opens downward.

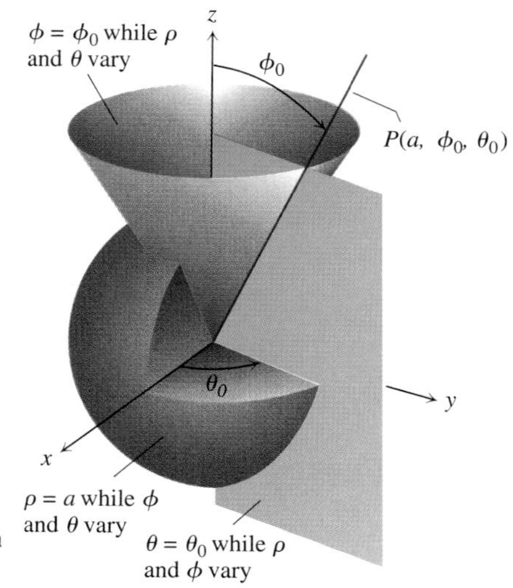

11.67 Constant-coordinate equations in spherical coordinates yield spheres, single cones, and half-planes.

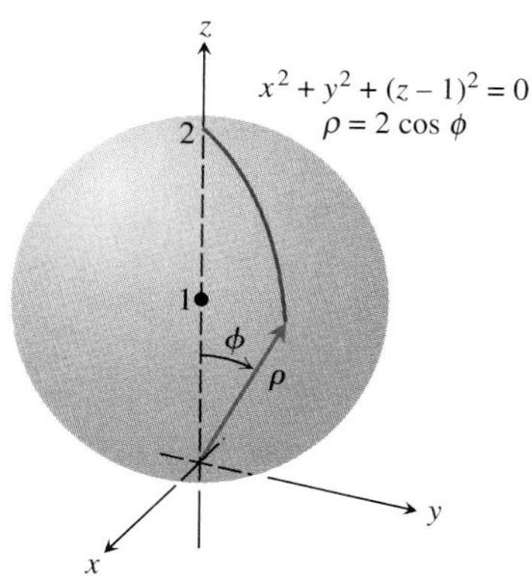

11.68 The sphere in Example 6.

Equations Relating Spherical Coordinates to Cartesian and Cylindrical Coordinates

$$\begin{aligned} r &= \rho \sin \phi, \qquad & x &= r \cos \theta = \rho \sin \phi \cos \theta, \\ z &= \rho \cos \phi, \qquad & y &= r \sin \theta = \rho \sin \phi \sin \theta, \\ & & \rho &= \sqrt{x^2 + y^2 + z^2} = \sqrt{r^2 + z^2} \end{aligned} \tag{2}$$

EXAMPLE 6 Find a spherical coordinate equation for the sphere

$$x^2 + y^2 + (z - 1)^2 = 1.$$

Solution We use Eqs. (2) to substitute for x, y, and z:

$$\begin{aligned} x^2 + y^2 + (z - 1)^2 &= 1 \\ \rho^2 \sin^2 \phi \cos^2 \theta + \rho^2 \sin^2 \phi \sin^2 \theta + (\rho \cos \phi - 1)^2 &= 1 \qquad \text{Eqs. (2)} \\ \rho^2 \sin^2 \phi \underbrace{(\cos^2 \theta + \sin^2 \theta)}_{1} + \rho^2 \cos^2 \phi - 2\rho \cos \phi + 1 &= 1 \\ \rho^2 \underbrace{(\sin^2 \phi + \cos^2 \phi)}_{1} &= 2\rho \cos \phi \\ \rho^2 &= 2\rho \cos \phi \\ \rho &= 2 \cos \phi \end{aligned}$$

See Fig. 11.68.

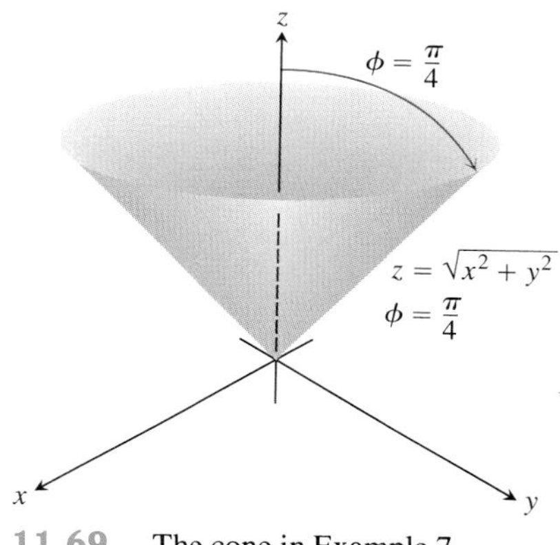

11.69 The cone in Example 7.

EXAMPLE 7 Find a spherical coordinate equation for the cone $z = \sqrt{x^2 + y^2}$ (Fig. 11.69).

Solution Use geometry. The cone is symmetric with respect to the z-axis and cuts the first quadrant of the yz-plane along the line $z = y$. The angle between the cone and positive z-axis is therefore $\pi/4$ radians. The cone consists of the points whose spherical coordinates have ϕ equal to $\pi/4$, so its equation is $\phi = \pi/4$.

Exercises 11.7

The following table gives the coordinates of specific points in space in one of three coordinate systems. In Exercises 1–10, find coordinates for each point in the other two systems. There may be more than one right answer because points in cylindrical and spherical coordinates may have more than one coordinate triple.

	Rectangular (x, y, z)	Cylindrical (r, θ, z)	Spherical (ρ, ϕ, θ)
1.	(0, 0, 0)		
2.	(1, 0, 0)		
3.	(0, 1, 0)		
4.	(0, 0, 1)		
5.		(1, 0, 0)	
6.		$(\sqrt{2}, 0, 1)$	
7.		$(1, \pi/2, 1)$	
8.			$(\sqrt{3}, \pi/3, -\pi/2)$
9.			$(2\sqrt{2}, \pi/2, 3\pi/2)$
10.			$(\sqrt{2}, \pi, 3\pi/2)$

In Exercises 11–36, translate the equations and inequalities from the given coordinate system (rectangular, cylindrical, spherical) into equations and inequalities in the other two systems. Also, identify the figure being defined.

11. $r = 0$

12. $x^2 + y^2 = 5$

13. $z = 0$

14. $z = -2$

15. $z = \sqrt{x^2 + y^2}, \quad z \le 1$

16. $z = \sqrt{x^2 + y^2}, \quad 1 \le z \le 2$

17. $\rho \sin \phi \cos \theta = 0$

18. $\tan^2 \phi = 1$

19. $x^2 + y^2 + z^2 = 4$

20. $x^2 + y^2 + \left(z - \frac{1}{2}\right)^2 = \frac{1}{4}$

21. $\rho = 5 \cos \phi$

22. $\rho = -6 \cos \phi$

23. $r = \csc \theta$

24. $r = -3 \sec \theta$

25. $\rho = \sqrt{2} \sec \phi$

26. $\rho = 9 \csc \phi$

27. $x^2 + y^2 + (z - 1)^2 = 1, \quad z \le 1$

28. $r^2 + z^2 = 4, \quad z \le -\sqrt{2}$

29. $\rho = 3, \quad \pi/3 \le \phi \le 2\pi/3$

30. $x^2 + y^2 + z^2 = 3, \quad 0 \le z \le \sqrt{3}/2$

31. $z = 4 - 4r^2, \quad 0 \le r \le 1$

32. $z = 4 - r, 0 \le r \le 4$

33. $\phi = 3\pi/4, \quad 0 \le \rho \le \sqrt{2}$

34. $\phi = \pi/2, 0 \le \rho \le \sqrt{7}$

35. $z + r^2 \cos 2\theta = 0$

36. $z^2 - r^2 = 1$

In Exercises 37–40, describe the set of points whose cylindrical coordinates satisfy the given equation. Sketch each set.

37. $r = -2 \sin \theta$

38. $r = 2 \cos \theta$

39. $r = 1 - \cos \theta$

40. $r = 1 + \sin \theta$

In Exercises 41 and 42, describe the set of points in space whose spherical coordinates satisfy the given equation. Sketch each set.

41. $\rho = 1 - \cos \phi$

42. $\rho = 1 + \cos \phi$

43. Find the rectangular coordinates of the center of the sphere

$$r^2 + z^2 = 4r \cos \theta + 6r \sin \theta + 2z.$$

44. Find the rectangular coordinates of the center of the sphere

$$\rho = 2 \sin \phi (\cos \theta - 2 \sin \theta).$$

45. *Horizontal Planes in Cylindrical and Spherical Coordinates.* (a) Show that the plane whose equation is $z = c$ $(c \ne 0)$ in rectangular and cylindrical coordinates has the equation $\rho = c \sec \phi$ in spherical coordinates. (b) Find an equation for the xy-plane in spherical coordinates.

46. *Vertical Circular Cylinders in Spherical Coordinates.* Find an equation of the form $\rho = f(\phi)$ for the cylinder $x^2 + y^2 = a^2$.

47. *Vertical Planes in Cylindrical Coordinates.* (a) Show that planes perpendicular to the x-axis have equations of the form $r = a \sec \theta$ in cylindrical coordinates. (b) Show that planes perpendicular to the y-axis have equations of the form $r = b \csc \theta$.

48. *Continuation of Exercise 47.* Find an equation of the form $r = f(\theta)$ in cylindrical coordinates for the plane $ax + by = c, c \ne 0$.

49. *Symmetry.* What symmetry will you find in a surface that has an equation of the form $r = f(z)$ in cylindrical coordinates? Give reasons for your answer.

50. *Symmetry.* What symmetry will you find in a surface that has an equation of the form $\rho = f(\phi)$ in spherical coordinates? Give reasons for your answer.

Writing for Your Own Knowledge

Answer the following questions in writing. Some answers will take only a sentence or two; others may require several paragraphs. Some explanations may also call for graphs or sketches.

1. What are cylindrical coordinates? What advantages do they offer? What restrictions, if any, are placed on the domains of these coordinates?
2. What are spherical coordinates? What advantages do they offer? What restrictions, if any, are placed on the domains of these coordinates?
3. What equations relate cylindrical and Cartesian coordinates? cylindrical and spherical coordinates? Cartesian and spherical coordinates?

For Your Review

Write brief paragraphs about the following topics and give examples.

Vector addition, subtraction, and scalar multiplication
Magnitude and direction
Dot products
Scalar and vector projections
Cross products
Triple scalar products
Equations for lines in the plane
Equations for lines in space
Equations for planes
Finding the distance from a point to a line
Finding the distance from a point to a plane
Equations for cylinders
Equations for quadric surfaces
Cylindrical coordinates
Spherical coordinates
Relations among space coordinate systems

Practice Exercises

1. Draw the unit vectors $\mathbf{u} = (\cos\theta)\,\mathbf{i} + (\sin\theta)\,\mathbf{j}$ for $\theta = 0, \pi/2, 2\pi/3, 5\pi/4$, and $5\pi/3$, together with the coordinate axes and unit circle.
2. Find the unit vector obtained by rotating
   a) $\mathbf{i}$ clockwise 45° b) $\mathbf{j}$ counterclockwise 120°.

In Exercises 3–4, find the unit vectors that are tangent and normal to the curve at point *P*.

3. $y = \tan x$, $P(\pi/4, 1)$
4. $x^2 + y^2 = 25$, $P(3, 4)$

Express the vectors in Exercises 5–8 in terms of their lengths and directions.

5. $\sqrt{2}\,\mathbf{i} + \sqrt{2}\,\mathbf{j}$
6. $-\mathbf{i} - \mathbf{j}$
7. $2\,\mathbf{i} - 3\,\mathbf{j} + 6\,\mathbf{k}$
8. $\mathbf{i} + 2\,\mathbf{j} - \mathbf{k}$
9. Find a vector 2 units long in the direction of $\mathbf{A} = 4\,\mathbf{i} - \mathbf{j} + 4\,\mathbf{k}$.
10. Find a vector 5 units long in the direction opposite to the direction of $\mathbf{A} = (3/5)\,\mathbf{i} + (4/5)\,\mathbf{k}$.
11. The accompanying figure shows parallelogram *ABCD* and the midpoint *P* of diagonal *BD*.
    a) Express $\overrightarrow{BD}$ in terms of $\overrightarrow{AB}$ and $\overrightarrow{AD}$.
    b) Express $\overrightarrow{AP}$ in terms of $\overrightarrow{AB}$ and $\overrightarrow{AD}$.
    c) Prove that *P* is also the midpoint of diagonal *AC*.

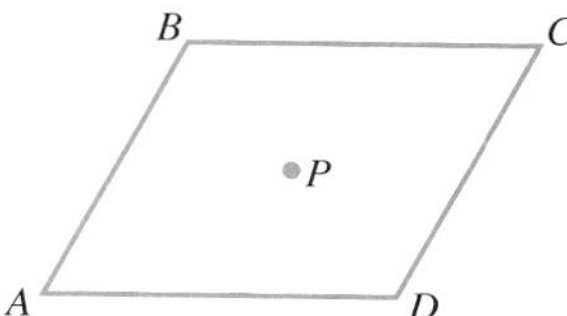

12. The points *O, A, B, C, D,* and *E* are vertices of the rectangular box shown here. Express $\overrightarrow{OD}$ and $\overrightarrow{OE}$ in terms of $\overrightarrow{OA}$, $\overrightarrow{OB}$, and $\overrightarrow{OC}$.

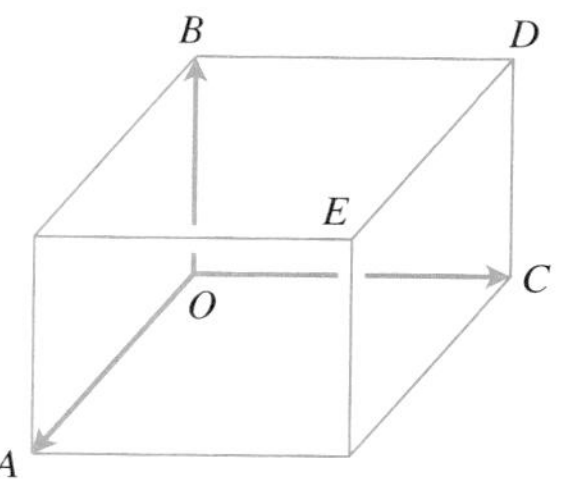

13. Copy the vectors **u** and **v** and sketch the vector projection of **v** onto **u**.

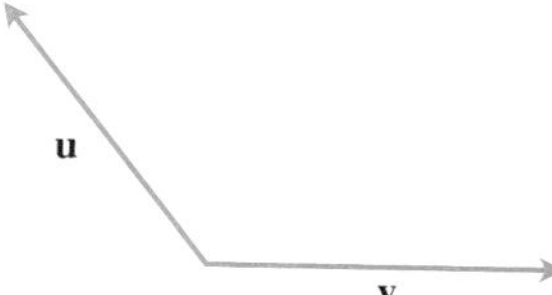

14. Express vectors **a**, **b**, and **c** in terms of **u** and **v**.

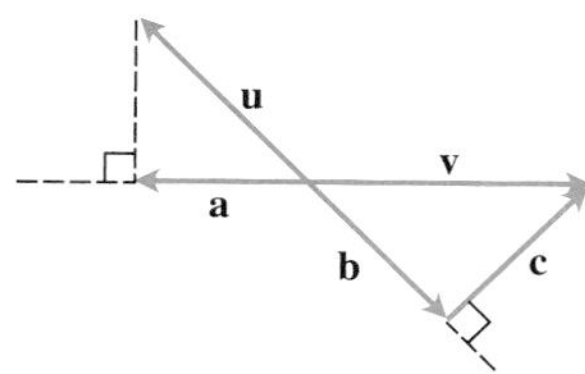

In Exercises 15 and 16, find $|\mathbf{A}|$, $|\mathbf{B}|$, $\mathbf{A}\cdot\mathbf{B}$, $\mathbf{B}\cdot\mathbf{A}$, $\mathbf{A}\times\mathbf{B}$, $\mathbf{B}\times\mathbf{A}$, $|\mathbf{A}\times\mathbf{B}|$, the angle between **A** and **B**, the scalar component of **B** in the direction of **A**, and the vector projection of **B** onto **A**.

15. $\mathbf{A} = \mathbf{i} + \mathbf{j}$,
    $\mathbf{B} = 2\,\mathbf{i} + \mathbf{j} - 2\,\mathbf{k}$
16. $\mathbf{A} = \mathbf{i} + \mathbf{j} + 2\,\mathbf{k}$
    $\mathbf{B} = -\mathbf{i} - \mathbf{k}$

In Exercises 17 and 18, write **B** as the sum of a vector parallel to **A** and a vector orthogonal to **A**.

17. $\mathbf{A} = 2\,\mathbf{i} + \mathbf{j} - \mathbf{k}$,
    $\mathbf{B} = \mathbf{i} + \mathbf{j} - 5\,\mathbf{k}$
18. $\mathbf{A} = \mathbf{i} - 2\,\mathbf{j}$,
    $\mathbf{B} = \mathbf{i} + \mathbf{j} + \mathbf{k}$

In Exercises 19 and 20, draw coordinate axes and then sketch **A**, **B**, and $\mathbf{A}\times\mathbf{B}$ as vectors at the origin.

19. $\mathbf{A} = \mathbf{i}$, $\mathbf{B} = \mathbf{i} + \mathbf{j}$
20. $\mathbf{A} = \mathbf{i} - \mathbf{j}$, $\mathbf{B} = \mathbf{i} + \mathbf{j}$
21. For any vectors **A** and **B**, show that $|\mathbf{A} + \mathbf{B}|^2 + |\mathbf{A} - \mathbf{B}|^2 = 2\,|\mathbf{A}|^2 + 2\,|\mathbf{B}|^2$.
22. Let *ABC* be the triangle determined by vectors **u** and **v**.
    a) Express the area of ΔABC in terms of **u** and **v**.
    b) Express the triangle's altitude *h* in terms of **u** and **v**.
    c) Find the area and altitude if $\mathbf{u} = \mathbf{i} - \mathbf{j} + \mathbf{k}$ and $\mathbf{v} = 2\,\mathbf{i} + \mathbf{k}$.

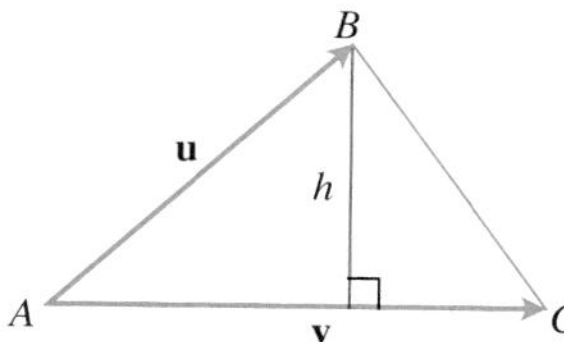

23. If $|\mathbf{v}| = 2$, $|\mathbf{w}| = 3$, and the angle between **v** and **w** is $\pi/3$, find $|\mathbf{v} - 2\mathbf{w}|$.
24. For what value or values of *a* will the vectors $\mathbf{u} = 2\,\mathbf{i} + 4\,\mathbf{j} - 5\,\mathbf{k}$ and $\mathbf{v} = -4\,\mathbf{i} - 8\,\mathbf{j} + a\,\mathbf{k}$ be parallel?
25. Suppose that **N** is normal to a plane and that **v** is parallel to the plane. Describe how you would find a vector **u** that is both perpendicular to **v** and parallel to the plane.
26. Find a vector in the plane parallel to the line $ax + by = c$.

In Exercises 27 and 28, find the distance from the point to the line in the xy-plane.

27. $(3, 2)$, $3x + 4y = 2$
28. $(-1, 1)$, $5x - 12y = 9$

In Exercises 29 and 30, find the distance from the point to the line.

29. $(2, 2, 0)$; $x = -t, \quad y = t, \quad z = -1 + t$

30. $(0, 4, 1)$; $x = 2 + t, \quad y = 2 + t, \quad z = t$

31. Find parametric equations for the line that passes through the point $(1, 2, 3)$ parallel to the vector $\mathbf{v} = -3\,\mathbf{i} + 7\,\mathbf{k}$.

32. Find parametric equations for the line segment joining the points $P(1, 2, 0)$ and $Q(1, 3, -1)$.

In Exercises 33 and 34, find the distance from the point to the plane.

33. $(6, 0, -6)$, $\quad x - y = 4$

34. $(3, 0, 10)$, $\quad 2x + 3y + z = 2$

35. Find an equation for the plane that passes through the point $(3, -2, 1)$ normal to the vector $\mathbf{N} = 2\,\mathbf{i} + \mathbf{j} - \mathbf{k}$.

36. Find an equation for the plane that passes through the point $(-1, 6, 0)$ perpendicular to the line $x = -1 + t$, $y = 6 - 2t$, $z = 3t$.

In Exercises 37 and 38, find an equation for the plane through points P, Q, and R.

37. $P(1, -1, 2)$, $\quad Q(2, 1, 3)$, $\quad R(-1, 2, -1)$

38. $P(1, 0, 0)$, $\quad Q(0, 1, 0)$, $\quad R(0, 0, 1)$

39. Find the points in which the line $x = 1 + 2t$, $y = -1 - t$, $z = 3t$ meets the three coordinate planes.

40. Find the point in which the line through the origin perpendicular to the plane $2x - y - z = 4$ meets the plane $3x - 5y + 2z = 6$.

41. Find the acute angle between the planes $x = 7$ and $x + y + \sqrt{2}z = -3$.

42. Find the acute angle between the planes $x + y = 1$ and $y + z = 1$.

43. Find parametric equations for the line in which the planes $x + 2y + z = 1$ and $x - y + 2z = -8$ intersect.

44. Show that the line in which the planes

$$x + 2y - 2z = 5 \quad \text{and} \quad 5x - 2y - z = 0$$

intersect is parallel to the line

$$x = -3 + 2t, \quad y = 3t, \quad z = 1 + 4t.$$

45. The planes $3x + 6z = 1$ and $2x + 2y - z = 3$ intersect in a line.

a) Show that the planes are orthogonal.
b) Find equations for the line of intersection.

46. Find an equation for the plane that passes through the point $(1, 2, 3)$ parallel to $\mathbf{u} = 2\,\mathbf{i} + 3\,\mathbf{j} + \mathbf{k}$ and $\mathbf{v} = \mathbf{i} - \mathbf{j} + 2\,\mathbf{k}$.

47. Is $\mathbf{v} = 2\,\mathbf{i} - 4\,\mathbf{j} + \mathbf{k}$ related in any special way to the plane $2x + y = 5$? Give reasons for your answer.

48. Is the line $x = 1 + 2t$, $y = -2 + 3t$, $z = -5t$ related in any way to the plane $-4x - 6y + 10z = 9$? Give reasons for your answer.

49. *Work.* Find the work done in pushing a car 250 m with a force of magnitude 160 N directed at an angle of $\pi/6$ rad downward from the horizontal against the back of the car.

50. *Torque.* The operator's manual for the Toro 21-in. lawnmower says "tighten the spark plug to 15 ft-lb (20.4 N · m)." If you are installing the plug with a 10.5-in. socket wrench that places the center of your hand 9 in. from the axis of the spark plug, about how hard should you pull? Answer in pounds.

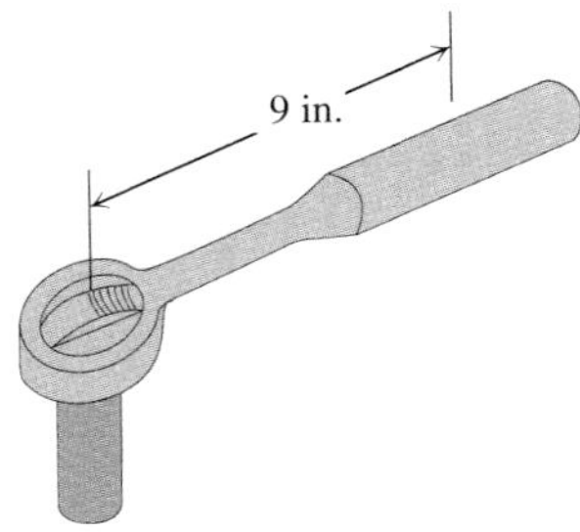

In Exercises 51 and 52, find (a) the area of the parallelogram determined by vectors $\mathbf{A}$ and $\mathbf{B}$, (b) the volume of the parallelepiped determined by the vectors $\mathbf{A}$, $\mathbf{B}$, and $\mathbf{C}$.

51. $\mathbf{A} = \mathbf{i} + \mathbf{j} - \mathbf{k}$, $\quad \mathbf{B} = 2\,\mathbf{i} + \mathbf{j} + \mathbf{k}$, $\quad \mathbf{C} = -\mathbf{i} - 2\,\mathbf{j} + 3\,\mathbf{k}$

52. $\mathbf{A} = \mathbf{i} + \mathbf{j}$, $\quad \mathbf{B} = \mathbf{j}$, $\quad \mathbf{C} = \mathbf{i} + \mathbf{j} + \mathbf{k}$

53. Which of the following are *always true*, and which are *not always true*? Give reasons for your answers.

a) $|\mathbf{A}| = \sqrt{\mathbf{A} \cdot \mathbf{A}}$ **b)** $\mathbf{A} \cdot \mathbf{A} = |\mathbf{A}|$
c) $\mathbf{A} \times \mathbf{0} = \mathbf{0} \times \mathbf{A} = \mathbf{0}$ **d)** $\mathbf{A} \times (-\mathbf{A}) = \mathbf{0}$
e) $\mathbf{A} \times \mathbf{B} = \mathbf{B} \times \mathbf{A}$
f) $\mathbf{A} \times (\mathbf{B} + \mathbf{C}) = \mathbf{A} \times \mathbf{B} + \mathbf{A} \times \mathbf{C}$
g) $(\mathbf{A} \times \mathbf{B}) \cdot \mathbf{B} = 0$ **h)** $(\mathbf{A} \times \mathbf{B}) \cdot \mathbf{C} = \mathbf{A} \cdot (\mathbf{B} \times \mathbf{C})$

54. Which of the following are *always true*, and which are *not always true*? Give reasons for your answers.

a) $\mathbf{A} \cdot \mathbf{B} = \mathbf{B} \cdot \mathbf{A}$ **b)** $\mathbf{A} \times \mathbf{B} = -(\mathbf{B} \times \mathbf{A})$
c) $(-\mathbf{A}) \times \mathbf{B} = -(\mathbf{A} \times \mathbf{B})$
d) $(c\mathbf{A}) \cdot \mathbf{B} = \mathbf{A} \cdot (c\mathbf{B}) = c(\mathbf{A} \cdot \mathbf{B})$ (any number c)
e) $c(\mathbf{A} \times \mathbf{B}) = (c\mathbf{A}) \times \mathbf{B} = \mathbf{A} \times (c\mathbf{B})$ (any number c)
f) $\mathbf{A} \cdot \mathbf{A} = |\mathbf{A}|^2$ **g)** $(\mathbf{A} \times \mathbf{A}) \cdot \mathbf{A} = 0$
h) $(\mathbf{A} \times \mathbf{B}) \cdot \mathbf{A} = \mathbf{B} \cdot (\mathbf{A} \times \mathbf{B})$

Sketch the quadric surfaces in Exercises 55–66.

55. $x^2 + y^2 + z^2 = 4$ **56.** $x^2 + (y - 1)^2 + z^2 = 1$

57. $4x^2 + 4y^2 + z^2 = 4$ **58.** $36x^2 + 9y^2 + 4z^2 = 36$

59. $z = -(x^2 + y^2)$ **60.** $y = -(x^2 + z^2)$

61. $x^2 + y^2 = z^2$ **62.** $x^2 + z^2 = y^2$

63. $x^2 + y^2 - z^2 = 4$ **64.** $4y^2 + z^2 - 4x^2 = 4$

65. $y^2 - x^2 - z^2 = 1$ **66.** $z^2 - x^2 - y^2 = 1$

The equations in Exercises 67–76 define sets both in the plane and in three-dimensional space. Identify both sets for each equation.

RECTANGULAR COORDINATES

67. $x = 0$ **68.** $x + y = 1$ **69.** $x^2 + y^2 = 4$

70. $x^2 + 4y^2 = 16$ **71.** $x = y^2$ **72.** $y^2 - x^2 = 1$

CYLINDRICAL COORDINATES

73. $r = 1 - \cos\theta$ **74.** $r = \sin\theta$

75. $r^2 = 2\cos 2\theta$ **76.** $r = \cos 2\theta$

Describe the sets defined by the spherical coordinate equations and inequalities in Exercises 77–82.

77. $\rho = 2$ **78.** $\theta = \pi/4$

79. $\phi = \pi/6$ **80.** $\rho = 1, \quad \phi = \pi/2$

81. $\rho = 1, \quad 0 \le \phi \le \pi/2$ **82.** $1 \le \rho \le 2$

The following table gives the coordinates of points in space in one of the three standard coordinate systems. In Exercises 83–88, find coordinates for each point in the other two systems. There may be more than one right answer because cylindrical and spherical coordinates are not unique.

	Rectangular (x, y, z)	Cylindrical (r, θ, z)	Spherical (ρ, ϕ, θ)
83.		$(1, 0, 0)$	
84.		$\left(1, \frac{\pi}{2}, 0\right)$	
85.			$\left(\sqrt{2}, \frac{\pi}{4}, \frac{\pi}{2}\right)$
86.			$\left(2, \frac{5\pi}{6}, 0\right)$
87.	$(-1, 0, -1)$		
88.	$(0, -1, 1)$		

In Exercises 89–100, translate the equations from the given coordinate system (rectangular, cylindrical, spherical) into the other two systems. Identify the set of points defined by the equation.

RECTANGULAR

89. $z = 2$

90. $z = \sqrt{3x^2 + 3y^2}$

91. $x^2 + y^2 + (z + 1)^2 = 1$

92. $x^2 + y^2 + (z - 3)^2 = 9$

CYLINDRICAL

93. $z = r^2$

94. $z = |r|$

95. $r = 7\sin\theta$

96. $r = 4\cos\theta$

SPHERICAL

97. $\rho = 4$

98. $\rho = \sqrt{3}\sec\phi$

99. $\phi = 3\pi/4$

100. $\rho\cos\phi + \rho^2\sin^2\phi = 1$

SKYWRITING

WAYNE MANSFIELD, owner of Aviad, Inc., in Andover, MA, produces and flies the world's largest aerial billboard, and has recently incorporated in Great Britain and the Czech Republic. If you saw a plane towing a billboard larger than the Goodyear blimp over the International Motorcycle Races in Brno, Czech Republic, in the fall of 1993, that was Wayne Mansfield at work.

Mansfield also works throughout the world as a skywriter. Skywriting, which exemplifies motion in space (the main topic of Chapter 12), was brought to the United States in 1924 by a former British World War I pilot, Major John Clifford Savage, according to the book *Skywriting and Skywriting Equipment* by Lieut. Joseph C. Mackey.

In skywriting, the letters are written upside down (to be read from below) in a horizontal plane about two miles up in the air.

As you fly, you must balance the forces of lift, gravity, thrust, and drag to keep the plane level and moving at a constant speed.

Wind is a consideration, too. It takes about a minute to write a letter (which can be a mile or more tall), and you want the completed message to be readable by the intended audience for as long as possible.

If the wind is blowing 15 mi/h, say, each letter will drift a quarter of a mile per minute after it is made. A message can usually be seen within a radius of 10 to 12 miles, and may remain readable for anywhere from 2 to 60 minutes.

12 Vector-Valued Functions

OVERVIEW

From the times of the ancient Greeks until the sixteenth century, it was widely believed by Western astronomers that the earth was the fixed center of the universe, with the heavenly bodies moving in circular orbits around it. In 1543 the Polish astronomer Nicolaus Copernicus disputed the prevailing theory by claiming that the earth and other planets move around the sun, although he still believed that the motions were basically circular and that each planet moved at a constant speed. In 1619, the German astronomer and mathematician Johannes Kepler correctly hypothesized that each planet's path is actually an ellipse with the sun at one focus and that each planet moves at a variable speed that enables the radius vector from the sun to the planet to sweep out equal areas in equal times (Section 12.5). Kepler's work was distinguished by his insistence that theory and observation be absolutely consistent. Later his work supported Newton's law of gravitational attraction, which set the stage for a new science of motion.

This chapter shows how we use calculus to determine the paths, velocities, and accelerations of moving bodies.

12.1 Vector-Valued Functions and Space Curves

To track a particle moving in space, we run a vector **r** from the origin to the particle (Fig. 12.1) and study the changes in **r**. If the particle's position coordinates are twice-differentiable functions of time, then so is **r** and we can find the particle's velocity and acceleration vectors at any time by differentiating **r**. Conversely, if we know either the particle's velocity vector or its acceleration vector as a continuous function of time, and if we have enough information about the particle's initial velocity and initial position, we can find **r** by integration.

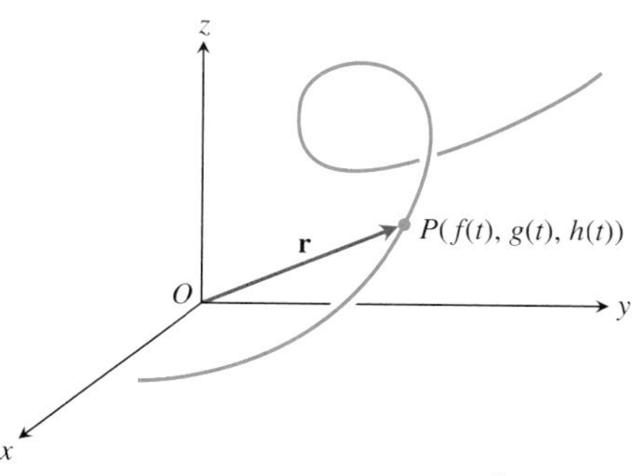

12.1 The position vector $\mathbf{r} = \overrightarrow{OP}$ of a particle moving through space is a function of time.

Definitions

When a particle moves through space during a time interval I, we think of the particle's coordinates as functions defined on I:

$$x = f(t), \qquad y = g(t), \qquad z = h(t), \qquad t \in I. \tag{1}$$

The points $(x, y, z) = (f(t), g(t), h(t))$, $t \in I$, make up the **curve** in space that we call the particle's path. The equations and interval in (1) **parametrize** the curve. The vector

$$\mathbf{r} = \overrightarrow{OP} = f(t)\,\mathbf{i} + g(t)\,\mathbf{j} + h(t)\,\mathbf{k} \tag{2}$$

from the origin to the particle's **position** $P(f(t), g(t), h(t))$ at time t is the particle's **position vector.** The functions f, g, and h are the **component functions** (**components**) of the position vector. We think of the particle's path as the curve traced by the tip of $\mathbf{r}$ during the time interval I.

Equation (2) defines $\mathbf{r}$ as a vector function of the real variable t on the interval I. More generally, a **vector function** or **vector-valued function** on a domain set D is a rule that assigns a vector in space to each element in D. For now, the domains will be intervals of real numbers. Later, in Chapter 15, the domains will be regions in the plane or in space. Vector functions will then be called "vector fields."

When we need to distinguish them from vector functions, we refer to real-valued functions as **scalar functions.** The components of $\mathbf{r}$ are scalar functions of t. When we define a vector-valued function by giving its component functions, we assume the vector function's domain to be the intersection of the domains of its component functions.

12.2 The upper half of the helix $\mathbf{r} = (\cos t)\,\mathbf{i} + (\sin t)\,\mathbf{j} + t\,\mathbf{k}$.

EXAMPLE 1 *A Helix.* The vector function

$$\mathbf{r} = (\cos t)\,\mathbf{i} + (\sin t)\,\mathbf{j} + t\,\mathbf{k}$$

is defined for all real values of t. The curve traced by $\mathbf{r}$ is a helix (from an old Greek word for spiral) that winds around the circular cylinder $x^2 + y^2 = 1$ (Fig. 12.2). The curve lies on the cylinder because the **i**- and **j**-components of $\mathbf{r}$, being the x- and y-coordinates of the tip of $\mathbf{r}$, satisfy the cylinder's equation:

$$x^2 + y^2 = (\cos t)^2 + (\sin t)^2 = 1.$$

The curve rises at a constant rate as the **k**-component $z = t$ increases. Each time t increases by 2π, the curve completes one turn around the cylinder. The equations

$$x = \cos t, \qquad y = \sin t, \qquad z = t$$

parametrize the helix, the interval $-\infty < t < \infty$ being understood. You will find more helices in Fig. 12.3.

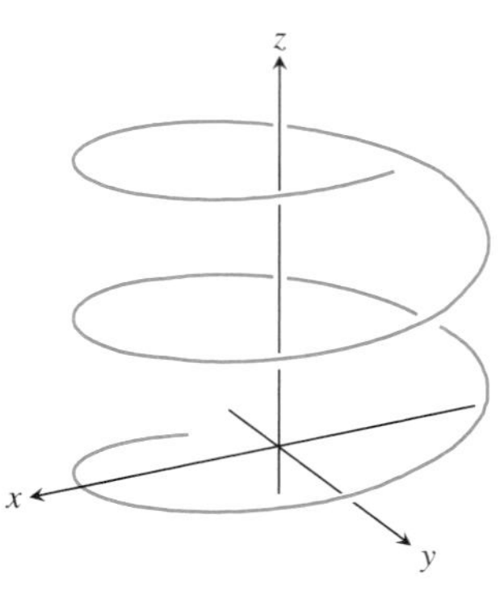

$\mathbf{r} = (\cos t)\mathbf{i} + (\sin t)\mathbf{j} + t\mathbf{k}$

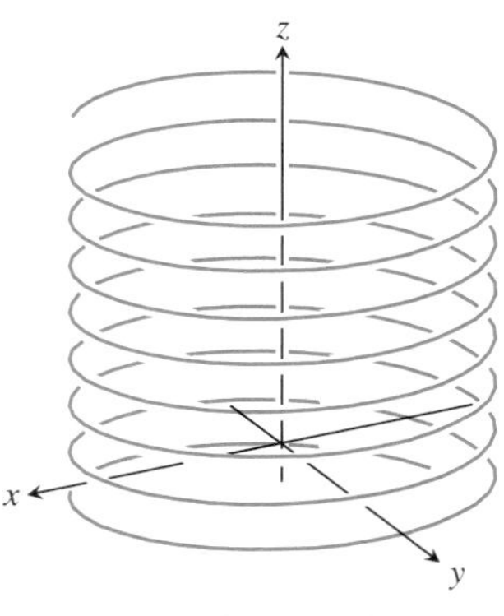

$\mathbf{r} = (\cos t)\mathbf{i} + (\sin t)\mathbf{j} + 0.3t\mathbf{k}$

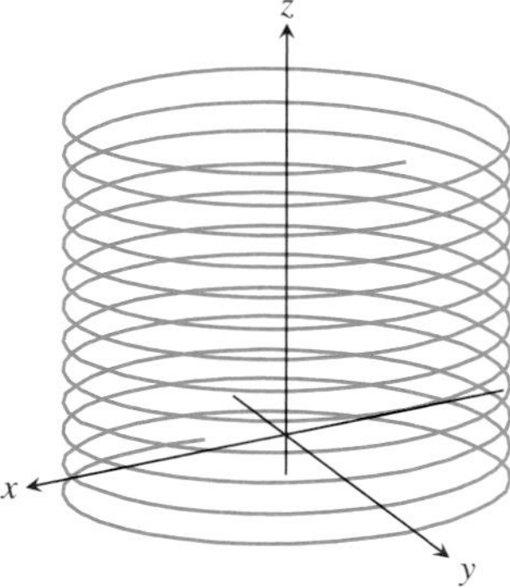

$\mathbf{r} = (\cos 5t)\mathbf{i} + (\sin 5t)\mathbf{j} + t\mathbf{k}$

(Generated by Mathematica)

12.3 Helices drawn by computer.

Limits and Continuity

We define limits of vector functions in terms of their scalar components.

DEFINITION

A vector function $\mathbf{r}$ defined by the rule $\mathbf{r}(t) = f(t)\,\mathbf{i} + g(t)\,\mathbf{j} + h(t)\,\mathbf{k}$ has **limit $\mathbf{L} = L_1\,\mathbf{i} + L_2\,\mathbf{j} + L_3\,\mathbf{k}$ as t approaches t_0** if

$$\lim_{t\to t_0} f(t) = L_1, \qquad \lim_{t\to t_0} g(t) = L_2, \qquad \text{and} \qquad \lim_{t\to t_0} h(t) = L_3. \tag{3}$$

We denote the existence of the limit in the usual way by writing

$$\lim_{t\to t_0} \mathbf{r}(t) = \mathbf{L}.$$

EXAMPLE 2 If $\mathbf{r}(t) = (\cos t)\,\mathbf{i} + (\sin t)\,\mathbf{j} + t\,\mathbf{k}$, then

$$\begin{aligned}\lim_{t\to\pi/4} \mathbf{r}(t) &= \left(\lim_{t\to\pi/4} \cos t\right)\mathbf{i} + \left(\lim_{t\to\pi/4} \sin t\right)\mathbf{j} + \left(\lim_{t\to\pi/4} t\right)\mathbf{k} \\ &= \frac{\sqrt{2}}{2}\,\mathbf{i} + \frac{\sqrt{2}}{2}\,\mathbf{j} + \frac{\pi}{4}\,\mathbf{k}.\end{aligned}$$

We define continuity for vector functions the same way we define continuity for scalar functions.

DEFINITION

A vector function $\mathbf{r}$ is **continuous at a point** $t = t_0$ in its domain if $\lim_{t\to t_0} \mathbf{r}(t) = \mathbf{r}(t_0)$. The function is **continuous** if it is continuous at every point in its domain.

Since limits are defined in terms of components, we can test vector functions for continuity by examining their components.

Component Test for Continuity at a Point

A vector function $\mathbf{r}$ defined by the rule $\mathbf{r}(t) = f(t)\,\mathbf{i} + g(t)\,\mathbf{j} + h(t)\,\mathbf{k}$ is continuous at $t = t_0$ if and only if f, g, and h are continuous at t_0.

EXAMPLE 3

a) The function

$$\mathbf{r} = (\cos t)\,\mathbf{i} + (\sin t)\,\mathbf{j} + t\,\mathbf{k}$$

is continuous because $\cos t$, $\sin t$, and t are continuous.

b) The function

$$\mathbf{r} = (\cos t)\,\mathbf{i} + (\sin t)\,\mathbf{j} + \lfloor t \rfloor\,\mathbf{k}$$

is discontinuous at every integer.

Derivatives and Motion

Suppose that $\mathbf{r} = f(t)\,\mathbf{i} + g(t)\,\mathbf{j} + h(t)\,\mathbf{k}$ is the position vector of a particle moving along a curve in space and that f, g, and h are differentiable functions of t. Then the difference between the particle's positions at time t and time $t + \Delta t$ is

$$\Delta\mathbf{r} = \mathbf{r}(t + \Delta t) - \mathbf{r}(t) \tag{4}$$

(Fig. 12.4). In terms of components,

$$\begin{aligned}\Delta\mathbf{r} &= \mathbf{r}(t + \Delta t) - \mathbf{r}(t)\\ &= [f(t + \Delta t)\,\mathbf{i} + g(t + \Delta t)\,\mathbf{j} + h(t + \Delta t)\,\mathbf{k}]\\ &\quad - [f(t)\,\mathbf{i} + g(t)\,\mathbf{j} + h(t)\,\mathbf{k}]\\ &= [f(t + \Delta t) - f(t)]\,\mathbf{i} + [g(t + \Delta t) - g(t)]\,\mathbf{j} + [h(t + \Delta t) - h(t)]\,\mathbf{k}.\end{aligned} \tag{5}$$

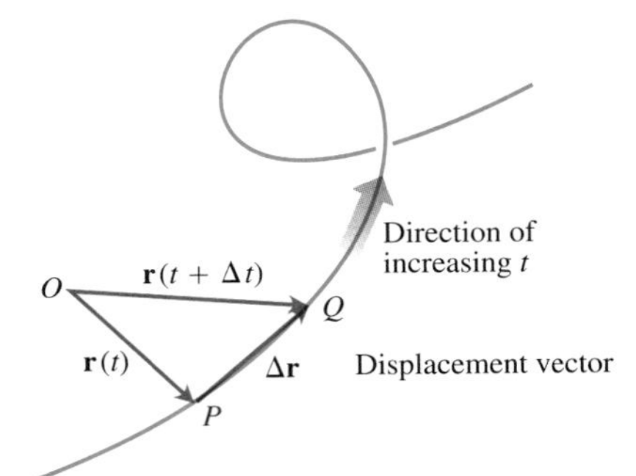

12.4 Between time t and time $t + \Delta t$, the particle moving along the path shown here undergoes the displacement $\overrightarrow{PQ} = \Delta\mathbf{r}$. The vector sum $\mathbf{r}(t) + \Delta\mathbf{r}$ gives the new position, $\mathbf{r}(t + \Delta t)$.

As Δt approaches zero, three things seem to happen simultaneously. First, Q approaches P along the curve. Second, the secant line PQ seems to approach a limiting position tangent to the curve at P. Third, the quotient $\Delta\mathbf{r}/\Delta t$ approaches the limit

$$\begin{aligned}\lim_{\Delta t \to 0} \frac{\Delta\mathbf{r}}{\Delta t} &= \left[\lim_{\Delta t \to 0} \frac{f(t + \Delta t) - f(t)}{\Delta t}\right]\mathbf{i} + \left[\lim_{\Delta t \to 0} \frac{g(t + \Delta t) - g(t)}{\Delta t}\right]\mathbf{j}\\ &\quad + \left[\lim_{\Delta t \to 0} \frac{h(t + \Delta t) - h(t)}{\Delta t}\right]\mathbf{k}\\ &= \left[\frac{df}{dt}\right]\mathbf{i} + \left[\frac{dg}{dt}\right]\mathbf{j} + \left[\frac{dh}{dt}\right]\mathbf{k}.\end{aligned} \tag{6}$$

We are therefore led by past experience to the following definition.

DEFINITIONS

The vector function $\mathbf{r} = f(t)\,\mathbf{i} + g(t)\,\mathbf{j} + h(t)\,\mathbf{k}$ is **differentiable at** $t = t_0$ if f, g, and h are differentiable at t_0. Also, $\mathbf{r}$ is said to be **differentiable** if it is differentiable at every point of its domain. At any point t at which $\mathbf{r}$ is differentiable, its **derivative** is the vector

$$\frac{d\mathbf{r}}{dt} = \lim_{\Delta t \to 0} \frac{\mathbf{r}(t + \Delta t) - \mathbf{r}(t)}{\Delta t} = \frac{df}{dt}\,\mathbf{i} + \frac{dg}{dt}\,\mathbf{j} + \frac{dh}{dt}\,\mathbf{k}.$$

The curve traced by $\mathbf{r}$ is **smooth** if $d\mathbf{r}/dt$ is continuous and never equal to $\mathbf{0}$, i.e., if f, g, and h have continuous first derivatives that are not simultaneously 0.

The vector $d\mathbf{r}/dt$, when different from $\mathbf{0}$, is also called the **tangent vector** to the curve. The **tangent line** to the curve at a point $(f(t_0), g(t_0), h(t_0))$ is defined to

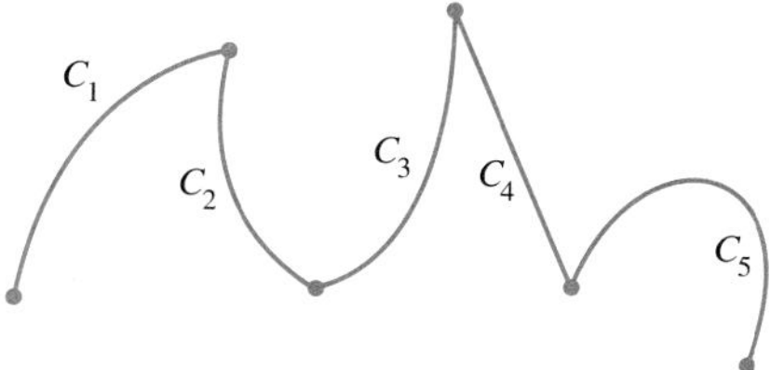

12.5 A piecewise-smooth curve made up of five smooth curves connected end to end in continuous fashion.

be the line through the point parallel to $d\mathbf{r}/dt$ at $t = t_0$. We require $d\mathbf{r}/dt \neq \mathbf{0}$ for a smooth curve to make sure the curve has a continuously turning tangent at each point. On a smooth curve there are no sharp corners or cusps.

A curve that is made up of a finite number of smooth curves pieced together in a continuous fashion so that the initial point of one curve is the terminal point of the immediately preceding one is called **piecewise smooth** (Fig. 12.5).

Look once again at Fig. 12.4. We drew the figure for Δt positive, so $\Delta\mathbf{r}$ points forward, in the direction of the motion. The vector $\Delta\mathbf{r}/\Delta t$ (not shown), having the same direction as $\Delta\mathbf{r}$, points forward too. Had Δt been negative, $\Delta\mathbf{r}$ would have pointed backward, against the direction of motion. The quotient $\Delta\mathbf{r}/\Delta t$, however, being a negative scalar multiple of $\Delta\mathbf{r}$, would once again have pointed forward. No matter how $\Delta\mathbf{r}$ points, $\Delta\mathbf{r}/\Delta t$ points forward and we expect the vector $d\mathbf{r}/dt = \lim_{\Delta t\to 0} \Delta\mathbf{r}/\Delta t$, when different from $\mathbf{0}$, to do the same. This means that the derivative $d\mathbf{r}/dt$ is just what we want for modeling a particle's velocity. It points in the direction of motion and gives the rate of change of position with respect to time. For a smooth curve the particle's velocity is never zero, so the particle does not stop along its path or reverse its direction.

DEFINITIONS

If $\mathbf{r}$ is the position vector of a particle moving along a smooth curve in space, then

$$\mathbf{v} = \frac{d\mathbf{r}}{dt}$$

is the particle's **velocity vector.** At any time t, the direction of $\mathbf{v}$ is the **direction of motion,** the magnitude of $\mathbf{v}$ is the particle's **speed,** and the derivative $\mathbf{a} = d\mathbf{v}/dt$, when it exists, is the particle's **acceleration vector.** In short,

1. Velocity is the derivative of position: $\mathbf{v} = \dfrac{d\mathbf{r}}{dt}$.
2. Speed is the magnitude of velocity: Speed $= |\mathbf{v}|$.
3. Acceleration is the derivative of velocity: $\mathbf{a} = \dfrac{d\mathbf{v}}{dt} = \dfrac{d^2\mathbf{r}}{dt^2}$.
4. The vector $\mathbf{v}/|\mathbf{v}|$ is the direction of motion at time t.

We use the following formula to express the velocity of a moving particle as the product of its speed and direction.

$$\text{Velocity} = |\mathbf{v}| \cdot \frac{\mathbf{v}}{|\mathbf{v}|} = (\text{Speed}) \cdot (\text{Direction}) \tag{7}$$

EXAMPLE 4 The vector

$$\mathbf{r} = (3\cos t)\,\mathbf{i} + (3\sin t)\,\mathbf{j} + t^2\,\mathbf{k}$$

gives the position of a moving body at time t. Find the body's speed and direction when $t = 2$. At what times, if any, are the body's velocity and acceleration orthogonal?

Solution

$$\mathbf{r} = (3\cos t)\,\mathbf{i} + (3\sin t)\,\mathbf{j} + t^2\,\mathbf{k}$$

$$\mathbf{v} = \frac{d\mathbf{r}}{dt} = -(3\sin t)\,\mathbf{i} + (3\cos t)\,\mathbf{j} + 2t\,\mathbf{k}$$

$$\mathbf{a} = \frac{d^2\mathbf{r}}{dt^2} = -(3\cos t)\,\mathbf{i} - (3\sin t)\,\mathbf{j} + 2\,\mathbf{k}$$

At $t = 2$, the body's speed and direction are

Speed: $$|\mathbf{v}(2)| = \sqrt{(-3\sin 2)^2 + (3\cos 2)^2 + (4)^2} = 5$$

Direction: $$\frac{\mathbf{v}(2)}{|\mathbf{v}(2)|} = -\left(\frac{3}{5}\sin 2\right)\mathbf{i} + \left(\frac{3}{5}\cos 2\right)\mathbf{j} + \frac{4}{5}\mathbf{k}.$$

To find the times when $\mathbf{v}$ and $\mathbf{a}$ are orthogonal, we look for values of t for which

$$\mathbf{v}\cdot\mathbf{a} = 9\sin t\cos t - 9\cos t\sin t + 4t = 4t = 0.$$

The only value is $t = 0$.

Differentiation Rules

Because the derivatives of vector functions are defined component by component, the rules for differentiating vector functions have the same form as the rules for differentiating scalar functions.

Differentiation Rules for Vector Functions

Constant Function Rule: $\dfrac{d}{dt}\mathbf{C} = \mathbf{0}$ (any constant vector $\mathbf{C}$)

If $\mathbf{u}$ and $\mathbf{v}$ are differentiable functions of t, then

Scalar Multiple Rule: $\dfrac{d}{dt}(c\,\mathbf{u}) = c\dfrac{d\mathbf{u}}{dt}$ (any number c)

Sum Rule: $\dfrac{d}{dt}(\mathbf{u} + \mathbf{v}) = \dfrac{d\mathbf{u}}{dt} + \dfrac{d\mathbf{v}}{dt}$

Difference Rule: $\dfrac{d}{dt}(\mathbf{u} - \mathbf{v}) = \dfrac{d\mathbf{u}}{dt} - \dfrac{d\mathbf{v}}{dt}$

Dot Product Rule: $\dfrac{d}{dt}(\mathbf{u}\cdot\mathbf{v}) = \dfrac{d\mathbf{u}}{dt}\cdot\mathbf{v} + \mathbf{u}\cdot\dfrac{d\mathbf{v}}{dt}$

Cross Product Rule: $\dfrac{d}{dt}(\mathbf{u}\times\mathbf{v}) = \dfrac{d\mathbf{u}}{dt}\times\mathbf{v} + \mathbf{u}\times\dfrac{d\mathbf{v}}{dt}$

Chain Rule (Short Form): If $\mathbf{r}$ is a differentiable function of t and t is a differentiable function of s, then

$$\frac{d\mathbf{r}}{ds} = \frac{d\mathbf{r}}{dt}\frac{dt}{ds}.$$

When you use the Cross Product Rule, remember to preserve the order of the factors. If **u** comes first on the left, it must also come first on the right or the signs will be wrong.

We will prove the Dot Product Rule and the Chain Rule but leave the rules for constants, scalar multiples, sums, and differences as exercises. The proof of the Cross Product Rule is cumbersome and we will omit it entirely.

Proof of the Dot Product Rule

Suppose that

$$\mathbf{u} = u_1(t)\,\mathbf{i} + u_2(t)\,\mathbf{j} + u_3(t)\,\mathbf{k}$$

and

$$\mathbf{v} = v_1(t)\,\mathbf{i} + v_2(t)\,\mathbf{j} + v_3(t)\,\mathbf{k}.$$

Then

$$\begin{aligned}\frac{d}{dt}(\mathbf{u}\cdot\mathbf{v}) &= \frac{d}{dt}(u_1 v_1 + u_2 v_2 + u_3 v_3)\\ &= \underbrace{u_1'v_1 + u_2'v_2 + u_3'v_3}_{\mathbf{u}'\cdot\mathbf{v}} + \underbrace{u_1 v_1' + u_2 v_2' + u_3 v_3'}_{\mathbf{u}\cdot\mathbf{v}'}.\end{aligned}$$

∎

Proof of the Chain Rule Suppose that $\mathbf{r} = f(t)\,\mathbf{i} + g(t)\,\mathbf{j} + h(t)\,\mathbf{k}$ is a differentiable vector function of t and that t is a differentiable scalar function of some other variable s. Then f, g, and h are differentiable functions of s and the Chain Rule for differentiable real-valued functions gives

$$\begin{aligned}\frac{d\mathbf{r}}{ds} &= \frac{df}{ds}\mathbf{i} + \frac{dg}{ds}\mathbf{j} + \frac{dh}{ds}\mathbf{k}\\ &= \frac{df}{dt}\frac{dt}{ds}\mathbf{i} + \frac{dg}{dt}\frac{dt}{ds}\mathbf{j} + \frac{dh}{dt}\frac{dt}{ds}\mathbf{k}\\ &= \left(\frac{df}{dt}\mathbf{i} + \frac{dg}{dt}\mathbf{j} + \frac{dh}{dt}\mathbf{k}\right)\frac{dt}{ds}\\ &= \frac{d\mathbf{r}}{dt}\frac{dt}{ds}.\end{aligned}$$

∎

Derivatives of Vectors of Constant Length

We might at first think that a vector whose length remained constant as time passed would have to have a zero derivative, but this is not the case. Think of a clock hand. Its length remains constant as time passes, but its direction still changes. What we *can* say about the derivative of a vector of constant length is that it is always orthogonal to the vector. Direction changes take place at right angles.

If **u** is a differentiable vector function of t of constant length, then

$$\mathbf{u}\cdot\frac{d\mathbf{u}}{dt} = 0. \tag{8}$$

To see why Eq. (8) holds, suppose that $\mathbf{u}$ is a differentiable function of t and that $|\mathbf{u}|$ is constant. Then $\mathbf{u} \cdot \mathbf{u} = |\mathbf{u}|^2$ is constant and we may differentiate both sides of this equation to get

$$\frac{d}{dt}(\mathbf{u} \cdot \mathbf{u}) = \frac{d}{dt}(\text{constant}) = 0$$

$$\frac{d\mathbf{u}}{dt} \cdot \mathbf{u} + \mathbf{u} \cdot \frac{d\mathbf{u}}{dt} = 0 \qquad \text{Dot Product Rule with } \mathbf{v} = \mathbf{u}$$

$$2\,\mathbf{u} \cdot \frac{d\mathbf{u}}{dt} = 0 \qquad \text{Dot multiplication is commutative.}$$

$$\mathbf{u} \cdot \frac{d\mathbf{u}}{dt} = 0.$$

EXAMPLE 5 Show that

$$\mathbf{u}(t) = (\sin t)\,\mathbf{i} + (\cos t)\,\mathbf{j} + \sqrt{3}\,\mathbf{k}$$

has constant length and is orthogonal to its derivative.

Solution

$$\mathbf{u}(t) = (\sin t)\,\mathbf{i} + (\cos t)\,\mathbf{j} + \sqrt{3}\,\mathbf{k}$$

$$|\mathbf{u}(t)| = \sqrt{(\sin t)^2 + (\cos t)^2 + (\sqrt{3})^2}$$

$$= \sqrt{1 + 3} = 2$$

$$\frac{d\mathbf{u}}{dt} = (\cos t)\,\mathbf{i} - (\sin t)\,\mathbf{j}$$

$$\mathbf{u} \cdot \frac{d\mathbf{u}}{dt} = \sin t \cos t - \sin t \cos t = 0$$

Integrals of Vector Functions

A differentiable vector function $\mathbf{R}(t)$ is an **antiderivative** of a vector function $\mathbf{r}(t)$ on an interval I if $d\mathbf{R}/dt = \mathbf{r}$ at each point of I. If $\mathbf{R}$ is an antiderivative of $\mathbf{r}$ on I, it can be shown, working one component at a time, that every antiderivative of $\mathbf{r}$ on I has the form $\mathbf{R} + \mathbf{C}$ for some constant vector $\mathbf{C}$ (Exercise 44). The set of all antiderivatives of $\mathbf{r}$ on I is the **indefinite integral** of $\mathbf{r}$ on I.

DEFINITION

The **indefinite integral** of $\mathbf{r}$ with respect to t is the set of all antiderivatives of $\mathbf{r}$, denoted by $\int \mathbf{r}(t)\,dt$. If $\mathbf{R}$ is any antiderivative of $\mathbf{r}$, then

$$\int \mathbf{r}(t)\,dt = \mathbf{R}(t) + \mathbf{C}. \tag{9}$$

The usual arithmetic rules for indefinite integrals apply.

EXAMPLE 6

$$\int ((\cos t)\,\mathbf{i} + \mathbf{j} - 2t\,\mathbf{k})\,dt$$

$$= \left(\int \cos t\,dt\right)\mathbf{i} + \left(\int dt\right)\mathbf{j} - \left(\int 2t\,dt\right)\mathbf{k} \qquad (10)$$

$$= (\sin t + C_1)\,\mathbf{i} + (t + C_2)\,\mathbf{j} - (t^2 + C_3)\,\mathbf{k} \qquad (11)$$

$$= (\sin t)\,\mathbf{i} + t\,\mathbf{j} - t^2\,\mathbf{k} + \mathbf{C} \qquad \mathbf{C} = C_1\,\mathbf{i} + C_2\,\mathbf{j} - C_3\,\mathbf{k}$$

As in the integration of scalar functions, we recommend that you skip the steps in (10) and (11) and go directly to the final form. Find an antiderivative for each component and add a constant vector at the end.

Definite integrals of vector functions are defined in terms of components.

DEFINITION

If the components of $\mathbf{r}(t) = f(t)\,\mathbf{i} + g(t)\,\mathbf{j} + h(t)\,\mathbf{k}$ are integrable over the interval $a \le t \le b$, then $\mathbf{r}$ is **integrable** over $[a, b]$ and the **definite integral** of $\mathbf{r}$ from a to b is

$$\int_a^b \mathbf{r}(t)\,dt = \left(\int_a^b f(t)\,dt\right)\mathbf{i} + \left(\int_a^b g(t)\,dt\right)\mathbf{j} + \left(\int_a^b h(t)\,dt\right)\mathbf{k}. \qquad (12)$$

The usual arithmetic rules for definite integrals apply (Exercise 42).

EXAMPLE 7

$$\int_0^{\pi} ((\cos t)\,\mathbf{i} + \mathbf{j} - 2t\,\mathbf{k})\,dt = \left(\int_0^{\pi} \cos t\,dt\right)\mathbf{i} + \left(\int_0^{\pi} dt\right)\mathbf{j} - \left(\int_0^{\pi} 2t\,dt\right)\mathbf{k}$$

$$= \Big[\sin t\Big]_0^{\pi}\,\mathbf{i} + \Big[t\Big]_0^{\pi}\,\mathbf{j} - \Big[t^2\Big]_0^{\pi}\,\mathbf{k}$$

$$= [0 - 0]\,\mathbf{i} + [\pi - 0]\,\mathbf{j} - [\pi^2 - 0^2]\,\mathbf{k}$$

$$= \pi\,\mathbf{j} - \pi^2\,\mathbf{k}$$

EXAMPLE 8 *Finding a Particle's Position Function from Its Velocity Function and Initial Position.* The velocity of a particle moving in space is

$$\frac{d\mathbf{r}}{dt} = (\cos t)\,\mathbf{i} - (\sin t)\,\mathbf{j} + \mathbf{k}.$$

Find the particle's position as a function of t if $\mathbf{r} = 2\,\mathbf{i} + \mathbf{k}$ when $t = 0$.

Solution Our goal is to solve the initial value problem that consists of

The differential equation: $\dfrac{d\mathbf{r}}{dt} = (\cos t)\,\mathbf{i} - (\sin t)\,\mathbf{j} + \mathbf{k}$

The initial condition: $\mathbf{r} = 2\,\mathbf{i} + \mathbf{k}$ when $t = 0$.

Integrating both sides of the differential equation with respect to t gives

$$\mathbf{r} = (\sin t)\,\mathbf{i} + (\cos t)\,\mathbf{j} + t\,\mathbf{k} + \mathbf{C}.$$

We then use the initial condition to find the right value for $\mathbf{C}$:

$$(\sin 0)\,\mathbf{i} + (\cos 0)\,\mathbf{j} + (0)\,\mathbf{k} + \mathbf{C} = 2\,\mathbf{i} + \mathbf{k} \qquad \mathbf{r} = 2\,\mathbf{i} + \mathbf{k} \text{ when } t = 0$$

$$\mathbf{j} + \mathbf{C} = 2\,\mathbf{i} + \mathbf{k}$$

$$\mathbf{C} = 2\,\mathbf{i} - \mathbf{j} + \mathbf{k}.$$

The particle's position as a function of t is

$$\mathbf{r} = (\sin t + 2)\,\mathbf{i} + (\cos t - 1)\,\mathbf{j} + (t + 1)\,\mathbf{k}.$$

To check (always a good idea), we can see from this formula that

$$\frac{d\mathbf{r}}{dt} = (\cos t + 0)\,\mathbf{i} + (-\sin t - 0)\,\mathbf{j} + (1 + 0)\,\mathbf{k} = (\cos t)\,\mathbf{i} - (\sin t)\,\mathbf{j} + \mathbf{k}$$

and that when $t = 0$,

$$\mathbf{r} = (\sin 0 + 2)\,\mathbf{i} + (\cos 0 - 1)\,\mathbf{j} + (0 + 1)\,\mathbf{k} = 2\,\mathbf{i} + \mathbf{k}.$$

Exercises 12.1

In Exercises 1–8, $\mathbf{r}$ is the position of a particle in space at time t. Find the particle's velocity and acceleration vectors. Then find the particle's speed and direction of motion at the given value of t and write the particle's velocity at that time as the product of its speed and direction.

1. $\mathbf{r} = (2\cos t)\,\mathbf{i} + (3\sin t)\,\mathbf{j} + 4t\,\mathbf{k}, \quad t = \pi/2$

2. $\mathbf{r} = (\sec t)\,\mathbf{i} + (\tan t)\,\mathbf{j} + \frac{4}{3}t\,\mathbf{k}, \quad t = \pi/6$

3. $\mathbf{r} = (t + 1)\,\mathbf{i} + (t^2 - 1)\,\mathbf{j} + 2t\,\mathbf{k}, \quad t = 1$

4. $\mathbf{r} = (1 + t)\,\mathbf{i} + \dfrac{t^2}{\sqrt{2}}\,\mathbf{j} + \dfrac{t^3}{3}\,\mathbf{k}, \quad t = 1$

5. $\mathbf{r} = (2\ln(t + 1))\,\mathbf{i} + t^2\,\mathbf{j} + \dfrac{t^2}{2}\,\mathbf{k}, \quad t = 1$

6. $\mathbf{r} = (e^{-t})\,\mathbf{i} + (2\cos 3t)\,\mathbf{j} + (2\sin 3t)\,\mathbf{k}, \quad t = 0$

7. *Motion in the xy-plane.* $\mathbf{r} = e^t\,\mathbf{i} + \frac{2}{9}e^{2t}\,\mathbf{j}, \quad t = \ln 3$

8. *Motion in the zy-plane.* $\mathbf{r} = (\cos 2t)\,\mathbf{j} + (2\sin t)\,\mathbf{k}, \quad t = 0$

In Exercises 9–12, $\mathbf{r}$ is the position of a particle in space at time t. Find the angle between the velocity and acceleration vectors at time $t = 0$.

9. $\mathbf{r} = (3t + 1)\,\mathbf{i} + \sqrt{3}t\,\mathbf{j} + t^2\,\mathbf{k}$

10. $\mathbf{r} = \left(\dfrac{\sqrt{2}}{2}t\right)\mathbf{i} + \left(\dfrac{\sqrt{2}}{2}t - 16t^2\right)\mathbf{j}$

11. $\mathbf{r} = (\ln(t^2 + 1))\,\mathbf{i} + (\tan^{-1} t)\,\mathbf{j} + \sqrt{t^2 + 1}\,\mathbf{k}$

12. $\mathbf{r} = \frac{4}{9}(1 + t)^{3/2}\,\mathbf{i} + \frac{4}{9}(1 - t)^{3/2}\,\mathbf{j} + \frac{1}{3}t\,\mathbf{k}$

In Exercises 13 and 14, $\mathbf{r}$ is the position vector of a particle in space at time t. Find the time or times in the given time interval when the velocity and acceleration vectors are orthogonal.

13. $\mathbf{r} = (t - \sin t)\,\mathbf{i} + (1 - \cos t)\,\mathbf{j}, \quad 0 \le t \le 2\pi$

14. $\mathbf{r} = (\sin t)\,\mathbf{i} + t\,\mathbf{j} + (\cos t)\,\mathbf{k}, \quad t \ge 0$

Evaluate the integrals in Exercises 15–20.

15. $\displaystyle\int_0^1 [t^3\,\mathbf{i} + 7\,\mathbf{j} + (t + 1)\,\mathbf{k}]\,dt$

16. $\displaystyle\int_1^2 \left[(6 - 6t)\,\mathbf{i} + 3\sqrt{t}\,\mathbf{j} + \left(\frac{4}{t^2}\right)\mathbf{k}\right]dt$

17. $\displaystyle\int_{-\pi/4}^{\pi/4} [(\sin t)\,\mathbf{i} + (1 + \cos t)\,\mathbf{j} + (\sec^2 t)\,\mathbf{k}]\,dt$

18. $\displaystyle\int_0^{\pi/3} [(\sec t \tan t)\,\mathbf{i} + (\tan t)\,\mathbf{j} + (2\sin t\cos t)\,\mathbf{k}]\,dt$

19. $\displaystyle\int_1^4 \left[\frac{1}{t}\,\mathbf{i} + \frac{1}{5 - t}\,\mathbf{j} + \frac{1}{2t}\,\mathbf{k}\right]dt$

20. $\displaystyle\int_0^1 \left[\frac{2}{\sqrt{1 - t^2}}\,\mathbf{i} + \frac{\sqrt{3}}{1 + t^2}\,\mathbf{k}\right]dt$

Exercises 21–24 give the position vectors of particles moving along various curves in the xy-plane. In each case, find the particle's velocity and acceleration vectors at the stated times and sketch them as vectors on the curve.

21. ***Motion on the Circle*** $x^2 + y^2 = 1$.

$$\mathbf{r} = (\sin t)\,\mathbf{i} + (\cos t)\,\mathbf{j}; \quad t = \pi/4 \text{ and } \pi/2$$

22. *Motion on the Circle $x^2 + y^2 = 16$.*

$$\mathbf{r} = \left(4\cos\frac{t}{2}\right)\mathbf{i} + \left(4\sin\frac{t}{2}\right)\mathbf{j}; \quad t = \pi \text{ and } 3\pi/2$$

23. *Motion on the Cycloid $x = t - \sin t$, $y = 1 - \cos t$.*

$$\mathbf{r} = (t - \sin t)\,\mathbf{i} + (1 - \cos t)\,\mathbf{j}; \quad t = \pi \text{ and } 3\pi/2$$

24. *Motion on the Parabola $y = x^2 + 1$.*

$$\mathbf{r} = t\,\mathbf{i} + (t^2 + 1)\,\mathbf{j}; \quad t = -1, 0, \text{ and } 1$$

Solve the initial value problems in Exercises 25–30 for $\mathbf{r}$ as a vector function of t.

25. Differential equation: $\dfrac{d\mathbf{r}}{dt} = -t\,\mathbf{i} - t\,\mathbf{j} - t\,\mathbf{k}$

Initial condition: $\mathbf{r} = \mathbf{i} + 2\,\mathbf{j} + 3\,\mathbf{k}$ when $t = 0$

26. Differential equation: $\dfrac{d\mathbf{r}}{dt} = (180t)\,\mathbf{i} + (180t - 16t^2)\,\mathbf{j}$

Initial condition: $\mathbf{r} = 100\,\mathbf{j}$ when $t = 0$

27. Differential equation: $\dfrac{d\mathbf{r}}{dt} = \dfrac{3}{2}(t + 1)^{1/2}\,\mathbf{i} + e^{-t}\,\mathbf{j} + \dfrac{1}{t + 1}\,\mathbf{k}$

Initial condition: $\mathbf{r} = \mathbf{k}$ when $t = 0$

28. Differential equation: $\dfrac{d\mathbf{r}}{dt} = (t^3 + 4t)\,\mathbf{i} + t\,\mathbf{j} + 2t^2\,\mathbf{k}$

Initial condition: $\mathbf{r} = \mathbf{i} + \mathbf{j}$ when $t = 0$

29. Differential equation: $\dfrac{d^2\mathbf{r}}{dt^2} = -32\,\mathbf{k}$

Initial conditions: $\mathbf{r} = 100\,\mathbf{k}$ and $\dfrac{d\mathbf{r}}{dt} = 8\,\mathbf{i} + 8\,\mathbf{j}$ when $t = 0$

30. Differential equation: $\dfrac{d^2\mathbf{r}}{dt^2} = -(\mathbf{i} + \mathbf{j} + \mathbf{k})$

Initial conditions: $\mathbf{r} = 10\,\mathbf{i} + 10\,\mathbf{j} + 10\,\mathbf{k}$ and $\dfrac{d\mathbf{r}}{dt} = \mathbf{0}$ when $t = 0$

31. A particle moves on a cycloid in the xy-plane in such a way that its position at time t is

$$\mathbf{r} = (t - \sin t)\,\mathbf{i} + (1 - \cos t)\,\mathbf{j},$$

as shown here for $t \geq 0$. Find the maximum and minimum values of $|\mathbf{v}|$ and $|\mathbf{a}|$. (*Hint:* Find the extreme values of $|\mathbf{v}|^2$ and $|\mathbf{a}|^2$ first and take square roots later.)

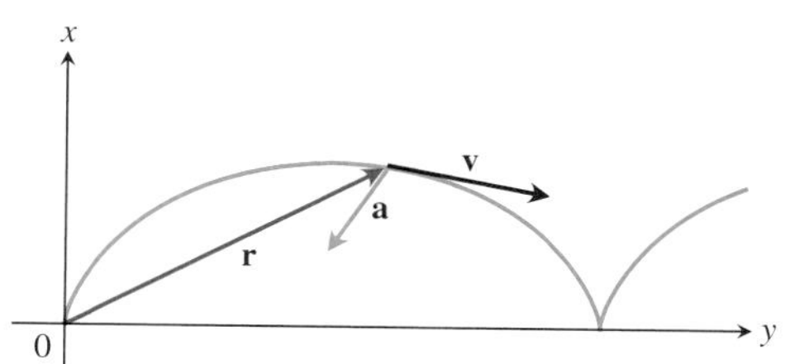

32. A particle moves around the ellipse $(y/3)^2 + (z/2)^2 = 1$ in the yz-plane in such a way that its position at time t is

$$\mathbf{r} = (3\cos t)\,\mathbf{j} + (2\sin t)\,\mathbf{k},$$

as shown here. Find the maximum and minimum values of $|\mathbf{v}|$ and $|\mathbf{a}|$. (*Hint:* Find the extreme values of $|\mathbf{v}|^2$ and $|\mathbf{a}|^2$ first and take square roots later.)

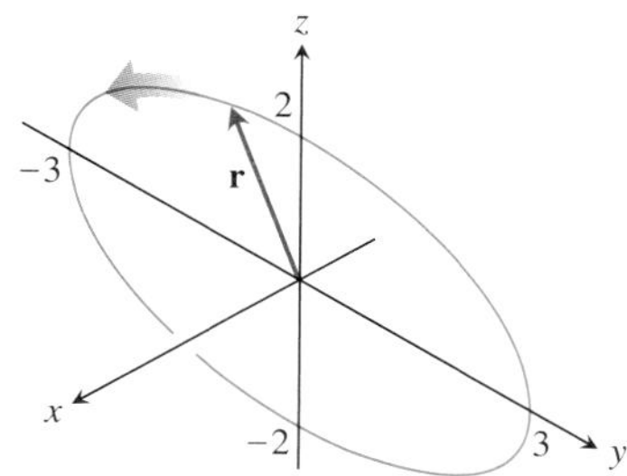

33. Suppose a particle moves on a sphere centered at the origin in such a way that its position vector $\mathbf{r}$ is a differentiable function of time, as shown here. Show that the particle's velocity is always orthogonal to $\mathbf{r}$.

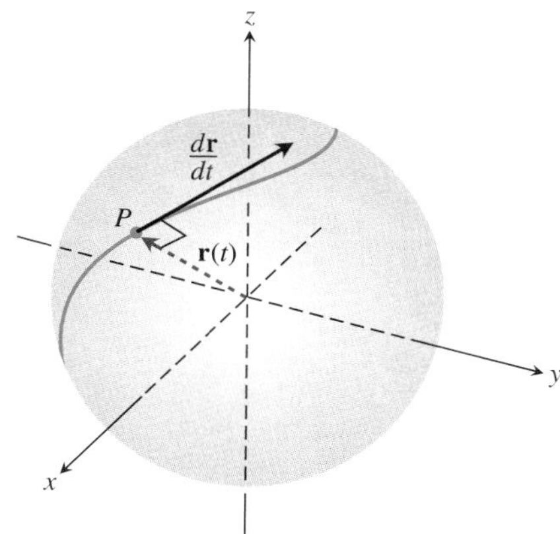

34. Let $\mathbf{v}$ be a differentiable vector function of t. If $\mathbf{v} \cdot (d\mathbf{v}/dt) = 0$ for all t, can anything be said about $|\mathbf{v}|$? Give reasons for your answer.

As mentioned in the text, the tangent line to a smooth curve $\mathbf{r} = f(t)\,\mathbf{i} + g(t)\,\mathbf{j} + h(t)\,\mathbf{k}$ at $t = t_0$ is the line that passes through the point $(f(t_0), g(t_0), h(t_0))$ parallel to $\mathbf{v}(t_0)$, the curve's velocity vector at t_0. In Exercises 35–38, find parametric equations for the line that is tangent to the given curve at the given parameter value $t = t_0$.

35. $\mathbf{r} = (\sin t)\,\mathbf{i} + (t^2 - \cos t)\,\mathbf{j} + e^t\,\mathbf{k}, \quad t_0 = 0$

36. $\mathbf{r} = (2\sin t)\,\mathbf{i} + (2\cos t)\,\mathbf{j} + 5t\,\mathbf{k}, \quad t_0 = 4\pi$

37. $\mathbf{r} = (a\sin t)\,\mathbf{i} + (a\cos t)\,\mathbf{j} + bt\,\mathbf{k}, \quad t_0 = 2\pi$

38. $\mathbf{r} = (\cos t)\,\mathbf{i} + (\sin t)\,\mathbf{j} + (\sin 2t)\,\mathbf{k}, \quad t_0 = \dfrac{\pi}{2}$

39. *The Constant Function Rule.* Prove that if $\mathbf{r}$ is the vector function with the constant value $\mathbf{C}$, then $d\mathbf{r}/dt = \mathbf{0}$.

40. *The Scalar Multiple Rule.* Prove that if $\mathbf{r}$ is a differentiable function of t and c is any real number, then

$$\frac{d(c\,\mathbf{r})}{dt} = c\frac{d\mathbf{r}}{dt}.$$

41. *The Sum and Difference Rules.* Prove that if $\mathbf{u}$ and $\mathbf{v}$ are differentiable functions of t, then

$$\frac{d}{dt}(\mathbf{u}+\mathbf{v}) = \frac{d\mathbf{u}}{dt} + \frac{d\mathbf{v}}{dt}$$

and

$$\frac{d}{dt}(\mathbf{u}-\mathbf{v}) = \frac{d\mathbf{u}}{dt} - \frac{d\mathbf{v}}{dt}.$$

42. Establish the following properties of integrable vector functions.

a) The *Constant Scalar Multiple Rule:*

$$\int_a^b k\,\mathbf{r}(t)\,dt = k\int_a^b \mathbf{r}(t)\,dt \qquad \text{(any scalar } k)$$

The *Rule for Negatives,*

$$\int_a^b (-\mathbf{r}(t))\,dt = -\int_a^b \mathbf{r}(t)\,dt,$$

is obtained by taking $k = -1$.

b) The *Sum and Difference Rules:*

$$\int_a^b (\mathbf{r}_1(t) \pm \mathbf{r}_2(t))\,dt = \int_a^b \mathbf{r}_1(t)\,dt \pm \int_a^b \mathbf{r}_2(t)\,dt$$

c) The *Constant Vector Multiple Rules:*

$$\int_a^b \mathbf{C}\cdot\mathbf{r}(t)\,dt = \mathbf{C}\cdot\int_a^b \mathbf{r}(t)\,dt \qquad \text{(any constant vector } \mathbf{C})$$

and

$$\int_a^b \mathbf{C}\times\mathbf{r}(t)\,dt = \mathbf{C}\times\int_a^b \mathbf{r}(t)\,dt \qquad \text{(any constant vector } \mathbf{C})$$

43. *Products of Scalar and Vector Functions.* Suppose that the scalar function $u(t)$ and the vector function $\mathbf{r}(t)$ are both defined for $a \le t \le b$.

a) Show that $u\,\mathbf{r}$ is continuous on $[a, b]$ if u and $\mathbf{r}$ are continuous on $[a, b]$.

b) If u and $\mathbf{r}$ are both differentiable on $[a, b]$, show that $u\,\mathbf{r}$ is differentiable on $[a, b]$ and that

$$\frac{d}{dt}(u\,\mathbf{r}) = u\frac{d\mathbf{r}}{dt} + \mathbf{r}\frac{du}{dt}.$$

44. *Antiderivatives of Vector Functions.*

a) Use Corollary 2 of the Mean Value Theorem for scalar functions to show that if two vector functions $\mathbf{R}_1(t)$ and $\mathbf{R}_2(t)$ have identical derivatives on an interval I, then the functions differ by a constant vector value throughout I.

b) Use the result in (a) to show that if $\mathbf{R}(t)$ is any antiderivative of $\mathbf{r}(t)$ on I, then every other antiderivative of $\mathbf{r}$ on I equals $\mathbf{R}(t) + \mathbf{C}$ for some constant vector $\mathbf{C}$.

Writing for Your Own Knowledge

Answer the following questions in writing. Some answers will take only a sentence or two; others may require several paragraphs. Some explanations may also call for graphs or sketches.

1. What are the rules for differentiating and integrating vector functions? How do they compare with the rules for differentiating and integrating real-valued functions of a single variable?
2. What is a smooth curve?
3. How do you find the velocity, speed, direction of motion, and acceleration of a body moving along a curve in space?
4. What is special about the derivative of a vector (function) of constant length?

12.2 Modeling Projectile Motion

To open the 1992 Summer Olympics in Barcelona, bronze medalist archer Antonio Rebollo lit the Olympic torch with a flaming arrow. The event was photographed in a time exposure revealing the arrow's path of motion (Fig. 12.6). The firing angle and speed of the arrow had to be precise—too large and fast and the arrow would fly too high over the cauldron to light it, too small and slow and the arrow would fly too low to hit the target. Rebollo had to do it right on his first try.

When we shoot a projectile into the air we usually want to know beforehand how far it will go (will it reach the target?), how high it will rise (will it clear the hill?), and when it will land (when do we get results?). We get this information from equations that calculate the answers we want from the direction and magnitude of the projectile's initial velocity vector, described in terms of the angle and

12.6 Spanish archer Antonio Rebollo lights the Olympic torch in Barcelona with a flaming arrow.

speed at which the projectile is fired. The equations come from combining calculus and Newton's second law of motion in vector form.

The Vector and Parametric Equations for Ideal Projectile Motion

To derive equations for projectile motion, we assume that the projectile behaves like a particle moving in a vertical coordinate plane and that the only force acting on the projectile during its flight is the constant force of gravity, which always points straight down. In practice, none of these assumptions really holds. The ground moves beneath the projectile as the earth turns, the air creates a frictional force that varies with the projectile's speed and altitude, and the force of gravity changes as the projectile moves along. All this must be taken into account by applying corrections to the predictions of the ideal equations we are about to derive. The corrections, however, are not the subject of this section.

We assume that our projectile is launched from the origin at time $t = 0$ into the first quadrant with an initial velocity $\mathbf{v}_0$ (Fig. 12.7). If α is the angle that $\mathbf{v}_0$ makes with the horizontal, then

$$\mathbf{v}_0 = \left(|\mathbf{v}_0| \cos \alpha\right) \mathbf{i} + \left(|\mathbf{v}_0| \sin \alpha\right) \mathbf{j}. \tag{1}$$

If we use the simpler notation v_0 for the initial speed $|\mathbf{v}_0|$, then

$$\mathbf{v}_0 = (v_0 \cos \alpha)\, \mathbf{i} + (v_0 \sin \alpha)\, \mathbf{j}. \tag{2}$$

The projectile's initial position is

$$\mathbf{r}_0 = 0\, \mathbf{i} + 0\, \mathbf{j} = \mathbf{0}. \tag{3}$$

If the only force acting on the projectile during its flight comes from a constant downward acceleration of gravity of magnitude g, then

$$\frac{d^2\mathbf{r}}{dt^2} = -g\, \mathbf{j}. \tag{4}$$

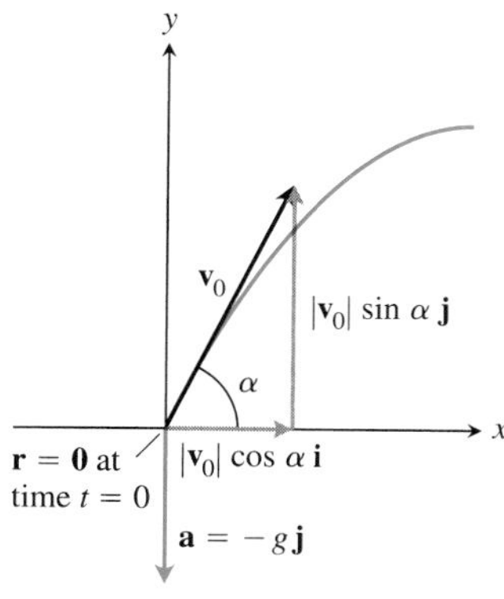

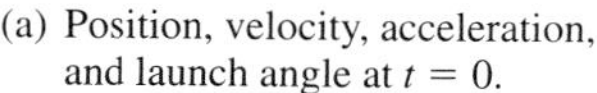

(a) Position, velocity, acceleration, and launch angle at $t = 0$.

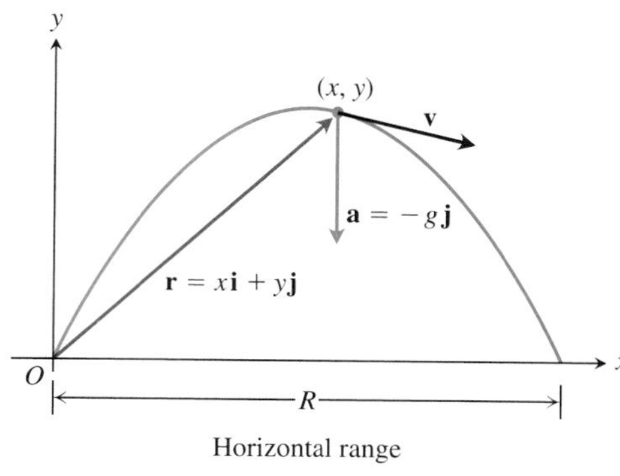

(b) Position, velocity, and acceleration at a later time t.

12.7 The flight of an ideal projectile.

We can find the projectile's position as a function of time t by solving the following initial value problem:

Differential equation: $\frac{d^2\mathbf{r}}{dt^2} = -g\,\mathbf{j}$

Initial conditions: $\mathbf{r} = \mathbf{0}$ and $\frac{d\mathbf{r}}{dt} = \mathbf{v}_0$ when $t = 0$.

The first integration of the differential equation gives

$$\frac{d\mathbf{r}}{dt} = -(gt)\,\mathbf{j} + \mathbf{v}_0. \tag{5}$$

A second integration gives

$$\mathbf{r} = -\frac{1}{2}gt^2\,\mathbf{j} + \mathbf{v}_0 t + \mathbf{r}_0. \tag{6}$$

Substituting the values of $\mathbf{v}_0$ and $\mathbf{r}_0$ from Eqs. (2) and (3) gives

$$\mathbf{r} = -\frac{1}{2}gt^2\,\mathbf{j} + \underbrace{(v_0\cos\alpha)t\,\mathbf{i} + (v_0\sin\alpha)t\,\mathbf{j}}_{\mathbf{v}_0 t} + \mathbf{0}$$

$$= (v_0\cos\alpha)t\,\mathbf{i} + \left[(v_0\sin\alpha)t - \frac{1}{2}gt^2\right]\mathbf{j}. \tag{7}$$

Equations for the Motion of an Ideal Projectile Fired from the Origin at $t = 0$

Vector form: $$\mathbf{r} = (v_0\cos\alpha)t\,\mathbf{i} + \left((v_0\sin\alpha)t - \frac{1}{2}gt^2\right)\mathbf{j} \tag{8}$$

Parametric form: $$x = (v_0\cos\alpha)t, \qquad y = (v_0\sin\alpha)t - \frac{1}{2}gt^2 \tag{9}$$

where α is the **firing angle (launch angle, angle of elevation)** and v_0 is the **initial speed.**

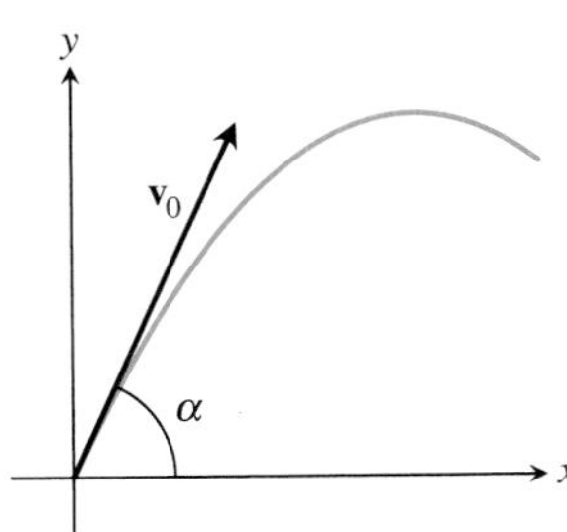

If we measure time in seconds and distance in meters, g is 9.8 m/sec^2 and Eqs. (9) give x and y in meters. If we measure time in seconds and distance in feet, then g is 32 ft/sec^2 and the equations in (9) give x and y in feet.

EXAMPLE 1 A projectile is fired from the origin over horizontal ground at an initial speed of 500 m/sec at an angle of elevation of 60°. Where will the projectile be 10 sec later?

Solution We use Eqs. (9) with $v_0 = 500$, $\alpha = 60°$, $g = 9.8$, and $t = 10$ to find the projectile's coordinates to the nearest meter 10 sec after firing:

$$x = (v_0 \cos \alpha)t = 500 \cdot \frac{1}{2} \cdot 10 = 2500 \text{ m}$$

$$\begin{aligned} y &= (v_0 \sin \alpha)t - \frac{1}{2}gt^2 \\ &= 500 \cdot \frac{\sqrt{3}}{2} \cdot 10 - \frac{1}{2} \cdot 9.8 \cdot (10)^2 \\ &= 2500\sqrt{3} - 490 \\ &\approx 3840 \text{ m.} \end{aligned}$$

Ten seconds after firing, the projectile is 3840 m in the air and 2500 m downrange.

Height, Flight Time, and Range

Equations (9) enable us to answer most questions about an ideal projectile fired from the origin.

The projectile reaches its highest point when its vertical velocity component is zero, that is, when

$$\frac{dy}{dt} = v_0 \sin \alpha - gt = 0, \qquad \text{or} \qquad t = \frac{v_0 \sin \alpha}{g}.$$

For this value of t, the value of y is

$$y_{\max} = (v_0 \sin \alpha)\left(\frac{v_0 \sin \alpha}{g}\right) - \frac{1}{2}g\left(\frac{v_0 \sin \alpha}{g}\right)^2 = \frac{(v_0 \sin \alpha)^2}{2g}. \tag{10}$$

To find when the projectile lands, if it is fired over horizontal ground, we set y equal to zero in Eqs. (9) and solve for t:

$$(v_0 \sin \alpha)t - \frac{1}{2}gt^2 = 0$$

$$t\left(v_0 \sin \alpha - \frac{1}{2}gt\right) = 0$$

$$t = 0, \quad t = \frac{2v_0 \sin \alpha}{g}. \tag{11}$$

Since 0 is the time the projectile is fired, $(2v_0 \sin \alpha)/g$ must be the time when the projectile strikes the ground.

To find the projectile's range R, the distance from the origin to the point of impact on horizontal ground, we find the value of x when $t = (2v_0 \sin \alpha)/g$:

$$x = (v_0 \cos \alpha)t$$

$$\begin{aligned} R &= (v_0 \cos \alpha)\left(\frac{2v_0 \sin \alpha}{g}\right) \\ &= \frac{v_0^2}{g}(2 \sin \alpha \cos \alpha) \\ &= \frac{v_0^2}{g} \sin 2\alpha. \end{aligned} \tag{12}$$

Notice that the range is largest when $\sin 2\alpha = 1$, or $\alpha = 45°$.

Height, Flight Time, and Range

For an ideal projectile fired from the origin over horizontal ground:

Maximum height: $$y_{max} = \frac{(v_0 \sin \alpha)^2}{2g} \tag{13}$$

Flight time (time to impact): $$t = \frac{2v_0 \sin \alpha}{g} \tag{14}$$

Range (distance to point of impact): $$R = \frac{{v_0}^2}{g} \sin 2\alpha \tag{15}$$

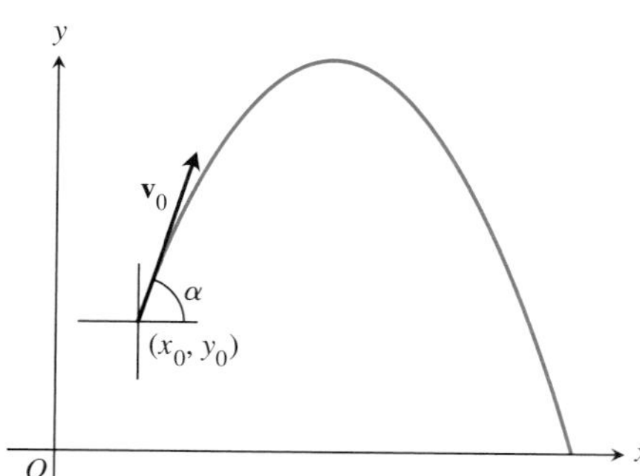

12.8 The path of a projectile fired from (x_0, y_0) with an initial velocity $\mathbf{v}_0$ at an angle of α degrees with the horizontal.

EXAMPLE 2 Find the maximum height, flight time, and range of a projectile fired from the origin over horizontal ground at an initial speed of 500 m/sec and a firing angle of 60° (same projectile as in Example 1).

Solution

Maximum height (Eq. 13): $$y_{max} = \frac{(v_0 \sin \alpha)^2}{2g} = \frac{(500 \sin 60°)^2}{2(9.8)}$$
$$\approx 9566 \text{ m}$$

Flight time (Eq. 14): $$t = \frac{2v_0 \sin \alpha}{g} = \frac{2(500) \sin 60°}{9.8}$$
$$\approx 88 \text{ sec}$$

Range (Eq. 15): $$R = \frac{{v_0}^2}{g} \sin 2\alpha = \frac{(500)^2 \sin 120°}{9.8}$$
$$\approx 22{,}092 \text{ m}$$

Firing from (x_0, y_0)

If we fire our ideal projectile from the point (x_0, y_0) instead of the origin (Fig. 12.8), the equations that replace Eqs. (9) are

$$x = x_0 + (v_0 \cos \alpha)t, \qquad y = y_0 + (v_0 \sin \alpha)t - \frac{1}{2}gt^2 \tag{16}$$

(Exercise 21).

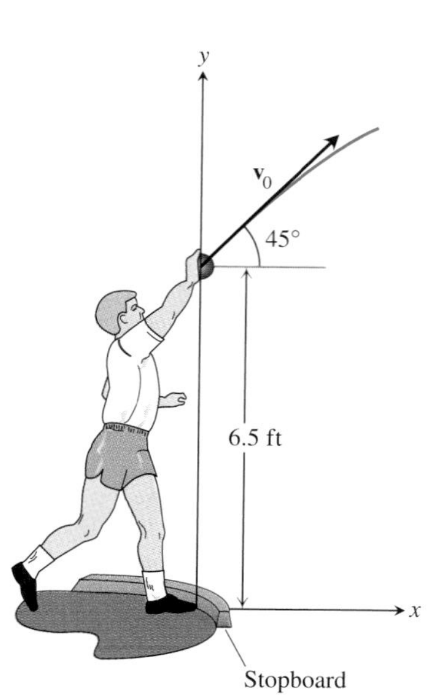

12.9 The shot put in Example 3. How far will the shot go?

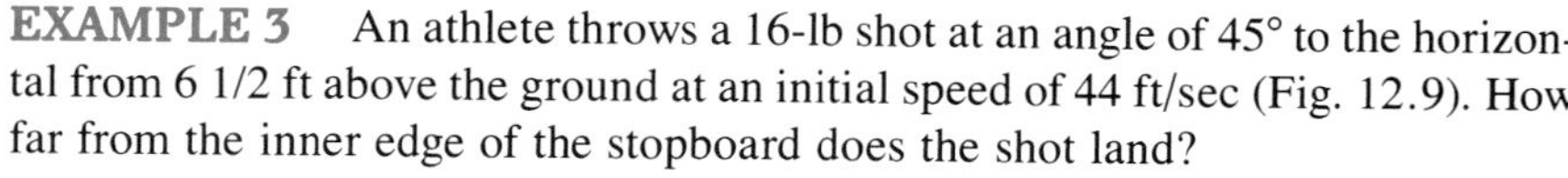
EXAMPLE 3 An athlete throws a 16-lb shot at an angle of 45° to the horizontal from 6 1/2 ft above the ground at an initial speed of 44 ft/sec (Fig. 12.9). How far from the inner edge of the stopboard does the shot land?

Solution We use a coordinate system in which the x-axis lies along the ground and the shot's coordinates at the time of launch ($t = 0$) are

$$x_0 = 0, \qquad y_0 = 6.5.$$

With these values for x_0 and y_0, and with $\alpha = 45°$, $v_0 = 44$ ft/sec, and $g = 32$ ft/sec^2, Eqs. (16) tell us that

$$x = 0 + (44 \cos 45°)t = 22\sqrt{2}t,$$
$$y = 6.5 + (44 \sin 45°)t - 16t^2 = 6.5 + 22\sqrt{2}t - 16t^2.$$

We find when the shot lands by setting y equal to zero and using the quadratic formula to solve for t, obtaining the positive solution

$$t = \frac{22\sqrt{2} + \sqrt{968 + 416}}{32} \approx 2.135 \text{ sec.}$$

We then find the value of x at this time from the equation $x = 22\sqrt{2}t$:

$$x = 22\sqrt{2}\,(2.135) \approx 66.43 \text{ ft.}$$

The shot lands about 66 ft. 5 in. from the stopboard. Air resistance, variations in gravity, and the rotation of the earth have little effect on a dense object, like a shot, that moves relatively slowly and for only a few seconds. In such cases, we expect good results from the ideal model.

EXAMPLE 4 Suppose that Antonio Rebollo (Fig. 12.6) wanted the flaming arrow to reach its maximum height exactly 4 ft above the center of the cauldron (Fig. 12.10).

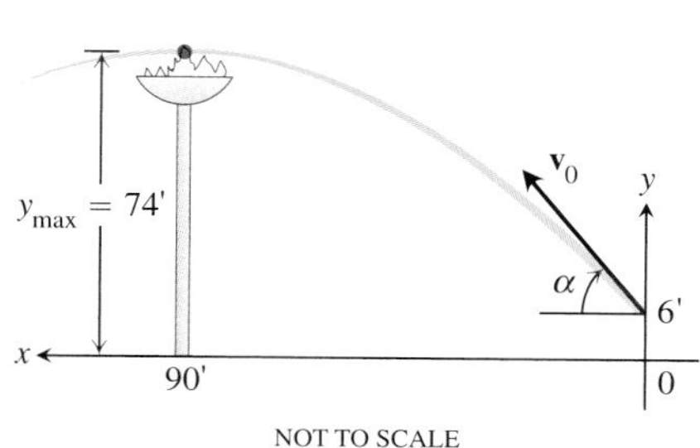

12.10 Path of the arrow that lit the Olympic torch.

a) If he shot the arrow at a height of 6 ft above ground level 30 yd from the 70-ft-high cauldron, express y_{max} in terms of the initial speed v_0 and firing angle α.

b) If $y_{max} = 74$ ft (Fig. 12.10), use the results of part (a) to find the value of $v_0 \sin \alpha$.

c) When the arrow reaches y_{max}, the horizontal distance traveled to the center of the cauldron is $x = 90$ ft. Use this fact to find the value of $v_0 \cos \alpha$.

d) Find the initial firing angle of the arrow.

Solution

a) We use a coordinate system in which the x-axis lies along the ground toward the left (to match the photograph in Fig. 12.6) and the coordinates of the flaming arrow at $t = 0$ are $x_0 = 0$ and $y_0 = 6$ (Fig. 12.10). We have

$$y = y_0 + (v_0 \sin \alpha)t - \frac{1}{2}gt^2 \qquad \text{Eqs. (16)}$$

$$= 6 + (v_0 \sin \alpha)\,t - \frac{1}{2}gt^2. \qquad y_0 = 6$$

We find when the arrow reaches its highest point by setting $dy/dt = 0$ and solving for t, obtaining

$$t = \frac{v_0 \sin \alpha}{g}.$$

For this value of t, the value of y is

$$y_{max} = 6 + (v_0 \sin \alpha)\left(\frac{v_0 \sin \alpha}{g}\right) - \frac{1}{2}g\left(\frac{v_0 \sin \alpha}{g}\right)^2 = 6 + \frac{(v_0 \sin \alpha)^2}{2g}.$$

b) Using $y_{max} = 74$ and $g = 32$, we see from part (a) that

$$74 = 6 + \frac{(v_0 \sin \alpha)^2}{(2)(32)}$$

or

$$v_0 \sin \alpha = \sqrt{(68)(64)} \approx 65.97 \text{ ft/sec.}$$

c) We substitute the time to reach y_{max} from part (a) and the horizontal distance $x = 90$ ft into Eqs. (16) to obtain

$$\begin{aligned} x &= x_0 + (v_0 \cos\alpha)t && \text{Eqs. (16)} \\ 90 &= 0 + (v_0 \cos\alpha)t && x = 90,\quad x_0 = 0 \\ &= (v_0 \cos\alpha)\left(\frac{v_0 \sin\alpha}{g}\right). && t = (v_0 \sin\alpha)/g \end{aligned}$$

Solving this equation for $v_0 \cos\alpha$ and using the result from part (b), we have

$$\begin{aligned} v_0 \cos\alpha &= \frac{90g}{v_0 \sin\alpha} \\ &= \frac{(90)(32)}{65.97} \approx 43.66 \text{ ft/sec.} && g = 32,\ v_0 \sin\alpha = 65.97 \end{aligned}$$

d) Parts (b) and (c) together tell us that

$$\tan\alpha = \frac{v_0 \sin\alpha}{v_0 \cos\alpha} = \frac{65.97}{43.66} \approx 1.51099$$

or

$$\alpha \approx \tan^{-1}(1.51099) \approx 57°.$$

This is Rebollo's firing angle.

Ideal Trajectories Are Parabolic

It is often claimed that water from a hose traces a parabola in the air, but anyone who looks closely enough will see this isn't so. The air slows the water down and its forward progress is too slow at the end to match the rate at which it falls.

What is really being claimed is that ideal projectiles move along parabolas, and this we can see from Eqs. (9). If we substitute $t = x/(v_0 \cos\alpha)$ from the first equation into the second, we obtain the Cartesian coordinate equation

$$y = -\left(\frac{g}{2{v_0}^2 \cos^2\alpha}\right)x^2 + (\tan\alpha)x. \tag{17}$$

This equation expresses y as a quadratic function of x, so its graph is a parabola.

Exercises 12.2

The projectiles in the following exercises are to be treated as ideal projectiles whose behavior is faithfully portrayed by the equations derived in the text. Most of the arithmetic, however, is realistic and is best done with a calculator. All launch angles are assumed to be measured from the horizontal. All projectiles are assumed to be fired from the origin over horizontal ground, unless stated otherwise.

1. A projectile is fired at a speed of 840 m/sec at an angle of 60°. How long will it take to get 21 km downrange?

2. Find the muzzle speed of a gun whose maximum range is 24.5 km.

3. A projectile is fired with an initial speed of 500 m/sec at an angle of elevation of 45°.
   a) When and how far away will the projectile strike?
   b) How high overhead will the projectile be when it is 5 km downrange?
   c) What is the highest the projectile will go?

4. A baseball is thrown from the stands 32 ft above the field at an angle of 30° up from horizontal. When and how far away will the ball strike the ground if its initial speed is 32 ft/sec?

5. Show that a projectile fired at an angle of α degrees, $0 < \alpha < 90$, has the same range as a projectile fired at the

same speed at an angle of $(90 - \alpha)$ degrees. (In models that take air resistance into account, this symmetry is lost.)

6. What two angles of elevation will enable a projectile to reach a target 16 km downrange on the same level as the gun if the projectile's initial speed is 400 m/sec?

7. A spring gun at ground level fires a golf ball at an angle of 45°. The ball lands 10 m away. What was the ball's initial speed? For the same initial speed, find the two firing angles that make the range 6 m.

8. An electron in a TV tube is beamed horizontally at a speed of 5×10^6 m/sec toward the face of the tube 40 cm away. About how far will the electron drop before it hits?

9. Laboratory tests designed to find how far golf balls of different hardness go when hit with a driver showed that a 100-compression ball hit with a club-head speed of 100 mph at a launch angle of 9° carried 248.8 yd. What was the launch speed of the ball? (It was more than 100 mph. At the same time the club head was moving forward, the compressed ball was kicking away from the club face, adding to the ball's forward speed.)

10. Show that doubling a projectile's initial speed at a given launch angle multiplies its range by 4. By about what percentage should you increase the initial speed to double the height and range?

11. Show that a projectile attains three-quarters of its maximum height in half the time it takes to reach the maximum height.

12. A human cannonball is to be fired with an initial speed of $v_0 = 80\sqrt{10/3}$ ft/sec. The circus performer (of the right caliber, naturally) hopes to land on a special cushion located 200 ft downrange. The circus is being held in a large room with a flat ceiling 75 ft high. Can the performer be fired to the cushion without striking the ceiling? If so, what should the cannon's angle of elevation be?

13. A golf ball leaves the ground at a 30° angle at a speed of 90 ft/sec. Will it clear the top of a 30-ft tree 135 ft away?

14. A golf ball is hit from the tee to an elevated green with an initial speed of 116 ft/sec at an angle of elevation of 45°, as shown in Fig. 12.11. Will the ball reach the pin?

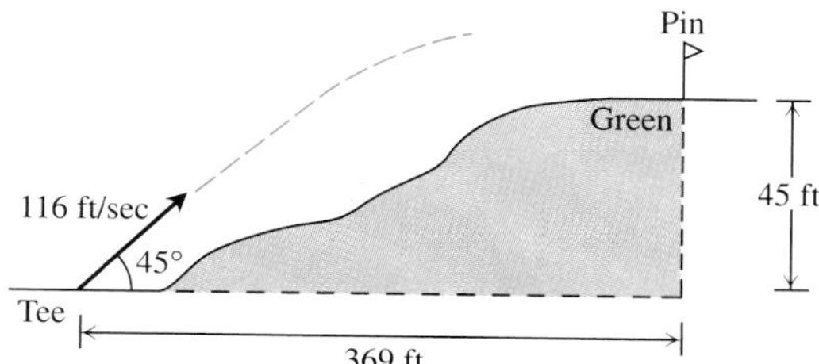

12.11 The tee and green in Exercise 14.

15. All other things being equal, the shot in Example 3 would have gone slightly farther if it had been launched at a 40° angle. How much farther? Answer in inches.

16. In Moscow in 1987, Natalya Lisouskaya set a women's world record by putting an 8-lb 13-oz shot 73 ft 10 in. Assuming that she launched the shot at a 40° angle to the horizontal 6.5 ft above the ground, what was the shot's initial speed?

17. A baseball hit by a Boston Red Sox player at a 20° angle from 3 ft above the ground just cleared the left end of the "Green Monster," the left-field wall in Fenway Park (Fig. 12.12). This wall is 37 ft high and 315 ft from home plate. About how fast was the ball going? How long did it take the ball to reach the wall?

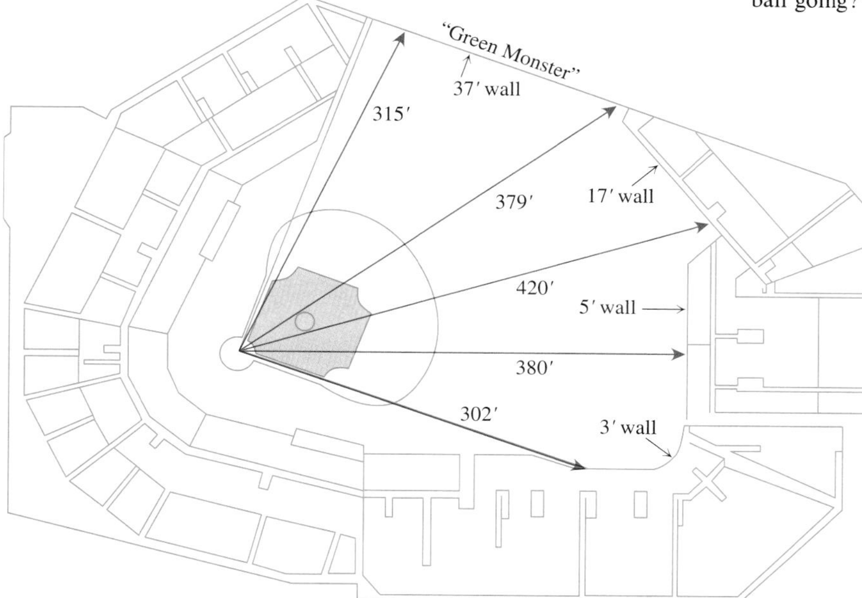

12.12 The "Green Monster," the left-field wall at Fenway Park in Boston (Exercise 17).

18. The multiflash photograph in Fig. 12.13 shows a model train engine moving at a constant speed on a straight track. As the engine moved along, a marble was fired into the air by a spring in the engine's smokestack. The marble, which continued to move with the same forward speed as the engine, rejoined the engine 1 sec after it was fired. Measure the angle the marble's path made with the horizontal and use the information to find how high the marble went and how fast the engine was moving.

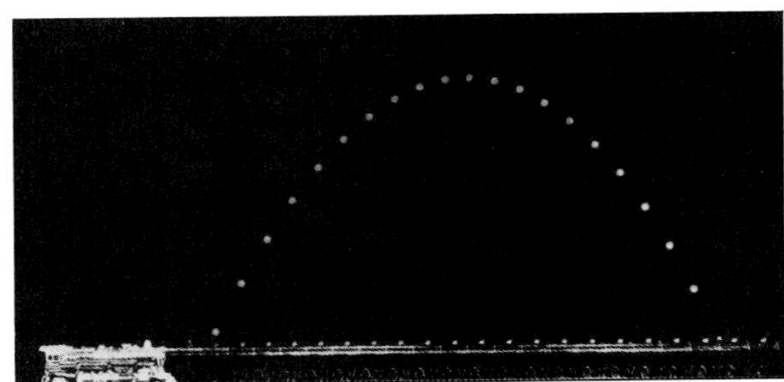

12.13 The train in Exercise 18.

19. Figure 12.14 shows an experiment with two marbles. Marble A was launched toward marble B with launch angle α and initial speed v_0. At the same instant, marble B was released to fall from rest $R \tan \alpha$ units directly above a spot R units downrange from A. The marbles were found to collide regardless of the value of v_0. Was this mere coincidence, or must this happen? Give reasons for your answer.

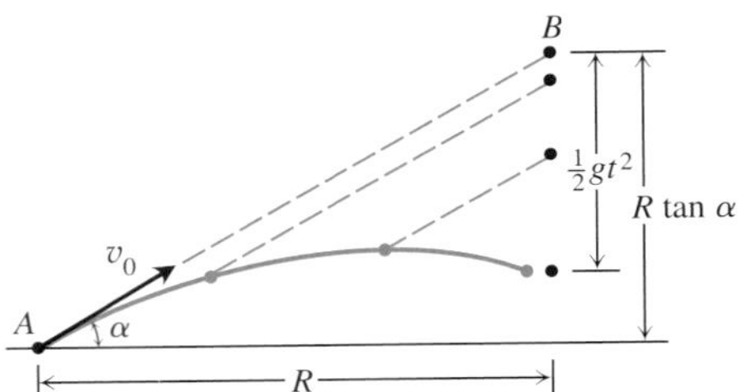

12.14 The marbles in Exercise 19.

20. An ideal projectile is launched straight down an inclined plane, as shown in profile in Fig. 12.15.

    a) Show that the greatest downhill range is achieved when the initial velocity vector bisects angle AOR.

    b) If the projectile were fired uphill instead of down, what launch angle would maximize its range? Give reasons for your answer.

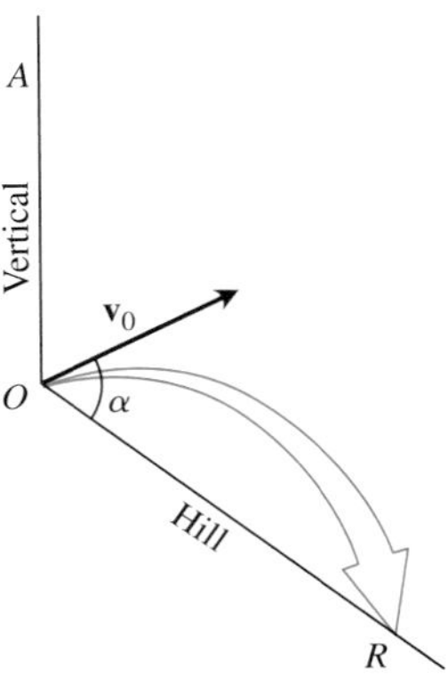

12.15 Maximum downhill range occurs when the velocity vector bisects angle AOR (Exercise 20).

21. Derive the equations

$$x = x_0 + (v_0 \cos \alpha)t$$

$$y = y_0 + (v_0 \sin \alpha)t - \frac{1}{2}gt^2$$

(Eqs. 16 in the text) by solving the following initial value problem for a vector $\mathbf{r}$ in the plane.

Differential equation: $\dfrac{d^2\mathbf{r}}{dt^2} = -g\,\mathbf{j}$

Initial conditions: $\mathbf{r} = x_0\,\mathbf{i} + y_0\,\mathbf{j}$

and

$$\frac{d\mathbf{r}}{dt} = (v_0 \cos \alpha)\,\mathbf{i} + (v_0 \sin \alpha)\,\mathbf{j}$$

when

$t = 0$

22. Using the firing angle $\alpha = 57°$ found in Example 4, find the speed with which the flaming arrow left Rebollo's bow. See Fig. 12.10.

23. The cauldron in Example 4 is 12 ft in diameter. Using Eqs. (16) and Example 4(c), find how long it takes the flaming arrow to cover the horizontal distance to the rim. How high is the arrow at that time? Does the arrow clear the edge of the cauldron? Give reasons for your answer.

24. If you have access to a parametric equation grapher and have not yet done Exercise 39 in Section 10.3, do it now. It is about ideal projectile motion.

Writing for Your Own Knowledge

Answer the following questions in writing. Some answers will take only a sentence or two; others may require several paragraphs. Some explanations may also call for graphs or sketches.

1. What are the equations for ideal projectile motion?
2. How do you find a projectile's maximum height, flight time, and range?

EXPLORER PROGRAM

Power Grapher	Traces the curves for $x = f(t)$, $y = g(t)$, and $\mathbf{r} = f(t)\,\mathbf{i} + g(t)\,\mathbf{j}$ in side-by-side displays as t increases through the parameter interval. Also graphs $\mathbf{r} = f(t)\,\mathbf{i} + g(t)\,\mathbf{j}$ in a separate display. Graphs different sets of parametric equations in a common display.

12.3 *Arc Length and the Unit Tangent Vector* $\boldsymbol{T}$

As you can imagine, differentiable curves, especially those with continuous first and second derivatives, have been subjects of intense study, for their mathematical interest as well as for their applications to motion in space. In this section and the next, we study some of the features that account for the importance of these curves.

Arc Length Along a Curve

One of the special features of smooth space curves is that they have a measurable length. This enables us to locate points along these curves by giving their directed distance s along the curve from some **base point,** the way we locate points on coordinate axes by giving their directed distance from the origin (Fig. 12.16). It might seem that time is the more natural parameter for describing the curve because differentiation with respect to time gives the velocity and acceleration of the particle as it moves along the curve. However, the geometric *shape* of the curve is quite independent of how fast the particle moves, and it turns out that s is the natural parameter for describing a curve's shape.

In the plane, we define the length of a parametrized curve $x = f(t)$, $y = g(t)$, $a \le t \le b$, by the formula

$$L = \int_a^b \sqrt{\left(\frac{dx}{dt}\right)^2 + \left(\frac{dy}{dt}\right)^2}\,dt. \tag{1}$$

In space, the analogous formula has an additional term for the third coordinate.

DEFINITION

The **length** of a smooth curve $\mathbf{r} = f(t)\,\mathbf{i} + g(t)\,\mathbf{j} + h(t)\,\mathbf{k}$, $a \le t \le b$, is

$$L = \int_a^b \sqrt{\left(\frac{dx}{dt}\right)^2 + \left(\frac{dy}{dt}\right)^2 + \left(\frac{dz}{dt}\right)^2}\,dt. \tag{2}$$

Just as for plane curves, we can calculate the length of a curve in space from any convenient parametrization as long as it is smooth. Again, we omit the proof.

Base point

12.16 Smooth curves can be scaled like coordinate axes or like tape measures that include negative numbers as well as positive numbers. The coordinate given to each point is its directed distance from the base point.

Notice that the square root in Eq. (2) is $|\mathbf{v}|$, the length of the velocity vector $d\mathbf{r}/dt$. This lets us write the equation a shorter way.

Length Formula (Short Form)

$$L = \int_a^b |\mathbf{v}|\, dt \tag{3}$$

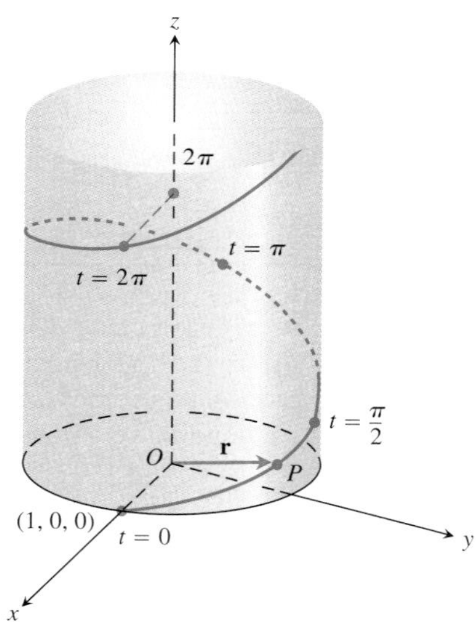

12.17 The helix $\mathbf{r} = (\cos t)\,\mathbf{i} + (\sin t)\,\mathbf{j} + t\,\mathbf{k}$ makes a complete turn in the interval from $t = 0$ to $t = 2\pi$. We calculate the distance traveled by P by integrating $|\mathbf{v}|$ from $t = 0$ to $t = 2\pi$ (Example 1).

EXAMPLE 1 Find the length of one turn of the helix

$$\mathbf{r} = (\cos t)\,\mathbf{i} + (\sin t)\,\mathbf{j} + t\,\mathbf{k}.$$

Solution Since the sine and cosine both have periods of 2π, the helix makes one full turn as t runs from 0 to 2π (Fig. 12.17). The length of this portion of the curve is

$$\begin{aligned} L &= \int_a^b |\mathbf{v}|\, dt \qquad \text{Eq. (3)} \\ &= \int_0^{2\pi} \sqrt{(-\sin t)^2 + (\cos t)^2 + (1)^2}\, dt \\ &= \int_0^{2\pi} \sqrt{2}\, dt = 2\pi\sqrt{2}. \end{aligned}$$

This is $\sqrt{2}$ times the length of the circle in the xy-plane over which the helix stands.

If we choose a base point $P(t_0)$ on a smooth curve $\mathbf{r} = f(t)\,\mathbf{i} + g(t)\,\mathbf{j} + h(t)\,\mathbf{k}$, we can define the associated **arc length function** $s(t)$ to be the integral of $|\mathbf{v}|$ from t_0 to t (Fig. 12.18). If $t > t_0$, the value of s is the distance from $P(t_0)$ to the point $P(t)$ along the curve. If $t < t_0$, $s(t)$ is the negative of the distance. We call s an **arc length parameter** for the curve. The parameter's value increases in the direction of increasing t.

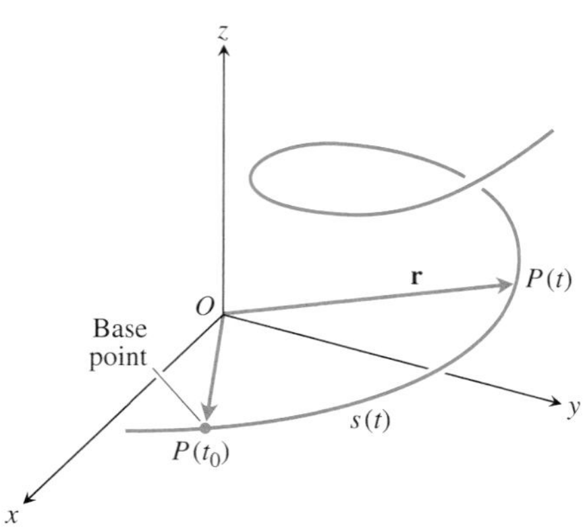

12.18 The arc length along the curve from $P(t_0)$ to any point $P(t)$ is

$$s(t) = \int_{t_0}^{t} |\mathbf{v}(\lambda)|\, d\lambda.$$

Arc Length Parameter along a Curve from t_0 to t

$$\begin{aligned} s(t) &= \int_{t_0}^{t} \sqrt{[x'(\lambda)]^2 + [y'(\lambda)]^2 + [z'(\lambda)]^2}\, d\lambda \\ &= \int_{t_0}^{t} |\mathbf{v}(\lambda)|\, d\lambda \end{aligned} \tag{4}$$

The letter λ ("lambda") is the Greek letter l ("ell").

EXAMPLE 2 If $t_0 = 0$, the arc length parameter along the helix

$$\mathbf{r} = (\cos t)\,\mathbf{i} + (\sin t)\,\mathbf{j} + t\,\mathbf{k}$$

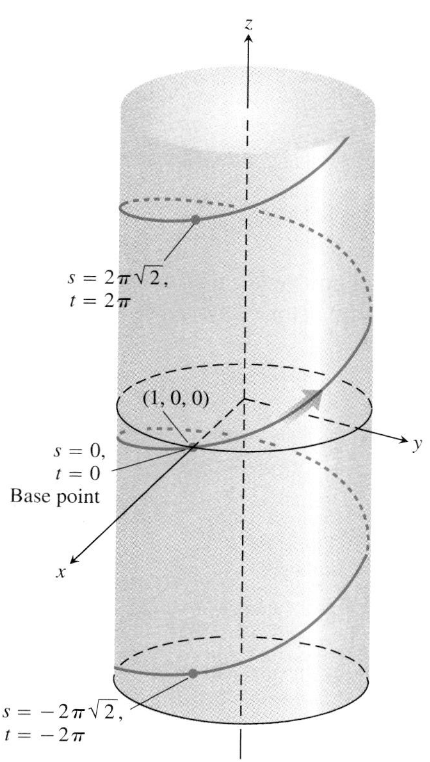

12.19 Arc length parameter values on the helix $\mathbf{r} = (\cos t)\,\mathbf{i} + (\sin t)\,\mathbf{j} + t\,\mathbf{k}$ (Example 2).

from t_0 to t is

$$\begin{aligned} s(t) &= \int_{t_0}^{t} |\mathbf{v}(\lambda)|\,d\lambda && \text{Eq. (4)} \\ &= \int_{0}^{t} \sqrt{2}\,d\lambda && \text{Value from Example 1} \\ &= \sqrt{2}t. \end{aligned}$$

Thus, $s(2\pi) = 2\pi\sqrt{2}$, $s(-2\pi) = -2\pi\sqrt{2}$, and so on (Fig. 12.19).

EXAMPLE 3 *Distance along a Line.* Show that if $\mathbf{u} = u_1\,\mathbf{i} + u_2\,\mathbf{j} + u_3\,\mathbf{k}$ is a unit vector, then the arc length parameter along the line

$$\mathbf{r} = (x_0 + tu_1)\,\mathbf{i} + (y_0 + tu_2)\,\mathbf{j} + (z_0 + tu_3)\,\mathbf{k}$$

from the point $P_0\,(x_0, y_0, z_0)$ where $t = 0$ is t itself.

Solution

$$\begin{aligned} \mathbf{v} &= \frac{d}{dt}(x_0 + tu_1)\,\mathbf{i} + \frac{d}{dt}(y_0 + tu_2)\,\mathbf{j} + \frac{d}{dt}(z_0 + tu_3)\,\mathbf{k} \\ &= u_1\,\mathbf{i} + u_2\,\mathbf{j} + u_3\,\mathbf{k} = \mathbf{u}, \end{aligned}$$

so

$$s(t) = \int_0^t |\mathbf{v}|\,d\lambda = \int_0^t |\mathbf{u}|\,d\lambda = \int_0^t 1\,d\lambda = t.$$

Since the derivatives beneath the radical in Eq. (4) are continuous, the Fundamental Theorem of Calculus, Part 1 (Section 5.4) tells us that s is a differentiable function of t, whose derivative is

$$\frac{ds}{dt} = |\mathbf{v}(t)|. \tag{5}$$

As we expect, the speed with which a particle moves along a path is the magnitude of $\mathbf{v}$.

Notice that while the base point $P(t_0)$ plays a role in defining the arc length parameter s in Eq. (4), it has no effect on Eq. (5). The speed ds/dt at which a moving particle traverses its path does not depend on the choice of the base point.

Notice also that ds/dt is always positive, since $|\mathbf{v}|$ is never zero for a smooth curve.

The Unit Tangent Vector T

Since ds/dt is positive for the smooth curves we are considering, s is one-to-one and has an inverse that gives t as a differentiable function of s (Section 6.2). The derivative of the inverse function is

$$\frac{dt}{ds} = \frac{1}{ds/dt} = \frac{1}{|\mathbf{v}|}. \tag{6}$$

This makes $\mathbf{r}$ a differentiable function of s whose derivative can be calculated

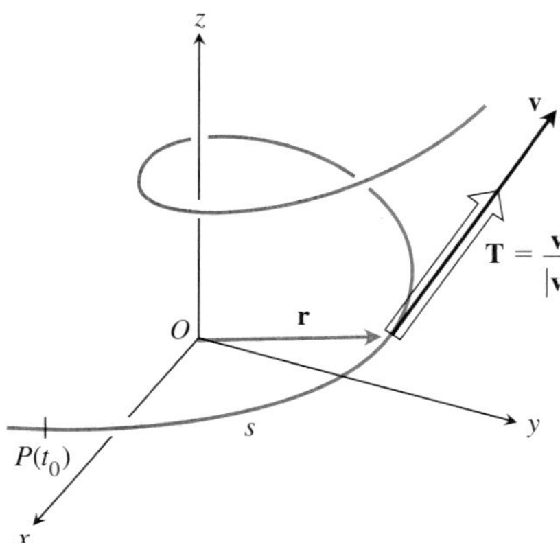

12.20 We find the unit tangent vector **T** by dividing **v** by $|\mathbf{v}|$.

with the Chain Rule for vector-valued functions as

$$\frac{d\mathbf{r}}{ds}=\frac{d\mathbf{r}}{dt}\frac{dt}{ds}=\mathbf{v}\left(\frac{1}{|\mathbf{v}|}\right)=\frac{\mathbf{v}}{|\mathbf{v}|}. \tag{7}$$

This tells us that $d\mathbf{r}/ds$ has the constant length

$$\left|\frac{d\mathbf{r}}{ds}\right|=\frac{1}{|\mathbf{v}|}|\mathbf{v}|=1. \tag{8}$$

Together, Eqs. (7) and (8) say that $d\mathbf{r}/ds$ is a unit vector that always points in the direction of **v**. We call $d\mathbf{r}/ds$ the unit tangent vector of the curve traced by **r** and denote it by **T** (Fig. 12.20).

DEFINITION

The **unit tangent vector** of a smooth curve $\mathbf{r}=f(t)\,\mathbf{i}+g(t)\,\mathbf{j}+h(t)\,\mathbf{k}$ is

$$\mathbf{T}=\frac{d\mathbf{r}}{ds}=\frac{d\mathbf{r}/dt}{ds/dt}=\frac{\mathbf{v}}{|\mathbf{v}|}. \tag{9}$$

The unit tangent vector **T** is a differentiable function of t whenever **v** is a differentiable function of t. As we will see in the next section, **T** is one of three unit vectors in a traveling reference frame that may be used to describe the motion of space vehicles and other bodies moving in three dimensions.

EXAMPLE 4 Find the unit tangent vector of the helix

$$\mathbf{r}=(\cos t)\,\mathbf{i}+(\sin t)\,\mathbf{j}+t\,\mathbf{k}$$

at any time t.

Solution

$$\mathbf{v}=(-\sin t)\,\mathbf{i}+(\cos t)\,\mathbf{j}+\mathbf{k}$$

$$|\mathbf{v}|=\sqrt{(-\sin t)^2+(\cos t)^2+(1)^2}=\sqrt{2}$$

$$\mathbf{T}=\frac{\mathbf{v}}{|\mathbf{v}|}=-\frac{\sin t}{\sqrt{2}}\,\mathbf{i}+\frac{\cos t}{\sqrt{2}}\,\mathbf{j}+\frac{1}{\sqrt{2}}\,\mathbf{k}.$$

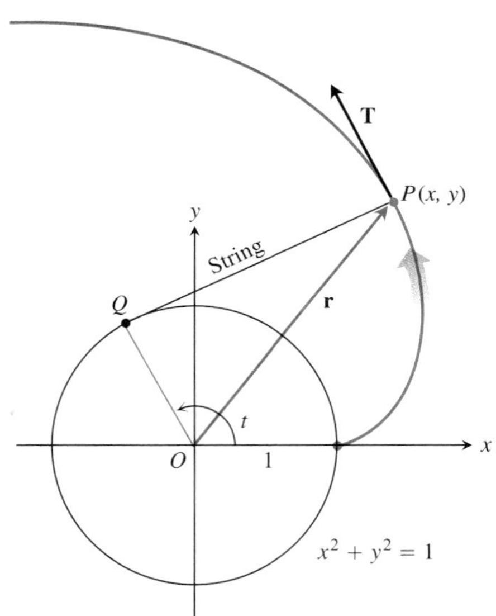

12.21 The *involute* of a circle is the path traced by the endpoint P of a string unwinding from a circle, here the unit circle in the xy-plane. The position vector of P can be shown to be

$$\mathbf{r}=(\cos t+t\sin t)\,\mathbf{i}+(\sin t-t\cos t)\,\mathbf{j},$$

where t is the angle from the positive x-axis to Q. Example 5 derives a formula for the curve's unit tangent vector **T** for $t>0$.

EXAMPLE 5 *The Involute of a Circle (Fig. 12.21).* Find the unit tangent vector of the curve

$$\mathbf{r}=(\cos t+t\sin t)\,\mathbf{i}+(\sin t-t\cos t)\,\mathbf{j},\qquad t>0.$$

Solution

$$\mathbf{v}=\frac{d\mathbf{r}}{dt}=(-\sin t+\sin t+t\cos t)\,\mathbf{i}+(\cos t-\cos t+t\sin t)\,\mathbf{j}$$

$$=(t\cos t)\,\mathbf{i}+(t\sin t)\,\mathbf{j}$$

$$|\mathbf{v}|=\sqrt{t^2\cos^2 t+t^2\sin^2 t}=\sqrt{t^2}=|t|=t \qquad |t|=t \text{ because } t>0$$

$$\mathbf{T}=\frac{\mathbf{v}}{|\mathbf{v}|}=\frac{\mathbf{v}}{t}=(\cos t)\,\mathbf{i}+(\sin t)\,\mathbf{j}$$

EXAMPLE 6 For the counterclockwise motion

$$\mathbf{r} = (\cos t)\,\mathbf{i} + (\sin t)\,\mathbf{j}$$

around the unit circle,

$$\mathbf{v} = (-\sin t)\,\mathbf{i} + (\cos t)\,\mathbf{j}$$

is already a unit vector, so $\mathbf{T} = \mathbf{v}$ (Fig. 12.22).

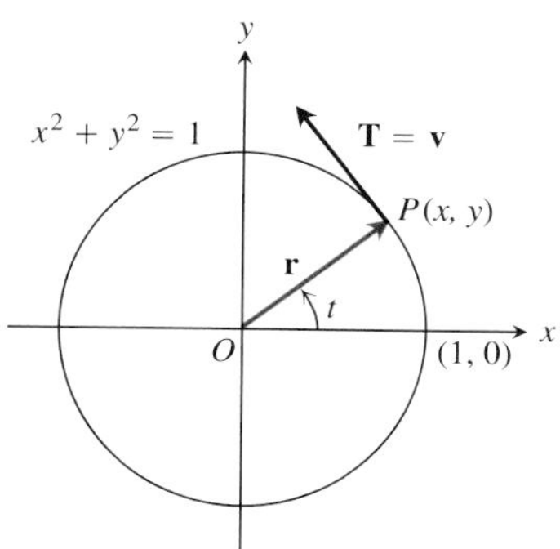

12.22 For the counterclockwise motion $\mathbf{r} = (\cos t)\,\mathbf{i} + (\sin t)\,\mathbf{j}$ about the unit circle, the unit tangent vector is $\mathbf{v}$ itself (Example 6).

Exercises 12.3

In Exercises 1–8, find the curve's unit tangent vector. Also, find the length of the indicated portion of the curve.

1. $\mathbf{r} = (2\cos t)\,\mathbf{i} + (2\sin t)\,\mathbf{j} + \sqrt{5}t\,\mathbf{k}, \quad 0 \le t \le \pi$

2. $\mathbf{r} = (6\sin 2t)\,\mathbf{i} + (6\cos 2t)\,\mathbf{j} + 5t\,\mathbf{k}, \quad 0 \le t \le \pi$

3. $\mathbf{r} = t\,\mathbf{i} + (2/3)t^{3/2}\,\mathbf{k}, \quad 0 \le t \le 8$

4. $\mathbf{r} = (\cos^3 t)\,\mathbf{j} + (\sin^3 t)\,\mathbf{k}, \quad 0 \le t \le \pi/2$

5. $\mathbf{r} = (2 + t)\,\mathbf{i} - (t + 1)\,\mathbf{j} + t\,\mathbf{k}, \quad 0 \le t \le 3$

6. $\mathbf{r} = 6t^3\,\mathbf{i} - 2t^3\,\mathbf{j} - 3t^3\,\mathbf{k}, \quad 1 \le t \le 2$

7. $\mathbf{r} = \left(t\cos t\right)\mathbf{i} + \left(t\sin t\right)\mathbf{j} + \left(2\sqrt{2}/3\right)t^{3/2}\,\mathbf{k}, \quad 0 \le t \le \pi$

8. $\mathbf{r} = (t\sin t + \cos t)\,\mathbf{i} + (t\cos t - \sin t)\,\mathbf{j}, \quad \sqrt{2} \le t \le 2$

In Exercises 9–12, find the arc length parameter along the curve from the point where $t = 0$ by evaluating the integral

$$s = \int_0^t |\mathbf{v}(\lambda)|\, d\lambda$$

from Eq. (3). Then find the length of the indicated portion of the curve.

9. $\mathbf{r} = (4\cos t)\,\mathbf{i} + (4\sin t)\,\mathbf{j} + 3t\,\mathbf{k}, \quad 0 \le t \le \pi/2$

10. $\mathbf{r} = (\cos t + t\sin t)\,\mathbf{i} + (\sin t - t\cos t)\,\mathbf{j}, \quad \pi/2 \le t \le \pi$

11. $\mathbf{r} = (e^t\cos t)\,\mathbf{i} + (e^t\sin t)\,\mathbf{j} + e^t\,\mathbf{k}, \quad -\ln 4 \le t \le 0$

12. $\mathbf{r} = (1 + 2t)\,\mathbf{i} + (1 + 3t)\,\mathbf{j} + (6 - 6t)\,\mathbf{k}, \quad -1 \le t \le 0$

13. Find the length of the curve

$$\mathbf{r} = \left(\sqrt{2}t\right)\mathbf{i} + \left(\sqrt{2}t\right)\mathbf{j} + \left(1 - t^2\right)\mathbf{k}$$

from $(0, 0, 1)$ to $(\sqrt{2}, \sqrt{2}, 0)$.

14. The length $2\pi\sqrt{2}$ of the turn of the helix in Example 1 is also the length of the diagonal of a square 2π units on a side. Show how to obtain this square by cutting away and flattening a portion of the cylinder around which the helix winds.

15. a) Show that the curve $\mathbf{r} = (\cos t)\,\mathbf{i} + (\sin t)\,\mathbf{j} + (1 - \cos t)\,\mathbf{k}$, $0 \le t \le 2\pi$ is an ellipse by showing that it is the intersection of a right circular cylinder and a plane. Find equations for the cylinder and plane.

b) Sketch the ellipse on the cylinder. Add to your sketch the unit tangent vectors at $t = 0$, $\pi/2$, π, and $3\pi/2$.

c) Show that the acceleration vector always lies parallel to the plane (orthogonal to a vector normal to the plane). Thus, if you draw the acceleration as a vector attached to the ellipse, it will lie in the plane of the ellipse. Add the acceleration vectors for $t = 0$, $\pi/2$, π, and $3\pi/2$ to your sketch.

d) Write an integral for the length of the ellipse. Do not try to evaluate the integral—it is nonelementary.

e) NUMERICAL INTEGRATOR Estimate the length of the ellipse to two decimal places.

16. *Length Is Independent of Parametrization.* To illustrate the fact that the length of a smooth space curve does not depend on the parametrization you use to compute it, calculate the length of one turn of the helix in Example 1 with the following parametrizations.

a) $\mathbf{r} = (\cos 4t)\,\mathbf{i} + (\sin 4t)\,\mathbf{j} + 4t\,\mathbf{k}, \quad 0 \le t \le \pi/2$

b) $\mathbf{r} = [\cos(t/2)]\,\mathbf{i} + [\sin(t/2)]\,\mathbf{j} + (t/2)\,\mathbf{k}, \quad 0 \le t \le 4\pi$

c) $\mathbf{r} = (\cos t)\,\mathbf{i} - (\sin t)\,\mathbf{j} - t\,\mathbf{k}, \quad -2\pi \le t \le 0$

Writing for Your Own Knowledge

Answer the following questions in writing. Some answers will take only a sentence or two; others may require several paragraphs. Some explanations may also call for graphs or sketches.

1. How do you find the length of a space curve?
2. What is a curve's unit tangent vector?

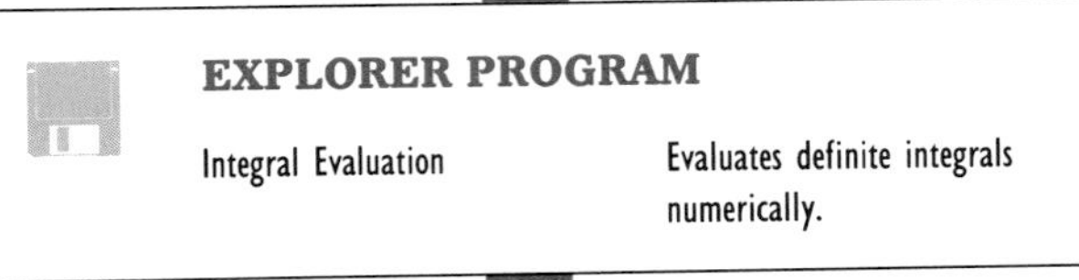

EXPLORER PROGRAM
Integral Evaluation
Evaluates definite integrals numerically.

12.4 Curvature, Torsion, and the TNB Frame

In this section we define a frame of mutually orthogonal unit vectors that always travels with a body moving along a curve in space (Fig. 12.23). The frame has three vectors. The first is $\mathbf{T}$, the unit tangent vector. The second is $\mathbf{N}$, the unit vector that gives the direction of $d\mathbf{T}/ds$. The third is $\mathbf{B} = \mathbf{T} \times \mathbf{N}$. These vectors and their derivatives, when available, give useful information about a vehicle's orientation in space and about how the vehicle's path turns and twists.

For example, the magnitude of the derivative $d\mathbf{T}/ds$ tells how much a vehicle's path turns to the left or right as it moves along; it is called the *curvature* of the vehicle's path. The number $-(d\mathbf{B}/ds) \cdot \mathbf{N}$ tells how much a vehicle's path rotates or twists as the vehicle moves along; it is called the *torsion* of the vehicle's path. Look at Fig. 12.23 again. If P is a train climbing up a curved track, the rate at which the headlight turns from side to side per unit distance is the curvature of the track. The rate at which the engine tends to twist out of the plane formed by $\mathbf{T}$ and $\mathbf{N}$ is the torsion.

The Curvature of a Plane Curve

As a particle moves along a smooth curve in the plane, the unit tangent vector $\mathbf{T}$ turns as the curve bends. Recall that $\mathbf{T} = d\mathbf{r}/ds$ is the derivative of the position vector $\mathbf{r}$ with respect to the arc length parameter. Since $\mathbf{T}$ is a unit vector, its length remains constant and only its direction changes as the particle moves along the curve. The rate at which the tangent vector turns per unit of length

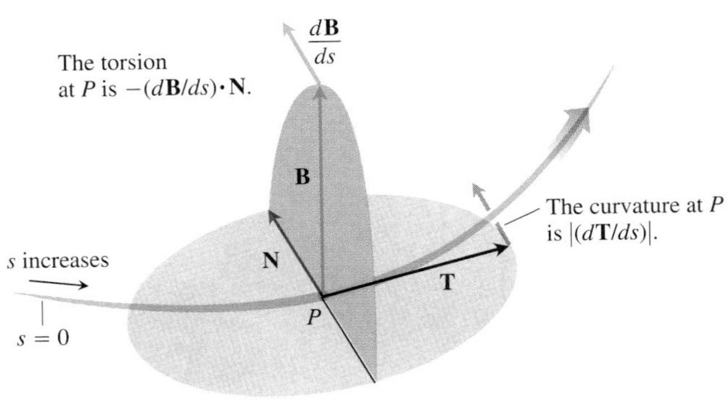

12.23 Every moving body travels with a **TNB** frame that completely characterizes the geometry of the path of motion.

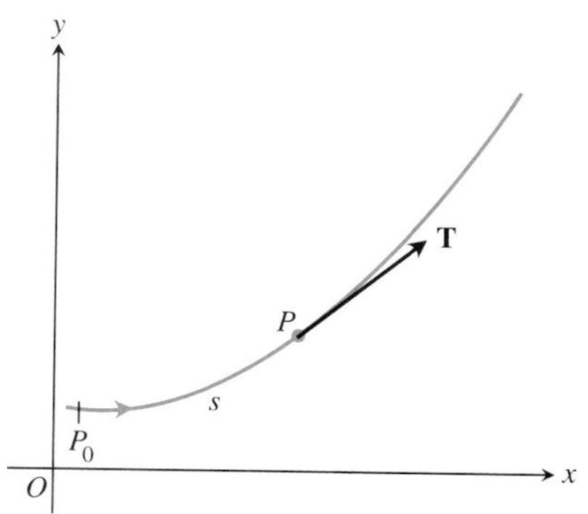

12.24 As P moves along the curve in the direction of increasing arc length, the unit tangent vector turns. The value of $|d\mathbf{T}/ds|$ at P is called the *curvature* of the curve at P.

along the curve is defined to be the **curvature** at the point P (Fig. 12.24). The traditional symbol for the curvature function is the Greek letter κ (kappa).

DEFINITION

If **T** is the unit tangent vector of a smooth curve, the **curvature** function of the curve is

$$\kappa = \left|\frac{d\mathbf{T}}{ds}\right|. \tag{1}$$

If $|d\mathbf{T}/ds|$ is large, **T** turns sharply as the particle passes through P, and the curvature at P is large. If $|d\mathbf{T}/ds|$ is close to zero, **T** turns more slowly and the curvature at P is smaller. On circles and lines, the curvature is constant, as we will see in Examples 1 and 2. On other curves, the curvature can change from place to place.

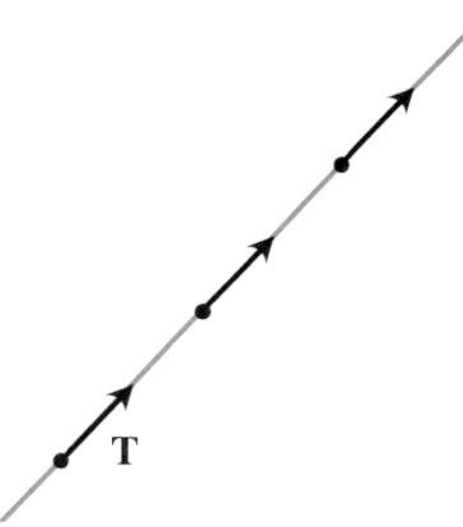

12.25 Along a straight line, the tangent vector **T** always points in the same direction from point to point and the curvature, $|d\mathbf{T}/ds|$, is zero (Example 1).

EXAMPLE 1 *The Curvature of a Straight Line Is Zero.* On a straight line, the unit tangent vector **T** always points in the same direction, so its components are constants. Therefore $|d\mathbf{T}/ds| = |\mathbf{0}| = 0$ (Fig. 12.25).

EXAMPLE 2 *The Curvature of a Circle of Radius a Is 1/a.* To see why (Fig. 12.26), start with the parametrization

$$\mathbf{r} = (a\cos\theta)\,\mathbf{i} + (a\sin\theta)\,\mathbf{j}$$

and substitute $\theta = s/a$ to obtain the arc length parametrization

$$\mathbf{r} = \left(a\cos\frac{s}{a}\right)\mathbf{i} + \left(a\sin\frac{s}{a}\right)\mathbf{j}.$$

Then

$$\mathbf{T} = \frac{d\mathbf{r}}{ds} = \left(-\sin\frac{s}{a}\right)\mathbf{i} + \left(\cos\frac{s}{a}\right)\mathbf{j}$$

and

$$\frac{d\mathbf{T}}{ds} = \left(-\frac{1}{a}\cos\frac{s}{a}\right)\mathbf{i} - \left(\frac{1}{a}\sin\frac{s}{a}\right)\mathbf{j}.$$

Hence,

$$\begin{aligned}\kappa &= \left|\frac{d\mathbf{T}}{ds}\right| \\ &= \sqrt{\frac{1}{a^2}\cos^2\left(\frac{s}{a}\right) + \frac{1}{a^2}\sin^2\left(\frac{s}{a}\right)} \\ &= \frac{1}{\sqrt{a^2}} = \frac{1}{|a|} = \frac{1}{a}. \qquad \text{Since } a > 0,\ |a| = a.\end{aligned}$$

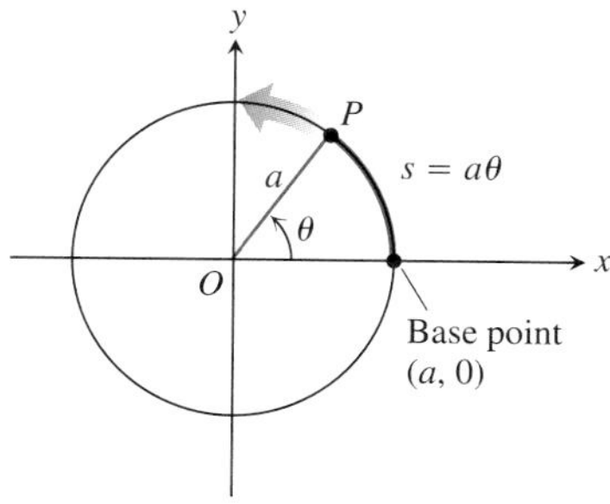

12.26 The point P has coordinates $(\cos\theta, \sin\theta)$ where $s = a\theta$ is the arc length measured counterclockwise from $(a, 0)$ to P (Example 2).

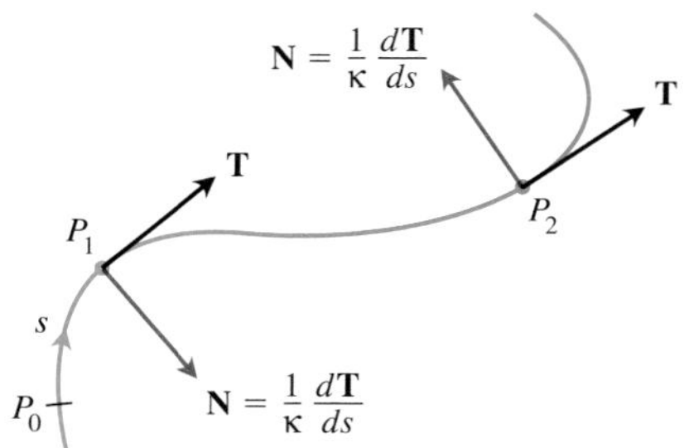

12.27 The vector $d\mathbf{T}/ds$, normal to the curve, always points inward toward the direction in which **T** is turning. The principal unit normal vector **N** is the direction of $d\mathbf{T}/ds$.

The Principal Unit Normal Vector for Curves in the Plane

The unit tangent vector $\mathbf{T} = d\mathbf{r}/ds$ is a unit vector that always points in the direction of the velocity vector **v**. Since

$$\mathbf{T} \cdot \mathbf{T} = 1, \tag{2}$$

we see that

$$\frac{d\mathbf{T}}{ds} \cdot \mathbf{T} + \mathbf{T} \cdot \frac{d\mathbf{T}}{ds} = 0 \qquad \text{Dot Product Derivative Rule}$$

or

$$2\,\mathbf{T} \cdot \frac{d\mathbf{T}}{ds} = 0. \tag{3}$$

Therefore, the vector $d\mathbf{T}/ds$ is always orthogonal to **T**. If we divide $d\mathbf{T}/ds$ by its length κ, we get a *unit* vector orthogonal to **T** (Fig. 12.27).

DEFINITION

The **principal unit normal** vector for a curve in the plane is

$$\mathbf{N} = \frac{1}{\kappa}\frac{d\mathbf{T}}{ds}. \tag{4}$$

The vector $d\mathbf{T}/ds$ points in the direction in which **T** turns as the curve bends. Therefore, if we face in the direction of increasing arc length, the vector $d\mathbf{T}/ds$ points toward the right if **T** turns clockwise and toward the left if **T** turns counterclockwise. In other words, the principal normal vector **N** will point toward the concave side of the curve (Fig. 12.27).

Because the arc length parameter for a smooth curve $\mathbf{r} = f(t)\,\mathbf{i} + g(t)\,\mathbf{j}$ is defined with ds/dt positive, $ds/dt = |ds/dt|$ and the Chain Rule gives

$$\begin{aligned}\mathbf{N} &= \frac{d\mathbf{T}/ds}{|d\mathbf{T}/ds|} = \frac{(d\mathbf{T}/dt)(dt/ds)}{|d\mathbf{T}/dt|\,|dt/ds|} \\ &= \frac{d\mathbf{T}/dt}{|d\mathbf{T}/dt|}.\end{aligned} \tag{5}$$

This formula enables us to find **N** without having to find κ and s first.

EXAMPLE 3 Find **T** and **N** for the circular motion

$$\mathbf{r} = (\cos 2t)\,\mathbf{i} + (\sin 2t)\,\mathbf{j}.$$

Solution We first find **T**:

$$\begin{aligned}\mathbf{v} &= -(2\sin 2t)\,\mathbf{i} + (2\cos 2t)\,\mathbf{j}, \\ |\mathbf{v}| &= \sqrt{4\sin^2 2t + 4\cos^2 2t} = 2, \\ \mathbf{T} &= \frac{\mathbf{v}}{|\mathbf{v}|} = -(\sin 2t)\,\mathbf{i} + (\cos 2t)\,\mathbf{j}.\end{aligned}$$

From this we find

$$\frac{d\mathbf{T}}{dt} = -(2\cos 2t)\,\mathbf{i} - (2\sin 2t)\,\mathbf{j},$$

$$\left|\frac{d\mathbf{T}}{dt}\right| = \sqrt{4\cos^2 2t + 4\sin^2 2t} = 2,$$

and

$$\mathbf{N} = \frac{d\mathbf{T}/dt}{|d\mathbf{T}/dt|}$$

$$= -(\cos 2t)\,\mathbf{i} - (\sin 2t)\,\mathbf{j}. \qquad \text{Eq. (5)}$$

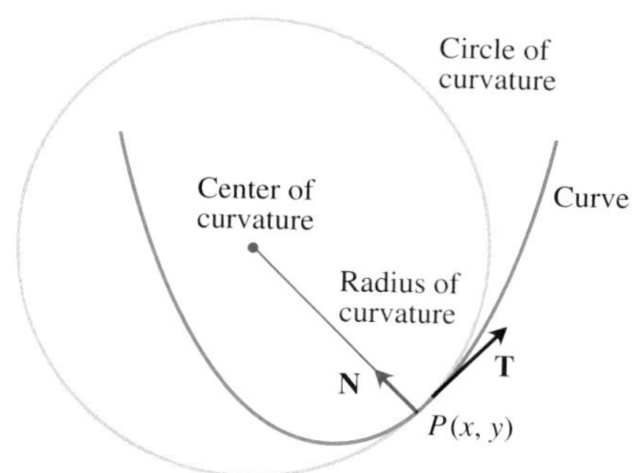

12.28 The osculating circle or circle of curvature at $P(x, y)$ lies toward the inner side of the curve.

Circle of Curvature and Radius of Curvature

The **circle of curvature** or **osculating circle** at a point P on a plane curve where $\kappa \neq 0$ is the circle in the plane of the curve that

1. is tangent to the curve at P (has the same tangent line the curve has);
2. has the same curvature the curve has at P; and
3. lies toward the concave or inner side of the curve (as in Fig. 12.28).

The **radius of curvature** of the curve at P is the radius of the circle of curvature, which, according to Example 2, is

$$\text{Radius of curvature} = \rho = \frac{1}{\kappa}. \tag{6}$$

To find ρ, we find κ and take the reciprocal. The **center of curvature** of the curve at P is the center of the circle of curvature.

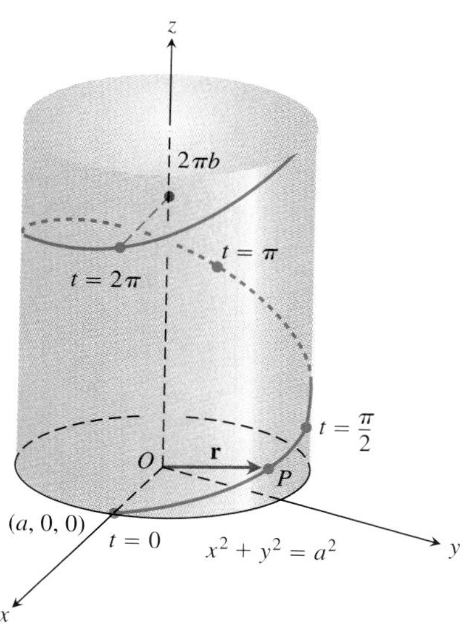

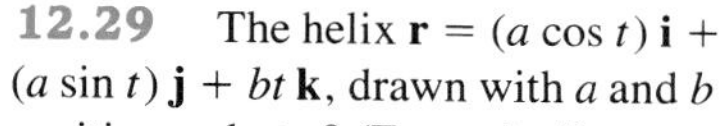

12.29 The helix $\mathbf{r} = (a\cos t)\,\mathbf{i} + (a\sin t)\,\mathbf{j} + bt\,\mathbf{k}$, drawn with a and b positive and $t \geq 0$ (Example 4).

Curvature and N for Curves in Space

Just as it does for a curve in the plane, the arc length parameter s gives the unit tangent vector $\mathbf{T} = d\mathbf{r}/ds$ for a smooth curve in space. We again define the curvature to be

$$\kappa = \left|\frac{d\mathbf{T}}{ds}\right|. \tag{7}$$

Since $\mathbf{T}$ is a unit vector, Eqs. (2) and (3) hold, as for plane curves. Thus $d\mathbf{T}/ds$ is orthogonal to $\mathbf{T}$ and we define the principal unit normal of a smooth curve in space in the same way:

$$\mathbf{N} = \frac{1}{\kappa}\frac{d\mathbf{T}}{ds} = \frac{d\mathbf{T}/dt}{|d\mathbf{T}/dt|}. \tag{8}$$

EXAMPLE 4 Find the curvature for the helix

$$\mathbf{r} = (a\cos t)\,\mathbf{i} + (a\sin t)\,\mathbf{j} + bt\,\mathbf{k} \qquad a, b \geq 0 \qquad \text{Fig. 12.29.}$$

Solution We calculate $\mathbf{T}$ from the velocity vector $\mathbf{v}$:

$$\mathbf{v} = -(a \sin t)\,\mathbf{i} + (a \cos t)\,\mathbf{j} + b\,\mathbf{k}$$

$$|\mathbf{v}| = \sqrt{a^2 \sin^2 t + a^2 \cos^2 t + b^2} = \sqrt{a^2 + b^2}$$

$$\mathbf{T} = \frac{\mathbf{v}}{|\mathbf{v}|} = \frac{1}{\sqrt{a^2 + b^2}}[-(a \sin t)\,\mathbf{i} + (a \cos t)\,\mathbf{j} + b\,\mathbf{k}].$$

Then, using the Chain Rule, we find $d\mathbf{T}/ds$ as

$$\begin{aligned}
\frac{d\mathbf{T}}{ds} &= \frac{d\mathbf{T}}{dt}\frac{dt}{ds} && \text{Chain Rule} \\
&= \frac{d\mathbf{T}}{dt} \cdot \frac{1}{|\mathbf{v}|} && \frac{ds}{dt} = |\mathbf{v}|, \text{ so } \frac{dt}{ds} = \frac{1}{|\mathbf{v}|} \\
&= \frac{1}{\sqrt{a^2 + b^2}}[-(a \cos t)\,\mathbf{i} - (a \sin t)\,\mathbf{j}] \cdot \left(\frac{1}{\sqrt{a^2 + b^2}}\right) \\
&= \frac{a}{a^2 + b^2}[-(\cos t)\,\mathbf{i} - (\sin t)\,\mathbf{j}].
\end{aligned}$$

Therefore,

$$\begin{aligned}
\kappa &= \left|\frac{d\mathbf{T}}{ds}\right| && \text{Eq. (7)} \\
&= \frac{a}{a^2 + b^2}\left|-(\cos t)\,\mathbf{i} - (\sin t)\,\mathbf{j}\right| \\
&= \frac{a}{a^2 + b^2}\sqrt{(\cos t)^2 + (\sin t)^2} = \frac{a}{a^2 + b^2}. && (9)
\end{aligned}$$

From Eq. (9) we see that increasing b for a fixed a decreases the curvature. Decreasing a for a fixed b eventually decreases the curvature as well. In other words, stretching a spring tends to straighten it.

If $b = 0$, the helix reduces to a circle of radius a and its curvature reduces to $1/a$, as it should. If $a = 0$, the helix becomes the z-axis, and its curvature reduces to 0, again as it should.

EXAMPLE 5 Find $\mathbf{N}$ for the helix in Example 4.

Solution We have

$$\begin{aligned}
\frac{d\mathbf{T}}{dt} &= -\frac{1}{\sqrt{a^2 + b^2}}[(a \cos t)\,\mathbf{i} + (a \sin t)\,\mathbf{j}] && \text{Example 4} \\
\left|\frac{d\mathbf{T}}{dt}\right| &= \frac{1}{\sqrt{a^2 + b^2}}\sqrt{a^2 \cos^2 t + a^2 \sin^2 t} = \frac{a}{\sqrt{a^2 + b^2}} \\
\mathbf{N} &= \frac{d\mathbf{T}/dt}{|d\mathbf{T}/dt|} && \text{Eq. (8)} \\
&= -\frac{\sqrt{a^2 + b^2}}{a} \cdot \frac{1}{\sqrt{a^2 + b^2}}[(a \cos t)\,\mathbf{i} + (a \sin t)\,\mathbf{j}] \\
&= -(\cos t)\,\mathbf{i} - (\sin t)\,\mathbf{j}.
\end{aligned}$$

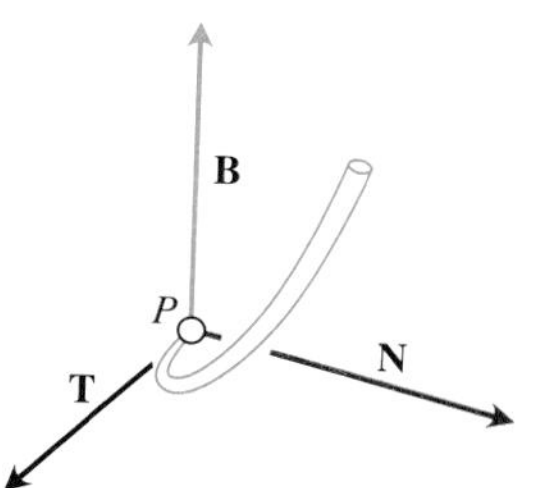

12.30 The vectors **T**, **N**, and **B** (in that order) make a right-handed frame of mutually orthogonal unit vectors in space. You can call it the **Frenet** (fre-*nay*) **frame** (after Jean-Frédéric Frenet, 1816–1900), or you can call it the **TNB frame.**

Torsion and the Binormal Vector

The **binormal vector** of a curve in space is the vector $\mathbf{B} = \mathbf{T} \times \mathbf{N}$, a unit vector orthogonal to both **T** and **N** (Fig. 12.30). Together **T**, **N**, and **B** define a moving right-handed vector frame that plays a significant role in calculating the flight paths of space vehicles.

From the rule for differentiating a cross product, we have

$$\frac{d\mathbf{B}}{ds} = \frac{d\mathbf{T}}{ds} \times \mathbf{N} + \mathbf{T} \times \frac{d\mathbf{N}}{ds}.$$

Since **N** is the direction of $d\mathbf{T}/ds$, $(d\mathbf{T}/ds) \times \mathbf{N} = \mathbf{0}$ and

$$\frac{d\mathbf{B}}{ds} = \mathbf{0} + \mathbf{T} \times \frac{d\mathbf{N}}{ds} = \mathbf{T} \times \frac{d\mathbf{N}}{ds}. \tag{10}$$

How does $d\mathbf{B}/ds$ behave in relation to **T**, **N**, and **B**? First observe that $d\mathbf{B}/ds$ is orthogonal to **T** since a cross product is orthogonal to its factors.

Because **N** is a unit vector, differentiation of $\mathbf{N} \cdot \mathbf{N} = 1$ gives

$$2\,\mathbf{N} \cdot \frac{d\mathbf{N}}{ds} = 0. \tag{11}$$

If we now dot the vector **B** with $d\mathbf{B}/ds$ from Eq. (10), we obtain

$$\begin{aligned}
\mathbf{B} \cdot \frac{d\mathbf{B}}{ds} &= \mathbf{B} \cdot \left(\mathbf{T} \times \frac{d\mathbf{N}}{ds}\right) \\
&= (\mathbf{B} \times \mathbf{T}) \cdot \frac{d\mathbf{N}}{ds} && \text{Triple scalar product} \\
&= \mathbf{N} \cdot \frac{d\mathbf{N}}{ds} && \mathbf{B} \times \mathbf{T} = \mathbf{N} \\
&= 0.
\end{aligned}$$

Therefore, $d\mathbf{B}/ds$ is also orthogonal to **B**. It follows that the vector $d\mathbf{B}/ds$ is orthogonal to the plane of **B** and **T**. In other words, $d\mathbf{B}/ds$ is parallel to **N**. This means that $d\mathbf{B}/ds$ is a scalar multiple of **N**. In symbols,

$$\frac{d\mathbf{B}}{ds} = -\tau\,\mathbf{N}. \tag{12}$$

The minus sign in Eq. (12) is traditional. The scalar τ (the Greek letter tau) is called the **torsion** along the curve. Unlike the curvature κ, which is always nonnegative, the torsion τ may be positive, negative, or zero.

Notice that

$$\begin{aligned}
\frac{d\mathbf{B}}{ds} \cdot \mathbf{N} &= -\tau\,\mathbf{N} \cdot \mathbf{N} && \text{Because } \frac{d\mathbf{B}}{ds} = -\tau\,\mathbf{N} \\
&= -\tau(1) = -\tau, && \mathbf{N} \cdot \mathbf{N} = 1
\end{aligned}$$

so that

$$\tau = -\frac{d\mathbf{B}}{ds} \cdot \mathbf{N}. \tag{13}$$

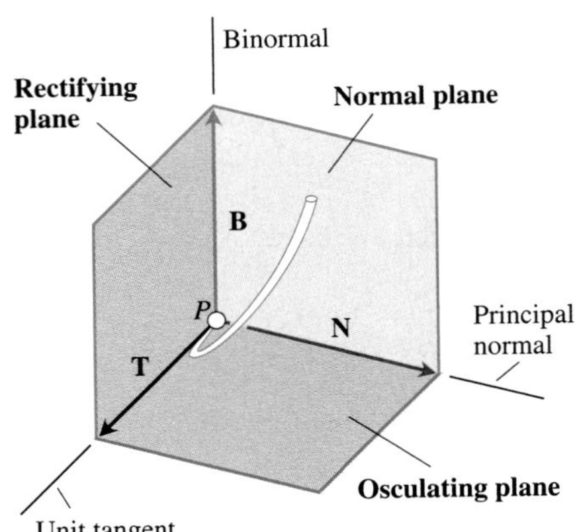

12.31 The names of the three planes determined by **T**, **N**, and **B**.

The three planes determined by **T**, **N**, and **B** are shown in Fig. 12.31. The curvature $\kappa = |d\mathbf{T}/ds|$ can be thought of as the rate at which the normal plane turns as the point P moves along the curve. Similarly, the torsion $\tau = -(d\mathbf{B}/ds) \cdot \mathbf{N}$ is the rate at which the osculating plane turns about **T** as P moves along the curve. It is a measure of how much the curve twists.

The Tangential and Normal Components of Acceleration

When a moving body is accelerated by gravity, brakes, a combination of rocket motors, or whatever, we usually want to know how much of the acceleration acts to move the body straight ahead in the direction of motion, that is, in the tangential direction **T**. We can find out if we use the Chain Rule to rewrite **v** as

$$\mathbf{v} = \frac{d\mathbf{r}}{dt} = \frac{d\mathbf{r}}{ds}\frac{ds}{dt} = \mathbf{T}\frac{ds}{dt} \tag{14}$$

and differentiate both ends of this string of equalities to get

$$\begin{aligned} \mathbf{a} &= \frac{d\mathbf{v}}{dt} = \frac{d}{dt}\left(\mathbf{T}\frac{ds}{dt}\right) = \frac{d^2s}{dt^2}\mathbf{T} + \frac{ds}{dt}\frac{d\mathbf{T}}{dt} \\ &= \frac{d^2s}{dt^2}\mathbf{T} + \frac{ds}{dt}\left(\frac{d\mathbf{T}}{ds}\frac{ds}{dt}\right) = \frac{d^2s}{dt^2}\mathbf{T} + \frac{ds}{dt}\left(\kappa\,\mathbf{N}\frac{ds}{dt}\right) \\ &= \frac{d^2s}{dt^2}\mathbf{T} + \kappa\left(\frac{ds}{dt}\right)^2\mathbf{N}. \end{aligned} \tag{15}$$

This is a remarkable equation. There is no binormal vector **B** in it. No matter how the path of the moving body we are watching may appear to twist and turn in space, the acceleration **a** always lies in the plane of **T** and **N** orthogonal to **B**. The equation also tells us exactly how much of the acceleration takes place tangent to the motion (d^2s/dt^2) and how much takes place normal to the motion $[\kappa(ds/dt)^2]$ (Fig. 12.32).

The **tangential** and **normal** scalar components of acceleration are

$$a_{\mathrm{T}} = \frac{d^2s}{dt^2} = \frac{d}{dt}|\mathbf{v}| \quad \text{and} \quad a_{\mathrm{N}} = \kappa\left(\frac{ds}{dt}\right)^2 = \kappa|\mathbf{v}|^2. \tag{16}$$

That is,

$$\mathbf{a} = \frac{d^2s}{dt^2}\mathbf{T} + \kappa\left(\frac{ds}{dt}\right)^2\mathbf{N}. \tag{17}$$

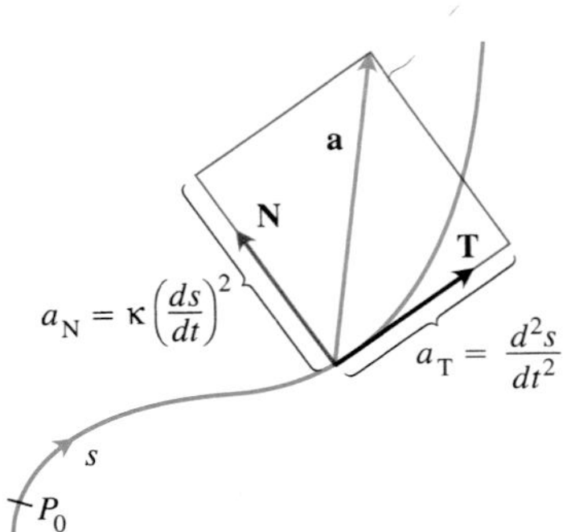

12.32 The tangential and normal components of acceleration. The acceleration vector **a** always lies in the plane of **T** and **N** orthogonal to **B**.

By definition, acceleration **a** is the rate of change of velocity **v**, and in general both the length and direction of **v** change as a body moves along its path. The tangential component of acceleration a_{T} measures the rate of change of the *length* of **v** (that is, the change in the speed). The normal component of acceleration a_{N} measures the rate of change of the *direction* of **v**.

Notice that the normal scalar component of the acceleration is the curvature

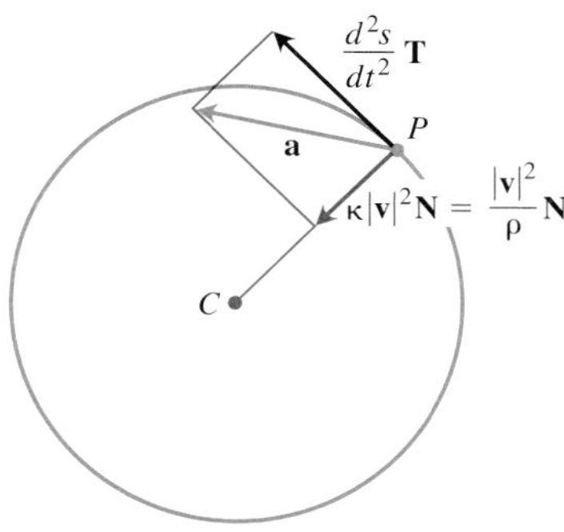

12.33 The tangential and normal components of the acceleration of a body that is speeding up as it moves counterclockwise around a circle of radius ρ.

times the square of the speed. This explains why you have to hold on when your car makes a sharp (large κ), high-speed (large $|\mathbf{v}|$) turn: If you double the speed of your car, you will experience four times the normal component of acceleration for the same curvature.

If a body moves in a circle at a constant speed, d^2s/dt^2 is zero and all the acceleration points along **N** toward the circle's center. If the body is speeding up or slowing down, **a** has a nonzero tangential component (Fig. 12.33).

To calculate a_{N} we usually use the formula

$$a_{\mathrm{N}} = \sqrt{|\mathbf{a}|^2 - a_{\mathrm{T}}^2}, \tag{18}$$

which comes from solving the equation $|\mathbf{a}|^2 = \mathbf{a}\cdot\mathbf{a} = a_{\mathrm{T}}^2 + a_{\mathrm{N}}^2$ for a_{N}. With this formula we can find a_{N} without having to calculate κ first.

EXAMPLE 6 Without finding **T** and **N**, write the acceleration of the motion

$$\mathbf{r} = (\cos t + t\sin t)\,\mathbf{i} + (\sin t - t\cos t)\,\mathbf{j}, \qquad t > 0$$

in the form $\mathbf{a} = a_{\mathrm{T}}\,\mathbf{T} + a_{\mathrm{N}}\,\mathbf{N}$. (The path of the motion is the involute of the circle in Fig. 12.34.)

Solution We use the first of Eqs. (16) to find a_{T}:

$$\mathbf{v} = (t\cos t)\,\mathbf{i} + (t\sin t)\,\mathbf{j} \qquad \text{Value from Section 12.3, Example 5}$$

$$|\mathbf{v}| = \sqrt{t^2\cos^2 t + t^2\sin^2 t} = \sqrt{t^2} = |t| = t \qquad t > 0$$

$$a_{\mathrm{T}} = \frac{d}{dt}|\mathbf{v}| = \frac{d}{dt}(t) = 1. \qquad \text{Eq. (16)}$$

Knowing a_{T}, we use Eq. (18) to find a_{N}:

$$\mathbf{a} = (\cos t - t\sin t)\,\mathbf{i} + (\sin t + t\cos t)\,\mathbf{j}$$

$$|\mathbf{a}|^2 = t^2 + 1 \qquad \text{After some algebra}$$

$$a_{\mathrm{N}} = \sqrt{|\mathbf{a}|^2 - a_{\mathrm{T}}^2} = \sqrt{(t^2+1) - (1)} = \sqrt{t^2} = t.$$

We then use Eq. (17) to find **a**:

$$\mathbf{a} = a_{\mathrm{T}}\,\mathbf{T} + a_{\mathrm{N}}\,\mathbf{N} = (1)\,\mathbf{T} + (t)\,\mathbf{N} = \mathbf{T} + t\,\mathbf{N}.$$

See Fig. 12.34.

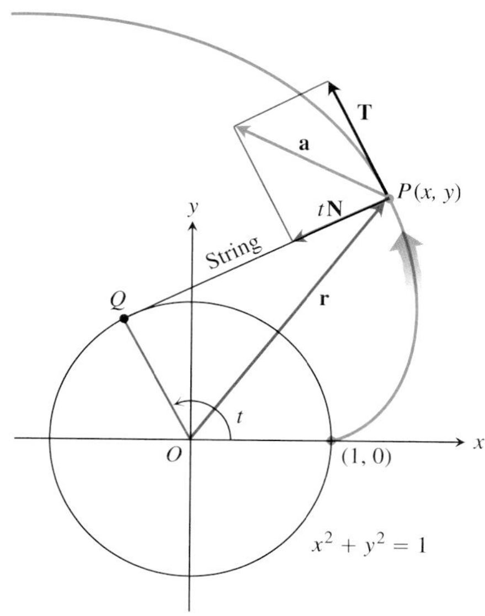

12.34 The tangential and normal components of the acceleration of the motion $\mathbf{r} = (\cos t + t\sin t)\,\mathbf{i} + (\sin t - t\cos t)\,\mathbf{j}$, for $t > 0$ (Example 6).

Formulas for Computing Curvature and Torsion

We now give some easy-to-use formulas for computing the curvature and torsion of a smooth curve. From Eq. (17) we have

$$\mathbf{v}\times\mathbf{a} = \left(\frac{ds}{dt}\mathbf{T}\right)\times\left[\frac{d^2s}{dt^2}\mathbf{T} + \kappa\left(\frac{ds}{dt}\right)^2\mathbf{N}\right] \qquad \text{From Section 12.3, Eq. (9), } d\mathbf{r}/dt = (ds/dt)\,\mathbf{T},\ \mathbf{v} = (ds/dt)\,\mathbf{T}$$

$$= \left(\frac{ds}{dt}\frac{d^2s}{dt^2}\right)(\mathbf{T}\times\mathbf{T}) + \kappa\left(\frac{ds}{dt}\right)^3(\mathbf{T}\times\mathbf{N})$$

$$= \kappa\left(\frac{ds}{dt}\right)^3\mathbf{B}. \qquad \mathbf{T}\times\mathbf{T} = \mathbf{0} \text{ and } \mathbf{T}\times\mathbf{N} = \mathbf{B}$$

It follows that

$$|\mathbf{v} \times \mathbf{a}| = \kappa \left|\frac{ds}{dt}\right|^3 |\mathbf{B}| = \kappa\, |\mathbf{v}|^3. \qquad \frac{ds}{dt} = |\mathbf{v}| \text{ and } |\mathbf{B}| = 1$$

Solving for κ gives the following formula.

A Vector Formula for Curvature

$$\kappa = \frac{|\mathbf{v} \times \mathbf{a}|}{|\mathbf{v}|^3} \tag{19}$$

Equation (19) calculates the curvature, a geometric property of the curve, from the velocity and acceleration of any vector representation of the curve in which $|\mathbf{v}|$ is different from zero. Take a moment to think about how remarkable this really is: From any formula for motion along a curve, no matter how variable the motion may be (as long as $\mathbf{v}$ is never zero), we can calculate a physical property of the curve that seems to have nothing to do with the way the curve is traversed.

The most widely used formula for torsion, derived in more advanced texts, is

$$\tau = \frac{\begin{vmatrix} \dot{x} & \dot{y} & \dot{z} \\ \ddot{x} & \ddot{y} & \ddot{z} \\ \dddot{x} & \dddot{y} & \dddot{z} \end{vmatrix}}{|\mathbf{v} \times \mathbf{a}|^2} \qquad (\text{if } \mathbf{v} \times \mathbf{a} \neq \mathbf{0}). \tag{20}$$

This formula calculates the torsion directly from the derivatives of the component functions $x = f(t)$, $y = g(t)$, $z = h(t)$ that make up $\mathbf{r}$. The determinant's first row comes from $\mathbf{v}$, the second row comes from $\mathbf{a}$, and the third row comes from $\dot{\mathbf{a}} = d\mathbf{a}/dt$.

Newton's Dot Notation for Derivatives

The dots in Eq. (20) denote differentiation with respect to t, one derivative for each dot. Thus, $\dot{x}$ ("x dot") means dx/dt, $\ddot{x}$ ("x double dot") means d^2x/dt^2, and $\dddot{x}$ ("x triple dot") means d^3x/dt^3. Similarly, $\dot{y} = dy/dt$ and so on.

EXAMPLE 7 Find the curvature and torsion of the helix

$$\mathbf{r} = (a \cos t)\,\mathbf{i} + (a \sin t)\,\mathbf{j} + bt\,\mathbf{k} \qquad (a, b \geq 0)$$

using Eqs. (19) and (20).

Solution We calculate the curvature with Eq. (19):

$$\mathbf{v} = -(a \sin t)\,\mathbf{i} + (a \cos t)\,\mathbf{j} + b\,\mathbf{k},$$

$$\mathbf{a} = -(a \cos t)\,\mathbf{i} - (a \sin t)\,\mathbf{j},$$

$$\mathbf{v} \times \mathbf{a} = \begin{vmatrix} \mathbf{i} & \mathbf{j} & \mathbf{k} \\ -a \sin t & a \cos t & b \\ -a \cos t & -a \sin t & 0 \end{vmatrix} = (ab \sin t)\,\mathbf{i} - (ab \cos t)\,\mathbf{j} + a^2\,\mathbf{k},$$

$$\kappa = \frac{|\mathbf{v} \times \mathbf{a}|}{|\mathbf{v}|^3} = \frac{\sqrt{a^2b^2 + a^4}}{(a^2 + b^2)^{3/2}} = \frac{a\sqrt{a^2 + b^2}}{(a^2 + b^2)^{3/2}} = \frac{a}{a^2 + b^2}. \tag{21}$$

Notice that Eq. (21) agrees with Eq. (9) in Example 4, where we calculated the curvature directly from its definition.

To evaluate Eq. (20) for the torsion, we find the entries in the determinant by differentiating $\mathbf{r}$. We already have $\mathbf{v}$ and $\mathbf{a}$, and

$$\dot{\mathbf{a}} = \frac{d\mathbf{a}}{dt} = (a \sin t)\,\mathbf{i} - (a \cos t)\,\mathbf{j}.$$

Hence,

$$\tau = \frac{\begin{vmatrix} \dot{x} & \dot{y} & \dot{z} \\ \ddot{x} & \ddot{y} & \ddot{z} \\ \dddot{x} & \dddot{y} & \dddot{z} \end{vmatrix}}{|\mathbf{v} \times \mathbf{a}|^2} = \frac{\begin{vmatrix} -a \sin t & a \cos t & b \\ -a \cos t & -a \sin t & 0 \\ a \sin t & -a \cos t & 0 \end{vmatrix}}{\left(a\sqrt{a^2 + b^2}\right)^2}$$

Value of $|\mathbf{v} \times \mathbf{a}|$ from Eq. (21)

$$= \frac{b(a^2 \cos^2 t + a^2 \sin^2 t)}{a^2(a^2 + b^2)}$$

$$= \frac{b}{a^2 + b^2}. \qquad (22)$$

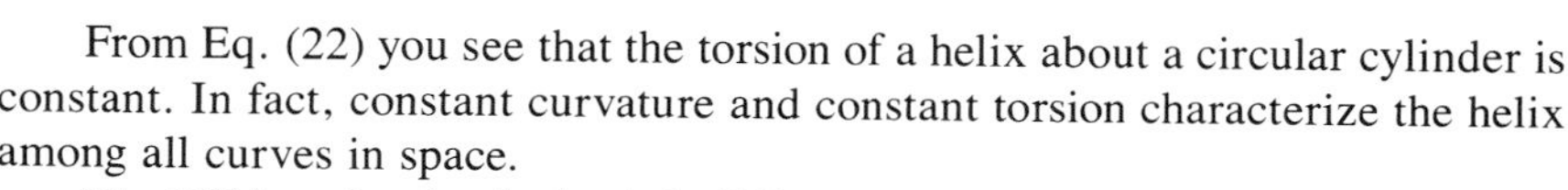

From Eq. (22) you see that the torsion of a helix about a circular cylinder is constant. In fact, constant curvature and constant torsion characterize the helix among all curves in space.

The DNA molecule, the basic building block of life forms, is designed in the form of two helices winding around each other, a little like the rungs and sides of a twisted rope ladder (Fig. 12.35). Not only is the space occupied by the DNA molecule very much smaller than it would be if it were unraveled, but when the molecule is damaged the imperfect piece can be snipped out by a kind of molecular scissors (because the curvature and torsion functions are constant) and the DNA made right again.

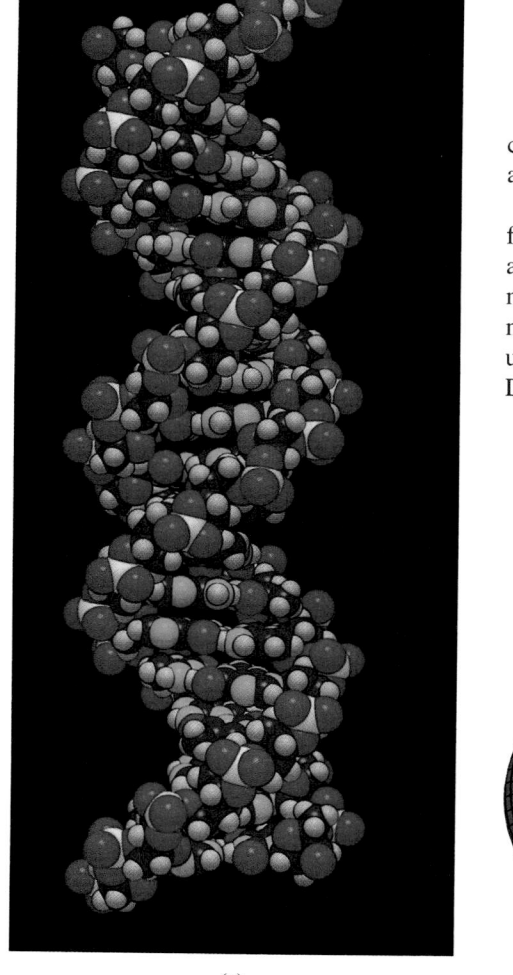

(a) (b) (c)

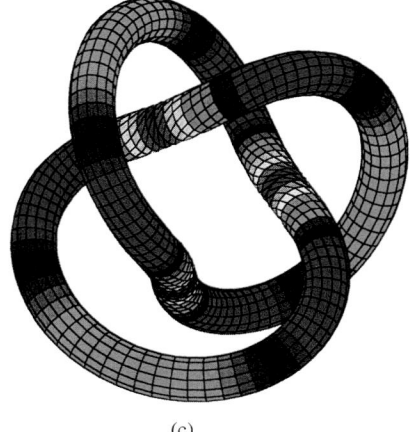

12.35 The helical shape of the DNA molecule (a) is characterized by its constant curvature and torsion. When a shape's curvature and torsion vary, geometers can sometimes use a computer to portray the variation with color. The plots in (b) and (c), provided by Alfred Gray, University of Maryland at College Park, show the variation in the curvature and torsion, respectively, of a knotted twisted tube.

Motion Formulas for Smooth Curves in Space

Unit tangent vector: $\mathbf{T} = \dfrac{\mathbf{v}}{|\mathbf{v}|}$

Principal unit normal vector: $\mathbf{N} = \dfrac{d\mathbf{T}/dt}{|d\mathbf{T}/dt|}$

Binormal vector: $\mathbf{B} = \mathbf{T} \times \mathbf{N}$

Curvature: $\kappa = \left|\dfrac{d\mathbf{T}}{ds}\right| = \dfrac{|\mathbf{v} \times \mathbf{a}|}{|\mathbf{v}|^3}$

Torsion: $\tau = -\dfrac{d\mathbf{B}}{ds} \cdot \mathbf{N} = \dfrac{\begin{vmatrix} \dot{x} & \dot{y} & \dot{z} \\ \ddot{x} & \ddot{y} & \ddot{z} \\ \dddot{x} & \dddot{y} & \dddot{z} \end{vmatrix}}{|\mathbf{v} \times \mathbf{a}|^2}$

Tangential and normal scalar components of acceleration: $\mathbf{a} = a_{\mathrm{T}}\,\mathbf{T} + a_{\mathrm{N}}\,\mathbf{N}$

$a_{\mathrm{T}} = \dfrac{d}{dt}|\mathbf{v}|$

$a_{\mathrm{N}} = \sqrt{|\mathbf{a}|^2 - a_{\mathrm{T}}^2}$

Exercises 12.4

Find $\mathbf{T}$, $\mathbf{N}$, and κ for the plane curves in Exercises 1–4.

1. $\mathbf{r} = t\,\mathbf{i} + (\ln \cos t)\,\mathbf{j}, \quad -\pi/2 < t < \pi/2$
2. $\mathbf{r} = (\ln \sec t)\,\mathbf{i} + t\,\mathbf{j}, \quad -\pi/2 < t < \pi/2$
3. $\mathbf{r} = (2t + 3)\,\mathbf{i} + (5 - t^2)\,\mathbf{j}$
4. $\mathbf{r} = (\cos t + t \sin t)\,\mathbf{i} + (\sin t - t \cos t)\,\mathbf{j}, \quad t > 0$

Find $\mathbf{T}$, $\mathbf{N}$, $\mathbf{B}$, κ, and τ for the space curves in Exercises 5–12.

5. $\mathbf{r} = (3 \sin t)\,\mathbf{i} + (3 \cos t)\,\mathbf{j} + 4t\,\mathbf{k}$
6. $\mathbf{r} = (\cos t + t \sin t)\,\mathbf{i} + (\sin t - t \cos t)\,\mathbf{j} + 3\,\mathbf{k}$
7. $\mathbf{r} = (e^t \cos t)\,\mathbf{i} + (e^t \sin t)\,\mathbf{j} + 2\,\mathbf{k}$
8. $\mathbf{r} = (6 \sin 2t)\,\mathbf{i} + (6 \cos 2t)\,\mathbf{j} + 5t\,\mathbf{k}$
9. $\mathbf{r} = (t^3/3)\,\mathbf{i} + (t^2/2)\,\mathbf{j}, \quad t > 0$
10. $\mathbf{r} = (\cos^3 t)\,\mathbf{i} + (\sin^3 t)\,\mathbf{j}, \quad 0 < t < \pi/2$
11. $\mathbf{r} = t\,\mathbf{i} + a(\cosh(t/a))\,\mathbf{j}, \quad a > 0$
12. $\mathbf{r} = (\cosh t)\,\mathbf{i} - (\sinh t)\,\mathbf{j} + t\,\mathbf{k}$

In Exercises 13–16, write $\mathbf{a}$ in the form $\mathbf{a} = a_{\mathrm{T}}\,\mathbf{T} + a_{\mathrm{N}}\,\mathbf{N}$ without finding $\mathbf{T}$ and $\mathbf{N}$.

13. $\mathbf{r} = (2t + 3)\,\mathbf{i} + (t^2 - 1)\,\mathbf{j}$
14. $\mathbf{r} = \ln(t^2 + 1)\,\mathbf{i} + (t - 2\tan^{-1} t)\,\mathbf{j}$
15. $\mathbf{r} = (a \cos t)\,\mathbf{i} + (a \sin t)\,\mathbf{j} + bt\,\mathbf{k}$
16. $\mathbf{r} = (1 + 3t)\,\mathbf{i} + (t - 2)\,\mathbf{j} - 3t\,\mathbf{k}$

In Exercises 17–20, write $\mathbf{a}$ in the form $\mathbf{a} = a_{\mathrm{T}}\,\mathbf{T} + a_{\mathrm{N}}\,\mathbf{N}$ at the given value of t without finding $\mathbf{T}$ and $\mathbf{N}$.

17. $\mathbf{r} = (t + 1)\,\mathbf{i} + 2t\,\mathbf{j} + t^2\,\mathbf{k}, \quad t = 1$
18. $\mathbf{r} = (t \cos t)\,\mathbf{i} + (t \sin t)\,\mathbf{j} + t^2\,\mathbf{k}, \quad t = 0$
19. $\mathbf{r} = t^2\,\mathbf{i} + (t + (1/3)t^3)\,\mathbf{j} + (t - (1/3)t^3)\,\mathbf{k}, \quad t = 0$
20. $\mathbf{r} = (e^t \cos t)\,\mathbf{i} + (e^t \sin t)\,\mathbf{j} + \sqrt{2}e^t\,\mathbf{k}, \quad t = 0$

In Exercises 21 and 22, find $\mathbf{r}$, $\mathbf{T}$, $\mathbf{N}$, and $\mathbf{B}$ at the given value of t. Then find equations for the osculating, normal, and rectifying planes at that value of t.

21. $\mathbf{r} = (\cos t)\,\mathbf{i} + (\sin t)\,\mathbf{j} - \mathbf{k}, \quad t = \pi/4$
22. $\mathbf{r} = (\cos t)\,\mathbf{i} + (\sin t)\,\mathbf{j} + t\,\mathbf{k}, \quad t = 0$
23. The speedometer on your car reads a steady 35 mph. Could you be accelerating? Explain.
24. Can anything be said about the acceleration of a particle that is moving at a constant speed? Give reasons for your answer.
25. Can anything be said about the speed of a particle whose acceleration is always orthogonal to its velocity? Give reasons for your answer.
26. What can be said about the torsion of a (sufficiently differentiable) plane curve $\mathbf{r} = f(t)\,\mathbf{i} + g(t)\,\mathbf{j}$? Give reasons for your answer.

27. *A Sometime Shortcut to Curvature.* If you already know $|a_N|$ and $|\mathbf{v}|$, then the formula $a_N = \kappa|\mathbf{v}|^2$ gives a convenient way to find the curvature. Use it to find the curvature and radius of curvature of the curve

$$\mathbf{r} = (\cos t + t \sin t)\,\mathbf{i} + (\sin t - t \cos t)\,\mathbf{j}, \quad t > 0.$$

(Take a_N and $|\mathbf{v}|$ from Example 6.)

28. Show that κ and τ are both zero for the line

$$\mathbf{r} = (x_0 + At)\,\mathbf{i} + (y_0 + Bt)\,\mathbf{j} + (z_0 + Ct)\,\mathbf{k}.$$

29. *Maximizing the Curvature of a Helix.* In Example 4, we found the curvature of the helix $\mathbf{r} = (a \cos t)\,\mathbf{i} + (a \sin t)\,\mathbf{j} + bt\,\mathbf{k}$ $(a, b \geq 0)$ to be $\kappa = a/(a^2 + b^2)$. What is the largest value κ can have for a given value of b? Give reasons for your answer.

30. *The Torsion of a Helix.* In Example 7, we found the torsion of the helix

$$\mathbf{r} = (a \cos t)\,\mathbf{i} + (a \sin t)\,\mathbf{j} + bt\,\mathbf{k}, \quad a, b \geq 0$$

to be $\tau = b/(a^2 + b^2)$. What is the largest value τ can have for a given value of a? Give reasons for your answer.

31. *Total Curvature.* We find the **total curvature** of the portion of a smooth curve that runs from $s = s_0$ to $s = s_1 > s_0$ by integrating κ from s_0 to s_1. If the curve has some other parameter, say t, then the total curvature is

$$K = \int_{s_0}^{s_1} \kappa\, ds = \int_{t_0}^{t_1} \kappa \frac{ds}{dt}\, dt = \int_{t_0}^{t_1} \kappa|\mathbf{v}|\, dt,$$

where t_0 and t_1 correspond to s_0 and s_1. Find the total curvature of the portion of the helix $\mathbf{r} = (3 \cos t)\,\mathbf{i} + (3 \sin t)\,\mathbf{j} + t\,\mathbf{k}$, $0 \leq t \leq 4\pi$.

32. *Continuation of Exercise 31.* Find the total curvatures of the following curves.

a) The involute of the unit circle: $\mathbf{r} = (\cos t + t \sin t)\,\mathbf{i} + (\sin t - t \cos t)\,\mathbf{j}$, $a \leq t \leq b$ $(a > 0)$. (Exercise 27 gives a convenient way to find κ. Use values from Example 6.)

b) The parabola $y = x^2$, $-\infty < x < \infty$

33. Find an equation for the circle of curvature of the curve $\mathbf{r} = t\,\mathbf{i} + (\sin t)\,\mathbf{j}$ at the point $(\pi/2, 1)$. (The curve parametrizes the graph of $y = \sin x$ in the xy-plane.)

34. a) Find an equation for the circle of curvature of the curve $\mathbf{r} = (2 \ln t)\,\mathbf{i} - [t + (1/t)]\,\mathbf{j}$, $e^{-2} \leq t \leq e^2$, at the point $(0, -2)$, where $t = 1$.

b) Find a cartesian equation for the curve in (a).

c) Graph the curve in (a) together with the circle of curvature.

35. *A Formula for the Curvature of the Graph of a Function in the xy-plane.*

a) The graph $y = f(x)$ in the xy-plane automatically has the parametrization $x = x$, $y = f(x)$, and the vector formula $\mathbf{r} = x\,\mathbf{i} + f(x)\,\mathbf{j}$. Use this formula to show that if f is a twice-differentiable function of x, then

$$\kappa = \frac{|f''(x)|}{[1 + (f'(x))^2]^{3/2}}.$$

b) Use the formula for κ in (a) to find the curvature of $y = \ln(\cos x)$, $-\pi/2 < x < \pi/2$. Compare your answer with the answer in Exercise 1.

c) Show that the curvature is zero at a point of inflection.

36. *A Formula for the Curvature of a Parametrized Plane Curve.*

a) Show that the curvature of a smooth curve $\mathbf{r} = f(t)\,\mathbf{i} + g(t)\,\mathbf{j}$ defined by twice-differentiable functions $x = f(t)$ and $y = g(t)$ is the formula

$$\kappa = \frac{|\dot{x}\ddot{y} - \dot{y}\ddot{x}|}{(\dot{x}^2 + \dot{y}^2)^{3/2}}.$$

Apply the formula to find the curvatures of the following curves.

b) $\mathbf{r} = t\,\mathbf{i} + (\ln \sin t)\,\mathbf{j}$, $0 < t < \pi$

c) $\mathbf{r} = [\tan^{-1}(\sinh t)]\,\mathbf{i} + (\ln \cosh t)\,\mathbf{j}$.

GRAPHER EXERCISES

The formula

$$\kappa(x) = \frac{|f''(x)|}{[1 + (f'(x))^2]^{3/2}},$$

derived in Exercise 35, expresses the curvature $\kappa(x)$ of a twice-differentiable plane curve $y = f(x)$ as a function of x. Find the curvature function of each of the curves in Exercises 37–40. Then graph $f(x)$ together with $\kappa(x)$ over the given interval. You will find some surprises.

37. $y = x^2$, $-2 \leq x \leq 2$

38. $y = x^4/4$, $-2 \leq x \leq 2$

39. $y = \sin x$, $0 \leq x \leq 2\pi$

40. $y = e^x$, $-1 \leq x \leq 2$

Writing for Your Own Knowledge

Answer the following questions in writing. Some answers will take only a sentence or two; others may require several paragraphs. Some explanations may also call for graphs or sketches.

1. How do you define the curvature of a curve in the plane?
2. What is a plane curve's principal unit normal vector? Which way does it point?
3. How do you define $\mathbf{N}$ and κ for curves in space? How are these quantities related?
4. What is a curve's binormal vector? Give an example. What is the relation of this vector to the curve's torsion?
5. What formulas are available for describing a body's acceleration as a sum of its tangential and normal components? Give an example. Why might one want to write the acceleration this way? What if the body moves at a constant speed? At a constant speed around a circle?
6. How do you calculate curvature and torsion using vectors?

12.5 Planetary Motion and Satellites

This section introduces the standard vector equations for motion in polar and cylindrical coordinates and discusses Kepler's three laws of planetary motion.

Vector Equations for Motion in Polar and Cylindrical Coordinates

When a particle moves along a curve in the polar coordinate plane, we express its position, velocity, and acceleration in terms of the moving unit vectors

$$\mathbf{u}_r = (\cos\theta)\,\mathbf{i} + (\sin\theta)\,\mathbf{j}, \qquad \mathbf{u}_\theta = -(\sin\theta)\,\mathbf{i} + (\cos\theta)\,\mathbf{j}, \tag{1}$$

shown in Fig. 12.36. The vector $\mathbf{u}_r$ points along the position vector $\overrightarrow{OP}$, so $\mathbf{r} = r\,\mathbf{u}_r$. The vector $\mathbf{u}_\theta$, orthogonal to $\mathbf{u}_r$, points in the direction of increasing θ.

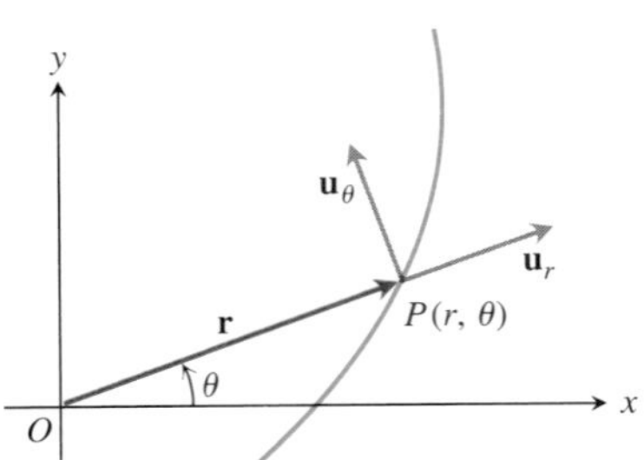

12.36 The length of the position vector $\mathbf{r}$ is the positive polar coordinate r of the point P. Thus, $\mathbf{u}_r$, which is $\mathbf{r}/|\mathbf{r}|$, is also $\mathbf{r}/r$. Equations (1) express $\mathbf{u}_r$ and $\mathbf{u}_\theta$ in terms of $\mathbf{i}$ and $\mathbf{j}$.

We find from (1) that

$$\frac{d\mathbf{u}_r}{d\theta} = -(\sin\theta)\,\mathbf{i} + (\cos\theta)\,\mathbf{j} = \mathbf{u}_\theta$$
$$\frac{d\mathbf{u}_\theta}{d\theta} = -(\cos\theta)\,\mathbf{i} - (\sin\theta)\,\mathbf{j} = -\mathbf{u}_r. \tag{2}$$

When we differentiate $\mathbf{u}_r$ and $\mathbf{u}_\theta$ with respect to t to find how they change with time, the Chain Rule gives

$$\frac{d\mathbf{u}_r}{dt} = \frac{d\mathbf{u}_r}{d\theta}\frac{d\theta}{dt} = \frac{d\theta}{dt}\mathbf{u}_\theta, \qquad \frac{d\mathbf{u}_\theta}{dt} = \frac{d\mathbf{u}_\theta}{d\theta}\frac{d\theta}{dt} = -\frac{d\theta}{dt}\mathbf{u}_r. \tag{3}$$

Hence,

$$\mathbf{v} = \frac{d\mathbf{r}}{dt} = \frac{d}{dt}(r\,\mathbf{u}_r) = \frac{dr}{dt}\mathbf{u}_r + r\frac{d\mathbf{u}_r}{dt} = \frac{dr}{dt}\mathbf{u}_r + r\frac{d\theta}{dt}\mathbf{u}_\theta. \tag{4}$$

See Fig. 12.37.

The acceleration is

$$\mathbf{a} = \frac{d\mathbf{v}}{dt} = \left(\frac{d^2r}{dt^2}\mathbf{u}_r + \frac{dr}{dt}\frac{d\mathbf{u}_r}{dt}\right) + \left(r\frac{d^2\theta}{dt^2}\mathbf{u}_\theta + \frac{dr}{dt}\frac{d\theta}{dt}\mathbf{u}_\theta + r\frac{d\theta}{dt}\frac{d\mathbf{u}_\theta}{dt}\right). \tag{5}$$

When Eqs. (3) are used to evaluate $d\mathbf{u}_r/dt$ and $d\mathbf{u}_\theta/dt$ and the components are separated, the equation for acceleration becomes

$$\mathbf{a} = \left(\frac{d^2r}{dt^2} - r\left(\frac{d\theta}{dt}\right)^2\right)\mathbf{u}_r + \left(r\frac{d^2\theta}{dt^2} + 2\frac{dr}{dt}\frac{d\theta}{dt}\right)\mathbf{u}_\theta. \tag{6}$$

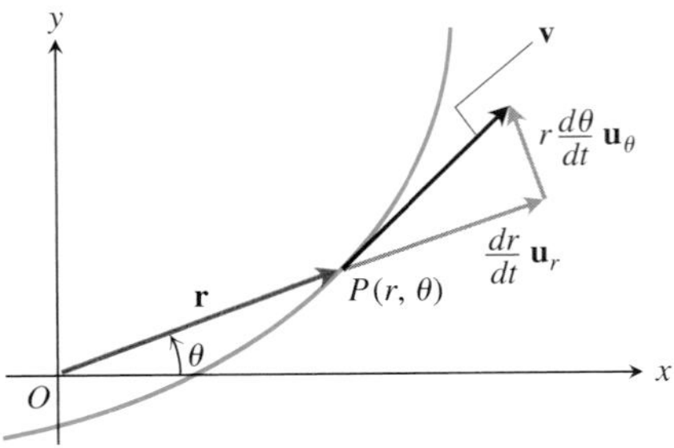

12.37 In polar coordinates, the velocity vector is

$$\mathbf{v} = (dr/dt)\,\mathbf{u}_r + r(d\theta/dt)\,\mathbf{u}_\theta.$$

To extend the equations of motion to space, we add $z\,\mathbf{k}$ to the right-hand side of the equation $\mathbf{r} = r\,\mathbf{u}_r$. Then, in cylindrical coordinates,

$$\mathbf{r} = r\,\mathbf{u}_r + z\,\mathbf{k} \tag{7}$$

$$\mathbf{v} = \frac{dr}{dt}\mathbf{u}_r + r\frac{d\theta}{dt}\mathbf{u}_\theta + \frac{dz}{dt}\mathbf{k} \tag{8}$$

$$\mathbf{a} = \left(\frac{d^2r}{dt^2} - r\left(\frac{d\theta}{dt}\right)^2\right)\mathbf{u}_r + \left(r\frac{d^2\theta}{dt^2} + 2\frac{dr}{dt}\frac{d\theta}{dt}\right)\mathbf{u}_\theta + \frac{d^2z}{dt^2}\mathbf{k}. \tag{9}$$

The vectors $\mathbf{u}_r$, $\mathbf{u}_\theta$, and $\mathbf{k}$ make a right-handed frame (Fig. 12.38) in which

$$\mathbf{u}_r \times \mathbf{u}_\theta = \mathbf{k}, \qquad \mathbf{k} \times \mathbf{u}_r = \mathbf{u}_\theta, \qquad \mathbf{u}_\theta \times \mathbf{k} = \mathbf{u}_r. \tag{10}$$

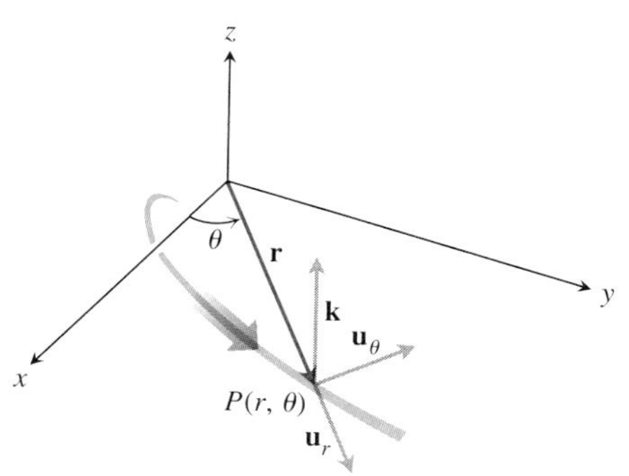

12.38 Motion in space with cylindrical coordinates.

Planets Move in Planes

Newton's law of gravitation says that if $\mathbf{r}$ is the radius vector from the center of a sun of mass M to the center of a planet of mass m, then the force $\mathbf{F}$ of the gravitational attraction between the planet and sun is given by the equation

$$\mathbf{F} = -\frac{GmM}{|\mathbf{r}|^2}\frac{\mathbf{r}}{|\mathbf{r}|} \tag{11}$$

(Fig. 12.39). The constant G is called the (universal) **gravitational constant.** If we measure the masses m and M in kilograms, time in seconds, force in newtons, and distance in meters, then G is about $6.6720 \times 10^{-11}\mathrm{Nm}^2\mathrm{kg}^{-2}$.

Combining Eq. (11) with Newton's second law of motion, $\mathbf{F} = m\, d^2\mathbf{r}/dt^2$, gives

$$m\frac{d^2\mathbf{r}}{dt^2} = -\frac{GmM}{|\mathbf{r}|^2}\frac{\mathbf{r}}{|\mathbf{r}|},$$

$$\frac{d^2\mathbf{r}}{dt^2} = -\frac{GM}{|\mathbf{r}|^3}\mathbf{r}. \tag{12}$$

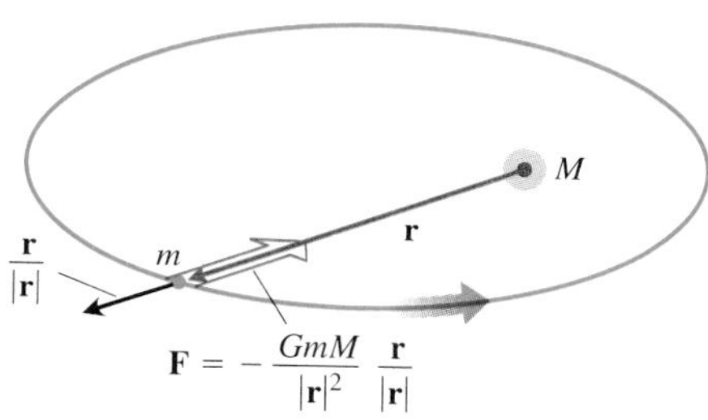

12.39 The force of gravity is directed along the line joining the centers of mass.

This is typical of a **central force,** one that points toward a fixed center at all times—in this case the center of the sun.

Equation (12) says that $d^2\mathbf{r}/dt^2$ is a scalar multiple of $\mathbf{r}$ and hence tells us that

$$\mathbf{r} \times \frac{d^2\mathbf{r}}{dt^2} = \mathbf{0}. \tag{13}$$

The left-hand side of this equation is the derivative of $\mathbf{r} \times d\mathbf{r}/dt$:

$$\begin{aligned}\frac{d}{dt}\left(\mathbf{r} \times \frac{d\mathbf{r}}{dt}\right) &= \frac{d\mathbf{r}}{dt} \times \frac{d\mathbf{r}}{dt} + \mathbf{r} \times \frac{d^2\mathbf{r}}{dt^2} && \text{Cross Product Rule}\\ &= \mathbf{0} + \mathbf{r} \times \frac{d^2\mathbf{r}}{dt^2} && \mathbf{A} \times \mathbf{A} = \mathbf{0} \text{ for any vector}\\ &= \mathbf{r} \times \frac{d^2\mathbf{r}}{dt^2}.\end{aligned} \tag{14}$$

Thus, Eq. (13) is equivalent to

$$\frac{d}{dt}\left(\mathbf{r} \times \frac{d\mathbf{r}}{dt}\right) = \mathbf{0},$$

which, in turn, says that

$$\mathbf{r} \times \frac{d\mathbf{r}}{dt} = \mathbf{C} \tag{15}$$

for some constant vector $\mathbf{C}$.

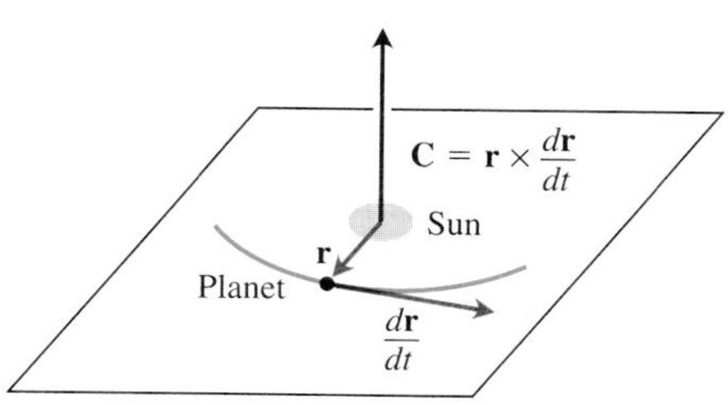

12.40 A planet that obeys Newton's laws of gravitation and motion travels in the plane through the sun's center of mass normal to $\mathbf{C} = \mathbf{r} \times d\mathbf{r}/dt$.

Equation (15) tells us that $\mathbf{r}$ and $d\mathbf{r}/dt$ always lie in a plane perpendicular to $\mathbf{C}$. Hence, the planet moves in a fixed plane through the center of its sun (Fig. 12.40).

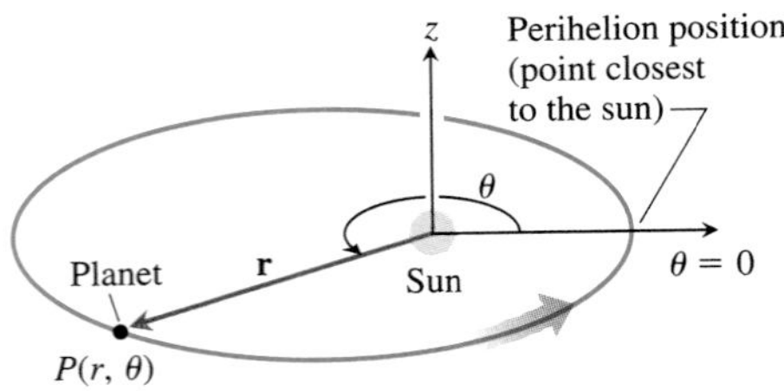

12.41 The coordinate system for planetary motion. The motion is counterclockwise when viewed from above, as it is here, and $d\theta/dt$ is positive.

Coordinates and Initial Conditions

We now introduce cylindrical coordinates in a way that places the origin at the sun's center of mass and makes the plane of the planet's motion the polar coordinate plane. This makes $\mathbf{r}$ the planet's polar coordinate position vector and makes $|\mathbf{r}|$ equal to r and $\mathbf{r}/|\mathbf{r}|$ equal to $\mathbf{u}_r$. We also position the z-axis to make $\mathbf{k}$ the direction of $\mathbf{C}$. Thus, $\mathbf{k}$ has the same right-hand relation to $\mathbf{r} \times d\mathbf{r}/dt$ that $\mathbf{C}$ does, and the planet's motion is counterclockwise when viewed from the positive z-axis. This makes θ increase with t, so that $d\theta/dt$ is positive for all t. Finally, we rotate the polar coordinate plane about the z-axis, if necessary, to make the initial ray coincide with the direction $\mathbf{r}$ has when the planet is closest to the sun. This runs the ray through the planet's **perihelion** position (Fig. 12.41).

If we now measure time so that $t = 0$ when the planet is at perihelion, we have the following initial conditions for the planet's motion:

1. $r = r_0$, the minimum radius, when $t = 0$

2. $\dfrac{dr}{dt} = 0$ when $t = 0$ (because r has a minimum value then)

3. $\theta = 0$ when $t = 0$

4. $|\mathbf{v}| = v_0$ when $t = 0$

Since

$$
\begin{aligned}
v_0 &= |\mathbf{v}|_{t=0} && \text{Standard notation}\\
&= \left|\frac{dr}{dt}\mathbf{u}_r + r\frac{d\theta}{dt}\mathbf{u}_\theta\right|_{t=0} && \text{Eq. (4)}\\
&= \left|r\frac{d\theta}{dt}\mathbf{u}_\theta\right|_{t=0} && \frac{dr}{dt} = 0 \text{ when } t = 0\\
&= \left|r\frac{d\theta}{dt}\right|\left|\mathbf{u}_\theta\right|_{t=0} &&\\
&= \left|r\frac{d\theta}{dt}\right|_{t=0} && |\mathbf{u}_\theta| = 1\\
&= \left(r\frac{d\theta}{dt}\right)_{t=0} && r \text{ and } d\theta/dt \text{ are both positive}
\end{aligned}
$$

we also know that

5. $r\dfrac{d\theta}{dt} = v_0$ when $t = 0$.

The German astronomer, mathematician, and physicist Johannes Kepler (1571–1630) was the first, and until Descartes the only, scientist to demand physical (as opposed to theological) explanations of celestial phenomena. His three laws of motion, the results of a lifetime of work, changed the course of astronomy forever and played a crucial role in the development of Newton's physics.

Statement of Kepler's First Law (The Conic Section Law)

Kepler's first law says that a planet's path is a conic section with the sun at one focus. The eccentricity of the conic is

$$e = \frac{r_0 v_0^2}{GM} - 1 \tag{16}$$

and the polar equation is

$$r = \frac{(1 + e)r_0}{1 + e\cos\theta}. \tag{17}$$

The derivation is involved and we will not give it here.

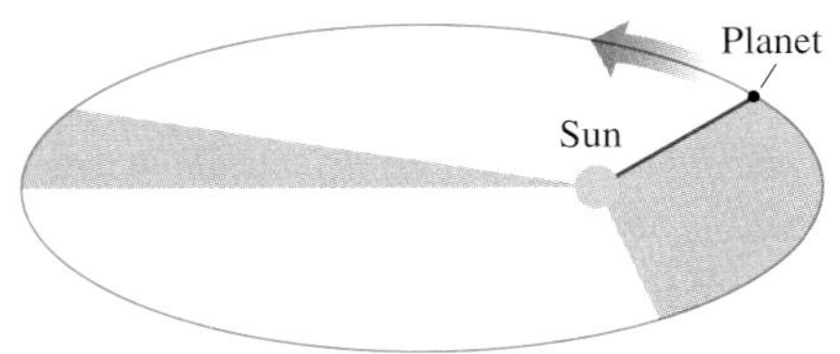

12.42 The line joining a planet to its sun sweeps over equal areas in equal times.

Kepler's Second Law (The Equal Area Law)

Kepler's second law says that the radius vector from a sun to a planet (the position vector **r** in our model) sweeps out equal areas in equal times (Fig. 12.42). To derive this law, we use Eq. (4) to evaluate the cross product in Eq. (15):

$$\begin{aligned}
\mathbf{C} &= \mathbf{r} \times \frac{d\mathbf{r}}{dt} && \text{Eq. (15)} \\
&= \mathbf{r} \times \mathbf{v} && \mathbf{v} = d\mathbf{r}/dt \\
&= r\,\mathbf{u}_r \times \left(\frac{dr}{dt}\,\mathbf{u}_r + r\frac{d\theta}{dt}\,\mathbf{u}_\theta\right) && \text{Eq. (4)} \\
&= r\frac{dr}{dt}\underbrace{\mathbf{u}_r \times \mathbf{u}_r}_{\mathbf{0}} + r\left(r\frac{d\theta}{dt}\right)\underbrace{\mathbf{u}_r \times \mathbf{u}_\theta}_{\mathbf{k}} \\
&= r\left(r\frac{d\theta}{dt}\right)\mathbf{k}.
\end{aligned} \tag{18}$$

Setting t equal to zero then shows that

$$\mathbf{C} = \left[r\left(r\frac{d\theta}{dt}\right)\right]_{t=0} \cdot \mathbf{k} = r_0 v_0\,\mathbf{k}. \tag{19}$$

Substituting this value for **C** in Eq. (18) gives

$$r_0 v_0\,\mathbf{k} = r^2\frac{d\theta}{dt}\,\mathbf{k} \qquad \text{or} \qquad r^2\frac{d\theta}{dt} = r_0 v_0. \tag{20}$$

Here is where the area comes in. From Section 10.8, the area differential in polar coordinates is

$$dA = \frac{1}{2}r^2\,d\theta.$$

Accordingly, dA/dt has the constant value

$$\frac{dA}{dt} = \frac{1}{2}r^2\frac{d\theta}{dt} = \frac{1}{2}r_0 v_0, \tag{21}$$

which is Kepler's second law.

For Earth, r_0 is about 150,000,000 km, v_0 is about 30 km/sec, and dA/dt is about 2,250,000,000 km^2/sec. Every time your heart beats, Earth advances 30 km along its orbit and the line joining Earth to the sun sweeps out 2,250,000,000 square kilometers.

Statement of Kepler's Third Law (The Time-Distance Law)

The time T it takes a planet to go around its sun once is the planet's **orbital period.** The semimajor axis a of the planet's orbit is the planet's **mean distance** from the sun. *Kepler's third law* says that T and a are related by the equation

$$\frac{T^2}{a^3} = \frac{4\pi^2}{GM}. \tag{22}$$

Since the right-hand side of this equation is constant within a given solar system, the ratio of T^2 to a^3 is the same for every planet in the system. The derivation of Eq. (22) can be found, along with the derivation of Kepler's first law, in more advanced texts.

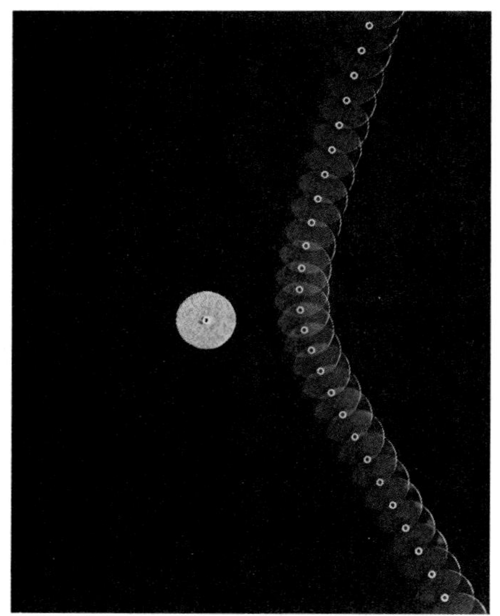

12.43 This multiflash photograph shows a body being deflected by an inverse square law force. It moves along a hyperbola.

Kepler's third law is the starting point for working out the size of our solar system. It allows the semimajor axis of each planetary orbit to be expressed in astronomical units, Earth's semimajor axis being one unit. The distance between any two planets at any time can then be predicted in astronomical units and all that remains is to find one of these distances in kilometers. This can be done by bouncing radar waves off Venus, for example. The astronomical unit is now known, after a series of such measurements, to be 149,597,870 km.

Astronomical Data

Although Kepler discovered his laws empirically and stated them only for the six planets known at the time, the modern derivations of Kepler's laws show that they apply to any body driven by a force that obeys an inverse square law. They apply to Halley's comet and the asteroid Icarus. They apply to the moon's orbit about Earth, and they applied to the orbit of the spacecraft *Apollo 8,* about the moon. They also applied to the air puck shown in Fig. 12.43 being deflected by an inverse square law force—its path is a hyperbola. Even charged particles fired at the nuclei of atoms scatter along hyperbolic paths.

Tables 12.1–12.3 give additional data for planetary orbits and for the orbits

TABLE 12.1
Values of a, e, and T for the major planets

Planet	Semimajor Axis $a^\dagger$	Eccentricity e	Period T
Mercury	57.95	0.2056	87.967 days
Venus	108.11	0.0068	224.701 days
Earth	149.57	0.0167	365.256 days
Mars	227.84	0.0934	1.8808 years
Jupiter	778.14	0.0484	11.8613 years
Saturn	1427.0	0.0543	29.4568 years
Uranus	2870.3	0.0460	84.0081 years
Neptune	4499.9	0.0082	164.784 years
Pluto	5909	0.2481	248.35 years

†Millions of kilometers

TABLE 12.2
Data on Earth's satellites

Name	Launch Date	Time or Expected Time Aloft	Weight at Launch (kg)	Period (min)	Perigee Height (km)	Apogee Height (km)	Semimajor Axis a (km)	Eccentricity
Sputnik 1	Oct. 1957	57.6 days	83.6	96.2	215	939	6,955	0.052
Vanguard 1	March 1958	300 years	1.47	138.5	649	4,340	8,872	0.208
Syncom 3	Aug. 1964	$>10^6$ years	39	1436.2	35,718	35,903	42,189	0.002
Skylab 4	Nov. 1973	84.06 days	13,980	93.11	422	437	6,808	0.001
Tiros 11	Oct. 1978	500 years	734	102.12	850	866	7,236	0.001
GOES 4	Sept. 1980	$>10^6$ years	627	1436.2	35,776	35,800	42,166	0.0003
Intelsat 5	Dec. 1980	$>10^6$ years	1,928	1417.67	35,143	35,707	41,803	0.007

TABLE 12.3
Numerical data

Gravitational constant: $G = 6.6720 \times 10^{-11}\ \mathrm{Nm^2kg^{-2}}$ (When you use this value of G in a calculation, remember to express force in newtons, distance in meters, mass in kilograms, and time in seconds.)
Sun's mass: 1.99×10^{30} kg
Earth's mass: 5.975×10^{24} kg
Equatorial radius of Earth: 6378.533 km
Polar radius of Earth: 6356.912 km
Earth's rotational period: 1436.1 min
Earth's orbital period: 1 year = 365.256 days

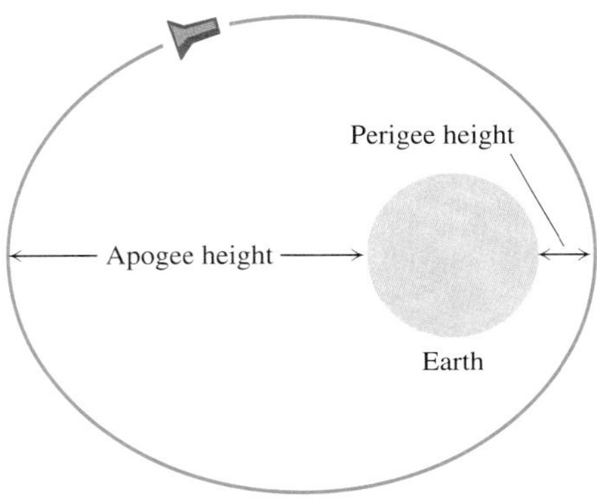

12.44 The orbit of an Earth satellite: $2a$ = Diameter of Earth + Perigee height + Apogee height.

of seven of Earth's artificial satellites (Fig. 12.44). *Vanguard 1* was nicknamed "Grapefruit." You will see why when you look at the photograph in Fig. 12.45. The data *Vanguard* sent back revealed differences among the levels of Earth's oceans and provided the first determination of the precise locations of some of the more isolated Pacific islands. The data also verified that the gravitation of the sun and moon would affect the orbits of Earth's satellites and that solar wind could exert enough pressure to deform an orbit.

Syncom 3 is one of a series of U.S. Department of Defense telecommunications satellites. *Tiros 11* (for "television infrared observation satellite") is one of a series of weather satellites. *GOES 4* (for "geostationary operational environmental satellite") is one of a series of satellites designed to gather information about Earth's atmosphere. Its orbital period, 1436.2 minutes, is nearly the same as Earth's rotational period of 1436.1 minutes, and its orbit is nearly circular ($e = 0.0003$). *Intelsat 5* is a heavy-capacity commercial telecommunications satellite.

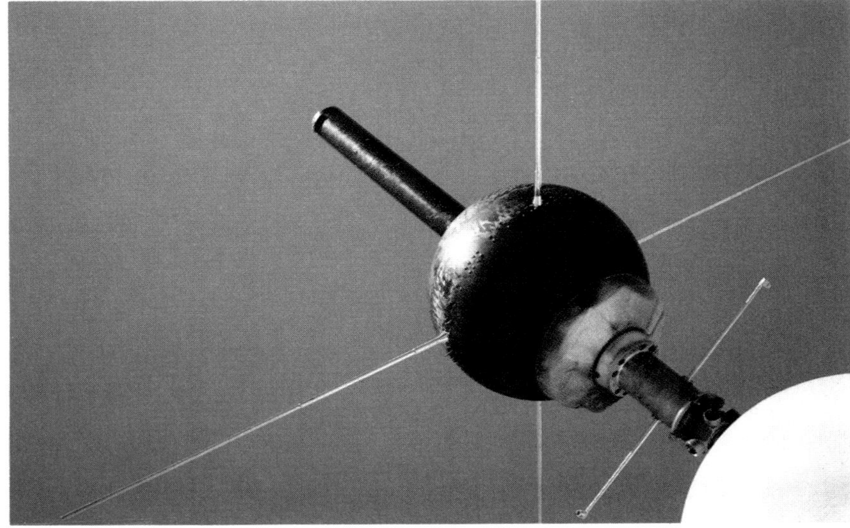

12.45 *Vanguard 1*, still in orbit, is so small it weighs only three and a quarter pounds.

Circular Orbits

For circular orbits, e is zero, $r = r_0$ is a constant, and Eq. (16) gives

$$r = r_0 = \frac{GM}{{v_0}^2}, \tag{23}$$

which reduces to

$$r = \frac{GM}{v^2} \tag{24}$$

because v is constant as well (Exercise 12). Kepler's third law becomes

$$\frac{T^2}{r^3} = \frac{4\pi^2}{GM} \tag{25}$$

because $a = r$.

Exercises 12.5

Reminder: When a calculation involves the gravitational constant G, express force in newtons, distance in meters, mass in kilograms, and time in seconds.

CALCULATOR EXERCISES

1. Since the orbit of *Skylab 4* had a semimajor axis of $a = 6808$ km, Kepler's third law with M equal to the earth's mass should give the period. Calculate it. Compare your result with the value in Table 12.2.

2. Earth's distance from the sun at perihelion is approximately 149,577,000 km, and the eccentricity of the earth's orbit about the sun is 0.0167. Find the velocity v_0 of Earth in its orbit at perihelion. (Use Eq. 16.)

3. In July 1965, the USSR launched *Proton I,* weighing 12,200 kg (at launch), with a perigee height of 183 km, an apogee height of 589 km, and a period of 92.25 min. Using the relevant data for the mass of Earth and the gravitational constant G, find the semimajor axis a of the orbit from Eq. (22). Compare your answer with the number you get by adding the perigee and apogee heights to the diameter of the earth.

4. a) The *Viking 1* orbiter, which surveyed Mars from August 1975 to June 1976, had a period of 1639 min. Use this and the fact that the mass of Mars is 6.418×10^{23} kg to find the semimajor axis of the *Viking 1* orbit.
   b) The *Viking 1* orbiter was 1499 km from the surface of Mars at its closest point and 35,800 km from the surface at its farthest point. Use this information together with the value you obtained in part (a) to estimate the average diameter of Mars.

5. The *Viking 2* orbiter, which surveyed Mars from September 1975 to August 1976, moved in an ellipse whose semimajor axis was 22,030 km. What was the orbital period? (Express your answer in minutes.)

6. *Geosynchronous Orbits.* Several satellites in the earth's equatorial plane have nearly circular orbits whose periods are the same as the earth's rotational period. Such orbits are called **geosynchronous** or **geostationary** because they hold the satellite over the same spot on Earth's surface.
   a) Approximately what is the semimajor axis of a geosynchronous orbit? Give reasons for your answer.
   b) About how high is a geosynchronous orbit above Earth's surface?
   c) Which of the satellites in Table 12.2 have (nearly) geosynchronous orbits?

7. The mass of Mars is 6.418×10^{23} kg. If a satellite revolving about Mars is to hold a stationary orbit (have the same period as the period of Mars's rotation, which is 1477.4 min), what must the semimajor axis of its orbit be? Give reasons for your answer.

8. The period of the moon's rotation about Earth is 2.36055×10^6 sec. About how far away is the moon?

9. A satellite moves around Earth in a circular orbit. Express the satellite's speed as a function of the orbit's radius.

10. If T is measured in seconds and a in meters, what is the value of T^2/a^3 for planets in our solar system? for satellites orbiting Earth? for satellites orbiting the moon? (The moon's mass is 7.354×10^{22} kg.)

NONCALCULATOR EXERCISES

11. For what values of v_0 in Eq. (16) is the orbit in Eq. (17) a circle? an ellipse? a parabola? a hyperbola?

12. Show that a planet in a circular orbit moves with a constant speed. (*Hint:* This is a consequence of one of Kepler's laws.)

Writing for Your Own Knowledge

Answer the following questions in writing. Some answers will take only a sentence or two; others may require several paragraphs. Some explanations may also call for graphs or sketches.

1. State Kepler's laws. To what do they apply?

2. Why do planets move in planes?

For Your Review

Write brief paragraphs about the following topics and give examples.

Position vector
Vector-valued function; component function
Limits and continuity of vector functions
Derivatives and integrals of vector functions
Smooth curve; piecewise-smooth curve
Tangent vectors and tangent lines
Velocity, speed, direction of motion, and acceleration
Equations for ideal projectile motion
Arc length parameter; length of a space curve
Unit tangent vector
Principal unit normal vector
Curvature
Circle and radius of curvature
Binormal vector
Torsion
Tangential and normal components of acceleration
Kepler's laws

Practice Exercises

Graph the curves in Exercises 1 and 2, and sketch their velocity and acceleration vectors at the given values of t.

1. $\mathbf{r} = (4\cos t)\,\mathbf{i} + (\sqrt{2}\sin t)\,\mathbf{j}, \quad t = 0$ and $\pi/4$

2. $\mathbf{r} = (\sqrt{3}\sec t)\,\mathbf{i} + (\sqrt{3}\tan t)\,\mathbf{j}, \quad t = 0$ and $\pi/6$

Evaluate the integrals in Exercises 3 and 4.

3. $\displaystyle\int_0^1 [(3 + 6t)\,\mathbf{i} + (4 + 8t)\,\mathbf{j} + (6\pi\cos \pi t)\,\mathbf{k}]\,dt$

4. $\displaystyle\int_e^{e^2} \left[\frac{2\ln t}{t}\,\mathbf{i} + \frac{1}{t\ln t}\,\mathbf{j} + \frac{1}{t}\,\mathbf{k}\right] dt$

Solve the initial value problems in Exercises 5–8.

5. $\dfrac{d\mathbf{r}}{dt} = -(\sin t)\,\mathbf{i} + (\cos t)\,\mathbf{j} + \mathbf{k}, \quad \mathbf{r} = \mathbf{j}$ when $t = 0$

6. $\dfrac{d\mathbf{r}}{dt} = \dfrac{1}{t^2+1}\,\mathbf{i} - \dfrac{1}{\sqrt{1-t^2}}\,\mathbf{j} + \dfrac{t}{\sqrt{t^2+1}}\,\mathbf{k}, \quad \mathbf{r} = \mathbf{j} + \mathbf{k}$ when $t = 0$

7. $\dfrac{d^2\mathbf{r}}{dt^2} = 2\,\mathbf{j}, \quad \dfrac{d\mathbf{r}}{dt} = \mathbf{k}$ and $\mathbf{r} = \mathbf{i}$ when $t = 0$

8. $\dfrac{d^2\mathbf{r}}{dt^2} = -2\,\mathbf{i} - 4\,\mathbf{j}, \quad \dfrac{d\mathbf{r}}{dt} = 4\,\mathbf{i}$ and $\mathbf{r} = 3\,\mathbf{i} + 3\,\mathbf{j}$ when $t = 1$

Find the lengths of the curves in Exercises 9 and 10.

9. $\mathbf{r} = (2\cos t)\,\mathbf{i} + (2\sin t)\,\mathbf{j} + t^2\,\mathbf{k}, \quad 0 \le t \le \pi/4$

10. $\mathbf{r} = (3\cos t)\,\mathbf{i} + (3\sin t)\,\mathbf{j} + 2t^{3/2}\,\mathbf{k}, \quad 0 \le t \le 3$

In Exercises 11–14, find **T**, **N**, **B**, κ, and τ at the given value of t.

11. $\mathbf{r} = \frac{4}{9}(1+t)^{3/2}\,\mathbf{i} + \frac{4}{9}(1-t)^{3/2}\,\mathbf{j} + \frac{1}{3}t\,\mathbf{k}, \quad t = 0$

12. $\mathbf{r} = (e^t\sin 2t)\,\mathbf{i} + (e^t\cos 2t)\,\mathbf{j} + 2e^t\,\mathbf{k}, \quad t = 0$

13. $\mathbf{r} = t\,\mathbf{i} + \frac{1}{2}e^{2t}\,\mathbf{j}, \quad t = \ln 2$

14. $\mathbf{r} = (3\cosh 2t)\,\mathbf{i} + (3\sinh 2t)\,\mathbf{j} + 6t\,\mathbf{k}, \quad t = \ln 2$

In Exercises 15 and 16, write **a** in the form $\mathbf{a} = a_{\mathrm{T}}\,\mathbf{T} + a_{\mathrm{N}}\,\mathbf{N}$ at $t = 0$ without finding **T** and **N**.

15. $\mathbf{r} = (2 + 3t + 3t^2)\,\mathbf{i} + (4t + 4t^2)\,\mathbf{j} - (6\cos t)\,\mathbf{k}$

16. $\mathbf{r} = (2 + t)\,\mathbf{i} + (t + 2t^2)\,\mathbf{j} + (1 + t^2)\,\mathbf{k}$

17. Find **T**, **N**, **B**, κ, and τ as functions of t if $\mathbf{r} = (\sin t)\,\mathbf{i} + (\sqrt{2}\cos t)\,\mathbf{j} + (\sin t)\,\mathbf{k}$.

18. The position of a particle in the plane at time t is

$$\mathbf{r} = \frac{1}{\sqrt{1+t^2}}\,\mathbf{i} + \frac{t}{\sqrt{1+t^2}}\,\mathbf{j}.$$

Find the particle's highest speed.

19. Suppose $\mathbf{r} = (e^t\cos\, t)\,\mathbf{i} + (e^t\sin\, t)\,\mathbf{j}$. Show that the angle between $\mathbf{r}$ and $\mathbf{a}$ never changes. What *is* the angle?

20. At what times in the interval $0 \le t \le \pi$ are the velocity and acceleration vectors of the motion $\mathbf{r} = \mathbf{i} + (5\cos t)\,\mathbf{j} + (3\sin t)\,\mathbf{k}$ orthogonal?

21. The position of a particle moving in space at time $t \ge 0$ is

$$\mathbf{r} = 2\,\mathbf{i} + \left(4\sin\frac{t}{2}\right)\mathbf{j} + \left(3 - \frac{t}{\pi}\right)\mathbf{k}.$$

Find the first time $\mathbf{r}$ is orthogonal to the vector $\mathbf{i} - \mathbf{j}$.

22. *Shot Put.* A shot leaves the thrower's hand 8 ft above the ground at a 45° angle at 44 ft/sec. Where is it 3 sec later?

23. *Javelin.* A javelin leaves the thrower's hand 7 ft above the ground at a 45° angle at 80 ft/sec. How high does it go?

24. *The Dictator.* The Civil War mortar Dictator weighed so much (17,120 lb) that it had to be mounted on a railroad car. It had a 13-in. bore and used a 20-lb powder charge to fire a 200-lb shell. The mortar was made by Mr. Charles Knapp in his ironworks in Pittsburgh, Pennsylvania, and was used by the Union army in 1864 in the siege of Petersburg, Virginia. How far did it shoot? Here we have a difference of opinion. The ordnance manual claimed 4325 yd, while field officers claimed 4752 yd. Assuming a 45° firing angle, what muzzle speeds are involved here?

25. *The World's Record for Popping a Champagne Cork.* The world's record for popping a champagne cork is 109 ft. 6 in., held by Captain Michael Hill of the British Royal Artillery (of course). Assuming Cpt. Hill held the bottle neck at ground level at a 45° angle, and the cork behaved like an ideal projectile, how fast was the cork going as it left the bottle?

26. *Javelin.* In Potsdam in 1988, Petra Felke of (then) East Germany set a women's world record by throwing a javelin 262 ft 5 in.

a) Assuming that Felke launched the javelin at a 40° angle to the horizontal 6.5 ft above the ground, what was the javelin's initial speed?

b) How high did the javelin go?

27. Find parametric equations for the line that is tangent to the curve $\mathbf{r} = e^t\,\mathbf{i} + (\sin\, t)\,\mathbf{j} + \ln\,(1-t)\,\mathbf{k}$ at $t = 0$.

28. Find parametric equations for the line tangent to the helix $\mathbf{r} = \left(\sqrt{2}\,\cos\, t\right)\mathbf{i} + \left(\sqrt{2}\,\sin\, t\right)\mathbf{j} + t\,\mathbf{k}$ at the point where $t = \pi/4$.

29. At point P, the velocity and acceleration of a particle moving in the plane are $\mathbf{v} = 3\,\mathbf{i} + 4\,\mathbf{j}$ and $\mathbf{a} = 5\,\mathbf{i} + 15\,\mathbf{j}$. Find the curvature of the particle's path at P.

30. Find the normal plane of the curve $\mathbf{r} = t\,\mathbf{i} + t\,\mathbf{j} + (2/3)t^{3/2}\,\mathbf{k}$ at the point $(1, 1, 2/3)$ (the plane of $\mathbf{B}$ and $\mathbf{N}$).

31. *The View from Skylab 4.* What percentage of Earth's surface area could the astronauts see when *Skylab 4* was at its apogee height, 437 km above the surface? To find out, model the visible surface as the surface generated by revolving the circular arc GT, shown here, about the y-axis. Then carry out these steps:

1. Use similar triangles in the figure to show that $y_0/6380 = 6380/(6380 + 437)$. Solve for y_0.
2. Calculate the visible area as
$$VA = \int_{y_0}^{6380} 2\pi x\,\sqrt{1 + \left(\frac{dx}{dy}\right)^2}\,dy.$$
3. Express the result as a percentage of Earth's surface area.

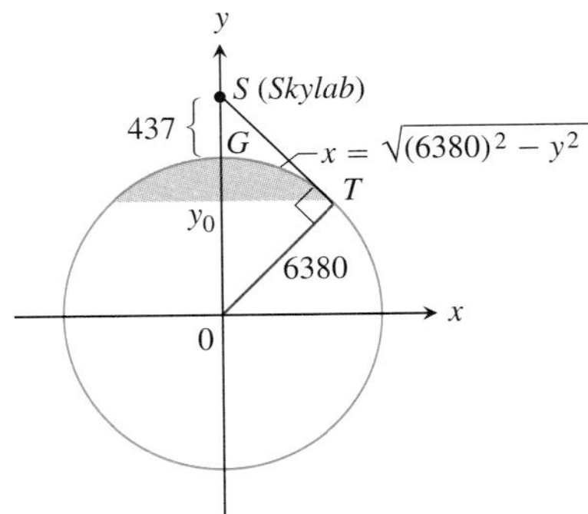

32. Deduce from the orbit equation

$$r = \frac{(1+e)r_0}{1 + e\cos\theta}$$

that a planet is closest to its sun when $\theta = 0$ and show that $r = r_0$ at that time.

33. *A Kepler Equation.* The problem of locating a planet in its orbit at a given time and date eventually leads to solving "Kepler" equations of the form

$$f(x) = x - 1 - \frac{1}{2}\sin x = 0.$$

a) Show that this particular equation has a solution between $x = 0$ and $x = 2$.
b) With your computer or calculator in radian mode, use Newton's method to find the solution to as many places as you can.

34. In Section 12.5, we found the velocity vector of a particle moving in a plane to be

$$\mathbf{v} = \frac{d\mathbf{r}}{dt} = \frac{dx}{dt}\mathbf{i} + \frac{dy}{dt}\mathbf{j}$$
$$= \frac{dr}{dt}\mathbf{u}_r + r\frac{d\theta}{dt}\mathbf{u}_\theta.$$

a) Express dx/dt and dy/dt in terms of dr/dt and $r\,d\theta/dt$ by computing $\mathbf{v}\cdot\mathbf{i}$ and $\mathbf{v}\cdot\mathbf{j}$.
b) Express dr/dt and $r\,d\theta/dt$ in terms of dx/dt and dy/dt by computing $\mathbf{v}\cdot\mathbf{u}_r$ and $\mathbf{v}\cdot\mathbf{u}_\theta$.

AIR DUCT SEALS

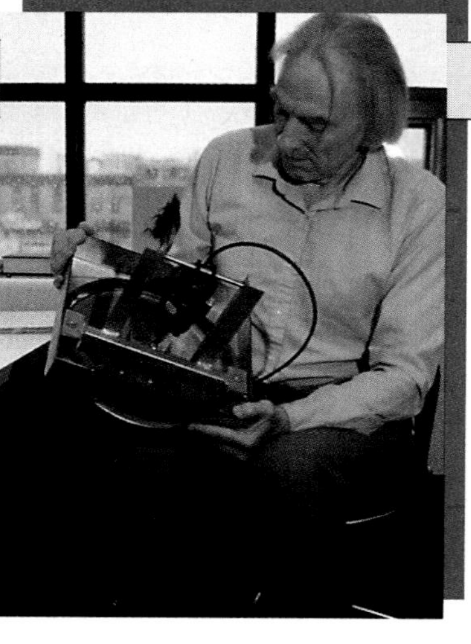

HERBERT WILLKE, an engineer at MITCO Corporation in East Boston, MA, designs dampers that can open and seal air ducts 3 ft in diameter in a fraction of a second.

Dampers like these are used to regulate ventilation in large buildings. They can also be installed as safety seals that can snap shut to prevent hazardous fumes from entering a building's air supply in the event of a fire or industrial accident. The damper is opened by a pneumatic piston that pops the damper up a few inches and then rotates it to a fully open position. A critical design variable is the height to which the damper must be lifted to ensure clearing the opening during rotation.

The height must provide adequate clearance, but not sacrifice speed and compactness. Another important variable is the distance from the piston's line of action to the damper's axis of rotation. The axis moves as the damper opens and the linkages controlling the damper's position must provide the proper distance at all times.

If the distance is too great at the beginning, the damper will rotate too soon. If the distance is too small toward the end, the damper may jam before it is fully rotated.

The height and distance variables are functions of eight other variables (locations of pivots, lengths of linkage bars) whose values must be chosen to minimize unwanted variation. The chosen values are, of course, ideal and cannot be produced exactly during manufacture. So Dr. Willke must also find out how sensitive the height and distance are to deviations from these ideal values and tell the manufacturer how much variation can be tolerated in machining each piece.

Ideal values and tolerances like these are found with partial derivatives, as you will see in Sections 13.4 and 13.7.

13 Partial Derivatives

OVERVIEW

Functions with two or more independent variables appear more often in science than functions of a single variable, and their calculus is even richer. Their derivatives are more varied and more interesting because of the different ways in which the variables can interact. Their integrals lead to a greater variety of applications. The studies of probability, statistics, fluid dynamics, and electricity, to mention only a few, all lead in natural ways to functions of more than one variable, and the mathematical analysis associated with these functions is one of the finest achievements in science.

13.1 Functions of Several Independent Variables

The values of many functions are determined by more than one independent variable. The function $V = \pi r^2 h$ calculates the volume of a right circular cylinder from its radius and height. The function $f(x, y) = x^2 + y^2$ calculates the height of the paraboloid $z = x^2 + y^2$ above the point $P(x, y)$ from the two coordinates of P. In this section, we define functions of more than one independent variable and discuss two ways to graph their values.

Functions and Variables

Real-valued functions of several independent real variables are defined much the way you would imagine from the single-variable case. The domains are sets of ordered pairs (triples, quadruples, whatever) of real numbers, and the ranges are sets of real numbers of the kind we have worked with all along.

DEFINITIONS

Suppose D is a set of n-tuples of real numbers $(x_1, x_2, \ldots, x_n)$. A **real-valued function** f on D is a rule that assigns a real number

$$w = f(x_1, x_2, \ldots, x_n)$$

to each element in D. The set D is the function's **domain.** The set of w-values taken on by f is the function's **range.** The symbol w is the **dependent variable** of f, and f is said to be a function of the n **independent variables** x_1 to x_n. We also call the x's the function's **input variables** and call w the function's **output variable.**

If f is a function of two independent variables, we usually call the independent variables x and y and picture the domain of f as a region in the xy-plane. If f is a function of three independent variables, we call the variables x, y, and z and picture the domain as a region in space.

When functions of more than one variable arise in applications, we tend to use letters that remind us of what the variables stand for. To say that the volume of a right circular cylinder is a function of its radius and height, we might write $V = f(r, h)$. To be more specific, we might replace the notation $f(r, h)$ by the formula that calculates the value of V from the values of r and h, and write $V = \pi r^2 h$. In either case, r and h would be the independent variables and V the dependent variable of the function.

As usual, we evaluate functions defined by formulas by substituting the values of the independent variables in the formula and calculating the corresponding value of the dependent variable.

EXAMPLE 1 The value of the function $f(x, y, z) = \sqrt{x^2 + y^2 + z^2}$ at the point (3, 0, 4) is

$$f(3, 0, 4) = \sqrt{(3)^2 + (0)^2 + (4)^2} = \sqrt{25} = 5.$$

Domains

In defining functions of more than one variable, we follow the usual practice of excluding inputs that lead to complex numbers or division by zero. If $f(x, y) = \sqrt{y - x^2}$, we do not allow y to be less than x^2. If $f(x, y) = 1/xy$, we do not allow xy to be zero.

These are the only restrictions, however, and the domains of functions are otherwise assumed to be the largest sets for which the defining rules generate real numbers.

EXAMPLE 2 *Functions of Two Variables*

Function	Domain	Range
$w = \sqrt{y - x^2}$	$y \geq x^2$	$w \geq 0$
$w = \dfrac{1}{xy}$	$xy \neq 0$	$w \neq 0$
$w = \sin xy$	Entire plane	$-1 \leq w \leq 1$
$w = -\dfrac{1}{x^2 + y^2}$	$(x, y) \neq (0, 0)$	$-\infty < w < 0$

EXAMPLE 3 *Functions of Three Variables*

Function	Domain	Range
$w = \sqrt{x^2 + y^2 + z^2}$	Entire space	$w \geq 0$
$w = \dfrac{1}{x^2 + y^2 + z^2}$	$(x, y, z) \neq (0, 0, 0)$	$0 < w < \infty$
$w = xy \ln z$	Half-space $z > 0$	$-\infty < w < \infty$

The domains of functions defined on portions of the plane can have interior points and boundary points just the way the domains of functions defined on intervals of the real line can.

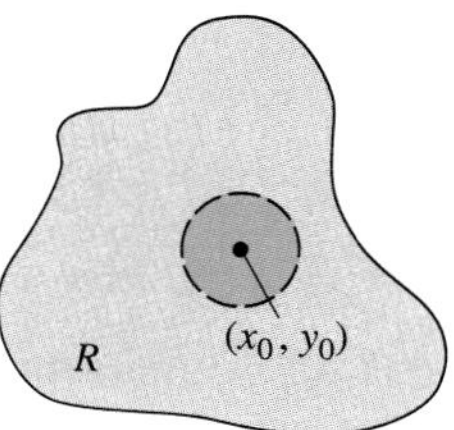

(a) Interior point

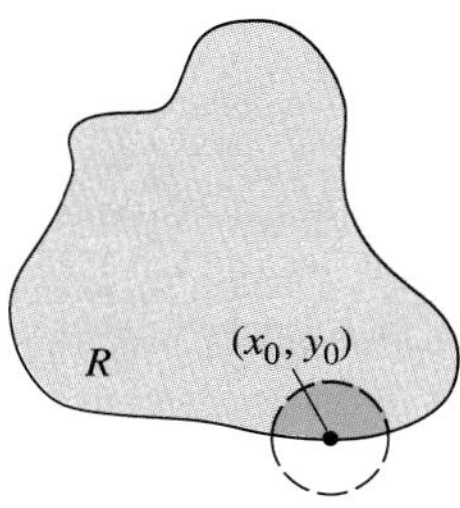

(b) Boundary point

13.1 Interior points and boundary points of a plane region R. An interior point is necessarily a point of R. A boundary point of R need not belong to R.

DEFINITIONS

A point (x_0, y_0) in a region (set) R in the xy-plane is an **interior point** of R if it is the center of a disk that lies entirely in R (Fig. 13.1). A point (x_0, y_0) is a **boundary point** of R if every disk centered at (x_0, y_0) contains points that lie outside of R as well as points that lie in R. (The boundary point itself need not belong to R.)

The interior points of a region, as a set, make up the **interior** of the region. The region's boundary points make up its **boundary**. A region is **open** if it consists entirely of interior points. A region is **closed** if it contains all of its boundary points (Fig. 13.2).

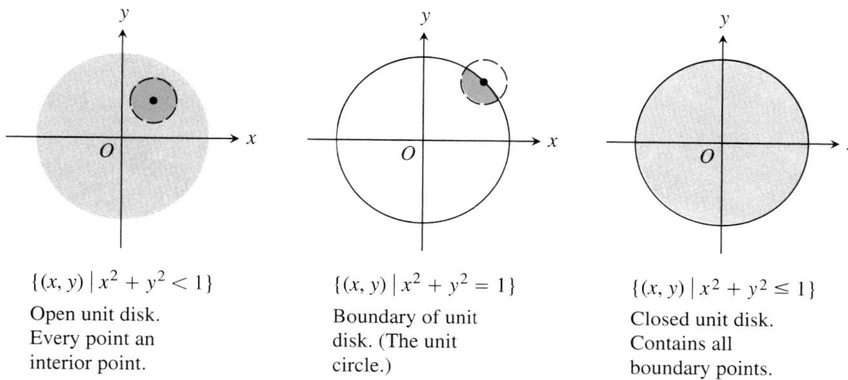

$\{(x, y) \mid x^2 + y^2 < 1\}$ Open unit disk. Every point an interior point.

$\{(x, y) \mid x^2 + y^2 = 1\}$ Boundary of unit disk. (The unit circle.)

$\{(x, y) \mid x^2 + y^2 \leq 1\}$ Closed unit disk. Contains all boundary points.

13.2 Interior points and boundary points of the unit disk in the plane.

As with intervals of real numbers, some regions in the plane are neither open nor closed. If you start with the open disk in Fig. 13.2 and add to it some but not all of its boundary points, the resulting set is neither open nor closed. The boundary points that *are* there keep the set from being open. The absence of the remaining boundary points keeps the set from being closed.

DEFINITIONS

A region in the plane is **bounded** if it lies inside a disk of fixed radius. A region is **unbounded** if it is not bounded.

EXAMPLE 4

Bounded sets in the plane:	Line segments, triangles, interiors of triangles, rectangles, disks
Unbounded sets in the plane:	Lines, coordinate axes, the graphs of functions defined on infinite intervals, quadrants, half-planes, the plane itself

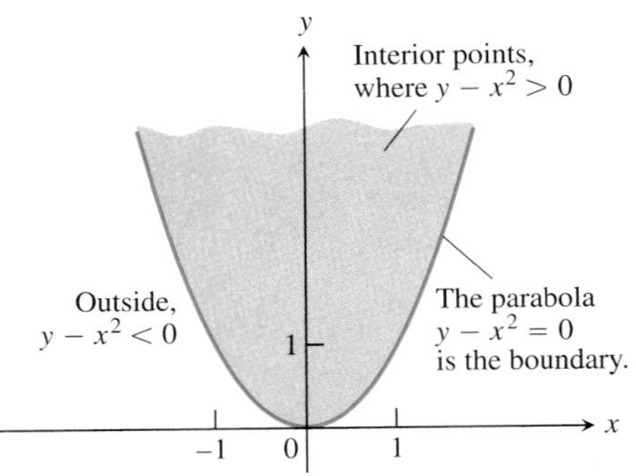

13.3 The domain of $f(x, y) = \sqrt{y - x^2}$ consists of the shaded region and its bounding parabola $y = x^2$.

EXAMPLE 5

The domain of the function $f(x, y) = \sqrt{y - x^2}$ is closed and unbounded (Fig. 13.3). The parabola $y = x^2$ is the boundary of the domain. The points above the parabola make up the domain's interior.

The definitions of interior, boundary, open, closed, bounded, and unbounded for regions in space are similar to those for regions in the plane. To accommodate the extra dimension, we use balls instead of disks. A **closed ball** consists of the region of points inside a sphere together with the sphere. An **open ball** is the region of points inside a sphere without the bounding sphere.

DEFINITIONS

A point (x_0, y_0, z_0) in a region D in space is an **interior point** of D if it is the center of a ball that lies entirely in D (Fig. 13.4). A point (x_0, y_0, z_0) is a **boundary point** of D if every sphere centered at (x_0, y_0, z_0) encloses points that lie outside D as well as points that lie inside D. The **interior** of D is the set of interior points of D. The **boundary** of D is the set of boundary points of D.

A region D is **open** if it consists entirely of interior points. A region is **closed** if it contains its entire boundary.

EXAMPLE 6

Open sets in space:	Open balls; the open half-space $z > 0$; the first octant (bounding planes absent); space itself
Closed sets in space:	Lines; planes; closed balls; the closed half-space $z \geq 0$; the first octant together with its bounding planes; space itself
Neither open nor closed:	A closed ball with part of its bounding sphere removed; solid cube with a missing face, edge, or corner point

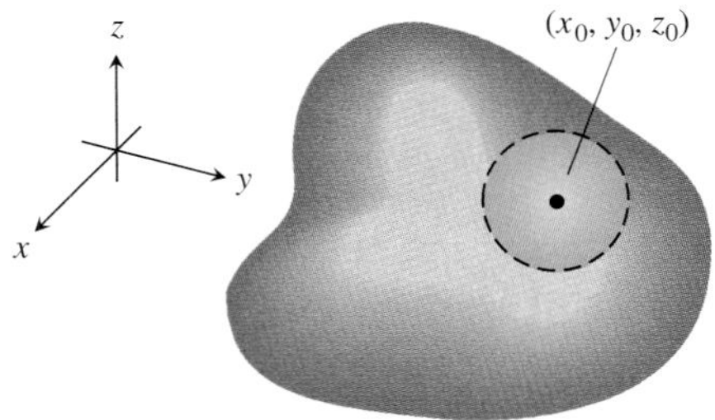

(a) Interior point

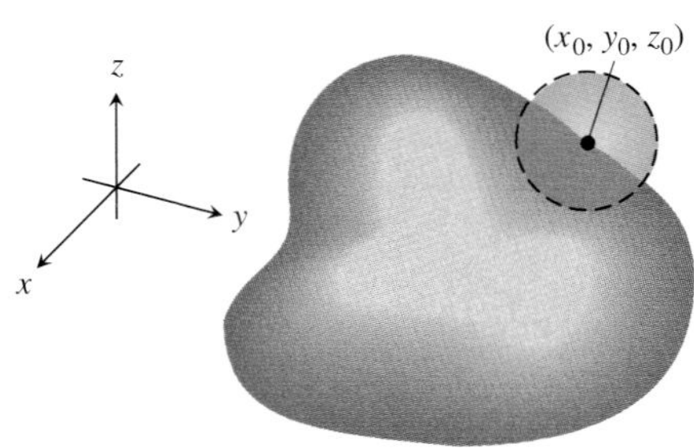

(b) Boundary point

13.4 Interior points and boundary points of a region in space.

Graphs and Level Curves of Functions of Two Variables

There are two standard ways to picture the values of a function $f(x, y)$. One is to draw and label curves in the domain on which f has a constant value. The other is to sketch the surface $z = f(x, y)$ in space.

DEFINITIONS

The set of points in the plane where a function $f(x, y)$ has a constant value $f(x, y) = c$ is called a **level curve** of f. The set of all points $(x, y, f(x, y))$ in space, for (x, y) in the domain of f, is called the **graph** of f. The graph of f is also called the **surface $z = f(x, y)$.**

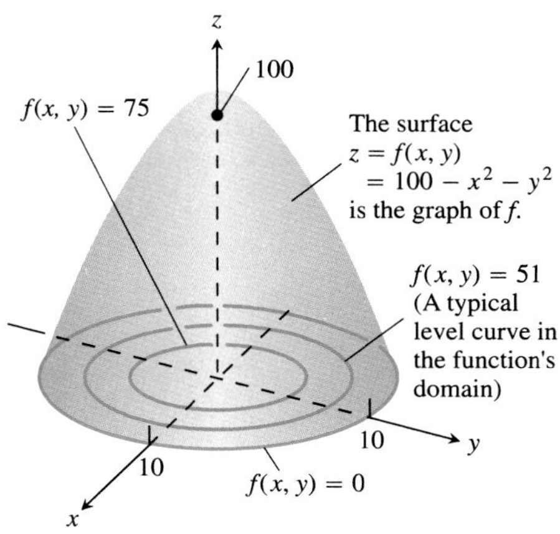

13.5 The graph and selected level curves of the function $f(x, y) = 100 - x^2 - y^2$.

EXAMPLE 7 Graph the function $f(x, y) = 100 - x^2 - y^2$ in space and plot the level curves $f(x, y) = 0$, $f(x, y) = 51$, and $f(x, y) = 75$ in the domain of f in the plane.

Solution The domain of f is the entire xy-plane, and the range of f is the set of real numbers less than or equal to 100. The graph is the paraboloid $z = 100 - x^2 - y^2$, a portion of which is shown in Fig. 13.5.

The level curve $f(x, y) = 0$ is the set of points in the xy-plane at which

$$f(x, y) = 100 - x^2 - y^2 = 0, \qquad \text{or} \qquad x^2 + y^2 = 100,$$

which is the circle of radius 10 centered at the origin (Fig. 13.5). Similarly, the level curves $f(x, y) = 51$ and $f(x, y) = 75$ are the circles

$$f(x, y) = 100 - x^2 - y^2 = 51, \qquad \text{or} \qquad x^2 + y^2 = 49,$$
$$f(x, y) = 100 - x^2 - y^2 = 75, \qquad \text{or} \qquad x^2 + y^2 = 25.$$

The level curve $f(x, y) = 100$ consists of the origin alone. (It is still called a level curve.)

Contour Lines

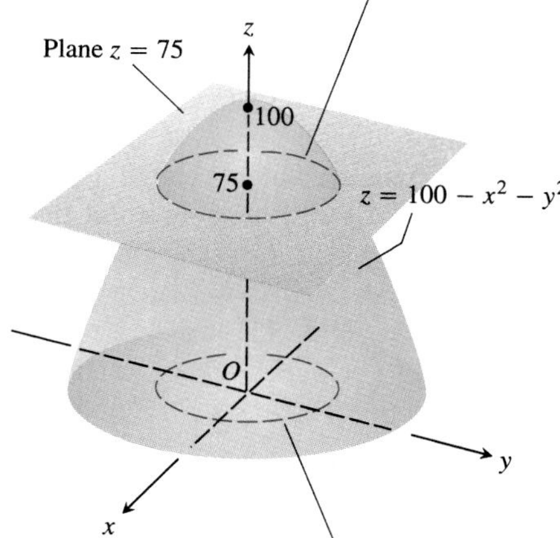

13.6 The graph of $f(x, y) = 100 - x^2 - y^2$ and its intersection with the plane $z = 75$.

The curve in space in which the plane $z = c$ cuts a surface $z = f(x, y)$ is made up of the points that represent the function value $f(x, y) = c$. It is called the **contour line** $f(x, y) = c$ to distinguish it from the level curve $f(x, y) = c$ in the domain of f. Figure 13.6 shows the contour line $f(x, y) = 75$ on the surface $z = 100 - x^2 - y^2$ defined by the function $f(x, y) = 100 - x^2 - y^2$. The contour line lies directly above the circle $x^2 + y^2 = 25$, which is the level curve $f(x, y) = 75$ in the function's domain.

Not everyone makes this distinction, however, and you may wish to call both kinds of curves by a single name and rely on context to convey which one you have in mind. On most maps, for example, the curves that represent constant elevation (height above sea level) are called contours, not level curves (Fig. 13.7).

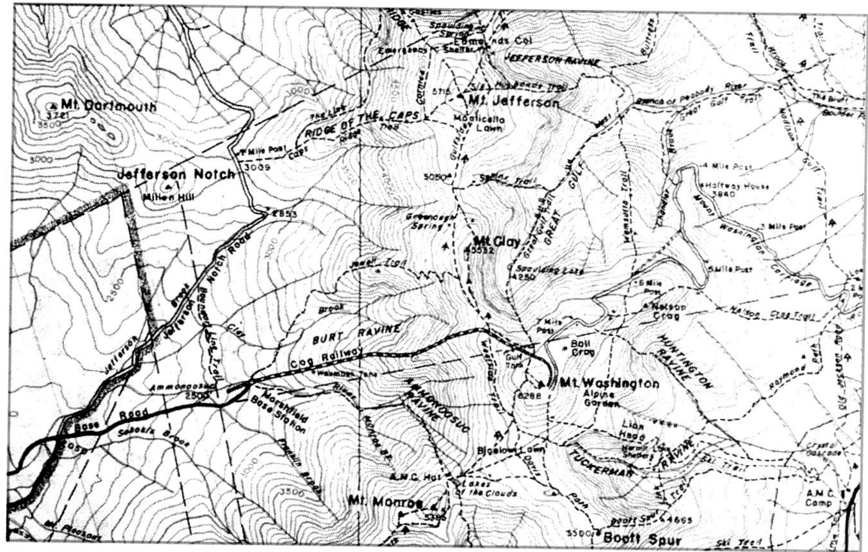

13.7 Contours on Mt. Washington in north-central New Hampshire. The streams, which follow paths of steepest descent, run perpendicular to the contours. So does the Cog Railway.

Level Surfaces of Functions of Three Variables

In the plane, the points at which a function of two independent variables has a constant value $f(x, y) = c$ make a curve in the function's domain. In space, the points where a function of three independent variables has a constant value $f(x, y, z) = c$ make a surface in the function's domain.

DEFINITION

The set of points (x, y, z) in space where a function of three independent variables has a constant value $f(x, y, z) = c$ is called a **level surface** of f.

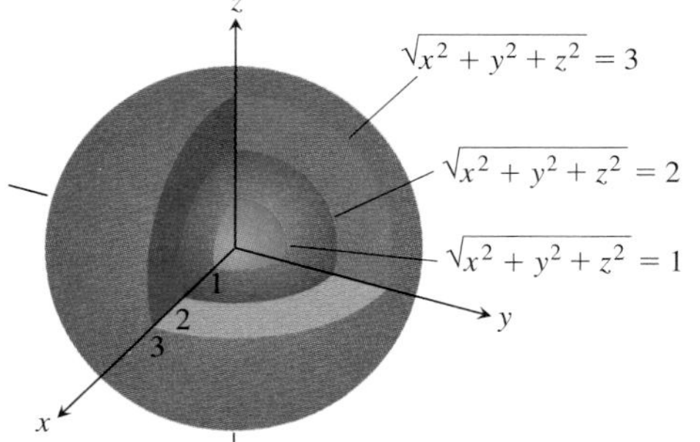

13.8 The level surfaces of $f(x, y, z) = \sqrt{x^2 + y^2 + z^2}$ are concentric spheres.

EXAMPLE 8 Describe the level surfaces of the function

$$f(x, y, z) = \sqrt{x^2 + y^2 + z^2}.$$

Solution The value of f is the distance from the origin to the point (x, y, z). Each level surface $\sqrt{x^2 + y^2 + z^2} = c$, $c > 0$, is a sphere of radius c centered at the origin. Figure 13.8 shows a cutaway view of three of these spheres. The level surface $\sqrt{x^2 + y^2 + z^2} = 0$ consists of the origin alone.

We are not graphing the function here. The graph of the function, made up of the points $(x, y, z, \sqrt{x^2 + y^2 + z^2})$, lies in a four-variable space. Instead, we are looking at level surfaces in the function's domain.

The function's level surfaces show how the function's values change as we move through its domain. If we remain on a sphere of radius c centered at the origin, the function maintains a constant value, namely c. If we move from one sphere to another, the function's value changes. It increases if we move away from the origin and decreases if we move toward the origin. The way the function's values change depends on the direction we take. The dependence of change on direction is important. We will return to it in Section 13.6.

Computer Graphing

The three-dimensional graphing programs for computers make it possible to graph functions of two variables with only a few keystrokes. We can often get information more quickly from a graph than we can from a formula.

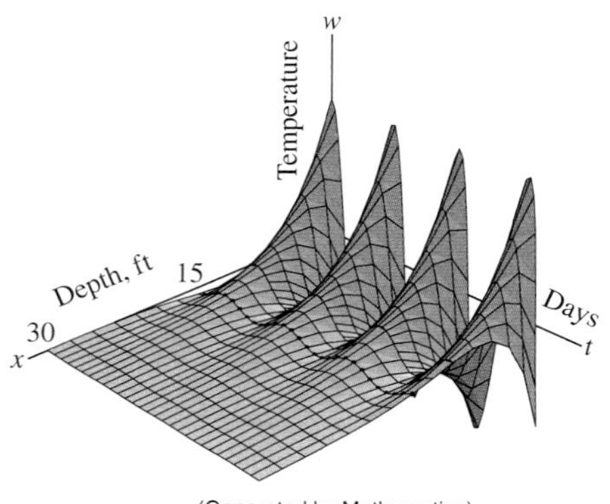

13.9 This computer-generated graph of

$$w = \cos(1.7 \times 10^{-2} t - 0.2x) e^{-0.2x}$$

shows the seasonal variation of the temperature below ground as a fraction of surface temperature. At $x = 15$ ft the variation is only 5% of the variation at the surface. At $x = 30$ ft the variation is less than 0.25% of the surface variation. (Adapted from art provided by Norton Starr for G. C. Berresford's "Differential Equations and Root Cellars," *The UMAP Journal*, Vol. 2, No. 3, [1981], pp. 53–75.)

EXAMPLE 9 Figure 13.9 shows a computer-generated graph of the function $w = \cos(1.7 \times 10^{-2} t - 0.2x) e^{-0.2x}$, where t is in days and x is in feet. The graph shows how the temperature beneath the earth's surface varies with time. The variation is given as a fraction of the variation at the surface. At a depth of 15 ft, the variation (change in vertical amplitude in the figure) is about 5 percent of the surface variation. At 30 ft, there is almost no variation in temperature during the year.

Another thing the graph shows that is not immediately apparent from the equation for f is that the temperature 15 ft below the surface is about half a year out of phase with the surface temperature. When the temperature is lowest on the surface (late January, say) it is at its highest 15 ft below. Fifteen feet below the ground, the seasons are reversed.

Exercises 13.1

In Exercises 1–8, find the function's domain and range and describe its level curves.

1. $f(x, y) = y - x$
2. $f(x, y) = \sqrt{y - x}$
3. $f(x, y) = \ln(x^2 + y^2)$
4. $f(x, y) = e^{-(x^2 + y^2)}$
5. $f(x, y) = xy$
6. $f(x, y) = y/x^2$
7. $f(x, y) = 4x^2 + 9y^2$
8. $f(x, y) = x^2 - y^2$

Exercises 17–22 show level curves for the functions graphed in (a)–(f). Match each set of curves with the appropriate function.

17.

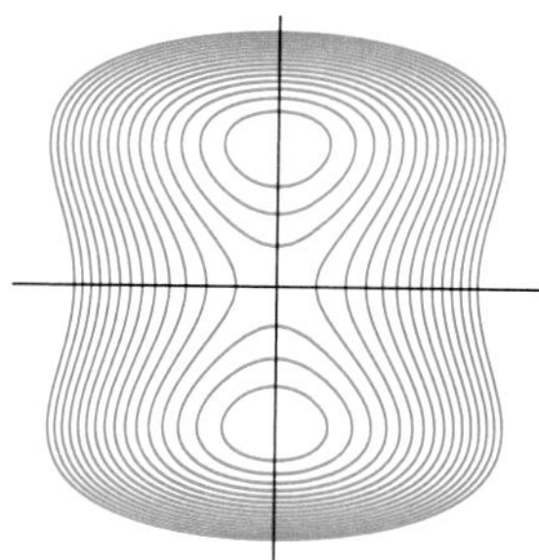

18.

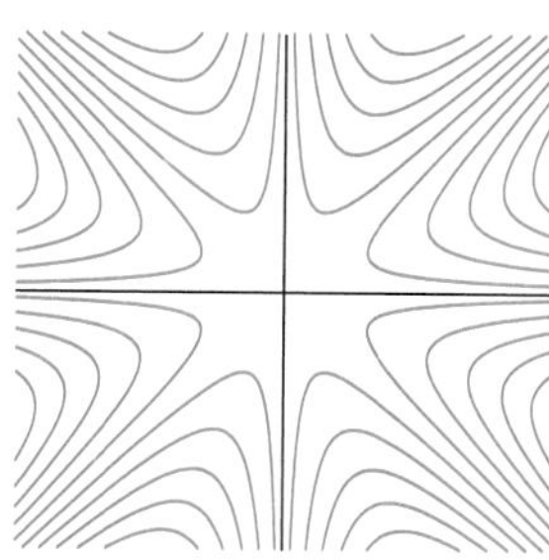

19.

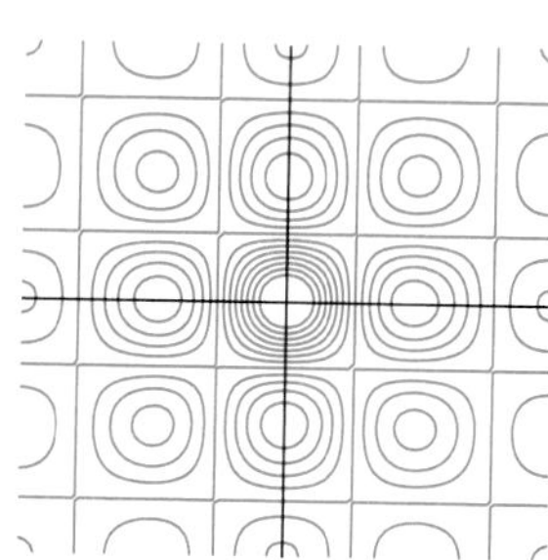

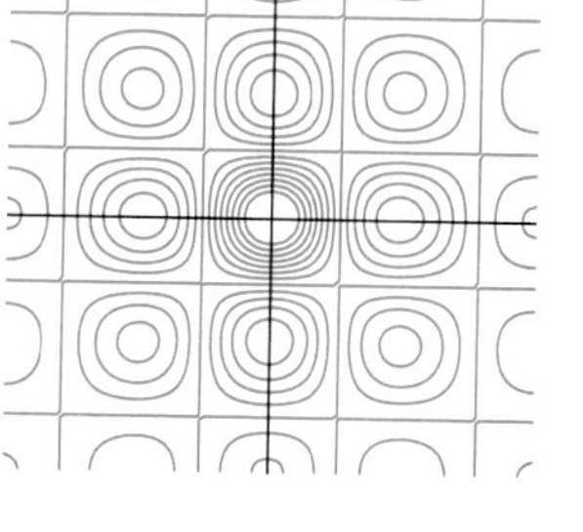

20.

21.

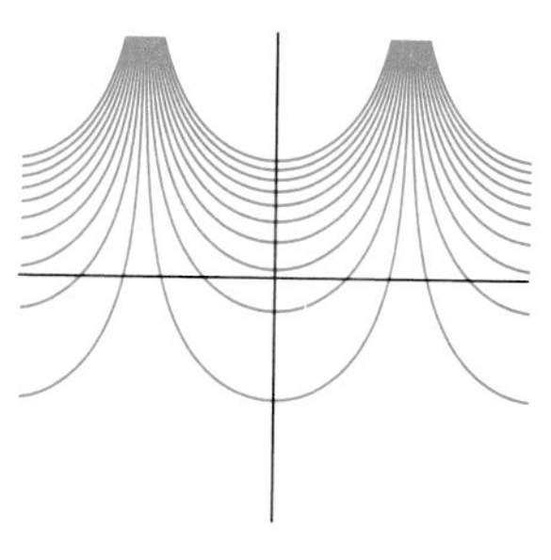

22.

Display the values of the functions in Exercises 9–16 in two ways: (a) by sketching the surface $z = f(x, y)$ and (b) by drawing an assortment of level curves in the function's domain. Label each level curve with its function value.

9. $f(x, y) = y^2$
10. $f(x, y) = 4 - y^2$
11. $f(x, y) = x^2 + y^2$
12. $f(x, y) = \sqrt{x^2 + y^2}$
13. $f(x, y) = -(x^2 + y^2)$
14. $f(x, y) = 4 - x^2 - y^2$
15. $f(x, y) = 4x^2 + y^2$
16. $f(x, y) = 4x^2 + y^2 + 1$

(a)

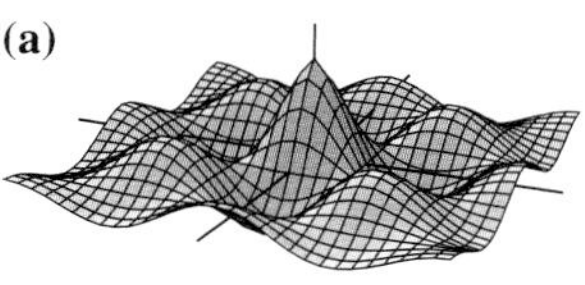

$z = (\cos x)(\cos y)\, e^{-\sqrt{x^2 + y^2}/4}$

(b)

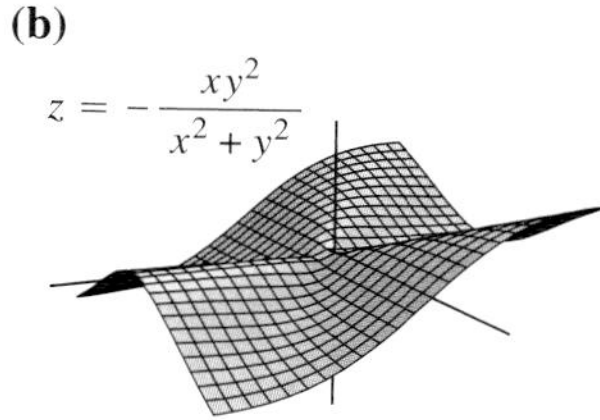

$z = -\dfrac{xy^2}{x^2 + y^2}$

(c)

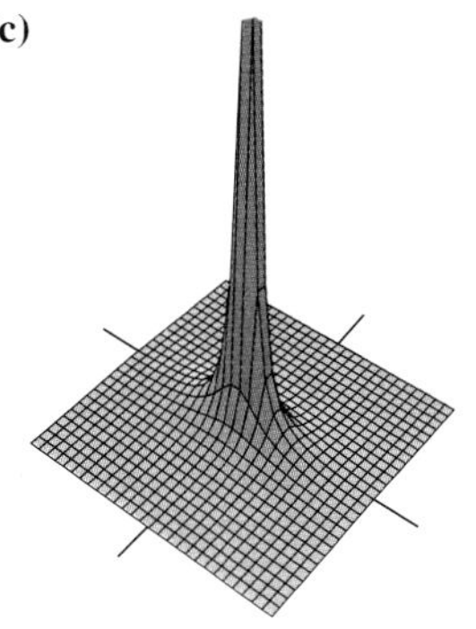

$z = \dfrac{1}{(4x^2 + y^2)}$

(d)

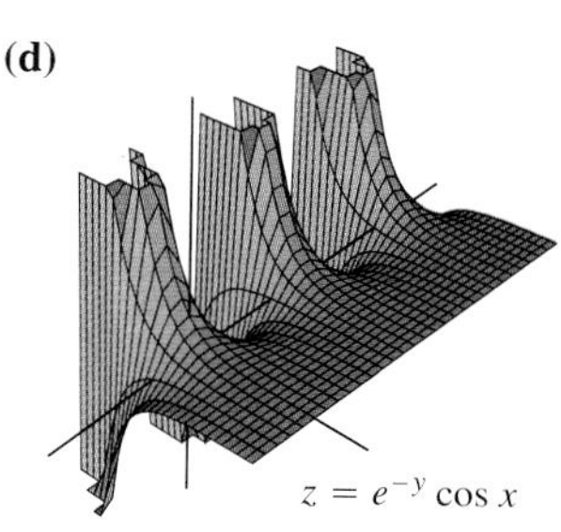

$z = e^{-y} \cos x$

(e)

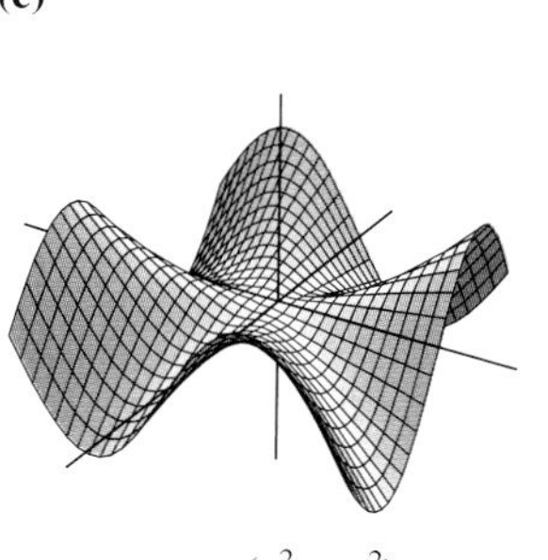

$z = \dfrac{xy(x^2 - y^2)}{(x^2 + y^2)}$

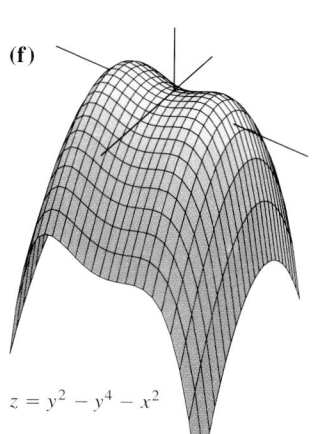

(f)

$z = y^2 - y^4 - x^2$

In Exercises 23–30, sketch a typical level surface for the function.

23. $f(x, y, z) = x^2 + y^2 + z^2$

24. $f(x, y, z) = \ln(x^2 + y^2 + z^2)$

25. $f(x, y, z) = x + z$

26. $f(x, y, z) = z$

27. $f(x, y, z) = x^2 + y^2$

28. $f(x, y, z) = y^2 + z^2$

29. $f(x, y, z) = z - x^2 - y^2$

30. $f(x, y, z) = (x^2/25) + (y^2/16) + (z^2/9)$

In Exercises 31 and 32, find an equation for the level curve of f through the given point.

31. $f(x, y) = 16 - x^2 - y^2, \quad (2\sqrt{2}, 2\sqrt{2})$

32. $f(x, y) = \sqrt{x^2 - 1}, \quad (1, 0)$

In Exercises 33 and 34, find an equation for the level surface of f through the given point.

33. $f(x, y, z) = \sqrt{x - y} - \ln z, \quad (3, -1, 1)$

34. $f(x, y, z) = \ln(x^2 + y + z^2), \quad (-1, 2, 1)$

35. *The Maximum Value of a Function on a Line in Space.* Does the function $f(x, y, z) = xyz$ have a maximum value on the line $x = 20 - t$, $y = t$, $z = 20$? If so, what is it? Give reasons for your answer. (*Hint:* Along the line, $w = f(x, y, z)$ is a differentiable function of t.)

36. *The Minimum Value of a Function on a Line in Space.* Does the function $f(x, y, z) = xy - z$ have a minimum value on the line $x = t - 1$, $y = t - 2$, $z = t + 7$? If so, what is it? Give reasons for your answer. (*Hint:* Along the line, $w = f(x, y, z)$ is a differentiable function of t.)

37. *The Concorde's Sonic Booms.* The width w of the region in which people on the ground hear the *Concorde*'s sonic boom directly, not reflected from a layer in the atmosphere, is a function of

T = air temperature at ground level (in degrees Kelvin),

h = the *Concorde*'s altitude (in km),

d = the vertical temperature gradient (temperature drop in degrees Kelvin per km).

The formula for w is

$$w = 4(Th/d)^{1/2}.$$

See Fig. 13.10.

The Washington-bound *Concorde* approaches the United States from Europe on a course that takes it south of Nantucket Island at an altitude of 16.8 km. If the surface temperature is 290 K and the vertical temperature gradient is 5 K/km, how many kilometers south of Nantucket must the plane be flown to keep its sonic boom carpet away from the island? (From "Concorde Sonic Booms as an Atmospheric Probe" by N. K. Balachandra, W. L. Donn, and D. H. Rind, *Science,* July 1, 1977, Vol. 197, p. 47.)

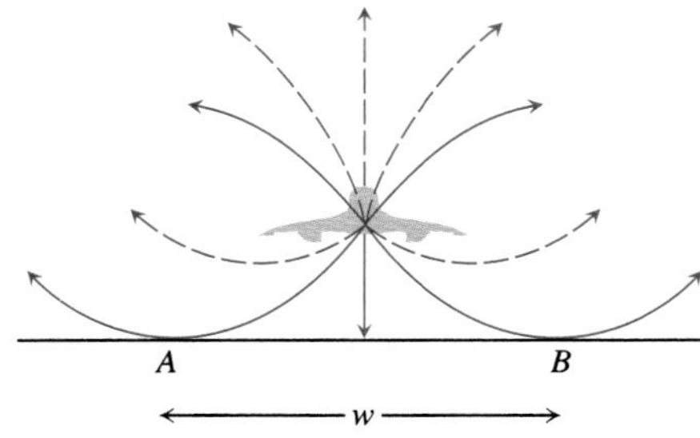

Sonic boom carpet

13.10 Sound waves from the *Concorde* bend as the temperature changes above and below the altitude at which the plane flies. The sonic boom carpet is the region on the ground that receives shock waves directly from the plane, not reflected from the atmosphere or diffracted along the ground. The carpet is determined by the grazing rays striking the ground from the point directly under the plane (Exercise 37).

38. As you know, the graph of a real-valued function of a single real variable is a set in a two-coordinate space. The graph of a real-valued function of two independent real variables is a set in a three-coordinate space. The graph of a real-valued function of three independent real variables is a set in a four-coordinate space. How would you define the graph of a real-valued function $f(x_1, x_2, x_3, x_4)$ of four independent real variables? How would you define the graph of a real-valued function $f(x_1, x_2, x_3, \ldots, x_n)$ of n independent real variables?

Writing for Your Own Knowledge

Answer the following questions in writing. Some answers will take only a sentence or two; others may require several paragraphs. Some explanations may also call for graphs or sketches.

1. What is a real-valued function of two independent variables? three independent variables?
2. What does it mean for sets in the plane or in space to be open? closed?
3. How can you display the values of a function $f(x, y)$ of two independent variables graphically?
4. How can you display the values of a function $f(x, y, z)$ of three independent variables graphically?

EXPLORER PROGRAM

3D Grapher	Graphs surfaces defined by equations of the form $z = f(x, y)$ over rectangular regions in the xy-plane.

Surfaces Defined by Functions of Two Variables

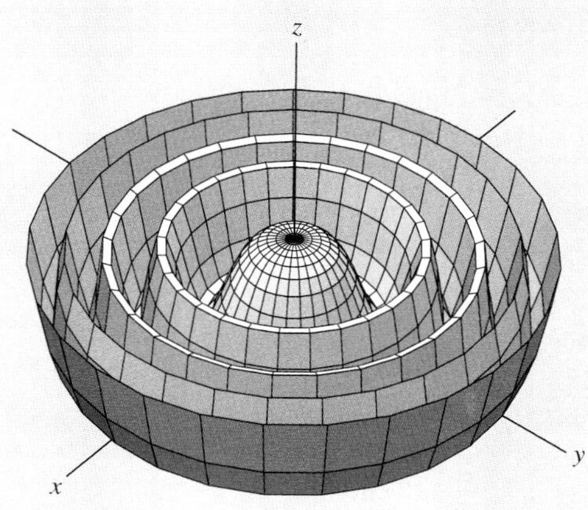

$z = 1 + \cos(x^2 + y^2)$

(Generated by Mathematica)

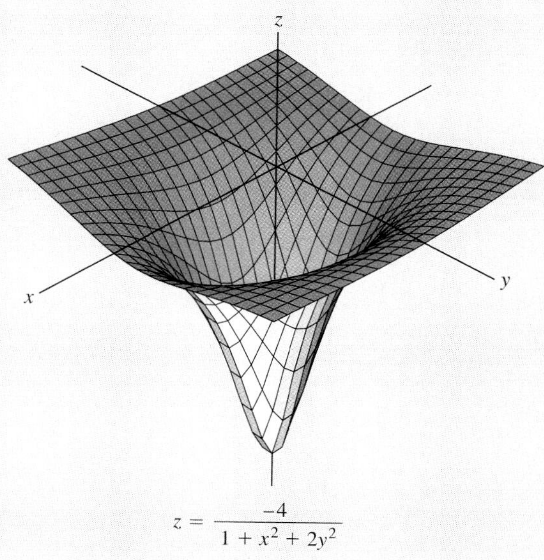

$z = \dfrac{-4}{1 + x^2 + 2y^2}$

(Generated by Mathematica)

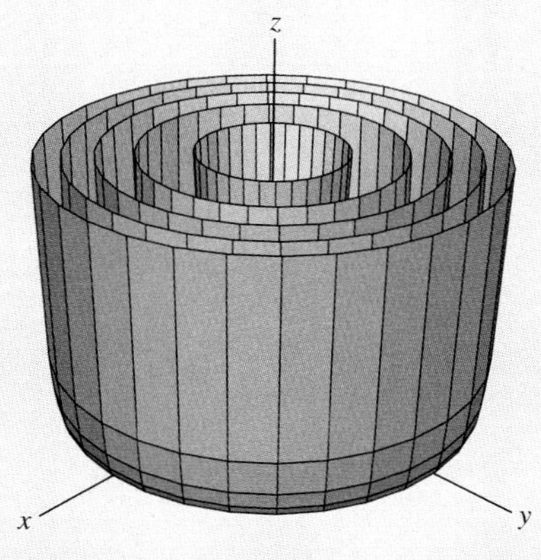

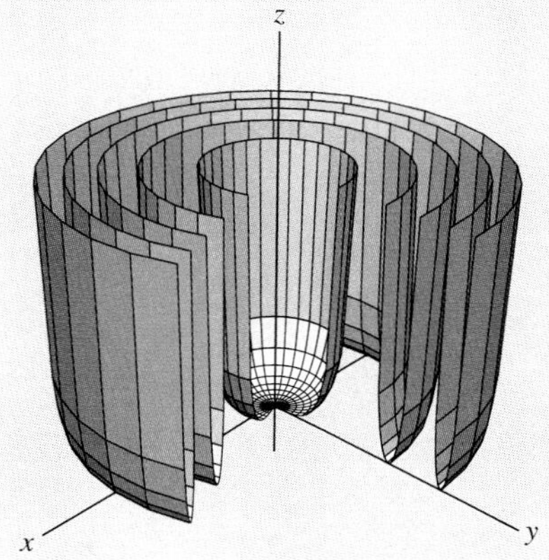

$z = \ln(\sec(x^2 + y^2))$

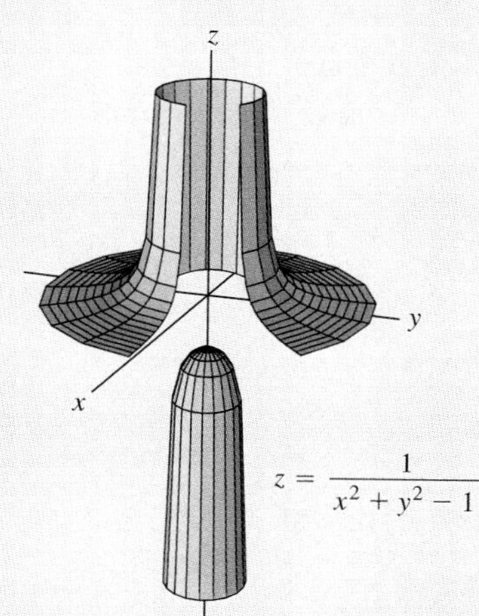

$z = \dfrac{1}{x^2 + y^2 - 1}$

13.2 Limits and Continuity

This section deals with limits and continuity of functions of more than one variable. The definitions are the same as for functions of a single variable, except that there are now more variables.

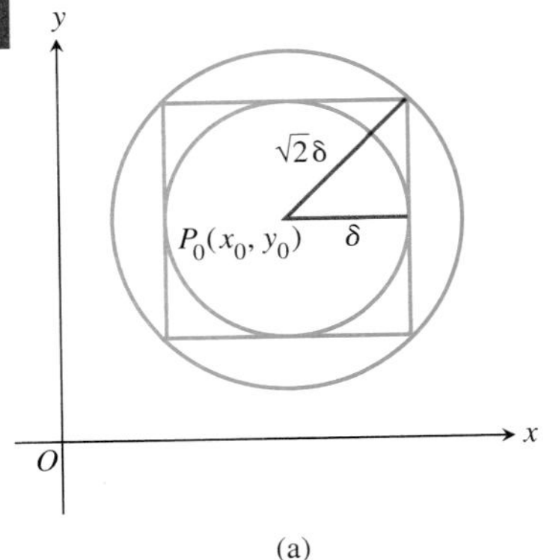

(a)

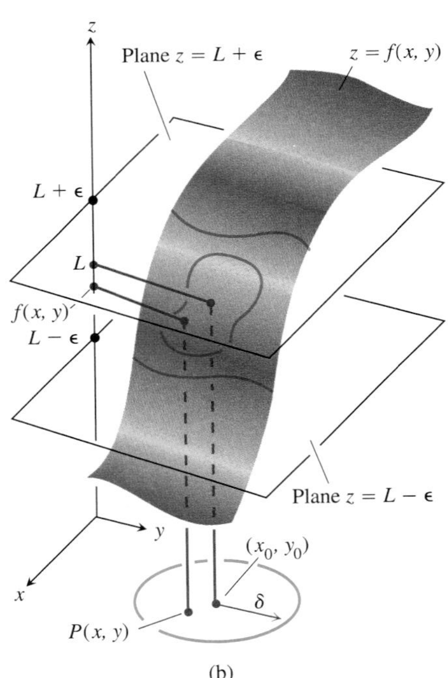

(b)

13.11 (a) The open square $|x - x_0| < \delta$, $|y - y_0| < \delta$ lies inside the open disk $\sqrt{(x - x_0)^2 + (y - y_0)^2} < \sqrt{2}\delta$ and contains the open disk $\sqrt{(x - x_0)^2 + (y - y_0)^2} < \delta$. Thus, we can make both $|x - x_0|$ and $|y - y_0|$ small by making $\sqrt{(x - x_0)^2 + (y - y_0)^2}$ small, and conversely. (b) For every point (x, y) within δ of (x_0, y_0), the value of $f(x, y)$ lies within ϵ of L.

Limits

If the values of a real-valued function $f(x, y)$ lie close to a fixed real number L for all points (x, y) sufficiently close to the point (x_0, y_0), but not equal to (x_0, y_0), we say that L is the limit of f as (x, y) approaches (x_0, y_0). In symbols, we write

$$\lim_{(x, y)\to(x_0, y_0)} f(x, y) = L, \tag{1}$$

and we say "the limit of f as (x, y) approaches (x_0, y_0) equals L." This is like the limit of a function of one variable, except that two independent variables are involved instead of one. In addition, if (x_0, y_0) is an interior point of f's domain, (x, y) can approach (x_0, y_0) from any direction. The direction of approach may turn out to be an issue, as some of the following examples show.

For (x, y) to be "close" to (x_0, y_0) means that the Cartesian distance $\sqrt{(x - x_0)^2 + (y - y_0)^2}$ is small in some sense. Since

$$|x - x_0| = \sqrt{(x - x_0)^2} \le \sqrt{(x - x_0)^2 + (y - y_0)^2} \tag{2}$$

and

$$|y - y_0| = \sqrt{(y - y_0)^2} \le \sqrt{(x - x_0)^2 + (y - y_0)^2}, \tag{3}$$

the inequality

$$\sqrt{(x - x_0)^2 + (y - y_0)^2} < \delta$$

for any value of δ implies that

$$|x - x_0| < \delta \quad \text{and} \quad |y - y_0| < \delta.$$

Conversely, if for some $\delta > 0$ both $|x - x_0| < \delta$ and $|y - y_0| < \delta$, then

$$\sqrt{(x - x_0)^2 + (y - y_0)^2} < \sqrt{\delta^2 + \delta^2} = \sqrt{2}\delta,$$

which is small if δ is small (Fig. 13.11). Thus, in calculating limits we may think either in terms of the distance in the plane or in terms of differences in individual coordinates.

DEFINITIONS

The **limit** of $f(x, y)$ as $(x, y)\to(x_0, y_0)$ is the number L if for any $\epsilon > 0$ there exists a $\delta > 0$ such that for all points $(x, y) \neq (x_0, y_0)$ in the domain of f, either

1. $\sqrt{(x - x_0)^2 + (y - y_0)^2} < \delta \quad \Rightarrow \quad |f(x, y) - L| < \epsilon$ or
2. $|x - x_0| < \delta$ and $|y - y_0| < \delta \quad \Rightarrow \quad |f(x, y) - L| < \epsilon$.

These equivalent definitions apply to boundary points as well as interior points of the domain of f. The only requirement is that the point (x, y) remain in the domain at all times.

It can be shown, as for functions of a single variable, that

$$\lim_{(x, y)\to(x_0, y_0)} x = x_0$$
$$\lim_{(x, y)\to(x_0, y_0)} y = y_0 \tag{4}$$
$$\lim_{(x, y)\to(x_0, y_0)} k = k. \qquad \text{(Any number } k)$$

It can also be shown that the limit of the sum of two functions is the sum of their limits (when they both exist), with similar results for the limits of the differences, products, constant multiples, and quotients.

THEOREM 1

Properties of Limits of Functions of Two Variables

The following rules hold if

$$\lim_{(x, y)\to(x_0, y_0)} f(x, y) = L_1 \quad \text{and} \quad \lim_{(x, y)\to(x_0, y_0)} g(x, y) = L_2.$$

1. *Sum Rule:* $\lim [f(x, y) + g(x, y)] = L_1 + L_2$
2. *Difference Rule:* $\lim [f(x, y) - g(x, y)] = L_1 - L_2$
3. *Product Rule:* $\lim f(x, y) \cdot g(x, y) = L_1 \cdot L_2$
4. *Constant Multiple Rule:* $\lim kg(x, y) = kL_2$ (Any number k)
5. *Quotient Rule:* $\lim \dfrac{f(x, y)}{g(x, y)} = \dfrac{L_1}{L_2}$ if $L_2 \neq 0$.

All limits are to be taken as $(x, y)\to(x_0, y_0)$, and L_1 and L_2 are to be real numbers.

When we apply Theorem 1 to the limits in Eqs. (4) we obtain the useful result that the limits of polynomials and rational functions as $(x, y)\to(x_0, y_0)$ may be calculated by evaluating the functions at the point (x_0, y_0). The only requirement is that the functions be defined at (x_0, y_0).

EXAMPLE 1

a) $\displaystyle\lim_{(x, y)\to(3, -4)} (x^2 + y^2) = (3)^2 + (-4)^2 = 9 + 16 = 25$

b) $\displaystyle\lim_{(x, y)\to(0, 1)} \frac{x - xy + 3}{x^2y + 5xy - y^3} = \frac{0 - 0(1) + 3}{(0)^2(1) + 5(0)(1) - (1)^3} = -3$

EXAMPLE 2 Find

$$\lim_{(x, y)\to(0, 0)} \frac{x^2 - xy}{\sqrt{x} - \sqrt{y}}.$$

Solution Since the denominator $\sqrt{x} - \sqrt{y}$ approaches 0 as $(x, y)\to(0, 0)$, we cannot use the Quotient Rule from Theorem 1. However, if we multiply numerator and denominator by $\sqrt{x}+\sqrt{y}$, we produce an equivalent fraction whose limit we *can* find with Theorem 1:

$$\begin{aligned}
\lim_{(x,y)\to(0,0)} \frac{x^2-xy}{\sqrt{x}-\sqrt{y}} &= \lim_{(x,y)\to(0,0)} \frac{\left(x^2-xy\right)\left(\sqrt{x}+\sqrt{y}\right)}{\left(\sqrt{x}-\sqrt{y}\right)\left(\sqrt{x}+\sqrt{y}\right)} \\
&= \lim_{(x,y)\to(0,0)} \frac{x\left(x-y\right)\left(\sqrt{x}+\sqrt{y}\right)}{x-y} && \text{Algebra} \\
&= \lim_{(x,y)\to(0,0)} x\left(\sqrt{x}+\sqrt{y}\right) && \text{Cancel the factor } (x-y) \\
&= 0\left(\sqrt{0}+\sqrt{0}\right) = 0
\end{aligned}$$

Continuity

The definition of continuity for functions of two variables is the same as for functions of a single variable.

DEFINITIONS

A function $f(x, y)$ is **continuous at the point (x_0, y_0)** if

1. f is defined at (x_0, y_0),
2. $\lim_{(x,y)\to(x_0,y_0)} f(x, y)$ exists,
3. $\lim_{(x,y)\to(x_0,y_0)} f(x, y) = f(x_0, y_0)$.

A function is **continuous** if it is continuous at every point of its domain.

As with the definition of limit, the definition of continuity applies at boundary points as well as interior points of the domain of f. The only requirement is that the point (x, y) remain in the domain at all times.

As you may have guessed, one of the consequences of Theorem 1 is that algebraic combinations of continuous functions are continuous at every point at which all the functions involved are defined. This means that sums, differences, products, constant multiples, and quotients of continuous functions are continuous where defined. In particular, polynomials and rational functions of two variables are continuous at every point at which they are defined.

If $z = f(x, y)$ is a continuous function of x and y, and $w = g(z)$ is a continuous function of z, then the composite $w = g(f(x, y))$ is continuous. Thus, composites like

$$e^{x-y}, \qquad \cos\frac{xy}{x^2+1}, \qquad \ln\left(1+x^2y^2\right)$$

are continuous at every point (x, y).

As with functions of a single variable, the general rule is that composites of continuous functions are continuous. The only requirement is that each function be continuous where it is applied.

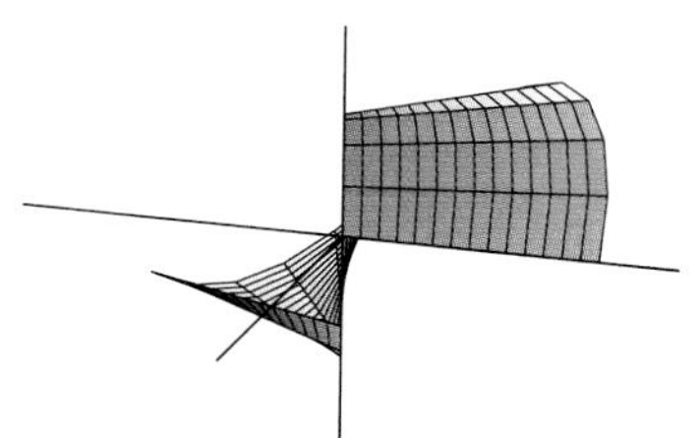
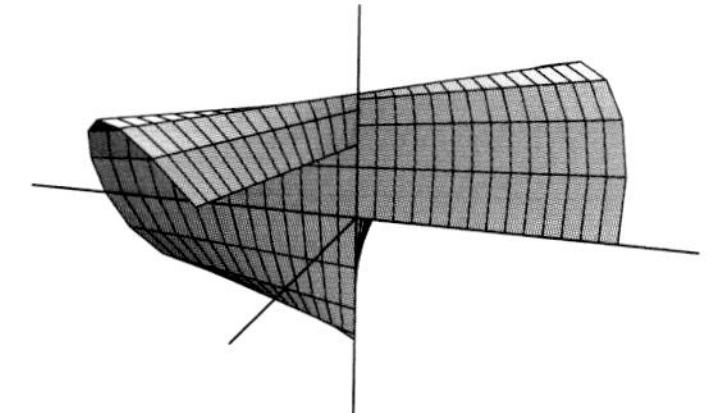
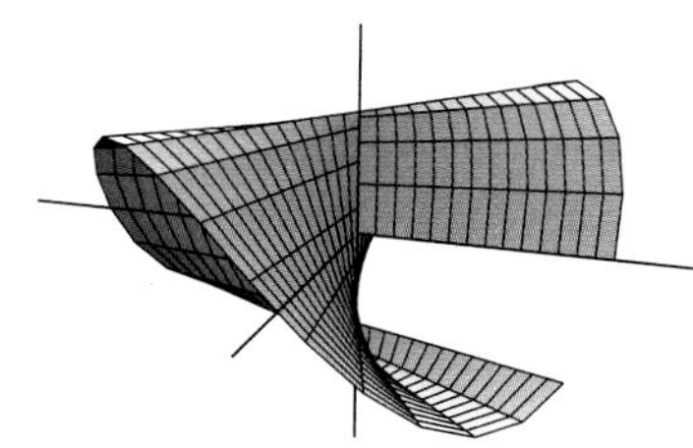

(a)

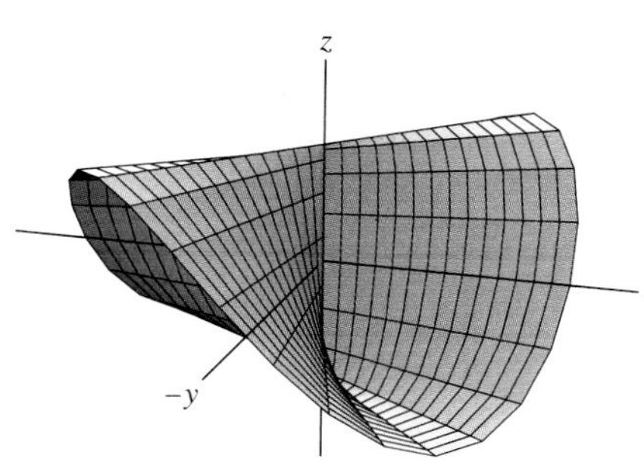

(Generated by Mathematica)

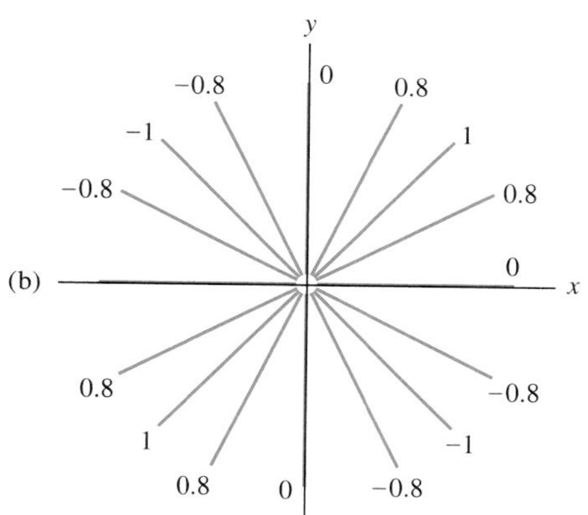

13.12 (a) Stages in a computer's construction of the graph of

$$f(x, y) = \begin{cases} \dfrac{2xy}{x^2 + y^2}, & (x, y) \neq (0, 0) \\ 0, & (x, y) = (0, 0) \end{cases}$$

The function is continuous at every point except the origin. (b) The level curves of f.

EXAMPLE 3 Show that

$$f(x, y) = \begin{cases} \dfrac{2xy}{x^2 + y^2}, & (x, y) \neq (0, 0) \\ 0, & (x, y) = (0, 0) \end{cases}$$

is continuous at every point except the origin (Fig. 13.12).

Solution The function f is continuous at any point $(x, y) \neq (0, 0)$ because its values are then given by a rational function of x and y.

At $(0, 0)$ the value of f is defined, but f, we claim, has no limit as $(x, y) \to (0, 0)$. The reason is that different paths of approach to the origin can lead to different results, as we will now see.

For every value of m, the function f has a constant value on the "punctured" line $y = mx$, $x \neq 0$, because

$$f(x, y)\Big|_{y = mx} = \frac{2xy}{x^2 + y^2}\Big|_{y = mx} = \frac{2x(mx)}{x^2 + (mx)^2} = \frac{2mx^2}{x^2 + m^2x^2} = \frac{2m}{1 + m^2}.$$

Therefore, f has this number as its limit as (x, y) approaches the origin along the line:

$$\lim_{\substack{(x, y) \to (0, 0) \\ \text{along } y = mx}} f(x, y) = \lim_{(x, y) \to (0, 0)} \left[f(x, y)\Big|_{y = mx} \right] = \frac{2m}{1 + m^2}.$$

This limit changes with m. There is therefore no single number we may call the limit of f as (x, y) approaches the origin. The limit fails to exist, and the function is not continuous.

Example 3 illustrates an important point about limits of functions of two variables (or even more variables, for that matter). For a limit to exist at a point, the limit must be the same along every approach path. Therefore, if we ever find paths with different limits, we know the function has no limit at the point they approach.

The Two-Path Test for Discontinuity

If a function $f(x, y)$ has different limits along two different paths as (x, y) approaches (x_0, y_0) then $\lim_{(x, y) \to (x_0, y_0)} f(x, y)$ does not exist.

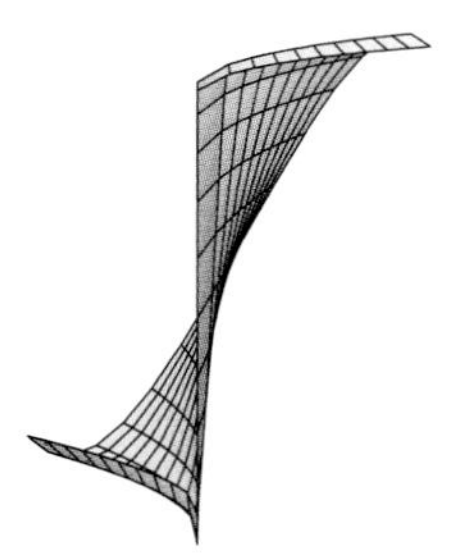

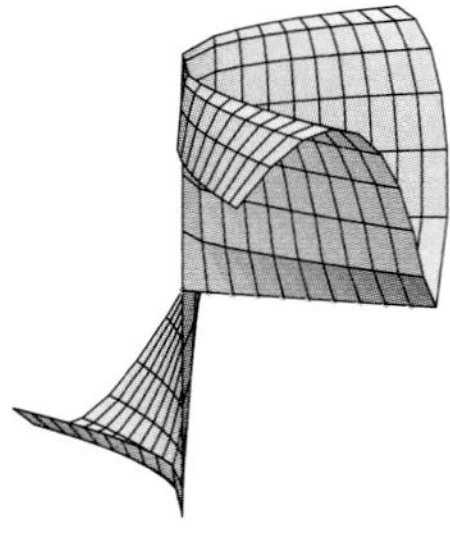

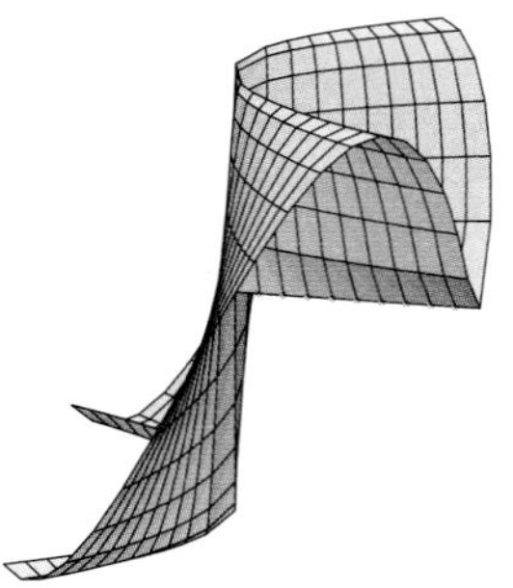

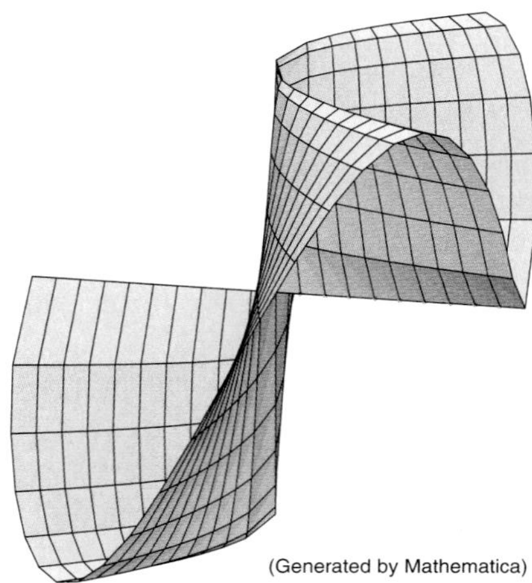

(a)

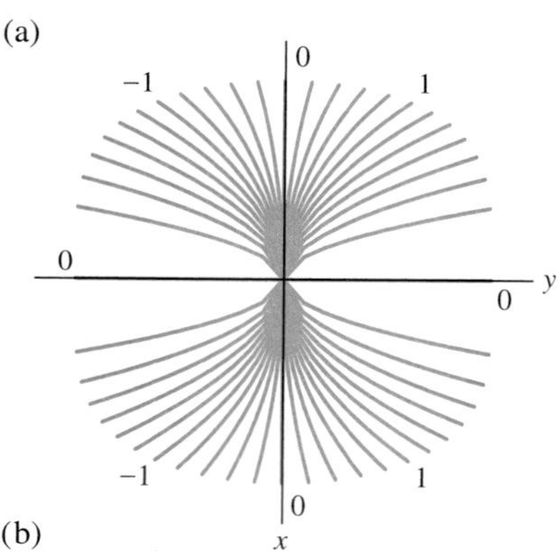

(b)

13.13 Stages in a computer's construction of the graph of $f(x, y) = 2x^2y/(x^4 + y^2)$. As the completed graph in (a) suggests and the level-curve values in (b) confirm,

$$\lim_{(x,y)\to(0,0)} f(x, y)$$

does not exist.

EXAMPLE 4 Show that the function

$$f(x, y) = \frac{2x^2y}{x^4 + y^2}$$

(Fig. 13.13) has no limit as (x, y) approaches $(0, 0)$.

Solution Along the curve $y = kx^2$, $x \neq 0$, the function has the constant value

$$f(x, y)\bigg|_{y=kx^2} = \frac{2x^2y}{x^4 + y^2}\bigg|_{y=kx^2} = \frac{2x^2(kx^2)}{x^4 + (kx^2)^2} = \frac{2kx^4}{x^4 + k^2x^4} = \frac{2k}{1 + k^2}.$$

Therefore,

$$\lim_{\substack{(x,y)\to(0,0)\\ \text{along } y=kx^2}} f(x, y) = \lim_{(x,y)\to(0,0)} \left[f(x, y)\bigg|_{y=kx^2} \right] = \frac{2k}{1 + k^2}.$$

This limit varies with the path of approach. If (x, y) approaches $(0, 0)$ along the parabola $y = x^2$, for instance, $k = 1$ and the limit is 1. If (x, y) approaches $(0, 0)$ along the x-axis, $k = 0$ and the limit is 0. By the two-path test, f has no limit as (x, y) approaches $(0, 0)$.

The language we use here may seem contradictory. You might well ask, "What do you mean f has no limit as (x, y) approaches the origin—it has lots of limits." But that's the point. There is no single path-independent limit, and therefore, by our definition, $\lim_{(x,y)\to(0,0)} f(x, y)$ does not exist. It is our translating this formal statement into the more colloquial "has no limit" that creates the apparent contradiction. The mathematics is fine. The problem arises in how we talk about it. In the crunch, we need the formality to keep things straight.

Functions of More Than Two Variables

The definitions of limit and continuity for functions of two variables and the conclusions about limits and continuity for sums, products, quotients, and composites all extend to functions of three or more variables. Functions like

$$\ln(x + y + z) \qquad \text{and} \qquad \frac{y \sin z}{x - 1}$$

are continuous throughout their domains, and limits like

$$\lim_{P\to(1,0,-1)} \frac{e^{x+z}}{z^2 + \cos\sqrt{xy}} = \frac{e^{1-1}}{(-1)^2 + \cos 0} = \frac{1}{2},$$

where P denotes the point (x, y, z), may be found by direct substitution.

Exercises 13.2

Find the limits in Exercises 1–12.

1. $\displaystyle\lim_{(x, y)\to(0, 0)} \frac{3x^2 - y^2 + 5}{x^2 + y^2 + 2}$

2. $\displaystyle\lim_{(x, y)\to(1, 1)} \ln|1 + x^2 y^2|$

3. $\displaystyle\lim_{(x, y)\to(0, \ln 2)} e^{x-y}$

4. $\displaystyle\lim_{(x, y)\to(0, 4)} \frac{x}{\sqrt{y}}$

5. $\displaystyle\lim_{(x, y)\to(3, 4)} \sqrt{x^2 + y^2 - 1}$

6. $\displaystyle\lim_{(x, y)\to(2, -3)} \left(\frac{1}{x} + \frac{1}{y}\right)^2$

7. $\displaystyle\lim_{(x, y)\to(0, \pi/4)} \sec x \tan y$

8. $\displaystyle\lim_{(x, y)\to(0, 0)} \cos \frac{x^2 + y^2}{x + y + 1}$

9. $\displaystyle\lim_{(x, y)\to(1, 1)} \cos \sqrt[3]{|xy| - 1}$

10. $\displaystyle\lim_{(x, y)\to(1, 0)} \frac{x \sin y}{x^2 + 1}$

11. $\displaystyle\lim_{(x, y)\to(0, 0)} \frac{e^y \sin x}{x}$

12. $\displaystyle\lim_{(x, y)\to(\pi/2, 0)} \frac{\cos y + 1}{y - \sin x}$

Find the limits in Exercises 13–20 by rewriting the fractions first.

13. $\displaystyle\lim_{\substack{(x, y)\to(1, 1)\\ x \ne y}} \frac{x^2 - 2xy + y^2}{x - y}$

14. $\displaystyle\lim_{\substack{(x, y)\to(1, 1)\\ x \ne y}} \frac{x^2 - y^2}{x - y}$

15. $\displaystyle\lim_{\substack{(x, y)\to(1, 1)\\ x \ne 1}} \frac{xy - y - 2x + 2}{x - 1}$

16. $\displaystyle\lim_{\substack{(x, y)\to(2, -4)\\ y \ne -4,\ x \ne x^2}} \frac{y + 4}{x^2 y - xy + 4x^2 - 4x}$

17. $\displaystyle\lim_{(x, y)\to(0, 0)} \frac{x - y + 2\sqrt{x} - 2\sqrt{y}}{\sqrt{x} - \sqrt{y}}$

18. $\displaystyle\lim_{(x, y)\to(2, 2)} \frac{x + y - 4}{\sqrt{x + y} - 2}$

19. $\displaystyle\lim_{(x, y)\to(2, 0)} \frac{\sqrt{2x - y} - 2}{2x - y - 4}$

20. $\displaystyle\lim_{(x, y)\to(4, 3)} \frac{\sqrt{x} - \sqrt{y + 1}}{x - y - 1}$

Find the limits in Exercises 21–26. In each exercise, P stands for the point (x, y, z).

21. $\displaystyle\lim_{P\to(2, 3, -6)} \sqrt{x^2 + y^2 + z^2}$

22. $\displaystyle\lim_{P\to(0, -2, 0)} \ln \sqrt{x^2 + y^2 + z^2}$

23. $\displaystyle\lim_{P\to(3, 3, 0)} (\sin^2 x + \cos^2 y + \sec^2 z)$

24. $\displaystyle\lim_{P\to(\pi, 0, 3)} ze^{-2y} \cos 2x$

25. $\displaystyle\lim_{P\to(-1/4, \pi/2, 2)} \tan^{-1} xyz$

26. $\displaystyle\lim_{P\to(1, -1, -1)} \frac{2xy + yz}{x^2 + z^2}$

At what points (x, y) in the plane are the functions in Exercises 27–30 continuous?

27. **a)** $f(x, y) = \sin(x + y)$ **b)** $f(x, y) = \ln(x^2 + y^2)$

28. **a)** $f(x, y) = \dfrac{x + y}{x - y}$ **b)** $f(x, y) = \dfrac{y}{x^2 + 1}$

29. **a)** $g(x, y) = \sin \dfrac{1}{xy}$ **b)** $g(x, y) = \dfrac{x + y}{2 + \cos x}$

30. **a)** $g(x, y) = \dfrac{x^2 + y^2}{x^2 - 3x + 2}$ **b)** $g(x, y) = \dfrac{1}{x^2 - y}$

At what points (x, y, z) in space are the functions in Exercises 31–34 continuous?

31. **a)** $f(x, y, z) = x^2 + y^2 - 2z^2$
    b) $f(x, y, z) = \sqrt{x^2 + y^2 - 1}$

32. **a)** $f(x, y, z) = \ln xyz$ **b)** $f(x, y, z) = e^{x+y} \cos z$

33. **a)** $h(x, y, z) = xy \sin \dfrac{1}{z}$ **b)** $h(x, y, z) = \dfrac{1}{x^2 + z^2 - 1}$

34. **a)** $h(x, y, z) = \dfrac{1}{|y| + |z|}$ **b)** $h(x, y, z) = \dfrac{1}{|xy| + |z|}$

By considering different paths of approach, show that the functions in Exercises 35–42 have no limit as $(x, y)\to(0, 0)$.

35. $f(x, y) = -\dfrac{x}{\sqrt{x^2 + y^2}}$

36. $f(x, y) = \dfrac{x^4}{x^4 + y^2}$

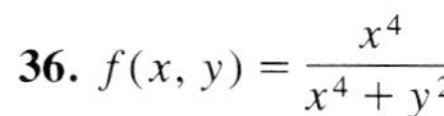

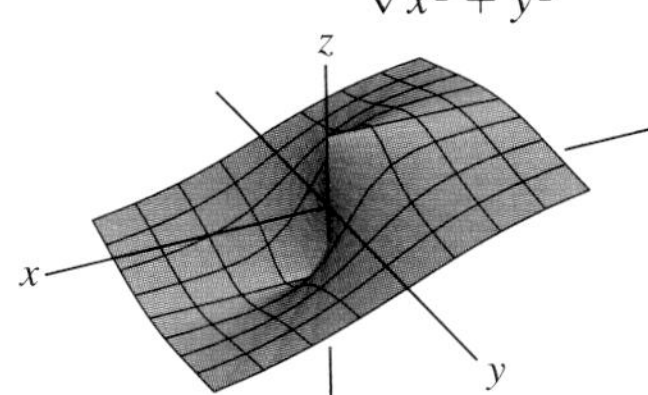

(Generated by Mathematica)

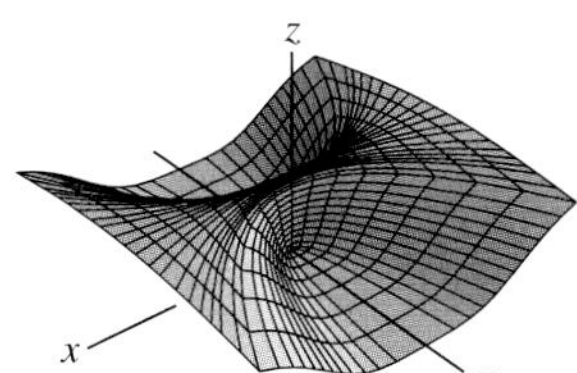

(Generated by Mathematica)

37. $f(x, y) = \dfrac{x^4 - y^2}{x^4 + y^2}$

38. $f(x, y) = \dfrac{xy}{|xy|}$

39. $g(x, y) = \dfrac{x - y}{x + y}$

40. $g(x, y) = \dfrac{x + y}{x - y}$

41. $h(x, y) = \dfrac{x^2 + y}{y}$

42. $h(x, y) = \dfrac{x^2}{x^2 - y}$

43. If $\lim_{(x, y)\to(x_0, y_0)} f(x, y) = L$, must f be defined at (x_0, y_0)? Give reasons for your answer.

44. If $f(x_0, y_0) = 3$, what can you say about

$$\lim_{(x, y)\to(x_0, y_0)} f(x, y)$$

if f is continuous at (x_0, y_0)? if f is not continuous at (x_0, y_0)? Give reasons for your answer.

The Sandwich Theorem for functions of two variables states that if $g(x, y) \leq f(x, y) \leq h(x, y)$ for all $(x, y) \neq (x_0, y_0)$ in a disk centered at (x_0, y_0) and if g and h have the same finite limit L as $(x, y) \to (x_0, y_0)$, then

$$\lim_{(x, y)\to(x_0, y_0)} f(x, y) = L.$$

Use this result to support your answers to the questions in Exercises 45–48.

45. Does knowing that

$$1 - \frac{x^2 y^2}{3} < \frac{\tan^{-1} xy}{xy} < 1$$

tell you anything about

$$\lim_{(x, y)\to(0, 0)} \frac{\tan^{-1} xy}{xy}?$$

Give reasons for your answer.

46. Does knowing that

$$2|xy| - \frac{x^2 y^2}{6} < 4 - 4\cos\sqrt{|xy|} < 2|xy|$$

tell you anything about

$$\lim_{(x, y)\to(0, 0)} \frac{4 - 4\cos\sqrt{|xy|}}{|xy|}?$$

Give reasons for your answer.

47. Does knowing that $|\sin(1/x)| \leq 1$ tell you anything about

$$\lim_{(x, y)\to(0, 0)} y \sin\frac{1}{x}?$$

Give reasons for your answer.

48. Does knowing that $|\cos(1/y)| \leq 1$ tell you anything about

$$\lim_{(x, y)\to(0, 0)} x \cos\frac{1}{y}?$$

Give reasons for your answer.

49. *Continuation of Example 3.*

a) Reread Example 3. Then substitute $m = \tan\theta$ into the formula

$$f(x, y)\Big|_{y = mx} = \frac{2m}{1 + m^2}$$

and simplify the result to show how the value of f varies with the line's angle of inclination.

b) Use the formula you obtained in (a) to show that the limit of f as $(x, y) \to (0, 0)$ along the line $y = mx$ varies from -1 to 1 depending on the angle of approach.

Writing for Your Own Knowledge

Answer the following questions in writing. Some answers will take only a sentence or two; others may require several paragraphs. Some explanations may also call for graphs or sketches.

1. What does it mean for a function $f(x, y)$ to have a limit as (x, y) approaches a point (x_0, y_0)?
2. What properties of limits enable you to go from knowing that $\lim_{(x, y)\to(x_0, y_0)} x = x_0$, $\lim_{(x, y)\to(x_0, y_0)} y = y_0$, and $\lim_{(x, y)\to(x_0, y_0)} k = k$ (k a constant) to being able to calculate limits of polynomials and rational functions of two independent variables?
3. What does it mean for a function $f(x, y)$ to be continuous?
4. What can be said about algebraic combinations of continuous functions? composites of continuous functions?
5. What is the two-path test for discontinuity?
6. If a function $f(x, y)$ has different limits as $(x, y) \to (x_0, y_0)$ along different paths, why can you say that f has *no* limit as $(x, y) \to (x_0, y_0)$?

13.3 *Partial Derivatives*

When we hold all but one of the independent variables of a function constant and differentiate with respect to that one variable, we get a "partial" derivative. This section shows how partial derivatives arise geometrically and how to calculate partial derivatives by applying the rules for differentiating functions of a single variable. We begin with functions of two independent variables.

Definitions and Notation

If (x_0, y_0) is a point in the domain of a function $f(x, y)$, the vertical plane $y = y_0$ will cut the surface $z = f(x, y)$ in the curve $z = f(x, y_0)$ (Fig. 13.14). This curve is the graph of the function $z = f(x, y_0)$ in the plane $y = y_0$. The horizontal coordinate in this plane is x; the vertical coordinate is z.

We define the partial derivative of f with respect to x at the point (x_0, y_0) as the ordinary derivative of $f(x, y_0)$ with respect to x at the point $x = x_0$.

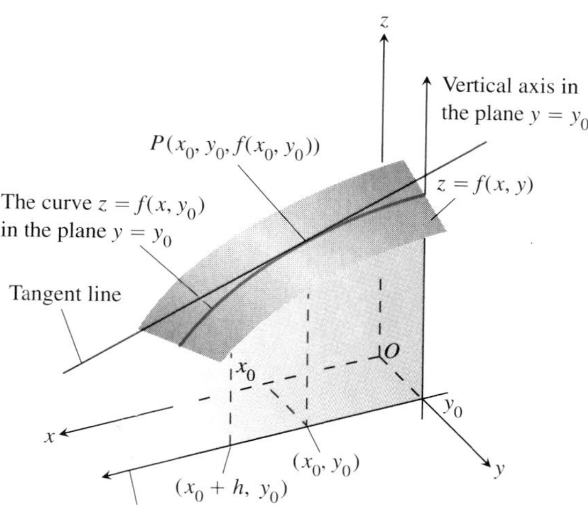

13.14 The intersection of the plane $y = y_0$ with the surface $z = f(x, y)$, viewed from a point above the first quadrant of the xy-plane.

DEFINITION

The **partial derivative of $f(x, y)$ with respect to x** at the point (x_0, y_0) is

$$\left.\frac{\partial f}{\partial x}\right|_{(x_0, y_0)} = \left.\frac{d}{dx} f(x, y_0)\right|_{x = x_0} = \lim_{h \to 0} \frac{f(x_0 + h, y_0) - f(x_0, y_0)}{h}, \tag{1}$$

provided the limit exists. (Think of ∂ as a kind of d.)

The slope of the curve $z = f(x, y_0)$ at the point $P(x_0, y_0, f(x_0, y_0))$ in the plane $y = y_0$ is the value of the partial derivative of f with respect to x at (x_0, y_0). The tangent line to the curve at P is the line in the plane $y = y_0$ that passes through P with this slope. The partial derivative $\partial f/\partial x$ at (x_0, y_0) gives the rate of change of f with respect to x when y is held fixed at the value y_0.

The notation we use for the partial derivative of f with respect to x depends on what aspect of the derivative we want to emphasize:

$\frac{\partial f}{\partial x}(x_0, y_0)$ or $f_x(x_0, y_0)$ — "Partial derivative of f with respect to x at (x_0, y_0)" or "f sub x at (x_0, y_0)." Convenient for stressing the point (x_0, y_0).

$\left.\frac{\partial z}{\partial x}\right|_{(x_0, y_0)}$ — "Partial derivative of z with respect to x at (x_0, y_0)." Common in science and engineering when you are dealing with variables and do not mention the function explicitly.

f_x, $\frac{\partial f}{\partial x}$, z_x, or $\frac{\partial z}{\partial x}$ — "Partial derivative of f (or z) with respect to x." Convenient when you regard the partial derivative as a function in its own right.

The definition of the partial derivative of $f(x, y)$ with respect to y at a point (x_0, y_0) is similar to the definition of the partial derivative of f with respect to x. We hold x fixed at the value x_0 and take the ordinary derivative of $f(x_0, y)$ with respect to y at y_0.

DEFINITION

The **partial derivative of $f(x, y)$ with respect to y** at the point (x_0, y_0) is

$$\left.\frac{\partial f}{\partial y}\right|_{(x_0, y_0)} = \left.\frac{d}{dy} f(x_0, y)\right|_{y = y_0} = \lim_{h \to 0} \frac{f(x_0, y_0 + h) - f(x_0, y_0)}{h}, \tag{2}$$

provided the limit exists.

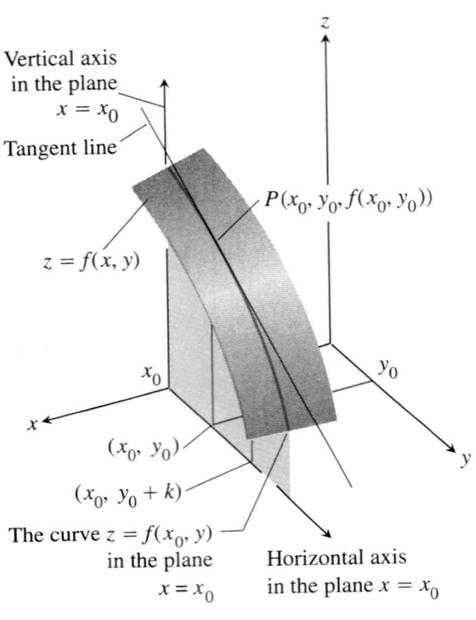

13.15 The intersection of the plane $x = x_0$ with the surface $z = f(x, y)$, viewed from above the first quadrant of the xy-plane.

The slope of the curve $z = f(x_0, y)$ at the point $P(x_0, y_0, f(x_0, y_0))$ in the vertical plane $x = x_0$ (Fig. 13.15) is the partial derivative of f with respect to y at (x_0, y_0). The tangent line to the curve at P is the line in the plane $x = x_0$ that passes through P with this slope. The partial derivative gives the rate of change of f with respect to y at (x_0, y_0) when x is held fixed at the value x_0.

The partial derivative with respect to y is denoted the same way as the partial derivative with respect to x:

$$\frac{\partial f}{\partial y}(x_0, y_0), \qquad f_y(x_0, y_0), \qquad \frac{\partial f}{\partial y}, \qquad f_y. \tag{3}$$

Notice that we now have two tangent lines associated with the surface $z = f(x, y)$ at the point $P(x_0, y_0, f(x_0, y_0))$ (Fig. 13.16). Is the plane they determine tangent to the surface at P? It would be nice if it were, but we have to learn more about partial derivatives before we can find out.

Calculations

As Eq. (1) shows, we calculate $\partial f/\partial x$ by differentiating f with respect to x in the usual way while treating y as a constant. As Eq. (2) shows, we can calculate $\partial f/\partial y$ by differentiating f with respect to y in the usual way while holding x constant.

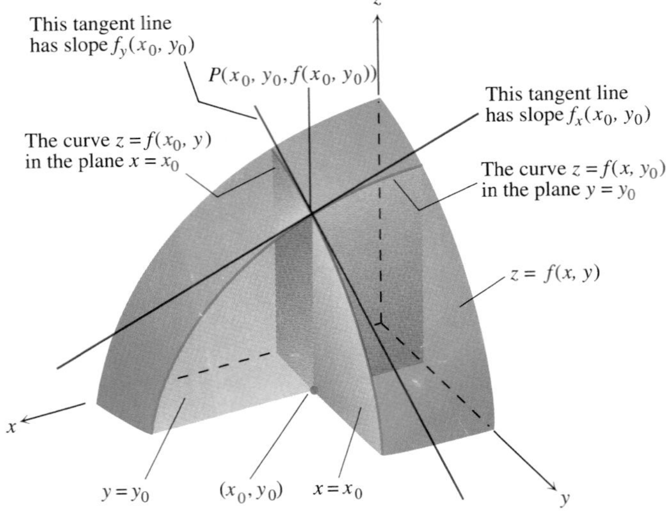

13.16 Figures 13.14 and 13.15 combined. The tangent lines at the point $(x_0, y_0, f(x_0, y_0))$ determine a plane that, in this picture at least, appears to be tangent to the surface.

EXAMPLE 1 Find the values of $\partial f/\partial x$ and $\partial f/\partial y$ at the point $(4, -5)$ if

$$f(x, y) = x^2 + 3xy + y - 1.$$

Solution To find $\partial f/\partial x$, we regard y as a constant and differentiate with respect to x:

$$\frac{\partial f}{\partial x} = \frac{\partial}{\partial x}(x^2 + 3xy + y - 1) = 2x + 3 \cdot 1 \cdot y + 0 - 0 = 2x + 3y.$$

The value of $\partial f/\partial x$ at $(4, -5)$ is $2(4) + 3(-5) = -7$.

To find $\partial f/\partial y$, we regard x as a constant and differentiate with respect to y:

$$\frac{\partial f}{\partial y} = \frac{\partial}{\partial y}(x^2 + 3xy + y - 1) = 0 + 3 \cdot x \cdot 1 + 1 - 0 = 3x + 1.$$

The value of $\partial f/\partial y$ at $(4, -5)$ is $3(4) + 1 = 13$.

EXAMPLE 2 Find $\partial f/\partial y$ if

$$f(x, y) = y \sin xy.$$

Solution We treat x as a constant and f as a product of y and $\sin xy$:

$$\begin{aligned}\frac{\partial f}{\partial y} &= \frac{\partial}{\partial y}(y \sin xy) = y \frac{\partial}{\partial y} \sin xy + (\sin xy) \frac{\partial}{\partial y}(y) \\ &= (y \cos xy) \frac{\partial}{\partial y}(xy) + \sin xy = xy \cos xy + \sin xy.\end{aligned}$$

EXAMPLE 3 Find f_x if

$$f(x, y) = \frac{2y}{y + \cos x}.$$

Solution We treat f as the quotient of $2y$ divided by $(y + \cos x)$. With y held constant, we get

$$\begin{aligned}f_x = \frac{\partial}{\partial x}\left(\frac{2y}{y + \cos x}\right) &= \frac{(y + \cos x)\frac{\partial}{\partial x}(2y) - 2y\frac{\partial}{\partial x}(y + \cos x)}{(y + \cos x)^2} \\ &= \frac{(y + \cos x)(0) - 2y(-\sin x)}{(y + \cos x)^2} = \frac{2y \sin x}{(y + \cos x)^2}.\end{aligned}$$

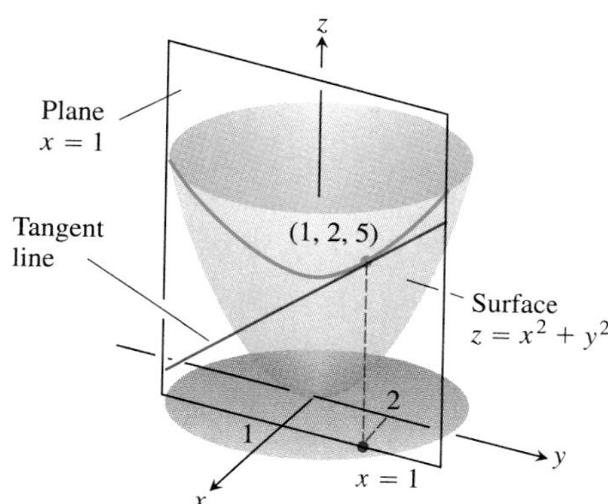

13.17 The tangent to the curve of intersection of the plane $x = 1$ and surface $z = x^2 + y^2$ at the point $(1, 2, 5)$ (Example 4).

EXAMPLE 4 The plane $x = 1$ intersects the paraboloid $z = x^2 + y^2$ in a parabola. Find the slope of the tangent to the parabola at the point $(1, 2, 5)$ (Fig. 13.17).

Solution The slope is the value of the partial derivative $\partial z/\partial y$ at $(1, 2)$:

$$\left.\frac{\partial z}{\partial y}\right|_{(1,2)} = \left.\frac{\partial}{\partial y}(x^2 + y^2)\right|_{(1,2)} = \left.2y\right|_{(1,2)} = 2(2) = 4.$$

As a check, we can treat the parabola as the graph of the single-variable function $z = (1)^2 + y^2 = 1 + y^2$ in the plane $x = 1$ and ask for the slope at $y = 2$. The slope, calculated now as an ordinary derivative, is

$$\left.\frac{dz}{dy}\right|_{y=2} = \left.\frac{d}{dy}(1+y^2)\right|_{y=2} = \left.2y\right|_{y=2} = 4.$$

The calculations agree, as they should.

Implicit differentiation works for partial derivatives the way it works for ordinary derivatives.

EXAMPLE 5 Find $\partial z/\partial x$ if the equation

$$yz - \ln z = x + y$$

defines z as a function of the two independent variables x and y and the partial derivative exists.

Solution We differentiate both sides of the equation with respect to x, holding y constant and treating z as a differentiable function of x:

$$\frac{\partial}{\partial x}(yz) - \frac{\partial}{\partial x}\ln z = \frac{\partial x}{\partial x} + \frac{\partial y}{\partial x}$$

$$y\frac{\partial z}{\partial x} - \frac{1}{z}\frac{\partial z}{\partial x} = 1 + 0 \qquad \text{With } y \text{ constant, } \frac{\partial}{\partial x}(yz) = y\frac{\partial z}{\partial x}.$$

$$\left(y - \frac{1}{z}\right)\frac{\partial z}{\partial x} = 1$$

$$\frac{\partial z}{\partial x} = \frac{z}{yz - 1}.$$

Functions of More Than Two Variables

The definitions of the partial derivatives of functions of more than two independent variables are like the definitions for functions of two variables. They are ordinary derivatives with respect to one variable, taken while the other independent variables are held constant.

EXAMPLE 6 If x, y, and z are independent variables and

$$f(x, y, z) = x \sin(y + 3z),$$

then

$$\frac{\partial f}{\partial z} = \frac{\partial}{\partial z}[x \sin(y + 3z)] = x\frac{\partial}{\partial z}\sin(y + 3z)$$

$$= x\cos(y + 3z)\frac{\partial}{\partial z}(y + 3z) = 3x\cos(y + 3z).$$

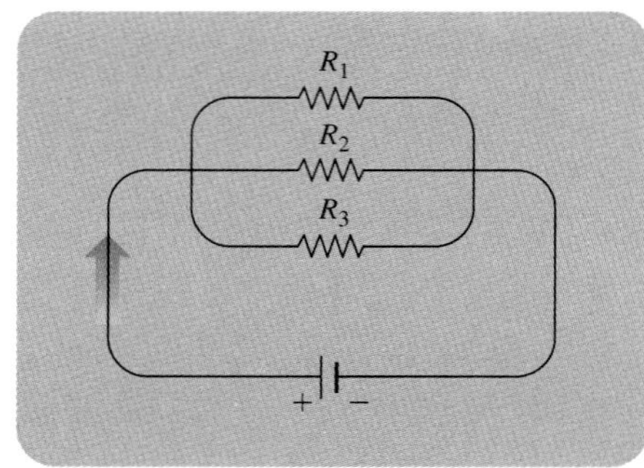

13.18 Resistors arranged this way are said to be connected in parallel (Example 7). Each resistor lets a portion of the current through. Their combined resistance R is calculated with the formula

$$\frac{1}{R} = \frac{1}{R_1} + \frac{1}{R_2} + \frac{1}{R_3}.$$

EXAMPLE 7 *Electrical Resistors in Parallel.* If resistors of R_1, R_2, and R_3 ohms are connected in parallel to make an R-ohm resistor, the value of R can be found from the equation

$$\frac{1}{R} = \frac{1}{R_1} + \frac{1}{R_2} + \frac{1}{R_3} \tag{4}$$

(Fig. 13.18). Find the value of $\partial R/\partial R_2$ when $R_1 = 30$, $R_2 = 45$, and $R_3 = 90$ ohms.

Solution To find $\partial R/\partial R_2$, we treat R_1 and R_3 as constants and differentiate both sides of Eq. (4) with respect to R_2:

$$\frac{\partial}{\partial R_2}\left(\frac{1}{R}\right) = \frac{\partial}{\partial R_2}\left(\frac{1}{R_1} + \frac{1}{R_2} + \frac{1}{R_3}\right)$$

$$-\frac{1}{R^2}\frac{\partial R}{\partial R_2} = 0 - \frac{1}{R_2{}^2} + 0$$

$$\frac{\partial R}{\partial R_2} = \frac{R^2}{R_2{}^2} = \left(\frac{R}{R_2}\right)^2.$$

When $R_1 = 30$, $R_2 = 45$, and $R_3 = 90$,

$$\frac{1}{R} = \frac{1}{30} + \frac{1}{45} + \frac{1}{90} = \frac{3+2+1}{90} = \frac{6}{90} = \frac{1}{15},$$

so $R = 15$ and

$$\frac{\partial R}{\partial R_2} = \left(\frac{15}{45}\right)^2 = \left(\frac{1}{3}\right)^2 = \frac{1}{9}.$$

The Relationship Between the Existence of Partial Derivatives and Continuity

A function $f(x, y)$ can have partial derivatives with respect to both x and y at a point without being continuous at that point. This is different from what we know about functions of a single variable, where the existence of a derivative implies continuity. However, if the partial derivatives of $f(x, y)$ exist and are continuous throughout a disk centered at (x_0, y_0), then f is continuous at (x_0, y_0), as we will see in the next section.

EXAMPLE 8 The function

$$f(x, y) = \begin{cases} 0, & xy \neq 0 \\ 1, & xy = 0 \end{cases}$$

(Fig. 13.19) is not continuous at the point (0, 0). The limit of f as (x, y) approaches (0, 0) along the line $y = x$ is 0, but $f(0, 0)$ itself is 1. The partial derivatives f_x and f_y, being the slopes of the horizontal lines L_1 and L_2 in Fig. 13.19, both exist at (0, 0).

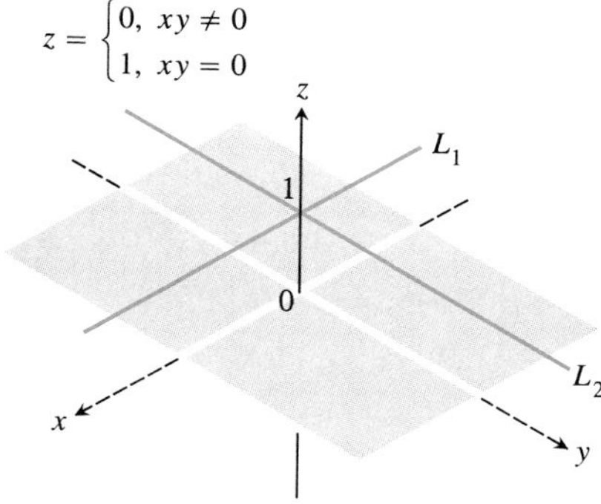

13.19 The graph of

$$f(x, y) = \begin{cases} 0, & xy \neq 0 \\ 1, & xy = 0 \end{cases}$$

consists of the lines L_1 and L_2 and the four open quadrants of the xy-plane. The function has partial derivatives at the origin but is not continuous there.

Second Order Partial Derivatives

When we differentiate a function $f(x, y)$ twice, we produce its second order derivatives. These derivatives are usually denoted by

$\frac{\partial^2 f}{\partial x^2}$	"*d* squared *f d x* squared"	or	f_{xx}	"*f* sub *x x*"
$\frac{\partial^2 f}{\partial y^2}$	"*d* squared *f d y* squared"		f_{yy}	"*f* sub *y y*"
$\frac{\partial^2 f}{\partial x \partial y}$	"*d* squared *f d x d y*"		f_{yx}	"*f* sub *y x*"
$\frac{\partial^2 f}{\partial y \partial x}$	"*d* squared *f d y d x*"		f_{xy}	"*f* sub *x y*"

The defining equations are

$$\frac{\partial^2 f}{\partial x^2} = \frac{\partial}{\partial x}\left(\frac{\partial f}{\partial x}\right), \qquad \frac{\partial^2 f}{\partial x\, \partial y} = \frac{\partial}{\partial x}\left(\frac{\partial f}{\partial y}\right),$$

and so on. Notice the order in which the derivatives are taken:

$\dfrac{\partial^2 f}{\partial x \partial y}$ Differentiate first with respect to y, then with respect to x.

$f_{yx} = (f_y)_x$ Means the same thing.

EXAMPLE 9 If $f(x, y) = x \cos y + ye^x$, then

$$\frac{\partial f}{\partial x} = \cos y + ye^x$$

$$\frac{\partial^2 f}{\partial y\, \partial x} = \frac{\partial}{\partial y}\left(\frac{\partial f}{\partial x}\right) = -\sin y + e^x$$

$$\frac{\partial^2 f}{\partial x^2} = \frac{\partial}{\partial x}\left(\frac{\partial f}{\partial x}\right) = ye^x.$$

Also,

$$\frac{\partial f}{\partial y} = -x \sin y + e^x$$

$$\frac{\partial^2 f}{\partial x\, \partial y} = \frac{\partial}{\partial x}\left(\frac{\partial f}{\partial y}\right) = -\sin y + e^x$$

$$\frac{\partial^2 f}{\partial y^2} = \frac{\partial}{\partial y}\left(\frac{\partial f}{\partial y}\right) = -x \cos y.$$

The Mixed Derivative Theorem

You may have noticed that the "mixed" second order derivatives

$$\frac{\partial^2 f}{\partial y\, \partial x} \quad \text{and} \quad \frac{\partial^2 f}{\partial x\, \partial y}$$

in Example 9 were equal. This was not a coincidence. They have to be equal whenever f, f_x, f_y, f_{xy}, and f_{yx} are continuous.

THEOREM 2

The Mixed Derivative Theorem (Euler's Theorem)

If $f(x, y)$ and its partial derivatives f_x, f_y, f_{xy}, and f_{yx} are defined throughout an open region containing a point (a, b) and are all continuous at (a, b), then

$$f_{xy}(a, b) = f_{yx}(a, b). \tag{5}$$

You can find proofs of Theorem 2 in most advanced calculus texts.

Theorem 2 says that when we want to calculate a mixed second order derivative we may differentiate in either order. This can work to our advantage, as the next example shows.

EXAMPLE 10 Find $\partial^2 w/\partial x\, \partial y$ if

$$w = xy + \frac{e^y}{y^2 + 1}.$$

Solution The symbol $\partial^2 w/\partial x\, \partial y$ tells us to differentiate first with respect to y and then with respect to x. However, if we postpone the differentiation with respect to y and differentiate first with respect to x, we can get the answer more quickly. In two steps,

$$\frac{\partial w}{\partial x} = y \quad \text{and} \quad \frac{\partial^2 w}{\partial y\, \partial x} = 1.$$

We are in for more work if we differentiate first with respect to y. (Just try it.)

Partial Derivatives of Still Higher Order

Although we will deal mostly with first and second order partial derivatives, because these appear the most frequently in applications, there is no theoretical limit to how many times we can differentiate a function as long as the derivatives involved exist. Thus we get third and fourth order derivatives denoted by symbols like

$$\frac{\partial^3 f}{\partial x\, \partial y^2} = f_{yyx},$$

$$\frac{\partial^4 f}{\partial x^2\, \partial y^2} = f_{yyxx},$$

and so on. As with second order derivatives, the order of differentiation is immaterial as long as the function and its derivatives through the order in question are continuous.

Exercises 13.3

In Exercises 1–18, find $\partial f/\partial x$ and $\partial f/\partial y$.

1. $f(x, y) = 2x$

2. $f(x, y) = -3y$

3. $f(x, y) = -4$

4. $f(x, y) = 2x - 3y - 4$

5. $f(x, y) = x(y - 1)$

6. $f(x, y) = x^2 + y^2$

7. $f(x, y) = x^2 - xy + y^2$

8. $f(x, y) = (x + 2)(y + 3)$

9. $f(x, y) = x^2(5y - 1)^3$

10. $f(x, y) = 1/(x + y)$

11. $f(x, y) = \sqrt{x^2 + y^2}$

12. $f(x, y) = x/(x^2 + y^2)$

13. $f(x, y) = (x + y)/(xy - 1)$

14. $f(x, y) = (y - x)e^x$

15. $f(x, y) = e^x \ln y$

16. $f(x, y) = \sin(x + y)$

17. $f(x, y) = e^x \sin(y + 1)$

18. $f(x, y) = \tan^{-1}(y/x)$

In Exercises 19–24, find f_x, f_y, and f_z.

19. $f(x, y, z) = xy + yz + zx$

20. $f(x, y, z) = 1 + y^2 + 2z^2$

21. $f(x, y, z) = (x^2 + y^2 + z^2)^{-1/2}$

22. $f(x, y, z) = x - \sqrt{y^2 + z^2}$

23. $f(x, y, z) = \sin(x + yz)$

24. $f(x, y, z) = \tan(x + y + z)$

In Exercises 25–30, find the partial derivative of the function with respect to each variable.

25. $f(t, \alpha) = \cos(2\pi t - \alpha)$

26. $g(u, v) = v^2 e^{(2u/v)}$

27. $h(\rho, \phi, \theta) = \rho \sin\phi \cos\theta$

28. $g(r, \theta, z) = r(1 - \cos\theta) - z$

29. *Work Done by the Heart* (Section 3.7, Exercise 48).

$$W(P, V, \delta, v, g) = PV + \frac{V\delta v^2}{2g}$$

30. *Wilson Lot Size Formula* (Section 4.5, Exercise 49).

$$A(c, h, k, m, q) = \frac{km}{q} + cm + \frac{hq}{2}$$

Find the second order partial derivatives of the functions in Exercises 31–36.

31. $f(x, y) = x + y + xy$

32. $f(x, y) = \sin xy$

33. $g(x, y) = x^2 y + \cos y + y \sin x$

34. $h(x, y) = xe^y + y + 1$

35. $r(x, y) = \ln(x + y)$

36. $s(x, y) = \tan^{-1}(y/x)$

In Exercises 37–40, verify that $w_{xy} = w_{yx}$.

37. $w = \ln(2x + 3y)$

38. $w = e^x + x \ln y + y \ln x$

39. $w = xy^2 + x^2y^3 + x^3y^4$

40. $w = x \sin y + y \sin x + xy$

41. Which order of differentiation will calculate f_{xy} faster: x first or y first? Try to answer without writing anything down.

a) $f(x, y) = x \sin y + e^y$
b) $f(x, y) = 1/x$
c) $f(x, y) = y + (x/y)$
d) $f(x, y) = y + x^2 y + 4y^3 - \ln(y^2 + 1)$
e) $f(x, y) = x^2 + 5xy + \sin x + 7e^x$
f) $f(x, y) = x \ln xy$

42. The fifth order partial derivative $\partial^5 f/\partial x^2 \partial y^3$ is zero for each of the following functions. To show this as quickly as possible, which variable would you differentiate with respect to first: x, or y? Try to answer without writing anything down.

a) $f(x, y) = y^2 x^4 e^x + 2$
b) $f(x, y) = y^2 + y(\sin x - x^4)$
c) $f(x, y) = x^2 + 5xy + \sin x + 7e^x$
d) $f(x, y) = xe^{y^2/2}$

43. Assume that the equation

$$x^3 z + z^3 x - 2yz = 0$$

defines z as a differentiable function of the two independent variables x and y. Find the value of $\partial z/\partial x$ at the point $(x, y, z) = (1, 1, 1)$.

44. Assume that the equation

$$xz + y \ln x - (9/z) = 0$$

defines x as a differentiable function of the two independent variables y and z. Find the value of $\partial x/\partial z$ at the point $(x, y, z) = (1, -1, -3)$.

LAPLACE EQUATIONS

The *three-dimensional Laplace equation*

$$\frac{\partial^2 f}{\partial x^2} + \frac{\partial^2 f}{\partial y^2} + \frac{\partial^2 f}{\partial z^2} = 0 \qquad (6)$$

is satisfied by steady-state temperature distributions $T = f(x, y, z)$ in space, by gravitational potentials, and by electrostatic potentials. The *two-dimensional Laplace equation*

$$\frac{\partial^2 f}{\partial x^2} + \frac{\partial^2 f}{\partial y^2} = 0, \qquad (7)$$

obtained by dropping the $\partial^2 f/\partial z^2$ term from Eq. (6), describes potentials and steady-state temperature distributions in a plane (Fig. 13.20).

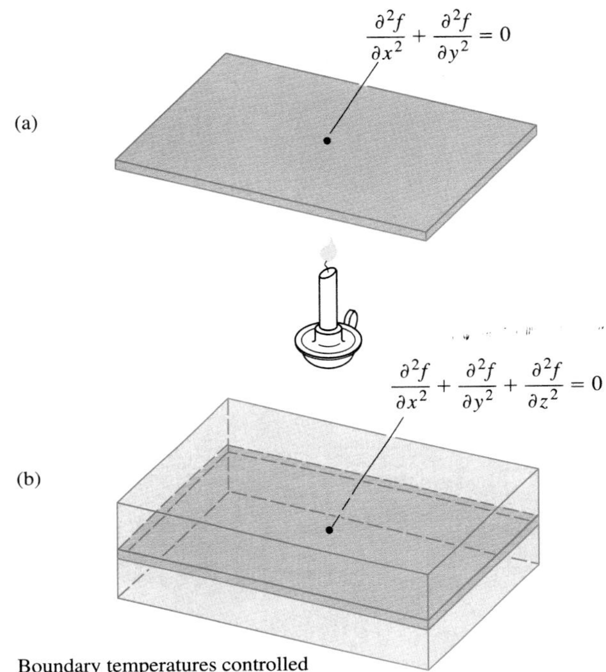

13.20 Steady state temperature distributions in planes and solids satisfy Laplace equations. The plane (a) may be treated as a thin slice of the solid (b) perpendicular to the z-axis.

Show that each function in Exercises 45–50 satisfies a Laplace equation.

45. $f(x, y, z) = x^2 + y^2 - 2z^2$

46. $f(x, y, z) = 2z^3 - 3(x^2 + y^2)z$

47. $f(x, y) = e^{-2y} \cos 2x$

48. $f(x, y) = \ln \sqrt{x^2 + y^2}$

49. $f(x, y, z) = (x^2 + y^2 + z^2)^{-1/2}$

50. $f(x, y, z) = e^{3x + 4y} \cos 5z$

THE WAVE EQUATION

If we stand on an ocean shore and take a snapshot of the waves, the picture shows a regular pattern of peaks and valleys in an instant of time (Fig. 13.21). We see periodic vertical motion in space, with respect to distance. If we stand in the water, we can feel the rise and fall of the water as the waves go by. We see periodic vertical motion in time. In physics, this beautiful symmetry is expressed by the *one-dimensional wave equation*

$$\frac{\partial^2 w}{\partial t^2} = c^2 \frac{\partial^2 w}{\partial x^2}, \tag{8}$$

where w is the wave height, x is the distance variable, t is the time variable, and c is the velocity with which the waves are propagated.

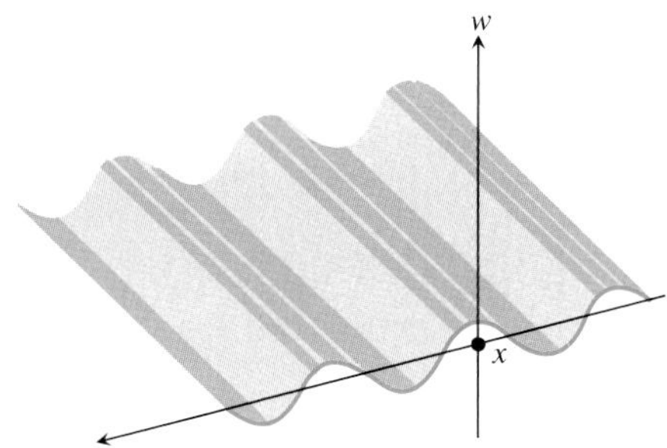

13.21 Waves in water at an instant in time. As time passes,

$$\frac{\partial^2 w}{\partial t^2} = c^2 \frac{\partial^2 w}{\partial x^2}.$$

In our example, x is the distance across the ocean's surface, but in other applications x might be the distance along a vibrating string, distance through air (sound waves), or distance through space (light waves). The number c varies with the medium and type of wave.

Show that the functions in Exercises 51–56 are all solutions of the wave equation.

51. $w = \sin(x + ct)$

52. $w = \cos(2x + 2ct)$

53. $w = \sin(x + ct) + \cos(2x + 2ct)$

54. $w = \ln(2x + 2ct)$

55. $w = \tan(2x - 2ct)$

56. $w = 5\cos(3x + 3ct) + e^{x+ct}$

Writing for Your Own Knowledge

Answer the following questions in writing. Some answers will take only a sentence or two; others may require several paragraphs. Some explanations may also call for graphs or sketches.

1. How are the partial derivatives $\partial f/\partial x$ and $\partial f/\partial y$ of a function $f(x, y)$ defined? What is their geometric meaning? What rates do they describe?
2. How are partial derivatives calculated?
3. How does the relation between first partial derivatives and continuity for real-valued functions of two independent variables differ from the relation between first derivatives and continuity for real-valued functions of a single independent variable?
4. How can Euler's theorem help in calculating derivatives?

13.4 *Differentiability, Linearization, and Differentials*

In this section, we define differentiability and proceed from there to linearizations and differentials. The mathematical results of the section stem from the Increment Theorem. As we will see in the next section, this theorem underlies the Chain Rule for multivariable functions.

Differentiability

Surprising as it may seem, the starting point for differentiability is not Fermat's difference quotient but rather the idea of increment. You may recall from our work with functions of a single variable that if $y = f(x)$ is differentiable at $x = x_0$, then the change in the value of f that results from changing x from x_0 to $x_0 + \Delta x$ is given by an equation of the form

$$\Delta y = f'(x_0)\Delta x + \epsilon\, \Delta x \tag{1}$$

in which $\epsilon \to 0$ as $\Delta x \to 0$. For functions of two variables, the analogous property becomes the definition of differentiability. The Increment Theorem (from advanced calculus) tells us when we may expect the property to hold.

THEOREM 3

The Increment Theorem for Functions of Two Variables

Suppose that the first partial derivatives of $f(x, y)$ are defined throughout an open region R containing the point (x_0, y_0) and that f_x and f_y are continuous at (x_0, y_0). Then the change

$$\Delta z = f(x_0 + \Delta x, y_0 + \Delta y) - f(x_0, y_0)$$

in the value of f that results from moving from (x_0, y_0) to another point $(x_0 + \Delta x, y_0 + \Delta y)$ in R satisfies an equation of the form

$$\Delta z = f_x(x_0, y_0)\Delta x + f_y(x_0, y_0)\Delta y + \epsilon_1 \Delta x + \epsilon_2 \Delta y, \tag{2}$$

in which $\epsilon_1, \epsilon_2 \to 0$ as $\Delta x, \Delta y \to 0$.

Similar results hold for functions of more than two variables.

DEFINITION

A function $f(x, y)$ is **differentiable at (x_0, y_0)** if $f_x(x_0, y_0)$ and $f_y(x_0, y_0)$ exist and Eq. (2) holds for f at (x_0, y_0). We call f **differentiable** if it is differentiable at every point in its domain.

In light of this definition, we have the immediate corollary of Theorem 3 that a function is differentiable if its first partial derivatives are *continuous*.

COROLLARY OF THEOREM 3

If the partial derivatives f_x and f_y of a function $f(x, y)$ are continuous throughout an open region R, then f is differentiable at every point of R.

If we replace the Δz in Eq. (2) by the expression $f(x, y) - f(x_0, y_0)$ and rewrite the equation as

$$f(x, y) = f(x_0, y_0) + f_x(x_0, y_0)\Delta x + f_y(x_0, y_0)\Delta y + \epsilon_1 \Delta x + \epsilon_2 \Delta y, \tag{3}$$

we see that the right-hand side of the new equation approaches $f(x_0, y_0)$ as Δx and Δy approach 0. This tells us that a function $f(x, y)$ is continuous at every point where it is differentiable.

THEOREM 4

If a function $f(x, y)$ is differentiable at (x_0, y_0), then f is continuous at (x_0, y_0).

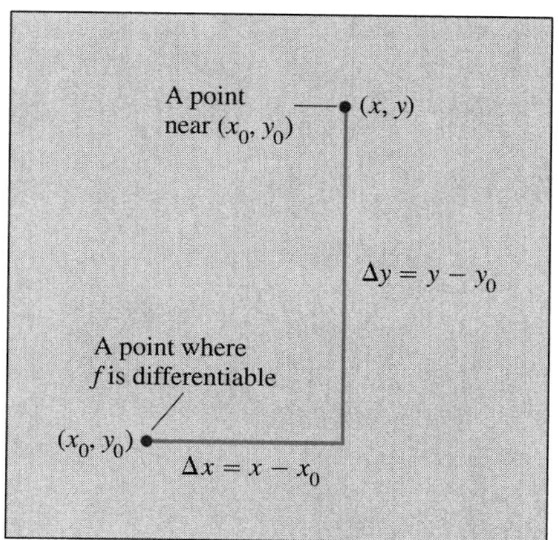

13.22 If f is differentiable at (x_0, y_0), then the value of f at any point (x, y) nearby is given by Eq. (4).

We can see from Theorems 3 and 4 that a function $f(x, y)$ is continuous at a point (x_0, y_0) if its first partial derivatives are continuous throughout some open region R containing the point. Our experience with functions of a single variable might tempt us to think that the mere existence of f_x and f_y at (x_0, y_0) would be enough to ensure the continuity of f at (x_0, y_0). After all, the existence of the derivative of a single-variable function at a point does ensure continuity. But here we have a departure from the single-variable theory. A function of two variables can be discontinuous at a point where its first partial derivatives exist, as we saw in the previous section (Fig. 13.19). Existence alone is not enough.

How to Linearize a Function of Two Variables

The functions of two variables that arise in science and mathematics can be complicated, and we sometimes need to replace them with simpler functions that give the accuracy required for specific applications without being so hard to work with. We do this in a way that is similar to the way we find linear replacements for functions of a single variable (Section 3.7). The source of the linear replacements, or linearizations as we again call them, is Eq. (3).

Suppose the function we wish to replace is $z = f(x, y)$ and that we want the replacement to be effective near a point (x_0, y_0) at which we know the values of f, f_x, and f_y and at which f is differentiable. Since f is differentiable, Eq. (3) holds for f at (x_0, y_0). Therefore, if we move from (x_0, y_0) to any point (x, y) by increments $\Delta x = x - x_0$ and $\Delta y = y - y_0$ (Fig. 13.22), the new value of f will be

$$\begin{aligned} f(x, y) = f(x_0, y_0) &+ f_x(x_0, y_0)(x - x_0) \\ &+ f_y(x_0, y_0)(y - y_0) + \epsilon_1 \Delta x + \epsilon_2 \Delta y, \end{aligned} \qquad \text{Eq. (3), with } \Delta x = x - x_0 \text{ and } \Delta y = y - y_0 \tag{4}$$

where $\epsilon_1, \epsilon_2 \to 0$ as $\Delta x, \Delta y \to 0$. If the increments Δx and Δy are small, the products $\epsilon_1 \Delta x$ and $\epsilon_2 \Delta y$ will be smaller still and we will have

$$f(x, y) \approx \underbrace{f(x_0, y_0) + f_x(x_0, y_0)(x - x_0) + f_y(x_0, y_0)(y - y_0)}_{L(x, y)}. \tag{5}$$

In other words, as long as Δx and Δy are small, f will have approximately the same value as the linear function L. When f is too hard to use, and our work can tolerate the error involved, we may safely replace f by L.

DEFINITIONS

The **linearization** of a function $f(x, y)$ at a point (x_0, y_0) where f is differentiable is the function

$$L(x, y) = f(x_0, y_0) + f_x(x_0, y_0)(x - x_0) + f_y(x_0, y_0)(y - y_0). \tag{6}$$

The approximation

$$f(x, y) \approx L(x, y) \tag{7}$$

is the **standard linear approximation** of f at (x_0, y_0).

In Section 13.7 we will see that the plane $z = L(x, y)$ is tangent to the surface $z = f(x, y)$ at the point (x_0, y_0). Thus, the linearization of a function of two variables is a tangent-*plane* approximation to the function in the same way that the linearization of a function of a single variable is a tangent-*line* approximation. Here is an example of a linearization.

EXAMPLE 1 Find the linearization of

$$f(x, y) = x^2 - xy + \frac{1}{2}y^2 + 3$$

at the point (3, 2).

Solution We evaluate Eq. (6) with

$$f(x_0, y_0) = \left(x^2 - xy + \frac{1}{2}y^2 + 3\right)_{(3,2)} = 8,$$

$$f_x(x_0, y_0) = \frac{\partial}{\partial x}\left(x^2 - xy + \frac{1}{2}y^2 + 3\right)_{(3,2)} = (2x - y)_{(3,2)} = 4,$$

$$f_y(x_0, y_0) = \frac{\partial}{\partial y}\left(x^2 - xy + \frac{1}{2}y^2 + 3\right)_{(3,2)} = (-x + y)_{(3,2)} = -1,$$

getting

$$\begin{aligned} L(x, y) &= f(x_0, y_0) + f_x(x_0, y_0)(x - x_0) + f_y(x_0, y_0)(y - y_0) \qquad \text{Eq. (6)} \\ &= 8 + (4)(x - 3) + (-1)(y - 2) = 4x - y - 2. \end{aligned}$$

The linearization of f at (3, 2) is $L(x, y) = 4x - y - 2$.

How Accurate Is the Standard Linear Approximation?

To find the error in the approximation $f(x, y) \approx L(x, y)$, we use the second order partial derivatives of f. Suppose that the first and second order partial derivatives of f are continuous throughout an open set containing a closed rectangular region R centered at (x_0, y_0) and given by the inequalities

$$|x - x_0| \le h, \qquad |y - y_0| \le k \tag{8}$$

(Fig. 13.23). A theorem from advanced calculus says that because R is closed and bounded, the second partial derivatives all take on absolute maximum values on R. Another theorem from advanced calculus says that if B is the largest of these values then the error $E(x, y) = f(x, y) - L(x, y)$ in the standard linear approximation satisfies the inequality

$$|E(x, y)| \le \frac{1}{2}B\left(|x - x_0| + |y - y_0|\right)^2 \tag{9}$$

throughout R.

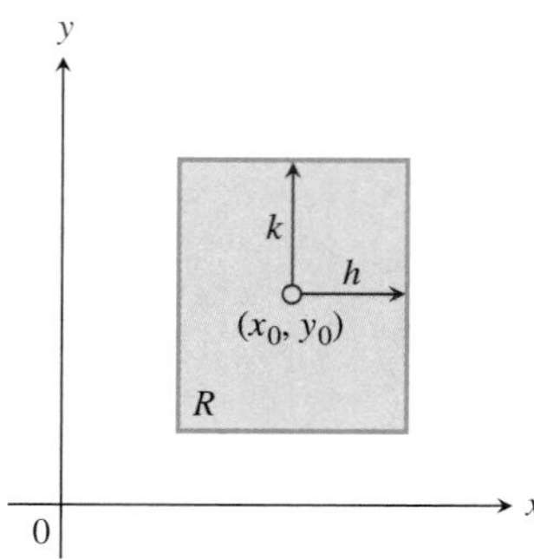

13.23 The rectangular region R: $|x - x_0| \le h$, $|y - y_0| \le k$ in the xy-plane. On this kind of region, we can find useful error bounds for our approximations.

When we use this inequality to estimate E, we usually cannot find the values of f_{xx}, f_{yy}, and f_{xy} that determine B and we have to settle for an upperbound or "worst-case" value instead. If M is any common upper bound for $|f_{xx}|$, $|f_{yy}|$, and $|f_{xy}|$ on R, then B will be less than or equal to M and we will know that

$$|E(x, y)| \le \frac{1}{2}M\left(|x - x_0| + |y - y_0|\right)^2. \tag{10}$$

This is the inequality we normally use in estimating E. When we need to make $|E(x, y)|$ small for a given M, we just make $|x - x_0|$ and $|y - y_0|$ small.

The Error in the Standard Linear Approximation of $f(x, y)$ near (x_0, y_0)

If f has continuous first and second partial derivatives throughout an open set containing a rectangle R centered at (x_0, y_0) and if M is any upper bound for the values of $|f_{xx}|$, $|f_{yy}|$, and $|f_{xy}|$ on R, then the error $E(x, y)$ incurred in replacing $f(x, y)$ on R by its linearization

$$L(x, y) = f(x_0, y_0) + f_x(x_0, y_0)(x - x_0) + f_y(x_0, y_0)(y - y_0) \qquad (11)$$

satisfies the inequality

$$|E(x, y)| \le \frac{1}{2} M(|x - x_0| + |y - y_0|)^2. \qquad (12)$$

EXAMPLE 2 In Example 1, we found the linearization of

$$f(x, y) = x^2 - xy + \frac{1}{2}y^2 + 3$$

at (3, 2) to be

$$L(x, y) = 4x - y - 2.$$

Find an upper bound for the error in the approximation $f(x, y) \approx L(x, y)$ over the rectangle

$$R: \quad |x - 3| \le 0.1, \quad |y - 2| \le 0.1.$$

Express the upper bound as a percentage of $f(3, 2)$, the value of f at the center of the rectangle.

Solution We use the inequality

$$|E(x, y)| \le \frac{1}{2} M(|x - x_0| + |y - y_0|)^2. \qquad \text{Eq. (12)}$$

To find a suitable value for M, we calculate f_{xx}, f_{xy}, and f_{yy}, finding, after a routine differentiation, that all three derivatives are constant, with values

$$|f_{xx}| = |2| = 2, \qquad |f_{xy}| = |-1| = 1, \qquad |f_{yy}| = |1| = 1.$$

The largest of these is 2, so we may safely take M to be 2. With $(x_0, y_0) = (3, 2)$, we then know that, throughout R,

$$|E(x, y)| \le \frac{1}{2}(2)(|x - 3| + |y - 2|)^2 = (|x - 3| + |y - 2|)^2.$$

Finally, since $|x - 3| \le 0.1$ and $|y - 2| \le 0.1$ on R, we have

$$|E(x, y)| \le (0.1 + 0.1)^2 = 0.04.$$

As a percentage of $f(3, 2) = 8$, the error is no greater than

$$\frac{0.04}{8} \times 100 = 0.5\%.$$

As long as (x, y) stays in R, the approximation $f(x, y) \approx L(x, y)$ will be in error by no more than 0.04, which is 1/2% of the value of f at the center of R.

Predicting Change with Differentials

Suppose we know the values of a differentiable function $f(x, y)$ and its first partial derivatives at a point (x_0, y_0) and we want to predict how much the value of f will change if we move to a point $(x_0 + \Delta x, y_0 + \Delta y)$ nearby. If Δx and Δy are small, f and its linearization will change by nearly the same amount, so the change in L will give a practical estimate of the change in f.

The change in f is

$$\Delta f = f(x_0 + \Delta x, y_0 + \Delta y) - f(x_0, y_0).$$

A straightforward calculation with Eq. (6), using the notation $x - x_0 = \Delta x$ and $y - y_0 = \Delta y$, shows that the corresponding change in L is

$$\begin{aligned} \Delta L &= L(x_0 + \Delta x, y_0 + \Delta y) - L(x_0, y_0) \\ &= f_x(x_0, y_0)\Delta x + f_y(x_0, y_0)\Delta y. \end{aligned} \tag{13}$$

The formula for Δf is usually as hard to work with as the formula for f. The change in L, however, is just a known constant times Δx plus a known constant times Δy.

The change ΔL is usually described in the more suggestive notation

$$df = f_x(x_0, y_0)\,dx + f_y(x_0, y_0)\,dy, \tag{14}$$

in which df denotes the change in the linearization that results from the changes dx and dy in x and y. As usual, we call dx and dy differentials of x and y, and call df the corresponding differential of f.

DEFINITION

If we move from (x_0, y_0) to a point $(x_0 + dx, y_0 + dy)$ nearby, the resulting differential in f is

$$df = f_x(x_0, y_0)\,dx + f_y(x_0, y_0)\,dy. \tag{15}$$

This change in the linearization of f is called the **total differential of f.**

EXAMPLE 3 *Sensitivity to Change.* Your company manufactures right circular cylindrical molasses storage tanks that are 25 ft high with a radius of 5 ft (Fig. 13.24). How sensitive are the tanks' volumes to small variations in height and radius?

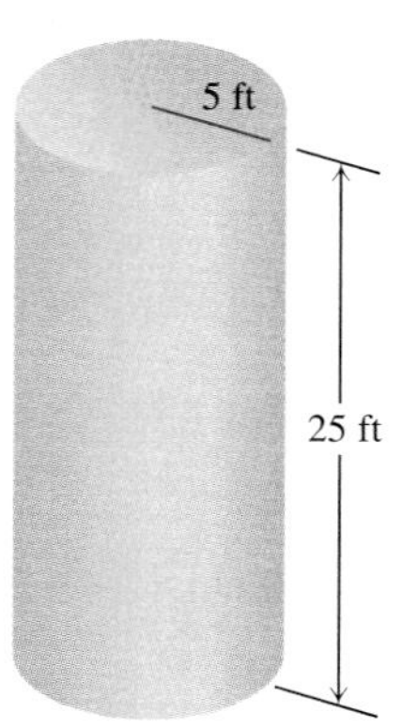

13.24 A small change in this tank's radius will change the volume 10 times as much as a change of the same size in the tank's height (Example 3).

Solution As a function of radius r and height h, the typical tank's volume is

$$V = \pi r^2 h.$$

The change in volume caused by small changes dr and dh in radius and height is approximately

$$\begin{aligned} dV &= V_r(5, 25)\,dr + V_h(5, 25)\,dh \\ &= (2\pi rh)_{(5,25)}\,dr + (\pi r^2)_{(5,25)}\,dh \\ &= 250\pi\,dr + 25\pi\,dh. \end{aligned}$$

Eq. (15) with $f = V$ and $(x_0, y_0) = (5, 25)$

Thus, a 1-unit change in r will change V by about 250π units. A 1-unit change in h will change V by about 25π units. The tank's volume is 10 times more sensitive to a small change in r than it is to a small change of equal size in h. As a

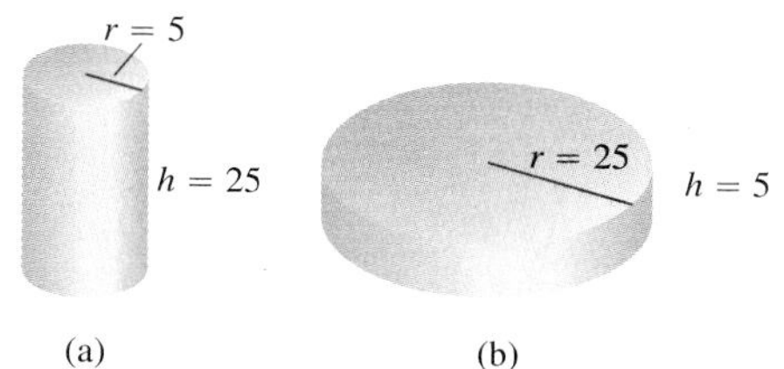

13.25 The volume of cylinder (a) is more sensitive to a small change in r than it is to an equally small change in h. The volume of cylinder (b) is more sensitive to small changes in h than it is to small changes in r.

quality control engineer concerned with being sure the tanks have the correct volume, you would want to pay special attention to their radii.

In contrast, if the values of r and h are reversed to make $r = 25$ and $h = 5$, then the total differential in V becomes

$$dV = (2\pi rh)_{(25,\,5)}\,dr + (\pi r^2)_{(25,\,5)}dh = 250\pi\,dr + 625\pi\,dh.$$

Now the volume is more sensitive to changes in h than to changes in r (Fig. 13.25).

The general rule to be learned from this example is that functions are most sensitive to small changes in the variables that generate the largest partial derivatives.

Absolute, Relative, and Percentage Change

When we move from (x_0, y_0) to a point nearby, we can describe the corresponding change in the value of a function $f(x, y)$ in three different ways.

	True	Estimate	
Absolute change:	Δf	df	
Relative change:	$\dfrac{\Delta f}{f(x_0, y_0)}$	$\dfrac{df}{f(x_0, y_0)}$	(16)
Percentage change:	$\dfrac{\Delta f}{f(x_0, y_0)} \times 100$	$\dfrac{df}{f(x_0, y_0)} \times 100$	

Absolute Change vs. Relative Change

If you measure a 20-volt potential with an error of 10 volts, your reading is probably too crude to be useful. You are off by 50%. But if you measure a 200,000-volt potential with an error of 10 volts, your reading is still within 0.005 percent of the true value. An absolute error of 10 volts is significant in the first case but of no consequence in the second because the relative error is so small.

In other cases, a small relative error—say, traveling a few meters too far in a journey of hundreds of thousands of meters—can have spectacular consequences.

EXAMPLE 4 Suppose that the variables r and h change from the initial values of $(r_0, h_0) = (1, 5)$ by the amounts $dr = 0.03$ and $dh = -0.1$. Estimate the resulting absolute, relative, and percentage changes in the values of the function $V = \pi r^2 h$.

Solution To estimate the absolute change in V, we evaluate

$$dV = V_r(r_0, h_0)\,dr + V_h(r_0, h_0)\,dh \tag{17}$$

to get

$$\begin{aligned} dV &= 2\pi r_0 h_0\,dr + \pi r_0^2\,dh = 2\pi(1)(5)(0.03) + \pi(1)^2(-0.1) \\ &= 0.3\pi - 0.1\pi = 0.2\pi. \end{aligned}$$

We divide this by $V(r_0, h_0)$ to estimate the relative change:

$$\frac{dV}{V(r_0, h_0)} = \frac{0.2\pi}{\pi r_0^2 h_0} = \frac{0.2\pi}{\pi(1)^2(5)} = 0.04.$$

We multiply this by 100 to estimate the percentage change:

$$\frac{dV}{V(r_0, h_0)} \times 100 = 0.04 \times 100 = 4\%.$$

EXAMPLE 5 The volume $V = \pi r^2 h$ of a right circular cylinder is to be calculated from measured values of r and h. Suppose that r is measured with an error of no more than 2% and h with an error of no more than 0.5%. Estimate the resulting possible percentage error in the calculation of V.

Solution We are told that

$$\left|\frac{dr}{r} \times 100\right| \le 2 \qquad \text{and} \qquad \left|\frac{dh}{h} \times 100\right| \le 0.5.$$

Since $$\frac{dV}{V} = \frac{2\pi rh\,dr + \pi r^2\,dh}{\pi r^2 h} = \frac{2\,dr}{r} + \frac{dh}{h},$$

we have $$\left|\frac{dV}{V} \times 100\right| = \left|2\frac{dr}{r} \times 100 + \frac{dh}{h} \times 100\right|$$

$$\le 2\left|\frac{dr}{r} \times 100\right| + \left|\frac{dh}{h} \times 100\right| \le 2(2) + 0.5 = 4.5.$$

We estimate the error in the volume calculation to be at most 4.5%.

How accurately do we have to measure r and h to have a reasonable chance of calculating $V = \pi r^2 h$ with an error, say, of less than 2%? Questions like this are hard to answer because there is usually no single right answer. Since

$$\frac{dV}{V} = 2\frac{dr}{r} + \frac{dh}{h},$$

we see that dV/V is controlled by a combination of dr/r and dh/h. If we can measure h with great accuracy, we might come out all right even if we are sloppy about measuring r. On the other hand, our measurement of h might have so large a dh that the resulting dV/V would be too crude an estimate of $\Delta V/V$ to be useful even if dr were zero.

What we do in such cases is look for a reasonable square about the measured values (r_0, h_0) in which V will not vary by more than the allowed amount from $V_0 = \pi r_0^2 h_0$. The next example shows how this is done.

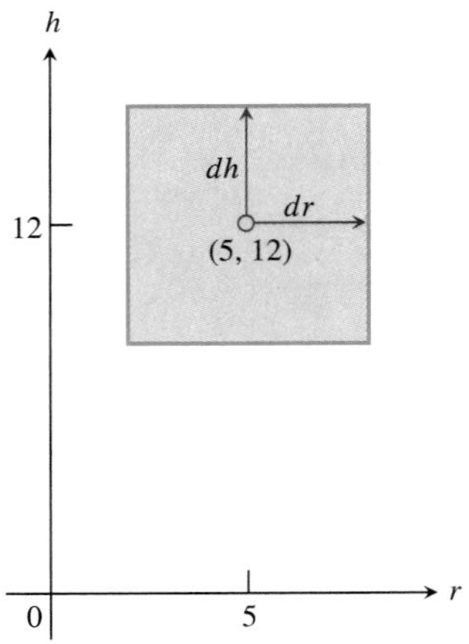

13.26 A small square about the point (5, 12) in the rh-plane (Example 6).

EXAMPLE 6 Find a reasonable square about the point $(r_0, h_0) = (5, 12)$ in which the value of $V = \pi r^2 h$ will not vary by more than ± 0.1.

Solution We approximate the variation ΔV by the differential

$$dV = 2\pi r_0 h_0\,dr + \pi r_0^2\,dh = 2\pi(5)(12)\,dr + \pi(5)^2\,dh = 120\pi dr + 25\pi dh.$$

Since the region to which we are restricting our attention is a square (Fig. 13.26), we may set $dh = dr$ to get

$$dV = 120\pi\,dr + 25\pi\,dr = 145\pi\,dr.$$

We then ask, How small must we take dr to be sure that $|dV|$ is no larger than 0.1? To answer, we start with the inequality

$$|dV| \le 0.1,$$

express dV in terms of dr,

$$|145\pi\,dr| \le 0.1,$$

and find a corresponding upper bound for dr:

$$|dr| \le \frac{0.1}{145\pi} \approx 2.1 \times 10^{-4}.$$ Rounding down to make sure dr won't accidentally be too big.

With $dh = dr$, then, the square we want is described by the inequalities

$$|r - 5| \le 2.1 \times 10^{-4}, \qquad |h - 12| \le 2.1 \times 10^{-4}.$$

As long as (r, h) stays in this square, we may expect $|dV|$ to be less than or equal to 0.1 and we may expect $|\Delta V|$ to be approximately the same size.

Exercises 13.4

In Exercises 1–6, find the linearization $L(x, y)$ of the given function at each point.

1. $f(x, y) = x^2 + y^2 + 1$ at (a) $(0, 0)$, (b) $(1, 1)$
2. $f(x, y) = x^3y^4$ at (a) $(1, 1)$, (b) $(0, 0)$
3. $f(x, y) = e^x \cos y$ at (a) $(0, 0)$, (b) $(0, \pi/2)$
4. $f(x, y) = (x + y + 2)^2$ at (a) $(0, 0)$, (b) $(1, 2)$
5. $f(x, y) = 3x - 4y + 5$ at (a) $(0, 0)$, (b) $(1, 1)$
6. $f(x, y) = e^{2y-x}$ at (a) $(0, 0)$, (b) $(1, 2)$

In Exercises 7–12, find the linearization $L(x, y)$ of the function $f(x, y)$ at P_0. Then use inequality (12) to find an upper bound for the magnitude $|E|$ of the error in the approximation $f(x, y) \approx L(x, y)$ over the rectangle R.

7. $f(x, y) = x^2 - 3xy + 5$ at $P_0(2, 1)$,
   R: $|x - 2| \le 0.1$, $|y - 1| \le 0.1$
8. $f(x, y) = (1/2)x^2 + xy + (1/4)y^2 + 3x - 3y + 4$ at $P_0(2, 2)$,
   R: $|x - 2| \le 0.1$, $|y - 2| \le 0.1$
9. $f(x, y) = 1 + y + x \cos y$ at $P_0(0, 0)$,
   R: $|x| \le 0.2$, $|y| \le 0.2$
   (Use $|\cos y| \le 1$ and $|\sin y| \le 1$ in estimating E.)
10. $f(x, y) = \ln x + \ln y$ at $P_0(1, 1)$,
    R: $|x - 1| \le 0.2$, $|y - 1| \le 0.2$
11. $f(x, y) = e^x \cos y$ at $P_0(0, 0)$,
    R: $|x| \le 0.1$, $|y| \le 0.1$
    (Use $e^x \le 1.11$ and $|\cos y| \le 1$ in estimating E.)
12. $f(x, y) = xy^2 + y \cos(x - 1)$ at $P_0(1, 2)$,
    R: $|x - 1| \le 0.1$, $|y - 2| \le 0.1$
13. You plan to calculate the area of a long, thin rectangle from measurements of its length and width. Which dimension should you measure more carefully? Give reasons for your answer.
14. a) Around the point $(1, 0)$, is $f(x, y) = x^2(y + 1)$ more sensitive to changes in x, or to changes in y? Give reasons for your answer.
    b) What ratio of dx to dy will make df equal zero at $(1, 0)$?
15. Suppose T is to be found from the formula $T = x(e^y + e^{-y})$ where x and y are found to be 2 and ln 2 with maximum possible errors of $|dx| = 0.1$ and $|dy| = 0.02$. Estimate the maximum possible error in the computed value of T.
16. About how accurately may $V = \pi r^2 h$ be calculated from measurements of r and h that are in error by 1%?
17. If $r = 5.0$ cm and $h = 12.0$ cm to the nearest millimeter, what should we expect the maximum percentage error in calculating $V = \pi r^2 h$ to be?
18. To estimate the volume of a cylinder of radius about 2 m and height about 3 m, about how accurately should the radius and height be measured so that the error in the volume estimate will not exceed 0.1 m³? Assume that the possible error dr in measuring r is equal to the possible error dh in measuring h.
19. Give a reasonable square centered at $(1, 1)$ over which the value of $f(x, y) = x^3y^4$ will not vary by more than ± 0.1.
20. *Variation in Electrical Resistance.* The resistance R produced by wiring resistors of R_1 and R_2 ohms in parallel (Fig. 13.27) can be calculated from the formula
$$\frac{1}{R} = \frac{1}{R_1} + \frac{1}{R_2}.$$
    a) Show that
$$dR = \left(\frac{R}{R_1}\right)^2 dR_1 + \left(\frac{R}{R_2}\right)^2 dR_2.$$
    b) You have designed a two-resistor circuit like the one in Fig. 13.27 to have resistances of $R_1 = 100$ ohms and $R_2 = 400$ ohms, but there is always some variation in manufacturing and the resistors received by your firm will probably not have these exact values. Will the value of R be more sensitive to variation in R_1, or to variation in R_2? Give reasons for your answer.
21. *Continuation of Exercise 20.* In another circuit like the one in Fig. 13.27, you plan to change R_1 from 20 to 20.1 ohms and R_2 from 25 to 24.9 ohms. By about what percentage will this change R?

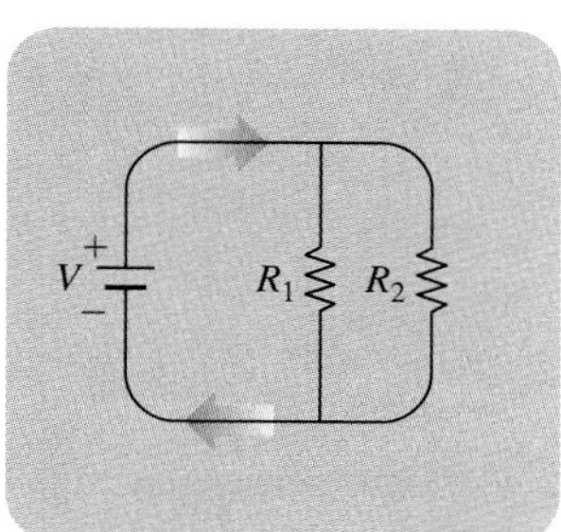

13.27 The circuit in Exercises 20 and 21.

22. *Error Carry-over in Coordinate Changes.*
    a) If $x = 3 \pm 0.01$ and $y = 4 \pm 0.01$, as shown here, with approximately what accuracy can you calculate the polar coordinates r and θ of the point $P(x, y)$ from the formulas $r^2 = x^2 + y^2$ and $\theta = \tan^{-1}(y/x)$? Express your estimates as percentage changes of the values that r and θ have at the point $(x_0, y_0) = (3, 4)$.
    b) At the point $(x_0, y_0) = (3, 4)$, are the values of r and θ more sensitive to changes in x, or to changes in y? Give reasons for your answer.

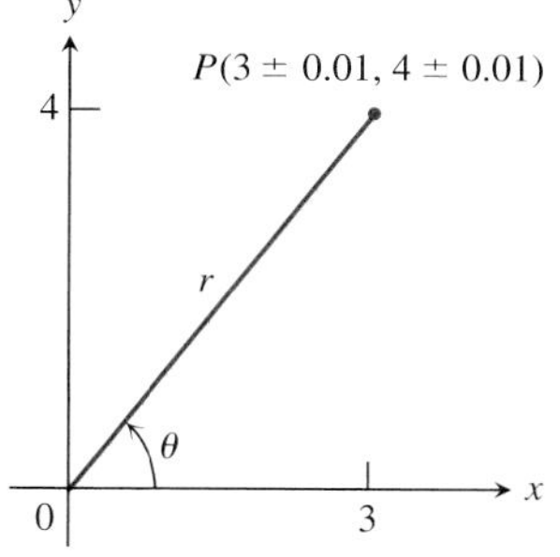

FUNCTIONS OF THREE VARIABLES

To get the linearization and total-differential formulas for a differentiable function $f(x, y, z)$, we add z-terms to the two-variable formulas:

Linearization of $f(x, y, z)$:

$$L(x, y, z) = f(x_0, y_0, z_0) + f_x(x_0, y_0, z_0)(x - x_0) + f_y(x_0, y_0, z_0)(y - y_0) + f_z(x_0, y_0, z_0)(z - z_0)$$

Total differential of $f(x, y, z)$:

$$df = f_x(x_0, y_0, z_0)\,dx + f_y(x_0, y_0, z_0)\,dy + f_z(x_0, y_0, z_0)\,dz$$

Similar results hold for functions of four or more variables.

Find the linearizations of the functions in Exercises 23–28 at the given points.

23. $f(x, y, z) = xy + yz + xz$ at
a) $(1, 1, 1)$ **b)** $(1, 0, 0)$ **c)** $(0, 0, 0)$

24. $f(x, y, z) = x^2 + y^2 + z^2$ at
a) $(1, 1, 1)$ **b)** $(0, 1, 0)$ **c)** $(1, 0, 0)$

25. $f(x, y, z) = \sqrt{x^2 + y^2 + z^2}$ at
a) $(1, 0, 0)$ **b)** $(1, 1, 0)$ **c)** $(1, 2, 2)$

26. $f(x, y, z) = (\sin xy)/z$ at
a) $(\pi/2, 1, 1)$ **b)** $(2, 0, 1)$

27. $f(x, y, z) = e^x + \cos(y + z)$ at
a) $(0, 0, 0)$ **b)** $\left(0, \frac{\pi}{2}, 0\right)$ **c)** $\left(0, \frac{\pi}{4}, \frac{\pi}{4}\right)$

28. $f(x, y, z) = \tan^{-1}(xyz)$ at
a) $(1, 0, 0)$ **b)** $(1, 1, 0)$ **c)** $(1, 1, 1)$

29. If $|a|$ is much greater than $|b|$, $|c|$, and $|d|$, to which of a, b, c, and d is the value of the determinant

$$f(a, b, c, d) = \begin{vmatrix} a & b \\ c & d \end{vmatrix}$$

most sensitive? Give reasons for your answer.

30. Estimate how strongly simultaneous errors of 2% in a, b, and c might affect the calculation of the product

$$p(a, b, c) = abc.$$

31. Estimate how much wood it takes to make a hollow rectangular box whose inside measurements are 5 ft long by 3 ft wide by 2 ft deep if the box is made of lumber 1/2-in. thick and the box has no top.

32. The area of a triangle is $(1/2)ab \sin C$, where a and b are the lengths of two sides of the triangle and C is the measure of the included angle. In surveying a triangular plot, you have measured a, b, and C to be 150 ft, 200 ft, and 60°, respectively. By about how much could your area calculation be in error if your values of a and b are off by half a foot each and your measurement of C is off by 2°? See the figure here. Remember to use radians.

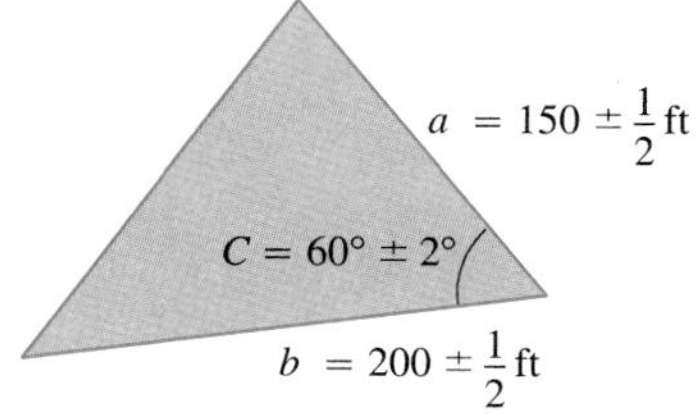

33. Suppose that $u = xe^y + y \sin z$ and that x, y, and z can be measured with maximum possible errors of ± 0.2, ± 0.6, and $\pm \pi/180$, respectively. Estimate the maximum possible error in calculating u from the measured values $x = 2$, $y = \ln 3$, $z = \pi/2$.

34. *The Wilson Lot Size Formula.* The Wilson lot size formula in economics says that the most economical quantity Q of goods (radios, shoes, brooms, whatever) for a store to order is given by the formula $Q = \sqrt{2KM/h}$, where K is the cost of placing the order, M is the number of items sold per week, and h is the weekly holding cost for each item (cost of space, utilities, security, and so on). To which of the variables K, M, and h is Q most sensitive near the point $(K_0, M_0, h_0) = (2, 20, 0.05)$? Give reasons for your answer.

35. Does a function $f(x, y)$ with continuous first partial derivatives throughout an open region R have to be continuous on R? Give reasons for your answer.

36. If a function $f(x, y)$ has continuous second partial derivatives throughout an open region R, must the first order partial derivatives of f be continuous on R? Give reasons for your answer.

Writing for Your Own Knowledge

Answer the following questions in writing. Some answers will take only a sentence or two; others may require several paragraphs. Some explanations may also call for graphs or sketches.

1. What does the Increment Theorem say?
2. What does it mean for a function $f(x, y)$ to be differentiable?
3. How can you sometimes decide from examining $\partial f/\partial x$ and $\partial f/\partial y$ that a function $f(x, y)$ is differentiable?
4. What relation holds between differentiability and continuity for a function $f(x, y)$?
5. How do you linearize a function of two independent variables? Why might you want to do this?
6. What can you say about the accuracy of linear approximations?
7. If (x, y) moves from (x_0, y_0) to a point $(x_0 + dx, y_0 + dy)$ nearby, how do you estimate the absolute change in the value of a differentiable function $f(x, y)$? How do you estimate the relative change? the percentage change?

13.5 The Chain Rule

When we are interested in the temperature $w = f(x, y, z)$ at points along a curve $x = g(t)$, $y = h(t)$, $z = k(t)$ in space, or in the pressure or density along a path through a gas or fluid, we may think of f as a function of the single variable t. For each value of t, the temperature at the point $(g(t), h(t), k(t))$ is the value of the composite function $f(g(t), h(t), k(t))$. If we then wish to know the rate at which f changes with respect to t along the path, we have only to differentiate this composite with respect to t, provided, of course, the derivative exists.

Sometimes we can find the derivative by substituting the formulas for g, h, and k into the formula for f and differentiating directly with respect to t. But we often have to work with functions whose formulas are too complicated for convenient substitution or for which formulas are not readily available. To find a function's derivatives under circumstances like these, we use the Chain Rule. The form the Chain Rule takes depends on how many variables are involved but, except for the presence of additional variables, it works just like the Chain Rule from Chapter 3.

The Chain Rule for Functions of Two Variables

In Chapter 3, we used the Chain Rule when $w = f(x)$ was a differentiable function of x and $x = g(t)$ was a differentiable function of t. This made w a differentiable function of t and the Chain Rule said that dw/dt could be calculated with the formula

$$\frac{dw}{dt} = \frac{dw}{dx}\frac{dx}{dt}.$$

The analogous formula for a function $w = f(x, y)$ of two independent variables is given in Theorem 5.

THEOREM 5

Chain Rule for Functions of Two Independent Variables

If $w = f(x, y)$ is differentiable and x and y are differentiable functions of t, then w is a differentiable function of t and

$$\frac{dw}{dt} = \frac{\partial f}{\partial x}\frac{dx}{dt} + \frac{\partial f}{\partial y}\frac{dy}{dt}. \tag{1}$$

Proof The proof consists of showing that if x and y are differentiable at $t = t_0$, then w is differentiable at t_0 and

$$\left(\frac{dw}{dt}\right)_{t_0} = \left(\frac{\partial w}{\partial x}\right)_{P_0}\left(\frac{dx}{dt}\right)_{t_0} + \left(\frac{\partial w}{\partial y}\right)_{P_0}\left(\frac{dy}{dt}\right)_{t_0}, \tag{2}$$

where $P_0 = (x(t_0), y(t_0))$.

Let Δx, Δy, and Δw be the increments that result from changing t from t_0 to $t_0 + \Delta t$. Since f is differentiable (remember the definition in Section 13.4),

$$\Delta w = \left(\frac{\partial w}{\partial x}\right)_{P_0}\Delta x + \left(\frac{\partial w}{\partial y}\right)_{P_0}\Delta y + \epsilon_1 \Delta x + \epsilon_2 \Delta y, \tag{3}$$

where $\epsilon_1, \epsilon_2 \to 0$ as $\Delta x, \Delta y \to 0$. To find dw/dt, we divide Eq. (3) through by Δt and let Δt approach zero. The division gives

$$\frac{\Delta w}{\Delta t} = \left(\frac{\partial w}{\partial x}\right)_{P_0} \frac{\Delta x}{\Delta t} + \left(\frac{\partial w}{\partial y}\right)_{P_0} \frac{\Delta y}{\Delta t} + \epsilon_1 \frac{\Delta x}{\Delta t} + \epsilon_2 \frac{\Delta y}{\Delta t}, \tag{4}$$

and letting Δt approach zero gives

$$\begin{aligned} \left(\frac{dw}{dt}\right)_{t_0} &= \lim_{\Delta t \to 0} \frac{\Delta w}{\Delta t} \\ &= \left(\frac{\partial w}{\partial x}\right)_{P_0} \left(\frac{dx}{dt}\right)_{t_0} + \left(\frac{\partial w}{\partial y}\right)_{P_0} \left(\frac{dy}{dt}\right)_{t_0} + 0 \cdot \left(\frac{dx}{dt}\right)_{t_0} + 0 \cdot \left(\frac{dy}{dt}\right)_{t_0}. \end{aligned} \tag{5}$$

This completes the proof. ■

The way to remember the Chain Rule is to picture the diagram below. To find dw/dt, start at w and read down each route to t, multiplying derivatives along the way. Then add the products.

Chain Rule

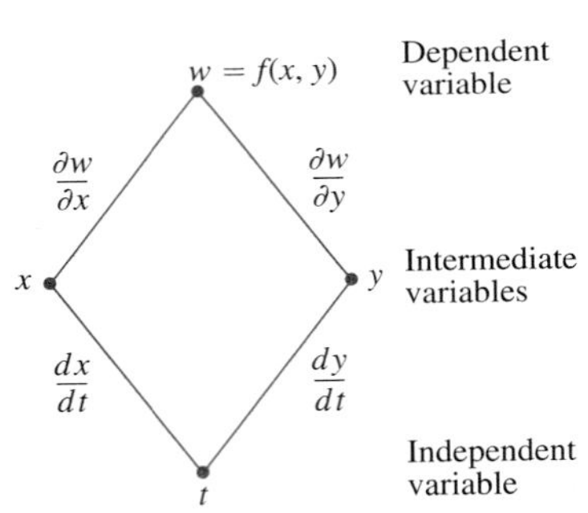

$$\frac{dw}{dt} = \frac{\partial w}{\partial x}\frac{dx}{dt} + \frac{\partial w}{\partial y}\frac{dy}{dt}$$

The accompanying tree diagram provides a convenient way to remember the Chain Rule. From the diagram you see that when $t = t_0$ the derivatives dx/dt and dy/dt are evaluated at t_0. The value of t_0 then determines the value x_0 for the differentiable function x and the value y_0 for the differentiable function y. The partial derivatives $\partial w/\partial x$ and $\partial w/\partial y$ (which are themselves functions of x and y) are evaluated at the point $P_0\ (x_0, y_0)$ corresponding to t_0. The "true" independent variable is t, while x and y are *intermediate variables* (controlled by t) and w is the dependent variable.

A more precise notation for the Chain Rule shows how the various derivatives are evaluated:

$$\frac{dw}{dt}(t_0) = \frac{\partial f}{\partial x}(x_0, y_0) \cdot \frac{dx}{dt}(t_0) + \frac{\partial f}{\partial y}(x_0, y_0) \cdot \frac{dy}{dt}(t_0). \tag{6}$$

However, Eq. (1) gives the shortest form of the Chain Rule. When we do not need to be told how each derivative is to be evaluated, it is preferable and easier to use Eq. (1).

EXAMPLE 1 Use the Chain Rule to find the derivative of

$$w = xy$$

with respect to t along the path $x = \cos t$, $y = \sin t$. What is the derivative's value at $t = \pi/2$?

Solution We evaluate the right-hand side of Eq. (1) with $w = xy$, $x = \cos t$, and $y = \sin t$:

$$\frac{\partial w}{\partial x} = y = \sin t, \qquad \frac{\partial w}{\partial y} = x = \cos t, \qquad \frac{dx}{dt} = -\sin t, \qquad \frac{dy}{dt} = \cos t$$

$$\begin{aligned} \frac{dw}{dt} &= \frac{\partial w}{\partial x}\frac{dx}{dt} + \frac{\partial w}{\partial y}\frac{dy}{dt} = (\sin t)(-\sin t) + (\cos t)(\cos t) \\ &= -\sin^2 t + \cos^2 t = \cos 2t. \end{aligned}$$

Eq. (1) with values from above

Notice in our calculation that we have substituted the functional expressions $x = \cos t$ and $y = \sin t$ in the partial derivatives $\partial w/\partial x$ and $\partial w/\partial y$. The resulting derivative dw/dt is then expressed in terms of the independent variable t (so the intermediate variables x and y do not appear).

Here we have three routes from w to t instead of two. But finding dw/dt is still the same. Read down each route, multiplying derivatives along the way; then add.

Chain Rule

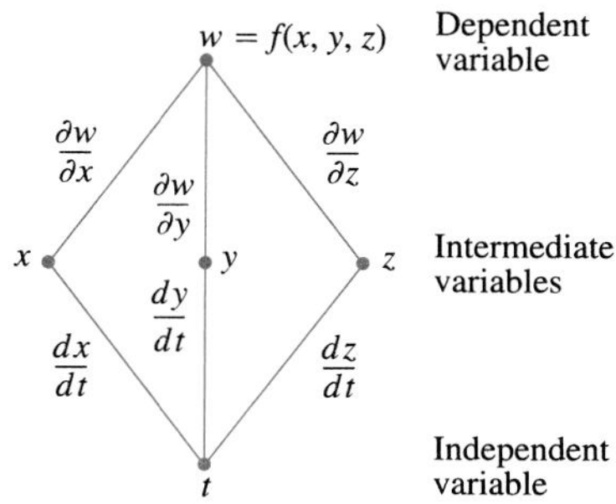

$$\frac{dw}{dt} = \frac{\partial w}{\partial x}\frac{dx}{dt} + \frac{\partial w}{\partial y}\frac{dy}{dt} + \frac{\partial w}{\partial z}\frac{dz}{dt}$$

In this example we can check the result with a more direct calculation. As a function of t,

$$w = xy = \cos t \sin t = \frac{1}{2}\sin 2t,$$

so

$$\frac{dw}{dt} = \frac{d}{dt}\left(\frac{1}{2}\sin 2t\right) = \frac{1}{2}\cdot 2\cos 2t = \cos 2t.$$

In either case,

$$\left(\frac{dw}{dt}\right)_{t=\pi/2} = \cos\left(2\cdot\frac{\pi}{2}\right) = \cos\pi = -1.$$

The Chain Rule for Functions of Three Variables

To get the Chain Rule for functions of three variables, we add another term to Eq. (1).

Chain Rule for Functions of Three Independent Variables

If $w = f(x, y, z)$ and f_x, f_y, and f_z are continuous, and if x, y, and z are differentiable functions of t, then w is a differentiable function of t and

$$\frac{dw}{dt} = \frac{\partial f}{\partial x}\frac{dx}{dt} + \frac{\partial f}{\partial y}\frac{dy}{dt} + \frac{\partial f}{\partial z}\frac{dz}{dt}. \tag{7}$$

The derivation is identical with the derivation of Eq. (1) except that there are now three intermediate variables instead of two. The diagram we use for remembering the new equation is similar as well.

EXAMPLE 2 *Changes in a Function's Values Along a Helix.* Find dw/dt if

$$w = xy + z, \qquad x = \cos t, \qquad y = \sin t, \qquad z = t$$

(Fig. 13.28). What is the derivative's value at $t = 0$?

Solution

$$\frac{dw}{dt} = \frac{\partial w}{\partial x}\frac{dx}{dt} + \frac{\partial w}{\partial y}\frac{dy}{dt} + \frac{\partial w}{\partial z}\frac{dz}{dt} \qquad \text{Eq. (7)}$$

$$= (y)(-\sin t) + (x)(\cos t) + (1)(1)$$

$$= (\sin t)(-\sin t) + (\cos t)(\cos t) + 1 \qquad \text{Substitute for the intermediate variables}$$

$$= -\sin^2 t + \cos^2 t + 1 = 1 + \cos 2t$$

$$\left(\frac{dw}{dt}\right)_{t=0} = 1 + \cos(0) = 2.$$

The helix
$\mathbf{r} = (\cos t)\mathbf{i} + (\sin t)\mathbf{j} + t\mathbf{k}$

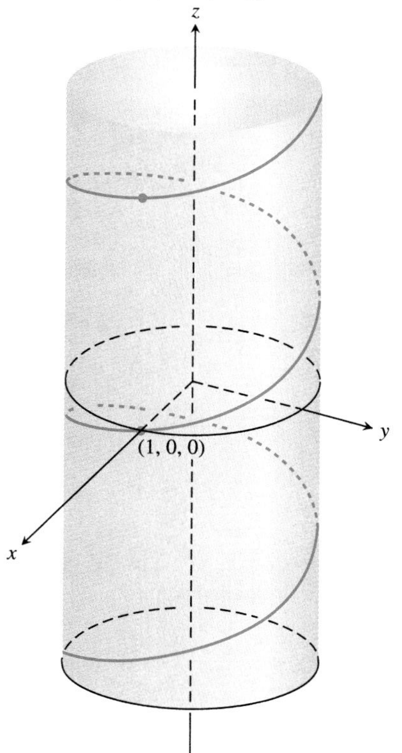

13.28 Example 2 shows how the values of $w = xy + z$ vary with t along this helix.

The Chain Rule for Functions Defined on Surfaces

If we are interested in the temperature $w = f(x, y, z)$ at points (x, y, z) on a globe in space, we might prefer to think of x, y, and z as functions of the variables r and s that give the points' longitudes and latitudes. If $x = g(r, s)$, $y = h(r, s)$, and $z = k(r, s)$, we could then express the temperature as a function

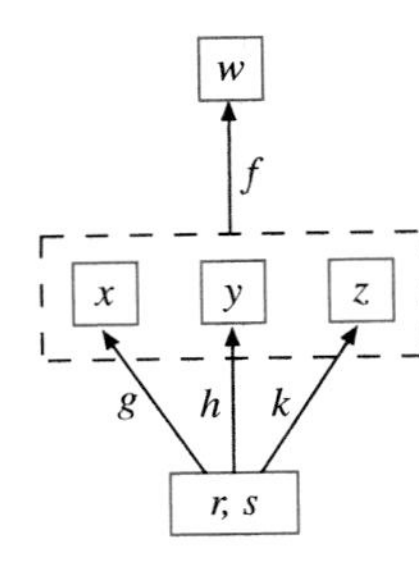

(a)

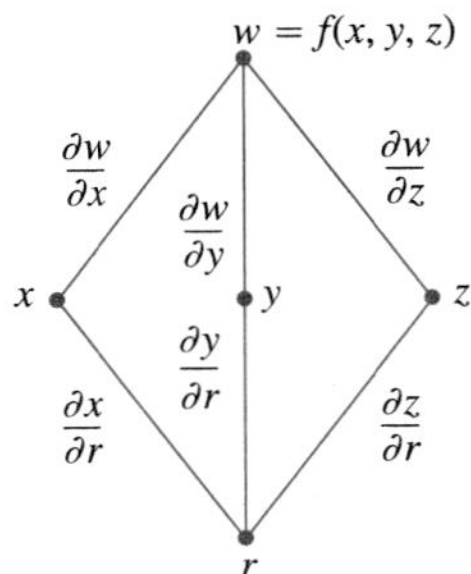

$$\frac{\partial w}{\partial r} = \frac{\partial w}{\partial x}\frac{\partial x}{\partial r} + \frac{\partial w}{\partial y}\frac{\partial y}{\partial r} + \frac{\partial w}{\partial z}\frac{\partial z}{\partial r}$$

(b)

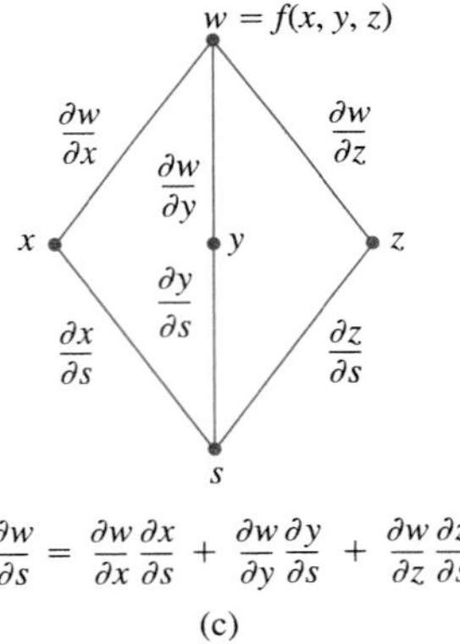

$$\frac{\partial w}{\partial s} = \frac{\partial w}{\partial x}\frac{\partial x}{\partial s} + \frac{\partial w}{\partial y}\frac{\partial y}{\partial s} + \frac{\partial w}{\partial z}\frac{\partial z}{\partial s}$$

(c)

13.29 Composite-function and tree diagrams for Eqs. (8) and (9).

of r and s with the composite function

$$w = f(g(r, s), h(r, s), k(r, s)).$$

Under the right conditions, w would have partial derivatives with respect to both r and s that could be calculated in the following way.

Chain Rule for Two Independent Variables and Three Intermediate Variables

Suppose that $w = f(x, y, z)$, $x = g(r, s)$, $y = h(r, s)$, and $z = k(r, s)$. If all four functions are continuous and have continuous first partial derivatives with respect to all their independent variables, then w has partial derivatives with respect to r and s, given by the formulas

$$\frac{\partial w}{\partial r} = \frac{\partial w}{\partial x}\frac{\partial x}{\partial r} + \frac{\partial w}{\partial y}\frac{\partial y}{\partial r} + \frac{\partial w}{\partial z}\frac{\partial z}{\partial r}, \tag{8}$$

$$\frac{\partial w}{\partial s} = \frac{\partial w}{\partial x}\frac{\partial x}{\partial s} + \frac{\partial w}{\partial y}\frac{\partial y}{\partial s} + \frac{\partial w}{\partial z}\frac{\partial z}{\partial s}. \tag{9}$$

Equation (8) can be derived from Eq. (7) by holding s fixed and setting r equal to t. Similarly, Eq. (9) can be derived by holding r fixed and setting s equal to t. The tree diagrams for Eqs. (8) and (9) are shown in Fig. 13.29.

EXAMPLE 3 Express $\partial w/\partial r$ and $\partial w/\partial s$ in terms of r and s if

$$w = x + 2y + z^2, \qquad x = \frac{r}{s}, \qquad y = r^2 + \ln s, \qquad z = 2r.$$

Solution

$$\frac{\partial w}{\partial r} = \frac{\partial w}{\partial x}\frac{\partial x}{\partial r} + \frac{\partial w}{\partial y}\frac{\partial y}{\partial r} + \frac{\partial w}{\partial z}\frac{\partial z}{\partial r} \qquad \text{Eq. (8)}$$

$$= (1)\left(\frac{1}{s}\right) + (2)(2r) + (2z)(2)$$

$$= \frac{1}{s} + 4r + (4r)(2) = \frac{1}{s} + 12r \qquad \text{Substitute for intermediate variable } z$$

$$\frac{\partial w}{\partial s} = \frac{\partial w}{\partial x}\frac{\partial x}{\partial s} + \frac{\partial w}{\partial y}\frac{\partial y}{\partial s} + \frac{\partial w}{\partial z}\frac{\partial z}{\partial s} \qquad \text{Eq. (9)}$$

$$= (1)\left(-\frac{r}{s^2}\right) + (2)\left(\frac{1}{s}\right) + (2z)(0) = \frac{2}{s} - \frac{r}{s^2}$$

If f is a function of two variables instead of three, Eqs. (8) and (9) become one term shorter, because the intermediate variable z doesn't appear.

If $w = f(x, y)$, $x = g(r, s)$, and $y = h(r, s)$, then

$$\frac{\partial w}{\partial r} = \frac{\partial w}{\partial x}\frac{\partial x}{\partial r} + \frac{\partial w}{\partial y}\frac{\partial y}{\partial r} \quad \text{and} \quad \frac{\partial w}{\partial s} = \frac{\partial w}{\partial x}\frac{\partial x}{\partial s} + \frac{\partial w}{\partial y}\frac{\partial y}{\partial s}. \tag{10}$$

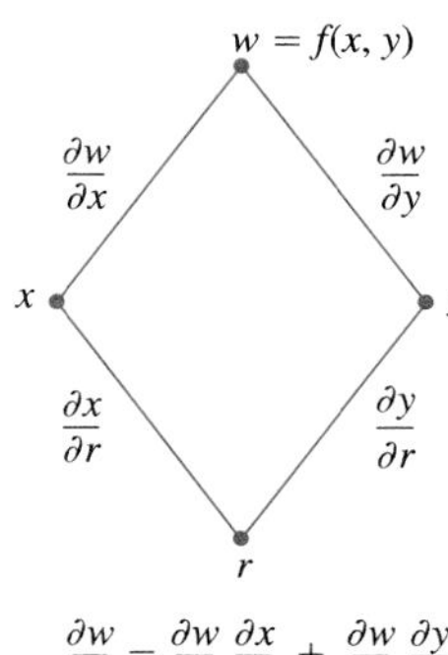

13.30 Tree diagram for the first of Eqs. (10).

Figure 13.30 shows the tree diagram for the first of Eqs. (10). The diagram for the second equation is similar—just replace r with s.

EXAMPLE 4 Express $\partial w/\partial r$ and $\partial w/\partial s$ in terms of r and s if

$$w = x^2 + y^2, \qquad x = r - s, \qquad y = r + s.$$

Solution We use Eqs. (10):

$$\begin{aligned} \frac{\partial w}{\partial r} &= \frac{\partial w}{\partial x}\frac{\partial x}{\partial r} + \frac{\partial w}{\partial y}\frac{\partial y}{\partial r} & \frac{\partial w}{\partial s} &= \frac{\partial w}{\partial x}\frac{\partial x}{\partial s} + \frac{\partial w}{\partial y}\frac{\partial y}{\partial s} \\ &= (2x)(1) + (2y)(1) & &= (2x)(-1) + (2y)(1) \\ &= 2(r - s) + 2(r + s) & &= -2(r - s) + 2(r + s) \\ &= 4r & &= 4s \end{aligned}$$

Substitute for the intermediate variables

If f is a function of x alone, Eqs. (8) and (9) simplify still further.

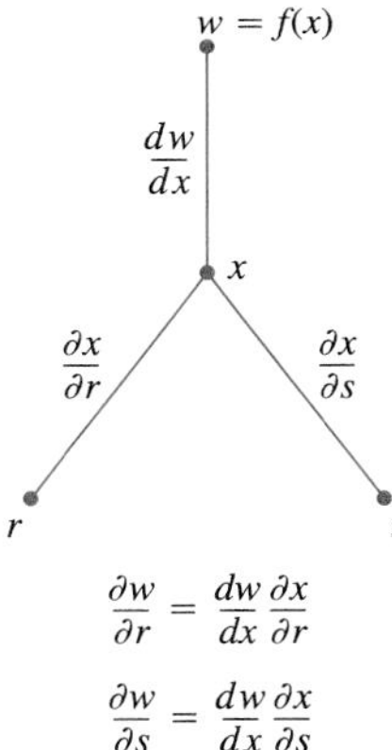

13.31 Tree diagram for Eqs. (11).

If $w = f(x)$ and $x = g(r, s)$, then

$$\frac{\partial w}{\partial r} = \frac{dw}{dx}\frac{\partial x}{\partial r} \quad \text{and} \quad \frac{\partial w}{\partial s} = \frac{dw}{dx}\frac{\partial x}{\partial s}. \tag{11}$$

Here dw/dx is the ordinary (single-variable) derivative (Fig. 13.31).

Implicit Differentiation (Continued from Chapter 3)

Believe it or not, the two-variable Chain Rule in Eq. (1) leads to a formula that takes most of the work out of implicit differentiation. The formula comes up in the following way. Suppose:

1. The function $F(x, y)$ is differentiable and
2. The equation $F(x, y) = 0$ defines y implicitly as a differentiable function of x, say $y = h(x)$.

Since $w = F(x, y) = 0$, the derivative dw/dx must be zero. Computing the derivative from the Chain Rule (tree diagram in Fig. 13.32), we find

$$0 = \frac{dw}{dx} = F_x\frac{dx}{dx} + F_y\frac{dy}{dx} \qquad \text{Eq. (1) with } t = x \text{ and } f = F$$

$$= F_x \cdot 1 + F_y \cdot \frac{dy}{dx}. \tag{12}$$

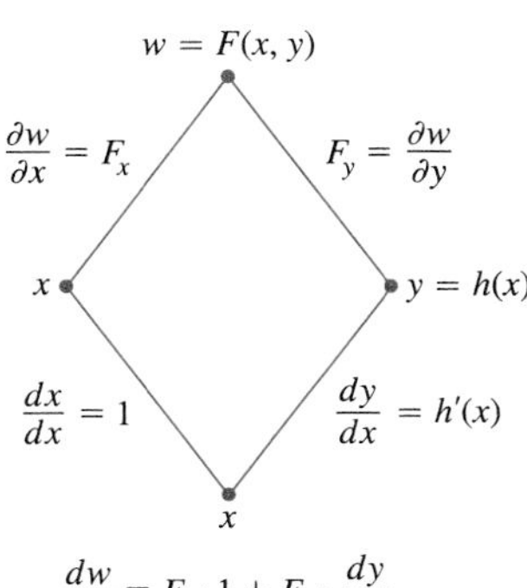

13.32 Tree diagram for Eq. (12).

If $F_y = \partial w/\partial y \neq 0$, we can solve Eq. (12) for dy/dx to get

$$\frac{dy}{dx} = -\frac{F_x}{F_y}. \tag{13}$$

Suppose that $F(x, y)$ is differentiable and that the equation $F(x, y) = 0$ defines y as a differentiable function of x. Then, at any point where $F_y \neq 0$,

$$\frac{dy}{dx} = -\frac{F_x}{F_y}. \tag{14}$$

EXAMPLE 5 Find dy/dx if $x^2 + \sin y - 2y = 0$.

Solution Take

$$F(x, y) = x^2 + \sin y - 2y.$$

Then

$$\frac{dy}{dx} = -\frac{F_x}{F_y} = -\frac{2x}{\cos y - 2}. \qquad \text{Eq. (14)}$$

This calculation is significantly shorter than the single-variable calculation with which we found dy/dx in Section 3.6, Example 3.

Remembering the Different Forms of the Chain Rule

How are we to remember all the different forms of the Chain Rule? The answer is that there is no need to remember them all. The best thing to do is to draw the appropriate tree diagram by placing the dependent variable on top, the intermediate variables in the middle, and the selected independent variable at the bottom. To find the derivative of the dependent variable with respect to the selected independent variable, start at the dependent variable and read down each branch of the tree to the independent variable, calculating and multiplying the derivatives along the branch. Then add the products you found for the different branches. Let's summarize this rule.

The Chain Rule for Functions of Many Variables

Suppose $w = f(x, y, \ldots, v)$ is a differentiable function of the variables $x, y, \ldots, v$ (a finite set) and the $x, y, \ldots, v$ are themselves differentiable functions of the variables $p, q, \ldots, t$ (another finite set). Suppose also that all the functions involved are continuous. Then w is a differentiable function of the variables p through t and the partial derivatives of w with respect to these variables are given by equations of the form

$$\frac{\partial w}{\partial p} = \frac{\partial w}{\partial x}\frac{\partial x}{\partial p} + \frac{\partial w}{\partial y}\frac{\partial y}{\partial p} + \cdots + \frac{\partial w}{\partial v}\frac{\partial v}{\partial p}. \tag{15}$$

The other equations are obtained by replacing p by $q, \ldots, t$, one at a time.

One way to remember Eq. (15) is to think of the right-hand side as the dot product of two vectors with components

$$\underbrace{\left(\frac{\partial w}{\partial x}, \frac{\partial w}{\partial y}, \ldots, \frac{\partial w}{\partial v}\right)}_{\substack{\text{Derivatives of } w \text{ with} \\ \text{respect to the} \\ \text{intermediate variables}}} \quad \text{and} \quad \underbrace{\left(\frac{\partial x}{\partial p}, \frac{\partial y}{\partial p}, \ldots, \frac{\partial v}{\partial p}\right)}_{\substack{\text{Derivatives of the intermediate} \\ \text{variables with respect to the} \\ \text{selected independent variable}}}. \tag{16}$$

Exercises 13.5

In Exercises 1–6, (a) express dw/dt as a function of t, both by using the Chain Rule and by expressing w in terms of t and differentiating directly with respect to t. Then (b) evaluate dw/dt at the given value of t.

1. $w = x^2 + y^2$, $x = \cos t$, $y = \sin t$; $t = \pi$
2. $w = x^2 + y^2$, $x = \cos t + \sin t$, $y = \cos t - \sin t$; $t = 0$
3. $w = \frac{x}{z} + \frac{y}{z}$, $x = \cos^2 t$, $y = \sin^2 t$, $z = 1/t$; $t = 3$
4. $w = \ln(x^2 + y^2 + z^2)$, $x = \cos t$, $y = \sin t$, $z = 4\sqrt{t}$; $t = 3$
5. $w = 2ye^x - \ln z$, $x = \ln(t^2 + 1)$, $y = \tan^{-1} t$, $z = e^t$; $t = 1$
6. $w = z - \sin xy$, $x = t$, $y = \ln t$, $z = e^{t-1}$; $t = 1$

In Exercises 7 and 8, (a) express $\partial z/\partial r$ and $\partial z/\partial\theta$ as functions of r and θ both by using the Chain Rule and by expressing z directly in terms of r and θ before differentiating. Then (b) evaluate $\partial z/\partial r$ and $\partial z/\partial\theta$ at the given point (r, θ).

7. $z = 4e^x \ln y$, $x = \ln(r\cos\theta)$, $y = r\sin\theta$; $(r, \theta) = (2, \pi/4)$
8. $z = \tan^{-1}(x/y)$, $x = r\cos\theta$, $y = r\sin\theta$; $(r, \theta) = (1.3, \pi/6)$

In Exercises 9 and 10, (a) express $\partial w/\partial u$ and $\partial w/\partial v$ as functions of u and v both by using the Chain Rule and by expressing w directly in terms of u and v before differentiating. Then (b) evaluate $\partial w/\partial u$ and $\partial w/\partial v$ at the given point (u, v).

9. $w = xy + yz + xz$, $x = u + v$, $y = u - v$, $z = uv$; $(u, v) = (1/2, 1)$
10. $w = \ln(x^2 + y^2 + z^2)$, $x = ue^v \sin u$, $y = ue^v \cos u$, $z = ue^v$; $(u, v) = (-2, 0)$

In Exercises 11 and 12, (a) express $\partial u/\partial x$, $\partial u/\partial y$, and $\partial u/\partial z$ as functions of x, y, and z both by using the Chain Rule and by expressing u directly in terms of p, q, and r before differentiating. Then (b) evaluate $\partial u/\partial x$, $\partial u/\partial y$, and $\partial u/\partial z$ at the given point (x, y, z).

11. $u = \frac{p - q}{q - r}$, $p = x + y + z$, $q = x - y + z$, $r = x + y - z$; $(x, y, z) = (\sqrt{3}, 2, 1)$
12. $u = e^{qr} \sin^{-1} p$, $p = \sin x$, $q = z^2 \ln y$, $r = 1/z$; $(x, y, z) = (\pi/4, 1/2, -1/2)$

In Exercises 13–24, draw a tree diagram and write a Chain Rule formula for each derivative.

13. $\frac{dz}{dt}$ for $z = f(x, y)$, $x = g(t)$, $y = h(t)$
14. $\frac{dz}{dt}$ for $z = f(u, v, w)$, $u = g(t)$, $v = h(t)$, $w = k(t)$
15. $\frac{\partial w}{\partial u}$ and $\frac{\partial w}{\partial v}$ for $w = h(x, y, z)$, $x = f(u, v)$, $y = g(u, v)$, $z = k(u, v)$
16. $\frac{\partial w}{\partial x}$ and $\frac{\partial w}{\partial y}$ for $w = f(r, s, t)$, $r = g(x, y)$, $s = h(x, y)$, $t = k(x, y)$
17. $\frac{\partial w}{\partial u}$ and $\frac{\partial w}{\partial v}$ for $w = g(x, y)$, $x = h(u, v)$, $y = k(u, v)$
18. $\frac{\partial w}{\partial x}$ and $\frac{\partial w}{\partial y}$ for $w = g(u, v)$, $u = h(x, y)$, $v = k(x, y)$
19. $\frac{\partial z}{\partial t}$ and $\frac{\partial z}{\partial s}$ for $z = f(x, y)$, $x = g(t, s)$, $y = h(t, s)$
20. $\frac{\partial y}{\partial r}$ for $y = f(u)$, $u = g(r, s)$
21. $\frac{\partial w}{\partial s}$ and $\frac{\partial w}{\partial t}$ for $w = g(u)$, $u = h(s, t)$
22. $\frac{\partial w}{\partial p}$ for $w = f(x, y, z, v)$, $x = g(p, q)$, $y = h(p, q)$, $z = j(p, q)$, $v = k(p, q)$
23. $\frac{\partial w}{\partial r}$ and $\frac{\partial w}{\partial s}$ for $w = f(x, y)$, $x = g(r)$, $y = h(s)$
24. $\frac{\partial w}{\partial s}$ for $w = g(x, y)$, $x = h(r, s, t)$, $y = k(r, s, t)$

Assuming that the equations in Exercises 25–28 define y as a differentiable function of x, use Eq. (14) to find the value of dy/dx at the given point.

25. $x^3 - 2y^2 + xy = 0$, $(1, 1)$
26. $xy + y^2 - 3x - 3 = 0$, $(-1, 1)$
27. $x^2 + xy + y^2 - 7 = 0$, $(1, 2)$
28. $xe^y + \sin xy + y - \ln 2 = 0$, $(0, \ln 2)$

Equation (14) can be generalized to functions of three variables and even more. The three-variable version goes like this:

If the equation $F(x, y, z) = 0$ determines z as a differentiable function of x and y, then, at points where $F_z \neq 0$,

$$\frac{\partial z}{\partial x} = -\frac{F_x}{F_z} \quad \text{and} \quad \frac{\partial z}{\partial y} = -\frac{F_y}{F_z}. \tag{17}$$

Use these equations to find the values of $\partial z/\partial x$ and $\partial z/\partial y$ at the points in Exercises 29–32.

29. $z^3 - xy + yz + y^3 - 2 = 0$, $(1, 1, 1)$
30. $\frac{1}{x} + \frac{1}{y} + \frac{1}{z} - 1 = 0$, $(2, 3, 6)$
31. $\sin(x + y) + \sin(y + z) + \sin(x + z) = 0$, (π, π, π)
32. $xe^y + ye^z + 2\ln x - 2 - 3\ln 2 = 0$, $(1, \ln 2, \ln 3)$

33. Find $\partial w/\partial r$ when $r = 1$, $s = -1$ if $w = (x + y + z)^2$, $x = r - s$, $y = \cos(r + s)$, $z = \sin(r + s)$.

34. Find $\partial w/\partial v$ when $u = -1$, $v = 2$ if $w = xy + \ln z$, $x = v^2/u$, $y = u + v$, $z = \sin u$.

35. Find $\partial w/\partial v$ when $u = 0$, $v = 0$ if $w = x^2 + (y/x)$, $x = u - 2v + 1$, $y = 2u + v - 2$.

36. Find $\partial z/\partial u$ when $u = 0$, $v = 1$ if $z = \sin xy + x \sin y$, $x = u^2 + v^2$, $y = uv$.

37. Find $\partial z/\partial u$ and $\partial z/\partial v$ when $u = \ln 2$, $v = 1$ if $z = 5 \tan^{-1} x$ and $x = e^u + \ln v$.

38. Find $\partial z/\partial u$ and $\partial z/\partial v$ when $u = 1$ and $v = -2$ if $z = \ln q$ and $q = \sqrt{v + 3} \tan^{-1} u$.

39. *Changing Voltage in a Circuit.* The voltage V in a circuit that satisfies the law $V = IR$ is slowly dropping as the battery wears out. At the same time, the resistance R is increasing as the resistor heats up. Use the equation

$$\frac{dV}{dt} = \frac{\partial V}{\partial I}\frac{dI}{dt} + \frac{\partial V}{\partial R}\frac{dR}{dt}$$

to find how the current is changing at the instant when $R = 600$ ohms, $I = 0.04$ amp, $dR/dt = 0.5$ ohm/sec, and $dV/dt = -0.01$ volt/sec.

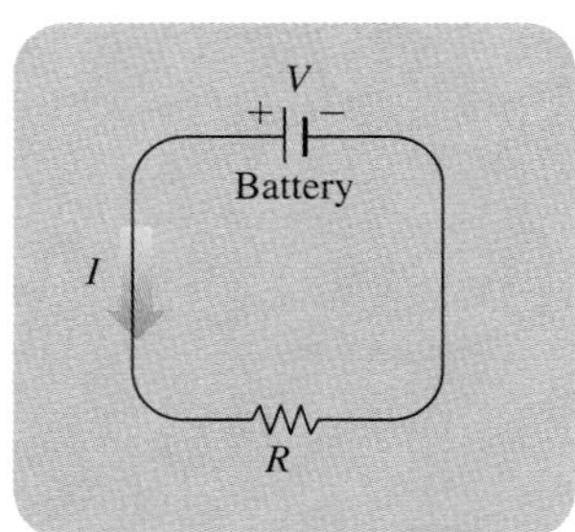

40. *Changing Dimensions in a Box.* The dimensions a, b, and c of the box shown here are changing with time. At the instant in question, $a = 1$ m, $b = 2$ m, $c = 3$ m, $da/dt = db/dt = 1$ m/sec, and $dc/dt = -3$ m/sec. At what rates are the box's volume V and surface area S changing at that instant? Are the box's diagonals increasing in length, or decreasing?

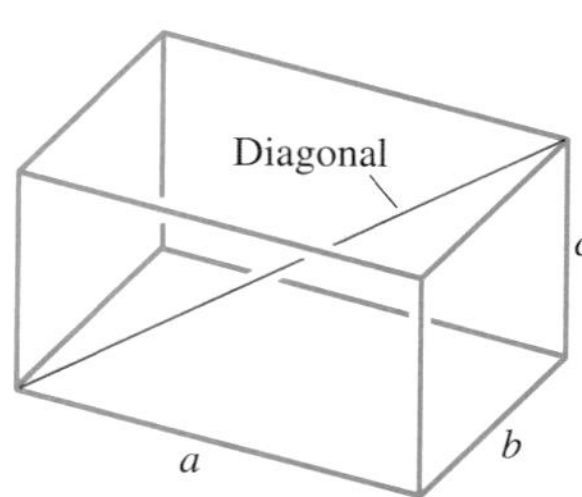

CHANGES IN FUNCTIONS ALONG CURVES

41. Suppose that the partial derivatives of a function $f(x, y, z)$ at points on the helix $x = \cos t$, $y = \sin t$, $z = t$ are

$$f_x = \cos t, \qquad f_y = \sin t, \qquad f_z = t^2 + t - 2.$$

At what points on the curve, if any, can f take on extreme values?

42. Let $w = x^2 e^{2y} \cos 3z$. Find the value of dw/dt at the point $(1, \ln 2, 0)$ on the curve $x = \cos t$, $y = \ln(t + 2)$, $z = t$.

43. Let $T = f(x, y)$ be the temperature at the point (x, y) on the circle $x = \cos t$, $y = \sin t$, $0 \le t \le 2\pi$, and suppose that

$$\frac{\partial T}{\partial x} = 8x - 4y, \qquad \frac{\partial T}{\partial y} = 8y - 4x.$$

a) Find where the maximum and minimum temperatures on the circle occur by examining the derivatives dT/dt and d^2T/dt^2.

b) Suppose $T = 4x^2 - 4xy + 4y^2$. Find the maximum and minimum values of T on the circle.

44. Let $T = g(x, y)$ be the temperature at the point (x, y) on the ellipse

$$x = 2\sqrt{2} \cos t, \qquad y = \sqrt{2} \sin t, \qquad 0 \le t \le 2\pi,$$

and suppose that

$$\frac{\partial T}{\partial x} = y, \qquad \frac{\partial T}{\partial y} = x.$$

a) Locate the maximum and minimum temperatures on the ellipse by examining dT/dt and d^2T/dt^2.

b) Suppose that $T = xy - 2$. Find the maximum and minimum values of T on the ellipse.

Writing for Your Own Knowledge

Answer the following questions in writing. Some answers will take only a sentence or two; others may require several paragraphs. Some explanations may also call for graphs or sketches.

1. What is the Chain Rule for functions of two independent variables? three independent variables? functions defined on surfaces? How do you diagram these rules?
2. How does the Chain Rule lead to a formula for implicit differentiation?
3. What general pattern enables one to remember all the different forms of the Chain Rule?

13.6 Directional Derivatives, Gradient Vectors, and Tangent Planes

We know from Section 13.5 that if $f(x, y)$ is differentiable, then the rate at which the values of f change with respect to t along a differentiable curve $x = g(t)$, $y = h(t)$ is

$$\frac{df}{dt} = \frac{\partial f}{\partial x}\frac{dx}{dt} + \frac{\partial f}{\partial y}\frac{dy}{dt}. \tag{1}$$

At any point $P_0(x_0, y_0) = P_0(g(t_0), h(t_0))$, Eq. (1) gives the rate of change of f with respect to increasing t and therefore depends, among other things, on the direction of motion along the curve. This observation is particularly important when the curve is a straight line and t is the arc length parameter along the line measured from P_0 in the direction of a given unit vector $\mathbf{u}$. For then df/dt is the rate of change of f with respect to distance in its domain in the direction of $\mathbf{u}$. By varying $\mathbf{u}$, we find the rates at which f changes with respect to distance as we move through P_0 in different directions. These "directional derivatives" have useful interpretations in science and engineering as well as in mathematics. This section develops a formula for calculating them and proceeds from there to find equations for tangent planes and normal lines on surfaces in space. We begin the discussion in the xy-plane.

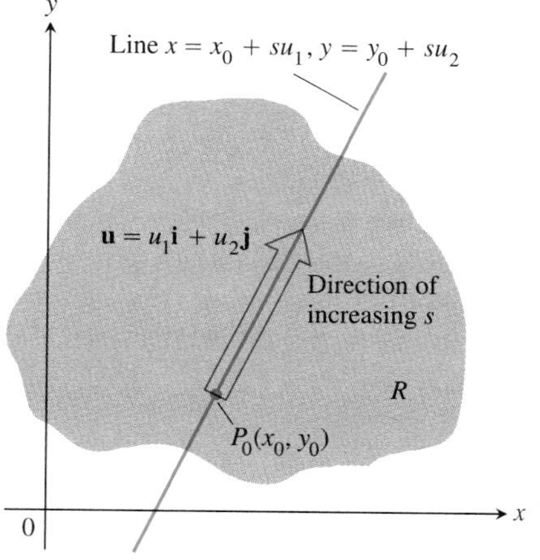

13.33 The rate of change of f in the direction of $\mathbf{u}$ at a point P_0 is the rate at which f changes along this line at P_0.

Directional Derivatives in the Plane

Suppose that the function $f(x, y)$ is defined throughout a region R in the xy-plane, that $P_0(x_0, y_0)$ is a point in R, and that $\mathbf{u} = u_1\,\mathbf{i} + u_2\,\mathbf{j}$ is a unit vector. Then the equations

$$x = x_0 + su_1, \qquad y = y_0 + su_2 \tag{2}$$

parametrize the line through P_0 parallel to $\mathbf{u}$. The parameter s measures arc length from P_0 in the direction of $\mathbf{u}$. We find the rate of change of f at P_0 in the direction of $\mathbf{u}$ by calculating df/ds at P_0 (Fig. 13.33):

DEFINITION

The **derivative of f at $P_0\ (x_0, y_0)$ in the direction of the unit vector $\mathbf{u} = u_1\,\mathbf{i} + u_2\,\mathbf{j}$** is the number

$$\left(\frac{df}{ds}\right)_{\mathbf{u},P_0} = \lim_{s\to 0}\frac{f(x_0 + su_1, y_0 + su_2) - f(x_0, y_0)}{s}, \tag{3}$$

provided the limit exists.

The directional derivative is also denoted by

$$(D_{\mathbf{u}}f)_{P_0}. \qquad \text{"The derivative of } f \text{ at } P_0 \text{ in the direction of } \mathbf{u}\text{"}$$

EXAMPLE 1 Find the derivative of

$$f(x, y) = x^2 + xy$$

at $P_0(1, 2)$ in the direction of the unit vector $\mathbf{u} = \left(1/\sqrt{2}\right)\mathbf{i} + \left(1/\sqrt{2}\right)\mathbf{j}$.

Solution

$$\begin{aligned}
\left(\frac{df}{ds}\right)_{\mathbf{u},P_0} &= \lim_{s\to 0}\frac{f(x_0+su_1,\, y_0+su_2)-f(x_0,y_0)}{s} \qquad \text{Eq. (3)}\\
&= \lim_{s\to 0}\frac{f\left(1+s\cdot\frac{1}{\sqrt{2}},\, 2+s\cdot\frac{1}{\sqrt{2}}\right)-f(1,2)}{s}\\
&= \lim_{s\to 0}\frac{\left(1+\frac{s}{\sqrt{2}}\right)^2+\left(1+\frac{s}{\sqrt{2}}\right)\left(2+\frac{s}{\sqrt{2}}\right)-(1^2+1\cdot 2)}{s}\\
&= \lim_{s\to 0}\frac{\left(1+\frac{2s}{\sqrt{2}}+\frac{s^2}{2}\right)+\left(2+\frac{3s}{\sqrt{2}}+\frac{s^2}{2}\right)-3}{s}\\
&= \lim_{s\to 0}\frac{\frac{5s}{\sqrt{2}}+s^2}{s} = \lim_{s\to 0}\left(\frac{5}{\sqrt{2}}+s\right) = \left(\frac{5}{\sqrt{2}}+0\right) = \frac{5}{\sqrt{2}}.
\end{aligned}$$

The rate of change of $f(x, y) = x^2 + xy$ at $P_0\,(1, 2)$ in the direction $\mathbf{u} = \left(1/\sqrt{2}\right)\mathbf{i} + \left(1/\sqrt{2}\right)\mathbf{j}$ is $5/\sqrt{2}$.

Geometric Interpretation of the Directional Derivative

The equation $z = f(x, y)$ represents a surface S in space. If $z_0 = f(x_0, y_0)$, then the point $P(x_0, y_0, z_0)$ lies on S. The vertical plane that passes through P and $P_0\,(x_0, y_0)$ parallel to $\mathbf{u}$ intersects S in a curve C (Fig. 13.34). The rate of change of f in the direction of $\mathbf{u}$ is the slope of the tangent to C at P.

Notice that when $\mathbf{u} = \mathbf{i}$ the directional derivative at P_0 is $\partial f/\partial x$ evaluated at (x_0, y_0). When $\mathbf{u} = \mathbf{j}$ the directional derivative at P_0 is $\partial f/\partial y$ evaluated at (x_0, y_0). The directional derivative generalizes the two partial derivatives. We can now ask for the rate of change of f in any direction $\mathbf{u}$, not just the directions $\mathbf{i}$ and $\mathbf{j}$.

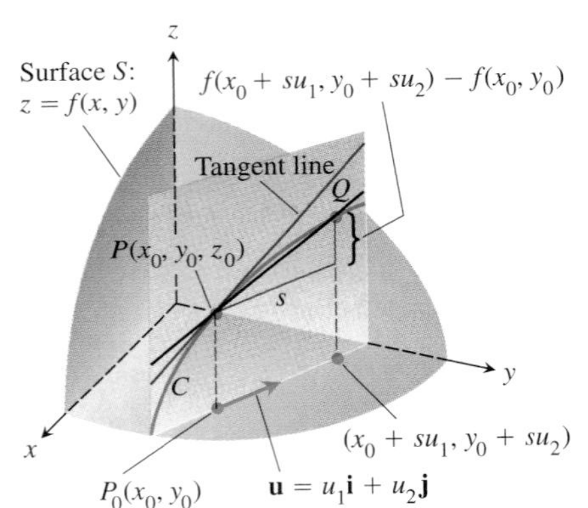

13.34 The slope of curve C at P_0 is

$$\lim_{Q\to P}\text{slope}(PQ) = \lim_{s\to 0}\frac{f(x_0+su_1,\, y_0+su_2)-f(x_0,y_0)}{s} = \left(\frac{df}{ds}\right)_{\mathbf{u},P_0}$$

Calculation

As you know, it is rarely convenient to calculate a derivative directly from its definition as a limit, and the directional derivative is no exception. We can develop a more efficient formula in the following way. We begin with the line

$$x = x_0 + su_1, \qquad y = y_0 + su_2, \tag{4}$$

through $P_0(x_0, y_0)$, parametrized with the arc length parameter s increasing in the direction of the unit vector $\mathbf{u} = u_1\,\mathbf{i} + u_2\,\mathbf{j}$. Then

$$\begin{aligned}
\left(\frac{df}{ds}\right)_{\mathbf{u},P_0} &= \left(\frac{\partial f}{\partial x}\right)_{P_0}\frac{dx}{ds}+\left(\frac{\partial f}{\partial y}\right)_{P_0}\frac{dy}{ds} \qquad \text{Chain Rule}\\
&= \left(\frac{\partial f}{\partial x}\right)_{P_0}\cdot u_1+\left(\frac{\partial f}{\partial y}\right)_{P_0}\cdot u_2 \qquad \text{From Eqs. (4), } dx/ds = u_1 \text{ and } dy/ds = u_2\\
&= \underbrace{\left[\left(\frac{\partial f}{\partial x}\right)_{P_0}\mathbf{i}+\left(\frac{\partial f}{\partial y}\right)_{P_0}\mathbf{j}\right]}_{\text{The gradient of } f \text{ at } P_0}\cdot\underbrace{\left[u_1\,\mathbf{i}+u_2\,\mathbf{j}\right]}_{\text{The direction } \mathbf{u}}.
\end{aligned} \tag{5}$$

The notation ∇f is read "grad f" as well as "gradient of f" and "del f." The symbol ∇ by itself is read "del." Another notation for the gradient is grad f, read the way it is written.

DEFINITION

The **gradient vector (gradient)** of $f(x, y)$ at a point $P_0\ (x_0, y_0)$ is the vector

$$\nabla f = \frac{\partial f}{\partial x}\,\mathbf{i} + \frac{\partial f}{\partial y}\,\mathbf{j} \tag{6}$$

obtained by evaluating the partial derivatives of f at P_0.

Equation (5) says that the derivative of f in the direction of $\mathbf{u}$ at P_0 is the dot product of $\mathbf{u}$ with the gradient of f at P_0.

THEOREM 6

If the partial derivatives of $f(x, y)$ are defined at $P_0(x_0, y_0)$, then

$$\left(\frac{df}{ds}\right)_{\mathbf{u}, P_0} = (\nabla f)_{P_0} \cdot \mathbf{u}, \tag{7}$$

the scalar product of the gradient f at P_0 and $\mathbf{u}$.

EXAMPLE 2 Find the derivative of

$$f(x, y) = xe^y + \cos(xy)$$

at the point (2, 0) in the direction of the vector $\mathbf{A} = 3\,\mathbf{i} - 4\,\mathbf{j}$.

Solution The direction of $\mathbf{A}$ is obtained by dividing $\mathbf{A}$ by its length:

$$|\mathbf{A}| = \sqrt{(3)^2 + (-4)^2} = \sqrt{25} = 5$$

$$\mathbf{u} = \frac{\mathbf{A}}{|\mathbf{A}|} = \frac{3}{5}\,\mathbf{i} - \frac{4}{5}\,\mathbf{j}.$$

The partial derivatives of f at (2, 0) are

$$f_x\,(2, 0) = (e^y - y \sin(xy))_{(2, 0)} = e^0 - 0 = 1$$

$$f_y\,(2, 0) = (xe^y - x\sin(xy))_{(2, 0)} = 2e^0 - 2 \cdot 0 = 2.$$

The gradient of f at (2, 0) is

$$\nabla f\Big|_{(2, 0)} = f_x\,(2, 0)\,\mathbf{i} + f_y\,(2, 0)\,\mathbf{j} = \mathbf{i} + 2\,\mathbf{j}$$

(Fig. 13.35). The derivative of f at (2, 0) in the direction of $\mathbf{A}$ is therefore

$$(D_{\mathbf{u}}f)\Big|_{(2, 0)} = \nabla f\Big|_{(2, 0)} \cdot \mathbf{u} \qquad \text{Eq. (7)}$$

$$= (\mathbf{i} + 2\,\mathbf{j}) \cdot \left(\frac{3}{5}\,\mathbf{i} - \frac{4}{5}\,\mathbf{j}\right) = \frac{3}{5} - \frac{8}{5} = -1.$$

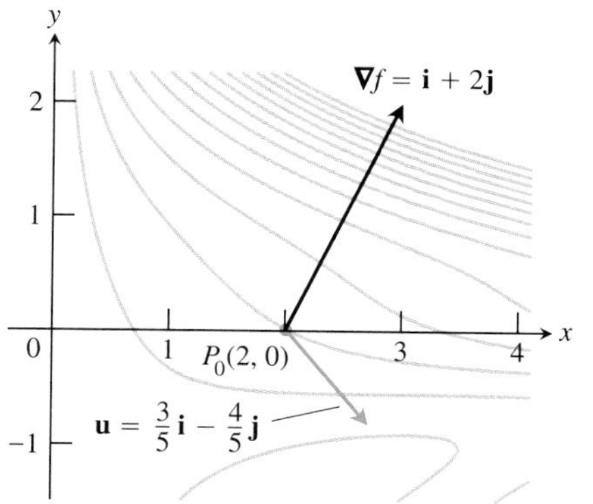

13.35 It is customary to picture ∇f as a vector in the domain of f. In the case of $f(x, y) = xe^y + \cos(xy)$, the domain is the entire plane. The rate at which f changes in the direction $\mathbf{u} = (3/5)\,\mathbf{i} - (4/5)\,\mathbf{j}$ is $\nabla f \cdot \mathbf{u} = -1$ (Example 2).

Properties of Directional Derivatives

Evaluating the dot product in the formula

$$D_{\mathbf{u}}f = \nabla f \cdot \mathbf{u} = |\nabla f|\,|\mathbf{u}| \cos\theta = |\nabla f| \cos\theta \tag{8}$$

reveals the following properties.

Properties of the Directional Derivative $D_{\mathbf{u}}f = \nabla f \cdot \mathbf{u} = |\nabla f| \cos \theta$

1. The function f increases most rapidly when $\cos \theta = 1$, or when $\mathbf{u}$ is the direction of ∇f. The derivative in this direction is
$$D_{\mathbf{u}}f = |\nabla f| \cos (0) = |\nabla f|.$$
2. Similarly, f decreases most rapidly in the direction of $-\nabla f$. The derivative in this direction is $D_{\mathbf{u}}f = |\nabla f| \cos (\pi) = -|\nabla f|$.
3. Any direction $\mathbf{u}$ orthogonal to the gradient is a direction of zero change in f because θ then equals $\pi/2$ and
$$D_{\mathbf{u}}f = |\nabla f| \cos (\pi/2) = |\nabla f| \cdot 0 = 0.$$

As we will discuss later, the properties just listed hold in three dimensions as well as two.

EXAMPLE 3 Find the directions in which $f(x, y) = (x^2/2) + (y^2/2)$ (a) increases most rapidly and (b) decreases most rapidly at the point $(1, 1)$. (c) What are the directions of zero change in f at $(1, 1)$?

Solution

a) The function increases most rapidly in the direction of ∇f at $(1, 1)$. The gradient is
$$(\nabla f)_{(1,1)} = (x\,\mathbf{i} + y\,\mathbf{j})_{(1,1)} = \mathbf{i} + \mathbf{j}.$$
Its direction is
$$\mathbf{u} = \frac{\mathbf{i} + \mathbf{j}}{|\mathbf{i} + \mathbf{j}|} = \frac{\mathbf{i} + \mathbf{j}}{\sqrt{(1)^2 + (1)^2}} = \frac{1}{\sqrt{2}}\mathbf{i} + \frac{1}{\sqrt{2}}\mathbf{j}.$$

b) The function decreases most rapidly in the direction of $-\nabla f$ at $(1, 1)$, which is
$$-\mathbf{u} = -\frac{1}{\sqrt{2}}\mathbf{i} - \frac{1}{\sqrt{2}}\mathbf{j}.$$

c) The directions of zero change at $(1, 1)$ are the two directions orthogonal to ∇f. These are
$$\mathbf{n} = -\frac{1}{\sqrt{2}}\mathbf{i} + \frac{1}{\sqrt{2}}\mathbf{j} \quad \text{and} \quad -\mathbf{n} = \frac{1}{\sqrt{2}}\mathbf{i} - \frac{1}{\sqrt{2}}\mathbf{j}.$$
See Fig. 13.36.

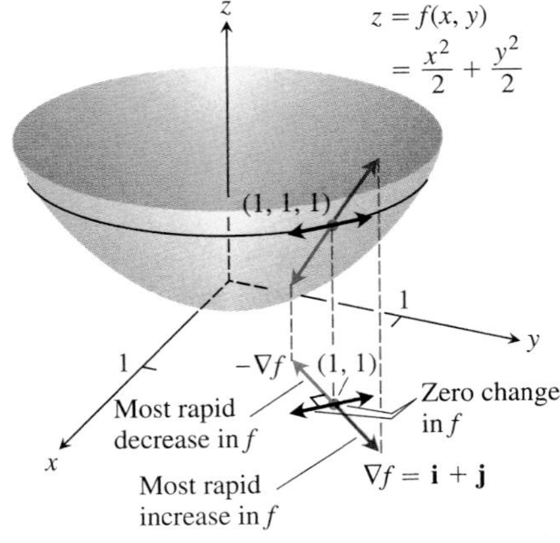

13.36 The direction in which $f(x, y) = (x^2/2) + (y^2/2)$ increases most rapidly at $(1, 1)$ is the direction of $\nabla f|_{(1,1)} = \mathbf{i} + \mathbf{j}$. It corresponds to the direction of steepest ascent on the surface at $(1, 1, 1)$.

Gradients and Tangents to Level Curves

If a differentiable function $f(x, y)$ has a constant value c along a smooth curve $\mathbf{r} = g(t)\,\mathbf{i} + h(t)\,\mathbf{j}$ (making the curve a level curve of f), then $f(g(t), h(t)) = c$.

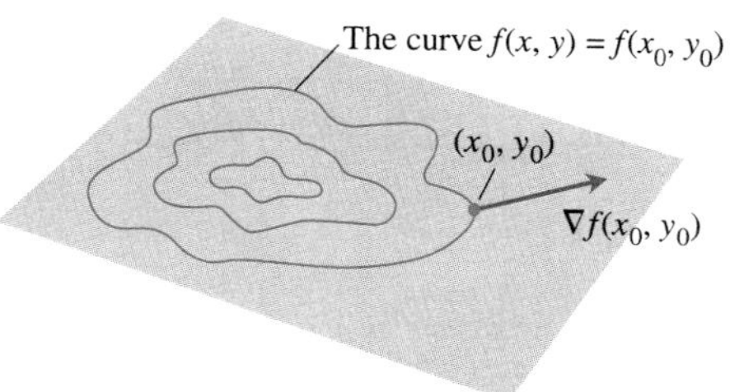

13.37 The gradient of a differentiable function of two variables is always normal to the function's level curves.

Differentiating both sides of this equation with respect to t leads to the equations

$$\frac{d}{dt}f(g(t), h(t)) = \frac{d}{dt}(c),$$

$$\frac{\partial f}{\partial x}\frac{dg}{dt} + \frac{\partial f}{\partial y}\frac{dh}{dt} = 0, \qquad \text{Chain Rule}$$

$$\underbrace{\left(\frac{\partial f}{\partial x}\mathbf{i} + \frac{\partial f}{\partial y}\mathbf{j}\right)}_{\nabla f} \cdot \underbrace{\left(\frac{dg}{dt}\mathbf{i} + \frac{dh}{dt}\mathbf{j}\right)}_{\frac{d\mathbf{r}}{dt}} = 0. \tag{9}$$

Equation (9) says that ∇f is normal to the tangent vector $d\mathbf{r}/dt$, so it is normal to the curve.

At every point (x_0, y_0) in the domain of $f(x, y)$, the gradient of f is normal to the level curve through (x_0, y_0) (Fig. 13.37).

This observation enables us to find equations for tangent lines to level curves. They are the lines normal to the gradients. As we saw in Section 11.3, the line through a point $P_0(x_0, y_0)$ normal to a vector $\mathbf{N} = A\,\mathbf{i} + B\,\mathbf{j}$ has the equation

$$A(x - x_0) + B(y - y_0) = 0. \qquad \text{Section 11.3, Eq. (19)}$$

If $\mathbf{N}$ is the gradient $(\nabla f)_{(x_0, y_0)} = f_x(x_0, y_0)\,\mathbf{i} + f_y(x_0, y_0)\,\mathbf{j}$, the equation becomes

$$f_x(x_0, y_0)(x - x_0) + f_y(x_0, y_0)(y - y_0) = 0.$$

The Tangent to a Level Curve

The tangent to the level curve $f(x, y) = f(x_0, y_0)$ at the point $P_0(x_0, y_0)$ is the line

$$f_x(x_0, y_0)(x - x_0) + f_y(x_0, y_0)(y - y_0) = 0. \tag{10}$$

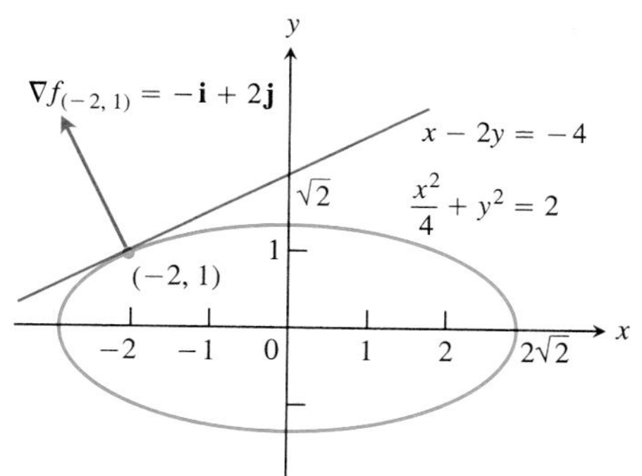

13.38 We can find the tangent to the ellipse $(x^2/4) + y^2 = 2$ by treating the ellipse as a level curve of the function $f(x, y) = (x^2/4) + y^2$ (Example 4).

EXAMPLE 4 Find an equation for the tangent to the ellipse

$$\frac{x^2}{4} + y^2 = 2$$

(Fig. 13.38) at the point $(-2, 1)$.

Solution The ellipse is a level curve of the function

$$f(x, y) = \frac{x^2}{4} + y^2.$$

The gradient of f at $(-2, 1)$ is

$$\nabla f\Big|_{(-2, 1)} = \left(\frac{x}{2}\mathbf{i} + 2y\,\mathbf{j}\right)_{(-2, 1)} = -\mathbf{i} + 2\,\mathbf{j}.$$

The tangent is the line

$$(-1)(x+2)+(2)(y-1)=0 \qquad \text{Eq. (10)}$$
$$x-2y=-4.$$

Functions of Three Variables

For functions of three variables, we get results much like the ones for functions of two variables. We obtain the three-variable formulas by adding the z-terms to the two-variable formulas. For a differentiable function $f(x, y, z)$ and a unit vector $\mathbf{u} = u_1\,\mathbf{i} + u_2\,\mathbf{j} + u_3\,\mathbf{k}$ in space, we have

$$\nabla f = \frac{\partial f}{\partial x}\,\mathbf{i} + \frac{\partial f}{\partial y}\,\mathbf{j} + \frac{\partial f}{\partial z}\,\mathbf{k} \tag{11}$$

and

$$D_{\mathbf{u}} f = \nabla f \cdot \mathbf{u} = \frac{\partial f}{\partial x} u_1 + \frac{\partial f}{\partial y} u_2 + \frac{\partial f}{\partial z} u_3. \tag{12}$$

The directional derivative can once again be written in the form

$$D_{\mathbf{u}} f = \nabla f \cdot \mathbf{u} = |\nabla f|\,|u| \cos\theta = |\nabla f| \cos\theta, \tag{13}$$

so the properties listed earlier for functions of two variables continue to hold. At any given point, f increases most rapidly in the direction of ∇f and decreases most rapidly in the direction of $-\nabla f$. In any direction orthogonal to ∇f, the derivative is zero.

EXAMPLE 5 **a)** Find the derivative of

$$f(x, y, z) = x^3 - xy^2 - z$$

at P_0 (1, 1, 0) in the direction of the vector $\mathbf{A} = 2\,\mathbf{i} - 3\,\mathbf{j} + 6\,\mathbf{k}$.

b) In what directions does f change most rapidly at P_0, and what are the rates of change in these directions?

Solution

a) The direction of **A** is obtained by dividing **A** by its length:

$$|\mathbf{A}| = \sqrt{(2)^2 + (-3)^2 + (6)^2} = \sqrt{49} = 7$$
$$\mathbf{u} = \frac{\mathbf{A}}{|\mathbf{A}|} = \frac{2}{7}\mathbf{i} - \frac{3}{7}\mathbf{j} + \frac{6}{7}\mathbf{k}.$$

The partial derivatives of f at P_0 are

$$f_x = 3x^2 - y^2\Big|_{(1,1,0)} = 2,$$
$$f_y = -2xy\Big|_{(1,1,0)} = -2, \qquad f_z = -1\Big|_{(1,1,0)} = -1.$$

The gradient of f at P_0 is

$$\nabla f\Big|_{(1,1,0)} = 2\,\mathbf{i} - 2\,\mathbf{j} - \mathbf{k}$$

(Fig. 13.39). The derivative of f at P_0 in the direction of **A** is therefore

$$(D_{\mathbf{u}} f)\Big|_{(1,1,0)} = \nabla f\Big|_{(1,1,0)} \cdot \mathbf{u} = (2\,\mathbf{i} - 2\,\mathbf{j} - \mathbf{k}) \cdot \left(\frac{2}{7}\mathbf{i} - \frac{3}{7}\mathbf{j} + \frac{6}{7}\mathbf{k}\right)$$
$$= \frac{4}{7} + \frac{6}{7} - \frac{6}{7} = \frac{4}{7}.$$

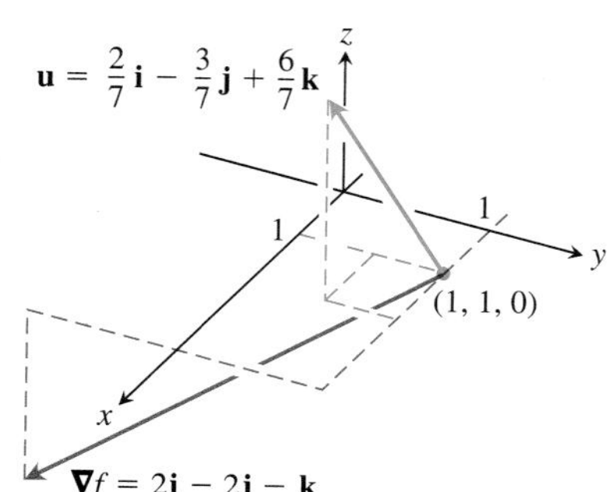

13.39 The change in f in the direction of **u** is $\nabla f \cdot \mathbf{u} = 4/7$ (Example 5).

b) The function increases most rapidly in the direction of $\nabla f = 2\,\mathbf{i} - 2\,\mathbf{j} - \mathbf{k}$, and decreases most rapidly in the direction of $-\nabla f$. The rates of change in the directions are, respectively,

$$|\nabla f| = \sqrt{(2)^2 + (-2)^2 + (-1)^2} = \sqrt{9} = 3 \quad \text{and} \quad -|\nabla f| = -3.$$

Equations for Tangent Planes and Normal Lines

If $\mathbf{r} = g(t)\,\mathbf{i} + h(t)\,\mathbf{j} + k(t)\,\mathbf{k}$ is a smooth curve on the level surface $f(x, y, z) = c$ of a differentiable function f, then $f(g(t), h(t), k(t)) = c$. Differentiating both sides of this equation with respect to t leads to the equations

$$\frac{d}{dt} f(g(t), h(t), k(t)) = \frac{d}{dt}(c),$$

$$\frac{\partial f}{\partial x}\frac{dg}{dt} + \frac{\partial f}{\partial y}\frac{dh}{dt} + \frac{\partial f}{\partial z}\frac{dk}{dt} = 0, \qquad \text{Chain Rule}$$

$$\underbrace{\left(\frac{\partial f}{\partial x}\mathbf{i} + \frac{\partial f}{\partial y}\mathbf{j} + \frac{\partial f}{\partial z}\mathbf{k}\right)}_{\nabla f} \cdot \underbrace{\left(\frac{dg}{dt}\mathbf{i} + \frac{dh}{dt}\mathbf{j} + \frac{dk}{dt}\mathbf{k}\right)}_{d\mathbf{r}/dt} = 0. \tag{14}$$

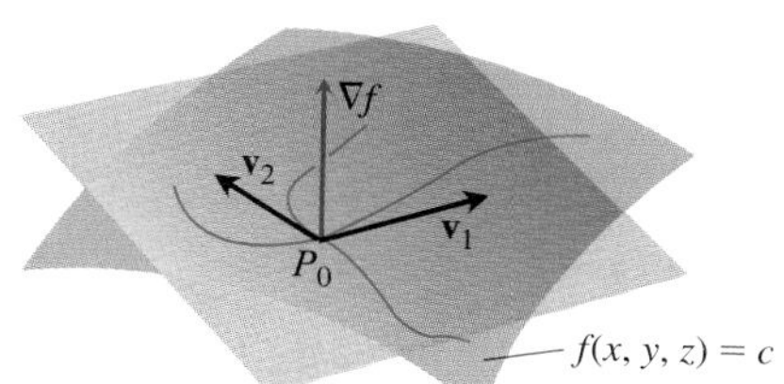

13.40 ∇f is orthogonal to the velocity vector of every smooth curve in the surface through P_0. The velocity vectors at P_0 therefore lie in a common plane, which we call the tangent plane at P_0.

Equation (14) says that at every point along the curve, ∇f is orthogonal to the curve's velocity vector.

Now let us restrict our attention to the curves that pass through P_0 (Fig. 13.40). All the velocity vectors at P_0 are orthogonal to ∇f at P_0, so the tangent lines to these curves lie in the plane through P_0 normal to ∇f. We call this plane the tangent plane of the surface at P_0. The line through P_0 perpendicular to the plane is the surface's normal line at P_0.

DEFINITIONS

The **tangent plane** at the point $P_0(x_0, y_0, z_0)$ on the level surface $f(x, y, z) = c$ is the plane

$$f_x(P_0)(x - x_0) + f_y(P_0)(y - y_0) + f_z(P_0)(z - z_0) = 0. \tag{15}$$

The **normal line** of the surface at P_0 is the line

$$x = x_0 + f_x(P_0)t, \qquad y = y_0 + f_y(P_0)t, \qquad z = z_0 + f_z(P_0)t. \tag{16}$$

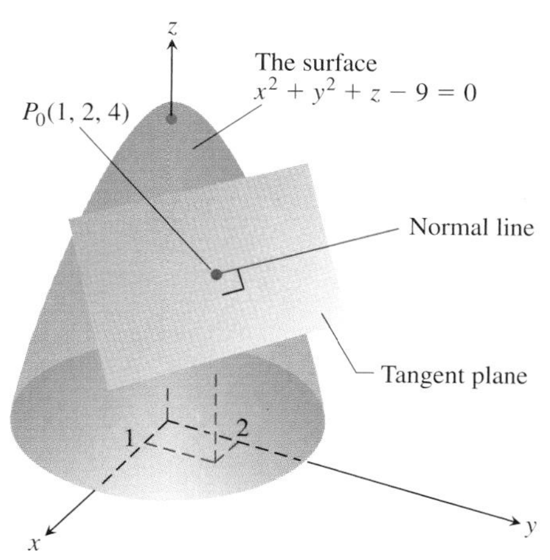

13.41 The tangent plane and normal line to the surface $x^2 + y^2 + z - 9 = 0$ at $P_0(1, 2, 4)$ (Example 6).

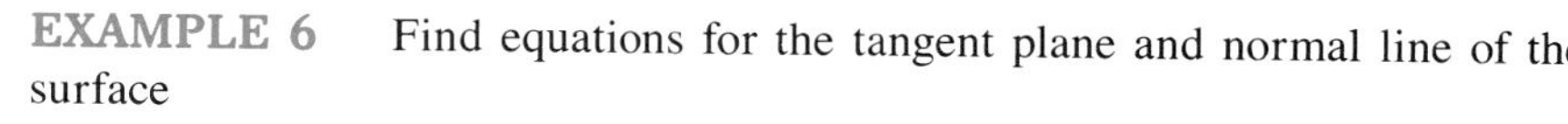

EXAMPLE 6 Find equations for the tangent plane and normal line of the surface

$$f(x, y, z) = x^2 + y^2 + z - 9 = 0 \qquad \text{A circular paraboloid}$$

at the point $P_0(1, 2, 4)$.

Solution The surface is shown in Fig. 13.41.

The tangent plane is the plane through P_0 perpendicular to the gradient of f at P_0. The gradient is

$$\nabla f\Big|_{P_0} = (2x\,\mathbf{i} + 2y\,\mathbf{j} + \mathbf{k})_{(1,2,4)} = 2\,\mathbf{i} + 4\,\mathbf{j} + \mathbf{k}.$$

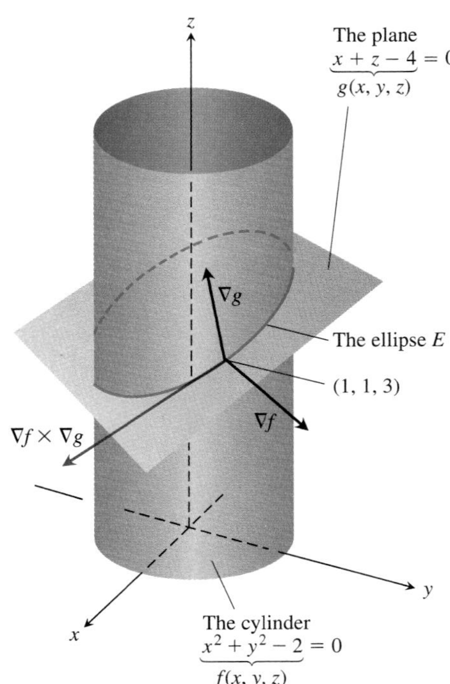

13.42 The cylinder $f(x, y, z) = x^2 + y^2 - 2 = 0$ and the plane $g(x, y, z) = x + z - 4 = 0$ intersect in an ellipse E. Any tangent to E will be orthogonal to ∇f and ∇g and hence parallel to $\nabla f \times \nabla g$ (Example 7).

The plane is therefore the plane

$$2(x - 1) + 4(y - 2) + (z - 4) = 0 \qquad \text{or} \qquad 2x + 4y + z = 14.$$

The line normal to the surface at P_0 is

$$x = 1 + 2t, \qquad y = 2 + 4t, \qquad z = 4 + t.$$

EXAMPLE 7 The surfaces

$$f(x, y, z) = x^2 + y^2 - 2 = 0 \qquad \text{A cylinder}$$

and

$$g(x, y, z) = x + z - 4 = 0 \qquad \text{A plane}$$

meet in an ellipse E (Fig. 13.42). Find parametric equations for the line tangent to E at the point $P_0(1, 1, 3)$.

Solution The tangent line is orthogonal to both ∇f and ∇g at P_0, and therefore parallel to $\mathbf{v} = \nabla f \times \nabla g$. The components of $\mathbf{v}$ and the coordinates of P_0 give us equations for the line. We have

$$\nabla f_{(1,1,3)} = (2x\,\mathbf{i} + 2y\,\mathbf{j})_{(1,1,3)} = 2\,\mathbf{i} + 2\,\mathbf{j}$$
$$\nabla g_{(1,1,3)} = (\mathbf{i} + \mathbf{k})_{(1,1,3)} = \mathbf{i} + \mathbf{k}$$
$$\mathbf{v} = (2\,\mathbf{i} + 2\,\mathbf{j}) \times (\mathbf{i} + \mathbf{k}) = \begin{vmatrix} \mathbf{i} & \mathbf{j} & \mathbf{k} \\ 2 & 2 & 0 \\ 1 & 0 & 1 \end{vmatrix} = 2\,\mathbf{i} - 2\,\mathbf{j} - 2\,\mathbf{k}.$$

The line is

$$x = 1 + 2t, \qquad y = 1 - 2t, \qquad z = 3 - 2t.$$

Planes Tangent to a Surface $z = f(x, y)$

To find an equation for the plane tangent to a surface $z = f(x, y)$ at a point $P_0(x_0, y_0, z_0)$ where $z_0 = f(x_0, y_0)$, we first observe that the equation $z = f(x, y)$ is equivalent to the equation $f(x, y) - z = 0$. The surface $z = f(x, y)$ is therefore the zero level surface of the function $F(x, y, z) = f(x, y) - z$. The partial derivatives of F are

$$F_x = \frac{\partial}{\partial x}(f(x, y) - z) = f_x - 0 = f_x,$$
$$F_y = \frac{\partial}{\partial y}(f(x, y) - z) = f_y - 0 = f_y,$$
$$F_z = \frac{\partial}{\partial z}(f(x, y) - z) = 0 - 1 = -1.$$

The formula

$$F_x(P_0)(x - x_0) + F_y(P_0)(y - y_0) + F_z(P_0)(z - z_0) = 0 \qquad \text{Eq. (15) restated for } F(x, y, z)$$

for the plane tangent to the level surface at P_0 therefore reduces to

$$f_x(x_0, y_0)(x - x_0) + f_y(x_0, y_0)(y - y_0) - (z - z_0) = 0. \tag{17}$$

The plane tangent to the surface $z = f(x, y)$ at the point $P_0(x_0, y_0, z_0) = (x_0, y_0, f(x_0, y_0))$ is

$$f_x(x_0, y_0)(x - x_0) + f_y(x_0, y_0)(y - y_0) - (z - z_0) = 0. \qquad (18)$$

EXAMPLE 8 Find an equation for the plane tangent to the surface

$$z = x\cos y - ye^x$$

at the origin.

Solution We calculate the partial derivatives of $f(x, y) = x\cos y - ye^x$ and use Eq. (18):

$$f_x(0, 0) = (\cos y - ye^x)_{(0,0)} = 1 - 0 \cdot 1 = 1$$
$$f_y(0, 0) = (-x\sin y - e^x)_{(0,0)} = 0 - 1 = -1.$$

The tangent plane is therefore

$$1 \cdot (x - 0) - 1 \cdot (y - 0) - (z - 0) = 0, \qquad \text{Eq. (18)}$$

or

$$x - y - z = 0.$$

Increments and Distance

The directional derivative plays the role of an ordinary derivative when we want to estimate how much a function f changes if we move a small distance ds from a point P_0 to another point nearby. If f were a function of a single variable, we would have

$$df = f'(P_0)\,ds. \qquad \text{Ordinary derivative} \times \text{increment}$$

For a function of two or more variables, we use the formula

$$df = (\nabla f|_{P_0} \cdot \mathbf{u})\,ds, \qquad \text{Directional derivative} \times \text{increment}$$

where $\mathbf{u}$ is the direction of the motion away from P_0.

Estimating the Change in f in a Direction $\mathbf{u}$

To estimate the change in the value of a function f when we move a small distance ds from a point P_0 in a particular direction $\mathbf{u}$, use the formula

$$df = \underbrace{(\nabla f|_{P_0} \cdot \mathbf{u})}_{\text{Directional derivative}} \cdot \underbrace{ds}_{\text{Distance increment}} \qquad (19)$$

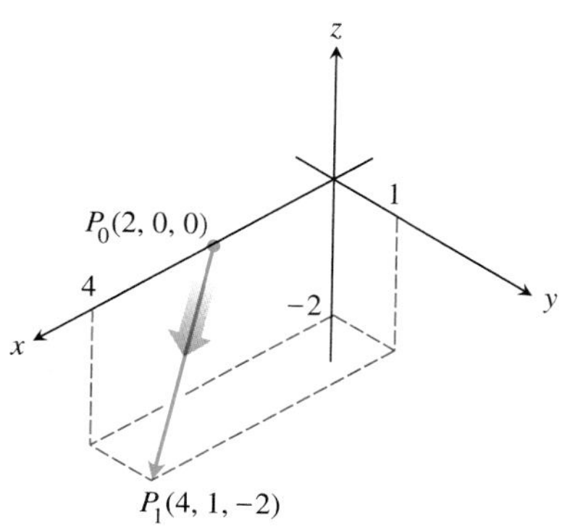

13.43 Example 9 shows how to estimate the change in $f(x, y, z) = xe^y + yz$ as (x, y, z) moves 0.1 unit from P_0 along the line toward P_1.

EXAMPLE 9 Estimate how much the value of

$$f(x, y, z) = xe^y + yz$$

will change if the point $P(x, y, z)$ moves 0.1 unit from $P_0(2, 0, 0)$ straight toward $P_1(4, 1, -2)$ (Fig. 13.43).

Solution We first find the derivative of f at P_0 in the direction of the vector

$$\overrightarrow{P_0P_1} = 2\,\mathbf{i} + \mathbf{j} - 2\,\mathbf{k}.$$

The direction of this vector is

$$\mathbf{u} = \frac{\overrightarrow{P_0P_1}}{|\overrightarrow{P_0P_1}|} = \frac{\overrightarrow{P_0P_1}}{3} = \frac{2}{3}\mathbf{i} + \frac{1}{3}\mathbf{j} - \frac{2}{3}\mathbf{k}.$$

The gradient of f at P_0 is

$$\nabla f|_{(2,0,0)} = (e^y\,\mathbf{i} + (xe^y + z)\,\mathbf{j} + y\,\mathbf{k})|_{(2,0,0)} = \mathbf{i} + 2\,\mathbf{j}.$$

Therefore,

$$\nabla f|_{P_0} \cdot \mathbf{u} = (\mathbf{i} + 2\,\mathbf{j}) \cdot \left(\frac{2}{3}\mathbf{i} + \frac{1}{3}\mathbf{j} - \frac{2}{3}\mathbf{k}\right) = \frac{2}{3} + \frac{2}{3} = \frac{4}{3}.$$

The change df in f that results from moving $ds = 0.1$ unit away from P_0 in the direction of $\mathbf{u}$ is approximately

$$df = (\nabla f|_{P_0} \cdot \mathbf{u})\,(ds) = \left(\frac{4}{3}\right)(0.1) \approx 0.13.$$

Algebra Rules for Gradients

If we know the gradients of two functions f and g, we automatically know the gradients of their constant multiples, sum, difference, product, and quotient.

Algebra Rules for Gradients

1. *Constant Multiple Rule:* $\nabla(kf) = k\nabla f$ (Any number k)
2. *Sum Rule:* $\nabla(f + g) = \nabla f + \nabla g$
3. *Difference Rule:* $\nabla(f - g) = \nabla f - \nabla g$
4. *Product Rule:* $\nabla(fg) = f\nabla g + g\nabla f$
5. *Quotient Rule:* $\nabla\left(\dfrac{f}{g}\right) = \dfrac{g\nabla f - f\nabla g}{g^2}$

These rules have the same form as the corresponding rules for derivatives, as they should. You will see where the rules come from if you do Exercise 58.

EXAMPLE 10 We illustrate the rules with

$$f(x, y, z) = x - y \qquad g(x, y, z) = z$$
$$\nabla f = \mathbf{i} - \mathbf{j} \qquad \nabla g = \mathbf{k}.$$

We have:

1. $\nabla\,(2f) = \nabla(2x - 2y) = 2\,\mathbf{i} - 2\,\mathbf{j} = 2\nabla f$
2. $\nabla\,(f + g) = \nabla\,(x - y + z) = \mathbf{i} - \mathbf{j} + \mathbf{k} = \nabla f + \nabla g$
3. $\nabla\,(f - g) = \nabla(x - y - z) = \mathbf{i} - \mathbf{j} - \mathbf{k} = \nabla f - \nabla g$
4. $\nabla\,(fg) = \nabla(xz - yz) = z\,\mathbf{i} - z\,\mathbf{j} + (x - y)\,\mathbf{k} = g\nabla f + f\nabla g$

$$5.\ \nabla\left(\frac{f}{g}\right) = \nabla\left(\frac{x-y}{z}\right) = \frac{\partial}{\partial x}\left(\frac{x-y}{z}\right)\mathbf{i} + \frac{\partial}{\partial y}\left(\frac{x-y}{z}\right)\mathbf{j} + \frac{\partial}{\partial z}\left(\frac{x-y}{z}\right)\mathbf{k}$$

$$= \frac{1}{z}\mathbf{i} - \frac{1}{z}\mathbf{j} + \frac{z\cdot 0 - (x-y)\cdot 1}{z^2}\mathbf{k}$$

$$= \frac{z\,\mathbf{i} - z\,\mathbf{j} - (x-y)\,\mathbf{k}}{z^2} = \frac{g\nabla f - f\nabla g}{g^2}$$

Exercises 13.6

In Exercises 1–4, find the gradient of the function at the given point. Then sketch the gradient together with the level curve that passes through the point.

1. $f(x, y) = y - x$, $(2, 1)$
2. $f(x, y) = \ln(x^2 + y^2)$, $(1, 1)$
3. $g(x, y) = y - x^2$, $(-1, 0)$
4. $g(x, y) = \frac{x^2}{2} - \frac{y^2}{2}$, $(\sqrt{2}, 1)$

In Exercises 5–8, find the gradient of the function at the given point.

5. $f(x, y, z) = x^2 + y^2 - 2z^2$, $(1, 1, 1)$
6. $f(x, y, z) = 2z^3 - 3(x^2 + y^2)z$, $(1, 1, 1)$
7. $h(x, y, z) = (x^2 + y^2 + z^2)^{-1/2}$, $(1, 2, -2)$
8. $h(x, y, z) = e^{x+y}\cos z$, $(0, 0, \pi/6)$

In Exercises 9–16, find the derivative of the function at P_0 in the direction of **A**.

9. $f(x, y) = x - (y^2/x)$, $P_0(1, 1)$, $\mathbf{A} = 12\,\mathbf{i} + 5\,\mathbf{j}$
10. $f(x, y) = 2x^2 + y^2$, $P_0(-1, 1)$, $\mathbf{A} = 3\,\mathbf{i} - 4\,\mathbf{j}$
11. $g(x, y) = x^2 + 2xy - 3y^2$, $P_0(1, 1)$, $\mathbf{A} = 3\,\mathbf{i} + 4\,\mathbf{j}$
12. $h(x, y) = x\tan^{-1}(y/x)$, $P_0(1, 1)$, $\mathbf{A} = 2\,\mathbf{i} - \mathbf{j}$
13. $f(x, y, z) = xy + yz + zx$, $P_0(1, -1, 2)$, $\mathbf{A} = 3\,\mathbf{i} + 6\,\mathbf{j} - 2\,\mathbf{k}$
14. $f(x, y, z) = x^2 + 2y^2 - 3z^2$, $P_0(1, 1, 1)$, $\mathbf{A} = \mathbf{i} + \mathbf{j} + \mathbf{k}$
15. $g(x, y, z) = 3e^x\cos yz$, $P_0(0, 0, 0)$, $\mathbf{A} = 2\,\mathbf{i} + \mathbf{j} - 2\,\mathbf{k}$
16. $h(x, y, z) = \cos xy + e^{yz} + \ln zx$, $P_0(1, 0, 1/2)$, $\mathbf{A} = \mathbf{i} + 2\,\mathbf{j} + 2\,\mathbf{k}$

In Exercises 17–22, find the directions in which the function increases and decreases most rapidly at P_0. Then find the derivatives of the function in these directions.

17. $f(x, y) = x^2 + xy + y^2$, $P_0(-1, 1)$
18. $f(x, y, z) = (x/y) - yz$, $P_0(4, 1, 1)$
19. $f(x, y) = x^2 + \sin y$, $P_0(1, 0)$
20. $f(x, y, z) = \sin x + \sin y + \sin z$, $P_0(0, 0, 0)$
21. $g(x, y, z) = xe^y + z^2$, $P_0(1, \ln 2, 1/2)$
22. $h(x, y, z) = \ln(x^2 + y^2 - 1) + y + 6z$, $P_0(1, 1, 0)$

23. By about how much will
$$f(x, y, z) = \ln\sqrt{x^2 + y^2 + z^2}$$
change if the point $P(x, y, z)$ moves from $P_0(3, 4, 12)$ a distance of $ds = 0.1$ unit in the direction of $3\,\mathbf{i} + 6\,\mathbf{j} - 2\,\mathbf{k}$?

24. By about how much will
$$f(x, y, z) = e^x\cos yz$$
change as the point $P(x, y, z)$ moves from the origin a distance of $ds = 0.1$ unit in the direction of $2\,\mathbf{i} + 2\,\mathbf{j} - 2\,\mathbf{k}$?

25. By about how much will
$$g(x, y, z) = x + x\cos z - y\sin z + y$$
change if the point $P(x, y, z)$ moves from $P_0(2, -1, 0)$ a distance of $ds = 0.2$ unit toward the point $P_1(0, 1, 2)$?

26. By about how much will
$$h(x, y, z) = \cos(\pi xy) + xz^2$$
change if the point $P(x, y, z)$ moves from $P_0(-1, -1, -1)$ a distance of $ds = 0.1$ unit toward the origin?

In Exercises 27–34, find equations for the (a) tangent plane and (b) normal line at the point P_0 on the given surface.

27. $x^2 + y^2 + z^2 = 3$, $P_0(1, 1, 1)$
28. $x^2 + y^2 - z^2 = 18$, $P_0(3, 5, -4)$
29. $2z - x^2 = 0$, $P_0(2, 0, 2)$
30. $x^2 + 2xy - y^2 + z^2 = 7$, $P_0(1, -1, 3)$
31. $\cos\pi x - x^2y + e^{xz} + yz = 4$, $P_0(0, 1, 2)$
32. $x^2 - xy - y^2 - z = 0$, $P_0(1, 1, -1)$
33. $x + y + z = 1$, $P_0(0, 1, 0)$
34. $x^2 + y^2 - 2xy - x + 3y - z = -4$, $P_0(2, -3, 18)$

In Exercises 35–38, find an equation for the plane that is tangent to the given surface at the given point.

35. $z = \ln(x^2 + y^2)$, $(1, 0, 0)$
36. $z = e^{-(x^2+y^2)}$, $(0, 0, 1)$
37. $z = \sqrt{y - x}$, $(1, 2, 1)$
38. $z = 4x^2 + y^2$, $(1, 1, 5)$

In Exercises 39–42, sketch the curve $f(x, y) = c$ together with ∇f and the tangent line at the given point. Then write an equation for the tangent line.

39. $x^2 + y^2 = 4$, $(\sqrt{2}, \sqrt{2})$
40. $x^2 - y = 1$, $(\sqrt{2}, 1)$

41. $xy = -4, \quad (2, -2)$

42. $x^2 - xy + y^2 = 7, \quad (-1, 2)$ (This is the curve in Section 3.6, Example 4.)

In Exercises 43–48, find parametric equations for the line tangent to the curve of intersection of the surfaces at the given point.

43. Surfaces: $x + y^2 + 2z = 4, \quad x = 1$
Point: $(1, 1, 1)$

44. Surfaces: $xyz = 1, \quad x^2 + 2y^2 + 3z^2 = 6$
Point: $(1, 1, 1)$

45. Surfaces: $x^2 + 2y + 2z = 4, \quad y = 1$
Point: $(1, 1, 1/2)$

46. Surfaces: $x + y^2 + z = 2, \quad y = 1$
Point: $(1/2, 1, 1/2)$

47. Surfaces: $x^3 + 3x^2y^2 + y^3 + 4xy - z^2 = 0,$
$x^2 + y^2 + z^2 = 11$
Point: $(1, 1, 3)$

48. Surfaces: $x^2 + y^2 = 4, \quad x^2 + y^2 - z = 0$
Point: $(\sqrt{2}, \sqrt{2}, 4)$

49. In what two directions is the derivative of $f(x, y) = xy + y^2$ equal to zero at the point (3, 2)? Give reasons for your answer. (Fig. 13.44.)

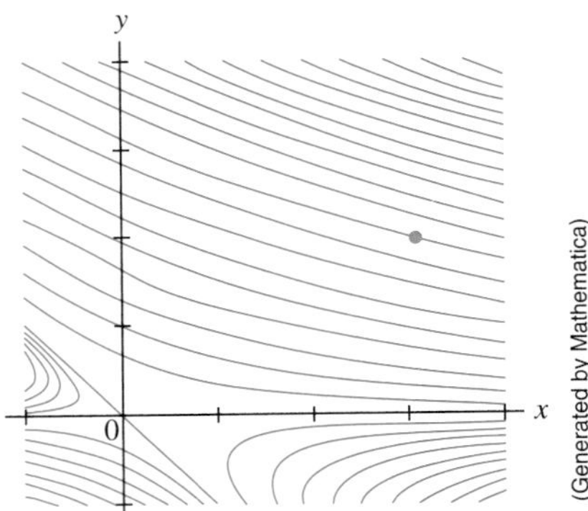

13.44 Level curves of $f(x, y) = xy + y^2$ (Exercise 49).

50. In what two directions is the derivative of $f(x, y) = (x^2 - y^2)/(x^2 + y^2)$ equal to zero at the point (1, 1)? Give reasons for your answer. (Fig. 13.45.)

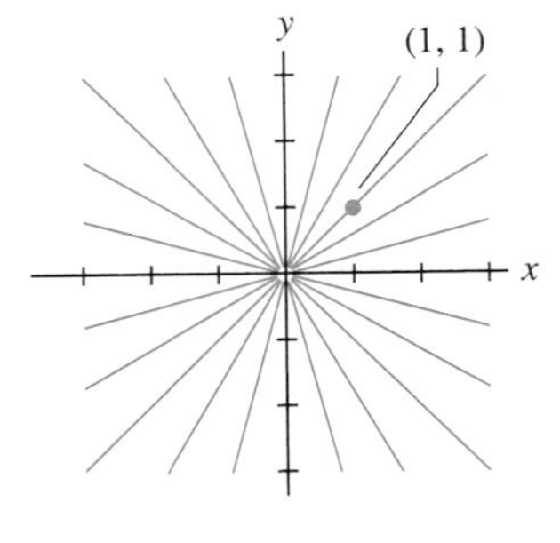

13.45 Level curves of

$$f(x, y) = \frac{x^2 - y^2}{x^2 + y^2}$$

(Exercise 50).

51. *Change Along a Helix.* Find the derivative of $f(x, y, z) = x^2 + y^2 + z^2$ in the direction of the unit tangent vector of the helix $\mathbf{r} = (\cos t)\,\mathbf{i} + (\sin t)\,\mathbf{j} + t\,\mathbf{k}$ at the points where $t = -\pi/4$, 0, and $\pi/4$. The function f gives the square of the distance from a point $P(x, y, z)$ on the helix to the origin. The derivatives calculated here give the rates at which the square of the distance is changing with respect to t as P moves through the points where $t = -\pi/4$, 0, and $\pi/4$.

52. *Change Along the Involute of a Circle.* Find the derivative of $f(x, y) = x^2 + y^2$ in the direction of the unit tangent vector of the curve

$$\mathbf{r} = (\cos t + t \sin t)\,\mathbf{i} + (\sin t - t \cos t)\,\mathbf{j}, \quad t > 0$$

(Fig. 13.46).

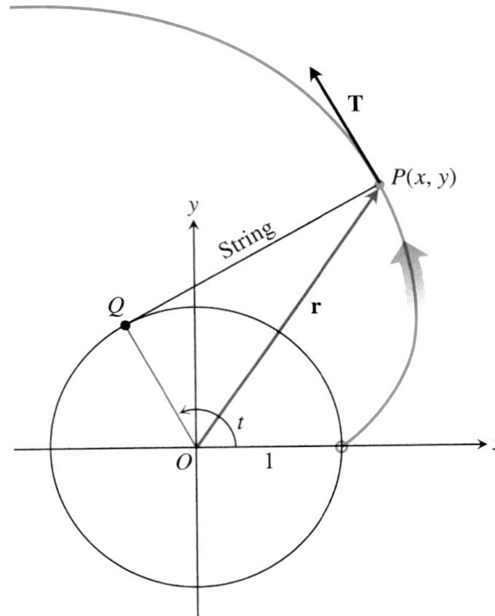

13.46 The involute of the unit circle from Section 12.3, Example 5. If you move out along the involute, covering distance along the curve at a constant rate, your distance from the origin will increase at a constant rate as well. (This is how to interpret the result of your calculation in Exercise 52.)

53. The derivative of $f(x, y)$ at $P_0(1, 2)$ in the direction of $\mathbf{i} + \mathbf{j}$ is $2\sqrt{2}$ and in the direction of $-2\,\mathbf{j}$ is -3. What is the derivative of f in the direction of $-\mathbf{i} - 2\,\mathbf{j}$? Give reasons for your answer.

54. The derivative of $f(x, y, z)$ at a point P is greatest in the direction of $\mathbf{A} = \mathbf{i} + \mathbf{j} - \mathbf{k}$. In this direction the value of the derivative is $2\sqrt{3}$.

a) What is ∇f at P? Give reasons for your answer.
b) What is the derivative of f at P in the direction of $\mathbf{i} + \mathbf{j}$?

55. *Directional Derivatives and Scalar Components.* How is the derivative of a differentiable function $f(x, y, z)$ at a point P_0 in the direction of a unit vector $\mathbf{u}$ related to the scalar component of $(\nabla f)_{P_0}$ in the direction of $\mathbf{u}$? Give reasons for your answer.

56. *Directional Derivatives and Partial Derivatives.* Assuming that the necessary derivatives of $f(x, y, z)$ are defined, how are $D_{\mathbf{i}}f$, $D_{\mathbf{j}}f$, and $D_{\mathbf{k}}f$ related to f_x, f_y, and f_z? Give reasons for your answer.

57. *Normal Curves and Tangent Curves.* A curve is *normal* to a surface $f(x, y, z) = c$ at a point of intersection if the curve's velocity vector is a scalar multiple of ∇f at the point. The curve is *tangent* to the surface at a point of intersection if its velocity vector is orthogonal to ∇f there.

a) Show that the curve

$$\mathbf{r} = \sqrt{t}\,\mathbf{i} + \sqrt{t}\,\mathbf{j} - \frac{1}{4}(t+3)\,\mathbf{k}$$

is normal to the surface $x^2 + y^2 - z = 3$ when $t = 1$.

b) Show that the curve

$$\mathbf{r} = \sqrt{t}\,\mathbf{i} + \sqrt{t}\,\mathbf{j} + (2t-1)\,\mathbf{k}$$

is tangent to the surface $x^2 + y^2 - z = 1$ when $t = 1$.

58. *The Algebra Rules for Gradients.* Given a constant k and the gradients

$$\nabla f = \frac{\partial f}{\partial x}\mathbf{i} + \frac{\partial f}{\partial y}\mathbf{j} + \frac{\partial f}{\partial z}\mathbf{k}$$

and

$$\nabla g = \frac{\partial g}{\partial x}\mathbf{i} + \frac{\partial g}{\partial y}\mathbf{j} + \frac{\partial g}{\partial z}\mathbf{k},$$

use the scalar equations

$$\frac{\partial}{\partial x}(kf) = k\frac{\partial f}{\partial x}, \qquad \frac{\partial}{\partial x}(f \pm g) = \frac{\partial f}{\partial x} \pm \frac{\partial g}{\partial x},$$

$$\frac{\partial}{\partial x}(fg) = f\frac{\partial g}{\partial x} + g\frac{\partial f}{\partial x}, \qquad \frac{\partial}{\partial x}\left(\frac{f}{g}\right) = \frac{g\dfrac{\partial f}{\partial x} - f\dfrac{\partial g}{\partial x}}{g^2},$$

and so on, to establish the following rules:

a) $\nabla(kf) = k\nabla f$

b) $\nabla(f + g) = \nabla f + \nabla g$

c) $\nabla(f - g) = \nabla f - \nabla g$

d) $\nabla(fg) = f\nabla g + g\nabla f$

e) $\nabla\left(\dfrac{f}{g}\right) = \dfrac{g\nabla f - f\nabla g}{g^2}$

Writing for Your Own Knowledge

Answer the following questions in writing. Some answers will take only a sentence or two; others may require several paragraphs. Some explanations may also call for graphs or sketches.

1. What is the derivative of a function $f(x, y)$ at a point P_0 in the direction of a unit vector $\mathbf{u}$? What rate does it describe? What geometric interpretation does it have?
2. What is the gradient of a function $f(x, y)$? How is it related to the function's directional derivatives?
3. How do you find tangents to the level curves of a function $f(x, y)$?
4. What is the gradient of a function $f(x, y, z)$ of three independent variables? How is it related to the function's directional derivatives?
5. How do you find the tangent plane and normal line at a point on a level surface of a differentiable function $f(x, y, z)$?
6. How do you find the tangent plane and normal line at a point on a surface $z = f(x, y)$?
7. How can you use a function's directional derivative to estimate how much the function's value will change if you move a small distance in a particular direction?
8. What are the algebra rules for gradients? How do they resemble the algebra rules for derivatives of functions of a single independent variable?

13.7 Maxima, Minima, and Saddle Points

As we mentioned in Section 13.4, continuous functions defined on closed bounded regions in the xy-plane take on absolute maximum values on these domains (Figs. 13.47 and 13.48 on the following page). They also take on absolute minimum values. It is important to be able to find these values and to know where they occur. For example, what are the highest and lowest temperatures on a heated metal plate and where are they taken on? How high does a surface rise above or fall below a given patch of the xy-plane? We can often answer questions like these by examining partial derivatives.

The Derivative Tests

To find the local extreme values of a function of a single variable, we look for points where the graph has a horizontal tangent line. At such points we then look for local maxima, local minima, and points of inflection. For a function $f(x, y)$

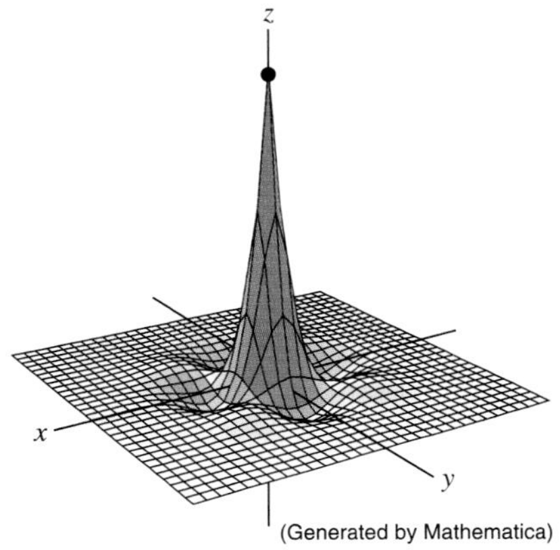

13.47 The function

$$z = (\cos x)(\cos y)e^{-\sqrt{x^2 + y^2}}$$

has a maximum value of 1 and a minimum value of about -0.067 on the square region $|x| \le 3\pi/2$, $|y| \le 3\pi/2$.

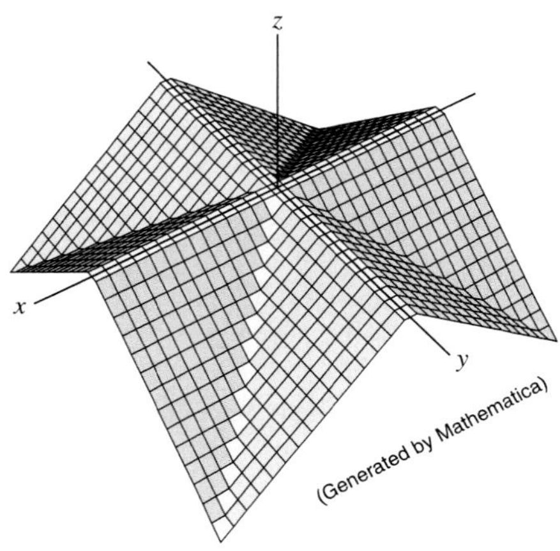

13.48 The "roof surface"

$$z = \frac{1}{2}\left(\left||x| - |y|\right| - |x| - |y|\right)$$

viewed from the point (10, 15, 20). The defining function has a maximum value of 0 and a minimum value of $-a$ on the square region $|x| \le a$, $|y| \le a$.

of two variables, we look for points where the surface $z = f(x, y)$ has a horizontal tangent *plane*. At such points we then look for local maxima, local minima, and saddle points (more about saddle points in a moment).

DEFINITION

Let $f(x, y)$ be defined on a region R containing the point (a, b). Then

1. $f(a, b)$ is a **local maximum** value of f if $f(a, b) \ge f(x, y)$ for all domain points (x, y) in an open disk centered at (a, b).
2. $f(a, b)$ is a **local minimum** value of f if $f(a, b) \le f(x, y)$ for all domain points (x, y) in an open disk centered at (a, b).

Local maxima correspond to mountain peaks on the surface $z = f(x, y)$ and local minima correspond to valley bottoms (Fig. 13.49). At such points the tangent planes are horizontal. Local extrema are also called **relative extrema.**

As with functions of a single variable, the key to identifying the local extrema is a first derivative test.

THEOREM 7

First Derivative Test for Local Extreme Values

If $f(x, y)$ has a local maximum or minimum value at an interior point (a, b) of its domain, and if the first partial derivatives exist there, then $f_x(a, b) = 0$ and $f_y(a, b) = 0$.

If we substitute the values $f_x(a, b) = 0$ and $f_y(a, b) = 0$ into the equation

$$f_x(a, b)(x - a) + f_y(a, b)(y - b) - (z - f(a, b)) = 0 \qquad (1)$$

for the tangent plane to the surface $z = f(x, y)$ at (a, b), the equation reduces to

$$0 \cdot (x - a) + 0 \cdot (y - b) - z + f(a, b) = 0 \qquad (2)$$

or

$$z = f(a, b). \qquad (3)$$

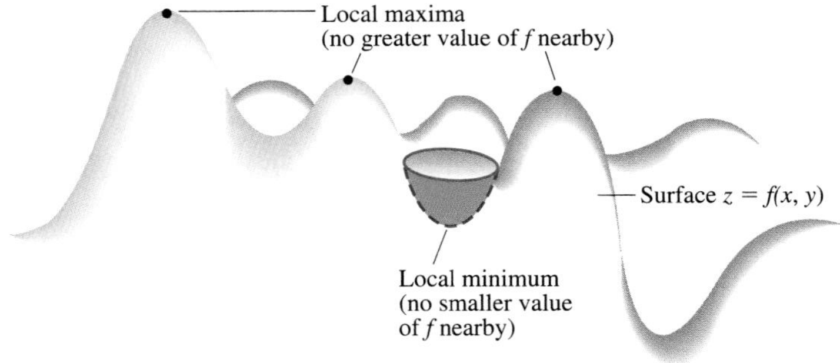

13.49 A local maximum is a mountain peak and a local minimum is a valley low.

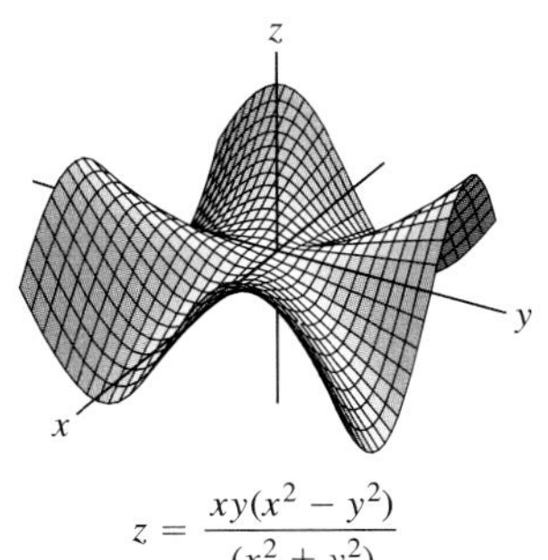

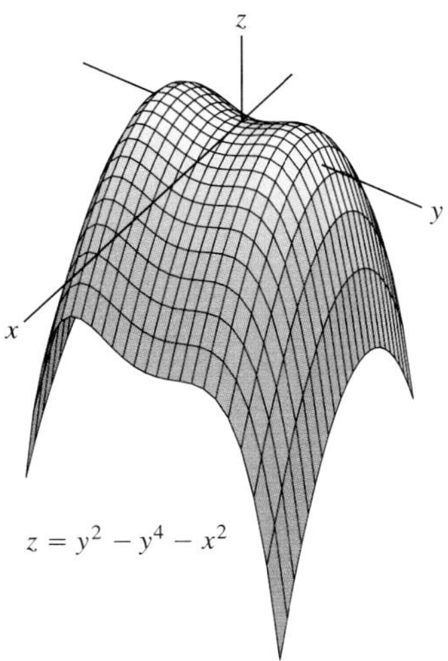

13.50 Each of these surfaces has a saddle point at the origin.

Thus, Theorem 7 says that the surface does indeed have a horizontal tangent plane at a local extremum, provided there is a tangent plane there.

As in the single-variable case, Theorem 7 says that the only places a function $f(x, y)$ can ever have an extreme value are

1. Interior points where $f_x = f_y = 0$,
2. Interior points where one or both of f_x and f_y do not exist,
3. Boundary points of the function's domain.

DEFINITION

An interior point of the domain of a function $f(x, y)$ where both f_x and f_y are zero or where one or both of f_x and f_y do not exist is a **critical point** of f.

Thus, the only points where a function $f(x, y)$ can assume extreme values are critical points and boundary points. As with differentiable functions of a single variable, not every critical point gives rise to a local extremum. A differentiable function of a single variable might have a point of inflection. A differentiable function of two variables might have a saddle point.

DEFINITION

A differentiable function $f(x, y)$ has a **saddle point** at a critical point (a, b) if in every open disk centered at (a, b) there are domain points (x, y) where $f(x, y) > f(a, b)$ and domain points (x, y) where $f(x, y) < f(a, b)$. The corresponding point $(a, b, f(a, b))$ on the surface $z = f(x, y)$ is called a saddle point of the surface (Fig. 13.50).

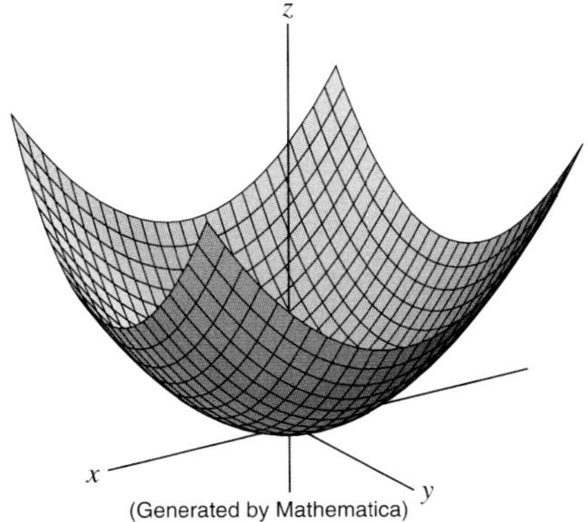

13.51 The graph of the function $f(x, y) = x^2 + y^2$ is the paraboloid $z = x^2 + y^2$. The function has only one critical point, the origin, which gives rise to a local minimum value of 0 (Example 1).

EXAMPLE 1 Find the local extreme values of $f(x, y) = x^2 + y^2$.

Solution The domain of f is the entire plane (so there are no boundary points) and the partial derivatives $f_x = 2x$ and $f_y = 2y$ exist everywhere. Therefore, local extreme values can occur only where

$$f_x = 2x = 0 \qquad \text{and} \qquad f_y = 2y = 0.$$

The only possibility is the origin, where the value of f is zero. Since f is never negative, we see that the origin gives a local minimum (Fig. 13.51).

EXAMPLE 2 Find the local extreme values (if any) of $f(x, y) = y^2 - x^2$.

Solution The domain of f is the entire plane (so there are no boundary points) and the partial derivatives $f_x = -2x$ and $f_y = 2y$ exist everywhere. Therefore, local extrema can occur only at the origin $(0, 0)$. However, along the positive x-axis f has the value $f(x, 0) = -x^2 < 0$; along the positive y-axis f has the

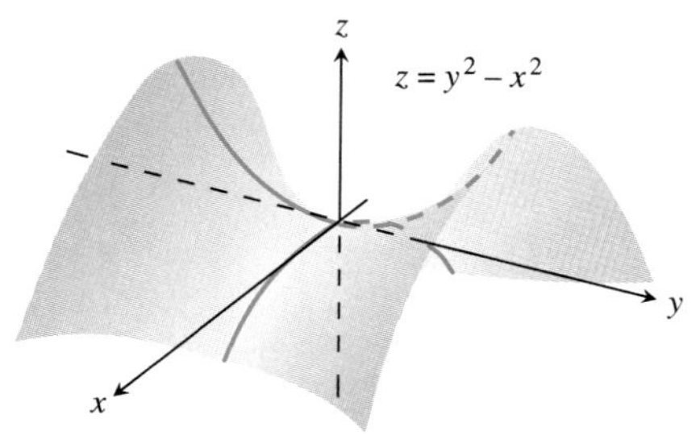

13.52 The origin is a saddle point of the function $f(x, y) = y^2 - x^2$. There are no local extreme values (Example 2).

value $f(0, y) = y^2 > 0$. Therefore every open disk in the xy-plane centered at $(0, 0)$ contains points where the function is positive and points where it is negative. The function has a saddle point at the origin (Fig. 13.52) instead of a local extreme value. We conclude that the function has no local extreme values.

The fact that $f_x = f_y = 0$ at an interior point (a, b) of R does not tell us enough to be sure f has an extreme value there. However, if f and its first and second partial derivatives are continuous on R, we may be able to learn the rest from the following test from advanced calculus.

THEOREM 8

Second Derivative Test

Suppose $f(x, y)$ and its first and second partial derivatives are continuous throughout a disk centered at (a, b) and that $f_x(a, b) = f_y(a, b) = 0$. Then

i) f has a **local maximum** at (a, b) if $f_{xx} < 0$ and $f_{xx}f_{yy} - f_{xy}^2 > 0$ at (a, b);

ii) f has a **local minimum** at (a, b) if $f_{xx} > 0$ and $f_{xx}f_{yy} - f_{xy}^2 > 0$ at (a, b);

iii) f has a **saddle point** at (a, b) if $f_{xx}f_{yy} - f_{xy}^2 < 0$ at (a, b).

iv) **The test is inconclusive** at (a, b) if $f_{xx}f_{yy} - f_{xy}^2 = 0$ at (a, b). In this case, we must find some other way to determine the behavior of f at (a, b).

The expression $f_{xx} f_{yy} - f_{xy}^2$ is called the **discriminant** of f. It is sometimes easier to remember in the determinant form

$$f_{xx} f_{yy} - f_{xy}^2 = \begin{vmatrix} f_{xx} & f_{xy} \\ f_{xy} & f_{yy} \end{vmatrix}.$$

Theorem 8 says that if the discriminant is positive at the point (a, b), then the surface curves the same way in all directions: downwards if $f_{xx} < 0$, giving rise to a local maximum, and upwards if $f_{xx} > 0$, giving a local minimum. On the other hand, if the discriminant is negative at (a, b), then the surface curves up in some directions and down in others, so we have a saddle point.

EXAMPLE 3 Find the local extreme values of the function

$$f(x, y) = xy - x^2 - y^2 - 2x - 2y + 4.$$

Solution The function is defined and differentiable for all x and y and its domain has no boundary points. The function therefore has extreme values only at the points where f_x and f_y are simultaneously zero. This leads to

$$f_x = y - 2x - 2 = 0, \qquad f_y = x - 2y - 2 = 0,$$

or

$$x = y = -2.$$

Therefore, the point $(-2, -2)$ is the only point where f may take on an extreme

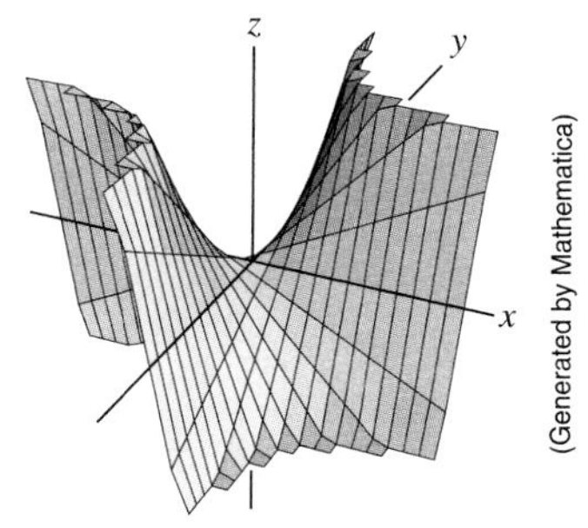

13.53 The surface $z = xy$ has a saddle point at the origin (Example 4).

value. To see if it does so, we calculate

$$f_{xx} = -2, \qquad f_{yy} = -2, \qquad f_{xy} = 1.$$

The discriminant of f at $(a, b) = (-2, -2)$ is

$$f_{xx} f_{yy} - f_{xy}^2 = (-2)(-2) - (1)^2 = 4 - 1 = 3.$$

The combination

$$f_{xx} < 0 \qquad \text{and} \qquad f_{xx} f_{yy} - f_{xy}^2 > 0$$

tells us that f has a local maximum at $(-2, -2)$. The value of f at this point is $f(-2, -2) = 8$.

EXAMPLE 4 Find the local extreme values of $f(x, y) = xy$.

Solution Since f is differentiable everywhere (Fig. 13.53), it can assume extreme values only where

$$f_x = y = 0 \qquad \text{and} \qquad f_y = x = 0.$$

Thus, the origin is the only point where f might have an extreme value. To see what happens there, we calculate

$$f_{xx} = 0, \qquad f_{yy} = 0, \qquad f_{xy} = 1.$$

The discriminant,

$$f_{xx} f_{yy} - f_{xy}^2 = -1,$$

is negative. Therefore the function has a saddle point at (0, 0). We conclude that $f(x, y) = xy$ has no local extreme values.

Absolute Maxima and Minima on Closed Bounded Regions

We organize the search for the absolute extrema of a continuous function $f(x, y)$ on a closed and bounded region R into three steps.

STEP 1: *List the interior points of R where f may have local maxima and minima and evaluate f at these points.* These are the points where $f_x = f_y = 0$ or where one or both of f_x and f_y fail to exist (the critical points of f).

STEP 2: *List the boundary points of R where f has local maxima and minima and evaluate f at these points.* We will show how to do this shortly.

STEP 3: *Look through the lists for the maximum and minimum values of f. These will be the absolute maximum and minimum values of f on R.* Since absolute maxima and minima are also local maxima and minima, the absolute maximum and minimum values of f already appear somewhere in the lists made in Steps 1 and 2. We have only to glance at the lists to see what they are.

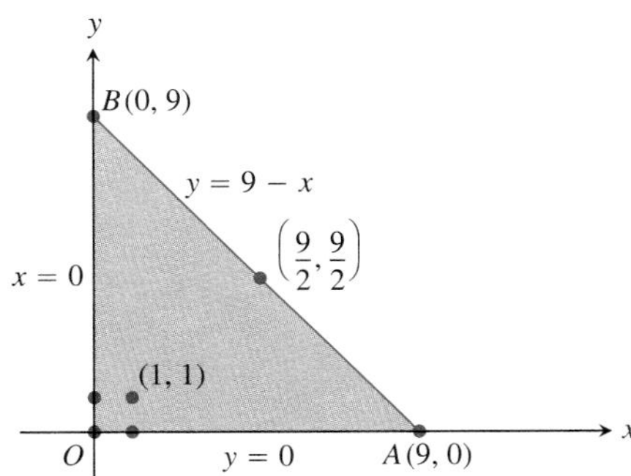

13.54 This triangular plate is the domain of the function in Example 5.

EXAMPLE 5 Find the absolute maximum and minimum values of

$$f(x, y) = 2 + 2x + 2y - x^2 - y^2$$

on the triangular plate in the first quadrant bounded by the lines $x = 0$, $y = 0$, $y = 9 - x$.

Solution Since f is differentiable, the only places where f can assume these values are points inside the triangle (Fig. 13.54) where $f_x = f_y = 0$ and points on the boundary.

Interior points. For these we have

$$f_x = 2 - 2x = 0, \qquad f_y = 2 - 2y = 0,$$

yielding the single point $(x, y) = (1, 1)$. The value of f there is

$$f(1, 1) = 4.$$

Boundary points. We take the triangle one side at a time:

1. On the segment OA, $y = 0$. The function

$$f(x, y) = f(x, 0) = 2 + 2x - x^2$$

may now be regarded as a function of x defined on the closed interval $0 \le x \le 9$. Its extreme values (we know from Chapter 4) may occur at the endpoints

$$\begin{aligned} x &= 0 \qquad \text{where} \quad f(0, 0) = 2, \\ x &= 9 \qquad \text{where} \quad f(9, 0) = 2 + 18 - 81 = -61, \end{aligned}$$

and at the interior points where $f'(x, 0) = 2 - 2x = 0$. The only interior point where $f'(x, 0) = 0$ is $x = 1$, where

$$f(x, 0) = f(1, 0) = 3.$$

2. On the segment OB, $x = 0$ and

$$f(x, y) = f(0, y) = 2 + 2y - y^2.$$

We know from the symmetry of f in x and y and from the analysis we just carried out that the candidates on this segment are

$$f(0, 0) = 2, \qquad f(0, 9) = -61, \qquad f(0, 1) = 3.$$

3. We have already accounted for the values of f at the endpoints of AB, so we need only look at the interior points of AB. With $y = 9 - x$, we have

$$f(x, y) = 2 + 2x + 2(9 - x) - x^2 - (9 - x)^2 = -61 + 18x - 2x^2.$$

Setting $f'(x, 9 - x) = 18 - 4x = 0$ gives

$$x = \frac{18}{4} = \frac{9}{2}.$$

At this value of x,

$$y = 9 - \frac{9}{2} = \frac{9}{2} \qquad \text{and} \qquad f(x, y) = f\left(\frac{9}{2}, \frac{9}{2}\right) = -\frac{41}{2}.$$

Summary. We list all the candidates:

$$4, \quad 2, \quad -61, \quad 3, \quad -\frac{41}{2}.$$

The maximum is 4, which f assumes at $(1, 1)$. The minimum is -61, which f assumes at $(0, 9)$ and $(9, 0)$.

Proof of the First Derivative Test (Theorem 7)

The assertion that a function $f(x, y)$ with defined first partial derivatives can have a local extreme value at an interior point of its domain only if f_x and f_y are both zero at that point seems reasonable when we think in terms of tangent lines.

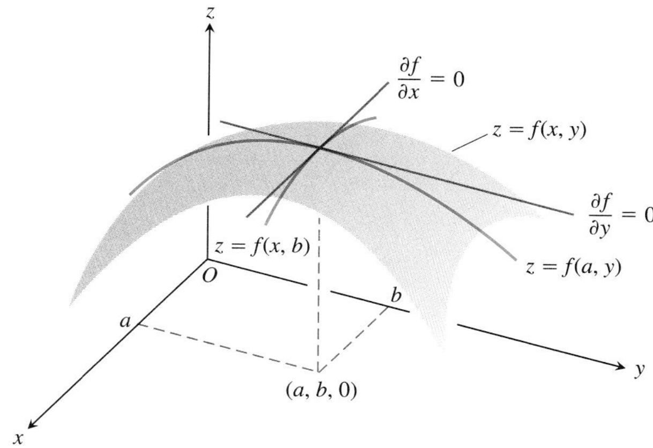

13.55 The maximum of f occurs at $x = a$, $y = b$.

How could the tangents at such a point be anything but horizontal? But we still need a proof, so let's begin by supposing that the value of f at (a, b) is a local maximum. Then

1. $x = a$ is an interior point of the domain of the curve $z = f(x, b)$ in which the plane $y = b$ cuts the surface $z = f(x, y)$ (Fig. 13.55).
2. The function $z = f(x, b)$ is a differentiable function of x at $x = a$ (the derivative is $f_x(a, b)$).
3. The function $z = f(x, b)$ has a local maximum value at $x = a$.
4. The value of the derivative of $z = f(x, b)$ at $x = a$ is therefore zero (Theorem 2, Section 4.2). Since this derivative is $f_x(a, b)$, we conclude that $f_x(a, b) = 0$.

A similar argument with the function $z = f(a, y)$ shows that $f_y(a, b) = 0$.

This proves the theorem for local maximum values. To prove it for local minimum values, replace f by $-f$ and run through the argument again. ■

Despite the power of Theorem 7, we urge you to remember its limitations. It does not apply to boundary points of a function's domain, where it is possible for a function to have extreme values along with nonzero derivatives. And it does not apply to points where either f_x or f_y fails to exist.

Summary of Max-Min Tests

The extreme values of $f(x, y)$ can occur only at

i) **boundary points** of the domain of f,

ii) **critical points** (interior points where $f_x = f_y = 0$ or points where f_x or f_y fail to exist).

If the first and second order partial derivatives of f are continuous throughout a disk centered at a point (a, b), and $f_x(a, b) = f_y(a, b) = 0$, you may be able to classify (a, b) with the ***second derivative test:***

i) $f_{xx} < 0$ and $f_{xx} f_{yy} - f_{xy}^2 > 0$ at (a, b) $\Rightarrow$ **local maximum,**

ii) $f_{xx} > 0$ and $f_{xx} f_{yy} - f_{xy}^2 > 0$ at (a, b) $\Rightarrow$ **local minimum,**

iii) $f_{xx} f_{yy} - f_{xy}^2 < 0$ at (a, b) $\Rightarrow$ **saddle point,**

iv) $f_{xx} f_{yy} - f_{xy}^2 = 0$ at (a, b) $\Rightarrow$ **test is inconclusive.**

Exercises 13.7

Find all the local maxima, local minima, and saddle points of the functions in Exercises 1–26.

1. $f(x, y) = x^2 + xy + y^2 + 3x - 3y + 4$
2. $f(x, y) = x^2 + 3xy + 3y^2 - 6x + 3y - 6$
3. $f(x, y) = 2xy - 5x^2 - 2y^2 + 4x + 4y - 4$
4. $f(x, y) = 2xy - 5x^2 - 2y^2 + 4x - 4$
5. $f(x, y) = x^2 + xy + 3x + 2y + 5$
6. $f(x, y) = y^2 + xy - 2x - 2y + 2$
7. $f(x, y) = 5xy - 7x^2 + 3x - 6y + 2$
8. $f(x, y) = 2xy - x^2 - 2y^2 + 3x + 4$
9. $f(x, y) = x^2 - 4xy + y^2 + 6y + 2$
10. $f(x, y) = 3x^2 + 6xy + 7y^2 - 2x + 4y$
11. $f(x, y) = 2x^2 + 3xy + 4y^2 - 5x + 2y$
12. $f(x, y) = 4x^2 - 6xy + 5y^2 - 20x + 26y$
13. $f(x, y) = x^2 - y^2 - 2x + 4y + 6$
14. $f(x, y) = x^2 - 2xy + 2y^2 - 2x + 2y + 1$
15. $f(x, y) = x^2 + 2xy$
16. $f(x, y) = 3 + 2x + 2y - 2x^2 - 2xy - y^2$
17. $f(x, y) = x^3 - y^3 - 2xy + 6$
18. $f(x, y) = x^3 + 3xy + y^3$
19. $f(x, y) = 6x^2 - 2x^3 + 3y^2 + 6xy$
20. $f(x, y) = 3y^2 - 2y^3 - 3x^2 + 6xy$
21. $f(x, y) = 9x^3 + y^3/3 - 4xy$
22. $f(x, y) = 8x^3 + y^3 + 6xy$
23. $f(x, y) = x^3 + y^3 + 3x^2 - 3y^2 - 8$
24. $f(x, y) = 2x^3 + 2y^3 - 9x^2 + 3y^2 - 12y$
25. $f(x, y) = 4xy - x^4 - y^4$
26. $f(x, y) = x^4 + y^4 + 4xy$

In Exercises 27–34, find the absolute maxima and minima of the functions on the given domains.

27. $f(x, y) = 2x^2 - 4x + y^2 - 4y + 1$ on the closed triangular plate bounded by the lines $x = 0$, $y = 2$, $y = 2x$ in the first quadrant
28. $D(x, y) = x^2 - xy + y^2 + 1$ on the closed triangular plate in the first quadrant bounded by the lines $x = 0$, $y = 4$, $y = x$
29. $f(x, y) = x^2 + y^2$ on the closed triangular plate bounded by the lines $x = 0$, $y = 0$, $y + 2x = 2$ in the first quadrant
30. $T(x, y) = x^2 + xy + y^2 - 6x$ on the rectangular plate $0 \le x \le 5$, $-3 \le y \le 3$
31. $T(x, y) = x^2 + xy + y^2 - 6x + 2$ on the rectangular plate $0 \le x \le 5$, $-3 \le y \le 0$
32. $f(x, y) = 48xy - 32x^3 - 24y^2$ on the rectangular plate $0 \le x \le 1$, $0 \le y \le 1$
33. $f(x, y) = (4x - x^2) \cos y$ on the rectangular plate $1 \le x \le 3$, $-\pi/4 \le y \le \pi/4$ (Fig. 13.56)

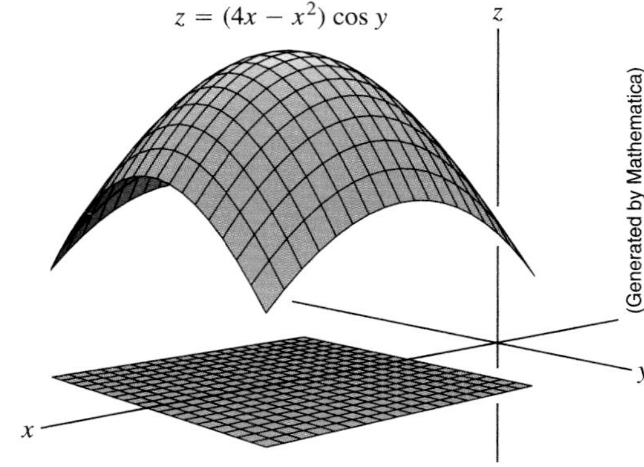

13.56 The function and domain in Exercise 33.

34. $f(x, y) = 4x - 8xy + 2y + 1$ on the triangular plate bounded by the lines $x = 0$, $y = 0$, $x + y = 1$ in the first quadrant
35. *Temperatures.* The flat circular plate in Fig. 13.57 has the shape of the region $x^2 + y^2 \le 1$. The plate, including the boundary where $x^2 + y^2 = 1$, is heated so that the temperature at the point (x, y) is
$$T(x, y) = x^2 + 2y^2 - x.$$
Find the temperatures at the hottest and coldest points on the plate.

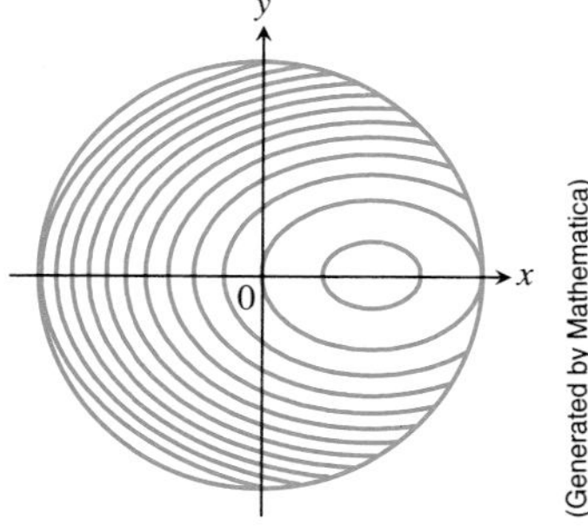

13.57 Curves of constant temperature are called isotherms. The figure shows isotherms of the temperature function $T(x, y) = x^2 + 2y^2 - x$ on the disk $x^2 + y^2 \le 1$ in the xy-plane. Exercise 35 asks you to locate the extreme temperatures.

36. Find the critical point of
$$f(x, y) = xy + 2x - \ln x^2 y$$

in the open first quadrant ($x > 0$, $y > 0$) and show that f takes on a minimum there (Fig. 13.58).

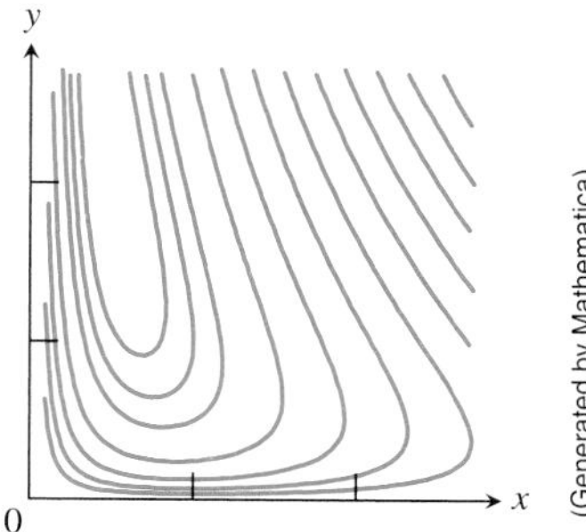

13.58 The function $f(x, y) = xy + 2x - \ln x^2 y$ (selected level curves shown here) takes on a minimum value somewhere in the open first quadrant $x > 0$, $y > 0$. Exercise 36 asks you to find where.

37. Find the maxima, minima, and saddle points of $f(x, y)$, if any, given that

a) $f_x = 2x - 4y$ and $f_y = 2y - 4x$
b) $f_x = 2x - 2$ and $f_y = 2y - 4$
c) $f_x = 9x^2 - 9$ and $f_y = 2y + 4$

Describe your reasoning in each case.

38. The discriminant $f_{xx} f_{yy} - f_{xy}^2$ is zero at the origin for each of the following functions, so the second derivative test fails there. Determine whether the function has a maximum, a minimum, or neither at the origin by imagining what the surface $z = f(x, y)$ looks like. Describe your reasoning in each case.

a) $f(x, y) = x^2 y^2$ **b)** $f(x, y) = 1 - x^2 y^2$
c) $f(x, y) = xy^2$ **d)** $f(x, y) = x^3 y^2$
e) $f(x, y) = x^3 y^3$ **f)** $f(x, y) = x^4 y^4$

39. Show that (0, 0) is a critical point of $f(x, y) = x^2 + kxy + y^2$ no matter what value the constant k has. (*Hint:* Consider two cases: $k = 0$ and $k \neq 0$.)

40. For what values of the constant k does the second derivative test guarantee that $f(x, y) = x^2 + kxy + y^2$ will have a saddle point at (0, 0)? a local minimum at (0, 0)? For what values of k is the second derivative test inconclusive? Give reasons for your answers.

41. If $f_x(a, b) = f_y(a, b) = 0$, must f have a local maximum or minimum value at (a, b)? Give reasons for your answer.

42. Can you conclude anything about $f(a, b)$ if f and its first and second partial derivatives are continuous throughout a disk centered at (a, b) and $f_{xx}(a, b)$ and $f_{yy}(a, b)$ differ in sign? Give reasons for your answer.

EXTREME VALUES ON PARAMETRIZED CURVES

To find the extreme values of a function $f(x, y)$ on a curve $x = x(t)$, $y = y(t)$, we treat f as a function of the single variable t and use the Chain Rule to find where df/dt is zero. As in any other single-variable case, the extreme values of f are then found among the values at the

a) critical points (points where df/dt is zero or fails to exist), and
b) endpoints of the parameter domain.

Find the absolute maximum and minimum values of the following functions on the given curves.

43. Functions:

a) $f(x, y) = x + y$ **b)** $g(x, y) = xy$
c) $h(x, y) = 2x^2 + y^2$

Curves:

i) The semicircle $x^2 + y^2 = 4$, $y \geq 0$
ii) The quarter circle $x^2 + y^2 = 4$, $x \geq 0$, $y \geq 0$

Use the parametric equations $x = 2 \cos t$, $y = 2 \sin t$.

44. Functions:

a) $f(x, y) = 2x + 3y$ **b)** $g(x, y) = xy$
c) $h(x, y) = x^2 + 3y^2$

Curves:

i) The semi-ellipse $(x^2/9) + (y^2/4) = 1$, $y \geq 0$
ii) The quarter ellipse $(x^2/9) + (y^2/4) = 1$, $x \geq 0$, $y \geq 0$

Use the parametric equations $x = 3 \cos t$, $y = 2 \sin t$.

45. Function: $f(x, y) = xy$
Curves:

i) The line $x = 2t$, $y = t + 1$
ii) The line segment $x = 2t$, $y = t + 1$, $-1 \leq t \leq 0$
iii) The line segment $x = 2t$, $y = t + 1$, $0 \leq t \leq 1$

46. Functions:

a) $f(x, y) = x^2 + y^2$ **b)** $g(x, y) = 1/(x^2 + y^2)$

Curves:

i) The line $x = t$, $y = 2 - 2t$
ii) The line segment $x = t$, $y = 2 - 2t$, $0 \leq t \leq 1$

LEAST SQUARES AND REGRESSION LINES

When we try to fit a line $y = mx + b$ to a set of numerical data points $(x_1, y_1), (x_2, y_2), \ldots, (x_n, y_n)$ (Fig. 13.59), we usually

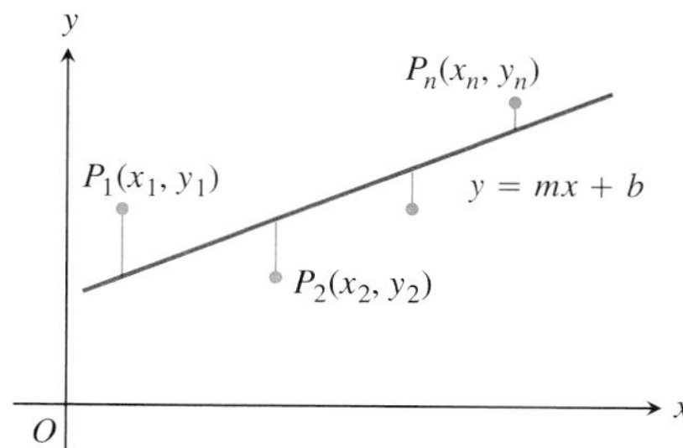

13.59 To fit a line to noncollinear points, we choose the line that minimizes the sum of the squares of the deviations.

choose the line that minimizes the sum of the squares of the vertical distances from the points to the line. In theory, this means finding the values of m and b that minimize the value of the function

$$w = (mx_1 + b - y_1)^2 + \cdots + (mx_n + b - y_n)^2. \tag{4}$$

The values of m and b that do this are found with the first and second derivative tests to be

$$m = \frac{\left(\sum x_k\right)\left(\sum y_k\right) - n \sum x_k y_k}{\left(\sum x_k\right)^2 - n \sum x_k{}^2}, \tag{5}$$

$$b = \frac{1}{n}\left(\sum y_k - m \sum x_k\right), \tag{6}$$

with all sums running from $k = 1$ to $k = n$. Many scientific calculators have these formulas built in, enabling you to find m and b with only a few key presses after you have entered the data.

The line $y = mx + b$ determined by these values of m and b is called the **least squares line, regression line,** or **trend line** for the data under study. Finding a least squares line lets you

1. summarize data with a simple expression,
2. predict values of y for other, experimentally untried values of x,
3. handle data analytically.

EXAMPLE Find the least squares line for the points (0, 1), (1, 3), (2, 2), (3, 4), (4, 5).

Solution We organize the calculations in a table:

k	x_k	y_k	$x_k{}^2$	$x_k y_k$
1	0	1	0	0
2	1	3	1	3
3	2	2	4	4
4	3	4	9	12
5	4	5	16	20
Σ	10	15	30	39

Then we find

$$m = \frac{(10)(15) - 5(39)}{(10)^2 - 5(30)} = 0.9 \qquad \text{Eq. (5) with } n = 5 \text{ and data from the table}$$

and use the value of m to find

$$b = \frac{1}{5}(15 - (0.9)(10)) = 1.2. \qquad \text{Eq. (6) with } n = 5,\ m = 0.9$$

The least squares line is $y = 0.9x + 1.2$ (Fig. 13.60).

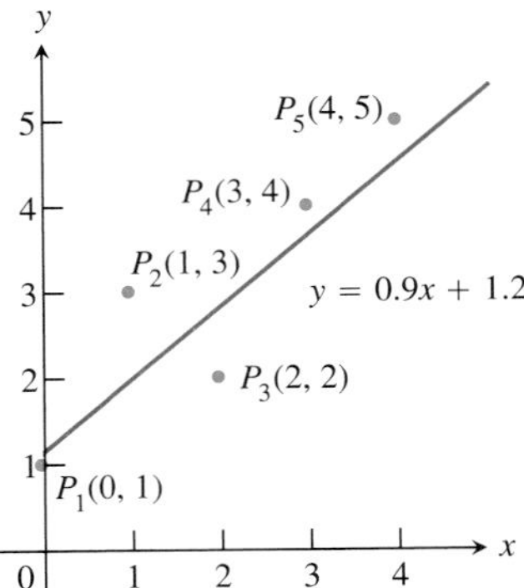

13.60 The least squares line for the data in the example.

In Exercises 47–50, use Eqs. (5) and (6) to find the least squares line for each set of data points. Then use the linear equation you obtain to predict the value of y that would correspond to $x = 4$.

47. $(-1, 2)$, $(0, 1)$, $(3, -4)$

48. $(-2, 0)$, $(0, 2)$, $(2, 3)$

49. $(0, 0)$, $(1, 2)$, $(2, 3)$

50. $(0, 1)$, $(2, 2)$, $(3, 2)$

51. Write a linear equation for the effect of irrigation on the yield of alfalfa by fitting a least squares line to the data in Table 13.1 (from the University of California Experimental Station, *Bulletin* No. 450, p. 8). Plot the data and draw the line.

TABLE 13.1
Growth of alfalfa

x (Total Seasonal Depth of Water Applied, in.)	y (Average Alfalfa Yield, Tons/Acre)
12	5.27
18	5.68
24	6.25
30	7.21
36	8.20
42	8.71

52. *Craters of Mars.* One theory of crater formation suggests that the frequency of large craters should fall off as the square of the diameter (Marcus, *Science,* June 21, 1968, p. 1334). Pictures from *Mariner IV* show the frequencies listed in Table 13.2. Fit a line of the form $F = m(1/D^2) + b$ to the data. Plot the data and draw the line.

TABLE 13.2
Crater sizes on Mars

Diameter in km, D	$1/D^2$ (For Left Value of Class Interval)	Frequency, F
32–45	0.001	53
45–64	0.0005	22
64–90	0.00025	14
90–128	0.000125	3

53. *Köchel Numbers.* In 1862, the German musicologist Ludwig von Köchel made a chronological list of the musical works of Wolfgang Amadeus Mozart. This list is the source of the Köchel numbers, or "K numbers," that now accompany the titles of Mozart's pieces (Sinfonia Concertante in E-flat major, K.364, for example). Table 13.3 gives the Köchel numbers and composition dates (y) of ten of Mozart's works.

a) Plot y vs. K to show that y is close to being a linear function of K.

b) Find a least squares line $y = m\text{K} + b$ for the data and add the line to your plot in (a).

c) K.364 was composed in 1779. What date is predicted by the least squares line?

TABLE 13.3
Compositions by Mozart

Köchel Number, K	Year Composed, y
1	1761
75	1771
155	1772
219	1775
271	1777
351	1780
425	1783
503	1786
575	1789
626	1791

54. *Submarine Sinkings.* The data in Table 13.4 show the results of a historical study of German submarines sunk by the U.S. Navy during 16 consecutive months of World War II. The data given for each month are the number of reported sinkings and the number of actual sinkings. The number of submarines sunk was slightly greater than the Navy's reports implied. Find a least squares line for estimating the number of actual sinkings from the number of reported sinkings.

TABLE 13.4
Sinkings of German submarines by U.S. during 16 consecutive months of WWII

Month	Guesses by U.S. (Reported Sinkings) x	Actual Number y
1	3	3
2	2	2
3	4	6
4	2	3
5	5	4
6	5	3
7	9	11
8	12	9
9	8	10
10	13	16
11	14	13
12	3	5
13	4	6
14	13	19
15	10	15
16	16	15
	123	140

Writing for Your Own Knowledge

Answer the following questions in writing. Some answers will take only a sentence or two; others may require several paragraphs. Some explanations may also call for graphs or sketches.

1. How do you define local maxima, local minima, and saddle points?
2. What derivative tests are available for determining the local extreme values of a function $f(x, y)$? How do they enable us to narrow our search for these values?
3. How do you find the absolute extrema of a continuous function $f(x, y)$ on a closed bounded region?

13.8 Lagrange Multipliers

As we saw in Section 13.7, we sometimes need to find the extreme values of a function whose domain is constrained to lie within some particular subset of the plane—a disk, for example, or a closed triangular region. But, as Fig. 13.61 suggests, a function may be subject to other kinds of constraints as well.

In this section, we explore a powerful method for finding extreme values of constrained functions: the method of *Lagrange multipliers*. Lagrange developed the method in 1755 to solve max-min problems in geometry. Today the method is important in economics, in engineering (where it is used in designing multistage rockets, for example), and in mathematics itself.

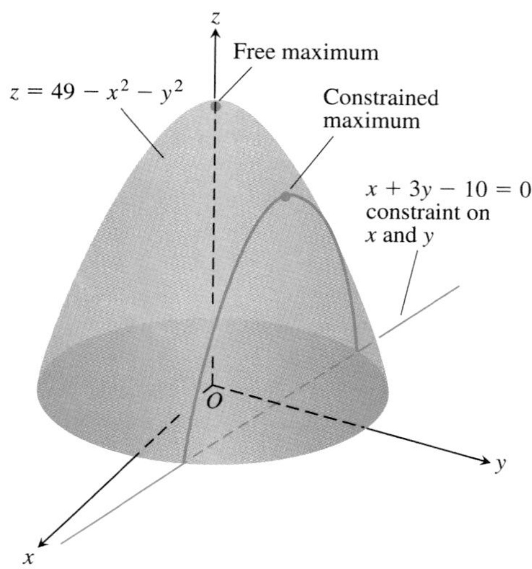

13.61 The function $f(x, y) = 49 - x^2 - y^2$, subject to the constraint $g(x, y) = x + 3y - 10 = 0$.

Constrained Maxima and Minima

EXAMPLE 1 Find the point $P(x, y, z)$ on the plane

$$2x + y - z - 5 = 0$$

that lies closest to the origin.

Solution The problem asks us to find the minimum value of the function

$$|\overrightarrow{OP}| = \sqrt{(x-0)^2 + (y-0)^2 + (z-0)^2} = \sqrt{x^2 + y^2 + z^2}$$

subject to the constraint that

$$2x + y - z - 5 = 0.$$

Since $|\overrightarrow{OP}|$ has a minimum value wherever the function

$$f(x, y, z) = x^2 + y^2 + z^2$$

has a minimum value, we may solve the problem by finding the minimum value of $f(x, y, z)$ subject to the constraint $2x + y - z - 5 = 0$. If we regard x and y as the independent variables in this equation and write z as

$$z = 2x + y - 5,$$

our problem reduces to one of finding the points (x, y) at which the function

$$h(x, y) = f(x, y, 2x + y - 5) = x^2 + y^2 + (2x + y - 5)^2$$

has its minimum value or values. Since the domain of h is the entire xy-plane, the first derivative test of Section 13.7 tells us that any minima that h might have must occur at points where

$$h_x = 2x + 2(2x + y - 5)(2) = 0, \qquad h_y = 2y + 2(2x + y - 5) = 0.$$

This leads to

$$10x + 4y = 20, \qquad 4x + 4y = 10,$$

and the solution

$$x = \frac{5}{3}, \qquad y = \frac{5}{6}.$$

We may apply a geometric argument together with the second derivative test to show that these values minimize h. The z-coordinate of the corresponding point on the plane $z = 2x + y - 5$ is

$$z = 2\left(\frac{5}{3}\right) + \frac{5}{6} - 5 = -\frac{5}{6}.$$

Therefore, the point we seek is

$$\text{Closest point:} \qquad P\left(\frac{5}{3}, \frac{5}{6}, -\frac{5}{6}\right).$$

The distance from P to the origin is $5/\sqrt{6} \approx 2.04$.

Attempts to solve a constrained maximum or minimum problem by substitution, as we might call the method of Example 1, do not always go smoothly. This is one of the reasons for learning the new method of this section.

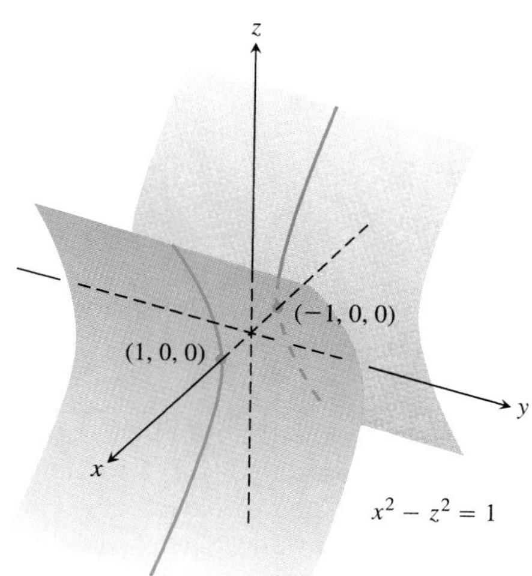

13.62 The hyperbolic cylinder $x^2 - z^2 - 1 = 0$ in Example 2.

EXAMPLE 2 Find the points on the hyperbolic cylinder

$$x^2 - z^2 - 1 = 0$$

closest to the origin.

Solution 1 The cylinder is shown in Fig. 13.62. We seek the points on the cylinder closest to the origin. These are the points whose coordinates minimize the value of the function

$$f(x, y, z) = x^2 + y^2 + z^2 \qquad \text{Square of the distance}$$

subject to the constraint that $x^2 - z^2 - 1 = 0$. If we regard x and y as independent variables in the constraint equation, then

$$z^2 = x^2 - 1$$

and the values of $f(x, y, z) = x^2 + y^2 + z^2$ on the cylinder are given by the function

$$h(x, y) = x^2 + y^2 + (x^2 - 1) = 2x^2 + y^2 - 1.$$

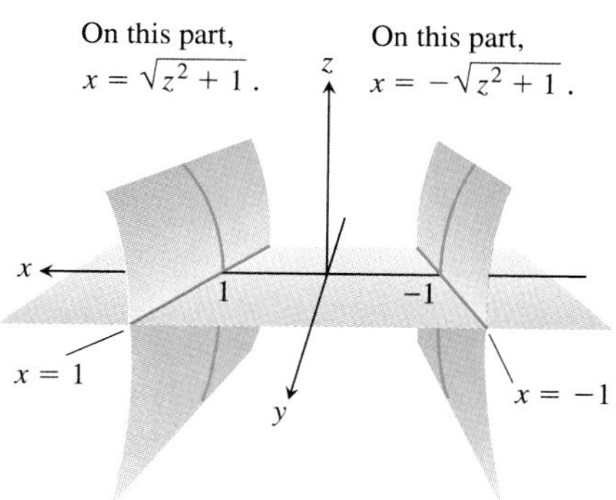

13.63 The region in the xy-plane from which the first two coordinates of the points (x, y, z) on the hyperbolic cylinder $x^2 - z^2 = 1$ are selected excludes the band $-1 < x < 1$ in the xy-plane.

To find the points on the cylinder whose coordinates minimize f, we look for the points in the xy-plane whose coordinates minimize h. The only extreme value of h occurs where

$$h_x = 4x = 0 \qquad \text{and} \qquad h_y = 2y = 0,$$

that is, at the point (0, 0). But now we're in trouble—there are no points on the cylinder where both x and y are zero. What went wrong?

What happened was that the first derivative test found (as it should have) the point *in the domain of* h where h has a minimum value. We, on the other hand, want the points *on the cylinder* where h has a minimum value. While the domain of h is the entire xy-plane, the domain from which we can select the first two coordinates of the points (x, y, z) on the cylinder is restricted to the "shadow" of the cylinder on the xy-plane; it does not include the band between the lines $x = -1$ and $x = 1$ (Fig. 13.63).

We can avoid this problem if we treat y and z as independent variables (instead of x and y) and express x in terms of y and z as

$$x^2 = z^2 + 1.$$

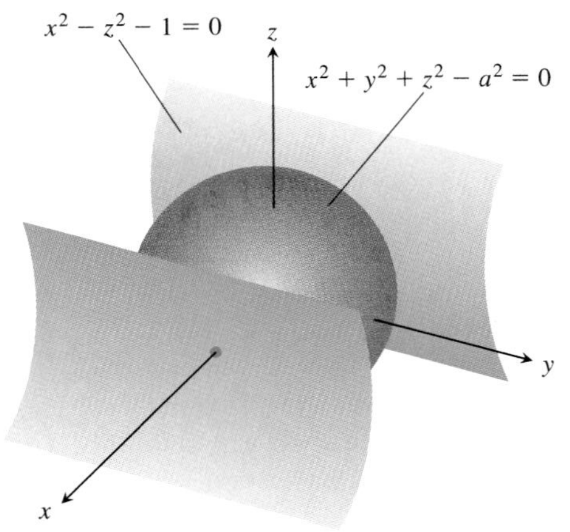

13.64 A sphere expanding like a soap bubble centered at the origin until it just touches the hyperbolic cylinder

$$x^2 - z^2 - 1 = 0.$$

See Solution 2 of Example 2.

With this substitution, $f(x, y, z) = x^2 + y^2 + z^2$ becomes

$$k(y, z) = (z^2 + 1) + y^2 + z^2 = 1 + y^2 + 2z^2$$

and we look for the points where k takes on its smallest value. The domain of k in the yz-plane now matches the domain from which we select the y- and z-coordinates of the points (x, y, z) on the cylinder. Hence, the points that minimize k in the plane will have corresponding points on the cylinder. The smallest values of k occur where

$$k_y = 2y = 0 \qquad \text{and} \qquad k_z = 4z = 0,$$

or where $y = z = 0$. This leads to

$$x^2 = z^2 + 1 = 1, \qquad x = \pm 1.$$

The corresponding points on the cylinder are $(\pm 1, 0, 0)$. We can see from the inequality

$$k(y, z) = 1 + y^2 + 2z^2 \geq 1$$

that the points $(\pm 1, 0, 0)$ give a minimum value for k. We can also see that the minimum distance from the origin to a point on the cylinder is 1 unit.

Solution 2 Another way to find the points on the cylinder closest to the origin is to imagine a small sphere centered at the origin expanding like a soap bubble until it just touches the cylinder (Fig. 13.64). At each point of contact, the cylinder and sphere have the same tangent plane and normal line. Therefore, if the sphere and cylinder are represented as the level surfaces obtained by setting

$$f(x, y, z) = x^2 + y^2 + z^2 - a^2 \qquad \text{and} \qquad g(x, y, z) = x^2 - z^2 - 1$$

equal to 0, then the gradients ∇f and ∇g will be parallel where the surfaces touch. At any point of contact we should therefore be able to find a scalar λ ("lambda") such that

$$\nabla f = \lambda \nabla g,$$

or

$$2x\,\mathbf{i} + 2y\,\mathbf{j} + 2z\,\mathbf{k} = \lambda(2x\,\mathbf{i} - 2z\,\mathbf{k}).$$

Thus, the coordinates x, y, and z of any point of tangency will have to satisfy the three scalar equations

$$2x = 2\lambda x, \qquad 2y = 0, \qquad 2z = -2\lambda z. \tag{1}$$

For what values of λ will a point (x, y, z) whose coordinates satisfy the equations in (1) also lie on the surface $x^2 - z^2 - 1 = 0$? To answer this question, we use the fact that no point on the surface has a zero x-coordinate to conclude that $x \neq 0$ in the first equation in (1). This means that $2x = 2\lambda x$ only if

$$2 = 2\lambda, \qquad \text{or} \qquad \lambda = 1.$$

For $\lambda = 1$, the equation $2z = -2\lambda z$ becomes $2z = -2z$. If this equation is to be satisfied as well, z must be zero. Since $y = 0$ also (from the equation $2y = 0$), we conclude that the points we seek all have coordinates of the form

$$(x, 0, 0).$$

What points on the surface $x^2 - z^2 = 1$ have coordinates of this form? The points $(x, 0, 0)$ for which

$$x^2 - (0)^2 = 1, \qquad x^2 = 1, \qquad \text{or} \qquad x = \pm 1.$$

The points on the cylinder closest to the origin are the points $(\pm 1, 0, 0)$.

The Method of Lagrange Multipliers

In Solution 2 of Example 2, we solved the problem by the **method of Lagrange multipliers.** In general terms, the method says that the extreme values of a function $f(x, y, z)$ whose variables are subject to a constraint $g(x, y, z) = 0$ are to be found on the surface $g = 0$ at the points where

$$\nabla f = \lambda \nabla g$$

for some scalar λ (called a **Lagrange multiplier**).

To explore the method further and see why it works, we first make the following observation, which we state as a theorem.

THEOREM 9

The Orthogonal Gradient Theorem

Suppose that $f(x, y, z)$ is differentiable in a region whose interior contains a smooth curve

$$C: \quad \mathbf{r} = g(t)\,\mathbf{i} + h(t)\,\mathbf{j} + k(t)\,\mathbf{k}.$$

If P_0 is a point on C where f has a local maximum or minimum relative to its values on C, then ∇f is orthogonal to C at P_0.

Proof We show that ∇f is orthogonal to the curve's velocity vector at P_0. The values of f on C are given by the composite $f(g(t), h(t), k(t))$, whose derivative with respect to t is

$$\frac{df}{dt} = \frac{\partial f}{\partial x}\frac{dg}{dt} + \frac{\partial f}{\partial y}\frac{dh}{dt} + \frac{\partial f}{\partial z}\frac{dk}{dt} = \nabla f \cdot \mathbf{v}.$$

At any point P_0 where f has a local maximum or minimum relative to its values on the curve, $df/dt = 0$, so

$$\nabla f \cdot \mathbf{v} = 0.$$

By dropping the z-terms in Theorem 9, we obtain a similar result for functions of two variables.

COROLLARY OF THEOREM 9

At the points on a smooth curve $\mathbf{r} = g(t)\,\mathbf{i} + h(t)\,\mathbf{j}$ where a differentiable function $f(x, y)$ takes on its local maxima and minima relative to its values on the curve, $\nabla f \cdot \mathbf{v} = 0$.

Theorem 9 is the key to the method of Lagrange multipliers. Suppose that $f(x, y, z)$ and $g(x, y, z)$ are differentiable and that P_0 is a point on the surface $g(x, y, z) = 0$ where f has a local maximum or minimum value relative to its other values on the surface. Then f takes on a local maximum or minimum at P_0 relative to its values on every differentiable curve through P_0 on the surface $g(x, y, z) = 0$. Therefore, ∇f is orthogonal to the velocity vector of every such differentiable curve through P_0. But so is ∇g (because ∇g is orthogonal to the level surface $g = 0$, as we saw in Section 13.6). Therefore, at P_0, ∇f is some scalar multiple λ of ∇g.

The Method of Lagrange Multipliers

Suppose that $f(x, y, z)$ and $g(x, y, z)$ are differentiable. To find the local maximum and minimum values of f subject to the constraint $g(x, y, z) = 0$, find the values of x, y, z, and λ that simultaneously satisfy the equations

$$\nabla f = \lambda \nabla g \quad \text{and} \quad g(x, y, z) = 0. \tag{2}$$

For functions of two independent variables, the appropriate equations are

$$\nabla f = \lambda \nabla g \quad \text{and} \quad g(x, y) = 0. \tag{3}$$

EXAMPLE 3 Find the greatest and smallest values that the function

$$f(x, y) = xy$$

takes on the ellipse (Fig. 13.65)

$$\frac{x^2}{8} + \frac{y^2}{2} = 1.$$

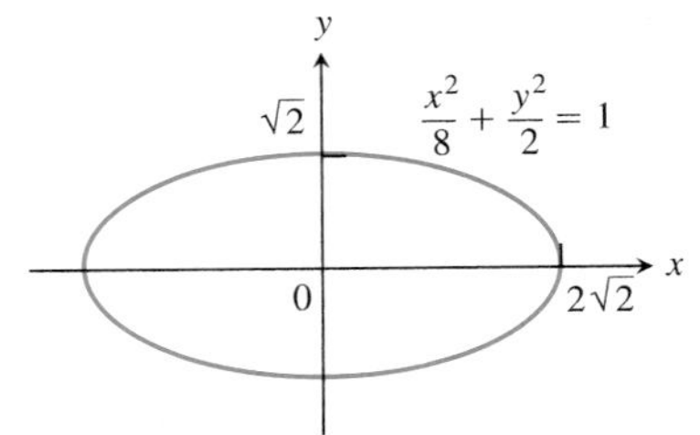

13.65 Example 3 shows how to find the largest and smallest values of the product xy on this ellipse.

Solution We are asked to find the extreme values of $f(x, y) = xy$ subject to the constraint

$$g(x, y) = \frac{x^2}{8} + \frac{y^2}{2} - 1 = 0.$$

To do so, we first find the values of x, y, and λ for which

$$\nabla f = \lambda \nabla g \quad \text{and} \quad g(x, y) = 0.$$

The gradient equation gives

$$y\,\mathbf{i} + x\,\mathbf{j} = \frac{\lambda}{4} x\,\mathbf{i} + \lambda y\,\mathbf{j},$$

from which we find

$$y = \frac{\lambda}{4} x, \qquad x = \lambda y, \qquad \text{and} \qquad y = \frac{\lambda}{4}(\lambda y) = \frac{\lambda^2}{4} y,$$

so that $y = 0$ or $\lambda = \pm 2$. We now consider these two cases.

CASE 1: If $y = 0$, then $x = y = 0$, but the point $(0, 0)$ is not on the ellipse. Hence, $y \neq 0$.

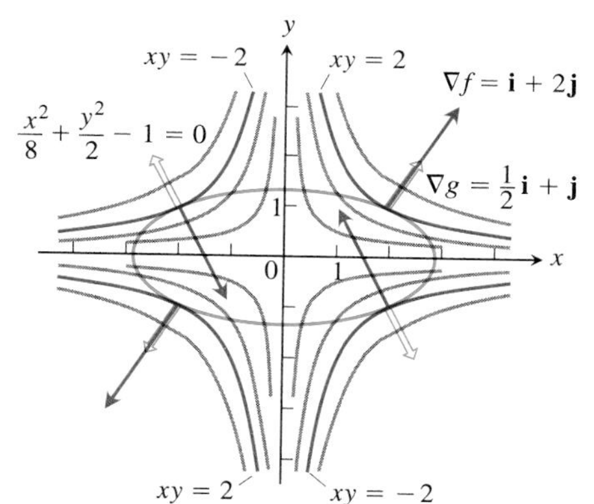

13.66 When subjected to the constraint $g(x, y) = x^2/8 + y^2/2 - 1 = 0$, the function $f(x, y) = xy$ takes on extreme values at the four points $(\pm 2, \pm 1)$. These are the points on the ellipse where ∇f (red) is a scalar multiple of ∇g (blue) (Example 3).

CASE 2: If $y \neq 0$, then $\lambda = \pm 2$ and $x = \pm 2y$. Substituting this in the equation $g(x, y) = 0$ gives

$$\frac{(\pm 2y)^2}{8} + \frac{y^2}{2} = 1, \qquad 4y^2 + 4y^2 = 8, \qquad \text{and} \qquad y = \pm 1.$$

The function $f(x, y) = xy$ therefore takes on its extreme values on the ellipse at the four points $(\pm 2, 1)$, $(\pm 2, -1)$. The extreme values are $xy = 2$ and $xy = -2$.

The Geometry of the Solution The level curves of the function $f(x, y) = xy$ are the hyperbolas $xy = c$ (Fig. 13.66). The farther the hyperbolas lie from the origin, the larger the absolute value of f. We want to find the extreme values of $f(x, y)$, given that the point (x, y) also lies on the ellipse $x^2 + 4y^2 = 8$. Which hyperbolas intersecting the ellipse lie farthest from the origin? The hyperbolas that just graze the ellipse, the ones that are tangent to it. At these points, any vector normal to the hyperbola is normal to the ellipse, so the gradient $\nabla f = y\,\mathbf{i} + x\,\mathbf{j}$ is a multiple ($\lambda = \pm 2$) of the gradient $\nabla g = (x/4)\,\mathbf{i} + y\,\mathbf{j}$. At the point $(2, 1)$, for example,

$$\nabla f = \mathbf{i} + 2\,\mathbf{j}, \qquad \nabla g = \frac{1}{2}\mathbf{i} + \mathbf{j}, \qquad \text{and} \qquad \nabla f = 2\nabla g.$$

At the point $(-2, 1)$,

$$\nabla f = \mathbf{i} - 2\,\mathbf{j}, \qquad \nabla g = -\frac{1}{2}\mathbf{i} + \mathbf{j}, \qquad \text{and} \qquad \nabla f = -2\nabla g.$$

EXAMPLE 4 Find the maximum and minimum values of the function $f(x, y) = 3x + 4y$ on the circle $x^2 + y^2 = 1$.

Solution We model this as a Lagrange multiplier problem with

$$f(x, y) = 3x + 4y, \qquad g(x, y) = x^2 + y^2 - 1$$

and look for the values of x, y, and λ that satisfy the equations

$$\begin{aligned} \nabla f = \lambda \nabla g: &\qquad 3\,\mathbf{i} + 4\,\mathbf{j} = 2x\lambda\,\mathbf{i} + 2y\lambda\,\mathbf{j}, \\ g(x, y) = 0: &\qquad x^2 + y^2 - 1 = 0. \end{aligned} \tag{4}$$

The gradient equation implies that $\lambda \neq 0$ and gives

$$x = \frac{3}{2\lambda}, \qquad y = \frac{2}{\lambda}.$$

These equations tell us, among other things, that x and y have the same sign. With these values for x and y, the equation $g(x, y) = 0$ gives

$$\left(\frac{3}{2\lambda}\right)^2 + \left(\frac{2}{\lambda}\right)^2 - 1 = 0,$$

so $\dfrac{9}{4\lambda^2} + \dfrac{4}{\lambda^2} = 1, \qquad 9 + 16 = 4\lambda^2, \qquad 4\lambda^2 = 25, \qquad \text{and} \qquad \lambda = \pm\dfrac{5}{2}.$

Thus, $x = \dfrac{3}{2\lambda} = \pm\dfrac{3}{5}, \qquad y = \dfrac{2}{\lambda} = \pm\dfrac{4}{5},$

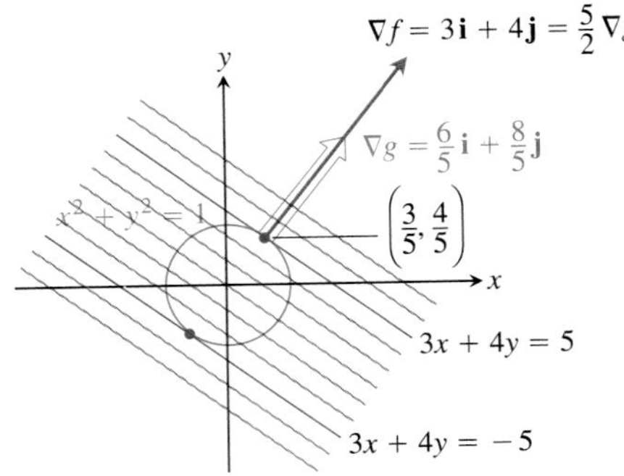

13.67 The function $f(x, y) = 3x + 4y$ takes on its largest value on the unit circle $g(x, y) = x^2 + y^2 - 1 = 0$ at the point $(3/5, 4/5)$ and its smallest value at the point $(-3/5, -4/5)$ (Example 4). At each of these points, ∇f is a scalar multiple of ∇g. The figure shows the gradients at the first point but not the second.

and $f(x, y) = 3x + 4y$ has extreme values at $(x, y) = \pm(3/5, 4/5)$.

By calculating the value of $3x + 4y$ at the points $\pm(3/5, 4/5)$, we see that its maximum and minimum values on the circle $x^2 + y^2 = 1$ are

$$3\left(\frac{3}{5}\right) + 4\left(\frac{4}{5}\right) = \frac{25}{5} = 5 \quad \text{and} \quad 3\left(-\frac{3}{5}\right) + 4\left(-\frac{4}{5}\right) = -\frac{25}{5} = -5.$$

The Geometry of the Solution (Fig. 13.67) The level curves of $f(x, y) = 3x + 4y$ are the lines $3x + 4y = c$. The farther the lines lie from the origin, the larger the absolute value of f. We want to find the extreme values of $f(x, y)$ given that the point (x, y) also lies on the circle $x^2 + y^2 = 1$. Which lines intersecting the circle lie farthest from the origin? The lines tangent to the circle. At the points of tangency, any vector normal to the line is normal to the circle, so the gradient $\nabla f = 3\,\mathbf{i} + 4\,\mathbf{j}$ is a multiple ($\lambda = \pm 5/2$) of the gradient $\nabla g = 2x\,\mathbf{i} + 2y\,\mathbf{j}$. At the point $(3/5, 4/5)$, for example,

$$\nabla f = 3\,\mathbf{i} + 4\,\mathbf{j}, \qquad \nabla g = \frac{6}{5}\mathbf{i} + \frac{8}{5}\mathbf{j}, \qquad \text{and} \qquad \nabla f = \frac{5}{2}\nabla g.$$

Lagrange Multipliers with Two Constraints

Many applied problems require us to find the extreme values of a differentiable function $f(x, y, z)$ whose variables are subject to two constraints. If the constraints on x, y, and z are

$$g_1(x, y, z) = 0 \quad \text{and} \quad g_2(x, y, z) = 0$$

and g_1 and g_2 are differentiable, with ∇g_1 not parallel to ∇g_2, we find the constrained local maxima and minima of f by introducing two Lagrange multipliers λ and μ (mu, pronounced "mew"). That is, we locate the points $P(x, y, z)$ where f takes on its constrained extreme values by finding the values of x, y, z, λ, and μ that simultaneously satisfy the equations

$$\nabla f = \lambda \nabla g_1 + \mu \nabla g_2, \qquad g_1(x, y, z) = 0, \qquad g_2(x, y, z) = 0. \tag{5}$$

The equations in (5) have a nice geometric interpretation. The surfaces $g_1 = 0$ and $g_2 = 0$ (usually) intersect in a smooth curve, say C (Fig. 13.68), and along this curve we seek the points where f has local maximum and minimum values relative to its other values on the curve. These are the points where ∇f is normal to C, as we saw in Theorem 9. But ∇g_1 and ∇g_2 are also normal to C at these points because C lies in the surfaces $g_1 = 0$ and $g_2 = 0$. Therefore ∇f lies in the plane determined by ∇g_1 and ∇g_2, which means that

$$\nabla f = \lambda \nabla g_1 + \mu \nabla g_2$$

for some λ and μ. Since the points we seek also lie in both surfaces, their coordinates must satisfy the equations $g_1(x, y, z) = 0$ and $g_2(x, y, z) = 0$, which are the remaining requirements in Eq. (5).

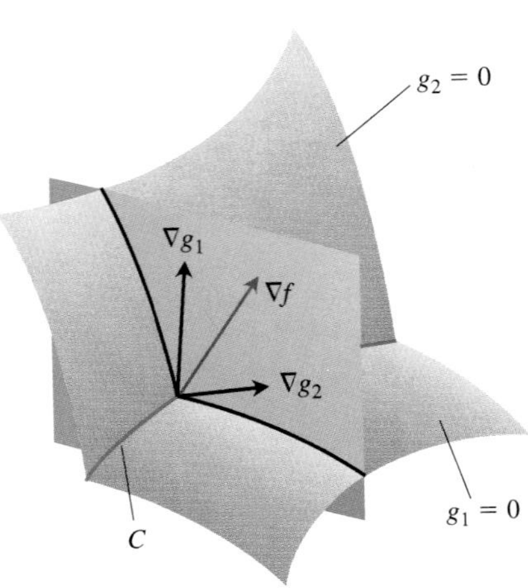

13.68 The vectors ∇g_1 and ∇g_2 lie in a plane perpendicular to the curve C because ∇g_1 is normal to the surface $g_1 = 0$ and ∇g_2 is normal to the surface $g_2 = 0$.

EXAMPLE 5 The plane $x + y + z = 1$ cuts the cylinder $x^2 + y^2 = 1$ in an ellipse (Fig. 13.69). Find the points on the ellipse that lie closest to and farthest from the origin.

Solution We model this as a Lagrange multiplier problem in which we find the extreme values of

$$f(x, y, z) = x^2 + y^2 + z^2$$

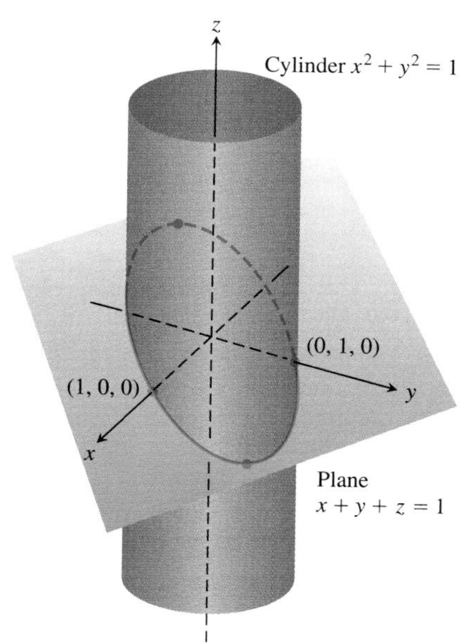

13.69 On the ellipse where the plane and cylinder meet, what are the points closest to and farthest from the origin (Example 5)?

(the square of the distance from (x, y, z) to the origin) subject to the constraints

$$g_1(x, y, z) = x^2 + y^2 - 1 = 0, \tag{6}$$

$$g_2(x, y, z) = x + y + z - 1 = 0. \tag{7}$$

The gradient equation in (5) then gives

$$\nabla f = \lambda \nabla g_1 + \mu \nabla g_2 \qquad \text{Eq. (5)}$$

$$2x\,\mathbf{i} + 2y\,\mathbf{j} + 2z\,\mathbf{k} = \lambda(2x\,\mathbf{i} + 2y\,\mathbf{j}) + \mu(\mathbf{i} + \mathbf{j} + \mathbf{k}) \tag{8}$$

$$2x\,\mathbf{i} + 2y\,\mathbf{j} + 2z\,\mathbf{k} = (2\lambda x + \mu)\,\mathbf{i} + (2\lambda y + \mu)\,\mathbf{j} + \mu\,\mathbf{k} \tag{9}$$

or

$$2x = 2\lambda x + \mu, \qquad 2y = 2\lambda y + \mu, \qquad 2z = \mu. \tag{10}$$

The scalar equations in (10) yield

$$\begin{aligned} 2x &= 2\lambda x + 2z \quad \Rightarrow \quad (1 - \lambda)x = z, \\ 2y &= 2\lambda y + 2z \quad \Rightarrow \quad (1 - \lambda)y = z. \end{aligned} \tag{11}$$

Equations (11) are satisfied simultaneously if either $\lambda = 1$ and $z = 0$ or $\lambda \neq 1$ and $x = y = z/(1 - \lambda)$.

If $z = 0$, then solving Eqs. (6) and (7) simultaneously to find the corresponding points on the ellipse gives the two points $(1, 0, 0)$ and $(0, 1, 0)$. This makes sense when you look at Fig. 13.69.

If $x = y$, then Eqs. (6) and (7) give

$$\begin{aligned} x^2 + x^2 - 1 &= 0 & \qquad x + x + z - 1 &= 0 \\ 2x^2 &= 1 & z &= 1 - 2x \\ x &= \pm\frac{\sqrt{2}}{2} & z &= 1 \mp \sqrt{2}. \end{aligned} \tag{12}$$

The corresponding points on the ellipse are

$$\left(\frac{\sqrt{2}}{2}, \frac{\sqrt{2}}{2}, 1 - \sqrt{2}\right) \quad \text{and} \quad \left(-\frac{\sqrt{2}}{2}, -\frac{\sqrt{2}}{2}, 1 + \sqrt{2}\right). \tag{13}$$

Again this makes sense when you look at Fig. 13.69.

The points on the ellipse closest to the origin are $(1, 0, 0)$ and $(0, 1, 0)$. The points on the ellipse farthest from the origin are the two points displayed in (13).

Exercises 13.8

1. Find the points on the ellipse $x^2 + 2y^2 = 1$ where $f(x, y) = xy$ has its extreme values.
2. Find the extreme values of $f(x, y) = xy$ subject to the constraint $g(x, y) = x^2 + y^2 - 10 = 0$.
3. Find the maximum value of $f(x, y) = 49 - x^2 - y^2$ on the line $x + 3y = 10$ (Fig. 13.61).
4. How close does the line $y = x + 1$ come to the parabola $y^2 = x$?
5. Find the local extreme values of $f(x, y) = x^2 y$ on the line $x + y = 3$.
6. Find the points on the curve $x^2 y = 2$ nearest the origin.
7. Use the method of Lagrange multipliers to find
   a) the minimum value of $x + y$, subject to the constraints $xy = 16$, $x > 0$, $y > 0$;
   b) the maximum value of xy, subject to the constraint $x + y = 16$.

   Comment on the geometry of each solution.
8. Find the points on the curve $x^2 + xy + y^2 = 1$ in the xy-plane that are nearest to and farthest from the origin.
9. Find the dimensions of the closed right circular cylindrical can of smallest surface area whose volume is 16π cm^3.
10. Use the method of Lagrange multipliers to find the dimensions

of the rectangle of greatest area that can be inscribed in the ellipse $x^2/16 + y^2/9 = 1$ with sides parallel to the coordinate axes.

11. The temperature at a point (x, y) on a metal plate is $T(x, y) = 4x^2 - 4xy + y^2$. An ant on the plate walks around the circle of radius 5 centered at the origin. What are the highest and lowest temperatures encountered by the ant?

12. Your firm has been asked to design a storage tank for liquid petroleum gas. The customer's specifications call for a cylindrical tank with hemispherical ends, and the tank is to hold 8000 m^3 of gas. The customer also wants to use the smallest amount of material possible in building the tank. What radius and height do you recommend for the cylindrical portion of the tank?

13. Find the maximum and minimum values of $x^2 + y^2$ subject to the constraint $x^2 - 2x + y^2 - 4y = 0$.

14. Find the point on the plane $x + 2y + 3z = 13$ closest to the point $(1, 1, 1)$.

15. Find the maximum and minimum values of

$$f(x, y, z) = x - 2y + 5z$$

on the sphere

$$x^2 + y^2 + z^2 = 30.$$

16. Find the minimum distance from the surface $x^2 + y^2 - z^2 = 1$ to the origin.

17. Find the point on the surface $z = xy + 1$ nearest the origin.

18. Find the points on the surface $z^2 = xy + 4$ closest to the origin.

19. Find the points on the sphere $x^2 + y^2 + z^2 = 25$ where $f(x, y, z) = x + 2y + 3z$ has its maximum and minimum values.

20. Find three real numbers whose sum is 9 and the sum of whose squares is as small as possible.

21. Find the largest product the positive numbers x, y, and z can have if $x + y + z^2 = 16$.

22. A space probe in the shape of the ellipsoid

$$4x^2 + y^2 + 4z^2 = 16$$

enters the earth's atmosphere and its surface begins to heat. After one hour, the temperature at the point (x, y, z) on the probe's surface is

$$T(x, y, z) = 8x^2 + 4yz - 16z + 600.$$

Find the hottest point on the probe's surface.

23. *An Example from Economics.* In economics, the usefulness or *utility* of amounts x and y of two capital goods G_1 and G_2 is sometimes measured by a function $U(x, y)$. For example, G_1 and G_2 might be two chemicals a pharmaceutical company needs to have on hand and $U(x, y)$ the gain from manufacturing a product whose synthesis requires different amounts of the chemicals depending on the process used. If G_1 costs a dollars per kilogram, G_2 costs b dollars per kilogram, and the total amount allocated for the purchase of G_1 and G_2 together is c dollars, then the company's managers want to maximize $U(x, y)$ given that $ax + by = c$. Thus, they need to solve a typical Lagrange multiplier problem.

Suppose that

$$U(x, y) = xy + 2x$$

and that the equation $ax + by = c$ simplifies to

$$2x + y = 30.$$

Find the maximum value of U and the corresponding values of x and y subject to this latter constraint.

24. You are in charge of erecting a radio telescope on a newly discovered planet. To minimize interference, you want to place it where the magnetic field of the planet is weakest. The planet is spherical, with a radius of 6 units. Based on a coordinate system whose origin is at the center of the planet, the strength of the magnetic field is given by $M(x, y, z) = 6x - y^2 + xz + 60$. Where should you locate the radio telescope?

25. *The Condition $\nabla f = \lambda \nabla g$ Is Not Sufficient.* While $\nabla f = \lambda \nabla g$ is a necessary condition for the occurrence of an extreme value of $f(x, y)$ subject to the condition $g(x, y) = 0$, it does not in itself guarantee that one exists. As a case in point, try using the method of Lagrange multipliers to find a maximum value of $f(x, y) = x + y$ subject to the constraint that $xy = 16$. The method will identify the two points $(4, 4)$ and $(-4, -4)$ as candidates for the location of extreme values. Yet the sum $(x + y)$ has no maximum value on the hyperbola $xy = 16$. The farther you go from the origin on this hyperbola in the first quadrant, the larger the sum $f(x, y) = x + y$ becomes.

26. *A Least Squares Plane.* The plane

$$z = Ax + By + C$$

is to be "fitted" to the following points (x_k, y_k, z_k):

$$(0, 0, 0), \quad (0, 1, 1), \quad (1, 1, 1), \quad (1, 0, -1).$$

Find the values of A, B, and C that minimize the sum

$$\sum_{k=1}^{4} (Ax_k + By_k + C - z_k)^2,$$

the sum of the squares of the deviations.

LAGRANGE MULTIPLIERS WITH TWO CONSTRAINTS

27. Find the point closest to the origin on the line of intersection of the planes $y + 2z = 12$ and $x + y = 6$.

28. Find the maximum value that $f(x, y, z) = x^2 + 2y - z^2$ can have on the line of intersection of the planes $2x - y = 0$ and $y + z = 0$.

29. Find the extreme values of $f(x, y, z) = x^2yz + 1$ on the intersection of the plane $z = 1$ with the sphere $x^2 + y^2 + z^2 = 10$.

30. **a)** Find the maximum value of $w = xyz$ on the line of intersection of the two planes $x + y + z = 40$ and $x + y - z = 0$.

b) Give a geometric argument to support your claim that you have found a maximum, and not a minimum, value of w.

31. Find the extreme values of the function $f(x, y, z) = xy + z^2$ on the circle in which the plane $y - x = 0$ intersects the sphere $x^2 + y^2 + z^2 = 4$.

Writing for Your Own Knowledge

Answer the following questions in writing. Some answers will take only a sentence or two; others may require several paragraphs. Some explanations may also call for graphs or sketches.

1. Describe the method of Lagrange multipliers for finding the extreme values of a differentiable function $f(x, y, z)$ subject to a constraint $g(x, y, z) = 0$ defined by a differentiable function g. What is the appropriate description for functions of two independent variables? What is going on geometrically in each case?

2. How does the method of Lagrange multipliers work for a function $f(x, y, z)$ subject to *two* constraints, $g_1(x, y, z) = 0$ and $g_2(x, y, z) = 0$? What is going on geometrically?

For Your Review

Write brief paragraphs about the following topics and give examples.

Functions of two and three (independent) variables
Level curves and surfaces
Limits of functions of two and three variables
Continuity of functions of two and three variables
First partial derivatives and their interpretation
Notation for higher order partial derivatives
The Mixed Derivative Theorem (Euler's theorem)
The Increment Theorem for functions of two variables
Differentiability
Linearization
Estimating change with differentials
Sensitivity of functions to changes in variables
The Chain Rule
Directional derivatives
The gradient of a function of two independent variables and its role in finding directional derivatives and tangent lines
The gradient of a function of three independent variables and its role in finding directional derivatives, tangent planes, and normal lines
Local extrema and saddle points of a continuous function $f(x, y)$, and how to find them
Finding extreme values of continuous functions on closed bounded regions in the plane
Extreme values of functions with constrained variables

Practice Exercises

In Exercises 1–4, find the domain and range of the given function and identify its level curves. Sketch a typical level curve.

1. $f(x, y) = 9x^2 + y^2$

2. $f(x, y) = e^{x+y}$

3. $g(x, y) = 1/xy$

4. $g(x, y) = \sqrt{x^2 - y}$

In Exercises 5–8, find the domain and range of the given function and identify its level surfaces. Sketch a typical level surface.

5. $f(x, y, z) = x^2 + y^2 - z$

6. $g(x, y, z) = x^2 + 4y^2 + 9z^2$

7. $h(x, y, z) = \dfrac{1}{x^2 + y^2 + z^2}$

8. $k(x, y, z) = \dfrac{1}{x^2 + y^2 + z^2 + 1}$

Find the limits in Exercises 9–14.

9. $\lim\limits_{(x, y) \to (\pi, \ln 2)} e^y \cos x$

10. $\lim\limits_{(x, y) \to (0, 0)} \dfrac{2 + y}{x + \cos y}$

11. $\lim\limits_{\substack{(x, y) \to (1, 1) \\ x \neq y}} \dfrac{x - y}{x^2 - y^2}$

12. $\lim\limits_{(x, y) \to (1, 1)} \dfrac{x^3 y^3 - 1}{xy - 1}$

13. $\lim\limits_{P \to (1, -1, e)} \ln|x + y + z|$

14. $\lim\limits_{P \to (1, -1, -1)} \tan^{-1}(x + y + z)$

By considering different paths of approach, show that the limits in Exercises 15 and 16 do not exist.

15. $\lim\limits_{\substack{(x, y) \to (0, 0) \\ y \neq x^2}} \dfrac{y}{x^2 - y}$

16. $\lim\limits_{\substack{(x, y) \to (0, 0) \\ xy \neq 0}} \dfrac{x^2 + y^2}{xy}$

In Exercises 17–22, find the partial derivative of the function with respect to each variable.

17. $g(r, \theta) = r\cos\theta + r\sin\theta$

18. $f(x, y) = \frac{1}{2}\ln(x^2 + y^2) + \tan^{-1}\frac{y}{x}$

19. $f(R_1, R_2, R_3) = \frac{1}{R_1} + \frac{1}{R_2} + \frac{1}{R_3}$

20. $h(x, y, z) = \sin(2\pi x + y - 3z)$

21. $P(n, R, T, V) = \frac{nRT}{V}$ (the Ideal Gas Law)

22. $f(r, l, T, w) = \frac{1}{2rl}\sqrt{\frac{T}{\pi w}}$

(the frequency of a struck piano string, Chapter 3, Practice Exercise 74)

Find the second order partial derivatives of the functions in Exercises 23–26.

23. $g(x, y) = y + \frac{x}{y}$

24. $g(x, y) = e^x + y\sin x$

25. $f(x, y) = x + xy - 5x^3 + \ln(x^2 + 1)$

26. $f(x, y) = y^2 - 3xy + \cos y + 7e^y$

In Exercises 27 and 28, find the linearization $L(x, y)$ of the function $f(x, y)$ at the point P_0. Then find an upper bound for the magnitude of the error E in the approximation $f(x, y) \approx L(x, y)$ over the rectangle R.

27. $f(x, y) = \sin x\cos y, \quad P_0(\pi/4, \pi/4)$

$R: \quad \left|x - \frac{\pi}{4}\right| \le 0.1, \quad \left|y - \frac{\pi}{4}\right| \le 0.1$

28. $f(x, y) = xy - 3y^2 + 2, \quad P_0(1, 1)$

$R: \quad |x - 1| \le 0.1, \quad |y - 1| \le 0.2$

Find the linearizations of the functions in Exercises 29 and 30 at the given points.

29. $f(x, y, z) = xy + 2yz - 3xz$ at $(1, 0, 0)$ and $(1, 1, 0)$.

30. $f(x, y, z) = \sqrt{2}\cos x\sin(y + z)$ at $(0, 0, \pi/4)$ and $(\pi/4, \pi/4, 0)$.

31. You plan to calculate the volume inside a stretch of pipeline that is about 36 in. in diameter and 1 mi long. With which measurement should you be more careful—the length, or the diameter? Give reasons for your answer.

32. Near the point $(1, 2)$, is $f(x, y) = x^2 - xy + y^2 - 3$ more sensitive to changes in x, or to changes in y? Give reasons for your answer.

33. Suppose that the current I (amperes) in an electrical circuit is related to the voltage V (volts) and the resistance R (ohms) by the equation $I = V/R$. If the voltage drops from 24 to 23 volts and the resistance drops from 100 to 80 ohms, will I increase, or decrease? By about how much? Express the changes in V and R and the estimated change in I as percentages of their original values.

34. If $a = 10$ cm and $b = 16$ cm to the nearest millimeter, what should you expect the maximum percentage error to be in the calculated area $A = \pi ab$ of the ellipse $x^2/a^2 + y^2/b^2 = 1$? Give reasons for your answer.

35. Find dw/dt at $t = 0$ if $w = \sin(xy + \pi)$, $x = e^t$, $y = \ln(t + 1)$.

36. Find dw/dt at $t = 1$ if $w = xe^y + y\sin z - \cos z$, $x = 2\sqrt{t}$, $y = t - 1 + \ln t$, $z = \pi t$.

37. Find $\partial w/\partial r$ and $\partial w/\partial s$ when $r = \pi$ and $s = 0$ if $w = \sin(2x - y)$, $x = r + \sin s$, $y = rs$.

38. Find $\partial w/\partial u$ and $\partial w/\partial v$ when $u = v = 0$ if $w = \ln\sqrt{1 + x^2} - \tan^{-1} x$ and $x = 2e^u\cos v$.

Assuming that the equations in Exercises 39 and 40 define y as a differentiable function of x, find the value of dy/dx at the given point.

39. $1 - x - y^2 - \sin xy = 0, \quad (0, 1)$

40. $2xy + e^{x+y} - 2 = 0, \quad (0, \ln 2)$

41. Find the value of the derivative of $f(x, y, z) = xy + yz + xz$ with respect to t on the curve $x = \cos t$, $y = \sin t$, $z = \cos 2t$ at the point where $t = 1$ (Fig. 13.70).

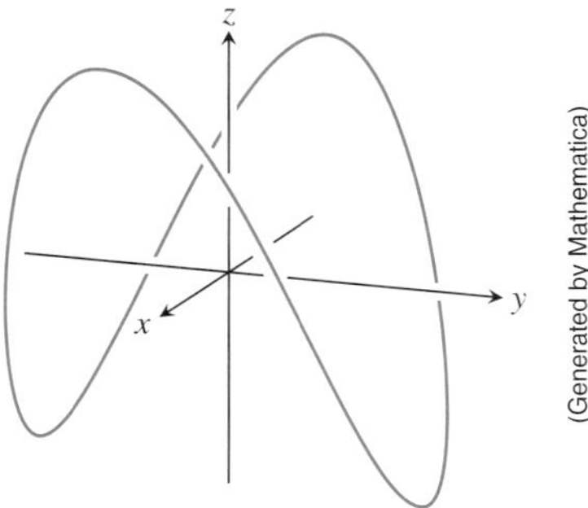

13.70 The curve in Exercise 41.

42. Show that if $w = f(s)$ is any differentiable function of s whatever, and $s = y + 5x$, then

$$\frac{\partial w}{\partial x} - 5\frac{\partial w}{\partial y} = 0.$$

In Exercises 43–46, find the directions in which f increases and decreases most rapidly at P_0 and find the derivative of f in each direction. Also, find the derivative of f at P_0 in the direction of the vector $\mathbf{A}$.

43. $f(x, y) = \cos x\cos y, \quad P_0(\pi/4, \pi/4), \quad \mathbf{A} = 3\mathbf{i} + 4\mathbf{j}$

44. $f(x, y) = x^2e^{-2y}, \quad P_0(1, 0), \quad \mathbf{A} = \mathbf{i} + \mathbf{j}$

45. $f(x, y, z) = \ln(2x + 3y + 6z), \quad P_0(-1, -1, 1)$, $\mathbf{A} = 2\mathbf{i} + 3\mathbf{j} + 6\mathbf{k}$

46. $f(x, y, z) = x^2 + 3xy - z^2 + 2y + z + 4, \quad P_0(0, 0, 0)$, $\mathbf{A} = \mathbf{i} + \mathbf{j} + \mathbf{k}$

In Exercises 47 and 48, sketch the surface $f(x, y, z) = c$ together with ∇f at the given points.

47. $x^2 + y + z^2 = 0$; $(0, -1, \pm 1)$, $(0, 0, 0)$

48. $y^2 + z^2 = 4$; $(2, \pm 2, 0)$, $(2, 0, \pm 2)$

In Exercises 49 and 50, find an equation for the plane tangent to the level surface $f(x, y, z) = c$ at the point P_0. Also, find parametric equations for the line that is normal to the surface at P_0.

49. $x^2 - y - 5z = 0$, $P_0(2, -1, 1)$

50. $x^2 + y^2 + z = 4$, $P_0(1, 1, 2)$

In Exercises 51 and 52, find an equation for the plane tangent to the surface $z = f(x, y)$ at the given point

51. $z = \ln(x^2 + y^2)$, $(0, 1, 0)$

52. $z = 1/(x^2 + y^2)$, $(1, 1, 1/2)$

In Exercises 53 and 54, find equations for the lines that are tangent and normal to the level curve $f(x, y) = c$ at the point P_0. Then sketch the lines and level curve together with ∇f at P_0.

53. $y - \sin x = 1$, $P_0(\pi, 1)$

54. $\frac{y^2}{2} - \frac{x^2}{2} = \frac{3}{2}$, $P_0(1, 2)$

In Exercises 55 and 56, find parametric equations for the line that is tangent to the curve of intersection of the surfaces at the given point.

55. Surfaces: $x^2 + 2y + 2z = 4$, $y = 1$
Point: $(1, 1, 1/2)$

56. Surfaces: $x + y^2 + z = 2$, $y = 1$
Point: $(1/2, 1, 1/2)$

57. What is the largest value that the directional derivative of $f(x, y, z) = xyz$ can have at the point $(1, 1, 1)$?

58. At the point $(1, 2)$ the function $f(x, y)$ has a derivative of 2 in the direction toward $(2, 2)$ and a derivative of -2 in the direction toward $(1, 1)$.
   a) Find $f_x(1, 2)$ and $f_y(1, 2)$.
   b) Find the derivative of f at $(1, 2)$ in the direction toward the point $(4, 6)$.

Test the functions in Exercises 59–64 for local maxima and minima and saddle points. Find each function's values at these points.

59. $f(x, y) = x^2 - xy + y^2 + 2x + 2y - 4$

60. $f(x, y) = 5x^2 + 4xy - 2y^2 + 4x - 4y$

61. $f(x, y) = 2x^3 + 3xy + 2y^3$

62. $f(x, y) = x^3 + y^3 - 3xy + 15$

63. $f(x, y) = x^3 + y^3 + 3x^2 - 3y^2$

64. $f(x, y) = x^4 - 8x^2 + 3y^2 - 6y$

In Exercises 65–70, find the absolute maximum and minimum values of f on the region R.

65. $f(x, y) = x^2 + xy + y^2 - 3x + 3y$
   R: The triangular region cut from the first quadrant by the line $x + y = 4$

66. $f(x, y) = x^2 - y^2 - 2x + 4y + 1$
   R: The rectangular region in the first quadrant bounded by the coordinate axes and the lines $x = 4$ and $y = 2$

67. $f(x, y) = y^2 - xy - 3y + 2x$
   R: The square region enclosed by the lines $x = \pm 2$ and $y = \pm 2$

68. $f(x, y) = 2x + 2y - x^2 - y^2$
   R: The square bounded by the coordinate axes and the lines $x = 2$, $y = 2$ in the first quadrant

69. $f(x, y) = x^2 - y^2 - 2x + 4y$
   R: The triangular region bounded below by the x-axis, above by the line $y = x + 2$, and on the right by the line $x = 2$

70. $f(x, y) = 4xy - x^4 - y^4 + 16$
   R: The triangular region bounded below by the line $y = -2$, above by the line $y = x$, and on the right by the line $x = 2$

71. Find the points nearest the origin on the curve $xy^2 = 54$.

72. Find the extreme values of $f(x, y) = x^3 + y^2$ on the circle $x^2 + y^2 = 1$.

73. Suppose that the temperature T (degrees) at the point (x, y, z) on the sphere $x^2 + y^2 + z^2 = 1$ is $T = 400\,xyz^2$. Locate the highest and lowest temperatures on the sphere.

74. Find the extreme values of $f(x, y) = x^2 + 3y^2 + 2y$ on the unit disk $x^2 + y^2 \leq 1$.

75. Find the point(s) on the surface $xyz = 1$ closest to the origin.

76. Suppose $\mathbf{r} = g(t)\,\mathbf{i} + h(t)\,\mathbf{j} + k(t)\,\mathbf{k}$ is a smooth curve in the domain of a differentiable function $f(x, y, z)$. Describe the relation between df/dt, ∇f, and $\mathbf{v} = d\mathbf{r}/dt$. What can be said about ∇f and $\mathbf{v}$ at interior points of the curve where f has extreme values relative to its other values on the curve? Give reasons for your answer.

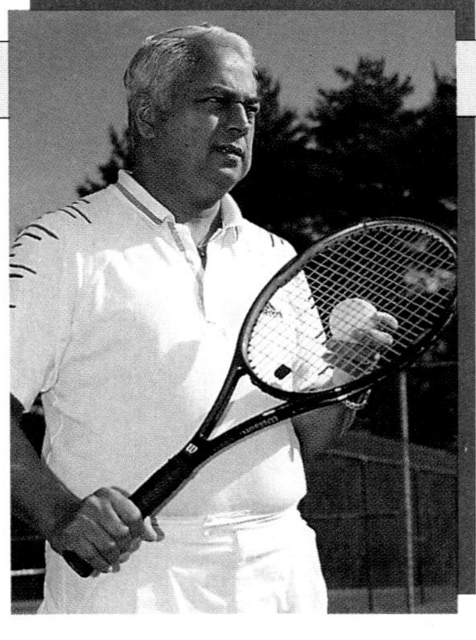

RUDRAPATNA V. RAMNATH, a Professor of Aeronautics and Astronautics at the Massachusetts Institute of Technology, is one of the pioneers of modern tennis racket design. "The sport is becoming more sophisticated," says Dr. Ramnath, "with more mathematics, physics, and technology involved in the production and use of advanced sports equipment."

Many tennis players, particularly beginners, have the problem that the racket turns in their hand. This happens when the ball is hit off center, away from the longitudinal axis of the racket, imparting a net angular impulse to the racket.

The farther from the axis the ball hits, the more the racket will tend to rotate on impact. This tendency can be reduced by increasing the polar moment of inertia of the racket about the axis (Section 14.2).

There are two ways to accomplish this. One is to increase the mass along the sides of the racket's head. The other (preferable, because it does not add to the racket's weight) is to move the head's mass farther away from the axis (in other words, make the racket head larger — a common practice in recent years).

If you want to see the polar moment of inertia at work, try the following experiment. Tape two coins to the ends of a pencil and twiddle the pencil about the center of mass.

The moment of inertia accounts for the resistance you feel to turning each time you change the direction of motion. Now move the coins an equal distance toward the center of mass and twiddle the pencil again. The system has the same mass and center of mass but now offers less resistance to changes in motion.

Increasing the polar moment of inertia is the right thing to do if you want your tennis racket to resist rotation on impact.

14 Multiple Integrals

OVERVIEW

This chapter complements the previous chapter on differentiation. The problems we can solve by integrating functions of two and three variables are similar to the problems solved by single-variable integration, but more general. For example, in Chapter 7 we calculated volumes of solids of revolution, whereas now we will learn how to calculate volumes of other solids, in a variety of coordinate systems. Earlier, we calculated the moments and centers of mass of rods and thin plates; now we will be able to handle plates more easily, work with more general density functions, and treat solids as well. As in the previous chapter, we can perform the necessary calculations by drawing on our experience with functions of a single variable. Multiple integrals also play important roles in statistics, electrical engineering, and the physical theory of electromagnetism, but we will not go into these applications here.

14.1 Double Integrals

We now show how to integrate a continuous function $f(x, y)$ over a bounded region in the xy-plane. We begin with rectangular regions and then proceed to bounded regions of a more general nature. There are many similarities between the "double" integrals we define here and the "single" integrals we defined in Chapter 5 for functions of a single variable. Indeed, the connection is very strong. The basic theorem for evaluating double integrals says that every double integral can be evaluated in stages, using the single-integration methods already at our command.

Double Integrals Over Rectangles

Suppose that $f(x, y)$ is defined on a rectangular region R given by

$$R: \qquad a \leq x \leq b, \quad c \leq y \leq d.$$

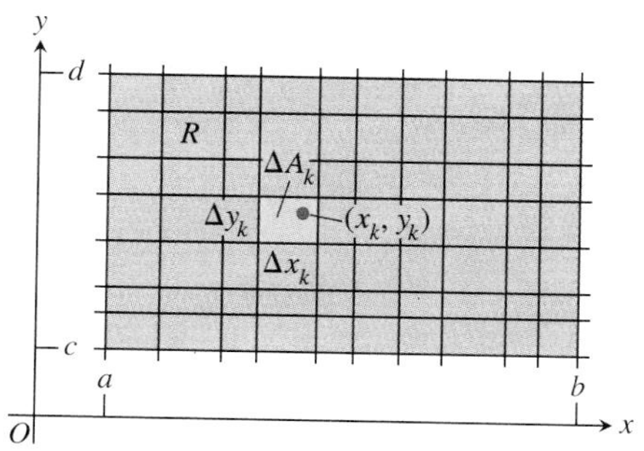

14.1 Rectangular grid partitioning the region R into small rectangles of area $\Delta A_k = \Delta x_k \Delta y_k$.

We imagine R to be covered by a network of lines parallel to the x- and y-axes (Fig. 14.1). These lines divide R into small pieces of area $\Delta A = \Delta x\, \Delta y$. We number these in some order $\Delta A_1, \Delta A_2, \ldots, \Delta A_n$, choose a point (x_k, y_k) in each piece ΔA_k, and form the sum

$$S_n = \sum_{k=1}^{n} f(x_k, y_k)\, \Delta A_k. \tag{1}$$

If f is continuous throughout R, then, as we refine the mesh width to make both Δx and Δy go to zero, the sums in (1) approach a limit called the **double integral** of f over R. The notation for it is

$$\iint_R f(x, y)\, dA \qquad \text{or} \qquad \iint_R f(x, y)\, dx\, dy.$$

Thus,

$$\iint_R f(x, y)\, dA = \lim_{\Delta A \to 0} \sum_{k=1}^{n} f(x_k, y_k)\, \Delta A_k. \tag{2}$$

As with functions of a single variable, the sums approach this limit no matter how the intervals $[a, b]$ and $[c, d]$ that determine R are partitioned, as long as the norms of the partitions both go to zero. The limit in (2) is also independent of the order in which the areas ΔA_k are numbered and independent of the choice of the point (x_k, y_k) within each ΔA_k. The values of the individual approximating sums S_n depend on these choices, but the sums approach the same limit in the end. The proof of the existence and uniqueness of this limit for a continuous function f is given in more advanced texts. The continuity of f is a sufficient condition for the existence of the double integral, but not a necessary one. The limit in question exists for many discontinuous functions as well.

Properties of Double Integrals

Like single integrals, double integrals of continuous functions have algebraic properties that are useful in computations and applications.

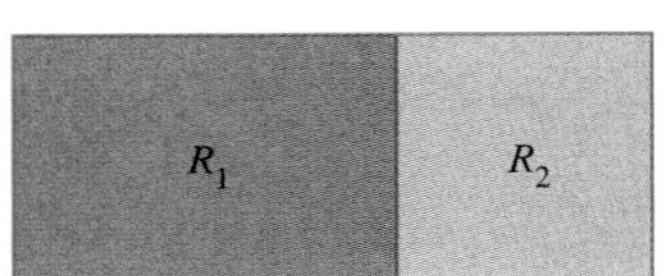

$$\iint_{R_1 \cup R_2} f(x, y)\, dA = \iint_{R_1} f(x, y)\, dA + \iint_{R_2} f(x, y)\, dA$$

14.2 Double integrals have the same kind of domain additivity property that single integrals have.

1. $\displaystyle\iint_R kf(x, y)\, dA = k \iint_R f(x, y)\, dA$ (any number k)
2. $\displaystyle\iint_R (f(x, y) \pm g(x, y))\, dA = \iint_R f(x, y)\, dA \pm \iint_R g(x, y)\, dA$
3. $\displaystyle\iint_R f(x, y)\, dA \geq 0$ if $f(x, y) \geq 0$ on R
4. $\displaystyle\iint_R f(x, y)\, dA \geq \iint_R g(x, y)\, dA$ if $f(x, y) \geq g(x, y)$ on R

These are like the single-integral properties in Section 5.3. There is also an additivity property:

5. $\displaystyle\iint_R f(x, y)\, dA = \iint_{R_1} f(x, y)\, dA + \iint_{R_2} f(x, y)\, dA.$

It holds when R is the union of two nonoverlapping rectangles R_1 and R_2 (Fig. 14.2). Again, we omit the proof.

Double Integrals as Volumes

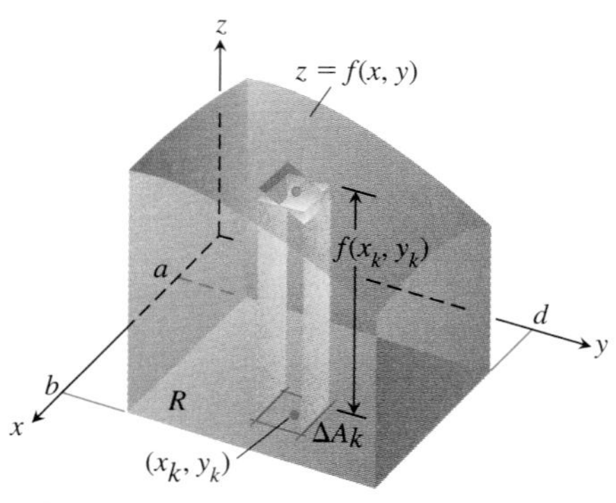

14.3 Approximating solids with rectangular prisms leads us to define the volumes of more general prisms as double integrals. The volume of the prism shown here is the double integral of $f(x, y)$ over the base region R.

When $f(x, y)$ is positive, we may interpret the double integral of f over a rectangular region R as the volume of the solid prism bounded below by R and above by the surface $z = f(x, y)$ (Fig. 14.3). Each term $f(x_k, y_k)\, \Delta A_k$ in the sum $S_n = \Sigma f(x_k, y_k)\, \Delta A_k$ is the volume of a vertical rectangular prism that approximates the volume of the portion of the solid that stands directly above the base ΔA_k. The sum S_n thus approximates what we want to call the total volume of the solid. We *define* this volume to be

$$\text{Volume} = \lim S_n = \iint_R f(x, y)\, dA. \tag{3}$$

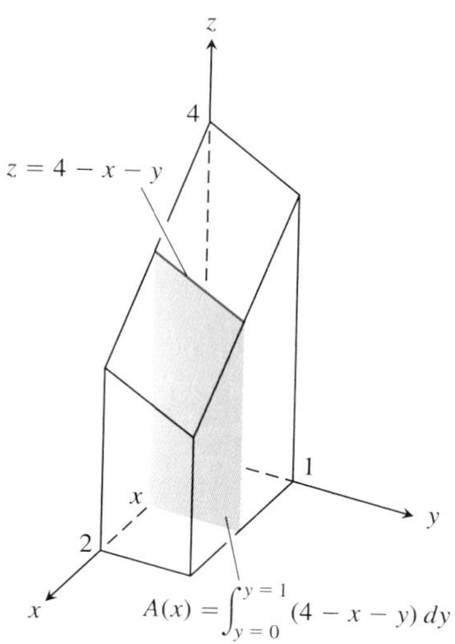

14.4 To obtain the cross-section area $A(x)$, we hold x fixed and integrate with respect to y.

As you might expect, this more general method of calculating volume agrees with the methods in Chapter 7 (it would be useless if it did not), but we will not prove this here.

Fubini's Theorem for Calculating Double Integrals

We are ready to calculate our first double integral.

Suppose we wish to calculate the volume under the plane $z = 4 - x - y$ over the rectangular region R: $0 \le x \le 2$, $0 \le y \le 1$ in the xy-plane. If we apply the method of slicing from Section 7.8, with slices perpendicular to the x-axis (Fig. 14.4), then the volume is

$$\int_{x=0}^{x=2} A(x)\, dx, \tag{4}$$

where $A(x)$ is the cross-section area at x. For each value of x we may calculate $A(x)$ as the integral

$$A(x) = \int_{y=0}^{y=1} (4 - x - y)\, dy, \tag{5}$$

which is the area under the curve $z = 4 - x - y$ in the plane of the cross section at x. In calculating $A(x)$, x is held fixed and the integration takes place with respect to y. Combining (4) and (5), we see that the volume of the entire solid is

$$\begin{aligned}\text{Volume} &= \int_{x=0}^{x=2} A(x)\, dx = \int_{x=0}^{x=2} \left(\int_{y=0}^{y=1} (4 - x - y)\, dy \right) dx \\ &= \int_{x=0}^{x=2} \left[4y - xy - \frac{y^2}{2} \right]_{y=0}^{y=1} dx = \int_{x=0}^{x=2} \left(\frac{7}{2} - x \right) dx = \left[\frac{7}{2}x - \frac{x^2}{2} \right]_0^2 = 5.\end{aligned} \tag{6}$$

If we had just wanted to write instructions for calculating the volume, without carrying out any of the integrations, we could write

$$\text{Volume} = \int_0^2 \int_0^1 (4 - x - y)\, dy\, dx.$$

The expression on the right, called an **iterated** or **repeated integral,** says that the volume is obtained by integrating $4 - x - y$ with respect to y from $y = 0$ to $y = 1$, holding x fixed, and then integrating the resulting expression in x with respect to x from $x = 0$ to $x = 2$.

What would have happened if we had calculated the volume by slicing with planes perpendicular to the y-axis (Fig. 14.5)? As a function of y, the typical cross-section area is

$$A(y) = \int_{x=0}^{x=2} (4 - x - y)\, dx = \left[4x - \frac{x^2}{2} - xy \right]_{x=0}^{x=2} = 6 - 2y. \tag{7}$$

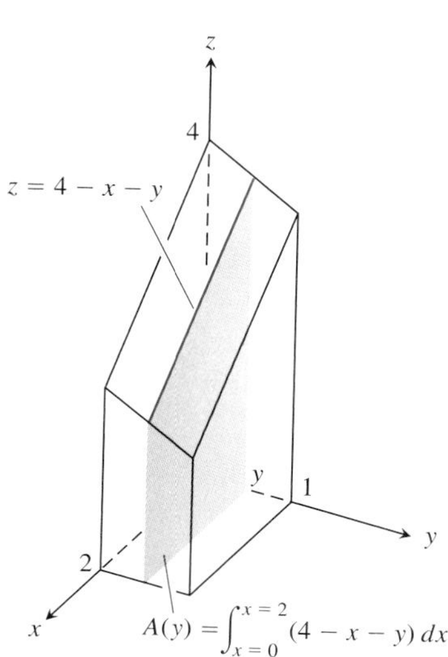

14.5 To obtain the cross-section area $A(y)$, we hold y fixed and integrate with respect to x.

The volume of the entire solid is therefore

$$\text{Volume} = \int_{y=0}^{y=1} A(y)\, dy = \int_{y=0}^{y=1} (6 - 2y)\, dy = \left[6y - y^2 \right]_0^1 = 5,$$

in agreement with our earlier calculation.

Again, we may give instructions for calculating the volume as an iterated integral by writing

$$\text{Volume} = \int_0^1 \int_0^2 (4 - x - y)\, dx\, dy.$$

The expression on the right says that we can find the volume by integrating $4 - x - y$ with respect to x from $x = 0$ to $x = 2$ (as in Eq. 7) and integrating the result with respect to y from $y = 0$ to $y = 1$. In this iterated integral the order of integration is first x and then y, the reverse of the order in Eq. (6).

What do these two volume calculations with iterated integrals have to do with the double integral

$$\iint_R (4 - x - y)\, dA$$

over the rectangle $R: 0 \leq x \leq 2,\ 0 \leq y \leq 1$? The answer is that they both give the value of the double integral. A theorem published in 1907 by Guido Fubini (1879–1943) says that the double integral of any continuous function over a rectangle can be calculated as an iterated integral in either order of integration. (Fubini proved his theorem in greater generality, but this is how it translates into what we're doing now.)

THEOREM 1

Fubini's Theorem (First Form)

If $f(x, y)$ is continuous on the rectangular region $R: a \leq x \leq b$, $c \leq y \leq d$, then

$$\iint_R f(x, y)\, dA = \int_c^d \int_a^b f(x, y)\, dx\, dy = \int_a^b \int_c^d f(x, y)\, dy\, dx.$$

Fubini's theorem says that double integrals over rectangles can be calculated as iterated integrals. This means we can evaluate a double integral by integrating one variable at a time, using the integration techniques we already know for functions of a single variable.

Fubini's theorem also says that we may calculate the double integral by integrating in *either* order, a genuine convenience, as we will see in Example 3. In particular, when we calculate a volume by slicing, we may use either planes perpendicular to the x-axis or planes perpendicular to the y-axis. We get the same answer either way.

Even more important is the fact that Fubini's theorem holds for *any* continuous function $f(x, y)$. In particular, f may have negative as well as positive values, and the integrals we calculate with Fubini's theorem may represent other things besides volumes (as we will see later).

EXAMPLE 1 Calculate $\iint_R f(x, y)\, dA$ for

$$f(x, y) = 1 - 6x^2y \quad \text{and} \quad R: \ 0 \leq x \leq 2, \quad -1 \leq y \leq 1.$$

Solution By Fubini's theorem,

$$\iint_R f(x\, y)\, dA = \int_{-1}^1 \int_0^2 (1 - 6x^2y)\, dx\, dy = \int_{-1}^1 \Big[x - 2x^3y\Big]_{x=0}^{x=2} dy$$

$$= \int_{-1}^1 (2 - 16y)\, dy = \Big[2y - 8y^2\Big]_{-1}^1 = 4.$$

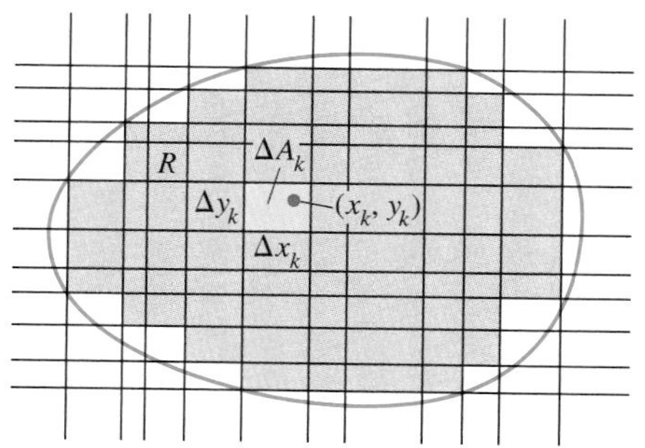

14.6 A rectangular grid partitioning a bounded nonrectangular region into cells.

Reversing the order of integration gives the same answer:

$$\int_0^2 \int_{-1}^1 (1 - 6x^2 y)\, dy\, dx = \int_0^2 \Big[y - 3x^2 y^2 \Big]_{y=-1}^{y=1} dx$$

$$= \int_0^2 \Big[(1 - 3x^2) - (-1 - 3x^2) \Big] dx = \int_0^2 2\, dx = 4.$$

Double Integrals over Bounded Nonrectangular Regions

To define the double integral of a function $f(x, y)$ over a bounded nonrectangular region, like the one shown in Fig. 14.6, we again imagine R to be covered by a rectangular grid, but we include in the partial sum only the small pieces of area $\Delta A = \Delta x \Delta y$ that lie entirely within the region (shaded in the figure). We number the pieces in some order, choose an arbitrary point (x_k, y_k) in each ΔA_k, and form the sum

$$S_n = \sum_{k=1}^{n} f(x_k, y_k)\, \Delta A_k.$$

The only difference between this sum and the one in Eq. (1) for rectangular regions is that now the areas ΔA_k may not cover all of R. But as the mesh becomes increasingly fine and the number of terms in S_n increases, more and more of R is included. If f is continuous and the boundary of R is made from the graphs of a finite number of continuous functions of x and/or continuous functions of y joined end to end, then the sums S_n will have a limit as the norms of the partitions that define the rectangular grid independently approach zero. We call the limit the **double integral** of f over R:

$$\iint_R f(x, y)\, dA = \lim_{\Delta A \to 0} \sum f(x_k, y_k)\, \Delta A_k.$$

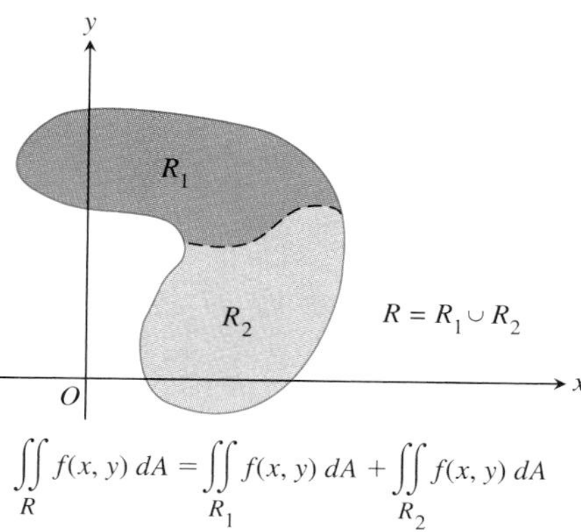

$\iint_R f(x, y)\, dA = \iint_{R_1} f(x, y)\, dA + \iint_{R_2} f(x, y)\, dA$

14.7 The additivity property for rectangular regions holds for regions bounded by continuous curves.

This limit may also exist under less restrictive circumstances, but we will not pursue the point here.

Double integrals of continuous functions over nonrectangular regions have the same algebraic properties as integrals over rectangular regions. The domain additivity property corresponding to property 5 says that if R is decomposed into nonoverlapping regions R_1 and R_2 with boundaries that are again made of a finite number of line segments or smooth curves (see Fig. 14.7 for an example), then

$$\iint_R f(x, y)\, dA = \iint_{R_1} f(x, y)\, dA + \iint_{R_2} f(x, y)\, dA.$$

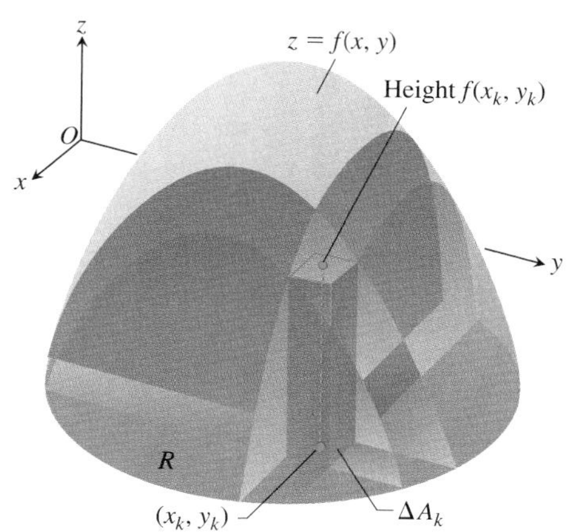

Volume $= \lim \Sigma f(x_k, y_k)\, \Delta A_k = \iint f(x, y)\, dA$

14.8 We define the volumes of solids with curved bases the same way we define the volumes of solids with rectangular bases.

If $f(x, y)$ is positive and continuous over R (Fig. 14.8), we define the volume of the solid region between R and the surface $z = f(x, y)$ to be $\iint_R f(x, y)\, dA$, as before.

If R is a region like the one shown in the xy-plane in Fig. 14.9 on the following page, bounded "above" and "below" by the curves $y = g_2(x)$ and $y = g_1(x)$ and on the sides by the lines $x = a$, $x = b$, we may again calculate the volume by the method of slicing. We first calculate the cross-section area

$$A(x) = \int_{y=g_1(x)}^{y=g_2(x)} f(x, y)\, dy$$

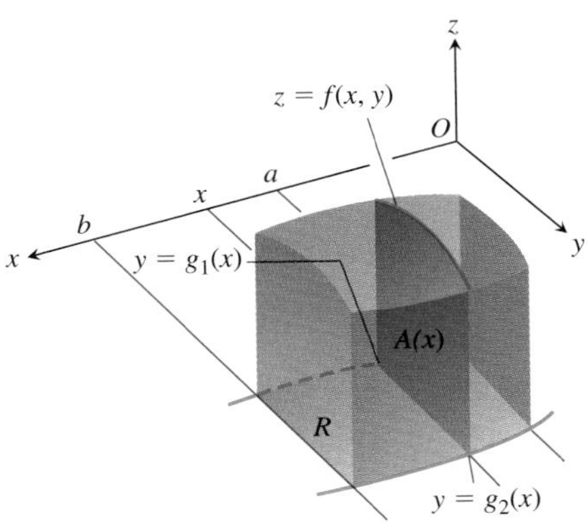

14.9 The area of the vertical slice shown here is

$$A(x) = \int_{g_1(x)}^{g_2(x)} f(x, y)\, dy.$$

To calculate the volume of the solid, we integrate this area from $x = a$ to $x = b$.

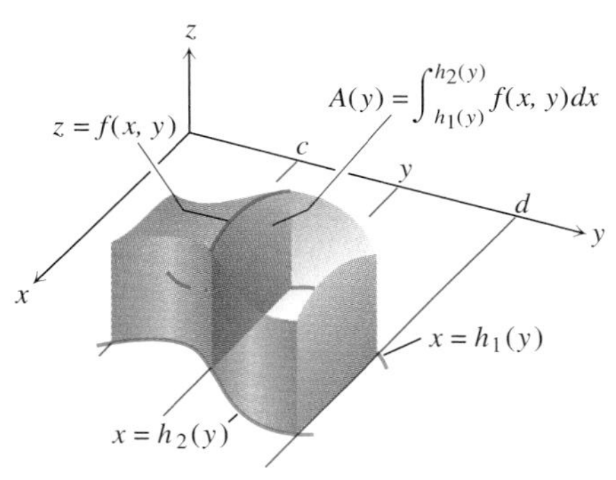

14.10 The volume of the solid shown here is

$$\int_c^d A(y)\, dy = \int_c^d \int_{h_1(y)}^{h_2(y)} f(x, y)\, dx\, dy.$$

and then integrate $A(x)$ from $x = a$ to $x = b$ to get the volume as an iterated integral:

$$V = \int_a^b A(x)\, dx = \int_a^b \int_{g_1(x)}^{g_2(x)} f(x, y)\, dy\, dx. \tag{8}$$

Similarly, if R is a region like the one shown in Fig. 14.10, bounded by the curves $x = h_2(y)$ and $x = h_1(y)$ and the lines $y = c$ and $y = d$, then the volume calculated by slicing is given by the iterated integral

$$\text{Volume} = \int_c^d \int_{h_1(y)}^{h_2(y)} f(x, y)\, dx\, dy. \tag{9}$$

The fact that the iterated integrals in Eqs. (8) and (9) both give the volume that we defined to be the double integral of f over R is a consequence of the following stronger form of Fubini's theorem.

THEOREM 2

Fubini's Theorem (Stronger Form)

Let $f(x, y)$ be continuous on a region R.

1. If R is defined by $a \le x \le b$, $g_1(x) \le y \le g_2(x)$, with g_1 and g_2 continuous on $[a, b]$, then
$$\iint_R f(x, y)\, dA = \int_a^b \int_{g_1(x)}^{g_2(x)} f(x, y)\, dy\, dx.$$
2. If R is defined by $c \le y \le d$, $h_1(y) \le x \le h_2(y)$, with h_1 and h_2 continuous on $[c, d]$, then
$$\iint_R f(x, y)\, dA = \int_c^d \int_{h_1(y)}^{h_2(y)} f(x, y)\, dx\, dy.$$

EXAMPLE 2 Find the volume of the prism whose base is the triangle in the xy-plane bounded by the x-axis and the lines $y = x$ and $x = 1$ and whose top lies in the plane

$$z = f(x, y) = 3 - x - y.$$

Solution See Fig. 14.11. For any x between 0 and 1, y may vary from $y = 0$ to $y = x$ (Fig. 14.11b). Hence,

$$\begin{aligned} V &= \int_0^1 \int_0^x (3 - x - y)\, dy\, dx \\ &= \int_0^1 \left[3y - xy - \frac{y^2}{2}\right]_{y=0}^{y=x} dx \\ &= \int_0^1 \left(3x - \frac{3x^2}{2}\right) dx = \left[\frac{3x^2}{2} - \frac{x^3}{2}\right]_{x=0}^{x=1} = 1. \end{aligned}$$

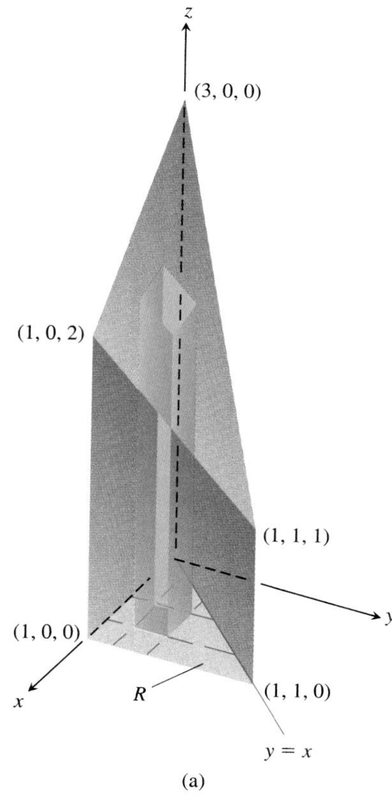

(a)

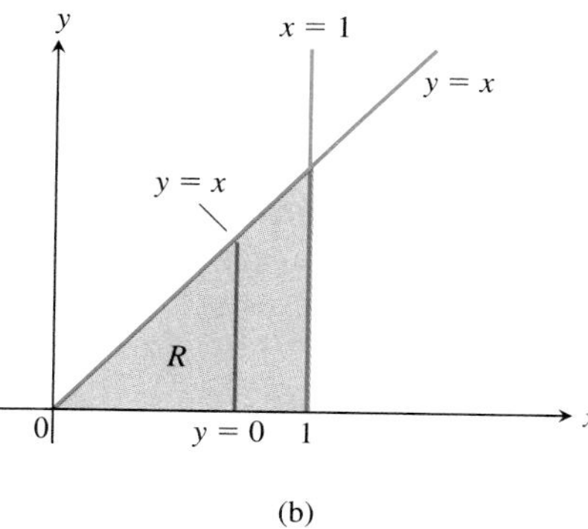

(b)

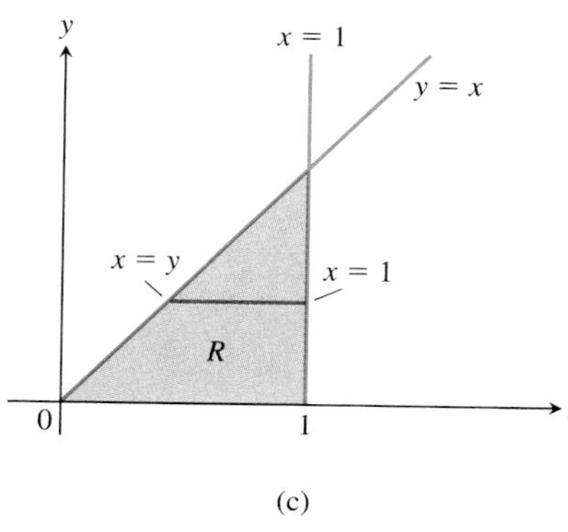

(c)

14.11 (a) Prism with a triangular base in the xy-plane. The volume of this prism is defined as a double integral over R. To evaluate it as an iterated integral, we may integrate first with respect to y and then with respect to x, or the other way around (Example 2).
(b) Integration limits of

$$\int_{x=0}^{x=1}\int_{y=0}^{y=x} f(x, y)\, dy\, dx.$$

If we integrate first with respect to y, we integrate along a vertical line through R and then integrate from left to right to include all the vertical lines in R.
(c) Integration limits of

$$\int_{y=0}^{y=1}\int_{x=y}^{x=1} f(x, y)\, dx\, dy.$$

If we integrate first with respect to x, we integrate along a horizontal line through R and then integrate from bottom to top to include all the horizontal lines in R.

When the order of integration is reversed (Fig. 14.11c), the integral for the volume is

$$\begin{aligned} V &= \int_0^1\int_y^1 (3 - x - y)\, dx\, dy \\ &= \int_0^1 \left[3x - \frac{x^2}{2} - xy\right]_{x=y}^{x=1} dy \\ &= \int_0^1 \left(3 - \frac{1}{2} - y - 3y + \frac{y^2}{2} + y^2\right) dy \\ &= \int_0^1 \left(\frac{5}{2} - 4y + \frac{3}{2}y^2\right) dy \\ &= \left[\frac{5}{2}y - 2y^2 + \frac{y^3}{2}\right]_{y=0}^{y=1} = 1. \end{aligned}$$

The two integrals are equal, as they should be.

While Fubini's theorem assures us that a double integral may be calculated as an iterated integral in either order of integration, the value of one integral may be easier to find than the value of the other. The next example shows how this can happen.

EXAMPLE 3 Calculate

$$\iint_R \frac{\sin x}{x}\, dA,$$

where R is the triangle in the xy-plane bounded by the x-axis, the line $y = x$, and the line $x = 1$.

Solution The region of integration is shown in Fig. 14.12 on the following page. If we integrate first with respect to y and then with respect to x, we find

$$\begin{aligned} \int_0^1\left(\int_0^x \frac{\sin x}{x}\, dy\right) dx &= \int_0^1 \left(y\frac{\sin x}{x}\right]_{y=0}^{y=x}\right) dx = \int_0^1 \sin x\, dx \\ &= -\cos(1) + 1 \approx 0.46. \end{aligned}$$

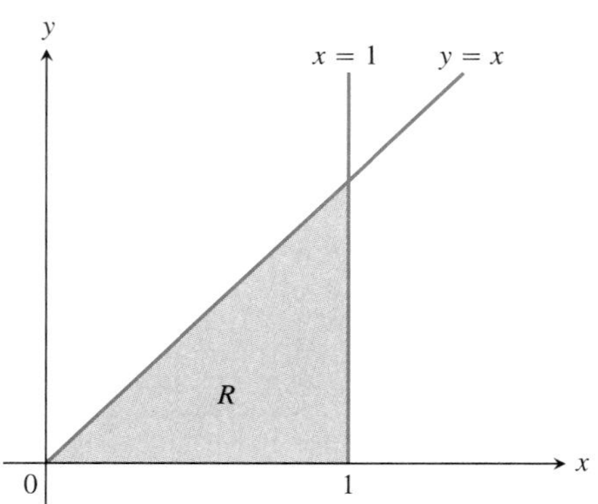

14.12 The region of integration in Example 3.

If we reverse the order of integration and attempt to calculate

$$\int_0^1 \int_y^1 \frac{\sin x}{x}\, dx\, dy,$$

we are stopped by the fact that $\int ((\sin x)/x)\, dx$ cannot be expressed in terms of elementary functions.

There is no general rule for predicting which order of integration will be the good one in circumstances like these, so don't worry about how to start your integrations. Just forge ahead and if the order you choose first doesn't work, try the other.

Finding the Limits of Integration

The hardest part of evaluating a double integral can be finding the limits of integration. Fortunately, there is a good procedure to follow.

Procedure for Finding Limits of Integration

A. To evaluate $\iint_R f(x, y)\, dA$ over a region R, integrating first with respect to y and then with respect to x, take the following steps:

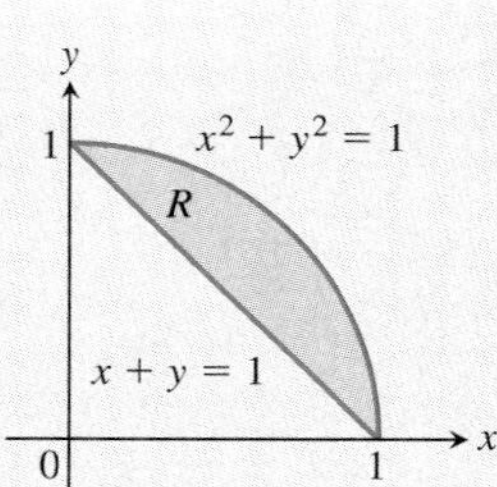

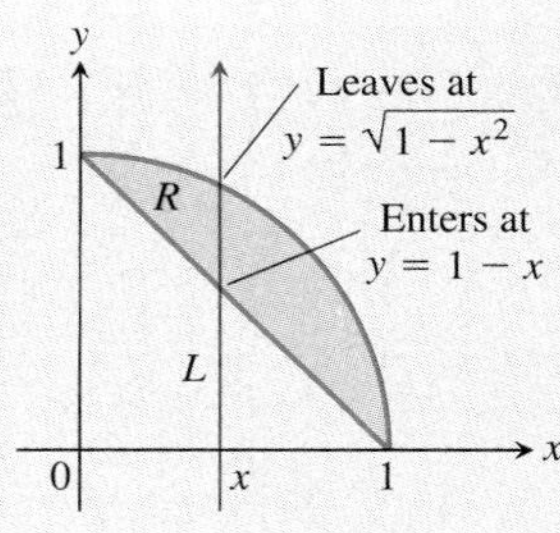

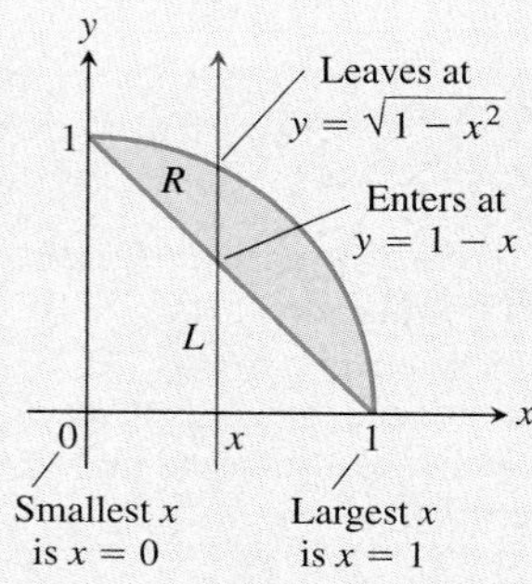

1. *A sketch.* Sketch the region of integration and label the bounding curves.

2. *The y-limits of integration.* Imagine a vertical line L cutting through R in the direction of increasing y. Mark the y-values where L enters and leaves. These are the y-limits of integration.

3. *The x-limits of integration.* Choose x-limits that include all the vertical lines through R. The integral is

$$\iint_R f(x, y)\, dA = \int_{x=0}^{x=1} \int_{y=1-x}^{y=\sqrt{1-x^2}} f(x, y)\, dy\, dx.$$

B. To evaluate the same double integral as an iterated integral with the order of integration reversed, use horizontal lines instead of vertical lines. The integral is

$$\iint_R f(x, y)\, dA = \int_0^1 \int_{1-y}^{\sqrt{1-y^2}} f(x, y)\, dx\, dy.$$

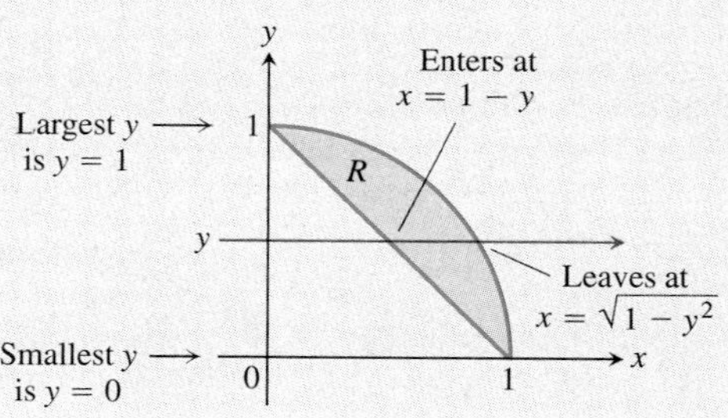

EXAMPLE 4 Sketch the region of integration for the integral

$$\int_0^2 \int_{x^2}^{2x} (4x + 2)\, dy\, dx$$

and write an equivalent integral with the order of integration reversed.

Solution The region of integration is given by the inequalities $x^2 \leq y \leq 2x$ and $0 \leq x \leq 2$. It is therefore the region bounded by the curves $y = x^2$ and $y = 2x$ between $x = 0$ and $x = 2$ (Fig. 14.13a).

To find the limits for integrating in the reverse order, we imagine a horizontal line passing from left to right through the region. It enters at $x = y/2$ and leaves at $x = \sqrt{y}$. To include all such lines, we let y run from $y = 0$ to $y = 4$ (Fig. 14.13b). The integral is

$$\int_0^4 \int_{y/2}^{\sqrt{y}} (4x + 2)\, dx\, dy.$$

The common value of these integrals is 8.

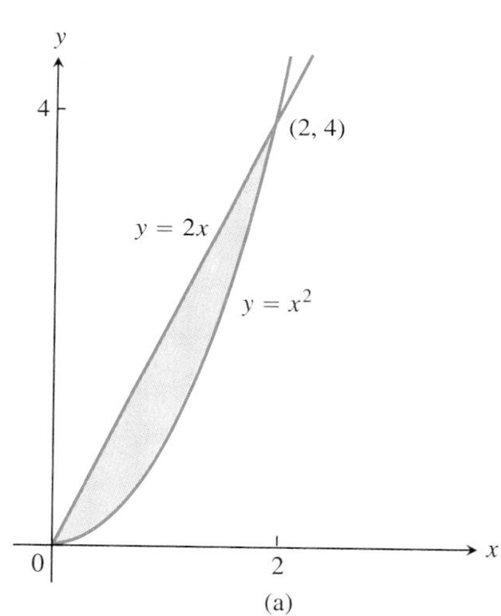

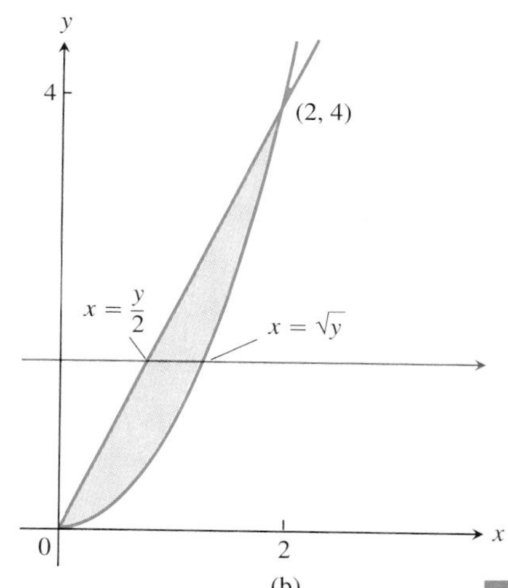

14.13 To write

$$\int_0^2 \int_{x^2}^{2x} (4x + 2)\, dy\, dx$$

as a double integral with the order of integration reversed, we (a) sketch the region of integration and (b) work out what the new limits of integration have to be. Example 4 gives the details.

Exercises 14.1

In Exercises 1–10, sketch the region of integration and evaluate the integral.

1. $\int_0^3 \int_0^2 (4 - y^2)\, dy\, dx$

2. $\int_0^3 \int_{-2}^0 (x^2 y - 2xy)\, dy\, dx$

3. $\int_{-1}^0 \int_{-1}^1 (x + y + 1)\, dx\, dy$

4. $\int_{\pi}^{2\pi} \int_0^{\pi} (\sin x + \cos y)\, dx\, dy$

5. $\int_0^{\pi} \int_0^x x \sin y\, dy\, dx$

6. $\int_0^{\pi} \int_0^{\sin x} y\, dy\, dx$

7. $\int_1^{\ln 8} \int_0^{\ln y} e^{x+y}\, dx\, dy$

8. $\int_1^2 \int_y^{y^2} dx\, dy$

9. $\int_0^1 \int_0^{y^2} 3y^3 e^{xy}\, dx\, dy$

10. $\int_1^4 \int_0^{\sqrt{x}} \frac{3}{2} e^{y/\sqrt{x}}\, dy\, dx$

In Exercises 11–16, integrate f over the given region.

11. $f(x, y) = x/y$ over the region in the first quadrant bounded by the lines $y = x$, $y = 2x$, $x = 1$, $x = 2$

12. $f(x, y) = 1/xy$ over the square $1 \le x \le 2$, $1 \le y \le 2$

13. $f(x, y) = x^2 + y^2$ over the triangular region with vertices $(0, 0)$, $(1, 0)$, and $(0, 1)$

14. $f(x, y) = y \cos xy$ over the rectangle $0 \le x \le \pi$, $0 \le y \le 1$

15. $f(u, v) = v - \sqrt{u}$ over the triangular region cut from the first quadrant of the uv-plane by the line $u + v = 1$

16. $f(s, t) = e^s \ln t$ over the region in the first quadrant of the st-plane that lies above the curve $s = \ln t$ from $t = 1$ to $t = 2$

Each of Exercises 17–20 gives an integral over a region in a Cartesian coordinate plane. Sketch the region and evaluate the integral.

17. $\int_{-2}^{0} \int_{v}^{-v} 2\, dp\, dv$ (the pv-plane)

18. $\int_0^1 \int_0^{\sqrt{1-s^2}} 8t\, dt\, ds$ (the st-plane)

19. $\int_{-\pi/3}^{\pi/3} \int_0^{\sec t} 3 \cos t\, du\, dt$ (the tu-plane)

20. $\int_0^3 \int_{-2}^{4-2u} \frac{4 - 2u}{v^2}\, dv\, du$ (the uv-plane)

In Exercises 21–30, sketch the region of integration and write an equivalent double integral with the order of integration reversed.

21. $\int_0^1 \int_2^{4-2x} dy\, dx$

22. $\int_0^2 \int_{y-2}^{0} dx\, dy$

23. $\int_0^1 \int_y^{\sqrt{y}} dx\, dy$

24. $\int_0^1 \int_{1-x}^{1-x^2} dy\, dx$

25. $\int_0^1 \int_1^{e^x} dy\, dx$

26. $\int_0^{\ln 2} \int_{e^y}^{2} dx\, dy$

27. $\int_0^{3/2} \int_0^{9-4x^2} 16x\, dy\, dx$

28. $\int_0^2 \int_0^{4-y^2} y\, dx\, dy$

29. $\int_0^1 \int_{-\sqrt{1-y^2}}^{\sqrt{1-y^2}} 3y\, dx\, dy$

30. $\int_0^2 \int_{-\sqrt{4-x^2}}^{\sqrt{4-x^2}} 6x\, dy\, dx$

In Exercises 31–38, sketch the region of integration and evaluate the integral.

31. $\int_0^{\pi} \int_x^{\pi} \frac{\sin y}{y}\, dy\, dx$

32. $\int_0^1 \int_y^1 x^2 e^{xy}\, dx\, dy$

33. $\int_0^2 \int_x^2 2y^2 \sin xy\, dy\, dx$

34. $\int_0^2 \int_0^{4-x^2} \frac{xe^{2y}}{4 - y}\, dy\, dx$

35. $\int_0^{2\sqrt{\ln 3}} \int_{y/2}^{\sqrt{\ln 3}} e^{x^2}\, dx\, dy$

36. $\int_0^{1/16} \int_{y^{1/4}}^{1/2} \cos (16\pi x^5)\, dx\, dy$

37. $\int_0^3 \int_{\sqrt{x/3}}^{1} e^{y^3}\, dy\, dx$

38. $\int_0^8 \int_{\sqrt[3]{x}}^{2} \frac{dy\, dx}{y^4 + 1}$

39. Find the volume of the solid whose base is the region in the xy-plane that is bounded by the parabola $y = 4 - x^2$ and the line $y = 3x$, while the top of the solid is bounded by the plane $z = x + 4$.

40. Find the volume of the solid in the first octant bounded by the coordinate planes, the cylinder $x^2 + y^2 = 4$, and the plane $z + y = 3$.

41. Find the volume of the solid in the first octant bounded by the coordinate planes, the plane $x = 3$, and the parabolic cylinder $z = 4 - y^2$.

42. Find the volume of the solid cut from the first octant by the surface $z = 4 - x^2 - y$.

43. Find the volume of the region that lies under the paraboloid $z = x^2 + y^2$ and above the triangle enclosed by the lines $y = x$, $x = 0$, and $x + y = 2$ in the xy-plane.

44. Find the volume of the solid that is bounded above by the parabolic cylinder (trough) $z = x^2$ and below by the region enclosed by the coordinate axes and the parabola $y = 4 - x^2$ in the first quadrant of the xy-plane.

45. What region R in the xy-plane maximizes the value of

$$\iint_R (4 - x^2 - 2y^2)\, dA?$$

Give reasons for your answer.

46. What region R in the xy-plane minimizes the value of

$$\iint_R (x^2 + y^2 - 9)\, dA?$$

Give reasons for your answer.

47. Is it all right to evaluate the integral of a continuous function $f(x, y)$ over a rectangular region in the xy-plane and get different answers depending on the order of integration? Give reasons for your answer.

48. How would you evaluate the double integral of a continuous function $f(x, y)$ over the region R in the xy-plane enclosed by the triangle with vertices $(0, 1)$, $(2, 0)$, and $(1, 2)$? Give reasons for your answer.

NUMERICAL EVALUATION

Just as there are methods for evaluating single integrals numerically, there are corresponding methods for the numerical evaluation of double integrals. If you have access to a double-integral evaluator, estimate the values of the integrals in Exercises 49–52.

49. $\int_1^3 \int_1^x \frac{1}{xy}\, dy\, dx$

50. $\int_0^1 \int_0^1 e^{-(x^2+y^2)}\, dy\, dx$

51. $\int_0^1 \int_0^1 \tan^{-1} xy\, dy\, dx$

52. $\int_{-1}^1 \int_0^{\sqrt{1-x^2}} 3\sqrt{1-x^2-y^2}\, dy\, dx$

Writing for Your Own Knowledge

Answer the following questions in writing. Some answers will take only a sentence or two; others may require several paragraphs. Some explanations may also call for graphs or sketches.

1. How do you define the double integral of a continuous function $f(x, y)$ over a closed bounded region in the xy-plane? How do you interpret the area element $dA = dy\, dx$?
2. What properties do double integrals have?
3. How can double integrals be interpreted geometrically?
4. What is Fubini's theorem?
5. How do you find appropriate limits of integration?
6. Why might you prefer one order of integration to another?

EXPLORER PROGRAM

Double Integral Evaluation — Evaluates integrals of the form

$$\int_a^b \int_{g(x)}^{h(x)} f(x, y)\, dy\, dx$$

by a variety of numerical methods.

14.2 *Areas, Moments, and Centers of Mass*

In this section we show how to use double integrals to define and calculate the areas of bounded regions in the plane and the masses, moments, centers of mass, and radii of gyration of thin plates covering these regions. The calculations are similar to the ones in Chapter 7, but now we can handle a greater variety of shapes.

Areas of Bounded Regions in the Plane

If we take $f(x, y) = 1$ in the definition of the double integral over a region R in the preceding section, the partial sums reduce to

$$S_n = \sum_{k=1}^{n} f(x_k, y_k)\Delta A_k = \sum_{k=1}^{n} \Delta A_k. \tag{1}$$

This approximates what we would like to call the area of R. As Δx and Δy approach zero, the coverage of R by the ΔA_k's (Fig. 14.14) becomes increasingly complete, and we define the area of R to be the limit

$$\text{Area} = \lim_{n\to\infty} \sum_{k=1}^{n} \Delta A_k = \iint_R dA. \tag{2}$$

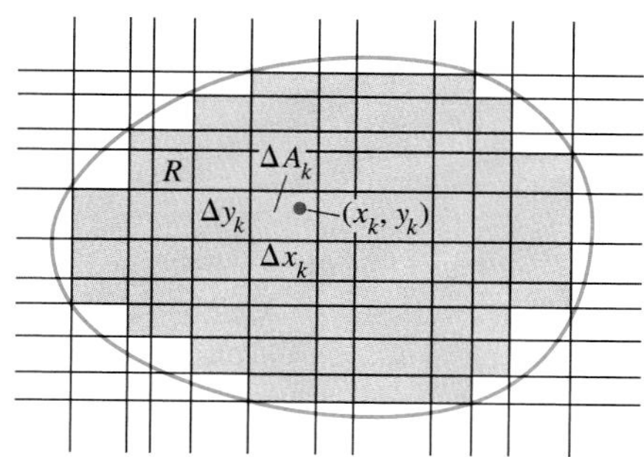

14.14 The first step in defining the area of a region is to partition the interior of the region into cells.

DEFINITION

The **area** of a closed bounded plane region R is

$$A = \iint_R dA. \tag{3}$$

As with the other definitions in this chapter, the definition here applies to a greater variety of regions than does the earlier single-variable definition of area, but it agrees with the earlier definition on regions to which they both apply.

To evaluate the integral in (3), we integrate the constant function $f(x, y) = 1$ over R.

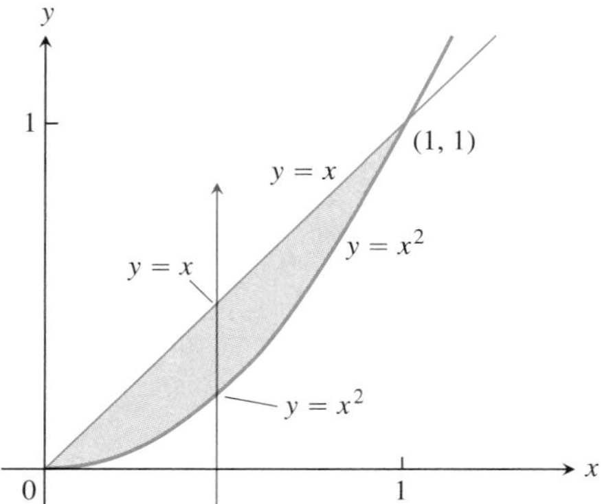

14.15 The area of the region between the parabola and the line in Example 1 is given by the double integral

$$\int_0^1 \int_{x^2}^x dy\, dx.$$

EXAMPLE 1 Find the area of the region R bounded by $y = x$ and $y = x^2$ in the first quadrant.

Solution We sketch the region (Fig. 14.15) and calculate the area as

$$A = \int_0^1 \int_{x^2}^x dy\, dx = \int_0^1 \Big[y\Big]_{x^2}^x dx = \int_0^1 (x - x^2)\, dx = \left[\frac{x^2}{2} - \frac{x^3}{3}\right]_0^1 = \frac{1}{6}.$$

EXAMPLE 2 Find the area of the region R enclosed by the parabola $y = x^2$ and the line $y = x + 2$.

Solution If we divide R into the regions R_1 and R_2 shown in Fig. 14.16a, we may calculate the area as

$$A = \iint_{R_1} dA + \iint_{R_2} dA = \int_0^1 \int_{-\sqrt{y}}^{\sqrt{y}} dx\, dy + \int_1^4 \int_{y-2}^{\sqrt{y}} dx\, dy.$$

On the other hand, reversing the order of integration (Fig. 14.16b) gives

$$A = \int_{-1}^2 \int_{x^2}^{x+2} dy\, dx.$$

This result is simpler and is the only one we would bother to write down in practice. The area is

$$A = \int_{-1}^2 \Big[y\Big]_{x^2}^{x+2} dx = \int_{-1}^2 (x + 2 - x^2)\, dx = \left[\frac{x^2}{2} + 2x - \frac{x^3}{3}\right]_{-1}^2 = \frac{9}{2}.$$

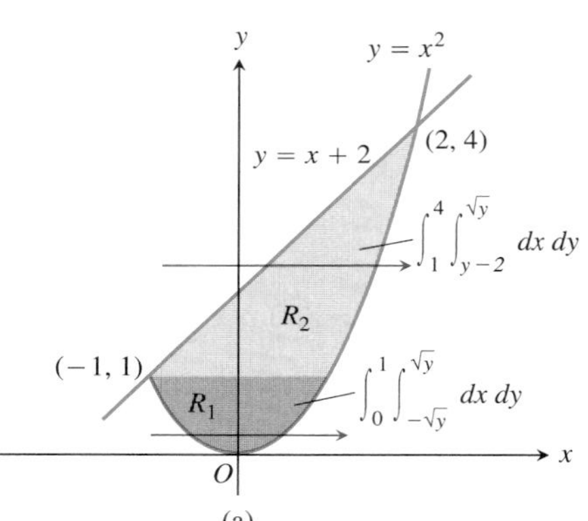

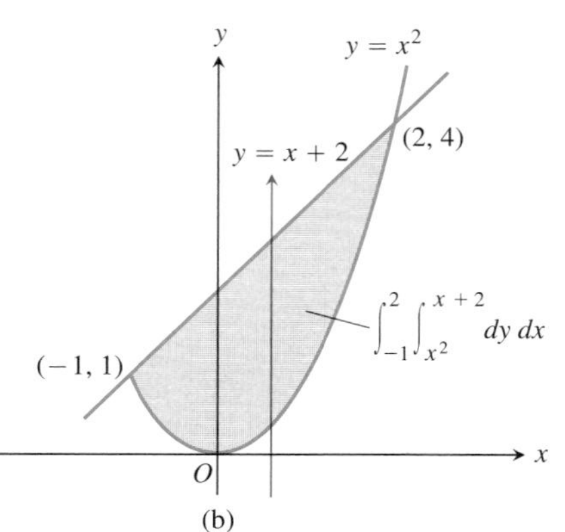

14.16 Calculating this area takes (a) two double integrals if the first integration is with respect to x, but (b) only one if the first integration is with respect to y (Example 2).

Average Value

The average value of an integrable function of a single variable on a closed interval is the integral of the function over the interval divided by the length of the interval. For an integrable function of two variables defined on a closed and bounded region that has a measurable area, the average value is the integral over the region divided by the area of the region. If f is the function and R the region, then

$$\textbf{Average value} \text{ of } f \text{ over } R = \frac{1}{\text{area of } R} \iint_R f\, dA. \tag{4}$$

If f is the area density of a thin plate covering R, then the double integral of f over R divided by the area of R is the plate's average density in units of mass per unit area. If $f(x, y)$ is the distance from the point (x, y) to a fixed point A, then the average value of f over R is the average distance of points in R from A.

EXAMPLE 3 Find the average value of

$$f(x, y) = x \cos xy$$

over the rectangle R: $0 \le x \le \pi$, $0 \le y \le 1$.

Solution The value of the integral of f over R is

$$\int_0^{\pi}\int_0^1 x\cos xy\,dy\,dx = \int_0^{\pi}\Big[\sin xy\Big]_{y=0}^{y=1}dx$$
$$= \int_0^{\pi}(\sin x - 0)\,dx$$
$$= -\cos x\Big]_0^{\pi}$$
$$= 1 + 1 = 2.$$

The area of R is π. The average value of f over R is $2/\pi$.

Moments of inertia are important in calculating the kinetic energies of rotating bodies. They also appear in formulas for the stiffness of beams.

First and Second Moments and Centers of Mass

To find the moments and centers of mass of thin sheets and plates, we use formulas similar to those in Chapter 7. The new formulas are given in Table 14.1.

The mathematical difference between the **first moments** M_x and M_y and the **moments of inertia,** or **second moments,** I_x and I_y is that the second moments use the *squares* of the "lever-arm" distances x and y.

The moment I_0 is also called the **polar moment** of inertia about the origin. It is calculated by integrating the density $\delta(x, y)$ times $r^2 = x^2 + y^2$, the square of the distance from a representative point (x, y) to the origin. Notice that $I_0 = I_x + I_y$; once we find two, we get the third free. (The moment I_0 is sometimes called I_z, for moment of inertia about the z-axis. The identity $I_z = I_x + I_y$ is then called the **Perpendicular Axis Theorem.**)

TABLE 14.1
Mass and moment formulas for thin plates covering regions in the xy-plane

Density: $\delta(x, y)$

Mass: $M = \iint \delta(x, y)\,dA$

First moments: $M_x = \iint y\delta(x, y)\,dA, \quad M_y = \iint x\delta(x, y)\,dA$

Center of mass: $\bar{x} = \dfrac{M_y}{M}, \quad \bar{y} = \dfrac{M_x}{M}$

Moments of inertia (second moments):

About the x-axis: $I_x = \iint y^2\delta(x, y)\,dA$

About the y-axis: $I_y = \iint x^2\,\delta(x, y)\,dA$

About the origin: $I_0 = \iint (x^2 + y^2)\,\delta(x, y)\,dA = I_x + I_y$

Radii of gyration:
About the x-axis: $R_x = \sqrt{I_x/M}$
About the y-axis: $R_y = \sqrt{I_y/M}$
About the origin: $R_0 = \sqrt{I_0/M}$

The examples that follow show how these formulas are used.

The **radius of gyration** R_x is defined by the equation

$$I_x = MR_x^2.$$

It tells how far from the x-axis the entire mass of the plate might be concentrated to give the same I_x. The radius of gyration gives a convenient way to express the moment of inertia in terms of a mass and a length. The radii R_y and R_0 are defined in a similar way:

$$I_y = MR_y^2 \qquad \text{and} \qquad I_0 = MR_0^2.$$

We take square roots to get the formulas in Table 14.1.

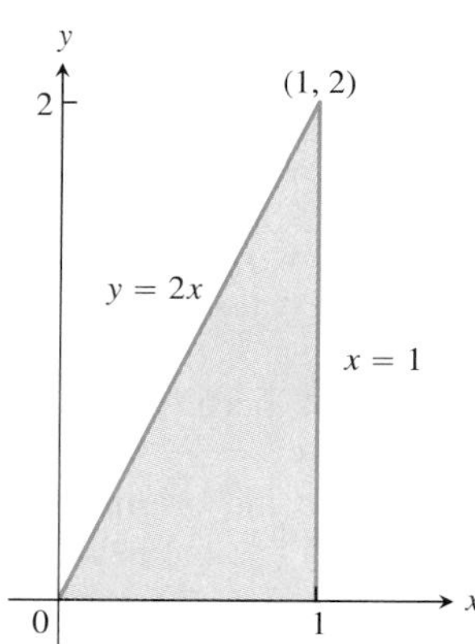

14.17 The triangular region covered by the plate in Example 4.

EXAMPLE 4 A thin plate covers the region bounded by the x-axis and the lines $x = 1$ and $y = 2x$ in the first quadrant. The plate's density at the point (x, y) is $\delta(x, y) = 6x + 6y + 6$. Find the plate's mass, first moments, center of mass, moments of inertia, and radii of gyration about the coordinate axes.

Solution We sketch the plate to find the limits of integration (Fig. 14.17).

The plate's mass is

$$\begin{aligned} M &= \int_0^1 \int_0^{2x} \delta(x, y)\, dy\, dx = \int_0^1 \int_0^{2x} (6x + 6y + 6)\, dy\, dx \\ &= \int_0^1 \Big[6xy + 3y^2 + 6y \Big]_{y=0}^{y=2x} dx = \int_0^1 (24x^2 + 12x)\, dx = \Big[8x^3 + 6x^2 \Big]_0^1 \\ &= 14. \end{aligned}$$

The first moment about the x-axis is

$$\begin{aligned} M_x &= \int_0^1 \int_0^{2x} y\delta(x, y)\, dy\, dx = \int_0^1 \int_0^{2x} (6xy + 6y^2 + 6y)\, dy\, dx \\ &= \int_0^1 \Big[3xy^2 + 2y^3 + 3y^2 \Big]_{y=0}^{y=2x} dx = \int_0^1 (28x^3 + 12x^2)\, dx \\ &= \Big[7x^4 + 4x^3 \Big]_0^1 = 11. \end{aligned}$$

A similar calculation gives

$$M_y = \int_0^1 \int_0^{2x} x\delta(x, y)\, dy\, dx = 10.$$

The coordinates of the center of mass are therefore

$$\bar{x} = \frac{M_y}{M} = \frac{10}{14} = \frac{5}{7}, \qquad \bar{y} = \frac{M_x}{M} = \frac{11}{14}.$$

The moment of inertia about the x-axis is

$$\begin{aligned} I_x &= \int_0^1 \int_0^{2x} y^2\delta(x, y)\, dy\, dx = \int_0^1 \int_0^{2x} (6xy^2 + 6y^3 + 6y^2)\, dy\, dx \\ &= \int_0^1 \Big[2xy^3 + \frac{3}{2}y^4 + 2y^3 \Big]_{y=0}^{y=2x} dx = \int_0^1 (40x^4 + 16x^3)\, dx \\ &= \Big[8x^5 + 4x^4 \Big]_0^1 = 12. \end{aligned}$$

Similarly, the moment of inertia about the y-axis is

$$I_y = \int_0^1 \int_0^{2x} x^2 \delta(x, y)\, dy\, dx = \frac{39}{5}.$$

Since we know I_x and I_y, we do not need to evaluate an integral to find I_0; we can use the equation $I_0 = I_x + I_y$ instead:

$$I_0 = 12 + \frac{39}{5} = \frac{60 + 39}{5} = \frac{99}{5}.$$

The three radii of gyration are

$$R_x = \sqrt{I_x/M} = \sqrt{12/14} = \sqrt{6/7},$$

$$R_y = \sqrt{I_y/M} = \sqrt{\left(\frac{39}{5}\right)/14} = \sqrt{39/70},$$

$$R_0 = \sqrt{I_0/M} = \sqrt{\left(\frac{99}{5}\right)/14} = \sqrt{99/70}.$$

Centroids of Geometric Figures

When the density of an object is constant, it cancels out of the numerator and denominator of the formulas for $\bar{x}$ and $\bar{y}$. Thus, when δ is constant, the location of the center of mass becomes a feature of the object's shape and not of the material of which it is made. In such cases, engineers may call the center of mass the **centroid** of the shape. To find a centroid, we just set δ equal to 1 and proceed to find $\bar{x}$ and $\bar{y}$ as before, by dividing first moments by masses.

EXAMPLE 5 Find the centroid of the region in the first quadrant that is bounded above by the line $y = x$ and below by the parabola $y = x^2$.

Solution We sketch the region and include enough detail to determine the limits of integration (Fig. 14.18). We then set δ equal to 1 and evaluate the appropriate formulas from Table 14.1:

$$M = \int_0^1 \int_{x^2}^{x} 1\, dy\, dx = \int_0^1 \Big[y \Big]_{y=x^2}^{y=x} dx = \int_0^1 (x - x^2)\, dx = \left[\frac{x^2}{2} - \frac{x^3}{3}\right]_0^1 = \frac{1}{6},$$

$$M_x = \int_0^1 \int_{x^2}^{x} y\, dy\, dx = \int_0^1 \left[\frac{y^2}{2}\right]_{y=x^2}^{y=x} dx = \int_0^1 \left(\frac{x^2}{2} - \frac{x^4}{2}\right) dx = \left[\frac{x^3}{6} - \frac{x^5}{10}\right]_0^1$$
$$= \frac{1}{15},$$

$$M_y = \int_0^1 \int_{x^2}^{x} x\, dy\, dx = \int_0^1 \Big[xy \Big]_{y=x^2}^{y=x} dx = \int_0^1 (x^2 - x^3)\, dx = \left[\frac{x^3}{3} - \frac{x^4}{4}\right]_0^1$$
$$= \frac{1}{12}.$$

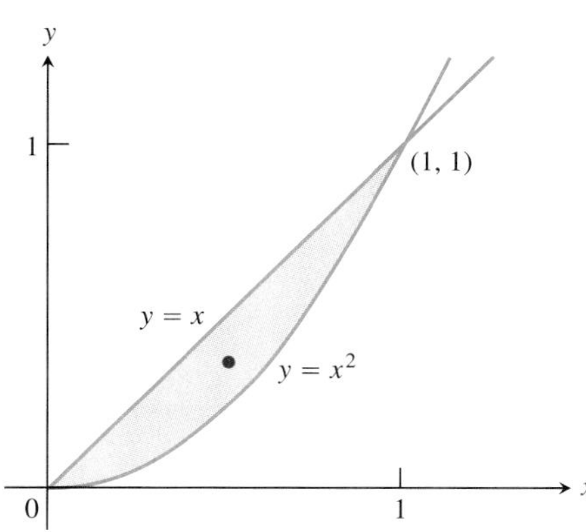

14.18 Example 5 calculates the coordinates of the centroid of the region shown here.

From these values of M, M_x, and M_y, we find

$$\bar{x} = \frac{M_y}{M} = \frac{1/12}{1/6} = \frac{1}{2} \quad \text{and} \quad \bar{y} = \frac{M_x}{M} = \frac{1/15}{1/6} = \frac{2}{5}.$$

The centroid is the point $\left(\frac{1}{2}, \frac{2}{5}\right)$.

Exercises 14.2

In Exercises 1–8, sketch the region bounded by the given lines and curves. Then express the region's area as an iterated double integral and evaluate the integral.

1. The coordinate axes and the line $x + y = 2$
2. The lines $x = 0$, $y = 2x$, and $y = 4$
3. The parabola $x = -y^2$ and the line $y = x + 2$
4. The parabola $x = y - y^2$ and the line $y = -x$
5. The curve $y = e^x$ and the lines $y = 0$, $x = 0$, and $x = \ln 2$
6. The curves $y = \ln x$ and $y = 2 \ln x$ and the line $x = e$, in the first quadrant
7. The parabolas $x = y^2$ and $x = 2y - y^2$
8. The parabolas $x = y^2 - 1$ and $x = 2y^2 - 2$

The integrals and sums of integrals in Exercises 9–14 give the areas of regions in the xy-plane. Sketch each region, label each bounding curve with its equation, and give the coordinates of the points where the curves intersect. Then find the area of the region.

9. $\int_0^6 \int_{y^2/3}^{2y} dx\, dy$
10. $\int_0^3 \int_{-x}^{x(2-x)} dy\, dx$
11. $\int_0^{\pi/4} \int_{\sin x}^{\cos x} dy\, dx$
12. $\int_{-1}^2 \int_{y^2}^{y+2} dx\, dy$
13. $\int_{-1}^0 \int_{-2x}^{1-x} dy\, dx + \int_0^2 \int_{-x/2}^{1-x} dy\, dx$
14. $\int_0^2 \int_{x^2-4}^0 dy\, dx + \int_0^4 \int_0^{\sqrt{x}} dy\, dx$
15. Find the average value of $f(x, y) = \sin(x + y)$ over
    a) the rectangle $0 \le x \le \pi$, $0 \le y \le \pi$;
    b) the rectangle $0 \le x \le \pi$, $0 \le y \le \pi/2$.
16. Which do you think will be larger, the average value of $f(x, y) = xy$ over the square $0 \le x \le 1$, $0 \le y \le 1$, or the average value of f over the quarter circle $x^2 + y^2 \le 1$ in the first quadrant? Calculate them to find out.
17. Find the average height of the paraboloid $z = x^2 + y^2$ over the square $0 \le x \le 2$, $0 \le y \le 2$.
18. Find the average value of $f(x, y) = 1/(xy)$ over the square $\ln 2 \le x \le 2 \ln 2$, $\ln 2 \le y \le 2 \ln 2$.
19. Find the center of mass of a thin plate of density $\delta = 3$ bounded by the lines $x = 0$, $y = x$, and the parabola $y = 2 - x^2$ in the first quadrant.
20. Find the moments of inertia and radii of gyration about the coordinate axes of a thin rectangular plate of constant density δ bounded by the lines $x = 3$ and $y = 3$ in the first quadrant.
21. Find the centroid of the region in the first quadrant bounded by the x-axis, the parabola $y^2 = 2x$, and the line $x + y = 4$.
22. Find the centroid of the triangular region cut from the first quadrant by the line $x + y = 3$.
23. Find the centroid of the semicircular region bounded by the x-axis and the curve $y = \sqrt{1 - x^2}$.
24. The area of the region in the first quadrant bounded by the parabola $y = 6x - x^2$ and the line $y = x$ is 125/6 square units. Find the centroid.
25. Find the centroid of the region cut from the first quadrant by the circle $x^2 + y^2 = a^2$.
26. Find the moment of inertia about the x-axis of a thin plate of density $\delta = 1$ bounded by the circle $x^2 + y^2 = 4$. Then use your result to find I_y and I_0 for the plate.
27. Find the centroid of the region between the x-axis and the arch $y = \sin x$, $0 \le x \le \pi$.
28. Find the moment of inertia with respect to the y-axis of a thin sheet of constant density $\delta = 1$ bounded by the curve $y = (\sin^2 x)/x^2$ and the interval $\pi \le x \le 2\pi$ of the x-axis.
29. *The Centroid of an Infinite Region.* Find the centroid of the infinite region in the second quadrant enclosed by the coordinate axes and the curve $y = e^x$. (Use improper integrals in the mass-moment formulas.)
30. *The First Moment of an Infinite Plate.* Find the first moment about the y-axis of a thin plate of density $\delta(x, y) = 1$ covering the infinite region under the curve $y = e^{-x^2/2}$ in the first quadrant.
31. Find the moment of inertia and radius of gyration about the x-axis of a thin plate bounded by the parabola $x = y - y^2$ and the line $x + y = 0$ if $\delta(x, y) = x + y$.
32. Find the mass of a thin plate occupying the smaller region cut from the ellipse $x^2 + 4y^2 = 12$ by the parabola $x = 4y^2$ if $\delta(x, y) = 5x$.
33. Find the center of mass of a thin triangular plate bounded by the y-axis and the lines $y = x$ and $y = 2 - x$ if $\delta(x, y) = 6x + 3y + 3$.
34. Find the center of mass and moment of inertia about the x-axis of a thin plate bounded by the curves $x = y^2$ and $x = 2y - y^2$ if the density at the point (x, y) is $\delta(x, y) = y + 1$.
35. Find the center of mass and the moment of inertia and radius of gyration about the y-axis of a thin rectangular plate cut from the first quadrant by the lines $x = 6$ and $y = 1$ if $\delta(x, y) = x + y + 1$.
36. Find the center of mass and the moment of inertia and radius of gyration about the y-axis of a thin plate bounded by the line $y = 1$ and the parabola $y = x^2$ if the density is $\delta(x, y) = y + 1$.
37. Find the center of mass and the moment of inertia and radius of gyration about the y-axis of a thin plate bounded by the x-axis, the lines $x = \pm 1$, and the parabola $y = x^2$ if $\delta(x, y) = 7y + 1$.
38. Find the center of mass and moment of inertia and radius of

gyration about the x-axis of a thin rectangular plate bounded by the lines $x = 0$, $x = 20$, $y = -1$, and $y = 1$ if $\delta(x, y) = 1 + (x/20)$.

39. Find the center of mass, the moments of inertia and radii of gyration about the coordinate axes, and the polar moment of inertia and radius of gyration of a thin triangular plate bounded by the lines $y = x$, $y = -x$, and $y = 1$ if $\delta(x, y) = y + 1$.

40. Repeat Exercise 39 for $\delta(x, y) = 3x^2 + 1$.

41. *Appliance Design.* When we design an appliance, one of the concerns is how hard the appliance will be to tip over. When tipped, it will right itself as long as its center of mass lies on the correct side of the *fulcrum,* the point on which the appliance is riding as it tips. Suppose the profile of an appliance of approximately constant density is parabolic, like an old-fashioned radio. It fills the region $0 \le y \le a(1 - x^2)$, $-1 \le x \le 1$, in the xy-plane (Fig. 14.19). What values of a will guarantee that the appliance will have to be tipped more than 45° to fall over?

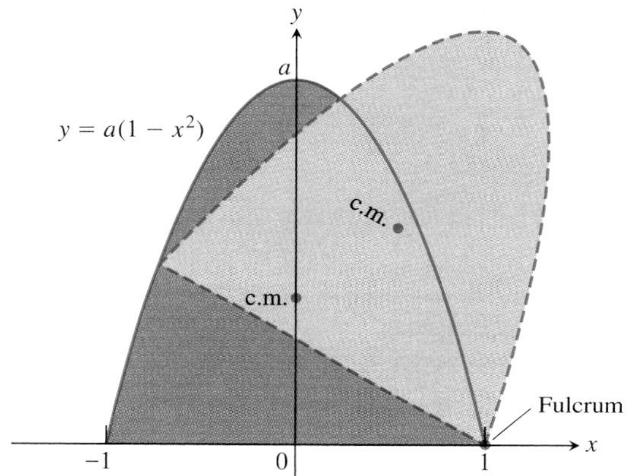

14.19 The profile of the appliance in Exercise 41.

42. *Minimizing a Moment of Inertia.* A rectangular plate of constant density $\delta(x, y) = 1$ occupies the region bounded by the lines $x = 4$ and $y = 2$ in the first quadrant. The moment of inertia I_a of the rectangle about the line $y = a$ is given by the integral

$$I_a = \int_0^4 \int_0^2 (y - a)^2 \, dy \, dx.$$

Find the value of a that minimizes I_a.

Writing for Your Own Knowledge

Answer the following questions in writing. Some answers will take only a sentence or two; others may require several paragraphs. Some explanations may also call for graphs or sketches.

1. How do you use double integrals to calculate areas, masses, moments, centers of mass, and radii of gyration?
2. What is the average value of a continuous function over a closed bounded region in the plane?
3. What is a centroid?

14.3 *Double Integrals in Polar Form*

Integrals are sometimes easier to evaluate if we change to polar coordinates. This section shows how to accomplish the change and how to evaluate integrals over regions whose boundaries are given by polar equations.

Integrals in Polar Coordinates

When we defined the double integral of a function over a region R in the xy-plane, we began by cutting R into rectangles whose sides were parallel to the coordinate axes. These were the natural shapes to use because their sides have either constant x-values or constant y-values. In polar coordinates, the natural shape is a "polar rectangle" whose sides have constant r- and θ-values.

Suppose that a function $f(r, \theta)$ is defined over a region R that is bounded by the rays $\theta = \alpha$ and $\theta = \beta$ and by the continuous curves $r = g_1(\theta)$ and $r = g_2(\theta)$. Suppose also that $0 \le g_1(\theta) \le g_2(\theta) \le a$ for every value of θ between α and β. Then R lies in a fan-shaped region Q defined by the inequalities $0 \le r \le a$ and $\alpha \le \theta \le \beta$. See Fig. 14.20 on the following page.

We cover Q by a grid of circular arcs and rays. The arcs are cut from circles centered at the origin, with radii $\Delta r, 2\Delta r, \ldots, m\Delta r$, where $\Delta r = a/m$. The rays

14.20 The region $R: g_1(\theta) \le r \le g_2(\theta)$, $\alpha \le \theta \le \beta$ is contained in the fan-shaped region $Q: 0 \le r \le a$, $\alpha \le \theta \le \beta$. The partition of Q by circular arcs and rays induces a partition of R.

are given by

$$\theta = \alpha, \quad \theta = \alpha + \Delta\theta, \quad \theta = \alpha + 2\Delta\theta, \quad \ldots, \quad \theta = \alpha + m'\Delta\theta = \beta,$$

where $\Delta\theta = (\beta - \alpha)/m'$. The arcs and rays partition Q into small patches called "polar rectangles."

We number the polar rectangles that lie inside R (the order does not matter), calling their areas $\Delta A_1, \quad \Delta A_2, \quad \ldots, \quad \Delta A_n$.

We let (r_k, θ_k) be the center of the polar rectangle whose area is ΔA_k. By "center" we mean the point that lies halfway between the circular arcs on the ray that bisects the arcs. We then form the sum

$$S_n = \sum_{k=1}^{n} f(r_k, \theta_k)\Delta A_k. \tag{1}$$

If f is continuous throughout R, this sum will approach a limit as we refine the grid to make Δr and $\Delta\theta$ go to zero. The limit is called the double integral of f over R. In symbols,

$$\lim_{n\to\infty} S_n = \iint_R f(r, \theta)\, dA.$$

To evaluate this limit, we first have to write the sum S_n in a way that expresses ΔA_k in terms of Δr and $\Delta\theta$. The radius of the inner arc bounding ΔA_k is $r_k - (\Delta r/2)$ (Fig. 14.21). The radius of the outer arc is $r_k + (\Delta r/2)$. The areas of the circular sectors subtended by these arcs at the origin are

$$\text{inner radius: } \frac{1}{2}\left(r_k - \frac{\Delta r}{2}\right)^2 \Delta\theta \qquad \text{outer radius: } \frac{1}{2}\left(r_k + \frac{\Delta r}{2}\right)^2 \Delta\theta. \tag{2}$$

Therefore,

$$\begin{aligned}\Delta A_k &= \text{Area of large sector} - \text{Area of small sector} \\ &= \frac{\Delta\theta}{2}\left[\left(r_k + \frac{\Delta r}{2}\right)^2 - \left(r_k - \frac{\Delta r}{2}\right)^2\right] = \frac{\Delta\theta}{2}(2r_k\,\Delta r) = r_k \Delta r \Delta\theta.\end{aligned}$$

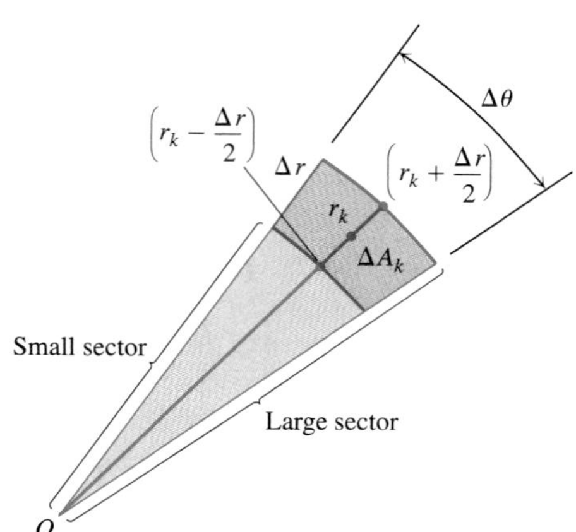

14.21 The observation that

$$\Delta A_k = \begin{pmatrix}\text{area of} \\ \text{large sector}\end{pmatrix} - \begin{pmatrix}\text{area of} \\ \text{small sector}\end{pmatrix}$$

leads to the formula $\Delta A_k = r_k \Delta r \Delta\theta$. The text explains why.

Combining this result with Eq. (1) gives

$$S_n = \sum_{k=1}^{n} f(r_k, \theta_k) r_k \Delta r \Delta\theta. \tag{3}$$

A version of Fubini's theorem now says that the limit approached by these sums can be evaluated by repeated single integrations with respect to r and θ as

$$\iint_R f(r, \theta)\, dA = \int_{\theta=\alpha}^{\theta=\beta} \int_{r=g_1(\theta)}^{r=g_2(\theta)} f(r, \theta)\, r\, dr\, d\theta. \tag{4}$$

Limits of Integration

The procedure for finding limits of integration in rectangular coordinates also works for polar coordinates.

How to Integrate in Polar Coordinates

To evaluate $\iint_R f(r, \theta)\, dA$ over a region R in polar coordinates, integrating first with respect to r and then with respect to θ, take the following steps.

1. *A sketch.* Sketch the region and label the bounding curves.

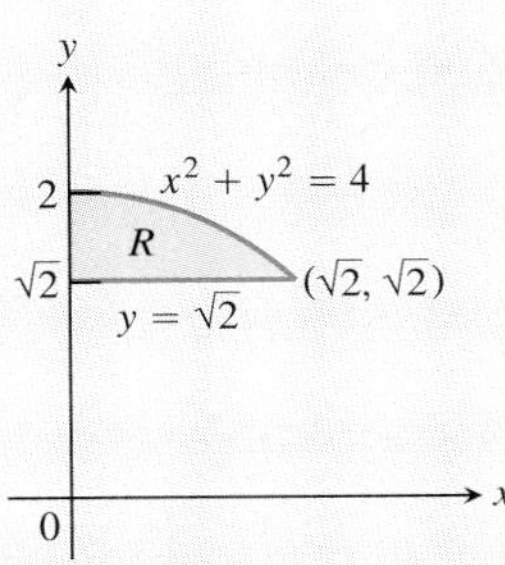

2. *The r-limits of integration.* Imagine a ray L from the origin cutting through R in the direction of increasing r. Mark the r-values where L enters and leaves R. These are the r-limits of integration. They usually depend on the angle θ that L makes with the positive x-axis.

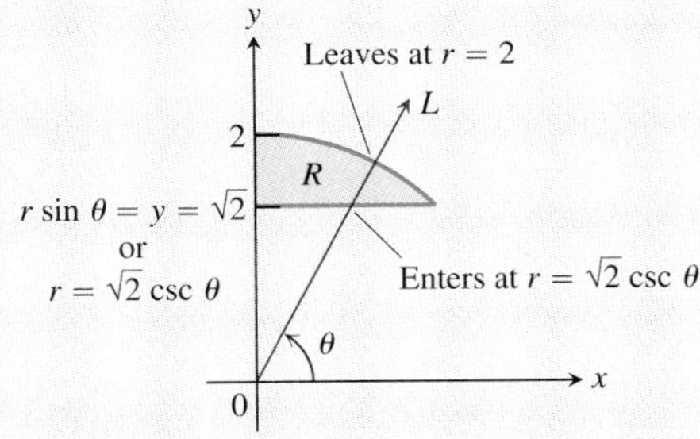

3. *The θ-limits of integration.* Find the smallest and largest θ-values that bound R. These are the θ-limits of integration.

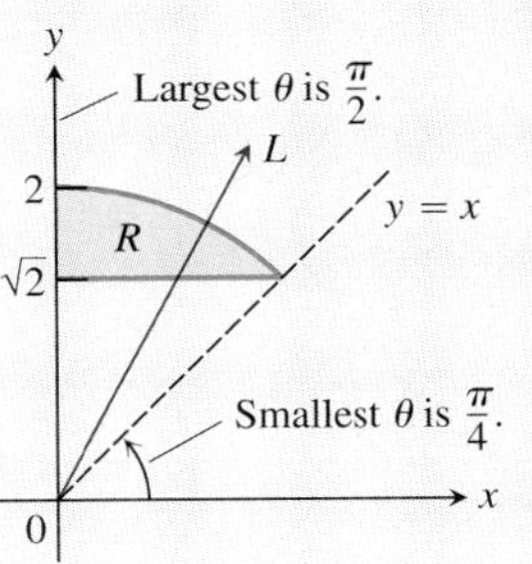

The integral is

$$\iint_R f(r, \theta)\, dA = \int_{\theta=\pi/4}^{\theta=\pi/2} \int_{r=\sqrt{2}\csc\theta}^{r=2} f(r, \theta)\, r\, dr\, d\theta.$$

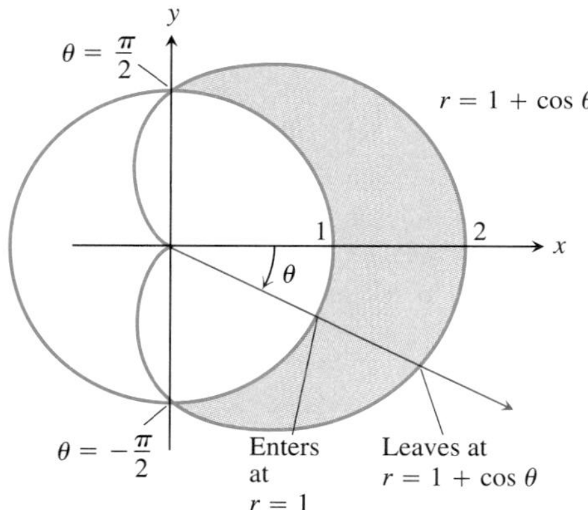

14.22 The sketch for Example 1.

EXAMPLE 1 Find the limits of integration for integrating $f(r, \theta)$ over the region R that lies inside the cardioid $r = 1 + \cos\theta$ and outside the circle $r = 1$.

Solution

STEP 1: *A sketch.* We sketch the region and label the bounding curves (Fig. 14.22).

STEP 2: *The r-limits of integration.* A typical ray from the origin enters R where $r = 1$ and leaves where $r = 1 + \cos\theta$.

STEP 3: *The θ-limits of integration.* The rays from the origin that intersect R run from $\theta = -\pi/2$ to $\theta = \pi/2$. The integral is

$$\int_{-\pi/2}^{\pi/2}\int_{1}^{1+\cos\theta} f(r, \theta)\, r\, dr\, d\theta.$$

If $f(r, \theta)$ is the constant function whose value is 1, then the integral of f over R is the area of R.

Area in Polar Coordinates

The area of a closed and bounded region R in the polar coordinate plane is

$$A = \iint_R r\, dr\, d\theta. \tag{5}$$

As you might expect, this formula for area is consistent with all earlier formulas, although we will not prove the fact.

EXAMPLE 2 Find the area enclosed by the lemniscate $r^2 = 4\cos 2\theta$.

Solution We graph the lemniscate to determine the limits of integration (Fig. 14.23) and see that the total area is four times the first-quadrant portion.

$$\begin{aligned} A &= 4\int_0^{\pi/4}\int_0^{\sqrt{4\cos 2\theta}} r\, dr\, d\theta = 4\int_0^{\pi/4}\left[\frac{r^2}{2}\right]_{r=0}^{r=\sqrt{4\cos 2\theta}} d\theta \\ &= 4\int_0^{\pi/4} 2\cos 2\theta\, d\theta = 4\sin 2\theta\Big]_0^{\pi/4} = 4. \end{aligned}$$

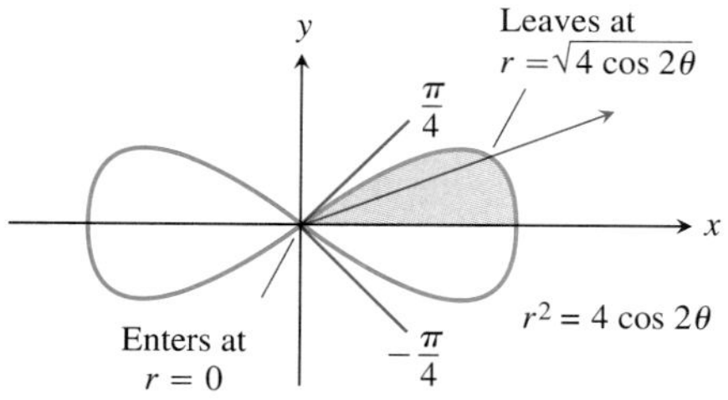

14.23 To integrate over the shaded region, we run r from 0 to $\sqrt{4\cos 2\theta}$ and θ from 0 to $\pi/4$ (Example 2).

Changing Cartesian Integrals into Polar Integrals

The procedure for changing a Cartesian integral $\iint_R f(x, y)\, dx\, dy$ into a polar integral has two steps.

STEP 1: Substitute $x = r\cos\theta$ and $y = r\sin\theta$, and replace $dx\, dy$ by $r\, dr\, d\theta$ in the Cartesian integral.

STEP 2: Supply polar limits of integration for the boundary of R.

The Cartesian integral then becomes

$$\iint_R f(x, y)\, dx\, dy = \iint_G f(r\cos\theta, r\sin\theta)\, r\, dr\, d\theta, \tag{6}$$

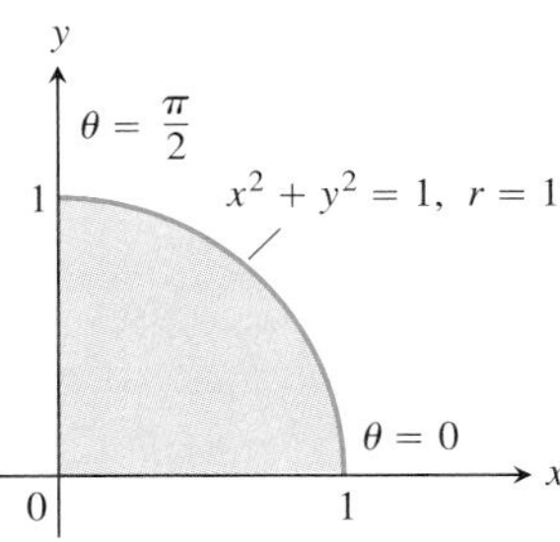

14.24 In polar coordinates, this region is described by simple inequalities:

$0 \le r \le 1$ and $0 \le \theta \le \pi/2$

(Example 3).

where G denotes the region of integration in polar coordinates. This is like the substitution method in Chapter 5 except that there are now two variables to substitute for instead of one. Notice that $dx\,dy$ is not replaced by $dr\,d\theta$ but by $r\,dr\,d\theta$. We will see why in Section 14.7.

EXAMPLE 3 Find the polar moment of inertia about the origin of a thin plate of density $\delta(x, y) = 1$ bounded by the quarter circle $x^2 + y^2 = 1$ in the first quadrant.

Solution We sketch the region of integration to determine the limits of integration (Fig. 14.24).

In Cartesian coordinates, the polar moment is the value of the integral

$$\int_0^1 \int_0^{\sqrt{1-x^2}} (x^2 + y^2)\,dy\,dx.$$

Integration with respect to y gives

$$\int_0^1 \left(x^2\sqrt{1 - x^2} + \frac{(1 - x^2)^{3/2}}{3} \right) dx,$$

an integral difficult to evaluate without tables.

Things go better if we change the original integral to polar coordinates. Substituting $x = r\cos\theta$, $y = r\sin\theta$, and replacing $dx\,dy$ by $r\,dr\,d\theta$, we get

$$\int_0^1 \int_0^{\sqrt{1-x^2}} (x^2 + y^2)\,dy\,dx = \int_0^{\pi/2} \int_0^1 (r^2)\,r\,dr\,d\theta$$

$$= \int_0^{\pi/2} \left[\frac{r^4}{4} \right]_{r=0}^{r=1} d\theta = \int_0^{\pi/2} \frac{1}{4}\,d\theta = \frac{\pi}{8}.$$

Why is the polar coordinate transformation so effective? One reason is $x^2 + y^2$ simplifies to r^2. Another is the limits of integration become constants.

EXAMPLE 4 Evaluate

$$\iint_R e^{x^2 + y^2}\,dy\,dx,$$

where R is the semicircular region bounded by the x-axis and the curve $y = \sqrt{1 - x^2}$ (Fig. 14.25).

Solution In Cartesian coordinates, the integral in question is a nonelementary integral and there is no direct way to integrate $e^{x^2 + y^2}$ with respect to either x or y. Yet this integral and others like it are important in mathematics—in statistics, for example—and we must find a way to evaluate it. Polar coordinates save the day. Substituting $x = r\cos\theta$, $y = r\sin\theta$, and replacing $dy\,dx$ by $r\,dr\,d\theta$ enables us to evaluate the integral as

$$\iint_R e^{x^2 + y^2}\,dy\,dx = \int_0^{\pi} \int_0^1 e^{r^2}\,r\,dr\,d\theta = \int_0^{\pi} \left[\frac{1}{2} e^{r^2} \right]_0^1 d\theta$$

$$= \int_0^{\pi} \frac{1}{2}(e - 1)\,d\theta = \frac{\pi}{2}(e - 1).$$

The r in the $r\,dr\,d\theta$ was just what we needed to integrate e^{r^2}. Without it we would have been stuck, as we were at the beginning.

14.25 The semicircular region in Example 4 is the region

$0 \le r \le 1$, $0 \le \theta \le \pi$.

Exercises 14.3

In Exercises 1–16, change the Cartesian integral into an equivalent polar integral. Then evaluate the polar integral.

1. $\int_{-1}^{1}\int_{0}^{\sqrt{1-x^2}} dy\,dx$

2. $\int_{-1}^{1}\int_{-\sqrt{1-x^2}}^{\sqrt{1-x^2}} dy\,dx$

3. $\int_{0}^{1}\int_{0}^{\sqrt{1-y^2}} (x^2+y^2)\,dx\,dy$

4. $\int_{-1}^{1}\int_{-\sqrt{1-y^2}}^{\sqrt{1-y^2}} (x^2+y^2)\,dx\,dy$

5. $\int_{-a}^{a}\int_{-\sqrt{a^2-x^2}}^{\sqrt{a^2-x^2}} dy\,dx$

6. $\int_{0}^{2}\int_{0}^{\sqrt{4-y^2}} (x^2+y^2)\,dx\,dy$

7. $\int_{0}^{6}\int_{0}^{y} x\,dx\,dy$

8. $\int_{0}^{2}\int_{0}^{x} y\,dy\,dx$

9. $\int_{-1}^{0}\int_{-\sqrt{1-x^2}}^{0} \frac{2\,dy\,dx}{1+\sqrt{x^2+y^2}}$

10. $\int_{-1}^{1}\int_{-\sqrt{1-y^2}}^{0} \frac{4\sqrt{x^2+y^2}\,dx\,dy}{1+x^2+y^2}$

11. $\int_{0}^{\ln 2}\int_{0}^{\sqrt{(\ln 2)^2-y^2}} e^{\sqrt{x^2+y^2}}\,dx\,dy$

12. $\int_{0}^{1}\int_{0}^{\sqrt{1-x^2}} e^{-(x^2+y^2)}\,dy\,dx$

13. $\int_{0}^{2}\int_{0}^{\sqrt{1-(x-1)^2}} 3\,xy\,dy\,dx$

14. $\int_{0}^{2}\int_{-\sqrt{1-(y-1)^2}}^{0} xy^2\,dx\,dy$

15. $\int_{-1}^{1}\int_{-\sqrt{1-y^2}}^{\sqrt{1-y^2}} \ln(x^2+y^2+1)\,dx\,dy$

16. $\int_{-1}^{1}\int_{-\sqrt{1-x^2}}^{\sqrt{1-x^2}} \frac{2\,dy\,dx}{(1+x^2+y^2)^2}$

17. Find the area of the region cut from the first quadrant by the curve $r = 2(2 - \sin 2\theta)^{1/2}$.

18. Find the area of the region that lies inside the cardioid $r = 1 + \cos\theta$ and outside the circle $r = 1$.

19. Find the area enclosed by one leaf of the rose $r = 12\cos 3\theta$.

20. Find the area of the region enclosed by the positive x-axis and spiral $r = 4\theta/3$, $0 \le \theta \le 2\pi$. The region looks like a snail shell.

21. Find the area of the region cut from the first quadrant by the cardioid $r = 1 + \sin\theta$.

22. Find the area of the region common to the interiors of the cardioids $r = 1 + \cos\theta$ and $r = 1 - \cos\theta$.

23. Integrate the function $f(x, y) = 1/(1 - x^2 - y^2)$ over the disk $x^2 + y^2 \le 3/4$.

24. Integrate the function $f(x, y) = [\ln(x^2 + y^2)]/(x^2 + y^2)$ over the region between the circles $x^2 + y^2 = 1$ and $x^2 + y^2 = e^2$.

25. Find the first moment about the x-axis of a thin plate of constant density $\delta(x, y) = 3$, bounded below by the x-axis and above by the cardioid $r = 1 - \cos\theta$.

26. Find the moment of inertia about the x-axis and the polar moment of inertia about the origin of a thin disk bounded by the circle $x^2 + y^2 = a^2$ if the disk's density at the point (x, y) is $\delta(x, y) = k(x^2 + y^2)$, k a constant.

27. Find the mass of a thin plate covering the region outside the circle $r = 3$ and inside the circle $r = 6\sin\theta$ if the plate's density function is $\delta(x, y) = 1/r$.

28. Find the polar moment of inertia about the origin of a thin plate covering the region that lies inside the cardioid $r = 1 - \cos\theta$ and outside the circle $r = 1$ if the plate's density function is $\delta(x, y) = 1/r^2$.

29. Find the centroid of the region enclosed by the cardioid $r = 1 + \cos\theta$.

30. Find the polar moment of inertia about the origin of a thin plate enclosed by the cardioid $r = 1 + \cos\theta$ if the plate's density function is $\delta(x, y) = 1$.

31. Find the average height of the hemisphere $z = \sqrt{a^2 - x^2 - y^2}$ above the disk $x^2 + y^2 \le a^2$ in the xy-plane.

32. Find the average height of the (single) cone $z = \sqrt{x^2 + y^2}$ above the disk $x^2 + y^2 \le a^2$ in the xy-plane.

33. Find the average distance from a point $P(x, y)$ in the disk $x^2 + y^2 \le a^2$ to the origin.

34. Find the average value of the *square* of the distance from the point $P(x, y)$ in the disk $x^2 + y^2 \le 1$ to the boundary point $A(1, 0)$.

Writing for Your Own Knowledge

Answer the following questions in writing. Some answers will take only a sentence or two; others may require several paragraphs. Some explanations may also call for graphs or sketches.

1. How do you define the double integral of a continuous function $f(r, \theta)$ over a region in the polar coordinate plane? How do you interpret the area element $dA = r\,dr\,d\theta$?
2. How do you find the limits of integration for a double integral in polar coordinates?
3. How do you change a Cartesian double integral into an equivalent polar double integral? Why might you want to do this?

14.4 Triple Integrals in Rectangular Coordinates

We use triple integrals to find the volumes of three-dimensional shapes, the masses and moments of solids, and the average values of functions of three variables. In Chapter 15, we will also see how these integrals arise in the studies of vector fields and fluid flow.

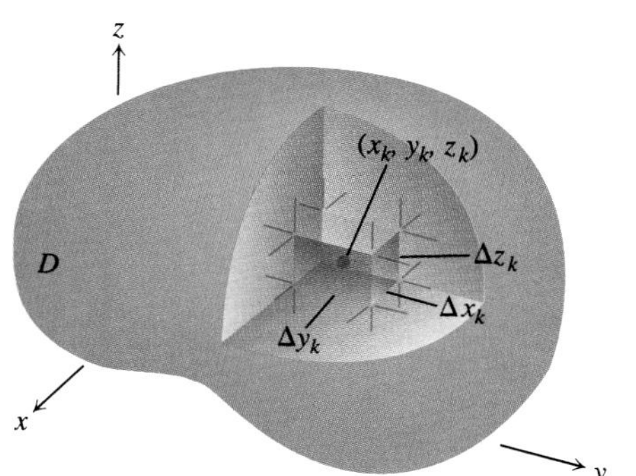

14.26 Partitioning a solid with rectangular cells of volume ΔV_k.

Triple Integrals

If $F(x, y, z)$ is a function defined on a closed bounded region D in space—the region occupied by a solid ball, for example, or a lump of clay—then the integral of F over D may be defined in the following way. We partition a rectangular region containing D into rectangular cells by planes parallel to the coordinate planes (Fig. 14.26). We number the cells that lie inside D from 1 to n in some order, a typical cell having dimensions Δx_k by Δy_k by Δz_k and volume ΔV_k. We choose a point (x_k, y_k, z_k) in each cell and form the sum

$$S_n = \sum_{k=1}^{n} F(x_k, y_k, z_k)\,\Delta V_k. \tag{1}$$

If F is continuous and the bounding surface of D is made of smooth surfaces joined along continuous curves, then as Δx_k, Δy_k, and Δz_k approach zero independently the sums S_n approach a limit

$$\lim_{n\to\infty} S_n = \iiint_D F(x, y, z)\, dV. \tag{2}$$

We call this limit the **triple integral of F over D.** The limit also exists for some discontinuous functions.

Properties of Triple Integrals

Triple integrals have the same algebraic properties as double and single integrals. If $F = F(x, y, z)$ and $G = G(x, y, z)$ are continuous, then

1. $\displaystyle\iiint_D kF\, dV = k\iiint_D F\, dV \qquad \text{(any number } k\text{)}$
2. $\displaystyle\iiint_D (F \pm G)\, dV = \iiint_D F\, dV \pm \iiint_D G\, dV$
3. $\displaystyle\iiint_D F\, dV \ge 0 \qquad \text{if } F \ge 0 \text{ on } D$
4. $\displaystyle\iiint_D F\, dV \ge \iiint_D G\, dV \qquad \text{if } F \ge G \text{ on } D.$

Triple integrals also have an additivity property, used in physics and engineering as well as in mathematics. If the domain D of a continuous function F is partitioned by smooth surfaces into a finite number of nonoverlapping cells D_1, $D_2, \ldots, D_n$, then

5. $\displaystyle\iiint_D F\, dV = \iiint_{D_1} F\, dV + \iiint_{D_2} F\, dV + \cdots + \iiint_{D_n} F\, dV.$

Volume of a Region in Space

If F is the constant function whose value is 1, then the sums in Eq. (1) reduce to

$$S_n = \sum F(x_k, y_k, z_k)\Delta V_k = \sum 1 \cdot \Delta V_k = \sum \Delta V_k. \tag{3}$$

As Δx, Δy, and Δz approach zero, the cells ΔV_k become smaller and more numerous and fill up more and more of D. We therefore define the volume of D to be the triple integral

$$\lim_{n\to\infty} \sum_{k=1}^{n} \Delta V_k = \iiint_D dV.$$

DEFINITION

The **volume** of a closed bounded region D in space is

$$V = \iiint_D dV. \tag{4}$$

As we will see in a moment, this integral enables us to calculate the volumes of solids enclosed by curved surfaces.

Evaluation

We seldom evaluate a triple integral from its definition as a limit. Instead, we apply a three-dimensional version of Fubini's theorem to evaluate it by repeated single integrations. As with double integrals, there is a geometric procedure for finding the limits of integration.

How to Find Limits of Integration in Triple Integrals

To evaluate

$$\iiint_D F(x, y, z)\, dV$$

over a region D, integrating first with respect to z, then with respect to y, finally with x, take the following steps.

1. *A sketch.* Sketch the region D along with its "shadow" R (vertical projection) in the xy-plane. Label the upper and lower bounding surfaces of D and the upper and lower bounding curves of R.

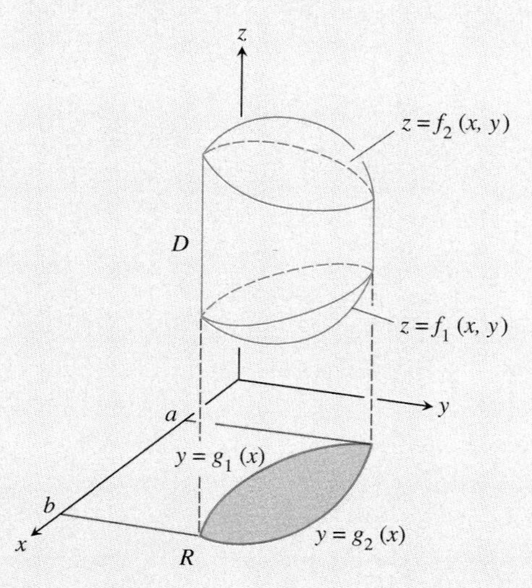

2. *The z-limits of integration.* Draw a line M passing through a typical point (x, y) in R parallel to the z-axis. As z increases, M enters D at $z = f_1(x, y)$ and leaves at $z = f_2(x, y)$. These are the z-limits of integration.

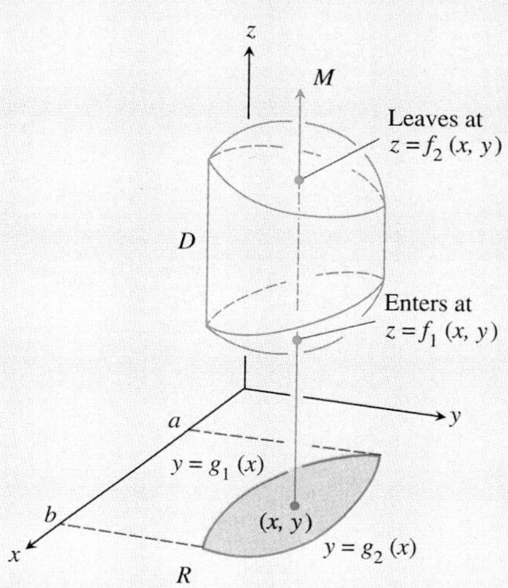

3. *The y-limits of integration.* Draw a line L through (x, y) parallel to the y-axis. As y increases, L enters R at $y = g_1(x)$ and leaves at $y = g_2(x)$. These are the y-limits of integration.

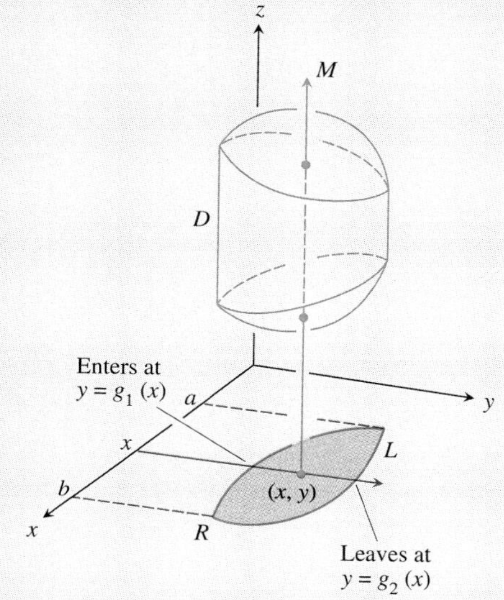

4. *The x-limits of integration.* Choose x-limits that include all lines through R parallel to the y-axis ($x = a$ and $x = b$ in the preceding figure). These are the x-limits of integration. The integral is

$$\int_{x=a}^{x=b} \int_{y=g_1(x)}^{y=g_2(x)} \int_{z=f_1(x,y)}^{z=f_2(x,y)} F(x, y, z)\, dz\, dy\, dx.$$

Follow similar procedures if you change the order of integration. The "shadow" of region D lies in the plane of the last two variables with respect to which the iterated integration takes place.

EXAMPLE 1 Find the volume of the region D enclosed by the surfaces $z = x^2 + 3y^2$ and $z = 8 - x^2 - y^2$.

Solution The volume is

$$V = \iiint_D dz\, dy\, dx,$$

the integral of $F(x, y, z) = 1$ over D. To find the limits of integration for evaluating the integral, we take these steps.

STEP 1: *A sketch.* The surfaces (Fig. 14.27 on the following page) intersect on the elliptical cylinder $x^2 + 3y^2 = 8 - x^2 - y^2$ or $x^2 + 2y^2 = 4$. The boundary of the region R, the projection of D onto the xy-plane, is an ellipse with the same equation: $x^2 + 2y^2 = 4$. The "upper" boundary of R is the curve $y = \sqrt{(4 - x^2)/2}$. The lower boundary is the curve $y = -\sqrt{(4 - x^2)/2}$.

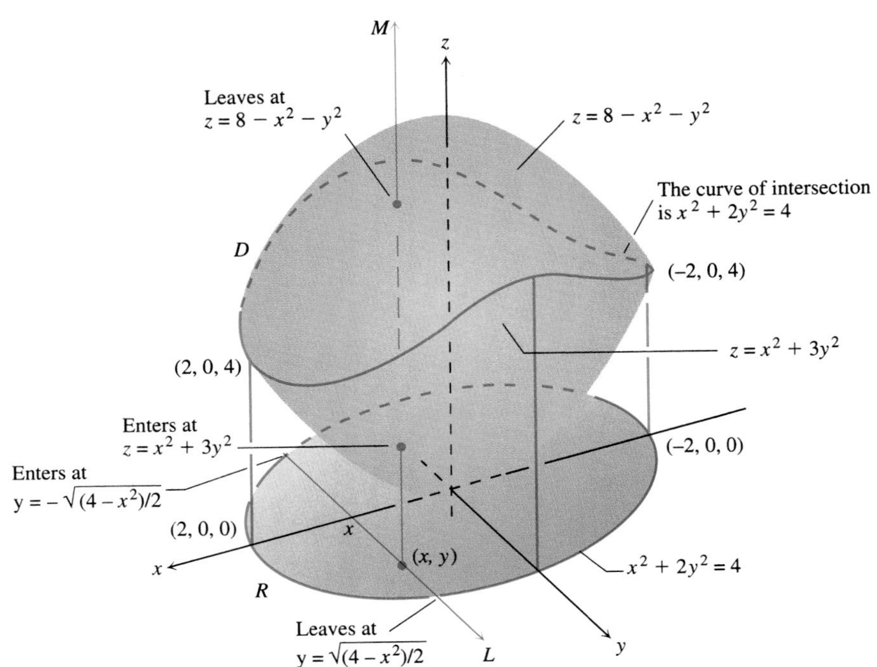

14.27 The volume of the region enclosed by these two paraboloids is calculated in Example 1.

STEP 2: *The z-limits of integration.* The line M passing through a typical point (x, y) in R parallel to the z-axis enters D at $z = x^2 + 3y^2$ and leaves at $z = 8 - x^2 - y^2$.

STEP 3: *The y-limits of integration.* The line L through (x, y) parallel to the y-axis enters R at $y = -\sqrt{(4 - x^2)/2}$ and leaves at $y = \sqrt{(4 - x^2)/2}$.

STEP 4: *The x-limits of integration.* As L sweeps across R, the value of x varies from $x = -2$ at $(-2, 0, 0)$ to $x = 2$ at $(2, 0, 0)$. The volume of D is

$$
\begin{aligned}
V &= \iiint_D dz\,dy\,dx \\
&= \int_{-2}^{2} \int_{-\sqrt{(4-x^2)/2}}^{\sqrt{(4-x^2)/2}} \int_{x^2+3y^2}^{8-x^2-y^2} dz\,dy\,dx \\
&= \int_{-2}^{2} \int_{-\sqrt{(4-x^2)/2}}^{\sqrt{(4-x^2)/2}} (8 - 2x^2 - 4y^2)\,dy\,dx \\
&= \int_{-2}^{2} \left[(8 - 2x^2)y - \frac{4}{3}y^3 \right]_{y=-\sqrt{(4-x^2)/2}}^{y=\sqrt{(4-x^2)/2}} dx \\
&= \int_{-2}^{2} \left(2(8 - 2x^2)\sqrt{\frac{4 - x^2}{2}} - \frac{8}{3}\left(\frac{4 - x^2}{2}\right)^{3/2} \right) dx \\
&= \int_{-2}^{2} \left[8\left(\frac{4 - x^2}{2}\right)^{3/2} - \frac{8}{3}\left(\frac{4 - x^2}{2}\right)^{3/2} \right] dx = \frac{4\sqrt{2}}{3} \int_{-2}^{2} (4 - x^2)^{3/2}\,dx \\
&= 8\pi\sqrt{2}. \qquad \text{After integration with the substitution } x = 2\sin u
\end{aligned}
$$

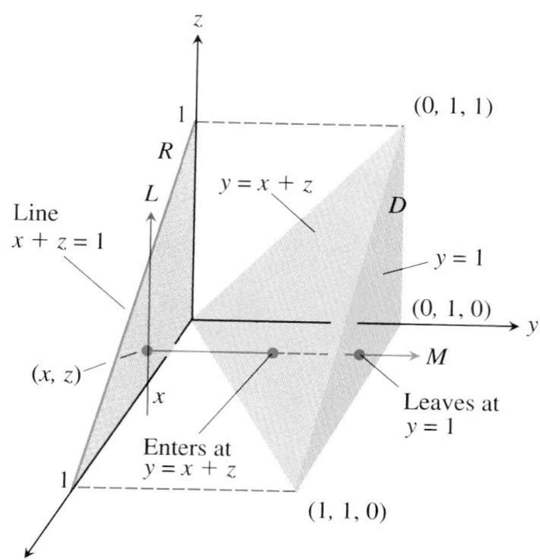

14.28 The tetrahedron in Example 2.

In the next example, we project D onto the xz-plane instead of the xy-plane.

EXAMPLE 2 Set up the limits of integration for evaluating the triple integral of a function $F(x, y, z)$ over the tetrahedron D with vertices $(0, 0, 0)$, $(1, 1, 0)$, $(0, 1, 0)$, and $(0, 1, 1)$.

Solution

STEP 1: *A sketch.* We sketch D along with its "shadow" R in the xz-plane (Fig. 14.28). The upper (right-hand) bounding surface of D lies in the plane $y = 1$. The lower (left-hand) bounding surface lies in the plane $y = x + z$. The upper boundary of R is the line $z = 1 - x$. The lower boundary is the line $z = 0$.

STEP 2: *The y-limits of integration.* The line through a typical point (x, z) in R parallel to the y-axis enters D at $y = x + z$ and leaves at $y = 1$.

STEP 3: *The z-limits of integration.* The line L through (x, z) parallel to the z-axis enters R at $z = 0$ and leaves at $z = 1 - x$.

STEP 4: *The x-limits of integration.* As L sweeps across R, the value of x varies from $x = 0$ to $x = 1$. The integral is

$$\int_0^1 \int_0^{1-x} \int_{x+z}^1 F(x, y, z)\, dy\, dz\, dx.$$

As we know, there are sometimes (but not always) two different orders in which the single integrations for evaluating a double integral may be worked. For triple integrals, there could be as many as *six*.

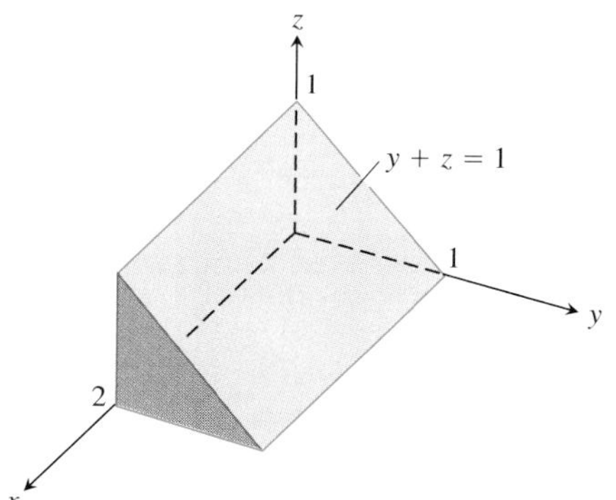

14.29 Example 3 gives six different iterated triple integrals for the volume of this prism.

EXAMPLE 3 Each of the following integrals gives the volume of the solid shown in Fig. 14.29.

a) $\int_0^1 \int_0^{1-z} \int_0^2 dx\, dy\, dz$ **b)** $\int_0^1 \int_0^{1-y} \int_0^2 dx\, dz\, dy$

c) $\int_0^1 \int_0^2 \int_0^{1-z} dy\, dx\, dz$ **d)** $\int_0^2 \int_0^1 \int_0^{1-z} dy\, dz\, dx$

e) $\int_0^1 \int_0^2 \int_0^{1-y} dz\, dx\, dy$ **f)** $\int_0^2 \int_0^1 \int_0^{1-y} dz\, dy\, dx$

Average Value of a Function in Space

The average value of a function F over a region D in space is defined by the formula

$$\textbf{Average value} \text{ of } F \text{ over } D = \frac{1}{\text{Volume of } D} \iiint_D F\, dV. \tag{5}$$

If $F(x, y, z) = \sqrt{x^2 + y^2 + z^2}$, then the average value of F over D is the average distance of points in D from the origin. If $F(x, y, z)$ is the density of a solid that occupies a region D in space, then the average value of F over D is the average density of the solid in units of mass per unit volume.

EXAMPLE 4 Find the average value of $F(x, y, z) = xyz$ over the cube bounded by the coordinate planes and the planes $x = 2$, $y = 2$, and $z = 2$ in the first octant.

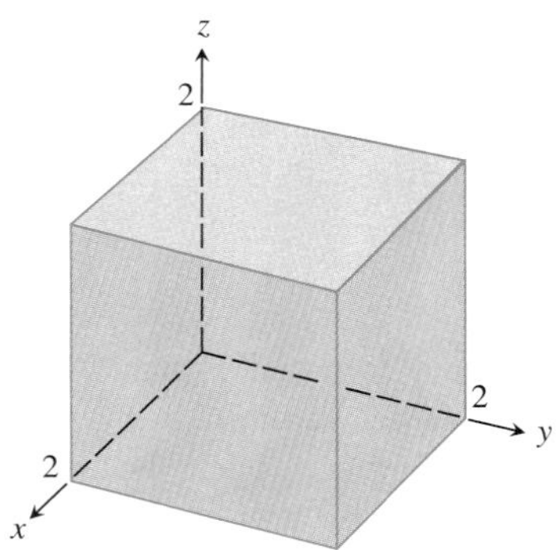

14.30 The region of integration in Example 4.

Solution We sketch the cube with enough detail to show the limits of integration (Fig. 14.30). We then use Eq. (5) to calculate the average value of F over the cube.

The volume of the cube is $(2)(2)(2) = 8$.

The value of the integral of F over the cube is

$$\int_0^2\int_0^2\int_0^2 xyz\,dx\,dy\,dz = \int_0^2\int_0^2\left[\frac{x^2}{2}yz\right]_{x=0}^{x=2} dy\,dz = \int_0^2\int_0^2 2yz\,dy\,dz$$

$$= \int_0^2\left[y^2z\right]_{y=0}^{y=2} dz = \int_0^2 4z\,dz = \left[2z^2\right]_0^2 = 8.$$

With these values, Eq. (5) gives

$$\begin{array}{c}\text{Average value of}\\ xyz \text{ over the cube}\end{array} = \frac{1}{\text{Volume}}\iiint_{\text{cube}} xyz\,dV = \left(\frac{1}{8}\right)(8) = 1.$$

In evaluating the integral, we chose the order dx, dy, dz, but any of the other five possible orders would have done as well.

Exercises 14.4

1. Find the common value of the integrals in Example 3.
2. Write six different iterated triple integrals for the volume of the rectangular solid in the first octant bounded by the coordinate planes and the planes $x = 1$, $y = 2$, and $z = 3$. Evaluate one of the integrals.
3. Write six different iterated triple integrals for the volume of the tetrahedron cut from the first octant by the plane $6x + 3y + 2z = 6$. Evaluate one of the integrals.
4. Write six different iterated triple integrals for the volume of the region in the first octant enclosed by the cylinder $x^2 + z^2 = 4$ and the plane $y = 3$. Evaluate one of the integrals.

Evaluate the integrals in Exercises 5–18.

5. $\displaystyle\int_0^1\int_0^1\int_0^1 (x^2 + y^2 + z^2)\,dz\,dy\,dx$

6. $\displaystyle\int_0^{\sqrt{2}}\int_0^{3y}\int_{x^2+3y^2}^{8-x^2-y^2} dz\,dx\,dy$

7. $\displaystyle\int_1^e\int_1^e\int_1^e \frac{1}{xyz}\,dx\,dy\,dz$

8. $\displaystyle\int_0^1\int_0^{3-3x}\int_0^{3-3x-y} dz\,dy\,dx$

9. $\displaystyle\int_0^1\int_0^\pi\int_0^\pi y\sin z\,dx\,dy\,dz$

10. $\displaystyle\int_{-1}^1\int_{-1}^1\int_{-1}^1 (x + y + z)\,dy\,dx\,dz$

11. $\displaystyle\int_0^3\int_0^{\sqrt{9-x^2}}\int_0^{\sqrt{9-x^2}} dz\,dy\,dx$

12. $\displaystyle\int_0^2\int_{-\sqrt{4-y^2}}^{\sqrt{4-y^2}}\int_0^{2x+y} dz\,dx\,dy$

13. $\displaystyle\int_0^1\int_0^{2-x}\int_0^{2-x-y} dz\,dy\,dx$

14. $\displaystyle\int_0^1\int_0^{1-x^2}\int_3^{4-x^2-y} x\,dz\,dy\,dx$

15. $\displaystyle\int_0^\pi\int_0^\pi\int_0^\pi \cos(u + v + w)\,du\,dv\,dw$ (uvw-space)

16. $\displaystyle\int_1^e\int_1^e\int_1^e \ln r\ln s\ln t\,dt\,dr\,ds$ (rst-space)

17. $\displaystyle\int_0^{\pi/4}\int_0^{\ln\sec v}\int_{-\infty}^{2t} e^x\,dx\,dt\,dv$ (tvx-space)

18. $\displaystyle\int_0^7\int_0^2\int_0^{\sqrt{4-q^2}} \frac{q}{r+1}\,dp\,dq\,dr$ (pqr-space)

19. Here is the region of integration of the integral $\displaystyle\int_{-1}^1\int_{x^2}^1\int_0^{1-y} dz\,dy\,dx.$

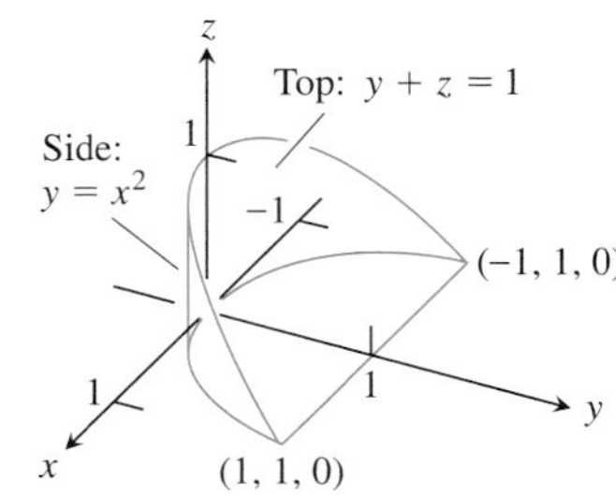

Rewrite the integral as an equivalent iterated integral in the order

a) $dy\,dz\,dx$ **b)** $dy\,dx\,dz$
c) $dx\,dy\,dz$ **d)** $dx\,dz\,dy$
e) $dz\,dx\,dy$

20. Here is the region of integration of the integral

$$\int_0^1 \int_{-1}^0 \int_0^{y^2} dz\,dy\,dx.$$

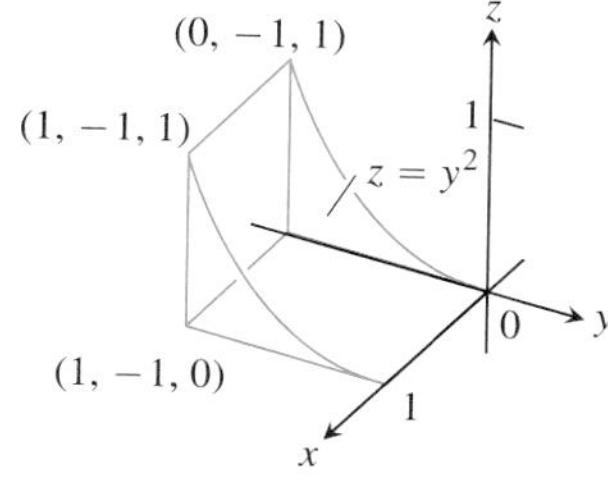

Rewrite the integral as an equivalent iterated integral in the order

a) $dy\,dz\,dx$ **b)** $dy\,dx\,dz$
c) $dx\,dy\,dz$ **d)** $dx\,dz\,dy$
e) $dz\,dx\,dy$

Find the volumes of the regions in Exercises 21–30.

21. The region between the cylinder $z = y^2$ and the xy-plane that is bounded by the planes $x = 0$, $x = 1$, $y = -1$, $y = 1$

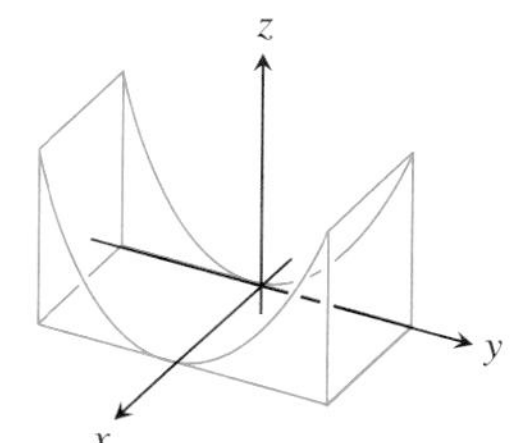

22. The region in the first octant bounded by the coordinate planes and the planes $x + z = 1$, $y + 2z = 2$

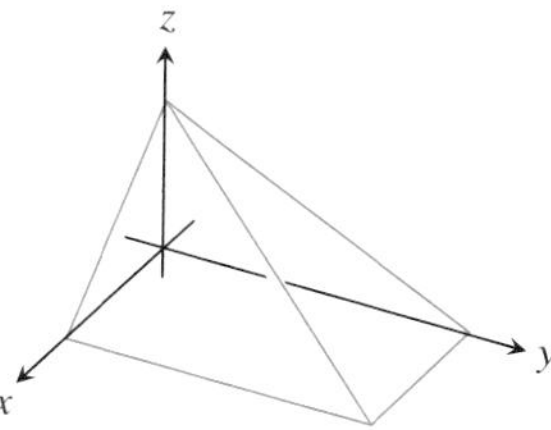

23. The region in the first octant bounded by the coordinate planes, the plane $y + z = 2$, and the cylinder $x = 4 - y^2$

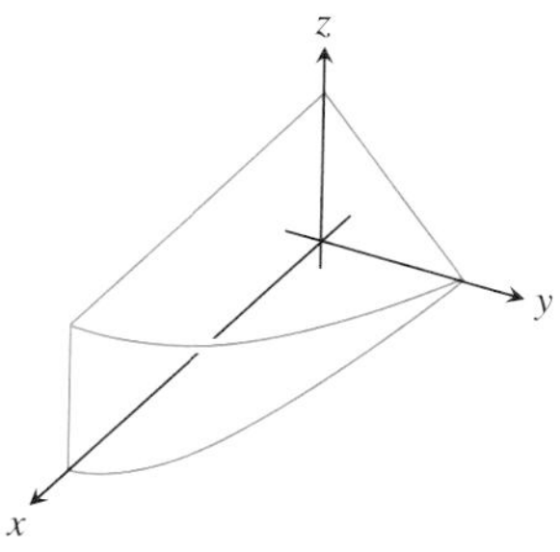

24. The wedge cut from the cylinder $x^2 + y^2 = 1$ by the planes $z = -y$ and $z = 0$

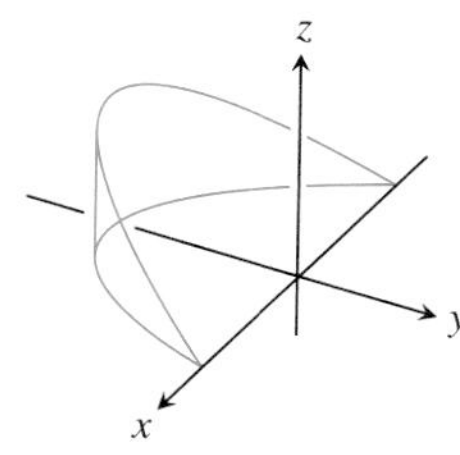

25. The tetrahedron in the first octant bounded by the coordinate planes and the plane $x + y/2 + z/3 = 1$

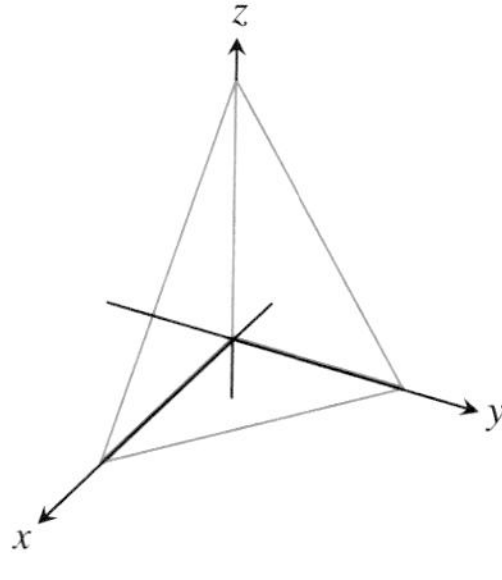

26. The region in the first octant bounded by the coordinate planes, the plane $y = 1 - x$, and the surface $z = \cos(\pi x/2)$, $0 \le x \le 1$

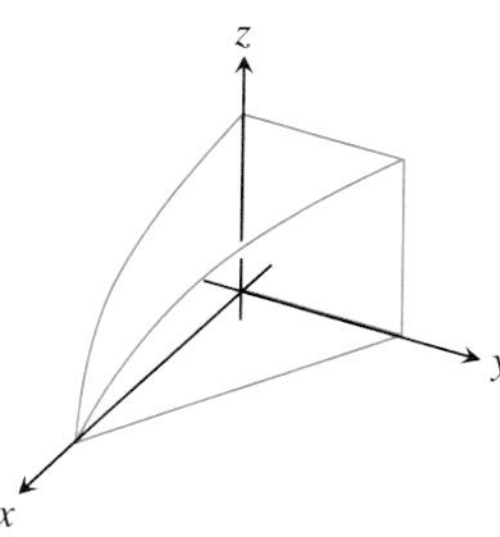

27. The region common to the interiors of the cylinders $x^2 + y^2 = 1$ and $x^2 + z^2 = 1$ (Fig. 14.31)

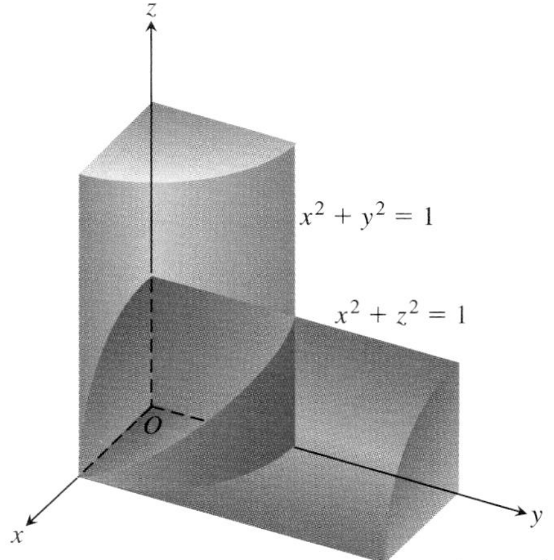

14.31 One-eighth of the region common to the cylinders $x^2 + y^2 = 1$ and $x^2 + z^2 = 1$ in Exercise 27.

28. The region in the first octant bounded by the coordinate planes and the surface $z = 4 - x^2 - y$

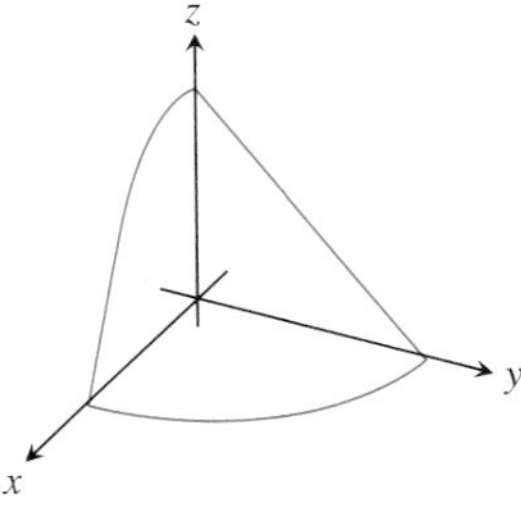

29. The region in the first octant bounded by the coordinate planes, the plane $x + y = 4$, and the cylinder $y^2 + 4z^2 = 16$

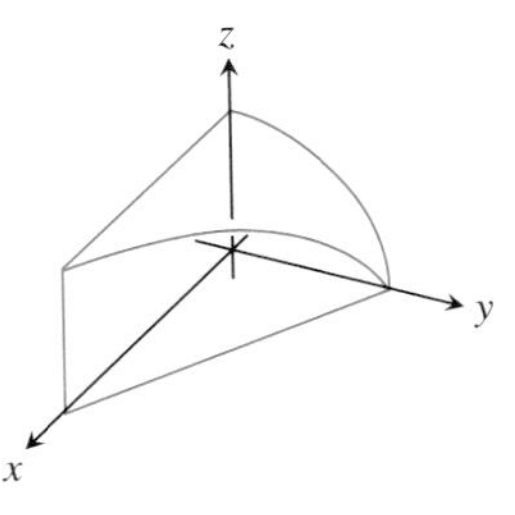

30. The region cut from the cylinder $x^2 + y^2 = 4$ by the plane $z = 0$ and the plane $x + z = 3$

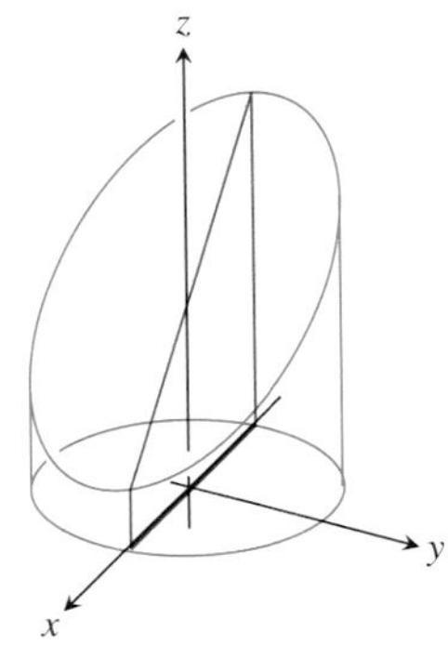

In Exercises 31–34, find the average value of $F(x, y, z)$ over the given region.

31. $F(x, y, z) = x^2 + 9$ over the cube in the first octant bounded by the coordinate planes and the planes $x = 2$, $y = 2$, and $z = 2$

32. $F(x, y, z) = x + y - z$ over the rectangular solid in the first octant bounded by the coordinate planes and the planes $x = 1$, $y = 1$, and $z = 2$

33. $F(x, y, z) = x^2 + y^2 + z^2$ over the cube in the first octant bounded by the coordinate planes and the planes $x = 1$, $y = 1$, and $z = 1$

34. $F(x, y, z) = xyz$ over the cube in the first octant bounded by the coordinate planes and the planes $x = 2$, $y = 2$, and $z = 2$

35. What domain D in space minimizes the value of the integral

$$\iiint_D (4x^2 + 4y^2 + z^2 - 4)\, dV?$$

Give reasons for your answer.

36. What domain D in space maximizes the value of the integral

$$\iiint_D (1 - x^2 - y^2 - z^2)\, dV?$$

Give reasons for your answer.

Writing for Your Own Knowledge

Answer the following questions in writing. Some answers will take only a sentence or two; others may require several paragraphs. Some explanations may also call for graphs or sketches.

1. How do you define the triple integral of a continuous function $F(x, y, z)$ over a closed bounded region in space? How do you interpret the volume element $dV = dx\, dy\, dz$?
2. What properties do triple integrals have?
3. How do you evaluate a triple integral? How do you find appropriate limits of integration?
4. How do you use triple integrals to calculate volumes and average values?

14.5 Masses and Moments in Three Dimensions

This section shows how to calculate the masses and moments of three-dimensional objects in Cartesian coordinates. The formulas are similar to those for two-dimensional objects. For calculations in spherical and cylindrical coordinates, see Section 14.6.

Masses and Moments

If $\delta(x, y, z)$ is the density of an object occupying a region D in space, the integral of δ over D gives the mass of the object. To see why, imagine partitioning the object into n mass elements like the one in Fig. 14.32. The object's mass is the limit

$$M = \lim_{n \to \infty} \sum_{k=1}^{n} \Delta m_k = \lim_{n \to \infty} \sum_{k=1}^{n} \delta(x_k, y_k, z_k) \Delta V_k = \iiint_D \delta(x, y, z)\, dV. \tag{1}$$

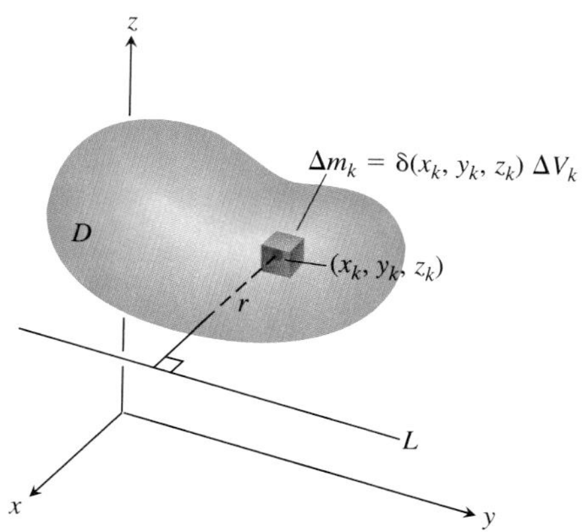

14.32 To define an object's mass and moment of inertia about a line, we first imagine it to be subdivided into a finite number of mass elements Δm_k.

If $r(x, y, z)$ is the distance from the point (x, y, z) in D to a line L, then the moment of inertia of the mass

$$\Delta m_k = \delta(x_k, y_k, z_k)\Delta V_k$$

about the line L (shown in Fig. 14.32) is approximately

$$\Delta I_k = r^2(x_k, y_k, z_k)\Delta m_k.$$

The moment of inertia of the entire object about L is

$$I_L = \lim_{n\to\infty} \sum_{k=1}^{n} \Delta I_k = \lim_{n\to\infty} \sum_{k=1}^{n} r^2(x_k, y_k, z_k)\delta(x_k, y_k, z_k)\Delta V_k = \iiint_D r^2\delta\, dV.$$

If L is the x-axis, then $r^2 = y^2 + z^2$ (Fig. 14.33) and

$$I_x = \iiint_D (y^2 + z^2)\delta\, dV.$$

Similarly,

$$I_y = \iiint_D (x^2 + z^2)\delta\, dV \qquad \text{and} \qquad I_z = \iiint_D (x^2 + y^2)\delta\, dV.$$

These and other useful formulas are summarized in Table 14.2.

TABLE 14.2
Mass and moment formulas for objects in space

Mass: $M = \iiint_D \delta\, dV \qquad (\delta = \text{density})$

First moments about the coordinate planes:

$$M_{yz} = \iiint_D x\delta\, dV, \qquad M_{xz} = \iiint_D y\delta\, dV, \qquad M_{xy} = \iiint_D z\delta\, dV$$

Center of mass:

$$\bar{x} = \frac{M_{yz}}{M}, \qquad \bar{y} = \frac{M_{xz}}{M}, \qquad \bar{z} = \frac{M_{xy}}{M}$$

Moments of inertia (second moments):

$$I_x = \iiint (y^2 + z^2)\delta\, dV,$$
$$I_y = \iiint (x^2 + z^2)\delta\, dV,$$
$$I_z = \iiint (x^2 + y^2)\delta\, dV$$

Moment of inertia about a line L:

$I_L = \iiint r^2\,\delta\, dV \qquad (r(x, y, z) = \text{Distance from points } (x, y, z) \text{ to line } L)$

Radius of gyration about a line L:

$$R_L = \sqrt{I_L/M}$$

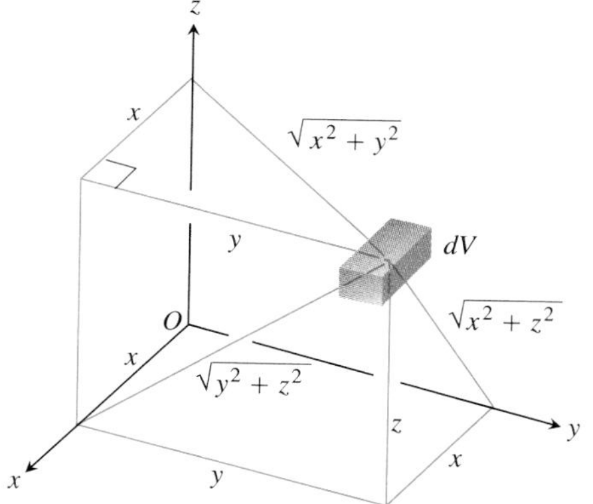

14.33 Distances from dV to the coordinate planes and axes.

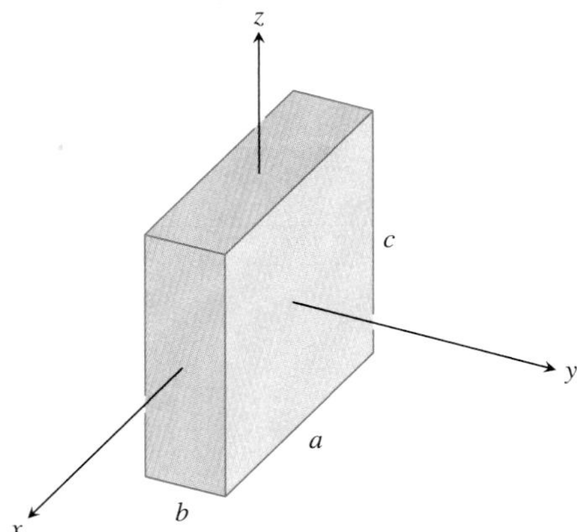

14.34 Example 1 calculates I_x, I_y, and I_z for the block shown here. The origin lies at the center of the block.

EXAMPLE 1 Find I_x, I_y, I_z for the rectangular solid of constant density δ shown in Fig. 14.34.

Solution The preceding formula for I_x gives

$$I_x = \int_{-c/2}^{c/2} \int_{-b/2}^{b/2} \int_{-a/2}^{a/2} (y^2 + z^2)\delta \, dx \, dy \, dz. \tag{2}$$

We can avoid some of the work of integration by observing that $(y^2 + z^2)\delta$ is an even function of x, y, and z and therefore

$$\begin{aligned} I_x &= 8 \int_0^{c/2} \int_0^{b/2} \int_0^{a/2} (y^2 + z^2)\delta \, dx \, dy \, dz = 4a\delta \int_0^{c/2} \int_0^{b/2} (y^2 + z^2) \, dy \, dz \\ &= 4a\delta \int_0^{c/2} \left[\frac{y^3}{3} + z^2 y \right]_{y=0}^{y=b/2} dz \\ &= 4a\delta \int_0^{c/2} \left(\frac{b^3}{24} + \frac{z^2 b}{2} \right) dz \\ &= 4a\delta \left(\frac{b^3 c}{48} + \frac{c^3 b}{48} \right) = \frac{abc\delta}{12}(b^2 + c^2) = \frac{M}{12}(b^2 + c^2). \end{aligned}$$

Similarly,

$$I_y = \frac{M}{12}(a^2 + c^2) \qquad \text{and} \qquad I_z = \frac{M}{12}(a^2 + b^2).$$

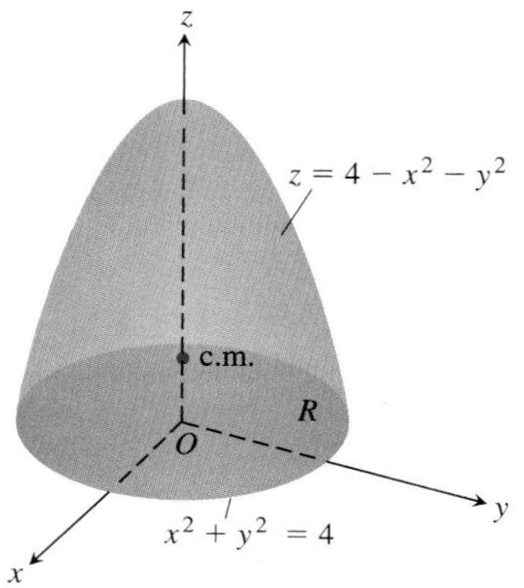

14.35 Example 2 calculates the coordinates of the center of mass of this solid.

EXAMPLE 2 Find the center of mass of a solid of constant density δ bounded below by the disk R: $x^2 + y^2 \leq 4$ in the plane $z = 0$ and above by the paraboloid $z = 4 - x^2 - y^2$ (Fig. 14.35).

Solution By symmetry, $\bar{x} = \bar{y} = 0$. To find $\bar{z}$ we first calculate

$$\begin{aligned} M_{xy} &= \iint_R \int_{z=0}^{z=4-x^2-y^2} z\,\delta \, dz \, dy \, dx = \iint_R \left[\frac{z^2}{2} \right]_{z=0}^{z=4-x^2-y^2} \delta \, dy \, dx \\ &= \frac{\delta}{2} \iint_R (4 - x^2 - y^2)^2 \, dy \, dx \\ &= \frac{\delta}{2} \int_0^{2\pi} \int_0^2 (4 - r^2)^2 \, r \, dr \, d\theta \qquad \text{Polar coordinates} \\ &= \frac{\delta}{2} \int_0^{2\pi} \left[-\frac{1}{6}(4 - r^2)^3 \right]_{r=0}^{r=2} d\theta = \frac{16\delta}{3} \int_0^{2\pi} d\theta = \frac{32\pi\delta}{3}. \end{aligned}$$

A similar calculation gives

$$M = \iint_R \int_0^{4-x^2-y^2} \delta \, dz \, dy \, dx = 8\pi\delta.$$

Therefore $\bar{z} = (M_{xy}/M) = 4/3$ and the center of mass is $(\bar{x}, \bar{y}, \bar{z}) = (0, 0, 4/3)$.

When the density of a solid object is constant (as in Examples 1 and 2), the center of mass is called the **centroid** of the object (as was the case for two-dimensional shapes in Section 14.2).

Exercises 14.5

The solids in Exercises 1–12 all have constant density $\delta = 1$.

1. Evaluate the integral for I_x in Eq. (2) directly to show that the shortcut in Example 1 gives the same answer. Use the results in Example 1 to find the radius of gyration of the rectangular solid about each coordinate axis.

2. The coordinate axes shown in Fig. 14.36 run through the centroid of a solid wedge parallel to the labeled edges. Find I_x, I_y, and I_z if $a = b = 6$ and $c = 4$.

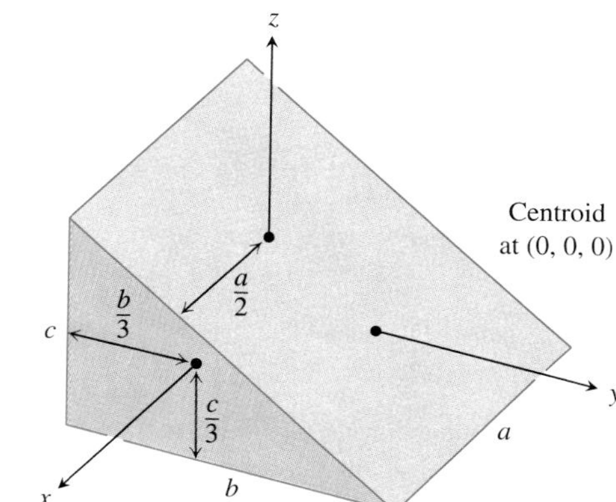

14.36 The figure for Exercise 2.

3. Find the moments of inertia of the rectangular solid shown in Fig. 14.37 with respect to its edges by calculating I_x, I_y, and I_z.

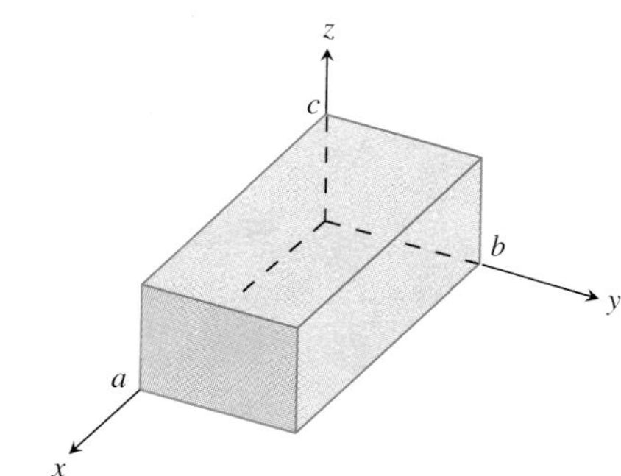

14.37 The solid in Exercise 3.

4. a) Find the centroid and the moments of inertia I_x, I_y, and I_z of the tetrahedron whose vertices are the points (0, 0, 0), (1, 0, 0), (0, 1, 0), and (0, 0, 1).
   b) Find the radius of gyration of the tetrahedron about the x-axis. Compare it with the distance from the centroid to the x-axis.

5. A solid "trough" of constant density is bounded below by the surface $z = 4y^2$, above by the plane $z = 4$, and on the ends by the planes $x = 1$ and $x = -1$. Find the center of mass and the moments of inertia with respect to the three axes.

6. A solid of constant density is bounded below by the plane $z = 0$, on the sides by the elliptic cylinder $x^2 + 4y^2 = 4$, and above by the plane $z = 2 - x$ (Fig. 14.38).
   a) Find $\bar{x}$ and $\bar{y}$.
   b) Evaluate the integral

$$M_{xy} = \int_{-2}^{2} \int_{-(1/2)\sqrt{4-x^2}}^{(1/2)\sqrt{4-x^2}} \int_{0}^{2-x} z\,dz\,dy\,dx,$$

using integral tables to carry out the final integration with respect to x. Then divide M_{xy} by M to verify that $\bar{z} = 5/4$.

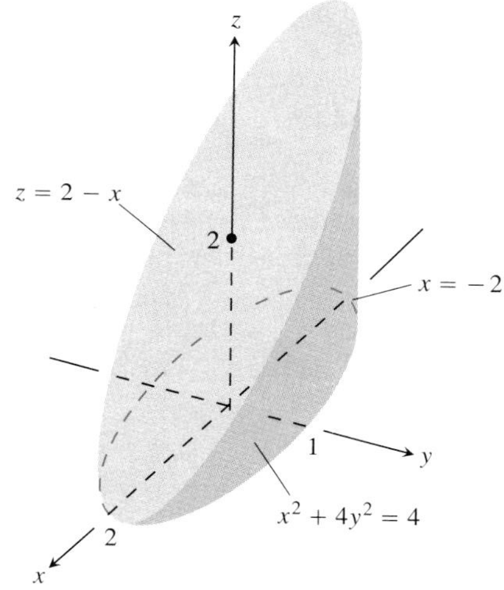

14.38 The solid in Exercise 6.

7. a) Find the center of mass of a solid of constant density bounded below by the paraboloid $z = x^2 + y^2$ and above by the plane $z = 4$.
   b) Find the plane $z = c$ that divides the solid into two parts of equal volume. This plane does not pass through the center of mass.

8. A solid cube, 2 units on a side, is bounded by the planes $x = \pm 1$, $z = \pm 1$, $y = 3$, and $y = 5$. Find the center of mass and the moments of inertia and radii of gyration about the coordinate axes.

9. A wedge shaped like the one in Fig. 14.36 has $a = 4$, $b = 6$, and $c = 3$. Make a quick sketch to check for yourself that the square of the distance from a typical point (x, y, z) of the wedge to the line L: $z = 0$, $y = 6$ is $r^2 = (y - 6)^2 + z^2$. Then calculate the moment of inertia and radius of gyration of the wedge about L.

10. A wedge shaped like the one in Fig. 14.36 has $a = 4$, $b = 6$, and $c = 3$. Make a quick sketch to check for yourself that the square of the distance from a typical point (x, y, z) of the

wedge to the line $L: x = 4, y = 0$ is $r^2 = (x - 4)^2 + y^2$. Then calculate the moment of inertia and radius of gyration of the wedge about L.

11. A rectangular solid like the one in Fig. 14.37 has $a = 4$, $b = 2$, and $c = 1$. Make a quick sketch to check for yourself that the square of the distance between a typical point (x, y, z) of the solid and the line $L: y = 2, z = 0$ is $r^2 = (y - 2)^2 + z^2$. Then find the moment of inertia and radius of gyration of the solid about L.

12. A rectangular solid like the one in Fig. 14.37 has $a = 4$, $b = 2$, and $c = 1$. Make a quick sketch to check for yourself that the square of the distance between a typical point (x, y, z) of the solid and the line $L: x = 4, y = 0$ is $r^2 = (x - 4)^2 + y^2$. Then find the moment of inertia and radius of gyration of the solid about L.

13. A solid region in the first octant is bounded by the coordinate planes and the plane $x + y + z = 2$. The density of the solid is $\delta(x, y, z) = 2x$. Find the center of mass.

14. A solid wedge shaped like the one in Fig. 14.36 has dimensions $a = 4$, $b = 6$, and $c = 3$. The density is $\delta(x, y, z) = x + 1$. Find the center of mass and the moments of inertia and radii of gyration about the coordinate axes. Notice that if the density is constant, the center of mass will be $(0, 0, 0)$.

15. A solid cube in the first octant is bounded by the coordinate planes and by the planes $x = 1$, $y = 1$, and $z = 1$. Find its center of mass and the moments of inertia and radii of gyration about the coordinate axes if

$$\delta(x, y, z) = x + y + z + 1.$$

16. A solid in the first octant is bounded by the planes $y = 0$ and $z = 0$ and by the surfaces $z = 4 - x^2$ and $x = y^2$ (Fig. 14.39).

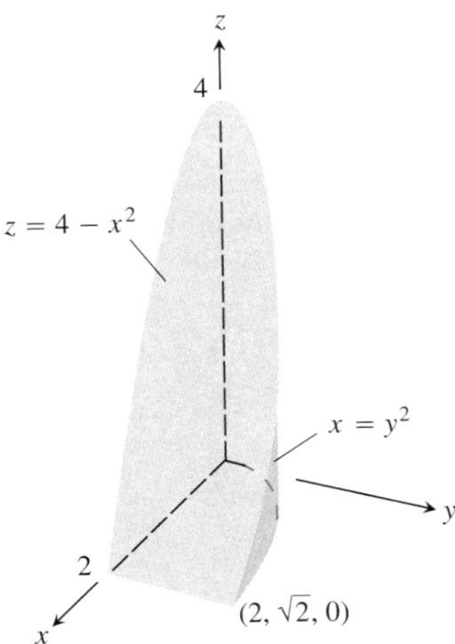

14.39 The solid in Exercise 16.

Its density function is $\delta(x, y, z) = kxy$.

a) Find the solid's mass.
b) Find $\bar{x}$.
c) Find $\bar{y}$.
d) Find $\bar{z}$.

Writing for Your Own Knowledge

Answer the following questions in writing. Some answers will take only a sentence or two; others may require several paragraphs. Some explanations may also call for graphs or sketches.

1. How do you use triple integrals in rectangular coordinates to calculate masses, moments, and centers of mass of three-dimensional objects?
2. How do you find the centroid of a geometric solid?

14.6 *Triple Integrals in Cylindrical and Spherical Coordinates*

When a calculation in physics, engineering, or geometry involves a cylinder, cone, or sphere, we can often simplify our work by using cylindrical or spherical coordinates.

Cylindrical Coordinates

Cylindrical coordinates (Fig. 14.40) are good for describing cylinders whose axes run along the z-axis and planes that either contain the z-axis or lie perpendicular to the z-axis. As we saw in Section 11.7, surfaces like these have equations of constant coordinate value:

$r = 4$	Cylinder, radius 4, axis the z-axis
$\theta = \dfrac{\pi}{3}$	Plane containing the z-axis
$z = 2$	Plane perpendicular to the z-axis

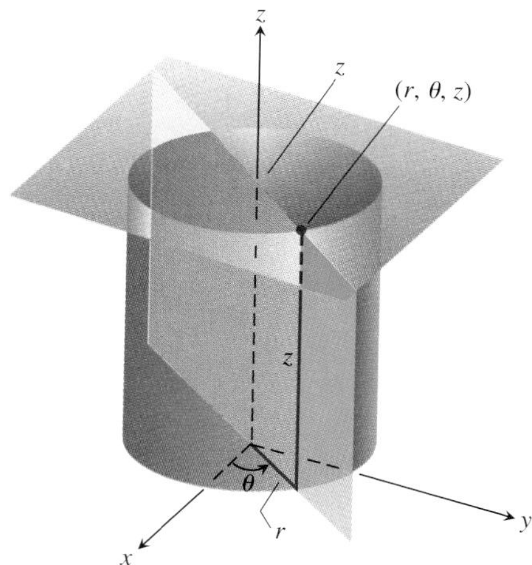

14.40 Cylindrical coordinates and typical surfaces of constant coordinate value.

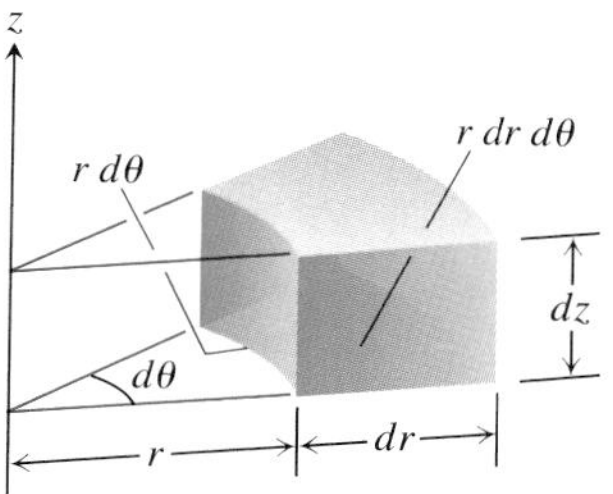

14.41 The volume element in cylindrical coordinates is $dV = dz\, r\, dr\, d\theta$.

The volume element for subdividing a region in space with cylindrical coordinates is

$$dV = dz\, r\, dr\, d\theta \tag{1}$$

(Fig. 14.41). Triple integrals in cylindrical coordinates are then evaluated as iterated integrals, as in the following example.

EXAMPLE 1 Find the limits of integration in cylindrical coordinates for integrating a function $f(r, \theta, z)$ over the region D bounded below by the plane $z = 0$, laterally by the circular cylinder $x^2 + (y-1)^2 = 1$, and above by the paraboloid $z = x^2 + y^2$.

Solution

STEP 1: *A sketch* (Fig. 14.42). The base of D is also the region's projection R on the xy-plane. The boundary of R is the circle $x^2 + (y-1)^2 = 1$. Its polar coordinate equation is

$$\begin{aligned} x^2 + (y-1)^2 &= 1 \\ x^2 + y^2 - 2y + 1 &= 1 \\ r^2 - 2r\sin\theta &= 0 \\ r &= 2\sin\theta. \end{aligned}$$

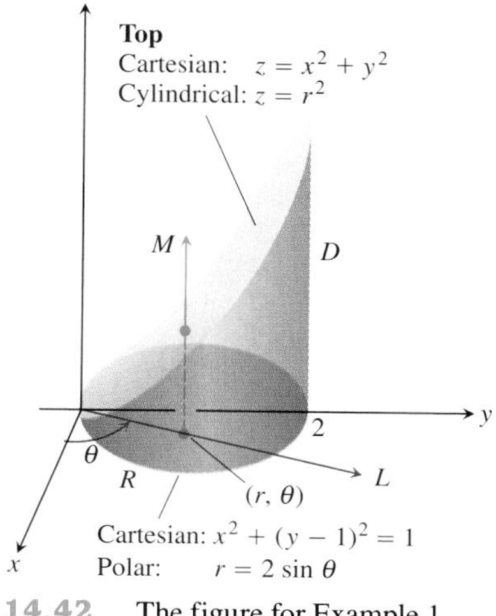

14.42 The figure for Example 1.

STEP 2: *The z-limits of integration.* A line M through a typical point (r, θ) in R parallel to the z-axis enters D at $z = 0$ and leaves at $z = x^2 + y^2 = r^2$.

STEP 3: *The r-limits of integration.* A ray L through (r, θ) from the origin enters R at $r = 0$ and leaves at $r = 2\sin\theta$.

STEP 4: *The θ-limits of integration.* As L sweeps across R, the angle θ it makes with the positive x-axis runs from $\theta = 0$ to $\theta = \pi$. The integral is

$$\iiint_D f(r, \theta, z)\, dV = \int_0^{\pi} \int_0^{2\sin\theta} \int_0^{r^2} f(r, \theta, z)\, dz\, r\, dr\, d\theta.$$

Example 1 illustrates a good procedure for finding limits of integration in cylindrical coordinates. The procedure is summarized on the following page.

How to Integrate in Cylindrical Coordinates

To evaluate

$$\iiint_D f(r, \theta, z)\, dV$$

over a region D in space in cylindrical coordinates, integrating first with respect to z, then with respect to r, and finally with respect to θ, take the following steps:

1. *A sketch.* Sketch the region D along with its projection R on the xy-plane. Label the surfaces and curves that bound D and R.

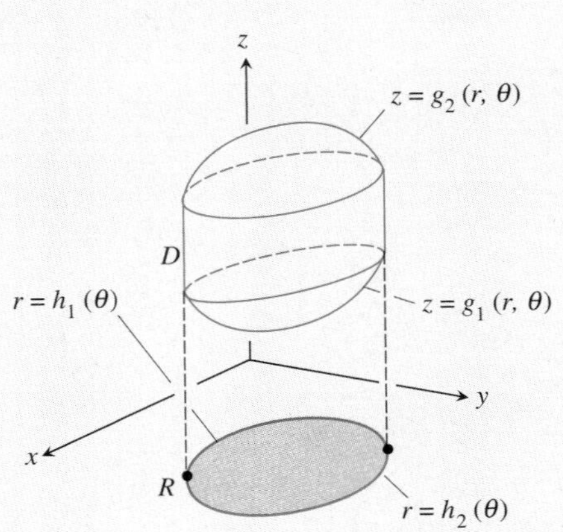

2. *The z-limits of integration.* Draw a line M through a typical point (r, θ) of R parallel to the z-axis. As z increases, M enters D at $z = g_1(r, \theta)$ and leaves at $z = g_2(r, \theta)$. These are the z-limits of integration.

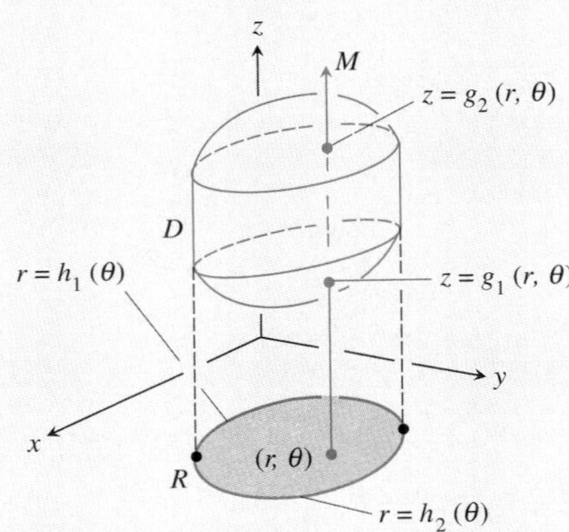

3. *The r-limits of integration.* Draw a ray L through (r, θ) from the origin. The ray enters R at $r = h_1(\theta)$ and leaves at $r = h_2(\theta)$. These are the r-limits of integration.

4. *The θ-limits of integration.* As L sweeps across R, the angle θ it makes with the positive x-axis runs from $\theta = \alpha$ to $\theta = \beta$. These are the θ-limits of integration. The integral is

$$\iiint_D f(r, \theta, z)\, dV = \int_{\theta=\alpha}^{\theta=\beta} \int_{r=h_1(\theta)}^{r=h_2(\theta)} \int_{z=g_1(r,\theta)}^{z=g_2(r,\theta)} f(r, \theta, z)\, dz\, r\, dr\, d\theta. \quad (2)$$

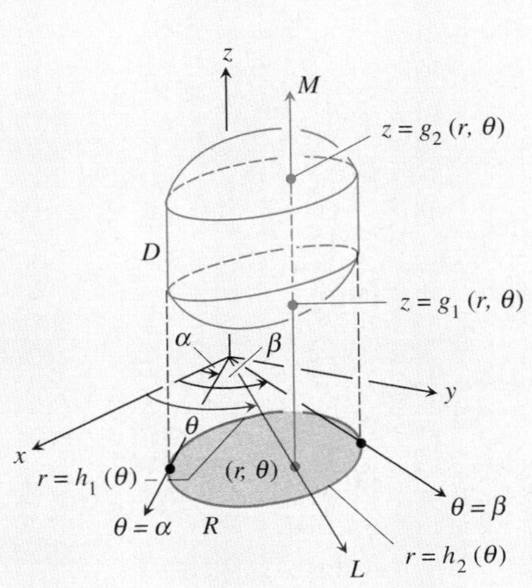

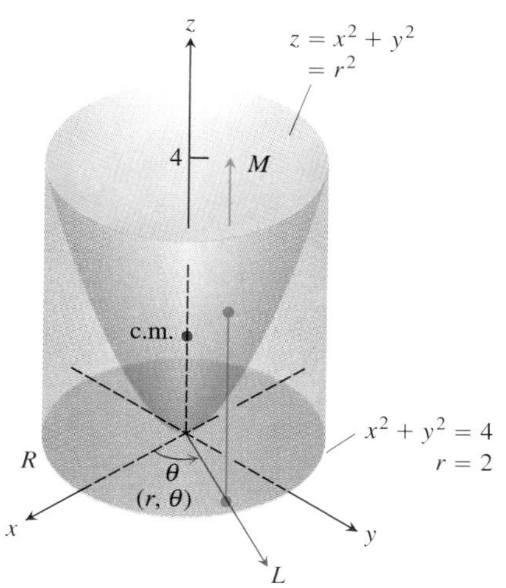

14.43 Example 2 shows how to find the centroid of this solid.

EXAMPLE 2 Find the centroid ($\delta = 1$) of the solid enclosed by the cylinder $x^2 + y^2 = 4$, bounded above by the paraboloid $z = x^2 + y^2$ and below by the xy-plane.

Solution We sketch the solid, bounded above by the paraboloid $z = r^2$ and below by the plane $z = 0$ (Fig. 14.43). Its base R is the disk $|r| \le 2$ in the xy-plane.

The solid's centroid $(\bar{x}, \bar{y}, \bar{z})$ lies on its axis of symmetry, here the z-axis. This makes $\bar{x} = \bar{y} = 0$. To find $\bar{z}$, we divide the first moment M_{xy} by the mass M.

To find the limits of integration for the mass and moment integrals, we continue with the four basic steps. We completed step 1 with our initial sketch. The remaining steps give the limits of integration.

STEP 2: *The z-limits.* A line M through a typical point (r, θ) in the base parallel to the z-axis enters the solid at $z = 0$ and leaves at $z = r^2$.

STEP 3: *The r-limits.* A ray L through (r, θ) from the origin enters R at $r = 0$ and leaves at $r = 2$.

STEP 4: *The θ-limits.* As L sweeps over the base like a clock hand, the angle θ it makes with the positive x-axis runs from $\theta = 0$ to $\theta = 2\pi$. The value of M_{xy} is

$$M_{xy} = \int_0^{2\pi}\int_0^2\int_0^{r^2} z\,dz\,r\,dr\,d\theta = \int_0^{2\pi}\int_0^2 \left[\frac{z^2}{2}\right]_0^{r^2} r\,dr\,d\theta$$

$$= \int_0^{2\pi}\int_0^2 \frac{r^5}{2}\,dr\,d\theta = \int_0^{2\pi}\left[\frac{r^6}{12}\right]_0^2 d\theta = \int_0^{2\pi}\frac{16}{3}\,d\theta = \frac{32\pi}{3}.$$

The value of M is

$$M = \int_0^{2\pi}\int_0^2\int_0^{r^2} dz\,r\,dr\,d\theta = \int_0^{2\pi}\int_0^2 \Big[z\Big]_0^{r^2} r\,dr\,d\theta$$

$$= \int_0^{2\pi}\int_0^2 r^3\,dr\,d\theta = \int_0^{2\pi}\left[\frac{r^4}{4}\right]_0^2 d\theta = \int_0^{2\pi} 4\,d\theta = 8\pi.$$

Therefore,

$$\bar{z} = \frac{M_{xy}}{M} = \frac{32\pi}{3}\frac{1}{8\pi} = \frac{4}{3},$$

and the centroid is (0, 0, 4/3).

Spherical Coordinates

Spherical coordinates (Fig. 14.44) are good for describing spheres centered at the origin, half-planes hinged along the z-axis, and single-nápped cones whose vertices lie at the origin and whose axes lie along the z-axis. Surfaces like these have equations of constant coordinate value:

$\rho = 4$	Sphere, radius 4, center at origin
$\phi = \dfrac{\pi}{3}$	Cone opening up from the origin, making an angle of $\pi/3$ radians with the positive z-axis
$\theta = \dfrac{\pi}{3}$	Half-plane, hinged along the z-axis, making an angle of $\pi/3$ radians with the positive x-axis

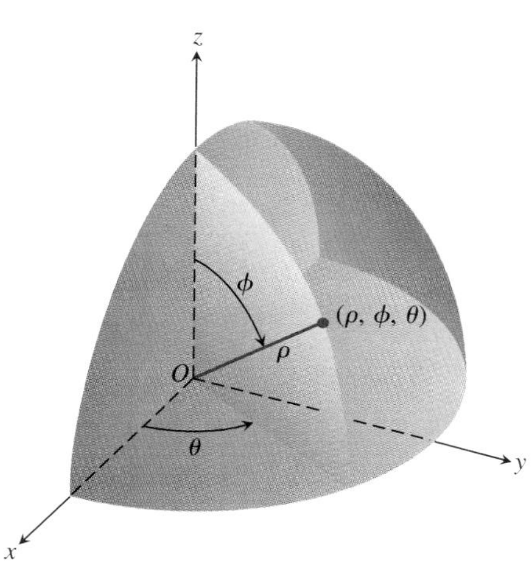

14.44 Spherical coordinates are measured with a distance and two angles.

The volume element in spherical coordinates is the volume of a **spherical wedge** defined by the increments $d\rho$, $d\phi$, and $d\theta$ (Fig. 14.45 on the following page). The wedge is approximately a rectangular box with one side a circular arc of

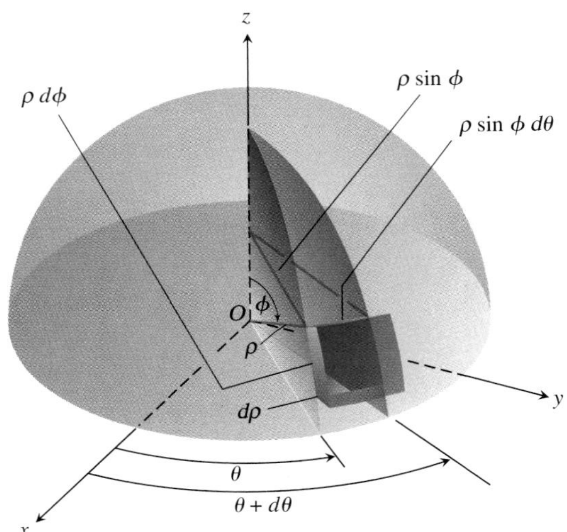

14.45 The volume element in spherical coordinates is

$$dV = d\rho \cdot \rho\, d\phi \cdot \rho \sin \phi\, d\theta = \rho^2 \sin \phi\, d\rho\, d\phi\, d\theta.$$

length $\rho\, d\phi$, another side a circular arc of length $\rho \sin \phi\, d\theta$, and thickness $d\rho$. Therefore the volume element in spherical coordinates is

$$dV = \rho^2 \sin \phi\, d\rho\, d\phi\, d\theta, \tag{3}$$

and triple integrals take the form

$$\iiint F(\rho, \phi, \theta)\, dV = \iiint F(\rho, \phi, \theta)\, \rho^2 \sin \phi\, d\rho\, d\phi\, d\theta. \tag{4}$$

To evaluate these integrals we usually integrate first with respect to ρ. The procedure for finding the limits of integration is shown in the following box. We restrict our attention to integrating over domains that are solids of revolution about the z-axis (or portions thereof) and for which the limits for θ and ϕ are constant.

How to Integrate in Spherical Coordinates

To evaluate

$$\iiint_D f(\rho, \phi, \theta)\, dV$$

over a region D in space in spherical coordinates, integrating first with respect to ρ, then with respect to ϕ, and finally with respect to θ, take the following steps.

STEP 1: *A sketch.* Sketch the region D along with its projection R on the xy-plane. Label the surfaces that bound D.

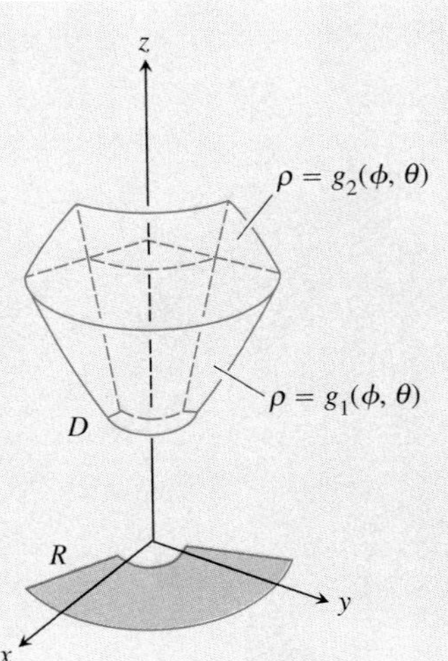

STEP 2: *The ρ-limits of integration.* Draw a ray M from the origin making an angle ϕ with the positive z-axis. Also draw the projection of M on the xy-plane (call the projection L). The ray L makes an angle θ with the positive x-axis. As ρ increases, M enters D at $\rho = g_1(\phi, \theta)$ and leaves at $\rho = g_2(\phi, \theta)$. These are the ρ-limits of integration.

STEP 3: *The ϕ-limits of integration.* For any given θ, the angle ϕ that M makes with the z-axis runs from $\phi = \phi_{\min}$ to $\phi = \phi_{\max}$. These are the ϕ-limits of integration.

STEP 4: *The θ-limits of integration.* The ray L sweeps over R as θ runs from α to β. These are the θ-limits of integration. The integral is

$$\iiint_D f(\rho, \phi, \theta)\, dV$$

$$= \int_{\theta=\alpha}^{\theta=\beta} \int_{\phi=\phi_{\min}}^{\phi=\phi_{\max}} \int_{\rho=g_1(\phi,\theta)}^{\rho=g_2(\phi,\theta)} f(\rho, \phi, \theta)\, \rho^2 \sin\phi \, d\rho\, d\phi\, d\theta. \quad (5)$$

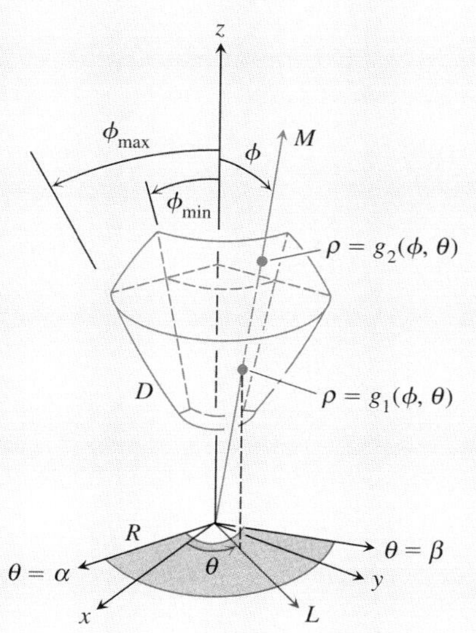

EXAMPLE 3 Find the volume of the upper region D cut from the solid sphere $\rho \le 1$ by the cone $\phi = \pi/3$.

Solution The volume is $V = \iiint_D \rho^2 \sin\phi\, d\rho\, d\phi\, d\theta$, the integral of $f(\rho, \phi, \theta) = 1$ over D.

To find the limits of integration for evaluating the integral, we take the following steps:

STEP 1: *A sketch.* We sketch D and its projection R on the xy-plane (Fig. 14.46).

STEP 2: *The ρ-limits of integration.* We draw a ray M from the origin making an angle ϕ with the positive z-axis. We also draw L, the projection of M on the xy-plane, along with the angle θ that L makes with the positive x-axis. Ray M enters D at $\rho = 0$ and leaves at $\rho = 1$.

STEP 3: *The ϕ-limits of integration.* The cone $\phi = \pi/3$ makes an angle of $\pi/3$ with the positive z-axis. For any given θ, the angle ϕ can run from $\phi = 0$ to $\phi = \pi/3$.

STEP 4: *The θ-limits of integration.* The ray L sweeps over R as θ runs from 0 to 2π. The volume is

$$V = \iiint_D \rho^2 \sin\phi\, d\rho\, d\phi\, d\theta = \int_0^{2\pi} \int_0^{\pi/3} \int_0^1 \rho^2 \sin\phi\, d\rho\, d\phi\, d\theta$$

$$= \int_0^{2\pi} \int_0^{\pi/3} \left[\frac{\rho^3}{3}\right]_0^1 \sin\phi\, d\phi\, d\theta = \int_0^{2\pi} \int_0^{\pi/3} \frac{1}{3} \sin\phi\, d\phi\, d\theta$$

$$= \int_0^{2\pi} \left[-\frac{1}{3}\cos\phi\right]_0^{\pi/3} d\theta = \int_0^{2\pi} \left(-\frac{1}{6} + \frac{1}{3}\right) d\theta = \frac{1}{6}(2\pi) = \frac{\pi}{3}.$$

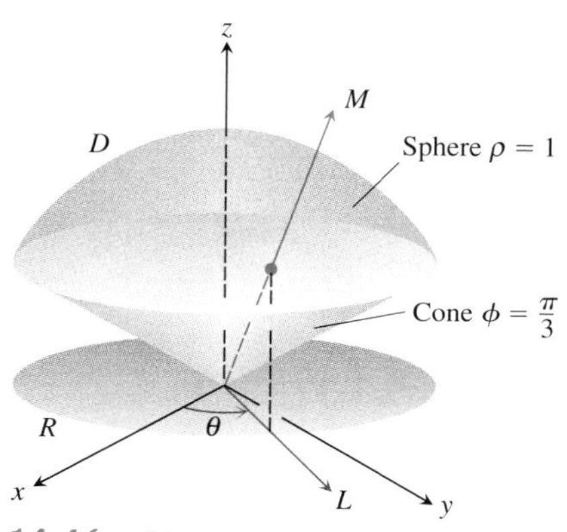

14.46 The solid in Example 3.

Coordinate Conversion Formulas (from Section 11.7)

Cylindrical to Rectanglar	Spherical to Rectangular
$x = r\cos\theta$	$x = \rho\sin\phi\cos\theta$
$y = r\sin\theta$	$y = \rho\sin\phi\sin\theta$
$z = z$	$z = \rho\cos\phi$

Spherical to Cylindrical

$r = \rho\sin\phi$
$z = \rho\cos\phi$
$\theta = \theta$

Corresponding volume elements

$$\begin{aligned} dV &= dx\,dy\,dz \\ &= dz\,r\,dr\,d\theta \\ &= \rho^2\sin\phi\,d\rho\,d\phi\,d\theta \end{aligned}$$

EXAMPLE 4 A solid of constant density $\delta = 1$ occupies the region D in Example 3. Find the solid's moment of inertia about the z-axis.

Solution In rectangular coordinates, the moment is

$$I_z = \iiint (x^2 + y^2)\,dV.$$

In spherical coordinates, $x^2 + y^2 = (\rho\sin\phi\cos\theta)^2 + (\rho\sin\phi\sin\theta)^2 = \rho^2\sin^2\phi$. Hence,

$$I_z = \iiint (\rho^2\sin^2\phi)\,\rho^2\sin\phi\,d\rho\,d\phi\,d\theta = \iiint \rho^4\sin^3\phi\,d\rho\,d\phi\,d\theta.$$

For the region in Example 3, this becomes

$$\begin{aligned} I_z &= \int_0^{2\pi}\int_0^{\pi/3}\int_0^1 \rho^4\sin^3\phi\,d\rho\,d\phi\,d\theta = \int_0^{2\pi}\int_0^{\pi/3}\left[\frac{\rho^5}{5}\right]_0^1 \sin^3\phi\,d\phi\,d\theta \\ &= \frac{1}{5}\int_0^{2\pi}\int_0^{\pi/3}(1-\cos^2\phi)\sin\phi\,d\phi\,d\theta = \frac{1}{5}\int_0^{2\pi}\left[-\cos\phi + \frac{\cos^3\phi}{3}\right]_0^{\pi/3} d\theta \\ &= \frac{1}{5}\int_0^{2\pi}\left(-\frac{1}{2} + 1 + \frac{1}{24} - \frac{1}{3}\right)d\theta \\ &= \frac{1}{5}\int_0^{2\pi}\frac{5}{24}\,d\theta = \frac{1}{24}(2\pi) = \frac{\pi}{12}. \end{aligned}$$

Exercises 14.6

Evaluate the cylindrical coordinate integrals in Exercises 1–6.

1. $\displaystyle\int_0^{2\pi}\int_0^1\int_r^{\sqrt{2-r^2}} dz\,r\,dr\,d\theta$

2. $\displaystyle\int_0^{2\pi}\int_0^3\int_{r^2/3}^{\sqrt{18-r^2}} dz\,r\,dr\,d\theta$

3. $\displaystyle\int_0^{2\pi}\int_0^{\theta/2\pi}\int_0^{3+24r^2} dz\,r\,dr\,d\theta$

4. $\displaystyle\int_0^{\pi}\int_0^{\theta/\pi}\int_{-\sqrt{4-r^2}}^{3\sqrt{4-r^2}} z\,dz\,r\,dr\,d\theta$

5. $\displaystyle\int_0^{2\pi}\int_0^1\int_r^{1/\sqrt{2-r^2}} 3\,dz\,r\,dr\,d\theta$

6. $\displaystyle\int_0^{2\pi}\int_0^1\int_{-1/2}^{1/2} (r^2\sin^2\theta + z^2)\,dz\,r\,dr\,d\theta$

Evaluate the spherical coordinate integrals in Exercises 7–12.

7. $\displaystyle\int_0^{\pi}\int_0^{\pi}\int_0^{2\sin\phi} \rho^2\sin\phi\,d\rho\,d\phi\,d\theta$

8. $\displaystyle\int_0^{2\pi}\int_0^{\pi/4}\int_0^2 (\rho\cos\phi)\,\rho^2\sin\phi\,d\rho\,d\phi\,d\theta$

9. $\displaystyle\int_0^{2\pi}\int_0^{\pi}\int_0^{(1-\cos\phi)/2} \rho^2\sin\phi\,d\rho\,d\phi\,d\theta$

10. $\displaystyle\int_0^{3\pi/2}\int_0^{\pi}\int_0^1 5\rho^3\sin^3\phi\,d\rho\,d\phi\,d\theta$

11. $\displaystyle\int_0^{2\pi}\int_0^{\pi/3}\int_{\sec\phi}^2 3\rho^2\sin\phi\,d\rho\,d\phi\,d\theta$

12. $\displaystyle\int_0^{2\pi}\int_0^{\pi/4}\int_0^{\sec\phi} (\rho\cos\phi)\,\rho^2\sin\phi\,d\rho\,d\phi\,d\theta$

The integrals we have seen so far suggest that there are preferred orders of integration for cylindrical and spherical coordinates, but this is not really the case. The other orders usually work well and are occasionally better. Evaluate the integrals in Exercises 13–20.

13. $\displaystyle\int_0^{2\pi}\int_0^3\int_0^{z/3} r^3\,dr\,dz\,d\theta$

14. $\displaystyle\int_{-1}^1\int_0^{2\pi}\int_0^{1+\cos\theta} 4r\,dr\,d\theta\,dz$

15. $\displaystyle\int_0^1\int_0^{\sqrt{z}}\int_0^{2\pi} (r^2\cos^2\theta + z^2)r\,d\theta\,dr\,dz$

16. $\int_0^2 \int_{r-2}^{\sqrt{4-r^2}} \int_0^{2\pi} (r \sin \theta + 1) r \, d\theta \, dz \, dr$

17. $\int_0^2 \int_{-\pi}^0 \int_{\pi/4}^{\pi/2} \rho^3 \sin 2\phi \, d\phi \, d\theta \, d\rho$

18. $\int_{\pi/6}^{\pi/3} \int_{\csc\phi}^{2\csc\phi} \int_0^{2\pi} \rho^2 \sin \phi \, d\theta \, d\rho \, d\phi$

19. $\int_0^1 \int_0^{\pi} \int_0^{\pi/4} 12\rho \sin^3 \phi \, d\phi \, d\theta \, d\rho$

20. $\int_{\pi/6}^{\pi/2} \int_{-\pi/2}^{\pi/2} \int_{\csc\phi}^{2} 5\rho^4 \sin^3 \phi \, d\rho \, d\theta \, d\phi$

21. Set up triple integrals for the volume of the sphere $\rho = 2$ in (a) spherical, (b) cylindrical, and (c) rectangular coordinates.

22. Let D be the region in the first octant that is bounded below by the cone $\phi = \pi/4$ and above by the sphere $\rho = 3$. Express the volume of D as an iterated triple integral in (a) cylindrical and (b) spherical coordinates. Then (c) find V.

23. Let D be the smaller cap cut from a solid ball of radius 2 units by a plane 1 unit from the center of the sphere. Express the volume of D as an iterated triple integral in (a) spherical, (b) cylindrical, and (c) rectangular coordinates. Then (d) find the volume by evaluating one of the three triple integrals.

24. Express the moment of inertia I_z of the solid hemisphere $x^2 + y^2 + z^2 \le 1$, $z \ge 0$, as an iterated integral in (a) cylindrical and (b) spherical coordinates. Then (c) find I_z.

CYLINDRICAL COORDINATES

In Exercises 25–30, set up the iterated integral for evaluating $\iiint_D f(r, \theta, z) \, dz \, r \, dr \, d\theta$ over the given region D.

25. D is the right circular cylinder whose base is the circle $r = 2 \sin \theta$ in the xy-plane and whose top lies in the plane $z = 4 - y$.

26. D is the right circular cylinder whose base is the circle $r = 3 \cos \theta$ and whose top lies in the plane $z = 5 - x$.

27. D is the solid right cylinder whose base is the region in the xy-plane that lies inside the cardioid $r = 1 + \cos \theta$ and outside the circle $r = 1$ and whose top lies in the plane $z = 4$.

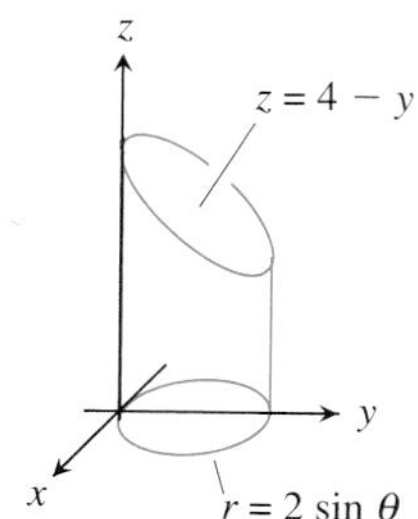

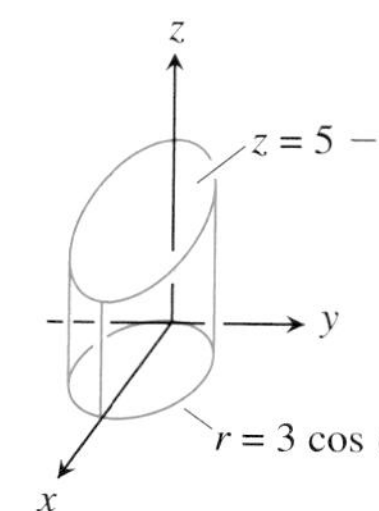

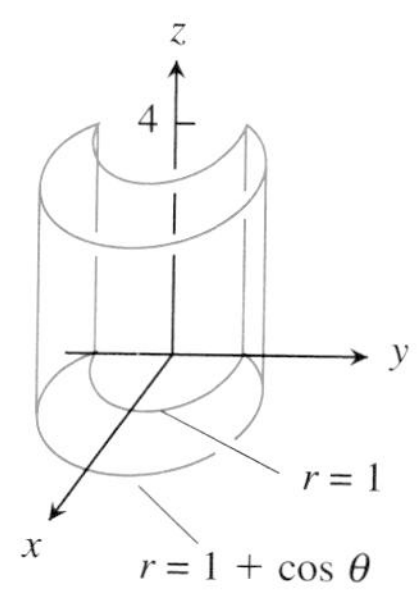

28. D is the solid right cylinder whose base is the region between the circles $r = \cos \theta$ and $r = 2 \cos \theta$, and whose top lies in the plane $z = 3 - y$.

29. D is the prism whose base is the triangle in the xy-plane bounded by the x-axis and the lines $y = x$ and $x = 1$ and whose top lies in the plane $z = 2 - y$.

30. D is the prism whose base is the triangle in the xy-plane bounded by the y-axis and the lines $y = x$ and $y = 1$ and whose top lies in the plane $z = 2 - x$.

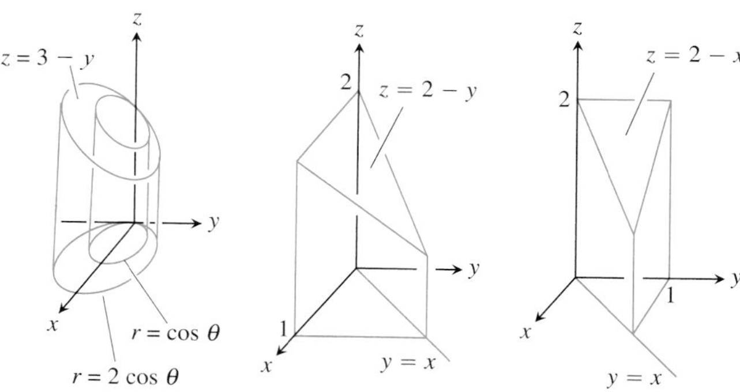

Find the volumes of the solids in Exercises 31–36.

31.

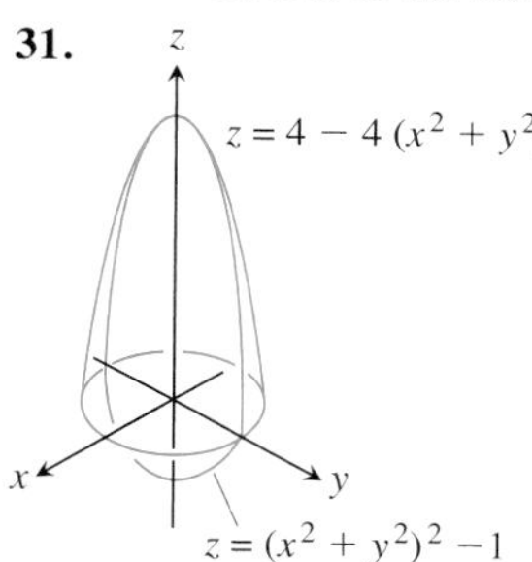

32.

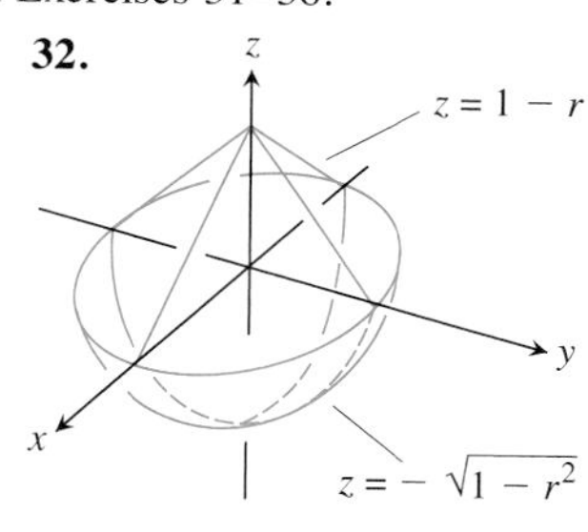

33.

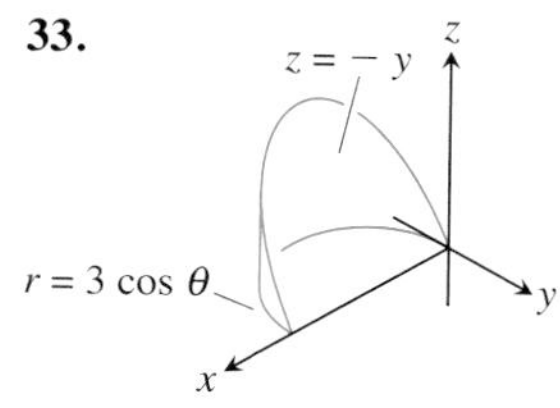

34.

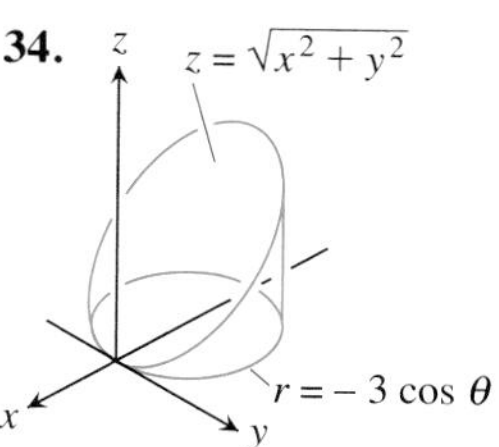

35.

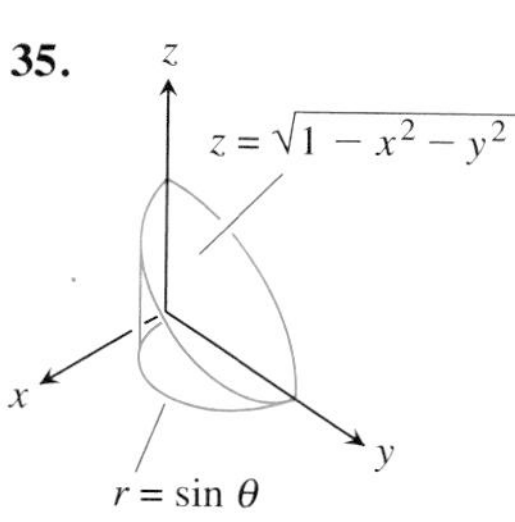

36.

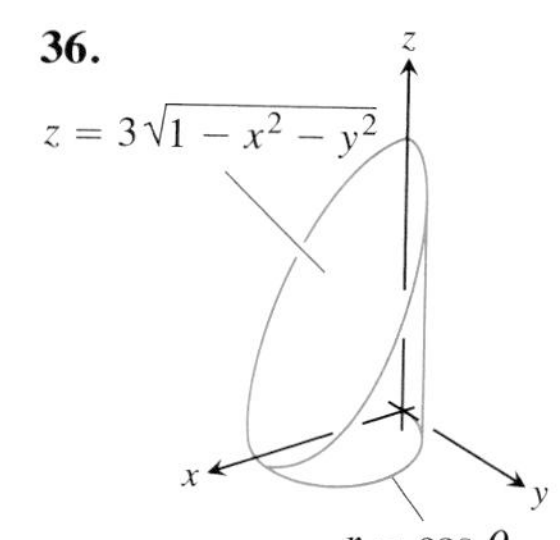

37. Find the volume of the region bounded below by the plane $z = 0$, laterally by the cylinder $x^2 + y^2 = 1$, and above by the paraboloid $z = x^2 + y^2$.

38. Find the volume of the region bounded below by the paraboloid $z = x^2 + y^2$, laterally by the cylinder $x^2 + y^2 = 1$, and above by the paraboloid $z = x^2 + y^2 + 1$.

39. Find the volume of the region enclosed by the cylinder $x^2 + y^2 = 4$ and the planes $z = 0$ and $y + z = 4$.

40. Find the volume of the region enclosed by the cylinder $x^2 + y^2 = 4$ and the planes $z = 0$ and $x + y + z = 4$.

41. Find the volume of the region bounded above by the paraboloid $z = 5 - x^2 - y^2$ and below by the paraboloid $z = 4x^2 + 4y^2$.

42. Find the volume of the region bounded above by the paraboloid $z = 9 - x^2 - y^2$, below by the xy-plane, and lying *outside* the cylinder $x^2 + y^2 = 1$.

43. Find the volume of the region cut from the solid cylinder $x^2 + y^2 \le 1$ by the sphere $x^2 + y^2 + z^2 = 4$.

44. Find the volume of the region bounded above by the sphere $x^2 + y^2 + z^2 = 2$ and below by the paraboloid $z = x^2 + y^2$.

45. Find the average value of the function $f(r, \theta, z) = r$ over the region bounded by the cylinder $r = 1$ between the planes $z = -1$ and $z = 1$.

46. Find the average value of the function $f(r, \theta, z) = r$ over the solid ball bounded by the sphere $r^2 + z^2 = 1$. (This is the sphere $x^2 + y^2 + z^2 = 1$.)

47. A solid is bounded below by the plane $z = 0$, above by the cone $z = r$, $r \ge 0$, and on the sides by the cylinder $r = 1$. Find the center of mass.

48. Find the centroid of the region in the first octant that is bounded above by the cone $z = \sqrt{x^2 + y^2}$, below by the plane $z = 0$, and on the sides by the cylinder $x^2 + y^2 = 4$ and the planes $x = 0$ and $y = 0$.

49. Find the centroid of the region that is bounded above by the surface $z = \sqrt{r}$, on the sides by the cylinder $r = 4$, and below by the xy-plane.

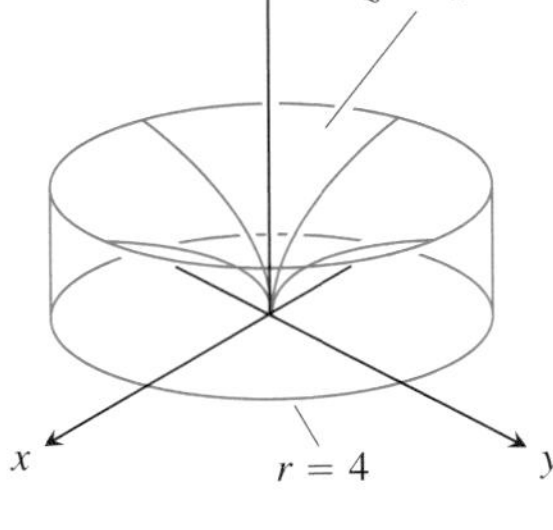

50. Find the moment of inertia and radius of gyration about the z-axis of a thick-walled right circular cylinder bounded on the inside by the cylinder $r = 1$, on the outside by the cylinder $r = 2$, and on the top and bottom by the planes $z = 4$ and $z = 0$. (Take $\delta = 1$.)

51. Find the moment of inertia of a solid circular cylinder of radius 1 and height 2 (a) about the axis of the cylinder, (b) about a line through the centroid perpendicular to the axis of the cylinder. (Take $\delta = 1$.)

52. Find the moment of inertia of a right circular cone of base radius 1 and height 1 about an axis through the vertex parallel to the base. (Take $\delta = 1$.)

53. Find the moment of inertia of a solid sphere of radius a about a diameter. (Take $\delta = 1$.)

54. Find the centroid of the region cut from the solid ball $r^2 + z^2 \le 1$ by the half-planes $\theta = -\pi/3$, $r \ge 0$ and $\theta = \pi/3$, $r \ge 0$.

SPHERICAL COORDINATES

In Exercises 55–60, (a) find the spherical coordinate limits for the integral that calculates the volume of the given solid, and (b) then evaluate the integral.

55. The solid between the sphere $\rho = \cos\phi$ and the hemisphere $\rho = 2$, $z \ge 0$

56. The solid bounded below by the hemisphere $\rho = 1$, $z \ge 0$ and above by the cardioid of revolution $\rho = 1 + \cos\phi$

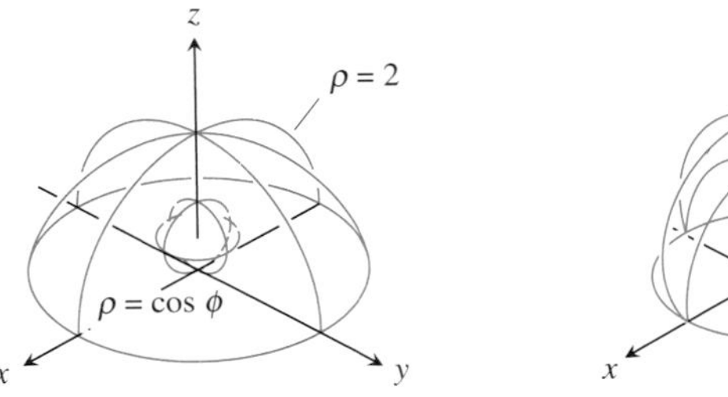

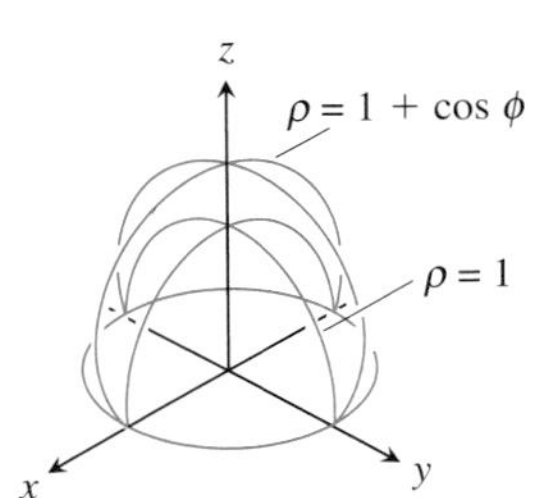

57. The solid enclosed by the cardioid of revolution $\rho = 1 - \cos\phi$

58. The upper portion cut from the solid in Exercise 57 by the xy-plane

59. The solid bounded below by the sphere $\rho = 2\cos\phi$ and above by the cone $z = \sqrt{x^2 + y^2}$

60. The solid bounded below by the xy-plane, on the sides by the sphere $\rho = 2$, and above by the cone $\phi = \pi/3$

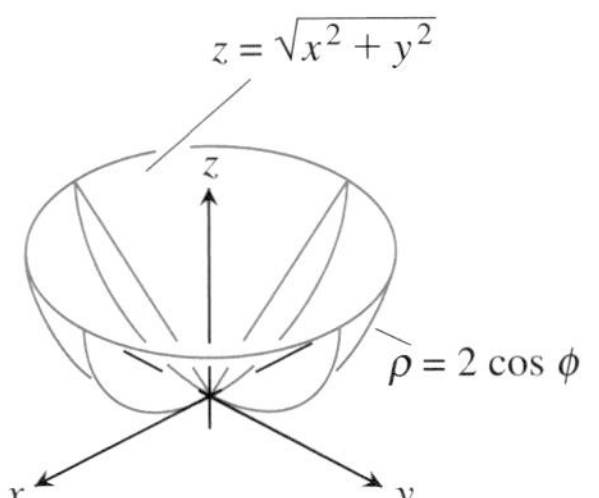

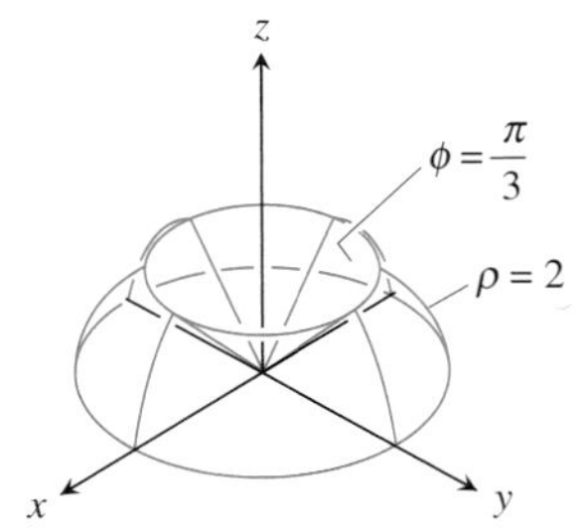

61. Find the volume of the portion of the solid sphere $\rho \le a$ that lies between the cones $\phi = \pi/3$ and $\phi = 2\pi/3$.

62. Find the volume of the region cut from the solid sphere $\rho \le a$ by the half-planes $\theta = 0$ and $\theta = \pi/6$ in the first octant.

63. Find the volume of the smaller region cut from the solid sphere $\rho \le 2$ by the plane $z = 1$.

64. Find the volume of the solid enclosed by the cone $z = \sqrt{x^2 + y^2}$ between the planes $z = 1$ and $z = 2$.

65. Find the volume of the solid cut from the thick-walled cylinder $1 \le x^2 + y^2 \le 2$ by the cones $z = \pm\sqrt{x^2 + y^2}$.

66. Find the volume of the region that lies inside the sphere $x^2 + y^2 + z^2 = 2$ and outside the cylinder $x^2 + y^2 = 1$.

67. Find the average value of the function $f(\rho, \phi, \theta) = \rho$ over the solid ball $\rho \le 1$.

68. Find the centroid of the solid in Exercise 60.

69. Find the centroid of the solid bounded above by the sphere $\rho = a$ and below by the cone $\phi = \pi/4$.

70. A solid ball is bounded by the sphere $\rho = a$. Find the moment of inertia and radius of gyration about the z-axis if the density is

a) $\delta(\rho, \phi, \theta) = \rho^2$, **b)** $\delta(\rho, \phi, \theta) = r = \rho \sin \phi$.

Writing for Your Own Knowledge

Answer the following questions in writing. Some answers will take only a sentence or two; others may require several paragraphs. Some explanations may also call for graphs or sketches.

1. How do you integrate in cylindrical coordinates?
2. How do you interpret the volume element $dV = dz\, r\, dr\, d\theta$?
3. What surfaces have relatively simple equations in cylindrical coordinates?
4. How do you integrate in spherical coordinates?
5. How do you interpret the volume element $dV = \rho^2 \sin \phi\, d\rho\, d\phi\, d\theta$?
6. What surfaces have relatively simple equations in spherical coordinates?
7. What equations do you use to convert from cylindrical to rectangular coordinates? from spherical to cylindrical coordinates? from spherical to rectangular coordinates?

14.7 *Substitutions in Multiple Integrals*

This section shows how to evaluate multiple integrals by substitution. As in single integration, the goal of substitution is to replace complicated integrals by ones that are easier to evaluate. Substitutions accomplish this by simplifying the integrand, the limits of integration, or both.

Substitutions in Double Integrals

The polar coordinate substitution of Section 14.3 is a special case of a more general substitution method for double integrals, a method that pictures changes in variables as transformations of regions.

Suppose that a region G in the uv-plane is transformed one-to-one into the region R in the xy-plane by equations of the form

$$x = g(u, v), \qquad y = h(u, v),$$

as suggested in Fig. 14.47. Then any function $f(x, y)$ defined on R can be thought of as a function $f(g(u, v), h(u, v))$ defined on G as well. How is the integral of $f(x, y)$ over R related to the integral of $f(g(u, v), h(u, v))$ over G?

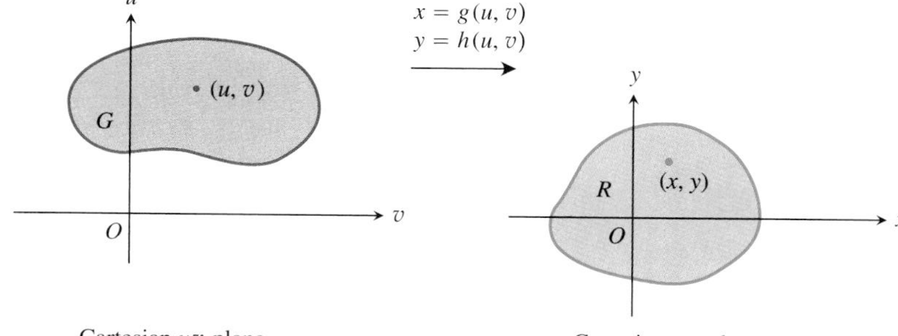

14.47 The equations $x = g(u, v)$ and $y = h(u, v)$ allow us to write an integral over a region R in the xy-plane as an integral over a region G in the uv-plane.

Notice the "Reversed" Order

The transforming equations $x = g(u, v)$ and $y = h(u, v)$ go from G to R, but we use them to change an integral over R into an integral over G.

The answer is: If g, h, and f have continuous partial derivatives and $J(u, v)$ (to be discussed in a moment) is zero only at isolated points, if at all, then

$$\iint_R f(x, y)\,dx\,dy = \iint_G f(g(u, v), h(u, v))\,|J(u, v)|\,du\,dv. \tag{1}$$

The factor $J(u, v)$, whose absolute value appears in Eq. (1), is called the *Jacobian* of the coordinate transformation, named after the mathematician Carl Jacobi.

DEFINITION

The **Jacobian determinant** or **Jacobian** of the coordinate transformation $x = g(u, v)$, $y = h(u, v)$ is

$$J(u, v) = \begin{vmatrix} \dfrac{\partial x}{\partial u} & \dfrac{\partial x}{\partial v} \\[2ex] \dfrac{\partial y}{\partial u} & \dfrac{\partial y}{\partial v} \end{vmatrix} = \frac{\partial x}{\partial u}\frac{\partial y}{\partial v} - \frac{\partial y}{\partial u}\frac{\partial x}{\partial v}. \tag{2}$$

The Jacobian is also denoted by

$$J(u, v) = \frac{\partial(x, y)}{\partial(u, v)}$$

to help remember how the determinant in Eq. (2) is constructed from the partial derivatives of x and y. The derivation of Eq. (1) is intricate and properly belongs to a course in advanced calculus. We will not give the derivation here.

For polar coordinates, we have r and θ in place of u and v. With $x = r\cos\theta$ and $y = r\sin\theta$, the Jacobian is

$$J(r, \theta) = \begin{vmatrix} \dfrac{\partial x}{\partial r} & \dfrac{\partial x}{\partial \theta} \\[2ex] \dfrac{\partial y}{\partial r} & \dfrac{\partial y}{\partial \theta} \end{vmatrix} = \begin{vmatrix} \cos\theta & -r\sin\theta \\ \sin\theta & r\cos\theta \end{vmatrix} = r(\cos^2\theta + \sin^2\theta) = r.$$

Hence, Eq. (1) becomes

$$\begin{aligned} \iint_R f(x, y)\,dx\,dy &= \iint_G f(r\cos\theta, r\sin\theta)\,|r|\,dr\,d\theta \\ &= \iint_G f(r\cos\theta, r\sin\theta)\,r\,dr\,d\theta, \qquad \text{If } r \ge 0 \end{aligned} \tag{3}$$

which is Eq. (7) in Section 14.3.

Figure 14.48 shows how the equations $x = r\cos\theta$, $y = r\sin\theta$ transform the rectangle G: $0 \le r \le 1$, $0 \le \theta \le \pi/2$ into the quarter circle R bounded by $x^2 + y^2 = 1$ in the first quadrant of the xy-plane.

Notice that the integral on the right-hand side of Eq. (3) is not the integral of $f(r\cos\theta, r\sin\theta)$ over a region in the polar coordinate plane. It is the integral of the product of $f(r\cos\theta, r\sin\theta)$ and r over a region G in the *Cartesian* $r\theta$-plane.

Here is an example of another substitution.

θ $\frac{\pi}{2}$ G O 1 r

Cartesian $r\theta$-plane

$x = r\cos\theta$
$y = r\sin\theta$

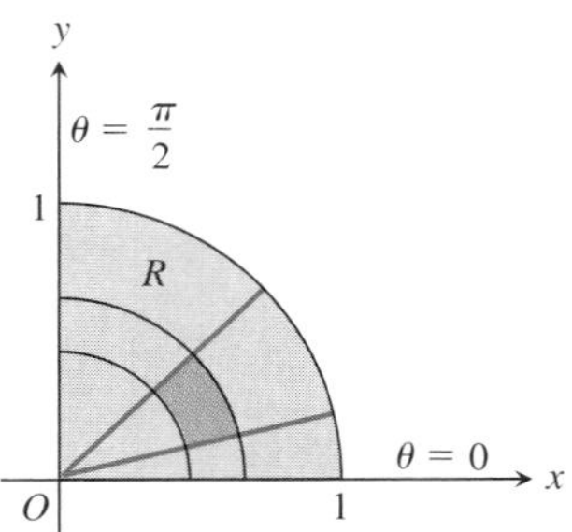

Cartesian xy-plane

14.48 The equations $x = r\cos\theta$, $y = r\sin\theta$ transform G into R.

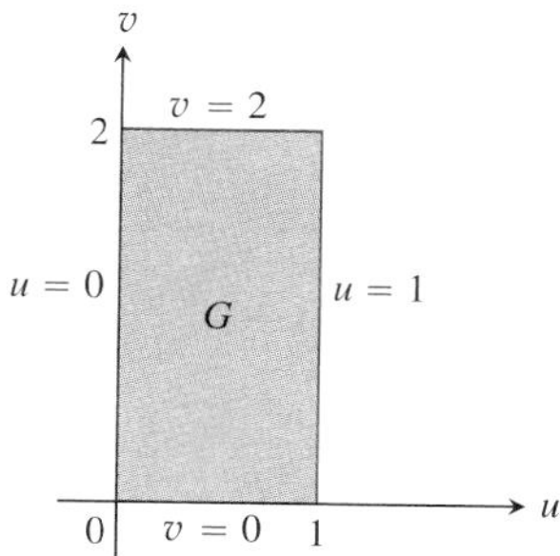

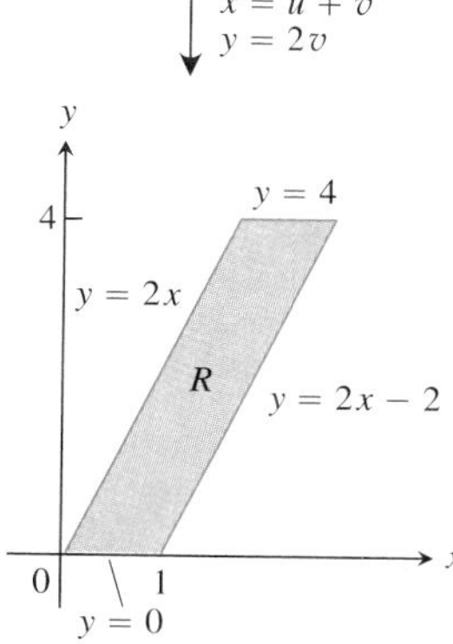

14.49 The equations $x = u + v$ and $y = 2v$ transform G into R. Reversing the transformation by the equations $u = (2x - y)/2$ and $v = y/2$ transforms R into G. See Example 1.

EXAMPLE 1 Evaluate

$$\int_0^4 \int_{x=y/2}^{x=(y/2)+1} \frac{2x - y}{2}\, dx\, dy$$

by applying the transformation

$$u = \frac{2x - y}{2}, \qquad v = \frac{y}{2} \tag{4}$$

and integrating over an appropriate region in the uv-plane.

Solution We sketch the region R of integration in the xy-plane and identify its boundaries (Fig. 14.49).

To apply Eq. (1), we need to find the corresponding uv-region G and the Jacobian of the transformation. To find them, we first solve Eqs. (4) for x and y in terms of u and v. Routine algebra gives

$$x = u + v, \qquad y = 2v. \tag{5}$$

We then find the boundaries of G by substituting these expressions into the equations for the boundaries of R (Fig. 14.49).

xy-equations for the boundary of R	Corresponding uv-equations for the boundary of G	Simplified uv-equations
$x = y/2$	$u + v = 2v/2 = v$	$u = 0$
$x = (y/2) + 1$	$u + v = (2v/2) + 1 = v + 1$	$u = 1$
$y = 0$	$2v = 0$	$v = 0$
$y = 4$	$2v = 4$	$v = 2$

The Jacobian of the transformation (again from Eqs. 5) is

$$J(u, v) = \begin{vmatrix} \dfrac{\partial x}{\partial u} & \dfrac{\partial x}{\partial v} \\ \dfrac{\partial y}{\partial u} & \dfrac{\partial y}{\partial v} \end{vmatrix} = \begin{vmatrix} \dfrac{\partial}{\partial u}(u + v) & \dfrac{\partial}{\partial v}(u + v) \\ \dfrac{\partial}{\partial u}(2v) & \dfrac{\partial}{\partial v}(2v) \end{vmatrix} = \begin{vmatrix} 1 & 1 \\ 0 & 2 \end{vmatrix} = 2.$$

We now have everything we need to apply Eq. (1):

$$\int_0^4 \int_{x=y/2}^{x=(y/2)+1} \frac{2x - y}{2}\, dx\, dy = \int_{v=0}^{v=2} \int_{u=0}^{u=1} u\,|J(u, v)|\, du\, dv$$

$$= \int_0^2 \int_0^1 (u)(2)\, du\, dv = \int_0^2 \Big[u^2\Big]_0^1 dv = \int_0^2 dv = 2.$$

EXAMPLE 2 Evaluate

$$\int_0^1 \int_0^{1-x} \sqrt{x + y}\,(y - 2x)^2\, dy\, dx.$$

Solution We sketch the region R of integration in the xy-plane and identify its boundaries (Fig. 14.50 on the following page). The integrand suggests the transformation $u = x + y$ and $v = y - 2x$. Routine algebra produces x and y as functions of u and v:

$$x = \frac{u}{3} - \frac{v}{3}, \qquad y = \frac{2u}{3} + \frac{v}{3}. \tag{6}$$

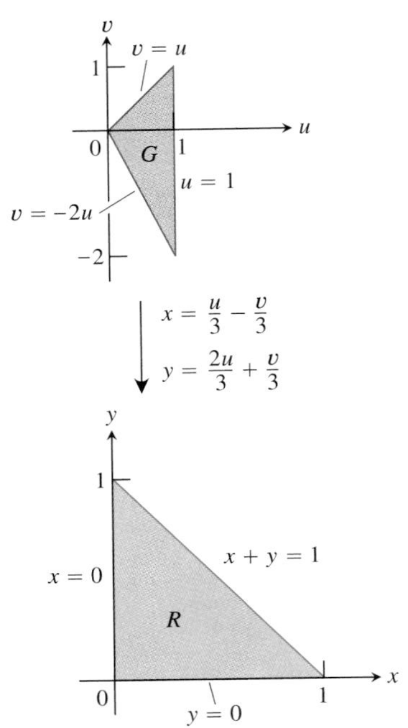

14.50 The equations $x = (u/3) - (v/3)$ and $y = (2u/3) + (v/3)$ transform G into R. Reversing the transformation by the equations $u = x + y$ and $v = y - 2x$ transforms R into G. See Example 2.

From Eqs. (6) we can find the boundaries of the uv-region G (Fig. 14.50).

xy-equations for the boundary of R	Corresponding uv-equations for the boundary of G	Simplified uv-equations
$x + y = 1$	$\left(\frac{u}{3} - \frac{v}{3}\right) + \left(\frac{2u}{3} + \frac{v}{3}\right) = 1$	$u = 1$
$x = 0$	$\frac{u}{3} - \frac{v}{3} = 0$	$v = u$
$y = 0$	$\frac{2u}{3} + \frac{v}{3} = 0$	$v = -2u$

The Jacobian of the transformation in Eq. (6) is

$$J(u, v) = \begin{vmatrix} \dfrac{\partial x}{\partial u} & \dfrac{\partial x}{\partial v} \\ \dfrac{\partial y}{\partial u} & \dfrac{\partial y}{\partial v} \end{vmatrix} = \begin{vmatrix} \dfrac{1}{3} & -\dfrac{1}{3} \\ \dfrac{2}{3} & \dfrac{1}{3} \end{vmatrix} = \frac{1}{3}.$$

Applying Eq. (1), we evaluate the integral:

$$\begin{aligned} \int_0^1 \int_0^{1-x} \sqrt{x+y}\,(y-2x)^2\,dy\,dx &= \int_{u=0}^{u=1} \int_{v=-2u}^{v=u} u^{1/2} v^2 |J(u, v)|\,dv\,du \\ &= \int_0^1 \int_{-2u}^{u} u^{1/2} v^2 \left(\frac{1}{3}\right) dv\,du \\ &= \frac{1}{3} \int_0^1 u^{1/2} \left(\frac{1}{3} v^3\right)\Big]_{v=-2u}^{v=u} du \\ &= \frac{1}{9} \int_0^1 u^{1/2} (u^3 + 8u^3)\,du \\ &= \int_0^1 u^{7/2}\,du = \frac{2}{9} u^{9/2} \Big]_0^1 = \frac{2}{9}. \end{aligned}$$

Substitutions in Triple Integrals

The cylindrical and spherical coordinate substitutions are special cases of a substitution method that pictures changes of variables in triple integrals as transformations of three-dimensional regions. The method is like the method for double integrals except that now we work in three dimensions instead of two.

Suppose that a region G in uvw-space is transformed one-to-one into the region D in xyz-space by differentiable equations of the form

$$x = g(u, v, w), \qquad y = h(u, v, w), \qquad z = k(u, v, w),$$

as suggested in Fig. 14.51. Then any function $F(x, y, z)$ defined on D can be thought of as a function

$$F(g(u, v, w), h(u, v, w), k(u, v, w)) = H(u, v, w)$$

defined on G. If g, h, and k have continuous first partial derivatives, then the integral of $F(x, y, z)$ over D is related to the integral of $H(u, v, w)$ over G by the

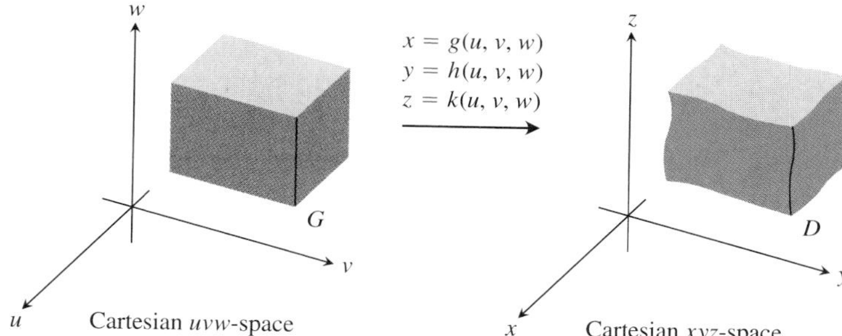

14.51 The equations $x = g(u, v, w)$, $y = h(u, v, w)$, and $z = k(u, v, w)$ allow us to write an integral over a region D in Cartesian xyz-space as an integral over a region G in Cartesian uvw-space.

equation

$$\iiint_D F(x, y, z)\, dx\, dy\, dz = \iiint_G H(u, v, w)\, |J(u, v, w)|\, du\, dv\, dw. \tag{7}$$

The factor $J(u, v, w)$, whose absolute value appears in this equation, is the **Jacobian determinant**

$$J(u, v, w) = \begin{vmatrix} \dfrac{\partial x}{\partial u} & \dfrac{\partial x}{\partial v} & \dfrac{\partial x}{\partial w} \\ \dfrac{\partial y}{\partial u} & \dfrac{\partial y}{\partial v} & \dfrac{\partial y}{\partial w} \\ \dfrac{\partial z}{\partial u} & \dfrac{\partial z}{\partial v} & \dfrac{\partial z}{\partial w} \end{vmatrix} = \frac{\partial(x, y, z)}{\partial(u, v, w)}. \tag{8}$$

As in the two-dimensional case, the derivation of the change-of-variable formula in Eq. (7) is complicated and we will not go into it here.

For cylindrical coordinates, r, θ, and z take the place of u, v, and w. The transformation from Cartesian $r\theta z$-space to Cartesian xyz-space is given by the equations

$$x = r\cos\theta, \qquad y = r\sin\theta, \qquad z = z$$

(Fig. 14.52). The Jacobian of the transformation is

$$J(r, \theta, z) = \begin{vmatrix} \dfrac{\partial x}{\partial r} & \dfrac{\partial x}{\partial \theta} & \dfrac{\partial x}{\partial z} \\ \dfrac{\partial y}{\partial r} & \dfrac{\partial y}{\partial \theta} & \dfrac{\partial y}{\partial z} \\ \dfrac{\partial z}{\partial r} & \dfrac{\partial z}{\partial \theta} & \dfrac{\partial z}{\partial z} \end{vmatrix} = \begin{vmatrix} \cos\theta & -r\sin\theta & 0 \\ \sin\theta & r\cos\theta & 0 \\ 0 & 0 & 1 \end{vmatrix}$$

$$= r\cos^2\theta + r\sin^2\theta = r.$$

The corresponding version of Eq. (7) is

$$\iiint_D F(x, y, z)\, dx\, dy\, dz = \iiint_G H(r, \theta, z)\, |r|\, dr\, d\theta\, dz. \tag{9}$$

We can drop the absolute value signs whenever $r \geq 0$.

For spherical coordinates, ρ, ϕ, and θ take the place of u, v, and w. The

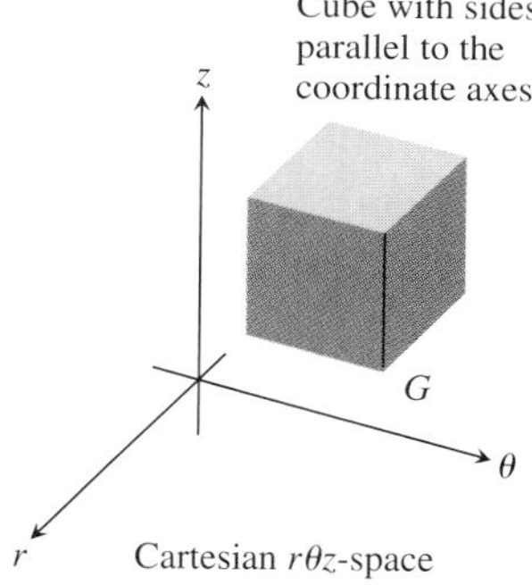

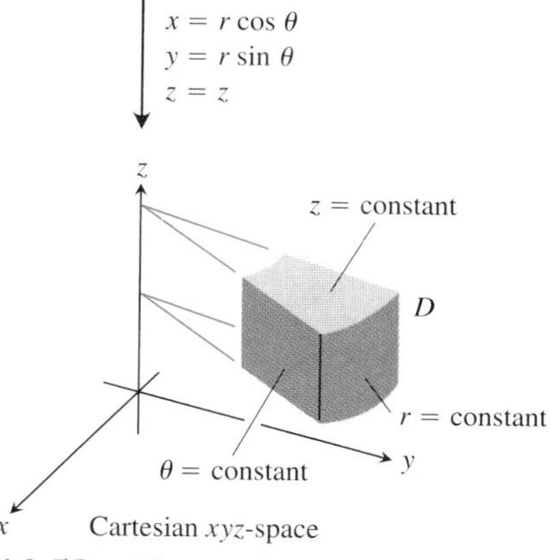

14.52 The equations $x = r\cos\theta$, $y = r\sin\theta$, and $z = z$ transform G into D.

14.53 The equations $x = \rho \sin \phi \cos \theta$, $y = \rho \sin \phi \sin \theta$, and $z = \rho \cos \phi$ transform G into D.

transformation from Cartesian $\rho\phi\theta$-space to Cartesian xyz-space is given by the equations

$$x = \rho \sin \phi \cos \theta, \qquad y = \rho \sin \phi \sin \theta, \qquad z = \rho \cos \phi$$

(Fig. 14.53). The Jacobian of the transformation is

$$J(\rho, \phi, \theta) = \begin{vmatrix} \dfrac{\partial x}{\partial \rho} & \dfrac{\partial x}{\partial \phi} & \dfrac{\partial x}{\partial \theta} \\ \dfrac{\partial y}{\partial \rho} & \dfrac{\partial y}{\partial \phi} & \dfrac{\partial y}{\partial \theta} \\ \dfrac{\partial z}{\partial \rho} & \dfrac{\partial z}{\partial \phi} & \dfrac{\partial z}{\partial \theta} \end{vmatrix} = \rho^2 \sin \phi \tag{10}$$

(Exercise 9). The corresponding version of Eq. (7) is

$$\iiint\limits_D F(x, y, z)\, dx\, dy\, dz = \iiint\limits_G H(\rho, \phi, \theta)\, |\rho^2 \sin \phi|\, d\rho\, d\phi\, d\theta. \tag{11}$$

We can drop the absolute value signs because $\sin \phi$ is never negative.

Here is an example of another substitution.

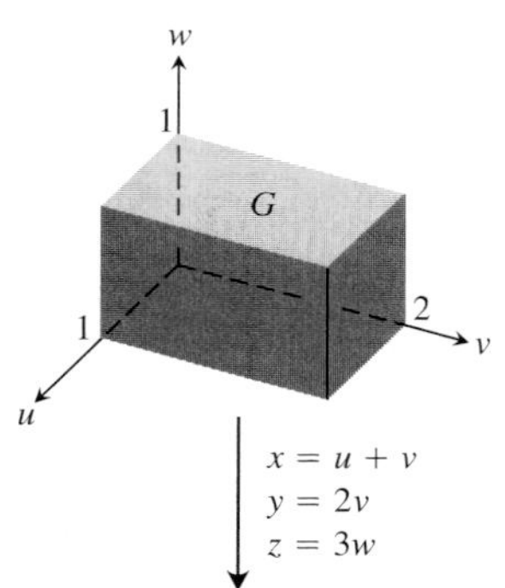

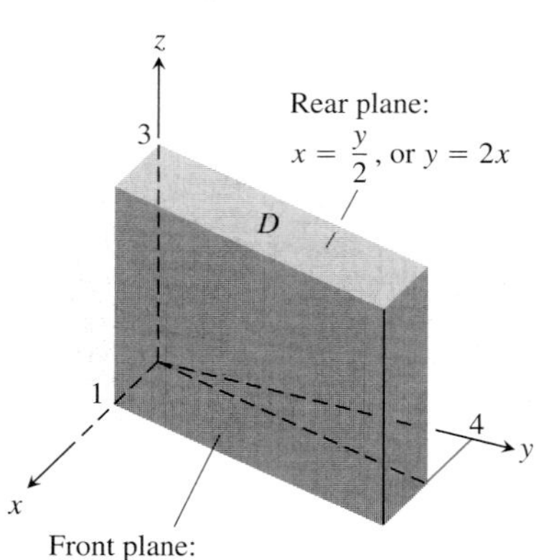

Front plane: $x = \frac{y}{2} + 1$, or $y = 2x - 2$

14.54 The equations $x = u + v$, $y = 2v$, and $z = 3w$ transform G into D. Reversing the transformation by the equations $u = (2x - y)/2$, $v = y/2$, and $w = z/3$ transforms D into G. See Example 3.

EXAMPLE 3 Evaluate

$$\int_0^3 \int_0^4 \int_{x = y/2}^{x = (y/2) + 1} \left(\frac{2x - y}{2} + \frac{z}{3}\right) dx\, dy\, dz$$

by applying the transformation

$$u = \frac{2x - y}{2}, \qquad v = \frac{y}{2}, \qquad w = \frac{z}{3} \tag{12}$$

and integrating over an appropriate region in uvw-space.

Solution We sketch the region D of integration in xyz-space and identify its boundaries (Fig. 14.54). In this case, the bounding surfaces are planes.

To apply Eq. (7), we need to find the corresponding uvw-region G and the Jacobian of the transformation. To find them, we first solve Eqs. (12) for x, y, and z in terms of u, v, and w. Routine algebra gives

$$x = u + v, \qquad y = 2v, \qquad z = 3w. \tag{13}$$

We then find the boundaries of G by substituting these expressions into the equations for the boundaries of D:

xyz-equations for the boundary of D	Corresponding uvw-equations for the boundary of G	Simplified uvw-equations
$x = y/2$	$u + v = 2v/2 = v$	$u = 0$
$x = (y/2) + 1$	$u + v = (2v/2) + 1 = v + 1$	$u = 1$
$y = 0$	$2v = 0$	$v = 0$
$y = 4$	$2v = 4$	$v = 2$
$z = 0$	$3w = 0$	$w = 0$
$z = 3$	$3w = 3$	$w = 1$

Carl Gustav Jacob Jacobi

Jacobi (1804–1851), one of nineteenth-century Germany's most accomplished scientists, developed the theory of determinants and transformations into a powerful tool for evaluating multiple integrals and solving differential equations. He also applied transformation methods to study nonelementary integrals like the ones that arise in the calculation of arc length. Like Euler, Jacobi was a prolific writer and an even more prolific calculator and worked in a variety of mathematical and applied fields.

The Jacobian of the transformation, again from Eqs. (13), is

$$J(u, v, w) = \begin{vmatrix} \dfrac{\partial x}{\partial u} & \dfrac{\partial x}{\partial v} & \dfrac{\partial x}{\partial w} \\ \dfrac{\partial y}{\partial u} & \dfrac{\partial y}{\partial v} & \dfrac{\partial y}{\partial w} \\ \dfrac{\partial z}{\partial u} & \dfrac{\partial z}{\partial v} & \dfrac{\partial z}{\partial w} \end{vmatrix} = \begin{vmatrix} 1 & 1 & 0 \\ 0 & 2 & 0 \\ 0 & 0 & 3 \end{vmatrix} = 6.$$

We now have everything we need to apply Eq. (7):

$$\int_0^3 \int_0^4 \int_{x=y/2}^{x=(y/2)+1} \left(\frac{2x - y}{2} + \frac{z}{3}\right) dx\, dy\, dz$$

$$= \int_0^1 \int_0^2 \int_0^1 (u + w)\, |J(u, v, w)|\, du\, dv\, dw$$

$$= \int_0^1 \int_0^2 \int_0^1 (u + w)(6)\, du\, dv\, dw = 6 \int_0^1 \int_0^2 \left[\frac{u^2}{2} + uw\right]_0^1 dv\, dw$$

$$= 6 \int_0^1 \int_0^2 \left(\frac{1}{2} + w\right) dv\, dw = 6 \int_0^1 \left[\frac{v}{2} + vw\right]_0^2 dw = 6 \int_0^1 (1 + 2w)\, dw$$

$$= 6\left[w + w^2\right]_0^1 = 6(2) = 12.$$

Exercises 14.7

DOUBLE INTEGRALS

1. Evaluate the integral

$$\int_0^4 \int_{x=y/2}^{x=(y/2)+1} \frac{2x - y}{2}\, dx\, dy$$

from Example 1 directly by integration with respect to x and y to confirm that its value is 2.

2. Find the Jacobian $\partial(x, y)/\partial(u, v)$ for the transformation

a) $x = u \cos v, \quad y = u \sin v,$
b) $x = u \sin v, \quad y = u \cos v.$

3. **a)** Solve the system

$$u = x - y, \qquad v = 2x + y$$

for x and y in terms of u and v. Then find the value of the Jacobian $\partial(x, y)/\partial(u, v)$.

b) Let R be the region in the first quadrant bounded by the lines $y = -2x + 4$, $y = -2x + 7$, $y = x - 2$, and $y = x + 1$. Evaluate

$$\iint_R (2x^2 - xy - y^2)\, dx\, dy$$

by changing variables with the equations in (a) and integrating over a region G in the uv-plane.

4. a) Find the Jacobian of the transformation $x = u$, $y = uv$, and sketch the region G: $1 \le u \le 2$, $1 \le uv \le 2$ in the uv-plane.
   b) Then use Eq. (1) to transform the integral

$$\int_1^2 \int_1^2 \frac{y}{x}\, dy\, dx$$

into an integral over G, and evaluate both integrals.

5. Let R be the region in the first quadrant of the xy-plane bounded by the hyperbolas $xy = 1$, $xy = 9$ and the lines $y = x$, $y = 4x$ (Fig. 14.55). Use the transformation $x = u/v$, $y = uv$ with $u > 0$ and $v > 0$ to rewrite

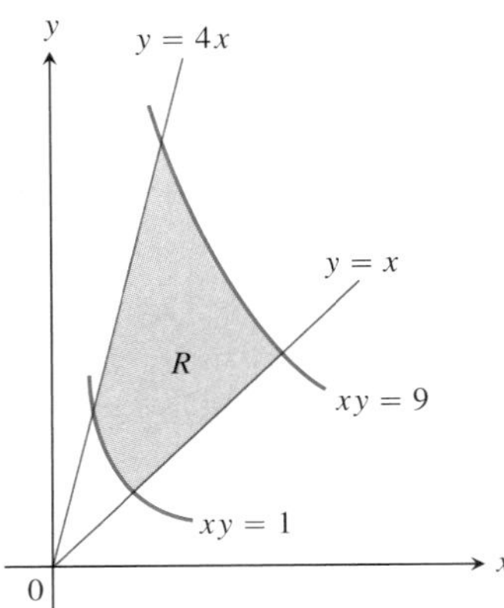

14.55 The xy-region in Exercise 5.

$$\iint_R \left(\sqrt{\frac{y}{x}} + \sqrt{xy}\right) dx\, dy$$

as an integral over an appropriate region G in the uv-plane. Then evaluate the uv-integral over G.

6. The area πab of the ellipse $x^2/a^2 + y^2/b^2 = 1$ can be found by integrating the function $f(x, y) = 1$ over the region bounded by the ellipse in the xy-plane. Evaluating the integral directly requires a trigonometric substitution. An easier way to evaluate the integral is to use the transformation $x = au$, $y = bv$ and evaluate the transformed integral over the disk G: $u^2 + v^2 \le 1$ in the uv-plane. Find the area this way.

7. A thin plate of constant density covers the region bounded by the ellipse $x^2/a^2 + y^2/b^2 = 1$ in the xy-plane. Find the first moment of the plate about the origin. (*Hint:* Use the transformation $x = ar \cos \theta$, $y = br \sin \theta$.)

8. Use the transformation $x = u + (1/2)\, v$, $y = v$ to evaluate the integral

$$\int_0^2 \int_{y/2}^{(y+4)/2} y^3(2x - y)e^{(2x-y)^2}\, dx\, dy$$

by first writing it as an integral over a region G in the uv-plane.

TRIPLE INTEGRALS

9. Evaluate the determinant in Eq. (10) to show that the Jacobian of the transformation from Cartesian $\rho\phi\theta$-space to Cartesian xyz-space is $\rho^2 \sin \phi$.

10. Evaluate the integral in Example 3 by integrating with respect to x, y, and z.

11. Find the volume of the ellipsoid

$$\frac{x^2}{a^2} + \frac{y^2}{b^2} + \frac{z^2}{c^2} = 1.$$

(*Hint:* Let $x = au$, $y = bv$, and $z = cw$. Then find the volume of an appropriate region in uvw-space.)

12. Evaluate

$$\iiint |xyz|\, dx\, dy\, dz$$

over the solid ellipsoid

$$\frac{x^2}{a^2} + \frac{y^2}{b^2} + \frac{z^2}{c^2} \le 1.$$

(*Hint:* Let $x = au$, $y = bv$, and $z = cw$. Then integrate over an appropriate region in uvw-space.)

13. Let D be the region in xyz-space defined by the inequalities

$$1 \le x \le 2, \qquad 0 \le xy \le 2, \qquad 0 \le z \le 1.$$

Evaluate

$$\iiint_D (x^2y + 3xyz)\, dx\, dy\, dz$$

by applying the transformation

$$u = x, \qquad v = xy, \qquad w = 3z$$

and integrating over an appropriate region G in uvw-space.

14. Assuming the result that the center of mass of a solid hemisphere lies on the axis of symmetry three-eighths of the way from the base toward the top, show, by transforming the appropriate integrals, that the center of mass of a solid semi-ellipsoid $(x^2/a^2) + (y^2/b^2) + (z^2/c^2) \le 1$, $z \ge 0$ lies on the z-axis three-eighths of the way from the base toward the top. (You can do this without evaluating any of the integrals.)

Writing for Your Own Knowledge

Answer the following questions in writing. Some answers will take only a sentence or two; others may require several paragraphs. Some explanations may also call for graphs or sketches.

1. How do you evaluate a double integral by substitution? How can you interpret the substitution geometrically?

2. What is the Jacobian of the transformation

$$x = r \cos \theta, \qquad y = r \sin \theta$$

from the Cartesian $r\theta$-plane to the Cartesian xy-plane? How is it related to integration in polar coordinates?

3. How do you evaluate a triple integral by substitution? How can you interpret the substitution geometrically?

4. What is the Jacobian of the transformation

$$x = \rho \sin \phi \cos \theta, \qquad y = \rho \sin \phi \sin \theta, \qquad z = \rho \cos \phi$$

from Cartesian $\rho\phi\theta$-space to Cartesian xyz-space? How is it related to integration in spherical coordinates?

5. What is the Jacobian of the transformation

$$x = r \cos \theta, \qquad y = r \sin \theta, \qquad z = z$$

from Cartesian $r\theta z$-space to Cartesian xyz-space? How is it related to integration in cylindrical coordinates?

6. Why might you want to evaluate an integral by substitution?

For Your Review

Write brief paragraphs about the following topics and give examples.

The double integral of a continuous function $f(x, y)$ over a closed bounded region in the coordinate plane
Geometric interpretations of double integrals
Evaluation of double integrals by repeated single integration
Masses, moments, centers of mass, and radii of gyration of thin plates
Double integrals in polar coordinates
Changing a double integral from rectangular to polar coordinates
The triple integral of a continuous function $f(x, y, z)$ over a closed bounded region in space
Calculating volume
Evaluation of triple integrals by repeated single integrations
Average values of continuous functions of two and three independent variables
Masses, moments, centers of mass, and radii of gyration of objects in space
Centroids of two- and three-dimensional shapes
Triple integrals in cylindrical coordinates
Triple integrals in spherical coordinates
Substitutions in multiple integrals and the Jacobian determinant of a coordinate transformation

Practice Exercises

In Exercises 1 and 2, sketch the regions of integration and then evaluate the integrals.

1. $\displaystyle\int_1^{10} \int_0^{1/y} y e^{xy}\, dx\, dy$

2. $\displaystyle\int_0^1 \int_0^{x^3} e^{y/x}\, dy\, dx$

In Exercises 3 and 4, sketch the region of integration and write an equivalent iterated integral with the order of integration reversed.

3. $\displaystyle\int_0^1 \int_{x^2}^{x} f(x, y)\, dy\, dx$

4. $\displaystyle\int_0^4 \int_y^{2\sqrt{y}} f(x, y)\, dx\, dy$

In Exercises 5 and 6, sketch the region of integration and write an equivalent integral with the order of integration reversed. Then evaluate both integrals.

5. $\displaystyle\int_0^{3/2} \int_{-\sqrt{9-4y^2}}^{\sqrt{9-4y^2}} y\, dx\, dy$

6. $\displaystyle\int_0^2 \int_0^{4-x^2} 2x\, dy\, dx$

Evaluate the integrals in Exercises 7–10.

7. $\displaystyle\int_0^1 \int_{2y}^2 4 \cos (x^2)\, dx\, dy$

8. $\displaystyle\int_0^2 \int_{y/2}^1 e^{x^2}\, dx\, dy$

9. $\displaystyle\int_0^8 \int_{\sqrt[3]{x}}^2 \frac{dy\, dx}{y^4 + 1}$

10. $\displaystyle\int_0^1 \int_{\sqrt[3]{y}}^1 \frac{2\pi \sin \pi x^2}{x^2}\, dx\, dy$

11. Find the volume under the paraboloid $z = x^2 + y^2$ above the triangle enclosed by the lines $y = x$, $x = 0$, and $x + y = 2$ in the xy-plane.

12. Find the volume under the parabolic cylinder $z = x^2$ above the region enclosed by the parabola $y = 6 - x^2$ and the line $y = x$ in the xy-plane.

13. Find the area of the region enclosed by the line $y = 2x + 4$ and the parabola $y = 4 - x^2$ in the xy-plane.

14. Find the area of the "triangular" region in the xy-plane that is bounded on the right by the parabola $y = x^2$, on the left by the line $x + y = 2$, and above by the line $y = 4$.

Find the average value of $f(x, y) = xy$ over the regions in Exercises 15 and 16.

15. The square bounded by the lines $x = 1$, $y = 1$ in the first quadrant

16. The quarter circle $x^2 + y^2 \le 1$ in the first quadrant

17. Find the centroid of the "triangular" region bounded by the lines $x = 2$, $y = 2$ and the hyperbola $xy = 2$ in the xy-plane.

18. Find the polar moment of inertia about the origin of a thin triangular plate of constant density $\delta = 3$, bounded by the y-axis and the lines $y = 2x$ and $y = 4$ in the xy-plane.

19. Find the polar moment of inertia about the center of a thin rectangular sheet of constant density $\delta = 1$ bounded by the lines

a) $x = \pm 2, \quad y = \pm 1$ in the xy-plane
b) $x = \pm a, \quad y = \pm b$ in the xy-plane

(*Hint:* Find I_x. Then use the formula for I_x to find I_y and add the two to find I_0.)

20. Find the moment of inertia and radius of gyration about the x-axis of a thin plate of constant density δ covering the triangle with vertices (0, 0), (3, 0), and (3, 2) in the xy-plane.

21. Find the mass and first moments about the coordinate axes of a thin square plate bounded by the lines $x = \pm 1$, $y = \pm 1$ in the xy-plane if the density is $\delta(x, y) = x^2 + y^2 + 1/3$.

22. Find the center of mass and the moments of inertia and radii of gyration about the coordinate axes of a thin plate bounded by the line $y = x$ and the parabola $y = x^2$ in the xy-plane if the density is $\delta(x, y) = x + 1$.

Evaluate the integrals in Exercises 23 and 24 by changing to polar coordinates.

23. $\displaystyle\int_{-1}^{1}\int_{-\sqrt{1-x^2}}^{\sqrt{1-x^2}} \frac{2\,dy\,dx}{(1 + x^2 + y^2)^2}$

24. $\displaystyle\int_{-1}^{1}\int_{-\sqrt{1-y^2}}^{\sqrt{1-y^2}} \ln(x^2 + y^2 + 1)\,dx\,dy$

25. Find the centroid of the region in the polar coordinate plane that lies inside the cardioid $r = 1 + \cos\theta$ and outside the circle $r = 1$.

26. Find the centroid of the region in the polar coordinate plane defined by the inequalities $0 \le r \le 3$ and $-\pi/3 \le \theta \le \pi/3$.

27. Find the centroid of the region in the first quadrant bounded by the rays $\theta = 0$ and $\theta = \pi/2$ and the circles $r = 1$ and $r = 3$.

28. The usual way to evaluate the improper integral

$$I = \int_0^{\infty} e^{-x^2}\,dx$$

is to calculate its square:

$$I^2 = \left(\int_0^{\infty} e^{-x^2}\,dx\right)\left(\int_0^{\infty} e^{-y^2}\,dy\right) = \int_0^{\infty}\int_0^{\infty} e^{-(x^2+y^2)}\,dx\,dy.$$

Introduce polar coordinates in the last expression and show that

$$I = \int_0^{\infty} e^{-x^2}\,dx = \frac{\sqrt{\pi}}{2}.$$

Evaluate the integrals in Exercises 29–32.

29. $\displaystyle\int_0^{\pi}\int_0^{\pi}\int_0^{\pi} \cos(x + y + z)\,dx\,dy\,dz$

30. $\displaystyle\int_{\ln 6}^{\ln 7}\int_0^{\ln 2}\int_{\ln 4}^{\ln 5} e^{(x+y+z)}\,dz\,dy\,dx$

31. $\displaystyle\int_0^{1}\int_0^{x^2}\int_0^{x+y} (2x - y - z)\,dz\,dy\,dx$

32. $\displaystyle\int_1^{e}\int_1^{x}\int_0^{z} \frac{2y}{z^3}\,dy\,dz\,dx$

33. Find the volume of the wedge-shaped region enclosed on the side by the cylinder $x = -\cos y$, $-\pi/2 \le y \le \pi/2$, on the top by the plane $z = -2x$, and below by the xy-plane.

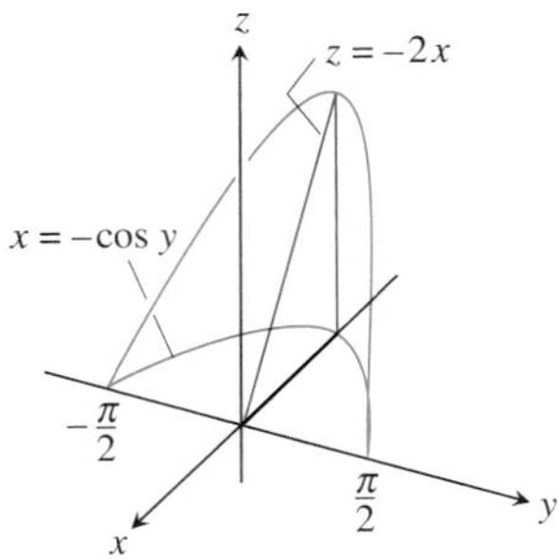

34. Find the volume of the solid that is bounded above by the cylinder $z = 4 - x^2$, on the sides by the cylinder $x^2 + y^2 = 4$, and below by the xy-plane.

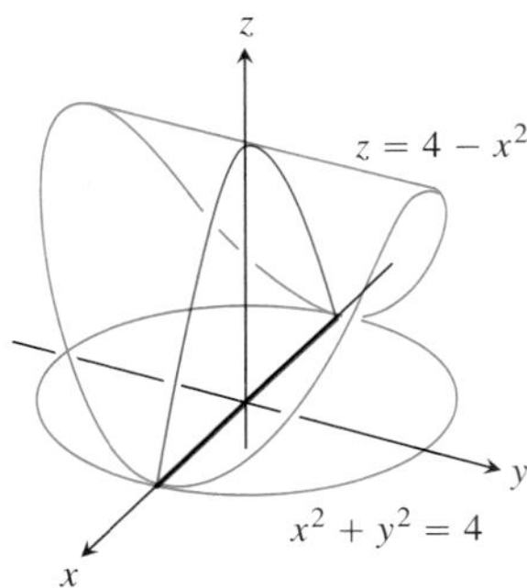

35. Find the average value of $f(x, y, z) = 30\,xz\sqrt{x^2 + y}$ over the rectangular solid in the first octant bounded by the coordinate planes and the planes $x = 1$, $y = 3$, $z = 1$.

36. Find the average value of ρ over the solid sphere $\rho \le a$ (spherical coordinates).

37. Convert

$$\int_0^{2\pi}\int_0^{\sqrt{2}}\int_r^{\sqrt{4-r^2}} 3\,dz\,r\,dr\,d\theta, \quad r \ge 0$$

to (a) rectangular coordinates with the order of integration

$dz\,dx\,dy$, and (b) spherical coordinates. Then (c) evaluate one of the integrals.

38. (a) Convert to cylindrical coordinates. Then (b) evaluate the new integral.

$$\int_0^1 \int_{-\sqrt{1-x^2}}^{\sqrt{1-x^2}} \int_{-(x^2+y^2)}^{(x^2+y^2)} 21xy^2\,dz\,dy\,dx.$$

39. (a) Convert to spherical coordinates. Then (b) evaluate the new integral.

$$\int_{-1}^1 \int_{-\sqrt{1-x^2}}^{\sqrt{1-x^2}} \int_{\sqrt{x^2+y^2}}^{1} dz\,dy\,dx.$$

40. Write an iterated triple integral for the integral of $f(x, y, z) = 6 + 4y$ over the region in the first octant bounded by the cone $z = \sqrt{x^2 + y^2}$, the cylinder $x^2 + y^2 = 1$, and the coordinate planes in (a) rectangular coordinates, (b) cylindrical coordinates, (c) spherical coordinates. Then (d) find the integral of f by evaluating one of the triple integrals.

41. Set up an integral in rectangular coordinates equivalent to the integral

$$\int_0^{\pi/2} \int_1^{\sqrt{3}} \int_1^{\sqrt{4-r^2}} r^3 \sin\theta \cos\theta\, z^2\,dz\,dr\,d\theta.$$

Arrange the order of integration to be z first, then y, then x.

42. The volume of a solid is

$$\int_0^2 \int_0^{\sqrt{2x-x^2}} \int_{-\sqrt{4-x^2-y^2}}^{\sqrt{4-x^2-y^2}} dz\,dy\,dx.$$

a) Describe the solid by giving equations for the surfaces that form its boundary.

b) Convert the integral to cylindrical coordinates but do not evaluate the integral.

43. Let D be the smaller spherical cap cut from a solid ball of radius 2 by a plane 1 unit from the center of the sphere. Express the volume of D as an iterated triple integral in (a) rectangular, (b) cylindrical, and (c) spherical coordinates. *Do not evaluate the integrals.*

44. Express the moment of inertia I_z of the solid hemisphere bounded below by the plane $z = 0$ and above by the sphere $x^2 + y^2 + z^2 = 1$ as an iterated integral in (a) rectangular, (b) cylindrical, and (c) spherical coordinates. *Do not evaluate the integrals.*

45. Find the volume of the region in the first octant that lies between the cylinders $r = 1$ and $r = 2$ and between the xy-plane and the surface $z = xy$.

46. Find the volume of the region bounded above by the sphere $x^2 + y^2 + z^2 = 2$ and below by the paraboloid $z = x^2 + y^2$.

47. Find the volume of the region bounded above by the paraboloid $z = 3 - x^2 - y^2$ and below by the paraboloid $z = 2x^2 + 2y^2$.

48. A hole is bored through a solid sphere, the axis of the hole being a diameter of the sphere. The volume of the solid remaining is

$$V = 2\int_0^{2\pi} \int_0^{\sqrt{3}} \int_1^{\sqrt{4-z^2}} r\,dr\,dz\,d\theta.$$

a) By inspecting the integral, find the radius of the hole and the radius of the sphere.

b) Evaluate the integral.

49. A solid is bounded on the top by the paraboloid $z = r^2$, on the bottom by the plane $z = 0$, and on the sides by the cylinder $r = 1$. Find the center of mass and the moment of inertia and radius of gyration about the z-axis if the density is (a) $\delta(r, \theta, z) = z$, (b) $\delta(r, \theta, z) = r$.

50. A solid is bounded below by the cone $z = \sqrt{x^2 + y^2}$ and above by the plane $z = 1$. Find the center of mass and the moment of inertia and radius of gyration about the z-axis if the density is (a) $\delta(r, \theta, z) = z$, (b) $\delta(r, \theta, z) = z^2$.

51. Find the volume of the region enclosed by the spherical coordinate surface $\rho = 2 \sin\phi$ (Fig. 14.56).

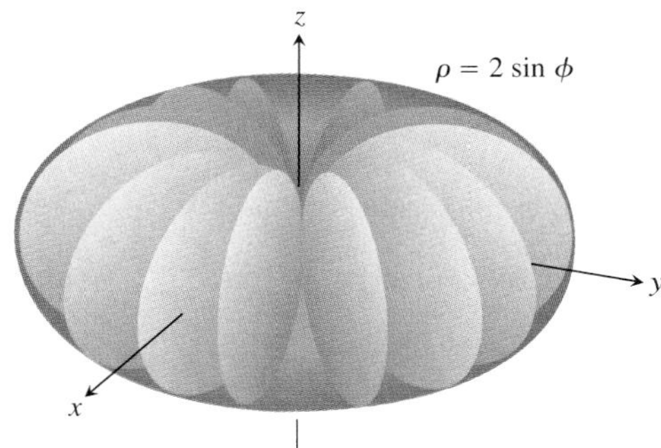

14.56 The surface $\rho = 2 \sin\phi$ in Exercise 51 is generated by revolving a circle of radius 1 about one of its tangents (in this case, the z-axis).

52. Find the moment of inertia about the z-axis of a solid of constant density $\delta = 1$ that is bounded above by the sphere $\rho = 2$ and below by the cone $\phi = \pi/3$ (spherical coordinates).

53. Use spherical coordinates to find the centroid of a solid hemisphere of radius a.

54. Find the moment of inertia and radius of gyration of a solid sphere of radius a and density $\delta = 1$ about a diameter of the sphere.

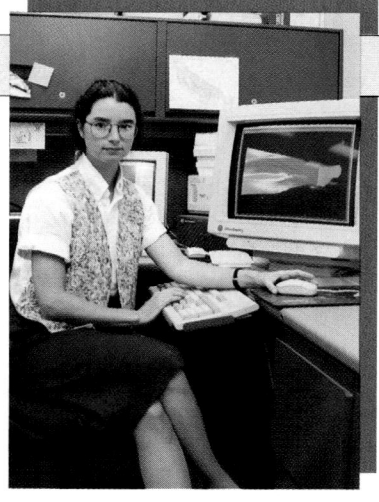

JULIA KIMBELL, research mathematician at the Chemical Industry Institute of Toxicology (CIIT) in Research Triangle Park, NC, uses a Cray supercomputer to model airflow in the upper respiratory tracts of rats.

The business of CIIT is finding out why toxic chemicals are toxic in the way they are. The traditional mode of research into a substance that may cause cancer is to expose animals to it, determine if cancer occurs and at what levels of exposure, and then extrapolate to human beings. But the accuracy of such extrapolation is often questionable. Take formaldehyde, for instance, a substance used in the manufacture of textiles and plywood.

Formaldehyde inhalation is suspected of being linked to lung cancer in humans, but in rodents at high exposure levels, it causes nasal cancer. Why? And what can rat nasal cancer possibly tell us about cancer in humans? The answer may lie not just in how air flows in the upper respiratory tract.

Gas and fluid flows in tubes are well understood (in part because of the mathematics of the present chapter). The answer may depend more on what happens when gas flows through tubes of complex structure with absorbing walls, and that is not as well understood.

Dr. Kimbell is developing a model for this kind of interactive flow in rats, animals about which there are already ample data against which to test the model's ability to predict. The next step will be to develop similar models for the noses of monkeys and, ultimately, people.

The figure here shows the computational grid used in modeling airflow in the rat nose, with vectors indicating air velocity at the grid's interior end. Once the model is fully developed, Kimbell hopes to understand exactly how breathing affects where injury and diseases such as cancer end up, not only in rats but also in people.

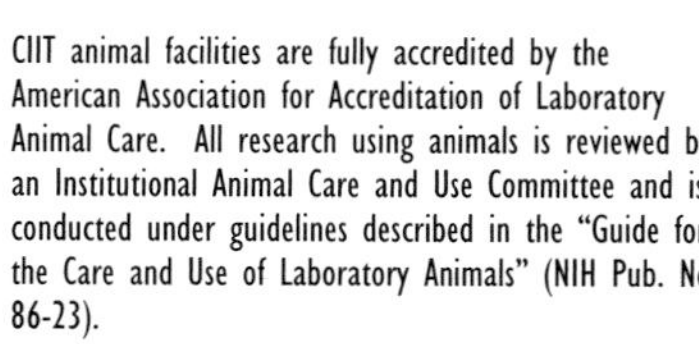

CIIT animal facilities are fully accredited by the American Association for Accreditation of Laboratory Animal Care. All research using animals is reviewed by an Institutional Animal Care and Use Committee and is conducted under guidelines described in the "Guide for the Care and Use of Laboratory Animals" (NIH Pub. No. 86-23).

OVERVIEW

This chapter combines derivatives, integrals, and vector functions to study integration in vector fields. The field concept has proved to be one of the most useful ideas in all of physical science. The mathematics in this chapter is the mathematics that is used to describe the properties of electromagnetism, explain the flow of heat in stars, and calculate the work it takes to put a satellite in orbit.

15 *Integration in Vector Fields*

15.1 *Line Integrals*

When a curve $\mathbf{r} = g(t)\,\mathbf{i} + h(t)\,\mathbf{j} + k(t)\,\mathbf{k}$, $a \leq t \leq b$, passes through the domain of a function $f(x, y, z)$ in space, the values of f along the curve are given by the composite function $f(g(t), h(t), k(t))$. If we integrate this composite with respect to arc length from $t = a$ to $t = b$, we calculate the so-called line integral of f along the curve. Despite the three-dimensional geometry, the line integral is an ordinary integral of a real-valued function over an interval of real numbers. We have evaluated such integrals ever since Chapter 5. The usual techniques apply and nothing new is needed.

The importance of line integrals lies in their application. These are the integrals with which we calculate the work done by variable forces along paths in space and the rates at which fluids flow along curves and across boundaries.

Definitions and Notation

Line integrals are integrals of functions over curves. We define them in the following way.

Suppose that $f(x, y, z)$ is a function whose domain contains the curve $\mathbf{r} = g(t)\,\mathbf{i} + h(t)\,\mathbf{j} + k(t)\,\mathbf{k}$, $a \leq t \leq b$. We partition the curve into a finite number of subarcs (Fig. 15.1). The typical subarc has length Δs_k. In each subarc we choose a point (x_k, y_k, z_k) and form the sum

$$S_n = \sum_{k=1}^{n} f(x_k, y_k, z_k)\,\Delta s_k. \tag{1}$$

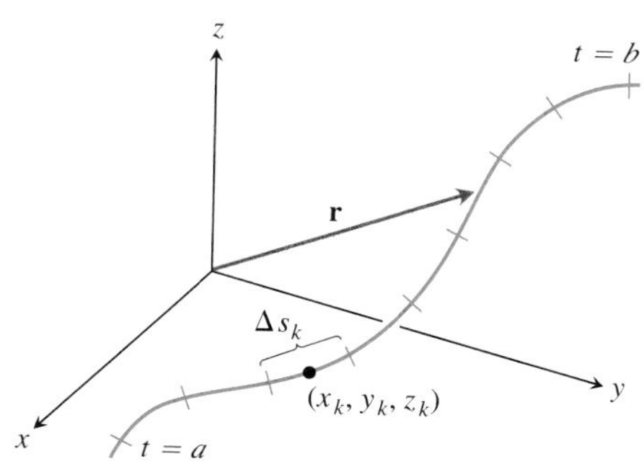

15.1 The curve $\mathbf{r} = g(t)\,\mathbf{i} + h(t)\,\mathbf{j} + k(t)\,\mathbf{k}$, partitioned into small arcs from $t = a$ to $t = b$. The length of a typical subarc is Δs_k.

If f is continuous and the functions g, h, and k have continuous first derivatives, then the sums in (1) approach a limit as n increases and the lengths Δs_k approach zero. We call this limit the **integral of f over the curve from a to b.** If the curve is denoted by a single letter, C for example, the notation for the integral is

$$\int_C f(x, y, z)\,ds \qquad \text{“The integral of } f \text{ over } C\text{”} \tag{2}$$

Evaluation for Smooth Curves

If $\mathbf{r}$ is smooth (f', g', and h' are continuous and $|d\mathbf{r}/dt| = |\mathbf{v}(t)|$ is never 0), we can use the equation

$$s(t) = \int_a^t |\mathbf{v}(\lambda)|\, d\lambda \qquad \text{Eq. (4) of Section 12.3, with } t_0 = a$$

to express the ds in Eq. (2) in terms of dt:

$$ds = |\mathbf{v}(t)|\, dt.$$

A theorem from advanced calculus says that we can then go on to evaluate the integral of f over C as

$$\int_C f(x, y, z)\, ds = \int_a^b f(g(t), h(t), k(t))|\mathbf{v}(t)|\, dt. \tag{3}$$

This formula will evaluate the integral correctly no matter what parametrization we use, as long as it is smooth.

How to Evaluate a Line Integral

To integrate a continuous function $f(x, y, z)$ over a curve C, take the following steps.

1. Find a smooth parametrization of C,
$$\mathbf{r} = g(t)\,\mathbf{i} + h(t)\,\mathbf{j} + k(t)\,\mathbf{k}, \quad a \le t \le b.$$
2. Evaluate the integral as
$$\int_C f(x, y, z)\, ds = \int_a^b f(g(t), h(t), k(t))\, |\mathbf{v}(t)|\, dt. \tag{4}$$

Notice that if f has the constant value 1, then the integral of f over C gives the length of C. We calculated lengths in Section 12.3 and will not repeat the calculations here.

EXAMPLE 1 Integrate $f(x, y, z) = x - 3y^2 + z$ over the line segment C joining the origin and the point $(1, 1, 1)$ (Fig. 15.2).

Solution We choose the simplest parametrization we can think of:

$$\mathbf{r} = t\,\mathbf{i} + t\,\mathbf{j} + t\,\mathbf{k}, \quad 0 \le t \le 1.$$

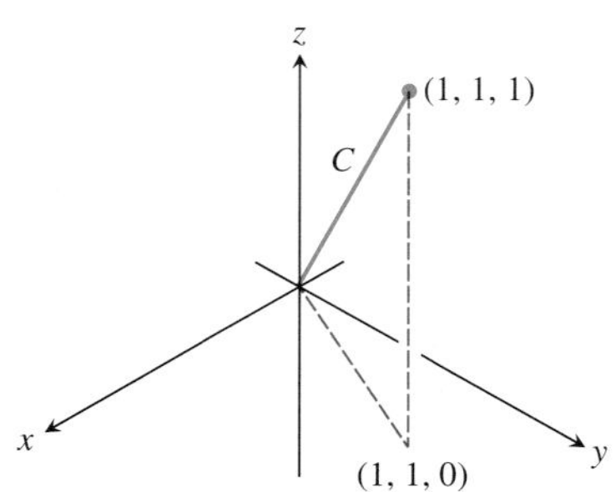

15.2 The integration path in Example 1.

The component functions have continuous first derivatives and $|\mathbf{v}(t)| = \sqrt{1^2 + 1^2 + 1^2} = \sqrt{3}$ is never 0, so the parametrization is smooth. The integral of f over C is therefore

$$\int_C f(x, y, z)\, ds = \int_0^1 f(t, t, t)\left(\sqrt{3}\right) dt \qquad \text{Eq. (4)}$$
$$= \int_0^1 (t - 3t^2 + t)\sqrt{3}\, dt$$
$$= \sqrt{3}\int_0^1 (2t - 3t^2)\, dt = \sqrt{3}\left[t^2 - t^3\right]_0^1 = 0.$$

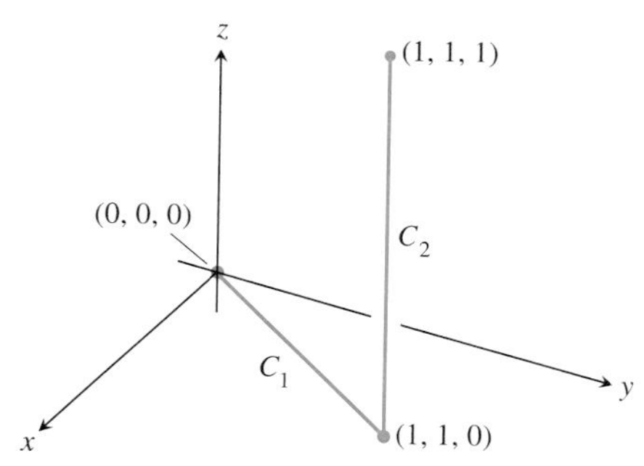

15.3 The path of integration in Example 2.

Additivity

Line integrals have the useful property that if a curve C is made by joining together a finite number of curves $C_1, C_2, \ldots, C_n$ end to end, then the integral of a function over C is the sum of the integrals over the curves that make it up:

$$\int_C f\,ds = \int_{C_1} f\,ds + \int_{C_2} f\,ds + \cdots + \int_{C_n} f\,ds. \tag{5}$$

EXAMPLE 2 Figure 15.3 shows another path connecting the origin to $(1, 1, 1)$, the union of two line segments, C_1 and C_2. Integrate

$$f(x, y, z) = x - 3y^2 + z$$

over $C_1 \cup C_2$.

Solution We choose the simplest parametrizations for C_1 and C_2 we can think of, checking the lengths of the velocity vectors as we go along:

$$C_1:\quad \mathbf{r} = t\,\mathbf{i} + t\,\mathbf{j},\quad 0 \le t \le 1;\quad |\mathbf{v}| = \sqrt{1^2 + 1^2} = \sqrt{2}$$

$$C_2:\quad \mathbf{r} = \mathbf{i} + \mathbf{j} + t\,\mathbf{k},\quad 0 \le t \le 1;\quad |\mathbf{v}| = \sqrt{0^2 + 0^2 + 1^2} = 1.$$

With these parametrizations we find that

$$\begin{aligned}
\int_{C_1 \cup C_2} f(x, y, z)\,ds &= \int_{C_1} f(x, y, z)\,ds + \int_{C_2} f(x, y, z)\,ds && \text{Eq. (5)}\\
&= \int_0^1 f(t, t, 0)\sqrt{2}\,dt + \int_0^1 f(1, 1, t)(1)\,dt && \text{Eq. (4)}\\
&= \int_0^1 (t - 3t^2 + 0)\sqrt{2}\,dt + \int_0^1 (1 - 3 + t)(1)\,dt\\
&= \sqrt{2}\int_0^1 (t - 3t^2)\,dt + \int_0^1 (t - 2)\,dt\\
&= \sqrt{2}\left[\frac{t^2}{2} - t^3\right]_0^1 + \left[\frac{t^2}{2} - 2t\right]_0^1 = -\frac{\sqrt{2}}{2} - \frac{3}{2}.
\end{aligned}$$

There are three things to notice about the integrations in Examples 1 and 2. First, as soon as the components of the appropriate curve were substituted into the formula for f, the integration became a standard integration with respect to t. Second, the integral of f over $C_1 \cup C_2$ was obtained by integrating f over each section of the path and adding the results. Third, the integrals of f over the paths C and $C_1 \cup C_2$ had different values. For most functions, the value of the integral along a path joining two points changes when you change the path between them. For some functions, however, the value remains the same, as we will see in Section 15.3.

Mass and Moment Calculations

We treat coil springs and wires like masses distributed along continuously differentiable curves in space. The distribution is described by a continuous density function $\delta(x, y, z)$. The spring's or wire's mass, center-of-mass coordinates, and moments are then calculated with the formulas in Table 15.1 on the following page. The formulas apply to thin rods as well as springs and wires.

TABLE 15.1
Mass and moment formulas for coil springs, thin rods, and wires lying along a curve C in space

Mass: $M = \int_C \delta(x, y, z)\, ds$

First moments about the coordinate planes:

$$M_{yz} = \int_C x\, \delta\, ds, \qquad M_{xz} = \int_C y\, \delta\, ds, \qquad M_{xy} = \int_C z\, \delta\, ds$$

Coordinates of the center of mass:

$$\bar{x} = M_{yz}/M, \qquad \bar{y} = M_{xz}/M, \qquad \bar{z} = M_{xy}/M$$

Moments of inertia:

$$I_x = \int_C (y^2 + z^2)\, \delta\, ds, \qquad I_y = \int_C (x^2 + z^2)\, \delta\, ds,$$

$$I_z = \int_C (x^2 + y^2)\, \delta\, ds, \qquad I_L = \int_C r^2\, \delta\, ds,$$

$r(x, y, z)$ = distance from point (x, y, z) to line L

Radius of gyration about a line L: $R_L = \sqrt{I_L/M}$

EXAMPLE 3 A coil spring lies along the helix

$$\mathbf{r} = (\cos 4t)\,\mathbf{i} + (\sin 4t)\,\mathbf{j} + t\,\mathbf{k}, \quad 0 \le t \le 2\pi.$$

The spring's density is a constant, $\delta = 1$. Find the spring's mass, the coordinates of the spring's center of mass, and the spring's moment of inertia and radius of gyration about the z-axis.

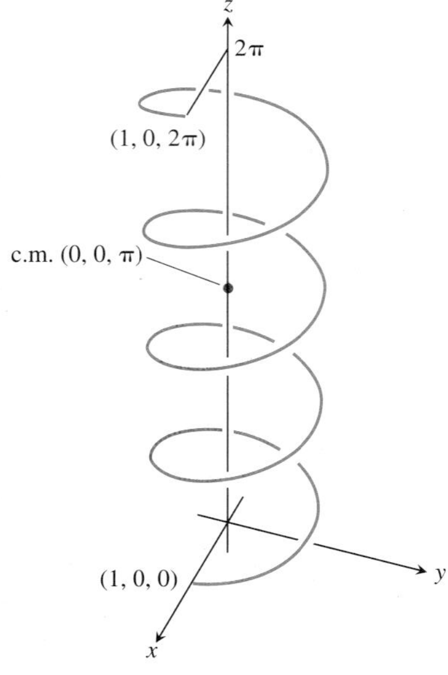

15.4 The helical spring in Example 3.

Solution We sketch the spring (Fig. 15.4). Because of the symmetries involved, the center of mass lies at the point $(0, 0, \pi)$ on the z-axis.

For the remaining calculations, we first find $|\mathbf{v}(t)|$:

$$|\mathbf{v}(t)| = \sqrt{\left(\frac{dx}{dt}\right)^2 + \left(\frac{dy}{dt}\right)^2 + \left(\frac{dz}{dt}\right)^2}$$
$$= \sqrt{(-4 \sin 4t)^2 + (4 \cos 4t)^2 + 1} = \sqrt{17}.$$

We then evaluate the formulas from Table 15.1 using Eq. (4):

$$M = \int_{\text{Helix}} \delta\, ds = \int_0^{2\pi} (1)\sqrt{17}\, dt = 2\pi\sqrt{17}$$

$$I_z = \int_{\text{Helix}} (x^2 + y^2)\delta\, ds = \int_0^{2\pi} (\cos^2 4t + \sin^2 4t)(1)\sqrt{17}\, dt$$
$$= \int_0^{2\pi} \sqrt{17}\, dt = 2\pi\sqrt{17}$$

$$R_z = \sqrt{I_z/M} = \sqrt{2\pi\sqrt{17}/(2\pi\sqrt{17})} = 1.$$

Notice that the radius of gyration about the z-axis is the radius of the cylinder around which the helix winds.

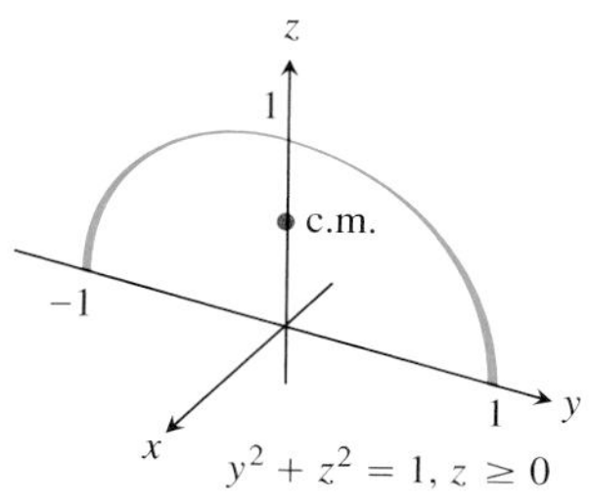

15.5 Example 4 shows how to find the center of mass of a circular arch of variable density.

EXAMPLE 4 A slender metal arch, denser at the bottom than at the top, lies along the semicircle $y^2 + z^2 = 1$, $z \geq 0$, in the yz-plane (Fig. 15.5). Find the center of the arch's mass if the density at the point (x, y, z) on the arch is $\delta(x, y, z) = 2 - z$.

Solution We know that $\bar{x} = 0$ and $\bar{y} = 0$ because the arch lies in the yz-plane with its mass distributed symmetrically about the z-axis. To find $\bar{z}$, we parametrize the circle as

$$\mathbf{r} = (\cos t)\,\mathbf{j} + (\sin t)\,\mathbf{k}, \quad 0 \leq t \leq \pi.$$

For this parametrization,

$$|\mathbf{v}(t)| = \sqrt{\left(\frac{dx}{dt}\right)^2 + \left(\frac{dy}{dt}\right)^2 + \left(\frac{dz}{dt}\right)^2} = \sqrt{(0)^2 + (-\sin t)^2 + (\cos t)^2} = 1.$$

The formulas in Table 15.1 then give

$$M = \int_C \delta\, ds = \int_C (2 - z)\, ds = \int_0^{\pi} (2 - \sin t)\, dt = 2\pi - 2$$

$$M_{xy} = \int_C z\,\delta\, ds = \int_C z(2 - z)\, ds = \int_0^{\pi} (\sin t)(2 - \sin t)\, dt$$

$$= \int_0^{\pi} (2 \sin t - \sin^2 t)\, dt = \frac{8 - \pi}{2}$$

$$\bar{z} = \frac{M_{xy}}{M} = \frac{8 - \pi}{2} \cdot \frac{1}{2\pi - 2} = \frac{8 - \pi}{4\pi - 4} \approx 0.57.$$

To the nearest hundredth, the center of mass is $(0, 0, 0.57)$.

Exercises 15.1

Match the vector equations in Exercises 1–8 on the following page with the graphs in Fig. 15.6.

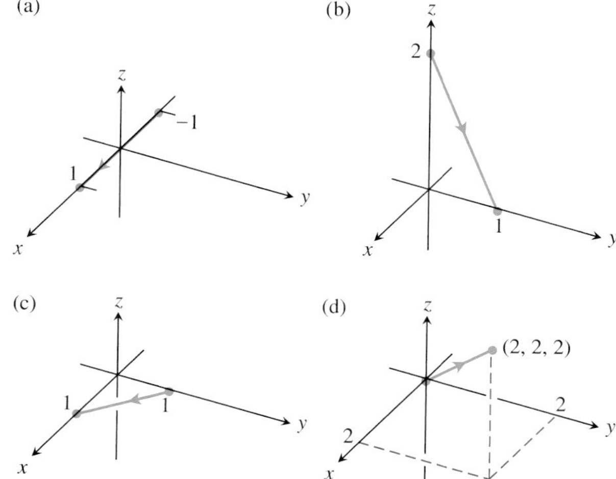

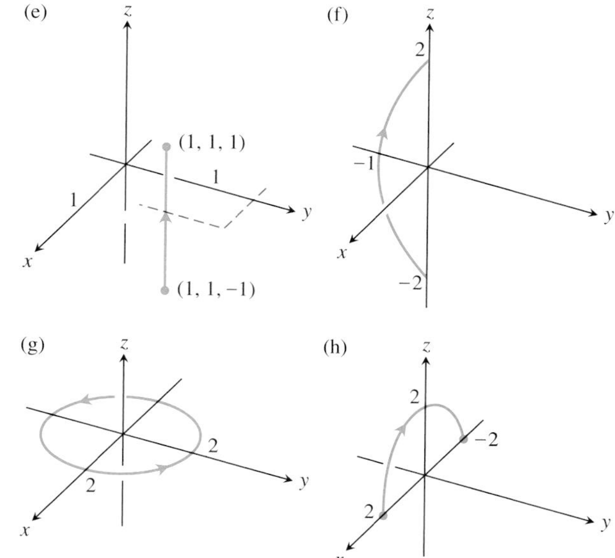

15.6 The graphs for Exercises 1–8.

1. $\mathbf{r} = t\,\mathbf{i} + (1-t)\,\mathbf{j}, \quad 0 \le t \le 1$

2. $\mathbf{r} = \mathbf{i} + \mathbf{j} + t\,\mathbf{k}, \quad -1 \le t \le 1$

3. $\mathbf{r} = (2\cos t)\,\mathbf{i} + (2\sin t)\,\mathbf{j}, \quad 0 \le t \le 2\pi$

4. $\mathbf{r} = t\,\mathbf{i}, \quad -1 \le t \le 1$

5. $\mathbf{r} = t\,\mathbf{i} + t\,\mathbf{j} + t\,\mathbf{k}, \quad 0 \le t \le 2$

6. $\mathbf{r} = t\,\mathbf{j} + (2-2t)\,\mathbf{k}, \quad 0 \le t \le 1$

7. $\mathbf{r} = (t^2-1)\,\mathbf{j} + 2t\,\mathbf{k}, \quad -1 \le t \le 1$

8. $\mathbf{r} = (2\cos t)\,\mathbf{i} + (2\sin t)\,\mathbf{k}, \quad 0 \le t \le \pi$

In Exercises 9–14, integrate f over the given curve.

9. $f(x, y, z) = x + y$
$\mathbf{r} = t\,\mathbf{i} + (1-t)\,\mathbf{j}, \; 0 \le t \le 1$

10. $f(x, y, z) = x - y + z - 2$
$\mathbf{r} = t\,\mathbf{i} + (1-t)\,\mathbf{j} + \mathbf{k}, \quad 0 \le t \le 1$

11. $f(x, y, z) = xy + y + z$
$\mathbf{r} = 2t\,\mathbf{i} + t\,\mathbf{j} + (2-2t)\,\mathbf{k}, \quad 0 \le t \le 1$

12. $f(x, y, z) = \sqrt{x^2+y^2}$
$\mathbf{r} = (4\cos t)\,\mathbf{i} + (4\sin t)\,\mathbf{j} + 3t\,\mathbf{k}, \quad -2\pi \le t \le 2\pi$

13. $f(x, y, z) = 3z\sqrt{3x^2+y^2+z^2}$
$\mathbf{r} = \mathbf{i} + \mathbf{j} + t\,\mathbf{k}, \quad -1 \le t \le 1$

14. $f(x, y, z) = \sqrt{3}/(x^2+y^2+z^2)$
$\mathbf{r} = t\,\mathbf{i} + t\,\mathbf{j} + t\,\mathbf{k}, \quad 1 \le t < \infty$

15. Integrate $f(x, y, z) = x + \sqrt{y} - z^2$ over the path from $(0, 0, 0)$ to $(1, 1, 1)$ (Fig. 15.7a) given by
C_1: $\mathbf{r} = t\,\mathbf{i} + t^2\,\mathbf{j}, \quad 0 \le t \le 1$
C_2: $\mathbf{r} = \mathbf{i} + \mathbf{j} + t\,\mathbf{k}, \quad 0 \le t \le 1$

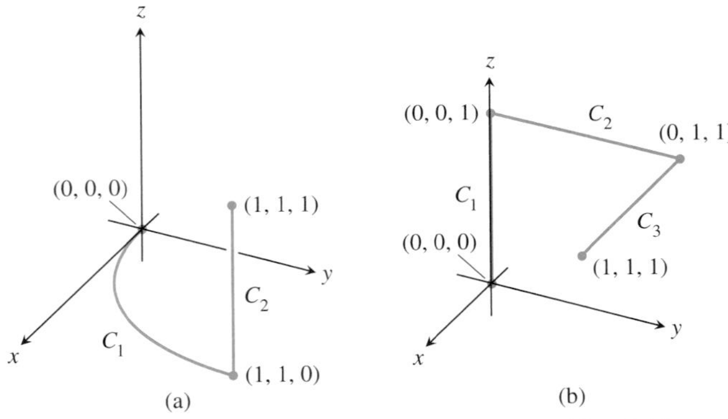

15.7 The paths of integration for Exercises 15 and 16.

16. Integrate $f(x, y, z) = x + \sqrt{y} - z^2$ over the path from $(0, 0, 0)$ to $(1, 1, 1)$ (Fig. 15.7b) given by
C_1: $\mathbf{r} = t\,\mathbf{k}, \quad 0 \le t \le 1$
C_2: $\mathbf{r} = t\,\mathbf{j} + \mathbf{k}, \quad 0 \le t \le 1$
C_3: $\mathbf{r} = t\,\mathbf{i} + \mathbf{j} + \mathbf{k}, \quad 0 \le t \le 1$

17. Integrate $f(x, y, z) = (x+y+z)/(x^2+y^2+z^2)$ over the path $\mathbf{r} = t\,\mathbf{i} + t\,\mathbf{j} + t\,\mathbf{k}$, $0 < a \le t \le b$.

18. Integrate $f(x, y, z) = -\sqrt{x^2+z^2}$ over the circle $\mathbf{r} = (a\cos t)\,\mathbf{j} + (a\sin t)\,\mathbf{k}$, $0 \le t \le 2\pi$.

19. Find I_x and R_x for the arch in Example 4.

20. Find the mass of a wire that lies along the curve $\mathbf{r} = (t^2-1)\,\mathbf{j} + 2t\,\mathbf{k}$, $0 \le t \le 1$, if the density is $\delta = (3/2)t$.

21. A circular wire hoop of constant density δ lies along the circle $x^2+y^2=a^2$ in the xy-plane. Find the hoop's moment of inertia and radius of gyration about the z-axis.

22. A slender rod of constant density lies along the line segment $\mathbf{r} = t\,\mathbf{j} + (2-2t)\,\mathbf{k}$, $0 \le t \le 1$ in the yz-plane. Find the moments of inertia and radii of gyration of the rod about the three coordinate axes.

23. A spring of constant density δ lies along the helix $\mathbf{r} = (\cos t)\,\mathbf{i} + (\sin t)\,\mathbf{j} + t\,\mathbf{k}$, $0 \le t \le 2\pi$.

a) Find I_z and R_z.

b) Suppose you have another spring of constant density δ that is twice as long as the spring in (a) and lies along the helix for $0 \le t \le 4\pi$. Do you expect I_z and R_z for the longer spring to be the same as those for the shorter one, or should they be different? Check your predictions by calculating I_z and R_z for the longer spring.

24. A wire of density $\delta(x, y, z) = 15\sqrt{y+2}$ lies along the curve $\mathbf{r} = (t^2-1)\,\mathbf{j} + 2t\,\mathbf{k}$, $-1 \le t \le 1$. Find its center of mass. Then sketch the curve and center of mass together.

25. *Continuation of Example 1.* The value of $\int_C f(x, y, z)\,ds$ has nothing to do with the direction in which C is traversed by the parametrization you choose. The only requirements are that the parametrization be smooth and that, having chosen the parametrization, you integrate with respect to increasing t. To emphasize this point, integrate $f(x, y, z) = x - 3y^2 + z$ over the line segment joining $(0, 0, 0)$ and $(1, 1, 1)$ using the parametrization

$$\mathbf{r} = (1-t)\,\mathbf{i} + (1-t)\,\mathbf{j} + (1-t)\,\mathbf{k}, \qquad 0 \le t \le 1.$$

You should get the same answer (0) even though the parametrization now traverses C from $(1, 1, 1)$ to $(0, 0, 0)$ instead of going from $(0, 0, 0)$ to $(1, 1, 1)$.

26. *Continuation of Exercise 25.* As a further illustration of the fact that the value of $\int_C f(x, y, z)\,ds$ is independent of the direction in which C happens to be traversed by the parametrization you use, evaluate the integral

$$\int_{C_1 \cup C_2} (x - 3y^2 + z)\,ds$$

of Example 2 using the parametrizations

C_1: $\mathbf{r} = t\,\mathbf{i} + t\,\mathbf{j}, \quad 0 \le t \le 1$

C_2: $\mathbf{r} = \mathbf{i} + \mathbf{j} + (1-t)\,\mathbf{k}, \quad 0 \le t \le 1.$

The parametrization of C_1 is the same as the one in Example 2, but the parametrization of C_2 now traverses C_2 from $(1, 1, 1)$ to $(1, 1, 0)$.

27. Suppose you integrate a continuous function $f(x, y, z)$ from $(0, 0, 0)$ to $(1, 1, 1)$ over two different paths and come up with two different answers. Does this necessarily mean you made a mistake? Give reasons for your answer.

28. Suppose you integrate a continuous function $g(x, y, z)$ over a curve C using two different smooth parametrizations (integrating with respect to increasing t) and come up with two different answers. Does this necessarily mean you made a mistake? Give reasons for your answer.

Writing for Your Own Knowledge

Answer the following questions in writing. Some answers will take only a sentence or two; others may require several paragraphs. Some explanations may also call for graphs or sketches.

1. What is a line integral?
2. How are line integrals evaluated?
3. How can you use line integrals to find the center of mass of a spring?

15.2 *Vector Fields, Work, Circulation, and Flux*

When we study physical phenomena that are represented by vectors, we replace integrals over closed intervals by integrals over paths through vector fields. We use such integrals to find the work done in moving an object along a path against a variable force (a vehicle sent into space against Earth's gravitational field). Or we might want to find the work done by a vector field in moving an object along a path through the field (the work done by a particle accelerator in raising the energy of a particle). We also use line integrals to find the rates at which fluids flow along and across curves.

Vector Fields

A **vector field** on a domain in the plane or in space is a function that assigns a vector to each point in the domain. A field of three-dimensional vectors might have a formula like

$$\mathbf{F} = M(x, y, z)\,\mathbf{i} + N(x, y, z)\,\mathbf{j} + P(x, y, z)\,\mathbf{k}. \tag{1}$$

The field is **continuous** if the **component functions** M, N, and P are continuous, **differentiable** if M, N, and P are differentiable, and so on. A field of two-dimensional vectors might have a formula like

$$\mathbf{F} = M(x, y)\,\mathbf{i} + N(x, y)\,\mathbf{j}. \tag{2}$$

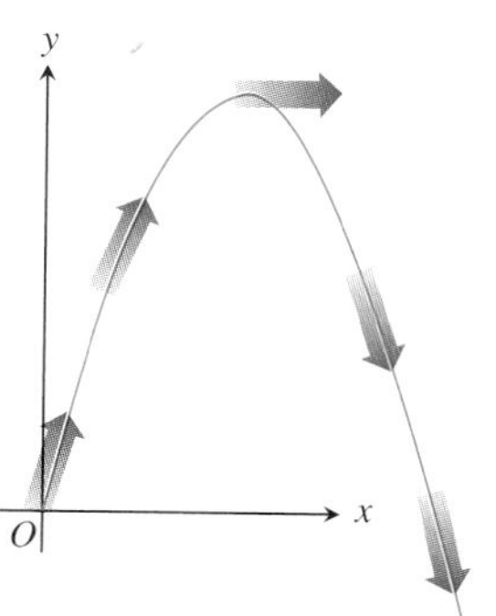

15.8 The velocity vectors $\mathbf{v}(t)$ of a projectile's motion make a vector field along the trajectory.

If we attach a projectile's velocity vector to each point of the projectile's trajectory in the plane of motion, we have a two-dimensional field defined along the trajectory. If we attach the gradient vector of a scalar function to each point of a level surface of the function, we have a three-dimensional field on the surface. If we attach the velocity vector to each point of a flowing fluid, we have a three-dimensional field defined on a region in space. These and other fields are illustrated in Figs. 15.8–15.16. Some of the illustrations give formulas for the fields as well.

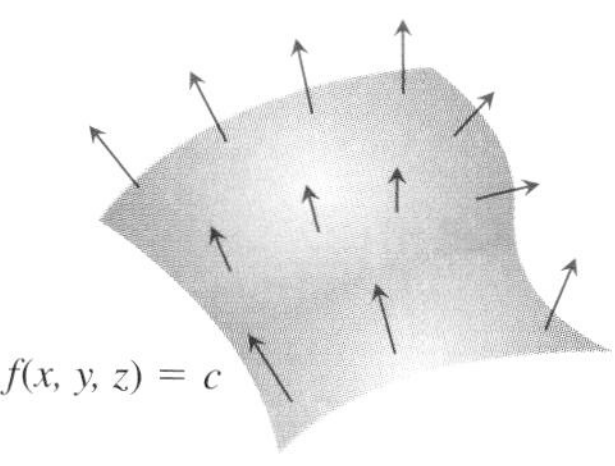

15.9 The field of gradient vectors ∇f on a surface $f(x, y, z) = c$.

To sketch the fields that had formulas, we picked a representative selection of domain points and sketched the vectors attached to them. Notice the convention that the arrows representing the vectors are drawn with their tails, not their heads, at the points where the vector functions are evaluated. This is different from the way we drew the position vectors of the planets and projectiles in Chapter 12, with their tails at the origin and their heads at the planet's and projectile's locations.

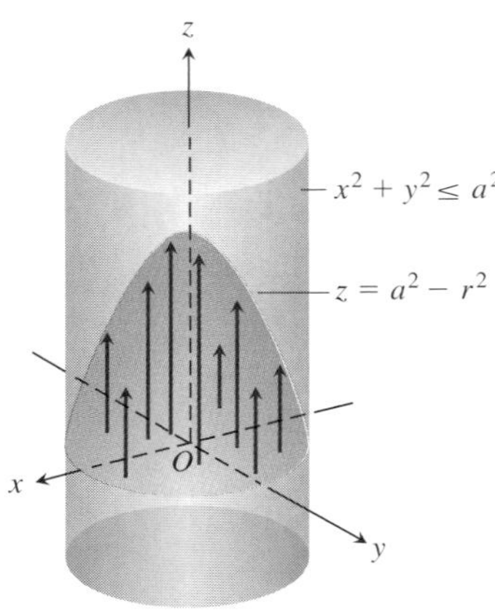

15.10 The flow of fluid in a long cylindrical pipe. The vectors $\mathbf{v} = (a^2 - r^2)\,\mathbf{k}$ inside the cylinder that have their bases in the xy-plane have their tips on the paraboloid $z = a^2 - r^2$.

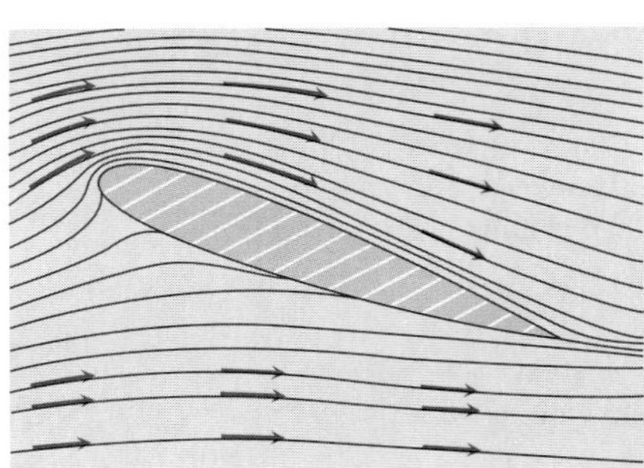

15.11 Velocity vectors of a flow around an airfoil in a wind tunnel. The streamlines were made visible by kerosene smoke. (Adapted from *NCFMF Book of Film Notes,* 1974, the MIT Press with Education Development Center, Inc., Newton, Massachusetts.)

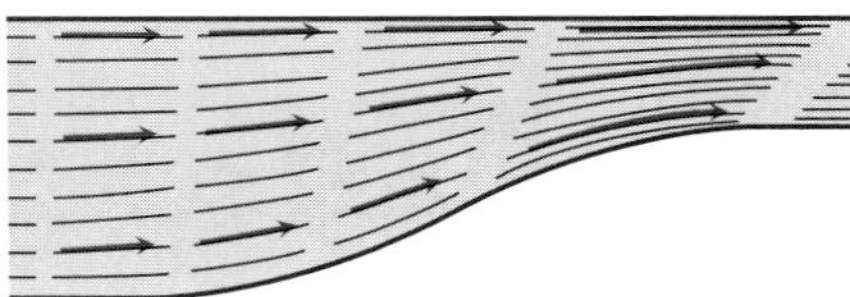

15.12 Streamlines in a contracting channel. The water speeds up as the channel narrows and the velocity vectors increase in length. (Adapted from *NCFMF Book of Film Notes,* 1974, the MIT Press with Education Development Center, Inc., Newton, Massachusetts.)

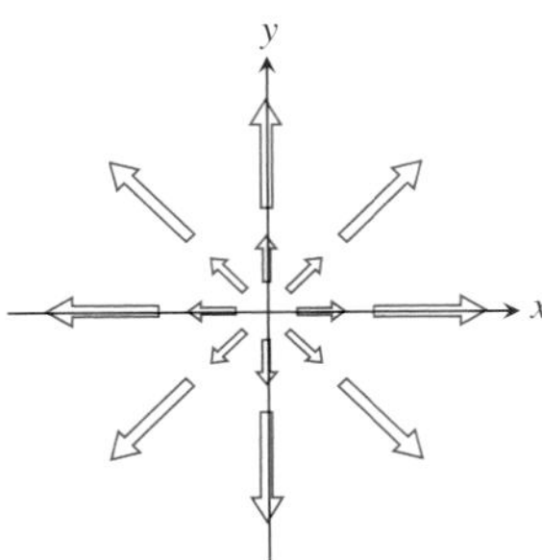

15.14 The radial field $\mathbf{F} = x\,\mathbf{i} + y\,\mathbf{j}$ of position vectors of points in the plane. Notice the convention that an arrow is drawn with its tail, not its head, at the point where $\mathbf{F}$ is evaluated.

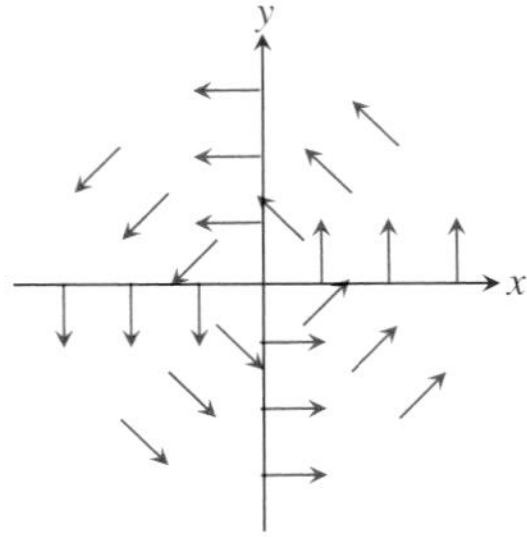

15.15 The circumferential or "spin" field of unit vectors

$$\mathbf{F} = (-y\,\mathbf{i} + x\,\mathbf{j})/(x^2 + y^2)^{1/2}$$

in the plane. The field is not defined at the origin.

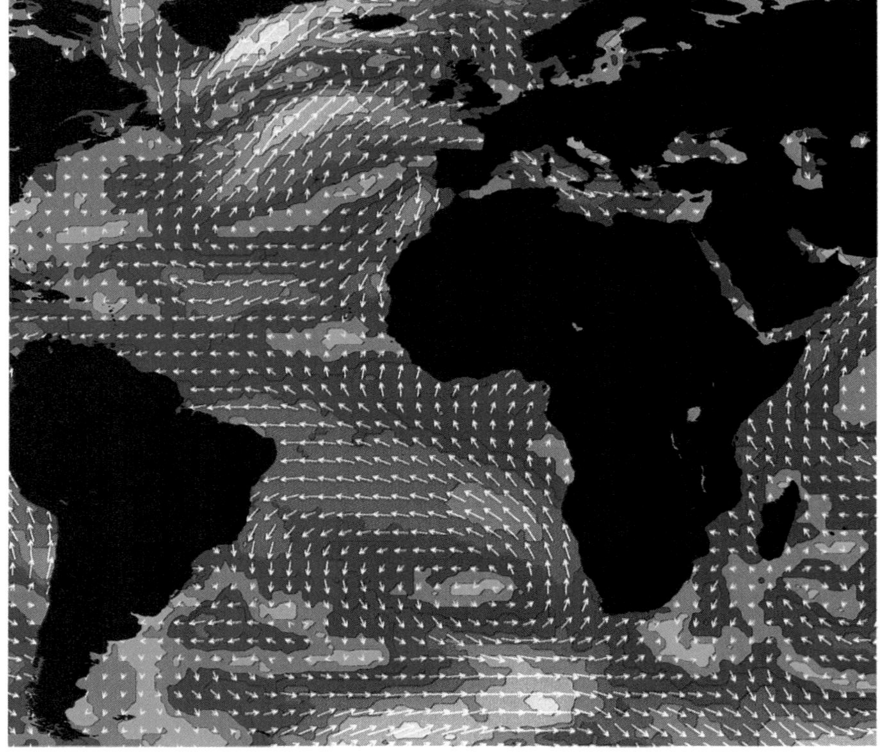

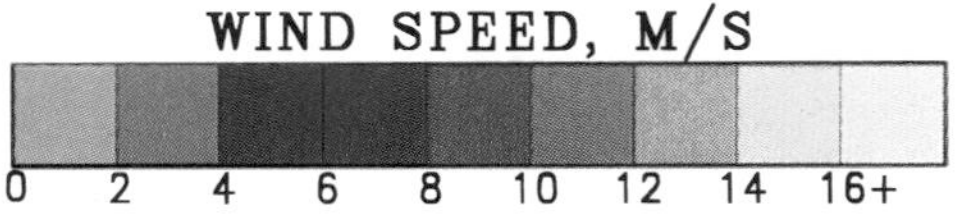

15.16 NASA's *Seasat* used radar during a 3-day period in September 1978 to take 350,000 wind measurements over the world's oceans. The arrows show wind direction; their length and the color contouring indicate speed. Notice the heavy storm south of Greenland.

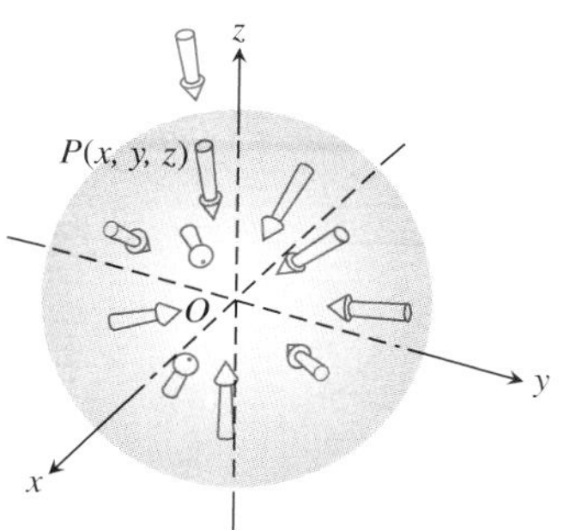

15.13 Vectors in the gravitational field

$$\mathbf{F} = -\frac{GM(x\,\mathbf{i} + y\,\mathbf{j} + z\,\mathbf{k})}{(x^2 + y^2 + z^2)^{3/2}}.$$

Gradient Fields

DEFINITION

The **gradient field** of a differentiable function $f(x, y, z)$ is the field of gradient vectors

$$\nabla f = \frac{\partial f}{\partial x}\,\mathbf{i} + \frac{\partial f}{\partial y}\,\mathbf{j} + \frac{\partial f}{\partial z}\,\mathbf{k}.$$

EXAMPLE 1 Find the gradient field of $f(x, y, z) = xyz$.

Solution The gradient field of f is the field

$$\mathbf{F} = \nabla f = yz\,\mathbf{i} + xz\,\mathbf{j} + xy\,\mathbf{k}.$$

As we will see in Section 15.3, gradient fields are of special importance in engineering, mathematics, and physics.

The Work Done by a Force over a Curve in Space

Suppose that the vector field $\mathbf{F} = M(x, y, z)\,\mathbf{i} + N(x, y, z)\,\mathbf{j} + P(x, y, z)\,\mathbf{k}$ represents a force throughout a region in space (it might be the force of gravity or an electromagnetic force of some kind) and that

$$\mathbf{r} = g(t)\,\mathbf{i} + h(t)\,\mathbf{j} + k(t)\,\mathbf{k}, \quad a \le t \le b,$$

is a smooth curve in the region. Then the integral of $\mathbf{F} \cdot \mathbf{T}$, the scalar component of $\mathbf{F}$ in the direction of the curve's unit tangent vector, over the curve is called the work done by $\mathbf{F}$ over the curve from a to b (Fig. 15.17).

DEFINITION

The **work** done by a (continuous) force

$$\mathbf{F} = M(x, y, z)\,\mathbf{i} + N(x, y, z)\,\mathbf{j} + P(x, y, z)\,\mathbf{k}$$

over a smooth curve $\mathbf{r} = g(t)\,\mathbf{i} + h(t)\,\mathbf{j} + k(t)\,\mathbf{k}$ from $t = a$ to $t = b$ is

$$W = \int_{t=a}^{t=b} \mathbf{F} \cdot \mathbf{T}\,ds. \tag{3}$$

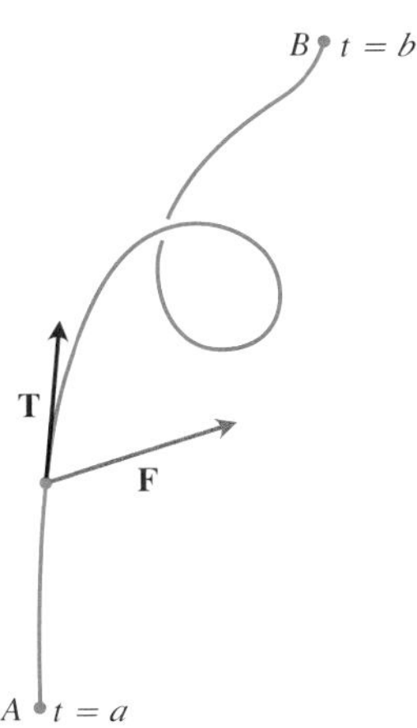

15.17 The work done by a continuous field $\mathbf{F}$ over a smooth path $\mathbf{r} = g(t)\,\mathbf{i} + h(t)\,\mathbf{j} + k(t)\,\mathbf{k}$ from A to B is the integral of $\mathbf{F} \cdot \mathbf{T}$ over the path from $t = a$ to $t = b$.

Notice how the numerical sign of the number we calculate in Eq. (3) depends on the direction in which the curve is traversed as t increases. If we reverse the direction of motion, we reverse the direction of $\mathbf{T}$ and change the sign of $\mathbf{F} \cdot \mathbf{T}$.

Notation and Evaluation

There are six standard ways to write the work integral in Eq. (3), as shown in Table 15.2 on the following page.

TABLE 15.2
Different ways to write the work integral

$\mathbf{W} = \int_{t=a}^{t=b} \mathbf{F} \cdot \mathbf{T}\, ds$	The definition
$= \int_{t=a}^{t=b} \mathbf{F} \cdot d\mathbf{r}$	Compact differential form
$= \int_a^b \mathbf{F} \cdot \frac{d\mathbf{r}}{dt}\, dt$	Expanded to include dt. Emphasizes the parameter t and velocity vector $d\mathbf{r}/dt$.
$= \int_a^b \left(M\frac{dg}{dt} + N\frac{dh}{dt} + P\frac{dk}{dt} \right) dt$	Emphasizes the component functions
$= \int_a^b \left(M\frac{dx}{dt} + N\frac{dy}{dt} + P\frac{dz}{dt} \right) dt$	Abbreviates the components of $\mathbf{r}$
$= \int_a^b M\, dx + N\, dy + P\, dz$	dt's canceled. The most common form.

Despite their variety, these formulas are all evaluated the same way.

How to Evaluate a Work Integral

To evaluate the work integral, take these steps:

1. Evaluate $\mathbf{F}$ on the curve as a function of the parameter t.
2. Find $d\mathbf{r}/dt$.
3. Dot $\mathbf{F}$ with $d\mathbf{r}/dt$.
4. Integrate from $t = a$ to $t = b$.

EXAMPLE 2 Find the work done by

$$\mathbf{F} = (y - x^2)\,\mathbf{i} + (z - y^2)\,\mathbf{j} + (x - z^2)\,\mathbf{k}$$

over the curve

$$\mathbf{r} = t\,\mathbf{i} + t^2\,\mathbf{j} + t^3\,\mathbf{k}, \quad 0 \le t \le 1,$$

from (0, 0, 0) to (1, 1, 1) (Fig. 15.18).

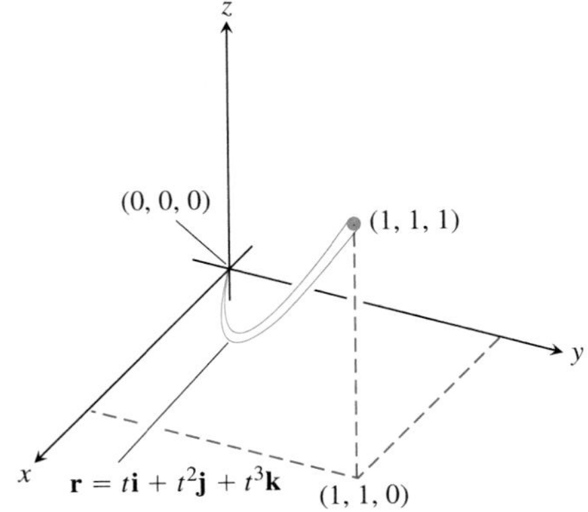

15.18 The curve in Example 2.

Solution

STEP 1: *Evaluate* $\mathbf{F}$ *on the curve.*

$$\begin{aligned}\mathbf{F} &= (y - x^2)\,\mathbf{i} + (z - y^2)\,\mathbf{j} + (x - z^2)\,\mathbf{k} \\ &= \underbrace{(t^2 - t^2)}_{0}\,\mathbf{i} + (t^3 - t^4)\,\mathbf{j} + (t - t^6)\,\mathbf{k}\end{aligned}$$

STEP 2: *Find* $d\mathbf{r}/dt$.

$$\frac{d\mathbf{r}}{dt} = \frac{d}{dt}(t\,\mathbf{i} + t^2\,\mathbf{j} + t^3\,\mathbf{k}) = \mathbf{i} + 2t\,\mathbf{j} + 3t^2\,\mathbf{k}$$

STEP 3: *Dot* **F** *with* $d\mathbf{r}/dt$.

$$\begin{aligned}\mathbf{F}\cdot\frac{d\mathbf{r}}{dt} &= [(t^3 - t^4)\,\mathbf{j} + (t - t^6)\,\mathbf{k}]\cdot(\mathbf{i} + 2t\,\mathbf{j} + 3t^2\,\mathbf{k})\\ &= (t^3 - t^4)(2t) + (t - t^6)(3t^2) = 2t^4 - 2t^5 + 3t^3 - 3t^8\end{aligned}$$

STEP 4: *Integrate from* $t = 0$ *to* $t = 1$.

$$\begin{aligned}\text{Work} &= \int_0^1 (2t^4 - 2t^5 + 3t^3 - 3t^8)\,dt\\ &= \left[\frac{2}{5}t^5 - \frac{2}{6}t^6 + \frac{3}{4}t^4 - \frac{3}{9}t^9\right]_0^1 = \frac{29}{60}.\end{aligned}$$

Flow Integrals and Circulation

Instead of being a force field, suppose that the vector field $\mathbf{F} = M\,\mathbf{i} + N\,\mathbf{j} + P\,\mathbf{k}$ represents the velocity field of a fluid flowing through a region in space (a tidal basin or the turbine chamber of a hydroelectric generator, for example). Under these circumstances, the integral of $\mathbf{F}\cdot\mathbf{T}$ along a curve in the region gives the fluid's flow along the curve.

DEFINITIONS

If $\mathbf{r} = g(t)\,\mathbf{i} + h(t)\,\mathbf{j} + k(t)\,\mathbf{k}$, $a \le t \le b$, is a smooth curve in the domain of a continuous velocity field $\mathbf{F} = M(x, y, z)\,\mathbf{i} + N(x, y, z)\,\mathbf{j} + P(x, y, z)\,\mathbf{k}$, the **flow** along the curve from $t = a$ to $t = b$ is the integral of $\mathbf{F}\cdot\mathbf{T}$ over the curve from a to b:

$$\text{Flow} = \int_a^b \mathbf{F}\cdot\mathbf{T}\,ds. \tag{4}$$

The integral in this case is called a **flow integral.** If the curve is a closed loop, the flow is called the **circulation** around the curve.

We evaluate flow integrals the same way we evaluate work integrals.

EXAMPLE 3 A fluid's velocity field is

$$\mathbf{F} = x\,\mathbf{i} + z\,\mathbf{j} + y\,\mathbf{k}.$$

Find the flow along the helix

$$\mathbf{r} = (\cos t)\,\mathbf{i} + (\sin t)\,\mathbf{j} + t\,\mathbf{k},\quad 0 \le t \le \pi/2.$$

Solution

STEP 1: *Evaluate* **F** *on the curve.*

$$\mathbf{F} = x\,\mathbf{i} + z\,\mathbf{j} + y\,\mathbf{k} = (\cos t)\,\mathbf{i} + t\,\mathbf{j} + (\sin t)\,\mathbf{k}$$

STEP 2: *Find* $d\mathbf{r}/dt$.

$$\frac{d\mathbf{r}}{dt} = (-\sin t)\,\mathbf{i} + (\cos t)\,\mathbf{j} + \mathbf{k}$$

STEP 3: *Find* $\mathbf{F}\cdot(d\mathbf{r}/dt)$.

$$\begin{aligned}\mathbf{F}\cdot\frac{d\mathbf{r}}{dt} &= (\cos t)(-\sin t) + (t)(\cos t) + (\sin t)(1)\\ &= -\sin t\cos t + t\cos t + \sin t\end{aligned}$$

STEP 4: *Integrate from* $t = a$ *to* $t = b$.

$$\begin{aligned}\text{Flow} &= \int_{t=a}^{t=b} \mathbf{F}\cdot\frac{d\mathbf{r}}{dt}\,dt = \int_0^{\pi/2} (-\sin t\cos t + t\cos t + \sin t)\,dt\\ &= \left[\frac{\cos^2 t}{2} + t\sin t\right]_0^{\pi/2} = \left(0 + \frac{\pi}{2}\right) - \left(\frac{1}{2} + 0\right) = \frac{\pi}{2} - \frac{1}{2}.\end{aligned}$$

EXAMPLE 4 Find the circulation of a fluid around the circle

$$\mathbf{r} = (\cos t)\,\mathbf{i} + (\sin t)\,\mathbf{j}, \quad 0 \le t \le 2\pi,$$

if the velocity field is $\mathbf{F} = (x - y)\,\mathbf{i} + x\,\mathbf{j}$.

Solution

1. On the circle, $\mathbf{F} = (x - y)\,\mathbf{i} + x\,\mathbf{j} = (\cos t - \sin t)\,\mathbf{i} + (\cos t)\,\mathbf{j}$.
2. $\dfrac{d\mathbf{r}}{dt} = (-\sin t)\,\mathbf{i} + (\cos t)\,\mathbf{j}$
3. $\mathbf{F}\cdot\dfrac{d\mathbf{r}}{dt} = -\sin t\cos t + \underbrace{\sin^2 t + \cos^2 t}_{1}$
4. $$\begin{aligned}\text{Circulation} &= \int_0^{2\pi} \mathbf{F}\cdot\frac{d\mathbf{r}}{dt}\,dt = \int_0^{2\pi} (1 - \sin t\cos t)\,dt\\ &= \left[t - \frac{\sin^2 t}{2}\right]_0^{2\pi} = 2\pi.\end{aligned}$$

Flux Across a Plane Curve

To find the rate at which a fluid is entering or leaving a region enclosed by a smooth curve C in the xy-plane, we calculate the line integral over C of $\mathbf{F}\cdot\mathbf{n}$, the scalar component of the fluid's velocity field in the direction of the curve's outward-pointing normal vector. The value of this integral is called the flux of $\mathbf{F}$ across C. *Flux* is Latin for *flow,* but many flux calculations involve no motion at all. If $\mathbf{F}$ were an electric field or a magnetic field, for instance, the integral of $\mathbf{F}\cdot\mathbf{n}$ would still be called the flux of the field across C.

DEFINITION

If C is a smooth closed curve in the domain of a continuous vector field $\mathbf{F} = M(x, y)\,\mathbf{i} + N(x, y)\,\mathbf{j}$ in the plane, and if $\mathbf{n}$ is the outward-pointing unit normal vector on C, the **flux** of $\mathbf{F}$ across C is given by the following line integral:

$$\text{Flux of } \mathbf{F} \text{ across } C = \int_C \mathbf{F}\cdot\mathbf{n}\,ds. \qquad (5)$$

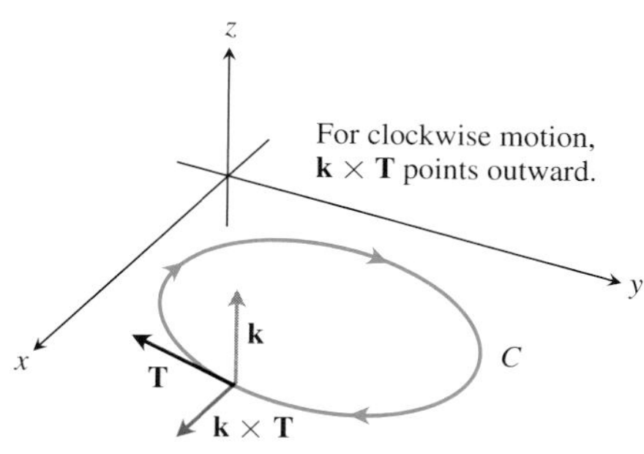

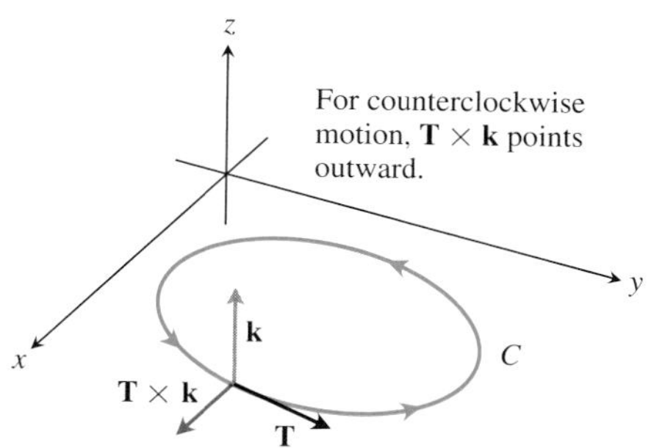

15.19 To find an outward unit normal vector for a smooth curve C in the xy-plane that is traversed counterclockwise as t increases, we take $\mathbf{n} = \mathbf{T} \times \mathbf{k}$.

Notice the difference between flux and circulation. The flux of $\mathbf{F}$ across C is the line integral with respect to arc length of $\mathbf{F} \cdot \mathbf{n}$, the scalar component of $\mathbf{F}$ in the direction of the outward normal. The circulation of $\mathbf{F}$ around C is the line integral with respect to arc length of $\mathbf{F} \cdot \mathbf{T}$, the scalar component of $\mathbf{F}$ in the direction of the unit tangent vector. Flux is the integral of the normal component of $\mathbf{F}$; circulation is the integral of the tangential component of $\mathbf{F}$.

To evaluate the integral in (5), we begin with a parametrization

$$x = g(t), \qquad y = h(t), \qquad a \le t \le b,$$

that traces the curve C exactly once as t increases from a to b. We can find the outward unit normal vector $\mathbf{n}$ by crossing the curve's unit tangent vector $\mathbf{T}$ with the vector $\mathbf{k}$. But which order do we choose, $\mathbf{T} \times \mathbf{k}$ or $\mathbf{k} \times \mathbf{T}$? Which one points outward? It depends on which way C is traversed as the parameter t increases. If the motion is clockwise, then $\mathbf{k} \times \mathbf{T}$ points outward; if the motion is counterclockwise, then $\mathbf{T} \times \mathbf{k}$ points outward (Fig. 15.19). The usual choice is $\mathbf{n} = \mathbf{T} \times \mathbf{k}$, the choice that assumes counterclockwise motion. Thus, while the value of the arc length integral in the definition of flux in Eq. (5) does not depend on which way C is traversed, the formulas we are about to derive for evaluating the integral in Eq. (5) will assume counterclockwise motion.

In terms of components,

$$\mathbf{n} = \mathbf{T} \times \mathbf{k} = \left(\frac{dx}{ds}\,\mathbf{i} + \frac{dy}{ds}\,\mathbf{j}\right) \times \mathbf{k} = \frac{dy}{ds}\,\mathbf{i} - \frac{dx}{ds}\,\mathbf{j}. \tag{6}$$

If $\mathbf{F} = M(x, y)\,\mathbf{i} + N(x, y)\,\mathbf{j}$, then

$$\mathbf{F} \cdot \mathbf{n} = M(x, y)\frac{dy}{ds} - N(x, y)\frac{dx}{ds}.$$

Hence,

$$\int_C \mathbf{F} \cdot \mathbf{n}\, ds = \int_C \left(M\frac{dy}{ds} - N\frac{dx}{ds}\right) ds = \oint_C M\,dy - N\,dx. \tag{7}$$

We put a directed circle $\circlearrowleft$ on the last integral as a reminder that the integration around the closed curve C is to be in the counterclockwise direction. To evaluate this integral, we express M, dy, N, and dx in terms of t and integrate from $t = a$ to $t = b$. We do not need to know either $\mathbf{n}$ or ds to find the flux.

The Formula for Calculating Flux Across a Smooth Closed Plane Curve

$$\text{Flux of } \mathbf{F} = M\,\mathbf{i} + N\,\mathbf{j} \text{ across } C = \oint M\,dy - N\,dx \tag{8}$$

The integral can be evaluated from any smooth parametrization $x = g(t)$, $y = h(t)$, $a \le t \le b$, that traces C counterclockwise exactly once. To evaluate the integral, express M, dy, N, and dx in terms of t and integrate from $t = a$ to $t = b$.

EXAMPLE 5 Find the flux of $\mathbf{F} = (x - y)\,\mathbf{i} + x\,\mathbf{j}$ across the circle $x^2 + y^2 = 1$ in the xy-plane.

Solution The parametrization

$$\mathbf{r} = (\cos t)\,\mathbf{i} + (\sin t)\,\mathbf{j}, \quad 0 \le t \le 2\pi,$$

traces the circle counterclockwise exactly once. We can therefore use this parametrization in Eq. (8). With

$$M = x - y = \cos t - \sin t \qquad dy = d(\sin t) = \cos t\, dt$$
$$N = x = \cos t \qquad dx = d(\cos t) = -\sin t\, dt,$$

we find

$$\text{Flux} = \int_C M\,dy - N\,dx = \int_0^{2\pi} (\cos^2 t - \sin t \cos t + \cos t \sin t)\,dt \qquad \text{Eq. (8)}$$
$$= \int_0^{2\pi} \cos^2 t\,dt = \int_0^{2\pi} \frac{1 + \cos 2t}{2}\,dt = \left[\frac{t}{2} + \frac{\sin 2t}{4}\right]_0^{2\pi} = \pi.$$

The flux of **F** across the circle is π. Since the answer is positive, the net flow across the curve is outward. A net inward flow would have given a negative flux.

Exercises 15.2

Find the gradient fields of the functions in Exercises 1–4.

1. $f(x, y, z) = (x^2 + y^2 + z^2)^{-1/2}$

2. $f(x, y, z) = \ln \sqrt{x^2 + y^2 + z^2}$

3. $g(x, y, z) = e^z - \ln (x^2 + y^2)$

4. $g(x, y, z) = xy + yz + xz$

In Exercises 5–10, find the work done by force **F** from (0, 0, 0) to (1, 1, 1) over each of the following paths (Fig. 15.20):

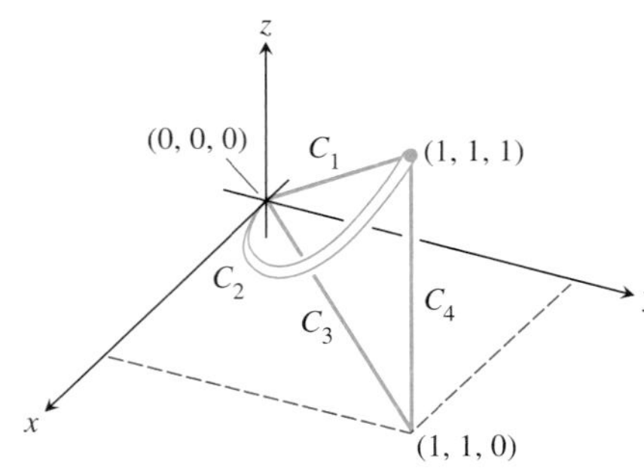

15.20 The paths from (0, 0, 0) to (1, 1, 1).

a) The straight-line path C_1: $\mathbf{r} = t\,\mathbf{i} + t\,\mathbf{j} + t\,\mathbf{k}, \quad 0 \le t \le 1$

b) The curved path C_2: $\mathbf{r} = t\,\mathbf{i} + t^2\,\mathbf{j} + t^4\,\mathbf{k}, \quad 0 \le t \le 1$

c) The path $C_3 \cup C_4$ consisting of the line segment from (0, 0, 0) to (1, 1, 0) followed by the line segment from (1, 1, 0) to (1, 1, 1)

5. $\mathbf{F} = 3y\,\mathbf{i} + 2x\,\mathbf{j} + 4z\,\mathbf{k}$

6. $\mathbf{F} = [1/(x^2 + 1)]\,\mathbf{j}$

7. $\mathbf{F} = \sqrt{z}\,\mathbf{i} - 2x\,\mathbf{j} + \sqrt{y}\,\mathbf{k}$

8. $\mathbf{F} = xy\,\mathbf{i} + yz\,\mathbf{j} + xz\,\mathbf{k}$

9. $\mathbf{F} = (3x^2 - 3x)\,\mathbf{i} + 3z\,\mathbf{j} + \mathbf{k}$

10. $\mathbf{F} = (y + z)\,\mathbf{i} + (z + x)\,\mathbf{j} + (x + y)\,\mathbf{k}$

In Exercises 11–14, find the work done by **F** over the curve in the direction of increasing t.

11. $\mathbf{F} = xy\,\mathbf{i} + y\,\mathbf{j} - yz\,\mathbf{k}$
$\mathbf{r} = t\,\mathbf{i} + t^2\,\mathbf{j} + t\,\mathbf{k}, \quad 0 \le t \le 1$

12. $\mathbf{F} = 2y\,\mathbf{i} + 3x\,\mathbf{j} + (x + y)\,\mathbf{k}$
$\mathbf{r} = (\cos t)\,\mathbf{i} + (\sin t)\,\mathbf{j} + (t/6)\,\mathbf{k}, \quad 0 \le t \le 2\pi$

13. $\mathbf{F} = z\,\mathbf{i} + x\,\mathbf{j} + y\,\mathbf{k}$
$\mathbf{r} = (\sin t)\,\mathbf{i} + (\cos t)\,\mathbf{j} + t\,\mathbf{k}, \quad 0 \le t \le 2\pi$

14. $\mathbf{F} = 6z\,\mathbf{i} + y^2\,\mathbf{j} + 12x\,\mathbf{k}$
$\mathbf{r} = (\sin t)\,\mathbf{i} + (\cos t)\,\mathbf{j} + (t/6)\,\mathbf{k}, \quad 0 \le t \le 2\pi$

In Exercises 15–18, **F** is the velocity field of a fluid flowing through a region in space. Find the flow along the given curve in the direction of increasing t.

15. $\mathbf{F} = -4xy\,\mathbf{i} + 8y\,\mathbf{j} + 2\,\mathbf{k}$
$\mathbf{r} = t\,\mathbf{i} + t^2\,\mathbf{j} + \mathbf{k}, \quad 0 \le t \le 2$

16. $\mathbf{F} = x^2\,\mathbf{i} + yz\,\mathbf{j} + y^2\,\mathbf{k}$
$\mathbf{r} = 3t\,\mathbf{j} + 4t\,\mathbf{k}, \quad 0 \le t \le 1$

17. $\mathbf{F} = (x - z)\,\mathbf{i} + x\,\mathbf{k}$
$\mathbf{r} = (\cos t)\,\mathbf{i} + (\sin t)\,\mathbf{k}, \quad 0 \le t \le \pi$

18. $\mathbf{F} = -y\,\mathbf{i} + x\,\mathbf{j} + 2\,\mathbf{k}$
$\mathbf{r} = (-2\cos t)\,\mathbf{i} + (2\sin t)\,\mathbf{j} + 2t\,\mathbf{k}, \quad 0 \le t \le 2\pi$

19. Find the circulation and flux of the fields

$$\mathbf{F}_1 = x\,\mathbf{i} + y\,\mathbf{j} \quad \text{and} \quad \mathbf{F}_2 = -y\,\mathbf{i} + x\,\mathbf{j}$$

around and across each of the following curves.

a) The circle $\mathbf{r} = (\cos t)\,\mathbf{i} + (\sin t)\,\mathbf{j}, \quad 0 \le t \le 2\pi$
b) The ellipse $\mathbf{r} = (\cos t)\,\mathbf{i} + (4 \sin t)\,\mathbf{j}, \quad 0 \le t \le 2\pi$

20. Find the flux of the fields

$$\mathbf{F}_1 = 2x\,\mathbf{i} - 3y\,\mathbf{j} \quad \text{and} \quad \mathbf{F}_2 = 2x\,\mathbf{i} + (x - y)\,\mathbf{j}$$

across the circle

$$\mathbf{r} = (a \cos t)\,\mathbf{i} + (a \sin t)\,\mathbf{j}, \quad 0 \le t \le 2\pi.$$

In Exercises 21–24, find the circulation and flux of the field $\mathbf{F}$ around and across the closed semicircular path that consists of the semicircular arch $\mathbf{r}_1 = (a \cos t)\,\mathbf{i} + (a \sin t)\,\mathbf{j}$, $0 \le t \le \pi$, followed by the line segment $\mathbf{r}_2 = t\,\mathbf{i}$, $-a \le t \le a$.

21. $\mathbf{F} = x\,\mathbf{i} + y\,\mathbf{j}$
22. $\mathbf{F} = x^2\,\mathbf{i} + y^2\,\mathbf{j}$
23. $\mathbf{F} = -y\,\mathbf{i} + x\,\mathbf{j}$
24. $\mathbf{F} = -y^2\,\mathbf{i} + x^2\,\mathbf{j}$

25. Draw the spin field

$$\mathbf{F} = -\frac{y}{\sqrt{x^2 + y^2}}\,\mathbf{i} + \frac{x}{\sqrt{x^2 + y^2}}\,\mathbf{j}$$

(see Fig. 15.15) along with its horizontal and vertical components at a representative assortment of points on the circle $x^2 + y^2 = 4$.

26. Draw the radial field

$$\mathbf{F} = x\,\mathbf{i} + y\,\mathbf{j}$$

(see Fig. 15.14) along with its horizontal and vertical components at a representative assortment of points on the circle $x^2 + y^2 = 1$.

27. a) Find a field $\mathbf{G} = P(x, y)\,\mathbf{i} + Q(x, y)\,\mathbf{j}$ in the xy-plane with the property that at any point $(a, b) \ne (0, 0)$, $\mathbf{G}$ is a vector of magnitude $\sqrt{a^2 + b^2}$ tangent to the circle $x^2 + y^2 = a^2 + b^2$ and pointing in the counterclockwise direction. (The field is undefined at (0, 0).)

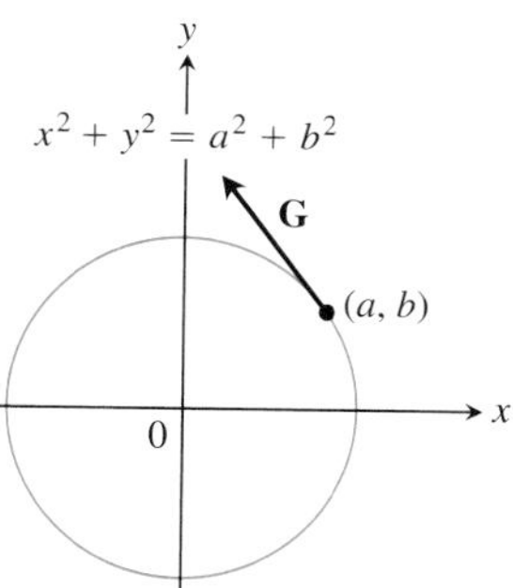

b) How is $\mathbf{G}$ related to the spin field $\mathbf{F}$ in Fig. 15.15?

28. a) Find a field $\mathbf{G} = P(x, y)\,\mathbf{i} + Q(x, y)\,\mathbf{j}$ in the xy-plane with the property that at any point $(a, b) \ne (0, 0)$, $\mathbf{G}$ is a unit vector tangent to the circle $x^2 + y^2 = a^2 + b^2$ and pointing in the clockwise direction.
b) How is $\mathbf{G}$ related to the spin field $\mathbf{F}$ in Fig. 15.15?

29. Find a field $\mathbf{F} = M(x, y)\,\mathbf{i} + N(x, y)\,\mathbf{j}$ in the xy-plane with the property that at each point $(x, y) \ne (0, 0)$, $\mathbf{F}$ is a unit vector pointing toward the origin. (The field is undefined at (0, 0).)

30. Find a field $\mathbf{F} = M(x, y)\,\mathbf{i} + N(x, y)\,\mathbf{j}$ in the xy-plane with the property that at each point $(x, y) \ne (0, 0)$, $\mathbf{F}$ points toward the origin and $|\mathbf{F}|$ is (a) the distance from (x, y) to the origin, (b) inversely proportional to the distance from (x, y) to the origin. (The field is undefined at (0, 0).)

31. Evaluate the flow integral of the velocity field $\mathbf{F} = (x + y)\,\mathbf{i} - (x^2 + y^2)\,\mathbf{j}$ along each of the following paths from (1, 0) to (−1, 0) in the xy-plane.

a) The upper half of the circle $x^2 + y^2 = 1$
b) The line segment from (1, 0) to (−1, 0)
c) The line segment from (1, 0) to (0, −1) followed by the line segment from (0, −1) to (−1, 0)

32. The field $\mathbf{F} = xy\,\mathbf{i} + y\,\mathbf{j} - yz\,\mathbf{k}$ is the velocity field of a flow in space. Find the flow from (0, 0, 0) to (1, 1, 1) along the curve of intersection of the cylinder $y = x^2$ and the plane $z = x$. (*Hint:* Use $t = x$ as the parameter.)

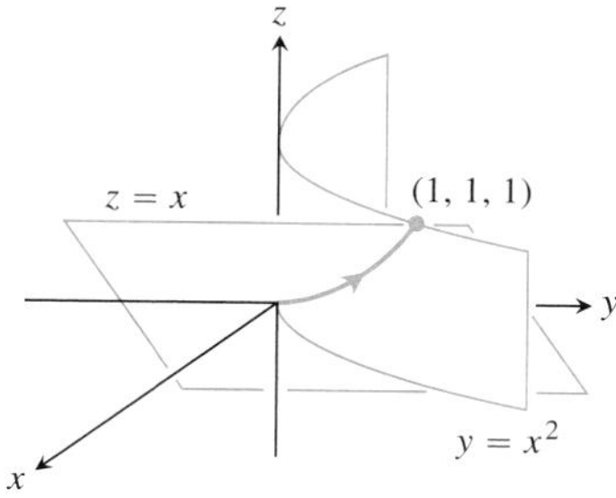

33. Find the circulation of $\mathbf{F} = 2x\,\mathbf{i} + 2z\,\mathbf{j} + 2y\,\mathbf{k}$ around the closed path consisting of the following three curves traversed in the direction of increasing t:

C_1: $\mathbf{r} = (\cos t)\,\mathbf{i} + (\sin t)\,\mathbf{j} + t\,\mathbf{k}, \quad 0 \le t \le \pi/2$
C_2: $\mathbf{r} = \mathbf{j} + (\pi/2)(1 - t)\,\mathbf{k}, \quad 0 \le t \le 1$
C_3: $\mathbf{r} = t\,\mathbf{i} + (1 - t)\,\mathbf{j}, \quad 0 \le t \le 1$

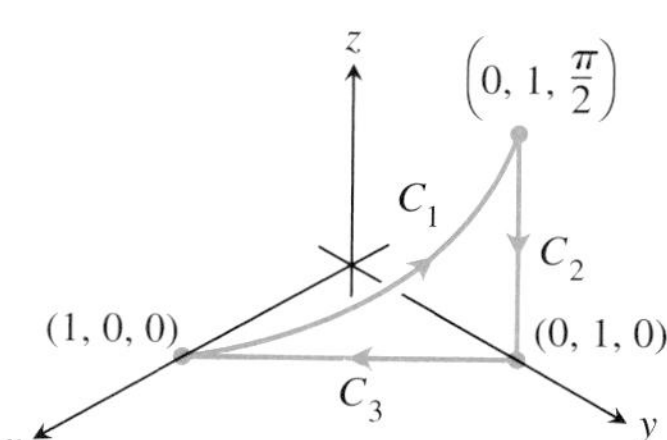

34. Suppose $f(t)$ is differentiable and is positive for $a \le t \le b$. Let C be the path $\mathbf{r} = t\,\mathbf{i} + f(t)\,\mathbf{j}$, $a \le t \le b$, and $\mathbf{F} = y\,\mathbf{i}$. Is there any relation between the value of the work integral

$$\int_C \mathbf{F} \cdot d\mathbf{r}$$

and the area of the region bounded by the t-axis, the graph of f, and the lines $t = a$ and $t = b$? Give reasons for your answer.

Writing for Your Own Knowledge

Answer the following questions in writing. Some answers will take only a sentence or two; others may require several paragraphs. Some explanations may also call for graphs or sketches.

1. What is a vector field?

2. Describe the gradient field of the function $f(x, y, z) = (x^2 + y^2 + z^2)/2$ on the sphere $x^2 + y^2 + z^2 = 1$.
3. How do you evaluate a work integral?
4. What are flow and circulation?
5. What is flux?

EXPLORER PROGRAM

Vector Fields	Pictures fields of the form $\mathbf{F} = M(x, y)\,\mathbf{i} + N(x, y)\,\mathbf{j}$ and integrates $\mathbf{F} \cdot \mathbf{n}$ over city-block paths in the plane.

15.3 Path Independence, Potential Functions, and Conservative Fields

In gravitational and electric fields, the amount of work it takes to move a mass or a charge from one point to another depends only on the object's initial and final positions and not on the path taken in between. This section discusses the notion of path independence of work integrals and describes the remarkable properties of fields in which work integrals are path independent.

Path Independence

If A and B are two points in an open region D in space, the work $\int \mathbf{F} \cdot d\mathbf{r}$ done in moving a particle from A to B by a field $\mathbf{F}$ defined on D usually depends on the path taken. For some special fields, however, the integral's value depends only on the points A and B and is the same for all paths from A to B. If this is true for all points A and B in D, we say that the integral $\int \mathbf{F} \cdot d\mathbf{r}$ is path independent in D and that $\mathbf{F}$ is conservative on D.

DEFINITIONS

Let $\mathbf{F}$ be a field defined on an open region D in space, and suppose that for any two points A and B in D the work $\int_A^B \mathbf{F} \cdot d\mathbf{r}$ done in moving from A to B is the same over all paths from A to B. Then the integral $\int \mathbf{F} \cdot d\mathbf{r}$ is **path independent in D** and the field $\mathbf{F}$ is **conservative on D**.

The word *conservative* comes from physics, where it refers to fields in which the principle of conservation of energy holds (it does, in conservative fields).

Under conditions normally met in practice, a field $\mathbf{F}$ is conservative if and only if it is the gradient field of a scalar function f; that is, if and only if $\mathbf{F} = \nabla f$ for some f. The function f is then called a potential function for $\mathbf{F}$.

DEFINITION

If $\mathbf{F}$ is a field defined on D and $\mathbf{F} = \nabla f$ for some scalar function f on D, then f is called a **potential function** for $\mathbf{F}$.

An electric potential is a scalar function whose gradient field is an electric field. A gravitational potential is a scalar function whose gradient field is a gravitational field, and so on. As we will see, once we have found a potential function f for a field $\mathbf{F}$, we can evaluate all the work integrals in the domain of $\mathbf{F}$ by

$$\int_A^B \mathbf{F} \cdot d\mathbf{r} = \int_A^B \nabla f \cdot d\mathbf{r} = f(B) - f(A). \tag{1}$$

Connected and simply connected.

Connected but not simply connected.

Connected and simply connected.

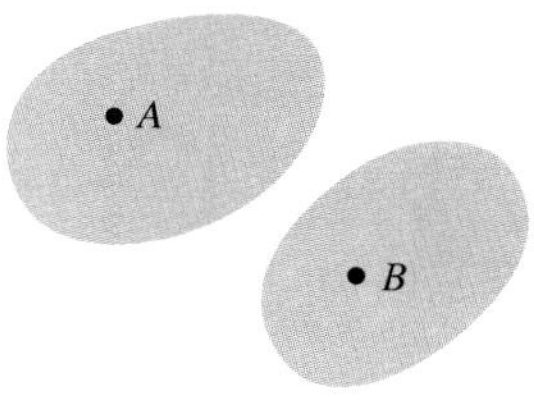

Simply connected but not connected. No path from A to B lies entirely in the region.

15.21 Connectivity and simple connectivity are not the same. Neither implies the other, as these pictures of plane regions illustrate. To make three-dimensional regions with these properties, thicken the plane regions into cylinders.

If you think of ∇f for functions of several variables as being something like the derivative f' for functions of a single variable, then you see that Eq. (1) is the vector calculus analogue of the Fundamental Theorem of Calculus equation

$$\int_a^b f'(x)\,dx = f(b) - f(a).$$

Conservative fields have other remarkable properties we will study as we go along. For example, saying that $\mathbf{F}$ is conservative on D is equivalent to saying that the integral of $\mathbf{F}$ around every closed path in D is zero. Naturally, we need to impose conditions on the curves, fields, and domains to make Eq. (1) and its implications hold.

We assume that all curves are **piecewise smooth,** i.e., made up of finitely many smooth pieces connected end to end, as discussed in Section 12.1. We also assume that the components of $\mathbf{F}$ are continuous and have continuous first partial derivatives. When $\mathbf{F} = \nabla f$, this continuity requirement guarantees that the mixed second derivatives of the potential function f are equal, a result we will find revealing in studying conservative fields $\mathbf{F}$.

We assume D to be an *open* region in space. This means that every point in D is the center of a ball that lies entirely in D. We also assume D to be **simply connected.** This means that every closed path in D can be contracted to a point in D without ever leaving D. If D consisted of space with a line removed, for example, D would not be simply connected. There would be no way to contract a loop around the line to a point without leaving D. On the other hand, space itself *is* simply connected.

Finally, we assume D to be **connected,** which in an open region means that every point can be connected to every other point by a smooth curve that lies in the region. See Fig. 15.21.

Line Integrals in Conservative Fields

The following result provides a convenient way to evaluate a line integral in a conservative field. The result establishes that the value of the integral depends only on the endpoints and not on the specific path joining them.

THEOREM 1

The Fundamental Theorem of Line Integrals

1. Let $\mathbf{F} = M\,\mathbf{i} + N\,\mathbf{j} + P\,\mathbf{k}$ be a vector field whose components are continuous throughout an open connected region D in space. Then there exists a differentiable function f such that

$$\mathbf{F} = \nabla f = \frac{\partial f}{\partial x}\,\mathbf{i} + \frac{\partial f}{\partial y}\,\mathbf{j} + \frac{\partial f}{\partial z}\,\mathbf{k}$$

   if and only if for all points A and B in D the value of $\int_A^B \mathbf{F}\cdot d\mathbf{r}$ is independent of the path joining A to B in D.

2. If the integral is independent of the path from A to B, its value is

$$\int_A^B \mathbf{F}\cdot d\mathbf{r} = f(B) - f(A).$$

Proof That $\mathbf{F} = \nabla f$ Implies Path Independence of the Integral Suppose that A and B are two points in D and that

$$C: \quad \mathbf{r} = g(t)\,\mathbf{i} + h(t)\,\mathbf{j} + k(t)\,\mathbf{k}, \quad a \le t \le b,$$

is a smooth curve in D joining A and B. Along the curve, f is a differentiable function of t and

$$\begin{aligned} \frac{df}{dt} &= \frac{\partial f}{\partial x}\frac{dx}{dt} + \frac{\partial f}{\partial y}\frac{dy}{dt} + \frac{\partial f}{\partial z}\frac{dz}{dt} && \text{Chain Rule} \\ &= \nabla f \cdot \left[\frac{dx}{dt}\mathbf{i} + \frac{dy}{dt}\mathbf{j} + \frac{dz}{dt}\mathbf{k}\right] = \nabla f \cdot \frac{d\mathbf{r}}{dt} = \mathbf{F} \cdot \frac{d\mathbf{r}}{dt}. && \text{Because } \mathbf{F} = \nabla f \end{aligned} \qquad (2)$$

Therefore,

$$\begin{aligned} \int_C \mathbf{F} \cdot d\mathbf{r} &= \int_{t=a}^{t=b} \mathbf{F} \cdot \frac{d\mathbf{r}}{dt}\,dt = \int_a^b \frac{df}{dt}\,dt \\ &= f(g(t), h(t), k(t))\Big]_a^b = f(B) - f(A). && \text{Eq. (2)} \end{aligned}$$

Thus, the value of the work integral depends only on the values of f at A and B and not on the path in between. This proves Part 2 as well as the forward implication in Part 1. The proof of the reverse implication is somewhat more technical. You can find it in Appendix 8. ∎

EXAMPLE 1 Find the work done by the conservative field

$$\mathbf{F} = yz\,\mathbf{i} + xz\,\mathbf{j} + xy\,\mathbf{k} = \nabla(xyz)$$

along any smooth curve C joining the point $(-1, 3, 9)$ to $(1, 6, -4)$.

Solution With $f(x, y, z) = xyz$, we have

$$\begin{aligned} \int_A^B \mathbf{F} \cdot d\mathbf{r} &= \int_A^B \nabla f \cdot d\mathbf{r} && \mathbf{F} = \nabla f \\ &= f(B) - f(A) && \text{Fundamental Theorem, Part 2} \\ &= xyz\Big|_{(1,6,-4)} - xyz\Big|_{(-1,3,9)} \\ &= (1)(6)(-4) - (-1)(3)(9) \\ &= -24 + 27 = 3. \end{aligned}$$

∎

THEOREM 2

The following statements are equivalent:

1. $\int \mathbf{F} \cdot d\mathbf{r} = 0$ around every closed loop in D.
2. The field $\mathbf{F}$ is conservative on D.

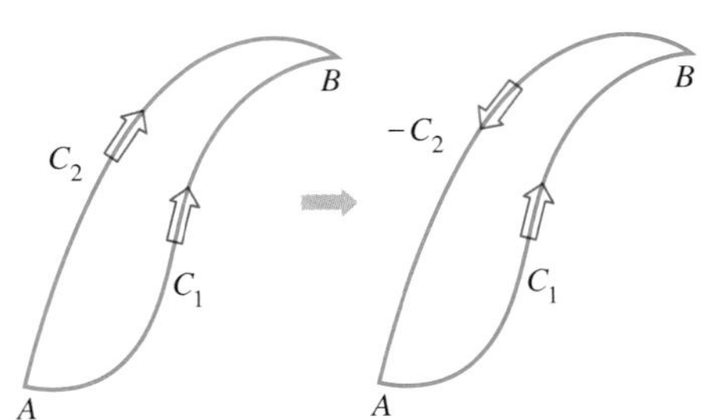

15.22 If we have two paths from A to B, one of them can be reversed to make a loop.

Proof That (1) ⇒ (2) We want to show that for any two points A and B in D the integral of $\mathbf{F} \cdot d\mathbf{r}$ has the same value over any two paths C_1 and C_2 from A to B. We reverse the direction on C_2 to make a path $-C_2$ from B to A (Fig. 15.22).

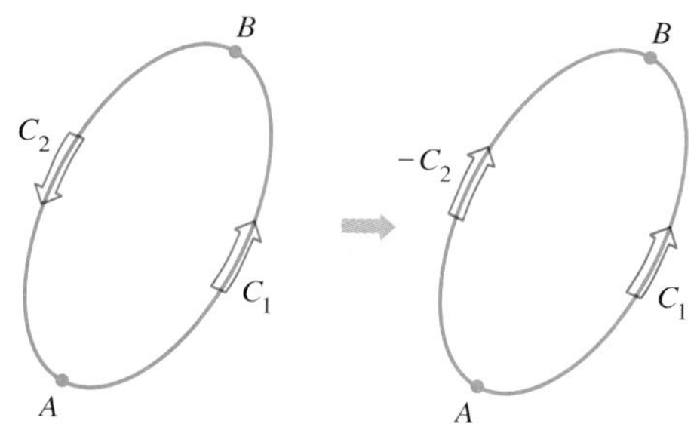

15.23 If A and B lie on a loop, we can reverse part of the loop to make two paths from A to B.

Together, C_1 and $-C_2$ make a closed loop C, and

$$\int_{C_1} \mathbf{F}\cdot d\mathbf{r} - \int_{C_2} \mathbf{F}\cdot d\mathbf{r} = \int_{C_1} \mathbf{F}\cdot d\mathbf{r} + \int_{-C_2} \mathbf{F}\cdot d\mathbf{r} = \int_{C} \mathbf{F}\cdot d\mathbf{r} = 0.$$

Thus the integrals over C_1 and C_2 give the same value.

Proof That (2) ⇒ (1) We want to show that the integral of $\mathbf{F}\cdot d\mathbf{r}$ is zero over any closed loop C. We pick two points A and B on C and use them to break C into two pieces: C_1 from A to B followed by C_2 from B back to A (Fig. 15.23). Then

$$\oint_C \mathbf{F}\cdot d\mathbf{r} = \int_{C_1} \mathbf{F}\cdot d\mathbf{r} + \int_{C_2} \mathbf{F}\cdot d\mathbf{r} = \int_A^B \mathbf{F}\cdot d\mathbf{r} - \int_A^B \mathbf{F}\cdot d\mathbf{r} = 0.$$

The following diagram summarizes the results of Theorems 1 and 2.

	Theorem 1		Theorem 2	
$\mathbf{F} = \nabla f$ on D	⇔	$\mathbf{F}$ conservative on D	⇔	$\oint_C \mathbf{F}\cdot d\mathbf{r} = 0$ over any closed path in D

Now that we see how convenient it is to evaluate line integrals in conservative fields, two questions remain:

1. How do we know when a given field $\mathbf{F}$ *is* conservative?
2. If $\mathbf{F}$ is in fact conservative, how do we find a potential function f (so that $\mathbf{F} = \nabla f$)?

Finding Potentials for Conservative Fields

The test for being conservative is this:

The Component Test for Conservative Fields

Let $\mathbf{F} = M(x, y, z)\,\mathbf{i} + N(x, y, z)\,\mathbf{j} + P(x, y, z)\,\mathbf{k}$ be a field whose component functions have continuous first partial derivatives. Then, $\mathbf{F}$ is conservative if and only if

$$\frac{\partial P}{\partial y} = \frac{\partial N}{\partial z}, \qquad \frac{\partial M}{\partial z} = \frac{\partial P}{\partial x}, \qquad \text{and} \qquad \frac{\partial N}{\partial x} = \frac{\partial M}{\partial y}. \tag{3}$$

Proof We show that Eqs. (3) must hold if $\mathbf{F}$ is conservative. There is a potential function f such that

$$\begin{aligned}\mathbf{F} &= M\,\mathbf{i} + N\,\mathbf{j} + P\,\mathbf{k}\\ &= \frac{\partial f}{\partial x}\,\mathbf{i} + \frac{\partial f}{\partial y}\,\mathbf{j} + \frac{\partial f}{\partial z}\,\mathbf{k}.\end{aligned}$$

Hence

$$\begin{aligned}\frac{\partial P}{\partial y} &= \frac{\partial}{\partial y}\left(\frac{\partial f}{\partial z}\right) = \frac{\partial^2 f}{\partial y\,\partial z}\\ &= \frac{\partial^2 f}{\partial z\,\partial y} && \text{Continuity implies that the mixed partial derivatives are equal.}\\ &= \frac{\partial}{\partial z}\left(\frac{\partial f}{\partial y}\right) = \frac{\partial N}{\partial z}.\end{aligned}$$

The other two equations in (3) are proved similarly.

The second half of the proof, that Eqs. (3) imply that **F** is conservative, is a consequence of Stokes's theorem, taken up in Section 15.7. ■

When we know that **F** is conservative, we usually want to find a potential function for **F**. This requires solving the equation $\nabla f = \mathbf{F}$ or

$$\frac{\partial f}{\partial x}\mathbf{i} + \frac{\partial f}{\partial y}\mathbf{j} + \frac{\partial f}{\partial z}\mathbf{k} = M\,\mathbf{i} + N\,\mathbf{j} + P\,\mathbf{k} \tag{4}$$

for f. We accomplish this by integrating the three equations

$$\frac{\partial f}{\partial x} = M, \qquad \frac{\partial f}{\partial y} = N, \qquad \frac{\partial f}{\partial z} = P \tag{5}$$

as in the following example.

EXAMPLE 2 Show that

$$\mathbf{F} = (e^x \cos y + yz)\,\mathbf{i} + (xz - e^x \sin y)\,\mathbf{j} + (xy + z)\,\mathbf{k}$$

is conservative and find a potential function for it.

Solution We apply the test in Eqs. (3) to

$$M = e^x \cos y + yz, \qquad N = xz - e^x \sin y, \qquad P = xy + z$$

and calculate

$$\frac{\partial M}{\partial z} = y = \frac{\partial P}{\partial x}, \qquad \frac{\partial N}{\partial z} = x = \frac{\partial P}{\partial y}, \qquad \frac{\partial M}{\partial y} = -e^x \sin y + z = \frac{\partial N}{\partial x}.$$

Together, these equalities tell us that there is a function f with $\nabla f = \mathbf{F}$.

We find f by integrating the equations

$$\frac{\partial f}{\partial x} = e^x \cos y + yz, \qquad \frac{\partial f}{\partial y} = xz - e^x \sin y, \qquad \frac{\partial f}{\partial z} = xy + z. \tag{6}$$

We integrate the first equation with respect to x, holding y and z fixed, to get

$$f(x, y, z) = e^x \cos y + xyz + g(y, z).$$

We write the constant of integration as a function of y and z because its value may change if y and z change. We then calculate $\partial f/\partial y$ from this equation and match it with the expression for $\partial f/\partial y$ in Eq. (6). This gives

$$-e^x \sin y + xz + \frac{\partial g}{\partial y} = xz - e^x \sin y,$$

so
$$\frac{\partial g}{\partial y} = 0.$$

Therefore, g is a function of z alone, and

$$f(x, y, z) = e^x \cos y + xyz + h(z).$$

We now calculate $\partial f/\partial z$ from this equation and match it to the formula for $\partial f/\partial z$ in Eq. (6). This gives

$$xy + \frac{dh}{dz} = xy + z, \qquad \text{or} \qquad \frac{dh}{dz} = z,$$

so
$$h(z) = \frac{z^2}{2} + C.$$

Hence,
$$f(x, y, z) = e^x \cos y + xyz + \frac{z^2}{2} + C.$$

We have found infinitely many potential functions for **F**, one for each value of C.

EXAMPLE 3 Show that $\mathbf{F} = (2x - 3)\,\mathbf{i} - z\,\mathbf{j} + (\cos z)\,\mathbf{k}$ is not conservative.

Solution We apply the component test in Eqs. (3) and find right away that

$$\frac{\partial P}{\partial y} = \frac{\partial}{\partial y}(\cos z) = 0, \qquad \frac{\partial N}{\partial z} = \frac{\partial}{\partial z}(-z) = -1.$$

The two are unequal, so **F** is not conservative. No further testing is required.

Exact Differential Forms

As we will see in the next section and again later on, it is often convenient to express work and circulation integrals in the "differential" form

$$\int_A^B M\,dx + N\,dy + P\,dz \tag{7}$$

mentioned in Section 15.2. Such integrals are relatively easy to evaluate if $M\,dx + N\,dy + P\,dz$ is the differential of a function f. For then

$$\begin{aligned} \int_A^B M\,dx + N\,dy + P\,dz &= \int_A^B \frac{\partial f}{\partial x}dx + \frac{\partial f}{\partial y}dy + \frac{\partial f}{\partial z}dz \\ &= \int_A^B \nabla f \cdot d\mathbf{r} \\ &= f(B) - f(A). \qquad \text{Theorem 1} \end{aligned} \tag{8}$$

Thus,

$$\int_A^B df = f(B) - f(A), \tag{9}$$

just as with differentiable functions of a single variable.

DEFINITIONS

The form

$$M(x, y, z)\,dx + N(x, y, z)\,dy + P(x, y, z)\,dz \tag{10}$$

is called a **differential form.** A differential form is **exact** on a domain D in space if

$$M\,dx + N\,dy + P\,dz = \frac{\partial f}{\partial x}\,dx + \frac{\partial f}{\partial y}\,dy + \frac{\partial f}{\partial z}\,dz = df \tag{11}$$

for some (scalar) function f throughout D.

Notice that if $M\,dx + N\,dy + P\,dz = df$ on D, then $\mathbf{F} = M\,\mathbf{i} + N\,\mathbf{j} + P\,\mathbf{k}$ is the gradient field of f on D. Conversely, if $\mathbf{F} = \nabla f$, then the form $M\,dx + N\,dy + P\,dz$ is exact. The test for the form's being exact is therefore the same as the test for $\mathbf{F}$'s being conservative.

The Test for Exactness of $M\,dx + N\,dy + P\,dz$

The differential form $M\,dx + N\,dy + P\,dz$ is exact if and only if

$$\frac{\partial P}{\partial y} = \frac{\partial N}{\partial z}, \qquad \frac{\partial M}{\partial z} = \frac{\partial P}{\partial x}, \qquad \text{and} \qquad \frac{\partial N}{\partial x} = \frac{\partial M}{\partial y}. \tag{12}$$

This is equivalent to saying that the field $\mathbf{F} = M\,\mathbf{i} + N\,\mathbf{j} + P\,\mathbf{k}$ is conservative.

EXAMPLE 4 Show that $y\,dx + x\,dy + 4\,dz$ is exact and evaluate the integral

$$\int_{(1,1,1)}^{(2,3,-1)} y\,dx + x\,dy + 4\,dz$$

over the line segment from $(1, 1, 1)$ to $(2, 3, -1)$.

Solution We let $M = y$, $N = x$, $P = 4$ and apply the test of Eq. (12):

$$\frac{\partial M}{\partial z} = 0 = \frac{\partial P}{\partial x}, \qquad \frac{\partial N}{\partial z} = 0 = \frac{\partial P}{\partial y}, \qquad \frac{\partial M}{\partial y} = 1 = \frac{\partial N}{\partial x}.$$

These equalities tell us that $y\,dx + x\,dy + 4\,dz$ is exact, so

$$y\,dx + x\,dy + 4\,dz = df$$

for some function f, and the integral's value is $f(2, 3, -1) - f(1, 1, 1)$.

We find f up to a constant by integrating the equations

$$\frac{\partial f}{\partial x} = y, \qquad \frac{\partial f}{\partial y} = x, \qquad \frac{\partial f}{\partial z} = 4. \tag{13}$$

From the first equation we get

$$f(x, y, z) = xy + g(y, z).$$

The second equation tells us that

$$\frac{\partial f}{\partial y} = x + \frac{\partial g}{\partial y} = x, \qquad \text{or} \qquad \frac{\partial g}{\partial y} = 0.$$

Hence, g is a function of z alone, and

$$f(x, y, z) = xy + h(z).$$

The third of Eqs. (13) tells us that

$$\frac{\partial f}{\partial z} = 0 + \frac{dh}{dz} = 4, \qquad \text{or} \qquad h(z) = 4z + C.$$

Therefore,

$$f(x, y, z) = xy + 4z + C,$$

and the value of the integral is

$$f(2, 3, -1) - f(1, 1, 1) = 2 + C - (5 + C) = -3.$$

Exercises 15.3

Which fields in Exercises 1–6 are conservative, and which are not?

1. $\mathbf{F} = yz\,\mathbf{i} + xz\,\mathbf{j} + xy\,\mathbf{k}$
2. $\mathbf{F} = (y \sin z)\,\mathbf{i} + (x \sin z)\,\mathbf{j} + (xy \cos z)\,\mathbf{k}$
3. $\mathbf{F} = y\,\mathbf{i} + (x + z)\,\mathbf{j} - y\,\mathbf{k}$
4. $\mathbf{F} = -y\,\mathbf{i} + x\,\mathbf{j}$
5. $\mathbf{F} = (z + y)\,\mathbf{i} + z\,\mathbf{j} + (y + x)\,\mathbf{k}$
6. $\mathbf{F} = (e^x \cos y)\,\mathbf{i} - (e^x \sin y)\,\mathbf{j} + z\,\mathbf{k}$

In Exercises 7–10, find a potential function f for the field $\mathbf{F}$.

7. $\mathbf{F} = 2x\,\mathbf{i} + 3y\,\mathbf{j} + 4z\,\mathbf{k}$
8. $\mathbf{F} = (y + z)\,\mathbf{i} + (x + z)\,\mathbf{j} + (x + y)\,\mathbf{k}$
9. $\mathbf{F} = e^{y+2z}(\mathbf{i} + x\,\mathbf{j} + 2x\,\mathbf{k})$
10. $\mathbf{F} = (y \sin z)\,\mathbf{i} + (x \sin z)\,\mathbf{j} + (xy \cos z)\,\mathbf{k}$

Evaluate the integrals in Exercises 11–20.

11. $\displaystyle\int_{(0,0,0)}^{(2,3,-6)} 2x\,dx + 2y\,dy + 2z\,dz$
12. $\displaystyle\int_{(1,1,2)}^{(3,5,0)} yz\,dx + xz\,dy + xy\,dz$
13. $\displaystyle\int_{(0,0,0)}^{(1,2,3)} 2xy\,dx + (x^2 - z^2)\,dy - 2yz\,dz$
14. $\displaystyle\int_{(1,1,1)}^{(1,2,3)} 3x^2\,dx + \frac{z^2}{y}\,dy + 2z \ln y\,dz$
15. $\displaystyle\int_{(1,0,0)}^{(0,1,1)} \sin y \cos x\,dx + \cos y \sin x\,dy + dz$
16. $\displaystyle\int_{(0,0,0)}^{(3,3,1)} 2x\,dx - y^2\,dy - \frac{4}{1 + z^2}\,dz$
17. $\displaystyle\int_{(0,2,1)}^{(1,\pi/2,2)} 2 \cos y\,dx + \left(\frac{1}{y} - 2x \sin y\right) dy + \frac{1}{z}\,dz$
18. $\displaystyle\int_{(1,2,1)}^{(2,1,1)} (2x \ln y - yz)\,dx + \left(\frac{x^2}{y} - xz\right) dy - xy\,dz$
19. $\displaystyle\int_{(1,1,1)}^{(2,2,2)} \frac{1}{y}\,dx + \left(\frac{1}{z} - \frac{x}{y^2}\right) dy - \frac{y}{z^2}\,dz$
20. $\displaystyle\int_{(-1,-1,-1)}^{(2,2,2)} \frac{2x\,dx + 2y\,dy + 2z\,dz}{x^2 + y^2 + z^2}$
21. Evaluate the integral

$$\int_{(1,1,1)}^{(2,3,-1)} y\,dx + x\,dy + 4\,dz$$

from Example 4 by finding parametric equations for the line segment from $(1, 1, 1)$ to $(2, 3, -1)$ and evaluating the line integral of $\mathbf{F} = y\,\mathbf{i} + x\,\mathbf{j} + 4\,\mathbf{k}$ along the segment. This is permissible because $\mathbf{F}$ is conservative and the integral is independent of the path.

22. Evaluate

$$\int_C x^2\,dx + yz\,dy + (y^2/2)\,dz$$

along the line segment C joining $(0, 0, 0)$ to $(0, 3, 4)$.

Show that the values of the integrals in Exercises 23 and 24 do not depend on the path taken from A to B.

23. $\int_A^B z^2\,dx + 2y\,dy + 2xz\,dz$

24. $\int_A^B \dfrac{x\,dx + y\,dy + z\,dz}{\sqrt{x^2+y^2+z^2}}$

In Exercises 25 and 26, express $\mathbf{F}$ in the form ∇f.

25. $\mathbf{F} = \dfrac{2x}{y}\,\mathbf{i} + \left(\dfrac{1-x^2}{y^2}\right)\mathbf{j}$

26. $\mathbf{F} = (e^x \ln y)\,\mathbf{i} + \left(\dfrac{e^x}{y} + \sin z\right)\mathbf{j} + (y\cos z)\,\mathbf{k}$

27. Find the work done by $\mathbf{F} = (x^2+y)\,\mathbf{i} + (y^2+x)\,\mathbf{j} + ze^z\,\mathbf{k}$ over the following paths from $(1, 0, 0)$ to $(1, 0, 1)$.

a) The line segment $x = 1,\ y = 0,\ 0 \le z \le 1$
b) The helix $\mathbf{r} = (\cos t)\,\mathbf{i} + (\sin t)\,\mathbf{j} + (t/2\pi)\,\mathbf{k},\ 0 \le t \le 2\pi$
c) The x-axis from $(1, 0, 0)$ to $(0, 0, 0)$ followed by the parabola $z = x^2,\ y = 0$ from $(0, 0, 0)$ to $(1, 0, 1)$

28. Evaluate $\int_C 2x\cos y\,dx - x^2\sin y\,dy$ along the following paths C in the xy-plane.

a) The parabola $y = (x-1)^2$ from $(1, 0)$ to $(0, 1)$
b) The line segment from $(-1, \pi)$ to $(1, 0)$
c) The x-axis from $(-1, 0)$ to $(1, 0)$
d) The astroid $\mathbf{r} = (\cos^3 t)\,\mathbf{i} + (\sin^3 t)\,\mathbf{j},\ 0 \le t \le 2\pi$, counterclockwise from $(1, 0)$ back to $(1, 0)$

29. Let $\mathbf{F} = \nabla(x^3y^2)$ and let C be the path in the xy-plane from $(-1, 1)$ to $(1, 1)$ that consists of the line segment from $(-1, 1)$ to $(0, 0)$ followed by the line segment from $(0, 0)$ to $(1, 1)$. Evaluate $\int_C \mathbf{F}\cdot d\mathbf{r}$ in two ways:

a) by finding parametrizations for the segments that make up C and evaluating the integral;
b) by using the fact that $f(x, y) = x^3y^2$ is a potential function for $\mathbf{F}$.

30. Find a potential function for the gravitational field

$$\mathbf{F} = -GmM\frac{x\,\mathbf{i} + y\,\mathbf{j} + z\,\mathbf{k}}{(x^2+y^2+z^2)^{3/2}}$$

(G, m, and M are constants).

31. You have been asked to find the path along which a force field $\mathbf{F}$ will perform the least work in moving a particle between two locations. A quick calculation on your part shows $\mathbf{F}$ to be conservative. How should you respond? Give reasons for your answer.

32. Through experimentation, you find that a force field $\mathbf{F}$ performs only half as much work in moving an object along path C_1 from A to B as it does in moving the object along path C_2 from A to B. What can you conclude about $\mathbf{F}$? Give reasons for your answer.

Writing for Your Own Knowledge

Answer the following questions in writing. Some answers will take only a sentence or two; others may require several paragraphs. Some explanations may also call for graphs or sketches.

1. What is special about path independent fields?
2. How can you tell when a field is conservative?
3. What is a potential function?
4. Show by example how to find a potential function for a conservative field.

EXPLORER PROGRAMS

Scalar Fields	Plots two-dimensional scalar fields and their associated gradient fields. Integrates $\nabla f \cdot d\mathbf{r}$ along line segments parallel to the coordinate axes.
Slope Fields	Graphs solutions of the initial value problem $y' = f(x, y)$, $y = y_0$ when $x = x_0$, for your choice of f, x_0, and y_0.

15.4 *Green's Theorem in the Plane*

We now come to a theorem that can be used to describe the relationship between the way an incompressible fluid flows along or across the boundary of a plane region and the way it moves inside the region. The connection between the fluid's boundary behavior and its internal behavior is made possible by the notions of divergence and curl. The divergence of a fluid's velocity field measures the rate at which fluid is being piped into or out of the region at any given point. The curl measures the fluid's rate of rotation at each point.

Green's theorem states that, under conditions usually met in practice, the outward flux of a vector field across the boundary of a plane region equals the double integral of the divergence of the field over the interior of the region. In another form, Green's theorem states that the counterclockwise circulation of a vector field around the boundary of a region equals the double integral of the curl of the vector field over the region.

Green's theorem is one of the great theorems of calculus. It is deep and surprising and has far-reaching consequences. In pure mathematics, it ranks in importance with the Fundamental Theorem of Calculus. In applied mathematics the generalizations of Green's theorem to three dimensions provide the foundation for theorems about electricity, magnetism, and fluid flow.

We talk in terms of velocity fields of fluid flows because fluid flows are easy to picture. We would like you to be aware, however, that Green's theorem applies to any vector field satisfying certain mathematical conditions. It does not depend for its validity on the field's having a particular physical interpretation.

Flux Density at a Point: Divergence

We need two new ideas for Green's theorem. The first is the idea of the flux density of a vector field at a point, which in mathematics is called the *divergence* of the vector field. We obtain it in the following way.

Suppose that

$$\mathbf{F}(x, y) = M(x, y)\,\mathbf{i} + N(x, y)\,\mathbf{j}$$

is the velocity field of a fluid flow in the plane and that the first partial derivatives of M and N are continuous at each point of a region R. Let (x, y) be a point in R and let A be a small rectangle with one corner at (x, y) that, along with its interior, lies entirely in R (Fig. 15.24). The sides of the rectangle, parallel to the coordinate axes, have lengths Δx and Δy. The rate at which fluid leaves the rectangle across the bottom edge is approximately

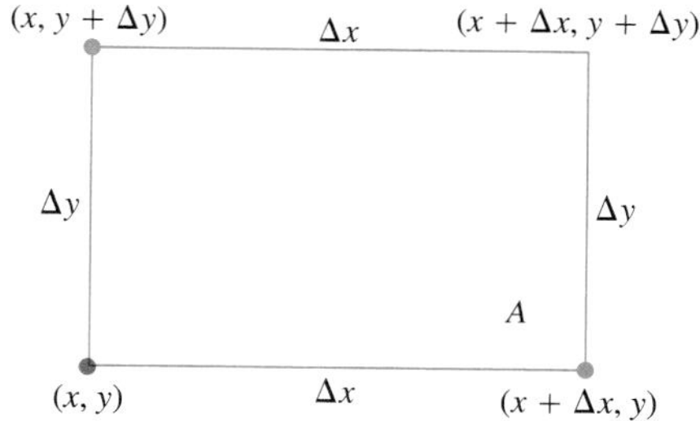

15.24 The rectangle for defining the flux density (divergence) of a vector field at a point (x, y).

$$\mathbf{F}(x, y) \cdot (-\mathbf{j})\,\Delta x = -N(x, y)\,\Delta x. \tag{1}$$

This is the scalar component of the velocity at (x, y) in the direction of the outward normal times the length of the segment. If the velocity is in meters per second, for example, the exit rate will be in meters per second times meters or square meters per second. The rates at which the fluid crosses the other three sides in the directions of their outward normals can be estimated in a similar way. All told, we have

$$\begin{aligned}
&\text{Top:} && \mathbf{F}(x, y + \Delta y) \cdot \mathbf{j}\,\Delta x = N(x, y + \Delta y)\,\Delta x \\
&\text{Bottom:} && \mathbf{F}(x, y) \cdot (-\mathbf{j})\,\Delta x = -N(x, y)\,\Delta x \\
&\text{Right:} && \mathbf{F}(x + \Delta x, y) \cdot \mathbf{i}\,\Delta y = M(x + \Delta x, y)\,\Delta y \\
&\text{Left:} && \mathbf{F}(x, y) \cdot (-\mathbf{i})\,\Delta y = -M(x, y)\,\Delta y.
\end{aligned} \tag{2}$$

Combining opposite pairs gives

$$\text{Top and bottom:} \quad (N(x, y + \Delta y) - N(x, y))\,\Delta x \approx \left(\frac{\partial N}{\partial y}\Delta y\right)\Delta x \tag{3}$$

$$\text{Right and left:} \quad (M(x + \Delta x, y) - M(x, y))\,\Delta y \approx \left(\frac{\partial M}{\partial x}\Delta x\right)\Delta y. \tag{4}$$

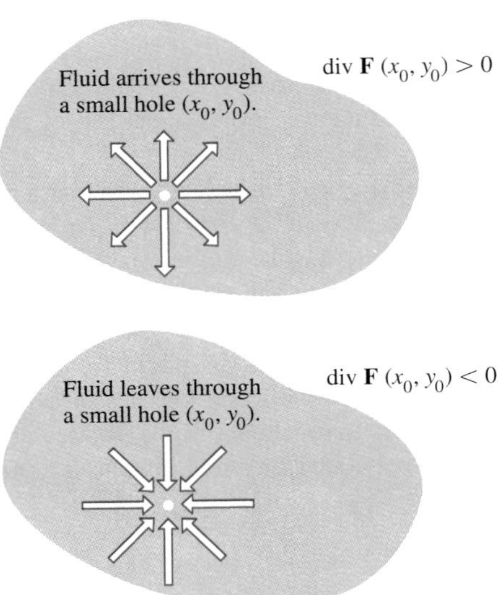

15.25 In the flow of an incompressible fluid across a plane region, the divergence is positive at a "source," a point where fluid enters the system, and negative at a "sink," a point where the fluid leaves the system.

Adding (3) and (4) gives

$$\text{Flux across rectangle boundary} \approx \left(\frac{\partial M}{\partial x} + \frac{\partial N}{\partial y}\right) \Delta x\, \Delta y. \tag{5}$$

We now divide by $\Delta x\, \Delta y$ to estimate the total flux per unit area or flux density for the rectangle:

$$\frac{\text{Flux across rectangle boundary}}{\text{Rectangle area}} \approx \left(\frac{\partial M}{\partial x} + \frac{\partial N}{\partial y}\right). \tag{6}$$

Finally, we let Δx and Δy approach zero to define what we call the *flux density* of **F** at the point (x, y).

In mathematics, we call the flux density the *divergence* of **F**. The symbol for it is div **F**, pronounced "divergence of **F**" or "div **F**."

DEFINITION

The **flux density** or **divergence** of a vector field $\mathbf{F} = M\mathbf{i} + N\mathbf{j}$ at the point (x, y) is

$$\text{div}\,\mathbf{F} = \frac{\partial M}{\partial x} + \frac{\partial N}{\partial y}. \tag{7}$$

Intuitively, if water were flowing into a region through a small hole at the point (x_0, y_0), the lines of flow would diverge there (hence the name) and, since water would be flowing out of a small rectangle about (x_0, y_0), the divergence of **F** at (x_0, y_0) would be positive. If the water were draining out instead of flowing in, the divergence would be negative. See Fig. 15.25.

EXAMPLE 1 Find the divergence of the vector field

$$\mathbf{F}(x, y) = (x^2 - y)\,\mathbf{i} + (xy - y^2)\,\mathbf{j}.$$

Solution We use the formula in Eq. (7):

$$\begin{aligned} \text{div}\,\mathbf{F} &= \frac{\partial M}{\partial x} + \frac{\partial N}{\partial y} = \frac{\partial}{\partial x}(x^2 - y) + \frac{\partial}{\partial y}(xy - y^2) \\ &= 2x + x - 2y = 3x - 2y. \end{aligned}$$

Circulation Density at a Point: The Curl

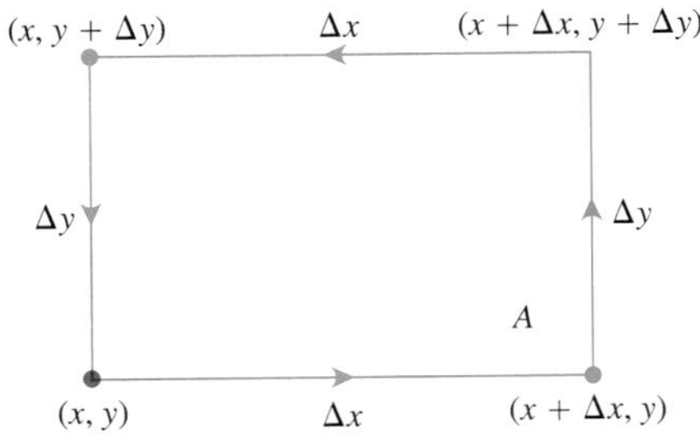

15.26 The rectangle for defining the circulation density (curl) of a vector field at a point (x, y).

The second of the two new ideas we need for Green's theorem is the idea of circulation density of a vector field **F** at a point, which in mathematics is called the *curl* of **F**. To obtain it, we return to the velocity field

$$\mathbf{F}(x, y) = M(x, y)\,\mathbf{i} + N(x, y)\,\mathbf{j} \tag{8}$$

and the rectangle A. The rectangle is redrawn here as Fig. 15.26.

The counterclockwise circulation of **F** around the boundary of A is the sum of flow rates along the sides. For the bottom edge, the flow rate is approximately

$$\mathbf{F}(x, y) \cdot \mathbf{i}\,\Delta x = M(x, y)\,\Delta x. \tag{9}$$

This is the scalar component of the velocity $\mathbf{F}(x, y)$ in the direction of the tangent vector $\mathbf{i}$ times the length of the segment. The rates of flow along the other sides in the counterclockwise direction are expressed in a similar way. In all, we have

$$\begin{aligned}
&\text{Top:} && \mathbf{F}(x, y + \Delta y) \cdot (-\mathbf{i})\, \Delta x = -M(x, y + \Delta y)\, \Delta x \\
&\text{Bottom:} && \mathbf{F}(x, y) \cdot \mathbf{i}\, \Delta x = M(x, y)\, \Delta x \\
&\text{Right:} && \mathbf{F}(x + \Delta x, y) \cdot \mathbf{j}\, \Delta y = N(x + \Delta x, y)\, \Delta y \\
&\text{Left:} && \mathbf{F}(x, y) \cdot (-\mathbf{j})\, \Delta y = -N(x, y)\, \Delta y.
\end{aligned} \tag{10}$$

We add opposite pairs to get

Top and bottom:

$$-(M(x, y + \Delta y) - M(x, y))\, \Delta x \approx -\left(\frac{\partial M}{\partial y}\, \Delta y\right) \Delta x \tag{11}$$

Right and left:

$$(N(x + \Delta x, y) - N(x, y))\, \Delta y \approx \left(\frac{\partial N}{\partial x}\, \Delta x\right) \Delta y. \tag{12}$$

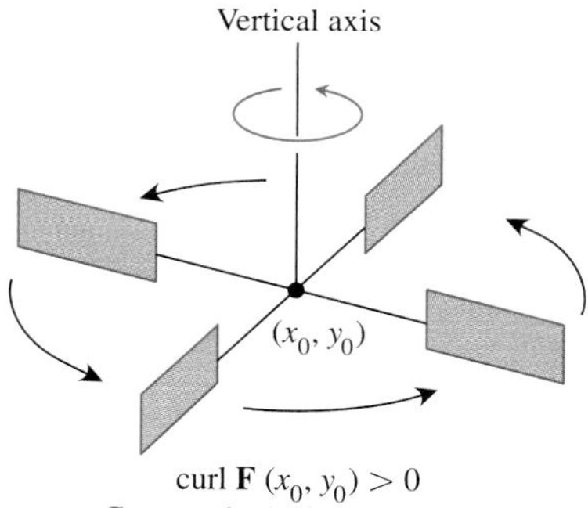

curl $\mathbf{F}\,(x_0, y_0) > 0$
Counterclockwise circulation

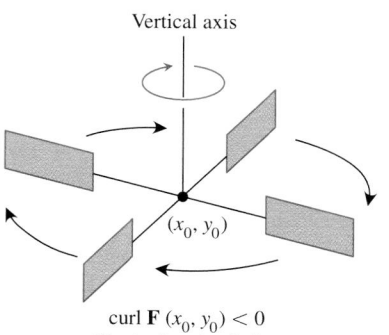

Vertical axis

(x_0, y_0)

curl $\mathbf{F}\,(x_0, y_0) < 0$
Clockwise circulation

15.27 In the flow of an incompressible fluid over a plane region, the curl measures the rate of the fluid's rotation at a point. The curl is positive at points where the rotation is counterclockwise and negative where the rotation is clockwise.

Adding (11) and (12) and dividing by $\Delta x\, \Delta y$ gives an estimate of the circulation density for the rectangle:

$$\frac{\text{Circulation around rectangle}}{\text{Rectangle area}} \approx \frac{\partial N}{\partial x} - \frac{\partial M}{\partial y}. \tag{13}$$

Finally, we let Δx and Δy approach zero to define what we call the *circulation density* of $\mathbf{F}$ at the point (x, y).

DEFINITION

The **circulation density** or **curl** of a vector field $\mathbf{F} = M\,\mathbf{i} + N\,\mathbf{j}$ at the point (x, y) is

$$\text{curl}\ \mathbf{F} = \frac{\partial N}{\partial x} - \frac{\partial M}{\partial y}. \tag{14}$$

If water is moving about a region in the xy-plane in a thin layer, then the circulation, or curl, at a point (x_0, y_0) gives a way to measure how fast and in what direction a small paddle wheel will spin if it is put into the water at (x_0, y_0) with its axis perpendicular to the plane (Fig. 15.27).

EXAMPLE 2 Find the curl of the vector field

$$\mathbf{F}(x, y) = (x^2 - y)\,\mathbf{i} + (xy - y^2)\,\mathbf{j}.$$

Solution We use the formula in Eq. (14):

$$\text{curl}\ \mathbf{F} = \frac{\partial N}{\partial x} - \frac{\partial M}{\partial y} = \frac{\partial}{\partial x}(xy - y^2) - \frac{\partial}{\partial y}(x^2 - y) = y + 1.$$

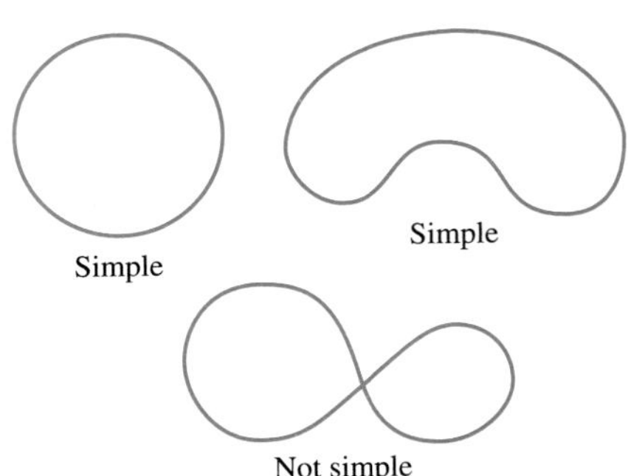

15.28 In proving Green's theorem, we distinguish between two kinds of closed curves, simple and not simple. Simple curves do not cross themselves. A circle is simple but a figure 8 is not.

Green's Theorem in the Plane

In one form, Green's theorem says that under suitable conditions the outward flux of a vector field across a simple closed curve in the plane (Fig. 15.28) equals the double integral of the divergence of the field over the region enclosed by the curve. Recall the formulas for flux in Eqs. (5) and (8) in Section 15.2.

THEOREM 3

Green's Theorem (Flux-Divergence or Normal Form)

The outward flux of a field $\mathbf{F} = M\,\mathbf{i} + N\,\mathbf{j}$ across a simple closed curve C equals the double integral of div $\mathbf{F}$ over the region R enclosed by C.

$$\underbrace{\oint_C \mathbf{F}\cdot\mathbf{n}\,ds}_{\text{Outward flux}} = \oint_C M\,dy - N\,dx = \underbrace{\iint_R \left(\frac{\partial M}{\partial x} + \frac{\partial N}{\partial y}\right) dx\,dy}_{\text{Divergence integral}} \qquad (15)$$

In another form, Green's theorem says that the counterclockwise circulation of a vector field around a simple closed curve is the double integral of the curl of the field over the region enclosed by the curve.

For a two-dimensional field $\mathbf{F} = M\,\mathbf{i} + N\,\mathbf{j}$, the integral in Eq. (4), Section 15.2, for circulation takes the equivalent form

$$\oint_C \mathbf{F}\cdot\mathbf{T}\,ds = \oint_C M\,dx + N\,dy.$$

THEOREM 4

Green's Theorem (Circulation-Curl or Tangential Form)

The counterclockwise circulation of a field $\mathbf{F} = M\,\mathbf{i} + N\,\mathbf{j}$ around a simple closed curve C in the plane equals the double integral of curl $\mathbf{F}$ over the region R enclosed by C.

$$\underbrace{\oint_C \mathbf{F}\cdot\mathbf{T}\,ds}_{\text{Counterclockwise circulation}} = \oint_C M\,dx + N\,dy = \underbrace{\iint_R \left(\frac{\partial N}{\partial x} - \frac{\partial M}{\partial y}\right) dx\,dy}_{\text{Curl integral}} \qquad (16)$$

The two forms of Green's theorem are equivalent. Applying Eq. (15) to the field $\mathbf{G}_1 = N\,\mathbf{i} - M\,\mathbf{j}$ gives Eq. (16), and applying Eq. (16) to $\mathbf{G}_2 = -N\,\mathbf{i} + M\,\mathbf{j}$ gives Eq. (15). We do not need to prove them both. We will prove the curl form shortly.

We need two kinds of assumptions for Green's theorem to hold. First, we need conditions on M and N to ensure the existence of the integrals. The usual assumptions are that M, N, and their first partial derivatives are continuous at every point of some open region containing C and R. Second, we need geometric conditions on the curve C. It must be simple, closed, and made up of pieces along which we can integrate M and N. The usual assumptions are that C is piecewise smooth. The proof we give for Green's theorem, however, assumes things about the shape of R as well. You can find proofs that are less restrictive in more advanced texts. First let's look at some examples.

EXAMPLE 3 Verify both forms of Green's theorem for the field

$$\mathbf{F}(x, y) = (x - y)\,\mathbf{i} + x\,\mathbf{j}$$

and the region R bounded by the unit circle

$$C: \quad \mathbf{r} = (\cos t)\,\mathbf{i} + (\sin t)\,\mathbf{j}, \quad 0 \le t \le 2\pi .$$

Solution We first express all functions, derivatives, and differentials in terms of t:

$$M = \cos t - \sin t, \qquad dx = d(\cos t) = -\sin t\,dt,$$
$$N = \cos t, \qquad dy = d(\sin t) = \cos t\,dt,$$
$$\frac{\partial M}{\partial x} = 1, \qquad \frac{\partial M}{\partial y} = -1, \qquad \frac{\partial N}{\partial x} = 1, \qquad \frac{\partial N}{\partial y} = 0. \tag{17}$$

The two sides of Eq. (15):

$$\oint_C M\,dy - N\,dx = \int_{t=0}^{t=2\pi} (\cos t - \sin t)(\cos t\,dt) - (\cos t)(-\sin t\,dt)$$
$$= \int_0^{2\pi} \cos^2 t\,dt = \pi$$
$$\iint_R \left(\frac{\partial M}{\partial x} + \frac{\partial N}{\partial y}\right) dx\,dy = \iint_R (1 + 0)\,dx\,dy$$
$$= \iint_R dx\,dy = \text{area of unit circle} = \pi .$$

The two sides of Eq. (16):

$$\oint_C M\,dx + N\,dy = \int_{t=0}^{t=2\pi} (\cos t - \sin t)(-\sin t\,dt) + (\cos t)(\cos t\,dt)$$
$$= \int_0^{2\pi} (-\sin t \cos t + 1)\,dt = 2\pi ,$$
$$\iint_R \left(\frac{\partial N}{\partial x} - \frac{\partial M}{\partial y}\right) dx\,dy = \iint_R (1 - (-1))\;dx\,dy = 2\iint_R dx\,dy = 2\pi .$$

Using Green's Theorem to Evaluate Line Integrals

If we construct a closed curve C by piecing a number of different curves end to end, the process of evaluating a line integral over C can be lengthy because there are so many different integrals to evaluate. However, if C bounds a region R to which Green's theorem applies, we can use Green's theorem to change the line integral around C into one double integral over R.

EXAMPLE 4 Evaluate the integral

$$\oint_C xy\,dy - y^2\,dx,$$

where C is the square cut from the first quadrant by the lines $x = 1$ and $y = 1$.

The Green of Green's Theorem

The Green of Green's theorem was George Green (1793–1841), a self-taught scientist in Nottingham, England. Green's work on the mathematical foundations of gravitation, electricity, and magnetism was published privately in 1828 in a short book entitled *An Essay on the Application of Mathematical Analysis to Electricity and Magnetism.* The book sold all of fifty-two copies (fewer than one hundred were printed), the copies going mostly to Green's patrons and personal friends. A few weeks before Green's death in 1841, William Thompson noticed a reference to Green's book and in 1845 was finally able to locate a copy. Excited by what he read, Thompson shared Green's ideas with other scientists and had the book republished in a series of journal articles. Green's mathematics provided the foundation on which Thompson, Stokes, Rayleigh, and Maxwell built the present-day theory of electromagnetism.

Solution We can use either form of Green's theorem to change the line integral into a double integral over the square.

1. *With Eq.* (15): Taking $M = xy$, $N = y^2$, and C and R as the square's boundary and interior gives

$$\oint_C xy\,dy - y^2\,dx = \iint_R (y + 2y)\,dx\,dy = \int_0^1\int_0^1 3y\,dx\,dy$$
$$= \int_0^1 \Big[3xy\Big]_{x=0}^{x=1} dy$$
$$= \int_0^1 3y\,dy = \frac{3}{2}y^2\Big]_0^1 = \frac{3}{2}.$$

2. *With Eq.* (16): Taking $M = -y^2$ and $N = xy$ gives the same result:

$$\oint_C -y^2\,dx + xy\,dy = \iint_R (y - (-2y))\,dx\,dy = \frac{3}{2}.$$

EXAMPLE 5 Calculate the outward flux of the field $\mathbf{F}(x, y) = x\,\mathbf{i} + y^2\,\mathbf{j}$ across the square bounded by the lines $x = \pm 1$ and $y = \pm 1$.

Solution Calculating the flux with a line integral would take four integrations, one for each side of the square. With Green's theorem, we can change the line integral to one double integral. With $M = x$, $N = y^2$, C the square, and R the square's interior, we have

$$\text{Flux} = \oint_C \mathbf{F}\cdot\mathbf{n}\,ds = \oint_C M\,dy - N\,dx$$
$$= \iint_R \left(\frac{\partial M}{\partial x} + \frac{\partial N}{\partial y}\right) dx\,dy \qquad \text{Green's theorem}$$
$$= \int_{-1}^1\int_{-1}^1 (1 + 2y)\,dx\,dy = \int_{-1}^1 \Big[x + 2xy\Big]_{x=-1}^{x=1} dy$$
$$= \int_{-1}^1 (2 + 4y)\,dy = \Big[2y + 2y^2\Big]_{-1}^1 = 4.$$

A Proof of Green's Theorem (Special Regions)

Let C be a smooth simple closed curve in the xy-plane with the property that lines parallel to the axes cut it in no more than two points. Let R be the region enclosed by C and suppose that M, N, and their first partial derivatives are continuous at every point of some open region containing C and R. We want to prove the circulation-curl form of Green's theorem,

$$\oint_C M\,dx + N\,dy = \iint_R \left(\frac{\partial N}{\partial x} - \frac{\partial M}{\partial y}\right) dx\,dy. \tag{18}$$

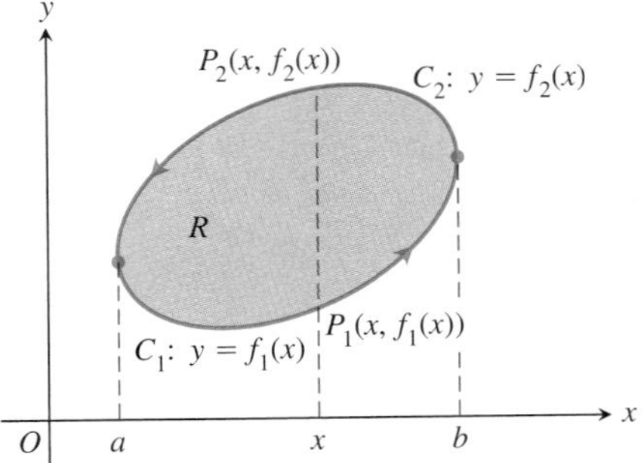

15.29 The boundary curve C is made up of C_1, the graph of $y = f_1(x)$, and C_2, the graph of $y = f_2(x)$.

Figure 15.29 shows C made up of two directed parts:

$$C_1:\quad y = f_1(x),\quad a \le x \le b, \qquad C_2:\quad y = f_2(x),\quad b \ge x \ge a.$$

For any x between a and b, we can integrate $\partial M/\partial y$ with respect to y from

$y = f_1(x)$ to $y = f_2(x)$ and obtain

$$\int_{f_1(x)}^{f_2(x)} \frac{\partial M}{\partial y}\,dy = M(x, y)\Big]_{y=f_1(x)}^{y=f_2(x)} = M(x, f_2(x)) - M(x, f_1(x)). \tag{19}$$

We can then integrate this with respect to x from a to b:

$$\begin{aligned}\int_a^b \int_{f_1(x)}^{f_2(x)} \frac{\partial M}{\partial y}\,dy\,dx &= \int_a^b [M(x, f_2(x)) - M(x, f_1(x))]\,dx \\ &= -\int_b^a M(x, f_2(x))\,dx - \int_a^b M(x, f_1(x))\,dx \\ &= -\int_{C_2} M\,dx - \int_{C_1} M\,dx \\ &= -\oint_C M\,dx.\end{aligned}$$

Therefore

$$\oint_C M\,dx = \iint_R \left(-\frac{\partial M}{\partial y}\right) dx\,dy. \tag{20}$$

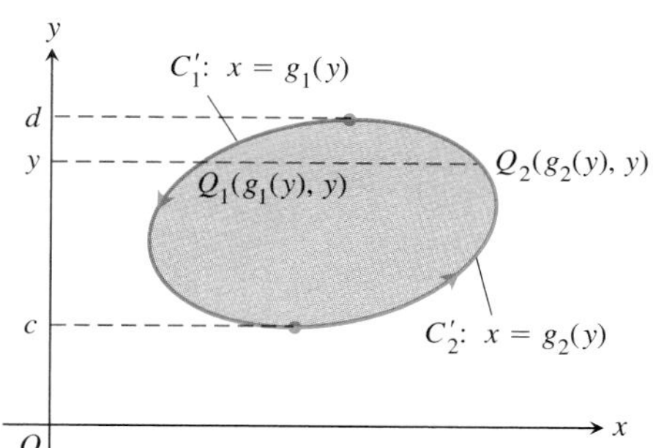

15.30 The boundary curve C is made up of C_1', the graph of $x = g_1(y)$, and C_2', the graph of $x = g_2(y)$.

Equation (20) is half the result we need for Eq. (18). We derive the other half by integrating $\partial N/\partial x$ first with respect to x and then with respect to y, as suggested by Fig. 15.30. This shows the curve C of Fig. 15.29 decomposed into the two directed parts

$$C_1': \quad x = g_1(y), \quad d \ge y \ge c, \qquad C_2': \quad x = g_2(y), \quad c \le y \le d.$$

The result of this double integration is

$$\oint_C N\,dy = \iint_R \frac{\partial N}{\partial x}\,dx\,dy. \tag{21}$$

Combining Eqs. (20) and (21) gives Eq. (18). This concludes the proof.

Extending the Proof to Other Regions

The argument we just gave does not apply directly to the rectangular region in Fig. 15.31 because the lines $x = a$, $x = b$, $y = c$, and $y = d$ meet the region's boundary in more than two points. However, if we divide the boundary C into four directed line segments,

$$\begin{aligned}&C_1: \quad y = c, \quad a \le x \le b, \qquad &&C_2: \quad x = b, \quad c \le y \le d,\\ &C_3: \quad y = d, \quad b \ge x \ge a, \qquad &&C_4: \quad x = a, \quad d \ge y \ge c,\end{aligned}$$

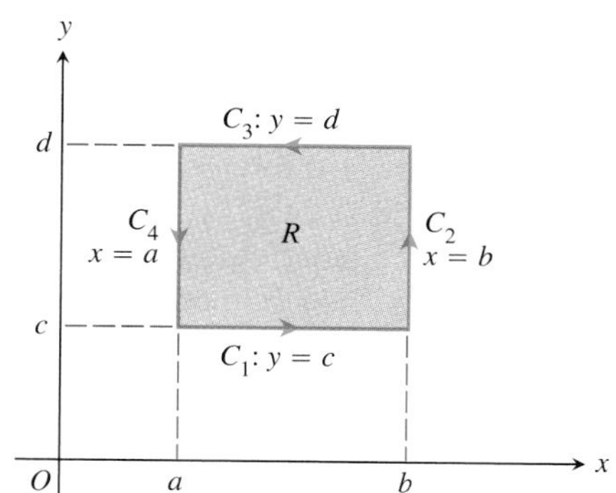

15.31 To prove Green's theorem for a rectangle, we divide the boundary into four directed line segments.

we can modify the argument in the following way.

Proceeding as in the proof of Eq. (21), we have

$$\begin{aligned}\int_c^d \int_a^b \frac{\partial N}{\partial x}\,dx\,dy &= \int_c^d (N(b, y) - N(a, y))\,dy \\ &= \int_c^d N(b, y)\,dy + \int_d^c N(a, y)\,dy \qquad (22) \\ &= \int_{C_2} N\,dy + \int_{C_4} N\,dy.\end{aligned}$$

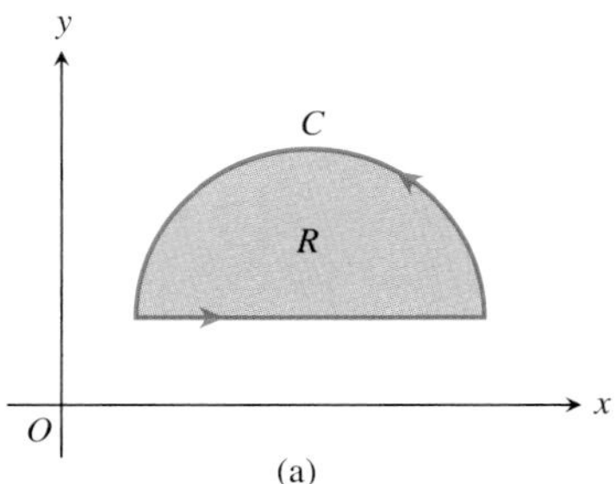

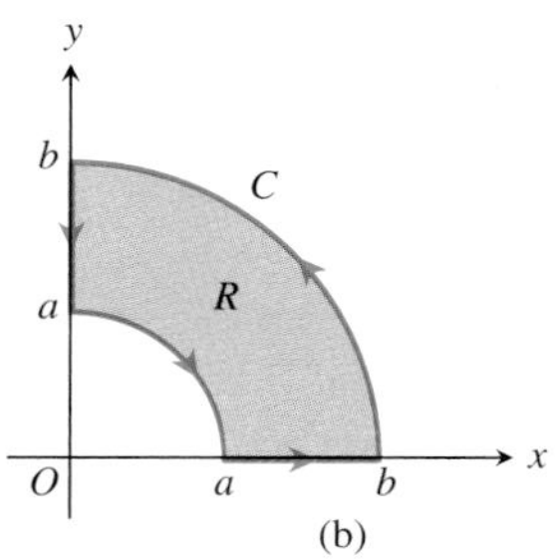

15.32 Other regions to which Green's theorem applies.

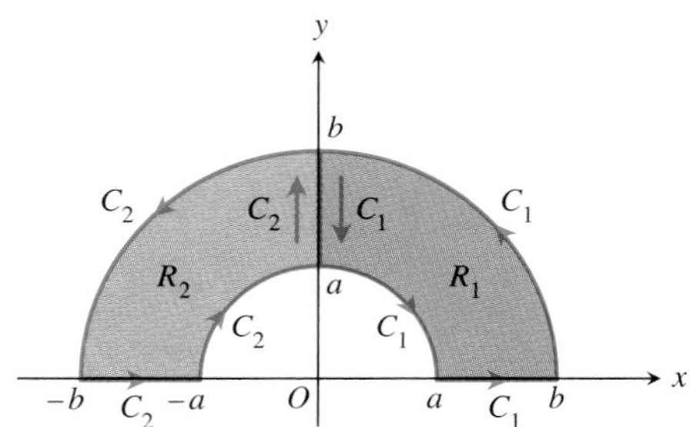

15.33 A region R that combines regions R_1 and R_2.

Because y is constant along C_1 and C_3,

$$\int_{C_1} N\,dy = \int_{C_3} N\,dy = 0,$$

so we can add

$$\int_{C_1} N\,dy + \int_{C_3} N\,dy$$

to the right-hand side of Eq. (22) without changing the equality. Doing so, we have

$$\int_c^d \int_a^b \frac{\partial N}{\partial x}\,dx\,dy = \oint_C N\,dy. \tag{23}$$

Similarly, we can show that

$$\int_a^b \int_c^d \frac{\partial M}{\partial y}\,dy\,dx = -\oint_C M\,dx. \tag{24}$$

Subtracting Eq. (24) from Eq. (23), we again arrive at

$$\oint_C M\,dx + N\,dy = \iint_R \left(\frac{\partial N}{\partial x} - \frac{\partial M}{\partial y}\right) dx\,dy.$$

Regions like those in Fig. 15.32 can be handled with no greater difficulty. Equation (18) still applies. It also applies to the horseshoe-shaped region R shown in Fig. 15.33, as we see by putting together the regions R_1 and R_2 and their boundaries. Green's theorem applies to C_1, R_1, and to C_2, R_2, yielding

$$\int_{C_1} M\,dx + N\,dy = \iint_{R_1} \left(\frac{\partial N}{\partial x} - \frac{\partial M}{\partial y}\right) dx\,dy$$

$$\int_{C_2} M\,dx + N\,dy = \iint_{R_2} \left(\frac{\partial N}{\partial x} - \frac{\partial M}{\partial y}\right) dx\,dy.$$

When we add these two equations, the line integral along the y-axis from b to a for C_1 cancels the integral over the same segment but in the opposite direction for C_2. Hence

$$\oint_C M\,dx + N\,dy = \iint_R \left(\frac{\partial N}{\partial x} - \frac{\partial M}{\partial y}\right) dx\,dy,$$

where C consists of the two segments of the x-axis from $-b$ to $-a$ and from a to b and of the two semicircles, and where R is the region inside C.

The device of adding line integrals over separate boundaries to build up an integral over a single boundary can be extended to any finite number of subregions. In Fig. 15.34(a), let C_1 be the boundary, oriented counterclockwise, of the region R_1 in the first quadrant. Similarly for the other three quadrants: C_i is the boundary of the region R_i, $i = 1, 2, 3, 4$. By Green's theorem,

$$\oint_{C_i} M\,dx + N\,dy = \iint_{R_i} \left(\frac{\partial N}{\partial x} - \frac{\partial M}{\partial y}\right) dx\,dy. \tag{25}$$

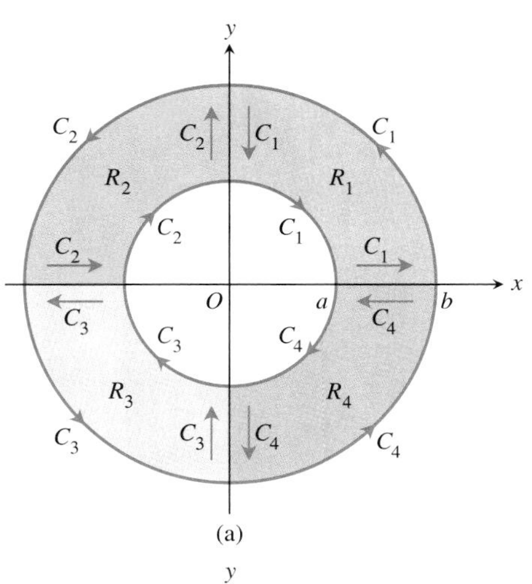

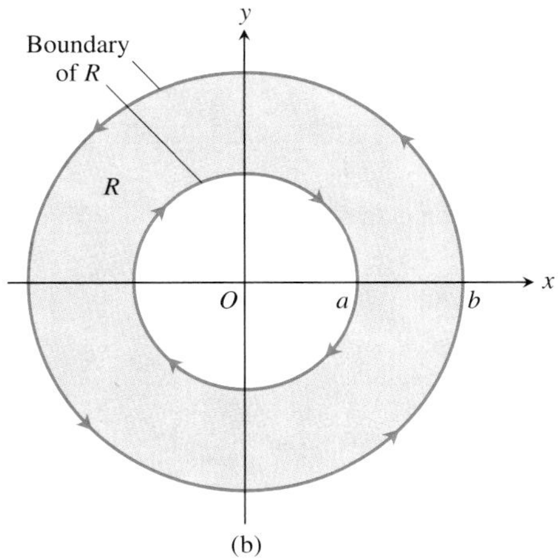

15.34 The annular region R combines four smaller regions. In polar coordinates, $r = a$ for the inner circle, $r = b$ for the outer circle, and $a \le r \le b$ for the region itself.

We add Eqs. (25) for $i = 1, 2, 3, 4$, and get (Fig. 15.34(b))

$$\oint_{r=b} (M\,dx + N\,dy) + \oint_{r=a} (M\,dx + N\,dy) = \iint_{a \le r \le b} \left(\frac{\partial N}{\partial x} - \frac{\partial M}{\partial y}\right) dx\,dy. \tag{26}$$

Equation (26) says that the double integral of $(\partial N/\partial x) - (\partial M/\partial y)$ over the annular ring R equals the line integral of $M\,dx + N\,dy$ over the complete boundary of R in the direction that keeps R on our left as we progress (Fig. 15.34b).

EXAMPLE 6 Verify the circulation form of Green's theorem (Eq. 16) on the annular ring R: $h^2 \le x^2 + y^2 \le 1$, $0 < h < 1$ (Fig. 15.35), if

$$M = \frac{-y}{x^2 + y^2}, \qquad N = \frac{x}{x^2 + y^2}.$$

Solution The boundary of R consists of the circle

$$C_1: \quad x = \cos t, \quad y = \sin t, \quad 0 \le t \le 2\pi,$$

traversed counterclockwise as t increases, and the circle

$$C_h: \quad x = h \cos \theta, \quad y = -h \sin \theta, \quad 0 \le \theta \le 2\pi,$$

traversed clockwise as θ increases. The functions M and N and their partial derivatives are continuous throughout R. Moreover,

$$\begin{aligned}\frac{\partial M}{\partial y} &= \frac{(x^2 + y^2)(-1) + y(2y)}{(x^2 + y^2)^2} \\ &= \frac{y^2 - x^2}{(x^2 + y^2)^2} = \frac{\partial N}{\partial x},\end{aligned}$$

so

$$\iint_R \left(\frac{\partial N}{\partial x} - \frac{\partial M}{\partial y}\right) dx\,dy = \iint_R 0\,dx\,dy = 0.$$

The integral of $M\,dx + N\,dy$ over the boundary of R is

$$\begin{aligned}\int_C M\,dx + N\,dy &= \oint_{C_1} \frac{x\,dy - y\,dx}{x^2 + y^2} + \oint_{C_h} \frac{x\,dy - y\,dx}{x^2 + y^2} \\ &= \int_0^{2\pi} (\cos^2 t + \sin^2 t)\,dt - \int_0^{2\pi} \frac{h^2(\cos^2 \theta + \sin^2 \theta)}{h^2}\,d\theta \\ &= 2\pi - 2\pi = 0.\end{aligned}$$

The functions M and N in Example 6 are discontinuous at $(0, 0)$, so we cannot apply Green's theorem to the circle C_1 and the region inside it. We must exclude the origin. We do so by excluding the points inside C_h.

We could replace the circle C_1 in Example 6 by an ellipse or any other simple closed curve K surrounding C_h (Fig. 15.36 on the following page). The result would still be

$$\oint_K (M\,dx + N\,dy) + \oint_{C_h} (M\,dx + N\,dy) = \iint_R \left(\frac{\partial N}{\partial x} - \frac{\partial M}{\partial y}\right) dy\,dx = 0,$$

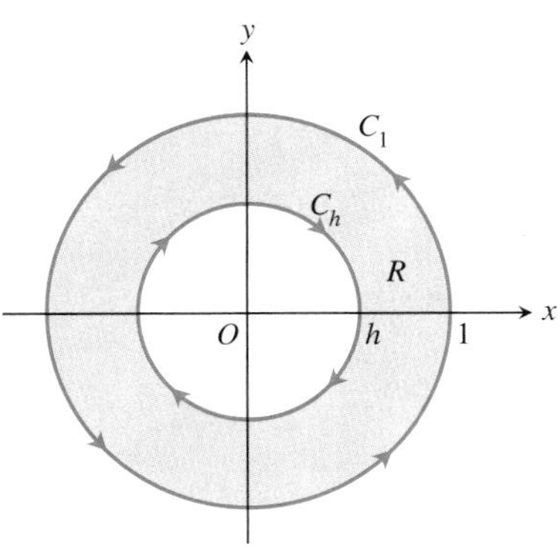

15.35 Green's theorem may be applied to the annular region R by integrating along the boundaries as shown (Example 6).

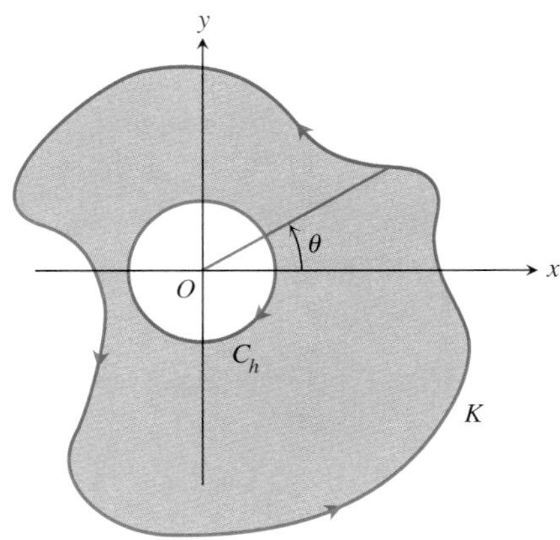

15.36 The region bounded by the circle C_h and the curve K.

which leads to the surprising conclusion that

$$\oint_K (M\,dx + N\,dy) = 2\pi$$

for any such curve K. We can explain this result by changing to polar coordinates. With

$$x = r\cos\theta \qquad y = r\sin\theta$$
$$dx = -r\sin\theta\,d\theta + \cos\theta\,dr, \qquad dy = r\cos\theta\,d\theta + \sin\theta\,dr,$$

we have

$$\frac{x\,dy - y\,dx}{x^2+y^2} = \frac{r^2(\cos^2\theta + \sin^2\theta)\,d\theta}{r^2} = d\theta,$$

and θ increases by 2π as we traverse K once counterclockwise.

Exercises 15.4

In Exercises 1–4, verify Green's theorem by evaluating both sides of Eqs. (15) and (16) for the field $\mathbf{F} = M\mathbf{i} + N\mathbf{j}$. Take the domains of integration in each case to be the disk R: $x^2 + y^2 \le a^2$ and its bounding circle C: $\mathbf{r} = (a\cos t)\,\mathbf{i} + (a\sin t)\,\mathbf{j}$, $0 \le t \le 2\pi$.

1. $\mathbf{F} = -y\,\mathbf{i} + x\,\mathbf{j}$

2. $\mathbf{F} = y\,\mathbf{i}$

3. $\mathbf{F} = 2x\,\mathbf{i} - 3y\,\mathbf{j}$

4. $\mathbf{F} = -x^2y\,\mathbf{i} + xy^2\,\mathbf{j}$

In Exercises 5–10, use Green's theorem to find the counterclockwise circulation and outward flux for the field **F** and curve C.

5. $\mathbf{F} = (x-y)\,\mathbf{i} + (y-x)\,\mathbf{j}$
C: The square bounded by $x = 0$, $x = 1$, $y = 0$, $y = 1$

6. $\mathbf{F} = (x^2 + 4y)\,\mathbf{i} + (x + y^2)\,\mathbf{j}$
C: The square bounded by $x = 0$, $x = 1$, $y = 0$, $y = 1$

7. $\mathbf{F} = (y^2 - x^2)\,\mathbf{i} + (x^2 + y^2)\,\mathbf{j}$
C: The triangle bounded by $y = 0$, $x = 3$, and $y = x$

8. $\mathbf{F} = (x + y)\,\mathbf{i} - (x^2 + y^2)\,\mathbf{j}$
C: The triangle bounded by $y = 0$, $x = 1$, and $y = x$

9. $\mathbf{F} = (x + e^x\sin y)\,\mathbf{i} + (x + e^x\cos y)\,\mathbf{j}$
C: The right-hand loop of the lemniscate $r^2 = \cos 2\theta$

10. $\mathbf{F} = \left(\tan^{-1}\frac{y}{x}\right)\mathbf{i} + \ln(x^2 + y^2)\,\mathbf{j}$
C: The boundary of the region defined by the polar coordinate inequalities $1 \le r \le 2$, $0 \le \theta \le \pi$

11. Find the counterclockwise circulation and outward flux of the field $\mathbf{F} = xy\,\mathbf{i} + y^2\,\mathbf{j}$ around and over the boundary of the region enclosed by the parabola $y = x^2$ and the line $y = x$ in the first quadrant.

12. Find the counterclockwise circulation and the outward flux of the field $\mathbf{F} = (-\sin y)\,\mathbf{i} + (x\cos y)\,\mathbf{j}$ around and over the square cut from the first quadrant by the lines $x = \pi/2$ and $y = \pi/2$.

13. Find the outward flux of the field

$$\mathbf{F} = \left(3xy - \frac{x}{1+y^2}\right)\mathbf{i} + (e^x + \tan^{-1}y)\,\mathbf{j}$$

across the cardioid $r = a(1 + \cos\theta)$, $a > 0$.

14. Find the counterclockwise circulation of the field $\mathbf{F} = (y + e^x\ln y)\,\mathbf{i} + (e^x/y)\,\mathbf{j}$ around the boundary of the region that is bounded above by the curve $y = 3 - x^2$ and below by the curve $y = x^4 + 1$.

Apply Green's theorem in one of its two forms to evaluate the line integrals in Exercises 15–20.

15. $\oint_C (y^2\,dx + x^2\,dy)$
C: The triangle bounded by $x = 0$, $x + y = 1$, $y = 0$

16. $\oint_C (3y\,dx + 2x\,dy)$
C: The boundary of $0 \le x \le \pi$, $0 \le y \le \sin x$

17. $\oint_C (6y + x)\,dx + (y + 2x)\,dy$
C: The circle $(x-2)^2 + (y-3)^2 = 4$

18. $\oint_C (2x + y^2)\,dx + (2xy + 3y)\,dy$
C: Any simple closed curve in the plane for which Green's theorem holds

19. $\oint_C 2xy^3\,dx + 4x^2y^2\,dy$

C: The boundary of the "triangular" region in the first quadrant enclosed by the x-axis, the line $x = 1$, and the curve $y = x^3$

20. $\oint_C (4x - 2y)\,dx + (2x - 4y)\,dy$

C: The circle $(x - 2)^2 + (y - 2)^2 = 4$

21. Let C be the boundary of a region on which Green's theorem holds. Use Green's theorem to calculate

a) $\oint_C f(x)\,dx + g(y)\,dy$,

b) $\oint_C ky\,dx + hx\,dy$ (k and h constants).

22. Show that the value of

$$\oint_C xy^2\,dx + (x^2y + 2x)\,dy$$

around any square depends only on the area of the square and not on its location in the plane.

23. What is special about the integral

$$\oint_C 4x^3y\,dx + x^4\,dy?$$

Give reasons for your answer.

24. What is special about the integral

$$\oint_C -y^3\,dx + x^3\,dy?$$

Give reasons for your answer.

25. Can anything be said about the curl of a conservative two-dimensional vector field? Give reasons for your answer.

26. Does Green's theorem give any information about the circulation of a conservative field? Does this agree with anything else you know? Give reasons for your answer.

CALCULATING AREA WITH GREEN'S THEOREM

If a simple closed curve C in the plane and the region R it encloses satisfy the hypotheses of Green's theorem, then the area of R is given by the following formula.

Green's Theorem Area Formula

$$\text{Area of } R = \frac{1}{2}\oint_C x\,dy - y\,dx \tag{27}$$

The reason is that by Eq. (15), run backward,

$$\text{Area of } R = \iint_R dy\,dx = \iint_R \left(\frac{1}{2} + \frac{1}{2}\right) dy\,dx$$
$$= \oint_C \frac{1}{2}x\,dy - \frac{1}{2}y\,dx.$$

Use the Green's theorem area formula (Eq. 27) to find the areas of the regions enclosed by the curves in Exercises 27–30.

27. The circle $\mathbf{r} = (a\cos t)\,\mathbf{i} + (a\sin t)\,\mathbf{j}$, $0 \le t \le 2\pi$

28. The ellipse $\mathbf{r} = (a\cos t)\,\mathbf{i} + (b\sin t)\,\mathbf{j}$, $0 \le t \le 2\pi$

29. The astroid (Fig. 10.37) $\mathbf{r} = (\cos^3 t)\,\mathbf{i} + (\sin^3 t)\,\mathbf{j}$, $0 \le t \le 2\pi$

30. The curve (Fig. 10.69) $\mathbf{r} = t^2\,\mathbf{i} + ((t^3/3) - t)\,\mathbf{j}$, $-\sqrt{3} \le t \le \sqrt{3}$

Writing for Your Own Knowledge

Answer the following questions in writing. Some answers will take only a sentence or two; others may require several paragraphs. Some explanations may also call for graphs or sketches.

1. How can you interpret the divergence of a two-dimensional vector field?
2. How can you interpret the curl of a two-dimensional vector field?
3. What is Green's theorem about?

EXPLORER PROGRAM

Vector Fields — Displays two-dimensional vector fields and integrates the curl over rectangular regions. Also calculates flux across rectangular boundaries.

15.5 *Surface Area and Surface Integrals*

We know how to integrate a function over a flat region in a plane, but what if the function is defined over a curved surface instead? How do we calculate its integral then? The trick to evaluating one of these so-called surface integrals is to rewrite it as a double integral over a region in a coordinate plane beneath the surface (Fig. 15.37 on the following page).

In Sections 15.7 and 15.8 we will see how surface integrals provide just

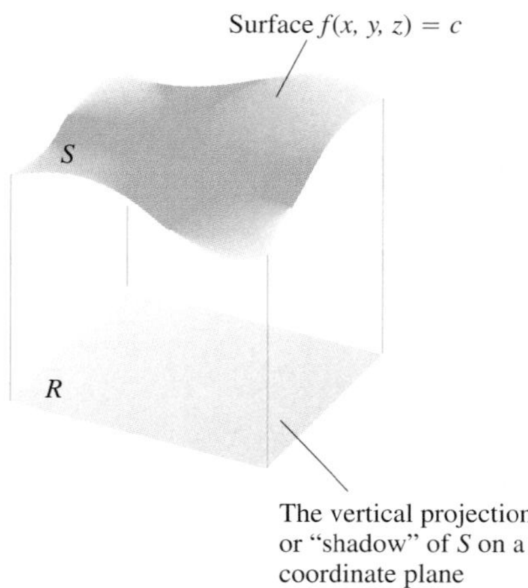

15.37 As we will soon see, the integral of a function $g(x, y, z)$ over a surface S in space can be calculated by evaluating a related double integral over the vertical projection or "shadow" of S on a coordinate plane.

what we need to generalize the two forms of Green's theorem to three dimensions. One of these generalizations will enable us to express the flux of a vector field through a closed surface as a triple integral over the three-dimensional region enclosed by the surface. The other will enable us to express the circulation of a vector field around a closed curve in space as an integral over a surface bounded by the curve.

The Definition of Surface Area

Figure 15.38 shows a surface S lying above its "shadow" region R in a plane beneath it. The surface is defined by the equation $f(x, y, z) = c$. If the surface is **smooth** (∇f is continuous and never vanishes on S), we can define and calculate its area as a double integral over R. It takes a while to derive the integral, but the integral itself is easy enough to work with.

The first step in defining the area of S is to partition the region R into small rectangles ΔA_k of the kind we would use if we were defining an integral over R. Directly above each ΔA_k lies a patch of surface $\Delta\sigma_k$ that we may approximate with a portion ΔP_k of the tangent plane. To be specific, we suppose that ΔP_k is a portion of the plane that is tangent to the surface at the point $T_k(x_k, y_k, z_k)$ directly above the back corner C_k of ΔA_k. If the tangent plane is parallel to R, then ΔP_k will be congruent to ΔA_k. Otherwise, it will be a parallelogram whose area is somewhat larger than the area of ΔA_k.

Figure 15.39 gives a magnified view of $\Delta\sigma_k$ and ΔP_k, showing the gradient vector $\nabla f(x_k, y_k, z_k)$ at T_k and a unit vector $\mathbf{p}$ that is normal to R. The figure also shows the angle γ_k between ∇f and $\mathbf{p}$. The other vectors in the picture, $\mathbf{u}$ and $\mathbf{v}$, lie along the edges of the patch ΔP_k in the tangent plane. Thus, both $\mathbf{u} \times \mathbf{v}$ and ∇f are normal to the tangent plane.

We now need the fact from advanced vector geometry that $|(\mathbf{u} \times \mathbf{v}) \cdot \mathbf{p}|$ is the area of the projection of the parallelogram determined by $\mathbf{u}$ and $\mathbf{v}$ onto any plane whose normal is $\mathbf{p}$. In our case, this translates into the statement

$$|(\mathbf{u} \times \mathbf{v}) \cdot \mathbf{p}| = \Delta A_k. \tag{1}$$

Now, $|\mathbf{u} \times \mathbf{v}|$ itself is the area ΔP_k (standard fact about cross products) so Eq. (1) becomes

$$\underbrace{|\mathbf{u} \times \mathbf{v}|}_{\Delta P_k}\;\underbrace{|\mathbf{p}|}_{1}\;\underbrace{|\cos(\text{angle between } \mathbf{u} \times \mathbf{v} \text{ and } \mathbf{p})|}_{\substack{\text{same as } |\cos \gamma_k| \text{ because} \\ \nabla f \text{ and } \mathbf{u} \times \mathbf{v} \text{ are both} \\ \text{normal to the tangent plane}}} = \Delta A_k \tag{2}$$

or

$$\Delta P_k |\cos \gamma_k| = \Delta A_k$$

or

$$\Delta P_k = \frac{\Delta A_k}{|\cos \gamma_k|},$$

provided $\cos \gamma_k \neq 0$. We will have $\cos \gamma_k \neq 0$ as long as ∇f is not parallel to the ground plane and $\nabla f \cdot \mathbf{p} \neq 0$.

Since the patches ΔP_k approximate the surface patches $\Delta\sigma_k$ that fit together to make S, the sum

$$\sum \Delta P_k = \sum \frac{\Delta A_k}{|\cos \gamma_k|} \tag{3}$$

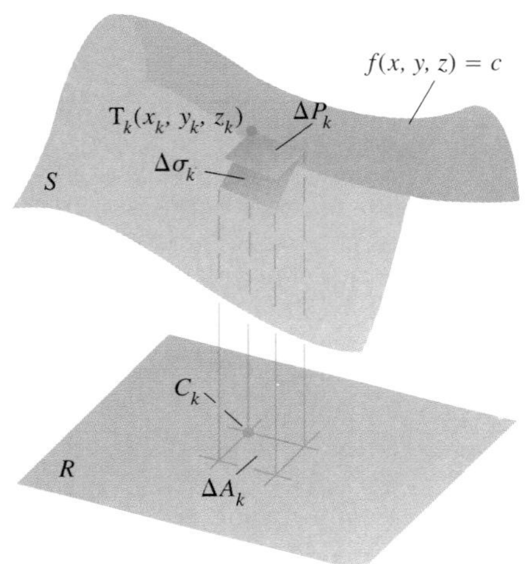

15.38 A surface S and its vertical projection onto a plane beneath it. You can think of R as the shadow of S on the plane. The tangent plate ΔP_k approximates the surface patch $\Delta\sigma_k$ above ΔA_k.

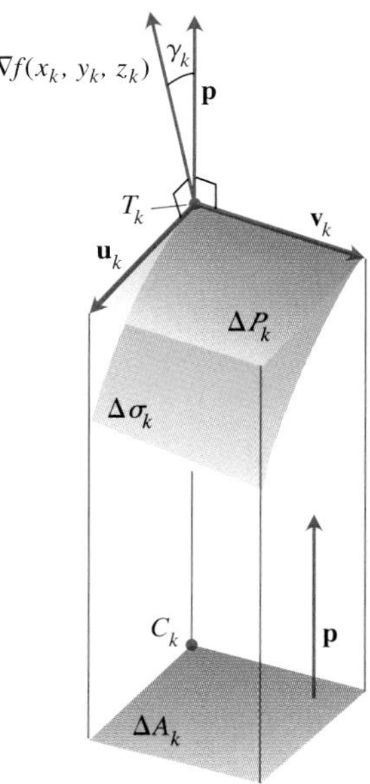

15.39 Magnified view from the preceding figure. The vector $\mathbf{u} \times \mathbf{v}$ (not shown) is parallel to the vector ∇f because both vectors are normal to the plane of ΔP_k.

looks like an approximation of what we might like to call the surface area of S. It also looks as if the approximation would improve if we refined the partition of R. In fact, the sums on the right-hand side of Eq. (3) are approximating sums for the double integral

$$\iint_R \frac{1}{|\cos \gamma|}\, dA. \tag{4}$$

We therefore define the **area** of S to be the value of this integral whenever it exists.

A Practical Formula

For any surface $f(x, y, z) = c$, we have $|\nabla f \cdot \mathbf{p}| = |\nabla f|\,|\mathbf{p}|\,|\cos \gamma|$, so

$$\frac{1}{|\cos \gamma|} = \frac{|\nabla f|}{|\nabla f \cdot \mathbf{p}|}.$$

This combines with Eq. (4) to give a practical formula for area.

The Formula for Surface Area

The area of the surface $f(x, y, z) = c$ over a closed and bounded plane region R is

$$\text{Surface area} = \iint_R \frac{|\nabla f|}{|\nabla f \cdot \mathbf{p}|}\, dA, \tag{5}$$

where $\mathbf{p}$ is a unit vector normal to R and $\nabla f \cdot \mathbf{p} \neq 0$.

Thus, the area is the double integral over R of the magnitude of ∇f divided by the magnitude of the scalar component of ∇f normal to R.

We reached Eq. (5) under the assumption that $\nabla f \cdot \mathbf{p} \neq 0$ throughout R and that ∇f is continuous. Whenever the integral exists, however, we define its value to be the area of the portion of the surface $f(x, y, z) = c$ that lies over R.

EXAMPLE 1 Find the area of the surface cut from the bottom of the paraboloid $x^2 + y^2 - z = 0$ by the plane $z = 4$.

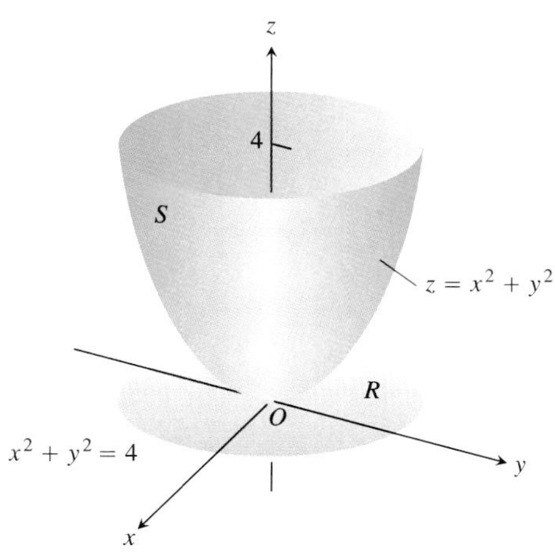

15.40 The area of this parabolic surface is calculated in Example 1.

Solution We sketch the surface S and the region R below it in the xy-plane (Fig. 15.40). The surface S is part of the level surface $f(x, y, z) = x^2 + y^2 - z = 0$, and R is the disk $x^2 + y^2 \leq 4$ in the xy-plane. To get a unit vector normal to the plane of R, we can take $\mathbf{p} = \mathbf{k}$.

At any point (x, y, z) on the surface, we have

$$\begin{aligned}
f(x, y, z) &= x^2 + y^2 - z \\
\nabla f &= 2x\,\mathbf{i} + 2y\,\mathbf{j} - \mathbf{k} \\
|\nabla f| &= \sqrt{(2x)^2 + (2y)^2 + (-1)^2} \\
&= \sqrt{4x^2 + 4y^2 + 1} \\
|\nabla f \cdot \mathbf{p}| &= |\nabla f \cdot \mathbf{k}| = |-1| = 1.
\end{aligned}$$

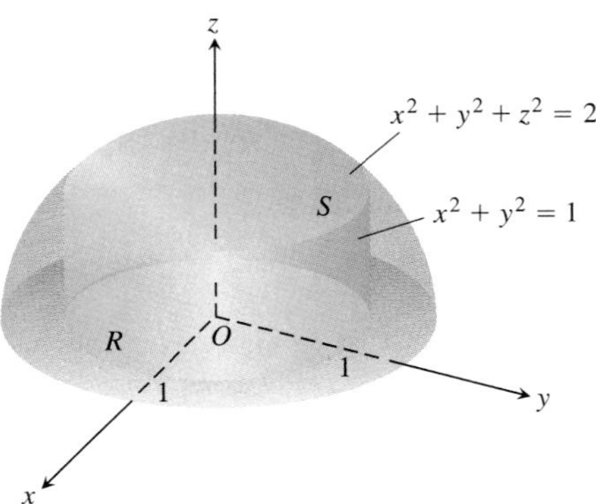

15.41 The cap cut from the hemisphere by the cylinder projects vertically onto the disk $R: x^2 + y^2 \leq 1$ (Example 2).

In the region R, $dA = dx\, dy$. Therefore,

$$\begin{aligned} \text{Surface area} &= \iint_R \frac{|\nabla f|}{|\nabla f \cdot \mathbf{p}|}\, dA && \text{Eq. (5)} \\ &= \iint_{x^2+y^2\leq 4} \sqrt{4x^2 + 4y^2 + 1}\, dx\, dy \\ &= \int_0^{2\pi}\int_0^2 \sqrt{4r^2+1}\, r\, dr\, d\theta && \text{Polar coordinates} \\ &= \int_0^{2\pi} \left[\frac{1}{12}(4r^2+1)^{3/2}\right]_0^2 d\theta \\ &= \int_0^{2\pi} \frac{1}{12}(17^{3/2} - 1)\, d\theta = \frac{\pi}{6}(17\sqrt{17} - 1). \end{aligned}$$

EXAMPLE 2 Find the area of the cap cut from the hemisphere $x^2 + y^2 + z^2 = 2$, $z \geq 0$, by the cylinder $x^2 + y^2 = 1$ (Fig. 15.41).

Solution The cap S is part of the level surface $f(x, y, z) = x^2 + y^2 + z^2 = 2$. It projects one-to-one onto the disk R: $x^2 + y^2 \leq 1$ in the xy-plane. The vector $\mathbf{p} = \mathbf{k}$ is normal to the plane of R.

At any point on the surface,

$$\begin{aligned} f(x, y, z) &= x^2 + y^2 + z^2 \\ \nabla f &= 2x\,\mathbf{i} + 2y\,\mathbf{j} + 2z\,\mathbf{k} \\ |\nabla f| &= 2\sqrt{x^2 + y^2 + z^2} = 2\sqrt{2} && \text{Because } x^2+y^2+z^2 = 2 \text{ at points of } S \\ |\nabla f \cdot \mathbf{p}| &= |\nabla f \cdot \mathbf{k}| = |2z| = 2z. \end{aligned}$$

Therefore,

$$\text{Surface area} = \iint_R \frac{|\nabla f|}{|\nabla f \cdot \mathbf{p}|}\, dA = \iint_R \frac{2\sqrt{2}}{2z}\, dA = \sqrt{2}\iint_R \frac{dA}{z}. \tag{6}$$

What do we do about the z?

Since z is the z-coordinate of a point on the sphere, we can express it in terms of x and y as

$$z = \sqrt{2 - x^2 - y^2}.$$

We continue the work of Eq. (6) with this substitution:

$$\begin{aligned} \text{Surface area} &= \sqrt{2}\iint_R \frac{dA}{z} = \sqrt{2}\iint_{x^2+y^2\leq 1} \frac{dA}{\sqrt{2 - x^2 - y^2}} \\ &= \sqrt{2}\int_0^{2\pi}\int_0^1 \frac{r\, dr\, d\theta}{\sqrt{2 - r^2}} && \text{Polar coordinates} \\ &= \sqrt{2}\int_0^{2\pi} \left[-(2 - r^2)^{1/2}\right]_{r=0}^{r=1} d\theta \\ &= \sqrt{2}\int_0^{2\pi} (\sqrt{2} - 1)\, d\theta \\ &= 2\pi(2 - \sqrt{2}). \end{aligned}$$

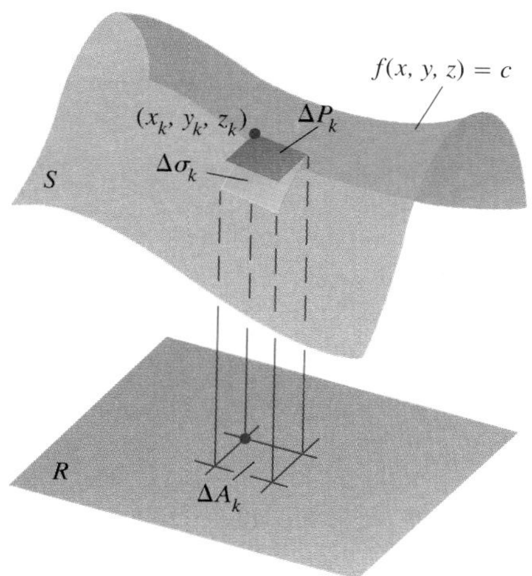

15.42 If we know how an electrical charge is distributed over a surface, we can find the total charge with a suitably modified surface integral.

Surface Integrals

We now show how to integrate a function over a surface, using the ideas we just developed for calculating surface area.

Suppose, for example, that we have an electrical charge distributed over a surface $f(x, y, z) = c$ like the one shown in Fig. 15.42 and that the function $g(x, y, z)$ gives the charge per unit area (charge density) at each point on S. Then we may calculate the total charge on S as an integral in the following way.

We partition the shadow region R on the ground plane beneath the surface into small rectangles of the kind we would use if we were defining the surface area of S. Then directly above each ΔA_k lies a patch of surface $\Delta\sigma_k$ that we approximate with a parallelogram-shaped portion of tangent plane, ΔP_k.

Up to this point the construction proceeds as in the definition of surface area, but now we take one additional step: We evaluate g at (x_k, y_k, z_k) and then approximate the total charge on the surface patch $\Delta\sigma_k$ by the product $g(x_k, y_k, z_k)\Delta P_k$. The rationale is that when the partition of R is sufficiently fine, the value of g throughout $\Delta\sigma_k$ is nearly constant and ΔP_k is nearly the same as $\Delta\sigma_k$. The total charge over S is then approximated by the sum

$$\text{Total charge} \approx \sum g(x_k, y_k, z_k)\,\Delta P_k = \sum g(x_k, y_k, z_k)\frac{\Delta A_k}{|\cos\gamma_k|}. \tag{7}$$

If f, the function defining the surface S, and its first partial derivatives are continuous, and if g is continuous over S, then the sums on the right-hand side of Eq. (7) approach the limit

$$\iint_R g(x, y, z)\frac{dA}{|\cos\gamma|} = \iint_R g(x, y, z)\frac{|\nabla f|}{|\nabla f\cdot\mathbf{p}|}\,dA \tag{8}$$

as the partition of R is refined in the usual way. This limit is called the integral of g over the surface S and is calculated as a double integral over R. The value of the integral is the total charge on the surface S.

As you might expect, the formula in Eq. (8) defines the integral of *any* function g over the surface S as long as the integral exists.

DEFINITIONS

If R is the shadow region of a surface S defined by the equation $f(x, y, z) = c$, and g is a continuous function defined at the points of S, then the **integral of g over S** is the integral

$$\iint_R g(x, y, z)\frac{|\nabla f|}{|\nabla f\cdot\mathbf{p}|}\,dA, \tag{9}$$

where $\mathbf{p}$ is a unit vector normal to R and $\nabla f\cdot\mathbf{p}\neq 0$. The integral itself is called a **surface integral.**

The integral in (9) takes on different meanings in different applications. If g has the constant value 1, the integral gives the area of S. If g gives the mass density of a thin shell of material modeled by S, the integral gives the mass of the shell.

Algebraic Properties: The Surface Area Differential

We can abbreviate the integral in (9) by writing $d\sigma$ for $(|\nabla f|/|\nabla f \cdot \mathbf{p}|)\, dA$.

The Surface Area Differential and the Differential Form for Surface Integrals

$$d\sigma = \frac{|\nabla f|}{|\nabla f \cdot \mathbf{p}|}\, dA \qquad\qquad \iint_S g\, d\sigma \tag{10}$$

surface area differential — differential formula for surface integrals

---

Surface integrals behave like other double integrals, the integral of the sum of two functions being the sum of their integrals and so on. The domain additivity property takes the form

$$\iint_S g\, d\sigma = \iint_{S_1} g\, d\sigma + \iint_{S_2} g\, d\sigma + \cdots + \iint_{S_n} g\, d\sigma.$$

The idea is that if S is partitioned by smooth curves into a finite number of nonoverlapping smooth patches (i.e., if S is **piecewise smooth**), then the integral over S is the sum of the integrals over the patches. Thus, the integral of a function over the surface of a cube is the sum of the integrals over the faces of the cube. We integrate over a turtle shell of welded plates by integrating one plate at a time and adding the results.

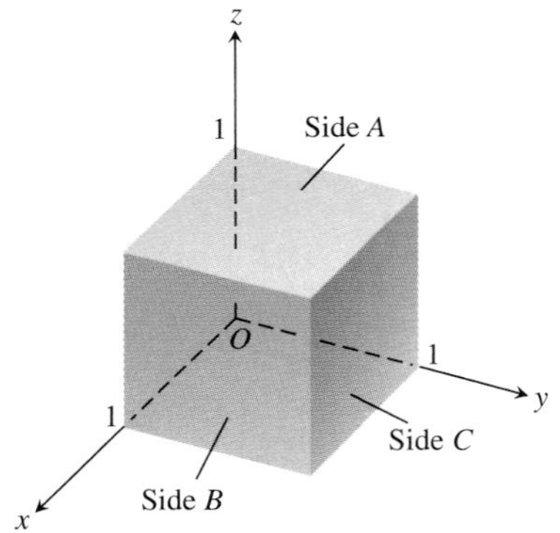

15.43 To integrate a function over the surface of a cube, we integrate over each face and add the results (Example 3).

EXAMPLE 3 Integrate $g(x, y, z) = xyz$ over the surface of the cube cut from the first octant by the planes $x = 1$, $y = 1$, and $z = 1$ (Fig. 15.43).

Solution We integrate xyz over each of the six sides and add the results. Since $xyz = 0$ on the sides that lie in the coordinate planes, the integral over the surface of the cube reduces to

$$\iint_{\substack{\text{cube}\\ \text{surface}}} xyz\, d\sigma = \iint_{\text{side } A} xyz\, d\sigma + \iint_{\text{side } B} xyz\, d\sigma + \iint_{\text{side } C} xyz\, d\sigma.$$

Side A is the surface $f(x, y, z) = z = 1$ over the square region $R_{xy}: 0 \le x \le 1$, $0 \le y \le 1$, in the xy-plane. For this surface and region,

$$\mathbf{p} = \mathbf{k}, \qquad \nabla f = \mathbf{k}, \qquad |\nabla f| = 1, \qquad |\nabla f \cdot \mathbf{p}| = |\mathbf{k} \cdot \mathbf{k}| = 1,$$

$$d\sigma = \frac{|\nabla f|}{|\nabla f \cdot \mathbf{p}|}\, dA = \frac{1}{1}\, dx\, dy = dx\, dy,$$

$$xyz = xy(1) = xy,$$

and

$$\iint_{\text{side } A} xyz\, d\sigma = \iint_{R_{xy}} xy\, dx\, dy = \int_0^1 \int_0^1 xy\, dx\, dy = \int_0^1 \frac{y}{2}\, dy = \frac{1}{4}.$$

Symmetry tells us that the integrals of xyz over sides B and C are also 1/4.

Hence,

$$\iint_{\substack{\text{cube}\\\text{surface}}} xyz\, d\sigma = \frac{1}{4} + \frac{1}{4} + \frac{1}{4} = \frac{3}{4}.$$

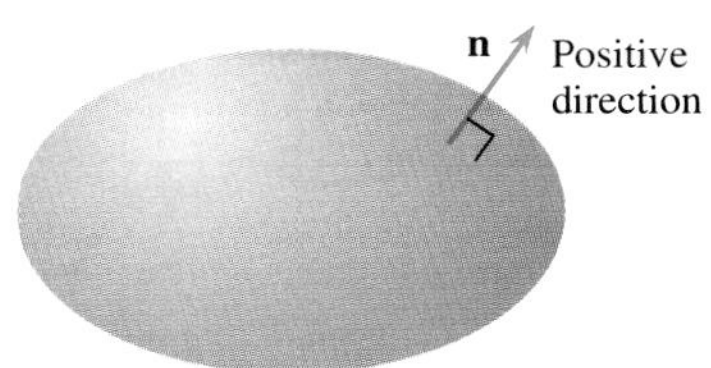

15.44 Smooth closed surfaces in space are orientable. The outward unit normal vector defines the positive direction at each point.

Orientation

We call a smooth surface S **orientable** or **two-sided** if it is possible to define a field $\mathbf{n}$ of unit normal vectors on S that varies continuously with position. Any patch or subportion of an orientable surface is orientable. Spheres and other smooth closed surfaces in space (smooth surfaces that enclose solids) are orientable. By convention, we choose $\mathbf{n}$ on a closed surface to point outward.

Once $\mathbf{n}$ has been chosen, we say that we have **oriented** the surface, and we call the surface together with its normal field an **oriented surface.** The vector $\mathbf{n}$ at any point is called the **positive direction** at that point (Fig. 15.44).

The Möbius band in Fig. 15.45 is not orientable. No matter where you start to construct a continuous unit normal field (shown as the shaft of a thumbtack in the figure), moving the vector continuously around the surface in the manner shown will return it to the starting point with a direction opposite to the one it had when it started out. The vector at that point cannot point both ways and yet it must if the field is to be continuous. We conclude that no such field exists.

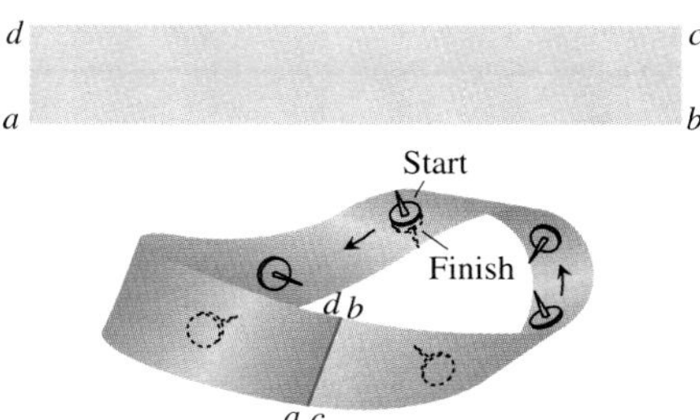

15.45 The Möbius band can be constructed by taking a rectangular strip of paper $abcd$, giving the end bc a single twist to interchange the positions of the vertices b and c, and then pasting the ends of the strip together to match a with c and b with d. The Möbius band is a nonorientable or one-sided surface.

The Surface Integral for Flux

Suppose that $\mathbf{F}$ is a continuous vector field defined over an oriented surface S and that $\mathbf{n}$ is the chosen unit normal field on the surface. We call the integral of $\mathbf{F}\cdot\mathbf{n}$ over S the flux across S in the positive direction. Thus, the flux is the integral over S of the scalar component of $\mathbf{F}$ in the direction of $\mathbf{n}$.

DEFINITION

The **flux** of a three-dimensional vector field $\mathbf{F}$ across an oriented surface S in the direction of $\mathbf{n}$ is given by the formula

$$\text{Flux} = \iint_S \mathbf{F}\cdot\mathbf{n}\, d\sigma. \tag{11}$$

This definition is analogous to the flux of a two-dimensional field $\mathbf{F}$ across a plane curve C. In the plane (Section 15.2), the flux is

$$\int_C \mathbf{F}\cdot\mathbf{n}\, ds,$$

the integral of the scalar component of $\mathbf{F}$ normal to the curve.

If $\mathbf{F}$ is the velocity field of a three-dimensional fluid flow, the flux of $\mathbf{F}$ across S is the net rate at which fluid is crossing S in the chosen positive direction. We will discuss such flows in more detail in Section 15.7.

If **S** is part of a level surface $g(x, y, z) = c$, then $\mathbf{n}$ may be taken to be one of the two fields

$$\mathbf{n} = \pm\frac{\nabla g}{|\nabla g|}, \tag{12}$$

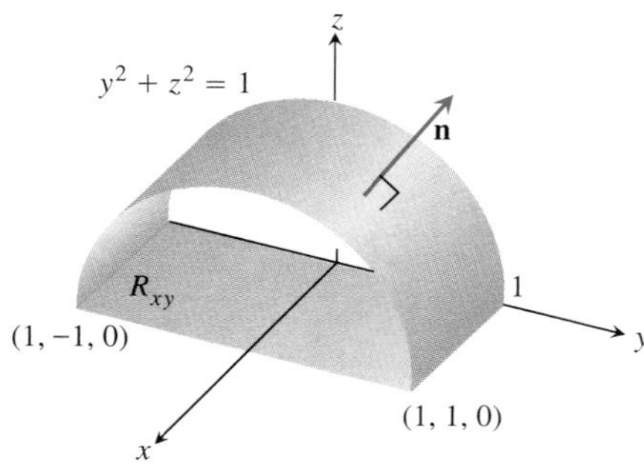

15.46 Example 4 calculates the flux of a vector field outward through this surface. The area of the shadow region R_{xy} is 2.

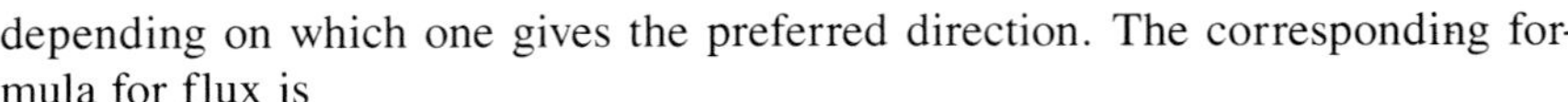
depending on which one gives the preferred direction. The corresponding formula for flux is

$$\text{Flux} = \iint_S \mathbf{F} \cdot \mathbf{n}\, d\sigma \qquad \text{Eq. (11)}$$

$$= \iint_R \left(\mathbf{F} \cdot \frac{\pm \nabla g}{|\nabla g|}\right) \frac{|\nabla g|}{|\nabla g \cdot \mathbf{p}|}\, dA \qquad \text{Eqs. (12) and (10)}$$

$$= \iint_R \mathbf{F} \cdot \frac{\pm \nabla g}{|\nabla g \cdot \mathbf{p}|}\, dA. \tag{13}$$

EXAMPLE 4 Find the flux of $\mathbf{F} = yz\,\mathbf{j} + z^2\,\mathbf{k}$ outward through the surface S cut from the semicircular cylinder $y^2 + z^2 = 1$, $z \geq 0$, by the planes $x = 0$ and $x = 1$.

Solution The outward normal field on S (Fig. 15.46) may be calculated from the gradient of $g(x, y, z) = y^2 + z^2$ to be

$$\mathbf{n} = +\frac{\nabla g}{|\nabla g|} = \frac{2y\,\mathbf{j} + 2z\,\mathbf{k}}{\sqrt{4y^2 + 4z^2}} = \frac{2y\,\mathbf{j} + 2z\,\mathbf{k}}{2\sqrt{1}} = y\,\mathbf{j} + z\,\mathbf{k}.$$

With $\mathbf{p} = \mathbf{k}$, we also have

$$d\sigma = \frac{|\nabla g|}{|\nabla g \cdot \mathbf{k}|}\, dA = \frac{2}{|2z|}\, dA = \frac{1}{z}\, dA.$$

We can drop the absolute value bars because $z \geq 0$ on S.

The value of $\mathbf{F} \cdot \mathbf{n}$ on the surface is given by the formula

$$\mathbf{F} \cdot \mathbf{n} = (yz\,\mathbf{j} + z^2\,\mathbf{k}) \cdot (y\,\mathbf{j} + z\,\mathbf{k})$$

$$= y^2 z + z^3 = z(y^2 + z^2)$$

$$= z. \qquad y^2 + z^2 = 1 \text{ on } S$$

Therefore, the flux of $\mathbf{F}$ outward through S is

$$\iint_S \mathbf{F} \cdot \mathbf{n}\, d\sigma = \iint_S (z)\left(\frac{1}{z}\, dA\right) = \iint_{R_{xy}} dA = \text{area } (R_{xy}) = 2.$$

Moments and Masses of Thin Shells

In engineering and physics, thin shells of material like bowls, metal drums, and domes are modeled with surfaces. Their moments and masses are calculated with the surface integral formulas in Table 15.3.

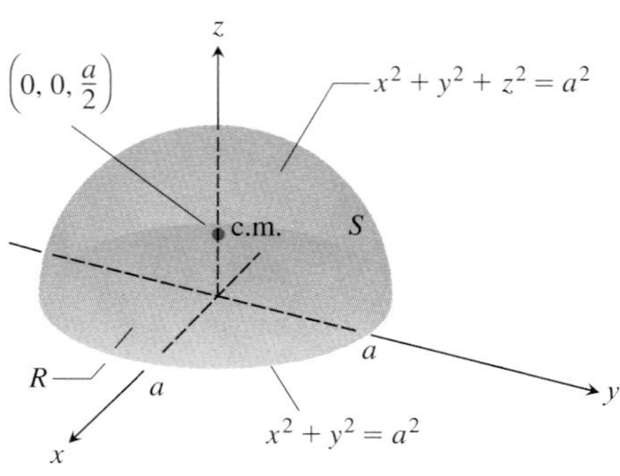

15.47 The center of mass of a thin hemispherical shell of constant density lies on the axis of symmetry halfway from the base to the top (Example 5).

EXAMPLE 5 Find the center of mass of a thin hemispherical shell of radius a and constant density δ.

Solution We model the shell with the hemisphere

$$f(x, y, z) = x^2 + y^2 + z^2 = a^2, \qquad z \geq 0$$

(Fig. 15.47). The symmetry of the surface about the z-axis tells us that $\bar{x} = \bar{y} = 0$. It remains only to find $\bar{z}$ from the formula $\bar{z} = M_{xy}/M$.

TABLE 15.3
Mass and moment formulas for very thin shells

Mass: $M = \iint_S \delta(x, y, z)\, d\sigma \qquad (\delta(x, y, z) = \text{density at } (x, y, z))$

First moments about the coordinate planes:

$$M_{yz} = \iint_S x\delta\, d\sigma, \qquad M_{xz} = \iint_S y\delta\, d\sigma, \qquad M_{xy} = \iint_S z\delta\, d\sigma$$

Coordinates of center of mass:

$$\bar{x} = M_{yz}/M, \qquad \bar{y} = M_{xz}/M, \qquad \bar{z} = M_{xy}/M$$

Moments of inertia:

$$I_x = \iint_S (y^2 + z^2)\, \delta\, d\sigma, \qquad I_y = \iint_S (x^2 + z^2)\, \delta\, d\sigma,$$

$$I_z = \iint_S (x^2 + y^2)\, \delta\, d\sigma, \qquad I_L = \iint_S r^2\, \delta\, d\sigma$$

$r(x, y, z) =$ distance from point (x, y, z) to line L

Radius of gyration about a line L: $R_L = \sqrt{I_L/M}$

The mass of the shell is

$$M = \iint_S \delta\, d\sigma = \delta \iint_S d\sigma = (\delta)(\text{area of } S) = 2\pi a^2 \delta.$$

To evaluate the integral for M_{xy}, we take $\mathbf{p} = \mathbf{k}$ and calculate

$$|\nabla f| = |2x\,\mathbf{i} + 2y\,\mathbf{j} + 2z\,\mathbf{k}| = 2\sqrt{x^2 + y^2 + z^2} = 2a$$

$$|\nabla f \cdot \mathbf{p}| = |\nabla f \cdot \mathbf{k}| = |2z| = 2z$$

$$d\sigma = \frac{|\nabla f|}{|\nabla f \cdot \mathbf{p}|}\, dA = \frac{a}{z}\, dA.$$

Then

$$M_{xy} = \iint_S z\delta\, d\sigma = \delta \iint_R z \frac{a}{z}\, dA = \delta a \iint_R dA = \delta a(\pi a^2) = \delta \pi a^3$$

$$\bar{z} = \frac{M_{xy}}{M} = \frac{\pi a^3 \delta}{2\pi a^2 \delta} = \frac{a}{2}.$$

The shell's center of mass is the point $(0, 0, a/2)$.

Exercises 15.5

SURFACE AREA

1. Find the area of the surface cut from the paraboloid $x^2 + y^2 - z = 0$ by the plane $z = 2$.

2. Find the area of the band cut from the paraboloid $x^2 + y^2 - z = 0$ by the planes $z = 2$ and $z = 6$.

3. Find the area of the region cut from the plane $x + 2y + 2z = 5$ by the cylinder whose walls are $x = y^2$ and $x = 2 - y^2$.

4. Find the area of the portion of the surface $x^2 - 2z = 0$ that lies above the triangle bounded by the lines $x = \sqrt{3}$, $y = 0$, and $y = x$ in the xy-plane.

5. Find the area of the surface $x^2 - 2y - 2z = 0$ that lies above the triangle bounded by the lines $x = 2$, $y = 0$, and $y = 3x$ in the xy-plane.

6. Find the area of the cap cut from the sphere $x^2 + y^2 + z^2 = 2$ by the cone $z = \sqrt{x^2 + y^2}$.

7. Find the area of the ellipse cut from the plane $z = cx$ by the cylinder $x^2 + y^2 = 1$.

8. Find the area of the upper portion of the cylinder $x^2 + z^2 = 1$ that lies between the planes $x = \pm 1/2$ and $y = \pm 1/2$.

9. Find the area of the portion of the paraboloid $x = 4 - y^2 - z^2$ that lies above the ring $1 \leq y^2 + z^2 \leq 4$ in the yz-plane.

10. Find the area of the surface cut from the paraboloid $x^2 + y + z^2 = 2$ by the plane $y = 0$.

SURFACE INTEGRALS

11. Integrate $g(x, y, z) = x + y + z$ over the surface of the cube cut from the first octant by the planes $x = a$, $y = a$, $z = a$.

12. Integrate $g(x, y, z) = y + z$ over the surface of the wedge in Fig. 15.48.

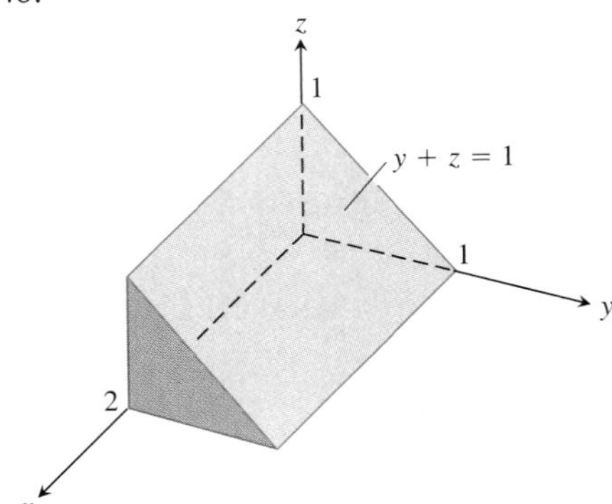

15.48 The wedge in Exercise 12.

13. Integrate $g(x, y, z) = xyz$ over the surface of the rectangular solid cut from the first octant by the planes $x = a$, $y = b$, and $z = c$.

14. Integrate $g(x, y, z) = xyz$ over the surface of the rectangular solid bounded by the planes $x = \pm a$, $y = \pm b$, and $z = \pm c$.

15. Integrate $g(x, y, z) = x + y + z$ over the portion of the plane $2x + 2y + z = 2$ that lies in the first octant.

16. Integrate $g(x, y, z) = x\sqrt{y^2 + 4}$ over the surface cut from the parabolic cylinder $y^2 + 4z = 16$ by the planes $x = 0$, $x = 1$, and $z = 0$.

FLUX ACROSS A SURFACE

In Exercises 17–22, find the flux of the field **F** across the portion of the sphere $x^2 + y^2 + z^2 = a^2$ in the first octant in the direction away from the origin.

17. $\mathbf{F}(x, y, z) = z\,\mathbf{k}$

18. $\mathbf{F}(x, y, z) = -y\,\mathbf{i} + x\,\mathbf{j}$

19. $\mathbf{F}(x, y, z) = y\,\mathbf{i} - x\,\mathbf{j} + \mathbf{k}$

20. $\mathbf{F}(x, y, z) = zx\,\mathbf{i} + zy\,\mathbf{j} + z^2\,\mathbf{k}$

21. $\mathbf{F}(x, y, z) = x\,\mathbf{i} + y\,\mathbf{j} + z\,\mathbf{k}$

22. $\mathbf{F}(x, y, z) = \dfrac{x\,\mathbf{i} + y\,\mathbf{j} + z\,\mathbf{k}}{\sqrt{x^2 + y^2 + z^2}}$

23. Find the flux of the field $\mathbf{F}(x, y, z) = z^2\,\mathbf{i} + x\,\mathbf{j} - 3z\,\mathbf{k}$ upward through the surface cut from the parabolic cylinder $z = 4 - y^2$ by the planes $x = 0$, $x = 1$, and $z = 0$.

24. Find the flux of the field $\mathbf{F}(x, y, z) = 4x\,\mathbf{i} + 4y\,\mathbf{j} + 2\,\mathbf{k}$ outward (away from the z-axis) through the surface cut from the bottom of the paraboloid $z = x^2 + y^2$ by the plane $z = 1$.

25. Let S be the portion of the cylinder $y = e^x$ in the first octant that projects parallel to the x-axis onto the rectangle R_{yz}: $1 \leq y \leq 2$, $0 \leq z \leq 1$ in the yz-plane (Fig. 15.49). Let **n** be the unit vector normal to S that points away from the yz-plane. Find the flux of the field $\mathbf{F}(x, y, z) = -2\,\mathbf{i} + 2y\,\mathbf{j} + z\,\mathbf{k}$ across S in the direction of **n**.

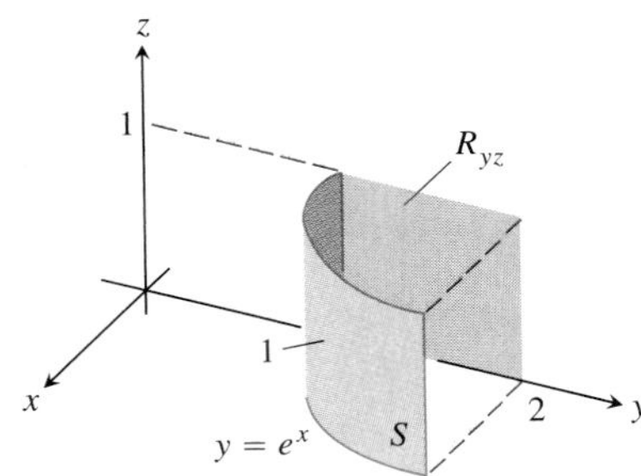

15.49 The surface and region in Exercise 25.

26. Let S be the portion of the cylinder $y = \ln x$ in the first octant whose projection parallel to the y-axis onto the xz-plane is the rectangle R_{xz}: $1 \leq x \leq e$, $0 \leq z \leq 1$. Let **n** be the unit vector normal to S that points away from the xz-plane. Find the flux of $\mathbf{F} = 2y\,\mathbf{j} + z\,\mathbf{k}$ through S in the direction of **n**.

27. Find the outward flux of the field $\mathbf{F} = 2xy\,\mathbf{i} + 2yz\,\mathbf{j} + 2xz\,\mathbf{k}$ across the surface of the cube cut from the first octant by the planes $x = a$, $y = a$, $z = a$.

28. Find the outward flux of the field $\mathbf{F} = xz\,\mathbf{i} + yz\,\mathbf{j} + \mathbf{k}$ across the surface of the upper cap cut from the solid sphere $x^2 + y^2 + z^2 \leq 25$ by the plane $z = 3$.

MOMENTS AND MASSES

29. Find the centroid of the portion of the sphere $x^2 + y^2 + z^2 = a^2$ that lies in the first octant.

30. Find the centroid of the surface cut from the cylinder $y^2 + z^2 = 9$, $z \geq 0$, by the planes $x = 0$ and $x = 3$ (resembles the surface in Example 4).

31. Find the center of mass and the moment of inertia and radius of gyration about the z-axis of a thin shell of constant density δ cut from the cone $x^2 + y^2 - z^2 = 0$ by the planes $z = 1$ and $z = 2$.

32. Find the moment of inertia about the z-axis of a thin shell of constant density δ cut from the cone $4x^2 + 4y^2 - z^2 = 0$, $z \geq 0$, by the circular cylinder $x^2 + y^2 = 2x$ (Fig. 15.50).

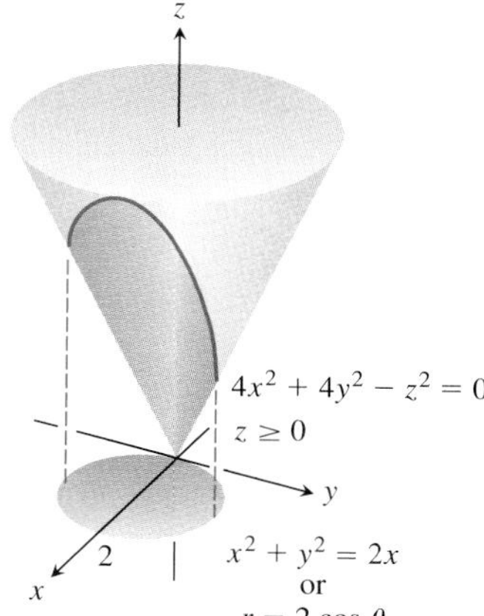

15.50 The surface in Exercise 32.

SPECIAL FORMULAS FOR SURFACE AREA

If S is the surface defined by a function $z = f(x, y)$ that has continuous first partial derivatives throughout a region R_{xy} in the xy-plane (Fig. 15.51), then S is also the level surface $F(x, y, z) = 0$ of the function $F(x, y, z) = f(x, y) - z$. Taking the unit normal to R_{xy} to be $\mathbf{p} = \mathbf{k}$ then gives

$$|\nabla F| = |f_x\,\mathbf{i} + f_y\,\mathbf{j} - \mathbf{k}| = \sqrt{f_x^2 + f_y^2 + 1},$$
$$|\nabla F \cdot \mathbf{p}| = |(f_x\,\mathbf{i} + f_y\,\mathbf{j} - \mathbf{k}) \cdot \mathbf{k}| = |-1| = 1,$$

and

$$A = \iint_{R_{xy}} \frac{|\nabla F|}{|\nabla F \cdot \mathbf{p}|}\,dA = \iint_{R_{xy}} \sqrt{f_x^2 + f_y^2 + 1}\;dx\,dy. \tag{14}$$

Similarly, the area of a smooth surface $x = f(y, z)$ over a region R_{yz} in the yz-plane is

$$A = \iint_{R_{yz}} \sqrt{f_y^2 + f_z^2 + 1}\;dy\,dz, \tag{15}$$

and the area of a smooth surface $y = f(x, z)$ over a region R_{xz} in the xz-plane is

$$A = \iint_{R_{xz}} \sqrt{f_x^2 + f_z^2 + 1}\;dx\,dz. \tag{16}$$

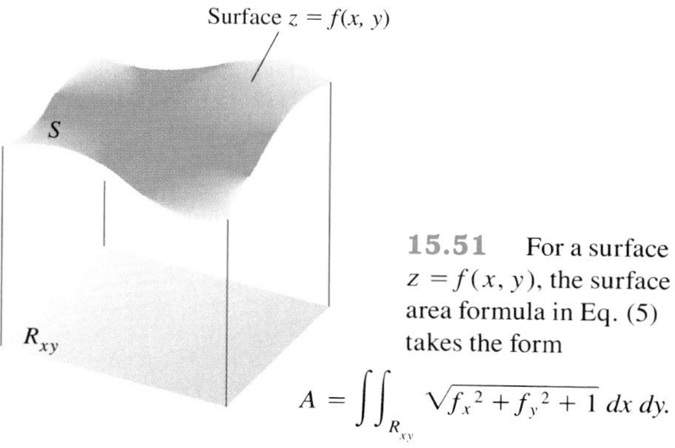

15.51 For a surface $z = f(x, y)$, the surface area formula in Eq. (5) takes the form

$$A = \iint_{R_{xy}} \sqrt{f_x^2 + f_y^2 + 1}\;dx\,dy.$$

Use Eqs. (14)–(16) to find the areas of the surfaces in Exercises 33–38.

33. The surface cut from the bottom of the paraboloid $z = x^2 + y^2$ by the plane $z = 3$

34. The portion of the cone $z = \sqrt{x^2 + y^2}$ that lies over the region between the circle $x^2 + y^2 = 1$ and the ellipse $9x^2 + 4y^2 = 36$ in the xy-plane. (*Hint:* Use formulas from geometry to find the area of the region.)

35. The surface cut from the bottom of the paraboloid $x = 1 - y^2 - z^2$ by the yz-plane

36. The triangle cut from the plane $2x + 6y + 3z = 6$ by the bounding planes of the first octant. Calculate the area three ways, once with each area formula.

37. The surface in the first octant cut from the cylinder $y = (2/3)\,z^{3/2}$ by the planes $x = 1$ and $y = 16/3$.

38. The portion of the plane $y + z = 4$ that lies above the region cut from the first quadrant of the xz-plane by the parabola $x = 4 - z^2$

Writing for Your Own Knowledge

Answer the following questions in writing. Some answers will take only a sentence or two; others may require several paragraphs. Some explanations may also call for graphs or sketches.

1. How do you calculate the area of a curved surface in space?
2. What is an oriented surface?
3. What are surface integrals? What sorts of things do you calculate with them?

15.6 *Parametrized Surfaces*

We have defined curves in the plane in three different ways:

$$\begin{aligned} &\text{Explicit form:} && y = f(x) \\ &\text{Implicit form:} && F(x, y) = 0 \\ &\text{Parametric vector form:} && \mathbf{r}(t) = f(t)\,\mathbf{i} + g(t)\,\mathbf{j}, \quad a \leq t \leq b. \end{aligned} \tag{1}$$

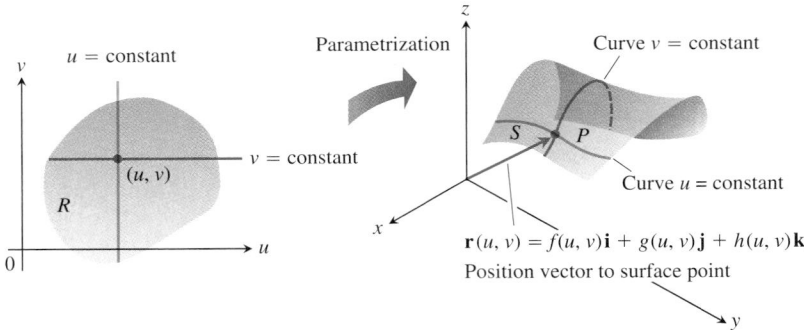

15.52 A parametrized surface.

We have analogous definitions of surfaces in space:

$$\begin{aligned} &\text{Explicit form:} \quad && z = f(x, y) \\ &\text{Implicit form:} \quad && F(x, y, z) = 0. \end{aligned} \tag{2}$$

There is also a parametric form that gives the position of a point on the surface as a vector function of two variables. The present section extends the investigation of surface area and surface integrals to surfaces in this new form.

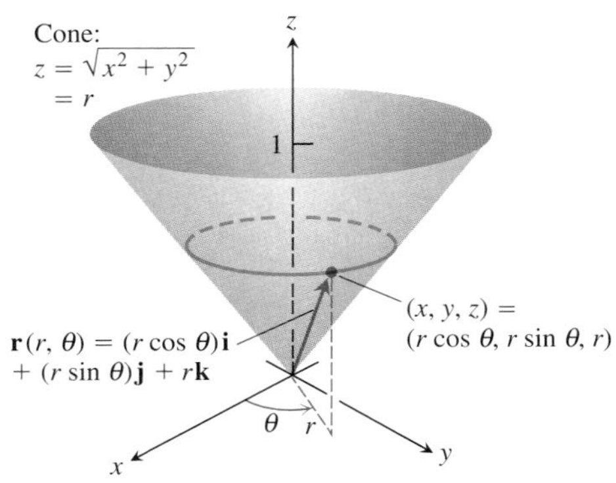

15.53 The cone in Example 1.

Parametrizations of Surfaces

Let

$$\mathbf{r}(u, v) = f(u, v)\,\mathbf{i} + g(u, v)\,\mathbf{j} + h(u, v)\,\mathbf{k} \tag{3}$$

be a continuous vector function that is defined on a region R in the uv-plane and one-to-one on the interior of R (Fig. 15.52). We call the range of $\mathbf{r}$ the **surface** S defined or traced by $\mathbf{r}$, and Eq. (3) together with the domain R constitute a **parametrization** of the surface. The variables u and v are the **parameters,** and R is the **parameter domain.** To simplify our discussion, we will take R to be a rectangle defined by inequalities of the form $a \le u \le b$, $c \le v \le d$. The requirement that $\mathbf{r}$ be one-to-one on the interior of R ensures that S does not cross itself. Notice that Eq. (3) is the vector equivalent of *three* parametric equations:

$$x = f(u, v), \qquad y = g(u, v), \qquad z = h(u, v). \tag{4}$$

EXAMPLE 1 Find a parametrization of the cone

$$z = \sqrt{x^2 + y^2}, \qquad 0 \le z \le 1.$$

Solution Here, cylindrical coordinates provide everything we need. A typical point (x, y, z) on the cone (Fig. 15.53) has $x = r\cos\theta$, $y = r\sin\theta$, and $z = \sqrt{x^2 + y^2} = r$, with $0 \le r \le 1$ and $0 \le \theta \le 2\pi$. Taking $u = r$ and $v = \theta$ in Eq. (3) gives the parametrization

$$\mathbf{r}(r, \theta) = (r\cos\theta)\,\mathbf{i} + (r\sin\theta)\,\mathbf{j} + r\mathbf{k}, \qquad 0 \le r \le 1, \quad 0 \le \theta \le 2\pi.$$

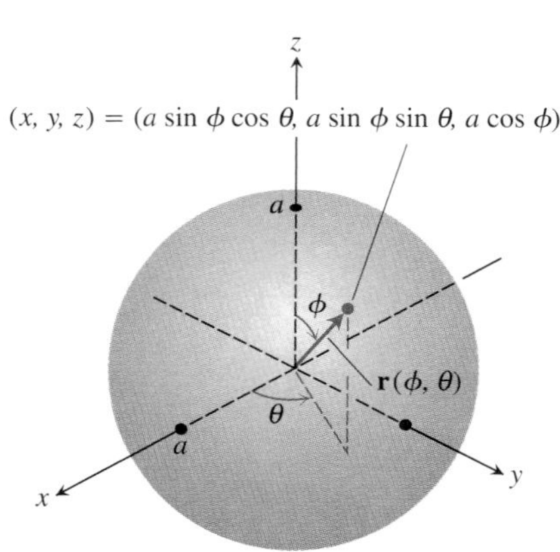

15.54 The sphere in Example 2.

EXAMPLE 2 Find a parametrization of the sphere $x^2 + y^2 + z^2 = a^2$.

Solution Spherical coordinates provide what we need. A typical point (x, y, z) on the sphere (Fig. 15.54) has $x = a\sin\phi\cos\theta$, $y = a\sin\phi\sin\theta$, and $z = a\cos\phi$, $0 \le \phi \le \pi$, $0 \le \theta \le 2\pi$. Taking $u = \phi$ and $v = \theta$ in Eq. (3) gives the

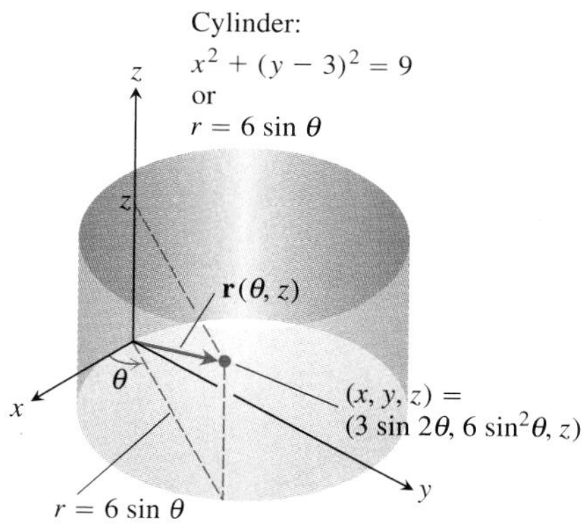

15.55 The cylinder in Example 3.

parametrization

$$\mathbf{r}(\phi, \theta) = (a \sin \phi \cos \theta)\, \mathbf{i} + (a \sin \phi \sin \theta)\, \mathbf{j} + (a \cos \phi)\, \mathbf{k},$$
$$0 \le \phi \le \pi, \quad 0 \le \theta \le 2\pi.$$

EXAMPLE 3 Find a parametrization of the cylinder

$$x^2 + (y - 3)^2 = 9, \qquad 0 \le z \le 5.$$

Solution In cylindrical coordinates, a point (x, y, z) has $x = r \cos \theta$, $y = r \sin \theta$, and $z = z$. For points on the cylinder $x^2 + (y - 3)^2 = 9$ (Fig. 15.55), $r = 6 \sin \theta$, $0 \le \theta \le \pi$ (Section 11.7, Example 5). A typical point on the cylinder therefore has coordinates

$$x = r \cos \theta = 6 \sin \theta \cos \theta = 3 \sin 2\theta$$
$$y = r \sin \theta = 6 \sin^2 \theta$$
$$z = z.$$

Taking $u = \theta$ and $v = z$ in Eq. (3) gives the parametrization

$$\mathbf{r}(\theta, z) = (3 \sin 2\theta)\, \mathbf{i} + (6 \sin^2 \theta)\, \mathbf{j} + z\, \mathbf{k},$$
$$0 \le \theta \le \pi, \quad 0 \le z \le 5.$$

Surface Area

Our goal is to find a double integral for calculating the area of a curved surface S based on the parametrization

$$\mathbf{r}(u, v) = f(u, v)\, \mathbf{i} + g(u, v)\, \mathbf{j} + h(u, v)\, \mathbf{k}, \qquad a \le u \le b, \quad c \le v \le d. \tag{5}$$

We need to assume that S is smooth enough for the construction we are about to carry out to work. The definition of smoothness involves the partial derivatives of $\mathbf{r}$ with respect to u and v:

$$\begin{aligned} \mathbf{r}_u &= \frac{\partial \mathbf{r}}{\partial u} = \frac{\partial f}{\partial u}\mathbf{i} + \frac{\partial g}{\partial u}\mathbf{j} + \frac{\partial h}{\partial u}\mathbf{k} \\ \mathbf{r}_v &= \frac{\partial \mathbf{r}}{\partial v} = \frac{\partial f}{\partial v}\mathbf{i} + \frac{\partial g}{\partial v}\mathbf{j} + \frac{\partial h}{\partial v}\mathbf{k}. \end{aligned} \tag{6}$$

DEFINITION

A parametrized surface $\mathbf{r}(u, v) = f(u, v)\, \mathbf{i} + g(u, v)\, \mathbf{j} + h(u, v)\, \mathbf{k}$ is **smooth** if $\mathbf{r}_u$ and $\mathbf{r}_v$ are continuous and $\mathbf{r}_u \times \mathbf{r}_v$ is never zero on the parameter domain.

Now consider a small rectangle ΔA_{uv} in R with sides on the lines $u = u_0$, $u = u_0 + \Delta u$, $v = v_0$, and $v = v_0 + \Delta v$ (Fig. 15.56 on the following page). Each side of ΔA_{uv} maps to a curve on the surface S, and together these four curves bound a "curved area element" $\Delta \sigma_{uv}$. In the notation of the figure, the side $v = v_0$ maps to curve C_1, the side $u = u_0$ maps to C_2, and their common vertex (u_0, v_0) maps to P_0. Figure 15.57 on the following page shows an enlarged view of $\Delta \sigma_{uv}$. The vector $\mathbf{r}_u(u_0, v_0)$ is tangent to C_1 at P_0. Likewise, $\mathbf{r}_v(u_0, v_0)$

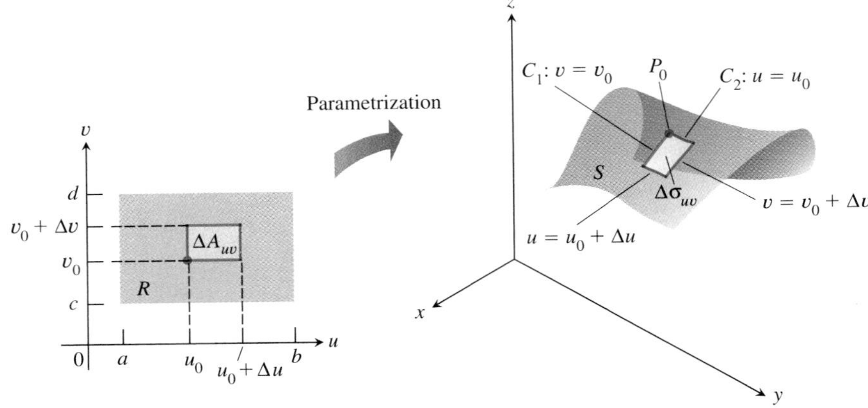

15.56 A rectangular area element ΔA_{uv} in the uv-plane maps onto a curved area element $\Delta \sigma_{uv}$ on S.

is tangent to C_2 at P_0. The cross product $\mathbf{r}_u \times \mathbf{r}_v$ is normal to the surface at P_0. (Here is where we begin to use the assumption that S is smooth. We want to be sure that $\mathbf{r}_u \times \mathbf{r}_v \neq \mathbf{0}$.)

We next approximate the surface element $\Delta\sigma_{uv}$ by the parallelogram on the tangent plane whose sides are determined by the vectors $\Delta u\, \mathbf{r}_u$ and $\Delta v\, \mathbf{r}_v$ (Fig. 15.58). The area of this parallelogram is

$$|\Delta u\, \mathbf{r}_u \times \Delta v\, \mathbf{r}_v| = |\mathbf{r}_u \times \mathbf{r}_v|\,\Delta u\, \Delta v. \tag{7}$$

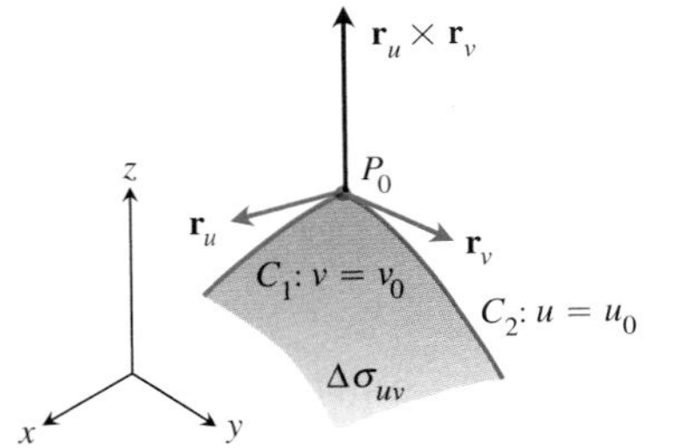

15.57 A magnified view of a surface area element $\Delta\sigma_{uv}$.

A partition of the region R in the uv-plane by rectangular regions ΔA_{uv} generates a partition of the surface S into surface area elements $\Delta\sigma_{uv}$. We approximate each surface element $\Delta\sigma_{uv}$ by the parallelogram area in Eq. (7) and sum these areas together to obtain an approximation of the area of S:

$$\sum_u \sum_v |\mathbf{r}_u \times \mathbf{r}_v|\, \Delta u\, \Delta v. \tag{8}$$

As Δu and Δv approach zero independently, the continuity of $\mathbf{r}_u$ and $\mathbf{r}_v$ guarantees that the sum in Eq. (8) approaches the double integral $\int_c^d \int_a^b |\mathbf{r}_u \times \mathbf{r}_v|\, du\, dv$. This double integral gives the area of the surface S.

Parametric Formula for the Area of a Smooth Surface

The area of the smooth surface

$$\mathbf{r}(u, v) = f(u, v)\,\mathbf{i} + g(u, v)\,\mathbf{j} + h(u, v)\,\mathbf{k}, \qquad a \le u \le b, \quad c \le v \le d$$

is

$$A = \int_c^d \int_a^b |\mathbf{r}_u \times \mathbf{r}_v|\, du\, dv. \tag{9}$$

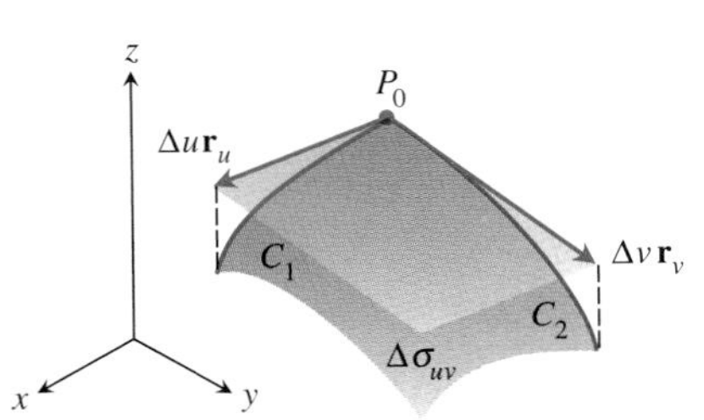

15.58 The parallelogram determined by the vectors $\Delta u\, \mathbf{r}_u$ and $\Delta v\, \mathbf{r}_v$ approximates the surface area element $\Delta\sigma_{uv}$.

This formula is consistent with other formulas for surface area, but we will omit the proof.

As in Section 15.5, we can abbreviate the integral in (9) by writing $d\sigma$ for $|\mathbf{r}_u \times \mathbf{r}_v|\, du\, dv$.

Surface Area Differential and the Differential Formula for Surface Area

$$d\sigma = |\mathbf{r}_u \times \mathbf{r}_v|\, du\, dv \qquad \iint_S d\sigma \tag{10}$$

surface area differential — differential formula for surface area

EXAMPLE 4 Find the surface area of the cone in Example 1 (Fig. 15.53).

Solution In Example 1 we found the parametrization

$$\mathbf{r}(r, \theta) = (r\cos\theta)\,\mathbf{i} + (r\sin\theta)\,\mathbf{j} + r\,\mathbf{k}, \qquad 0 \le r \le 1, \quad 0 \le \theta \le 2\pi.$$

To apply Eq. (9) we first find $\mathbf{r}_r \times \mathbf{r}_\theta$:

$$\mathbf{r}_r \times \mathbf{r}_\theta = \begin{vmatrix} \mathbf{i} & \mathbf{j} & \mathbf{k} \\ \cos\theta & \sin\theta & 1 \\ -r\sin\theta & r\cos\theta & 0 \end{vmatrix}$$

$$= -(r\cos\theta)\,\mathbf{i} - (r\sin\theta)\,\mathbf{j} + \underbrace{(r\cos^2\theta + r\sin^2\theta)}_{r}\,\mathbf{k}.$$

Thus, $\quad |\mathbf{r}_r \times \mathbf{r}_\theta| = \sqrt{r^2\cos^2\theta + r^2\sin^2\theta + r^2} = \sqrt{2r^2} = \sqrt{2}\,r.$

The area of the cone is

$$A = \int_0^{2\pi}\int_0^1 |\mathbf{r}_r \times \mathbf{r}_\theta|\, dr\, d\theta \qquad \text{Eq. (9) with } u = r,\ v = \theta$$

$$= \int_0^{2\pi}\int_0^1 \sqrt{2}\, r\, dr\, d\theta = \int_0^{2\pi} \frac{\sqrt{2}}{2}\, d\theta = \frac{\sqrt{2}}{2}(2\pi) = \pi\sqrt{2}.$$

EXAMPLE 5 Find the surface area of a sphere of radius a.

Solution We use the parametrization from Example 2:

$$\mathbf{r}(\phi, \theta) = (a\sin\phi\cos\theta)\,\mathbf{i} + (a\sin\phi\sin\theta)\,\mathbf{j} + (a\cos\phi)\,\mathbf{k},$$
$$0 \le \phi \le \pi, \quad 0 \le \theta \le 2\pi.$$

For $\mathbf{r}_\phi \times \mathbf{r}_\theta$ we get

$$\mathbf{r}_\phi \times \mathbf{r}_\theta = \begin{vmatrix} \mathbf{i} & \mathbf{j} & \mathbf{k} \\ a\cos\phi\cos\theta & a\cos\phi\sin\theta & -a\sin\phi \\ -a\sin\phi\sin\theta & a\sin\phi\cos\theta & 0 \end{vmatrix}$$

$$= (a^2\sin^2\phi\cos\theta)\,\mathbf{i} + (a^2\sin^2\phi\sin\theta)\,\mathbf{j} + (a^2\sin\phi\cos\phi)\,\mathbf{k}.$$

Thus,

$$|\mathbf{r}_\phi \times \mathbf{r}_\theta| = \sqrt{a^4\sin^4\phi\cos^2\theta + a^4\sin^4\phi\sin^2\theta + a^4\sin^2\phi\cos^2\phi}$$
$$= \sqrt{a^4\sin^4\phi + a^4\sin^2\phi\cos^2\phi}$$
$$= \sqrt{a^4\sin^2\phi(\sin^2\phi + \cos^2\phi)}$$
$$= a^2\sqrt{\sin^2\phi} = a^2\sin\phi,$$

since $\sin\phi \geq 0$ for $0 \leq \phi \leq \pi$. Therefore the area of the sphere is

$$\begin{aligned} A &= \int_0^{2\pi}\int_0^{\pi} a^2 \sin\phi \, d\phi \, d\theta \\ &= \int_0^{2\pi}\left[-a^2\cos\phi\right]_0^{\pi} d\theta \\ &= \int_0^{2\pi} 2a^2 \, d\theta = 4\pi a^2, \end{aligned}$$

in agreement with the standard formula from geometry.

Surface Integrals

Having found the formula for calculating the area of a parametrized surface, we can now integrate a function over the surface using the parametrized form.

DEFINITION

If S is a smooth surface defined parametrically as $\mathbf{r}(u, v) = f(u, v)\,\mathbf{i} + g(u, v)\,\mathbf{j} + h(u, v)\,\mathbf{k}$, $a \leq u \leq b$, $c \leq v \leq d$, and $G(x, y, z)$ is a continuous function defined on S, then the **integral of G over S** is

$$\iint_S G(x, y, z)\, d\sigma = \int_c^d \int_a^b G(f(u, v), g(u, v), h(u, v))\, |\mathbf{r}_u \times \mathbf{r}_v|\, du\, dv. \tag{11}$$

EXAMPLE 6 Integrate $G(x, y, z) = x^2$ over the cone $z = \sqrt{x^2 + y^2}$, $0 \leq z \leq 1$.

Solution Continuing the work in Examples 1 and 4, we have

$$|\mathbf{r}_r \times \mathbf{r}_\theta| = \sqrt{2}\, r$$

and

$$\begin{aligned} \iint_S x^2 \, d\sigma &= \int_0^{2\pi}\int_0^1 (r^2\cos^2\theta)(\sqrt{2}\, r)\, dr\, d\theta \qquad x = r\cos\theta \\ &= \sqrt{2}\int_0^{2\pi}\int_0^1 r^3 \cos^2\theta \, dr\, d\theta \\ &= \frac{\sqrt{2}}{4}\int_0^{2\pi} \cos^2\theta \, d\theta = \frac{\sqrt{2}}{4}\left[\frac{\theta}{2} + \frac{1}{4}\sin 2\theta\right]_0^{2\pi} = \frac{\pi\sqrt{2}}{4}. \end{aligned}$$

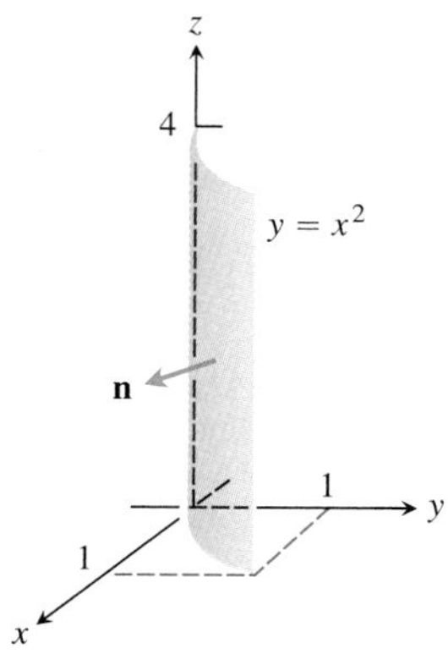

15.59 The parabolic surface in Example 7.

EXAMPLE 7 Find the flux of $\mathbf{F} = yz\,\mathbf{i} + x\,\mathbf{j} - z^2\,\mathbf{k}$ outward through the parabolic cylinder $y = x^2$, $0 \leq x \leq 1$, $0 \leq z \leq 4$ (Fig. 15.59).

Solution On the surface we have $x = x$, $y = x^2$, and $z = z$, so we automatically have the parametrization

$$\mathbf{r}(x, z) = x\,\mathbf{i} + x^2\,\mathbf{j} + z\,\mathbf{k}, \qquad 0 \leq x \leq 1, \quad 0 \leq z \leq 4.$$

The cross product of the tangent vectors is

$$\mathbf{r}_x \times \mathbf{r}_z = \begin{vmatrix} \mathbf{i} & \mathbf{j} & \mathbf{k} \\ 1 & 2x & 0 \\ 0 & 0 & 1 \end{vmatrix} = 2x\,\mathbf{i} - \mathbf{j}.$$

The unit normal pointing outward from the surface is

$$\mathbf{n} = \frac{\mathbf{r}_x \times \mathbf{r}_z}{|\mathbf{r}_x \times \mathbf{r}_z|} = \frac{2x\mathbf{i} - \mathbf{j}}{\sqrt{4x^2 + 1}}.$$

On the surface, $y = x^2$, so the vector field is

$$\mathbf{F} = yz\,\mathbf{i} + x\mathbf{j} - z^2\,\mathbf{k} = x^2 z\,\mathbf{i} + x\,\mathbf{j} - z^2\,\mathbf{k}.$$

Thus, $$\mathbf{F} \cdot \mathbf{n} = \frac{1}{\sqrt{4x^2+1}}\left[(x^2 z)(2x) + (x)(-1) + 0\right] = \frac{2x^3 z - x}{\sqrt{4x^2+1}}.$$

The flux of $\mathbf{F}$ outward through the surface is

$$\begin{aligned}
\iint_S \mathbf{F} \cdot \mathbf{n}\, d\sigma &= \int_0^4 \int_0^1 \frac{2x^3 z - x}{\sqrt{4x^2+1}} |\mathbf{r}_x \times \mathbf{r}_z|\, dx\, dz \\
&= \int_0^4 \int_0^1 \frac{2x^3 z - x}{\sqrt{4x^2+1}} \sqrt{4x^2+1}\, dx\, dz \\
&= \int_0^4 \int_0^1 (2x^3 z - x)\, dx\, dz = \int_0^4 \left[\frac{1}{2}x^4 z - \frac{1}{2}x^2\right]_{x=0}^{x=1} dz \\
&= \int_0^4 \frac{1}{2}(z-1)\, dz = \frac{1}{4}(z-1)^2\Big|_0^4 = \frac{1}{4}(9) - \frac{1}{4}(1) = 2.
\end{aligned}$$

EXAMPLE 8 Find the center of mass of a thin shell of constant density δ cut from the cone $z = \sqrt{x^2 + y^2}$ by the planes $z = 1$ and $z = 2$ (Fig. 15.60).

Solution The symmetry of the surface about the z-axis tells us that $\bar{x} = \bar{y} = 0$. We find $\bar{z} = M_{xy}/M$. Working as in Examples 1 and 4 we have

$$\mathbf{r}(r, \theta) = r\cos\theta\,\mathbf{i} + r\sin\theta\,\mathbf{j} + r\mathbf{k}, \qquad 1 \le r \le 2, \quad 0 \le \theta \le 2\pi,$$

and $$|\mathbf{r}_r \times \mathbf{r}_\theta| = \sqrt{2}\, r.$$

Therefore,

$$\begin{aligned}
M &= \iint_S \delta\, d\sigma = \int_0^{2\pi} \int_1^2 \delta\sqrt{2}\, r\, dr\, d\theta \\
&= \delta\sqrt{2} \int_0^{2\pi} \left[\frac{r^2}{2}\right]_1^2 d\theta = \delta\sqrt{2}\int_0^{2\pi}\left(2 - \frac{1}{2}\right) d\theta \\
&= \delta\sqrt{2}\left[\frac{3\theta}{2}\right]_0^{2\pi} = 3\pi\,\delta\sqrt{2},
\end{aligned}$$

$$\begin{aligned}
M_{xy} &= \iint_S \delta z\, d\sigma = \int_0^{2\pi}\int_1^2 \delta r\sqrt{2}\, r\, dr\, d\theta \\
&= \delta\sqrt{2}\int_0^{2\pi}\int_1^2 r^2\, dr\, d\theta = \delta\sqrt{2}\int_0^{2\pi}\left[\frac{r^3}{3}\right]_1^2 d\theta \\
&= \delta\sqrt{2}\int_0^{2\pi} \frac{7}{3}\, d\theta = \frac{14}{3}\pi\,\delta\sqrt{2},
\end{aligned}$$

$$\bar{z} = \frac{M_{xy}}{M} = \frac{14\pi\,\delta\sqrt{2}}{3(3\pi\,\delta\sqrt{2})} = \frac{14}{9}.$$

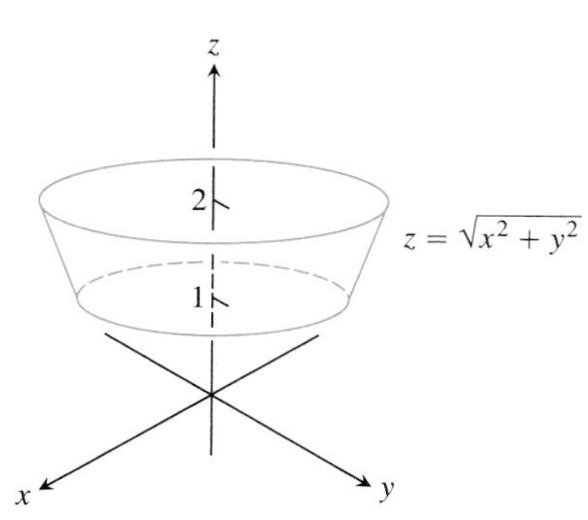

15.60 The cone frustum in Example 8.

The shell's center of mass is the point (0, 0, 14/9).

Exercises 15.6

In Exercises 1–16, find a parametrization of the surface. (There are many correct ways to do these, so your answers may not be the same as those in the back of the book.)

1. The paraboloid $z = x^2 + y^2$, $z \le 4$
2. The paraboloid $z = 9 - x^2 - y^2$, $z \ge 0$
3. The first-octant portion of the cone $z = \sqrt{x^2 + y^2}/2$ between the planes $z = 0$ and $z = 3$
4. The portion of the cone $z = 2\sqrt{x^2 + y^2}$ between the planes $z = 2$ and $z = 4$
5. The cap cut from the sphere $x^2 + y^2 + z^2 = 9$ by the cone $z = \sqrt{x^2 + y^2}$
6. The portion of the sphere $x^2 + y^2 + z^2 = 4$ in the first octant between the xy-plane and the cone $z = \sqrt{x^2 + y^2}$
7. The portion of the sphere $x^2 + y^2 + z^2 = 3$ between the planes $z = \sqrt{3}/2$ and $z = -\sqrt{3}/2$
8. The upper portion cut from the sphere $x^2 + y^2 + z^2 = 8$ by the plane $z = -2$
9. The surface cut from the parabolic cylinder $z = 4 - y^2$ by the planes $x = 0$, $x = 2$, and $z = 0$
10. The surface cut from the parabolic cylinder $y = x^2$ by the planes $z = 0$, $z = 3$, and $y = 2$
11. The portion of the cylinder $y^2 + z^2 = 9$ between the planes $x = 0$ and $x = 3$
12. The portion of the cylinder $x^2 + z^2 = 4$ above the xy-plane between the planes $y = -2$ and $y = 2$
13. The portion of the plane $x + y + z = 1$
    a) inside the cylinder $x^2 + y^2 = 9$
    b) inside the cylinder $y^2 + z^2 = 9$
14. The portion of the plane $x - y + 2z = 2$
    a) inside the cylinder $x^2 + z^2 = 3$
    b) inside the cylinder $y^2 + z^2 = 2$
15. The portion of the cylinder $(x - 2)^2 + z^2 = 4$ between the planes $y = 0$ and $y = 3$
16. The portion of the cylinder $y^2 + (z - 5)^2 = 25$ between the planes $x = 0$ and $x = 10$

In Exercises 17–26, use a parametrization to express the area of the surface as a double integral. Then evaluate the integral. (There are many correct ways to set up the integrals, so your integrals may not be the same as those in the back of the book. They should have the same values, however.)

17. The portion of the plane $y + 2z = 2$ inside the cylinder $x^2 + y^2 = 1$
18. The portion of the plane $z = -x$ inside the cylinder $x^2 + y^2 = 4$
19. The portion of the cone $z = 2\sqrt{x^2 + y^2}$ between the planes $z = 2$ and $z = 6$
20. The portion of the cone $z = \sqrt{x^2 + y^2}/3$ between the planes $z = 1$ and $z = 4/3$
21. The portion of the cylinder $x^2 + y^2 = 1$ between the planes $z = 1$ and $z = 4$
22. The portion of the cylinder $x^2 + z^2 = 10$ between the planes $y = -1$ and $y = 1$
23. The cap cut from the paraboloid $z = 2 - x^2 - y^2$ by the cone $z = \sqrt{x^2 + y^2}$
24. The portion of the paraboloid $z = x^2 + y^2$ between the planes $z = 1$ and $z = 4$
25. The lower portion cut from the sphere $x^2 + y^2 + z^2 = 2$ by the cone $z = \sqrt{x^2 + y^2}$
26. The portion of the sphere $x^2 + y^2 + z^2 = 4$ between the planes $z = -1$ and $z = \sqrt{3}$

In Exercises 27–34, integrate the given function over the given surface.

27. $G(x, y, z) = x$, over the parabolic cylinder $y = x^2$, $0 \le x \le 2$, $0 \le z \le 3$
28. $G(x, y, z) = z$, over the cylindrical surface $y^2 + z^2 = 4$, $z \ge 0$, $1 \le x \le 4$
29. $G(x, y, z) = x^2$, over the unit sphere $x^2 + y^2 + z^2 = 1$
30. $G(x, y, z) = z^2$, over the hemisphere $x^2 + y^2 + z^2 = a^2$, $z \ge 0$
31. $F(x, y, z) = z$, over the portion of the plane $x + y + z = 4$ that lies above the square $0 \le x \le 1$, $0 \le y \le 1$, in the xy-plane
32. $F(x, y, z) = z - x$, over the cone $z = \sqrt{x^2 + y^2}$, $0 \le z \le 1$
33. $H(x, y, z) = x^2\sqrt{5 - 4z}$, over the parabolic dome $z = 1 - x^2 - y^2$, $z \ge 0$
34. $H(x, y, z) = yz$, over the part of the sphere $x^2 + y^2 + z^2 = 4$ that lies above the cone $z = \sqrt{x^2 + y^2}$

In Exercises 35–44, use a parametrization to find the flux $\iint_S \mathbf{F} \cdot \mathbf{n}\, d\sigma$ across the surface in the given direction.

35. $\mathbf{F} = z^2\mathbf{i} + x\mathbf{j} - 3z\mathbf{k}$ outward (normal away from the x-axis) through the surface cut from the parabolic cylinder $z = 4 - y^2$ by the planes $x = 0$, $x = 1$, and $z = 0$
36. $\mathbf{F} = x^2\mathbf{j} - xz\mathbf{k}$ outward (normal away from the yz-plane) through the surface cut from the parabolic cylinder $y = x^2$, $-1 \le x \le 1$, by the planes $z = 0$ and $z = 2$
37. $\mathbf{F} = z\mathbf{k}$ across the portion of the sphere $x^2 + y^2 + z^2 = a^2$ in the first octant in the direction away from the origin
38. $\mathbf{F} = x\mathbf{i} + y\mathbf{j} + z\mathbf{k}$ across the sphere $x^2 + y^2 + z^2 = a^2$ in the direction away from the origin
39. $\mathbf{F} = 2xy\mathbf{i} + 2yz\mathbf{j} + 2xz\mathbf{k}$ upward across the portion of the plane $x + y + z = 2a$ that lies above the square $0 \le x \le a$, $0 \le y \le a$, in the xy-plane

40. $\mathbf{F} = x\,\mathbf{i} + y\,\mathbf{j} + z\,\mathbf{k}$ outward through the portion of the cylinder $x^2 + y^2 = 1$ cut by the planes $z = 0$ and $z = a$

41. $\mathbf{F} = xy\,\mathbf{i} - z\,\mathbf{k}$ outward (normal away from the z-axis) through the cone $z = \sqrt{x^2 + y^2}$, $0 \le z \le 1$

42. $\mathbf{F} = y^2\,\mathbf{i} + xz\,\mathbf{j} - \mathbf{k}$ outward (normal away from the z-axis) through the cone $z = 2\sqrt{x^2 + y^2}$, $0 \le z \le 2$

43. $\mathbf{F} = -x\,\mathbf{i} - y\,\mathbf{j} + z^2\,\mathbf{k}$ outward (normal away from the z-axis) through the portion of the cone $z = \sqrt{x^2 + y^2}$ between the planes $z = 1$ and $z = 2$

44. $\mathbf{F} = 4x\,\mathbf{i} + 4y\,\mathbf{j} + 2\,\mathbf{k}$ outward (normal away from the z-axis) through the surface cut from the bottom of the paraboloid $z = x^2 + y^2$ by the plane $z = 1$

45. Find the centroid of the portion of the sphere $x^2 + y^2 + z^2 = a^2$ that lies in the first octant.

46. Find the center of mass and the moment of inertia and radius of gyration about the z-axis of a thin shell of constant density δ cut from the cone $x^2 + y^2 - z^2 = 0$ by the planes $z = 1$ and $z = 2$.

47. Find the moment of inertia about the z-axis of a thin spherical shell $x^2 + y^2 + z^2 = a^2$ of constant density δ.

48. Find the moment of inertia about the z-axis of a thin conical shell $z = \sqrt{x^2 + y^2}$, $0 \le z \le 1$, of constant density δ.

TANGENT PLANES

The tangent plane at a point $P_0\,(f(u_0, v_0), g(u_0, v_0), h(u_0, v_0))$ on a parametrized surface $\mathbf{r}(u, v) = f(u, v)\,\mathbf{i} + g(u, v)\,\mathbf{j} + h(u, v)\,\mathbf{k}$ is the plane through P_0 normal to the vector $\mathbf{r}_u(u_0, v_0) \times \mathbf{r}_v(u_0, v_0)$, which is the cross product of the tangent vectors $\mathbf{r}_u(u_0, v_0)$ and $\mathbf{r}_v(u_0, v_0)$ at P_0. In Exercises 49–52, find an equation for the plane that is tangent to the surface at the given point P_0. Then find a Cartesian equation for the surface and sketch the surface and tangent plane together.

49. The cone $\mathbf{r}(r, \theta) = (r\cos\theta)\,\mathbf{i} + (r\sin\theta)\,\mathbf{j} + r\,\mathbf{k}$, $r \ge 0$, $0 \le \theta \le 2\pi$ at the point $P_0\left(\sqrt{2}, \sqrt{2}, 2\right)$ corresponding to $(r, \theta) = (2, \pi/4)$

50. The hemisphere surface $\mathbf{r}(\phi, \theta) = (4\sin\phi\cos\theta)\,\mathbf{i} + (4\sin\phi\sin\theta)\,\mathbf{j} + (4\cos\phi)\,\mathbf{k}$, $0 \le \phi \le \pi/2$, $0 \le \theta \le 2\pi$, at the point $P_0\left(\sqrt{2}, \sqrt{2}, 2\sqrt{3}\right)$ corresponding to $(\phi, \theta) = (\pi/6, \pi/4)$

51. The circular cylinder $\mathbf{r}(\theta, z) = (3\sin 2\theta)\,\mathbf{i} + (6\sin^2\theta)\,\mathbf{j} + z\,\mathbf{k}$, $0 \le \theta \le \pi$, at the point $P_0\left(\frac{3\sqrt{3}}{2}, \frac{9}{2}, 0\right)$ corresponding to $(\theta, z) = (\pi/3, 0)$ (See Example 3.)

52. The parabolic cylinder surface $\mathbf{r}(x, y) = x\,\mathbf{i} + y\,\mathbf{j} - x^2\,\mathbf{k}$, $-\infty < x < \infty$, $-\infty < y < \infty$, at the point $P_0\,(1, 2, -1)$ corresponding to $(x, y) = (1, 2)$

Writing for Your Own Knowledge

Answer the following questions in writing. Some answers will take only a sentence or two; others may require several paragraphs. Some explanations may also call for graphs or sketches.

1. What is a parametrized surface?
2. How do you find the area of a parametrized surface?
3. How do you integrate a function over a parametrized surface?

15.7 *Stokes's Theorem*

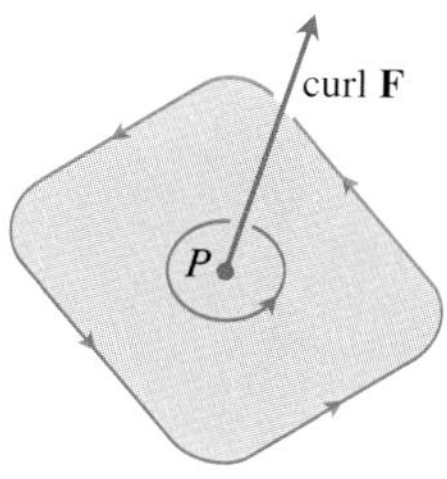

15.61 The circulation vector at a point P in a plane in a three-dimensional fluid flow. Notice its right-hand relation to the circulation line.

As we saw in Section 15.4, the circulation density or curl of a two-dimensional field $\mathbf{F} = M\,\mathbf{i} + N\,\mathbf{j}$ at a point (x, y) is described by the scalar quantity $(\partial N/\partial x - \partial M/\partial y)$. In three dimensions, the circulation around a point P in a plane is described with a vector. This vector is normal to the plane of the circulation (Fig. 15.61) and points in the direction that gives it a right-hand relation to the circulation line. The length of the vector gives the rate of the fluid's rotation, which usually varies as the circulation plane is tilted about P. It turns out that the vector of greatest circulation in a flow with velocity field $\mathbf{F} = M\mathbf{i} + N\mathbf{j} + P\mathbf{k}$ is

$$\text{curl}\,\mathbf{F} = \left(\frac{\partial P}{\partial y} - \frac{\partial N}{\partial z}\right)\mathbf{i} + \left(\frac{\partial M}{\partial z} - \frac{\partial P}{\partial x}\right)\mathbf{j} + \left(\frac{\partial N}{\partial x} - \frac{\partial M}{\partial y}\right)\mathbf{k}. \qquad (1)$$

We get this information from Stokes's theorem, the generalization of the circulation-curl form of Green's theorem to space.

In this section we present Stokes's theorem and investigate what it says about circulation. We also see how Stokes's theorem sometimes enables us to evaluate a line integral around a loop in space by calculating an easier surface integral. This is similar to the way we use Green's theorem to evaluate a line integral over a complicated curve in the plane by calculating an easier double integral over the region enclosed by the curve. In addition, we will conclude our discussion of conservative fields.

George Gabriel Stokes

Sir George Gabriel Stokes (1819–1903), one of the most influential scientific figures of his century, was Lucasian Professor of Mathematics at Cambridge University from 1849 until his death in 1903. His theoretical and experimental investigations covered hydrodynamics, elasticity, light, gravity, sound, heat, meteorology, and solar physics. He left electricity and magnetism to his friend William Thomson, Baron Kelvin of Largs. It is another one of those delightful quirks of history that the theorem we call Stokes's theorem isn't his theorem at all. He learned of it from Thomson in 1850 and a few years later included it among the questions on an examination he wrote for the Smith Prize. It has been known as Stokes's theorem ever since. As usual, things have balanced out. Stokes was the original discoverer of the principles of spectrum analysis that we now credit to Bunsen and Kirchhoff.

Del Notation

The formula for curl **F** in Eq. (1) is usually written in a shorter form, using the symbolic operator

$$\nabla = \mathbf{i}\frac{\partial}{\partial x} + \mathbf{j}\frac{\partial}{\partial y} + \mathbf{k}\frac{\partial}{\partial z}. \tag{2}$$

(The symbol ∇ is pronounced "del.") The curl of **F** is $\nabla \times \mathbf{F}$:

$$\begin{aligned}\nabla \times \mathbf{F} &= \begin{vmatrix} \mathbf{i} & \mathbf{j} & \mathbf{k} \\ \dfrac{\partial}{\partial x} & \dfrac{\partial}{\partial y} & \dfrac{\partial}{\partial z} \\ M & N & P \end{vmatrix} \\ &= \left(\frac{\partial P}{\partial y} - \frac{\partial N}{\partial z}\right)\mathbf{i} + \left(\frac{\partial M}{\partial z} - \frac{\partial P}{\partial x}\right)\mathbf{j} + \left(\frac{\partial N}{\partial x} - \frac{\partial M}{\partial y}\right)\mathbf{k} \qquad (3) \\ &= \operatorname{curl} \mathbf{F}.\end{aligned}$$

$$\operatorname{curl} \mathbf{F} = \nabla \times \mathbf{F} \tag{4}$$

EXAMPLE 1 Find the curl of $\mathbf{F} = (x^2 - y)\,\mathbf{i} + 4z\,\mathbf{j} + x^2\,\mathbf{k}$.

Solution

$$\begin{aligned}\operatorname{curl} \mathbf{F} = \nabla \times \mathbf{F} &= \begin{vmatrix} \mathbf{i} & \mathbf{j} & \mathbf{k} \\ \dfrac{\partial}{\partial x} & \dfrac{\partial}{\partial y} & \dfrac{\partial}{\partial z} \\ x^2 - y & 4z & x^2 \end{vmatrix} \qquad \text{Eq. (4)} \\ &= \left(\frac{\partial}{\partial y}(x^2) - \frac{\partial}{\partial z}(4z)\right)\mathbf{i} - \left(\frac{\partial}{\partial x}(x^2) - \frac{\partial}{\partial z}(x^2 - y)\right)\mathbf{j} \\ &\qquad + \left(\frac{\partial}{\partial x}(4z) - \frac{\partial}{\partial y}(x^2 - y)\right)\mathbf{k} \\ &= (0 - 4)\,\mathbf{i} - (2x - 0)\,\mathbf{j} + (0 + 1)\,\mathbf{k} \\ &= -4\,\mathbf{i} - 2x\,\mathbf{j} + \mathbf{k}\end{aligned}$$

As we will see, the operator ∇ has a number of other applications. For instance, when applied to a scalar function $f(x, y, z)$, it gives the gradient of f:

$$\nabla f = \frac{\partial f}{\partial x}\,\mathbf{i} + \frac{\partial f}{\partial y}\,\mathbf{j} + \frac{\partial f}{\partial z}\,\mathbf{k}.$$

This may now be read as "del f" as well as "grad f."

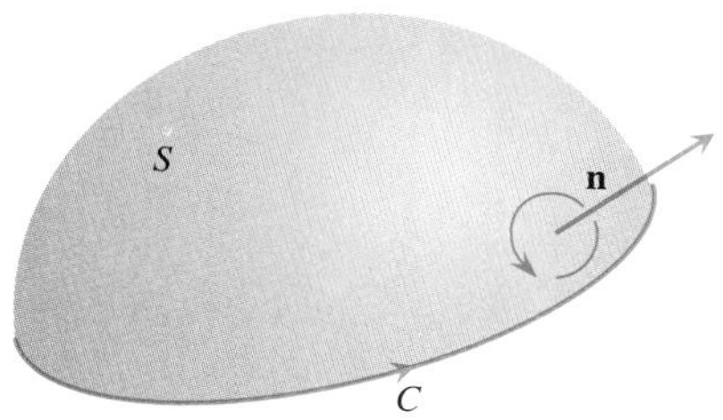

15.62 The orientation of the bounding curve C gives it a right-handed relation to the normal field $\mathbf{n}$.

Stokes's Theorem

Stokes's theorem says that, under conditions normally met in practice, the circulation of a vector field around the boundary of an oriented surface in space in the direction counterclockwise with respect to the surface's unit normal vector field $\mathbf{n}$ (Fig. 15.62) is equal to the double integral of the normal component of the curl of the field over the surface.

THEOREM 5

Stokes's Theorem

The circulation of $\mathbf{F} = M\mathbf{i} + N\mathbf{j} + P\mathbf{k}$ around the boundary C of an oriented surface S in the direction counterclockwise with respect to the surface's unit normal vector $\mathbf{n}$ equals the integral of $\nabla \times \mathbf{F} \cdot \mathbf{n}$ over S.

$$\underbrace{\oint_C \mathbf{F} \cdot d\mathbf{r}}_{\text{counterclockwise circulation}} = \underbrace{\iint_S \nabla \times \mathbf{F} \cdot \mathbf{n}\, d\sigma}_{\text{curl integral}} \tag{5}$$

Notice from Eq. (5) that if two different oriented surfaces S_1 and S_2 have the same boundary C, then their curl integrals are equal:

$$\iint_{S_1} \nabla \times \mathbf{F} \cdot \mathbf{n}_1\, d\sigma = \iint_{S_2} \nabla \times \mathbf{F} \cdot \mathbf{n}_2\, d\sigma.$$

Both curl integrals equal the counterclockwise circulation integral on the left side of Eq. (5) as long as the unit normal vectors $\mathbf{n}_1$ and $\mathbf{n}_2$ correctly orient the surfaces.

Naturally, we need some mathematical restrictions on $\mathbf{F}$, C, and S to ensure the existence of the integrals in Stokes's equation. The usual restrictions are that all the functions and derivatives involved be continuous.

If C is a curve in the xy-plane, oriented counterclockwise, and R is the region in the xy-plane bounded by C, then $d\sigma = dx\, dy$ and

$$(\nabla \times \mathbf{F}) \cdot \mathbf{n} = (\nabla \times \mathbf{F}) \cdot \mathbf{k} = \left(\frac{\partial N}{\partial x} - \frac{\partial M}{\partial y}\right). \tag{6}$$

Under these conditions, Stokes's equation becomes

$$\oint_C \mathbf{F} \cdot d\mathbf{r} = \iint_R \left(\frac{\partial N}{\partial x} - \frac{\partial M}{\partial y}\right) dx\, dy,$$

which is the circulation-curl form of the equation in Green's theorem. Conversely, by reversing these steps we can rewrite the circulation-curl form of Green's theorem for two-dimensional fields in del notation as

$$\oint_C \mathbf{F} \cdot d\mathbf{r} = \iint_R \nabla \times \mathbf{F} \cdot \mathbf{k}\, dA. \tag{7}$$

See Fig. 15.63.

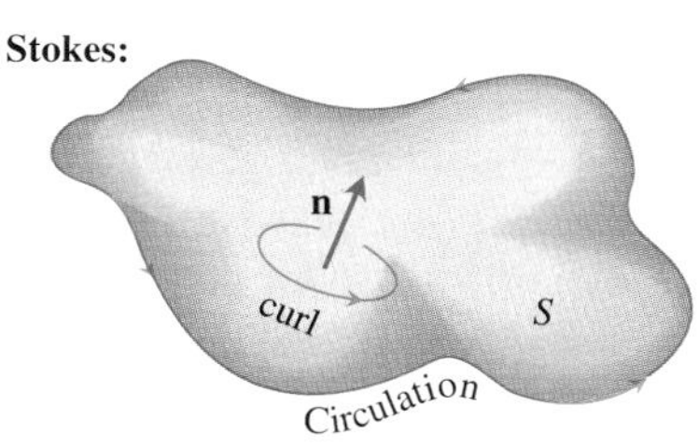

15.63 Green's theorem vs. Stokes's theorem.

EXAMPLE 2 Evaluate the two integrals in Stokes's theorem for the hemisphere S: $x^2 + y^2 + z^2 = 9$, $z \geq 0$, its bounding circle C: $x^2 + y^2 = 9$, $z = 0$, and the field

$$\mathbf{F} = y\,\mathbf{i} - x\,\mathbf{j}.$$

Solution We calculate the counterclockwise circulation around C (as viewed from above) using the parametrization

$$\mathbf{r} = (3\cos\theta)\,\mathbf{i} + (3\sin\theta)\,\mathbf{j}, \quad 0 \leq \theta \leq 2\pi.$$

We have

$$\begin{aligned}
d\mathbf{r} &= (-3\sin\theta\,d\theta)\,\mathbf{i} + (3\cos\theta\,d\theta)\,\mathbf{j} \\
\mathbf{F} &= y\,\mathbf{i} - x\,\mathbf{j} = (3\sin\theta)\,\mathbf{i} - (3\cos\theta)\,\mathbf{j} \\
\mathbf{F}\cdot d\mathbf{r} &= -9\sin^2\theta\,d\theta - 9\cos^2\theta\,d\theta = -9\,d\theta \\
\oint_C \mathbf{F}\cdot d\mathbf{r} &= \int_0^{2\pi} -9\,d\theta = -18\pi.
\end{aligned}$$

For the curl integral of $\mathbf{F}$, we have

$$\begin{aligned}
\nabla\times\mathbf{F} &= \left(\frac{\partial P}{\partial y} - \frac{\partial N}{\partial z}\right)\mathbf{i} + \left(\frac{\partial M}{\partial z} - \frac{\partial P}{\partial x}\right)\mathbf{j} + \left(\frac{\partial N}{\partial x} - \frac{\partial M}{\partial y}\right)\mathbf{k} \\
&= (0-0)\,\mathbf{i} + (0-0)\,\mathbf{j} + (-1-1)\,\mathbf{k} = -2\,\mathbf{k} \\
\mathbf{n} &= \frac{x\,\mathbf{i} + y\,\mathbf{j} + z\,\mathbf{k}}{\sqrt{x^2+y^2+z^2}} = \frac{x\,\mathbf{i} + y\,\mathbf{j} + z\,\mathbf{k}}{3} \qquad \text{Outer unit normal} \\
d\sigma &= \frac{3}{z}\,dA \qquad \text{Section 15.5, Example 5, with } a = 3 \\
\nabla\times\mathbf{F}\cdot\mathbf{n}\,d\sigma &= -\frac{2z}{3}\frac{3}{z}\,dA = -2\,dA
\end{aligned}$$

and

$$\iint_S \nabla\times\mathbf{F}\cdot\mathbf{n}\,d\sigma = \iint_{x^2+y^2\leq 9} -2\,dA = -18\pi.$$

The circulation around the circle equals the integral of the curl over the hemisphere, as it should.

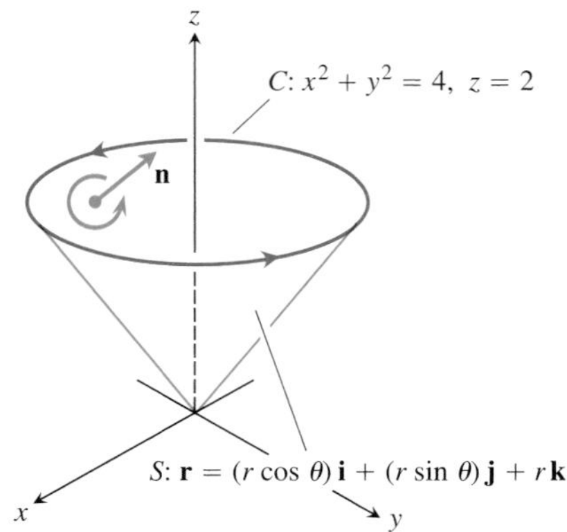

15.64 The curve C and cone S in Example 3.

EXAMPLE 3 Find the circulation of the field $\mathbf{F} = (x^2 - y)\,\mathbf{i} + 4z\,\mathbf{j} + x^2\,\mathbf{k}$ around the curve C in which the plane $z = 2$ meets the cone $z = \sqrt{x^2 + y^2}$, counterclockwise as viewed from above (Fig. 15.64).

Solution Stokes's theorem enables us to find the circulation by integrating over the surface of the cone. Traversing C in the counterclockwise direction viewed from above corresponds to taking the *inner* normal $\mathbf{n}$ to the cone (which has a positive z-component).

We parametrize the cone as

$$\mathbf{r} = (r\cos\theta)\,\mathbf{i} + (r\sin\theta)\,\mathbf{j} + r\,\mathbf{k}, \qquad 0 \leq r \leq 2, \quad 0 \leq \theta \leq 2\pi.$$

We then have

$$\begin{aligned}
\mathbf{n} &= \frac{\mathbf{r}_r \times \mathbf{r}_\theta}{|\mathbf{r}_r \times \mathbf{r}_\theta|} \\
&= \frac{-(r\cos\theta)\,\mathbf{i} - (r\sin\theta)\,\mathbf{j} + r\,\mathbf{k}}{r\sqrt{2}} && \text{Section 15.6, Example 4} \\
&= \frac{1}{\sqrt{2}}(-(\cos\theta)\,\mathbf{i} - (\sin\theta)\,\mathbf{j} + \mathbf{k}) \\
d\sigma &= r\sqrt{2}\,dr\,d\theta && \text{Section 15.6, Example 4} \\
\nabla \times \mathbf{F} &= -4\,\mathbf{i} - 2x\,\mathbf{j} + \mathbf{k} && \text{Example 1} \\
&= -4\,\mathbf{i} - 2r\cos\theta\,\mathbf{j} + \mathbf{k}. && x = r\cos\theta
\end{aligned}$$

Accordingly,

$$\begin{aligned}
\nabla \times \mathbf{F} \cdot \mathbf{n} &= \frac{1}{\sqrt{2}}(4\cos\theta + 2r\cos\theta\sin\theta + 1) \\
&= \frac{1}{\sqrt{2}}(4\cos\theta + r\sin 2\theta + 1)
\end{aligned}$$

and the circulation is

$$\begin{aligned}
\oint_C \mathbf{F} \cdot d\mathbf{r} &= \iint_S \nabla \times \mathbf{F} \cdot \mathbf{n}\,d\sigma && \text{Stokes's theorem} \\
&= \int_0^{2\pi}\int_0^2 \frac{1}{\sqrt{2}}\big(4\cos\theta + r\sin 2\theta + 1\big)\big(r\sqrt{2}\,dr\,d\theta\big) \\
&= 4\pi.
\end{aligned}$$

An Interpretation of $\nabla \times \mathbf{F}$

Stokes's theorem provides a visual interpretation of $\nabla \times \mathbf{F}$. Suppose that $\mathbf{v}(x, y, z)$ is the velocity of a moving fluid whose density at (x, y, z) is $\delta(x, y, z)$, and let $\mathbf{F} = \delta\mathbf{v}$. Then

$$\oint_C \mathbf{F} \cdot d\mathbf{r}$$

is the circulation of the fluid around the closed curve C. By Stokes's theorem, the circulation is equal to the flux of $\nabla \times \mathbf{F}$ through a surface S spanning C:

$$\oint_C \mathbf{F} \cdot d\mathbf{r} = \iint_S \nabla \times \mathbf{F} \cdot \mathbf{n}\,d\sigma.$$

Suppose we fix a point Q in the domain of $\mathbf{F}$ and a direction $\mathbf{u}$ at Q. Let C be a circle of radius ρ, with center at Q, whose plane is normal to $\mathbf{u}$. If $\nabla \times \mathbf{F}$ is continuous at Q, then the average value of the $\mathbf{u}$-component of $\nabla \times \mathbf{F}$ over the circular disk S bounded by C approaches the $\mathbf{u}$-component of $\nabla \times \mathbf{F}$ at Q as $\rho \to 0$:

$$(\nabla \times \mathbf{F} \cdot \mathbf{u})_Q = \lim_{\rho \to 0} \frac{1}{\pi\rho^2} \iint_S \nabla \times \mathbf{F} \cdot \mathbf{u}\,d\sigma. \tag{8}$$

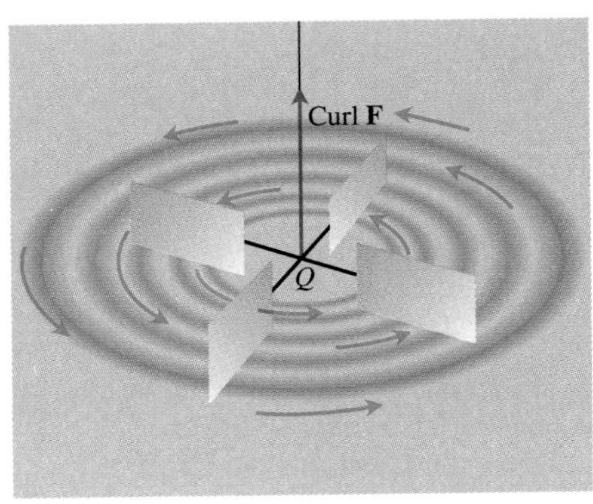

15.65 The paddle wheel interpretation of curl **F**.

If we replace the double integral on the right-hand side of Eq. (8) by the circulation, we get

$$(\nabla \times \mathbf{F} \cdot \mathbf{u})_Q = \lim_{\rho \to 0} \frac{1}{\pi \rho^2} \oint_C \mathbf{F} \cdot d\mathbf{r}. \tag{9}$$

The left-hand side of Eq. (9) has its maximum value when $\mathbf{u}$ is the direction of $\nabla \times \mathbf{F}$. When ρ is small, the limit on the right-hand side of Eq. (9) is approximately

$$\frac{1}{\pi \rho^2} \oint_C \mathbf{F} \cdot d\mathbf{r},$$

which is the circulation around C divided by the area of the disk (circulation density). Suppose that a small paddle wheel of radius ρ is introduced into the fluid at Q, with its axle directed along $\mathbf{u}$. The circulation of the fluid around C will affect the rate of spin of the paddle wheel. The wheel will spin fastest when the circulation integral is maximized; therefore it will spin fastest when the axle of the paddle wheel points in the direction of $\nabla \times \mathbf{F}$ (Fig. 15.65).

EXAMPLE 4 A fluid of constant density δ rotates around the z-axis with velocity $\mathbf{v} = \omega(-y\,\mathbf{i} + x\,\mathbf{j})$, where ω is a positive constant called the *angular velocity* of the rotation (Fig. 15.66). If $\mathbf{F} = \delta\mathbf{v}$, find $\nabla \times \mathbf{F}$ and show its relation to the circulation density.

Solution With $\mathbf{F} = \delta\mathbf{v} = -\delta\omega y\,\mathbf{i} + \delta\omega x\,\mathbf{j}$,

$$\begin{aligned}\nabla \times \mathbf{F} &= \left(\frac{\partial P}{\partial y} - \frac{\partial N}{\partial z}\right)\mathbf{i} + \left(\frac{\partial M}{\partial z} - \frac{\partial P}{\partial x}\right)\mathbf{j} + \left(\frac{\partial N}{\partial x} - \frac{\partial M}{\partial y}\right)\mathbf{k} \\ &= (0 - 0)\,\mathbf{i} + (0 - 0)\,\mathbf{j} + (\delta\omega - (-\delta\omega))\,\mathbf{k} \\ &= 2\,\delta\omega\,\mathbf{k}.\end{aligned}$$

By Stokes's theorem, the circulation of $\mathbf{F}$ around a circle C of radius ρ bounding a disk S in a plane normal to $\nabla \times \mathbf{F}$, say the xy-plane, is

$$\oint_C \mathbf{F} \cdot d\mathbf{r} = \iint_S \nabla \times \mathbf{F} \cdot \mathbf{n}\, d\sigma = \iint_S 2\,\delta\omega\,\mathbf{k} \cdot \mathbf{k}\, dx\, dy = (2\,\delta\omega)(\pi\rho^2).$$

Thus,

$$(\nabla \times \mathbf{F}) \cdot \mathbf{k} = 2\,\delta\omega = \frac{1}{\pi\rho^2} \oint_C \mathbf{F} \cdot d\mathbf{r},$$

in agreement with Eq. (9) with $\mathbf{u} = \mathbf{k}$.

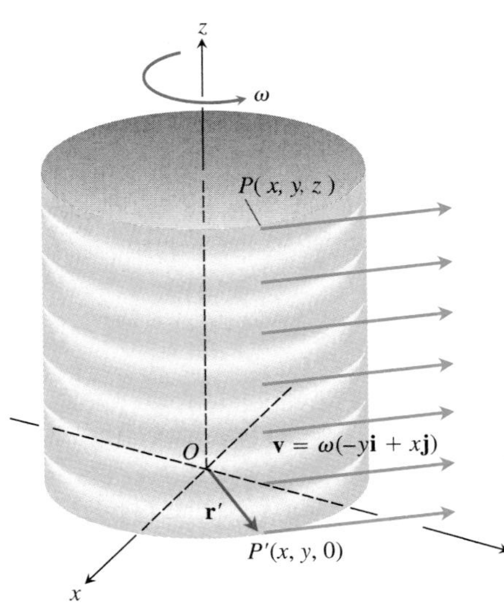

15.66 A steady rotational flow parallel to the xy-plane, with constant angular velocity ω in the positive (counterclockwise) direction.

EXAMPLE 5 Use Stokes's theorem to evaluate $\int_C \mathbf{F} \cdot d\mathbf{r}$, if $\mathbf{F} = xz\,\mathbf{i} + xy\,\mathbf{j} + 3xz\,\mathbf{k}$ and C is the boundary of the portion of the plane $2x + y + z = 2$ in the first octant, traversed counterclockwise as viewed from above (Fig. 15.67).

Solution The plane is the level surface $f(x, y, z) = 2$ of the function $f(x, y, z) = 2x + y + z$. The unit normal vector

$$\mathbf{n} = \frac{\nabla f}{|\nabla f|} = \frac{(2\,\mathbf{i} + \mathbf{j} + \mathbf{k})}{|2\,\mathbf{i} + \mathbf{j} + \mathbf{k}|} = \frac{1}{\sqrt{6}}(2\,\mathbf{i} + \mathbf{j} + \mathbf{k})$$

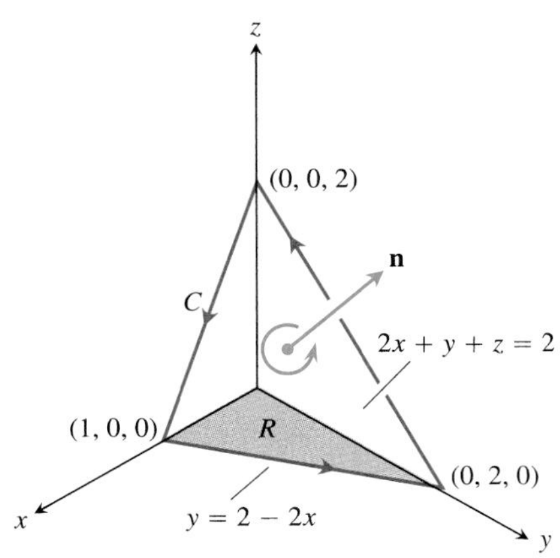

15.67 The planar surface in Example 5.

is consistent with counterclockwise motion around C (Fig. 15.67). To apply Stokes's theorem, we find

$$\operatorname{curl} \mathbf{F} = \nabla \times \mathbf{F} = \begin{vmatrix} \mathbf{i} & \mathbf{j} & \mathbf{k} \\ \dfrac{\partial}{\partial x} & \dfrac{\partial}{\partial y} & \dfrac{\partial}{\partial z} \\ xz & xy & 3xz \end{vmatrix} = (x - 3z)\,\mathbf{j} + y\,\mathbf{k}.$$

On the plane, z equals $2 - 2x - y$, so

$$\nabla \times \mathbf{F} = (x - 3(2 - 2x - y))\,\mathbf{j} + y\,\mathbf{k} = (7x + 3y - 6)\,\mathbf{j} + y\,\mathbf{k}$$

and
$$\nabla \times \mathbf{F} \cdot \mathbf{n} = \frac{1}{\sqrt{6}}(7x + 3y - 6 + y) = \frac{1}{\sqrt{6}}(7x + 4y - 6).$$

The surface area element is

$$d\sigma = \frac{|\nabla f|}{|\nabla f \cdot \mathbf{k}|}\,dA = \frac{\sqrt{6}}{1}\,dx\,dy.$$

The circulation is

$$\begin{aligned} \oint_C \mathbf{F} \cdot d\mathbf{r} &= \iint_S \nabla \times \mathbf{F} \cdot \mathbf{n}\,d\sigma \qquad \text{Stokes's theorem} \\ &= \int_0^1 \int_0^{2-2x} \frac{1}{\sqrt{6}}(7x + 4y - 6)\sqrt{6}\,dy\,dx \\ &= \int_0^1 \int_0^{2-2x} (7x + 4y - 6)\,dy\,dx \\ &= -1. \end{aligned}$$

Proof of Stokes's Theorem for Polyhedral Surfaces

Let S be a polyhedral surface consisting of a finite number of plane regions. (Think of one of Buckminster Fuller's geodesic domes.) We apply Green's theorem to each separate panel of S. There are two types of panels:

1. those that are surrounded on all sides by other panels, and
2. those that have one or more edges that are not adjacent to other panels.

The boundary Δ of S consists of those edges of the type 2 panels that are not adjacent to other panels. In Fig. 15.68, the triangles EAB, BCE, and CDE represent a part of S, with $ABCD$ part of the boundary Δ. Applying Green's theorem to the three triangles in turn and adding the results, we get

$$\left(\oint_{EAB} + \oint_{BCE} + \oint_{CDE}\right)\mathbf{F} \cdot d\mathbf{r} = \left(\iint_{EAB} + \iint_{BCE} + \iint_{CDE}\right)\nabla \times \mathbf{F} \cdot \mathbf{n}\,d\sigma. \tag{10}$$

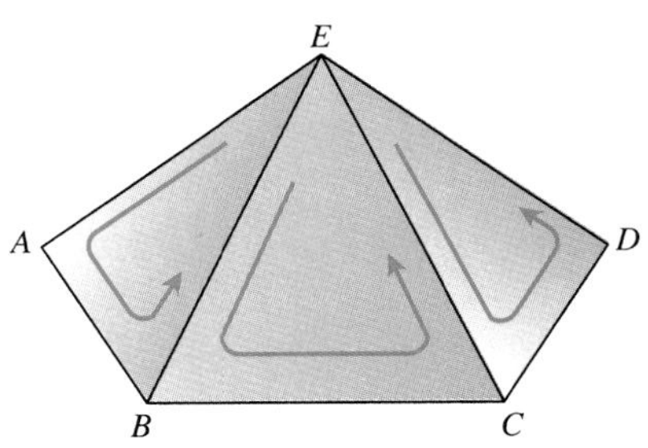

15.68 Part of a polyhedral surface.

The three line integrals on the left-hand side of Eq. (10) combine into a single line integral taken around the periphery $ABCDE$ because the integrals along interior segments cancel in pairs. For example, the integral along segment BE in triangle ABE is opposite in sign to the integral along the same segment in triangle EBC. Similarly for segment CE. Hence (10) reduces to

$$\oint_{ABCDE} \mathbf{F} \cdot d\mathbf{r} = \iint_{ABCDE} \nabla \times \mathbf{F} \cdot \mathbf{n}\,d\sigma.$$

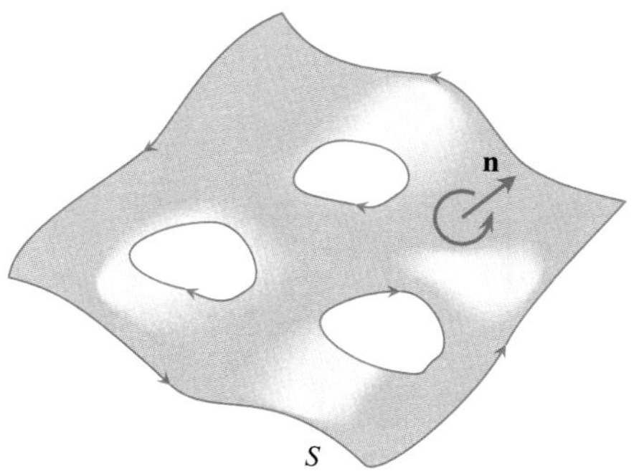

15.69 Stokes's theorem also holds for oriented surfaces with holes.

When we apply Green's theorem to all the panels and add the results, we get

$$\oint_{\Delta} \mathbf{F} \cdot d\mathbf{r} = \iint_{S} \nabla \times \mathbf{F} \cdot \mathbf{n} \, d\sigma. \tag{11}$$

This is Stokes's theorem for a polyhedral surface S. You can find proofs for more general surfaces in advanced calculus texts. ■

Stokes's Theorem for Surfaces with Holes

Stokes's theorem can be extended to an oriented surface S that has one or more holes in it (like a curved slice of Swiss cheese), in a way exactly analogous to the extension of Green's theorem: The surface integral over S of the normal component of $\nabla \times \mathbf{F}$ is equal to the sum of the line integrals around all the boundaries of S (including boundaries of the holes) of the tangential component of $\mathbf{F}$, where the boundary curves are to be traced in the positive direction induced by the positive orientation of S (Fig. 15.69).

An Important Identity

The identity

$$\text{curl grad} f = \mathbf{0} \qquad \text{or} \qquad \nabla \times \nabla f = \mathbf{0} \tag{12}$$

arises frequently in mathematics and the physical sciences. (We will use it ourselves in a moment.) It holds for any continuous function $f(x, y, z)$ whose first and second partial derivatives are continuous. The proof goes like this:

$$\nabla \times \nabla f = \begin{vmatrix} \mathbf{i} & \mathbf{j} & \mathbf{k} \\ \dfrac{\partial}{\partial x} & \dfrac{\partial}{\partial y} & \dfrac{\partial}{\partial z} \\ \dfrac{\partial f}{\partial x} & \dfrac{\partial f}{\partial y} & \dfrac{\partial f}{\partial z} \end{vmatrix} = (f_{zy} - f_{yz})\,\mathbf{i} - (f_{zx} - f_{xz})\,\mathbf{j} + (f_{yx} - f_{xy})\,\mathbf{k}. \tag{13}$$

When f and its first and second partial derivatives are continuous, the mixed second derivatives in parentheses are equal (Euler's theorem, Section 13.3) and the vector is zero.

Conservative Fields and Stokes's Theorem

In Section 15.3 we found that saying that a field $\mathbf{F}$ is conservative on an open region D in space is equivalent to saying that the integral of $\mathbf{F}$ around every closed loop in D is zero. This, in turn, is equivalent in a great many domains to saying that $\nabla \times \mathbf{F} = \mathbf{0}$, as we will now show.

THEOREM 6

If $\nabla \times \mathbf{F} = \mathbf{0}$ at every point of a simply connected open region D in space, then

$$\oint_{C} \mathbf{F} \cdot d\mathbf{r} = 0$$

on any piecewise smooth closed path C in D.

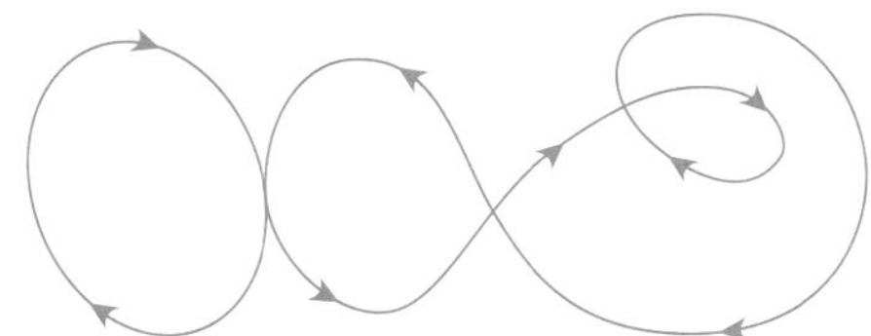

15.70 In a simply connected open region in space, differentiable curves that cross themselves can be divided into loops to which Stokes's theorem applies.

Sketch of a Proof Theorem 6 is usually proved in two steps. The first step is for simple closed curves. A theorem from topology, a branch of advanced mathematics, states that every differentiable simple closed curve C in a simply connected open region D is the boundary of a smooth two-sided surface S that also lies in D. Hence, by Stokes's theorem,

$$\oint_C \mathbf{F} \cdot d\mathbf{r} = \iint_S \nabla \times \mathbf{F} \cdot \mathbf{n}\, d\sigma = 0.$$

The second step is for curves that cross themselves, like the one in Fig. 15.70. The idea is to break these into simple loops spanned by orientable surfaces, apply Stokes's theorem one loop at a time, and add the results. ∎

The following diagram summarizes all of our results on conservative fields.

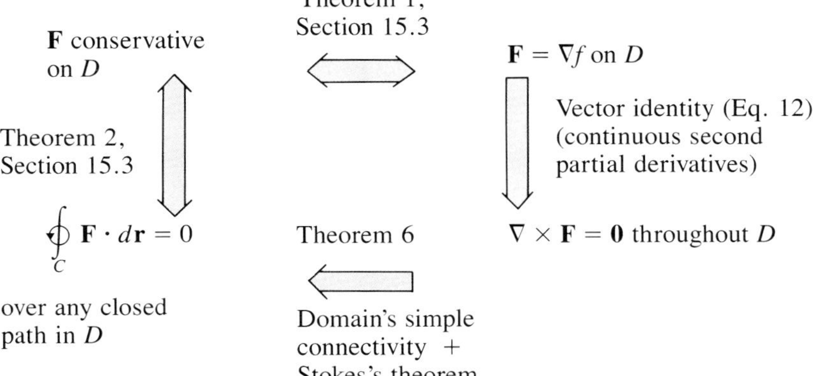

Exercises 15.7

In Exercises 1–6, use the surface integral in Stokes's theorem to calculate the circulation of the field $\mathbf{F}$ around the curve C in the indicated direction.

1. $\mathbf{F} = x^2\,\mathbf{i} + 2x\,\mathbf{j} + z^2\,\mathbf{k}$
C: The ellipse $4x^2 + y^2 = 4$ in the xy-plane, counterclockwise when viewed from above

2. $\mathbf{F} = 2y\,\mathbf{i} + 3x\,\mathbf{j} - z^2\,\mathbf{k}$
C: The circle $x^2 + y^2 = 9$ in the xy-plane, counterclockwise when viewed from above

3. $\mathbf{F} = y\,\mathbf{i} + xz\,\mathbf{j} + x^2\,\mathbf{k}$
C: The boundary of the triangle cut from the plane $x + y + z = 1$ by the first octant, counterclockwise when viewed from above

4. $\mathbf{F} = (y^2 + z^2)\,\mathbf{i} + (x^2 + z^2)\,\mathbf{j} + (x^2 + y^2)\,\mathbf{k}$
C: The boundary of the triangle cut from the plane $x + y + z = 1$ by the first octant, counterclockwise when viewed from above

5. $\mathbf{F} = (y^2 + z^2)\,\mathbf{i} + (x^2 + y^2)\,\mathbf{j} + (x^2 + y^2)\,\mathbf{k}$
C: The square bounded by the lines $x = \pm 1$ and $y = \pm 1$ in the xy-plane, counterclockwise when viewed from above

6. $\mathbf{F} = x^2y^3\,\mathbf{i} + \mathbf{j} + z\,\mathbf{k}$
C: The boundary of the circle $x^2 + y^2 = a^2$ in the xy-plane, counterclockwise when viewed from above

7. Let $\mathbf{n}$ be the outer unit normal of the elliptical shell

$$S:\quad 4x^2 + 9y^2 + 36z^2 = 36, \quad z \geq 0,$$

and let

$$\mathbf{F} = y\,\mathbf{i} + x^2\,\mathbf{j} + (x^2 + y^4)^{3/2} \sin e^{\sqrt{xyz}}\,\mathbf{k}.$$

Find the value of

$$\iint_S \nabla \times \mathbf{F} \cdot \mathbf{n}\, d\sigma.$$

(*Hint:* One parametrization of the ellipse at the base of the shell is $x = 3\cos t$, $y = 2\sin t$, $0 \leq t \leq 2\pi$.)

8. Let $\mathbf{n}$ be the outer unit normal (normal away from the origin) of the parabolic shell

$$S:\quad 4x^2 + y + z^2 = 4, \quad y \geq 0$$

and let

$$\mathbf{F} = \left(-z + \frac{1}{2 + x}\right)\mathbf{i} + (\tan^{-1} y)\,\mathbf{j} + \left(x + \frac{1}{4 + z}\right)\mathbf{k}.$$

Find the value of

$$\iint_S \nabla \times \mathbf{F} \cdot \mathbf{n}\, d\sigma.$$

9. Let S be the cylinder $x^2 + y^2 = a^2$, $0 \le z \le h$, together with its top, $x^2 + y^2 \le a^2$, $z = h$. Let $\mathbf{F} = -y\,\mathbf{i} + x\,\mathbf{j} + x^2\mathbf{k}$. Use Stokes's theorem to calculate the flux of $\nabla \times \mathbf{F}$ outward through S.

10. Evaluate

$$\iint_S \nabla \times (y\,\mathbf{i}) \cdot \mathbf{n}\, d\sigma,$$

where S is the hemisphere $x^2 + y^2 + z^2 = 1$, $z \ge 0$.

11. Show that

$$\iint_S \nabla \times \mathbf{F} \cdot \mathbf{n}\, d\sigma$$

has the same value for all oriented surfaces S that span C and that induce the same positive direction on C.

12. Show that if $\mathbf{F} = x\,\mathbf{i} + y\,\mathbf{j} + z\,\mathbf{k}$, then $\nabla \times \mathbf{F} = \mathbf{0}$.

13. Use the identity $\nabla \times \nabla f = \mathbf{0}$ (Eq. 12 in the text) and Stokes's theorem to show that the circulations of the following fields around the boundary of any smooth orientable surface in space are zero.

a) $\mathbf{F} = 2x\,\mathbf{i} + 2y\,\mathbf{j} + 2z\,\mathbf{k}$

b) $\mathbf{F} = \nabla(xy^2z^3)$

c) $\mathbf{F} = \nabla \times (x\,\mathbf{i} + y\,\mathbf{j} + z\,\mathbf{k})$

d) $\mathbf{F} = \nabla f$

14. Let $f(x, y, z) = (x^2 + y^2 + z^2)^{-1/2}$. Show that the clockwise circulation of the field $\mathbf{F} = \nabla f$ around the circle $x^2 + y^2 = a^2$ in the xy-plane is zero

a) by taking $\mathbf{r} = (a \cos t)\,\mathbf{i} + (a \sin t)\,\mathbf{j}$, $0 \le t \le 2\pi$, and integrating $\mathbf{F} \cdot d\mathbf{r}$ over the circle, and

b) by applying Stokes's theorem.

15. Let C be a simple closed smooth curve in the plane $2x + 2y + z = 2$, oriented as in Fig. 15.71. Show that

$$\oint_C 2y\,dx + 3z\,dy - x\,dz$$

depends only on the area of the region enclosed by C and not on the position or shape of C.

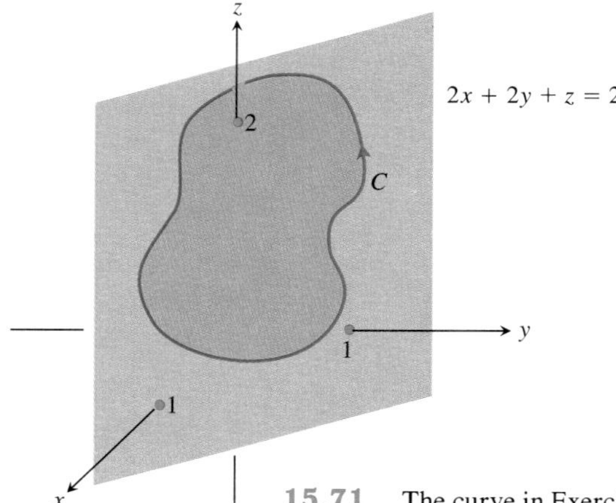

15.71 The curve in Exercise 15.

16. Let $\mathbf{F}$ be a differentiable vector field defined on a region containing a smooth closed oriented surface S and its interior. Let $\mathbf{n}$ be the unit normal vector field on S. Suppose that S is the union of two surfaces S_1 and S_2 joined along a smooth simple closed curve C. Can anything be said about

$$\iint_S \nabla \times \mathbf{F} \cdot \mathbf{n}\, d\sigma?$$

Give reasons for your answer.

17. Does Stokes's theorem say anything special about circulation in a field whose curl is zero? Give reasons for your answer.

18. Let R be a region in the xy-plane that is bounded by a piecewise smooth simple closed curve C, and suppose that the moments of inertia of R about the x- and y-axes are known to be I_x and I_y. Evaluate the line integral

$$\oint_C \nabla(r^4) \cdot \mathbf{n}\, ds,$$

where $r = \sqrt{x^2 + y^2}$, in terms of I_x and I_y.

19. Show that the curl of

$$\mathbf{F} = \frac{-y}{x^2 + y^2}\,\mathbf{i} + \frac{x}{x^2 + y^2}\,\mathbf{j} + z\,\mathbf{k}$$

is zero but that

$$\int_C \mathbf{F} \cdot d\mathbf{r}$$

is not zero if C is the circle $x^2 + y^2 = 1$ in the xy-plane. (Theorem 6 does not apply here because the domain of $\mathbf{F}$ is not simply connected. The field $\mathbf{F}$ is not defined along the z-axis so there is no way to contract C to a point without leaving the domain of $\mathbf{F}$.)

Writing for Your Own Knowledge

Answer the following questions in writing. Some answers will take only a sentence or two; others may require several paragraphs. Some explanations may also call for graphs or sketches.

1. What is Stokes's theorem about?
2. How can you interpret $\nabla \times \mathbf{F}$?
3. Summarize the chapter's results on conservative fields.

EXPLORER PROGRAM

Vector Fields	Displays two-dimensional vector fields and integrates the curl over rectangular regions. Also calculates flux across rectangular boundaries.

15.8 The Divergence Theorem

The divergence form of Green's theorem in the plane states that the net outward flux of a vector field across a simple closed curve can be calculated by integrating the divergence of the field over the region enclosed by the curve. The corresponding theorem in three dimensions, called the Divergence Theorem, states that the net outward flux of a vector field across a closed surface in space can be calculated by integrating the divergence of the field over the region enclosed by the surface. In this section, we prove the Divergence Theorem and show how it simplifies the calculation of flux. We also derive Gauss's law for flux in an electric field.

Divergence in Three Dimensions

The **divergence** of a vector field $\mathbf{F} = M(x, y, z)\,\mathbf{i} + N(x, y, z)\,\mathbf{j} + P(x, y, z)\,\mathbf{k}$ is the scalar function

$$\operatorname{div} \mathbf{F} = \nabla \cdot \mathbf{F} = \frac{\partial M}{\partial x} + \frac{\partial N}{\partial y} + \frac{\partial P}{\partial z}. \tag{1}$$

The symbol "div **F**" is read as "divergence of **F**" or "div **F**." The notation $\nabla \cdot \mathbf{F}$ is read "del dot **F**."

Div **F** has the same physical interpretation in three dimensions that it does in two. If **F** is the velocity field of a fluid flow, the value of div **F** at a point (x, y, z) is the rate at which fluid is being piped in or drained away at (x, y, z). The divergence is the flux per unit volume or flux density at the point.

EXAMPLE 1 Find the divergence of $\mathbf{F} = 2xz\,\mathbf{i} - xy\,\mathbf{j} - z\,\mathbf{k}$.

Solution The divergence of **F** is

$$\nabla \cdot \mathbf{F} = \frac{\partial}{\partial x}(2xz) - \frac{\partial}{\partial y}(xy) - \frac{\partial}{\partial z}(z) = 2z - x - 1.$$

The Divergence Theorem

The Divergence Theorem says that under suitable conditions the outward flux of a vector field across a closed surface (oriented outward) equals the triple integral of the divergence of the field over the region enclosed by the surface.

THEOREM 7

The Divergence Theorem

The flux of a vector field $\mathbf{F} = M\,\mathbf{i} + N\,\mathbf{j} + P\,\mathbf{k}$ across a closed oriented surface S in the direction of the surface's outward unit normal field **n** equals the integral of $\nabla \cdot \mathbf{F}$ over the region D enclosed by the surface:

$$\underbrace{\iint_S \mathbf{F} \cdot \mathbf{n}\, d\sigma}_{\text{outward flux}} = \underbrace{\iiint_D \nabla \cdot \mathbf{F}\, dV.}_{\text{divergence integral}} \tag{2}$$

The Divergence Theorem

Mikhail Vassilievich Ostrogradsky (1801–1862) was the first mathematician to publish a proof of the Divergence Theorem. Upon being denied his degree at Kharkhov University by the minister for religious affairs and national education (for atheism), Ostrogradsky left Russia for Paris in 1822, attracted by the presence of Laplace, Legendre, Fourier, Poisson, and Cauchy. While working on the theory of heat in the mid-1820s, he formulated the Divergence Theorem as a tool for converting volume integrals to surface integrals.

Carl Friedrich Gauss (1777–1855) had already proved the theorem while working on the theory of gravitation, but his notebooks were not to be published until many years later. (The theorem is sometimes called Gauss's theorem.) The list of Gauss's accomplishments in science and mathematics is truly astonishing, ranging from the invention of the electric telegraph (with Wilhelm Weber in 1833) to the development of a wonderfully accurate theory of planetary orbits and to work in non-Euclidean geometry that later became fundamental to Einstein's general theory of relativity.

EXAMPLE 2 Evaluate both sides of Eq. (2) for the field $\mathbf{F} = x\,\mathbf{i} + y\,\mathbf{j} + z\,\mathbf{k}$ over the sphere $x^2 + y^2 + z^2 = a^2$.

Solution The outer unit normal to S, calculated from the gradient of $f(x, y, z) = x^2 + y^2 + z^2 - a^2$, is

$$\mathbf{n} = \frac{2(x\,\mathbf{i} + y\,\mathbf{j} + z\,\mathbf{k})}{\sqrt{4(x^2 + y^2 + z^2)}} = \frac{x\,\mathbf{i} + y\,\mathbf{j} + z\,\mathbf{k}}{a}.$$

Hence,
$$\mathbf{F} \cdot \mathbf{n}\, d\sigma = \frac{x^2 + y^2 + z^2}{a}\, d\sigma = \frac{a^2}{a}\, d\sigma = a\, d\sigma$$

because $x^2 + y^2 + z^2 = a^2$ on the surface. Therefore

$$\iint_S \mathbf{F} \cdot \mathbf{n}\, d\sigma = \iint_S a\, d\sigma = a \iint_S d\sigma = a(4\pi a^2) = 4\pi a^3.$$

The divergence of $\mathbf{F}$ is

$$\nabla \cdot \mathbf{F} = \frac{\partial}{\partial x}(x) + \frac{\partial}{\partial y}(y) + \frac{\partial}{\partial z}(z) = 3,$$

so
$$\iiint_D \nabla \cdot \mathbf{F}\, dV = \iiint_D 3\, dV = 3\left(\frac{4}{3}\pi a^3\right) = 4\pi a^3.$$

EXAMPLE 3 Calculate the flux of the field $\mathbf{F} = xy\,\mathbf{i} + yz\,\mathbf{j} + xz\,\mathbf{k}$ outward through the surface of the cube cut from the first octant by the planes $x = 1$, $y = 1$, and $z = 1$.

Solution The Divergence Theorem says that instead of calculating the flux as a sum of six separate integrals, one for each face of the cube, we can calculate the flux by integrating the divergence

$$\nabla \cdot \mathbf{F} = \frac{\partial}{\partial x}(xy) + \frac{\partial}{\partial y}(yz) + \frac{\partial}{\partial z}(xz) = y + z + x$$

over the cube's interior:

$$\begin{aligned}
\text{Flux} &= \iint_{\substack{\text{cube}\\ \text{surface}}} \mathbf{F} \cdot \mathbf{n}\, d\sigma \\
&= \iiint_{\substack{\text{cube}\\ \text{interior}}} \nabla \cdot \mathbf{F}\, dV && \text{The Divergence Theorem} \\
&= \int_0^1 \int_0^1 \int_0^1 (x + y + z)\, dx\, dy\, dz \\
&= \frac{3}{2}. && \text{Routine integration}
\end{aligned}$$

Proof of the Divergence Theorem (Special Regions)

To prove the Divergence Theorem, we assume that the components of $\mathbf{F}$ have continuous first partial derivatives. We also assume that D is a convex region with no holes or bubbles, such as a solid sphere, cube, or ellipsoid, and that S is

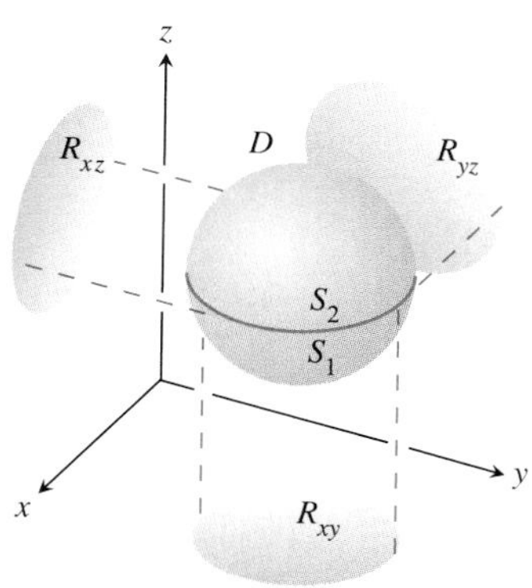

15.72 We first prove the Divergence Theorem for the kind of three-dimensional region shown here. We then extend the theorem to other regions.

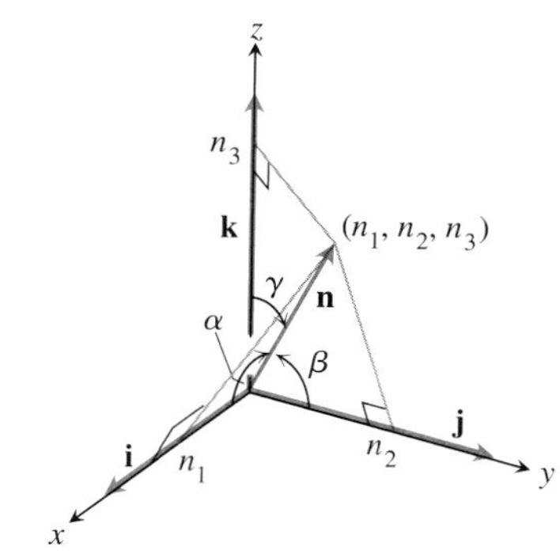

15.73 The scalar components of a unit normal vector **n** are the cosines of the angles α, β, and γ that it makes with **i, j,** and **k**.

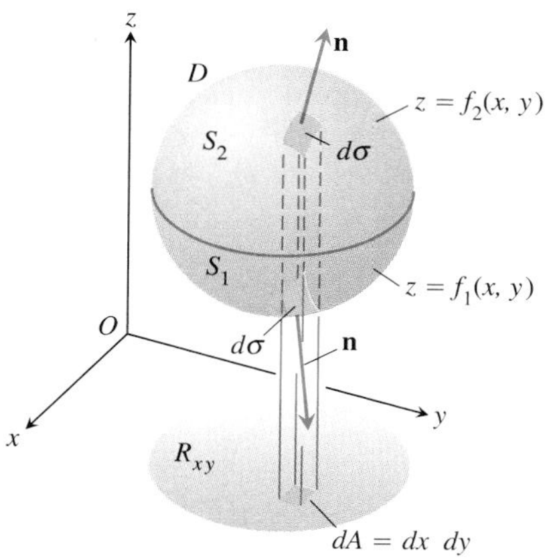

15.74 The three-dimensional region D enclosed by the surfaces S_1 and S_2 shown here projects vertically onto a two-dimensional region R_{xy} in the xy-plane.

a piecewise smooth surface. In addition, we assume that any line perpendicular to the xy-plane at an interior point of the region R_{xy} that is the projection of D on the xy-plane intersects the surface S in exactly two points, producing surfaces S_1 and S_2:

$$S_1:\quad z = f_1(x, y), \quad (x, y) \text{ in } R_{xy}$$
$$S_2:\quad z = f_2(x, y), \quad (x, y) \text{ in } R_{xy},$$

with $f_1 \le f_2$. We make similar assumptions about the projection of D onto the other coordinate planes. See Fig. 15.72.

The components of the unit normal vector $\mathbf{n} = n_1\,\mathbf{i} + n_2\,\mathbf{j} + n_3\,\mathbf{k}$ are the cosines of the angles α, β, and γ that **n** makes with **i**, **j**, and **k** (Fig. 15.73). This is true because all the vectors involved are unit vectors. We have

$$\begin{aligned} n_1 &= \mathbf{n}\cdot\mathbf{i} = |\mathbf{n}|\,|\mathbf{i}|\cos\alpha = \cos\alpha \\ n_2 &= \mathbf{n}\cdot\mathbf{j} = |\mathbf{n}|\,|\mathbf{j}|\cos\beta = \cos\beta \\ n_3 &= \mathbf{n}\cdot\mathbf{k} = |\mathbf{n}|\,|\mathbf{k}|\cos\gamma = \cos\gamma. \end{aligned} \tag{3}$$

Thus,

$$\mathbf{n} = (\cos\alpha)\,\mathbf{i} + (\cos\beta)\,\mathbf{j} + (\cos\gamma)\,\mathbf{k}$$

and

$$\mathbf{F}\cdot\mathbf{n} = M\cos\alpha + N\cos\beta + P\cos\gamma.$$

In component form, the Divergence Theorem states that

$$\iint_S (M\cos\alpha + N\cos\beta + P\cos\gamma)\,d\sigma = \iiint_D \left(\frac{\partial M}{\partial x} + \frac{\partial N}{\partial y} + \frac{\partial P}{\partial z}\right) dx\,dy\,dz. \tag{4}$$

We prove the theorem by proving three separate equalities that add up to Eq. (4):

$$\iint M\cos\alpha\,d\sigma = \iiint \frac{\partial M}{\partial x}\,dx\,dy\,dz \tag{5}$$

$$\iint N\cos\beta\,d\sigma = \iiint \frac{\partial N}{\partial y}\,dx\,dy\,dz \tag{6}$$

$$\iint P\cos\gamma\,d\sigma = \iiint \frac{\partial P}{\partial z}\,dx\,dy\,dz \tag{7}$$

We prove Eq. (7) by converting the surface integral on the left to a double integral over the projection R_{xy} of D on the xy-plane (Fig. 15.74). The surface S consists of an upper part S_2 whose equation is $z = f_2(x, y)$ and a lower part S_1 whose equation is $z = f_1(x, y)$. On S_2, the outer normal **n** has a positive **k**-component and

$$\cos\gamma\,d\sigma = dx\,dy \quad\text{because}\quad d\sigma = \frac{dA}{|\cos\gamma|} = \frac{dx\,dy}{\cos\gamma}. \tag{8}$$

See Fig. 15.75 (on the following page). On S_1, the outer normal **n** has a negative **k**-component and

$$\cos\gamma\,d\sigma = -dx\,dy. \tag{9}$$

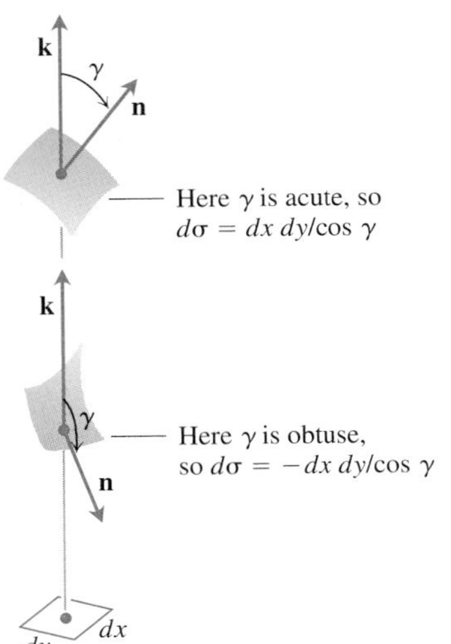

15.75 An enlarged view of the area patches in Fig. 15.74. The relations $d\sigma = \pm\, dx\, dy/\cos\gamma$ are derived in Section 15.5.

Therefore,

$$\begin{aligned}\iint_S P\cos\gamma\, d\sigma &= \iint_{S_2} P\cos\gamma\, d\sigma + \iint_{S_1} P\cos\gamma\, d\sigma \\ &= \iint_{R_{xy}} P(x, y, f_2(x, y))\, dx\, dy - \iint_{R_{xy}} P(x, y, f_1(x, y))\, dx\, dy \\ &= \iint_{R_{xy}} [P(x, y, f_2(x, y)) - P(x, y, f_1(x, y))]\, dx\, dy \\ &= \iint_{R_{xy}} \left[\int_{f_1(x,y)}^{f_2(x,y)} \frac{\partial P}{\partial z}\, dz\right] dx\, dy = \iiint_D \frac{\partial P}{\partial z}\, dz\, dx\, dy.\end{aligned} \tag{10}$$

This proves Eq. (7).

The proofs for Eqs. (5) and (6) follow the same pattern; or just permute x, y, z; M, N, P; α, β, γ, in order, and get those results from Eq. (7).

The Divergence Theorem for Other Regions

The Divergence Theorem can be extended to regions that can be partitioned into a finite number of simple regions of the type just discussed and to regions that can be defined as limits of simpler regions in certain ways. For example, suppose that D is the region between two concentric spheres and that $\mathbf{F}$ has continuously differentiable components throughout D and on the bounding surfaces. Split D by an equatorial plane and apply the Divergence Theorem to each half separately. The bottom half, D_1, is shown in Fig. 15.76. The surface that bounds D_1 consists of an outer hemisphere, a plane washer-shaped base, and an inner hemisphere. The Divergence Theorem says that

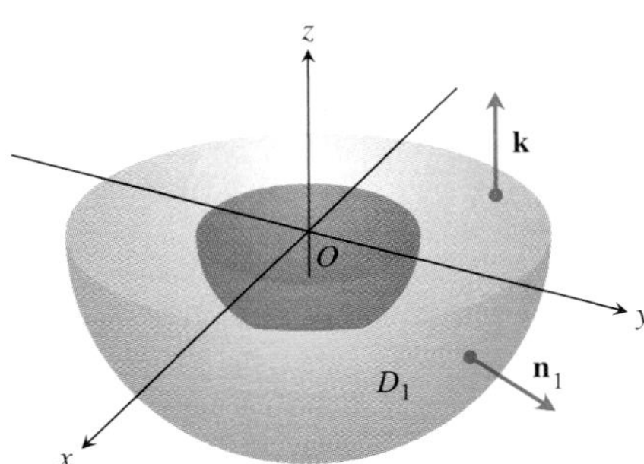

15.76 The lower half of the solid region between two concentric spheres.

$$\iint_{S_1} \mathbf{F}\cdot\mathbf{n}_1\, d\sigma_1 = \iiint_{D_1} \nabla\cdot\mathbf{F}\, dV_1. \tag{11}$$

The unit normal $\mathbf{n}_1$ that points outward from D_1 points away from the origin along the outer surface, equals $\mathbf{k}$ along the flat base, and points toward the origin along the inner surface. Next apply the Divergence Theorem to D_2, as shown in Fig. 15.77:

$$\iint_{S_2} \mathbf{F}\cdot\mathbf{n}_2\, d\sigma_2 = \iiint_{D_2} \nabla\cdot\mathbf{F}\, dV_2. \tag{12}$$

As we follow $\mathbf{n}_2$ over S_2, pointing outward from D_2, we see that $\mathbf{n}_2$ equals $-\mathbf{k}$ along the washer-shaped base in the xy-plane, points away from the origin on the outer sphere, and points toward the origin on the inner sphere. When we add Eqs. (11) and (12), the integrals over the flat base cancel because of the opposite signs of $\mathbf{n}_1$ and $\mathbf{n}_2$. We thus arrive at the result

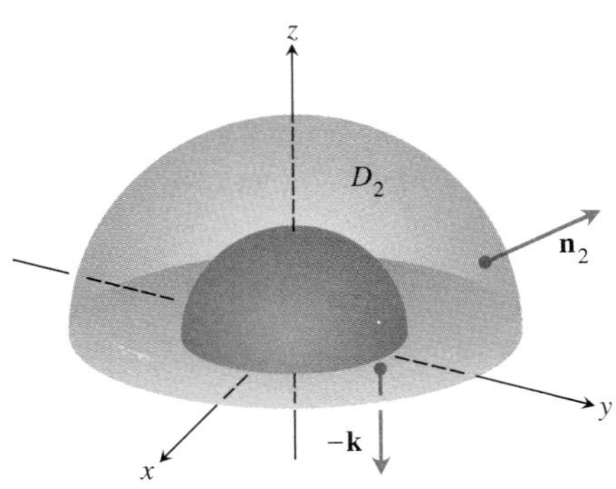

15.77 The upper half of the solid region between two concentric spheres.

$$\iint_S \mathbf{F}\cdot\mathbf{n}\, d\sigma = \iiint_D \nabla\cdot\mathbf{F}\, dV, \tag{13}$$

with D the region between the spheres, S the boundary of D consisting of two spheres, and $\mathbf{n}$ the unit normal to S directed outward from D.

EXAMPLE 4 Find the net outward flux of the field

$$\mathbf{F} = \frac{x\,\mathbf{i} + y\,\mathbf{j} + z\,\mathbf{k}}{\rho^3}, \qquad \rho = \sqrt{x^2 + y^2 + z^2}$$

across the boundary of the region D: $0 < a^2 \le x^2 + y^2 + z^2 \le b^2$.

Solution The flux can be calculated by integrating $\nabla \cdot \mathbf{F}$ over D. We have

$$\frac{\partial \rho}{\partial x} = \frac{1}{2}(x^2 + y^2 + z^2)^{-1/2}(2x) = \frac{x}{\rho}$$

and
$$\frac{\partial M}{\partial x} = \frac{\partial}{\partial x}(x\rho^{-3}) = \rho^{-3} - 3x\rho^{-4}\frac{\partial \rho}{\partial x} = \frac{1}{\rho^3} - \frac{3x^2}{\rho^5}.$$

Similarly,
$$\frac{\partial N}{\partial y} = \frac{1}{\rho^3} - \frac{3y^2}{\rho^5} \quad \text{and} \quad \frac{\partial P}{\partial z} = \frac{1}{\rho^3} - \frac{3z^2}{\rho^5}.$$

Hence,
$$\text{div}\,\mathbf{F} = \frac{3}{\rho^3} - \frac{3}{\rho^5}(x^2 + y^2 + z^2) = \frac{3}{\rho^3} - \frac{3\rho^2}{\rho^5} = 0$$

and
$$\iiint_D \nabla \cdot \mathbf{F}\, dV = 0.$$

So the integral of $\nabla \cdot \mathbf{F}$ over D is zero and the net outward flux across the boundary of D is zero. But there is more to learn from this example. The flux leaving D across the inner sphere S_a is the negative of the flux leaving D across the outer sphere S_b (because the sum of these fluxes is zero). This means that the flux of $\mathbf{F}$ across S_a in the direction away from the origin equals the flux of $\mathbf{F}$ across S_b in the direction away from the origin. Thus, the flux of $\mathbf{F}$ across a sphere centered at the origin is independent of the radius of the sphere. What is this flux?

To find it, we evaluate the flux integral directly. The outward unit normal on the sphere of radius a is

$$\mathbf{n} = \frac{x\,\mathbf{i} + y\,\mathbf{j} + z\,\mathbf{k}}{\sqrt{x^2 + y^2 + z^2}} = \frac{x\,\mathbf{i} + y\,\mathbf{j} + z\,\mathbf{k}}{a}.$$

Hence, on the sphere,

$$\mathbf{F} \cdot \mathbf{n} = \frac{x\,\mathbf{i} + y\,\mathbf{j} + z\,\mathbf{k}}{a^3} \cdot \frac{x\,\mathbf{i} + y\,\mathbf{j} + z\,\mathbf{k}}{a} = \frac{x^2 + y^2 + z^2}{a^4} = \frac{a^2}{a^4} = \frac{1}{a^2}$$

and
$$\iint_{S_a} \mathbf{F} \cdot \mathbf{n}\, d\sigma = \frac{1}{a^2}\iint_{S_a} d\sigma = \frac{1}{a^2}(4\pi a^2) = 4\pi.$$

The outward flux of $\mathbf{F}$ across any sphere centered at the origin is 4π. ■

Gauss's Law—One of the Four Great Laws of Electromagnetic Theory

There is still more to be learned from Example 4. In electromagnetic theory, the electric field created by a point charge q located at the origin is the inverse square field

$$\mathbf{E}(x, y, z) = \frac{q}{|\mathbf{r}|^2}\left(\frac{\mathbf{r}}{|\mathbf{r}|}\right) = q\frac{\mathbf{r}}{|\mathbf{r}|^3} = q\frac{x\,\mathbf{i} + y\,\mathbf{j} + z\,\mathbf{k}}{\rho^3},$$

where $\mathbf{r}$ is the position vector of the point (x, y, z) and $\rho = |\mathbf{r}| = \sqrt{x^2 + y^2 + z^2}$. In the notation of Example 4,

$$\mathbf{E} = q\mathbf{F}.$$

The calculations in Example 4 show that the outward flux of $\mathbf{E}$ across any sphere centered at the origin is $4\pi q$. But this result is not confined to spheres. The outward flux of $\mathbf{E}$ across any surface S that encloses the origin (and to which the Divergence Theorem applies) is also $4\pi q$. To see why, we have only to imagine a large sphere S_a centered at the origin and enclosing the surface S. Since

$$\nabla \cdot \mathbf{E} = \nabla \cdot q\mathbf{F} = q\,\nabla \cdot \mathbf{F} = 0$$

when $\rho > 0$, the integral of $\nabla \cdot \mathbf{E}$ over the region D between S and S_a is zero. Hence, by the Divergence Theorem,

$$\iint_{\substack{\text{boundary}\\ \text{of } D}} \mathbf{E} \cdot \mathbf{n}\, d\sigma = 0,$$

and the flux of $\mathbf{E}$ across S in the direction away from the origin must be the same as the flux of $\mathbf{E}$ across S_a in the direction away from the origin, which is $4\pi q$. This statement, called *Gauss's law,* applies to much more general charge distributions than the one we have assumed here, as you will see in nearly any college physics text.

Gauss's Law

$$\iint_S \mathbf{E} \cdot \mathbf{n}\, d\sigma = 4\pi q \tag{14}$$

Unifying the Integral Theorems

If we think of a two-dimensional field $\mathbf{F} = M(x, y)\,\mathbf{i} + N(x, y)\,\mathbf{j}$ as a three-dimensional field whose $\mathbf{k}$-component is zero, then

$$\nabla \cdot \mathbf{F} = \frac{\partial M}{\partial x} + \frac{\partial N}{\partial y}$$

and the normal form of Green's theorem can be written as

$$\oint_C \mathbf{F} \cdot \mathbf{n}\, ds = \iint_R \left(\frac{\partial M}{\partial x} + \frac{\partial N}{\partial y}\right) dx\, dy = \iint_R \nabla \cdot \mathbf{F}\, dA. \tag{15}$$

Similarly,

$$\nabla \times \mathbf{F} \cdot \mathbf{k} = \left(\frac{\partial N}{\partial x} - \frac{\partial M}{\partial y}\right),$$

so the tangential form of Green's theorem can be written as

$$\oint_C \mathbf{F} \cdot d\mathbf{r} = \iint_R \left(\frac{\partial N}{\partial x} - \frac{\partial M}{\partial y}\right) dx\, dy = \iint_R \nabla \times \mathbf{F} \cdot \mathbf{k}\, dA. \tag{16}$$

With equations of Green's theorem now in del notation, we can see their relationships to the equations in Stokes's theorem and the Divergence Theorem.

The Equations from Green's Theorem and Their Generalizations to Three Dimensions

Normal form of Green's theorem:	$\oint_C \mathbf{F}\cdot\mathbf{n}\,ds = \iint_R \nabla\cdot\mathbf{F}\,dA$
Divergence Theorem:	$\iint_S \mathbf{F}\cdot\mathbf{n}\,d\sigma = \iiint_D \nabla\cdot\mathbf{F}\,dV$
Tangential form of Green's theorem:	$\oint_C \mathbf{F}\cdot d\mathbf{r} = \iint_R \nabla\times\mathbf{F}\cdot\mathbf{k}\,dA$
Stokes's theorem:	$\oint_C \mathbf{F}\cdot d\mathbf{r} = \iint_S \nabla\times\mathbf{F}\cdot\mathbf{n}\,d\sigma$

Notice how Stokes's theorem generalizes the curl form of Green's theorem from a flat surface in the plane to a surface in three-dimensional space. In each case, the integral of the normal component of curl **F** over the interior of the surface equals the circulation of **F** around the boundary.

Likewise, the Divergence Theorem generalizes the flux form of Green's theorem from a two-dimensional region in the plane to a three-dimensional region in space. In each case, the integral of $\nabla\cdot\mathbf{F}$ over the interior of the region equals the total flux of the field across the boundary.

There is still more to be learned here. All of these results can be thought of as forms of a *single fundamental theorem.* Think back to the Fundamental Theorem of Calculus in Section 5.4, which says that if $f(x)$ is differentiable on $[a, b]$, then

$$\int_a^b \frac{df}{dx}\,dx = f(b) - f(a). \tag{17}$$

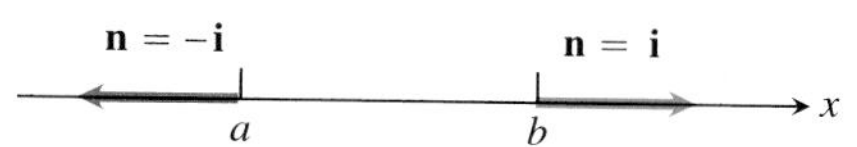

15.78 The outward unit normals at the boundary of $[a, b]$ in one-dimensional space.

If we let $\mathbf{F} = f(x)\,\mathbf{i}$ throughout $[a, b]$, then $(df/dx) = \nabla\cdot\mathbf{F}$. If we also define the unit vector **n** normal to the boundary of $[a, b]$ to be **i** at b and $-\mathbf{i}$ at a (Fig. 15.78), then

$$\begin{aligned} f(b) - f(a) &= f(b)\,\mathbf{i}\cdot(\mathbf{i}) + f(a)\,\mathbf{i}\cdot(-\mathbf{i}) \\ &= \mathbf{F}(b)\cdot\mathbf{n} + \mathbf{F}(a)\cdot\mathbf{n} \\ &= \text{total outward flux of } \mathbf{F} \text{ across the boundary of } [a, b]. \end{aligned} \tag{18}$$

The Fundamental Theorem now says that

$$\int_{[a,b]} \nabla\cdot\mathbf{F}\,dx = \text{total outward flux of } \mathbf{F} \text{ across the boundary.} \tag{19}$$

The Fundamental Theorem of Calculus, the flux form of Green's theorem, and the Divergence Theorem all say that the integral of the differential operator $\nabla\cdot$ operating on a field **F** over a region equals the sum of the normal field components over the boundary of the region.

Stokes's theorem and the circulation form of Green's theorem say that, when things are properly oriented, the integral of the normal component of the curl operating on a field equals the sum of the tangential field components on the boundary of the surface.

The beauty of these interpretations is the observance of a marvelous underlying principle, which we might state as follows:

The integral of a differential operator acting on a field over a region equals the sum of the field components appropriate to the operator over the boundary of the region.

Exercises 15.8

In Exercises 1–4, find the divergence of the field.

1. The spin field in Fig. 15.15
2. The radial field in Fig. 15.14
3. The gravitational field in Fig. 15.13
4. The velocity field in Fig. 15.10

In Exercises 5–16, use the Divergence Theorem to find the outward flux of **F** across the boundary of the region D.

5. $\mathbf{F} = (y - x)\,\mathbf{i} + (z - y)\,\mathbf{j} + (y - x)\,\mathbf{k}$
D: The cube bounded by the planes $x = \pm 1$, $y = \pm 1$, and $z = \pm 1$

6. $\mathbf{F} = x^2\,\mathbf{i} + y^2\,\mathbf{j} + z^2\,\mathbf{k}$

a) D: The cube cut from the first octant by the planes $x = 1$, $y = 1$, and $z = 1$

b) D: The cube bounded by the planes $x = \pm 1$, $y = \pm 1$, and $z = \pm 1$

c) D: The region cut from the solid cylinder $x^2 + y^2 \le 4$ by the planes $z = 0$ and $z = 1$

7. $\mathbf{F} = y\,\mathbf{i} + xy\,\mathbf{j} - z\,\mathbf{k}$
D: The region inside the solid cylinder $x^2 + y^2 \le 4$ between the plane $z = 0$ and the paraboloid $z = x^2 + y^2$

8. $\mathbf{F} = x^2\,\mathbf{i} + xz\,\mathbf{j} - 3z\,\mathbf{k}$
D: The solid sphere $x^2 + y^2 + z^2 \le 4$

9. $\mathbf{F} = x^2\,\mathbf{i} - 2xy\,\mathbf{j} + 3xz\,\mathbf{k}$
D: The region cut from the first octant by the sphere $x^2 + y^2 + z^2 = 4$

10. $\mathbf{F} = (6x^2 + 2xy)\,\mathbf{i} + (2y + x^2z)\,\mathbf{j} + 4x^2y^3\,\mathbf{k}$
D: The region cut from the first octant by the cylinder $x^2 + y^2 = 4$ and the plane $z = 3$

11. $\mathbf{F} = 2xz\,\mathbf{i} - xy\,\mathbf{j} - z^2\,\mathbf{k}$
D: The wedge cut from the first octant by the plane $y + z = 4$ and the elliptical cylinder $4x^2 + y^2 = 16$

12. $\mathbf{F} = x^3\,\mathbf{i} + y^3\,\mathbf{j} + z^3\,\mathbf{k}$
D: The solid sphere $x^2 + y^2 + z^2 \le a^2$

13. $\mathbf{F} = \sqrt{x^2 + y^2 + z^2}\,(x\,\mathbf{i} + y\,\mathbf{j} + z\,\mathbf{k})$
D: The region $1 \le x^2 + y^2 + z^2 \le 2$

14. $\mathbf{F} = (x\,\mathbf{i} + y\,\mathbf{j} + z\,\mathbf{k})/\sqrt{x^2 + y^2 + z^2}$
D: The region $1 \le x^2 + y^2 + z^2 \le 4$

15. $\mathbf{F} = (5x^3 + 12xy^2)\,\mathbf{i} + (y^3 + e^y \sin z)\,\mathbf{j} + (5z^3 + e^y \cos z)\,\mathbf{k}$
D: The solid region between the spheres $x^2 + y^2 + z^2 = 1$ and $x^2 + y^2 + z^2 = 2$

16. $\mathbf{F} = \ln(x^2 + y^2)\,\mathbf{i} - \left(\dfrac{2z}{x}\tan^{-1}\dfrac{y}{x}\right)\mathbf{j} + z\sqrt{x^2 + y^2}\,\mathbf{k}$
D: The thick-walled cylinder $1 \le x^2 + y^2 \le 2$, $-1 \le z \le 2$

17. Let **F** be a field whose components have continuous first partial derivatives throughout a portion of space containing a region D bounded by a smooth closed surface S. If $|\mathbf{F}| \le 1$, can any bound be placed on the size of

$$\iiint_D \nabla \cdot \mathbf{F}\, dV?$$

Give reasons for your answer.

18. The base of the closed cubelike surface shown here is the unit square in the xy-plane. The four sides lie in the planes $x = 0$, $x = 1$, $y = 0$, and $y = 1$. The top is an arbitrary smooth surface whose exact identity is unknown. Let $\mathbf{F} = x\,\mathbf{i} - 2y\,\mathbf{j} + (z + 3)\,\mathbf{k}$, and suppose the outward flux of **F** through side A is 1 and through side B is -3. Can you conclude anything about the outward flux through the top? Give reasons for your answer.

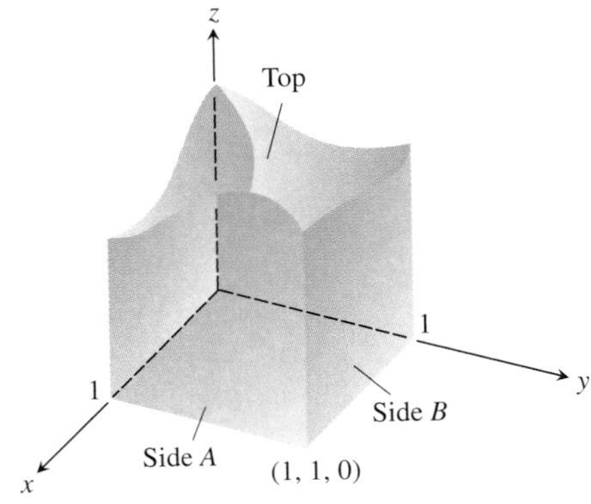

19. Can anything be said about the flux of a constant vector field $\mathbf{F} = \mathbf{C}$ across a closed surface? Give reasons for your answer.

20. Is there any relationship between the flux of $\mathbf{F} = x\,\mathbf{i} + y\,\mathbf{j} + z\,\mathbf{k}$ across a smooth closed surface S and the volume of the region D enclosed by the surface? Give reasons for your answer.

21. *div (curl G) = 0.*

a) Show that if the necessary partial derivatives of the components of the field $\mathbf{G} = M\,\mathbf{i} + N\,\mathbf{j} + P\,\mathbf{k}$ are continuous, then $\nabla \cdot \nabla \times \mathbf{G} = 0$.

b) What, if anything, can you conclude about the flux of the field $\nabla \times \mathbf{G}$ across a closed surface? Give reasons for your answer.

22. Among all rectangular solids defined by the inequalities $0 \le x \le a$, $0 \le y \le b$, $0 \le z \le 1$, find the one for which the total flux of $\mathbf{F} = (-x^2 - 4xy)\,\mathbf{i} - 6yz\,\mathbf{j} + 12z\,\mathbf{k}$ outward through the six sides is greatest. What *is* the maximum flux?

23. *Basic Properties of Curl and Divergence.* Let $g(x, y, z)$ be a differentiable scalar function, let $\mathbf{F}$, $\mathbf{F}_1$, and $\mathbf{F}_2$ be differentiable vector fields, and let a and b be arbitrary real constants. Verify the following identities.

a) $\nabla \cdot (a\mathbf{F}_1 + b\mathbf{F}_2) = a\,\nabla \cdot \mathbf{F}_1 + b\,\nabla \cdot \mathbf{F}_2$

b) $\nabla \times (a\mathbf{F}_1 + b\mathbf{F}_2) = a\,\nabla \times \mathbf{F}_1 + b\,\nabla \times \mathbf{F}_2$

c) $\nabla \cdot (g\mathbf{F}) = g\,\nabla \cdot \mathbf{F} + \nabla g \cdot \mathbf{F}$

d) $\nabla \times (g\mathbf{F}) = g\,\nabla \times \mathbf{F} + \nabla g \times \mathbf{F}$

e) $\nabla \cdot (\mathbf{F}_1 \times \mathbf{F}_2) = \mathbf{F}_2 \cdot \nabla \times \mathbf{F}_1 - \mathbf{F}_1 \cdot \nabla \times \mathbf{F}_2$

24. *Harmonic Functions.* A function $f(x, y, z)$ is said to be **harmonic** in a region D in space if it satisfies the Laplace equation

$$\nabla^2 f = \nabla \cdot \nabla f = \frac{\partial^2 f}{\partial x^2} + \frac{\partial^2 f}{\partial y^2} + \frac{\partial^2 f}{\partial z^2} = 0$$

throughout D.

a) Suppose that f is harmonic throughout a bounded region D enclosed by a smooth surface S and that $\mathbf{n}$ is the chosen unit normal vector on S. Show that the integral over S of $\nabla f \cdot \mathbf{n}$, the derivative of f in the direction of $\mathbf{n}$, is zero.

b) Show that if f is harmonic on D, then

$$\iint_S f\nabla f \cdot \mathbf{n}\, d\sigma = \iiint_D |\nabla f|^2\, dV.$$

Writing for Your Own Knowledge

Answer the following questions in writing. Some answers will take only a sentence or two; others may require several paragraphs. Some explanations may also call for graphs or sketches.

1. What is the Divergence Theorem about?
2. How does the Divergence Theorem generalize Green's theorem?
3. How does Stokes's theorem generalize Green's theorem?

For Your Review

Write brief paragraphs about the following topics and give examples.

Line integrals
Vector fields
Work and circulation
Flux across a closed curve in the plane
The Fundamental Theorem of Line Integrals
Properties of conservative fields
Potential functions and how to find them
Exact differential forms
Finding the area of a surface $f(x, y, z) = c$
Integration over a surface $f(x, y, z) = c$
Parametrized surfaces
Finding areas of parametrized surfaces
Integration over parametrized surfaces
The flux density of a two-dimensional vector field
The circulation density of a two-dimensional vector field
The relationship between flux and divergence in the plane; in space
The relationship between circulation and curl in the plane; in space

Practice Exercises

1. Figure 15.79 shows two polygonal paths in space joining the origin to the point (1, 1, 1). Integrate $f(x, y, z) = 2x - 3y^2 - 2z + 3$ over each path.

2. Figure 15.80 (on the following page) shows three polygonal paths joining the origin to the point (1, 1, 1). Integrate $f(x, y, z) = x^2 + y - z$ over each path.

3. Integrate $f(x, y, z) = \sqrt{x^2 + z^2}$ over the circle $\mathbf{r} = (a \cos t)\,\mathbf{j} + (a \sin t)\,\mathbf{k}$, $0 \le t \le 2\pi$.

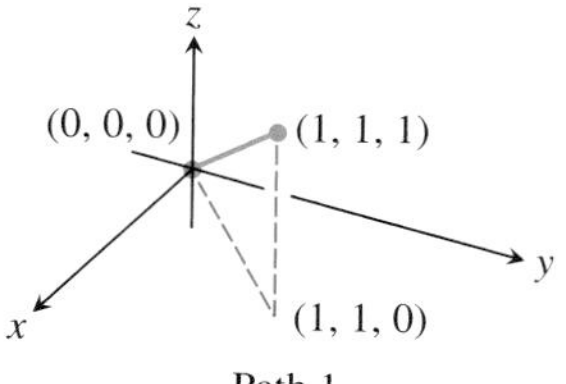

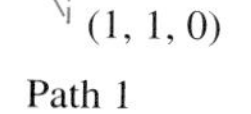

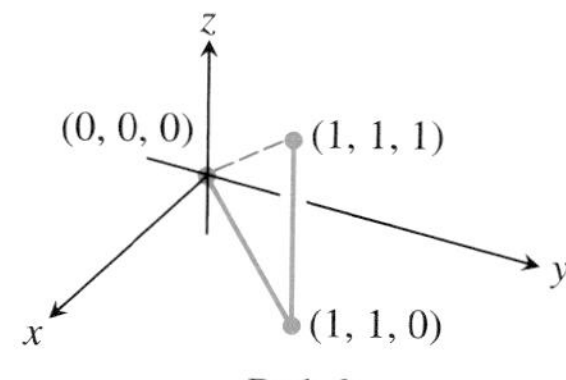

15.79 The paths in Exercise 1.

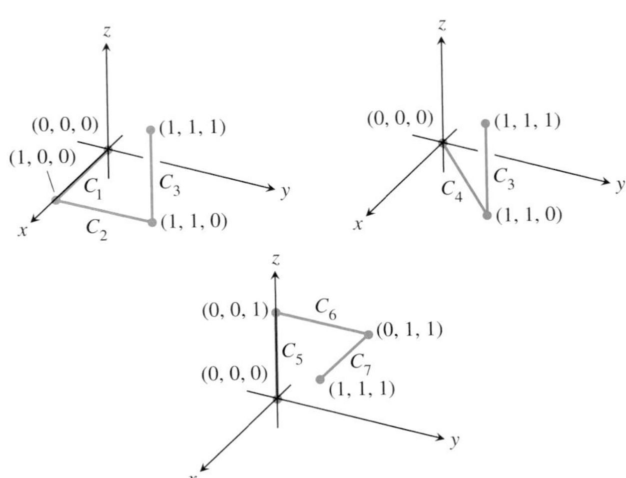

15.80 The paths in Exercise 2.

4. Integrate $f(x, y, z) = \sqrt{x^2 + y^2}$ over the involute curve $\mathbf{r} = (\cos t + t \sin t)\,\mathbf{i} + (\sin t - t \cos t)\,\mathbf{j}$, $0 \le t \le \sqrt{3}$. (Figure 12.21 shows the curve.)

5. Find the mass of a thin wire lying along the curve $\mathbf{r} = \sqrt{2}\,t\,\mathbf{i} + \sqrt{2}\,t\,\mathbf{j} + (4 - t^2)\,\mathbf{k}$, $0 \le t \le 1$, if the density at t is (a) $\delta = 3t$, (b) $\delta = 1$.

6. Find the center of mass of a thin wire lying along the curve $\mathbf{r} = t\,\mathbf{i} + 2t\,\mathbf{j} + (2/3)t^{3/2}\,\mathbf{k}$, $0 \le t \le 2$, if the density at t is $\delta = 3\sqrt{5 + t}$.

7. Find the center of mass and the moments of inertia and radii of gyration about the coordinate axes of a thin wire lying along the curve

$$\mathbf{r} = t\,\mathbf{i} + \frac{2\sqrt{2}}{3}t^{3/2}\,\mathbf{j} + \frac{t^2}{2}\mathbf{k}, \quad 0 \le t \le 2,$$

if the density at t is $\delta = 1/(t + 1)$.

8. A wire of constant density $\delta = 1$ lies along the curve $\mathbf{r} = (t \cos t)\,\mathbf{i} + (t \sin t)\,\mathbf{j} + (2\sqrt{2}/3)t^{3/2}\,\mathbf{k}$, $0 \le t \le 1$. Find $\bar{z}$, I_z, and R_z.

9. Suppose $\mathbf{F}(x, y) = (x + y)\,\mathbf{i} - (x^2 + y^2)\,\mathbf{j}$ is the velocity field of a fluid flowing across the xy-plane. Find the flow along each of the following paths from $(1, 0)$ to $(-1, 0)$.
   a) The upper half of the circle $x^2 + y^2 = 1$
   b) The line segment from $(1, 0)$ to $(-1, 0)$
   c) The line segment from $(1, 0)$ to $(0, -1)$ followed by the line segment from $(0, -1)$ to $(-1, 0)$

10. Find the circulation of $\mathbf{F} = 2x\,\mathbf{i} + 2z\,\mathbf{j} + 2y\,\mathbf{k}$ along the closed path consisting of the helix $\mathbf{r}_1 = (\cos t)\,\mathbf{i} + (\sin t)\,\mathbf{j} + t\,\mathbf{k}$, $0 \le t \le \pi/2$, followed by the line segments $\mathbf{r}_2 = \mathbf{j} + (\pi/2)(1 - t)\,\mathbf{k}$, $0 \le t \le 1$, and $\mathbf{r}_3 = t\,\mathbf{i} + (1 - t)\,\mathbf{j}$, $0 \le t \le 1$.

Which of the fields in Exercises 11–14 are conservative and which are not?

11. $\mathbf{F} = x\,\mathbf{i} + y\,\mathbf{j} + z\,\mathbf{k}$

12. $\mathbf{F} = (x\,\mathbf{i} + y\,\mathbf{j} + z\,\mathbf{k})/(x^2 + y^2 + z^2)^{3/2}$

13. $\mathbf{F} = x\,e^y\,\mathbf{i} + y\,e^z\,\mathbf{j} + z\,e^x\,\mathbf{k}$

14. $\mathbf{F} = (\mathbf{i} + z\,\mathbf{j} + y\,\mathbf{k})/(x + yz)$

Find potential functions for the fields in Exercises 15 and 16.

15. $\mathbf{F} = 2\,\mathbf{i} + (2y + z)\,\mathbf{j} + (y + 1)\,\mathbf{k}$

16. $\mathbf{F} = (z \cos xz)\,\mathbf{i} + e^y\,\mathbf{j} + (x \cos xz)\,\mathbf{k}$

Evaluate the integrals in Exercises 17 and 18.

17. $\displaystyle\int_{(-1,1,1)}^{(4,-3,0)} \frac{dx + dy + dz}{\sqrt{x + y + z}}$

18. $\displaystyle\int_{(1,1,1)}^{(10,3,3)} dx - \sqrt{\frac{z}{y}}\,dy - \sqrt{\frac{y}{z}}\,dz$

In Exercises 19 and 20, find the work done by each field along the paths from $(0, 0, 0)$ to $(1, 1, 1)$ in Fig. 15.79.

19. $\mathbf{F} = 2xy\,\mathbf{i} + \mathbf{j} + x^2\,\mathbf{k}$

20. $\mathbf{F} = 2xy\,\mathbf{i} + x^2\,\mathbf{j} + \mathbf{k}$

21. Let C be the ellipse in which the plane $2x + 3y - z = 0$ meets the cylinder $x^2 + y^2 = 12$. Show, without evaluating either line integral directly, that the circulation of the field $\mathbf{F} = x\,\mathbf{i} + y\,\mathbf{j} + z\,\mathbf{k}$ around C in either direction is zero.

22. Find the flow of the field $\mathbf{F} = \nabla(xy^2z^3)$
   a) once around the curve C in Exercise 21, clockwise as viewed from above,
   b) along the line segment from $(1, 1, 1)$ to $(2, 1, -1)$.

23. Find the work done by

$$\mathbf{F} = \frac{x\,\mathbf{i} + y\,\mathbf{j}}{(x^2 + y^2)^{3/2}}$$

over the plane curve $\mathbf{r} = (e^t \cos t)\,\mathbf{i} + (e^t \sin t)\,\mathbf{j}$ from the point $(1, 0)$ to the point $(e^{2\pi}, 0)$ in two ways:
   a) by using the parametrization of the curve to evaluate the work integral,
   b) by evaluating a potential function for f.

24. Integrate $\mathbf{F} = -(y \sin z)\,\mathbf{i} + (x \sin z)\,\mathbf{j} + (xy \cos z)\,\mathbf{k}$ around the circle cut from the sphere $x^2 + y^2 + z^2 = 5$ by the plane $z = -1$, clockwise as viewed from above.

Use Green's theorem to find the counterclockwise circulation and outward flux for the fields and curves in Exercises 25 and 26.

25. $\mathbf{F} = (2xy + x)\,\mathbf{i} + (xy - y)\,\mathbf{j}$
   C: The square bounded by $x = 0$, $x = 1$, $y = 0$, $y = 1$

26. $\mathbf{F} = (y - 6x^2)\,\mathbf{i} + (x + y^2)\,\mathbf{j}$
   C: The triangle made by the lines $y = 0$, $y = x$, and $x = 1$

27. Show that

$$\oint_C \ln x \sin y\,dy - \frac{\cos y}{x}\,dx = 0$$

for any closed curve C to which Green's theorem applies.

28. **a)** Show that the outward flux of the position vector field $\mathbf{F} = x\,\mathbf{i} + y\,\mathbf{j}$ across any closed curve to which Green's

theorem applies is twice the area of the region enclosed by the curve.

b) Let **n** be the outward unit normal vector to a closed curve to which Green's theorem applies. Show that it is not possible for $\mathbf{F} = x\,\mathbf{i} + y\,\mathbf{j}$ to be orthogonal to **n** at every point of C.

Use Green's theorem to evaluate the line integrals in Exercises 29 and 30.

29. $\displaystyle\int_C 8x \sin y\, dx - 8y \cos x\, dy$

C is the square cut from the first quadrant by the lines $x = \pi/2$ and $y = \pi/2$.

30. $\displaystyle\int_C y^2\, dx + x^2\, dy$

C is the circle $x^2 + y^2 = 4$.

Find parametrizations for the surfaces in Exercises 31–36. (There are many correct ways to do these, so your answers may not be the same as those in the back of the book.)

31. The portion of the sphere $x^2 + y^2 + z^2 = 36$ between the planes $z = -3$ and $z = 3\sqrt{3}$

32. The portion of the paraboloid $z = -(x^2 + y^2)/2$ above the plane $z = -2$

33. The cone $z = 1 + \sqrt{x^2 + y^2}$, $z \le 3$

34. The portion of the plane $4x + 2y + 4z = 12$ that lies above the square $0 \le x \le 2$, $0 \le y \le 2$ in the first quadrant

35. The portion of the paraboloid $y = 2(x^2 + z^2)$, $y \le 2$, that lies above the xy-plane

36. The portion of the hemisphere $x^2 + y^2 + z^2 = 10$, $y \ge 0$, in the first octant

37. Find the area of the elliptical region cut from the plane $x + y + z = 1$ by the cylinder $x^2 + y^2 = 1$.

38. Find the area of the cap cut from the paraboloid $y^2 + z^2 = 3x$ by the plane $x = 1$.

39. Find the area of the cap cut from the top of the sphere $x^2 + y^2 + z^2 = 1$ by the plane $z = \sqrt{2}/2$.

40. Find the area of the surface cut from the hemisphere $x^2 + y^2 + z^2 = 4$, $z \ge 0$, by the cylinder $x^2 + y^2 = 2x$ (Fig. 15.81).

41. Find the area of the triangle in which the plane $(x/a) + (y/b) + (z/c) = 1$ $(a, b, c > 0)$ intersects the first octant. Check your answer with an appropriate vector calculation.

42. Let S be the surface that is bounded on the left by the hemisphere $x^2 + y^2 + z^2 = a^2$, $y \le 0$, in the middle by the cylinder $x^2 + z^2 = a^2$, $0 \le y \le a$, and on the right by the plane $y = a$. Find the flux of the field $\mathbf{F} = y\,\mathbf{i} + z\,\mathbf{j} + x\,\mathbf{k}$ outward across S.

43. Integrate

a) $g(x, y, z) = \dfrac{yz}{\sqrt{4y^2 + 1}}$ b) $g(x, y, z) = \dfrac{z}{\sqrt{4y^2 + 1}}$

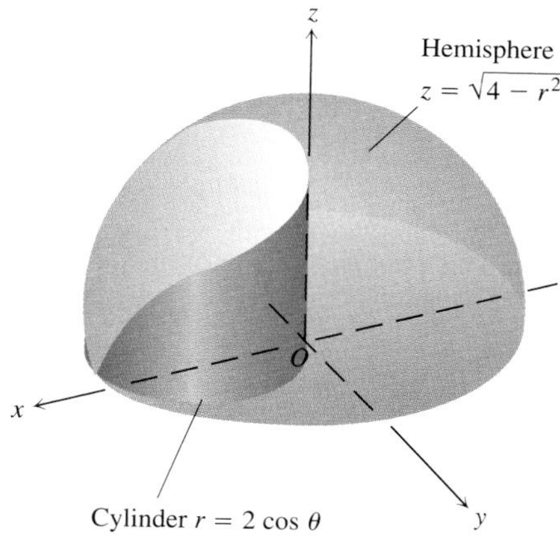

15.81 The surface cut from the hemisphere $x^2 + y^2 + z^2 = 4$, $z \ge 0$, by the cylinder $x^2 + y^2 = 2x$ in Exercise 40.

over the surface cut from the parabolic cylinder $y^2 - z = 1$ by the planes $x = 0$, $x = 3$, and $z = 0$.

44. Integrate $g(x, y, z) = x^4 y(y^2 + z^2)$ over the portion of the cylinder $y^2 + z^2 = 25$ that lies in the first octant between the planes $x = 0$ and $x = 1$ and above the plane $z = 3$.

45. Find I_z, R_z, and the center of mass of a thin shell of density $\delta(x, y, z) = z$ cut from the upper portion of the sphere $x^2 + y^2 + z^2 = 25$ by the plane $z = 3$.

46. Find the moment of inertia about the z-axis of the surface of the cube cut from the first octant by the planes $x = 1$, $y = 1$, and $z = 1$ if the density is $\delta = 1$.

In Exercises 47–50, find the outward flux of **F** across the boundary of D.

47. $\mathbf{F} = 2xy\,\mathbf{i} + 2yz\,\mathbf{j} + 2xz\,\mathbf{k}$

D: The cube cut from the first octant by the planes $x = 1$, $y = 1$, $z = 1$

48. $\mathbf{F} = xz\,\mathbf{i} + yz\,\mathbf{j} + \mathbf{k}$

D: The entire surface of the upper cap cut from the solid sphere $x^2 + y^2 + z^2 \le 25$ by the plane $z = 3$

49. $\mathbf{F} = -2x\mathbf{i} - 3y\mathbf{j} + z\,\mathbf{k}$

D: The upper region cut from the solid sphere $x^2 + y^2 + z^2 \le 2$ by the paraboloid $z = x^2 + y^2$

50. $\mathbf{F} = (6x + y)\,\mathbf{i} - (x + z)\,\mathbf{j} + 4yz\,\mathbf{k}$

D: The region in the first octant bounded by the cone $z = \sqrt{x^2 + y^2}$, the cylinder $x^2 + y^2 = 1$, and the coordinate planes

51. Find the outward flux of the field $\mathbf{F} = 3xz^2\,\mathbf{i} + y\,\mathbf{j} - z^3\,\mathbf{k}$ across the surface of the solid in the first octant that is bounded by the cylinder $x^2 + 4y^2 = 16$ and the planes $y = 2z$, $x = 0$, and $z = 0$.

52. Find the flux of $\mathbf{F} = (3z + 1)\,\mathbf{k}$ upward across the hemisphere $x^2 + y^2 + z^2 = a^2$, $z \geq 0$ (a) with the Divergence Theorem, (b) by evaluating the flux integral directly.

In Exercises 53 and 54, use the surface integral in Stokes's theorem to find the circulation of the field $\mathbf{F}$ around the curve C in the indicated direction.

53. $\mathbf{F} = y^2\,\mathbf{i} - y\,\mathbf{j} + 3z^2\,\mathbf{k}$
C: The ellipse in which the plane $2x + 6y - 3z = 6$ meets the cylinder $x^2 + y^2 = 1$, counterclockwise as viewed from above

54. $\mathbf{F} = (x^2 + y)\,\mathbf{i} + (x + y)\,\mathbf{j} + (4y^2 - z)\,\mathbf{k}$
C: The circle in which the plane $z = -y$ meets the sphere $x^2 + y^2 + z^2 = 4$, counterclockwise as viewed from above

FINDING AREAS WITH GREEN'S THEOREM

Use the Green's theorem area formula, Eq. (27) in Exercises 15.4, to find the areas of the regions enclosed by the curves in Exercises 55–58.

55. The limaçon $x = 2\cos t - \cos 2t$, $y = 2\sin t - \sin 2t$, $0 \leq t \leq 2\pi$

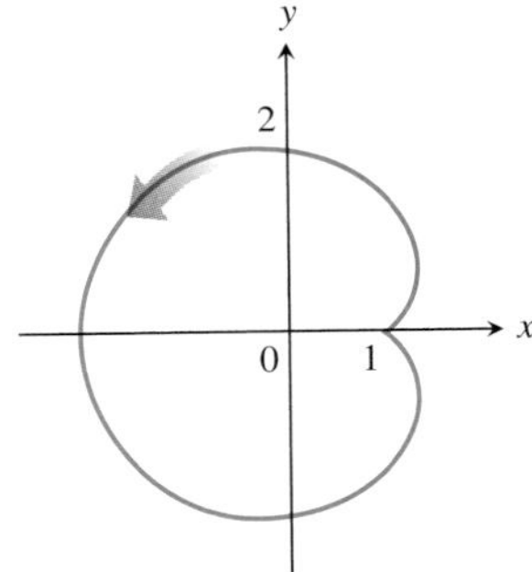

56. The deltoid $x = 2\cos t + \cos 2t$, $y = 2\sin t - \sin 2t$, $0 \leq t \leq 2\pi$

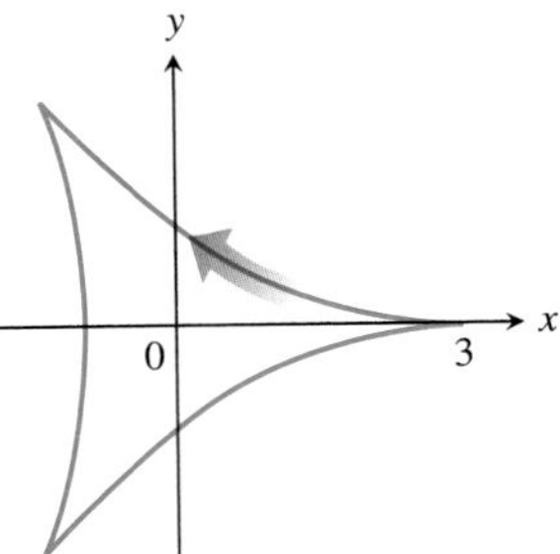

57. The eight curve $x = (1/2)\sin 2t$, $y = \sin t$, $0 \leq t \leq \pi$ (one loop)

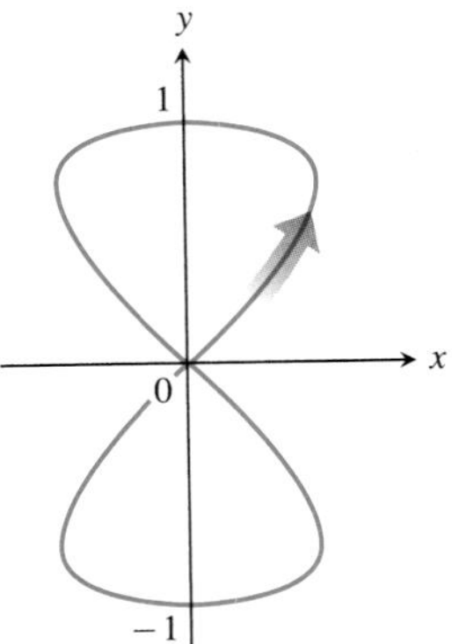

58. The teardrop $x = 2a\cos t - a\sin 2t$, $y = b\sin t$, $0 \leq t \leq 2\pi$

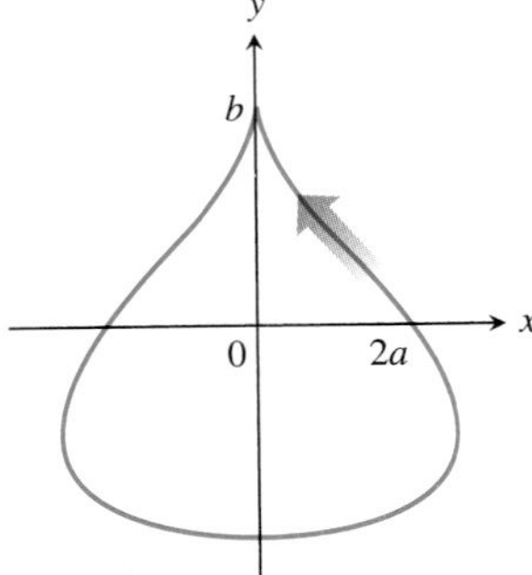

Appendices

A.1 Formulas from Precalculus Mathematics

Algebra

1. Laws of Exponents

$$a^m a^n = a^{m+n}, \quad (ab)^m = a^m b^m, \quad (a^m)^n = a^{mn}, \quad a^{m/n} = \sqrt[n]{a^m}$$

If $a \neq 0$,

$$\frac{a^m}{a^n} = a^{m-n}, \quad a^0 = 1, \quad a^{-m} = \frac{1}{a^m}.$$

2. Zero Division by zero is not defined.

If $a \neq 0$: $\quad \frac{0}{a} = 0, \quad a^0 = 1, \quad 0^a = 0$

For any number a: $\quad a \cdot 0 = 0 \cdot a = 0$

3. Fractions

$$\frac{a}{b} + \frac{c}{d} = \frac{ad + bc}{bd}, \qquad \frac{a}{b} \cdot \frac{c}{d} = \frac{ac}{bd}, \qquad \frac{a/b}{c/d} = \frac{a}{b} \cdot \frac{d}{c}, \qquad \frac{-a}{b} = -\frac{a}{b} = \frac{a}{-b},$$

$$\frac{(a/b) + (c/d)}{(e/f) + (g/h)} = \frac{(a/b) + (c/d)}{(e/f) + (g/h)} \cdot \frac{bdfh}{bdfh} = \frac{(ad + bc)fh}{(eh + fg)bd}$$

4. The Binomial Theorem

For any positive integer n,

$$(a + b)^n = a^n + na^{n-1}b + \frac{n(n-1)}{1 \cdot 2} a^{n-2} b^2$$
$$+ \frac{n(n-1)(n-2)}{1 \cdot 2 \cdot 3} a^{n-3} b^3 + \cdots + nab^{n-1} + b^n.$$

For instance,

$$(a + b)^1 = a + b,$$
$$(a + b)^2 = a^2 + 2ab + b^2,$$
$$(a + b)^3 = a^3 + 3a^2b + 3ab^2 + b^3,$$
$$(a + b)^4 = a^4 + 4a^3b + 6a^2b^2 + 4ab^3 + b^4.$$

5. Difference of Like Integer Powers, $n > 1$

$$a^n - b^n = (a - b)(a^{n-1} + a^{n-2}b + a^{n-3}b^2 + \cdots + ab^{n-2} + b^{n-1})$$

For instance,

$$a^2 - b^2 = (a - b)(a + b),$$
$$a^3 - b^3 = (a - b)(a^2 + ab + b^2),$$
$$a^4 - b^4 = (a - b)(a^3 + a^2b + ab^2 + b^3).$$

6. Completing the Square

If $a \neq 0$, we can rewrite the quadratic $ax^2 + bx + c$ in the form $au^2 + C$ by a process called completing the square:

$$ax^2 + bx + c = a\left(x^2 + \frac{b}{a}x\right) + c$$
Factor a from the first two terms.

$$= a\left(x^2 + \frac{b}{a}x + \frac{b^2}{4a^2} - \frac{b^2}{4a^2}\right) + c$$
Add and subtract the square of half the coefficient of x.

$$= a\left(x^2 + \frac{b}{a}x + \frac{b^2}{4a^2}\right) + a\left(-\frac{b^2}{4a^2}\right) + c$$
Bring out the $-b^2/4a^2$.

$$= \underbrace{a\left(x^2 + \frac{b}{a}x + \frac{b^2}{4a^2}\right)}_{\text{This is } \left(x + \frac{b}{2a}\right)^2.} + \underbrace{c - \frac{b^2}{4a}}_{\text{Call this part } C.}$$

$$= au^2 + C$$
$u = x + b/2a$

7. The Quadratic Formula

By completing the square on the first two terms of the equation

$$ax^2 + bx + c = 0$$

and solving the resulting equation for x (details omitted), we obtain the formula

$$x = \frac{-b \pm \sqrt{b^2 - 4ac}}{2a}.$$

This equation is called the **quadratic formula.**

The solutions of the equation $2x^2 + 3x - 1 = 0$ are

$$x = \frac{-3 \pm \sqrt{(3)^2 - 4(2)(-1)}}{2(2)} = \frac{-3 \pm \sqrt{9 + 8}}{4},$$

or $$x = \frac{-3 + \sqrt{17}}{4} \quad \text{and} \quad x = \frac{-3 - \sqrt{17}}{4}.$$

The solutions of the equation $x^2 + 4x + 6 = 0$ are

$$x = \frac{-4 \pm \sqrt{(4)^2 - 4 \cdot 1 \cdot 6}}{2} = \frac{-4 \pm \sqrt{16 - 24}}{2}$$

$$= \frac{-4 \pm \sqrt{-8}}{2} = \frac{-4 \pm 2\sqrt{2}\sqrt{-1}}{2} = -2 \pm \sqrt{2}\, i.$$

The solutions are the complex numbers $-2 + \sqrt{2}\, i$ and $-2 - \sqrt{2}\, i$. Appendix A.9 has more on complex numbers.

Geometry

(A = area, B = area of base, C = circumference, S = lateral area or surface area, V = volume)

1. Triangle

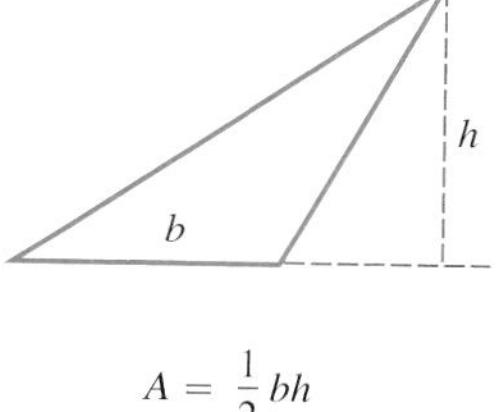

$A = \frac{1}{2}bh$

2. Similar Triangles

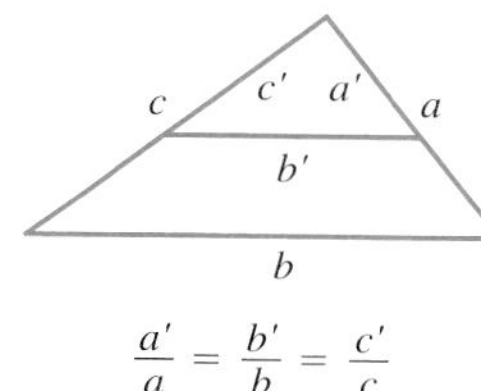

$\frac{a'}{a} = \frac{b'}{b} = \frac{c'}{c}$

3. Pythagorean Theorem

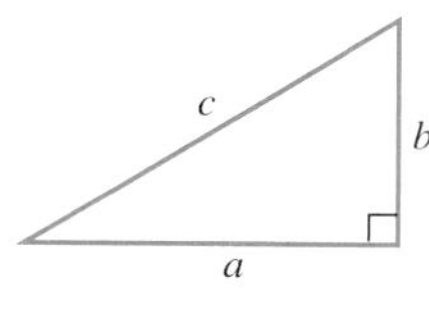

4. Parallelogram

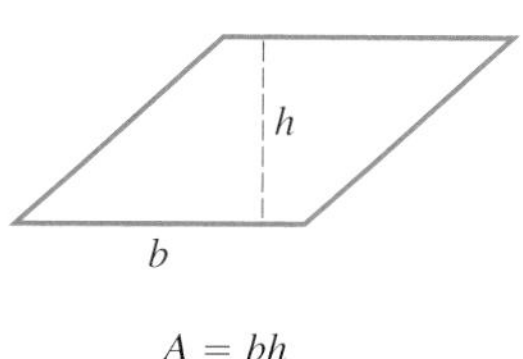

$A = bh$

5. Trapezoids

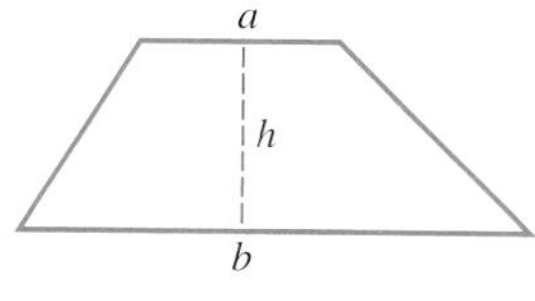

$A = \frac{1}{2}(a + b)h$

h_1, h_2, b

$A = b\,\frac{h_1 + h_2}{2}$

6. Circle

r

$A = \pi r^2$
$C = 2\pi r$

7. Circle Sector

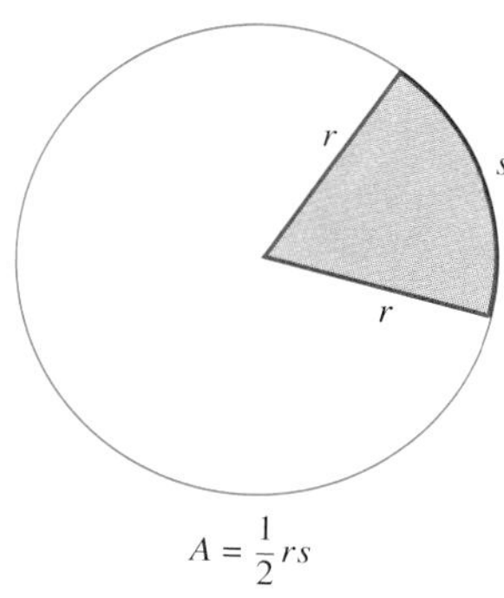

$A = \frac{1}{2}rs$

$p = s + 2r$

8. Any Cylinder or Prism with Parallel Bases

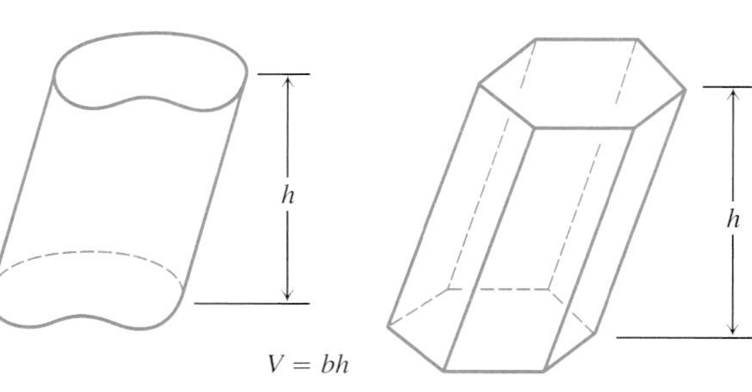

$V = bh$

9. Right Circular Cylinder

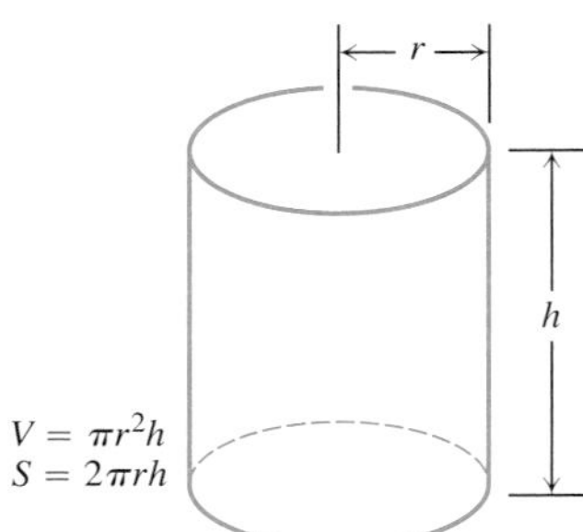

$V = \pi r^2 h$
$S = 2\pi r h$

10. Any Cone or Pyramid

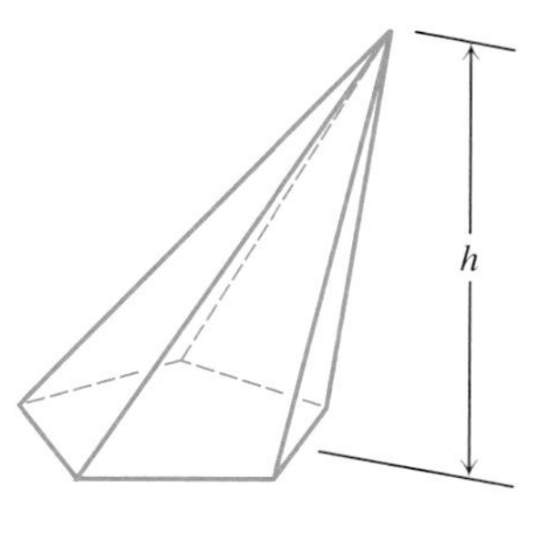

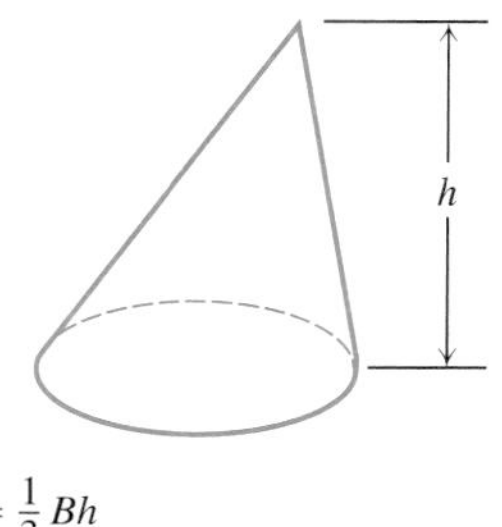

$V = \frac{1}{3} Bh$

11. Right Circular Cone

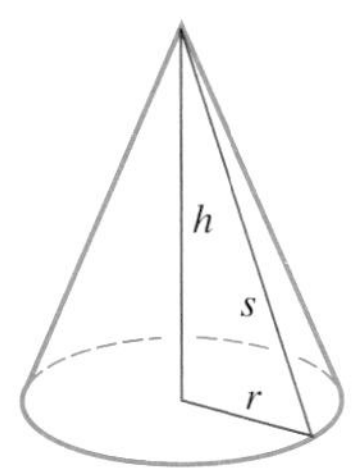

$V = \frac{1}{3}\pi r^2 h, \quad S = \pi r s$

12. Frustum of a Right Circular Cone

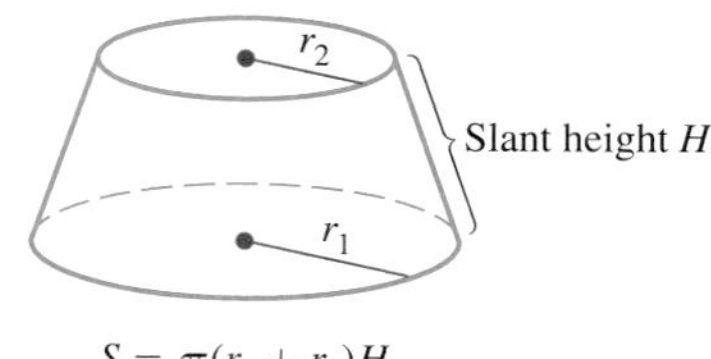

$S = \pi(r_1 + r_2)H$

13. Sphere

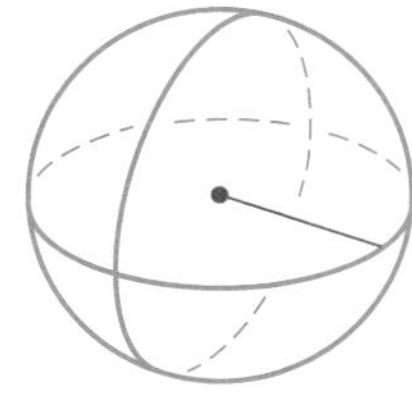

$V = \frac{4}{3}\pi r^3, \quad S = 4\pi r^2$

Trigonometry

1. Definitions and Fundamental Identities

Sine: $\sin\theta = \dfrac{y}{r} = \dfrac{1}{\csc\theta}$

Cosine: $\cos\theta = \dfrac{x}{r} = \dfrac{1}{\sec\theta}$

Tangent: $\tan\theta = \dfrac{y}{x} = \dfrac{1}{\cot\theta}$

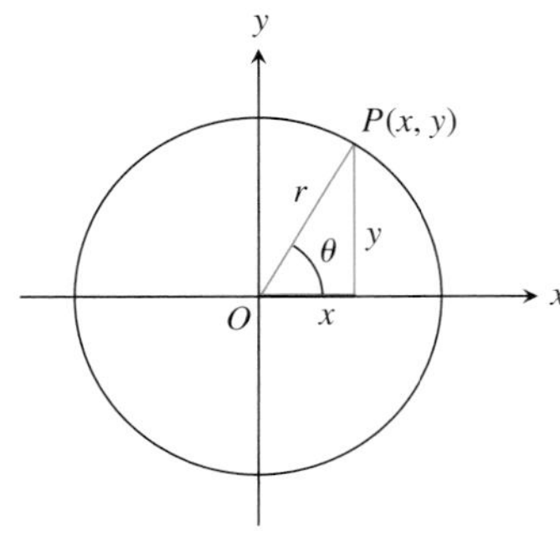

2. Identities

$\sin(-\theta) = -\sin\theta, \qquad \cos(-\theta) = \cos\theta$

$\sin^2\theta + \cos^2\theta = 1, \qquad \sec^2\theta = 1 + \tan^2\theta, \qquad \csc^2\theta = 1 + \cot^2\theta$

$\sin 2\theta = 2\sin\theta\cos\theta, \qquad \cos 2\theta = \cos^2\theta - \sin^2\theta$

$\cos^2\theta = \dfrac{1 + \cos 2\theta}{2}, \qquad \sin^2\theta = \dfrac{1 - \cos 2\theta}{2}$

$$\sin(A+B) = \sin A \cos B + \cos A \sin B$$
$$\sin(A-B) = \sin A \cos B - \cos A \sin B$$
$$\cos(A+B) = \cos A \cos B - \sin A \sin B$$
$$\cos(A-B) = \cos A \cos B + \sin A \sin B$$

$$\tan(A+B) = \frac{\tan A + \tan B}{1 - \tan A \tan B}$$

$$\tan(A-B) = \frac{\tan A - \tan B}{1 + \tan A \tan B}$$

$$\sin\left(A - \frac{\pi}{2}\right) = -\cos A, \qquad \cos\left(A - \frac{\pi}{2}\right) = \sin A$$

$$\sin\left(A + \frac{\pi}{2}\right) = \cos A, \qquad \cos\left(A + \frac{\pi}{2}\right) = -\sin A$$

$$\sin A \sin B = \tfrac{1}{2}\cos(A-B) - \tfrac{1}{2}\cos(A+B)$$
$$\cos A \cos B = \tfrac{1}{2}\cos(A-B) + \tfrac{1}{2}\cos(A+B)$$
$$\sin A \cos B = \tfrac{1}{2}\sin(A-B) + \tfrac{1}{2}\sin(A+B)$$

$$\sin A + \sin B = 2\sin\tfrac{1}{2}(A+B)\cos\tfrac{1}{2}(A-B)$$
$$\sin A - \sin B = 2\cos\tfrac{1}{2}(A+B)\sin\tfrac{1}{2}(A-B)$$

$$\cos A + \cos B = 2\cos\tfrac{1}{2}(A+B)\cos\tfrac{1}{2}(A-B)$$
$$\cos A - \cos B = -2\sin\tfrac{1}{2}(A+B)\sin\tfrac{1}{2}(A-B)$$

3. Common Reference Triangles

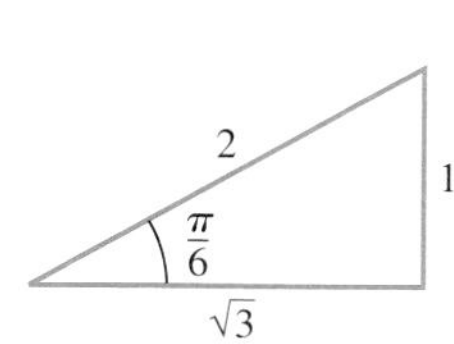

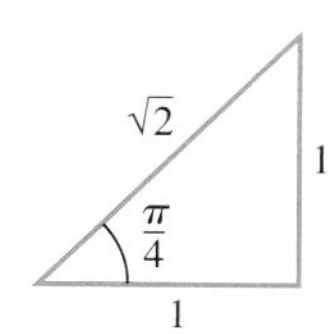

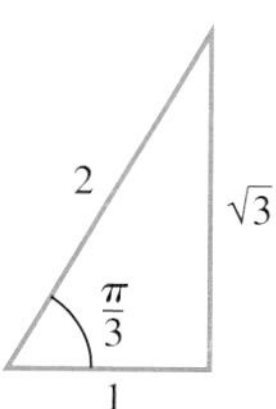

4. Angles and Sides of a Triangle

Law of cosines: $c^2 = a^2 + b^2 - 2ab\cos C$

Law of sines: $\dfrac{\sin A}{a} = \dfrac{\sin B}{b} = \dfrac{\sin C}{c}$

$$\text{Area} = \frac{1}{2}bc\sin A = \frac{1}{2}ac\sin B = \frac{1}{2}ab\sin C$$

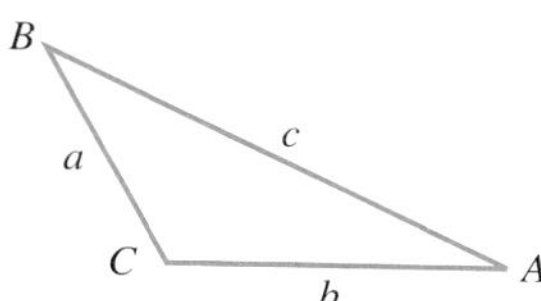

A.2 Proofs of the Limit Theorems in Chapter 2

This appendix furnishes the ϵ-δ proofs for Theorems 1 and 6 in Chapter 2.

THEOREM 1 (SECTION 2.1)

The following rules hold if $\lim_{x\to c} f(x) = L_1$ and $\lim_{x\to c} g(x) = L_2$. (L_1 and L_2 are real numbers.)

1. *Sum Rule:* $\lim_{x\to c} (f(x) + g(x)) = L_1 + L_2$
2. *Difference Rule:* $\lim_{x\to c} (f(x) - g(x)) = L_1 - L_2$
3. *Product Rule:* $\lim_{x\to c} f(x) \cdot g(x) = L_1 \cdot L_2$
4. *Constant Multiple Rule:* $\lim_{x\to c} k \cdot g(x) = k \cdot L_2$ (any number k)
5. *Quotient Rule:* $\lim_{x\to c} \dfrac{f(x)}{g(x)} = \dfrac{L_1}{L_2}$ if $L_2 \neq 0$

We proved the Sum Rule in Section 2.5. We obtain the Difference Rule by replacing $g(x)$ by $-g(x)$ and L_2 by $-L_2$ in the Sum Rule. The Constant Multiple Rule is the special case $f(x) = k$ of the Product Rule. This leaves only the Product and Quotient Rules to prove.

Proof of the Limit Product Rule We need to show that for any $\epsilon > 0$ there exists a $\delta > 0$ such that for all x in the functions' common domain,

$$0 < |x - c| < \delta \quad \Rightarrow \quad |f(x)\,g(x) - L_1 L_2| < \epsilon. \tag{1}$$

Suppose then that ϵ is a positive number, and write $f(x)$ and $g(x)$ as

$$f(x) = L_1 + (f(x) - L_1) \qquad \text{and} \qquad g(x) = L_2 + (g(x) - L_2).$$

Multiply these expressions together and subtract $L_1 L_2$:

$$\begin{aligned} f(x)\cdot g(x) - L_1L_2 &= (L_1 + (f(x) - L_1))(L_2 + (g(x) - L_2)) - L_1L_2 \\ &= L_1L_2 + L_1(g(x) - L_2) + L_2(f(x) - L_1) \\ &\quad + (f(x) - L_1)(g(x) - L_2) - L_1L_2 \\ &= L_1(g(x) - L_2) + L_2(f(x) - L_1) + (f(x) - L_1) \\ &\quad \times (g(x) - L_2). \end{aligned} \tag{2}$$

Since f and g have limits L_1 and L_2 as $x \to c$, there exist positive numbers δ_1, δ_2, δ_3, and δ_4 such that for all x,

$$\begin{aligned} 0 < |x - c| < \delta_1 &\quad \Rightarrow \quad |f(x) - L_1| < \sqrt{\epsilon/3}, \\ 0 < |x - c| < \delta_2 &\quad \Rightarrow \quad |g(x) - L_2| < \sqrt{\epsilon/3}, \\ 0 < |x - c| < \delta_3 &\quad \Rightarrow \quad |f(x) - L_1| < \epsilon/(3(1 + |L_2|)), \\ 0 < |x - c| < \delta_4 &\quad \Rightarrow \quad |g(x) - L_2| < \epsilon/(3(1 + |L_1|)). \end{aligned} \tag{3}$$

All four of the inequalities on the right-hand side of (3) will hold for $0 < |x - c| < \delta$ if we take δ to be the smallest of the numbers δ_1 through δ_4. Therefore, for all x, $0 < |x - c| < \delta$ implies

$$|f(x) \cdot g(x) - L_1 L_2|$$
$$\leq |L_1|\,|g(x) - L_2| + |L_2|\,|f(x) - L_1| + |f(x) - L_1|\,|g(x) - L_2|$$

Triangle inequality applied to Eq. (2)

$$\leq (1 + |L_1|)|g(x) - L_2| + (1 + |L_2|)|f(x) - L_1| + |f(x) - L_1|\,|g(x) - L_2|$$

$$\leq \frac{\epsilon}{3} + \frac{\epsilon}{3} + \sqrt{\frac{\epsilon}{3}}\sqrt{\frac{\epsilon}{3}} = \epsilon. \qquad \text{Values from (3)}$$

This completes the proof of the Limit Product Rule. ■

Proof of the Limit Quotient Rule We show that

$$\lim_{x \to c} \frac{1}{g(x)} = \frac{1}{L_2}.$$

Then we can apply the Limit Product Rule to show that

$$\lim_{x \to c} \frac{f(x)}{g(x)} = \lim_{x \to c} f(x) \cdot \frac{1}{g(x)} = \lim_{x \to c} f(x) \cdot \lim_{x \to c} \frac{1}{g(x)} = L_1 \cdot \frac{1}{L_2} = \frac{L_1}{L_2}.$$

To show that $\lim_{x \to c} (1/g(x)) = 1/L_2$, we need to show that for any $\epsilon > 0$ there exists a $\delta > 0$ such that for all x.

$$0 < |x - c| < \delta \quad \Rightarrow \quad \left|\frac{1}{g(x)} - \frac{1}{L_2}\right| < \epsilon.$$

Since $|L_2| > 0$, there exists a positive number δ_1 such that for all x,

$$0 < |x - c| < \delta_1 \quad \Rightarrow \quad |g(x) - L_2| < \frac{|L_2|}{2}. \tag{4}$$

For any numbers A and B it can be shown that $|A| - |B| \leq |A - B|$ and $|B| - |A| \leq |A - B|$, from which it follows that

$$||A| - |B|| \leq |A - B|. \tag{5}$$

With $A = g(x)$ and $B = L_2$, the inequality in (5) gives

$$||g(x)| - |L_2|| \leq |g(x) - L_2|,$$

which we can combine with the right-hand inequality in (4) to get, in turn,

$$||g(x)| - |L_2|| < \frac{|L_2|}{2},$$

$$-\frac{|L_2|}{2} < |g(x)| - |L_2| < \frac{|L_2|}{2},$$

$$\frac{|L_2|}{2} < |g(x)| < \frac{3|L_2|}{2}, \tag{6}$$

$$|L_2| < 2|g(x)| < 3|L_2|,$$

$$\frac{1}{|g(x)|} < \frac{2}{|L_2|} < \frac{3}{|g(x)|}.$$

Therefore $0 < |x - c| < \delta_1$, implies that

$$\left|\frac{1}{g(x)} - \frac{1}{L_2}\right| = \left|\frac{L_2 - g(x)}{L_2 g(x)}\right| \le \frac{1}{|L_2|} \cdot \frac{1}{|g(x)|} \cdot |L_2 - g(x)|$$
$$< \frac{1}{|L_2|} \cdot \frac{2}{|L_2|} \cdot |L_2 - g(x)|. \qquad \text{Eq. (6)}$$

Suppose now that ϵ is an arbitrary positive number. Then $\frac{1}{2}|L_2|^2 \epsilon > 0$, so there exists a number $\delta_2 > 0$ such that for all x,

$$0 < |x - c| < \delta_2 \quad \Rightarrow \quad |L_2 - g(x)| < \frac{\epsilon}{2}|L_2|^2. \tag{7}$$

The conclusions in (6) and (7) both hold for all x such that $0 < |x - c| < \delta$ if we take δ to be the smaller of the positive values δ_1 and δ_2. Combining (6) and (7) then gives

$$0 < |x - c| < \delta \quad \Rightarrow \quad \left|\frac{1}{g(x)} - \frac{1}{L_2}\right| < \epsilon. \tag{8}$$

This concludes the proof of the Limit Quotient Rule. ■

THEOREM 6 (SECTION 2.3)

The Sandwich Theorem

Suppose that $g(x) \le f(x) \le h(x)$ for all $x \ne c$ in some interval about c and that $\lim_{x\to c} g(x) = \lim_{x\to c} h(x) = L$. Then $\lim_{x\to c} f(x) = L$.

Proof for Right-hand Limits Suppose $\lim_{x\to c^+} g(x) = \lim_{x\to c^+} h(x) = L$. Then for any $\epsilon > 0$ there exists a $\delta > 0$ such that for all x the inequality $c < x < c + \delta$ implies

$$L - \epsilon < g(x) < L + \epsilon \quad \text{and} \quad L - \epsilon < h(x) < L + \epsilon. \tag{9}$$

These inequalities combine with the inequality $g(x) \le f(x) \le h(x)$ to give

$$\begin{aligned} L - \epsilon < g(x) \le f(x) \le h(x) < L + \epsilon, \\ L - \epsilon < f(x) < L + \epsilon, \\ -\epsilon < f(x) - L < \epsilon. \end{aligned} \tag{10}$$

Therefore, for all x, the inequality $c < x < c + \delta$ implies $|f(x) - L| < \epsilon$. ■

Proof for Left-hand Limits Suppose $\lim_{x\to c^-} g(x) = \lim_{x\to c^-} h(x) = L$. Then for any $\epsilon > 0$ there exists a $\delta > 0$ such that for all x the inequality $c - \delta < x < c$ implies

$$L - \epsilon < g(x) < L + \epsilon \quad \text{and} \quad L - \epsilon < h(x) < L + \epsilon. \tag{11}$$

We conclude as before that for all x the inequality $c - \delta < x < c$ implies $|f(x) - L| < \epsilon$. ■

Proof for Two-sided Limits If $\lim_{x\to c} g(x) = \lim_{x\to c} h(x) = L$, then $g(x)$ and $h(x)$ both approach L as $x \to c^+$ and as $x \to c^-$; so $\lim_{x\to c^+} f(x) = L$ and $\lim_{x\to c^-} f(x) = L$. Hence $\lim_{x\to c} f(x)$ exists and equals L. ∎

Exercises A.2

1. Suppose that functions $f_1(x)$, $f_2(x)$, and $f_3(x)$ have limits L_1, L_2, and L_3, respectively, as $x \to c$. Show that their sum has limit $L_1 + L_2 + L_3$. Use mathematical induction (Appendix A.4) to generalize this result to the sum of any finite number of functions.

2. Use mathematical induction and the Limit Product Rule in Theorem 1 to show that if functions $f_1(x), f_2(x), \ldots, f_n(x)$ have limits $L_1, L_2, \ldots, L_n$ as $x \to c$, then

$$\lim_{x\to c} f_1(x) f_2(x) \cdot \cdots \cdot f_n(x) = L_1 \cdot L_2 \cdot \cdots \cdot L_n.$$

3. Use the fact that $\lim_{x\to c} x = c$ and the result of Exercise 2 to show that $\lim_{x\to c} x^n = c^n$ for any integer $n > 1$.

4. *Limits of Polynomials.* Use the fact that $\lim_{x\to c} (k) = k$ for any number k together with the results of Exercises 1 and 3 to show that $\lim_{x\to c} f(x) = f(c)$ for any polynomial function

$$f(x) = a_0 x^n + a_1 x^{n-1} + \cdots + a_{n-1} x + a_n.$$

5. *Limits of Rational Functions.* Use Theorem 1 and the result of Exercise 4 to show that if $f(x)$ and $g(x)$ are polynomial functions and $g(c) \neq 0$, then

$$\lim_{x\to c} \frac{f(x)}{g(x)} = \frac{f(c)}{g(c)}.$$

6. *Composites of Continuous Functions.* Figure A.1 gives the diagram for a proof that the composite of two continuous functions is continuous. Reconstruct the proof from the diagram. The statement to be proved is this: If g is continuous at $x = c$ and f is continuous at $g(c)$, then $f \circ g$ is continuous at c.

   Assume that c is an interior point of the domain of g and that $g(c)$ is an interior point of the domain of f. This will make the limits involved two-sided. (The arguments for the cases that involve one-sided limits are similar.)

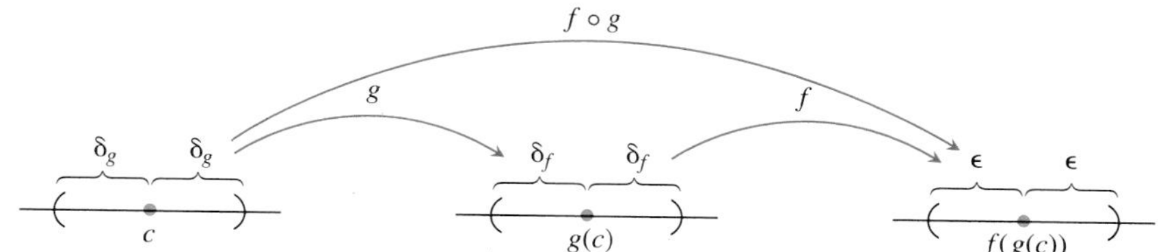

A.1 The diagram for a proof that the composite of two continuous functions is continuous. The continuity of composites holds for any finite number of functions. The only requirement is that each function be continuous where it is applied. In the figure, g is to be continuous at c and f at $g(c)$.

A.3

A Proof of the Chain Rule for Functions of a Single Variable

Our goal is to show that if $f(u)$ is a differentiable function of u and $u = g(x)$ is a differentiable function of x then the composite $y = f(g(x))$ is a differentiable function of x. More precisely, if g is differentiable at x_0 and f is differentiable at $g(x_0)$, then the composite is differentiable at x_0 and

$$\left.\frac{dy}{dx}\right|_{x=x_0} = f'(g(x_0)) \cdot g'(x_0). \tag{1}$$

Suppose that Δx is an increment in x and that Δu and Δy are the corresponding increments in u and y. As you can see in Fig. A.2 (on the following page),

$$\left.\frac{dy}{dx}\right|_{x=x_0} = \lim_{\Delta x\to 0} \frac{\Delta y}{\Delta x},$$

so our goal is to show that this limit is $f'(g(x_0)) \cdot g'(x_0)$.

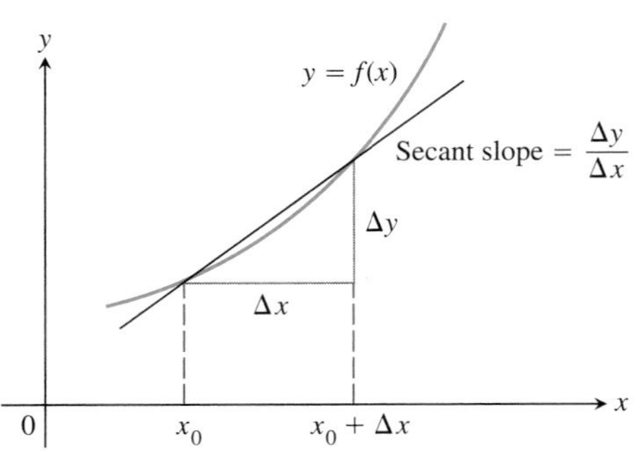

A.2 The graph of y as a function of x. The derivative of y with respect to x at $x = x_0$ is $\lim_{\Delta x \to 0} \Delta y/\Delta x$.

By virtue of Eq. (11) in Section 3.7,

$$\Delta u = g'(x_0)\,\Delta x + \epsilon_1\,\Delta x = (g'(x_0) + \epsilon_1)\,\Delta x,$$

where $\epsilon_1 \to 0$ as $\Delta x \to 0$. Similarly,

$$\Delta y = f'(u_0)\,\Delta u + \epsilon_2\,\Delta u = (f'(u_0) + \epsilon_2)\,\Delta u,$$

where $\epsilon_2 \to 0$ as $\Delta u \to 0$. Combining the equations for Δu and Δy gives

$$\Delta y = (f'(u_0) + \epsilon_2)(g'(x_0) + \epsilon_1)\,\Delta x, \tag{2}$$

so

$$\frac{\Delta y}{\Delta x} = f'(u_0)g'(x_0) + \epsilon_2\,g'(x_0) + f'(u_0)\epsilon_1 + \epsilon_2\epsilon_1.$$

Since ϵ_1 and ϵ_2 go to zero as Δx goes to zero, the three terms on the right vanish in the limit and

$$\lim_{\Delta x \to 0} \frac{\Delta y}{\Delta x} = f'(u_0)g'(x_0) = f'(g(x_0)) \cdot g'(x_0).$$

This concludes the proof. ■

A.4 Mathematical Induction

Many formulas, like

$$1 + 2 + \cdots + n = \frac{n(n+1)}{2},$$

can be shown to hold for every positive integer n by applying an axiom called the *mathematical induction principle*. A proof that uses this axiom is called a *proof by mathematical induction* or a *proof by induction*.

The steps in proving a formula by induction are the following.

STEP 1: Check that it holds for $n = 1$.

STEP 2: Prove that if it holds for any positive integer $n = k$, then it also holds for the next integer, $n = k + 1$.

Once these steps are completed (the axiom says), we know that the formula holds for all positive integers n. By step 1 it holds for $n = 1$. By step 2 it holds for $n = 2$, and therefore by step 2 also for $n = 3$, and by step 2 again for $n = 4$, and so on. If the first domino falls, and the kth domino always knocks over the $(k + 1)$st when it falls, all the dominoes fall.

From another point of view, suppose we have a sequence of statements

$$S_1, S_2, \ldots, S_n, \ldots,$$

one for each positive integer. Suppose we can show that assuming any one of the statements to be true implies that the next statement in line is true. Suppose that we can also show that S_1 is true. Then we may conclude that the statements are true from S_1 on.

EXAMPLE 1 Show that for every positive integer n,

$$1 + 2 + \cdots + n = \frac{n(n+1)}{2}.$$

Solution We accomplish the proof by carrying out the two steps of mathematical induction.

STEP 1: The formula holds for $n = 1$ because

$$1 = \frac{1(1+1)}{2}.$$

STEP 2: If the formula holds for $n = k$, does it also hold for $n = k + 1$? The answer is yes, and here's why: If

$$1 + 2 + \cdots + k = \frac{k(k+1)}{2},$$

then

$$\begin{aligned} 1 + 2 + \cdots + k + (k+1) &= \frac{k(k+1)}{2} + (k+1) = \frac{k^2 + k + 2k + 2}{2} \\ &= \frac{(k+1)(k+2)}{2} = \frac{(k+1)((k+1)+1)}{2}. \end{aligned}$$

The last expression in this string of equalities is the expression $n(n+1)/2$ for $n = (k+1)$.

The mathematical induction principle now guarantees the original formula for all positive integers n.

Notice that all *we* have to do is carry out steps 1 and 2. The mathematical induction principle does the rest.

EXAMPLE 2 Show that for all positive integers n,

$$\frac{1}{2^1} + \frac{1}{2^2} + \cdots + \frac{1}{2^n} = 1 - \frac{1}{2^n}.$$

Solution We accomplish the proof by carrying out the two steps of mathematical induction.

STEP 1: The formula holds for $n = 1$ because

$$\frac{1}{2^1} = 1 - \frac{1}{2^1}.$$

STEP 2: If

$$\frac{1}{2^1} + \frac{1}{2^2} + \cdots + \frac{1}{2^k} = 1 - \frac{1}{2^k},$$

then

$$\begin{aligned} \frac{1}{2^1} + \frac{1}{2^2} + \cdots + \frac{1}{2^k} + \frac{1}{2^{k+1}} &= 1 - \frac{1}{2^k} + \frac{1}{2^{k+1}} = 1 - \frac{1 \cdot 2}{2^k \cdot 2} + \frac{1}{2^{k+1}} \\ &= 1 - \frac{2}{2^{k+1}} + \frac{1}{2^{k+1}} = 1 - \frac{1}{2^{k+1}}. \end{aligned}$$

Thus, the original formula holds for $n = (k + 1)$ whenever it holds for $n = k$.

With these steps verified, the mathematical induction principle now guarantees the formula for every positive integer n.

Other Starting Integers

Instead of starting at $n = 1$, some induction arguments start at another integer. The steps for such an argument are as follows.

STEP 1: Check that the formula holds for $n = n_1$ (whatever the appropriate first integer is).

STEP 2: Prove that if the formula holds for any integer $n = k \geq n_1$, then it also holds for $n = (k + 1)$.

Once these steps are completed, the mathematical induction principle guarantees the formula for all $n \geq n_1$.

EXAMPLE 3 Show that $n! > 3^n$ if n is large enough.

Solution How large is large enough? We experiment:

n	1	2	3	4	5	6	7
$n!$	1	2	6	24	120	720	5040
3^n	3	9	27	81	243	729	2187

It looks as if $n! > 3^n$ for $n \geq 7$. To be sure, we apply mathematical induction. We take $n_1 = 7$ in step 1 and try for step 2.

Suppose $k! > 3^k$ for some $k \geq 7$. Then

$$(k + 1)! = (k + 1)(k!) > (k + 1)3^k > 7 \cdot 3^k > 3^{k+1}.$$

Thus, for $k \geq 7$,

$$k! > 3^k \quad \Rightarrow \quad (k + 1)! > 3^{k+1}.$$

The mathematical induction principle now guarantees $n! \geq 3^n$ for all $n \geq 7$.

Exercises A.4

1. Assuming that the triangle inequality $|a + b| \leq |a| + |b|$ holds for any two numbers a and b, show that
$$|x_1 + x_2 + \cdots + x_n| \leq |x_1| + |x_2| + \cdots + |x_n|$$
for any n numbers.

2. Show that if $r \neq 1$, then
$$1 + r + r^2 + \cdots + r^n = \frac{1 - r^{n+1}}{1 - r}$$
for every positive integer n.

3. Use the Product Rule,
$$\frac{d}{dx}(uv) = u\frac{dv}{dx} + v\frac{du}{dx},$$
and the fact that
$$\frac{d}{dx}(x) = 1$$
to show that
$$\frac{d}{dx}(x^n) = nx^{n-1}$$
for every positive integer n.

4. Suppose that a function $f(x)$ has the property that $f(x_1x_2) = f(x_1) + f(x_2)$ for any two positive numbers x_1 and x_2. Show that
$$f(x_1 x_2 \cdots x_n) = f(x_1) + f(x_2) + \cdots + f(x_n)$$
for the product of any n positive numbers $x_1, x_2, \ldots, x_n$.

5. Show that

$$\frac{2}{3^1}+\frac{2}{3^2}+\cdots+\frac{2}{3^n}=1-\frac{1}{3^n}$$

for all positive integers n.

6. Show that $n! > n^3$ if n is large enough.

7. Show that $2^n > n^2$ if n is large enough.

8. Show that $2^n \geq 1/8$ for $n \geq -3$.

9. *Sums of Squares.* Show that the sum of the squares of the first n positive integers is

$$\frac{n\left(n+\frac{1}{2}\right)(n+1)}{3}.$$

10. *Sums of Cubes.* Show that the sum of the cubes of the first n positive integers is $(n(n+1)/2)^2$.

11. *Rules for Finite Sums.* Show that the following finite sum rules hold for every positive integer n.

a) $\sum_{k=1}^{n}(a_k+b_k)=\sum_{k=1}^{n}a_k+\sum_{k=1}^{n}b_k$

b) $\sum_{k=1}^{n}(a_k-b_k)=\sum_{k=1}^{n}a_k-\sum_{k=1}^{n}b_k$

c) $\sum_{k=1}^{n}ca_k=c\cdot\sum_{k=1}^{n}a_k$ (Any number c)

d) $\sum_{k=1}^{n}a_k=n\cdot c$ if a_k has the constant value c

12. *Sums of Products of Consecutive Positive Integers.* You are probably already familiar with the sums

$$\sum_{k=1}^{n}k^0=\sum_{k=1}^{n}1=\frac{n}{1}\quad\text{and}\quad\sum_{k=1}^{n}k=\frac{n(n+1)}{2}.$$

Show that

a) $\sum_{k=1}^{n}k(k+1)=\frac{n(n+1)(n+2)}{3}$

b) $\sum_{k=1}^{n}k(k+1)(k+2)=\frac{n(n+1)(n+2)(n+3)}{4}$

c) $\sum_{k=1}^{n}k(k+1)(k+2)(k+3)=$

$$\frac{n(n+1)(n+2)(n+3)(n+4)}{5}$$

Then show, in general, that if m and n are integers with $m \geq 0$ and $n \geq 1$, then

d) $\sum_{k=1}^{n}\left(\prod_{j=0}^{m}(k+j)\right)=\frac{1}{m+2}\prod_{j=0}^{m+1}(n+j)$

A.5 Simpson's One-Third Rule

Simpson's rule for approximating $\int_a^b f(x)\,dx$ is based on approximating f with quadratic polynomials instead of linear polynomials. We approximate the graph of f with parabolic arcs instead of line segments.

The area of the shaded region under the parabola in Fig. A.3 is

$$\text{Area}=\frac{h}{3}(y_0+4y_1+y_2), \tag{1}$$

which is known as Simpson's one-third rule.

A.3 Simpson's rule approximates short stretches of curve with parabolic arcs.

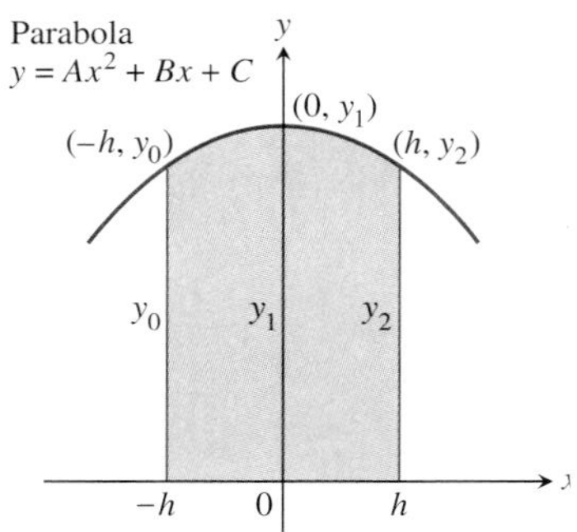

A.4 By integrating from $-h$ to h, the shaded area is found to be

$$\frac{h}{3}(y_0 + 4y_1 + y_2).$$

We can derive this formula as follows. To simplify the algebra, we use the coordinate system shown in Fig. A.4. The area under the parabola is the same no matter where the y-axis is, as long as we preserve the vertical scale. The parabola has an equation of the form $y = Ax^2 + Bx + C$, so the area under it from $x = -h$ to $x = h$ is

$$\begin{aligned} \text{Area} = \int_{-h}^{h} (Ax^2 + Bx + C)\,dx &= \left[\frac{Ax^3}{3} + \frac{Bx^2}{2} + Cx\right]_{-h}^{h} \\ &= \frac{2Ah^3}{3} + 2Ch = \frac{h}{3}(2Ah^2 + 6C). \end{aligned} \tag{2}$$

Since the curve passes through $(-h, y_0)$, $(0, y_1)$, and (h, y_2), we also have

$$y_0 = Ah^2 - Bh + C, \qquad y_1 = C, \qquad y_2 = Ah^2 + Bh + C.$$

From these equations we obtain

$$\begin{aligned} C &= y_1, \\ Ah^2 - Bh &= y_0 - y_1, \\ Ah^2 + Bh &= y_2 - y_1, \\ 2Ah^2 &= y_0 + y_2 - 2y_1. \end{aligned} \tag{3}$$

These substitutions for C and $2Ah^2$ give

$$\text{Area} = \frac{h}{3}(2Ah^2 + 6C) = \frac{h}{3}((y_0 + y_2 - 2y_1) + 6y_1) = \frac{h}{3}(y_0 + 4y_1 + y_2). \tag{4}$$

A.6 Limits That Arise Frequently

This appendix verifies the limits in Table 9.1 of Section 9.1.

1. $\displaystyle\lim_{n\to\infty} \frac{\ln n}{n} = 0$

2. $\displaystyle\lim_{n\to\infty} \sqrt[n]{n} = 1$

3. $\displaystyle\lim_{n\to\infty} x^{1/n} = 1 \quad (x > 0)$

4. $\displaystyle\lim_{n\to\infty} x^n = 0 \quad (|x| < 1)$

5. $\displaystyle\lim_{n\to\infty} \left(1 + \frac{x}{n}\right)^n = e^x \quad (\text{any } x)$

6. $\displaystyle\lim_{n\to\infty} \frac{x^n}{n!} = 0 \quad (\text{any } x)$

In Eqs. (3)–(6), x remains fixed while n varies.

1. $\displaystyle\lim_{n\to\infty} \frac{\ln n}{n} = 0$ We proved this in Section 9.1, Example 9.

2. $\displaystyle\lim_{n\to\infty} \sqrt[n]{n} = 1$ Let $a_n = n^{1/n}$. Then

$$\ln a_n = \ln n^{1/n} = \frac{1}{n}\ln n \to 0. \tag{1}$$

Applying Theorem 3, Section 9.1, with $f(x) = e^x$ gives

$$n^{1/n} = a_n = e^{\ln a_n} = f(\ln a_n) \to f(0) = e^0 = 1. \tag{2}$$

3. If $x > 0$, $\lim_{n\to\infty} x^{1/n} = 1$ Let $a_n = x^{1/n}$. Then

$$\ln a_n = \ln x^{1/n} = \frac{1}{n} \ln x \to 0 \tag{3}$$

because x remains fixed as $n \to \infty$. Applying Theorem 3, Section 9.1, with $f(x) = e^x$ gives

$$x^{1/n} = a_n = e^{\ln a_n} \to e^0 = 1. \tag{4}$$

4. If $|x| < 1$, $\lim_{n\to\infty} x^n = 0$ We need to show that to each $\epsilon > 0$ there corresponds an integer N so large that $|x^n| < \epsilon$ for all n greater than N. Since $\epsilon^{1/n} \to 1$, while $|x| < 1$, there exists an integer N for which

$$\epsilon^{1/N} > |x|. \tag{5}$$

In other words,

$$|x^N| = |x|^N < \epsilon. \tag{6}$$

This is the integer we seek because, if $|x| < 1$, then

$$|x^n| < |x^N| \quad \text{for all } n > N. \tag{7}$$

Combining (6) and (7) produces

$$|x^n| < \epsilon \quad \text{for all } n > N, \tag{8}$$

and we're done.

5. For any number x, $\lim_{n\to\infty} \left(1 + \frac{x}{n}\right)^n = e^x$ Let

$$a_n = \left(1 + \frac{x}{n}\right)^n.$$

Then

$$\ln a_n = \ln \left(1 + \frac{x}{n}\right)^n = n \ln \left(1 + \frac{x}{n}\right) \to x,$$

as we can see by the following application of l'Hôpital's rule, in which we differentiate with respect to n:

$$\lim_{n\to\infty} n \ln \left(1 + \frac{x}{n}\right) = \lim_{n\to\infty} \frac{\ln (1 + x/n)}{1/n}$$

$$= \lim_{n\to\infty} \frac{\left(\dfrac{1}{1 + x/n}\right) \cdot \left(-\dfrac{x}{n^2}\right)}{-1/n^2} = \lim_{n\to\infty} \frac{x}{1 + x/n} = x.$$

Apply Theorem 3, Section 9.1, with $f(x) = e^x$ to conclude that

$$\left(1 + \frac{x}{n}\right)^n = a_n = e^{\ln a_n} \to e^x.$$

6. For any number x, $\lim_{n\to\infty} \frac{x^n}{n!} = 0$ Since

$$-\frac{|x|^n}{n!} \le \frac{x^n}{n!} \le \frac{|x|^n}{n!},$$

all we need to show is that $|x|^n/n! \to 0$. We can then apply the Sandwich Theorem for Sequences (Section 9.1, Theorem 2) to conclude that $x^n/n! \to 0$.

The first step in showing that $|x|^n/n! \to 0$ is to choose an integer $M > |x|$, so that

$$\frac{|x|}{M} < 1 \quad \text{and} \quad \left(\frac{|x|}{M}\right)^n \to 0.$$

We then restrict our attention to values of $n > M$. For these values of n, we can write

$$\frac{|x|^n}{n!} = \frac{|x|^n}{1 \cdot 2 \cdot \cdots \cdot M \cdot \underbrace{(M+1)(M+2) \cdot \cdots \cdot n}_{(n-M)\text{ factors}}}$$

$$\leq \frac{|x|^n}{M!M^{n-M}} = \frac{|x|^n M^M}{M!M^n} = \frac{M^M}{M!}\left(\frac{|x|}{M}\right)^n.$$

Thus,

$$0 \leq \frac{|x|^n}{n!} \leq \frac{M^M}{M!}\left(\frac{|x|}{M}\right)^n.$$

Now, the constant $M^M/M!$ does not change as n increases. Thus the Sandwich Theorem tells us that

$$\frac{|x|^n}{n!} \to 0 \quad \text{because} \quad \left(\frac{|x|}{M}\right)^n \to 0.$$

A.7 Determinants and Cramer's Rule

A rectangular array of numbers like

$$A = \begin{bmatrix} 2 & 1 & 3 \\ 1 & 0 & -2 \end{bmatrix}$$

is called a **matrix.** We call A a 2 by 3 matrix because it has two rows and three columns. An m by n matrix has m rows and n columns, and the **entry** or **element** (number) in the ith row and jth column is often denoted by a_{ij}:

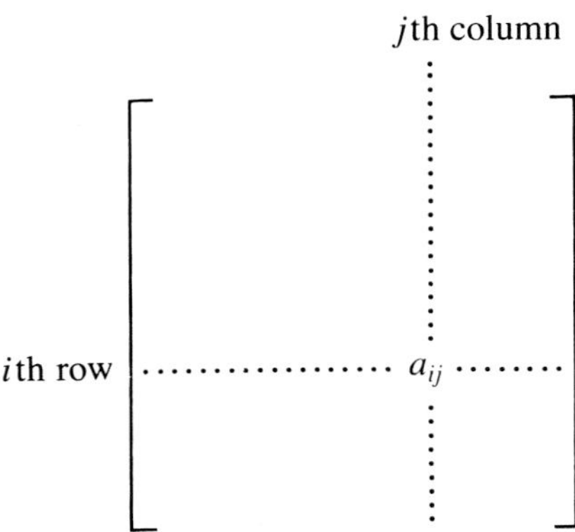

The matrix

$$A = \begin{bmatrix} 2 & 1 & 3 \\ 1 & 0 & -2 \end{bmatrix}$$

has

$$a_{11} = 2, \qquad a_{12} = 1, \qquad a_{13} = 3,$$
$$a_{21} = 1, \qquad a_{22} = 0, \qquad a_{23} = -2.$$

A matrix with the same number of rows as columns is a **square matrix.** It is a **matrix of order *n*** if the number of rows and columns is n.

With each square matrix A we associate a number det A or $|a_{ij}|$, called the **determinant** of A, calculated from the entries of A in the following way. (The vertical bars in the notation $|a_{ij}|$ do not mean absolute value.) For $n = 1$ and $n = 2$, we define

$$\det [a] = a, \tag{1}$$

$$\det \begin{bmatrix} a_{11} & a_{12} \\ a_{21} & a_{22} \end{bmatrix} = a_{11}a_{22} - a_{21}a_{12}. \tag{2}$$

For a matrix of order 3, we define

$$\det A = \det \begin{bmatrix} a_{11} & a_{12} & a_{13} \\ a_{21} & a_{22} & a_{23} \\ a_{31} & a_{32} & a_{33} \end{bmatrix} = \begin{array}{l} \text{Sum of all signed products} \\ \text{of the form } \pm\, a_{1i}a_{2j}a_{3k}, \end{array} \tag{3}$$

where i, j, k is a permutation of 1, 2, 3 in some order. There are $3! = 6$ such permutations, so there are six terms in the sum. The sign is positive when the index of the permutation is even and negative when the index is odd.

DEFINITION

Index of a Permutation

Given any permutation of the numbers 1, 2, 3, . . . , n, denote the permutation by $i_1, i_2, i_3, \ldots, i_n$. In this arrangement, some of the numbers following i_1 may be less than i_1, and the number of these is called the **number of inversions** in the arrangement pertaining to i_1. Likewise, there is a number of inversions pertaining to each of the other i's; it is the number of indices that come after that particular i in the arrangement and are less than it. The **index** of the permutation is the sum of all of the numbers of inversions pertaining to the separate indices.

EXAMPLE 1 For $n = 5$, the permutation

$$5 \quad 3 \quad 1 \quad 2 \quad 4$$

has

4 inversions pertaining to the first element, 5,

2 inversions pertaining to the second element, 3,

and no further inversions, so the index is $4 + 2 = 6$.

The following table shows the permutations of 1, 2, 3, the index of each permutation, and the signed product in the determinant of Eq. (3).

Permutation	Index	Signed product
1 2 3	0	$+a_{11}a_{22}a_{33}$
1 3 2	1	$-a_{11}a_{23}a_{32}$
2 1 3	1	$-a_{12}a_{21}a_{33}$
2 3 1	2	$+a_{12}a_{23}a_{31}$
3 1 2	2	$+a_{13}a_{21}a_{32}$
3 2 1	3	$-a_{13}a_{22}a_{31}$

(4)

The sum of the six signed products is

$$a_{11}(a_{22}a_{33}-a_{23}a_{32})-a_{12}(a_{21}a_{33}-a_{23}a_{31})+a_{13}(a_{21}a_{32}-a_{22}\,a_{31})$$

$$=a_{11}\begin{vmatrix}a_{22}&a_{23}\\a_{32}&a_{33}\end{vmatrix}-a_{12}\begin{vmatrix}a_{21}&a_{23}\\a_{31}&a_{33}\end{vmatrix}+a_{13}\begin{vmatrix}a_{21}&a_{22}\\a_{31}&a_{32}\end{vmatrix}=\begin{vmatrix}a_{11}&a_{12}&a_{13}\\a_{21}&a_{22}&a_{23}\\a_{31}&a_{32}&a_{33}\end{vmatrix}. \quad (5)$$

The formula

$$\begin{vmatrix}a_{11}&a_{12}&a_{13}\\a_{21}&a_{22}&a_{23}\\a_{31}&a_{32}&a_{33}\end{vmatrix}=a_{11}\begin{vmatrix}a_{22}&a_{23}\\a_{32}&a_{33}\end{vmatrix}-a_{12}\begin{vmatrix}a_{21}&a_{23}\\a_{31}&a_{33}\end{vmatrix}+a_{13}\begin{vmatrix}a_{21}&a_{22}\\a_{31}&a_{32}\end{vmatrix} \quad (6)$$

reduces the calculation of a 3 by 3 determinant to the calculation of three 2 by 2 determinants.

Many people prefer to remember the following scheme for calculating the six signed products in the determinant of a 3 by 3 matrix:

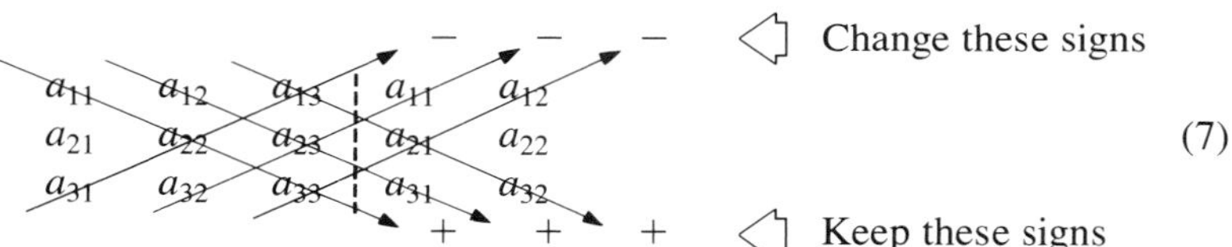

(7)

Minors and Cofactors

The second order determinants on the right-hand side of Eq. (6) are called the **minors** (short for "minor determinants") of the entries they multiply. Thus,

$$\begin{vmatrix}a_{22}&a_{23}\\a_{32}&a_{33}\end{vmatrix} \text{ is the minor of } a_{11},$$

$$\begin{vmatrix}a_{21}&a_{23}\\a_{31}&a_{33}\end{vmatrix} \text{ is the minor of } a_{12},$$

and so on. The minor of the element a_{ij} in a matrix A is the determinant of the matrix that remains after we delete the row and column containing a_{ij}:

$$\begin{vmatrix}a_{11}&a_{12}&a_{13}\\a_{21}&a_{22}&a_{23}\\a_{31}&a_{32}&a_{33}\end{vmatrix}. \qquad \text{The minor of } a_{22} \text{ is } \begin{vmatrix}a_{11}&a_{13}\\a_{31}&a_{33}\end{vmatrix}.$$

$$\begin{vmatrix}a_{11}&a_{12}&a_{13}\\a_{21}&a_{22}&a_{23}\\a_{31}&a_{32}&a_{33}\end{vmatrix}. \qquad \text{The minor of } a_{23} \text{ is } \begin{vmatrix}a_{11}&a_{12}\\a_{31}&a_{32}\end{vmatrix}.$$

The **cofactor** A_{ij} of a_{ij} is $(-1)^{i+j}$ times the minor of a_{ij}. Thus,

$$A_{22} = (-1)^{2+2}\begin{vmatrix} a_{11} & a_{13} \\ a_{31} & a_{33} \end{vmatrix} = \begin{vmatrix} a_{11} & a_{13} \\ a_{31} & a_{33} \end{vmatrix},$$

$$A_{23} = (-1)^{2+3}\begin{vmatrix} a_{11} & a_{12} \\ a_{31} & a_{32} \end{vmatrix} = -\begin{vmatrix} a_{11} & a_{12} \\ a_{31} & a_{32} \end{vmatrix}.$$

The factor $(-1)^{i+j}$ changes the sign of the minor when $i + j$ is odd. There is a checkerboard pattern for remembering these changes.

$$\begin{matrix} + & - & + \\ - & + & - \\ + & - & + \end{matrix}$$

In the upper left corner, $i = 1$, $j = 1$ and $(-1)^{1+1} = +1$. In going from any cell to an adjacent cell in the same row or column, we change i by 1 or j by 1, but not both, so we change the exponent from even to odd or from odd to even, which changes the sign from $+$ to $-$ or from $-$ to $+$.

When we rewrite Eq. (6) in terms of cofactors we get

$$\det A = a_{11}A_{11} + a_{12}A_{12} + a_{13}A_{13}. \tag{8}$$

EXAMPLE 2 Find the determinant of

$$A = \begin{bmatrix} 2 & 1 & 3 \\ 3 & -1 & -2 \\ 2 & 3 & 1 \end{bmatrix}.$$

Solution 1 The cofactors are

$$A_{11} = (-1)^{1+1}\begin{vmatrix} -1 & -2 \\ 3 & 1 \end{vmatrix}, \qquad A_{12} = (-1)^{1+2}\begin{vmatrix} 3 & -2 \\ 2 & 1 \end{vmatrix},$$

$$A_{13} = (-1)^{1+3}\begin{vmatrix} 3 & -1 \\ 2 & 3 \end{vmatrix}.$$

To find det A, we multiply each element of the first row of A by its cofactor and add:

$$\begin{aligned} \det A &= 2\begin{vmatrix} -1 & -2 \\ 3 & 1 \end{vmatrix} + (-1)\begin{vmatrix} 3 & -2 \\ 2 & 1 \end{vmatrix} + 3\begin{vmatrix} 3 & -1 \\ 2 & 3 \end{vmatrix} \\ &= 2(-1+6) - 1(3+4) + 3(9+2) = 10 - 7 + 33 = 36. \end{aligned}$$

Solution 2 From (7) we find

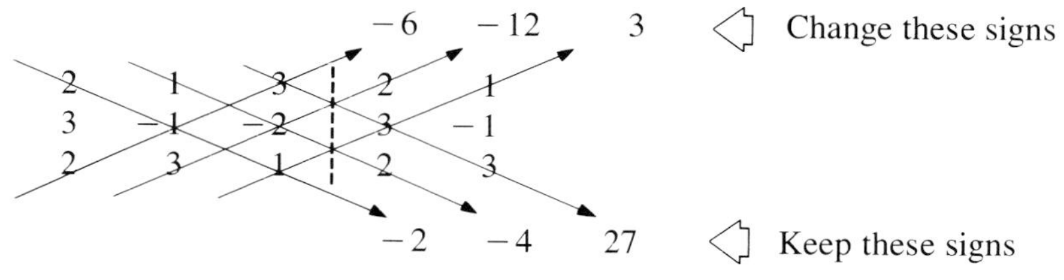

$$\det A = -(-6) - (-12) - 3 + (-2) + (-4) + 27 = 36$$

Expanding by Columns or by Other Rows

The determinant of a square matrix can be calculated from the cofactors of any row or any column.

If we were to expand the determinant in Example 2 by cofactors according to elements of its third column, say, we would get

$$+3\begin{vmatrix} 3 & -1 \\ 2 & 3 \end{vmatrix} - (-2)\begin{vmatrix} 2 & 1 \\ 2 & 3 \end{vmatrix} + 1\begin{vmatrix} 2 & 1 \\ 3 & -1 \end{vmatrix}$$

$$= 3(9 + 2) + 2(6 - 2) + 1(-2 - 3) = 33 + 8 - 5 = 36.$$

Useful Facts About Determinants

FACT 1: If two rows (or columns) are identical, the determinant is zero.

FACT 2: Interchanging two rows (or columns) changes the sign of the determinant.

FACT 3: The determinant is the sum of the products of the elements of the ith row (or column) by their cofactors, for any i.

FACT 4: The determinant of the transpose of a matrix is the same as the determinant of the original matrix. (The **transpose** of a matrix is obtained by writing the rows as columns.)

FACT 5: Multiplying each element of some row (or column) by a constant c multiplies the determinant by c.

FACT 6: If all elements above the main diagonal (or all below it) are zero, the determinant is the product of the elements on the main diagonal. (The **main diagonal** is the diagonal from upper left to lower right.)

EXAMPLE 3

$$\begin{vmatrix} 3 & 4 & 7 \\ 0 & -2 & 5 \\ 0 & 0 & 5 \end{vmatrix} = (3)(-2)(5) = -30$$

FACT 7: If the elements of any row are multiplied by the cofactors of the corresponding elements of a different row and these products are summed, the sum is zero.

EXAMPLE 4 If A_{11}, A_{12}, A_{13} are the cofactors of the elements of the first row of $A = (a_{ij})$, then the sums

$$a_{21}A_{11} + a_{22}A_{12} + a_{23}A_{13}$$

(elements of second row times cofactors of elements of first row) and

$$a_{31}A_{11} + a_{32}A_{12} + a_{33}A_{13}$$

are both zero.

FACT 8: If the elements of any column are multiplied by the cofactors of the corresponding elements of a different column and these products are summed, the sum is zero.

FACT 9: If each element of a row is multiplied by a constant c and the results added to a different row, the determinant is not changed. A similar result holds for columns.

EXAMPLE 5 If we start with

$$A = \begin{bmatrix} 2 & 1 & 3 \\ 3 & -1 & -2 \\ 2 & 3 & 1 \end{bmatrix}$$

and add -2 times row 1 to row 2 (subtract 2 times row 1 from row 2), we get

$$B = \begin{bmatrix} 2 & 1 & 3 \\ -1 & -3 & -8 \\ 2 & 3 & 1 \end{bmatrix}.$$

Since det $A = 36$ (Example 2), we should find that det $B = 36$ as well. Indeed we do, as the following calculation shows:

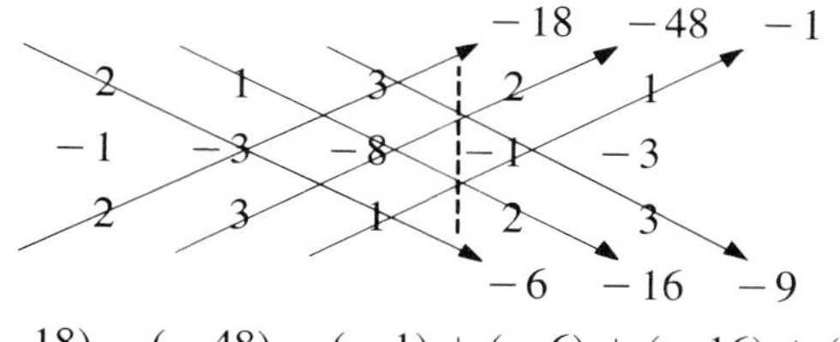

$$\begin{aligned} \det B &= -(-18) - (-48) - (-1) + (-6) + (-16) + (-9) \\ &= 18 + 48 + 1 - 6 - 16 - 9 = 67 - 31 = 36. \end{aligned}$$

EXAMPLE 6 Evaluate the fourth order determinant

$$D = \begin{vmatrix} 1 & -2 & 3 & 1 \\ 2 & 1 & 0 & 2 \\ -1 & 2 & 1 & -2 \\ 0 & 1 & 2 & 1 \end{vmatrix}.$$

Solution We subtract 2 times row 1 from row 2 and add row 1 to row 3 to get

$$D = \begin{vmatrix} 1 & -2 & 3 & 1 \\ 0 & 5 & -6 & 0 \\ 0 & 0 & 4 & -1 \\ 0 & 1 & 2 & 1 \end{vmatrix}.$$

We then multiply the elements of the first column by their cofactors to get

$$D = \begin{vmatrix} 5 & -6 & 0 \\ 0 & 4 & -1 \\ 1 & 2 & 1 \end{vmatrix} = 5(4 + 2) - (-6)(0 + 1) + 0 = 36.$$

Cramer's Rule

If the determinant

$$D = \det A = \begin{vmatrix} a_{11} & a_{12} \\ a_{21} & a_{22} \end{vmatrix}$$

of the coefficient matrix of the system

$$\begin{aligned} a_{11}x + a_{12}y &= b_1, \\ a_{21}x + a_{22}y &= b_2 \end{aligned} \tag{9}$$

of linear equations is 0, the system has either infinitely many solutions or no solution at all. The system

$$x + y = 0,$$
$$2x + 2y = 0$$

whose determinant is $D = \begin{vmatrix} 1 & 1 \\ 2 & 2 \end{vmatrix} = 2 - 2 = 0$

has infinitely many solutions. We can find an x to match any given y. The system

$$x + y = 0,$$
$$2x + 2y = 2$$

has no solution. If $x + y = 0$, then $2x + 2y = 2(x + y)$ cannot be 2.

If $D \neq 0$, the system (9) has a unique solution, and Cramer's rule states that it may be found from the formulas

$$x = \frac{\begin{vmatrix} b_1 & a_{12} \\ b_2 & a_{22} \end{vmatrix}}{D}, \qquad y = \frac{\begin{vmatrix} a_{11} & b_1 \\ a_{21} & b_2 \end{vmatrix}}{D}. \tag{10}$$

The numerator in the formula for x comes from replacing the first column in A (the x-column) by the column of constants b_1 and b_2 (the b-column). Replacing the y-column by the b-column gives the numerator of the y-solution.

EXAMPLE 7 Solve the system

$$3x - y = 9,$$
$$x + 2y = -4.$$

Solution We use Eqs. (10). The determinant of the coefficient matrix is

$$D = \begin{vmatrix} 3 & -1 \\ 1 & 2 \end{vmatrix} = 6 + 1 = 7.$$

Hence,

$$x = \frac{\begin{vmatrix} 9 & -1 \\ -4 & 2 \end{vmatrix}}{D} = \frac{18 - 4}{7} = \frac{14}{7} = 2,$$

$$y = \frac{\begin{vmatrix} 3 & 9 \\ 1 & -4 \end{vmatrix}}{D} = \frac{-12 - 9}{7} = \frac{-21}{7} = -3.$$

Systems of three equations in three unknowns work the same way. If the determinant

$$D = \det A = \begin{vmatrix} a_{11} & a_{12} & a_{13} \\ a_{21} & a_{22} & a_{23} \\ a_{31} & a_{32} & a_{33} \end{vmatrix}$$

of the system

$$\begin{aligned} a_{11}x + a_{12}y + a_{13}z &= b_1, \\ a_{21}x + a_{22}y + a_{23}z &= b_2, \\ a_{31}x + a_{32}y + a_{33}z &= b_3 \end{aligned} \tag{11}$$

is zero, the system has either infinitely many solutions or no solution at all. If $D \neq 0$, the system has a unique solution, given by Cramer's rule:

$$x = \frac{1}{D}\begin{vmatrix} b_1 & a_{12} & a_{13} \\ b_2 & a_{22} & a_{23} \\ b_3 & a_{32} & a_{33} \end{vmatrix}, \qquad y = \frac{1}{D}\begin{vmatrix} a_{11} & b_1 & a_{13} \\ a_{21} & b_2 & a_{23} \\ a_{31} & b_3 & a_{33} \end{vmatrix},$$

$$z = \frac{1}{D}\begin{vmatrix} a_{11} & a_{12} & b_1 \\ a_{21} & a_{22} & b_2 \\ a_{31} & a_{32} & b_3 \end{vmatrix}.$$

The pattern continues in higher dimensions.

Exercises A.7

Evaluate the following determinants.

1. $\begin{vmatrix} 2 & 3 & 1 \\ 4 & 5 & 2 \\ 1 & 2 & 3 \end{vmatrix}$

2. $\begin{vmatrix} 2 & -1 & -2 \\ -1 & 2 & 1 \\ 3 & 0 & -3 \end{vmatrix}$

3. $\begin{vmatrix} 1 & 2 & 3 & 4 \\ 0 & 1 & 2 & 3 \\ 0 & 0 & 2 & 1 \\ 0 & 0 & 3 & 2 \end{vmatrix}$

4. $\begin{vmatrix} 1 & -1 & 2 & 3 \\ 2 & 1 & 2 & 6 \\ 1 & 0 & 2 & 3 \\ -2 & 2 & 0 & -5 \end{vmatrix}$

Evaluate the following determinants by expanding according to the cofactors of (a) the third row and (b) the second column.

5. $\begin{vmatrix} 2 & -1 & 2 \\ 1 & 0 & 3 \\ 0 & 2 & 1 \end{vmatrix}$

6. $\begin{vmatrix} 1 & 0 & -1 \\ 0 & 2 & -2 \\ 2 & 0 & 1 \end{vmatrix}$

7. $\begin{vmatrix} 1 & 1 & 0 & 0 \\ 0 & 0 & -2 & 1 \\ 0 & -1 & 0 & 7 \\ 3 & 0 & 2 & 1 \end{vmatrix}$

8. $\begin{vmatrix} 0 & 1 & 0 & 0 \\ 0 & 1 & 1 & 0 \\ 1 & 1 & 1 & 1 \\ 1 & 1 & 0 & 0 \end{vmatrix}$

Solve the following systems of equations by Cramer's rule.

9. $\begin{aligned} x + 8y &= 4 \\ 3x - y &= -13 \end{aligned}$

10. $\begin{aligned} 2x + 3y &= 5 \\ 3x - y &= 2 \end{aligned}$

11. $\begin{aligned} 4x - 3y &= 6 \\ 3x - 2y &= 5 \end{aligned}$

12. $\begin{aligned} x + y + z &= 2 \\ 2x - y + z &= 0 \\ x + 2y - z &= 4 \end{aligned}$

13. $\begin{aligned} 2x + y - z &= 2 \\ x - y + z &= 7 \\ 2x + 2y + z &= 4 \end{aligned}$

14. $\begin{aligned} 2x - 4y \qquad &= 6 \\ x + y + z &= 1 \\ 5y + 7z &= 10 \end{aligned}$

15. $\begin{aligned} x \qquad - z &= 3 \\ 2y - 2z &= 2 \\ 2x \qquad + z &= 3 \end{aligned}$

16. $\begin{aligned} x_1 + x_2 - x_3 + x_4 &= 2 \\ x_1 - x_2 + x_3 + x_4 &= -1 \\ x_1 + x_2 + x_3 - x_4 &= 2 \\ x_1 \qquad + x_3 + x_4 &= -1 \end{aligned}$

17. Find values of h and k for which the system

$$2x + hy = 8,$$
$$x + 3y = k$$

has (a) infinitely many solutions, (b) no solution at all.

18. For what value of x will

$$\begin{vmatrix} x & x & 1 \\ 2 & 0 & 5 \\ 6 & 7 & 1 \end{vmatrix} = 0?$$

19. Suppose u, v, and w are twice-differentiable functions of x that satisfy the relation $au + bv + cw = 0$, where a, b, and c are constants, not all zero. Show that

$$\begin{vmatrix} u & v & w \\ u' & v' & w' \\ u'' & v'' & w'' \end{vmatrix} = 0.$$

20. *Partial Fractions.* Expanding the quotient

$$\frac{ax + b}{(x - r_1)(x - r_2)}$$

by partial fractions calls for finding the values of C and D that make the equation

$$\frac{ax + b}{(x - r_1)(x - r_2)} = \frac{C}{x - r_1} + \frac{D}{x - r_2}$$

hold for all x.

a) Find a system of linear equations that determines C and D.

b) Under what circumstances does the system of equations in part (a) have a unique solution? That is, when is the determinant of the coefficient matrix of the system different from zero?

A.8 Path Independence of $\int \mathbf{F}\cdot d\mathbf{r}$ Implies $\mathbf{F} = \nabla f$

This appendix completes the proof of Theorem 1 in Section 15.3 by showing that, under the mathematical hypotheses discussed there, path independence of the integral $\int \mathbf{F}\cdot d\mathbf{r}$ throughout D implies that $\mathbf{F}$ is the gradient of a scalar function f defined on D.

Proof That Path Independence of $\int \mathbf{F}\cdot d\mathbf{r}$ Implies $\mathbf{F} = \nabla f$

We need to show that if $\mathbf{F} = M\,\mathbf{i} + N\,\mathbf{j} + P\,\mathbf{k}$ is conservative on D, then there exists a scalar function f defined on D for which

$$\frac{\partial f}{\partial x} = M, \qquad \frac{\partial f}{\partial y} = N, \qquad \text{and} \qquad \frac{\partial f}{\partial z} = P. \tag{1}$$

To define f, we choose an arbitrary basepoint A in D. We define the value of f at A to be zero and the value of f at every other point B of D to be the value of the integral of $\mathbf{F}\cdot d\mathbf{r}$ along some smooth path in D from A to B. Such paths exist because D is a connected open region, and all such paths assign the same value of $f(B)$ because the integral of $\mathbf{F}\cdot d\mathbf{r}$ is path independent in D. Since the integral of $\mathbf{F}\cdot d\mathbf{r}$ from A to A is zero, the values of f are all defined by the single equation

$$f(B) = \int_A^B \mathbf{F}\cdot d\mathbf{r}. \tag{2}$$

One consequence of this definition is that for any points B and B_0 in D,

$$\begin{aligned} f(B) - f(B_0) &= \int_A^B \mathbf{F}\cdot d\mathbf{r} - \int_A^{B_0} \mathbf{F}\cdot d\mathbf{r} \\ &= \int_{B_0}^A \mathbf{F}\cdot d\mathbf{r} + \int_A^B \mathbf{F}\cdot d\mathbf{r} \\ &= \int_{B_0}^B \mathbf{F}\cdot d\mathbf{r}. \end{aligned} \tag{3}$$

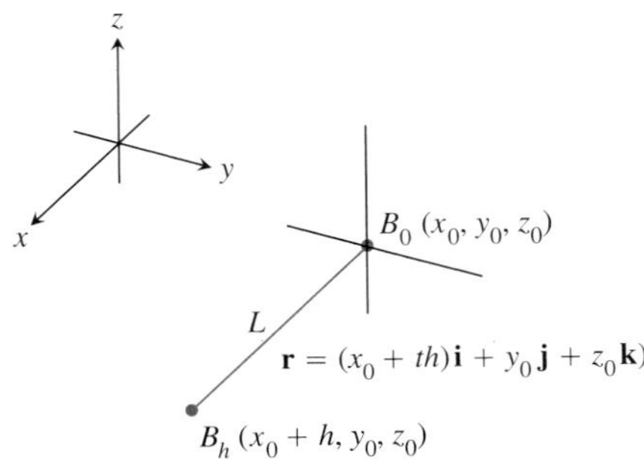

A.5 The line segment L from B_0 to B_h lies parallel to the x-axis. The partial derivative with respect to x of the function

$$f(x, y, z) = \int_A^{(x,y,z)} \mathbf{F}\cdot d\mathbf{r}$$

at B_0 is the limit of $(1/h)\int_L \mathbf{F}\cdot d\mathbf{r}$ as $h \to 0$.

Let us now show that f has partial derivatives that give the components of $\mathbf{F}$ at every point $B_0(x_0, y_0, z_0)$ in D.

Since D is open, B_0 is the center of a solid sphere that lies entirely in D. We can therefore find a positive number h (it might be small) for which the point $B_h(x_0 + h, y_0, z_0)$ and the line segment L joining B_0 to B_h both lie in D (Fig. A.5). When we calculate the value of the integral of $\mathbf{F}\cdot d\mathbf{r}$ along L with the parametrization

$$\mathbf{r} = (x_0 + th)\,\mathbf{i} + y_0\,\mathbf{j} + z_0\,\mathbf{k}, \qquad 0 \le t \le 1, \tag{4}$$

we find that

$$\begin{aligned} \int_{B_0}^{B_h} \mathbf{F}\cdot d\mathbf{r} &= \int_0^1 (M\mathbf{i} + N\mathbf{j} + P\mathbf{k})\cdot(h\,dt\,\mathbf{i}) \\ &= h\int_0^1 M(x_0 + th, y_0, z_0)\,dt. \end{aligned} \tag{5}$$

The difference quotient for defining $\partial f/\partial x$ at B_0 is therefore

$$\begin{aligned}\frac{f(x_0+h, y_0, z_0) - f(x_0, y_0, z_0)}{h} &= \frac{f(B_h) - f(B_0)}{h} \\ &= \frac{1}{h}\int_{B_0}^{B_h} \mathbf{F}\cdot d\mathbf{r} && \text{Eq. (3)} \\ &= \int_0^1 M(x_0 + th, y_0, z_0)\, dt. && \text{Eq. (5)}\end{aligned}$$

Since M is continuous, given any $\epsilon > 0$ there exists a $\delta > 0$ such that

$$|th| < \delta \quad \Rightarrow \quad |M(x_0 + th, y_0, z_0) - M(x_0, y_0, z_0)| < \epsilon.$$

This implies that whenever $|h| < \delta$

$$\begin{aligned}&\left|\int_0^1 M(x_0 + th, y_0 z_0)\, dt - M(x_0, y_0, z_0)\right| \\ &\qquad = \left|\int_0^1 (M(x_0 + th, y_0, z_0) - M(x_0, y_0, z_0))\, dt\right| \\ &\qquad \le \int_0^1 \left| M(x_0 + th, y_0, z_0) - M(x_0, y_0, z_0)\right| dt < \int_0^1 \epsilon\, dt = \epsilon.\end{aligned}$$

We can find such a positive δ for every positive ϵ, so

$$\begin{aligned}\left.\frac{\partial f}{\partial x}\right|_{(x_0, y_0, z_0)} &= \lim_{h\to 0}\int_0^1 M(x_0 + th, y_0, z_0)\, dt \\ &= M\ (x_0, y_0, z_0). \qquad (6)\end{aligned}$$

In other words, the partial derivative of f with respect to x exists at B_0 and equals the value of M at B_0. Since B_0 was chosen arbitrarily, we can conclude that $\partial f/\partial x$ exists and equals M at every point of D.

The equations $\partial f/\partial y = N$ and $\partial f/\partial z = P$ are derived in a similar way. This concludes the proof. ■

A.9 Complex Numbers

Complex numbers are numbers of the form $a + bi$, where a and b are real numbers and $i = \sqrt{-1}$. The number a is the **real part** of $a + bi$, and b is the **imaginary part.**

Complex numbers $a + bi$ and $c + di$ are equal if and only if $a = c$ and $b = d$. In particular, $a + bi = 0$ if and only if $a = 0$ and $b = 0$ or, equivalently, if and only if $a^2 + b^2 = 0$.

We add and subtract complex numbers by adding and subtracting their real and imaginary parts:

$$(a + bi) + (c + di) = (a + c) + (b + d)i,$$
$$(a + bi) - (c + di) = (a - c) + (b - d)i.$$

We multiply complex numbers the way we multiply other binomials, using the

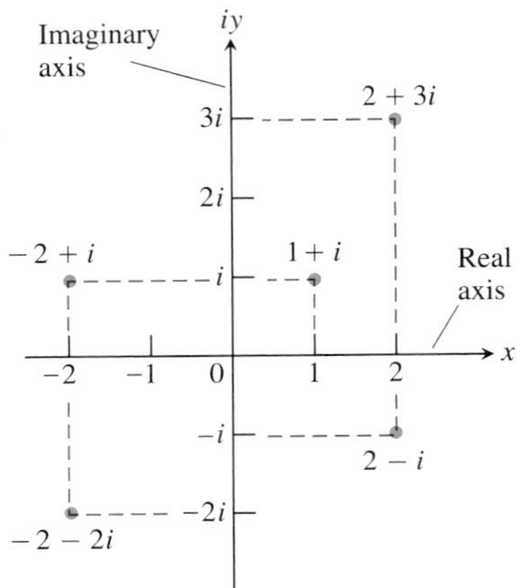

A.6 Numbers in the complex plane.

fact that $i^2 = -1$ to simplify the final result:

$$\begin{aligned}(a+bi)(c+di) &= ac + adi + bci + bdi^2 \\ &= ac + adi + bci - bd \qquad i^2 = -1 \\ &= (ac - bd) + (ad + bc)i, \qquad \text{Real and imaginary parts combined}\end{aligned}$$

To divide a complex number $c + di$ by a nonzero complex number $a + bi$, multiply the numerator and denominator of the quotient by $a - bi$ (the number $a - bi$ is the **complex conjugate** of $a + bi$):

$$\begin{aligned}\frac{c+di}{a+bi} &= \frac{c+di}{a+bi}\,\frac{a-bi}{a-bi} \qquad \text{Multiply numerator and denominator by the complex conjugate of } a+bi. \\ &= \frac{ac - bci + adi - bdi^2}{a^2 - abi + abi - b^2i^2} \\ &= \frac{(ac+bd) + (ad - bc)i}{a^2 + b^2} \\ &= \frac{ac+bd}{a^2+b^2} + \frac{ad-bc}{a^2+b^2}\,i.\end{aligned}$$

EXAMPLE

a) $(2+3i) + (6-2i) = (2+6) + (3-2)i = 8 + i$

b) $(2+3i) - (6-2i) = (2-6) + (3-(-2))i = -4 + 5i$

c) $(2+3i)(6-2i) = (2)(6) + (2)(-2i) + (3i)(6) + (3i)(-2i)$
$$= 12 - 4i + 18i - 6i^2 = 12 + 14i + 6 = 18 + 14i$$

d)
$$\begin{aligned}\frac{2+3i}{6-2i} &= \frac{2+3i}{6-2i}\,\frac{6+2i}{6+2i} \\ &= \frac{12 + 4i + 18i + 6i^2}{36 + 12i - 12i - 4i^2} \\ &= \frac{6+22i}{40} = \frac{3}{20} + \frac{11}{20}i\end{aligned}$$

We plot complex numbers as points in a plane by identifying the number $x + iy$ with the point (x, y) in the Cartesian plane. We then call the x-axis the **real axis**, the y-axis the **imaginary axis** (sometimes, ***iy*-axis**), and the relabeled plane the **complex plane** (Fig. A.6).

A.10 *Tables for* sin *x*, cos *x*, tan *x*, e^x, e^{-x}, *and* ln *x*

The following tables give first quadrant values of $\sin x$, $\cos x$, and $\tan x$; selected values of e^x and e^{-x} for $0 \le x \le 10$; and selected values of $\ln x$ for $0 < x \le 100$. Except for a few obvious entries, all values have been rounded.

TABLE 1
Natural trigonometric functions

Angle		Sine	Cosine	Tangent
Degree	Radian			
0°	0.000	0.000	1.000	0.000
1°	0.017	0.017	1.000	0.017
2°	0.035	0.035	0.999	0.035
3°	0.052	0.052	0.999	0.052
4°	0.070	0.070	0.998	0.070
5°	0.087	0.087	0.996	0.087
6°	0.105	0.105	0.995	0.105
7°	0.122	0.122	0.993	0.123
8°	0.140	0.139	0.990	0.141
9°	0.157	0.156	0.988	0.158
10°	0.175	0.174	0.985	0.176
11°	0.192	0.191	0.982	0.194
12°	0.209	0.208	0.978	0.213
13°	0.227	0.225	0.974	0.231
14°	0.244	0.242	0.970	0.249
15°	0.262	0.259	0.966	0.268
16°	0.279	0.276	0.961	0.287
17°	0.297	0.292	0.956	0.306
18°	0.314	0.309	0.951	0.325
19°	0.332	0.326	0.946	0.344
20°	0.349	0.342	0.940	0.364
21°	0.367	0.358	0.934	0.384
22°	0.384	0.375	0.927	0.404
23°	0.401	0.391	0.921	0.424
24°	0.419	0.407	0.914	0.445
25°	0.436	0.423	0.906	0.466
26°	0.454	0.438	0.899	0.488
27°	0.471	0.454	0.891	0.510
28°	0.489	0.469	0.883	0.532
29°	0.506	0.485	0.875	0.554
30°	0.524	0.500	0.866	0.577
31°	0.541	0.515	0.857	0.601
32°	0.559	0.530	0.848	0.625
33°	0.576	0.545	0.839	0.649
34°	0.593	0.559	0.829	0.675
35°	0.611	0.574	0.819	0.700
36°	0.628	0.588	0.809	0.727
37°	0.646	0.602	0.799	0.754
38°	0.663	0.616	0.788	0.781
39°	0.681	0.629	0.777	0.810
40°	0.698	0.643	0.766	0.839
41°	0.716	0.656	0.755	0.869
42°	0.733	0.669	0.743	0.900
43°	0.750	0.682	0.731	0.933
44°	0.768	0.695	0.719	0.966
45°	0.785	0.707	0.707	1.000
46°	0.803	0.719	0.695	1.036
47°	0.820	0.731	0.682	1.072
48°	0.838	0.743	0.669	1.111
49°	0.855	0.755	0.656	1.150
50°	0.873	0.766	0.643	1.192
51°	0.890	0.777	0.629	1.235
52°	0.908	0.788	0.616	1.280
53°	0.925	0.799	0.602	1.327
54°	0.942	0.809	0.588	1.376
55°	0.960	0.819	0.574	1.428
56°	0.977	0.829	0.559	1.483
57°	0.995	0.839	0.545	1.540
58°	1.012	0.848	0.530	1.600
59°	1.030	0.857	0.515	1.664
60°	1.047	0.866	0.500	1.732
61°	1.065	0.875	0.485	1.804
62°	1.082	0.883	0.469	1.881
63°	1.100	0.891	0.454	1.963
64°	1.117	0.899	0.438	2.050
65°	1.134	0.906	0.423	2.145
66°	1.152	0.914	0.407	2.246
67°	1.169	0.921	0.391	2.356
68°	1.187	0.927	0.375	2.475
69°	1.204	0.934	0.358	2.605
70°	1.222	0.940	0.342	2.748
71°	1.239	0.946	0.326	2.904
72°	1.257	0.951	0.309	3.078
73°	1.274	0.956	0.292	3.271
74°	1.292	0.961	0.276	3.487
75°	1.309	0.966	0.259	3.732
76°	1.326	0.970	0.242	4.011
77°	1.344	0.974	0.225	4.332
78°	1.361	0.978	0.208	4.705
79°	1.379	0.982	0.191	5.145
80°	1.396	0.985	0.174	5.671
81°	1.414	0.988	0.156	6.314
82°	1.431	0.990	0.139	7.115
83°	1.449	0.993	0.122	8.144
84°	1.466	0.995	0.105	9.514
85°	1.484	0.996	0.087	11.43
86°	1.501	0.998	0.070	14.30
87°	1.518	0.999	0.052	19.08
88°	1.536	0.999	0.035	28.64
89°	1.553	1.000	0.017	57.29
90°	1.571	1.000	0.000	

TABLE 2
Exponential functions

x	e^x	e^{-x}	x	e^x	e^{-x}
0.00	1.0000	1.0000	2.5	12.182	0.0821
0.05	1.0513	0.9512	2.6	13.464	0.0743
0.10	1.1052	0.9048	2.7	14.880	0.0672
0.15	1.1618	0.8607	2.8	16.445	0.0608
0.20	1.2214	0.8187	2.9	18.174	0.0550
0.25	1.2840	0.7788	3.0	20.086	0.0498
0.30	1.3499	0.7408	3.1	22.198	0.0450
0.35	1.4191	0.7047	3.2	24.533	0.0408
0.40	1.4918	0.6703	3.3	27.113	0.0369
0.45	1.5683	0.6376	3.4	29.964	0.0334
0.50	1.6487	0.6065	3.5	33.115	0.0302
0.55	1.7333	0.5769	3.6	36.598	0.0273
0.60	1.8221	0.5488	3.7	40.447	0.0247
0.65	1.9155	0.5220	3.8	44.701	0.0224
0.70	2.0138	0.4966	3.9	49.402	0.0202
0.75	2.1170	0.4724	4.0	54.598	0.0183
0.80	2.2255	0.4493	4.1	60.340	0.0166
0.85	2.3396	0.4274	4.2	66.686	0.0150
0.90	2.4596	0.4066	4.3	73.700	0.0136
0.95	2.5857	0.3867	4.4	81.451	0.0123
1.0	2.7183	0.3679	4.5	90.017	0.0111
1.1	3.0042	0.3329	4.6	99.484	0.0101
1.2	3.3201	0.3012	4.7	109.95	0.0091
1.3	3.6693	0.2725	4.8	121.51	0.0082
1.4	4.0552	0.2466	4.9	134.29	0.0074
1.5	4.4817	0.2231	5	148.41	0.0067
1.6	4.9530	0.2019	6	403.43	0.0025
1.7	5.4739	0.1827	7	1096.6	0.0009
1.8	6.0496	0.1653	8	2981.0	0.0003
1.9	6.6859	0.1496	9	8103.1	0.0001
2.0	7.3891	0.1353	10	22026	0.00005
2.1	8.1662	0.1225			
2.2	9.0250	0.1108			
2.3	9.9742	0.1003			
2.4	11.023	0.0907			

TABLE 3
Natural logarithms

x	$\ln x$	x	$\ln x$	x	$\ln x$
0.0	*	4.5	1.5041	9.0	2.1972
0.1	7.6974	4.6	1.5261	9.1	2.2083
0.2	8.3906	4.7	1.5476	9.2	2.2192
0.3	8.7960	4.8	1.5686	9.3	2.2300
0.4	9.0837	4.9	1.5892	9.4	2.2407
0.5	9.3069	5.0	1.6094	9.5	2.2513
0.6	9.4892	5.1	1.6292	9.6	2.2618
0.7	9.6433	5.2	1.6487	9.7	2.2721
0.8	9.7769	5.3	1.6677	9.8	2.2824
0.9	9.8946	5.4	1.6864	9.9	2.2925
1.0	0.0000	5.5	1.7047	10	2.3026
1.1	0.0953	5.6	1.7228	11	2.3979
1.2	0.1823	5.7	1.7405	12	2.4849
1.3	0.2624	5.8	1.7579	13	2.5649
1.4	0.3365	5.9	1.7750	14	2.6391
1.5	0.4055	6.0	1.7918	15	2.7081
1.6	0.4700	6.1	1.8083	16	2.7726
1.7	0.5306	6.2	1.8245	17	2.8332
1.8	0.5878	6.3	1.8405	18	2.8904
1.9	0.6419	6.4	1.8563	19	2.9444
2.0	0.6931	6.5	1.8718	20	2.9957
2.1	0.7419	6.6	1.8871	25	3.2189
2.2	0.7885	6.7	1.9021	30	3.4012
2.3	0.8329	6.8	1.9169	35	3.5553
2.4	0.8755	6.9	1.9315	40	3.6889
2.5	0.9163	7.0	1.9459	45	3.8067
2.6	0.9555	7.1	1.9601	50	3.9120
2.7	0.9933	7.2	1.9741	55	4.0073
2.8	1.0296	7.3	1.9879	60	4.0943
2.9	1.0647	7.4	2.0015	65	4.1744
3.0	1.0986	7.5	2.0149	70	4.2485
3.1	1.1314	7.6	2.0281	75	4.3175
3.2	1.1632	7.7	2.0412	80	4.3820
3.3	1.1939	7.8	2.0541	85	4.4427
3.4	1.2238	7.9	2.0669	90	4.4998
3.5	1.2528	8.0	2.0794	95	4.5539
3.6	1.2809	8.1	2.0919	100	4.6052
3.7	1.3083	8.2	2.1041		
3.8	1.3350	8.3	2.1163		
3.9	1.3610	8.4	2.1282		
4.0	1.3863	8.5	2.1401		
4.1	1.4110	8.6	2.1518		
4.2	1.4351	8.7	2.1633		
4.3	1.4586	8.8	2.1748		
4.4	1.4816	8.9	2.1861		

*Subtract 10 from $\ln x$ entries for $x < 1.0$.

Answers

Chapter 1

Section 1.1, pp. 9–11

1. $\sqrt{2}$ **3.** 6 **5.** $\sqrt{a^2 + b^2}$

7. $\Delta x = 2, \Delta y = -4$ **9.** $\Delta x = -4.9, \Delta y = 0$

11.

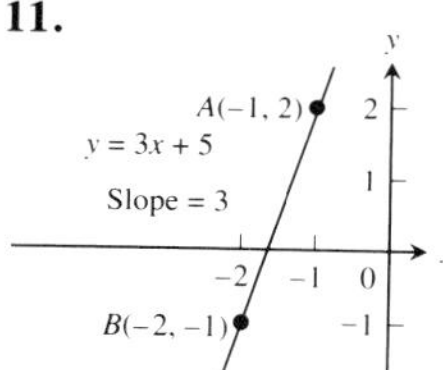

13.

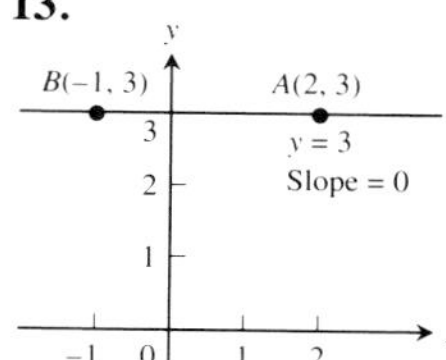

15. a) $x = -1$ b) $y = 4/3$

17. a) $x = 0$ b) $y = -\sqrt{2}$

19. $y = -x$ **21.** $y = -\dfrac{x}{5} + \dfrac{23}{5}$ **23.** $y = -\dfrac{5}{4}x + 6$

25. $y = -9$ **27.** $y = 4x + 4$ **29.** $y = -\dfrac{2}{5}x + 1$

31. $y = -\dfrac{x}{2} + 12$

33. x-intercept = 4, y-intercept = 3

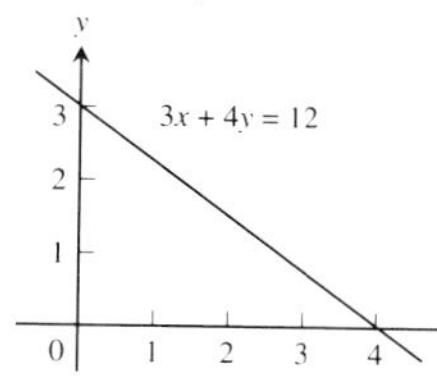

35. x-intercept = $\sqrt{3}$, y-intercept = $-\sqrt{2}$

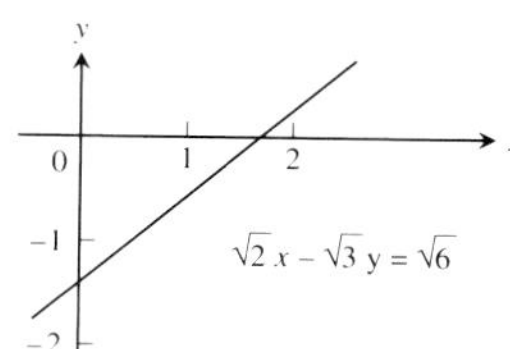

39. $(3, -3)$ **41.** $(-2, -9)$

43. a) ≈ -2.5 degrees/in. b) ≈ -16.1 degrees/in. c) ≈ -8.3 degrees/in.

45. $-40°$ **47.** a) $y = x - 1$, b) $y = (\sqrt{3}/3)x - 1$

49. Yes **51.** a) $(3, -7)$ and $(-4, -2)$, b) 35 **53.** $b = 2$

55.

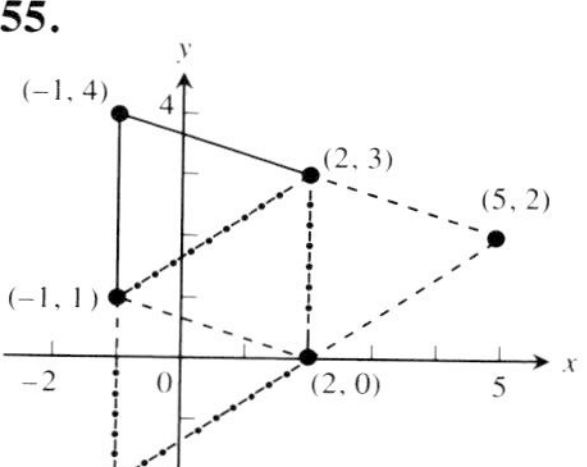

57. Perpendicular for $k = -2$; parallel for $k = 2$

Section 1.2, pp. 19–22

1. $P(s) = 4s$ **3.** $V(r) = (4/3)\pi r^3$

5. $D: -\infty < x < \infty, R: y \le 0$, symmetric with respect to the y-axis

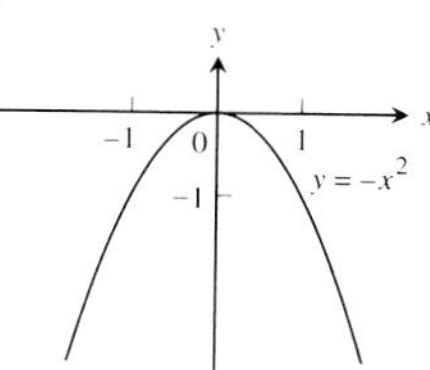

7. $D: x \ne 0, R: y \ne 0$, symmetric with respect to the origin

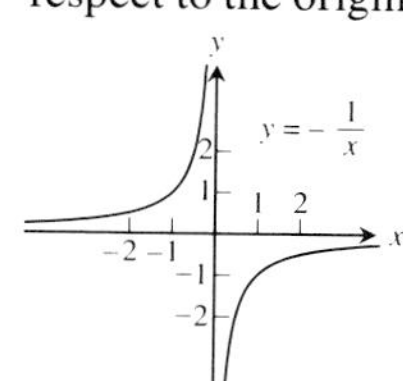

9. $D: x \ge 0, R: y \ge 0$, no symmetry

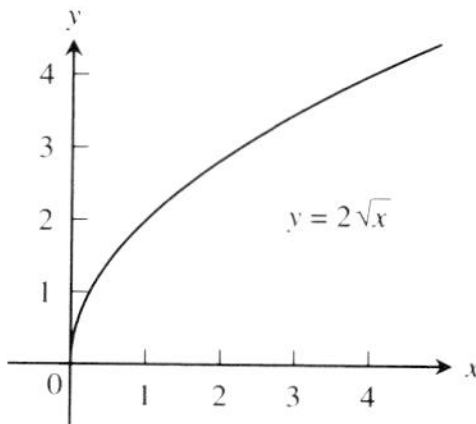

11. $D: x \ge 0, R: y \le 0$, no symmetry

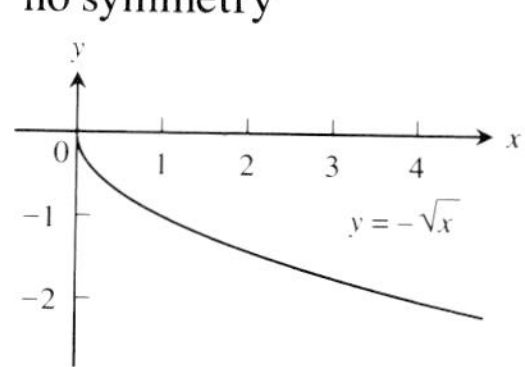

13. $D: x \geq 0$, $R: y \leq 0$, no symmetry

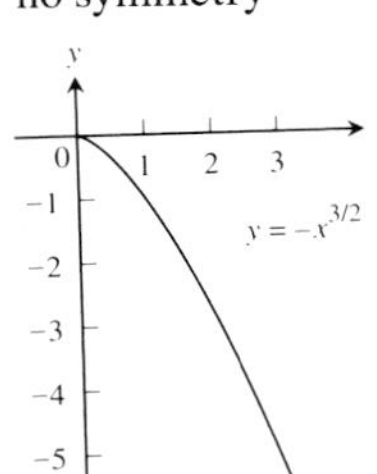

15. $D: -\infty < x < \infty$, $R: y \geq 0$, symmetric with respect to the y-axis

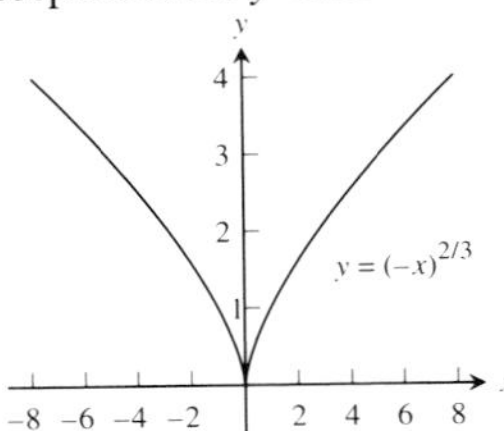

17. $D: -\infty < x < \infty$, $R: -\infty < y < \infty$, symmetric with respect to the origin

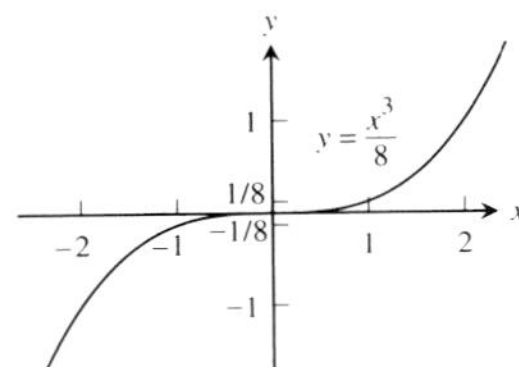

19. a) No b) No c) $D: x > 0$, $R: y > 0$
21. Even **23.** Odd **25.** Neither **27.** Even **29.** Even
31. Odd **33.** $D: -\infty < x < \infty$, $R: y$ is an integer.

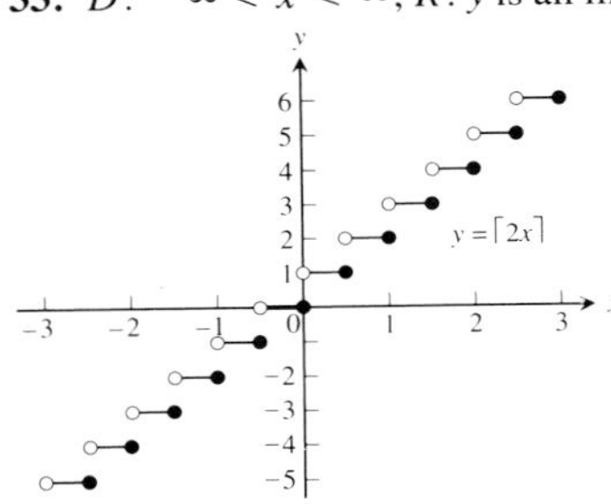

35. $D: -\infty < x < \infty$, $R: y$ is an integer.

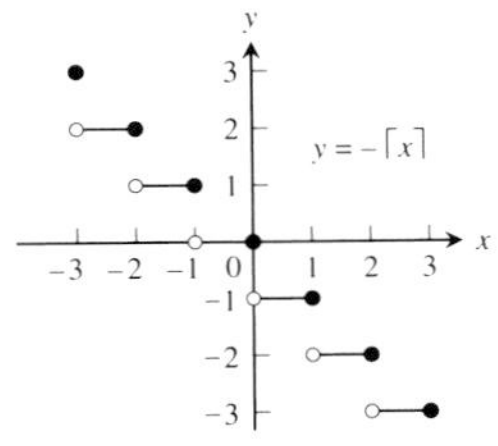

37. $D: -\infty < x < \infty$, $R: y = n/2$ for some integer n.

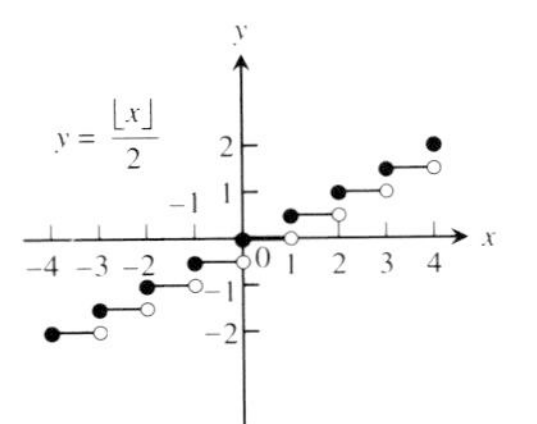

39. a)

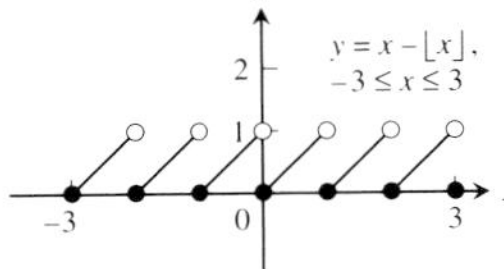

b)

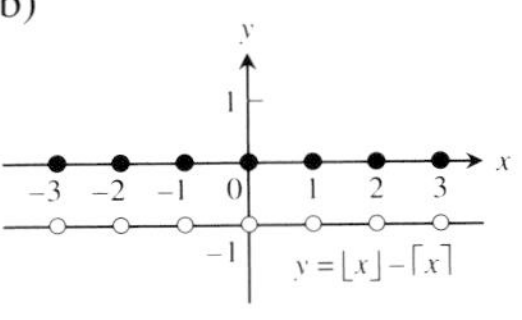

41.

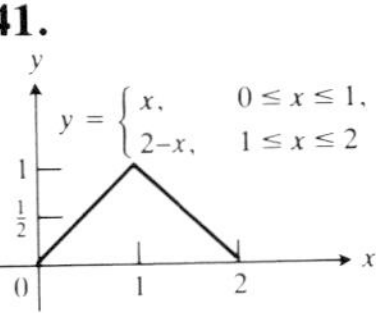

43.

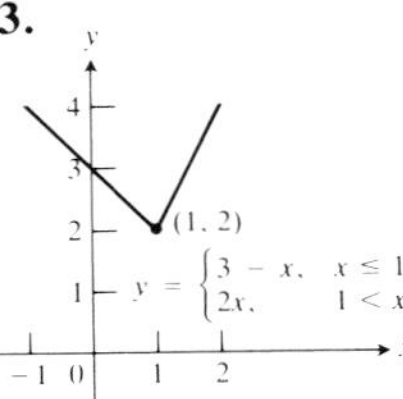

45.

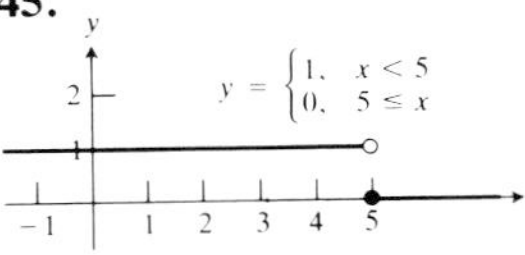

47. a) $y = \begin{cases} x, & 0 \leq x \leq 1 \\ 2 - x, & 1 < x \leq 2 \end{cases}$

b) $y = \begin{cases} 2, & 0 \leq x < 1 \text{ or } 2 \leq x < 3 \\ 0, & 1 \leq x < 2 \text{ or } 3 \leq x \leq 4 \end{cases}$

49. $D_f: -\infty < x < \infty$, $D_g: x \geq 1$, $R_f: -\infty < y < \infty$, $R_g: y \geq 0$, $D_{f+g} = D_{f \cdot g} = D_g$, $R_{f+g}: y \geq 1$, $R_{f \cdot g}: y \geq 0$

51. $D_f: -\infty < x < \infty$, $D_g: -\infty < x < \infty$, $R_f: y = 2$, $R_g: y \geq 1$, $D_{f/g}: -\infty < x < \infty$, $R_{f/g}: 0 < y \leq 2$, $D_{g/f}: -\infty < x < \infty$, $R_{g/f}: y \geq 1/2$

53. a) 2 b) 22 c) $x^2 + 2$ d) $x^2 + 10x + 22$ e) 5 f) -2 g) $x + 10$ h) $x^4 - 6x^2 + 6$

55. a) $\frac{4}{x^2} - 5$ b) $\frac{4}{x^2} - 5$ c) $\left(\frac{4}{x} - 5\right)^2$ d) $\left(\frac{1}{4x - 5}\right)^2$ e) $\frac{1}{4x^2 - 5}$ f) $\frac{1}{(4x - 5)^2}$

57. a) $f(g(x))$ b) $j(g(x))$ c) $g(g(x))$ d) $j(j(x))$ e) $g(h(f(x)))$ f) $h(j(f(x)))$

59.

	$g(x)$	$f(x)$	$(f \circ g)(x)$
a)	$x - 7$	$\sqrt{x}$	$\sqrt{x - 7}$
b)	$x + 2$	$3x$	$3x + 6$
c)	x^2	$\sqrt{x - 5}$	$\sqrt{x^2 - 5}$
d)	$\frac{x}{x - 1}$	$\frac{x}{x - 1}$	x
e)	$\frac{1}{x - 1}$	$1 + \frac{1}{x}$	x
f)	$\frac{1}{x}$	$\frac{1}{x}$	x

61. a)

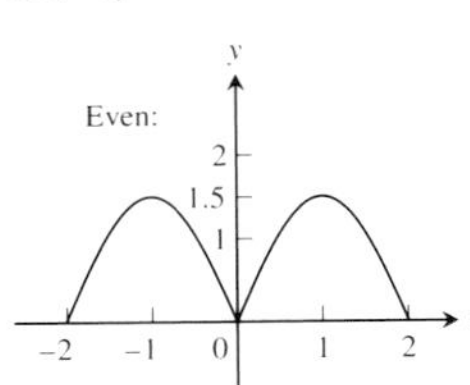

b)

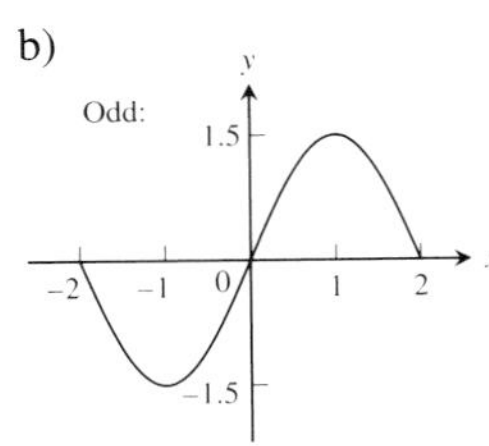

63. a)

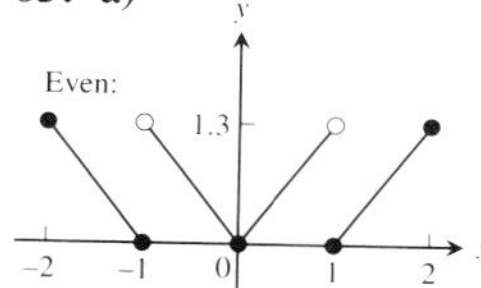

b)

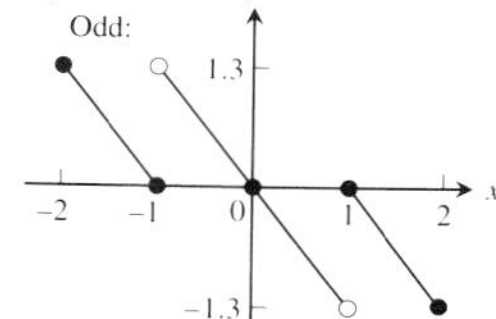

65. a) Take $g(x) = -\dfrac{1}{x}$

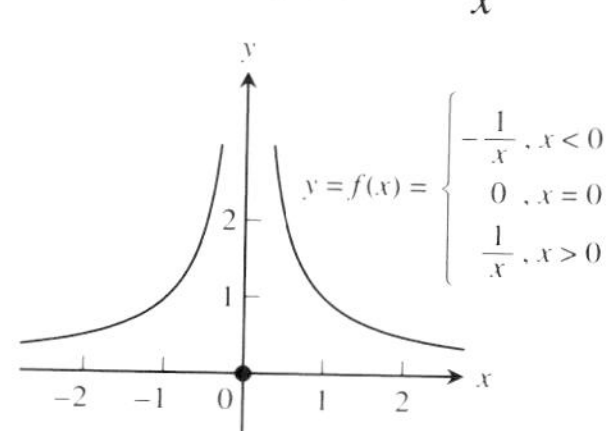

b) Take $g(x) = \dfrac{1}{x}$

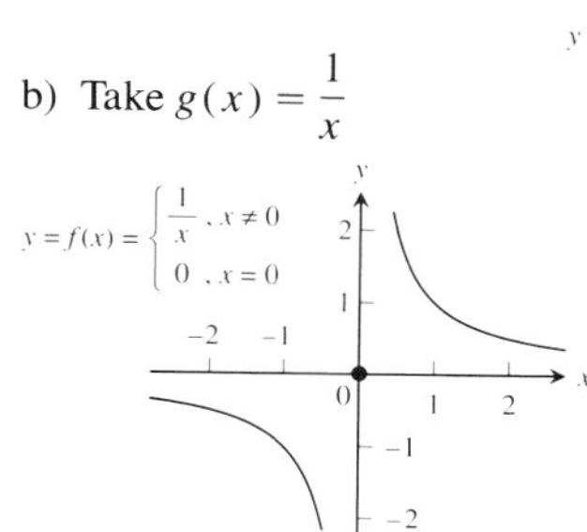

67. a) Take $g(x) = x^{2/3}$

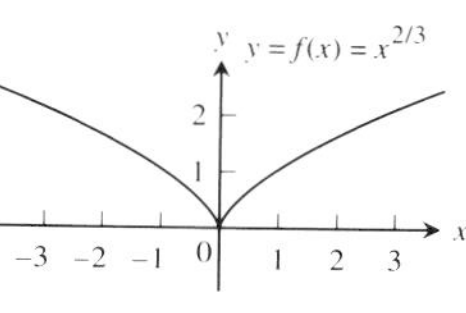

b) Take $g(x) = -x^{2/3}$

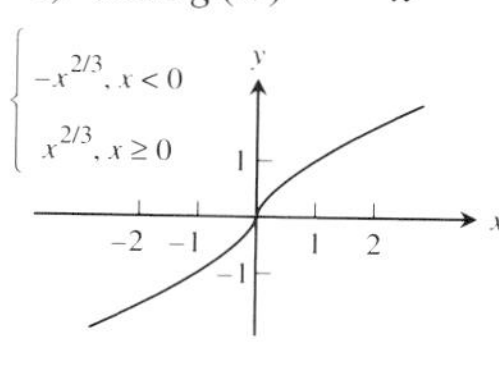

Section 1.3, pp. 29–30

1. a) $\dfrac{2\pi}{3}$ b) $\dfrac{3\pi}{2}$ c) $-\dfrac{\pi}{3}$ d) -3π

3. a) $120°$ b) $135°$ c) $-315°$ d) $-630°$

5. a) 8π m b) $\dfrac{55\pi}{9}$ m **7.** 8.4 in.

9.

θ	$-\pi$	$-2\pi/3$	0	$\pi/2$	$3\pi/4$
$\sin\theta$	0	$-\dfrac{\sqrt{3}}{2}$	0	1	$\dfrac{1}{\sqrt{2}}$
$\cos\theta$	-1	$-\dfrac{1}{2}$	1	0	$-\dfrac{1}{\sqrt{2}}$
$\tan\theta$	0	$\sqrt{3}$	0	UND	-1
$\cot\theta$	UND	$\dfrac{1}{\sqrt{3}}$	UND	0	-1
$\sec\theta$	-1	-2	1	UND	$-\sqrt{2}$
$\csc\theta$	UND	$-\dfrac{2}{\sqrt{3}}$	UND	1	$\sqrt{2}$

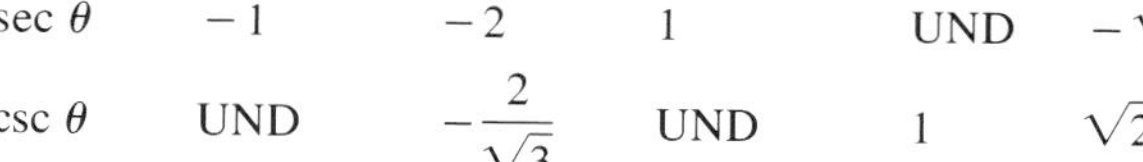

11.

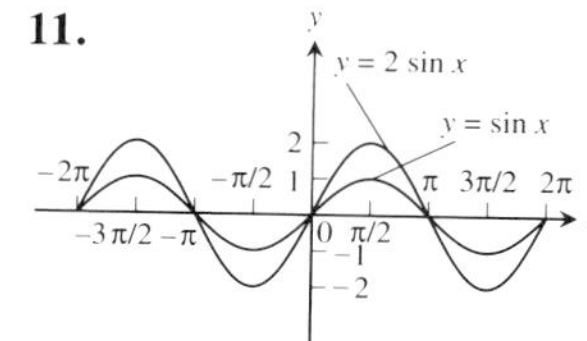

13.

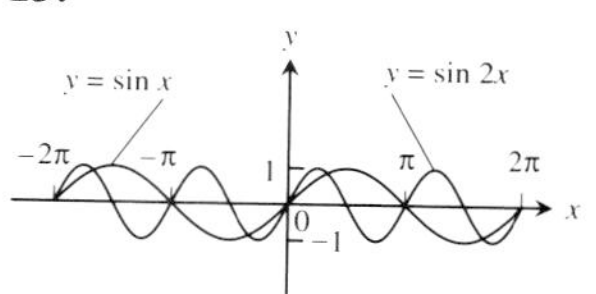

15.

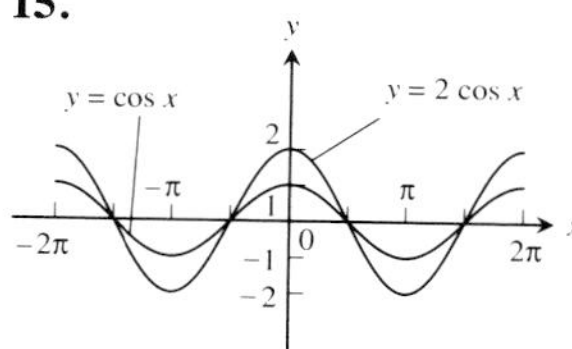

17.

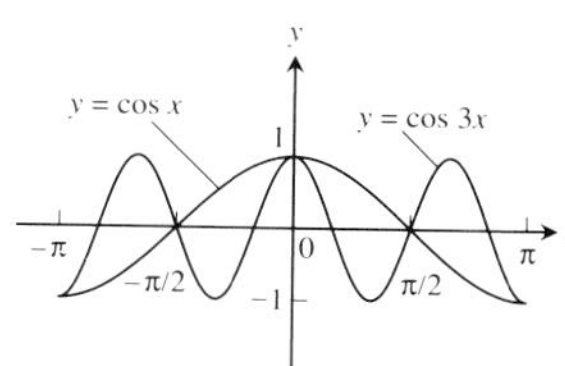

19.

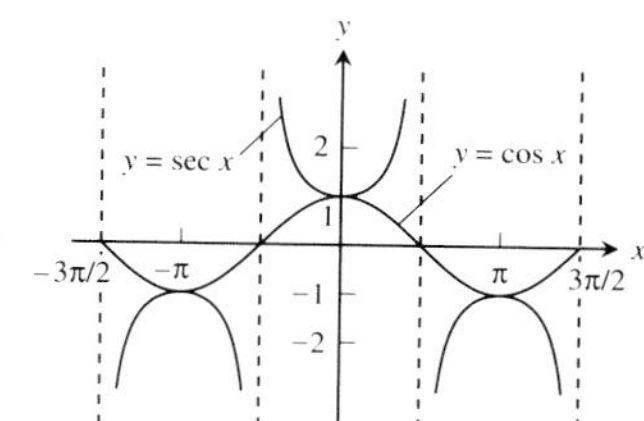

21. Symmetric with respect to the origin

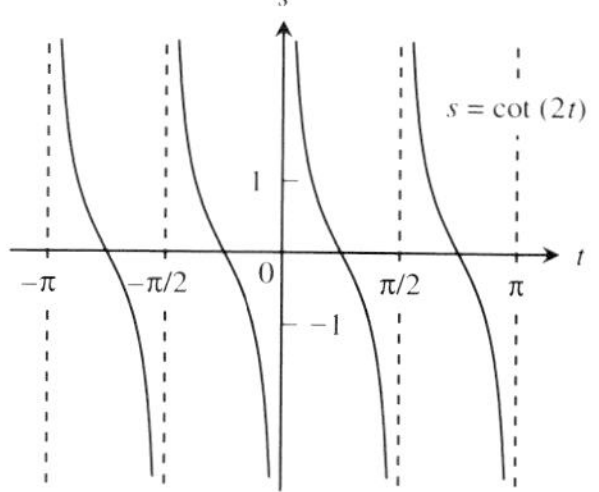

23. Symmetric with respect to the y-axis

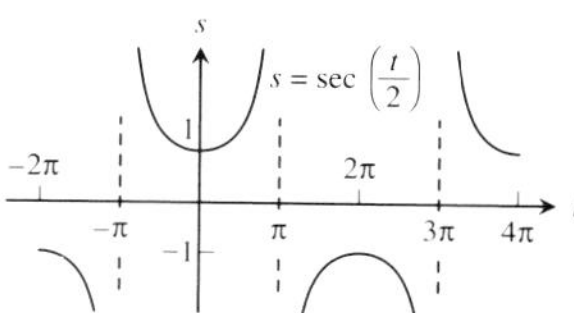

25. Symmetric with respect to the origin

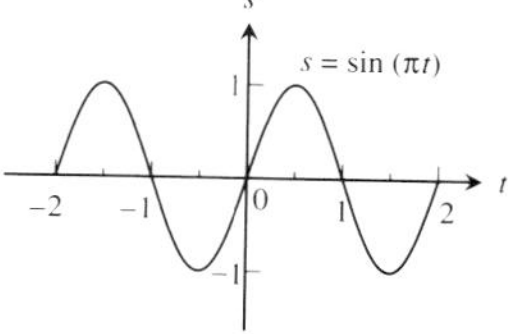

27. Symmetric with respect to the y-axis

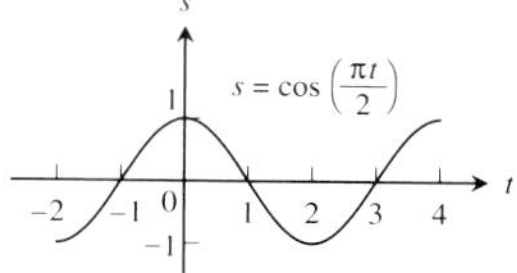

29. D: $-\infty < x < \infty$, R: $y = -1, 0, 1$

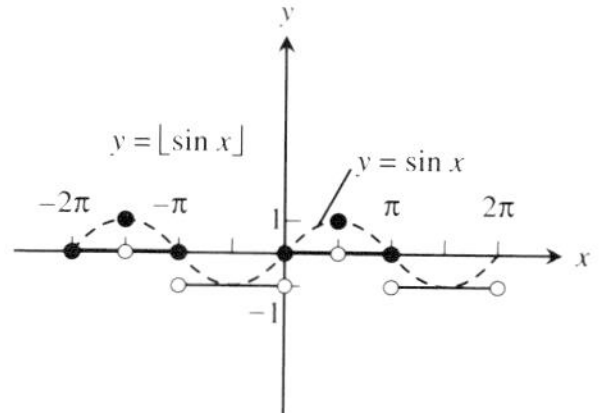

31. a) 1, −1 b) 1, 0 c) $D: -\infty < x < \infty$, $R: 0 \le y \le 1$

33. $\sec^2\theta = \dfrac{r^2}{x^2} = \dfrac{x^2+y^2}{x^2} = 1 + \dfrac{y^2}{x^2} = 1 + \left(\dfrac{y}{x}\right)^2 = 1 + \tan^2\theta$

35. If $B = \dfrac{\pi}{2}$, $\cos\left(A - \dfrac{\pi}{2}\right) = \cos A \cos\dfrac{\pi}{2} + \sin A \sin\dfrac{\pi}{2} = \sin A$

37. If $B = \dfrac{\pi}{2}$, $\sin\left(A + \dfrac{\pi}{2}\right) = \sin A \cos\dfrac{\pi}{2} + \cos A \sin\dfrac{\pi}{2} = \cos A$

39. Replacing B by $-B$ in Eq. (11) gives

$$\begin{aligned}\cos(A - B) &= \cos A\cos(-B) - \sin A\sin(-B)\\ &= \cos A\cos B - \sin A(-\sin B)\\ &= \cos A\cos B + \sin A\sin B\end{aligned}$$

43. $\dfrac{\sqrt{6}+\sqrt{2}}{4}$ **45.** $\dfrac{\sqrt{6}+\sqrt{2}}{4}$ **47.** $\dfrac{2+\sqrt{2}}{4}$ **49.** $\dfrac{2-\sqrt{3}}{4}$

Section 1.4, pp. 37–40

1. a) $y = -(x+7)^2$, b) $y = -(x-4)^2$

3. a) Position 4, b) Position 1, c) Position 2, d) Position 3

5. $x^2 + y^2 = 4$ **7.** $(x-3)^2 + (y-3)^2 = 9$

9. $x^2 + (y-2)^2 = 4$

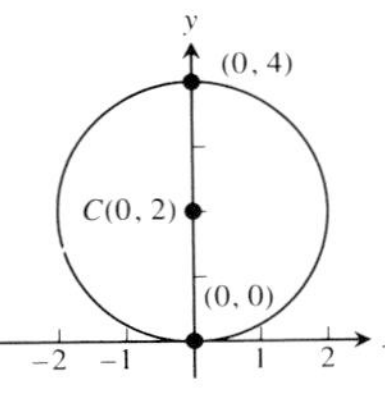

11. $(x+1)^2 + (y-5)^2 = 9/4$

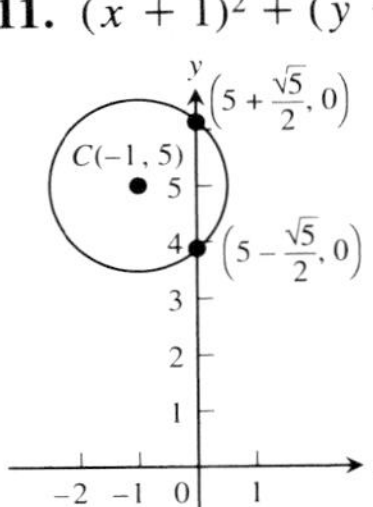

13. $(x + \sqrt{3})^2 + (y+2)^2 = 4$

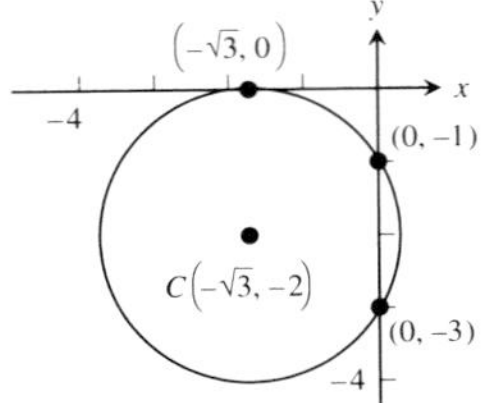

15. $(x+2)^2 + (y+3)^2 = 49$

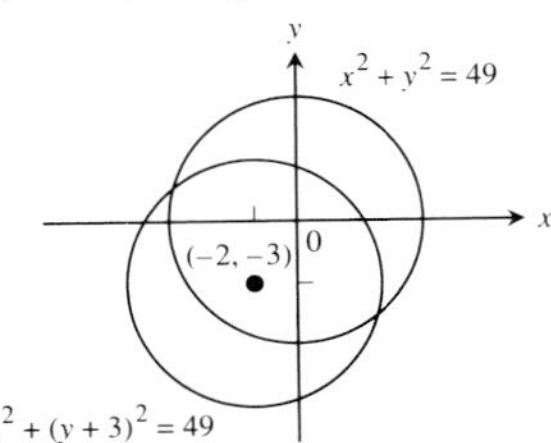

17. $y + 1 = (x+1)^3$

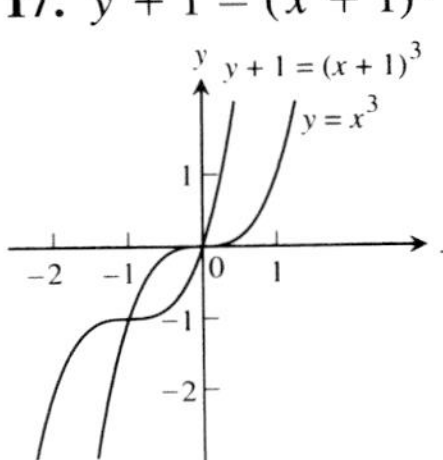

19. $y = \sqrt{x + 0.81}$

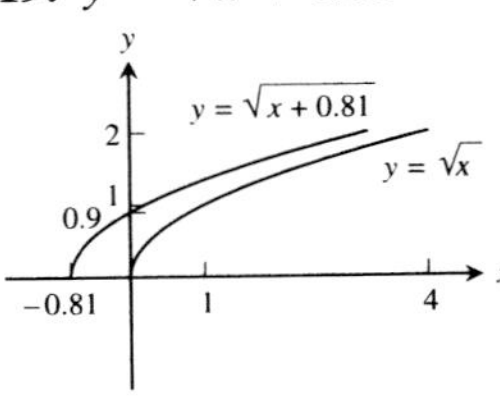

21. $y = 2x$

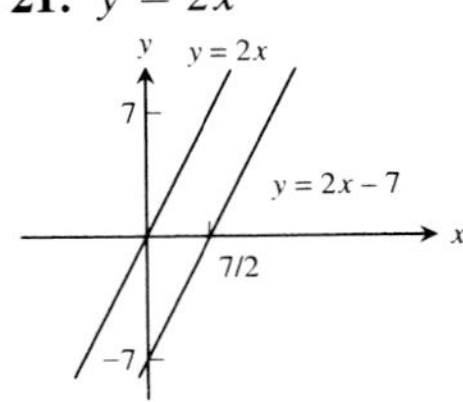

23. $x + 1 = y^2$

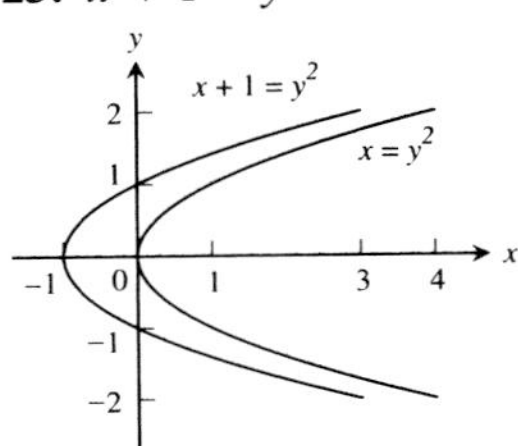

25. $y - 1 = \dfrac{1}{x-1}$

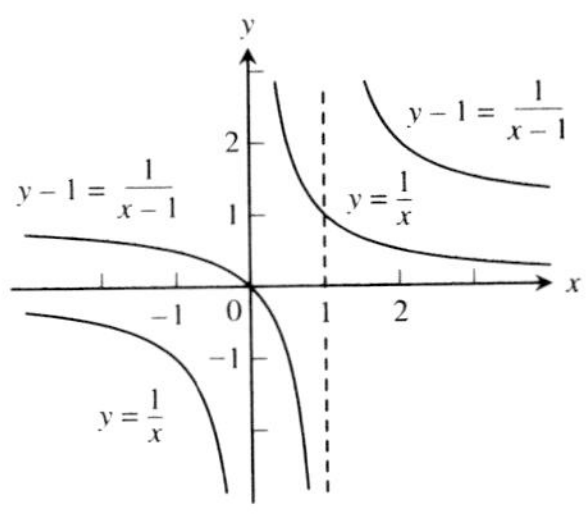

27. $D: x \ge -4$, $R: y \ge 0$

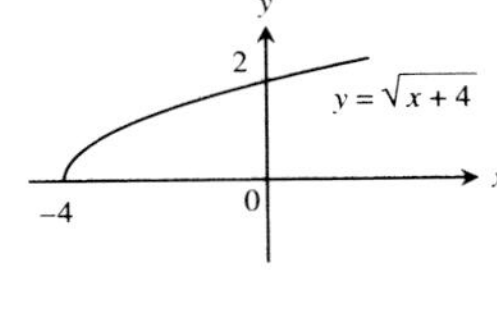

29. $D: x \le 4$, $R: y \ge 0$

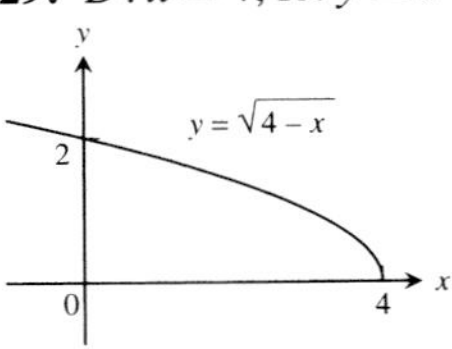

31. $D: x \ge 1$, $R: y \ge 1$

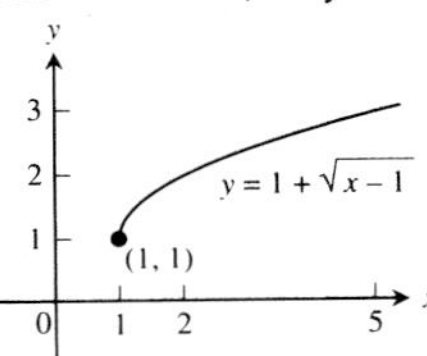

33. $D: -\infty < x < \infty$, $R: y \ge 0$

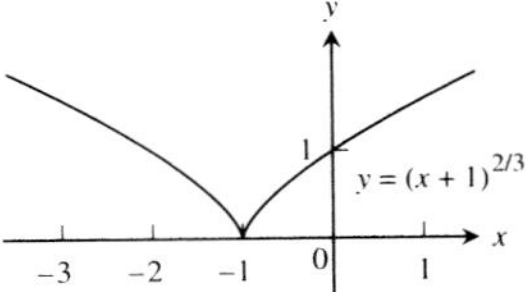

35. $D: -\infty < x < \infty$, $R: y \le 1$

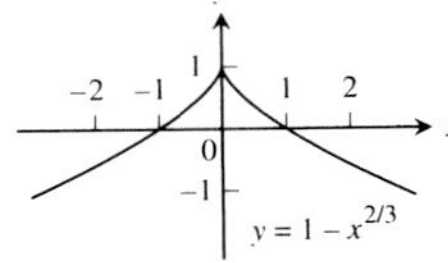

37. $D: -\infty < x < \infty$, $R: -\infty < y < \infty$

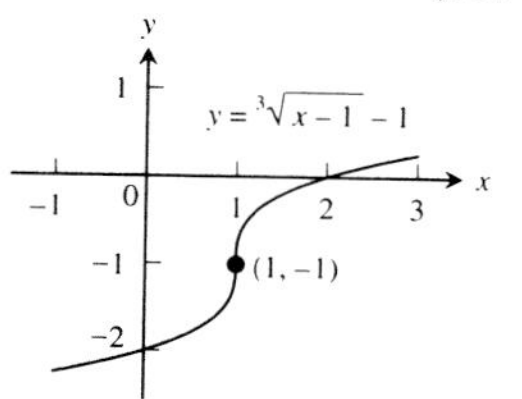

39. $D: x \neq 2$, $R: y \neq 0$

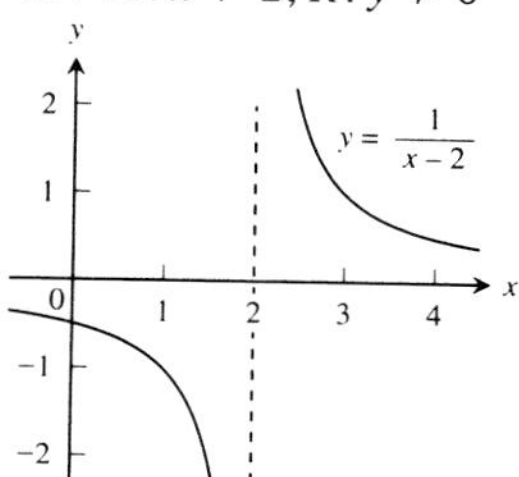

41. $D: x \neq 0$, $R: y \neq 2$

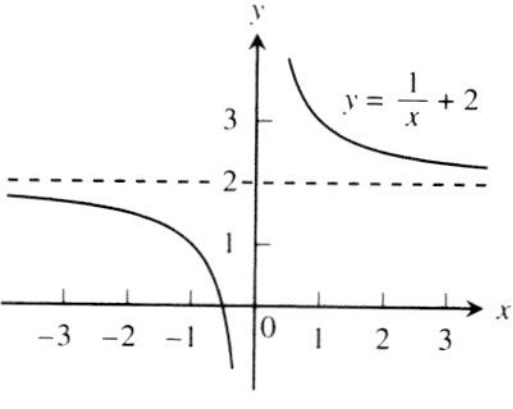

43. $D: x \neq 1, y > 0$

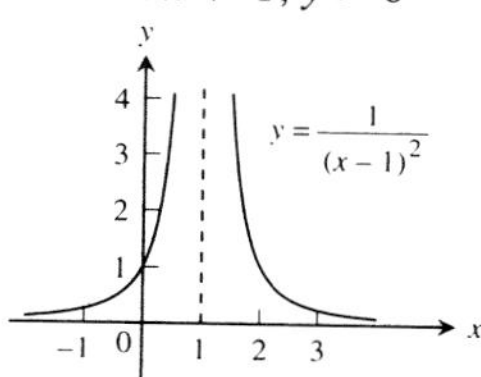

45. $D: x \neq 0$, $R: y > 1$

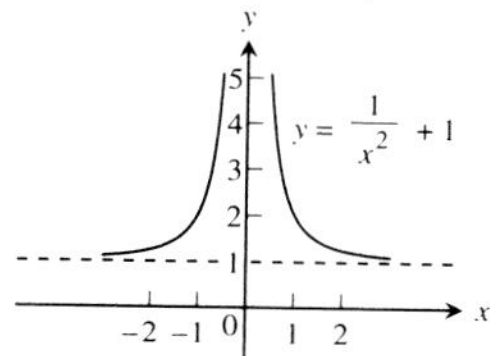

47.

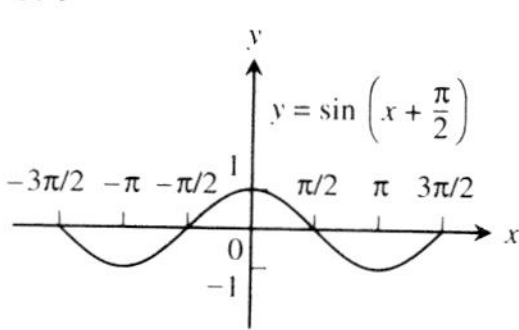

49.

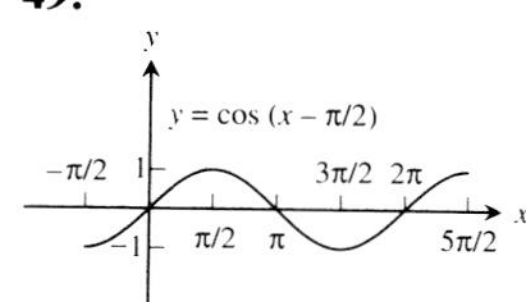

51.

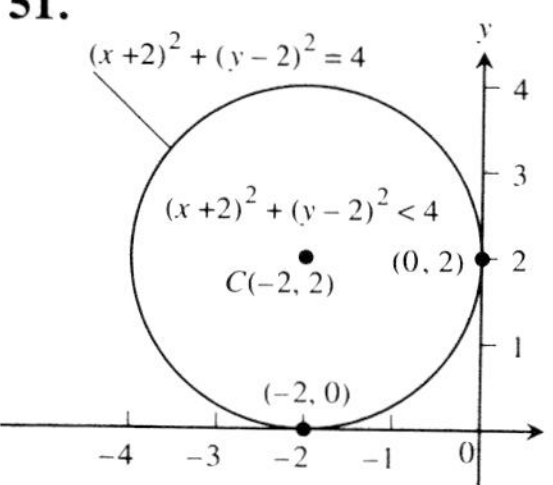

53.

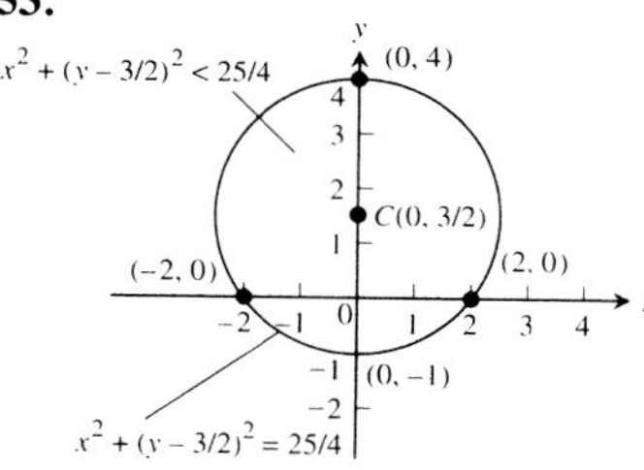

55.

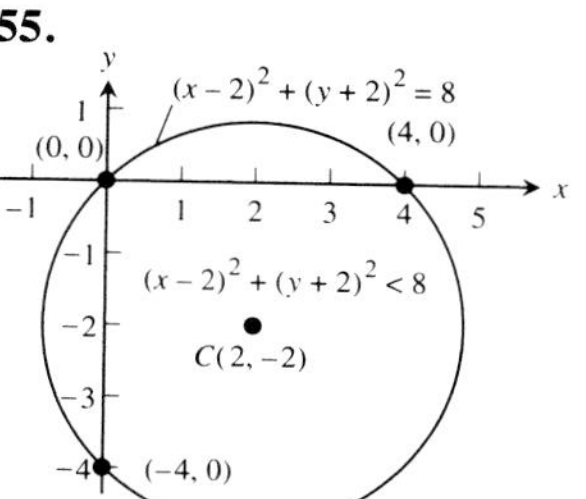

57.

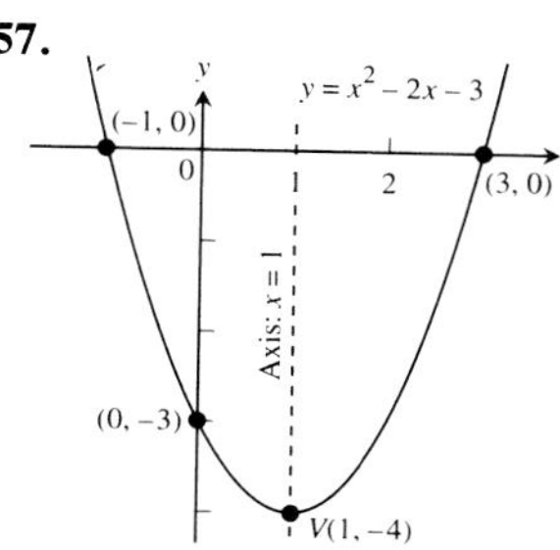

59.

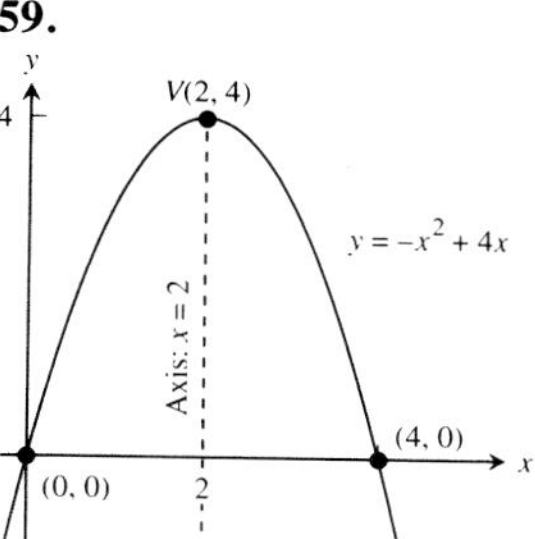

61.

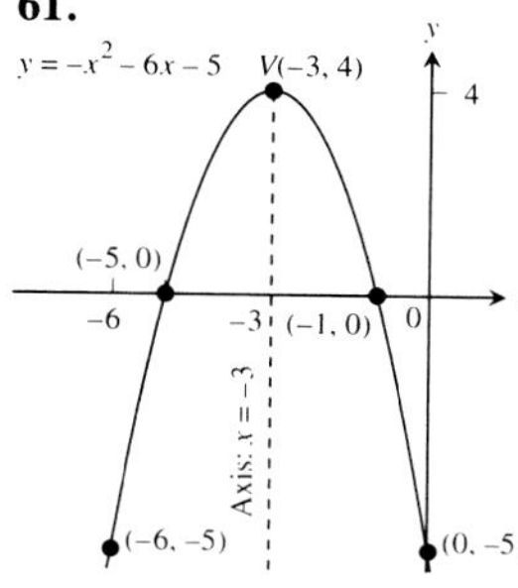

63.

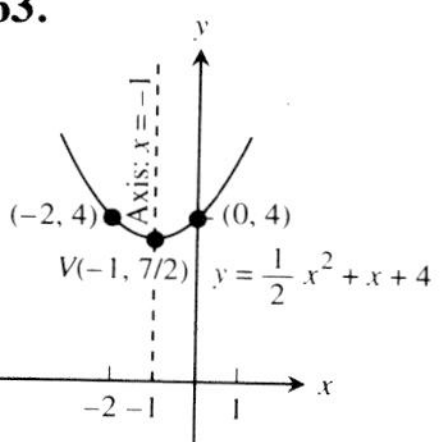

65. Domain and range of $f(x) = \sqrt{x - x^2}$: $D: 0 \leq x \leq 1$, $R: 0 \leq y \leq \frac{1}{2}$

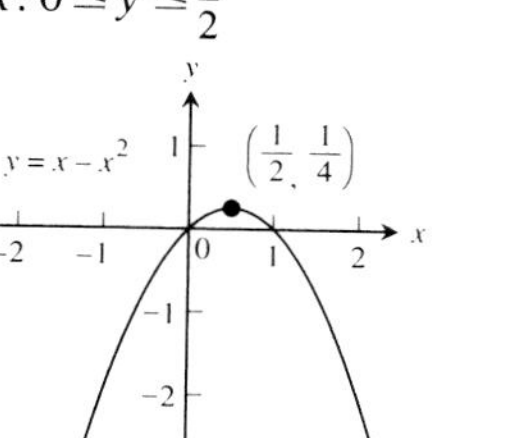

67. a) Exterior of the unit circle centered at the origin

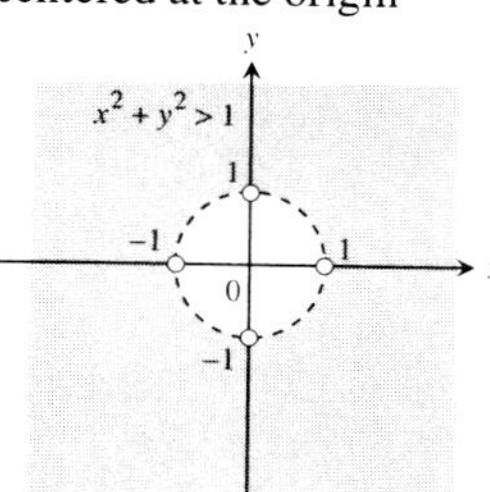

b) Interior of the circle of radius 2 centered at the origin

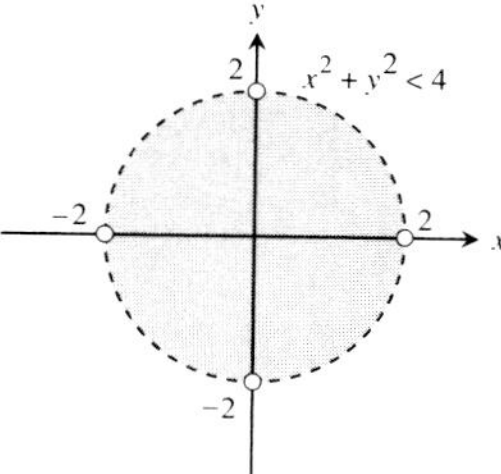

c) The region between the circles $x^2 + y^2 = 1$ and $x^2 + y^2 = 4$

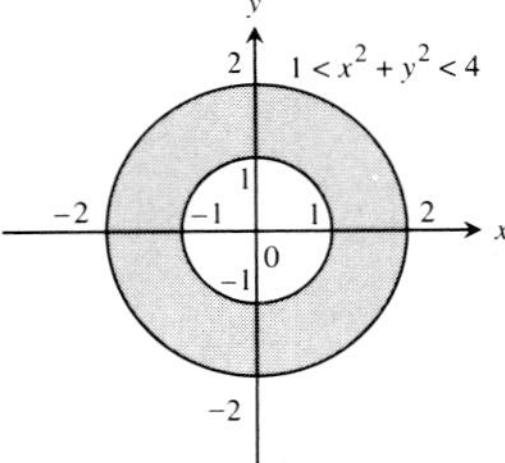

69. a) The points above both the line and the parabola

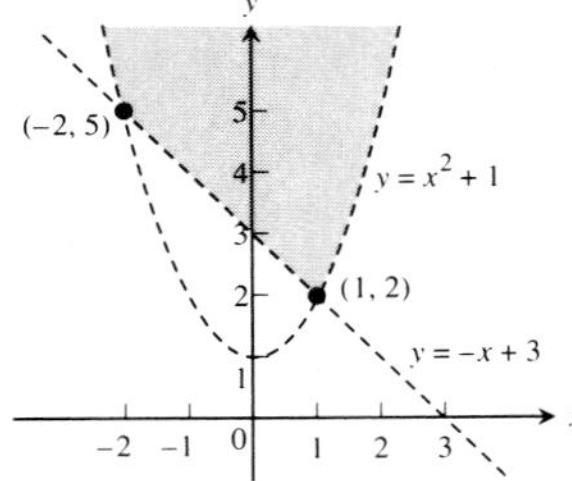

b) The points above the line but below the parabola

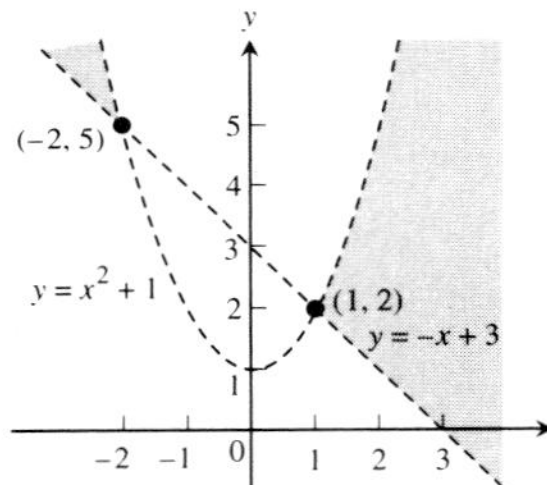

c) The points below the line but above the parabola

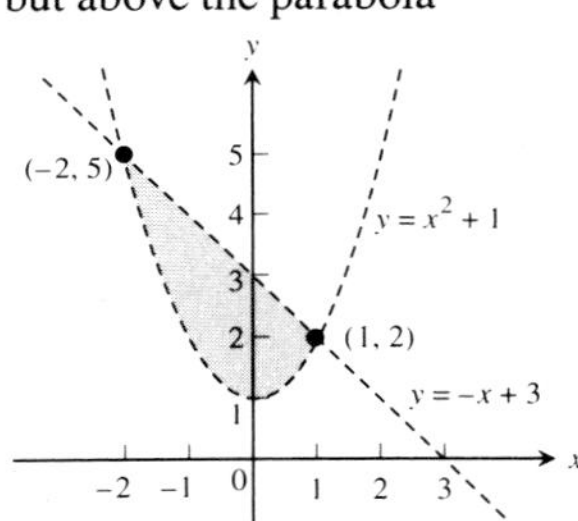

d) The points below both the line and the parabola

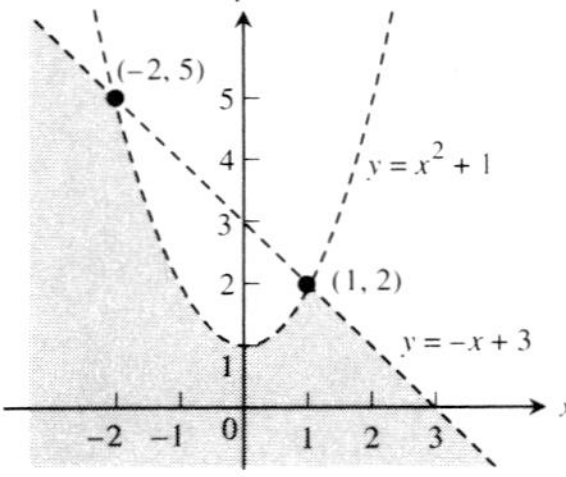

71. a) The points above both parabolas

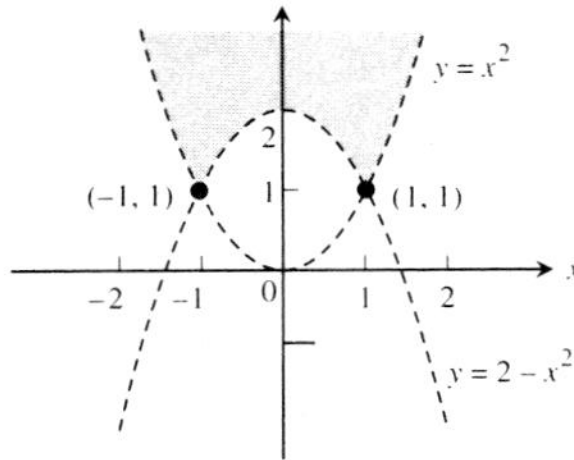

b) The points above the parabola $y = x^2$ but below the parabola $y = 2 - x^2$

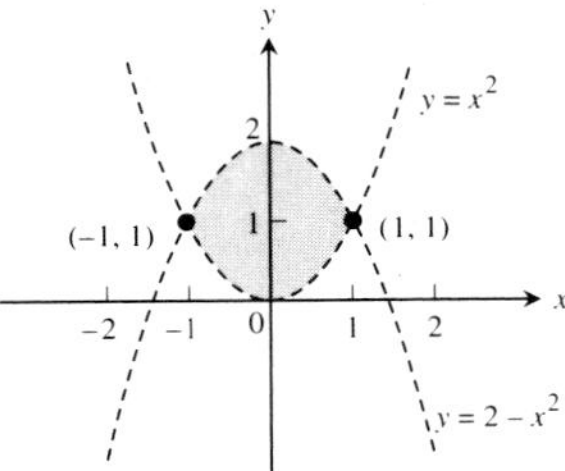

c) The points below the parabola $y = x^2$ but above the parabola $y = 2 - x^2$

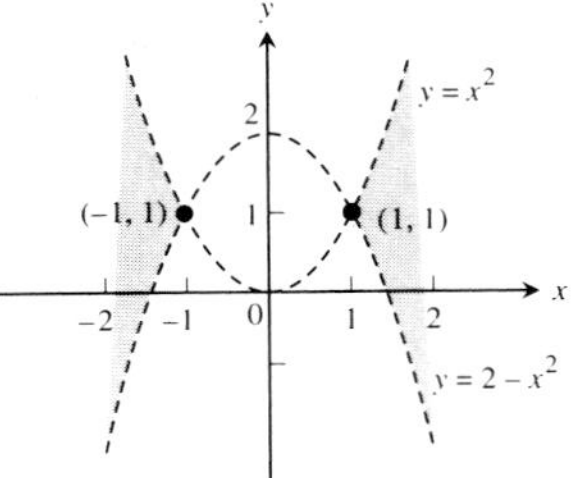

d) The points below both parabolas

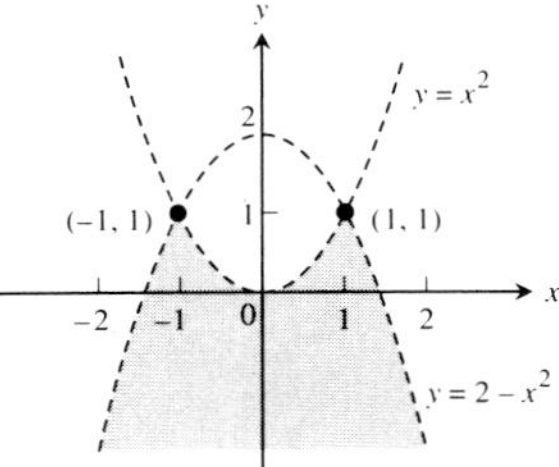

75. a) 37 b) 365 c) Right 101 d) Up 25

Section 1.5, pp. 46–48

1. a) Answers vary b) $e^{-1} = 0.367879441171$, $e^{-10} = 4.53999297625 \times 10^{-5}$, $e^{-100} = 3.72007597602 \times 10^{-44}$, $e^{-1000} = 0$ (answers vary with the calculator used)

3. Answers vary, $x^* = \pi$ **5.** $y = x$

7. Difference $= 1$ for $x \neq -1$

9. Difference $= 2$ for $x \neq n\pi/2$, n an odd integer

11. Difference $= \ln 2 \approx 0.7$ for $x > 0$

13. a) $\sqrt{3} = 1.732050808$, $\sqrt{1.732050808} = 1.14720269$, etc. b) $\sqrt{5} = 2.236067978$, $\sqrt{2.236067978} = 1.495348781$, $\sqrt{1.495348781} = 1.222844545$, etc.

15. $\sqrt[10]{2} = 1.071773463$, $\sqrt[10]{1.071773463} = 1.00695555$ $\sqrt[10]{1.00695555} = 1.000693387$, $\sqrt[10]{1.000693387} = 1.000069317$, etc.

17. $x_0 = 1$, $x_1 = 1.540302306$, $x_2 = 1.570791601$, $x_3 = 1.570796327$, $x_4 = 1.570796327$, etc.

19. a) $\left(\frac{1}{10}\right)^{1/(\ln 10)} = 0.367879441$, $\left(\frac{1}{100}\right)^{1/(\ln 100)} = 0.367879441$, etc.
b) $y = 0.367879441171$
21. 0.8391 **23.** Min: 17°, Max: 48°

Section 1.6, pp. 55–58

1. a) 5 b) 1.2315 c) 4.1 **3.** ± 2 **5.** $-1/2, -9/2$
7. $-1/3, 17/3$ **9.** a) False b) True c) True d) True e) True f) True g) True h) True
11. e **13.** b **15.** b **17.** $-2 < y < 2$ **19.** $-1 \le r \le 3$
21. $5/3 < s < 3$ **23.** $0 \le t \le 4$ **25.** $|x - 6| < 3$
27. $|x + 1| < 4$ **29.** $\sqrt{99} < x < \sqrt{101}$
31. $22.21 < x < 23.81$ **33.** $20 < x < 30$ **35.** $|x - 3| < 0.5$
37. $|x - 6| < 1$ **39.** $|x - 2| < \dfrac{0.03}{|m|}$ **41.** $|x - 1| < \dfrac{0.05}{|m|}$
43. $|x - 3.385| \le 0.002$ **45.** a) iii b) iv c) i d) ii
47.

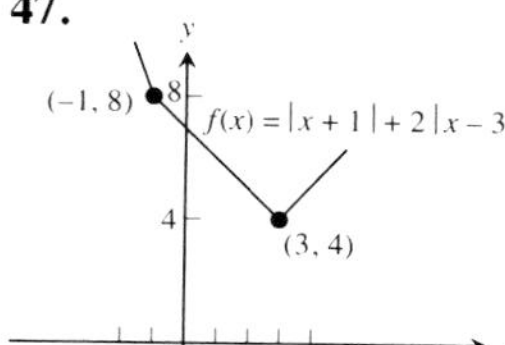

49.

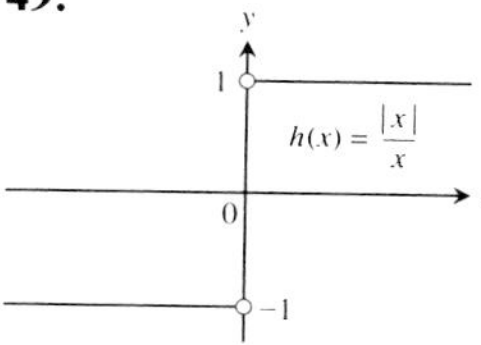

51.

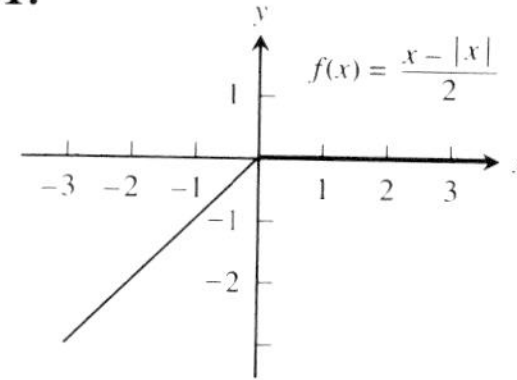

53. Domains: $-\infty < x < \infty$ versus $x \ge 0$; Ranges: Both $y \ge 0$
55. $g(x) = \sqrt{x}$
57. a) $D: -4 \le x \le 4$, $R: 0 \le y \le 2$ b) $D: x = 0$, $R: y = 0$

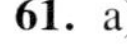
61. a)

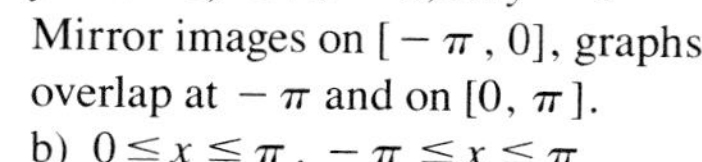
Mirror images on $[-\pi, 0]$, graphs overlap at $-\pi$ and on $[0, \pi]$.
b) $0 \le x \le \pi$, $-\pi \le x \le \pi$

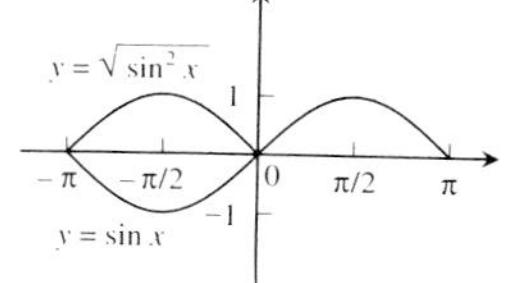

63. $D: -\infty < x < \infty$, $R: 0 \le y \le 2$

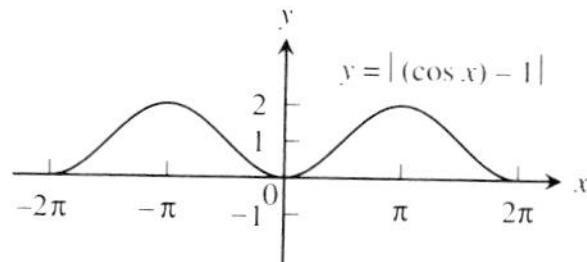

65. $d = 7$ at $x = 2$

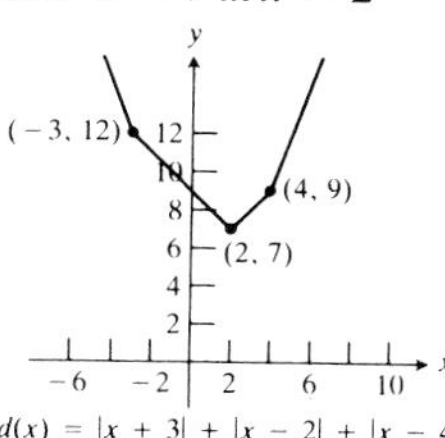

67. Minimum value is 17 when $x = 2$; place the table at 2.

Chapter 1 Practice Exercises, pp. 58–61

1. $y = -2x + 7$ **3.** $y = x/3$ **5.** $y = (5/3)x + (4/3)$
7. $y = -(5/4)x + 7$ **9.** $y = 10$ **11.** $y = (4/3)x - 4$
13. $y = 2x - 12$ **15.** $y = (3/4)x - 15$
17. $D: -\infty < x < \infty$, $R: y \ge 0$

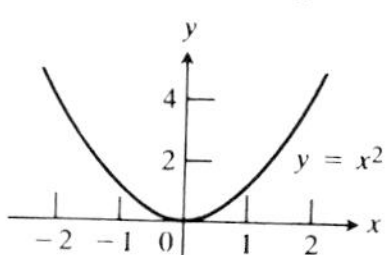

19. $D: -\infty < x < \infty$, $R: y \ge 0$

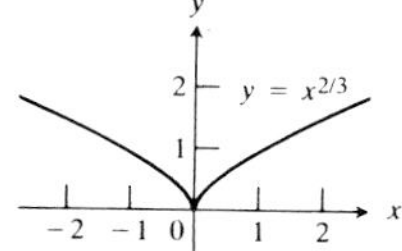

21. $D: -\infty < x < \infty$, $R: -\infty < y < \infty$

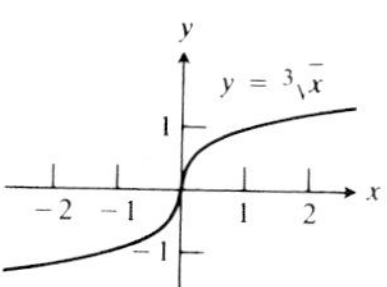

23. $D: x \ne 0$, $R: y > 0$

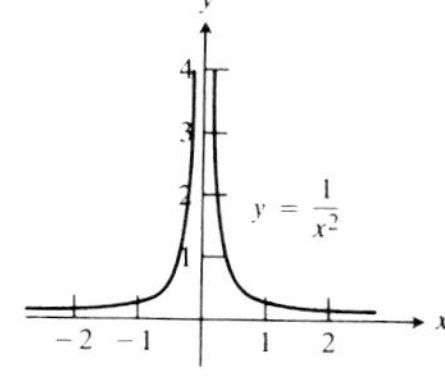

25. $D: -\infty < x < \infty$, R: y is an integer

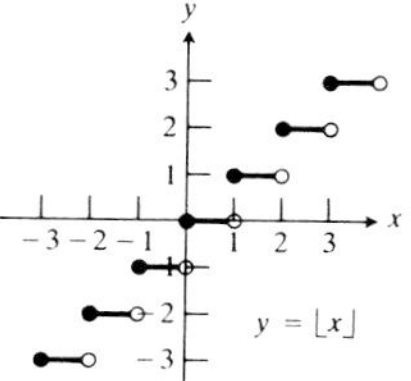

27. $D: -\infty < x < \infty$, $R: -1 \le y \le 1$

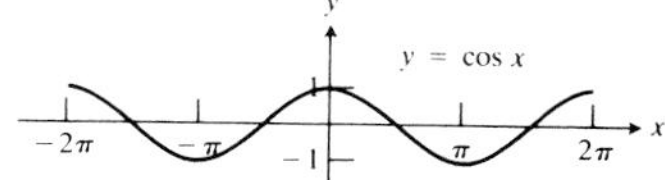

29. $D: x \neq \dfrac{n\pi}{2}$, n an odd integer, $R: -\infty < y < \infty$

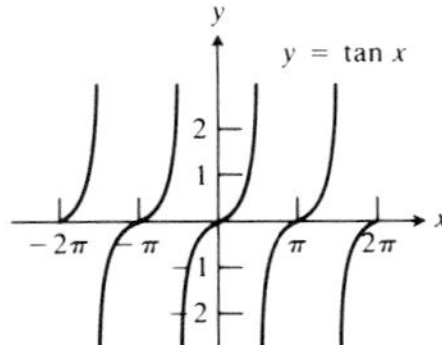

31. $D: x \neq \dfrac{n\pi}{2}$, n an odd integer, $R: y \leq -1$ or $y > 1$

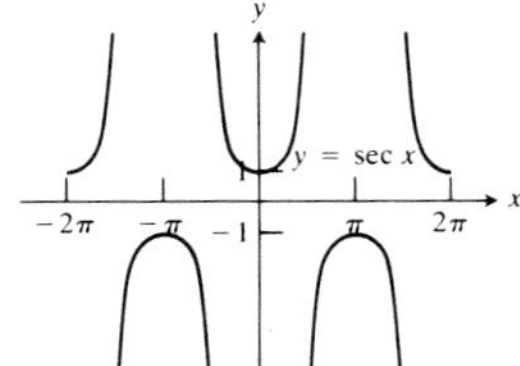

33. a) Even b) Even c) Even **35.** a) Even b) Odd c) Odd
37. a) Even b) Odd

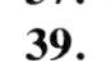

39.

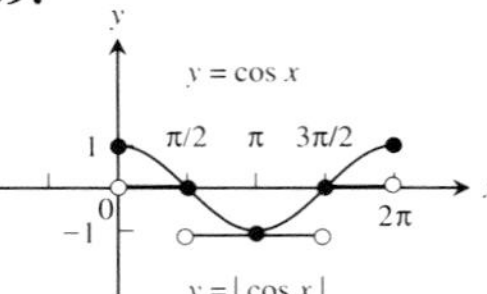

43.

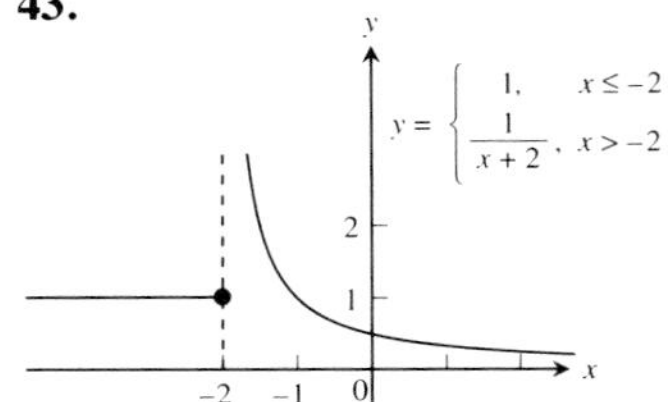

45. $y = \begin{cases} -x + 1, & 0 \leq x \leq 1 \\ -x + 2, & 1 < x \leq 2 \end{cases}$

47. a) $f(g(t))$ b) $f(g(v(t)))$ c) $v(u(t))$ d) $g(v(u(t)))$
e) $g(g(t))$ f) $g(g(g(t)))$ g) $u(g(t))$ h) $u(g(f(t)))$

49. a) $y + 1 = (x - 2)^2$ b) $y = (x + 2)^2$

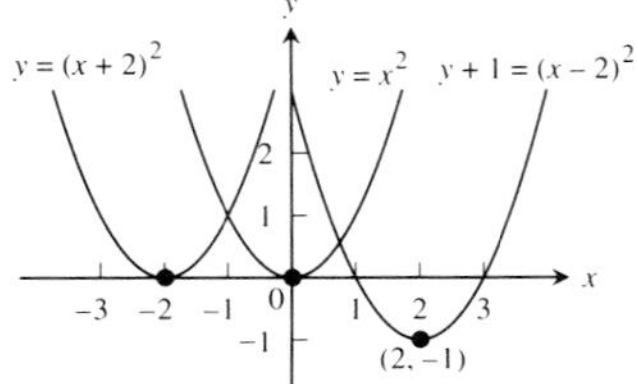

51. a) $y = \sin(x - \pi/2)$ b) $y - 1 = \sin(x - \pi)$

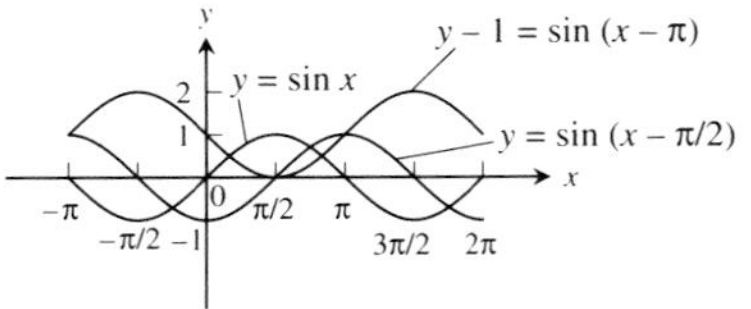

53. a) $y = \sqrt{x - 2}$ b) $y = \sqrt{x + 2}$

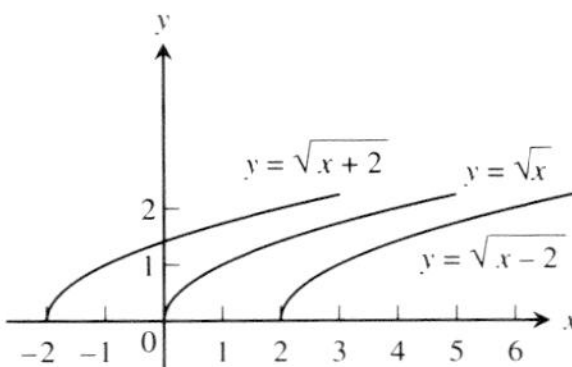

55. a)

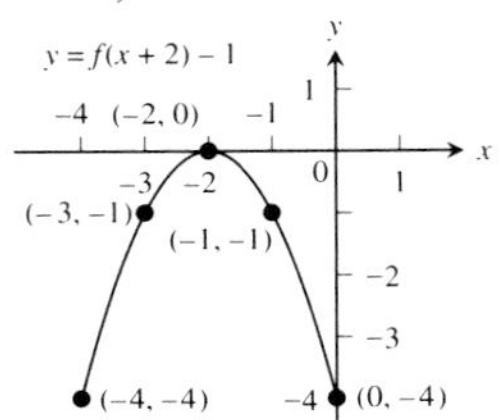

b)

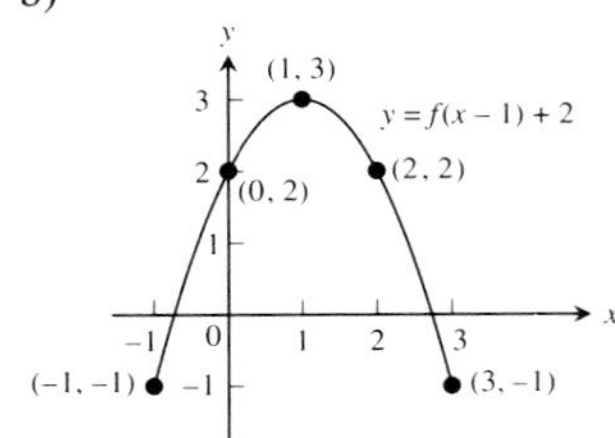

57. $y - 3 = f(x + 5)$ **59.** $(x - 1)^2 + (y - 1)^2 = 1$
61. $(x - 2)^2 + (y + 3)^2 = 1/4$ **63.** $C(3, -5); a = 4$
65. $C(0, 5); a = \sqrt{2}$ **67.**

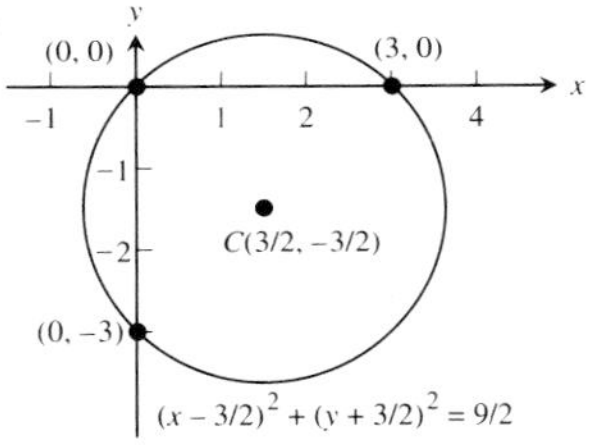

(0, 0) (3, 0) C(3/2, −3/2) (0, −3) $(x - 3/2)^2 + (y + 3/2)^2 = 9/2$

69.

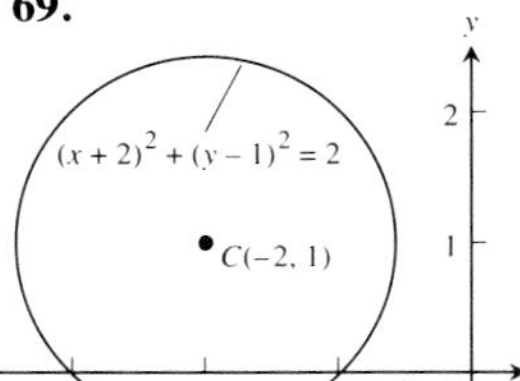

71.

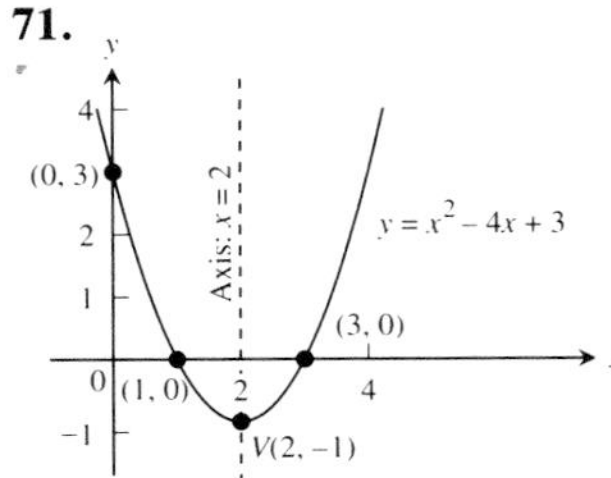

73.

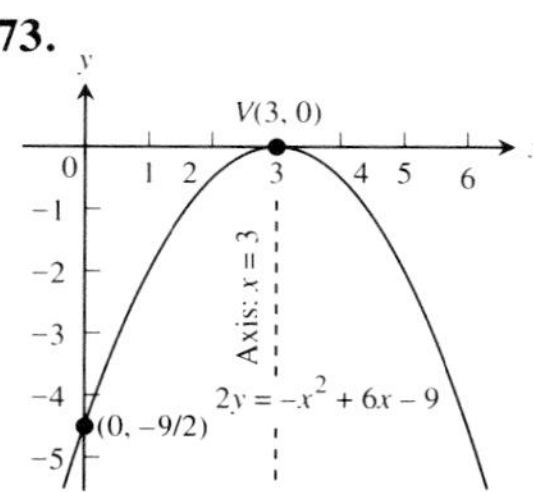

75. a) $(x-2)^2+(y-3)^2<4$ b) $(x-2)^2+(y-3)^2\le 4$
77. $y< -x^2+4x$ and $y>x$
79. $x=3/2$ or $1/2$
81. $s=15$ or -20

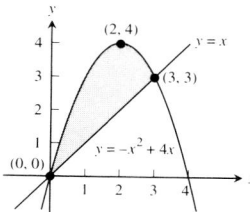

83. $-\frac{5}{2}\le x\le -\frac{3}{2}$ **85.** $-\frac{1}{5}<y<1$ **87.** $|x-7|<4$
89. $|y-3|<4$ **91.** $|x-2|<1$ **93.** $|x-15|<8$
95.

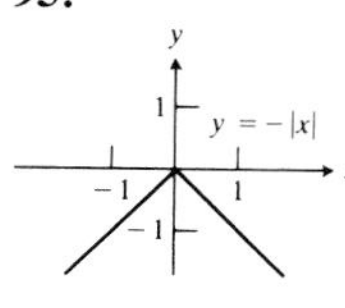

97.

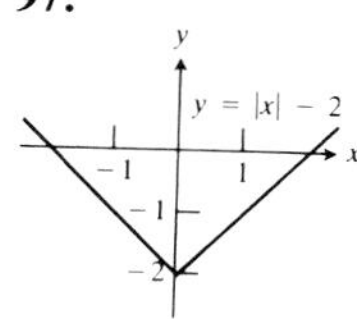

99.

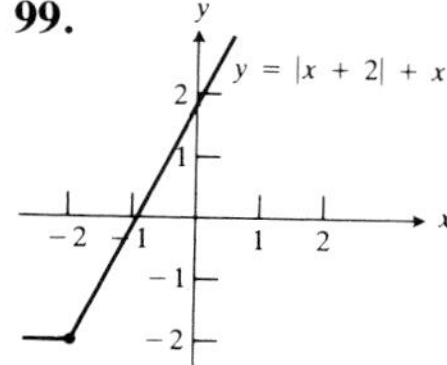

101. For $E=0.2$, $2.56<x<5.76$; for $E=0.1$, $3.24<x<4.84$

Chapter 2

Section 2.1, pp. 72–75

1.

x	3.9	3.99	3.999	4.001	4.01	4.1
$f(x)$	8.9	8.99	8.999	9.001	9.01	9.1

$\lim_{x\to c} f(x)=9$

3.

x	−1.1	−1.01	−1.001	−0.999	−0.99	−0.9
$f(x)$	2.1	2.01	2.001	1.999	1.99	1.9

$\lim_{x\to c} f(x)=2$

5. 2 **7.** a) 1 b) −1 **9.** 3/4 **11.** 3/4
13. a) True b) True c) False d) True e) True f) True g) False h) False i) False j) False
15. a) 2, 1 b) No, $\lim_{x\to 2^+} f(x)\ne \lim_{x\to 2^-} f(x)$ c) 3, 3 d) Yes, 3
17. a)

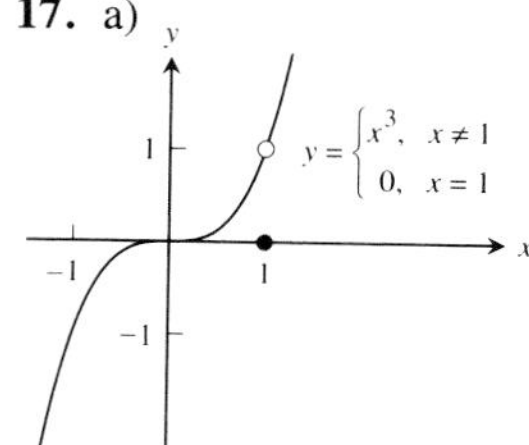

b) $\lim_{x\to 1^-} f(x)=1$, $\lim_{x\to 1^+} f(x)=1$
c) Yes, $\lim_{x\to 1^-} f(x)=\lim_{x\to 1^+} f(x)=1$

19. a) $D: 0\le x\le 2$, $R: 0<y\le 1$ and $y=2$
b) $(0,1)\cup(1,2)$ c) $x=2$ d) $x=0$

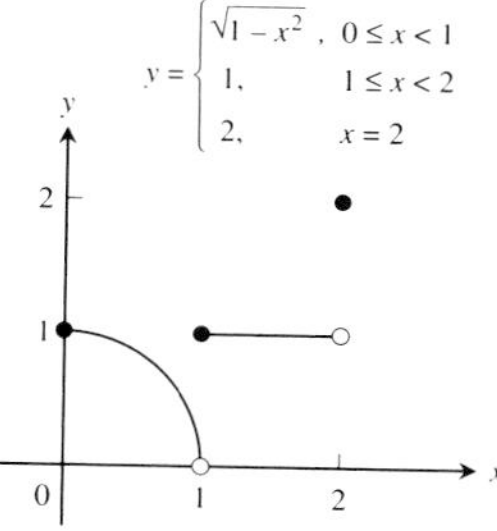

21. a) No b) Yes, 0 c) No **23.** −9 **25.** 4 **27.** −15
29. 0 **31.** −5 **33.** 27 **35.** 45 **37.** 5/8 **39.** −2
41. 5/2 **43.** 2 **45.** 3/2 **47.** 3 **49.** 1 **51.** −2
53. 1/10 **55.** −7 **57.** 3/2 **59.** −1/2 **61.** 4/3
63. a) −10 b) −20 c) −1 d) 5/7
65. a) 4 b) −21 c) −12 d) −7/3 **67.** 3/4 **69.** $\frac{1}{2\sqrt{2}}$

75. a)

x	$x^{1/(x-1)}$
1.1	2.59374
1.01	2.70481
1.001	2.71692
0.999	2.71964
0.99	2.73200
0.9	2.86797

b) 2.71828

77. a)

x	$\frac{1-\cos x}{x^2}$
0.1	.49958
0.01	.499996
0.001	.50000
−0.1	.49958
−0.01	.499996
−0.001	.50000

b) −1/2

Section 2.2, pp. 81–83

1. a) −3 b) −3 **3.** a) 1/2 b) 1/2
5. a) 0 b) 0 **7.** a) 2/5 b) 2/5 **9.** a) 0 b) 0
11. a) $-\infty$ b) $+\infty$ **13.** a) $+\infty$ b) $-\infty$
15. a) 0 b) 0 **17.** a) 7 b) 7 **19.** a) −2/3 b) −2/3
21. 0 **23.** $+\infty$ **25.** 1 **27.** $+\infty$ **29.** $+\infty$ **31.** $+\infty$
33. $-\infty$ **35.** a) ∞ b) $-\infty$ **37.** ∞ **39.** 1/2 **41.** 1
43. $+\infty$ **45.** −1/2 **47.** −1 **49.** −1
51. a) $+\infty$ b) $-\infty$ c) $-\infty$ d) $+\infty$
53. a) $+\infty$ b) $-\infty$ c) $+\infty$ d) $-\infty$
55. a) $+\infty$ b) 0 **57.** Here is one possibility.

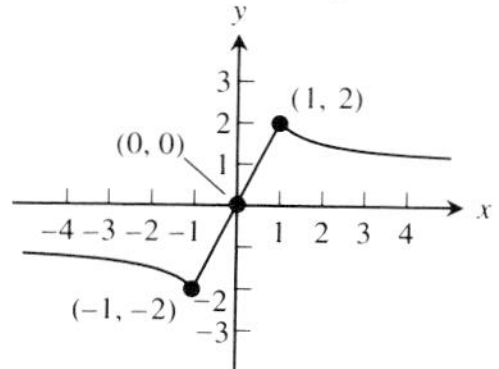

59. Here is one possibility.

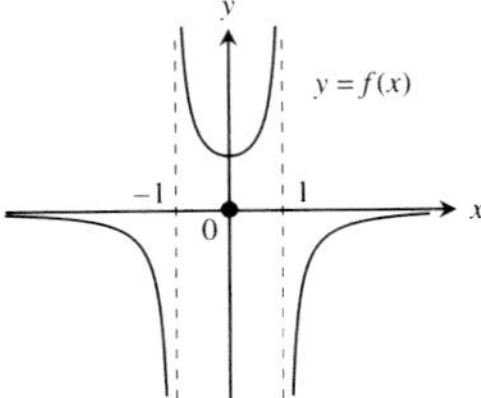

65. $p > 0$, $p = 0$, $p < 0$

69. a)

x	10	100	1000
$\left(1+\frac{1}{x}\right)^x$	2.5937	2.7048	2.7169

71. 2.3025 85092 299 . . . (ln 10)

Section 2.3, pp. 89–90

1. 1 **3.** 1 **5.** 2 **7.** 1 **9.** 1 **11.** 2 **13.** −1
15. 2 **17.** 1 **19.** 1 **21.** 1 **23.** 1/2 **25.** 2/3
27. 0 **29.** 2 **31.** 1 **33.** 1 **35.** $+\infty$ **37.** $-\infty$
39. 2 **43.** 1/2

Section 2.4, pp. 99–100

1. No, discontinuous at $x = 2$, not defined at $x = 2$
3. Continuous **5.** a) Yes b) Yes c) Yes d) Yes
7. a) No b) No **9.** a) 0 b) 0 **11.** No
13. 2, nonremovable **15.** 1, nonremovable; 0, removable
17. Continuous at $(-\infty, 0) \cup (0, 1) \cup (1, \infty)$; discontinuous at $x = 0$, $x = 1$; continuous only from the right at $x = 0$

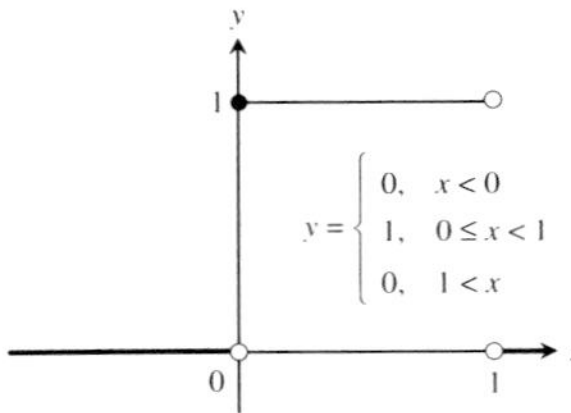

19. $x = 2$ **21.** $x = 3, x = 1$ **23.** None **25.** $x = 0$
27. $x = (n\pi)/2$, n any integer **29.** None **31.** Yes
33. $f(1) = 2$ **35.** $h(2) = 7$ **37.** $f(2) = 1$ **39.** $h(0) = 4$
41. 0 **43.** −1 **45.** 1 **47.** $\sqrt{2}/2$
49. Intermediate Value Theorem

Section 2.5, pp. 107–108

1. $\delta = 2$ **3.** $\delta = 1/2$ **5.** $\delta = 2$ **7.** $\delta = 1/18$ **9.** $\delta = 0.1$
11. $\delta = \sqrt{5} - 2$ **13.** $\delta = 7/16$ **15.** $2.99 < x < 3.01$
17. $\sqrt{8.95} < x < \sqrt{9.05}$ and $-\sqrt{9.05} < x < -\sqrt{8.95}$
19. $2.7591 < x < 3.2391$ **21.** $10/41 < x < 10/39$
23. $L = 5, \delta \le 0.005$ **25.** $L = 0, \delta \le 0.005$
27. $L = 4, \delta \le 0.05$ **29.** $L = 2, \delta \le .0399$ **31.** $L = 2, \delta \le 1/3$
33. $\epsilon = 0.01 \Rightarrow \delta = 0.01$; $\epsilon = 0.001 \Rightarrow \delta = 0.001$; $\epsilon = 0.0001 \Rightarrow \delta = 0.0001$; $\delta = \epsilon$
35. $\delta = \epsilon^2$, $\lim_{x\to 5^+} \sqrt{x-5} = 0$ **37.** $\delta = \epsilon/6$

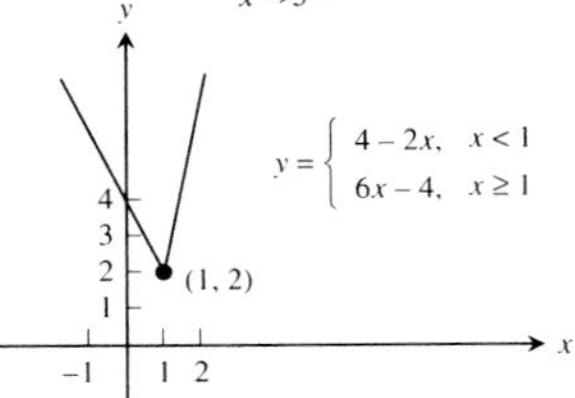

Chapter 2 Practice Exercises, pp. 109–111

1. 1 **3.** −4 **5.** $\sqrt{3}$ **7.** −2/3 **9.** −1 **11.** 1/4
13. $2/\sqrt{5}$ **15.** −3 **17.** 2 **19.** 1/5 **21.** 2/5
23. 0 **25.** $-\infty$ **27.** $+\infty$ **29.** $+\infty$
31. a) $+\infty$ b) $-\infty$ **33.** $+\infty$ **35.** k **37.** 1
39. 4 **41.** 0 **43.** a) $+\infty$ b) $-\infty$ **47.** No
49. a) $f(x)$ approaches 0 as $x \to 0$, $f(x)$ approaches 0 as $x \to \infty$
51. a) −21 b) 49 c) 0 d) 1 e) 1 f) 7 **53.** 0
55. 0 **57.** 1
59. a) Right: 1, 0, 1; Left: 1, 0, −1 b) 1, 0, does not exist
c) $x = -1$, removable, $f(-1) = 1$; $x = 0$, removable, $f(0) = 0$; $x = 1$, nonremovable
61. a)

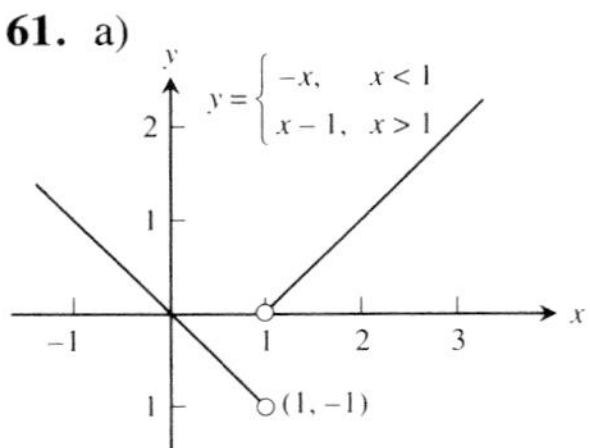

b) No **63.** Yes, $k = -6$ **65.** Yes, $k = 1/2$
67. Yes **69.** Yes **73.** $\delta \le \epsilon/2$ **75.** $L = 5, \delta \le 0.01$
77. $L = -5, \delta \le 0.01$ **79.** $L = 2, \delta \le 3$
81. $L = 1, \delta \le 2/11$

Chapter 3

Section 3.1, pp. 124–125

1. P_1: $m_1 = 1$, P_2: $m_2 = 5$ **3.** P_1: $m_1 = 5/2$, P_2: $m_2 = -1/2$
5. $-3, m = -3$ **7.** $4x, m = 12$ **9.** $4x - 13, m = -1$

11. $-2/x^2, m = -2/9$ **13.** $\dfrac{1}{(x+1)^2}, m = \dfrac{1}{16}$

15. $\dfrac{1}{2\sqrt{x}}, m = \dfrac{1}{2\sqrt{3}}$ **17.** $\dfrac{1}{2\sqrt{x+1}}, m = \dfrac{1}{4}$

19. $\dfrac{-5}{2(x-2)^{3/2}}, m = -\dfrac{5}{2}$

21. $y = 2x + 5$

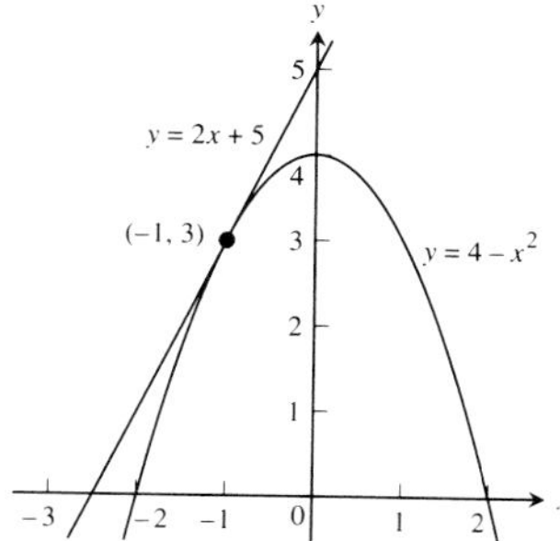

23. $y = x + 1$

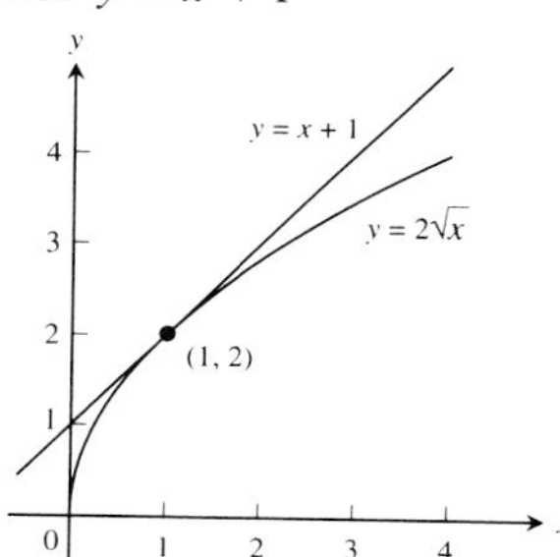

25. $y = \dfrac{3}{2}x + 2$

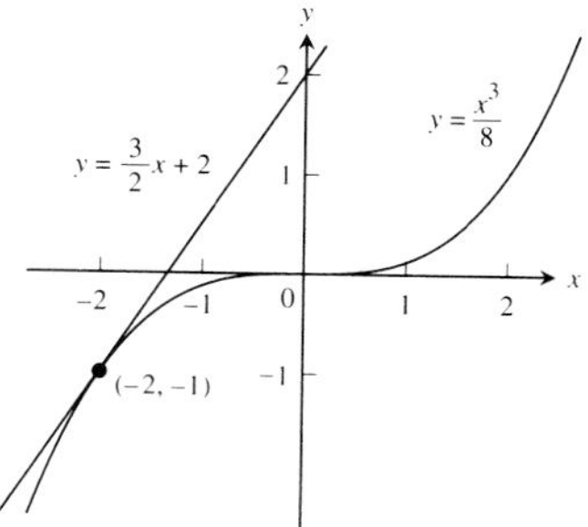

27. a) $y' = -2x$

b)

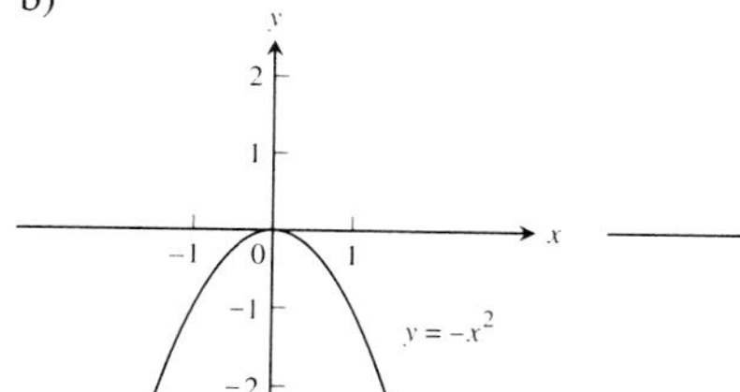

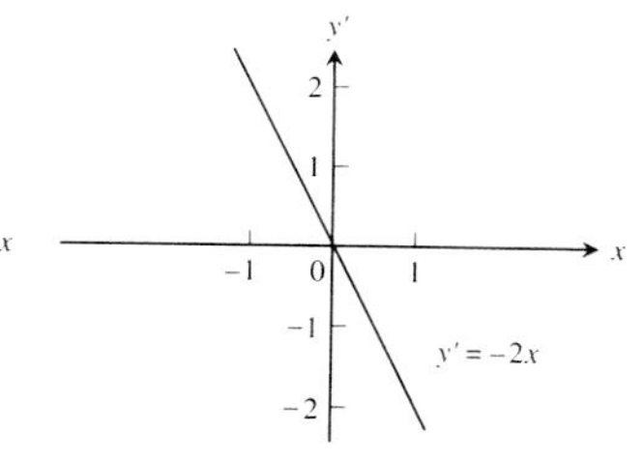

c) $x < 0; x = 0; x > 0$ d) $-\infty < x < 0; 0 < x < \infty$

29. a) $y' = x^2$

b)

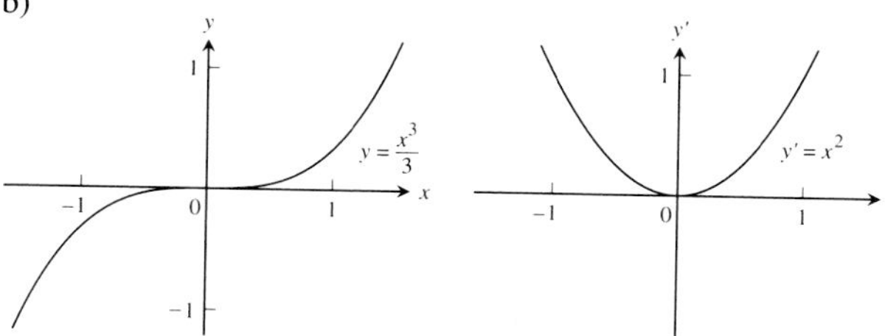

c) $x \neq 0; x = 0$; none d) $-\infty < x < \infty$; none

31. 0 **33.** -1 **35.** $-1/54$

37. a) $-3 \leq x \leq 2$ b) None c) None

39. a) $-3 \leq x < 0, 0 < x \leq 3$ b) None c) $x = 0$

41. a) $-1 \leq x < 0, 0 < x \leq 2$ b) $x = 0$ c) None

43. Since $\lim_{x \to 0^+} f'(x) = 1$ while $\lim_{x \to 0^-} f'(x) = 0$, $f(x)$ is not differentiable at $x = 0$.

45. Since $\lim_{x \to 1^+} f'(x) = 2$ while $\lim_{x \to 1^-} f'(x) = 1/2$, $f(x)$ is not differentiable at $x = 1$.

Section 3.2, pp. 135–137

1. $-2x, -2$ **3.** $15x^2 - 15x^4, 30x - 60x^3$ **5.** $4x^2 - 1, 8x$

7. $-6/x^3, 18/x^4$ **9.** $1/x^2, -2/x^3$

11. $12x - 10 + \dfrac{10}{x^3}, 12 - \dfrac{30}{x^4}$ **13.** $-\dfrac{2}{3x^3} + \dfrac{5}{2x^2}, \dfrac{2}{x^4} - \dfrac{5}{x^3}$

15. $9 - \dfrac{1}{x^2}, \dfrac{2}{x^3}$ **17.** a) $3(2x+5) + 2(3x-1)$ b) $12x + 13$

19. a) $2x(x^3 - 1) + x^2(3x^2)$ b) $5x^4 - 2x$

21. a) $2x\left(x + 5 + \dfrac{1}{x}\right) + x^2\left(1 - \dfrac{1}{x^2}\right)$ b) $3x^2 + 10x + 1$

23. $y' = \dfrac{-19}{(3x-2)^2}$ **25.** $y' = \dfrac{x^2 + x + 4}{(x + (1/2))^2}$

27. $y' = \dfrac{1 - 3x^2 - 4x^3}{(x^2 - 1)^2(x^2 + x + 1)^2}$ **29.** $y' = \dfrac{x^2 - 2x - 1}{(1 + x^2)^2}$

31. $y' = \dfrac{-5}{\sqrt{x}\left(\sqrt{x} - 4\right)^2}$ **33.** $y' = 1/\left(\sqrt{x}\left(\sqrt{x} + 1\right)^2\right)$

35. $y' = \left(2\sqrt{x} - 1\right)/x^2$ **37.** $y' = 2x - (7/x^2), y'' = 2 + (14/x^3)$

39. $y' = 3/x^4, y'' = -12/x^5$

41. $y' = 2x - 1, y'' = 2, y^{(n)} = 0$ for $n > 2$

43. $y' = 2x^3 - 3x - 1, y'' = 6x^2 - 3, y''' = 12x, y^{(4)} = 12$, $y^{(n)} = 0$ for $n > 4$

45. $s' = -1 + 2t - 3t^2, s'' = 2 - 6t, s''' = -6, s^{(n)} = 0, n \geq 4$

47. $\dfrac{dr}{d\theta} = \dfrac{\theta^2 + 2\theta}{(1 + \theta + \theta^2)^2}$ **49.** $\dfrac{dw}{dz} = -1 - \dfrac{1}{z^2}, \dfrac{d^2w}{dz^2} = \dfrac{2}{z^3}$

51. $\dfrac{dp}{dq} = \dfrac{q}{6} + \dfrac{1}{6q^3} + \dfrac{1}{q^5}, \dfrac{d^2p}{dq^2} = \dfrac{1}{6} - \dfrac{1}{2q^4} - \dfrac{5}{q^6}$

53. a) 13 b) -7 c) $7/25$ d) 20 **55.** $y = 3x + 2$

57. a) $y = -\dfrac{x}{8} + \dfrac{5}{4}$ b) $m = -4$ at $(0, 1)$

c) $y = 8x - 15, y = 8x + 17$

59. $(2, 0), (-1, 27)$ **61.** $y = 4x, y = 2$

63. a) $y = 2x + 2$ c) $x = 2$ **65.** $\frac{dP}{dv} = -\frac{nRT}{(V - nb)^2} + \frac{2an^2}{V^3}$
71. Let $y = (u + v)$, then $y' = u' + v'$; let $y = (u - v)$, then $y' = u' - v'$; let $y = \left(\frac{u}{v}\right)$, then $y' = \frac{vu' - uv'}{v^2}$

Section 3.3, pp. 147–151

1. a) 80 m, 8 m/sec b) 0 m/sec, 16 m/sec; 1.6 m/sec^2, 1.6 m/sec^2
3. a) 0 m, 0 m/sec b) 2 m/sec, 2 m/sec; 6 m/sec^2, -6 m/sec^2
5. a) -20 m, -5 m/sec b) 45 m/sec, 1/5 m/sec; 140 m/sec^2, 4/25 m/sec^2
7. a) 2 m, 2/3 m/sec b) 0 m/sec, 1 m/sec; 1 m/sec^2, 1/8 m/sec^2
9. Mars: 4.46 sec; Jupiter: 0.726 sec
11. a) $24 - 9.8t$ m/sec, -9.8 m/sec^2 b) 2.4 sec c) 29.4 m d) 0.7 sec going up, 4.2 sec going down e) 4.9 sec
13. 320 sec on the moon, 52 sec on the earth
15. a) $(t/12) - 1$ b) Fastest ($dy/dt = -1$ m/h) when $t = 0$; slowest ($dy/dt = 0$ m/h) when $t = 12$
17. a) \$110/machine b) \$80 c) \$79.90
19. a) -6 m/sec^2, 6 m/sec^2 b) 3 m/sec
21. a) $t = 2, t = 7$ b) $3 \le t \le 6$
c)

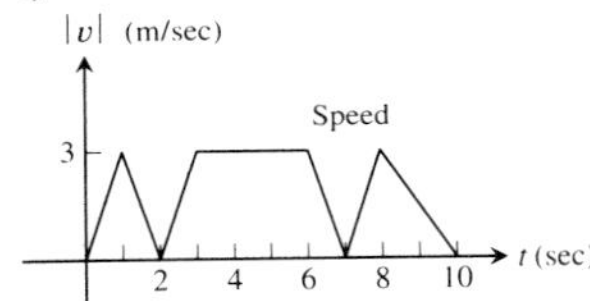

23. a) 190 ft/sec b) 2 sec c) 8 sec, 0 ft/sec d) 10.8 sec, 90 ft/sec e) 2.8 sec f) Greatest acceleration happens 2 sec after launch. g) Constant acceleration between 2 and 10.8 sec, -32 ft/sec^2 **25.** $9.8t$ m/sec b) 9.8 m/sec^2
27. a) 0, 0 b) 1700 rabbits, ≈ 1400 rabbits **29.** b **31.** d
35. a)

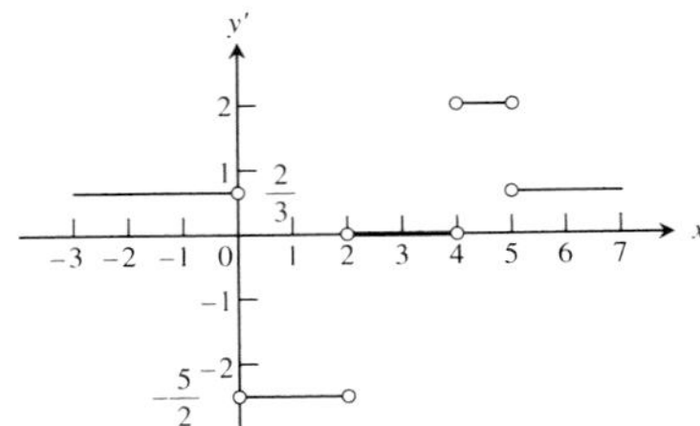

b) 0, 2, 4, and 5 **37.** a)

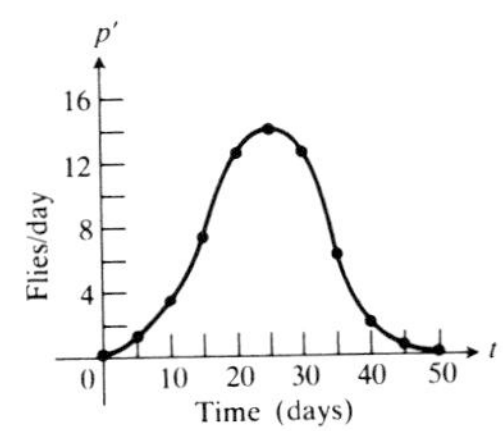

b) Fastest on day 25, slowest on first and last days

Section 3.4, pp. 157–159

1. $-10 - 3 \sin x$ **3.** $-(2/x^2) + \sin x$
5. $-\csc x \cot x - (2/\sqrt{x})$ **7.** $-x^2 \csc^2 x + 2x \cot x + (2/x^3)$
9. 0 **11.** $\frac{-\csc^2 x}{(1 + \cot x)^2}$ **13.** $4 \tan x \sec x - \csc^2 x$ **15.** $x^2 \cos x$
17. $\sec^2 t - 1$ **19.** $\frac{-2 \csc t \cot t}{(1 - \csc t)^2}$ **21.** $-\theta(\theta \cos \theta + 2 \sin \theta)$
23. $\sec \theta \csc \theta (\tan \theta - \cot \theta) = \sec^2 \theta - \csc^2 \theta$ **25.** $\sec^2 q$
27. $\sec^2 q$ **29.** a) $2 \csc^3 x - \csc x$ b) $2 \sec^3 x - \sec x$
31.

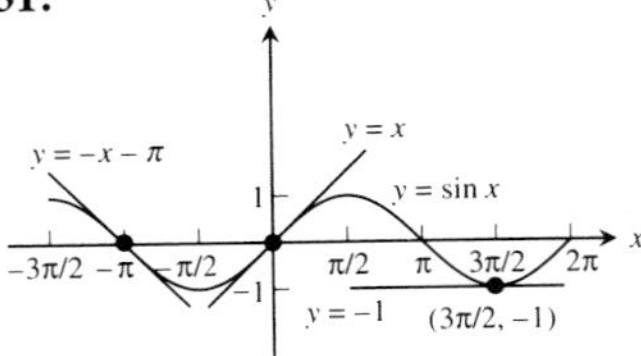

33.

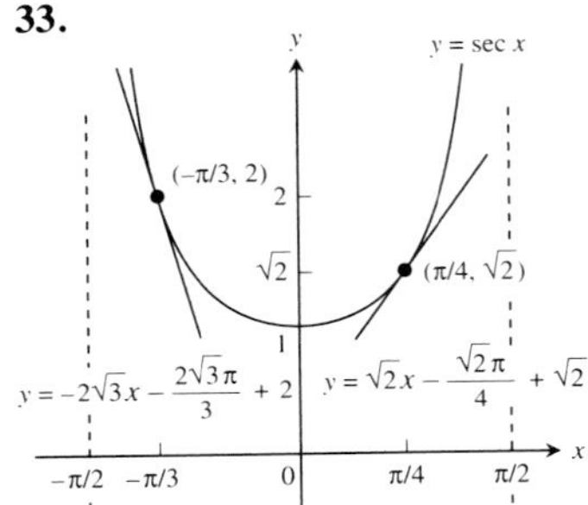

35. $y'(0) = \sec 0 \tan 0 = 0$, $y'(0) = -\sin 0 = 0$
37. Yes, at $x = \pi$ **39.** Yes, at $x = \pi/2$ **41.** 0 **43.** -1
45. Yes, $b = 1$
47. $-\sqrt{2}$ m/sec, $\sqrt{2}$ m/sec, $\sqrt{2}$ m/sec^2, $\sqrt{2}$ m/sec^3
49. $(-\pi/4, -1)$; $(\pi/4, 1)$

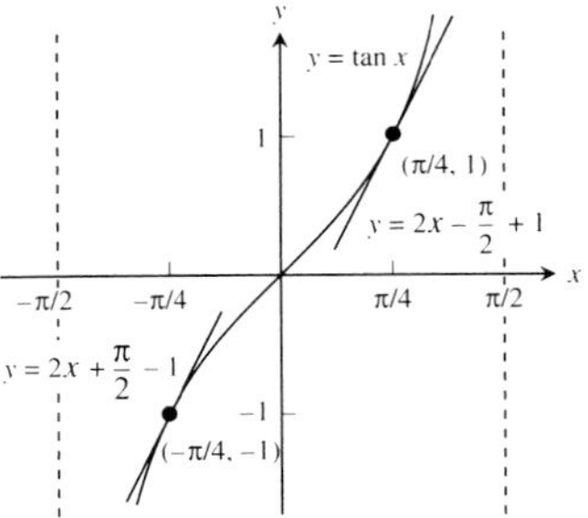

51. a) $y = -x + (\pi/2) + 2$ b) $y = 4 - \sqrt{3}$
55. The derivative of $\sin x$ would be $(\pi/180) \cos x$.

Section 3.5, pp. 165–168

1. $12x^3$ **3.** $3 \cos (3x + 1)$ **5.** $\frac{1}{3} \sin\left(-\frac{x}{3}\right)$
7. $(2 - 3x^2) \sec^2 (2x - x^3)$ **9.** $2x \sec(x^2 + \sqrt{2}) \tan(x^2 + \sqrt{2})$
11. $(2x + 7) \csc (x^2 + 7x) \cot (x^2 + 7x)$ **13.** $(10/x^2) \csc^2(2/x)$

15. $10(2x+1)^4$ **17.** $-6x(x^2+1)^{-4}$ **19.** $\dfrac{-5}{(5x-7)^2}$

21. $\left(1-\dfrac{x}{7}\right)^{-8}$ **23.** $4\left(\dfrac{x^2}{8}+x-\dfrac{1}{x}\right)^3\left(\dfrac{x}{4}+1+\dfrac{1}{x^2}\right)$

25. $\csc x(\csc x+\cot x)^{-1}$ **27.** $4\sin^3 x\cos x+2\cos^{-3}x\sin x$

29. $5x^4-5\cos(x/5)$ **31.** $3x\sec^2(3x)+\tan(3x)$

33. $(3x-2)^6-\dfrac{1}{x^3\left(4-\dfrac{1}{2x^2}\right)^2}$ **35.** $x^2(2x-5)^3(14x-15)$

37. $\dfrac{(4x+3)^3(4x+7)}{(x+1)^4}$ **39.** $\dfrac{2\sin x}{(1+\cos x)^2}$ **41.** $\dfrac{3(x-1)^2}{x^4}$

43. $4\sin^3 x\sec^2(4x)+3\sin^2 x\cos x\tan(4x)$

45. $3\sin(\pi/2-3t)$ **47.** $(4/\pi)\cos(3t)-(4/\pi)\sin(5t)$

49. $-\sec^2(2-\theta)$ **51.** $\theta^2\cos(\theta^2/2)+\sin(\theta^2/2)$

53. $2\pi\sin(\pi t-2)\cos(\pi t-2)$ **55.** $\dfrac{8\sin(2t)}{(1+\cos 2t)^5}$

57. $-\sin(\sin t)\cos t$ **59.** $-2\cos(\cos(2t-5))(\sin(2t-5))$

61. $[1+\tan^4(t/12)]^2[\tan^3(t/12)\sec^2(t/12)]$

63. $2\csc^2(3x-1)\cot(3x-1)$ **65.** $5/2$ **67.** $-\pi/4$

69. 0 **71.** a) $(-\sin u)\cdot\dfrac{du}{dx}=-\sin(6x+2)\cdot\dfrac{d}{dx}(6x+2)$
$=-6\sin(6x+2)$

b) $\left(-\sin(2u)\cdot\dfrac{d}{du}(2u)\right)\cdot\dfrac{du}{dx}=-2\sin(2u)\cdot\dfrac{du}{dx}=$
$-2\sin(2(3x+1))\cdot\dfrac{d}{dx}(3x+1)=-6\sin(6x+2)$

73. a) 1 b) 1 **75.** 5 **77.** a) $y=\pi x+2-\pi$ b) $\pi/2$

79. a) 2/3 b) $2\pi+5$ c) $15-8\pi$ d) 37/6 e) -1
f) $\sqrt{2}/24$ g) 5/32 h) $-5/(3\sqrt{17})$

81. It multiplies the velocity, acceleration, and jerk by 2, 4, and 8 respectively.

Section 3.6, pp. 174–176

1. $(9/4)x^{5/4}$ **3.** $2^{1/3}/3x^{2/3}$ **5.** $\dfrac{7}{2(x+6)^{1/2}}$ **7.** $-(2x+5)^{-3/2}$

9. $\dfrac{2x^2+1}{(x^2+1)^{1/2}}$ **11.** $\dfrac{9\cot x}{2(\csc x)^{3/2}}$ **13.** $-\dfrac{8\pi}{7}(\cos\pi x)^{1/7}(\sin\pi x)$

15. $\dfrac{-1}{4\sqrt{x}\sqrt{1-\sqrt{x}}}$ **17.** $\dfrac{-2xy-y^2}{x^2+2xy}$

19. $\dfrac{1-2y}{2x+2y-1}$ **21.** $\dfrac{-2x^3+3x^2y-xy^2+x}{x^2y-x^3+y}$

23. $\dfrac{1}{y(x+1)^2}$ **25.** $\cos^2 y$ **27.** $\dfrac{-\cos^2(xy)-y}{x}$

29. $\dfrac{-y^2}{y\sin\left(\dfrac{1}{y}\right)-\cos\left(\dfrac{1}{y}\right)+xy}$ **31.** $\sqrt{r}/\sqrt{\theta}$ **33.** $\dfrac{-r}{\theta}$

35. $y'=-\dfrac{x}{y}$, $y''=\dfrac{-y^2-x^2}{y^3}$

37. $y'=\dfrac{x+1}{y}$, $y''=\dfrac{y^2-(x+1)^2}{y^3}$ **39.** -2

41. a) $y=\dfrac{7}{4}x-\dfrac{1}{2}$ b) $y=-\dfrac{4}{7}x+\dfrac{29}{7}$

43. a) $y=3x+6$ b) $y=-\dfrac{1}{3}x+\dfrac{8}{3}$

45. a) $y=\dfrac{6}{7}x+\dfrac{6}{7}$ b) $y=-\dfrac{7}{6}x-\dfrac{7}{6}$

47. a) $y=-\dfrac{\pi}{2}x+\pi$ b) $y=\dfrac{2}{\pi}x-\dfrac{2}{\pi}+\dfrac{\pi}{2}$

49. a) $y=2\pi x-2\pi$ b) $y=-\dfrac{x}{2\pi}+\dfrac{1}{2\pi}$

51. Points: $(-\sqrt{7},0)$ and $(\sqrt{7},0)$, slope: -2

53. $m=-1$ at $(\sqrt{3}/4,\sqrt{3}/2)$, $m=\sqrt{3}$ at $\left(\sqrt{3}/4,\dfrac{1}{2}\right)$

55. a) False b) True c) True d) True

57. $v\big|_{t=6}=2/5$ m/sec, $a\big|_{t=6}=-4/125$ m/sec^2

61. a) $\pm\dfrac{x-2}{\sqrt{4-(x-2)^2}}$, $\dfrac{-(x-2)}{y}$; yes, when $y=\pm\sqrt{4-(x-2)^2}$ is substituted

Section 3.7, pp. 185–187

1. $4x-3$ **3.** $2x-2$ **5.** $\dfrac{1}{4}x+1$ **7.** $2x$ **9.** -5

11. $(1/12)x+4/3$

13. $L(x)=x$

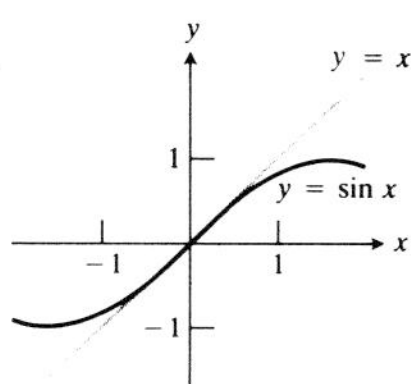

15. $L(x)=-x+\pi$

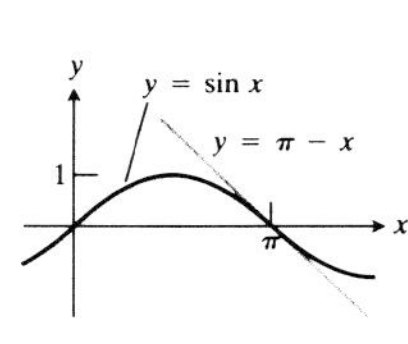

17. $L(x)=2x+1-\pi/2$

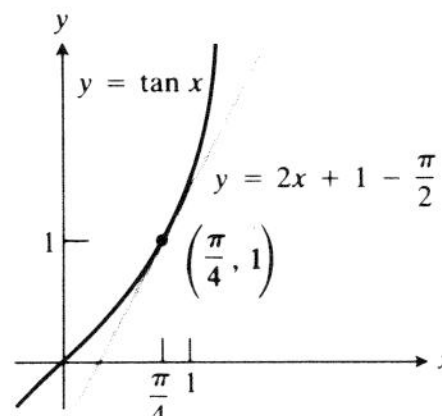

19. a) $1+2x$ b) $1-5x$ c) $2+2x$ d) $1-6x$
e) $3+x$ f) $1-x/2$

21. $(3/2)x+1$; it is equal to their sum.

25. a) .21 b) .2 c) .01

27. a) .231 b) .2 c) .031 **29.** a) $-1/3$ b) $-2/5$ c) $1/15$

31. $dV=4\pi r_0^2\,dr$ **33.** $dV=3x_0^2\,dx$ **35.** $dV=2\pi r_0 h\,dr$

37. a) $.08\pi$ m^2 b) 2% **39.** 3% **41.** 3% **43.** 1/3%

45. .05% **53.** $\left(3x^2-\dfrac{3}{2\sqrt{x}}\right)dx$ **55.** $\dfrac{2-2x^2}{(1+x^2)^2}\,dx$

57. $\dfrac{1-y}{3\sqrt{y}+x}\,dx$ **59.** $\dfrac{5}{2\sqrt{x}}\cos(5\sqrt{x})\,dx$

61. $(4x^2)\sec^2(x^3/3)\,dx$

63. $(3/\sqrt{x})\left(\csc(1-2\sqrt{x})\cot(1-2\sqrt{x})\right)dx$

Section 3.8, pp. 191–193

1. $x_2 = .61905, -1.66667$ **3.** $x_2 = 1.16542, -1.64516$
5. $x_2 = 1.1935$ **9.** $x \approx 0.45$
11.

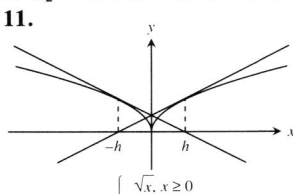

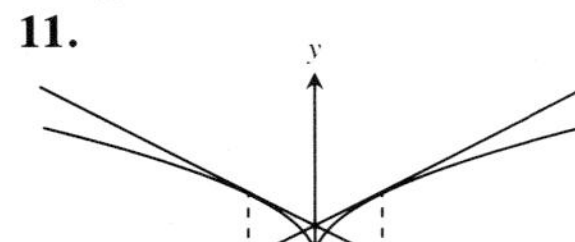

13. The root is 1.17951.
15. $x_1 = 1.49870$
17. 1.1655 61185
19. a) Two b) 0.3500 35015 05249 and -1.0261 73161 5301
21. ± 1.3065 62964 8764, ± 0.5411 96100 14619
23. Answers will vary with the machine used.

Chapter 3 Practice Exercises, pp. 195–199

1. $5x^4 - .25x + .25$ **3.** $3x(x-2)$
5. $2(x+1)(2x^2+4x+1)$ **7.** $3(x^2+x+1)^2(2x+1)$
9. $2\sin(1-2x)$ **11.** $2\sec^2 x \tan x$ **13.** $\dfrac{-2\sin x}{(\cos x - 1)^2}$
15. $-\dfrac{1}{2x^2\left(1+\dfrac{1}{x}\right)^{1/2}}$ **17.** $-\dfrac{y+2}{x+3}$ **19.** $\dfrac{-3x^2-4y+2}{4x-4y^{1/3}}$
21. $-y/x$ **23.** $\dfrac{1}{2y(x+1)^2}$ **25.** $\dfrac{(5x^2+2x)^{1/2}(5x+1)}{2y}$
27. $3\sqrt{2x+1}$ **29.** $5\csc^5(1-x)\cot(1-x)$
31. $x\csc\left(\dfrac{2}{x}\right) + \csc\left(\dfrac{2}{x}\right)\cot\left(\dfrac{2}{x}\right)$
33. $\dfrac{\sec(2x)}{2\sqrt{x^3}}(4x\tan(2x)-1)$ **35.** $-10x\csc^2 x^2$
37. $8x^3\sin(2x^2)\cos(2x^2) + 2x\sin^2(2x^2)$ **39.** $\dfrac{1}{2\sqrt{t}\,(1+\sqrt{t})^2}$
41. $\dfrac{-(t+1)}{8t^3}$ **43.** $\dfrac{\theta\cos\theta + \sin\theta}{\sqrt{2\theta}\sin\theta}$ **45.** $\dfrac{\cos\sqrt{2\theta}}{\sqrt{2\theta}}$
47. a)

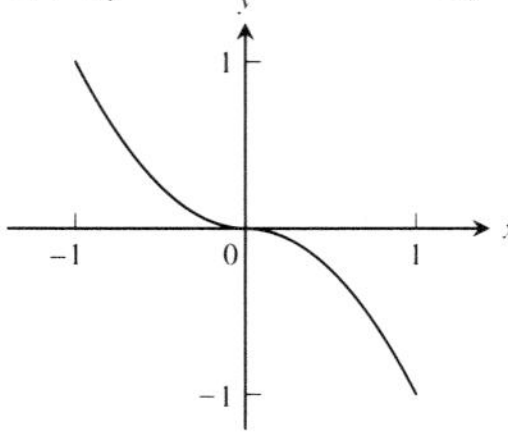

b) Yes c) Yes

49. a)

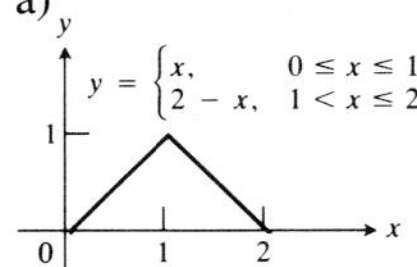

b) Yes c) No

51. a) $(2, 0), (-1, 27)$ b) $(0, 20), (1, 7)$
55. a) $\dfrac{10}{\sqrt{2}}$ b) Left: -10, right: 10 c) Left: $v = 0, a = 10$, right: $v = 0, a = -10$ d) When $t = \pi/4$, $v = -10$, $|v| = 10$, $a = 0$.
57. a) 4/7 sec, 280 cm/sec b) 560 cm/sec, 980 cm/sec^2 c) 29.75 flashes/sec
59. a) iii b) i c) ii
61.

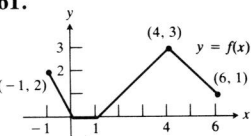

63. Yes, the curve has an infinite number of horizontal tangents.
65. a) 1 b) 6 c) 1 d) $-1/9$ e) $-40/3$ f) 2 g) $-4/9$
67. $\sin(-\theta) = -\sin\theta$; $-\cos(-\theta) = -\cos\theta$; $\cos(-\theta) = \cos\theta$
69. $\sin 2\theta = 2\sin\theta\cos\theta$; $2\cos 2\theta = 2\sin\theta(-\sin\theta) + \cos\theta(2\cos\theta)$; $2\cos 2\theta = -2\sin^2\theta + 2\cos^2\theta$; $\cos 2\theta = \cos^2\theta - \sin^2\theta$
71. 0 **73.** $\sqrt{3}$ **75.** $(0, 1), (-4, 0)$ **77.** $(-13/4, 17/16)$
79.

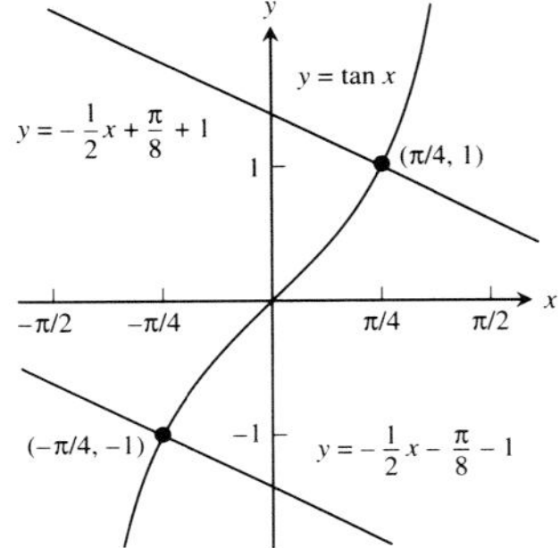

81. $y = -(1/4)x + (17/4)$, $y = 4x$ **83.** 3 ft
85. a) $\dfrac{d^2y}{dx^2} = \dfrac{-2xy^3 - 2x^4}{y^5}$ b) $\dfrac{d^2y}{dx^2} = \dfrac{-2xy^2 - 1}{x^4y^3}$
87. a) $\dfrac{d^2y}{dx^2} = \dfrac{-1}{\sqrt{(2x+7)^3}}$ b) $\dfrac{d^2y}{dx^2} = \dfrac{-1}{y^3}$
89. a) $L(x) = 2x + (\pi - 2)/2$

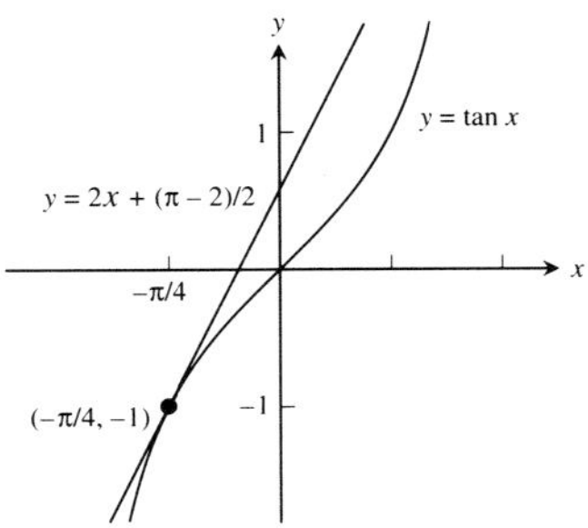

b) $L(x) = -\sqrt{2}x + \sqrt{2}(4 - \pi)/4$

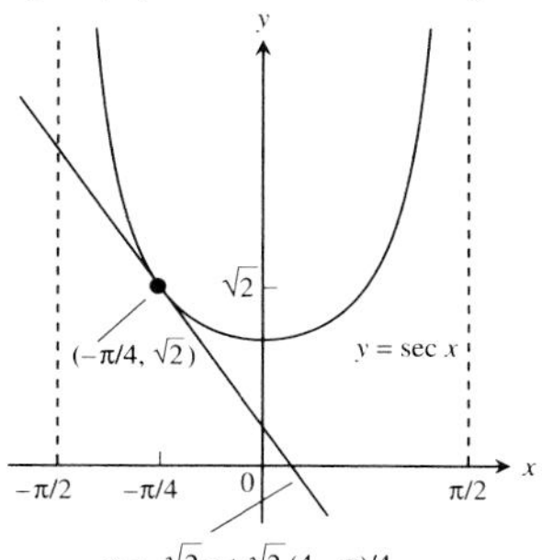

91. $dV = \frac{2}{3}\pi r_0 h\, dr$ **93.** a) Error $<$ 1% b) 3%

95. $dh \approx \pm 2.3271$ ft **97.** 2.19582 **99.** 0.82836

Chapter 4

Section 4.1, pp. 206–209

1. $\frac{dA}{dt} = 2\pi r \frac{dr}{dt}$ **3.** a) $\frac{dV}{dt} = \pi r^2 \frac{dh}{dt}$ b) $\frac{dV}{dt} = 2\pi hr \frac{dr}{dt}$

c) $\frac{dV}{dt} = \pi r^2 \frac{dh}{dt} + 2\pi hr \frac{dr}{dt}$ **5.** a) $\frac{dA}{dt} = \frac{1}{2} ab \cos\theta \frac{d\theta}{dt}$

b) $\frac{dA}{dt} = \frac{1}{2} ab \cos\theta \frac{d\theta}{dt} + \frac{1}{2} b \sin\theta \frac{da}{dt}$

c) $\frac{dA}{dt} = \frac{1}{2} ab \cos\theta \frac{d\theta}{dt} + \frac{1}{2} b \sin\theta \frac{da}{dt} + \frac{1}{2} a \sin\theta \frac{db}{dt}$

7. a) $\frac{dS}{dt} = \frac{x}{\sqrt{x^2 + y^2}} \frac{dx}{dt}$

b) $\frac{dS}{dt} = \frac{x}{\sqrt{x^2 + y^2}} \frac{dx}{dt} + \frac{y}{\sqrt{x^2 + y^2}} \frac{dy}{dt}$ c) $\frac{dx}{dt} = -\frac{y}{x} \frac{dy}{dt}$

9. π cm²/min **11.** a) 14 cm²/sec, increasing
b) 0 cm/sec, constant c) −14/13 cm/sec, decreasing

13. −680 mph **15.** ≈0.064 mm/min

17. a) $\frac{dh}{dt} = 11.19$ cm/min b) $\frac{dr}{dt} = 14.92$ cm/min

19. a) $\frac{-1}{24\pi}$ m/min b) $r = \sqrt{26y - y^2}$ m

c) $\frac{dr}{dt} = -\frac{5}{288\pi}$ m/min

21. 1 ft/min, 40π ft²/min **23.** 11 ft/sec **25.** 80%/min

27. 1 rad/sec **29.** a) 0.3, 0.9, 0.6 b) −1.5625, 3.5, 5.0625

31. −1500 ft/sec **33.** $\frac{5}{72\pi}$ in./min, $\frac{10}{3}$ in²/min **35.** 7.1 in./min

37. 29.5 knots

Section 4.2, pp. 216–218

1. Absolute minimum at $x = C_2$, absolute maximum at $x = b$

3. Absolute maximum at $x = c$, no absolute minimum

5. Absolute minima at $x = a$ and $x = b$, absolute maximum at $x = c$

7. Absolute maximum: −3, absolute minimum: −19/3

9. Absolute maximum: 3, absolute minimum: −1

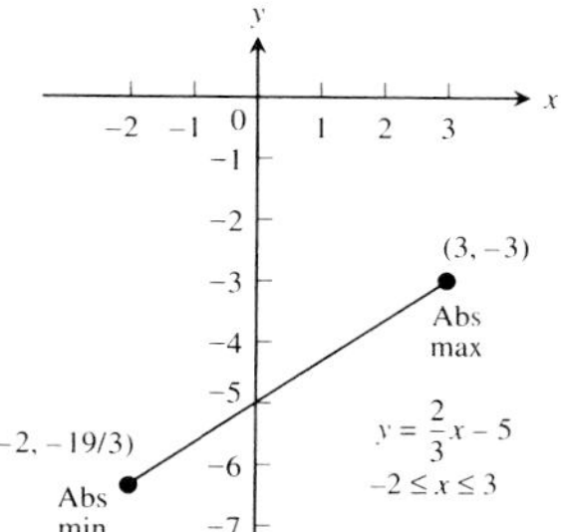

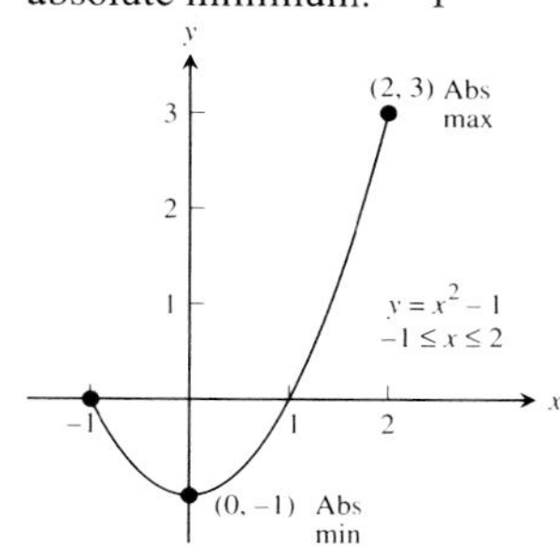

11. Absolute maximum: −0.25, absolute minimum: −4

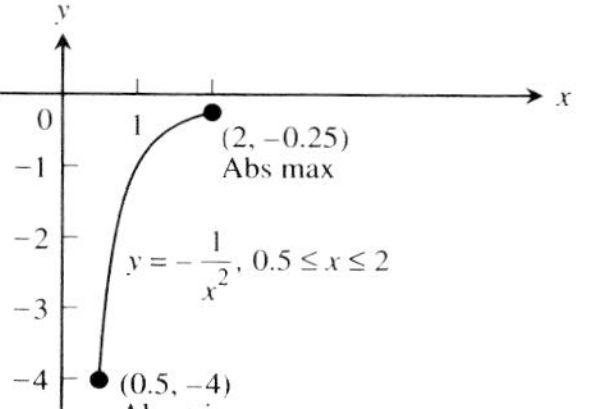

13. Absolute maximum: 2, absolute minimum: −1

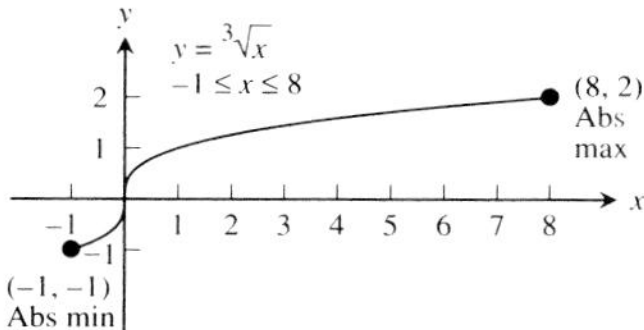

15. Absolute maximum: 2, absolute minimum: 0

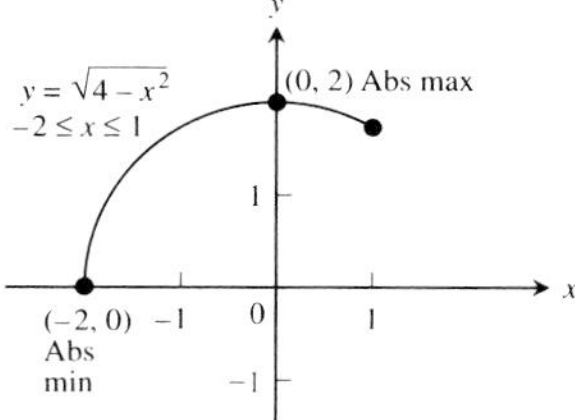

17. Absolute maximum: 1, absolute minimum: −1

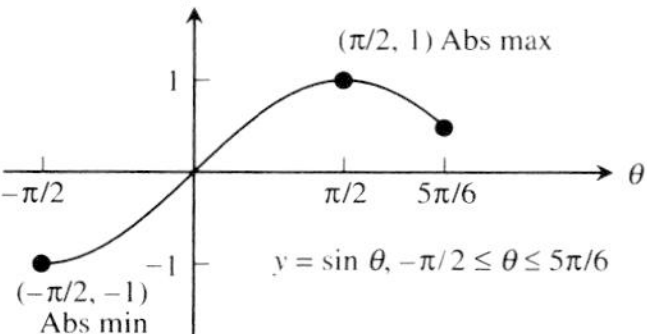

19. Absolute maximum: $2/\sqrt{3}$, absolute minimum: 1

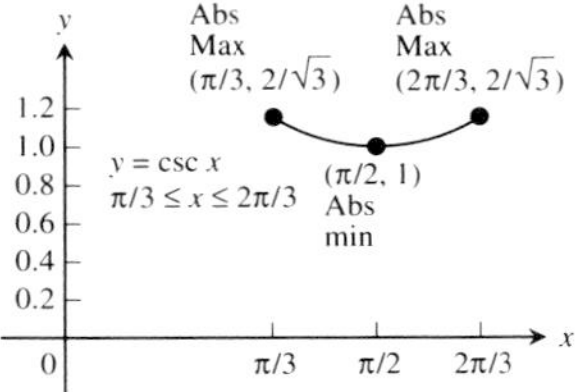

21. Absolute maximum: 2, absolute minimum: -1

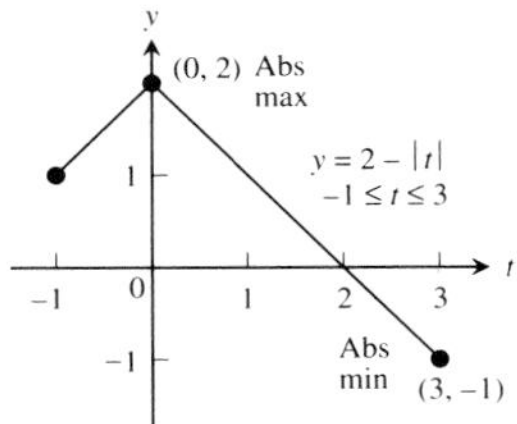

23. Increasing on (0, 8), decreasing on $(-1, 0)$, absolute maximum: 16 at $x = 8$, absolute minimum: 0 at $x = 0$
25. Increasing on $(-32, 1)$, absolute maximum: 1 at $\theta = 1$, absolute minimum: -8 at $\theta = -32$
27. a) 0, 1 b) Increasing on $(-\infty, 0)$ and $(1, \infty)$, decreasing on (0, 1) c) Local maximum at $x = 0$, local minimum at $x = 1$
29. a) -2, 1
b) Increasing on $(-2, 1)$ and $(1, \infty)$, decreasing on $(-\infty, -2)$
c) No local maximum, local minimum at $x = -2$
31. a) $-2, 1, 3$
b) Increasing on $(-2, 1)$ and $(3, \infty)$, decreasing on $(-\infty, -2)$ and (1, 3)
c) Local maximum at $x = 1$, local minima at $x = -2, 3$
33. a) $-2, 0$
b) Increasing on $(-\infty, -2)$ and $(0, \infty)$, decreasing on $(-2, 0)$
c) Local maximum at $x = -2$, local minimum at $x = 0$
35. Increasing on $(-\infty, -1.5)$, decreasing on $(-1.5, \infty)$, local maximum: 5.25 at $t = -1.5$
37. Decreasing on $(-\infty, 0)$, increasing on (0, 4/3), decreasing on $(4/3, \infty)$, local minimum at $x = 0$ (0, 0), local maximum at $x = 4/3$ (4/3, 32/27)
39. Decreasing on $(-\infty, 0)$, increasing on (0, 1/2), decreasing on $(1/2, \infty)$, local minimum at $\theta = 0$ (0, 0), local maximum at $\theta = 1/2$ (1/2, 1/4)
41. Increasing on $(-\infty, \infty)$, never decreasing, no local extrema
43. Increasing on $(-2, 0)$ and $(2, \infty)$, decreasing on $(-\infty, -2)$ and (0, 2), local maximum: 16 at $x = 0$, local minimum: 0 at $x = \pm 2$
45. Increasing on $(-\infty, -1)$, decreasing on $(-1, 0)$, increasing on (0, 1), decreasing on $(1, \infty)$, local maximum at $x = \pm 1$ (1, 0.5) $(-1, 0.5)$, local minimum at $x = 0$ (0, 0)
47. Decreasing on $(-2\sqrt{2}, -2)$, increasing on $(-2, 2)$, decreasing on $(2, 2\sqrt{2})$, local minimum at $x = -2$ $(-2, -4)$, local maximum at $x = 2$ (2, 4)
49. Increasing on $(-\infty, 1)$, decreasing when $1 < x < 2$, decreasing when $2 < x < 3$, discontinuous at $x = 2$, increasing on $(3, \infty)$, local minimum at $x = 3$ (3, 6), local maximum at $x = 1$ (1, 2)
51. a) Increasing on $(-2, 0)$ and $(0, \infty)$, decreasing on $(-\infty, -2)$
b) Local minimum: -7.56 at $x = -2$
53. a) Increasing on $(-\infty, -2/\sqrt{7})$ and $(2/\sqrt{7}, \infty)$, decreasing on $(-2/\sqrt{7}, 0)$ and $(0, 2/\sqrt{7})$ b) local maximum ≈ 3.12 at $x = -2/\sqrt{7}$, local minimum ≈ -3.12 at $x = 2/\sqrt{7}$
55. Local maximum: 1 at $x = 1$, local minimum: 0 at $x = 2$
57. Local maximum: 1 at $x = 1$, local minimum: 0 at $x = 2$
59. Local maxima: -9 at $t = -3$ and 16 at $t = -2$, local minimum: -16 at $t = 2$
61. Local minimum: 0 at $x = 0$
63. Local maxima: $4\sqrt{2}$ at $x = -\sqrt{2}$ and -4 at $x = 2$, local minima: 4 at $x = -2$ and $-4\sqrt{2}$ at $x = \sqrt{2}$
65. Local maximum: 1 at $x = 1$, local minima: -7 at $x = -1$ and -16 at $x = 2$
67. a) Local minimum: $(\pi/3) - \sqrt{3}$ at $x = \dfrac{2\pi}{3}$, local maximum: 0 at $x = 0$, local maximum: π at $x = 2\pi$
69. a) Local minimum: 0 at $x = \pi/4$
71. Local maximum: 3 at $\theta = 0$, local minimum: -3 at $\theta = 2\pi$
73. a) Local maximum: 0 at $x = \pm 2$, local minimum: -4 at $x = 0$, absolute maximum: 0, absolute minimum: -4
b) Local maximum: 0 at $x = -2$, local minimum: -4 at $x = 0$, absolute maximum: 0, absolute minimum: -4
c) No local maximum, local minimum: -4 at $x = 0$, absolute minimum: -4
d) Local maximum: 0 at $x = -2$, local minimum: -4 at $x = 0$, absolute minimum: -4
e) No local extrema, no absolute extrema
75.

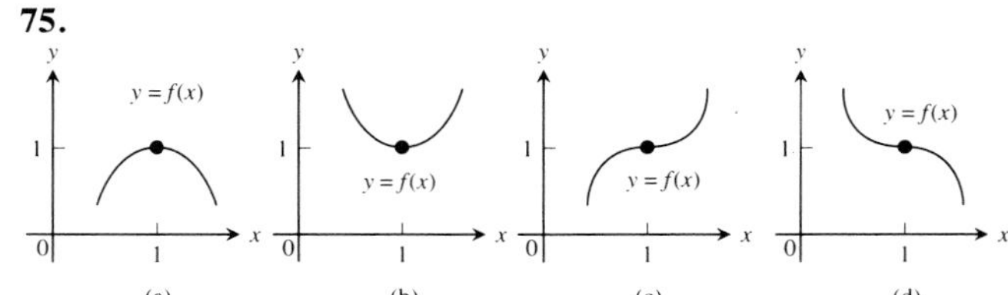

77. Rising **79.** Yes

Section 4.3, pp. 224–227

1. Local maximum: 3/2 at $x = -1$, local minimum: -3 at $x = 2$, point of inflection at $(1/2, -3/4)$, rising on $(-\infty, -1)$ and $(2, \infty)$, falling on $(-1, 2)$, concave up on $(1/2, \infty)$, concave down on $(-\infty, 1/2)$
3. Local maximum: 3/4 at $x = 0$, local minimum: 0 at $x = \pm 1$, points of inflection at $\left(-\sqrt{3}, \dfrac{3\sqrt[3]{4}}{4}\right)$ and $\left(\sqrt{3}, \dfrac{3\sqrt[3]{4}}{4}\right)$, rising on $(-1, 0)$ and $(1, \infty)$, falling on $(-\infty, -1)$ and (0, 1), concave up on $(-\infty, -\sqrt{3})$ and $(\sqrt{3}, \infty)$, concave down on $(-\sqrt{3}, \sqrt{3})$
5. Local maxima: $-2\pi/3 + \sqrt{3}/2$ at $x = -2\pi/3$, $\dfrac{\pi}{3} + \dfrac{\sqrt{3}}{2}$ at $x = \dfrac{\pi}{3}$, local minima: $-\dfrac{\pi}{3} - \dfrac{\sqrt{3}}{2}$ at $x = -\dfrac{\pi}{3}$, $2\pi/3 - \sqrt{3}/2$ at

$x = \dfrac{2\pi}{3}$, points of inflection at $(-\pi/2, -\pi/2)$, $(0, 0)$, and $(\pi/2, \pi/2)$, rising on $(-\pi/3, \pi/3)$, falling on $(-2\pi/3, -\pi/3)$ and $(\pi/3, 2\pi/3)$, concave up on $(-\pi/2, 0)$ and $(\pi/2, 2\pi/3)$, concave down on $(-2\pi/3, -\pi/2)$ and $(0, \pi/2)$

7. Local maxima: 1 at $x = -\dfrac{\pi}{2}$ and $x = \dfrac{\pi}{2}$, 0 at $x = -2\pi$ and $x = 2\pi$, local minima: -1 at $x = -\dfrac{3\pi}{2}$ and $x = \dfrac{3\pi}{2}$, 0 at $x = 0$, points of inflection at $(-\pi, 0)$ and $(\pi, 0)$, rising on $(-3\pi/2, -\pi/2)$, $(0, \pi/2)$, and $(3\pi/2, 2\pi)$, falling on $(-2\pi, -3\pi/2)$, $(-\pi/2, 0)$, and $(\pi/2, 3\pi/2)$, concave up on $(-2\pi, -\pi)$ and $(\pi, 2\pi)$, concave down on $(-\pi, \pi)$

9.

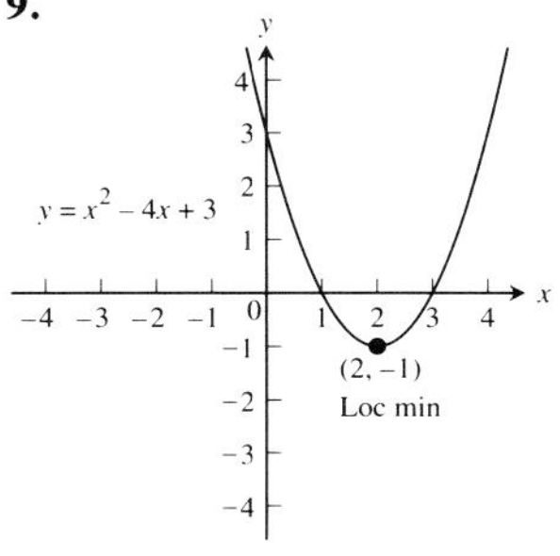

11.

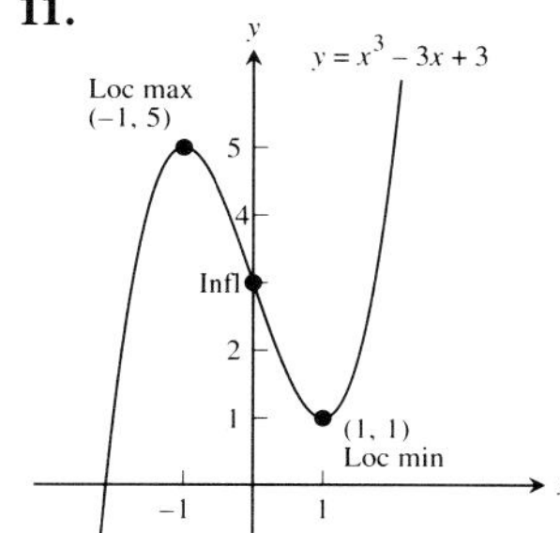

13.

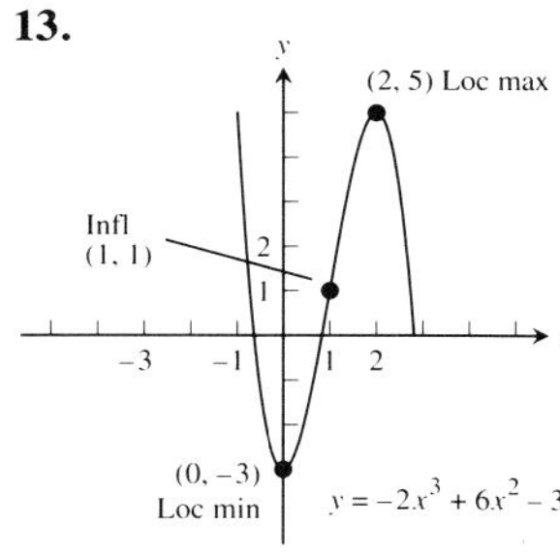

15.

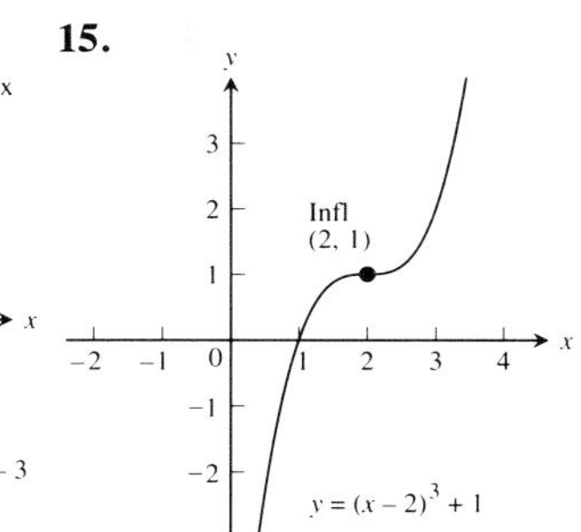

17.

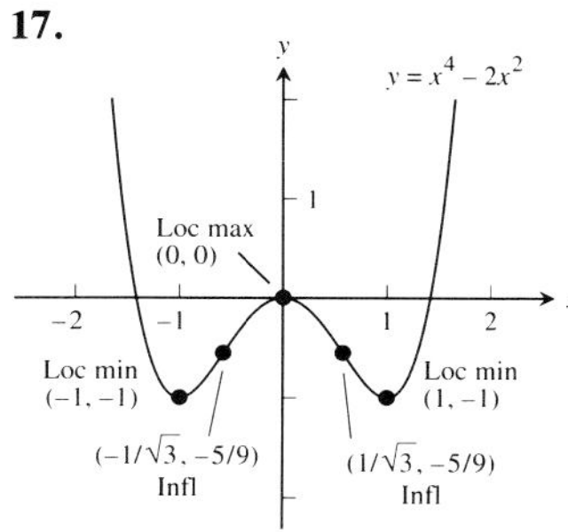

19. **21.**

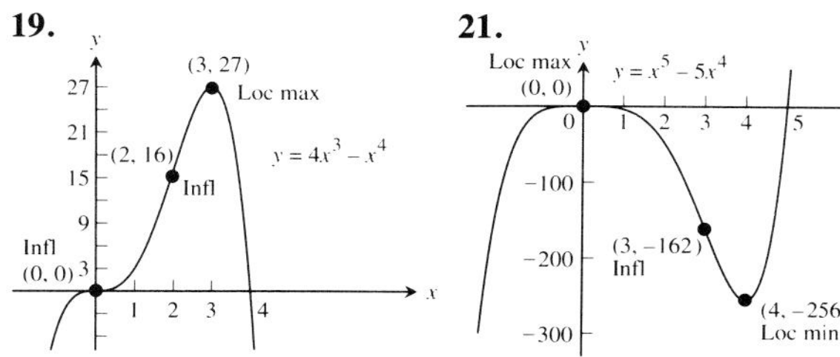

23. **25.**

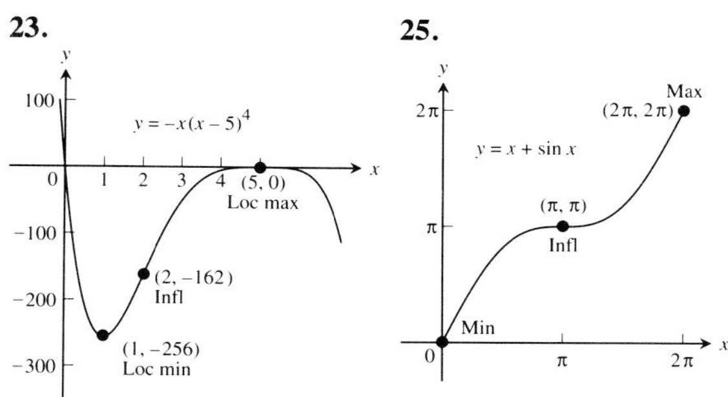

27. **29.**

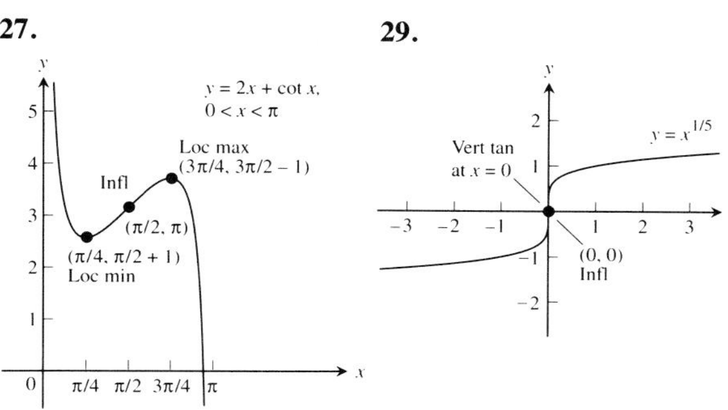

31. **33.**

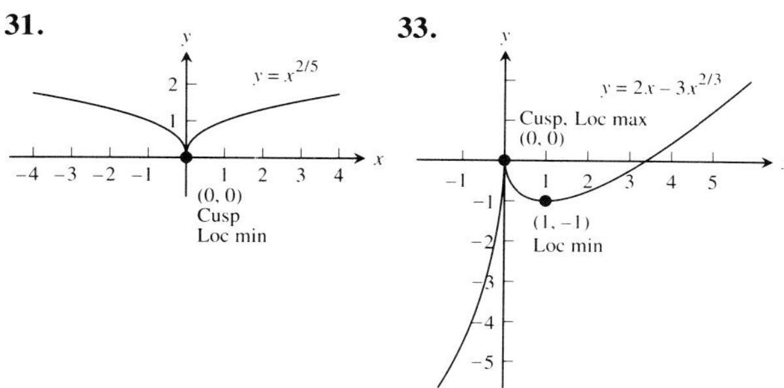

35. **37.**

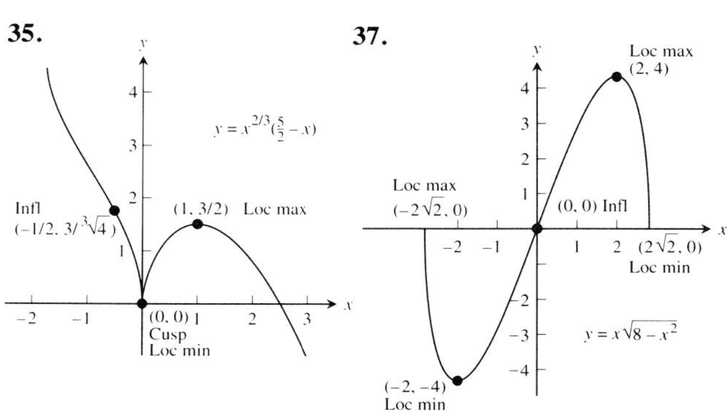

39.

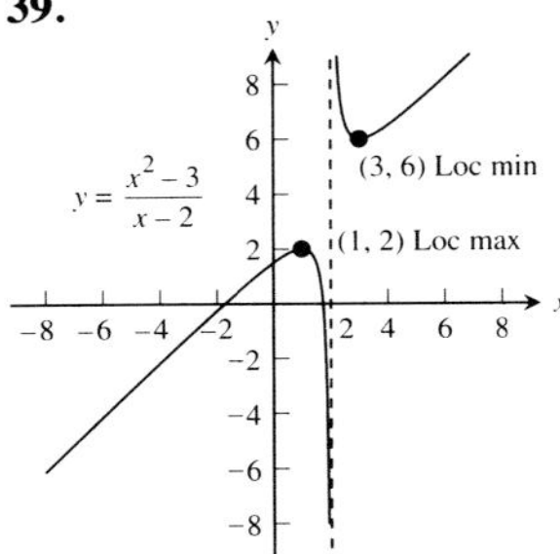

41.

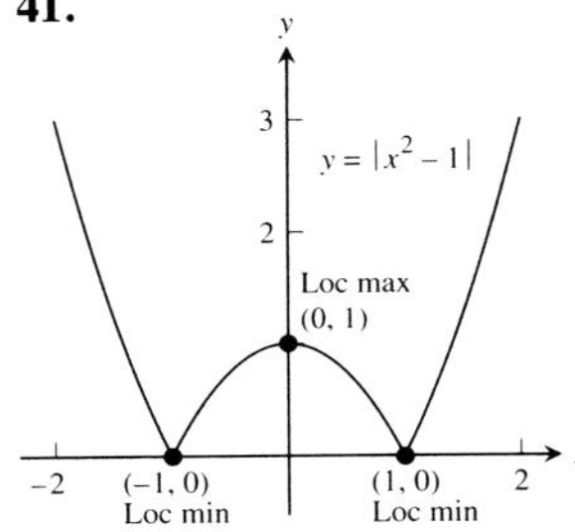

55. $y'' = -\frac{1}{2}\csc^2\frac{\theta}{2}, 0 < x < 2\pi$

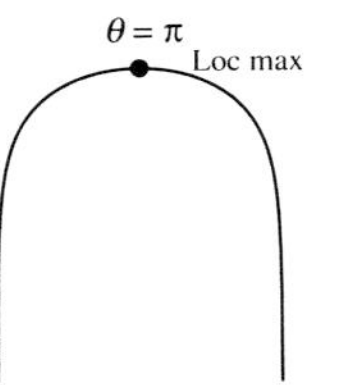

43.

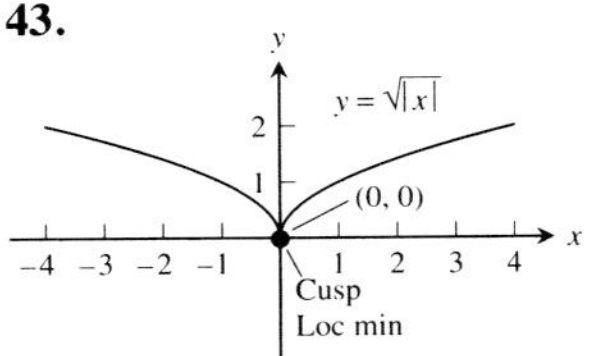

45. $y'' = 1 - 2x$

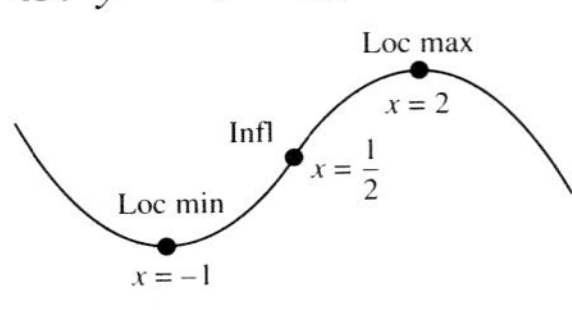

57. $y'' = 2\tan\theta\sec^2\theta, -\frac{\pi}{2} < \theta < \frac{\pi}{2}$

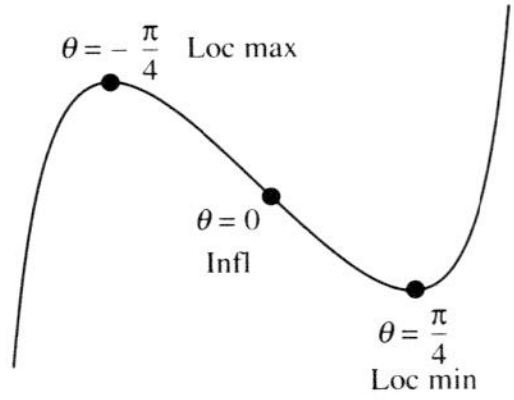

59. $y'' = -\sin t, 0 \le t \le 2\pi$

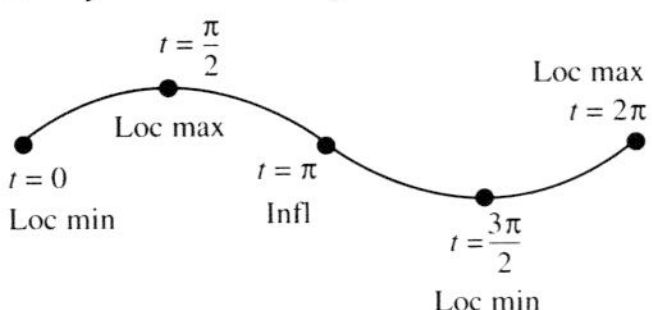

47. $y'' = 3(x - 3)(x - 1)$

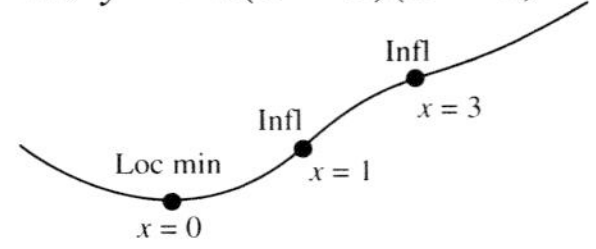

61. $y'' = -\frac{2}{3}(x + 1)^{-5/3}$

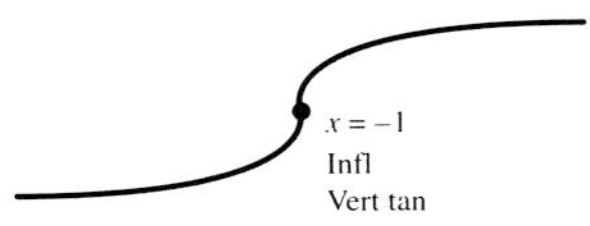

49. $y'' = 3(x - 2)(x + 2)$

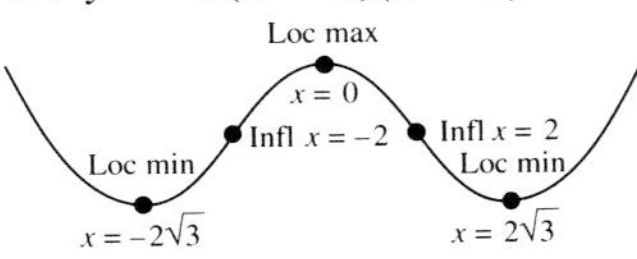

63. $y'' = \frac{1}{3}x^{-2/3} + \frac{2}{3}x^{-5/3}$

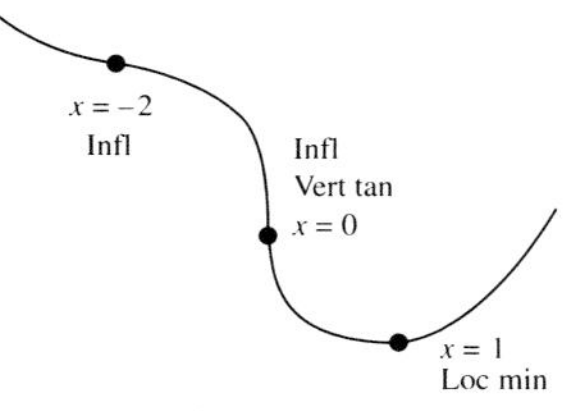

51. $y'' = 4(4 - x)(5x^2 - 16x + 8)$

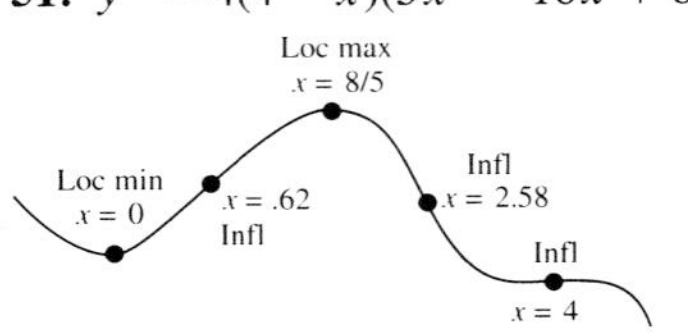

53. $y'' = 2\sec^2 x\tan x$

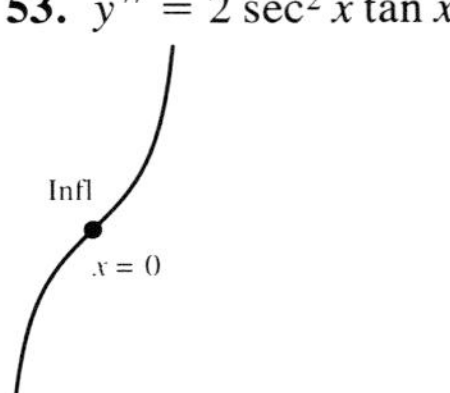

65. $y'' = \begin{cases} -2, & x \le 0 \\ 2, & x > 0 \end{cases}$

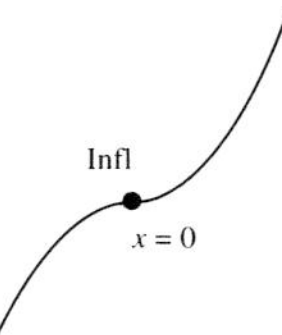

67. a) $0 < t < 2$ and $6 < t < 9.5$, $2 < t < 6$ and $9.5 < t < 15$
b) 2 sec, 6 sec, 9.5 sec, c) 4 sec, 7.5 sec, 12.5 sec
d) $4 < t < 7.5$ and $12.5 < t < 15$, $0 < t < 4$ and $7.5 < t < 12.5$ **69.** $\approx 60{,}000$ units

71.

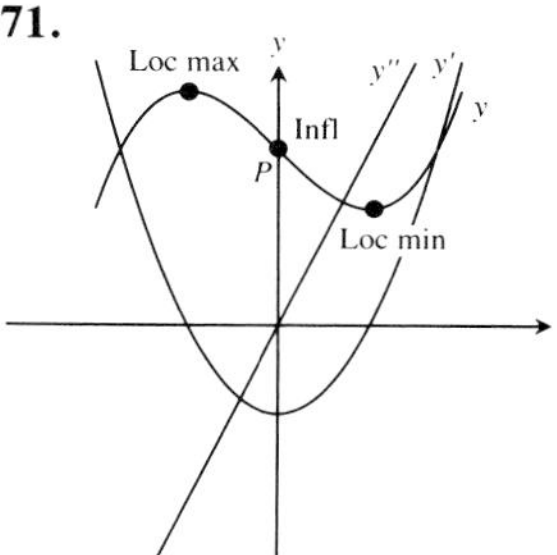

73.

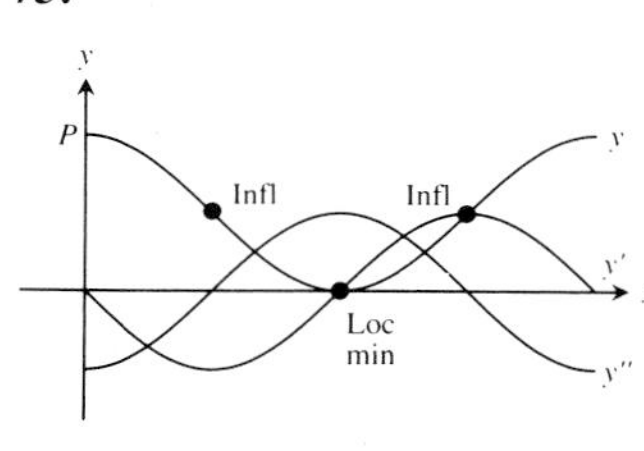

75. $b = -3$
83. b) $f'(x) = 3x^2 + k$, $-12k$, positive if $k < 0$, negative if $k > 0$, 0 if $k = 0$, f' has two zeros if $k < 0$, one zero if $k = 0$, no zeros if $k > 0$
85. b) A cusp since $\lim_{x\to 0^-} y' = \infty$ and $\lim_{x\to 0^+} y' = -\infty$

Section 4.4, pp. 233–234

1.

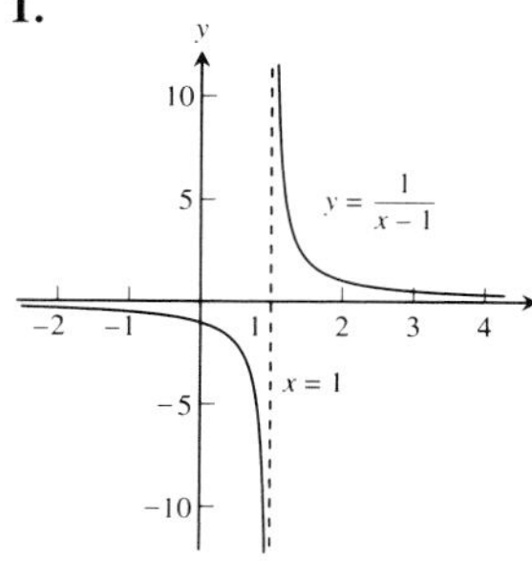

3.

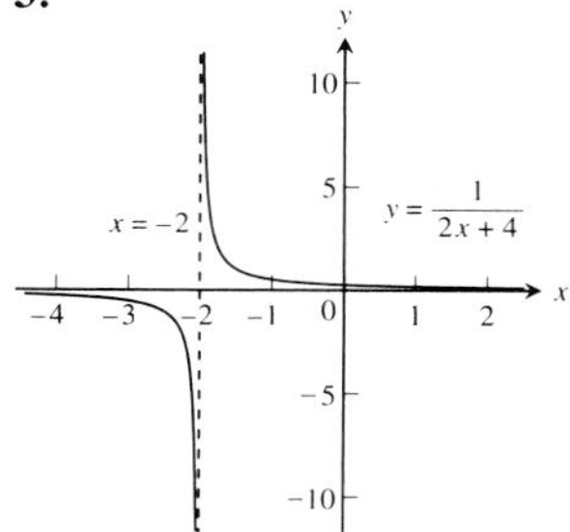

5.

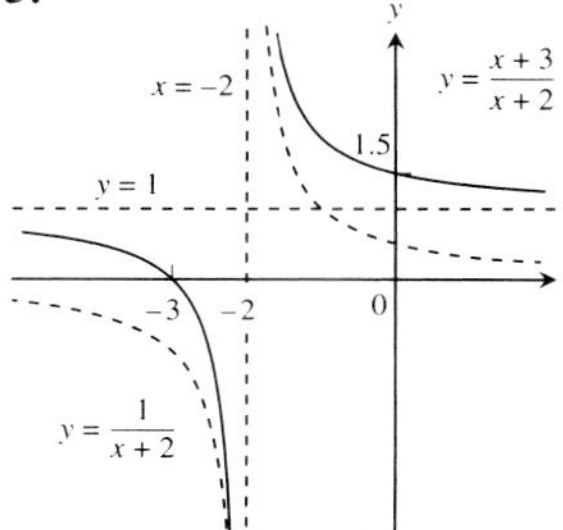

7.

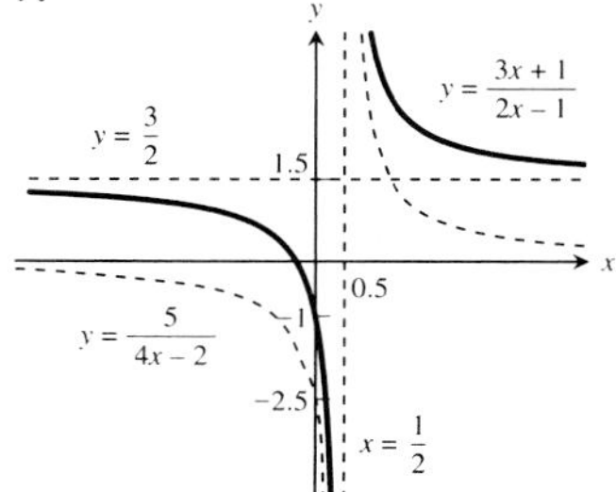

9.

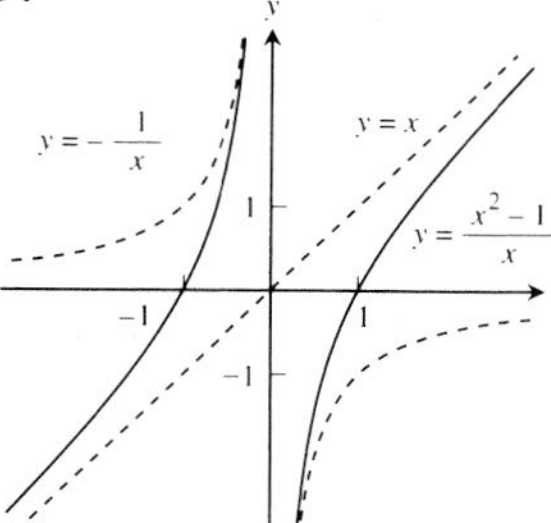

11.

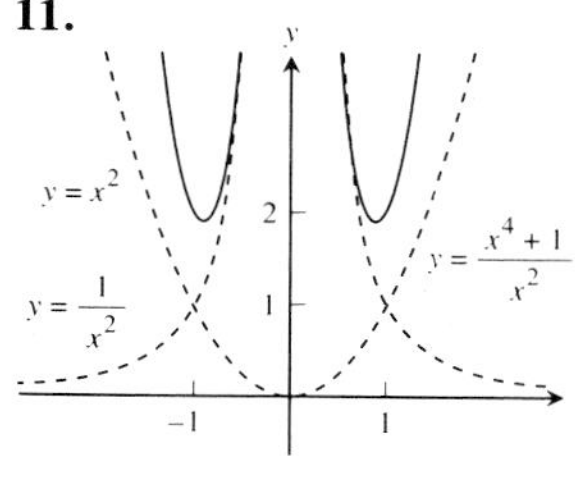

13.

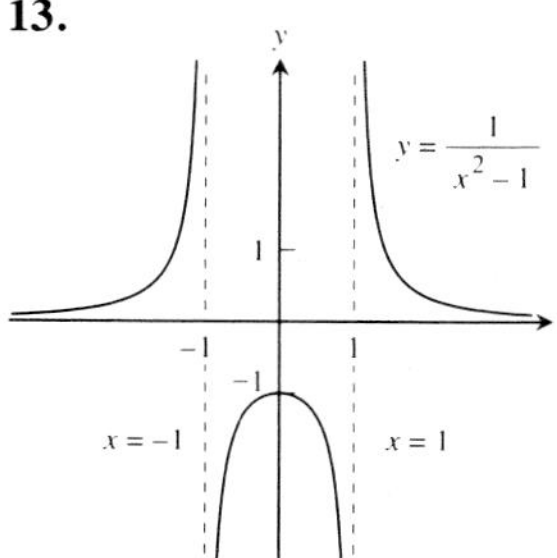

15.

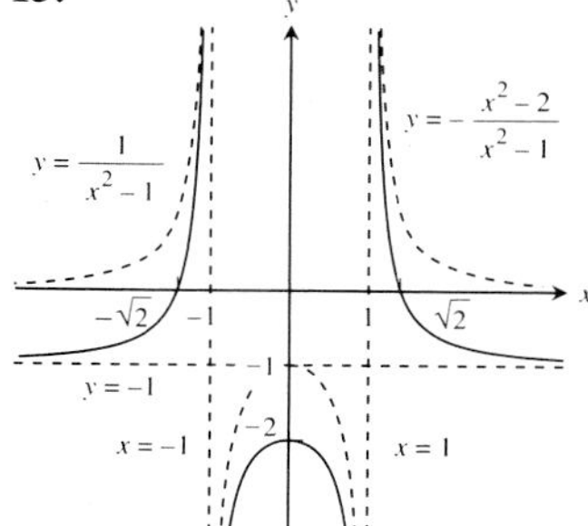

17.

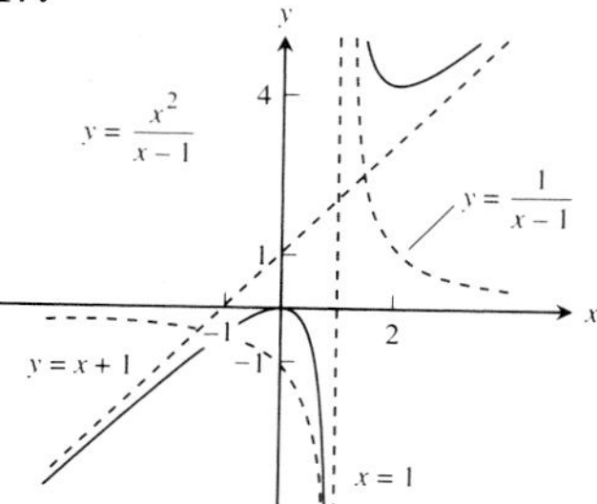

19.

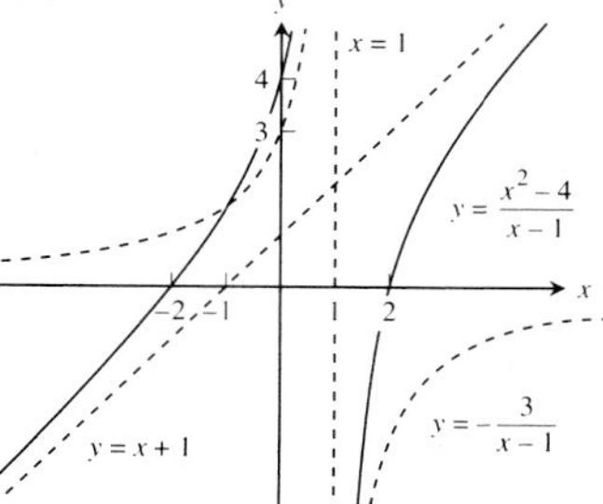

21.

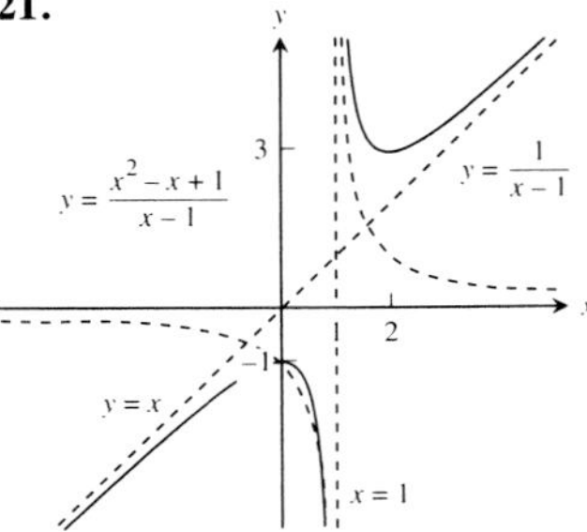

23.

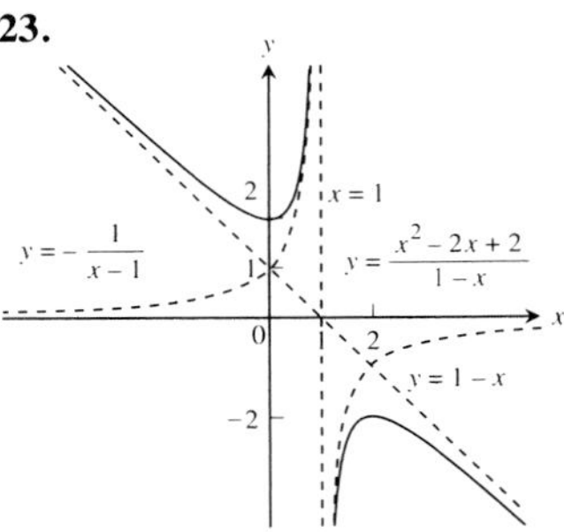

25.

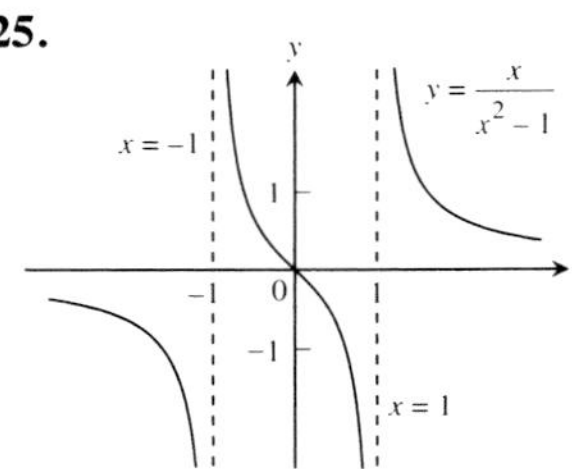

27.

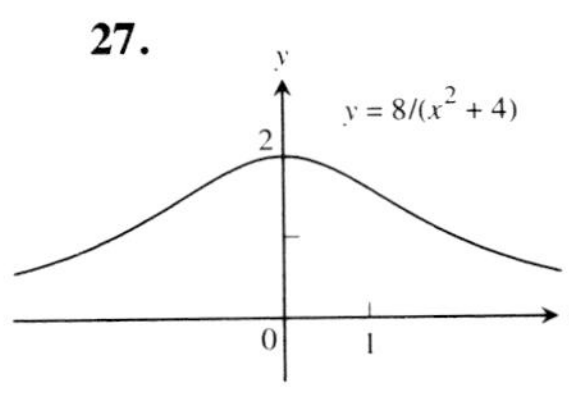

29.

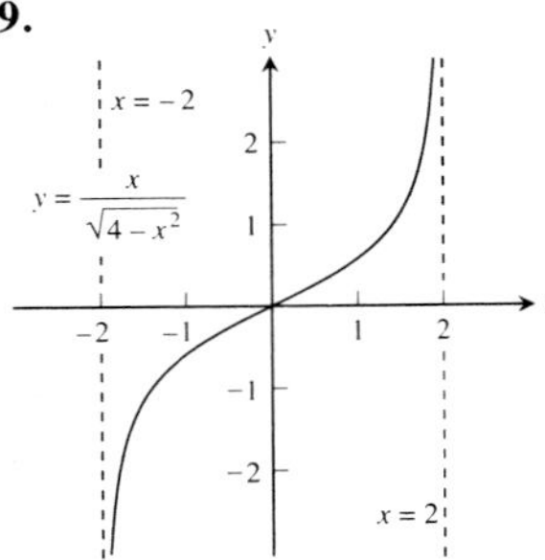

31.

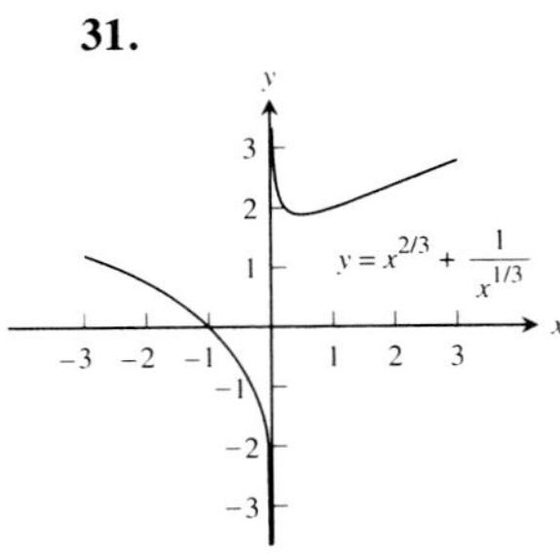

33.

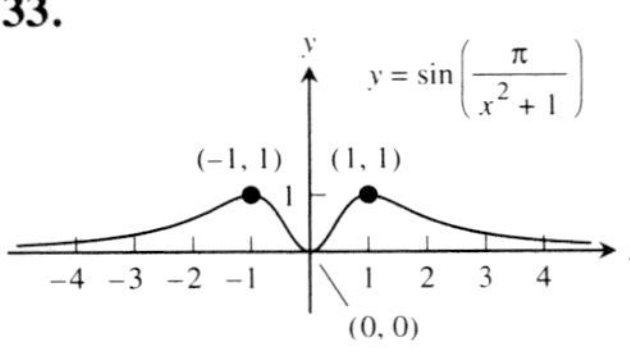

35.

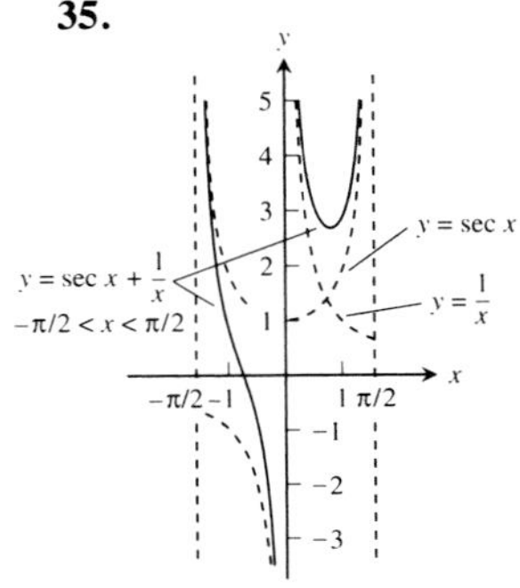

37.

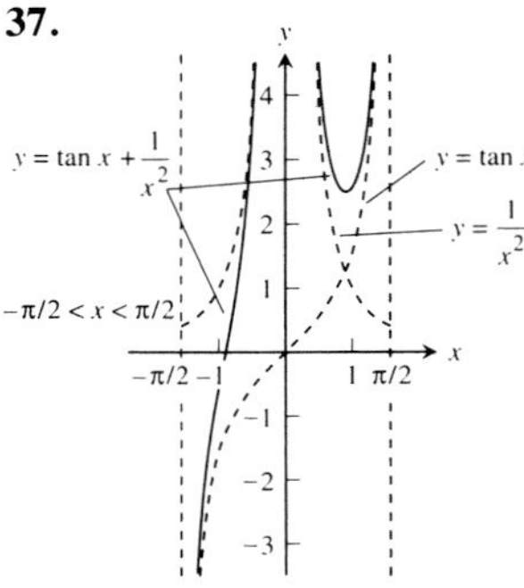

43. $x = -1, y = 1 - x$ **45.** $x = 1, x = -1, y = x - 1$
53. a) $y \to \infty$ b) $y \to \infty$ c) Cusp at $x = \pm 1$
55. b) $x = 1, x = -2$, $x - 1$ is a factor of $x^3 - 3x^2 + 3x - 1$
c) $y = x - 4$
57. The distance in part (c) is so great that small movements are not visible.

Section 4.5, pp. 242–246

1. a) 0 and 20, 10 and 10 b) 1/4 and $19\frac{3}{4}$, 0 and 20 **3.** 16 in.
5. a) $(x, 1 - x)$ b) $A(x) = 2x(1 - x)$ c) 1/2 square units
7. $(14/3) \times (35/3) \times (5/3)$ in. **9.** 80,000 m^2
11. Base: 10 ft, height: 5 ft **13.** 9×18 in. **15.** $\pi/2$
17. $r = h = 10/\sqrt[3]{\pi}$ cm **19.** a) $18 \times 18 \times 36$ in.
21. a) 12 cm, 6 cm b) 12 cm, 6 cm **23.** a) 16 b) -1
25. a) $a = -3, b = -9$ b) $a = -3, b = -24$
27. a) $4\sqrt{3} \times 4\sqrt{6}$ in. **29.** $2\sqrt{2}$ **31.** a) $y = -1$ **33.** $\sqrt{5}/2$
37. a) When t is an integer multiple of π
b) $t = \frac{2\pi}{3}, t = \frac{4\pi}{3}, 3\frac{\sqrt{3}}{2}$ **39.** $\pi/6$ **43.** $x = a/2, (ka^2)/4$
47. $(c/2) + 50$ **49.** $\sqrt{\frac{2km}{h}}$

Section 4.6, pp. 252–253

1. 1/2 **3.** 1 **5.** Does not; f is not differentiable at the interior domain point $x = 0$.
7. Does
23. a)

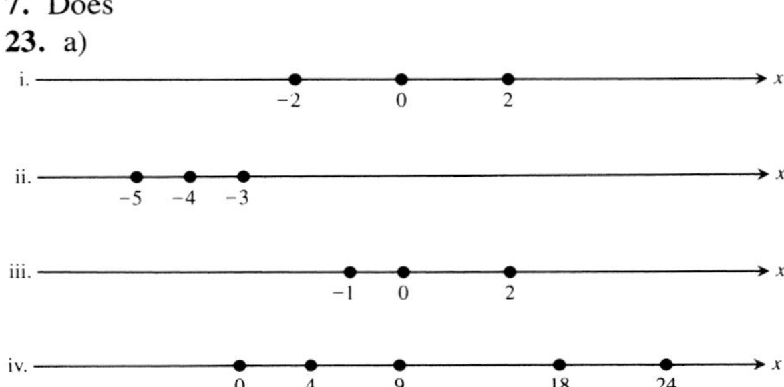

29. 1.1 **33.** Yes

Section 4.7, pp. 262–265

1. a) $x^2 + C$ b) $(x^3/3) + C$ c) $(x^3/3) - x^2 + x + C$

3. a) $x^{-3} + C$ b) $-\frac{1}{3}x^{-3} + C$ c) $-\frac{1}{3}x^{-3} + x^2 + 3x + C$

5. a) $-\frac{1}{x} + C$ b) $-\frac{5}{x} + C$ c) $2x + \frac{5}{x} + C$

7. a) $\sqrt{x^3} + C$ b) $\sqrt{x} + C$ c) $\frac{2\sqrt{x^3}}{3} + 2\sqrt{x} + C$

9. a) $\frac{3}{4}x^{2/3} + C$ b) $x^{-1/2} + C$ c) $x^{-3/2} + C$

11. a) $\cos(\pi x) + C$ b) $-3\cos x + C$
c) $-\frac{1}{\pi}\cos(\pi x) + \cos(3x) + C$

13. a) $\tan x + C$ b) $2\tan\left(\frac{x}{3}\right) + C$ c) $-\frac{2}{3}\tan\frac{3x}{2} + C$

15. a) $-\csc x + C$ b) $\frac{1}{5}\csc(5x) + C$ c) $2\csc\left(\frac{\pi x}{2}\right) + C$

17. $x + \frac{\cos(2x)}{2} + C$

19. a) $-\sqrt{x} + C$ b) $x + C$ c) $\sqrt{x} + C$ d) $-x + C$
e) $-\sqrt{x} + x + C$ f) $-3\sqrt{x} - 2x + C$ g) $(x^2/2) - \sqrt{x} + C$
h) $-3x + C$ **21.** b **23.** $y = x^2 - 7x + 10$

25. $y = -(1/x) + (x^2/2) - (1/2)$ **27.** $y = 2x^{3/2} - 50$

29. $s = t + \sin t + 4$ **31.** $r = \cos(\pi\theta) - 1$

33. $v = \frac{1}{2}\sec t + \frac{1}{2}$ **35.** $y = x^2 - x^3 + 4x + 1$

37. $r = (1/t) + 2t - 2$ **39.** $y = x^3 - 4x^2 + 5$

41. $y = -\sin t + \cos t + t^3 - 1$ **43.** $s = 4.9t^2 + 5t + 10$

45. $s = \frac{1 - \cos(\pi t)}{\pi}$ **47.** $s = 16t^2 + 20t + 5$

49. $s = \sin(2t) - 3$ **51.** $y = 2x^{3/2} - 50$

53. $r(x) = x^3 - 3x^2 + 12x$ **55.** 48 m/sec **57.** 14 m/sec

59. a) $2y^{1/2} + C_1 = -kt + C_2$ b) $y = \frac{(C - kt)^2}{4}$

c) $y = \frac{1}{4}\left(6 - \frac{t}{10}\right)^2$, 1 h **61.** 1.24 sec

63. a) 1: 33.2 units, 2: 33.2 units, 3: 33.2 units

65.

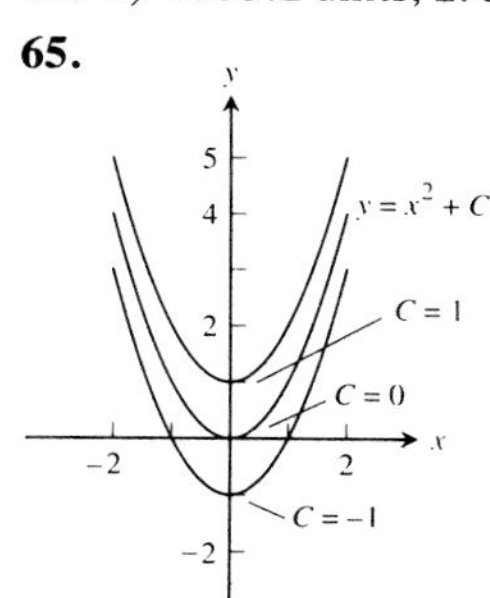

67.

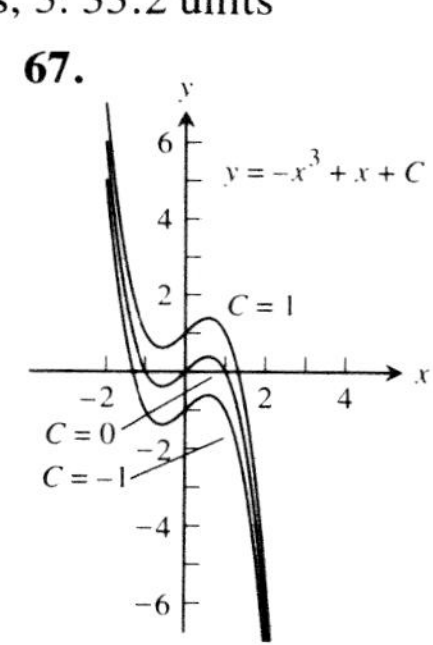

69.

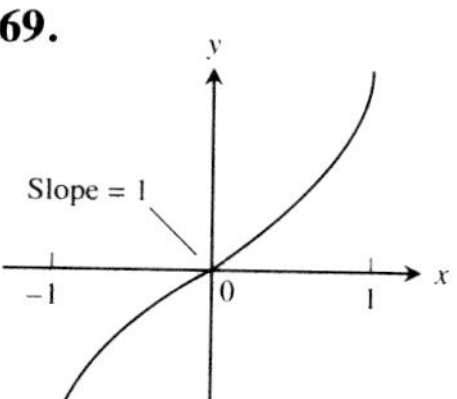

71.

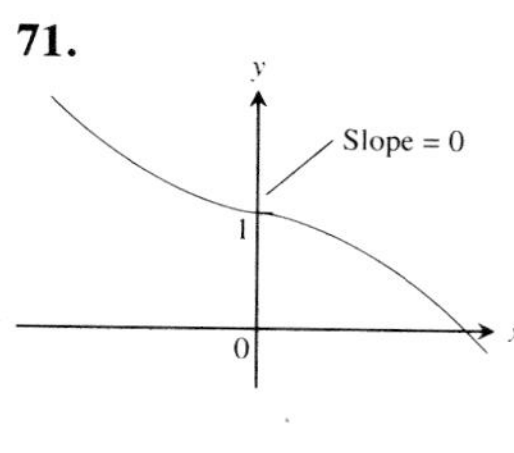

Chapter 4 Practice Exercises, pp. 266–269

1. a) $\frac{dS}{dt} = (4\pi r + 2\pi h)\frac{dr}{dt}$ b) $\frac{dS}{dt} = 2\pi r\frac{dh}{dt}$

c) $\frac{dS}{dt} = (4\pi r + 2\pi h)\frac{dr}{dt} + 2\pi r\frac{dh}{dt}$ d) $\frac{dr}{dt} = -\frac{r}{2r + h}\frac{dh}{dt}$

3. -40 m²/sec **5.** 0.02 ohm/sec **7.** 5 m/sec² **9.** a) $r = \frac{2}{5}h$,

b) $-\frac{125}{144\pi}$ ft/min **11.** 2 rad/sec, 1 rad/sec

13. No **15.** b) One **17.** No

21.

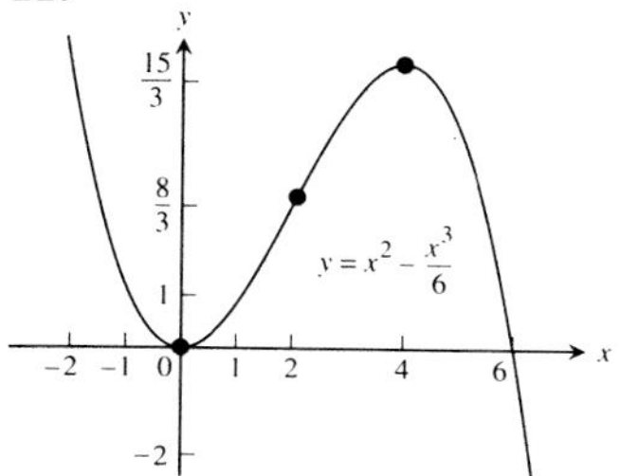

23.

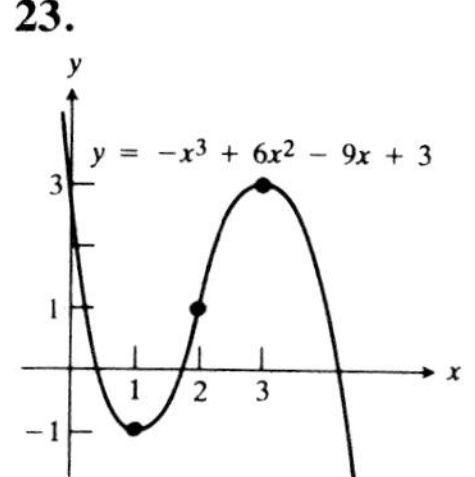

25.

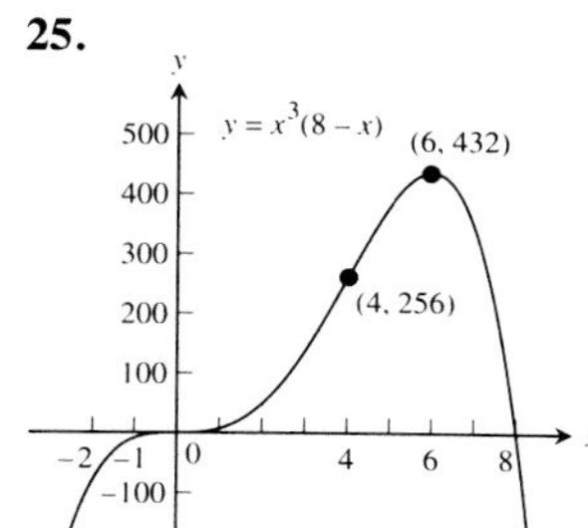

27.

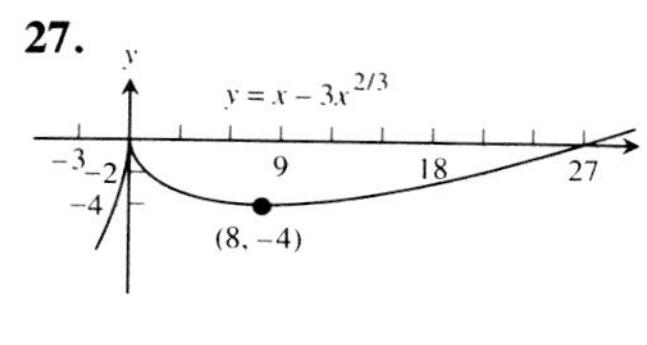

29.

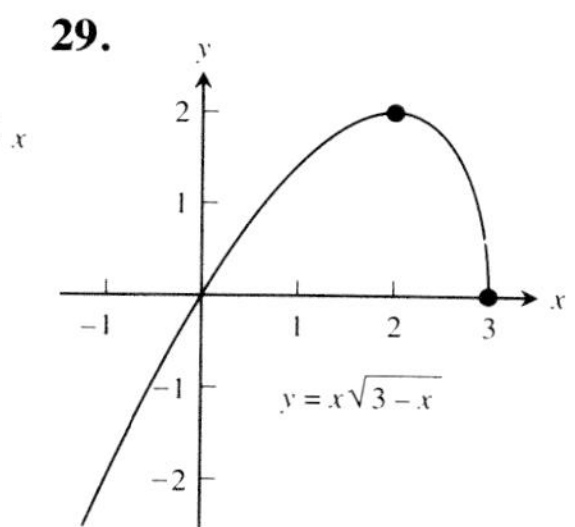

31. a) Local maximum at $x=4$, local minimum at $x=-4$, inflection point at $x=0$
b)

Loc max $x=4$; $x=0$ Infl; Loc min $x=-4$

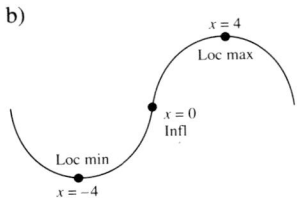

33. a) Local maximum at $x=0$, local minima at $x=-1$ and $x=2$, inflection points at $x=(1\pm\sqrt{7})/3$
b)

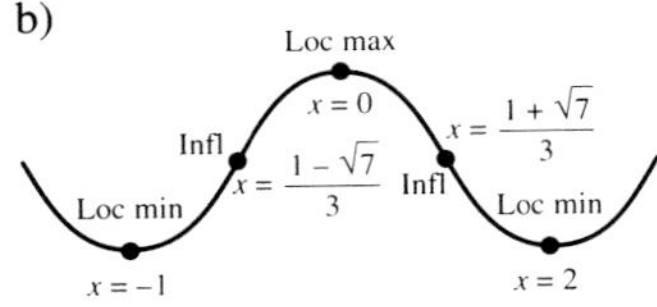

35. a) Local maximum at $x=-\sqrt{2}$, local minimum at $x=\sqrt{2}$, inflection points at $x=\pm 1$ and 0
b)

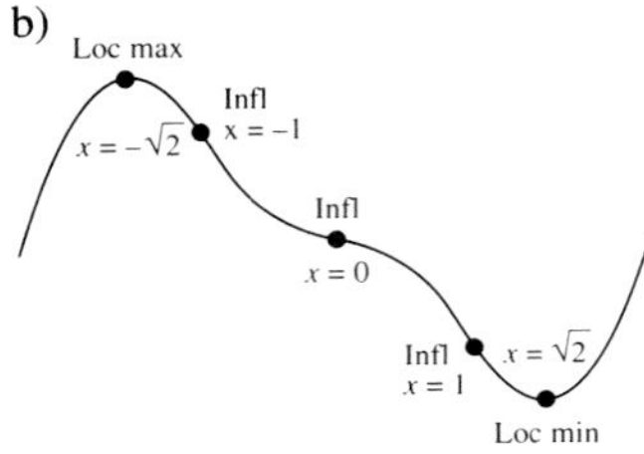

37. a) $t=0, 6, 12$ b) $t=3, 9$ c) $6<t<12$
d) $0<t<6$, $12<t<14$
39. a) T b) P

45.

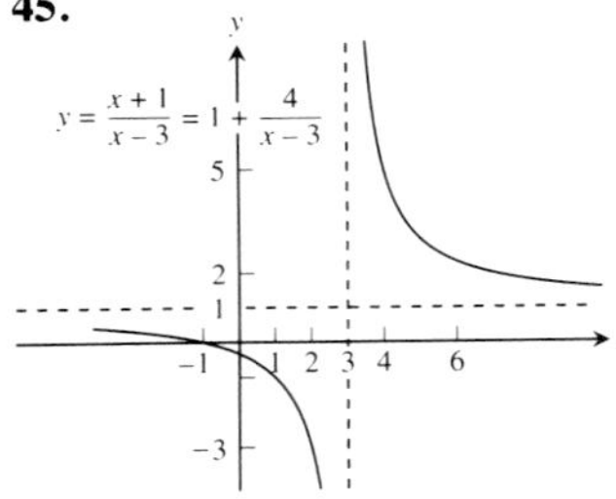

47.

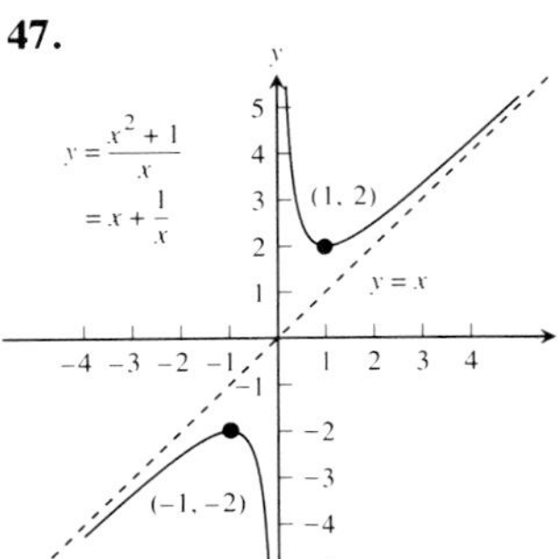

49.

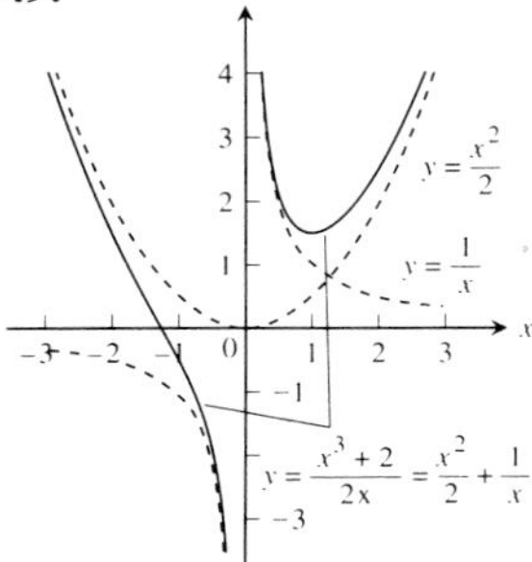

51.

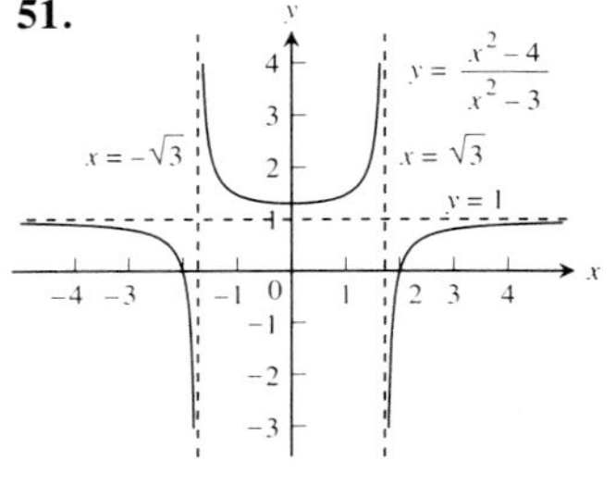

53.

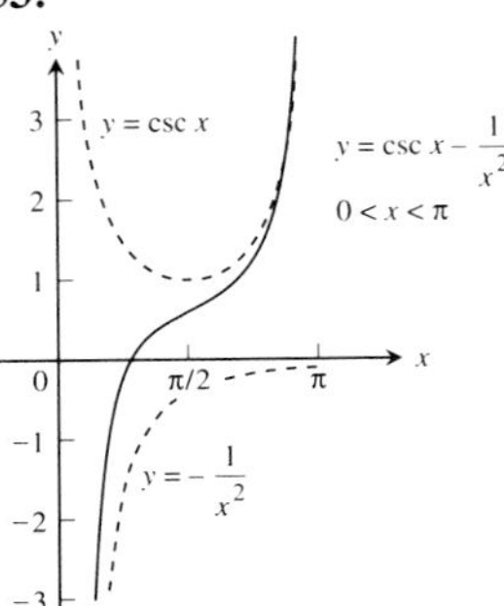

55. $a=1, b=0, c=1$ **59.** a) 0, 36 b) 18, 18
61. $r=25$ ft, $s=50$ ft **63.** Side base is 6 ft, height is 3 ft
65. Height = 2, radius = $\sqrt{2}$ **67.** $x=15$ mi, $y=9$ mi
69. $x=5-\sqrt{5}$ hundred ≈ 276 tires, $y=2(5-\sqrt{5})$ hundred ≈ 553 tires
71. c) 0.79762 **73.** Yes, these are the only functions.
75. a) C b) $\dfrac{x^2}{2}+C$ c) $\dfrac{x^{11}}{11}+C$ d) $-\dfrac{x^{-4}}{4}+C$
e) $\frac{3}{7}x^{7/3}+C$ f) $\frac{7}{4}x^{4/7}+C$ g) $-\cos x+C$ h) $\tan x+C$
i) $\sec x+C$ **77.** $x^3+\dfrac{5x^2}{2}-7x+C$ **79.** $\dfrac{2\sqrt{x^3}}{3}+2\sqrt{x}+C$
81. $\sin(\sqrt{5}\,x)-16\cos\left(\dfrac{x}{2}\right)+C$ **83.** $\frac{2}{3}t^{3/2}+\frac{5}{2}\sin(2t)+C$
85. $3\tan x+(1/x)+C$ **87.** $3\sec(\theta/3)+5\theta+C$
89. $\tan(x)-x+C$ **91.** $x-(1/2)\sin(2x)+C$
93. $y=x+(x^2/2)+(x^3/6)+1$ **95.** $y=x-(1/x)-1$
97. $y=\sin x$ **99.** $y=x$ **101.** Duck! **103.** $f=g$
105.

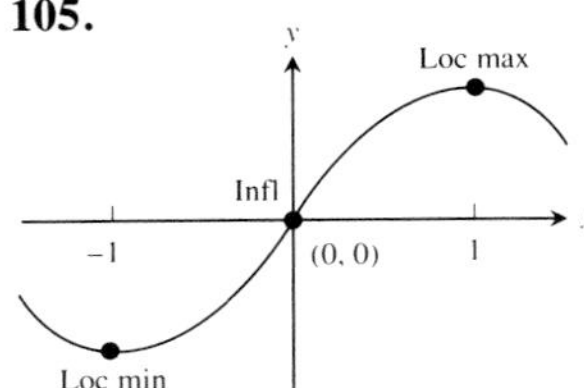

Chapter 5

Section 5.1, pp. 278–281

1. a) 87 in. b) 87 in. **3.** a) 3490 ft b) 3840 ft
5. $\approx$44.8, 6.7 L/min **7.** 20π **9.** a) 24.4 b) 3%
11. a) 96π b) 13% **13.** a) 292π b) 1%
15. a) 108π, 1% b) 107π, 0% **17.** a) left $\approx 15{,}465$ ft^3
b) right $\approx 16{,}515$ ft^3 **19.** 31/16 **21.** 1 **23.** 2
25. $\dfrac{4-\pi}{4}$ **27.** 37.5 mi/h

Section 5.2, pp. 292–294

1. $\frac{6(1)}{1+1}+\frac{6(2)}{2+1}=7$
3. $\cos(1)\pi+\cos(2)\pi+\cos(3)\pi+\cos(4)\pi=0$
5. $\sin\pi-\sin\frac{\pi}{2}+\sin\frac{\pi}{3}=\frac{\sqrt{3}-2}{2}$ **7.** All of them
9. b **11.** $\sum_{k=1}^{6} k$ **13.** $\sum_{k=1}^{4}\frac{1}{2^k}$ **15.** $\sum_{k=1}^{5}(-1)^{k+1}\frac{1}{k}$
17. a) -15 b) 1 c) 1 d) -11 e) 16 **19.** a) 55 b) 385 c) 3025 **21.** -56 **23.** -73 **25.** 240 **27.** 3376
29. a)

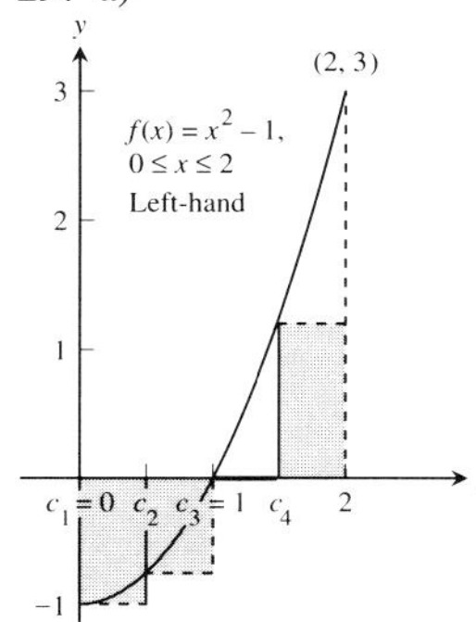

b)

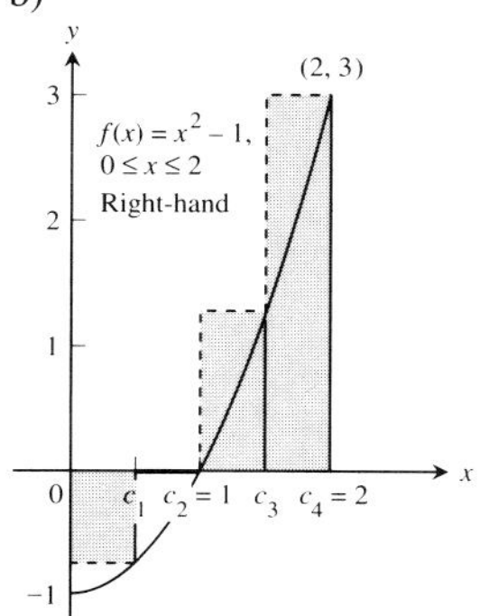

c)

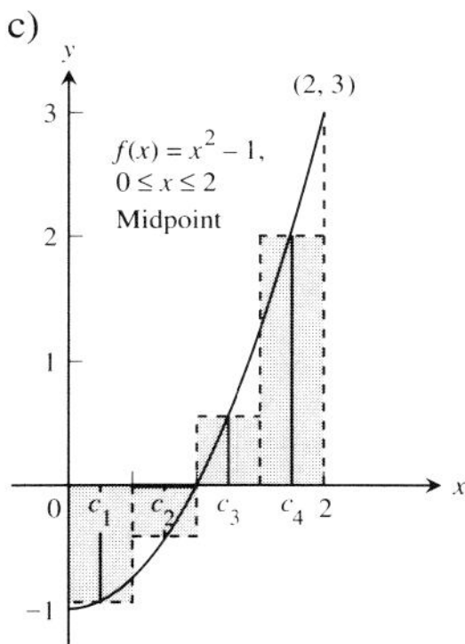

31. a)

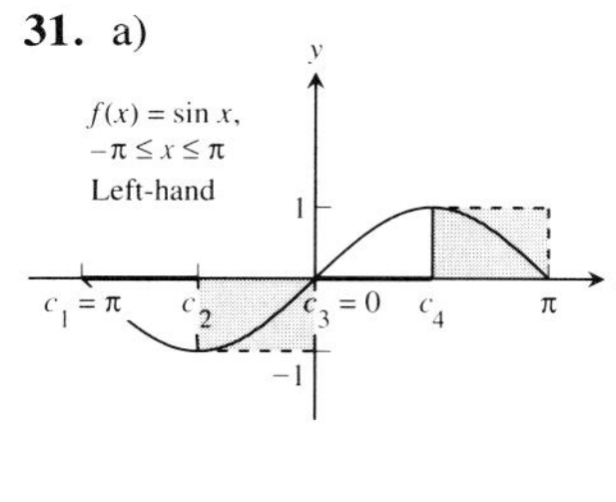

b)

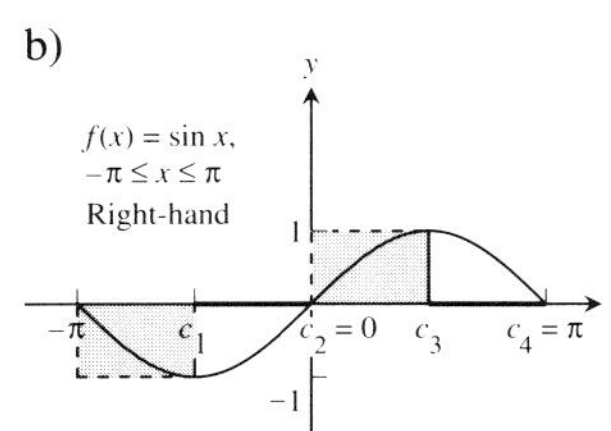

c)

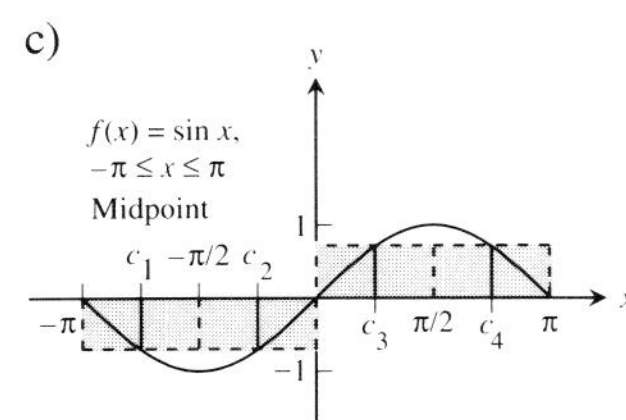

33. 1.2 **35.** $\int_0^2 x^2\,dx$ **37.** $\int_{-7}^{5}(x^2-3x)\,dx$ **39.** $\int_2^3\frac{1}{1-x}\,dx$
41. $\int_{-\pi/4}^{0}\sec x\,dx$ **43.** Area = 21 square units
45. Area = $9\pi/2$ square units **47.** Area = $2\frac{1}{2}$ square units
49. Area = 3 square units **51.** 1/2 **53.** $3\pi^2/2$ **55.** 7/3
57. 1/24 **59.** $3a^2/2$ **61.** $b/3$ **63.** 2/3 **65.** 2/3 **67.** 4/3
69. 15 **71.** -480 **73.** 2.75 **75.** $b^2/2$ **77.** b^2-a^2
79. Using n subintervals of length $\Delta x=b/n$ and right-endpoint values:

$$\text{Area}=\int_0^b 3x^2\,dx=b^3$$

81. Using n subintervals of length $\Delta x=b/n$ and right-endpoint values: Area $=\int_0^b 2x\,dx=b^2$

Section 5.3, pp. 300–302

1. a) 0 b) -8 c) -12 d) 10 e) -2 f) 16
3. a) 5 b) 5 c) -5 d) -5 **5.** a) 4 b) -4
7. -14 **9.** 10 **11.** -2 **13.** $-7/4$ **15.** 7 **17.** 0
19. $5\frac{1}{3}$ **21.** 19/3 **23.** b) 6 c) $7\frac{1}{3}$
25. b) 0, c) 8/3 **27.** av(f) = 0, assumed at $x=1$
29. av(f) = -2, assumed at $x=\sqrt{3}/3$
31. av(f) = 0, assumed at $t=0$, π, and 2π
33. a) av(f) = $-1/2$, assumed at $x=\pm 1/2$
b) av(f) = 1, assumed at $x=2$
c) av(f) = 1/4, assumed at $x=5/4$
35. Upper bound = 1, lower bound = 1/2
43. Upper bound = 1/2

Section 5.4, pp. 309–312

1. 6 **3.** 8 **5.** 1 **7.** 5/2 **9.** 2 **11.** $2\sqrt{3}$ **13.** 0 **15.** $-\pi/4$
17. $2\pi^3/3$ **19.** $-8/3$ **21.** $-3/4$ **23.** $\sqrt{2}-\sqrt[4]{8}+1$
25. 28/3 **27.** 1/2 **29.** 51/4 **31.** π **33.** $\sqrt{2}\pi/2$
35. $(\cos\sqrt{x})\left(\frac{1}{2\sqrt{x}}\right)$ **37.** $4t^5$ **39.** $\sqrt{1+x^2}$
41. $\frac{1}{2}x^{-1/2}\sin x$ **43.** 1 **45.** d **47.** b **49.** $y=\int_2^x\sec t\,dt+3$
51. $s=\int_{t_0}^{t}f(x)\,dx+s_0$ **57.** b) $V_{\max}=240\sqrt{2}$
59. a) \$9.00 b) \$10.00 **61.** 600, \$18.00 **63.** 300, \$6.00
65. $64\pi/3$ **67.** $128\pi/3$ **71.** $-3x+5$
73. a) True b) True c) True d) False e) True f) False g) True

Section 5.5, pp. 319–321

1. $(x^2/2)+x+C$ **3.** $t^3+(t^2/4)+C$
5. $(x^4/2)-(5x^2/2)+7x+C$ **7.** $-(1/x)-(x^3/3)-(x/3)+C$
9. $\frac{3}{2}x^{2/3}+C$ **11.** $\frac{2}{3}x^{3/2}+\frac{3}{4}x^{4/3}+C$ **13.** $4y^2-\frac{8}{3}y^{3/4}+C$
15. $x^2+(2/x)+C$ **17.** $2\sqrt{t}-(2/\sqrt{t})+C$ **19.** $-2\sin t+C$
21. $-3\cos(\theta/3)+C$ **23.** $3\cot x+C$ **25.** $-\frac{1}{2}\csc\theta+C$
27. $4\sec x-2\tan x+C$ **29.** $-\frac{1}{2}\cos 2x+\cot x+C$
31. $2y-\sin 2y+C$ **33.** $\frac{t}{2}+\frac{\sin 4t}{8}+C$ **35.** $\tan\theta+C$
37. $-\cot x-x+C$

43. $\frac{d}{dx}\left(\frac{-1}{x+1}+C\right)=(-1)(-1)(x+1)^{-2}=\frac{1}{(x+1)^2}dx$

45. a) Wrong: $\frac{d}{dx}\left(\frac{x^2}{2}\sin x+C\right)=\frac{2x}{2}\sin x+\frac{x^2}{2}\cos x=$ $x\sin x+\frac{x^2}{2}\cos x$ b) Wrong: $\frac{d}{dx}(-x\cos x+C)=-\cos x+$ $x\sin x$

c) Right: $\frac{d}{dx}(-x\cos x+\sin x+C)=-\cos x+x\sin x+$ $\cos x=x\sin x$

47. a) Wrong: $\frac{d}{dx}\left(\frac{(2x+1)^3}{3}+C\right)=\frac{3(2x+1)^2(2)}{3}=2(2x+1)^2$

b) Wrong: $\frac{d}{dx}((2x+1)^3+C)=3(2x+1)^2(2)=6(2x+1)^2$

c) Right: $\frac{d}{dx}((2x+1)^3+C)=6(2x+1)^2$

49. $y=2x^{3/2}-50$ **51.** $y=\cos(\pi t)-1$ **53.** $y=2x+5$
55. $y=x^3+\cos x-5x+1$ **57.** $y=x-x^{4/3}+(1/2)$
59. $y=-\sin x-\cos x-2$
61. a) $v=10t^{3/2}-6t^{1/2}$ b) $s=4t^{5/2}-4t^{3/2}$

Section 5.6, pp. 329–330

1. $-\frac{1}{3}\cos 3x+C$ **3.** $\frac{1}{2}\sec 2t+C$ **5.** $-(7x-2)^{-4}+C$
7. $-6(1-r^3)^{1/2}+C$
9. a) $-\frac{1}{4}(\cot^2 2\theta)+C$ b) $-\frac{1}{4}(\csc^2 2\theta)+C$
11. $\frac{2}{5}(5s+4)^{1/2}+C$ **13.** $-\frac{1}{3}(3-2x)^{3/2}+C$
15. $-\frac{2}{5}(1-\theta^2)^{5/4}+C$ **17.** $-\frac{1}{3}(7-3y^2)^{3/2}+C$
19. $\frac{1}{3}\sin(3z+4)+C$ **21.** $\frac{1}{3}\tan(3x+2)+C$
23. $\frac{1}{2}\sin^6\left(\frac{x}{3}\right)+C$ **25.** $\left(\frac{r^3}{18}-1\right)^6+C$
27. $-\frac{2}{3}\cos(x^{3/2}+1)+C$ **29.** $\sec\left(v+\frac{\pi}{2}\right)+C$
31. $\frac{1}{2\cos(2t+1)}+C$ **33.** $-\frac{2}{3}(\cot^3 y)^{1/2}+C$
35. $\frac{3}{4}\left(1-\frac{1}{x}\right)^4+C$ **37.** $-\sin\left(\frac{1}{t}-1\right)+C$
39. $\frac{(s^3+2s^2-5s+5)^2}{2}+C$ **41.** a) 14/3 b) 2/3 **43.** a) 1/2 b) $-1/2$ **45.** a) 15/16 b) 0 **47.** a) 0 b) 1/8 **49.** a) 4 b) 0 **51.** a) 1/6 b) 1/2 **53.** a) 0 b) 0 **55.** $2\sqrt{3}$ **57.** 3/4 **59.** $9^{5/4}-1$ **61.** 3 **63.** 16/3 **65.** $2^{5/2}$
69. $s=(3t^2-1)^4-1$ **71.** $s=-6\cos(t+\pi)-6$
73. a) 1 b) 1 c) 1

Section 5.7, pp. 338–342

1. I: a) 1.5, 0 b) 1.5, 0 c) 0%; II: a) 1.5, 0 b) 1.5, 0 c) 0%
3. I: a) 2.75, 0.08 b) 2.67, 0.08 c) 0.0312 ≈ 3%; II: a) 2.67, 0 b) 2.67, 0 c) 0%
5. I: a) 6.25, 0.5 b) 6, 0.25 c) 0.0417 ≈ 4%; II: a) 6, 0 b) 6, 0 c) 0%
7. I: a) 0.509, 0.03125 b) 0.5, 0.009 c) 0.018 ≈ 2%; II: a) 0.5, 0.002604 b) 0.5, 0 c) 0%
9. I: a) 1.8961, 0.161 b) 2, 0.1039 c) 0.052 ≈ 5%; II: a) 2.0045, 0.0066 b) 2, 0.00454 c) 0%
11. a) 0.319287 b) 0.3281208 c) 0.333333, 0.014045, 0.00521
13. a) 1.9564307 b) 2.00420521 c) 2, 0.0435693, 0.00420521
15. a) 1 b) 2 **17.** a) 116 b) 2 **19.** a) 283 b) 2 **21.** a) 71 b) 10 **23.** a) 75 b) 12 **25.** a) 82 b) 8
27. 1013 **29.** 56.86 kw/weekday **31.** 4, 4
33. a) 3.11571 b) 0.02588 c) With $M=3.11$, we get $|E_T|\le(\pi^3/1200)(3.11)<0.081$.
37. 1.08943 **39.** 0.82812

Chapter 5 Practice Exercises, pp. 342–345

1. About 686 ft **3.** a) $-1/2$ b) 31 c) 13 d) 0
5. $\int_1^5(2x-1)^{-1/2}dx=2$ **7.** $\int_{-\pi}^{0}\cos\frac{x}{2}dx=2$ **9.** a) 4 b) 2 c) -2 d) -2π e) 8/5 **11.** 8/3 **13.** 62
17. $y=\int_5^x\left(\frac{\sin t}{t}\right)dt-3$ **19.** $\frac{x^4}{4}+\frac{5}{2}x^2-7x+C$
21. $2t^{3/2}-(4/t)+C$ **23.** $-\frac{1}{2(r^2+5)}+C$
25. $-(2-\theta^2)^{3/2}+C$ **27.** $\frac{1}{3}(1+x^4)^{3/4}+C$
29. $\frac{1}{10}\tan\frac{s}{10}+C$ **31.** $-\frac{1}{\sqrt{2}}\csc\sqrt{2}\,\theta+C$
33. $\frac{1}{2}x-\sin\frac{x}{2}+C$ **35.** $-4(\cos x)^{1/2}+C$
37. $\theta^2+\theta+\sin(2\theta+1)+C$ **39.** $(t^3/3)+(4/t)+C$
41. 16 **43.** 2 **45.** 1 **47.** 8 **49.** $27\sqrt{3}/160$ **51.** 2/5
53. $\sqrt{3}$ **55.** $6\sqrt{3}-2\pi$ **57.** -1 **59.** 2 **61.** -2
63. 1 **65.** a) b b) b **73.** Cost ≈ \$12,518.10; no
75. At least 16 **77.** $T=\pi$, $S=\pi$

Chapter 6

Section 6.1, pp. 353–354

1.

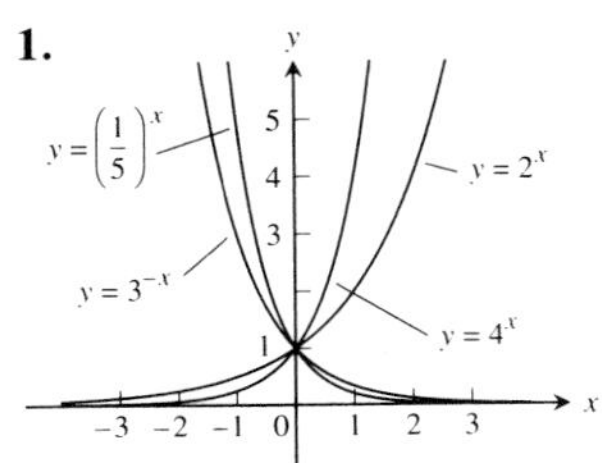

3.

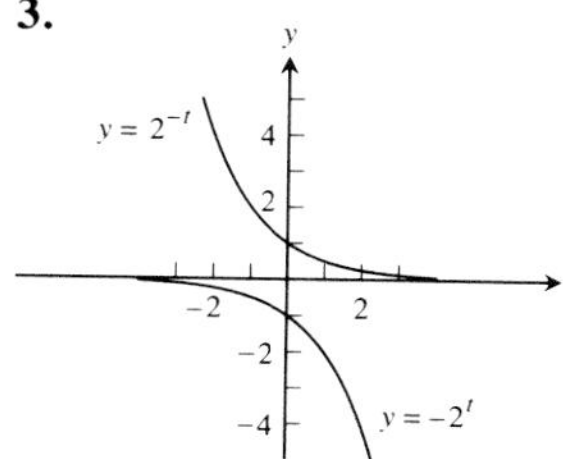

5.

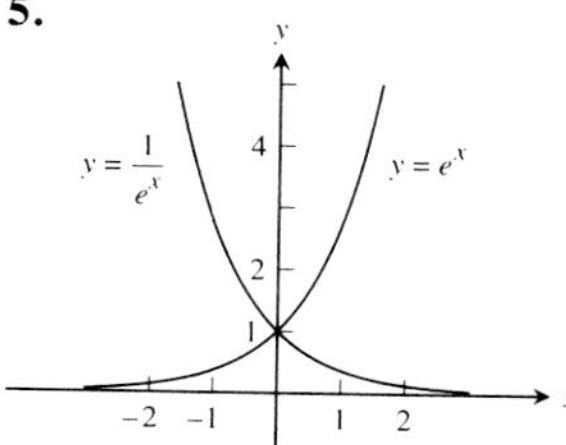

7.

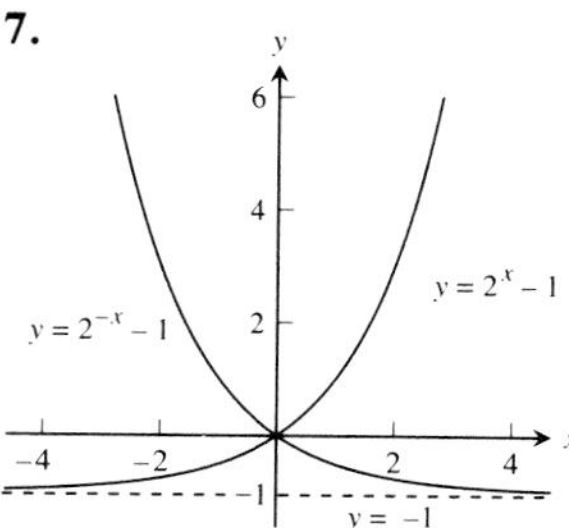

9.

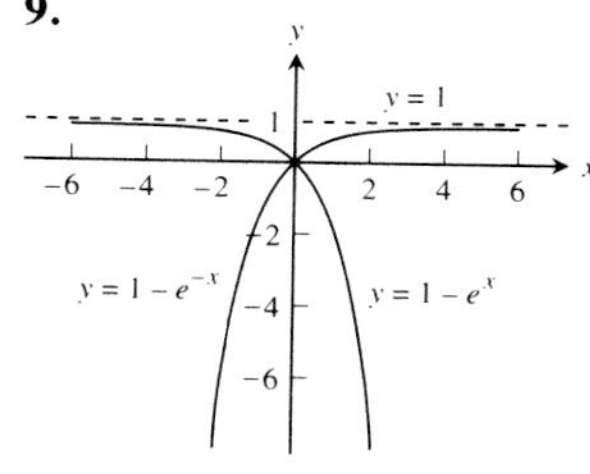

11. a) ∞ b) 0 **13.** 4 **15.** 3/2 **17.** $16^{1/4} = 2$
19. $4^{1/2} = 2$ **21.** 5 **23.** $14^{\sqrt{3}}$ **25.** 4 **27.** $-5/e^{5x}$
29. $\frac{2}{3}e^{(2x)/3}$ **31.** $e^{x+\sqrt{2}}$ **33.** $6xe^{3x^2}$
35. $(10t - 7)(e^{5t^2 - 7t})$ **37.** $2\sec^2\theta\, e^{\tan\theta}$ **39.** $xe^x + e^x$
41. xe^x **43.** $12e^{2x}(x^2 + 2x + 1)$ **45.** $\dfrac{te^{\sqrt{t}}}{\sqrt{t}} + 2e^{\sqrt{t}}$
47. $\dfrac{e^x + 2}{(e^{-x} + 1)^2}$ **49.** $-\sin\theta\cos\theta\, e^{\cos\theta}$ **51.** $e^t\cos t$
53. $e^{-x}\cos 2x$ **55.** xe^{ax} **57.** $\dfrac{2e^{2\theta}}{(e^{2\theta} + 1)^2}$
59. Absolute max $= 1/\sqrt{2e}$ at $x = 0.5$, absolute min $= 0$ at $x = 0$
61.

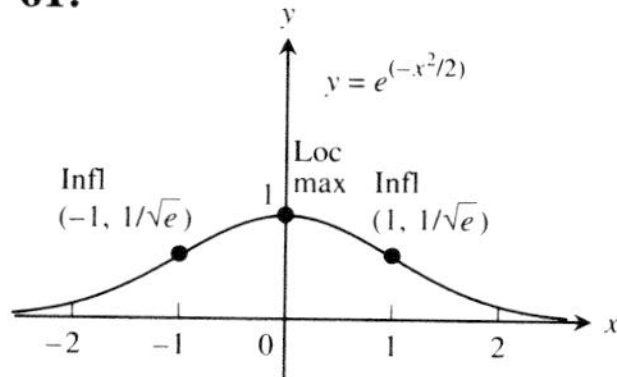

63. Where $\cos(x/2) = 0$. This happens at odd-integer multiples of π. The extreme values are $2e$ and $2/e$.
65. Absolute max of $\sqrt{e}$ at $x = 1$, absolute min of $1/\sqrt{e}$ at $x = -1$
67. Absolute max of e^2 at $t = \sqrt{2}$, absolute min of $1/e^2$ at $t = -\sqrt{2}$
69. $dy/dt = ky$ **71.** $dp/dt = kp$ **73.** $x + 1$
77. a) $\lim_{h\to 0}\dfrac{4^h - 1}{h} = f'(0)$ b) $L \approx 1.4$ **79.** $t = 0.69$

Section 6.2, pp. 359–361

1. One-to-one **3.** Not one-to-one **5.** One-to-one
7. $f^{-1}(x) = \sqrt{x - 1}$ **9.** $f^{-1}(x) = \sqrt[3]{x + 1}$
11. $f^{-1}(x) = \sqrt{x} - 1$
13.

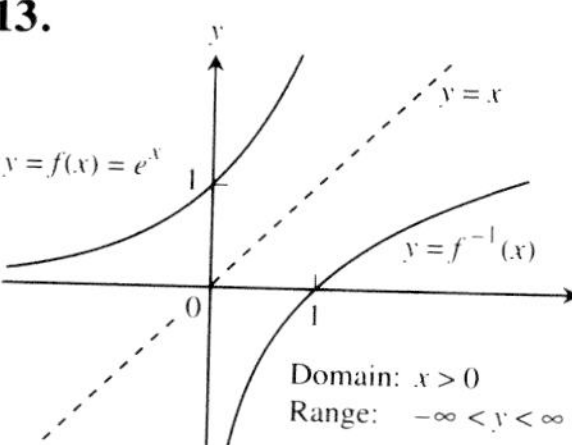

15.

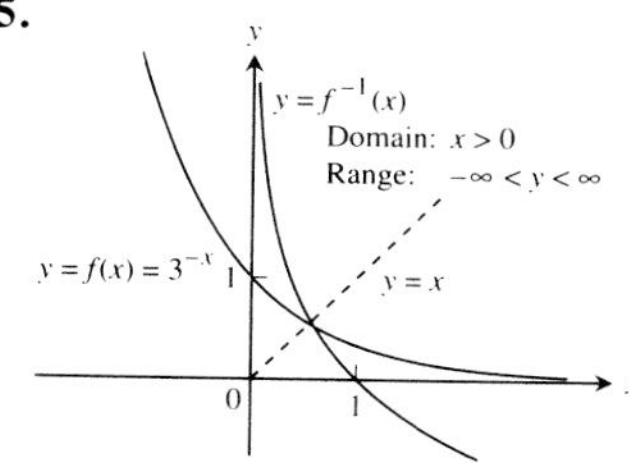

17.

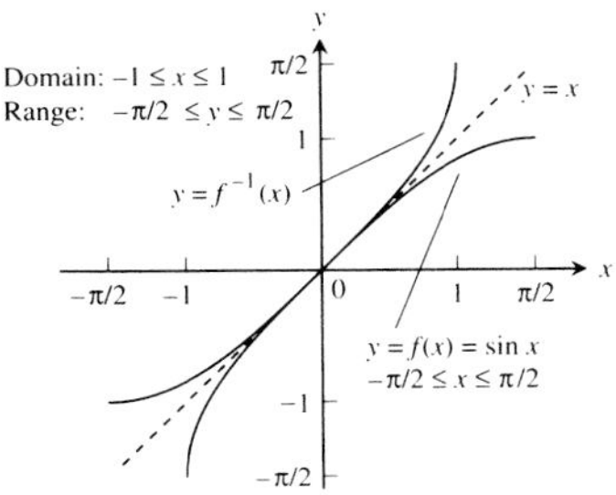

19. $f^{-1}(x) = \sqrt[5]{x}$, domain: $-\infty < x < \infty$, range: $-\infty < y < \infty$
21. $f^{-1}(x) = \sqrt[3]{x - 1}$, domain: $-\infty < x < \infty$, range: $-\infty < y < \infty$
23. $f^{-1}(x) = \dfrac{1}{\sqrt{x}}$, domain: $x > 0$, range: $y > 0$
25. a) $f^{-1}(x) = (x/2) - (3/2)$
b)

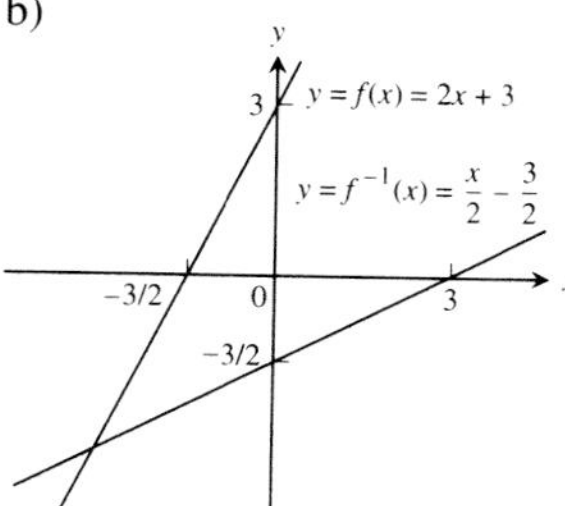

c) 2, 1/2
27. a) $f^{-1}(x) = 5x - 35$
b)

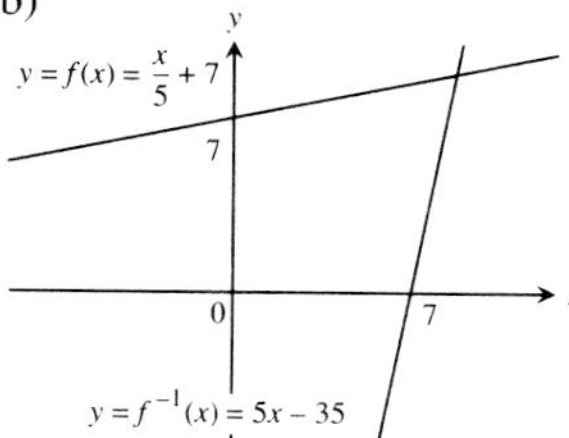

c) 1/5, 5

29. b)

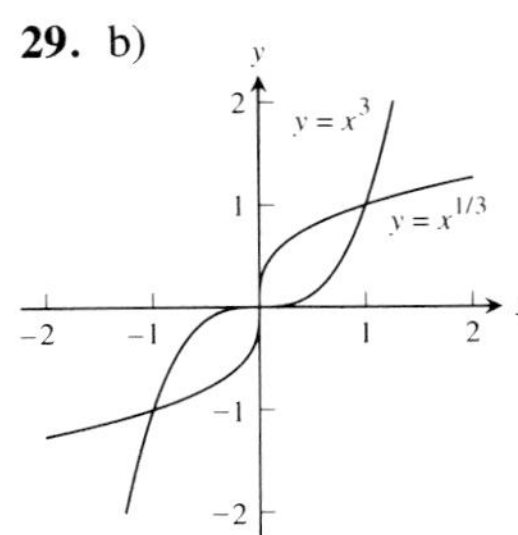

c) Slope of f at $(1, 1)$: 3, slope of g at $(1, 1)$: 1/3, slope of f at $(-1, -1)$: 3, slope of g at $(-1, -1)$: 1/3
d) $y = 0$ is tangent to $y = x^3$ at $x = 0$; $x = 0$ is tangent to $y = \sqrt[3]{x}$ at $x = 0$.
31. 1/9 **33.** 3
35. a) Symmetric about the line $y = x$

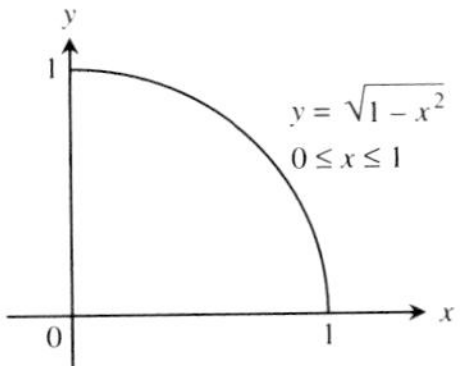

37. a) $f^{-1}(x) = \frac{1}{m}x$ b) The graph of f^{-1} is the line through the origin with slope $1/m$.

Section 6.3, pp. 370–372

1. a) 7.2 b) $1/x^2$ c) x/y **3.** a) 1 b) 1 c) $-x^2 - y^2$ **5.** e^{2t+4} **7.** $e^{5t} + 40$ **9.** $y = 2xe^x + 1$ **11.** a) $k = \ln 2$ b) $k = 1/10 \ln 2$ c) $k = 1000 \ln a$ **13.** a) $t = -10 \ln 3$ b) $t = -\frac{\ln 2}{k}$ c) $t = \frac{\ln .4}{\ln .2}$

15. a) $\ln 3 - \ln 4$ b) $2(\ln 2 - \ln 3)$ c) $-\ln 2$ d) $\frac{2}{3}\ln 3$ e) $\ln 3 + \frac{1}{2}\ln 2$ f) $\frac{1}{2}(3\ln 3 - \ln 2)$

17. a) $\ln 5$ b) $\ln(x - 3)$ c) $\ln(t^2)$ **19.** $1/x$ **21.** $2/t$ **23.** $-1/x$ **25.** $1/(\theta + 1)$ **27.** $x^3 \ln x$ **29.** $2(\ln t) + (\ln t)^2$ **31.** $\frac{1 - \ln t}{t^2}$ **33.** $\frac{1}{x(1 + \ln x)^2}$ **35.** $\frac{1 - t}{t}$ **37.** $\frac{1}{1 + e^\theta}$

39. $-\csc\theta$ **41.** $\frac{1}{2}\sqrt{x(x + 1)}\left(\frac{1}{x} + \frac{1}{x + 1}\right) = \frac{2x + 1}{2\sqrt{x(x + 1)}}$

43. $\frac{1}{2}\sqrt{\frac{t}{t + 1}}\left(\frac{1}{t} - \frac{1}{t + 1}\right) = \frac{1}{2\sqrt{t}(t + 1)^{3/2}}$

45. $\sqrt{\theta + 3}\,(\sin\theta)\left(\frac{1}{2(\theta + 3)} + \cot\theta\right)$

47. $t(t + 1)(t + 2)\left[\frac{1}{t} + \frac{1}{t + 1} + \frac{1}{t + 2}\right] = 3t^2 + 6t + 2$

49. $\frac{\theta + 5}{\theta\cos\theta}\left[\frac{1}{\theta + 5} - \frac{1}{\theta} + \tan\theta\right]$

51. $\frac{x\sqrt{x^2 + 1}}{(x + 1)^{2/3}}\left[\frac{1}{x} + \frac{x}{x^2 + 1} - \frac{2}{3(x + 1)}\right]$ **53.** a) 7 b) $\sqrt{2}$ c) 75 d) 2 e) 0.5 f) -1 **55.** $x = 12$ **57.** $x = 3$ or $x = 2$ **59.** $\frac{1}{\theta\ln 2}$ **61.** $\frac{3}{x\ln 4}$ **63.** $\frac{2(\ln r)}{r(\ln 2)(\ln 4)}$ **65.** $\frac{-2}{(x + 1)(x - 1)}$

67. $2^x \ln 2$ **69.** $-3^{-x}(\ln 3)$ **71.** $\left(\frac{\ln 5}{2\sqrt{s}}\right)5^{\sqrt{s}}$

73. $7^{\sec\theta}(\ln 7)^2(\sec\theta\tan\theta)$ **75.** $(3\cos 3t)(2^{\sin 3t})\ln 2$ **77.** a) $\ln 2$ b) $\ln 5$ **79.** $\pi x^{(\pi - 1)}$ **81.** $(3 - \sqrt{2})t^{(2 - \sqrt{2})}$ **83.** $-\sqrt{2}\cos\theta^{(\sqrt{2} - 1)}\sin\theta$

85. $(x + 1)^x\left(\frac{x}{x + 1} + \ln(x + 1)\right)$ **87.** $(\sqrt{t})^t\left(\frac{\ln t}{2} + \frac{1}{2}\right)$

89. $(\sin x)^x(\ln\sin x + x\cot x)$ **91.** Max $= 1/(2e)$ at $x = 1/\sqrt{e}$

93.

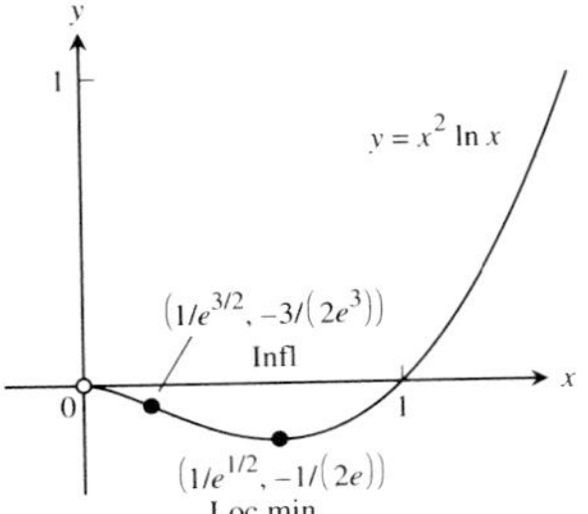

95. $[10^{-7.44}, 10^{-7.37}]$ **97.** $k = 10$ **99.** a) -0.22314 b) 10.32 years **105.** $x \approx -0.76666$

Section 6.4, pp. 377–379

1. $\frac{1}{3}e^{3x} - 5e^{-x} + C$ **3.** 1 **5.** $8e^{(x + 1)} + C$ **7.** 2 **9.** $2e^{\sqrt{r}} + C$ **11.** $-e^{-t^2} + C$ **13.** $-e^{1/x} + C$ **15.** e **17.** $\frac{1}{\pi}e^{\sec\pi t} + C$ **19.** 1 **21.** $\frac{5^x}{\ln 5} + C$ **23.** $\frac{1}{2\ln 2}$ **25.** $\frac{1}{\ln 2}$

27. $6/(\ln 7)$ **29.** $\ln(2/3)$ **31.** $\frac{1}{2}\ln|2x - 5| + C$ **33.** $\ln(2/5)$

35. $\ln|x^2 - 25| + C$ **37.** $\ln(1/3)$ **39.** $\frac{1}{6}(\ln x)^2 + C$

41. $-\frac{4}{\ln x} + C$ **43.** 1 **45.** $-10\left[\ln\left|\cos\frac{\theta}{2}\right|\right] + C$

47. $-\ln\sqrt{2}$ **49.** $\left(-\frac{2}{\pi}\right)\ln\left(\frac{\sqrt{2}}{2}\right)$ **51.** $\frac{(\ln x)^2}{2\ln 7} + C$

53. $2\ln 10$ **55.** $\frac{7}{3}\ln 2$ **57.** $(\ln 10)\ln|\ln x| + C$

59. $\frac{3x^{(\sqrt{3} + 1)}}{\sqrt{3} + 1} + C$ **61.** $3^{\sqrt{2} + 1}$ **63.** $\ln(\ln x), x > 1$ **65.** $-\ln x$ **67.** $y = x + \ln(x) + 2$ **69.** $y = -\cos(e^t - 2) + 1$ **71.** $y = \ln|\sec\theta| + \theta$ **73.** $2\ln 5$ **75.** b) $L(x) = x - 1$ c) $0.1 - \ln 1.1 \approx 0.00469$ (rounded up to be safe) **77.** $\ln\left(\frac{81}{16}\right) + 1$ **79.** b) $\frac{1}{e - 1}$

Section 6.5, pp. 385–388

1. a) -0.00001 b) 10,536 years c) 82% **3.** 54.88 g

5. 59.8 ft **7.** 2.8147497×10^{14} **9.** a) 8 years b) 32.02 years **11.** 15.28 years **13.** a) $A_0 e^{0.2}$ b) 17.33 years c) 27.47 years **15.** 4.50% **17.** 0.585 day **21.** a) 17.5 min b) 13.26 min **23.** -3°C **25.** About 6658 years **27.** 41 years old

Section 6.6, pp. 393–394

1. 1/4 **3.** $-23/7$ **5.** 5/7 **7.** 0 **9.** -16 **11.** -2 **13.** 1/4 **15.** 2 **17.** 3 **19.** -1 **21.** ln 3 **23.** $\dfrac{1}{\ln 2}$ **25.** ln 2 **27.** 1 **29.** 1/2 **31.** ln 2 **33.** 0 **35.** $-1/2$ **37.** $1/e$ **39.** 1 **41.** $1/e$ **43.** $e^{1/2}$ **45.** 1 **47.** 3 **49.** 1 **51.** b is correct **53.** d is correct **55.** $c = 27/10$

Section 6.7, pp. 399–401

1. a) Slower b) Slower c) Slower d) Faster e) Slower f) Slower g) Same h) Slower
3. a) Same b) Faster c) Same d) Same e) Slower f) Faster g) Slower h) Same
5. a) Same b) Same c) Same d) Faster e) Faster f) Same g) Slower h) Faster
7. d, a, c, b
11. a) False b) False c) True d) True e) True f) True g) False h) True
15. b) $\ln(e^{17000000}) = 17{,}000{,}000 < (e^{17 \times 10^6})^{1/10^6} = e^{17} \approx 24{,}154{,}952.75$ c) $x \approx 3.4306311 \times 10^{15}$ d) They cross at $x \approx 3.4306311 \times 10^{15}$.
17. a) The algorithm that takes $O(n \log_2 n)$ steps
19. It could take one million for a sequential search; at most 20 steps for a binary search.
23. When the degree of f is less than the degree of g
25. b) The rates are the same.

Section 6.8, pp. 407–409

1. a) $\pi/4$ b) $-\pi/3$ c) $\pi/6$
3. a) $-\pi/6$ b) $\pi/4$ c) $-\pi/3$
5. a) $\pi/3$ b) $3\pi/4$ c) $\pi/6$ **7.** $3\pi/4$ b) $\pi/6$ c) $2\pi/3$
9. a) $\pi/4$ b) $-\pi/3$ c) $\pi/6$
11. a) $3\pi/4$ b) $\pi/6$ c) $2\pi/3$
13. $\cos\alpha = 12/13$, $\tan\alpha = 5/12$, $\sec\alpha = 13/12$, $\csc\alpha = 13/5$, $\cot\alpha = 12/5$
15. $\sin\alpha = 2/\sqrt{5}$, $\cos\alpha = -1/\sqrt{5}$, $\tan\alpha = -2$, $\csc\alpha = \sqrt{5}/2$, $\cot\alpha = -1/2$
17. $1/\sqrt{2}$ **19.** $-1/\sqrt{3}$ **21.** $\dfrac{4+\sqrt{3}}{2\sqrt{3}}$ **23.** 1 **25.** $-\sqrt{2}$
27. $\pi/6$ **29.** $\sqrt{x^2+4}/2$ **31.** $\sqrt{9y^2-1}$ **33.** $\sqrt{1-x^2}$
35. $\sqrt{x^2-2x}/(x-1)$ **37.** $\sqrt{9-4y^2}/3$ **39.** $\sqrt{x^2-16}/x$
41. $\pi/2$ **43.** $\pi/2$ **45.** $\pi/2$ **47.** 0 **51.** 42.23°
53. a) 0.84107 b) -0.72973 c) 0.46365
55. a) Defined; there is an angle whose tangent is 2. b) Not defined; there is no angle whose cosine is 2.
57. a) Not defined; no angle has secant 0. b) Not defined; no angle has sine $\sqrt{2}$.

59. a) Domain: all real numbers except those having the form $(\pi/2) + k\pi$ where k is an integer; range: $-(\pi/2) < y < (\pi/2)$ b) Domain: $-\infty < x < \infty$, range: $-\infty < y < \infty$
61. a) Domain: $-\infty < x < \infty$, range: $0 \le x \le \pi$ b) Domain: $-1 \le x \le 1$, range: $-1 \le x \le 1$

Section 6.9, pp. 414–415

1. $-2x/\sqrt{1-x^4}$ **3.** $\sqrt{2}/\sqrt{1-2t^2}$ **5.** $1/\left(|2s+1|\sqrt{s^2+s}\right)$
7. $-2x/\left((x^2+1)\sqrt{x^4+2x^2}\right)$ **9.** $-1/\sqrt{1-t^2}$
11. $-1/\left(2\sqrt{t}(1+t)\right)$ **13.** $1/\left((\tan^{-1}x)(1+x^2)\right)$
15. $\dfrac{-e^t}{|e^t|\sqrt{(e^t)^2-1}} = \dfrac{-1}{\sqrt{e^{2t}-1}}$ **17.** $-2s^2/\sqrt{1-s^2}$
19. 0 **21.** $\sin^{-1}x$ **27.** $\sin^{-1}\dfrac{x}{3} + C$
29. $\dfrac{1}{\sqrt{17}}\tan^{-1}\dfrac{x}{\sqrt{17}} + C$ **31.** $\dfrac{1}{\sqrt{2}}\sec^{-1}\left|\dfrac{5x}{\sqrt{2}}\right| + C$ **33.** $2\pi/3$
35. $\pi/16$ **37.** $-\pi/12$ **39.** $\dfrac{3}{2}\sin^{-1}2(r-1) + C$
41. $\dfrac{\sqrt{2}}{2}\tan^{-1}\left(\dfrac{x-1}{\sqrt{2}}\right) + C$ **43.** $\dfrac{1}{4}\sec^{-1}\left(\dfrac{2x-1}{2}\right) + C$
45. π **47.** $\pi/12$ **49.** $\dfrac{1}{2}\sin^{-1}y^2 + C$ **51.** $\sin^{-1}(x-2) + C$
53. π **55.** $\dfrac{1}{2}\tan^{-1}\left(\dfrac{y-1}{2}\right) + C$ **57.** 2π
59. $\sec^{-1}(x+1) + C$ **61.** $e^{\sin^{-1}x} + C$ **63.** $\dfrac{1}{3}(\sin^{-1}x)^3 + C$
65. $\ln|\tan^{-1}y| + C$ **67.** 1 **69.** 5 **71.** 2 **73.** $3\sqrt{5}$ ft
75. $y = \sin^{-1}(x)$ **77.** $y = \sec^{-1}(x) + (2\pi/3)$
79. Yes, $\sin^{-1}(x)$ and $\cos^{-1}(x)$ differ by the constant $\pi/2$.

Section 6.10, pp. 421–424

1. $\cosh x = 5/4$, $\tanh x = -3/5$, $\coth x = -5/3$, $\operatorname{sech} x = 4/5$, $\operatorname{csch} = -4/3$
3. $2\cosh(\ln x) = 2\left(\dfrac{e^{\ln x} + e^{-\ln x}}{2}\right) = x + (1/x)$
5. $(\sinh(x) + \cosh(x))^4 = \left(\dfrac{e^x - e^{-x}}{2} + \dfrac{e^x + e^{-x}}{2}\right)^4 = (e^x)^4 = e^{4x}$
7. $2\cosh(x/3)$ **9.** $\operatorname{sech}^2\sqrt{t} + \dfrac{\tanh\sqrt{t}}{\sqrt{t}}$ **11.** $\coth z$
13. $(\ln \operatorname{sech}\theta)(\operatorname{sech}\theta\tanh\theta)$ **15.** $\tanh^3 v$ **17.** 2
19. $\dfrac{1}{2\sqrt{x(1+x)}}$ **21.** $\dfrac{1}{1+\theta} - \tanh^{-1}\theta$
23. $\dfrac{1}{2\sqrt{t}} - \coth^{-1}\sqrt{t}$ **25.** $-\operatorname{sech}^{-1}x$ **27.** $\dfrac{\ln 2}{\sqrt{1+(1/2)^{2\theta}}}$
29. $|\sec x|$ **35.** $\dfrac{\cosh 2x}{2} + C$ **37.** $12\sinh((x/2) - \ln 3) + C$
39. $7\ln|e^{x/7} + e^{-x/7}| + C$ **41.** $\tanh(x - 1/2) + C$
43. $-2\operatorname{sech}\sqrt{t} + C$ **45.** $\ln(5/2)$ **47.** $(3/32) + \ln 2$
49. $e - e^{-1}$ **51.** 3/4 **53.** $(3/8) + \ln\sqrt{2}$ **55.** $\ln(2/3)$

57. $\dfrac{-\ln 3}{2}$ **59.** $\ln 3$ **61.** a) $\sinh^{-1}\sqrt{3}$ b) $\ln(\sqrt{3}+2)$
63. a) $\coth^{-1} 2 - \coth^{-1}(5/4)$ b) $(1/2)\ln(1/3)$
65. a) $-\operatorname{sech}^{-1}(12/13) + \operatorname{sech}^{-1}(4/5)$
b) $-\ln\left(\dfrac{1+\sqrt{1-(12/13)^2}}{(12/13)}\right) + \ln\left(\dfrac{1+\sqrt{1-(4/5)^2}}{(4/5)}\right) =$
$-\ln(3/2) + \ln(2) = \ln(4/3)$
67. a) 0 b) 0 **71.** b) $\sqrt{mg/k}$ c) $80\sqrt{5} \approx 178.89$ ft/sec
73. $y = \operatorname{sech}^{-1} x - \sqrt{1-x^2}$

Section 6.11, pp. 431–434

9. $\frac{2}{3}y^{3/2} - x^{1/2} = C$ **11.** $e^y - e^x = C$
13. $-e^{-y} - e^{\sin x} = C$ **15.** $y = e^{-x} + Ce^{-2x}$
17. $y = \dfrac{-\cos x}{x^3} + \dfrac{C}{x^3}$ **19.** $s = \dfrac{t^3}{3(t-1)^4} - \dfrac{t}{(t-1)^4} + \dfrac{C}{(t-1)^4}$
21. $r = \csc\theta(\ln|\sec\theta| + C)$ **23.** $y = -e^{-x}\operatorname{sech} x + C\operatorname{sech} x$
25. $y = \frac{1}{2}t - \frac{1}{4} + \frac{5}{4}e^{-2t}$ **27.** $y = -\dfrac{1}{\theta}\cos\theta + \dfrac{\pi}{2\theta}$
29. $y = 6e^{x^2} - \dfrac{e^{x^2}}{x+1}$ **31.** b is correct, but a is not.
33. $y = y_0 e^{kt}$ **35.** a) $c = \dfrac{G}{100Vk} + \left(c_0 - \dfrac{G}{100Vk}\right)e^{-kt}$
b) $\dfrac{G}{100Vk}$ **37.** a) 550 ft b) $25\ln 22 \approx 77$ sec
39. $t = \dfrac{L}{R}\ln 2$ sec
41. a) $i = \dfrac{V}{R} - \dfrac{V}{R}e^{-3} = \dfrac{V}{R}(1-e^{-3}) \approx 0.95\dfrac{V}{R}$ amp b) 86%
43. a) 10 lb/min b) $100 + t$ gal c) $4\left(\dfrac{y}{100+t}\right)$ lb/min
d) $\dfrac{dy}{dt} = 10 - \dfrac{4y}{100+t}$, $y(0) = 50$, $y = 2(100+t) - \dfrac{150}{\left(1+\dfrac{t}{100}\right)^4}$
e) Concentration $= \dfrac{y(25)}{\text{amt brine in tank}} = \dfrac{188.6}{125} \approx 1.5$ lb/gal
45. $y(27.8) \approx 14.8$ lb, $t \approx 27.8$ min

Chapter 6 Practice Exercises, pp. 435–437

1. $-2e^{-x/5}$ **3.** xe^{4x} **5.** $\dfrac{2\sin\theta\cos\theta}{\sin^2\theta} = 2\cot\theta$ **7.** $\dfrac{2}{(\ln 2)x}$
9. $-8^{-t}(\ln 8)$ **11.** $18x^{2.6}$ **13.** $(x+2)^{x+2}(\ln(x+2)+1)$
15. $-\dfrac{1}{\sqrt{1-u^2}}$ **17.** $\dfrac{1-z}{\sqrt{z^2-1}} + \sec^{-1} z$
19. $\tan^{-1}(t) + \dfrac{t}{1+t^2} - \dfrac{1}{2t}$ **21.** $\dfrac{\sec^{-1}\sqrt{x}}{\sqrt{x-1}} + \dfrac{1}{x}$
23. $y' = \dfrac{2(x^2+1)}{\sqrt{\cos 2x}}\left[\dfrac{2x}{x^2+1} + \tan 2x\right]$
25. $y' = 5\left[\dfrac{(x+5)(x-1)}{(x-2)(x+3)}\right]^5\left(\dfrac{1}{x+5} + \dfrac{1}{x-1} - \dfrac{1}{x-2} - \dfrac{1}{x-3}\right)$
29. $-\cos e^x + C$ **31.** $\tan(e^x - 7) + C$ **33.** $e^{\tan x} + C$

35. $\dfrac{-\ln 7}{3}$ **37.** $\ln 8$ **39.** $\ln(9/25)$ **41.** $-(\ln|\cos(\ln v)|) + C$
43. $-\frac{1}{2}(\ln x)^{-2} + C$ **45.** $-\cot(1+\ln r) + C$
47. $\dfrac{1}{2\ln 3}\left(3^{x^2}\right) + C$ **49.** $3\ln 7$ **51.** $(15/16) + \ln 2$
53. $e - 1$ **55.** 1/6 **57.** 9/14
59. $\frac{1}{3}[(\ln 4)^3 - (\ln 2)^3]$ or $\frac{7}{3}(\ln 2)^3$ **61.** $\dfrac{9\ln 2}{4}$ **63.** π
65. $\pi/\sqrt{3}$ **67.** $\sec^{-1} 2y + C$ **69.** $\pi/12$
71. $\sin^{-1}(x+1) + C$ **73.** $\pi/2$ **75.** $\frac{1}{3}\sec^{-1}\left(\frac{t+1}{3}\right) + C$
77. $y = \dfrac{\ln 2}{\ln(3/2)}$ **79.** $y = \ln x - \ln 3$ **81.** $y = \dfrac{1}{1-e^x}$
83. $\ln 10$ **85.** $\ln 2$ **87.** 5 **89.** 2 **91.** 1 **93.** e^3
95. 1/3
97. Absolute max $= 0$ at $x = e/2$, absolute min $= -0.5$ at $x = 0.5$
99. $1/e$ m/sec
101. $1/\sqrt{2}$ units long by $1/\sqrt{e}$ units high, $A = 1/\sqrt{2e} \approx 0.43$ square units
103. $h = \sqrt{e}$ cm **107.** $\ln(5x) - \ln(3x) = \ln(5/3)$
109. a) $f(x) = \dfrac{\ln 2}{\ln x}$, $g(x) = \dfrac{\ln x}{\ln 2}$ c) $(0.5, -1)$ and $(2, 1)$
111. 18,935 years **113.** a) Same rate b) Same rate c) Faster d) Faster e) Same rate f) Same rate
115. a) True b) False c) False d) True e) True f) True
121. $y = \ln(-e^{-x-2} + 2e^{-2})$
123. $y = \dfrac{1}{(x+1)^2}\cdot\left(\dfrac{x^3}{3} + \dfrac{x^2}{2} + 1\right)$

Chapter 7

Section 7.1, pp. 444–446

1. 2 **3.** 2 **5.** $\pi/2$ **7.** 1/12 **9.** 5/6 **11.** $(4/3) - (\pi/4)$
13. 32/3 **15.** 48/5 **17.** 8/3 **19.** 18 **21.** 243/8 **23.** 8/3
25. 104/15 **27.** 56/15 **29.** 4 **31.** $(4/3) - (4/\pi)$ **33.** $\pi/2$
35. 2 **37.** 38/3 **39.** 49/6 **41.** 1/2 **43.** $(3/2) - \ln 2$
45. a) $(\pm\sqrt{c}, c)$ b) $c = 4^{2/3}$ c) $c = 4^{2/3}$

Section 7.2, pp. 453–455

1. $2\pi/3$ **3.** $4 - \pi$ **5.** $\pi\ln 3$ **7.** 4π **9.** $32\pi/5$ **11.** 36π
13. π **15.** $\pi\left(-2\ln\dfrac{2}{\sqrt{2}} + 1\right)$ **17.** 2π **19.** 2π
21. $4\pi\ln 4$ **23.** $\pi[\ln 4 - 1]$ **25.** $2\pi/3$ **27.** 2π
29. $117\pi/5$ **31.** $\pi(\pi - 2)$ **33.** $\pi\left(\dfrac{\pi}{2} + \ln 4 - 2\right)$ **35.** $4\pi/3$
37. 8π **39.** $\pi(\sqrt{3})$ **41.** $7\pi/6$ **43.** $\pi^2 - 2\pi$ **45.** a) $\dfrac{11\pi}{3}$
b) $\pi[4\ln(4) - 3]$ c) $\pi(4\ln 4 - 5)$
47. a) 8π b) $32\pi/5$ c) $8\pi/3$ d) $224\pi/15$
49. a) $16\pi/15$ b) $56\pi/15$ c) $64\pi/15$ **51.** $V = 1053\pi$ cm^3
53. a) $c = 2/\pi$ b) $c = 0$ **55.** a) 1 b) $\pi/2$ c) π

Section 7.3, pp. 460–462

1. $4\pi/3$ **3.** $8\pi/3$ **5.** 6π **7.** 2π **9.** 8π **11.** $5\pi/6$
13. 3π **15.** $(16\pi/15)(3\sqrt{2}+5)$ **17.** $8\pi/3$
19. $4\pi/3$ **21.** $16\pi/3$ **23.** $14\pi/3$ **25.** 10π
27. $2\pi[8-(\ln 10)^2+(\ln 2)^2]$
29. a) $6\pi/5$ b) $4\pi/5$ c) 2π d) 2π
31. a) $\pi\ln 4$ b) $\pi(4\pi/3-\ln 4)$ c) $\pi(2\pi+\ln 4)$
33. a) $5\pi/3$ b) $4\pi/3$ c) 2π d) $2\pi/3$
35. a) $11\pi/15$ b) $97\pi/105$ c) $121\pi/210$ d) $23\pi/30$
37. a) $512\pi/21$ b) $832\pi/21$ **39.** a) $\pi/6$ b) $\pi/6$
41. a) $\left(\ln 4-\frac{3}{4}\right)\pi$ b) $\left(\ln 4-\frac{3}{4}\right)\pi$ **43.** b) 4π
45. Disk: 2 integrals; washer: 2 integrals; shell: 1 integral

Section 7.4, pp. 468–471

1. $L=\int_{-1}^{2}\sqrt{1+4x^2}\,dx$ **3.** $L=\int_{0}^{\pi}\sqrt{1+\cos^2 y}\,dy$
5. $L=\int_{0}^{\pi/6}\sec x\,dx$ **7.** $S=2\pi\int_{-\pi/4}^{\pi/4}\tan x\sqrt{1+\sec^4 x}\,dx$
9. $S=2\pi\int_{1}^{2}\frac{1}{y}\sqrt{1+y^{-4}}\,dy$
11. $S=2\pi\int_{1}^{4}\left(3-\sqrt{x}\right)^2\sqrt{1+(1-3x^{-1/2})^2}\,dx$
13. 12 **15.** 53/6 **17.** 123/32 **19.** 99/8 **21.** $6+\ln 2$
23. 2 **25.** $\pi/3$ **27.** $y=e^x$ **29.** $4\pi\sqrt{5}$ **31.** $3\pi\sqrt{5}$
33. $98\pi/81$ **35.** 2π **37.** $\frac{\pi\left(\sqrt{8}-1\right)}{9}$ **39.** $\frac{35\pi\sqrt{5}}{3}$
45. Order 226.2 liters of each color. **49.** 21.07 in. **51.** 14.4
53. 54.9 **55.** 99 **57.** $((455/18)+4\ln 36)\,2\pi$

Section 7.5, pp. 477–479

1. 400 ft · lb **3.** 780 J **5.** 72,900 ft · lb **7.** 4 cm, 0.08 J
9. a) 7238 lb/in. b) 904.78 in · lb, 2714.25 in · lb
11. a) 1,497,600 ft · lb
b) 1 hr, 39.8 min d) At 62.26 lb/ft³: a) 1,494,240 ft · lb
b) 1 hr, 39.6 min; at 62.59 lb/ft³: a) 1,502,160 ft · lb,
b) 1 hr, 40.1 min **13.** 38,484,510 J
15. 7,238,229.48 ft · lb
17. 91.32 in · oz **19.** 21,446,605.9 J
21. 967,610 ft · lb, at a cost of \$4838.05 **23.** 5.144×10^{10} J

Section 7.6, pp. 484–486

1. 114,511,052 lb, 28,627,763 lb **5.** 2808 lb **7.** a) 1164.8 lb
b) 1194.7 lb **9.** a) 374.4 lb b) 7.5 in. c) No
11. 2,261,952 lb **13.** 4.2 lb **15.** 41.6 lb
17. a) 93.33 lb b) 3 ft **19.** 1035.27 ft³ **21.** $wb/2$

Section 7.7, pp. 495–497

1. 4 ft **3.** $M_0=8, M=8, \bar{x}=1$
5. $M_0=15/2, M=9/2, \bar{x}=5/3$
7. $M_0=21/2, M=3+\ln 4, \bar{x}=\frac{21}{6+\ln 16}$
9. $M_0=3, M=3, \bar{x}=1$ **11.** $\bar{x}=0, \bar{y}=12/5$
13. $\bar{x}=1, \bar{y}=-3/5$ **15.** $\bar{x}=16/105, \bar{y}=8/15$
17. $\bar{x}=0, \bar{y}=\pi/8$ **19.** $\bar{x}=1, \bar{y}=-2/5$ **21.** $\bar{x}=\bar{y}=\frac{2}{4-\pi}$
23. a) $\bar{x}=\frac{1}{\ln 2}, \bar{y}=\frac{1}{\ln 16}$
b)

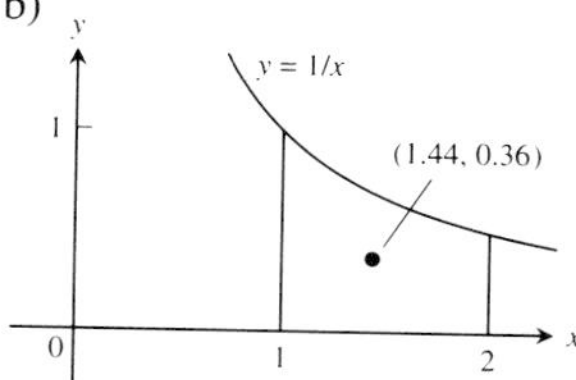

25. $\bar{x}=14/9, \bar{y}=(\ln 4)/3$
27. a) $224\pi/3$ b) $\bar{x}=3/\ln 4, \bar{y}=0$
c)

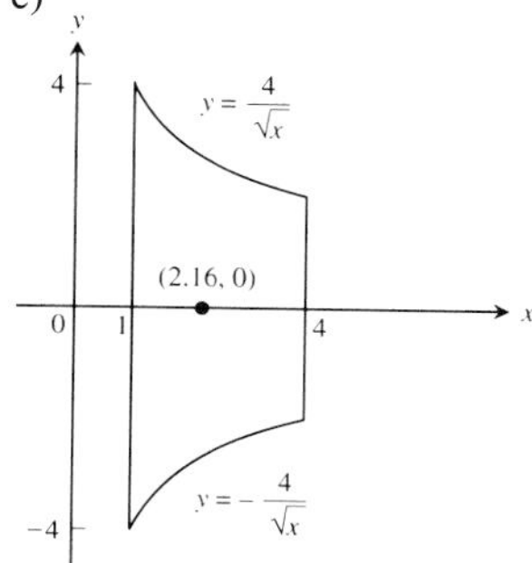

29. $\bar{x}=0, \bar{y}=1$ **31.** $\bar{x}=\bar{y}=a/3$
33. $V=32\pi, S=32\sqrt{2}\,\pi$ **35.** $4\pi^2$ **37.** $\bar{x}=0, \bar{y}=2a/\pi$

Section 7.8, pp. 504–506

1. 16 **3.** 16/3 **5.** a) $\frac{\pi}{4}\left(4\sqrt{3}-\frac{2\pi}{3}\right)$ b) $4\sqrt{3}-\frac{2\pi}{3}$
7. a) $\pi^2/2$ b) 2π **9.** 8π **11.** a) s^2h b) s^2h
15. b) 20 m c) 0 m **17.** b) 6 m c) 2 m
19. b) 245 m c) 0 m **21.** b) 6 m c) 4 m
23. b) $2<t<4$ c) 6 m d) 22/3 m
25. a) Total distance = 7, displacement = 3
b) Total distance = 19.5, displacement = −4.5
27. About 70% **29.** $\sqrt{3}\,\pi$ **31.** a) 210 ft³ b) 13,440 lb

Chapter 7 Practice Exercises, pp. 507–509

1. 1 **3.** 1/6 **5.** 18 **7.** 9/8 **9.** $(\pi^2/32)+\left(\sqrt{2}/2\right)-1$
11. 4 **13.** $\frac{8\sqrt{2}-7}{6}$ **15.** 3
17. a) 2π b) $10\pi/3$ c) $64\pi/5$ d) $128\pi/15$
19. a) 2π b) $26\pi/5$ c) π

21. a) $\pi((4\pi/3) - \sqrt{3})$ b) $\pi[(2\pi/3) + \sqrt{3}(1 - \ln 4)]$
23. a) $\pi \ln 16$ b) $\pi(12 - \ln 16)$ **25.** $28\pi/3$ **27.** $13/12$
29. $15 + \dfrac{\ln 2}{4}$ **31.** $28\pi\sqrt{2}/3$ **33.** 4π **35.** 4640 J
37. 10 ft · lb, 30 ft · lb **39.** 418,208.81 ft · lb **41.** 332.8 lb
43. 2200 lb **45.** $\bar{x} = 0, \bar{y} = 8/5$ **47.** $\bar{x} = 3/2, \bar{y} = 12/5$
49. $\bar{x} = 0, \bar{y} = 1/(4 \ln 2)$ **51.** $9\pi/280$ **53.** π^2 **55.** $72\pi/35$
57. a) 64/3 m b) 0 ft **59.** a) 15 m b) −5 m

Chapter 8

Section 8.1, pp. 515–516

1. $2\sqrt{8x^2+1} + C$ **3.** $2(\sin v)^{3/2} + C$ **5.** $\ln 5$
7. $2\ln(\sqrt{x}+1) + C$ **9.** $-\frac{1}{7}(\ln|\sin(3-7x)| + C$
11. $-\ln|\csc(e^\theta+1) + \cot(e^\theta+1)| + C$
13. $3\left(\ln\left|\sec\frac{t}{3} + \tan\frac{t}{3}\right|\right) + C$
15. $-\ln|\csc(s-\pi) + \cot(s-\pi)| + C$ **17.** 1
19. $e^{\tan v} + C$ **21.** $\dfrac{3^{(x+1)}}{\ln 3} + C$ **23.** $\dfrac{2^{\sqrt{w}}}{\ln 2} + C$
25. $3(\tan^{-1}3u) + C$ **27.** $\pi/18$ **29.** $\sin^{-1}s^2 + C$
31. $6\sec^{-1}|5x| + C$ **33.** $\sin^{-1}\left(\dfrac{x+1}{2}\right) + C$
35. $\tan^{-1}\left(\dfrac{t+1}{8}\right) + C$ **37.** $\sec^{-1}\left|\dfrac{x-1}{7}\right| + C$
39. $\tan x - 2\ln|\csc x + \cot x| - \cot x - x + C$
41. $\ln|\sin x| + \ln|\cos x| + C$ **43.** 4 **45.** $\sqrt{2}$ **47.** 2
49. $\ln|\sqrt{2}+1| - \ln|\sqrt{2}-1|$
51. $x - \ln|x+1| + C$ **53.** $7 + \ln 8$
55. $2t^2 - t + 2\tan^{-1}\left(\dfrac{t}{2}\right) + C$ **57.** $\sin^{-1}(x) + \sqrt{1-x^2} + C$
59. $\sqrt{2}$ **61.** $\dfrac{-2}{\tan(x/2)+1} + C$ **63.** $\ln|1+\sin\theta| + C$
65. $\cot x + x + \csc x + C$
67. a) $\sin\theta - \frac{1}{3}\sin^3\theta + C$
b) $\sin\theta - \frac{2}{3}\sin^3\theta + \frac{1}{5}\sin^5\theta + C$
c) $\int \cos^9\theta\, d\theta = \int \cos^8\theta(\cos\theta)\, d\theta = \int (1-\sin^2\theta)^4(\cos\theta)\, d\theta$
69. a) $\int \tan^3\theta\, d\theta = \frac{1}{2}\tan^2\theta - \int \tan\theta\, d\theta = \frac{1}{2}\tan^2\theta + \ln|\cos\theta| + C$
b) $\int \tan^5\theta\, d\theta = \frac{1}{4}\tan^4\theta - \int \tan^3\theta\, d\theta$
c) $\int \tan^7\theta\, d\theta = \frac{1}{6}\tan^6\theta - \int \tan^5\theta\, d\theta$
d) $\int \tan^{2k+1}\theta\, d\theta = \frac{1}{2k}\tan^{2k}\theta - \int \tan^{2k-1}\theta\, d\theta$
71. $2\sqrt{2} - \ln(3+2\sqrt{2})$ **73.** π^2 **75.** $\ln(2+\sqrt{3})$
77. $\bar{x} = 0, \bar{y} = \dfrac{1}{\ln(2\sqrt{2}+3)}$

Section 8.2, pp. 522–524

1. $-2x\cos(x/2) + 4\sin(x/2) + C$
3. $t^2\sin t + 2t\cos t - 2\sin t + C$ **5.** $\ln 4 - (3/4)$
7. $z\tan^{-1}(z) - \ln\sqrt{1+z^2} + C$ **9.** $x\tan x + \ln|\cos x| + C$
11. $(x^3 - 3x^2 + 6x - 6)e^x + C$ **13.** $(x^2 - 7x + 7)e^x + C$
15. $(x^5 - 5x^4 + 20x^3 - 60x^2 + 120x - 120)e^x + C$
17. $\dfrac{\pi^2-4}{8}$ **19.** $\dfrac{5\pi - 3\sqrt{3}}{9}$
21. $\frac{1}{2}[-e^\theta\cos\theta + e^\theta\sin\theta] + C$
23. $\dfrac{e^{2x}}{13}(3\sin 3x + 2\cos 3x) + C$
25. $\frac{2}{3}\left(\sqrt{3s+9}\,e^{\sqrt{3s+9}} - e^{\sqrt{3s+9}}\right) + C$
27. $\dfrac{\pi\sqrt{3}}{3} - \ln(2) - \dfrac{\pi^2}{18}$
29. $\frac{1}{2}[-x\cos(\ln x) + x\sin(\ln x)] + C$ **33.** $2\pi(1 - \ln 2)$
35. a) $\pi(\pi - 2)$ b) 2π
37. a) $\bar{x} = \dfrac{6-2e}{e-2}, \bar{y} = \dfrac{e^2-3}{8(e-2)}$
b)

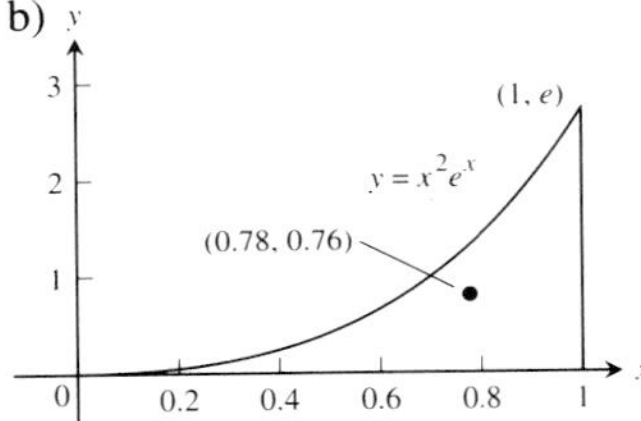

39. $\pi^2 + \pi - 4$ **41.** a) $\dfrac{1}{2\pi}\left(1 - e^{-2\pi}\right)$
43. $x\cos^{-1}x - \sqrt{1-x^2} + C$ **45.** $x\sinh^{-1}x - \sqrt{1+x^2} + C$
47. $x\tanh^{-1}x + \frac{1}{2}\ln(1-x^2) + C$

Section 8.3, pp. 527–529

1. $\dfrac{2}{x-3} + \dfrac{3}{x-2}$ **3.** $\dfrac{1}{x+1} + \dfrac{3}{(x+1)^2}$
5. $\dfrac{-2}{x} + \dfrac{-1}{x^2} + \dfrac{2}{x-1}$ **7.** $1 + \dfrac{17}{x-3} + \dfrac{-12}{x-2}$
9. $\frac{1}{2}[\ln|1+x| - \ln|1-x|] + C$
11. $\frac{1}{7}\ln|(x+6)^2(x-1)^5| + C$ **13.** $(\ln 15)/2$
15. $-\frac{1}{2}\ln|t| + \frac{1}{6}\ln|t+2| + \frac{1}{3}\ln|t-1| + C$ **17.** $3\ln 2 - 2$
19. $\frac{1}{4}\ln\left|\dfrac{x+1}{x-1}\right| - \dfrac{x}{2(x^2-1)} + C$
21. $\dfrac{(\tan^{-1}2x)^2}{4} - 3\ln|x-2| + \dfrac{6}{x-2} + C$
23. $x - \frac{3}{2}\tan^{-1}\frac{2}{3}x + C$ **25.** $\dfrac{y^2}{2} - \ln|y| + \frac{1}{2}\ln(1+y^2) + C$

27. $(\pi + 2\ln 2)/8$

29. $8\tan^{-1}\left(\frac{\theta}{2}\right) + \ln|\theta^2+4| + \frac{\theta^3}{3} - 4\theta + C$

31. $\tan^{-1} y - \frac{1}{y^2+1} + C$

33. $-(s-1)^{-2} + (s-1)^{-1} + \tan^{-1} s + C$

35. $\frac{-1}{\theta^2+2\theta+2} + \ln|\theta^2+2\theta+2| - \tan^{-1}(\theta+1) + C$

37. $\ln\left|\frac{e^t+1}{e^t+2}\right| + C$ **39.** $\frac{1}{5}\ln\left|\frac{\sin y - 2}{\sin y + 3}\right| + C$

41. $-x + 4\sqrt{x} - 4\ln(\sqrt{x}+1) + C$

43. $\frac{t^2\ln(t+5)}{2} + \frac{5t}{2} - \frac{t^2}{4} - \frac{25}{2}\ln|t+5| + C$ **45.** $3\pi\ln 25$

47. $(15\pi/4) + 2\pi\ln 4$ **49.** 1.10

51. a) $x = \frac{1000e^{4t}}{499+e^{4t}}$
b) 1.55 days **53.** $x = \ln|t-2| - \ln|t-1| + \ln 2$

55. $x = \frac{6t}{t+2} - 1$ **57.** a) $\frac{22}{7} - \pi$ b) 0.04%

Section 8.4, pp. 533–534

1. $\ln\left|\sqrt{9+y^2}+y\right| + C$ **3.** $\frac{1}{3}(x^2+4)^{3/2} - 4\sqrt{x^2+4} + C$

5. $\frac{-2\sqrt{4-w^2}}{w} + C$ **7.** $\frac{25}{2}\sin^{-1}\left(\frac{t}{5}\right) + \frac{t\sqrt{25-t^2}}{2} + C$

9. $\frac{\sqrt{x^2-1}}{x} + C$ **11.** $\frac{1}{2}\ln\left|\frac{2x}{7} + \frac{\sqrt{4x^2-49}}{7}\right| + C$

13. $\ln(1+\sqrt{2})$ **15.** $4\sqrt{3} - (4\pi/3)$ **17.** $-\frac{x}{\sqrt{x^2-1}} + C$

19. $1/\sqrt{2}$ **21.** $-\frac{1}{5}\left(\frac{\sqrt{1-x^2}}{x}\right)^5 + C$

23. $7\left[\frac{\sqrt{y^2-49}}{7} - \sec^{-1}\left(\frac{y}{7}\right)\right] + C$

25. $2\tan^{-1}2x + \frac{4x}{(4x^2+1)} + C$ **27.** $\frac{1}{3}\left(\frac{v}{\sqrt{1-v^2}}\right)^3 + C$

29. $\sec^{-1}|x| + C$ **31.** $\sqrt{x^2-1} + C$ **33.** $3\pi/4$

35. $y = 2\left[\frac{\sqrt{x^2-4}}{2} - \sec^{-1}\left(\frac{x}{2}\right)\right]$ **37.** $\frac{2}{1-\tan(x/2)} + C$

39. 1 **41.** $\frac{\sqrt{3}\,\pi}{9}$ **43.** $\frac{1}{\sqrt{2}}\ln\left|\frac{\tan(x/2)+1-\sqrt{2}}{\tan(x/2)+1+\sqrt{2}}\right| + C$

Section 8.5, pp. 540–542

1. $\frac{2}{\sqrt{3}}\left(\tan^{-1}\sqrt{\frac{x-3}{3}}\right) + C$ **3.** $\sqrt{x-2}\left(\frac{2(x-2)}{3} + 4\right) + C$

5. $\frac{(2x-3)^{3/2}(x+1)}{5} + C$

7. $\frac{-\sqrt{9-4x}}{x} - \frac{2}{3}\ln\left|\frac{\sqrt{9-4x}-3}{\sqrt{9-4x}+3}\right| + C$

9. $\frac{(x+2)(2x-6)\sqrt{4x-x^2}}{6} + 4\sin^{-1}\left(\frac{x-2}{2}\right) + C$

11. $-\frac{1}{\sqrt{7}}\ln\left|\frac{\sqrt{7}+\sqrt{7+x^2}}{x}\right| + C$

13. $\sqrt{4-x^2} - 2\ln\left|\frac{2+\sqrt{4-x^2}}{x}\right| + C$

15. $\frac{p}{2}\sqrt{25-p^2} + \frac{25}{2}\sin^{-1}\frac{p}{5} + C$

17. $2\sin^{-1}\frac{r}{2} - \frac{1}{2}r\sqrt{4-r^2} + C$

19. $-\frac{1}{3}\tan^{-1}\left[\frac{1}{3}\tan\left(\frac{\pi}{4}-\theta\right)\right] + C$

21. $\frac{e^{2t}}{13}(2\cos 3t + 3\sin 3t) + C$

23. $\frac{x^2}{2}\cos^{-1}(x) + \frac{1}{4}\sin^{-1}(x) - \frac{1}{4}x\sqrt{1-x^2} + C$

25. $\frac{x}{18(9-x^2)} + \frac{1}{108}\ln\left|\frac{x+3}{x-3}\right| + C$

27. $-\frac{\sqrt{4x+9}}{x} + \frac{2}{3}\ln\left|\frac{\sqrt{4x+9}-3}{\sqrt{4x+9}+3}\right| + C$

29. $2\sqrt{3x-4} - 4\tan^{-1}\sqrt{\frac{3x-4}{4}} + C$

31. $\frac{x^3}{3}\tan^{-1}x - \frac{x^2}{6} + \frac{1}{6}\ln(1+x^2) + C$

33. $\frac{1}{2}\ln|x^2+1| + \frac{x}{2(1+x^2)} + \frac{1}{2}\tan^{-1}x + C$

35. $\left(x - \frac{1}{2}\right)\sin^{-1}\sqrt{x} + \frac{1}{2}\sqrt{x-x^2} + C$

37. $\sin^{-1}\sqrt{x} - \sqrt{x}\sqrt{1-x} + C$

39. $\sqrt{1-\sin^2 t} - \ln\left|\frac{1-\sqrt{1+\sin^2 t}}{\sin t}\right| + C$

41. $\ln\left|\ln y + \sqrt{3+(\ln y)^2}\right| + C$ **43.** $\ln\left|3r + \sqrt{9r^2-1}\right| + C$

45. $\left[-\frac{\sin^4 2x\cos 2x}{10} - \frac{2\sin^2 2x\cos 2x}{15} - \frac{4\cos 2x}{15}\right] + C$

47. $\frac{\cos^3 2\pi t\sin 2\pi t}{\pi} + \frac{3}{2}\,\frac{\cos 2\pi t\sin 2\pi t}{\pi} + 3t + C$

49. $-\frac{\cos 5x}{10} - \frac{\cos x}{2} + C$ **51.** $8\left[\frac{\sin(7t/2)}{7} - \frac{\sin(9t/2)}{9}\right] + C$

53. $6\sin(\theta/12) + \frac{6}{7}\sin(7\theta/12) + C$

55. $\frac{\sin^3 2\theta\cos^2 2\theta}{10} + \frac{\sin^3 2\theta}{15} + C$ **57.** $\frac{2}{3}\sin^3 x + \cos^{-3} x + C$

59. $\tan^2 2x - 2\ln|\sec 2x| + C$

61. $8\left[-\frac{1}{3}\cot^3 t + \cot t + t\right] + C$

63. $\frac{(\sec\pi x)(\tan\pi x)}{\pi} + \frac{1}{\pi}\ln|\sec\pi x + \tan\pi x| + C$

65. $\frac{\sec^2 3x\tan 3x}{3} + \frac{2}{3}\tan 3x + C$

67. $\frac{-\csc^3 x\cot x}{4} - \frac{3\csc x\cot x}{8} - \frac{3}{8}\ln|\csc x + \cot x| + C$

69. $16\left(\frac{x^4(\ln x)^2}{4} - \frac{x^4(\ln x)}{8} + \frac{x^4}{32}\right) + C$ **71.** $\frac{e^{3x}}{9}(3x - 1) + C$
73. $2x^3 e^{x/2} - 12x^2 e^{x/2} + 96e^{x/2}((x/2) - 1) + C$
75. $\frac{x^2 2^x}{\ln 2} - \frac{2}{\ln 2}\left[\frac{x2^x}{\ln 2} - \frac{2^x}{(\ln 2)^2}\right] + C$ **77.** $\frac{x\pi^x}{\ln \pi} - \frac{\pi^x}{(\ln \pi)^2} + C$
79. $\sqrt{2} + \ln\left(\sqrt{2} + 1\right)$ **81.** $\pi/3$
83. $\frac{1}{2}\left[\sec(e^t - 1)\tan(e^t - 1) + \ln|\sec(e^t - 1) + \tan(e^t - 1)|\right] + C$
85. $x\cos^{-1}\sqrt{x} + \frac{1}{2}\sin^{-1}\sqrt{x} - \frac{1}{2}\sqrt{x}\sqrt{1 - x} + C$
95. $\pi\left(2\sqrt{3} + \sqrt{2}\ln(\sqrt{2} + \sqrt{3})\right)$ **97.** $\bar{x} = 4/3, \bar{y} = \ln\sqrt{2}$
99. 7.62

Section 8.6, pp. 550–551

1. $\pi/2$ **3.** $\ln 3$ **5.** 4 **7.** 1000 **9.** 6 **11.** 0
13. $\ln\left(1 + \frac{\pi}{2}\right)$ **15.** -1 **17.** $\pi/2$ **19.** $\pi/3$ **21.** 6 **23.** 2
25. $-1/4$ **27.** $\ln 4$ **29.** $\ln 2$ **31.** Diverges **33.** Converges
35. Converges **37.** Converges **39.** Diverges **41.** Converges
43. Converges **45.** Diverges **47.** Converges **49.** Converges
51. Diverges **53.** Converges **55.** Diverges **57.** Converges
59. Converges **65.** 1 **67.** 2π **69.** $\ln 2$

Chapter 8 Practice Exercises, pp. 552–555

1. $\frac{1}{12}(4x^2 - 9)^{3/2} + C$ **3.** $\frac{(2x + 1)^{5/2}}{10} - \frac{(2x + 1)^{3/2}}{6} + C$
5. $\frac{\sqrt{8x^2 + 1}}{8} + C$ **7.** $\frac{1}{2}\ln|25 + y^2| + C$
9. $\frac{-\sqrt{9 - 4t^4}}{8} + C$ **11.** $\frac{9}{25}(z^{5/3} + 1)^{5/3} + C$
13. $-\frac{1}{2(1 - \cos 2\theta)} + C$ **15.** $-\frac{1}{4}\ln|3 + 4\cos t| + C$
17. $-\frac{1}{2}e^{\cos 2x} + C$ **19.** $-\frac{1}{3}\cos^3(e^\theta) + C$ **21.** $\frac{2^{x-1}}{\ln 2} + C$
23. $\ln(\ln v) + C$ **25.** $\ln|2 + \tan^{-1} x| + C$
27. $\sin^{-1}(2x) + C$ **29.** $\frac{1}{3}\sin^{-1}\left(\frac{3t}{4}\right) + C$
31. $\frac{1}{3}\tan^{-1}\left(\frac{t}{3}\right) + C$ **33.** $\frac{1}{5}\sec^{-1}\left(\frac{5x}{4}\right) + C$
35. $\sin^{-1}\left(\frac{x - 2}{2}\right) + C$ **37.** $\frac{1}{2}\tan^{-1}\left(\frac{y - 2}{2}\right) + C$
39. $\sec^{-1}(x - 1) + C$ **41.** $\frac{x}{2} - \frac{\sin 2x}{4} + C$
43. $-\frac{2}{3}\sin^2\left(\frac{\theta}{2}\right)\cos\left(\frac{\theta}{2}\right) - \frac{4}{3}\cos\left(\frac{\theta}{2}\right) + C$
45. $\frac{\tan^2(2t)}{4} - \frac{1}{2}\ln|\sec 2t| + C$
47. $-\frac{1}{2}\ln|\csc(2x) + \cot(2x)| + C$ **49.** $\ln\sqrt{2}$ **51.** 2
53. $2\sqrt{2}$ **55.** $x - 2\tan^{-1}\left(\frac{x}{2}\right) + C$
57. $x + x^2 + 2\ln|2x - 1| + C$
59. $\ln|y^2 + 4| - \frac{1}{2}\tan^{-1}\left(\frac{y}{2}\right) + C$
61. $-\sqrt{4 - t^2} + 2\sin^{-1}\left(\frac{t}{2}\right) + C$
63. $2\left[\sin\left(\frac{x}{2}\right) - \cos\left(\frac{x}{2}\right)\right] + C$ **65.** $x - \tan x + \sec x + C$
67. $-\frac{1}{3}\ln|\sec(5 - 3x) + \tan(5 - 3x)| + C$
69. $4\ln\left|\sin\left(\frac{x}{4}\right)\right| + C$
71. $-2\left[\frac{(\sqrt{1 - x})^3}{3} - \frac{(\sqrt{1 - x})^5}{5}\right] + C$
73. $[(x + 1)(\ln(x + 1)) - (x + 1)] + C$
75. $x\tan^{-1}(3x) - \frac{1}{6}\ln(1 + 9x^2) + C$ **77.** $\frac{(\ln x)^2}{2} + C$
79. $(x + 1)^2 e^x - 2(x + 1)e^x + 2e^x + C$
81. $2\ln|x - 2| - \ln|x - 1| + C$
83. $\ln x - \ln(x + 1) + \frac{1}{x + 1} + C$
85. $-\frac{1}{3}\ln\left|\frac{\cos\theta - 1}{\cos\theta + 2}\right| + C$
87. $4\ln x - \frac{1}{2}\ln|x^2 + 1| + 4\tan^{-1} x + C$
89. $\frac{1}{16}\ln\left|\frac{(v - 2)^5(v + 2)}{v^6}\right| + C$
91. $\frac{1}{2}\tan^{-1} t - \frac{\sqrt{3}}{6}\tan^{-1}\frac{t}{\sqrt{3}} + C$
93. $\frac{x^2}{2} + \frac{4}{3}\ln|x + 2| + \frac{2}{3}\ln|x - 1| + C$
95. $\frac{x^2}{2} - \frac{9}{2}\ln|x + 3| + \frac{3}{2}\ln|x + 1| + C$
97. $\ln\left|\frac{x}{(3\sqrt{x} + 1)^2}\right| + C$ **99.** $\ln|1 - e^{-x}| + C$
101. $\frac{1}{2}\left[z\sqrt{z^2 + 1} + \ln\left|z + \sqrt{z^2 + 1}\right|\right] + C$
103. $\ln\left|y + \sqrt{25 + y^2}\right| + C$ **105.** $\frac{-\sqrt{1 - x^2}}{x} + C$
107. $\frac{\sin^{-1} x}{2} - \frac{x\sqrt{1 - x^2}}{2} + C$ **109.** $\ln\left|\frac{x}{3} + \frac{\sqrt{x^2 - 9}}{3}\right| + C$
111. $\sqrt{w^2 - 1} - \sec^{-1}|w| + C$ **113.** $\pi/2$ **115.** 6 **117.** $\ln 3$
119. 2 **121.** $\pi/6$ **123.** Diverges **125.** Converges
127. Converges
129. $\frac{2x^{3/2}}{3} - x + 2\sqrt{x} - 2\ln\left(\sqrt{x} + 1\right) + C$
131. $\ln\left|\frac{x}{\sqrt{x^2 + 1}}\right| - \frac{1}{2}\left(\frac{x}{\sqrt{x^2 + 1}}\right)^2 + C$

133. $\sin^{-1}(x+1)+C$ **135.** $\ln\left|u+\sqrt{1+u^2}\right|+C$
137. $-2\cot x-\ln|\csc x+\cot x|+\csc x+C$
139. $\frac{1}{12}\ln\left|\frac{3+v}{3-v}\right|+\frac{1}{6}\tan^{-1}\frac{v}{3}+C$
141. $\frac{\theta\sin(2\theta+1)}{2}+\frac{\cos(2\theta+1)}{4}+C$
143. $\frac{x^2}{2}+2x+3\ln|x-1|-\frac{1}{x-1}+C$
145. $-\cos 2\sqrt{x}+C$ **147.** $-\ln|\csc(2y)+\cot(2y)|+C$
149. $\frac{1}{2}\tan^2 x+C$ **151.** $-\sqrt{4-(r+2)^2}+C$ **153.** $\frac{1}{4}\sec^2\theta$
155. $\frac{\sqrt{2}}{2}$ **157.** $2\left[\frac{\left(\sqrt{2-x}\right)^3}{3}-2\sqrt{2-x}\right]+C$
159. $\tan^{-1}(y-1)+C$ **161.** $\frac{1}{3}\ln|\sec\theta^3|+C$
163. $\frac{1}{4}\ln|z|-\frac{1}{4z}-\frac{1}{4}\left[\frac{1}{2}\ln|z^2+4|+\frac{1}{2}\tan^{-1}\left(\frac{z}{2}\right)\right]+C$
165. $-\frac{1}{4}\sqrt{9-4t^2}+C$ **167.** $\ln|\sin\theta|-\frac{1}{2}\ln(1+\sin^2\theta)+C$
169. $\ln|\sec\sqrt{y}|+C$ **171.** $-\theta+\ln\left|\frac{\theta+2}{\theta-2}\right|+C$
173. $\sin e^x+C$ **175.** $-\frac{\cos x}{2}+C$ **177.** $\ln|1+e^t|+C$
179. 1/4 **181.** $\ln(\ln\sin v)+C$ **183.** $\frac{2}{3}x^{3/2}+C$
185. $-\frac{1}{5}\tan^{-1}\cos(5t)+C$ **187.** $\frac{1}{3}\left[\frac{27^{3\theta}+1}{\ln 27}\right]+C$
189. $2\sqrt{r}-2\ln\left|1+\sqrt{r}\right|+C$
191. $\ln\left|\frac{y}{y+2}\right|+\frac{2}{y}-\frac{2}{y^2}+C$ **193.** $4\sec^{-1}\left(\frac{7m}{2}\right)+C$
195. $-\sqrt{16-y^2}+C$ **197.** $-\frac{1}{2}\ln|4-x^2|+C$
199. 1 **201.** $32\pi/35$ **203.** 2π **205.** a) π b) $\pi(2e-5)$
207. b) $\pi\left(\frac{8(\ln 2)^2}{3}-\frac{16(\ln 2)}{9}+\frac{16}{27}\right)$ **209.** $\bar{x}=2/\pi,\ \bar{y}=0$
211. 6

Chapter 9

Section 9.1, pp. 564–566

1. $a_1=0,\ a_2=-1/4,\ a_3=-2/9,\ a_4=-3/16$
3. $a_1=1,\ a_2=-1/3,\ a_3=1/5,\ a_4=-1/7$
5. $a_n=(-1)^{n+1}$ **7.** $a_n=(-1)^{n+1}(n)^2$ **9.** $a_n=n^2-1$
11. $a_n=4n-3$ **13.** $1, \frac{3}{2}, \frac{7}{4}, \frac{15}{8}, \frac{31}{16}, \frac{63}{32}, \frac{127}{64}, \frac{255}{128}, \frac{511}{256}, \frac{1023}{512}$
15. $2, 1, -\frac{1}{2}, -\frac{1}{4}, \frac{1}{8}, \frac{1}{16}, -\frac{1}{32}, -\frac{1}{64}, \frac{1}{128}, \frac{1}{256}$
17. 1, 1, 2, 3, 5, 8, 13, 21, 34, 55 **19.** Converges, 2
21. Converges, -1 **23.** Converges, -5 **25.** Diverges
27. Diverges **29.** Converges, 1/2 **31.** Converges, 0
33. Converges, 0 **35.** Converges, $\sqrt{2}$ **37.** Converges, $\pi/2$
39. Converges, 0 **41.** Converges, 0 **43.** Converges, 1
45. Converges, e^7 **47.** Diverges **49.** Converges, 1
51. Converges, 1 **53.** Diverges **55.** Converges, 0
57. Converges, 0 **59.** Converges, e^{-1} **61.** Diverges
63. Converges, 1 **65.** Converges, 1 **67.** Converges, 0
69. Converges, 1/2 **73.** $N=692$ **75.** $N=65$
77. a) No
b) $a_1=\$1002.15$, $a_2=\$1004.31$, $a_3=\$1006.47$, $a_4=\$1008.64$, $a_5=\$1010.81$, $a_6=\$1012.98$, $a_7=\$1015.17$, $a_8=\$1017.35$, $a_9=\$1019.54$, $a_{10}=\$1021.73$ **79.** $x_n=2^{n-2}$ for $n\geq 2$
81. a) Converges, $\approx\sqrt{2}$ b) Converges, $\approx\pi/4$ c) Diverges

Section 9.2, pp. 574–576

1. $s_n=\frac{2(1-(1/3)^n)}{1-(1/3)}, 3$ **3.** $s_n=\frac{1-(-1/2)^n}{1-(-1/2)}, 2/3$
5. $s_n=\frac{1}{2}-\frac{1}{n+2}, \frac{1}{2}$ **7.** $1-\frac{1}{4}+\frac{1}{16}-\frac{1}{64}+\cdots, \frac{4}{5}$
9. $\frac{7}{4}+\frac{7}{16}+\frac{7}{64}+\cdots, \frac{7}{3}$
11. $(5+1)+\left(\frac{5}{2}+\frac{1}{3}\right)+\left(\frac{5}{4}+\frac{1}{9}\right)+\left(\frac{5}{8}+\frac{1}{27}\right)+\cdots, \frac{23}{2}$
13. $(1+1)+\left(\frac{1}{2}-\frac{1}{5}\right)+\left(\frac{1}{4}+\frac{1}{25}\right)+\left(\frac{1}{8}-\frac{1}{125}\right)+\cdots, \frac{17}{6}$
15. 1 **17.** 5 **19.** Converges, $2+\sqrt{2}$ **21.** Converges, 1
23. Diverges **25.** Converges, $\frac{e^2}{e^2-1}$ **27.** Diverges
29. Converges, 3/2 **31.** Diverges **33.** Diverges
35. Converges, 1 **37.** Converges, $-\frac{1}{\ln 2}$
39. $a=1,\ r=-x,\ |x|<1$
41. $a=3,\ r=(x-1)/2,\ -1<x<3$ **43.** 23/99
45. 7/9 **47.** 1/15 **49.** 41333/33300 **51.** 28 m
53. a) $\sum_{n=-2}^{\infty}\frac{1}{(n+4)(n+5)}$ b) $\sum_{n=0}^{\infty}\frac{1}{(n+2)(n+3)}$
c) $\sum_{n=5}^{\infty}\frac{1}{(n-3)(n-2)}$ **55.** 8 m²
57. a) $3\left(\frac{4}{3}\right)^{n-1}$ b) The area enclosed by C_n, $n\geq 2$, is $A_n=A+\frac{1}{3}A+\frac{1}{3}\left(\frac{4}{9}\right)A+\cdots+\frac{1}{3}\left(\frac{4}{9}\right)^{n-2}A$, where $A=\sqrt{3}/4$ is the area of C_1. $\lim_{n\to\infty}A_n=2\sqrt{3}/5$.

Section 9.3, pp. 584–585

1. Converges; geometric series, $r=\frac{1}{10}<1$
3. Diverges; $\lim_{n\to\infty}\frac{n}{n+1}=1\neq 0$
5. Diverges; compare with $\sum\frac{1}{n^{1/2}}$
7. Converges; compare with $\sum\frac{1}{2^n}$

9. Converges; geometric series, $r = 1/8 < 1$
11. Diverges; compare with $\Sigma\ 1/n$
13. Converges; geometric series, $r = 2/3 < 1$
15. Diverges; compare with $\Sigma\ 1/(n+1)$
17. Diverges; $\lim_{n\to\infty} \frac{2^n}{n+1} \neq 0$
19. Converges; compare with $\sum \frac{1}{n^{3/2}}$
21. Diverges; $\frac{1}{n} \le \frac{\sqrt{n}}{n} \le \frac{\sqrt{n}}{\ln n}$ for $n \ge 2$
23. Diverges; direct comparison to $\Sigma(1/n)$
25. Converges; limit comparison with $\Sigma(1/n^2)$
27. Diverges; $3n > n\sqrt[n]{n} \Rightarrow \frac{1}{3n} < \frac{1}{n\sqrt[n]{n}} \Rightarrow \sum_{n=1}^{\infty} \frac{1}{n\sqrt[n]{n}}$ diverges
29. Diverges; $\lim_{n\to\infty}\left(1+\frac{1}{n}\right)^n = e \neq 0$
31. Converges; $\frac{1}{n2^n} < \frac{1}{2^n}$
33. Diverges; geometric series, $r = \frac{1}{\ln 2} > 1$
35. Converges; $\frac{1}{3^{n-1}+1} < \frac{1}{3^{n-1}}$
37. Diverges; limit comparison with $\Sigma(1/n)$
39. Diverges; nth-Term Test
41. Converges; compare with $\Sigma\ 4\pi/(1+n^2)$ or use Integral Test
43. Converges; compare with $\Sigma\ 1/n^2$
45. Converges; $\frac{\tan^{-1} n}{n^{1.1}} < \frac{\pi/2}{n^{1.1}}$ **47.** Converges; Integral Test
49. Converges; compare with $\sum \frac{1}{e^n}$
51. Converges; compare with $\sum \frac{1}{e^n}$
53. Converges; compare with $\sum \frac{1}{n^2}$ **55.** b) About 41.55
61. b) By the Integral Test, the series would converge if $p > 1$ and diverge if $p \le 1$.

Section 9.4, p. 590

1. Converges; Ratio Test **3.** Diverges; Ratio Test
5. Converges; Ratio Test
7. Converges; compare with $\Sigma\ 3/(1.25)^n$
9. Diverges; $\lim_{n\to\infty}\left(1-\frac{3}{n}\right)^n = e^{-3} \neq 0$
11. Converges; compare with $\Sigma\ 1/n^2$
13. Diverges; $\sum_{n=1}^{\infty} \frac{n-1}{n^2} = \sum_{n=1}^{\infty} \frac{1}{n} - \sum_{n=1}^{\infty} \frac{1}{n^2}$. The difference between a divergent and a convergent series diverges.
15. Diverges; compare with $\Sigma\ 1/n$ **17.** Converges; Ratio Test
19. Converges; Ratio Test **21.** Converges; Ratio Test
23. Converges; Root Test **25.** Converges; compare with $\Sigma\ 1/n^2$
27. Converges; Ratio Test **29.** Diverges; Ratio Test
31. Converges; Ratio Test **33.** Converges; Ratio Test
35. Diverges; $a_n = (1/3)^{(1/n!)} \to 1$ **37.** Converges; Ratio Test
39. Diverges; Root Test **41.** Converges; Root Test

Section 9.5, pp. 596–597

1. Converges by Theorem 8 **3.** Diverges, $a_n \not\to 0$
5. Converges by Theorem 8 **7.** Diverges, $a_n \to 1/2$
9. Converges by Theorem 8
11. Converges absolutely. Series of absolute values is a convergent geometric series.
13. Converges conditionally; $1/\sqrt{n} \to 0$ but $\sum_{n=1}^{\infty} \frac{1}{\sqrt{n}}$ diverges.
15. Converges absolutely; compare with $\Sigma_{n=1}^{\infty}\ 1/n^2$
17. Converges conditionally; $1/(n+3) \to 0$ but $\Sigma_{n=1}^{\infty} \frac{1}{n+3}$ diverges (compare with $\Sigma_{n=1}^{\infty}\ 1/n$)
19. Diverges; $\frac{3+n}{5+n} \to 1$
21. Converges conditionally; $\left(\frac{1}{n^2}+\frac{1}{n}\right) \to 0$ but $(1+n)/n^2 > 1/n$
23. Converges absolutely; Root Test
25. Converges absolutely by Integral Test **27.** Diverges, $a_n \not\to 0$
29. Converges absolutely by the Ratio Test
31. Converges absolutely; $\frac{1}{n^2+2n+1} < \frac{1}{n^2}$
33. Converges absolutely since $\left|\frac{\cos n\pi}{n\sqrt{n}}\right| = \left|\frac{(-1)^{n+1}}{n^{3/2}}\right| = \frac{1}{n^{3/2}}$ (convergent p-series)
35. Converges absolutely by Root Test **37.** Diverges; $a_n \to \infty$
39. Converges conditionally; $\sqrt{n+1} - \sqrt{n} = 1/(\sqrt{n} + \sqrt{n+1}) \to 0$, but series of absolute values diverges (compare with $\Sigma(1/\sqrt{n})$)
41. Converges absolutely; $\operatorname{sech} n = \frac{2}{e^n + e^{-n}} = \frac{2e^n}{e^{2n}+1} < \frac{2e^n}{e^{2n}} = \frac{2}{e^n}$, a term from a convergent geometric series
43. $|\text{error}| < 0.2$ **45.** $|\text{error}| < 2 \times 10^{-11}$ **47.** 0.54030
49. a) The condition that $a_n \ge a_{n+1}$ for all n fails to hold because $1/3^n < 1/2^n$ for $n \ge 1$. b) $-1/2$

Section 9.6, pp. 604–605

1. a) $1, -1 < x < 1$ b) $-1 < x < 1$ c) None
3. a) $1/4, -1/2 < x < 0$ b) $-1/2 < x < 0$ c) None
5. a) $10, -8 < x < 12$ b) $-8 < x < 12$ c) None
7. a) $1, -1 < x < 1$ b) $-1 < x < 1$ c) None
9. a) $3, -3 \le x \le 3$ b) $-3 \le x \le 3$ c) None
11. a) ∞, for all x b) For all x c) None
13. a) ∞, for all x b) For all x c) None
15. a) $1, -1 \le x < 1$ b) $-1 < x < 1$ c) $x = -1$
17. a) $5, -8 < x < 2$ b) $-8 < x < 2$ c) None
19. a) $3, -3 < x < 3$ b) $-3 < x < 3$ c) None
21. a) $1, -1 < x < 1$ b) $-1 < x < 1$ c) None
23. a) $0, x = 0$ b) $x = 0$ c) None
25. a) $2, -4 < x \le 0$ b) $-4 < x < 0$ c) $x = 0$
27. a) $1, -1 \le x \le 1$ b) $-1 \le x \le 1$ c) None
29. a) $1, 1 \le x \le 3/2$ b) $1 \le x \le 3/2$ c) None
31. a) $1, (-1-\pi) \le x < (1-\pi)$

b) $(-1-\pi) < x < (1-\pi)$ c) $x = -1-\pi$
33. $-1 < x < 3,\ 4/(3+2x-x^2)$ **35.** $0 < x < 16,\ 2/(4-\sqrt{x})$
37. $-\sqrt{2} < x < \sqrt{2},\ 3/(2-x^2)$
39. $1 < x < 5,\ 2/(x-1),\ 1 < x < 5,\ -2/(x-1)^2$
41. a) $\frac{x^2}{2} + \frac{x^4}{12} + \frac{x^6}{45} + \frac{17x^8}{2520} + \frac{31x^{10}}{14175},\ -\frac{\pi}{2} < x < \frac{\pi}{2}$
b) $1 + x^2 + \frac{2x^4}{3} + \frac{17x^6}{45} + \frac{62x^8}{315} + \cdots,\ -\frac{\pi}{2} < x < \frac{\pi}{2}$

Section 9.7, pp. 617–618

1. $P_0(x) = 0,\ P_1(x) = x-1,\ P_2(x) = (x-1) - \frac{1}{2}(x-1)^2,$
$P_3(x) = (x-1) - \frac{1}{2}(x-1)^2 + \frac{1}{3}(x-1)^3$
3. $P_0(x) = \frac{1}{2},\ P_1(x) = \frac{1}{2} - \frac{1}{4}(x-2),\ P_2(x) = \frac{1}{2} - \frac{1}{4}(x-2) + \frac{1}{8}(x-2)^2,\ P_3(x) = \frac{1}{2} - \frac{1}{4}(x-2) + \frac{1}{8}(x-2)^2 - \frac{1}{16}(x-2)^3$
5. $P_0(x) = \frac{\sqrt{2}}{2},\ P_1(x) = \frac{\sqrt{2}}{2} + \frac{\sqrt{2}}{2}\left(x-\frac{\pi}{4}\right),\ P_2(x) = \frac{\sqrt{2}}{2} + \frac{\sqrt{2}}{2}\left(x-\frac{\pi}{4}\right) - \frac{\sqrt{2}}{4}\left(x-\frac{\pi}{4}\right)^2,\ P_3(x) = \frac{\sqrt{2}}{2} + \frac{\sqrt{2}}{2}\left(x-\frac{\pi}{4}\right) - \frac{\sqrt{2}}{4}\left(x-\frac{\pi}{4}\right)^2 - \frac{\sqrt{2}}{12}\left(x-\frac{\pi}{4}\right)^3$
7. $P_0(x) = 2,\ P_1(x) = 2 + \frac{1}{4}(x-4),\ P_2(x) = 2 + \frac{1}{4}(x-4) - \frac{1}{64}(x-4)^2,\ P_3(x) = 2 + \frac{1}{4}(x-4) - \frac{1}{64}(x-4)^2 + \frac{1}{512}(x-4)^3$
9. $\sum_{n=0}^{\infty} \frac{(-x)^n}{n!} = 1 - x + \frac{x^2}{2!} - \frac{x^3}{3!} + \frac{x^4}{4!} - \cdots$
11. $\sum_{n=0}^{\infty} \frac{(-1)^n 3^{2n+1} x^{2n+1}}{(2n+1)!}$ **13.** $7\sum_{n=0}^{\infty} \frac{(-1)^n x^{2n}}{(2n)!}$
15. $\sum_{n=0}^{\infty} \frac{(-1)^n x^n}{(2n)!}$ **17.** $x + x^2 + \frac{x^3}{2!} + \frac{x^4}{3!} + \frac{x^5}{4!} + \cdots$
19. $1 - \frac{x^2}{3!} + \frac{x^4}{5!} - \frac{x^6}{7!} + \cdots$ **21.** $\frac{x^4}{4!} - \frac{x^6}{6!} + \frac{x^8}{8!} - \frac{x^{10}}{10!} + \cdots$
23. $1 - \frac{(2x)^2}{2\cdot 2!} + \frac{(2x)^4}{2\cdot 4!} - \frac{(2x)^6}{2\cdot 6!} + \frac{(2x)^8}{2\cdot 8!} - \cdots$
25. $1 + \frac{x^2}{2!} + \frac{x^4}{4!} + \frac{x^6}{6!} + \cdots$
27. $1 + x + \frac{x^2}{2} + \frac{f'''(c)}{3!}x^3$, where c is between 0 and x
29. $-\frac{x^2}{2} + \frac{f'''(c)}{3!}x^3$, where c is between 0 and x
31. $x + \frac{f'''(c)}{3!}x^3$, where c is between 0 and x
35. $|x| < (0.06)^{1/5} < 0.56968$
37. $|\text{error}| < (10^{-3})^3/6 < 1.67 \times 10^{-10},\ -10^{-3} < x < 0$
39. $|\text{error}| < (3^{0.1})(0.1)^3/6 < 1.87 \times 10^{-5}$
41. $\sin x,\ x = 0.1,\ \sin(0.1)$

45. $2x - \frac{8x^3}{3!} + \frac{32x^5}{5!} - \frac{128x^7}{7!} + \frac{512x^9}{9!} - \cdots$
51. a) -1 b) $(1/\sqrt{2})(1+i)$ c) $-i$
55. $x + x^2 + \frac{1}{3}x^3 - \frac{1}{30}x^5 \cdots$; will converge for all x

Section 9.8, p. 625

1. $1 + \frac{x}{2} - \frac{x^2}{8} + \frac{x^3}{16}$ **3.** $1 + x - x^2 + \frac{5x^3}{3}$
5. $1 - x + \frac{3x^2}{4} - \frac{x^3}{2}$ **7.** $1 - \frac{x^3}{2} + \frac{3x^6}{8} - \frac{5x^9}{16}$
9. $1 + \frac{1}{2x} - \frac{1}{8x^2} + \frac{1}{16x^3}$
11. $(1+x)^4 = 1 + 4x + 6x^2 + 4x^3 + x^4$
13. $(1-2x)^3 = 1 - 6x + 12x^2 - 8x^3$ **15.** 0.00267
17. 0.00033 **19.** 0.36331 **21.** 0.1 **23.** 0.0999 44461 1
25. 0.1000 01 **29.** 500 terms **31.** 3 terms
33. a) $x + \frac{x^3}{6} + \frac{3x^5}{40} + \frac{5x^7}{112}, 1$ b) $\frac{\pi}{2} - x - \frac{x^3}{6} - \frac{3x^5}{40} - \frac{5x^7}{112}$
35. $1 - 2x + 3x^2 - 4x^3 + \cdots$ **37.** $y = \sum_{n=0}^{\infty} \frac{(-1)^n}{n!}x^n = e^{-x}$
39. $y = \sum_{n=1}^{\infty} x^n/n! = e^x - 1$ **41.** $y = \sum_{n=0}^{\infty} \frac{2^n}{n!}x^n = e^{2x}$
43. $y = \sum_{n=2}^{\infty} x^n/n! = e^x - x - 1$
45. $y = \sum_{n=2}^{\infty} \frac{(-1)^n}{n!}x^n = e^{-x} + x - 1$

Chapter 9 Practice Exercises, pp. 626–627

1. Converges to 1 **3.** Converges to -1 **5.** Diverges
7. Converges to 0 **9.** Converges to 1 **11.** Converges to e^5
13. Converges to 3 **15.** Diverges **17.** 1/6 **19.** 3/2
21. $e/(e-1)$ **23.** Diverges **25.** Converges conditionally
27. Converges conditionally **29.** Converges absolutely
31. Converges absolutely **33.** Converges absolutely
35. Converges absolutely **37.** Converges absolutely
39. a) $3,\ -7 \le x < -1$ b) $-7 < x < -1$ c) $x = -7$
41. a) $1/3,\ 0 \le x \le 2/3$ b) $0 \le x \le 2/3$ c) None
43. a) ∞, for all x b) For all x c) None
45. a) $\sqrt{3},\ -\sqrt{3} < x < \sqrt{3}$ b) $-\sqrt{3} < x < \sqrt{3}$ c) None
47. b) $|\text{error}| < |\sin(1/41)| < 0.02439$; an overestimate because the remainder is negative
49. $\frac{1}{1+x}, \frac{1}{4}, \frac{4}{5}$ **51.** $\sin x,\ \pi,\ 0$ **53.** e^x, ln 2, 2
55. $2 - \frac{(x+1)}{2\cdot 1!} + \frac{3(x+1)^2}{2^3\cdot 2!} + \frac{9(x+1)^3}{2^5\cdot 3!} + \cdots$
57. $\sum_{n=0}^{\infty} 2^n x^n$ **59.** $\sum_{n=0}^{\infty} \frac{(-1)^n \pi^{2n+1} x^{2n+1}}{(2n+1)!}$ **61.** $\sum_{n=0}^{\infty} \frac{(-1)^n x^{5n}}{(2n)!}$
63. $\sum_{n=0}^{\infty} \frac{((\pi x)/2)^n}{n!}$ **65.** 0.4849 17143 1

67. Diverges. The nth partial sum $\ln\left(\frac{1}{2}\right) + \ln\left(\frac{2}{3}\right) + \cdots + \ln\left(\frac{n-1}{n}\right) + \ln\left(\frac{n}{n+1}\right) = \ln\left(\frac{1}{2}\cdot\frac{2}{3}\cdot \cdots \cdot \frac{n-1}{n}\cdot\frac{n}{n+1}\right) = \ln\left(\frac{1}{n+1}\right)$ approaches $-\infty$ as $n \to \infty$.

73. $y = \sum_{n=0}^{\infty} \frac{(-1)^{n+1}}{n!} x^n = -e^{-x}$

75. $y = 1 + x + 2\sum_{n=0}^{\infty} x^n/n! = 2e^x - 1 - x$

21. $e = 1/\sqrt{3}$ **23.** $e = \sqrt{3}/3$

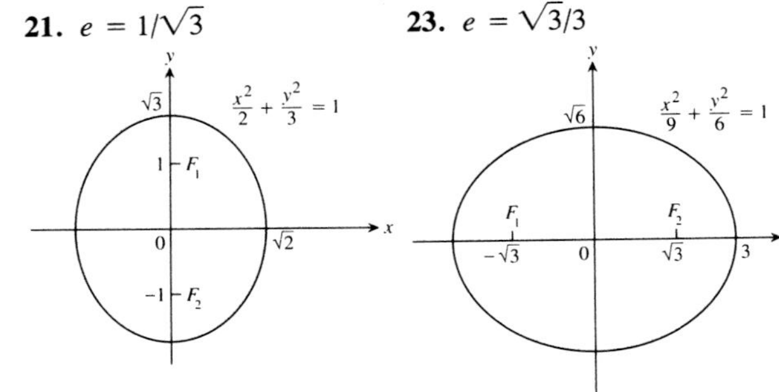

Chapter 10

Section 10.1, pp. 641–644

1. $y^2 = 8x$, $F(2, 0)$; Directrix; $x = -2$

3. $x^2 = -6y$, $F(0, -3/2)$; Directrix: $y = 3/2$

5. $x^2/4 - y^2/9 = 1$, $F(\pm\sqrt{13}, 0)$, $e = \sqrt{13}/2$; Directrices: $x = \pm 4/\sqrt{13}$; Asymptotes: $y = \pm\frac{3}{2}x$

7. $x^2/2 + y^2 = 1$, $F(\pm 1, 0)$, $e = 1/\sqrt{2}$; Directrices: $x = \pm 2$

9.

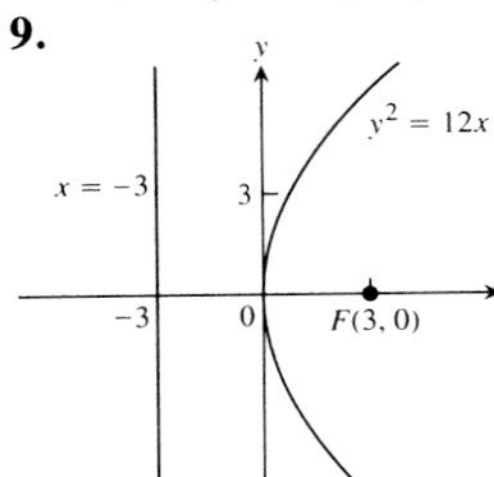

11.

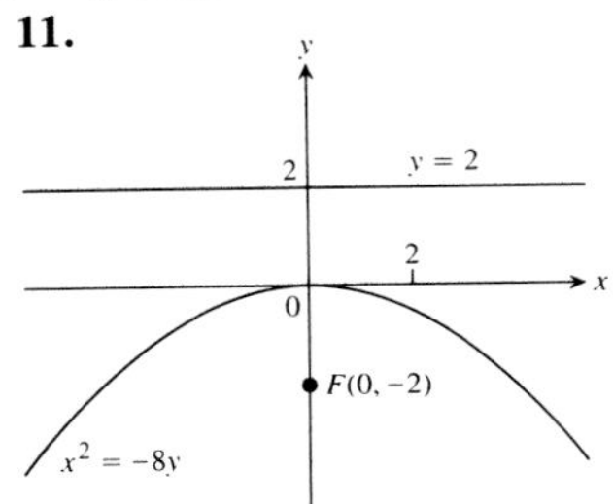

13. **15.**

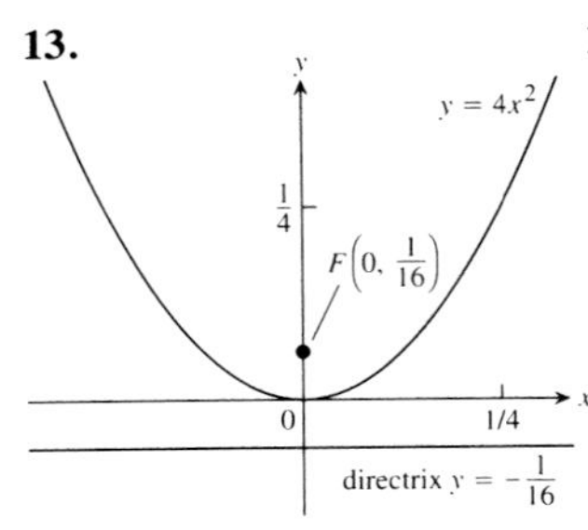

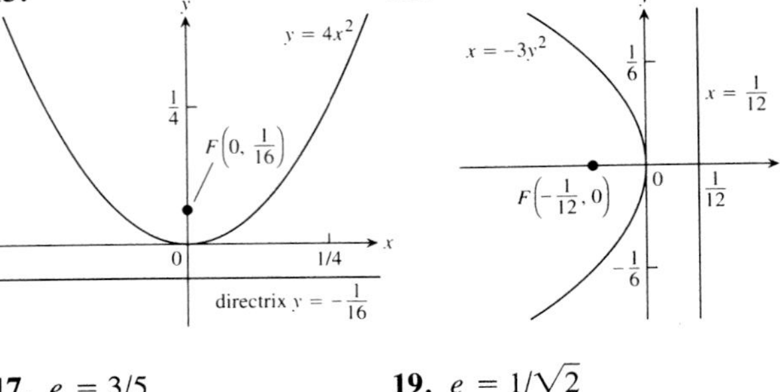

17. $e = 3/5$ **19.** $e = 1/\sqrt{2}$

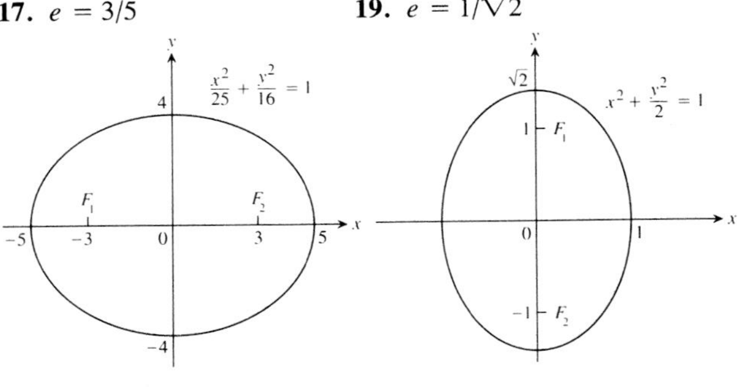

25. $e = \sqrt{2}$; Asymptotes: $y = \pm x$

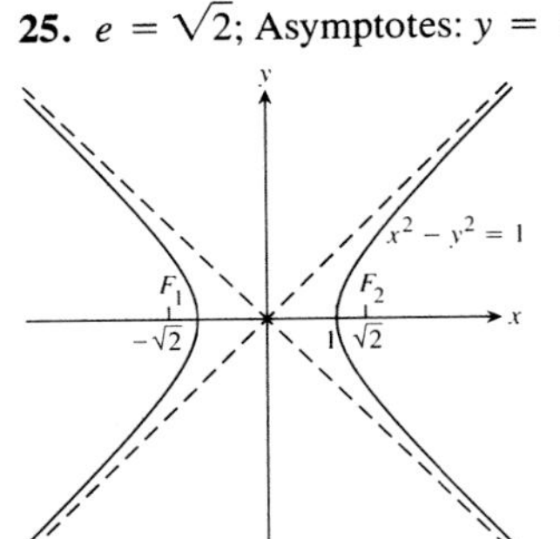

27. $e = \sqrt{2}$; Asymptotes: $y = \pm x$

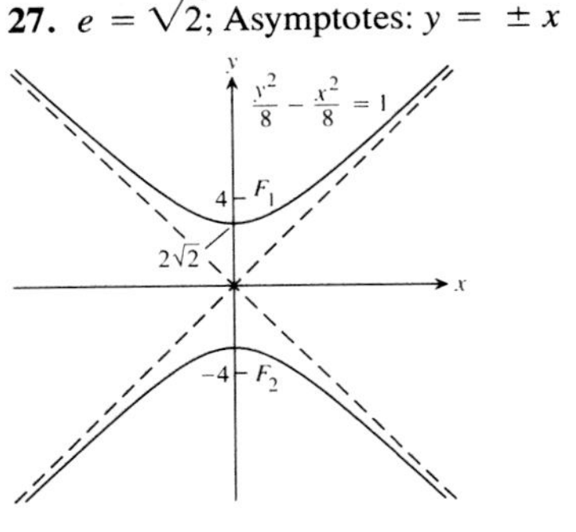

29. $e = \sqrt{5}$; Asymptotes: $y = \pm 2x$

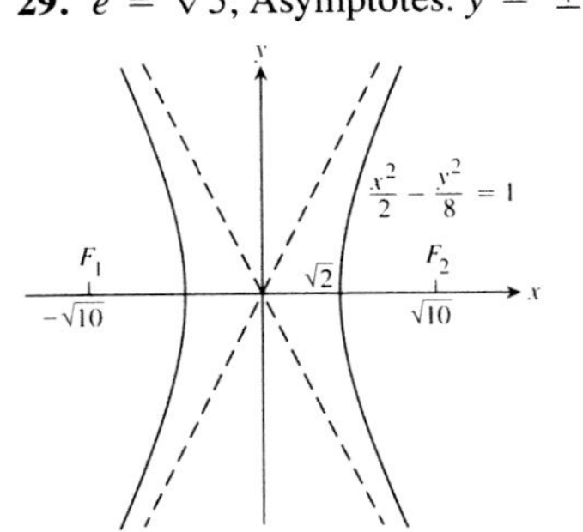

31. $e = \sqrt{5}$; Asymptotes: $y = \pm x/2$

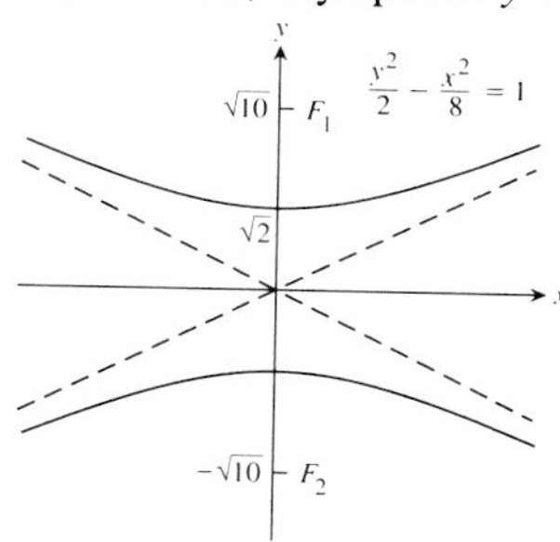

35. Length $= 2\sqrt{2}$, Width $= \sqrt{2}$, Area $= 4$ **37.** 24π

47. a) Vertex: $(1, -2)$; Focus: $(3, -2)$; Directrix: $x = -1$

b)

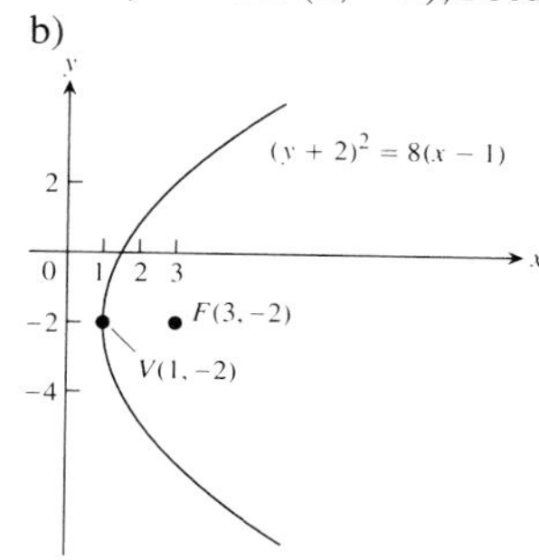

49. a) Foci: $(4 \pm \sqrt{7}, 3)$; Vertices: $(8, 3)$ and $(0, 3)$; Center: $(4, 3)$

b)

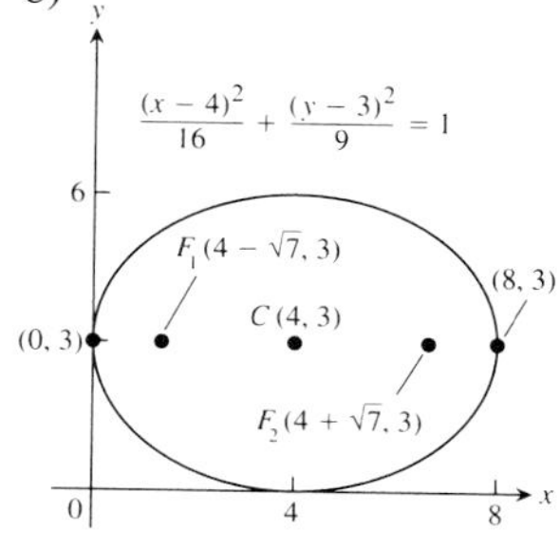

51. a) Center: $(2, 0)$; Foci: $(7, 0)$ and $(-3, 0)$; Vertices: $(6, 0)$ and $(-2, 0)$; Asymptotes: $y = \pm\frac{3}{4}(x - 2)$

b)

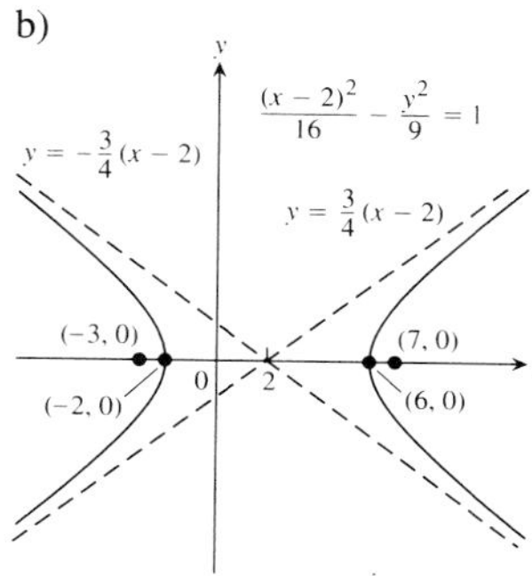

53. $(y + 3)^2 = 4(x + 2)$, $V(-2, -3)$, $F(-1, -3)$; Directrix: $x = -3$

55. $(x - 1)^2 = 8(y + 7)$, $V(1, -7)$, $F(1, -5)$; Directrix: $y = -9$

57. $\frac{(x + 2)^2}{6} + \frac{(y + 1)^2}{9} = 1$, $F(-2, \pm\sqrt{3} - 1)$, $V(-2, \pm 3 - 1)$, $C(-2, -1)$

59. $\frac{(x - 2)^2}{3} + \frac{(y - 3)^2}{2} = 1$, $F(3, 3)$ and $F(1, 3)$, $V(\pm\sqrt{3} + 2, 3)$, $C(2, 3)$

61. $\frac{(x - 2)^2}{4} - \frac{(y - 2)^2}{5} = 1$, $C(2, 2)$, $F(5, 2)$ and $F(-1, 2)$, $V(4, 2)$ and $V(0, 2)$; Asymptotes: $(y - 2) = \pm\frac{\sqrt{5}}{2}(x - 2)$

63. $(y + 1)^2 - (x + 1)^2 = 1$, $C(-1, -1)$, $F(-1, \sqrt{2} - 1)$ and $F(-1, -\sqrt{2} - 1)$, $V(-1, 0)$ and $V(-1, -2)$; Asymptotes: $(y + 1) = \pm(x + 1)$

65. Ellipse: $\frac{(x + 2)^2}{5} + y^2 = 1$, $C(-2, 0)$, $F(0, 0)$ and $F(-4, 0)$, $V(\sqrt{5} - 2, 0)$ and $V(-\sqrt{5} - 2, 0)$

67. Ellipse: $\frac{(x - 1)^2}{2} + (y - 1)^2 = 1$, $C(1, 1)$, $F(2, 1)$ and $F(0, 1)$, $V(\sqrt{2} + 1, 1)$ and $V(-\sqrt{2} + 1, 1)$

69. Hyperbola: $(x - 1)^2 - (y - 2)^2 = 1$, $C(1, 2)$, $F(1 + \sqrt{2}, 2)$ and $F(1 - \sqrt{2}, 2)$, $V(2, 2)$ and $V(0, 2)$; Asymptotes: $(y - 2) = \pm(x - 1)$

71. Hyperbola: $\frac{(y - 3)^2}{6} - \frac{x^2}{3} = 1$, $C(0, 3)$, $F(0, 6)$ and $F(0, 0)$, $V(0, \sqrt{6} + 3)$ and $V(0, -\sqrt{6} + 3)$; Asymptotes: $y = \sqrt{2}x + 3$ or $y = -\sqrt{2}x + 3$

Section 10.2, pp. 649–650

1. Hyperbola **3.** Ellipse **5.** Parabola **7.** Parabola **9.** Hyperbola **11.** Hyperbola **13.** Ellipse **15.** Ellipse **17.** $x'^2 - y'^2 = 4$, hyperbola **19.** $4x'^2 + 16y' = 0$, parabola **21.** $y'^2 = 1$, parallel lines **23.** $2\sqrt{2}x'^2 + 8\sqrt{2}y' = 0$, parabola **25.** $4x'^2 + 2y'^2 = 19$, ellipse **27.** $A' = 0.88$, $B' = 0.00$, $C' = 3.10$, $D' = 0.74$, $E' = -1.20$, $F' = -3$, $0.88x'^2 + 3.10y'^2 + 0.74x' - 1.20y' - 3 = 0$, ellipse **29.** $A' = 0.00$, $B' = 0.00$, $C' = 5.00$, $D' = 0$, $E' = 0$, $F' = -5$, $5.00y'^2 - 5 = 0$ or $y' = \pm 1.00$, parallel lines **31.** $A' = 5.05$, $B' = 0.00$, $C' = -0.05$, $D' = -5.07$, $E' = -6.18$, $F' = -1$, $5.05x'^2 - 0.05y'^2 - 5.07x' - 6.18y' - 1 = 0$, hyperbola **33.** a) $\frac{x'^2}{b^2} + \frac{y'^2}{a^2} = 1$ b) $\frac{y'^2}{a^2} - \frac{x'^2}{b^2} = 1$ c) $x'^2 + y'^2 = a^2$ d) $y' = -\frac{1}{m}x'$ e) $y' = -\frac{1}{m}x' + \frac{b}{m}$

35. a) $x'^2 - y'^2 = 2$ b) $x'^2 - y'^2 = 2a$

Section 10.3, pp. 654–656

1.

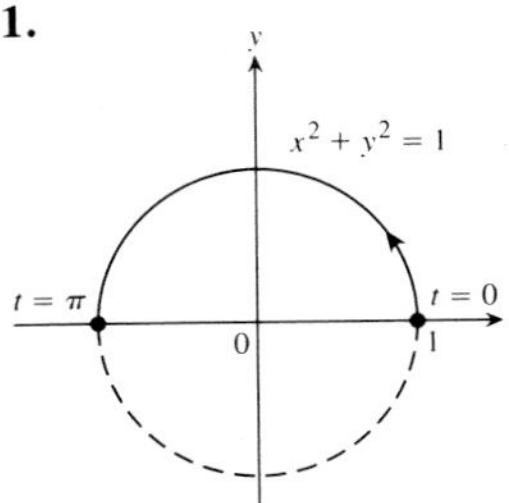

3.

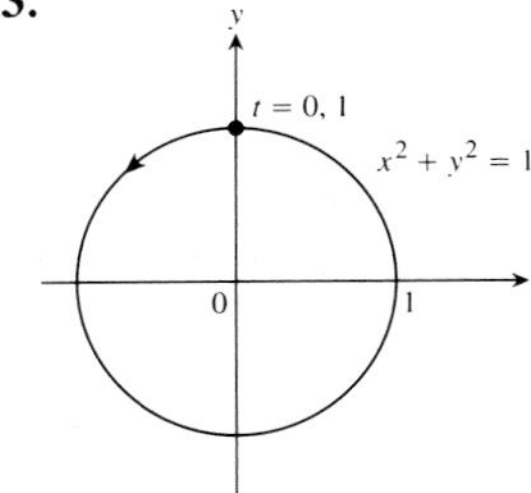

5.

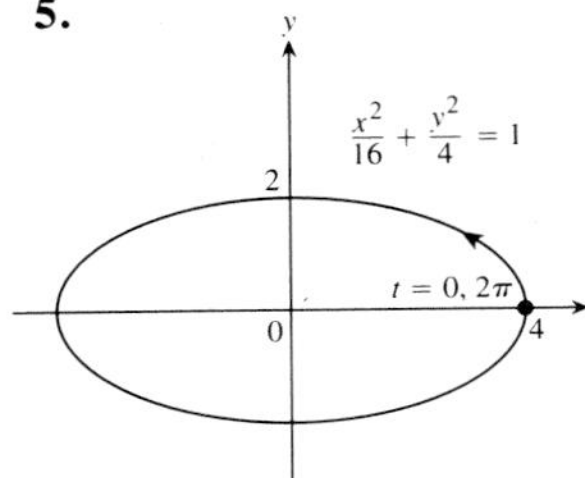

7.

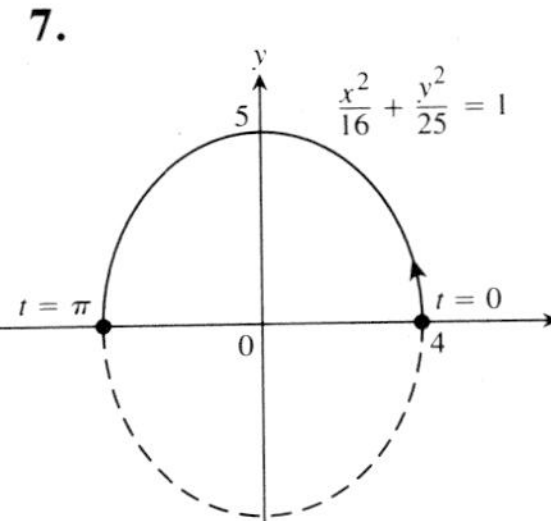

9.

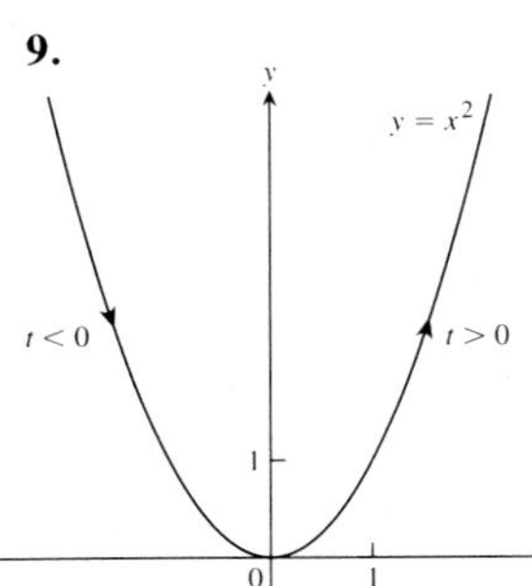

11.

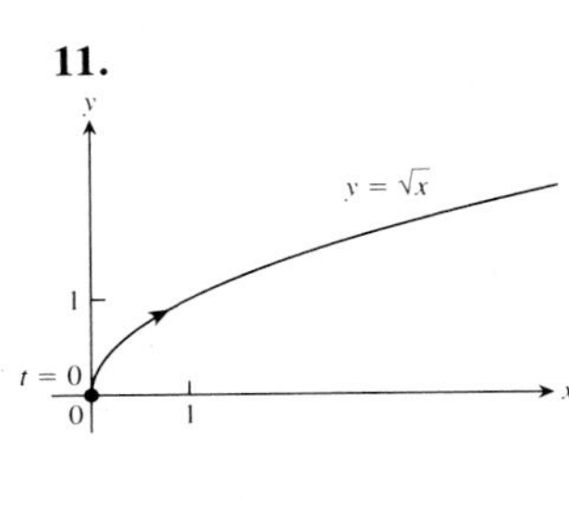

13.

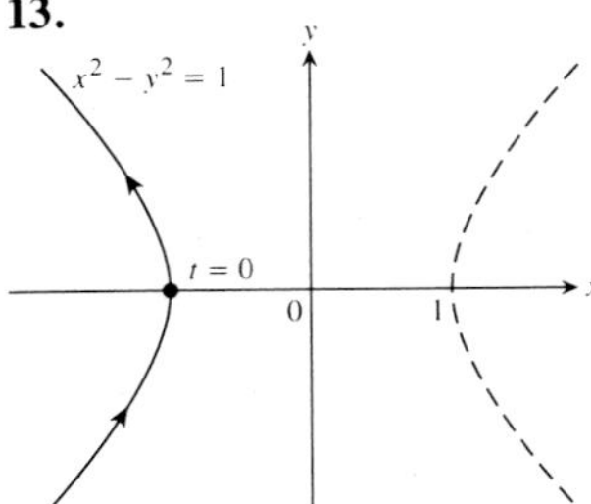

15.

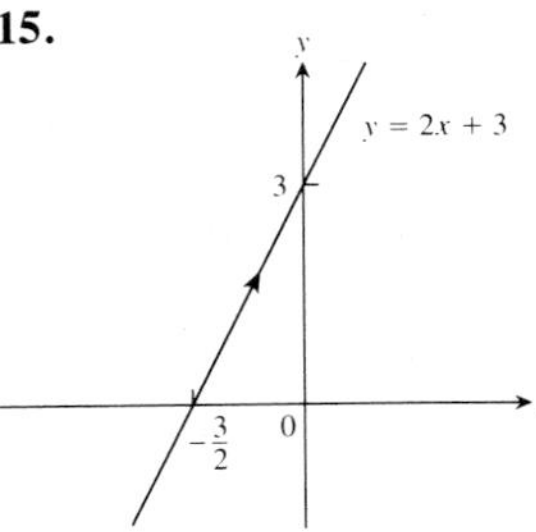

17.

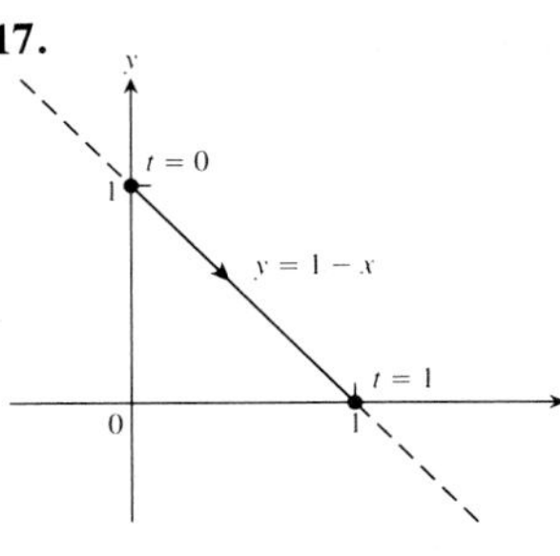

19.

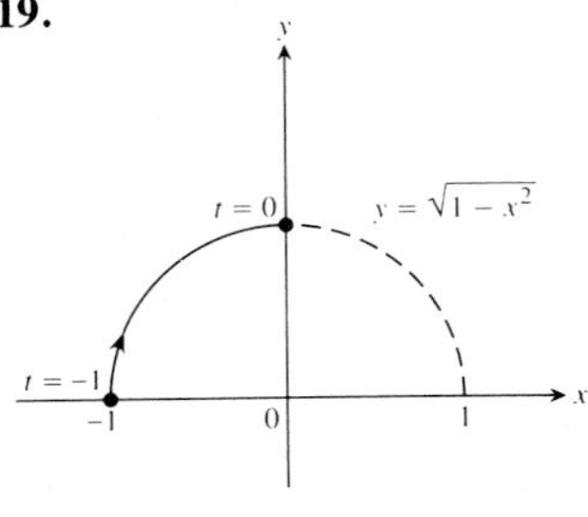

21.

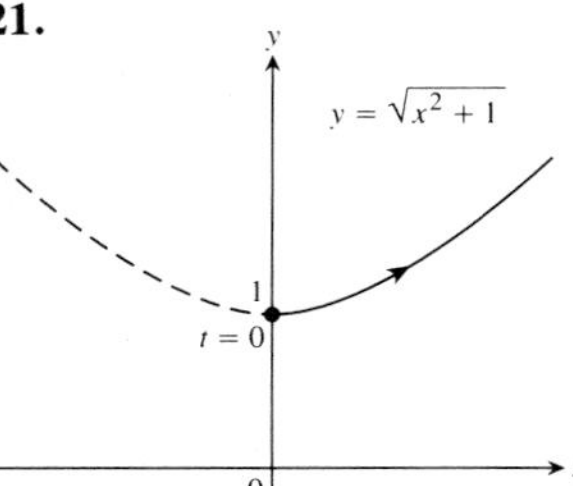

23.

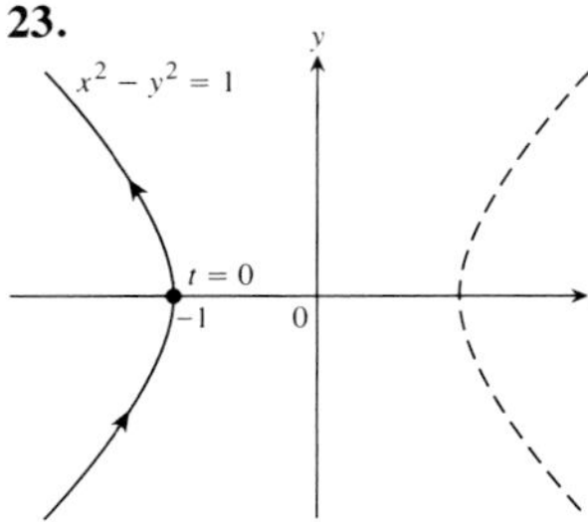

25. a) $x = a\cos t, \quad y = -a\sin t, \quad 0 \le t \le 2\pi$
b) $x = a\cos t, \quad y = a\sin t, \quad 0 \le t \le 2\pi$
c) $x = a\cos t, \quad y = -a\sin t, \quad 0 \le t \le 4\pi$
d) $x = a\cos t, \quad y = a\sin t, \quad 0 \le t \le 4\pi$ **29.** $(1, 1)$
31. b) $x = x_1 t, y = y_1 t$ (Answer not unique)
c) $x = -1 + t, y = t$ (Answer not unique)

Section 10.4, pp. 660–661

1. $y = -x + 2\sqrt{2}, \dfrac{d^2y}{dx^2} = -\sqrt{2}$

3. $y = -\dfrac{1}{2}x + 2\sqrt{2}, \dfrac{d^2y}{dx^2} = -\dfrac{\sqrt{2}}{4}$

5. $y = x + \dfrac{1}{4}, \dfrac{d^2y}{dx^2} = -2$ **7.** $y = 2x - \sqrt{3}, \dfrac{d^2y}{dx^2} = -3\sqrt{3}$

9. $y = x - 4, \dfrac{d^2y}{dx^2} = \dfrac{1}{2}$ **11.** $y = \sqrt{3}x - \dfrac{\pi\sqrt{3}}{3} + 2, \dfrac{d^2y}{dx^2} = -4$

13. 0 **15.** -6 **17.** 4 **19.** 12 **21.** π^2 **23.** $8\pi^2$

25. $\dfrac{52}{3}\pi$ **27.** $3\pi\sqrt{5}$ **29.** a) π b) π

33. $\left(\dfrac{\sqrt{2}}{2}, 1\right)$, $y = 2x$ at $t = 0$, $y = -2x$ at $t = \pi$

Section 10.5, pp. 666–667

1. a, c; b, d; e, k; g, j; h, f; i, l; m, o; n, p
3.

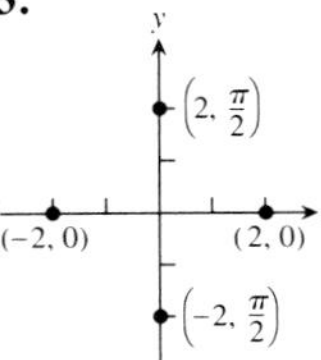

a) $\left(2, \dfrac{\pi}{2} + 2n\pi\right)$ and $\left(-2, \dfrac{\pi}{2} + (2n + 1)\pi\right)$, n an integer
b) $(2, 2n\pi)$ and $(-2, (2n + 1)\pi)$, n an integer
c) $\left(2, \dfrac{3\pi}{2} + 2n\pi\right)$ and $\left(-2, \dfrac{3\pi}{2} + (2n + 1)\pi\right)$, n an integer
d) $(2, (2n + 1)\pi)$ and $(-2, 2n\pi)$, n an integer
5. a) $(1, 1)$ b) $(1, 0)$ c) $(0, 0)$ d) $(-1, -1)$
e) $\left(\dfrac{3\sqrt{3}}{2}, -\dfrac{3}{2}\right)$ f) $(3, 4)$ g) $(1, 0)$ h) $(-\sqrt{3}, 3)$

7.

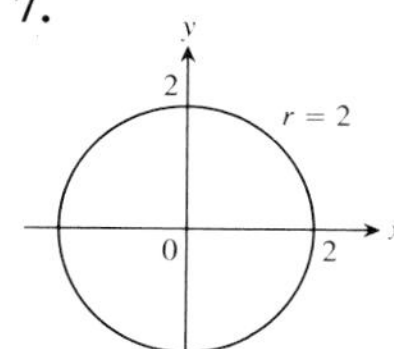

9.

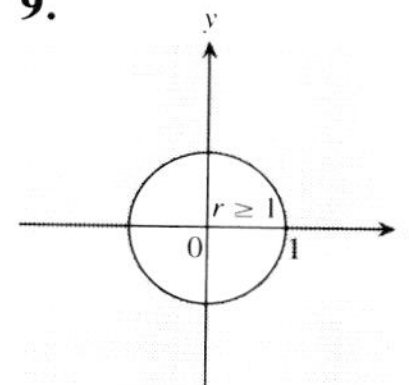

11.

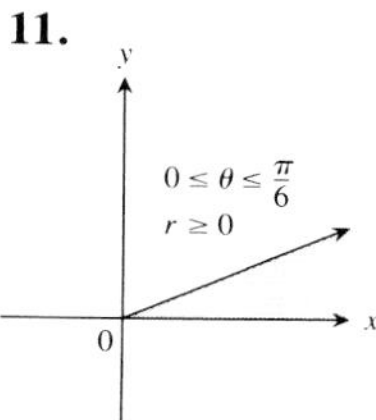

13.

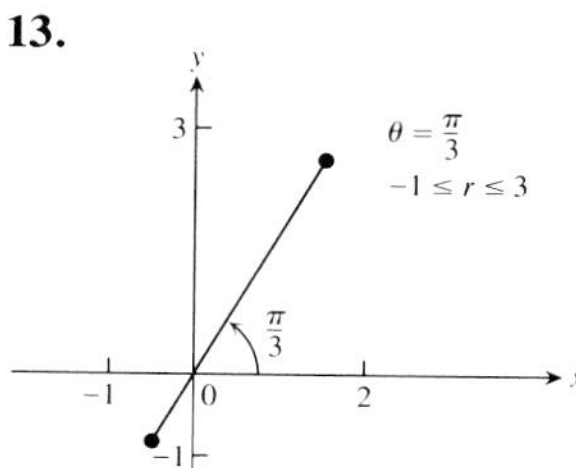

15.

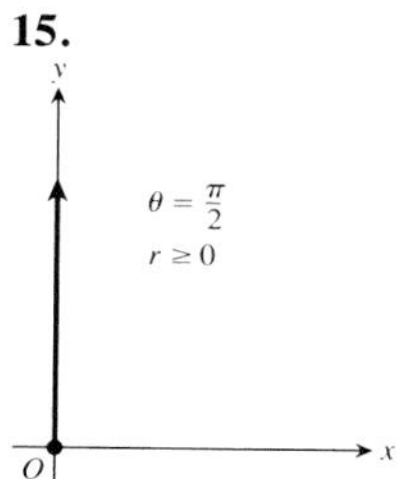

17.

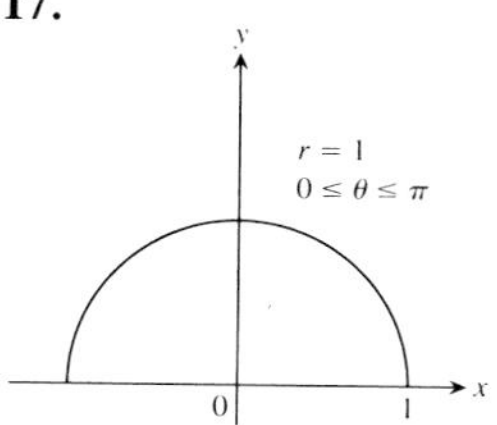

19.

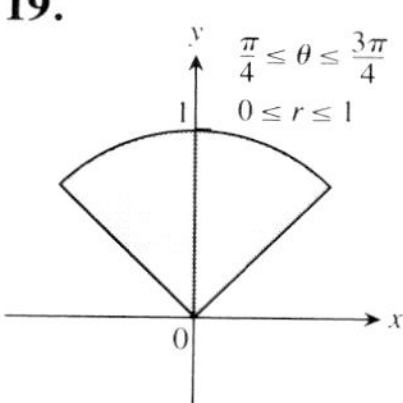

21.

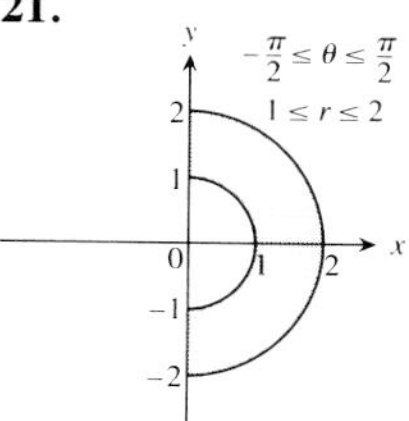

23. $x = 2$, vertical line through $(2, 0)$ **25.** $y = 0$, the x-axis
27. $y = 4$, horizontal line through $(0, 4)$
29. $x + y = 1$, line, $m = -1$, $b = 1$
31. $x^2 + y^2 = 1$, circle, $C(0, 0)$, radius 1
33. $y - 2x = 5$, line, $m = 2$, $b = 5$
35. $y^2 = x$, parabola, vertex $(0, 0)$, opens right
37. $y = e^x$, graph of natural exponential function
39. $x + y = \pm 1$, two straight lines of slope -1, y-intercepts $b = \pm 1$
41. $(x + 2)^2 + y^2 = 4$, circle, $C(-2, 0)$, radius 2
43. $x^2 + (y - 4)^2 = 16$, circle, $C(0, 4)$, radius 4
45. $(x - 1)^2 + (y - 1)^2 = 2$, circle, $C(1, 1)$, radius $\sqrt{2}$
47. $r \cos \theta = 7$ **49.** $\theta = \pi/4$ **51.** $r = 2$ or $r = -2$
53. $4r^2 \cos^2 \theta + 9r^2 \sin^2 \theta = 36$ **55.** $r \sin^2 \theta = 4 \cos \theta$
57. $r = 4 \sin \theta$ **59.** $r^2 = 6r \cos \theta - 2r \sin \theta - 6$
61. a) Every vertical line has a Cartesian equation $x = a$. The corresponding polar equation, for $-\pi/2 < \theta < \pi/2$, is $r \cos \theta = a$ or $r = a/\cos \theta = a \sec \theta$. b) $r = b \csc \theta$

Section 10.6, p. 673

1. x-axis

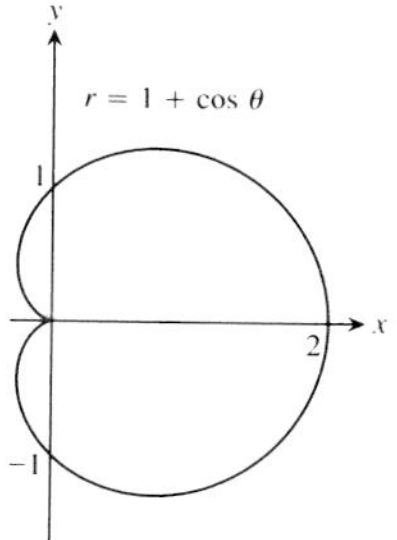

3. y-axis

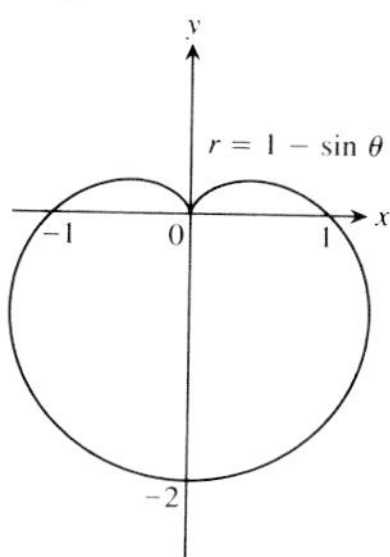

5. y-axis

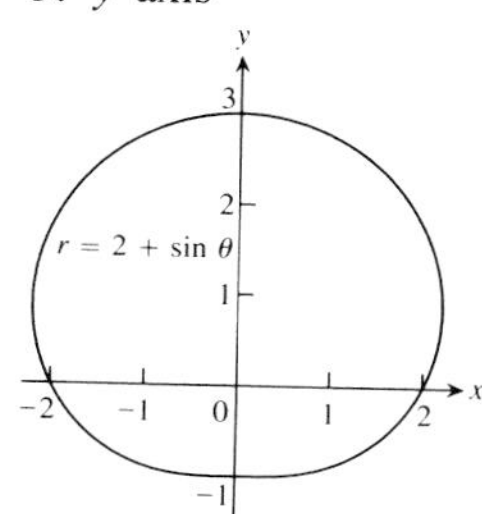

7. x-axis

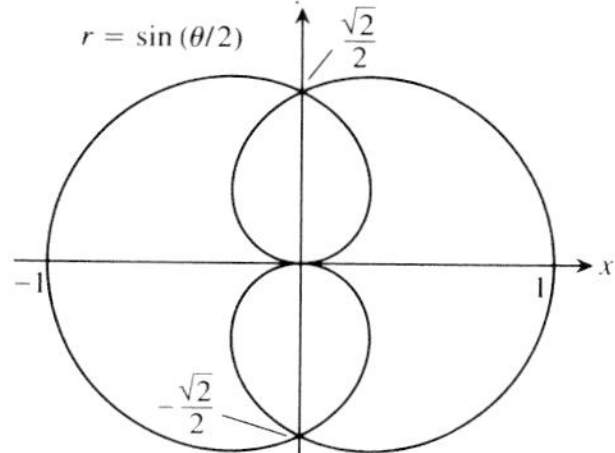

9. x-axis, y-axis, origin

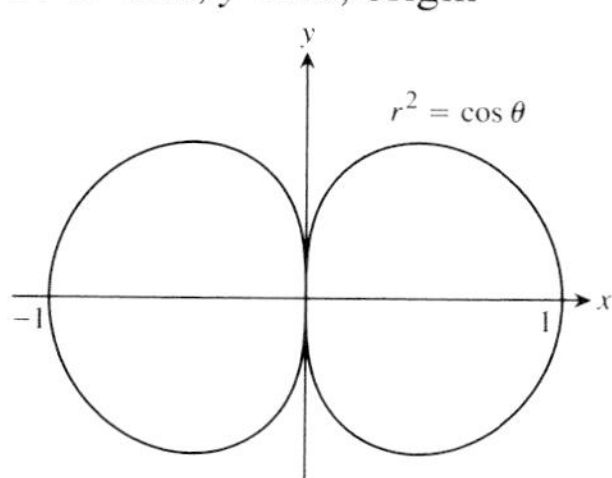

11. y-axis, x-axis, origin

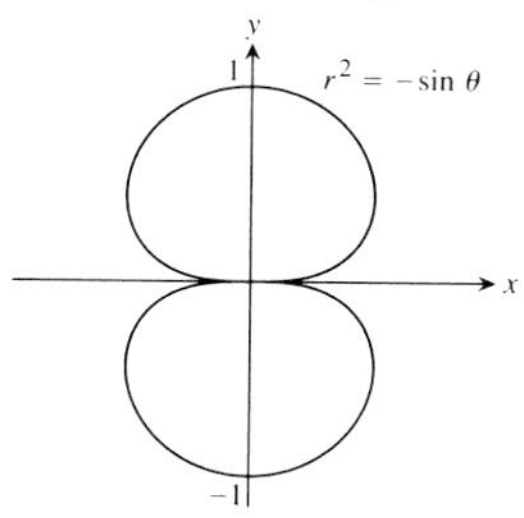

13.

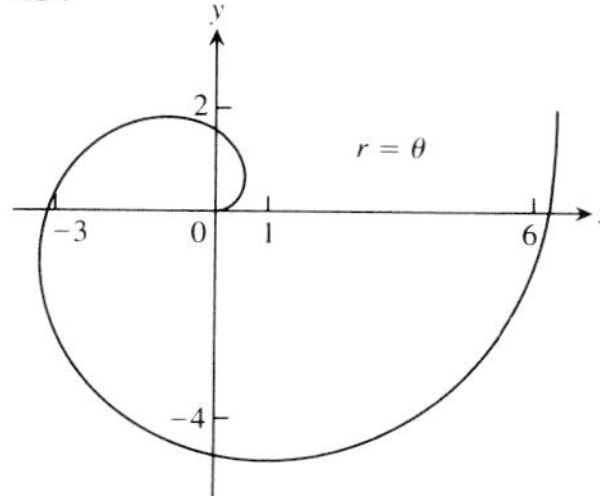

15. The slope at $(-1, \pi/2)$ is -1, at $(-1, -\pi/2)$ is 1.

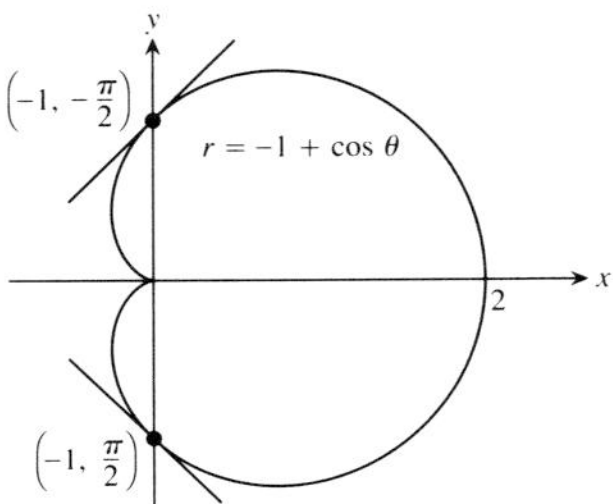

17. The slope at $(1, \pi/4)$ is -1, at $(-1, -\pi/4)$ is 1, at $(-1, 3\pi/4)$ is 1, at $(1, -3\pi/4)$ is -1.

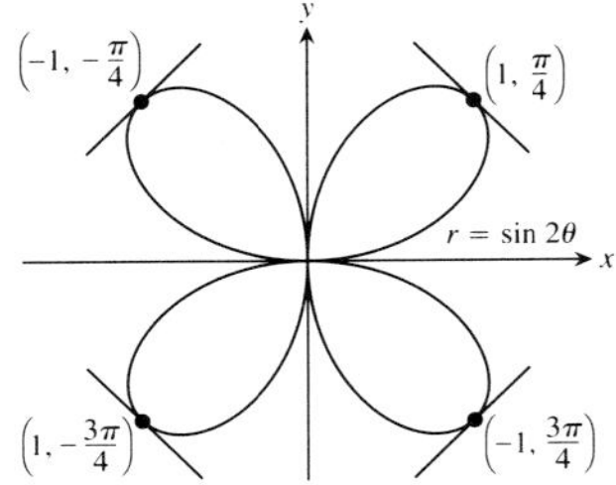

19. x-axis, y-axis, origin

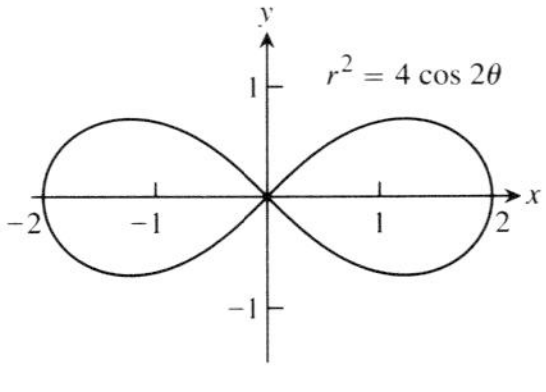

21. Origin

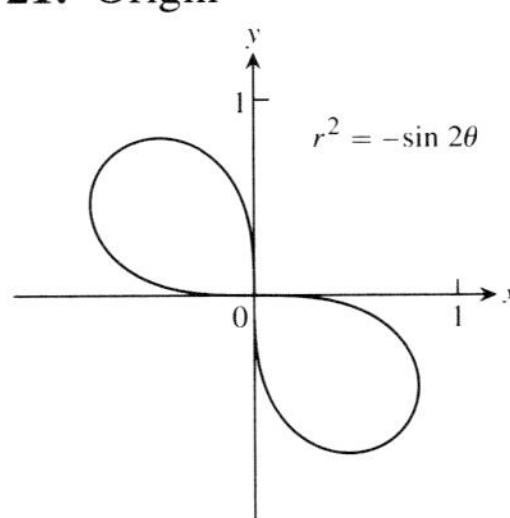

23. a)

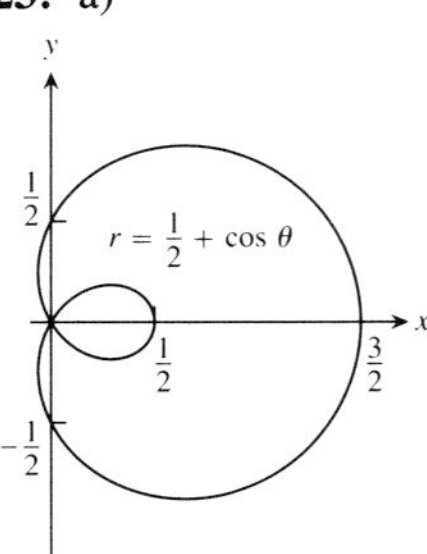

b)

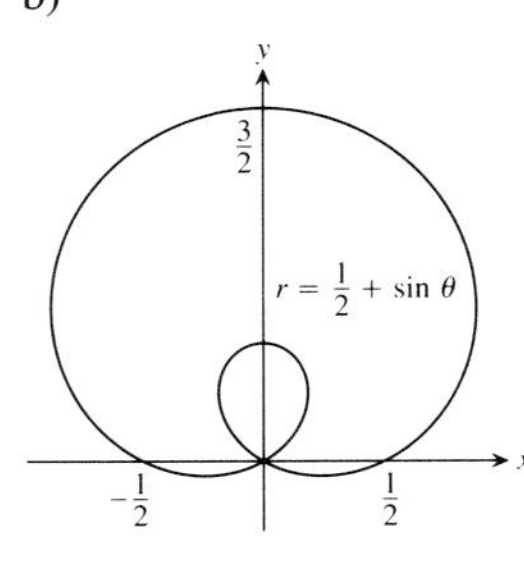

25. a)

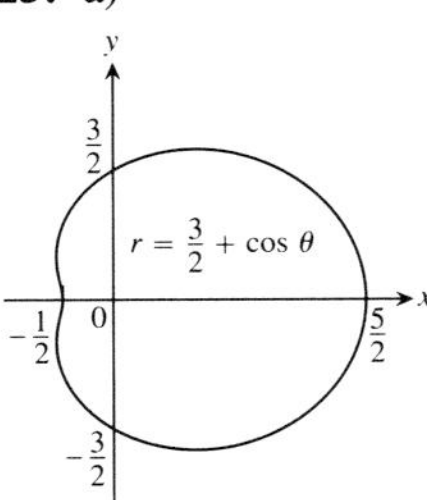

b)

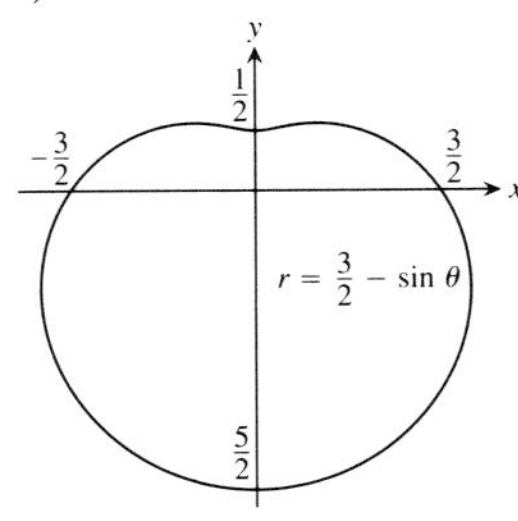

27.

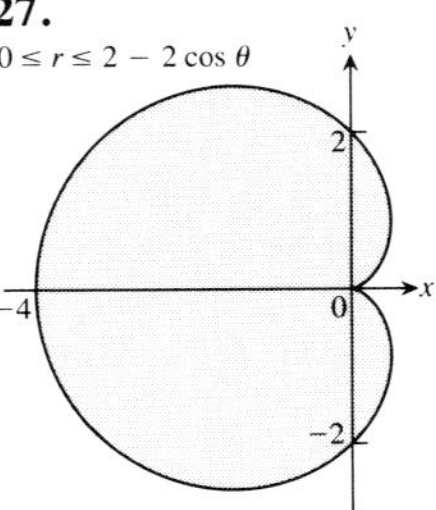

31. $(0, 0), (1, \pi/2), (1, 3\pi/2)$
33. $(0, 0), (\sqrt{3}, \pi/3), (-\sqrt{3}, -\pi/3)$
35. $(\sqrt{2}, \pm\pi/6), (\sqrt{2}, \pm 5\pi/6)$ **37.** $(1, \pi/12), (1, 5\pi/12), (1, 13\pi/12), (1, 17\pi/12)$

Section 10.7, pp. 678–680

1. $r\cos(\theta - \pi/6) = 5$, $y = -\sqrt{3}\,x + 10$
3. $r\cos(\theta - 4\pi/3) = 3$, $y = -(\sqrt{3}/3)x - 2\sqrt{3}$
5. $y = 2 - x$ **7.** $y = (\sqrt{3}/3)x + 2\sqrt{3}$ **9.** $r = 8\cos\theta$
11. $r = 2\sqrt{2}\sin\theta$

13.

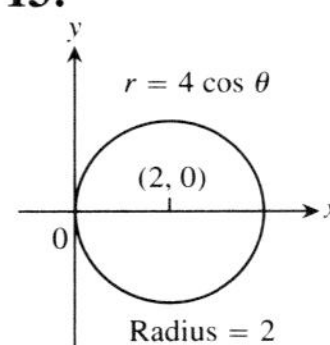

15.

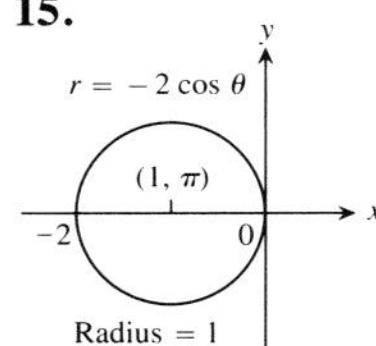

17. $(x - 6)^2 + y^2 = 36$, $r^2 = 12r\cos\theta$
19. $x^2 + (y - 5)^2 = 25$, $r^2 = 10r\sin\theta$
21. $(x + 1)^2 + y^2 = 1$, $r^2 = -2r\cos\theta$
23. $x^2 + (y + 1/2)^2 = 1/4$, $r^2 = -r\sin\theta$
25. $r = 2/(1 + \cos\theta)$ **27.** $r = 8/(1 + 2\cos\theta)$
29. $r = 1/(2 + \cos\theta)$ **31.** $r = 10/(5 - \sin\theta)$

33.

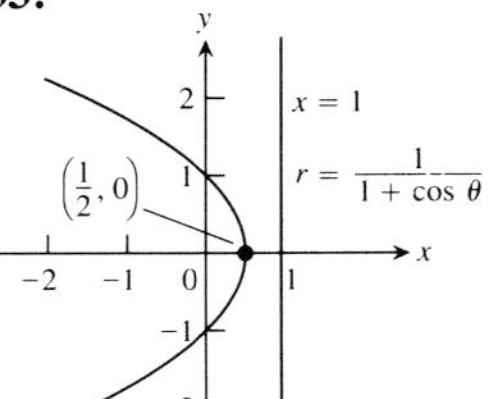

35.

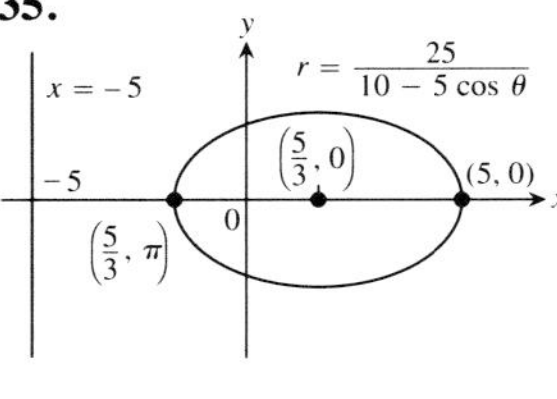

37.

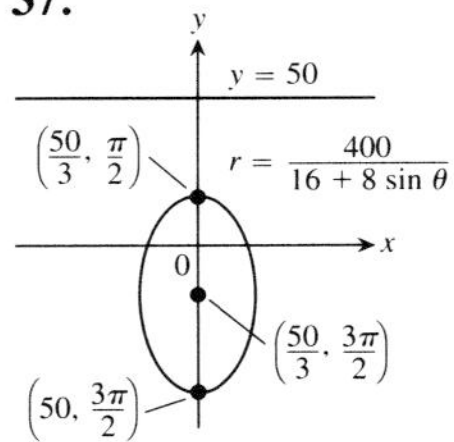

39.

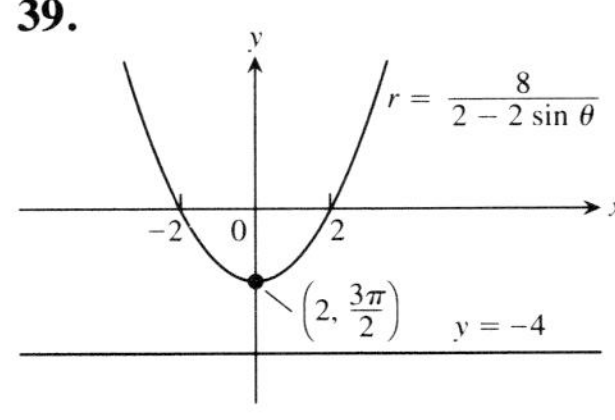

41.

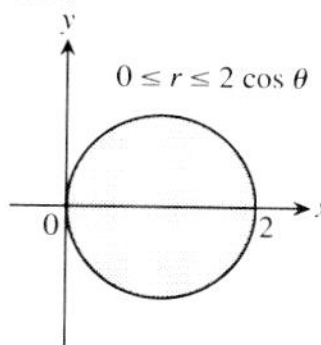

43. a) Perihelion $= a - ae = a(1 - e)$, Aphelion $= ea + a = a(1 + e)$

b)

Planet	Perihelion	Aphelion
Mercury	0.3075 AU	0.4667 AU
Venus	0.7184 AU	0.7282 AU
Earth	0.9833 AU	1.0167 AU
Mars	1.3817 AU	1.6663 AU
Jupiter	4.9512 AU	5.4548 AU
Saturn	9.0210 AU	10.0570 AU
Uranus	18.2977 AU	20.0623 AU
Neptune	29.8135 AU	30.3065 AU
Pluto	29.6549 AU	49.2251 AU

45. a) $x^2 + (y - 2)^2 = 4$, $x = \sqrt{3}$
b)

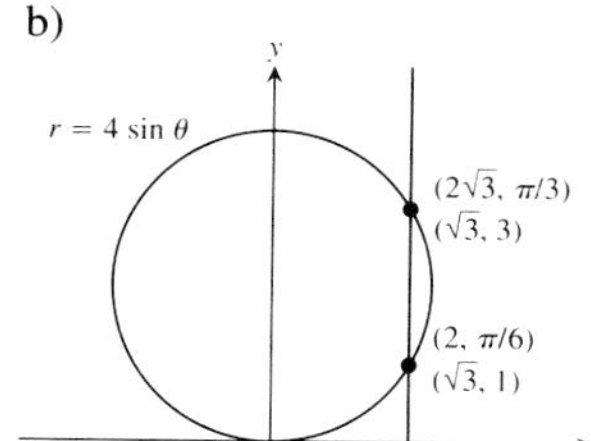

47. $r = 4/(1 + \cos\theta)$

Section 10.8, pp. 685–686

1. $\sqrt{2}$ **3.** $-\frac{3\pi}{4} + \pi e + \frac{\pi}{4}e^2$

5. 18π **7.** $\pi/8$ **9.** 2 **11.** $\frac{\pi}{2} - 1$

13. $5\pi - 8$ **15.** $3\sqrt{3} - \pi$ **17.** $\frac{\pi}{3} + \frac{\sqrt{3}}{2}$

19. $12\pi - 9\sqrt{3}$ **21.** a) $\frac{3}{2} - \frac{\pi}{4}$ **23.** 19/3

25. 8 **27.** $\frac{\pi}{8} + \frac{3}{8}$ **29.** 2π

31. $\pi\sqrt{2}$ **33.** $2\pi(2 - \sqrt{2})$

Chapter 10 Practice Exercises, pp. 687–689

1.

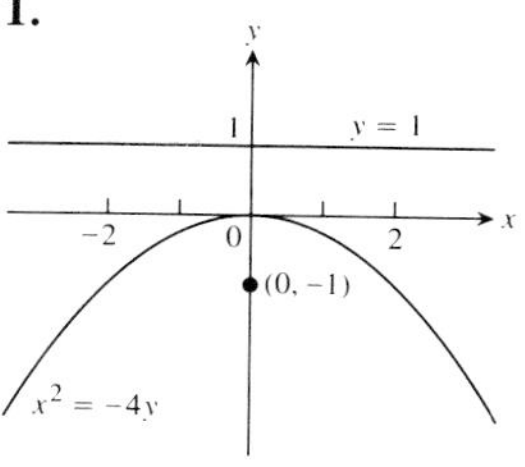

3.

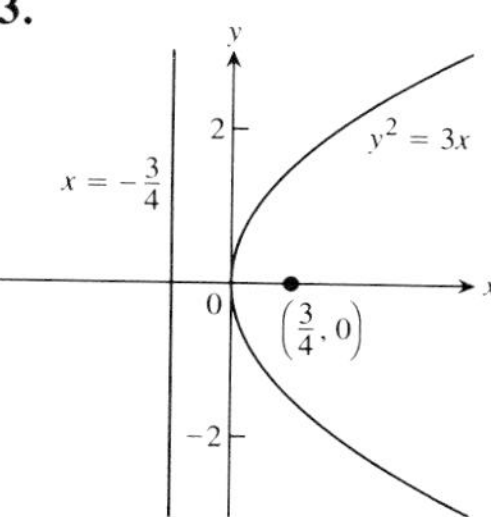

5. $e = 3/4$

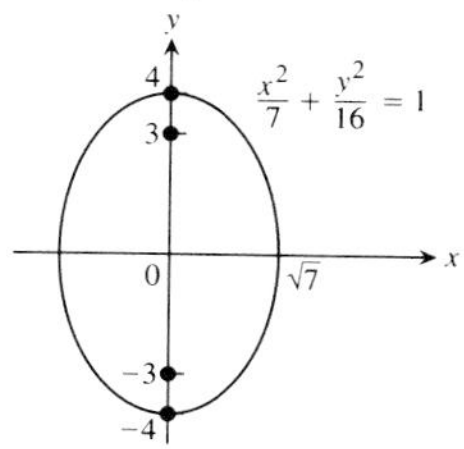

7. $e = 2$

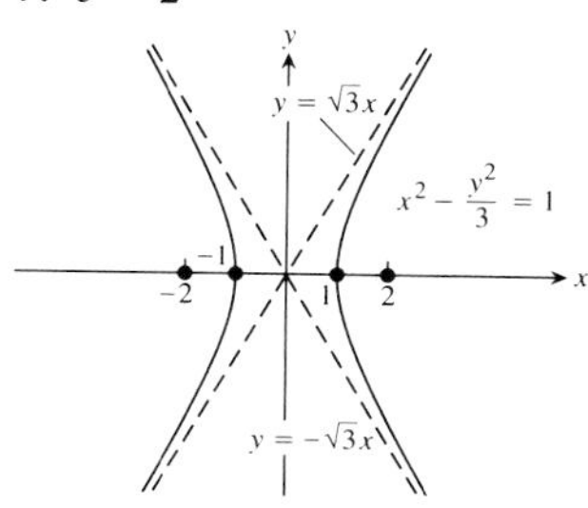

9. $(x - 2)^2 = -12(y - 3)$, $V(2, 3)$, $F(2, 0)$, Directrix: $y = 6$

11. $\frac{(x + 3)^2}{9} + \frac{(y + 5)^2}{25} = 1$, $C(-3, -5)$, $V(-3, 0)$ and $V(-3, -10)$, $F(-3, -1)$ and $F(-3, -9)$

13. $\frac{(y - 2\sqrt{2})^2}{8} - \frac{(x - 2)^2}{2} = 1$, $C(2, 2\sqrt{2})$, $V(2, 4\sqrt{2})$ and $V(2, 0)$, $F(2, \sqrt{10} + 2\sqrt{2})$ and $F(2, -\sqrt{10} + 2\sqrt{2})$; Asymptotes: $y = 2x - 4 + 2\sqrt{2}$ and $y = -2x + 4 + 2\sqrt{2}$

15. Hyperbola: $\frac{(x - 2)^2}{4} - y^2 = 1$, $F(2 \pm \sqrt{5}, 0)$, $V(2 \pm 2, 0)$, $C(2, 0)$; Asymptotes: $y = \pm(1/2)(x - 2)$

17. Parabola: $(y - 1)^2 = -16(x + 3)$, $V(-3, 1)$, $F(-7, 1)$; Directrix: $x = 1$

19. Ellipse: $\frac{(x + 3)^2}{16} + \frac{(y - 2)^2}{9} = 1$, $F(\pm\sqrt{7} - 3, 2)$, $V(\pm 4 - 3, 2)$, $C(-3, 2)$

21. Circle: $(x - 1)^2 + (y - 1)^2 = 2$, $C(1, 1)$, radius $= \sqrt{2}$

23. Ellipse **25.** Hyperbola **27.** Line

29. Ellipse, $5x'^2 + 3y'^2 - 30 = 0$

31. Hyperbola, $y'^2 - x'^2 = 2$ **33.** a) 24π b) 16π

35.

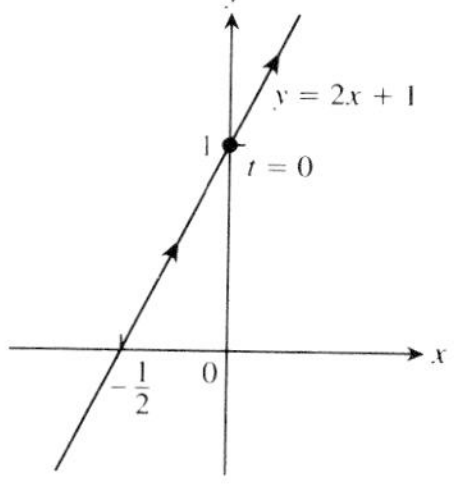

37.

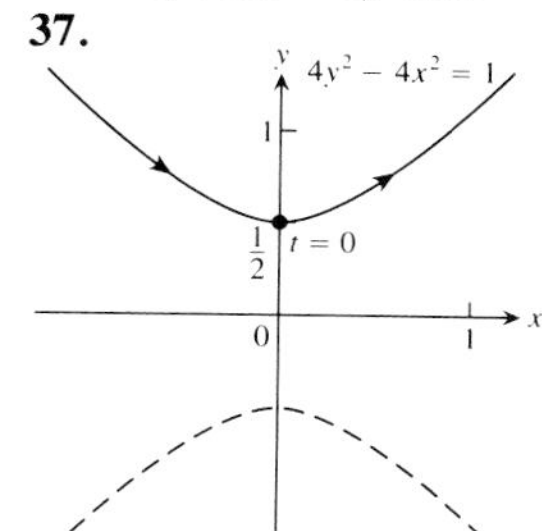

39.

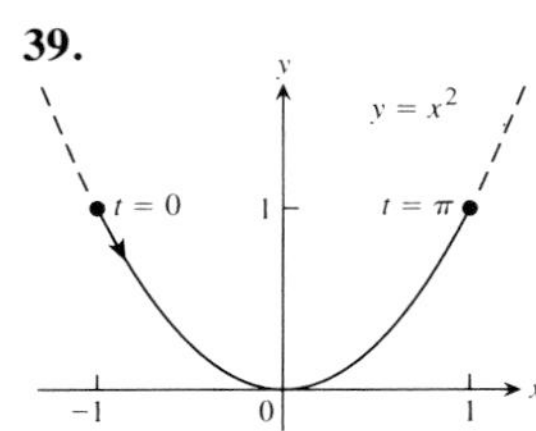

41. $x = 3\cos t,\ y = 4\sin t,\ 0 \le t \le 2\pi$ **43.** $y = \frac{\sqrt{3}}{2}x + \frac{1}{4}, \frac{1}{4}$

45. $3 + \frac{\ln 2}{8}$ **47.** $\frac{76\pi}{3}$

49.

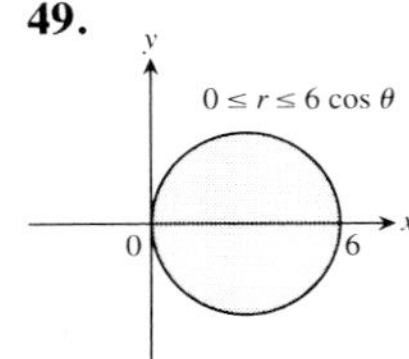

51. d **53.** l **55.** k **57.** i **59.** $(0, 0)$ **61.** $(0, 0), (1, \pm\pi/2)$
63. The graphs coincide. **65.** $(\sqrt{2}, \pi/4)$ **67.** $y = x, y = -x$
69. At $(1, \pi/4)$: $r\cos(\theta - \pi/4) = 1$; at $(1, 3\pi/4)$: $r\cos(\theta - 3\pi/4) = 1$; at $(1, 5\pi/4)$: $r\cos(\theta - 5\pi/4) = 1$; at $(1, 7\pi/4)$: $r\cos(\theta - 7\pi/4) = 1$
71. $y = (\sqrt{3}/3)x - 4$ **73.** $x = 2$ **75.** $y = -3/2$
77. $r = -5\sin\theta$ **79.** $r = 3\cos\theta$ **81.** $x^2 + (y + 2)^2 = 4$
83. $(x - \sqrt{2})^2 + y^2 = 2$
85. **87.**

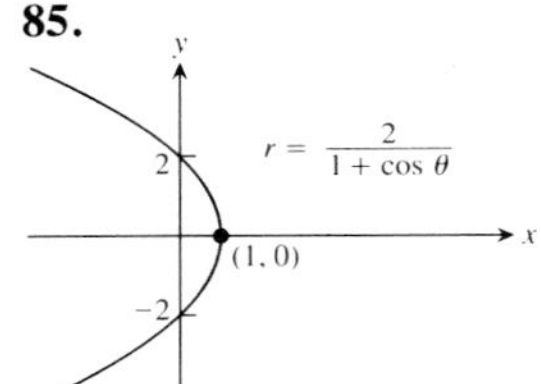

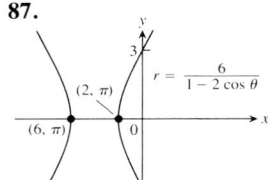

89. $r = \frac{4}{1 + 2\cos\theta}$ **91.** $r = \frac{2}{2 + \sin\theta}$ **93.** $\frac{9}{2}\pi$ **95.** $2 + \pi/4$
97. 8 **99.** $\pi - 3$ **101.** $(2 - \sqrt{2})\pi$
103. Each portion of the wave front will reflect to the other focus, and, since the wave front travels at a constant speed as it expands, the different portions will arrive at the second focus simultaneously.

Chapter 11

Section 11.1, pp. 698–700

1. a) b)

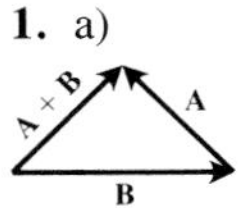

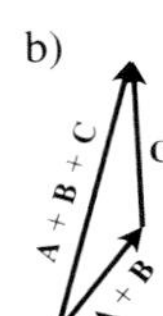

c) d)

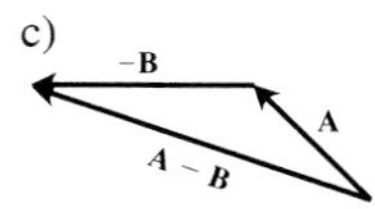

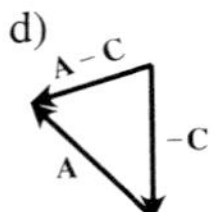

3. $\overrightarrow{DA} = -(\mathbf{u} + \mathbf{w}),\ \overrightarrow{DP} = -\left(\frac{\mathbf{u} + \mathbf{w}}{2}\right)$

5. a) $\mathbf{w} = \mathbf{v} + \mathbf{u}$ b) $\mathbf{v} = \mathbf{w} - \mathbf{u}$ **7.** $\mathbf{a} = \frac{\mathbf{u} + \mathbf{w}}{2}$

9. $3\mathbf{i} - \mathbf{j}$ **11.** $-\mathbf{i}$ **13.** $-(\ln 2)\mathbf{i} + (2 - \pi)\mathbf{j}$
15. $\mathbf{i} - 4\mathbf{j}$ **17.** $-2\mathbf{i} - 3\mathbf{j}$
19.

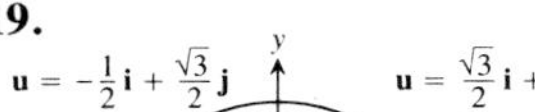

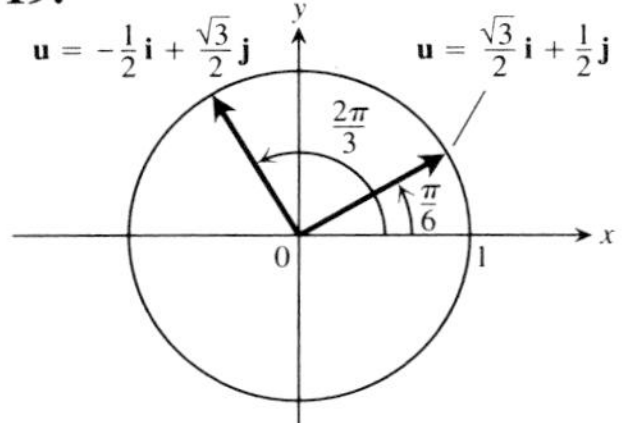

21.

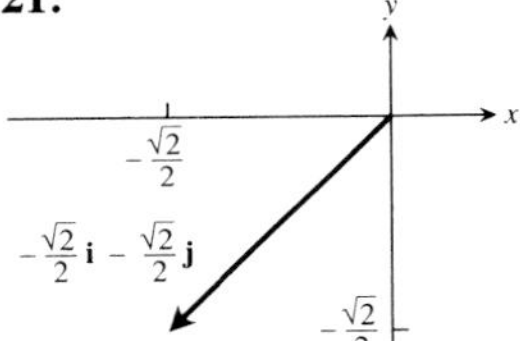

23. $5\sqrt{3}\,\mathbf{i}, 5\mathbf{j}$ **25.** $94\mathbf{i}, -34.2\mathbf{j}$ **27.** $\sqrt{2}\left(\frac{1}{\sqrt{2}}\mathbf{i} + \frac{1}{\sqrt{2}}\mathbf{j}\right)$

29. $2\left(\frac{\sqrt{3}}{2}\mathbf{i} + \frac{1}{2}\mathbf{j}\right)$ **31.** $13\left(\frac{5}{13}\mathbf{i} + \frac{12}{13}\mathbf{j}\right)$

33.

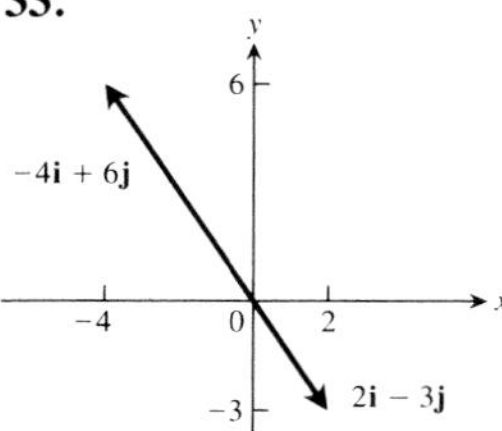

35. $-\sqrt{2}\,\mathbf{i} - \sqrt{2}\,\mathbf{j}$

37. $\mathbf{u} = \frac{1}{\sqrt{17}}\mathbf{i} + \frac{4}{\sqrt{17}}\mathbf{j}$,

$-\mathbf{u} = -\frac{1}{\sqrt{17}}\mathbf{i} - \frac{4}{\sqrt{17}}\mathbf{j}$,

$\mathbf{n} = \frac{4}{\sqrt{17}}\mathbf{i} - \frac{1}{\sqrt{17}}\mathbf{j}$,

$-\mathbf{n} = -\frac{4}{\sqrt{17}}\mathbf{i} + \frac{1}{\sqrt{17}}\mathbf{j}$

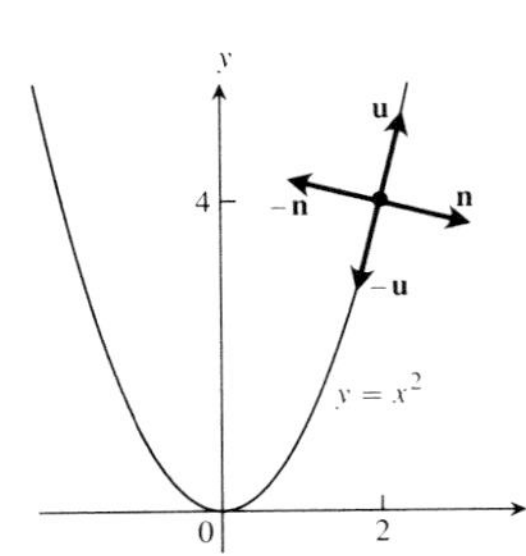

39. $\mathbf{u} = \frac{1}{\sqrt{2}}(\mathbf{i} - \mathbf{j}),\ -\mathbf{u} = \frac{1}{\sqrt{2}}(-\mathbf{i} + \mathbf{j}),$
$\mathbf{n} = \frac{1}{\sqrt{2}}(\mathbf{i} + \mathbf{j}),\ -\mathbf{n} = \frac{1}{\sqrt{2}}(-\mathbf{i} - \mathbf{j})$

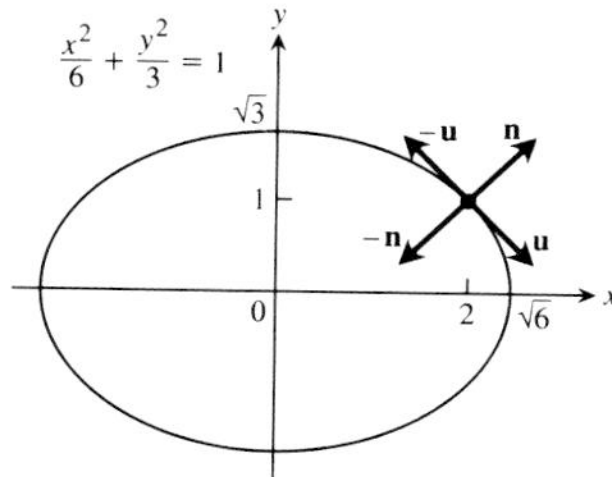

41. $\mathbf{u} = \frac{1}{\sqrt{5}}(2\,\mathbf{i} + \mathbf{j}),\ -\mathbf{u} = \frac{1}{\sqrt{5}}(-2\,\mathbf{i} - \mathbf{j}),\ \mathbf{n} = \frac{1}{\sqrt{5}}(-\mathbf{i} + 2\,\mathbf{j}),$
$-\mathbf{n} = \frac{1}{\sqrt{5}}(\mathbf{i} - 2\,\mathbf{j})$

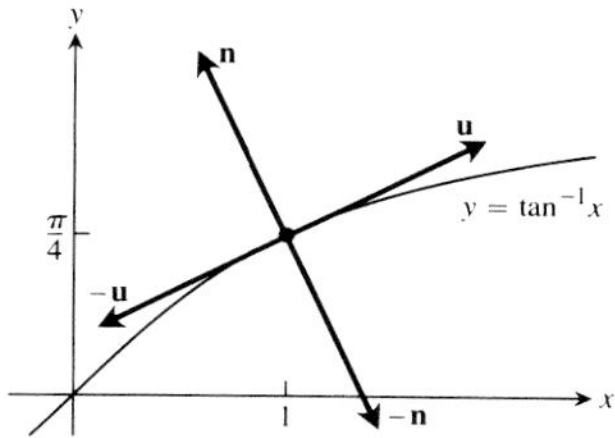

Section 11.2, pp. 708–710

1. The line through the point (2, 3, 0) parallel to the z-axis
3. The x-axis **5.** The circle $x^2 + y^2 = 4$ in the xy-plane
7. The circle $x^2 + z^2 = 4$ in the xz-plane
9. The circle $y^2 + z^2 = 1$ in the yz-plane
11. The circle $x^2 + y^2 = 16$ in the xy-plane
13. a) The first quadrant of the xy-plane
b) The fourth quadrant of the xy-plane
15. a) The ball of radius 1 centered at the origin
b) All points greater than 1 unit from the origin
17. a) The upper hemisphere of radius 1 centered at the origin
b) The solid upper hemisphere of radius 1 centered at the origin **19.** a) $x = 3$ b) $y = -1$ c) $z = -2$
21. a) $z = 1$ b) $x = 3$ c) $y = -1$
23. a) $x^2 + (y - 2)^2 = 4,\ z = 0$ b) $(y - 2)^2 + z^2 = 4,\ x = 0$
c) $x^2 + z^2 = 4,\ y = 2$
25. a) $y = 3,\ z = -1$ b) $x = 1,\ z = -1$ c) $x = 1,\ y = 3$
27. $x^2 + y^2 + z^2 = 25,\ z = 3$ **29.** $0 \le z \le 1$
31. $z \le 0$ **33.** a) $(x - 1)^2 + (y - 1)^2 + (z - 1)^2 < 1$
b) $(x - 1)^2 + (y - 1)^2 + (z - 1)^2 > 1$ **35.** $3\left(\frac{2}{3}\mathbf{i} + \frac{1}{3}\mathbf{j} - \frac{2}{3}\mathbf{k}\right)$
37. $9\left(\frac{1}{9}\mathbf{i} + \frac{4}{9}\mathbf{j} - \frac{8}{9}\mathbf{k}\right)$ **39.** $5(\mathbf{k})$ **41.** $1\left(\frac{3}{5}\mathbf{i} + \frac{4}{5}\mathbf{k}\right)$
43. $\sqrt{\frac{1}{2}}\left(\frac{1}{\sqrt{3}}\mathbf{i} - \frac{1}{\sqrt{3}}\mathbf{j} - \frac{1}{\sqrt{3}}\mathbf{k}\right)$
45. a) 3 b) $\frac{2}{3}\mathbf{i} + \frac{2}{3}\mathbf{j} - \frac{1}{3}\mathbf{k}$ c) (2, 2, 1/2)
47. a) 7 b) $\frac{3}{7}\mathbf{i} - \frac{6}{7}\mathbf{j} + \frac{2}{7}\mathbf{k}$ c) (5/2, 1, 6)
49. a) $2\sqrt{3}$ b) $\frac{1}{\sqrt{3}}\mathbf{i} - \frac{1}{\sqrt{3}}\mathbf{j} - \frac{1}{\sqrt{3}}\mathbf{k}$ c) $(1, -1, -1)$
51. a) $2\,\mathbf{i}$ b) $-\sqrt{3}\,\mathbf{k}$ c) $\frac{3}{10}\mathbf{j} + \frac{2}{5}\mathbf{k}$ d) $6\,\mathbf{i} - 2\,\mathbf{j} + 3\,\mathbf{k}$
53. $\frac{7}{13}(12\,\mathbf{i} - 5\,\mathbf{k})$ **55.** $-\frac{10}{7}\mathbf{i} + \frac{15}{7}\mathbf{j} - \frac{30}{7}\mathbf{k}$
57. $C(-2, 0, 2),\ a = 2\sqrt{2}$ **59.** $C(\sqrt{2}, \sqrt{2}, -\sqrt{2}),\ a = \sqrt{2}$
61. $(x - 1)^2 + (y - 2)^2 + (z - 3)^2 = 14$
63. $(x + 2)^2 + y^2 + z^2 = 3$ **65.** $C(-2, 0, 2),\ a = \sqrt{8}$
67. $C\left(-\frac{1}{4}, -\frac{1}{4}, -\frac{1}{4}\right),\ a = \frac{5\sqrt{3}}{4}$
69. a) $\sqrt{y^2 + z^2}$ b) $\sqrt{x^2 + z^2}$ c) $\sqrt{x^2 + y^2}$

Section 11.3, pp. 716–718

	A · B	|A|	|B|	cos θ	|B| cos θ	Proj$_{\mathbf{A}}$ B
1.	-25	5	5	-1	-5	$-2\,\mathbf{i} + 4\,\mathbf{j} - \sqrt{5}\,\mathbf{k}$
3.	25	15	5	1/3	5/3	$\frac{1}{9}(10\,\mathbf{i} + 11\,\mathbf{j} - 2\,\mathbf{k})$
5.	0	$\sqrt{53}$	1	0	0	$\mathbf{0}$
7.	2	$\sqrt{34}$	$\sqrt{3}$	$\frac{2}{\sqrt{3}\sqrt{34}}$	$\frac{2}{\sqrt{34}}$	$\frac{1}{17}(5\,\mathbf{j} - 3\,\mathbf{k})$
9.	10	$\sqrt{13}$	$\sqrt{26}$	$\frac{10}{13\sqrt{2}}$	$\frac{10}{\sqrt{13}}$	$\frac{10}{13}(3\,\mathbf{i} + 2\,\mathbf{j})$
11.	$\sqrt{3} - \sqrt{2}$	$\sqrt{2}$	3	$\frac{\sqrt{3} - \sqrt{2}}{3\sqrt{2}}$	$\frac{\sqrt{3} - \sqrt{2}}{\sqrt{2}}$	$\frac{\sqrt{3} - \sqrt{2}}{2}(-\mathbf{i} + \mathbf{j})$

13. $\left(\frac{3}{2}\mathbf{i}+\frac{3}{2}\mathbf{j}\right)+\left(-\frac{3}{2}\mathbf{i}+\frac{3}{2}\mathbf{j}+4\,\mathbf{k}\right)$

15. $\left(\frac{14}{3}\mathbf{i}+\frac{28}{3}\mathbf{j}-\frac{14}{3}\mathbf{k}\right)+\left(\frac{10}{3}\mathbf{i}-\frac{16}{3}\mathbf{j}-\frac{22}{3}\mathbf{k}\right)$

17. $x + 2y = 4$ **19.** $-2x + y = -3$

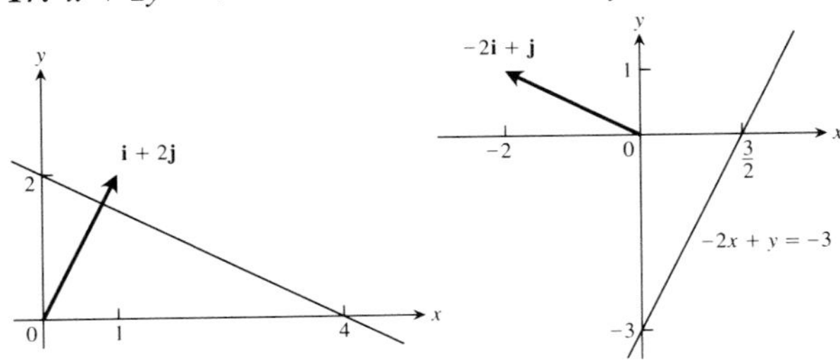

21. $2\sqrt{10}$ **23.** $\sqrt{2}$ **25.** $2/\sqrt{13}$ **31.** a **39.** $\tan^{-1}\sqrt{2}$
41. 0.75 rad **43.** 1.77 rad
45. $\angle A \approx 1.24$ rad, $\angle B \approx 0.66$ rad, $\angle C \approx 1.24$ rad **47.** 0.62 rad
49. 5 J **51.** 3464.10 J **53.** $\pi/4$ **55.** $\pi/6$ **57.** 0.14 rad
59. $\pi/3$ and $2\pi/3$ at each point
61. At (0, 0): $\pi/2$; at (1, 1): $\pi/4$ and $3\pi/4$

Section 11.4, pp. 723–724

1. $|\mathbf{A}\times\mathbf{B}| = 3$, direction is $\frac{2}{3}\mathbf{i}+\frac{1}{3}\mathbf{j}+\frac{2}{3}\mathbf{k}$; $|\mathbf{B}\times\mathbf{A}| = 3$, direction is $-\frac{2}{3}\mathbf{i}-\frac{1}{3}\mathbf{j}-\frac{2}{3}\mathbf{k}$
3. $|\mathbf{A}\times\mathbf{B}| = 0$, no direction; $|\mathbf{B}\times\mathbf{A}| = 0$, no direction
5. $|\mathbf{A}\times\mathbf{B}| = 6$, direction is $-\mathbf{k}$; $|\mathbf{B}\times\mathbf{A}| = 6$, direction is $\mathbf{k}$
7. $|\mathbf{A}\times\mathbf{B}| = 6\sqrt{5}$, direction is $\frac{1}{\sqrt{5}}\mathbf{i}-\frac{2}{\sqrt{5}}\mathbf{k}$; $|\mathbf{B}\times\mathbf{A}| = 6\sqrt{5}$, direction is $-\frac{1}{\sqrt{5}}\mathbf{i}+\frac{2}{\sqrt{5}}\mathbf{k}$

9.

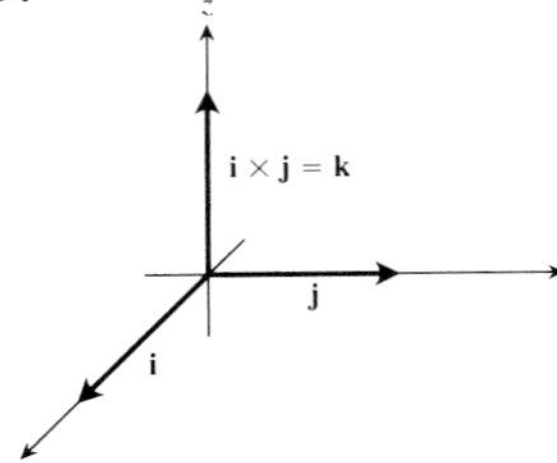

11.

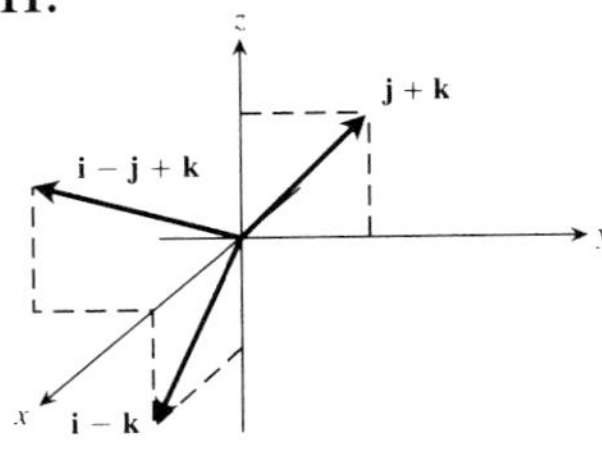

13.

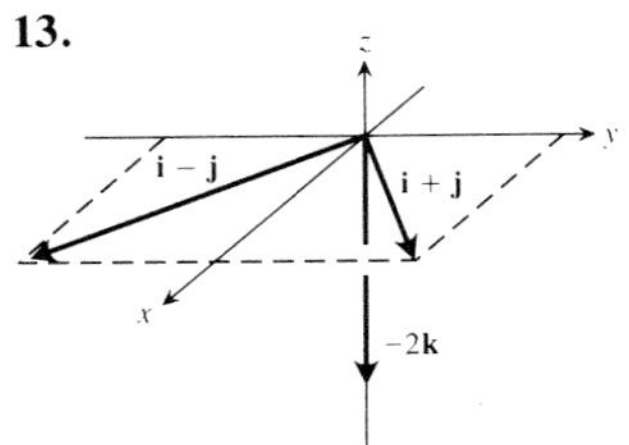

15. a) $2\sqrt{6}$ b) $\pm\frac{1}{\sqrt{6}}(2\mathbf{i}+\mathbf{j}+\mathbf{k})$
17. a) $\frac{\sqrt{2}}{2}$ b) $\pm\frac{1}{\sqrt{2}}(\mathbf{i}-\mathbf{j})$ **19.** a) None b) **A** and **C**
21. $10\sqrt{3}$ ft · lb **23.** 8 **25.** 7 **27.** 3
29. a) $\text{proj}_{\mathbf{B}}\mathbf{A} = \frac{\mathbf{A}\cdot\mathbf{B}}{\mathbf{B}\cdot\mathbf{B}}\mathbf{B}$ b) $\pm\,\mathbf{A}\times\mathbf{B}$ c) $\pm\,(\mathbf{A}\times\mathbf{B})\times\mathbf{C}$ d) $|(\mathbf{A}\times\mathbf{B})\cdot\mathbf{C}|$ **33.** 2 **35.** 13 **37.** 11/2 **39.** 25/2

Section 11.5, pp. 730–731

1. $x = 3 + t,\ y = -4 + t,\ z = -1 + t$
3. $x = -2 + 5t,\ y = 5t,\ z = 3 - 5t$ **5.** $x = 0,\ y = 2t,\ z = t$
7. $x = 1,\ y = 1,\ z = 1 + t$ **9.** $x = t,\ y = -7 + 2t,\ z = 2t$
11. $x = t,\ y = 0,\ z = 0$
13. $x = t,\ y = t,\ z = \frac{3}{2}t,\ 0 \le t \le 1$

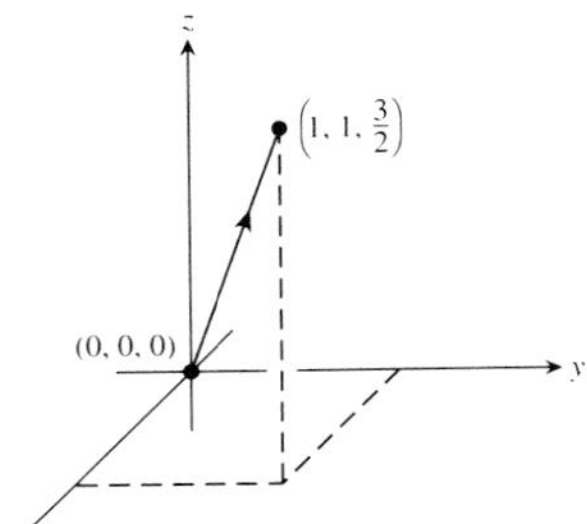

15. $x = 1,\ y = 1 + t,\ z = 0,\ -1 \le t \le 0$

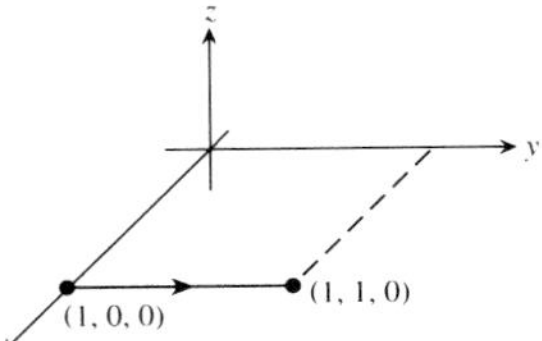

17. $x = 0,\ y = 1 - 2t,\ z = 1,\ 0 \le t \le 1$

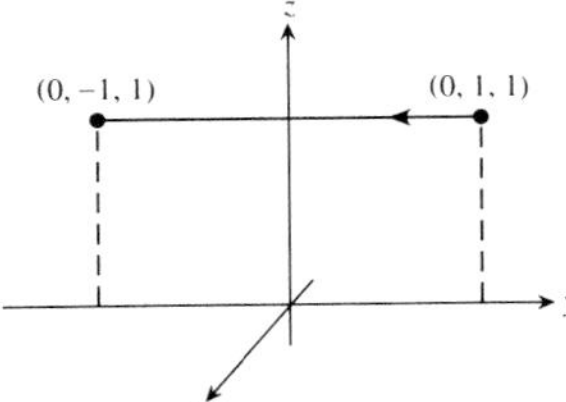

19. $x = 2 - 2t,\ y = 2t,\ z = 2 - 2t,\ 0 \le t \le 1$

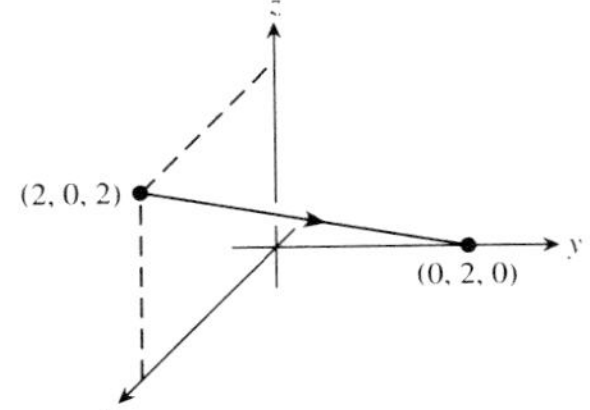

21. $3x - 2y - z = -3$ **23.** $7x - 5y - 4z = 6$
25. $x + 3y + 4z = 34$ **27.** $4x - y - 12z = -34$
29. $x = 2 + 2t,\ y = -4 - t,\ z = 7 + 3t;\ x = -2 - t,$
$y = -2 + (1/2)t,\ z = 1 - (3/2)t$
31. $2\sqrt{30}$ **33.** 0 **35.** $\dfrac{9\sqrt{42}}{7}$ **37.** 3 **39.** 19/5 **41.** 5/3
43. $\left(\dfrac{3}{2}, -\dfrac{3}{2}, \dfrac{1}{2}\right)$ **45.** $(1, 1, 0)$ **47.** $\pi/4$ **49.** 1.76 rad
51. 0.82 rad **53.** $x = 1 - t,\ y = 1 + t,\ z = -1$
55. $x = 4,\ y = 3 + 6t,\ z = 1 + 3t$
57. $\left(0, -\dfrac{1}{2}, -\dfrac{3}{2}\right), (-1, 0, -3), (1, -1, 0)$ **61.** $y + z = 3$
63. $L1$ intersects $L2$, $L2$ is parallel to $L3$, $L1$ and $L3$ are skew

Section 11.6, pp. 740–741

1. d, ellipsoid **3.** a, cylinder **5.** l, hyperbolic paraboloid
7. b, cylinder **9.** k, hyperbolic paraboloid **11.** h, cone

13.

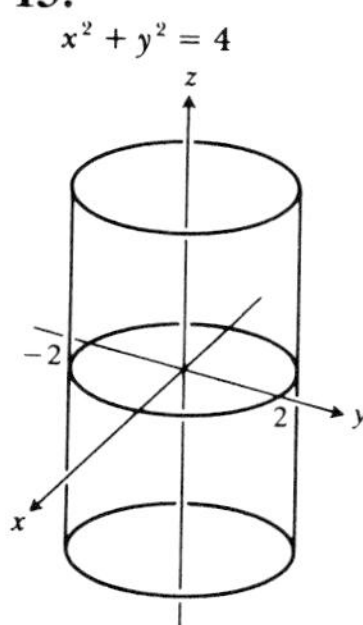

15.

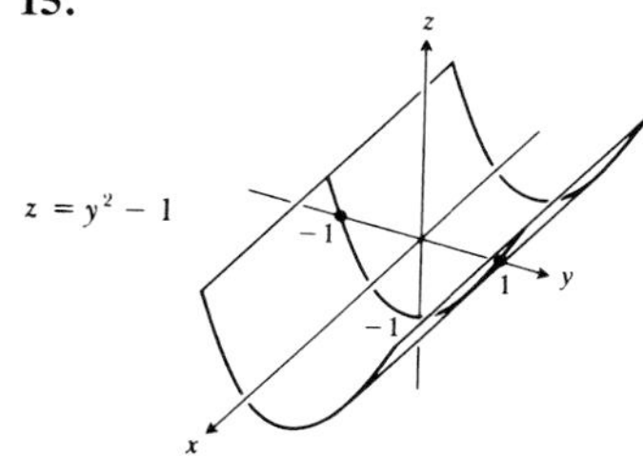

17.

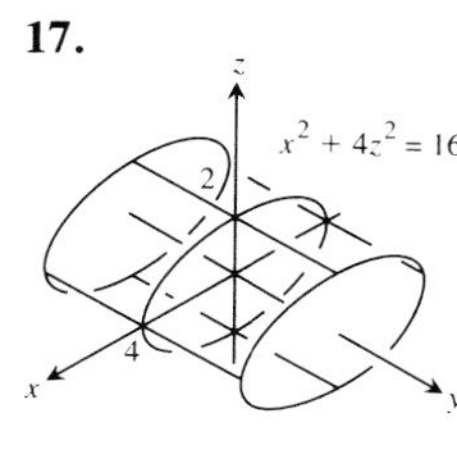

19.

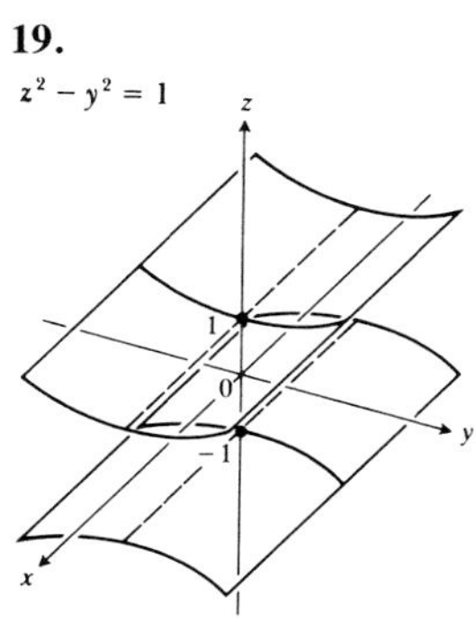

21.

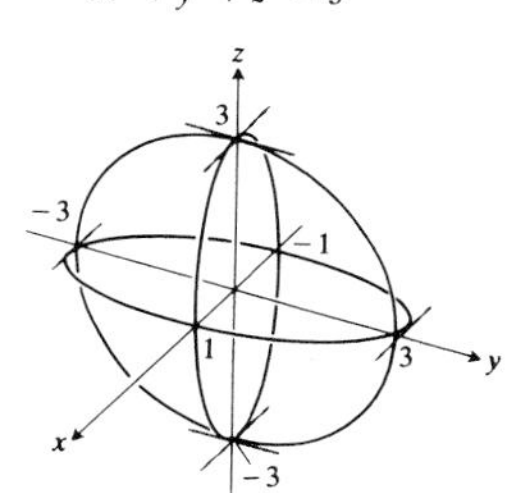

23.

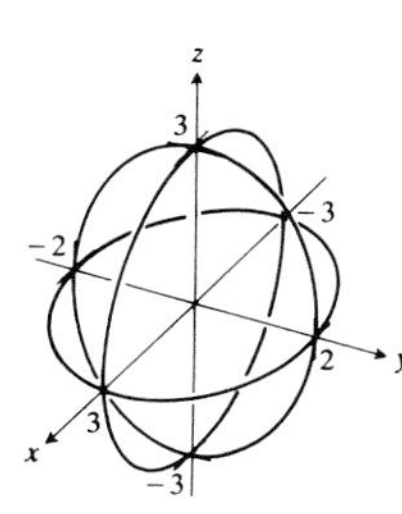

25.

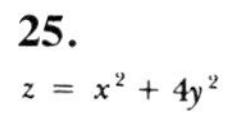

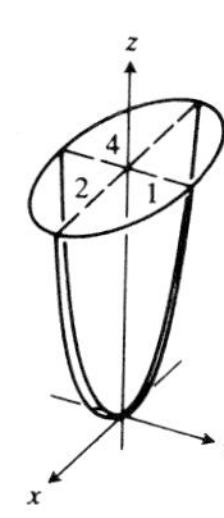

27.

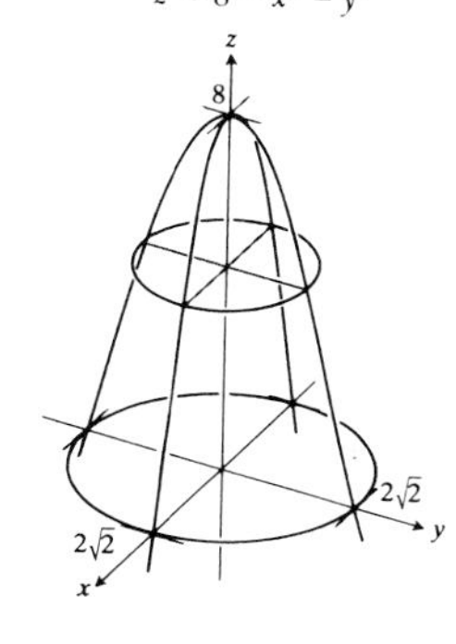

29.

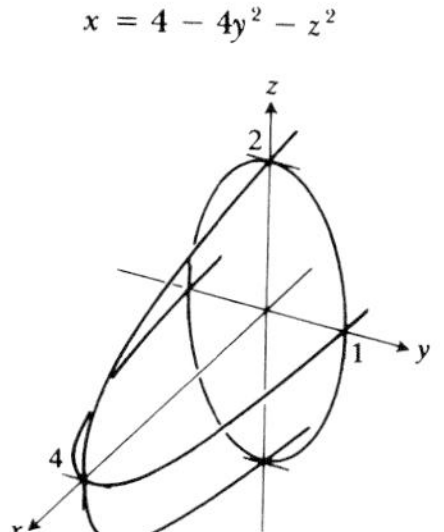

31.

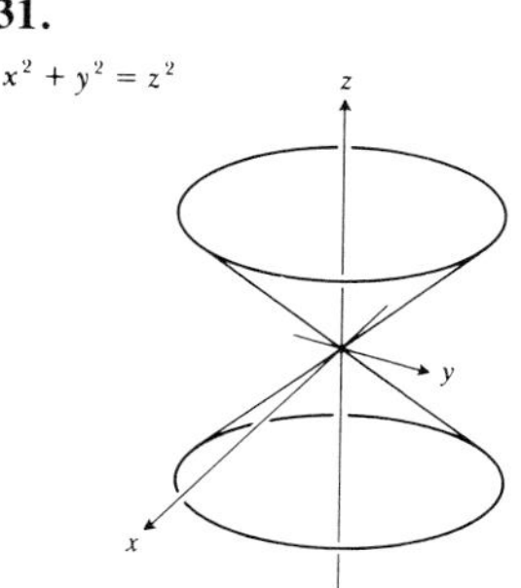

33.

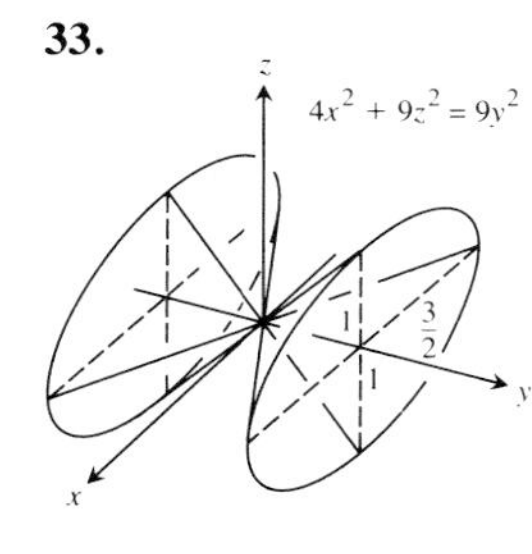

35.

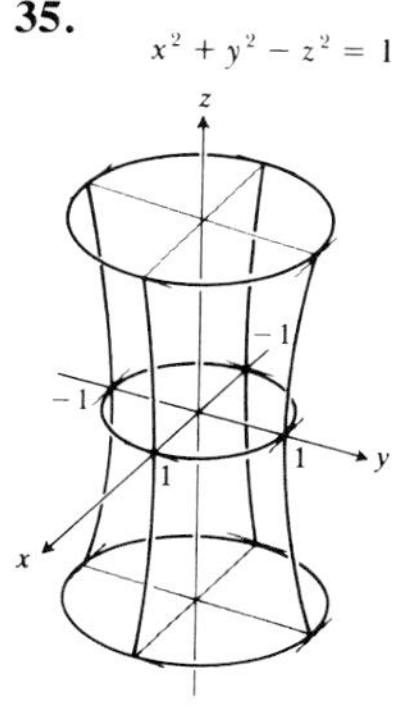

37.

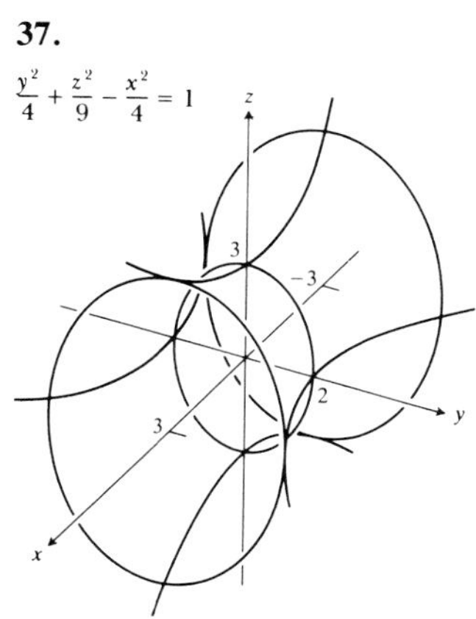

39.

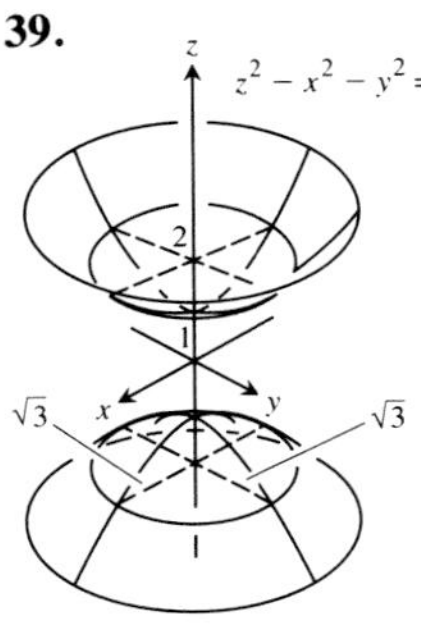

41.

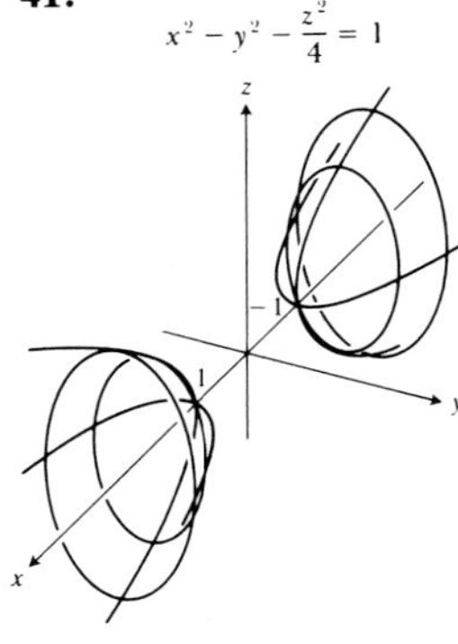

43.

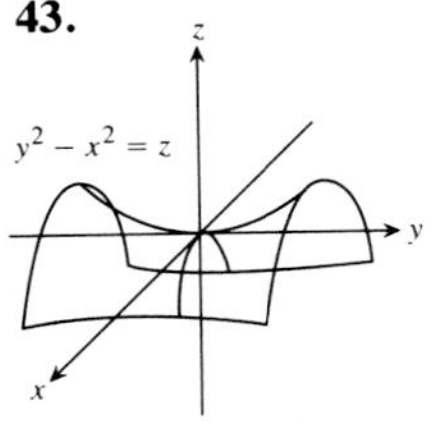

45.

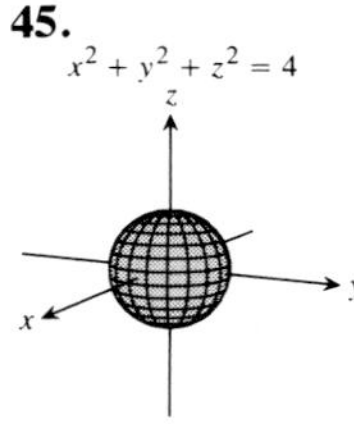

47.

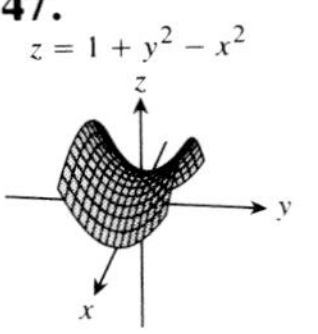

49.

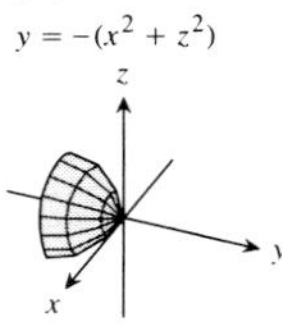

51.

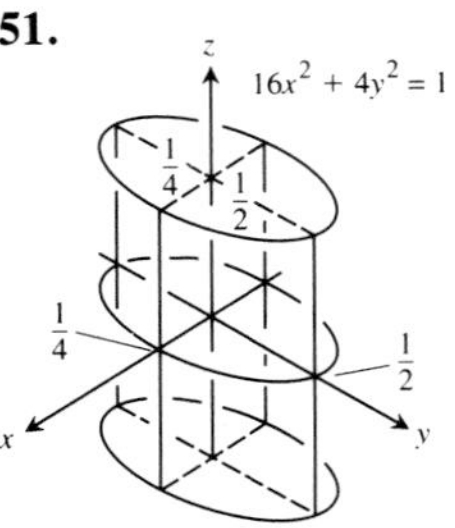

53.

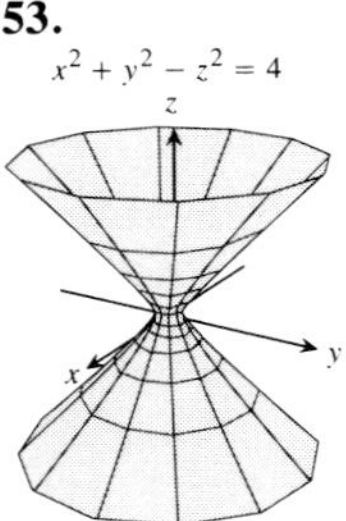

55.

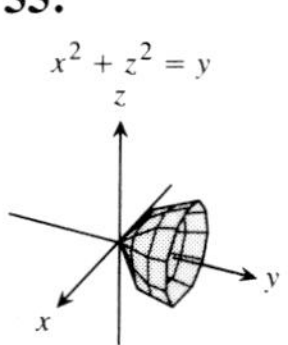

57.

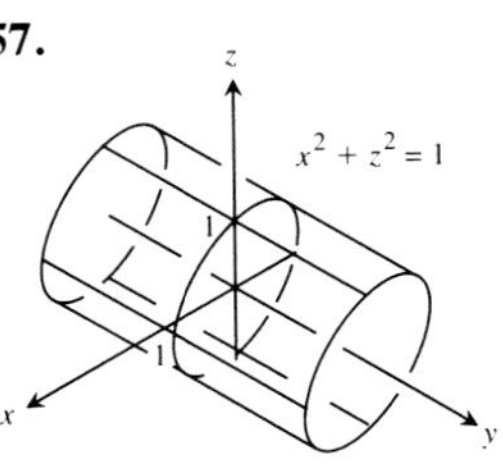

59.

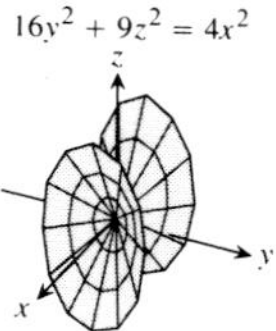

61.

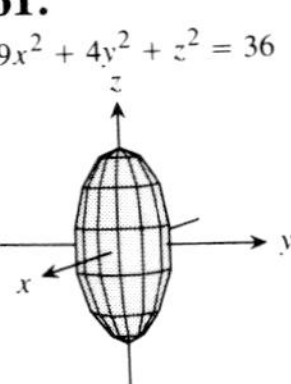

63.

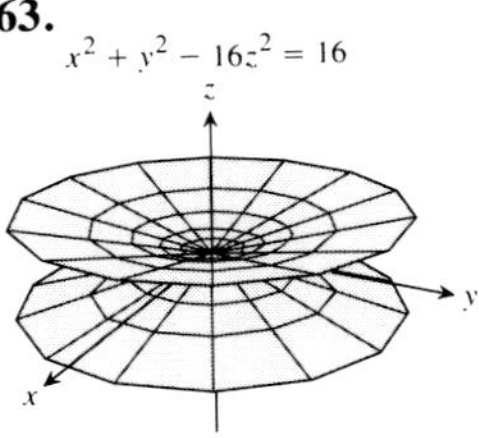

65.

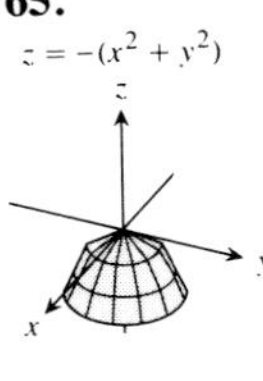

67.

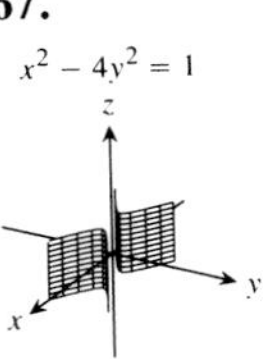

69.

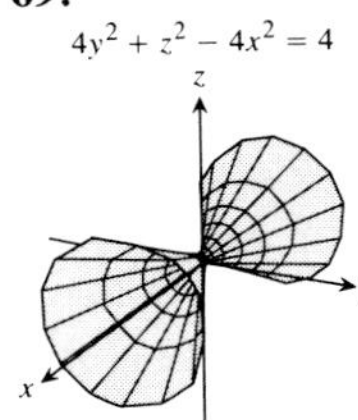

71.

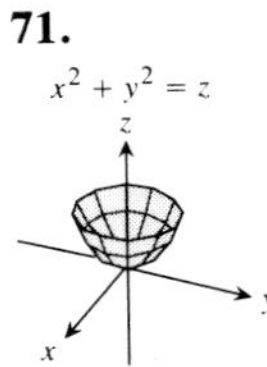

73.

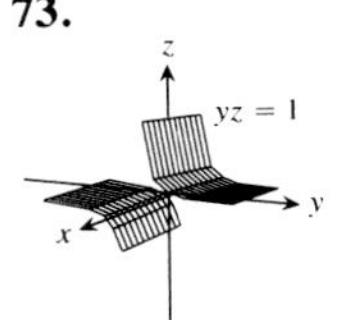

2

75.

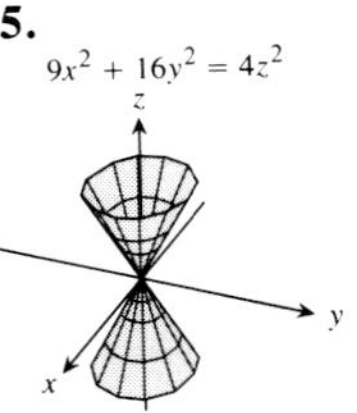

77. a) $\dfrac{2\pi(9 - c^2)}{9}$ b) 8π c) $\dfrac{4\pi abc}{3}$

Section 11.7, pp. 745–746

Rectangular	Cylindrical	Spherical
1. $(0, 0, 0)$	$(0, 0, 0)$	$(0, 0, 0)$
3. $(0, 1, 0)$	$(1, \pi/2, 0)$	$(1, \pi/2, \pi/2)$
5. $(1, 0, 0)$	$(1, 0, 0)$	$(1, \pi/2, 0)$
7. $(0, 1, 1)$	$(1, \pi/2, 1)$	$(\sqrt{2}, \pi/4, \pi/2)$
9. $(0, -2\sqrt{2}, 0)$	$(2\sqrt{2}, 3\pi/2, 0)$	$(2\sqrt{2}, \pi/2, 3\pi/2)$

11. $x^2 + y^2 = 0$, $\theta = 0$ or $\theta = \pi$, the z-axis
13. $z = 0$, $\phi = \pi/2$, the xy-plane
15. $z = r$, $0 \le r \le 1$; $\phi = \pi/4$, $0 \le \rho \le \sqrt{2}$; a (finite) cone
17. $x = 0$, $\theta = \pi/2$, the yz-plane
19. $r^2 + z^2 = 4$, $\rho = 2$, sphere of radius 2 centered at the origin
21. $x^2 + y^2 + \left(z - \frac{5}{2}\right)^2 = \frac{25}{4}$, $r^2 + z^2 = 5z$, sphere of radius 5/2 centered at (0, 0, 5/2) (rectangular)
23. $y = 1$, $\rho \sin\phi \sin\theta = 1$, the plane $y = 1$
25. $z = \sqrt{2}$, the plane $z = \sqrt{2}$
27. $r^2 + z^2 = 2z$, $z \le 1$; $\rho = 2\cos\phi$, $\pi/4 \le \phi \le \pi/2$; lower half (hemisphere) of the sphere of radius 1 centered at (0, 0, 1) (rectangular)
29. $x^2 + y^2 + z^2 = 9$, $-3/2 \le z \le 3/2$; $r^2 + z^2 = 9$, $-3/2 \le z \le 3/2$; the portion of the sphere of radius 3 centered at the origin between the planes $z = -3/2$ and $z = 3/2$
31. $z = 4 - 4(x^2 + y^2)$, $0 \le z \le 4$; $\rho\cos\phi = 4 - 4\rho^2 \sin^2\phi$, $0 \le \phi \le \pi/2$; the upper portion cut from the paraboloid $z = 4 - 4(x^2 + y^2)$ by the xy-plane
33. $z = -\sqrt{x^2 + y^2}$, $-1 \le z \le 0$; $z = -r$, $0 \le r \le 1$; cone, vertex at origin, base the circle $x^2 + y^2 = 1$ in the plane $z = -1$
35. $z + x^2 - y^2 = 0$ or $z = y^2 - x^2$, $\cos\phi + \rho\sin^2\phi\cos 2\theta = 0$, hyperbolic paraboloid
37. Right circular cylinder parallel to the z-axis generated by the circle $r = -2\sin\theta$ in the $r\theta$-plane

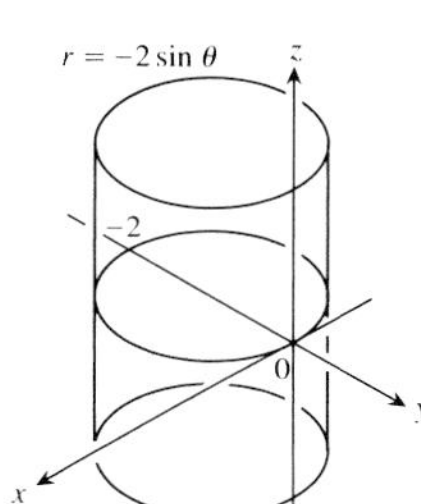

39. Cylinder of lines parallel to the z-axis generated by the cardioid $r = 1 - \cos\theta$ in the $r\theta$-plane

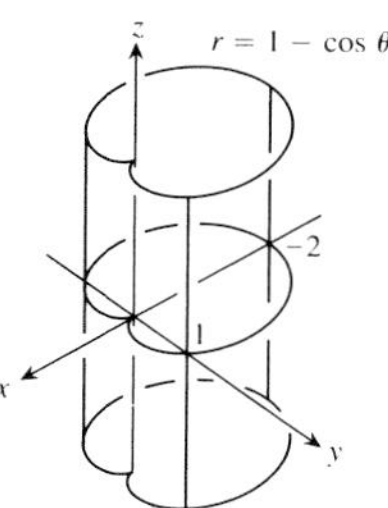

41. Cardioid of revolution symmetric about the y-axis, cusp at the origin pointing down

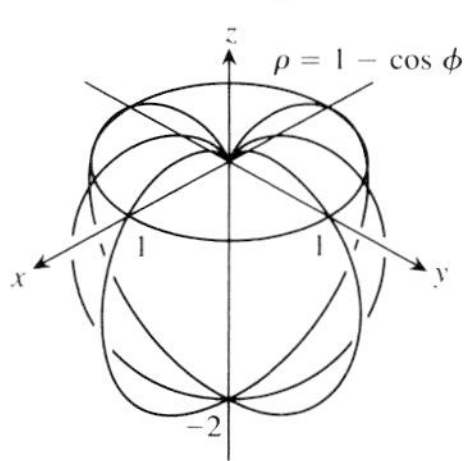

43. (2, 3, 1) **45.** b) $\phi = \pi/2$

49. The surface's equation $r = f(z)$ tells us that the point $(r, \theta, z) = (f(z), \theta, z)$ will lie on the surface for all θ. In particular $(f(z), \theta + \pi, z)$ lies on the surface whenever $(f(z), \theta, z)$ lies on the surface, so the surface is symmetric with respect to the z-axis.

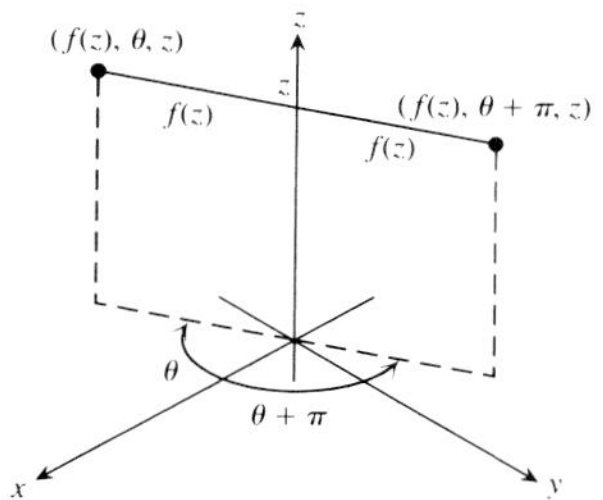

Chapter 11 Practice Exercises, pp. 747–749

1.

θ	**u**
0	**i**
$\pi/2$	**j**
$2\pi/3$	$-(1/2)\,\mathbf{i} + (\sqrt{3}/2)\,\mathbf{j}$
$5\pi/4$	$-(1/\sqrt{2})\,\mathbf{i} - (1/\sqrt{2})\,\mathbf{j}$
$5\pi/3$	$(1/2)\,\mathbf{i} - (\sqrt{3}/2)\,\mathbf{j}$

3. Unit tangents $\pm\left(\frac{1}{\sqrt{5}}\mathbf{i} + \frac{2}{\sqrt{5}}\mathbf{j}\right)$, unit normals $\pm\left(-\frac{2}{\sqrt{5}}\mathbf{i} + \frac{1}{\sqrt{5}}\mathbf{j}\right)$

5. $2 \cdot \left(\frac{1}{\sqrt{2}}\mathbf{i} + \frac{1}{\sqrt{2}}\mathbf{j}\right)$ **7.** $7 \cdot \left(\frac{2}{7}\mathbf{i} - \frac{3}{7}\mathbf{j} + \frac{6}{7}\mathbf{k}\right)$

9. $\frac{8}{\sqrt{33}}\mathbf{i} - \frac{2}{\sqrt{33}}\mathbf{j} + \frac{8}{\sqrt{33}}\mathbf{k}$

11. a) $\overrightarrow{BD} = \overrightarrow{AD} - \overrightarrow{AB}$ b) $\overrightarrow{AP} = \frac{1}{2}\left(\overrightarrow{AB} + \overrightarrow{AD}\right)$

13.

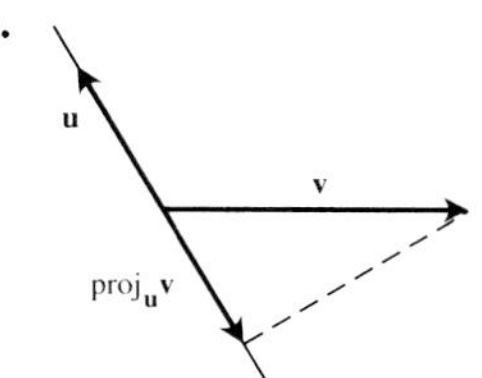

15. $|\mathbf{A}| = \sqrt{2}$, $|\mathbf{B}| = 3$, $\mathbf{A} \cdot \mathbf{B} = \mathbf{B} \cdot \mathbf{A} = 3$, $\mathbf{A} \times \mathbf{B} = -2\,\mathbf{i} + 2\,\mathbf{j} - \mathbf{k}$, $\mathbf{B} \times \mathbf{A} = 2\,\mathbf{i} - 2\,\mathbf{j} + \mathbf{k}$, $|\mathbf{A} \times \mathbf{B}| = 3$, $\theta = \pi/4$, $|\mathbf{B}| \cos\theta = 3/\sqrt{2}$, $\text{proj}_{\mathbf{A}}\mathbf{B} = (3/2)(\mathbf{i} + \mathbf{j})$

17. $\frac{4}{3}(2\mathbf{i} + \mathbf{j} - \mathbf{k}) - \frac{1}{3}(5\mathbf{i} + \mathbf{j} + 11\mathbf{k})$

19.

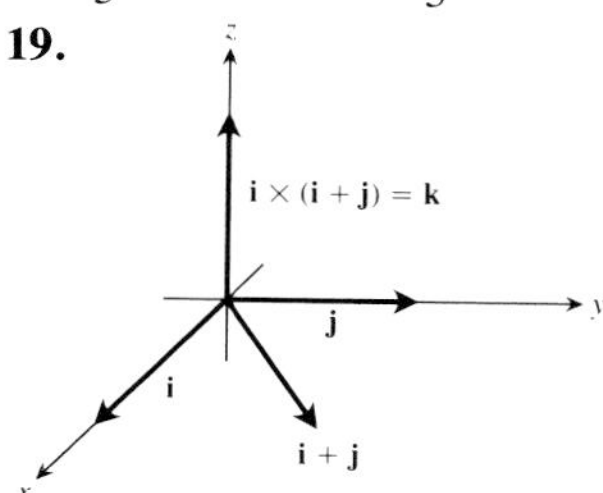

23. $2\sqrt{7}$ **27.** 3 **29.** $\sqrt{78}/3$
31. $x = 1 - 3t$, $y = 2$, $z = 3 + 7t$ **33.** $\sqrt{2}$
35. $2x + y - z = 3$ **37.** $-9x + y + 7z = 4$
39. $\left(0, -\frac{1}{2}, -\frac{3}{2}\right)$, $(-1, 0, -3)$, $(1, -1, 0)$
41. $\pi/3$ **43.** $x = -5 + 5t$, $y = 3 - t$, $z = -3t$
45. b) $x = -12t$, $y = 19/12 + 15t$, $z = 1/6 + 6t$
47. Yes; **v** is parallel to the plane. **49.** $\approx 34{,}641$ J
51. a) $A = \sqrt{14}$ b) $V = 1$
53. a) True b) Not always true c) True d) True e) Not always true f) True g) True h) True

55.

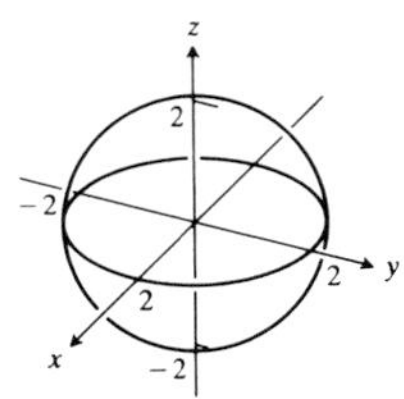

57.

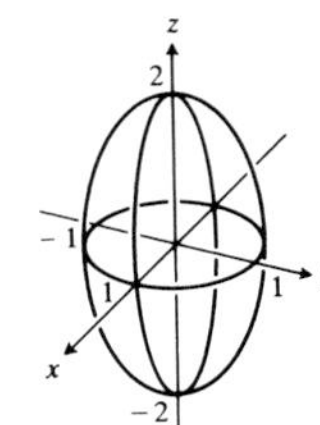

59.

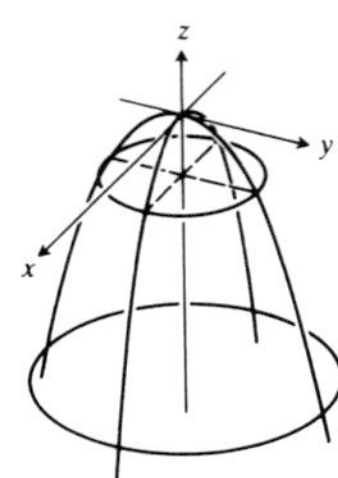

61.

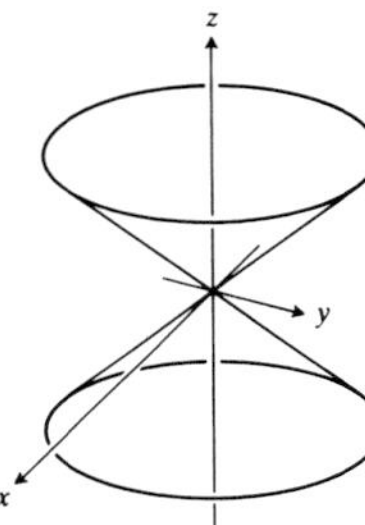

63.

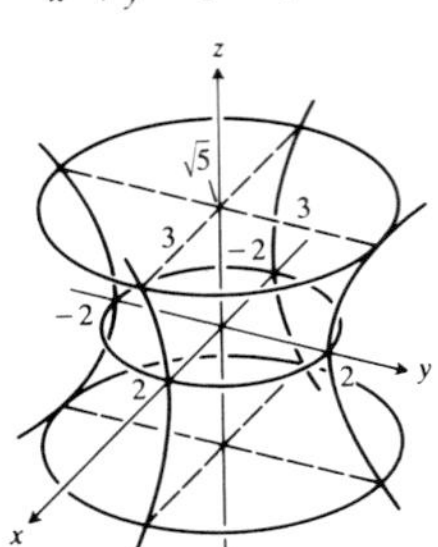

65.

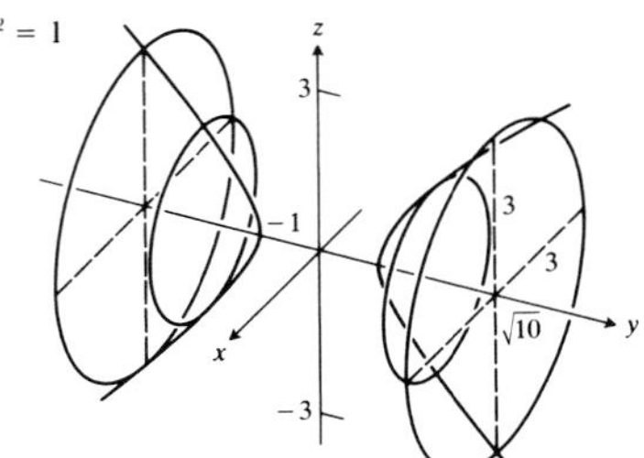

67. The y-axis in the xy-plane; the yz-plane in three-dimensional space
69. The circle centered at (0, 0) with radius 2 in the xy-plane; the cylinder parallel to the z-axis in three-dimensional space with the circle as a generating curve
71. The parabola $x = y^2$ in the xy-plane; the cylinder parallel to the z-axis in three-dimensional space with the parabola as a generating curve
73. A cardioid in the $r\theta$-plane; a cylinder parallel with the z-axis in three-dimensional space with the cardioid as a generating curve
75. A horizontal lemniscate of length $2\sqrt{2}$ in the $r\theta$-plane; the cylinder parallel to the z-axis in three-dimensional space with the lemniscate as a generating curve
77. The sphere of radius 2 centered at the origin
79. The upper nappe of the cone having its vertex at the origin and making a $\pi/6$ angle with the z-axis
81. The upper hemisphere of the sphere of radius 1 centered at the origin

	Rectangular	Cylindrical	Spherical
83.	(1, 0, 0)	(1, 0, 0)	$(1, \pi/2, 0)$
85.	(0, 1, 1)	$(1, \pi/2, 1)$	$(\sqrt{2}, \pi/4, \pi/2)$
87.	$(-1, 0, -1)$	$(1, \pi, -1)$	$(\sqrt{2}, 3\pi/4, \pi)$

89. Cylindrical: $z = 2$; spherical: $\rho \cos \phi = 2$; a plane parallel with the xy-plane
91. Cylindrical: $r^2 + z^2 = -2z$; spherical: $\rho = -2 \cos \phi$; sphere of radius 1 centered at $(0, 0, -1)$ (rectangular)
93. Rectangular: $z = x^2 + y^2$; spherical: $\rho = 0$ or $\rho = \dfrac{\cos \phi}{\sin^2 \phi}$ when $0 < \phi < \pi/2$; paraboloid symmetric to the z-axis, opening upward, vertex at the origin
95. Rectangular: $x^2 + (y - 7/2)^2 = 49/4$; spherical: $\rho \sin \phi = 7 \sin \theta$; cylinder parallel to the z-axis generated by the circle
97. Rectangular: $x^2 + y^2 + z^2 = 16$; cylindrical: $r^2 + z^2 = 16$; sphere of radius 4 centered at the origin
99. Rectangular: $-\sqrt{x^2 + y^2} = z$; cylindrical: $z = -r$, $r \geq 0$; single cone making an angle of $3\pi/4$ with the positive z-axis, vertex at the origin

Chapter 12

Section 12.1, pp. 760–762

1. $\mathbf{v} = (-2 \sin t)\mathbf{i} + (3 \cos t)\mathbf{j} + 4\mathbf{k}$; $\mathbf{a} = (-2 \cos t)\mathbf{i} - (3 \sin t)\mathbf{j}$; speed: $2\sqrt{5}$; direction: $(-1/\sqrt{5})\mathbf{i} + (2/\sqrt{5})\mathbf{k}$; $\mathbf{v}(\pi/2) = 2\sqrt{5}[(-1/\sqrt{5})\mathbf{i} + (2/\sqrt{5})\mathbf{k}]$
3. $\mathbf{v} = \mathbf{i} + 2t\mathbf{j} + 2\mathbf{k}$; $\mathbf{a} = 2\mathbf{j}$; speed: 3; direction: $\frac{1}{3}\mathbf{i} + \frac{2}{3}\mathbf{j} + \frac{2}{3}\mathbf{k}$; $\mathbf{v}(1) = 3\left(\frac{1}{3}\mathbf{i} + \frac{2}{3}\mathbf{j} + \frac{2}{3}\mathbf{k}\right)$
5. $\mathbf{v} = \left(\dfrac{2}{t+1}\right)\mathbf{i} + 2t\mathbf{j} + t\mathbf{k}$; $\mathbf{a} = \left(\dfrac{-2}{(t+1)^2}\right)\mathbf{i} + 2\mathbf{j} + \mathbf{k}$;

speed: $\sqrt{6}$; direction: $\frac{1}{\sqrt{6}}\mathbf{i}+\frac{2}{\sqrt{6}}\mathbf{j}+\frac{1}{\sqrt{6}}\mathbf{k}$;

$\mathbf{v}(1)=\sqrt{6}\left(\frac{1}{\sqrt{6}}\mathbf{i}+\frac{2}{\sqrt{6}}\mathbf{j}+\frac{1}{\sqrt{6}}\mathbf{k}\right)$

7. $\mathbf{v}=e^t\mathbf{i}+\frac{4}{9}e^{2t}\mathbf{j}$; $\mathbf{a}=e^t\mathbf{i}+\frac{8}{9}e^{2t}\mathbf{j}$; speed: 5; direction: $\frac{3}{5}\mathbf{i}+\frac{4}{5}\mathbf{j}$; $\mathbf{v}(\ln 3)=5\left[\frac{3}{5}\mathbf{i}+\frac{4}{5}\mathbf{j}\right]$ **9.** $\pi/2$ **11.** $\pi/2$ **13.** $t=0,\pi,2\pi$

15. $(1/4)\mathbf{i}+7\mathbf{j}+(3/2)\mathbf{k}$ **17.** $\left(\frac{\pi+2\sqrt{2}}{2}\right)\mathbf{j}+2\mathbf{k}$

19. $(\ln 4)\mathbf{i}+(\ln 4)\mathbf{j}+(\ln 2)\mathbf{k}$

21. $t=\frac{\pi}{4}$: $\mathbf{v}=\frac{\sqrt{2}}{2}\mathbf{i}-\frac{\sqrt{2}}{2}\mathbf{j}$, $\mathbf{a}=\frac{-\sqrt{2}}{2}\mathbf{i}-\frac{\sqrt{2}}{2}\mathbf{j}$;

$t=\frac{\pi}{2}$: $\mathbf{v}=-\mathbf{j}$, $\mathbf{a}=-\mathbf{i}$

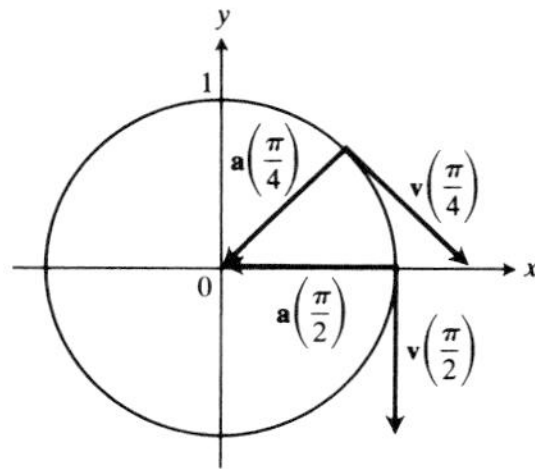

23. $t=\pi$: $\mathbf{v}=2\mathbf{i}$, $\mathbf{a}=-\mathbf{j}$; $t=\frac{3\pi}{2}$: $\mathbf{v}=\mathbf{i}-\mathbf{j}$, $\mathbf{a}=-\mathbf{i}$

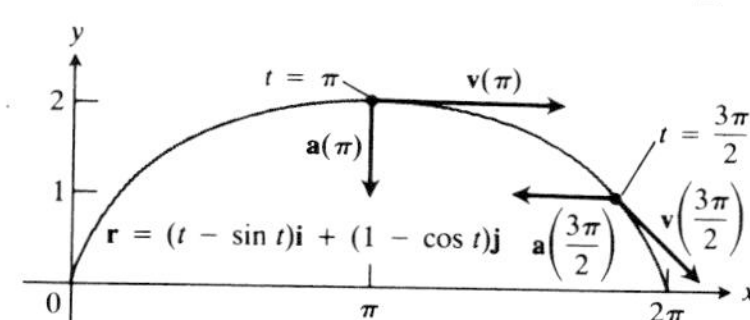

25. $\mathbf{r}=\left(\frac{-t^2}{2}+1\right)\mathbf{i}+\left(\frac{-t^2}{2}+2\right)\mathbf{j}+\left(\frac{-t^2}{2}+3\right)\mathbf{k}$

27. $\mathbf{r}=[(t+1)^{3/2}-1]\mathbf{i}+(-e^{-t}+1)\mathbf{j}+[\ln(t+1)+1]\mathbf{k}$

29. $\mathbf{r}=8t\,\mathbf{i}+8t\,\mathbf{j}+(-16t^2+100)\mathbf{k}$

31. $\max|\mathbf{v}|=2$, $\max|\mathbf{a}|=1$; $\min|\mathbf{v}|=0$, $\min|\mathbf{a}|=1$

35. $x=t,\ y=-1,\ z=1+t$

37. $x=at,\ y=a,\ z=2\pi b+bt$

Section 12.2, pp. 768–770

1. 50 sec **3.** a) 72.2 sec, 25,510 m b) 4020 m c) 6378 m

7. $v_0=9.9$ m/sec, $\alpha=18.4°$ or $71.6°$ **9.** 190 mph

13. The golf ball will clip the leaves at the top.

15. About 1 in. **17.** 149 ft/sec, 2.25 sec

23. 1.92 sec, 73.7 ft (approx.), yes

Section 12.3, p. 775

1. $\mathbf{T}=\left(-\frac{2}{3}\sin t\right)\mathbf{i}+\left(\frac{2}{3}\cos t\right)\mathbf{j}+\frac{\sqrt{5}}{3}\mathbf{k}$, 3π

3. $\mathbf{T}=\frac{1}{\sqrt{1+t}}\mathbf{i}+\frac{\sqrt{t}}{\sqrt{1+t}}\mathbf{k}$, $\frac{52}{3}$

5. $\mathbf{T}=\frac{1}{\sqrt{3}}\mathbf{i}-\frac{1}{\sqrt{3}}\mathbf{j}+\frac{1}{\sqrt{3}}\mathbf{k}$, $3\sqrt{3}$

7. $\mathbf{T}=\left(\frac{\cos t-t\sin t}{t+1}\right)\mathbf{i}+\left(\frac{\sin t+t\cos t}{t+1}\right)\mathbf{j}+\left(\frac{\sqrt{2}t^{1/2}}{t+1}\right)\mathbf{k}$, $\frac{\pi^2}{2}+\pi$ **9.** $s(t)=5t$, $L=\frac{5\pi}{2}$

11. $s(t)=\sqrt{3}e^t-\sqrt{3}$, $L=\frac{3\sqrt{3}}{4}$ **13.** $\sqrt{2}+\ln(1+\sqrt{2})$

15. a) Cylinder is $x^2+y^2=1$, plane is $x+z=1$.

b)

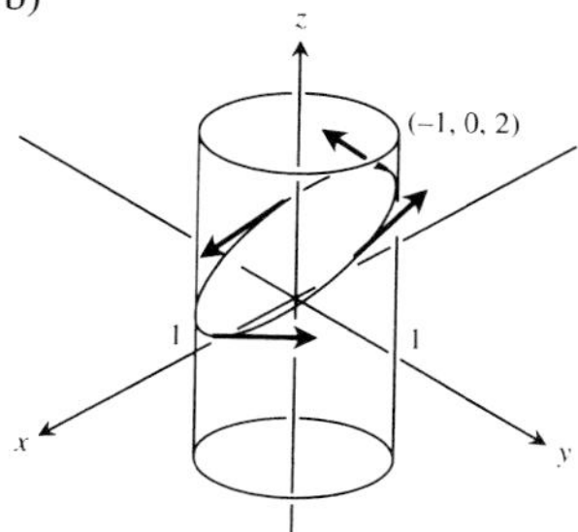

c)

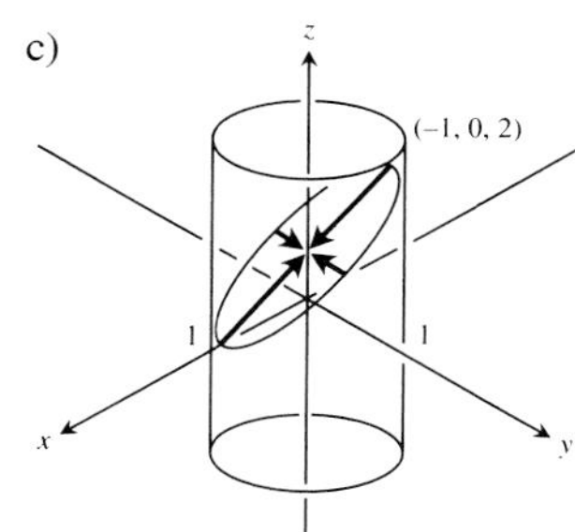

d) $L=\int_0^{2\pi}\sqrt{1+\sin^2 t}\,dt$ e) $L\approx 7.64$

Section 12.4, pp. 786–787

1. $\mathbf{T}=(\cos t)\mathbf{i}-(\sin t)\mathbf{j}$, $\mathbf{N}=(-\sin t)\mathbf{i}-(\cos t)\mathbf{j}$, $\kappa=\cos t$

3. $\mathbf{T}=\frac{1}{\sqrt{1+t^2}}\mathbf{i}-\frac{t}{\sqrt{1+t^2}}\mathbf{j}$, $\mathbf{N}=\frac{-t}{\sqrt{1+t^2}}\mathbf{i}-\frac{1}{\sqrt{1+t^2}}\mathbf{j}$, $\kappa=\frac{1}{2(\sqrt{1+t^2})^3}$

5. $\mathbf{T}=\frac{3\cos t}{5}\mathbf{i}-\frac{3\sin t}{5}\mathbf{j}+\frac{4}{5}\mathbf{k}$, $\mathbf{N}=(-\sin t)\mathbf{i}-(\cos t)\mathbf{j}$, $\mathbf{B}=\left(\frac{4}{5}\cos t\right)\mathbf{i}-\left(\frac{4}{5}\sin t\right)\mathbf{j}-\frac{3}{5}\mathbf{k}$, $\kappa=\frac{3}{25}$, $\tau=-\frac{4}{25}$

7. $\mathbf{T}=\left(\frac{\cos t-\sin t}{\sqrt{2}}\right)\mathbf{i}+\left(\frac{\cos t+\sin t}{\sqrt{2}}\right)\mathbf{j}$, $\mathbf{N}=\left(\frac{-\cos t-\sin t}{\sqrt{2}}\right)\mathbf{i}+\left(\frac{-\sin t+\cos t}{\sqrt{2}}\right)\mathbf{j}$, $\mathbf{B}=\mathbf{k}$, $\kappa=\frac{1}{e^t\sqrt{2}}$, $\tau=0$ **9.** $\mathbf{T}=\frac{t}{\sqrt{t^2+1}}\mathbf{i}+\frac{1}{\sqrt{t^2+1}}\mathbf{j}$, $\mathbf{N}=\frac{\mathbf{i}}{\sqrt{t^2+1}}-\frac{t\,\mathbf{j}}{\sqrt{t^2+1}}$, $\mathbf{B}=-\mathbf{k}$, $\kappa=\frac{1}{t(t^2+1)^{3/2}}$, $\tau=0$

11. $\mathbf{T} = \left(\operatorname{sech}\frac{t}{a}\right)\mathbf{i} + \left(\tanh\frac{t}{a}\right)\mathbf{j}$, $\mathbf{N} = \left(-\tanh\frac{t}{a}\right)\mathbf{i} + \left(\operatorname{sech}\frac{t}{a}\right)\mathbf{j}$,

$\mathbf{B} = \mathbf{k}$, $\kappa = \frac{1}{a}\operatorname{sech}^2\frac{t}{a}$, $\tau = 0$

13. $\mathbf{a} = \frac{2t}{\sqrt{1+t^2}}\mathbf{T} + \frac{2}{\sqrt{1+t^2}}\mathbf{N}$ **15.** $\mathbf{a} = |a|\,\mathbf{N}$

17. $\mathbf{a}(1) = \frac{4}{3}\mathbf{T} + \frac{2\sqrt{5}}{3}\mathbf{N}$ **19.** $\mathbf{a}(0) = 2\mathbf{N}$

21. $\mathbf{r}\left(\frac{\pi}{4}\right) = \frac{\sqrt{2}}{2}\mathbf{i} + \frac{\sqrt{2}}{2}\mathbf{j} - \mathbf{k}$, $\mathbf{T}\left(\frac{\pi}{4}\right) = -\frac{\sqrt{2}}{2}\mathbf{i} + \frac{\sqrt{2}}{2}\mathbf{j}$,

$\mathbf{N}\left(\frac{\pi}{4}\right) = -\frac{\sqrt{2}}{2}\mathbf{i} - \frac{\sqrt{2}}{2}\mathbf{j}$, $\mathbf{B}\left(\frac{\pi}{4}\right) = \mathbf{k}$; osculating plane: $z = -1$;
normal plane: $-x + y = 0$; rectifying plane: $x + y = \sqrt{2}$

23. Yes. If the car is moving on a curved path ($\kappa \neq 0$), then $a_N = \kappa|\mathbf{v}|^2 \neq 0$ and $\mathbf{a} \neq \mathbf{0}$.

27. $\kappa = 1/t$, $\rho = t$ **29.** $1/(2b)$ **31.** $12\pi/\sqrt{10}$

33. $\left(x - \frac{\pi}{2}\right)^2 + y^2 = 1$ **35.** (b) $\kappa(x) = \cos x$

37. $\kappa(x) = 2/(1+4x^2)^{3/2}$ **39.** $\kappa(x) = |\sin x|/(1+\cos^2 x)^{3/2}$

Section 12.5, p. 794–795

1. $T = 93.2$ min **3.** $a = 6763$ km **5.** $T = 1655$ min

7. $a = 20{,}430$ km **9.** $|v| = 1.9966 \times 10^7 r^{-1/2}$ m/sec

11. Circle: $v_0 = \sqrt{\frac{GM}{r_0}}$; ellipse: $\sqrt{\frac{GM}{r_0}} < v_0 < \sqrt{\frac{2GM}{r_0}}$;
parabola: $v_0 = \sqrt{\frac{2GM}{r_0}}$; hyperbola: $v_0 > \sqrt{\frac{2GM}{r_0}}$

Chapter 12 Practice Exercises, pp. 795–797

1. $\frac{x^2}{16} + \frac{y^2}{2} = 1$

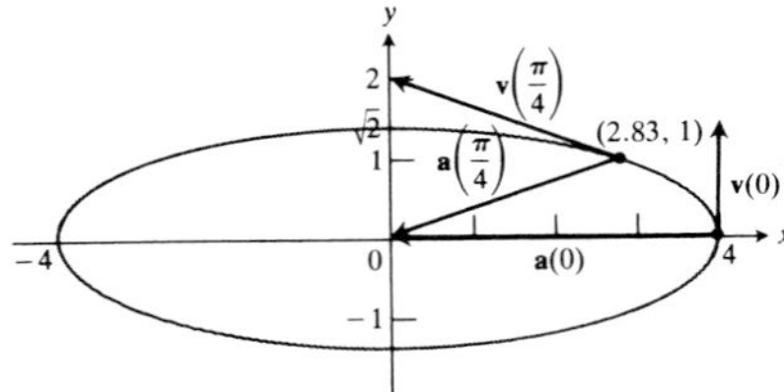

3. $6\mathbf{i} + 8\mathbf{j}$

5. $\mathbf{r} = [(\cos t) - 1]\,\mathbf{i} + [(\sin t) + 1]\,\mathbf{j} + t\,\mathbf{k}$ **7.** $\mathbf{r} = \mathbf{i} + t^2\mathbf{j} + t\,\mathbf{k}$

9. Length $= \frac{\pi}{4}\sqrt{1 + \frac{\pi^2}{16}} + \ln\left(\frac{\pi}{4} + \sqrt{1 + \frac{\pi^2}{16}}\right)$

11. $\mathbf{T}(0) = \frac{2}{3}\mathbf{i} - \frac{2}{3}\mathbf{j} + \frac{1}{3}\mathbf{k}$; $\mathbf{N}(0) = \frac{1}{\sqrt{2}}\mathbf{i} + \frac{1}{\sqrt{2}}\mathbf{j}$; $\mathbf{B}(0) =$
$-\frac{1}{3\sqrt{2}}\mathbf{i} + \frac{1}{3\sqrt{2}}\mathbf{j} + \frac{4}{3\sqrt{2}}\mathbf{k}$; $\kappa = \frac{\sqrt{2}}{3}$; $\tau = \frac{1}{6}$

13. $\mathbf{T}(\ln 2) = \frac{1}{\sqrt{17}}\mathbf{i} + \frac{4}{\sqrt{17}}\mathbf{j}$; $\mathbf{N}(\ln 2) = -\frac{4}{\sqrt{17}}\mathbf{i} + \frac{1}{\sqrt{17}}\mathbf{j}$;
$\mathbf{B}(\ln 2) = \mathbf{k}$; $\kappa = \frac{8}{17\sqrt{17}}$; $\tau = 0$

15. $\mathbf{a}(0) = 10\,\mathbf{T} + 6\,\mathbf{N}$

17. $\mathbf{T} = \left(\frac{1}{\sqrt{2}}\cos t\right)\mathbf{i} - (\sin t)\,\mathbf{j} + \left(\frac{1}{\sqrt{2}}\cos t\right)\mathbf{k}$; $\mathbf{N} =$
$\left(-\frac{1}{\sqrt{2}}\sin t\right)\mathbf{i} - (\cos t)\,\mathbf{j} - \left(\frac{1}{\sqrt{2}}\sin t\right)\mathbf{k}$; $\mathbf{B} = \frac{1}{\sqrt{2}}\mathbf{i} - \frac{1}{\sqrt{2}}\mathbf{k}$;
$\kappa = \frac{1}{\sqrt{2}}$; $\tau = 0$

19. $\pi/2$ for all t **21.** $\pi/3$ **23.** 57 ft **25.** 59.19 ft/sec

27. $x = 1 + t$, $y = t$, $z = -t$ **29.** $\kappa = 1/5$

31. 5971 miles; 16,395,469 km²; 3.21% visible

33. b) $\approx 1.4987\ 01133\ 5179$

Chapter 13

Section 13.1, pp. 805–806

1. Domain: All points in the xy-plane
Range: All reals
Level curves: the lines $y - x = c$.

3. Domain: $(x, y) \neq (0, 0)$
Range: All reals
Level curves: the circles with center $(0, 0)$ and radii >0.

5. Domain: All points in the xy-plane
Range: All reals
Level curves: for $f(x, y) = 0$, the x- and y-axes; for $f(x, y) \neq 0$, hyperbolas with the x- and y-axes as asymptotes

7. Domain: All points in the xy-plane
Range: The nonnegative real numbers
Level curves: for $f(x, y) = 0$, the origin; for $f(x, y) \neq 0$, ellipses with center $(0, 0)$ and major and minor axes along the x- and y-axes, respectively

9. a)

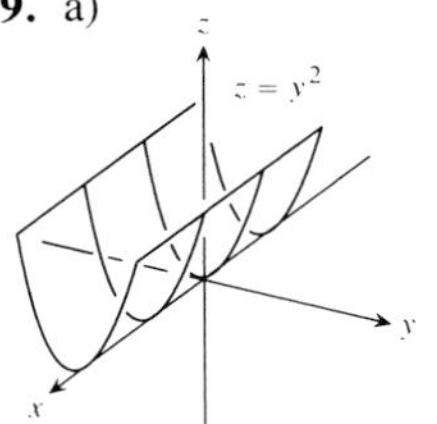

b)

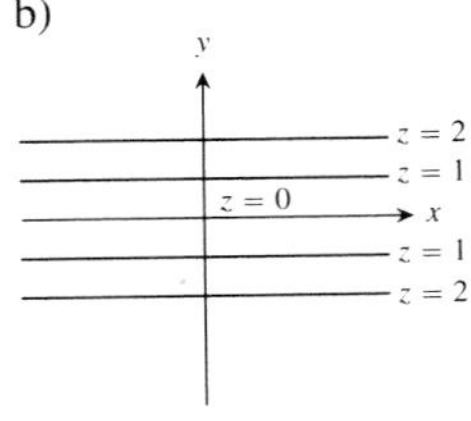

11. a)

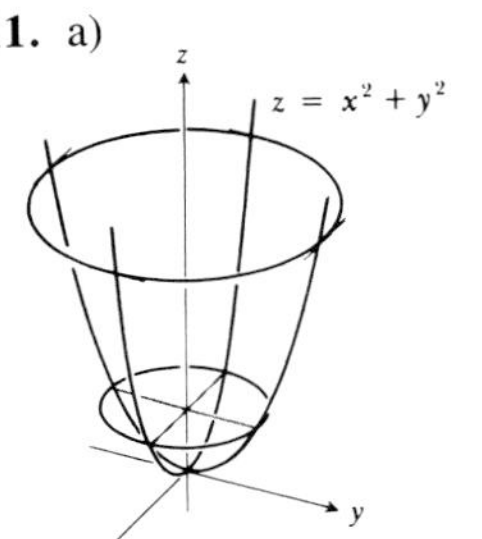

b)

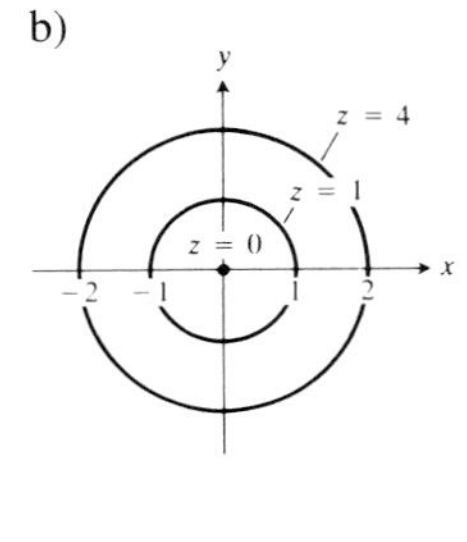

13. a)

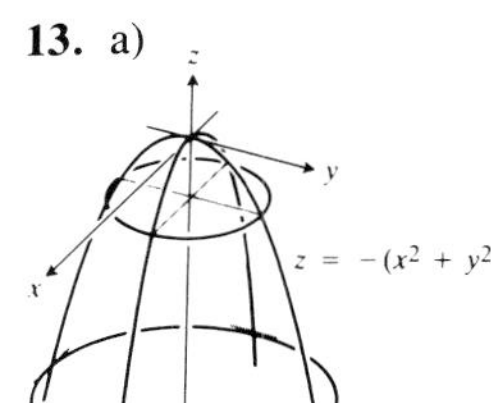

b)

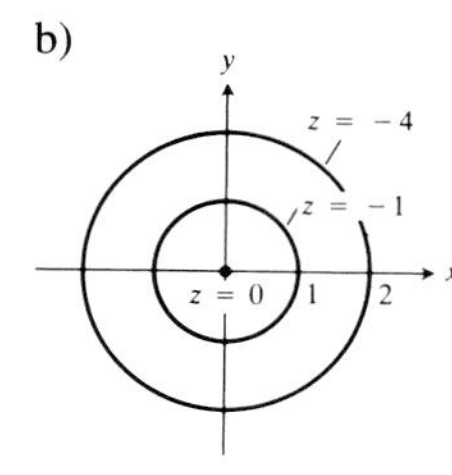

15. a)

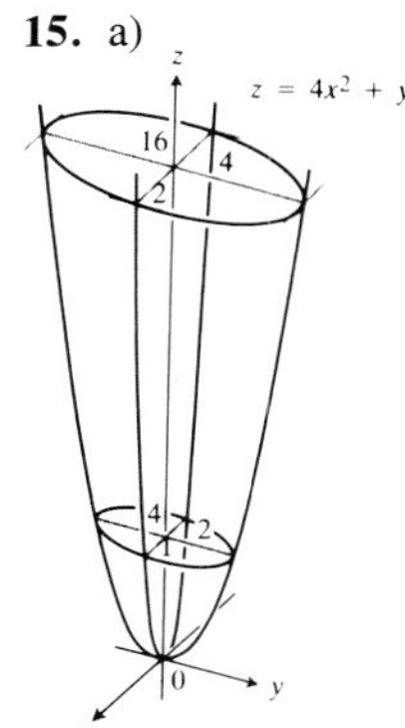

b)

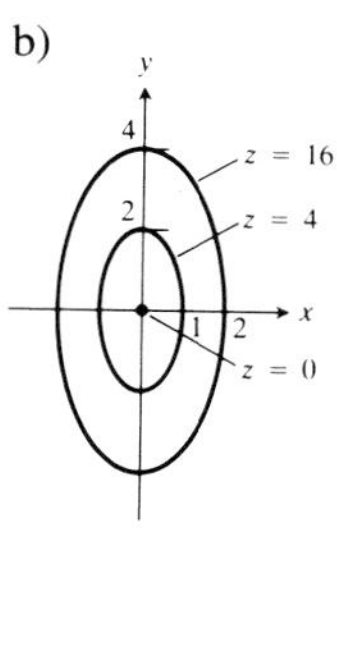

17. f **19.** a **21.** d

23.

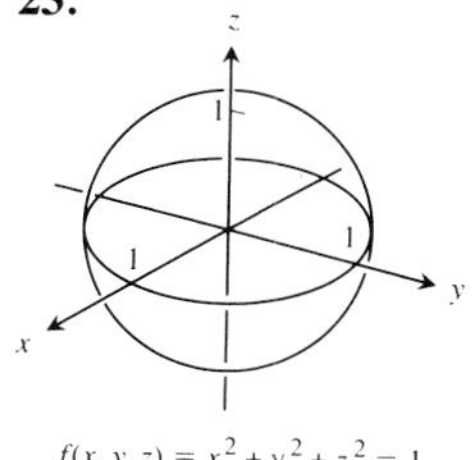

25.

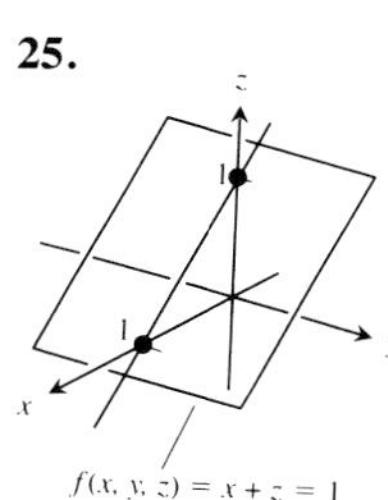

27.

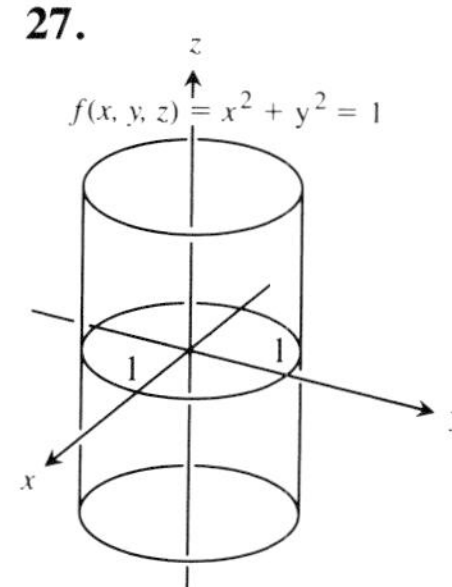

29.

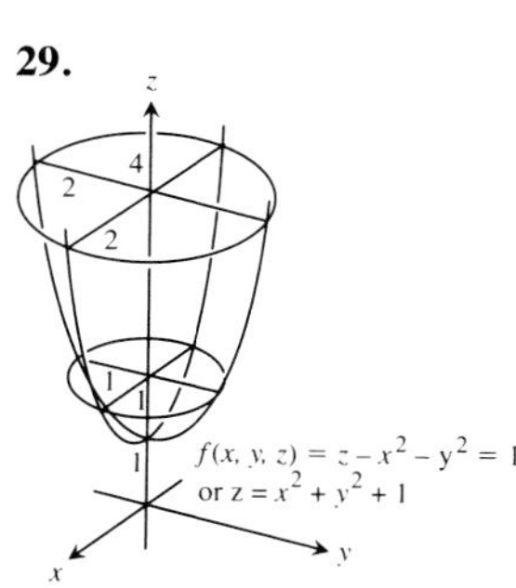

31. $x^2 + y^2 = 16$ **33.** $\sqrt{x - y} - \ln z = 2$ **35.** Yes; 2000
37. About 62.43 km

Section 13.2, pp. 813–814

1. 5/2 **3.** 1/2 **5.** $2\sqrt{6}$ **7.** 1 **9.** 1 **11.** 1 **13.** 0
15. −1 **17.** 2 **19.** 1/4 **21.** 7 **23.** 2 **25.** $\tan^{-1}\left(-\frac{\pi}{4}\right)$
27. a) All (x, y) b) All (x, y) except $(0, 0)$
29. a) All (x, y) except where $x = 0$ or $y = 0$ b) All (x, y)
31. a) All (x, y, z) b) All (x, y, z) except the interior of the cylinder $x^2 + y^2 = 1$
33. a) All (x, y, z) with $z \neq 0$ b) All (x, y, z) with $x^2 + z^2 \neq 1$
35. Consider paths along $y = x, x > 0$, and along $y = x, x < 0$
37. Consider the paths $y = kx^2$, k a constant
39. Consider the paths $y = mx$, m a constant, $m \neq -1$
41. Consider the paths $y = kx^2$, k a constant, $k \neq 0$
45. The limit is 1. **47.** The limit is 0.
49. a) $f(x, y)\big|_{y = mx} = \sin 2\theta$ where $\tan \theta = m$

Section 13.3, pp. 821–823

1. $\frac{\partial f}{\partial x} = 2, \frac{\partial f}{\partial y} = 0$ **3.** $\frac{\partial f}{\partial x} = 0, \frac{\partial f}{\partial y} = 0$
5. $\frac{\partial f}{\partial x} = y - 1, \frac{\partial f}{\partial y} = x$ **7.** $\frac{\partial f}{\partial x} = 2x - y, \frac{\partial f}{\partial y} = -x + 2y$
9. $\frac{\partial f}{\partial x} = 2x(5y - 1)^3, \frac{\partial f}{\partial y} = 15x^2(5y - 1)^2$
11. $\frac{\partial f}{\partial x} = x(x^2 + y^2)^{-1/2}, \frac{\partial f}{\partial y} = y(x^2 + y^2)^{-1/2}$
13. $\frac{\partial f}{\partial x} = \frac{-y^2 - 1}{(xy - 1)^2}, \frac{\partial f}{\partial y} = \frac{-x^2 - 1}{(xy - 1)^2}$
15. $\frac{\partial f}{\partial x} = e^x \ln y, \frac{\partial f}{\partial y} = \frac{e^x}{y}$
17. $\frac{\partial f}{\partial x} = e^x \sin(y + 1), \frac{\partial f}{\partial y} = e^x \cos(y + 1)$
19. $f_x = y + z, f_y = x + z, f_z = y + x$
21. $f_x = -x(x^2 + y^2 + z^2)^{-3/2}, f_y = -y(x^2 + y^2 + z^2)^{-3/2}$, $f_z = -z(x^2 + y^2 + z^2)^{-3/2}$
23. $f_x = \cos(x + yz), f_y = z\cos(x + yz), f_z = y\cos(x + yz)$
25. $\frac{\partial f}{\partial t} = -2\pi \sin(2\pi t - \alpha), \frac{\partial f}{\partial \alpha} = \sin(2\pi t - \alpha)$
27. $\frac{\partial h}{\partial \rho} = \sin\phi \cos\theta, \frac{\partial h}{\partial \phi} = \rho\cos\phi\cos\theta$, $\frac{\partial h}{\partial \theta} = -\rho\sin\phi\sin\theta$
29. $\frac{\partial W}{\partial P} = V, \frac{\partial W}{\partial V} = P + \frac{\delta v^2}{2g}, \frac{\partial W}{\partial \delta} = \frac{Vv^2}{2g}, \frac{\partial W}{\partial v} = \frac{V\delta v}{g}$, $\frac{\partial W}{\partial g} = \frac{-V\delta v^2}{2g^2}$
31. $\frac{\partial^2 f}{\partial x^2} = 0, \frac{\partial^2 f}{\partial y^2} = 0, \frac{\partial^2 f}{\partial y \partial x} = \frac{\partial^2 f}{\partial x \partial y} = 1$
33. $\frac{\partial^2 g}{\partial x^2} = 2y - y\sin x, \frac{\partial^2 g}{\partial y^2} = -\cos y$, $\frac{\partial^2 g}{\partial y \partial x} = \frac{\partial^2 g}{\partial x \partial y} = 2x + \cos x$
35. $\frac{\partial^2 r}{\partial x^2} = \frac{-1}{(x + y)^2}, \frac{\partial^2 r}{\partial y^2} = \frac{-1}{(x + y)^2}, \frac{\partial^2 r}{\partial y \partial x} = \frac{\partial^2 r}{\partial x \partial y} = \frac{-1}{(x + y)^2}$
37. $\frac{\partial^2 w}{\partial y \partial x} = \frac{\partial^2 w}{\partial x \partial y} = \frac{-6}{(2x + 3y)^2}$ **39.** $\frac{\partial^2 w}{\partial y \partial x} = \frac{\partial^2 w}{\partial x \partial y} = 2y + 6xy^2 + 12x^2y^3$
41. a) x first b) y first c) x first d) x first e) y first f) y first
43. −2

Section 13.4, pp. 831–832

1. a) $L(x, y) = 1$ b) $L(x, y) = 2x + 2y - 1$
3. a) $L(x, y) = 1 + x$ b) $L(x, y) = -y + (\pi/2)$
5. a) $L(x, y) = 3x - 4y + 5$ b) $L(x, y) = 3x - 4y + 5$
7. $L(x, y) = 7 + x - 6y; 0.06$ **9.** $L(x, y) = x + y + 1; 0.08$
11. $L(x, y) = 1 + x; 0.0222$
13. Pay more attention to the smaller of the two dimensions. It will generate the larger partial derivative.
15. Maximum error (estimate) ≤ 0.31 in magnitude
17. Maximum percentage error $= \pm 4.83\%$
19. Let $|x - 1| \leq 0.014$, $|y - 1| \leq 0.014$ **21.** $\approx 0.1\%$
23. a) $L(x, y, z) = 2x + 2y + 2z - 3$ b) $L(x, y, z) = y + z$ c) $L(x, y, z) = 0$
25. a) $L(x, y, z) = x$ b) $L(x, y, z) = \frac{1}{\sqrt{2}}x + \frac{1}{\sqrt{2}}y$
c) $L(x, y, z) = \frac{1}{3}x + \frac{2}{3}y + \frac{2}{3}z$
27. a) $L(x, y, z) = 2 + x$ b) $L(x, y, z) = x - y - z + (\pi/2) + 1$ c) $L(x, y, z) = x - y - z + (\pi/2) + 1$
31. 47/24 ft³
33. Magnitude of possible error ≤ 4.8

Section 13.5, pp. 839–840

1. $\frac{dw}{dt} = 0, \frac{dw}{dt}(\pi) = 0$ **3.** $\frac{dw}{dt} = 1, \frac{dw}{dt}(3) = 1$

5. $\frac{dw}{dt} = 4t \tan^{-1} t + 1, \frac{dw}{dt}(1) = \pi + 1$

7. a) $\frac{\partial z}{\partial r} = 4 \cos \theta \ln (r \sin \theta) + 4 \cos \theta; \frac{\partial z}{\partial \theta} = -4r \sin \theta \ln (r \sin \theta) + \frac{4r \cos^2 \theta}{\sin \theta}$ b) $\frac{\partial z}{\partial r} = \sqrt{2}(\ln 2 + 2); \frac{\partial z}{\partial \theta} = -2\sqrt{2} \ln 2 + 4\sqrt{2}$

9. a) $\frac{\partial w}{\partial u} = 2u + 4uv; \frac{\partial w}{\partial v} = -2v + 2u^2$ b) $\frac{\partial w}{\partial u} = 3; \frac{\partial w}{\partial v} = -\frac{3}{2}$

11. a) $\frac{\partial u}{\partial x} = 0; \frac{\partial u}{\partial y} = \frac{z}{(z - y)^2}; \frac{\partial u}{\partial z} = \frac{-y}{(z - y)^2}$
b) $\frac{\partial u}{\partial x} = 0; \frac{\partial u}{\partial y} = 1; \frac{\partial u}{\partial z} = -2$

13. $\frac{dz}{dt} = \frac{\partial z}{\partial x}\frac{dx}{dt} + \frac{\partial z}{\partial y}\frac{dy}{dt}$

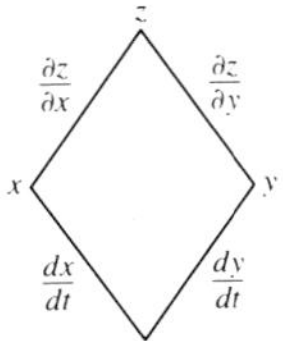

15. $\frac{\partial w}{\partial u} = \frac{\partial w}{\partial x}\frac{\partial x}{\partial u} + \frac{\partial w}{\partial y}\frac{\partial y}{\partial u} + \frac{\partial w}{\partial z}\frac{\partial z}{\partial u}$

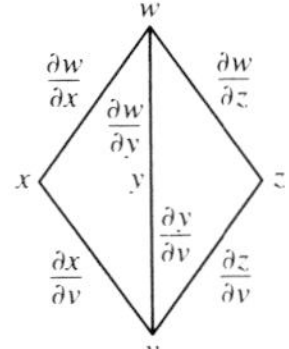

$\frac{\partial w}{\partial v} = \frac{\partial w}{\partial x}\frac{\partial x}{\partial v} + \frac{\partial w}{\partial y}\frac{\partial y}{\partial v} + \frac{\partial w}{\partial z}\frac{\partial z}{\partial v}$

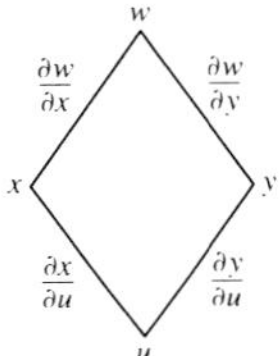

17. $\frac{\partial w}{\partial u} = \frac{\partial w}{\partial x}\frac{\partial x}{\partial u} + \frac{\partial w}{\partial y}\frac{\partial y}{\partial u}$

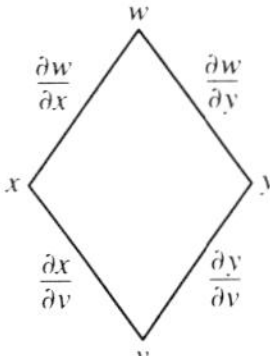

$\frac{\partial w}{\partial v} = \frac{\partial w}{\partial x}\frac{\partial x}{\partial v} + \frac{\partial w}{\partial y}\frac{\partial y}{\partial v}$

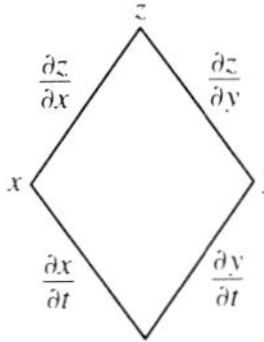

19. $\frac{\partial z}{\partial t} = \frac{\partial z}{\partial x}\frac{\partial x}{\partial t} + \frac{\partial z}{\partial y}\frac{\partial y}{\partial t}$

$\frac{\partial z}{\partial s} = \frac{\partial z}{\partial x}\frac{\partial x}{\partial s} + \frac{\partial z}{\partial y}\frac{\partial y}{\partial s}$

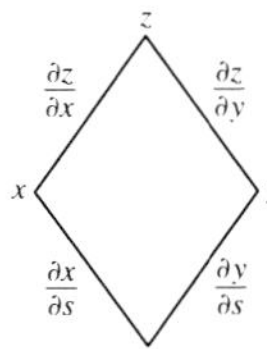

21. $\dfrac{\partial w}{\partial s} = \dfrac{dw}{du}\dfrac{\partial u}{\partial s}$ $\qquad$ $\dfrac{\partial w}{\partial t} = \dfrac{dw}{du}\dfrac{\partial u}{\partial t}$

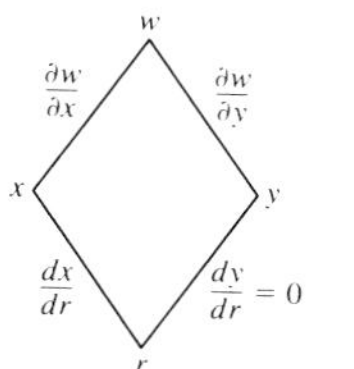

23. $\dfrac{\partial w}{\partial r} = \dfrac{\partial w}{\partial x}\dfrac{dx}{dr} + \dfrac{\partial w}{\partial y}\dfrac{dy}{dr} = \dfrac{\partial w}{\partial x}\dfrac{dx}{dr}$ since $\dfrac{dy}{dr} = 0$

$\dfrac{\partial w}{\partial s} = \dfrac{\partial w}{\partial x}\dfrac{dx}{ds} + \dfrac{\partial w}{\partial y}\dfrac{dy}{ds} = \dfrac{\partial w}{\partial y}\dfrac{dy}{ds}$ since $\dfrac{dx}{ds} = 0$

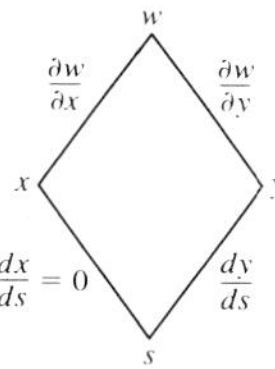

25. 4/3 **27.** − 4/5 **29.** $\dfrac{\partial z}{\partial x} = \dfrac{1}{4}, \dfrac{\partial z}{\partial y} = -\dfrac{3}{4}$

31. $\dfrac{\partial z}{\partial x} = -1, \dfrac{\partial z}{\partial y} = -1$ **33.** 12 **35.** −7

37. $\partial z/\partial u = 2; \partial z/\partial v = 1$ **39.** − 0.00005 amps/sec

41. $(\cos 1, \sin 1, 1)$ and $(\cos(-2), \sin(-2), -2)$

43. a) Maximum at $\left(-\dfrac{\sqrt{2}}{2}, \dfrac{\sqrt{2}}{2}\right)$ and $\left(\dfrac{\sqrt{2}}{2}, -\dfrac{\sqrt{2}}{2}\right)$, minimum at $\left(\dfrac{\sqrt{2}}{2}, \dfrac{\sqrt{2}}{2}\right)$ and $\left(-\dfrac{\sqrt{2}}{2}, -\dfrac{\sqrt{2}}{2}\right)$ b) Max = 6, min = 2

Section 13.6, pp. 851–853

1.

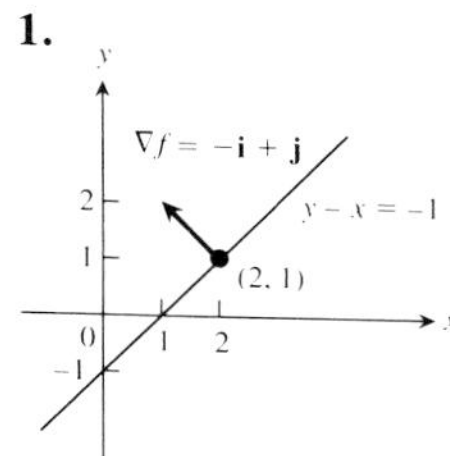

3.

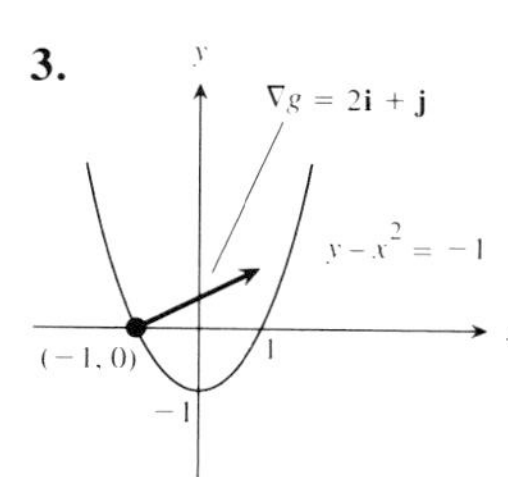

5. $\nabla f = 2\mathbf{i} + 2\mathbf{j} - 4\mathbf{k}$ **7.** $\nabla h = \dfrac{-1}{27}\mathbf{i} - \dfrac{2}{27}\mathbf{j} + \dfrac{2}{27}\mathbf{k}$

9. $(D_{\mathbf{u}}f) = 14/13$ **11.** $(D_{\mathbf{u}}g) = -4/5$ **13.** $(D_{\mathbf{u}}f) = 3$

15. $(D_{\mathbf{u}}g) = 2$

17. f increases most rapidly in the direction $\mathbf{u} = -\dfrac{1}{\sqrt{2}}\mathbf{i} + \dfrac{1}{\sqrt{2}}\mathbf{j}$; decreases most rapidly in the direction $-\mathbf{u} = \dfrac{1}{\sqrt{2}}\mathbf{i} - \dfrac{1}{\sqrt{2}}\mathbf{j}$; $(D_{\mathbf{u}}f) = \sqrt{2}, (D_{-\mathbf{u}}f) = -\sqrt{2}$.

19. f increases most rapidly in the direction $\mathbf{u} = \dfrac{2}{\sqrt{5}}\mathbf{i} + \dfrac{1}{\sqrt{5}}\mathbf{j}$; decreases most rapidly in the direction $-\mathbf{u} = -\dfrac{2}{\sqrt{5}}\mathbf{i} - \dfrac{1}{\sqrt{5}}\mathbf{j}$; $(D_{\mathbf{u}}f) = \sqrt{5}, (D_{-\mathbf{u}}f) = -\sqrt{5}$.

21. g increases most rapidly in the direction $\mathbf{u} = \frac{2}{3}\mathbf{i} + \frac{2}{3}\mathbf{j} + \frac{1}{3}\mathbf{k}$; decreases most rapidly in the direction $-\mathbf{u} = -\frac{2}{3}\mathbf{i} - \frac{2}{3}\mathbf{j} - \frac{1}{3}\mathbf{k}$; $(D_{\mathbf{u}}g) = 3, (D_{-\mathbf{u}}g) = -3$. **23.** $df = \dfrac{9}{910} \approx 0.01$

25. $dg = 0$

27. Tangent: $x + y + z = 3$
Normal line: $x = 1 + 2t, y = 1 + 2t, z = 1 + 2t$

29. Tangent: $2x - z - 2 = 0$
Normal line: $x = 2 - 4t, y = 0, z = 2 + 2t$

31. Tangent: $2x + 2y + z - 4 = 0$
Normal line: $x = 2t, y = 1 + 2t, z = 2 + t$

33. Tangent: $x + y + z - 1 = 0$
Normal line: $x = t, y = 1 + t, z = t$

35. $2x - z - 2 = 0$ **37.** $x - y + 2z - 1 = 0$

39. **41.**

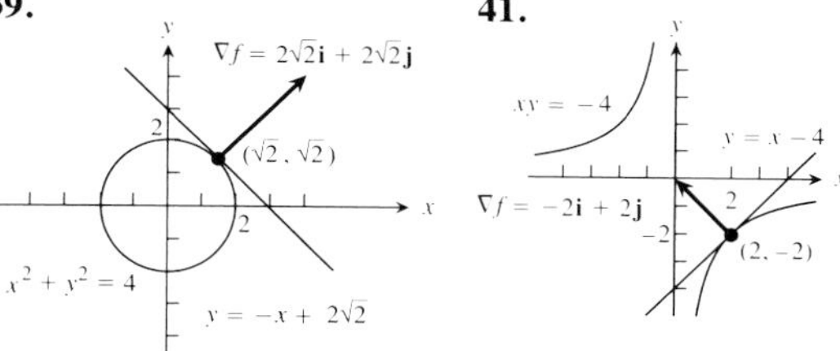

43. $x = 1, y = 1 + 2t, z = 1 - 2t$

45. $x = 1 - 2t, y = 1, z = (1/2) + 2t$

47. $x = 1 + 90t, y = 1 - 90t, z = 3$

49. $\mathbf{u} = \dfrac{7}{\sqrt{53}}\mathbf{i} - \dfrac{2}{\sqrt{53}}\mathbf{j}; -\mathbf{u} = -\dfrac{7}{\sqrt{53}}\mathbf{i} + \dfrac{2}{\sqrt{53}}\mathbf{j}$

51. At $-\dfrac{\pi}{4}, -\dfrac{\pi}{2\sqrt{2}}$; at 0, 0; at $\dfrac{\pi}{4}, \dfrac{\pi}{2\sqrt{2}}$ **53.** $-\dfrac{7}{\sqrt{5}}$

Section 13.7, pp. 860–863

1. $f(-3, 3) = -5$, local minimum **3.** $f\left(\dfrac{2}{3}, \dfrac{4}{3}\right) = 0$, local maximum

5. $f(-2, 1)$, saddle point **7.** $f\left(\dfrac{6}{5}, \dfrac{69}{25}\right)$, saddle point

9. $f(2, 1)$, saddle point

11. $f(2, -1) = -6$, local minimum **13.** $f(1, 2)$, saddle point

15. $f(0, 0)$, saddle point

17. $f(0,0)$, saddle point; $f\left(-\frac{2}{3}, \frac{2}{3}\right) = \frac{170}{27}$, local maximum
19. $f(0,0) = 0$, local minimum; $f(1,-1)$, saddle point
21. $f(0,0)$, saddle point; $f\left(\frac{4}{9}, \frac{4}{3}\right) = -\frac{64}{81}$, local minimum
23. $f(0,0)$, saddle point; $f(0,2) = -12$, local minimum; $f(-2,0) = -4$, local maximum; $f(-2,2)$, saddle point
25. $f(0,0)$, saddle point; $f(1,1) = 2, f(-1,-1) = 2$, local maxima
27. Absolute maximum: 1 at $(0,0)$; absolute minimum: -5 at $(1,2)$
29. Absolute maximum: 4 at $(0,2)$; absolute minimum: 0 at $(0,0)$
31. Absolute maximum: 11 at $(0,-3)$; absolute minimum: -10 at $(4,-2)$
33. Absolute maximum: 4 at $(2,0)$; absolute minimum: $\frac{3\sqrt{2}}{2}$ at $(3,-\pi/4)$, $(3,\pi/4)$, $(1,-\pi/4)$, and $(1,\pi/4)$
35. Hottest: 2.25° at $(-1/2, \sqrt{3}/2)$ and $(-1/2, -\sqrt{3}/2)$; coldest: -0.25° at $(1/2, 0)$
37. a) $f(0,0)$, saddle point b) $f(1,2)$, local minimum c) $f(1,-2)$, local minimum; $f(-1,-2)$, saddle point
43. a) On the semicircle, $\max f = 2\sqrt{2}$ at $t = \pi/4$, $\min f = -2$ at $t = \pi$. On the quarter circle, $\max f = 2\sqrt{2}$ at $t = \pi/4$, $\min f = 2$ at $t = 0, \pi/2$ b) On the semicircle, $\max g = 2$ at $t = \pi/4$, $\min g = -2$ at $t = 3\pi/4$. On the quarter circle, $\max g = 2$ at $t = \pi/4$, $\min g = 0$ at $t = 0, \pi/2$ c) On the semicircle, $\max h = 8$ at $t = 0, \pi$, $\min h = 4$ at $t = \pi/2$. On the quarter circle, $\max h = 8$ at $t = 0$, $\min h = 4$ at $t = \pi/2$
45. i) $\min f = -1/2$ at $t = -1/2$; no max
ii) $\max f = 0$ at $t = -1, 0$; $\min f = -1/2$ at $t = -1/2$
iii) $\max f = 4$ at $t = 1$; $\min f = 0$ at $t = 0$
47. $y = -\frac{20}{13}x + \frac{9}{13}; y\big|_{x=4} = -\frac{71}{13}$ **49.** $y = \frac{3}{2}x + \frac{1}{6}; y\big|_{x=4} = \frac{37}{6}$
51. $y = 0.122x + 3.58$

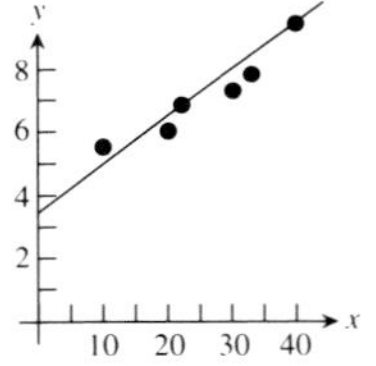

53. a)

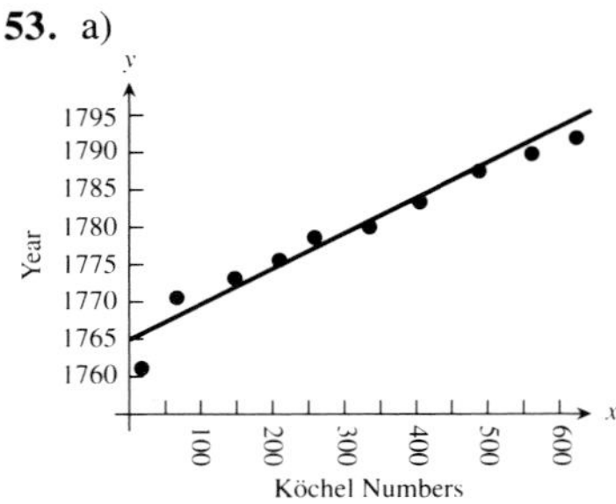

b) $y = 0.0427K + 1764.8$ c) 1780

Section 13.8, pp. 871–873

1. $(\pm\sqrt{2}, 1/2), (\pm\sqrt{2}, -1/2)$ **3.** 39
5. $f(0,3) = 0, f(2,1) = 4$
7. a) 8 b) 64 **9.** $r = 2$ cm, $h = 4$ cm
11. Minimum $= 0°$, maximum $= 125°$
13. $f(0,0) = 0$ is minimum, $f(2,4) = 20$ is maximum.
15. $f(1,-2,5) = 30$ is maximum, $f(-1,2,-5) = -30$ is minimum.
17. $(0,0,1)$
19. $f\left(\frac{5}{\sqrt{14}}, \frac{10}{\sqrt{14}}, \frac{15}{\sqrt{14}}\right) = 5\sqrt{14}$ is maximum, $f\left(-\frac{5}{\sqrt{14}}, -\frac{10}{\sqrt{14}}, -\frac{15}{\sqrt{14}}\right) = -5\sqrt{14}$ is minimum.
21. $\frac{4096}{25\sqrt{5}}$ **23.** $U(8,14) = \$128$ **27.** $(2,4,4)$
29. Maximum is $1 + 6\sqrt{3}$ at $(\pm\sqrt{6}, \sqrt{3}, 1)$, minimum is $1 - 6\sqrt{3}$ at $(\pm\sqrt{6}, -\sqrt{3}, 1)$.
31. Maximum is 4 at $(0, 0, \pm 2)$, minimum is 2 at $(\pm\sqrt{2}, \pm\sqrt{2}, 0)$

Chapter 13 Practice Exercises, pp. 873–875

1.

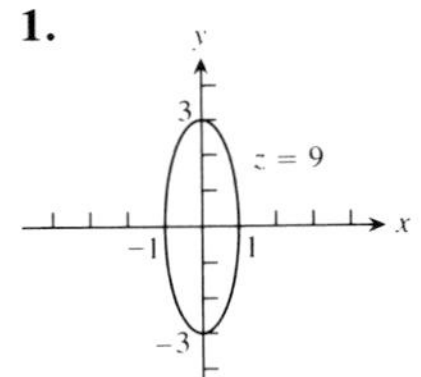

Domain: All points in the xy-plane
Range: $z \geq 0$
Level curves are ellipses with major axis along the y-axis and minor axis along the x-axis.

3.

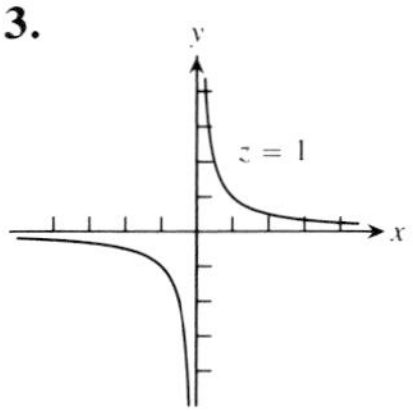

Domain: All (x, y) such that $x \neq 0$ and $y \neq 0$
Range: $z \neq 0$
Level curves are hyperbolas with the x- and y-axes as asymptotes.

5.

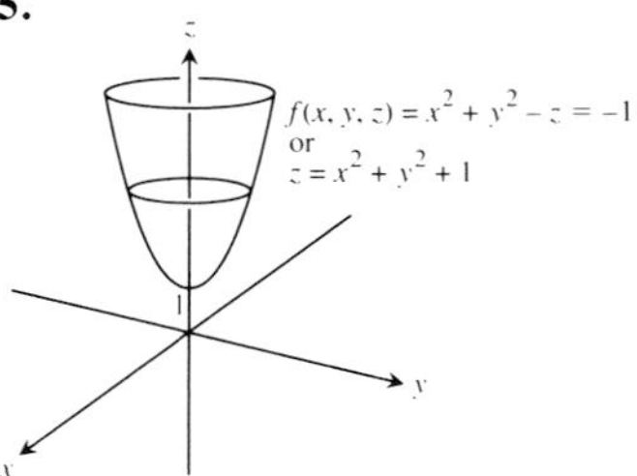

Domain: All points (x, y, z)
Range: All real numbers
Level surfaces are paraboloids of revolution with the z-axis as axis.

7.

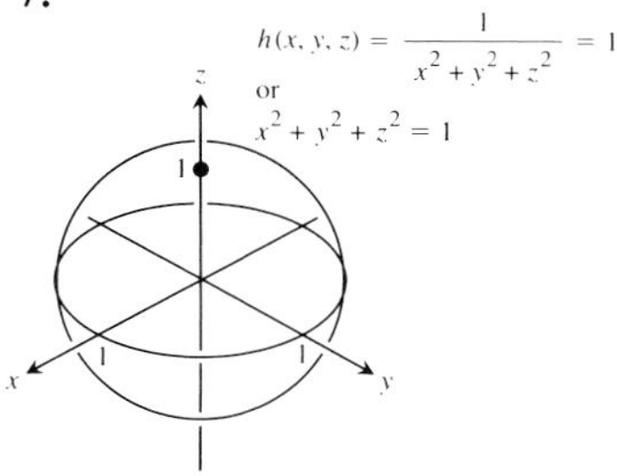

Domain: All (x, y, z) such that $(x, y, z) \neq (0, 0, 0)$
Range: Positive real numbers
Level surfaces are spheres with center $(0, 0, 0)$ and radius $r > 0$.

9. -2 **11.** $1/2$ **13.** 1 **15.** Let $y = kx^2, k \neq 1$

17. $\dfrac{\partial g}{\partial r} = \cos\theta + \sin\theta,\ \dfrac{\partial g}{\partial \theta} = -r\sin\theta + r\cos\theta$

19. $\dfrac{\partial f}{\partial R_1} = -\dfrac{1}{R_1{}^2},\ \dfrac{\partial f}{\partial R_2} = -\dfrac{1}{R_2{}^2},\ \dfrac{\partial f}{\partial R_3} = -\dfrac{1}{R_3{}^2}$

21. $\dfrac{\partial P}{\partial n} = \dfrac{RT}{V},\ \dfrac{\partial P}{\partial R} = \dfrac{nT}{V},\ \dfrac{\partial P}{\partial T} = \dfrac{nR}{V},\ \dfrac{\partial P}{\partial V} = -\dfrac{nRT}{V^2}$

23. $\dfrac{\partial^2 g}{\partial x^2} = 0,\ \dfrac{\partial^2 g}{\partial y^2} = \dfrac{2x}{y^3},\ \dfrac{\partial^2 g}{\partial y\,\partial x} = \dfrac{\partial^2 g}{\partial x\,\partial y} = -\dfrac{1}{y^2}$

25. $\dfrac{\partial^2 f}{\partial x^2} = -30x + \dfrac{2-2x^2}{(x^2+1)^2},\ \dfrac{\partial^2 f}{\partial y^2} = 0,\ \dfrac{\partial^2 f}{\partial y\,\partial x} = \dfrac{\partial^2 f}{\partial x\,\partial y} = 1$

27. $L(x, y) = (1/2)(x - y + 1)$. The upper bound found for $|E|$ will depend on the upper bound used for $|f_{xx}|, |f_{xy}|, |f_{yy}|$. With $M = \sqrt{2}/2$, $|E| \le 0.0142$. With $M = 1$, $|E| \le 0.02$.

29. $L(x, y, z) = y - 3z$, $L(x, y, z) = x + y - z - 1$

31. Diameter

33. Increases by 0.038 amp; percentage change in $V = -4.17\%$; percentage change in $R = -20\%$; estimated percentage change in $I = 15.83\%$

35. $\left.\dfrac{dw}{dt}\right|_{t=0} = -1$ **37.** $\left.\dfrac{\partial w}{\partial r}\right|_{(r,s)=(\pi,0)} = 2,\ \left.\dfrac{\partial w}{\partial s}\right|_{(r,s)=(\pi,0)} = 2 - \pi$

39. $\left.\dfrac{dy}{dx}\right|_{(x,y)=(0,1)} = -1$ **41.** $\left.\dfrac{df}{dt}\right|_{t=1} = -(\sin 1 + \cos 2)\sin 1 + (\cos 1 + \cos 2)\cos 1 - 2(\sin 1 + \cos 1)\sin 2$

43. f increases most rapidly in the direction $\mathbf{u} = -\dfrac{\sqrt{2}}{2}\mathbf{i} - \dfrac{\sqrt{2}}{2}\mathbf{j}$; decreases most rapidly in the direction $-\mathbf{u} = \dfrac{\sqrt{2}}{2}\mathbf{i} + \dfrac{\sqrt{2}}{2}\mathbf{j}$; $D_{\mathbf{u}}f = \dfrac{\sqrt{2}}{2}, D_{-\mathbf{u}}f = -\dfrac{\sqrt{2}}{2}, D_{\mathbf{u}_1}f = -\dfrac{7}{10}$

45. f increases most rapidly in the direction $\mathbf{u} = \frac{2}{7}\mathbf{i} + \frac{3}{7}\mathbf{j} + \frac{6}{7}\mathbf{k}$; decreases most rapidly in the direction $-\mathbf{u} = -\frac{2}{7}\mathbf{i} - \frac{3}{7}\mathbf{j} - \frac{6}{7}\mathbf{k}$; $D_{\mathbf{u}}f = 7, D_{-\mathbf{u}}f = -7, D_{\mathbf{u}_1}f = 7$

47.

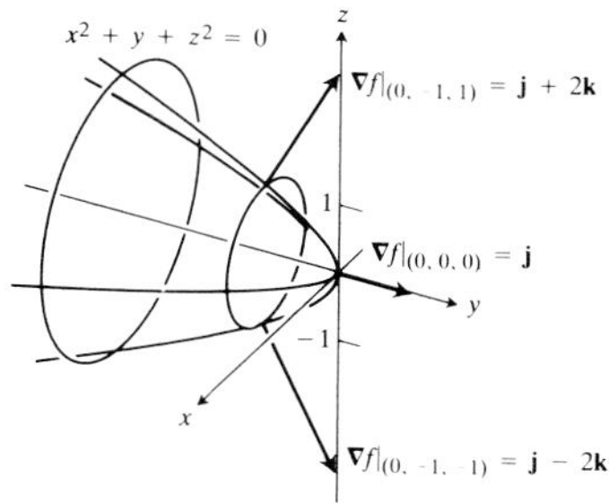

49. Tangent: $4x - y - 5z = 4$
Normal line: $x = 2 + 4t, y = -1 - t, z = 1 - 5t$

51. $2y - z - 2 = 0$

53. Tangent: $x + y = \pi + 1$
Normal: $y = x - \pi + 1$

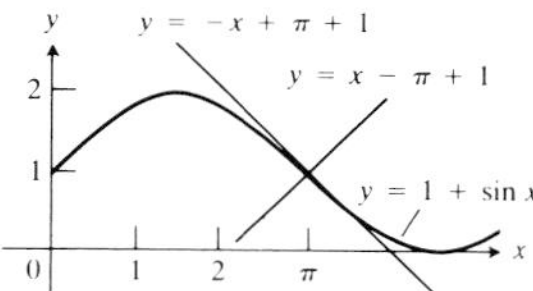

55. $x = 1 - 2t, y = 1, z = \frac{1}{2} + 2t$ **57.** $\sqrt{3}$

59. Local minimum of -8 at $(-2, -2)$

61. Saddle point at $(0, 0), f(0, 0) = 0$; local maximum of $\frac{1}{4}$ at $\left(-\frac{1}{2}, -\frac{1}{2}\right)$

63. Saddle point at $(0, 0), f(0, 0) = 0$; local minimum of -4 at $(0, 2)$; local maximum of 4 at $(-2, 0)$; saddle point at $(-2, 2)$, $f(-2, 2) = 0$

65. Absolute maximum: 28 at $(0, 4)$; absolute minimum: $-\frac{9}{4}$ at $\left(\frac{3}{2}, 0\right)$

67. Absolute maximum: 18 at $(2, -2)$; absolute minimum: $-\frac{17}{4}$ at $\left(-2, \frac{1}{2}\right)$

69. Absolute maximum: 8 at $(-2, 0)$; absolute minimum: -1 at $(1, 0)$

71. $(3, 3\sqrt{2}), (3, -3\sqrt{2})$

73. 50 is maximum, -50 is minimum.

75. $(1, 1, 1), (1, -1, -1), (-1, -1, 1), (-1, 1, -1)$

Chapter 14

Section 14.1, pp. 885–887

1. 16

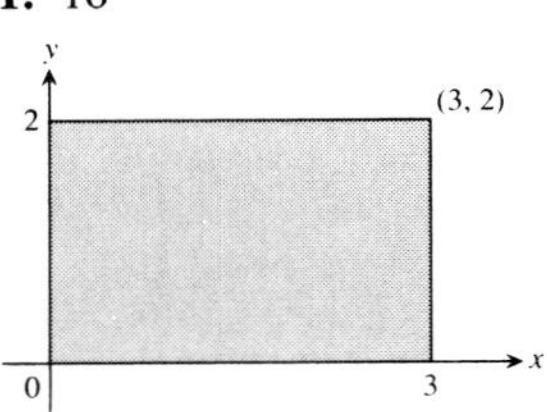

3. 1

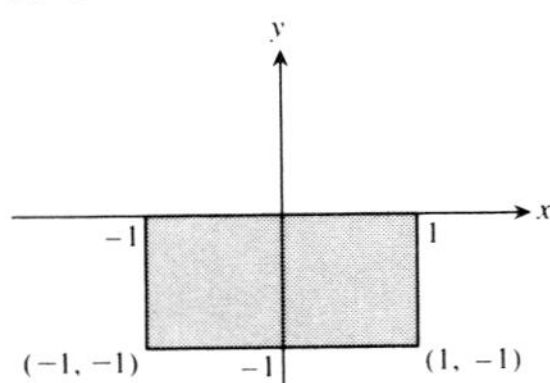

5. $\frac{\pi^2}{2} + 2$

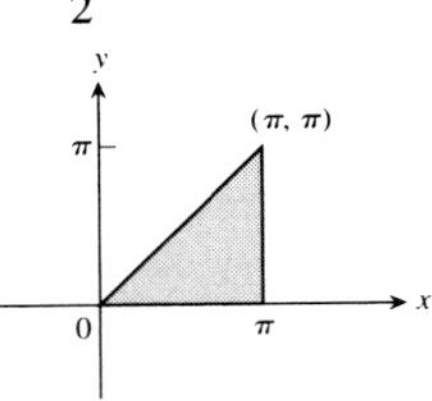

7. $8 \ln 8 - 16 + e$

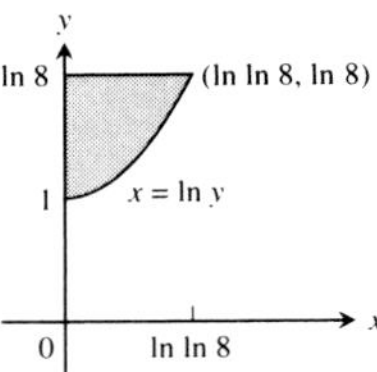

9. $e - 2$

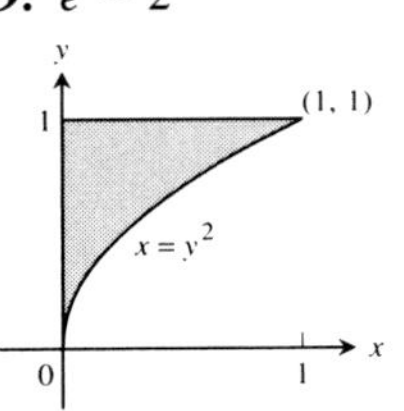

11. $\frac{3}{2} \ln 2$ **13.** 1/6 **15.** −1/10

17. 8

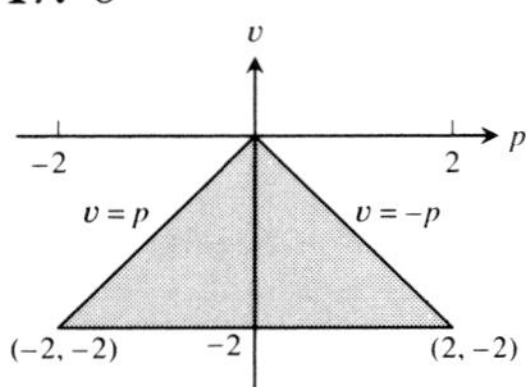

19. 2π

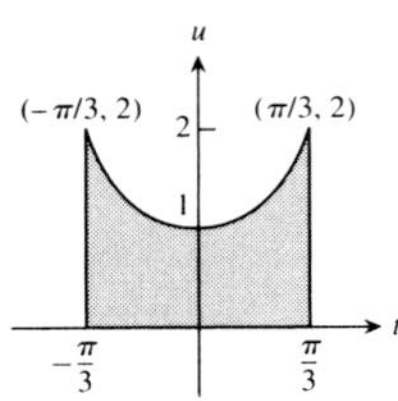

21. $\int_2^4 \int_0^{(4-y)/2} dx\, dy$

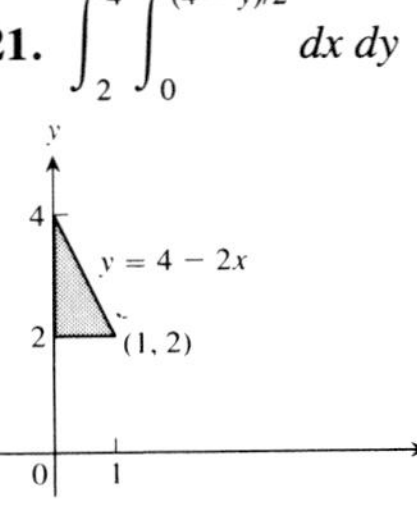

23. $\int_0^1 \int_{x^2}^{x} dy\, dx$

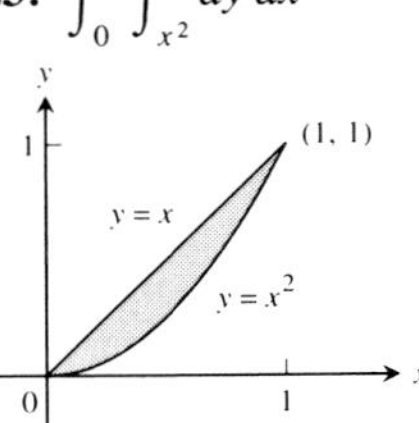

25. $\int_1^e \int_{\ln y}^{1} dx\, dy$

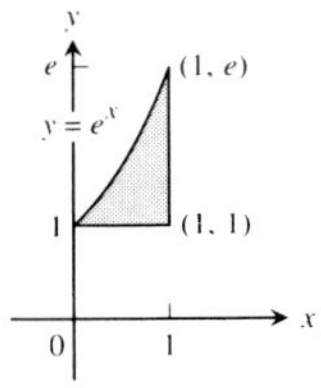

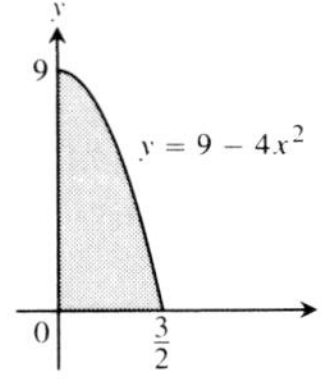

27. $\int_0^9 \int_0^{(\sqrt{9-y})/2} 16x\, dx\, dy$

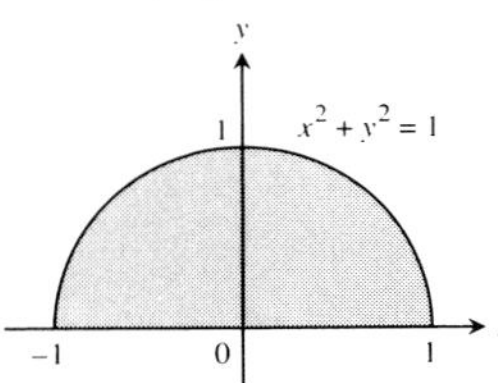

29. $\int_{-1}^1 \int_0^{\sqrt{1-x^2}} 3y\, dy\, dx$

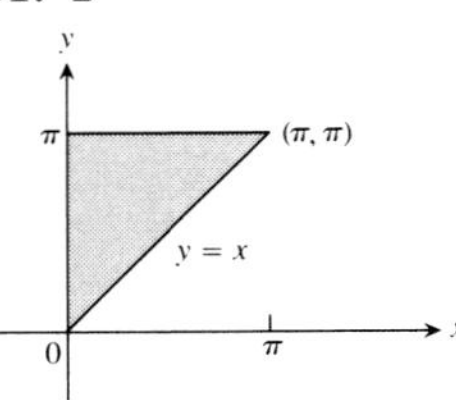

31. 2

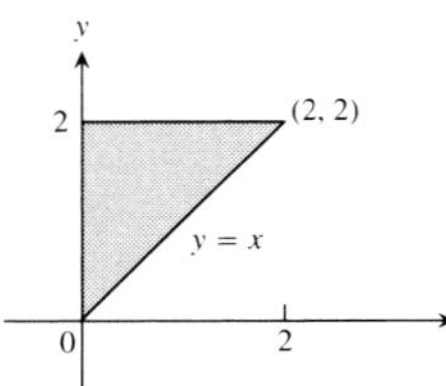

33. $4 - \sin 4$

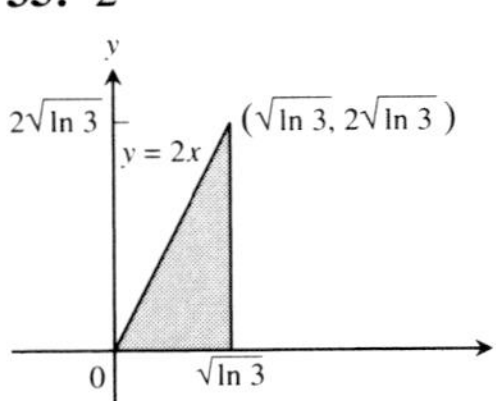

35. 2

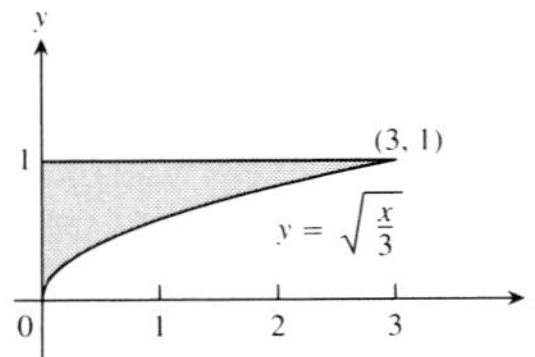

37. $e - 1$

39. $\frac{625}{12}$ **41.** 16 **43.** 4/3 **49.** 0.603 **51.** 0.233

Section 14.2, pp. 892–893

1. $\int_0^2 \int_0^{2-x} dy\,dx = 2$ or $\int_0^2 \int_0^{2-y} dx\,dy = 2$

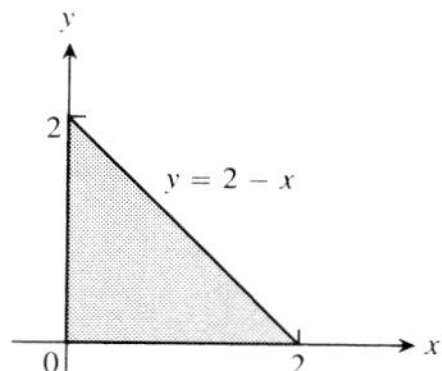

3. $\int_{-2}^{1} \int_{y-2}^{-y^2} dx\,dy = 9/2$ **5.** $\int_0^{\ln 2} \int_0^{e^x} dy\,dx = 1$

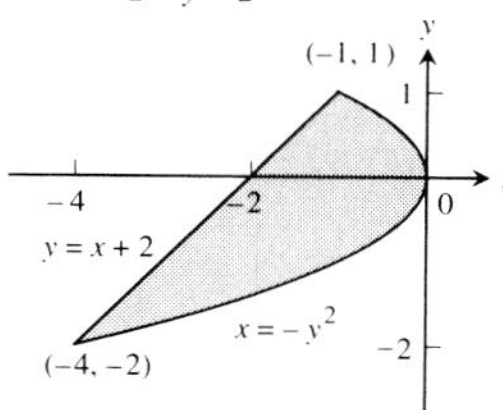

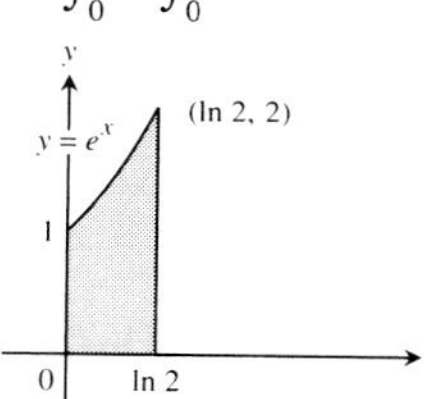

7. $\int_0^1 \int_{y^2}^{2y-y^2} dx\,dy = 1/3$ **9.** 12

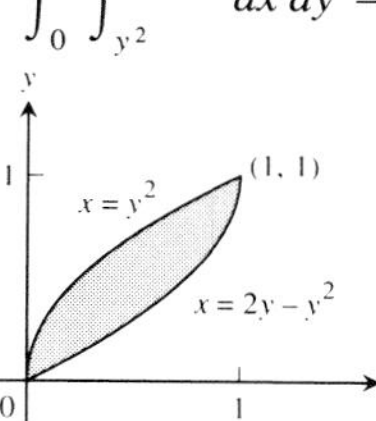

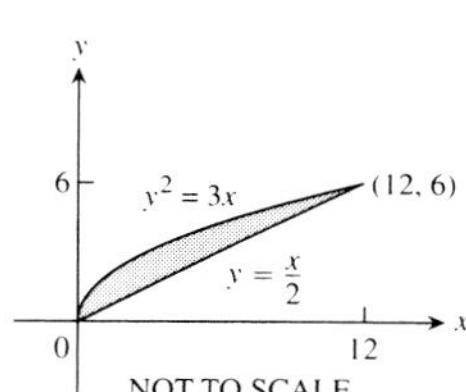

11. $\sqrt{2} - 1$ **13.** 3/2

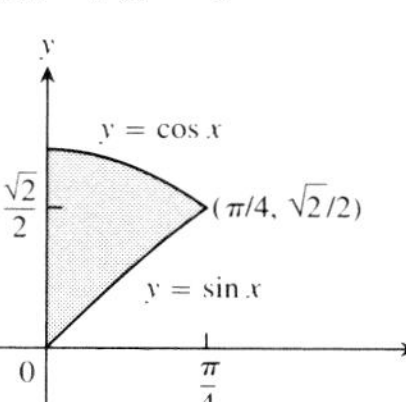

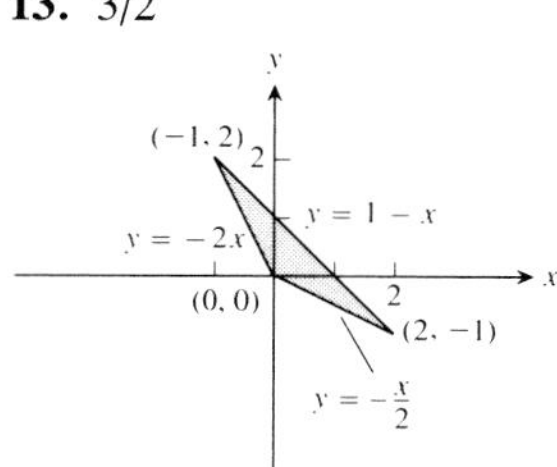

15. a) 0, b) $4/\pi^2$ **17.** 8/3 **19.** $\bar{x} = \frac{5}{14}, \bar{y} = \frac{38}{35}$

21. $\bar{x} = \frac{64}{35}, \bar{y} = \frac{5}{7}$ **23.** $\bar{x} = 0, \bar{y} = \frac{4}{3\pi}$

25. $\bar{x} = \bar{y} = \frac{4a}{3\pi}$ **27.** $\bar{x} = \frac{\pi}{2}, \bar{y} = \frac{\pi}{8}$

29. $\bar{x} = -1, \bar{y} = \frac{1}{4}$ **31.** $I_x = \frac{64}{105}$, $R_x = 2\sqrt{\frac{2}{7}}$

33. $\bar{x} = \frac{3}{8}, \bar{y} = \frac{17}{16}$ **35.** $\bar{x} = \frac{11}{3}, \bar{y} = \frac{14}{27}, I_y = 432, R_y = 4$

37. $\bar{x} = 0, \bar{y} = \frac{13}{31}, I_y = \frac{7}{5}, R_y = \sqrt{\frac{21}{31}}$

39. $\bar{x} = 0, \bar{y} = 7/10; I_x = 9/10, I_y = 3/10, I_0 = 6/5; R_x = \frac{3\sqrt{6}}{10}$, $R_y = \frac{3\sqrt{2}}{10}, R_0 = \frac{3\sqrt{2}}{5}$

41. If $0 < a < 5/2$, the appliance will have to be tipped more than 45° to fall over.

Section 14.3, p. 898

1. $\pi/2$ **3.** $\pi/8$ **5.** πa^2 **7.** 36 **9.** $(1 - \ln 2)\pi$
11. $(2\ln 2 - 1)(\pi/2)$ **13.** 2 **15.** $\pi(\ln(4) - 1)$
17. $2(\pi - 1)$ **19.** 12π **21.** $\frac{3\pi}{8} + 1$ **23.** $\pi \ln 4$ **25.** 4
27. $6\sqrt{3} - 2\pi$ **29.** $\bar{x} = 5/6, \bar{y} = 0$ **31.** $2a/3$ **33.** $2a/3$

Section 14.4, pp. 904–906

1. 1 **3.** $\int_0^1 \int_0^{2-2x} \int_0^{3-3x-3y/2} dz\,dy\,dx$,
$\int_0^2 \int_0^{1-y/2} \int_0^{3-3x-3y/2} dz\,dx\,dy$, $\int_0^1 \int_0^{3-3x} \int_0^{2-2x-2z/3} dy\,dz\,dx$,
$\int_0^3 \int_0^{1-z/3} \int_0^{2-2x-2z/3} dy\,dx\,dz$, $\int_0^2 \int_0^{3-3y/2} \int_0^{1-y/2-z/3} dx\,dz\,dy$,
$\int_0^3 \int_0^{2-2z/3} \int_0^{1-y/2-z/3} dx\,dy\,dz$. The value of all six integrals is 1.

5. 1 **7.** 1 **9.** $\left(\frac{\pi^3}{2}\right)(1 - \cos 1)$

11. 18 **13.** 7/6 **15.** 0 **17.** $\frac{1}{2} - \frac{\pi}{8}$

19. a) $\int_{-1}^{1} \int_0^{1-x^2} \int_{x^2}^{1-z} dy\,dz\,dx$ b) $\int_0^1 \int_{-\sqrt{1-z}}^{\sqrt{1-z}} \int_{x^2}^{1-z} dy\,dx\,dz$

c) $\int_0^1 \int_0^{1-z} \int_{-\sqrt{y}}^{\sqrt{y}} dx\,dy\,dz$

d) $\int_0^1 \int_0^{1-y} \int_{-\sqrt{y}}^{\sqrt{y}} dx\,dz\,dy$ e) $\int_0^1 \int_{-\sqrt{y}}^{\sqrt{y}} \int_0^{1-y} dz\,dx\,dy$

21. 2/3 **23.** 20/3 **25.** 1 **27.** 16/3 **29.** $8\pi - \frac{32}{3}$
31. 31/3 **33.** 1

Section 14.5, pp. 909–910

1. $R_x = \sqrt{\frac{b^2 + c^2}{12}}, R_y = \sqrt{\frac{a^2 + c^2}{12}}, R_z = \sqrt{\frac{a^2 + b^2}{12}}$

3. $I_x = \frac{M}{3}(b^2 + c^2), I_y = \frac{M}{3}(a^2 + c^2), I_z = \frac{M}{3}(a^2 + b^2)$

5. $\bar{x} = \bar{y} = 0, \bar{z} = \frac{12}{5}, I_x = \frac{7904}{105} \approx 75.28, I_y = \frac{4832}{63} \approx 76.70,$
$I_z = \frac{256}{45} \approx 5.69$

7. a) $\bar{x} = \bar{y} = 0, \bar{z} = \frac{8}{3}$, b) $c = 2\sqrt{2}$

9. $I_L = 1386, R_L = \sqrt{\frac{77}{2}}$

11. $I_L = \frac{40}{3}, R_L = \sqrt{\frac{5}{3}}$ **13.** $\bar{x} = \frac{4}{5}, \bar{y} = \bar{z} = \frac{2}{5}$

15. $\bar{x} = \bar{y} = \bar{z} = \frac{8}{15}; I_x = I_y = I_z = \frac{11}{6}; R_x = R_y = R_z = \sqrt{\frac{11}{15}}$

Section 14.6, pp. 916–919

1. $\frac{4\pi(\sqrt{2}-1)}{3}$ **3.** $\frac{17\pi}{5}$ **5.** $\pi(6\sqrt{2}-8)$

7. π^2 **9.** $\pi/3$ **11.** 5π

13. $3\pi/10$ **15.** $\pi/3$ **17.** 2π **19.** $\left(\frac{8-5\sqrt{2}}{2}\right)\pi$

21. a) $8\int_0^{\pi/2}\int_0^{\pi/2}\int_0^2 \rho^2 \sin\phi \, d\rho \, d\phi \, d\theta$

b) $8\int_0^{\pi/2}\int_0^2\int_0^{\sqrt{4-r^2}} r \, dz \, dr \, d\theta$

c) $8\int_0^2\int_0^{\sqrt{4-x^2}}\int_0^{\sqrt{4-x^2-y^2}} dz \, dy \, dx$

23. a) $\int_0^{2\pi}\int_0^{\pi/3}\int_{\sec\phi}^2 \rho^2 \sin\phi \, d\rho \, d\phi \, d\theta$

b) $\int_0^{2\pi}\int_0^{\sqrt{3}}\int_1^{\sqrt{4-r^2}} r \, dz \, dr \, d\theta$

c) $\int_{-\sqrt{3}}^{\sqrt{3}}\int_{-\sqrt{3-x^2}}^{\sqrt{3-x^2}}\int_1^{\sqrt{4-x^2-y^2}} dz \, dy \, dx$ d) $\frac{5\pi}{3}$

25. $\int_0^{\pi}\int_0^{2\sin\theta}\int_0^{4-r\sin\theta} f(r,\theta,z) \, dz \, r \, dr \, d\theta$

27. $\int_{-\pi/2}^{\pi/2}\int_1^{1+\cos\theta}\int_0^4 f(r,\theta,z) \, dz \, r \, dr \, d\theta$

29. $\int_0^{\pi/4}\int_0^{\sec\theta}\int_0^{2-r\sin\theta} f(r,\theta,z) \, dz \, r \, dr \, d\theta$

31. $8\pi/3$ **33.** 9/4 **35.** $(3\pi - 4)/18$

37. $\pi/2$ **39.** 16π **41.** $5\pi/2$ **43.** $\frac{4\pi(8-3\sqrt{3})}{3}$

45. 2/3 **47.** $\bar{x} = \bar{y} = 0, \bar{z} = 3/8$ **49.** $\bar{x} = \bar{y} = 0, \bar{z} = 5/6$

51. a) π, b) $7\pi/6$ **53.** $\frac{8\pi a^5}{15}$

55. $\int_0^{2\pi}\int_0^{\pi/2}\int_{\cos\phi}^2 \rho^2 \sin\phi \, d\rho \, d\phi \, d\theta = \frac{31\pi}{6}$

57. $\int_0^{2\pi}\int_0^{\pi}\int_0^{1-\cos\phi} \rho^2 \sin\phi \, d\rho \, d\phi \, d\theta = \frac{8\pi}{3}$

59. $\int_0^{2\pi}\int_{\pi/4}^{\pi/2}\int_0^{2\cos\phi} \rho^2 \sin\phi \, d\rho \, d\phi \, d\theta = \frac{\pi}{3}$ **61.** $\frac{2\pi a^3}{3}$

63. $5\pi/3$ **65.** $\frac{4(2\sqrt{2}-1)\pi}{3}$ **67.** 3/4

69. $\bar{x} = \bar{y} = 0, \bar{z} = \frac{3(2+\sqrt{2})a}{16}$

Section 14.7, pp. 925–926

3. a) $x = \frac{u+v}{3}, y = \frac{v-2u}{3}; J(u,v) = \frac{1}{3}$; b) $\frac{33}{4}$

5. $\int_1^2\int_1^3 (u+v)\frac{2u}{v} \, du \, dv = 8 + \frac{52}{3}\ln 2$

7. $\frac{\pi ab(a^2+b^2)}{4}$ **11.** $\frac{4\pi abc}{3}$

13. $\int_0^3\int_0^2\int_1^2 \left(\frac{v}{3} + \frac{vw}{3u}\right) du \, dv \, dw = 2 + \ln 8$

Chapter 14 Practice Exercises, pp. 927–929

1. $9e - 9$ **3.** $\int_0^1\int_y^{\sqrt{y}} f(x,y) \, dx \, dy$

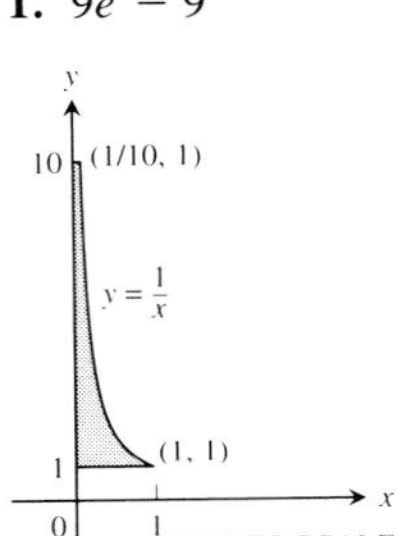

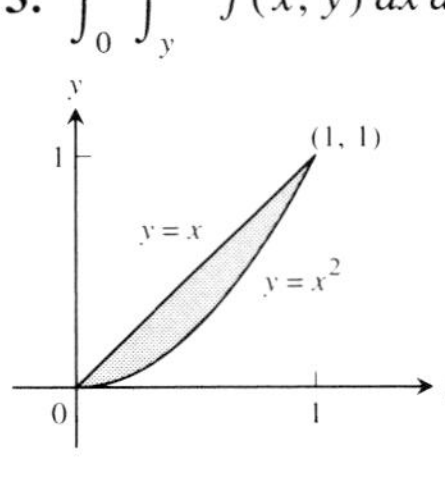

5. $\int_{-3}^3\int_0^{(1/2)\sqrt{9-x^2}} y \, dy \, dx$; $\frac{9}{2}$

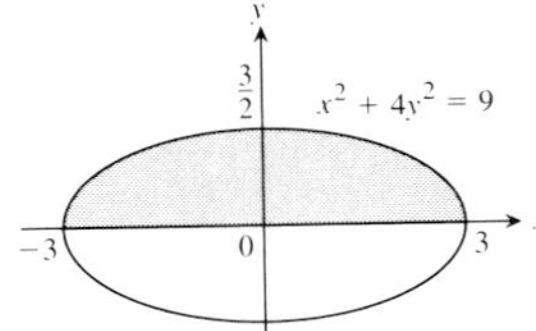

7. sin 4 **9.** $\frac{\ln 17}{4}$ **11.** 4/3 **13.** 4/3 **15.** 1/4

17. $\bar{x} = \bar{y} = \frac{1}{2 - \ln 4}$

19. a) $I_0 = \frac{40}{3}$, b) $I_0 = \frac{4ab(b^2+a^2)}{3}$

21. $M = 4, M_x = 0, M_y = 0$ **23.** π

25. $\bar{x} = \frac{15\pi + 32}{6\pi + 48}, \bar{y} = 0$

27. $\bar{x} = \bar{y} = \frac{13}{3\pi}$ **29.** 0 **31.** 8/35 **33.** $\pi/2$

35. $\frac{2(31 - 3^{5/2})}{3}$

37. a) $\int_{-\sqrt{2}}^{\sqrt{2}}\int_{-\sqrt{2-y^2}}^{\sqrt{2-y^2}}\int_{\sqrt{x^2+y^2}}^{\sqrt{4-x^2-y^2}} 3\,dz\,dx\,dy$

b) $\int_0^{2\pi}\int_0^{\pi/4}\int_0^2 3\,\rho^2 \sin\phi\,d\rho\,d\phi\,d\theta$ c) $2\pi(8-4\sqrt{2})$

39. $\int_0^{2\pi}\int_0^{\pi/4}\int_0^{\sec\phi} \rho^2\sin\phi\,d\rho\,d\phi\,d\theta = \frac{\pi}{3}$

41. $\int_0^1\int_{\sqrt{1-x^2}}^{\sqrt{3-x^2}}\int_1^{\sqrt{4-x^2-y^2}} z^2xy\,dz\,dy\,dx\ +$

$\int_1^{\sqrt{3}}\int_0^{\sqrt{3-x^2}}\int_1^{\sqrt{4-x^2-y^2}} z^2xy\,dz\,dy\,dx$

43. a) $\int_{-\sqrt{3}}^{\sqrt{3}}\int_{-\sqrt{3-x^2}}^{\sqrt{3-x^2}}\int_1^{\sqrt{4-x^2-y^2}} dz\,dy\,dx$

b) $\int_0^{2\pi}\int_0^{\sqrt{3}}\int_1^{\sqrt{4-r^2}} r\,dz\,dr\,d\theta$

c) $\int_0^{2\pi}\int_0^{\pi/3}\int_{\sec\phi}^{2} \rho^2\sin\phi\,d\rho\,d\phi\,d\theta$

45. $\frac{15}{8}$

47. $3\pi/2$

49. a) $\bar{x}=\bar{y}=0,\ \bar{z}=1/2;\ I_z=\frac{\pi}{8},\ R_z=\frac{\sqrt{3}}{2}$

b) $\bar{x}=\bar{y}=0,\ \bar{z}=5/14;\ I_z=\frac{2\pi}{7},\ R_z=\sqrt{\frac{5}{7}}$

51. $2\pi^2$

53. $\bar{x}=\bar{y}=0,\ \bar{z}=\frac{3a}{8}$

Chapter 15

Section 15.1, pp. 935–937

1. c **3.** g **5.** d **7.** f **9.** $\sqrt{2}$ **11.** 13/2 **13.** 0
15. $(1/6)(5\sqrt{5}+9)$ **17.** $\sqrt{3}\ln(b/a)$
19. $I_x = 2\pi - 2,\ R_x = 1$ **21.** $I_z = 2\pi\,\delta a^3,\ R_z = a$
23. a) $I_z = 2\pi\sqrt{2}\,\delta,\ R_z = 1$ b) $I_z = 4\pi\sqrt{2}\,\delta,\ R_z = 1$

Section 15.2, pp. 944–945

1. $\nabla f = -(x\mathbf{i}+y\mathbf{j}+z\mathbf{k})(x^2+y^2+z^2)^{-3/2}$
3. $\nabla g = -(2x/(x^2+y^2))\,\mathbf{i} - (2y/(x^2+y^2))\,\mathbf{j} + e^z\mathbf{k}$
5. a) 9/2 b) 13/3 c) 9/2 **7.** a) 1/3 b) −1/5 c) 0
9. a) 2 b) 3/2 c) 1/2 **11.** 1/2 **13.** $-\pi$ **15.** 48
17. π **19.** a) $\text{Circ}_1 = 0,\ \text{Circ}_2 = 2\pi,\ \text{Flux}_1 = 2\pi,\ \text{Flux}_2 = 0$
b) $\text{Circ}_1 = 0,\ \text{Circ}_2 = 8\pi,\ \text{Flux}_1 = 8\pi,\ \text{Flux}_2 = 0$
21. Circ = 0, Flux = $a^2\pi$ **23.** Circ = $a^2\pi$, Flux = 0

25.

27. a) $\mathbf{G} = -y\,\mathbf{i} + x\,\mathbf{j}$ b) $\mathbf{G} = \sqrt{x^2+y^2}\,\mathbf{F}$
29. $\mathbf{F} = -(x\,\mathbf{i}+y\,\mathbf{j})/\sqrt{x^2+y^2}$
31. a) $-\pi/2$ b) 0 c) 1 **33.** 0

Section 15.3, pp. 953–954

1. Conservative **3.** Not conservative **5.** Not conservative
7. $f(x,y,z) = x^2 + \frac{3y^2}{2} + 2z^2 + C$
9. $f(x,y,z) = xe^{y+2z} + C$ **11.** 49 **13.** −16 **15.** 1
17. $\ln(\pi/2)$ **19.** 0 **21.** −3 **25.** $\mathbf{F} = \nabla\left(\frac{x^2-1}{y}\right)$
27. a) 1 b) 1 c) 1 **29.** a) 2 b) 2

Section 15.4, pp. 964–965

1. Flux = 0, Circ = $2\pi a^2$ **3.** Flux = $-\pi a^2$, Circ = 0
5. Flux = 2, Circ = 0 **7.** Flux = −9, Circ = 9
9. Flux = 1/2, Circ = 1/2 **11.** Flux = 1/5, Circ = −1/12
13. 0 **15.** 0 **17.** -16π **19.** 2/33
21. a) 0 b) $(h-k)$(area of the region) **27.** πa^2
29. $(3/8)\pi$

Section 15.5, pp. 973–975

1. $(13/3)\pi$ **3.** 4 **5.** $6\sqrt{6}-2\sqrt{2}$ **7.** $\pi\sqrt{c^2+1}$
9. $(\pi/6)(17\sqrt{17}-5\sqrt{5})$ **11.** $9a^3$ **13.** $(abc/4)(ab+ac+bc)$
15. 2 **17.** $(\pi a^3)/6$ **19.** $(\pi a^2)/4$ **21.** $(\pi a^3)/2$ **23.** −32
25. −4 **27.** $3a^4$ **29.** $(a/2, a/2, a/2)$
31. $(\bar{x},\bar{y},\bar{z}) = (0, 0, 14/9),\ I_z = \frac{15\pi\sqrt{2}\delta}{2},\ R_z = \sqrt{\frac{5}{2}}$
33. $(\pi/6)(13\sqrt{13}-1)$ **35.** $(\pi/6)(5\sqrt{5}-1)$
37. $(2/3)(5\sqrt{5}-1)$

Section 15.6, pp. 982–983

1. $\mathbf{r}(r,\theta) = (r\cos\theta)\,\mathbf{i} + (r\sin\theta)\,\mathbf{j} + r^2\mathbf{k},\ 0\le r\le 2,\ 0\le\theta\le 2\pi$
3. $\mathbf{r}(r,\theta) = (r\cos\theta)\,\mathbf{i} + (r\sin\theta)\,\mathbf{j} + (r/2)\,\mathbf{k},\ 0\le r\le 6,$
$0\le\theta\le\pi/2$
5. $\mathbf{r}(r,\theta) = (r\cos\theta)\,\mathbf{i} + (r\sin\theta)\,\mathbf{j} + \sqrt{9-r^2}\,\mathbf{k},$
$0\le r\le 3\sqrt{2}/2,\ 0\le\theta\le 2\pi$. Also, $\mathbf{r}(\phi,\theta) = (3\sin\phi\cos\theta)\,\mathbf{i}\ +$
$(3\sin\phi\sin\theta)\,\mathbf{j} + (3\cos\phi)\,\mathbf{k},\ 0\le\phi\le\pi/4,\ 0\le\theta\le 2\pi$
7. $\mathbf{r}(\phi,\theta) = (\sqrt{3}\sin\phi\cos\theta)\,\mathbf{i} + (\sqrt{3}\sin\phi\sin\theta)\,\mathbf{j}\ +$
$(\sqrt{3}\cos\phi)\,\mathbf{k},\ \pi/3\le\phi\le 2\pi/3,\ 0\le\theta\le 2\pi$
9. $\mathbf{r}(x,y) = x\,\mathbf{i} + y\,\mathbf{j} + (4-y^2)\,\mathbf{k},\ 0\le x\le 2,\ -2\le y\le 2$

11. $\mathbf{r}(u, v) = u\mathbf{i} + (3\cos v)\mathbf{j} + (3\sin v)\mathbf{k}, 0 \le u \le 3,$ $0 \le v \le 2\pi$

13. a) $\mathbf{r}(r, \theta) = (r\cos\theta)\mathbf{i} + (r\sin\theta)\mathbf{j} + (1 - r\cos\theta - r\sin\theta)\mathbf{k}, 0 \le r \le 3, 0 \le \theta \le 2\pi$ b) $\mathbf{r}(u, v) = (1 - u\cos v - u\sin v)\mathbf{i} + (u\cos v)\mathbf{j} + (u\sin v)\mathbf{k}, 0 \le u \le 3,$ $0 \le v \le 2\pi$

15. $\mathbf{r}(u, v) = (4\cos^2 v)\mathbf{i} + u\mathbf{j} + (4\cos v\sin v)\mathbf{k}, 0 \le u \le 3,$ $-(\pi/2) \le v \le (\pi/2)$. Another way: $\mathbf{r}(u, v) = (2 + 2\cos v)\mathbf{i} + u\mathbf{j} + 2\sin v\,\mathbf{k}, 0 \le u \le 3, 0 \le v \le 2\pi$

17. $\displaystyle\int_0^{2\pi}\int_0^1 \frac{\sqrt{5}}{2} r\,dr\,d\theta = \frac{\pi\sqrt{5}}{2}$

19. $\displaystyle\int_0^{2\pi}\int_1^3 r\sqrt{5}\,dr\,d\theta = 8\pi\sqrt{5}$ **21.** $\displaystyle\int_0^{2\pi}\int_1^4 1\,du\,dv = 6\pi$

23. $\displaystyle\int_0^{2\pi}\int_0^1 u\sqrt{4u^2+1}\,du\,dv = \frac{\pi}{6}\left(5\sqrt{5} - 1\right)$

25. $\displaystyle\int_0^{2\pi}\int_{\pi/4}^{\pi} 2\sin\phi\,d\phi\,d\theta = \left(4 + 2\sqrt{2}\right)\pi$

27. $\displaystyle\iint_S x\,d\sigma = \int_0^3\int_0^2 u\sqrt{4u^2+1}\,du\,dv = \frac{17\sqrt{17} - 1}{4}$

29. $\displaystyle\iint_S x^2\,d\sigma = \int_0^{2\pi}\int_0^{\pi} \sin^3\phi\cos^2\theta\,d\phi\,d\theta = \frac{4\pi}{3}$

31. $\displaystyle\iint_S z\,d\sigma = \int_0^1\int_0^1 (4 - u - v)\sqrt{3}\,dv\,du = 3\sqrt{3}$

(for $x = u, y = v$)

33. $\displaystyle\iint_S x^2\sqrt{5 - 4z}\,d\sigma =$

$\displaystyle\int_0^1\int_0^{2\pi} u^2\cos^2 v \cdot \sqrt{4u^2+1} \cdot u\sqrt{4u^2+1}\,dv\,du =$

$\displaystyle\int_0^1\int_0^{2\pi} u^3(4u^2+1)\cos^2 v\,dv\,du = (11\pi)/12$

35. -32 **37.** $\pi a^3/6$ **39.** $13a^4/6$ **41.** $2\pi/3$ **43.** $-73\pi/6$
45. $(a/2, a/2, a/2)$ **47.** $8\delta\pi a^4/3$

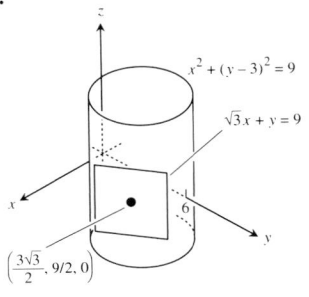

49.

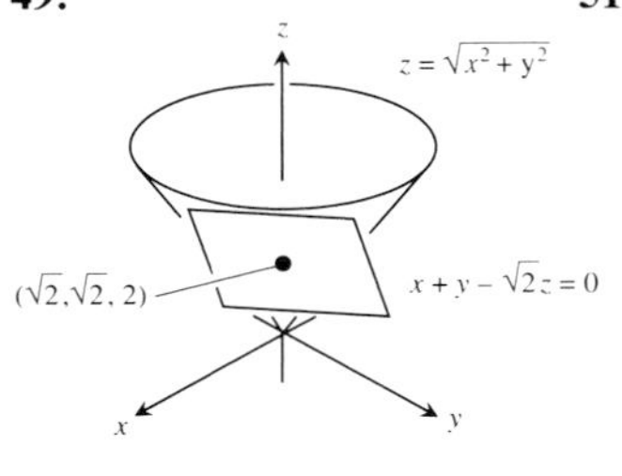

51.

z
$x^2 + (y-3)^2 = 9$
$\sqrt{3}x + y = 9$
x
6
y
$\left(\frac{3\sqrt{3}}{2}, 9/2, 0\right)$

Section 15.7, pp. 991–992

1. 4π **3.** $-5/6$ **5.** 0 **7.** -6π **9.** $2\pi a^2$

Section 15.8, pp. 1000–1001

1. 0 **3.** 0 **5.** -16 **7.** -8π **9.** 3π **11.** $-40/3$
13. 12π **15.** $12\pi\left(4\sqrt{2} - 1\right)$

Chapter 15 Practice Exercises, pp. 1001–1004

1. Path 1: $2\sqrt{3}$; Path 2: $1 + 3\sqrt{2}$ **3.** $4a^2$
5. a) $4\sqrt{2} - 2$, b) $\sqrt{2} + \ln(1 + \sqrt{2})$
7. $(\bar{x}, \bar{y}, \bar{z}) = (1, 8/15, 2/3)$; $I_x = 232/45$, $I_y = 64/15$, $I_z = 56/9$; $R_x = \sqrt{116/45}$, $R_y = \sqrt{32/15}$, $R_z = \sqrt{28/9}$
9. a) $-\pi/2$, b) 0, c) 1 **11.** Conservative
13. Not conservative **15.** $f(x, y, z) = y^2 + yz + 2x + z$
17. 0 **19.** Path 1: 2; Path 2: 8/3
23. a) $1 - e^{-2\pi}$, b) $1 - e^{-2\pi}$
25. Flux: 3/2, Circ: $-1/2$ **29.** 0
31. $\mathbf{r}(\phi, \theta) = (6\sin\phi\cos\theta)\mathbf{i} + (6\sin\phi\sin\theta)\mathbf{j} + (6\cos\phi)\mathbf{k}$, $(\pi/6) \le \phi \le 2\pi/3, 0 \le \theta \le 2\pi$
33. $\mathbf{r}(r, \theta) = (r\cos\theta)\mathbf{i} + (r\sin\theta)\mathbf{j} + (1 + r)\mathbf{k}, 0 \le r \le 2,$ $0 \le \theta \le 2\pi$
35. $\mathbf{r}(u, v) = (u\cos v)\mathbf{i} + 2u^2\mathbf{j} + (u\sin v)\mathbf{k}, 0 \le u \le 1,$ $0 \le v \le \pi$ **37.** $\pi\sqrt{3}$ **39.** $2\pi\left(1 - (1/\sqrt{2})\right)$
41. $\dfrac{abc}{2}\sqrt{\dfrac{1}{a^2} + \dfrac{1}{b^2} + \dfrac{1}{c^2}}$ **43.** a) 0, b) -4
45. $(\bar{x}, \bar{y}, \bar{z}) = (0, 0, 49/12)$; $I_z = 640\pi$; $R_z = 2\sqrt{2}$
47. 3 **49.** $(2\pi/3)(7 - 8\sqrt{2})$ **51.** 8/3 **53.** 0
55. 6π **57.** 2/3

Appendices

Appendix A.7, p. A-23

1. -5 **3.** 1 **5.** -7 **7.** 38 **9.** $x = -4, y = 1$
11. $x = 3, y = 2$ **13.** $x = 3, y = -2, z = 2$
15. $x = 2, y = 0, z = -1$
17. a) $h = 6, k = 4$ b) $h = 6, k \ne 4$

Index

Note: Numbers in parentheses refer to exercises on the pages indicated.

Absolute convergence, 593 ff.
Absolute maximum/minimum, 211, 857
Absolute value, 48
  and distance, 50
  and intervals, 50 ff.
Acceleration, 142
  due to gravity, 138
  tangential and normal components, 782
  vector, 755
AGNESI, MARIA GAETANA (1718–1799), 654
Algorithm, 188
Alternating series estimation theorem, 592
Angle(s), between curves, 718(59–62)
  of inclination, 4
  between lines, 717(53–56)
  between planes, 729
  between vectors, 711
Antiderivative(s), 254 ff.
  of continuous functions, 303
  general, 254
  of vector functions, 758, 762(44)
Aphelion, 678
Arbitrary constant, 254
Arc length, along a curve, 771 ff.
  function, 772
  parameter, 772
Archimedes, area formula, 310(54)
  spiral, 689(106)
  volume formula, 642(33)
Area(s), of bounded plane regions, 887 ff.
  between curves, 439 ff.
  of ellipse, 926(6)
  under a graph, 288 ff.
  and Green's theorem, 965, 1004(55–58)
  and integrals, 296 ff.
  of parallelogram, $|\mathbf{A} \times \mathbf{B}|$, 720
  of parallelogram's projection on a plane, 966
  in the plane, 724(33–41)
  in polar coordinates, 680 ff., 896
  surfaces of revolution, 465 ff., 659, 683 ff.
Asymptotes, 227 ff.
  horizontal and vertical, 228
  of hyperbolas, 635
  oblique, 229
Autocatalytic reactions, 245(43)
Average daily holding cost, 311
Average daily inventory, 311
Average rate of change, 113 ff., 143
Average value of a function, 276 ff., 686(36), 888, 903 ff.

Bacterial growth, unchecked, 262
BARROW, ISAAC (1630–1677), 44
Basic trigonometric functions, 24
BERNOULLI, JOHN (1667–1748), 390
Best location for a factory assembly table, 57(65)
Binomial series, 619 ff., 624
Binomial theorem, A–1
Binormal vector **B**, 781
BOND, HENRY (ca. 1640), 44
Boundary point, 13, 801
Bounded and unbounded regions, 801
Bowditch curves (Lissajous figures), 661(33–41)
BUNSEN, ROBERT WILHELM EBERHARD (1811–1899), 984

Calculator(s), 41 ff.
  accuracy, 41
Carbon-14 dating, 383
Cardiac output, 208(26), 273
Cardioid(s), 668 ff.
Cartesian (rectangular) coordinates, in the plane, 1 ff.
  in space, 700 ff.
Catalyst, 245(43)
Catenaries, 471
Cauchy condensation test, 585
CAVALIERI, BONAVENTURA (1598–1647), 500
Cavalieri's theorem, 500
Celsius vs. Fahrenheit, 7, 10(45)
Center of curvature, 779
Center(s) of mass, 486 ff., 488 ff., 889 ff., 906 ff., 933 ff., 972 ff. *See also* Centroids
  of a linear distribution, 486 ff.
  objects in space, 907
  of a thin plate, 491, 889
Central force, 789
Centroid(s), 494, 891, 908
  of a triangle, 496(29–32)
Chain rule(s), functions defined on surfaces, 835 ff.
  functions of many variables, 838
  functions of a single variable, 160 ff.
  functions of three independent variables, 835
  functions of two or more variables, 833 ff.
  and implicit differentiation, 837
  repeated use, 163 ff.
Change (absolute, relative, percentage), 181 ff., 829 ff.
Circle(s), 32, 629, 651
  involute, 655(28)
  polar, 675
  standard parametrization, 654
Circle of curvature (osculating circle), 779
Circular orbits, 794
Circular paraboloid, 735
Circulation, 941
  density/curl, 956 ff.
  of fluid, 941, 987
Cissoid of Diocles, 175(54)
Closed and open, balls, 802
  regions, 709(34), 801
Cofactor, A–18 ff.
COLSON, JOHN (d. 1760), 654
Completing the square. A–2
Complex numbers, A–25 ff.
Composite functions, 18, 95 ff.
Compound interest, continuously compounded, 110(50), 381 ff.
Concavity, 219
  second derivative test, 219
Cone(s), elliptic, 735
Conic sections, 629 ff.
  circle, 32, 629
  classified by eccentricity, 640
  discriminant test, 647 ff.
  eccentricity, 637 ff.
  ellipse, 632 ff.
  focus-directrix equation, 640
  hyperbola, 634 ff.
  parabola, 34 ff., 630
  polar equations, 674 ff.
  reflective properties, 640
  shifting, 644
Connected, graph, 97
  region, 947
Conservative fields, 946
  component test, 949
  and path independence, 946
  and Stokes's theorem, 990 ff.
Constant functions, 291 ff.
Constant multiple rule, 127
Continuity, 92 ff., 810 ff.
  and differentiability, 122 ff., 824
  at an end point, 92
  vs. having a limit, 98
  at an interior point, 92
  test for, 92
  of vector functions, 753
Continuous extension, 95
Continuous function(s), 90 ff., 810
  algebraic combinations, 94
  defined, 92
  intermediate value theorem, 96
  max-min theorem, 211
  nowhere differentiable, 122
Contour lines, 803
Convergence tests, for improper integrals, 547 ff.
Cost/revenue, 238 ff.
  and profit, 239
Cramer's rule, A–21 ff.
Critical points, 212, 855
Curl of vector field, 956
  paddle-wheel interpretation, 988
Curvature, 776 ff.
  center of, 779

Curvature *(Cont.)*
circle of, 779
of a circle, 777
function, 777
of graphs in the *xy*-plane, 787(35)
and **N**, 779
of a plane curve, 776 ff.
radius of, 779
of a straight line, 777
total, 787(31)
Curve(s) (graphs), concave up or down, 219 ff.
differentiable, 118, 656, 754
length of, 462 ff., 658, 682, 771
infinite length, 464, 575(57)
parametrized, 650 ff.
piecewise smooth, 755, 947
simple closed, 958
smooth, 462, 754
space, 751 ff.
Cusp, 223
Cycloid(s), 653 ff.
standard parametrization, 654
Cylinder(s), 731 ff.
drawing, 733
Cylindrical coordinates, 741 ff.

Daedelus, 145 ff.
Decibel scale, 367
Definite integrals, 287 ff.
domination inequality, 300
evaluation, 305 ff.
existence of, 288
integrand, 288
limits of integration, 288
max-min inequality, 299
mean value theorem, 298
properties, 294 ff.
variable of integration, 288
of vector functions, 759
Del notation, 984
DELESSE, ACHILLE ERNEST (ca. 1840), 503
Delesse's rule, 501 ff.
Density, 488
Dependent variable, 12
Derivative(s), 117 ff., 814 ff. *See also* Differentiation
of composite functions. *See* Chain Rule
of a constant, 126
directional, 841 ff.
first, 134
higher order, 134
intermediate value property, 123, 219
interpretations, 142
of inverse functions, 357 ff.
left-hand, 121
of $\log_a u$, 366
nonexistence, 121 ff.
one- or two-sided, 121
partial, 814 ff.
power functions, 369
right-hand, 121
second and higher orders, 134
of trigonometric functions, 152 ff.
inverse trigonometric functions, 409 ff.
DESCARTES, RENÉ (1596–1650), 1, 790

Determinant(s), A–16 ff.
facts about, A–20
minor, A–18 ff.
Difference quotient, 117
Differentiability, 823 ff.
and continuity, 122 ff., 824
Differential(s), 180 ff., 828 ff.
of a function, 180, 828
Differential equations, 256 ff., 424 ff.
first order, 424 ff.
initial condition, 256
integrating factor, 427
linear, first order, 426
mixture problems, 433
power series solutions, 622
separable first order, 425
solution(s), general, 256
particular, 256
solution (integral) curve, 259, 321
Differential form, 952
Differentiation. *See also* Derivatives
implicit, 168 ff., 837 ff.
logarithmic, 364
power rule, 126, 133, 162, 172, 369
rules, 126 ff.
of vector functions, 754 ff.
Direct comparison test, for improper integrals, 547
for infinite series, 579
Directional derivatives, 841 ff.
calculation, 842
geometric interpretation, 842
properties, 844
in space, 846
Discontinuities, 92
removable and nonremovable, 95
two-path test for, 811
Discriminant, of $f(x,y)$, 856
of a general quadratic equation, 648
Displacement, 139
vs. distance traveled, 500 ff.
Distance, in the plane, 2
from point to line, 714, 726
from point to plane, 728
in space, 704 ff.
traveled, 271 ff., 500 ff.
Divergence, in three dimensions, 993
in two dimensions, 955 ff.
Divergence theorem, 993 ff.
DNA, 785
Dominant terms, 231
Double integrals, 877 ff.
over bounded nonrectangular regions, 881 ff.
Cartesian into polar, 896 ff.
finding limits of integration, 884, 895
Fubini's theorem, 879 ff.
numerical evaluation, 886 ff.
order of integration, 880 ff.
polar form, 893 ff.
properties, 878
over rectangles, 877
substitutions in, 919 ff.
as volumes, 878 ff.
Drosophila. *See* Fruit flies

e (Euler's number), 350
$e = \lim_{x \to 0^+} (1 + x)^{1/x}$, 392
e^x, 349 ff.
Eccentricity, 637 ff.
of planetary orbits, 638
space engineer's formula, 679(49)
Eight curve, 175(53)
Ellipse(s), 632 ff.
area formulas, 926(6)
axes, 633
drawing, 632, 633
eccentricity, 637, 677
equations, standard form, 634
polar equations, 676 ff.
standard parametrization, 654
Ellipsoid(s), 734
Elliptic cone, 735
Elliptic integral(s), 661(30)
Elliptic paraboloid, 735 ff.
Estimating, change with differentials, 180 ff., 828 ff.
change in f in direction **u**, 849
f' from graph of f, 145 ff.
with finite sums, 271 ff.
EULER, LEONHARD (1707–1783), 12
Euler's formula, 616
Euler's identities, 618(52)
Euler's theorem, 820
Exact differential forms, 951 ff.
Exactness, test for, 952
Exponential change, 351 ff.
law, 379 ff.
Exponential function, 347 ff., 367 ff.
base of, 348
tables, A–26 ff.
Exponents, laws of, 348
Extreme values of functions, 209 ff., 853 ff.
on closed bounded regions, 857
on closed intervals, 213
first derivative test, 214, 854
first derivative theorem, 212
second derivative test, 221, 856

Factorial notation($n!$), 561
FERMAT, PIERRE DE (1601–1665), 45
Fermat's difference quotient, 117
Fermat's principle, 245 (41)
Fibonacci numbers, 561
Finite sums, 271 ff., 282 ff.
First derivative test, for increasing/ decreasing, 213
for local extreme values, 214, 854
First derivative theorem for local extreme values, 212
Flow integrals and circulation, 941
Fluid force, 479 ff.
Fluid pressures, 479 ff.
Flux, across an oriented surface, 971
across a plane curve, 942 ff.
Flux density/divergence, 955 ff.
Force constant, 474
Fractal coastline, 465
FRANKLIN, BENJAMIN (1706–1790), 386(15)
Free fall, 138
Galileo's formula, 149(25)
from Tower of Pisa, 149(26)

FRENET, JEAN-FRÉDÉRIC (1816–1900), 781
Frenet frame, 781
Fruit flies, 114
FUBINI, GUIDO (1879–1943), 880
Fubini's theorem, 879 ff.
Function(s), 12
  absolute value, 48
  composition of, 18
  continuous, 90 ff., 810
  differentiable, 118, 754, 824
    on closed interval, 121
  even and odd, 16
  exponential, 347 ff., 367 ff.
  extreme values, 209 ff., 853 ff.
  greatest integer, 17
  inverse, 355 ff.
  inverse hyperbolic, 418 ff.
  inverse trigonometric, 401 ff.
  least integer, 17
  logarithmic, 361 ff.
  one-to-one, 355, 361(41, 42)
  periodic, 26 ff.
  rational, 70
  scalar, 752
  several independent variables, 799
  smooth, 462
  step, 17
  trigonometric, 22 ff.
  of two or more variables, 799 ff.
  vector-valued, 751 ff.
Function table generator, 14
Fundamental theorem of calculus, 302 ff., 999

GAUSS, CARL FRIEDRICH (1777–1855), 284, 993
Gauss's law, 997 ff.
General linear equation, 7
General sine function, 40
Geosynchronous orbit, 794(6)
GIBBS, JOSIAH WILLARD (1839–1903), 714
Gradient, 843
  algebra rules, 850
  and level curves, 844
Gradient field, 939
Graphs, 14
  of inverse functions, 356
  of rational functions, 227 ff.
Graphing, 221 ff.
  in polar coordinates, 670 ff.
  strategy, 222
GRASSMAN, HERMANN (1809–1877), 714
Gravitational constant (universal), 789
GREEN, GEORGE (1793–1841), 960
Green's theorem, 954 ff.
  area formula, 965, 1004(55–58)
  generalized, 999
  normal form, 958
  tangential form, 958
GREGORY, JAMES (1638–1675), 44, 613
Growth and decay, 379 ff.

HALLEY, EDMUND (1656–1742), 639
Halley's comet, 639
HAMILTON, SIR WILLIAM (1805–1865), 714
Hanging cable, 471
Harmonic series, 579
Heat transfer, 384 ff.
HEAVISIDE, OLIVER (1850–1925), 714
Hooke's law, 474
Horizontal line test, 355
Human powered airplane, 145
HUYGENS, CHRISTIAAN (1629–1695), 653
Huygens's clock, 653
Hyperbola(s), 634 ff.
  asymptotes, 635 ff.
  drawing, 636
  eccentricity of, 639
  equations for, 636
  polar, 676
  and hyperbolic functions, 423(74)
Hyperbolic cosines, 471
Hyperbolic functions, 416 ff.
  derivatives, 417
  evaluation with logarithms, 422
  identities, 416
  integrals, 418
  inverses, 418 ff.
Hyperbolic paraboloid, 738
Hyperboloid, one sheet, 736 ff.
  two sheets, 737 ff.

Identity function, 356
Implicit differentiation, 168 ff., 837 ff.
Improper integrals, 542 ff.
  tests for convergence/divergence, 547 ff.
  types of, 549
Increasing/decreasing functions, 213, 251, 361(41, 42)
Increment theorem for functions of two variables, 824
Increments, 3
  and distance, 849
Indefinite integrals, 313 ff. *See also* Integrals
  rules, 315
Independent variable, 12
Indeterminate forms, 388 ff.
  products and differences, 391
Indeterminate powers, 391 ff.
Index of permutation, A–17
Inequalities (properties of), 55
Infinite series, 567 ff. *See also* Series
Inflection points, 219 ff., 227(88)
Initial value problems, 256
  with indefinite integrals, 317 ff.
  power series solutions, 622
  uniqueness of solutions, 265(64)
Instantaneous rate of change, 115, 143
Integrable function, 287
Integral(s). *See also* Definite integrals, Integration
  and area, 296
  cot x, 375
  over a curve, 931
  double, 919 ff.
  of exponential functions, 373 ff.
  improper, 542 ff., 549
  indefinite, 313 ff.
  iterated/repeated, 879
  leading to logarithms, 373 ff.
  modeling applications, 487 ff.
  multiple, 877 ff.
  nonelementary, 538
  surface, 969 ff.
  tables, T-1
    how to use, 534 ff.
  tan x, 375
  triple, 899 ff., 910 ff.
  of vector functions, 758 ff.
Integral curves, 321
Integrating factor, 427
Integration. *See also* Integrals
  basic formulas, 511 ff.
  in cylindrical coordinates, 912
  general procedures for indefinite integrals, 539 ff.
  limits (finding), 884, 900, 912, 914 ff.
  numerical, 331 ff.
  partial fraction method, 524 ff.
  by parts, 517 ff.
  in polar coordinates, 680 ff., 895
  of rational functions, 524 ff.
  by reduction formulas, 536 ff.
  in spherical coordinates, 914 ff.
  by substitution, 322 ff.
  using tables, 534 ff.
  tabular, 521 ff.
  term-by-term, 316 ff.
  trigonometric substitutions, 529 ff.
    $z = \tan(x/2)$, 533 ff.
  in vector fields, 931 ff.
Interior point, 13, 801
Intermediate value property, 96
  of derivatives, 123, 219
Intermediate Value Theorem for continuous functions, 96
Intervals, 13
Inverse functions, 355 ff.
Inverse hyperbolic functions, 418 ff.
  derivatives, 420
  evaluating, 422
  integrals leading to, 420
Inverse trigonometric functions, 401 ff.
  the "arc" in arc sine and arc cosine, 406
  derivatives and related integrals, 409 ff.
Inverses, 356 ff.
Involute of circle, 655(28), 774, 852(52)
Irreducible quadratic polynomial, 526
Iteration, 188

JACOBI, CARL GUSTAV JACOB (1804–1851), 920, 925
Jacobian determinant, 920, 923
Jerk, 155
Joule, 472

KELVIN, Lord (WILLIAM THOMSON) (1824–1907), 960, 984
KEPLER, JOHANNES (1571–1630), 790
Kepler's laws of motion, 790 ff.
KIRCHHOFF, GUSTAV ROBERT (1824–1887), 984
KOCH, HELGA VON, 172, 984
KÖCHEL, LUDWIG VON (1800–1877), 863(53)

LAGRANGE, JOSEPH LOUIS (1736–1813), 864
Lagrange multipliers, 864 ff.
Lagrange multipliers with two constraints, 870 ff.
Laplace equations, 822
Laws of exponents, 348, A–1
Least squares/regression lines, 862
LEIBNIZ, Baron GOTTFRIED WILHELM (1646–1716), 288, 302
Lemniscate(s), 670
Length, of a curve $r = f(\theta)$, 686(35)
  of parametrized curves, 658 ff.
  of plane curve(s), 462 ff., 658, 682 ff.
  of space curves, 771
Level curves, 802
  tangents to, 845
Level surfaces, 804
l'HÔPITAL, GUILLAUME FRANÇOIS ANTOINE DE (1661–1704), 388, 390, 654
l'Hôpital's rule, 388 ff.
$\text{Lim}_{h \to 0}\,(a^h - 1)/h$, geometric significance of, 351
  value of, 368
Limaçon(s), 673(23–26)
Limit(s), 63 ff., 76 ff., 101 ff., 753, 808 ff.
  calculation rules, 68, 809
  and continuity, 808 ff.
  defining formally, 101 ff.
  of functions of two variables, 808 ff.
  infinite, 76 ff.
  informal definition, 65
  left-hand/right-hand, 66, 106
  one- or two-sided, 66, 106
  of polynomials, 70
  properties of, 68, 809
  of rational functions, 70, 79 ff.
  of a sequence, 557 ff.
  of vector functions, 753
  as $x \to \pm\infty$, 77
Line(s), in the plane, 5 ff., 714
  polar equations, 674
  in space, 724 ff.
Line integrals, 931 ff.
  in conservative fields, 947 ff.
  fundamental theorem, 947
  path independence, 946
Linear approximation(s), common, 178
  error, 183, 827
  standard, 177
Linear approximations and differentials, 825 ff. *See also* Linearization
Linearization(s), 176 ff., 825 ff.
  at inflection points, 227(88)
Lissajous figures (Bowditch curves), 661(33–41)
ln *x*, 362 ff.
  integral formula, 376
Logarithms. *See also* ln *x*
  base *a*, 365 ff.
    evaluation, 365
  base 10, 366 ff.
  common, 366
  natural, 362 ff.
  properties, 363
Logarithmic differentiation, 364 ff.
Logarithmic functions, 361 ff.

MACLAURIN, COLIN (1698–1746), 613
Maclaurin series, 605 ff.
  frequently used, 624
  generated by a power series, 618(57)
Marginal cost, 143
Marginal revenue, 144
Marginal value, 143
Mass vs. weight, 430, 486
Masses and moments, 486 ff., 889 ff., 906 ff., 934, 972 ff.
Mathematical induction, A–11 ff.
Mathematical modeling, 241, 260 ff., 497, 762
Matrix, A–16 ff.
  main diagonal, A–20
  transpose, A–20
Max/min, 209 ff.
  absolute, 210, 857
  constrained, 864 ff.
  extrema, 210
  first derivative test, 214, 854
  local, 210, 854
  relative, 210
  and saddle points, 853 ff.
  second derivative test, 221, 856
  strategy, 237
Maximizing profit, 239
MAXWELL, JAMES CLERK (1831–1879), 960
Mean life of radioactive nucleus, 387(19)
Mean Value Theorem for derivatives, 248 ff.
  corollaries, 250 ff.
  for definite integrals, 298
  physical interpretation, 250
MENDEL, GREGOR JOHANN (1822–1884), 143
Midpoint of line segment, 708
Minimal surface, 471(57)
Mixed derivative theorem, 820
Mixture problems, 433
Möbius band, 971
Model rocket, 148(23)
Modeling. *See* Mathematical modeling
Molasses (great flood), 480
Moments, 487, 489, 889
  first and second, 889, 907, 934, 973
  of inertia, 889, 907, 934, 973
  polar, 889
  of thin shells, 972 ff.
Motion, planetary, 788 ff.
  of a projectile, 762 ff.
  in space, 754 ff.
  vector formulas, 786
MOZART, WOLFGANG AMADEUS (1756–1791), 863(53)

NAPIER, JOHN (1550–1617), 363, 386(14)
Natural domain, 13
Natural logarithm, 362 ff. *See also* ln *x*
Newton (unit of force), 472
NEWTON, SIR ISAAC (1642–1727), 302
Newton's dot notation, 784
Newton's law(s), of cooling, 384 ff.
  of gravitation, 789
  of motion, second, 789
Newton's method (Newton–Raphson), 187 ff.
  computer program, 193 ff.
Nondecreasing sequence theorem, 578
Nondecreasing sequences, 577 ff.
Nonelementary integrals, 538
Norm of a partition, 287
Normal (perpendicular), 171
  curves, 853(57)
  line, 170, 847
  to a surface, 170, 847
Normal plane, 782
Numerical integration, 331 ff.

Odd functions. *See* Functions, even and odd
Open region, 709(34), 801
  connected, 947
  simply connected, 947
Optimization, 234 ff.
Orbital period, 791
Orbits, circular, 794
  geosynchronous, 794(6)
Order of growth, 397 ff.
Order of magnitude ("little oh" and "big oh"), 397
Order and Oh-notation, 397 ff.
ORESME, NICOLE (1320–1382), 579
Orthogonal gradient theorem, 867
Osculating circle, 779
Osculating plane, 782
OSTROGRADSKY, MIKHAIL (1801–1862), 993

Pappus's theorems, surface area–centroid, 496
  volume–centroid, 496
Parabola(s), 34 ff., 630
  drawing, 643(45)
  eccentricity, 640
  focal length, 631
  polar equation, 676
Paraboloid, circular, 735
  elliptic, 734 ff.
  hyperbolic, 738
  of revolution, 735
Parallelepiped, 722
Parametrization(s), curves in the plane, 650 ff.
  curves in space, 751 ff.
  cycloids, 653 ff.
  lines in the plane, 655(31)
  lines in space, 724 ff.
  surfaces, 975 ff.
Parametrized curves, differentiable, 656
  dy/dx, 657
  d^2y/dx^2, 657
  length, 658 ff.
  slope, 656 ff.
  smooth, 656
Parametrized surfaces, 975 ff.
  smooth, 977
  tangent planes, 983
Partial derivatives, 799 ff., 814 ff.
  chain rule, 833 ff.
  and continuity, 819

and differentiability, 824
second order and higher, 819 ff., 821
Partial fractions, 524 ff.
Partition of [a,b], 284 ff.
norm of, 287
Path independence, 946 ff.
Perihelion, 678, 790
Period, of periodic function, 27
orbital, 791
Permutation, A–17
Perpendicular axis theorem, 889
Planes, 727 ff.
drawing, 706
equations for, 727
line of intersection, 729
Planetary motion, 788 ff.
Planetary orbits, 679(44)
data on, 638, 679, 792
Planets, mean distances from sun, 791
POISEUILLE, JEAN LEONARD MARIE (1797–1869), 182
Polar coordinates, 662 ff.
area in the plane, 680 ff., 896
area of a surface of revolution, 684
integration, 680 ff., 895
length of a plane curve, 682 ff.
Polar equations, for circles, 675
ellipses/parabolas/hyperbolas, 674 ff.
for lines, 674
Polar graphs, 667 ff.
intersection points, 670
slope, 668
symmetry tests, 667
Polynomials, degree of, 80
leading coefficient of, 81
Position vector, 702, 751
Potential functions, 946
for conservative fields, 949
Power Chain Rule, 162
Power series, 597 ff. *See also* Series; Taylor series
binomial, 619 ff.
convergence at endpoints, 605(45)
convergence tests (summary), 595
convergence theorem, 600
interval of convergence, 601
Maclaurin, 605 ff.
multiplication, 603 ff.
radius of convergence, 601
solutions of initial value problems, 622
Taylor, 605 ff.
Taylor's formula, 611
Taylor's theorem, 609
term-by-term differentiation, 602
term-by-term integration, 603
truncation error, 614
uniqueness, 605(43)
Precalculus formulas, A–1 ff.
Principal unit normal vector **N**, 778 ff.
Product rule, for derivatives, 130
generalized, 137(69)
Projectile motion, 762 ff.
angle of elevation, 764
equations, 764
height/flight time/range, 765
ideal trajectory, 768
Quadratic approximations, 617(27–32)
Quadratic curves, 645
Quadratic equations in x and y, 645 ff.
cross product term, 645
discriminant test, 647 ff.
graphs of, 647
rotation of axes, 645
Quadratic formula, A–2
Quadric surfaces, 734 ff.
drawing, 739
Quotient rule for derivatives, 132 ff.

Rabbits and foxes, 149(27, 28)
Radian measure, 22 ff.
in calculus, 153
Radioactive, decay, 382
half-life, 382
Radius of gyration, 889, 907, 934, 973
Rates of change, average/instantaneous, 113, 115, 143
related, 201 ff.
Rates of growth, e^x vs. polynomials, 400(14)
ln x vs. polynomials, 400(16)
relative, 395 ff.
Rational functions, 70
continuity, 93
graphs of, 227 ff.
integration of, 524 ff.
RAYLEIGH, Lord (1842–1919), 960
Real variable, 13
Rectangular coordinates, 1, 700
Rectifying plane, 782
Recursion formula, 560
Reduction formulas, 536 ff.
Reflective properties of conic sections, 640
Region, boundary of, 801, 802
boundary/interior points, 801, 802
bounded/unbounded, 801
closed/open, 801, 802
connected, 947
interior of, 801, 802
simply connected, 947
Related rates of change, 201 ff.
strategy for problem solving, 203
Regression line, 862
Repeating decimals, 570
Resistance proportional to velocity, 429 ff.
Richter scale, 366
RIEMANN, GEORG F. B. (1826–1866), 285
Riemann sums, 284 ff.
RL circuits, 430 ff.
steady-state solution, 431
time constant, 443(41)
transient solution, 431
ROLLE, MICHEL (1652–1719), 248
Rolle's theorem, 247 ff.
Root (zero), 97
Root finding, 97, 187 ff.
Rotation of axes formula, 645

Saddle point, 855
Sandwich theorem, 85
for functions of two variables, 814
for sequences, 562
Satellites, 788 ff.
data on, 792
Scalar components, 693
Scalar functions, 752
Scalars (scalar multiples of vectors), 692
Search (sequential vs. binary), 398 ff.
Secant, 114
Second derivative test for local extreme values, 221, 856
Sensitivity to change, 143, 183, 828
Sequence(s) (infinite), 557 ff.
bounded from above, 577
Fibonacci, 561
limits, 557 ff.
limits that arise frequently, 564
nondecreasing, 577 ff.
nonincreasing, 584(59)
recursive definition, 560, 566
Sandwich Theorem, 562
subsequence, 561
tail, 560
Series (infinite), 567 ff. *See also* Power series; Taylor series
absolute convergence, 593
adding and deleting terms, 573 ff.
alternating, 591
estimation theorem, 591
harmonic, 591
Leibniz's theorem, 591
p-series, 594
binomial, 619 ff., 624
Cauchy condensation test, 585(60)
conditional convergence, 593
converge/diverge, 568
direct comparison test, 580 ff.
evaluating nonelementary integrals, 620
geometric, 568 ff.
harmonic, 579
integral test, 580 ff.
limit comparison test, 582 ff.
simplified, 583
logarithmic p-series, 585(61)
Maclaurin. *See* Maclaurin series
nth root test, 588 ff.
nth term test (divergence), 571 ff.
necessary condition for convergence, 571
p-series, 581
partial sums, 567
ratio test, 585 ff.
reindexing, 574
sum/difference/constant multiple, 573
summary of tests for convergence and divergence, 595
telescoping, 570 ff.
Shifts, 30 ff.
conic sections, 644
formulas, 31
Sigma (Σ) notation, 282
Simple harmonic motion, 154
SIMPSON, THOMAS (1720–1761), 335
Simpson's rule, 335 ff.
error estimate, 336
(sin θ)/θ, 86 ff.
Skew lines, 731
Slope, of curve, 115 ff.
of line, 8
of parametrized curves, 656 ff.

Slope *(Cont.)*
of polar curves, 668
of a vector, 697
Smooth, function, 462
parametrized curve, 754
parametrized surface, 977
plane curve, 462
space curve, 754
surface, 966
Snowflake curve, 172, 464, 575(57)
Solar-powered car, 339(28)
Solids of revolution, 446 ff.
Solution curve, 259 ff.
sketching, 259 ff.
Space curves, 751 ff.
Speed, 141, 755
Spheres, standard equation, 705
Spherical coordinates, 744 ff.
Spring constant, 474
Standard linear approximation, 177, 825
error in, 183, 827
Step size, 331
STOKES, SIR GEORGE GABRIEL (1819–1903), 960, 984
Stokes's theorem, 983 ff.
and conservative fields, 990 ff.
Subintervals, 284
Substitutions, in definite integrals, 327
in multiple integrals, 919 ff.
Sum formula for positive integers, 284
Surface(s), 731 ff., 802
orientable/two-sided, 971
oriented, 971
parametrized, 975 ff.
piecewise smooth, 970
positive direction on, 971
quadric, 734 ff.
smooth, 966
Surface area, 465 ff., 659, 683 ff., 965 ff.
cylindrical vs. conical bands, 503
differential, 970, 979
differential formula, 979
parametric formula, 978
special formulas, 975
Surface integrals, 969 ff., 980ff.
differential form, 970
parametric form, 980
Symmetry, in the polar coordinate plane, 667
in the xy-plane, 16
System torque, 486

Tables of values of sin x, cos x, tan x, e^x, e^{-x}, and ln x, A–26 ff.
Tangent(s), curves, 853(57)
to a curve, 115 ff.
to level curves, 844 ff.
line, 754
planes, 847, 983
vector, 754
Target values, 52 ff.
TAYLOR, BROOK (1685–1731), 613
Taylor polynomials, 607 ff.
Taylor series, 605 ff.
arctangents, 621
calculations with, 619 ff.
combining, 616
evaluating nonelementary integrals, 620
remainder estimation, 612
Taylor's formula, 611
Taylor's theorem, 609
THOMSON, WILLIAM (LORD KELVIN) (1824–1907), 960, 984
Tin pest, 245(43)
TNB frame, 781
Torque, 486, 718, 720
Torsion, 781
Total curvature, 787(31)
Total differential, 828
Tower of Pisa, 149(26), 151(38)
Trans-Alaska Pipeline, 39 ff.
Translation. *See* Shifts
Trapezoidal rule, 331 ff.
error, 333
Trend line, 862
Triangle inequality, 50
Trigonometric functions, 22 ff., A–4 ff.
basic, 24
continuity of, 157
derivatives, 152 ff.
Trigonometric substitutions, 529 ff.
Trigonometric tables, A–27 ff.
Trigonometry, formulas and identities, A–4 ff.
review, 22 ff.
Triple integrals, 899 ff., 910 ff.
in cylindrical coordinates, 910 ff.
integration, 912
evaluation of, 900
finding limits of integration, 900, 912, 914
properties of, 899
in spherical coordinates, 913 ff.
integration, 914 ff.
substitutions in, 922 ff.
Triremes, 252

Unit tangent vector **T**, 773 ff.
Upper bound, 577

Variable(s), 12, 799
Vector(s), 691 ff.
acceleration, 755
addition and subtraction, 693 ff., 702
angle between, 711
basic, 692, 702
binormal **B**, 781
box product $\mathbf{A} \cdot \mathbf{B} \times \mathbf{C}$, 722 ff.
components, 693
of constant length, 757
cross (or vector) product $\mathbf{A} \times \mathbf{B}$, 718 ff.
determinant formula, 720 ff.
direction, 696, 704, 755
dot (or scalar) product $\mathbf{A} \cdot \mathbf{B}$, 710 ff.
magnitude (length), 694, 703
normal, 697
orthogonal, 712 ff.
parallel, 697
parallelogram law of addition, 692
in the plane, 691 ff.
principal unit normal **N**, 778 ff.
projections, 712 ff.
scalar components, 712 ff.
scalar multiplication, 692, 695, 702
scalar product, 710 ff.
slope, 697
as sum of orthogonal vectors, 713 ff.
tangent, 697, 754
torque, 718
triple scalar (box) product $\mathbf{A} \cdot \mathbf{B} \times \mathbf{C}$, 722 ff.
unit, 695 ff.
unit tangent **T**, 773
vector product $\mathbf{A} \times \mathbf{B}$, 718 ff.
velocity, 755
zero, 695
Vector fields, 937 ff.
component functions, 937
conservative, 946
continuous/differentiable, 937
curl, 956
divergence of $\mathbf{F}(x, y)$, 955 ff.
divergence of $\mathbf{F}(x, y, z)$, 993
gradient, 939
gravitational, 939, 954(30)
path independent (conservative), 946
radial, 938
spin, 938
Vector functions (vector-valued), 751 ff.
antiderivative, 758
continuous, 753
derivative, 754
differentiable, 754
differentiation rules, 756
integrals of, 758 ff.

Velocity. *See also* Vectors
average, 139
instantaneous, 139
VERMEER (1632–1675), 388(27)
Volume(s), arbitrary solids, 497 ff.
cylindrical shell method, 456 ff.
disk method, 447 ff.
of a parallelepiped, 722
of a region in space, 900
shell method, 456 ff.
slicing method, 497 ff.
solids of known cross section area, 499
solids of revolution, 446 ff.
washer method, 450 ff.
washers vs. shells, 459

Wave equation, 822 ff.
WEBER, WILHELM (1804–1891), 993
WEIERSTRASS, KARL (1815–1897), 122
Weierstrass's nowhere differentiable continuous functions, 122
Weight densities, 480
Weight vs. mass, 430, 486
Weight of water, 477
Whales, 439
Witch of Agnesi, 654, 655(27)
Work, constant force, 472, 715
done in pumping liquids, 475 ff.
done by a variable-force along a line, 472
as dot product, 715
integral evaluation, 940
over smooth curve in space, 939 ff.

$y = a^x$, 367 ff.

Zero of a function (root), 97

A Brief Table of Integrals

1. $\int u\,dv = uv - \int v\,du$

2. $\int a^u\,du = \frac{a^u}{\ln a} + C, \qquad a \neq 1, \qquad a > 0$

3. $\int \cos u\,du = \sin u + C$

4. $\int \sin u\,du = -\cos u + C$

5. $\int (ax+b)^n\,dx = \frac{(ax+b)^{n+1}}{a(n+1)} + C, \qquad n \neq -1$

6. $\int (ax+b)^{-1}\,dx = \frac{1}{a}\ln|ax+b| + C$

7. $\int x(ax+b)^n\,dx = \frac{(ax+b)^{n+1}}{a^2}\left[\frac{ax+b}{n+2} - \frac{b}{n+1}\right] + C, \qquad n \neq -1, -2$

8. $\int x(ax+b)^{-1}\,dx = \frac{x}{a} - \frac{b}{a^2}\ln|ax+b| + C$

9. $\int x(ax+b)^{-2}\,dx = \frac{1}{a^2}\left[\ln|ax+b| + \frac{b}{ax+b}\right] + C$

10. $\int \frac{dx}{x(ax+b)} = \frac{1}{b}\ln\left|\frac{x}{ax+b}\right| + C$

11. $\int \left(\sqrt{ax+b}\right)^n dx = \frac{2}{a}\frac{\left(\sqrt{ax+b}\right)^{n+2}}{n+2} + C, \qquad n \neq -2$

12. $\int \frac{\sqrt{ax+b}}{x}\,dx = 2\sqrt{ax+b} + b\int \frac{dx}{x\sqrt{ax+b}}$

13. (a) $\int \frac{dx}{x\sqrt{ax+b}} = \frac{2}{\sqrt{-b}}\tan^{-1}\sqrt{\frac{ax+b}{-b}} + C, \qquad \text{if } b < 0$

(b) $\int \frac{dx}{x\sqrt{ax+b}} = \frac{1}{\sqrt{b}}\ln\left|\frac{\sqrt{ax+b}-\sqrt{b}}{\sqrt{ax+b}+\sqrt{b}}\right| + C, \qquad \text{if } b > 0$

14. $\int \frac{\sqrt{ax+b}}{x^2}\,dx = -\frac{\sqrt{ax+b}}{x} + \frac{a}{2}\int \frac{dx}{x\sqrt{ax+b}} + C$

15. $\int \frac{dx}{x^2\sqrt{ax+b}} = -\frac{\sqrt{ax+b}}{bx} - \frac{a}{2b}\int \frac{dx}{x\sqrt{ax+b}} + C$

16. $\int \frac{dx}{a^2+x^2} = \frac{1}{a}\tan^{-1}\frac{x}{a} + C$

17. $\int \frac{dx}{(a^2+x^2)^2} = \frac{x}{2a^2(a^2+x^2)} + \frac{1}{2a^3}\tan^{-1}\frac{x}{a} + C$

18. $\int \frac{dx}{a^2-x^2} = \frac{1}{2a}\ln\left|\frac{x+a}{x-a}\right| + C$

19. $\int \frac{dx}{(a^2-x^2)^2} = \frac{x}{2a^2(a^2-x^2)} + \frac{1}{2a^2}\int \frac{dx}{a^2-x^2}$

20. $\int \frac{dx}{\sqrt{a^2+x^2}} = \sinh^{-1}\frac{x}{a} + C = \ln\left(x + \sqrt{a^2+x^2}\right) + C$

21. $\int \sqrt{a^2+x^2}\,dx = \frac{x}{2}\sqrt{a^2+x^2} + \frac{a^2}{2}\ln\left(x + \sqrt{a^2+x^2}\right) + C$

22. $\int x^2\sqrt{a^2+x^2}\,dx = \frac{x}{8}(a^2+2x^2)\sqrt{a^2+x^2} - \frac{a^4}{8}\ln\left(x + \sqrt{a^2+x^2}\right) + C$

23. $\int \frac{\sqrt{a^2+x^2}}{x}\,dx = \sqrt{a^2+x^2} - a\ln\left|\frac{a+\sqrt{a^2+x^2}}{x}\right| + C$

24. $\int \frac{\sqrt{a^2+x^2}}{x^2}\,dx = \ln\left(x+\sqrt{a^2+x^2}\right) - \frac{\sqrt{a^2+x^2}}{x} + C$

25. $\int \frac{x^2}{\sqrt{a^2+x^2}}\,dx = -\frac{a^2}{2}\ln\left(x+\sqrt{a^2+x^2}\right) + \frac{x\sqrt{a^2+x^2}}{2} + C$

26. $\int \frac{dx}{x\sqrt{a^2+x^2}} = -\frac{1}{a}\ln\left|\frac{a+\sqrt{a^2+x^2}}{x}\right| + C$

27. $\int \frac{dx}{x^2\sqrt{a^2+x^2}} = -\frac{\sqrt{a^2+x^2}}{a^2x} + C$

28. $\int \frac{dx}{\sqrt{a^2-x^2}} = \sin^{-1}\frac{x}{a} + C$

29. $\int \sqrt{a^2-x^2}\,dx = \frac{x}{2}\sqrt{a^2-x^2} + \frac{a^2}{2}\sin^{-1}\frac{x}{a} + C$

30. $\int x^2\sqrt{a^2-x^2}\,dx = \frac{a^4}{8}\sin^{-1}\frac{x}{a} - \frac{1}{8}x\sqrt{a^2-x^2}\,(a^2-2x^2) + C$

31. $\int \frac{\sqrt{a^2-x^2}}{x}\,dx = \sqrt{a^2-x^2} - a\ln\left|\frac{a+\sqrt{a^2-x^2}}{x}\right| + C$

32. $\int \frac{\sqrt{a^2-x^2}}{x^2}\,dx = -\sin^{-1}\frac{x}{a} - \frac{\sqrt{a^2-x^2}}{x} + C$

33. $\int \frac{x^2}{\sqrt{a^2-x^2}}\,dx = \frac{a^2}{2}\sin^{-1}\frac{x}{a} - \frac{1}{2}x\sqrt{a^2-x^2} + C$

34. $\int \frac{dx}{x\sqrt{a^2-x^2}} = -\frac{1}{a}\ln\left|\frac{a+\sqrt{a^2-x^2}}{x}\right| + C$

35. $\int \frac{dx}{x^2\sqrt{a^2-x^2}} = -\frac{\sqrt{a^2-x^2}}{a^2x} + C$

36. $\int \frac{dx}{\sqrt{x^2-a^2}} = \cosh^{-1}\frac{x}{a} + C = \ln\left|x+\sqrt{x^2-a^2}\right| + C$

37. $\int \sqrt{x^2-a^2}\,dx = \frac{x}{2}\sqrt{x^2-a^2} - \frac{a^2}{2}\ln\left|x+\sqrt{x^2-a^2}\right| + C$

38. $\int \left(\sqrt{x^2-a^2}\right)^n dx = \frac{x\left(\sqrt{x^2-a^2}\right)^n}{n+1} - \frac{na^2}{n+1}\int \left(\sqrt{x^2-a^2}\right)^{n-2} dx, \quad n \neq -1$

39. $\int \frac{dx}{\left(\sqrt{x^2-a^2}\right)^n} = \frac{x\left(\sqrt{x^2-a^2}\right)^{2-n}}{(2-n)a^2} - \frac{n-3}{(n-2)a^2}\int \frac{dx}{\left(\sqrt{x^2-a^2}\right)^{n-2}}, \quad n \neq 2$

40. $\int x\left(\sqrt{x^2-a^2}\right)^n dx = \frac{\left(\sqrt{x^2-a^2}\right)^{n+2}}{n+2} + C, \quad n \neq -2$

41. $\int x^2\sqrt{x^2-a^2}\,dx = \frac{x}{8}(2x^2-a^2)\sqrt{x^2-a^2} - \frac{a^4}{8}\ln\left|x+\sqrt{x^2-a^2}\right| + C$

42. $\int \frac{\sqrt{x^2-a^2}}{x}\,dx = \sqrt{x^2-a^2} - a\sec^{-1}\left|\frac{x}{a}\right| + C$

43. $\int \frac{\sqrt{x^2-a^2}}{x^2}\,dx = \ln\left|x+\sqrt{x^2-a^2}\right| - \frac{\sqrt{x^2-a^2}}{x} + C$

44. $\int \frac{x^2}{\sqrt{x^2-a^2}}\,dx = \frac{a^2}{2}\ln\left|x+\sqrt{x^2-a^2}\right| + \frac{x}{2}\sqrt{x^2-a^2} + C$

45. $\int \frac{dx}{x\sqrt{x^2-a^2}} = \frac{1}{a}\sec^{-1}\left|\frac{x}{a}\right| + C = \frac{1}{a}\cos^{-1}\left|\frac{a}{x}\right| + C$

46. $\int \frac{dx}{x^2\sqrt{x^2-a^2}} = \frac{\sqrt{x^2-a^2}}{a^2x} + C$

47. $\int \frac{dx}{\sqrt{2ax-x^2}} = \sin^{-1}\left(\frac{x-a}{a}\right) + C$

48. $\int \sqrt{2ax-x^2}\,dx = \frac{x-a}{2}\sqrt{2ax-x^2} + \frac{a^2}{2}\sin^{-1}\left(\frac{x-a}{a}\right) + C$

49. $\int \left(\sqrt{2ax-x^2}\right)^n dx = \frac{(x-a)\left(\sqrt{2ax-x^2}\right)^n}{n+1} + \frac{na^2}{n+1}\int \left(\sqrt{2ax-x^2}\right)^{n-2} dx$

50. $\int \frac{dx}{\left(\sqrt{2ax-x^2}\right)^n} = \frac{(x-a)\left(\sqrt{2ax-x^2}\right)^{2-n}}{(n-2)a^2} + \frac{(n-3)}{(n-2)a^2}\int \frac{dx}{\left(\sqrt{2ax-x^2}\right)^{n-2}}$

51. $\int x\sqrt{2ax-x^2}\,dx = \frac{(x+a)(2x-3a)\sqrt{2ax-x^2}}{6} + \frac{a^3}{2}\sin^{-1}\left(\frac{x-a}{a}\right) + C$

52. $\int \frac{\sqrt{2ax-x^2}}{x}\,dx = \sqrt{2ax-x^2} + a\sin^{-1}\left(\frac{x-a}{a}\right) + C$

53. $\int \frac{\sqrt{2ax-x^2}}{x^2}\,dx = -2\sqrt{\frac{2a-x}{x}} - \sin^{-1}\left(\frac{x-a}{a}\right) + C$

54. $\int \frac{x\,dx}{\sqrt{2ax-x^2}} = a\sin^{-1}\left(\frac{x-a}{a}\right) - \sqrt{2ax-x^2} + C$

55. $\int \frac{dx}{x\sqrt{2ax - x^2}} = -\frac{1}{a}\sqrt{\frac{2a - x}{x}} + C$

56. $\int \sin ax\, dx = -\frac{1}{a}\cos ax + C$

57. $\int \cos ax\, dx = \frac{1}{a}\sin ax + C$

58. $\int \sin^2 ax\, dx = \frac{x}{2} - \frac{\sin 2ax}{4a} + C$

59. $\int \cos^2 ax\, dx = \frac{x}{2} + \frac{\sin 2ax}{4a} + C$

60. $\int \sin^n ax\, dx = -\frac{\sin^{n-1} ax \cos ax}{na} + \frac{n-1}{n}\int \sin^{n-2} ax\, dx$

61. $\int \cos^n ax\, dx = \frac{\cos^{n-1} ax \sin ax}{na} + \frac{n-1}{n}\int \cos^{n-2} ax\, dx$

62. (a) $\int \sin ax \cos bx\, dx = -\frac{\cos(a+b)x}{2(a+b)} - \frac{\cos(a-b)x}{2(a-b)} + C, \quad a^2 \neq b^2$

(b) $\int \sin ax \sin bx\, dx = \frac{\sin(a-b)x}{2(a-b)} - \frac{\sin(a+b)x}{2(a+b)} + C, \quad a^2 \neq b^2$

(c) $\int \cos ax \cos bx\, dx = \frac{\sin(a-b)x}{2(a-b)} + \frac{\sin(a+b)x}{2(a+b)} + C, \quad a^2 \neq b^2$

63. $\int \sin ax \cos ax\, dx = -\frac{\cos 2ax}{4a} + C$

64. $\int \sin^n ax \cos ax\, dx = \frac{\sin^{n+1} ax}{(n+1)a} + C, \quad n \neq -1$

65. $\int \frac{\cos ax}{\sin ax}\, dx = \frac{1}{a}\ln|\sin ax| + C$

66. $\int \cos^n ax \sin ax\, dx = -\frac{\cos^{n+1} ax}{(n+1)a} + C, \quad n \neq -1$

67. $\int \frac{\sin ax}{\cos ax}\, dx = -\frac{1}{a}\ln|\cos ax| + C$

68. $\int \sin^n ax \cos^m ax\, dx = -\frac{\sin^{n-1} ax \cos^{m+1} ax}{a(m+n)} + \frac{n-1}{m+n}\int \sin^{n-2} ax \cos^m ax\, dx, \; n \neq -m$

(If $n = -m$, use No. 86.)

69. $\int \sin^n ax \cos^m ax\, dx = \frac{\sin^{n+1} ax \cos^{m-1} ax}{a(m+n)} + \frac{m-1}{m+n}\int \sin^n ax \cos^{m-2} ax\, dx, \; m \neq -n$

(If $m = -n$, use No. 87.)

70. $\int \frac{dx}{b + c\sin ax} = \frac{-2}{a\sqrt{b^2 - c^2}}\tan^{-1}\left[\sqrt{\frac{b-c}{b+c}}\tan\left(\frac{\pi}{4} - \frac{ax}{2}\right)\right] + C, \quad b^2 > c^2$

71. $\int \frac{dx}{b + c\sin ax} = \frac{-1}{a\sqrt{c^2 - b^2}}\ln\left|\frac{c + b\sin ax + \sqrt{c^2 - b^2}\cos ax}{b + c\sin ax}\right| + C, \quad b^2 < c^2$

72. $\int \frac{dx}{1 + \sin ax} = -\frac{1}{a}\tan\left(\frac{\pi}{4} - \frac{ax}{2}\right) + C$

73. $\int \frac{dx}{1 - \sin ax} = \frac{1}{a}\tan\left(\frac{\pi}{4} + \frac{ax}{2}\right) + C$

74. $\int \frac{dx}{b + c\cos ax} = \frac{2}{a\sqrt{b^2 - c^2}}\tan^{-1}\left[\sqrt{\frac{b-c}{b+c}}\tan\frac{ax}{2}\right] + C, \quad b^2 > c^2$

75. $\int \frac{dx}{b + c\cos ax} = \frac{1}{a\sqrt{c^2 - b^2}}\ln\left|\frac{c + b\cos ax + \sqrt{c^2 - b^2}\sin ax}{b + c\cos ax}\right| + C, \quad b^2 < c^2$

76. $\int \frac{dx}{1 + \cos ax} = \frac{1}{a}\tan\frac{ax}{2} + C$

77. $\int \frac{dx}{1 - \cos ax} = -\frac{1}{a}\cot\frac{ax}{2} + C$

78. $\int x\sin ax\, dx = \frac{1}{a^2}\sin ax - \frac{x}{a}\cos ax + C$

79. $\int x\cos ax\, dx = \frac{1}{a^2}\cos ax + \frac{x}{a}\sin ax + C$

80. $\int x^n \sin ax\, dx = -\frac{x^n}{a}\cos ax + \frac{n}{a}\int x^{n-1}\cos ax\, dx$

81. $\int x^n \cos ax\, dx = \frac{x^n}{a}\sin ax - \frac{n}{a}\int x^{n-1}\sin ax\, dx$

82. $\int \tan ax\, dx = \frac{1}{a}\ln|\sec ax| + C$

83. $\int \cot ax\, dx = \frac{1}{a}\ln|\sin ax| + C$

84. $\int \tan^2 ax\, dx = \frac{1}{a}\tan ax - x + C$

85. $\int \cot^2 ax\, dx = -\frac{1}{a}\cot ax - x + C$

86. $\int \tan^n ax\, dx = \frac{\tan^{n-1} ax}{a(n-1)} - \int \tan^{n-2} ax\, dx, \quad n \neq 1$

87. $\int \cot^n ax\, dx = -\frac{\cot^{n-1} ax}{a(n-1)} - \int \cot^{n-2} ax\, dx, \quad n \neq 1$

88. $\int \sec ax\,dx = \frac{1}{a}\ln|\sec ax + \tan ax| + C$

89. $\int \csc ax\,dx = -\frac{1}{a}\ln|\csc ax + \cot ax| + C$

90. $\int \sec^2 ax\,dx = \frac{1}{a}\tan ax + C$

91. $\int \csc^2 ax\,dx = -\frac{1}{a}\cot ax + C$

92. $\int \sec^n ax\,dx = \frac{\sec^{n-2} ax \tan ax}{a(n-1)} + \frac{n-2}{n-1}\int \sec^{n-2} ax\,dx, \qquad n \neq 1$

93. $\int \csc^n ax\,dx = -\frac{\csc^{n-2} ax \cot ax}{a(n-1)} + \frac{n-2}{n-1}\int \csc^{n-2} ax\,dx, \qquad n \neq 1$

94. $\int \sec^n ax \tan ax\,dx = \frac{\sec^n ax}{na} + C, \qquad n \neq 0$

95. $\int \csc^n ax \cot ax\,dx = -\frac{\csc^n ax}{na} + C, \qquad n \neq 0$

96. $\int \sin^{-1} ax\,dx = x\sin^{-1} ax + \frac{1}{a}\sqrt{1-a^2x^2} + C$

97. $\int \cos^{-1} ax\,dx = x\cos^{-1} ax - \frac{1}{a}\sqrt{1-a^2x^2} + C$

98. $\int \tan^{-1} ax\,dx = x\tan^{-1} ax - \frac{1}{2a}\ln(1+a^2x^2) + C$

99. $\int x^n \sin^{-1} ax\,dx = \frac{x^{n+1}}{n+1}\sin^{-1} ax - \frac{a}{n+1}\int \frac{x^{n+1}\,dx}{\sqrt{1-a^2x^2}}, \qquad n \neq -1$

100. $\int x^n \cos^{-1} ax\,dx = \frac{x^{n+1}}{n+1}\cos^{-1} ax + \frac{a}{n+1}\int \frac{x^{n+1}\,dx}{\sqrt{1-a^2x^2}}, \qquad n \neq -1$

101. $\int x^n \tan^{-1} ax\,dx = \frac{x^{n+1}}{n+1}\tan^{-1} ax - \frac{a}{n+1}\int \frac{x^{n+1}\,dx}{1+a^2x^2}, \qquad n \neq -1$

102. $\int e^{ax}\,dx = \frac{1}{a}e^{ax} + C$

103. $\int b^{ax}\,dx = \frac{1}{a}\frac{b^{ax}}{\ln b} + C, \qquad b > 0, \quad b \neq 1$

104. $\int xe^{ax}\,dx = \frac{e^{ax}}{a^2}(ax-1) + C$

105. $\int x^n e^{ax}\,dx = \frac{1}{a}x^n e^{ax} - \frac{n}{a}\int x^{n-1}e^{ax}\,dx$

106. $\int x^n b^{ax}\,dx = \frac{x^n b^{ax}}{a\ln b} - \frac{n}{a\ln b}\int x^{n-1}b^{ax}\,dx, \qquad b > 0, \quad b \neq 1$

107. $\int e^{ax}\sin bx\,dx = \frac{e^{ax}}{a^2+b^2}(a\sin bx - b\cos bx) + C$

108. $\int e^{ax}\cos bx\,dx = \frac{e^{ax}}{a^2+b^2}(a\cos bx + b\sin bx) + C$

109. $\int \ln ax\,dx = x\ln ax - x + C$

110. $\int x^n(\ln ax)^m\,dx = \frac{x^{n+1}(\ln ax)^m}{n+1} - \frac{m}{n+1}\int x^n(\ln ax)^{m-1}\,dx, \qquad n \neq -1$

111. $\int x^{-1}(\ln ax)^m = \frac{(\ln ax)^{m+1}}{m+1} + C, \qquad m \neq -1$

112. $\int \frac{dx}{x\ln ax} = \ln|\ln ax| + C$

113. $\int \sinh ax\,dx = \frac{1}{a}\cosh ax + C$

114. $\int \cosh ax\,dx = \frac{1}{a}\sinh ax + C$

115. $\int \sinh^2 ax\,dx = \frac{\sinh 2ax}{4a} - \frac{x}{2} + C$

116. $\int \cosh^2 ax\,dx = \frac{\sinh 2ax}{4a} + \frac{x}{2} + C$

117. $\int \sinh^n ax\,dx = \frac{\sinh^{n-1} ax \cosh ax}{na} - \frac{n-1}{n}\int \sinh^{n-2} ax\,dx, \qquad n \neq 0$

118. $\int \cosh^n ax\,dx = \frac{\cosh^{n-1} ax \sinh ax}{na} + \frac{n-1}{n}\int \cosh^{n-2} ax\,dx, \qquad n \neq 0$